THE OXFORD GUIDE TO
AMERICAN LAW

THE OXFORD GUIDE TO
AMERICAN LAW

Editor in Chief

Kermit L. Hall

Editors

David S. Clark, James W. Ely, Jr.,
Joel Grossman, N. E. H. Hull

OXFORD
UNIVERSITY PRESS

Oxford New York
Auckland Cape Town Dar es Salaam Hong Kong Karachi
Kuala Lumpur Madrid Melbourne Mexico City
Nairobi New Delhi Shanghai Taipei Toronto

and an associated company in
Berlin

Copyright © 2002 by Oxford University Press, Inc.

Originally published in 2002 as *The Oxford Companion to American Law*.

Published by Oxford University Press, Inc.
198 Madison Avenue, New York, New York, 10016-4314

www.oup.com

Oxford is a registered trademark of Oxford University Press

ISBN: 978-0-19-534090-7

CONTENTS

INTRODUCTION

The great Prussian statesman Otto von Bismarck is said to have observed, "If you like laws and sausages, you should never watch either one being made." That is hardly a comforting insight, although doubtless a realistic one, for Americans, who perhaps more than any other people on earth live by the law. This is because in America law has emerged as a form of civic religion, a set of values, ideals, and processes to which the American people have been as committed as they have been to any spiritual code. This book is about that civic religion, the law.

But what is law? Once again Bismarck's insight proves helpful, because it so clearly links the untidy processes of society and politics with law. The contemporary definitions of law fully stress its connections to society, as does this book. Most dictionaries, for example, describe law as "a rule established by authority, society, or custom . . . governing the affairs of man within a community or among states." The legal scholar Donald Black offered an even shorter definition. He described law as "governmental social control." In fine, law is best understood as a system of social choice, one in which government provides for the allocation of resources, the legitimate use of violence, and the structuring of social relationships.

Without society we need no law; without law we cannot produce society. The rules of behavior for both government and individuals take on meaning as they affect and are affected by the social order. When we think about Bismarck and his sausage metaphor, we are reminded that the process by which we build and implement these rules is often chaotic, almost always freighted with contending views of what constitutes the just society, and inevitably subject to change. We tend to think of the law as complex, something that only lawyers, judges, and legal educators can comprehend. Making sense of sausage, too, can be a tough business. Yet an understanding of the internal workings of the law offers a beginning, not an ending. Law is, after all else, a humanistic institution, and that is why it can be at once so disorderly and so systematic, reflecting as it does the often competing human tendencies to exercise free will while searching for order. The history of the law, for example, can be viewed as a tale of human choices. Its abstract rules deal with the most central of human issues: the preservation of life, the protection of property, the exercise of individual liberty, the fashioning of creative knowledge, the allocation of scarce resources, and the limiting of the authority of lawmakers themselves through constitutional processes.

This last point has particular resonance in the American experience. "If one man can be allowed to determine for himself what is law, every man can," Felix Frankfurter once observed. "That means first chaos, then tyranny," he continued, and the prevention of both meant that the "[l]egal process is an essential part of the democratic process." American liberty has been nourished by the traditions of constitutional law, meaning those rules, enshrined in both the federal Constitution and state constitutions, that specify the bounds of governmental authority, especially as they apply to the power of the government to intrude on individual liberty. Hence, American law has a particularly rich public law culture that goes hand-in-hand with an equally powerful private law tradition.

The story of American law, however, extends far beyond constitutions and law, whether common or positive. It is also very much about the formal institutions through which the law operates. Supreme Court Justice David J. Brewer once observed that America is the paradise of lawyers. For some critics of the American bar, of course, Brewer's comment offers an explanation of why Bismarck might have reached the conclusion that he did. Yet a more balanced approach quickly reveals that lawyers have been an essential and often defining part of the legal culture. Almost all judicial positions since independence have been filled by lawyers, and that connection has meant that legal expertise has been a qualification for interpreting the law. Lawyers have played a disproportionate role in legislatures, however, both state and federal. And the high incidence of lawyers in politics has meant that law and politics have been intimately related, both yesterday and today.

As this volume makes clear, the institutions of the law include much more than the bench and bar. They extend to police and prisons and to informal mechanisms of dispute resolution. Moreover, law is much more than the black letters in the court reports and statutes; it is also the popular perspectives that the American people have held about the law and the sociopolitical context from which they approach it.

Given this perspective, we have organized this volume to stress the concept of governance, the ways and means by which lawmakers go about using law to exert the power of government. Hence, we have included an essay on governance, but we have also provided detailed essays about the executive, legislative, and judicial branches, both federal and state. One of the virtues of this approach is that it helps the reader understand that law is the work of more than just courts, judges, and lawyers. It is the product of lawmakers, of persons engaged in the political process who, through the exercise of their constitutional authority, shape and then reshape the law. We have, as a result, paid attention to such basic concepts as separation of powers and federalism, since both have had important consequences for the scope and direction of American law.

This *Companion* offers a comprehensive guide to the development and current status of American law. It does so through an alphabetical organization that comprises several broad categories of entries. Biographical entries explore the personal and professional careers of the nation's important lawyers, judges, and legal educators, including some of the members of the Supreme Court. Many of the biographical entries provide information about the education, formative influences, and substantive legal and judicial careers of these figures, and the reasons they attained eminence in the galaxy of American law. The editors realize that our list could have been expanded considerably, but limitations of space precluded us from doing so. There are, moreover, several other excellent biographical reference works that detail the lives of a much larger number of lawyers and judges than was possible here. John R. Vile, for example, has edited *Great American Lawyers: An Encyclopedia* (2 vols., 2001) and Melvin I. Urofsky has produced *The Supreme Court Justices: A Biographical Dictionary* (1994). We felt no compunction to duplicate their work in this volume.

Another category of entries treats concepts central to the American legal experience. These include such protean areas as contracts, torts, property, both real and personal, equity, and much more. Typically, these kinds of entries define the concept and then trace its historical origins and development and explore its contemporary status.

A special emphasis of this volume is on explaining the ways in which law, legal actors, and legal institutions have been understood in the day-to-day lives of Americans. Hence, there are entries on current controversies surrounding such matters as abortion and reproductive rights, the right to bear arms, affirmative action, and freedom of speech and the press. These entries have a particularly strong constitutional law component, although this volume is not designed, as was *The Oxford Companion to the Supreme Court of the United States*, to provide anything like a full account of the development of either American constitutional law or the high court. There are also entries dealing with the popular perception of lawyers and judges that speak to the way in which American culture has enshrined the law as a civic culture, and often simultaneously valorized and demonized the persons associated with it. Finally, in underscoring the day-to-day operations of the law, we have given particular attention to institutions, individuals, and processes through which the law operates. Such entries include items on bounty hunters, detectives, the highway patrol and state police, paralegals, and the Federal Bureau of Investigation.

The law often operates through cases, of course, and no task proved more vexing for the editors than attempting to distill from the American experience the handful of most important cases. Some of the great chestnuts of American legal history are included, such as the Supreme Court cases *Marbury* v. *Madison* (1803), *Dred Scott* v. *Sandford* (1857), and *Roe* v. *Wade* (1973). We consciously decided not to include a large number of state cases as direct entries in the *Companion;* instead, we have left those items to appear in the entries dealing with such concepts as contracts and torts. A case index provides quick reference to these cases. We have, however, included a handful of notable nonfederal cases, especially those that have drawn substantial popular attention. These range from the trial of John Peter

Zenger to the Scottsboro Trials, and more recently to the sagas of Rodney King and O. J. Simpson. These and similar cases, we believe, are important to understanding the connection between American social and legal development and, almost always, the ways in which politics and law have converged. For information on a wide range of cases, both federal and nonfederal, we recommend John W. Johnson's remarkable volume, *Historic U.S. Court Cases: An Encyclopedia* (2001). For concise explanations of leading Supreme Court cases the reader will find *The Oxford Companion to the Supreme Court of the United States* and *The Oxford Guide to Supreme Court Decisions* both invaluable.

Also included in this volume are broad interpretive entries. First, a wide range of essays sums up developments in important substantive and procedural areas of American law. For example, there are essays dealing with legal education, employment discrimination, privacy, gender, due process both procedural and substantive, civil and criminal procedure, and the appellate process. Essays such as these form a coherent overview of major bodies of American law.

Second, along with these substantive essays is a large category of "and law" entries, such as "Medicine and Law," "Sociology and Law," and "Economics and Law." The editors consider these essays among the most important in the volume. They are particularly important because they explore the dynamic relationship between society and law and the ways in which social demands are often mediated into legal responses.

Third, American law has not historically been independent, nor does it today exist in isolation from legal developments in other countries and at the international level. The editors believe strongly in the concept of legal culture, and with it the notion that law should not be viewed simply as an official enterprise of the state. Such an approach means, as the entries indicate, that there are alternatives to formal law, whether through processes of alternative conflict resolution or acts of wild justice. Many contributors, therefore, have approached their subjects from a cultural, comparative, and international perspective.

There is also another category of broad essays, those dealing with the "History of Law." This one large essay, which is composed of five sub-essays, provides an overview of crucial developments during the entire course of the nation's history. Taken as a whole, these essays explain how the process of social demand and legal response has become such an integral feature of the nation's legal development. Also included in the volume is an array of articles on historical subjects of particular significance, including, for example, slavery, the militia movement, the impeachment of Andrew Johnson, and the Sedition Act Trials.

A final category of entries explains vocabulary and phrases. These brief entries provide direct definitions of such technical terms as injunction and fault liability.

In creating this *Companion*, the editors wished to make authoritative information about American law widely available in a readily accessible form. That means that the volume is directed at a broad and diverse audience, one that includes students, general readers, scholars in law, the social sciences, the humanities, the sciences, and some professions. It is also designed to serve a readership of lawyers, judges, journalists, public servants, and others. There is a virtual Niagara of writing about American law, but much of it is directed toward the professional bar and is often highly technical in character. The editors, then, have sought to fill what they view as a void for a widely available, authoritative reference on all aspects of American law. In the end, more than three hundred contributors have brought to the volume the insights of many disciplines, including law, political science, history, anthropology, sociology, philosophy, and literature. As well, practicing lawyers and judges have contributed to the volume. All of the contributors were encouraged to make their entries accessible to a general readership, by offering historical and interpretive background to their subjects and by avoiding the use of arcane legal terminology.

The editors hope that all readers will benefit from our efforts to cast subjects in broad terms, to do more than present the law. Throughout, contributors have sought to approach the law as a symbol of the values of American culture. The essay on "Family Law," for example, connects the changing nature of the American family from the nineteenth to the twentieth centuries with the development of laws more sensitive to the needs of both mother and father and far more attentive to the interests of children, whether natural or adopted. The essay on "Civil Rights and Civil Liberties" ranges across the entire history of the nation and makes the basic point that both rights and liberties depend on the courage of individual citizens, and the efforts of groups such as the American Civil Liberties Union and the National Association for the Advancement of Colored People, to make their case. We hope that the *Companion* will serve all of its readers well.

How to Use This Companion

The *Companion* is organized alphabetically, with several kinds of cross-references. These cross-references form a carefully planned pattern of articles designed to guide the reader to topics of related interest, and from these to topics of general interest. Each element of the *Companion* is meant to complement the others and to facilitate the user's search for information.

The highest level of cross-references involves blind entries. These entries appear within the alphabetical range of headwords, and, for synonyms, related subjects, inverted terms, and larger topics, refer the reader to the actual entry term under which the topic is discussed. For example, the blind entry "Carjacking" refers the reader to the main entry "Automobiles and Crime."

Within the body of an article, cross-references may also be denoted by insertion of a star before the relevant word. Topics marked in this way will be found elsewhere in the volume as separate entries. For example, in the entry "Civil Rights and Civil Liberties," the terms desegregation and race are preceded by stars, meaning that the reader may wish to look up the entries under "Desegregation" and "Race." An item marked with a star may not exactly match the form of the entry term. For example, the concept substantive due process of law is mentioned several times in the *Companion*, but the entry term of this article is inverted as "Due Process, Substantive." When a cross-reference is being made to this entry in another article, the phrase appears as "substantive *due process," which leads the reader to the article "Due Process, Substantive." Note as well that there is a separate entry titled "Due Process, Procedural."

Finally, at the end of many entries there are cross-references that direct the user to related or expanded discussions found in other entries. For example, a reader interested in "Abortion and Reproductive Decisions" would find references at the end of that article to "Privacy," "Gender and Law," and "*Roe* v. *Wade*."

Two other items follow at the end of each entry. Many entries list bibliographical references that users may find helpful if they wish to learn more about the topic in question; longer essays are typically supported by the most bibliographical material. Every effort has been made to include in the bibliographies nontechnical literature that is readily available in a good public library. We have given special attention to books because they are, on balance, usually more accessible than are specialized journals in law, social science, and the humanities. The second item at the end of an entry is the name of the article's author. To find all articles in the *Companion* by a particular contributor, readers may consult the Directory of Contributors following this introduction.

Each case included as an entry opens with standard information. After the name of the case, readers will find, for federal cases, the official *United States Reports* citation—for example, the case of *Swift* v. *Tyson* can be found at 41 U.S. 1, meaning the case appeared in volume 41 of *United States Reports* and that it begins on page 1. The year the case was decided follows in parentheses. The article goes on to provide information about the vote, the justices who participated, and the ways in which they participated.

The analytical power of the *Companion* is enhanced by two indexes. The first is an index of every case mentioned in the *Companion* along with its proper citation. In the instance of Supreme Court cases the citation is to *United States Reports* rather than the nominative reports, such as Dallas, Cranch, and Wheaton. The only exception to the use of *United States Reports* occurs when recently decided cases were available at the time of publication only through the unofficial *Supreme Court Reports*, *Lawyers Edition*, or *U.S. Law Week*. The decisions of lower federal courts are cited in *Federal Cases* for reports in the district and circuit courts up to 1880; the *Federal Supplement* for district cases since 1880 and circuit cases from 1880 to 1932; and the *Federal Reporter* for circuit court and U.S. Court of Appeals decisions since 1932. When citing state cases, the editors have relied on the official reports, which are issued by the courts themselves as the authoritative text of their decisions, rather than the widely used but unofficial reports of West Group (National Reporter System) and Lawyers Co-operative

Publishing Company *(American Law Reports)*. Some states, however, have ceased issuing their own reports and have instead adopted the National Reporter System as their official reporter. The case index covers more than just the cases listed as entries; it encompasses all of the cases mentioned anywhere in the volume. Thus, even if a case is not covered as an entry, it may well appear somewhere in the volume, and the case index is the best way to find it.

The *Companion* also has a topical index that directs readers to concepts, persons, places, and institutions mentioned in the text. The topical index supplements and reinforces the system of cross-references employed in the main body of the work, and provides access to detailed points of information that are not themselves the subjects of independent entries.

Acknowledgments. The *Companion* is the work of many people. The Directory of Contributors provides the names and institutional affiliations of the more than three hundred persons whose scholarship, learning, and erudition made this volume possible. We are grateful for the support of colleagues in such a wide array of disciplines and professions.

Along the way we received excellent research assistance from Tricia Randall of Utah State University, and Seth Whitaker, a graduate of North Carolina State University and currently a student at the University of Virginia Law School. Rose Marie A. Ernstrom and Teresa Denton should be commended for expert administrative support.

This *Companion* was the inspiration of Linda Halvorson Morse, now at the University of Chicago Press, and more recently of Nancy Toff. We are grateful for the assistance of Catherine Carter during the early and middle stages of this project, and we are especially grateful for the heroic efforts of Katherine Adzima to pull the intellectual pieces and the contributors to the *Companion* together at the end of the process.

Kermit L. Hall
Editor-in-Chief

David S. Clark
James W. Ely, Jr.
Joel B. Grossman
N. E. H. Hull
Editors
December 2001

ABOUT THE EDITORS

~

EDITOR IN CHIEF

Kermit L. Hall is President of Utah State University and Professor of History. He holds an undergraduate degree from the University of Akron, a Ph.D. from the University of Minnesota, and an MSL from the Yale Law School. President Hall has published widely in American constitutional and legal history, including *The Politics of Justice: Federal Judicial Selection in the Second American Party System* (1979) and *The Magic Mirror: Law in American History* (1989). He has edited or co-edited twelve other books, including *The Oxford Guide to Supreme Court Decisions* (1999), and served as the editor-in-chief of the award winning *Oxford Companion to the Supreme Court of the United States* (1992). President Hall has held fellowships from the National Endowment for the Humanities, the American Council of Learned Societies, the American Bar Foundation, and the Fulbright Education Foundation. The American Library Association bestowed the James Madison Award on him in 1999 for his service on the five-member John F. Kennedy Assassination Records Review Board, to which he was appointed by President Bill Clinton and confirmed by the Senate. He is currently a member of the Advisory Commission of the Standing Committee of Public Education of the American Bar Association.

EDITORS

David S. Clark is Maynard and Bertha Wilson Professor of Law at Willamette University. He earned his A.B., J.D., and J.S.M. degrees at Stanford University. Clark is a member of the California Bar and vice president of the American Society of Comparative Law. He has taught in Europe, Latin America, and Asia and held the Alexander von Humboldt and Max Planck Society research fellowships. Clark previously taught at the universities of Colorado, Houston, Louisiana State, and Tulsa. He was the Inns of Court Fellow at Inner Temple (London) (2000), the Fulbright Chair in Comparative Law at Trento University (1999), the Wing Tat Lee Visiting Professor of Comparative and International Law at Loyola University Chicago (1996), and the Dan Hopson Distinguished Visiting Professor of Law at Southern Illinois University (1987). He has authored or edited several books on comparative law, law and society, and procedural law and teaches in those areas.

James W. Ely, Jr. is Milton R. Underwood Professor of Law and Professor of History at Vanderbilt University. A graduate of Princeton University, he received his L.L.B. from Harvard Law School and his Ph.D. in history from the University of Virginia. Ely is the author of numerous books, including *The Guardian of Every Other Right: A Constitutional History of Property Rights, The Chief Justiceship of Melville W. Fuller, 1888–1910,* and *Railroads and American Law.* He is also an editor of *The Oxford Companion to the Supreme Court of the United States.*

Joel B. Grossman is Professor of Political Science at Johns Hopkins University. Previously he was Professor of Political Science and Law at the University of Wisconsin-Madison, where he taught for many years. His teaching and writing focuses on American constitutional law, constitutional theory, and legal institutions and processes. He has been Chair of the Wisconsin Judicial Commission, chair of the political science departments at both Hopkins and Wisconsin, and editor of *Law & Society Review.*

N. E. H. Hull is Distinguished Professor of Law and a member of the graduate faculty in history at Rutgers University, Camden. She has written *Female Felons: Women and Serious Crime in Colonial Massachusetts* (1987) and co-authored *Impeachment in America, 1635–1805* (1984); *Murdering Mothers: Infanticide in England and New England, 1558–1803* (1981); and *Roe v. Wade: The Abortion Rights Controversy in American History* (2001).

DIRECTORY OF CONTRIBUTORS

~

Howard Abadinsky, *Professor of Criminal Justice, Saint Xavier University, Chicago, Ill.*
PROBATION AND PAROLE

Philip Abbott, *Distinguished Graduate Professor, Wayne State University, Detroit, Mich.*
SECESSION

David Adamany, *Laura Carnell Professor of Law and Political Science, and President, Temple University, Philadelphia, Pa.*
JUDICIAL REVIEW

Charles W. Adams, *Professor of Law, University of Tulsa College of Law, Okla.*
REMEDIES: PRETRIAL

S. L. Alexander, *Coordinator, Communications Law, Loyola University, New Orleans, La.*
SUNSHINE LAWS

Michael S. Ariens, *Professor of Law, St. Mary's University of San Antonio, Tex.*
LEGAL PRACTICE, FORMS OF; PARALEGAL AND LEGAL SECRETARY; SOLE PRACTITIONERS

Robert H. Aronson, *Professor of Law, University of Washington School of Law, Seattle*
FEES, ATTORNEY

Michael Asimow, *Professor of Law, Emeritus, University of California, Los Angeles, School of Law*
LAWYERS, POPULAR PERCEPTIONS OF

Tracy L. Bach, *Assistant Professor of Legal Writing, Vermont Law School, South Royalton*
MEDICINE AND LAW: MEDICINE AND LAW

Ronald J. Bacigal, *Professor of Law, University of Richmond School of Law, Va.*
ASSAULT AND BATTERY; MAYHEM

Gordon Bakken, *Professor of History, California State University, Fullerton*
OUTLAWS, POPULAR

Gloria J. Banks, *Associate Professor of Law, Widener University School of Law, Harrisburg, Pa.*
MEDICINE AND LAW: MEDICAL MALPRACTICE

Carol M. Bast, *Associate Professor of Legal Studies, University of Central Florida, Orlando*
WIRETAPPING AND ELECTRONIC EAVESDROPPING

William Beard, *Independent scholar*
LINCOLN, ABRAHAM

Mary Becker, *Professor of Law, DePaul University College of Law, Chicago, Ill.*
FEMINIST LEGAL THEORY

Michal R. Belknap, *Professor of Law, California Western School of Law, San Diego; Adjunct Professor of History, University of California, San Diego*
AMERICAN JUDICATURE SOCIETY; CHICAGO CONSPIRACY CASE; DENNIS, EUGENE, TRIAL OF; HISS, ALGER, TRIAL OF; LINCOLN ASSASSINATION TRIALS; ROSENBERG ESPIONAGE TRIAL

Michael Les Benedict, *Professor of History, The Ohio State University, Columbus*
HISTORY OF AMERICAN LAW: GILDED AGE TO THE GREAT DEPRESSION (1877–1929); JOHNSON, ANDREW, IMPEACHMENT TRIAL OF

Harold J. Berman, *Robert W. Woodruff Professor of Law, Emory University, Atlanta, Ga.; James Barr Ames Professor of Law, Emeritus, Harvard University, Cambridge, Mass.*
LEGAL SYSTEMS

Roger Bernhardt, *Professor of Law, Golden Gate University School of Law, San Francisco, Calif.*
PROPERTY, REAL

Christopher L. Blakesley, *J. Y. Sanders Professor of International and Comparative Criminal Law, Paul M. Hebert Law Center, Louisiana State University, Baton Rouge*
EXTRADITION; KIDNAPPING

Brian A. Blum, *Professor of Law, Northwestern School of Law, Lewis and Clark College, Portland, Oreg.*
BANKRUPTCY: PROCEDURES; DEBTOR AND CREDITOR

Matthew H. Bosworth, *Assistant Professor of Political Science, Winona State University, Winona, Minn.*
WITNESS, RIGHT TO CONFRONT

Kathleen F. Brickey, *James Carr Professor of Criminal Jurisprudence, Washington University School of Law, St. Louis, Mo.*
WHITE COLLAR CRIME

Richard Briffault, *Vice-Dean & Joseph P. Chamberlain Professor of Legislation, Columbia University Law School, New York, N.Y.*
FEDERALISM

John Brigham, *Professor, Political Science Department, University of Massachusetts, Amherst*
POLITICAL SCIENCE AND LAW; POLITICS AND THE LAW

Margaret F. Brinig, *Edward A. Howry Professor of Law, University of Iowa College of Law, Iowa City*
ADOPTION AND TERMINATION OF PARENTAL RIGHTS; ADULTERY; CHILD CUSTODY

R. Ben Brown, *Visiting Scholar, Center for the Study of Law and Society, Boalt Hall, University of California, Berkeley*
POWER OF ATTORNEY; *YOUNGSTOWN SHEET & TUBE CO. V. SAWYER*

Rebecca L. Brown, *Professor of Law, Vanderbilt University Law School, Nashville, Tenn.*
DUE PROCESS: PROCEDURAL

W. Elliot Brownlee, *Professor of History, University of California, Santa Barbara*
TAXATION: OVERVIEW; TAXATION: INCOME TAXES

William Hamilton Bryson, *Professor of Law, The T. C. Williams School of Law, University of Richmond, Va.*
EDUCATOR, LEGAL

Barlow Burke Jr., *Professor of Law, Washington College of Law, American University, Washington, D.C.*
PROPERTY, PERSONAL

Ann M. Burkhart, *Professor of Law, University of Minnesota Law School, Minneapolis*
MORTGAGE

David L. Callies, *Benjamin A. Kudo Professor of Law, William S. Richardson School of Law, The University of Hawaii at Manoa*
ZONING

David T. Canon, *Professor of Political Science, University of Wisconsin, Madison*
CONGRESS

Robert A. Carp, *Professor of Political Science, University of Houston, Texas*
COURTS, UNITED STATES: FEDERAL COURTS

J. Dean Carro, *Professor of Clinical Law, Dean's Club Professor of Law, University of Akron School of Law, Akron, Ohio*
SHEPPARD, SAM, CASE OF

Robert C. Casad, *John H. and John M. Kane Professor Emeritus, University of Kansas School of Law, Lawrence*
JUDGMENTS

Bill F. Chamberlin, *Joseph L. Brechner Eminent Scholar of Mass Communications, College of Journalism and Communications, University of Florida, Gainesville*
FREEDOM OF INFORMATION ACT; MEDIA AND THE LAW

John Whiteclay Chambers II, *Professor of History, Rutgers University, New Brunswick, N.J.*
MILITARY POLICE

Sandra F. Chance, *Associate Professor of Journalism; Director, Brechner Center for Freedom of Information, College of Journalism and Communications, University of Florida, Gainesville*
SUNSET LAWS

Anthony Chase, *Professor of Law, Nova Southeastern University Law Center, Fort Lauderdale, Fla.*
KING, RODNEY, CASE OF

Edward E. Chase, *Professor of Law, Rutgers University School of Law, Camden, N.J.*
LANDLORD-TENANT

David S. Clark, *Maynard and Bertha Wilson Professor of Law, Willamette University College of Law, Salem, Oreg.*
ACTUS REUS; APPEALS; ATTACHMENT; ATTEMPT; CIVIL LAW; COMPARATIVE LAW; COMPLICITY; COSTS; COURT; DAMAGES; GARNISHMENT; INJUNCTIONS; LITIGIOUSNESS; MENS REA; REFORMATION; RELIANCE; REPLEVIN; RESCISSION; RES JUDICATA; RESTRAINING ORDER; SPECIFIC PERFORMANCE; SUMMARY JUDGMENTS; VERDICTS

Cornell W. Clayton, *Professor of Political Science, Washington State University, Pullman*
ATTORNEY GENERAL; JUSTICE, UNITED STATES DEPARTMENT OF

Robert Clinton, *Department of Political Science, Southern Illinois University, Carbondale*
MARBURY V. MADISON; MCCULLOCH V. MARYLAND

Michael L. Closen, *Professor of Law, The John Marshall Law School, Chicago, Ill.*
EDUCATION, LEGAL

Wendy Collins Perdue, *Associate Dean for the J. D. Program and Professor of Law, Georgetown University Law Center, Washington, D.C.*
ERIE RAILROAD V. TOMPKINS

Stephen A. Conrad, *Professor of Law, Indiana University School of Law, Bloomington*
CITIZENSHIP

Saul Cornell, *Associate Professor of American History, Ohio State University, Columbus*
MILITIA MOVEMENT

Robert N. Covington, *Professor of Law, Vanderbilt University Law School, Nashville, Tenn.*
LABOR LAW: WORKPLACE ISSUES

Gregg Crane, *Assistant Professor of English, Miami University, Oxford, Ohio*
LAW AND LITERATURE, THEORY OF

Thomas E. Cronin, *President, Whitman College, Walla Walla, Wash.*
EXECUTIVE POWER (co-author)

Nathan M. Crystal, *Class of 1969 Professor of Professional Responsibility and Contract Law, University of South Carolina School of Law, Columbia*
ETHICS AND PROFESSIONAL RESPONSIBILITY, LEGAL

Michael Kent Curtis, *Professor of Law, Wake Forest University School of Law, Winston-Salem, N.C.*
FOURTEENTH AMENDMENT

Anthony D'Amato, *Leighton Professor of Law, Northwestern University, Evanston, Ill.*
INTERNATIONAL LAW

David Danelski, *Professor Emeritus, Stanford Law School, Stanford, Calif.*
DOUGLAS, WILLIAM ORVILLE

Stephen Daniels, *Senior Research Fellow, American Bar Foundation, Chicago, Ill.*
PERSONAL INJURY LAW PRACTICE

Sheldon Danziger, *Henry J. Meyer Collegiate Professor of Social Work and Public Policy, University of Michigan, Ann Arbor*
WELFARE (co-author)

Roger H. Davidson, *Professor Emeritus of Government and Politics, University of Maryland, College Park*
LEGISLATIVE POWER; LEGISLATIONAL LAWMAKING

Thomas Y. Davies, *Associate Professor of Law, University of Tennessee College of Law, Knoxville*
INCORPORATION DOCTRINE; SEARCH AND SEIZURE

Richard Delgado, *Jean Lindsley Professor of Law, University of Colorado School of Law, Boulder*
CRITICAL RACE THEORY (co-author); HATE CRIMES

Neal Devins, *Goodrich Professor of Law; Professor of Government, College of William and Mary, Williamsburg, Va.*
GOVERNMENT LAWYERS

John L. Diamond, *Professor of Law, University of California, Hastings College of the Law, San Francisco*
BURGLARY; LARCENY; TRESPASS

Leonard Dinnerstein, *Professor of History, University of Arizona, Tucson*
FRANK, LEO, CASE OF

Brian Dirck, *Assistant Professor of History, Anderson University, Anderson, Ind.*
CIVIL WAR, LEGAL IMPACT OF

Nelson C. Dometrius, *Professor of Political Science, Texas Tech University, Lubbock*
GOVERNOR

Nancy E. Dowd, *Chesterfield Smith Professor of Law, Fredric G. Levin College of Law, University of Florida, Gainesville*
GENDER AND LAW

Donald A. Downs, *Professor of Political Science, Law, and Journalism, University of Wisconsin, Madison*
ASSEMBLY AND ASSOCIATION; FAIR TRIAL, CRIMINAL (co-author)

Markus Dirk Dubber, *Professor of Law and Director, Buffalo Criminal Law Center, State University of New York Buffalo Law School*
CRIMINAL LAW; MODEL PENAL CODE; MORALS OFFENSES

Mary L. Dudziak, *Professor of Law and History, University of Southern California Law School, Los Angeles*
DISCRIMINATION

Lauren Dundes, *Assistant Professor of Sociology, Western Maryland College, Westminster*
JUVENILE LAW

Steven J. Eagle, *Professor of Law, George Mason University School of Law, Arlington, Va.*
PROPERTY; TAKINGS

Linda Henry Elrod, *Distinguished Professor of Law, Washburn University School of Law, Topeka, Kans.*
DIVORCE AND ANNULMENT; FAMILY LAW; FAMILY LAW PRACTICE

James W. Ely Jr., *Milton R. Underwood Professor of Law and Professor of History, Vanderbilt University Law School, Nashville, Tenn.*
COOLEY, THOMAS; FRANCHISE; JACKSON, ROBERT HOUGHWOUT; KENT, JAMES; LIABILITY; PROPERTY RIGHTS

Mark Engsberg, *Assistant Librarian for International Law, Lillian Goldman Law Library, Yale Law School, New Haven, Conn.*
COMPUTERIZED RESEARCH (co-author)

Lee Epstein, *Edward Mallinckrodt Distinguished University Professor of Political Science and Professor of Law, Washington University, St. Louis, Mo.*
GREGG V. GEORGIA

Samuel Estreicher, *Director, The Institute of Judicial Administration; Director, The Center for Labor and Employment; and Professor of Law, New York University*
LABOR LAW: LABOR RELATIONS

Robert K. Faulkner, *Professor of Political Science, Boston College, Chestnut Hill, Mass.*
BURR, AARON, TRIAL OF

Malcolm M. Feeley, *Claire Sanders Clements Dean's Chair, University of California School of Law, Berkeley (Boalt Hall)*
PRISONERS' RIGHTS

Floyd F. Feeney, *Professor of Law, University of California, Davis, School of Law*
AUTOMOBILES AND CRIME; INITIATIVE; REFERENDUM

Jay M. Feinman, *Distinguished Professor of Law, Rutgers School of Law, Camden, N.J.*
STRICT LIABILITY; TORTS

Stephen M. Feldman, *Professor of Law, College of Law, and Associate Member of Political Science, University of Tulsa, Okla.*
HISTORY AND LAW

Peter J. Ferrara, *Associate Professor of Law, George Mason University School of Law, Arlington, Va.*
ENTITLEMENTS

Paul Finkelman, *Chapman Distinguished Professor of Law, University of Tulsa College of Law, Okla.*
AMERICAN REVOLUTION, LEGAL IMPACT OF; BROWN, JOHN, TRIAL OF; CHASE, SALMON PORTLAND; DAVIS, JOHN W.; *DRED SCOTT* V. *SANDFORD*; MANN ACT; *NEW YORK TIMES CO.* V. *SULLIVAN*; SEGREGATION; SLAVERY, LAW OF; STORY, JOSEPH; TANEY, ROGER BROOKE; WARREN, EARL; ZENGER, PETER, TRIAL OF

Glenn W. Fisher, *Regents' Professor Emeritus, Wichita State University, Kans.*
TAXATION: PROPERTY TAXES

Louis Fisher, *Senior Specialist in Separation of Powers, Congressional Research Service, The Library of Congress, Washington, D.C.*
PRESIDENCY OF THE UNITED STATES; SEPARATION OF POWERS

Edith Elisabeth Flynn, *Professor Emeritus of Criminal Justice, Northeastern University, Lexington, Mass.*
PRISONS AND JAILS (co-author)

Lorien Foote, *Assistant Professor of History, University of Central Arkansas, Conway*
CHOATE, RUFUS

Richard S. Frase, *Benjamin N. Berger Professor of Law, University of Minnesota Law School, Minneapolis*
CRIMINAL PUNISHMENTS

Richard D. Freer, *Robert Howell Hall Professor of Law, Emory University, Atlanta, Ga.*
BUSINESS ORGANIZATIONS

Tony A. Freyer, *University Research Professor of History and Law, University of Alabama School of Law, Tuscaloosa*
BLACK, HUGO LAFAYETTE

Steven F. Friedell, *Professor of Law, Rutgers University Law School, Camden, N.J.*
ADMIRALTY AND MARITIME JURISDICTION

Barry Friedman, *Professor of Law, New York University School of Law*
PENNZOIL V. TEXACO

Lawrence A. Frolik, *Professor of Law, University of Pittsburgh School of Law, Penn.*
AGING AND THE LAW; DOMESTIC VIOLENCE: ELDER ABUSE; ELDERLAW

Kenneth S. Gallant, *Professor and Director of Clinical Programs, University of Arkansas at Little Rock William H. Bowen School of Law*
EX POST FACTO LAWS

Alfredo Garcia, *Professor of Law, St. Thomas University School of Law, Miami, Fla.*
BAIL, PRACTICE OF; FORFEITURE; SEARCH WARRANT

Martin R. Gardner, *Stienhart Foundation Professor of Law, University of Nebraska College of Law, Lincoln*
FELONY AND MISDEMEANOR

Leonard Garment, *Of Counsel, Verner, Liipfert, Bernhard, McPherson & Hand, Chartered, Washington, D.C.*
WATERGATE

M. David Gelfand, *Ashton Phelps Chair and Professor of Constitutional Law, Tulane University School of Law, New Orleans, La.*
TAXATION: SALES TAX (co-author)

Howard Gillman, *Professor of Political Science, University of Southern California, Los Angeles*
BUSH V. GORE

John Goldberg, *Professor of Law, Vanderbilt University Law School, Nashville, Tenn.*
BLACKSTONE'S *COMMENTARIES ON THE LAWS OF ENGLAND*; PALSGRAF V. LONG ISLAND RAILROAD COMPANY; TRAYNOR, ROGER

Sally F. Goldfarb, *Associate Professor, Rutgers University School of Law, Camden, N.J.*
MALPRACTICE

Leslie Goldstein, *Department of Political Science, University of Delaware, Newark*
ROE V. WADE

Mark A. Graber, *Assistant Professor of Government and Politics, University of Maryland, College Park*
COURT SYSTEMS; PRIVILEGES AND IMMUNITIES

Mark F. Grady, *Dean and Professor of Law, George Mason University School of Law, Arlington, Va.*
FAULT LIABILITY

Ronald C. Griffin, *Professor of Law, Washburn University School of Law, Topeka, Kans.*
ALCOHOL, TOBACCO, AND FIREARMS, BUREAU OF

Joanna L. Grossman, *Associate Professor of Law, Hofstra University, Hempstead, N.Y.*
HARASSMENT; SEXUAL HARASSMENT

Lakshman D. Guruswamy, *Professor of Law, School of Law, University of Colorado, Boulder*
ENVIRONMENTAL LAW: INTERNATIONAL ENVIRONMENTAL LAW IN THE U.S.

Kermit L. Hall, *President, Utah State University, Logan*
HISTORY OF AMERICAN LAW: ANTEBELLUM THROUGH RECONSTRUCTION (1801–1877); HUGHES, CHARLES EVANS; LOCKWOOD, BELVA; MANSFIELD, ARABELLA; STONE, HARLAN FISKE

Melinda Gann Hall, *Professor of Political Science, Michigan State University, East Lansing*
COURTS, UNITED STATES: STATE AND LOCAL COURTS

Leslie J. Harris, *Dorothy Kliks Fones Professor of Law, University of Oregon, Eugene*
CHILDREN'S RIGHTS; MARRIAGE; SPOUSAL SUPPORT

Roger E. Hartley, *Assistant Professor of Public Administration and Policy, University of Arizona, Tucson*
ARBITRATION AND MEDIATION

Grant M. Hayden, *Associate Professor of Law, Hofstra Law School, Hempstead, N.Y.*
VOTING AND POLITICAL PARTICIPATION

Thomas Lee Hazen, *Cary C. Boshamer Distinguished Professor of Law, University of North Carolina School of Law, Chapel Hill*
SECURITIES LAW

Steven A. Hetcher, *Associate Professor of Law, Vanderbilt University Law School, Nashville, Tenn.*
PROPERTY, INTELLECTUAL

Milton Heumann, *Professor and Chair, Department of Political Science, Rutgers University, New Brunswick, N.J.*
PROSECUTOR (co-author)

Walter L. Hixson, *Professor of History, University of Akron, Ohio*
BORDEN, LIZZIE, CASE OF; LINDBERGH KIDNAPPING CASE; SIMPSON, O.J., TRIALS OF

Charles F. Hobson, *Editor, The Papers of John Marshall, Omohundro Institute of Early American History and Culture, College of William and Mary, Williamsburg, Va.*
MARSHALL, JOHN

Michael H. Hoeflich, *John H. and John M. Kane Distinguished Professor of Law, University of Kansas School of Law, Lawrence*
GERMAN LEGAL PHILOSOPHY, INFLUENCE OF; HOLMES, OLIVER WENDELL, JR.; JURISPRUDENCE, AMERICAN: EUROPEAN INFLUENCE AND 19TH CENTURY AMERICAN JURISPRUDENCE; NATURAL LAW THEORY

Peter Hoffer, *Professor of History, University of Georgia, Athens*
ABORTION AND REPRODUCTIVE DECISIONS; HISTORY OF AMERICAN LAW: COLONIAL PERIOD; HUTCHINSON, ANN, TRIALS OF; SALEM WITCHCRAFT TRIALS

Williamjames Hull Hoffer, *Golieb Fellow, New York University School of Law*
FRANKFURTER, FELIX; PROMISSORY ESTOPPEL

Herbert Hovenkamp, *Professor of Law and History, University of Iowa, Iowa City*
DUE PROCESS: SUBSTANTIVE; ECONOMICS AND LAW

Philip K. Howard, *Vice-Chairman, Covington & Burling, New York, N.Y.*
HISTORY OF AMERICAN LAW: SINCE 1968

Timothy Huebner, *Assistant Professor of History, Rhodes College, Memphis, Tenn.*
CALHOUN, JOHN C.; JUDGE; REGIONALISM

N. E. H. Hull, *Distinguished Professor of Law, Rutgers University School of Law, Camden, N.J.*
AMERICAN LAW INSTITUTE; JURISPRUDENCE, AMERICAN: THE REVOLT AGAINST FORMALISM; LLEWELLYN, KARL NICKERSON; POUND, (NATHAN) ROSCOE

John P. Husmann, *Ph.D. candidate in history, University of Nebraska, Lincoln*
CHEROKEE NATION V. GEORGIA (co-author); NATIVE AMERICANS AND THE LAW: HISTORY (co-author)

Gregg Ivers, *Professor of Government, American University, Washington, D.C.*
CHURCH AND STATE

Mark Weston Janis, *William F. Starr Professor of Law, University of Connecticut School of Law, Hartford*
HUMAN RIGHTS, INTERNATIONAL LAW AND

Robert H. Jerry II, *Floyd R. Gibson Missouri Endowed Professor of Law, University of Missouri-Columbia School of Law*
INSURANCE

Robert D. Joffe, *Presiding Partner, Cravath, Swaine & Moore, New York, N.Y.*
CRAVATH, PAUL DRENNAN

John W. Johnson, *Professor and Head, Department of History, University of Northern Iowa, Cedar Falls*
THAYER, JAMES BRADLEY

Kevin R. Johnson, *Associate Dean for Academic Affairs and Professor of Law and Chicana/o Studies, University of California, Davis, School of Law*
IMMIGRATION LAW PRACTICE

Daniel Kanstroom, *Professor of Law and Director, Boston College Immigration and Asylum Project, Boston College Law School, Newton, Mass.*
IMMIGRATION

Andrew Karmen, *Professor of Sociology, John Jay College of Criminal Justice, New York, N.Y.*
VICTIMLESS CRIME

Ethan Katsh, *Professor of Legal Studies, University of Massachusetts, Amherst*
TECHNOLOGY AND LAW

S. Blair Kauffman, *Law Librarian and Professor of Law, Yale Law School, New Haven, Conn.*
COMPUTERIZED RESEARCH (co-author)

Andrew L. Kaufman, *Charles Stebbins Fairchild Professor of Law, Harvard Law School, Cambridge, Mass.*
CARDOZO, BENJAMIN NATHAN

Robert J. Kelly, *Broeklundian Professor, Emeritus, Brooklyn College and the Graduate Center, City University of New York*
ORGANIZED CRIME

Paul Kens, *Professor of Political Science, Southwest Texas State University, Austin*
FIELD, DAVID DUDLEY, JR.; FIELD, STEPHEN JOHNSON; LOCHNER V. NEW YORK

Judith Kilpatrick, *Associate Professor of Law, University of Arkansas School of Law, Fayetteville*
ASSOCIATION OF TRIAL LAWYERS OF AMERICA

Andrew J. King, *Professor of Law, University of Maryland School of Law, Baltimore*
WEBSTER, DANIEL

Nancy Jean King, *Professor of Law, Vanderbilt University Law School, Nashville, Tenn.*
CRIMINAL PROCEDURE, FEDERAL RULES OF

Kit Kinports, *Professor of Law, University of Illinois College of Law, Champaign*
SEX OFFENSES

Frederic L. Kirgis, *Law School Association Alumni Professor, Washington and Lee University School of Law, Lexington, Va.*
UNITED NATIONS, U.S. OBLIGATIONS TO

Neil G. Kornze, *London School of Economics*
EXECUTIVE POWER (co-author)

Candace Saari Kovacic-Fleischer, *Professor of Law, Washington College of Law at American University, Washington, D.C.*
REMEDIES: LEGAL AND EQUITABLE

Margaret Bull Kovera, *Associate Professor of Psychology, Florida International University, Miami*
PSYCHOLOGY AND LAW

Stefan H. Krieger, *Professor of Law, Hofstra University School of Law, Hempstead, N.Y.*
LEGAL REASONING

Daniel R. Krislov, *Professor of Political Science, University of Minnesota, Minneapolis*
HABEAS CORPUS

Samuel Krislov, *Professor Emeritus of Political Science and Law, University of Minnesota, Minneapolis*
GOVERNANCE

Ronald J. Krotoszynski Jr., *Ethan Allen Faculty Fellow and Associate Professor of Law, Washington and Lee University School of Law, Lexington, Va.*
CIVIL DISOBEDIENCE

John Q. La Fond, *Edward A. Smith/Missouri Chair in Law, the Constitution, and Society, University of Missouri-Kansas City School of Law*
CRIMINAL LAW PRINCIPLES: DEFENSE PRINCIPLES; CRIMINAL LAW PRINCIPLES: LEGALITY PRINCIPLES

David J. Langum, *Professor of Law, Cumberland School of Law of Samford University, Birmingham, Ala.*
JACKSON, HOWELL EDMUNDS; KUNSTLER, WILLIAM

Edward Larson, *Richard B. Russell Professor of History and Law, University of Georgia, Athens*
DARROW, CLARENCE; SCOPES TRIAL

Stanley K. Laughlin Jr., *Professor of Law, Ohio State University, Columbus*
TERRITORIES AND POSSESSIONS

Robert Laurence, *Robert A. Leflar Professor of Law, University of Arkansas School of Law, Fayetteville*
NATIVE AMERICANS AND THE LAW: NATIVE AMERICAN LAW AND TRIBAL SOVEREIGNTY

Jeffrey S. Lehman, *Dean of the Law School and Professor of Public Policy, University of Michigan, Ann Arbor*
WELFARE (co-author)

Kevin B. Leonard, *Northwestern University, University Archives, Evanston, Ill.*
WIGMORE, JOHN HENRY

James P. Levine, *Dean of Graduate Studies and Research, John Jay College of Criminal Justice, The City University of New York*
JURY: JURIES; JURY: RIGHT TO A JURY TRIAL

Sanford Levinson, *W. St. John Garwood and W. St. John Jr. Regents Chair in Law, University of Texas Law School, Austin*
ARMS, RIGHT TO BEAR

Janet K. Levit, *Assistant Professor of Law, University of Tulsa School of Law, Okla.*
GAMBLING; SEDITION

Anthony Lewis, *Columnist,* The New York Times
GIDEON V. WAINWRIGHT

Tobe Liebert, *Director of Public Services, Tarlton Law Library, University of Texas School of Law, Austin*
PUBLISHING, LAW (co-author)

Michael S Lief, *Senior Deputy District Attorney, Ventura County, California*
ORATORY, LEGAL

Margit Livingston, *Professor of Law, DePaul University College of Law, Chicago, Ill.*
CONTEMPT, CIVIL AND CRIMINAL

Gordon Lloyd, *Professor of Public Policy, School of Public Policy, Pepperdine University, Malibu, Calif.*
BILLS OF RIGHTS

John E. Lopatka, *Alumni Professor of Law, University of South Carolina School of Law, Columbia*
IBM LITIGATION

George I. Lovell, *Assistant Professor of Political Science, University of Washington, Seattle*
LEGISLATIVE POWER: LEGISLATION, FEDERAL

L. Randolph Lowry, *Director, Straus Institute for Dispute Resolution and Professor of Law, Pepperdine University School of Law, Malibu, Calif.*
NEGOTIATION

Jonathan Lurie, *Professor of History, Rutgers University, Newark, N.J.*
MILITARY JUSTICE

Donald S. Lutz, *Department of Political Science, University of Houston, Tex.*
CONSTITUTIONS, UNITED STATES; LIBERTY; SOVEREIGNTY

Hugh Macgill, *Professor of Law, University of Connecticut School of Law, Hartford*
COURT PACKING; *SWIFT V. TYSON*

Thomas C. Mackey, *Associate Professor of History, University of Louisville, Ky.*
TAFT, WILLIAM HOWARD

Tayyab Mahmud, *Professor of Law, Cleveland-Marshall College of Law, Cleveland State University, Ohio*
TREASON

John Anthony Maltese, *Associate Professor, Department of Political Science, University of Georgia, Athens*
RELIGION

Paul Marcus, *Haynes Professor of Law, College of William and Mary, Williamsburg, Va.*
CONSPIRACY

Richard L. Marcus, *Horace O. Coil ('57) Chair in Litigation Distinguished Professor of Law, University of*

California, Hastings College of the Law, San Francisco
COMPLEX LITIGATION

James P. May, *Professor of Law, Washington College of Law, American University, Washington, D.C.*
ANTITRUST LAW

David N. Mayer, *Professor of Law and History, Capital University Law School, Columbus, Ohio*
JEFFERSON, THOMAS

Mary Brigid McManamon, *Associate Professor of Law, Widener University School of Law, Wilmington, Del.*
VANDERBILT, ARTHUR T.

Genna Rae McNeil, *Professor of History, University of North Carolina, Chapel Hill*
HOUSTON, CHARLES H.

Daniel J. Meador, *James Monroe Professor of Law Emeritus, University of Virginia, Charlottesville*
PROCEDURE, COURT

R. Shep Melnick, *Thomas P. O'Neill, Jr. Professor of American Politics, Boston College, Bedford, Mass.*
REGULATION

Carrie Menkel-Meadow, *Professor of Law, Georgetown University Law Center, Washington, D.C.*
ALTERNATIVE DISPUTE RESOLUTION; LAWYERS

Elizabeth B. Mensch, *Professor of Law, State University of New York, Buffalo, Law School*
JURISPRUDENCE, AMERICAN: 1945–1970

Roy M. Mersky, *Harry M. Reasoner Regents Chair in Law and Director of Research, University of Texas School of Law, Jamail Center for Legal Research, Austin*
PUBLISHING, LAW (co-author)

Linda R. Meyer, *Professor of Law, Quninnipiac School of Law, Hamden, Conn.*
PROCEDURE, CRIMINAL: PRETRIAL

Susan Gluck Mezey, *Professor of Political Science, Loyola University of Chicago*
COURTS, UNITED STATES: JUVENILE COURTS

Matthew J. Middleton, *Legal scholar*
LEGISLATIVE POWER: LEGISLATION, STATE AND LOCAL

Gary Minda, *Professor of Law, Brooklyn Law School, New York*
MARXIST AND POST-MARXIST THEORIES OF LAW

Joel Mintz, *Professor of Law, Nova Southeastern University Shepard Broad Law Center, Fort Lauderdale, Fla.*
TAXATION: SALES TAXES (co-author)

Jennifer L. Mnookin, *Associate Professor of Law, University of Virginia School of Law, Charlottesville*
SCIENCE AND LAW

Carl C. Monk, *Executive Vice President and Executive Director, Association of American Law Schools, Washington, D.C.*
ASSOCIATION OF AMERICAN LAW SCHOOLS

Thomas H. Morawetz, *Tapping Reeve Professor of Law and Ethics, University of Connecicut School of Law, Hartford*
HOMICIDE

Myron Moskovitz, *Professor of Law, Golden Gate University, San Francisco, Calif.*
INTERROGATION AND CONFESSION; LINEUP; *MAPP V. OHIO; MIRANDA V. ARIZONA*

Thomas Moyer, *Chief Justice, Ohio Supreme Court*
EXTRALEGALITY

John F. Murphy, *Villanova University School of Law, Villanova, Pa.*
TERRORISM

John E. B. Myers, *Professor of Law, University of the Pacific, Sacramento, Calif.*
DOMESTIC VIOLENCE: CHILD ABUSE

James A. R. Nafziger, *Thomas B. Stoel Professor of Law, Willamette University College of Law, Salem, Oreg.*
EXECUTIVE AGREEMENTS; TREATIES

Richard A. Nagareda, *Professor of Law, Vanderbilt University Law School, Nashville, Tenn.*
TOBACCO LITIGATION

Eva Nilsen, *Associate Clinical Professor, Boston University School of Law, Mass.*
DRUGS, ILLEGAL

Raymond T. Nimmer, *University of Houston Law Center*
BANKRUPTCY: BUSINESS; BANKRUPTCY: PERSONAL

Michael F. Noone, *Professor of Law, The Catholic University of America, Columbus School of Law, Washington, D.C.*
MARTIAL LAW

David M. O'Brien, *Leone Reaves and George Spicer Professor, University of Virginia, Charlottesville*
CONSTITUTIONAL COMMENTATORS; SUPREME COURT OF THE UNITED STATES

A. Samuel Oddi, *Giles Sutherland Rich Professor in Intellectual Property, University of Akron School of Law, Ohio*
PATENT LAW PRACTICE

Ladislas Örsy, *Professor Emeritus of Canon Law, The Catholic University of America; Visiting Professor of Law, Georgetown University, Washington, D.C.*
CANON LAW

John V. Orth, *William Rand Kenan, Jr., Professor of Law, University of North Carolina at Chapel Hill*
COMMON LAW; *COMMONWEALTH V. HUNT;* PROBATE; TRUST; WILL

William H. Page, *Marshall M. Criser Eminent Scholar, University of Florida, Levin College of Law, Gainesville*
AT&T LITIGATION

David Ray Papke, *Professor of Law, Marquette University Law School, Milwaukee, Wisc.*
CODIFICATION; DETECTIVE; LAW DAY

Margaret L. Paris, *Associate Professor of Law, University of Oregon School of Law, Eugene*
ARREST

Wendy E. Parmet, *Professor of Law, Northeastern University School of Law, Newton, Mass.*
HEALTH LAW

David F. Partlett, *Dean and Professor of Law, Washington and Lee University School of Law, Lexington, Va.*
EQUITY

John J. Patrick, *Professor, School of Education, Indiana University, Bloomington*
BURGER, WARREN EARL

Dennis M. Patterson, *Distinguished Professor of Law, Rutgers University, School of Law, Camden, N.J.*
COMMERCIAL LAW; JURISPRUDENCE, AMERICAN: 1970–PRESENT; STATUTE OF FRAUDS

Robert V. Percival, *University of Maryland Law School, Baltimore*
ENVIRONMENTAL LAW: UNITED STATES ENVIRONMENTAL LAW

Joseph M. Perillo, *Distinguished Professor of Law, Fordham University School of Law, New York, N.Y.*
WILLISTON, SAMUEL R.

Carl A. Pierce, *Associate Professor of Law, University of Tennessee College of Law, Knoxville*
BAR ASSOCIATIONS; BAR EXAMINATION

Tamara Piety, *Visiting Assistant Professor, University of Tulsa College of Law, Okla.*
BURDEN OF PROOF, CRIMINAL AND CIVIL; ROBBERY; THEFT

Brian Pinaire, *Ph.D. candidate, Department of Political Science, Rutgers University, New Brunswick, N.J.*
PROSECUTOR (co-author)

Daniel Pinello, *Associate Professor of Government, John Jay College of Criminal Justice of the City University of New York*
HOMOSEXUALITY AND THE LAW

Ronald M. Pipkin, *Professor of Legal Studies, University of Massachusetts, Amherst*
LAW AND SOCIETY ASSOCIATION

Helle Porsdam, *Associate Professor of American Studies, University of Southern Denmark*
ARTS, POPULAR CULTURE, AND LAW

John W. Poulos, *Professor of Law, University of California, Davis, Law School*
ARSON

Walter F. Pratt Jr., *Associate Dean and Professor of Law, Notre Dame Law School, Notre Dame, Ind.*
BALDWIN, SIMEON; DOE, CHARLES; RUFFIN, THOMAS; SHAW, LEMUEL

Stephen B. Presser, *Raoul Berger Professor of Legal History, Northwestern University School of Law, Chicago, Ill.*
CHASE, SAMUEL, IMPEACHMENT TRIAL OF; CORPORATIONS: FOR-PROFIT CORPORATIONS; CORPORATIONS: NONPROFIT CORPORATIONS; SEDITION ACT TRIALS

David Kenneth Pye, *Ph.D. candidate in history, University of California, San Diego*
NATIONAL BAR ASSOCIATION

Eric Rakowski, *Halbach Professor of Trust & Estates Law, University of California at Berkeley School of Law*
TAXATION: ESTATE AND GIFT TAXES

Alison Dundes Renteln, *Associate Professor of Political Science, University of Southern California, Los Angeles*
ANTHROPOLOGY AND LAW; CULTURE AND LAW; CUSTOM; RACE AND ETHNICITY

Glenn H. Reynolds, *University of Tennessee College of Law, Knoxville*
SPACE LAW

Donald Ritchie, *Associate Historian, U.S. Senate Historical Office*
GOVERNMENT, UNITED STATES

Gary Roberts, *Tulane University Law School*
SPORTS LAW

Thomas E. Roberts, *Professor of Law, Wake Forest University School of Law, Winston-Salem, N.C.*
WATER RIGHTS

Lindsay Robertson, *Associate Professor of Law, History & Native American Studies, University of Oklahoma College of Law, Tulsa*
NATIVE AMERICANS AND THE LAW: NATIVE AMERICANS UNDER CURRENT UNITED STATES LAW

David W. Rohde, *Professor of Political Science, Michigan State University, East Lansing*
LEGISLATURES, STRUCTURE OF

Gerald N. Rosenberg, *Associate Professor of Political Science and Lecturer in Law, University of Chicago, Ill.*
BROWN V. BOARD OF EDUCATION

Arthur I. Rosett, *Professor of Law, University of California, Los Angeles, School of Law*
PLEA BARGAINING (co-author)

William G. Ross, *Professor of Law, Cumberland School of Law of Samford University, Birmingham, Ala.*
FIRMS, LAW; HAYMARKET TRIALS; LEOPOLD AND LOEB CASE; RICO; SACCO AND VANZETTI CASE

Nicolas Rostow, *General Counsel and Senior Policy Advisor to the U.S. Permanent Representative to the United Nations; Former Charles H. Stockton Professor International Law, U.S. Naval War College, Newport, R.I.*
ARMS CONTROL LAW

Mitchel P. Roth, *Associate Professor of Criminal Justice, Sam Houston State University, Huntsville, Tex.*
POLICE

Cristina M. Ruggiero
FAIR TRIAL, CRIMINAL (co-author)

Catherine E. Rymph, *Assistant Professor, University of Missouri, Columbia*
EQUAL RIGHTS AMENDMENT

Michael J. Saks, *Professor of Law, Arizona State University College of Law, Tempe*
EVIDENCE

Rebecca Mae Salokar, *Associate Professor of Political Science, Florida International University, Miami*
SOLICITOR GENERAL

Austin Sarat, *William Nelson Cromwell Professor of Jurisprudence & Political Science, Amherst College, Amherst, Mass.*
CRUEL AND UNUSUAL PUNISHMENT

Stuart A. Scheingold, *Professor Emeritus of Political Science, University of Washington, Seattle*
CAUSE LAWYERS

John Henry Schlegel, *Professor of Law, State University of New York, Buffalo, School of Law*
CRITICAL LEGAL STUDIES; LEGAL REALISM

Lorraine A. Schmall, *Northern Illinois University College of Law, De Kalb*
PARDON, REPRIEVE, AND COMMUTATION (co-author)

Patrick Schmidt, *John Adams Research Fellow, Centre for Socio-Legal Studies and Nuffield College, University of Oxford*
BAIL BONDSMEN; IMPEACHMENT

Howard Schweber, *Assistant Professor of Political Science, University of Wisconsin, Madison*
AFFIRMATIVE ACTION

Robert A. Sedler, *Distinguished Professor of Law and Walter Gibbs Chair in Civil Rights and Civil Liberties, Wayne State University, Detroit, Mich.*
CIVIL RIGHTS LEGISLATION

John E. Semonche, *Professor of History, University of North Carolina at Chapel Hill*
CIVIL RIGHTS AND CIVIL LIBERTIES

Edward F. Sherman, *Professor of Law, Tulane University School of Law, New Orleans, La.*
CLASS ACTIONS

Gene R. Shreve, *Richard S. Melvin Professor of Law, School of Law, Indiana University, Bloomington*
PROCEDURE, CIVIL: APPEALS; PROCEDURE, CIVIL: PRETRIAL; PROCEDURE, CIVIL: TRIAL

Stephen Siegel, *Professor of Law, DePaul University College of Law, Chicago, Ill.*
PROSSER, WILLIAM; SOCIOLOGICAL JURISPRUDENCE

Norman I. Silber, *Professor of Law, Hofstra University Law School, Hempstead, N.Y.*
CONSUMER LAW

Susan S. Silbey, *Professor of Sociology and Anthropology, Massachusetts Institute of Technology, Cambridge*
LAW AND SOCIETY MOVEMENT

David A. Sklansky, *Professor of Law, University of California, Los Angeles, School of Law*
PLEA BARGAINING (co-author); PRIVATE SECURITY SERVICES

Christopher Slobogin, *University of Florida College of Law, Gainesville*
POLICE PROCEDURES

Lionel S. Sobel, *Editor,* Entertainment Law Reporter
ENTERTAINMENT LAW

Ann Southworth, *Professor of Law, Case Western Reserve University School of Law, Cleveland, Ohio*
LEGAL SERVICES, PROVISION OF; NATIONAL LAWYERS GUILD

Clyde Spillenger, *University of California, Los Angeles, School of Law*
SPEECH AND THE PRESS, FREEDOM OF

Jean Stefancic, *Senior Research Associate in Law, University of Colorado School of Law, Boulder*
CRITICAL RACE THEORY (co-author)

Otis H. Stephens, *Professor and Resident Scholar of Constitutional Law, University of Tennessee College of Law, Knoxville*
EQUAL PROTECTION

James R. Stoner, *Associate Professor of Political Science, Louisiana State University, Baton Rouge*
STATES' RIGHTS

Rennard Strickland, *Dean and Philip H. Knight Professor of Law, University of Oregon School of Law, Eugene*
NATIVE AMERICAN REMOVAL; *WORCESTER V. GEORGIA*

Philippa, Strum, *Director, Division of United States Studies, Woodrow Wilson International Center for Scholars, Washington, D.C.*
BRANDEIS, LOUIS DEMBITZ; PRIVACY

Charles A. Sullivan, *Professor of Law, Seton Hall Law School, Newark, N.J.*
DISABILITIES LAW

Robert Samuel Summers, *McRoberts Research Professor of Law, Cornell University Law School, Ithaca, N.Y.*
CONTRACT LAW

Symeon Symeonides, *Dean and Professor of Law, Willamette University College of Law, Salem, Oreg.*
CONFLICT OF LAWS

Susette Talarico, *Professor of Political Science and Director, Criminal Justice Studies, University of Georgia, Athens*
COUNSEL, RIGHT TO

Eric L. Talley, *Professor of Law, University of Southern California Law School, Los Angeles*
LAW AND ECONOMICS, THEORY OF

Brian Z. Tamanaha, *St. John's University Law School*
SOCIOLOGY AND LAW

G. Alan Tarr, *Director, Center for State Constitutional Studies, Rutgers University, Camden, N J*
SUPREME COURTS, STATE

Andrew Eric Taslitz, *Professor of Law, Howard University School of Law, Washington, D.C.*
CRIMINAL LAW PRACTICE; MOB VIOLENCE AND VIGILANTISM

Melissa L. Tatum, *Associate Professor of Law; Co-Director, Native American Law Center, University of Tulsa College of Law, Okla.*
INDIGENOUS PEOPLE'S RIGHTS, INTERNATIONAL LAW OF

Jon C. Teaford, *Professor of History, Purdue University, West Lafayette, Ind.*
MAYOR

Steven Theide
PARDON, REPRIEVE, AND COMMUTATION (co-author)

Athan G. Theoharis, *Professor of History, Marquette University, Milwaukee, Wisc.*
FEDERAL BUREAU OF INVESTIGATION

Joseph P. Tomain, *Dean and Nippert Professor of Law, University of Cincinnati College of Law, Ohio*
ENERGY AND NATURAL RESOURCES LAW

John O. Tomasi, *Professor of Political Science, Brown University, Providence, R.I.*
JUSTICE

Mark Tunick, *Associate Professor of Political Science, The Honors College, Florida Atlantic University, Jupiter*
ETHICS, MORALITY, AND LAW

Mark Tushnet, *Carmack Waterhouse Professor of Constitutional Law, Georgetown University Law Center, Washington, D.C.*
MARSHALL, THURGOOD

Melvin I. Urofsky, *Professor of History and Public Policy, and Director, Doctoral Program in Public Policy and Administration, Center for Policy Study, Virginia Commonwealth University, Richmond*
HAND, LEARNED; HISTORY OF AMERICAN LAW: GREAT DEPRESSION TO 1968; RIGHT TO DIE

Sandra F. VanBurkleo, *Associate Professor of History and Adjunct Professor of Law, Wayne State University, Detroit, Mich.*
ANTHONY, SUSAN B., TRIAL OF; JAY, JOHN

James Etienne Viator, *Professor of Law, Loyola University School of Law, New Orleans, La.*
SOCIAL DIMENSIONS OF LAW

John R. Vile, *Department of Political Science, Middle Tennessee State University, Murpheesboro*
BAKER V. CARR; CONSTITUTIONAL AMENDMENTS

Kathleen Waits, *Associate Professor of Law, University of Tulsa College of Law, Okla.*
DOMESTIC VIOLENCE: PARTNER ABUSE

Christopher Waldrep, *Jamie and Phyllis Pasker Professor of History, San Francisco State University, Calif.*
BLACK CODES; SCOTTSBORO TRIALS

David Weiner, *Legal scholar*
JAPANESE INTERNMENT

Richard Weisberg, *Floersheimer Professor of Constitutional Law, Cardozo Law School, Yeshiva University, New York, N.Y*
LITERATURE AND LAW

Stephen J. Wermeil, *Associate Professor of Law, American University, Washington College of Law, Washington, D.C.*
BRENNAN, WILLIAM J., JR.

Seth Whitaker
ELECTRIC CHAIR; SHERIFF

Charles H. Whitebread II, *George T. and Harriet E. Pfleger Professor of Law, University of Southern California Law School, Los Angeles*
PROCEDURE, CRIMINAL: APPEALS; PROCEDURE, CRIMINAL: TRIAL

Robert Whitman, *Professor of Law, University of Connecticut School of Law, Hartford*
CORBIN, ARTHUR

Ralph U. Whitten, *Professor Law, Creighton University Law School, Omaha, Nebr.*
FULL FAITH AND CREDIT CLAUSE

William Wiecek, *Syracuse University College of Law*
FRANK, JEROME

Lou Falkner Williams, *Associate Professor of History, Kansas State University, Manhattan*
PLESSY V. FERGUSON

John R. Wunder, *Professor, Department of History, University of Nebraska, Lincoln*
CHEROKEE NATION V. GEORGIA (co-author); NATIVE AMERICANS AND THE LAW: HISTORY (co-author)

David Alistair Yalof, *Assistant Professor of History, University of Connecticut, Storrs*
BAIL; COURT OFFICERS; DOUBLE JEOPARDY; INDEPENDENT COUNSEL; MEDICAL EXAMINER; SELF-INCRIMINATION, PRIVILEGE AGAINST

Tinsley Yarbrough, *Professor of Political Science, East Carolina University, Greenville, N.C.*
HARLAN, JOHN MARSHALL; HARLAN, JOHN MARSHALL II

Christopher S. Yoo, *Assistant Professor of Law, Vanderbilt University Law School, Nashville, Tenn.*
CLERK, LAW

Margaret Zahn, *Dean, College of Humanities and Social Sciences, North Carolina State University, Raleigh*
PRISONS AND JAILS (co-author)

Jamil Zainaldin, *President, Georgia Humanities Council, Atlanta*
AMERICAN BAR ASSOCIATION

Rex J. Zedalis, *Professor of Law and Director, Comparative and International Law Center, University of Tulsa, Okla.*
FOREIGN TRADE AND INVESTMENT LAW; WAR, LAW OF

Nicholas S. Zeppos, *Professor of Law, Vanderbilt University Law School, Nashville, Tenn.*
ADMINISTRATIVE LAW JUDGE; LEGISLATIVE VETO

Franklin E. Zimring, *William G. Simon Professor of Law and Director, Earl Warren Legal Institute, University of California School of Law, Berkeley*
CAPITAL PUNISHMENT

Matthew Zingraff, *Associate Dean for Research and Professor of Sociology, College of Humanities and Social Sciences, North Carolina State University, Raleigh*
HIGHWAY PATROL; INVESTIGATION, STATE BUREAUS OF

Hiller B. Zobel
ADAMS, JOHN; BOSTON MASSACRE TRIALS

Todd J. Zywicki, *Associate Professor of Law, George Mason University School of Law, Arlington, Va.*
CORPORATE LAW PRACTICE

A

ABORTION AND REPRODUCTIVE DECISIONS. Abortion law in the United states is the product of a unique legal, political, religious, and social history. In other countries today, abortion is widely practiced. The state either does not take such interest in it, or simply regulates abortions to protect the *health and welfare of the mother. In the United States, by contrast, the focus of the law has long been the fetus rather than the woman, the subject is one of major political importance, and official intervention has resulted in a bewildering variety of state and federal rulings and laws.

Until the middle of the nineteenth century, in line with the long-standing notion that the victim in an abortion was the woman, abortion or attempted abortion that harmed or killed the pregnant woman was a statutory offense in a handful of states including Connecticut, Missouri, and New York. Conviction required proof that the woman was actually pregnant, but was hard to obtain if the woman had solicited or consented to the abortion. If a fetus was born and then died as the result of the abortion or attempted abortion, the abortionist was liable to criminal punishment as well, but the fetus was not considered a person in law or in *religion until quickening (about twenty-four weeks into the pregnancy) or in modern terms, viability. In 1828, New York law also provided the first "doctor's law" regarding abortion, allowing therapeutic abortions when the doctor and patient agreed that her health was at stake in the continued pregnancy.

A campaign by doctors and religious leaders in the middle of the nineteenth century, along with an apparent rise in the activity of abortionists and those who sold abortifacients, convinced state legislatures to shift the emphasis of the law. In 1845, New York State was the first to change its laws to penalize a woman who sought an abortion and to indicate that the fetus was the victim of the offense. Other states soon followed suit. The new laws also dropped the distinction based on quickening, but most states retained some version of the therapeutic exception, at least to save the life of a woman when the pregnancy endangered it.

In 1873, the federal government made any attempt to send information on abortion or abortifacients through the mails a crime. The law, framed by New York reformer Anthony Comstock, likened all forms of birth control to abortion and barred the former as well as the latter. Many states passed their own "Comstock" laws, forbidding all but doctors from offering counsel on birth control of any kind. Some states, notably Connecticut, even forbade doctors from so advising their patients. By the beginning of the twentieth century no state allowed abortion at will.

The laws against abortion did not prevent women from attempting to end their pregnancies, particularly when the pregnancy was out of wedlock, the woman or her *family could not support the child, the pregnancy was the result of rape or incest, or the mother's health was endangered by the pregnancy.

Often, the woman herself attempted the abortion. Poverty was the greatest cause of such attempted abortions, and during the Great Depression of 1929–39, experts estimated that over six hundred thousand abortions took place each year in the United States. Although authorities refused to reform the laws to allow these women legal and safe abortions, their attitude on birth control changed. In 1936, over the objections of some doctors and the Roman Catholic church, the American Medical Association urged states to make birth control legal. In *United States* v. *One Package* (1935), the federal courts ruled that the Comstock laws against the mailing of birth control information were unconstitutional. By the end of the 1930s, there were hundreds of birth control clinics operating in the country. The last state law against the dissemination of birth control information fell in *Griswold* v. *Connecticut* (1965). A 7–2 majority of the U.S. Supreme Court found that the right of married couples to decide whether and when to have children was protected by the Ninth Amendment, the *Fourteenth Amendment, and the "penumbras" of the rights in the other provisions of the *Bill of Rights. *Privacy in reproductive decisions was extended to unmarried people in *Baird* v. *Eisenstadt* (1972).

The privacy right did not yet extend to abortions, but many of the leaders of the birth control movement, as well as doctors who treated women who were harmed during abortions and lawyers who saw the impossibility of enforcing the antiabortion statutes as they stood wanted reform. In 1962, the *American Law Institute's draft *Model Penal Code proposed an extension of the therapeutic exception to all women whose health might be harmed by continued pregnancy, as well as those women whose pregnancies had resulted from incest or rape. Attempts to adopt some version of the code in state laws languished until 1967, when Colorado acceded, followed thereafter by Maryland, Georgia, and California. Typically, these states required a panel of doctors to agree that the procedure was medically appropriate (see MEDICINE AND LAW). In 1970, New York, whose legislature had introduced the penalization of women and the concept that human life began with conception, narrowly passed a bill that allowed abortion at will up to the twenty-fourth week of pregnancy. Other states, like Texas, rejected all attempts at reform.

Not all attempts to legalize abortion came from doctors or lawyers, nor were they directed at the legislative process. The National Organization for Women, created in 1966, made abortion rights a major cause. So did the so-called "women's liberation movement." In the late 1960s, these advocates of women's right to abortions selected the word "choice" to promote their cause. The word became the centerpiece of a new paradigm of women's place in the law, in which women's rights grew out of women's experiences, and therein the differences between women and men, rather than being privileges granted by men. Feminists argued that access to a safe, legal abortion was all about choice, about women's right to determine what happened inside their own bodies. Women leaders of the movement joined with doctors and birth control clinics to file federal lawsuits against state abortion laws. These suits argued that the abortion laws were vague and overbroad, offering no guidance to doctors, and that they violated women's rights to privacy under the Bill of Rights and the Fourteenth Amendment. Some state courts—for example, in California and Missouri—overturned antiabortion laws on the grounds of vagueness of the laws, but state courts did not find the right to choose an abortion to be a fundamental one.

Inspired by traditional religious ideals and conservative views of women's domestic roles, antiabortion advocates responded to the pro-choice label by selecting their own key word: "life." The linking of life to traditional maternal roles further argued that abortion violated the most basic of women's duties to children. By 1971, the Catholic National Right to Life committee brought together many of these groups to lobby legislatures against changing antiabortion laws and file amicus briefs in state and federal courts supporting existing laws.

The key concepts of choice and life, along with the constitutional principles, on the one hand, of a fundamental right to privacy under the Ninth and Fourteenth Amendments, and on the other of the state's claim that fetuses were human beings from conception and had a legitimate right to the protection of the state, came face to face in *Roe* v. *Wade*, a Texas abortion rights case. Texas had not changed its law since 1857, and women seeking voluntary abortions had to leave the state to get them. Bringing suit for a pregnant woman who wished to be able to gain a safe and legal abortion in the state, and a couple who wished to be able to obtain such an abortion should the wife become pregnant, Texas attorneys Linda Coffee and Sarah Weddington convinced a federal district court that the Texas law violated the women's privacy rights. The federal panel found grounds in the Ninth and Fourteenth Amendments for the right to choose an abortion. States needed a compelling reason to deny such a fundamental right. The Texas statute offered no such compelling reason. But the court did not issue the injunction to the state that the plaintiffs sought, forbidding enforcement of the law. Both sides appealed.

In the meantime, a federal panel in the Georgia abortion rights case of *Doe* v. *Bolton* adopted similar reasoning to strike down that state's recently passed reform statute. Again the court refused to issue the injunction sought. As in *Roe*, both sides appealed. Other federal panels in Ohio and Louisiana disagreed with the outcome in *Roe* and *Doe*. In split decisions, the judges in the former cases found the state statutes valid—the state having a legitimate interest in protecting unborn life and the language of their laws neither vague nor overbroad.

The U.S. Supreme Court concurred with the *Roe* panel. In a 7–2 opinion authored by Justice Harry Blackmun, the Court found that the right to choose an abortion was constitutionally protected, but conceded that the state had an interest in potential life as well. Blackmun drew upon his reading in the medical literature to introduce a trimester formula, in the first of which, before viability, the state needed a compelling reason to intervene in a pregnancy. In effect, only the patient and the doctor need agree to the abortion. In the second and third trimesters, the state could take steps to regulate the abortion practice, so long as those steps did not harm the woman. Justices Byron White and William Rehnquist dissented, neither finding any language in the Constitution that conferred the right to an abortion on a woman. Justice White averred that the fetus was a potential human being from conception and thus entitled to the protection of its fundamental rights by the state. Justice Rehnquist thought the matter best left to the state legislatures.

The political and popular furor over the decision was immediate and lasting. The opposition was led by Protestant evangelical groups and Roman Catholic organizations. In Congress, the so-called Hyde Amendment, first introduced in 1976 by Illinois Congressman Henry Hyde, denied federal funding to all but a handful of medically necessary abortions. Many states opted not to use any public funds or facilities for abortion. At first, lower federal courts disagreed, but a sharply divided U.S. Supreme Court permitted states to use their funds as they saw fit and in 1980 upheld the constitutionality of the Hyde Amendment.

Up to 1988, a variety of state regulations including parental and spousal notification, informed-consent waivers designed to discourage the patient from electing the abortion, viability tests, and denial of access to hospitals were struck down by the Court. In *Webster* v. *Reproductive Health Services* (1989) and *Planned Parenthood* v. *Casey* (1992), however, the Court reversed itself and found many of the same restrictions did not contradict the basic holding in *Roe*. Although by a narrow majority the Court refused to overturn *Roe*, it did replace the trimester formula with one based on a test for the "undue burden" any regulation might place on the women's choice. In the process, the state no longer had the job of showing that it had a compelling reason for its regulations. Chief Justice Rehnquist and Justice Antonin Scalia

argued that the decisions had so weakened *Roe* that it was little more than a facade, but the majority argued that so many women had come to rely on *Roe* that it should not be discarded.

The current state of abortion law is tangled. Sixteen states and the District of Columbia have never officially repealed the laws that criminalized abortion before *Roe*. *Casey* held that such absolute restrictions were still constitutionally invalid. Both cases allowed states to regulate abortion practice and access to abortions, the former under the trimester formula, the latter under the undue burden test. Forty states and the District of Columbia currently have laws banning post-viability abortions. Eighteen states bar the dilation and extraction (sometimes called "partial-birth") abortion method at any time in the pregnancy, athough the U.S. Supreme Court in *Stenberg* has ruled these restrictions an undue burden, as they prevent doctors from employing what doctors see as the safest method for the pregnant woman. Three state legislatures (Illinois, Kentucky, and Louisiana) have declared that if *Roe* is overturned, leaving it up to the states to determine the legality of abortion at any time, they will ban it totally. Four states (Connecticut, Maine, Maryland, and Washington) have passed laws affirming the right to an abortion before viability and permission for abortions after viability to preserve the life or health of the mother. Four states have laws requiring tests for viability, but two of these have been ruled unconstitutional by lower courts.

Ten states have laws mandating some form of spousal consent or notice, ignoring the Court's rejection of the spousal consent requirement in *Casey*. Thirty-eight states insist that parents of a minor seeking an abortion be notified or give consent, although provisions for "judicial bypass" hearings are included. Empirical evidence has shown that these hearings are cumbersome and often result in denial of the bypass, however. Twenty-eight of the states with such laws strictly enforce them. One state's supreme court (California) has found the state's law unconstitutional under the state constitution. Eighteen states have mandatory waiting periods, ranging from one to two days, but only eleven of these states strictly enforce this provision.

Thirty states have informed-consent rules that differ from those in other surgeries (including, for example, the requirement that the notice be read to a patient by a doctor and the inclusion of alternatives to the procedure, such as adoption). Five states have laws that ban state-funded care providers and counselors from mentioning abortion or giving abortion referrals. One of the state's laws (North Dakota) has been found unconstitutional. Forty-three states limit abortion practice to licensed doctors. Forty-six states permit doctors and other care providers to refuse to take part in any abortion on the grounds of conscience or religious affiliation.

Missouri prohibits any state employee from taking part in any abortion, even to save the life of the mother. Five states, including Missouri, have laws prohibiting the use of public facilities for abortions. Thirty states will fund abortion when the pregnant woman's life is in danger, and twenty-seven will also fund abortion when the pregnancy was the result of rape or incest. Four states (Iowa, New Mexico, Virginia, and Wisconsin) will fund abortions for a wide variety of health reasons, and sixteen states and the District will fund it in most all circumstances (before viability).

In the meantime, *Roe* v. *Wade* and its companion cases remain the most divisive and controversial judicial decisions of the twentieth century. The raised voices of advocates and opponents of *Roe* in judges' chambers and legislative halls have spilled into the streets, causing state and federal lawmakers to debate and federal courts to adjudicate rules separating pro-abortion rights and antiabortion demonstrators from one another. Twelve states prohibit protestors from blocking clinic entrances and four states have declared their abhorrence of violence against clinics or their personnel, a limitation on *speech and *assembly that the U.S. Supreme Court has upheld. Police forces continue to search for the sniper who killed a doctor in his own home because the doctor performed abortions. While most antiabortion rights spokespersons have called the murder of doctors immoral, more than a few have called the murderers heroes, saving thousands of lives of the unborn by taking the life of the abortionist.

[*See also* Gender and Law; Privacy; *Roe* v. *Wade*]

—Peter Charles Hoffer and N. E. H. Hull

ACCIDENTS. *See* Torts.

ACTUS REUS. Every crime has two parts: (1) *actus reus*, or an objective part, the criminal act; and (2) *mens rea*, or a subjective part, the criminal defendant's culpable state of mind. The criminal act (or omission if there is a duty to act) must be voluntary, overt conduct (not merely thoughts) that exactly fits the crime's definition and causes harmful results.

[*See also* Criminal Law Principles; Mens Rea]

—David S. Clark

ADAMS, JOHN. Born 30 October 1735 in Braintree (now Quincy), Massachusetts, and died there on 4 July 1826. After graduating from Harvard in 1755, he kept school in Worcester, Massachusetts for a year, then studied law there with James Putnam. He was admitted to practice at Boston (the Inferior Court of Common Pleas, November 1758; the Superior Court of Judicature, November 1761).

Throughout his legal career, indeed, during his entire life, Adams followed advice he received "to pursue the study of the law rather than the gain of it." From his earliest days at the bar, Adams read widely, not only in common-law treatises and reports, but also discourses on the civil law and on maritime commerce, and, especially, in political science.

Although Adams practiced productively, including the successful defense in the *Boston Massacre trials, and helped found a forerunner of the Boston *Bar Association, his chief contribution to the law came through his writings: primarily, the oddly named *Dissertation on the Canon and Feudal Law* (1765) (which argued powerfully against parliamentary authority) and *A Defense of the Constitution and Government of the United States* (1787).

After 1774, Adams's service in the Continental Congress and abroad on various diplomatic missions diverted him from the law (and from serving as chief justice of Massachusetts). He did return in 1779, long enough to draft the Massachusetts Constitution, prescribing "a government of laws, not men."

Adams was in England representing the United States during the Philadelphia convention. Fourteen years later, however, he contributed significantly albeit indirectly to American constitutional law: as president, he appointed John *Marshall as chief justice of the Supreme Court.

[*See also* Lawyers]

• L. Kinvin Wroth and Hiller B. Zobel, eds., *John Adams*, 3 vols., 1965. David McCullough, *Legal Papers of John Adams*, 2001.

—Hiller B. Zobel

ADMINISTRATIVE AGENCIES. *See* Regulation.

ADMINISTRATIVE LAW. *See* Regulation.

ADMINISTRATIVE LAW JUDGE. The twentieth century marked a dramatic shift in the structure of American law. Traditionally, an independent judicial branch, with the aid of a jury, enforced rights created by *common law, supplemented at times by statutes. Increasingly, however, Congress and state legislatures displaced this scheme by empowering administrative agencies to enforce laws and adjudicate disputes. Agencies designated judicial officers to conduct hearings and undertake factual findings. Sometimes these judicial officers had the power to issue final orders, while on other occasions they could make recommended decisions to be reviewed by the head of the agency and eventually a court. These judicial officers were originally referred to as hearing officers or examiners. Consistent with their increased power, Congress changed their name to administrative law judge.

Administrative adjudication is a controversial issue. Opponents argue that administrative judges are not independent since they have neither life tenure nor the protection against diminution of salary provided federal judges by Article III of the Constitution. Moreover, administrative judges are perceived to be under the control of the agency litigating in the dispute. Finally, administrative law judges act as the initial finder of fact, thus displacing the jury in the American legal system. Congress attempted to address some of these concerns in the Administrative Procedure Act (1946), which secures the independence of administrative law judges and mandates that the administrative judge presiding at a hearing be insulated from agency personnel prosecuting the matter. Yet these congressional actions did not address all the concerns because to do so would have required an elimination of this new system of administrative adjudication. The Supreme Court ultimately held that the trial of matters before an administrative law judge within an agency did not violate either the Seventh Amendment right to *jury or the guarantees to a life-tenured judge in Article III of the Constitution.

Administrative law judges adjudicate cases that cover the entire range of substantive law. It is safe to say that no part of American government operates without having disputes heard before administrative law judges. The most pervasive public benefits program in this country—Social Security—initially resolves almost all disputes through administrative law judges. Additionally, many health, safety, and employment matters on the state and federal level are adjudicated before administrative law judges. Apart from their broad substantive scope, administrative law judges have powers to issue a broad array of remedial measures. Administrative law judges award benefits

paid from the public fisc. They may also issue decisions that can lead to severe sanctions. For example, in financial and securities regulation, administrative law judges are authorized to recommend civil monetary penalties or orders of restitution that involve millions of dollars, and may also adjudicate disputes that lead to debarment from a chosen business profession. In almost all cases, however, the law authorizes *judicial review of the matter including the decision of the administrative law judge. This avenue for judicial review is believed to protect the right of the individual to an independent judicial forum.

[See also Regulation]

• Antonin Scalia, "The ALJ Fiasco," *University of Chicago Law Review* (1979): 57. Stephen G. Breyer, Richard B. Stewart, Cass R. Sunstein, and Matthew L. Spitzer, *Administrative Law and Regulatory Policy*, 4th ed., 1999.

—Nicholas S. Zeppos

ADMINISTRATIVE PROCEDURES ACTS. *See*

ADMIRALTY AND MARITIME JURISDICTION. Article III of the United States *Constitution empowers the federal courts to hear "all cases of admiralty and maritime jurisdiction." These terms are nowhere defined in the Constitution or in any statute. The federal courts have largely defined for themselves the territorial scope of the jurisdiction, the types of claims that may be brought, and the relief that may be sought. Congress has on occasion expanded the federal courts' admiralty jurisdiction, and the Federal Rules of Civil Procedure provide some unique rules for admiralty cases. By statute certain admiralty claims can only be maintained in federal court, and states have no power generally to hear in rem actions. State courts maintain concurrent jurisdiction over most admiralty claims. The substantive law applied in an admiralty case is generally federal law. But in some instances when the state interest is strong, state law is applied. For example, state law is applied to supplement federal *regulations where pollution from a vessel threatens a state's air or water.

The framers of the Constitution conferred admiralty jurisdiction on the federal courts because of the vital importance of interstate and international shipping to the nation. The national interest in maritime matters transcended local interests.

American admiralty law, both in terms of substance and procedure, is derived from the practice of the English High Court of Admiralty. That court was a civil law court, unlike the *common law courts of Kings Bench, Common Pleas and

Exchequer. Aside from a difference in terminology (e.g., instead of a "lawsuit" filed by a "plaintiff's lawyer," in admiralty a "libelant's proctor" filed a "libel"), the outstanding feature of the admiralty practice was the proceeding in rem. This procedure allowed the plaintiff to sue a vessel directly as if it were the defendant. The plaintiff was not required to provide notice to the owners of the vessel. To this day the suit in rem remains a useful device where the owners of a vessel may be hard to ascertain or difficult to sue, or where there is a threat that the vessel may leave the district and deprive the plaintiff of security for its claim. After the vessel has been arrested, the Federal Rules of Civil Procedure require that notice of the seizure be provided in a newspaper of general circulation in the district where the vessel is seized.

In a series of cases, mostly decided before the Civil War, the *Supreme Court expanded the admiralty jurisdiction beyond the English precedents. In England, the admiralty jurisdiction was generally limited to cases arising on the seas or within the ebb and flow of the tide. It excluded *contracts that were made on land or were to be performed on land, and it excluded *tort claims arising on the rivers. The Supreme Court rejected most of these limitations, overcoming strong opposition from those opposed to federal intervention in local matters. For example, in *Genesee Chief* v. *Fitzhugh* (1851), the Court held that the admiralty jurisdiction extended to the Great Lakes and to any other navigable waterway connecting different states or nations. In *Insurance Co.* v. *Dunham* (1870), the Court ruled that marine *insurance contracts are maritime even though they are made on land and are performed on land. They are maritime because they cover a maritime risk. Similarly the Court has held that charter parties, maritime bills of lading, and contracts to repair vessels are maritime. More recently, in *Exxon Corp.* v. *Central Gulf Lines* (1991), the Court has expanded the admiralty jurisdiction to include at least some contracts between shipowners and their agents. In so doing it stressed that the reason for admiralty jurisdiction was "the protection of maritime commerce." Nonetheless admiralty law still excludes several contracts that have important federal concerns. Contracts to sell or build a vessel are regarded as being non-maritime. Moreover, state substantive law governs much of the rights and liabilities of parties to marine insurance contracts.

For most of our history, admiralty jurisdiction over torts applied only to injuries occurring on navigable waters. This presented difficulties when injuries occurred near the water's edge, as they frequently do when goods are loaded or unloaded from vessels or when passengers board or disembark. In 1948 the Congress corrected this problem by extending admiralty jurisdiction to any injury "caused by a vessel on navigable water, notwithstanding that such damage or injury be done or consummated on land." Many thought that the admiralty tort jurisdiction was too broad, as it included airplane crashes occurring on the Great Lakes, collisions between swimmers on a navigable water, and collisions between automobiles on a ferry boat. Although these accidents have a maritime dimension, there is no federal interest in resolving them. Responding to this concern, the Supreme Court in *Executive Jet Aviation, Inc.* v. *Cleveland* (1972), required that in addition to the locality requirement, a tort must bear a substantial connection to traditional maritime activity for it to be within the admiralty jurisdiction. In several cases since that decision, the Court has had difficulty drawing the line. It seems that any tort caused by a vessel on navigable water will ordinarily be maritime. This has included damage to buildings in the Chicago Loop caused by a barge being used as a work platform that was replacing pilings to a pier on the Chicago River (*Jerome B. Grubart, Inc.* v. *Great Lakes Dredge & Dock Corp.*, (1995)). By contrast, product *liability claims by shipyard workers for damage caused by exposure to asbestos on board seagoing vessels are non-maritime (*Oman* v. *Johns-Manville Corp.* (4th Cir. 1985)).

For most of our history, American admiralty judges thought that they lacked jurisdiction to provide equitable relief. Some believed that since England maintained separate courts for admiralty and *equity, that an American admiralty court must lack equitable powers. Others reasoned that an admiralty court, whose jurisdiction is based on the suit in rem, cannot provide equitable relief that is normally given in personam. Perhaps there was also a concern that *injunctions and other equitable *remedies issuing from federal courts would interfere with states' rights. Whatever the original basis, the *courts of appeal have concluded that they have the power to provide equitable relief in admiralty. This view seems correct. The Constitution did not establish a separate admiralty court. Rather it authorized federal courts to exercise all of their power in a variety of cases including admiralty cases. Such relief is necessary if the court is to fulfill its role protecting maritime commerce.

Because state and federal governments each have power to make some admiralty law, and because of the power of the legislatures and the courts to develop legal rules, some of the law has been complex. The subject of wrongful death in admiralty is one such area. Overruling lower court precedent, the Supreme Court decided in *The Harrisburg* (1886) that there was no right to recover for wrongful death in admiralty in the absence of a statute. Wrongful death plaintiffs relied on state statutes to provide relief. In 1920 Congress provided a wrongful death action for seamen, the Jones Act. The same year it also created a right for anyone to recover for wrongful death resulting from injuries on the high seas. State law continued to apply to deaths occurring from injuries within the territorial waters. This patchwork system did not work satisfactorily. The statutes provide different types of remedies, create different classes of beneficiaries, and apply to different types of conduct. In *Moragne* v. *States Marine Lines, Inc.* (1970), the Supreme Court overruled *The Harrisburg* and created a right to recover in admiralty for wrongful death. Later cases have generally limited this right, however. In case of the death of a seaman, for example, the Jones Act's limitations on damages are controlling. The Supreme Court also held that the *Moragne* remedy does not apply when in conflict with the Death on the High Seas Act. The Supreme Court and Congress have added to the patchwork quality. The Court has declared in *Yamaha Motor Corp.* v. *Calhoun* (1996) that in the case of nonseafarers, state wrongful death acts may supplement the *Moragne* remedy. *Yamaha* involved the death of a twelve-year-old child who was killed while riding a jet ski. Congress in 2000 amended the Death on the High Seas Act so that it would not apply to commercial aviation accidents within 12 nautical miles of the United States and so that it would allow additional compensation for nonpecuniary damages (but not punitive damages) in cases of commercial aviation accidents occurring beyond the 12 nautical mile limit.

Despite its complexities and anomalies, the admiralty jurisdiction remains a vital part of this country's interest in maritime commerce.

• David W. Robertson, *Admiralty and Federalism*, 1970. Grant Gilmore and Charles L. Black Jr., *The Law of Admiralty*, 2d ed., 1975. Thomas J. Schoenbaum, *Admiralty and Maritime Law*, 2d ed., 1994. Robert M. Jarvis, *An Admiralty Law Anthology*, 1995. Erastus Cornelius Benedict, *Benedict On Admiralty*, 7th ed. rev., 1958– (plus supplements).   —Steven F. Friedell

ADOPTION AND TERMINATION OF PARENTAL RIGHTS. Relationships come in many varieties, but only two flavors are legally families: connections of consanguinity (ties of blood) and connections of affinity (ties based on emotional relationships and sanctioned by law, such as *marriage and adoption) In most families, children are children "by blood" and are reared by their birth parents. Adoption creates a bond between parent and child by operation of law. Although adoption of adult heirs was common in ancient Rome, adoption of children is relatively recent in both England and the United States. Because the legal practice dates only from the mid-nineteenth century, it is not part of the common-law heritage. Consequently, courts granting adoptions must have special jurisdiction and must follow statutory formulations. As stated in many adoption cases, "adoption is a creature of statute."

Because all children are born into families and legally can possess only one set of parents at a time, adoption involves two steps: the breakage of ties to the birth parents and the legal forging of bonds to the new, or adoptive, parents.

Most decisions to terminate parental rights are voluntary; that is, they involve the consent of the birth parents. As provided by Colo. Rev. Stat. § 19-1-103 (1999) subsection 28: " 'Consent' means voluntary, informed, written consent." Older cases involve duress or fraud that might have led to unwise consent (e.g., *Huebert* v. *Marshall* (1971)). In more recent cases, unwed fathers seek to block their children's adoption, alleging that they have not given consent. Some well-known such cases are *Michael H.* v. *Gerald D.* (1989), holding that the birth father of a child conceived in an adulterous relationship does not have the constitutional right to establish legal fatherhood when California law has conclusively presumed the husband is the child's father; *In re Clausen* (1993), Baby Jessica case; and *In re Petition of Doe* (1994), the Baby Richard case. Where an unwed father has established (or has attempted to establish) a relationship with the child before the mother gave consent for adoption, the father has constitutional liberty interests requiring procedural protections before an adoption is valid (*Lehr* v. *Robertson* (1983)).

In a smaller number of cases, the state terminates parental rights because the parents are unfit; that is, they have abused, neglected, or abandoned the child. Because the termination decision is final and threatens the constitutional liberty interests of the parents, a series of U.S. Supreme Court decisions has granted the contesting parent substantial procedural rights, including a heightened *burden of proof, access to counsel (in some cases at government expense), and a free transcript on appeal (*M.L.B.* v. *S.L.J.* (1996), reviewing the earlier cases). Recently, the pendulum has swung from attempting to preserve families even when the parents were earlier found unfit and the child placed in foster care to promoting swift adoption and ensuring child safety (Adoption and Safe Families Act of 1997, 42 U.S.C. § 671 and ff.).

The second step in adoption, placement with a new family, has always been heavily regulated. Not only must the court granting adoption create the legal relationship, but statutes require that adoptions be "in the best interests of the child." This gives the state or its agency delegates power to investigate adoptive parents for fitness and to ration children on the basis of such parental characteristics as stability, *race, and religion. Though race cannot be the sole criterion in adoption cases (Multiethnic Placement Act of 1996, 42 U.S.C. § 671[a]), in some states, such as Minnesota (Minn. Stat. § 259.29), strong efforts are made to ensure that the child's cultural heritage, including racial or ethnic identity, is preserved. Particularly strong safeguards under the Indian Child Welfare Act (25 U.S.C. §§ 1901-63) maintain exclusive jurisdiction in Indian tribes for cases of placement in foster care, termination of parental rights, or adoption where adults or children have strong connections with the tribe (see NATIVE AMERICANS AND THE LAW). *In re Adoption No. 12612 in the Circuit Court for Montgomery County* (1999) involved both transracial adoption and the question of preserving a family in which the birth mother had earlier killed one sibling of the child and neglected another.

In addition to race and religion, contemporary courts face other pluralism questions in deciding which of several persons should adopt. One of the most common issues is adoption by gay or lesbian partners of a natural parent. For example, a Massachusetts court finalized an adoption in *Adoption of Tammy* (1993) in which both women in question were biologically related to the five-year-old child. The court further held that "when a natural parent is a party to a joint adoption petition, that parent's legal relationship to the child does not terminate on entry of the adoption decree." In *In re Adoption of B.L.V.B.* (1993), the court held that "when the family unit is comprised of the natural mother and her [lesbian] partner, and the adoption [by the partner] is in the best interests of the children, terminating the natural mother's right is

unreasonable and unnecessary." A psychologist who had evaluated the family unit in this case testified that "it was essential for the children to be assured of a continuing relationship" and recommended that the "adoptions be allowed for the psychological and emotional protection of the children." A recent contested case involved the rights of a lesbian former partner who was not the child's biological parent but who was allowed visitation (*V.C.* v. *M.L.B.* (2000)) (see HOMOSEXUALITY AND THE LAW).

Despite the shortage of healthy infant children available for adoption, many children are not adopted even after their birth parents' rights end. These "special needs" children may be nonwhite, older, or in large sibling groups that need placement together. Most often, though, they are disabled in some way. In a market for babies these children would fetch a negative price—adoptive parents would be paid to take them. In the adoption market, where explicit pricing is prohibited, agencies may attempt to portray these children in a more desirable light than the adoptive parents find justifiable—hence the problem of "wrongful adoption." Once the child is placed "wrongfully" with the adoptive parents and the parents discover a major problem, the question becomes one of remedy. In some cases, adoptions are annulled because of agency misrepresentation or nondisclosure. In a growing number of wrongful adoption cases, the adoption remains intact but the distressed adoptive parents sue the placing agency.

Even when adoptions are finalized, all contacts with the birth family do not necessarily end. For example, increasing numbers of states are allowing contact with natural grandparents under statutes permitting the grandparents to get court-ordered visitation following divorce or death of a natural parent (e.g., *In re Nearhoof* (1987)). One court permitted visitation of her former foster children by a foster mother who was unable to adopt the children because her husband had died during the period when the social services department attempted to terminate the natural mother's rights (*In re Francisco A.* (1993)).

In matters of inheritance, many state statutes permit adopted children to inherit from their birth parents under intestate succession, particularly when the adoption is by a blood relative or stepparent. This may raise the problem of "dual inheritance," since the child might receive two shares of the deceased's *estate. The problem (under a now defunct statute) is illustrated in *In re Estate of Cregar* (1975), which allowed recovery through both natural and adoptive parents. In contrast, *Hall* v. *Vallandingham* (1988) barred the adopted child's inheritance from the natural parent.

In order to facilitate inheritance from adoptive parents, as well as to make useful information available to natural parents and adopted children and to satisfy their curiosity, more states are permitting natural parents to leave identifying information with adoption agencies (e.g., Va. Code Ann. § 63.1-236). The Second Circuit Court has held, however, that adoption agencies have no constitutional right to receive such identifying information (*Alma Society* v. *Mellon* (1979)). *Roger B.* has a similar holding: that the adoptee has no constitutional right to obtain identifying information about the natural parents (*In re Roger B.* (1981)).

Another question surrounding the effect of adoption involves the remedy called "equitable adoption," which permits children who placed for adoption but were never adopted to claim the benefits they would have received if a legal adoption had taken place. Usually such children seek recovery from their would-be parents when these parents die. However, in *Estate of McConnell* (1967), the "sisters" of Edward McConnell, who thought he had been adopted as a child, sued his estate. These women were the natural children of a couple who did not fulfill their promise to adopt Edward McConnell. The women were the only living "relatives" of McConnell, who died wealthy and intestate. The "sisters" were not permitted to inherit the estate. The right to claim equitable adoption belongs only to the wronged person, not to those claiming through the parents who did not fulfill their obligations.

[*See also* Child Custody; Spousal Support]

• Elisabeth Landes and Richard Posner, "The Economics of the Baby Shortage," *Journal of Legal Studies* 7 (1978): 323–48. David Chambers and Michael Wald, "*Smith* v. *Offer*: A Case Study of Children in Foster Care," in *In the Interests of Children* (Robert Mnookin, ed.), 1985. June Carbone, *From Partners to Parents*, 1999. Lynn C. Franklin and Elizabeth Ferber, *May the Circle Be Unbroken: An Intimate Journal into the Heart of Adoption*, 1999. Michael Shapiro, *Solomon's Sword: Two Families and the Children the State Took Away*, 1999. Marsha Garrison, "Law Making for Baby-Making: An Interpretive Approach to the Determination of Legal Parentage," *Harvard Law Review* 113 (2000): 835–920.

—Margaret F. Brinig

ADULTERY. Adulterous conduct has violated both criminal and marital law at least since Biblical times. According to historian James A. Brundage, by the Reformation, Roman Catholic countries made adultery a cause for legal separation, while Protestant countries allowed *divorce and remarriage. In England, until 1857 an absolute divorce required an Act of Parliament, and this was true in some of the American colonies and states; after independence, the former American colonies required a bill of divorce obtained from state legislatures until the mid-nineteenth century. As Brundage notes, records more frequently reveal public humiliation of adulterers when divorce was difficult to obtain. The earliest secular objections to infidelity arose from the threat posed to lineage and hence to the entire property system. From the inception of the notion of adultery, then, women committing adultery were treated more severely than were men.

As affections became more important to *marriage and as married women became their own legal persons, the legal rules were more evenhanded. Nevertheless, because proof of adultery can affect or even bar alimony (granted primarily to wives) and because a parent's moral behavior continues to affect *child custody awards, even today the legal consequences of adultery remain more serious for women than for men. As of early 2001, adultery was grounds for divorce in thirty-one states, barred alimony in six, and was a crime in twenty-four. Because of the severe consequences, the *burden of proof required has always been more substantial than for other divorce cases. The party proving adultery must show "opportunity and inclination" and must have corroborating *evidence.

The actual incidence of adultery remains unknown. In 1995, state vital statistics records revealed that less than 1 percent of Virginia divorces were granted on grounds of adultery, and even when marriages dissolved and the spouse seeking divorce knew about the behavior, the no-fault ground was used far more often. Further, not all adultery is discovered, sometimes the behavior is forgiven (the legal defense of condonation), sometimes it occurs at the request of one spouse (connivance), and sometimes both spouses engage in it (recrimination). In the days before no-fault divorce, many states made adultery the only cause of action for divorce, so evidence was frequently fabricated (collusion).

States continuing to consider adultery as grounds for divorce note "it is the one act most likely to frustrate and prevent a reconciliation" (*Mayhugh* v. *Mayhugh* (1997)). Adultery cases are more difficult to mediate than other divorce cases, because these marriages establish a pattern of secrecy and because the uninvolved spouse feels particularly angry.

Since the advent of no-fault divorce grounds, twenty states have made adultery irrelevant for both property distribution and alimony. In many other states that retain consideration of marital fault for the financial ramifications of divorce, alimony may be called into question, limited, or barred entirely only if the spouse seeking alimony was comparatively more at fault than the other spouse or if the adultery actually caused the destruction of the marriage. Some legal academics now urge that adultery be irrelevant in custody proceedings as well, and many cases now conclude that moral conduct, including adultery, should be considered only if it directly affects the child.

[*See also* Divorce and Annulment]

• James A. Brundage, *Law, Sex and Christian Society in Medieval Europe*, 1987. Mary Beth Norton, *Founding Mothers and Fathers: Gendered Power and the Forming of American Society*, 1996. American Law Institute, *Principles of Family Dissolution: Analysis and Recommendations*, 2001.   —Margaret F. Brinig

ADVERSARIAL SYSTEM. *See* Ethics and Professional Responsibility, Legal; Legal Systems; Procedure, Court.

ADVERSE POSSESSION. *See* Property, Real.

ADVERTISING, LEGAL. *See* Ethics and Professional Responsibility, Legal.

AFFIRMATIVE ACTION. The phrase affirmative action was first used by President John F. Kennedy in 1961, in an executive order that prohibited federal government contractors from discriminating on the basis of "race, creed, color, or national origin," and required them "to take affirmative action" to prevent such *discrimination. The concept and its primary justification were further developed by President Lyndon Johnson, most famously in a speech at Howard University in 1965. "[F]reedom is not enough. You do not wipe away the scars of centuries by saying: Now you are free to go where you want, do as you desire, and choose the leaders you please. You do not take a person who, for years, has been hobbled by chains and liberate him, bring him up to the starting line of a race and then say 'You are free to compete with all the others' and still justly believe that you have been completely fair." That same year, President Johnson issued an executive order extending the principles of nondiscrimination to federal employment, which led to congressional action creating the Equal Employment Opportunity Commission by Congress, and by the 1970s to the

creation of federal regulations creating timetables and goals for increasing minority representation in federal employment and contracting. At its root, then, the idea of affirmative action began as an attempt to remedy the effects of past discrimination, primarily racial discrimination against African Americans in the form of *segregation laws and unfair government practices that were widely practiced until the enactment of *civil rights legislation in the 1960s. Later programs extended the principles of affirmative action to women, again on the principle that there was a long and recent history of discrimination against women by state agencies.

The federal lead was followed by states and cities, which experimented with a wide variety of programs designed to remedy the effects of past discrimination through affirmative action. Universities, too, began to implement programs designed to increase minority representation. These three areas—government contracting, government employment and promotion, and access to higher education—have been the most important areas of affirmative action efforts, and consequently the areas in which the debates over affirmative action have been carried out. By the mid-1970s, however, the original justification for affirmative action had been joined by a separate argument. This was the idea that government has an affirmative, legitimate interest in fostering diversity in areas like employment, contracting, and education, either as a means of improving the social circumstances of minority populations or by virtue of the benefit that diversity brings to the affected institutions. Universities, in particular, argued that promoting racial diversity among the student body was a positive good that served their educational mission. This argument took on constitutional as well as political dimensions, since the existence of a valid and sufficiently important government purpose can justify a law that would otherwise be unconstitutional.

The primary argument against affirmative action was that it sacrificed individual fairness—in the form of objective measurement of qualifications—in the name of conferring benefits to racially defined groups. As a constitutional matter, it was argued that this deprived individuals who were not members of recognized minority groups of their rights under the *equal protection and *due process clauses of the *Fourteenth Amendment. The argument reached the Supreme Court in 1975, in *Regents of the University of California v. Bakke* (1978). Alan Bakke challenged the University of California, Davis medical school's policy of reserving sixteen out of one hundred slots for "disadvantaged" minority students (defined as students of African-American, Hispanic, Asian, or Native American descent) on the grounds that the policy violated his constitutional right to an equal chance at a publicly supported education. The university argued that the Court should take into account the fact that the purpose of their program was "benign." Writing for a plurality, Justice Lewis Powell concluded that strict constitutional scrutiny should be applied in any case of racial classification, regardless of whether the purpose of the classification was "benign" or "invidious." "The guarantee of equal protection," he wrote, "cannot mean one thing when applied to one individual and something else when applied to a person of another color." Powell found that the University of California's practice did not survive strict scrutiny. "If petitioner's purpose is to assure within its student body some specified percentage of a particular group merely because of its race or ethnic origin, such a preferential purpose must be rejected. . . . Preferring members of any one group for no reason other than race or ethnic origin is discrimination for its own sake. This the Constitution forbids."

On the other hand, Powell also stated that it was perfectly permissible for universities to use *race as one "plus" factor among many in the admissions process, in order to further racial diversity among the student population. And he sharply distinguished the justification of promoting diversity from cases involving remedial actions taken in response to a record of discrimination by the particular institution in question. There were two other "camps" in the case: Justices Stevens, *Burger, Stewart, and Rehnquist found the California program to be in violation of federal statutes, and thus avoided the constitutional issue, while Justices *Brennan, White, *Marshall, and Blackmun would have recognized the difference between benign and invidious racial discrimination, and reviewed the case under an intermediate standard of review.

Powell's opinion in Bakke, despite the fractured nature of the plurality for which he was writing, defined the Court's approach to affirmative action through the 1980s. Remedial policies could make use of goals and timetables, while nonremedial forms of affirmative action could treat race only as one factor among many, and in all cases strict scrutiny should be applied. In Fullilove v. Klutznick (1980), the Court upheld a 1977 law that re-

quired that 10 percent of public works go to "minority business enterprises" on the grounds that it was a remedial statute, based in part on the idea that the Court owed special deference to Congress' determination of legislative purpose. The same reasoning was the basis for upholding an FCC program that set aside a portion of licenses for minority-owned stations in order to foster racial diversity in broadcasting on the basis of the "special institutional competence" of Congress. Metro Broadcasting, Inc. v. FCC (1990). In the employment area, two cases illustrate the two points of Powell's Bakke analysis in practice. In Local 28 of the Sheet Metal Workers v. EEOC (1986), the Court, in a plurality opinion written by Justice Brennan, upheld a 29 percent minority hiring goal on the grounds that the measure was designed to remedy previous discrimination, while in Johnson v. Transportation Agency of Santa Clara (1987), a solid six-member majority upheld a promotion program that gave a preference to female applicants in traditionally segregated job classifications. The program in Johnson was not purely remedial, but it also did not involve any specific quotas or goals, and treated *gender as only one among many factors in the decision process. On the other hand, in Wygant v. Jackson Board of Education (1986), in a plurality opinion written by Justice Powell, a plan that was not strictly remedial was struck down where it required that white teachers should be laid off in preference to minority teachers with less seniority.

In the 1990s, however, the Court began to reconsider the theory of Bakke. In City of Richmond v. Croson (1989) and Adarand v. Pena (1995), the Court reconsidered its approach to affirmative action in the context of government contracts. Croson involved a set-aside program by the City of Richmond to remedy racial discrimination in the building trades by requiring nonminority contractors to subcontract 30 percent of their work to minority subcontractors. Adarand concerned a federal law, the Small Business Act, that promoted subcontracting to businesses owned by minorities. Both programs were struck down. The Richmond set-aside was found to be insufficiently narrowly tailored to its goal. Justice O'Connor, writing for the majority, held that a history of discrimination in an industry was not enough. "[A]n amorphous claim that there has been past discrimination in a particular industry cannot justify the use of an unyielding racial quota." And in Adarand, a five-member majority of the Court essentially did away with the distinctions in Bakke altogether. Identifying three critical principles of "skepticism," "consistency," and "congruence," the Court concluded that "all racial classifications, imposed by whatever federal, state, or local governmental actor, must be analyzed . . . under strict scrutiny."

In recent cases, the *Adarand* rule has become the basis for lower federal courts to revisit the use of race as a favorable factor in university admissions. In *Hopwood* v. *Texas* (2000), the Fifth Circuit struck down a University of Texas law school program that made race a factor in admissions decision; the Supreme Court refused to review the decision. Applying strict scrutiny, the court in *Hopwood* declared that *Bakke* was not binding precedent, and ruled that neither attaining a diverse student body nor remedying the effects of past discrimination were compelling government interests. Similarly, in *Johnson* v. *Regents of University of Georgia* (2001), the 11th Circuit Court of Appeals declared that "racial diversity alone is not necessarily the hallmark of a diverse student body." *Johnson*, in particular, turned on the argument that diversity cannot be defined by race. "[A] white applicant from a disadvantaged rural area in Appalachia may well have more to offer a Georgia public university such as UGA—from the standpoint of diversity—than a nonwhite applicant from an affluent family and a suburban Atlanta high school." Furthermore, said the court in Johnson, "the constitutional viability of student body diversity as a compelling interest is an open question." Thus there are two important questions that have been raised in this area: whether diversity is a legitimate goal that can justify affirmative action; and, if so, whether "diversity" can include racial diversity. It appears likely that both these questions will be addressed by the Supreme Court in the near future.

[*See also* Civil Rights and Civil Liberties]

• Stephen Carter, *Reflections of an Affirmative Action Baby*, 1991. Dinesh D'Souza, *Illiberal Education: The Politics of Race and Sex on Campus*, 1991. Nicolaus Mills, ed., *Debating Affirmative Action: Race, Gender, Ethnicity and the Politics of Inclusion*, 1994. Akhil Reed Amar and Neal Kumar Katyal, "Bakke's Fate," *UCLA Law Review* 43 (1996). George E. Curry, ed., *The Affirmative Action Debate*, 1996. Richard D. Kahlenberg, *The Remedy: Class, Race and Affirmative Action*, 1996. Charles R. Lawrence III and Mari Matsuda, *We Won't Go Back: Making the Case for Affirmative Action*, 1997. William G. Bowen and Derek Bok, *The Shape of the River: Long-term Consequences of Considering Race in College and University Admissions*, 1998. Bryan Grapes, ed., *Affirmative Action*, 2000.   —Howard Schweber

AGENCY, LAW OF. *See* Power of Attorney.

AGENCY RULEMAKING. *See* Regulation.

AGING AND THE LAW. Over the last thirty years, the United States has experienced an unprecedented growth in its older population. In 1970, approximately 10 percent of Americans, or twenty million in all, were sixty-five years of age or older. By 2000, the number had reached almost 13 percent, or more than thirty-five million. And the number will continue to rise with the aging of the "baby boomers," those born between 1945 and 1964. By 2020, more than 16 percent of the U.S. population will be sixty-five or older. The fastest growing age cohort, however, is those age eighty-five and older: in 2000, over four million Americans were in this age group. The aging of the population affects almost all industrialized nations. For example, soon 20 percent or more of the populations of Japan, France, Italy, and Germany will be age sixty-five or older. In all these nations, aging populations create critical challenges and stresses for law and legal institutions.

Aging is, of course, associated with advancing chronological age, but it is better understood as comprising a variety of factors, such as changing functional capacity and physical and mental health. Law, however, generally favors the use of chronological age to identify the old, because this measure has the advantage of providing a bright-line test: either an individual meets the chronological age requirement or she does not. For example, in the United States, Social Security retirement benefits begin at age sixty-five rather than at a subjective age when an individual is "old." By using age sixty-five as an objective and universal requirement for eligibility, the government is spared the cost and complexity of making determinations about each individual applicant. For the law, then, "old" means having reached a certain age.

Characteristics of Aging. Although individuals age at different rates, certain broad generalizations about the aging process are relevant to the law. Aging is inevitably accompanied by physical decline. Muscles atrophy, bones become brittle, vision weakens, and hearing becomes less acute. Many older individuals have chronic health conditions such as arthritis. As a consequence of physical decline, many elderly persons are unable to care for themselves. And because of dementia or other mental disabilities, many also suffer a loss of mental capacity and some lose the ability to care for themselves. In response to these declines in physical and mental ability, most industrialized nations have adopted social benefit programs for the elderly and have created legal institutions and laws to confront the legal problems associated with the physical and mental consequences of aging.

Income Benefits for the Elderly. In part because of declining physical and mental capabilities, and in part because of social customs, most elderly persons are retired from the workforce. In the United States, less than 15 percent of those age sixty-five and older are gainfully employed. Retirees depend on their savings and on employer-provided pensions for income. But less than half of all retired workers receive a pension and many older married women have never worked outside the home. To provide at least a minimum income for older retirees, the federal government provides Social Security. Initiated in 1935, Social Security is a universal benefit program that provides a publicly financed pension for workers, their spouses, and their dependents. In 2000, Social Security paid retirement benefits to over thirty-one million persons.

Government's financial support of older persons does not stop with Social Security. As individuals live longer (the average additional life expectancy at age sixty-five is more than fifteen years for men and almost twenty years for women), the need for long-term retirement income is critical. Employer-provided pensions are mandated in some countries, but in the United States they are voluntary, with the result that only about half of all retirees receive an employer-provided pension. To promote the provision of pensions, the government grants employers significant income tax advantages, which has resulted in very detailed and convoluted income tax laws governing pensions. The favorable tax advantages are counterbalanced by complex laws designed to ensure that private pension plans, which control trillions of dollars, meet their obligations to employees and retirees. The enforcement of these complicated laws governing private pensions has spawned a new category of "pension law," which covers governmental regulatory agencies, company lawyers, and plaintiffs' lawyers, who represent aggrieved retirees. It serves as a textbook example of how the aging of the population has created a social problem—the lack of adequate retirement income—which necessitated the creation of new laws and regulations, which in turn created a new legal specialty and numerous high-stake lawsuits.

The aging of the population also prompted the passage in 1967 of the federal Age Discrimination in Employment Act (ADEA) to fight elder poverty by making it easier for older workers to continue work. The statute prohibits discrimination in the hiring or retention of individuals age forty or older by most employers with twenty or more employees. Many states have similar laws that apply to employers with even fewer employees. Although older individuals are quite capable of performing most jobs, the common social attitude that the elderly are incapable of being productive workers creates a powerful barrier to employment of older persons. In the past, mandatory retirement was common, and employers would not consider hiring an older job applicant. To circumvent the prejudices about older workers, the ADEA makes it illegal for an employer to discriminate against an employee or job applicant merely because of his or her age. Thus mandatory retirement on account of age is no longer legal. The ADEA, of course, does not merely state the law; it also affects how the elderly are perceived. As more older individuals continue to work, social attitudes about what is "normal" or what can be expected of an older person will gradually shift. The social construction of aging thus both creates law and is in turn a creature of the law.

In years past, impoverished older persons often received financial support from their children. Many states even required children to support their parents in order to relieve the state government of that burden. Today, however, these family support laws are in general disfavor. Social Security provides at least minimum financial support for most elderly persons, and the federal Supplemental Security Income program helps the poorest elderly. Other federal and state aid programs also support the elderly in a variety of ways, including subsidized housing, free meals, subsidized public transportation, and, most importantly, subsidized medical care. As a result, U.S. law now sees the elderly as autonomous individuals, with rights and benefits, who no longer must look to their children for support. For example, Medicaid is a joint federal and state program that pays for about one-half the cost of nursing home care and prohibits states from using family support laws to seek reimbursement from children for the cost of care provided to their parents as Medicaid beneficiaries.

Health Care. The decline of family support laws is evidence of the changing legal status of the elderly. Elders are no longer supplicants or marginalized members of the society; rather, they are citizens with rights and entitlements that include financial support from the government. Chief among these entitlements is subsidized medical care. Federal subsidized medical care began in

1965 with the enactment of Medicare. Originally proposed in the 1930s as a companion to Social Security, subsidized medical care for the elderly was strongly resisted by the American Medical Association, but it was finally adopted during the Great Society years under President Lyndon Johnson. Along with the adoption of the ADEA, Medicare was promoted as an attack on poverty among the elderly. Because aging is almost inevitably accompanied by a greater need for acute health care, older persons, absent Medicare, found themselves either devoting more of their income to health care costs or going without. The former impoverished them; the latter put them at risk for poor health or even premature death.

Because Medicare has become the single largest payer of medical care, it has had a profound effect on the delivery of medical care for both the elderly and the young. Its attempts to control costs have led to increased regulation of physicians, hospitals, and other health care providers. The necessary legal apparatus in the form of laws and regulations, lawyers, and legal doctrines is so ubiquitous that entire law firms now promote themselves as specialists in *"health law." Thus the growth in the number of elderly and their increasing political power has led to the adoption of government programs that result in the creation of a new practice of law.

Health law concerns more than just Medicare and other payment programs. It also includes treatment issues that grow ever more important in an aging society. Concurrent with the increasing number of older persons has been the adoption of the health care doctrine of informed consent, which gives the patient the ultimate responsibility for his or her health decisions. The doctrine, which requires that the patient be informed of the risks and benefits of a proposed health care treatment, naturally assumes that the patient is capable of understanding the choice to be made. With the exception of the mentally disabled, almost all adults are legally empowered to participate in their health care decisions. However, as a practical matter, many older patients cannot. Some suffer from diminished mental functioning because of dementia or other brain diseases. Others, ravaged by illness or incapacitated by medication or other treatments, are unable to comprehend the options presented to them.

Older patients are not alone in possibly lacking the necessary ability to give informed consent, but because of their greater likelihood of experiencing severe acute illness and chronic conditions and their vulnerability to dementia, they are much more likely to be unable to participate fully in complex health care decisions. Consequently, the law has been forced to empower surrogate decision-makers who can make health care decisions on behalf of mentally incapacitated elders. Every state has enacted legislation authorizing advance health care directives that permit individuals to name surrogate decision-makers who can make decisions on their behalf if they become mentally incapacitated. Still, most persons, including the elderly, fail to name a surrogate. For these persons, should the need arise, many states by statute create proxy health care decision-makers. In the absence of a state law–created proxy, the only alternative for a mentally incapacitated person in need of health care who has not signed an advance health care directive is a court-appointed guardian.

Health care decision-making for the elderly creates complex legal issues. The threshold question is: who decides what is appropriate care? Custom and law determine whether the patient, the physician, or the family decides. While the United States permits the patient to decide, other nations give the physician and the family more rights in the final decision. For elderly patients, the need for health care decision-making is both more common (because of more illness) and more problematic, because older patients may be unable to make a reasoned decision or may prefer to defer to the wishes of their medical provider or their family. For elderly patients who cannot participate in their health care decisions, the common solutions are to rely on a previously designated surrogate health care decision-maker, ask a court to appoint a substitute decision-maker, or, as is often the case—although not sanctioned by law—merely permit the spouse or other family member to decide.

The most perplexing legal issue is whether to continue life-sustaining treatment for a terminally ill patient. Termination of futile care is legal even though the discontinuation of care shortens the patient's life, but there is less unanimity on the conditions that justify discontinuation of life support for an unconscious, comatose, or mentally incapacitated patient for whom there is no hope of recovery, but who may be kept alive indefinitely. Nor is there agreement as to who can make the decision to terminate life support care and hasten the death of a mentally incapacitated patient. These questions are even more difficult when the patient is very old and the quality of life is very low. Death is never welcome, but for the very old, death may be preferable to a marginal life maintained only by extraordinary medical procedures. And the cost of those procedures cannot be ignored. The question is: what does society owe to a very old and very ill individual? As a society we must make normative decisions about how many resources to devote to the very old who are very sick, and then we must translate those values into law and legal procedures.

The law has also been challenged by terminally ill individuals who demand the right to terminate their lives, in part because they do not want to undergo a painful process of dying and wish to control the manner and means of their death. Whether individuals have the right to terminate their lives is controversial. The right of a patient to terminate an intolerable life—or as it is generally known, the right to assisted suicide—has many supporters. In 1994, the voters of Oregon, by referendum, legalized a restrictive form of physician-assisted suicide. Most states, however, have outlawed assisting another person to commit suicide. In 1997, the U.S. Supreme Court upheld the constitutionality of state laws that criminalize physician-assisted suicide. In contrast, in the Netherlands, physicians are not prosecuted for assisting patients to die.

The need of many frail, ill, or demented elderly for long-term care creates the need for yet another system of public subsidies. To meet these needs, most economically advanced countries have created programs that subsidize long-term care for the elderly. These programs include mandatory long-term care insurance, innovative housing to shelter dependent elders, family-support programs to encourage voluntary care of the elderly, and economic need–based assistance programs. In the United States, Medicaid, the federal and state assistance program, requires a recipient to show financial need. As noted above, Medicaid pays for almost one-half of all nursing home costs for the elderly. Because of the complexity of the assistance program, many who apply for Medicaid seek out legal assistance. As a result, the practice of *"elderlaw" has arisen to help with obtaining Medicaid and with other related legal needs. Aging and the government response have conspired to create yet another field of law.

Aging, Diminished Capacity, and the Law. For those age eighty-five and older, the incidence of dementia rises sharply. It is estimated that one-half of this age group will incur some form of dementia or other brain disease. As the number of Americans in this group rapidly increases, so does the number of older, mentally incapacitated adults. Of course, dementia can occur at much younger ages, and other physical and mental ailments, such as strokes and clinical depression, can cause a loss of mental capacity. Not surprisingly, many younger persons mistakenly equate being old with a significant loss of memory, cognition, and judgment. But the proportion of elderly with impaired mental functioning is high enough to make the problem of mental incapacity among older persons a serious challenge.

The law and legal institutions are founded on the belief that adults can make rational decisions and can act in their own best interests. These assumptions break down in the case of mentally incapacitated individuals. For these persons to be represented in the legal system, someone must make decisions for them. The need for substitute decision-makers is not new. For over five hundred years, the Anglo-American legal tradition has permitted the state, acting through the courts, to appoint substitute decision-makers known as guardians or conservators. Every state has a statute that defines who is mentally incapacitated, the legal procedures for declaring that person incapacitated, the appointment of a guardian, the powers of the guardian, and the legal rights of the person under guardianship (the ward). But as the number of incapacitated elders rises, the guardianship system comes under increasing pressure. While the volume of cases stresses the court system, the greater challenge is the demand for greater protection of the wards. When guardianships were less common and wards tended not to live too long, few worried about whether the guardian was ensuring that the ward was properly cared for. But as the numbers of guardians increased and as wards lived longer, apprehension about the behavior of guardians escalated. And as aging wards had more assets and more income, concern also grew about the use and preservation of their assets. Finally, with the expansion of the doctrine of informed consent, guardians were making critical health care decisions about wards, often with no court supervision. All these factors, combined with the growing belief in individual autonomy and the promotion of individual preferences even of persons with diminished capacities, brought the guardianship system under closer scrutiny and criticism. This led to a seemingly endless number of "reforms." In the past decade, state after state has amended its laws to address such issues as: should the ward be represented by counsel at the guardianship hearing, what is an appropriate definition of mental incapacity, and how should guardians be monitored?

Traditional guardianship may simply be too cumbersome and too antiquated to meet the needs of our aging society. We may need a much more streamlined and responsive legal answer that balances the conflicting values of protecting the person and property of incapacitated individuals and preserving their right to autonomy and self-determination. The law must somehow distinguish between the eccentric or irrational but competent individual and the mentally incapacitated person unable to make rational decisions, and it must reconcile an individual's right to self-determination with the legal need for rational actors.

Generational Justice. The growth in the number of elders and the corresponding expansion of government programs for the elderly raise the fundamental question of generational justice: how much do the young owe the old? Whether the issue is pensions, medical care, or housing, the underlying—though not necessarily expressed—issue is: who is responsible for the well-being of the elderly? Some would argue that individuals should save enough when young to meet their needs when they are older. Because old age, retirement, poor health, and possible mental incapacity are predictable, everyone should prepare for these eventualities. This model of self-sufficiency, while not adopted in its pure form, does affect the structure of our laws, in that Social Security is thought of as a safety net than rather than an adequate source of retirement income. Even direct-aid programs, such as Medicaid, use means testing to create eligibility. Still, it is taxpayers, most of whom are below age sixty-five, who must bear the burden. Of course, the young who pay taxes for the support of the old are in a way merely prepaying the cost of their own old age. When they become old, they in turn will be supported by the next generation of young taxpayers. It is the wealthier young who disproportionately support the old, because they pay more as taxpayers than they (as a group) will receive in benefits in later years. Like other government assistance programs, aid to the elderly is less a wealth transfer between generations than an income redistribution program from the "haves" to the "have nots."

[See also Civil Rights and Civil Liberties]

• Alan Meisel, *The Right to Die*, 2d ed., 1995. Mark E. Williams, *The American Geriatrics Society's Complete Guide to Aging and Health*, 1995. Marilyn Moon, *Medicare Now and in the Future*, 2d ed., 1996. Michael Smyer, K. Warner Schaie, and Marshall B. Kapp, *Older Adults' Decision-Making and the Law*, 1996. Steven A. Sass, *The Promise of Private Pensions: The First Hundred Years*, 1997. William C. Cockerham, *This Aging Society*, 2d ed., 1997. Harold Cox, ed., *Aging*, 12th ed., 1998. Charles P. Sabatino and Nancy M. Coleman, *The American Bar Association Legal Guide for Older Americans: The Law Every American over Fifty Needs to Know*, 1998. Dean Baker and Mark Weisbrot, *Social Security: The Phony Crisis*, 1999. Lawrence A. Frolik, ed., *Aging and the Law: An Interdisciplinary Reader*, 1999. Michael J. Graetz and Jerry L. Mashaw, *True Security: Rethinking American Social Insurance*, 1999. Lawrence A. Frolik and Melissa C. Brown, *Advising the Elderly or Disabled Client*, 2d ed., 2000.   —Lawrence A. Frolik

AID, LEGAL. *See* Procedure, Criminal.

AIDS. *See* Health Law.

ALCOHOL, TOBACCO, AND FIREARMS, BUREAU OF. The United States Bureau of Alcohol, Tobacco, and Firearms (ATF) is one of the Treasury Department's tax collecting, enforcement, and regulatory arms. A Treasury Department order separates the ATF from the Internal Revenue Service.

The ATF traces its roots across two hundred years of American history. In 1789, Congress imposed a tax upon imported spirits to offset a portion of the revolutionary war debt accepted by the states. The Treasury Department assumed administration of that duty. In 1791, the import tax was augmented by a congressionally inspired tax on domestic alcohol production.

Taxpayers grumbled over import duties. Some of them greeted the domestic levy with political resistance. In the end, both revenue sources survived domestic rebellion. Although these particular taxes lost favor in Congress, similar devices for revenue came and went as needed until 1862. In that year Congress created the Office of Internal Revenue within the Treasury Department. It charged the commissioner with the collection of taxes on distilled spirits and tobacco products. The commissioner was authorized to hire three detectives to aid in the prevention, detection, and punishment of tax evaders.

In 1886, an employee from the Department of Agriculture was added to the Bureau of Internal Revenue under the Oleomargarine Act. This act was the progenitor of the sophisticated chemistry labs and staff (chemists, document analysts, latent print specialists, firearm and toolmaker examiners) doing ATF work in several locations in the United States.

The nation's ratification of the Eighteenth Amendment, in combination with Congress's promulgation of the 1919 Volstead Prohibition Enforcement Act, enlarged the task assigned to federal officers charged with investigating criminal violations of the internal revenue law. They dealt with the illicit manufacture, sale, and transportation of intoxicating liquors. In 1927, the Treasury Department elevated this enforcement unit to bureau status and in 1930, Congress transferred the penal provisions of the Volstead Act from Treasury's enforcement unit to a new Bureau of Prohibition in the Department of Justice. The Treasury Department was left with authority over tax-related and regulatory activities housed with the Bureau of Industrial Alcohol.

The Twenty-first Amendment ended Prohibition in 1933. To manage a burgeoning alcohol industry, President Franklin Roosevelt established the Federal Alcohol Control Administration (FACA). In cooperation with the Departments of Agriculture and the Treasury, FACA policed wineries and distilleries under a system based upon the industry's voluntary code of fair competition. The FACA was replaced by an entity called the Federal Alcohol Administration (FAA) under the 1935 Federal Alcohol Administrative Act.

In 1934, the Department of Justice's prohibition enforcement unit's duties were folded into the infant Alcohol Tax Unit (ATU), Bureau of Internal Revenue, Department of the Treasury. At the same time, the FAA, functioning independently within Treasury, carried forward its mandate to collect data, establish license requirements, and define regulations to ensure an open, fair marketplace for the alcohol industry and consumers. In 1940 the FAA merged with the ATU, but to this day the FAA Act remains a foundation stone for the ATF.

National dismay over the weaponry wielded by gangsters during Prohibition led to the passage of the 1934 National Firearms Act. Additional legislation directed the Miscellaneous Tax Unit in the Treasury Department to collect taxes on gun sales. In 1942, the enforcement of that duty fell to the ATU.

There was a major overhaul and reorganization of Internal Revenue in 1952. The Bureau became the Internal Revenue Service (IRS). The ATU was renamed the Alcohol and Tobacco Tax Division. The ATF was born under the 1968 Gun Control Act. Title XI of the 1970 Organized Crime Control Act formalized the ATF. The IRS's powers and duties relating to alcohol, tobacco, firearms, and explosives were transferred to the ATF.

While the ATF received political, law enforcement, and media praise for its work in the 1993 terrorist bombing of the New York World Trade Center and the 1995 bombing of the federal building in Oklahoma City, the agency's work in some recent situations have put it in a negative light.

These situations include the raid on a religious cult in Waco, Texas and the agency's botched attempt to arrest a part-time illegal gun dealer in Ruby Ridge, Idaho.

• Jon Kerr, "Treasury Department Establishes Policy on Use of Force," *West's Legal News*, 1995 WL 910782 (October 26, 1995). "Ruby Ridge: Report of the Senate Judiciary Committee Subcommittee on Terrorism, Technology and Government," 1995 WL 13701496 (December 21, 1995). "Investigation into the Activities of Federal Law Enforcement Agencies toward the Branch Davidians," House Report No. 104–749, 1996 WL 688841 (August 2, 1996). David B. Kopek and Paul M. Blackman, "Can Soldiers be Peace Officers? The Waco Disaster and the Militarization of American Law Enforcement," 30 *Akron Law Review* 619 (1997). "A Brief History of ATF: 1789–1998," <http://www.atf.treas.gov/ycgii/kids/burearu/history.htm>.

—Ronald C. Griffin

ALIMONY. *See* Divorce and Annulment; Spousal Support.

ALTERNATIVE DISPUTE RESOLUTION. The term alternative dispute resolution (ADR) describes processes used to resolve disputes, either within or outside of the formal legal system, without formal adjudication and decision by an officer of the state. The term appropriate dispute resolution is used to express the idea that different kinds of disputes may require different kinds of processes—there is no one legal or dispute resolution process that serves for all kinds of human disputing. ADR includes a variety of different processes including *mediation*, which is a process in which a third party (usually neutral and unbiased) facilitates a negotiated consensual agreement among parties, without rendering a formal decision, and *arbitration*, which resembles formal adjudication in which a third party or panel of arbitrators, most often chosen by the parties themselves, renders a decision, in terms less formal than a court, often without a written or reasoned opinion and without formal rules of *evidence being applied. As noted later, the full panoply of processes denominated under the rubric of ADR now includes a variety of primary and hybrid processes, with elements of dyadic negotiation, facilitative, advisory, and decisional action by a wide variety of third-party neutrals, sometimes combined with each other to create new form of dispute processing.

ADR: What It Is. In an era characterized by a wide variety of processes for resolving disputes among individuals, organizations, and nations, process pluralism has become the norm in both formal disputing systems, such as legal systems and *courts, and in more informal, private settings, as in private *contracts and transactions, family disputes, and internal organizational grievance systems. A number of factors determine the kinds of processes that parties may choose or may be ordered to use under rules of law, court, or contract.

The "primary" processes consist of individual action (self-help, avoidance), dyadic bargaining (negotiation), and third-party facilitated approaches (mediation) or third-party decisional formats (arbitration and adjudication). "Hybrid" or "secondary" processes combine elements of these processes, and include med-arb (facilitated negotiation followed by decision), mini-trials (shortened evidentiary proceedings followed by negotiation), summary jury/judge trials (use of mock jurors or judges to hear evidence and issue "advisory" verdicts to assist in negotiation, often conducted within the formal court system), and early neutral evaluation (third parties, usually lawyers or other experts, who hear arguments and evidence and "advise" about the issues or values of the dispute, for purposes of facilitating settlement or structuring the dispute process). Increasing judicial involvement in dispute settlement suggests that judicial, and often mandatory, settlement conferences, under Rule 16 of the Federal Rules of Civil Procedure (see PROCEDURE, CIVIL), are another form of hybrid dispute mechanism. Retired judges provide a hybrid form of arbitration or adjudication in private "rent-a-judge" schemes that are sometimes authorized by the state.

Dispute processes are also characterized by the extent to which they are voluntary and consensual (whether in pre-dispute contract agreements, ADR *ex ante*, or voluntarily undertaken after the dispute ripens, ADR *ex post*), or whether they are mandated (by a pre-dispute contract commitment), or by court rule or referral. Several federal statutes now require consideration of some form of ADR in all ninety-four federal district courts (Alternative Dispute Resolution Act of 1998, 28 U.S. Code sect. 651–658; Civil Justice Reform Act of 1990, 28 U.S. Code sect. 471–482). The use of a hybrid form of ADR, negotiated rule-making, is authorized for federal administrative agencies in the Administrative Dispute Resolution Act of 1996, 5 U.S. Code sect. 571–584. Many states also either require or strongly recommend the use of some form of ADR once a case is filed in court.

The ideology that contributed to the founding of modern mediation urges that mediation be vol-untarily entered into and all agreements be arrived at consensually. Nevertheless, as courts have increasingly sought to "manage" or reduce their caseloads, and have looked to ADR processes as a means of diverting cases to other forums, even mediation may be "mandated," although it is usually participation in, not substantive agreement, that is required.

The taxonomy of different dispute processes also differentiates between binding and nonbinding processes. Arbitration, for example, can be structured either way. Under some contractual and statutory schemes (such as the American Federal Arbitration Act, 9 U.S. Code sect. 1 et. seq. (1925)), decisions by private arbitrators are final and binding on the parties and subject to very limited court review, including only such claims as fraud, corruption of the arbitrator, or, in a few jurisdictions, serious errors of law or extreme "miscarriages of justice." Nonbinding processes, including nonbinding decisions in some arbitrations, allow appeals or follow-through to other processes, such as mediation or full trial. Many court-annexed arbitration programs (for example, mandated and voluntary arbitration of cases, usually by lawyers, which have been filed as lawsuits and are pending for decision in a court, but may be assigned by court rule or judicial order to a court sponsored arbitration program) allow a de novo trial following an arbitration if one party seeks it, often requiring that party to post a bond or deposit for costs. The process of mediation itself is nonbinding in that, as a consensual process, a party may exit at any time; on the other hand, once an agreement in mediation is reached, a "binding" contract may be signed, enforceable in a court of law.

Finally, dispute processes are often subject to different requirements depending on whether they are used in private settings (by contract, in employment, or other organizational settings) or in public arenas such as courts. Court related or "court-annexed" ADR programs, now encompassing the full panoply of dispute processes, may be subject to greater legal regulation, including selection, training, and credentialing of the arbitrators or mediators, ethics, *confidentiality and conflicts of interest rules, as well as providing for greater immunity from legal *liability.

ADR processes are often differentiated from each other by the degree of control the third-party neutral has over both the process (the rules of proceedings), the substance (decision, advice, or facilitation), and the formality of the proceeding (whether held in private or public settings, with or without formal rules of evidence, informal separate meetings, or "caucuses" with the parties, and with or without participation of more than the principal disputants). ADR processes are increasingly being applied to diverse kinds of conflicts, disputes, and transactions, some requiring expertise in the subject matter (such as scientific and policy disputes) and spawning new hybrid processes such as "consensus-building," which engage multiple parties in complex, multi-issue problem-solving, drawing on negotiation, mediation, and other non-adjudicative processes.

Historical Background. The modern growth of arbitration, mediation, and other ADR processes can be attributed to at least two different animating concerns. On the one hand, scholars, practitioners, consumers, and advocates for justice in the 1960s and 1970s noted the lack of responsiveness of the formal judicial system, and sought better "quality" processes and outcomes for members of society seeking to resolve disputes with each other, with the government, or with private organizations. This strand of concern with the "quality" of dispute-resolution processes sought deprofessionalization of judicial processes (a reduction of the lawyer monopoly over dispute representation), with greater access to more locally based institutions, such as neighborhood "justice centers," which utilized community members, as well as those with expertise in particular problems, with the hope of generating greater party participation in dispute-resolution processes. Others sought better outcomes than those commonly provided by the formal justice system, which tend toward the binary, polarized results of litigation in which one party is declared a loser, while the other is, at least nominally, a winner. More flexible and party-controlled processes were believed to deliver the possibility of more creative solutions that were geared to joint outcomes, reduction of harm or waste to as many parties as possible, improvement of long-term relationships, and greater responsiveness to the underlying needs and interests of the parties, rather than to the stylized arguments and "limited remedial imaginations" of courts and the formal justice system. Some ADR processes (such as arbitration) are rule-based, but others (negotiation and mediation) are thought to provide individualized solutions to problems, rather than generalized notions of "justice."

A second strand of argument contributing to the development of ADR was more quantitatively or efficiency-based. Judicial officers argued that the excessive cost and delay in the litigation system required devices that would divert cases from courts and reduce caseloads, as well as provide other and more efficient ways of providing access to justice. This efficiency-based impetus behind ADR encouraged both court-mandated programs such as court-annexed arbitration for cases with lower economic stakes, and encouraged contractual requirements to arbitrate any and all disputes arising from services and products provided in banking, *health care, *consumer, *securities, educational, and communication-based industries.

Modern ADR structures are only loosely related to their historical antecedents. Arbitration had its origins in private commercial arbitrations, outside the formal court structure, and was used principally by merchants in disputes with each other. *Labor arbitration developed in order to secure "labor peace" as well as to develop a specialized substantive law of the "shop floor."

Early use of mediation or conciliation occurred in some courts and communities seeking both to reduce caseloads and provide more consensual agreements in ethnically or religiously homogeneous areas. Indeed, mediation and other consensually based processes are thought to work best in regimes where there are shared values, whether based on common ethnicity, communitarian, or political values. In some nations, such as China, mediation, as a preferred form of dispute resolution, has been used for system or political regime purposes beyond resolving the disputes of the parties.

Key Concepts and Usages. Each of the ADR processes have their own logic, purposes, and jurisprudential justifications. Mediation and conciliation are often used to improve communications between parties, especially those with preexisting relationships, to "reorient the parties to each other," and to develop future-oriented solutions to broadly defined conflicts. Arbitration, on the other hand, being more like adjudication, is used more often to definitively resolve a concrete dispute about an event that has transpired and requires fact-finding, interpretation of contractual terms, or application of legal principles.

These basic forms have been adapted to a number of subject areas and dispute sites. As regular use of these formats of dispute resolution becomes more common, mediation seems to be overtaking arbitration as a preferred method of dispute resolution (because of the ideology of party self-determination and the flexibility of agreements). Arbitration, still most commonly used in labor disputes, is now the method of choice in form contracts signed by consumers as well as merchants. Arbitration has thus far been the mode of choice for resolving international commercial, investment, and trade disputes, such as in the World Trade Organization (WTO) and the General Agreement on Tariffs and Trade (GATT). Arbitration has also been deployed in new forms of disputes developing under both domestic and international intellectual *property regimes. Various forms of mediation and arbitration are also increasingly being used to resolve transnational disputes of various kinds (political, economic, natural resource allocation, and ethnic violence) and are employed by international organizations such as the United Nations and the Organization of American States, as well as multinational trade and treaty groups (NAFTA, the European Union, and Mercosur) and non-governmental organizations in human rights and other issue-related disputes.

Increasingly, mass injury (class action) cases, both involving personal and property damages, have been allocated to ADR claims facilities, utilizing both arbitral and mediative forms of individual case processing. Family disputes are increasingly assigned to mediative processes, both for *child custody and support and maintenance issues. In many nations, this growth in family mediation has spurred the development of a new profession of mediators, drawn from social work or psychology, who sometimes compete with lawyers, both in private practice and as court officers.

In many jurisdictions, some form of referral to ADR is now required before a case may be tried. Increasingly, however, parties to particularly complex disputes, such as environmental, mass torts, or governmental budgeting, may convene their own ADR processes, with a third-party neutral facilitating a new form of public participatory process that combines negotiation, fact-finding, mediation, and joint problem-solving. Such "consensus-building" processes have also been applied to the administrative tribunal processes of both rule-making and administrative adjudication in a new process called "reg-neg" (negotiated rule-making or regulation).

Controversies. The use of mediation, arbitration, and ADR processes, in lieu of more traditional adjudication, has not been without its controversies, which are reviewed briefly in this section.

Privatization of Jurisprudence. With the increased use of negotiated settlements, mediation, and private arbitration, there has been concern that fewer and fewer cases will be available in the public arena for the making of precedent and debate about, and creation of rules and political values for, the larger community. As settlements are conducted in private, and often have confidentiality or secrecy clauses attached to them, others will not learn about wrongs committed by defendants, and information that might otherwise be discoverable will be shielded from public view. Settlements may be based on nonlegal criteria, threatening compliance with and enforcement of the law. Claims are more likely to be individualized than collectivized.

Related concerns about the privatization of the judicial system include increased indirect state intervention in the affairs of the citizenry through more disputing institutions, at the same time that the exit of wealthier litigants gives them less of a stake in the quality and financing of public justice systems. The debate centers on whether dispute-resolution systems can simultaneously serve the private interests of disputants before them, and the polity's need for the articulation of publicly enforced norms and values.

Inequalities of Bargaining Power. A number of critics have suggested that less powerful members of society, particularly those subordinated by race, ethnicity, class, or gender, will be disproportionately disadvantaged in ADR processes, where there are no judges, formal rules, or, in some cases, even legal representatives to protect the parties and advise them of their legal entitlements. Responses from ADR theorists suggest that there is little empirical evidence that less-advantaged individuals or groups necessarily fare better in the formal justice system, and that sophisticated mediators and arbitrators are indeed sensitive to power imbalances and can be trained to "correct" for them without endangering their "neutrality" in the ADR process. Many private ADR organizations have begun developing standards for good practices and due process protocols to protect the parties and ensure the integrity of the process.

Evaluation and Empirical Verification of Effectiveness. There are few robust research findings with respect to the effectiveness of ADR in meeting its claimed advantages. Recent findings from studies of ADR in U.S. federal courts have been contradictory about whether or not arbitration, mediation, and some forms of early neutral evaluation do decrease case-processing time or costs, either for the parties or the system. Yet studies continue to demonstrate high satisfaction rates of users of arbitration and mediation programs and higher compliance rates with mediated outcomes than traditional adjudication.

Distortions and Deformations of ADR Processes.

Within the nascent ADR profession there is concern that the early animating ideologies of ADR are being distorted by their assimilation into the conventional justice system. Within a movement that sought to deprofessionalize conflict resolution, there are now competing professional claims for control of standards, ethics, credentialing, and quality control between lawyers and nonlawyers. Processes such as mediation that were conceived as voluntary and consensual are now being mandated by court rules and contracts. Processes that were supposed to be creative, flexible, and facilitative are becoming more rigid and rule- and law-based, and judicialized as more common law about ADR is created by courts and more laws are passed by legislatures. The overall concern is that a set of processes that were developed to be "alternatives" to the traditional judicial system are themselves being coopted by the traditional judicial process with its overwhelming adversary culture. Policymakers and practitioners in the field are concerned about whether a private market in ADR is good for "disciplining" and competing with the public justice system, or whether there will be insufficient accountability within a private market of dispute resolution.

The Future of ADR. There is no question that the use of a variety of different processes to resolve individual, organizational, and international problems is continuing to expand. New hybrid forms of ADR (as in mediation on the Internet) are developing to help resolve new problems with greater participation by more parties. Large organizations are creating their own internal dispute-resolution systems. There are clearly trends in favor of mediation and arbitration in the international arena, where globalization of enterprises and governmental interests require creative and simple processes that are not overly attached to any one jurisdiction's substantive law to promote goals of efficiency, fairness, clarity, and legitimacy, particularly in regimes with underdeveloped formal legal systems. It is also clear that there is competition over who will control such processes and which processes will dominate in which spheres of human disputing and deal-making. The likely result is that the creative pluralism and flexibility of ADR will be increasingly subject to its own forms of formality and regulation in an effort to keep its promises of efficiency, participation, better quality outcomes, and justice.

[See also Arbitration and Mediation]

• Jerold Auerbach, *Justice Without Law?*, 1983. Roger Fisher, William Ury, and Bruce Patton, *Getting To Yes: Negotiating Agreement Without Giving In*, 2d.ed., 1991.

Carrie Menkel-Meadow, *Mediation: Theory, Practice and Policy*, 2001. Carrie Menkel-Meadow, "When Dispute Resolution Begets Disputes of Its Own: Conflicts Among Dispute Professionals," *UCLA Law Review* 44 (1997): 1871–1933. Jacqueline M. Nolan-Haley, *Alternative Dispute Resolution*, 1992. Michael Palmer and Simon Roberts, *ADR and the Primary Processes of Decision-Making*, 1998. Frank Sander, "Varieties of Dispute Processing," *Federal Rules Decisions* 70 (1976): 111–134. Frank Sander and Stephen Goldberg, "Fitting the Forum to the Fuss: A User Friendly Guide to Selecting an ADR Procedure," *Negotiation Journal* 10 (1994): 49–68. Lawrence Susskind, Sarah McKearnan, Jennifer Thomas-Larmer, eds., *The Consensus Building Handbook: A Comprehensive Guide to Reaching Agreement*, 1999.

—Carrie Menkel-Meadow

AMENDMENTS, CONSTITUTIONAL. *See* Bill of Rights; Constitutional Amendments; Fourteenth Amendment.

AMERICAN BAR ASSOCIATION. On the eve of the founding of the American Bar Association in 1878, the status of education and preparation for the bar in the United States was rudimentary at best. The Jacksonian era's aversion to privilege had lifted many of the local restrictions to the bar and the bench, effectively democratizing the profession of law. Preparation for the bar was almost exclusively through apprenticeship, and law practice itself was predominantly court-and advocacy-based; in 1860 as few as nine of the nation's thirty-nine jurisdictions required some formal preparation for admission to the bar. In 1878 only a handful of local and state *bar associations were meeting (fifteen in all). The first modern law school had been founded only seven years earlier at Harvard, with the appointment of Christopher Columbus Langdell as dean. Against this backdrop, the social, demographic, and economic transformation of American society in the post–Civil War era—with its regional, national, and international financial and industrial concerns—posed new demands on law and its practitioners. These changes brought to the forefront issues of professional training and competence, *ethics, the quality of judicial administration, and the rationality and uniformity of laws.

Simeon E. Baldwin was a distinguished Connecticut lawyer, early practitioner of corporate law, and leader in the Connecticut Bar Association. As a member of the Yale Law School faculty and a person keenly interested in legal reform and good government, Baldwin issued a circular to some of the "best men of the bar" in America inviting them to a meeting in Saratoga Springs, New York, to consider the founding of an American bar association. The gathering at the New York resort in 1878, attracting seventy-five lawyers from twenty-one states (at this time the United States had sixty thousand lawyers), was a congenial meeting of like minds. The lawyers approved a constitution (drafted by Baldwin) with a unanimous vote, and the American Bar Association (ABA) was launched.

The emergence of the ABA, far from being a self-interested enterprise of a handful of lawyers, was part of an emerging culture of professionalism. In the same era, librarians, scholars, social workers, economists, chemists, teachers, medical doctors, and others formed specialized national membership organizations. The ABA's mission was to "advance the science of jurisprudence, promote the administration of justice and uniformity in legislation throughout the union, uphold the honor of the profession of law, and encourage cordial intercourse among the members of the American bar."

The growth in membership was slow (reaching 1,718 in 1902). Yet Baldwin was a skillful organizer, and the association busied itself with the appointment of standing and special committees, reports, sections, and conferences. The uniformity of laws was a uniquely national concern, and in 1892 the ABA formed the National Conference of Commissioners on Uniform State Laws. The association invited delegations from state and local bar associations to its meetings and soon spun off a new, partner organization, the *Association of American Law Schools (1900). In 1908 the ABA enacted a canon of professional ethics, which state bar associations adopted or modified. By 1920 its membership had grown to just under four thousand, but it asserted an influence that belied its size and reflected the perspectives of the profession's elite, which made up its membership.

Until 1936 an assembly of members attending the annual meeting governed the ABA, an organizational structure unchanged since the association's founding. That year, as membership reached almost thirty thousand, the ABA undertook a major reorganization as part of an effort to broaden its base and operate more effectively. (It retained its system of sections and committees through which the organization accomplishes much of its work.) It added a house of delegates composed of affiliated organizations, state delegates, representatives of state and local bar associations, juridical groups, and others. Together with a board of governors, the federated structure of governance set up in 1936 has continued to serve the association while its membership has grown to four hundred

thousand (a little less than half of all lawyers in the country). It is the largest professional voluntary association in the world and is the official voice and representative of the profession in the United States.

The ABA, as a membership association, historically has found itself pulled in different directions. Despite the perception that the organization has become more political in recent years, the ABA has always lived with the tension between its public and professional responsibilities and the political and personal interests of its members— and the challenge of understanding specifically where the line between the two is drawn.

The association's extensive law reform efforts have been effective and generally have enjoyed broad support within the profession. These notably include the formulation of the Federal Rules of Civil Procedure, creation of the Administrative Office of the United States Courts, development of a separate federal *courts of appeal, and the more specific contributions of its specialized sections to substantive law. It has provided for continuing legal education, guarded judicial independence and integrity, and prescribed ethical standards and procedures for enforcement. Not least significant, the ABA has helped shape the modern profession through its long-term emphasis on standards and education.

Another aspect of the ABA's professional service (and perhaps its most public) began in 1946, when the association created the Standing Committee on the Federal Judiciary to assess the professional qualifications of nominations for the federal bench. Since 1948, the Senate has invited the ABA's assessment of individuals nominated for a federal judicial appointment. In 1952 President Harry Truman consulted the committee, a precedent that every president since has followed. Not until 1969 and 1970, with the nominations of Judge Clement F. Haynesworth and Judge Harold D. Carswell to the Supreme Court, were the committee's recommendations publicly questioned. The nomination of Judge Robert H. Bork in 1987 led to the most controversial assessment yet. A minority report by the ABA's standing committee objected to his nomination based on his lack of compassion and sensitivity as an element of judicial temperament. The Bork nomination heightened the conversation in the association, begun in 1969, about the place of politics and ideology in the assessment of a candidate's qualifications (a complex issue) and set a new precedent in the involvement of the public in the debate. Despite the challenges of the questions posed in these cases and the diversity of views within the ABA, the association remains indispensable to the process of federal judicial appointment.

The ABA's activities have also extended into areas that have on occasion sparked internal disagreement and brought down public accusations of partisanship. As early as 1908, an editorial in the *American Lawyer* argued that the association should become involved in the formulation of public policy—and indeed, many lawyers had been involved as opponents of populist reforms and progressive legislation. In 1912 the ABA took its first public position and opposed the ratification of the Sixteenth Amendment (1913), which allowed for a national income tax, as an "encroachment on private wealth." In 1916 Elihu Root, president of the ABA, and several former association presidents, including William Howard *Taft, sharply attacked President Woodrow Wilson's nomination of Louis D. *Brandeis to the Supreme Court, an action interpreted as politically motivated. In 1924 the association launched a public campaign in opposition to a *constitutional amendment that would prohibit child labor, creating public concern. Its running battle with President Franklin Roosevelt in the 1930s kept the ABA in the news. In the 1950s, at the beginning of the Cold War, the association vigorously supported loyalty oaths and advocated the exclusion of communists and persons of Marxist-Leninist persuasion from the profession.

The ABA's activism, however, is not easily pigeonholed. In 1903 it condemned *trusts; in 1912, endorsed state laws modeled on federal food and drug legislation; and in the 1920s, advocated government regulation of air navigation and income tax deductions for charitable contributions. While it visibly and adamantly opposed the "Child Labor Amendment," it urged adoption by the states of a uniform child labor law.

A new phase of activism, begun in the 1970s and continuing to the present, has led to the adoption of official positions in areas (*abortion, sexual orientation, AIDS, homelessness, hunger, artistic freedom) that raise issues of discrimination, access, *privacy rights, intellectual and artistic freedom, and ethics in government. The ABA has positions on over seven hundred standing legislative provisions, and since 1957, in addition to its headquarters in Chicago, the organization has operated an office in Washington, D.C.

The extent to which members' views are represented in the association's formally adopted positions, and the appropriateness of action in areas perceived as political, are not new concerns. Internal dissent in the 1930s culminated in an effort to create a counter-organization, the *National Lawyers Guild, by ABA members unhappy with the association's perceived partisan stance toward the New Deal and its record in defense of civil rights and civil liberties. (The Guild failed.) Chief Justice Earl *Warren resigned his membership in the ABA over displeasure with the association's positions on free speech. In his 1965 address, ABA president Lewis Powell warned that if the association strayed too far from its core professional purpose of "administration of justice" to express views on controversial or political issues, it would "fractionate" the profession.

The American Bar Association's historical challenge has been to balance the interests of its members with the responsibility of serving the public. The goals of the association in 2001 remain largely consistent with those of its founders, but it has broadened its membership base while evolving new values of justice and inclusion. Education, administration of justice, legal improvements, ethics, and professional competence and integrity remain important goals. They are supplemented by a more recent commitment to "full and equal participation in the legal profession by minorities, women, and persons with disabilities" and "meaningful access to legal representation and the American system of justice for all persons regardless of their economic or social condition." The ABA's capacity for growth, change, and service remains its strongest asset.

[*See also* Bar Associations; National Lawyers' Guild]

• James Willard Hurst, *The Growth of American Law: The Law Makers*, 1950. Edson R. Sunderland, *History of the American Bar Association and Its Work*, 1953. Edythe Keshner, *Check List: Publications of Sections and House of Delegates—American Bar Association*, 1961. Lawrence M. Friedman, *A History of American Law*, 1973. Burton J. Bledstein, *The Culture of Professionalism: The Middle Class and the Development of Higher Education in America*, 1976. Gerard W. Gawalt, ed., *The New High Priests: Lawyers in Post–Civil War America*, 1984. Kermit L. Hall, *The Magic Mirror: Law in American History*, 1989. Federalist Society for Law and Public Policy Studies, *The ABA in Law and Social Policy: What Role?*, 1994.

—Jamil Zainaldin

AMERICAN JUDICATURE SOCIETY. A nonpartisan organization consisting of judges, lawyers, and lay people who share an interest in improving the administration of justice. The American Judicature Society (AJS) seeks to ensure the independence of the judiciary, improve judicial selection and ethics, upgrade court administration and the performance of juries, and enhance public understanding of the justice system through research, public education programs, and publications.

A product of early twentieth-century Progressivism, AJS was founded in 1913 by Herbert Lincoln Harley, a lawyer turned journalist, with financial backing from Charles Ruggles, an eccentric lumberman who hated courts. Harley tapped into the widespread dissatisfaction with the judicial system that Professor Roscoe *Pound had highlighted in a famous 1906 speech condemning its archaic organization and procedures. Seeking to solve those problems and get the judiciary out of politics, Harley spent about a year touring the country, soliciting ideas on how to make the courts more efficient, and enlisting support from the legal community. Then, on October 7, 1912, he sent out a circular letter, proposing creation of a permanent national organization to reform the administration of justice. The enthusiastic support it elicited led to the official launching of AJS on April 5, 1913 in Chicago.

The organization devoted most of the next dozen years to publishing a series of bulletins that outlined possible causes of popular disaffection with the legal system and proposed ways to eliminate them. AJS also drafted model rules of civil procedure and launched a journal. By 1925 it was becoming moderately influential, and some of the reforms it championed were winning adoption.

In the mid-1920s Ruggles withdrew his financial support. After nearly folding, in 1928 AJS reorganized into what was essentially a letterhead organization, nominally headed by prominent figures, such as Charles Evans Hughes and Newton Baker, but actually consisting of little more than Harley himself. In 1931, after feuding with the dean of the Northwestern University School of Law, which had housed AJS since 1916, he moved AJS to the University of Michigan School of Law, where it remained until 1953, when it returned to Chicago at the invitation of the American Bar Foundation.

A 1935 grant from the Carnegie Corporation revitalized AJS financially. Under the leadership of Harley and Glenn Winters, who succeeded him as secretary-treasurer in 1945, AJS expanded its membership and saw Missouri adopt the reform with which it was most closely identified, the merit selection of judges.

Long merely a source of ideas and an information clearing house, during the 1960s AJS plunged into the active promotion of reform. Working with like-minded groups under the umbrella of the Joint Committee for the Effective Administration of Justice, AJS successfully promoted reforms in judicial selection and tenure and the creation of unified state courts. It also sponsored research, publications, and citizens conferences across the country. Its membership expanded, and its volunteer leadership came to exercise greater control over its affairs.

That leadership replaced Winters with Frederick D. Lewis Jr. in 1974, but his inept administration lasted only two years. In 1982 an Internal Revenue Service ruling that money derived from insurance AJS had been making available to members was taxable income nearly destroyed the organization financially. It took a number of years for Executive Directors George H. Williams and Frances Zemans, with substantial assistance from volunteer leaders, to rebuild AJS into a viable and active organization.

[See also Judge]

• Michal R. Belknap, *To Improve the Administration of Justice: A History of the American Judicature Society*, 1992.   —Michal R. Belknap

AMERICAN LAW INSTITUTE. The American Law Institute (ALI) is an independent, nongovernmental, nonprofit organization dedicated to the improvement of the law. Its members include law professors, practicing lawyers, and judges.

The impetus for the organization of the ALI came from the *Association of American Law Schools (AALS). For a number of years, dating back to before the First World War, reformist and liberal law professors had debated the possibility of organizing a "juristic center" dedicated to improving American law. Some of the law professors who championed such a center wanted to bring order to what they saw as the complexity and lack of uniformity in the American legal system. To some extent they were inspired by the success of the National Conference of Commissioners on Uniform State Laws (NCCUSL), which was founded in the late nineteenth century with the aim of promoting uniform state laws through model laws that its members would lobby state legislatures to adopt. The juristic center the AALS law professors discussed would, they hoped, bring the same sort of order to the *common law.

When the AALS convened for its annual meeting at the end of 1920, the charged political events surrounding the first Red Scare, and the response of the practicing bar during the previous twelve months, had placed the creation of a national juristic center in a new light. A number of the reformist law professors backing the creation of the juristic center now hoped that it would promote a more liberal legal atmosphere, less antipathetic toward social reform in an era when courts, particularly the federal courts, regularly oppressed or ganized labor and overturned Progressive social legislation.

It was at this juncture that William Draper Lewis, former dean of the University of Pennsylvania Law School, an ardent Progressive, and a member of the committee charged by the AALS to study the question of founding a juristic center, took the project "on his own responsibility," to New York lawyer Elihu Root. Root was the acknowledged leader of the American bar, a former U.S. senator, secretary of war under McKinley and secretary of state under Theodore Roosevelt, and a Nobel Peace Prize Winner. His endorsement of the ALI was important to the inauguration of the enterprise.

Lewis sent out invitations at the end of April 1922 to a select list of practitioners on behalf of the AALS Committee and included a copy of the 1921 AALS resolution to establish a permanent institution for the improvement of law. Lewis's letter concluded by mentioning that Root, James Byrne (president of both the Association of the Bar of the City of New York and the Harvard Club of New York), and George S. Wickersham (a leading corporate counsel and attorney general under President Taft) all planned to attend. Though the AALS committee was the official host for the meeting, it was thus also sponsored by the leaders of the New York corporate legal community.

Twenty-three invitees met on May 10, 1922, at the headquarters of the Association of the Bar of the City of New York. This preliminary gathering of bar luminaries and AALS committee members agreed to the creation of an institute for the improvement of law, authorized the writing of a report to state its case, and voted to convene a general meeting of founders the next year.

On February 23, 1923, the cream of the American legal establishment convened in Washington, D.C., to found the ALI. Among those attending were three U.S. Supreme Court justices, five judges of the U.S. Circuit Court of Appeals, twenty-seven state supreme court justices, the presidents or representatives of seventeen state bar associations, the president and twenty-one General Council members of the American Bar Association, the president of the National Conference and twenty-one state Commissioners on Uniform State Laws, twenty-three law school deans or professors representing the Association of American Law Schools, and nearly two hundred "specially invited" practitioners and law professors from twenty-eight states and the District of Co-

lumbia. The *New York Times* reported the next day that the meeting was "probably the most distinguished gathering of the legal profession in the history of the country." Elihu Root commented at the close of the meeting that "I have been fifty-six years at the American bar, and that I have never seen so distinguished and competent meeting of the bench and bar as this."

The first major project of the new organization was a Restatement of the principles and rules of the common law. This turned out to be a massive undertaking encompassing ten subject areas ranging from the law of agency to the laws of contract, property, and torts. The preliminary budget of $15,000, plus an additional $10,000 of anticipated future expenses, would be raised by applying to the Carnegie Corporation. A complete list of the subjects, volumes, and participants who helped write or advise on this first Restatement project fills twenty pages. The first volume (on the subject of contract law) appeared in 1932, and the final volume was not published until 1944 (the last volume of the Restatement of the law of property).

Even before the original Restatement project was completed—a second Restatement with additional subject areas was begun in 1952 and completed in the 1980s, and an even more ambitious third Restatement is currently under way)—the ALI branched out in several directions. Early projects included a Code of Criminal Procedure (1930), a report on the Administration of the Criminal Law's Double Jeopardy rule (1935), a Youth Correction Authority Act (1940), and a Model Code of Evidence (1942). The Institute also sponsored the drafting of a Statement of Essential Human Rights in the 1940s that became the model for the United Nations Declaration of Human Rights.

By far the most successful and significant of the ALI's extra-Restatement undertakings were The Uniform Commercial Code (UCC) (first draft completed in 1952 and final version adopted in 1963) and the *Model Penal Code (MPC)(1962). The UCC was a fairly comprehensive code intended for legislative adoption. It went far beyond the earlier Uniform Sales Act to regulate commercial activity in banking, secure transactions, and sales. The MPC was just that, an ambitious model for statutory reform of criminal law and corrections. Both the UCC and the MPC were immensely successful; the UCC has been adopted in whole or in part by every state in the Union (Louisiana has not adopted its sales provisions) and the MPC is the model for criminal law reform for most states and the federal government.

[*See also* Codification; Llewellyn, Karl Nickerson]

• William Draper Lewis, *History of the American Law Institute and the First Restatement of the Law, "How We Did It,"* 1945. Herbert F. Goodrich and Paul A. Wolkin, *The Story of the American Law Institute,* 1961. N. E. H. Hull, "Restatement and Reform: A New Perspective on the Origins of the American Law Institute," *Law and History Review* (1990): 55. N. E. H. Hull, "Back to the 'Future of the Institute': William Draper Lewis's Vision of the ALI's Mission During Its First Twenty-Five Years and the Implications for the Institute's Seventy-Fifth Anniversary," *The American Law Institute's Seventy-Fifth Anniversary,* 1998.   —N. E. H. Hull

AMERICAN REVOLUTION, LEGAL IMPACT OF.

The Revolution affected American law in numerous ways. It liberated Americans from their ties to Britain, and thus allowed changes in law that would have previously been disallowed because they violated British Imperial policy. For example, in the period before the Revolution, Virginia attempted to prohibit the importation of new slaves from Africa, but London disallowed the laws because they would have undermined the Royal Africa Company and harmed overall mercantile policy. Once the Revolution began, Virginia and other states were able to implement this new policy. The Revolution also allowed for a reform of English *common law to make it more compatible with American circumstances. In the years following the Revolution the common law was "Americanized" through judicial interpretation and legislative action. The abolition of entail and primogeniture by Virginia and other states illustrates this. Similarly, all of the northern states rejected English *divorce law and allowed courts to grant full divorces, rather than simply granting legal separations.

The humanitarian impulses of the Revolution had an immediate affect on *criminal law. Some older laws, such as those punishing premarital fornication, either ceased to be enforced or disappeared altogether. In most states the number of capital offenses rapidly diminished, stimulated by a dramatic change in ideology that led to a liberalization of law to reflect new humanitarian concerns. A number of states reduced their capital offenses to just three: murder, rape, and treason. In 1796 Virginia abolished *capital punishment for all crimes committed by whites except premeditated murder. At the same time, almost all states prohibited *cruel and unusual punishments for whites. Rejecting whipping and other forms of physical punishment, many of the new states created penitentiaries, as part of an ideological commitment to reforming criminals, rather than using punishment as a form of vengeance or to make examples of criminals. Criminal law reform even affected slavery. Some slave states banned maiming, castration, and other barbaric punishment for slaves. In 1791 North Carolina declared that anyone convicted of "wilfully and maliciously killing a slave" would be "guilty of murder."

Humanitarian reform also affected *slavery more directly. During the Revolution every state suspended or banned the African slave trade, and only Georgia and South Carolina later reopened the trade. Meanwhile, between 1780 and 1804 all of the northern states either ended slavery outright, through constitutional provision, or phased it out through gradual emancipation statutes. The preamble to Pennsylvania's Gradual Abolition Act of 1780, written by Tom Paine, incorporated revolutionary rhetoric and idealism, making a reference to the "tyranny of Great-Britain." The southern states continued to maintain slavery, but Virginia and Maryland liberalized their laws to allow for private manumission. The creation of written *constitutions was a profoundly important innovation of the Revolution. By the end of the period every state but Rhode Island and Connecticut had written a constitution. So too had the new national government. The constitutions not only set out a framework for creating a republican form of government throughout the United States, but also provided specific protections of basic civil and political liberties in the new nation. Especially important were guarantees for a fair judicial process and the protections of freedom of the press and the free exercise of *religion. Through constitutional provision and statute a number of states, as well as the national government, jettisoned their colonial heritage of state-supported religion. Many states expanded legal and political rights, including the right of suffrage. Some states removed property restrictions on *voting, all removed any remaining religious disabilities for voting, although only two did for office holding, and most of the northern states, as well as North Carolina, extended the franchise to all free males, without any racial barriers. New Jersey, in a remarkable and short-lived experiment, extended the franchise to women.

The culmination of legal change in the Revolutionary period came with the development of American legal texts. Zephaniah Swift's *A System of the Laws of the State of Connecticut* (1795) was the first American legal text of the period. More important was Saint George Tucker's American edition of *Blackstone's Commentaries* (1803). Tucker noted that although law students studied Blackstone, they in fact only learned "what the *law had been*," and "to know *what it is now*" the law student had to "resort to very different sources of information." Tucker used these sources—cases, statutes, and Constitutions—to show the world what had happened in his country since 1775: that a new, American law had been created, based on Republican values, written constitutions, and a federal system of states working with a national government.

• William E. Nelson, *The Americanization of the Common Law*, 1975. Morton Horwitz, *The Transformation of American Law*, 1977. Linda Kerber, *Women of the Republic: Intellect and Ideology in Revolutionary America*, 1980. A. G. Roeber, *Faithful Magistrates and Republican Lawyers: Creators of Virginia Legal Culture, 1680–1810*, 1981. Paul Finkelman and David Cobin, eds., *Tucker's Blackstone*, 1996. Sandra F. VanBurkleo, *Belonging to the World: Women's Rights and American Constitutional Culture*, 2001. Melvin Urofsky and Paul Finkelman, *A March of Liberty: A Constitutional History of the United States*, 2002.   —Paul Finkelman

AMERICANS WITH DISABILITIES ACT (ADA). *See* Disabilities Law; Discrimination.

ANNOYANCE. *See* Harassment.

ANNULMENT. *See* Canon Law in America; Divorce and Annulment.

ANTHONY, SUSAN B., TRIAL OF (1873). On the last day of registration for the presidential elections of 1872, suffragist Susan B. Anthony and her three sisters tried to register to vote. At least fifty other women in Rochester, New York, followed suit, as did a significant number of would-be female voters in other cities and towns throughout the nation. These actions were part of a suffragist strategy to win the vote by means of a test case. When election judges rejected Anthony's registration, she demonstrated *citizenship and asserted a right to vote under the *Fourteenth Amendment. Anthony also threatened to sue the election judges personally. After consulting a lawyer and learning that punishments would fall on the women if they voted, the judges allowed registration. On November 5, 1872, Anthony cast a ballot. "Well, I have been & gone & done it!" she wrote to Elizabeth Cady Stanton. "Positively voted the Republican ticket—strait—this A.M. at 7 o'clock & swore my vote in."

On November 28, 1872, Anthony was arrested, with fourteen other Rochester women, for the federal crime of unlawfully casting a ballot in a presidential election. Determined to transform her arrest into a public trial of the woman suffrage question, Anthony refused bail; without her knowledge, her attorney put up the amount, thereby sacrificing a chance to get the case before the Supreme Court. Anthony was outraged.

On January 22, 1873, a grand jury indicted Anthony under an 1870 federal statute; in March, she voted in a local election. At the same time, she undertook a lecture series throughout the county to educate "possible jurymen," mobilize public support for suffragism, encourage women to storm the polls, and castigate public officials for tampering with citizens' natural rights. Perceiving rightly that Anthony's speeches had influenced public opinion, authorities moved her trial to Canandaigua, in Ontario County.

Anthony's trial commenced on June 17, 1873, with Supreme Court justice Ward Hunt presiding. Prosecutors argued that Anthony was a woman and had voted illegally. She insisted that the Constitution of the United States, as amended in 1868 and 1870, permitted and even required universal suffrage. In an opinion prepared in advance of trial, Hunt argued (in keeping with the implications of the Supreme Court's ruling in the 1873 *Slaughterhouse Cases*) that suffrage was not one of the *privileges and immunities of federal citizenship. When Anthony tried to speak, Hunt silenced her. In the end, Hunt directed a verdict of guilty and imposed a fine of $100, which Anthony refused to pay.

In January, 1874, delegates to the annual convention of the National Woman Suffrage Association meeting in Washington, D.C., condemned Hunt's "grossly partial course," underscored the unconstitutional denial of Anthony's right to a trial by her peers, and urged women's rights activists to engage in *civil disobedience. Congress ultimately spread over the record a petition containing Anthony's constitutional arguments and, in lieu of a Supreme Court appeal, remitted her fine. The Anthony case was an important milestone in securing eventual adoption of the Nineteenth Amendment.

[*See also* Voting and Political Participation]

• Kathleen Barry, *Susan B. Anthony: A Biography*, 1988. Sandra F. VanBurkleo, *"Belonging to the World": Women's Rights and American Constitutional Culture*, 2001.   —Sandra F. VanBurkleo

ANTHROPOLOGY AND LAW. Anthropological jurisprudence focuses on the ways in which various groups settle their disputes. Legal anthropologists argue for a contextual understanding of legal institutions, processes, and behaviors. Because anthropologists have been steeped in cultural relativism as part of their professional training, they generally describe a particular legal system in its entirety in an ethnography, on the basis of extensive fieldwork. They view the legal systems of smaller-scale societies as juridical forms, unlike legal positivists, who presume that only state law deserves to be considered law. Because the codes of conduct among these societies are often unwritten, scholars have had to document the customary law of various groups.

A few pivotal intellectual figures stand out in the vast scholarship in the field of legal anthropology. Sir Henry Maine's *Ancient Law* set forth a stage theory of legal evolution: as societies evolve, their legal systems become more modern. Malinowski's *Crime and Custom in Savage Society* emphasized the importance of reciprocal relations in social life. Westermarck's encyclopedic study, *The Origin and Development of Moral Ideas,* contains the legal customs of many groups. Many important works afford insight into the proper use of force in various societies, for example, the studies of the blood feud or vendetta by Boehm, Colson, Hasluck, Karsten, and others.

The recording of actual cases represented a methodological innovation in the discipline. One leading U.S. study is *Llewellyn and Hoebel's compilation of cases in *The Cheyenne Way.* Another is Max Gluckman's landmark study of Barotse jurisprudence in Africa, in which he contends that the *kuta,* the Barotse "court," invoked the "reasonable man" standard in the disposition of cases. Gluckman's claim that finding the European reasonable man standard in Africa demonstrated that it was a universal concept was itself controversial. It also led to other debates such as whether researchers should use conceptual categories from their own legal systems, or use folk terms, as Paul Bohannan argued, to describe the processes they observed. A serious criticism of the case method has been its excessive attention to the "trouble" case. By ignoring "troubleless" cases, researchers give a distorted impression of what transpires in legal systems. Another issue has been whether to rely on informants' accounts of cases or whether it is preferable to observe cases in person.

In the 1960s legal anthropologists in the United States played a crucial role in the formation of the *law and society association. With their insistence on studying law in context, they helped shift attention away from "law on the books" to "law in action." The entire thrust of the discipline was based on this more empirical orientation. Anthropology played a decisive role in emphasizing that law is not autonomous; law is part of society. In the late twentieth century some scholars began to emphasize the more ideological functions law serves, for example, Laura Nader in *Harmony Ideology.* Other contemporary works, such as *History and Power in the Study of Law* (Starr and Collier, eds.) also question the utility of traditional approaches.

Anthropologists' knowledge about groups' ways of life has been considered in various types of cases in the United States. Anthropologists were involved in the litigation to vindicate the rights of ethnic minorities and indigenous peoples (see RACE AND ETHNICITY). For instance, Robert Redfield testified in *Sweatt* v. *Painter,* a lawsuit involving a challenge to the "separate but equal" doctrine. John Hostetler was the key expert witness in *Wisconsin* v. *Yoder,* the case in which the Amish won the right to take their children out of school after eighth grade, so that the children would not be exposed to "worldly" values, which would undermine their way of life. Anthropologists have also testified in environmental litigation about the impact development projects on sacred sites would have on indigenous groups. In criminal cases, anthropologists' testimony has sometimes been considered during the trial as part of a defense, and other times during sentencing as a mitigating factor.

[*See also* Law and Society Movement]

• Karl Llewellyn and E. A. Hoebel, *The Cheyenne Way: Conflict and Case Law in Primitive Jurisprudence,* 1941. Max Gluckman, *Judicial Process among the Barotse of Northern Rhodesia,* 1955. Laura Nader and Harry F. Todd Jr., eds., *The Disputing Process: Law in Ten Societies,* 1978. E. Adamson Hoebel, *The Law of Primitive Man: A Study in Comparative Legal Dynamics,* 1979. Laura Nader, *Harmony Ideology: Justice and Control in a Zapotec Mountain Village,* 1990. Peter Sack and Jonathan Aleck, eds., *Law and Anthropology,* 1992. Alison Dundes Renteln and Alan Dundes, eds., *Folk Law: Essays on the Theory and Practice of Lex Non Scripta,* 1995.

—Alison Dundes Renteln

ANTITRUST LAW consists of a body of statutes, judicial decisions, and enforcement activities designed to check business activities posing a threat to free-market competition. The core antitrust concern with competition reflects a fundamental belief that economic questions are generally best determined in the American economy through a process of independent, competitive decision-making by profit-seeking firms striving to serve customers who seek maximum satisfaction through their choices among market alternatives. Antitrust law aims to protect economic competition by prohibiting collusive, exclusionary, and monopolistic practices that restrain competition and thereby pose a danger of increased prices and reduced output, quality, and innovation. It contrasts with other forms of economic *regulation that directly prescribe the number, rates, and service offerings of particular firms, for example, in "natural monopoly" settings where economies of scale are thought to preclude active multifirm competition.

Basic Provisions and Long-run Patterns. Antitrust law originated in reaction to tremendous economic changes in late nineteenth- and early twentieth-century America. Since that time, federal antitrust developments have dominated the field, although state antitrust efforts also were prominent prior to World War I and have regained significance in recent years. Federal antitrust law is founded on three main enactments. Section 1 of the Sherman Act of 1890, the most important of these acts, focuses on group behavior in broadly banning "[e]very contract, combination . . . or conspiracy" in restraint of interstate or foreign trade or commerce; Section 2 primarily targets the activities of individual firms in its prohibition of monopolization and attempted monopolization. The Clayton Act of 1914 specifically addresses the competitive dangers arising from price discrimination, "tying" arrangements, exclusive dealing, mergers, and interlocking directorates. The Federal Trade Commission Act of 1914 sweepingly empowers the administrative agency it establishes to police "unfair methods of competition."

Violations of the Sherman Antitrust Act are punishable by substantial criminal penalties. In addition, private parties as well as the United States Department of Justice can seek injunctive relief against threatened violations of either the Sherman or Clayton Acts. The Federal Trade Commission is authorized to issue cease and desist orders ultimately enforceable through the federal courts to remedy breaches of either the Clayton Act or Federal Trade Commission Act. The United States and private parties also can collect three times the amount of the actual damages they have suffered as a result of conduct prohibited by the Sherman or Clayton Acts. Under *parens patriae* legislation passed in 1976, individual states can seek treble damages on behalf of natural persons residing within their borders who have been injured by Sherman Act violations.

Although grounded in legislative enactments, substantive antitrust doctrine since its inception has developed primarily through Supreme Court interpretation of federal antitrust statutes. Indeed, the centrality of the Court's doctrinal role and the widespread belief that these measures are fundamental to the maintenance of the American free enterprise system often have prompted suggested parallels between constitutional and antitrust jurisprudence.

Over time, antitrust enforcement and interpretation repeatedly have changed course, reflecting larger changes and patterns in American economic, political, and intellectual life. Ever since the first antitrust acts were passed, moreover, the nature and purpose of antitrust law have been the subject of recurring debate. Some jurists, scholars, and enforcement officials have stressed as antitrust goals fairer wealth distribution, the preservation of individual business opportunity, and the protection of political freedom from potential threats posed by increased concentrations of private economic power. Others have conceived of antitrust law's protection of competition solely or primarily as a means to enhance economic efficiency and the overall maximization of social wealth. This latter perspective predominates today with respect to all four of the main types of conduct addressed by antitrust law: horizontal agreements among competitors, single-firm activities directed toward the acquisition or maintenance of monopoly power, vertical arrangements among firms in a supplier-purchaser relationship, and mergers.

Origins and Early Development. Late-nineteenth-century antitrust legislation and case law built upon earlier English and American *common-law precedents on agreements in restraint of trade. These precedents varied significantly among state jurisdictions and over time.

As American markets expanded geographically in the post–Civil War decades, new technological innovations repeatedly boosted productivity in excess of demand, contributing to a sharp intensification of competitive rivalry in many lines of business. These developments prompted large numbers of late-nineteenth- and early-twentieth-century American businesses to seek greater security and higher returns through various forms of multifirm combination. At first turning primarily to loose arrangements such as simple cartels, American businesses increasingly embraced tighter, more fully integrated combinations such as trusts, holding companies, and mergers beginning in the 1880s. Public concerns, which earlier had centered on anticompetitive and discriminatory railroad practices, then shifted to focus more broadly on predatory business behavior, cartelization, and industrial concentration in general, prompting a burst of new antitrust activity at the state level. The perceived practical and legal limitations of state efforts, however, soon led to mounting popular pressure for new federal antitrust legislation, resulting in adoption of the Sherman Act of 1890.

In the debates preceding passage of the act, congressmen expressed strong support for the protection of competition and concerns to safeguard economic opportunity, fair consumer prices, efficiency, and political liberty. Scholars have long debated which of these values Congress primarily or even exclusively sought to promote. In late-nineteenth-century thinking, however, these goals and values typically were thought to be largely complementary so that most congressmen may well have hoped to serve all of these ends simultaneously.

Neither the statute itself nor the congressional debates provided any detailed guidance as to the practical application of the Act's general language. Congress generally sought to incorporate the traditional common-law restraint of trade approaches of the state courts, without any detailed understanding of what those doctrines had become by 1890. Congress intended to delegate significant authority to the federal courts to develop more precise doctrine. Passage of the act was an important symbolic affirmation of the basic ideal of competitive free markets, and the statute's enforcement provisions went substantially beyond earlier common-law doctrines that provided merely for the legal unenforceability of restrictive trade agreements.

The first decade after passage of the act saw only limited federal enforcement, partly as a result of the Supreme Court's restrictive reading of congressional commerce-clause authority in its rejection of a challenge to a monopolistic merger of sugar refineries in *United States* v. *E. C. Knight Co.* (1895), the Court's first consideration of the statute. Within a few years, however, the Court strongly supported the application of the act in a variety of other contexts, beginning with cases against railroad cartels in the late 1890s. A dramatic acceleration in the growth of overall economic concentration as a result of a wave of mergers in the late 1890s and early 1900s heightened public apprehension and led to increased federal enforcement efforts under Presidents Theodore Roosevelt and William Howard Taft. These efforts produced a number of Supreme Court victories,

climaxing in the Court's decisions in *Standard Oil Co.* v. *United States* (1911) and *United States* v. *American Tobacco Co.* (1911). In those cases, the Court ordered the dissolution of two of the greatest industrial combinations of the day to remedy violations of the Sherman Act, although that did not effectively dissipate the concentrated economic power established by those combinations.

During these years, the Supreme Court debated the proper general standard of Sherman Act analysis. Initially dominant was Justice Rufus W. Peckham's rejection of any defense of "reasonableness" for challenged restraints. Chief Justice Edward D. White was the chief proponent of the alternative "rule of reason" position that ultimately triumphed in the Court's *Standard Oil* and *American Tobacco* opinions. Despite its name, Chief Justice White's framework contemplated that certain types of agreements, because of their inherent nature, could be summarily condemned as anticompetitive without any extended inquiry into reasonableness. This aspect of the opinion foreshadowed the Court's subsequent, more extensive development of the central, but often troubled, antitrust distinction between activities condemnable "per se" and those to be judged only after a lengthier "rule of reason" examination of purposes, market power, effects, and possible less restrictive alternatives available to achieve particular legitimate ends.

The Supreme Court's affirmation of a "rule of reason" approach revitalized political controversy over antitrust law. This subject became a main focus of the three-way presidential race between Roosevelt, Taft, and Woodrow Wilson in 1912. Following Wilson's election, efforts to buttress the Sherman Act resulted in the 1914 passage of the Clayton and Federal Trade Commission Acts.

During World War I and the 1920s, concern over anticompetitive and monopolistic behavior substantially declined as Americans came to accept the increased level of economic concentration established during the Progressive Era, associating it with heightened economic prosperity. In these years, federal officials and the Supreme Court continued to condemn nakedly anticompetitive arrangements such as price fixing but encouraged other forms of cooperation among competing businesses such as the sharing of general data on business conditions.

From the New Deal to the 1970s. Public confidence in business and in the health of American markets collapsed with the stock market crash of 1929. Yet the federal government in the early years of President Franklin D. Roosevelt's New Deal turned not to renewed antitrust enforcement but instead to expanded business cooperative efforts under the National Industrial Recovery Act. The Supreme Court declared that act unconstitutional in 1935, however, and later New Deal efforts proceeded in a very different direction. Spurred by a new economic downturn in 1937, concerns over the consequences of contemporary cartelization in Europe, and growing economic scholarship criticizing concentrated markets as typically productive of troublesome economic performance, federal antitrust activity soon expanded greatly. The intensified antitrust efforts begun in the later 1930s did not result in any significant rollback of the levels of economic concentration established in the early years of the twentieth century. They did, however, set the stage for a continued, bipartisan commitment in the succeeding decades to a much higher level of antitrust activity than had prevailed before the New Deal.

In this setting of expanded enforcement, antitrust case law grew substantially. In numerous decisions through the early 1970s the Supreme Court strongly supported the vigorous application of federal antitrust law, repeatedly displaying substantial skepticism toward cooperative business agreements, single-firm activities promoting market preeminence, and mergers. While the court continued to acknowledge that certain types of cooperation among competitors, such as general data dissemination or reasonably limited joint ventures, could improve efficiency and competitive performance in particular circumstances, the Supreme Court greatly increased its use of summary, per se rules to condemn such collective agreements as price fixing, output limitation, market division, and concerted refusals to deal, as well as vertical resale price maintenance agreements, non-price restrictions imposed by individual manufacturers on dealers, and most tying arrangements whereby the purchase of one good is conditioned on the simultaneous purchase of another.

The Court strongly endorsed the landmark monopolization opinion in *United States* v. *Aluminum Co. of America (Alcoa)* (2d Cir., 1945), which exhibited considerable suspicion of the legitimacy of dominating market power in general and stressed the social and political as well as economic importance of antitrust law. While requiring both dominant market power and its acquisition or maintenance through wrongful conduct distinguishable from competition on the merits as elements of Sherman Act monopolization, the *Al-coa* decision limited the range of conduct deemed to be mere skill, foresight, and industry to a very narrow ambit.

Supreme Court merger decisions in the post–New Deal decades initially departed from these trends, permitting very large acquisitions under the Sherman Act. The Clayton Act's original 1914 ban on anticompetitive mergers rarely was invoked because it applied only to stock and not asset acquisitions and did not extend beyond horizontal mergers to reach vertical and conglomerate acquisitions. Renewed economic, social, and political concerns for rising economic concentration in the 1940s, however, prompted Congress to amend the act to close these loopholes in 1950, thus leading the Court to limit permissible mergers by the 1960s. The Court then greatly limited the range of permissible merger activity, for example, condemning horizontal mergers creating companies with combined market shares as low as 5 percent. Exhibiting strong concerns for even early market trends toward increasing concentration, the Court acted to protect smaller competitors endangered by the creation of new, more efficient merged entities even where such protection sacrificed new cost savings and lower consumer prices potentially obtainable through the mergers the Court condemned.

Modern Antitrust Law. Over the last quarter-century, major changes in the structure and patterns of global and national economic life have combined with fundamental shifts in the scholarly analysis of market behavior to alter antitrust enforcement and interpretation dramatically. Many areas of economic life have become more globalized, intensifying the competition faced by many firms in the United States at the same time that sentiment supporting government regulation in general has declined. Beginning in the latter half of the 1970s, the Supreme Court, lower federal courts, and federal enforcement agencies increasingly embraced economic critiques of previously prevailing antitrust doctrine that were urged most prominently by economists and law professors associated with the University of Chicago. These critiques heavily stressed the efficiency-enhancing potential of diverse activities previously viewed with considerable suspicion or hostility in antitrust law, and reflected a fundamental belief that in general markets powerfully tend to remain competitive without the need for potentially counterproductive government intervention.

Such neoclassical economic critiques powerfully continue to hold sway over much of current antitrust doctrine and enforcement philosophy. Over the last decade, however, the continuing evolution of economic life and scholarly outlook have generated additional new developments in antitrust thinking. For example, antitrust scholars, enforcers, and courts have focused intently on the applicability of antitrust law to high-technology companies in a new "information age" economy in which intellectual property development and protection have assumed magnified importance. At the same time, scholars, enforcers, and courts have debated the desirability of refining antitrust doctrine further in light of still-developing "post-Chicago" economic perspectives. These perspectives posit a greater prevalence of market imperfections facilitating anticompetitive behavior than has been acknowledged by leading Chicago School theorists. To date, such post-Chicago analyses have influenced the work of scholars and government enforcement agencies more than they have the opinions of judges.

In the realm of case law, the Supreme Court over the last twenty-five years has retreated substantially, but not completely, from the invocation of per se rules for judging horizontal and vertical agreements. The court's movement away from per se analysis was signaled in its landmark opinion overturning the Court's decade-old per se condemnation of nonprice vertical restrictions on dealers (*Continental T.V., Inc.* v. *GTE Sylvania, Inc.* (1977)). The Court found that such "intrabrand" restraints pro-competitively can induce more aggressive interbrand promotional efforts by dealers desiring to reap the benefits of their own promotional efforts, by restricting the intensity of intrabrand rivalry and eliminating "free riders" who costlessly might take advantage of other dealers' expensive promotional activity.

The Court similarly has narrowed the scope of per se treatment for horizontal agreements. While stressing that Sherman Act analysis focuses narrowly on whether a challenged restraint promotes or suppresses competition, the Court nevertheless has looked not simply to whether any business rivalry has been tempered, but also to whether any such effects have been offset by new gains in efficiency and output. At the same time, government criminal enforcement efforts against naked cartel restraints, which remain subject to per se condemnation, have intensified since the early 1980s. The number of prosecutions brought annually has increased greatly and government prosecutors recently have won convictions against long-standing global cartels generating enormous illegal profits. Government prosecutors also successfully have pushed for the imposition of sub-

stantially increased fines and jail sentences for criminal antitrust convictions. In the merger area, the Supreme Court in the mid-1970s substantially altered its previously restrictive approach to mergers, requiring a more thorough economic assessment of the likely competitive impact of particular acquisitions before mergers could be declared unlawful (see *United States* v. *General Dynamics Corp.* (1974)). Since then, the Supreme Court largely has left further development of merger law to the lower federal courts. The federal courts of appeal have undermined previous reliance on presumptions from market share and concentration data in merger cases, and have emphasized that strong evidence of relatively easy new entry into a market will undercut inferences that a merger in that market will increase market power or facilitate its exercise.

Much of the change in the antitrust treatment of mergers since the 1970s has resulted from changes in federal enforcement policy. Although still reflecting concern that particular mergers may increase the risks of multi-firm collusion or single-firm market power, the revised merger guidelines adopted by the Department of Justice in the 1980's emphasized the potential economic benefits of merger activities and established substantially higher thresholds for antitrust challenges than had prevailed in earlier case law and department philosophy. The 1992 joint Department of Justice/Federal Trade Commission revised Guidelines heightened the emphasis given to the unilateral exercise of market power by newly merged entities and provided more detailed guidance for assessing the potential for new entry to counteract the adverse effects of a merger. More recent Guidelines revisions expressed a greater willingness to allow otherwise problematic mergers where sufficiently strong evidence demonstrates that a merger likely would generate important, otherwise unattainable, efficiency gains.

In its limited modern treatment of monopolization issues, the Supreme Court contributed to continuing controversy over the extent of any obligation to cooperate with smaller rivals, the legality of various practices raising rivals' costs, and the appropriate treatment of claims of predatory pricing. The Court has held, for example, that a dominant firm may not severely disadvantage a smaller competitor by discontinuing a long established cooperative marketing arrangement, at least in the absence of any plausible efficiency justification (*Aspen Skiing* v. *Aspen Highlands Skiing Corp.* (1985)). On the other hand, the Court has tightened the criteria for proving unlawful predatory pricing, requiring more careful attention to both market structure and the relationship between a defendant firm's costs and the prices it charged during the period of alleged predation.

Two major milestones in government antimonopolization efforts were reached in 1982. In that year, the government dismissed its multiyear suit against the International Business Machines Corporation and settled its suit against the American Telephone and Telegraph Company. The latter settlement resulted in the largest divestiture in antitrust history, separating the company's long distance service from its local operating companies. The *AT&T litigation stood as the government's last major monopolization case until the mid-1990s, when the United States and several states charged the Microsoft corporation with illegal monopolization and other antitrust violations.

The Microsoft case captured public attention as only relatively few cases, like the *Standard Oil* case of 1911, had in the history of antitrust law. The case highlighted the rise of expanded concerns over the applicability of antitrust law to "new economy," high-technology industries in which "network effects" (or "scale economies of consumption") play a central role. In "network" industries, where the consumer value of a particular product, such as a telephone or a personal computer operating system, increases as the number of consumers using that product increases, firms have a tremendous incentive to compete to have their own product accepted as the industry standard. Once a standard is established, however, it may be difficult for other firms to challenge a dominant industry incumbent.

At its core, the complaint against Microsoft charged that the company had engaged in a variety of practices not justified as means to further business efficiency, that were undertaken with the aim of thwarting the possible rise of effective new competition to Microsoft's monopoly in operating systems for Intel-based personal computers. The United States District Court hearing the case found Microsoft guilty of illegal monopolization and ordered the parties to submit plans for the break up of the company into an operating system company and a software applications firm. The United States Court of Appeals for the D.C. Circuit upheld the great majority of the district court's findings as to liability, concluding that Microsoft had failed to rebut government prima facie showings of exclusionary conduct through demonstration of efficiency justifications for Microsoft's challenged conduct. After the Court of Appeals remanded the case for further proceedings

as to remedy, the federal government and most, but not all, of the state plaintiffs joined in a proposed settlement limiting Microsoft's conduct but not requiring corporate restructuring. As of this writing, the proposed settlement has yet to receive court approval.

While most antitrust cases today still are brought by private parties rather than by government enforcers, the Supreme Court since the 1970s has made the maintenance of private antitrust actions more difficult by tightening standing requirements and encouraging lower courts to screen out more cases on the ground that the plaintiff's theory is economically implausible. At the same time, the efforts of federal antitrust enforcers have been supplemented by the antitrust enforcement activities of attorneys general in various states and, in a global context, by the efforts of antitrust enforcement officials in other nations. More and more nations now have adopted their own antitrust laws, and in recent years there has been substantially increased cooperation among antitrust authorities in various countries designed to check more effectively anticompetitive activity crossing national borders.

Conclusion. Although the major developments discussed here have dominated antitrust law since the late nineteenth century, antitrust analysis also has focused on such other important issues as the scope of various exceptions to antitrust coverage. Today, in the midst of ongoing debate over economic analysis and substantive doctrine, the meaning of antitrust law's protection of competition continues to evolve as American economic, intellectual, and political contexts continue to change.

[*See also* Commercial Law; Economics and Law; IBM Litigation]

• Hans Thorelli, *The Federal Antitrust Policy: Origination of an American Tradition*, 1955. Phillip Areeda and Donald Turner, *Antitrust Law: An Analysis of Antitrust Principles and Their Application*, 1978. Robert Bork, *The Antitrust Paradox: A Policy at War with Itself*, 1978. James May, "Antitrust in the Formative Era: Political and Economic Theory in Constitutional and Antitrust Analysis, 1880–1918," *Ohio State Law Journal* 50 (1989): 257–395. Ernest Gellhorn and William Kovacic, *Antitrust Law and Economics*, 4th ed., 1994. Herbert Hovenkamp, *Federal Antitrust Policy: The Law of Competition and Its Practice*, 2d ed., 1999.

—James May

APPEALS. All jurisdictions, federal and state, generally make appellate review for correctness from the civil or criminal judgments of trial courts available in some form. Most states and the federal system provide two tiers of potential review, with the last tier reserved for discretionary review, normally of legal issues, before a supreme court.

[*See also* Courts, United States: Federal Courts]

—David S. Clark

APPRENTICESHIP, LEGAL. *See* Education, Legal.

ARBITRATION, LABOR. *See* Arbitration and Mediation; Labor Law; Labor Relations.

ARBITRATION AND MEDIATION. Two forms of alternative dispute resolution (ADR) commonly used in the United States and internationally, arbitration and mediation were "rediscovered" in the 1970s as ways to resolve disputes outside of the more formal, adversarial system found in courts. Some have even compared arbitration and mediation to *negotiation, a very common method of resolving disputes inside the formal justice system. However, mediation and arbitration are not new to the United States and their procedures differ from negotiations. Some scholars, in fact, suggest that the differences in procedures found in these forms of ADR satisfy different goals and can even lead to different resolutions of disputes than the common methods employed in litigation.

Procedures. Mediation and arbitration are both informal processes for resolving disputes that involve the use of a neutral third party. However, there are differences between them. In mediation, the parties to a dispute (or disputants) voluntarily agree to bring their dispute before a mediator (they can also be ordered to do so by a court official). The mediator's role is to encourage communication between the parties to tell their story, and to aid the parties in reaching an agreement. The mediator may use a variety of communication techniques including caucusing with each disputant privately in order to generate alternatives for an agreement. Thus, in mediation, the parties only come to an agreement if they are willing to agree and the mediator has no authority to make a decision. In addition, the ethics of mediation often include that the mediator should not coerce disputants into an agreement that they are not comfortable with signing and should not allow an agreement to be signed when one party is coercing the other into the agreement. But it is not the mediator's responsibility to ensure a just or fair outcome. This is left to the choice of the party in the dispute. In practice, mediation is used in a wide variety of dispute types including domestic,

torts, contract, labor, environmental, and even criminal disputes.

An arbitrator, on the other hand, acts as a "quasi-judge" and is given the power to make a decision. While there are a number of variations in the procedures of arbitration, most focus on allowing each side to be "heard" and to present evidence in an informal manner. Thus, while discovery, witnesses, and cross-examination of witnesses can be introduced into arbitration by agreement of the parties, the process is usually limited in order to keep the process speedy and efficient. Once the process, as agreed to by the participants, is finished, the arbitrator makes a judgment in the form of a very simple written statement that includes the judgment and the award. This award is enforceable in a court of law and in the law of contracts.

Although voluntary arbitration rulings are typically binding and can be appealed only in rare instances, there is some disagreement about whether court-ordered arbitration is binding or not. The United States Constitution provides citizens the right to a *jury trial. In addition, some federal and state statutes (e.g., discrimination laws) provide citizens a right to sue for relief on the basis of individual and civil rights. Mandatory and binding arbitration would allow the subversion of these rights. As a result, most mandatory mediations allow for an *appeal for a trial de novo if a party is unsatisfied with a ruling. However, many courts with mandatory arbitration have rules that make it difficult or costly for participants to appeal. Arbitration, like mediation, is also used in a very wide variety of dispute types, but the most common are contracts involving labor, commercial, consumer, and business disputes.

Justice without Law. Mediation and arbitration in the United States are not new. Since the seventeenth century, there has been a pattern of resolving disputes "outside of law." Legal historian Jerold Auerbach traces this history in *Justice Without Law (1983)*, and argues that mediation and arbitration have always been found in America, but neither overcame the American legal system and the individual pursuit of litigation. The movement of mediation and arbitration began in early America and was practiced within religious, utopian, ethnic, and business communities. The common thread among each of these societies was to contain and take ownership over disputes and resolve them within their own cultures. Therefore, merchants, religious societies, ethnic groups, and utopian communities could exert power over disputants, could keep disputes within their communities, and could resolve disputes privately rather than in public forums.

Court-Connected ADR: A New Movement. While mediation and arbitration have always existed in American society, Auerbach (1983) argues that neither has become a substitute for litigation, in part, because American culture is individualistic, competitive, and decidedly not communal in nature. Therefore, individuals always sought out courts in order to pursue their individual rights, against others or against those in power. Despite the fact that formal law "wins out" in America, the use of mediation and arbitration has continued, giving rise to a more recent and different movement in the 1970s.

The use of mediation in the 1960s and 1970s could be described as being based on goals of community empowerment and emphasized "peacemaking" in the face of conflict in urban and labor settings. Arbitration was also used to find a more informal manner to resolve disputes, a process that would be private and would benefit disputants by using neutrals that had expertise in the type of dispute. In each, the common goal was to resolve disputes outside of the eye of the public and the combative forum of courts and litigation, and in a less costly manner. However, in the 1980s, another movement for the use of mediation and arbitration began that emphasized their uses within court systems and for the purposes of improving court efficiency and access to justice. Beginning with the 1976 National Conference on the Causes of Popular Dissatisfaction with the Administration of Justice, sponsored by the American Bar Association, there was a heightened concern that the courts faced a crisis of litigation that threatened their legitimacy (see LITIGIOUSNESS). The predominant message at the conference was that the courts were overloaded with disputes, the public had become dissatisfied with courts, and the courts needed reform to improve their efficiency.

Scholars today suggest that this began a discussion and a movement toward the use of arbitration and mediation, not for communal goals, but for reform and efficiency purposes. Some scholars, such as Auerbach (1983) and Elizabeth Ellen Gordon (1999), even suggest the interest of the legal community in ADR was, in part, to co-opt the earlier movements of ADR before dissatisfaction with the legal system took individuals away from courts and lawyers. This more recent adoption of ADR by the legal community was a form of co-optation, controlled and regulated by legal community itself, a practice observed in past legal reforms in the United States.

Along with settling cases through negotiation, mediation and arbitration provide additional avenues for resolving disputes before trial. Reformers argued that these procedures would save court resources, would save time and money for attorneys and litigants, and would improve satisfaction with the American court system. In the late 1970s and early 1980s, Congress created several "Neighborhood Justices Centers" (NJCs) around the country that took case referrals from local judges and prosecutors and provided services such as mediation and arbitration.

Court-Annexed (Connected) Mediation and Arbitration. In the 1980s and 1990s, the use of mediation and arbitration within federal and state courts systems in the United States increased exponentially. This new movement of ADR is commonly called court-annexed or court-connected ADR, and requires that certain types of cases must go to mediation or arbitration before proceeding into the legal system. In some cases, statutes or local court rules give the court or a court official the discretion to send a case to ADR.

Although many forms of voluntary mediation and arbitration are common in the United States, court-annexed arbitration and mediation are mandatory and are often nonbinding. A 1996 study by Plapinger and Stienstra found that thirty-three states and twenty-two federal district courts provided mandatory court-annexed arbitration. A large number of states and federal courts also refer cases to mandatory mediation (Goldberg, Sander, Rogers, 1999).

[*See also* Alternative Dispute Resolution]

• Jerold S. Auerbach, *Justice Without Law? Resolving Disputes Without Lawyers*, 1983. John S. Murry, Alan Scott Rau, and Edward F. Sherman, *Processes of Dispute Resolution: The Role of Lawyers*, 2d ed., 1996. Stephen B. Goldberg, Frank E. A. Sander, and Nancy H. Rogers, *Dispute Resolution: Negotiation, Mediation, and Other Processes*, 3d ed., 1999. Elizabeth Ellen Gordon, "Why Attorneys Support Mandatory Mediation," *Judicature* (1999): 224–31.   —Roger E. Hartley

ARMS, RIGHT TO BEAR. Three questions are raised by the somewhat mysterious words of the Second Amendment of the U.S. *Constitution: "A well regulated Militia, being necessary to the security of a free State, the right of the people to keep and bear Arms, shall not be infringed." 1) What was its most likely meaning in 1791, when it was added to the Constitution? 2) What was its most likely meaning in 1868, when, according to many scholars, the Fourteenth Amendment made the *Bill of Rights applicable to the States?

3) What should it mean to us today, when circumstances may be strikingly different from those that existed in either 1791 or 1868? All of these questions are the subject of significant, sometimes acrimonious, debate.

For some scholars, the key to the Amendment is its "preamble," with its reference to militias. They argue that the Amendment was designed only to reassure states that they could not be prevented from organizing their own militias. Other scholars point out that the word "militia" in much eighteenth-century discourse referred to the general population of law-abiding citizens, as opposed to a "select militia" similar to today's national guard. The right of individuals to keep their own arms served as a practical way of preventing governmental tyranny precisely insofar as it threatened the possibility of popular uprising should government become viewed as tyrannical (as, of course, happened in 1775). Critics of this argument note that states sometimes regulated access to firearms, though one response is that the Amendment, however silent with regard to state regulation, prohibited any national regulation, given the fear by supporters of the Bill of Rights of specifically Federal suppression of rights. A 1939 decision by the Supreme Court, *U.S.* v. *Miller,* left things somewhat confused; even while upholding the conviction of someone for possessing a sawed-off shotgun, the majority opinion emphasized that it was not a "military weapon" appropriate for use by a militia. (*Miller* is the last decision by the Supreme Court that analyzes the Second Amendment at any length, and most lower courts have viewed it as licensing a wide degree of Federal regulation.)

Constitutional provisions scarcely receive static readings. Whatever the 1791 meaning, Yale professor Akhil Reed Amar argues that by the time of the proposal and ratification of the Fourteenth Amendment, there was a general understanding, first, that the Second Amendment indeed protected an individual right of citizens, including, for example, newly freed African Americans who needed arms to protect themselves against the terroristic Ku Klux Klan; and, second, that the Fourteenth Amendment was designed to extend the protections of the Bill of Rights against both state and national hostile action. Although the Supreme Court initially rejected any such "incorporationist" thesis (see INCOPORATION DOCTRINE), the twentieth century featured making most of the Bill of Rights applicable against the States. This has not, however, included the Second Amendment.

An obvious reason for the nonincorporation of the Amendment is a widespread belief that the private possession of guns poses great danger and, therefore, should be subject to widespread regulation, whether by the national or local governments. Although some supporters of guns ardently believe that the greater danger is a disarmed populace maximally vulnerable to governmental abuses, probably more supporters emphasize the utility of guns in allowing vulnerable people to defend themselves against criminals. There is no reason to believe that the debate about gun control (and its constitutional implications) will be resolved in the foreseeable future.

[*See also* Bills of Rights; Constitutions, United States]

• Robert Cottrol, ed., *Gun Control and the Constitution: The Modern Debate on Gun Control,* 1993. Akhil Reed Amar, *The Bill of Rights,* 1998. Michael A. Bellesiles, *Arming America: The Origins of a National Gun Culture,* 1999.   —Sanford Levinson

ARMS CONTROL LAW is concerned with weapons, usually those used by government armed forces, including the police and paramilitary forces. Public pressure to limit armaments has been constant in international politics since World War I. U.S. arms control law has developed as new treaties and statutes were adopted and international custom was recognized, all of which have created legal obligations. This will continue in an ever more technologically complex environment.

Arms control law is tied to other areas of the law, including the laws of *war, international humanitarian law, and the law of armed conflict. Customary *international law in part governs the use of force, and U.S. statutes are also important. Each might affect the kinds of weapons usable in a given situation.

Statutes may implement *treaties or control the way the United States accepts international arms control obligations. For example, Congress in 1963 enacted a law prohibiting the United States from incurring obligations "to reduce or limit the Armed Forces or armaments of the United States in a militarily significant manner" other than by treaty, requiring the advice and consent of the Senate, or by specific legislation.

The United States has long supported legal restrictions on armaments. It originated the law governing the conduct of military operations and, in particular, the treatment of prisoners. U.S. citizens and government officials participated in the international movement a century ago to mitigate suffering caused by war, by prohibiting such weapons as dumdum bullets (1899), poisonous gases

(1925), and the like. The United States accepted the ban on dumdum bullets as part of the customary law of war; it was not a party to the 1899 declaration.

The United States is a party to a number of multilateral treaties related to arms control. These include the Environmental Modification Convention (1977), prohibiting among other things the use of weather modification as a weapon, the Conventional Weapons Convention of 1980 and its protocols, the Chemical (1997) and Biological (1972) Weapons Conventions, as well as conventions prohibiting the use of Antarctica (1959) and the Moon (1967) for military purposes. Congress formally incorporated prohibitions contained in the Chemical Weapons Convention into U.S. criminal law.

In the realm of nuclear weapons, the United States recommended international control in 1946 and then settled for bilateral agreements with the Soviet Union. These include the Limited Test Ban Treaty (1963), the Anti-Ballistic Missile (ABM) Treaty (1972), a series of agreements on offensive weapons, including the Treaty on Intermediate and Shorter-Range Missiles (1987), and the important multilateral Non-Proliferation Treaty (NPT) (1968). The NPT's preamble commits all parties to seek complete nuclear disarmament as part of the arrangement by which most countries forswore nuclear weapons.   —Nicholas Rostow

ARREST. An arrest occurs when a person is taken into custody, or forcibly restrained, by legal authority. Law enforcement officers, who are government employees such as local *police officers and federal agents, make most arrests. These "government actor" arrests are often accompanied by *searches that may uncover evidence to be used in the prosecution of criminal charges. Such a "search incident to arrest" is limited to the arrested person and that person's "wingspan." Government actor arrests are also often followed by *interrogation. Statements made under interrogation by an arrested person can be used against him in a criminal case, so long as he waived his rights under *Miranda v. Arizona (1966). As a result, government actors often read Miranda warnings to persons they place under arrest.

Government actor arrests must comply with the "reasonableness" requirement of the Fourth Amendment to the United States Constitution. That amendment applies whenever a person reasonably believes that a government actor has limited his freedom of movement in a significant way. Under the Fourth Amendment, an arrest is reasonable in two different sets of circumstances. First, the police may have "probable cause" to believe that the arrested person committed a crime, and use only the amount of force necessary to make the arrest, avoiding deadly force unless it is necessary to prevent the escape of a dangerous felon. Second, the police may have a valid warrant authorizing the arrest, and execute the warrant promptly and reasonably—for instance, in the day time after knocking and announcing their presence. The warrant requirement is relaxed when police make arrests in public places. In public places, felony arrests do not require warrants. Misdemeanor arrests may be warrantless if the police witnessed the offense. Some jurisdictions allow all warrantless misdemeanor arrests in public places; the Supreme Court has not spoken definitively about this issue. The warrant requirement also is relaxed if circumstances make it impractical for police to obtain a warrant.

The Fourth Amendment also imposes a reasonableness requirement on police detentions that fall short of arrests, because these impose significant deprivations on freedom of movement. For example, when a police officer pulls over a car to issue a traffic citation to the driver, the Fourth Amendment applies even though the encounter does not constitute an arrest. Here, the constitutional requirements are lower, and the police need only (1) have "reasonable suspicion" to believe the person committed an offense, (2) limit the detention to the brief amount of time it reasonably takes to complete the transaction, and (3) use minimal force to detain the person.

The Fourth Amendment generally does not apply when government actors recapture escaped prisoners. Recapture is considered an extension of the original imprisonment.

Government actor arrests that violate the Fourth Amendment are illegal, and persons aggrieved by them may seek remedies. An aggrieved person may sue for damages (some state officials may be immune from such lawsuits) and for a court order prohibiting the use of the illegal practices in the future. Using the "exclusionary rule," a person may also move to suppress any "fruits" of the arrest that the government seeks to use against the person in a criminal action, including evidence found during a search incident to arrest and statements made by the arrested person. Government officials who engage in illegal arrests may face criminal charges under state and federal laws that prohibit the use of excessive force and violations of civil rights. For example, in 1992, Los Angeles Police Department officers were *prosecuted after they beat and kicked Rodney King while arresting him. They were convicted of federal civil rights violations, and served prison sentences.

Private persons sometimes make what are called "citizen's arrests"—for example, when an individual restrains a burglar until police arrive. Private actors do not have to comply with federal constitutional requirements, but they must comply with state laws. Although these laws vary, citizens generally are permitted to make arrests for crimes committed in their presence, although some jurisdictions limit these crimes to felonies and breaches of the peace. If someone makes an arrest that is not permitted under applicable law, the arrestee may collect tort damages for false arrest or false imprisonment. The private actor also might face criminal charges, and is also limited in the manner in which the arrest can be made. Generally, persons may use only such force as is reasonably necessary to make the arrest. In most states, private actors may not use deadly force unless they would be justified in doing so by state laws regarding self-defense. Those laws typically prohibit the use of deadly force unless it is necessary to repel an imminent threat of death or serious bodily injury.

Citizen's arrests were common in the American colonies, because organized police forces did not exist in most areas until the middle of the nineteenth century. Ordinary citizens were expected to serve as daytime volunteer constables or night watchmen. When these volunteers discovered a serious crime, they would raise a "hue and cry," which obligated other citizens to arm themselves and give pursuit. Although these practices ended when police forces became professional, private persons remain heavily involved in law enforcement as private security guards and bounty hunters. Neither of these are subject to federal constitutional requirements, but private security guards are limited by the same state laws as other private actors. State law restrictions generally do not apply to bounty hunters, who track down escaped prisoners and "bail jumpers"—that is, criminal defendants who were released after signing bail bonds in which they promised to appear for trial. A bail bond usually contains a defendant's waiver of all claims against wrongful arrest in the event of the defendant's failure to appear.

[See also Criminal Law Practice; Criminal Law Principles; Criminal Procedure, Federal Rules of]

• American Law Institute, Model Penal Code, 1962. Lawrence M. Friedman, Crime and Punishment in American History, 1993. Jonathan Drimmer, "When Man Hunts Man," Houston Law Review 33 (1996): 731–91.

Andrew E. Taslitz and Margaret L. Paris, Constitutional Criminal Procedure, 1997. Wayne R. LaFave, Jerold H. Israel, and Nancy J. King, Criminal Procedure, 3d ed., 2000.
—Margaret L. Paris

ARSON. The earliest *common law cases and commentaries announce that a person's home is her castle. This was understood to mean that the common law gave special protection to the personal security of a dweller from a variety of intrusions into her home. Arson is one of the several felony offenses created by the common law judges to further this goal.

The earliest written references define arson as the malicious burning of the dwelling house of another. In essence, arson protects our personal security by seeking to prevent the burning of our homes by others, either intentionally or by extreme recklessness.

With the rise of the industrial revolution, the growth of the market economy, and the heightened concerns for personal security that marked the latter half of the twentieth century, legislatures began expanding the common law offense by statute. This expansion took place in two periods. In the first period, which begins in the early sixteenth century and continues to the middle of the twentieth century, the focus of arson reform was on the protection of *property, although common law arson was always retained in the statutory scheme. In this period, arson was expanded by statute to protect a variety of property from damage or destruction by fire or explosion; and most statutes prohibited the burning of any property, including one's own property, if done to collect insurance for the loss.

The last period in the development of arson begins in the middle of the twentieth century. Although property was widely protected, the arson statutes offered minimal protection from the danger of death or bodily injury by fire or explosion beyond that provided by the common law offense. Recognizing that we now spent the majority of our waking hours in buildings other than our homes, American legislatures expanded arson to provide personal security outside the home from the risk of death or bodily harm caused by a fire or an explosion.

Today, although there is considerable variation in the state statutes, statutory arson is a complex offense that protects people and property. In its essential form, contemporary arson may be defined as intentionally or recklessly starting a fire or causing an explosion in the following situations: (1) when it places another person in danger of death or bodily injury; (2) when it damages or destroys the property of another; and (3) when it damages or destroys any property, including the incendiary's property, to collect insurance on the claimed loss. Exactly which types of property are afforded protection by the modern arson statutes varies from state to state.

Convicted arsonists were burned alive at common law; but by the sixteenth century, the punishment was changed to death by hanging. Following the common law pattern, arson remains a felony today; but it is now punished by a term of imprisonment. In most American jurisdictions, the length of imprisonment depends upon the type of arson committed. Person-endangering arson is more severely punished than the other varieties of this offense.

• The American Law Institute, *Model Penal Code And Commentaries*, Part II, Article 220, pp. 1–35 (1980). John W. Poulos, "The Metamorphosis of The Law Of Arson," *Missouri Law Review* 51 (1986): 295–456.

—John W. Poulos

ARTS, POPULAR CULTURE, AND LAW. In classical sculpture, women were often made to stand for virtuous abstractions. The words for virtue, justice, faith, hope, charity, and the seven liberal arts in Latin and Greek are all feminine, and this may have prompted a tendency to identify virtues with the female form. Thus, in Archaic art, Dike, the daughter of Zeus and Themis and the personification of Justice, is sitting beside Zeus. Reporting men's wrongdoing to him, she punishes Injustice. Later, she is shown with a sword in Underworld scenes. The Roman equivalent of Dike is Iustitia. Roman poets sang about her in their poetry and Emperor Augustus built her a temple, which was inaugurated on 8 January A.D. 13.

The association between women and the abstract names of the virtues was passed down to the Renaissance. In Renaissance art we meet Iustitia (justice) as the personification of one of the four so-called cardinal virtues, the other three being *Fortitudo* (perseverance), *Temperantia* (temperance), and *Prudentia* (wisdom). On the sepulchral monument in Roskilde Cathedral in Denmark, for example, dedicated to King Frederick II who died in 1588, there is a sculpture of Iustitia, holding a sword and a pair of scales. The United States inherited this pattern of association between the female and the virtuous. One of the artists responsible for this was Frederic-Auguste Bartholdi, whose work—notably the Statue of Liberty—was steeped in the classical tradition. On the day of

Liberty's dedication, 22 October 1886, the celebrations included all the traditional elements of democratic ritual—a parade, speeches, and fireworks—and the statue eventually became an all-encompassing national symbol of liberty, justice, and democracy. Fifty-three years later, at the 1939 New York World's Fair, Leo Friedlander continued where Bartholdi left off by creating four statues representing the "Four Freedoms": freedom of speech, religion, press, and assembly. The statues stood on Constitution Mall behind the statue of George Washington, and with the exception of "Freedom of Speech," all the statues were female. It is interesting to note that the concept of the four freedoms was "in the air" two years before it was made immortal by Franklin D. Roosevelt in his annual message to Congress in 1941. Foreign observers of American culture have always been puzzled by the invocation of judicial authority in all kinds of unlikely contexts, as well as of the constant reference to personal rights and freedoms. Permeating as it does all levels of American society and culture, the law makes an obvious area of study for anyone interested in the United States. In America, wrote French aristocrat Hector St. John de Crèvecoeur (1735–1813), who emigrated to the New World in the middle of the eighteenth century, "we have no princes, for whom we toil, starve, and bleed; we are the most perfect society now existing in the world. Here man is as free as he ought to be" (text from *The Heath Anthology of American Literature*, Vol. I). In his letters to his family and friends back home, Crèvecoeur attempted to explain what was different about the American, this "new man." He summed up his observations by saying that citizenship constituted the most important difference. Being a citizen of a country that had no aristocracy and other feudal authorities and institutions meant that the average American had certain rights, most importantly those outlined in the Bill of Rights. Another French aristocrat, Alexis de Tocqueville, who toured the United States in the 1830s to appraise the meaning of democracy, found the judicial organization of the United States confusing. He concluded that judges must be very important players in American politics because people deferred to their authority in various political contexts.

American courts have played a major role in deciding who can and cannot become an American citizen. It has also been the courts that have defined what the Constitution and its various amendments mean in practice. What, more than anything else, made the courts, and especially the Supreme Court, a force to be reckoned with was the explosion of *judicial review in the nineteenth century. Judicial review was first asserted in the 1803 landmark decision *Marbury* v. *Madison*, in which Chief Justice John *Marshall and his colleagues declared an act of Congress unconstitutional.

The degree of power exercised by the courts, and especially the Supreme Court, is unique in judicial history: no other country has given its courts such extraordinary power. In deciding who belonged (and especially who did *not* belong), the nine justices on the Supreme Court have had a major say in defining "Americanness." The language used has been that of the law. Discussions about national identity—what it means to be an American—have consequently become inseparably bound up with law, and the Supreme Court has become the "translator" into every day life of the American dream of respect for the individual and his or her freedom.

One of the reasons for the Supreme Court's becoming such an important player in cultural and political life is the fact that the United States has always been a multicultural country. With the exception of Native Americans, who were there long before European Americans arrived on the scene, and African Americans who came to America as slaves, many American families consist of immigrants. The actual immigration could well have taken place several generations ago, but it is there in the family history somewhere.

The nine justices on the Supreme Court are not elected directly by the people. They are nominated by the president and subsequently approved by the Congress. The founding fathers wanted to make sure that some government officials would be independent of the will of the majority. By not being elected directly, such officials would be better suited to honor the wishes of America's various minorities.

The role performed by the law and the legal system in the United States is somewhat different from that of other countries. Whereas in most countries with civil law, the law is viewed primarily as a technical means to achieving a certain end, for Americans the law, in addition to performing such a technical function, also carries a very important symbolic meaning. Down through American history, but perhaps especially after the Second World War, Americans have used their legal system to seek empowerment. To be able to turn to the law, though the matter at hand may seem small, to have one's day in court, is considered one of the most important democratic rights.

But it is not simply that the legal dimension of affairs is particularly prominent in the United States, nor that people turn to the courts more often, on more matters, than elsewhere. Americans seem to turn to the courts with a particular kind of faith, and hope, that survives at a deep level despite all the disappointments and frustrations of the legal process. This underlying faith in litigation as a remedy for all injustice is reflected in the cultural life of the nation. A cursory look at the number of films, television series, and books produced and written immediately confirms the United States as a thoroughly law-permeated country. In many of these cultural products, there is an element of utopian hope—a commitment to law, all complaints about litigiousness, greedy lawyers, and the adversary system run wild notwithstanding. People know that real life is different from life on the screen or in a novel; in real life, the "good guy" does not always win. Yet there is an underlying yearning in these cultural products for the active inclusion of everyone, by law, into community life. This somewhat utopian concept of the law as a unifying discourse and the legal system as a meeting point for people with widely different backgrounds and values is something we recognize from international human rights discourses. These discourses too are characterized by a yearning for something universal, something that may transcend cultural differences.

Within the academy, the past twenty years have seen many important works on the role of law in American culture. They may be divided roughly into three categories: *law and literature, law and *history, and law and popular culture. The category of law and literature is the most well established of the three, and many of the discussions going on in law and history and law and popular culture have their origins in debates taking place within law and literature. In practice, of course, these discussions overlap, so that it is not always possible, nor indeed desirable, to say that a particular issue "belongs" in one category or another.

Contemporary legal scholarship often expresses a narrative impulse. This impulse has been gaining prominence through the writing of *Feminist Legal Theory and *Critical Race Theory scholars. Within the past ten years, intellectuals and writers have produced a significant amount of "different," often very personal, writing about gender, race, and law. This writing, which includes personal essays and memoirs, is often written for a broader audience than that of traditional legal scholarship. In using storytelling as a way to alert lawyers and nonlawyers alike to the fact that laws have a profound impact on people who do not participate [in their textual production], Critical Race Theory scholars build on and further develop concerns that have been present within the law and literature movement since its tentative beginnings in the 1970s.

Law and literature is a project that may be defined as a process of reading and comparing literary and legal texts for the knowledge that each may provide of the other. Roughly speaking, the movement consists of two different enterprises or concerns: "law-in-literature" and "law-as-literature." The distinction is Robert Weisberg's, and was introduced in his influential and much-quoted article, "The Law-Literature Enterprise" from 1988 (*Yale Journal of Law and the Humanities* 1:1). As Weisberg himself points out, it is useful mostly in terms of sorting out existing scholarship in the field. In practice, the work of both enterprises tends to converge.

Law-in-literature scholars pursue the study of specific authors and texts for the light they shed on legal issues and their impact on our lives. The area is not new. In the nineteenth century, English lawyers were interested in the ways in which Shakespeare, Dickens, and others wrote about the legal system. In an American context, it is only more recently that critics have realized the prominent part law plays in American letters. Underlying, and to some extent shaping, the discourse of law-in-literature is the view that law and legal thinking has always been or is increasingly becoming too rigid and technical, and that it is necessary to supplement its professionally detached and rational voice with a more human and passionate one. In *Law and Literature: A Misunderstood Relation* (1988), Richard A. Posner, one of the key early players in the law-in-literature debate points to a number of important connections between law and literature: the issue of interpretations is central to both; legal texts resemble literary texts in being highly rhetorical; literature is subject to legal regulation under such rubrics as defamation, obscenity, and copyright; and judicial opinions often employ literary devices. Finally, the legal process has a significant theatrical dimension to it that is attractive to writers of literature.

The law-as-literature part of the law-literature enterprise is more elusive and hard to define. Its essence is the suggestion that the techniques and methods of literary theory and practice may be useful to people involved with legal scholarship. Law-as-literature scholars have pursued two different areas of inquiry: hermeneutics and rhetoric. As some scholars see it, questions relating to the interpretation of legal texts are the most pressing. Inspired by post-structuralist and deconstructionist thinking, these scholars have stressed that any critical approach is at bottom a textual one—that the literature of law is inevitable, so to speak. To other scholars, the ways in which the law manages to cover up how it works and manipulates is more important. Legal writing is open to the uses and misuses of power as is any kind of writing, and it is only by emphasizing the dimension of figurative description or style that we may successfully expose legal writing as a vehicle for the distribution and use of power.

Law and history is not a movement or even a field in the same way that law and literature is. In one sense, historians have always been aware of the importance of law in American history. For example, Perry Miller in his seminal 1965 work *The Life of the Mind in America*, talks about the rise of a legal mentality among Americans. As a field in its own right, however, legal history only dates back to the late 1950s. At the beginning, historians preoccupied themselves with statutes and doctrines, appellate judicial opinions, and other material internal to the legal system. To some, it was the whole institutional process concerning the passage of laws and statutes that merited the attention of historians. Others found the legal profession itself and its role in American society interesting, and concentrated their efforts on describing the origins and status of lawyers and writing biographies of great American jurists. A third group of legal historians investigated issues relating to the police and the enforcement of laws—issues that led in turn to an interest in crime levels and social deviance.

In the 1970s and 1980s, social historians began looking beyond legal statutes and doctrine and toward legal records of all kinds. Court cases and legal codes were now of interest, less for what they might reveal about the working of the judicial system itself than for what they might tell us about the general history and development of the United States. Whether the specific area of interest was the origins of slavery and segregation in general, bastardy and bridal pregnancy, privacy, family and gender relations, or legal reform movements, law codes and court cases were perceived as sources for social history. The preoccupation of the older generation of legal historians with the highest levels of the American judicial system, moreover, was viewed as too narrow. From now on, every level of the judicial system, from the Supreme Court to local common councils, would be seen as worthy of investigation. From the insistence of the new social history on recovering legal records of all kinds and from all levels of society, it was but a short jump to the interdisciplinary orientation of recent legal historiography in which no concern, topic, or element, however trivial, is off-limits to the legal historiographer.

When we consider the emerging field of law and popular culture, it no longer makes sense to use categories such as literature and history. Law and popular culture is an interdisciplinary endeavor; its practitioners consciously seek to blur the boundaries between older, more traditional fields of study. What gave rise to it was the realization that there is a complex relationship between popular culture, the day-to-day operation of the legal system, and the ideas that books, films, and television shows attempt to convey. Most Americans learn about their legal system indirectly, from mystery novels and perhaps most of all from films and television. These are the media that tell those legal stories that may put us in touch with popular beliefs about law and social justice in our time.

Legal storytelling merits our attention for several reasons. First, what people consider necessary, acceptable, or just may form the basis for their support of the legal system. If we concentrate our efforts at understanding the place of law in society on the reading of specific legal rules and the operation of the legal system, we miss out on one very important source of law: the popular imagination. Second, and not unrelated, the popular myths, images, and storytelling conventions that help shape the popular imagination serve to remind us that we are surrounded by a plurality of legal meanings. For legal officials and law professors, whose professional lives are intimately related to law, legal ideas and symbols are bound to have a different meaning than the one they carry for the lay person. Similarly, various groups within a nation or culture may experience, and therefore think, very differently about the law and its practitioners.

Participants in the field of law and popular culture believe that important and innovative interdisciplinary work may result when they venture into this recent addition to American Studies. Parameters are not yet fixed; opinions as to how the domain is constructed—what and whom it includes and excludes—and how it is approached vary. As Steve Redhead argues in *Unpopular Cultures: The Birth of Law and Popular Culture* (1995), for example, the disciplinary terrain of "popular cultural studies" is shown where law and popular culture meet, and he proposes three areas of study as particularly relevant to the field of law and popular culture: the role of law in licensing popular entertainment and regulating public spaces, the role of legal institutions in the changing forms of ownership and control of cultural goods and services, and the involvement of law in moral censure, particularly in the domains of domesticity and sexuality. For Richard Sherwin and Stewart Macauley, the worlds of law, film, and television increasingly overlap, and this calls for a careful examination of the images and stories furnished by popular culture. David Ray Papke's research reflects a basic interest in the dominant American culture's most basic law-related faith, institutions, motifs, and disbelievers. It is, he has argued, in paying attention to cultural configurations and conventions such as courtroom trials, lawyer novels, and films that the analysis of law and popular culture must begin. John Denvir has concentrated his scholarly efforts on Hollywood films. Unabashedly products of "mass" culture, Hollywood films turn out to provide a comparative advantage over "serious" narrative texts in that they make use of a broader variety of communicative tools than novels and therefore more easily reach us emotionally.

Finally, several scholars have concentrated on how law and lawyers are represented in popular culture. Are lawyers seen as heroes or villains? Is the legal system portrayed as a well-functioning part of the American democracy or as a part that may no longer be trusted to work fairly and impartially? What role do gender, race, or class play in the day-to-day operation of the American justice system, and how is this reflected in the media? These are but some of the questions raised by law and popular culture scholars. As these scholars see it, representations in popular culture of law and lawyers are a cultural barometer that may provide useful information about current norms and values, as well as about alternative normative possibilities and ways of thinking about law and lawyers. And precisely because the law is such an important cultural factor in American history and society, law and popular culture scholars feel a need to "intrude" on the kind of scholarship traditionally undertaken by legal scholars.

[*See also* Culture and Law]

• Robert A. Ferguson, *Law and Letters in American Culture*, 1984. Kermit L. Hall, *The Magic Mirror: Law in American History*, 1989. Kenneth L. Karst, *Belonging to America: Equal Citizenship and the Constitution*, 1989. Mary Ann Glendon, *Rights Talk*, 1991. Michael Kammen, *A Machine That Would Go of Itself: The Constitution in American Culture*, 1993. Richard Delgado and Jean Stefancio, eds., *Critical Race Theory: The Cutting

Edge, 2d ed., 1995. John Denvir, ed., *Legal Reelism: Movies As Legal Texts*, 1996. David Ray Papke, *Heretics in the Temple: Americans Who Reject the Nation's Legal Faith*, 1998. Michael Schudson, *The Good Citizen: A History of American Civic Life*, 1998. David Alan Black, *Law in Film: Resonance and Representation*, 1999. Helle Porsdam, *Legally Speaking: Contemporary American Culture and the Law*, 1999. Richard K. Sherwin, *When Law Goes Pop: The Vanishing Line Between Law and Popular Culture*, 2000.

—Helle Porsdam

ASSAULT AND BATTERY. In English *common law, assault and battery were discrete crimes. Today, although some jurisdictions have merged the two crimes into a single offense, all jurisdictions recognize forms of aggravated assault and battery such as mayhem, malicious wounding, or felonious assault.

Battery is defined as an unlawful touching. The touching need not cause physical injury, thus caressing a stranger's buttocks is an offensive and unlawful touching. A touching may be of the person's body or items attached to the body, such as a shoulder bag or necktie. Touching may involve either body-to-body contact or may occur through use of an instrumentality, such as a thrown object or a dog ordered to attack the victim.

A touching is unlawful in the absence of justification, excuse, or consent. For example, police are legally justified in using reasonable force to apprehend criminals; striking another in self-defense is an excusable touching; and adults may consent to certain forms of touching. Although people may consent to an embrace or to a simple fistfight, they cannot consent to a duel or any form of serious injury. The law also mandates consent to certain inconsequential touchings, such as the incidental jostling that occurs in a crowded hallway.

The criminal state of mind required for battery is that the defendant either act with an intent to strike another person (such as a well-aimed punch in the nose) or perform a reckless act that results in a touching (shooting off a sky rocket that falls into a crowd).

Assault is defined as either an attempted battery or placing another in apprehension of an imminent battery. An attempted battery requires that the defendant intend to and come close to touching another person. For example, an attempted battery occurs when a defendant strikes at and misses someone, even though the intended victim is unaware of the failed attack. This form of assault focuses on the defendant's mental state and physical act, while ignoring the victim's state of mind.

In contrast to an attempted battery, the "offer" type of assault requires that the victim be placed in reasonable apprehension of an unwanted touching. The apprehension must be reasonable and it must be in anticipation of an imminent touching. Someone who merely scowls at another does not create reasonable apprehension of a battery; just as someone threatening to shoot another next week does not threaten imminent harm. Threats of future harm are not an assault, although they are often covered by statutes that criminalize communicating a threat. The modern movement toward "stalking laws" is another use of statutes to prohibit menacing conduct not amounting to a traditional assault.

An offer type of assault occurs when the defendant either intends to frighten the victim or recklessly causes the victim to apprehend an imminent touching. Thus a defendant who waives a gun in another's face intends to frighten that person. A defendant randomly firing a weapon in public may not intend to frighten anyone, but may recklessly cause a nearby person to fear imminent harm.

[*See also* Criminal Law Practice; Criminal Law Principles; Criminal Procedure, Federal Rules of]

• Wayne R. LaFave, *Criminal Law*, 3rd ed., 2000.

—Ronald J. Bacigal

ASSEMBLY AND ASSOCIATION. Freedom of assembly and association is indispensable to self-government. Assembly is a public act by a group to convey a message; association is often an element of assembly, but it also pertains to the private right of individuals to form an organization or community based on their own vision. While the First Amendment of the United States Constitution and state *constitutions expressly protect the right of assembly, these instruments are silent about the right of association. Nonetheless, the Supreme Court has recognized a constitutional right of association (*NAACP* v. *Alabama* (1958)) and linked it to the rights of *speech and assembly, and also to the implied constitutional right of privacy (*Griswold* v. *Connecticut* (1965)). The two rights raise different legal questions, and reflect the two major concepts of *citizenship in liberal theory: those derived from John Locke, which emphasize private rights against the state, and those traced from Aristotle and Jean-Jacques Rousseau, which stress republicanism and active political participation (see VOTING AND PUBLIC PARTICIPATION).

The Supreme Court has held that such public areas as streets, parks, sidewalks, and related places are "public forums" for vibrant assembly and protest (see *Edwards* v. *South Carolina* (1963)). Because assembly can involve conduct that harms valid social interests ("speech-plus"), courts have developed special tests for the public forum that balance the expressive interests at stake with societal interests. For example, the Supreme Court permits such reasonable "time, place, and manner" regulations as antinoise and anticongestion provisions as long as such regulations do not discriminate against speakers because of their viewpoint or unnecessarily restrict the availability of speech (see, e.g., *Clark* v. *Community for Creative Non-Violence* (1984)). Licensing is also allowed if it is not a smokescreen for inhibiting or discriminating against expression. Courts have also distinguished lawful, peaceful picketing from picketing that violates property rights or is disruptive in nature. In 1994, the Supreme Court dealt with many of these issues in a complex case dealing with court-ordered restrictions of anti-abortion protesters (*Madsen* v. *Women's Health Center, Inc.* (1994)).

Another important assembly issue concerns access to private *property to convey a message. The Supreme Court limits First Amendment rights to claims against the government. Accordingly, First Amendment jurisprudence does not require owners of such private property as shopping centers to provide access to speakers. But six state supreme courts have held that their state constitutions require such access, at least on a limited basis. For example, the New Jersey Supreme Court has declared that the state constitution grants private groups the right to distribute leaflets in private shopping centers, and that a private citizen had the right to protest labor issues on the private property of Princeton University (*New Jersey Coalition Against War in the Middle East* v. *J.M.B. Realty Corp.* (1994) and *State* v. *Schmid* (1980)).

The right of association protects private groups in forming their own communities of meaning (what Robert Cover calls the pursuit of "nomos"). The right has two major applications. First, groups have a right to protect their private affairs from unnecessary state scrutiny. For example, the Supreme Court does not allow governments to harass associations by requiring them to provide membership lists or related information unless there is substantial evidence that the group is involved in subversive or other illegal activity (*NAACP* v. *Alabama* (1958)). Second, private groups have a right to control their own membership, and may even engage in racial or gender discrimination. But the Supreme Court has allowed states and municipalities to prohibit certain

private organizations from discriminating in this manner if the groups are sufficiently large in size and are nonexclusive (compare *Roberts* v. *U.S. Jaycees* (1984) with *Boy Scouts of America* v. *Dale* (2000)).

[*See also* Bills of Rights]

• M. Glenn Abernathy, *The Right of Assembly and Association*, 2d. rev. ed., 1981. Robert Cover, "Forward: Nomos and Narrative," *Harvard Law Review* 97 (1983).

—Donald A. Downs

ASSOCIATION OF AMERICAN LAW SCHOOLS. The Association of American Law Schools was founded in 1900, with thirty-two law schools as charter members, for the purpose of improving the legal profession through legal *education. The association pursues this objective through the establishment and enforcement of membership requirements for law schools, and through providing various types of professional development programs for law school faculty, staff, and deans. Today one hundred sixty-four of the nation's accredited law schools (about 85 percent) are members of the association, which works with the *American Bar Association in reviewing the quality of law schools. The six core values of the association are: quality of teaching, scholarly research, a diverse intellectual community, academic freedom, faculty governance, and a commitment to justice and public service.

From its inception, the association has provided programs for professional development: in the early years, plenary session roundtable discussions with faculty who attended the association's annual meeting, and publication of selected writings and essays on various topics. The association has published the *Journal of Legal Education* since 1948.

As the association has grown in size, the type and variety of professional development programs have changed dramatically. The annual meeting now attracts about three thousand law professors, and programs offered by eighty different sections have replaced plenary session roundtable discussions About six "stand-alone" programs each year are offered, which began with a series of "teaching clinics" in the late 1960s. Today, programs are offered for faculty who teach virtually every major subject in the law school curriculum; programs are also offered for professors who share similar interests and experiences, such as women and minority law professors. The association has been instrumental in fostering the growth of clinical legal education by offering an annual program for clinical law faculty since 1977. Annual workshops for new law teachers and occasional workshops on new ideas for experienced teachers contribute to developing more effective and innovative pedagogy.

The association has fostered racial diversity in legal education dating back to the early 1950s when membership requirements first prohibited race discrimination and the association began filing amicus briefs in important civil rights cases. The association has also played a leadership role in providing opportunities for women in legal education, and in prohibiting discrimination on other bases, including religion, age, disability, and sexual orientation.

Through its membership in groups like the Consortium of Social Science Associations and American Council of Learned Societies, the association seeks to foster more interdisciplinary instruction and research, and more international collaboration. In May 2000 a groundbreaking conference of international legal *educators was held at Villa La Pietra in Florence, Italy, with fifty representatives from about thirty different countries; follow-up international conferences are anticipated.

A national office was established in 1963 with Professor Michael Cardozo as the founding executive director. Leaders of the association have included distinguished law professors who later became significant public figures in American law, including Roscoe *Pound, Harlan Fiske *Stone, Erwin Griswold, Wade H. McCree Jr., Drew S. Days III, and Ruth Bader Ginsburg.

• Warren A. Seavey "The Association in Retrospect," *Journal of Legal Education* 3 (1950–51): 153–73. Michael Cardozo, "The Association Process: 1963–1973," *Association of American Law Schools–1975 Annual Meeting Proceedings* (1973–75): 1–86. —Carl C. Monk

THE ASSOCIATION OF TRIAL LAWYERS OF AMERICA (ATLA),

a not-for-profit voluntary association, was created in 1946 by workers' compensation attorneys. It quickly expanded its membership to include all trial lawyers who represent plaintiffs in tort-law claims or defendants in criminal cases. Today, ATLA membership includes virtually anyone who is interested in its activities. General goals of the organization include protection of the public, preservation of the administration of justice and the right to *jury trial, and a forum for the *education, exchange of ideas, and mutual support of plaintiff's trial lawyers. As of 2001, ATLA has approximately 60,000 members, many of whom are part of 100 subspecialty Sections and Litigation Groups. It operates through a 136-member Board of Governors, an 18-member Executive Committee, and a 150-person staff that includes approximately 30 lawyers. In addition, ATLA works with state and local trial lawyer associations and law student chapters in many law schools.

The impetus for such an organization came from the perception that *personal injury plaintiff's lawyers were at a disadvantage against lawyers representing defendants, especially large corporate entities. Injured plaintiffs bring individual claims, while defendants often face multiple similar claims each year. Defense lawyers are able to develop an expertise in specific tort law by virtue of their repeated involvement in similar cases. This is unlikely for the average plaintiff's attorney. For example, the lawyer representing a railroad would encounter hundreds of injury claims each year while those claimants would be represented by numerous attorneys who might handle such a case once in their career. Also, plaintiffs and their attorneys rarely have financial resources comparable to those of major corporate defendants.

ATLA, the remedy for such disparity, focuses on specific member benefits: its National College of Advocacy (NCA) produces and presents more than eighty continuing legal education programs each year, on both substantive and practice-skills topics. The programs are geared toward different levels of skill, from neophytes to highly specialized practitioners. ATLA also produces books, magazines, and articles containing information and practice tips for plaintiff's lawyers. A majority of the education programs and legal publications are available to all interested parties. The monthly publication, *TRIAL Magazine*, is widely distributed. Technology advances have allowed ATLA to make benefits available to members through a computer research entity, the ATLA Exchange, which maintains a database containing more than 500,000 records that contain thousands of briefs, depositions, and court orders that can aid the lawyer handling his or her first major case. An ATLA member with a new case can obtain information, advice, and research from attorneys who have handled similar cases.

ATLA also is directly involved in grassroots and national political action through its full-time lobbyists and political action committee (PAC). At twice-yearly conventions, ATLA coordinates member activities on a national basis. Through its Civil Justice Foundation, ATLA supports local organizations across the country that are actively working to prevent injuries—for example, handgun violence and worker safety. At its national headquarters in Washington, D.C., ATLA works to inform and influence legislators in numerous *consumer-rights areas. Over the years, the organization has had a significant impact on the development of tort law in product liability, comparative negligence standards, and damage awards. The ATLA Legal Affairs Department places the organization in the courts through constitutional challenges of laws that limit the legal rights of citizens and the authority of juries; amicus curiae, or "friend of the court" briefs in significant cases affecting the integrity of the civil justice system; and direct support for member attorneys.

[*See also* Criminal Law Practice]

• "ATLA: The First Fifty Years," 32 *Trial* 40 (July 1996). Judith Kilpatrick, "Specialty Lawyer Associations: Their Role in the Socialization Process," 33 *Gonzaga L. Rev.* 502 (No. 3, 1997/1998). ATLA Web site: *http://www.atlanet.org.*   —Judith Kilpatrick

AT&T LITIGATION was a federal *antitrust case that produced the historic 1982 consent decree known as the "MFJ" (Modified Final Judgment), which broke up the Bell System. Before the MFJ, "Ma Bell"—the American Telephone and Telegraph Company (AT&T) and its subsidiaries—controlled most of the U.S. telephone system: Western Electric manufactured equipment, Bell Laboratories developed new technologies, the Long Lines Department carried long-distance calls at prices regulated by the Federal Communications Commission (FCC), and the twenty-two Bell Operating Companies provided local service at prices regulated by state public utility commissions. This arrangement assumed that telephone service was a natural monopoly, best provided by an integrated system with price and service obligations policed by regulatory agencies. Critics argued, however, that the arrangement unjustifiably sacrificed the benefits of competition in favor of an inefficient mix of regulated and unregulated monopolies.

In the 1950s, technological innovations such as microwave transmission made competition in long-distance service possible, and the FCC began to remove regulatory barriers to entry in the long-distance service and equipment markets. Using its advantages as the dominant provider, AT&T fought back against fledgling rivals such as Litton Industries and Microwave Communications, Inc. (MCI). In the 1970s, both the rival companies and the Justice Department filed antitrust lawsuits charging that AT&T was using its monopoly of local exchanges to block competition in the equipment and long-distance service markets—for example, by preferring Western Electric's equipment to its rivals' and refusing to grant long-distance rivals interconnection with local networks on nondiscriminatory terms. The government suit sought divestiture of the regulated local operating companies from AT&T's competitive arms. President Ronald Reagan's first antitrust chief, William Baxter, pursued the case despite vehement opposition within the administration. After suffering defeats in some of the private suits, AT&T acceded to the government's requested relief. The MFJ went into effect in 1984, giving the federal district court control over much of U.S. telephony for twelve years.

Under the MFJ, AT&T retained Long Lines, Western Electric, and Bell Labs but divested its local networks to seven Regional Bell Operating Companies (RBOCs), such as Bell Atlantic. The decree freed AT&T to compete in long-distance service and in computer services. Significantly, however, the RBOCs remained regulated monopolies and came under "quarantines" blocking them from manufacturing telephone equipment and from providing long-distance service between (though not within) "local access and transport areas" defined by the court. The quarantines were designed to prevent RBOCs from reprising AT&T's strategy by using their protected local monopolies to favor their own long-distance service and equipment operations. But the quarantines also limited competition in important ways and were later challenged by new communication technologies (such as mobile phones) and further regulatory reforms. The 1996 Telecommunications Act, which finally displaced the MFJ, was designed to introduce competition in the local exchange and to allow the descendants of the Bell operating companies to enter long-distance service.

[*See also* Anti-Trust Law]

• Steve Coll, *The Deal of the Century: The Breakup of AT&T*, 1986. Jim Chen, "The Legal Process and Political Economy of Telecommunications Reform," *Columbia Law Review* 97 (1997): 835–73.

—William H. Page

ATROCITY, WAR. *See* War, Law of.

ATTACHMENT is a form of preliminary relief in civil actions. The plaintiff asks a *sheriff to seize some of the defendant's property, such as a bank account, so that the asset will be available to pay the plaintiff's claim if he wins. Attachment may also serve as the basis for a court's limited jurisdiction.

[*See also* Procedure, Civil]

—David S. Clark

ATTEMPT may be a crime when it involves the defendant's intent to do an act that goes beyond mere preparation or to cause a consequence that constitutes a substantive crime.

[*See also* Criminal Law Principles]

—David S. Clark

ATTORNEY. *See* Lawyers.

ATTORNEY, POWER OF. *See* Power of Attorney.

ATTORNEY FEES. *See* Fees, Attorney.

ATTORNEY GENERAL. The attorney general is the chief law-enforcement officer of the United States. The office serves as the head of the Department of *Justice and is responsible for representing the federal government in judicial proceedings, advising the president and the executive branch on legal matters, and administering most federal policing and correctional agencies.

The attorney general's office originated in England in 1472, and it became part of America's colonial heritage. The federal office was established under the Judiciary Act of 1789, and Edmund Randolph served as its first incumbent. Attorneys general are appointed by the president and confirmed by the Senate. The modern office is a member of the president's Cabinet and a key adviser on judicial selection and administration policy.

During its early years, the attorney general's office operated as a part-time, quasi-judicial institution. Most attorneys general maintained private practices in addition to their official duties and did not view their office as part of the president's administration. Over time the office's duties expanded and the office's relationship to the presidency was transformed. By the time Caleb Cushing left the office in 1857, it had become a full-time position in the executive branch with a set of conventionally defined norms and duties. Nevertheless, this transformation left deep tensions in the office's role in American government, and complicates its operation during periods of interbranch legal conflicts when its loyalty to the president is a source of tension.

Historically, presidents have appointed close friends or trusted political advisers to the office. President John F. Kennedy appointed his own brother, Robert, to the office in 1961. During the *Watergate scandal in the early 1970s, Attorney General John Mitchell's ties to President Nixon became a central focus of corruption charges. A watershed in the development of the attorney generalship occurred in 1870, when Congress established the Department of Justice (DOJ). Creation of the DOJ elevated the attorney general's office to Cabinet-level status and transformed what had been an elite barristers' office into the administrator of a large legal bureaucracy. Today the DOJ has more than 250,000 employees, housed in six separate legal divisions and numerous law enforcement and policing agencies, including: the *Federal Bureau of Investigation, the Immigration and Naturalization Service, the Bureau of Prisons, and the Drug Enforcement Administration. In few other nations is a single officer responsible for both the lawyering (litigation, legal advising, etc.) and nonlawyering (policing, investigations, corrections, etc.) functions connected to law enforcement.

The 1870 act also helped consolidate the office's control over the federal government's legal work. Today the DOJ conducts most federal litigation and prosecutions, while agency legal counsel advise their respective agencies on routine legal matters. Official opinions of the attorney general, however, are binding on executive-branch departments and agencies, though not on the courts.

Similar offices are also found in each of the fifty states. In many, the state attorney general also administers a state department of law or justice. Two important differences distinguish state offices from their federal counterpart, however: first, in most states the attorney general is popularly elected and politically independent from the state's governor and the state legislature. Second, responsibility for nonlawyering functions, such as police, prisons, and most criminal prosecutions, is not usually under the control of the attorney general, but under the control of other state-level administrators or locally elected prosecutors.

[*See also* Executive Power]

• Luther Huston, Arthur Miller, Samuel Krislov, and Robert Dixon, *Roles of the Attorney General of the United States*, 1968. Cornell W. Clayton, *The Politics of Justice: The Attorney General and the Making of Legal Policy*, 1992. Nancy Baker, *Conflicting Loyalties: Law and Politics in the Attorney General's Office, 1789–1990*, 1993.

—Cornell W. Clayton

AUTOMOBILE INSURANCE. *See* Insurance.

AUTOMOBILES AND CRIME. Although a relatively new invention, automobiles and other motor vehicles play a pervasive role in modern life.

They profoundly impact criminal justice—as objects of *theft and other crimes, as instruments for committing crimes, and as the stimulus for crimes such as drunk driving and vehicular *homicide that are designed to prevent deaths and other harms that can result from their improper use.

More than 2.6 million motor vehicles in the United States suffered break-ins, vandalism, or the theft of outer parts in 1998. Over 1.2 million were reported stolen. Although fewer than 1 percent of all registered vehicles are stolen each year, and 60 percent of these are recovered, vehicle thefts feed a huge market for stolen cars and parts and result in enormous losses—over five billion dollars in 1998. Fraud in the sale of new and used cars, phony theft and accident *insurance claims, and other criminal acts add to the economic impact of automobile crimes.

Motor vehicle thefts usually fit general theft definitions. Most states, however, punish such thefts under separate vehicle theft statues. "Carjackings," in which the thief uses a gun or some other weapon to force the driver to give up the vehicle, can be punished as *robbery. By creating a separate carjacking crime, however, many states punish this frightening form of vehicle theft even more seriously. On the other hand, many states provide lesser punishment for "joyriding," typically juveniles temporarily taking an automobile. Federal laws punish motor vehicle thefts that cross state lines.

Criminals use thousands of automobiles in the commission of crimes. Bootleggers, drug runners, bank robbers, and other types of lawbreakers need cars to carry things and to escape the police and rival criminals. Cars can also be used to kill or injure. When used as instruments for the commission of crime, vehicles may be seized by the government and subjected to *forfeiture proceedings.

By far the largest number of vehicular crimes involve illegal driving. Although millions of parking offenses have been downgraded to civil violations, speeding and other minor traffic offenses usually remain low-level crimes. More serious traffic offenses are generally misdemeanors, but some are felonies. The most common felony is driving under the influence of alcohol or drugs (1.4 million arrests in the United States in 1998). Other frequent felonies include reckless driving and hit-and-run, when these involve bodily injury.

Driving under the influence of alcohol or drugs has long been a felony under American law. In earlier times, however, it was not considered particularly serious and was usually punished with a fine. Following European examples and pushed by victims' rights groups such as Mothers Against Drunk Driving, American states began in the 1970s to increase punishments and to strengthen the laws themselves. Initially, many states created a rebuttable presumption that a person with a blood alcohol content of 0.10 percent or more was under the influence of alcohol. Under these laws drivers could escape criminal *liability by showing that their drinking had not impaired their driving. Concerned about studies suggesting that nearly half of all motor vehicle fatalities were attributable to drunk drivers, Congress pressured the states to eliminate this loophole and create a zero tolerance for drinking by teenage drivers. Between 1982 and 1998, these new, stronger laws helped reduce fatalities per mile driven by more than 40 percent and the proportion of fatalities involving drinking drivers from 39 to 23 percent. (Greater use of seat belts, air bags, and other safety measures also played a role in reducing fatalities.) In the late 1990s, Congress began to encourage states to reduce the blood alcohol limit to 0.08 percent.

With millions of people driving billions of miles each year in the United States, accidents, serious injuries, and deaths on the road are inevitable. More than forty-one thousand Americans lost their lives as a result of motor vehicle accidents in 1998. At least one driver was at fault in over 60 percent of these fatalities. As two-thirds of those killed were drivers, often in one-car accidents, many of those causing accidents were beyond the reach of criminal prosecution.

When a careless driver causes a death, the driver is normally civilly liable to the victim's family. Whether the driver is also criminally liable depends upon the degree of the driver's fault and the law of the state where the incident occurred. Neither American nor English criminal law generally punishes the killing of another person through ordinary negligence. Both do, however, punish as involuntary manslaughter the killing of another when the negligence (i.e., the risk of causing death) is greater ("gross"). In addition to requiring a great risk of causing death, American states often require that the driver be aware of the risk created. A declining number of states still punish any death that results from illegal driving as involuntary manslaughter, whether great risk was created or not.

Because juries are sometimes reluctant to convict careless drivers of a crime as serious as involuntary manslaughter, some states have created a lesser crime. Frequently called "vehicular homicide," this crime punishes ordinary negligence while driving and has a lesser penalty than involuntary manslaughter.

Deaths caused by extremely risky driving may be punished as murder. Most states punish these deaths as murder only when the driver was subjectively aware of the risk. A few states do so if a reasonable person would have been aware of the risk. Occasionally a prosecutor argues that a death occurring in the course of drunken driving or some other driving felony should be punished as murder solely because the death occurred during the commission of the felony. Of the nation's three thousand five hundred or so annual arrests for homicide involving some kind of criminal fault, experts believe that only a tiny percentage result in murder convictions.

Criticizing traditional approaches as lacking in clarity, the American Law Institute's *Model Penal Code urges states to limit a charge of murder to those reckless acts manifesting an "extreme indifference to the value of human life." It recommends that "involuntary manslaughter" be limited to reckless conduct in which the actor is aware of the risk created, and suggests a new crime called "negligent homicide" based on gross negligence under circumstances in which the actor "should have been" aware of the risk created. The code rejects punishing deaths caused by ordinary negligence. It also rejects the felony murder rule and other theories not closely tied to the creation of actual risks.

[See also Criminal Law; Federal Bureau of Investigation]

• American Law Institute, *Model Penal Code and Commentaries*, 1980, esp. §§ 210–210.4. Michael D. Lawrence, John R. Snortum, and Franklin E. Zimring, eds., *Social Control of the Drinking Driver*, 1988. James B. Jacobs, *Drunk Driving: An American Dilemma*, 1989. H. Lawrence Ross, *Confronting Drunk Drivers*, 1992. National Highway Traffic Safety Administration, *Traffic Safety Facts 1998*, 1999. Wayne LaFave, *Criminal Law*, 3d ed., 2000, esp. §§ 7.4, 7.12, 7.13.

—Floyd Feeney

AUTOPSY. *See* Medical Examiner; Medicine and Law.

B

BAD FAITH. *See* Insurance.

BAIL. The Eighth Amendment's admonishment that "Excessive Bail shall not be required . . ." requires that the state balance defendants' interests in freedom before trial against the public's interest that they actually appear at trial. The traditional approach to bail under the English *common law and in early America required the defendant to simply produce a "surety"—a friend or neighbor who would promise to see that the defendant would appear. By the late nineteenth century, however, money bail had emerged to become the dominant approach in the United States: a defendant was obliged to put up cash that was subject to forfeiture in the event he failed to appear at trial. Today a vast majority of defendants (over 85 percent) are released before trial—a substantial percentage of those either provide their own cash bail to the court, or borrow money from *bail bondsmen, third-party agents who commercially guarantee the defendant's appearance for a fixed fee.

Bail supports a fair criminal justice system by (1) minimizing the detention of persons who may later be proven innocent; (2) preventing hardship to families dependent on the accused; and (3) enabling defendants to look for necessary documents, consult a lawyer, or do whatever else is necessary to put on a strong defense. Additionally, the state maintains its own practical interest in bail as a means of keeping the costs of detention relatively low.

During the 1960s, the prevailing bail system came under attack from critics who charged that cash bail levels imposed by judges discriminate against the poor and minority groups. Major American cities thus adopted procedures that allowed a defendant to be released on one's own recognizance ("ROR"), which amounted to the simple promise from a defendant charged with a minor crime that he appear for trial. A pretrial release agency normally interviews the defendant to determine whether he maintains strong "community ties" before issuing a recommendation either for or against releasing the defendant on his own recognizance.

By the 1970s, fears grew that the pendulum had swung too far in favor of liberal bail procedures, as increased numbers of defendants committed crimes while on pretrial release. In response, a majority of states authorized judges, in setting release conditions, to consider both the likelihood of appearance *and* the defendant's "dangerousness" to himself or the community. In 1984 Congress passed its own Bail Reform Act, which allows judges to order the "preventative detention" of certain types of dangerous defendants before trial, without the possibility of bail. In 1987 the U.S. Supreme Court upheld the controversial law in *U.S.* v. *Salerno*, ruling that "nothing in the text of the [Eight Amendment's] Bail Clause limits permissible government considerations solely to questions of flight." Thus, notwithstanding the clear language of the Excessive Bail Clause, judges may (under certain conditions) require extremely high bail, and in some cases, deny bail altogether.

In recent years bail reformers have objected to judicial reliance on certain characteristics (race, class, etc.) in making pretrial release and detention decisions. Also controversial has been the wide disparity in release conditions and bail amounts imposed by different judges. Unfortunately, proposals to institute more explicit and universal bail guidelines have met with only limited success to date.

[*See also* Criminal Law Practice]

• Wayne H. Thomas Jr., *Bail Reform in America*, 1976. John S. Goldkamp, *Two Classes of Accused: A Study of Bail and Detention in American Justice*, 1979.

—David A. Yalof

BAIL, PRACTICE OF. A person who is arrested on suspicion of having committed a crime is typically transported to a police station, booked, and detained. Bail affords the individual the opportunity of release from confinement pending resolution of the charges against him. It is derived from the English practice that gave the detainee the option of being released—or "bailed"—to the custody of a third party. Both the English Bill of Rights (1689), as well as the United States Constitution, speak of an accused person's right not to be detained because of "excessive" bail. Indeed, the U.S. Constitution's Eighth Amendment provides that "excessive bail shall not be required." Bail, moreover, is the remedy for the inherent disadvantages attendant upon pretrial confinement: (1) inability to meaningfully assist counsel in defending against the charges (for example, locating witnesses); (2) financial and emotional harm flowing from the incapacity to earn a living, support a family, or to enjoy the emotional support of relatives and friends; (3) and interference with the *liberty of a person who has not been convicted of a crime.

Although the concept of "bail" is deeply ingrained in the American legal tradition, several contentious issues have enveloped its practice. Does the constitutional prohibition against excessive bail mean that an individual must not be denied bail, however heinous a crime he might have committed? If the overarching goal of setting bail is to assure the accused's presence at relevant pretrial proceedings, at trial, and at sentencing, does the countervailing need to protect the community from potentially dangerous offenders furnish a valid reason for denying bail? What conditions are appropriate for setting bail that are consistent with the Constitution? These questions have framed the social and political debate over the appropriate role of bail in the American criminal justice system.

Beginning with *Stack* v. *Boyle* (1952), the Supreme Court expressed a preference for pretrial release of suspects in unequivocal terms, noting the accused's "traditional right to freedom before conviction." The Court defined the purpose of bail as assuring the presence of the defendant at trial and sentencing. Accordingly, an amount of bail that went beyond the scope of securing the accused's presence was "excessive" and therefore unconstitutional. In the same year, the Court in *Carlson* v. *Landon* (1952) strongly intimated that the Constitution's bar against excessive bail did not "accord a right to bail in all cases." This pronouncement was consistent with historical practice, which traditionally denied bail for capital crimes when the proof of the crime was "evident."

Traditionally, bail was conditioned on a third party's responsibility for the accused's appearance at all scheduled court hearings. With the advent of urbanization, however, money became the principal condition imposed to ensure the defendant's presence. The emergence of *bailbondsmen, who typically charge a nonrefundable ten percent of the bond set for the suspect's release (plus collateral for the remainder), raised the question whether indigent suspects might suffer adverse consequences stemming from their inability to pay. In the 1960s a reform movement attempted to correct this inequity and to diminish, if not eradicate, the role of money bail and thus the bondsmen from the criminal process. The Vera Institute's Manhattan Bail Project, initiated in 1961, aimed to identify suspects who posed a low flight risk and to weigh criteria designed to release detainees on their own recognizance under carefully supervised terms.

The logical outgrowth of the Manhattan Project was the Federal Bail Reform Act (1966) and a series of state statutes modeled upon it. Seeking to eliminate the need for money bail for noncapital crimes, the act stipulated that persons accused of noncapital offenses should be released on their recognizance, or under unsecured bonds, unless the judicial officer determined that such conditions would not "reasonably assure the appearance of the person as required." Furthermore, the act delineated the relevant considerations that the judge should take into account in determining whether a person should be afforded pretrial release: (1) the nature and circumstances of the offense charged; (2) the weight of the evidence against the accused; (3) his ties to the community and his family; (4) his prior criminal record, if any; and (4) his record of appearing at scheduled court hearings. In effect, the act represented an effort to tailor pretrial release to the personal and situational characteristics of the accused, favoring release over pretrial detention. Other jurisdictions followed this trend of bail reform by replacing bailbondsmen with court-administered bail. Thus, in *Schilb* v *Kuebel*, the Supreme Court upheld, against an *equal protection challenge, a state statute that allowed the defendant either to post the entire amount of the bail set by the court or, alternatively, to post 10 percent of the bond with the court, which would be returned minus an administrative fee upon the defendant's appearance at trial and sentencing.

Within less than two decades after the passage of the Bail Reform Act (1966), a countertrend emerged, largely fueled by a "law and order" mentality that derived from the war on drugs and the upsurge in the rate of violent crimes. Reversing the 1966 act's presumption in favor of pretrial release, the Federal Bail Reform Act (1984) provided for preventive detention of those offenders who by commission of certain crimes or by the potential of posing danger to the community were not candidates for release pending trial or sentencing. In brief, the 1984 act permitted, upon proper proof, the pretrial detention of: those accused of crimes punishable by life imprisonment or death, crimes of violence, and serious drug offenses; persons who had previously been convicted of those offenses, and who posed a threat to others in the community upon release; and persons who posed a high risk of flight. In *United States* v. *Salerno* (1992) the Supreme Court rejected a constitutional challenge to the 1984 act. The Court held that the act did not impose punishment before the defendant was adjudicated guilty, but was merely a regulatory measure designed to protect the public. Similarly, the Court rejected the notion that the Constitution prohibited pretrial detention to deter the commission of potential crimes by the accused.

[*See also* Criminal Law Practice]

• Caleb Foote, ed., *Studies on Bail*, 1966. Paul B. Wice, *Freedom for Sale: A National Survey of Pretrial Release*, 1974. Wayne H. Thomas, *Bail Reform in America*, 1976. Kenneth Berg, "The Bail Reform Act of 1984," *Emory Law Journal* (1985): 685–740.   —Alfredo Garcia

BAIL BONDSMEN. In many states, the most common way for defendants to raise *bail and secure release from jail pending trial is to hire private bail bondsmen. In a typical bail bonding arrangement, the bail bondsman issues the necessary bond to the court on the defendant's behalf, while the defendant pays the bondsman a nonrefundable fee, typically 10 percent of the bond, and agrees to appear in court as required for hearings and trial. The bondsman, usually backed by a surety company, becomes liable to the court for the whole amount of the bail if the defendant fails to return, and so has strong incentives to monitor defendants and ensure their return. Bail bondsmen have the discretion to refuse clients they believe pose too great a risk of fleeing, or they may ask for collateral (such as property) from defendants.

Bail bondsmen generally provide an important service by making possible the pretrial release of most accused criminals, especially those without independent means to post bail. Although commercial bail bondsmen are virtually unique to the United States, their role in the judicial process grew directly out of the English system. Historically, a family member or trusted member of the community (the "surety") would assume responsibility for an accused person released on bail (the "principal"). Greater mobility in the United States made these relationships less reliable and encouraged the rise of commercial bail bondsmen in the nineteenth century. The rights and powers of commercial bail bondsmen nevertheless trace directly to the *common law, which recognized no difference between the powers of a surety over a principal and a *sheriff recapturing an escaped prisoner.

When defendants fail to appear in court, bail bondsmen typically hire bounty hunters to pursue, arrest, and return fugitives. Viewing the relationship between bail bondsmen and defendants as a private contract, courts have given bounty hunters much wider latitude than police to capture those who "skip" bail, including freedom from Fourth, Fifth, and Sixth-Amendment constraints. In *Taylor* v. *Taintor* (1873), the Supreme Court reaffirmed the idea that bail bondsmen and bounty hunters "have their principal on a string, and may pull the string whenever they please. . . ." Courts have generally followed *Taylor* in allowing bounty hunters to pursue defendants across state lines, seize and imprison them at any time, break and enter houses without a warrant, and use any necessary force.

Traditionally loose state regulations of bail bondsmen and bounty hunters have been strengthened in response to highly publicized cases of abuse by bounty hunters, as well as to concerns that bail bondsmen are a source of corruption. Since the 1960s, reforms in a few states have effectively eliminated commercial bail bonding by making it easier for defendants to gain release with little or no bail. More recently, some states have placed limits on the discretion of bounty hunters, many of whom are ex-convicts and have no formal training. Most states have been reluctant to eliminate bail bondsmen entirely, however, because they have proven cheaper and more effective than police in capturing the thousands of defendants who flee bail each year.

[*See also* Criminal Law Practice]

• Jonathan Drimmer, "When Man Hunts Man: The Rights and Duties of Bounty Hunters in the American Criminal Justice System," 33 *Houston Law Review* 731 (1996).   —Patrick Schmidt

BAILIFF. See Court Officers.

BAILMENT. See Property, Personal.

BAKER V. CARR, 369 U.S. 186 (1962). In a decision that Chief Justice Earl *Warren later identified as the most important of his tenure, *Baker* v. *Carr* (1962) decided that the issue of state legislative apportionment was justiciable. *Baker* thus paved the way for decisions like *Gray* v. *Sanders* (1963), where the Supreme Court developed and applied the "one person, one vote" standard to statewide elections and *Wesberry* v. *Sanders* (1964) and *Reynolds* v. *Sims* (1964), applying this standard to congressional districts and to both state legislative houses.

Baker v. Carr arose in Tennessee, where neither legislative house had been reapportioned since 1901. Advancing urbanization resulted in significant population disparities among districts with equal representation. In *Colegrove* v. *Green* (1946), a plurality of the Supreme Court had ruled that such disputes were "political questions" under the Guarantee Clause in Article IV for the elected branches to resolve; in *Baker*, Solicitor General Archibald Cox intervened for the Kennedy administration on behalf of voters from urban districts.

Justice William *Brennan wrote the opinion for six justices reversing *Colegrove* and deciding both that the Court had jurisdiction of voters' claims that their votes were unconstitutionally devalued and that remedies were available under the *equal protection clause. In a still definitive interpretation of the political questions doctrine, Brennan outlined six criteria identifying such questions. All involved *separation of powers issues among the three branches of the national government rather than federal concerns. Minimizing concerns that equal protection standards were vague, Brennan remanded the case for equitable relief to the three-judge U.S. district court that had dismissed it.

Justice William O. *Douglas's concurring opinion relied upon previous judicial interventions in state voting controversies, whereas Justice Tom Clark's argued that the Tennessee system was a patchwork with no rational basis, and, absent a state initiative or referendum mechanism, little other hope for redress. Justice Potter Stewart's concurring opinion stressed the limited nature of the Court's ruling as to justiciability.

Justice Felix *Frankfurter's dissent labeled the decision as a novel departure from precedent and warned against judicial involvement in such political questions. Justice John Marshall *Harlan's dissent also denied that the equal protection clause had been designed to address such apportionment issues.

Senator Everett Dirksen (R.-Ill.) led unsuccessful congressional calls for a constitutional convention to overturn the Court's decisions. *Baker* remains an example of the use of *judicial review, like that presaged in paragraph two of footnote 4 of the *Carolene Products* Case (1938), and defended in John Hart Ely's *Democracy and Distrust*, designed to clear democratic channels.

[*See also* Civil Rights and Civil Liberties; Voting and Political Participation]

• Richard C. Cortner, *The Apportionment Cases*, 1970. Jene Graham, *One Man, One Vote: Baker v. Carr and the American Levellers*, 1972.   —John R. Vile

BALDWIN, SIMEON EBEN (1840–1927), lawyer, judge, founder, and later president of the *American Bar Association.

Baldwin lived almost his entire life in New Haven, Connecticut. A graduate of Yale University, Baldwin attended Yale Law School for a year and spent a few months at Harvard Law School. He developed a lucrative practice, primarily representing railroad corporations. In 1869, Baldwin led two other New Haven attorneys in reviving the law school at Yale, where he taught on a part-time basis until 1919. He took the lead in urging that legal *education should be graduate education. Even so, his influence waned early in the twentieth century, when the school turned toward the case method of instruction, a move that Baldwin resisted.

Baldwin played a key role in the formation of the American Bar Association (ABA) in 1878. Motivated by the desire to bring the country together and by the hope of increasing standards within the legal profession, Baldwin inspired the Connecticut Bar Association to form a committee in 1877 to investigate the formation of a national *bar association. As chair of the committee, Baldwin undertook to write hundreds of letters to leaders of the bar in other states. The result of Baldwin's invitations was a meeting in Saratoga Springs, New York, in 1878, where the ABA was formed. Baldwin played an active role in the organization, serving as president in 1890–91, being the first editor of the *ABA Journal*.

In 1893, Baldwin was elected to serve on the state's highest court, the Supreme Court of Errors, a position he held until 1910.

Baldwin's opinions were known as competent, thorough analyses of the law but with little rhetorical flourish. The one opinion that attracted the most attention was *Hoxie* v. *The New York, New Haven, and Hartford Railroad Co.* (1909). Writing for a unanimous court, Baldwin held that the 1908 Federal Employers' Liability Act was unconstitutional because it violated the liberty of *contract guaranteed by *due process. Although the U.S. Supreme Court eventually rejected that view, former President Theodore Roosevelt castigated Baldwin for the opinion. The exchange between Roosevelt and Baldwin dominated much of public life in the United States in 1909 and 1910, with Baldwin threatening to sue Roosevelt for libel. In 1910 Baldwin was elected governor of Connecticut. In his later life, he became increasingly interested in international law.

[See also American Bar Association]

• Frederick H. Jackson, Simeon Eben Baldwin: Lawyer, Social Scientist, Statesman, 1955. Charles C. Goetsch, Essays on Simeon E. Baldwin, 1981.

—Walter F. Pratt Jr.

BANKRUPTCY

Procedures
Personal
Business

BANKRUPTCY: PROCEDURES

Bankruptcy is a system of laws and procedures designed to deal with the management and settlement of the debts of either an individual (a natural person) or a corporate entity that is in serious financial difficulty. Bankruptcy law seeks to balance debtor relief against creditor protection by giving the debtor respite from creditor pressure while preserving the assets of the *estate and providing for the orderly and evenhanded settlement of claims. This goal is accomplished by the creation of a bankruptcy estate, consisting of all the *property owned by the debtor at the commencement of the case, which is administered by a trustee under court control to maximize the value of assets or income for the payment of claims.

Because bankrupt debtors are usually insolvent (their liabilities exceed their assets), most claims are not fully paid. The extent to which a creditor shares in the estate depends on the nature and status of that creditor's claim. Secured claims—those protected by a valid lien in property—are paid to the extent of the value of the creditor's interest in the property (collateral). Priority unsecured claims—those accorded priority treatment in bankruptcy law—are paid in rank order. Unsecured general creditors, with no security or priority, share what is left and often receive little or no payment.

History and Federal Nature of the Law. Bankruptcy procedures existed in Roman law and were revived in medieval Europe. The earliest English bankruptcy statute was enacted in the sixteenth century. Originally, English bankruptcy law was solely aimed at creditor relief, often with harsh consequences for the debtor. The use of bankruptcy for the debtor's benefit arose only in the eighteenth century. The American colonies adopted English *common law, including its bankruptcy law. Colonial bankruptcy law then developed differently in the various colonies. By the time of the Constitutional Convention, debt-enforcement laws were a patchwork of local rules and procedures. Because the framers were concerned that interstate commerce would be hampered by the lack of a nationwide bankruptcy law, they gave Congress the power to establish uniform bankruptcy laws (U.S. Constitution, Art. 1, § 8). Therefore, once a bankruptcy petition is filed, federal bankruptcy law preempts state law, and the bankruptcy case is governed by federal law and adjudicated by federal courts.

Although Congress made sporadic attempts at bankruptcy legislation during the nineteenth century, no stable bankruptcy statute was passed until 1898. This statute lasted (with significant amendment and judicial embellishment) until 1978, when it was replaced by the current Bankruptcy Code (Title 11 of the U.S. Code). The 1978 code built on but substantially reformed the old law. Although Congress has not undertaken such extensive revision since 1978, the Bankruptcy Code has been amended significantly several times. The issue of properly balancing debtor and creditor interests has often motivated amendments and continues to generate controversy.

Process. The administration and adjudication of bankruptcy cases is dealt with through a specialized system in which a bankruptcy trustee administers the estate under the supervision of a public official, the U.S. trustee, and judicial proceedings are brought in bankruptcy courts. Because bankruptcy judges are not appointed with life tenure (U.S. Constitution, Art. III), they must operate under the control of the federal district courts. Although this is awkward and constitutionally tenuous, it has worked for many years.

A case is initiated by the filing of a petition in a federal bankruptcy court. Most bankruptcies are voluntary—the financially troubled debtor files the petition seeking bankruptcy relief. In limited circumstances, qualified creditors may force the debtor into bankruptcy through an involuntary petition. A voluntary petition automatically places the debtor in bankruptcy, but involuntary bankruptcy requires court adjudication. Immediately upon the filing of the petition, all creditors are bound to bankruptcy's collective proceeding and are forbidden, by an automatic stay, from taking any further action to collect their claims outside the bankruptcy proceeding. They submit their claims to the estate to be handled by the trustee in accordance with bankruptcy law.

Liquidation and Reorganization. Liquidation and reorganization are the two distinct forms of bankruptcy relief provided in the Bankruptcy Code and governed by different code chapters. Chapter 7 is used to liquidate the debtor's estate. The trustee realizes the debtor's non-exempt pre-petition property and distributes its proceeds to creditors in accordance with the rank of claims. The effect of liquidation differs for individuals and corporations. An individual debtor is entitled to claim specified property as exempt, thereby excluding it from the liquidation. Exempt property, combined with earnings and property acquired by the debtor after the petition was filed, forms the debtor's new estate, which is not subject to pre-petition claims. A corporation receives no exemptions and becomes defunct after liquidation.

If the purpose of the bankruptcy is to rehabilitate rather than liquidate the debtor, one of the reorganization chapters is used. The most common of these are Chapter 11, suitable for corporations or for individuals with substantial debt, and Chapter 13, available only for voluntary petitions by individuals whose debts are relatively small. Although Chapter 11 is more complex than Chapter 13, they have a similar basic structure: the debtor is able to keep certain assets in return for a commitment under a plan to distribute money or property to creditors. Distributions are typically made in installments over a period of time and are derived, for example, from income earned by the debtor during that period. (Some distinctive features of Chapter 11 are that the debtor assumes the trustee function, creditors vote on the plan following extensive disclosure, and the reorganization process can take much longer.) The value of the distribution is decided under complex standards. As a general rule it must be at least equal to what creditors would have received in a liquidation. However, the ideal is that rehabilitation will enhance creditor recovery, so the code encourages it as being in both the debtor's and the creditors' best interests. There is some controversy over whether current rehabilitation procedures generally achieve this goal.

Discharge. The fresh start of an honest debtor is a fundamental aim of bankruptcy. Therefore, bankruptcy discharges (releases) a debtor who has complied with the law from the unpaid balance of all or most of the pre-petition debt handled in the case. An individual debtor is entitled to a discharge in both liquidation and reorganization bankruptcy, but a corporation is discharged only if reorganized, and it does not survive liquidation.

[*See also* Economics and Law]

• Teresa A. Sullivan, Elizabeth Warren, and Jay Lawrence Westbrook, *As We Forgive Our Debtors: Bankruptcy and Consumer Credit in America*, 1989. Charles Jordan Tabb, "The History of the Bankruptcy Laws in the United States," *American Bankruptcy Institute Law Review* 3 (1995): 5-51. Eric A. Posner, "The Political Economy of the Bankruptcy Reform Act of 1978," *Michigan Law Review* 96 (1997): 47. Brian Anthony Blum, *Bankruptcy and Debtor/Creditor: Examples and Explanations*, 2d ed., 1999. Douglas G. Baird, *Elements of Bankruptcy*, 3d ed., 2001. —Brian A. Blum

BANKRUPTCY: PERSONAL

The Constitution gives Congress the right to establish uniform laws on bankruptcy. The earliest American bankruptcy laws were extensions of older English practices of debt slavery and imprisonment, emphasizing the obligation to pay, rather than the right to relief from debts. Procedures were primarily creditor initiated as an adjunct of debt collection. Concessions to *debtors began to come grudgingly in English law in the 1700s in the form of very limited exemptions of assets and the creation of limited procedures to allow third-party handling of assets for the benefit of creditors. The first American bankruptcy act in 1800 followed that model.

In the 1800s, several American states enacted constitutional provisions that prohibited imprisonment for debt. This was followed by the Bankruptcy Act of 1841 setting out voluntary procedures for individuals and largely ending imprisonment except in cases of fraud. This act expanded exemptions and allowed discharge of debts unless the majority of creditors objected; however it was repealed one year after enactment in the face of objections to the extent of debtor protection. A similar act was passed in 1867 but repealed twenty years later.

The tension that shapes bankruptcy policy thus entails a conflict between emphasis on ensuring repayment of valid debts and emphasis on protecting honest debtors overburdened with debts. As the credit economy burgeoned, the focus of bankruptcy law inexorably shifted toward debtor protection to sustain that system and cure some of its malfunctions. The Bankruptcy Act of 1898 set out a body of law that lasted for almost a century. It provided for discharge of debtors and exemption of assets pursuant to state law. Creditors could not block discharge except on the basis of specific statutory criteria. This statute was replaced by the Bankruptcy Code of 1978 which expanded consumer protection significantly.

Consumer bankruptcy law in the early twenty-first century emphasizes protection of the individual by creating a "fresh-start," consisting of relief from most debts incurred prior to the bankruptcy, and enabling the consumer to reconstruct an economic future unburdened by a failed past. This is offset in part by considerations of fairness for creditors and the argument that debt relief should not be too easily available. Over the years, the competing policies resulted in different balances. The debtor protection view reached a zenith in the 1978 code. Subsequently, there has been some erosion of consumer protection, but consumer bankruptcy remains primarily concerned with giving consumers an economic fresh start.

Bankruptcy is federal law that preempts contrary state law, such as by discharging debts enforceable under state law. Additionally, bankruptcy filing places an automatic stay on collection efforts by creditors. This shields consumers faced with aggressive debt collectors. Relief from the stay can only be granted by the bankruptcy court.

While creditors may file a bankruptcy petition against the debtor, virtually all consumer bankruptcies are made voluntarily by the debtor. The debtor chooses between two types of bankruptcy. Chapter 7 bankruptcies are liquidation proceedings; a debtor's nonexempt assets are sold by a trustee with proceeds distributed to creditors under statutory priority rules. Chapter 7 proceedings are by far the most common form of bankruptcy.

In Chapter 13 bankruptcies, in contrast, the debtor proposes a plan of payment to creditors from the debtor's future income, while retaining all assets. The plan is not effective unless approved by the bankruptcy court. The least that the creditor can receive is payments whose present value when the plan is approved equals what the creditor would receive in a Chapter 7. Chapter 7 is open to all debtors, while Chapter 13 has dollar limits on the debt involved and requires that the debtor have income.

Chapter 7 and a Chapter 13 differ in the source from which creditors are paid. Depending on the debtor's economic condition, one or the other may benefit creditors. One debate in bankruptcy policy is whether the debtor's choice should be limited to that option that gives the greatest return to creditors. That rule is rejected under the code as inconsistent with the freedom of choice implicit in the modern law and the idea that an honest debtor has a right to relief by giving up his nonexempt assets. That, of course, represents a full circle from early emphasis on debt collection. Over the years since 1978, however, some limited new rules have constrained debtor choice. For example, a court can dismiss a consumer Chapter 7 if granting relief would be a substantial abuse of bankruptcy. Few cases use this remedy to preclude an individual with income from using a Chapter 7, however.

For the consumer, the fees she pays and assets she relinquishes measure the tangible cost. The debt relief measures the tangible benefit. Each aspect of the tangible trade-off represents a policy choice; the balance defines the overall character of consumer bankruptcy law. The code does not deal with the moral cost of not paying debts.

Chapter 7 provides the economic baseline. A bankruptcy filing creates an *estate consisting of all the debtor's existing property. The debtor must provide a list of assets and the assets are administered by a trustee. The trustee represents the unsecured creditors with the goal to optimize return for them.

The debtor in Chapter 7 retains exempt assets. What assets are exempt depends on whether the debtor chooses state law exemptions (the state of its domicile) or federal alternative exemptions. The federal exemptions were created to standardize exemptions nationally and to override law in those states with narrow exemptions unprotective of consumers. State laws vary; states such as Texas and Florida allow debtors to retain a home worth over one million dollars, while other states give few exemptions of small value. Whether such variation and such broad exemptions should be allowed has been another point of conflict. Overriding state exemption laws, however, encroaches into state's rights in the federal system and has been resisted on that ground also.

The trustee in Chapter 7 also may not be able to sell assets that are subject to a valid security interest. A secured creditor has a right to the value of its secured claim (e.g., what it could collect from the collateral). Often, the debt exceeds the value of the collateral; no value will be left for unsecured creditors. Very often, the issue is between the secured creditor and the consumer on whether the consumer can retain the asset (e.g., a car or a home) by reinstating the secured debt.

These rules and the simple fact that most consumers who file bankruptcy lack assets means that most consumer bankruptcies are "no asset" cases: there are no assets distributed to unsecured creditors. In terms of tangible cost, other than fees the debtor pays nothing for bankruptcy relief. Creditors receive nothing for their claims.

What assets are available does not affect the debtor's relief. The norm is that a Chapter 7 bankruptcy discharges all debts that exist at bankruptcy filing, but has no effect on debts incurred after filing. A discharge is a statutory injunction barring the creditor from any act to collect the debt in the future. The debtor may voluntarily repay. The debtor may reaffirm a debt, but only under judicial supervision. By and large, debts are discharged.

Some debts are exempt from the discharge by statute, with the exceptions being greater in Chapter 7 than Chapter 13. The exceptions cover two types of issues. The first is where the debtor acted improperly in incurring the debt and the creditor proves that fact during a bankruptcy hearing on dischargeability of the debt. Included are fraudulently incurred debts. The second type of exception involves creditors singled out for protection as a matter of policy, such as alimony payments and recent tax debts. In some cases, for misconduct or misjudgment, the debtor may be denied discharge of all debts. For example, no discharge can be granted if the debtor obtained bankruptcy relief under Chapter 7 within six years before the current case.

Although exceptions to discharge are significant, in most consumer cases, there are no applicable exceptions. With the exception of some secured debt, the debtor leaves bankruptcy with a clean slate. This is the fresh start that serves as a primary baseline of bankruptcy policy, that is, fresh in terms of existing debt burdens.

[See also Economics and Law]

• William Miller Collier, Collier on Bankruptcy, 1903. Countryman, "A History of American Bankruptcy Law," Comm. Law Journal 81 (1976): 226.

—Raymond T. Nimmer

BANKRUPTCY: BUSINESS

The Constitution gives Congress the right to set uniform laws on bankruptcy. The earliest bankruptcy laws focused on remedies such as imprisonment for debt—acting as an adjunct of enforcing debt collection controlled by creditors. By the early 1800s, however, several states prohibited imprisonment for debt. Ultimately, the increased importance of credit led to a series of bankruptcy acts that offered relief for *debtors, balanced against creditor rights, culminating in the Bankruptcy Act of 1898.

These early laws dealt mostly with individuals as debtors, while the world of business began to be dominated by corporate and other entities. The Chandler Act (1938) detailed the treatment of bankruptcy for such business entities. In entity-based bankruptcies, policy issues not only focus on the debtor (a legal entity) and its creditors, but also on *equity holders and business managers.

Chapter X and Chapter XI of the Chandler Act contemplated reorganization preserving the ongoing business as an alternative to liquidation under Chapter 7. Reorganization allows restructuring of debts and, even, ownership without a sale of assets. The policy basis for this approach to bankruptcy emphasized that preserving an ongoing business was a valuable social goal that benefits employees, users of the business, and the community. There was also a belief that preserving the company preserved value for creditors as compared to a liquidation that sold assets piecemeal. The social context of these and subsequent laws included the increasing importance of corporate entities as debtors and as organizations the continuation of which affected many people (see BUSINESS ORGANIZATIONS).

Reorganization, however, involves risks of abuse. The company must be run by someone, and the natural choice is the preexisting management who best know the business, but who also may have brought it to an economic impasse. There is also a risk that insiders may act in ways that are adverse to creditors or public interest holders. Reflecting this, Chapter X, which dealt with publicly held companies, circumscribed the redistribution of assets to prevent abuse. One rule was that equity owners could retain no interest in the company unless senior claimants were fully repaid. This rule of absolute priority often eliminated prior owners. Chapter X also contemplated oversight by the SEC to protect against management acts adverse to public debt and equity holders, and authorized appointment of a trustee to run the business; in most cases, trustees were appointed. Chapter XI, in contrast, focused on reorganization of privately held companies, providing far fewer restrictions because the interested groups could protect themselves, but giving debtors fewer rights to control the terms of the reorganization.

The goal of the reorganization procedures was to preserve the value and ongoing existence of companies while providing safeguards for claimants. In practice, however, most public companies that opted for reorganization used Chapter XI, which was less costly, more flexible, and did not cause appointment of a trustee to run the company. Chapter XI, however, unlike Chapter X, lacked any means to alter debts of secured creditors without consent, and consequently gave those creditors great control. Preservation goals were not effectively realized.

The Chandler Act gave businesses a choice between liquidating a company under Chapter 7 or reorganizing it and its debts. Liquidation was, and continues to be, a simple resolution of debt problems: the assets of the company are collected, sold, and the proceeds distributed in a format that pays secured claims first, then distributes assets pro rata under a statutory priority system. A business shell may be left, but without assets. A total revision of law occurred in the 1978 Bankruptcy Code. The code preserved the different types of reorganization, but changed reorganization law to encourage successful use. The code created Chapter 11 bankruptcy, a proceeding that entails flexibility. The ordinary rule in Chapter 11 is that the debtor retains control of the business and, initially, the sole right to propose reorganization plans. The "debtor" here refers to management. The presumption is that business people are best able to assess the options for the company. The debtor acts as a "debtor-in-possession," a role that entails semi-trustee status as the entity with operating control of a bankruptcy estate formed for the benefit of all claimants and consisting of all of the original debtor's assets. In effect, the managers no longer owe sole allegiance to equity owners.

The debtor's actions are subject to overview and often prior approval by the court. A trustee generally supervises all pending cases. Unsecured creditors, equity interest holders, and other interest groups are represented through committees appointed by the court.

Chapter 11 creates an environment for negotiation in which the parties determine the reorganization subject to judicial oversight, rather than control, while the business continues to operate. The various interest groups have different leverage in negotiation, generally reflecting their position if the company were liquidated.

The assumption is that this interaction can best determine the future of the company, but that while the interaction occurs, the company should be kept in business and the economic interests of the claimants generally protected. How this works can be seen in terms of two different functions in a reorganization case. The first occurs during the preliminary part of the case, while assets are re-arranged and the business maintained. During this time, creditors are subject to an automatic stay that prevents action to enforce debts against the debtor. The stay continues unless removed by the court. Mere nonpayment is not generally a reason to remove the stay. Generally, secured creditors continue subject to the stay as long as they receive adequate protection of their economic interest in the collateral. Unsecured creditors do not have even that right. Parties holding mutually unperformed contracts with the debtor are subject to the debtor's decision to accept (perform) or reject (breach) the *contract, a choice that often need not be made until a reorganization plan is proposed, although some contractors have special protection requiring earlier decisions.

The premise is that a business should be allowed to continue if feasible and that the debtor has discretion to rearrange assets to optimize the business. The claims against the debtor are protected in general, but many creditors remain unpaid throughout this period. Ultimately, this practice is derived from a belief that managers are best able to make business judgments, subject to judicial overview, to prevent self-dealing or to end the process when no business options are feasible.

The second function entails development of a reorganization plan. The plan can restructure all debts and ownership of the company. Chapter 11 reorganization plans approved by an appropriate majority of each interest group are confirmed by the court in the absence of collusion, subject to economic restrictions that protect minority voters by assuring their equal treatment and at least what they would receive in a liquidation. Most importantly, however, the negotiation occurs in a setting where there is a right in law to obtain confirmation of a plan over dissent of an entire class of claims or interests, aslong as economic conditions are met.

The resulting negotiation delivers the end product of reorganization (a plan confirmed by the court) or, failing to do so, leads to liquidation of the company. This principle allows for self-determination in a context where the claimants can maintain the business as an ongoing concern because this yields greater value to all. In practice, however, large Chapter 11 proceedings are expensive and lengthy. The true measure of their economic effect as compared to a simple liquidation remains to be assessed.

[See also Economics and Law]

• William Miller Collier, Collier on Bankruptcy, 1903. Raymond T. Nimmer, "Secured Creditors and the Automatic Stay: Variable Bargain Models of Fairness,"

Minnesota Law Review (1983): 1 Raymond T. Nimmer, "Negotiated Bankruptcy Reorganization Plans: Absolute Priority and New Capital Contributions," *Emory Law Journal* (1988): 1010. Raymond T. Nimmer, "Chapter 11 Business Governance: Fiduciary Duties and Business Judgment," *Bankruptcy Developments Journal* 1(1989): 6.

—Raymond T. Nimmer

BAR ASSOCIATIONS. The first bar associations in America consisted of self-selected groups of socially well-connected eighteenth-century lawyers who joined together on a local basis for social events, group study, and debate, and to address their common concerns about the practice of law, including the regulation of admission to the bar and the fees to be charged their clients. Lawyer interest in bar associations waned during the first half of the nineteenth century, but was rekindled after the Civil War, when in 1870, "leading" lawyers in New York formed the Association of the Bar of the City of New York for the primary purpose of fighting corruption in local government that the lawyers associated with Boss Tweed. Similarly, in 1874, lawyers in Chicago formed the Chicago Bar Association to fight the unauthorized practice of law. Then, in 1878, a group of well-heeled lawyers summering in Saratoga Springs, New York, formed the *American Bar Association to advance the science of law, improve the administration of justice, enhance the honor and prestige of the legal profession, and provide opportunities for lawyers to socialize with each other.

Thereafter, there was a steady increase in the number of bar associations, until by 1925 there was a statewide bar association in every state or territory. By 1930, it was estimated there were more than 1,100 city or county bar associations. This proliferation of bar associations was one facet of what has been called the "organizational revolution" in America. Although at first most of these associations had restrictive, invitation-only membership policies that precluded the participation of many lawyers, eligibility requirements were gradually relaxed. As a result, the percentage of lawyers belonging to at least one bar association climbed from 30 percent in 1915 to 60 percent in 1930. Starting in the 1920s, some states decided to require that all lawyers join the statewide bar association, which in turn was delegated significant responsibility for the regulation of the legal profession. In more than one-half of the states, lawyers are now required to belong to what is variously referred to as a "mandatory," "unified," or "integrated" bar association.

Of the voluntary bar associations, the American Bar Association (ABA) is now the largest and most influential. Over the past several decades, 45–55 percent of the country's lawyers have belonged to the ABA. There are also other important bar associations, such as the *National Bar Association for black attorneys, the American Trial Lawyers Association for plaintiffs personal injury lawyers, the American Corporate Counsel Association for in-house counsel, and the *National Lawyer's Guild for lawyers committed to the political, economic, and legal empowerment of the poor.

What do bar associations do? One objective of the early bar associations was simply to promote social interaction among lawyers. But all bar associations included among their objectives both the promotion of the professional interests of their members and the furtherance of the profession's commitment to public service. Bar associations serve their members by offering continuing legal *education courses, providing practice management services, and arranging for group discounts on various products and services. Public service activities include efforts to improve the law—most typically technical issues about which lawyers have special knowledge and issues related to the administration of justice. While most members approve of such law reform initiatives, many will balk if a bar association attempts to wield its influence on controversial questions of public policy about which the legal profession, as such, has no peculiar interest or special expertise.

Along with their goal of improving the administration of justice, bar associations have sought to provide disinterested information about the professional qualifications of nominees for judicial office. Until the Bush administration terminated the practice in 2001, the ABA played an official role in the evaluation of nominees for federal judgeships. In connection with local elections of judges, many local bar associations survey their members about the qualifications of the candidates and publish the results for consideration by the voters. Of equal importance has been the effort of the ABA and state bar associations to promote the adoption throughout the country of its Model Code of Judicial Conduct.

Much of the energy of both the ABA and the state bar associations has been directed to the regulation of the legal profession. With respect to bar admission, for example, the ABA led a long, eventually successful fight to increase the educational requirements for admission to the bar, and in the process earned a formal role in the bar admission process of the many states that now require graduation from a law school that has been accredited by the ABA. As part of this initiative, bar associations also sought the adoption and enforcement of laws broadly defining the practice of law and imposing strict penalties for its unauthorized practice.

The ABA also undertook to regulate the conduct of lawyers when in 1908 it adopted its Canons of Ethics and required its members to abide by them. In 1969, the ABA replaced the Canons with a Code of Professional Responsibility, and once again conditioned membership on compliance with the Code. When the Justice Department contended that ABA enforcement of some of the rules might violate the antitrust laws, the ABA dropped the requirement that its members abide by the Code, and redirected its energy to securing adoption of the Model Code by the various state supreme courts. With the support of state bar associations, the Model Code was adopted in all but one of the states. In 1979, the ABA also promulgated its Standards for Lawyer Disciplinary and Disability Proceedings. Bar associations continue to pay considerable attention to these issues, as evidenced by the ABA's adoption in 1983 of new Model Rules of Professional Conduct, which have been followed closely by both state and local bar associations, and the fact that some important ABA proposals were neither supported by state bar associations nor adopted by their supreme courts. This process is underway once again as the ABA is considering significant changes to the Model Rules proposed by a blue-ribbon Commission on Evaluation of the Rules of Professional Conduct, also known as the Ethics 2000 Commission.

Many lawyers think that bar associations have served the public well. They emphasize the numerous public service activities, with special emphasis on the efforts to improve the law and the administration of justice, and to establish standards of conduct for both judges and lawyers. But bar associations also have their critics, who view them as nothing more than guilds or trade associations, the primary purpose of which is to further the economic interests of their members by promulgating and securing judicial approval of anticompetitive rules and rules of professional conduct that favor lawyers at the expense of both their clients and the public. Early bar associations have also been criticized for their political and social conservatism, elitism, racism, sexism, xenophobia, and anti-Semitism. It remains undeniable,

however, that national, state, and local bar associations have played an important, and at times controversial, role in the history of American law and the history of the legal profession. It is also likely that bar associations will continue to do so in the years to come.

[See also Ethics and Professional Responsibility, Legal; Lawyers]

• James W. Hurst, *The Growth of American Law*, 1950. Roscoe Pound, *The Lawyer from Antiquity to Modern Times*, 1953. Jerold Auerbach, *Unequal Justice: Lawyers and Social Change in Modern America*, 1976. John P. Heinz, Edward O. Laumann, Charles L. Cappell, Terence C. Halliday, and Michael Schallman, "The Organized Bar," in John P. Heinz and Edward O. Laumann, *Chicago Lawyers*, 232–73, 1982. Charles W. Wolfram, *Modern Legal Ethics*, 1986. Michael Powell, *From Patrician to Professional Elite: The Transformation of the New York City Bar Association*, 1988. Richard L. Abel, *American Lawyers*, 1989.
                                                        —Carl A. Pierce

BAR EXAMINATION. For the past 175 years, the bar examination has been used to protect consumers of legal services by assuring that each applicant for admission to the bar demonstrates that he or she is at least minimally competent to practice law. It has also been argued, however, that the legal profession has used the bar examination to restrict entry to the profession for the purpose of reducing competition and preserving the racial, ethnic, and religious homogeneity of the bar.

Until the 1870s, the bar examination was typically taken after an apprenticeship with a practicing lawyer. It was administered orally and on an ad hoc basis by a local judge or lawyer, and was unlikely to be comprehensive or rigorous. Almost all who completed an apprenticeship passed the bar examination.

With the passage of a hundred years, however, much has changed. Almost all applicants for admission to the bar are required to take a bar examination after their graduation from an accredited four-year college or university and an accredited law school. Most also take an extensive and expensive bar review course. Gone is the oral quizzing by a local judge or lawyer. Administered on a statewide basis by Boards of Law Examiners, the bar examination now extends over two or three days and includes written essay and multiple choice questions. On the essay portion, the applicant must identify and resolve legal problems raised by hypothetical situations, thereby demonstrating adequate knowledge of the state's law and an adequate ability to reason logically about the application of the law to the facts presented. In most states, the multiple choice portion of the exam consists of the Multi-State Bar Examination (MBE), which is prepared under the auspices of the National Conference of Bar Examiners and tests knowledge of core subjects, such as Contracts and Torts, that are commonly taught in all law schools without regard to state variations. Most states also require applicants to take the Multi-State Professional Responsibility Examination (MPRE).

The movement toward a centrally administered written bar examination as a core component of the bar admission process coincided with the initiatives of newly emergent bar associations to "professionalize" the practice of law by heightening the educational standards for admission to the bar and otherwise regulating the conduct of lawyers. The first written bar examination was in 1870. The first Board of Law Examiners was established in 1878. The National Conference of Bar Examiners was established in 1931. The *American Bar Association vigorously championed the bar examinations. By 1937, written examinations were the norm, and 37 states had established statewide Boards Law Examiners. During these years, however, there was a tension between those who saw legal *education as the core component of the qualification process and wanted to encourage law school attendance by exempting graduates of approved law schools from the bar examination, and those who wanted to retain and strengthen the bar examination as an additional centralized vehicle for controlling admission to the bar. In 1890, sixteen states conferred such a "diploma privilege" upon the graduates of twenty-six approved law schools. Those opposed to the diploma privilege actively campaigned for its repeal, and by the 1930s only 10 percent of those admitted to the bar had not been required to take a bar examination, and by the 1960s the figure was 2 percent. One other noticeable change is that the modern bar examination is more difficult to pass than its nineteenth-century forbear. Since World War II, for example, the failure rate nationwide ranged from a high of 44 percent in 1954 to a low of 24 percent in 1974. In 1985, 34 percent failed the examination. Repeat attempts are allowed, however, and in the end, it is estimated that over 90 percent of those who take the bar examination will eventually pass it.

Another key question is just how difficult it should be to pass the bar examination. The issue was treated differently in different states and at different times, and the variance in the passage rate has given rise to questions about whether the bar examination was being used as a fair measure of competency or rather was being used to restrict admission to the bar because those already admitted thought there were too many lawyers. Related to this was the question of whether strict bar passage standards were part of a program intended to prevent members of ethnic, religious, and racial minorities from becoming lawyers. These questions cannot be answered with any degree of certainty, but commentators have noted that bar passage rates in many states dropped significantly during the Depression, and that the states with consistently lower pass rates were those with large cities, many immigrants, a large number of lawyers, and a large number of applicants for admission to the bar. In the end, though, the bar examination has proved more likely to delay than to prevent admission to the bar.

Although conscientiously administered with considerable attention to quality control, with respect to both question design and grading protocols, and staunchly defended by many lawyers as providing ease of skill assessment and a needed incentive for law students to fully engage in their studies, the bar examination remains controversial. Some lawyers question whether lawyers licensed in one state should be required to take the bar examination when they move to another state or whether they should instead be admitted "by motion." Underlying this issue is the question of whether the bar examination is really necessary to protect the public against incompetency or whether the real reason for it is to protect the state's lawyers from the added competition. More generally, there have been calls for a single national bar exam, the passage of which would entitle the lawyer to practice throughout the United States. Minority applicants have challenged the bar examination, as well as other standardized examinations such as the Law School Admission Test, as racially discriminatory. Others have contended that bar examination procedures deprive them of *due process of law. Finally, the bar examination has been criticized as an unnecessary burden that merely replicates the tests the bar applicant passed to graduate from law school. Such critics also contend that the bar examination does not adequately measure the competencies actually needed for success in the practice of law. While there surely will be changes in the bar examination to reflect changes in the profession and the society it serves, it seems very unlikely that this rite of passage into the legal profession will meet the same fate as its primary historical predecessors, the apprenticeship and the diploma privilege.

[*See also* Lawyers]

• James W. Hurst, *The Growth of American Law,* 1950. Michael Bard and Barbara A. Bamford, "The Bar: Professional Association or Medieval Guild," *Catholic University Law Review* 19 (1970): 393. George N. Stevens, "Diploma Privilege, Bar Examination or Open Admission," *Bar Examiner* 46 (1977): 15. Stuart Duhl, ed., *The Bar Examiner's Handbook,* 2d ed., 1980. Richard L. Abel, *American Lawyers,* 1989. Linda Wightman, *LSAC National Longitudinal Bar Passage Study,* 1998.

—Carl A. Pierce

BARRISTERS. *See* Legal Practice, Forms of.

BASHING, LAWYER. *See* Lawyers, Popular Perceptions of.

BATTERED WOMAN SYNDROME. *See* Criminal Law Principles: Defense Principles.

BATTERY. *See* Assault and Battery.

BILLS OF RIGHTS. Prior to declaring independence from Britain, the Second Continental Congress issued a "Resolve" to the thirteen Colonial Assemblies: "adopt such a government as shall, in the opinion of the representatives of the people, best conduce to the happiness and safety of their constituents in particular, and America in general." Between 1776 and 1780, elected representatives met in deliberative bodies and chose a republican form of government for the newly created states. Connecticut and Rhode Island decided to retain their colonial charters, but the other eleven explicitly reaffirmed the American covenanting tradition by creating republican governments dedicated to securing both traditional *common law rights and newly articulated natural rights. Rights that were secure for generations under an empire of monarchy were now deemed to be secure only with the adoption of a republican form of government. The *constitutions of the eleven states relied, for the most part, on bicameralism: *separation of powers with legislative dominance, a weak executive, an independent judiciary, and representatives elected by a democratic suffrage, for short duration, subject to recall and rotation, and limited to the exercise of delegated powers. And this concept of limited government was reinforced by the notion that individual rights were made more secure by "writing rights down."

Declarative statements were a vital part of Anglo-American legal history. The Magna Carta (1215) proclaimed the principle of no *taxation without representation and incorporated the right to *due process of law, trial by *jury, and no *cruel punishments as part of a sixty-three–chapter proclamation instigated by nobles to restrain monarchs to "reasonable conduct." In 1628, Parliament petitioned Charles I to adhere to the "Rights of Englishmen" articulated in the Magna Carta as well as the right to petition for redress of grievances, the right to *habeas corpus relief, and additional safeguards for private *property. The 1689 English Bill of Rights, issued by Parliament, listed twelve indictments against King James II and reaffirmed the ancient Rights of Englishmen, including an expectation that the rule of law shall prevail in the creation and implementation of public policy and that "excessive bail ought not to be required, nor excessive fines imposed, nor cruel and unusual punishment inflicted."

The notion that a documentary record stating fundamental traditional rights would protect the many from the arbitrary behavior of the one or the few in power took root in colonial America. But the enforcement mechanism relied upon was something peculiarly American: "the people" made mutual promises in the presence of God, through a written and signed covenant, reinforced by a system of popular representation and institutional checks and balances. The Virginia Charter (1606) went beyond securing the Rights of Englishmen; local legislatures were empowered to pass laws to secure "Liberties, franchises, and Immunities." In 1620, Puritan immigrants signed, "in the presence of God," the Mayflower Compact, dedicated to enacting "just and equal laws." This gave birth to what Alexis de Toqueville called a "full-grown" democracy. Similarly, in 1635, Massachusetts immigrants to Connecticut established "an orderly and decent Government . . . according to God."

Seven of the eleven constitution states attached a separate Declaration of Rights to their constitutions: Virginia, Delaware, Pennsylvania, Maryland, North Carolina, Massachusetts, and New Hampshire. Today, we are used to seeing a Bill of Rights attached at the end of the United States Constitution in the form of ten amendments (see CONSTITUTIONAL AMENDMENTS). But that is an accident of politics rather than a matter of principle. In each of the seven states, the constitutions were preceded by a bill of rights. Declarations formed preambles to the state constitutions, outlining the purposes of republican government. In Virginia and Delaware, the bill of rights was actually written chronologically as well as conceptually prior to the constitution.

There is a remarkable uniformity among the seven states with regard to the kinds of civil and criminal rights that were to be secured. The Virginia, Pennsylvania, and Massachusetts declarations capture both the similarity, and the subtle differences, in the coverage given to freedom of press (see SPEECH AND THE PRESS, FREEDOM OF), the right to petition, the right to bear *arms, the quartering of troops, protection from unreasonable *searches and seizures, the centrality of trial by jury, the right to confrontation of *witnesses and the right to *counsel, the importance of *"due process of law," and the protection against excessive fines and cruel and unusual punishment. Most of the civil rights and criminal procedures listed were an accepted part of the Americanization of the Rights of Englishmen.

To be sure, each of the other four states can make a legitimate claim to being unique, in the sense of being the "first" to anticipate one or more of the civil or criminal rights found in the other states' lists and in the 1791 federal Bill of Rights: Delaware for the *ex-post facto clause, Maryland for the bill of attainder clause, North Carolina for the grand jury indictment clause, and New Hampshire for the *double jeopardy clause. Nevertheless, they were each modeled on one or more of the "big three": Virginia, Pennsylvania, and Massachusetts. In fact, as John Adams correctly observed with respect to Pennsylvania, the state bill of rights is "taken almost verbatim from that of Virginia."

Englishmen did not have the right to choose their form of government nor to practice the free exercise of *religion. But such rights were very much part of an American covenanting tradition that incorporated an appeal to both natural right and divine support. Accordingly, there was also little variation from state to state concerning the inclusion of these foundational rights. Interestingly, Americans were engaged in a conscious effort to synthesize the natural rights doctrine of Locke, the teachings of scripture, the skepticism of Hume, and the common law approach of *Blackstone.

Englishmen also lacked the right to the nonestablishment of religion. Not surprisingly, there is disparity among the states when they turn to this subject. Again, Virginia, Pennsylvania, and Massachusetts capture the range of possibilities. An established religious education had an important part to play in securing what section fifteen of the Virginia Declaration of Rights referred to as "a firm adherence to justice, moderation, temperance, frugality, and virtue," without which free government cannot be preserved. This association between religious education and republican institutions was central to the following question: what support should government give to religion? Should a state name a particular sect as the officially established church? Only Virginia followed this traditional English model, until the Anglican Church was disestablished in 1779. Should a state name a specific religion—Protestant Christianity—as the officially established religion, but give *"equal protection" to each sect? This model of "neutrality" toward each sect was adopted in Maryland, Massachusetts, South Carolina, and New Hampshire. Should the legislature approve a tax for the support of the established religion with the understanding that the individual taxpayer can designate the sect that shall receive the individual's contribution? The 1780 Massachusetts Declaration of Rights duplicated the language of Virginia's section fifteen and provided for a general tax to support religious sects. Moreover, Maryland empowered the legislature, at its discretion, to "lay a general and equal tax, for the support of the Christian religion." On the other hand, neither Pennsylvania nor Delaware addressed directly the issue of religious establishment; both explicitly state, however, that to require an individual to support "any ministry contrary to or against his own free will and consent" is a violation of the "natural and unalienable right to worship" God in accordance with the dictates of one's own conscience. And Delaware, following the example of Pennsylvania, not only excluded the possibility of a legislatively approved discretionary tax to support religion, but also omitted any reference to the beneficial association between the existence of religious sects and the future of republican institutions.

The Federalist, however, downplays the extent to which states adopted a bill of rights. In *The Federalist* 24, Alexander Hamilton criticizes the Antifederalists for "a deliberate intention to deceive" the public: "New York has no bill of rights," says Hamilton, and "no bills of rights appear annexed to the constitutions of the other States, except" Pennsylvania, North Carolina, New Hampshire, Massachusetts, Delaware, and Maryland. Hamilton has exaggerated the minority status of the bill of rights. Strictly speaking, the charter states, Rhode Island and Connecticut, should not be counted in the tabulation, and he omitted Virginia from his list of states with a bill of rights! The more telling figure should be that only four states declined to "annex" a bill of rights to their constitutions: New Jersey, Georgia, New York, and

South Carolina. But each of these four states not only had prefaces confirming the authority of the covenanting tradition and the dignity of enlightenment principles—essential to the bill of rights story—they also incorporated into the body of their constitutions essential features of the bill of rights found in those states that had a separately annexed bill of rights. Civil rights and criminal procedure are addressed in four of the thirty-nine articles in the 1776 New Jersey constitution. Twenty-one of the sixty-three articles of the 1777 Georgia constitution directly concern individual rights. Four of the forty-five articles of the South Carolina constitution address the issue of civil rights and criminal procedures and are grouped together in the main body of the document. Hamilton is correct: the 1777 New York constitution excluded a prefatory bill of rights. Nevertheless, the entire Declaration of Independence is incorporated into the preamble that precedes the constitution. Furthermore, seven of the forty-two articles of the constitution deal specifically with civil rights and criminal procedures.

The Second Continental Congress also created the first continent-wide system of *governance. The Articles of Confederation guaranteed a preeminent position to the states and there is no mention of a bill of rights. But there was no need for one because the Articles did not create a government over individuals; instead it created a nation of states. One consequence is that the American discussion of individual rights becomes entangled with the question of *states' rights. A full nationwide conversation over a bill of rights began with the Constitutional Convention of 1787, which met to alter the Articles. The Virginia Plan removes the states from their preeminent position and proposes a government over individuals instead. The Plan reflects Madison's attempt to secure private rights by means of an extended political orbit and institutional checks and balances rather than by "parchment barriers." Moreover the Plan reflects his position that the greatest danger to private rights came from state legislatures whose independence was protected by the Articles. Madison was not successful in his attempt to structurally remove the states from the scheme of representation and he was forced to accept the Connecticut Compromise, which provides representation for both the people and the states. He was also unsuccessful in permitting Congress to "legislate in all cases to which the separate states are incompetent." Nevertheless, the Constitution points away from a mere confederation and in the direction of a government. And this raises the question: shouldn't there be a bill of rights to restrain the government?

The powers of Congress are enumerated in Article 1, Section 8 of the Constitution. And with the enumeration of powers, an enumeration of rights isn't far behind. Article 1, Section 9 places limits on Congress in the areas of habeas corpus, ex post facto laws, bills of attainder, and titles of nobility, and outlines rights retained by the states. Similar restraints were placed on the states in Article 1, Section 10 with an additional provision concerning obligation of contracts. During the final week of the Convention, George Mason, author of the Virginia Bill of Rights, expressed his wish that "the plan had been prefaced with a Bill of Rights . . . [It] would give great quiet to the people" and would be easy to prepare given the presence of state declarations. His motion was deemed unnecessary and dangerous, a theme that proponents of the Constitution returned to frequently during the ratification controversy.

During the summer of 1787, the Confederation Congress also passed the Northwest Ordinance. This document is a continent-wide expression of the rights of Americans: free exercise of religion, benefit of habeas corpus, trial by jury, access to the judicial system, no cruel and unusual punishments, due process of law, just compensation and the right to "proportionate representation" in the Assembly. And a firm stand was taken in abolishing *slavery from the territory. Finally, the Ordinance repeats the ambiguity concerning the establishment of religion. Article III states that "religion, morality, and knowledge being necessary to good government and the happiness of mankind, schools and the means of education shall forever be encouraged." But the Ordinance is silent on how this encouragement is to be achieved.

Opponents of ratification of the Constitution argued that the absence of a bill of rights demonstrated that rights were insecure under the proposed Constitution. They considered the proponents' arguments to be ingenuous at best: how could the Constitution be a bill of rights, yet include certain rights and then ignore such fundamental rights as freedom of religion, freedom of the press, and trial by jury? How could one grant Congress the power of governing and constitutional supremacy over state laws, and still argue that the Constitution is a document in which "everything which is not given, is reserved"? But that is what the leading proponents argued.

The fate of the Constitution turned on a compromise made in the Massachusetts, New Hampshire, Virginia, and New York ratifying conventions. The compromise—"ratify now, amend later"—involved two distinguishable kinds of recommendations: 1) an attachment, or inclusion, of a bill of rights and 2) amendments that would alter the structure and powers of the general government. With the adoption of the Constitution, Representative Madison urged the First Congress to adopt a bill of rights and reject amendments that would radically change the Constitution. He argued that enumerating rights was not dangerous if there were a stipulation that the list "shall not be construed to deny or disparage others retained by the people." This is the reasoning undergirding the ninth amendment in the federal Bill of Rights. And for prudential reasons a bill of rights was necessary to conciliate "honorable and patriotic opponents."

Madison recommended that the representatives open up the Constitution and insert specific rights limiting the power of Congress in Article 1, Section 9. Seven of these limitations became part of the ten amendments adopted by the state legislatures in 1791. He also suggested the inclusion of the following in Article 1, Section 10: "No State shall violate the equal right of conscience, freedom of the press, or trial by jury." This would test the sincerity of the claim that "every government" should be limited by a bill of rights. Madison's attempt to incorporate the Bill of Rights into the main body of the Constitution, and to insert the Declaration of Independence into the Preamble, was rejected by the House; they voted instead to send seventeen "supplements" to the Constitution to the Senate for consideration. Thus the Bill of Rights went forward as amendments to be attached to the end of the Constitution. The Senate, in turn, reduced the number to twelve, and excluded Madison's three restrictions on state governments, which, ironically, was fourteenth on the list, and would become the Fourteenth Amendment. Congress finally submitted the twelve amendments to the states for ratification, the last ten of which were approved. With the exception of the numerous changes made to the establishment of religion clause, the deliberations indicate a broad consensus over what to include on the list.

The American story of the origin of the federal Bill of Rights involves a conceptual shift of immense consequences: what began as a protection of the many against the unreasonable conduct of the one or the few had, by 1791, become a protection of the minority against a tyrannical Congressional majority. And with this conceptual shift, there is also an institutional shift away from the legislative branch as the enforcer of rights to the states and the courts as the primary guardians. In the nineteenth century, the legislative branch asserted the right to declare null and void Acts of Congress that were deemed unconstitutional. With the passage of the 14th Amendment in 1868, which prohibited states from depriving "any person of life liberty and property without due process of law," the groundwork was laid for another remarkable development in the twentieth century. The courts began "incorporating" the 1791 Bill of Rights, originally designed to limit Congress, into the *due process clause of the *14th Amendment in *Gitlow* v. *New York* (1925), and thus applied the federal Bill of Rights to governmental agencies at the state level. Not surprisingly, the most contentious *incorporation disputes have involved the establishment of religion clause.

Also of considerable interest has been the export of the American Bill of Rights to the international community. In 1948, the United Nations created a Universal Declaration of Human Rights in which there is an appeal to "equal and inalienable rights" of all members of the human race. But a subtle change in the meaning of rights has taken place, both at home and abroad, in the last part of the twentieth century: peace, security, employment, health care, and the right to self-determination—the social issues—replace liberty, freedom, and the consent of the governed. It is no longer sufficient that government secure the conditions that "best conduce" to an individual exercising the right to pursue happiness; rather, governments must actively provide substantial well-being because individuals are now deemed to have a right to happiness and not simply its pursuit.

[*See also* Civil Rights and Civil Liberties]

• Irving Brandt, *The Bill of Rights: Its Origin and Meaning*, 1965. Stephen L. Schechter and Richard B. Bernstein, *Contexts of The Bill of Rights*, 1990. Eugene W. Hickok, *The Bill of Rights: Original Meaning and Current Understanding*, 1991. Helen E. Veit, Kenneth R. Bowling, and Charlene Bangs Brickford, *Creating the Bill of Rights: The Documentary Record from the First Federal Congress*, 1991. Patrick T. Conley and John P. Kaminski, *The Bill of Rights and the States: The Colonial and Revolutionary Origins of American Liberties*, 1992. Bernard Schwartz, *The Great Rights of Mankind: A History of the American Bill of Rights*, 1992. Neil H. Cogan, *The Complete Bill of Rights: The Drafts, Debates, Sources, and Origins*, 1997. Gordon Lloyd and Margie Lloyd, *The Essential Bill of Rights*, 1998.   —Gordon Lloyd

BIOETHICS. *See* Science and Law.

BLACK, HUGO LAFAYETTE (1886–1971). Black rose from a locally respectable family in the isolated hill community of Clay County, Alabama, to be among the most significant justices ever to sit on the U.S. *Supreme Court. Small-town family life intensified Black's perception that individual responsibility and community obligation existed in continuing tension. Graduating in 1906 from the state law school, Black entered practice in Alabama's industrial center, Birmingham. By the early 1920s he was a leading trial lawyer and supporter of Progressive Reform. An extraordinarily effective advocate, Black defended African Americans and southern values of white supremacy with equal fervor. Even so, the Ku Klux Klan's influence over local juries led Black to join the Invisible Empire in 1923; three years later his membership helped bring about his election to the U.S. Senate. By the time of his reelection in 1932 during the Great Depression, Black had left the Klan, becoming a loyal, active proponent of Democrat Franklin D. Roosevelt's liberal New Deal. Accordingly, Black was Roosevelt's first appointment to the Supreme Court, serving from 1937 to 1971.

His small-town origins and law practice fostered Black's support for the Court's expansion of the commerce and taxing powers to uphold New Deal liberalism's regulation of corporate capitalism. In World War II his majority opinion upheld the internment of tens of thousands innocent American citizens of *Japanese ancestry for reasons of military necessity; during the Korean conflict, however, his majority decision overturned the president's efforts to exercise war powers without a declaration of war. Once on the Court, Black's ambivalent background concerning racial equality resulted in vigorous advocacy of interpreting the *Fourteenth and Fifteenth Amendments to end the South's system of racial *segregation, which finally prevailed between the 1954 *Brown decision and the civil rights movement of the 1960s. His 1947 dissent favoring the standard of one person, one vote to overcome unfairly apportioned voting districts also gained a Court majority during the sixties.

Black's most important constitutional principle was that all of the Bill of Rights limited state authorities through the *due process clause of the Fourteenth Amendment. He also propounded the principle, initially in dissent, that the First Amendment's guarantees of free *speech, press, and *assembly were absolute. In large part, these became established constitutional doctrine by the 1960s. Yet when the Court sustained forms of symbolic expression, Black again dissented. Perhaps his most controversial decision—which nonetheless also became an enduring precedent—held that

prayer in public schools violated the First Amendment's establishment of *religion clause. Similarly, his efforts to balance the application of Bill of Rights provisions pertaining to state law enforcement, especially indigent's right to *counsel and what *evidence may be excluded from jury trials, continued to guide the Court at the millennium. His dissenting position rejecting the right of *privacy received more support after his death in 1971, although not a Court majority. What explained the ongoing timeliness of Black's principles was the fervent search for balance within the fundamentals of American constitutional governance, a search rooted firmly in his Alabama past.

[*See also* Court Packing; Courts, United States: Federal Courts]

• Tony Freyer, *Hugo L. Black and the Dilemma of American Liberalism*, 1990. Roger K. Newman, *Hugo Black: A Biography*, 1994.   —Tony A. Freyer

BLACK CODES. Months after the end of the Civil War, Mississippi, followed by other southern states, began passing laws designed to control newly freed slaves through the legal system. Under *slavery, whites had disciplined blacks primarily outside the law, through extralegal whippings administered by slave owners and their overseers. After emancipation, panicky whites feared that the end of plantation slavery would unleash blacks' alleged criminality. White men feared for the safety of their wives and daughters and sought protection for their property.

While some white southerners thought African Americans were best controlled by vigilantes, others proposed using courts and the law. On 22 November 1865, the Mississippi legislature passed a law directing civil officers to hire out orphaned minor "freedmen, free negroes, and mulattoes." This law allowed "moderate corporal chastisement," forbade the orphans to leave their masters, and made it a crime for anyone to "entice" an apprenticed orphan from his or her employer.

Soon thereafter the Mississippi legislature also established a system of county courts to punish persons charged with minor offenses. The authors of this law intended to control blacks and allowed judges to hang convicted thieves by their thumbs. Mississippi also passed an extensive vagrancy law, defining vagrants to include not only common drunkards, dissipated persons, beggars, jugglers, lascivious persons, and brawlers but workers who "neglect their calling or employment [or] misspend what they earn."

In addition, the Mississippi legislature passed an act to "Confer Civil Rights on Freedmen and for other Purposes." This law allowed blacks to sue and be sued and to intermarry, but it also required that they carry written evidence of employment at all times, similar to the old pass system under slavery.

On 1 December 1865, the Chicago *Tribune* published an angry editorial denouncing the Mississippi "civil rights" law as a "Black Code of Mississippi." The *Tribune* told "the white men of Mississippi that the men of the North will convert the State of Mississippi into a frog-pond before they allow any such law to disgrace one foot of soil in which the bones of our soldiers sleep and over which the flag of freedom waves." The *Tribune* editorial did not prevent other states from passing their own "Black Codes." Alabama, Georgia, and Louisiana soon followed suit. On 19 December 1865, South Carolina passed the only true "code," an encyclopedic set of laws designed to control the behavior of black persons. Florida, Tennessee, Virginia, and North Carolina enacted similar laws early in 1866.

Northerners saw the discriminatory laws as an attempt to return black people to bondage. In the resulting uproar, Congress passed the Civil Rights Act of 1866, defining citizenship and making discriminatory state laws illegal. Southern states responded by repealing their Black Codes, only to pass a new wave of "nondiscriminatory" legislation that permitted local officials to discriminate quietly, without specific statutory instruction. Many southern whites saw the new laws as a failed effort, proof that blacks could be "disciplined" only outside the law.

[*See also* Fourteenth Amendment; History of American Law: Antebellum Through Reconstruction (1801–1877); Race and Ethnicity; Segregation]

• Theodore Brantner Wilson, *The Black Codes of the South*, 1965. Christopher Waldrep, *Roots of Disorder: Race and Criminal Justice in the American South, 1817–80*, 1998.   —Christopher Waldrep

BLACKSTONE'S COMMENTARIES ON THE LAWS OF ENGLAND (1756–1759).

Sir William Blackstone was born in London in 1723. After graduating from Oxford he endured the lonely, unsupervised course of law study then provided by Middle Temple. In 1745, he was elected a fellow of Oxford's All Souls College. An excellent administrator, he improved the business affairs of both the college and the University's press. He also helped enliven the moribund university with a popular course of undergraduate lectures on English law. In 1758, Blackstone was awarded the Vinerian Chair, the first Oxford chair for the study of domestic (as opposed to Roman or Civil) law. However, his attentions were soon diverted, first to law practice, and then to his duties as a Member of Parliament (1761–70). In 1770, he was appointed to the Court of Common Pleas, in which office he served until his death in 1780.

In 1756, Blackstone published *An Analysis of the Laws of England*, a schematic of his lecture course that drew its inspiration from Matthew Hale's *Analysis of the Law* (1713). From 1761–65, Blackstone converted his *Analysis* into a rich and readable treatise: the four-volume, 2,000-page *Commentaries on the Laws of England*. The *Commentaries* were designed to provide a guide for the British elite to English public and private law. They further aimed to demonstrate that the ancient, unwritten customary law of England had evolved into a complex and ingenious scheme for the protection of liberty—one that deserved loyalty and only the most thoughtful reform. The *Commentaries* proved to be hugely popular, running through eight editions in the remaining fourteen years of Blackstone's life. For the next century, they served as the most influential general treatment of Anglo-American law.

Blackstone organized the *Commentaries* around a simple division between "Rights" and "Wrongs," devoting two books to each subject. After a cursory discussion of the nature of law—an effort that left the young Jeremy Bentham apoplectic—Book I endorses the basic proposition of classical liberal theory, that is, that the point of government is to protect the individual's fundamental rights of security, *liberty, and *property ownership. The remainder of Book I sets out how England's unwritten constitution protects those rights by allocating powers among the various officials that make up the government. To American eyes, the most notable feature of this treatment was the ascription to King-in-Parliament of "sovereign and uncontrollable power" to legislate. Book II, still within the heading of "rights," is devoted to untangling the *common-law rules empowering persons to own and transfer interests in real and personal property, and to establishing that these rules, although feudal in origin, served modern, liberal ends.

Books III and IV address, respectively, the common law of civil ("private") and criminal ("public") wrongs. The former focuses on civil *procedure and *remedies, as well as *torts. Its broadest aim is to explain that the myriad overlapping jurisdictions within the English judicial system, and its unruly catalogue of causes of action, provides a rational system for vindicating individual rights against invasion by other private citizens. Book IV identifies the various criminal offenses and quietly makes a case for reform and greater leniency. The *Commentaries* conclude with a brief exercise in Whig history that exhorts the English elite to observe their duty to protect and advance the cause of British liberty through careful attention to law.

Across the Atlantic, the *Commentaries* have always received a mixed reception. As an M.P., Blackstone vigorously denounced the movement for American independence. Indeed, the *Commentaries* went so far as to deny that the colonists possessed any of the rights enjoyed by Englishmen. Not surprisingly, then, the man and his work drew the ire of leading American revolutionaries. Supreme Court Justice James Wilson gave a series of lectures devoted to disproving Blackstone's attribution of sovereignty to Parliament rather than the People. Thomas *Jefferson warned young lawyers not to rely on the *Commentaries*' treatment of particular subjects for fear that they surreptitiously advanced an antidemocratic agenda.

For all this, the *Commentaries* were probably as significant in the new republic as in England. Speaking on behalf of conciliation with the colonies, Edmund Burke famously observed that nearly as many copies of the *Commentaries* had been sold in the former as the latter. Even if not strictly accurate, the point is sound: the lawyer-elite of the founding era knew their Blackstone. Subsequent generations likewise learned law through the *Commentaries*, either as a basic law school text (often in the form of St. George Tucker's Americanized edition) or as an on-the-job guide for practitioners (including, most famously, Abraham *Lincoln). American law on basic matters such as property, crime, and procedure largely tracked English law and, in the absence of widespread access to law libraries, the *Commentaries* served as an invaluably comprehensive yet portable survey of that law. Moreover, nineteenth-century American lawyers, no less than their English counterparts, accepted Blackstone's basic claim that the common law reflected a commitment to the liberal rights of life, liberty, and property.

By the turn of the twentieth century, Blackstone's status as leading legal light was turned against him: he became a convenient foil for American scholars looking to articulate alternative conceptions of constitutionalism, law, and government. In Edward Corwin's ode to the American "higher law" tradition, Blackstone's commitment to parliamentary sovereignty is taken to treat liberties not as bounds on legislative authority, but

as mere creatures of positive law subject to arbitrary and tyrannical incursions at the whim of legislative majorities. In Daniel Boorstin's analysis of the "mysterious science" of law, Blackstone's attempt to find animating principles within the common law is cast as a feeble attempt at rationalizing his non-rational embrace of the *status quo* of his time. In Duncan Kennedy's hands, the *Commentaries* are said to reveal "inherent" contradictions within liberal political theory.

For the most part, these treatments tell us more about Blackstone's critics than about his own thinking. Kennedy's is not so much a close reading of the *Commentaries*, as an expression of the tendency among scholars in the *Critical Legal Studies movement to find deep 'contradictions' in political ideologies. Boorstin's portrayal mostly reflects the arrogance of a generation that regarded the common law and traditional legal reasoning as "transcendental nonsense" destined to be overcome by "functional" or "scientific" analysis. Finally, *contra* Corwin, Blackstone's recognition of King-in-Parliament as sovereign was not driven by a statist commitment to legislative supremacy. Blackstone believed that he had accurately located the *de facto* sovereign within the English system of government, and that this system was likely most conducive to the protection of liberty. Hence, the importance to his mind of the *Commentaries* themselves: their very point was to ensure that future M.P.s would understand the reasons why so immense a power had been conferred on them. If they shirked their duty by legislating tyrannically, the solution was not judicial nullification on the basis of "higher law," but citizen petition, or, in the worst case, Lockean resistance and the establishment of a new sovereign.

[*See also* Constitutional Commentators]

• Daniel Boorstin, *The Mysterious Science of the Law: An Essay on Blackstone's Commentaries*, 1941. Edward S. Corwin, *The "Higher Law" Background of American Constitutional Law*, 1955. David Lieberman, *The Province of Legislation Determined: Legal Theory in Eighteenth-Century Britain*, 1989. S. F. C. Milsom, "The Nature of Blackstone's Achievement," in *Studies in the History of the Common Law* (1985): 197–208. Dennis R. Nolan, "Sir William Blackstone and the New American Republic: A Study of Intellectual Impact," *N.Y.U. Law Review* 51 (1976): 731–68. James Stoner, *Common Law and Liberal Theory: Coke, Hobbes and the Origins of American Constitutionalism*, 1992.

—John C. P. Goldberg

BLOCKADE. *See* War, Law of.

BLUE LAWS. *See* Morals Offenses; Religion and Law.

BORDEN, LIZZIE, CASE OF. One of the most notorious crimes in American history occurred on 4 August 1892, in Fall River, Massachusetts, when Lizzie Andrew Borden allegedly bludgeoned her parents to death in their downtown home, delivering thirty-one blows in all (not the "forty whacks" of the popular Victorian ditty). Although evidence against Lizzie Borden was compelling, an all-male jury acquitted her of the murder charges in June 1893.

The prosecution attempted to prove that Ms. Borden, thirty-two years old at the time of the murders, bitterly resented her father and her stepmother, Andrew and Abby Durfee Borden, for failing to share more of the family's wealth with Lizzie and her older sister, Emma. The sisters—both "spinsters" and thus compelled to remain under their father's roof—wished, among other things, to live in the Hill district of Fall River, a neighborhood more suited to the family's economic standing than the downtown dwelling where they resided in a state of perpetual tension. Andrew Borden, a wealthy businessman but a frugal Yankee of the first order, refused to move into a better home, although he certainly never denied his family the necessities of life. Lizzie, a known shoplifter and apparently emotionally unstable, lashed out in a paroxysm of violence, according to the prosecution.

Victorian gender mores, combined with popular anxieties about the reputation of a burgeoning mill town, overshadowed the evidence of Lizzie Borden's guilt. To have acknowledged Lizzie Borden's guilt would have been to shatter Victorian convictions of female piety and passionlessness. Such a verdict would have done violence to the prevailing myth that the home represented a separate sphere, a sanctuary from the harsh realities of the world, a place where the moral superiority of women held sway. A guilty verdict in such a high-profile case would have contravened the Victorian image of the middle-class woman as the vital center of the nuclear family structure. If an apparently loving daughter and good Christian community woman could commit such crimes, the entire social order would be called into question. Better that a guilty woman go free.

While thus highly revealing with respect to gender and culture, the Borden case established no significant legal precedents. The three-judge panel, however, showed a marked bias for the defense, skillfully conducted by a former governor of Massachusetts, George D. Robinson. The judges threw out Lizzie Borden's incriminating testimony at an inquest, as well as evidence that she had attempted to purchase a deadly poison the day before the hatchet murders. Prosecutor William H. Moody—later associate justice of the U.S. Supreme Court—bitterly condemned the judges' decisions, but to no avail. Judge Justin Dewey delivered a loaded charge that virtually commanded the jury to return a not-guilty verdict.

The public, initially jubilant over the acquittal of "Miss Lizzie," soon turned against her. Lizzie Borden became a pariah in the community, no longer welcome at church and seldom venturing beyond the confines of the new home she had purchased in the Hill district with the inheritance from her father's estate. Lizzie Borden died on 2 June 1927, but the Borden case continued to fascinate through the next century, spurring hundreds of songs, poems, plays, books, conferences, articles, an opera, and even a journal devoted to the woman and the infamous crimes.

[See also Criminal Law]

• Cara W. Robertson, "Representing 'Miss Lizzie': Cultural Convictions in the Trial of Lizzie Borden," *Yale Journal of Law and the Humanities* 8 (Summer 1996): 351–416. Walter L. Hixson, *Murder, Culture, and Injustice: Four Sensational Cases in American History*, 2001.

—Walter L. Hixson

THE BOSTON MASSACRE TRIALS. The British Government's effort to generate revenue from colonial America by increasing colonial customs duties and strengthening the enforcement apparatus led in 1768 to the arrival of four infantry regiments in Boston. Friction between troops and the customs establishment on the one hand, and townspeople and maritime interests on the other, artfully stimulated by Samuel Adams and a radical "caucus," ultimately produced bloodshed. On March 5, 1770, a mob of Bostonians, sailors, and boys attacked the lone sentry at the Customs House and besieged the seven-man party that Captain Thomas Preston of the 29th Regiment led down King (now State) Street to the sentry's aid. In the uproar, amid shouting, clanging bells, snowballs, and brickbats, the troops fired, leaving five men dead or dying.

A grand jury returned murder indictments against Preston, the soldiers, and four civilians (accused of firing from a Customs House window). Although the radicals pressed for a speedy resolution, the justices of the Superiour Court of Judicature, who would preside, en banc, managed to postpone the trials until late fall. Meanwhile both sides published eyewitness "affidavits" calculated to turn public opinion. The radicals scored the biggest propaganda coup with the famous Paul Revere print, which seared into America's unconscious the image of military brutality. Meanwhile, under circumstances never fully explained, Preston and the soldiers secured as counsel two of the radical party, John *Adams and Josiah Quincy.

A conflict soon arose between the soldiers and Preston. They insisted that they had fired only at his command; he denied having given any such order. The men even petitioned, apparently without counsel's knowledge and in any event vainly, to be tried with their officer.

Preston's case went to trial first, on October 24, 1770. Assisted by the courtroom advice of a Tory sympathizer, the defense managed to seat a jury that contained five Loyalists. With this advantage, and a lack of evidence that Preston had ordered the firing, the six-day trial (the first in Massachusetts history to last beyond one day) ended in acquittal.

The soldiers' trial began on November 27, 1770, before a jury devoid of Bostonians. Adams and Quincy adopted a simple defense: the mob having threatened the soldiers' lives, the law allowed them to kill in self-defense. This, however, meant conceding that the Boston crowd was out of control (something the radicals generally liked to deny). Moreover, the eighteenth-century rule placed the *burden of proof on the defense.

Thanks to shrewd presentation of the evidence and brilliant arguments by both lawyers, the jury, after a week of trial, took two-and-one-half hours to acquit six of the soldiers completely, and to convict two others of manslaughter. These, after branding on the thumb, were also released.

A stenographic report of the trial has survived. It contains the first recorded use by an American judge of "reasonable doubt" as a standard of proof.

The four civilians went to trial immediately thereafter. Only four witnesses testified; the jury acquitted all the defendants without even leaving the box. Despite the outcome of the trials, the Boston Massacre helped to shape anti-British attitudes in the years before the Revolution.

[See also History of American Law, Colonial Period]

• L. Kinvin Wroth and Hiller B. Zobel, eds., *Legal Papers of John Adams*, 3 vols., 1965. Hiller B. Zobel, *The Boston Massacre*, 1970.
—Hiller B. Zobel

BOYCOTT, LABOR. *See* Labor Law: Labor Relations.

BRANDEIS, LOUIS DEMBITZ (1856–1941), attorney and justice of the U.S. Supreme Court, 1916–39. Brandeis was born in Louisville, Kentucky, the child of immigrants from Prague. He was educated in Louisville's public schools and then in Germany at Dresden's Annen-Realschule. At age eighteen he enrolled in Harvard Law School, where he received a bachelor's degree— and the highest grades ever awarded by that institution—in 1877; he remained at the school for a year of graduate work.

After practicing for a few months in St. Louis, in 1879 Brandeis joined a Harvard classmate in the new Boston law firm of Warren & Brandeis. There, Brandeis began his career as the representative of small business with a fervent belief in unbridled capitalism. He changed his views, however, after negotiating with union leaders on behalf of his clients, and he gradually became an advocate first of unionism and then of worker-management (that is, participation by workers in the decisions made by management) and worker profit sharing. The Homestead strike of 1892, in which the Carnegie steel works hired Pinkertons to fire on unarmed strikers, and the New York garment workers' strike of 1910, which Brandeis successfully mediated, convinced him that unilateral control of economic resources was dangerous for political as well as economic democracy. Workers without power would lack leisure and resources. This would prevent them from continuing to educate themselves to become intelligent voters and well-rounded human beings and from participating actively in the political life of the community.

Brandeis argued that citizens of a democracy had the responsibility to participate; without citizens' participation, democracy could not thrive. Working for no fee, and in fact reimbursing his law firm for the hours in which he was not generating income, he created a system of sliding-scale utility rates that tied higher dividends to lower rates, invented savings bank life insurance, and fought for conservation of natural resources and against transportation monopolies. Above all, he campaigned against bigness in government and economics, writing and lecturing extensively about the corruption of excessive power and the inability of human beings to manage overly large institutions intelligently. His public service endeavors and life-long crusade against the trusts earned him the popular sobriquet the "People's Attorney." His example, and his warnings about the legal profession's becoming no more than a handmaiden to big business, were crucial in creating an American pro bono bar.

His experiences as an attorney and negotiator taught Brandeis that law must embody rational solutions to societal problems and would do so only if it was based on thorough examination of the facts. He based his brief in *Muller* v. *Oregon* (1908) on that theory, offering the Supreme Court only two pages of legal precedents and over a hundred pages of factual support for his argument in favor of maximum-hour laws for women. The "Brandeis brief," as presented in that case, is now the norm in constitutional adjudication.

Brandeis carried his fact-based *jurisprudence to the U.S. Supreme Court, to which President Woodrow Wilson appointed him in 1916. There he repeatedly voted against bigness in both government (*Myers* v. *US* (1927); *Louisville* v. *Radford* (1935)) and business (*Bedford* v. *Journeymen* (1927); *Quaker City Cab* v. *Pennsylvania* (1928)), while maintaining that state governments needed the freedom to experiment with solutions to contemporary societal problems (*Liggett* v. *Lee* (1933)). He favored judicial restraint and, in *Ashwander* v. *TVA* (1936), established tightly self-limiting criteria for Supreme Court involvement in constitutional litigation.

Back in 1890, Warren & Brandeis had reacted to journalistic intrusions upon socialite Warren's privacy by writing a pathbreaking article arguing that the law must protect individual *privacy and the right "to be let alone." Brandeis extended and applied this thinking in *Olmstead* v. *United States* (1929). The best known of Brandeis's judicial opinions, however, may be his concurrence in *Whitney* v. *California* (1929), eloquently asserting protections for *speech beyond those accepted by the Court of his day. His view ultimately was endorsed in *Brandenburg* v. *Ohio* (1969) and is the philosophical basis for the uniquely permissive modern speech jurisprudence in the United States.

[*See also* Supreme Court of the United States]

• Philippa Strum, *Louis D. Brandeis: Justice for the People*, 1984. Vincent Blasi, "The First Amendment and the Ideal of Civic Courage: The Brandeis Opinion in *Whitney* v. *California*," *William and Mary Law Review* 29 (1988): 653–97.   —Philippa Strum

BRENNAN, WILLIAM J. JR. (1906–1997), justice of the U. S. Supreme Court, 1956–90. Brennan was the son of Irish immigrant parents, the second of eight children. His father rose through labor ranks to become a leader and a popular, elected police commissioner of Newark. Brennan graduated from the University of Pennsylvania, and from Harvard Law School, where he represented indigent clients through the Legal Aid Bureau. Brennan became a successful Newark lawyer, representing companies in labor law disputes. His involvement in court reform in 1947 led to a spot

on the state superior court in 1949 and the New Jersey Supreme Court in 1952. A Democrat, Brennan was nominated by Republican President Eisenhower to the U.S. Supreme Court in September 1956. He became one of the most important justices of the twentieth century, a leader of the view that the Supreme Court should adapt the Constitution to changing times. He wrote *New York Times Co. v. Sullivan* (1964), ruling that the First Amendment limits the power of states to punish libelous *speech about public officials. His opinion in *Baker* v. *Carr* (1962) exposed state legislative apportionments to *judicial review under the *equal protection clause of the *Fourteenth Amendment. In *Craig* v. *Boren* (1976), Brennan led the Court in bringing gender discrimination under the purview of the equal protection clause. He wrote several decisions upholding *affirmative action and others holding government officials liable for damages for violating the rights of individuals. Brennan retired in July 1990.

[*See also* Supreme Court of the United States]

• Stephen J. Wermiel, "William Joseph Brennan, Jr.," in *The Supreme Court Justices: A Biographical Dictionary* (Melvin I. Urofsky, ed.), 1994. E. Joshua Rosenkrantz and Bernard Schwartz, eds., *Reason and Passion: Justice Brennan's Enduring Influence*, 1997.

—Stephen J. Wermiel

BROWN, JOHN, TRIAL OF. John Brown is one of the most compelling figures of the nineteenth century. Born in 1800, he lived in New York, Connecticut, and Ohio in his early years, spent time in Kansas, and was eventually executed in Virginia. He was famous—or, rather, infamous—for his activities in Kansas during the mid–1850s. There he was involved in a number of violent encounters, including the killing of proslavery settlers along the Pottowatomie Creek. He then planned an invasion of the South in 1859, which led to his capture at Harpers Ferry and his execution.

He was captured on 18 October 1859 by U.S. Marines, under the command of Robert E. Lee. Virginia indicted him for *treason, although this was a crime he surely had not committed: he should have been charged with *homicide and tried in a Virginia court, or with treason against the United States and tried in a federal court. Severely wounded before his capture, Brown was carried into court and lay on a cot for most of his trial. The judge would not even delay the proceedings a day to allow Brown's lawyer to arrive. Throughout the trial Brown denied the legitimacy of the charge, but the outcome of the trial in the heated atmosphere of pre–Civil War Virginia was a foregone conclusion. He was convicted and sentenced to death on 2 November.

Before sentencing, Brown told the court that his actions against *slavery were consistent with God's commandments. "I believe," he said in a speech that electrified many northerners who later read it, "that to have interfered as I have done in behalf of His despised poor, is no wrong, but right. Now, if it is deemed necessary that I should forfeit my life for the furtherance of the ends of justice, and mingle my blood with the blood of millions in this slave country whose rights are disregarded by wicked, cruel, and unjust enactments, I say let it be done."

In the time between his capture and execution Brown transformed himself into a martyr dying for the cause of the slave by writing hundreds of letters to supporters, especially in the North. Brown rejected offers to help him either escape from jail or be pardoned, telling one friend "I am worth now infinitely more to die than to live." He was hanged on 2 December 1859. Before his execution he left his jailer a note, predicting that "the crimes of this *guilty, land: will* never be purged *away*, but with Blood."

In the North, he was seen as a Christ-like martyr for freedom, in the South, a supreme villain. His trial, which was a sham, proved to many northerners, not only the injustice of slavery, but also the fundamental lawlessness of the South. Within two years soldiers would march off to fight the South, and slavery, singing about Brown's heroism.

[*See also* Treason]

• Paul Finkelman, ed. *His Soul Goes Marching On: Responses to John Brown and the Harpers Ferry Raid*, 1995.

—Paul Finkelman

BROWN V. BOARD OF EDUCATION, 347 U.S. 483 (1954); 349 U.S. 294 (1955).

Brown v. *Board of Education* is generally considered one of the most important U.S. Supreme Court decisions of the twentieth century, and perhaps of all time. It is a symbol of America's commitment to racial equality and constitutional rights (see RACE AND ETHNICITY). *Brown* dealt with racial *segregation of public schools. The plaintiffs were represented by the NAACP and its lead attorney and later the first African-American Supreme Court justice, Thurgood *Marshall.

On 17 May 1954, Chief Justice Earl *Warren delivered the unanimous opinion of the Court, holding racial segregation of public schools unconstitutional. Chief Justice Warren's opinion

made four main arguments. First, he wrote that the history of the Fourteenth Amendment was "inconclusive" as to the intent of the framers regarding school segregation. Second, Warren rejected earlier decisions upholding segregation, stressing that the Constitution must be interpreted in light of modern conditions. Third, he emphasized the importance of education in modern America. Fourth, he argued that segregation denied African Americans an equal education because it created feelings of inferiority. He appended a footnote to this claim, citing several social science studies. Finally, he concluded, "in the field of public education the doctrine of 'separate but equal' has no place. Separate educational facilities are inherently unequal."

The Court held four days of re-argument to consider the remedy. On 31 May 1955, the Court announced its decision (*Brown II*), holding that because the challenge of ending segregation varied, the lower federal courts were in the best position to assure compliance. They were ordered to act with "all deliberate speed".

Brown was savagely criticized. Segregationists around the country denounced the decision as political, not legal, pointing to, among other criticisms, its rejection of precedent and its reliance on social science evidence. Legal academics from leading liberal law schools such as Harvard, Yale, and Columbia, criticized the decision as unprincipled. Politically, the decision was met with open defiance. In 1956, 101 members of the Congress signed a document known as the Southern Manifesto pledging resistance to the decision. President Dwight D. Eisenhower refused to endorse the decision. Southern states enacted hundreds of new laws strengthening school segregation. Thus, little changed. By the 1963–64 school year, nearly a decade after the decision, barely one in a hundred African-American schoolchildren in the states of the old Confederacy was in a school with whites. Despite *Brown*, desegregation did not occur until the late 1960s and early 1970s, a full fifteen years after the decision, as a result of Congressional action.

The opinion has also been criticized by proponents of racial equality who point out that it did not address *de facto* segregation where racially segregated housing, not state law, produces racially segregated schools. Others maintain that the decision itself was based on biased notions of African-American inferiority. What African-American children need, these critics argue, is not white schoolmates but dollars sufficient to hire well-trained teachers and place them in fully resourced schools. Despite these criticisms, *Brown* v. *Board of Education* is a constitutional landmark, one of the Supreme Court's most noble acts.

[*See also* Race and Ethnicity; Segregation; Warren, Earl]

• Richard Kluger, *Simple Justice: The History of Brown v. Board of Education,* 1976. Mark Tushnet, *The NAACP's Legal Strategy Against Segregated Education, 1925–1950,* 1987.   —Gerald N. Rosenberg

BURDEN OF PROOF, CRIMINAL AND CIVIL

Burden of proof is an evidentiary and procedural concept. It refers to the quantum of evidence necessary for a party to prevail on a claim or defense. The law provides for a range of burdens, from low to high, depending on the nature of the case. And allocations of the burden of proof, from one party to another, affect the likely outcomes of particular classes of cases by making cases harder or easier to prove. However, burdens of proof, although stated in fairly simple terms such as "beyond a reasonable doubt," are attempts to capture an essentially elusive idea—how much *evidence will be demanded to reconstruct a past that may defy all attempts at conclusive proof? As a consequence, it is not clear that these burdens work as intended or reliably influence outcomes in the way often assumed.

All legal systems operate under a necessity to resolve cases. In the United States, courts and juries cannot refuse to decide cases when they feel they do not know who is right. Thus, the rules concerning burdens of proof operate as rules of decision in the face of such uncertainty. In addition, the burden of proof concept is not limited to the ultimate disposition of a case. It permeates all stages of a case. Any lawsuit involves evidentiary decisions that must be made at several stages. And each one of these decisions involves burden of proof questions.

Furthermore, the burden of proof is broken down into two subparts—the burden of production and the burden of persuasion. Each is an aspect of the burden of proof. The burden of production refers to a party's duty to come forward with evidence, and is of primary interest in the pleading and discovery stage of a lawsuit. Procedural rules provide for a number of ways to dispose of a case before it gets to trial, many of which turn on whether or not a party has met its burden of production. Usually this burden initially rests on the plaintiff or other proponent of a claim or defense, and typically the burden is a minimal one. A party need only come up with some evidence in order to move its case forward. It need not be conclusive evidence. However, failure to meet the burden of production can result in an early dismissal or summary judgment of the case.

Once a party makes a prima facie case, the burden of production may shift to the opponent to offer contrary evidence. Many laws provide for rebuttable presumptions that set up such burden shifting. If such contrary evidence is forthcoming, the burden may then shift back again until it reaches that stage at which the finder of fact (a jury or, in most cases, a judge) must decide which of the parties has carried the burden of persuasion. The burden of persuasion refers to the responsibility to persuade the trier of fact after all the evidence is considered. Each party generally carries the burden of persuasion on its own claims or defenses.

Criminal Cases. The burden of proof is also a device through which various value preferences, social policies, and priorities find expression. Nowhere is this more apparent than in the criminal law. Here the Constitution requires the government to meet a very high burden for the successful prosecution of those accused of a crime. This high burden is ostensibly represented by the "beyond a reasonable doubt" standard. This standard is of constitutional dimension to the extent that the *due process clauses in the Fifth and Fourteenth Amendments are understood to encompass the Anglo-American tradition that "beyond a reasonable doubt" is the appropriate standard for criminal cases. Although this standard is deemed the highest burden that can be imposed on a party, there is some evidence that in fact juries find the criminal standard easier to satisfy than the supposedly less rigorous "clear and convincing evidence" standard. Moreover, the rigors of meeting the criminal burden are offset somewhat by a number of social factors that tend to favor the government, as well as by decisions to allow the burden of proof to shift to the defendant for some affirmative defenses.

Civil Proceedings. In contrast to the criminal law, in civil cases there is greater flexibility in burdens of proof, and an array of standards exist— from what amounts to a "probable cause" standard for defaults, to "preponderance" of the evidence standard, to the "clear and convincing" standard. Moreover, states are afforded a fair amount of leeway in adjusting the burdens of proof as they see fit to try to manage the amount and the success rates of various types of civil actions. Some of the areas in which both the states and the federal government have sought to achieve substantive policy goals by the manipulation of burdens of proof are punitive damages, fraud, civil rights, civil forfeiture, libel, and defamation.

Similarly, certain types of relief, such as temporary *restraining orders or other injunctive remedies, are disfavored, and subject to higher burdens of proof than ordinary civil cases. These remedies are subject to higher burdens of proof on the theory that making the burden higher will make it harder for plaintiffs to prevail; thus in turn will result in fewer law suits seeking this sort of relief and fewer successes among those suits filed. Whether or not burdens of proof actually have this effect, as an empirical matter, or whether shifting burdens of proof is necessary to achieve policy goals is subject to debate. However, as with criminal cases, the significance of burden of proof verbal formulations may be as much, if not more, aspirational than practical. Seen in this light, burden of proof is an expression of the political and social will.

[*See also* Criminal Law Practice]

• Edward W. Cleary, "Presuming and Pleading: An Essay on Juristic Immaturity," *Stanford Law Review* 12 (1959): 5. John Kaplan, "Decision Theory and the Fact-finding Process," *Stanford Law Review* 20 (1968): 1065. Barbara D. Underwood, "The Thumb on the Scales of Justice: Burdens of Persuasion in Criminal Cases," *Yale Law Journal* 86 (1977): 1299. John Calvin Jeffries and Paul B. Stephan III, "Defenses, Presumptions & Burdens of Proof in the Criminal Law," *Yale Law Journal* 88 (1979): 1325. Bruce L. Hay and Kathryn E. Spier, "Burdens of Proof in Civil Litigation: An Economic Perspective," *Journal of Legal Studies* 26 (1997): 413. Lawrence M. Solan, "Refocusing the Burden of Proof in Criminal Cases: Some Doubt About Reasonable Doubt," *Texas Law Review* 78 (1999): 105.

—Tamara Piety

BURGER, WARREN EARL (b. St. Paul, Minn., 17 September 1907; d. Washington, D.C., 25 June 1995) was the fifteenth chief justice of the U. S. Supreme Court, and served in this position longer than all but three of his predecessors.

From 1925–27, he studied at the University of Minnesota. In 1931 he graduated from St. Paul College of Law (now William Mitchell College of Law), where he was awarded his LL.B. *magna cum laude*. From 1931–53, Burger practiced law in St. Paul and participated in Republican party politics. From 1953–55, he served as an assistant attorney general in the U.S. Department of Justice. In 1956, President Dwight Eisenhower named Burger to the U.S. Court of Appeals for the District of Columbia Circuit, where he served until 1969, when President Richard Nixon appointed him chief justice of the United States on 21 May.

Burger's most important opinions pertained to separation of powers. In *United States* v. *Nixon* (1974), his opinion for the unanimous Court rejected President Nixon's claim of executive privilege as a reason for withholding tape recordings of private conversations from use in a criminal conspiracy trial. The Court ordered the president to turn over the tapes, which established an important limitation on the chief executive's power. In *Immigration and Nationalization Service* v. *Chadha* (1983), Burger wrote the Court's opinion that declared unconstitutional the Congress's use of the legislative veto against decisions of federal agencies.

In cases involving criminal justice and the rights of the accused, Burger's opinions tended to support the side of the police and prosecutors. He moved away from the more expansive interpretations of Fifth and Sixth Amendment rights by the Court under his immediate predecessor, Earl Warren.

Burger retired from the Court in 1986 to become chairman of the Commission on the Bicentennial of the United States Constitution. His greatest legacy as chief justice was reform of the ways the federal judicial system works. He reorganized many procedures for keeping records and executing more efficiently the business of the federal courts.

• Earl M. Maltz, *The Chief Justiceship of Warren Burger, 1969–1986*, 2000. Tinsley E. Yarbrough, *The Burger Court, Justices, Rulings, and Legacy*, 2000.

—John J. Patrick

BURGLARY is a classic *felony, subject to *capital punishment until modern times. It is now often expanded to encompass petty shoplifting. Traditionally, burglary required the following elements: (1) breaking (2) and entering (3) a dwelling (4) of another (5) at nighttime (6) with the intent to commit a felony. The common law crime was against the sanctity and security of the home. The perpetrator had to break into the dwelling, and not merely walk through an open door or window. On the other hand, opening an unlocked door or fraudulently gaining admission constituted a sufficient "breaking" to constitute burglary. These technicalities persuaded most American states to dispense with the breaking requirement, although some utilize it as a prerequisite to first-degree burglary.

The "entering" element has also been expanded. Any instrument under the perpetrator's control often constitutes an entry. Consequently, inserting a card into a cash machine constitutes an entry when the cash machine is attached to the outside of a building.

Historically, burglary required entry into a residence, although the occupants need not be present at the time. Today, many states accept entry into any structure suitable for occupancy as sufficient, including a car (or its trunk) or a telephone booth. For first-degree burglary, the historical requirement of a dwelling is still often utilized. One prosecutor vainly argued that the deceased's apartment was still a dwelling, since his body had not been removed.

Modern burglary statutes still routinely require that the perpetrator's intrusion be in "another's" structure to avoid the anomaly of prosecuting one who entered his own home to utilize illicit drugs or engage in other criminal acts.

Traditionally, burglary must have occurred at "nighttime," when natural light was insufficient to recognize a face. Today, nighttime is required in some first-degree burglary statutes.

Finally, burglary traditionally required that the perpetrator intend to commit a felony when entering the dwelling. Consequently, burglary is complete once the entry occurs with the requisite intent, even if the perpetrator does not commit the crime or even attempt to commit it inside the structure. It is also not burglary if the perpetrator forms the intent to commit the crime only after entering the structure. When an intruder entered Buckingham Palace and visited the Queen's bedroom, prosecutors were unable to prosecute for burglary, absent proof of felonious intent. Some modern statutes have expanded this element to encompass the intent to commit non-felonies, such as misdemeanor *larceny. The *Model Penal Code proposes that the intent to commit any crime should suffice.

Under common expansions of burglary's elements, an individual entering a store during business hours with the intent to steal an ice cream bar is guilty of burglary, even if he ultimately renounced his intent once he enters the store. The Model Penal Code, concerned about expansion, limits burglary to trespassory intrusions where the perpetrator has no legal right to be present. Burglary's enlargement has prompted many states to dramatically reduce the crime's penalties. On the other hand, burglary is often included as a qualifying crime in "three-strike" statutes, which impose life imprisonment on offenders who are convicted three successive times of specified crimes.

Perpetrators who commit burglary can also be punished for the attempted or completed crimes—such as the theft—that motivated the burglary.

Scholars debate whether the additional crime of burglary, now extended in many jurisdictions to most "inside" crime, is appropriate, since outside crimes are punished less.

[See also Criminal Law; Criminal Law Principles]

• Wayne R. LaFave and Austin W. Scott Jr., Criminal Law, 3rd ed., 1982. Rollin M. Perkins and Ronald N. Boyce, Criminal Law, 3rd ed., 1982.

—John L. Diamond

BURR, AARON, TRIAL OF. The trial of Aaron Burr for *treason in 1807 is perhaps the formative political trial in American history and certainly the one that fixed strict constitutional and judicial limits on prosecutions for treason. The defendant was famously controversial. Burr was vice-president during Thomas *Jefferson's first term and twice a failed candidate for governor of New York. He was also betrayer of Jefferson (snatching at the Presidency itself as Congress decided the election of 1800) and murderer of Alexander Hamilton (in a duel). To recoup his fortunes Burr organized in 1806 a little semi-military expedition down the Mississippi. He was arrested and charged with treason on orders of Jefferson himself. It remains disputed whether Burr aimed at rebellion—at separating the region west of the Appalachians from the Union—but he was surely plotting to attack Spain's possessions and erect his own empire over Mexico. Jefferson, fearing an American Napoleon, stood forth as the people's executive protecting the people's government. Burr, he declared to Congress, was "guilty beyond question."

The judge was Chief Justice John *Marshall, on federal circuit in Richmond, Virginia, and the trial renewed the confrontation between the Republican executive under Jefferson and the judiciary under the old Federalist Marshall. While the proceedings stretched on from March to September, with Marshall doubting from the start evidence of treason, the important events were the convening of the grand jury, which charged Burr with treason, and the treason trial itself. An important ruling in the grand jury phase limited "executive privilege"—the president's right to keep executive documents confidential—when such papers are relevant to a defendant's guilt or innocence (see EXECUTIVE POWER). This subordination of executive to judiciary infuriated Jefferson. Yet it led to a statesmanlike dialogue of the giants, which has been called superior to the recent discussions in U.S. v. Nixon and Clinton v. Jones. Each side maintained his branch's final authority to decide which papers had to be supplied. But Marshall allowed that the president need not answer a *sub poena* in person, and might, for cause, keep some materials confidential. Jefferson, quietly warning the court not to insist upon his presence, sent the materials in question, albeit with omissions.

The crucial question all along was whether the prosecution could prove what the Constitution required to convict for treason: an "overt Act" of "levying war" attested by two witnesses (Art. 3, sect. 3). The prosecution could prove that Burr procured an ambiguous little assembly on the Ohio. But procuring an overt act is not itself the warlike overt act, Marshall held, and if it were, the procuring must itself be attested by two witnesses. Such evidence was lacking. So constrained, the jury reluctantly acquitted. Thus Marshall rejected conspiracy to commit treason as itself treason in the constitutional sense, and he rejected too such *common law doctrines as "constructive presence" and "in treason all are principals." His opinion, the longest of his career, accords with what seems the framers' intent: to replace old customs, which made prosecution for treason easy, with a strict and explicit restriction drawn from the humane Montesquieu. Political partisans were thus restrained from playing with dangerous fire.

[*See also* Treason]

• John C. Yoo, "The First Claim: The Burr Trial, *United States* v. *Nixon*, and Presidential Power," *Minnesota Law Review* 83: 1435–79.   —Robert K. Faulkner

BUSH V. GORE, 531 U.S. __ (2000). The accusation of partisan decision making on the U.S. Supreme Court was never more intense than in the wake of the decision in *Bush* v. *Gore,* when five conservative justices relied on innovative readings of the Constitution in order to resolve the 2000 presidential election dispute in favor of the more conservative candidate.

The outcome of the election between Vice President Al Gore (D) and Texas Governor George W. Bush (R) came down to an unbelievably close vote in Florida. Trailing by just a few hundred votes, the Gore campaign requested hand recounts of ballots in four Democratic counties, arguing that manual inspections might lead to the discovery of legal votes that were inadvertently uncounted by the vote-tabulating machines. The strategy of the Bush campaign was to mobilize all political resources and sympathetic office-holders to block all efforts at hand recounts.

Bush v. *Gore* arose at the end of the recount saga, after the Florida Supreme Court ruled that

state law required a statewide manual recount of all ballots in which a machine failed to register a vote for president. Less than twenty-four hours later, the five most conservative justices on the U.S. Supreme Court issued an emergency injunction halting this recount, with Justice Scalia explaining that the review of these ballots threatened "irreparable harm to [Bush], and to the country, by casting a cloud upon what he claims to be the legitimacy of his election." The four dissenters, led by Justice Stevens, responded that "counting every legally cast vote cannot constitute irreparable harm."

Oral arguments were held two days later, and late the following day, on December 12, the same five justices ruled that no more recounting could take place. They noted that the Florida Supreme Court did not articulate a more specific standard for determining a legitimate vote than the statutory standard of "clear intent of the voter," and this made it possible that identical ballots would be treated differently in different parts of the state. This, they said, violated the equal protection clause of the Fourteenth Amendment. They did not explain what this innovative interpretation might mean more generally for vote-counting in American elections, or even how it applied to the original vote totals in Florida, where balloting and counting practices varied widely from county to county. Instead, the majority said simply, "our consideration is limited to the present circumstances, for the problem of equal protection in election processes generally presents many complexities."

While under different circumstances it might have been possible to remand the case back to the Florida Supreme Court so that it might create a more explicit counting standard, the majority announced that it was their belief that Florida intended to resolve all disputes by December 12 so that the state would benefit from a federal law that ensured the state's electoral college votes would not be challenged in the Congress. Because their decision was handed down on the evening of the 12th the majority invoked this deadline in support of their conclusion that there was no time left to count votes in Florida.

Three members of the majority—Chief Justice Rehnquist and Justices Scalia and Thomas—added a concurring opinion in which they argued that the state's election statutes did not support the remedy of a statewide recount under these circumstances, and thus the Florida Supreme Court's decision violated Article II of the U.S. Constitution, which gives to the state *legislature* the exclusive authority to determine the manner by which presidential electors will be chosen.

Each of the four dissenters wrote separately to argue that the U.S. Supreme Court had no business interfering in this presidential election dispute. Two of the dissenters, Justices Breyer and Souter, expressed some sympathy for the equal protection argument, but they stressed that these issues were more properly addressed by the state and (if necessary) Congress. They argued it would have been best to remand the case to the Florida Supreme Court as the institution authorized to determine whether Florida should continue counting under a more explicit recount standard. Justices Stevens and Ginsburg emphasized that the Florida Supreme Court's interpretation of the state statute was completely defensible and that the majority's opinion was inconsistent with the previously expressed views of those justices on equal protection and federalism. The practical effect of this decision was to declare Bush the president-elect. Gore conceded the election the following day. While the majority insisted that its intervention was an "unsought responsibility," the most frequently cited language in the *Bush* v. *Gore* opinions belonged to Justice Stevens, who lamented that the actual loser of this presidential election was "the Nation's confidence in the judge as an impartial guardian of the rule of law."

• Howard Gillman, *The Votes that Counted: How the Courts Decided the 2000 Presidential Election*, 2001.

—Howard Gillman

BUSINESS CULTURE. *See* Economics and Law.

BUSINESS ORGANIZATIONS. Persons setting up any business must address certain core questions, including (1) who will own the business, (2) who will manage it, (3) who will reap any profit, (4) who will bear the risk of any loss, and (5) who will pay income tax on any business profit. In the simplest of business arrangements—the sole proprietorship—the proprietor does all these things herself. The development of other forms of business organization in the United States is largely the story of attempting to maximize benefit while reducing risk. One example might be assessing the possibility of whether an owner could limit his liability for business debts while sharing in profits and decision-making.

Sole Proprietorship. The sole proprietorship is as old as business itself. With it, one person owns the enterprise, is responsible for management decisions, receives all profit, and bears all loss. The business is indistinguishable from its proprietor. Business income is part of the proprietor's taxable income for federal and state personal income tax purposes. The law imposes no formalities for forming a sole proprietorship. The proprietor simply owns and operates a business, which is a sole proprietorship even if the proprietor is unaware of that fact.

Often, the proprietor is the only person involved in the enterprise. But the proprietor may hire as many employees as needed to help run the business. Thus, at least in theory, a sole proprietorship may have thousands of employees. The determinative factor remains that one person owns the business, makes the management decisions, receives the profits, holds the risk of loss, and pays the income taxes.

The relationship between the sole proprietor and employees—including such issues as job responsibility and compensation—is subject to *contract. Because the employees often deal with third parties, however, there may be questions of whether the proprietor is liable for the employees' acts or omissions. These questions are governed by principles of agency law.

The proprietor is the principal and the employees are her agents. The principal may give the agent actual authority to bind her in dealings with third parties. For example, if the principal empowers the agent to purchase supplies for the business, the principal will be liable for the employee's purchases on that account. In addition, the agent may have implied authority to bind the principal. Such authority is created not by an express grant of power, but by the principal's holding the agent out to the third party as having the authority to bind her. If the principal indicates to a third party that the agent has the authority to bind her, the authority exists, even though the principal never expressly indicated to the agent that it existed.

In addition, the proprietor may be vicariously liable in *tort for the acts or omissions of her employees. The law protects the third party by permitting it to recover directly against the proprietor in cases of torts committed by an employee. A prudent proprietor will deal with the threat posed by such vicarious liability through insurance.

Partnership. The partnership essentially extends the sole proprietorship to multiple owners. The universal American definition of a partnership is "an association of two or more persons to carry on as co-owners a business for profit." As with the sole proprietorship, the law imposes no formalities for forming a partnership. The partnership exists by conduct, and is formed when two or more persons act in a way that satisfies the definition of partnership, even if they are unaware that they have formed a partnership.

Partnerships may be simple two-person affairs or may be very complex arrangements with numerous partners. Most American law firms—some of which have over a thousand members—are partnerships. The fact that no formalities are required to form a partnership does not mean that the parties may not fashion a formal working arrangement; most partnerships have a partnership agreement, which may be oral or written. Absent agreement, the basic model of partnership gives each partner an equal ownership interest in the business; an equal voice in management; an equal right to share in profits; and an equal risk of loss. But American legislation governing partnerships permits partners to customize their arrangement by agreement.

The partnership developed in English *common law, and was firmly rooted in the common law of the United States throughout the eighteenth and nineteenth centuries. Early in the twentieth century, however, state legislatures undertook to codify partnership law. In 1914, the Commission on Uniform State Laws promulgated the Uniform Partnership Act (UPA). In 1994, the same group promulgated the Revised Uniform Partnership Act (RUPA). Every American state has adopted some version of UPA or RUPA. Although there are differences in approach between UPA and RUPA (one of which will be addressed below), the acts set out rules of internal governance which the parties are free to change by agreement. In other words, the acts provide default rules, and not immutable prescriptions.

The resultant flexibility is important, and reflects the clear policy choice that businesspeople should be left to structure their relationship as best suits them. For example, suppose three people form a partnership. Alpha contributes 70 percent of the capital to start the business, while Beta and Omega each contribute 15 percent. Because of her larger investment and risk, Alpha may naturally expect that she should have the authority to make major business decisions. Similarly, Alpha may naturally expect to receive 70 percent of any profits. Unless such understandings are reflected in a partnership agreement, however, Alpha is subject to the default rules of the UPA and RUPA, which provide that management decisions are to be made by majority vote of the partners and that profits will be shared equally.

There is surprising disagreement about the legal nature of a partnership. Specifically, is it an entity (with legal existence separate from those who manage it), or is it a combination, or "aggregate," of its partners? English and American courts have failed to resolve the issue definitively. Legislative approaches also have been inconsistent. The UPA largely embraced the aggregate theory, and did not treat the partnership as an entity. It was difficult, however, to reconcile this theory with the desire to have some characteristics of an entity. For instance, it is preferable to consider property owned by the business as owned by an entity, rather than as jointly owned by all the partners. Similarly, it is desirable to allow the partnership to sue and be sued as an entity, rather than having to join all partners in litigation. Because of problems such as these, the RUPA reflects a different policy choice, and clearly adopts the "entity" theory. Under it, the partnership is a thing, a legal person, separate from the partners.

Despite this declaration, however, the modern American partnership is still seen as an aggregate of its partners in important ways, which reflect some of the major advantages and disadvantages of this business form. With regard to *taxation, the aggregate theory is advantageous. Because the partnership (for this purpose) is not considered an entity, it is not taxed on its income. Instead, partners are taxed individually on profits they receive from the business. This "flow-through" taxation is a distinct benefit compared to the corporation, which must pay income taxes as an entity before making distributions to stockholders, who then pay taxes on the distributions.

But in other particulars, adherence to the aggregate theory creates disadvantages. First, the death or other withdrawal of a partner causes dissolution of the partnership, although the parties can, by agreement, arrange for the other partners to take over operation of the business. Withdrawal of one partner can change the partnership and requires machinations that could be avoided were the business seen as an entity. Second, although the partners can agree to limit risk of *liability among themselves, third parties must be protected. As with the sole proprietorship, agency principles govern. In conducting the enterprise's business, each partner is an agent of the partnership. Thus, misfeasance or nonfeasance by one partner might be seen as putting the partnership, as the principal, at risk of liability. But here, too, the partnership is not considered an entity. Each partner is responsible for liability in tort or contract for the acts and omissions of her partners.

The personal liability of partners (and sole proprietors) for the acts or debts of the business was probably the greatest incentive for the development of other forms of business structure. The goal of the law is at once straightforward and somewhat contradictory: to create a vehicle for investment without risk of personal liability, while at the same time protecting the public that deals with the business.

Limited Partnerships. The first step toward achieving this goal came with the limited partnership. This form of business developed in the United States from the European *société en commandite* ("limited company") that allowed passive investors to escape personal liability for business debts. New York enacted the first American limited partnership statute in 1822. The major legislative incentive came in 1916, however, with the promulgation of the Uniform Limited Partnership Act (ULPA). In 1976, a Revised Uniform Limited Partnership Act (RULPA) was drafted. Every American state has adopted some form of one of these uniform acts. These acts provide default provisions which in most instances can be tailored by the parties. Unlike a partnership, however, a limited partnership can be formed only by filing appropriate documents with a state official.

A limited partnership has two types of partners, general and limited. As to general partners, the ordinary rules of partnership law govern. Thus, a general partner has a role in management and retains personal liability for business losses and debts. The limited partner, in contrast, invests in the business and is entitled to a share of the profits. But she has no voice in management. Moreover, in return for giving up control, the limited partner is not liable to third parties for business debts. The limited partner thus looks less like a partner and more like the stockholder of a corporation. She is a passive investor: she may lose her investment; but she is not otherwise at risk of loss should the business incur a debt or obligation.

Importantly, however, the status of the limited partner is part of an exchange. She enjoys limited liability because she is willing to forego a voice in management. Many cases address whether a limited partner has exerted such control over the business as to lose her limited liability. The ULPA and RULPA attempt to delineate how much control is too much, but the issue is a lurking danger for limited partners who wish to manage.

Corporations. The corporation is the most popular business form for passive investment. The status of the corporation is clear. It is an entity, separate from the people who manage and who own it. It is formed only by satisfying formalities that differ slightly from state to state, but which universally require filing documents with a state agency and performing periodic requirements such as filing reports and paying franchise fees.

The corporation's entity status carries positive consequences. The most important advantage is limited liability. Like limited partners, stockholders in a corporation are not liable for acts or debts of the business. (There is an exception for extraordinary circumstances that justify "piercing the corporate veil" and holding the stockholders liable for the business debts. Courts occasionally find such circumstances.) More interestingly, even the managers of the corporation are not liable for business debts. This situation differs from the limited partnership, in which general partners bear potential risk of the enterprise's loss. In the partnership, those who govern must bear the risk of loss. Limited liability in the corporation is not the result of eschewing managerial prerogative; rather, it is the result of the business's entity status. The entity is liable for its own debts.

Stockholders are the owners of the corporation. Largely, they are passive investors, although the corporate governance model does repose in them significant power in two instances. First, by electing the board of directors, they are responsible for selecting the business managers. Second, stockholders must approve fundamental changes in the corporation's structure, such as mergers or sales of all the assets. On the other hand, the directors are the managers of the business, making the policy decisions that drive the corporation.

This corporate model of organization reflects the American embrace of the republican form of government. In it, the owners elect those who make the management decisions, the directors, and may remove them with or without cause. The directors hire and monitor the officers, who implement the directors' management decisions. In turn, the officers, who hire and monitor lower level employees, are agents of the corporation. Their actions, if made within the scope of their authority, will bind the entity, just as an employee's act might bind a sole proprietor or a partner's act might bind other partners.

Statutes governing incorporation have evolved in ways that reflect fundamental changes in the societal view of corporations. For decades after the founding of the United States, each state followed the English model, under which corporate charters were granted by legislative act. To form a corporation, then, the proprietors had to convince the legislature to pass a special bill granting them an individual charter. In the early nineteenth century, states moved away from this model. In 1811, New York passed the first general incorporation law, which permitted parties to form a corporation by meeting specific requirements, without an individual legislative grant. Other states soon accepted the notion. This trend clearly reflected an American sense of democracy—the privilege of operating a corporation should be available to the people, and not simply to the few influential enough to garner direct legislative favor.

At the same time the young country was nervous about concentration of economic power. To curb potential abuse, state legislatures placed in the general incorporation statutes significant restrictions on the amount of capital corporations could raise, on their temporal duration, and on the activities corporations could undertake. Yet over time, these restrictions melted away. Some were the victims of judicial craftsmanship. Mostly, however, legislatures concluded that such restrictions were inappropriate as a matter of policy. Their actions reflected a growing belief in the inevitability and benefit of economic concentration, and the conviction that any anticompetitive effects of economic concentration should be addressed through the *antitrust laws, and not by imposing additional restrictions on the corporation.

As a result, state laws governing incorporation became less prescriptive and more flexible. States saw opportunities for generating fees, franchise taxes, and income taxes by giving businesspeople an incentive to incorporate under their laws. Although New Jersey passed the first modern, liberalized incorporation law, Delaware soon took over as the leading state for incorporation. Through the years, states competed for business by providing more liberal, flexible provisions, and allowing greater prerogatives to the corporate managers. Some feared that this competition was a "race to the bottom" in which states would abdicate too much control to managerial prerogative. In a famous dissenting opinion in *Louis K. Liggett Co.* v. *Lee* (1933), Justice Louis D. *Brandeis decried what he called the "race . . . of laxity" in corporate law.

Despite these concerns, the competition among states for corporate charters continues. Although states are free to experiment with their own laws in this regard, the late twentieth century saw greater uniformity, as a result of the widespread embrace of the Model Business Corporation Act and the Revised Model Business Corporation Act. The latter looks very much like the UPA, providing a set of default rules, and giving the parties leeway in structuring and managing the corporation. This strong modern trend in incorporation laws reflects the victory of the contract theory of the corporation over the regulatory theory, meaning that those forming and managing the business ought to be free to make major decisions with minimal state-imposed restriction.

In many ways, then, the corporation seems ideal for maximizing the benefits and avoiding the potential liabilities of business. Owners can be passive and need take no role in management. Barring rare circumstances, they will not be liable for the acts or debts of the business. They can share in any profit (as long as the management declares distributions). Stockholders also enjoy free transferability of ownership, and can sell their stock without harming the entity. Indeed, the entity can have infinite duration. But the corporation has drawbacks. It is relatively difficult to form and requires periodic filings with the state. In addition, as noted it presents the problem of double taxation; the corporation pays income tax on profits, and stockholders pay tax on distributions.

Limited Liability Company. Such drawbacks led to the emergence in the 1990s of yet another business form, the limited liability company (LLC). Now available in a majority of states, the LLC may represent the optimal combination of business characteristics. The LLC is an entity, and thus features limited liability to its owners, just as a corporation does. Unless the entity requests otherwise, however, the entity does not pay income taxes on its profits. Thus, it carries the benefit of flow-through taxation, just as a partnership does. Unlike a partnership or limited partnership, no individual need be liable for business acts or debts. Moreover, although there are governing statutes, LLCs allow great flexibility; operation of the LLC can be governed by the "operating agreement" among the stockholders. The remaining drawback of the LLC is the formal nature of its formation, but such obeisance to the state seems small price to pay for such an efficacious combination of features.

Business Organizations as a Healthy Development. The development of various business organizations in the United States reflects a consistent effort of businesspeople to maximize the advantages (such as sharing in profits and exercising management prerogatives) and to minimize the disadvantages (such as liability for losses and taxation) that are inherent in any business. It also reflects changes in the societal view of aggregation of capital and increasing acceptance of the notion that the state should facilitate the desires of those who are engaged in the business, while retaining some prescriptions for the protection of the public.

[*See also* Corporations: For-Profit Corporations]

• Larry E. Ribstein, *Unincorporated Business Entities,* 1996. James D. Cox, Thomas Lee Hazen, and F. Hodge O'Neal, *Corporations,* 1997. Franklin A Gevurtz, *Corporation Law,* 2000.   —Richard D. Freer

BUSINESS REORGANIZATION. *See* Bankruptcy: Business.

C

CALHOUN, JOHN C. (1782–1850), vice president (1825–32) of the United States and United States senator (1832–43, 1845–50), was born 18 March 1782 in the District of Ninety-six (later Abbeville), South Carolina, the son of Patrick Calhoun and Martha Caldwell. After graduating from Yale in 1804, he moved to Charleston to read law, and subsequently studied at the Litchfield Law School in Connecticut. In 1806 Calhoun returned to South Carolina, where he set up a practice and entered politics.

Initially a nationalist, Calhoun became the foremost champion of *states' rights constitutional thought. Elected vice president in 1824, he opposed increases in the federal tariff that year and again four years later. In 1828, Calhoun wrote the paper "South Carolina Exposition and Protest," where he articulated his compact theory of government and doctrine of nullification. The Constitution, he argued, was a compact among several equal, sovereign states. These states established the federal government, but that government possessed only those powers specifically enumerated in the Constitution. When the federal government exceeded its constitutional authority, a state possessed the power to nullify an act of Congress— to declare the operation of the law void in that state. These ideas came to fruition in 1832, when Calhoun resigned the vice presidency to serve in the U.S. Senate and South Carolina nullified the tariff. President Andrew Jackson vigorously opposed the state's actions, but Congress resolved the crisis by reducing the tariff.

Calhoun's theories increasingly became linked to the defense of *slavery. By the late 1830s he described the institution as a "positive good," used state *sovereignty to justify restrictions on abolitionist literature, and defended the holding of slave property on the basis of the Constitution's Fifth Amendment. Fearing that northern states would gain control of the federal government and emancipate slaves, Calhoun devoted the last years of his life to developing a theory of minority rights to protect southern interests within the Union. His "Disquisition on Government" and "Discourse on the Constitution" dealt with these issues. He died on 31 March, just before the passage of the Compromise of 1850, but only the Civil War would resolve the questions of state sovereignty, slavery, and minority rights that consumed his career.

• John A. Niven, *John C. Calhoun and the Price of Union*, 1988. —Timothy S. Huebner

CANON LAW refers to the legal systems of some Christian churches; namely, the Roman Catholic, Orthodox, and Anglican (Episcopalian). Other Christian denominations prefer to speak of "church order" when they refer to their organizational structures and operational norms.

Canon law belongs to the family of legal systems that have their origin in classical Roman law. Its specific religious content emerged from three principal sources: enactments by episcopal councils, especially by universally recognized ecumenical councils; decrees by the papacy; and customs and usages developed through ecclesiastical courts and offices as well as through the people's common observance.

There was one body of canon law until the separation of the churches of the East (Constantinople) and the West (Rome) in the eleventh century; afterwards, and even more so following the Reformation in the sixteenth century, independent branches developed differently according to the nature of the churches and their relationship to secular government.

The bulk of Roman Catholic church law is found today in the *Code of Canon Law* (1983). The *Code of Canons* (1990) of the Eastern churches is modeled on the former; it is applicable to all the churches that do not follow the Roman rite of worship but accept the overall jurisdiction of the bishop of Rome.

The codes are intended to regulate the operations of the church. They are not meant to establish norms of morality (for instance, concerning divorce, birth control, or abortion). They leave such issues to the teaching authority of the popes, bishops, or councils. The codes, however, contain provisions for both the preservation of traditional doctrine and for research to assure progressive development.

The content of canon law is well illustrated by listing the topics covered by the codes:

- modalities of legislation and the norms for the interpretation of laws;
- creation of ecclesiastical corporations and their functions;
- appointment to offices of different ranks; fundamental rights and duties of the faithful;
- the church's hierarchical organization;
- tasks of the pope, bishops, priests, deacons, and councils (local, provincial, general);
- the composition, life, and work of religious orders; the right to form associations within the church; preservation of traditional beliefs, including the preaching and teaching of Christian doctrine; institutions of education and health care;
- promotion of common worship through the administration of the sacraments;
- protection of the church's assets, especially real property;
- definitions of criminal and disciplinary offenses with their appropriate sanctions;
- judicial processes that include special procedures, trials, and criminal prosecutions.

In addition to the codes, canon law includes statutory norms for special institutions and activities, such as election of the pope, appointment of local bishops, organization of executive departments assisting the pope, sending and receiving ambassadors by the Holy See, and the relationship with other Christian churches. The internal law of the Vatican City State, however, is not part of canon law.

Following the break with Rome in the eleventh century, the autonomous Orthodox churches developed their laws on the basis of one common tradition, but independently from each other. Today, they tend to put less emphasis on law than the Roman church does and are more generous in allowing exceptions.

After the repudiation of papal jurisdiction in the sixteenth century, the Church of England acknowledged the supreme authority of the king and Parliament; its canon law has since taken on the character of "royal legislation for the church." Today other churches of the "Anglican communion" worldwide are autonomous and regard the creation and administration of their laws as being entirely within the domain of their religious jurisdiction.

In the Middle Ages canon law was a powerful force in shaping the cultures of European nations and people; it had a strong impact on the development of English law mainly through the procedures of the chancery court that created equitable remedies.

In the United States the internal organization and religious activity of Christian churches follow their own canon law and "order"; no community denies the competency of the secular government in nonreligious matters. The U.S. Constitution's first amendment, which grants religious freedom and prevents Congress from establishing a state religion, proved to be a sound foundation not only for peaceful co-existence but also for a productive cooperation among various religious bodies and secular government.

[See also Comparative Law; Religion]

• Harold J. Berman, *Law and Revolution: The Formation of the Western Legal Tradition,* 1983. Ladislas Orsy, *Marriage in Canon Law,* 1986. R. H. Helmholz, *Canon Law and the Law of England,* 1987. John H. Erickson, *The Challenge of our Past: Studies in Orthodox Canon Law and Church History,* 1991. Norman Doe, *The Legal Framework of the Church of England: A Critical Study in a Comparative Context,* 1996. John P. Beal, James A. Coriden, and Thomas G. Green, eds., *New Commentary on the Code of Canon Law,* with a revised translation of the code, 2000.   —Ladislas M. Orsy, S. J.

CAPACITY, DIMINISHED. *See* Criminal Law Principles: Defense Principles.

CAPITAL PUNISHMENT. At the beginning of the twenty-first century, the position of the United States on the law and practice of capital punishment is singular. Alone among the Western democracies, state governments in the United States authorize and conduct executions as *criminal punishment and show no clear indication of a willingness to stop doing so. Alone among nations with strong traditions of due process in criminal procedure, criminal justice systems in the United States attempt to merge a system of extensive procedures and review with execution as a legal outcome. It has been an impossible task. The result has been a frustrating and lengthy process that combines all of the disadvantages of procedural regularity with unprincipled and arbitrary outcomes.

The Death Penalty in Recent History. As recently as the end of World War II, the overwhelming majority of nations, including all of the major Western democracies, retained execution as a criminal punishment. Prior to that, two centuries of debate about the justification of death as a punishment had reduced both the number of offences for which death was a penalty and the number of executions conducted in most countries, but the abolition of capital punishment had been achieved *de jure* only in Scandinavia and in parts of Latin America. The post–World War II abolition of capital punishment in Europe began in the 1940s with the successor regimes in Italy and Germany and spread throughout western Europe during the 1960s and 1970s. After that, condemnation of the death penalty quickly achieved the status of *human rights orthodoxy with the members of the Council of Europe. Most British Commonwealth nations embraced the abolition of capital punishment at roughly the same time, including New Zealand, Australia, and Canada. A burst of abolition in central and eastern European nations emerging from Soviet domination produced reports in the 1990s by international human rights organizations that over half of the world's governments had ceased executions. While the number of countries not using execution as a criminal punishment has increased substantially over time, it is not clear that the number of executions occurring worldwide has decreased at anywhere near the same rate. Most of the nations that have abolished capital punishment were responsible for only a small number of executions in the modern era. By contrast, the People's Republic of China, with an estimated volume of executions of five thousand in the 1980s, would conduct more executions in a month at that rate than any western European nation experienced during the second half of the twentieth century. And those countries with the highest volume of executions are also the least reliable sources of information on execution numbers. Worldwide trends in the number of capital sentences actually carried out are not known. But the legislative and judicial trends on capital punishment are clear and important. The regional pattern shows executing nations clustered in Asia, the Islamic Middle East, and parts of Africa. The socioeconomic profile of executing versus nonexecuting nations reveals a clear developmental divide, with all but two of the fully developed nations having ceased executions, while capital punishment continues as criminal justice policy in upwards of seventy less developed nations. (The two executing exceptions to this developmental divide are Japan and the United States.) The political distribution of capital punishment policy reveals a cleavage as clear as the economic profile. Executing regimes are with very few exceptions undemocratic governments with poor human rights records. Nonexecution of offenders is a *sine qua non* for nations with ambitions to achieve high standing in the community of nations concerned with human rights. Two points about the worldwide trends in capital punishment policy are necessary to put the American situation in appropriate perspective. The first point is that the abhorrence of capital punishment, which is now orthodox in developed nations in the human rights community, is of recent origin. The elimination of capital punishment as government policy in western Europe was not complete until the last quarter of the twentieth century. If one consults the statute book, the guillotine was an official instrument of the French justice system as recently as 1980. While the foundations for opposition to execution can be traced back much further, the now orthodox position of the developed nations did not emerge until after 1975. It is in fact astonishing how quickly after capital punishment was abandoned as a domestic policy that objections to executions hardened into a moral absolute in Europe and the Commonwealth countries and was judged suitable for worldwide export.

The Singular American Present. While the current conditions in the United States are sharply different from those in the rest of the developed West, this contrast turns out to be of surprisingly recent origin also. For the first half of the postwar period, policy in the United States seemed to be on track toward an end of executions in much the same pattern found in France, England, and the Commonwealth countries. Figure 1 profiles executions over time in the United States, by year, combining execution totals from all states conducting them into a national aggregate. Between 1950 and 1965 executions steadily diminished from over one hundred a year to under ten.

By 1967, federal courts had imposed a prohibition on execution so that a series of challenges to the principles and procedures of capital punishment could be decided. The nationwide judicial moratorium on executions would last a decade, during which the U. S. Supreme Court would tiptoe to the brink of judicial abolition of capital punishment in 1972 and then pull back four years later to allow states to reinstitute regimes of capital punishment in a series of decisions issued in 1976. All of the divergent elements of American policy that are evident in current international comparisons are based on changes in policy in the United States that have occurred since those 1976 decisions. While the rest of the Western world has been creating and attempting to enforce nonexecution as a human rights orthodoxy, the policy of the national government in the United States has shifted to the toleration of capital punishment by the states, and a series of capital crimes have been added by the federal Congress for the limited jurisdiction of the federal government. The result of these shifts in policy are reflected in the trends in the number of executions by year since 1977, displayed on the right-hand side of Figure 1. By the year 2000 the volume of executions by American states had bounced back to levels quite close to those experienced during the 1950s. The crude visual impression of Figure 1 is of an almost symmetrical policy pattern in the United States, with declines to zero in the first half of the post-war period and a return to a level of execution in the late 1990s quite close to the historical pattern of fifty years before. There is a kernel of truth to this visual impression of decline and regression to a previous equilibrium, but the national aggregate pattern over time conveys two false impressions. In the first place, aggregate criminal execution levels for the United States as a whole hide the huge variations among regions and individual states that are one of the chief characteristics of American capital punishment. Twelve of the fifty states

provide no death penalty in their criminal statutes, and other states have conducted no executions. South Dakota and New Hampshire are death penalty states that have had no executions in over half a century. The populous state of New Jersey legislated a death penalty in 1980, but has not produced an execution in its first two decades. The states of the American south are at the other extreme in the distribution of American executions. In the year 2000 for example, seventy-six of the eighty-five executions taking place in the United States (89 percent of the total) were in the south, even though that region accounts for about one-third of the United States population and about 40 percent of the American states that authorize a death penalty. During the year 2000, two-thirds of all American executions were conducted in just three of the thirty-eight American states that authorize executions: Texas, Oklahoma, and Virginia. The state of Texas alone currently executes more people (forty in 2000) each year than have been executed in the last quarter of a century in the four most populous northern states that have had any executions: California (eight), Illinois (twelve), Ohio (one), and Pennsylvania (three).

The second respect in which the similarity in numbers of executions between the 1950s and the late 1990s might be misleading is that the capital punishment systems that produce these superficially similar numbers of executions have changed drastically. The total population of condemned prisoners awaiting execution in the United States during the late 1950s was about 220 (that was the 1960 total). Indeed, five years after the federal

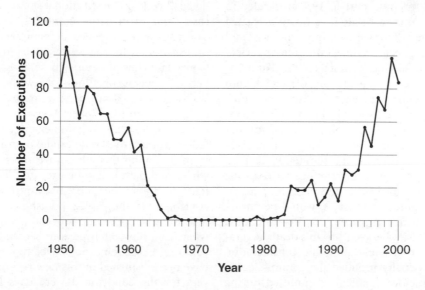

Figure 1: U.S. Executions by Year, 1950–2000
Source: Bureau of Justice Statistics, U.S. Department of Justice, *Capital Punishment 1999* (2000).

courts imposed a moratorium on executions in 1967, 620 persons awaiting execution created an unprecedented "pile-up" in death row populations. In the year 2000, by contrast, the eighty-five persons executed were drawn from a population of persons under sentence of death that exceeded 3,500, a forty-year supply at the current rate of execution. The circumstances of capital punishment in the United States are therefore distinguished from earlier eras by huge death row populations, long delays between the sentence of death and the earliest that an execution might occur, and a relatively small likelihood at current rates that a particular death sentence will lead to an execution. The delay and uncertainty of the current system have produced citizen anger and frustration. Appellate review in state or federal courts invalidated about 70 percent of death sentences, but these aggregate figures also hide wide variation among American states. The current circumstances of capital punishment are hated in equal measure by the opponents of capital punishment systems and by those who support execution but desire more certainty and less delay.

The Legal Framework. The current circumstances of law and procedure that have produced the high rates of death sentences, the substantial delays, and the variations among states are the product of substantive legal rules and procedures created by the U.S. Supreme Court over the past thirty years. This federal constitutional framework is the product of two contrasting precedents of the 1970s and a long series of subsidiary high court decisions.

The U.S. Supreme Court in 1972 first ruled in *Furman* v. *Georgia* that state laws which delegated to the jury the choice between imprisonment and execution for specific crimes without any clear guidelines were unconstitutional as *cruel and unusual punishment in violation of the Eighth Amendment. Four years later the Supreme Court ruled that legislative standards that provided mandatory death penalties for some types of murder were also unconstitutional. But in *Gregg* v. *Georgia* (1976) the Court held that statutes which provided a series of aggravating circumstances in the commission of murders to be weighed by juries, against listed mitigating factors, would be an acceptable structure for guiding the jury to choose in individual cases between life and death. Aggravating factors that could allow the consideration of the death penalty included the commission of multiple homicides, homicide committed during other felonies, premeditation, and the personal dangerousness of the offender. Mitigating circumstances that could allow juries and judges to choose imprisonment rather than death included youth, mental and emotional disturbance, and other factors. The result of this search for guided discretion was a patchwork of decisions on a wide variety of topics in which some rules were clear and others decidedly vague. States were allowed substantial variations of the circumstances that they could select to aggravate and mitigate murders, but the ultimate standards were matters of federal law and the ultimate judgment was that of federal courts.

The problem with approving the results in both the 1972 *Furman* decision and the 1976 *Gregg* approval of guided discretion is that there are no observable differences between outcomes in the "standardless" discretion disapproved in *Furman* and the "guided discretion" approved in *Gregg*. It is much easier to support the result in one case or the other than to approve of both, but both decisions remain precedent. One result of the decisions in *Furman* and *Gregg* was that federal courts became the ultimate authority on what circumstances and procedures could be used by the states in death cases. Whereas the Supreme Court of the United States had only rarely reviewed state death sentences in the century before the *Furman* decision, the substantive law and procedure in state death cases became the most frequent business of that Court in the two decades after 1976. But death penalty jurisprudence was not a specialization that Supreme Court justices welcomed. Most of the justices who heard cases in the last quarter of the twentieth century disliked administering a detailed code of constitutional standards for death cases, and particularly resented serving as a last resort for appeals lodged by prisoners on the eve of execution. In the early 1980s the Supreme Court launched a campaign to loosen the links between federal constitutional law and the administration of the death penalty by the states, a judicial program that Robert Weisberg labeled "Deregulating Death." To some extent, the easing of federal control over state capital punishment came from loosening the substantive rules that govern who could permissibly be executed. For the most part, however, the Supreme Court loosened its controls over the capital punishment process by instituting or approving procedural limits on how, when, and how often persons sentenced to death could raise legal objections. Death penalty appeals have been dismissed in this new regime when lawyers for the condemned were days late in presenting an issue for review in a state court. Since the issue had not been properly presented before the state court, the U.S. Supreme Court ruled in *Coleman* v. *Thompson* (1991) that it could not be later entertained by any federal court. Whether the attorney who missed the deadline was sanctioned is not known; the client was executed.

The Death Penalty and American Legal Values. Twenty-five years after the U.S. Supreme Court allowed the reintroduction of capital punishment, the controversy surrounding the administration of the death penalty is more acute than ever before in American history. Because an execution cannot take place until all legal appeals have been decided, those who desire prompt execution are frustrated and angered by the years that pass before the punishment of death is inflicted. This frustration inspired the passage of federal laws that attempt to reduce delays in execution by requiring that prisoners must raise legal issues within a short time or forfeit the opportunity to have their claims heard.

These attempts to streamline the path to execution illustrate the tension between American legal values about fairness and procedural *due process and the pressure to execute. No nation other than the United States has ever attempted to combine meticulous due process of law and regular executions: the passage by the U.S. Congress of "The Federal Death Penalty Act of 1994," (1994 & Supp. 1999) is a tacit admission that full legal procedures cannot be accommodated in a system that uses execution as a penal sanction. At the same time that attempts are being made to streamline executions by reducing judicial scrutiny of death cases, investigative reporting and DNA testing caused a scandal in Illinois, where several innocent men had been sentenced to death. The governor of that state suspended executions and appointed a commission of inquiry. Legislation to facilitate DNA testing has been proposed in many American states and enacted in several. There are, however, a large number of capital cases where DNA crime scene evidence is not available, and the mechanism to test the validity of death sentences in these circumstances is not obvious. What does seem clear is that any attempt to "streamline" the criminal justice process to facilitate more and faster executions will make it more likely that wrongly convicted persons are executed, and any serious attempt to identify and protect the wrongly convicted will add delay and additional judicial inquiry to the appellate process. A nation can have full and fair criminal procedures, or it can have a regularly functioning process of executing prisoners, but it cannot have both. This conflict underscores the ultimate stakes in the struggle over capital punishment in the United States, and they are high stakes indeed. Either the execution system will be brought to a standstill by good lawyers and full procedural inquiry or the justice system itself will have to be deconstructed to accommodate the executioner's demands.

[*See also* Criminal Law; Electric Chair]

• Robert Weisberg, "Deregulating Death," *The Supreme Court Review* (1983): 305–95. Franklin E. Zimring and Gordon Hawkins, *Capital Punishment and the American Agenda*, 1986. Roger G. Hood, *The Death Penalty: A World-Wide Perspective*, 1996. Hugo A. Bedeau, *The Death Penalty in America: Current Controversies*, 1997. Amnesty International, "The Death Penalty: Arbitrary, Unfair and Racially Biased," in *Rights for All*, ch. 6, 1998. Available online at *http://www.rightsforall-usa.org/info/report/r06.htm#*. Bureau of Justice Statistics, U.S. Department of Justice, *Capital Punishment 1999*, 2000. James Liebman, Jeffrey Fagan, Valerie West, and Jonathan Lloyd, "Capital Attrition: Error Rates in Capital Cases," *Texas Law Review* 78 (2000): 1839–65.

—Franklin E. Zimring and Gordon Hawkins

CAPTURE, REGULATORY. *See* Regulation.

CARDOZO, BENJAMIN NATHAN, (1870–1938). Benjamin Nathan Cardozo chief judge of the New York Court of Appeals and justice of the United States *Supreme Court, lived from just after the Civil War until just before World War II. By common consent, he was the most outstanding state court judge of that period, and his judicial reputation was second only to that of Oliver Wendell *Holmes. Cardozo came from a well-established, pre-Revolutionary War Sephardic Jewish family. Just after Ben was born, his father, Albert Cardozo, one of Boss Tweed's judges, resigned his state judgeship as the New York legislature was about to impeach him. Ben's mother was chronically ill, and he was raised in large part by his older sister, Nellie, with whom he lived for the whole of her life.

Cardozo was tutored for Columbia College by Horatio Alger, and he was an outstanding student at college. He studied for two years at Columbia Law School before entering practice in his father's old firm. He was an excellent trial and appellate lawyer for twenty-three years before being elected to the New York Supreme Court as part of a reform Fusion ticket in 1913. Designation by Governor Glynn to the Court of Appeals followed one month later. A few years later, he was elected to the Court of Appeals, and he was elected chief judge in 1926. After eighteen years as a New York judge, he was appointed to the United States Supreme Court in 1932 by Herbert Hoover to replace Holmes. Cardozo served for six years during the critical time when the Supreme Court was at the center of controversy because it overturned so much New Deal legislation, usually with him in dissent, but he lived just long enough to see the Court change course.

After Cardozo had been on the bench for seven years, he undertook the task of explaining what judges did in his Yale Lectures entitled *The Nature of the Judicial Process*. A major thesis, exemplified also in his state and federal opinions, was the progressive idea that judges *make* law, for which he offered a stirring defense. A second thesis was that in making law, judges are restrained by history, precedent, and the powers and responsibilities of the other branches of government. Cardozo believed that the major role in guiding social change in a democracy belonged to the legislature and the executive. Thus, he innovated most when the step to be taken was modest and when the innovation did not violate what he saw as the prerogatives of other institutions of government—ideally when the legislative or executive branch had already pointed the way. While Cardozo often adapted law to new social conditions, as in his famous opinion in *MacPherson* v. *The Buick Co.* (N.Y., 1916), he also often declined to make such adaptations, as in another famous opinion in *Palsgraf* v. *Long Island Railroad Co.* (N.Y., 1928). And good lawyer that he was, his decisions often turned on his vision of the underlying factual situation.

In his day, Cardozo was lionized, especially by academia, as a progressive judge who cast off the shackles of nineteenth-century mechanical jurisprudence and formalism in order to modernize legal doctrine (see JURISPRUDENCE, AMERICAN-THE REVOLT AGAINST FORMALISM). He wrote numerous memorable opinions that exposed troublesome legal issues in a striking style. He had an ear for the illuminating phrase. His thoughtful, dispassionate approach to legal issues, the ambiguity of his resolution of the competing themes of his messages, and his distinctive literary style all contributed to his enduring reputation as one of the nation's great judges.

• Richard A. Posner, *Cardozo: A Study in Reputation*, 1990. Andrew L. Kaufman, *Cardozo*, 1998.

—Andrew L. Kaufman

CARJACKING. *See* Automobiles and Crime.

CAUSE LAWYERS. Cause lawyering is a concept that brings together a number of modes of *legal practice (public interest lawyering, civil rights and civil liberties lawyering, feminist lawyering, pov-

erty lawyering, and the like under a single terminological umbrella). The common bond among these lawyers is a commitment to use their legal skills to promote social and political causes they believe in (see POLITICS AND THE LAW). It is this commitment that distinguishes them from, and puts them ethically at odds with, the vast majority of lawyers, who see their primary responsibility as serving individual clients, not causes. Whereas service to clients is an end in itself for conventional lawyers, cause lawyers view clients more as a means to achieve broader social and political goals.

Conventional and cause lawyering ordinarily entail contrasting styles of representation. Conventional representation calls on lawyers to serve clients in a vigorous but neutral and detached fashion, whereas cause lawyers tend to identify closely with their clients. According to conventional ethical precepts, such identification with clients compromises the attorney's professional judgment and therefore imperils effective representation. Cause lawyers reject this claim—arguing that an alliance with clients, rooted in common values and interests, enhances the kind of mutuality that is conducive to authentic and resolute representation. Critics of cause lawyering counter that a preoccupation with causes can tempt cause lawyers to give priority to the cause itself at the expense of the client's interest. Whatever the truth of these claims and counterclaims, cause lawyering emerges as an ethically suspect mode of legal practice with a relatively low standing among conventional practitioners. Not surprisingly, cause lawyers are not among the higher paid members of the legal profession (see ETHICS AND PROFESSIONAL RESPONSIBILITY, LEGAL).

Nonetheless, cause lawyering can be found in the full range of professional venues in the United States and around the world. It is practiced in large and small private *firms, and on a salaried basis in national and transnational nongovernmental organizations and in publicly funded governmental and quasi-governmental agencies. Full-time cause lawyering is found principally in salaried practices for privately funded social action organizations and publicly funded legal services agencies. For lawyers in private practice, cause lawyering is necessarily a part-time activity funded by more lucrative forms of practice. In some small firms with heavy caseloads, cause lawyering may account for upward of 50 percent of their work. At the other end of the scale, pro bono programs funded by large corporate firms allow associates, but seldom partners, to devote 5 to 10 percent of their billable hourly targets to serving causes. Only in personal injury practices based on contingent fees is cause lawyering sometimes self-financing. For firms in private practice, the choice of causes is also constrained by conflicts with the representation of paying clients.

Cause lawyering has flourished in the United States at least since the 1960s. This has been due in large part to the successes of the civil rights movement and to the work of a number of well-established social advocacy organizations such as the NAACP Legal Defense Fund, the Environmental Defense Fund, the Center for Constitutional Rights, and many others. In recent years, the practice of cause lawyering has also been documented in parts of Europe, Asia, Latin America, the Middle East, and Africa. The expansion of cause lawyering throughout the world is due to a combination of factors, including local problems and opportunities, transnational human rights networks, and the influence of the U.S. model and U.S. legal training. And while cause lawyering is most likely to be found in mature, democratic regimes, it has also been found in nascent democracies and even in authoritarian countries.

How is the persistence of cause lawyering to be explained? First, while cause lawyering for individual practitioners is not associated with either high status or high income, there are other attractions. The primary motivation is idealism. Cause lawyering is, as some cause lawyers put it, driven by the desire to give something back, or, as others are inclined to think of it, by a desire to maximize the harmony between their personal convictions and their professional lives. And cause lawyering often provides opportunities for young lawyers working in the lower reaches of large corporate law firms to take the lead in handling noteworthy cases. As such, it can sometimes bring both personal satisfaction and enhanced career prospects.

It is important to realize that cause lawyering is not entirely unwelcome to *mainstream* professionals. The mainstream includes the leadership of the organized legal profession as well as the vast majority of lawyers who are themselves indifferent, at least as lawyers, to political and social causes. The bar leadership sees cause lawyers as fortuitous allies in the defense and enhancement of the profession's social capital. To the public, after all, lawyers typically appear to be no more than hired guns—using suspect means to defend sometimes unsavory clients, and profiting handsomely from doing so. Accordingly, cause lawyers, with their penchant for doing good, can add some luster to the often-tarnished public image of the legal pro-

fession. There is also a kind of tacit quid pro quo between cause lawyers and conventional practitioners. Cause lawyers generally represent the impecunious, and in so doing assume a burden that mainstream professionals are, according to their own ethical precepts, supposed to shoulder but are more than happy to leave to others.

How all of this plays out depends a great deal on what kind of cause lawyering is practiced. *Traditional* cause lawyers, who pursue so-called "first generation" rights—closely linked to the rule of law and to liberal social contract theory—primarily through litigation, can gain significant prestige within the legal profession. Much the same can be said of *conservative* cause lawyers, who are becoming increasingly prominent in the United States. They serve causes such as the property rights and right-to-life movements and they tend to work for, and on behalf of, relatively well-funded foundations such as the Manhattan Institute or the Mountain States Legal Defense Fund. Over the long haul, conservative cause lawyering may well enhance one's status and career prospects within corporate America and perhaps within corporate law firms. Conversely, *transgressive* cause lawyering on behalf of "second-generation" rights such as minimum income, health care, and housing, particularly when combined with grassroots organizing and other unconventional tactics, is likely to marginalize a practitioner professionally. Indeed, because second-generation rights are rooted in social democratic traditions with redistributive implications, transgressive cause lawyers are sometimes deemed subversive, and may find themselves marginalized politically as well as professionally.

[*See also* Civil Rights and Civil Liberties; Lawyers, Popular Perceptions of]

• David Luban, *Lawyers and Justice: An Ethical Study*, 1988. Gerald P. Lopez, *Rebellious Lawyering: One Chicano's Vision of Progressive Law Practice*, 1992. Michael J. Kelly, *Lives of Lawyers: Journeys in the Organizations of Practice*, 1994. Austin Sarat and Stuart Scheingold, eds., *Cause Lawyering: Political Commitments and Professional Responsibility,* 1998. William H. Simon, *The Practice of Justice: A Theory of Lawyers' Ethics,* 1998. Austin Sarat and Stuart Scheingold, eds., *Cause Lawyering and the State in a Global Era,* 2001.

—Stuart A. Scheingold

CENSORSHIP. *See* Speech and the Press, Freedom of.

CEREMONY, COURT. *See* Judge.

CHAIN GANG. *See* Prisons and Jails.

CHARTER, CORPORATE. *See* Corporation.

CHASE, SALMON PORTLAND, born in Cornish, New Hampshire, 13 January 1808, died in New York, New York, 7 May 1873. Chase was a successful lawyer in Cincinnati, Ohio and an unrelenting opponent of *slavery. From the 1830s onward he represented numerous fugitive slaves and their abolitionist allies, and by the late 1840s was known as the "attorney general for fugitive slaves." His most successful effort involved the defense of the abolitionist publisher James G. Birney, who was charged with harboring a fugitive slave.

From 1842 until 1847 Chase was involved in the defense of John Van Zandt, an abolitionist convicted in a civil trial for helping fugitive slaves who had crossed into Ohio. His brief in the case, running more than 100 pages, was widely distributed as a pamphlet entitled, *Reclamation of Fugitive From Service* (1847). In *Jones* v. *Van Zandt* (1847) the *Supreme Court rejected his arguments that the 1793 fugitive slave law was unconstitutional. In other cases in the federal courts in Ohio, Chase used procedures rules to frustrate masters trying to sue abolitionists for the value of lost slaves. In 1849 a handful of free soilers held the balance of power in the Ohio legislature. They agreed to support the Democrats in organizing the Ohio House, in return for a repeal of the state's black laws and the election of Chase to the United States Senate.

At the end of his six-year term in the Senate Chase became governor of Ohio, where he refused to return to Kentucky a free black who had helped a slave escape to Ohio. This set the stage for the Supreme Court's decision in *Kentucky* v. *Dennison* (1861). Chase sought the Republican presidential nomination, but lost to Abraham Lincoln, who named him secretary of the treasury. In 1864 Lincoln appointed Chase chief justice of the United States, replacing Roger B. *Taney. Chase resisted presiding over the *treason trial of Jefferson Davis, and on circuit voted to quash the indictment. He subsequently presided over the impeachment trial of Andrew *Johnson, but proved to be a weak Chief Justice. He mustered a slim majority to overturn the Legal Tender Act of 1863, only to see his position reversed and legal tender held constitutional in *Knox* v. *Lee* and *Parker* v. *Davis* (1871). In the *Slaughterhouse Cases* (1873), he was unable to construct a majority for his expansive views of the *Fourteenth Amendment.

[*See also* Slavery, Law of; Supreme Court of the United States]

• Frederick Blue, *Salmon P. Chase: A Life in Politics*, 1987. John Niven, *Salmon P. Chase: A Biography*, 1995.
　　　　　　　　　　　　　　　—Paul Finkelman

CHASE, SAMUEL, IMPEACHMENT TRIAL OF. (February–March 1805) Samuel Chase, a signer of the Declaration of Independence from Maryland, a principal author of the Maryland Constitution of 1776, and an associate justice of the U.S. Supreme Court from 1796 to 1811, is remembered as the only Supreme Court justice ever to have been impeached. Following his acquittal, Chase's reputation cycled through the nineteenth century, when he was regarded as one of Maryland's greatest lawyers, and the twentieth century, during most of which he was regarded as the most prejudiced man ever to sit on the high bench. An objective assessment of Chase would recognize his considerable intellectual ability, his conservative philosophy, and his ardent patriotism, but would also note Chase's nearly pathological ability to enrage his foes.

Chase was the most vigorous champion on the circuit court benches of the 1798 Alien and Sedition Act; he sought sternly to punish the perpetrators of the 1799 rebellion in Eastern Pennsylvania; he actually campaigned for John *Adams while he served as a Supreme Court justice; and he complained, in his grand jury charges following Thomas *Jefferson's election, that the president's party was committed to subverting the Constitution. This did not sit well with the new president, who was already disturbed by the fact that there were so many Federalist holdovers on the nation's courts. Jefferson turned the matter over to his allies in Congress, and sought to preserve a sort of plausible deniability, in his efforts to appear presidentially above the fray. It seemed evident that if the Jeffersonians succeeded in removing Chase, appointed Chief Justice John *Marshall would probably have been their next target.

On March 12, 1804, the House of Representatives voted to impeach Chase, and the House committee presented seven articles of *impeachment that essentially charged Chase with conduct too partisan to be tolerable in a judge. Most of the articles had to do with legal rulings in criminal cases, some against Jeffersonian partisans, in which Chase had excluded allegedly exculpatory evidence, or had restrained the arguments of zealous defense counsel. Perhaps the most important of the charges was that Chase's criticism of the Jeffersonians in a Grand Jury charge had gone too far to go unpunished.

John Randolph handled the prosecution at the Senate trial, and his arguments were generally to the effect that judges needed to be nonpartisan. Still, it was evident that the charges against Chase were also based on ideas about the proper role of judges, juries, and the rule of law that were simply different from Chase's. In other words, he was being impeached for his jurisprudential views and perhaps his assertiveness as a judge, and not because of any crimes he had committed. Chase had superb counsel provided by Federalist lawyers Robert Goodloe Harper and Luther Martin, among others, and they presented a convincing case that whatever Chase's failings as a judge, his conduct could not be construed as the kind of "treason, bribery, or other High Crime or Misdemeanor" the Constitution required for removal. Randolph was capable of occasionally florid denunciations of the Justice, but seemed generally flustered and had little more than a political attack to offer.

Chase effectively testified in his own defense, suggesting that his tormentors were trying to remove him simply because they believed his legal rulings, though made in good faith, were incorrect. To allow them to succeed, Chase and his counsels argued, would be to endanger any judge who sought to apply the law in the face of political pressure. John Marshall testified as a witness for Chase, although he was not particularly forceful, and, at about the time of the proceedings, suggested that perhaps review of the Constitutionality of statutes ought to be for Congress and not the courts, thus engaging in a surprising *volte-face* from his views in *Marbury*. Marshall was concerned about his ability to preserve the Court from the political forces arrayed against it. Although most of the Jeffersonian senators voted against Chase, some did not, and in the final vote of the Senate, the two-thirds majority was not achieved to convict Chase. It would have taken twenty-three votes for conviction, but none of the charges garnered more than nineteen votes.

The flamboyant Chase was somewhat subdued by the experience, and from that time to this no Supreme Court justice has been impeached. The conventional wisdom is that the Chase acquittal stands for the proposition that criminal conduct is requisite for impeachment and removal, but, in the aftermath of the trial, John Marshall's Supreme Court seemed consciously to seek to appear less partisan. Chase and his pre-Marshall colleagues had sought to be "Republican Schoolmasters," warning the people against the perils of demagoguery and the need to preserve wisdom and virtue, but following his impeachment, and until the late twentieth century, judges came to be seen more as politically neutral expositors of the law than active participants in the formation of political philosophy.

[*See also* Impeachment]

• Ralph Lerner, "The Supreme Court as Republican Schoolmaster," *Sup. Ct. Rev.* (1967): 127. Richard E. Ellis, *The Jeffersonian Crisis: Courts and Politics in the Young Republic*, 1971. Stephen B. Presser, *The Original Misunderstanding: The English, the Americans, and the Dialectic of Federalist Jurisprudence*, 1991.

—Stephen B. Presser

CHECKS AND BALANCES. *See* Separation of Powers; Sovereignty.

CHEROKEE NATION V. GEORGIA, 30 U.S. 1 (1831). Prompted in the late 1820s by discoveries of gold, the state of Georgia adopted statutes putting territory possessed by the Cherokee Indians under county court jurisdictions and rendering Cherokee law void. Georgia's aggressive actions clearly threatened tribal *sovereignty. Exacerbating the Cherokees' situation, Congress passed the Indian Removal Act of 1830, which allowed the federal government to force eastern indigenous nations onto lands beyond the Mississippi River. The Cherokees resisted tribal dispossession, and contested Georgia's actions in the federal courts, employing the legal talents of William Wirt and John Sergeant. The Cherokees' legal strategy aimed at constructing a case before the United States *Supreme Court challenging Georgia's assertion of sovereignty over Cherokee lands. The Cherokees directly appealed to the Supreme Court for an injunction against Georgia's actions. Their brief relied upon the Supreme Court's original jurisdiction in cases involving foreign entities. The case encapsulated two key objectives for the Cherokees: federal recognition of Cherokee sovereignty and the protection of it against state government encroachments. Georgia presented no argument while Wirt maintained that the Cherokees constituted a sovereign nation. Writing the majority opinion of the Court, however, Chief Justice John *Marshall denied the Cherokee request for an *injunction. Instead, he described the Cherokees as a "domestic dependent nation," a dubious status for the Cherokees, and Indians in general, that denied them full sovereignty and defined them in relation to the United States as "a ward to his guardian."

Outlining a procedure by which the Cherokees could bring their grievances to the Supreme Court through an appeal from a lesser court, Marshall left an opening for the Cherokees to challenge Georgia's impositions. More importantly, Marshall encouraged two dissenting justices to publish their views. Justice Smith Thompson constructed an argument for Cherokee sovereignty as a foreign nation largely from Wirt's oral arguments. Thompson's dissent would become the basis for the majority opinion the next year in *Worcester* v. *Georgia* (1832), an opinion that acknowledged Cherokee sovereignty.

Cherokee Nation v. *Georgia* has shaped basic American Indian law. The limbo in which this case left American Indian sovereignty attests to its inconstancy as a jurisprudential concept in today's American legal system.

[*See also* Native Americans and the Law; Native American Law and Tribal Sovereignty]

• J. C. Burke, "The Cherokee Cases: A Study in Law, Politics, and Morality," *Stanford Law Review* (1969): 500–31. Jill Norgren, *The Cherokee Cases: The Confrontation of Law and Politics*, 1996.

—John R. Wunder and John P. Husmann

CHICAGO CONSPIRACY CASE. The most important political trial of the Vietnam War era, the Chicago Conspiracy case was a product of four days of riotous demonstrations during the 1968 Democratic National Convention. Approximately ten thousand opponents of the war marched through Chicago, rallied, vandalized property, and taunted police, who retaliated by beating them. Although Democratic Attorney General Ramsey Clark concluded there was no basis for legal action against the demonstrators, under his Republican successor, John Mitchell, a federal grand jury indicted eight of them.

Those it charged were a microcosm of American dissidence in the 1960s. David Dellinger and Rennie Davis were leaders of the National Mobilization Committee to End the War in Vietnam, which had organized the demonstrations. Tom Hayden, a New Left activist and founder of the Students for a Democratic Society, played a prominent role in the protests. Bobby Seale, a last-minute substitute for another speaker, did not, but he was a leader of the dreaded Black Panther party. Jerry Rubin and Abbie Hoffman represented the Youth International Party (Yippies), a manifestation of the dropout culture. John Froines and Lee Weiner were obscure academics who exemplified campus protest. They were charged with teaching the use of incendiary devices. All eight defendants were accused of conspiring to cross state lines with the intent to incite a riot, teach the use of incendiary devices, and obstruct law enforcement.

Their trial was a chaotic spectacle, that featured repeated clashes between the defendants and their lawyers and Judge Julius Hoffman, a thin-skinned septuagenarian. One of these confrontations, triggered by Hoffman's refusal to delay the trial until Seale's attorney could recover from surgery, ended with the Black Panther leader being bound and gagged, given a four-year contempt sentence, and severed from the other defendants. The now Chicago Seven engaged in flamboyant behavior, which included repeated mocking of the judge. Abbie Hoffman even threw judicial robes on the floor and walked on them. The defendants also sought to use the trial as a political forum, countering a prosecution case based mainly on testimony from undercover policemen and a journalism student, with a parade of scholars, artists, and politicians, who represented them as victims of an effort to stifle antiwar dissent.

Their behavior alienated some members of the jury, which initially split eight to four for conviction. On 18 February 1970, jurors returned a compromise verdict, exonerating Froines and Weiner entirely, while convicting the other defendants of crossing state lines with intent to incite a riot but acquitting them of *conspiracy. In addition, Judge Hoffman found the defendants and their lawyers guilty of multiple instances of *contempt, sentencing them to prison terms ranging up to more than four years for lead defense attorney William Kuntsler.

The Seventh Circuit reversed all of these contempt judgments. After a new hearing before a different judge, Kuntsler, Dellinger, Rubin, and Abbie Hoffman were again found guilty but they received no additional jail time. The Court of Appeals also overturned the crossing-state-lines convictions because of errors and misconduct by Judge Hoffman and the prosecutors. The government elected not to retry those five defendants or to bring Seale to trial again. To avoid complying with an order to let him inspect electronic surveillance logs, it also dropped the contempt case against Seale.

[*See also* Kuntsler, William]

• John Schultz, *The Chicago Conspiracy Trial*, 1993. James W. Ely Jr., The Chicago Conspiracy Case," in *American Political Trials* (Michal R. Belknap, ed.), 1995.

—Michal R. Belknap

CHILD ABUSE. *See* Children's Rights; Domestic Violence: Child Abuse; Sex Offenses.

CHILD CUSTODY. For many years, English law followed the Roman tradition of treating minor children as their father's responsibility. Because he was responsible for their support, education, and protection, the father had a right to his child's wages, services, and obedience. Divorce was such a rarity until the nineteenth century that no special rule on child custody was necessary. If the husband deserted the wife for another place or another woman, the child's mother had custody by default. If she deserted, was unfaithful, or simply refused to move when the husband established a new domicile, her violation of marital vows was equated with bad parenting and the mother lost custody.

With the industrial revolution, men more frequently left home to work and child rearing became increasingly women's work. Because divorce, though still rare, was increasing, the early to mid-nineteenth century saw more custody cases. The now ubiquitous language of the "best interests of the child" dates from this period. Custody was associated less often with a paternal right and more often, at least in theory, with marital faithfulness. By the mid-twentieth century, the emphasis was shifting again, this time to the child's need for stability and nurturing. Although still couched in terms of "best interests," cases began to include reference to a "tender years presumption"—that is, the young child's interests would best be served in the mother's care. When working women, who in the 1950s had dropped out of the paid employment market on becoming mothers, began to remain in the labor force after having children, the statutes changed again. In keeping with other legislation written during the mid-1970s' "divorce revolution," these statutes rejected the "tender years" or "maternal presumption" in favor of strict gender equality: "Neither parent is presumed to have any right to custody that is superior to the right of the other parent." (Md. Fam. Code § 5-203(d)(2)).

At the same time, experience with decades of relatively common divorce has revealed the weaknesses of any system that results in the child's effectively losing one parent and of the indeterminacy of the "best interests" standard. Increasingly, states have sought to make both parents responsible, if not for the physical care of the child, then at least for major decision-making. Joint custody, in which the child spends significant time with each parent, has its own costs as well. Frequent meaningful time with both mother and father requires that the parents live in close proximity, a need that may conflict with employment or other goals. Residence with both parents requires a duplication of furniture, playthings, and space that many families cannot afford. Perhaps most problematic, joint custody arrangements require the parents to cooperate in minimizing the disruption to the child. Some of the initial enthusiasm with shared or joint parenting has faded, and a number of states now presume this is best only when both parents agree to it.

West Virginia (followed for a short time by Minnesota) took a different approach to custody, awarding sole custody to the "primary caretaker" parent. Minnesota abandoned this approach in favor of a joint custody presumption, while West Virginia's Code (§§ 48-11-101 to 48-11-604 [2000]) adopted the American Law Institute's approximation formula, awarding custody to parents who cannot come to an agreement on custody in rough proportion to the time each cared for the child prior to separation. The most popular statutes currently mention both the best interests of the child and a need to spend time with both parents. Although most physical custody awards go to mothers, courts usually award joint legal custody. Nationwide, fathers receive physical custody in about 10 percent of cases. A minority of states award joint physical custody in approximately equal shares, i.e., joint physical custody with each parent living with the child approximately half the time.

Child custody rules can advance a number of goals. At different times, these have included the best interests of the child, fairness between the parents, sexual equality, stability for the child, and creation of appropriate parental incentives. An additional concern, which first surfaced in the academic literature in 1979, was more procedural in character. Law professors Mnookin and Kornhauser reasoned that because most divorces are resolved through settlement rather than litigated in court, the vaguer the standard, the more the divorcing parents would be tempted to trade custody time for money. Women, who might be more "risk averse"—that is, more apt to accept unfair bargains in order to avoid the risk of losing custody completely—could be disadvantaged by such trades. Although subsequent empirical work, including that of Mnookin, has not revealed such trading, the concern continues to lurk in the background of custody reform, particularly for feminists. The case of *Garska* v. *McCoy* (1981), in which West Virginia moved to the "primary caretaker" presumption, was based primarily on this reasoning. Custody rules also should minimize litigation itself, since litigation involves expensive expert testimony, results in particularly acrimonious post-divorce relationships, and can be very traumatic for the child or children involved, especially if they are asked to testify.

In the typical case, physical custody is awarded to one parent and the other receives "liberal visitation" rights. "Liberal visitation" usually means one evening during the school week, every other weekend, alternating holidays, and two weeks during the summer. If the parents live too far apart for such an arrangement, visitation may be less frequent and for longer times. Some parents frequently litigate the timing and detail of visitation. Reported cases particularly involve religious training and practices during visitation when the parents are of different religions. Increasingly, the custodial parent wishes to relocate for job or other reasons. Most states grant permission for such a move so long as it is for a legitimate purpose. If the relocating parent can afford it, he or she may have to bear some of the transportation expense to accommodate visitation by the other parent.

Some cases and some academic writing have suggested tying the issues of visitation and child support. Most courts are unwilling to do this and continue to permit visitation by parents who are behind or delinquent in child support payments as well as to require payment even if the custodial parent limits visitation or makes it difficult. In some egregious cases of obstruction of visitation, the courts have ordered changes in custody. Tort actions may also be available when one parent takes the child out of the country and refuses to return the child.

Historically, courts were very concerned about the morality of the parents in child custody cases. In particular, *adultery or promiscuity meant an award of custody to the other parent. The modern rule is to change custody (or limit visitation) on moral grounds only when the complaining parent can show the behavior adversely affects the child. Although states are not uniform in their treatment of this issue, the same rules generally apply to heterosexual and same-sex conduct. Racial differences usually cannot be considered in making custody determinations since the Supreme Court case of *Palmore* v. *Sidoti* (1984). The exception to this rule is the Indian Child Welfare Act (25 U.S.C. §§ 1901-1963), which gives tribal courts custody jurisdiction when at least one parent shows ties to the tribe (see NATIVE AMERICANS AND THE LAW). Finally, domestic violence continues to be relevant, and in some states determinative, for child custody outcomes. Violence or sexual abuse directed against the child demonstrates unfitness. Physical violence directed against the other parent certainly makes continued parental interaction problematic. If the minor child has witnessed the violence, the trend is to sharply restrict the perpetrator's custody, in part because marital violence has intergenerational effects, and in part because children of parents who are violent with each other tend to become victims of parental abuse

themselves (see DOMESTIC VIOLENCE: PARTNER ABUSE; DOMESTIC VIOLENCE: CHILD ABUSE).

Beginning with the Supreme Court case of *Stanley* v. *Illinois* (1972), unmarried fathers who have established relationships with their children (and who therefore have constitutional rights to assume parental rights and responsibilities) have increasingly become custodial parents. Before the decision in *Troxel* v. *Granville* (2000), many states allowed visitation rights for grandparents, stepparents, and other third parties. Since *Troxel*, some statutes have been rewritten to circumscribe access and others have been found unconstitutional because they interfere with parental autonomy.

Although the Supreme Court has made it clear that fit parents have constitutional rights to custody, states continue to implement procedures to enhance the child's right to the best custodial situation. Statutes frequently spell out a list of factors the judge must consider in deciding which parent should be awarded custody. The guardian *in litem* is a special representative for the child whose role differs from that played by an advocate for the child. The guardian *in litem* does not necessarily do what the child wants, but what is in the child's best interests. The guardian may independently speak with experts or access the child's records, may speak to the child, the parents and teachers, and may examine the various proposed living situations. The guardian may be paid for by both parents or by the court, but is to operate as independently as possible of parental interests. Because custody litigation itself potentially harms children, many states mandate alternative processes such as conciliation or mediation. Others require the parents to view films on post-divorce parenting or on the harm of continued conflict between divorcing adults. A few states have longer waiting periods before no-fault divorces in cases where minor children may be affected.

[*See also* Family Law]

• Joseph Goldstein, Anna Freud, and Albert Solnit, *Beyond the Best Interests of the Child*, 1973. Robert H. Mnookin and Lewis Kornhauser, "Bargaining in the Shadow of the Law: The Case of Divorce," *Yale Law Journal* 88 (1979): 950–99. Jamil Zainaldin, "The Emergence of a Modern American Family Law: Child Custody, Adoption, and the Courts, 1796–1851," *Northwestern University Law Review* 73 (1979): 1038–89. Michael Grossberg, *Governing the Hearth: Law and the Family in Nineteenth-Century America*, 1988. Trina Grillo, "The Mediation Alternative: Process Dangers for Women," *Yale Law Journal* 100 (1991): 1545–1610. Elizabeth S. Scott, "Pluralism, Parental Preference, and Child Custody," *California Law Review* 80 (1992): 615–

72. Mary Ann Mason, *From Father's Property to Children's Rights*, 1994. American Law Institute, *Principles of Family Dissolution: Analysis and Recommendations*, ch. 2, 2001.
— Margaret F. Brinig

CHILD LABOR. *See* Labor Law: Workplace Issues.

CHILDREN'S RIGHTS. In virtually every legal realm in which adults are regarded as having rights, children's rights are recognized as well. However, children's rights are typically not coextensive with those of adults because of perceived differences between adults and children and because of social interests that are particularly affected by state recognition of children's rights. Generally, rights can be divided into two categories. "Welfare rights" are rights to be provided for or taken care of; "autonomy rights" are rights to make choices and decisions for oneself. Children receive much greater legal protection for welfare rights than do adults, but often their autonomy rights are more limited. Similar justifications are given for both kinds of differences.

First, by comparison with adults, children are generally regarded as dependent, immature, and having diminished capacity for reasoning and judgment. Therefore they have greater claims against others to be provided for, but less claim to autonomy. This empirically based argument certainly contains much truth. No one seriously doubts that young children cannot provide for their basic needs and are unable to make decisions about important matters that are consistent with their own interests. On the other hand, empirical studies show that by the time children reach early adolescence, their ability to make many kinds of decisions approximates that of adults. Yet adolescents' autonomy is still limited compared with that of adults, and they still have welfare claims that adults do not have.

Second, children's rights are different from those of adults because society advances other interests by making the distinction. Recognition of children's welfare rights and limitations on their autonomy are often justified as necessary to protect social interests in ensuring that the children grow into healthy, productive adult citizens. Limitations on children's autonomy are also justified as protecting parents' interests in raising their children as they see fit (*Prince* v. *Massachusetts* (1944)). This interest in turn is protected for several reasons: to encourage and facilitate parents' discharge of their responsibility to take care of children, to advance parents' own interest in expressing themselves through parenthood, and to promote diversity as a cultural and political value.

Welfare rights include the right to food, shelter, medical care, education, and the like. All states impose obligations on parents to provide these basics for their children until the age of majority. However, parents have substantial discretion about how to satisfy this duty, and ordinarily the state does not intervene to supervise parental choices unless the child is subject to sufficient harm to be regarded as abused or neglected. With regard to medical care, parents may not withhold lifesaving, efficacious medical care from their children, even in the name of religion. In other situations, parents generally may choose from among all medically approved courses, even when their doctor strongly disagrees with them.

The state supplements parental efforts to provide for children through *welfare cash assistance, Medicaid, Head Start, and other programs. Probably the most important state-provided benefit is education. All states, by constitution or legislation, provide that children have a right to education through high school. While there is no federal constitutional right to an education, Supreme Court decisions establish that where states provide education, they must do so consistently with *due process (*Brown* v. *Board of Education* (1954); *Goss* v. *Lopez* (1975)). Federal legislation requires states to provide free, appropriate education to children with *disabilities (Individuals with Disabilities Education Act, 20 U.S. Code §§ 1400-1485).

By comparison with many other countries, the United States gives parents greater authority over their children and imposes fewer obligations on states to provide for the welfare of children. This is one reason that the United States has not ratified the UN Convention on the Rights of the Child, which was unanimously adopted by the UN General Assembly in 1989 (UN Doc. A/Res/44/25, available at *http://www.unhchr.ch/html/menu3/b/k2crc.htm*).

Children's authority to make decisions for themselves, and *liability for the consequences of those decisions, is recognized, but also limited. While we generally regard the age of majority as the point at which children acquire the right to make their own choices, legal recognition of children's autonomy in fact develops through adolescence. For example, people are entitled to vote when they become eighteen, but in most states they can drive at fifteen or sixteen, though they may not be able to drink until they are twenty-one. Minors younger than eighteen usually cannot enter into legally enforceable *contracts, which means that they can disavow contracts they do purport to enter. However, minors may still be required to pay the fair value of good or services they receive in such transactions. Minors cannot sue or be sued in court in their own name, but they may participate in litigation with the assistance of adults appointed to protect their interests.

The Supreme Court has resoundingly rejected the traditional notion that children may be denied legal protection for autonomy interests until they attain the age of majority. In *In re Gault* (1967), the Court rejected the state's argument that minors charged in *juvenile court as delinquents are not entitled to the protections of the *due process clause because children are always in someone's custody and therefore have no right to liberty. While subsequent cases have upheld state choices to limit some rights of minors in delinquency proceedings, courts have continued to affirm that minors are "persons" for purposes of the Constitution, and are entitled to its protections.

Similarly, the Court in *Parham* v. *J.R.* (1979) recognized that minors have a constitutionally protected interest in physical freedom that is infringed by confinement in a mental hospital, and are entitled to due process safeguards against erroneous commitment. However, the Court concluded that when commitment is initiated by parents, minors are not entitled to the procedural protections given to adults, out of deference to parental authority and to the state interest in ensuring that minors receive needed mental health treatment. With regard to other forms of medical care, state law varies, but ordinarily gives adolescents the right to consent to certain kinds of medical care for themselves, including mental health and drug treatment, treatment for venereal disease, and contraception. In some states, any "mature minor" can consent to other medical care as well.

The Supreme Court has recognized substantial constitutional protection for minors with regard to matters of reproductive choice. In *Carey* v. *Population Services International* (1977), the Court held that a complete ban on the distribution of contraceptives to minors violates due process. A year earlier, in *Planned Parenthood of Central Missouri* v. *Danforth* (1976), the Court held that a complete ban on minors' access to *abortion also violates the Constitution, saying, "Constitutional rights do not mature and come into being magically only when one attains the state-defined age of majority" (428 U.S. Code at 74). In *Bellotti* v. *Baird* (1979), however, the Court upheld rules that limit minors' right to consent to abortions. It recognized that state interests in protecting minors from their own immaturity and supporting parental authority sometimes justify the requirement of parental consent to minors' abortions. However, the Court held that the state could not assume that all minors below a particular age lack the capacity to make decisions for themselves, and required procedures for individualized determinations into the maturity of young women who seek abortions without parental consent. This decision is widely understood as expressing the Court's recognition of minors' gradually emerging autonomy.

The Supreme Court has also recognized that the First Amendment protects minors' rights to freedom of expression in a variety of contexts. In 1943, in *West Virginia State Board of Education* v. *Barnette*, the Court held that Jehovah's Witness children were constitutionally entitled not to say the Pledge of Allegiance. Twenty-five years later, *Ginsberg* v. *New York* (1968) held that minors have constitutionally protected interests in access to information. However, the Court held that their constitutional rights are not coextensive with those of adults, and approved the concept of variable obscenity. Under this concept, a state may define materials as obscene for minors even when the same materials cannot be regarded as obscene for adults. The distinction is based on society's interests in the well-being of children and in supporting parents' decisions about what kinds of materials their children should see. In *FCC* v. *Pacifica* (1978), the Court also upheld federal regulations limiting the broadcasting of material not obscene for adults to times when children were less likely to be in the audience, on a similar rationale. However, in *Reno* v. *American Civil Liberties Union* (1997), the Court held unconstitutional portions of the Communications Decency Act of 1996, which criminalized the knowing transmission of obscene or indecent messages to persons under eighteen. The Court distinguished the case from *Ginsberg* and *Pacifica*, partly on the grounds that the Communications Decency Act banned the distribution of materials that were not obscene for adults, rather than merely channeling their distribution so as to limit minors' access to them.

Several other Supreme Court decisions concern minors' First Amendment Rights within school. While these cases affirm that "Children do not shed their rights at the schoolhouse gate" (*Tinker* v. *Des Moines School District* (1969)), they also uphold limitations on minors' expression that would not be permissible for adults. In *Tinker*, the Court emphatically rejected a school's effort to limit students' political speech. It held that even elementary school children were entitled to express views in opposition to the Vietnam War, saying that the state could impose limits only to protect against significant disruption or invasion of the rights of others. However, in subsequent cases, the Court granted schools greater control over minors' expression in the context of school-sponsored activities. In *Bethel School District No. 403* v. *Fraser* (1986) and *Hazelwood School District* v. *Kuhlmeier* (1988), the Court upheld limits on adolescents' *speech and press rights, which were justified as part of the schools' educational missions. *Fraser* held that imposing school sanctions on a student who gave a vulgar, racy speech during an assembly was justified in order to teach students lessons in civility, and *Kuhlmeier* upheld a principal's censorship of the school newspaper published as part of a journalism class. In both cases, the Court accorded substantial deference to school officials' judgment about what is educationally appropriate and to society's interests in the socialization of children through the public schools. The Court held that school rules that limit student speech are not subject to the same exacting scrutiny that is applied to state-imposed limits on adults' speech and press rights. However, in *Board of Education* v. *Pico* (1982), the Court imposed limits on school board authority to ban books from school libraries, finding that students' First Amendment rights should receive greater protection when they are exercised within the school but outside the classroom. Together, these cases indicate that the Constitution permits schools significantly greater leeway to limit students' expressive rights in the classroom and with regard to curriculum than in the libraries and hallways of the school.

Other Supreme Court decisions recognize the special interest of schools in controlling their students. In two cases, the Court has upheld school searches against Fourth Amendment challenges that would likely have been held unconstitutional in other settings. In *New Jersey* v. *T.L.O.* (1985), the Court held that while the Fourth Amendment protects schoolchildren, searches in school by school officials do not have to satisfy the standards required for police searches. As long as an official reasonably suspects that a student is breaking a school rule or the law, the *search is legal. In *Vernonia School District 47J* v. *Acton* (1995), the Court relied on *T.L.O.* to uphold a school rule requiring all student athletes to submit to random drug testing as a condition of participating in school programs.

[*See also* Civil Rights and Civil Liberties]

• Bruce C. Hafen, "Children's Liberation and the New Egalitarianism: Some Reservations about Abandoning Youth To Their 'Rights,' *Brigham Young University Law* *Review* (1976): 605. Robert H. Mnookin, *In the Interest of Children*, 1985. Barbara Bennett Woodhouse, "Hatching the Egg: A Child-Centered Perspective on Parents' Rights," *Cardozo Law Review* 14 (1993): 1747. Samuel M. Davis, Elizabeth S. Scott, Walter Wadlington, and Charles H. Whitebread, *Children in the Legal System*, 2d. ed., 1997. Douglas E. Abrams and Sarah H. Ramsey, *Children and the Law*, 2000. Robert H. Mnookin and D. Kelly Weisberg, *Child, Family, and State*, 2000. Leslie J. Harris and Lee E. Teitelbaum, *Children and the Law*, 2002.   —Leslie J. Harris

CHILD SUPPORT. *See* Child Custody; Divorce and Annulment; Family Law; Spousal Support.

CHOATE, RUFUS (born 1 October 1799 in Essex County, Massachusetts; died 13 July 1859 in Halifax, Nova Scotia), attorney. With his theatrical style, Rufus Choate was New England's premier trial lawyer and America's first celebrated defense attorney. Rufus was the fourth of Miriam Foster and David Choate's six children. He graduated from Dartmouth in 1819 and attended Harvard Law School. His interest in law stemmed from an encounter with Daniel *Webster, Dartmouth's attorney during the college's 1815 legal controversy with the state legislature of New Hampshire. Choate studied law under William Wirt, then attorney general of the United States, and returned to Massachusetts to prepare for the bar. In September 1823, Choate began a thirty-six-year career during which he accepted a staggering number of cases that covered nearly every aspect of law. Choate specialized in criminal cases, building a reputation as a master defense lawyer who could command a jury. Through a series of widely publicized cases, Choate perfected defense strategies that would later become commonplace. His most celebrated trial was his 1846 defense of Albert J. Tirrell, accused of murdering his mistress in a brothel. Taking advantage of the prosecution's circumstantial case, Choate presented the jury with alternative theories of the crime. In cross-examination he undermined the credibility of prosecution witnesses, an art he mastered over the course of his career. In two widely covered 1857 cases, *Shaw* v. *Boston and Worcester Railroad* and the Dalton divorce trial, he cultivated a theatrical oratorical style designed to influence the juries and used exaggerated rhetoric and humor to discredit opposing witnesses and his opponents' claims. In every case, Choate marshaled as much evidence as possible on points of law. An active Whig who served briefly in the U.S. House of Representatives (1831–34) and the U.S. Senate (1841–45), Choate delivered a eulogy for Daniel Webster that contemporaries lauded as one of the era's great pieces of rhetoric. Webster and Choate were frequent opponents and partners; they teamed for the landmark legal case *Norris* v. *Boston* in 1842, part of the U.S. Supreme Court's *Passenger Cases*. Averaging seventy cases a year by the last decade of his practice, Choate packed courtrooms with observers and reporters while achieving a notoriety unusual for lawyers before the Civil War. His reputation and the proliferation of newspapers in antebellum America helped to create the American taste for courtroom drama. After Rufus Choate, infamous trials became an important part of the emerging mass media and culture of nineteenth-century America.

[*See also* Lawyers]

• Samuel Gilman Brown, *The Works of Rufus Choate, with a Memoir of His Life*, 1862. Jean V. Matthews, *Rufus Choate: The Law and Civic Virtue*, 1980.

—Lorien Foote

CHOICE OF LAW. *See* Conflict of Laws.

CHURCH AND STATE. The U.S. *Constitution does not mention God, Christianity, or anything else even remotely connected with any one church or particular *religion. The only references the Constitution makes to religion actually *constrain* government power to act on behalf or against religion. Article 4 states that "no religious Test shall ever be required as a Qualification to any Office or public Trust under the United States." This provision, also known as the *Test Oath Clause*, deprived the federal government of a potentially quite powerful tool of *discrimination. The framers held many different conceptions of what religious *liberty meant, and those differences emerged with great force during the debate over the language of the *Establishment and Free Exercise Clauses of the First Amendment*. But none of the delegates to the Constitutional Convention of 1787 contested the Test Oath Clause; few Americans during the period leading up to the ratification of the Constitution believed the federal government should have any power over religion.

Likewise, the First Amendment provides an explicit constraint on the federal government's power to interfere with religious liberty. Historian Thomas Curry has noted that the states would have been unable to reach agreement on a single definition of religious liberty, but, as with the Test Oath Clause, they agreed that Congress should have no power to meddle in the affairs of religion. Beyond a consensus that Congress and, by extension, the federal government, should steer clear of religion, Americans, including several key framers of the First Amendment, held wildly varying conceptions of the proper relationship between church and state. To some, establishment of religion meant placing state authority behind a single religion (*preferential establishment*), taxing citizens to support its churches and ministerial functions, and allowing a single religious denomination to maintain control over state and local political arrangements. But it was completely acceptable to permit "multiple establishments of religion (*nonpreferential establishment*), or state laws that provided general aid to religion. Many Americans, however, disagreed with both preferential and nonpreferential forms of religious establishment, believing that neither the federal government nor the states should support religion on any level. Yet almost all Americans understood freedom of religion as most Protestant Christian reformers had defined it over the years: the freedom to follow one's conscience to the truth of Christ.

On the other hand, the framers took great care to extend religious liberty to groups beyond the Protestant majority. Catholics, Jews, Mormons, and other religions "peculiar" and "foreign" to the Protestant sensibilities of the framers were denied civil and political rights, such as the right to vote and the right to hold public office, from the colonial period until the late nineteenth century. More generally, they were viewed as something less than American by many Protestants. But the right of persons to worship according to the dictates of their conscience was protected. Only in cases when religious conduct breached the civil peace were state governments permitted to limit liberty of conscience. In sum, the Constitution did not require American citizens to believe in God, to profess faith in Christianity, or to support any religion, including their own, with tax dollars.

Of course, most Americans did believe in God and professed faith in Christianity when the Constitution and the *Bill of Rights were ratified, leading some scholars to conclude that the new constitutional relationship between church and state was designed to do little more than protect the diverse and flourishing arrangement of Protestant religious life. Any benefit that flowed to Catholics, Jews, and other non-Protestant or non-Christian religions was purely incidental. But one such incidental benefit was *religious tolerance*, an attitude that over time blossomed into an understanding of the First Amendment that respected the religious liberty of all faiths. The framers and their generation generally did not consider Jews, Catholics, Mormons, and others outside the "Cope of

Heaven" the equals of Protestants, but they also recognized that establishing an official religion was a recipe for civil strife. James Madison, in *Federalist* 51, acknowledged as much when he wrote, "In a free government, the security for civil rights must be the same as for religious rights. It consists in the one case in the multiplicity of interests, and in the other, in the multiplicity of sects." The Test Oath Clause and the First Amendment thus can be understood to embody articles of faith and articles of peace.

Was there something contradictory about the First Amendment's clear intent to prohibit the establishment of a national religion and yet at the same time to permit continued support for religion in state constitutions? By contemporary standards, yes. By the standards emerging in the late 1700s and early 1800s, the answer is less clear. In 1776, only four colonies, Rhode Island, Pennsylvania, Delaware, and New Jersey, had never supported the establishment of religion in any form. New York, Massachusetts, Connecticut, and New Hampshire, on the other hand, practiced what was then a uniquely American Model of religious establishment. Civil authorities in the states protected and supported multiple churches. Respect for multiple establishments of religion offered a marked contrast to the European model with which most Americans were familiar, such as the Anglican Church, the officially established church of Great Britain. Only the Southern colonies, Georgia, Virginia, North Carolina, South Carolina, and Maryland, had established religion in the European sense. In these colonies, the Anglican Church received the support of government authorities.

After the 1776 Revolution, religious freedom in the United States slowly moved toward complete *disestablishment*, or the removal of government support for religion. In 1777, New York repudiated all establishments of religion. In 1833, Massachusetts repealed its state constitutional provision establishing religion, beginning the process of disestablishment throughout the region. In the Southern states, the European model soon collapsed entirely; by 1810, Georgia, Maryland, and South Carolina had all withdrawn their legal and financial support for multiple establishments of religion. South Carolina even guaranteed the free exercise of religion for Jews and Catholics. But the most dramatic exercise in religious disestablishment in the early Republic came in Virginia, the home of the First Amendment's two key architects, James Madison and Thomas *Jefferson.

In 1779, Jefferson introduced his Bill Establishing Religious Freedom in the Virginia legislature. The bill prohibited the government from compelling any person "to frequent or support any religious worship, place or ministry whatsoever." Although Jefferson certainly respected the rights of persons to follow their conscience free from government's corrupting influence, he was just as leery—perhaps more so—of a state-sponsored religion's potentially disruptive impact on the secular state. Historians have pointed out that Jefferson made his case for disestablishment, and later a "wall of separation" separating church and state, by using language claiming to free religion in order to help religion. In this sense, Jefferson's arguments were close to those of Roger Williams, the New England preacher who carried the torch of religious liberty in colonial Rhode Island. In 1644, Williams had used the "wall of separation" metaphor to argue against the enforced uniformity of religious belief, writing that government support for an established religion offered the "greatest occasion of civill Warre." Jefferson, in his famous 1802 letter to the Danbury Connecticut Baptist Association, wrote: "I contemplate with sovereign reverence the act of the whole American people which declared that their legislature should 'make no law respecting an establishment of religion, or prohibiting the free exercise thereof,' thus building a wall of separation between church and state."

Whether Jefferson was motivated primarily to help religion, or to protect government from what he believed were the failed lessons of past experiments with support for established churches, is a question that continues to draw the attention of scholars. But few question the tremendous influence that his Virginia legislation had on Madison's equally important statement on church-state relations, the *Memorial and Remonstrance Against Religious Assessments*. Madison wrote the *Memorial and Remonstrance* in response to a countermeasure introduced by Patrick Henry in 1779 that would have permitted a general assessment against Virginia citizens to support teachers in all Protestant churches. Sensing that Baptists, Methodists, and Presbyterians would rise up against what had been the established Episcopal Church, Madison organized a massive drive to defeat the Assessment Bill in 1785. "[T]he same authority which can force a citizen to contribute three pence only of his property for the support of any one establishment," wrote Madison, "may force him to conform to any other establishment in all cases." The *Memorial and Remonstrance* soon became—and has remained—a classic statement of religious freedom in the United States. In 1786, the Virginia legislature enacted Jefferson's Bill Establishing Religious Freedom.

Madison and Jefferson's writings on religious freedom, their prominence in the battle to disestablish religion in Virginia, and their role in crafting the First Amendment have all featured prominently in the Supreme Court's modern interpretation of the constitutional boundaries separating church and state. The Court did not begin to nationalize the principle of church-state separation until the mid-twentieth century. In *Everson* v. *Board of Education* (1947), Justice Hugo *Black, writing for a 5-4 majority, held that "neither a state nor the Federal Government can set up a church. Neither can pass laws which aid one religion, aid all religions, or prefer one religion over another . . . In the words of Jefferson, the clause against establishment of religion by law was intended to erect a wall of separation between church and state." But Black concluded that the New Jersey law contested in that case did not violate the Establishment Clause by providing general transportation subsidies to school-age children, including those attending parochial schools. In concluding that "the wall" separating church and state must remain "high and impregnable," but reaching a result that seemed contrary to his firm *dicta* endorsing the separating principle, Black laid the foundation for future church-state litigation. The Court's posture, however, took a much different turn after *Everson*: by the late 1960s, the Court struck down state-sponsored prayer and bible reading in the public schools (*Engel* v. *Vitale* (1962); *Abington* v. *Schempp* (1963)), banned religious tests to hold public office (*Torcaso* v. *Watkins* (1961)), allowed nonreligious conscientious objections to military service, and prohibited direct subsidies for parochial schools and pervasively religious organizations (*Lemon* v. *Kurtzman* (1971)). The Court's decisions during this time had two important additional consequences for American constitutional law and politics. First, the Court sent a clear signal that state constitutions must conform to a constitutional guarantee that was now firmly national in scope. Second, the qualities of church-state litigation took on an increasingly interest-group driven and directed quality, a dynamic that has become even more plural and contentious over time.

Beginning in the mid-1980s, the Court began to retreat from the separationist impulses that had guided its decisions after *Everson*. In *Lynch* v. *Donnelly* (1984), the Court upheld the right of a municipality to display privately owned religious symbols, including a Nativity scene, on public property. The Court continued to reject efforts to overturn *Engel* and *Abington*, holding in *Wallace* v. *Jaffree* (1985), *Lee* v. *Weisman* (1992), and *Sante Fe School District* v. *Doe* (2000) that state-sponsored prayer in or out of the classroom was unconstitutional, and a majority gradually emerged that was willing to revisit and in some cases overturn its decisions prohibiting governmental financial aid to religion. In *Zobrest* v. *Catalina Foothills School District* (1993), *Rosenberger* v. *Virginia* (1995), *Agostini* v. *Felton* (1997), and *Mitchell* v. *Helms* (2000), the Court narrowed or overruled several key decisions that placed tight reigns on the authority of government to provide financial aid to religion. These decisions took place, perhaps not coincidentally, in a political environment in which conservative religious organizations had assumed a much more powerful position in public policy debates and legislative law making than during the heyday of the Court's commitment to a more absolutist interpretation of the separation principle.

Scholars such as Garry Wills have suggested that Madison and Jefferson would have applauded the Court's decisions limiting government power to support or aid religion and frowned upon its more recent decisions lowering the metaphorical wall between church and state. Both men embraced a vision of religious liberty that went beyond mere "toleration" for less favored religions to one that embraced the equal standing of all religious denominations with special status for none. Other scholars have insisted that neither man ever intended to divorce religion completely from state support and that the First Amendment offered nothing more than a release of federal control over religion with no accompanying substantive definition of religious freedom. Even constitutional scholars sympathetic to Madison and Jefferson as firm church-state separationists have argued that the history of the Establishment Clause permits no clear generalization of what was meant by an establishment of religion. Moreover, the disestablishment of religion in the early Republic was not accompanied by the withering of Protestant values in education and civic life. Religion was also a moral force in early reform movements in American politics, such as temperance, equal rights for women, and the abolition of slavery.

Today, Americans continue to debate the role of religion in public life. The intent of the framers is invoked to justify both support for and opposition to prayer in the public schools, government aid to pervasively religious institutions, and the right of religious ideas to command a place in making public policy. The same themes that occupied the minds of Americans during the formative period of religious disestablishment—religious purity, civic peace, toleration, equality of social status and religion as a moral compass in the secular state—continue to find a prominent place in the Court's decisions involving the constitutional relationship between church and state.

[See also Civil Rights and Civil Liberties; Religion]

• Anson Phelps Stokes, *Church and State in the United States*, 1960. Leo Pfeffer, *Church, State and Freedom*, 1967. Leonard Levy, *The Establishment Clause*, 1985. Thomas J. Curry, *The First Freedoms: Church and State in America to the Passage of the First Amendment*, 1986. Garry Wills, *Under God*, 1990. Stephen Feldman, *Please Don't Wish Me a Merry Christmas: A Critical History of the Separation of Church and State*, 1997. Stephen V. Monsma and Christopher J. Soper, *Equal Treatment of Religion in a Pluralistic Society*, 1998.

—Gregg Ivers

CINEMA. *See* Arts, Popular Culture, and Law: Entertainment Law; Media and the Law.

CITIZEN'S ARREST. *See* Arrest.

CITIZENSHIP. Throughout American history, citizenship has proved to be an indeterminate legal concept. In general theory, the modern concept of citizenship broadly denotes membership in a political community whereby the individual citizen has rights in, and corresponding duties to, that community. But in the contemporary United States, even as a matter of law, the incidence of important rights and corresponding duties has become significantly dissociated from the legal status of citizenship, in principle and in practice.

At least as a matter of legal terminology, however, it is important to distinguish the status of the citizen from that of, respectively, the subject, the national, and the alien. Even today in most monarchies—for example, the United Kingdom—the traditional term *subject* is often used to mean largely what the term *citizen* means in the United States and other republics. The term *subject* distinctively signifies an individual's subordination to the monarch as the head of state. But because in most constitutional monarchies such as the United Kingdom the monarch no longer retains any superiority to its subjects in any important civic capacity, there generally remains little practical difference between the terms *subject* and *citizen*. In America during the British colonial period, most important civic rights and duties were identified with Americans' status as subjects of the British crown. And although there had been some prefiguring developments in the colonial period, the modern American civic ideal of an essentially voluntaristic and egalitarian concept of citizenship emerged only with the American Revolution and its aftermath.

As for the term *national*, in the parlance of modern international relations it is often used indistinguishably from *citizen*. Strictly speaking, however, the term *national* applies to every individual in a territorial nation-state who has a duty of permanent allegiance to that state. Under American law today, not all nationals are citizens, the chief examples being the native inhabitants of American Samoa, Wake Island, or Midway Island, who are classified as American nationals and who do not have all the rights of American citizens. Nevertheless, full citizenship is accorded not only to anyone (except the children of diplomats) born in any of the fifty United States, but also to anyone born in Puerto Rico, Guam, the former Panama Canal Zone, or the U.S. Virgin Islands, and to anyone born into any of the native American tribes or peoples (including Eskimos and Aleuts).

As in most countries, in the United States the term *alien* generally encompasses all persons within its borders who are thereby subject to the authority of its laws but who remain either foreign citizens or foreign nationals and who therefore owe the United States no duty of permanent allegiance.

As a matter of legal terminology, it is also important to note that under certain circumstances the term *citizen* is applied to entities other than individual persons. For purposes of jurisdiction of the federal courts (under Article III, Section 2, of the Constitution), the term is applied to United States *corporations. Moreover, municipalities and some other local governments (but not state governments) are deemed corporations at law.

Whether an individual is a citizen of the United States or of some other country is a question of *international law as typically given effect in American law by the terms of a treaty. International law includes "the law of the flag," which, as recognized under American law, determines whether someone born on the high seas is an American citizen.

As suggested above, American citizenship is most often legally conferred as a birthright, on the basis of place of birth or on the basis of parentage, and thus with reference to the two basic principles of the international jurisprudence of citizenship: the *ius soli* (right of land, or ground) and the *ius sanguinis* (right of blood).

Citizenship is also often acquired by naturalization, a legal process that has proved especially important to the United States in its historic character as a nation of immigrants. The United States Constitution (Article I, Section 8) authorizes Congress to enact uniform national laws for naturalization. These laws have thus historically reflected prevailing *national immigration policy, taking into account changing concerns and attitudes about matters ranging from labor supply, national security, and public health to ethnicity, foreign nationality, and other factors, political or more broadly cultural. These laws are implemented and administered, under rules set by the attorney general, by the Immigration and Naturalization Service, on whose recommendations citizenship is officially conferred on qualifying petitioners by a federal court. To qualify for naturalization, an immigrant must typically meet the following requirements: lawful entry into the United States for the purpose of "permanent residence"; ensuing residence in the United States for five years (three years for spouses of American citizens); residence of six months in the federal judicial district of naturalization; and demonstration of good moral character, devotion to the Constitution, and sufficient basic knowledge of American history, government, and the English language. Traditionally, however, there have been various special exceptions to these requirements—for example for military veterans or for other special classes of persons as designated from time to time by Congress or the State Department.

Although today everyone within the jurisdiction of the United States is accorded most of the rights and protections of the Constitution, certain rights have been traditionally associated with—even when not conferred with or reserved to—American citizenship. These include the right to vote, to own and convey property, and to serve in government offices and other public employment. Some of these rights, and some important privileges of foreign travel and extraterritorial protections, have been or continue to be denied to legal aliens, regardless of their period of residence in the United States. Nevertheless, all "permanent resident aliens" share with citizens the duty to contribute to the defense of the United States against foreign enemies, to pay applicable taxes, and to obey the law. Only citizens are subject to jury duty.

The sole express distinction in the Constitution between naturalized and natural born citizens is that naturalized citizens are disqualified from the office of president (Article II, Section 1). But historically, Congress has made, and the federal courts have upheld, distinctions subjecting naturalized citizens to loss of citizenship on grounds not applied to the natural born. For example, until recently, the Immigration and Nationality Act of 1952 (often referred to as the "McCarran-Walter Act") subjected to loss of American citizenship any naturalized citizen who resided in any foreign country for five years or in his country of birth or previous nationality for three years. The policy underlying these provisions for denaturalization was to revoke the citizenship of any naturalized citizen who called into question the good faith of his earlier transfer of fundamental allegiance to the United States. But the United States Supreme Court has in recent years found that the Constitution significantly restricts denaturalization, even in some cases of evident disloyalty or foreign allegiance.

The volitional essence of American citizenship has been historically evident in the various legal grounds that have been adduced for the loss of citizenship of any citizen, whether nauturalized or natural born. These grounds have included the following voluntary actions: becoming a naturalized citizen of any foreign country, serving without American authorization in any foreign military, working for any foreign government in any other unauthorized capacity, voting in any foreign election, renouncing (except in some circumstances) American nationality, being convicted of *treason against the United States, impermissibly avoiding military conscription, and deserting military service. But not only has the United States Supreme Court held some of these provisions unconstitutional, it has questioned the constitutionality of any legal provision for the forfeiture of American citizenship, by either a natural born or naturalized citizen, unless the government meets exacting standards of proof of the specific intent of the individual to abandon, relinquish, or renounce his citizenship (*Afroyim* v. *Rusk* (1967)).

Unlike some other countries, the United States has traditionally recognized among the rights of American citizenship the affirmative right to relinquish citizenship through voluntary expatriation. Indeed, this distinctive recognition of the volitional essence of American citizenship became manifest in 1868 when Congress declared the right of expatriation to be a fundamental right of citizenship.

As a matter of international relations, the status of dual (or even multiple) nationality or citizenship can result from the conflicting nationality and citizenship laws of respective nation states. Numerous provisions of international law already address problems posed by such conflicting laws. And although the United States government has discouraged such dual/multiple nationality and citizenship, it has customarily tolerated them, and even afforded them legal protections.

Given the structure of the United States as a federal union, the instrinsically dual citizenship of individuals—both in the nation and in one of the constituent states—became a problematic constitutional norm from the outset. Although, at the late-eighteenth-century founding the Constitution placed exclusive authority for naturalization in the national government, the Constitution otherwise left the law of citizenship to the respective state governments. Thus there was at least, in principle, the problem that while every citizen of a state was also a citizen of the United States, a naturalized American citizen might never become a legal citizen of any of the states constituting the federal union. And every state had the authority to grant state citizenship without regard to United States citizenship. Such problematics reached a historic climax in the case of *Dred Scott* v. *Sanford,* (1857), in which the United States Supreme Court decided that under the Constitution no American "Negro, slave or free, was a citizen, nor could the national or any state government make a Negro a citizen. This landmark judicial decision became important in the events leading up to the Civil War; and it ultimately led to the adoption in 1868 of the *Fourteenth Amendment, which provides that, "All persons born or naturalized in the United States, and subject to the jurisdiction thereof, are citizens of the United States and of the State wherein they reside." But the Amendment itself does nothing to define the substantive meaning of American citizenship in general.

Nor does the original Constitution, as ratified in 1791. It does, however, include four express references to citizenship: Article I requires that all members of Congress be citizens of the United States. Article II requires that the President be a "natural born" citizen. Article III grants to the federal courts jurisdiction over all United States citizens. And Article IV guarantees to the "Citizens of each State . . . all Privileges and Immunities of Citizens in the Several states."

Subsequent to the Fourteenth Amendment, four additional amendments added express references to citizenship, whereby a citizen's right to vote is guaranteed without regard to *race (Fifteenth Amendment), *gender (Nineteenth Amendment), payment of a poll tax (Twenty-fourth Amendment), or age if eighteen or older (Twenty-sixth Amendment).

Despite the many cases that have variously called for interpretation of the references to citizenship in the text of the Constitution, the United States Supreme Court has not played much of a role in giving substantive legal meaning to the concept of citizenship. The Court has typically left it to Congress to determine, as a matter of contingent policy rather than fundamental principle, what it means in terms of rights and duties to be a member of the American community. Moreover, in its decision in the *Slaughterhouse Cases* (1873), the Court held that all *"privileges and immunities" that are predicated on state citizenship are, under the Fourteenth Amendment, beyond the reach of any branch of the national government. The only ordinary legal duty of American citizenship to perform a public service is the adventitious duty to serve on a jury, and the only rights constitutionally reserved to American citizenship concern two discretionary, although basic, political activities—*voting and office-holding.

The sovereign constitutive agency of American constitutionalism has remained from the outset not the American citizenry, as it has been variously reconstructed over time in positive law by Congress and the federal courts; rather, as the very Preamble of the Constitution declares, sovereign authority remains ultimately and exclusively with "the People of the United States." Accordingly, the most fundamental political and civil rights of individuals have been held to be constitutionally secured—most notably in the Bill of Rights—to all "people" or "persons" in America, without regard to citizenship status. And in interpreting the constitutional principles of *due process and *equal protection, which shape so much of the contemporary legal American culture of rights, the United States Supreme Court has even extended the rights of every American person, citizen or noncitizen, to include some important economic rights. For example, the Court has held that the states, solely in consideration of citizenship status, cannot deny access to public education, certain state-licensed professions, or certain permanent civil service jobs.

Congressional *welfare reform legislation in 1996, denying federal welfare benefits to future immigrants, evinces a historic challenge to the modern American constitutionalization of important economic as well as political and *civil rights for all members of American society regardless of citizenship. Whether or not this legislation augurs further changes in national policy, in principle contemporary American civic culture would seem to be generally oriented toward ideals and practices of political, social, and economic community in which the legal status of citizenship per se means, and counts for, less and less.

The concept of citizenship in Anglo-American constitutional culture has now long been generalized beyond its traditional associations with formal legal status. This broadening of the civic meaning of citizenship—beyond the matter of strictly legal status in a national state—has come from wide-ranging consideration of what constitutes both effective and affective membership in a modern political community. This functional meaning of American citizenship as membership in the American community is evident in the development of constitutional jurisprudence at least as far back as the Civil War era. And the same functional, developmental approach to understanding what citizenship means in terms of a widening range of operative rights is at the heart of the classic general theory of modern citizenship formulated by the English sociologist T. H. Marshall.

Most notably in his 1949 essay "Citizenship and Social Class," Marshall approached the modern concept of citizenship as comprising three analytically distinct elements: the "civil" (or legal), the political, and the "social" (or socioeconomic). And taking citizenship to be essentially a "principle" of equality and social class to be, by definition, a "system" of variable inequality, he traced the historical development of modern citizenship, from its early-modern origins in "civil" (that is, legal) rights to its increasing modern significance in terms of political rights and then also social and economic rights.

This functional, historical approach—emphasizing the importance of the changing political, social, and economic contexts of law—has for some time come to shape the concept of American citizenship. But the prevalence of functional, *de facto* concepts of citizenship—what citizenship means in practice, in fact—has not marked the end of traditional concern over what citizenship means and could mean *de jure*—at least as a civic ideal. Indeed, there is today much interest in developing modern concepts of citizenship as a civic identity that could play an important part in promoting other traditional American civic ideals such as equality, national solidarity, democratic self-

government, and individual self-determination. There is also particular interest in how legal or legalistic re-conceptions of citizenship could reform constitutional jurisprudence in such matters as immigration, civil rights, and *federalism. And, more broadly, there have been re-conceptualizations of citizenship in order to promote a vision of increased popular participation in political life and a reorientation of political discourse away from shared interests and toward shared fundamental values.

Such lively debate—distinctively focusing on the concept of citizenship and drawing on distinctive American traditions of volitional and egalitarian citizenship—testifies to the continuing importance of the concept. And in continuing to dissociate citizenship from narrow conceptions of legal status, this debate reflects the indeterminacy of what the concept of citizenship has meant, means today, and might come to mean.

[*See also* Governance; Social Dimensions of Law]

• John P. Roche, *The Early Development of United States Citizenship*, 1949. T. H. Marshall, "Citizenship and Social Class," in *Class, Citizenship, and Social Development: Essays by T. H. Marshall*, 1964. James H. Kettner, *The Development of American Citizenship, 1608–1870*, 1978, repr. 1984. Peter H. Schuck and Rogers M. Smith, *Citizenship Without Consent: Illegal Aliens in the American Polity*, 1986. W. R. Brubaker, ed., *Immigration and the Politics of Citizenship in Europe and North America*, 1989. Judith N. Shklar, *American Citizenship*, 1991. Bruce A. Ackerman, *We the People*, 2 vols., 1991–98. Richard C. Sinopoli, *The Foundations of American Citizenship: Liberalism, the Constitution, and Civic Virtue*, 1992. Samuel H. Beer, *To Make a Nation: The Rediscovery of American Federalism*, 1993. Martin Bulmer and Anthony M. Rees, eds., *Citizenship Today: The Contemporary Relevance of T. H. Marshall*, 1996. Rogers M. Smith, *Civic Ideals: Conflicting Visions of Citizenship in U.S. History*, 1997.

—Stephen A. Conrad

CIVIL DISOBEDIENCE. Since the American Revolution, civil disobedience has been a recurring theme in the nation's history. The Boston Tea Party of December 1773 provides a well-known example of the citizenry's zest for such disobedience. Indeed, one could reasonably argue that the Revolution of 1776 was itself a well-organized and large-scale act of civil disobedience.

Supporters of the abolition of *slavery often asserted that laws requiring the involuntary return of fugitive slaves violated *natural law and therefore did not command obedience. Abolitionists routinely flouted federal laws requiring the return of escaped slaves from free states. Some state governments were themselves intransigent regarding enforcement of the Fugitive Slave Clause of the U.S. Constitution (Art. IV, §2, cl. 3) and federal legislation enforcing this clause. Abolitionists argued that efforts to require complicity in the continuing practice of human slavery were fundamentally unjust and, therefore, void.

More recently, civil disobedience played a central role in the efforts of African Americans to end racial *segregation in the South. Organizations such as the Southern Christian Leadership Conference (SCLC) and the National Association for the Advancement of Colored People (NAACP) often engaged in acts of civil disobedience to protest the systematic denial of basic human rights to literally millions of African-American citizens.

The Vietnam War era featured a continuation and expansion of acts of civil disobedience to protest government policies. The ubiquitous burning of draft cards and college campus sit-ins characterized this period.

The American penchant for lawbreaking as a means of calling attention to perceived injustices continues. Antiabortion protestors and members of the self-described "militia" movement routinely engage in acts of civil disobedience to call attention to their causes. For the antiabortion movement, acts of civil disobedience run from the relatively mundane (such as impeding access to family planning clinics) to the egregious (such as killing physicians who perform abortions). Members of the *militia movement and Christian Identity movements similarly have embraced acts of domestic terrorism to get their viewpoints across when government, in their view, has failed to respect their policy preferences.

Currently, leftwing protestors concerned about globalization and the increasing power of transnational corporations have disrupted meetings of the World Bank and World Trade Organization. Greenpeace routinely engages in unlawful protest activities to advance its environmentalist agenda. In sum, civil disobedience as a form of direct political action is alive and well in the contemporary United States.

Many people commonly assume that the U.S. legal system facilitates acts of civil disobedience by excusing, or at least treating less harshly, otherwise unlawful acts undertaken to advance a political or ideological cause. As a formal matter, this is simply not the case. U.S. law, both at the federal and state level, does not excuse unlawful activities because the person responsible for the activities

wishes to communicate a grievance. As a matter of law, a person engaged in acts of civil disobedience risks the full sanction of criminal and civil laws.

However, governmental institutions and personnel charged with enforcing the law can (and sometimes do) turn a blind eye toward acts of civil disobedience. Jury nullification presents the most basic, and perhaps most common, example of this phenomenon. In most U.S. jurisdictions, and in both federal and state courts, juries may refuse to convict criminal defendants for reasons wholly unrelated to the strength or weakness of the government's case. If a jury disagrees with the application of the law in some particular context, its members have the raw power to acquit defendants notwithstanding the evidence against them.

Of course, jury nullification is hardly an unqualified social good. For example, racist jurors in the 1960s (and before) would often refuse to convict defendants charged with criminal *civil rights violations, including assault, battery, and even murder. In some important ways, jury nullification not only facilitates civil disobedience, but itself constitutes a legally sanctioned form of civil disobedience.

Prosecutors also may excuse civil disobedients from answering legally for their unlawful actions. Because state prosecutors are almost always popularly elected officials, groups engaged in civil disobedience in the service of a politically popular cause are unlikely to be prosecuted, even if the police arrest them. Politically astute prosecutors simply decline to press criminal charges for the unlawful behavior. Of course, such leniency would not likely be forthcoming for politically disfavored groups.

Even when prosecutors elect to bring cases against people engaged in civil disobedience, judges sometimes bend the rules to avoid punishing them if they are associated with causes that the judges believe to be just. For example, in *Brown v. Louisiana* (1966), the United States Supreme Court struck down criminal breach of the peace convictions associated with a sit-in at a segregated public library in Clinton, Louisiana. Strictly speaking, the arrests were perfectly lawful: a group of African-American young men refused to leave the library after being instructed to do so by the librarian on duty. Instead, the group stood by the circulation desk in a silent protest against the town's policy of segregation.

The Supreme Court, sympathetic to the protestors, characterized the trespass as expressive conduct, and held it to be protected under the First Amendment's guarantee of freedom of *speech. The Supreme Court was, however, not always so sympathetic toward minorities challenging segregation through direct action.

In *Adderly* v. *Florida* (1966), a protest outside a Florida county jail resulted in mass arrests for criminal trespass. The protestors were attempting to call attention to racist practices by local law enforcement personnel in Tallahassee, Florida. Notwithstanding the unconstitutional nature of the police practices, the criminal convictions stood. The Supreme Court was less willing to tolerate mass protests outside a county jail than in a public library. In a facile move, the justices found mass protest at a county jail to be unprotected conduct, while characterizing a civil rights protest in a local public library as protected speech activity.

Even pure speech activity can serve as the basis for criminal prosecution when the speakers lack the appropriate permits for a particular demonstration. In *Walker* v. *City of Birmingham* (1967), the Supreme Court upheld contempt of court convictions against SCLC civil rights protestors who violated a state court injunction enforcing an unconstitutionally vague permit requirement. Although the justices undoubtedly sympathized with the SCLC's cause, they could not bring themselves to excuse a flagrant disregard of a direct court order (albeit an order that itself could not withstand constitutional scrutiny). *Walker* helps to illustrate the general reluctance of judges, even federal judges, to create legal excuses for acts of civil disobedience.

Although there are numerous rationales for engaging in acts of civil disobedience, Dr. Martin Luther King Jr., offered one of the most persuasive theories in his 1963 "Letter from a Birmingham Jail." Dr. King posited the existence of two basic types of laws: "just laws" and "unjust laws." Just laws incorporate and reflect "the moral law or the law of God." Conversely, an unjust law contradicts the moral law. King argued that just laws "uplift human personality" whereas unjust laws "degrade" human personality. King asserted that laws creating and enforcing policies of segregation constituted plainly "unjust" laws and therefore did not command obedience.

Members of the political majority write both just and unjust laws—the key distinction between them rests on the scope of their application. Just laws apply to all persons within the community evenly, whereas unjust laws apply only to selected groups within the community King meant that laws should not treat citizens differently for reasons that do not advance a legitimate government purpose. In his view, the distinction between just and unjust laws was the difference between "sameness made legal" and "difference made legal." Of course, a just law could prove to be unjust in its application.

Dr. King advocated disregarding only unjust laws. King emphatically decried any general intention to break the law, for doing so would be on a moral plane with the rabid segregationist and would put the entire community on a path toward "anarchy." In the absence of direct action, entrenched power will not respond to calls for a more just ordering of the community. Because freedom is never voluntarily given by the oppressor, King embraced the necessity of direct action (i.e., disregard of unjust laws on a massive scale).

Dr. King believed that elites within the community are unlikely to make concessions to racial or ethnic minorities in the absence of effective pressure for reform. At the same time, however, his definition of just and unjust laws arguably invites individual citizens to make subjective evaluations of the moral status of every local, state, and federal law. Each and every citizen potentially becomes self-sovereign and has no obligation to obey laws that do not comport with his particular understanding of the moral universe.

Many members of the contemporary antiabortion movement and the militia movement view a good number of current laws and policies as immoral and unjust. Of course, if citizens may disregard at will laws they deem unjust, chaos seems a likely result.

Dr. King's theory, however, contains two important limitations. The most important is his insistence that one who violates an unjust law stand ready to accept the law's sanction for the transgression. Dr. King never suggested that civil authorities should decline to enforce unjust laws; instead, he argued that a person breaking the law must accept the penalty for doing so.

The second limiting principle involves King's definition of unjust laws as those written by the majority, but not binding on the majority. This restates one version of Immanuel Kant's famous categorical imperative: one should always act in such a way that he could will his behavior as a universal principle applicable to all. If the majority writes a law that its members do not plan themselves to observe, the law would be unjust. Such a law would be an attempt to bind some, but not all, members of the community for reasons unrelated to any legitimate governmental policy.

More radical theories of civil disobedience reject Dr. King's insistence that the civil disobedient accept the legal consequences of his actions. For example, certain extremist elements of the antiabortion movement freely advocate the assassination of medical personnel providing abortion services. Moreover, they assert that those who kill abortion service providers should not be subject to legal punishment for murder. In the same way that Abolitionists refused to submit to what they perceived to be a thoroughly unjust and evil legal order, so too the more extreme members of the antiabortion movement embrace a "by any means necessary" ethic.

The formal response of the U.S. legal system will, for the most part, remain one of formal disapproval accompanied by isolated efforts to leaven the harsher effects of the law for certain civil disobedients (i.e., those whose causes seem particularly compelling to judges, juries, and prosecutors). One could not realistically expect a different response, because the Rule of Law itself simply cannot acknowledge a generalized personal right to disregard the law without consequence. As the famed civil rights judge Frank M. Johnson Jr., once explained, "civil disobedience is simply not like other acts in which men stand up courageously for their principles." This is so because "[c]ivil disobedience necessarily involves *violation of the law,* and the law can make no provision for its violation except to hold the offender liable for punishment."

[*See also* Civil Rights and Civil Liberties; Extralegality]

• Henry David Thoreau, *Walden and On Civil Disobedience* (Owen Thomas, ed.), 1966. Bernard Bailyn, *The Ideological Origins of the American Revolution,* 1967. Judge Frank M. Johnson Jr., "Civil Disobedience and the Law," *Tulane Law Review* 44 (1969): 1. William O. Douglas, *Points of Rebellion,* 1970. Alfred H. Kelly, et al., *The American Constitution: Its Origins and History,* 6th ed., 1983. David J. Garrow, *Bearing the Cross: Martin Luther King, Jr. and the Southern Christian Leadership Conference,* 1986. Martin Luther King Jr., *I Have A Dream; Writings and Speeches that Changed the World,* James M. Washington, ed., 1992. Malcolm X, *By Any Means Necessary,* 2d ed., 1992. Harold Holzer, ed., *The Lincoln–Douglas Debates,* 1993. Stephen L. Carter, *The Dissent of the Governed: A Meditation on Law, Religion, and Loyalty,* 1998.   —Ronald J. Krotoszynski Jr.

CIVIL LAW IN AMERICA

English Common Law. The two principal legal traditions in the contemporary world—the civil law and the *common law—derive from European history. Conventional wisdom states that those countries that trace their legal system to their colonial experience with England, including the United States, have the common law. This overgeneralization hides important civil law influences on American legal history.

The common law became distinct from the historical roots of civil law beginning in the thirteenth century, when England succeeded in developing a judicial organization and procedure that was successful throughout the Anglo-Norman realm. By the fourteenth century, the royal courts, centered in London and also dispensing justice elsewhere via circuit-riding judges and local juries, had the best lawyers in England, trained at the London Inns of Court, and the confidence of the landowning class. Glanvill and Bracton wrote treatises that gave the common law a reasonable coherence, and the judges' wrote opinions reported in yearbooks that kept legal information current.

Roman Law and Canon Law. On the continent of Europe at the time, the main organizing force for law was at university law faculties, which numbered about 50 by 1500. Scholars called "glossators" restored the text of the Roman Emperor Justinian's sixth century *Corpus juris civilis,* and later commentators wrote treatises and provided *consilia,* or opinions, to emperors, kings, judges, baronial families, and prosperous merchants. This gave Roman law a second life, while its inherent system and reason (*ratio scripta*) made it attractive as the authority to resolve disputes appropriate for secular jurisdictions.

Parallel to this development was the emergence of the Roman church's *canon law and court system. Canon law had its own faculty at the university. After Gratian, who prepared the compilation *Concordia discordantium canonum* (1140), sometimes called *Decretum Gratiani* and which systematized the church's rules or canons, scholars worked to refine a rational legal system for the spiritual realm. These two universal systems—Roman and canon law—influenced each other. Canon law was dominant in *family relations, inheritance, and personal *property, but also significant for *contracts and *procedure.

Europe's Reception of Roman Law. The sixteenth century was crucial for the separation of English common law from continental Roman and canon law. By 1500, canon law had been accepted by all Christian peoples because of their allegiance to the Roman church, whose ecclesiastical courts applied it, along with the provision of the right of *appeal to the Rota in Rome. Revived Roman law was easily integrated into the legal systems of southern Europe—Italy, southern France, and the Iberian peninsula—because it had never completely disappeared. Medieval Roman law compilations had helped to preserve Roman law as the personal law of those peoples. Further north, the issue of "reception" of Roman law was debated. Although in German lands the assertion of imperial continuity (*jus scriptum*) with the Roman Caesars was acceptable to the German emperor, Roman law elsewhere was received in its university-developed form as *ratio scripta*, so that by the eighteenth century, shortly before the age of *codification, one could speak (less so in Scandinavia) of a European-wide common law.

England as the Partial Exception. Although the English royal courts were successful in fostering a rational bar and bench, the procedural system—based on writs that had become rigid in the face of social change—needed reform. It was here in the fifteenth and sixteenth centuries that the introduction of Romano-canonical procedure revived English law. First, the English crown's chancellor exercised his equitable jurisdiction in the Court of Chancery to correct deficiencies in the common law courts with remedies such as injunction, specific performance, and contract or will reformation. The chancellor, as a bishop, borrowed liberally from canonical remedies and procedure, using witness interrogation but rejecting the emotional and sometimes-intimidated jury. Second, the English Court of Admiralty used Continental commercial court procedure influenced by the summary ecclesiastical process. As a result, civil law influence in England was significant, continuing in important ways in the seventeenth and eighteenth centuries, and providing a basis for further civil law transplantation into America after United States independence.

The United States at Independence. Although some of the American republic's founding fathers were familiar with European civil law and Roman legal history, most American lawyers knew only English law. But Americans had revolted from a colonial master, and events leading to the War of 1812 maintained a certain Anglophobia, so there was no rush to import English public law, although English private law presented fewer ideological hurdles. Even there, however, federal and state legislatures and courts were pragmatic about which doctrines to accept. English entail—maintaining land with male family heirs, for instance—was rejected as inappropriate for a vast new region in which farmers worked their own land or needed marketable title to generate economic growth.

United States law spread west from the original thirteen colonies. New states borrowed law from older states. Almost everywhere, American settlers pushed the native peoples out and rejected their customs. Louisiana was an exception, since Spanish and French traditions were strong and would not yield easily to the common law. The Louisiana 1808 Digest, derived from Spanish and French legal sources, was an important step in establishing a civil law presence in the United States. Spanish (and later Mexican) law flavored the territories the United States absorbed after the 1846–48 Mexican–American War: Texas, New Mexico, California, and other western states. However, as frontier outposts of the Spanish colonial legal system, the territories' civil law tradition was too weak to survive intact from the English-speaking onslaught, although certain substantive civil law rules such as those for community property and water law were maintained in order to retain settled property rights. Community property has now spread to other states as a superior form of marital property arrangement by comparison with the English separate-property regime.

Two examples of civil law influence in common law states—codification and legal *education reform—will illustrate America's pragmatism toward legal development.

Pre–Civil War Law Reform and Civil Law Codification. By the 1820s, Americans had a substantial body of indigenous legal materials. Joseph *Story (1779–1845) addressed the Suffolk, Massachusetts Bar in 1821 and complained that legal source materials were growing too fast and were too diverse. Story counted 250 volumes of American case law (probably only 170) and feared that they threatened Americans with "being buried alive, not in the catacombs, but in the labyrinths of the law." He also worried about the diversity inherent in each state's independent development of the common law.

Industrialization and westward expansion were well underway by the 1820s. Some jurists criticized English law as unnecessarily mysterious and uncertain, and poorly suited to fit American legal needs. William Sampson (1764–1836), an exiled Irish patriot, denounced the common law before the New York Historical Society in 1823 as "Norman subtleties" and "Saxon barbarity," and called for the enactment of a code. Other lawyers, such as Edward Livingston (1764–1836), a New Yorker who had moved to Louisiana in 1804, condemned *judge-made law as capricious. He believed that judges had too much discretion and had to be restrained by definitive written laws.

These critics spearheaded the notion of law reform through codification. Most early interest focused on the French substantive codes, a product of the intellectual forces responsible for the French Revolution. Both the French Penal Code and French Commercial Code were translated into English in 1811. Henry Dwight Sedgwick (1785–1831) and Joseph Story both favored the French methodology of expressing law as exemplified in the 1804 Napoleonic Code. The French codes also directly affected Louisiana's codification efforts, especially the successor to the 1808 Digest, the Louisiana Civil Code (1825), as well its Code of Practice (1825), both available to common-law jurisdictions in English.

The general American interest in codification was especially strong in New York, which was emerging as the nation's premier commercial center and whose population had tripled between 1800 and 1820. When David Dudley *Field (1805–1894) began his New York law apprenticeship, he studied French and Spanish and traveled for over a year in Europe in the 1830s, observing the continental legal systems. Field's greatest law reform success came as the key member of the New York Commission on Practice and Pleadings, which submitted its draft 391 section Code of Civil Procedure to the New York state legislature in 1848. The French and Spanish influence on both the form and substance of the new Code is significant, and probably made its way to New York through the cultural intermediary of Louisiana and its codes. The New York Code was enacted into law, and together with revisions proposed by the Commission in 1849 became the final 473 section New York Code of Procedure.

The Code's influence, in one of its versions, was pervasive. It was revolutionary because it abolished the English feudal writ and bill system of pleading, replacing it with a single civil action guided by "code" pleading. It implemented the merger of law and *equity—a distinction unknown to civilian procedure, and a source of great confusion and delay. By 1873, more than half the American states and territories had adopted civil procedure codes based on one of the New York versions or the California model. Field's legacy was renewed during the next wave of procedural reform, and emerged in code-like form as the 1938 Federal Rules of Civil Procedure.

Post–Civil War University Legal Education Reform. Prior to 1865, the intellectual origins of American legal training were predominantly English, since most lawyers learned law through the apprenticeship system. But there were still subtle civil influences, such as those that had affected William *Blackstone's (1723–1780) four-volume *Commentaries on the Laws of England*, widely used in American editions and emulated in American law commentaries. The two most important commentators in particular frequently cited Roman and civil law sources. James *Kent (1763–1847), chancellor of New York and a Columbia law professor, published his four volume *Commentaries on American Law* between 1826 and 1830. Joseph Story published nine "Commentaries" on various aspects of American law between 1832 and 1845.

Civil law found its way into the new American law schools. Harvard Law School's rise to prominence in the 1870s was due primarily to the appointment of Charles Eliot (1834–1926) as university president in 1869. He actively initiated reform throughout the university, especially in the undergraduate science curriculum and the law and medical schools. Eliot drew heavily on the German university model, the world's most prestigious in the nineenth century, which he had come to know during his two years of European travels. In appointing Christopher Langdell (1826–1906) as dean in 1870, Eliot found someone who believed that law was a science. The appointment appealed to Eliot's background in chemistry and was consistent with the excitement he had seen in German law faculties with introduction of the Pandectist legal science that would lead to the German Civil Code.

The first fifteen years of Langdell's deanship under Eliot's leadership institutionalized important changes, including a research function similar to that existing in German universities, and the introduction of an instructional method utilizing Socratic dialogue to discuss appellate court cases. Justified as a scientific process to elaborate general, organic principles of the common law, it supplanted lecturing and recitation based on treatises. The reforms of Eliot and Langdell, inspired by the civil law approach to legal education, spread everywhere in the United States, and became the dominant model in the twentieth century. When Prince Henry of Prussia visited Harvard in 1902 to present an art collection to the University's new Germanic Museum, Eliot in his ceremonial remarks acknowledged Germany's contribution to America's universities.

The Twentieth Century. From the end of the nineteenth century until World War I there was an active interchange between German and American legal academics that significantly influenced American *jurisprudence. Roscoe *Pound (1870–1964) was the principal transmitter of German law, which he used to build his theory of sociological jurisprudence.

The *American Law Institute (ALI), created in 1923, took off where legal education ended in trying to make the common law more scientific and less complex. Through its restatements and unification of law projects, the ALI has continued the impulse that first motivated Field in the nineteenth century. Over the years, there have been numerous foreign law influences on several important ALI projects. The best known example is that of Karl *Llewellyn (1893–1962), chief reporter of the Uniform Commercial Code (UCC), and the German law influence on the sale-of-goods Article in the Code. In 1931, Llewellyn had become a member, with Ernst Rabel (1874–1955), of the committee of the Rome International Institute for the Unification of Private Law studying a uniform international sale of goods law, whose 1939 draft uniform law had many similarities to the 1949 draft UCC Article 2 (sale of goods).

From 1933 to 1935, German law faculties lost a third of their members solely because each scholar (or his wife) was Jewish. Some of these legal scholars, such as Friedrich Kessler, Heinrich Kronstein, Stephan Kuttner, Arthur Nussbaum, Max Rheinstein, Stefan Reisenfeld, and Rudolf Schlesinger, emigrated to the United States, where they made major contributions in the fields of *antitrust, *bankruptcy, contracts, *commercial law, *conflict of laws, *family law, *comparative law, canon law, and Roman law.

After World War II, about a score of civilian-trained lawyers emigrated to the United States and took positions on American law faculties, often teaching comparative law as well as bringing their insights to American legal subjects.

The Twenty-First Century. The impact in the twenty-first century of the civil law tradition may be greater, even if unacknowledged, than in earlier centuries. Puerto Rico, an American semi-colony since it was acquired from Spain after the 1898 Spanish–American War, could become a state, bringing with it a complete civil law system with Spanish as an official governmental language. Future waves of non-English speaking immigrants (like the Germans of the 1930s) may also make subtle improvements in areas of the law that are impossible to predict. And certain values inherent in law as a system, such as uniformity, favor the civilian solution of codification. Looking back, one can see that the American approach to law has never been one of blind adherence to one so-called legal tradition or another, but rather to carve out its own solution, piece by piece, as a pragmatic response to economic, political, and social forces.

[See also Common Law; Comparative Law]

• Harold J. Berman, *Law and Revolution: The Formation of the Western Legal Tradition*, 1983. John Henry Merryman, *The Civil Law Tradition: An Introduction to the Legal Systems of Western Europe and Latin America*, 2d ed., 1985. Marcus Lutter, Ernst C. Stiefel, and Michael H. Hoeflich, eds., *Der Einfluß deutscher Emigranten auf die Rechtsentwicklung in den USA und in Deutschland*, 1993. Mathias Reimann, ed., *The Reception of Continental Ideas in the Common Law World: 1820–1920*, 1993. John Henry Merryman, David S. Clark, and John O. Haley, *The Civil Law Tradition: Europe, Latin America, and East Asia*, 1994. David S. Clark, "Tracing the Roots of American Legal Education—A Nineteenth–Century German Connection," *Rabels Zeitschrift für ausländisches und internationales Privatrecht* 51 (1987): 313–33. Id., "The Civil Law Influence on David Dudley Field's Code of Civil Procedure," in Reimann, supra at 63–87. Id., "The Influence of Ernst Rabel on American Law," in Lutter et al., supra at 107–26. Id., "The Stool's Third Leg: Unification of Law in Berlin, Rome, and Washington from the 1920s to the 1940s," in *Aufbruchnach Europa: 75 Jahre Max-Planck-Institut für Privatrecht* 39–50, 2001.
—David S. Clark

CIVIL LIBERTIES. *See* Civil Rights and Civil Liberties.

CIVIL RIGHTS AND CIVIL LIBERTIES. Civil rights and civil liberties should be distinguished. Civil rights are those rights we have, as individuals, to be treated equally with others. Civil liberties are those rights incumbent on government to respect. So, the right not to be discriminated against because of your sex is a civil right, enforceable not only against governmental officials but also against non-governmental parties as well. However, a right to free *speech is a civil liberty protected only from governmental interference. Civil rights are premised on equality or equal treatment; civil liberties are premised on individual freedom or the *liberty to be unequal or different. Their stories are so intertwined that they are often treated together.

As framed in 1787 and ratified by the states, the United States *Constitution protected both civil liberties and civil rights. As for civil liberties, both the new federal government and the states were prohibited from passing bills of attainder or *ex post facto laws. States were also prohibited from jeopardizing individual *property rights by "impairing the obligation of contracts." As for civil rights, although each state determined what individual rights to respect, Section IV of the Constitution stipulated that "The citizens of each State shall be entitled to all privileges and immunities of citizens in the several States."

The absence of a *bill of rights in the Constitution engendered opposition, and supporters in the state ratifying conventions were forced to consent to proposed amendments to accompany the state's ratification. James Madison, as a Congressman fulfilling a promise made in the Virginia convention, guided amendment proposals through the House of Representatives. The one he favored most would have protected liberty of conscience, free press, and trial by jury from abridgement by *both* federal and state governments. Although the House concurred, the Senate did not. The result was ten amendments that embraced civil liberties but, as Chief Justice John *Marshall would rule in the case of *Barron* v. *Baltimore* (1833), that interposed no bar to state action.

There matters stood until after the *Civil War when Southern resistance to making the former slaves equal citizens led Congress to begin the process of Reconstruction. The Civil Rights Act of 1866, the first such legislation in the nation's history, asserted that all those born in the United States and subject to its jurisdiction were United States citizens. These new citizens had the right to make *contracts, to have access to the courts, and to have all the property rights and security enjoyed by whites.

Worries about the constitutionality of the statute led Congress to propose another constitutional amendment. It would embed in the fundamental law the primacy of federal *citizenship and limit the states' ability to discriminate among their citizens. Making the amendment's acceptance a condition of being accepted back into the Union, Congress succeeded in getting the states to ratify the *Fourteenth Amendment. The highly significant first section contained not only the citizenship clause but also three other clauses. States were now denied authority to "deprive any person of life, liberty, or property," as was the federal government under the Fifth Amendment. In addition, states were not to "make any law which shall abridge the privileges or immunities of citizens of the United States; . . . nor deny to any person . . . the equal protection of the laws." With the concluding empowerment clause, the federal government seemed to have new wide-ranging power to protect both civil rights and civil liberties from state abridgement.

The negative idea of liberty—that government was the potential enemy—gave way to a positive idea—that one government could act to ensure the individual's protection from another. Working out this mammoth change in the nature of American federalism required a century, but the basis for the change had been laid in the Fourteenth Amendment.

The Fourteenth Amendment had reversed the decision in *Barron* v. *Baltimore*, because the *due process clause was now written into the new amendment and made binding on the states. The remaining question was whether the amendment's first section imposed any more of the Bill of Rights guarantees on the states. Scholars have continued to wrangle over this issue, but the United States Supreme Court passed judgment on the *"privileges and immunities" clause just five years after the amendment had become fundamental law.

In the *Slaughterhouse Cases* (1873), butchers claimed that a Louisiana law granting a company a monopoly on the slaughtering business deprived them of their ability to work at a lawful occupation, a right they claimed as federal citizens. A bare majority of the Court expressed horror at the breadth of the claim, seeing it sounding the death knell of the federal system. Although the argument touched all the clauses of the Fourteenth Amendment's first section, the greatest hope had been placed on the privileges and immunities clause. The Court's refusal to find such meaning in those words forced future advocates to rely on the due process and *equal protection clauses.

When the Court in 1883 invalidated the Civil Rights Act of 1875 (the first federal public accommodations act) because it sought to regulate individual and not state action, and when the Court in 1896 found that Jim Crow laws did not violate the equal protection clause, the advancement toward the equality of black citizens was substantially halted. Laws that clearly discriminated on the basis of race were invalidated, but custom and official discretion filled in the gaps and permitted such *discrimination to continue. The Fifteenth Amendment, which barred race as a voting qualification, did not prevent the disenfranchisement of blacks in the last decade of the nineteenth century. Although the Supreme Court had no trouble invalidating grandfather clauses, it did approve locally administered literacy tests and poll taxes. Civil rights had suffered a substantial setback.

As blacks were being remanded to the tender mercies of state governments, corporate interests seeking to avoid or limit government *regulation sought protection under the Fourteenth Amendment. By the end of the nineteenth century, the due process clause had been expanded beyond its pre–Civil War procedural meaning to embrace substantive results as well. A Supreme Court that rejected claims that property could not be regulated by government eventually subscribed to the view that the constitutional clause did require that government allow property-holders a fair return on their investment. Government was thus limited in its ability to regulate the individual's property.

The justices also discovered a liberty of contract in the due process clause that further limited governmental regulation.

John Marshall *Harlan, who protested that a color-blind Constitution necessitated the voiding of *segregation laws and the upholding of the Civil Rights Act of 1875, was the first justice to argue that the Fourteenth Amendment's clauses protected far more than property and commercial liberty. In a series of cases, he insisted that all the civil liberty guarantees of the Bill of Rights were made binding on the states by the Fourteenth Amendment. During his long tenure on the Court, Harlan's interpretation received no support.

Throughout the first quarter of the twentieth century, the civil liberties individuals enjoyed still differed from state to state. At times, state courts, in interpreting their own constitutions, afforded individuals certain protections that only later would be nationalized by the United States Supreme Court opinions. Prior to World War I, when the Court began to interpret the free speech and free press clauses in the First Amendment, it heard relatively few cases dealing with the Bill of Rights. The paucity of cases reflected the limited activity of the federal government.

Prior to the Court's beginning a process of case-by-case application of Bill of Rights guarantees to the states, the justices gave a creative reading to the due process clause in two decisions in the early 1920s. Targeting Catholic parochial schools, the Oregon legislature had required all children in the state to attend public schools. In a number of Midwestern states, as a result of anti-German feeling, legislatures had prohibited teaching in any language other than English. The Court invalidated such laws as an infringement of the liberty protected by the Fourteenth Amendment. In the word "liberty," the justices found certain protected rights of parents and teachers.

In 1925, the Court began to make the protections of the Bill of Rights binding on the states by announcing that the free speech clause in the First Amendment now also applied to state action. Opening this door, the justices proceeded to nationalize certain guarantees of the Bill of Rights. By 1937, most of the protections of the First Amendment and the right to *counsel (at least in capital cases) were applied to the states. In that year, the Court tried to sum up why certain parts of the Bill of Rights had been nationalized and other parts had not. Justice Benjamin *Cardozo, in rejecting the argument that the Fifth Amendment's protection against *double jeopardy bound the states, said that it was not fundamental in the

sense that its violation did not shock our sense of justice.

After the Court majority had shifted to favor New Deal and state measures to cope with depressed economic conditions, Justice Harlan Fiske *Stone in 1938 tried to distinguish the Court's new role from its old one. He acknowledged that he and his colleagues would now presume the constitutionality of economic regulations, thereby stripping the individual's property right of any federal constitutional protection. However, legislation that fell within the purview of the protections of the Bill of Rights or that clogged the political process, either by making change difficult or by discriminating against religious, ethnic, or racial minorities, would not be accorded this accommodating presumption. This announcement, made in a footnote to a rather routine case, would characterize the reshaped Court's work into the indefinite future.

The justices' announced willingness to review the way racial minorities were treated resulted not only in the expansion of civil liberties, such as providing a right to counsel and finding that coerced confessions violated due process, but also in a new sympathy to claims that blacks were not being treated the same as whites. As early as 1914, the justices had ruled that economic excuses for failing to provide equal facilities under the separate but equal standard were unacceptable. In the 1930s, the National Association for the Advancement of Colored People (NAACP) began a campaign to expose the inequality of educational opportunities in higher education. In a series of cases, the Court agreed with the NAACP, and made the cost of separateness high indeed. Then, in *Brown v. Board of Education (1954), the justices unanimously abandoned the separate but equal standard.

Compliance was slow in coming, and not until the administrations of John F. Kennedy and Lyndon Baines Johnson in the 1960s did the Executive Department get behind the Court initiative to desegregate the nation's schools. Also in the decade, Congress passed a series of civil rights acts, the most significant of which was the wide-ranging act of 1964 that included a public accommodations section. Legislation dealing with voting rights and housing followed.

Eliminating racial discrimination by law did not reach the vestiges of that discrimination, which were embedded in the society. To combat this discrimination, *affirmative action measures were instituted not only by federal and state governments but also by private corporations. Such action provided real difficulty for the Supreme Court, charged with interpreting a Constitution that respected individual, not group, rights. Affirmative action was based less on actual discrimination suffered by an individual than it was on pervasive societal discrimination affecting all the members of the group. Such programs benefited individuals because of their race; some observers claimed this was only fair; others cried reverse discrimination. The Supreme Court tended to uphold such programs into the mid-1990s, but the new century promised a more searching inquiry into the constitutional justification of such preferences.

What the civil rights movement did was stir other groups in society to seek, through both the judicial and the legislative branches, an end to discrimination based on matters extraneous to individual merit and ability. The most obvious beneficiaries were women. Having only been enfranchised since 1920 with the Nineteenth Amendment, women now attacked sexual discrimination in statutory law. An *equal rights amendment to the Constitution failed, but the Fourteenth Amendment's equal protection clause and the Civil Rights Act of 1964 provided support for their claims to equality. Subsequent modifications of the latter act, along with the supportive work of the Executive branch, have gone far to equalize opportunities in employment and education, including the ability to compete in collegiate team sports.

This focus on the equal protection clause led some legal observers to see a shift in the Court's interpretation of that clause from procedural to substantive, similar to its earlier interpretation of the due process clause. From asking for an equal start, some were now asking for an equal finish.

In 1990, Congress passed the Americans with Disabilities Act, seeking to strike down barriers preventing the disabled from becoming more productive and valued members of society. Access to public places was mandated, and ramps increasingly replaced stairs. When a physically disabled golfer challenged the Professional Golf Association's ban on golf carts, the Court ruled in *PGA Tour, Inc.* v. *Martin* in 2001, that the act required the PGA to make a reasonable accommodation of its rules to allow the golfer to compete in its tournaments (see DISABILITIES LAW).

Beginning, then, with the civil rights crusade of blacks, other groups have sought to have their members accepted as equal partners within the society. The fight along these lines continues. Gays and lesbians strive to overcome prejudice through the force of law, and the United States Supreme Court invalidated a state constitutional amendment that sought to prevent localities in a state from passing regulations designed to prevent discrimination based on sexual preference.

This latter case, *Romer* v. *Evans* (1996), illustrates how the majority is limited in our democratic system. Here the Court overrode the verdict of Colorado voters, ruling that they could not discriminate against a minority. Claims that the democratic majority should have its way and not be impeded by too great a sensitivity for individual rights have often been rejected not only in favor of civil rights but also in favor of civil liberties. The right of the majority or the community, the critics of the Court would say, should be taken into account and balanced against the claims of dissenting individuals, whether the matter be the rights of an accused criminal, the rights of an outspoken prejudiced person, or the rights of an atheist.

Picking up the story of civil liberties where we left it in the late 1930s, the next thirty-two years would see substantial nationalization of the Bill of Rights. The pace picked up in the 1960s with the Earl *Warren Court. Within a period of eight years, the exclusionary rule of the Fourth Amendment, the prohibition against *cruel and unusual punishment, the widening of a right to counsel, and generally the important parts of the Fifth and Sixth Amendments, including in 1969 the protection against double jeopardy, were all made applicable to the states.

Already under attack because of *Brown* and a string of allegedly pro-communist rulings, the Warren Court found its vulnerability increasing with this spate of decisions on the rights of accused criminals. Law enforcement groups argued that their job had been made more difficult and that the social order was threatened. Critics called for justices who would be more sensitive to the rights of the vast majority of law-abiding citizens to be safe in their homes and on their streets.

Changes in the Court's personnel prevented the expansion of some civil liberty guarantees, and, at times, defendants found more extensive protection of their rights in sympathetic interpretations of similar state constitutional protections. However, the Court headed by Warren *Burger in 1972 did find that *capital punishment as applied by the states was "cruel and unusual," and, a year later, building on a right of *privacy the justices first invoked in 1965, that women had the right to choose to have an abortion. This latter decision, *Roe* v. *Wade* (1973), has been the occasion for a searching inquiry into what the Court's role should be. Presidents Ronald Reagan and George Bush (Sr.) sought in their appointments to overturn the abortion decision. Despite this concerted attempt, three of their appointees joined two holdovers from earlier administrations to uphold *Roe* in 1992.

Unlike a right of privacy, the right of free speech is spelled out in the Constitution, but its reach is subject to interpretation. For instance, the Warren Court was skeptical about whether the act of burning the American flag could be considered free speech, but in 1989 and 1990 the Court headed by William Rehnquist found that such burnings were protected speech. When the subject was nude dancing, a bare majority of justices found no protected speech, though attempts to regulate the Internet to protect children from sexually explicit material were deemed to be invasive of free speech.

Feminists and others have questioned the primacy of the free speech protection in American life, arguing that sexually explicit material tends to demean women and that words do indeed wound. Courts have generally not been sympathetic to such attempts to limit free speech, whether the initiative comes from women's groups or those seeking to create a politically correct environment.

Recent controversy has also swirled around another First Amendment freedom—the free exercise of *religion. When the Supreme Court seemed to limit the range of this freedom, Congress passed the Religious Freedom Restoration Act in 1993. Four years later, the Court invalidated the legislation because it had invaded judicial authority to interpret the Constitution. Since the First Amendment contains two religion clauses, the second prohibiting an establishment of religion, federal government action to protect the individual right of free exercise gives rise to a constitutional problem not encountered when nationalizing other individual rights. If the government acts to widen the area of free exercise, does it not prefer religion in a way that runs afoul of the establishment clause? For this reason, the justices, when they can, prefer to treat religious issues as matters of free speech.

Some critics have argued that the emphasis on individual rights in the United States works against the creation of a wholesome community; others have maintained that the community, as much as it can exist in a pluralistic society, must in fact be built on a tolerance for the diversity that the exercise of individual rights ensures. For instance, renewed attention has been focused on the individual's right to own and use property, as some critics call for a revival of federal constitutional protection for a right they see as being imperiled by the representatives of the majority.

Controversy there will be, for the Constitution was framed to house a diverse people, but the survival of the American experiment in nation building necessitates continuing compromise—between the majority and minorities, between equality and individuality, and between claims of civil rights and claims of civil liberty.

[*See also* Children's Rights; Civil Disobedience; Homosexuality and the Law]

• Richard Kluger, *Simple Justice: The History of Brown v. Board of Education and Black America's Struggle for Equality*, 2 vols., 1975. Michael Kent Curtis, *No State Shall Abridge: The Fourteenth Amendment and the Bill of Rights*, 1986. James MacGregor Burns and Stewart Burns, *A People's Charter: The Pursuit of Rights in America*, 1991. Mary Ann Glendon, *Rights Talk: The Impoverishment of Political Discourse*, 1991. Donald W. Jackson, *Even the Children of Strangers: Equality Under the U.S. Constitution*, 1992. Catharine A. MacKinnon, *Only Words*, 1993. Ronald Dworkin, *Freedom's Law: The Moral Reading of the American Constitution*, 1996. Henry J. Abraham and Barbara A. Perry, *Freedom and the Court: Civil Rights and Liberties in the United States*, 7th ed., 1998. Akhil Reed Amar, *The Bill of Rights: Creation and Reconstruction*, 1998. James W. Ely Jr., *The Guardian of Every Other Right: A Constitutional History of Property Rights*, 2d ed., 1998. David A. J. Richards, *Women, Gays and the Constitution: The Grounds for Feminism and Gay Rights in Culture and Law*, 1998. John E. Semonche, *Keeping the Faith: A Cultural History of the U.S. Supreme Court*, 1998.
                                        —John E. Semonche

CIVIL RIGHTS LEGISLATION. Civil rights legislation serves two important functions in the American legal system. First, it provides a remedy for the violation of constitutional rights by governmental officials. Second, it prohibits and provides *remedies for certain kinds of *discrimination committed by private entities and by the government.

In the period following the *Civil War, Congress enacted a number of laws designed to protect the civil rights of the newly emancipated African-American citizens. While some of these laws were later repealed by Congress or invalidated by the U.S. Supreme Court, the two major laws of this period remain in effect today. The Civil Rights Act of 1871 (1983), which is perhaps the Nation's most important civil rights law, provides relief against "persons acting under color of state law" for a claimed violation of federal constitutional and statutory rights. This law enables people to challenge the constitutionality of state laws in the federal courts and to obtain redress against state officials who have violated their federally protected rights. The scope of this law is illustrated by *Monroe* v. *Pape* (1961), holding that the police are liable to the victims of an unlawful home invasion that violated the Fourth Amendment's prohibition against unreasonable *searches and seizures. Although there is no federal equivalent of this law, the Supreme Court has held that the federal courts are empowered to grant relief to persons whose constitutional rights have been violated by federal officials *(Bivens* v. *Six Unknown Federal Narcotics Agents* (1971)).

The other law from this period is the Civil Rights Act of 1866 (1982), which gives "all persons" in the United States "the same right to make and enforce contracts" and to "inherit, purchase, lease, sell, hold and convey real and personal property" "as is enjoyed by white citizens." This law lay dormant for many years because of questions about Congress's power to enact it. However, in *Jones* v. *Alfred H. Mayer Co.* (1968), the Supreme Court held that Congress, acting under its Thirteenth-Amendment power to eliminate all "badges and incidents of slavery," could prohibit racial discrimination in contracting and housing by private persons.

From the end of Reconstruction through the first half of the twentieth century, Congress was completely indifferent to the widespread racial discrimination existing throughout the United States. The Supreme Court decision in *Brown* v. *Board of Education* (1954), which held that state-imposed racial *segregation in the public schools was unconstitutional, sparked the civil rights movement and the demand for racial equality in the United States. Congress responded hesitatingly, but beginning with the Voting Rights Act of 1957, attempted to deal with the long-standing denial of *voting rights to African Americans in the southern states. This culminated with the Voting Rights Act of 1965 (1973), which not only provided for federal officials to oversee the voting registration of African Americans in these states, but required the approval of the U.S. Department of Justice or a federal court for any change in voting laws that would have the effect of diluting minority political power. In 1982, Congress extended the Act to prohibit any state from adopting a law or practice that had the effect of diluting minority political power. Today there is a detailed body of federal law protecting minority voting rights (see *Thornburg* v. *Gingles* (1986)), and any form of racial discrimination in voting is subject to legal challenge.

In the Civil Rights Act of 1964, Congress responded to the demand for racial equality by enacting a comprehensive law prohibiting racial, national origin, and religious discrimination by private persons in places of public accommodation (Title II) and employment (Title VII), and by private persons and governmental agencies in all federally funded programs and activities (Title VI). Opponents of the law tried to defeat it by including a prohibition against employment discrimination on the basis of sex, but the law passed nonetheless, and this kind of employment discrimination also became prohibited. In 1968, following the assassination of civil rights leader Martin Luther King Jr., the law was extended to prohibit discrimination in housing on the basis of race, national origin, religion, sex, handicap, and familial status (Title VIII). In 1972, Congress expanded the law to prohibit employment discrimination by federal, state, and local governments. Congress also prohibited sex discrimination in federally funded education programs (Title IX).

The Civil Rights Act of 1964 has been broadly interpreted to accomplish its remedial purposes. The public accommodation provisions of Title II reach any facility open to the public, such as a community swimming pool (*Tillman* v. *Wheaton-Haven Recreation Ass'n.* (1973)). The employment discrimination provisions of Title VII reach not only intentional discrimination, but any employment practice that has a "disparate impact" on minorities and other protected groups (*Griggs* v. *Duke Power Co.* (1971)). This has resulted in the invalidation of tests and employment requirements that disproportionately excluded minorities and women and were not shown to be job related. The Supreme Court has also upheld the use of court-imposed affirmative hiring and promotional requirements designed to remedy an employer's past systematic discrimination against minorities and women (*United States* v. *Paradise* (1987)). At the same time the Court has held that since the underlying purpose of Title VII was to increase employment opportunities for minorities and women in jobs from which they traditionally had been excluded, Title VII permitted employers to provide hiring and promotion preferences for minorities and women in order to alleviate manifest imbalance in traditionally segregated job categories. These preferences must be reasonable and must not "unfairly trammel" the interests of white or male employees (*United Steelworkers* v. *Weber* (1971); *Johnson* v. *Transportation Agency of Santa Clara* (1987)).

In the late 1980s, the Supreme Court rendered a series of decisions that were generally perceived as making it more difficult for minorities and women to establish "disparate impact" discrimination claims against employers. Congress responded by enacting the Civil Rights Act of 1991, which, although not overruling many parts of these and other decisions, added a number of provisions that significantly expanded Title VII's protections against employment discrimination.

Title VII's prohibition of sexual discrimination in employment reaches what is commonly known as *"sexual harassment." This discrimination may take the form of "quid pro quo" harassment, where the employee's submission to an employer's or supervisor's sexual demands is made a condition for conferring or withholding employment benefits, and the employee either submits or suffers tangible employment harm. It may also take the form of "hostile environment" harassment, where the employer is responsible for or fails to correct sexually objectionable behavior in the workplace that is so "severe or pervasive as to alter the conditions of the victim's employment and create an abusive working environment" (*Meritor Savings Bank* v. *Vinson* (1986); *Harris* v. *Forklift Systems, Inc.* (1993)).

Congress has subsequently extended the scope of civil rights laws to prohibit discrimination against other groups. The Age Discrimination in Employment Act, first enacted in 1967 and expanded by later amendments, prohibits employment discrimination against persons forty and older on the basis of their age. Its most significant effect has been to prohibit virtually all mandatory retirement. The law, however, does not prohibit practices based on neutral factors that correlate with age, such as reducing costs by replacing higher-paid employees with lower-paid ones (*Hazen Paper Co.* v. *Biggins* (1993)) (see AGING AND THE LAW).

The Americans with Disabilities Act of 1990 protects persons with disabilities against discrimination in the receipt of public services, in employment, and in access to places of public accommodations. The focus of the law is on requiring a "reasonable accommodation" for persons with disabilities. There has been extensive litigation over who is a "person with disabilities" (see *Bragdon* v. *Abbott* (1998), holding that a person infected with HIV is a "person with disabilities,") and over what is a "reasonable accommodation" (see *PGA Tour* v. *Martin* (2001), holding that the sponsors of a golf tournament were required to permit a professional golfer with a degenerative circulatory disorder to use a golf cart during the competition) (see DISABILITIES LAW).

Today, there are many state and municipal civil rights laws, generally prohibiting the same kinds of discrimination prohibited by federal law. The remedies provided under these laws are sometimes more extensive, and sometimes less extensive than the remedies provided by federal law. Some states and municipalities also prohibit discrimination on the basis of sexual orientation, but most do not, and Congress has not yet added sexual orientation to the many forms of discrimination prohibited by federal law.

[*See also* Civil Rights and Civil Liberties; Congress; Race and Ethnicity]

• Sheldon H. Nahmod, ed., *A Section 1983 Civil Rights Anthology*, 1993. Bonnie P. Tucker and Bruce A. Goldstein, *Legal Rights of Persons with Disabilities*, 1995. Derrick Bell, *Race, Racism and American Law*, 4th ed., 2000. Harold S. Lewis and Elizabeth J. Norman, *Employment Discrimination Law and Practice*, 2001.

—Robert A. Sedler

CIVIL WAR, LEGAL IMPACT OF. After the Confederate assault on Fort Sumter on 12–13 April 1861, Abraham *Lincoln faced three legal questions. First, what was the precise legal nature of the Confederate States of America? Second, what internal security measures could he enact? Third, what measures could he take to end the legal status of chattel *slavery?

Where the nature of the Confederacy was concerned, Lincoln faced difficult choices. His war policies were predicated on the assumption that the Confederacy had no legal existence as a sovereign nation; rather, it was merely a collection of rebellious Americans that could have no standing in an American court or in international law. At the same time, however, the exigencies of war dictated that he treat the Confederacy as a de facto legal entity, particularly in his imposition of a blockade along the Southern coast. Lincoln's response was pragmatic: throughout the war, he treated the Confederacy as a lawful nation when necessary—for example, he considered captured Confederate soldiers to be legitimate prisoners of war rather than treasonous brigands subject to execution—but otherwise avoided, in speeches or public documents, references to the Confederacy as anything other than a sham nation with no legal existence.

In confronting the various threats to the North's internal security, Lincoln was likewise pragmatic. He suspended the writ of *habeas corpus when he thought it was imperative for him to do so, particularly in those areas threatened by pro-Confederate saboteurs. Congress supported him, and in 1863 passed the Habeas Corpus Act, which granted Lincoln broad discretionary powers to suspend the writ, and protected from lawsuits those military officers who carried out internal security policies. Congress also supported Lincoln's declarations of *martial law as necessary internal security measures in wartime. Modern historians agree that Lincoln's use of these powers was restrained and legally defensible.

Nevertheless, the president's habeas corpus policies provoked the ire of Southern sympathizers and libertarian-minded Northerners. Supreme Court Chief Justice Roger B. *Taney, author of the *Dred Scott decision (1857) and no friend of the Lincoln administration, was perhaps Lincoln's most prominent critic in this regard. Following suspension of the writ in Maryland in May 1861, Taney seized upon the arrest of a pro-Southern saboteur named John Merryman to lecture the president on the limits of his authority. In *ex parte Merryman* (1866), Taney informed Lincoln that his internal security measures constituted a despotic exercise of *executive power that threatened American democracy by substituting presidential fiat for judicial authority and by subverting the various constitutional safeguards for citizens' civil liberties. Lincoln responded that suspension of the writ was a hard but necessary measure, legal under the Constitution and required by the dangerous crisis of civil war. Lincoln continued to pursue these policies throughout the war, ignoring Taney's opinion and rendering *ex parte Merryman* largely moot.

The first blows at slavery's legal status were struck by the North's confiscation acts. The First Confiscation Act, passed in the summer of 1861, allowed advancing Union armies to seize weapons, horses, vehicles, and other paraphernalia employed by the Confederate military. It also allowed the army to take any slave who was being used for military purposes, and stated that the slave's owner had "forfeit[ed] his claim to such labor, any law of the State or the United States to the contrary notwithstanding." Whether this translated into outright emancipation was unclear. The Second Confiscation Act, passed in July of 1862, was less ambivalent. It declared that all slaves of persons aiding the Rebellion who escaped or were captured were "captives of war," and "forever free of their servitude."

Two months later the president declared that emancipation was official Union policy, and in January of 1863 he issued the Emancipation Proclamation. As a political document, the Proclamation was revolutionary; as a legal document, it was transitory and problematic. As Lincoln himself pointed out, the Proclamation was grounded in the president's warmaking powers, and possessed unambiguous legal authority only for the duration of the war. Once the Confederacy surrendered, it could easily be revoked by a future executive. Consequently, Lincoln and his Republican allies in Congress labored hard for the passage of the Thirteenth Amendment, which forever outlawed slavery and involuntary servitude. The amendment was ratified in December, 1865.

After Roger Taney's death in 1863, the Supreme Court vindicated Lincoln's answers to nearly all of the war's legal questions. In their most important ruling of the war, the Court held in *The Prize Cases* (1863) that Lincoln was justified in taking whatever measures he deemed necessary, without prior Congressional approval, to suppress the Rebellion, and that the North could wage war without explicitly recognizing the Confederacy as a sovereign nation. In *ex parte Vallandigham* (1864) the Court supported the Lincoln administration's trial by military tribunal of Clement Vallandigham, a prominent Northern Confederate sympathizer. No case directly involving the shifting wartime legal status of slavery came before the Court, but the fact that Taney's replacement, Chief Justice Salmon *Chase, was a well-known antislavery Republican, and the admittance of John Rock, an African-American attorney, to practice before the Court suggested its general sympathy for Lincoln's emancipation policies.

Despite their protestations of moral superiority where the law and constitutional rights were concerned, Confederates took similarly pragmatic approaches to the legal questions arising from the war. Jefferson Davis's strict constructionist constitutionalism did not prevent him from centralizing power in the hands of the Richmond government. This included suspensions of the writ of habeas corpus and declarations of martial law which, while less frequent than those of the Lincoln administration, were nevertheless significant departures from the South's antebellum libertarianism. The Confederacy also enacted strong property confiscation and impressment measures, and created the first military conscription law in American history.

Like his Northern counterpart, Davis was subjected to severe criticism for exceeding his lawful authority; and like Lincoln, Davis vigorously defended his actions as necessary and lawful extensions of his war-making powers. Probably most Americans North and South agreed with their respective leaders, suggesting that, in the end, the fundamental effect of the Civil War on American law was to highlight the pragmatic, flexible nature of the American constitution and legal institutions in wartime.

[*See also* Constitutional Amendments; Fourteenth Amendment]

• Harold M. Hyman, *A More Perfect Union: The Impact of the Civil War and Reconstruction on the Constitution*, 1973. Phillip S. Paludan, *A Covenant With Death: The Constitution, Law, and Equality in the Civil War Era*, 1975. Herman Belz, *Emancipation and Equal Rights: Politics and Constitutionalism in the Civil War Era*, 1978. Mark E. Neely Jr., *The Fate of Liberty: Abraham Lincoln and Civil Liberties*, 1991. Mark E. Neely Jr., *Southern Rights: Political Prisoners and the Myth of Confederate Constitutionalism*, 1999.   —Brian Dirck

CLASS ACTIONS. The class action is a uniquely American procedural device. It allows plaintiffs to sue not only for injury done to themselves but also on behalf of other persons similarly situated for injury done to them. It serves the interests of economy by avoiding trying the same issues again and again in separate cases. It serves the interests of consistency and finality by avoiding the possibility of inconsistent outcomes in separate jury trials and by resolving the claims in a single case that is binding on all class members. It can also affect the bargaining power of the parties, enabling plaintiffs to command greater litigation resources by combining their cases and giving them greater leverage by greatly compounding the defendant's risk of loss. On the other hand, if there is insufficient commonality of interests between class members, class treatment can unfairly deprive them and the defendant of individualized determinations of their disputes.

The American class action was the invention of *equity procedure. When the Federal Rules of Civil Procedure were adopted in 1938, the equitable class action was extended to all actions in federal courts under the merger of law and equity; similar rules have been adopted by states to apply in state courts.

One or more persons begin a class action by filing suit as the class representative for a defined class. After holding a hearing, a judge will rule on whether the suit can be certified as a class action. Four conditions must be satisfied: numerosity—the class is so numerous that joinder of all class members is impracticable (at least twenty-five); commonality—a common question of law or fact; typicality—the class representative's claims have the same general characteristics as those of the class; representativeness—the named party is ded-icated to pursuing the litigation in the interests of the class, class counsel is competent and financially able to conduct the litigation, and there are no antagonisms between the interests of the representative and the class members.

In 1966, Federal Rule 23 amendments opened the door to the greater use of class actions, creating three kinds of action that are distinguished by functional tests, and are not mutually exclusive.

A (b)(2) class seeks injunctive or declaratory relief against a party who has acted or refused to act on grounds generally applicable to the class. This type of action included civil rights suits in the 1960s and 1970s, which brought an end to segregation and enforced the new federal civil rights acts, and "institutional reform" suits of the 1970s and 1980s, which enforced a wide range of constitutional and statutory standards against institutions such as prisons and mental hospitals.

A (b)(1)(A), or "incompatible standards" class, is allowed if separate suits would risk inconsistent adjudications that establish incompatible standards for the party opposing the class. For example, separate suits by quarrelling beneficiaries of a *trust might impose incompatible standards on the trustee concerning distributions to the beneficiaries. A (b)(1)(B), or "impeding of interests" class, is applicable if separate suits would, as a practical matter, dispose of the interests of non-party class members or impede their ability to protect their interests. The classic example is the "limited fund" situation in which the claims of all class members exceed the defendant's assets and separate suits could exhaust the assets and leave nothing for other class members.

A (b)(3) class involves a lesser identity of interests, requiring only that questions of law or fact predominate over questions affecting individual class members and that a class action be superior to other available methods for the fair and efficient adjudication of the controversy. Unlike the first two kinds of class actions, members of this class must be given (1) "the best notice practicable" that a class action is proposed, and (2) a right to "opt out" of the class if they choose.

Rule 23(b)(3) class actions have been subject to much criticism. They are brought for money damages, and thus can offer attractive incentives to both class members and attorneys who promote class action litigation. In *consumer cases, class members often only recover small sums of money while the class attorneys may receive millions of dollars in fees. But the advisory committee that drafted the 1966 rules noted that class actions provide a means for vindicating the rights of people who individually would lack effective strength to bring their opponents into court. Thus the "superiority" of a (b)(3) class action may be based on the fact that (1) there is little incentive for class members to sue individually for small sums (for example, for overcharges on utility bills averaging $100 per customer) and, (2) without class treatment, defendants may not be deterred from improper practices or have to disgorge ill-gotten gains.

After the 1966 amendments, the most class actions for monetary damages were brought under federal *antitrust, *securities, and *civil rights laws. These were often national classes not presenting serious problems as to *conflict of laws, commonality of interests, or determination of damages. Since the late 1970s, consumer class actions have blossomed (against practices in such industries as insurance, banking, credit cards, and telecommunications). They are generally brought under state laws, raising conflict of laws problems for national or multistate classes, and commonality problems as to such individualized elements as reliance in fraud or breach of contract. Courts differ markedly in their willingness to certify such class actions.

Perhaps the most contentious arena for class actions involves *tort law, including mass accidents (plane or railway crashes or the collapse of a building), environmental disasters (escape of toxic chemicals into the air or water), and defective products (asbestos, prescription drugs, appliances, vehicles, or computer hardware or software). The drafters' notes to the 1966 amendments said that mass torts are inappropriate for class certification, but situations in which large numbers of individuals are harmed by the same conduct, condition, or product have led many courts to certify such classes.

In the mid-1990s, several federal appellate courts, increasingly followed by state courts, took a more critical view of class actions. One court commented on the "blackmail" impact that loose class certification standards could have on defendants, rejecting a class action on behalf of hemophiliacs who had become infected with HIV from tainted blood manufactured by the defendant companies. The battleground is now often over whether common issues actually do "predominate" and whether the case is "manageable" as a class action. This depends heavily on courts' assessment of what evidence will be adduced at trial and whether an adequate "trial plan" can be devised.

The U.S. Supreme Court has largely left the parameters of class action rules to the lower courts, but did step in to curb abuses in the settlement of class actions. Although defendants may initially oppose class certification, they are often willing to settle upon certification of an extremely broad class that will preclude any litigation by class members in the future. In *Amchem Products, Inc. v. Windsor* (1997), the Court vacated a class settlement that included hundreds of thousands of persons who had been exposed to the defendants' asbestos products, but had not manifested harmful effects. It found that such "futures" class actions failed to satisfy the Rule 23 class action requirements. Two years later, in *Ortiz* v. *Fibreboard Corp.* (1999), the Court rejected a global settlement of an asbestos class action brought as a mandatory "limited fund" class, finding the unequal disposition of funds to different class members to be improper. Similarly, the Texas Supreme Court refused to approve a class action settlement that only gave the class members "coupons" of little value while the class attorneys received large cash fees.

[*See also* Procedure, Civil]

• *Manual for Complex Litigation*, 3d ed., 1995. Jack B. Weinstein, *Individual Justice in Mass Tort Litigation: The Effect of Class Actions, Consolidations, and Other Multiparty Devices*, 1995. Richard L. Marcus and Edward F. Sherman, *Complex Litigation: Cases and Materials on Advanced Civil Procedure*, 3d ed., 1998. Robert H. Klonoff, *Class Actions (Nutshell)*, 1998. James Wm. Moore et al., *Moore's Federal Practice*, 3d ed., 1999.

—Edward F. Sherman

CLAYTON ACT. *See* Anti-Trust Law.

CLEAN HANDS DOCTRINE. *See* Equity.

CLERK, COURT. *See* Court Officers.

CLERK, LAW. The term "law clerk" once referred to a law student or recent graduate who spent time prior to his or her admission to the bar working in the office of a practicing attorney. In recent years, it has come to refer more particularly to a person hired by a judge to serve as a personal and legal assistant.

The practice began in 1875 when Horace Gray hired at his own expense a recent law-school graduate to help him discharge his responsibilities as Chief Justice of the Massachusetts Supreme Judicial Court of Errors. Gray maintained the practice after his appointment to the U.S. Supreme Court in 1882. Other Supreme Court justices also began to hire legal assistants of their own following the enactment of legislation in 1886 authorizing each of them to hire a "stenographic clerk." Clerkships became a more widespread and permanent feature of the federal judiciary when Congress authorized law clerks for the lower federal courts in the 1930s. Rising caseloads have led the number of state courts employing clerks to increase steadily over the years as well.

Clerkships typically last for one or two years shortly after graduation from law school. The roles that law clerks play vary widely with the traditions of particular courts and with the preferences of particular judges. Typical responsibilities include conducting legal research, reviewing the arguments advanced by the parties, preparing memoranda organizing the facts and legal issues in a case, attending court sessions and conferences with counsel, preparing and editing drafts of opinions and orders, and assisting with administrative matters. Judges often also use their clerks as sounding boards and are typically quite generous in serving as professional mentors. All work is necessarily done under the judge's strict supervision, and all communications are regarded as confidential.

Clerkships have become a mark of considerable professional distinction that enhances the clerk's career opportunities. The number of distinguished judges, government officials, and legal academics who have clerked are too many to mention. To cite but one particular set of examples, the present Supreme Court includes three active justices who are former Supreme Court clerks (William H. Rehnquist for Robert H. *Jackson, John Paul Stevens for Wiley B. Rutledge, and Stephen G. Breyer for Arthur J. Goldberg), another who is a former district court clerk (Ruth Bader Ginsburg for Edmund L. Palmieri), as well as one retired justice who clerked for the Supreme Court (Byron R. White for Fred M. Vinson).

Clerkships have at times been the subject of some criticism. For example, a series of articles appearing in the 1950s suggested that law clerks exert too much influence over judicial decision-making. In more recent years, criticism has focused on the role that clerks play in reviewing petitions for certiorari requesting that the Supreme Court review a particular case and on the hiring patterns of particular judges and justices. As a general matter, however, these criticisms have not altered the consensus view that on balance law clerks play an important and constructive role in promoting the administration of justice.

[See also Legal Practice, Forms of]

• John Bilyeu Oakley and Robert S. Thompson, *Law Clerks and the Judicial Process*, 1980. Richard A. Posner, *The Federal Courts*, 1996.   —Christopher S. Yoo

CLINICS, LAW SCHOOL. *See* Codification; Legal Services, Provision of.

CODIFICATION. Codification is the systematic development, organization, and enactment of legal codes, most commonly by legislative bodies. While these codes are usually statutory, many individual statutes are not part of more structured and coherent codes. In the United States codification has frequently been held out as an alternative to the *common law articulated by appellate courts.

As early as the seventeenth century, American colonists turned to codification in both criminal and civil areas. Distant from their homeland, the colonists found it especially difficult to follow and even to know the English common law. Codes also seemed to them more easily tailored for the concerns of the New World. When colonists from one colony found a code from another colony appealing, they borrowed freely. Massachusetts in the North and Virginia in the South were major sources of codes in their respective regions.

After the founding of the Republic, reformers found codification attractive for various reasons. The English thinker Jeremy Bentham influenced some with his enthusiasm for codification, and in 1811 Bentham himself proposed a comprehensive federal code to President James Madison. The idea never caught fire, but the Massachusetts lawyer Robert Rantoul and Supreme Court Justice Joseph *Story also supported codification. Rantoul, a Jacksonian Democrat, argued that the unpredictable and sometimes contradictory common law was inaccessible to the average citizen and gave too much power to *judges. Story cared less about average citizens but was troubled that a lack of certainty and uniformity in American law would stifle economic development.

The most famous nineteenth-century champion of codification was David Dudley *Field. Enamored of the French codes that originated in the Napoleonic era, Field accepted a charge from the New York legislature to codify the state's civil law. He was disappointed when the legislature failed to enact his draft, but it did in 1848 adopt his Code of Civil Procedure. The so-called "Field Code" was subsequently adopted in whole or in part in twenty-four other states, England, and Ireland. All of Field's codes—the two previously mentioned, a penal code, a political code, and a code of criminal *procedure—were adopted in California, in part owing to the influence of his brother Stephen *Field, then a member of the California Supreme Court and later of the United States Supreme Court.

As the New York legislature's rejection of Field's first code suggests, codification drives are not necessarily popular movements. Field was a self-styled expert and angry when the legislature refused to defer to his expertise. Codifiers might have been leery of appellate judges purporting to articulate and apply the vague common law, but many codifiers were also skeptical of the partisan give-and-take of the legislative process.

During the twentieth century the *National Conference of Commissioners of Uniform State Laws and the *American Law Institute drove the codification movement. The former, with support of the *American Bar Association, generated a series of model codes and then called on the various states to adopt them. The American Law Institute—an organization of distinguished legal academics, judges, and practitioners—produced a series of authoritative restatements of the major branches of the common law: agency, *contracts, *property, *torts, *trusts, and so on. Although not adopted by state legislatures, these restatements resembled codes and were designed to help judges and lawyers properly understand the common law.

The most successful joint codification project of the Conference of Commissioners and the American Law Institute was the Uniform Commercial Code. Calls for a *commercial code dated back at least to Justice Story, but powerful momentum for the project did not build until the 1940s. Prominent law professor and legal theorist Karl Llewellyn became the chief reporter. The wide-ranging and widely respected Uniform Commercial Code is today the leading commercial legislation in forty-nine of the fifty states. Louisiana is the exception; ironically, from the perspective of codification, it is also the state whose law is most influenced by the Napoleonic codes of the nineteenth century.

At the beginning of the twenty-first century codification continues to figure in American lawmaking. Proposals such as the American Law Institute's *Model Penal Code are quite respected, albeit not necessarily enacted state-by-state, as was the Uniform Commercial Code. The United States Congress has codified large bodies of law concerning *bankruptcy, *criminal procedure, *taxation, and other matters. Many individual states have reorganized all of their statutes and called them a "code," e.g., the Indiana Code.

Yet the self-conscious drive for codification has waned. Given the immense variety of law enacted and articulated by assorted legal institutions on different governmental levels, law reformers are less likely to look at codification per se as a pan-acea. Good codes are useful, but the relationships between laws and society are too complex for codification to spark the enthusiasm and rallying cries of earlier eras.

[See also Field, David Dudley]

• Alison Reppy, ed., David Dudley Field: Centenary Essays Celebrating One Hundred Years of Legal Reform, 1949. Karl Llewellyn, "Why a Commercial Code?" Tennessee Law Review 22 (1953). Robert Braucher, "The Legislative History of the Uniform Commercial Code," Harvard Law Review 58 (1958). S. J. Stoljar, ed., Problems of Codification, 1977. Daun Van Ee, David Dudley Field and the Reconstruction of the Law, 1986. Casaba Varga, Codification as a Socio-Historical Phenomenon, 1991. Philip Schofield and Jonathan Harris, eds., Legislator of the World: Writings on Codification, Law, and Education, 1998.   —David Ray Papke

COLLECTIVE BARGAINING. See Labor Law: Labor Relations.

COMMERCIAL LAW. For an American lawyer, commercial law is comprised of two principal sources. First, and foremost, is the Uniform Commercial Code. The second principal source of commercial law is the *common law of *contracts, particularly as found in the Restatement (Second) of Contracts. Complicating this picture of commercial law is the necessary inclusion of many distinct bodies of law (e.g., *consumer law; *antitrust; and *bankruptcy law) which are often found in commercial-law disputes. In addition to these fields, one may add restitution, *equity, and agency. Taken together, these norms—and the conflicts between them—comprise commercial law.

The code, the principal source of contemporary American commercial law, was drafted in part by one of America's leading legal theorists, Karl Nickerson *Llewellyn, and represents one of the most far-reaching accomplishments of the American Legal Realist Movement (see LEGAL REALISM). No understanding of the code is complete without discussion of some of the jurisprudential ideas that underpin both its general and particular aspects. Especially significant here are the jurisprudential views of Llewellyn, who, together with New York lawyer William Schnader created the first unified commercial law statute in North America. Before their work on the code, commercial law was a hodgepoge of rules, statutes, and cases. The law of each state was often different on key points of law. The necessity for uniform law was evident to all, but it was Schnader who began the project; it was he who brought in Llewellyn. Together they created a statute that has endured for over a half century.

The initial version of the code was completed in the early 1950s and immediately adopted in Pennsylvania. Upon its review by the New York legislature, however, numerous difficulties were noticed and, as a result, hearings were held in New York to devise plans for revision. Significant political negotiation ensued, much of which was orchestrated by Llewellyn's wife and colleague, Soia Mentschikoff. Subsequently, the code was adopted by most American states during the 1960s.

Structural Features. The code has certain unique structural features that require comment. The code is not a "code" in the European sense of the word. Unlike civil-law systems, the United States has a common (judge-made) private law. The common law of contracts is directly related to the code via Section 1–103 of the Code. This section incorporates all noncontradictory common law, including the law of equity. Speaking metaphorically, the code "sits atop" or "floats" on the common law. The common law of contracts is as much a part of the code as any of its substantive provisions.

The code exists in a "pure" form only in statute books studied by law students. There are more than a few state-law variations on the uniform text: several of these merit attention. The first type of variation occurs in the text of the code itself. Several of its sections provide separate alternatives for enacting legislatures. For example, § 2–318, which governs third-party beneficiaries of the seller's warranty liability, provides three separate alternatives. The text of the code also makes room for lesser variations, including bracketed language that is optional and blank spaces where state legislatures are to enter monetary amounts, time periods and the names of relevant local statutes. Second, many of the states have not adopted the most recent revisions, and therefore different versions of several of the articles are currently in force in different states. Finally, many states have adopted nonuniform amendments to the code.

Another divergence from the European approach to codes is the fact that the code governs both civil and commercial transactions; for example, both sales to end users and sales for resale. On the one hand, it includes a number of provisions specific to the situation in which one or both of the parties are merchants (so-called "Merchant Rules"), while, on the other, the current revisions to several of the articles contain provisions protecting consumers.

Partly as a result of Llewellyn's influence, the code—especially in the Sales Article—fails to provide specific answers to the critical questions that arise in commercial disputes. Instead, the code often responds with a question of its own: asking the courts to determine what would be "reasonable in the circumstances." For example, when one looks at Article 2 to find the seller's obligations under a typical shipping contract, one finds in § 2–504(a) that the seller must "put the goods in the possession of such a carrier and make such a contract for the transportation as may be reasonable having regard for the nature of the goods and the other circumstances of the case. . . ." The open texture of these provisions (in other words, their explicit reference to an assessment of the specific transaction involved) is a leitmotif in the code.

Each of the sections of the code is accompanied by an official comment. Although the comments are not enacted into law—state legislatures enact only the black letter—the comments are, nonetheless, often authoritative statements concerning the intent of the drafters. In many cases however the comments go beyond the clear mandate of the section provision, sometimes indicating that the reporter for that provision failed to convince the membership of the "ALI" or the "NCCUSL" that the Reporter's position should be anchored in the substantive text. Care must therefore be used in reading the comments as they occasionally represent little more than wishful thinking.

Jurisprudence. There is a vast literature on Llewellyn's general jurisprudential views and their influence on the Code. Of late, it has become almost fashionable to question the degree to which Llewellyn's jurisprudence has or should have continuing influence on judges and legislators. Whatever the merits of these claims, there is little doubt that the present text of the code bears the marks of Llewellyn's continuing influence. A few aspects of this influence are worth mentioning.

Llewellyn's commercial law jurisprudence is at bottom a substantive theory of the relation of legal doctrine to social facts. Llewellyn's legal philosophy evolved as a reaction to the then-prevailing jurisprudence of formalism. From the late nineteenth to the early twentieth century, theoretical reflection on law was dominated by a model advanced by the first dean of the Harvard Law School, Christopher Columbus Langdell. Langdell believed the task of legal theory to be identification of the small number of principles which both organize a doctrinal field and lie immanent to or behind the flurry of decided cases. For Langdell, the "scientific" aspect of law is a process of reason. With sufficient effort, a legal theorist could identify the half-dozen or so principles that underlie a particular field of law. Thus, to discern the law on any given question is not a matter of reading cases but was the product of reflection on doctrine. Pure reason was, for Langdell, the engine of legal understanding.

Llewellyn rejected the idea of reason, juridical or otherwise, as the key to law. Llewellyn believed that much of the "law" of commercial law was a matter of how businesspersons conducted their affairs. In short, Llewellyn believed that the practice of business was a source of legal normativity. In this regard, one of the principal jurisprudential contributions of Llewellyn to the code is the idea of business norms. Known in the code as "Trade Usage" (section 1–205[2]), the practices and forms of business are directly made part of the meaning of the parties' "Agreement" (section 1–201[3]) or "Contract" (Section 1–201[11]). In advancing the concept of trade usage, Llewellyn was making a point about the very idea of agreement or contract.

Despite the clarity with which Llewellyn advanced his conception of agreement, the question of the proper understanding of the meaning of agreement remains quite controversial. The ongoing question is whether the express terms of an agreement may be subordinated to any of the elements of the parties' Agreement. The controlling section of the code is section 1–205(4). It reads:

> The express terms of an agreement and any applicable course of dealing or usage of trade shall be construed wherever reasonable as consistent with each other; but when such a construction is unreasonable, express terms control both course of dealing and usage of trade and course of dealing controls usage of trade.

Some commentators, judges, and scholars argue that express terms can never be contradicted by course of dealing, course of performance, or usage of trade. In other words, where express terms conflict with any other element of the parties' agreement, express terms control. The problem with the argument is that it cannot be sustained, even at the level of the text of the code. If express terms always control course of dealing and usage of trade, then why does the statute direct that express terms, course of dealing, and usage of trade "shall be construed wherever reasonable as consistent with each other . . . ?" Only after finding such a construction unreasonable is a court justified in interpreting the parties' agreement in accordance with the statutory maxim "express terms control

both course of dealing and usage of trade and course of dealing controls usage of trade." To claim, as some do, that no reasonable way exists to override express terms by a contradictory set of terms imposed by a course of dealing or usage of trade is to argue with the ordinary meaning of the statutory language. The code's interpretive methodology is clear: first, make an honest attempt to construe all sources of the meaning of the parties' agreement. Failing that, go to the second step in the analysis: express terms control all others.

In sum, it is fair to say that Llewellyn's concept of agreement integrates trade usage, course of dealing (a prior course of dealing between the parties), and course of performance (the parties conduct after contract formation) with the written terms of the parties' agreement. Now, it is no longer possible to answer the question of what the parties meant by their agreement without first understanding the meaning of the commercial practice from which their agreement arose. A related issue, and one equally as controversial as the question of the meaning of the parties' agreement, is the obligation of good faith and fair dealing. Under section 1–203, the code imposes a nondisclaimable duty of good faith on the performance and enforcement of "[e]very contract or duty within this Act [the code]." After nearly twenty years of sustained litigation over the meaning of good faith, the question that remains is whether the good-faith obligation ever overrides the express language of the parties' agreement. An example is termination clauses. Where a contract has a clause expressly permitting termination of the contract by one party, the question is whether the exercise of that right is reached and regulated by the good-faith obligation. There is simply no settled answer to the question.

The Revision Process. While the code has seen some revision since it was first enacted, the code has—until recently—been little changed from the time of the New York Law Revision Commission hearings. In the early twenty-first century, the code is undergoing substantial revision. Many of the articles have been thoroughly revised and are pending before state legislatures. The sales article has been a subject of much dispute and has not yet been approved. There are very few cases decided on the basis of revised provisions of the code. As a result, the Code references in many cases do not by and large correspond to the code as revised. Given the usual delays in the legislative process, it will be quite some time before the revised code becomes uniform law.

Whereas, as mentioned above, the original code

tended to present an open texture providing flexibility to the courts to decide cases on their individual facts in the best Realist tradition, the new code rejects that vision of the purpose of a code. Current jurisprudential thinking downplays the role of judges in commercial decision-making. Instead, the goal is to provide clear answers to as many of the potential issues as possible in the text of the statute. Since, however, there is considerable disagreement among the different groups as to what constitutes a fair result in any particular situation, the individual provisions are all too frequently the source of political contention. As a result, they present technically—often technocratically—worded compromises. Those compromises may be difficult to understand for those who were not in the room on the day the wording was adopted.

International Conventions. There is little doubt that the globalization of commerce adds considerably to the scope and depth of commercial law. There is an emerging *international law of commercial transactions that, to varying degrees, displaces part of the UCC. We shall briefly examine two of the most interesting sources of law relating to international trade: the Convention on Contracts, the International Sale of Goods (variously called the Sales Convention, the Vienna Convention, or CISG) and UNIDROIT's Principles of International Commercial Contracts (known as the "UNIDROIT Principles" or just the "Principles").

The Sales Convention is the product of a long history of attempts to unify the law governing the international sale of goods, perhaps the most frequent type of international transaction. The modern history of these efforts began with the International Institute for the Unification of Private Law (UNIDROIT), a creation of the short-lived League of Nations. As one of its first projects, UNIDROIT commissioned Ernst Rabel, perhaps the leading comparative scholar of his day, to prepare a draft convention on the topic. The study he prepared, with the assistance of members of the Kaiser-Wilhelm Institut in Berlin, which he directed (forerunner of the Max Planck Institut in Hamburg) was published in two volumes and represents still today the most insightful discussion of the comparative law of sales. On the basis of his comparative investigations, Rabel prepared a draft convention that ultimately evolved into two Hague conventions—the Uniform Law for International Sales (ULIS) and the Uniform Law for the Formation of International Sales Contracts (ULF). These two conventions were approved in the Hague in 1964 but never gained wide adherence.

Almost immediately upon the completion of these two conventions, the United Nations Commission on International Trade Law (UNCITL) began to think of revising them in order to broaden the acceptance of uniform sales law. That resulted in the approval of the Sales Convention at an international conference in Vienna in 1980. CISG entered into force on 1 January 1988 by the United States and ten other countries. It counts today more than fifty parties, including most of this country's principal trading partners, though not yet Japan.

What is important about the sales convention from the point of view of an American lawyer is that it automatically applies (unless excluded by the contract) to contracts for the sale of goods concluded between a merchant located in the United States and another merchant located in any of the other sixty countries that have ratified or acceded to the convention. In other words, it is just as much the law of every American jurisdiction as is the code.

Future Directions. Commercial law is a highly specialized area of legal practice. Consistently good practice in commercial matters requires knowledge of heterogeneous statutory schemes, common law, and business practices. Academic scholarship in commercial law reflects these complexities, although much work in commercial law scholarship is devoted to economic analysis of law. Despite this emphasis, significant doctrinal scholarship continues to be produced by leading scholars. Finally, longstanding calls for more empirical scholarship have finally been heard. It seems realism—at least as an approach to doctrine—is alive and well.

Code Subject Matter by Article
Article 1: General Provisions
Article Two: Sales
Article 2A: Leases
Article 3: Negotiable Instruments
Article 4: Bank Deposits and Collections
Article 4A: Funds Transfers
Article 5: Letters of Credit
Article Six: Repealer of Article 6 as well as a Revised Article 6
Article 7: Warehouse Receipts, Bills of Lading and Other Documents of Title
Article 8: Investment Securities
Article Nine: Secured Transactions

[*See also* Economics and Law; *Erie Railroad* v. *Tompkins* (1938); *Swift* v. *Tyson* (1842)]

• Richard Danzig, "A Comment on the Jurisprudence of the Uniform Commercial Code," *Stanford Law Review* (1975): 621. Zipporah B. Wiseman, "The Limits of

Vision: Karl Llewellyn and the Merchant Rules," *Harvard Law Review* (1987): 65. Dennis Patterson, "Good Faith, Lender Liability and Discretionary Acceleration: Of Llewellyn, Wittgenstein and the Uniform Commercial Code," *Texas Law Review* (1989): 169. Thomas Quinn, *Uniform Commercial Code Commentary and Case Digest*, 2d ed., 1991. J. J. White and Robert Summers, *Uniform Commercial Code*, 4th ed., 1995. Richard Hyland and Dennis Patterson, *An Introduction to Commercial Law*, 1999.   —Dennis Patterson

COMMON LAW. Originating in the decisions of English judges of the early Middle Ages and systematically developed since the twelfth century, the common law eventually spread with English settlements throughout much of the world. Once referred to as "unwritten law" (*lex non scripta*), the common law was, in fact, gathered from the written reports of judicial decisions and in consequence was also called case law as opposed to law found in legislative enactments or statute law. Common law is sometimes contrasted with *equity, the distinctive rights and remedies historically administered by the English Court of Chancery; today the administration of law and equity are merged in England and most American states.

Historical Roots. In medieval England royal courts dispensed *justice in cases in which important national interests were at stake, such as the ownership of landed estates or violations of the King's peace. Lesser or local disputes were resolved by other courts, often applying their own special rules. Common to the whole country, the decisions of the royal courts laid the foundations of the English legal system prior to the adoption of any statutes. King Henry II in the twelfth century provided the institutional framework for regular development by organizing an integrated judicial system. Eventually three common law courts emerged: the Court of Common Pleas, the Court of King's Bench, and the Court of Exchequer—an arrangement that endured until the nineteenth century when the Judicature Acts (1873–75) put the English court system on its modern basis.

The oldest book on the common law, a brief treatise *On the Laws and Customs of England*, written in Latin, dates to the twelfth century and is attributed to Ranulf de Glanvill, an important figure in King Henry's government. In keeping with the common law's origin in judicial decisions, the book is organized around writs, the forms used to initiate legal proceedings and define remedies for specific wrongs. Glanvill includes much information about medieval litigation and is an early example of the common law's characteristic method of reasoning, posing hypothetical cases and seeking guidance from prior decisions. The impressive progress of the common law over the next hundred years is evident from another monumental work, also in Latin and also entitled *On the Laws and Customs of England*, composed in the mid-thirteenth century and attributed to Henry de Bracton, a royal judge. Although obviously acquainted with ancient Roman law and the latest developments in *canon law, Bracton largely reflects the indigenous development of English law in the work of the courts. Singling out for special study the decisions of one or two judges, Bracton illustrates the heroic role assigned to the *judge in the *literature of the common law. Five hundred years were to pass before another systematic exposition of the common law appeared, this time in English: Sir William *Blackstone's four-volume *Commentaries on the Laws of England* (1765–69).

During the centuries between Bracton and Blackstone, the makers of the common law concentrated on filling in the details, especially the almost incredible complexities of the law of real *property. Typical of the new emphasis was Sir Thomas Littleton's short treatise *On Tenures*, published in 1481. Not in English or even in Latin but in Law French, the argot of English lawyers for centuries after the Norman Conquest, Littleton offered a scientific account of English land law, long the heart of the common law. Practical in organization and emphasis, Littleton was inward looking, wholly unaffected by non-English influences— the perfect example of the common law's hermetic tendencies. After a century and a half, Littleton's *On Tenures* was updated in a voluminous commentary by Sir Edward Coke; *Coke on Littleton* quickly became a classic of the common law. Displaying an astounding mastery of ancient precedent and an uncanny ability to restate it in a manner relevant to current conditions, Coke's work ensured that modern Anglo-American property law would be erected on firm medieval foundations. In commentaries on the statutes, criminal law, and the courts, Coke also developed the concept of *due process and emphasized the political implications of the rule of law as a restraint on arbitrary power.

Centered on judicial decisions, the common law early developed a tradition of case reports, beginning with the medieval Year Books in Law French. Modern law reporting began in the sixteenth century with the immensely influential reports in English prepared by Sir Edward Coke, the source for such arcana of the common law as the Rule in Shelley's Case and the Rule in Wild's Case. Access to the reports was facilitated by a series of books known as "abridgements," which catalogued cases under topics arranged alphabetically, the ancestors of modern legal encyclopedias such as *Halsbury's Laws of England* and *American Jurisprudence*.

Born in the decisions of individual cases, the common law continued into the modern period to be developed more by judicial decision than by legislation. Property law, the primary legal interest of the landed aristocracy, evolved slowly as entails gave way to strict settlements, and mortgages facilitated the economic exploitation of land. With the growth of the British Empire and the spread of international trade, novel questions of *commercial law required the renovation of the common law of *contracts and the development of new legal arrangements such as *insurance and joint ventures. Lord Mansfield, chief justice of the Court of King's Bench in the late eighteenth century, exploited the common law's flexibility to the full and laid down new law to deal with the unprecedented new realities.

From the beginning, the English legal profession was divided into barristers and solicitors. Barristers had a monopoly on practice before the common law courts, and from their ranks the judges were recruited, forging the link between practice and judging that distinguishes the common law to this day. Legal advice on family settlements, property transactions, and business in general was the preserve of solicitors, earlier referred to as attorneys. Legal *education necessarily followed this functional division. Barristers were trained in the Inns of Court, medieval hostelries that developed into a combination law school and professional club. Solicitors had comparable but less prestigious accommodations. After the medieval period the educational functions of the Inns atrophied, although students, including numerous framers of the United States Constitution, continued to visit frequently. Realistically, a form of professional apprenticeship was the only means of legal education until organized curricula in law appeared at English universities in the nineteenth century. Although the professional division into barristers and solicitors was briefly attempted in some of the older American colonies like Virginia, it proved too costly and too deeply rooted in English institutions to survive transplantation to America where a unified bar became the norm.

Relation to Civil Law. Although common law is often divided into criminal and *civil law, the former concerned with public order and the latter with private rights such as property and contracts, civil law has also another and different meaning: the entire legal system derived from Roman law as expressed in the *Corpus juris civilis*, the definitive summation promulgated by the Emperor Jus-

tinian in the sixth century. Roman law was never entirely forgotten in Europe, and the Church through its own canon law and general Latin culture kept alive some knowledge of the Roman past. Clerically trained English jurists like Bracton were obviously familiar with Roman law, and in Britain the Scottish legal system was (and remains) a civil law system with its own distinct forms and terminology. But the common law generally developed in isolation from these influences and was already fully formed when in the fifteenth century, during the Renaissance, classical sources were rediscovered. The logical arrangement and cultural prestige of the rediscovered *Corpus juris civilis* attracted academic English attention but was far less significant an influence on English law than on European legal systems. In America, Louisiana alone among the states retains an integrated civil law system, one based on Spanish and French colonial traditions, but many Western states preserve some civil law contributions, such as the community property system whereby husbands and wives are presumed to share equally in property acquired during marriage.

Revived interest in the *Corpus juris civilis* resulted eventually in the adoption by various European countries of legal codes, rigorously logical statements of basic rules and practices, such as the French Code Civil adopted after the French Revolution and often referred to as the Code Napoleon. In England *codification was championed by Jeremy Bentham, a radical critic of the common law. In America codification was associated with a demand for intellectual liberation from England and the past, Robert Rantoul famously proclaiming in a Fourth of July oration that "All American Law must be statute law" (Oration at Scituate, 4 July 1836). Despite the seemingly democratic appeal of enacted statutes over decided cases as the source of law, American legislatures in the nineteenth century proved unable and to some extent unwilling to assume control over legal development. Despite the logical charms systematic codification exerted over academically inclined lawyers, neither in England nor America did the codification movement make more than limited gains. Civil *procedure was codified successfully in the nineteenth century by David Dudley Field, beginning in New York and spreading to many other states despite the opposition of practitioners trained in old-style pleading. In the twentieth century the Uniform Commercial Code (see COMMERCIAL LAW) eventually gained acceptance in all states, but the common law assimilated the codes rather than yielded to them.

Common Law and United States Legal Tradition. Although some English settlers in the New World may have come in search of a purer law both ecclesiastical and secular, many instinctively turned to the common law when legal rules were needed; it was, after all, the system they knew best. When Britain eventually realized and rationalized its imperial responsibilities, the common law and its institutions were systematically extended to America, at least insofar as appropriate to frontier conditions. Many colonial assemblies passed explicit reception statutes declaring the common law in force; even in the absence of statutes, colonial judges routinely applied the common law.

After American Independence, reception statutes were often reenacted, and are generally still in effect. North Carolina's Act of 1778 is typical, declaring in force "so much of the common law as . . . has not otherwise been provided for in whole or in part, not abrogated, repealed, or become obsolete." The common law, in other words, was presumed to govern in the absence of indications to the contrary. While legislatures could certainly modify the received law, eliminating primogeniture from the law of inheritance, for example, the judges retained their role as arbiters of the common law. An interesting debate at the time of reception concerned the extent to which ancient or fundamental English statutes, such as Magna Carta or various acts concerning real property, were included in the reception; so completely had jurists like Sir Edward Coke melded these statutes with the nonstatutory common law that they too were generally "received." In ascertaining the content of the common law, Blackstone's *Commentaries*, published on the eve of American Independence and widely read in the colonies, proved particularly useful.

As it was understood in the seventeenth and eighteenth centuries, the common law was seen as a bulwark of individual rights against *executive power, and the founders routinely asserted their supposedly ancient rights against what they saw as examples of modern tyranny. The Continental Congress in 1774 expressly laid claim to "the rights of life, liberty, and property, and the common law of England." (*Journal of Congress*, 14 October 1774). The Declaration of Independence placed particular emphasis on the procedural safeguards enshrined in the common law, specifically charging that King George III "has combined with others to subject us to a jurisdiction foreign to our constitutions and unacknowledged by our laws . . . for depriving us in many cases of the benefits of trial by jury." The Federal Constitution routinely used common law terms, for example, guaranteeing "the writ of *habeas corpus" and prohibiting the enactment of any *"ex post facto law." The Bill of Rights constitutionalizes a host of common law procedures for the prosecution and punishment of crime, such as the privilege against *self-incrimination in the Fifth Amendment and the prohibition of *"cruel and unusual punishments" in the Eighth Amendment. Perhaps the most noticeable instance of wholesale incorporation of the common law, however, occurs in the Seventh Amendment, concerning civil procedure: "In suits at common law, where the value in controversy shall exceed twenty dollars, the right of trial by *jury shall be preserved, and no fact tried by a jury shall be otherwise re-examined in any court of the United States, than according to the rules of the common law."

As it had grown over the centuries in England, so the common law continued to grow when it was transplanted in the new soil of America. In 1735 a colonial lawyer had argued at the trial of John Peter Zenger that common law rules on the periphery of the British Empire might not be identical with those at home in England. A century later the United States Supreme Court declared in *Van Ness* v. *Packard* (1829), a case involving the law of trade fixtures, that "[t]he common law of England is not to be taken in all respects to be that of America." Rules suitable to a settled society with established patterns of land management were not always appropriate to the conditions of settlement in America; trees on estates in England, for instance, might be viewed as growing timber that could not be cut by tenants without the permission of the owner of the freehold, while on the American frontier clearing trees could be regarded as an improvement. Industrialization created risks of a quality or quantity unknown to the common law; railroads, for example, created multiple hazards for passengers, workers, shippers, and landowners along the right-of-way. Rules appropriate to earlier means of transportation had to be urgently re-evaluated. Rooted in tradition yet capable of growth, the common law proved readily adaptable to the new conditions of an expanding society.

Although remodeling the common law was still largely the work of the judges, systematic reporting of their decisions was slow to develop in America. English reports continued to circulate after the Revolution and remained influential even after American reports became common in the mid-nineteenth century. Although law libraries were few, legal treatises were especially important as handy guides to case law. Blackstone's *Commentaries* continued to be updated in new editions throughout the nineteenth century, but in America it generally yielded to James *Kent's four-volume *Commentaries on American Law*, first published in 1826–30. Kent's *Commentaries* went through many subsequent editions, the definitive one being the twelfth edition produced by Oliver Wendell *Holmes a half century later. Joseph *Story, a seemingly indefatigable justice of the Supreme Court, turned out a series of influential commentaries on specialized topics, mostly commercial, beginning with *Bailments* in 1832, including *Agency* (1839), *Partnership* (1841), *Bills of Exchange* (1843), and *Promissory Notes* (1845)—testimony to the increased pace of economic development.

American conditions were especially conducive to the rapid growth of the common law. All the states except Louisiana had received the common law at one remove or another, and as law reporting improved, a sort of market for legal developments emerged. Practicing lawyers and academic commentators constantly observed the degree to which states adhered to or remodeled traditional rules and applauded or deplored the results. The Constitution, itself a dramatic innovation in the history of the common law, was quickly assimilated by strong judges imbued with the idea that "it is emphatically the province and duty of the judicial department to say what the law is." (*Marbury* v. *Madison* (1803)). *Judicial review, the judges' prerogative to rule on the constitutionality of federal and state statutes, while not a necessary development of the common law—it failed to establish itself in England—was nonetheless not a radical departure.

Until its legal abolition by the Thirteenth Amendment in 1865, *slavery proved an indigestible lump in American common law. Because of Lord Mansfield's decision in *Sommersett's case* (1772), slavery had no basis in English common law but existed in various parts of the British Empire, including the colonies that later became parts of the United States, only by local law or *custom. After American Independence, Southern states provided some legislative basis for the "peculiar institution," but state judges struggled to reconcile slavery with the existing common law. The difficulty of the undertaking is testimony to the extent to which the common law embodied concepts of individual autonomy and personal worth.

American legal education carried forward the common law's inveterate emphasis on cases and the judicial function. At first, apprenticeship remained the primary route to legal practice, but after the Civil War formal legal education began to develop as a new seriousness pervaded the learned professions. Beginning in 1871 the Harvard Law School under its reformist dean, Charles C. Langdell, became a model for law schools throughout the country. Langdell's legal pedagogy, based on a close reading of the written opinions of appellate judges (the case method) and expounded by posing a series of sequenced questions (the Socratic dialogue), brought the method of the courtroom into the classroom and helped ensure the continued primacy of the common law.

In one sense the triumph of the common law tradition in legal education was ironic: just as the Harvard model was spreading, the creative function of the judges was beginning to wane, rivaled by the legislatures' newfound interest in law reform. If the period from 1830 to 1890 was the golden age of American common law, the years thereafter witnessed a new emphasis on statute law. Case reports increasingly had to share the primacy with statute books, and the law schools struggled, at first with only limited success, to adapt their methods to the new legislative materials. After the turn of the century, uniform acts began to be proposed by the *National Conference of Commissioners on Uniform State Laws, determined in the interests of efficiency to eliminate confusing differences that had developed among the states. The Uniform Sales Act, commended to the attention of the legislatures in 1906, was extensively adopted and paved the way for the eventual triumph of the Uniform Commercial Code later in the twentieth century. Starting in 1923 the *American Law Institute began its monumental project of "restatements of the law," intended not for legislative adoption but to stabilize and standardize the common law as applied by the judges.

The rise of the law school marked the debut of a new force in the common law: the law professor. Joining the judges and the legislators as shapers of the common law, law professors provided a useful new perspective on rules and procedures. Freed from the agenda of the court docket and the self-interested demands of political constituents, law professors offered logical critiques of existing law, disinterested proposals for reform, and occasional academic faddism. To a great extent law professors supplied the legal literature of the twentieth century and staffed the commissions that proposed uniform acts and drafted restatements.

The apparent displacement of the common law

tradition was, however, more illusory than real. The new legal materials often simply incorporated the common law rules, and the legislative role in such law reform was often limited to adoption without amendment of comprehensive and complicated statutes barely understood by many legislators. Sometimes important statutes were little more than invitations to the judges to develop the common law in certain directions; the Sherman Antitrust Act of 1890, for example, simply declared "combinations in restraint of trade" illegal, leaving it up to the judges to define essential terms and make necessary exceptions. The common law way with statutes was to treat them very much like precedents, subject to close reading and extended or distinguished in keeping with judicial notions of public policy. Harvard Law School professor John Chipman Gray went so far in 1906 as to imply that statutes were not law, limiting law to rules that the judges actually apply in deciding cases; in that sense, legislation was only one of several "sources of the law."

Throughout its long history the common law was shaped by great judges; their rulings provided the substance of the law, their written opinions formed its basic texts, their sayings and idiosyncrasies became its lore. Promotion to the bench was the crown of many careers in law; recruitment from the ranks of practicing lawyers and successful politicians—often one and the same—linked the judiciary and the world of practical affairs. Coming from such backgrounds, common law judges were often impatient with purely abstract concepts and naturally inclined to consider practical results. Custodianship of the Constitution endowed them not only with awesome power but also with a sense of high purpose. Ordering an end to racial segregation in public schools, Supreme Court Chief Justice Earl *Warren discarded the legal fiction of "separate but equal" and declared that "separate educational facilities are inherently unequal," setting off a social revolution that spread far beyond the classrooms. (*Brown v. Board of Education (1954)).

In its essence the common law remains a set of rules for resolving disputes, many of them unchanged since the Middle Ages. The principal purpose of legal rules is to direct the attention of the judge away from the particularities of the parties and the specifics of the given dispute and toward the generalized social problem involved in the case. Training in the common law is unusually effective in inducing judges to subordinate their personal preferences to the preferences expressed in the impersonal tradition. While not susceptible to easy generalization, the common law's preferences include a protective attitude toward private property, a reluctance to impose affirmative duties on individuals, and a respect for personal autonomy.

More than a set of ancient rules, the common law also became a set of procedures guaranteeing fairness in the resolution of disputes. Although procedural regularity is most important in criminal law, where the individual faces the might of the state, it is important in civil litigation as well. The ability of the common law over the centuries to command the respect of the public was largely dependent on the widespread perception of its fundamental fairness. The popularity of the common law at the time of American Independence derived from its historic association with due process, the legal code word for fair play. Rules may often be settled one way or another; the common law and the civil law, for example, reach opposing results in numerous cases. In the abstract it is usually difficult to develop enthusiasm for one rule over another, but a reputation for impartial decision making after an opportunity to be heard is what grounds a legal system in popular esteem. The common law in the Anglo-American world is synonymous for most people with the rule of law.

Beyond specific rules and procedures, the common law also embodies a certain way of handling legal problems. Born in the courts, the common law was always primarily focused on resolving individual disputes. Judge-centered in the sense that it was historically expressed in the decisions of the judges, the common law is in another sense centered on the litigants. The parties generally control the presentation of their own cases, and the judge plays a relatively passive role, limited by and large to deciding which side has the better argument. In consequence, the common law developed a deep-seated attachment to the adversarial process, which in turn fostered a frame of mind that assumes two sides to every case.

A product of the age of feudalism, the common law survived the complete overthrow of the feudal system of property. A product of royal courts under the direction of a powerful king, the common law, at least in America, long outlived monarchism. A product of an hierarchical society, the common law survived, even encouraged, the development of individualism and demonstrated a capacity to foster civil liberty—it proved itself compatible with, if not actually conducive to, industrial and social revolution. Through it all, the common law retained a tie with the remote past that cloaked its intense practicality with an unmistakable air of majesty.

[*See also* Blackstone's *Commentaries on the Laws of England*; Civil Law in America]

• William Blackstone, *Commentaries on the Laws of England*, 4 vols., 1765–69. Oliver Wendell Holmes, *The Common Law*, 1881. Frederick Pollock and Frederic W. Maitland, *The History of English Law*, 2 vols., 2d ed., 1898. William S. Holdsworth, *A History of English Law*, 17 vols., 1903–66. John Chipman Gray, *The Nature and Sources of the Law*, 2d ed., 1927. Karl N. Llewellyn, *The Common Law Tradition: Deciding Appeals*, 1960. Grant Gilmore, *The Ages of American Law*, 1977. Morton J. Horwitz, *The Transformation of American Law*, 2 vols., 1977, 1992. Guido Calabresi, *A Common Law for the Age of Statutes*, 1982. Harold J. Berman, *Law and Revolution: The Formation of the Western Legal Tradition*, 1983. Lawrence M. Friedman, *A History of American Law*, 2d ed., 1985. Kermit L. Hall, *The Magic Mirror: Law in American History*, 1989.   —John V. Orth

COMMON LAW SPOUSE. *See* Divorce and Annulment; Domestic Violence: Partner Abuse; Family Law; Marriage; Spousal Support.

COMMONWEALTH V. HUNT, 45 MASS. 111 (1842). In a landmark victory for American labor, the Massachusetts Supreme Judicial Court under its influential Chief Justice Lemuel *Shaw held in 1842 that labor unions were not criminal *conspiracies. John Hunt and six others, leaders of the Boston bootmakers' union, had been prosecuted for leading a strike against employers that hired laborers who did not belong to the union, demanding what today would be called a "closed shop." Convicted by a municipal court judge, who ruled that the *common law as inherited from England prohibited all combinations in restraint of trade, the labor leaders appealed to the state's highest court. They were ably represented by Robert Rantoul, well known as a radical critic of the common law. Chief Justice Shaw, no radical, had only recently ruled (*Farwell* v. *Boston & Worcester RR*, 45 Mass. 49 (1842)) that employers were not liable to workers injured on the job by fellow servants. Nonetheless, Shaw reversed the bootmakers' conviction, holding that neither the end (a closed shop) nor the means (a strike) was illegal at common law.

In terms of legal history, Shaw was on shaky ground; the precedents in both England and America were sparse but contrary. The product of a regulated society and economy, the common law could be interpreted to forbid individual workers from uniting to coerce their employers or fellow employees. Class bias by judges and legislators also encouraged anti-union results. But in terms of public policy, Shaw's decision indicated a different role for the courts, one only imperfectly realized over the ensuing century: neutral judges overseeing an unending struggle between labor and capital.

[*See also* Labor Law]

• Leonard W. Levy, *The Law of the Commonwealth and Chief Justice Shaw*, 1957. Christopher Tomlins, *Law, Labor and Ideology in the Early American Republic*, 1993.

—John V. Orth

COMMUNES, LAW. *See* Legal Services, Provision of.

COMMUNITY SERVICE. *See* Criminal Punishments.

COMMUTATION. *See* Pardon, Reprieve, and Commutation.

COMPARATIVE LAW. Contemporary comparative law in America and worldwide has three dimensions or aims: (1) professional or practical; (2) scientific or sociological; and (3) cultural. As an organized discipline within legal education and among jurists, with its own associations, conferences, journals, and courses, comparative law dates from the mid-nineteenth century, but its known origins are rooted in the beginnings of western law.

Origins. The essence of comparative law is comparison. We imagine some ancient peoples concerned with the rules regulating human behavior in their own societies were curious about an idealized law of nature (originally tied to religion) or about the laws of neighboring societies. Specialists in the law compared what was foreign to them—that is, foreign law—usually for some practical purpose. As trade and relations among different ethnic or language groups developed, law was often considered personal to a people so that towns might consist of persons who could rely on the laws of their own group. These differences in laws stimulated comparison, again with a practical objective. It was only with the Enlightenment that the sociological and cultural aims of comparative law became significant.

Classification of Legal Systems. Comparatists are often interested in classifying *legal systems to clarify their work. Classical Greeks made the earliest recorded efforts explicitly classifying legal systems as a result of their philosophical speculation about law. For instance, Plato (429–348 BCE) in his *Laws* discussed the rules of several Greek and other city-states in formulating his ideal code and legal institutions for Magnesia. Aristotle (384–322 BCE) examined many legal structures in his *Politics* before settling on the three preferred categories of kingship, aristocracy, and constitutional government with their deviant siblings tyranny, oligarchy, and democracy.

In Rome jurists' interest in foreign law was more practical, particularly with the creation of the office of *praetor peregrinus* in 242 BCE. This official supervised jurisdiction over disputes involving non-Romans. It was here that the mixture of a less formalistic Roman *ius civile*, Greek law, and other foreign legal norms led to an internationalized *ius gentium*. Roman jurists did not have a philosophical interest in studying and classifying foreign legal systems because they believed in the superiority of their own law.

In the early modern era some natural law jurists such as Hugo Grotius (1583–1645), Samuel Pufendorf (1632–94), and Baron Charles Louis de Montesquieu (1689–1755) used the comparative law method to provide empirical backing for *natural-law principles. Others such as William *Blackstone (1723–80) had the additional objective of providing prestige for their national law: Blackstone's four-volume *Commentaries on the Laws of England* (1765–69) emphasized the similarities in English *common law, Roman law, and natural law.

Montesquieu's extensive speculation about the relation of law to natural and social forces, and explicit classification of legal systems emphasized the distinct manners of a particular people in a particular era. His *Lettres Persanes* (1721) used the satiric device of two Persians traveling in Europe who commented on the customs of French and European society. They pointed to the abuses and cruelties of criminal justice systems and argued for a rational theory of punishment adjusted to the settled sensibilities of the people.

Montesquieu's relativist view of humans' ability to achieve justice was further developed in *De l'esprit des lois* (1748), which drew upon causative factors such as climate, soil, population size, a people's morals and customs, religion, and commerce. He classified governments along with the appropriate principle for their constitutive societies. Thus, democracy required civic virtue; aristocracy, moderation against the people; monarchy, honor for the law and intermediate institutions; and despotism, fear to maintain order. He found different mechanisms for lawmaking and adjudication in the first three types of legal systems, but pointed out that law was not necessary for despotism.

This set the stage for much more elaborate comparative law classifications beginning with nineteenth-century evolutionary theorists. Law in these schemes was part of the larger social system that changed over time. For instance, Sir Henry Maine (1822–1888), interested in the striking parallels between the development of English common law and classical Roman law, posited in *Ancient Law* (1861) stages of social development common to different peoples that could be correlated with particular instruments of legal growth. Legal systems could be characterized by whether social change was primarily dealt with by legal fictions, equity or natural law, or conscious creative legislation.

Max Weber (1864–1920) used many of the same historical sources as legal evolutionists, but in *Wirtschaft und Gesellschaft* (1922) constructed ideal types to facilitate the comparison of actual social and legal systems in trying to explain the rise of industrial capitalism. His four-cell typology for lawmaking and law application considered the rationality or irrationality of legal thought as well as whether the legal norms and decision-making were highly differentiated from religion, ideology, or emotion. He argued that the category of formal autonomous rationality with a consistent body of general legal norms provided the predictability facilitating modern capitalism.

In an effort to make American lawyers less parochial, John Henry *Wigmore published the three-volume *A Panorama of the World's Legal Systems* (1928). He covered sixteen historic and contemporary legal systems by the pictorial method, using between twenty and fifty pictures accompanied by text for each legal system to enliven its justice buildings, principal legal actors, and characteristic legal materials. Organized historically these systems included the Egyptian, Mesopotamian, Chinese, Hindu, Hebrew, Greek, maritime, Roman, Celtic, Germanic, *canon, Japanese, Mohammedan (Islam), Slavic, Romanesque (civil law), and Anglican.

Contemporary classifications of legal systems attempt to make the criteria of division clear and to assimilate, simplify, and comprehend the great wealth of legal minutiae existing in individual systems. The dominant comparative law approach is to identify legal families, styles, or traditions. The two dominant worldwide legal traditions today are the common law and the *civil law. Beyond the aim of simplification, the idea of legal traditions permits a clearer understanding of pluralistic legal systems with an official, dominant legal tradition that also includes the customary law of indigenous communities or canon law, Muslim law, Hindu law, or Jewish law used by communities lacking a sovereign political organization.

The Development of American Comparative Law. Although the early systematic development of comparative law as a discipline occurred in nineteenth-century Europe, especially in Germany and France, Americans participated at that time in European congresses concerned with improving legislation, facilitating *codification, and recognizing foreign legal entities such as corporations and foreign legal acts such as judgments. The renowned 1900 Paris International Congress of Comparative Law received five American delegates and helped to set the comparative law agenda for the first half of the twentieth century. Besides civil and commercial law, the Congress broadly dealt with procedure, economic and social legislation, public law, and criminology. Jurists supported comparative methods derived from the fields of history, sociology and anthropology, as well as so-called doctrinal legal science.

The first American comparative law congress on the European model was held in 1904 in St. Louis. This Universal Congress of Lawyers and Jurists emphasized courts, procedure, and practical lawyering with some discussion of legal harmonization. Reflecting America's more pragmatic legal culture, lawyers and judges (Associate Justice David J. Brewer of the U.S. Supreme Court was president) ran the Congress, with a smaller representation from academia. Delegates from seventeen countries attended, but the large majority of the 481 participants were from the United States. American professors from twenty-six law schools participated, including such leading comparatists as Munroe Smith (Columbia) and John Wigmore (Northwestern) and other juristic luminaries such as Nathan Abbott (Stanford), James Barr Ames and Samuel Williston (Harvard), and Joseph Beale (Chicago).

Because of the First World War, the next International Congress of Comparative Law was held in 1932 at the Hague. It was the first in the current series organized by the Académie internationale de droit comparé (itself founded in 1924), which sponsored the XVIth Congress in Brisbane, Australia, in 2002. Already in 1932 the American position in comparative law was much more important than in 1900. Of the thirty academy titular

members, five were Americans, including Edwin Borchard (Yale), Roscoe *Pound (Harvard, dean, named president of the Anglo-American group in 1927), Harlan F. *Stone (Columbia, former dean, named U.S. Supreme Court associate justice in 1925 and chief justice in 1941), and John Wigmore (Northwestern). Fully twenty percent of the delegates at the academy's 1932 meeting were Americans.

However, it was only after the Second World War that American professors created the organizational framework that would permit comparative law to securely establish itself in legal *education. In 1951 representatives from fourteen law schools and the American Foreign Law Association established the American Association for the Comparative Study of Law (today the American Society of Comparative Law), which in 1952 began publishing the *American Journal of Comparative Law*. Several of these representatives were immigrants who had fled Germany in the 1930s. Today the society has about one hundred law school members (some with multiple representatives) and ten foreign corresponding institutional members. Its journal has the largest worldwide circulation of any comparative law publication. Moreover, comparative law and specific foreign law courses are now taught at most U.S. law schools; many of these schools have their own student-run comparative and international law journal and maintain summer and even semester programs abroad.

Practicing lawyers and judges support comparative law through many national organizations, including the American Society of International Law and the *American Bar Association's Section on International Law and Practice, both of which have divisions for those interested in foreign and comparative law. American lawyers and judges encounter foreign law issues every day, as globalization characterizes the legal culture of the twenty-first century.

Comparative Lawyers as Cultural Brokers. Certain tasks loosely associated with comparative law actually involve no comparison. This is illustrated by lawyers who investigate a foreign-law issue and scholars who describe some part of a foreign legal system. Such activity may provide the basis for comparison, but is not itself comparative. In fact, most foreign legal system description employs comparison as a method to add meaning to the description. Comparative law requires that the lawyer or scholar is familiar with at least two legal systems, which are normally the jurist's home law as well as the foreign jurisdiction's law. The comparative task is then to communicate to a home audience the meaningful details about some part of a foreign legal system in the language and conceptual framework familiar to the home audience, or vice versa. Where rules, concepts, or institutions have no analogue in the home legal system, the foreign term should be retained and special care taken to avoid mischaracterizing the foreign situation.

Practical Comparative Law. There are many types of practical comparative law, by far the most common objective in the United States. First, one may distinguish between lawyers, in the transnational context, involved with transactions and those concerned with litigation or arbitration. Most international business requires lawyers trained in more than one jurisdiction or multiple lawyers that can cooperate and understand each other in completing a commercial transaction. Lawyers representing individuals with interests in more than one country handle estate planning, tax questions, and family law matters.

Foreign law is increasingly used in American courts (and arbitral tribunals) due to the internationalization of civil and criminal *procedure. This internationalization arises out of the growth of transnational activities and manifests itself when the American court must deal with a foreign substantive law issue, collect evidence abroad, extradite a fugitive, obtain jurisdiction over a foreign country defendant, or enforce a foreign country judgment. The court's involvement with a foreign element will at least implicitly force the judge to face the matter comparatively: how does the foreign law or legal system differ from the American approach? Both lawyers and foreign-law scholars assist the judge in answering this question.

Second, comparative law studies may assist an American legislature or supreme court to reform a legal rule or institution. This type of legal transplant has been common, and in an age of global communication should remain so. The underlying premise to this use of comparative law is that more rather than less information improves rule-making and policy development.

Third, some comparative lawyers work toward the goal of international harmonization or unification of law. This activity is based on the premise that it will improve efficiency or cooperation among people. In Europe this process accelerated after the 1991 Treaty on European Union (at Maastricht), which extended European Community (EC) competency in several fields, including consumer protection. The EC has begun to build, partly by using comparative law studies, a body of

European private law through the use of directives and soft law. The latter includes EC Parliament, Council, and Commission recommendations and opinions, plus member state resolutions and guidelines, which together produce practical effects even though not legally binding. Harmonization is also promoted by developing principles, law restatements, and model laws that will be voluntarily adopted due to their superior formulation. Two recent sets of contract principles are the UNIDROIT Principles of International Commercial Contracts (1994) and Principles of European Contract Law (2000).

This use of comparative law has been successful in the United States in the harmonization of state laws through the efforts of the *American Law Institute with its restatements and the National Conference of Commissioners on Uniform State Laws. Even with NAFTA (1994), however, legal harmonization involving the United States on the supranational level has been disappointing. On the international level, the United Nations Convention on Contracts for the International Sale of Goods (1980) is a success. The United States and twenty-nine other countries have ratified this multilateral treaty, which applies to international sales contracts.

Sociological Comparative Law. Empirical observation for the purpose of generating or testing general explanatory propositions is the essence of the scientific method. When these propositions are about some aspect of at least two legal systems, we can call the enterprise sociological comparative law, although the methodology may borrow from other social sciences such as anthropology, economics, and psychology. Some legal sociologists are interested in establishing general principles about the role of law in society; others may desire to learn more about legal professions or courts in comparative perspective.

This comparative law objective is useful to the formulation of public policy, since it is only when the functions of law and legal institutions are fully understood that policymakers may achieve their goals.

Cultural Comparative Law. Cultural comparative law often strives to break down parochialism and nationalism by providing meaningful information about other legal systems. Many believe that international understanding will promote cooperation and that ignorance breeds distrust. Others are interested in foreign law for the nonutilitarian purpose of education for the sheer joy of learning.

Non-European and Religious Legal Traditions.

The civil law and common law traditions embody concepts and institutions that were developed in the context of European history and culture. Elements shared by both traditions constitute the principles of western law, which have affected all contemporary legal systems including the international law system. But the extent of these principles' penetration into non-European societies differs widely, depending on the strength of indigenous traditions and the broader institutional and cultural influence of European immigrant communities.

The major competing legal influences in the Middle East, Africa, and South and Southeast Asia are the religious legal traditions of Islamic, Jewish, and Hindu law and the variety of indigenous legal cultures often called customary or tribal law. For East Asia there is the residual influence of the imperial Chinese legal tradition. In addition, some Latin American nations have significant indigenous populations that have retained customary law. A few comparatists undertake the difficult task of studying these non-western legal systems. This work involves multidisciplinary skills, but the insight gained from the effort often provides a fresh perspective on one's own legal system.

[See also Civil Law in America; Conflict of Laws; International Law]

• John Henry Merryman and David S. Clark, Comparative Law: Western European and Latin American Legal Systems, 1978. Harold J. Berman, Law and Revolution: The Formation of the Western Legal Tradition, 1983. John Henry Merryman, The Civil Law Tradition: An Introduction to the Legal Systems of Western Europe and Latin America, 2d ed., 1985. John Henry Merryman, David S. Clark and John O. Haley, The Civil Law Tradition: Europe, Latin America, and East Asia, 1994. David S. Clark, "The Use of Comparative Law by American Courts," American Journal of Comparative Law (Supp. 1994): 23–40. Rudolf B. Schlesinger et al., Comparative Law, 1998. Konrad Zweigert and Hein Kötz, Introduction to Comparative Law, translated by Tony Weir, 3d ed., 1998. David S. Clark, "Comparing the Work and Organization of Lawyers Worldwide: The Persistence of Legal Traditions," in Lawyers' Practice and Ideals: A Comparative View (John J. Barceló III and Roger C. Cramton, eds.) 1999, 9–155. Mary Ann Glendon, Michael Wallace Gordon and Paolo G. Carozza, Comparative Legal Traditions in a Nutshell, 2d ed. 1999. David S. Clark, "Nothing New in 2000?: Comparative Law in 1900 and Today," Tulane Law Review (2001): 871–912.

—David S. Clark

COMPENSATION, WORKERS. See Labor Law: Workplace Issues.

COMPLEX LITIGATION. Cases generally become complex because of some combination of difficult legal or factual issues, large numbers of parties, and large amounts of money at stake. Even the authoritative Manual for Complex Litigation has vacillated among definitions for "complex" in its various editions. By the 1990s, complex cases involved claims and settlements running into billions of dollars, and large enterprises—sometimes whole industries—are sometimes said to be put at risk.

The received wisdom is that until the middle of the twentieth century almost all civil litigation in American courts was "simple" in that it involved one plaintiff, one defendant, and relatively straightforward legal issues. That description probably overlooked many more intricate legal proceedings, but it is beyond doubt that the tenor changed after the Second World War, and that the dominant themes of U.S. civil litigation during the twentieth century's second half emerged from complex litigation. Economic, procedural, and political developments have contributed to the growing importance of complex litigation.

The economic developments might now be labeled "globalization." Throughout the twentieth century, American commerce became increasingly dominated by firms that marketed products throughout the nation and beyond. National markets meant that legal claims arising from product distribution—whether they were for price-fixing, product defects, or *securities violations—could be asserted on behalf of large numbers of claimants from across the country.

Mid-century procedural developments facilitated litigation that encompassed multiparty claims. Personal jurisdiction limits, fairly strict at the end of the nineteenth century in requiring the defendant to be a resident or present in the jurisdiction, became much looser in the wake of the Supreme Court's adoption of a "minimum contacts" approach in International Shoe Co. v. Washington (1945). The adoption of the Federal Rules of Civil Procedure in 1938 relaxed prior limitations on party joinder in a single lawsuit, providing a procedural format for adding claims against or by numerous parties who could be joined under the expansive attitude toward personal jurisdiction. The Federal Rules also introduced unprecedented broad opportunities for *evidence discovery.

Political developments that contributed to the growth of complex litigation largely focused on the rights of the disadvantaged. With *Brown v. Board of Education (1954), the Supreme Court committed the courts to a course of mandating public school integration. Later cases broadened occasions for "structural litigation," in which plaintiffs sought to persuade judges to revise (and sometimes to oversee) the operation of large public institutions. Meanwhile, legislation expanded protections against employment *discrimination and for consumers, all of which might often be asserted in large, multiparty lawsuits.

These developments gathered considerable momentum due to further procedural innovations during the 1960s. In 1966, the federal *class action rule was amended to broaden its potential operation. Two years later, Congress passed the Multidistrict Litigation Act, which permitted the combination of federal court cases from across the nation into a single proceeding before a designated federal judge. And many federal judges started using the "single assignment" system, under which they took control of cases from start to finish. Together, these procedural changes meant that federal judges appeared to wield unprecedented power in a wide array of cases. One leading scholar even proclaimed that "public law litigation" had transformed the role of the judge.

Consequently, a backlash emerged. Many decried the "blackmail" possibilities afforded by broad litigation opportunities in *antitrust and securities cases and urged that class actions be curtailed. "Consumer" class actions, initially conceived as devices that would provide otherwise unavailable legal relief to those swindled of small amounts, but in large numbers, came into disfavor. It seemed that settlements enriched lawyers who brought the suits, but did nothing for class members, who often got only coupons or discounts for further purchases of the offending defendants' products. Thus, there came to be increasing uneasiness about the "enabling" features of complex litigation—particularly class actions—because they might enable lawyers to use essentially meritless claims to exact large fees or settlements.

By the 1980s, mass *tort litigation emerged as a major concern, especially the tens of thousands of *personal injury suits by workers exposed to asbestos. Mass tort class actions were attempted by both plaintiffs and defendants. Plaintiffs sought to bring class actions on behalf of all users of a supposedly injurious product, and defendants resisted on the ground that the claims of the various plaintiffs were too different from each other to be combined in a single case. Defendants, on the other hand, sought to use class action settlements as a method of achieving "global peace" in connection with potential tort litigation. Defendants presented judges with proposals approved by plaintiff lawyers that would require all prospective plaintiffs to pursue out-of-court remedies, arguing that the plaintiffs' differences would not matter because of the settlement.

Altogether, these pressures made the 1990s a decade of debate about reforming complex litigation. In 1995, Congress passed the Private Securities Litigation Reform Act to curtail securities fraud class actions. New proposals to amend the federal class-action rule were circulated in 1996, but thus far these have led only to adding a provision for immediate appeal of decisions about whether a case is a proper class action. Two decisions by the Supreme Court—*Amchem Products, Inc.* v. *Windsor* (1997) and *Ortiz* v. *Fibreboard Corp.* (1999)—emphasized the need for careful attention to differences among class members' tort claims in connection with global peace settlements.

In the twenty-first century, therefore, complex litigation looms large in a variety of areas—mass torts, consumer rights, securities fraud, and antitrust. Billion-dollar settlements have become renowned, if not commonplace, and in *tobacco litigation plaintiff attorneys might receive fees exceeding $1 billion. Efforts to reform class actions continue, including proposals published in 2001, but these present difficult problems about balancing the rights of defendants and plaintiffs. In addition, there is the question whether reform should come from Congress (which acted unilaterally in regard to securities class actions) or from the rule amendment process managed by the judicial branch. Thus, although complex litigation will clearly continue to play an important role in the American economy, the path to further reform is far from clear.

[*See also* Procedure, Civil; Torts]

• Abram Chayes, "The Role of the Judge in Public Law Litigation," *Harvard Law Review* (1976): 1281–1316. *Manual for Complex Litigation*, 3d ed., 1995. Linda Mullenix, *Mass Tort Litigation*, 1996. Richard L. Marcus and Edward F. Sherman, *Complex Litigation*, 3d ed., 1998. Jay Tidmarsh and Roger Trangsrud, *Complex Litigation and the Adversary System*, 1999.

—Richard L. Marcus

COMPLICITY. Derived from the same root word as "accomplice," "complicity," in most states today, refers to all persons who are accountable for crimes committed by another, regardless of whether or not they were present when the crimes were committed.

[*See also* Criminal Law Principles]

—David S. Clark

COMPUTERIZED RESEARCH. The use of computers for the storing and retrieval of legal information is a relatively new but essential tool for legal research. The traditional bibliographic tools for legal research were primarily developed near the end of the nineteenth century. Near the end of the twentieth century the volume of case and statutory materials amassed in the U.S. was so great that lawmakers, legal scholars, and practitioners desperately needed a new method to record, store, and retrieve this material. The computer solved problems of both storage (space) and access. By the late twentieth century digitized databases containing whole bodies of law, many of which received daily or hourly updates, new search methodologies to access that information, and the hardware in which to house them were in place. The development of computerized legal research was a blend of private and government initiatives. One of the earliest computerized legal research systems was developed by the U.S. military in the late 1960s. A huge database of federal case and statutory law, it could not be searched remotely; rather, queries were sent to a computer operator, who would then search the database. Much of the primary source material that was converted to machine-readable format was later acquired by commercial systems (primarily LEXIS) to seed their initial databases.

LEXIS began as a nonprofit venture of the Ohio Bar Association. It sold its product to the Mead Corporation, a paper manufacturer alarmed by the prospect of a "paperless society" In 1980, the Mead Data Corporation launched NEXIS, a full-text database of secondary source information—primarily newspapers. The academic publishing giant, Reed-Elsevier, would later acquire LEXIS-NEXIS as part of the large consolidation of legal publishers in the 1990s.

West, the venerable behemoth of legal publishing, allowed LEXIS to make major inroads into their traditional market before responding with a system of its own, WESTLAW. West took tentative initial steps in the new realm of electronic media, primarily because it was concerned about competing with its own print products. Consequently, the first version of WESTLAW provided access to West headnotes only. To develop its system, West employed software developed by the Canadian academic Hugh Lawford for a Canadian electronic legal research system known as Quick Law. This first version of WESTLAW, launched in 1976, was a flop. LEXIS, with its full-text database, was considered far superior.

In another move, West struck a deal with the U.S. Department of Justice, which had developed its own full-text system, JURIS. Much of the JURIS database was given to WESTLAW in exchange for the right to use copyrighted West materials. The next version of WESTLAW added full-text capabilities and began replicating many of the search features offered on LEXIS. Meanwhile, VU/TEXT, a major database of Knight-Ridder–owned newspapers, was made available via WEST LAW, to compete with the NEXIS portion of LEXIS. Even with these enhancements, it took another full decade to catch up with the LEXIS market lead.

By the mid- to late-1980s WESTLAW and LEXIS-NEXIS had established themselves as the leading purveyors of electronic legal research tools. Initially, LEXIS and WESTLAW were accessible only through special dedicated terminals, using 300 baud modems (300 bits of information per second). The early terminals were huge, cumbersome machines, and their relative speed of access was frustratingly slow compared to early-twenty-first computers, which operate at speeds of 56,000 up to 10,000,000 bits per second, depending on the type of connection they employ. Eventually, LEXIS launched the Ubiq terminal, a smaller model that would fit on a desktop. The introduction of the personal computer in the early 1980s gave a boost to computer-assisted legal research. Law offices switched from dedicated word processing equipment to personal computers that were multifunctional. Adding a modem and some communications software transformed the personal computer into a workstation for computer-assisted legal research. This made it possible to download research material directly into documents simultaneously being created on the personal computer.

From the early 1990s, the Internet has provided another electronic platform from which to conduct legal research. The Internet's importance as a resource for law firms, legal publishers, and researchers cannot be emphasized enough. For large firms with multinational and international offices, the Internet has provided swifter communication. For publishers, the Internet has helped improve the speed of access to the major commercial systems such as LEXIS and WESTLAW. For individual researchers, the Internet makes a huge array of legal research materials available quickly and conveniently.

In more general terms, the Internet has greatly enhanced the speed of disseminating all kinds of legal information. For example, at the United States Supreme Court, Project Hermes puts the full text of U.S. Supreme Court opinions on the Internet within about twenty minutes after they are handed down. Prior to Project Hermes, the loose-leaf U.S. Law Week was the fastest way to get access to the full text of a newly announced Supreme Court decision. Before the Internet, access to other court decisions often took months. Now, many other courts have followed the example of the U.S. Supreme Court and are posting their opinions on the Internet soon after they are handed down. Legislatures and administrative agencies also are posting new laws and regulations on the Internet directly. The U.S. Supreme Court and many other courts and government agencies publish primary source materials on the Internet.

New avenues of competition for both entrepreneurial and established publishers have opened: a host of new commercial publishers have emerged on the Internet, several are competing directly with print publishers for market share. Some of these newer publishers originated in CD-ROM publishing; others simply make information available for free to end users (see PUBLISHING, LAW).

The CD-ROM is another important element of electronic legal research. The CD-ROM was introduced in the mid-1980s as a medium for distributing music. It quickly became clear that this new format held immediate application for distributing practically any other form of digitized information. West Publishing entered the CD-ROM market for legal publishing early, but, similar to its early experience with WESTLAW, it was challenged by having to compete with its own print sales; accordingly, West set prices artificially high. New entries into this market were more successful, most notably LOISLAW.

These new electronic means of organizing, storing, accessing, and sharing legal information have had an enormous impact on the American legal profession. Computerized legal research has effected the distribution and access to legal information, the publication of traditional print resources, legal *education and scholarship, contemporary legal practice, access to legal services, and employment opportunities within the legal profession. Traditional print publications have become less important for some types of material, most notably case law. Print resources currently remain the preferred format for statutes, monographs, and many other secondary materials. This may change with time, but today, effective legal research requires knowledge of and access to research materials published in all formats.

In terms of legal education and scholarship, access to computerized information is vital, although contemporary legal practice in every venue demands that law students can efficiently use both print and online research sources. In fact, contemporary legal ethics make it nearly impossible to do effective legal research without some access to computer-assisted systems. Failure to do so could be considered malpractice in some situations.

The breadth and depth of computerized legal research tools and their many capabilities have engendered a spirit of experimentation among some legal educators. At least one law school has attempted to operate solely over the Internet, but accreditation officials have not endorsed the idea. In contrast, many legal academicians are cautious about fully endorsing these new technologies, at least in professorial contexts. Although legal scholarship is widely distributed online, law school faculties remain reluctant to accept nonprint materials to satisfy tenure requirements. This is likely to change with time.

Among contemporary legal practitioners, computerized legal research resources have enabled some firms to reduce the size of their libraries. In many cases, costs for legal research have switched from being built into firm overhead to being billed directly to clients, sometimes with markup. Closely tied to changes in the practice of law is the notion of access to legal services. Although computerized legal research has had little impact on access to legal services, some lawyers are attempting to expand their practice via the Internet. And some smaller firms have been able to gain quick access to large databases of legal information previously only available to larger law firms. This in turn has expanded the opportunities for information professionals in the legal profession, including librarians and computer professionals. Law firm librarians now constitute the single largest constituency of the law library profession, whereas just twenty years ago, only the very largest law firms employed librarians.

A host of allied computer-related technologies have initiated innovations in hardware and software, and their implementation in legal education and practice contexts. Necessary additions and amendments to laws and regulations must respond to these changes. The developments in computerized legal research outlined above have created many crucial changes—it is an exciting time to be studying and practicing law.

[See also Legal Practice, Forms of]

• M. Ethan Katsh, Law in a Digital World, 1995. Robert C. Berring, "Legal Information and the Search for Cognitive Authority," California Law Review (2000): 1673–1708.
—Mark Engsberg

COMPUTERS. See Computerized Research; Property, Intellectual; Technology and Law.

CONCILIATION. See Arbitration and Mediation.

CONCURRENT OWNERSHIP. *See* Property, Real.

CONFESSION. *See* Interrogation and Confession.

CONFIDENTIALITY, LAWYER-CLIENT. *See* Ethics and Professional Responsibility, Legal.

CONFIDENTIALITY OF SOURCES. *See* Media and the Law; Speech and the Press, Freedom of.

CONFLICT OF LAWS

   Introduction. Conflict of laws is the body of law that deals with disputes that implicate the laws of more than one country or state because some of their constituent elements are connected with more than one jurisdiction. These elements may be the events that give rise to the dispute, the location of its object, or the nationality, citizenship, domicile, residence, or other affiliation of the parties. Thus, a *contract dispute between citizens of different countries or domiciliaries of different American states, or a *property dispute between residents of one state regarding assets situated in another state, or a *tort resulting from conduct occurring in one state and causing injury in another state are all examples of disputes that fall within the subject of conflict of laws.

   Implicit in conflict of laws is the assumption that each state involved has a claim to apply its own law, thus producing the conflict. While this assumption is debatable, what is not debatable is that this subject does not encompass disputes between countries as such, when acting in the exercise of pure governmental authority. These disputes fall within the scope of public *international law, as opposed to private international law—another name by which conflicts law is known in most countries outside the United States. Although this name may give the impression that conflicts law emanates from some international source, in reality it is part of national law. Each country determines for itself how best to resolve international conflicts of laws, subject only to mild restraints imposed by customary international law and treaty.

   In the United States, conflict of laws encompasses at least three categories of conflict, the first of which is intranational and the second two, international. In descending order of frequency, these are (1) conflicts between the laws of states of the United States (interstate conflicts); (2) conflicts between the law of a state of the United States and the law of a foreign country; and (3) conflicts between American federal law and the law of a foreign country. Conflicts of the first two categories are governed by state law, and largely by the same principles, subject only to mild restraints imposed by federal law, primarily constitutional law. The third category is governed by federal law that has to a great extent developed out of state law principles and continues to be influenced by it. A fourth category of conflicts, discussed elsewhere, concerns "vertical conflicts" between federal law and state law. These conflicts are governed by federal law, which, when applicable, preempts state law. When federal law is silent, these conflicts are resolved under principles of *federalism, which may or may not coincide with general-conflicts principles.

   All four categories of conflict may be adjudicated in either state or federal courts. The applicable conflicts law depends not on whether the adjudicating court is state or federal, but rather to which of the above categories the conflict belongs. For example, if the conflict belongs to a category governed by state law, such as the vast majority of interstate conflicts, then state conflicts law will be binding even on a federal court, at least when the court's jurisdiction is based on the parties' diversity of citizenship.

   The Three Parts of Conflicts Law. Conflicts law consists of three parts: (1) jurisdiction, which deals with the question of which of the involved states' courts or other organs will adjudicate the dispute; (2) choice of law, which deals with the question of whether the merits of the dispute will be resolved under the substantive law of the state of adjudication or under the law of another involved state; and (3) judgment-recognition, which deals with the requirements under which the courts of one state will recognize and enforce a judgment rendered in another state.

   The jurisdictional question and the choice-of-law question are analytically distinct, although in many cases they are practically interrelated. The jurisdictional question focuses on the relationship between the defendant and the forum state, and asks whether that relationship is sufficiently close as to fairly subject the defendant to litigation in that state and to justify utilizing that state's judicial resources to adjudicate the particular dispute. The choice-of-law question focuses on both parties and their dispute and seeks to identify that state, be it the forum state or another state, whose relationship to the dispute is such as to render most appropriate the application of its law to the merits of the dispute. In many cases, the same relationship that forms the basis of a state's jurisdiction to adjudicate the case can also be the basis for applying that state's law to the merits. This is by no means true in all cases.

   In public-law disputes—disputes involving a

state in the exercise of governmental authority, such as in the enforcement of its criminal laws— all three of the above questions are merged into one—the question of jurisdiction. When a state has jurisdiction to try a criminal case, that state applies its own law and enforces the resulting judgment. It does not apply the criminal laws nor enforce the criminal judgments of another state. Cases in which more than one state has concurrent jurisdiction, such as cases involving transborder crimes, are addressed and resolved as jurisdictional conflicts—for example through *extradition—rather than as choice-of-law conflicts.

Jurisdiction. In its broadest sense, jurisdiction is the power of a decision-maker to resolve a dispute in a binding manner. When the decision-maker is a court or other tribunal, the dispute is resolved through adjudication, and the power to do so is called judicial jurisdiction. It can be contrasted with legislative, or prescriptive, jurisdiction, which is the power to enunciate norms governing the merits of the dispute. The source of judicial jurisdiction is the law that constitutes the particular court, and thus it is a national or state law rather than international law. In some countries the exercise of jurisdiction is restricted by international treaties, such as the Brussels-Lugano conventions among several European countries; in some federal systems, such as the United States, the exercise of jurisdiction by the constituent states must conform to certain outer limits imposed by federal law, primarily the *due process clause of the federal constitution. This clause requires that the state that asserts jurisdiction have sufficient contacts with the defendant or the transaction from which the claim arises or with the property that is the subject of the litigation. In addition, the defendant must be given sufficient notice and opportunity to defend.

Subject to these limitations, each state itself delineates the bases on which its courts are authorized to adjudicate cases with nonlocal elements (jurisdiction in the international sense), and then allocates that authority internally among the various geographical subdivisions or judicial districts within that state (local jurisdiction or venue) and among its various general or specialized courts, tribunals, or other adjudicating agencies in each locality (competence or subject-matter jurisdiction). To render a valid judgment, a court must, in the absence of acquiescence by the defendant, satisfy all three types of jurisdiction.

In the United States, for historical reasons, a state court's interstate or international jurisdiction is divided into personal jurisdiction (*in personam*) and jurisdiction over things (*in rem*). Personal jurisdiction, which is the power to determine the rights and duties of the parties and to bind them personally, is further subdivided into general and specific jurisdiction. General jurisdiction exists when the defendant is domiciled, incorporated, has its principal place of business, or conducts "continuous and systematic" business in the forum state. Historically, service of process on the defendant within the territory of the court was also a basis of general jurisdiction, but the constitutionality of this basis is now questionable, at least when it is not supported by other defendant contacts. When a court has general jurisdiction, it may adjudicate any claims against the defendant, even claims unrelated to the defendant's contacts with, or activity in, that state. In contrast, when a court has only specific jurisdiction, it may only adjudicate claims against the defendant that arise from the defendant's specific contacts with, or activity in, the forum state. These contacts need not be as pervasive as those supporting general jurisdiction, but must satisfy a certain "minimum" and be of the type that makes it foreseeable that the defendant would be subject to litigation in the forum state and reasonable for that state to do so.

Jurisdiction over property or things is based on the presence of a thing within the territory of the forum state, and is subdivided into jurisdiction *in rem* and *quasi in rem*. When a lawsuit seeks to determine the parties' rights in, or relating to, that thing, the court is exercising *in rem* jurisdiction, and may adjudicate those rights even if it does not have personal jurisdiction over the defendant. In contrast, when the lawsuit seeks to vindicate claims against the defendant that are unrelated to that thing, the court is exercising *quasi in rem* jurisdiction. Since 1977, this basis of jurisdiction is— in the absence of other defendant contacts—constitutionally insufficient unless the claim has been previously reduced to a judgment rendered by another court that had jurisdiction over the defendant.

The defendant's consent is a sufficient basis of jurisdiction that may be manifested in different ways, including an express agreement to that effect. Through such an agreement (forum-selection clause), the parties agree to submit their present or future disputes (exclusively or nonexclusively) to a designated court that may or may not otherwise have jurisdiction. Such clauses are much more common in recent years, and are generally enforceable in the absence of contractual defects such as duress or serious overreaching.

In many multistate situations, the courts of more than one state may have concurrent jurisdiction to adjudicate the same dispute. In such a case, the plaintiff, who always has the choice of where to file the lawsuit, may shop for the most advantageous forum, a technique known as forum shopping. One of the mechanisms devised in the United States and in other *common-law systems to discourage this technique is the doctrine of *forum non conveniens*, which allows a court to decline to adjudicate the suit if, despite the existence of jurisdiction, litigation in that state would be seriously inconvenient and burdensome, and if another, more convenient, forum is available to the plaintiff.

Choice of Law. When a court exercises its jurisdiction to adjudicate a case with foreign elements, the court applies its own procedural law to the proceedings before it. With regard to the merits of the case, however, the court may or may not apply its own substantive law. This is the choice-of-law question, which may be answered legislatively as in most civil-law systems, or through judicial precedent, as in most common-law systems, including those of the United States. These rules may point to the law of either the forum state or to another state, depending on each state's pertinent contacts with the case. For example, in tort cases, these rules may point to the state where the tort was committed or the injury occurred (*lex loci delicti*), in contract cases to the state where the contract was made (*lex loci contractus*), and in cases involving land, to the state where the property is situated (*lex rei sitae*).

The above three rules are typical of what is usually referred to as a traditional choice-of-law system. In the United States, this system was enshrined in the First Conflicts Restatement drafted in 1933 by Professor Henry Beale under the auspices of the *American Law Institute. For much of the twentieth century, these rules and others like them were more or less uniformly followed in all states. This places a high premium on providing certainty and predictability in the choice of the governing law, leaving little room for judicial discretion. These rules give no preference to the forum state, and indeed they aspire to produce international or interstate uniformity—that is, make it more likely that each multistate case will be governed by the same law regardless of where the case is litigated. The choice of the governing law is based not on the content of the laws of the involved states, but rather on the territorial or other factual contacts of those states to the case at hand. Once a state is found to have the predesignated contact, such as the place of the injury, that state's law is applied almost automatically and—save for

some limited exceptions—regardless of its content, its underlying policy, or the substantive quality of the result that such application produces. Indeed, the objective of the traditional choice-of-law process is not supposed to be to ensure a substantively "just" result (material justice), but rather to ensure the application of the spatially appropriate law (conflicts justice).

Traditional choice-of-law rules such as those described above continue to be followed in many countries, including some states of the United States. However, in the 1960s, a movement emerged in the United States that has been characterized as a "conflicts revolution," which denounced both the specific rules and the general aspirations of the traditional choice-of-law process. At least in tort and contract conflicts, which are the most frequent conflicts, preconceived choice-of-law rules were abandoned in favor of various "approaches," such as Brainerd Currie's governmental interest analysis, Robert Leflar's choice-influencing considerations or better-law approach, and the Second Conflicts Restatement's (1971) most-significant relationship approach. By the beginning of the twenty-first century, all but about a dozen states have abandoned the traditional system in favor of one of the above approaches or a combination thereof, with the majority opting for the Second Restatement. Although different in many respects, these approaches reject the notion of preselecting the applicable law on the basis of a single territorial contact, and instead leave the selection to the court on a case-by-case basis. The choice is to be based on multiple contacts and factors, such as the content of the conflicting substantive laws and their underlying policies, the presumed "interests" or claims of the involved states to apply their respective laws, and the substantive quality of the result that the chosen law will produce in the individual case.

As a result of conflicts-resolution, the choice-of-law process today is more flexible, less predictable, and more forum-biased than it was only one generation earlier. The possibility that the forum state will apply its own law to most multistate cases adjudicated by its courts is now greater than in much of the twentieth century, especially in the United States. In turn, this increases the possibility that a given case will be governed by a different substantive law depending on where it is litigated, which in turn reinforces the incentive for forum shopping described earlier.

The United States Constitution provides certain means for restraining the freedom of states to make choice-of-law decisions through the due process, *full faith and credit, *privileges and immunities, and *equal protection clauses. However, as presently interpreted by the U.S. Supreme Court, these clauses amount to very modest restraints. For example, the due process and full faith and credit clauses are interpreted as allowing the application of the law of any state that has "a significant contact or significant aggregation of contacts, creating state interests, such that choice of its law is neither arbitrary nor fundamentally unfair" *(Allstate Insurance Co.* v. *Hague* (1981)). While the qualifier "significant" would seem to be a sufficient safeguard, in practice it can be satisfied rather easily, at least in the case of corporations with nationwide business.

While the conflicts laws of most states have been gradually diverging, they have also been converging in at least one important respect. Most of them now recognize the principle of party autonomy—namely, the notion that parties to a contractual relationship should have the power to agree in advance on the law that will govern disputes arising from that relationship. Although this is a principle whose origin can be traced back to ancient Greece, it was only in the second half of the twentieth century that it acquired the status of an almost universal principle sanctioned in most countries, including the United States. It is now followed not only in ordinary contracts, but also in matrimonial agreements, other *family-law agreements, and even in unilateral juridical acts such as testaments.

The use of a choice-of-law clause, especially when combined with a choice-of-forum clause or an *arbitration clause, can provide parties with a modicum of predictability. This is a good antidote to the uncertainty generated by conflicts-resolution, but it is an antidote that can only work in some cases. For example, the principle of party autonomy is not available in cases such as torts in which the disputants are not parties to a preexisting relationship. And while this principle is recognized in most countries, it is also subject to several limitations and exceptions that differ from country to country. Thus, there is the possibility of a different outcome, depending on where the case is litigated.

Recognition and Enforcement of Judgments. One of the many differences between local and multistate cases is the increased possibility that in multistate cases, a *judgment may have to be enforced in a state other than the one in which it was rendered. This will be the case if the defeated litigant (judgment debtor) does not voluntarily comply with the judgment and does not have sufficient assets in the forum state against which the successful litigant (judgment creditor) can execute the judgment. In such a case, the creditor will seek to have the judgment recognized and enforced in another state that has jurisdiction over the *debtor and in which the debtor has sufficient assets.

As between states of the United States, the recognition requirements are prescribed by federal law, primarily the Constitution's full faith and credit clause. This clause requires each state to give to a judgment of a sister state the same effect that the judgment had in the state of rendition, provided that the judgment is "final," "on the merits," and rendered by a court that had jurisdiction under its own law, which must conform with federal due process standards. Once these requirements are met, the judgment must be recognized, and may not be reviewed on the merits, even if it applied the wrong law or reached a result that contravenes the public policy of the second state. The reason for this strict regime is the national policy of finality embodied in the doctrine of *res judicata*, which seeks to conserve judicial resources and protect party expectations by prohibiting relitigation of disputes that have been finally decided.

The full faith and credit clause does not apply to foreign-country judgments, and thus American courts are not constitutionally compelled to enforce them. Nevertheless, as a matter of international comity, American courts recognize foreign-country judgments that meet the requirements for recognizing sister-state judgments, but also reserve the right to refuse recognition on certain grounds. For example, recognition may be refused if the judgment does not satisfy American jurisdictional standards, even if it does satisfy the foreign-law standards; if it is one for taxes or penalties; if it offends the recognizing court's public policy; or if it was rendered in a system that does not provide impartial tribunals or does not satisfy certain minimum standards of procedural fairness.

In many countries, foreign judgments are recognized under similar but somewhat less hospitable standards. For example, in some countries, recognition depends on whether the rendering court had applied the law that would have been chosen under the choice-of-law rules of the recognizing court or had reached a substantially equivalent result. In other countries, recognition is usually denied on public policy grounds to judgments awarding "excessive" sums of money, especially American judgments imposing punitive damages. Finally, some countries condition recognition on reciprocity-that is, on whether the country of rendition would recognize similar judgments from the second country—while other countries refuse recognition outright in the absence of a treaty requiring such recognition.

[See also Comparative Law]

• Brainerd Currie, Selected Essays on the Conflict of Laws, 1963. David F. Cavers, The Choice of Law Process, 1965. American Law Institute, Restatement of the Law Second: Conflict of Laws 2d, 3 vols., 1971. Albert A. Ehrenzweig, Private International Law, 1972. Robert A. Leflar, Luther L. McDougal, and Robert L. Felix, American Conflicts Law, 4th ed., 1986. Friedrich K. Juenger, Choice of Law and Multistate Justice, 1993. William M. Richman and William L. Reynolds, Understanding Conflict of Laws, 2d ed., 1993. Gene R. Shreve, A Conflict-of-Laws Anthology, 1997. Symeon C. Symeonides, Wendy Collins Perdue, and Arthur T. von Mehren, Conflict of Laws: American, Comparative, International, 1998. Symeon C. Symeonides, Private International Law at the End of the 20th Century: Progress or Regress? 1999. Eugene F. Scoles, Peter Hay, Patrick J. Borchers, and Symeon C. Symeonides, Conflict of Laws, 3d ed., 2000. Russell J. Weintraub, Commentary on the Conflict of Laws, 4th ed., 2001.

—Symeon C. Symeonides

CONGRESS. Decisions about Congress's place within the political system were at the center of the debates at the Constitutional Convention concerning national power versus state power, majority tyranny and individual rights, and the checks and balances of institutional power. The Anti-Federalists fought for a strong Congress that would check the *president, whom they feared might become a king. One proposal even had Congress electing the president. However, the compromise that resulted in the creation of the Electoral College provided the desired distance between the president and the people, while denying Congress a potentially crucial source of power. The "Great Compromise," which divided *legislative power between the House and the Senate, also reflected a balance between those who wanted stronger representation for national interests over local interests. In Federalist 56, Madison avowed that "it is a sound and important principle that the representative ought to be acquainted with the interests and circumstances of his constituents." The two-year House term was specifically intended to tie legislators to public sentiment, while the Senate, with its six-year term and indirect election, was to be the "saucer that cooled the hot tea" of the more volatile House and able to speak for the national interest. At the same time, the equal representation that smaller states received in the Senate provided the assurance that they would not be trampled on by the large states.

On balance, Congress was clearly the "first branch" in the early decades of the nation's history. It was given the leading role in a vast array of explicitly enumerated powers, including regulating commerce, coining money, raising and supporting armies, creating the federal courts, establishing post offices and roads, declaring war, and levying taxes. The "elastic clause," which gave Congress the power "to make all laws which shall be necessary and proper for carrying into execution the foregoing powers," gave it a vast range of implicit powers.

The president, in contrast, was given few explicit powers, and played a much less visible role in the early years of our history than he does today. In the first 125 years of U.S. history, several great presidents left their mark on national *politics (Washington, Jackson, and Lincoln, among others), but Congress dominated much of the day-to-day politics. With a relatively limited range of national powers and a small international role, national politics revolved around such issues as tariffs, slavery, and internal improvements. Given its tendency to address these issues with patronage and the pork barrel, Congress was better suited for the task than the president. Congressional giants such as Henry Clay, John *Calhoun, and Daniel *Webster also contributed to the institution's clout. Congress reached the peak of its power during the "Golden Age of Congress" from Reconstruction through World War I. Speakers Thomas Reed and Joseph Cannon ruled the House with an iron fist at the close of the nineteenth century through the early part of the twentieth. No president between *Lincoln and Theodore Roosevelt substantially challenged Congress's central role in the policymaking process.

While TR and Woodrow Wilson redressed the balance to some extent, it was not until Franklin D. Roosevelt that the presidency supplanted Congress as the "first branch." The economic crisis of the Great Depression called for the kind of swift action that Congress typically was unable to provide. FDR's leadership in creating the "New Deal" cemented the president's place at the center of national policymaking. World War II further solidified that position. Lyndon Johnson's "Great Society" programs of the 1960s, including Medicare, Medicaid, the Civil Rights Act, and the Voting Rights Act, maintained the president's leadership role. It was not until Congress reasserted its power in the 1970s, including its investigation of the Watergate scandal (which led to Richard Nixon's resignation), the War Powers Act (1973), the Budget and Impoundment Control Act (1974), and substantial internal reforms, that the balance of power was restored. More recently, in 1994, the "Gingrich Revolution" and "The Contract with America" produced the first Republican Congress in more than forty years. Additional reforms aimed at restoring public confidence in the institution had some positive effect, but Republican leaders overplayed their hand and Democrats picked up seats in the House and Senate in the 1998 midterm elections, something that had not happened in the president's party since 1934. However, Bill Clinton's impeachment prevented him from taking advantage of these gains by his party. Further gains by the Democrats in 2000 reduced the Republicans to razor-thin majorities (with a 50–50 tie in the Senate producing a historic power-sharing arrangement on Senate committees). The close margins in the Congress will ensure that the institution will play a central role in the policy-making process for the next several years.

The Institutional Development of Congress. Despite the vast transformation of modern politics, Congress is relatively unchanged as an institution. Henry Clay or Joe Cannon could slip onto the floor of the House today and have a pretty good sense of what was going on. They would be mystified by the C-SPAN cameras and other electronic gadgets, but the essence of the process would be very familiar. While the basic contours are the same, there have been important developments in the staff, parties and leadership, and the committee system.

The size of personal and committee staff exploded in the 1970s and 1980s (total congressional staff is more than four times as big as it was 40 years ago and the size of committee staff increased by three-fold in the 1970s alone). Part of the motivation for the growth was to reduce the gap between the policymaking capability of Congress and the president, especially with regard to fiscal policy. The larger committee staffs gave members of Congress independent sources of information and expertise with which they could challenge the president. The other motivation was electoral. By increasing the size of their personal staff, members were able to open multiple district offices and expand the opportunities for casework. One of the reforms of the Republican Congress in 1995 was to cut committee staff by one-third, but personal staff was left untouched.

Political parties in Congress have typically reflected the individualism of the institution. Compared with the parliamentary systems of Western Europe, Congressional parties are very weak. With the exception of the "czarist rule" of Speakers Reed and Cannon at the turn of the twentieth century, leaders do not impose a party line and penalize members who vote against the party. Indeed, they have virtually no ability to impose electoral sanctions (such as denying the party's nomination) on renegade members. Though there are strong party differences on many issues, a majority of both parties is on the same side on about half of all roll call votes in most Congresses. Despite the obvious weakness of parties in Congress, partisanship reached its highest levels in the mid-1980s through the late 1990s, as the proportion of party votes (votes in which a majority of one party opposes a majority of the other party) and party unity soared, especially in the House. David Rohde (1991) has shown that the Democratic party has become much more cohesive because Southern Democrats, partly because of the increasing importance of African-American voters in the South, are starting to vote more like their Northern counterparts.

Modern party leaders in Congress employ a "service oriented" leadership, recognizing that their power is only as strong as the leeway granted them by the rank-and-file membership. A leader's primary responsibility is to get his party's legislative agenda through Congress. Most leadership success depends on personal skills, ability to communicate, and trust. Some of the most successful leaders, such as Lyndon Johnson and Sam Rayburn, kept in touch with key members on a daily basis. Leaders also provide many favors for members (such as making campaign appearances for members, helping them with fundraising, making contributions to their campaigns, helping them get a desired committee assignment, or helping to see a pet project through the legislative process). In this way, the members feel personally obligated to the leadership when it needs a key vote.

The system of standing committees is where the bulk of the legislative work gets done. It did not always work this way. In the late eighteenth and early nineteenth centuries, every bill was sent to a separate select committee, which had little autonomous decision-making power. These committees reported to the Committee of the Whole, which was viewed as the ultimate decision-making body. The standing committee system evolved first in the House, and was quickly followed by the Senate. By the 1820s, a committee system that closely resembles the modern system was already in place. Seniority norms and partisan control of committees were firmly established a few decades later. The number of committees has dramatically fluctuated over the years, and the division of labor that is created by the system facilitates specialization and credit-claiming, serving the members' career goals of getting reelected.

Constitutional Issues. The focus here has been on the internal operations of Congress and its position within the broader political system. However, the courts have also influenced Congress's role in the policymaking process. Since the landmark *Marbury* v. *Madison* decision (1803), which established the practice of *judicial review, the Supreme Court has been an active player in shaping national policy. While an even cursory review of the constitutional struggles between Congress and the Courts would be impossible here, three areas where battles have been waged—the commerce clause, war powers, and redistricting—are discussed next.

Early decisions, such as *McCulloch* v. *Maryland* (1819) and *Gibbons* v. *Ogden* (1824), gave Congress substantial power to regulate interstate commerce through the principles of "implied powers" and "national supremacy" (for example, the power to establish a national bank). Later in the nineteenth century, the Court relied on a distinction between *inter*state commerce and *intra*state commerce to limit Congress's ability to regulate the economy (in such areas as child labor, fraud, the production of impure goods, and worker safety). This distinction was also used to strike down many of the laws passed in the early days of the New Deal. Finally, in 1937, the Court embraced the broader notion of interstate commerce in *NLRB* v. *Jones and Laughlin Steel Corporation*. The Court did not again challenge Congress's authority to regulate interstate commerce for more than a half century, until *U.S.* v. *Lopez* (1995).

For the first 150 years of the nation's history, the Court endorsed the founders' view that Congress and the president should share the war-making powers. The president as commander in chief, and Congress through its power to declare war and raise and support armies, could each stake a legitimate claim. However, in *United States* v. *Curtiss-Wright Export Corp.* (1936), the Court started to view the entire field of foreign affairs as controlled by the president. The Court briefly returned to a more balanced view in *Youngstown Sheet and Tube Co.* v. *Sawyer* (1952), in which the Court said that President Truman did not have the authority to seize the steel mills during the Korean War. But in a series of decisions since that time, the Court has returned to endorsing executive-centered leadership in foreign policy.

Another important area in which Congress and the Courts have tussled is redistricting. The Court traditionally avoided this "political thicket" (see *Colegrove* v. *Green*, 1946), but this changed with *Baker* v. *Carr* (1962) and *Wesberry* v. *Sanders* (1964). These decisions established the principle of "one person, one vote" and struck down legislative districts that had unequal populations. Recently, the Court has become even more active in this area with a series of cases stemming from the landmark case *Shaw* v. *Reno* (1993), which challenged the practice of creating black majority Congressional districts. In *Miller* v. *Johnson* (1995), however, the Court held that race could not be "the predominant factor" in drawing district lines.

[*See also* Governance]

• Richard F. Fenno, *Congressmen in Committees*, 1973. David R. Mayhew, *Congress: The Electoral Connection*, 1974. Douglas Arnold. *The Logic of Congressional Action*, 1990. David W. Rohde, *Parties and Leaders in the Postreform House*, 1991. Gary W. Cox and Mathew D. McCubbins. *Legislative Leviathan: Party Government in the U.S. House*, 1993. Richard L. Hall, *Participation in Congress*, 1996. Gary C. Jacobson, *The Politics of Congressional Elections*, 4th ed., 1997. Keith Krehbiel, *Pivotal Politics: A Theory of U.S. Lawmaking*, 1998. David T. Canon, *Race, Redistricting and Representation: The Unintended Consequences of Black Majority Districts*, 1999.

—David Canon

CONSCIENTIOUS OBJECTION. *See* Civil Disobedience; Ethics, Morality, and Law; Religion; War, Law of.

CONSERVATION. *See* Energy and Natural Resources Law; Environmental Law.

CONSPIRACY. The concept of criminal conspiracy has its earliest roots in fourteenth century English *common law. At that time, it saw limited use as a legal theory. It became more broadly applied in the United States in the nineteenth century, though still the scope of prosecutions was not wide. Today, however, conspiracy is a far-reaching legal principle, embracing *antitrust actions, an enormous number of more traditional criminal cases, and even *tort lawsuits. It is the basis of prosecutions dealing with, among other crimes, drug violations, *securities fraud, murder for hire, bank robbery, and extortion.

The basic criminal conspiracy principle is simple to state, but often difficult to apply. Conspiracy is an agreement by two or more people to commit a crime. In practice, many complex matters are often raised. One is the manner in which the crime is proved at trial. Agreement among conspirators is central to the offense, yet rarely is there clear and direct evidence of an agreement, such as a written statement, a videotaped meeting, or a tape-recorded conversation. As one judge has put it, "A conspiracy is seldom born of open covenants openly arrived at." Courts normally allow circumstantial evidence to be offered at trial so that the trier of fact can infer from particular facts (e.g., the presence of the parties, their relationship, later activities, profits received) the existence of a criminal agreement, even among a large group of individuals.

Another difficult issue concerns the type of evidence which will be admissible against specific defendants in proving their intentional membership in the agreement. Questions are raised, in particular, with respect to out-of-court statements made by coconspirators that are used against all members of the conspiracy, and also as to whether activities before the conspiracy was formed demonstrate a purpose or motive to enter into the later agreement.

Constitutional challenges to conspiracy law are often made, but rarely succeed. The earliest and most fundamental claimed that the crime as charged necessarily violates First Amendment freedom of *speech, for it may focus almost exclusively on a form of pure speech—an agreement to commit a crime. Because the agreement is directed to immediate criminal action, however, courts have consistently rejected the notion that such speech is protected under the Constitution. Narrower challenges have also been made, under the *double jeopardy clause of the Fifth Amendment and the confrontation clause of the Sixth Amendment. Regarding the former, defendants have asserted that they are being punished twice for the same action when they are convicted of the conspiracy to commit a crime and then the crime itself. As conspiracy has at its core an agreement, which the completed crime does not, courts have viewed these crimes as separate offenses, so that punishment for both offenses is not prohibited by the Fifth Amendment. Making the Sixth Amendment challenge, defendants have argued that confessions by one conspirator cannot be allowed in evidence against all parties, for the confessing party may not be available to be challenged at trial. This argument has been more successful; the *Supreme Court has scrutinized such confessions with care and prohibited their use against all except the confessing conspirator.

Conspiracy as a basis for criminal prosecution remains controversial in the twenty-first century. Critics contend that conspiracy trials are too large, often containing as many as ten to fifteen individuals tried jointly. Others wonder about the constitutionality and wisdom of prosecuting some defendants far from their homes because other members of the conspiracy committed acts, furthering the scheme, in distant places. Perhaps the most telling critique raises the question whether conspiracy is needed at all, or at least in many instances in which it is currently utilized. Stiff penalties exist for serious crimes. Most state and federal jurisdictions allow punishment of those who aid and assist in criminal endeavors. Thus, it has been contended that the justice system could do away with the problems associated with conspiracy theory and lose little prosecutorial effectiveness if the crime of conspiracy were either wholly eliminated or sharply restricted in practice. This view has not prevailed. Instead, throughout the United States, in state and federal courts, conspiracy is broadly used in a diverse pool of cases often with quite severe punishments imposed for both the conspiracy and any attempted or completed crimes.

[See also Criminal Law; Criminal Law Principles; Labor Law]

• Philip E. Johnson, "The Unnecessary Crime of Conspiracy," California Law Review 61 (1973): 11–88. Paul Marcus, The Prosecution and Defense of Criminal Conspiracy Cases (1978 and supp. 2000). Paul Marcus, "Conspiracy: The Criminal Agreement in Theory and in Practice," Geo. L. J. 65(1977): 925–67. Paul Marcus, "Conspiracy Law: Time to Turn Back From an Ever Expanding, Ever More Troubling Area," W. & Mary Bill of Rights Law Journal 1 (1992): 1–45.

—Paul Marcus

CONSTABULARY. See Police.

CONSTITUTIONAL AMENDMENTS. Political thinkers have long recognized the desirability of balancing the need for legal stability against the corresponding need for accommodating change. Individuals who feel unable to secure rights constitutionally may engage, like the American colonists, in revolution. Moreover, constitutions, like the Articles of Confederation of 1781, that are too difficult to amend—the Articles required that amendments proposed by Congress had to be approved unanimously by the states—might lead, as the Articles did, to extralegal measures for calling a new constitutional convention and ratifying a new document.

States began writing new *constitutions even before the Articles of Confederation were adopted. Of the nine states with amending mechanisms in 1787, four relied on legislative action, three on constitutional conventions, and two on councils of censors that met periodically to review and revise the documents. Fearful that the later innovation would encourage undue change and undermine faith in the document; the framers of the U.S. Constitution relied instead on the other two mechanisms.

The U.S. Constitution was designed to be paramount law, superior to ordinary acts of legislation and unchangeable by ordinary legislative means. The Constitutional Convention provided, in Article V of the Constitution, for two methods of proposing amendments and two ways of ratifying them. Article V specifies that two-thirds majorities of both Houses of Congress, or (in a still unused mechanism) a special convention called by Congress at the request of two-thirds of the states, are needed to propose amendments. Congress then stipulates whether amendments will be ratified by three-fourths of the state legislatures or by conventions in three-fourths of the states. Desirous of preserving the Connecticut Compromise of 1787, by which states with large and small populations had each protected their interest in one house of Congress, Article V provided an entrenchment clause prohibiting any state from being deprived of its equal representation in the Senate without its consent.

The wisdom of the amending process became evident during debates between Federalist proponents and Anti-Federalist opponents of the new constitution, over the necessity and/or propriety of a *bill of rights like that already found in many state constitutions. As Anti-Federalists proposed calling a second convention to remedy this perceived defect, prominent Federalists, including James Madison, indicated their willingness to accept amendments once the Constitution was ratified. Madison subsequently became the leading sponsor of the first ten amendments in the first Congress, where it was decided that such amendments would be added to the end of the document rather than being incorporated within the text. Madison avoided major structural changes in the new document, focusing instead primarily on protecting personal liberties from abuses by the new national government (he was unsuccessful in getting adoption of an amendment that would also limit the states). Three-fourths of the state legislatures ratified ten of the twelve proposals. The scope of these ten amendments was significantly widened in the twentieth century, when U.S. courts applied these provisions through the *due process clause of the *Fourteenth Amendment to limit state actions as well.

The Eleventh and Twelfth Amendments were adopted relatively soon after the Bill of Rights. The Eleventh Amendment, limiting suits against the states by out-of-state citizens, overturned a Supreme Court decision in *Chisholm* v. *Georgia* (1793) and thus demonstrated that the amending process was integral to the system of checks and balances incorporated into the Constitution. In turn, the Twelfth Amendment remedied a problem that developed in the electoral college as a result of political party tickets by providing for electors to cast separate ballots for president and vice-president, thus making a tie, such as occurred in the election of 1800, unlikely.

No amendments were adopted from 1804 to 1865, but states ratified three amendments from 1865 to 1870, all in response to problems that had precipitated the Civil War. The Thirteenth Amendment permanently outlawed slavery. The Fourteenth Amendment overturned *Dred Scott* v. *Sandford* (1857) by defining citizenship to include all who were born or naturalized in the United States. It further guaranteed *privileges and immunities, rights of *due process, and *equal protection of the law to all citizens, although the judicial branch interpreted the first such guarantee narrowly, and the other two provisions did not significantly aid the cause of African Americans until well into the next century. Also evaded for decades by such stratagems as poll taxes, literacy tests, physical intimidation, and understanding clauses, the Fifteenth Amendment prohibited deprivation of the right to vote on the basis of *race.

Like the period from 1804 to 1865, that from 1870 to 1913 saw no new amendments, but from 1913 to 1919, states ratified four amendments reflecting prominent themes of the Progressive Era. The Sixteenth Amendment reversed the Supreme Court decision invalidating the national income tax in *Pollock* v. *Farmers' Loan & Trust Co.* (1895); such taxes expanded the revenue base of the national government and permitted some income redistribution. The Seventeenth Amendment provided for direct election of U.S. senators, who had previously been selected by state legislatures.

The Eighteenth Amendment instituted national alcohol prohibition. Culminating a movement begun at the Seneca Falls Convention in 1848 but frustrated by the Fourteenth Amendment, the Nineteenth Amendment extended suffrage to women.

States ratified two amendments in 1933. The Twentieth Amendment dealt with the problem of "lame-duck" presidents and members of Congress by establishing earlier dates for the installation of new office-holders, and addressed presidential succession. The Twenty-first Amendment, the first and only amendment ever ratified by state ratifying conventions, repealed national alcohol prohibition.

States ratified five amendments from 1951 to 1971. The Twenty-second Amendment was adopted in reaction to Franklin Roosevelt's unprecedented election to four terms. It formalized the previous unwritten understanding that a president would serve no more than two full terms or ten years. The Twenty-third Amendment provided representation in the electoral college for the District of Columbia, whose residents were previously disenfranchised because it was not a state. The Twenty-fourth Amendment prohibited the payment of poll taxes as a condition of voting in national elections. The Twenty-fifth Amendment dealt with presidential disability and provided for filling vacancies in the vice-presidency. The Twenty-sixth Amendment extended the right to vote (previously set by most states at twenty-one) to eighteen-year-olds, after the Supreme Court decided in *Oregon* v. *Mitchell* (1970) that Congress could not change state election requirements through ordinary legislation.

The Twenty-seventh Amendment, ratified in 1992, has an unusual history. Originally proposed as one of twelve amendments submitted to the states in 1789, it provides that pay raises shall not go into effect for members of Congress until an intervening election. Originally ratified by six states, only a few other states had added ratifications when Gregory Watson, a state legislative aide, launched a crusade in the 1980s to ratify the amendment. Despite questions over the validity of ancient ratifications, the National Archivist certified the amendment, and Congress agreed.

In one of a number of cases addressing the amending process, the Supreme Court had decided in *Dillon* v. *Gloss* (1921) that ratification of amendments needed to reflect a contemporary consensus, but in *Coleman* v. *Miller* (1939), the Court also ruled that this and other amending issues were "political questions" for other branches of government to decide. Although states have ratified amendments they had previously rejected, no case has conclusively established whether states can rescind ratification of a pending amendment. Many questions—including state representation, procedures, the possibility of limitations on subject matter—continue to surround the unused convention method for proposing constitutional amendments.

The difficulty of the national amending process is attested to by the fact that, of more than 10,000 amending proposals (most redundant) introduced in Congress, it has proposed only 33 by the necessary majorities, and only 27 have been ratified. Unratified proposals include amendments designed to: alter congressional representation, penalize individuals accepting foreign titles of nobility, freeze slave relations into place prior to the Civil War, ban child labor, treat the District of Columbia as a state for purposes of representation, and grant equal rights to women (see EQUAL RIGHTS AMENDMENT).

Partly because amendments have been so infrequent, the Constitution has been shaped by presidential practices, congressional usages, and most notably, by court decisions. Although such changes may not be as durable as those enacted through amendments, the Supreme Court has sometimes been likened to a continuing constitutional convention.

State constitutions are typically much longer than the federal one and have many more amendments. Most states require a majority or supermajority of the state legislature to propose amendments (sometimes in two successive sessions), which are then ratified by the people. Many also allow amendments to be proposed through initiative mechanisms or by state conventions or commissions. States, particularly in the South, have often had a succession of constitutions that reflected various movements for reform, or retrenchment, in American history. By contrast, the nation continues under the amended Constitution adopted in 1789.

• Alan P. Grimes, *Democracy and the Amendments to the Constitution*, 1978. Russell L. Caplan, *Constitutional Brinksmanship: Amending the Constitution by National Convention*, 1988. John R. Vile, *The Constitutional Amending Process in American Political Thought*, 1992. Richard B. Bernstein with Jerome Agel, *Amending America: If We Love the Constitution So Much, Why Do We Keep Trying to Change It?*, 1993. Sanford Levinson, ed., *Responding to Imperfection: The Theory and Practice of Constitutional Amendment*, 1995. David E. Kyvig, *Explicit & Authentic Acts: Amending the U.S. Constitution 1776–1995*, 1996. John R. Vile, *Encyclopedia of Constitutional Amendments, Proposed Amendments, and Amending Issues, 1789–1995*, 1996. *The Book of the States, 2000–01 Edition*, Vol. 33, 2000. Kris E. Palmer, *Constitutional Amendments: 1789 to the Present*, 2000.

—John R. Vile

CONSTITUTIONAL COMMENTATORS. During the debates over the ratification of the Constitution the first great commentators emerged: writing anonymously under the name of Publius in a series of newspaper articles, Alexander Hamilton, James Madison, and John *Jay produced *The Fed-

eralist Papers, a defense of the new Constitution and a classic of American legal and political thought. They did so in response to articles written by opponents of ratification, who became known as the anti-federalists. Thus, from the outset the Constitution invited commentaries and debate that have been central to the development of constitutional law—and, indeed, constitutionalism and the rule of law—as well as reflected the great socioeconomic and political changes in the country.

In the early nineteenth century, however, there were relatively few commentators—principally, reporters, members of the Supreme Court, and law professors—and little public means of communication. Following the tradition of English reporting, Alexander James Dallas began reporting the decisions of courts in Pennsylvania and in 1790 added the *opinions of the Supreme Court. This tradition of private reporting and publication for personal gain continued until 1816 when the Supreme Court appointed its first official reporter, and ended in 1874 when Congress appropriated money for the publication of the *United States Reports.* Another important source of decisions and commentary, along with other governmental documents, was the *Niles Register.* A weekly newspaper published by Hezeckiah Niles, a Jeffersonian Republican, between 1811 and 1849, it had the second highest circulation of all newspapers and magazines at the time.

Among the prominent early scholarly commentators was James Wilson, a critic of the 1776 Pennsylvania constitution and of the Articles of Confederation, who attended the 1787 constitutional convention and later served on the Supreme Court (1789–98). As a professor of law at the College of Philadelphia, Wilson delivered in 1790 and 1791 his famous "Lectures on Law," expounding his constitutional theory of nationalism and popular sovereignty. In 1803, St. George Tucker published his *View of the Constitution of the United States,* the first extensive and systematic commentary.

The preeminent constitutional commentator in the early nineteenth century, though, was Joseph *Story, who served simultaneously as an associate justice of the Supreme Court (1811–45) and as Dane Professor at Harvard Law School. Along with a dozen books on public and private law, Story produced three volumes of *Commentaries on the Constitution* in 1833. In the tradition of Sir William *Blackstone's *Commentaries on the Laws of England* (1765–69), Story's work was influential and provided a model for later treatises on the Constitution. Although disavowing any novel theory of constitutional interpretation, as an ardent

nationalist, Story aimed to preserve the doctrinal purity of the Marshall Court (1801–35) (see MARSHALL, JOHN) in the Age of Jackson and against the mounting pressures for more democracy and *"states' rights."

Several other justices wrote major works on the Constitution and courts, including Justices Henry Baldwin (1830–1844), Benjamin Curtis (1851–1857), and Samuel Miller (1862–1877), as well as several twentieth-century justices: Hugo L. *Black (1937–1971), William O. *Douglas (1939–1975), Robert H. *Jackson (1941–1954), and Chief Justice William H. Rehnquist (1972–).

In 1868, Thomas M. *Cooley published his widely used *Treatise on the Constitutional Limitations which Rest upon the Legislative Power of the States of the American Union.* As a professor at the University of Michigan Law School and a member of the Michigan Supreme Court, Cooley championed judicial protection of *property rights and the doctrine of liberty of contract, while also remaining concerned about the growth of corporate power during the Industrial Revolution. Another influential late-nineteenth-century constitutional authority was Harvard Law School professor James Bradley *Thayer, who along with Christopher Columbus Langdell and John Chipman Gray developed the "case method" of modern legal education. By this time, *The Harvard Law Review,* along with *The North American Review,* were also well established as respected sources of constitutional commentary.

The early twentieth century brought a wave of constitutional reinterpretation and revisionism, led by Progressive historians Charles A. Beard, J. Allen Smith, and Vernon Louis Parrington. In 1922, Charles Warren published his three-volume *The Supreme Court in United States History.* Subsequently, provisions of the Constitution, periods of constitutional development, and doctrinal trends, became a staple of constitutional historians and legal scholars like Charles Fairman, Leonard W. Levy, William E. Leuchtenburg, Robert G. McCloskey, and Jack N. Rakove, among others.

A leading early- and mid-twentieth-century authority on constitutional law and political history was Princeton University political scientist Edward S. Corwin. He became publicly embroiled in the constitutional crisis of 1937 over Democratic president Franklin D. Roosevelt's *"Court-packing plan" and effort to secure a majority on the Court supportive of the New Deal. His *Constitution and What It Means Today* (1920) remains in print and updated by Jack W. Peltason and Sue Davis. One of Corwin's students, Alpheus T. Mason, pioneered the writing of judicial biographies based on the justices' private papers and illuminated their constitutional philosophies. Judicial biographies remain an important body of work; Howard Ball, Ed Cray, Dennis J. Hutchinson, John C. Jeffries Jr., G. Edward White, Juan Williams, and Tinsley Yarbrough, for instance, produced acclaimed biographies. In the tradition of Corwin and Mason, Bernard Schwartz, Mark V. Tushnet, and many others, wrote articles and books emphasizing the political struggles over and historical context of evolving constitutional law.

Constitutional commentaries in the twentieth century, nonetheless, fundamentally changed in several ways due to intellectual forces and struggles over expanding *civil rights and liberties. During the Progressive era emerged a diverse group of scholars at Yale, Columbia, and Johns Hopkins, calling themselves "American legal realists." Besides debunking the legal formalism and laissez-faire capitalism doctrines of the pre-1937 Court, they revolutionized legal thinking by highlighting the indeterminacy of legal facts and rules, thereby underscoring that judges make law. Karl *Llewellyn, one of the most influential, brought these insights to bear on constitutional interpretation in calling for "jurisprudence of a living Constitution." Roscoe Pound, the founder of "sociological jurisprudence" and dean of Harvard Law School, encouraged the use of sociology and advocated that judges be "social engineers."

As a result of American *legal realism, constitutional interpretation was candidly conceded to be a lawmaking process and commentators increasingly debated what Yale Law School professor Alexander Bickel termed "the Madisonian dilemma," or problem of reconciling "the countermajoritarian difficulty" of *judicial review with democratic self-governance. That debate became a preoccupation in the wake of the landmark school desegregation decision in *Brown v. Board of Education* (1954) and other rulings of the *Warren Court (1953–69) that forged a "reapportionment revolution" and a "due process revolution."

Constitutional commentators in turn increasingly championed specialized theories of constitutional interpretation. Some sought to reconcile the Court's decisions and judicial review with democracy in terms of "the reasoned elaboration of judicial decisions." Others, like Herbert Wechsler, Henry Hart, and John Hart Ely, advocated various versions of process-oriented theories of judicial review that reinforced the operation of democracy. Still others, like Laurence H. Tribe, Michael J. Perry, and Charles L. Black Jr., more or less followed Ronald Dworkin, one of the most well known liberal legal philosophers, and his 1977

Taking Rights Seriously, in defending the Court's expansive reading of the *Bill of Rights and of substantive yet unenumerated constitutional rights, like the right to *privacy, based on theories of "constitutional morality" and moral and political philosophy.

By the late 1970s and 1980s the outpouring of liberal legal commentary inspired a reaction and formidable criticism from conservative legal scholars and politicians, including legal scholar Raoul Berger; Justice Antonin Scalia, whom Republican President Ronald Reagan appointed in 1986; Robert H. Bork, who was nominated and defeated for his views for a seat on the Court in 1987; and political theorists Harry Jaffa and Walter Berns, among others. They advocated returning to a "jurisprudence of original intentions," and ignited a continuing debate with other legal scholars and historians.

In the late twentieth century, constitutional commentaries also proliferated with the increasing number of law schools and student-edited law reviews. In addition, constitutional commentaries tended to become not only more specialized but also more interdisciplinary and multicultural. Drawing on political science, some scholars advanced a "political jurisprudence," combining normative theory and empirical studies of the Court. Others, along with Judge Richard A. Posner, forged a "law and economics movement." Still others, including James Boyd White, Stanley Fish, and Sanford Levinson, took a linguistic turn with the "law and literature movement." Feminist jurisprudence emerged with the women's movement and from the pioneering work in the 1970s of Ruth Bader Ginsburg, for which Democratic President Bill Clinton appointed her to the Court in 1993; as well as other law school professors, notably, Catharine MacKinnon, Kimberly Crenshaw, and Wendy W. Williams. Progressive scholarship also continued with *Critical Legal Studies and *Critical Race Theory, focusing on the persistent legal problems of racism and poverty in works like Randall Kennedy's *Race, Crime, and the Law* (1997). And by the end of the twentieth century there was a growing body of gay and lesbian legal scholarship, as well as increasing attention given to developments in comparative constitutionalism.

[See also Cooley, Thomas; Kent, James; Story, Joseph]

• Ronald Dworkin, *Taking Rights Seriously,* 1977. Harvard Law Review, *CLS: Essays on Critical Legal Studies,* 1986. Catharine A. MacKinnon, *Feminism Unmodified: Discourses on Life and Law,* 1987. Sanford Levinson and Steve Mailloux, eds., *Interpreting Law and Literature,*

1988. Robert H. Bork, *The Tempting of America: The Political Seduction of the Law*, 1990. William W. Fisher III, Morton J. Horwitz, and Thomas A. Reed, eds., *American Legal Realism*, 1993. Jack N. Rakove, *Original Meanings: Politics and Ideas in the Making of the Constitution*, 1996. Daniel A. Farber and Suzanna Sherry, *Beyond All Reason: The Radical Assault on Truth in American Law*, 1997. Randall Kennedy, *Race, Crime, and the Law*, 1997.

—David M. O'Brien

CONSTITUTION DAY. *See* Public Ritual, Law and.

CONSTITUTIONS, UNITED STATES. Since 1776, Americans have adopted 2 national and almost 150 state constitutions. The written constitution is an American invention that predates 1776, however, and is a compound of English constitutionalism, covenant theology, European political philosophy, and colonial experience. Almost all nations now have a written constitution derived from the American example, but American state and national constitutions in their several variations reflect both the unique mix that emerged from pre-independence influences and the course of American history since independence.

Although constitutionalism as an idea can be traced back to classical Greece and Rome, American constitutions are specifically rooted in an English constitutionalism based on the rule of law. Rule of law, at a minimum, excludes the exercise of arbitrary power, and is generally held to imply that citizens and government officials are equally subject to the ordinary law administered by the ordinary courts. Implicit in this minimal notion of rule of law are the notions of procedural political rights and substantive rights that limit the operation of government. By the time Englishmen began migrating to America in the early 1600s, trial by a *jury of one's peers and no *taxation without consent were firmly in place as operational manifestations of the rule of law. Both were embedded in a *common law that served as the functional equivalent of a written constitution, so English colonists were used to the idea that political processes were to be defined by a set of rules written prior to the operation of those processes. Because most of English common law related to matters pertaining to the aristocracy and the status of the Church of England, and because it failed to address the dramatically different living conditions of the colonists, which included the absence of an aristocracy and the general absence of an established Church of England, the colonists began immediately to define their own common law through documents peculiar to themselves. One

set of documents was comprised of the charters that established each colony; another set was written in America by the colonists as a result of charter provisions that allowed for the creation of local legislatures and guaranteed the colonists the rights of Englishmen. Colonists thereby became deeply conditioned to the existence of explicit founding documents—a charter and a local political compact.

The form and content of the local compact varied from colony to colony. The New England use of the covenant form derived from dissenting Protestantism was highly influential in the long run, but other colonies used a more secular form of agreement, sometimes mimicking a business contract. The use of property requirements found in English common law to define the colonial electorate, because of plentiful and cheap land in America, resulted in the enfranchisement of up to ten times the percentage of adult males as found in Britain. This produced a high level of popular consent for local government, and the consequent expectation that all legislation and not just matters involving taxation should be based on relatively direct consent given through frequent elections. Rule of law, and thus constitutionalism, for American colonists, began to include the ability of a community to frame its own local institutions and basic laws, as well as to hold representatives close to the popular will through frequent elections.

By the time of the war for American independence, the colonists argued that the original charter, plus the local compact, comprised for each colony a constitution defining their legal political status, a status that had been violated by the Crown and Parliament and thereby justified independence. To this constitutional argument were added philosophical concepts, such as natural rights, that had been learned from many thinkers, including John Locke, Algernon Sidney, Baron de Montesquieu, Trenchard and Gordon, William *Blackstone, and a host of others now identified with either republican or liberal political theory. The ideas of these Europeans were selectively appropriated by Americans to underwrite institutions and practices they had independently developed for pragmatic reasons, including legislative supremacy, bicameralism, *separation of powers, popular *sovereignty, *federalism, and codified *bills of rights.

That American constitutionalism derived from colonial experience can be illustrated in a number of ways. While the Pilgrim Code of Law (1636) should probably be considered the first modern written constitution, the Fundamental Orders of

Connecticut (1639) had a history that makes its constitutional status clear. The Fundamental Orders effectively received royal sanction as the Charter of 1662, which John Winthrop convinced the king to sign after the English Civil War ended. This charter was readopted in 1776 as the Connecticut Constitution after simply removing all references to the Crown, and served as the state's constitution until replaced in 1818. The Rhode Island Charter of 1663 did likewise for the locally adopted Acts and Orders of 1647, and served as the constitution of Rhode Island until 1842. The Massachusetts Charter of 1725 continued as the Massachusetts Constitution until 1780 without readoption. The other states, as they adopted constitutions in the 1770s, reproduced their colonial institutional and legal structures. Furthermore, of the twenty-six discrete rights contained in the U.S. *Bill of Rights, only seven can be found in English previous common law documents, whereas all twenty-six can be found in colonial codes of law and in the bills of rights of pre-1789 state constitutions. Indeed, sixteen of these rights can be found in the Massachusetts Body of Liberties (1641), which alone contained the first historical statement of eight rights found in the U.S. Bill of Rights—more than was generated by all of English common law.

In addition to having a form and content developed on American shores, state constitutions written in the 1770s and 1780s worked from a coherent political theory that was decisively American. Based on popular sovereignty rather than parliamentary sovereignty, this theory blended European republican and liberal political thought in a way that undergirded political institutions developed during the colonial era. General commitments to *liberty, political equality, majority rule, limited government, federalism, and separation of powers were codified and operationalized in a sensationally broad electorate [for the times], frequent elections, independent executives and judiciaries, bicameralism, checks and balances, and written bills of rights containing the provisions that are now familiar to us.

The underlying assumptions and institutional implications of this theory were used to generate the first national constitution, the Articles of Confederation, and would later be defended in detail by the Antifederalists. American constitutionalism in the 1770s was much more strongly localist and communitarian than it is today, which is a major reason why the national government produced by the Articles was so weak. The colonies, and the resulting states, had been built federally from below by the local communities that comprised each of them. The desire to preserve local communities made a national government highly suspect, and the preference for local community was reflected in the turnout for local elections during the 1790s, averaging almost three times the turnout for national elections—the opposite of what we have today. It remained for the Federalists to alter American republican theory somewhat to generate at the national level the kind of government found at the state level. As a consequence of Federalist success, the constitution closest to that of the Unites States is the Massachusetts Constitution of 1780—itself the oldest constitution in the world.

There is little in the U.S. Constitution not found in the state constitutions written before it. Even an electoral college had been used in Maryland. Also, most of the Articles of Confederation ended up in the Constitution, to which we can attribute such things as the general organization of the Constitution, the admission of new states on an equal footing, and the "dual citizenship," "republican guarantee," *"full faith and credit," and *"privileges and immunities" clauses. Madison's famous theory of the extended republic articulated in *Federalist Paper* No. 10 is found institutionally in the Articles of Confederation, with one crucial change. The size of the United States was the same under the Articles as it was in 1790 under the U.S. Constitution, so the extent of the country was the same under both documents. Rather, the major change was the creation of an extended *republic*. According to republican theory, one could not be taxed without one's consent, and since the national legislature under the Articles was not directly elected by the people, it could not tax them as individuals. The Federalists altered this situation by essentially retaining the state-elected Continental Congress in the form of the U.S. Senate, and adding the directly elected House of Representatives. The direct election of the House brought with it the ability of the U.S. government to act directly on individual citizens with respect to taxation and anything else within its competency. With this fundamental alteration, the U.S. government, which already oversaw an extended nation, became a republic, and the alteration placed the state governments on the same footing vis a vis the national government as that between the states and their respective towns and counties.

The Virginia Plan, adopted after several weeks of discussion at the 1787 Constitutional Convention, would have created a kind of parliamentary system. It proposed that a directly elected lower house select the upper house of a bicameral legislature, and that these two houses in turn choose the executive and members of the Supreme Court. During debates over the summer, the independent executive and judiciary with which we are now familiar emerged. As these more independent branches were pulled away from complete Congressional dominance, the members of the convention became increasingly worried about their possible use of arbitrary power, so the delegates added more and more checks over these branches. If one lists all the checks in the U.S. Constitution, one can see that they are designed primarily to permit Congress to rein in the other two branches. The president can veto legislation, but Congress can override the veto, reject treaties and presidential appointments, impeach members of the executive and judicial branches, create and destroy executive bureaucratic offices and lower courts, set the salaries for the other two branches, alter the size of the Supreme Court, and create or eliminate the appellate jurisdiction of the Courts beyond the minimal list found in Article III. The checks are not "balanced," but rather skewed in favor of legislative dominance (see LEGISLATIVE POWER). The so-called balances—bicameralism, different terms of office for the three branches and two houses, and different constituencies for each—are designed to make it difficult for a passionate national majority to gain control of the government without sufficient passage of time for the passions to wear off. A "balance," in the understanding of the time, was derived from the balance mechanism used in watches and steam or water-driven machinery that slowed down the main spring or power wheel so that it turned at a regular rate—neither too quickly nor too slowly. Thus, the three separate branches were not balanced in power. The executive and judicial branches were quite weak, and George Washington, among others, worried about their long-term survival. Even today, with what to us seems like a powerful presidency, the American executive is rated among the weakest in the world when it comes to constitutional power. The executive's power today, as well as the enhanced power of the national government, rests heavily on extra-constitutional factors rather than on formal provisions granting these powers (see EXECUTIVE POWER).

On the other hand, the states have relied almost entirely on the formal amendment and replacement of their constitutions to produce similar changes, and the reasons for the difference are instructive. Because of an overriding desire to create a unified nation that did not have significant geographical gaps, the framers decided that ratification would require nine states rather than a simple majority of seven. This number was selected, in part, because experience with voting patterns in the Continental Congress showed that whenever nine states agreed, the three largest—Virginia, Pennsylvania, and Massachusetts—were always included; and when these three agreed, so did almost all of the other states. Unanimity could not be used, since it was certain that Rhode Island would, at least initially, say no. After deciding on the ratification process, the delegates to the Convention understood that in order to amend the constitution it would be necessary to return to the same level of consent as that used for ratification. Nine out of thirteen states is a 70 percent majority, which is half way between a two-thirds and three-fourths majority, so the amendment process uses a combination of two-thirds and three-fourths ratification. However, this combination produced the second most difficult amendment process ever devised for a national constitution, and the difficulty of formal amendment has led to the use of other means for altering the institutional system to respond to changing circumstances and values—primarily through Supreme Court interpretation and interpolation.

The states, on the other hand, have invariably used something close to a two-thirds legislative approval plus plurality approval in a popular referendum, which is a much easier hurdle. The states, therefore, in contrast with federal practice, rely on formal mechanisms of revision—formal amendment and replacement. The state constitutions have thus been more frequently amended, and rarely use judicial interpretation. State constitutions have historically averaged four times the length of the national document and have on average been replaced twice. Still, despite what at first looks to be an invidious comparison, state constitutions have generally proven to be quite durable. Nineteen states are still operating under their original constitutions, and thirty-four constitutions are more than a century old, with an average age of 135 years. Indeed, two state constitutions were adopted before the U.S. Constitution, and one four years later in 1793. With a current average age of 102 years for all state documents, American state constitutions comprise twenty-two of the twenty-five oldest constitutions in the world.

The average 121 amendments per state constitution do not result simply from differences in the amendment process. State constitutions are longer to begin with because states have many more policy areas to deal with than the national government does, and because state legislatures have plenary powers, whereas Congress, even with its greatly expanded powers, does not. Section 8 of Article I of the U.S. Constitution has a straightforward and limited list of national powers, whereas state constitutions need to specifically exclude or regulate many policy areas from a potentially unlimited list of state competencies, especially with respect to local government, education, and the police power.

The brevity of the U.S. Constitution and the length of state constitutions are related. The national document can be brief only because it is an incomplete constitution, that depends for its operation on state constitutions that complete and consequently form a part of the national constitution. For example, the original federal Constitution did not need to define voting qualifications because state constitutions had already done so. The national document refers directly or indirectly to the states at least fifty times in forty-two separate sections, and without the existence of state documents would have to address these topics. Partly for this reason, only Iceland today has a briefer national constitution, and the average democracy has a national constitution that is seven times the length of the U.S. document and 50 percent longer than the average state constitution. These other democracies also amend their respective national constitutions at twice the rate of that found among the American states.

Any people who take constitutionalism seriously will engage in constitutional revision in the face of changes thrust upon them by history. The states use formal amendment and replacement, but at the national level, the formal amendment process has been supplemented by extra-constitutional means. Bruce Ackerman has been prominent in suggesting that the United States has actually had three different national constitutions since 1789 as a result of extra-constitutional changes. Who would doubt that the Civil War and post–Civil War amendments, coupled with the rise of mass political parties, produced a considerably altered national constitution. It is also evident that the New Deal, Supreme Court decisions since the 1930s, the enhancement of national power during World War II and the Cold War, and the rise of the mass media have together produced a constitutional system that operates in ways significantly different from what came before. Whether these amount to the equivalent of constitutional replacement is a matter of continuing debate. Certainly the growing concern for the founders' "original intent" indicates that the alterations have not

been minor, and are not always obvious from the amended text of the document. Even without an activist Court, the cumulative impact of the sixteenth and seventeenth amendments, plus the changes in the electoral college that produce almost direct election of the president, have fundamentally altered the U.S. Constitution. The national Constitution serves as a legitimating symbol as well as a super-legal text, and the controversies over its meaning indicate that constitutionalism in general, and the U.S. Constitution in particular, are still taken seriously.

For more than two hundred years, the states have had the primary responsibility for carrying these burdens: the continuous influx of massive numbers of immigrants, the move from an agrarian to an urban society, the industrialization of the economy, the rise of mass political parties, and the effects of many technological developments. It is not surprising, then, that they have also altered their constitutions accordingly. The surprise is how little change there has been in basic institutions. The original formulation put in place during the eighteenth century remains, but has been modified in ways that reflect the times. The pre–Civil War state constitutions continue to be among the briefest and least amended. Those written between the Civil War and World War I are invariably the longest because they reflect the concerns of the Populist and Grange movements, as well as the consequences of urbanization and industrialization that pleaded for greater regulation of social and economic matters. Post–World War II constitutions have tended to be briefer and less concerned with these matters, since they reflected a more modern "managerial" approach to problem solving. Although every state but one has split the executive branch into multiple elective offices, the managerial approach has resulted in stronger executives than is found at the national level, whereas pre–World War I documents generally continue to work with weaker executives, although the item veto is now common.

One difference between national and state constitutions has remained prominent. States invariably have long preambles and bills of rights at the beginning of their constitutions. States thus have much higher symbolic content and often stronger legal protection of rights that requires much less judicial interpretation and more routine legal enforcement. The states have also continued to be more relevant to everyday life through regulation of a broader range of activities than the U.S. government. Finally, some states, such as Louisiana, Georgia, South Carolina, Florida, Alabama, Virginia, and Arkansas have replaced and amended their constitutions at such a high rate that constitutional issues have virtually become part of everyday politics. Other states with high amendment rates include California, Hawaii, North Carolina, and Texas. The overall geographical bias in this pattern is interesting, but whether high or low in amendment and replacement rate, the apparent seriousness with which constitutional politics is viewed at the national and state levels indicates the continuing importance of constitutions in America.

[*See also* Constitutional Amendments]

• Max Farrand, ed., *The Records of the Federal Convention of 1787,* 4 vols., 1966. Daniel J. Elazar, *American Federalism: A View from the States,* 1984. Jack P. Greene, *Center and Periphery: Constitutional Development in the Extended Polities of the British Empire and the United States,* 1986. Donald S. Lutz, *The Origins of American Constitutionalism,* 1988. Kermit Hall, *The Magic Mirror: Law in American History,* 1989. Jack Rakove, *Interpreting the Constitution: The Debate Over Original Intent,* 1990. Bruce Ackerman, *We the People: Foundations,* 1991. Stephen M. Griffin, *American Constitutionalism: From Theory to Politics,* 1996. G. Alan Tarr, *Understanding State Constitutions,* 1998.
                                             —Donald S. Lutz

CONSTRUCTIVE TRUST. *See* Equity.

CONSUMER LAW. Consumer laws govern personal, household, and family transactions in the marketplace. They provide avenues for the protection and vindication of consumers, as well as opportunities for producers to standardize their operations and insulate themselves from many liabilities. Broadly considered, consumer laws affect every aspect of the relationship between noncommercial buyers and sellers.

Consumer laws are created and enforced by private understandings and by public institutions and agencies. They are both formal and informal in nature, and they range in geographical scope from the local to the global. Private rules and informal trade customs, including voluntary industry standards, establish the context in which everyday consumer transactions take place. In many places, for example, local customs permit us to take a bite out of an apple in the vegetable market before we decide to buy. Standards-setting bodies (for example, the Society of Automotive Engineers or the National Association of Broadcasters) develop widely adhered-to standards for manufacturing, distributing, and retailing.

Public legislative acts embody state-sanctioned rules for buying and selling, thereby legislating rules for commercial behavior and for the quality of goods. Some consumer legislation has gained general approval from economists and consumer affairs professionals for its positive impact on the conditions and safety of the marketplace. Historically, however, many laws designated by their sponsors as "protecting" or "informing" consumers have been, by design or accident, unhelpful or even damaging.

Among the first consumer protection laws passed in Colonial America were ones enacted to alleviate problems connected with monopoly pricing (then referred to as "engrossing"), short weighting, and adulteration, as well as laws setting the hours during which some goods could be purchased. In some places laws restricted the consumption of certain goods (for example, tobacco and alcohol) and services (for example, abortions) on public health, religious, and moral grounds.

Court-fashioned or *"common law" rules regarding consumer transactions evolved from, and reinforced, customary rules about purchase transactions. In the absence of blatant fraud or deception, many early judicial rulings supported the maxim "caveat emptor" or "let the buyer aware." That maxim justified a multitude of sins—it presumed that buyers could and should inform themselves about the risks attached to purchasing decisions, and bargain. Until the late nineteenth century there were few special rules to distinguish consumer buyers from commercial buyers.

Accepting caveat emptor, however, never signified that fraud, misrepresentation, or negligent conduct was condoned by American consumer law. Determining what a consumer is entitled to recover as damages for a wrong depends upon the nature of the claim that has been brought and the type of losses suffered. If outright fraud, misrepresentation, or actionable negligence can be proven, the law of *torts (nonconsensual injuries) might return victims of nonconsensual injuries to their pre-injury state. *Contract law, including the common law interpretations of warranties, might award an aggrieved consumer with sums to compensate for the difference between the value of a product as received and the value as it was represented and agreed on. A fraudulently induced contract, or one tainted by bad faith in its performance, might be rescinded (abrogated or repealed). Consumers might be excused from meeting their payment obligations; or they might recover, in addition to direct costs, costs that were the forseeable consequences of a seller's wrong or act of neglect.

The legal requirements that nineteenth- and early twentieth-century common law courts traditionally applied to the complaints of aggrieved consumers often involved an excessively exacting presentation of proof. For example, a consumer trying to avoid a contract for a used automobile because of a misrepresentation that led her to purchase a car with much more mileage on it than she thought, would have to show not only that she had sustained an injury after she relied on the seller's misrepresentation, but also that the reliance was justified—that the seller made an actual representation of a present fact that was material and false, and was known or recklessly assumed to be false, and was made for the purpose of inducing the buyer to buy (*Jones* v. *West Side Buick Auto Co.* (1936)).

The common law rules, furthermore, made a direct connection between individual sellers and buyers that was virtually indispensible to recovery through the courts. Where consumers were injured by manufactured products, neither the law of contracts and warranties nor the law of torts would permit a consumer to recover from any contractor or supplier of a seller, except in rare instances. Requirements such as these might be relaxed under special circumstances, but these legal rules made elements of proof difficult for consumers to satisfy.

The differences between ordinary household consumer transactions and typical commercial transactions (in which the buyers were typically companies) became more pronounced as manufacturing processes grew more complicated, and as selling techniques became more sophisticated. Commercial entities retained specialized purchasing expertise while most household consumption was undertaken individually without effective laws that might disclose information that would allow for meaningful analysis and comparison.

Until the nineteenth century, handcrafted goods generated nonuniform product defects and idiosyncratic misrepresentations; thereafter, a defect in a single product's design might be multiplied through techniques of mass-production and mass consumption into hundreds of thousands of defective products and sold (and sometimes misrepresented) nationally to millions of people under advertised brand names.

Disparities in bargaining power, in the inability to estimate the risk of entering into a transaction, and in the costs associated with obtaining information about a product became wider than before. Doctrines of privity (connectedness between the parties) generally insulated remote manufacturers from suit by consumers when they bought from intermediary retailers.

Sellers developed many protective contractual provisions, and other legal tools that helped them to enforce consumer payment obligations. For example, rules governing the ability of creditors to take most kinds of property as "security" or "collateral" and to enforce judgments against consumers for nonpayment of debts permitted wage garnishments, liens on the property of consumer debtors, forclosures and self-help repossession of collateral such as houses (via the law of real property), and personal property including vehicles, furniture, and other consumer goods (via Article 9 of the Uniform Commercial Code, concerned with secured transactions).

By the late nineteenth century, older common law remedies for consumer problems seemed to many to be patently inadequate. Some higher courts and legislatures departed from the traditional approaches. Legislatures tried to curb monopolistic and other anti-competitive behavior through laws aimed at unfair and deceptive trade practices, and through independent regulatory agencies. Courts developed relational theories of contracting, in which the relative strength of the parties could affect the enforceability of an agreement, and modified classical exchange doctrines in recognition of modern merchandising realities: individual consumers often had neither the bargaining power nor the information they needed to give informed and meaningful consent to the terms of a bargain and accept all the risks attached to it. In *Delancey* v. *Insurance Co.* (1873), for example, Chief Justice Doe of New Hampshire determined that the boilerplate language of an insurance contract had worked a fraud on the payer of a premium: "It was printed in such small type, and in lines so long and so crowded, that the perusal of it was made physically difficult, painful and injurious. Seldom has the art of typography been so successfully diverted from the diffusion of knowledge to the suppression," the chief justice wrote.

In *MacPherson* v. *Buick Motor Co.* (1916), a breakthrough case in the law of products liability, Judge *Cardozo held that the Buick Motor Company was responsible for an injury to a driver that resulted from a defective wheel manufactured by one of Buick's suppliers. Buick "was not at liberty to put the finished product on the market without subjecting the component parts to ordinary and simple tests," the Judge wrote. Doctrines of *strict liability and implied warranty were broadened in the law of products *liability to make manufacturers and some other remote producers responsible for the physical injury caused by the dangerous products that they had manufactured, regardless of the manufacturers' good intentions, reasonable care, or remoteness from the seller.

Even as common law doctrines recognized important distinctions between consumer contracts and other types of doctrines, the court-fashioned remedies were proving to be inherently inadequate to the task of providing legal *regulation of consumer transactions. Judicial opinions, after all, were promulgated post hoc. They were uncodified, and nonuniform among the states. Thus, statutes and regulatory agencies were created—according to their political sponsors, to create better rules and enforcement procedures than common law jurisprudence allowed. Major federal departments and agencies charged with consumer protection responsibilities were generated by federal statutes. These established different sorts of legal standards—for minimum quality, minimum disclosure, or merchandising conduct—in connection with different kinds of consumer goods and services.

Significant laws and amendments passed in the first half of the twentieth century to regulate consumer transactions include: the Mail Fraud Act (1872), prohibiting the use of the mails to conduct fraudulent sales activities; the Meat Inspection Act (1904), establishing a system for government inspection of conditions under which meat was manufactured and sold; the Food and Drugs Act (1906), creating an agency to enforce minimum food and drug standards; the Federal Trade Commission Act (1914), charged with preventing unfair and deceptive trade practices; the Food, Drug and Cosmetic Act (1938), setting standards for truth in pharmaceutical labeling; the Securities Act (1933), mandating disclosure standards for certain investment instruments; the Flammable Fabrics Act (1953), requiring the use of fire-retardant fabrics in certain clothing; and the Food Additives Amendments to the FDA (1958), mandating that food additives generally be recognized as safe prior to their use.

President Kennedy, in 1960, reflected the emerging social concern for consumer legal rights by asserting that consumers had at least four of them: a right to safety, to be informed, to choose, and to be heard. And so, as the movement grew during the 1960s, laws to promote consumer welfare in the marketplace multiplied. Those who were injured by the unfair or deceptive practices of a seller did not need, after the late 1960s, to be concerned with the many burdens of proving a court action at common law. By then, every state in the union had passed antifraud legislation which did not require that sellers have an evil in-

tent, nor that consumers were justified in relying on a deceptive representation.

Congress adopted significant consumer protection legislation at a record pace during 1960s and 1970s. This legislation included the Hazardous Substances Labeling Act (1960), setting disclosure rules for dangerous household and other products; the Kefauver-Harris Drug Amendments (1962), promoting competition in the pharmaceutical industry; the Fair Packaging and Labeling Act (1965), providing standardized disclosure rules for many foods and other products; the National Traffic and Motor Vehicle Safety Act (1966), setting vehicle safety standards and creating an agency charged with the same; the Cigarette Labeling Act (1966), mandating warnings to consumers about the perils of smoking; the Truth in Lending Act (1968), requiring the disclosure of information about the costs associated with consumer debt transactions; the Toy Safety Act (1969), permitting government to monitor the children's toy market; the Fair Credit Reporting Act (1970), controlling information contained in consumer credit reports and the conditions for their release; the Equal Credit Opportunity Act (1974), barring certain kinds of discrimination in the extension of credit by lenders; the Magnuson-Moss Warranty Act (1975), regulating disclosure and certain substantive aspects of warrantees; and the Fair Debt Collection Practices Act (1978), designed to discourage excessive collection efforts.

Although the pace of consumer reform legislation slowed after 1980, various laws deregulated the economy (for example the Airline Deregulation Act (1978)); increased the nutritional information available (the Nutrition Labeling and Education Act (1990)); and broadened services and incentives available to serve consumer needs in the face of licensed monopolies (the Consumer Cable Communications Law (1993)). Over the ensuing decade, special problem areas for consumers led to national proposals to more effectively regulate managed health care, bankruptcy, electronic privacy, abusive lending practices, and fraud on the Internet.

State and local laws were enforced by state attorney generals, consumer affairs departments, and other bodies. Whether such state laws were preempted by the federal laws through the Supremacy Clause of the U.S. Constitution became a major point of contention in many consumer law disputes. Some state laws allowed consumers to act as private attorneys general by bringing actions individually, and to recover attorneys' fees, court costs, and punitive damages. Rules of evidence and procedure in several states permitted representative parties to file *class action lawsuits. In cases involving serious injuries caused by defective mass-produced products and devices, or in cases involving collectively large but individually minor overcharges, common questions of law and fact made class actions a superior method for recovery.

Numerous uniform state laws, including the Uniform Commercial Code, the Uniform Consumer Credit Code, and others, established imperfectly uniform rules for consumer transactions on the state and local levels. Broadly consistent standards of legal interpretation in consumer disputes developed only through professionally drafted restatements of law in such areas as torts, contracts, agency, and suretyship (guarantees of performance). These standards helped to determine when agreements were so one-sided as to be unconscionable, whether sellers performed their part of a bargain in bad faith, or whether consumers were acting the way reasonably prudent persons would act.

Standards by which consumer laws are interpreted, and the laws themselves, are being transformed continually by public and private bodies. New "topical" statutes, which deal with particular types of abuse, are frequently proposed. New approaches to consumer dispute resolution, especially provisions in standard form contracts that mandate binding consumer *arbitration, have become more common, despite the controversy they have aroused.

Regulatory consumer law appears destined to forever be playing catch-up with changing methods of selling, and with changing products and service delivery systems. The marketplace, furthermore, has become a global one, requiring global consumer protection rules. The "harmonization" of U.S. consumer laws with the laws of other nations and international bodies continues to raise difficult problems of protection and reconciliation.

• Norman Silber, *Test and Protest: The Influence of Consumers Union*, 1983. John A. Spanogle, et al., *Consumer Law*, 1991. Colston E. Warne, *The Consumer Movement* (Richard L. D. Morse, ed.), 1993. Michael Greenfield, *Consumer Law: A Guide for Those Who Represent Sellers, Lenders, and Consumers*, 1995. Stephen Brobeck, ed., *Encyclopedia of the Consumer Movement*, 1997.

—Norman I. Silber

CONTEMPT, CIVIL AND CRIMINAL. Contempt represents the power of a governmental body to compel enforcement of its decrees and orders. Most commonly, contempt refers to the authority of a court to punish or coerce individuals who violate its commands or offend the dignity of the judicial process. The term "contempt" is also used to refer to the disobedient or disrespectful behavior itself (e.g., "the defendant committed contempt by refusing to obey the court order"). American legislative bodies, such as Congress, also possess the power to hold witnesses before them in contempt for failing to answer questions or to produce required papers.

American courts after the Revolutionary War rested their authority to hold individuals in contempt upon the inherent contempt power claimed by the earlier English courts. For centuries English courts had asserted the ability to punish those who disobeyed a lawful court order or who disrupted judicial proceedings. In 1831, however, Congress passed a statute defining the exact scope of the criminal contempt power for American federal courts. Under this statute, which remains in effect today, a federal court may punish by fine or imprisonment only misbehavior in or near the court's presence, misbehavior of a court officer in an official transaction, or disobedience of a lawful court writ, rule, or order. 18 U.S.C. § 401 (1994).

Modern judicial contempt can be divided into four categories: direct contempt, indirect criminal contempt, coercive civil contempt, and remedial civil contempt. Any court of general jurisdiction, state or federal, normally has the power to impose any of the forms of contempt, provided that the court follows the appropriate procedures. Direct contempt constitutes disruptive or disrespectful behavior committed in the presence of the court or so near the court's presence as to disrupt the administration of justice. Thus shouting, cursing, and insulting the judge are examples of disruptive acts that could constitute criminal contempt. When direct contempt occurs, a court may summarily punish the individual committing the contempt by imposing a fine or term of imprisonment. Although normally *due process requires that an individual must have notice of the offense charged and an opportunity to be heard by the court, direct contempt of court may be punished without a hearing for two reasons: (1) the court must be able to punish disruptive or disrespectful behavior immediately to keep control over the proceedings before it, and (2) because the judge presumably witnessed the contemptuous behavior, there is no need for a hearing to establish the offender's guilt.

Indirect contempt usually consists of disobedience to a court order outside the court's presence, and can be either civil or criminal. Indirect civil contempt is further divided into two categories: remedial and coercive. Remedial civil contempt serves to compensate plaintiffs for damages suffered because of the defendant's disobedience of a court order. Remedial civil contempt is merely another form of compensatory damages, and plaintiffs must ordinarily prove their pecuniary loss as they would in any legal action for damages. For example, if the court orders the defendant not to destroy the plaintiff's fence and the defendant disobeys the order, the plaintiff can recover the value of the destroyed fence as compensatory civil contempt. Coercive civil contempt also exists primarily for the benefit of the plaintiff. It is designed to force a reluctant defendant to comply with a court order. In this context the court often imposes either a daily fine or an indefinite term of imprisonment; in either case the defendant can stop the accruing fine or get out of prison by obeying the court order. For example, if the court orders the defendant to disclose the location of his child and he refuses to do so, the court, using coercive civil contempt, can put the defendant into prison until he complies with the order.

Because coercive contempt and remedial contempt are considered civil in nature, they require only an ordinary civil hearing. Civil contempt is imposed as part of an action in *equity, and so no jury trial is available. Civil contempt also falls away if the underlying order is vacated. For example, if an appellate court invalidates a lower court's order, the plaintiff is no longer considered entitled to compensation for the defendant's violation of the order nor is the defendant subject to being coerced to obey an invalid order.

Indirect criminal contempt, like direct criminal contempt, serves to vindicate the court's authority and to punish defendants who disregard that authority. But indirect criminal contempt, unlike direct contempt, is committed outside the court's presence and usually involves disobedience of a court order. The punishment for criminal contempt often involves a fixed fine or a fixed term of imprisonment. Several states limit by statute the maximum amount of the fine or prison term that a court may impose for criminal contempt.

Today most state and federal courts are required to employ full-blown criminal procedures before imposing criminal contempt sanctions. These procedures include the privilege against self-incrimination, the right to counsel, the presumption of innocence, proof of the violation beyond a reasonable doubt, and the right to a jury trial for serious sanctions. Unlike civil contempt, criminal contempt is also prosecuted separately from the underlying equitable action and requires a showing of willful disobedience of the court order. Unlike civil contempt, criminal contempt survives the subsequent invalidation of the underlying court order. If the order turns out to be invalid the court is still entitled to have its orders obeyed until they are overturned on appeal. Thus if defendants disobey a court order that is later reversed, they may still be subject to criminal contempt sanctions.

Starting in the early twentieth century, American courts began to voice their concerns about the potential for judicial abuse of the contempt power. A large part of this concern stemmed from the excesses practiced on labor unions under the guise of judicial authority. The public and lawmakers came to regard the federal district courts as captives of industry in its struggle with the nascent labor movement. Businesses were often able to obtain *injunctions and contempt penalties from lower federal courts to stifle strikes and labor organizing at their inception. In 1932 Congress finally intervened and passed the Norris-LaGuardia Act, which essentially eliminated the federal district courts' ability to enjoin strikes.

In deciding contempt cases throughout the twentieth century, the United States Supreme Court most often focused on procedural issues. In 1900 many trial courts did not accord defendants full criminal procedural protections before sanctioning them with criminal contempt fines or incarceration. The Supreme Court, in a series of cases beginning with *Gompers* v. *Bucks Stove & Range Co.* (1911), gradually enlarged the procedural protections accorded criminal contemnors. That series of cases culminated with *Bloom* v. *Illinois* (1968), in which the Court held that defendants being tried for criminal contempt were entitled to a jury trial if the potential sanction was serious.

More recently, the Supreme Court has continued to express its concern over the possible judicial abuse of the contempt power, especially the ability of a trial court to label its contempt sanctions as civil and thereby to avoid affording the defendant full criminal procedural protections. In *International Union, United Mine Workers of America* v. *Bagwell* (1994), the Court held that the "character and purpose" of the contempt sanctions determine whether they are civil or criminal. In distinguishing between criminal contempt and coercive civil contempt in particular, the Court stated that the lower courts should examine whether the defendant has the ability to avoid an announced sanction by complying with the court. If the defendant can avoid the sanction through compliance, the contempt is civil in nature. Otherwise, the contempt is criminal. In *Bagwell*, the Court specifically held that where the lower court had announced in advance that it would impose a specific fine on the defendant labor union if it did not comply with the court order, the fine imposed for later violations of the order was a criminal contempt. At the point that the court imposed the fine, the defendant could no longer avoid it through complying with the court order. Because the lower court had not accorded the defendant full criminal procedural protections before imposing the fine, the Supreme Court held that the contempt fine had to be vacated.

Congress and state legislative bodies also possess contempt powers. Under federal statute the House of Representatives, the Senate, and any of their committees have the authority to cite individuals for contempt if they refuse to answer questions or to produce required papers. Congress, however, cannot hold someone in contempt unless it has the power to conduct the investigation during which the contemptuous act was committed. Similarly, a Congressional committee cannot impose contempt sanctions unless Congress gave the committee proper authority to conduct the particular investigation at issue.

[*See also* Procedure, Civil; Procedure, Criminal]

• Stewart Rapalje, *A Treatise on Contempt,* 1890. Ronald L. Goldfarb, *The Contempt Power,* 1963. Richard B. Kuhns, "The Summary Contempt Power: A Critique and a New Perspective," *Yale Law Journal* (1978):1–123. Doug Rendleman, "Compensatory Contempt: Plaintiff's Remedy When Defendant Violates an Injunction," *University of Illinois Law Forum* (1980): 971–1010. Owen M. Fiss and Doug Rendleman, *Injunctions,* 2d ed., 1984. Dan B. Dobbs, *Law of Remedies,* 2d ed., 1993. Earl C. Dudley Jr., "Getting Beyond the Civil/Criminal Distinction: A New Approach to the Regulation of Indirect Contempts," *Virginia Law Review* (1993): 1025–98. Margit Livingston, "Disobedience and Contempt," *Washington Law Review* (2000): 345–428.

—Margit Livingston

CONTINGENCY FEES. *See* Fees, Attorney.

CONTRACEPTION. *See* Abortion and Reproductive Decisions; Canon Law in America.

CONTRACT, LIBERTY OF. *See* Contract Law.

CONTRACT LAW. A contract is a legally valid agreement for either a present or future exchange, and is legally enforceable. If the contract is broken, the aggrieved party will usually be entitled to a judicial remedy of *damages, or, in exceptional cases, a court order requiring the breaching party to perform. The legal recognition of contracts and of *remedies for their breach is of ancient origin, and all Western systems of law enforce contracts. This is not difficult to explain. Individuals and entities are regularly motivated to enter into exchange relations—to exchange their services for money, to exchange money for goods, to exchange promises of money for title to real estate, and so on. Individuals and entities are not self-sufficient, and so must get what they need or want at least partly through exchanges with others. They enter particular exchanges because they value what they are to receive more than what they are to give up. Money greatly facilitates contractual exchange for it provides a common measure of value. But, even in a modern society, the mere barter of one object for another without the use of money also occurs.

The general economic importance of free contractual exchange goes well beyond the satisfaction of the immediate needs and wants of particular individuals in two-party contexts. It also gives rise to competitive markets in which individuals and entities can register their preferences in monetary terms for objects of value. This in turn induces producers to allocate resources to their highest valued uses in light of what participants in the relevant markets are willing to pay for the objects in question. Contractual exchange thus contributes to overall economic efficiency. Private contractual exchange is also generally more efficient than state manufacture and distribution of objects of value. This is partly because private producers responding to market demand can usually create the relevant objects of value more cheaply than state functionaries.

The moral and political rationales for legal recognition of free contractual exchange are no less important than the economic ones. In a society in which people provide for their own needs and wants through contractual exchange, people thereby determine the course of their own lives in such matters as education, employment, residence, lifestyle, and so on. People are thus relatively autonomous beings exercising wide freedom of contractual choice subject to the constraints of their own resources. They are not mere recipients of state distributions of objects, with little choice in what these objects are to be.

Yet the state participates in a system of contractual exchange as well. It must, through its legislature and its court system, create and administer a general body of contract law recognizing contractual exchanges and providing remedies for breach. This is a major function of the legal order in a market-oriented system such as that of the United States. A related function is that of affirmatively facilitating contractual exchange through the provision of money ("legal tender"), a standardized system of weights and measures, the regulation of communication and of transportation, a central banking system, laws recognizing and protecting rights of ownership, laws forbidding the imposition of tariffs by one state on goods from another, laws against private monopolistic practices, and so on. Thus the state plays a major role in creating and maintaining a general legal and economic environment and also particular markets in which contractual exchange can flourish (see ECONOMICS AND LAW).

The law of contract is a discrete branch of law within the general law of a society. In the United States, contract law is made largely by the legislatures and the courts of each of the fifty states, rather than by the federal government. The early American law of contract was mostly imported from England in the form of *"common law" made by judges deciding disputes between particular parties. These judges set forth their decisions and their reasoning in judicial opinions, which then became precedents for future similar cases. In colonial times and in nineteenth-century America, the judges often had to travel to the locales of disputes by horseback. Many of them carried in their saddlebags English treatises such as William *Blackstone's *Commentaries of the Laws of England* (1765). The early American law of contract often consisted largely of efforts to apply the principles of the English common law of contract. Eventually, each state judiciary came to develop its own body of contractual common law, and judges began the practice of borrowing from earlier opinions of judges in sister states.

The subject matter of contract disputes in the courts of the colonies and in the various states as they evolved was highly varied. Disputes arose in regard to employer-employee relations, the sale of goods, the sale or lease of land, the construction of buildings, the insuring of *property of all kinds, the use of negotiable instruments, and more. Disputes arose over contract formation, interpretation, breach, remedies, and virtually all aspects of contractual interaction. In these disputes, the trial and appellate courts of each state drew on prior common law and fashioned principles that comprise the primary basis of the general common law of contract today. This law, as it has evolved, applies today in the absence of statute or Code to the contrary. The leading twentieth-century treatises on the common law of contract are S. *Williston and G. J. Thompson, *Treatise on The Law of Contract*, 3rd ed., 1965; Arthur L. *Corbin, *Corbin on Contracts*, rev. ed., 1970, and E. Allan Farnsworth, *Contracts*, 3rd ed., 1999. These treatises were all written by professors of law—Williston was at Harvard Law School, Thompson at Cornell Law School, Corbin at Yale Law School, and Farnsworth at Columbia Law School.

The law of contract today is not entirely in the form of common law made by courts. In the last decade of the nineteenth century, all of the American state legislatures adopted the same body of general statute law on negotiable instruments such as checks and promissory notes, which came to be widely used as "substitutes for money." This new body of statute law was called the "Uniform Negotiable Instruments Law," and was drafted largely by professors of law and sponsored by the National Conference of Commissioners on Uniform State Laws. The state-by-state adoption of this body of law marked the beginning of the "uniform laws movement" in the United States, followed in the twentieth century by adoption in most states of separate bodies of uniform law for many other contractual subjects that had theretofore been largely the province of the common law, including the sale of goods, personal property security interests, bank collections, and warehouse receipts.

In the mid-1940s, Professor Karl N. *Llewellyn, then of Columbia, and William Schnader, President of the Conference of Commissioners on Uniform State Law, conceived the idea of a single Uniform Commercial Code that would draw together and modernize the various uniform laws, and, like those laws, be adopted by the legislatures in each of the various states. The *American Law Institute—a group of law professors, judges, and practicing lawyers—became cosponsors of this project. In 1952, the first official text of the Uniform Commercial Code appeared, as promulgated by the Commissioners and the Institute. It was eventually adopted (with a few amendments in some states) by nearly all state legislatures. There have been various official revisions of the text since, and some version of the Uniform Commercial Code has today been enacted and reenacted in revised form in all American states. This body of law displaces much of what would have been left solely to the common law of contract. Yet each state has its own general common law of contract, except insofar as superceded by the Uniform Commercial Code and other statutes. In various major fields such as employer-employee contracts, land-sale contracts (in many states), and insurance contracts, the common law of contracts makes up the vast bulk of the relevant law.

There is now a large body of case law interpreting the Uniform Commercial Code, and this law is not always consistent from state to state. The most widely cited scholarly work on the Uniform Commercial Code is a four-volume treatise: J. White and R. Summers, *The Uniform Commercial Code*, 4th ed., 1995. Professor White is at the University of Michigan School of Law, Summers is at Cornell Law School.

In addition to the "uniform laws movement" and the works of scholars in universities, another major and continuing influence on the law of contract in the twentieth century consists of the first and the second *Restatement of Contracts* promulgated by the American Law Institute in 1932 and in 1981, respectively. The "Chief Reporter" for the 1932 version was Samuel Williston, and of the 1981 version, Professor Robert Braucher of Harvard and Professor E. Allan Farnsworth of Columbia. Each Restatement purported to "restate" generally prevailing rules and principles of the common law of contract as a single body of general law in the United States as a whole, without regard to specific variations between the states. The Restatements also purported to adopt the "better view" in those instances in which the law of the various states was in conflict. The *Restatement of Contracts* is frequently cited in American courts, and is much studied in American law schools as well.

The ideas influencing the evolution of the general law of contract, in its common law, statutory, and code forms over the last hundred years, are not, in general, difficult to identify. The power of the idea of freedom of contract has been central and enduring. It is enshrined in all of the foregoing forms of law. At the same time it has been subjected to significant limitations. A major limitation is the doctrine that an unconscionable term or contract is not enforceable, as provided in section 2-302(1) of the Uniform Commercial Code, and in related law:

> If the court as a matter of law finds the contract or any clause of the contract to have been unconscionable at the time it was made the court may refuse to enforce the contract, or it may enforce the remainder of the contract without the unconscionable clause, or it may so limit the application of any unconscionable clause as to avoid any unconscionable result.

Other major limits on freedom of contract include doctrines making certain bargains illegal, protecting minors from their own improvidence, protecting persons not fully competent mentally, protecting against misrepresentation, fraud and duress in the bargaining process, and protecting parties to standardized form contracts from unfair surprise. Concerning the latter, a provision of the second *Restatement of Contracts* that has been the focus of much attention and controversy is section 211, which states:

> (1) Except as stated in Subsection (3), where a party to an agreement signs or otherwise manifests assent to a writing and has reason to believe that like writings are regularly used to embody terms of agreements of the same type, he adopts the writing as an integrated agreement with respect to the terms included in the writing.
> (2) Such a writing is interpreted wherever reasonable as treating alike all those similarly situated, without regard to their knowledge or understanding of the standard terms of the writing.
> (3) Where the other party has reason to believe that the party manifesting such assent would not do so if he knew that the writing contained a particular term, the term is not part of the agreement.

Another leading principle of general contract law is that the formation of a valid agreement is "objective." That is, although the law recognizes a "subjective concurrence of the wills" of the parties as the standard example of contract formation, the law does not require this for valid contract formation. A contract can be validly formed if party A believes, and has reason to believe from party B, that B intends to enter the relationship, even though party B may actually privately intend otherwise.

In regard to contract formation, another leading principle requires that the parties to a valid contract give "consideration." As the *Restatement of Contracts* (second), section 71, puts it, consideration requires that the parties enter a bargained-for exchange. A major rationale for this requirement is that bargaining between the parties usually signifies that they were in a cautionary state of mind when they reached agreement.

A further leading principle of contract formation is that many types of contracts must be partly in writing to be valid, a principle that is subject to various exceptions. The law here is complex, and derives from the 1677 English *"Statute of Frauds." A vast amount of American case law has arisen under the various versions of this early English statute adopted in the American states.

With the rise of contracting through the use of

computers, many states have enacted, or are in the course of enacting, new laws, or revising old laws, to deal with this mode of contracting. Among other things, the National Conference of Commissioners on Uniform State Laws has proposed new uniform laws in this area, as well as revising the proposed new official text of Article Two of the Uniform Commercial Code. For example, contracts that had to be in writing can now be in electronic form. Other issues concern the matter of when an electronic message can be properly attributed to a party, and problems, arising from mistaken electronic messages. Two proposed uniform statutes dealing with these issues are the Uniform Electronic Transactions Act (UETA) and the Uniform Computer Information Transactions Act (UCITA).

The most common source of disputes in the field of general contract law arises from the interpretation of contract terms. As a result, a large body of principles has now evolved governing such issues. The best summation of these principles is to be found in the *Restatement of Contracts* (second) at sections 200–204.

Breach of contract consists of a breach of one or more duties of performance arising under the contract, duly interpreted, and may entitle the aggrieved party to various remedies, provided the other party has no defense. A major current controversy rages over whether the law should recognize "efficient breach" of contract, all things considered. Economics-minded scholars have argued on both sides. See R. Posner, *Economic Analysis of Law*, 89–90, 2nd ed., 1977, and compare Friedmann, "The Efficient Breach Fallacy," *Journal Legal Studies* 18 (1989).

Contractual rights to performance and to remedies for breach are defeasible. That is, the nonperforming party may have a defense. I have already identified some of these defenses: unconscionability, illegality, and fraud, for example. There are still other defenses such as impossibility of performance and mutual mistake.

In the most influential single scholarly article of the twentieth century in the field of contracts, "The Reliance Interest in Contract Damages" (*Yale Law Journal* 46 (1936): 52), Lon L. Fuller of Harvard Law School differentiated and analyzed three major contract "interests," corresponding to the three most fundamental monetary remedies an aggrieved party may assert for breach: expectancy, reliance, and restitution. The first—lost expectancy damages—places the aggrieved party in the monetary position that this party would have been

in had the contract been performed as promised. Lost expectancy is sometimes not available because this expectancy cannot be proved, as in the case of uncertain lost profits. Here, the aggrieved party may, as an alternative, choose to recover expenditures incurred in reliance on the contract—that is, "reliance" damages. Another alternative, "restitutionary" damages, accords the aggrieved party the value of any benefit that this party has conferred on the other party.

Instead of monetary recovery, the aggrieved may, in a limited class of cases, secure a court decree ordering the breaching party to perform the very acts called for by the contract. In the United States and England, unlike in some Continental countries, this remedy of "specific performance" is available only in very exceptional cases, as in a sale-of-goods dispute, for example, where the goods are unique (such as an heirloom) and so cannot be procured on the open market, or in a contract for the purchase of land, where the aggrieved purchaser wants the very land in question—land being unique.

In the field of contractual interactions, American law recognizes several general theories of obligation. Under the leading theory, obligation arises from a valid agreement with "consideration," the principal focus of this discussion. Another basic theory of obligation is called *"promissory estoppel." Here, the aggrieved party has justifiably relied on a promise of the other party, suffered a detriment, and is seeking recovery therefor, even though unable to prove a valid agreement with consideration. A further theory of obligation is called "unjust enrichment." When this theory applies, the aggrieved party may recover the value of any benefit conferred on the breaching party. Indeed, under American law, if a party substantially breaches a contract, and the aggrieved party has conferred a benefit on the breacher pursuant to the contract, the aggrieved party may, in most states, recover the market value of the benefit conferred even if this amount exceeds the contract price the parties had placed on the benefit. Still another theory of obligation is *"tort." Various torts may be committed in contractual interactions. A common tort of this kind is negligent performance of a contract. In many states, if the contractual duty so broken is also one imposed by general law, as in the case of an engineer required to exercise due care in the practice of his profession, the aggrieved party may sue in tort and even recover punitive damages in an amount well beyond any lost expectancy or reliance, recovery for breach of contract, or restitutionary recovery for any unjust enrichment.

[See also Consumer Law]

—Robert S. Summers

CONTRACTS OPTIONS. See Contract Law.

COOLEY, THOMAS MCINTYRE (b. Attica, N.Y., 6 January 1824; d. Ann Arbor, Mich., 12 September 1898), treatise writer and jurist. Born into a farm family, Cooley was educated at a rural academy and began to study law with a local attorney. He moved to Michigan in 1843, completed his legal training there, and was admitted to the Michigan bar in 1846. Although he became a Republican in the mid-1850s, Cooley was always strongly influenced by the tenets of Jacksonian democracy, which he had absorbed in his youth.

During the 1860s Cooley served as a law professor at the University of Michigan and as a reporter for the state supreme court. Becoming a member of the Michigan Supreme Court in 1865, he remained on the bench until 1885, when he was defeated for reelection. As a judge he relied heavily on precedent and the *common law in rendering decisions. During these years he also served as a railroad receiver and became an authority on railroad issues.

In 1868, Cooley published his influential and widely cited treatise *The Constitutional Limitations Which Rest Upon the Legislative Power of the States of the American Union.* Much of his reputation is based upon this significant work. Cooley's primary goal was to fashion limits on arbitrary legislative action. He fused the Jacksonian principles of equal rights and hostility to special economic privilege with *due process protection of *property rights. Cooley endorsed a broad reading of due process as a substantive restraint on *legislative power, defining *liberty as encompassing the right to make *contracts and hold *property. Moreover, he assailed class legislation—laws that benefit one segment of society at the expense of others. Cooley's work provided much of the intellectual underpinning for judicial actions that fashioned the due process clause of the Fourteenth Amendment into a formidable protector of economic rights in the late nineteenth century.

Cooley was equally concerned, however, with the growth of monopoly and concentration of economic power. He opposed the use of public resources to subsidize private enterprise; in *People v. Salem* (1870), writing for the Michigan Supreme Court, he invalidated state laws authorizing financial assistance to railroad companies, ruling that *taxation could be imposed only for a public purpose. Cooley's defense of individual rights, though, was not limited to economic matters. He saw no dichotomy between property rights, and other individual liberties; thus, he was supportive of freedom of expression and religious liberty.

Cooley made other contributions to American law. He wrote treatises dealing with the law of taxation and of *torts, as well as numerous articles. His hopes for an appointment to the United States Supreme Court would never be realized, but in 1887 President Cleveland named Cooley to the newly formed Interstate Commerce Commission. Cooley pursued a generally conservative course as chairman of the commission, and has received high marks for his efforts to make it effective in eliminating railroad abuses while respecting the interests of all parties. In poor health, Cooley resigned from the ICC in 1891.

[See also Constitutional Commentators; Judge]

• Clyde Edward Jacobs, *Law Writers and the Courts: The Influence of Thomas M. Cooley, Christopher Tiedman, and John F. Dillon Upon American Constitutional Law,* 1954. Alan R. Jones, *The Constitutional Conservatism of Thomas McIntyre Cooley,* 1987.

—James W. Ely Jr.

COPYRIGHT. See Property, Intellectual.

CORBIN, ARTHUR LINTON (1874–1966), one of the most revered law professors of the twentieth century. Corbin was born in Cripple Creek, Colorado. After receiving his B.A. from the University of Kansas, he entered Yale Law School in 1897 and completed his legal education in two years. After graduation, Corbin practiced law in Cripple Creek until 1903, when he was hired by Yale as an instructor of contracts. In 1909 Yale named Corbin Professor of Contracts, a title he held with great distinction until his formal retirement (on reaching the mandatory retirement age) in 1943. As professor emeritus, Corbin remained active at Yale Law School until his death.

At least five superb accomplishments underlie Professor Corbin's status as an outstanding law professor. The first was his multivolume treatise on *contracts, published in 1950. This seminal work, fifty-plus years in the making, was described by his colleague Grant Gilmore as "the greatest lawbook ever written." Corbin set in motion trends that led to the modernization of contract theory. Rather than blindly accepting and reporting contract case precedents, he became an innovative thinker in the field. His ability as an "imaginative reformer" also spearheaded the drive at Yale to replace lectures delivered by law professors with casebooks and the Socratic method of teaching.

Second, Corbin's groundbreaking scholarship included more than twenty-five articles published in the *Yale Law Journal*. Third, he helped found and shape *legal realism. Corbin's ideas were transmitted to his protégés, who with his help founded the American legal realist school of *jurisprudence, with which the Yale Law School became closely associated. Fourth, Corbin guided numerous students in the art of legal thinking, many of whom went on to high positions in law, government, and industry. Finally, Corbin devoted himself to building the Yale Law School. In many ways, he stood out as an exemplary symbol of the school.

Arthur Corbin, a man of great physical and intellectual vigor, was well liked and respected by his students, his colleagues, and the entire legal community. He stands as a paradigm of the great law professor.   —Robert Whitman

CORONER. *See* Medical Examiner.

CORPORATE LAW PRACTICE. The practice of law in the United States is conventionally divided into two broad categories: litigation and "transactional" law. The public perception of practicing lawyers is often one of litigators arguing in court, but this perception does not accurately describe the practice of transactional lawyers. Transactional lawyers advise their clients in *negotiations and in drafting documents as they relate to economic transactions, such as *contracts, *wills, and sales of real *property. They also provide advice both as to the interpretation of documents as well as to the relevant laws that govern the client's affairs.

Corporate law is one major area of transactional law practice. Corporate lawyers represent *corporations in conducting their business affairs, as well as advising managers and members of the board of directors as to the legal obligations they owe the company, its shareholders, and the public. Corporate law practice includes further subcategories of practice, including general corporate law, *securities law, *bankruptcy law, and mergers and acquisitions.

Corporate law has traditionally been practiced in private law firms. Corporate law clients are almost exclusively private businesses seeking representation in the drafting of corporate documents, contracts to buy and sell goods and services, and negotiating the terms of business deals. Corporate lawyers practice in law firms of various sizes. Most small-firm corporate lawyers engage in general corporate law practice, representing small corporations and the owner-managers of those companies. Large-firm corporate lawyers represent more sizeable corporations, which have complicated legal issues and business arrangements. Very large corporations that issue publicly held stock have extraordinarily complicated legal arrangements that require ongoing representation in order to avoid legal problems and to conduct the business operations of the company.

Some corporate lawyers are direct employees of corporations, representing the corporation in negotiations over contracts, but also monitoring and advising outside lawyers on the larger issues for which those lawyers have been retained. Most of these "in-house" corporate lawyers begin their careers in private law firms. A large business may have dozens of lawyers working full-time for the corporation in its general counsel's office.

Highly specialized areas of corporate law practice, such as securities law and mergers and acquisitions, are practiced primarily by lawyers working in law firms with as many as a thousand lawyers. Some of the most elite corporate law practitioners practice in so-called "boutique" law firms that specialize in discrete areas of corporate law, most notably mergers and acquisitions and bankruptcy law.

Corporate lawyers practice in cities of all sizes throughout the country, representing local clients in their various business dealings. A "mom-and-pop" restaurant in a small town needs a corporate lawyer to draft its articles of incorporation, file the necessary paperwork with the government to do business as a corporate entity, and represent it in business matters that may arise. Because many corporations are headquartered in large cities, however, most corporate law practice is found in urban areas. New York's "Wall Street" law firms have represented America's leading corporations for generations. Important other strongholds of corporate law practice are Atlanta, Boston, Chicago, Houston, Los Angeles, and San Francisco.

Perhaps the fastest growing geographical areas for corporate law practice are in the centers of the "new economy," such as Silicon Valley in California and the high-technology region of Northern Virginia. The rapid growth of the biotechnology and telecommunications industries in these areas has spawned dramatic changes not only in the American economy as a whole, but also in the practice of corporate law. Companies in these industries compete in rapidly changing and highly competitive markets that place a premium on adaptability, creativity, and problem-solving. The new economy companies have also created numerous new problems in corporate finance. Traditional corporations were structured around large investments in factories and machines that required huge capital investments to build and maintain. By contrast, the new economy firms have little in the way of tangible physical capital. Instead, their primary assets are in the "human capital," education, and creativity of their employees. This has caused a dramatic shift not only in the structure of business enterprises but also in the financing of these enterprises. The further development of new economy firms promises to present new challenges and opportunities for corporate lawyers in the future.

The growth of international trade and communications technology in recent decades has also made corporate law practice increasingly international in scope. American businesses are entering into mergers and business partnerships with companies in Europe and Latin America. Issues such as international cooperation and negotiation will become increasingly important as the globalization of business continues. Moreover, American corporate lawyers are much more involved in planning and negotiating business dealings on behalf of their clients than are European lawyers, illustrating the substantial cultural differences in the nature of corporate law practice between these societies.

Many corporate lawyers engage in general corporate representation. This includes drafting the internal corporate documents of a business enterprise, such as the corporate charter and bylaws, as well as complying with all necessary government rules for conducting business. General corporate lawyers may also represent their business clients when they seek a bank loan or in major contract negotiations. Equally, many lawyers also represent banks in matters of commercial lending.

Most general corporate representation is continuous, assisting and advising business clients on business matters and helping them run their businesses smoothly and avoid legal problems. Unlike litigators, who generally enter the picture after a problem has arisen, corporate lawyers strive to keep their clients from running into problems in the first place. Thus, much of the practice of general corporate lawyers provides guidance, judgment, and wisdom to their clients, and not merely legal expertise.

The best general corporate lawyers are those who maintain a continuous relationship with their clients over years, or even decades. Representing a long-term client requires an intimate understanding of the client's business and industry, and the business's goals and challenges. In turn, this requires an understanding of economics, finance, and accounting in order to be of value to the client in a counseling capacity. General corporate lawyers must therefore not only be legal specialists but also conversant with the realities of business.

Corporate lawyers have traditionally studied the same law school curriculum as lawyers who plan on becoming litigation specialists. In recent years, however, law schools have come to recognize the need to adapt their educational curriculums to meet the challenges confronting modern corporate lawyers. Law schools now include courses that focus on the negotiation and drafting of corporate documents as well as providing a background in economics, finance, and accounting for students interested in pursuing a career in corporate law. Some law schools have even added courses tailored to specific specialties within corporate law, such as entrepreneurship or commercial lending (see EDUCATION, LEGAL).

In addition to general corporate law, there are a number of related specialty areas of law in which the actual practice varies dramatically from the counseling and negotiation practice of general corporate law. For example, securities lawyers advise clients on the complex rules governing public offerings of corporate stock and the various reporting requirements associated with compliance with securities laws.

Bankruptcy law is also a growing area of corporate law specialization. Bankruptcy lawyers deal with the resolution of the financial problems of bankrupt corporations. Changes to the federal bankruptcy laws in 1978 made bankruptcy more common even among well-known companies. For example, many major airlines have been through bankruptcy reorganizations. Bankruptcy law has also dealt with many of the major issues of product liability law in recent years, including defective products such as silicone implants and asbestos. The 1978 Bankruptcy Code also modified the compensation mechanism for bankruptcy professionals, so that today they are paid at a rate comparable to practitioners in other areas of law. As a result, almost all major law firms have large and established corporate bankruptcy practices. Moreover, in contrast to other areas of corporate law practice, bankruptcy lawyers often appear in court.

Bankruptcy law practice is also distinct in that the need for swift resolution of the problems of a company facing a financial crisis makes the practice fast-paced and informal in nature, and places a high premium on the ability to adapt and solve problems quickly. Whereas general corporate law practice and securities law practice tend to rise and fall with the business cycle, bankruptcy law practice tends to be countercyclical. Thus, even traditional corporate lawyers are developing expertise as bankruptcy lawyers in order to be able to continue their work during economic downturns.

[*See also* Law Practice, Forms of]

• Bryan Burrough and John Helyar, *Barbarians at the Gate: The Fall of RJR Nabisco*, 1990. "Symposium on Business Lawyering and Value Creation for Clients," *Oregon Law Review*, 74, No. 1 (Spring 1995). "Symposium on The Essays of Warren Buffett: Lessons for Corporate America," *Cardozo Law Review*, 19, Nos. 1–2 (Sept.–Nov. 1997).   —Todd J. Zywicki

CORPORATIONS

For-Profit Corporations
Nonprofit Corporations

CORPORATIONS: FOR-PROFIT CORPORATIONS

Probably the most important contribution of nineteenth- and twentieth-century American legal history was the creation of the modern business corporation. The corporate form, or something close to it, had existed in law at least since the time of the Romans, and was borrowed by America from British practice. But in America, the corporation was refined into the premier means for concentrating capital and management into an effective *commercial investment vehicle. In 1911, Nicholas Murray Butler, President of Columbia University, declared that "[T]he limited liability corporation is the greatest single discovery of modern times [and that] even steam and electricity are far less important . . . and they would be reduced to comparative impotence without it . . . It makes possible huge economy in production and in trading . . . it means the only possible engine for carrying on international trade on a scale commensurate with modern needs and opportunities." Butler's claim remains valid today, and it is likely that the twenty-first century will see the American business corporation, or something close to it, continue to be the dominant form for doing business around the globe.

This essay describes the principal characteristics of the corporation in American law, the roles played by Officers, Directors, and shareholders, and the influence of state and federal law on the corporation; some of the most important legal issues involving the corporation, including the rights and responsibilities of shareholders, and the fiduciary duties of corporate Officers and Directors, will be briefly treated.

It is virtually impossible to overstate the importance of the corporation to current American legal theory and practice; indeed, it is usual to describe the training given in modern law schools as fitting people for the practice of "corporate law," and that practice is the nearly exclusive concern of most of the great urban law firms that now dominate American law. Legal treatises and statutory codes on corporations run into the thousands of pages, and hundreds of thousands of judicial opinions have been rendered on the topic.

Characteristics of the Corporation. American law generally divides corporations into two basic categories: "for profit" corporations (usually called "corporations" or "business corporations") and "nonprofit corporations." The analysis here concerns "for profit" or "business" corporations. Such a corporation is generally understood to exhibit five important characteristics: (1) artificial legal personality, (2) centralized management, (3) perpetual life, (4) free transferability of ownership, and (5) limited *liability of the owners for the corporation's debts.

A corporation is created by filing the appropriate documents, usually with a state official, by paying a filing fee, and by designating officials to act for the corporation as Officers and Directors. Ownership in the corporation is in the hands of "shareholders," who contribute the capital necessary for the corporation to conduct business, and who are given an opportunity to share in corporate profits through dividends and to control the corporations through voting. Shareholders may be individuals or themselves be corporations. Where a corporate shareholder owns another corporation, the corporate shareholder owner is referred to as the "parent" corporation, and the owned entity is called a "subsidiary" corporation.

The shareholders elect the Board of Directors, who have the responsibility of monitoring the affairs of the corporation and the conduct of the Officers, who are selected by the Board. The Officers are charged with the day-to-day running of the corporation. In a general partnership, every partner shares the responsibility for the conduct of the entity, but in a corporation, management is in the hands, not of all the owners, but of the Board of Directors and the Officers. Shareholders may thus be little more than passive investors in the enterprise. There are generally state minimum capital requirements for corporations. Originally there were restrictions on the amount of capital a corporation could possess, but these were eliminated in the late nineteenth century. Though corporations may employ thousands of individuals, have millions of shareholders, and have their affairs directed by dozens of officials, the law treats the corporation as if it were a single individual. It is able to own property, enter into contracts, and sue and be sued in its own name. In this, the law treats corporations differently from the way partnerships are treated (although this is now changing), because partnerships are regarded as aggregations of individuals rather than entities.

Similarly, while partnerships end any time any of the partners withdraw from the business, corporations are recognized to have the potential to live forever, as shares are transferred from one stockholder to another, as the stockholders select new members for the Board of Directors, as the Directors fill vacancies on the Board when they occur between shareholder meetings, and as the Directors name new officers to run the corporation. In the general law regarding partnerships, no partner can be admitted without the consent of all the other partners, but, as a general rule, no permission is required from other shareholders for any shareholder to sell his or her shares to another person.

Finally, whereas in a partnership or a sole proprietorship each investor is generally liable to third parties for all of the debts of the business, in a corporation the liability of shareholders is limited to the original capital contribution (sometimes called a "subscription") that he or she makes to the corporation. This "limited liability" investment feature of corporations has come to be the single most important characteristic of the corporation, although it did not develop in its modern form until the middle of the nineteenth century. Limited liability was then universally adopted by the state legislatures on the joint theories that (1) limiting investor liability would increase investment in America's then capital-scarce economy, and (2) that by limiting the liability of shareholders, investors of modest means would be able to participate in corporations without risking the loss of all their financial resources. These economic and democratic justifications for shareholder limited liability are still invoked in support of the doctrine, although limited shareholder liability periodically comes under attack by critics of corporations.

Limited shareholder liability is generally recognized to be a privilege accorded by the state, but it is a privilege that can be lost if it is abused. Abuses by a shareholder (whether that shareholder is an individual or a corporation) that result in the loss of limited liability are usually referred to as "piercing the corporate veil." Piercing the corporate veil results in the imposition of liability for the debts of the corporation on individuals or parent corporations. There are probably more cases involving piercing the corporate veil than in any other area of corporate law, and it is usually described as an elusive doctrine. Nevertheless, certain clear factual situations justify piercing the corporate veil, and lend some coherence to the cases. In particular, where a shareholder treats the assets of the corporation as if they were his or her own, and drains the corporation of resources to meet its existing obligations and appropriates those resources for personal benefit, limited liability will have been lost, and the corporate veil will be pierced.

In another classic formulation of the piercing of the corporate veil doctrine, it was said that "[A] corporation will be looked upon as a legal entity [responsible for its own debts] as a general rule, and until sufficient reason to the contrary appears; but, when the notion of legal entity is used to defeat public convenience, justify wrong, protect fraud, or defend crime, the law will regard the corporation as an association of persons [and will impose liability for the corporate debts on them]." (*U.S.* v. *Milwaukee Refrigerator Transit Co.* (1905)).

State and Federal Law Regarding Conduct of Corporations and Corporate Actors. The internal affairs of the corporation—the rights, responsibilities, and duties of shareholders, directors, and officers—are regulated by the law of the state in which a corporation has been incorporated. While other states in which a corporation operates may regulate its external conduct (its entering into contracts, committing torts or crimes, or other aspects of the way it does business), the *"full faith and credit" clause of the United States Constitution requires each state to defer to the state of incorporation on internal corporate questions. Accordingly, the choice of the state of incorporation is crucial for determining matters of importance to investors and others who deal with corporations. Competition among the states has resulted in different policies, often reflecting the influence of powerful groups on the state's government. For example, New York corporate law is generally friendlier to corporate employees, California law is friendlier to corporate creditors, and Delaware, which is generally recognized as the most important jurisdiction for incorporation, has the friendliest law for corporate managers and majority shareholders.

For most of the twentieth century, Delaware's statutory corporate scheme was regarded as the most developed, and most of the nation's important business corporations were Delaware corporations. There were occasional charges that this was harmful to shareholders, and in one famous academic broadside, Yale Law Professor and one-time chairman of the Securities and Exchange Commission (SEC) William Cary charged that the law of Delaware "watered down the rights of shareholders to a thin gruel." It is true that the law of Delaware allows majority shareholders, Directors, and Officers the most unfettered control of any state. While many states require supermajority shareholder or Board votes for major corporate changes or for the issuance of new shares of stock, Delaware allows such organic changes to be accomplished by only a majority vote of shares followed by a majority vote of the Board of Directors. Delaware also goes further than any other state in holding Officers and Directors harmless for the decisions they reach when acting on behalf of the corporation, and makes it easier than any other state for the corporation to declare dividends. Many states have elaborate mechanisms for shareholder and Director voting, but Delaware has streamlined the process substantially.

The result of the refinement of Delaware Corporate law has been the construction of a statutory scheme that allows Directors and Officers the greatest freedom to take financial risks. This greater ability to take risks has, in the main, resulted in higher returns to the shareholders of Delaware corporation. Thus, paradoxically, while minority shareholders have relatively little influence over the conduct of Delaware corporations, their individual shares are more highly valued by the marketplace. Corporations may leave their original state of incorporation to "reincorporate" in another state, and there is much more movement into Delaware than out of it. Accordingly, the long-term trend in individual state corporate law appears to be to imitate the law of Delaware, and for the most part one can speak about state corporate law rules in generalities, using Delaware as a model. Perhaps the most important of those rules, apart from those establishing the corporate characteristics mentioned earlier, are those that set forth the "fiduciary" responsibilities of Officers, Directors, and majority shareholders. A "fiduciary" is one whom the law deems, because of the special power to control the disposition of finances and assets possessed by such a person, to have a responsibility to those affected by that con-

trol. In the case of corporate fiduciaries, it is their responsibility not to put their personal interests ahead of those of the corporation. This fiduciary responsibility is generally described under two rubrics: "the duty of care" and the "duty of loyalty."

Pursuant to the duty of care, Officers and Directors are required to perform their tasks with ordinary prudence and in the manner a reasonably prudent person would. Failure to act when a prudent person would have acted—for example in gathering sufficient information before deciding to make a major corporate decision—may result in the Officer or Director's being liable to shareholders for harm caused as a result of neglect. There is a major qualification to this rule of liability for negligence. This is the so-called "business judgment" rule, which forbids imposing liability on an Officer or Director, when such a person makes a decision on a corporate matter, provided (1) sufficient information has been gathered, (2) there is no conflict of interest involved in the decision, and (3) the decision was made in good faith and in a manner the Officer or Director rationally believed to be in the best interests of the corporation. The "business judgment" rule, which exists in order to encourage creativity and risk-taking on the part of corporate managers, is a difficult concept to grasp, but essentially it provides that if a corporate decision, in light of subsequent developments, appears to have been negligent or unreasonable, the decision-makers will not be liable for the adverse financial consequences to shareholders as long as the three requirements enumerated above have been satisfied.

Duty of loyalty applies in conflict-of-interest situations, and enforces the rule that corporate fiduciaries may not put their personal interests ahead of those of the corporation. Duty of loyalty has many aspects, but they add up to the proposition that transactions may be set aside, or those subject to a conflict of interest may be liable for damages to the corporation (if it is injured in a transaction with an interested Officer or Director), unless (1) the details of the transaction and the conflict of interest have been fully disclosed, (2) the decision to go ahead with the transaction has been made by a disinterested corporate actor, and (3) the transaction is, taking all of the circumstances into account, "fair" to the corporation. If a transaction involving a conflict of interest has not been accompanied by full disclosure, the transaction can usually be set aside as presumptively unfair, and the burden of proving the fairness of the transaction is usually placed on the party with the conflict of interest. Where there has been approval by a disinterested corporate decision-maker, however, and where there has been full disclosure, the burden of proving unfairness is placed on any party challenging the transaction.

Perhaps because of a perception that the state law rules (1) regarding fiduciary responsibility, and (2) giving Officers and Directors great power (particularly Delaware's), inadequately safeguarded the interests of individual shareholders, there has been continual pressure on the federal government to formulate rules to protect shareholders. The federal government's response has been in the area of interstate trading in corporate securities, and is codified in the Federal Securities Act of 1933 and the Federal Securities and Exchange Act of 1934.

The 1933 Act is concerned with new issues of stock. It requires that certain written materials must accompany or precede any interstate offering of *securities, and imposes federal criminal penalties as well as civil liability for misstatements or omissions in the offering materials.

The 1934 Act, which set up the SEC, the principal agency charged with the enforcement of federal securities laws, regulates interstate trading in existing securities, particularly trading by corporate "insiders" (Officers, Directors and controlling shareholders), and imposes both civil and criminal penalties for fraudulent practices in connection with the trading of already-issued securities. Other provisions of the 1934 Act require that communications involving means or instrumentalities of interstate commerce between a corporation and its shareholders in connection with shareholder votes on elections to the Board of Directors or for other matters of corporate change requiring shareholder vote be reviewed by the SEC. Failure to submit such materials for review, or the making of false or misleading statements in connection with such shareholder solicitation can result in criminal or civil liability. Revisions to the 1934 Act also impose federal regulation on tender offers and takeovers (ways to shift control of corporations that gained wide popularity in the late twentieth century).

It is not clear whether each provision of the federal securities laws actually serves to protect shareholders, but it is clear that the provisions of the 1934 and 1933 Acts have resulted in many thousands of criminal and civil cases being litigated. If piercing the corporate veil is the most litigated issue in state corporate law, then insider liability for trading in securities is the most litigated issue under federal law. Many of the lawsuits brought under these provisions may lack merit, and the costs of defending against them are substantial, leading Congress to periodically seek to review the regulations and restrict opportunities for frivolous litigation. Nevertheless, it does appear that the federal regulatory scheme, insofar as it promotes regular disclosure and imposes heavy civil and criminal penalties for fraud and misstatements, has resulted in an improved climate that encourages both foreign and domestic investment in the shares of domestic corporations.

Other State and Federal Issues of Corporate Law. Space here does not permit a detailed treatment of many other important and changing issues of corporate law. These include (1) when a shareholder may bring litigation in the name of his or her corporation, asserting an interest belonging not to him or her individually, but to the corporation generally; (2) how a corporation is taxed by the state and federal governments; and (3) the differences in state and federal law treatment of "publicly held" or "closely held" corporations. Publicly held corporations are generally required to adhere to greater corporate formalities, and are more subject to double-taxation than are closely held corporations. The latter are generally treated by both state and federal governments more as if they were partnerships than corporations.

The American business corporation will for the forseeable future remain the most important business form for investment and for large-scale transactions, both domestically and internationally. Still, it is likely that newer business forms, such as the Limited Liability Company (LLC) and The Limited Liability Partnership (LLP), which seek to combine the informality and tax advantages of the partnership with the limited liability of the corporation, will compete with the business corporation for investment. These new entities, as they develop, will also result in the creation of substantial bodies of state, national, and international law, which can be expected to borrow from the corporate law rules.

[*See also* Economics and Law]

• William L. Cary, "Federalism and Corporate Law: Reflections on Delaware," 83 Yale Law Journal (1974): 663. William Meade Fletcher, *Fletcher [Cyclopedia] of Private Corporations*, 35 vols., updated annually. Robert M. Hamilton, *Hamilton's Law of Corporations in A Nutshell*, 5th ed., 1996. Stephen B. Presser, *Piercing the Corporate Veil*, updated annually.   —Stephen B. Presser

CORPORATIONS: NONPROFIT CORPORATIONS

Nonprofit corporations, sometimes referred to as "charitable corporations" or "eleemosynary corporations," are the predominant form of charitable organization in the United States. While a "for-profit corporation" (also referred to as a "business corporation" or merely as a "corporation") exists for the purpose of increasing the wealth of its shareholders, a nonprofit corporation's objectives must not include pecuniary gain for its members. Organizing as a nonprofit corporation offers many of the same advantages possessed by business corporations, including artificial legal personality, centralized management, potentially perpetual life, and limited *liability for officers, directors, and others involved with the nonprofit. Limited liability can be lost, and personal liability for the debts of the nonprofit imposed on officers, directors, or members (those who form a nonprofit) if the corporate form is abused for personal purposes. The rules applied in "piercing the corporate veil" of a nonprofit are the same as for a "for-profit" corporation.

If a nonprofit corporation meets the tests laid out in Section 501(c)(3) of the United States Internal Revenue Code, the nonprofit gains four advantages not available to "for-profit corporations": (1) exemption from federal and state *taxation for the income and property of the nonprofit, (2) the ability of donors to the nonprofit to deduct their contributions on their individual income tax returns as charitable donations, (3) the opportunity to seek grants and funding from private, state, and federal agencies, and (4) the opportunity to take advantage of lower postage rates for nonprofits.

Most of the law regarding nonprofit corporations, especially insofar as it turns on 501(c)(3) tax considerations, is of very recent vintage, and is almost entirely a product of the twentieth century. The law of charitable corporations is somewhat chaotic in origin and expression, since it has moved from its English statutory and common law associations with the charitable trust, and now seems poised uneasily between state corporation law and federal tax law.

Because it was uncertain whether the English statutory law regarding charitable trusts would be applicable in America, corporations by the nineteenth century were becoming the preferred vehicle for accomplishing charitable goals. The organizational advantages of the form received a tremendous boost in the famous case of *Dartmouth College* v. *Woodward* (1819). That case, of profound importance for "for-profit" corpora-

tions, held that corporate charters, once granted, could not be altered by the state. New Hampshire had sought, in effect, to convert the College from a private to a public institution. Chief Justice John *Marshall's opinion for the court stated that the grant of a charter was a *contract that could not be changed unilaterally by the state without violating the contract clause of the Constitution. New Hampshire had argued that a corporation that served the public (what we might today regard as a "charitable" corporation) should be subject to alteration of its charter any time the public interest required it, but Justice Joseph *Story made clear in his concurring opinion that this should not be the case if the corporation's donors were private individuals. Both Marshall and Story emphasized that donations to charitable corporations might be discouraged if charters could be altered unilaterally by the states.

Many states responded to *Dartmouth College* by reserving the right to alter subsequently granted charters when the public interest required it, but with regard to existing corporations, no such alterations could be made. In any event, the court's holding established a powerful precedent for the autonomy of private charitable corporations, even if they were operated for public purposes. By emphasizing the importance of the source of a corporation's funding for the sanctity of its charter, the *Dartmouth College* decision also laid the foundation for legally similar treatment of charitable and for-profit corporations. Since that time, business corporation law has to a great extent provided a model for the internal operating rules of nonprofit corporations.

The procedures for forming a nonprofit corporation are similar to those for for-profit corporations. A Certificate of Incorporation ("charter") is granted by the state of incorporation, upon application and the payment of the designated fee. A charter and bylaws must be drawn up. These documents will specify the purposes for which the organization is incorporated, and supply other basic information such as the identity of the incorporators, the manner of choosing directors and officers, and names and addresses for the organization, its officers, and its agents. In Delaware, for example, the Certificate of Incorporation will clearly identify the organization as a nonprofit corporation.

501(c)(3) provides that a corporation seeking to maintain tax-exempt status must be "organized and operated exclusively for religious, charitable, scientific, testing for public safety, literary, or educational purposes, or to foster national or international amateur sports competition, or for the prevention of cruelty to children or animals." Further, "no part of the net earnings [of the corporation may inure] to the benefit of any private shareholder or individual." Finally, 501(c)(3) states that "no substantial part of the activities of [the corporation may include] carrying on propaganda, or otherwise attempting, to influence legislation . . . and [the corporation may] not participate in, or intervene in (including the publishing or distributing of statements), any political campaign on behalf of (or in opposition to) any candidate for public office."

Still another requirement for the maintenance of nonprofit and tax-exempt status under state and federal law, which supplements the "nondistribution constraint" preventing a nonprofit from distributing its net earnings to those in control of the corporation, is the proviso that if the corporation should cease its operations, its assets must not go to its members. Instead, the assets must be distributed to some other exempt organization that will employ them for one or more of the designated nonprofit purposes, or the assets must be distributed to the federal, state, or local government, to be used for a public purpose. As one might expect, all of these essentially vague provisions of 501(c)(3) have been the subject of extensive litigation and the issuance of supplemental federal regulations.

State law requires directors of nonprofit corporations to adhere to the same duty of care and loyalty to which for-profit directors are subject. Applying these laws in a stringent manner tends to discourage nonprofit directors, so some states may apply the rules a bit more leniently. Nevertheless, the problem of self-dealing by directors and officers with regard to the assets of a nonprofit can be as real as for a for-profit corporation. Because nonprofits are not subject to the same kind of reporting requirements that bind publicly traded for-profit corporations, such misconduct may go unpunished. As the Internal Revenue Service has limited resources to police compliance with its nonprofit requirements, and as the only sanction available to it is removal of the tax-exempt status of the nonprofit (a remedy that punishes the entire corporation and not just an individual violator), ensuring adherence to fiduciary standards for nonprofits may be even more difficult than for-profit corporations.

• Howard Leoner Oleck, *Nonprofit Corporations, Organizations & Associations*, 6th ed., 1994. James J. Fishman and Stephen Schwartz, *Nonprofit Organizations: Cases and Materials*, 2000. Internal Revenue Service, United States Department of the Treasury, *Tax Exempt Status for Your Organization*, (Government Printing Office, IRS Publication 557, Cat. No. 46573C, Rev. July, 2001).

—Stephen B. Presser

COSA NOSTRA. *See* Organized Crime.

COSTS, COURT. Court costs refer to civil litigation taxable costs listed by statute, other than attorney *fees. These are normally recoverable by the winning party, although the judge may determine otherwise. Typical costs include expenses for filing, service of process, witnesses, and court reporters.

[*See also* Procedure, Court]

—David S. Clark

COUNSEL, RIGHT TO. The Sixth Amendment to the Constitution dictates that "[i]n all criminal prosecutions, the accused shall . . . have the Assistance of Counsel for his defense." For the better part of American history, the guarantee assured that those persons who could afford counsel would have one. Over time the Supreme Court has interpreted this Sixth Amendment provision in an expansive way, first by adding requirements to provide counsel and second by specifying the stages where counsel is required. There is no constitutional right to counsel in most civil cases.

The Court began to expand the class of defendants entitled to legal counsel in criminal cases with its decision in *Powell* v. *Alabama* (1932), where it ruled that defendants in state capital cases were entitled to legal assistance. Six years later in *Johnson* v. *Zerbst*, the Court ruled that the Sixth Amendment required the appointment of counsel for all felony defendants in federal courts. In a break from this expansive pattern, the Court rejected a similar mandate for state felony courts in *Betts* v. *Brady* (1942), where it held that the appointment of counsel for indigents in state felony cases should be dictated by circumstances for the case. *Betts* was overruled twenty-one years later in one of the Supreme Court's most important decisions, *Gideon* v. *Wainwright* (1963). The Court ruled that counsel is required for defendants in all state felony cases. This guarantee was extended to misdemeanors in *Argersinger* v. *Hamlin* (1979), although the Court concluded that misdemeanor courts are not required to appoint counsel where imprisonment is possible but not specified.

Related to the Court's requirement of counsel for indigents are the specifications regarding the stages in criminal *procedure where counsel is required. The Sixth Amendment holds that the assistance of counsel is required in all criminal prosecutions. In several twentieth-century decisions the Court has interpreted this to include arraignment, trial, and sentencing. Specifically, the right to counsel is mandated for lineups (*U.S.* v. *Wade*, 1967) [but not for blood or handwriting samples], for pretrial arraignments (*Hamilton* v. *Alabama*, 1961), for preliminary hearings (*Coleman* v. *Alabama*, 1970), for trials (*Gideon* v. *Wainwright* (1963), *Argersinger* v. *Hamlin* (1972), *Scott* v. *Illinois* (1979)), for sentencing (*Mempa* v. *Rhay*, 1967), and at first, automatic appeals (*Douglas* v. *California*, 1963). The right to counsel mandated by the Court for police *interrogations in the famous *Miranda* v. *Arizona* decision of 1966 derived from the Fifth Amendment's privilege against *self-incrimination, and not the Sixth Amendment's guarantee. In contrast to these expansive holdings, the Court has declined to extend the right to counsel to grand jury processes (*U.S.* v. *Scarpelli*, 1973; *Morrissey* v. *Brewer*, 1972).

Recent holdings have upheld the constitutionality of self-representation. In *Faretta* v. *California* (1975), the Court, in effect, accepted the idea that "fools" may choose to represent themselves. The quality of legal representation is also an issue. The central holding on this point is *Strickland* v. *Washington* (1984), where the Court ruled that the Sixth Amendment right to counsel can be infringed upon by incompetent counsel. Here defendants must establish that the counsel's performance was deficient, that that performance prejudiced the case, and that were it not for that deficiency, the defendant would have been acquitted. It is not easy to meet this burden.

In spite of the Supreme Court's expansive interpretation of the Sixth Amendment right to counsel, several issues remain. The Court has offered no standards related to indigency nor has it required any particular system for public assistance. In spite of this silence, it is clear that the Supreme Court's decisions relative to right to counsel constitute important precedents for criminal procedure. The assistance of counsel, more than any other dimension of *due process, evokes general American support for fair play and reflects the centrality of attorneys in the adversarial tradition of countries with common law.

[*See also* Civil Rights and Civil Liberties]

—Suzette M. Talarico

COURT COSTS. See Costs, Court.

COURT OFFICERS. Most courtrooms in America are loosely organized around a network of critical actors. The most visible members of this network are the judges, the litigants that stand before them, and their lawyers. Equally crucial to the success of these loosely formed organizations are the various court officers—bailiffs, court clerks, marshals, and court reporters. Unlike clients, witnesses, and even jurors—whose activities in court are usually short-lived—court officers are fully integrated and permanent fixtures in the daily work of the court itself.

Some scholars have likened the work of the court as an organizational unit to the teamwork approach of other multiservice units such as hospitals, where relatively little formal or external coordination normally exists. Rather, the court relies on each of its officers to exhibit a considerable degree of self-direction, functional interdependence, and self-coordination in performing their respective tasks. And while American courts vary substantially in the size of their workloads and the character of their respective dockets, nearly every court tends to rely heavily on a model of work organization in which court officers enjoy considerable influence over court access, docket control, and other critical court functions.

Bailiffs. Serving mostly in state or local jurisdictions, a bailiff is one of the few court officials who enjoys personal contact with the judge, attorneys, litigants, and even jurors. Outside the courtroom, the bailiff often assists other court officers by procuring files and exhibits from the appropriate offices. As the official custodian of the courtroom itself, the bailiff also serves an especially important function during judicial proceedings. Before the judge arrives, the bailiff ascertains that the counsel and parties are present and ready to proceed. During the hearing or trial itself, the bailiff is responsible for the maintenance of order in the court. When a jury has been selected, the bailiff essentially safeguards the jury process, protecting the sanctity of its deliberations from outside influences. And while bailiffs generally remain outside the jury room during jury deliberations, they are on call to convey any messages from the jury foreman to the judge. In some rural areas, the local sheriff or deputy sheriff serves as the bailiff for all court proceedings.

Court Clerks. The clerk of the court runs the court office where all court records are maintained. Although all federal court clerks and many state court clerks are appointed by and serve at the pleasure of the court, in some jurisdictions they are elected officials. Except in the handful of jurisdictions that maintain an official "court administrator" or "executive," the clerk of the court also serves as chief operating officer and administrator, working under the supervision of the chief judge or justice of that court. Accordingly, his official responsibilities may include (1) maintaining the budget for the court's operations, (2) collecting and analyzing statistical data that reflect the performance of the court, (3) managing the jury selection process, (4) serving as liaison with all branches of the court and related government agencies, and (5) preparing and disseminating reports or other official information concerning the work of the court. Local practice varies widely as to what part (if any) the court clerk plays within the courtroom itself. Finally, the clerk of the court should never be confused with a judge's own personal law *clerks, who are generally distinguished law school graduates hired by a judge (usually for a short term only) to do legal research and draft opinions on his behalf.

Marshals. U.S. Marshals are appointed for a term of four years to each judicial district by the President, with the advice and consent of the U.S. Senate. U.S. Marshals in turn appoint their own deputies to serve at their pleasure. As a subdivision of the Department of Justice, the U.S. Marshal's service is responsible for (1) moving prisoners, (2) supervising the Justice Department's Witness Security Program, (3) apprehending fugitives, (4) executing court orders, and (5) providing security to the court and its personnel. U.S. Marshals also manage security at federal courthouses: they are authorized to carry firearms and make arrests. Marshals are even in charge of federal juries. As such, the duties of U.S. Marshals at the federal level can be likened to those of sheriffs and bailiffs in state and local courts. U.S. Marshals may also, under certain circumstances, be authorized to serve summons and complaints.

Court Reporters. Court reporters are responsible for recording all court proceedings verbatim (either by shorthand or by electronic means), and then transcribing them as required by statute, or upon request of the judge and/or the parties. The use of shorthand by court reporters dates back to eighteenth-century England; a century later, Miles Bartholomew (a court reporter from Illinois) patented the first stenotype machine in the United States. Improved versions of Bartholomew's invention eventually took hold in American courtrooms by the turn of the twentieth century. Today, court reporting has adopted high technology, with computer-aided transcription, audio recording technology (including voicewriters), and video technology nudging the stenotype machine aside in many instances. Spurred by these developments, word-to-word accuracy represents the

standard for reporting practices in all United States courts today. By contrast, generalized court records and brief summaries of court testimony remain the norm in many other legal systems around the world.

Although most court reporters have at least a high school education, large numbers have gone to college, and many have attended specialized reporting schools for two or more years. The National Shorthand Reporters Association instills professionalism in the reporters' field by certifying reporters, including video specialists. The practice of assigning court reporters varies widely: some courts require reporters to work for the court as a whole (in a pooling arrangement); in other courts, individual court reporters work mainly in the courtroom of one specific judge. Most official court reporters receive a set salary, and collect additional fees for transcripts prepared exclusively at the request of parties. In the case of trials, transcripts are usually prepared only after a trial is completed and an appeal has been filed; litigants may, however, request daily transcripts by giving notice in advance.

[See also Courts, United States; *Gideon* v. *Wainwright* (1963)]

• David J. Saari, *The Court and Free-Lance Reporter Profession: Improved Management Strategies,* 1988. Wolf Heydebrand and Carroll Seron, *Rationalizing Justice: The Political Economy of Federal District Courts,* 1990. Federal Judicial Center, *Chambers Handbook for Judges' Law Clerks and Secretaries,* 1994.

—David A. Yalof

COURT OF INTERNATIONAL TRADE. *See* Labor Law: Labor Relations.

COURT PACKING. In 1937, Franklin Roosevelt proposed the appointment of one justice to the *Supreme Court for each justice who failed to retire after becoming eligible to do so at the age of seventy, up to a limit of six additional justices. The proposal failed, in a storm of controversy without precedent in the history of the Supreme Court.

The premise of Roosevelt's New Deal, that the powers of the national government must be broad enough to meet the economic and social challenges of the Great Depression, contrasted so sharply with the Supreme Court's limited view of national power that a collision was bound to arise.

The administration was uncertain of its course in the event of conflict. The average age of the justices was unprecedentedly high; if argument alone failed to shift the balance of a Court that often was divided narrowly, one or more Roosevelt appointees would accomplish the same result.

Perhaps the administration could simply wait the Court out. The government prevailed in the first cases challenging New Deal legislation, but press rumors of a plan to enlarge the Supreme Court to fifteen justices appeared as early as 1934.

In a string of decisions in 1935 and 1936, the Court affirmed its narrow view of Congress's powers, its broad view of the protection against federal encroachment afforded states by the Tenth Amendment, and its conception of individual liberty of *contract as a limitation on governmental powers. Some statutes survived, but significant pieces of the New Deal were struck down and prospects for the National Labor Relations Act and the Social Security Act, critical to Roosevelt's agenda, were dim.

In Congress, proposals were offered to limit the jurisdiction of the Supreme Court, impose mandatory retirement, enlarge the bench, require a supermajority for the invalidation of federal statutes, and to amend the Constitution itself to reverse the Court's decisions. The press derided the Court as "The Nine Old Men," and its four most conservative justices as "The Four Horsemen" of the Apocalypse. Roosevelt, however, held his fire, and refused to make the Court an issue in the 1936 election.

With a triumphant reelection and enormous majorities in both houses of Congress, Roosevelt reviewed proposals generated by the attorney general for reforming the Court. The plan he sent to Congress early in 1937 was based on a memorandum concerning the lower courts prepared in 1913 by then—Attorney General McReynolds, subsequently one of the Four Horsemen. Roosevelt's principal justification for the plan—the need to help the Court keep abreast of its work—was disingenuous, and was widely so perceived. Even New Dealers wholly out of sympathy with the Court's decisions rallied to the Court as an institution. Congressional mail ran 9–1 against Roosevelt's plan; one of his principal allies in the Senate led the opposition to it. Justice Van Devanter announced he would retire at the end of the term, creating the long-awaited vacancy. Chief Justice *Hughes, in a letter read to the Senate Judiciary Committee, denied that the Court was behind in its work and doubted that efficiency would be enhanced by enlarging the bench. A week later the Court upheld a state minimum wage law, putting an end to liberty of contract. In April and May it upheld the constitutionality of the National Labor Relations Act and the Social Security Act, a timely switch by Justice Roberts supplying the critical vote for an expansive reading of the federal government's commerce and general welfare powers. Roberts made the fifth vote. Van Devanter's successor would make a sixth. The battle, if not the war, was over.

In June the Judiciary Committee declared in its report that the court packing plan violated "every sacred principle of American democracy" and should be "so emphatically rejected that its parallel will never again be presented to the free representatives of the free people of America." That astonishing language, addressed to a president at the peak of his popularity by members of his own party, is a measure of Roosevelt's failure to understand the almost mystical prestige of the Supreme Court in American public life. Even so, Roosevelt had five appointments to the Court in the following two years, and there were no significant invalidations of federal statutes for nearly two decades. It was now obvious that the justices make law rather than discover it, and virtually certain that their number was forever fixed at nine.

[*See also* Courts, United States]

• Joseph Alsop and Turner Catledge, *The 168 Days*, 1938. William E. Leuchtenberg, "Franklin D. Roosevelt's Court 'Packing' Plan," in *Essays on the New Deal* (Harold M. Hollingsworth and William F. Holmes, eds.) pp. 69–115 (1969).   —Hugh C. Macgill

COURTROOM NOVEL. *See* Literature and Law.

COURT RULES. *See* Procedure, Court.

COURTS, UNITED STATES

Federal Courts
State and Local Courts
Juvenile Courts

COURTS, UNITED STATES: FEDERAL COURTS

The United States is under a system of governance founded as a federalist system. We have one tier of government that encompasses each state, made up of executive, legislative, and judicial branches of the state tree. These three branches of state government form the policies and laws for each state. Additionally, we also have executive, legislative, and judicial branches at the federal level responsible to every citizen in the nation. Of these three federal branches, it is the federal judiciary that is responsible for defining and interpreting our Constitution and numerous laws enacted by the legislative branch. This federal judiciary has three levels: the United States District Courts at the bottom, the United States Courts of Appeal in the middle, and the United States *Supreme Court at the top.

The Constitution itself created the Supreme Court, and authorized Congress to create a system of lower courts. Article III of the Constitution begins with the clause "[t]he judicial Power of the United States, shall be vested in one supreme Court, and in such inferior Courts as the Congress may from time to time ordain and establish." Thus, once the Constitution was ratified in 1787, the Supreme Court was formed, but no other federal courts had yet been established. In 1789, Congress enacted the Judiciary Act, ordaining and establishing two additional levels of courts under the Supreme Court—the United States District Courts and what is now known as the United States Courts of Appeal. In addition to these three constitutional courts, Congress has also established a variety of less known courts. These legislative or Article I courts, such as the United States Court of Military Appeals and the United States Tax Court, serve both quasi-legislative and judicial duties. Further, these courts are primarily created to administer a specific congressional statute, such as the bankruptcy code, while the constitutional courts are established to handle litigation, such as traditional lawsuits.

All federal judges appointed under the provisions of Article III of the Constitution hold office during good behavior. This means they are in effect life tenured unless they choose to step down. The only way they can be removed from the bench is by *impeachment. In accordance with the constitutional requirements for Supreme Court justices and the legislative requirements for district court and court of appeals judges, impeachment may occur for treason, bribery, or other high Crimes and Misdemeanors. An impeached judge would face trial in the Senate, which could convict by a vote of two-thirds of the members present. Since 1789, the House of Representatives has impeached thirteen judges, but only seven have been convicted by the Senate and removed from office.

The United States District Courts are trial courts. Trial courts, as opposed to appellate courts, are courts that hear both civil and criminal cases through examination and cross-examination by attorneys. These Courts have original jurisdiction over matters involving federal questions or matters of diversity of citizenship. Original jurisdiction, as the name suggests, is the court where a case is initially filed. This means that no other trier of fact or law will have heard the issues before. In contrast, appellate jurisdiction allows a court to review the findings of other courts, and decide if the issues of fact and law were decided correctly. Diversity of *citizenship involves a controversy be-

tween a resident of one state and a citizen or government of another state, or between an American citizen and a foreign country, or a foreign citizen, where the amount in controversy exceeds $75,000. A federal question involves issues surrounding the Constitution and various laws enacted by Congress, as well as treaties. The Federal District Courts also hear matters involving *habeas corpus writs. Habeas corpus literally means "have the body," and is utilized when one is seeking to be released from custody. For example, if an individual is arrested for a crime, he or she will go to trial in a United States District Court. Since this would be the first time a judge or jury is hearing the case, the court will be exercising its original jurisdiction. However, in the instance that the individual is convicted, he can appeal the case to a Court of Appeal or file a writ of habeas corpus. The writ of habeas corpus asks the court to force the people who have the detained individual to set him free.

Each United States District Court is presided over by at least one judge who resides in the district. Originally, the districts were defined by state boundaries, but with the current level of the nation's population, some states have several districts. For example, California, New York, and Texas each have four districts, Pennsylvania and North Carolina each have three districts, Michigan and Wisconsin each have two districts, and Oregon and South Dakota each have one district. Additionally, the District of Columbia and the territories of Guam, Puerto Rico, the Virgin Islands, and the Northern Mariana Islands each have one United States District Court.

The judge presides over two different types of trials—bench trials and *jury trials. The jury trial is the type of trial that is most familiar to people. In a jury trial, randomly selected members of the public are chosen to be jurors, and assigned a time and date to appear at the courthouse. All of these potential jurors are then placed into a large jury pool and brought into the courtroom. Once there, the judge will address the potential jurors regarding their duties as jurors if they are selected to be on the jury. After the judge is finished, each attorney asks the potential jurors questions in what is referred to as voir dire. During voir dire, the attorneys evaluate which jurors would be more advantageous to their case. Once a jury is agreed upon, it sits as a petit jury and decides the issues of guilt or innocence in a criminal case, or *liability or no liability in a civil case. In either a bench or jury trial, it is always the judge who decides issues of law. For example, in a case involving a breach of contract, the judge would decide if there were a legally enforceable contract, while the jury would decide whether or not it was breached. In a bench trial, the judge decides issues of both fact and law.

During the course of the trial, the jury listens to the *evidence and the judge makes rulings on various issues of law that arise during the trial, such as whether a certain piece of evidence should be allowed into the case for the jury to evaluate or whether it should be excluded. The judge remains a neutral third-party while the attorneys ask questions of witnesses. This is different than in most other trial court systems. Only *common law countries, such as the United States and Great Britain, have a neutral third-party judge who does not usually ask questions. In many other countries, such as France, a civil law format is followed, allowing the judge to ask questions of the witnesses while still remaining a neutral third-party.

For the fiscal year 1999, about 320,000 cases were commenced in the United States District Courts. This figure has fluctuated somewhat over the past five years, ranging from a high of 322,390 cases in 1997 to a low of 294,123 cases in 1995. Criminal cases accounted for roughly 19 percent of the district courts' docket in 1999. As with the total docket, the number of criminal cases has increased steadily over the past five years, rising from 45,788 cases in 1995 to 59,923 cases in 1999. Criminal cases, while fewer in number than civil cases, are generally more time consuming for the courts. Drug cases, which abound in some of the federal district courts in states bordering international boundaries, are especially complex, and often involve multiple defendants.

Civil cases far outnumber criminal cases, making up 81 percent of the district court docket in 1999. Civil case filings have also fluctuated over the years. From 248,335 in 1995, they increased to a high of 272,027 in 1997, before declining to 256,787 in 1998.

In an effort to help district judges deal with these increased workloads, Congress passed the Federal Magistrates Act in 1968. This legislation created the office of United States Magistrate. In 1990, with the passage of the Judicial Improvements Act, that title was changed to United States Magistrate Judge. Magistrate judges are formally appointed by the judges of the district court for eight-year terms, although they can be removed for good cause before the expiration of the term.

The magistrate judge system constitutes a structure that responds to each district court's specific needs and circumstances. Within guidelines set by the Federal Magistrate Acts of 1968, 1976, and 1979, the judges in each district court establish the duties and responsibilities of their magistrate judges. Most significantly, the 1979 legislation permits a magistrate judge, with the consent of the involved parties, to conduct all proceedings in a jury or bench civil matter and enter a *judgment in the case, and to conduct a trial of persons accused of misdemeanors committed within the district, provided the defendant consents.

The Courts of Appeal are the primary appellate courts in the federal system. They receive less media coverage than the Supreme Court, partly because their activities are not as dramatic. After the Judiciary Act of 1789 created the Courts of Appeal, known as Circuit Courts until 1891, each court consisted of two United States Supreme Court justices and one United States District Court judge. In 1793, Congress altered this situation, allowing the court to include one United States Supreme Court justice and one United States District Court judge. In 1801, Congress authorized sixteen new appellate judgeships and relieved the Supreme Court justices of their circuit-riding responsibilities. This law was repealed in 1802, only to be changed again the same year to allow the circuit to be presided over by one United States District Court judge. In an effort to handle the rising tide of litigation, Congress in 1869 approved a measure that authorized the appointment of nine new circuit judges and reduced the Supreme Court justices' circuit duty to one term every two years.

Major changes in the United States Court of Appeals took place in 1891. The 1891 Evarts Act created new courts, resulting in two trial tribunals and two appellate tribunals. This confusing situation was resolved in 1911 with the elimination of one of the appellate courts, and by the 1948 Judicial Code, which established 179 authorized United States Courts of Appeal judges. There are currently eleven appellate districts encompassing the states, and one for the District of Columbia, none of which have any original jurisdiction. The main duty of the twelve courts is to review cases appealed from the United States Districts Courts and from United States administrative agencies, such as the Environmental Protection Agency, within their boundaries.

The first thing a United States Court of Appeal does when a case is appealed to it is to screen the case. During the screening stage, the judges decide whether to give an *appeal full review or to dispose of it in some other way. Those cases given full treatment are normally considered by panels of three judges, rather than by all of the judges in the court. This means that several cases can be heard at the same time by different three-judge panels often sitting in different cities throughout the circuit.

Occasionally, different three-judge panels within the same circuit may reach conflicting decisions in similar cases. To resolve such conflicts and to promote circuit unanimity, federal statutes provide for an en banc procedure in which all of the circuit's judges decide a case together. The en banc procedure may also be used when the case concerns an issue of extraordinary importance.

Cases that have survived the screening process and have not been settled by the litigants can be scheduled for oral argument. Attorneys for each side are given a short time to discuss the points made in their written briefs and to answer questions from the judges. Following oral argument, the judges confer, and if they are in agreement, they may announce their decision immediately. Otherwise, a decision will be announced only after the they have confered at greater length. Following the conference, some decisions will be announced with a brief order. Some decisions will be accompanied by a longer, signed opinion, though in recent years there has been a decrease in the number of published opinions. In 1999, 54,693 appeals were filed in the Courts of Appeal, up from 50,072 in 1995.

The basic framework for selecting federal judges is the same for all levels of the federal judiciary. All nominations are made by the president after due consultation with the White House staff, the attorney general's office, and other political leaders. After the nomination is announced to the public, various interest groups that believe they have a stake in the appointment may lobby for or against the candidate. The candidate's qualifications will also be evaluated by a committee of the *American Bar Association or another legally related entity such as the Federalist Society. The candidate's name is then sent to the Senate Judiciary Committee, which conducts an investigation of the nominee's fitness for the post. If the committee's vote is favorable, the nomination is sent to the floor of the Senate, where it is either approved or rejected by a simple majority vote.

Americans frequently view the appellate courts, notably the United States Supreme Court, as the most likely to be involved in policymaking. The trial courts, on the other hand, are frequently seen as norm enforcers rather than policymakers. Given this traditional view, the picture that often emerges is one in which the United States Su-

preme Court makes a decision that is then implemented by a lower court. In short, some envision a judicial bureaucracy with a hierarchy of courts much like the functioning of rank in the military. However, the United States District Courts and United States Courts of Appeal may in fact be less dependeant on the United States Supreme Court than people think. Many decisions of the United States Supreme Court do not provide ample guidance as to how they should be implemented. This lack of well-established guidelines occasionally allows the lower courts the policymaking freedom to implement United States Supreme Court decisions and decide to whom the decisions apply.

[*See also* Judge; Procedure, Court]

• Jeffrey Allan Segal and Harold J. Spaeth, *The Supreme Court and the Attitudinal Model*, 1993. David W. Neubauer, *Judicial Process*, 2d ed., 1997. Henry J. Abraham, *The Judicial Process*, 7th ed., 1998. Lawrence Baum, *American Courts*, 7th ed., 1998. Robert A. Carp and Ronald Stidham, *The Federal Courts*, 3rd ed., 1998. Robert A. Carp and Ronald Stidham, *Judicial Process in America*, 5th ed., 2001.   —Robert A. Carp

COURTS, UNITED STATES: STATE AND LOCAL COURTS

State courts resolve most of the nation's legal disputes. Although the federal courts process several hundred thousand cases annually, the state courts handle almost one hundred million. Moreover, such important matters as the prosecution of criminal defendants and the resolution of family issues remain largely within the purview of the states. State courts resolve disputes between private citizens in their daily interactions, between citizens and the government, and among the various branches and agencies of government. In the aggregate, these decisions have a profound impact on the distribution of wealth and power in the United States.

Organization of State and Local Courts. In the United States, state and federal courts operate simultaneously yet independently of each other, although the jurisdiction of these systems is concurrent in some situations (such as diversity of citizenship cases). State *constitutions and other state laws govern the structure and operation of each state court system, within the general bounds set by the United States Constitution and federal law. Consequently, the fifty states have developed court systems reflective of their own unique political conflicts and culture, and as a consequence no two state court systems are exactly alike.

However, state court systems share some common organizational features. Each state operates trial courts of limited and general jurisdiction, which collectively processed 91.5 million filings in 1999 (National Center for State Courts 2000). Courts with limited jurisdiction have authority over particular subsets of cases, while general jurisdiction courts hear all matters not delegated to the specialized courts. In some states, the limited jurisdiction trial courts are integrated into the state judicial hierarchy, and are financed and supervised centrally by the state. In other states, local governments operate these courts, with little or no central management. Further, the states range from having highly efficient jurisdictional arrangements among their trial courts to having complicated concurrent or overlapping jurisdictions.

Limited and general jurisdiction trial courts utilize different procedures for resolving disputes. Limited jurisdiction trial courts commonly use abbreviated procedures for conducting trials, sometimes exclude attorneys, and rarely utilize juries, largely because of the large volumes of civil and criminal matters not very significant or complex (e.g., minor traffic violations). Most courts in the United States fall into this category, and most cases are handled by these courts.

General jurisdiction trial courts are much more formal, necessitating the expertise of attorneys. These courts are the major trial courts in the United States and hear the most important criminal and civil disputes. In 1999, the number of judges per state staffing general jurisdiction trial courts ranged from 16 in Maine to 864 in Illinois (Council of State Governments 1999). These figures, however, do not include commissioners or magistrates who assist the judges with their routine duties.

Additionally, all states have at least one appellate court, while most have intermediate appellate courts and a court of last resort. In the eleven states (Delaware, Maine, Montana, Nevada, New Hampshire, North Dakota, Rhode Island, South Dakota, Vermont, West Virginia, Wyoming) without intermediate appellate courts, the sole venue for *appeal is the state high court, usually called the state supreme court.

Intermediate appellate courts have mandatory dockets and usually decide cases using three-judge panels, though occasionally these courts sit en banc. The total number of judges on each state's intermediate appellate bench ranges in size from three (Alaska and Idaho) to eighty-eight (California). In 1999, these courts processed 195,738 filings.

Courts of last resort are composed of five to nine members, though the most common size is seven. These courts almost always sit en banc. Oklahoma and Texas each have separate courts of last resort for the civil and criminal appeals. In states with an intermediate appellate bench, courts of last resort have discretionary dockets, although they may be required by state law to review some highly restricted categories of cases (e.g., death penalty cases). Without intermediate appellate courts, the court of last resort (as the only appellate court in the state) has a mandatory docket. Furthermore, all state courts of last resort have original jurisdiction in a limited range of cases (e.g., disciplinary action over members of the bar). In 1999, state high courts collectively processed 96,616 filings (National Center for State Courts 2000).

As with court size, substantial variations exist among the states in the compensation paid to judges. Generally, movement up the judicial hierarchy results in increased compensation. In 1999, according to the Council of State Governments, salaries for justices in state courts of last resort ranged from $77,092 (Montana) to $137,314 (Florida) annually. Compensation for intermediate appellate court judges ranged from $79,413 (New Mexico) to $124,200 (New Jersey). Finally, salaries in the general jurisdiction trial courts ranged from $72,042 (Montana) to $115,300 (Delaware).

Selection, Retention, and Removal of State Court Judges. Each American state decides how their *judges will be initially selected and subsequently retained. Currently, five basic methods are used. First: state court judges are elected in partisan elections, in which candidates appear on the ballot with their partisan affiliations listed. Typically, candidates are nominated in partisan primaries. Second: judges are elected in nonpartisan elections, in which candidates are listed on the general election ballot without partisan labels, although they may have been nominated in partisan primaries. Nonpartisan elections seek to encourage voters to cast ballots on the basis of the candidates' professional qualifications rather than their partisan affiliations, and also attempt to reduce party control over the selection process. Third, states use the Missouri Plan, or the "Merit" Plan, to staff the state bench. The Missouri Plan is a combination of appointment and election. While there are significant variations from state to state in actual operation, the basic process begins with the governor appointing a judicial nominating commission, which screens and recommends candidates for each vacancy. The commission typically presents a list of three candidates for each vacancy to the governor, who must appoint one of the three. Upon appointment, the nominee immediately assumes office. Shortly thereafter, usually in the next general election, the candidate must win voter approval in a retention election. If voters approve, the judge begins a regular term of office, facing subsequent retention elections at the end of every term. If voters disapprove, the process begins anew. Fourth: governors in selected states appoint judges, usually with the approval of the state senate. Some of these states restrict the governor's choices to nominees approved by a judicial nominating commission, while others allow the governor complete discretion. Finally, a handful of states empower their legislatures to select judges. Each chamber of the legislature has a committee to handle judicial appointments, and nominees are approved or rejected through the normal legislative process. Choices are not subject to veto by the governor.

Rather than utilizing one particular plan exclusively, numerous states use several methods of selection, depending upon the court being staffed. For instance, some states utilize partisan or nonpartisan elections for choosing trial court judges, and the Missouri Plan for the court of last resort. Overall, for staffing the court of last resort, nine states utilize partisan elections, thirteen states use nonpartisan elections, sixteen states employ the Missouri Plan, eight states utilize gubernatorial appointment, and four states use legislative election.

Selection systems are complex and varied in practice. For example, high court justices in some states are elected from districts (Illinois, Louisiana, Mississippi, Kentucky, Maryland, Nebraska, Oklahoma, South Dakota); justices in other states are elected statewide. Also, there can be substantial differences between formal selection mechanisms and informal practice. For instance, every state has a procedure for filling vacancies that occur during a term, usually by allowing the governor to appoint someone to fill the vacancy until the expiration of the term. Because judges sometimes resign or retire during a term if their political party controls the governorship, many judges in elective systems get their jobs initially through appointment rather than election. Through strategic retirements and ad interim appointments, the political party retains control of the office and the new appointee gains the advantage of running as an incumbent in the next election. In short, gubernatorial appointment is much more widely used as a means of initial accession than formal descriptions indicate, and seemingly straightforward

selection procedures can be manipulated to achieve political goals.

Concerning terms, the states differ substantially at all levels of the judiciary, although appellate court judges generally enjoy longer terms than trial court judges. Also, terms for judicial office at all levels tend to be longer than terms for most other state and federal political offices. More specifically, across the fifty states, terms in courts of last resort range from six years to life, while terms for intermediate appellate courts and general jurisdiction trial courts range from four years to life.

Does any particular selection system produce a better-qualified bench? Based on the evidence accumulated to date, the answer seems to be no. In a comprehensive study of the background characteristics of state supreme court justices, Henry R. Glick and Craig Emmert (1987) concluded that the credentials and backgrounds of justices are quite similar, regardless of the method of selection.

Also important is the issue of whether electoral politics affect judicial decisions. The answer to this question is a highly qualified yes. There is some evidence that, at least on the issue of the death penalty, supreme court justices facing competitive electoral conditions in conservative constituencies are not likely to reverse death sentences, all things considered (Hall 1987, 1992, 1995). The extent to which elected justices respond to constituencies on other matters of public policy, especially issues not salient to voters, remains unknown.

State court judges face a high degree of formal accountability. Across the nation, judges can be removed by their supreme courts (forty-eight states), impeached (forty-five states), subject to legislative address (sixteen states), and recalled (six states). The specific grounds for removal vary by method and across the states. And, of course, elected judges can be voted out of office. From 1980 through 1995, 45 of 541 (8.3 percent) supreme court justices seeking reelection were defeated (Hall 2001). Finally, all states but one have judicial disciplinary commissions that may recommend the removal of judges for misconduct.

Decision-Making Propensities in State Supreme Courts. A preliminary version of the State Supreme Court Data Project, sponsored by the National Science Foundation under the direction of Paul Brace and Melinda Gann Hall facilitates a comparison of state high courts on some important dimensions. This dataset contains decisions of state courts of last resort in 1995 and 1996, which produced opinions of at least five paragraphs.

First, the dockets of state high courts differ substantially. Overall, litigation can be classified into five basic categories: criminal, civil-government (i.e., civil cases in which governments are litigants), civil-private (i.e., civil cases involving private parties), juvenile, and nonadversarial. Using this classification, twenty-two states (Alabama, Alaska, Delaware, Indiana, Iowa, Louisiana, Maine, Maryland, Michigan, Montana, Nebraska, Nevada, New Jersey, New Mexico, North Dakota, Oklahoma, South Dakota, Tennessee, Utah, Virginia, West Virginia, Wyoming) devote the largest proportions of their dockets to civil–private cases. Eighteen states (Arizona, Arkansas, California, Florida, Georgia, Hawaii, Illinois, Indiana, Kansas, Massachusetts, Mississippi, New Hampshire, New York, North Carolina, Pennsylvania, Rhode Island, Texas, Washington) focus on criminal cases. Finally, nine states (Colorado, Connecticut, Kentucky, Minnesota, Montana, Ohio, Oregon, South Carolina, Wisconsin) decide larger proportions of civil-government cases. In Vermont, the state high court docket is evenly divided between civil-private and civil-government claims. Across all the states, juvenile and non-adversarial matters capture little docket space in supreme courts, at least with respect to cases decided with opinion.

Further, dissent rates, or the proportion of cases in which at least one justice openly expressed disagreement with the court's decision, vary across the states. While one might expect dissent to result simply from the failure to agree with the majority's treatment of the case, dissent rates are determined by a complex variety of factors, including the court's docket type, internal operating rules, and conditions in the external environment.

Among state supreme courts, Michigan ranks highest in levels of dissent (63 percent), while Rhode Island ranks lowest (2.9 percent). Three states (Louisiana, Michigan, Oklahoma) produce dissent in more than half their cases, while thirteen states (Delaware, Hawaii, Iowa, Kansas, Maine, Massachusetts, New Mexico, North Dakota, Rhode Island, South Carolina, Tennessee, West Virginia, Wisconsin) produce dissent in less than 10 percent of the cases. Overall, supreme court justices disagree about 21 percent of the time.

Finally, state supreme courts differ in how frequently they exercise the power of *judicial review and overturn state statutes. In 1995 and 1996, state supreme courts received 1,063 requests to invalidate state statutes in the cases granted review. Of the occasions involving federal law, 58 of 431 requests were granted, or 13.5 percent. Of the 632

requests under state law, 111 (17.6 percent) were granted. Although there were significant variations among the states in the number of laws challenged and the percent invalidated, state supreme courts, on average, invalidated about 1.69 laws per court per year.

The Impact of State Courts. State courts are important, sometimes aggressive players in state politics. State judiciaries handle a huge and diverse caseload. The judges who decide these cases are closely connected to the political culture of the state through their upbringing and educational experiences, and in most cases are linked directly to the voters through the electoral process. State courts also have opportunities to interact with the other branches of state government and frequently do so in an active manner. In short, the courts in the American states are fascinating political institutions with a resounding impact on the landscape of American politics.

• Henry R. Glick and Craig Emmert, "Selection Systems and Judicial Characteristics: The Recruitment of State Supreme Court Justices," *Judicature* (1987): 28–235. Melinda Gann Hall, "Constituent Influence in State Supreme Courts: Conceptual Notes and a Case Study," *Journal of Politics* (1987): 1117–24. Paul Brace and Melinda Gann Hall, 1990. "Neo-Institutionalism and Dissent in State Supreme Courts," *Journal of Politics* (1990): 4–70. Melinda Gann Hall, "Electoral Politics and Strategic Voting in State Supreme Courts." *Journal of Politics* (1992): 427–46. Paul Brace and Melinda Gann Hall, "Integrated Models of Judicial Dissent," *Journal of Politics* (1993): 914–35. Melinda Gann Hall, "Justices as Representatives: Elections and Judicial Politics in the American States," *American Politics Quarterly* (1995): 485–503. Council of State Governments, 1999. *Book of the States, 1998–99 Edition,* 1999. National Center for State Courts, *State Court Caseload Statistics, 1999–2000,* 2000. Melina Gann Hall, "State Supreme Courts in American Democracy: Probing the Myths of Judicial Reform." *American Political Science Review* (2001): 315–30.

—Melinda Gann Hall

COURTS, UNITED STATES: JUVENILE COURTS

During the 1980s and 1990s, government officials sought to address a perceived rise in juvenile crime by transferring youthful offenders into the adult criminal justice system. Contrary to popular belief, however, juvenile crime rates have declined over the last few years. Statistics from the Office of Juvenile Justice and Delinquency Prevention (OJJDP) and the National Center for Juvenile Justice (NCJJ) indicate a decrease in arrests of juveniles for violent crimes from 1995 to 1999. These data show that incidents of juvenile violence declined substantially from 1993 to 1997 and that most of the decrease in violent crimes committed by juveniles stems from a drop in the number of serious assaults.

In large part, lawmakers' actions were triggered by their distrust of the juvenile court system, viewing it as too soft and too deeply imbued with notions of coddling young "criminals." Thus, after a century of belief in the benefits of a separate justice system for children, the concern for laxness in the juvenile courts led to youthful offenders being increasingly judged under adult laws and imprisoned in adult settings, often serving adult sentences.

The Illinois Juvenile Court Act of 1899, establishing the first specialized court for juvenile offenders in the United States, created the Juvenile Court of Cook County. Arising out of the Progressive reform movement, and reflecting the turn of the century belief in rehabilitation rather than punishment of children, the Chicago juvenile court served as a model for other states. Guided by the common law doctrine of parens patriae (the state as parent), the juvenile court was founded on the principle that the state should be permitted to intervene in the family to promote the best interests of the child. By 1945, all states had followed Illinois' lead, with the juvenile courts reflecting a philosophy of flexibility, a nonpunitive atmosphere, and confidentiality. Hearings were informal, civil rather than criminal in nature; dispositions were rarely fixed in time, with judges determining the outcome believed to be in the child's best interests. Because the court's primary purpose was to rehabilitate rather than ascertain guilt or innocence, the relationship between the child and the state was considered non-adversarial. But despite good intentions, children were deprived of evolving constitutional protections afforded adults in the criminal justice system, and, under the best interests approach, were sometimes punished even more harshly than adults for the same offenses.

By the 1950s, reformers became aware that the original goals of the juvenile court movement were often thwarted, and turned to the United States Supreme Court for relief. A trio of juvenile justice decisions by the Supreme Court from 1966 to 1970 set in motion wholesale changes in the juvenile court system by creating procedural safeguards for youthful offenders: Kent v. United States (1966), In re Gault (1967), and In re Winship (1970).

In these cases, the Court noted that the juvenile court system had been intended to insulate juveniles from the harshness of the criminal courts and apply justice in a non-adversarial setting. The Court feared that if due process guarantees were imposed on juvenile hearings, they would become more adversarial and the best interests of the child would no longer remain in the forefront. But, for the most part, the Court felt that certain due process protections should be imported into the juvenile justice system, and expressed the hope that juvenile courts would retain an appropriate balance between non-adversariness and due process.

Kent marked the beginning of the nation's new approach to juvenile justice procedures, with the Court requiring more formal arrangements, including a waiver hearing with a written statement of judicial findings, when seeking to transfer juveniles to adult criminal court. In Gault, the most significant of these cases, the Supreme Court was squarely faced with the need to decide whether *due process rights in juvenile courts would subvert the desired goal of rehabilitation. The Court altered the adjudicatory phase of delinquency hearings by importing four constitutional due process principles into the juvenile court system: a right to notice of the charges, a right to *counsel, a right against compulsory *self-incrimination, and a right to confront and cross-examine *witnesses.

Subsequently, In re Winship required states to abandon the civil litigation standard of a "preponderance of the evidence" for a finding of delinquency to the "guilt beyond a reasonable doubt" standard used in adult criminal prosecutions.

Thus, while acknowledging the advantages inherent in a separate juvenile court system, the Court held that the Constitution required states to incorporate into it many of the procedural safeguards of the Fifth, Sixth, and *Fourteenth Amendments. The Court stopped short of imposing the entire panoply of due process protections on the juvenile court system. For example, in McKeiver v. Pennsylvania (1971), it held that *jury trials would interfere with the social service function of the juvenile court system, and ruled that states were not required to provide such trials in delinquency hearings.

Despite the due process revolution in juvenile rights, some argue that the juvenile justice system has not changed much in practice. First, they cite evidence of a low level of compliance by juvenile court judges, especially in rural areas; second, because Gault only dealt with the adjudicatory phase of the delinquency hearing, it addressed neither the pre-adjudicatory stage nor procedures regarding dispositions, *appeals, or conditions of confinement. More broadly, *Gault* did not, nor was it intended to, provide relief for the myriad social, behavioral, and emotional problems that children in the juvenile court system typically confront.

Most juvenile court systems have jurisdiction over delinquency (offenses that would be classified as crimes if committed by adults), non-criminal status offenses (such as truancy, curfew violation, or running away from home), and dependency (primarily, victims of abuse and neglect). Although the age at which minors are considered juveniles for purposes of juvenile court jurisdiction may vary, most states set a maximum age for juvenile offenders at seventeen—that is, juvenile courts have jurisdictions over youths who were younger than eighteen at the time the offense was committed. Some states have established higher age levels for certain status offenses or dependency matters.

The federal government's involvement in the juvenile justice system increased when Congress enacted the Juvenile Justice and Delinquency Prevention Act in 1974, in part as a reaction to several *class-action suits charging states with violating the Eighth Amendment for the conditions under which juveniles were confined. The goal of the 1974 law was to have states maintain separate facilities for juvenile offenders, or at least keep them apart from adults in the same facility, and end the common practice of imprisoning status offenders. Congress also provided financial incentives for states to divert children from the court system and create community-based treatment programs to avoid institutionalization, especially for status and other non-violent offenders.

Following the arrest of a juvenile, law enforcement officers may either send the case to juvenile court or divert the case out of the system. Although most cases are routed into the courts, substantial numbers of youths are released following their arrest. For cases directed to the juvenile courts, an initial decision is made about whether to proceed to a formal hearing, dismiss the case, or handle the matter informally, perhaps through referral to a social service agency. A large number of cases are dealt with informally, often ending in dismissal or an agreement between the juvenile and the court. A formal procedure involves either a waiver hearing to determine whether the juvenile should be ordered to stand trial in adult criminal court or an adjudicatory hearing before the juvenile court judge.

By 1997, forty-six states and the District of Columbia allowed juveniles charged with certain crimes to be tried in the criminal courts as adults, although a number retained restrictions on sentencing and conditions of confinement. Variations exist among the states, but there are generally three means by which juveniles are transferred into adult courts: judicial waiver, statutory exclusion, or concurrent jurisdiction. Also varying by state, decisions to waive the jurisdiction of the juvenile system may be made by juvenile court judges, prosecutors, or by state legislators through automatic transfer statutes. Whatever the method, the transfer of juveniles to criminal courts is typically based on the nature and severity of the crime charged as well as the nature of the alleged offender, including the record of prior offenses. Over the last decade, through a variety of means, almost all states have facilitated the transfer of juveniles into adult court.

Some argue that more resources should be committed to the juvenile justice system and that automatic transfers should be reduced so that judges have more discretion over waiver decisions. States such as Maryland and Massachusetts have created special programs for youthful offenders, especially nonviolent ones, to carry out the juvenile court's goals of rehabilitation and training. At the same time, proposals to abolish the juvenile court system and merge it with the adult criminal system have arisen from both sides of the ideological spectrum. On one side, critics argue that integrating the juvenile court into the criminal justice system will expand the procedural safeguards offered children. Others maintain that juvenile courts are too lenient with juvenile offenders and that consolidating the two courts will lead to more fitting punishments for juveniles. As the juvenile court enters its second century, the debate continues.

• Thomas J. Bernard, *The Cycle of Juvenile Justice*, 1992. Barry Feld, *Justice for Children: The Right to Counsel and the Juvenile Courts*, 1993. Susan Guarino-Ghezzi and Edward J. Loughran, *Balancing Juvenile Justice*, 1996. Christopher P. Manfredi, *The Supreme Court and Juvenile Justice*, 1997. John C. Watkins Jr., *The Juvenile Justice Century: A Sociolegal Commentary on American Juvenile Courts*, 1998. Preston Elrod and R. Scott Ryder, *Juvenile Justice: A Social, Historical, and Legal Perspective*, 1999. Simon I. Singer, "Juvenile Court and its Systems of Juvenile Justice," in *Handbook of Youth and Justice*, Susan O. White, ed., 2001.

—Susan Gluck Mezey

COURT SYSTEMS in the United States have evolved from simplicity to complexity. The earliest colonial political institutions combined legislative and judicial functions. The same body often made laws in the morning, then decided criminal cases in the afternoon. Three hundred years of mostly gradual jurisdictional developments have yielded a distinctive and often highly specialized *legal system. These developments were partly inspired by founding commitments to the *separation of powers, partly by the need to promote judicial efficiency, and partly as a result of numerous political agendas that have influenced courts throughout American history. The expansion of the power of the federal judiciary, in particular, is best understood as one aspect of the general expansion of federal power that has been taking place in the United States since the end of the Civil War.

Political institutions in seventeenth-century American did not have distinctive functions, even by seventeenth-century standards. Distinctive criminal and civil courts existed in England and on the European continent long before those institutions were clearly established in the United States. Criminal and civil cases in early colonial America were often judged by legislative bodies. The judges on the General Court of Massachusetts during the time of King Phillip's War—1675–76, last Indian resistance to the colonists in Southern New England—were the governor of the colony and his elected assistants. That body both made laws for the colony and adjudicated, with the help of juries, the major legal cases of the time. Lesser offenses were heard by local courts that were more confined to judicial functions.

The eighteenth century witnessed the gradual modernization of colonial legal systems in response to the modernization of political and economic life. By the eve of independence, the highest court in most colonies was not simply a subset of the colonial legislature. Still, those courts were hardly distinctive or autonomous judicial institutions. Colonial legislatures frequently overruled colonial courts, and *appeals were taken to the English parliament rather than to the English Court system. Little changed in the immediate wake of independence. The Articles of Confederation made no provision at all for a national judiciary. The framers of the original state constitutions were primarily concerned with the legislative and executive branches of government. State judiciaries were considered less important governing institutions, though in the 1780s, several declared state practices unconstitutional, precipitating substantial, though inconclusive, debates over the virtues of judicial independence.

The Constitution of 1787 made provision for a formal national judiciary. Article III established the *Supreme Court of the United States and gave Congress the power to establish a system of lower federal courts. Federal *judges would hold life tenure and their salaries could not be reduced while they were on the bench. Section 2 declared that federal jurisdiction would exist in all cases raising issues of federal constitutional law, federal statutory law, federal treaties, and diversity cases, most notably cases between "citizens of different states," and cases affecting "public Ministers and Consuls." Congress immediately exercised its power to create a federal judiciary. The Judiciary Act of 1789 established a Supreme Court with six justices, three federal circuit courts, and fourteen district courts. Each state had at least one district court, which was staffed by a single district court judge. No distinctive circuit court judgeships were created, however. Instead, the circuit courts were staffed by two Supreme Court justices and the local district court judge. The Judiciary Act of 1789 also established the jurisdiction of all federal courts. Minor cases were given to the district court, with the circuit courts given original jurisdiction over more controversial diversity cases. Plaintiffs in those cases, however, were also given the choice of seeking justice in a state forum. Remarkably, Congress vested state courts with original jurisdiction over cases raising questions of federal law. Although some prominent antebellum commentators, most notably Joseph *Story, insisted that federal courts had to have general jurisdiction over all federal questions, this position was rejected. Instead, the Supreme Court was able to hear appeals from state courts only when the state court declared a federal law unconstitutional or decided against a claim of federal constitutional right.

Two elements of this federal court system proved to be particularly controversial. Both the justices and their Federalist party supporters complained bitterly about the obligation of a Supreme Court justice to ride circuit twice, later once, a year. Congress created distinctive federal circuit court judgeships in 1802, but that bill was immediately repealed the following year. All Supreme Court justices would ride circuit until after the Civil War. Many Jeffersonians, Spencer Roane of Virginia in particular, repeatedly challenged the power of the Supreme Court to hear appeals from state courts. Congress from 1815 until 1832 consistently debated a variety of measures to limit the capacity of the federal courts to reverse state court decisions, but no proposal to strip federal courts of that jurisdiction passed. Rather, federal jurisdiction gradually increased both before and after the *Civil War. The Force Act of 1833 removed suits against federal officials to federal courts. The

Judiciary Act of 1867 permitted state prisoners with claims under federal law to obtain writs of *habeas corpus in federal courts. Fears that the court would declare Reconstruction measures unconstitutional led Congress to repeal an important section of the Habeas Act in 1868. That repeal was upheld in *Ex parte McCardle* (1868). Jurisdiction was quickly restored once the issues of Reconstruction faded. Congress also increased the number of federal courts. As new states were added to the Union, the number of federal circuit courts increased from three to six and to ten by the Civil War.

Several pieces of federal legislation passed during the late nineteenth and early twentieth centuries proved to be particularly important in establishing the contemporary federal court system. The Judiciary Acts of 1869 and 1891 first modified, then ended, the practice of circuit court riding by Supreme Court justices, establishing nine circuit courts of appeals with distinctive judgeships. The Removal Act of 1875 gave federal courts original jurisdiction over all federal questions. This and related measures enabled federal courts to hear most of the major federal questions of the day. The resulting burden on the Supreme Court resulted in the Judiciary Act of 1925. That bill dramatically reduced the number of appeals the Supreme Court was required to adjudicate by requiring most petitioners to secure a discretionary writ of certiorari from the justices in order for their appeal to be considered. When, for any reason, the justices elected not to hear a case, they could simply avoid making a decision by declining to issue the writ of certoirari. Later legislation expanded the discretionary jurisdiction of the Supreme Court to the point where now virtually all cases adjudicated by the Court require the writ of certiorari.

The federal judiciary presently consists of a Supreme Court, composed of a chief justice and eight associate justices, twelve regional circuit courts of appeals and the circuit court of appeals for the District of Columbia, and ninety-four federal district courts. The lower courts have the power to hear all issues of federal law and various diversity cases. Congress has also established a series of Article I, legislative courts, most notably the United States Court of Claims. Unlike justices on Article III courts, justices on Article I courts do not have tenure during good behavior. Decisions by Article I courts are subject in some instances to review by Congress.

State judiciaries mirror the federal court system to a fair degree. The bottom rung of the judicial hierarchy in the states tends to be more specialized than in the federal judiciary. Federal district courts handle the full spectrum of federal cases, but most states have distinctive courts for criminal litigation, *probate, civil litigation, and family matters. Above these tribunals lies a series of appellate courts. Most states have two layers of appellate courts, though a few states have only one. Most often the highest court in a state is called the "Supreme Court," but the "Court of Appeals" in New York is higher than the "Supreme Court" of that state. Some state appellate courts are more specialized than federal circuit court of appeals. Texas, for example, has a "second supreme court," a special appellate court that only hears criminal appeals.

State decisions on state law are final and cannot be reversed by a federal court unless reversal is warranted by a distinctive federal issue. Federal courts may not decide that a state court has misinterpreted state law. Persons may claim that the state court misapplied federal law, but when doing so they must demonstrate that no adequate or independent state ground exists for the state decision. Should a state court declare that the death penalty violates the state constitution, that decision will stand even if the state court also mistakenly declares that the death penalty violates the federal constitution. Litigants in state courts must typically exhaust their appeals in the state court system before seeking federal review of a federal question. Although exceptions exist, federal courts will typically hear an appeal from a state court case only after that appeal is rejected by the highest court in the state.

The primary difference between court systems in the United States and court systems in other countries is the existence of special constitutional courts in most countries. Constitutional issues in the United States are adjudicated in the course of ordinary litigation, and may normally be adjudicated in any court. A traffic court in rural Mississippi may issue a ruling, subject to appeal, that the local speed limit is unconstitutional when asked to do so by a person protesting a ten dollar speeding ticket. European practice is quite different. Most European countries have special constitutional courts authorized to hear only constitutional cases. In some instances, lower courts do not rule on constitutional issues, but certify the matter to the constitutional courts. Moreover, these constitutional courts need not wait for actual litigation. Legislatures may ask constitutional courts for rulings on the constitutionality of proposed legislation or legislation that has been passed but not yet implemented. The Supreme Court of the United States declared some aspects of a federal campaign finance law unconstitutional only after private citizens challenged that law. The Supreme Court in Spain declared a similar measure unconstitutional after being asked to review the matter by the national legislature.

[See also Courts, United States]

• Stanley I. Kutler, *Judicial Power and Reconstruction Politics*, 1968. Edward A. Purcell Jr., *Litigation and Inequality: Federal Diversity Jurisdiction in Industrial America, 1870–1958*, 1992. Edward A. Purcell Jr., *Brandeis and the Progressive Constitution: Erie, the Judicial Power, and the Politics of the Federal Courts in Twentieth Century America*, 2000. Yasuhide Kawashima, *Igniting King Phillip's War: The John Sassamon Murder Trial*, 2001.

—Mark A. Graber

COVENANT, RESTRICTIVE. *See* Segregation.

COVENANTS. *See* Property, Real.

CRAVATH, PAUL DRENNAN (1861–1940), lawyer. Born in Berlin Heights, Ohio, Cravath spent most of his childhood in Nashville, Tennessee, where his father was the first president of Fisk University. Later, he attended Brooklyn Polytechnic Institute and subsequently received his A.B. degree from Oberlin in 1882. Cravath pursued his ambition to become a lawyer by studying in a law office in Minneapolis and later became a salesman for an oil company, where after a year and a half, he had earned enough to be able to attend Columbia Law School. Although a less-than-stellar student in college, at Columbia Cravath ranked at the top of his class and received his LL.B. in 1886, *cum laude*. After receiving admission to the New York bar, Cravath began his practice as a clerk at Carter, Hornblower & Bryne. It was Walter Carter's practice of taking and training graduates with the best academic records from Columbia or Harvard that Cravath later incorporated into the "Cravath system." In 1899, at thirty-seven, Cravath joined Seward, Guthrie & Steele, the firm known today as Cravath, Swaine & Moore, as a partner. At the time Cravath joined the firm, like most other top firms, partners worked independently with their own clients and associates, and associates were not paid a salary but earned fees by developing their own clients. Cravath set out to make fundamental changes to the organization and structure of the firm, creating an institution that functioned with the efficiency of a business corporation. As the authoritative head of the firm until his death in 1940, he insisted that the firm hire only graduates with top academic records, that partners operate collectively in the firm's work, and that associates be paid a salary. Young associates were trained as generalists before specializing by watching senior attorneys break down a large problem into component parts and being given one of the small parts to handle thoroughly. Associate responsibilities were increased as soon as competency was demonstrated. With an "up or out" philosophy, Cravath believed that with few exceptions, no associate should be permitted to stay with the firm for more than six years unless admitted to the partnership. Cravath demanded a work ethic that results be achieved regardless of what was involved and how much inconvenience it might cause, even if it took all night. He had little patience for incompetence, inefficiency, and mediocrity. Adopting these approaches, Cravath systematically molded the firm into an entity that was competent, efficient, and completed work as nearly perfectly as possible. Other firms were quick to follow this system of organizing the law *firm, and the Cravath system in most ways has endured today. In his law practice, Cravath dominated discussions with his driven personality, persuasiveness, and respect for the opinions of others. Though he rarely appeared in a courtroom, he was particularly adept at creating solutions to complex mixed business and legal problems. Cravath continued at the firm until his death in 1940, advising clients including Westinghouse, Royal Dutch-Shell, Goodyear Tire & Rubber, and General Motors. Cravath was one of the founders of the Council on Foreign Relations in 1919 and served as President of the Metropolitan Opera during a critical period for the company.

[See also Corporate Law Practice; Lawyer]

• "Profiles: Public Man Paul D. Cravath," *The New Yorker*, 2 January 1932. Robert T. Swaine, *The Cravath Firm and Its Predecessors, 1819–1947*, Vol. I, 1946 and Vol. II, 1948.

—Robert D. Joffe

CREDITOR. *See* Debtor and Creditor.

CRIME COMMISSIONS. *See* Police.

CRIMINAL LAW. American criminal law comes in all shapes and sizes. There are federal crimes, state crimes, and local crimes. Although federal criminal law has expanded significantly since its humble beginnings, criminal law remains by and large a state affair. Local municipalities also define a host of crimes of their own, in city charters, administrative codes, and town ordinances.

Starting at the top in the hierarchy of sources of law, the U.S. Constitution, in Article III, defines the crime of *treason; analogous definitions also appear in various state constitutions. Then there are statutory compilations specifically dedicated to the criminal law, the criminal codes. These codes include, in what is often called by scholars their "special part," definitions of such traditional crimes as murder and *theft, and less traditional ones such as computer tampering or harassment of a rent-regulated tenant. They may also, in their "general part," spell out some basic principles of criminal *liability such as the requirements of *actus reus* and *mens rea (criminal intent)*, and defenses such as insanity or self-defense.

The majority of crimes, surprisingly, can be found in codes devoted to other subjects. Thus, codes of *environmental law, traffic law, or *securities law tend to feature criminal provisions, usually as supplements to noncriminal liability rules. An environmental code, for instance, might impose a civil fine on various logging practices, and provide that a second violation, or a first "willful" violation, amount to a crime, subject to *criminal punishment, perhaps even imprisonment.

Offenses defined in noncriminal codes tend to be minor—for example, misdemeanors, violations, or infractions. Many serious offenses, called *felonies, appear in criminal codes. Misdemeanors are generally punishable by incarceration of up to a year, often in a jail. Felonies are punishable by incarceration of one year or more, usually in a prison, or by capital punishment. Criminal violations, or infractions, may be punishable by a short confinement or by a fine. Many jurisdictions further differentiate between different classes (or degrees) of felonies, and even of misdemeanors (gross and petty). New York, for example, recognizes no fewer than five classes of felonies (A through E) and two classes of misdemeanors (A and B).

Definiting a crime is not limited to the legislative branch. Executive agencies, at both the federal and the state level, promulgate rules, regulations, and orders, violations of which are often punished as crimes. Criminalization here works in much the same way as in noncriminal codes passed directly by the legislature. Thus an administrative code might contain a clause stating that noncompliance with certain of its regulations shall constitute a misdemeanor.

The judiciary also has played a central, though diminishing, role in shaping American criminal law. Unlike the executive, whose power is thought to be delegated by the legislature, the judiciary has traditionally claimed independent authority to define crimes. In fact, until the 1960s, the judiciary

was the branch most closely associated with the making of American criminal law. It was only the promulgation of the *American Law Institute's *Model Penal Code in 1962, and the widespread reforms it inspired throughout the United States, that firmly placed the power to make criminal law in the hands of the legislature (see LEGISLATIVE POWER).

American criminal law was originally not a species of statutory law, based on legislative codes of one form or another, but of judge-made *common law. Here, American law followed English practice. (England to this day does not have a comprehensive criminal code.) Even after the Revolution, American criminal law continued to draw heavily on English precedent. The single most important work on American criminal law, other than the Model Penal Code, remains a pre-Revolutionary work on English law written by an Englishman: "Public Wrongs," volume 4 of *Commentaries on the Laws of England*, published by William *Blackstone in 1769.

Under the common law regime, judges were entitled to define new offenses, called common law misdemeanors. As late as 1964, a Pennsylvania trial court created, and then proceeded to enforce, the offense of "indecent disposition of a dead body," a crime not recognized by statute or in prior court opinions (*Commonwealth* v. *Keller* (PA Ct. Common Pleas, 1964)). Since then, the courts of most American jurisdictions, and even English courts, have either renounced their power to generate new crimes, or have been stripped of that power by statute. The Model Penal Code, for example, declares outright that "[n]o conduct constitutes an offense unless it is a crime or violation under this Code or another statute of this State" (*Model Penal Code* §1.05 (1)). The federal courts never enjoyed the power to create common law crimes (*United States* v. *Hudson & Goodwin* (1812)).

American courts, however, continue to shape the criminal law in other significant ways, particularly in the absence of specific legislative guidelines. For example, few legislatures set out to codify all of the prerequisites of criminal liability. The federal criminal code, in fact, has no real general part. It is therefore largely up to the courts to define precisely what sort of behavior amounts to the requisite *actus reus*, or which—if any—type of *mens rea* is required for criminal liability. Courts also struggle to determine just what sort of causal connection must exist between a defendant's conduct and some criminal harm (say, death), what constitutes consent (and whether consent matters), or whether duress should count as a defense in *homicide cases. In the special part of criminal law, courts are often faced with barebones criminal statutes they must either fill in, or strike down as unconstitutionally vague or overbroad.

Constitutional limitations on criminal law include, besides the prohibition against vague or overbroad statutes, the prohibition against *ex post facto (retroactive) criminal laws, and more generally the prohibition against *cruel and unusual punishment in the Eighth Amendment to the U.S. Constitution and its various state analogues.

The American law of criminal *procedure, which governs the application and enforcement of the provisions of substantive criminal law, is largely of constitutional origin. The U.S. Supreme Court, under the leadership of Chief Justice Earl *Warren, began in the late 1950s to turn to the Fourth, Fifth, and Sixth Amendments to the U.S. Constitution as the sources of an increasingly elaborate system of rules governing every aspect of the criminal process, from investigation and adjudication to the eventual infliction of punishment, primarily in prisons.

The American *prison and jail population in 2000 stood at 2 million, with another 4.5 million Americans on probation or parole, amounting to 3 percent of the adult American population. The overall incarceration rate was 699 per 100,000 residents, the highest in the world. Ten percent of black males between the ages of twenty-five and twenty-nine were in prison, compared with 1 percent of whites in the same age group. American exceptionalism in criminal law is not limited to the sanction of incarceration. The United States is also the only Western country that retains *capital punishment, and is one of a handful of countries that permit the execution of persons who are mentally retarded or who were under the age of eighteen at the time of their offense.

[See also Criminal Law Practice; Criminal Law Principles]

• William Blackstone, Commentaries on the Laws of England, vol. 4, 1769. Henry M. Hart Jr., "The Aims of the Criminal Law," Law & Contemporary Problems (1958): 401–41. President's Commission on Law Enforcement and Administration of Justice, The Challenge of Crime in a Free Society, 1967. Herbert L. Packer, The Limits of the Criminal Sanction, 1968. American Law Institute, Model Penal Code: Official Draft and Revised Commentaries, 1980. Samuel Walker, Popular Justice: A History of American Criminal Justice, 1980. Wayne R. LaFave and Austin W. Scott Jr., Substantive Criminal Law, 2d ed., 1986. Lawrence M. Friedman, Crime and Punishment in American History, 1993. Michael Tonry, Malign Neglect: Race, Crime, and Punishment in America, 1995. Roger Hood, "The Death Penalty: The USA in World Perspective," Journal of Transnational and Policy 6 (1997): 517–41. Leo Katz et al., eds., Foundations of Criminal Law, 1999. Ted Conover, Newjack: Guarding Sing Sing, 2000. Charles H. Whitebread and Christopher Slobogin, Criminal Procedure: An Analysis of Cases and Concepts, 2000. Bureau of Justice Statistics, U.S. Department of Justice, Prisoners in 2000, August 2001.

—Markus Dirk Dubber

CRIMINAL LAW PRACTICE. The criminal defense lawyer's task is to equalize the struggle between the individual and the state. The American justice system is an adversarial one, which assumes that a battle between highly motivated, equally matched opponents will produce both true and just outcomes via fair procedures. The criminal defense lawyer serves this overriding goal even in the many instances when his client is guilty of at least some charge. Our system requires that no person be deprived of life or liberty without substantial proof—proof beyond a reasonable doubt— that he committed the crime charged (see BURDEN OF PROOF, CRIMINAL AND CIVIL). The defense lawyer challenges the strength of the prosecution's case, for example, by cross-examining witnesses to challenge their credibility (they may be lying, mistaken, or confused) or by pointing out gaps in the *evidence or prosecutorial misinterpretations of the law.

Even when a client is convicted, the defense counsel's efforts may result in a conviction on a lesser charge, such as manslaughter, rather than the greater one actually charged, such as murder. Similarly, a client may have committed a seemingly criminal act, perhaps shooting and killing his alleged victim. But defense counsel might offer evidence supporting an affirmative defense—one that the law imposes on the defendant to prove— such as insanity, resulting in an acquittal. Additionally, when there is a conviction, defense counsel can offer mitigating evidence in favor of a lesser sentence than the one the prosecutor proposes. An offender may be in treatment for the drug problem that led him to act, or he may take a job to earn the money to compensate his victims, or he may be incorrectly portrayed by the state as a repeat offender when the records of previous convictions were simply wrong. Any of these options may lower the sentence.

Defense attorneys also challenge unfair procedures inconsistent with constitutional or statutory rights. Was the defendant's home searched by the police without probable cause and a warrant? Was his confession coerced or obtained without his being aware of his right to remain silent? Was he speedily tried? Was an unfairly suggestive identification procedure used, such as the production by the police of a single African-American male in handcuffs before a groggy white robbery victim and asking, "Is he the one?" Were all potential jurors of the defendant's race excluded from serving?

By posing these sorts of questions, defense counsel asserts rights that protect the innocent and guilty alike. No one wants the police to invade his home without good reason and the approval of a neutral magistrate. Nor would anyone want to languish in jail for months or years without a chance to contest the charges against him. Furthermore, no one would want, nor should the system approve, convictions based on coerced confessions, tainted lineups, or racially prejudiced juries. Evidence so obtained may be unreliable. Even if it is reliable, the means of getting it violates the dignity of, and respect for, individuals, perhaps involving the state itself in criminal conduct, such as the police beating a suspect to make him confess.

Thus the defense lawyer ideally serves as a monitor of the honesty and fairness of the state. Even well-meaning and hardworking prosecutors and police can make mistakes or overlook options when blinded by an overzealous belief in the suspect's guilt. The defense lawyer explores these risks that authority will be abused, reflecting Americans' deeply held belief that unrestrained state power becomes dangerous to all. Because society's politically weakest members face the greatest risk of state abuse, defense lawyers also often see themselves as in the forefront of the fight for the despised and dispossessed of society.

So deeply engrained is defense counsel's role in equalizing the individual's struggle with the state, that the right to the effective assistance of counsel is enshrined in the U.S. Constitution's Sixth Amendment. Although it originally applied only to the federal government, the *Fourteenth Amendment had the effect of applying the Sixth Amendment and most of the remaining provisions of the Bill of Rights to the states. The right to *counsel applies to every post-charge critical stage of a criminal prosecution, ensuring counsel's likely presence at lineups, arraignments, *bail hearings, hearings on motions to suppress evidence as unconstitutionally obtained, preliminary hearings, and trials. In the landmark case, *Gideon v. Wainwright (1963), the U.S. Supreme Court held that the state is obligated in most cases to provide counsel free of charge to an indigent accused. That led to an enormous increase in the number of criminal defense counsel and of the state's role in compensating them.

Theory and practice in the United States do not, however, always match up. The American criminal defense bar is diverse, and the extent to which it succeeds in creating a fair fight with the state varies with the type of practice, the locality, and the particular lawyer. On balance, however, the state often seems unwilling to spend the money necessary for an adequate defense of the indigent.

*White-collar criminal defense lawyers—those representing nonviolent offenders who sought financial gain by means of deception and who often have abused a position of trust to commit the criminal act—are an exception to this unwillingness to expend resources. These lawyers often practice in large law *firms as one part of the firm's varied practice, or in smaller "boutique" white-collar criminal defense firms. White-collar clients are often wealthy individuals or are well-funded entities such as corporations. These clients can afford to pay their privately retained counsel high fees and reimburse them for the cost of in-depth private investigation. They are also usually from the same income class as their lawyers, easing communication between them. White-collar defense counsel often graduate from the most prestigious law schools and have honed their skills in well-respected positions, including stints as prosecutors in United States Attorneys' offices or in public corruption units in top-flight state or county prosecutors' offices.

White-collar attorney work is intellectually challenging and varied. These attorneys write briefs, interview witnesses, argue *appeals, review documents, and try cases. They generally have sufficient time to thoroughly prepare their cases with a staff of younger attorneys, well-trained *paralegals, in-house law librarians, and seasoned secretaries. They spend more of their time in offices than in courtrooms. They also counsel clients on how to avoid criminal liability or how to react if they become enmeshed in a criminal investigation. They sit at the top of the prestige/compensation pyramid for the criminal defense bar and near the top in the legal profession as a whole.

Lawyers primarily handling street crimes, from theft and narcotics sales to arson, rape, and murder, usually fare less well in both income and prestige, though their lot is diverse. Privately retained lawyers, hired by clients who can afford to pay their fees, currently handle only 34 percent of federal felony defendants and 18 percent of felony defendants in large state courts; the remaining cases are handled by public defenders or court-appointed lawyers. Private counsel often work as solo practitioners or in small firms specializing at least partly in criminal law. Many carry heavy ca-seloads, receiving a relatively small fee per case. Fees often vary based on whether the case goes to trial or results in a *plea bargain. Since the bulk of criminal cases are disposed of by plea bargain, much of these lawyers' time is spent conducting investigation and negotiating with prosecutors. Many street crime cases raise routine legal issues that require little research, though a significant number of cases do involve sophisticated consti-tutional, statutory, and evidentiary issues that competent counsel should address. Private coun-sel, especially *sole practitioners, may supplement their income by taking court-appointed cases. In many jurisdictions, some of the indigent are rep-resented by private counsel appointed and paid by the state. State-financed fees are often extraordi-narily low, though counsel are frequently paid more for time in trial than for time spent prepar-ing for trial or on other tasks performed outside the courtroom. The result is to create a disincen-tive for counsel to take cases to trial or to prepare cases thoroughly. The out-of-pocket costs, or in-come lost from not working on better-paying mat-ters, can also far exceed the minimal fee paid to a lawyer who devotes substantial time to a case. This financial squeeze creates an ethical conflict of in-terest between the lawyer's financial self-interest and the client's need for representation. Some pri-vate lawyers, however, handle a mix of white col-lar, well-paying street cases (for example, where the client is a narcotics dealer) and low-paying court-appointed cases.

Public defenders handle most indigent defense work. In large cities, public defender offices in-clude hundreds of attorneys and specialized units, in a mirror image of the organization of many prosecutors' offices. Large public defender offices also employ professional investigators and a social services staff of social workers and psychologists. The social services staff seeks to place clients in rehabilitation programs and to evaluate their men-tal competency. Social services staff members may also testify at bail hearings, sentencing hearings, competency to stand trial hearings, or at trials raising the insanity defense or some other defense based on mental state. Like many of their private bar counterparts, assistant public defenders often have caseloads so heavy that these often extremely talented lawyers simply cannot provide each client the level of representation that is most desirable. Given the unpopularity of their clients, defenders' offices may sometimes be significantly under-funded, not only in an absolute sense but relative to prosecutors' offices. Some public defenders

have refused to take on additional cases or have filed lawsuits challenging the underfunding as en suring deprivation of their clients' Sixth Amend-ment right to the effective assistance of counsel.

Nevertheless, public defenders' offices have some significant advantages over many small or sole practitioner firms primarily handling street crime. Notably, the sheer size of the office allows for a degree of specialization in both substantive legal areas and skills, permitting one defender to call on a fellow defender's expertise. Assistant de-fenders also have the financial security of a fixed salary and medical benefits, rather than relying on obtaining enough higher-paying clients to survive.

Various troubling ethical issues plague both de-fenders and all other criminal practitioners. Cli-ents are frequently guilty of at least some offense, albeit not necessarily the one charged. Clients of-ten lie to their lawyers. A lawyer may not know-ingly use perjured testimony or false evidence. Yet a lawyer is also generally prohibited from revealing a client's privileged conversations. If a client therefore admits guilt to his lawyer, but insists on denying that guilt on the witness stand, the lawyer faces conflicting obligations.

Commentators and state codes offer unclear guidance to the lawyer, and suggest disparate so lutions. All recommend trying first to persuade the client not to lie. If the client insists on pro-ceeding, a minority of commentators counsel the lawyer to proceed just as he would were the client truthful. Others counsel the lawyer to let the client offer his own narrative, prompted by few ques-tions from the lawyer and with the lawyer prohib-ited from relying on the client's testimony in his closing argument. Most state codes require the lawyer to withdraw from such representation if it will remedy the problem, or, failing that, to advise the court of the perjury. The trial judge then de-cides what to do to correct the deception—make a statement to the jury, order a mistrial, or do nothing.

The problem is easier when the client does not take the stand but seeks to call phony alibi wit-nesses. The lawyer must refuse to call such wit-nesses, and is generally able to do so without re-vealing client confidences.

Some lawyers try to avoid these ethical prob-lems by never asking their clients whether they are guilty or what happened. Rather, they simply ask, "What do the police say that you did?" or "Whom would you want called to the stand and what would he say?" Thus the lawyer does not "know" whether a witness is lying. The tactical wisdom of this solution is subject to some debate, because the client is often an excellent source of information, though many skilled defense lawyers believe they can carefully frame their questions to get complete information necessary for the best defense without pushing their client to choose between outright confession or denial of the crime.

These ethical dilemmas illustrate why defense lawyers drawn to the job by the prospect of freeing the innocent are likely to face disappointment or burnout. Some lawyers may find great satisfaction in defending even a small number of innocent clients or in defending the many clients whose innocence or guilt the lawyer is uncertain about. More often, lawyers drawn by a passion for helping the poor, a distrust of state authority, an intellectual fascination with criminal law issues, a love of the trial spotlight, or simply a nonjudgmental approach to people in trouble, are likely to fare far better.

[See also Law Practice, Forms of]

• Kenneth Mann, *Defending White Collar Crime: A Portrait of Attorneys at Work*, 1985. Barbara Babcock, book review: James Kunin, "How Can You Defend a Criminal Lawyer," *George Washington Law Review* 53 (1985): 53. Thomas Geraghty, book review: Lisa McIntyre, "The Care and Feeding of Defender Offices: A Review of the Public Defender: The Practice of Law in the Shadows of Disrepute," *Northwestern University Law Review* 82 (1988): 1255. Abbe Smith, "When Ideology and Duty Conflict," in *Ethical Problems Facing The Criminal Defense Lawyer*, Rodney J. Uphoff, ed., 1995. Kim Taylor-Thompson, "Individual Actor v. Institutional Player: Alternating Visions of the Public Defender," *Georgetown Law Journal* 84 (1996): 2419. Andrew E. Taslitz & Margaret L. Paris, *Constitutional Criminal Procedure*, 1997, and 2001 Supplement. John M. Burkoff, *Criminal Defense Ethics: Law and Liability*, 2000. Caroline Wolf Harlow, "Bureau of Justice Statistics Special Report: Defense Counsel in Criminal Cases," NCJ 179023, November 2000.

—Andrew E. Taslitz

CRIMINAL LAW PRINCIPLES

Legality Principles
Defense Principles

CRIMINAL LAW PRINCIPLES: LEGALITY PRINCIPLES

Initially, the new American colonies based their criminal law on the English *common law, a term generally used to describe how *judges could create or define a crime when they decided a case and also use that new crime to convict and punish the defendant in the same case. In the centuries preceding colonization, English judges had developed definitions for numerous crimes and there was little need for American judges to begin again in developing their own criminal law.

Early on state legislators, elected in the new American democracy to represent the will of the people, began enacting statutes that defined specific crimes. Sometimes the statutory crime would simply adopt the common law definition. Other times, the statute would redefine the crime. Judges, as an educated elite, still created new crimes in the common law tradition well into the nineteenth century. Today, however, the people's elected representatives through the legislative process create virtually all crimes in the United States.

Following the English common law tradition, most crimes are divided into two categories: misdemeanors and *felonies. Misdemeanors are considered minor crimes and carry a relatively small maximum punishment, usually confinement for no longer than one year. Felonies are considered serious crimes and carry harsher punishment ranging from imprisonment for at least one year up to death (see CRIMINAL PUNISHMENT).

Crimes can also be categorized as *mala in se* or *mala prohibita*. *Mala in se* refers to crimes that have traditionally been considered inherently wrong and morally worthy of punishment in most societies. Murder of a human being or theft of another's property would fit in this category. In contrast, *mala probibita* refers to certain crimes of modern origin that do not share these characteristics. Instead, they are crimes only because legislatures criminalized these activities to address new problems generated by a complex modern capitalist society in which widespread economic activity creates serious risk of harm to many people. Selling contaminated food or agreeing with other businesses to form a monopoly to drive up prices are examples of this type of crime

Criminal Law Variety and Evolution. Every state in America (and many counties, cities, and towns) and the federal government now have their own statutory criminal law. Thus, criminal law, including definitions of crimes, varies widely in the United States. There are, however, some pressures for uniformity in American criminal law. In the 1960s the *American Law Institute (ALI), a prestigious group of lawyers, judges, and scholars, prepared the *Model Penal Code (MPC). It is a systematic criminal code, which includes definitions for many crimes. States and other jurisdictions may adopt it if they choose. Many states have adopted significant sections of the MPC, although none has adopted it in its entirety. In addition, states often copy criminal laws enacted by other states.

Courts, of course, continue to interpret criminal statutes when necessary. This allows judges to have the "last word" on the meaning of a criminal statute (unless the legislature subsequently changes the statute.) It is important that crimes be defined as precisely as possible because jurors in criminal cases are given "jury instructions" that explain the law. Jurors use them to determine whether the defendant is guilty or innocent

Common Law Crimes. Common law or judge-made crimes have some obvious advantages. They ensure that criminal law is always available to punish harmful conduct even though the legislature did not anticipate the harm and pass a law specifically proscribing that type of behavior. Judge-made law may also deter some imaginative individuals from exploiting "loopholes" in the law, which could cause serious damage. The power of judges to create law "on the spot", so to speak, also provides timely flexibility to deal with novel or unexpected situations.

Common law crimes also have serious weaknesses. First, people may not know that their behavior is criminal until a judge says it is. Thus, someone may reasonably believe that he was engaged in perfectly lawful conduct only to find out—after the fact—that he has committed a crime. This type of indeterminate legal system may make people guess whether they are breaking the law, making it more difficult to predict the future consequences of one's behavior. Second, the government's power to punish citizens is not limited under the common law. By deciding that a person committed a "new" crime a court expands the power of the government and, correspondingly, reduces individual freedom. This uncertainty allows the government to use criminal law's crushing power either to stifle certain types of behavior (such as political protests or labor strikes) or to punish individuals or groups (such as immigrants), which it disfavors. Finally, the absence of clear rules prohibiting conduct and the resulting uncertainty undermines the moral justifications for punishment, all of which assume that the criminal chose to engage in unlawful conduct.

Judicial Creation of Criminal Defenses. Although no longer allowed to create new crimes, American judges still retain substantial authority to create defenses, which are claims by a defendant that may prevent him from being convicted of criminal charges. Thus, a judge may alter the law in unusual circumstances, but only if the change favors the defendant by preventing his conviction.

Justification, one kind of defense, is a claim recognized by the law that, although the defendant did a harmful act that normally would be considered a crime, under the circumstances, his actions were the "right" thing to do. Thus, he was "justified" and should not be punished. Excuses, unlike justification, include a defendant's defense that, though he committed a crime, he should not be condemned and punished because of his unusual characteristics or the unusual situation. An excuse can also be partial, reducing the degree of the crime or the amount of punishment.

Self-defense is a good example of justification. A woman attacked by a mugger brandishing a knife can intentionally shoot and even kill her attacker. Although intentionally taking another human's life would normally be a *homicide, in this unusual situation the woman may kill the aggressor to save her own life. In killing him she has preserved the life of an "innocent" person (herself) and properly shifted the loss to the mugger. Society is better off because an "innocent" life has been saved. Moreover, she did what any other reasonable person would have done in the situation. Thus, the criminal law should not condemn this act of killing in self-preservation.

Insanity is a classic example of a legal excuse. A defendant charged with a crime may avoid criminal responsibility completely if he can establish that he was legally insane at the time of the crime. A person found not guilty by reason of insanity is usually committed to a secure mental health facility and held there until he is no longer mentally ill or dangerous. Most states today and the federal government use a form of the *M'Naghten* test of legal insanity, which was created in a case by that name in the English House of Lords in 1843. Under that test the defendant must prove that, at the time of the crime, as a result of a mental disorder he did not know what he was doing or that it was wrong. Though the legal tests may be somewhat complicated and at times difficult for juries to understand, the rationale of the insanity defense is straightforward. The criminal law does not want to condemn or punish an individual who, through no fault of his own, suffered from a mental illness that seriously impaired his ability to obey the law. Although his behavior was harmful, he is not morally blameworthy. Instead, he should be hospitalized until he no longer poses a serious threat of harm to society.

Judges can take into account new knowledge and create new defenses, thus allowing the criminal law to evolve. For instance, many American courts in the 1980s recognized the "battered woman" defense. Experts, who studied a number of battered women, concluded that many women who had experienced violent beating by men over a period of time suffered from "learned helplessness," which made it difficult for them to leave their batterers. These women could also predict when their batterer was going to attack them, even though the man did not expressly threaten death or serious bodily injury. Based on this social science research many courts allowed female defendants charged with killing or seriously injuring their batterers to present expert testimony on their claim of self-defense. This testimony would help juries understand why the woman was not at fault for staying with her violent husband or lover, and why she reasonably perceived that another violent attack was "imminent," even though no specific threats of violence had yet occurred

The Indispensable Notice Requirement. The shift in the United States to legislation as virtually the exclusive basis for prohibiting conduct as criminal was motivated in significant part by the modern principle of "legality." This principle (often expressed in the Latin maxim, *nullum crimen nulla poena sine lege* ["no crime without law; no punishment without law"]) is a basic premise of contemporary American criminal law. It ensures that no one can be convicted or punished for a crime unless the law forbidding the conduct has been enacted in advance.

This principle implements a collective sense of American justice that everyone deserves the protection provided by clearly announced rules that provide notice of what conduct will be punished. The principle of legality protects individual autonomy, an important American value, by allowing and protecting all conduct by individuals that is not specifically forbidden. It also limits the authority of the government. In the United States no one can be charged and convicted of a crime for conduct unless the legislature has previously passed a law defining that conduct as a crime. American criminal law implements the principle of legality in several different ways.

Prohibition of Ex Post Facto Laws. First, the United States Constitution has a specific provision (art. I, § 9) that prohibits both Congress and state legislatures from enacting *ex post facto* criminal laws. Some states also have a similar provision in their state constitutions. This prohibition is limited to legislation rather than to judicial decisions. It means that a legislature may not: criminalize acts that were innocent when the defendant did them; increase either the seriousness of the crime (from a misdemeanor to a felony, for example) or the amount of punishment after the defendant committed the crime; or change the legal rules of evidence in effect when the crime was committed

to convict the defendant (*Calder* v. *Bull* (1798)). Simply put, the U.S. Constitution forbids a retroactive criminal law.

This prohibition serves several purposes. First, it ensures that criminal statutes give "fair warning of their effect and permit individuals to rely on their meaning until explicitly changed." *Weaver* v. *Graham* (1981). Second, the prohibition limits the power of government by preventing arbitrary or vindictive legislation. Third, it allows the legislature to use the criminal law to punish only when deterrence could have been furthered. Without advance notice of what conduct is criminal, individuals cannot be deterred by the threat of criminal conviction and punishment.

Laws Void for Vagueness. The Fifth and *Fourteenth Amendments of the U.S. Constitution also protect legality and individual liberty by ensuring that the government cannot deprive a person of life, liberty, or property without *due process of law. The U.S. Supreme Court has consistently relied on these provisions to ensure that every criminal law provides fair notice of when conduct is criminal. It has struck down as unconstitutional criminal laws that are so vague that ordinary people could not determine what actions are criminal and laws that give police officers too much discretion in deciding arbitrarily which people they will arrest. In *Papachristou* v. *City of Jacksonville* (1972) the Court has struck down a vagrancy law, used for centuries in England for social control of laborers and others, because it allowed police officers to select offenders for arrest based on their race or ethnicity.

The Rule of Lenity. Because the meaning of criminal statutes is often unclear, courts must interpret them and provide authoritative explanation for future use by prosecutors, defense lawyers, judges, and juries. Though the *ex post facto* prohibition does not apply to judicial decisions, American courts, nonetheless, will often construe an ambiguous criminal statute, in the words of the California Supreme Court in *Keeler* v. *Superior Court* (1970), "as favorably to the defendant as its language and the circumstances of its application may reasonably permit." In *Keeler* the court interpreted the California murder statute to not include the deliberate destruction by a man of a viable, thirty-five-week-old fetus in the mother's womb. It concluded that the statute required the fetus to be "born alive" before it was protected by the homicide law. American courts often use the rule of lenity to interpret a criminal statute to benefit the defendant and to avoid an interpretation that would violate either the *ex post facto* or due process provisions of the U.S. Constitution.

[*See also* Procedure, Criminal]

• H. L. Hart, *Law, Liberty and Morality*, (1963). Anthony G. Amsterdam, "Federal Constitutional Restrictions on the Punishment of Crimes of Status, Crimes of General Obnoxiousness, Crimes of Displeasing Police Officers and the Like," *Criminal Law Bulletin* (1967): 205–42. John J. Jeffries Jr., "Legality, Vagueness and the Construction of Penal Statutes," *Virginia Law Review* (1985): 189. Robert Batey, "Vagueness and Construction of Criminal Statutes-Balancing Acts," *Virginia Journal of Social Policy and Law* (1997): 1–96. Wayne A. Logan, "The Ex Post Facto Clause and the Jurisprudence of Punishment," *American Criminal Law Review* (1998): 1261–1318. Wayne A. LaFave, *Criminal Law*, 3d ed., 2000.   —John Q. La Fond

CRIMINAL LAW PRINCIPLES: DEFENSE PRINCIPLES

Under the United States Constitution, every person charged with a crime is presumed innocent until the government proves him guilty beyond a reasonable doubt. The state may not take away a person's *liberty unless it convincingly demonstrates that he has committed a crime, thereby depriving him of his right to freedom.

The Constitution's Fifth Amendment expressly protects a criminal defendant from being compelled to testify against himself. Thus, he cannot be required to testify under oath at trial.

Elements of a Crime. To convict someone, the prosecutor generally must prove that the defendant committed a voluntary act (*actus reus*) with a criminal state of mind (*mens rea*). The statute defining the offense will specify what actions and what mental states—usually called "elements"—constitute the particular crime. A jury may convict the defendant only if the prosecutor proves all elements beyond a reasonable doubt.

Defenses. Even though the defendant may intentionally have harmed another person or property, he may claim that his case was an "exception" to the general principles of criminal responsibility and that, consequently, he should not be convicted and punished. There are invariably unusual situations in which people intentionally cause harm, but the purposes of punishment would not be furthered in these cases. Also, some individuals, through no fault of their own, do not have the necessary intellectual or psychological capacity to be criminally blamed for their harmful conduct. Consequently, to accommodate both types of cases, defendants can avoid criminal responsibility by presenting defenses. Defenses are generally classified as "justifications" or "excuses."

Affirmative Defenses and the Privilege against Self-Incrimination. When a defendant attempts to do more than simply negate one or more of the crime's elements, he must usually present *evidence establishing that defense. In most cases, the defendant must also persuade the jury, by at least a preponderance of the evidence (more than 50 percent certainty), that his defense is true. This is called an "affirmative" defense.

Though not required to testify when presenting an affirmative defense, many defendants, as a practical matter, do testify under oath and explain to the jury what they did and why they did it. The prosecutor can then cross-examine them, thus undermining the privilege against *self-incrimination.

The prosecutor still must prove all elements of the offenses charged in order to convict the defendant. The jury only considers an affirmative defense if it first finds that the government has established these elements beyond a reasonable doubt.

Justification. A justification defense, in effect, asserts that the defendant did the morally right thing under unusual circumstances. Thus, he is not blameworthy, did not commit a crime, and should not be punished. Most claims of justification arise from a situation of "necessity," which requires the defendant to make a "choice of evils." Necessity occurs when the defendant had to commit what otherwise would be a crime because an emergency situation left him with no other socially desirable choice. In this situation, the defendant can lawfully commit an intentional harm in order to avoid a more serious harm.

But necessity justifies what otherwise would be a crime only under certain conditions. First, there must be an imminent threat to person or property. At *common law, the peril had to originate in nature rather than in human action, although the modern view also allows the latter. Second, the defendant must not have been at fault in creating the peril. Third, there must be no reasonable alternative response other than the commission of the crime. Fourth, the defendant's crime must have prevented an even greater harm or, put another way, he must have chosen the "lesser of two evils." Fifth, the law must not expressly preclude his defense. Notice that reasonable belief does not justify the general defense of necessity—there must be an actual threat, and the defendant must have chosen the lesser of the two evils.

A concrete example illustrates these principles. A large dam is about to burst as a result of a record rainfall, with the inevitable destruction of hundreds of townspeople downstream. There is no time for repair or evacuation. Can a citizen deliberately make a small breach in the dam so that the floodwater is diverted away from the town toward a farmhouse where a family will be drowned? The criminal law would allow someone who intentionally breached the dam and thereby killed the family to raise the justification of "necessity."

The defendant would claim that there was an imminent choice of evils, he did not create the emergency, his actions were reasonable and there was no other alternative, anyone else in that situation might well have done the same thing, he chose the lesser evil, and the legislature has not excluded the justification claim.

His actions (when viewed from the perspective of a utilitarian calculation) were socially desirable. His conduct resulted in a net saving of lives (hundreds of townspeople lived, while a family perished), thus minimizing the loss suffered by society. Though harmful to some and arguably violating their right to life, his actions were life-saving to many. He has preserved the maximum human lives—the very reason for having a murder statute. His conduct was not morally blameworthy in this exceptional situation.

Justification defenses are allowed because otherwise the general purposes of *criminal punishment would not be served. Neither specific nor general deterrence would be advanced in such cases. Not only would the threat of punishment not deter the actor; it would not deter most members of the community. Moreover, there is no need for rehabilitation; the actor did the "right" thing. Nor is there a need to incapacitate him since he is not dangerous. Finally, the actor did not choose to commit a morally blameworthy act; thus, he does not deserve retribution.

Self-Defense. Self-defense is a common example of justification. Ordinarily it is a crime to intentionally kill or physically harm another human being. But what should a person do when he sees someone coming at him with a knife, and yelling, "I am going to kill you"? Most people would certainly take all reasonable steps to save their own lives even if it meant killing or seriously injuring the aggressor.

A person is lawfully entitled to use deadly force to defend himself (or another) when he reasonably believes that someone threatens him (or another) with imminent death or serious bodily injury and that the use of deadly force is necessary to prevent such injury. Some jurisdictions are more restrictive; a person may use deadly force in self-defense

only if he is attacked with deadly force. A person may use non-deadly force to defend himself (or another) if he reasonably believes that the aggressor threatens him (or another) with bodily injury.

Notice how the violent response by the victim must be proportional to the threat posed by the aggressor. A person may not intentionally shoot and kill his attacker if he is only threatened with a simple *assault. He may only use non-deadly force. Notice also that the threat of harm must be imminent. This ensures that the need to act could not have been avoided.

If the victim can, with complete safety, avoid choosing the lesser of two evils (perhaps by running away), then the law generally requires him to flee unless he is in his own residence. He is not required to die or suffer a serious injury if he cannot escape; on the contrary, he may intentionally harm the aggressor and thereby terminate the threat. Most people would do the same thing under these exceptional circumstances; even the threat of possible future punishment would not deter someone from acting in his own defense. Moreover, the life of an innocent person should be protected at the cost of the life of the aggressor, who has by his own violent act forfeited the law's protection. Thus, there is no retributive purpose to be served by punishing the victim.

Excuses. Unlike a justification, an excuse is a claim by the defendant that although he committed a crime, he should not be convicted and punished because of his unusual personal characteristics or because of the unusual situation. An excuse can be complete, avoiding conviction and punishment entirely, or it can be partial, reducing the degree of the crime and the severity of punishment.

Duress allows the defendant to prove that he committed a crime only because he reasonably believed that another person threatened him (or a close relative) with imminent death or serious bodily injury and he had no alternative, such as going to the police. Threats of less serious harm (such as blackmail) will not support a claim of duress. Thus the bank manager who opens the bank safe and gives the money to a robber pointing a loaded pistol at his head and threatening to kill him may claim duress. The manager did not "freely choose" to help the robber steal the bank's money. Most people would have made the same choice. Under common law, duress was not a defense to murder, but modern law allows it, and sometimes does not require the threat to be "imminent."

The Insanity Defense. Perhaps the most controversial legal excuse in the United States today is the insanity defense. Even when the prosecutor proves all the elements of the charged offense, a defendant may avoid conviction and punishment if he can prove that he was legally insane at the time of the crime. If successful, he will be found "not guilty by reason of insanity" and, in most cases, committed to a secure mental health facility until he is no longer mentally ill or dangerous.

Most states at present use a form of the 1843 *M'Naghten* test, which finds a person legally insane and not responsible for his crime if he can prove that he suffered from a mental disorder that left him unable to know what he was doing or that his act was wrong. A few states have added an additional component (the irresistible impulse) to the *M'Naghten* test. A defendant will be found legally insane even if he knew what he was doing and that it was wrong, if he can prove that he could not stop himself from committing the crime.

Some states use the American Law Institute (ALI) test set forth in the *Model Penal Code (§4.01). The ALI is a prestigious group of judges, scholars, and lawyers that writes model legislation, which states may adopt in whole or in part. Under the ALI test, the defendant must prove by a preponderance of the evidence that at the time of the crime, because of a mental disorder, he lacked "substantial capacity either to appreciate the criminality of his conduct or to conform his conduct to the requirements of law." This test is more favorable to defendants because it excuses a defendant if either his cognitive *or* volitional capacity was substantially impaired; it does not require complete impairment.

In 1981, John Hinckley tried to assassinate President Ronald Reagan. As a result of his acquittal by reason of insanity, Congress enacted a tough insanity test that is used in all federal criminal prosecutions. It is less favorable for defendants than the *M'Naghten* test because it requires a "serious" mental disease or defect.

Four states have abolished the insanity defense. Someone who suffers from a serious mental disorder can be convicted of a crime and punished even if he did not realize that his conduct was criminal.

Partial Defenses. Some excuses do not eliminate all criminal responsibility. Instead, they may reduce the seriousness of the crime used to convict, or the severity of the punishment. A modern partial excuse is the diminished capacity defense. A defendant may prove that because he was mentally ill, voluntarily intoxicated, or had consumed drugs, he did not act with the necessary criminal state of mind (*mens rea*) required for conviction of the charged offense. Often the defendant is then convicted of a lesser offense. Most states do not allow this defense.

Hybrid Defenses: Justification and Excuse. "Heat of passion" is a classic example of a partial excuse. An intentional killing that might otherwise result in a conviction of first- or second-degree murder may be reduced to voluntary manslaughter. The defendant must prove that he acted in response to sudden and adequate provocation without a sufficient cooling-off period. In some states, a man who finds his wife in a sexual act with another man, and kills him, may persuade a jury that the situation was exceptional and caused him (and would cause a reasonable person) to lose his normal power of self-control. From this perspective, heat of passion can be considered an excuse. From another perspective, the deceased is considered partially at fault for his own death because most husbands would have responded with deadly force. On this analysis, the defense may be a partial justification.

Feminists and others have criticized the law for allowing men to use the heat-of-passion defense in cases involving sexual conduct by their wives or lovers. In their view, this out-dated rule embodies and perpetuates an inappropriate male norm that wives are male possessions and that men may use violence to protect their "property."

[*See also* Burden of Proof, Criminal and Civil; Procedure, Criminal]

• George P. Fletcher, "The Individualization of Excusing Conditions," *Southern California Law Review* 47 (1974): 1269–1309. David L. Bazelon, "The Morality of the Criminal Law," *Southern California Law Review* 49 (1976): 385–405. Peter A. Arenella, "The Diminished Capacity Defense and Diminished Responsibility Defenses: Two Children of a Doomed Marriage," *Columbia Law Review* 77 (1977): 827–65. George P. Fletcher, *Rethinking Criminal Law*, 1978. Joshua Dressler, "Rethinking Heat of Passion: A Defense in Search of a Rationale," *Journal of Criminal Law and Criminology* 73 (1982): 421–70. Paul H. Robinson, *Criminal Law Defenses*, 1984. Sanford H. Kadish, *Excusing Crime*, California Law Review 75 (1987): 257–89. Wayne A. LaFave, *Criminal Law*, 3d ed., 2000.   —John Q. La Fond

CRIMINAL PROCEDURE. *See* Procedure, Criminal.

CRIMINAL PROCEDURE, FEDERAL RULES OF. The Federal Rules of Criminal Procedure are comprehensive standards governing procedure in federal court criminal cases. The Rules are just one of several sources of law regulating the process. The Constitution's *Bill of Rights provides the accused with rights to *due process, *counsel, freedom from unreasonable *searches and seizures, a public trial by an impartial *jury, and other important guarantees. *Arrest, *bail, venue, *plea, trial, *sentencing, *appeal, and other matters are regulated by federal statute. The Rules build on these constitutional and statutory standards, but also deal with additional subjects, such as pleading and motion practice.

The Rules were part of the reform effort to unify and simplify American procedural law that began in the nineteeenth century. Opposed by bench and bar, legislative reform of criminal procedure lagged behind similar efforts in civil procedure. By the late 1800s, one attempt to bring order to the complexity of criminal procedure law, Field's proposed Code of Criminal Procedure, developed by New York lawyer David Dudley *Field, was eventually adopted by several state legislatures. But in most jurisdictions, *common-law decisions continued to regulate the criminal process until the early decades of the twentieth century, when legislative reform accelerated.

At the federal level, congressional control of criminal procedure began with ad hoc statutes regulating appeal and indictment. In 1933, *Congress authorized the U.S. Supreme Court to prescribe rules for procedure following the verdict of a jury or judge. Seven years later, Congress passed a statute authorizing the promulgation of rules for earlier stages of the process. These two provisions (later combined) paved the way for the development of the original Federal Rules.

The Rules took shape during World War II. An advisory committee was appointed by the Court in 1941 to draft procedural rules prior to the verdict or the defendant's plea. Led by Arthur *Vanderbilt—one of the leading court reformers of the time—and aided by a research staff housed in the Supreme Court building, the prestigious committee included Herbert Wechsler, who later drafted the influential Model Penal Code, and Lester Orfield, a distinguished federal procedure scholar. The group labored over ten separate drafts. In 1944, a divided Supreme Court ordered the committee's final draft to be amended, then transmitted to Congress. Combined with additional rules promulgated by the Court governing proceedings after the verdict, these recommendations took effect in 1946.

The original Rules made several important changes in federal criminal case processing. These changes included extended territorial limits for service of warrants, simplified indictments and pretrial motions, provision for defense waiver of indictment in favor of information, limited pretrial discovery, presentence investigations in all cases, expanded time periods for raising motions for a new trial and for filing an *appeal, new procedures for cross-district arrest of defendants, *search warrants and their suppression, and more generous bail provisions.

By 1958, Congress had authorized the Judicial Conference of the United States to create advisory committees to assist the Court in revising federal rules to respond to the changing legal and social landscape. This revision process remains in place today: the committee's recommendations, once approved by the Judicial Conference, are submitted for approval by the Court, and then become law absent congressional action. In 1966, in the midst of the *Warren Court's "revolution" extending the Bill of Rights' criminal procedure guarantees by judicial decision, the Rules were extensively amended. Ever since, the Rules have been revised in some way almost every year.

Over the years, many states have turned to the Federal Rules as they sought to reform criminal procedure. Today, roughly half the states have court rules or statutory codes of criminal procedure that borrow heavily from the Rules. A handful of these lifted nearly all of the Rules and subsequent amendments; others have incorporated the basic concepts of the federal scheme. This tendency to adopt federal law is striking, considering the differing caseloads, types of crime, administrative settings, and resources of state and federal criminal justice systems. Nevertheless, states have adopted the Rules because they are accessible, designed to comply with constitutional requirements that govern state as well as federal courts, have been screened by several groups of lawyers and judges as well as Congress, and come with their own handy guide to interpretation—federal case law.

Although the Federal Rules have profoundly influenced the shape of criminal procedure, they have yet to be as widely adopted as the companion Federal Rules of Civil Procedure or Federal Rules of Evidence, both of which have been embraced by all but about a dozen states. A significant number of states have chosen instead not to adopt a comprehensive criminal procedure code or set of rules, or have modeled at least some of their rules on the ABA Standards of Criminal Justice (see AMERICAN BAR ASSOCIATION), another monumental effort in the reform of criminal procedure. A response to what the drafters termed the "crisis in our courts occasioned by overwhelming caseloads, recidivism, and a seeming incapacity of the system to respond to the challenges of the Sixties," the effort to write the Standards, chaired by Chief Justice Warren *Burger, spanned a decade, producing a comprehensive set of recommendations by 1973 for every aspect of criminal procedure. Although many of the recommended Standards duplicate federal law, several Standards differ significantly from the Rules.

Federal Rule 16 illustrates the incomplete hegemony of the Rules. Originally allowing defense discovery of only certain documents, it was criticized as encouraging "trial by surprise," and by 1975 had been amended to provide for broader defense access to various statements, reports, and objects. Nevertheless, many states, less concerned than Congress about the risks of defense fabrication and witness intimidation, followed instead the broader ABA Standards, which recommended pretrial disclosure of prosecution witnesses' names and statements. Another example is grand jury review, regulated by Federal Rule 6, which is a constitutional right for federal defendants, but is virtually extinct in some states. Even in states where the indictment alternative is common, grand jury practice often differs dramatically from the federal model.

[See also Procedure, Criminal]

• Lester B. Orfield, "The Federal Rules of Criminal Procedure," *California Law Review* 33 (1945): 543. Lester B. Orfield, "Early Federal Criminal Procedure," *Wayne Law Review* 1 (1961): 503. Symposium Issue, "The ABA Standards for Criminal Justice," *American Criminal Law Review* 12 (1974): no. 2. Wayne La Fave, Jerold Israel, and Nancy King, *Criminal Procedure* 1 §§ 1.2, 1.5, 1.6 (2d ed., 1999). Charles Alan Wright, *Federal Practice and Procedure: Criminal* 1 3d §§ 1–40 (1999).

—Nancy Jean King

CRIMINAL PUNISHMENTS are measures, usually designed to be unpleasant, which are imposed by governmental authorities on persons who have been convicted of violating provisions of applicable *criminal laws. Similar deprivations of *property and *liberty may also be imposed under civil or regulatory laws (taxes, civil fines and forfeitures, punitive damages, involuntary civil commitment, the military draft, immigration detention, and deportation). Thus, what principally distinguishes criminal punishment is its peculiar stigmatizing quality. Criminal sanctions have traditionally been viewed as expressing society's strong moral condemnation of the defendant's behavior.

Purposes of Punishment. The moral condemnation and stigmatizing effect of criminal penalties is related to one of the traditional purposes and limitations of criminal punishment: to exact retribution by imposing "deserved" punishment in proportion to the offender's blameworthiness. The theory of retribution (or "just deserts") views punishment as being proper either for its own sake, or for the sake of fairness to the victims of crime; to law-abiding offenders; to other offenders who have been punished for the same offense; and to this offender (who deserves to be punished no more severely than is warranted by his culpability, and also no more severely than other, similar offenders were punished). There are several versions of retributive theory. What some have called "defining" retributivism seeks to impose penalties which are directly proportional to the seriousness of the offense and the offender's blameworthiness. A more modest version of desert theory, "limiting" retributivism, merely sets upper and lower bounds—sentences must not be excessively severe or unduly lenient; within these outer limits, punishment is scaled according to what is needed to achieve the other purposes of punishment discussed below, and should be the least severe sanction necessary to achieve all of these other punishment goals (a concept sometimes referred to as sentencing parsimony).

Most nonretributive theories of punishment view criminal penalties as justified on the basis of the desirable consequences (other than fairness) which are intended to be achieved—in particular, the prevention of future criminal acts by this offender or other would-be offenders. These theories are sometimes collectively referred to as utilitarian, consequentialist, or instrumental theories of punishment. Four such theories are commonly recognized: rehabilitation, incapacitation, deterrence, and denunciation. Rehabilitation is designed to prevent or lessen this offender's future criminal behavior by addressing the causes of that behavior (through counseling, treatment, education, or training). Incapacitation prevents crime by imprisoning or executing dangerous offenders, thus physically restraining them from committing crimes against the public. Deterrence discourages future crimes by this offender ("special" deterrence) and by other likely offenders ("general" deterrence), by instilling and reinforcing fear of punishment. Lastly, the theory of denunciation (sometimes referred to as the expressive function of punishment, indirect general prevention, or affirmative general prevention) views criminal penalties as a means of defining and reinforcing important social norms of appropriate behavior. Given the many difficulties of preventing crime by rehabilitation, incapacitation, or deterrent threats (in particular: the fact that so few offenders are actually caught and convicted), normreinforcement may be one of the most important crime-preventive effects of punishment.

In addition to the traditional theories outlined above, courts and other officials have recently begun to apply the theory of restorative justice. This new paradigm seeks to obtain restitution or other satisfaction for the victim or the community, promote victim-offender reconciliation and healing, and provide more opportunities for victims and community representatives to participate in the adjudication, sentencing, and punishment processes. In pursuing these additional goals, restorative justice programs give little emphasis to assessments of deserved punishment; however, such programs are still compatible with the more flexible, "limiting" theory of retribution, described above.

A flexible notion of "just deserts" is also a practical, administrative necessity. The entire criminal justice process, from investigation through punishment, relies heavily on the defendant's cooperation (for instance: in providing testimony against other offenders; pleading guilty or waiving jury trial or other legal rights; maintaining good conduct in prison; and cooperating with treatment and with conditions of release). Cooperation is induced by giving defendants leniency in the form of lower charges and/or less severe penalties, even if such leniency results in punishment which is less than the offender deserves for his present or past crimes.

The definition and application of punishment purposes is highly problematic. Since these purposes are rarely specified in detail, criminal justice agents may apply differing purposes, thus producing disparate results for similarly situated offenders; indeed, the same agent may act inconsistently in different cases. Another source of disparity is that the traditional goals of punishment often conflict with each other, posing difficult tradeoffs. For example, increased rates of imprisonment may increase the general deterrent effect on other would-be offenders, yet some of the incarcerated offenders may be made substantially worse (more dangerous, less able to cope with freedom) than they were before entering prison (an effect know as prisonization). An offender's mental illness or addiction to drugs reduces his or her capacity to obey the law, thus making the offender less deter-

able and less blameworthy, but more dangerous and in need of incapacitation and treatment. Several sentencing purposes require assessments of the offender's dangerousness or amenability to treatment, yet these assessments and resulting measures inevitably produce disparate sentences for equally culpable offenders, thus violating at least a "defining" theory of retribution. Given all of these inherently conflicting values and goals, it is no wonder that many persons both inside and outside of the criminal justice system are strongly critical of punishment decisions.

Punishment in Historical Perspective. Four hundred years ago corporal punishment was the accepted method of punishment, and confinement was the exception. Since that time, rehabilitation has on several occasions been viewed as the main goal of punishment. But the predominant purposes of punishment today are, as they were four hundred years ago, retribution, deterrence, and incapacitation.

In seventeenth- and eighteenth-century England, confinement as a means of punishment was rare; jails were mainly used to hold those who were awaiting trial or punishment. Punishments consisted of flogging, the stocks, and hanging. Most of these punishments were carried out publicly, and the public nature of the punishment was its most important characteristic. At a hanging in London, the condemned would be paraded through the streets to the scaffold, local magistrates would attend, and the city's religious leaders would pray. The hanging was a public production that helped bolster the power of the monarchy and the magistrates. It was a theater of righteousness and authority, sending a warning to all that observed it. Changing perceptions led to the downfall of theatrical punishment. The lower classes who were the target audience of this theater began to treat it more as merriment and a mockery of the law than as a grave warning. At the same time, the upper classes were slowly growing more sensitive to the cruelty of physical pain. The death penalty began to be used less frequently, corporal punishment was more often carried out privately, and the use of imprisonment grew.

As an alternative to imprisonment or corporal punishment for felons, the English during most of the eighteenth century preferred transportation. Prisoners were sent to the United States until it gained independence, and then to Australia. By 1772, three-fifths of male convicts were being transported, while only one-tenth were sent to prison. But these practices then began to change rapidly, and by 1800 two-thirds of male convicts were sentenced to prison.

For minor offenders, imprisonment as punishment had started much earlier. In 1557, the first English House of Corrections was established in Bridewell palace, designed to reform and train minor offenders such as prostitutes, beggars, vagrants, and debtors. It enforced a work ethic on its inhabitants in the belief that these offenders' inappropriate social behavior was due to a lack of moral discipline and job skills.

In eighteenth-century America, although corporal punishment was also the chief means of punishment, more humane methods were normally used, mostly for economic reasons. Unlike the situation in Europe, Americans needed labor to build the growing colonies. The colonial governments wanted to keep their population alive and healthy, so the methods of corporal punishment were less severe and included public humiliation such as dunking and the stocks.

After the Revolutionary War, imprisonment became the dominant method of punishment in the United States. Two competing prison systems developed during this time, both designed to achieve rehabilitation, but with different methods. In Pennsylvania, the Quakers turned the Walnut Street Jail into the first penitentiary, founded on the idea that complete isolation and hard work would reform prisoners. Inmates worked, lived, and ate by themselves in their cells, and complete silence was maintained. In Auburn, New York, the more economical congregate system was developing. As in the Walnut Street Jail, prisoners had individual cells and maintained complete silence, but they worked together. The latter system made it easier to exploit inmate labor, so that system was adopted as more prisons were built.

*Prisons quickly became overcrowded and the isolation broke down as cells began to hold two or more prisoners. Guards became more brutal in their attempts to enforce order and silence. However, even as the system broke down, confinement remained the punishment of choice in the United States. Some believed that confinement itself would reform inmates. Others believed that it was impossible to reform most prisoners, and that they were unworthy of concern. For much of the nineteenth century, the labor of inmates was leased to private contractors, but this system often led to corruption and mistreatment of prisoners.

For the remainder of the nineteenth and all of the twentieth century, incarceration was the dominant form of punishment, with only moderate reforms. During the late nineteenth century juveniles were removed to separate courts and institutions, and the concepts of *probation and parole arrived. The former option recognized that some criminals needed very little rehabilitation, and for those who did, prison was often not the best place to achieve it. Parole reflected the belief that the hope of early release would motivate prisoners to improve themselves, or at least cooperate with prison rules. Some prisons began to teach prisoners skills they would need upon their release.

In the 1910s and 1920s, prisons began limited use of psychologists or psychiatrists to help inmates change their ways. Also, during these years, there was an increase in the use of "indeterminate" sentencing—lengthy prison terms subject to broad parole discretion. Under this so-called medical model, the warden or parole board would decide when a prisoner was reformed and ready to rejoin the outside world.

During the mid-twentieth century, prison systems began the classification of prisoners. By identifying those in need of minimum, medium, or maximum security, inmates could be more effectively treated, and money could be saved by avoiding unneeded security measures. Mentally disabled prisoners also began to be removed from prisons, and there was an increase in psychological treatment of prisoners. Rehabilitation became the main goal of imprisonment. But in practice, prisons remained predominately punitive rather than therapeutic institutions.

In the 1960s, courts abandoned their previous, "hands-off" approach and began to recognize a variety of *prisoners' rights. This change reflected broader movements for *civil rights on behalf of the poor and minorities, as well as an increase in public concern and press attention to the treatment of inmates, in the wake of numerous prison riots. In the 1970s, the rehabilitative ideal and indeterminate sentencing laws came under widespread attack. Some critics argued that the broad discretion exercised by judges and parole boards permitted substantial disparities in the sentencing of offenders convicted of similar crimes, that case-specific assessments of offender treatment needs and dangerousness were unreliable, and that few treatment programs had been shown to be effective. Other critics felt that judges and parole boards had used their discretion to impose unduly lenient sentences. Sentencing laws were changed in most states, reducing or eliminating judicial and parole discretion, and generally increasing sentencing severity. By the end of the twentieth century, prisons were serving the same purposes as the theatrical corporal and *capital punishment did in the seventeenth and eighteenth centuries—retribution, deterrence, and incapacitation.

Contemporary Punishment Laws and Practices. Many of the exotic penalties applied in former times are no longer practiced in the United States, but a wide variety of criminal punishments are available. The death penalty is authorized in over three-quarters of the states and in federal courts, although only about half of the states have carried out executions in recent decades, and less than a dozen do so with any regularity. Death penalties are provided for a variety of crimes, but in recent years have only actually been imposed for murder. Other authorized punishments include imprisonment in a regional prison or locally operated jail, fines, and probationary supervision (which may be combined with a suspended sentence of prison, jail, or a fine that will not be carried out if the defendant complies with certain conditions). The requirements of probation or a conditional sentence may include periodic reports to a probation officer or other supervisor; limitations on travel, place of residence, or associates; home detention and/or electronic monitoring; abstinence from liquor or drugs; periodic tests for drug or alcohol use; restitution to the victim; community-service work; participation in educational, counseling, or medical treatment programs; and refraining from further criminal behavior.

Persons convicted of crimes may also lose certain privileges or suffer other disabilities, either automatically or at the discretion of various officials. These include revocation or denial of a driver's license or other permit; ineligibility for government or private employment, public office-holding, and government programs or contracts; loss of voting and other civil or family rights; forfeiture of property gained from or used to commit the crime; and loss of credibility as a witness, through rules permitting impeachment by prior convictions.

Punishments are limited by both procedural and substantive legal safeguards. Under the Sixth Amendment to the U.S. Constitution, defendants may not receive a custody sentence unless they had (or waived) retained or appointed *counsel at their trial and sentencing hearing; many states have laws granting broader appointed counsel rights (e.g., for all offenses punishable with incarceration, regardless of the sentence imposed). Much more limited rights to appointed counsel apply at probation and parole revocation hearings,

prison disciplinary proceedings, and other critical stages of the correctional process. The rules of *evidence and *proof applied at sentencing hearings are more flexible than at trial; hearsay is often admissible, and most facts bearing only on the choice of sentence (not on proof of the charged offense) need only be proven by a preponderance of the evidence. Judges are generally not required to state specific reasons for the sentence imposed, except when departing from any applicable sentencing guidelines.

Substantively, offenders are protected by constitutional prohibitions against retroactive (*ex post facto) punishment; multiple prosecutions or punishments (*double jeopardy) for the same offense; *cruel and unusual punishments; excessive fines; and penalties for the exercise of free *speech or other constitutionally protected rights. Prohibited ex post facto penalties include laws that criminalize conduct which was not defined as criminal at the time of the alleged crime, or that increase the authorized punishment after the offender's conduct. However, offenders do not receive the benefit of post-offense reductions in the penalty unless the legislature so provides. Double Jeopardy rules prohibit successive prosecutions by the same jurisdiction, but not by two different states, or state and federal prosecutors, having criminal jurisdiction over the same offense, for example, a crime begun in one state and completed in another (however, state and federal statutes or regulations sometimes bar such multiple prosecutions). Nor do double jeopardy rules bar cumulative punishment in a single trial for versions of the same offense, provided there is clear legislative intent to permit this result (however, statutory "merger" provisions in many states limit cumulative punishment in such cases). Punishments deemed "cruel and unusual" include most forms of painful corporal punishment, imposition of the death penalty in an excessive or arbitrary manner, and prison sentences that are grossly disproportionate to the current offense (a standard which Supreme Court cases suggest will rarely be met). Some conditions of prison confinement have also been found unconstitutionally cruel (e.g., deliberate denial of medical care or sanitation; failure to protect from assaults) or a violation of First Amendment or other civil rights retained by prisoners.

Punishments are further regulated by state and federal statutes, rules of criminal procedure, and case law. Statutes defining crimes specify the allowable punishments, and sometimes also specify a particular required punishment (for instance: life imprisonment without parole, for some forms of murder), or a certain required minimum penalty (for instance: a "mandatory minimum" prison term of at least five years, for specified drug offenses). Where more than the one penalty is authorized, the punishment to be imposed on a given offender is selected by the *judge, following entry of the court's judgment of conviction. In some states, sentences are recommended or selected by the *jury, and death penalties often require jury approval.

The degree of choice allowed to the court or jury depends not only on the applicable criminal law, but also on the sentencing system used in that jurisdiction—in particular, whether the jurisdiction has sentencing guidelines. Most states have no such guidelines; judges have broad discretion to impose any sentence up to the statutory maximum, with little or no appellate review of the sentence imposed. In many of these states, parole boards have equally broad discretion to decide how much of any prison sentence must be served. These discretionary powers are based on the view that the most important goals of punishment are to incapacitate, deter, and (perhaps) rehabilitate offenders, and that these goals require sentences to be tailored to the particular risks and treatment needs of each offender, while also taking into account the seriousness of the offense and the need for deterrence. These assessments are often made with the aid of a presentence report prepared by a probation officer. The judge must first decide whether the offender is amenable to treatment in the community, and whether a jail or prison sentence is needed due to the seriousness of the offense. If the offender is employed or in school or outpatient treatment, a sentence in a local jail may be combined with daytime release. If a prison term is imposed, the parole board will then determine when the offender may be released, given the seriousness of his crime and the degree of danger he would pose if released.

A number of states retain broad sentencing discretion for judges, but have limited or abolished parole release discretion for some or all crimes. In such "truth in sentencing" systems, offenders serve most of any prison term imposed by the court, with only minor reductions allowed as a reward for good conduct in prison.

As noted earlier, highly discretionary sentencing and parole release began to fall out of favor in the 1970s. A number of reforms, including greatly narrowed sentencing ranges, abolition of parole, mandatory minimum prison terms, and sentencing guidelines were proposed as a means of reducing disparities in punishment. In some courts, judges began experimenting with voluntary guidelines.

In 1980, Minnesota became the first jurisdiction to enact statewide, legally binding sentencing guidelines for all felonies, and by the end of the 1990s, the federal courts and about one-third of the states had followed suit. Most guidelines have been written, implemented, and monitored by a full-time sentencing commission. This approach permits sentencing policy to be developed in a comprehensive manner, avoiding inconsistent, ad hoc responses to "the crime of the week," setting priorities in the use of limited correctional resources, and avoiding prison overcrowding by making detailed forecasts of future prison populations (and, if necessary, scaling back some guidelines sentences until adequate prison space can be built).

State and federal guidelines systems are quite varied. Over one-third of the state systems retain parole release discretion and only use guidelines to regulate judicial sentencing decisions. In more than half of the state systems, the recommended sentences are not legally binding (either because the guidelines are voluntary, or because departures from the guidelines are not closely reviewed by appellate courts). Only about half of the guidelines systems regulate the conditions of probation and other nonprison sentences. Almost all state guidelines apply only to felonies, and retain some version of indeterminate sentencing for misdemeanors (see FELONY AND MISDEMEANOR).

Opinions vary as to the desirability and effectiveness of sentencing guidelines. The federal guidelines have been widely criticized by judges, defense lawyers, and academics, whereas state guidelines have generally found broader acceptance. Legally binding guidelines have succeeded in changing sentencing norms and practices, in accordance with the goals of reformers in each system (in federal courts, sending many more white collar and drug offenders to prison; in state systems, imprisoning more violent and fewer property offenders). Evaluations of several state systems have found that sentencing disparities were reduced, but disparities may remain in unregulated charging and plea bargaining practices.

With or without guidelines, the most common punishment imposed for violent felonies is a prison sentence or, less frequently, a jail sentence (about 80 percent of violent offenders receive one or the other). Jail sentences are usually for one year or less; prison terms are often much longer, and the average length of time actually served varies from about three years, for felony assault, to eleven years, for murder. Between 50 and 70 percent of property, drug, weapons, and other felony offenders receive a custody sentence, with prison and jail sentences about equally common; average prison time served for these offenses is one and a half to two years. For misdemeanor crimes, the most common punishments are short jail terms, probation, and fines. Traffic violations are usually punished with a fine and/or loss of driving privileges.

International comparisons are particularly instructive in the field of punishment. Although data limitations and differences in offense definitions make precise comparisons difficult, numerous comparative studies agree that noncustodial sanctions, especially fines and community service, are used much more frequently in other Western countries, particularly for nonviolent crimes. It should also be noted that international *human rights norms impose many limitations on punishment which are not recognized under U.S. state and federal laws (in particular: forbidding capital punishment or adult prosecution for *juvenile offenders; giving all offenders the benefit of post-offense penalty reductions; requiring compensation for unlawful arrest, detention, or miscarriage of justice; viewing treatment and rehabilitation as the essential aim of prisons; and requiring appellate review of sentences).

Punishment Trends and Controversies. The final decades of the twentieth century witnessed a dramatic rise in American prison and jail populations. Between 1980 and 2000, jail populations tripled, and prison populations quadrupled. Much of this increase reflected the effects of the War on Drugs and other increases in law enforcement activity and criminal caseloads. However, adult arrest rates leveled off after 1989, but inmate populations continued to rise—prison populations almost doubled, in the following decade. Through most of the 1980s and 1990s, crime and punishment were important political issues, and elected officials became extremely reluctant to support any policy that an opponent could characterize as "soft on crime." Crime stories in the media also became much more frequent during this period, creating the false impression that crime rates were rising. All of these forces led many states, in the early 1990s, to adopt much more punitive sentencing laws, particularly for violent crimes and repeat offenders.

These massive increases in prison and jail populations are controversial, given their substantial human and social costs, and the lack of demon-

strated crime-control need or effect (crime rates rose and fell between 1980 and 2000, with no discernable relationship to inmate populations). But an even more troubling aspect of these increases was their disproportionate impact on racial and ethnic minorities. For instance, although African Americans make up less than 15 percent of the U.S. population, by the late 1980s they accounted for more prison admissions, and more inmates held in prisons and jails, than whites. At least some of this disproportionality is due, not to racial differences in offending, but rather to law enforcement policies—racial profiling (stopping suspects because of their race), heavy emphasis on street-level drug enforcement, and the disparate impact of pretrial release and sentencing policies which disfavor low-income defendants, many of whom are nonwhite. Another controversial trend is the growing use of measures outside of the criminal law, such as civil forfeitures of property supposedly used or derived from illegal activities, indefinite civil commitment of sex offenders, and lengthy detention and deportation of noncitizens. Although such measures can be very severe, and may even have a significant stigmatizing effect, the Supreme Court has generally viewed them as regulatory or preventive, not "punishment," which means that they do not require proof beyond reasonable doubt and other procedural and substantive safeguards applied to criminal punishments.

[*See also* Electric Chair]

• Jeremy Bentham, *An Introduction to the Principles of Morals and Legislation*, 1789. Herbert L. A. Hart, *Punishment and Responsibility*, 1968. Nigel Walker, *Why Punish?*, 1991. Andrew von Hirsch, *Censure and Sanctions*, 1993. Norval Morris and David J. Rothman, eds, *Oxford History of the Prison*, 1995. Michael Tonry, *Malign Neglect: Race, Crime and Punishment in America*, 1995. Franklin Zimring and Gordon Hawkins, *Incapacitation: Penal Confinement and the Restraint of Crime*, 1995. Michael Tonry, *Sentencing Matters*, 1996. Richard S. Frase, "Sentencing Principles in Theory and Practice," *Crime and Justice: A Review of Research*, (1997): 363–433. U.S. Department of Justice, Bureau of Justice Statistics, *Felony Sentences in State Courts 1996*, 1999. Kent Greenawalt, "Punishment," in *Encyclopedia of Crime and Justice, Revised Edition*, 2001. Michael Tonry and Richard S. Frase, eds., *Sentencing and Sanctions in Western Counties*, 2001.
                                      —Richard S. Frase

CRITICAL LEGAL STUDIES (CLS) is best understood both as a movement in legal thought and as a group of law teachers—identified with Harvard, Wisconsin, Buffalo, and Stanford but also including scholars from many other schools—who are associated with the Conference on Critical Legal Studies. Individuals whose work is often identified with CLS include Richard Abel, C. Edwin Baker, Gary Bellow, James Boyle, Kenneth Casebeer, Jean Charn, Anthony Chase, Clare Dalton, Jay Feinman, Michael Fischl, Alan Freeman, Gerald Frug, Mary Jo Frug, Peter Gabel, Robert Gordon, Thomas Heller, Wythe Holt, Morton Horwitz, Alan Hyde, David Kairys, Al Katz, Mark Kelman, David Kennedy, Duncan Kennedy, Karl Klare, Elizabeth Mensch, Gary Minda, Frances Olsen, Gary Peller, Joel Rogers, Rand Rosenblatt, John Henry Schlegel, William Simon, Joseph Singer, Kathy Stone, David Trubek, Mark Tushnet, and Roberto Unger.

First coming to the attention of legal scholars in the mid-1970s and often seen as a revival of American *legal realism, CLS is better understood as a reaction by the political left to the legal-process *jurisprudence dominant in law schools through the 1970s and to the focus on rights associated with the work of Ronald Dworkin—jurisprudential positions that CLS usually lumped together as "liberal legalism"—as well as to the rise of the *law and economics movement in the late 1960s. CLS scholars drew from an extremely diverse range of intellectual sources, including classic European Marxism, the neo-Marxism of Antonio Gramsci and György Lukács, the existential Marxism of Jean-Paul Sartre, the revived critical theory of Jürgen Habermas and Herbert Marcuse, the structuralism of Claude Levi-Strauss and Ferdinand de Saussure, the post-structuralism of Michel Foucault, the deconstructionism of Jacques Derrida, the anti-foundationalism of Thomas Kuhn and Richard Rorty, and the historical scholarship of E. P. Thompson.

Critical legal studies is best known for four assertions. The first—the indeterminacy thesis—holds that law, as a structure of binary opposites, always allows two opposed conclusions in any significantly litigated case. This binary opposition was often seen as pitting individualistic considerations, the claim of the liberal self to protection from community demands for conformity with its values, against altruistic considerations, the claim of the community to solidarity among its members in the pursuit of its interests. The indeterminacy thesis was offered in opposition to liberal legalism's claim that legal doctrine was determinate and so yielded only one, or one best, answer to any contested proposition.

The second assertion—the critique of rights—holds that, since legal doctrine does not provide determinate answers in contested cases, the choice of individuals to rely on rights for protection from

the actions of others or of the state is based on a false hope, because rights can and will be manipulated in the interest of the dominant forces in a given society. The critique of rights was offered in opposition to liberal legalism's claim that the New Deal and the *civil rights revolution had provided significant protection for the interests of workers and African Americans.

Both assertions were buttressed with research into legal doctrine, contemporary and historical. They were drawn together in the phrase "law is politics," which conveys the idea that the choices always available in legal doctrine make it possible, indeed inevitable, that the results in individual cases will reflect not the neutral application of correct legal "policy" but rather the same range of considerations regularly brought to bear in partisan political dispute. From this understanding came a third assertion—legitimation—which holds that legal doctrine and process, rather than being in opposition to political process, as liberal legalism asserted, are better viewed as a practice of legitimation designed to affirm the inevitability and disinterestedness of partisan choices to favor individual interests, choices that are in fact neither inevitable nor disinterested.

A fourth assertion of CLS was directed not at liberal legalism but at the claim by scholars in the law and economics movement that economic analysis regularly identified the most efficient legal rule—the outcome that secured the maximum of consumer welfare at the lowest possible cost. Here CLS relied on the work of the Columbia law professor Robert Lee Hale (who denied there was anything that could qualify as "the free market") to support two assertions. First, CLS argued that efficiency is not a concept endogenous to law by which legal results could be measured but is simply the set of economic results that the market produces given any particular set of legal rights and any set of initial entitlements. Second, and somewhat contradictorily, CLS argued that the concept of efficiency was no more determinate than any legal concept, so that buried within it were the outcomes purportedly derived from economic analysis.

Critical legal studies brought forth significant negative reaction from within the legal academy. Though some reactions were directed at the accuracy of the scholarship and others at its occasionally polemical tone, most simply reflected hostility to the notion that, given no theoretical difference between law and *politics, law was not directed toward securing a definable public interest. While some of this opposition called for members of the group to leave the legal academy, most centered on the assertion that CLS did not present actual proposals for reform of law and legal institutions. This claim ignored the positive proposals CLS did offer by dismissing them as vague or impractical.

After about fifteen years, critical legal studies died out as a force in legal thought. Several factors contributed to its death. First, most major voices of the CLS movement were opposed to conscious action directed toward building an intellectual program. Second, CLS never succeeded in offering additional insights about law that built on the indeterminacy thesis, the critique of rights, and legitimation. Third, CLS was politically unable to respond to critiques offered by scholars who later created the *feminist law movement and *critical race theory and, in trying to accommodate both, CLS lost its distinctive voice. Finally, as a result of the hostility the group engendered, younger adherents of CLS had some difficulty getting hired and tenured.

[*See also* Jurisprudence, American; Law and Society Movement]

• Roberto Mangabeira Unger, *Knowledge and Politics*, 1975. Alan Freeman, "Legitimating Racial Discrimination through Anti-Discrimination Law," *Minnesota Law Review* 62 (1978): 1049–1119. Duncan Kennedy, "The Structure of Blackstone's Commentaries," *Buffalo Law Review* 28 (1979): 205–382. David Kairys, ed., *The Politics of Law: A Progressive Critique*, 1982. Mark Tushnet, "Critical Legal Studies: A Political History," *Yale Law Journal* 100 (1991): 1515–44. Neil Duxbury, *Patterns of American Jurisprudence*, 1995.

—John Henry Schlegel

CRITICAL RACE THEORY (CRT) is a movement among legal academics and activist lawyers who wish to understand and transform the racial situation in the United States. CRT began in the late 1970s, when astute observers such as Derrick Bell and Alan Freeman realized that the gains of the *civil rights movement had stalled and in many cases were being rolled back. New approaches were needed to come to terms with subtle, institutional, or unconscious racism. Building on the insights of critical legal studies and the work of European writers such as Antonio Gramsci and Jacques Derrida, and drawing from American radical traditions exemplified by Sojourner Truth, Frederick Douglass, W. E. B. Du Bois, Martin Luther King Jr., and Cesar Chavez, critical race theorists began exploring the relationships among *race, racism, knowledge, and power.

The CRT movement, which holds periodic workshops and public conferences, also serves as an umbrella organization for a number of spin-off groups, such as Latino critical scholarship (LatCrit), critical Asian scholarship, and critical race feminism, which hold occasional meetings and publish law review symposia and readers explaining their basic concepts.

Supported by a loosely organized collection of scholars and lawyers, critical race theory features no specific credo or set of tenets that all members would subscribe to. But a number of themes play an important role. First is the belief that race is central, not peripheral, to American thought and life. Second is the notion that racism is common and ordinary rather than rare and episodic, so that a great deal of Americans' social life is affected by it. A third strand is material determinism, or interest convergence—the idea that racial relations maintain a white-over-black/brown hierarchy that provides benefits and profits to elite groups in the majority race and are for that reason difficult to reform. A fourth feature, which critical race theorists hold in common with many social scientists, is the social construction thesis, according to which races are products of social thought and invention, not objective or biologically real. Races are categories that society conjures up, deploys, and retires when convenient. Although humans do of course exhibit minor, heritable physical differences in skin color and hair texture, these constitute only a tiny proportion of our genetic makeup and have little, if anything, to do with higher-order human capabilities such as intelligence, personality, and moral behavior.

A final theme of CRT that is now emerging is the idea of differential racialization, the notion that U.S. society racializes different groups—that is, constructs and treats them in different ways. For African Americans, the formative experience was *slavery and Jim Crow. But other groups are racialized through other means, including perceived foreignness, conquered status, accent and foreign language, and, in some cases, *religion. Because the forms of racialization vary, they give rise to differing media stereotypes and majority-group pressures that change over time. In one era, African Americans are seen as threats to dominant interest groups; the corresponding stereotype may be that of the bestial black who merits segregated housing and schools. In another era, Latinos are seen as sources of necessary farm labor, but as an unassimilable group requiring close supervision and, possibly, deportation.

The reception of critical race theory by the academy and mainstream media was generally favorable in the early years, but recent critical response has been more mixed. While conservative columnists and traditional legal scholars criticize the movement for being overly preoccupied with race and for eschewing hard legal analysis in favor of autobiography and storytelling, other aspects of CRT have been well received. Some judges have begun incorporating CRT themes and ideas into opinions in such areas as racial profiling, hate speech, and hostile environments.

[*See also* Law and Society Movement]

• Richard Delgado and Jean Stefancic, eds., *Critical Race Theory: The Cutting Edge*, 2d ed., 2000. Richard Delgado and Jean Stefancic, *Critical Race Theory: An Introduction*, 2001.   —Richard Delgado and Jean Stefancic

CRUEL AND UNUSUAL PUNISHMENT. In the United States, opposition to the death penalty has traditionally been expressed in several guises. Some have opposed the death penalty in the name of the sanctity of life (Camus and Koestler, 1958). Even the most heinous criminals, so this argument goes, are entitled to be treated with dignity. In this view, there is nothing that anyone can do to forfeit the "right to have rights" (*Furman* v. *Georgia* (1972)) Others have emphasized the moral horror, the "evil," of the state's willfully taking the lives of any of its citizens (Kateb, 1992: 191–92). Still others believe that death as a punishment is always cruel, and, as such, is incompatible with the Eighth Amendment prohibition against cruel and unusual punishment (Bedau, 1987).

Each of these arguments has been associated with, and is an expression of, humanist liberalism or political radicalism. Each represents a frontal assault on the simple and appealing retributivist rationale for *capital punishment. Each has put the opponents of the death penalty on the side of society's most despised and notorious criminals. Thus it is not surprising that while traditional abolitionist arguments have been raised repeatedly in philosophical commentary, political debate, and legal cases, none of them has ever carried the day in the debate about capital punishment in the United States (Zimring and Hawkins, 1986).

In February 1994, Justice Harry Blackmun of the United States Supreme Court announced that "From this day forward I no longer shall tinker with the machinery of death" (*Callins* v. *Collins* (1994)). This dramatic proclamation capped his evolution from long-time supporter of the death penalty to tinkerer with various procedural schemes and devices designed to rationalize death sentences to outright abolitionist. Twenty-two years before his abolitionist announcement, he dissented in *Furman* v. *Georgia*, refusing to join the majority of his colleagues in what he labeled the "legislative" act of finding execution, as then administered, cruel and unusual punishment. Four years after *Furman*, he joined the majority in *Gregg* v. *Georgia* (1976), deciding to reinstate the death penalty in the United States. However, by the time he underwent his abolitionist conversion, Blackmun had left a trail of judicial opinions, moving gradually, but inexorably, away from this early embrace of death as a constitutionally legitimate punishment. As a result, the denunciation of capital punishment that he offered in 1994 was most significant as a moment in the transformation of abolitionist politics and as an example of "the new abolitionism."

Blackmun's abolitionism found its locus neither in liberal humanism nor in radicalism, nor even in the defense of the most indefensible among us. It was, instead, firmly rooted in mainstream legal values of *due process and *equal protection. Blackmun did not reject the death penalty because of its violence, argue against its appropriateness as a response to heinous criminals, or criticize its futility as a tool in the war against crime. Instead, harkening back to *Furman*, as if rewriting his opinion in that case, he focused on the procedures through which death sentences were decided. ". . . [D]espite the efforts of the States and the courts," Blackmun noted, "to devise legal formulas and procedural rules . . . , the death penalty remains fraught with arbitrariness, discrimination, caprice, and mistake. . . . Experience has taught us that the constitutional goal of eliminating arbitrariness and discrimination from the administration of death . . . can never be achieved without compromising an equally essential component of fundamental fairness—individualized sentencing" (*Callins* (1994)).

Two things stand out in Blackmun's argument. First, he acknowledges the law's effort to purge death sentences of any taint of procedural irregularity. As he sees it, the main implication of *Furman* is that a death penalty is constitutional only if it *can be* administered in a manner compatible with the guarantees of due process and equal protection. Here Blackmun moves the debate away from the question of whether capital punishment is cruel or whether it can be reconciled with society's evolving standards of decency. Second, Blackmun identified a constitutional conundrum in which consistency and individualization—the twin commands of the Supreme Court's post-*Furman* death penalty jurisprudence—could not be achieved simultaneously. As a result, Blackmun concluded that "the death penalty cannot be administered in accord with our Constitution." (*Callins* (1994)).

The new abolitionism that Blackmun championed presents itself as a reluctant abolitionism, one rooted in acceptance of the damage that capital punishment does to central legal values and to the legitimacy of the law itself (Sarat, 2001, chapter 10). It finds its home in an embrace, not a critique, of those values. "Rather than continue to coddle the Court's delusion that the desired level of fairness has been achieved...," Blackmun stated, "I feel morally and intellectually obligated simply to concede that the death penalty experiment has failed. It is virtually self-evident to me now that no combination of procedural rules or substantive regulations ever can save the death penalty from its inherent constitutional deficiencies" (*Callins* (1994)).

Blackmun's brand of abolitionism opened an important new avenue for engagement in the political struggle against capital punishment, providing abolitionists a position of political respectability while simultaneously allowing them to change the subject from the legitimacy of execution to the imperatives of due process. The rhetoric that Blackmun made available to opponents of capital punishment enabled them not to respond to the overwhelming political consensus in favor of death as a punishment; they no longer had to take on that consensus frontally. Instead, they could say that the most important issue in the debate about capital punishment is one of fairness, not one of sympathy for murderers; they could position themselves as defenders of law itself.

Just three years to the month after Blackmun's dissent in *Callins*, the *American Bar Association issued a call for a moratorium on executions in the United States (American Bar Association, 1997). Taking us back to *Furman*'s condemnation of the death penalty as "then administered," the ABA proclaimed that the death penalty as "currently administered" is not compatible with central values of our Constitution. Since *Furman*, the effort to produce a constitutionally acceptable death penalty has, in the view of the ABA, been to no avail.

The new abolitionism promoted by Blackmun and the ABA seems to be gaining momentum. While public opinion polls continue to register the support of the overwhelming majority of Americans for capital punishment, growing evidence of failures in the criminal justice system revealed by the increased availability of DNA testing has been particularly consequential in making this new situation possible. This fact has made it possible for politicians seeking to remain in the mainstream to embrace the new abolitionism.

A remarkable moment for the new abolitionism occurred on January 31, 2000, when Governor George Ryan of Illinois, a longtime supporter of capital punishment, announced plans to block all executions in that state by granting stays before any scheduled lethal injections are administered. His act effectively imposed a moratorium on the death penalty, the first time this had been done in any state. Following Ryan's announcement, the United States Department of Justice initiated its own review "to determine whether the federal death penalty system unfairly discriminates against racial minorities." Moreover, legislation was introduced in Congress to lessen the chances of unfairness and deadly error by making DNA testing available to both state and federal inmates, and by setting national standards to ensure that competent lawyers were appointed for capital defendants. Other legislation would suspend all executions at the federal and state levels while a national blue ribbon commission reviewed the administration of the death penalty. In May 2000, the New Hampshire Legislature became the first to vote for repeal of the death penalty in more than two decades. Although this legislation was subsequently vetoed by Governor Jeanne Shaheen, much of its support reflected new abolitionist sentiment. Finally, new and unexpected voices—including such prominent conservatives as the Reverend Pat Robertson and newspaper columnist George Will—have spoken out against what they see as inequality and racial *discrimination in the administration of executions and in favor of a moratorium.

Despite these developments, the new abolitionism is still a very long way from bringing an end to executions. Yet, as United States Senator Russ Feingold of Wisconsin noted, "At the end of 1999, as we enter a new millennium, our society is still far from fully just. The continued use of the death penalty demeans us. The death penalty is at odds with our best traditions.... And it's not just a matter of morality...the continued viability of our justice system as a truly just system requires that we do so" (Feingold, 1999). For Senator Feingold, as for Justice Blackmun, the ABA, Governor Ryan, and others, the rejection of the death penalty takes the form of an effort to prevent the erosion of the boundaries between state violence and its extra-legal counterpart. This recaptures the spirit of *Furman* and perhaps even radicalizes it by suggesting that it may never be possible to reconcile capital punishment with constitutional procedures.

[See also Civil Rights and Civil Liberties; Criminal Law Principles]

• Albert Camus and Arthur Koestler, Reflections on the Guillotine, 1958. Franklin Zimring and Gordon Hawkins, Capital Punishment and the American Agenda, 1986. Hugo Adam Bedau, Death Is Different: Studies in the Morality, Law and Politics of Capital Punishment, 1987. George Kateb, The Inner Ocean: Individualism and Democratic Culture, 1992. American Bar Association, Recommendation 107, ABA House of Delegates, February 3, 1997. Russell Feingold, "Statement Introducing the Federal Death Penalty Abolition Act of 1999," November 10, 1999, http://www.senate.gov/~feingold/issuearea/abolitionbill.html. Austin Sarat, ed., The Killing State: Capital Punishment in Law, Politics, and Culture, 1999. Austin Sarat, When the State Kills: Capital Punishment and the American Condition, 2001.

—Austin Sarat

CULTURE AND LAW. Culture is an elusive concept whose meaning is difficult to define with precision. It can refer to high culture—literature, opera, and ballet—or mass or popular culture—comic books, films, pulp fiction, and television. Another sense of culture commonly employed by anthropologists is traditional culture, which refers to the entire way of life of a particular group. George Peter Murdock's Outline of Cultural Materials, part of the Human Relations Area Files project at Yale University, represents one attempt to delineate all elements of culture. In anthropological jurisprudence, references to culture are frequently allusions to a "way of life." In many cases litigants refer to their cultural background in order to influence judicial decision-making to their advantage.

Because the American legal system reflects the melting pot ideology, or cultural assimilation, American *jurisprudence reveals little effort to accommodate the rights of ethnic or religious minorities by allowing the consideration of their cultural claims in the courtroom. With few exceptions, existing principles such as the right to religious liberty, the right to a fair trial, equal protection, and the right to culture have not been construed to vindicate the rights of these groups.

Historically, when the free exercise of *religion clause of the First Amendment has been interpreted by judges, they have invoked a so-called belief-action distinction, according to which beliefs are absolutely protected, but actions are not. Religiously motivated conduct, for the most part, is not protected under the free exercise clause. This has meant, for example, that Mormons could not practice plural marriage, Pentecostals could not handle snakes during religious ceremonies, and Native Americans could not use peyote in religious ceremonies except under carefully circumscribed conditions. Although U.S. courts have seldom authorized religious practices, the famous exception is Wisconsin v. Yoder (1972), in which the U.S. Supreme Court permitted the Amish to take their children out of school after eighth grade so they would not be exposed to worldly values which it was claimed would undermine the Amish way of life. The Court's unwillingness to extend the logic of this decision to allow other religious exemptions from statutes has led to considerable controversy.

When the government has protected religious communities through law, such as the authorization of a Hasidic Jewish school district or an executive order protecting sacred sites on federal lands, some have argued that policies such as these violate the establishment clause, which has been interpreted to require the separation of church and state. The interpretation of the two religion clauses makes it unlikely that religious liberty can be invoked to ensure adequate consideration of cultural circumstances in U.S. litigation.

The common attitude of American judges that culture is not "relevant" to legal proceedings has created evidentiary obstacles to the consideration of culture. For example, in criminal cases defendants sometimes claim they were provoked to kill by specific gestures or verbal insults which are not comprehensible to mainstream Americans. When they invoke the provocation defense in an attempt to reduce a murder change to manslaughter, they encounter difficulty because they cannot show that what provoked them would have provoked the so-called "objective, reasonable person." Because courts have declined to modify the standard to what the culturally specific reasonable person would do under the circumstances, defendants from other cultural backgrounds usually cannot succeed when they avail themselves of this defense. It has been suggested that the inability of cultural defendants to use the provocation defense when mainstream defendants can do so constitutes a violation of equal protection

Another illustration of the difficulty of bringing cultural evidence into the courtroom occurs during the sentencing phase of a trial, when information might influence a jury to spare a defendant's life. In some cases defendants have not displayed any emotion during sentencing, and juries have interpreted their demeanor as signifying a lack of remorse. American juries generally require a showing of remorse in order not to impose the death penalty. Where the lawyer neglects to explain to juries that individuals in some societies are socialized to have a stoic demeanor even when they are under extreme emotional stress, courts have occasionally held that this constitutes a violation of the Sixth Amendment right: effective assistance of counsel (e.g., *Mak* v. *Blodgett,* 1993). Whether the failure to consider cultural evidence occurs during the guilt or penalty phase, this arguably violates the defendant's right to a fair trial.

Not only crucial to the disposition of criminal cases, culture can also affect the disposition of civil proceedings. In litigation plaintiffs sometimes allege that the emotional distress suffered was greater because of their cultural or religious background. For example, in Spokane, Washington, after a Gypsy household was subjected to an illegal police search, the young unmarried girls in the family were said to be *marime,* or unmarriageable, as a result of being touched by men to whom they were not married. As a consequence, the Gypsies filed a lawsuit requesting forty million dollars in damages. In lawsuits where unauthorized autopsies are performed, members of religious minorities opposed to postmortem operations also argue for larger damage awards in light of their religious worldviews.

No matter what type of litigation, there will be problems of proof. Courts have to ensure the veracity of cultural claims presented, as claims can be spurious. Indeed, in the absence of any formal policy guidelines including uniform, patterned jury instructions, it is exceedingly difficult for judges to guarantee the validity of the information introduced in court. The ascertainment of customs supposedly involved in the case can be a nearly insuperable problem.

Even assuming a standard procedure existed by which to evaluate cultural claims, there would be still be the question of who is the appropriate person to speak on behalf of the group. Although expert witnesses are often asked to testify about the cultural tradition at issue, this may be offensive to members of the group who could explain the significance of the practice at least as well as experts. Not only is there the issue of whose voice should be heard in the courtroom, but there is the possibility that the custom may be contested. Insofar as some members of the group want to discard a tradition, it may well be dangerous to presume unanimous support for the practice. Assuming that the court overcomes the problems of proof and that the tradition is established, the court may be disinclined to protect it if the court

cannot be persuaded that it is central to the way of life. This centrality criterion is found in decisions concerning the protection of endangered species and of sacred sites.

Cultural autonomy is important to certain communities. Sometimes cultural communities, such as Orthodox Jews, the Hmong, and others, prefer to resolve disputes within their own traditional dispute resolution mechanisms. Although not known to most Americans, separate courts exist throughout the United States for this purpose, such as the *kris* of the Gypsies. A question that sometimes arises is whether U.S. courts should exercise jurisdiction over these legal orders. On occasion the U.S. Supreme Court has declined to consider issues regarded as more properly settled in other courts. For example, in *Santa Clara Pueblo* v. *Martinez* (1977), a case involving whether or not a challenge to a Pueblo ordinance that denied tribal membership to children of female members who married outside the tribe on the grounds that it violated the Indian Civil Rights Act of 1968, Justice Thurgood *Marshall held that federal courts lacked jurisdiction—the matter was best decided in tribal courts (see NATIVE AMERICANS AND THE LAW).

If the legal system takes account of diverse cultural groups, who will decide which groups deserve protection? Some worry that subcultures such as gangs, right-wing groups, and others would be entitled to seek a reduction in punishment based on their codes of conduct. With respect to subcultures, there is little reason to think that the approach will become widely used or that juries would accept the argument. A similar strategy, the "rotten social background defense" championed by Judge Bazelon, was attempted in the 1970s but won few supporters.

Because the U.S. has ratified the International Covenant on Civil and Political Rights, which guarantees the right to culture in Article 27, courts are, at least in principle, obligated to take cultural considerations into account. Unfortunately, most American law schools have yet to acknowledge the complex realities of American legal experience, including the existence of multiple legal systems, known as legal pluralism. If they were to expose students to the cultural forces that influence legal processes, their students would be better prepared for the practice of law. In the twenty-first century the vindication of fundamental principles of law as they relate to ethnic minority groups will become increasingly important.

[*See also* Anthropology and Law; Arts, Popular Culture, and Law; Race and Ethnicity]

• Richard Delgado, "'Rotten Social Background': Should the Criminal Law Recognize a Defense of Severe Environmental Deprivation," *Law & Inequality: A Journal of Theory and Practice* 3 (1985): 9–90. Edwin Brown Firmage and Richard Collin Mangrum, *Zion in the Courts; A Legal History of the Church of Jesus Christ of Latter-day Saints, 1830–1900,* 1988. Judith Resnik, "Dependent Sovereigns: Indian Tribes, States, and the Federal Courts," *University of Chicago Law Review* 56 (1989): 671–759. Omer C. Stewart, "Peyote and the Law," in *Handbook of American Indian Religious Freedom* (Christopher Vecsey, ed.), 1991. Carlos Villarreal, "Culture in Law Making: A Chicano Perspective," *University of California Davis Law Review* 24 (1991): 1193–1242. Walter Otto Weyrauch and Maureen Anne Bell, "Autonomous Lawmaking: The Case of the 'Gypsies'," *Yale Law Journal* 103 (1993): 323–99. Alison Dundes Renteln, "Raising Cultural Defenses," *Cultural Issues in Criminal Law*, James G. Connell III and Rene L. Valladares, eds., 2000.   —Alison Dundes Renteln

CUSTOM. Custom refers to patterns of behavior that come to be expected of or by a group. Although many terms are used as synonyms for custom, including culture, tradition, and usage, there may be subtle differences in meaning among them. Anthropologists such as Ruth Benedict and Edward Sapir consider culture to be a more "scientific" term for custom. A custom that has existed for a long period of time is a tradition; hence a tradition is an older sort of custom. Other terms are so similar to custom that one finds them used interchangeably with it. Rather than considering custom a synonym for culture, it might be better it to consider custom one component of the totality of culture.

Anthropologists often use the term custom in connection with patterns of behavior tied to belief systems. For example, Ruth Benedict, in her essay "The Science of Custom," analyzed the concept emphasizing the experiential aspect: "... [t]raditional custom is a mass of detailed behavior." Individuals are socialized to believe that they should follow customs.

Various misconceptions exist about the degree to which customs are accepted by any social group. Some theorists assume without empirical demonstration that customs are more important to "primitive" groups than to "modern" societies. It may be that members of "advanced" societies "... resisted the implication that their culture belonged to a series that included the customs of lesser people" or simply do not see the lens through which they look (Benedict). Moreover, in more "complex" social systems, customs may not be followed by all segments of the society.

A debate has raged over how to distinguish law from custom. One famous attempt to solve this analytic problem is Paul Bohannan's theory of law as the "double institutionalization" of custom. According to his analysis, custom is a social institution, and when a social institution is deemed important enough to be designated as law, the custom is "double-institutionalized," although the process by which this occurs is not delineated. Ordinarily, the notion that custom is different from law hinges on the legal positivist assumption that law is written and custom is unwritten. But if one accepts the proposition that unwritten norms can be legally binding, a proposition which is relatively uncontroversial considering how much of the world follows the *common law tradition, this distinction is rendered meaningless. Because of the intellectual confusion over how to distinguish between law and custom, the term customary law is inadvisable. For this reason, some prefer to use "folk law."

Examples of American folk law include sayings such as "Finders keepers, losers weepers" and "First come, first served." They are customs which affect social life, though they appear not to have the force of law. Such customs can be contrasted with legal proverbs that are incorporated into judicial decisions, which makes them part of the corpus of the common law. For instance, "A man's home is his castle" or the "castle doctrine" has been cited in landmark constitutional cases.

Attempts to codify important customary norms merit consideration. One scholarly project exemplifying this practice is the Restatement of African Customary Law undertaken by Anthony Allott and his colleagues at the School of Oriental and African Studies of the University of London. This effort, as well as other academic works such as treatises that sought to record folk law, have been subject to the criticism that their interpretations of customary principles contained a colonial bias. Moreover, although the rationale for the ascertainment endeavor was that African customary laws were disappearing, it was unclear for whose benefit these initiatives were made, as the Africans already knew what their legal standards were. A further concern was that writing down the norms would "freeze" them in time, thereby limiting their ability to evolve. This was regarded as a problem by some because the dynamic nature of folk law has always been considered one of its principal advantages over positive law.

Also worthy of note are legislative efforts, of which the most significant are found in ancient law. The desire for certainty in legal standards led to many codes incorporating customary law norms, such as the Assyrian Code of Hammurabi, the Greek Codes of Draco and Solon, the Twelve Tables of Rome, Justinian's Code, and the Napoleonic Code. The codes reflected customs existing during their respective eras. Sometimes legislation was enacted in order to change custom. For instance, provisions in colonial legal systems known as "repugnancy clauses" prohibited customs deemed "repugnant to natural justice." Examples of customs to which these clauses were applied include female circumcision, polygamy, suttee, and witchcraft. The effort to discourage custom through statutes generally met with limited success.

In the late twentieth century, ethnic minority customs were sometimes misinterpreted as crimes and those following traditions were subject to prosecution. For example, Vietnamese refugees rely on a form of folk medicine known as "coining" or "cao gio" to cure the flu and other types of physical ailments. The coin massage leaves bruises that appear to the untrained eye as child abuse.

Some groups' own customs can at times be problematic. As customs sometimes fall into disfavor, political campaigns emerge to mobilize opposition to them, such as the move to ban female genital cutting in Africa, Europe, and North America.

Custom is one of the major sources of law and the basis for many of the leading cases in international law. An indicatioin of its importance as a source is the fact that it is mentioned in the Statute of the International Court of Justice. Although it often takes time to establish new rules of customary law, customary international law has emerged quickly in such fields as international environmental law, international human rights law, and the law governing outer space.

Although definitional difficulties plague the analysis of custom and although its status as law is debatable, there is no question that custom influences American jurisprudence and legal systems across the globe.

[See also Anthropology and Law; Codification]

• Ruth Benedict, "The Science of Custom," The Century Magazine 117/6 (1929): 641–49. Edward Sapir, "Custom," in Encyclopedia of the Social Sciences, Vol. 4, 1931. Ake Hultkrantz, General Ethnological Concepts, 1960. Paul Bohannan, "The Differing Realms of the Law," in Law and Warfare (Paul Bohannan, ed.), 1967. Donald R. Kelley, " 'Second Nature': The Idea of Custom in European Law, Society and Culture," in The Transmission of Culture in Early Modern Europe (Anthony Grafton and Ann Blair, eds.), (1990): 131–72. E. P. Thompson, Customs in Common, 1991. Alison Dundes Renteln and Alan Dundes, eds., Folk Law: Essays on the Theory and Practice of Lex Non Scripta, 1995.

—Alison Dundes Renteln

CUSTOMARY LAW. *See* Legal Systems.

CYBERSPACE REGULATION. *See* Technology and Law.

D

DAMAGES. Money damages are an attempt to compensate the plaintiff for harm suffered. The types and measure of damages vary according to the nature of the claim, and may include pecuniary (loss of income, medical expenses), nonpecuniary (pain and suffering), and punitive (to deter wrongful conduct) damages.

[*See also* Remedies]   —David S. Clark

DARROW, CLARENCE (1857–1938). Clarence Darrow was a criminal defense lawyer, orator, and author born into a working-class family in tiny Kinsman, Ohio in 1857. He grew up in the traditions of nineteenth-century rationalism as propounded by his father, Amirus Darrow, a college-educated craftsman, and mother, Emily Eddy, a bookish homemaker. Darrow attended local public schools, Allegheny College, and one year at University of Michigan Law School before reading law and joining the Ohio bar in 1878. He practiced in Ashtabula County, Ohio, for nine years until he was inspired by reading a scathing critique of the criminal justice system by Chicago jurist John Peter Altgeld. Bored by small-town practice and leaving his wife and young child behind, Darrow moved to Chicago in 1887 to work with Altgeld.

Darrow threw himself into the life of the city and, with Altgeld's support, flourished there. He held a succession of public and private posts that left him free to promote radical political and social causes. He found his voice as a public speaker and his identity in opposing governmental and religious limits on individual freedom. He built a national reputation as a lawyer in defending American Railway Union president Eugene Debs against criminal charges growing out of the famed Pullman strike in 1894, but was upset in a race for Congress two years later. His family joined him in Chicago, but the marriage soon failed. Darrow later married journalist Ruby Hamerstrom.

From 1898 to 1911, Darrow devoted himself to defending organized labor in a series of criminal cases throughout the United States, such as his 1908 defense of Western Federation of Miners leader Big Bill Haywood, accused of murdering Idaho's governor. This phase of Darrow's career ended in 1911, with his defense of two Los Angeles union officials who killed twenty-two people in a strike-related bombing. Labor had lionized the defendants until Darrow plead them guilty, then turned on both them and their lawyer. Further harming his reputation, Darrow was charged with jury tampering in the case, a charge that recent scholarship supports. After two trials, the prosecution ended with a hung jury.

Returning to Chicago in 1913, Darrow slowly rebuilt his legal practice with high-paying criminal cases and high-visibility cause lawyering. He was again America's most famous criminal lawyer by the 1920s, when in a succession of sensational trials he defended the wealthy teenage murderers Nathan *Leopold and Richard Loeb (1924), John *Scopes for teaching evolution in Tennessee (1925), and the Sweet brothers for murder in the protection of their home from a racist Detroit mob (1926). Lawyers particularly admired his innovative techniques of selecting jurors, interrogating hostile witnesses, and making closing arguments. He also mastered a realist style of public speaking and writing that was widely imitated. Growing ever more skeptical of governmental power, he concluded his public career as a critic of New Deal programs during the 1930s. He died an invalid in his rented Chicago apartment in 1938.

[*See also* Criminal Law Practice; Lawyers; Lawyers, Popular Perceptions of]

• Kevin Tierney, *Darrow: A Biography*, 1979. Arthur Weinberg and Lila Weinberg, *Clarence Darrow: A Sentimental Rebel*, 1980.   —Edward J. Larson

DAVIS, JOHN W. (1873–1955), lawyer, was born in Clarksburg, West Virginia, the son of Anna

Kennedy Davis and John James Davis, a former Congressmen. John W. graduated from college (1892) and law school (1895) at Washington and Lee University; practiced law in West Virginia, representing mining and railroad interests; and served in Congress (1911–13) but left when, in his second term, he successfully prosecuted Judge Robert W. Archbald. He then became *solicitor general, arguing a number of important U.S. Supreme Court cases, successfully opposing the use of the "grandfather clause" to prevent blacks from *voting in Oklahoma in *Guinn* v. *U.S.* (1915), and unsuccessfully defending the federal ban on child labor in *Hammer* v. *Dagenhart* (1917). In 1918 Wilson appointed him ambassador to Great Britain. In 1921 he returned to the United States, where he became the named partner in Davis, Polk, Wardwell, an elite Wall Street firm, representing many of the richest and most powerful companies in the United States. He was elected president of the *American Bar Association in 1922, but declined to be considered for the U.S. Supreme Court. In 1924 he was the Democratic nominee for president. For the rest of his career Davis remained in private practice, where he was considered a "lawyer's lawyer." He won the *Steel Seizure Case* in 1952, his most important victory since leaving government service. In 1954 he represented South Carolina before the U.S. Supreme Court in *Brown* v. *Board of Education*. There he argued for the constitutionality of *segregation. Davis took this case without fee, thus ending his career arguing against civil rights, fundamental justice, and racial fairness.

[*See also* Corporate Law Practice; Lawyers]

• William H. Harbough, *Lawyer's Lawyer: The Life of John W. Davis,* 1973.   —Paul Finkelman

DEATH PENALTY. *See* Capital Punishment.

DEBTOR AND CREDITOR. In law, "debt" usually means a monetary obligation. If a debt is unpaid when due, the creditor may elect to use legal processes to enforce payment. Unless a debtor is bankrupt and subject to federal *bankruptcy jurisdiction, state law governs debt collection. This law derives from English *common law adopted at the time of colonization or statehood and further developed by judicial decision and legislation. One of the most notable reforms was the abolition of imprisonment for debt during the nineteenth century.

A creditor often can obtain payment of an overdue debt by demand or *negotiation. However, if informal collection is ineffective, payment is enforceable by legal procedures. This is expensive and not always successful. The process of debt enforcement depends on whether the debt is "secured" or "unsecured." Security gives the creditor important advantages in collecting payment.

Secured Debt. A debt is secured if the creditor's monetary claim is reinforced by an interest (generically termed a "lien") in property of the debtor ("collateral"), entitling the creditor to sell or keep the property to satisfy the debt upon the debtor's default. A lien may be created by *contract, such as a mortgage on real *property, or a consensual security interest in personal property (goods and other movable things) or intangible rights. A lien may also be created by law without the debtor's consent—for example, if the creditor has repaired or improved the property. To make the lien effective against third parties, the lienholder must perform an act of validation (called "perfection"), typically by filing the lien in public records or by taking possession of the collateral.

If the debtor fails to pay the debt when due, the lien can be enforced by foreclosure. The creditor seizes and sells the property, applying the proceeds to payment of the debt; more rarely, the creditor is permitted to keep the property in settlement of the debt. In qualified circumstances, the creditor is allowed to foreclose by taking control of the property on its own, without a court order ("self-help"), but a judicial foreclosure decree is usually required. If property is subject to more than one lien, they are satisfied in order of priority, usually based on the chronological sequence of perfection. If the proceeds of the collateral are insufficient to satisfy a lien, the unpaid balance of the debt ("deficiency") is unsecured. In some types of lien, any deficiency is forfeited.

Unsecured Debt. The enforcement of delinquent unsecured debt is by suit, judgment, and execution. If the debtor does not defend the suit, the creditor may obtain judgment by default. In qualifying cases, the creditor may be able to obtain a provisional seizure of property before judgment. Such prejudgment *remedies (e.g., *attachment—the court-authorized prejudgment seizure of property of the defendant) place the property in the custody of a court official, usually the sheriff, pending judgment. The seizure creates a lien on the property to secure the ultimate judgment. Because prejudgment remedies deprive the debtor of the power to use or dispose of his property before final adjudication on the claim, they are subject to rigorous safeguards. They are available only in selected circumstances; the creditor must establish grounds for the remedy; the debtor has due process rights to pre-seizure notice and a hearing; and the creditor must post a bond to assure the debtor's compensation if judgment is not ultimately obtained.

Irrespective of any provisional remedy, after judgment is granted a writ is issued and delivered to the *sheriff. Writs of execution are founded on the ancient writs of *fieri facias* for personal property and *elegit* for real property. The sheriff levies the writ by physical seizure of personal property or by recording the writ against the title to real property. If there was prejudgment levy, that property is now subjected to execution. In the absence of prejudgment levy, property of the debtor must be found. Levied property is sold at public auction and the proceeds applied to the debt. If they are insufficient, additional writs may be issued.

*"Garnishment" is a form of execution used when the property is an intangible right of the debtor (e.g., an employer's debt to the debtor for wages earned) or is tangible property of the debtor in the possession of a third party. The writ of garnishment orders the third party to pay the debt into court or to deliver the property to the sheriff for sale.

"Judicial liens" arise in property subjected to the enforcement process. Recording of the judgment in the real estate registry creates a judgment lien on all the debtor's real property in that locality. The levy of attachment, execution, or garnishment creates a lien on the levied property.

Successful execution depends on finding executable property. Even if none exists at the first attempt, the judgment remains effective for a period of years (as determined by state statute), and future execution may be possible. As an aid to execution, the creditor may examine the debtor in court to ascertain the existence or whereabouts of property. If the debtor has transferred property fraudulently to insulate it from execution, the creditor can sue to avoid the transfer. However, if the debtor has no assets and never acquires any, the judgment is uncollectable. Even if the debtor has assets, some or all may be exempt from execution. Exemption statutes, traceable to early common law, permit an individual debtor (not a corporation) to claim exemptions in specified property, usually of limited value. Exemptions aim to protect the debtor from penury and shelter property to the extent deemed vital for the debtor's basic sustenance.

Insolvency Procedures. State law provides some means for a financially troubled debtor to avert execution through the collective management and settlement of debt. A "composition and extension" is a contract between the debtor and creditors to reduce and extend the payment of debts. Creditors may be motivated to enter such an agreement to prevent a race for assets and to allow for even-handed claim treatment. Alternatively, a debtor who desires orderly liquidation may transfer all executable property in trust to an assignee for the benefit of creditors, for realization and distribution to creditors. Although these collective procedures have some similarity to bankruptcy, they are less formal, depend on creditor cooperation, and do not assure the debtor's release from unpaid debt balances. For most debtors, bankruptcy is a more effective means of settling overwhelming debt.

If the debtor becomes bankrupt, federal bankruptcy law preempts state debt-collection law. Bankruptcy stays the enforcement of claims under state law and overturns payments and liens obtained by a creditor in the period (in most cases, ninety days) immediately preceding the bankruptcy filing.

[*See also* Commercial Law; Contract Law; Garnishment]

• Stefan A. Reisenfeld, "Enforcement of Money Judgments in Early American History," *Michigan Law Review* 71 (1973): 691–728. Jay Cohen, "The History of Imprisonment for Debt and Its Relation to the Development of Discharge in Bankruptcy," *Journal of Legal History* 3 (1982): 152–69. Brian Anthony Blum, *Bankruptcy and Debtor/Creditor: Examples and Explanations*, 2d ed., 1999. William L. Norton III and Roger G. Jones, *Norton Creditors' Rights Handbook*, 1999.

—Brian A. Blum

DECLARATION OF WAR. *See* War, Law of.

DECLARATORY JUDGMENT. *See* Judgments.

DEFAMATION. *See* Torts.

DEFAULT JUDGMENT. *See* Judgments.

DELEGATION DOCTRINE. *See* Regulation.

DELINQUENCY, JUVENILE. *See* Courts, United States: Juvenile Courts; Juvenile Law.

DEMOGRAPHICS OF THE BAR. *See* Lawyers.

DEMONSTRATIONS. *See* Civil Disobedience.

DENNIS, EUGENE, TRIAL OF. The 1949 trial of Dennis and other top leaders of the Communist Party of the United States of America (CPUSA) led to a decision by the U.S. Supreme Court that significantly reduced the extent to which the First Amendment protected dissident political expression. The defendants were charged with violation of the Smith Act, a *sedition statute that proscribed conspiring to teach and advocate the violent overthrow of the government and setting up an organization to do so. They had allegedly violated that law by reconstituting the CPUSA (which had dissolved briefly during World War II) in order to promote Marxism-Leninism. Those indicted on that charge in 1948 were the members of the Party's National Board, headed by its National Secretary, William Z. Foster. Originally known as *United States* v. *Foster,* the case was restyled *United States* v. *Dennis* (for General Secretary Eugene Dennis) after Foster was severed prior to trial because of heart trouble.

The indictment of the *Dennis* defendants was a political byproduct of the Cold War. Although the target of those who secured enactment of the Smith Act in 1940, the CPUSA avoided prosecution during World War II because the United States and the Soviet Union were allies. When relations between the two countries later deteriorated into a tense confrontation, President Harry Truman sought to rally support for his anti-Soviet policies by characterizing the enemy as "communism." That rendered his Democratic administration vulnerable to Republican attacks based on its alleged failure to combat Communists at home. To counter such allegations, in February 1948 Attorney General Tom Clark moved against the CPUSA with the Smith Act. The FBI, which wanted such a prosecution to educate the public about the menace of communism, had already collected and summarized much of the evidence needed to bring it.

The result was a nine-month trial in New York. Both sides exploited this proceeding for propaganda purposes. Rather than presenting much evidence against the defendants, prosecutors concentrated on building a case against the Communist party. Implementing the "labor defense" strategy it had long advocated, the CPUSA filed motions and presented evidence intended to present itself in a positive light while discrediting American society and government. The trial ended in October 1949 with the conviction of all defendants. Judge Harold Medina sentenced them to prison and also jailed their lawyers (along with Dennis, who had acted as his own attorney) for *contempt because of their conduct during the trial.

The Court of Appeals for the Second Circuit and the U.S. Supreme Court upheld both the convictions and the contempt citations. Both courts rejected the contention that the Smith Act violated the First Amendment. Under existing doctrine, *speech could be punished only if it created a "clear and present danger" of some serious substantive evil. The government had presented no evidence that Communist teaching was about to lead to revolutionary action, so in order to uphold the convictions, Judge Learned *Hand of the Court of Appeals had to modify this rule. He held that the more grave the evil, the less likely it had to be that it would actually occur. The Supreme Court adopted Hand's new "grave and probable danger" test.

[*See also* Civil Rights and Civil Liberties]

• Michal R. Belknap, *Cold War Political Justice: The Smith Act, the Communist Party and American Civil Liberties,* 1977. Peter L. Steinberg, *The Great "Red Menace": United States Prosecution of American Communists, 1947–1952,* 1984.
—Michal R. Belknap

DETECTIVE. The detective profession has two branches in the United States. One branch consists of special plainclothes officers in federal, state, and especially local law enforcement agencies. These officers investigate and gather evidence in criminal matters. The second branch consists of private operatives, many of whom previously worked as either policemen or detectives in public agencies. These detectives sometimes call themselves "private investigators," and they charge their clients a fee to investigate civil or criminal matters.

The public branch of the profession originated in the West in the seventeenth century. In France Cardinal Mazarin, the king's chief minister, hired one hundred "exempts" in 1645. Leaders of the French Revolution abolished the detective force, but Napoleon created a new force. France's most famous detective of the early nineteenth century was François Vidocq, a former convict who asserted that it took a thief to catch a thief. England was more leery of state detectives than France, but during the Elizabethan period and later any citizen could become a self-styled "thief-taker." Such persons apprehended criminals and recovered stolen property in return for rewards and a percentage of the property. London established a detective unit in its *police force in 1842, but did not acknowledge it until 1878.

The United States shared some of the British leeriness of detectives, but after consolidated urban police forces emerged in the middle of the nineteenth century, those forces quickly came to include detective units. Heads of some detective units, such as New York City's Thomas Byrnes, achieved great prominence, and in the 1890s a police department's top detective was sometimes second in command to the chief of police. In 1924 the *Federal Bureau of Investigation (established in 1908 as the Bureau of Investigation) became a detective force on the national level, and detectives have remained important components in state and local law enforcement.

Uniformed police often seek promotion to detective—but enjoying their plainclothes, higher salaries, and degree of autonomy within the paramilitary organization of police departments, few detectives long for their days in the uniformed ranks. In the larger police departments, precincts may have their own detectives, but detectives more commonly work in detective divisions or in special units addressing *arson, consumer fraud, *homicide, *organized crime, or vice.

Vice squad detectives investigate prostitution, *gambling, and illegal *drugs. This work unfortunately invites bribery and extortion, and during the final decades of the twentieth century investigators, some of whom were themselves detectives, exposed rampant corruption among vice squad detectives in New York, Chicago, Los Angeles, and other cities.

While these scandals suggest intrigue and excitement, detective work can also be tedious. While detectives do in fact search crime scenes, gather evidence, and interview witnesses and suspects, a Rand Institute study found that only 7 percent of detectives' time is devoted to identifying and finding criminals. Writing detailed investigation reports for prosecutors and others may be the most important part of contemporary public detective work.

Private detectives have operated in the United States since the beginning of the Republic. Business proprietors and the well-to-do turned to detectives primarily to recover stolen property. These "private police," as they were sometimes known, cultivated contacts with thieves, pawnbrokers, and others and frequently employed the roughest of methods. By the 1840s private detectives' advertisements were common in assorted newspapers and journals, most notably the *National Police Gazette*. In New York City dozens of detectives had offices on Broadway, with some specializing in the investigation and, on occasion, fabrication of domestic infidelity.

In the final decades of the nineteenth century private detectives also investigated bank and train robberies and infiltrated labor organizations. Jurisdictional restrictions and the nascent state of federal investigation gave the larger agencies veritable control of interstate matters. The Pinkerton National Detective Agency, the largest national concern, counted the Jewelers' Union and American Bankers' Association as clients and also guarded property and replacement workers during strikes. The agency distributed wanted posters, developed the world's largest rogues' gallery, and convinced the International Association of Police Chiefs to pool criminal photographs. When detectives in the profession's private branch labeled themselves, they invoked the Pinkerton trademark and went as "private eyes."

Small local detective agencies and national concerns continue to thrive today. The widespread acceptance of no-fault *divorce deprived private detectives of one source of income, but they have found many new sources: pre-employment screening, workplace surveillance, missing persons searches, *child custody contests, and asset checks in conjunction with prenuptial negotiations. So-called "private investigators" also sometimes combine investigations for a fee with polygraph services, debt collection, repossession, and insurance adjustment.

Detective novels, Hollywood movies, and prime-time television have perhaps unduly romanticized the often tedious work of public and private detectives. Detectives "solve" only a small percentage of American crimes. But detectives continue to provide important services in a materialistic and often morally conflicted society.

[*See also* Criminal Law; Police]

• Jurgen Thorwald, *The Century of the Detective*, 1965. V. A. Leonard, *The Police Detective Function*, 1970. Richard V. Ericson, *Making Crime; A Study of Detective Work*, 1981. Frank Morn, *"The Eye that Never Sleeps": A History of the Pinkerton National Detective Agency*, 1982. Jan Chaiken, Peter Greenwood, and Joan Petersilia, eds., *Thinking About Police*, 1983. William Parkhurst, *True Detectives: The Real World of Today's P.I.*, 1989.
—David Ray Papke

DETECTIVE NOVEL. *See* Literature and Law.

DEVELOPMENT. *See* Environmental Law; Property Rights; Takings; Zoning.

DIMINISHED CAPACITY. *See* Criminal Law Principles: Defense Principles.

DIRECTORS, CORPORATE. *See* Corporation.

DISABILITIES LAW. Although the federal Rehabilitation Act addressed disability *discrimination as early as 1973, it did so in a very limited fashion, essentially reaching only federal employment, federal programs, and government contracts. It was not until the passage of the Americans with Disabilities Act of 1990 that a comprehensive national policy dealing with discrimination against those with disabilities emerged. The ADA, coupled with the Rehabilitation Act and analog state legislation, provides a comprehensive approach to dealing with disability discrimination.

The centerpiece of any discrimination legislation is employment discrimination, and Title I prohibits most employers from discriminating against qualified individuals with disabilities. Title II also prohibits disability discrimination in public services (although the Eleventh Amendment bars *all* private ADA suits against state governments). Title III prohibits discrimination in public accommodations.

Protecting individuals with disabilities from discrimination in employment poses difficult practical and legal problems. The primary practical difficulty is the scope and severity of discrimination on the basis of disability. In passing the ADA, Congress recognized "staggering levels of unemployment and poverty" among individuals with disabilities. A House committee report concluded that "Two-thirds of all disabled Americans between the age of 16 and 64 are not working at all; yet, a large majority of those not working say that they want to work" (1990). Congress also relied on an earlier report of the U.S. Commission on Civil Rights, which concluded that "only in a tiny percentage of cases is inability to perform a regular, full-time job the reason a handicapped person is not employed." Further, "The majority of unemployed handicapped people, if given the chance, are quite capable of taking their places in the job market" (1983).

The legal problems associated with ending disability discrimination result primarily from the fact that disabilities are sometimes relevant to an individual's ability to work. Some disabilities deprive people of the physical and/or mental prerequisites to perform essential job functions. Prohibiting "discrimination" against such individuals would unduly interfere with employers' selection of a qualified work force. Other disabled individuals may be qualified to work, but only if the employer "accommodates" their disability in some way. These individuals, unlike most other statutorily protected groups, require some form of accommodation—different treatment—in order to enjoy equal access to employment opportunities.

The ADA deals with the disability discrimination in two conflicting ways. First, while it generally prohibits disability discrimination, it broadens the defenses available to employers as compared with other antidiscrimination statutes. Employers are permitted to engage in disparate treatment on the basis of disability if the disabled employee is unable to perform the essential functions of the job. Second, to counterbalance this, disabled individuals have rights beyond those granted to other groups protected by antidiscrimination legislation. The centerpiece of disability discrimination law is the employer's duty to provide "reasonable accommodation" to ensure that individuals with disabilities secure equal employment opportunities. The focus of the duty to accommodate is on equal employment opportunity, rather than equal treatment. However, since accommodation can be costly for employers, the ADA includes an "undue hardship" defense, making cost an express statutory limitation on the duty to accommodate.

As a result, employers are legally obligated to treat covered employees equally or differently than nondisabled workers depending on the circumstances: employers *must treat individuals with disabilities equally* if they are qualified and their disabilities do not require accommodation; employers are *permitted to treat such individuals differently* if their disabilities cannot be accommodated; and employers *are required to treat such individuals differently* if reasonable accommodations are necessary to ensure equal employment opportunity.

These principles are applied in a deceptively simple way. Title I of the ADA prohibits discrimination against a "*qualified individual with a disability*." In contrast to other statutes prohibiting discrimination in employment, the threshold of membership in the ADA's protected classification is often the most difficult part of any disability discrimination question. To claim protection under the ADA, a person must first be an "individual with a disability." The statute defines "disability" as

1. a physical or mental impairment that substantially limits one or more of the major life activities of . . . [an] individual;
2. a record of such an impairment; or
3. being regarded as having such an impairment.

However, other sections expressly exclude certain conditions from this definition, including *homosexuality, pedophilia, compulsive *gambling, kleptomania, and disorders resulting from the current illegal use of psychoactive *drugs. The statute does, however, protect alcoholics and those who are addicted to drugs but not a person "who is currently engaging in the illegal use of drugs." Governing administrative agency regulations broadly define the terms "physical or mental impairment" and "major life activities." An individual is substantially limited if totally or significantly restricted in her ability to perform major life activities in comparison with "the average person in the general population" (2001). Further, an individual who has a "record" of a physical or mental impairment that substantially limits a major life activity is within the statute even if that person does not currently have such an impairment or was previously misclassified as having such an impairment. Finally, a person is protected if an employer regards her as having a disability, even if she is not in fact disabled.

For example, the U.S. Supreme Court has held that a person with tuberculosis is disabled (1987), as is a person who is HIV-positive (*Bragdon v. Abbott* (1998)). However, serious impairments are not necessarily disabilities. Individuals with impairments that can be controlled or corrected by medication or other ameliorative measures are not disabled within the meaning of the statute (*Sutton v. United Air Lines, Inc.* (1999)). Further, a person may not be disabled if a particular employer excludes her because of a physical condition, but most jobs remain open to her. Such a person is not "substantially limited" in "a major life activity" merely by being excluded from a narrow range of jobs. Finally, temporary impairments are not viewed as disabilities: the person who is fired because a skiing injury incapacitates him for a month or two has no claim (*Sanders v. Arneson Prods. Inc.* (9th Cir. 1996), (three-and-a-half-month impairment with minimal residual effects not substantially limiting; and 1997 "temporary, non-chronic impairments of short duration, with little or no long term or permanent impact, are usually not disabilities").

Even if a person is "disabled" within the meaning of the statute, the ADA does not prohibit discrimination against him unless he is a "*qualified* individual with a disability." In this context, "qualified" means a person who, "with or without reasonable accommodation, can perform the essential functions of the employment position that such individual holds or desires."

Thus, determining an individual has a disability is only the first step in the analysis. *Arline*, for example, found that the plaintiff's tuberculosis was a disability but remanded to determine if that condition posed a health threat to her students. If so, she would not be a qualified individual with a disability. The ADA explicitly provides that an employer may adopt standards requiring that "an individual shall not pose a direct threat to the health

or safety of other individuals in the workplace." Direct threat is defined by §101(3) as a "significant risk to the health or safety of others" that cannot be eliminated by a reasonable accommodation.

Determining whether a person is "qualified" is obviously highly contextual, and turns on the functions of the job, the condition of the plaintiff, and the availability and cost of accommodations. In *Southeastern Community College* v. *Davis* (1979), the Court held that a business does not have to change its fundamental operation in order to accommodate an individual with a disability. Numeous disability cases turn on what counts as the essential function of the job. For example, courts have held that regular and timely attendance at work is an essential job function and, therefore, a disabled individual who cannot meet that requirement is not "qualified" within the meaning of the ADA (see, e.g., *Waggoner* v. *Olin Corp.;* (1999)). The Sixth Circuit has cautioned, however, that a presumption that uninterrupted attendance is an essential job requirement improperly avoids the individualized assessment of accommodations required by the ADA (see *Cehrs* v. *Northeast Ohio Alzheimer's Research Ctr.* (1998)). It also seems likely that quantity or quality of work produced may be an essential function of the job. Thus, it may be permissible to discriminate against those whose disabilities prevent them from working as fast as others (see *Milton* v. *Scrivner, Inc.* (1995)).

Disability rights advocates hailed the passage of the ADA as a major step forward. More recently, however, court decisions have constricted the promise of the ADA. In large part this may be because of the amorphous, highly contextual, and often socially constructed meaning of the term "disability."

[*See also* Civil Liberties and Civil Rigths; Health Law]

• Pamela S. Karlan and George Rutherglen, "Disabilities, Discrimination, and Reasonable Accommodation," *Duke Law Journal* 46 (1996): 1. Jane Byeff Korn, "Fat," *Boston University Law Review* 77 (1997): 25. Samuel R. Bagenstos, "Subordination, Stigma, And "Disability," *Virginia Law Review* 86 (2000): 397. Robert Silverstein, "An Overview of the Emerging Disability Policy Framework: A Guidepost for Analyzing Public Policy, *Iowa Law Review* 85 (2000): 1757. Samuel Issacharoff and Justin Nelson, "Discrimination with a Difference: Can Employment Discrimination Law Accommodate the Americans with Disabilities Act?" *North Carolina Law Review* 79 (2001): 307. Jane Byeff Korn, "Cancer and the ADA: Rethinking Disability," *Southern California Law Review* 74 (2001): 339.

—Charles A. Sullivan

DISCOVERY. *See* Procedure, Civil; Procedure, Criminal.

DISCRETION, PROSECUTORIAL. *See* Procedure, Criminal.

DISCRIMINATION. The United States Constitution has become an important source of protection against discrimination, but those protections primarily stem from the amendments, not from the original text of the Constitution. As the American colonies were on the verge of independence, discrimination was on the minds of some observers. Abigail Adams corresponded with her husband, John, while he served as a delegate to the Continental Congress in 1776. "In the new Code of Laws," she urged, "I desire you would Remember the Ladies, and be more generous and favourable to them than your ancestors." Married women's legal status in eighteenth-century America was defined by the law of coverture. Their entire legal identity was subsumed under that of their husbands, so that married women could not enter *contracts or own *property.

The framers of the Constitution did not take up the question of sex discrimination but they did address another form of unequal treatment: *slavery. While not using the word "slave," they crafted a constitution that accommodated the practice. For the purpose of apportionment, slaves would count as three fifths of a person, slaves who escaped to non-slave states were to be returned to their owners, and Congress could not end the slave trade before 1808. Only after the Civil War was the Constitution amended, outlawing slavery under the Thirteenth Amendment, requiring that states not deny *"due process" and *"equal protection of the laws" under the *Fourteenth Amendment, and prohibiting (for men) discrimination in voting on the basis of *race or previous condition of servitude under the Fifteenth Amendment. While the Fourteenth Amendment did not explicitly mention race or slavery, it was understood that the amendment was intended especially to overcome discrimination against former slaves. In later years, the equal protection clause would be applied to other groups.

Congress also enacted important *civil rights legislation after the Civil War. One statute, the Civil Rights Act of 1875, forbade discrimination on the basis of race, color, and previous condition of servitude in public accommodations. In the *Civil Rights Cases* (1883), the Supreme Court struck down the statute on the basis that it exceeded Congress's power to enforce the Thirteenth

and Fourteenth Amendments. It would not be until 1957 that another civil rights bill would be enacted by Congress. In *Plessy* v. *Ferguson* (1896), the Supreme Court held that a state law requiring segregated railroad accommodations did not violate the equal protection clause. In a landmark dissent, Justice John Marshall *Harlan proclaimed that "in view of the Constitution, in the eye of the law, there is in this country no superior, dominant, ruling class of citizens. . . . Our Constitution is color-blind, and neither knows nor tolerates classes among citizens." *Plessy*'s "separate but equal" doctrine would remain the law for many years.

Legislative reforms eased some of the burdens of coverture for women by the late nineteenth century. However, women's status was still restricted by the idea that men and women had different duties in life. In *Bradwell* v. *Illinois* (1873), the Supreme Court upheld Illinois' refusal to grant Myra Bradwell a license to practice law because she was a woman. Justice Joseph P. Bradley wrote in his concurrence that "the paramount destiny and mission of woman are to fulfill the noble and benign offices of wife and mother." The source of women's role was in "the nature of things," and "the law of the Creator." In 1920, after a decades-long campaign for woman suffrage, the Nineteenth Amendment was adopted, guaranteeing women the right to vote. Feminist activists also advocated an *Equal Rights Amendment, which would prohibit other forms of discrimination on the basis of sex, but the amendment was never ratified.

World War II was a watershed in the development of American equality. The United States was fighting the Nazi dictatorship, yet if the purpose of the war was to uphold democracy, many wondered how the United States could tolerate antidemocratic practices at home. African Americans engaged in a "double-V" campaign: for victory abroad against fascism, and victory at home against racism. Under pressure from A. Philip Randolph's March on Washington Movement, President Franklin D. Roosevelt issued an executive order banning *segregation in defense industries. The Supreme Court took steps to advance equality as well. In *Smith* v. *Allwright* (1944), the Court took an important step toward enfranchising African-American voters by striking down the "white primary" system in the South. Because of Democratic Party dominance in the South, the Democratic primary nominee was inevitably elected, so segregated primaries kept African Americans from *voting the only time it really counted. The Court also held that states had to provide the educational opportunities for African Americans that it provided to whites, and could not comply with the "separate but equal" doctrine by sending an African-American student to an out-of-state law school (*Missouri ex rel. Gaines* v. *Canada* (1938)). Yet the war years were also a time of civil rights restrictions. Viewing Japanese Americans as inherently disloyal, the U.S. government relocated Japanese Americans from the west coast and placed them in internment camps in remote locations. The Supreme Court upheld their relocation in *Korematsu* v. *United States* (1944). Internment posed a hardship, Justice Hugo *Black acknowledged, but "hardships are part of war."

In the postwar years the Supreme Court played a major role in developing antidiscrimination law. The Court chipped away at "separate but equal," ruling that segregating black graduate and professional students from their white classmates created an unequal educational environment, which violated the equal protection clause (*McLaurin* v. *Oklahoma* (1950); *Sweatt* v. *Painter* (1952)). Then, in *Brown* v. *Board of Education* (1954), the Court took up the question of whether segregation *per se* violated the rights of African-American school children. Chief Justice Earl *Warren, in his opinion for a unanimous Court, did not discuss the legacy of racism that gave rise to segregation, but instead relied on social science evidence showing that present-day segregation harmed African-American children. The Court ruled that school segregation was unconstitutional, and the decision was soon applied to other areas of life where segregation was enforced by law. In *Brown* v. *Board of Education II* (1955), however, the Court held that school districts could desegregate "with all deliberate speed." School boards took this to mean that delay was permissible. Not until the 1960s, in the context of an intensified civil rights movement, and with the enactment of new civil rights statutes, would meaningful school desegregation be accomplished.

During the early 1960s, the civil rights movement captured the attention of the nation and the world. As peaceful demonstrators were brutalized by segregationist mobs and government officials, a broad coalition of Americans came to support civil rights reform. Because racism damaged the United States's image around the world, many also believed that race discrimination harmed U.S. world leadership during the Cold War. President John F. Kennedy called for the passage of civil rights legislation in 1963. The civil rights movement then pressed for reform through a massive March on Washington. Following Kennedy's assassination later that year, President Lyndon Baines Johnson took up the issue of civil rights as a means to honor Kennedy's memory and also to leave his own mark on the presidency. The landmark Civil Rights Act of 1964 has a number of important provisions. Title II revisited the issue posed in the *Civil Rights Cases* in 1883: discrimination in public accommodations. The 1964 Act was based on Congress's power under the Commerce Clause, as well as the Fourteenth Amendment, and the Supreme Court upheld the Act as an appropriate means of regulating interstate commerce in *Heart of Atlanta Motel, Inc.* v. *United States* (1964) and *Katzenbach* v. *McClung* (1964). Title VI of the Civil Rights Act allowed the federal government to bring suit against segregated school systems, and authorized the government to cut off federal education funds to segregated schools. By giving the federal government meaningful enforcement power, Title VI significantly aided progress in school desegregation. Title VII of the Act prohibited employment discrimination on the basis of race, color, religion, sex, or national origin, and this section was the only part that prohibited sex discrimination. In subsequent litigation, courts held that individuals could bring suit against an employer if they had evidence that they had been intentionally discriminated against, or when employment practices had a broad-based discriminatory impact. In 1965, Congress passed a Voting Rights Act aimed at undercutting pervasive disenfranchisement on the basis of race in particular areas of the nation.

Congress took other steps to protect women from discrimination. The Equal Pay Act, enacted in 1963, required equal pay for equal work, invalidating the common practice of paying men more than women when they performed the same job. In 1971, the Supreme Court for the first time struck down a state statute because it violated women's equal protection rights (*Reed* v. *Reed*). The Court went on to develop a *gender equality jurisprudence that allowed governments to treat men and women differently when they took into account "real differences," such as women's ability to bear children, and struck down statutes that reinforced old stereotypes, such as the idea that women were not breadwinners for their families. Whereas race discrimination was subjected to "strict scrutiny" under the Fourteenth Amendment, and therefore practices that discriminated on the basis of race were nearly always unconstitutional, sex discrimination was subjected to "intermediate scrutiny." Simply having a "rational" reason for treating women differently was no longer enough. In 1972, Congress extended protection against sex discrimination in Title IX, which prohibits sex discrimination in educational institutions that received federal funds. Title IX revolutionized college sports for women, because it required that schools provide equal opportunities in sports for women and men.

In extending the principles of antidiscrimination law, both the Supreme Court and Congress took up areas of discrimination that had not been recognized in the law before. The Court outlawed some forms of discrimination against noncitizens (*Graham* v. *Richardson* 1971)). In 1967, Congress passed the Age Discrimination in Employment Act, protecting older workers from discrimination based on age. The Supreme Court declined to hold that the poor were entitled to higher scrutiny under the equal protection clause, upholding a state educational financing scheme that resulted in great funding disparities based on the wealth of the property tax base (*San Antonio School District* v. *Rodriguez* (1973)). Some state courts then held that unequal school funding violated their state constitutions.

The Supreme Court has allowed states great leeway in the area of disability, but the Court still struck down a zoning ordinance under the Equal Protection clause because it was motivated by prejudice against mentally disabled people (*City of Cleburne* v. *Cleburne Living Well Center* (1985)). More extensive protection for disability rights came from Congress. Section 504 of the Rehabilitation Act of 1973 prohibits discrimination on the basis of disability in federally funded programs. Because most colleges and universities receive federal funds, this law opened the doors of higher education to persons with *disabilities. In 1990, a more far-reaching statute, the Americans with Disabilities Act, was passed, outlawing discrimination on the basis of disability in public accommodations and employment by private entities.

The civil rights revolution of the 1960s had a broad impact, yet some forms of discrimination remained resistant to change. In *Bowers* v. *Hardwick* (1986), the Supreme Court held that due process was not violated when a man was arrested for consensual oral sex with another man. In *Romer* v. *Evans* (1996), which invalidated a Colorado state initiative that prohibited local communities from banning sexual orientation discrimination, the Court signaled broader constitutional protection of sexual minorities. In 2000, Vermont passed a "Civil Unions" law that granted same-sex couples nearly all the rights provided by the state to married couples, except the title of "married," while other states continued to criminalize consensual gay sex. Under President Bill Clinton, the U.S. adopted a "don't ask, don't tell" policy, allowing homosexuals to serve in the military as long as they did not disclose their sexual identity. Although ostensibly less harsh, the policy led to a greater number of dismissals than had been the case under the earlier ban on gay and lesbian service.

While equality rights expanded through much of the twentieth century, competing visions of equality remain, as well as differences over the best means of social change. *Affirmative action programs, seen by many as a necessary means to remedy decades of exclusion, came under fire from opponents who viewed them as "reverse discrimination." Ultimately the Supreme Court heavily restricted affirmative action, holding that any race-based policy was constitutionally suspect, even if it was intended as a remedy for discrimination (*Adarand Constructors, Inc.* v. *Pena* (1995)). As voters approved some state antiaffirmative action initiatives, state policymakers scrambled to find race-neutral means to maintain integration on college campuses. In his 1896 *Plessy* dissent, Justice Harlan's call for a "color-blind" constitution sought to overcome an entrenched racial hierarchy. As the twentieth century came to a close, color-blindness had ironically become the justification to dismantle programs that had been established to overcome vestiges of discrimination.

[*See also* Civil Rights and Civil Liberties]

• Harold M. Hyman and William M. Wiecek, *Equal Justice under Law: Constitutional Development 1835–1875,* 1982. Hugh Davis Graham, *The Civil Rights Era: Origins and Development of National Policy, 1960–1972,* 1990. Theodore Eisenberg, *Civil Rights Legislation: Cases and Materials,* 1996. Rogers Smith, *Civic Ideals: Conflicting Visions of Citizenship in U.S. History,* 1997. William Eskridge Jr., *Gaylaw: Challenging the Apartheid of the Closet,* 1999. Linda K. Kerber, *No Constitutional Right To Be Ladies: Women and the Obligations of Citizenship,* 1999. Paul Brest, Sanford Levinson, Jack Balkin, and Akhil Amar, *Processes of Constitutional Decisionmaking: Cases and Materials,* 4th ed., 2000. Mary L. Dudziak, *Cold War Civil Rights: Race and the Image of American Democracy,* 2000. James T. Patterson, *Brown v. Board of Education: A Civil Rights Milestone and its Troubled Legacy,* 2001.
—Mary L. Dudziak

DISCRIMINATION, REVERSE. *See* Affirmative Action; Discrimination.

DISOBEDIENCE, CIVIL. *See* Civil Disobedience.

DISTRICT ATTORNEY. *See* Prosecutor.

DIVORCE AND ANNULMENT.

Divorce. Although Roman law by the third century allowed divorce at the will of either party, *canon law influenced the law of England and made divorce virtually nonexistent until 1857. *Marriage as a divine institution was a sacrament and fell within the province of the ecclesiastical courts. Exclusive ecclesiastical court jurisdiction over all aspects of marriage and annulment affected the law for centuries. English law did recognize an action called divorce *a mensa et thoro*, which allowed the parties to live apart if one party was guilty of extreme cruelty or committed *adultery. Parliament could grant a divorce for adultery after a successful suit for criminal conversation against the co-respondent, but the time and expense resulted in few divorces.

Most American colonies did not transport the strict prohibitions on divorce; the earliest reported divorce was in Massachusetts in 1661. South Carolina, however, did not provide for divorce until 1942 and adultery was the only ground for divorce in New York until 1966. The states considered marriage to be a status—an institution with fixed rights and obligations as well as a civil contract. The state has an interest in promoting and preserving marriage. Until the 1960s a court could grant a divorce only if the party seeking a divorce could prove that the other spouse was guilty of marital misconduct such that the court should allow the wronged party out of the marriage. The typical grounds for divorce were adultery, impotence, physical or mental cruelty, habitual drunkenness, desertion, or gross neglect of duty.

Domicile was seen as the basis for seeking the court's jurisdiction to adjudicate divorce. Most states had long residency requirements of one year before an action could be filed. A state had the jurisdiction to adjudicate marriage status even if only one party was a resident of the state. During the years following World War II, the population became more mobile and more women joined the work force because inflation made two-wage-earner families necessary. More parties sought divorces, often by agreement of both parties. If marriage is a voluntary union not necessarily expected to last forever, people wanted to be able to obtain a divorce without great legal impediments.

Divorce reforms moved to shorten the residency requirements and to eliminate fault from the law of divorce. "No-fault" divorce was supposed to eliminate from the courtroom the detailing of all the horrible things either spouse had done during the marriage, especially if the divorce was mutually agreeable. In 1969 California became the first state to allow a divorce for irreconcilable differences that have caused irremediable breakdown of the marriage. After the Uniform Marriage and Divorce Act in 1970 recommended irretrievable breakdown of the marriage as the sole ground for divorce, no-fault divorce statutes appeared across the country. By 1985 all fifty states had adopted at least one no-fault ground. No-fault divorce is available in all states either as the sole ground for divorce (eighteen states) or in addition to traditional grounds. Some states require living apart pursuant to an agreement for one year.

In place of the traditional insistence on domicile, most states now allow a person to file for divorce with six-months-or-less residency. Some states have placed comprehensive jurisdiction over family-law matters in family courts. A few states are experimenting with more of an administrative process for consensual divorces, so the parties do not even have to appear in front of a judge.

Annulment. Annulment is a judicial determination to set aside a marriage that was invalid at its inception because of some defect existing at the time of the marriage. The ecclesiastical courts at *common law granted annulments, called a divorce *a vinculo matrimonii*, for centuries before divorce was recognized in England in 1857.

The ecclesiastical court could only annul the marriage while the parties lived and only for canonical disabilities such as physical impotence, consanguinity, and affinity. These disabilities rendered the marriage voidable. At common law there were four civil disabilities that made a marriage void without any court action: an existing marriage, parties under the age of capacity (twelve for females and fourteen for males), lack of mental competency, and lack of parental consent. If the marriage were void, it could be attacked collaterally by anyone at any time. No judicial decree of nullity was required. If the marriage were only voidable, only the parties could attack the marriage while they lived and it was necessary to have a judicial decree annulling the marriage.

In the United States there were no comparable ecclesiastical courts. If a state had no statute, annulment was recognized to be within the inherent equitable powers of the court. The void/voidable distinction has partially blurred but remains in many jurisdictions. Because marriage is considered a status and a *contract, it requires the mutual consent of the parties. A marriage may be annulled if the consent to marry was obtained by force, duress, coercion, or fraud. Generally the fraud must pertain to the essentials of the marriage.

Today with unilateral divorce available, annulments are not sought as often as they once were. Many of the common-law negative effects, such as making children illegitimate and the inability to get maintenance, or to have a determination of custody and support, have disappeared and an annulment action is similar to a divorce action.

Although a divorce terminates an existing marriage and annulment finds that no marriage existed, in most states today the law uses the same procedures for division of property, awarding maintenance, and awarding custody and support of children (see CHILD CUSTODY). The advantage of getting an annulment is that the law treats the marriage as if it never took place, so some people prefer an annulment for social, religious, or other reasons.

[See also Family Law]

• Homer Clark, Law of Domestic Relations, 2d ed., 1988. Harry Krause, Linda Elrod, Marsha Garrison, and Tom Oldham, Principles of Family Law, 4th ed., 1998.

—Linda Henry Elrod

DNA. See Police Procedures; Science and Law.

DOE, CHARLES (1830–1896), lawyer, chief justice of the New Hampshire Supreme Court, 1876–1896. Charles Doe was one of the most important state court judges of the late nineteenth century. Educated at Exeter and at Dartmouth College, Doe studied law in the office of a prominent New Hampshire attorney before being admitted to the bar in 1854. Averse to sectional politics, Doe broke his affiliation with the Democrats, and in 1859 earned nomination by the Republican governor to the state's highest court. Doe served there with little distinction until 1874, when a shift in state political power led to the abolition of his court. Two years later, another shift returned him to the court, as chief justice, an office that he held until his death.

Doe's judicial service was marked by his active use of the *common-law process, by which courts, not legislatures, make changes in the law, and by his lack of respect for judicial precedent. He was prepared to openly make new law, whereas most judges of the era asserted that they did not create law. Consequently, Doe's decisions were highly personal, drawing on his own sense of what was "just" for a New Hampshire society that retained its homogeneous, rural character throughout Doe's life. Although not confronted with the divisive issues posed elsewhere by an industrializing society, Doe's active use of judicial power stood out at a time when much of the American legal system was turning to legislatures for reform. Doe's reputation is built on his success in anticipating the trend of history—reforming the rules of *procedure in courts, much of *tort law, and rules of *evidence and criminal responsibility, as well as ruling in favor of the admission of women to the practice of law.

[See also Courts, United States: State and Local]

• John Phillip Reid, Chief Justice: The Judicial World of Charles Doe, 1967.   —Walter F. Pratt Jr.

DOMESTIC PARTNERS. See Domestic Violence: Partner Abuse; Family Law; Homosexuality and the Law; Marriage.

DOMESTIC VIOLENCE

Partner Abuse
Child Abuse
Elder Abuse

DOMESTIC VIOLENCE: PARTNER ABUSE

The modern effort to stop domestic violence originated with the feminist movement of the 1970s. Feminists and their nonfeminist allies have insisted that partner abuse is a serious social and legal problem and not a trivial "private family matter."

Some claim that men and women are equally violent in intimate relationships, but this is simply not true. Study after study has shown that in heterosexual couples, perpetrators are overwhelmingly men and victims are overwhelmingly women. Domestic violence also occurs in gay and lesbian relationships. Domestic violence often involves sexual assault (See SEX OFFENSES) and stalking.

Physical violence and the threat of physical violence are just part of an overall pattern of power and control. Batterers' methods of control include degradation, isolation, financial control, destruction of property and pets, and controlling jealousy, as well as physical and sexual violence. In evaluating domestic violence cases, the law and legal actors must therefore view both parties' acts contextually.

The batterer's need for power and control also explains why leaving the abuser is often dangerous for women and their children. Whether victims leave the relationship or stay in it, victims' safety must be the top priority for everyone in the legal system.

An important tool in addressing domestic violence has been civil protective orders. Contrary to the idea that protective orders are "just pieces of paper," studies have shown that they empower victims and have a genuine deterrent effect against some batterers.

Every jurisdiction in the United States has some kind of protective order statute, setting forth the grounds under which a victim may seek injunctive relief from an abuser. The details of protective order statutes vary greatly from state to state. In all jurisdictions, however, a victim may seek an *ex parte* emergency protective order, and later, following notice to the defendant and a hearing, receive a permanent protective order. The Violence Against Women Act of 1994 (VAWA) provides that properly entered orders be given full faith and credit throughout the United States.

Unfortunately, judges have sometimes entered mutual protective orders, under which the victim as well as the perpetrator is ordered to stay away from the partner. To deter wrongful entry of mutual protective orders, VAWA provides that such orders are enforceable against the original petitioner only if the respondent filed a separate petition seeking protection and the issuing court specifically found that the respondent was legally entitled to the protective order.

Vigorous enforcement of protective orders is critical to battered women's safety. Courts can use their civil and criminal *contempt powers to ensure compliance with protective orders.

Arrest and criminal prosecution play an important role in a coordinated community response to domestic violence. Unfortunately, many police and prosecutors continue to assign a low priority to domestic violence cases. However, with adequate resources and a full understanding of the issues, a high percentage of abused women will participate in the prosecution of their batterers. Further, even in cases where the victim does not wish to testify, convictions may be obtained through "evidence-based prosecution." With adequate training of police and a proper understanding of the evidence issues presented, defendants can often be convicted or convinced to plea bargain even without the victim's testimony. When a victim asks that criminal charges be dropped, prosecutors must consider whether prosecution will enhance the continued safety of a woman and her children.

Prosecution of domestic violence defendants is often deferred, with the abuser agreeing to attend a batterers' intervention program. Even those who are convicted of domestic violence assaults are usually sentenced to an intervention program rather than jail. Intervention programs may be effective with some batterers. However, they can only work if there is some guarantee that failure

to attend or further assaults will have serious legal consequences, including jail. Some abusers are so dangerous that jail time is the only appropriate response.

Another important issue is the treatment of domestic violence in *family law matters. Many studies show that children are harmed by the abuse of their mother, even if the children are not physically or sexually assaulted themselves. There is also a substantial overlap between partner abuse and abuse of children. Child protection agencies sometimes focus on the mother's "failure to protect" the children from the abuser. Instead, authorities should consider ways to keep both women and children safe, and to hold abusers accountable for their violence.

Many batterers use custody and visitation to engage in ongoing acts of control and abuse against both their former partner and their children. A number of states have a rebuttable presumption against joint or sole custody for a parent who has engaged in domestic violence. Still, many judges continue to ignore or minimize domestic violence evidence when dealing with custody and visitation issues (see CHILD CUSTODY).

Virtually all domestic violence advocates, as well as many mediators, believe that mediation is inappropriate in *divorce cases involving domestic violence. A number of states have adopted statutes excluding domestic violence cases from divorce mediation.

Special issues arise when abused women are charged with crimes. Sometimes, women assault or kill their batterers. There is no "battered women's defense"; however, many such cases can be fitted into traditional criminal law doctrines such as self-defense and diminished capacity (see CRIMINAL LAW PRINCIPLES). In trying to explain the woman's actions to a jury, most courts have allowed the introduction of expert testimony on why the victim endured the abuse, and did not leave. While women's response is sometimes labeled "battered women's syndrome," many authorities in the field believe that battered women's response to abuse is neither pathological nor uniform Still, expert testimony can often help the factfinder understand why a particular woman responded as she did.

Many battered women are forced by their batterers to commit crimes, such as prostitution, drug crimes, property crimes, and even tax fraud. When abuse is present, defenses such as duress and lack of intent may be appropriate, and the abuse can be argued as a basis for mitigation and sentence reduction.

Because some batterers are men of means, victims should consider suing their batterers in tort. Generally, states have abolished interspousal *tort immunity for intentional torts. VAWA provided a federal tort remedy for plaintiffs victimized by "a crime of violence motivated by gender." However, the United Supreme Court in *United States* v. *Morrison* (2000) declared the VAWA civil tort remedy unconstitutional as a violation of *federalism.

[*See also* Family Law; Gender and Law]

• Fredrica L. Lehrman, *Domestic Violence Practice and Procedure*, 1996. Beth E. Richie, *Compelled to Crime : The Gender Entrapment of Battered, Black Women*, 1996. Patricia G. Barnes, ed., *Domestic Violence: From a Private Matter to a Federal Offense*, 1998. Elizabeth Schneider, *Battered Women and Feminist Lawmaking*, 2000. Clare Dalton and Elizabeth Schneider, *Battered Women and the Law*, 2001. Nancy K. D. Lemon, *Domestic Violence Law*, 2001.   —Kathleen Waits

DOMESTIC VIOLENCE: CHILD ABUSE

Most children grow up free from abuse or neglect. For too many youngsters, however, childhood is marred by physical abuse, sexual abuse, emotional maltreatment, or neglect. The true incidence of child abuse is impossible to determine, because abuse occurs behind closed doors. Researchers estimate that 20 to 25 percent of females and 5 to 15 percent of males in the United States experience some type of developmentally inappropriate sexual event during childhood, ranging from mild to extremely damaging (see SEX OFFENSES). The most prevalent form of child maltreatment is neglect, in which caretakers fail to provide for a child's basic need for nutrition, shelter, or love. Physical abuse afflicts thousands of children and ranges from minor bruises to life-threatening injury. Approximately two thousand children die each year in the United States as a result of physical abuse or neglect. The majority of these children are younger than five years, and 40 percent of fatalities are babies. Most American parents use some form of corporal punishment, and physical abuse is often "discipline" gone awry. Psychological maltreatment, at the core of most child maltreatment, is toxic for children's development.

The law plays a critical role in responding to child abuse, but it does not have all the answers for coping with this abuse. Judges, lawyers, and police officers work closely with social workers, physicians, psychologists, and policymakers to shape society's response to child abuse. At the federal level, Congress provides millions of dollars each year to support states' efforts to protect children. The federal government provides financial support for research on the abuse of children. Congress and experts from the executive branch play a major role in shaping national policy on child abuse.

Most law on child abuse is state law. The primary laws covering this area are (1) criminal statutes; (2) laws creating the child protection system, including the juvenile court and foster care systems; and (3) laws requiring professionals who work with children to report suspected abuse and neglect.

Although legal definitions vary slightly from one state to another, physical abuse and sexual abuse are crimes in every state. Severe neglect is also a crime. Physical abuse is prosecuted criminally under special child abuse statutes as well as under generally applicable criminal laws punishing *assault, battery, and *homicide. Similarly, sexual abuse is prosecuted under special child sexual abuse statutes as well as under generally applicable criminal laws punishing rape and sexual assault. The crime of statutory rape occurs when a person has consensual sexual intercourse with a minor.

Every state has a complex system intended to protect children from abuse and neglect. As part of this system, professionals who work with children (e.g., doctors, nurses, psychologists, teachers) are required by law to report suspected abuse or neglect to law enforcement or child protective services (CPS) agencies. CPS agencies are staffed by social workers, who on receiving reports of abuse and neglect conduct the necessary investigations. CPS social workers do not bring all cases to juvenile court. For many troubled families, social workers are able to prevent maltreatment of the children by supporting the family with therapy and other social services. When a child is harmed, however, or when the risk of harm is imminent, CPS social workers, working with police, can remove children from their parents and place them in emergency protective custody.

As soon as a child is placed in custody, or if a child needs protection for other reasons, CPS social workers turn to the juvenile court. Every state has a juvenile court, the first of which were established in Denver and Chicago in 1899. In most states the court is formally known as the Juvenile Court; in a small number of states, it is known as the Family Court. The juvenile court has responsibility for three groups of children: (1) juvenile delinquents, children who commit criminal acts; (2) status offenders, children who are truant from school, run away from home, violate curfew laws, or cannot be managed by their parents (so-called ungovernable children); and (3) abused and neglected children in need of protection. Juvenile court proceedings are civil rather than criminal. The purpose of abuse and neglect proceedings is to protect the child, not punish the parents. In most cases the ultimate goal is to strengthen the family and reunify children with parents.

Juvenile court protection proceedings occur in three, sometimes four, phases. First, when a child is removed from his or her parents and taken into emergency protective custody, a prompt judicial hearing is required to determine whether the child should remain in protective custody or be returned to the parents pending further proceedings. Second, following the initial decision about the child's safety, a trial (usually called an adjudicatory hearing) is scheduled in the juvenile court. The purpose of the adjudicatory hearing is to determine whether the parents committed the suspected abuse or neglect. At the hearing, the CPS agency accusing the parents of maltreatment is represented by a government lawyer. The parents may retain their own lawyer or, if they cannot afford to do so, the judge appoints a lawyer for them. In some states, the child has a lawyer; in others, the child's interests are protected by a guardian *ad litem*, who is not a lawyer. In most states there is no jury in juvenile court. The judge hears the evidence, including the testimony of witnesses, and determines whether the allegations of maltreatment are true. If the allegations are not proven, the judge dismisses the case. If the allegations are proven, the judge proceeds to the next phase, disposition. Most juvenile court cases do not proceed all the way to adjudicatory hearing. Like other forms of litigation, most juvenile court cases are settled before trial. In a typical case the parents admit some form of maltreatment and agree to accept services such as substance abuse treatment or classes on effective parenting.

In the third, disposition phase, the judge hears evidence and decides what disposition will serve the child's best interests. In some cases the child remains at home under CPS supervision. If the home is unsafe, the child is placed with members of her or his extended family or with licensed foster parents. Some abused and neglected children require institutional care. When children are removed from home, the goal is usually to reunify the family following services designed to reduce the risk of further maltreatment. The court holds periodic hearings to measure progress and to prevent children from getting "lost" in the foster care system.

The fourth phase occurs in a relatively small percentage of cases when parents cannot or will not provide a safe home for children, and legal action is taken to terminate the legal relationship between parent and child. With parental rights terminated, the child can be adopted by another family (see ADOPTION AND TERMINATION OF PARENTAL RIGHTS).

• Mary E. Helfer, Ruth S. Kempe, and Richard D. Krugman, eds., *The Battered Child*, 5th ed., 1997. John E. B. Myers, *Legal Issues in Child Abuse and Neglect Practice*, 2d ed., 1998. Howard Dubowitz, ed., *Neglected Children: Research, Practice, and Policy*, 1999. Robert M. Reece, ed., *Treatment of Child Abuse: Common Ground for Mental Health, Medical, and Legal Practitioners*, 2000. John E. B. Myers, Lucy Berliner, John Briere, Terry Hendrix, Carole Jenny, and Theresa Reid, eds., *The APSAC Handbook on Child Maltreatment*, 2d ed., 2001.

—John E. B. Myers

DOMESTIC VIOLENCE: ELDER ABUSE

Older Americans are extremely vulnerable to abuse, neglect, and exploitation. Because of declining physical and mental abilities, many elders are targeted by criminals, friends, family members, and even spouses as persons who are easily victimized. The widespread abuse of the elderly was little recognized until the 1970s and 1980s, when a number of studies and congressional hearings raised public awareness. In 1987 federal definitions of elder abuse were added to the amendments to the Older Americans Act, which greatly increased public recognition of the problem.

Each state has its own statutory definitions of elder abuse, neglect, and exploitation, definitions which overlap but are not identical. While every state includes physical harm as abuse, not all recognize mental anguish or psychological injury as abuse. A few states include unreasonable physical confinement as a form of abuse, and sexual abuse can be included in the general abuse definition or separately defined. Almost all states recognize neglect of the elderly as an offense. Neglect, defined as the deprivation of basic needs such as food, adequate shelter, clothing, and medical care, can be defined as intentional neglect or, under some state statutes, negligent failure to provide the needed assistance. To be guilty of neglect, the accused individual must have a duty to care for the abused person or must have created a reliance on or expectation of care on the part of the older person. "Exploitation" usually refers to financial exploitation by the theft or improper use of the income or assets of a vulnerable older person. It includes telemarketing frauds, securities scams, and other forms of consumer fraud. Some commentators also classify self-neglect as a form of elder abuse, although it is better understood as evidence of mental illness such as depression or dementia.

Elder abuse may be committed in the household by the spouse, children, or other family members. Some elder abuse is merely the continuation of spousal abuse. However, in many instances the spousal abuse begins only as the couple ages and is a direct result of the caregiving responsibility assumed by the healthier spouse. Adult children and other relatives, such as nieces and nephews, may abuse or exploit dependent older family members. Interestingly, adult children who abuse their parents were often abused as children.

The extent of elder abuse is uncertain, because of differing definitions, lack of centralized reporting, and, most importantly, underreporting by abused elderly. Most abused elders never report the abuse. The reasons are varied. Many of the elderly suffering abuse have diminished mental capacity and are unable to communicate or even understand their plight. Others, abused by caregivers, fear retaliation. Some elderly persons in institutions, such as nursing homes or personal care homes (also called board and care homes), may not know to whom they should complain or may not realize they are receiving abusive care. Elderly victims of neglect are often isolated in the home and too weak, frail, or demented to seek help. Older persons who are victims of consumer fraud, such as by a telemarketer, often are so chagrined that they will not report the crime to the authorities.

Domestic caregivers are the most frequent abusers of the elderly. More than 1.5 million elders are abused by caregivers every year. Women over the age of seventy-five who are dependent on the abuser for care are the most likely victims. Not only do caregivers have the opportunity, but they also can block attempts by the elderly person to seek help. Because the abusing caregiver provides day-to-day assistance, the older person is often afraid of complaining, fearful that in doing so she or he will lose the help of the caregiver. For example, a mother who lives with a physically abusive son may not report his abuse to the police for fear that if she does, her son will be criminally prosecuted and she will have no one to care for her.

Some elderly persons in institutions are victims of physical abuse or have their property or cash stolen. Institutional abuse is not uncommon. The low wages, insufficient training, and inadequate supervision of institutional staff are cited as the causes of abuse. A few nursing homes, and more personal care homes, are guilty of systemic abuse, with management either deliberately abusing the residents or grossly negligent. Institutional abuse occurs in part because many of the residents have diminished mental capacity and are isolated and dependent. Unfortunately, many institutionalized elders have few if any visitors and thus no one to look after their interests. The high incidence of diminished mental capacity among residents also protects abusers from disclosure.

Institutional abuse and neglect are best combated by informing management and the state authorities. Complaints about staff members' infractions or their failure to provide appropriate care should be reported to management. All states have an ombudsman and usually an elder-abuse hot line to which family, friends, and staff can report suspected cases of abuse and neglect. Reporting to the local police, who can investigate whether the abuse violates criminal assault laws, is another possibility.

Governmental response to elder abuse has been spurred by a series of congressional hearings that began in 1981. In 1992, the Older Americans Act, a source of federal money for state initiatives for community-based assistance to the elderly, was amended to encourage states to create adult protective service systems. Today every state has adopted some form of adult protective services designed to prevent the abuse and neglect of vulnerable persons by providing supportive services in the person's home or, if necessary, by removing the person from the abusers. Protective services range from home visits by visiting nurses to filing for guardianship proceedings to physical removal of the elderly person to a safe environment. Many state protective service statutes specifically designate elder abuse as a crime or provide civil penalties for the abuse or neglect of older, vulnerable adults.

Protective service laws are not without critics who object to such features as mandatory reporting of suspected abuse by physicians and other professionals, excessive reliance on confidential or anonymous reports of abuse, the right to intervene over the objections of the elderly person, and the too frequent resort to imposing guardianship upon vulnerable elders.

Protecting older persons from telemarketing, home-repair, securities, sweepstakes, and home-employment fraud has proven difficult. Despite state and federal laws against such fraud and enhanced penalties for victimizing older persons, professional con artists continue to prey upon unsuspecting elderly. Often older victims do not want to report the scam because they are ashamed about being taken in by the fraudulent activity. Sometimes the elderly victims are not even aware that they have been defrauded. Informing the elderly about the prevalent frauds and conducting aggressive legal action against activities such as sweepstakes and fraudulent telemarketing have had only limited success.

[See also Aging and the Law; Family Law]

• Melanie J. Flesser, *The Elderly Consumer: Legal Protection in an Evolving Market*, 1992. Tanya Fusco Johnson, ed., *Elder Mistreatment: Ethical Issues, Dilemmas, and Decisions*, 1995. Lorin A. Baumhover and S. Colleen Beall, eds., *Abuse, Neglect, and Exploitation of Older Persons: Strategies for Assessment and Intervention*, 1996. Mary Joy Quinn and Susan K. Tomita, eds., *Elder Abuse and Neglect: Causes, Diagnosis, and Intervention Strategies*, 2d ed., 1997. Frances Merchant Carp, *Elder Abuse in the Family: An Interdisciplinary Approach*, 2000.

—Lawrence A. Frolik

DOUBLE JEOPARDY. The premise that no person shall be "twice put in jeopardy of life and limb" for the same offense is enshrined in the Fifth Amendment of the U.S. Constitution, as well as in a substantial majority of state constitutions. Although the principle itself dates back to ancient Greek and Roman law, it did not become a fixture in the English *common law until 1642, when Sir Edward Coke articulated the basis for double jeopardy principles in his First and Second *Institutes of the Law of England*. Over a century later, Sir William *Blackstone reaffirmed the principles in his *Commentaries*, although limiting their application to a ban against multiple prosecutions of *felony cases only. In the United States, James Madison is credited with having included a prohibition against double jeopardy in the proposed Bill of Rights that was ratified in 1791.

Because the Fifth Amendment technically acts as a limitation on federal authorities only, defendants in state courts have looked to state constitutions for protection against double jeopardy violations during much of this nation's history. Not all state constitutions were equally helpful in this regard: as late as the 1960s, seven state constitutions provided protection against subsequent trials only in the case of prior jury acquittals; other states simply relegated double jeopardy protection to the "common law." In 1937 the Supreme Court rejected efforts to impose federal standards of double jeopardy on states as an aspect of *"due process" in the landmark case of *Palko* v. *Connecticut*. However, thirty-two years later the Court reversed course and lent some measure of uniformity to double jeopardy principles in state courts.

In *Benton* v. *Maryland* (1969), the Court held that double jeopardy was a "fundamental protection," and was thus afforded protection as an aspect of the *Fourteenth Amendment's due process clause. All states were thereafter required to satisfy the minimum double jeopardy standards guaranteed by the Fifth Amendment.

Various justifications have been offered in support of a robust prohibition against double jeopardy. First, double jeopardy principles guard against undue prosecutorial harassment of a defendant. When a defendant is acquitted on the merits at an initial trial, or when a conviction is followed by an especially light sentence, prosecutors might otherwise "keep trying" in hopes of securing a more favorable outcome. Second, double jeopardy provides a sense of closure in criminal matters, and thus serves a function similar to that of a statute of limitations. Once a defendant has been acquitted or convicted of an offense, he should be able to consider the matter closed and plan the rest of his life without the looming threat of prosecution and possible imprisonment. Other objectives commonly cited include the avoidance of social stigma to a defendant who must undergo repeated criminal trials; preserving the integrity of jury verdicts; and economy of time and money for the defendant as well as the government.

Stripped to its bare bones, the contours of the Fifth Amendment right against double jeopardy appear self-evident: the amendment prevents the government from trying a defendant for a specific statutory offense if that defendant has already been convicted or acquitted of having committed that same offense. Upon closer examination, however, the ambiguities inherent within the provision become more apparent.

Certainly no defendant already convicted or acquitted of one offense can be prosecuted in another criminal trial for the identical offense. But what about a subsequent charge brought for the same criminal act, but based on a separate statute? For example, can a defendant already acquitted of felony murder committed during an act of kidnapping be brought to a second trial for the kidnapping offense alone? Although some scholars have argued for a restrictive view which would limit the double jeopardy clause to trials for identical offenses only, the U.S. Supreme Court has adopted a "lesser included offense rule," prohibiting multiple prosecutions only when the proof of offenses at the second trial requires the same showing of proof as that required at the first trial.

Equally uncertain is the issue of when jeopardy "attaches" at the first trial. Certainly a defendant acquitted at trial may not be retried, no matter how erroneous the first verdict may have been. Less obvious is the legal effect carried by a dismissal of the charges or a mistrial. Although double jeopardy standards in this area remain a source of considerable confusion, a few rules of thumb have taken hold. As a general matter, jeopardy attaches in a jury trial when the jury is first sworn in; in a bench trial it attaches as soon as the first witness has been sworn. There is no jeopardy bar to a new trial when the jury hung at the first trial, or following appellate reversal on any grounds other than sufficiency of evidence. By contrast, guilty pleas and other abbreviated determinations of blameworthiness do bar subsequent prosecutions for the same offense. And if a conviction on a lesser included offense is set aside on appeal, the defendant may not be subsequently prosecuted for the greater offense.

Finally, the double jeopardy clause does not prevent different sovereign authorities from trying the same defendant for the same exact offense. Such a "dual sovereignty" approach to the clause occasionally proves controversial when a criminal act violates both federal and state laws (see sovereignty). In some high profile cases, such as the prosecution of noted attorney Clark Clifford for corruption in the Bank of Credit and Commerce International (BCCI) banking scandal of the early 1990s, federal and state authorities openly battled over the right to try Clifford first.

Controversy will forever surround the double jeopardy clause, due to the wide range of interpretations the clause invites. Increased codification of the criminal law has slowed the proliferation of overlapping and duplicative offenses that make double jeopardy violations more likely. Still, more can be done to limit the ambiguous nature of the clause. Some scholars have urged that Congress and state legislatures more specifically state in criminal statutes whether newly created offenses are intended to be "different" than other offenses already on the books, at least for double jeopardy purposes. (Although such a direct expression of legislative intent would not necessarily bind a court interpreting the Fifth Amendment, it might well prove authoritative in most cases.) Others have suggested that more states pass a "mandatory joinder law," which would require that prosecutors join in one trial all charges resulting from the same "criminal transaction," as long as those potential charges were known to the police or prosecutor at the time the trial begins. Such a rule would prevent prosecutors from taking advantage of (and perhaps abusing) the complicated rule

structure that determines what constitutes the "same offense" for double jeopardy purposes. Critics of mandatory joinder counter (with some justification) that the rule thereby "places a premium upon the inefficiency or ineptitude of the police or the prosecutor" in learning of alleged crimes, because their failure to do so in a timely manner would actually be rewarded.

[See also Criminal Law Principles]

• Jay A. Sigler, *Double Jeopardy: the Development of a Legal and Social Policy*, 1969. Peter Westen and Richard Drubel, "Toward a General Theory of Double Jeopardy," *Supreme Court Review* (1978): 81. George C. Thomas III, *Double Jeopardy: The History, the Law*, 1998.

—David A. Yalof

DOUGLAS, WILLIAM ORVILLE (1898–1980), associate justice of the U.S. *Supreme Court, 1939–75. Nominated to the Supreme Court by Franklin D. Roosevelt on March 20, 1939, Douglas was the youngest nominee in 128 years. He was also the first member of the Court who had been trained from the beginning in realistic legal analysis. A controversial judge, he publicly expressed unconventional views, wrote thirty books, engaged in political activity to preserve wilderness areas, served as president (with pay) of an educational foundation, traveled to the ends of the earth in search of adventure, and married four times. He survived two *impeachment attempts and retired from the bench on November 12, 1975, after serving longer than any other justice in the Court's history.

Douglas was born in a small crossroads settlement in western Minnesota. His father, Rev. William Douglas, was the pastor of the local Presbyterian church; his mother, Julia Bickford Fisk, was the church organist. When he was three, his family moved west, and he grew up in Yakima, Washington. He then worked his way through Whitman College, from which he graduated Phi Beta Kappa in 1920, and Columbia University Law School, from which he graduated second in his class in 1925.

He briefly practiced at a Wall Street law firm, and he taught law at Columbia and Yale from 1926 to 1934. Influenced by Underhill Moore at Columbia, he developed a realistic approach to law in teaching courses on bankruptcy, corporations, and corporate reorganization. His approach, which was policy oriented, took social and economic forces into account and focused on institutional functions, practices, and processes rather than legal definitions and doctrine, which he called "legal theology." Among his colleagues at

Yale whose ideas he shared were Jerome *Frank, Thurman Arnold, Charles Clark, and Walton Hamilton.

In 1934, Douglas went to Washington to conduct an investigation for the newly created Securities and Exchange Commission (SEC). He became a member of the SEC in 1936 and its chairman in 1937. His most important accomplishment at the SEC was reform of the New York Stock Exchange.

Soon after Douglas came to the Supreme Court in 1939, he established himself intellectually with his colleagues in a series of economics cases. Among those cases were *United States* v. *Socony Vacuum Oil Co.* (1940), which involved price fixing, and *Federal Power Commission* v. *Hope Natural Gas Co.* (1944), which established ratemaking standards. In the 1940s, he often voted for civil liberties claims, usually with his colleague, Hugo *Black, but it was not until the McCarthy era in the early 1950s that he became one of the Court's leading proponents of civil liberties. His most powerful statements supporting liberty were dissenting opinions in such cases as *Dennis* v. *United States* (1951), in which he defended freedom of *speech and association, and *Ullmann* v. *United States* (1956), in which he defended the privilege against *self-incrimination. His most important civil liberties opinions for the Court were in *Skinner* v. *Oklahoma* (1942), which established strict scrutiny in *equal protection cases involving fundamental rights, and *Griswold* v. *Connecticut* (1965), which established the right to *privacy.

Douglas left only a small doctrinal legacy, which is not surprising given his distrust of doctrine in deciding cases. Yet he ranks high among the Supreme Court justices of his era because of his understanding of the operation of law in society, his commitment to the constitutional values of freedom, privacy, equality, and fair procedure, and his courage, particularly in the McCarthy era, in defending these values.

• James F. Simon, *Independent Journey: The Life of William O. Douglas,* 1980. Stephen L. Wasby, ed., *"He Shall Not Pass This Way Again": The Legacy of William O. Douglas,* 1990.
—David J. Danelski

DOWER AND CURTSEY. *See* Family Law.

DRAFT, MILITARY. *See* War, Law of.

DRED SCOTT V. SANDFORD, 60 U.S. 393 (1857). In 1850 a Missouri trial court declared Dred Scott to be free because his late owner, Dr. Emerson, had taken him to the free state of Illinois and later to Fort Snelling in the Wisconsin Territory (present-day Minnesota), where Congress had prohibited *slavery under the Missouri Compromise of 1820. This decision was consistent with a long line of Missouri cases dating from 1824 that held that residence in a free jurisdiction led to the emancipation of a slave.

The Missouri Supreme Court reversed this result in *Scott* v. *Emerson* (1852), rejecting its precedents because of the "dark and fell spirit" of abolitionism, which the court claimed had taken over the North. In 1854 Scott began a new suit in federal court against his new owner, John F. A. Sanford (his name is misspelled as Sandford in the official report of the case). Scott sued on the basis of diversity of *citizenship, claiming he was a "citizen of Missouri" and noting Sanford was a "citizen of New York." Sanford denied Scott's right to sue him, arguing that because "Dred Scott, is not a citizen of the State of Missouri, as alleged in his declaration, because he is a negro of African descent; his ancestors were of pure African blood, and were brought into this country and sold as negro slaves."

United States District Judge Robert W. Wells rejected Sanford's theory, concluding that *if* Dred Scott was free, then he could sue in federal court as a citizen of Missouri. However, after hearing all the evidence, Wells charged the jury to uphold Scott's slave status, based on the earlier Missouri decision that Scott was still a slave.

Scott appealed to the U.S. Supreme Court, where he lost in a 7-2 decision. In his "Opinion of the Court," Chief Justice Roger B. *Taney ruled that the Missouri Compromise, under which Scott claimed to be free, unconstitutionally deprived southerners of their property in slaves without *due process of law or just compensation, in violation of the Fifth Amendment. This decision shocked northerners, who had long seen the Missouri Compromise as a central piece of legislation for organizing the settlement of the West and for accommodating differing sectional interests.

Taney also denied that blacks could ever be citizens of the United States, rhetorically declaring:

The question is simply this: Can a negro, whose ancestors were imported into this country, and sold as slaves, become a member of the political community formed and brought into existence by the Constitution of the United States, and as such become entitled to all the rights, and privileges, and immunities, guaranteed by that instrument to the citizen? One of which rights is the privilege of suing in a court of the United States in the cases specified in the Constitution.

Ignoring the right of free black men (in most of the northern states, as well as North Carolina) to vote at the time of the ratification of the Constitution, Taney declared that African-Americans

> are not included, and were not intended to be included, under the word 'citizens' in the Constitution, and can therefore claim none of the rights and privileges which the instrument provides and secures to citizens of the United States. On the contrary, they were at that time [1787–1788] considered as a subordinate and inferior class of beings who had been subjugated by the dominant *race, and, whether emancipated or not, yet remained subject to their authority, and had no rights or privileges but such as those who held the power and Government might choose to grant them.

According to Taney blacks were "so far inferior, that they had no rights which the white man was bound to respect."

Taney's opinion outraged many northerners, especially members of the new Republican Party. Abraham *Lincoln attacked the decision throughout his debates with Stephen A. Douglas in 1858 and again during the presidential campaign of 1860. The decision led many Republicans to support black citizenship and fundamental rights for blacks, and others to argue for black equality and suffrage.

The Lincoln Administration and the *Civil War Congress ignored the decision, banning slavery in all the western territories, despite Taney's assertation that such an act was unconstitutional. In 1866 Congress adopted the *Fourteenth Amendment, which declared that all persons born in the nation were citizens of the United States and of the state in which they lived. The ratification of this amendment in 1868 made the *civil rights aspects of *Dred Scott* a dead letter. The decision nevertheless remains a potent symbol of the denial of civil rights and the constitutionalization of racism under the Constitution of 1787.

[See also Fourteenth Amendment; Race and Ethnicity; Slavery, Law of]

- Don E. Fehrenbacher, *The Dred Scott Case: Its Significance in American Law and Politics,* 1978. Paul Finkelman, Dred Scott *v.* Sandford: *A Brief History With Documents,* 1997.   —Paul Finkelman

DRUGS, ILLEGAL. The history of drug prohibition in America is one of profound ambivalence, and the questions stirring drug policy debates today are as salient as they were a century ago. Should an individual be free to choose whether or not to take a mind-altering substance? If not, should drug use be viewed as criminal behavior to be punished by the law, or should it be viewed as a public *health problem and dealt with in ways that minimize the harms it causes? And in either case, should the goal be total eradication of drug use in the United States; or, should society tolerate some drug use as inevitable and address only the aspects that are socially disruptive or that significantly harm individual health?

America's answers to these questions have varied. Whether a particular substance has been subject to *regulation or prohibition has depended on if it was perceived as medically useful, a threat to social order, or dangerous to the user. Tobacco, for example, has been touted for its curative properties, protested by the Temperance movement, banned in some states, viewed as a symbol of sophistication, and subject to the Surgeon General's health warnings and the Cigarette Labeling and Advertising Act (1965). Since the 1990s cigarette smoking has become increasingly socially unacceptable and, due to associated health costs, the subject of major lawsuits.

Alcohol has had a similar history of acceptance and rejection in public opinion and in government regulation. In 1919 the federal government, through the Constitution's Eighteenth Amendment and the implementation of the Volstead Act, banned the use, production, and sale of alcohol, the most frequently used drug in the United States. This dramatic action culminated years of campaigning by clergy, social workers, middle-class Protestants, and organizers from the Women's Christian Temperance Union, for whom alcohol symbolized eastern, urban predominance and the decline of a traditional rural way of life.

*Organized crime gangs, who produced and sold alcohol to an eager and thirsty public, were the unintended consequence. The Eighteenth Amendment's repeal in 1933 was a Depression-era judgment that tax revenues were more important to the country than prohibition's cultural values. Alcohol use was, and continues to be, deeply embedded in the social culture of Americans despite the tremendous costs associated with its abuse.

In the last forty years, however, Americans have concentrated their regulatory efforts primarily on marijuana, opiates, cocaine, amphetamines, and hallucinogens. The Opium Exclusion Act (1909) made the importation of opium illegal, but it was still available through local production and continued to be used in patent *medicine. The Harrison Act (1914) further limited opium's availability to small amounts prescribed by licensed physicians, who were required to register and pay taxes on the drugs they prescribed. These laws marked the beginning of federal policing of the narcotics trade. Cocaine, like opium, gained popularity for its medicinal properties. Doctors prescribed it for depression, pain, heroin addiction, and lethargy. Additionally, it was one of the original ingredients in Coca Cola™ and was popular in wine. However, as its use and abuse spread, most states by 1916 had laws prohibiting the sale of opiates, even as a black market emerged.

In 1915 California enacted the first laws prohibiting marijuana, and by 1937 many states and the federal government had laws against it, such as the Marijuana Tax Stamp Act (1937). Widespread drug use in America gained attention in the 1960s as marijuana and other drugs gained popularity in the youth culture. Additionally, the war in Vietnam introduced hundreds of thousands of American soldiers to marijuana and heroin, and helped spawn a counterculture in which drug use became part of the more widespread rejection of authority. President Richard M. Nixon's concerns about drug-related crime led to passage of the Comprehensive Drug Abuse Prevention and Control Act (1970) and creation of the office of Drug Czar.

The states soon followed suit. In 1973 Governor Nelson D. Rockefeller of New York instituted what remain some of the toughest drug laws in the country, with mandatory prison sentences of fifteen years to life for selling small quantities of heroin or cocaine. Other politicians recognized the political capital to be gleaned from being tough on drug crime, and so began the escalating state and federal drug penalties that exist today.

In the 1970s prevention, education, and treatment garnered an equal or better share of government expenditures. Courts and policymakers considered drug addiction to be a medical issue. By the 1980s, this moderate approach shifted rapidly, and drug policy since has eschewed a public health model in favor of a punishment model.

During the Reagan administration, federal support for treatment diminished by 25 percent, reflecting the view that tax dollars should not be spent on drug addicts whose problems were thought to be self-inflicted. Congress eagerly adopted the punitive approach and passed the federal Anti-Drug Abuse Acts of 1986 and 1988, which remain the most comprehensive drug laws to date. They include a wide array of mandatory penalties and expand the government's ability to forfeit assets believed to be drug related. These laws redefined organized crime to include drug kingpins and reintroduced the death penalty into federal law by including it as punishment for drug-related killings. They created financial incentives for state and federal cooperation in drug law enforcement, expanded border patrols, and offered assistance in prison building. The anticrack cocaine hysteria of the 1980s lead to harsh and drastically disparate sentences (100:1 ratio) for cocaine charges, depending on whether the drug was in smokable "crack" or powder form. These tough antidrug laws reflected a national policy aimed at reducing supply and punishing demand. Former federal Drug Czar William Bennett in 1990 characterized drug use as a *moral evil that had to be stopped, and vigorously defended employing the death penalty for certain drug related homicides. The Supreme Court reflected this attitude toward drug crime in *Harmelin* v. *Michigan* (1991), when it compared the drug dealer's culpability to that of a murderer and held that a mandatory life sentence without the possibility of parole for selling cocaine was not *cruel and unusual punishment despite the fact that the defendant had no prior criminal record.

The combined state and federal drug policy expenditures are about $40 billion and growing. The treatment and education portions of the budget remain half of that used for law enforcement and interdiction, despite studies by the Rand Corporation showing that treatment produces a dramatic reduction in drug use and drug related crime at far less cost. Interdiction has been expanded beyond U.S. borders, most recently to Colombia, where in 2000 Congress approved a $1.3 billion effort to "eradicate" drug production machinery in Colombia partly by using U.S.-made helicopters. Nevertheless, today drugs are more plentiful, purer, and cheaper than ever. Although cocaine addiction is down, casual drug use is up, heroin addiction is up, and hard-core drug users number about four million. Nearly two million people are in America's jails and *prisons, 400,000 of them for drug offenses; this prison population is disproportionately ethnic minority. Constitutional protections, particularly those involving the Fourth Amendment's protection against unlawful *search and seizure, have been narrowed by the courts and, many have argued, ignored by the *police. Evidence of both police corruption and racial profiling in drug enforcement is a staple of the daily media. The enormity of the problem is exemplified by a government finding that a drug trafficker can afford to lose 90 percent of his product and still turn a profit.

The public may be more willing than politicians

to experiment with new approaches to the nation's drug problems—approaches aimed at the demand side rather than the supply side of the problem. In 2000, voters in five states approved referenda on drug related issues, with California passing an initiative mandating treatment rather than jail for charges of drug possession. Oregon and Utah altered provisions of *forfeiture laws by raising the government's *burden of proof and redirecting the seized assets away from law enforcement's own budget. Nevada and Colorado joined seven other states in approving measures that allow doctors to prescribe marijuana as a treatment for various illnesses. Even though doctors have long been permitted to prescribe opiates in pharmaceutical dosages, federal authorities are loathe to extend this policy to marijuana, which they see as a step toward legalization.

Another local initiative enjoying some success is the diversion of certain drug cases to specialized drug courts that utilize intensive probation, random drug testing, and frequent monitoring as an alternative to incarceration. Although the federal government has failed to endorse needle exchange programs, despite recommendations that these programs prevent the spread of human immunodeficiency virus (HIV), many states and localities have adopted such programs. It may be that such pragmatic experimentation on the state level will lead to a thorough reexamination of the national war on drugs.

A harm reduction policy based on the consequences of drug use would look very different. Treatment would receive more funds than incarceration. Inner city devastation caused by the crack epidemic of the 1980s and 1990s would be seen as a tear in the social fabric in need of mending rather than a problem solvable by imprisoning thousands of young minority men. Drug addicts would be coaxed into compliance with treatment incentives rather than harsh punishments. Medical programs would exist to help pregnant drug addicts avoid passing drugs on to their unborn babies in place of law enforcement efforts to test pregnant women for drugs with subsequent prosecution.

Nowhere else does one find the equivalent of the American government's wholesale demonization of the drug user. Many European countries have implemented a medical/harm reduction approach. Drug use and sale is illegal in most European Union countries, but enforcement of drug laws is not a high priority and the punishments are minimal. Laws or enforcement practices distinguish between hard and soft drugs; between those who possess small quantities for personal use and those who have larger quantities for sale; and between quiet use and disruptive use. At root, these policies assume that some individuals will always engage in risky behavior, and that the best a government can do is to raise awareness of health issues, encourage treatment and minimize harm to the individual user and to the public. In 2000, for example, The Netherlands decriminalized the use of psychedelic mushrooms, following a report by the Dutch Ministry of Health that found alcohol many times more damaging than drugs in that country. In Switzerland a three-year program providing prescription heroin to addicts had dramatically successful results including improved health of the addicts, a rise in their legitimate employment, decreased drug-related crime, and a general stabilization of their lives. These countries approach drug abuse as a public health problem to be dealt with by containment, education, prevention, treatment, and, only in extreme cases, punishment.

[See also Criminal Law]

• Joseph R. Gusfield, Symbolic Crusade, Status Politics and the American Temperance Movement, 2d ed., 1963, 1986. National Drug Control Strategy, Office of National Drug Control Policy, Washington, D.C., 1989, 1990, 1999. Zimring and Hawkins, The Search for Rational Drug Control, 1992. Juan R. Torruella (Hon.), One Judge's Attempt at a Rational Discussion of the So-called War on Drugs, 1996. Eric Blumenson and Eva Nilsen, "Policing for Profit: The Drug War's Hidden Economic Agenda," Chicago Law Review (1998). Michael Massing, The Fix, 1998. David Musto, The American Disease, 1999. Ethan Nadelman, "Commonsense Drug Policy," Foreign Affairs (1998): 111–26. Steven R. Belenko, Drugs and Drug Policy in America, 2000.

—Eva S. Nilsen

DRUNK DRIVING. See Automobiles and Crime.

DUELING. See Extralegality; Homicide.

DUE PROCESS

Procedural
Substantive

DUE PROCESS: PROCEDURAL

The term "due process" appears in two places in the United States Constitution, in the Fifth Amendment and the *Fourteenth Amendment, both of which prohibit deprivation of "life, liberty or property" without due process of law. But its meaning to American law goes back farther in time than the federal Constitution, and has a much broader reach, even today. It was Sir Edward

Coke who in 1641 explicitly equated the term "due process of law" with the older "law of the land." The latter phrase had appeared in the Magna Carta (1215), where it was set forth as a limitation on the ability of the king to take, imprison, or disseize a person of *property "except by the lawful judgment of his peers or by the law of the land."

Coke's conception of due process of law, which embraced procedural safeguards to check arbitrary exercise of governmental power as well as substantive limitation on the power of government, was extremely influential in the development of constitutional principle in the American colonies. Due process, to the colonists, provided a wide yet indefinite buffer zone of protection for individuals. It was, and remains, a notion of obligation on the government to act fairly, impartially, and rationally. The term "embodies a system of rights based on moral principles so deeply embedded in the traditions and feelings of our people as to be deemed fundamental to a civilized society as conceived by our whole history. Due Process is that which comports with the deepest notions of what is fair and right and just." (*Solesbee* v. *Balkcom*, 1950, Frankfurter, J., dissenting). The scope and application of the doctrine have been considerably refined and developed.

The core application of due process is in criminal *procedure. Those charged with criminal offenses are entitled to basic judicial procedures designed to increase the fairness of the adjudication. Some of those procedures, including right to *counsel and trial by *jury, are specifically guaranteed by other provisions of the Constitution. The due process clause performs two important additional functions: First, it renders most of the provisions of the *Bill of Rights applicable to state as well as federal prosecutions, and second, it imposes an independent right to "fundamental fairness" in the criminal setting. The latter is the source, for example, of the standard of proof applicable in criminal cases, requiring the prosecution to prove a defendant's guilt "beyond a reasonable doubt"—a very high standard. Criminal defendants also enjoy other independent rights under the umbrella of due process, including the right to an impartial decision-maker, to present a defense, and to disclosure of exculpatory *evidence, among others.

The reach of the due process clause is not limited to criminal adjudication. Litigants in civil proceedings are also entitled to certain basic guarantees of fairness by virtue of due process. Due process constrains, for example, a court's power to exercise personal jurisdiction in a civil case over a defendant who does not reside within the boundaries of the court's jurisdiction. In addition, even in civil cases due process is violated if the decision-maker has monetary, professional, or personal incentives to be partial. The basic components of due process in civil cases include reasonable notice of anticipated government action against a person and an opportunity to be heard.

Nor is the due process clause confined to the judicial branch of government. A very important focus of due process protection since the middle of the twentieth century has been the development of procedural principles to govern the actions of government agencies, which are typically part of the executive branch of either federal or state government. (Due process protections have not been applied to the procedures employed by legislatures, which do not typically act with respect to individuals.) A person appearing before an administrative agency has the following basic due process rights: to receive notice of the issues involved in the case; to present evidence and argument; to rebut adverse evidence; to appear with counsel; to have a decision based on the record; and to obtain access to the record. The federal Administrative Procedure Act (APA), enacted in 1946, reflects these and other procedures firmly in place in the federal administrative system. More than half the states have adopted codes based on the Uniform Law Commissioners' Model State Administrative Procedure Act, which is similar to the federal APA. These laws are designed to ensure, among other goals, compliance with due process imperatives in the administration of state agency action.

The trigger for any due process protection is a government effort to deprive a person (or entity) of life, *liberty, or property. While the notion of "life" has remained substantially unchanged, the meanings of "liberty" and "property" have continued to expand in modern interpretation. Threatened loss of physical liberty, the oldest and most widely acknowledged trigger for application of the clause, still presents the strongest case for due process protections. Even restraints on physical liberty that are not criminal in nature give rise to high levels of due process protection. Thus, any type of involuntary commitment for therapeutic or public-safety reasons must be preceded by a fair hearing to determine that the lawful grounds for such loss of liberty are established. In the case of adults, these grounds must be established to a "clear and convincing" certainty; children and adolescents, however, may be taken into state custody on a lesser showing, for nonpunitive reasons.

The notion of "liberty" is no longer confined, however, to mere lack of physical restraint. The *Supreme Court's cases suggest that any time the government takes action that significantly limits the freedom of a person to engage in an important activity, due process will require some sort of procedure to assure fairness in any underlying factual determinations. For example, the government may not deny a professional license without a showing that the applicant is unfit to hold the license. The granting, revocation, and suspension of driver's licenses, for the same reason, trigger a need for some kind of procedure to prevent arbitrary deprivation of liberty.

The term "property" has experienced the most dramatic growth. In a series of cases beginning in the 1960s, the Supreme Court recognized a new group of interests, described quite famously by one scholar as "The New Property," which, for the first time, were subject to due process protections even though they had previously been considered merely benefits or privileges, rather than rights. The types of benefits affected by this new analysis include welfare, social security, student financial aid, housing subsidies, food stamps, and a host of other government *"entitlements" established by statute, with stated criteria for eligibility. Once a federal or state law makes a person's entitlement to a benefit contingent on the satisfaction of specified criteria, then some sort of fair proceeding will be required if the government wishes to assert that a person once eligible no longer meets the criteria. The individual's interest rises to the level of a protected property interest only if it goes beyond mere expectancy, based on the terms of the law creating the interest. If a dispositive factual issue is in dispute, then some procedure will likely be required to resolve it fairly.

Once an individual has alleged a deprivation of an interest in life, liberty, or property sufficient to trigger due process protections, the question remains what process is "due" under the clause. It is clear that not all interests under the due process clause are entitled to the same procedures. Indeed, there is an array of possible procedures, ranging from the minimum of mere notice of an impending action, to a simple right to submit written documentation, all the way to a full, live evidentiary hearing with right to jury and counsel. Another important issue from the individual's perspective is the timing of this procedure, whether before or after the government takes its adverse action. The Supreme Court has established a balancing test designed to address these issues. Under *Mathews* v. *Eldridge* (1976), a court considers three factors in determining what process is required: first, the gravity of the individual's interest that the government action affects; second, the risk of error inherent in the existing procedures and the probable increase in accuracy to be expected by imposing additional procedures; and third, the interest of the government, including the fiscal and other burdens that additional procedures would entail.

Most states have due process clauses of their own, reflecting the tradition, since long before the drafting of the federal Constitution, of protecting due process. Of the fifty state constitutions, forty-six contain provisions identical or substantially similar to the federal due process clause. Because the states are already bound by the federal provision in the Fourteenth Amendment, these do not necessarily add to the procedural obligations on state governments. They do, however, provide the opportunity for states to afford greater procedural protections than the federal courts do, if state courts should choose to develop their own standards.

[*See also* Civil Liberties and Civil Rights; Economics and Law]

• Rodney L. Mott, *Due Process of Law,* 1926. Charles A. Reich, "The New Property," *Yale Law Journal* 73 (1964): 733–87. Richard B. Stewart, "The Reformation of American Administrative Law," *Harvard Law Review* 88 (1975): 1667–1813. Laurence H. Tribe, "Structural Due Process," *Harvard Civil Rights-Civil Liberties Law Review* 10 (1975): 269–321. Jerry L. Mashaw, *Due Process in the Administrative State,* 1985. Wayne R. LaFave & Jerold H. Israel, *Criminal Procedure,* 2d ed., 1992.

—Rebecca L. Brown

DUE PROCESS: SUBSTANTIVE

Substantive due process originated in the state *courts in the mid-nineteenth century and achieved fruition in the United States *Supreme Court during the early twentieth century, surviving in its original form until the Roosevelt *Court-packing controversy of 1937. In its federal version, the Supreme Court derived a test from the due process clause of the *Fourteenth Amendment for evaluating economic regulations such as wage and hour laws, product quality laws, licensing restrictions, and price regulation. Individuals were said to possess a "liberty of contract," which gave them freedom from governmental interference in decisions affecting individual economic status. This contrasted with the merely procedural rights intended by the framers of the *Constitution's due process clauses, as well as to the vested rights conceptions of the early nineteenth century, which gave such rights constitutional recognition only when they had been established in a binding *contract which the Constitution's contract clause said the state could not impair.

As Justice George Sutherland wrote in *Adkins* v. *Children's Hospital* (1923), which struck down a minimum wage statute, "the right to contract about one's affairs is a part of the liberty of the individual protected by [the due process] clause." The best-known federal decision invoking substantive due process is *Lochner* v. *New York* (1905), in which the Supreme Court overturned a state law establishing the maximum hours that New York bakers could work.

Early critics such as Roscoe *Pound and historians in the Progressive tradition viewed substantive due process as a dry legal formalism, in which the judges derived legal rules from worn-out principles. Later historians, particularly Morton White, Richard Hoftstadter, and Henry Steele Commager, believed that substantive due process was a manifestation of Social Darwinism in American legal thought.

More recent historians have challenged both of these views. Contrary to the legal formalism theory, the substantive due process era was a period of unprecedented judicial creativity. First, both state and federal courts reversed a long-standing policy of judicial deference to legislation and began striking down economic legislation on a large scale. Second, substantive due process judges produced some of the most creative, unconventional decisions ever known. One example is *Ex parte Young* (1908), which held that Eleventh Amendment sovereign immunity does not apply when a private party seeks to prohibit a state official from enforcing an unconstitutional rate regulation. Indeed, substantive due process was highly creative at its core, devising constitutional economic rules nowhere specified in the Constitution. The legislative history of the Fourteenth Amendment was all but irrelevant in substantive due process cases. The judges practiced aggressive, noninterpretivism equal to anything known in the 1960s and after. Tellingly, a bible of substantive due process jurisprudence was Christopher Tiedeman's *Unwritten Constitution of United States* (1890). Tiedeman argued that an "unwritten constitution" condemned state attempts to "protect the weak against the shrewdness of the stronger, to determine what wages a workman shall receive for his labor, and how many hours he shall labor."

Substantive due process was hardly a manifestation of Social Darwinism, although it received that appellation from a high source: in his dissenting opinion in *Lochner* Justice Oliver Wendell *Holmes Jr., accused the Court's majority of using the Fourteenth Amendment to "enact Mr. Herbert Spencer's Social Statics"—a naked accusation that they had incorporated Darwinian political philosophy into constitutional interpretation. There is little evidence, however, that any member of the Supreme Court was Social Darwinist, or even Darwinian. The Supreme Court's continuous citation in liberty of contract cases to "just equivalence" and "moral requirements" and "natural" or "inherent" rights was a reflection of Protestant orthodoxy and Scottish common sense realism.

The best ideological explanation of substantive due process is that it was a mixture of Protestant orthodoxy and classical political economy, much like the political philosophy of the curriculum of American colleges through the middle of the nineteenth century. These views have been confirmed in the many studies that have found the origins of substantive due process not in federal decisions of the late nineteenth and early twentieth centuries, but rather in state court decisions that stretch back to the highly evangelical Jacksonian era. The 1830s and 1840s witnessed the twin impulses of moral reform and economic individualism that culminated in substantive due process. Indeed, the ideology of substantive due process resembles the intensely religious moral philosophy more than the secularized thought of a Spencer or William Graham Sumner. Many Americans in the Protestant orthodox tradition developed systems of both moral philosophy and political economy that emphasized the strong role of the state in regulating morals, but insisted that individuals be the regulators of their own economic destinies. America's conservative judiciary perceived itself as the strongest defender of this moral brand of self-reliance. It often believed the new interventionist politics of the Progressive era as the biggest threat to liberty.

Substantive due process in the U.S. Supreme Court came to an abrupt end in 1937 when President Franklin D. Roosevelt proposed his Court-packing plan. While the plan itself failed, the almost immediate result was Justice Owen Roberts' change of sides coupled with several resignations that gave the Court a New Deal stamp by the early 1940s.

But substantive due process has never completely died. It has resurfaced time and again when the Supreme Court has seen fit to declare certain rights free from government interference even though they are not expressly granted by any clause in the Constitution. Rather, they are thought to be part of the basic liberties that democratic government must protect. Among these are the right to marry, even someone of a different race (*Loving* v. *Virginia* (1967)); a woman's right to obtain an *abortion (*Roe* v. *Wade* (1973)); the right to live with members of one's own extended family (*Moore* v. *East Cleveland* (1977)); the right not to be charged excessive punitive damages (*BMW* v. *Gore* (1996)). In most of these cases the Supreme Court has insisted that before the substantive due process right will be recognized, the person seeking to challenge it must show that the right was traditionally protected or recognized by the government, and that the statute under consideration deviates from that traditional view. For that reason in *Bowers* v. *Hardwick* (1986), the Supreme Court refused to find that consenting adults had a substantive due process right to engage in homosexual relations. In general, the trend since the 1990s has been toward a narrowing of substantive due process rights.

• Lawrence M. Friedman, "Freedom of Contract and Occupational Licensing 1890–1910: A Legal and Social Study," *California Law Review* 53 (1965): 487–534. William E. Nelson, "The Impact of the Antislavery Movement upon Styles of Judicial Reasoning in Nineteenth Century America," *Harvard Law Review* 87 (1974): 513–66. Laurence H. Tribe and Michael C. Dorf, "Levels of Generality in the Definition of Rights," *University Chicago Law Review* 57 (1990) 1057–1108. Herbert Hovenkamp, *Enterprise and American Law: 1836–1937*, 1991. William J. Novak, *The People's Welfare: Law and Regulation in Nineteenth-Century America*, 1996. Laurence H. Tribe, *American Constitutional Law*, 3d ed., 2000.

—Herbert Hovenkamp

DUI. *See* Automobiles and Crime.

DURABLE POWER OF ATTORNEY. *See* Power of Attorney.

E

EASEMENTS. *See* Property, Real.

EAVESDROPPING, ELECTRONIC. *See* Wiretapping and Electronic Eavesdropping.

ECONOMICS AND LAW. Since its Colonial inception, the United States has been largely, but not exclusively, a market economy. While "mercantilist" economic conceptions envisioning more active governmental *regulation were present during the seventeenth and eighteenth centuries, by the 1820s the new nation had an economy based on classical free-market principles. The legal system reflected this commitment, generally preferring market approaches over those that depend on government command and control of economic resources. One manifestation was a strong doctrine of liberty of *contract that after 1800 was loathe to interfere in freely made bargains.

Another manifestation of the free market was the rise of the "classical" concept of the business *corporation during the Jacksonian era. Classical political economists such as Adam Smith and John Stuart Mill believed that capital would flow naturally toward investments that promised to be profitable, provided that the government kept its hands off. Under classicism, the corporation was no longer conceived as a special prerogative of the mercantilist Crown, but rather as an ordinary device for assembling large amounts of capital so that it could be controlled efficiently by a few active managers. The classical business corporation began to emerge early in the post-Federalist Supreme Court. For example, Jackson appointee Chief Justice Roger B. *Taney declared in the *Charles River Bridge* case (1837) that a monopoly privilege would not be implied in a bridge corporation's charter, thus ending the view that corporate status implied special economic *privileges.

The developing model of the classical corporation included two fundamental premises: (1) the corporate form is not a special privilege from the state, but merely one of many forms of *business organization; (2) in a market economy, the peculiar advantage of the corporation that the law should encourage is its unique ability to raise and direct capital efficiently.

The states generally adopted a hands-off policy toward the business corporation, an attitude that eventually led to problems. The corporation worked most efficiently when decision-making was confined to a small number of coordinated managers. As the number of shareholders in American business corporations grew, and their relative involvement in daily corporate affairs diminished, the corporation experienced the "separation of ownership and control" that New Deal scholars such as Adolf Berle and Gardiner Means lamented. They argued that most stockholders had little to say about the real management of the corporation's affairs. Such decisions were in the hands of managers, whose ownership interest was generally small. Further, the interest of managers and the interest of stockholders often diverged. As a result, the corporation could not be expected to behave in the public interest.

Further, the corporation had become very large, thanks to its ability to reduce costs by large-scale production. The disadvantage of this, however, was that markets were widely perceived as being less competitive than they had been in the past. The result was the death of the classical corporation and the rise of large-scale business regulation during the New Deal, in particular the Securities and Securities Exchange Acts of 1933 and 1934, expansion of the *antitrust laws and the *labor exemption from them, and wholesale federal regulation of industries thought to be inherently monopolistic.

By the end of the New Deal, little was left of the classical corporation. Its internal dealings with shareholders were substantially regulated by the federal *securities acts. Its labor relations were regulated by the new federal labor laws. Its relations with *consumers and suppliers became increasingly regulated by the antitrust laws and the Federal Trade Commission (FTC), which tried to impose a duty on it to engage only in "fair" competition. In 1938, the Federal Trade Commission Act was amended to establish the FTC's jurisdiction over a firm's "unfair or deceptive acts or practices." For the emerging category of utilities and "public service" companies, regulation was even more complete, including restrictions on entry and price controls.

The origins of the modern *Law and Economics movement lay in this same reaction to economic classicism. Wide-ranging economic analysis of legal policy in the United States was first undertaken during the Progressive Era, roughly 1900 to 1920. An important pioneer in this work was Henry Carter Adams, whose classic essay, *The Relation of the State to Industrial Action* (1887), redefined regulatory policy toward the business firm by relating the appropriate degree of regulation to the presence of economies of scale that required business firms to be very large.

The early practitioners of Law and Economics were hostile toward classical political economy, and generally embraced the economic theory of the day, which espoused significant state intervention. For example, Thomas Nixon Carver employed Anglo-American "neoclassical" economics to make a social welfare argument for the graduated income tax. Edwin R. A. Seligman became a prominent authority on progressive income taxation, and was widely cited by the courts on questions of tax policy. Thorstein Veblen wrote the first economic analysis of the business firm shortly after the turn of the twentieth century. Veblen's work was elaborated with great brilliance by his student John R. Commons in the 1920s. Progressive economists such as Richard T. Ely wrote sizable books on the relationship between contract and *property law and the distribution of wealth, concluding that these legal areas required a larger measure of government regulation than the common law provided.

In sum, Law and Economics during the Progressive Era was robust and lively and encompassed a wide range of legal inquiries. However, its practitioners were distinguished from post-1960s Law and Economics in two respects. First, the earlier group believed that interpersonal comparisons of utility were possible, and justified broad-based policies of wealth redistribution. Second, Progressives engaged in Law and Economics were generally more interested in legislation than in *common-law rules, and tended to be optimistic about the use of regulation to achieve goals in the public interest.

The academic foundation of Progressive Era Law and Economics crumbled with the rise of "ordinalism" in the 1930s and after. The Progressives had assumed that economists could make interpersonal comparisons of utility. For example, they believed that a wealthy person placed low utility on each additional, or "marginal," dollar in his bank account because he already had so many. By contrast, a poor person valued each dollar very highly. As a result, transfers of wealth away from the affluent and toward the poor were believed to increase the total amount of utility in the economy. But in 1932, British economist Lionel Robbins showed that there was no empirical basis for quantifying and comparing the amount of utility held by one person with that held by another. Then, in the 1950s, Kenneth Arrow showed that democratic voting could also not be shown to produce wealth-distribution decisions that increased overall social utility. This revolution in welfare economics led to the view that economics should restrict its conclusions to the "efficiency," or overall size, of the economic pie. Economics had little to say about questions of wealth distribution. This paved the way for an aggressive restoration of free-market principles, and the rise of the modern Law and Economics movement.

No matter how one dates the revival of Law and Economics, much of the credit must be given to the law school and economics department of the University of Chicago. The "Chicago School" stands for an approach to Law and Economics that is rigorously neoclassical in the sense that it rests on strong assumptions of utility and profit maximization, traditionally ordinalist, and positivistic in its methodology. Its approach is also highly analytical and somewhat ahistorical.

The new Law and Economics movement can be said to have begun in 1960, with Ronald H. Coase's publication of "The Problem of Social Cost." Just as Lionel Robbins' work sharply reduced the domain of welfare economics to the study of markets and efficiency, Coase's work reduced the domain of Law and Economics to the study of the implications of the Coase Theorem for legal rule-making.

The Coase Theorem says that in a well-functioning market (one with minimal transaction, or bargaining, costs, and freely transferable interests), bargainers will reach a result that is both (1) efficient and (2) invariant to the underlying common-law rule. To illustrate, suppose that the operation of Λ's grinding machine benefits A by $40, but its noise causes $25 in annoyance to neighbor B. Suppose that B sued A for a nuisance, and B won. Then A would pay B some amount between $25 and $40 for the right to continue grinding, and both parties would be better off. By contrast, suppose that B lost his nuisance case. B would then be willing to pay A up to $25 for A to discontinue the noise, but A would not accept anything less than $40, so the transaction would not occur. In sum, whether or not the law recognizes the grinding as a nuisance, it will continue ("invariance thesis"), and in both cases the outcome is efficient because it preserves the $40 value at the expense of the $25 value, assuming that no one else has an interest one way or the other ("efficiency thesis").

As Coase himself saw the Theorem, it was designed to encourage the study of the role of transaction costs in our legal system. Once bargaining is costly, as in many cases involving complex or unique interests, then it can no longer be trusted to give the correct result. In sum, Coase intended his Theorem less as a normative argument for free markets than as a device for shifting the study of legal rules toward the role of transaction costs.

The neoclassical interpretation of the Coase Theorem, which is dominant in Law and Economics today, sees its real brilliance in the analysis of disputes between two persons (or firms) over legal *entitlements—precisely the kind of dispute that forms the setting for most common-law disputes. This connection between Law and Economics and the common-law system of structuring legal rights cannot be exaggerated. Neoclassical Law and Economics generally believes that the institution of the common law, with its elaborate toleration of private settlements of disputes, is nothing more than a market.

The Coase Theorem has many important implications for the economic analysis of legal rules. If the goal of law is allocative efficiency, then legal policy should do two things. First, it should leave the market to determine outcomes wherever the market functions well. Second, the law should minimize the effects of transaction costs by selecting a rule that would approximate the result of bargaining in a world without transaction costs. To take a simple example, consider the legal rule concerning whether trains or automobiles must stop at grade crossings. One might imagine a "market" in which the automobile driver would call out a price to the approaching train—"I'll give you $1.00 if you stop." The parties would hope-

fully agree on a price and assignment of the right to proceed before a collision occurred. In the real world, bargaining in this situation is impossible, so the legal system assigns the right to proceed to the train, for it has the highest stopping costs. This outcome maximizes social value. If the parties could have bargained in a perfectly functioning market, this would have been the outcome in any event.

Law and Economics has been ubiquitous in legal scholarship since the 1980s, touching every area of law. A summary of a few major themes follows.

Coase's work initially inspired an outpouring of literature concerned with property and *tort law. For example, several scholars explored the Coasian assumption of zero transaction costs, and the consequences of relaxing the assumption. This led to analysis of the types of legal rules best calculated to yield efficient solutions in various markets. A *"liability" rule is a rule that protects by an action for damages. A "property" rule is one that protects by an action for an injunction, but the parties can bargain around the subject of the injunction. An "inalienability" rule is also protected by an injunction, but the condemned act is positively illegal, and cannot be authorized by the parties through a private settlement. Guido Calabresi and A. Douglas Melamed argued that damages rules should be preferred in cases where valuations are easily made. Liability (injunction) rules are better where valuation is uncertain and the transaction costs of negotiating outcomes are very high. Inalienability rules might be thought to be most appropriate where the costs of assembling all those affected by a practice is very high. For example, pollution may injure a large number of people, but only a few could effectively bargain about their interests, and holdout problems could be significant. In that case, a regulation stipulating the amount of pollution or the amount of permissible injury might be better.

Law and Economics has produced a highly generalized theory of tort law. For example, an act causing harm is deemed "negligent" if the cost of the precaution not taken is less than the amount of the injury multiplied by the probability that the injury will occur. Further, the rule of contributory negligence says that the party to the accident who can avoid the mishap at the lowest cost should be the one to take the necessary precaution. For example, if the expected cost of the accident is $100, and the defendant could have prevented the accident at a cost of $80, he will be liable. But if the plaintiff could have prevented the accident at a cost of $60, the defendant will not be held liable. Finally, *strict liability (liability without fault) is appropriate when the best way to avoid losses is to reduce the level of activity rather than the level of care with which the activity is exercised. This might occur when the activity is especially hazardous, such as the storage of explosives in a residential area.

Law and Economics has also produced a theory of *criminal punishment, in which the optimal criminal sanction is a fine that is just sufficient to deter the criminal from engaging in the harmful activity. If the sanction is any harsher, then a criminal may not be constrained from committing a greater offense. For example, if both robbery and murder are punishable by death, the robber who had committed the first crime would not be constrained from also committing the second. An efficiently proportioned legal rule would be precise enough to make the crime unprofitable, allowing for the risk of nondetection. For example, if the value of the theft to the criminal is $100 and the probability of detection is ⅓, then the optimal penalty would be a fine of approximately $301, or just enough to make the theft unprofitable.

Although this rule may make considerable sense when applied to business criminals, applying it to biological persons is much more speculative. For example, criminals often obtain satisfaction from their crimes that are unrelated to the financial gain. In many situations, such as rape or child molestation, the criminal may not reap any *financial* gains at all. In that case, the optimal sanction must deprive the criminal of an amount of *utility* that, when discounted by the risk of detection, will make the crime unattractive to the criminal. Clearly, however, calculating the optimal sanction even for a single criminal now provokes serious problems of measurement. How does one balance the disutility of a given amount of incarceration against the utility derived from a particular crime? Coming up with a generalized punishment requires interpersonal utility comparisons of the grossest sort.

The same problems arise with respect to *family law. Some of the most interesting work in Law and Economics analogizes the family to a business firm. But the argument can be pushed only so far without running into problems of interpersonal utility comparisons. The device that has facilitated the expansion of economic inquiries into this area is the concept of "human capital," which turns the family into a kind of business firm in order to make economic analysis possible. Richard Posner, probably the best known writer on Law and Eco-

nomics, begins his analysis of family law with the observation "that the household is not merely a consuming, but more importantly a producing, unit in society." In this model, "the food, clothing, furniture, medicines, and other market commodities that the household purchases are inputs into the production of nourishment, warmth, affection, children, and other tangible and intangible goods that constitute the output of the household." One powerful argument in Law and Economics, particularly in the Chicago School, is that the common law is a more efficient mechanism for allocating resources than are most forms of government regulation. The argument really consists of two quite distinct parts. The first part argues that the common law is efficient because free markets are efficient, and the common law seeks to further market outcomes. This argument has been subject to numerous variations. Among the most prominent are that efficient common-law rules tend to outlast inefficient rules because inefficient ones are more costly and thus more likely to be challenged. Thus the common law "evolves" toward greater efficiency.

The other part of the argument is that government regulation is largely inefficient. In some cases, it is calculated to transfer wealth to small, well-organized interest groups. In other cases, regulation produced within the democratic system produces such haphazard results that they simply cannot be justified on efficiency grounds. This view is hostile toward government regulation, and its proponents sometimes argue that judicial power and even the Constitution should be used to preserve market outcomes over those prescribed by inefficient legislation.

While the Chicago School of Law and Economics has always been criticized, any talk of a "post-Chicago" Law and Economics might seem premature. Indeed, two Chicago architects of Law and Economics have won the economics Nobel Prize (Ronald Coase, 1991; Gary Becker, 1992). One of the consequences of the great success of the Law and Economics movement is that its influence and fundamental disciplinary approaches have spread widely, taking in many who do not have the same ideological commitments as those commonly associated with the University of Chicago. Ideological diversity seems to be a consequence of the great success of Law and Economics rather than of its failure.

Whatever the reason, many writers are departing from the perceived Chicago orthodoxy. Some have argued that whatever role the concept of the rational actor may have in formal economic analysis, legal analysis requires a richer, more substantive notion of what rationality means. Apropos of this, Law and Economics should accommodate other social sciences, such as psychology, much more readily. Others have argued that the Chicago-inspired dichotomy between efficiency and distribution is wrong-headed, and that often the efficiency of legal outcomes cannot be studied apart from consequences for the distribution of wealth. Yet others have argued that Chicago-style Law and Economics uses two inconsistent conceptions of rationality—an optimistic robust concept in its discussion of market efficiency, and a much weaker and more pessimistic concept in its discussion of rational democratic decision-making.

Other critiques are not "post-Chicago" at all, but may actually precede it. For example, libertarians have long been critical of Law and Economics for being too willing to subordinate fundamental questions about justice and property rights to a kind of cost-benefit analysis where nothing is considered as "fundamental."

Notwithstanding, Law and Economics has acquired a permanent place in law school curricula and has had a significant influence on both judicial and legislative decision-making.

[*See also* Due Process; Law and Economics, Theory of]

• Henry Carter Adams, "The Relation of the State to Industrial Action," *Publications of the American Economics Association* 1 (1887): 472. Adolf A. Berle Jr., and Gardiner C. Means, *The Modern Corporation and Private Property*, 1932. Ronald H. Coase, "The Nature of the Firm," *Economica* 4 (1937) (n.s.): 386. Ronald H. Coase, "The Problem of Social Cost," *Journal of Law & Economics* 3 (1960): 1. Kenneth J. Arrow, *Social Choice and Individual Values*, 2d ed., 1963. Guido Calabresi and A. Douglas Melamed, "Property Rules, Liability Rules, and Inalienability: One View of the Cathedral," *Harvard Law Review* 85 (1972): 1089. Gary S. Becker, *The Economic Approach to Human Behavior*, 1976. William M. Landes and Richard A. Posner, *The Economic Structure of Tort Law*, 1987. Daniel A. Farber and Philip P. Frickey, *Law and Public Choice: a Critical Introduction*, 1991. Herbert Hovenkamp, *Enterprise and American Law, 1836–1937*, 1991. Herbert Hovenkamp, "Law and Economics in the United States: A Brief Historical Survey," *Cambridge Journal of Economics* 19 (1995): 331. Richard A. Posner, *The Economic Analysis of Law*, 5th ed., 1998.

—Herbert Hovenkamp

ECOTAGE. *See* Environmental Law.

EDUCATION, LEGAL

Law Schools. The first American law school, the Litchfield Law School, was founded sometime between 1774 and 1784 and lasted for fifty to sixty years. The course of study was based on a series of lectures on forty-eight subjects presented over a period of fourteen months. The method of instruction was strictly the lecture. At about the same time that the Litchfield Law School was founded, chairs of law were being established at American colleges: in 1779 at the College of William and Mary, in 1790 at the College of Philadelphia, in 1793 at Columbia College, in 1799 at Transylvania University, in 1801 at Yale, and in 1815 at Harvard. Again, as at the Litchfield Law School, the method of instruction was lecture.

During the mid-nineteenth century, more university-affiliated law schools were established. In 1850, fifteen law schools awarded degrees. By 1870 the number had grown to thirty-one, and by 1890, sixty-one. In 1900, 102 law schools were in operation in thirty-three states. Very few law schools were not affiliated with universities. In the late nineteenth and early twentieth century, the Young Men's Christian Association (YMCA) established fourteen law schools. Universities eventually absorbed most of the unaffiliated and YMCA schools. To put the dramatic growth of law school education into perspective, consider that in the sixty years from 1850 to 1910 about seventy-five law schools opened, on average more than one new school each year, and by 1910 there were almost twenty thousand law students in the United States. This explosive growth spawned the need for an organization of law schools, and the *Association of American Law Schools (AALS) was formed by thirty charter member schools in 1900.

With the emergence of the unaffiliated and YMCA schools, which provided part-time legal education, most often in the evenings, a substantial debate developed over the goals of legal education and the content of the law school curriculum. Some of the established university-affiliated law schools excluded minorities (religious and ethnic/racial), women, and immigrants and their children, openly questioning the character of these groups and their competence to practice law effectively and ethically. In response, Notre Dame and Georgetown established law schools in 1869 and 1890, respectively, for Roman Catholic students. Howard University opened a law school in 1869 for African-American students. Portia Law School (now New England School of Law in Boston) opened in 1909 as an unaffiliated law school exclusively for female students. Many of the programs open to people of color, women, and immigrants were conducted part-time, often through evening course work. This schedule allowed students to work full-time day jobs to finance their legal studies, and incidentally allowed the schools to draw their faculty members from the ranks of practicing lawyers and sitting judges (rather than having to hire full-time academics to teach law).

Some of the university law schools questioned the quality of part-time education and the tendency of the unaffiliated and YMCA schools to emphasize a practical rather than academic legal education. The debate about part-time legal education, admissions practices, the content of the curriculum, and teaching methods that surfaced in the mid-nineteenth century continued with varying degrees of intensity into the mid-twentieth century. Today, the debate has been largely resolved by the positions taken by the Section on Legal Education and Admissions to the Bar of the *American Bar Association (ABA). The ABA currently is the principal accrediting agency of law schools. It sets the standards for accreditation and conducts periodic inspections of schools to ensure that they comply with its standards. In 2000, the ABA accredited 184 law schools. Membership in the AALS also requires schools to submit to and pass a rigorous inspection and review process and to be periodically reinspected. Several schools are accredited by the ABA but are not members of the AALS. All states except Alaska and New Hampshire currently have at least one law school.

The ABA created the Section on Legal Education and Admissions to the Bar in 1893—the first section created by the ABA. In 1896 the section engaged in serious debate about the criteria for admission to law school and the method of instruction. The debate within the section on whether the content of legal education should emphasize an academic or a practical curriculum was constant and heated.

This debate about legal education continued without resolution until 1921, when the Section on Legal Education and Admissions to the Bar proposed its first standards for admission to law school. The standards were a mix of general principles and specific requirements. Over the next few decades, the section developed detailed standards that covered various aspects of legal education— a process often embroiled in controversy. The section also actively engaged in the founding of the National Conference of Bar Examiners (NCBE) in 1931 and development of the Law School Admission Test (LSAT) in 1948. The goal of the NCBE was to increase the efficiency and effectiveness of state boards of admission to the bar and to improve the quality of legal education. The purpose of the LSAT was to provide better measures of the ability of applicants to successfully complete law school.

In 1956 the Section on Legal Education and Admissions to the Bar decided to reinspect law schools every seven years to ensure that they were meeting accreditation standards beyond their initial approval. After some controversy, in 1973 the section adopted a set of standards for accreditation, which, with some modification, are still in force today. In addition to the criteria for admission to law school, the standards set the criteria for the school's faculty, administration, organization, curriculum, and library. The importance of ABA accreditation is that graduates of an ABA-accredited law school are eligible to take the *bar exam in every state and territory in the union. Graduates of a law school not accredited by the ABA do not have this privilege.

Admissions and the Law Programs. The American Bar Association standards set the general criteria for accreditation by the association. Unlike most law schools in Europe and Asia, American law schools require a bachelor's degree for admission to their doctor of law (Juris Doctor; J.D.) programs. The J.D. is the first degree in law (the first degree was formerly bachelor of laws, LL.B., which is still granted occasionally in the United States). Higher degrees (LL.M. and S.J.D.) are discussed below ("Graduate and Joint Degree Programs").

The usual course of study for a J.D. takes three academic years or six semesters; it may take four years of part-time study (usually through evening programs). A J.D. at most schools requires eighty-five to ninety semester units of academic credit. The course of study covers the basic areas of the law such as *contracts and *commercial law, *criminal law and *procedure, *torts, *property, constitutional law (see CONSTITUTIONS, UNITED STATES), *evidence, *ethics, and skills in drafting documents and presenting cases in courts and administrative agencies.

In addition to holding a bachelor's degree, applicants for law school admission must take an examination that measures their potential for successfully completing the J.D. degree. The Law School Admissions Test is universally relied upon by law schools to satisfy this requirement. The LSAT, first used in 1948 on a limited scale, was initially developed and administered for testing the suitability of law school applicants from lesser known universities with unrecognized academic programs. It was administered by a loose association of law schools active in the ABA and AALS. The group was incorporated in 1968 and named the Law School Admissions Council (LSAC). Since its incorporation, the LSAC has continued to refine and administer the LSAT and engage in empirical studies on legal education.

In selecting applicants for admission, most law schools follow a similar process. First, they set the criteria they will use to accept applicants. They select or rank universities and colleges from which they wish to select their students, choose the undergraduate grade point average (GPA) and majors they expect of their students, and then decide what LSAT score is acceptable. Second, law schools usually sort the applicants into three pools. The first pool consists of applicants the school clearly wishes to accept, if not solicit. The second pool consists of applicants they clearly will reject. The final pool includes the applicants they may accept after further investigation so as to fill their enrollment. The applications from this group are studied and some applicants are interviewed to ascertain which of them possess the skills and character necessary for successfully completing law school.

The admissions criteria vary greatly among the schools. In addition to criteria based on academic achievements, some schools actively seek out women, minorities, and other groups who were once excluded from law schools and the bar. The law schools may offer various financial incentives to students who are highly sought after for admission, such as tuition waivers, low-interest loans, and scholarship funds.

Teaching Methods. As legal education moved into the academic institutions, the first teaching method was necessarily the lecture, the method used by experienced lawyers and judges in presenting oral summaries on various legal subjects. Occasionally, moot courts were also conducted, in which students argued mock cases before their teachers and fellow students. Soon, however, another teaching method was to develop, in somewhat the same way that common law develops— one case at a time, with due respect accorded to legal precedents (called *stare decisis*).

Credit for the founding of the case method of study and the casebook in American legal education belongs to Professor Christopher Columbus Langdell of Harvard. His belief was that law is a science and should be studied in a manner akin to the study of the natural sciences. The vehicle for legal study was the body of case law. By examining a series of cases tracing the development of a principle, a student of the law could gain a proper understanding of that principle.

Langdell prepared the first real casebook, *A Se-lection of Cases on the Law of Contracts,* which he employed in his classroom in advance sheet form in 1870; it was published in 1871. Preparation of the casebook allowed Langdell to teach by the case method, for without casebooks there was an enormous practical barrier to the systematic study of cases (professors would assign a series of cases to a class of students, each of whom would need the same books from the university's law library at the same time). The earliest casebooks were simply compilations of large numbers of unedited case decisions separated only by subject-matter headings.

Development of the case method of instruction and the casebook sparked a serious debate that lasted at least forty years, and surfaces occasionally today. The opponents were the proponents of the lecture method, but the latter was eventually replaced by the case method. Originally, the case method was intended to involve exclusively the study of a series of cases, but it has evolved into a mixture of lecture, problem-solving, and study of statutes and other materials, as well as the study of cases. Today, the mix of teaching methods in law schools includes on-line instruction and increased opportunities for practical training in legal research and writing, trial and appellate litigation, alternative dispute-resolution methods, and commercial transactional practice (including negotiation and drafting exercises). Just as there is an evolutionary process for the curricula and teaching methods in elementary schools and beyond, so too law schools engage in continuing debate over what and how to teach, including the same cyclical refrains about returning to "the basics."

Law Reviews. An important part of legal education and the practice of law involves law reviews. The first legal periodical in the United States, published in 1808, was the *American Law Journal and Miscellaneous Repertory,* usually known simply as the *Repertory.* This legal periodical (not edited by students) appeared after the development of case reporter publications but before legal magazines. The *Repertory* contained lengthy excerpts of judicial opinions, a short biography, notices and descriptions of recent law books, and an editorial section. It was published until 1817. Other similar journals were published in the early nineteenth century, but these were short-lived because they were very similar to the numerous case law reporters and their attempts to attract a wide readership made them too general for practicing attorneys and too technical for lay people.

The next type of American legal periodical made its appearance in 1829 with publication of the *United States Law Intelligencer and Review*, the antecedent of the modern legal magazine. This journal contained lead articles and case reports, but ceased publication after only three volumes because of financial problems. Its failure was typical for that period. Approximately thirty law journals had been launched by 1850, but only ten had survived.

A new kind of law journal emerged in the mid-nineteenth century: nationally oriented publications. Two journals of this new type were the *American Law Register*, which began in 1852, and the *American Law Review*, in 1866. At their inception, these journals were not edited by students. The *American Law Register* was a monthly publication that contained more scholarly articles than did other journals. In 1945 it evolved to its present form, the *University of Pennsylvania Law Review*. This law review is the oldest continuously published legal periodical in the United States. The *American Law Review*, a quarterly publication, was similar to modern law reviews. It contained lead articles, book reviews, news of regional and national legal events, and other contributions from practitioners and scholars. The *American Law Review* was one of the most important legal periodicals of the nineteenth century and served as a model for the student-edited law reviews of the late nineteenth and early twentieth centuries.

A slightly different type of legal periodical began gaining prominence in the 1870s. Rather than publishing articles with a strong academic orientation as did the *American Law Review* and the *American Law Register*, these new periodicals were designed to provide practical information. Their articles discussed "recent decisions, developments in law and legal education, efforts at codification, and news in a journalistic rather than in a scholarly style." These "practitioner-oriented" journals did not have many "lead" articles, because the articles were placed in the middle, not at the beginning, of the journal. Rather, they "typically began with comments or editorials, followed by brief articles, case reports, digests, and concluded with book notices."

One of the most successful of the practitioner-oriented journals was the *Albany Law Journal*, which began weekly publication in 1870 and continued for almost forty years. The *Albany Law Journal* had the largest circulation of any legal periodical of its time and was a tremendous success. Similar journals appeared in the 1870s. Interestingly, the 1870s saw the rise of specialized journals similar to those growing rapidly today. Examples included the *Insurance Law Journal* and the *Medico-Legal Journal*. In 1870 there were seventeen legal periodicals, and by 1886, forty-two.

The first American law periodical to be published by students instead of by practitioners was the *Albany Law School Journal*, beginning in 1875. However, this journal lasted only one academic year. The second student-run legal periodical appeared at the Columbia Law School, the *Columbia Jurist*; this lasted only two years. Today, there are more than four hundred student-edited law reviews centered in the nation's law schools. About half of them are general law reviews, and about half are specialty reviews (specializing in particular topic areas such as tax law, health law, labor law, and so on). Law reviews are significant components of legal education for those students who become part of the reviews' editorial staffs, and these reviews also constitute significant elements of the programs of their parent law schools. Law reviews can have a substantial influence on the development of law and policy and bring considerable prestige to their sponsoring schools (see PUBLISHING, LAW).

In the mid-twentieth century, an organization of law reviews called the National Conference of Law Reviews was established. Many, though by no means all, of the law reviews are members of the conference. The conference hosts an annual educational meeting for law review staff members, and in the 1990s it adopted a Model Code of Ethics for both law review authors and the law reviews themselves.

Graduate and Joint Degree Programs. Historically, law schools granted two graduate degrees beyond the J.D. degree. The first graduate degree in law is the LL.M., a master's degree. Admission to an LL.M. program generally requires a J.D.; some foreign law graduates or foreign-licensed lawyers may also be admitted. The course of study is usually one year in a full-time program, or about twenty-four hours of academic credits. The LL.M. was once a means for lawyers to enhance their academic credentials, especially for a teaching position, and was to a lesser extent a means of developing a specialty in areas of law less fully developed in the J.D. program. Limited specialty areas such as *patent law, *taxation, maritime law (see ADMIRALTY AND MARITIME JURISDICTION), and *labor law were commonplace in the earlier graduate study of law. Today, the LL.M. offerings have expanded dramatically. Hundreds of LL.M. programs are in place in American law schools, providing specialty training in greatly expanded subject areas, such as *health law, *technology and *privacy law, *comparative law, real estate law, legal advocacy, *environmental law, and so forth.

The second graduate degree in law is the S.J.D., a doctor of science in the law (doctor of juridical science), almost exclusively sought by persons with a J.D. and perhaps an LL.M. as a means of obtaining an academic appointment. Very few S.J.D. degrees are now awarded. The fact that all law degrees in the United States are postgraduate degrees is merely a reflection of the history of legal education. When the undergraduate LL.B. was abandoned in American universities in favor of three-year postgraduate study for a J.D., the LL.M. and S.J.D. remained as degrees to be sought after completion of the J.D.

The ABA involves itself minimally in graduate law programs. It is merely interested in whether a graduate program adversely affects a school's J.D. program. To this extent, the ABA does not accredit the graduate law program; it rather "acquiesces" in the program. Thus, each law school is left to establish the criteria by which it admits applicants and structures its graduate law program. The typical criteria for admission of an American law graduate are a J.D. from an ABA-accredited law school and an acceptable law school GPA. The admission criteria for a foreign law graduate are an LL.B. from a recognized university and an acceptable score on the Test of English as a Foreign Language (TOEFL). Publications are available to assist graduate program administrators in American law schools in academically ranking foreign universities and rating their academic programs.

In addition to graduate law degrees, many schools offer interdisciplinary programs and combined degrees. The interdisciplinary programs range from course offerings to programs or centers. The combined degrees include J.D.s or LL.M.s combined with doctoral or master's degrees in other disciplines. The interdisciplinary programs and combined degrees recognize that law is just one of many disciplines that affect or regulate conduct in society and is often intertwined with other disciplines.

Interdisciplinary programs cover a broad range of topics, from such popular subjects as social work, housing, and employment to philosophy, anthropology, and literature. In part the programs reflect the place of legal study within the liberal arts (where it was located historically in the universities) and also a modern world in which no one discipline can be isolated from others.

Combined degrees gained popularity in the latter part of the twentieth century. One of the earliest and most popular of the combined degrees is the J.D./M.B.A. (law and business). The vast majority of law schools grant a J.D./M.B.A. either directly or indirectly through a business school. Other degrees combine law with public administration, social work, land use, economics, and other topics. This broadening range of combined degrees indicates a recognition by law schools that the law is not an insular discipline: it is a functional discipline that interacts with others, which together affect both society and individuals.

Bar Examinations. After completing the academic study of law and earning a J.D. or LL.B., the graduate must pass an examination in order to practice law (except in Wisconsin: students who have graduated from a Wisconsin law school are admitted to practice in that state without having to pass a bar exam). Each state determines who shall have the right to practice law within the state. The highest court of the state, through an appointed agency, administers an examination that tests the applicant's knowledge of various legal subjects, including legal ethics, and investigates the applicant's moral character.

Historically, the bar exam to test professional competence was an oral exam administered by a judge of the court before which the lawyer wished to practice. Later, the written bar exam consisted of essay questions prepared by court-appointed bar examiners in each state who also administered and graded the examination, assisted by clerical personnel in administering the exam and by lawyers in grading it. However, as the number of applicants for a law license increased, preparing, administering, and grading the exam became unmanageable. Thus the National Conference of Bar Examiners was created to assist the state bar examiners. Over time, the NCBE developed different types of tests: first, an objective-style test on six basic subject areas; second, an objective-format test on professional responsibility; third, an essay examination on another six categories of substantive topics; and finally, a written performance exam designed to test lawyering skills. Most jurisdictions administer one or more segments, and many administer all four.

State bar examiners are still deeply involved in administering the bar exams. In most states the examiners still prepare some essay questions designed to test basic areas of the law. Many states still use questions prepared by the NCBE. All state bar exams are written examinations, usually consisting of four parts. Most include a six-hour exam with two hundred multiple-choice questions. This test, the Multistate Bar Examination (MBE), is prepared by the NCBE. The MBE covers six fundamental areas of the law: constitutional law, contracts, criminal law, evidence, property, and torts.

The essay test, the Multistate Essay Examination (MEE), covers six broad areas of the law: *business organizations, *conflict of laws, *commercial transactions, *family law, federal civil *procedure, and *estate planning. It is typically a three-hour exam with six essay questions. Recently, state bar exams have begun to include a performance test that evaluates applicants' fundamental lawyering skills. This test, the Multistate Performance Test (MPT), is also prepared by the NCBE. The test requires an applicant to complete a lawyering task that a lawyer should be able to perform, such as drafting a legal memorandum or document, using materials that are provided and are relevant to the task. The MPT consists of two ninety-minute tasks. Some state exams use both questions, others use only one. The most commonly used test on ethics is the Multistate Professional Responsibility Examination (MPRE), prepared by the NCBE.

State bar exams are designed to test applicants' minimum competence to practice law. Continuing legal education programs are designed to maintain and enhance that competence.

Continuing Legal Education. As early as the 1930s, both law practitioners and academicians recognized the need for continuing legal education. The ABA in 1936 adopted a resolution encouraging continuing education, and in 1937 it delegated to the Section on Legal Education and Admissions to the Bar the responsibility for implementing it. The section undertook to devise and administer a voluntary program, which met with moderate success until 1942, when it was abandoned. In 1947 the ABA and the *American Law Institute (ALI) entered into an agreement by which the ALI would undertake to institute, develop, and maintain a national program of continuing legal education. Since that time the ALI has regularly published works on the law and proposed statutes and conducted annual national meetings on continuing legal education.

Most states also have adopted programs for compulsory continuing legal education. The programs are mandated by the states' supreme courts, and a specified number of hours of attendance are required for lawyers to maintain their license to practice. In order to get credit for continuing legal education, a lawyer must attend a conference sponsored by an approved agency, usually a *bar association or a law school. The subject matter of the conferences varies greatly, allowing lawyers to choose a topic of interest or practical value. In many states, a lawyer is required to attend a specified number of hours covering the subject of attorney ethics.

The purpose of continuing legal education is twofold. It helps lawyers both to maintain the knowledge and skills they acquired in law school and to stay abreast of the ever-changing law and technology so as to enhance their professionalism. Short of reexamination to maintain a law license, continuing legal education is the only formal means of maintaining the quality of the profession.

Substantial continuing legal education programs are also provided for both law school professors and state and federal judges. For many years, the AALS has conducted such courses for law faculty members, and since the 1990s the Institute for Law School Teaching, centered at Gonzaga University School of Law, in Spokane, Washington, has offered an annual series of programs. The various court systems develop and offer continuing education seminars for their judges, and the National Judicial College, in Reno, Nevada, is an important source of educational classes for both new and experienced judges.

Modern Legal Education. Contemporary legal education reflects the myriad influences affecting other fields of higher education. Thus, costs have skyrocketed: construction and maintenance costs for law school facilities; salaries and benefits for law school administrators, faculty, and staff; and the costs to students of a legal education. Issues of reasonable access to legal education for women, people of color, and individuals with disabilities remain somewhat unsettled, and questions of access to positions on law school faculties and administrations for such persons are particularly unresolved.

Presently, in the face of market conditions adversely affecting employment prospects for new attorneys, the bar exam pass rates have been reduced in virtually all jurisdictions, sometimes to all-time low levels. Simultaneously, the bar exams are placing greater emphasis on testing for practical skills (performance testing has been added in many states) and on legal ethics. Law schools are struggling to formulate responses to both market conditions and the decline in bar exam pass rates.

An important focus of current legal education is practical training for lawyers, in both transactional and litigation practices. Hence, the typical law school curriculum includes several opportunities for students to participate in practice experiences. Many schools sponsor one or more pro bono legal clinics in which students assist clients in real legal matters. Similarly, law students can obtain real-life experiences by serving as legal externs in the public and private sectors (such as by clerking for judges, government agencies, or public-interest law firms). Law school courses in legal research and writing and in trial and appellate practice have expanded markedly. Extracurricular opportunities for students to participate in intraschool and interscholastic mock trial and moot court (appellate arguments) have multiplied. Many of today's law students also work part-time during the school year, and especially in the summers, conducting law-related activities for a wide range of employers, including private law firms and business entities.

The Future of Legal Education. Certain features of future legal education are almost certainly assured. There will be no shortage of law schools, of those interested in teaching in them, or of lawyers. Even as the employment market for new attorneys and the pass rates on bar exams in most jurisdictions are at all-time lows, new law schools continue to open. For fifty years, network television has featured programs about law and lawyering, indirectly encouraging viewers of all ages to attend law school. And increasing numbers of television series about attorneys and law practice are scheduled. The numbers of law school applicants remain high, several times the number of places available in entering classes. And the number of attorneys seeking full-time teaching positions is many times the relatively small number of vacancies on law school faculties.

The American Bar Association, and secondarily the Association of American Law Schools, will almost certainly continue to serve the function of oversight and regulation of legal education, given their well-established roles in the law school accreditation process. No other private entities have the expertise to establish and implement detailed standards for the initial approval and continuing review of schools, nor are they likely to commit the substantial resources necessary to do so. Only the federal Department of Education might have the capability to take on the law school accreditation role.

The most significant changes in the future of legal education, and in lawyering generally, will result from advances in technology. Off-site and on-line instructional opportunities are fundamentally changing the physical facilities and methods of administration of academic programs at law schools. Some schools will be virtual law schools, with no classrooms, no libraries, no law reviews, and no casebooks in the traditional sense. A model courtroom will be needed to conduct mock trial practice courses, but such classes can be conducted in an accelerated mode requiring students to be in residence for only brief periods of time. One way or another, an expansive system of legal education will continue to be necessary to fill the fundamental need for lawyers in government and commerce to develop and enforce the rule of law.

• Michael L. Closen, "Teaching with Recent Decisions: A Survey of Past and Present Practices," *Florida State University Law Review* 11 (1983): 289–338. Robert Stevens, *Law School: Legal Education in America from the 1850s to the 1980s,* 1983. Susan K. Boyd, *The ABA's First Section: Assuring a Qualified Bar,* 1993. Alberto Bernabe-Riefkohl, "Tomorrow's Law Schools: Globalization and Legal Education," *San Diego Law Review* 32 (1995): 137–62. Michael L. Closen and Robert J. Dzielak, "The History and Influence of the Law Review Institution," *Akron Law Review* 30 (1996): 15–53. Michael L. Closen and Robert M. Jarvis, "National Conference of Law Reviews Model Code of Ethics," *Marquette Law Review* 75 (1996): 509–28. Robert M. Jarvis, "An Anecdotal History of the Bar Exam," *Georgetown Journal of Legal Ethics* 9 (1996): 359–412. Linda R. Crane, "Graduate Law Degree Programs and Interdisciplinary Combined Degree Programs with Law: History and Trends," *John Marshall Law Review* 33 (1999): 47–80. Stephen Sheppard, ed., *The History of Legal Education in the United States,* vols. I and II, 1999. Debra Pogrund Stark, "See Jane Graduate: Why Can't Jane Negotiate a Business Transaction?" *St. John's Law Review* 73 (1999): 447–93. Linda R. Crane, "Grading Law School Examinations: Making a Case for Objective Exams to Cure What Ails 'Objectified' Exams," *New England Law Review* 34 (2000): 785–808. American Bar Association Section on Legal Education and Admissions to the Bar, *1999–2000 Annual Report of the Consultant on Legal Education to the American Bar Association,* 2001.

—Michael L. Closen and R. Gilbert Johnston

EDUCATOR, LEGAL. In colonial America, law was learned by self-directed reading of law books or by apprenticeship to a practicing lawyer—by reading his law books, and by observing proceedings in court. It was not until 1779 that Thomas *Jefferson as rector of the board of visitors of the College of William and Mary added a law course to the curriculum of his alma mater. In that year, George Wythe was appointed professor of law at William and Mary; Wythe used William *Blackstone's lectures on law as the foundation of his own lectures. Since that time, legal education has developed primarily as an academic discipline within the university setting. More recently, beginning with Dean Christopher C. Langdell's trans formation of the Harvard Law School at the end of the nineteenth century, the study of law has become a graduate course of study.

Legal educators today employ a wide variety of teaching methods, which vary not only according to the teacher's personal style but also according to the level of the students' experience and the subject matter to be taught. The Socratic method is used primarily in the first year of law school to teach analytical thinking, usually in conjunction with the case method, in which primary legal authorities (chiefly the decisions of appellate courts) are considered, rather than legal commentators. The emphasis on legal analysis results in a limited coverage of legal material. It requires diligent preparation and active classroom participation by both teacher and student and is much more effective in small classes than in large ones. In upper-level law courses, the problem method is often used; here, the class is presented with a legal problem to solve, which demonstrates the principles to be learned. The legal educator also conducts seminars in which the students present their own legal research and work product.

On the other hand, much complicated legal information is best conveyed in a straightforward course of lectures. This is a method of teaching that has its origin in former times when students could not afford to own books they could read for themselves. This method permits a broader coverage of material than any other, and was the predominant methodology in the nineteenth century and before. It is the only method used in Europe, where the law students are undergraduates today. Finally, there is clinical legal education, in which the legal educator works with a client experiencing a legal problem. Here, the student participates in the teacher's legal representation of the client and learns by close observation and by helping the teacher. This method is a costly but pale imitation of current medical clinical education; it looks back to the apprenticeship method of legal education, which was generally rejected a century ago.

The legal educator is also a legal scholar. One cannot teach a subject unless one has a thorough understanding of it. To publish scholarship sharpens one's knowledge and analysis of the subject. The legal educator has a professional responsibility not only to students in the classroom, but also to the legal profession in general. Practicing *lawyers' role is to solve the legal problems their clients bring to them. *Judges' role is to adjudicate, giving legal reasons, the issues presented to them. Neither have the opportunity to survey the legal scene as a whole; this is the traditional role of the academic

legal community. In Europe, many professors of law have achieved greater recognition than any judge or legislator, and this was certainly so in the Middle Ages. In the Anglo-American legal world, Sir William Blackstone, Justice Joseph *Story, and many others distinguished themselves by their activities in this direction.

The legal educator also participates in the governance of the law school and of the university. In the present era university leaders' are heavily concerned with fundraising, it is therefore vital that those who actually do the work of teaching keep the educational goals and needs of the institution before university decision-makers. Those educators who leave teaching to become administrators take their experiences as teachers with them, and this is a good thing.

Some law school teachers have a private legal practice in addition to their teaching job. In the nineteenth century, most American law professors did this because they could not live on their salaries or fees as teachers alone; many, in fact, were practitioners or judges who taught law on the side. The danger of this arrangement is that even those who have a practice in transactional law will become bound to put their clients' call on their time before that of the law school. It would be impossible to have a litigation practice without substantial prejudice to one's law students, because litigators must arrange their time around court schedules. On the other hand, close contact with current problems and issues of the law does broaden one's professional understanding.

Legal educators also perform a useful function by their participation in general bar activities. The academic legal perspective being broader than the selfish desires of the clients of the practicing bar, legal scholars can influence proposals for legislative changes and direct continuing legal education in productive ways that is beneficial to the common good. Legal academics, along with the judges, can help prevent the organizations of the bar from sliding into mere self-serving activities.

Through all of these endeavors, the legal educator participates in the strengthening and furtherance of the rule of law, thus participating in the advance of civilization and earning his or her place in society.

[See also Education, Legal]

• Alfred Zantzinger Reed, Training for the Public Profession of the Law, 1921. Herbert L. Packer and Thomas Ehrlich, New Directions in Legal Education, 1972. W. R. Johnson, Schooled Lawyers: A Study in the Clash of Professional Cultures, 1978. Robert B. Stevens, Law School: Legal Education in America from the 1850s to the 1980s,

1983. William P. LaPiana, *Logic and Experience: The Origin of Modern American Legal Education*, 1994. W. Hamilton Bryson, *Essays on Legal Education in Nineteenth Century Virginia*, 1998.   —W. H. Bryson

ELDERLAW. The branch of law that specializes in the legal concerns and needs of older persons, generally those age sixty-five or older, has become known as elderlaw. Elderlaw, however, is defined less by clients' age than by legal needs directly related to *aging. Individuals can have legal problems at any age, of course, but in the United States old age is often accompanied by unique financial, *health, and personal care issues that can create legal problems. Lawyers whose practice encompasses the range of legal problems associated with old age commonly refer to themselves as elderlaw attorneys. Elderlaw is a holistic approach to older clients and their many possible legal needs that is practiced by attorneys who attempt to offer integrated solutions to the interrelated problems that can beset the elderly.

The practice of elderlaw differs from traditional *estate planning, with its emphasis on transferring wealth at death, because elderlaw focuses on the legal problems of the living. The elderlaw attorney not only can draft *wills and *trusts but also is knowledgeable about planning for legal problems specific to the older client during her lifetime. Estate planners, on the other hand, focus on the legal issues created by death. But what most distinguishes the practice of elderlaw, and some would say what inspired it, is the client's need for advice on how to pay for nursing home care.

Over 3 million older Americans who need medical and custodial care live in nursing homes. The cost of this care to the individual is staggering, ranging from $50,000 to $90,000 a year and averaging about $65,000. Some nursing home residents can absorb that expense for several years, but for many the cost soon depletes their assets, leaving them destitute. Fortunately, the Medicaid program will pay the cost of nursing home care to the extent that the resident is unable to do so. As a result, approximately one-half of all nursing home expenses in the United States are paid for by Medicaid. A joint federal and state program, Medicaid is a complex statute, interpreted through voluminous regulations and administered on a state-by-state basis. Consequently, many older persons or their family members seek out legal assistance to help them retain as many assets as possible while still qualifying for Medicaid. The lawyers who first responded to this need began to refer to themselves as elderlaw attorneys.

While elderlaw now encompasses a much wider legal practice, at its core it still emphasizes advice to clients on how to qualify for Medicaid coverage of the cost of nursing home or other long-term care.

Concerns about nursing home care do not end with payment. Elderlaw also includes the legal rights of nursing home residents on admission to the home, during their residence therein, and on discharge and transfer. The quality of care provided in nursing homes and other institutional providers of care, such as assisted-living facilities, continuing care communities, and personal care homes, often does not meet the resident's needs or expectations. Protecting the rights of the institutionalized elderly is an important aspect of elderlaw. While both federal and state law provide significant protection, particularly for residents of nursing homes, the enforcement of those rights often requires a knowledgeable lawyer who can aggressively advocate on behalf of the older resident.

One of the most common fears about growing older is the possible loss of mental abilities. While old age does not necessarily translate into diminished mental capacity, certainly the longer one lives, the greater is the possibility of dementia or some other form of mental disability. Older clients seek out lawyers to help them plan for that contingency. Elderlaw thus includes the drafting of *powers of attorney and the use of trusts as means of managing property in the event of mental disability, while informing clients of the value and pitfalls of placing property in joint ownership. If the client is already incapacitated, the elderlaw attorney may be asked to seek court approval of guardianship or conservatorship. If the older individual objects to having a guardian, or if a family member objects to the appointment of a particular person as guardian, the elderlaw attorney can represent the interests of the older person and attempt to resist the imposition of guardianship or to affect who is appointed as guardian.

Other property issues in elderlaw include planning for the economic consequences of a later-life second or subsequent marriage. Those who remarry often wish to protect their property for the children from an earlier marriage in the event of death or divorce. Or children or other family members may not wish to be liable for the long-term care costs of the new spouse. The legal solutions to these problems are part of elderlaw.

The practice of elderlaw also includes an understanding of Medicare, the federal program that provides subsidized health care to individuals age sixty-five and older. While most disputes over

Medicare can be handled by the individual, at times the complexity of the problem or the amount of money at stake require the skills of a lawyer who is conversant with this complicated government program.

The housing needs of the elderly also can create legal concerns, which, too, are part of elderlaw. Older home owners may need advice on the wisdom of giving their home to their children or making a child a co-owner. Some seek legal advice about the wisdom of using their house as collateral for a reverse mortgage, by which they borrow a fixed sum each month repayable upon their death or the sale of the house in order to augment their income. Others need to give away the house or place it in trust as a means of avoiding federal estate taxes. Some older persons wish to enter into an agreement with one of their children, another relative, or even a stranger to provide them with lifetime caregiving in exchange for a promise to bequeath the house to the caregiver. Such arrangements are best made in consultation with an elderlaw attorney. Other elders merely wish to hire a household companion and need legal advice on the hiring contract and employment tax considerations.

With the average age of retirement in the United States now sixty-three and with less than 15 percent of those over age sixty-five employed, financial security is a major concern of elders. Although some elderly persons continue paid work, most depend on savings, a pension, and Social Security. Elderlaw includes legal advice on how to maximize income during retirement. Collecting Social Security benefits rarely requires the assistance of an attorney, but concerns about pension rights often do require legal help. Many retirees are the beneficiaries of defined-contribution plans, which require the employee, on retirement, to make critical decisions about when and how to draw down the money in the account. Elderlaw attorneys can advise retirees about the alternative ways of taking a pension, such as accepting a lump sum or an annuity or rolling over the pension into an individual retirement account. Not surprisingly, pension planning often leads to estate planning, another major aspect of elderlaw.

Planning for the disposition of property at death is fundamental to elderlaw. The drafting of wills and trusts, planning for various contingencies, and crafting of a plan to minimize federal and state death taxes are major aspects of legal planning for the elderly (see TAXATION: ESTATE AND GIFT TAXES). In the past such work was referred to as estate planning, and lawyers who specialized

in this area as estate planners. Today, many estate planners have broadened their practices to include other elderlaw issues. And as elderlaw attorneys increasingly engage in complex estate planning, the two practices often overlap.

Planning for health care decision-making in the event of mental incapacity is also fundamental to the practice of elderlaw. Every individual, but particularly the elderly, should plan for the possibility of becoming mentally incapacitated and unable to participate in health care decision-making. The doctrine of informed consent requires that either the patient or an authorized representative of the patient make health care decisions. Thus, individuals need to execute an advance health care directive that names the person who should make health care decisions for them if they become mentally incapacitated and contains instructions on whether to continue life-sustaining treatment if they become terminally ill.

Not every legal issue associated with growing older is considered part of elderlaw. Age discrimination in employment, for example, tends to be the provenance of labor or employment law attorneys. Personal injury claims are not normally thought of as elderlaw even when the victim is elderly. Claims against nursing homes for injury or neglect are often handled by personal injury or medical malpractice lawyers, although some elderlaw attorneys do take on such cases.

Elder abuse and neglect, however, are considered part of elderlaw (see DOMESTIC VIOLENCE: ELDER ABUSE). An older person who believes that he or she is being abused, neglected, or financially exploited—or someone who becomes aware of such an occurrence—would be well advised to seek the advice of an elderlaw attorney; these lawyers understand the unique psychological, economic, and legal realities of this area. Abused elders have recourse to both civil and criminal law remedies, and a knowledgeable elderlaw attorney can advise on the best manner to obtain relief and recourse for the injuries suffered.

Other legal issues identified as part of elder law include life *insurance, long-term care insurance, special planning concerns for older persons with disabled adult children, hospital discharge planning, the services of state and federal assistance programs operated through area agencies on aging, and the rights of members of health maintenance organizations. Ethical issues that arise when attorneys deal with individuals of diminished mental capacity are also integral to an elderlaw practice.

The confluence of an aging population, complex government programs, and the concerns of elders and their families with health and financial matters has created the expanding field of elderlaw. This relatively new field of legal practice is certain to flourish in the years to come.

[See also Civil Rights and Civil Liberties]

• Louis A. Mezzullo and Mark Woolpert, Advising the Elderly Client, 1998. Lawrence A. Frolik and Richard L. Kaplan, Elder Law in a Nutshell, 2d ed., 1999. Thomas D. Begley Jr. and Jo-Anne Herina Jeffreys, Representing the Elderly Client: Law and Practice, 2000. Lawrence A. Frolik and Melissa C. Brown, Advising the Elderly and Disabled Client, 2000. Joan M. Krauskopf, Robert N. Brown, Karen L. Tokartz, and Allan D. Bogutz, Elderlaw: Advocacy for the Aging, 2000. John J. Regan, Rebecca C. Morgan, and David M. English, Tax, Estate, and Financial Planning for the Elderly, 2000.

—Lawrence A. Frolik

ELECTRIC CHAIR. The electric chair was devised in the late nineteenth century to serve as a more humane and practical means of executing criminals condemned to death than existing methods. Present-day use of the chair involves placement of electrodes on the condemned prisoner's body and applying an electrical potential in excess of 2,000 volts, with a current of 5 to 7 amperes.

Since the first unsuccessful legal challenge to the use of the electric chair, its advocates and opponents have disagreed whether its use constitutes *"cruel and unusual punishment" within the meaning of the Eighth Amendment. In the case of In re Kemmler (1890), the Supreme Court refused relief to William Kemmler, the New York prisoner who would become the first American criminal executed by electrocution. The Court stated that the electric chair was not a "cruel" punishment and was therefore a constitutional means of execution since it produced "instantaneous" and "painless" death. In Louisiana ex rel. Francis v. Resweber (1947), the Court found that a mechanical failure in the chair did not make a subsequent second attempt at execution "cruel and unusual."

The courts have summarily relied on the Kemmler precedent to uphold the constitutionality of the electric chair. The Supreme Court found in Trop v. Dulles (1958) that a particular method of execution must meet "evolving standards of decency" in order to avoid being considered "cruel and unusual." A great deal of medical evidence now suggests that the electric chair does not produce the instantaneous, painless death presumed in Kemmler. A number of states have dropped the electric chair as a means of execution in favor of other methods such as lethal injection or lethal gas. The Supreme Court, however, has decided no further cases challenging the constitutionality of the electric chair.

[See also Capital Punishment; Criminal Punishments]

• Craig Brandon, The Electric Chair: An Unnatural American History, 1999.
—Seth W. Whitaker

EMBARGO. See War, Law of.

EMBEZZLEMENT. See Theft; White Collar Crime.

EMINENT DOMAIN. See Property, Real.

EMPLOYMENT AT WILL DOCTRINE. See Labor Law: Labor Relations.

ENERGY AND NATURAL RESOURCES LAW. Natural resources used in the production of energy constitute a fuel cycle, with environmental effects, from the exploration and extraction of resources through their consumption and use. It would seem, then, that a body of law should address the whole fuel cycle—however, such is not the case. Instead, natural resources and energy law, as well as *environmental law, consist of a wide variety of state, local, and federal laws, encompassing cases, statutes, orders, regulations, and constitutional provisions. In addition, this body of law is historically contingent, geographically specific, industry-oriented, and administered by several agencies. Still, a general national energy policy exists that favors large-scale energy development and the traditional use of fossil fuels rather than alternative energy resources.

Public Lands. The *regulation of public lands tells a story that includes gold mining, homesteading, railroad construction, and range wars. This story is one of westward expansion as the federal government encouraged migration to the Pacific Ocean. The legal system assisted with land giveaways, cheap mining rights, grazing permits, and water allocations. By the end of the nineteenth century, once the western United States was settled and images of nature captured the country's collective imagination, the basic tension in public lands law was formed: between the development of public lands and the preservation of fragile ecosystems and pristine wilderness. Yet, public land policy is not so simplistic. Rather, it must mediate multiple claims, such as those among ranchers, farmers, American Indian tribes, developers, and recreational users as well as local, state, and federal officials.

The federal government owns approximately 30 percent of the lands in the United States, mostly west of the Mississippi River, and excluding the outer continental shelf. The Department of the Interior is the key administrative agency responsible for seven major resources, including water, minerals, timber, range, wildlife, recreation, and preservation. The actions of the Army Corps of Engineers, the Agriculture Department, the Environmental Protection Agency, and the Energy Department also affect federal public lands.

Water as a natural resource is treated differently in the eastern and western United States. In the east, water is plentiful and must be protected from environmental degradation through such acts as the Federal Clean Water Act. In the west, water allocation involves hard-fought and controversial issues that only intensify as the population continues to grow and water resources diminish. For example, water allocation for golf courses in Palm Springs and orange groves in southern California compete with the needs of ranchers and preservationists.

Historically, water was allocated through a system of riparian rights or prior appropriation adopted from English *common law. Adjacent landowners acquired water rights through a riparian system, and first users through the doctrine of prior appropriation. As demand for water increased, the federal 1902 Reclamation Act regulated irrigation and agriculture. In addition, federal support assisted the construction of a series of dams for uses such as flood control, hydroelectricity production, and recreation.

Federal mineral lands contain most notably gold, oil, and natural gas, but also coal and copper. The 1872 General Mining Law is the basic statute which promoted the development of mining resources as it moved from a system of free access to a low-fee permit system. The 1920 Mineral Leasing Act subjected oil and gas to federal jurisdiction. In addition, the 1953 Outer Continental Shelf Lands Act regulated oil and gas lying from three to two hundred miles seaward from the coastline.

The federal government owns about 18 percent of the country's timberlands, which is primarily in national forests. Some people are against permitting the policies of cultivating timber in large areas or harvesting old growth timber. The Bureau of Land Management allows grazing on over 170 million acres of land, also mostly in national forests. Historically, these lands were grazed as a "commons," which meant that the lands were overused. In 1934, Congress passed the Taylor Grazing Act to regulate competition for range lands and to prevent overgrazing and soil erosion.

Federal lands contain valuable wildlife habitat such as wild turkey, moose, elk, mountain sheep, bears, wolves, and eagles. Fundamental U.S. policy involves balancing wildlife protection, grazing, timber, and other uses on public lands, as seen in the 1960 Multiple-use, Sustained-yield Act, later incorporated into the 1976 Federal Land Policy Management Act.

Development, preservation, and recreation on public lands are not only matters of policy, they are matters of culture. Ansel Adams' photographs capture that culture. National parks, wilderness preservation, and species protection have a long history of champions such as John Muir, Aldo Leopold, and Justice William *Douglas as well as Presidents Teddy Roosevelt and William Taft who withdrew federal lands from development at the turn of the twentieth century.

Private Enterprise and Natural Resources, Energy, and the Environment. United States energy production is principally executed by private enterprise, which has common law antecedents. As long as the resources are found, used, and consumed locally, basic *property laws govern, and there is no reason for complex regulatory schemes. For most of the nineteenth century, energy was generated from renewable natural resources such as running water, wind, coal, wood, and whale oil. With Colonel Drake's discovery of petroleum in Titusville, Pennsylvania, in 1859 and Thomas Edison's generation and distribution of electricity at Pearl Street Station in 1882, the United States experienced a transition from wood and other renewable resources to our present pattern of energy, which relies on fossil fuels and electricity. The period from the late nineteenth century until 1970 witnessed the development and institutionalization of a dominant energy policy. After 1970, energy production and consumption underwent a radical change as that dominant policy no longer served the demands of a changing and environmentally sensitive economy.

The Dominant Energy Policy. In the early part of the twentieth century, local and state rules regulated the natural gas and electricity industries. As both industries consolidated, consumer and shareholder abuses occurred giving rise to leasing and conservation laws. Leasing laws promoted exploration and extraction, and established a royalty system. Conservation laws limited extraction to stabilize market prices as well as conserve resources.

The federal government played little role during this time, save for the occasional *antitrust case such as *Standard Oil Co.* v. *United States* (1911), which forced the breakup of John D. Rockefeller's monopolistic oil company. There were occasional federal interventions, such as the 1906 Hepburn Act, which curtailed "Big Oil's" control of interstate pipelines and the 1920 Federal Power Act, which promoted hydroelectricity use.

During the First World War, the federal government established the United States Fuel Administration, which had the power to regulate prices and distribute resources, but did not exercise those powers. Instead it promoted the private oil industry. Coal was the most significant energy industry and it was left unregulated. The 1920s were important years for energy policy as huge discoveries of natural gas and petroleum, particularly in Texas and Louisiana, drove prices downward giving rise to the Federal Oil Conservation Board, which promoted an oil depreciation allowance and opened up public lands for oil exploration. By the end of the 1920s, the fossil fuel industries of oil, natural gas, and coal were well entrenched.

The New Deal had a profound effect on energy industries. In 1935, the Federal Power Act regulated the interstate transportation of electricity through cost-of-service ratemaking. The Federal Trade Commission issued a report warning of monopoly concentration of natural gas pipelines, which led to the passage of the 1938 Natural Gas Act. Both the Federal Power Act and the Natural Gas Act gave the then Federal Power Commission (FPC), now the Federal Energy Regulatory Commission, the authority to set rates for gas and electricity sold in interstate commerce. In exchange, utilities were given exclusive service territories and saddled with the obligation to serve.

This method of traditional rate regulation worked well until the 1970s, as both the electricity and natural gas industries continued to expand on a predictable basis to support an expanding economy. It was an article of *economic faith that as energy production expanded, so too would the economy, which was illustrated by the 1954 Atomic Energy Act. This moved nuclear power out of military hands into private commercial power generation. The cost-of-service ratemaking formula rewarded utilities for their continued investment in capital expansion, and improvements helping build the nation's energy infrastructure. Two things happened, however, to change that pattern. First, the regulation of the natural gas industry started to unravel. In 1954, the Supreme Court in *Phillips Petroleum Co.* v. *Wisconsin* (1954), required the FPC to set rates of individual producers in the field who dedicated their gas in interstate commerce. The *Phillips* decision had two

consequences. First, the FPC could not hold hearings for individual producers, and rates had to be set, first on a regional basis, and then nationally. Second, the federal rates were based on historic average costs, which created a dual market leading to a natural gas shortage. The second dislocation occurred in the electric industry as it reached a technological plateau, complicated by unanticipated problems in the construction of commercial nuclear power plants. In short, electricity became more expensive to produce.

The 1970s began a tumultuous decade for energy industries. The 1970 National Environmental Policy Act changed the nation's outlook on natural resources and energy. In addition, the Vietnam War's effect on the economy, dramatic inflation, and the 1973 OPEC oil embargo created economic dislocations that threatened U.S. oil independence. This raised national security concerns, as well as energy prices, eroding confidence in traditional regulatory forms. The nuclear power industry collapsed during this period. All nuclear plants ordered after 1974 were canceled, as utilities experienced cost overruns, delays, and cash flow problems.

President Jimmy Carter's 1978 National Energy Act was an attempt to correct those economic dislocations by promoting conservation, reducing dependence on foreign oil, eliminating a dual natural gas market, eliminating rate structures in electricity that promoted consumption rather than conservation, and looking for new energy resources. The National Energy Act was bold, but it was not comprehensive. Although alternative energy sources were addressed in the 1980 Energy Security Act to promote renewable resources such as biomass, wind power, and solar power, as well as the alternative fossil fuels of oil shale, tar sands, and coal gasification, these alternatives were not sustained by the market.

Fossil fuels, for the most part, are dirty fuels with severe environmental consequences. To address those consequences, the 1970s saw the passage of the Clean Air Act, the Clean Water Act, the Endangered Species Act, and the Surface Mining Control and Reclamation Act. Also during that period, nongovernmental organizations such as the Sierra Club, the Environmental Defense Fund, the Natural Resources Defense Council, and the Nature Conservancy became effective advocates for environmental policy, and became increasingly involved with energy policies. The system that regulated energy for most of the twentieth century developed our nation's energy infrastructure, but reached the end of its useful life. This gave way to more market-based regulations, as energy production confronted environmental protection and resource conservation.

Sustainable Development in the 21st Century. Once the infrastructure for the production, distribution, and transportation of energy was established, the need for tight government controls lessened. In the last two decades, the natural gas and electricity industries have started to deregulate. Two problems remain for this transition. First, investments in old regulatory requirements must be recouped. Second, transportation bottlenecks exist, making it difficult to get energy resources from producers to the desired consumers.

The Federal Energy Regulatory Commission has favored deregulation efforts by state legislatures. Deregulation in natural gas continues and electricity deregulation was proceeding apace until 2000. California was the first state to deregulate at the retail level for electricity, which was a dismal failure as rates multiplied with an insufficient amount of new capacity coming on line to generate electricity.

The new era of natural resources and energy law has a new label—sustainable development. In 1987, the World Commission on Environment and Development published the report *Our Common Future*, which popularized the idea that resources will be exploited and investments directed in ways consistent with future as well as present needs. In short, energy policy and environmental protection should be united into a single coherent vision. Sustainable development has been part of the international environmental law culture and is becoming a part of our domestic policy.

The history of energy and natural resources law in the United States has been one in which individual industries are regulated in uncoordinated ways by different agencies inconsistently over different periods. The reason for this lack of coordination is embedded in the very nature of our polity. As a capitalist democracy, with faith in property and individual ingenuity, private competition is the preferred form of social ordering over government regulation. Nevertheless, from a broad perspective, energy policy favors large-scale, capital intensive development and the production of fossil fuels and electricity, rather than softer, renewable resources. This policy will continue until alternative sources are supported by the market.

[*See also* Environmental Law]

• Leonard S., Andrew S., and Robert C. Hyman, *America's Electric Utilities: Past, Present and Future,* 7th ed., 1920. Richard H. K. Vietor, *Energy Policy in America Since 1945: A Study in Business and Government Relations,* 1984. John G. Clark, *Energy and the Federal Government: Fossil Fuel Policies, 1900–1946,* 1987. Joseph P. Tomain, *Nuclear Power Transformation,* 1987. Jan G. Laitos and Joseph P. Tomain, *Energy and Natural Resources Law,* 1992. David Howard Davis, *Energy Politics,* 4th ed., 1993. Fred Bosselman, Jim Rossi, and Jacqueline Lang Weaver, *Energy, Economics and the Environment,* 2000. Energy Law Group, *Energy Law and Policy for the 21st Century,* 2000. George Cameron Coggins, Charles F. Wilkinson, and John D. Leshy, *Federal Public Land and Resources Law,* 4th ed., 2001.

—Joseph P. Tomain

ENGLISH LAW. *See* Common Law; History of American Law: English Design of American Law.

ENTERTAINMENT LAW is a crazy quilt. Its patches are cut from many legal fabrics, including copyright, right of publicity, *defamation, *privacy, *contract, *labor, *antitrust, international trade, and even constitutional law. The reason for this unusual mix: entertainment has five distinctive characteristics, each of which requires its own legal tools.

Entertainment is intangible. Entertainment is produced from intangible raw materials. All productions require the personal services of talented people, and many use preexisting literary, dramatic, musical and artistic works. Though entertainment productions also use tangible items like costumes and sets, even their value comes from an intangible—design—rather than from physical characteristics.

Law plays a central role in the production of entertainment, because intangibles cannot be possessed. In order to be certain that those who provide personal services (or preexisting works) are rewarded for doing so, it is necessary to have enforceable rules concerning payment.

The basic terms of most talent contracts are bargained for collectively by unions representing talent, and employer associations representing producers, within a legal framework imposed by federal labor law. Thus, professional football players had been awarded a sizeable amount in an antitrust case involving a dispute over the salaries of practice squad players. But the *Supreme Court, in *Brown* v. *Pro Football, Inc.* (1996), reversed, holding that the dispute should have been resolved in collective bargaining between the Players Association and the National Football League.

Federal copyright law provides the framework for a producer's use of literary, dramatic, musical, and artistic works. It gives authors, composers and artists the exclusive right to reproduce, publicly perform, distribute, and create new versions of their works. A producer wishing to make a movie based on a novel, must first get copyright permission (known as a "license"). In the first entertainment law case it ever decided, the Supreme Court held, in *Kalem Co.* v. *Harper & Bros.* (1911), that a movie company infringed the copyright to Lew Wallace's 1880 historical novel *Ben-Hur* by making a movie from it without permission, even though the film featured only prominent scenes from the book and, being silent, therefore did not include any of the novel's words.

The commercial use of a celebrity's name or likeness is regulated by "right of publicity" law. Found primarily in state statutes and judicial rulings, this prohibits advertisers and product manufacturers from using celebrity identities without permission. Thus, singer-actress Bette Midler was awarded $400,000 in a lawsuit against Ford and its advertising agency, because they used a singer who closely imitated Midler's voice in a television commercial, after Midler had declined an offer to make the commercial herself.

Most right of publicity cases involve advertising uses, but the only case decided to date by the Supreme Court involved a television station's news broadcast of a videotape of the entire fifteen-second act of a "human cannonball". The Court held, in *Zacchini* v. *Scripps-Howard Broadcasting* (1977), that the First Amendment did not give the station the right to broadcast the performance without consent, even though it presented it as news.

Entertainment is uncertain. The entertainment business is uncertain. Consumer preferences are unknown and constantly changing. Aggregate demand is irrelevant, because most of it is for a small number of highly successful productions. Each production has the potential for huge financial gain, but runs the risk of huge losses.

Uncertainty thus dominates the terms of virtually all employment and licensing agreements.

Producers offer up-front and guaranteed payments that are as small as possible, and often propose contracts that give them the option for lengthy periods of time, but not the obligation, to employ talent or use literary works. On the other hand, talent and owners of literary (and other) works seek large up-front and guaranteed payments, and short-term contracts that give them the right to make new, better-paying deals, if success strikes. Arrangements that make compensation contingent on success are common. The con-

flicting desires of the parties on these points are usually resolved in contract *negotiations, and the enforcement of their deals is a matter of contract law.

In some cases, however, legislatures have imposed mandatory standards that even override the terms of contracts the parties may have signed. A California statute, for example, limits employment agreements to seven years. Actress Olivia DeHaviland successfully used this statute to get out of a long-term contract with Warner Bros. in the 1940s; comedian Redd Foxx utilized it to escape a long-term contract with Dootone Records in the 1960s (*DeHaviland* v. *Warner Bros.* (1944); *Foxx* v. *Williams* (1966)).

Federal copyright law contains provisions that prevent producers from acquiring perpetual ownership or usage rights to authors' literary works, even if perpetual rights are granted by contract. The law provides that pre-1978 copyrights automatically revert to authors' heirs under certain circumstances, and gives authors (or their heirs) the right to terminate post-1977 assignments and licenses after thirty-five years. As a result, the Supreme Court, in *Stewart* v. *Abend* (1990), ruled that Universal must stop distributing the movie *Rear Window* after the death of the author of the short story on which the movie was based, because the author's successor refused to grant Universal a new license when copyright reverted to him.

Technology has created a gap. Though *technology has not reduced the cost of producing most entertainment, it has dramatically lowered the cost of copying and distributing it. The gap thus created has prompted the development of two new strands of entertainment law. One seeks to control technologies that are used primarily to copy or distribute copyrighted works without authorization. The other recognizes the inevitability of unauthorized copying and distribution, and—under specific circumstances—either gives people permission to do so for free, or grants statutory licenses that permit them to do so in return for royalties set by law (rather than by negotiation).

The Digital Millennium Copyright Act of 1998 contains an example of the first strand. Its anticircumvention provisions prohibit the distribution of technologies designed to defeat measures used to prevent unauthorized copying of works.

The Audio Home Recording Act of 1992 is an example of the second strand. It permits consumers to make free copies of music recordings for noncommercial purposes. It also requires digital audiotape recorders to be designed so they cannot copy tapes that are themselves copies. It also requires those who make digital audiotape recorders to pay royalties, at rates set by law, that are distributed to recording artists, songwriters, record companies, and music publishers.

Entertainment sometimes offends. Entertainment ranks well behind food and shelter as a necessity of life. Yet in economically developed societies, it is pervasive and a key feature of the society's culture. For these reasons, entertainment has an enormous capacity to offend people.

Critics complain most often about sex and violence. Federal, state and municipal legislatures have responded by enacting a thicket of laws banning the "obscene," and sometimes the merely "indecent." Although these laws frequently run afoul of First Amendment guarantees, they remain a significant concern to producers—even those who make mainstream, non-pornographic entertainment—because most entertainment is intended for nationwide distribution, while the Supreme Court has permitted local community standards to be considered in deciding whether particular productions are "obscene."

The movie *Carnal Knowledge* was caught in this legal paradox. A Georgia jury found it to be obscene, even though *Carnal Knowledge* was on many "Ten Best" lists the year it was released. The Supreme Court reversed that judgment in *Jenkins* v. *Georgia* (1973), ruling—on First Amendment grounds—that the movie was not obscene.

Sex and violence are not the only things that offend people. Charges of blasphemy were leveled against *The Last Temptation of Christ* in unsuccessful efforts to have that movie banned. Here too the First Amendment had to be summoned in order to protect the movie.

Entertainment is international. The marketplace for entertainment is *international. American movies, in particular, are popular around the world. Since entertainment is an aspect of local culture, however, as well as a source of local employment, many countries have enacted laws designed to limit the inflow of entertainment from other nations. Local-content broadcast quotas and movie-theater screen-time quotas are stark examples of laws this type. In response to these and certain international copyright issues, entertainment law now involves international trade treaties.

The most significant of these treaties is the 1994 agreement that created the World Trade Organization. The WTO agreement enabled the United States to compel Japan to grant copyright protection to American recordings released before 1971 (which had been in the public domain in Japan).

It also enabled the U.S. to compel Canada to eliminate restrictions on *Sports Illustrated* and other American magazines.

Membership in the WTO has required significant changes in U.S. entertainment law, too. Federal law had to be amended to prohibit the bootlegging (unauthorized recording) of live musical performances. The United States also had to restore copyright protection to countless foreign works that had been in the public domain in this country.

Moreover, at the request of Irish songwriters, the European Union sued the United States in the WTO, complaining about a provision of American law that exempts thousands of bars, restaurants and retail stores from the requirement that they pay royalties when they publicly perform songs (by playing radio or television receivers). Because the WTO agreement requires the payment of royalties to songwriters and music publishers under those circumstances, the EU prevailed.

[*See also* Contract Law]

• Donald C. Farber (General Editor), *Entertainment Industry Contracts*, 1986. J. Thomas McCarthy, *The Rights of Publicity and Privacy*, 2nd ed., 2000. Melville B. Nimmer and David Nimmer, *Nimmer on Copyright*, 2000. Al Kohn and Bob Kohn, *Kohn on Music Licensing*, 3rd ed., 2000. Donald S. Passman, *All You Need to Know about the Music Business*, 4th ed., 2000. Donald E. Biederman, et al., *Law and Business of the Entertainment Industries*, 4th ed., 2001.   — Lionel S. Sobel

ENTITLEMENTS. Government entitlement programs arose during President Franklin D. Roosevelt's New Deal in the 1930s, and were expanded greatly during President Lyndon Johnson's Great Society in the 1960s. Entitlement programs provide government benefits based on established criteria fixed by statute. Everyone who meets the criteria is entitled to receive the benefits, which are also specified in the statute.

The largest entitlement program is Social Security, which provides retirement, survivors, and disability benefits. Everyone who meets the qualification criteria of the program receives the benefits calculated under formulas, specified in the Social Security statute, based on past income and other factors.

The second largest entitlement program is Medicare, which pays for private sector *health care for retirees and the disabled. Other entitlement programs provide *welfare benefits targeted to low income families. Medicaid pays for health care expenses for the poor, while food stamps provide assistance to pay for food. For sixty years, dating from the 1930s, the now reformed Aid to Families with Dependant Children program (AFDC) was the core entitlement program for the poor, paying cash assistance to families with children.

Based on Supreme Court precedents, constitutional law recognizes entitlement benefits as a form of *property with protections analogous to those provided to private property. The landmark case is *Goldberg* v. *Kelly* (1970), which required prior notice and a hearing before benefits under the AFDC program could be terminated for recipients believed to no longer qualify for the program. The Court grounded its decision in the protections for property in the *due process clause of the Fourteenth Amendment, declaring that termination of such benefits involves important rights. The justices added:

> "It may be realistic today to regard welfare benefits more like 'property' than a 'gratuity'. Much of the existing wealth in this country takes the form of rights that do not fall within traditional common law concepts of property." 397 U.S. 262 fn 8.

Similarly, in *Goss* v. *Lopez* (1975), the Court held that a student could not be temporarily suspended from public school without at least prior notice of the grounds for the suspension and a hearing of the student's response. It ruled that a student's entitlement to a public education was a property right that could not be ended for misconduct without adherence to fair procedures.

But the Constitutional protections apply only to the benefits specified by statute. In *O'Bannon* v. *Town Court Nursing Center* (1980), low-income residents of a nursing home were subsidized by Medicaid. When the nursing home was terminated from the program for various inadequacies, the residents sued claiming they had a right to prior notice and a hearing before such termination. The Court denied their claim, holding that the Medicaid statute gave them only the right to benefits for residence in a nursing home qualified for the program, not any nursing home of their choice.

Moreover, Congress is not prevented from changing, reducing, or eliminating entitlement benefits by amending the statute providing for such benefits. In *Flemming* v. *Nestor* (1960) the Court upheld a new statutory provision cutting off Social Security benefits for deported communists. Taxpayers and beneficiaries have no protected property or contractual right to prevent such legislative changes to entitlement benefits. The Court said, "To engraft upon the Social Security system

a concept of accrued property rights would deprive it of the flexibility and boldness in adjustment to ever changing conditions which it demands."

In other words, the protected property rights to entitlement benefits are defined by the statute specifying the benefits. Congress remains free to amend the statute to change the benefit scheme, which would redefine the protected property interest to apply to the newly specified benefits.

Economic Cost and Social Change. Entitlement programs have now grown to consume a dominant portion of government spending. Social Security alone now accounts for about 23 percent of all federal spending. Medicare accounts for another 13 percent. Medicaid and food stamps consume another 8 percent. These four programs alone consequently account for about 44 percent of the entire federal budget, and there are many other smaller entitlement programs.

Moreover, after the baby boom generation begins to retire in ten to fifteen years, this entitlement spending will undoubtedly soar further, particularly for Social Security and Medicare. Without reforms, in coming decades entitlement programs will account for well over 50 percent of federal spending.

Besides the financial burdens these programs impose, they have come under strong criticism over the last twenty-five years for negative and counterproductive economic and social effects on the intended beneficiaries, as well as society overall. Critics argue that welfare entitlements entail a moral hazard problem, as subsidies targeted to poor and low income workers encourage reduced work effort and reduced education and training. Such effects harm the intended beneficiaries as well as the general taxpayer, for lower income individuals tend to become mired in long-term dependency and poverty.

Critics also argue that welfare benefits targeted to single mothers with children encourage illegitimacy and family breakup. The funding alone makes such conduct more financially viable, and the program qualifications often provide strong incentives for the mother not to marry the father or any working male. In 1984, Charles Murray stirred welfare reform movement with his startling book *Losing Ground*, which argued that welfare entitlement programs, among other factors, produced counterproductive effects.

In addition, reformers argue that workers today would get far higher returns and benefits paying into personal private sector investment accounts rather than Social Security. Such reform would greatly expand ownership of capital and, through increased saving and investment, enhance general economic growth.

Reforms. These critiques have begun to produce reforms. In 1996, AFDC, the most venerable welfare entitlement, was replaced with a nonentitlement program, Temporary Assistance for Needy Families (TANF). The new program provides grants to states to address low-income needs, without any provision for automatic eligibility for benefits. Instead, the reforms strongly encourage states to require the able-bodied to work in a government-backed job in return for their benefits, if efforts to find private employment failed.

These and similar welfare reforms in the 1990s have produced dramatic results, with welfare rolls across the country reduced by 50 percent on average. These former recipients are now privately employed, with some increase in marriage as well. The work requirements changed the incentives faced by recipients, as they no longer receive long-term benefits without work. The block grants changed the incentives faced by the state administrators since, with fixed federal block grant funds, the states now bore the full cost of more expensive welfare systems, and reaped the gains of less expensive systems. These changed incentives produced the changed results.

Similarly, several countries around the world have now adopted personal investment account systems to replace part or all of their traditional Social Security entitlement programs. In 1981 Chile was the first to do so, granting workers the choice of a private, personal, investment account system to replace all of the benefits of the old system. Over 90 percent of workers chose the new account system, which has borne out claims of much higher benefits for much lower costs.

Chile's reforms were recognized as such an economic and political success that seven other Latin American countries have now adopted similar reforms. But the reform movement has now spread well beyond Latin America. In Great Britain, close to 80 percent of workers have opted into personal accounts or other private investment systems in place of most of the old social security program's benefits. In 1991, Australia adopted personal investment accounts to replace its old program entirely. In the United States, President George W. Bush appointed a commission in 2001 to consider a personal account option for the U.S. Social Security system.

[*See also* Welfare]

• Charles A. Reich, "The New Property," *Yale Law Journal* (1964): 773–87. Peter Ferrara, *Social Security: The Inherent Contradiction*, 1980. Charles Murray, *Losing Ground,* 1984. The World Bank, *Averting the Old-Age Crisis,* 1994. William W. Beach and Gareth G. Davis, *Social Security's Rate of Return,* 1998. Peter Ferrara and Michael Tanner, *A New Deal for Social Security,* 1998.

—Peter J. Ferrara

ENTRAPMENT. *See* Police Procedures.

ENVIRONMENTAL LAW

United States Environmental Law
International Environmental Law in the U.S.

ENVIRONMENTAL LAW: UNITED STATES ENVIRONMENTAL LAW

Environmental law has grown, from a sparse set of *common-law precedents and local ordinances, to encompass a vast body of national regulatory legislation to protect human health and to preserve natural resources for future generations. Numerous federal and state agencies now implement these laws through *regulations that affect virtually every aspect of our economic lives (see ECONOMICS AND LAW). The global growth of environmental concern also is serving as a catalyst for the development of new regimes of *international law.

The Common-Law Roots of Environmental Law. While United States environmental law is now dominated by federal regulatory programs enacted during the 1970s and 1980s, its roots run deeper. For centuries common-law courts wrestled with conflicts that invariably arise when human activity interferes with the interests of others in the quality of their physical surroundings. Using doctrines of public and private nuisance, courts sought to protect communities and *property owners from the most egregious consequences of industrial activity.

Early in the seventeenth century, English courts recognized that even nontrespassory invasions of property could be actionable as nuisances. *Aldred's Case* (1611) established that even a lawful use of property, such as the construction of a pig sty, could be a nuisance if it was located next to a private home where their stench interfered with the neighbor's quiet use and enjoyment of their land. Courts adopted the Latin maxim *sic utere tuo ut alienum non laedas,* or "every man must so use his own as not to damnify another." The *sic utere* principle—that no one has the right to use their property in a manner that causes foreseeable harm to the property of others—became a universal tenet of the common law of environmental protection.

A separate branch of nuisance law, derived from the common law of crimes, deems actions that cause substantial harm to the commons (property owned by the government) to be public nuisances.

Public nuisance actions can be brought only by government entities or by private parties who have suffered special harm due to damage to the commons.

By itself, the *sic utere* principle does not go very far toward resolving environmental disputes. It does not specify how substantial harm must be before it is actionable or what remedy courts should impose to rectify it. Although courts can issue *injunctions requiring abatement of nuisances, they often are reluctant to do so when offending activities have great economic value. For example, in *Madison* v. *Ducktown Sulphur, Copper & Iron Co.* (1904), the Tennessee Supreme Court refused to require a copper smelter to reduce pollution that severely damaged nearby farmland for fear of destroying enterprises that were the primary source of wealth and employment in the community. The court instead required the company to pay *damages to compensate the owners of the farmland for injuries caused by the pollution.

Uncertainty about the fate and transport of pollutants and their ultimate environmental consequences also makes it difficult for courts to resolve environmental disputes.

Although the common law could provide redress when a single source of particularly egregious pollution visibly alters the surrounding landscape, it proved to be a crude vehicle for preventing harm caused by the cumulative impact of more diffuse pollutants. The common law's requirement that plaintiffs prove causal injury is often difficult to satisfy, particularly when there are multiple sources of pollution. During the early 1900s, the state of Missouri tried to prove that raw sewage dumped by the city of Chicago was contaminating drinking water hundreds of miles downstream in St. Louis, harming the health of its citizens. Despite years of investigation, extensive expert testimony and experiments supervised by a special master, the U.S. Supreme Court ultimately ruled that Missouri had failed to prove causal injury, particularly when the state's own cities dumped their untreated sewage upstream of St. Louis (*Missouri* v. *Illinois* (1906)).

Nuisance law probably did encourage sources of pollution to locate in areas where they would do less damage and, at least in some cases, the threat of injunction helped stimulate the development of improved pollution control technology. When the state of Georgia brought a public nuisance action against the copper smelter that had been held liable only for damages in the *Madison* litigation, the U.S. Supreme Court issued an injunction limiting the smelter's emissions (*Georgia* v. *Tennessee Copper Co.* (1907)). This helped spur the development of a new technology for removing sulfur from the smelter's emissions and using it to make sulfuric acid. With continued growth in population and industry, human exposure to multiple sources of pollution became more ubiquitous and the reach of environmental problems more frequently exceeded the common law's grasp.

The Rise of the Conservation Movement. In the early years of the republic, environmental protection was rarely a concern of the federal government. Following the Louisiana Purchase, the United States was thought to possess seemingly limitless natural resources. The focus of federal policy was to encourage resource exploitation by transferring land in the public domain to private parties. When the Department of Interior was established in 1849, a large part of its initial mission was to help process federal land transfers. The Homestead Act of 1862 and the Mining Act of 1872 allowed private parties to acquire title to federal land and the mineral resources found on it. But the seeds of a new conservation movement had been planted as popular travel literature extolled the virtues of outdoor recreation. As art and literature celebrated the wonders of the American West, the public began to appreciate the natural world as a source of inspiration and spiritual renewal.

Concern about the environmental consequences of unbridled development began to appear in the work of George Perkins Marsh and Henry David Thoreau. Several states adopted measures to protect fish and wildlife and Congress in 1870 enacted legislation to regulate hunting of Pacific fur seals in Alaska. The following year, Congress asked President Ulysses Grant to investigate why the nation's fisheries were in decline.

After lengthy debate, Congress in 1872 adopted one of the most important innovations of U.S environmental law when it passed legislation establishing Yellowstone as the first national park. The movement to provide permanent protection for certain natural areas also affected the states. In 1885 New York State established the Adirondack Forest Preserve and decreed that it be kept "forever wild," protections later embedded in the state constitution. In 1891 Congress established the national forest system by enacting the Forest Reserve Act, which gave the president authority to withdraw forest reserves from the public domain.

As the conservation movement gained momentum, grassroots groups began to organize at the national level, forming organizations that became powerful influences on the development of environmental law. In 1892 the Sierra Club was founded by John Muir and friends. In 1901, the American Scenic and Historic Preservation Society was established from state-level organizations that promoted preservation of nature and culture. The National Association of Audubon Societies for the Protection of Wild Birds and Animals was founded in 1905, uniting numerous state organizations that had been voices for conservation since 1896.

Efforts to develop the American West included a failed effort to forest the Great Plains and legislation that brought federal irrigation projects to arid lands. The Newlands Reclamation Act of 1902 dedicated money from the sale of public lands in the West to fund construction of irrigation works, altering the landscape by providing federally subsidized water to agriculture interests.

When Theodore Roosevelt assumed the presidency in 1901 upon the death of President William McKinley, the conservation movement gained an outspoken presidential champion. Roosevelt convened a national governors' conference on conservation at the White House and he pioneered the use of executive orders to protect federal lands. Beginning with his order creating the Pelican Island bird sanctuary in Florida, Roosevelt issued 53 executive orders establishing national wildlife refuges. In 1906 Congress enacted the American Antiquities Act, which authorizes the president to set aside federal lands as national monuments to preserve "features of historic, prehistoric, and scientific interest." Roosevelt used this authority to establish Devil's Tower as the first national monument. He later designated the Grand Canyon as a national monument, the first of many monuments that later became national parks.

Beginning in 1908, the Sierra Club waged an aggressive national campaign opposing construction of a dam in the Hetch Hetchy Valley, a wilderness preserve that was part of Yosemite National Park. This battle exposed sharp differences between preservationists like John Muir who wanted wilderness protected for its own sake and conservationists like Gifford Pinchot who supported conserving public lands to maximize their consumption value. While the preservationists ultimately lost the fight, their campaign gave environmental concerns national visibility. While Hetch Hetchy was flooded to provide power to San Francisco, Congress continued to create national parks, and in 1916 it established the National Park Service as part of the Department of Interior.

The Federalization of U.S. Environmental Law.

Federal responsibility for environmental protection evolved gradually. In 1918 Congress adopted legislation to protect migratory birds to implement a treaty negotiated with Canada. States challenged this legislation as an infringement of their Tenth Amendment rights (see STATES' RIGHTS), but the Supreme Court upheld the law as a valid exercise of federal authority, citing the supremacy of federal law under the constitution (*Missouri* v. *Holland* (1920)).

In the decades that followed, concern for the impact of environmental conditions on human health spawned efforts to improve sewage disposal and to control smoke pollution in urban areas. Prior to the Second World World War, these concerns were regarded as the responsibility of state and local governments. Congress had adopted legislation regulating waste disposal in navigable waters in the Rivers and Harbors Act of 1899, but this law was designed to prevent obstruction of navigation rather than to protect the national environment. The federal Insecticide Act of 1910 prohibited the sale of misbranded pesticides to prevent consumer fraud rather than to control environmental risks. When deaths of workers from exposure to toxic substances grabbed national headlines, the Surgeon General convened national conferences of experts to investigate how to improve workplace safety. But it was not until the 1970s that Congress established national regulatory programs to protect public health from environmental risks.

President Franklin D. Roosevelt's New Deal programs of the 1930s laid the groundwork for the greater federal role in protecting consumer and environmental interests that Congress ultimately assumed in the 1970s. The Civilian Conservation Corps helped to restore public lands and to promote outdoor recreation. The Duck Stamp Act of 1934 provided additional funds for wildlife refuges through a federal licensing fee on hunters.

After the Second World War, the federal government assumed an active role encouraging states to adopt environmental protection measures. The Federal Water Pollution Control Act of 1948 provided federal funding to assist states in developing pollution control programs. In 1956 Congress overrode President Dwight Eisenhower's veto to launch a massive program to fund the construction of municipal sewage treatment plants. During the 1960s Congress prodded states to adopt air pollution controls in the Clean Air Act of 1963 and to develop programs to handle waste disposal problems in the Solid Waste Disposal Act of 1965.

The popularity of outdoor recreation and concern over the environmental effects of toxic chemicals helped spawn a powerful national environmental movement during the 1960s. To preserve wilderness areas on public land, Congress enacted the Wilderness Act of 1964, which directed that such areas be protected to preserve their "primeval character and influence" and "natural condition" with motorized equipment, roads and commercial enterprises prohibited. In 1964 Congress also created the Land and Water Conservation Fund, funded in part by royalties from the use of public lands, which has provided critical funding for federal and state land acquisition programs.

The roots of the modern environmental movement usually are traced to the publication of Rachel Carson's work *Silent Spring* in 1962. Carson issued a stern warning about the environmental harm that could occur from a buildup of persistent toxins in the food chain as a result of pesticide use. Her warnings helped mobilize a national environmental movement. Concerned scientists formed the Environmental Defense Fund, which launched a successful campaign to have the insecticide DDT banned. Another new group, the Natural Resources Defense Council, challenged the refusal of the Federal Power Commission to consider environmental concerns when it licensed environmentally destructive power projects.

Congress responded to the burgeoning environmental movement with a remarkable burst of legislation establishing national regulatory programs. The laws adopted during the 1970s created the federal regulatory infrastructure that remains in place today. Congress first directed all federal agencies to make environmental protection an important part of their mission when it enacted the National Environmental Policy Act (NEPA). Signed into law by President Richard M. Nixon on New Year's Day 1970, NEPA requires all agencies to assess the environmental impacts of their actions before making any decisions likely to have a significant effect on the environment.

Later in 1970, Congress enacted the Clean Air Act, which requires EPA to establish uniform national air quality standards to ensure protection of public health. It also mandated that automobile manufacturers dramatically reduce emissions from mobile sources. In 1972, Congress tackled national water pollution problems when it adopted the Federal Water Pollution Control Act, now known as the Clean Water Act. The act created a national permit program that requires all point sources of water pollution to comply with technology-based regulations for reducing pollution (see TECHNOLOGY AND LAW).

In 1973 Congress adopted the Endangered Species Act, which prohibits actions that harm species in danger of extinction. A year later it enacted the Safe Drinking Water Act, which requires EPA to set limits on levels of contaminants in water supplied by public water supply systems. In 1976 Congress adopted the Resource Conservation and Recovery Act, which required EPA to regulate the management of hazardous waste from "cradle to grave." The Toxic Substances Control Act, also enacted in 1976, gives EPA broad authority to ban or regulate any chemical substance found to pose an unreasonable risk to public health or the environment (see HEALTH LAW).

These and other federal environmental laws seek to prevent harm before it occurs by regulating pollutants, products, and practices that make environmental damage more likely to occur. Unlike the common law, which requires individual victims to prove what caused their particular harm, the environmental statutes authorize preventive regulation in circumstances where it would not be possible to meet the common law's requirement of individualized proof of causal injury. Except in the case of pesticides, the environmental laws require government regulators to make some threshold showing of potential for harm before substances or activities can be regulated. The Federal Insecticide, Fungicide and Rodenticide Act, adopted in 1972, places the burden on pesticide manufacturers to convince EPA that their products will not have unreasonable adverse effects before they can be marketed.

The judiciary played a major role in the development of environmental law by opening the courthouse doors to citizens seeking to require agencies to implement the new regulatory programs. In 1972 the Supreme Court ruled that environmental and aesthetic interests were no less deserving of judicial protection than economic interests for purposes of assessing whether plaintiffs had sufficient "injury in fact" to give them standing to sue (*Sierra Club* v. *Morton* (1972)). Because they contained provisions authorizing citizen suits and judicial review, the new environmental laws allowed the public to go to court repeatedly to force reluctant officials to implement the laws. The message that the new regulatory programs were to be taken seriously was delivered by the Supreme Court in 1978 when it halted construction of nearly completed dam in order to protect the snail darter, a tiny fish listed as endangered under the new Endangered Species Act (*TVA* v. *Hill* (1978)).

As agencies implemented the new regulatory programs, they faced legal challenges at every turn.

An early landmark decision upholding regulations limiting the amount of lead additives in gasoline illustrated how the new laws differed from the common law (*Ethyl Corporation* v. *EPA* (D.C. Cir. 1976)), rejecting industry arguments that lead additives could not be regulated until they had been proven to cause actual harm to individuals.

> Where a statute is precautionary in nature, the evidence difficult to come by, uncertain, or conflicting because it is on the frontiers of scientific knowledge, the regulations designed to protect the public health, and the decision that of an expert administrator, we will not demand rigorous step-by-step proof of cause and effect.

This did not mean that regulators could act on the basis of "hunches or wild guesses," as the Supreme Court later confirmed when it required the Occupational Safety and Health Administration to assess risks and to determine that they were significant before tightening limits on worker exposure to benzene.

When Congress reauthorized the first generation of federal environmental laws during the 1980s, it strengthened their requirements, set new deadlines for agencies to implement them, and increased penalties for violators. Congress also added some new weapons to the environmental protection arsenal. In the Superfund legislation (the Comprehensive Environmental Response, Compensation and Liability Act) enacted in 1980, Congress imposed strict, joint and several *liability for cleanup costs on broad classes of parties associated with releases of hazardous substances. In 1986 Congress adopted the Emergency Planning and Community Right-to-Know Act (EPCRA), which gives citizens the right to know about the types and volumes of toxic chemicals released in the environment each year. The 1990 Clean Air Act Amendments mandated sharp reductions in sulfur dioxide emissions from power plants while creating an emissions trading program that allows companies to buy and sell emissions allowances to reduce compliance costs.

States also generated important innovations in environmental law. These include California's Proposition 65, which prohibits companies from exposing the public without warning to significant quantities of substances that cause cancer or reproductive toxicity. By placing the burden on companies to decide whether to warn or to eliminate the risk, the law avoids the need for government regulators to make difficult judgments about the significance of risks and the best means for controlling them.

Significant Themes. As environmental law matures, important patterns have become evident. First: the initial generation of federal environmental laws adopted breathtakingly ambitious goals coupled with seemingly impossible mandates directed primarily at large industries. Despite protestations that what the laws required was technologically impossible, or impossibly costly, they helped spawn the development of new technology that has greatly reduced the costs, while improving the effectiveness, of pollution controls. Although these laws generally have succeeded in controlling large point sources of pollution, nonpoint source pollution remains a significant problem.

Second: an essential element of the success of the environmental laws is due to their profound commitment to involving the public in the development, implementation and enforcement of regulatory policy. NEPA's environmental impact assessment requirement, which now has been emulated in more than 130 countries, gave the public an important tool for ensuring that agencies considered the environmental consequences of their actions. Because Congress incorporated citizen suit and *judicial review provisions into virtually all the federal regulatory statutes, the public repeatedly has been able to go to court to ensure that the laws are implemented and enforced.

Third: Congress sought to enlist the states in cooperative partnerships to achieve the goals of the environmental laws while respecting federalism concerns. Thus, it largely eschewed federal preemption of state regulation (except for pesticide labeling, and chemical regulation), and concentrated on providing a federally guaranteed minimum level of environmental protection, while leaving states free to adopt more stringent regulations if they chose. However, environmental regulation remains a subject of considerable friction between federal and state officials.

Fourth: because of the vast range of industries and activities they regulate, the environmental laws rely heavily on self-monitoring and self-reporting for compliance. While violations often go undetected, the laws employ criminal penalties to deter intentional violations.

Fifth: while the initial generation of environmental laws focused on prescriptive requirements (sometimes referred to as "command and control" regulation), more recent initiatives seek to change behavior through information disclosure and market-based approaches that reduce the cost of emissions reductions. EPCRA's toxics release inventory and right-to-know requirements have created a powerful tool for encouraging emissions reductions, while the Clean Air Act's emissions trading program has demonstrated that substantial emissions reductions can be achieved at moderate cost.

Issues in the Twenty-First Century. Despite broad public support for the environmental laws, they remain a subject of vigorous debate. Critics of environmental regulation maintain that it is inefficient and unnecessarily costly because it often targets trivial risks while imposing excessively prescriptive requirements. EPA has found that its regulatory priorities are directed more toward risks the public considers to be significant than to the risks that concern expert risk assessors. Some argue that more environmental protection could be achieved at far lower cost if agencies were given complete freedom to set regulatory priorities while being required to base all regulations on cost-benefit analysis. Others argue that regulatory priorities should be responsive to public concerns and that greater reliance on cost-benefit analysis is a prescription for regulatory paralysis in light of the enormous uncertainties that surround efforts to estimate risks and the costs and benefits of regulation. The Supreme Court unanimously rejected industry claims that EPA should be required to set national air quality standards on the basis of cost-benefit analysis rather than a purely health-based approach (*Whitman* v. *American Trucking Associations* (2001)).

Issues of fairness are at the forefront of some current environmental policy debates. The environmental justice movement argues that environmental risks are disproportionately concentrated in poor and minority communities. Data show that members of minority groups and the poor have higher levels of lead in their blood than the rest of the population and that hazardous waste dumpsites and incinerators tend to be disproportionately located in poor and minority communities. Although there is some dispute whether undesirable land uses are sited in a discriminatory manner initially, there is little doubt that minorities and the poor are exposed to greater risks than the rest of the population. Executive Order 12,898 directs federal agencies to identify and address environmental justice problems, but vigorous debate continues over how to improve the fairness of environmental policy.

A different set of fairness issues are raised by property owners who claim that environmental regulations that significantly reduce the value of their property are *takings of their property rights for which just compensation must be paid under the Fifth Amendment to the U.S. Constitution.

Regulatory takings claims generally arise when new regulatory schemes are adopted that prohibit actions that previously were legal (e.g., building on beachfront property, filling wetlands) or when conditions are discovered that subject previously unregulated property to preexisting regulations (e.g., discovering the presence of an endangered species on private property). The Supreme Court has held that regulations that deprive a property owner of all economically beneficial use of land are regulatory takings unless the restrictions prohibit actions that would be common law nuisances (*Lucas* v. *South Carolina Coastal Council* (1992)). Although environmental regulations now are frequently challenged as takings, situations where regulations deny property owners all economically beneficial use of their land are relatively rare. Federal environmental regulation continues to raise significant issues concerning the appropriate division of power between federal and state governments. EPA relies heavily on states to help administer and enforce federal regulatory programs, but there are important constitutional limits on federal authority, as the Supreme Court has emphasized. The Supreme Court has held that Congress cannot simply require the states to regulate in a certain manner because such "commandeering" of state legislative choices impermissibly infringes the states' Tenth Amendment rights (*New York* v. *United States* (1992)). However, Congress can condition the receipt of federal funds on state agreement to regulate in a certain manner and it can give the states a choice of regulating in accordance with federal standards or having state law preempted by federal regulation. While these are the means the federal environmental laws typically employ to enlist states in the administration and enforcement of federal programs, state officials maintain that they should be given greater freedom to make regulatory choices.

The Supreme Court's revival of constitutional limits on federal regulatory authority has raised some questions concerning the limits of federal environmental regulation. The Court has held that an intrastate activity must "substantially affect" interstate commerce before Congress can use its commerce clause powers to regulate it directly (*United States* v. *Lopez* (1995)). When commercial activities are regulated, the Court assesses the cumulative impact of individual activities on interstate commerce. Because most activities regulated by the federal environmental laws involve commercial activities (e.g., emissions from an industrial facility), there is little question concerning Congress's authority to regulate them. However, when environmental laws restrict arguably non-commercial activities (e.g., the killing of an endangered species or the filling of a wetland on private land), courts have to determine whether the environmental consequences of the activities (e.g., loss of biodiversity, reduction of migratory bird habitat) have sufficient effects on interstate commerce to justify federal regulation. Controversy persists over federal management of natural resources on public lands. After shifting away from its initial focus on unbridled development, federal policy now seeks to promote "multiple uses" of vast tracts of federal land. This understandably had fostered conflict as federal officials seek to balance the competing demands of ranchers and farmers, timber and mining companies, fishers, hunters, hikers, and other recreational users. Environmentalists argue that mining, timber, and grazing interests have overexploited public lands due to government subsidies. Communities dependent on such industries fiercely resist efforts to tighten environmental standards or to charge market prices for access to resources on public lands. The intensity of these conflicts is illustrated by the response of some of the more radical groups on both sides. Some loggers have defied court orders and bulldozed illegal roads on federal property. Members of some groups like Earth First! have chained themselves to trees or have placed spikes in them to make it hazardous to cut, a practice dubbed "ecotage" in Edward Abbey's novel *The Monkey Wrench Gang*.

A final set of issues involves the future of efforts to combat global environmental problems and the impact of globalization on domestic environmental law. International agreements have enabled the nations of the world to halt trade in endangered species and to phase out chemicals destroying the earth's protective ozone layer. But the problems of global warming and climate change are proving to be far more difficult to combat. Efforts to restrict emissions of greenhouse gases contributing to global warming and climate change raise far more difficult political problems because they involve a much broader and more diffuse set of emission sources and sinks. Global trade liberalization has generated opposition from some environmentalists who fear that it will undermine domestic environmental standards that may be considered unfair trade practices by the World Trade Organization if they are deemed to operate in a discriminatory manner.

[*See also* Energy and Natural Resources Law]

• Joseph L. Sax, *Defending the Environment: A Strategy for Citizen Action*, 1971. Christopher D. Stone, "Should Trees Have Standing? Toward Legal Rights for Natural Objects," *Southern California Law Review* (1972): 450. Joel Brenner, "Nuisance Law and the Industrial Revolution," *Journal of Legal Studies* (1974): 403. Laurence H. Tribe, "Ways Not to Think About Plastic Trees: New Foundations for Environmental Law," *Yale Law Journal* (1974): 131. Roderick Nash, *Wilderness and the American Mind*, 1982. Robert L. Rabin, "Federal Regulation in Historical Perspective," *Stanford Law Review* (1986): 1189. Richard Revesz, "Rehabilitating Interstate Competition: Rethinking the 'Race to-the-Bottom' Rationale for Federal Environmental Regulation," *New York University Law Review* (1992): 1210. Robert V. Percival, "Environmental Federalism: Historical Roots and Contemporary Models," *Maryland Law Review* (1995): 1141. Daniel C. Esty and Marian R. Chertow, eds., *Thinking Ecologically: The Next Generation of Environmental Policy*, 1997. Robert V. Percival and Dorothy C. Alevizatos, eds., *Law and the Environment: A Multidisciplinary Reader*, 1997. Lisa Heinzerling, "Regulatory Costs of Mythic Proportions," *Yale Law Journal* (1998): 1981. Robert V. Percival, Alan S. Miller, Christopher H. Schroeder, and James P. Leape, *Environmental Regulation: Law, Science and Policy*, 3d ed., 2000.

—Robert V. Percival

ENVIRONMENTAL LAW: INTERNATIONAL ENVIRONMENTAL LAW IN THE UNITED STATES

International environmental law (IEL) is primarily a branch of public *international law, a body of law created by nation-states to govern problems that arise between nations. IEL endeavors to control global, regional, and interstate pollution, and the depletion of natural resources within a framework of sustainable development. Sustainable development may be defined as economic and social growth that does not damage the environment, yet meets the present generation's needs without incapacitating future generations.

Environmental problems, whether arising from air and water pollution, land use, or the extraction and use of natural resources and minerals, are experienced by almost all nations. Environmental abuses produce similar biophysical reactions wherever they occur, and thus have given rise to analogous preventive, mitigative, and remedial controls in various regions of the world.

The geopolitical ramifications of environmental problems are new to the international arena. However, nations have coped with similar internal environmental problems with various domestic laws and policies for years. These national environmental laws address problems arising from toxic and hazardous substances, land use, air and water pollution, conservation of resources, and nuclear power.

Although IEL deals primarily with nations, this situation has been attenuated by an emerging global civil society consisting of groups and participants who fall outside government entities. This civil society encompasses political parties and interest groups that include both for-profit and not-for-profit groups. Labor unions, professional associations, chambers of commerce, ethical and religious groups, and nongovernmental organizations (NGOs) all participate. Consequently, while the international community historically consisted only of nations, its embrace now extends to a nascent global civil society.

While IEL is rooted in the experience of national legislation, the formal legal sources of IEL are found in international law. They consist primarily of *treaties. A treaty is an agreement entered into between states, and typically does not enter into force unless it is ratified, and deposits of such ratifications reach the minimum number stipulated in the treaty. For example, the 1992 Convention on Biological Diversity requires 30 ratifications, and the 1997 Kyoto Protocol requires 55 parties accounting for a large percentage of carbon dioxide emissions. Most multilateral IEL treaties have been adopted within the last twenty-five years.

The formidable corpus of treaties includes those dealing with global warming and biodiversity in addition to toxic and hazardous substances, such as the 1989 Basel Convention on Transboundary Movements of Hazardous Wastes and their Disposal. They address pollution of varying kinds. These antipollution treaties deal with land based pollution (1982 United Nations Convention on the Law of the Sea), air pollution (1979 Convention on Long Range Transboundary Air Pollution), and water pollution (1997 Convention on the Law of the Non-Navigational Uses of International Watercourses). Other treaties deal with the conservation of resources (1980 Convention on the Conservation of Antarctic Marine Resources), and nuclear power (1994 Convention on Nuclear Safety). Another source of IEL is customary law. This refers largely to unwritten law inferred from the conduct of states undertaken in the belief that they were bound to do so by law.

The acceptance of a legal obligation in a treaty or in customary law is typically the first step in responding to an environmental challenge. A nation agrees to implement the treaty when it accepts its obligations. Such implementation first involves the state but then grows to embrace a cluster of other actors including corporations, individuals, and agencies whose behavior must now change to conform with IEL. The monitoring of state action to implement a treaty is undertaken typically through government reporting to and review by the international agency set up under the treaty. IEL implementation may also involve domestic measures to ensure that nations actually take steps to achieve treaty objectives. In practice, implementation has typically been confined to the first process, but the growth of an international "civil society," and the increasing power of NGOs, have resulted in accelerated scrutiny of the actual effectiveness of domestic measures taken to implement a treaty. For example, the 1993 North American Agreement on Environmental Cooperation allows NGOs and private parties to vindicate environmental rights.

In addressing global environmental problems the control of ozone pollution has become the most successful chapter of IEL for a number of socioeconomic reasons. These include the limited economic impact of the pollutant, the small number of states involved, and the fact that ozone producers, such as the United States, have found substitutes for it. Climate change or global warming and biodiversity have proven more difficult to address. The United States has not ratified the Convention on Biological Diversity or the Kyoto Protocol, calling for reductions in carbon dioxide by industrial countries.

Overall, while remaining a tributary of international law, IEL possesses its own characteristics. Its uniqueness arises as much from its relatively communal subject matter, the environment, as well as the substantial influence of domestic environmental law.

• Lakshman Guruswamy and Brent Hendricks, *International Environmental Law in a Nutshell*, 1997. Lakshman Guruswamy et al., *Supplement of Basic Documents to International Environmental Law and World Order*, 2d ed., 1999.   —Lakshman Guruswamy

ENVIRONMENTAL PROTECTION AGENCY. *See* Environmental Law; Regulation.

EPA. *See* Environmental Law; Regulation.

EQUAL OPPORTUNITY EMPLOYMENT COMMISSION. *See* Discrimination; Regulation.

EQUAL PROTECTION. The idea that all persons are equal before the law is a central tenet of American constitutional democracy. Traceable to the classical writings of Aristotle and social contract theorists such as John Locke, the equality principle is embodied in the Declaration of Independence and is implicit in a number of provisions of the United States *Constitution. This fundamental principle is stated explicitly in Section 1 of the *Fourteenth Amendment, which provides, among other things, that no state shall "deny to any person within its jurisdiction the equal protection of the laws." In essence the Equal Protection Clause requires that the government accord similar treatment to people who are similarly situated. This provision applies only to state and local governments. However, the Supreme Court has concluded that the values underlying the equal-protection guarantee are embraced within the *Due Process Clause of the Fifth Amendment and are thus applicable also to the federal government. Although a majority of state constitutions do not contain provisions identical to the Equal Protection Clause of the Fourteenth Amendment, these documents broadly endorse the principle of equality before the law.

Opposing this lofty ideal, and rooted in the fundamental commitment to *liberty, is the reality of widespread inequalities in American society, past and present. For example, Thomas *Jefferson and many of his contemporaries strongly defended an institution of *slavery based explicitly on assumptions of racial inferiority. Likewise, women were denied legal and political equality. Nevertheless, the ideal of equality before the law has persisted, and since the middle of the twentieth century it has become a dominant theme of American constitutional interpretation.

The Equal Protection Clause was written by members of Congress primarily concerned with safeguarding the *civil rights of several million African Americans who had recently been "freed" from slavery. In spite of this immediate and pervasive concern, the Equal Protection Clause makes no reference to *race. The text of the Fourteenth Amendment simply refers to "any person" within the jurisdiction of a state. Although Section 5 explicitly grants Congress power to enforce the provisions of the Fourteenth Amendment, the Supreme Court assumed the authority to determine the meaning and scope of the Equal Protection Clause and related guarantees of due process and *privileges and immunities specified in Section 1. The Court at first attempted to limit the Fourteenth Amendment to discrimination claims brought by African Americans. Writing for the majority in the *Slaughter-House Cases* (1873), Justice Samuel Miller identified "the one pervading purpose" underlying the post–Civil War Amendments as "the freedom of the slave race, the security and firm establishment of that freedom, and the protection of the newly made freeman and citizen from the oppressions of those who had formerly exercised unlimited dominion over him." The Court expressed similar concerns a few years later when, in *Strauder* v. *State of West Virginia* (1879), it invalidated a West Virginia law prohibiting blacks from serving on juries.

Within a few years, however, the Court moved beyond this exclusive emphasis on the historical context of the post–Civil War Amendments. It began to apply the Equal Protection Clause as a restriction against "irrational" *discrimination aimed at any identifiable group of persons. Moreover, in *Santa Clara County* v. *Southern Pacific Railroad Co.* (1886), the term "person" was extended to include *corporations.

The Equal Protection Clause was sometimes used in the late nineteenth and early twentieth centuries as a basis for invalidating business *regulations that the Court found to be unreasonably discriminatory. This provision, however, was largely eclipsed by the Due Process Clause as a substantive limitation on the states in the field of economic legislation. Justice Oliver Wendell *Holmes trivialized the significance of the Equal Protection Clause during the laissez-faire period of Supreme Court history by characterizing it, in *Buck* v. *Bell* (1927), as "the usual last resort of constitutional arguments."

The Supreme Court recognized as early as the 1880s that equal protection was more than a simple guarantee of procedural regularity. Thus it declared unconstitutional a San Francisco ordinance that required any person operating a laundry in a wooden building to obtain the consent of the local board of supervisors. Although this ordinance was "fair on its face," the Court concluded that it was administered in a racially discriminatory manner with the result that Chinese persons were forced to give up their laundry businesses while non-Oriental persons operating similar laundry facilities were exempted from the permit requirement.

Over the years the Supreme Court has articulated a set of standards for judging the constitutionality of laws challenged on equal-protection grounds. Most legislation classifies or discriminates among people by granting benefits or imposing burdens on some but not others. Most classifications present no serious constitutional problems. In addressing challenges to their validity, the Court has traditionally applied a deferential "rational basis" test and has usually upheld the classifications. This test places the burden of persuasion on the party challenging the classification or discrimination to show that its purpose is an illegitimate state objective and that the means employed by the state are not rationally related to the achievement of that objective (see, for example, *Gulf, C. & S. F. Ry.* v. *Ellis* (1897)).

The rational basis test, with its modest limitations on legislative choice, stands in sharp contrast to the standard of "strict scrutiny," first articulated in the 1940s and fully developed by the *Warren Court in the 1960s. In the course of this development the Equal Protection Clause served as the basis for the Court's monumental decision in *Brown v. Board of Education (1954) overturning the "separate but equal" doctrine (see *Plessy v. Ferguson (1896)) and holding that racially segregated public schools are "inherently unequal." In the companion case of Bolling v. Sharpe (1954) the justices held that the operation of segregated schools in the District of Columbia violated the Due Process Clause of the Fifth Amendment. While the Court retained the old rational basis test with its deference to most economic and social legislation, the "new equal protection" revolutionized this field of *jurisprudence by finding certain classifications inherently "suspect" and subjecting them to far more searching judicial examination.

Operationally this strict scrutiny approach reverses the ordinary presumption of constitutionality accorded to challenged legislation. The government has the burden of convincing the Court that the classification under review is constitutional. To carry this burden the government must show that its policy is "necessary" to the achievement of a "compelling state interest" and that it is narrowly tailored to attain that objective. The suspect classification/strict scrutiny formula has been applied to classifications based on race, ethnicity, and *religion, almost always resulting in the invalidation of such classifications. One notable exception is in the area of *affirmative action, where the Supreme Court, while moving far in the direction of a "color-blind" Constitution, in Adarand Constructors, Inc. v. Pena (1995) refused to bar all federal programs targeted to assist previously disadvantaged racial and ethnic minorities.

During the 1970s the *Burger Court continued the crafting of new equal-protection standards by modifying the strict scrutiny test. The result was the creation of a level of review falling somewhere between the rational basis test and the suspect classification doctrine. This approach, labeled "heightened" or "intermediate" scrutiny, has been applied most prominently but not exclusively to issues of gender discrimination. It has also been used to invalidate classifications targeting illegitimate children and illegal aliens. This level of scrutiny requires the government to show that a challenged policy bears a "substantial" relationship to an "important" government interest. The Court has ruled in Mississippi University for Women v. Hogan (1982) and United States v. Virginia (1996) that a gender-based classification cannot be upheld unless it is based on "an exceedingly persuasive justification." Some legal scholars have argued

that this standard closely approaches the "compelling state interest" test.

Although discrimination based on wealth has not been held inherently suspect, the Court has invalidated forms of economic discrimination that prevent individuals from exercising their constitutional rights. Wealth-based discriminations that burden such fundamental rights as *voting have been subjected to strict scrutiny, as in Harper v. Virginia Board of Elections (1966). Economic classifications not involving fundamental rights are reviewed under the traditional rational basis test.

The Court's choice to apply either rational basis or strict scrutiny to particular classifications can obviously have profound implications for litigants. For example, the Court has applied the rational basis test in reviewing classifications based on age and disability. Ironically, because the Court refused to view these classifications as suspect, a five-member majority ruled in Kimel v. Florida Board of Regents (2000) and Board of Trustees of the University of Alabama v. Garrett (2001) that Congress could not abolish state immunity against suits brought by individuals claiming discrimination based on age and disability.

In recent years several justices have expressed growing dissatisfaction with what they regard as the Court's unduly rigid approach to equal-protection questions. Justice Thurgood *Marshall, in San Antonio Independent School Dist. v. Rodriguez (1973), advocated adoption of a "sliding scale" that would embrace a "spectrum of standards" of review. Justice John Paul Stevens, in City of Cleburne v. Cleburne Living Well Center (1985), urged the Court to give more rigorous application to the rational basis test, which he deems adequate to invalidate all invidious forms of discrimination. Others on the Court, including Chief Justice William Rehnquist, are critical of the special solicitude that the post–New Deal Court has given to discrete and insular minorities. In the light of growing criticisms within an increasingly conservative Court, we can expect further changes in equal-protection analysis.

The history and application of the Equal Protection Clause implies a strong commitment to the fundamental value of racial equality. In recent years strong arguments have been advanced in support of the view that other fundamental values are also implicit in the equal-protection concept. These arguments emphasize the view that people are entitled to respect as individuals and to treatment as equals. For example, the Court has invoked the Equal Protection Clause in safeguarding the right to vote; protecting against diluting the value of a vote; and, as in Bush v. Gore, guaranteeing the right to have one's vote recounted in accordance with uniform statewide standards (see *Harper* v. *Virginia Board of Elections*, *Reynolds* v. *Sims* (1964), and *Bush* v. *Gore* (2000)). Recognition of the fundamental rights component of equal-protection jurisprudence is also evident in the Court's invalidation of a Colorado constitutional amendment that prohibited all state and local government action aimed at protecting homosexuals. Justice Anthony Kennedy, writing for the majority, found that this amendment imposed "a broad and undifferentiated disability on a single named group" that seemed "inexplicable by anything but animus toward the class that it affects." The Court held that a state could not thus "deem a class of persons a stranger to its laws." (See *Romer* v. *Evans* (1996)). It is significant that in declaring the Colorado amendment unconstitutional, the Court purported to apply the traditional rational basis test, thus indicating that some government action can fail to satisfy even this minimal standard of review.

Despite the Court's growing recognition of a variety of fundamental values implicit in the equal-protection concept, the legitimacy of this aspect of equal-protection interpretation remains controversial. Peter Westen has argued forcefully that the proposition that people who are alike should be treated alike is tautological and should be banished from moral and legal discourse as an explanatory norm. In response, others have argued that the concept of equality creates a presumption favoring equal treatment of all persons, departures from which must be justified.

It is axiomatic that state courts must recognize U.S. Supreme Court decisions interpreting the Fourteenth Amendment's Equal Protection Clause as threshold requirements. But while they may not narrow or evade federal standards, state courts have discretion to broaden the scope of equal-protection guarantees. For example, the California Supreme Court held in *Hardy* v. *Stumpf* (1978) that sex discrimination is subject to a standard of strict scrutiny more demanding than the heightened scrutiny required by the U.S. Supreme Court. The Vermont Supreme Court recently ruled in *Baker* v. *State* (1999) that same-sex couples are entitled to the benefits and protections that marriage affords to different-sex couples. This decision was based on the "common benefits" clause, the Vermont Constitution's counterpart to the Equal Protection Clause of the Fourteenth Amendment.

The financing of public education is among the most important issues of equality coming before

state courts since the late 1960s. In 1973 the U.S. Supreme Court, in *San Antonio Independent School District* v. *Rodriguez*, reversing a trend in state court decisions, refused to recognize education as a fundamental right and held that the Fourteenth Amendment did not require equal statewide funding of public schools. Following this ruling, a number of state courts, such as California in *Serrano* v. *Priest* (1977), recognized a right to education. In doing so, it and other courts have relied either on equal-protection analysis or on education provisions of state constitutions. These and a wide array of other state court decisions contribute to the dynamism of the equality principle as a source of modern constitutional interpretation.

[*See also* Affirmative Action; Civil Rights and Civil Liberties]

• Joseph Tussman and Jacobus tenBroek, "The Equal Protection of the Laws," *California Law Review* 37 (1949): 341. Gerald Gunther, "Forword: In Search of Evolving Doctrine on a Changing Court: A Model for a Newer Equal Protection," *Harvard Law Review* 86 (1972): 1. Peter Westen, "The Empty Idea of Equality," *Harvard Law Review* 95 (1982): 537. Judith A. Baer, *Equality under the Constitution: Reclaiming the Fourteenth Amendment*, 1983. Kenneth L. Karst, "Why Equality Matters," *Georgia Law Review* 17 (1983): 245. Robert F. Williams, "The Emergence of State Constitutional Law: Equality Guarantees in State Constitutional Law," *Texas Law Review* 63 (1985): 1195. J. R. Pole, *The Pursuit of Equality in American History*, 1993. Neal Devins and Davison M. Douglas, eds., *Redefining Equality*, 1998. Helen Hershkoff, "Positive Rights and State Constitutions: The Limits of Federal Rationality Review," *Harvard Law Review* 112 (1999): 1132. Mark Strasser, "Equal Protection at the Crossroads: On *Baker*, Common Benefits, and Facial Neutrality," *Arizona Law Review* 42 (2000): 935.   —Otis H. Stephens

EQUAL RIGHTS AMENDMENT. After the Nineteenth Amendment was ratified in 1920, suffragists regrouped for their next struggle. The Nineteenth Amendment stated that *voting rights could not be denied on the basis of sex. Yet states did not automatically grant women voters the right to hold political office or to serve on juries; women's civic identity in many ways continued to be defined through their husbands; and female workers were governed by various industrial regulations that did not apply to men.

Some suffragists, notably Alice Paul of the National Woman's Party, insisted that an Equal Rights Amendment was necessary to eliminate inequality. They faced opposition from other women's rights advocates who shared some, but not all, of Paul's concerns. In recent decades, the

U.S. Supreme Court had struck down laws regulating the conditions under which all workers labored, but had accepted arguments, as in *Muller v. Oregon* (1908), that women's weaker physiology and childbearing capacities permitted some sex specific regulations. Many suffragists, including Florence Kelley, rejected the ERA because it would undermine these "protective" labor laws, which they thought crucial to the welfare of poor women.

Paul's version of the ERA was first introduced to Congress in 1923. It stated: "Men and women shall have equal rights throughout the United States and every place subject to its jurisdiction." The ERA did not pass in the 1920s, due partly to conservative attacks on feminism but also because many post-suffrage women's organizations, incuding the League of Women Voters, actively opposed it.

Throughout the 1930s, women trade unionists and reformers, including Eleanor Roosevelt, continued to oppose the ERA. The ERA's supporters (in the NWP and some professional women's organizations) tended to be Republicans. During the 1940s, the GOP and the Democrats endorsed the ERA in their platforms. This support was of little consequence, however, as there was no broad movement demanding passage.

In the post–World War II period, several factors coincided to generate new interest in the ERA. The wartime mobilization of women workers raised new concerns about the discriminatory implications of "protective labor law." And Alice Paul, having returned from an extended stay in London, reinvigorated the movement. As before, however, definitions of "equal rights" had to accommodate widely accepted understandings of the special needs of women as a group. Supporters of protective legislation sought to finesse the Amendment by endorsing an alternative known as the "Status Bill" (introduced in 1947), which would have prohibited laws discriminating on the basis of sex, except those justified by differences in physiology, biology, and social funtion. Congress chose instead to pursue the ERA. Yet when the ERA did pass the Senate in 1950 and 1953 it was with the addition of the "Hayden rider," stating that the ERA would not be interpreted as overturning laws benefiting women. ERA supporters blocked this version in the House.

In 1964, Congress passed the *Civil Rights Act, which included Title VII, banning employment *discrimination on the basis of race, creed, and sex. Within a few years, pressure from the newly formed National Organization for Women, as well as the numerous discrimination complaints filed by women, forced the EEOC (after initial reluctance) to take seriously Title VII's sex discrimination prohibitions. The EEOC began striking down protective labor laws as violating Title VII. As these laws fell away, traditional opponents (such as the LWV) dropped their opposition. Key organizations of the resurgent women's rights movement made passage of the ERA the focus of the new feminism.

In the wake of the movement for black civil rights, which emphasized that different treatment was incompatible with equality, the ERA was now widely viewed as a logical, inevitable reform. Congress easily passed the ERA in 1972, rejecting efforts to attach riders pertaining to women and military service, *homosexuality, and the *family. The text that passed was simple and unqualified: Section 1 read: "Equality of rights under the law shall not be denied or abridged by the United States or by any State on account of sex."

By the end of 1973, thirty state legislatures had ratified the ERA. New sources of opposition mobilized, however, most notably the "ordinary housewives" led by Phyllis Schlafly who articulated fears about the disintegration of traditional families and concerns about their own economic vulnerability. Also opposing the ERA were overlapping constituencies who disliked the federal intervention implied in the ERA's Congressional enabling section, and who linked the ERA to *abortion after the *Roe v. Wade decision (1973). In the end, only thirty-five of the necessary thirty-eight state legislatures ratified ERA, notwithstanding Congress granting a five-year extension (until 1982) for ratification.

Despite its defeat, the movement for the ERA contributed to important revisions in American law. During the 1970s, feminist legislators helped write new laws addressing discrimination in the Social Security system, in banking and credit, and in educational funding. And feminist litigators, notably Ruth Bader Ginsburg, convinced the courts—in groundbreaking decisions such as *Reed v. Reed* (1970) and *Frontiero* v. *Richardson* (1973)—to reinterpret the *Equal Protection clause of the *Fourteenth Amendment as requiring greater scrutiny of gender distinctions in the law.

ERA, while not currently a high-profile issue, continues to be introduced regularly before Congress. Many of the inequalities that the ERA would have eliminated, were it ratified in the early 1970s, have been addressed in a more piecemeal fashion. Yet supporters argue that ERA nonetheless would have more than symbolic importance because it would establish a constitutional principle of equality (already present in a number of state constitutions) that would guide the courts in the future.

[*See also* Constitutional Amendments]

• Jane J. Mansbridge, *Why We Lost the ERA*, 1986. Nancy F. Cott, *The Grounding of Modern Feminism*, 1987. Cynthia Harrison, *On Account of Sex: The Politics of Women's Issues, 1945–1968*, 1988. Donald G. Mathews and Jane Sherron De Hart, *Sex, Gender and the Politics of ERA: A State and the Nation*, 1990. Joan Hoff, *Law, Gender and Injustice: A Legal History of U.S. Women*, 1991. Martha Craig Daughtrey, "Women and the Constitution: Where We Are at the End of the Century," *New York University Law Review* 75:1 (April 2000), 1–25.   —Catherine E. Rymph

EQUITY. In Anglo-American law "equity" derives from the historical jurisdiction of the medieval English Chancery Court. The concept of "equity" flows from the Aristotelian conception of equity as "a rectification of law where the law falls short by reason of its universality." In this Aristotelean vein, equity in Roman and English law created a remedy in face of law's failure and it worked to give relief from harsh application of legal rules in particular cases. Anglo-American law treated equity as a distinct source of law. Equity did not appear merely as a concept by which to interpret the law, but as a separate body of law with separate courts that had the potential to conflict with, and complement, the *common law.

The Chancery Court. The separateness of equity arose because in medieval law the chancellor was a powerful actor in the King's Council who had the authority to issue writs for unusual relief. The Chancery Court was known as a court of conscience. It developed remedies and substantive law doctrines that differed from common law in numerous ways. The chancellor exercised power over persons and could issue orders requiring a party to do or to refrain from doing certain specific acts. This authority to grant *injunctions was in marked contrast to the common-law courts, which were largely confined to the award of monetary damages. The Chancery Court also fashioned the law of trusts and enforced fiduciary obligations.

Important for later transplant in the American colonies, the chancellor was a trier of both fact and law. In contrast to the common law, no jury was utilized that would require the precise delineation of fact and law. Equity then was much more fluid than the common law. Such discretion residing in judges drew much hostility from some of the American colonies. As the chancery court in the seventeenth century grew more involved with *property matters, predictability became important. Adherence to precedent with the reporting of cases became a central aspect of dispensing justice according to conscience. Hence, a series of chancellors promoted equity as a systematic and principled body of law.

American Law. The introduction of equity into American *jurisprudence occurred during a period when equity was becoming rigid. Equity's ample discretion was seen as a flaw. Ideas of conscience were wrung out of it, to be replaced by a set of rules. Joseph *Story, the American expositor of equity jurisprudence, looked to equity as a disciplined body of law. The discretion inherent in equity, with its authority bestowed on judges, was a subject of debate at the framing of the United States Constitution. As part of the law reform movement in the late nineteenth century, law and equity were generally merged throughout the Anglo-American legal system. The reforms revitalized equity.

Maxims of Equity. The maxims of equity were developed in the late seventeenth and early eighteenth centuries just at the time of the movement toward more certainty. Of these distillations of the principles inherent in equity, the most significant are as follows:

- Equity looks on as done that which ought to be done.
- Equity follows the law.
- He or she who comes into equity must come with clean hands.
- He or she who seeks equity must do equity.
- Equity does not allow a statute to be made an instrument of fraud.
- Equality is equity.
- Equity acts in personam.
- Equity will not assist a volunteer.
- Equity looks to intent not form.
- Equity will not suffer a wrong to be without a remedy.
- Where the equities are equal, the law prevails.
- Where the equities are equal, the first in time prevails.
- Equity aids the diligent not the tardy.

The maxims have been applied in numerous cases and created distinct bodies of law that are at the center of what is viewed as modern equity.

Two equitable defenses are the clean hands doctrine (the third maxim above) and laches. It also analyses two substantive equitable doctrines, estoppel and constructive trust. The selection provides a sense of how equity operates in the law.

Clean Hands. Where a person has engaged in improper conduct in a transaction and seeks equitable relief in respect to that transaction, a court applying this maxim will refuse relief. The maxim is a reflection of the principle of that equity operated as a court of conscience. A court cannot be used to promote or condone crimes or breaches of public morality. Thus, if a person seeks to set aside a transaction on the ground of fraud he must be free of any participation in the fraud. The maxim constitutes a defense only to equitable *remedies, injunction, and specific performance, for example. It does not apply to common-law remedies.

Laches. This defense is associated with maxim: "Equity aids the vigilant." Broadly defined, "laches" is any unreasonable delay by a person possessing a legal right in enforcing that legal right that produces prejudice to the person against whom the legal right is being enforced. In addition, the holder of a right may by his conduct be fairly regarded as waiving that right. A court will not grant an equitable remedy in favor of a person whose conduct amounts to laches or acquiescence. The prejudice following from the delay may be to third parties.

Estoppel. Estoppel is a substantive equitable principle that precludes a party to a legal proceeding from asserting against another facts, rights, or absence of legal rights. The object of estoppel is to preclude unconscionable departure by a person for an assumption for which he or she bears responsibility and that has been adopted by another as a basis for action or inaction, to his detriment. Estoppel existed as common law, as well as in equity. Equitable estoppel precluded the enforcement of equitable relief.

The major development was *promissory estoppel in which one party to a *contract who represents he will not enforce his rights, will be precluded from that enforcement. In this form estoppel remains a defense and this is properly described as equitable. The courts, however, in Anglo-American law began to accept that promissory estoppel could be cause of action where one party makes a representation to another which is relied upon to his detriment.

Constructive Trust. The courts of equity devised the institution of the *trust. Trusts are often expressly created by parties. A trustee holds property for the benefit of another, the beneficiary. The trustee holds the legal estate, the beneficiary, the equitable estate. Equity imposes exacting obligations on the trustee to handle the property for the benefit of the beneficiary.

A constructive trust is imposed where it would be unconscionable for the legal owner to retain the benefit of the equitable estate. The constructive trust is remedial in nature, although it effects a change in the nature of property. Constructive trusts are imposed for a number of reasons including giving recognition of a preexisting property right, enforcing equitable principles, encouraging observance of equitable obligations, deterrence of breaches of fiduciary duties and remedying unconscionable behavior including unjust enrichment. The constructive trust is a discretionary remedy, the imposition of which turns on the courts review of the rights of third parties and the conduct of the parties—it is a powerful remedy. The constructive trust gives a property interest enforceable against purchases to the beneficiary who has notice of the circumstances leading to the imposition of the constructive trust. The equity courts allowed holders of equitable rights to trace that as property into the hands of others. Like the express trustee, a constructive trustee is personally liable to compensate the beneficiary for losses caused in mishandling the property and to account for any profits made for its use.

In these maxims, defenses, and institutions of equity the common theme is that equity will not allow legal rights to be enforced in a harsh and unconscionable way, and will create remedies, like constructive trust, to more thoroughly and flexibly deliver just results beyond the parameters of legal rights and remedies.

[*See also* Procedure, Civil]

• Jairus W. Perry, ed. *Story's Equity Jurisprudence,* 12th ed., 1877. J. H. Baker, *An Introduction to English Legal History,* 3d ed., 1990. P. C. Hoffer, *The Law's Conscience: Equitable Constitutionalism in America,* 1990. D. Parkinson, *The Principles of Equity,* 1996.

—David F. Partlett

EQUITY JURISDICTION. *See* Equity.

ERIE RAILROAD V. TOMPKINS 304 U.S. 64 (1938), limited the power of federal courts to create judge-made law that would displace state law. Jurists view the Supreme Court's decision both a modern cornerstone of American judicial *federalism and an example of legal realism's influence.

Prior to *Erie,* federal *courts applied state statutory law, but did not feel bound to apply state *common law rules in areas of general law, such as torts and contracts. Instead, federal courts created their own common law in these areas. This was not viewed as displacing state authority because law, from a jurisprudential standpoint, was thought to exist independently of any sovereign; thus, federal courts were as competent as state courts to ascertain the true common law. The *Erie* decision reflected growing concern about the unfairness of having different legal principles apply solely on the basis of whether the plaintiff brought the case in state or federal court. It also reflected legal realism's emergence as a jurisprudential theory and a rejection of the notion that common law is a transcendental body of law existing independently of any sovereign. The *Erie* holding that federal courts do not have the power to create general common law reflects the realist understanding that, if a federal court announces a common law rule, it is creating federal law and must have a basis of authority in the U.S. *Constitution. The Court found no such general authority, although federal courts can develop their own rules of procedure.

[*See also* Commercial Law; *Swift* v. *Tyson* (1842)]

• John H. Ely, "The Irrepressible Myth of Erie," *Harvard Law Review* 87 (1974): 693–740.

—Wendy C. Perdue

ESTATE

Testate Esates
Intestate Estates

ESTATE: TESTATE ESTATES

The owner of *property may dispose of it at death by a *will. The will is a formal document signed by the property owner, the "testator," and witnessed at its signing by two individuals. At the testator's death the will is submitted to a court to establish its validity. This is referred to as the "probate" (proving) of the will. The testator is said to die "testate."

The will was part of the English legal heritage of the American colonists. It was recognized by the English Statute of Wills (1540), a law based on existing customs. During the nineteenth century, American states tended to adopt more formal rules governing the execution of wills, and they treated land and personal property as the same for the purpose of disposition by will. Generally, only wealthy persons made wills in the nineteenth century, and wills were prepared by testators on their deathbed more frequently than in modern practice, with its focus on estate planning. After 1900, wealthy testators began to engage in careful planning of will provisions in order to minimize estate taxes and provide for future contingencies.

The will usually designates an executor, who during probate is appointed by the court to administer the estate of the testator. The executor collects the assets of the testator, pays the testator's creditors, the administration expenses, and any estate taxes owed by the estate, and distributes the remainder to those named in the will. The executor functions under the supervision of the court. The law of the state in which the testator was a resident at the time of death governs the will and the administration of the estate, except that federal estate taxes may be applicable to the estate.

In order to execute a valid will a testator must have the requisite mental capacity. This requirement is important because many testators are elderly. The testator must have the capacity to know the nature of his property, know the natural objects of his bounty, form an orderly disposition, and understand the disposition in his will. In addition, the testator must be free from undue influence in the execution of his will. An elderly testator may become subject to the influence of a person to such an extent that he cannot resist doing what that person wants him to do. This may result in executing a will that makes a disposition of property to such person that is unusual. If undue influence is judged to exist, the provisions of the will that are the product of undue influence are invalid. The circumstances that may give rise to a presumption of undue influence are a testator who is known to be susceptible to undue influence, a confidential relationship between the testator and the person allegedly exercising the influence, and a provision for the confidant in the will that is unusual.

The will has no legal effect during the life of the testator. It can be amended at any time or revoked in its entirety by a subsequent writing executed by the testator in accordance with the formalities required for a will. A will can also be revoked by the testator by destruction or by drawing lines across its face with the intention to revoke the will. The testator may execute a new will any number of times.

The will may contain several different types of gifts. With the "specific gift" the testator disposes of specifically described land or jewelry or other property. A testator who makes such a gift assumes that she will own that property at her death; if she does not, the gift may fail. Another form of gift is the "general gift," in which the testator disposes of a certain sum of money to a person. If there is insufficient cash in the estate to pay the gift, the executor sells assets of the estate to produce cash sufficient to pay the gift. A third form of gift is the "residuary gift." When the testator executes a will, she does not know exactly what she will own at the time of her death. This circumstance calls for a provision that disposes of all the rest and residue of her property that remains after all specific and general gifts are paid. Usually the bulk of the estate passes under the residuary clause.

A person must survive the testator in order to take under a will. If he does not survive, the gift is said to lapse. Often the will contains a provision for an alternative taker in the event that the first designated person predeceases the testator. If no alternative taker is named, an anti-lapse statute may take effect. The application of the anti-lapse statute is subject to the expression by the testator in her will that is not to apply.

The testator has great freedom in the disposition of her estate. The only limitation is that she cannot disinherit her spouse. The surviving spouse is entitled to a certain fraction of the estate, which he may claim if the testator makes no provision or inadequate provision for him in the will. This is called the surviving spouse's "elective share." In all other respects the testator is entitled to leave her property to charity or to strangers, even if this results in disinheritance of her children or other relatives. Historically, the surviving spouse had no elective share. Instead the surviving spouse was entitled to a lifetime interest in land, or a portion of the land, owned by the decedent spouse.

There are two methods other than a will of disposing of property at death. One is the "will substitute," by which the property owner in an informal manner designates who is to receive certain property. For example, an owner of a life *insurance policy may designate the beneficiary of the proceeds by completing a form provided by the insurance company; and the owner of a bank account may designate the person to receive the balance in the account at death by completing a form provided by the bank. Will substitute property passes directly to the named beneficiary, not to the executor, although it may be subject to the claims of the testator's creditors. Will substitutes are frequently subject to the surviving spouse's elective share.

Property may also be disposed of at death by law. To the extent that a property owner does not dispose of his property by will or will substitute, the property passes by intestacy to those specified in a statute in the state in which the property owner was resident at death. These statutes vary from state to state, but generally they provide for the property to pass to the surviving spouse and descendants in specified proportions, or if there is no surviving spouse, to the surviving descendants entirely, or if there is no surviving spouse or descendants, to other relatives. Intestate property is subject to estate administration, just as is testate property.

Two distinctive forms of property ownership bear upon the disposition of property at death: the joint tenancy and the *trust. Two people, usually husband and wife, may place land, corporate stock, or bonds in their names as joint tenants. This means that each person is entitled to a one-half interest in the property while both are alive. Upon the death of one person, the survivor automatically becomes the sole owner of the entire property. Nothing passes through the estate of the first to die. While both are alive, however, either party may sever the joint tenancy and take one-half as his absolute property. The other one-half remains the property of the other party to the ownership.

When a property owner places property in trust, he transfers legal title in the property to one party, the "trustee," and beneficial ownership of the property to others, the "beneficiaries." The trustee holds the title as a fiduciary and manages the property for the exclusive benefit of the beneficiaries. As an example, a property owner may transfer legal title to corporate stock to a bank, as trustee, to pay the income to his wife for her life and, upon her death, to transfer the legal title to the property to the property owner's children, thereby terminating the trust. The trustee receives a fee for the performance of its role.

A trust may be created during the property owner's lifetime or at his death under the terms of a will. There are several reasons for creating a trust rather than giving the property outright. First, continuing the example of the trust to pay income to the wife for her life and, upon her death, to transfer the legal title to the children, the property owner may not have confidence that his wife would properly manage the property. Second, the property owner may wish to be assured that the property will be preserved to benefit his children. Third, there often are estate tax reasons for creating a trust.

A trust created during the property owner's lifetime may be made subject to a power of revocation by the property owner. This means that the property owner can change her mind, terminate the trust, and take the property back at any time. If the property owner does not revoke, the trust continues in accordance with its terms after her death. This becomes a form of will substitute if the property owner does not exercise her power of revocation.

Nine states have a system of property ownership between husband and wife called "community property," which radically affects the power of disposition. In a large majority of states, husband and wife own property as do unmarried persons: whatever the husband earns is his and whatever the wife earns is hers. In community property states, the earnings of the spouses, and property acquired from such earnings, are owned one-half by each spouse. If the husband works and gets paid and the wife works as homemaker, the wife owns one-half of her husband's earnings. The earnings during *marriage and the property acquired by such earnings are community property. The property owned by a spouse prior to marriage, on the other hand, is not community property; it is "separate property" and remains individually owned. Property acquired by gift or inheritance during marriage is also separate property.

When a husband or wife is resident in a community property state at the time of death, he or she has the power to dispose of only one-half of the community property by will because that is all he or she owns. The other one-half of the community property belongs to the surviving spouse. If the decedent dies without a will, only one-half of the community property passes by intestacy. The decedent, however, retains full dispositive power over his or her separate property.

The community property system is derived from the Spanish and French property traditions. The individual ownership of property in the marital relationship is derived from the English property tradition. The community property states include California and Texas; the system is applicable to about one-fourth of the U.S. population.

[*See also* Probate]

• William M. McGovern Jr., Sheldon F. Kurtz, and Jan Ellen Rein, *Wills, Trusts, and Estates,* 1988. Paul G. Haskell, *Preface to Wills, Trusts, and Administration,* 2d ed., 1994. Lawrence W. Waggoner, Gregory S. Alexander, and Mary Louise Fellows, *Family Property Law,* 2d ed., 1997. Jesse Dukeminier and Stanley M. Johanson, *Wills, Trusts, and Estates,* 6th ed., 2000.

—James W. Ely Jr.

ESTATE: INTESTATE ESTATES

A person can dispose of *property at death by a *will, a formal document signed by the property owner in the presence of individuals who sign their names as witnesses. Some forms of property, however, can be disposed of at death informally by designating in writing who is to succeed to the property; this is called a "will substitute." Examples are life *insurance for which the property owner designates on a form provided by the insurance company who is to receive the insurance proceeds, and bank accounts for which the property owner designates on a form provided by the bank who is to receive the balance in the accounts at her death. The property owner may die leaving will substitutes and a will in which she disposes of all property other than the property covered by the will substitutes.

A property owner who dies without disposing of her property by will or will substitute is said to die intestate. In this case property passes to individuals designated by a statute in the state in which the property owner was resident at the time of death. A property owner may die partially intestate, leaving a will that disposes of specified property but does not cover other property owned at the time of death. The law of each state governs the passing of property at death, although federal estate taxes may be applicable.

The American colonists, early on, moved away from the English *common law governing intestate succession. They rejected the doctrine of primogeniture, under which the land of a father who died intestate passed to the oldest son. The colonists favored partible inheritance, giving equal shares to all children. Intestate estates were historically common. Estimates suggest that in the nineteenth century, 90 percent of people died without wills.

Modern intestacy statutes vary from state to state, but they generally follow a pattern. If a decedent is survived by a spouse and descendants (children, grandchildren, great-grandchildren), her property will pass to them in specified shares. If a decedent is survived by descendants but not by a spouse, the descendants receive all the property. If a decedent is survived by a spouse and a parent but no descendants, the spouse and parents share in specified portions. If the decedent is survived by a spouse and no parent or descendant, the spouse receives all the property. If the decedent is survived by a parent and no spouse or descendant, the parent takes all. In the absence of surviving spouse, descendant, or parent, the surviving siblings or surviving descendants of deceased siblings take all. The property of the decedent does not pass immediately to the heirs. The court in the state in which the decedent died resident first appoints a person to be administrator of the estate. The administrator collects the decedent's property, pays the decedent's creditors, the administration expenses, and whatever estate taxes are due from the estate, and distributes the remaining property to the heirs. The administrator is subject to the oversight of the court. Property that passes by will substitute goes directly to the beneficiary, not through estate administration, although it may be subject to the claims of the decedent's creditors.

Historically, the surviving spouse was not an heir to the land of the decedent spouse. The court in the state in which the decedent died resident first appoints a person to be administrator of the estate. Today the surviving spouse is an heir to all property of the decedent spouse.

For intestacy purposes, an adopted child is the child of the adoptive parents and ceases to be the child of her natural parents. If the spouse of the natural parent adopts the child, however, the adopted child remains the child of the natural parent for intestacy purposes. For example, if the father dies, the mother remarries, and the new husband adopts the child, the relationship of heirship between mother and child remains.

Historically, a child born out of wedlock was not an heir of her parents and the parents were not heirs of the child. That has now changed: the nonmarital child is the heir of the mother and is also the heir of the father, subject to proof of parentage.

In most states a person who commits murder cannot be an heir of the murdered person, and in some states an abandoning spouse cannot be an heir of the victimized spouse.

In the past, although a person named in a will could decline the gift, a person designated as an heir by statute could not refuse to accept his interest. He was the holder of title by statute, meaning that the property was subject to the claims of his creditors. If he did not want the property, he had to make a gift of it to another, which might be subject to a gift tax. Today the heir may refuse to accept the intestate property, just as the person provided for in a will may refuse to accept the provision in the will.

[See also Marriage]

• William M. McGovern Jr., Sheldon F. Kurtz, and Jan Ellen Rein, *Wills, Trusts, and Estates*, 1988. Paul G. Haskell, *Preface To Wills, Trusts, and Administration*, 2d ed., 1994. Lawrence W. Waggoner, Gregory S. Alexander, and Mary Louise Fellows, *Family Property Law*, 2d ed., 1997. Jesse Dukeminier and Stanley M. Johanson, *Wills, Trusts, and Estates*, 6th ed., 2000.

—James W. Ely Jr.

ESTATE TAX. *See* Taxation: Estate and Gift Taxes.

ESTOPPEL. *See* Equity.

ETHICS, MEDICAL. *See* Medicine and Law.

ETHICS, MORALITY, AND LAW. Morality concerns how one ought to live one's life, and ethics refers to the codes of conduct governing social interactions. To live morally or ethically is to adhere to standards of right conduct, to act well, to be a good person. Law is also a code of conduct. Ethics, morality, and law constrain what individuals may do, but in different ways. That an act is immoral or unethical is for many people sufficient reason not to commit it. For others, only the threat of legal punishment is sufficient. Laws are enforced by punishment or *damage awards, executed after a judicial determination according to procedures laid out by an authoritative governing body. Moral laws or principles have no similar enforcement mechanism, relying instead on individual conscience, social pressure, or perhaps the fear of God, although the philosopher Immanuel Kant (*Groundwork of the Metaphysics of Morals*, 1785) held that if you refrain from acting badly because you fear God or legal punishment, you are not really acting morally—a moral act must be done for the sake of morality.

The relation between morality and law is complex and a matter of considerable disagreement. To what extent do or should they coincide? Some have argued that law properly targets immoral or unethical conduct. For example, in 1977 the United States enacted the Foreign Corrupt Practices Act, making illegal the bribery of foreign officials. Recently the United States has urged other nations to follow suit. But many resist the view that government should use law to coerce people into being moral, and argue that law and morality must be separate and distinct; if we believe abortions are immoral, it does not necessarily follow that they should be illegal.

*Natural law theorists regard law and morality as connected; law is not simply whatever legislatures enact in statutes. If what is called a law fails to meet the features that all morally proper laws should have, then it is called law only by mistake, and has no authority. For St. Thomas Aquinas (1226–1274), insofar as human law deviates from the law of nature, or reason, it is no law at all, but a perversion of law (*Summa Theologica*, Question 95).

Appeal to a higher moral law, or a sense of fundamental fairness, has been used in American law to override enacted legislation, following the example of Justice Samuel *Chase, who wrote in *Calder* v. *Bull* (1798) that "[t]here are certain vital principles in our free republican governments, which will determine and overrule an apparent and flagrant abuse of legislative power.... An act of the legislature (for I cannot call it a law), contrary to the great first principles of the social compact, cannot be considered a rightful exercise of legislative authority." Appeal to a higher, natural law has been strongly criticized, however, on the ground that reasonable people disagree about which moral principles are valid; lacking objective means of resolving this disagreement, whether something truly accords with a higher moral law is a subjective judgment.

Another criticism of natural law theory is that law seems distinct from morality. Not everything that is illegal, for example, driving a few miles above the speed limit in sparse traffic, is immoral; not everything that is immoral, for example, breaking a promise to pick up a friend at the airport, is or should be illegal. An alternative theory of law, called "legal positivism," emphasizes the separation between law and morality. According to legal positivists, law is manmade and defined, or "posited," by the legislature or law-creating authority; one cannot say, with natural law theorists, that there is a law against X but you may still do X with impunity. We can challenge laws by appealing to moral or religious principles, but until a duly enacted law is changed, it remains law.

How does the positivist distinguish commands that count as law from commands that do not, without appealing to morality? The British theorist John Austin argues that law is distinguished from other commands by being the command of the sovereign; the gunman's command lacks this pedigree (see The Province of Jurisprudence Determined (1832) and Lectures on Jurisprudence (1869)). Who is sovereign? Not someone who has a right to rule, or who rules legitimately, for this would interject morality into the law. Rather, it is someone who is sovereign, who is in fact obeyed.

But this makes the legal system nothing more than a gunman writ large, responds H. L. A. Hart, who answers the question of how we distinguish laws from other commands by viewing law as a union of primary and secondary rules (The Concept of Law, 1961). Laws consist largely of primary rules, or basic commands that impose duties: keep off the grass, do not steal, drive within the speed limit. But why is a society bound by these rules and not others? The natural law theorist explains this by appealing to a natural moral order. Hart rejects this position, and appeals instead to what he calls "secondary rules": "While primary rules are concerned with the actions that individuals must or must not do, secondary rules are all concerned with the primary rules themselves. They specify the ways in which the primary rules may

be conclusively ascertained, introduced, eliminated, varied, and the fact of their violation conclusively determined." Primary rules are valid even if they are not obeyed, insofar as they are duly created through the system of secondary rules. How do we know the secondary rules are the right ones? Here Hart, much like Austin, must appeal to the fact that they are regarded as such.

Legal positivism regards law as a system of clearly defined rules. But this view of law seemed misguided to many lawyers, judges, and social scientists who have studied or worked within the American legal system. For *legal realists such as Oliver Wendell *Holmes (The Common Law, 1923), if the law were merely a system of rules, we would not need lawyers doing battle, for judges could just apply the rules. In fact judges have discretion with which they can decide a case in a number of ways, and factors such as the judge's temperament, or social class, or political ideology, may determine the outcome.

On another theory, called purposive adjudication, defended by Ronald Dworkin (Law's Empire, 1986), law is not merely a set of rules, but of rules as well as underlying principles, and judges should appeal to these principles—to the spirit or purpose of the law—not just narrowly to the law's letter. This is different from appealing to a natural moral order. The judge appeals to moral values, but these values must inhere in the law which the judge is authorized to interpret, and as such, these values are not entirely subjective.

Skepticism as to a natural moral order that regulates all human beings, and the fact that reasonable people disagree about what morality requires, raise the concern that law not be used to impose one conception of morality on those with a different but reasonable conception. According to the political theory of liberalism, which seeks to promote as much individual *liberty as is compatible with everyone else having the same liberty, the state should not use the criminal law to prevent immoral conduct that does not cause harm or offense to others. (See John Stuart Mill, On Liberty (1859) and Joel Feinberg, The Moral Limits of the Criminal Law (4 vols. 1984–88)). The theory of legal moralism, in contrast, holds that the law reflects society's moral standards and can be used to coerce people into conforming with these standards. The Supreme Court, in Bowers v. Hardwick (1986), upheld a Georgia criminal statute prohibiting homosexual sodomy. In dissent, Justice Blackmun criticized the decision, rejecting legal moralism. He acknowledged that government may legitimately ban public sexual activity to protect people from unwilling exposure to the sexual activities of others. But, he added, "The mere fact that intimate behavior may be punished when it takes place in public cannot dictate how States can regulate intimate behavior that occurs in intimate places." Liberalism demands that so long as individuals do not harm others, they be free to make their own choices about how to live their lives, even if their choices are at odds with the moral sensibilities of a majority: "The fact that individuals define themselves in a significant way through their intimate sexual relationships with others," Blackmun writes, "suggests, in a Nation as diverse as ours, that there may be many "right" ways of conducting those relationships, and that much of the richness of a relationship will come from the freedom an individual has to choose the form and nature of these intensely personal bonds."

Those who defend the liberal view that law should not be used to prohibit immoral conduct that does not harm others need not be legal positivists. While liberals want to restrict the law from forcing certain moral or religious codes of conduct on citizens, they do support the use of law to impose one particular moral conception that holds that all individuals have liberty interests and rights and that it is wrong to violate these rights by causing harm to others.

There is a genuine tension between the desire not to use the law to impose a particular moral code on everyone and the desire that law accord with *justice. Many defenders of punishment, often labeled retributivists, argue that the primary purpose of punishing those who break the law is not to deter crime or rehabilitate the offender, but to mete out justice; the criminal has violated society's conception of right, and punishment vindicates right and expresses society's condemnation. Sentences generally are set to match the culpability of the criminal, and American law allows defenses that excuse defendants or mitigate their punishment if we feel they are not fully blameworthy or morally accountable. If the law is separate from morality, as some positivists contend, many versions of retribution, and many features of the *criminal law, may be incoherent.

The argument of those who believe there is a separation between law and morality, that not everything that is illegal is immoral, assumes that it is not always immoral to break the law. Yet some philosophers argue that breaking the law, even pointless laws, is morally wrong, and that in doing so one acts badly; the law presents itself as a seamless web, and its subjects are not permitted to select which ones they ought to obey. A number of

reasons have been offered as to why one is morally obligated to obey law. One reason appeals to the contagion argument: if we allowed some violations of law, lawbreaking could spread, resulting in social disorder. One problem with this argument is that widespread disobedience does occur in some cases, such as speeding on highways, without leading to social unrest. A second argument is that people who benefit from laws have an obligation, of fairness or gratitude, to contribute to the cooperative venture providing the benefits by obeying the law. Still another argument is that we are morally obligated to obey laws because by consenting to government we have promised that we will; violating a law is immoral in the way breaking a promise is.

A number of philosophers, rejecting these arguments, have defended selective disobedience. M. B. E. Smith, for example, says that "[f]or most people, violation of the law becomes a matter for moral concern only when it involves an act which is believed to be wrong on grounds apart from its illegality" ("Is there a prima facie obligation to obey the law?" *Yale Law Journal* 82 (1973): 950–76).

The demands of morality and ethics create tensions for professionals practicing law. For example, a criminal lawyer is bound to defend a client known to be guilty, and doing this effectively may require saying things in court that ordinarily are regarded as misleading. The adversarial system functions well only when individuals adhere to their roles, and this requires the defense attorney to present the strongest case, even if it entails defending immoral conduct. The *American Bar Association's Model Rules of Professional Conduct however, clearly oppose legal argument based on a knowingly false representation of law or fact.

[*See also* Culture and Law]

• H. L. A. Hart, *The Concept of Law*, 1961. Lon Fuller, *The Morality of Law*, 1969. Monroe Freedman, *Lawyers' Ethics in an Adversary System*, 1975. A. J. Simmons, *Moral Principles and Political Obligations*, 1979. P. S. Atiyah, *Promises, Morals, and Law*, 1981. Charles Fried, *Contract as Promise*, 1981. Joel Feinberg, *The Moral Limits of the Criminal Law*, 4 vols., 1984–88. Kenneth Kipnis, *Legal Ethics*, 1986. Mark Tunick, *Practices and Principles: Approaches to Ethical and Legal Judgment*, 1998.

ETHICS AND PROFESSIONAL RESPONSIBILITY, LEGAL. In 1817 David Hoffman, a Baltimore lawyer and educator, published *Fifty Resolutions in Regard to Professional Deportment*, the earliest statement in the United States of lawyers' professional ethics. In 1854 George Sharswood, a Philadelphia judge, delivered a set of lectures on professional responsibility. Sharswood's lectures became the basis of the first formal code of lawyers' ethics, adopted by the Alabama Bar Association in 1887.

*Bar associations were common in the early part of the nineteenth century, declined in significance during the middle of the century as admission to the profession became more open, and experienced a revival in the last quarter of the century as part of an effort to raise professional standards. In 1878 a group of lawyers met to form a national organization, the *American Bar Association (ABA). The ABA has no formal power to regulate the legal profession; that power resides in the courts before which lawyers practice, usually in the highest court in each state. The ABA has nonetheless become a major force in drafting codes of ethics for courts to adopt.

Strongly influenced by the Alabama Code of 1887, the ABA adopted its first set of professional standards, the Canons of Ethics, in 1908. In 1969 the ABA replaced the Canons with the Model Code of Professional Responsibility (the code)—a significant departure from the canons. While the canons offered guidance for professional conduct, they were intended to be persuasive rather than to have the force of law. The drafters of the Code intended both to guide and to regulate the behavior of lawyers. Although the Code was widely adopted, many lawyers and judges found its tripartite organization into Canons, disciplinary rules, and ethical considerations confusing. Further, the Code focused on ethical obligations of litigators, largely ignoring ethics in business practice.

In 1977 the ABA appointed a Commission on Evaluation of Professional Standards, commonly known as the Kutak Commission, to recommend revisions of the Code. The commission ultimately decided to jettison the Code and replace it with a set of rules, followed by comments. A number of recommendations made by the Kutak Commission, particularly its proposals to expand exceptions to the duty of confidentiality, were controversial. With substantial modifications of the commission's proposals, the ABA in 1983 adopted the Model Rules of Professional Conduct. The Model Rules, with some variations, are in force in more than forty states. California continues to follow its own rules of conduct, and New York has a set of rules that uses the structure of the Code but incorporates many substantive provisions from the Model Rules.

Another round of rules revision began in 1997, when the president of the ABA appointed an Ethics 2000 Commission to recommend modifications of the Model Rules. The commission has decided to retain the structure of the Model Rules but has proposed a number of significant substantive changes.

The Canons of Ethics, the Model Code of Professional Responsibility, and the Model Rules of Professional Conduct have been the most important sources of professional obligations for lawyers, but other sets of standards have also become influential. The "professionalism movement" represents one strand in the development of supplementary standards of conduct. In 1984, as a result of a recommendation by United States Supreme Court Chief Justice Warren *Burger, the ABA appointed a commission to study the issue of professionalism. The Stanley Commission's 1986 report concluded that profound changes had affected the profession in the last quarter-century, and it recommended a series of steps by bar associations, courts, and law schools to promote lawyer professionalism. The commission noted that the disciplinary focus of both the Model Code and the Model Rules had made lawyers more attentive to professional duties but at the same time less concerned with aspirational standards. To promote higher standards, the ABA and other professional organizations have approved standards or creeds of professionalism for lawyers. The creeds are intended to emphasize the broader obligations that lawyers have to the system of justice, to other lawyers, and to third parties.

The Stanley Commission also stressed the importance of professional conduct within areas of legal specialization. Today, few lawyers conduct a general practice; most specialize in areas such as family, tax, labor, criminal defense, intellectual property, and so on. Specialty organizations of lawyers have developed standards of conduct that supplement the Model Rules by focusing on the problems that lawyers encounter in particular areas of practice.

Recurring Issues: Confidentiality, Commercialization, and Delivery of Legal Services. In 1975, two New York lawyers were accused of misconduct when they did not disclose the location of the bodies of several murder victims revealed to them by a client they were representing in another murder case. The Lake Pleasant Bodies Case (*People* v. *Belge* (1975)), dramatically illustrates the issue of the scope of lawyers' duty of confidentiality. In *Belge*, disclosure by the lawyers would not have prevented the defendant's crime but it would have alleviated the suffering of the victims' family members. In other situations, however, a lawyer's disclosure of confidential information could have prevented a wrongfully convicted person from imprisonment or even death. Issues of lawyer confidentiality also arise in business transactions when a lawyer learns that a client has committed or may be planning to commit a financial fraud.

The scope of the lawyer's duty of confidentiality has been a recurring source of debate and controversy within the profession. The historical trend in the ABA's codes has been toward greater protection of confidentiality, limiting the situations in which lawyers could disclose information to prevent or to rectify wrongful client conduct. Canon 41 of the 1908 Canons of Ethics provided that when a lawyer discovers that some fraud or deception has been practiced on a court or party, the lawyer should attempt to persuade the client to rectify the matter, but if unable to do so, the lawyer should promptly inform either the injured person or his lawyer. The 1969 Code of Professional Responsibility narrowed exceptions to the duty of confidentiality, and when the ABA adopted the Model Rules in 1983, it limited the exceptions even more. Lawyers were allowed to reveal a future client's crime only when the crime involved "imminent death or substantial bodily harm" (ABA Model Rule 1.6(b)(1)). Lawyers could reveal fraud on a person or tribunal only when necessary to prevent assisting the client's wrongdoing (ABA Model Rules 3.3(a)(2) and 4.1(b)). The rules generally prohibited lawyers from revealing wrongdoing that had already occurred. While the ABA has been moving toward greater protection of client confidentiality, many state supreme courts have been unwilling to follow ABA recommendations. In some states, rules allow or require lawyers to reveal confidential information in situations where the ABA rules would prohibit disclosure. For example, in Florida lawyers are required (rather than simply permitted) to reveal confidential information to prevent a client from committing any crime. In addition, controversy continues within the ABA ranks over whether confidentiality rules should be changed to provide greater protection to people who may be harmed by client conduct.

Commercialization has been another major topic of debate and controversy within the profession. The practice of law is a profession in which lawyers assist in important social activities, including dispute resolution and structuring of personal and business relationships, but the practice is also a business from which lawyers earn their livelihood. Traditionally, the profession has been opposed to commercial advertising or solicitation (ABA Canon 27 (1908)). Change has come as a result of the U.S. Supreme Court's decisions holding that lawyer advertising is entitled to substantial constitutional protection. Beginning with *Bates* v. *State Bar of Arizona* (1977), the Court has recognized and expanded the First Amendment right of lawyers to advertise their services. States retain substantial authority, however, over lawyers' commercial speech. The Court has ruled that states may prohibit in-person solicitation because it poses substantial risks not present with advertising. States may also outlaw false or inherently deceptive advertising and direct-mail advertising to accident victims within thirty days after the accident. But a number of constitutional issues remain unanswered, such as whether advertising on television is subject to regulation or is instead entitled to broad First Amendment protection.

Another aspect of the debate over commercialization has involved multidisciplinary practice. Accounting and consulting firms have expanded the range of services they offer to include legal services. In many countries, rules regulating lawyers allow combinations of professional services, but in the United States such affiliations violate prohibitions on partnerships and fee splitting between lawyers and nonlawyers. In 2000 an ABA commission recommended relaxation of these rules to allow lawyers to enter into multidisciplinary practices, but the ABA rejected this proposal. Debate and proposals for dealing with the issue continue (see LEGAL PRACTICE, FORMS OF).

Lawyer advertising and multidisciplinary practices are directed at clients who can afford to pay legal fees, but many potential clients for legal services are indigent or have only modest incomes. While the Supreme Court has recognized a constitutional right to appointed counsel in serious criminal cases, a general right to appointed counsel does not exist in civil proceedings, even in fundamental cases such as ones seeking termination of parental rights. Through the Legal Services Corporation, the federal government provides limited funding for representation of indigents in civil cases, but the demand is much greater than the funded services. A number of studies have documented the existence of a vast unmet need for legal services among low- and moderate-income individuals. To address this need some states have considered proposals for mandatory pro bono work. A typical proposal would require lawyers to provide forty to fifty hours per year of legal services to indigents. None of these proposals has been accepted, however, and the amount of lawyers' pro bono representation is voluntary.

Underlying Problems: The Morality of Professional Work, Discrimination, and Self-Regulation. Throughout most of the nineteenth century, lawyers received their professional training through apprenticeship in the offices of other lawyers. In the latter part of the century, universities and freestanding law schools began providing legal *education. In the early twentieth century, the Carnegie Foundation study, *Training for the Public Profession of the Law* (1921) by Alfred Reed, led to higher standards for education and admission of lawyers to practice. In most states, graduation from an ABA-accredited law school is now a requirement for admission to practice.

Movement of legal education from law offices to universities has led to a broader perspective on professional ethics and regulation. Until the last twenty-five years, the relationship between professional regulation and general moral philosophy was largely ignored. Since the 1970s, however, scholars have increasingly focused on the moral significance of lawyer ethics. David Luban, William Simon, Deborah Rhode, and other critics of professional conduct have called on lawyers to adhere to principles of morality or justice in their representation of clients, rather than to an "ideology of advocacy" under which many lawyers believe they may properly do anything on behalf of a client so long as their conduct does not clearly violate the law or specific rules of professional conduct.

The legal profession, like most American social institutions, has a sorry history of discrimination. African Americans, women, gays and lesbians, and other minorities were long excluded from the profession and still suffer discrimination in professional opportunities. While the ABA and other professional organizations have recently made some efforts to address these issues, much remains to be done.

One of the defining characteristics of a profession is self-regulation. Professions claim that they have the expertise and the will to regulate themselves in the public interest. The history of self-regulation by the legal profession, especially on such issues as confidentiality, delivery of legal services, and discrimination, raises substantial questions about whether the profession is capable of regulating itself in the public interest or whether the rules adopted by the profession have served the interests of its dominant groups and have changed only as a result of pressure from forces outside the legal profession itself.

[*See also* Lawyers]

• Jerold S. Auerbach, *Unequal Justice: Lawyers and Social Change in Modern America*, 1976. Richard L. Abel, *American Lawyers*, 1989. Monroe H. Freedman, *Understanding Lawyers' Ethics*, 1990. Anthony T. Kronman, *The Lost Lawyer: Failing Ideals of the Legal Profession*, 1993. Nathan M. Crystal, *An Introduction to Professional Responsibility*, 1998. William Simon, *The Practice of Justice: A Theory of Lawyers' Ethics*, 1998. Richard Zitrin and Carol M. Langford, *The Moral Compass of the American Lawyer: Truth, Justice, Power, and Greed*, 1999. Deborah L. Rhode, *In the Interests of Justice: Reforming the Legal Profession*, 2000. Geoffrey C. Hazard III and W. William Hodes, *Law of Lawyering: A Handbook on the Model Rules of Professional Conduct*, 3d ed., 2000.

—Nathan M. Crystal

ETHNICITY. *See* Race and Ethnicity.

EUTHANASIA. *See* Homicide; Medicine and Law.

EVIDENCE. Trials are fought with facts supplied by witnesses and with inferences drawn from those facts. The rules of evidence control what kinds of facts witnesses may present to a trial court. These rules are largely exclusionary, that is, they operate by filtering out certain facts and opinions (inferences made and offered by witnesses). Each exclusionary rule of evidence reflects the rulemakers' belief that lay jurors (and perhaps *judges) would not make what the rulemaker thinks is the correct evaluation of a class of evidence.

Though judges are the gatekeepers—deciding whether an item of evidence must be excluded—a judge will not rule on the admissibility of evidence unless an attorney first raises an objection to the evidence. This reflects the adversary nature of Anglo-American trials. Each side of a dispute, through its attorneys, develops and presents the evidence for their case; when asked to do so, judges rule on the admissibility of evidence; and juries draw inferences from the evidence and decide what verdict the evidence best supports. The rules of evidence function most effectively through exactly just such a division of responsibility: the judge decides what evidence is admissible and the *jury bases its decision on the admissible evidence. A single person, the judge, cannot consider the admissible evidence without awareness of the inadmissible evidence as well. Anglo-American evidence rules are complex and extensive, whereas the evidence codes of civil-law countries are far more concise. One theory attributes the difference to the existence of the jury, contending that while judges can discount or disregard weak or misleading evidence, lay jurors cannot and so it is necessary to screen the evidence for them. A second theory argues that the adversary system itself necessitates the exclusion of shoddy evidence, which zealous advocates will be tempted to offer. Though the rules of evidence have their origins in English *common law dating back many centuries, recent historical scholarship has found that the development of the strongly exclusionary features that characterize modern evidence doctrine coincided with the evolution of the adversary mode of trial, in the late eighteenth century—rather than with the rise of the jury centuries earlier.

Though evidence doctrine is largely the creation of common-law judges, in 1975 the United States codified these into the Federal Rules of Evidence. Though the federal rules apply only to proceedings in federal courts, most states have copied them, sometimes with variations, as their own evidence code. In addition, several important evidentiary rules arise from the Constitution and apply to both state and federal courts. Most notable of these, the exclusionary rule restricts the admissibility of evidence gathered in violation of a defendant's rights against unreasonable *search and seizure under the Fourth Amendment. Evidence that violates a defendant's Fifth Amendment privilege against *self-incrimination or Sixth Amendment right of confrontation also is excluded (see WITNESS, RIGHT TO CONFRONT).

Following are thumbnail sketches of some of the fundamental doctrines of evidence law.

Relevance. The cornerstone of evidence doctrine is relevance. Only relevant evidence is admissible, and all relevant evidence is admissible unless excluded by a specific rule. Relevant evidence is evidence that has "any" tendency to make the existence of a fact that logically matters to the verdict more probable or less probable than it would be without the evidence. Deciding whether something is or is not relevant usually requires thoughtful analysis of the particular item of evidence in relation to other case facts and to the substantive law applicable to the case.

Rule 403. The first and most important rule of exclusion of relevant evidence gives broad discretion to judges to exclude evidence which, though relevant, does more to impede than to advance rational decision-making. Evidence can be excluded if its probative value is "substantially outweighed" by the risk that it will unfairly prejudice, confuse, mislead, cause undue delay, or waste time.

Policy-based Exclusions. Certain rules reflect social policy preferences to exclude evidence in certain situations notwithstanding its relevance. Among these are rules excluding evidence of repairs made by a defendant following an accident, offers made to reach a settlement or a *plea bargain, payment by the defendant of the plaintiff's medical expenses, and whether the defendant has liability insurance. These rules aim to encourage desirable behavior such as repairing dangerous situations, engaging in settlement and plea negotiations, and so on, by not allowing evidence of those socially desirable acts to be used against a party in trial.

Privileges. Similarly, the law is willing to forego evidence that it wishes to protect from disclosure so as to promote certain relationships. These privileged communications are not specified in the code, but are allowed to evolve by common law rulemaking. Among the most familiar of these "privileges" are communications with one's lawyer, spouse, clergy person, and trade and state secrets.

Character, Habit, Routine Practice. We might assume that people are more likely to behave in a manner consistent with their "character" traits or their habits. But character traits are generally inadmissible as evidence to prove specific conduct. Without this rule, someone could be found criminally or civilly liable, based not on evidence that he engaged in the prohibited conduct but on evidence that he is the "sort of person" who does such things. Exceptions to the rule permit character evidence under certain circumstances, and complex rules govern when and how character evidence may be presented. In contrast, a person's habit or the routine practice of a business are admissible as tending to prove they behaved in a particular way on a particular occasion.

Original Writing. Because written documents and other recording media can be so influential to the outcome of legal proceedings, and yet can easily be falsified, the rules express a strong preference for original documents and other recordings. Under certain circumstances, however, the rule allows alternative evidence of their contents. This also is known as the "best evidence" rule.

Hearsay. Statements made outside of court, and then offered to a court as evidence of the truth of what the out-of-court statement asserts, are hearsay. For example, a month after a car crash someone says to a coworker: "I saw that crash and it happened because the blue car went through a red light." Suppose that at trial the person who uttered those words cannot be found but the coworker is offered to testify to what the absent person said—that is hearsay. Its central defect is that the absent person whose purported observations are offered as evidence cannot be cross-examined to test the reliability of the evidence. The original observer might have had a poor opportunity to observe, might be remembering incorrectly, or might for some reason be lying. Or the in-court witness might have misunderstood what the out-of-court declarant actually said. Because its reliability cannot be evaluated, hearsay generally is inadmissible. However, there are twenty-eight exceptions to the rule excluding hearsay. These exceptions identify classes of hearsay which are believed to be so reliable that they can be admitted anyway. For example, a statement describing an event made by a person while observing the event is admissible even if it is hearsay. Moreover, there is a "residual" exception under which judges can at their discretion admit hearsay they believe to be reliable. Consequently, much hearsay is admissible—so much so that inadmissible hearsay is said to be a small island surrounded by a sea of admissible hearsay.

Witnesses and Impeachment. All persons are presumed to be competent and may serve as witnesses. Challenges for lack of competency, on such grounds as that a witness is retarded or too young to testify accurately, may be brought in individual instances. In addition, the testimony of every witness is subject to impeachment on a variety of grounds as a means of challenging the witness's credibility.

Scientific and Other Expert Witnesses. The most active area of evolution of the rules of evidence has been those governing the admissibility of expert testimony. Unlike other witnesses, "experts" are permitted to offer opinions on matters which judges and jurors, even if they had access to all of the underlying data, would not be able to interpret as meaningfully as an expert can. Anyone with specialized knowledge not found in the general population is likely to be an expert on something. Beginning in 1993, the U.S. Supreme Court issued a series of unanimous rulings which have transformed the test of admissibility from the question of whether a consensus exists among a community of experts to whether the courts can find good grounds for believing the proffered opinions are valid. These cases were *Daubert* v. *Merrell Dow Pharmaceuticals* (proof of a valid basis is a precondition for admission of an asserted expertise), *General Electric* v. *Joiner* (the expert's assertion is not a sufficient basis for admission; appellate courts must review trial court admission

decisions deferentially), and *Kumho Tire Co.* v. *Carmichael* (*Daubert's* evidentiary reliability requirement applies to all fields of expert evidence, not only science). These rules have had their greatest impact on product liability and toxic tort plaintiffs and have started a small revolution in the evaluation of forensic science.

The rules of evidence have evolved more or less continuously for centuries and will continue to do so. Scholars raise new methods of analysis of evidence and challenge the assumptions underlying existing rules. Also, as in the past, societal concerns create pressures to change the rules in ways that will advance some interests and impede others.

[*See also* Criminal Law Principles]

• John Henry Wigmore, *A Treatise on the Anglo-American System of Evidence in Trials at Common Law*, 1923 (and various supplements). Weinstein and Berger, *Weinstein's Federal Evidence*, 2d ed., 1997. Lempert, Gross, and Liebman, *A Modern Approach to Evidence*, 3d ed., 2000. Faigman, Kaye, Saks, and Sanders, *Modern Scientific Evidence: The Law and Science of Expert Testimony*, 2d ed., 2002.   —Michael J. Saks

EXCLUSIVE POSSESSION. *See* Property, Real.

EXCUSE. *See* Criminal Law Principles: Defense Principles.

EXECUTION. *See* Capital Punishment; Criminal Punishments; Electric Chair.

EXECUTION, PUBLIC. *See* Law and Public Ritual.

EXECUTIVE AGREEMENTS. Most international agreements to which the United States is a party are entered into by the executive branch without the advice and consent of the Senate, which the *Constitution requires for a treaty. The subject matter of these executive agreements includes, for example, trade, air transport, the mails, settlement of international claims, arms control and disarmament, ceasefires, military cooperation, the status of United States armed forces abroad, and extradition.

Although the Constitution does not expressly empower the president to enter into executive agreements, it seems to recognize that not all binding instruments between the United States and foreign countries are *"treaties" in the constitutional sense. For example, states of the Union, with the consent of *Congress, may enter into an "agreement or compact with another State, or with a foreign power," but may not enter into a "treaty, alliance or confederation" (U.S. Const. art. I, §10). The president's specific authority to enter into executive agreements is derived from any of three sources: treaty provisions (treaty-authorized agreements); express constitutional powers (sole executive agreements); and Congressional authorization, either before or after an agreement is signed (congressional-executive agreements). The president has no authority to do by executive agreement what he cannot otherwise do by executive proclamation (see EXECUTIVE POWER).

A treaty-authorized executive agreement has the same validity, effect, and constitutional limitations as the treaty itself. Examples include several status-of-forces agreements that establish the terms of United States military bases abroad under the North Atlantic Treaty Organization (NATO).

Sole executive agreements are based on the president's exercise of any of five constitutional powers—(1) to "take care that the laws be faithfully executed" (U.S. Const. art. II, §3); (2) to conduct foreign relations generally (an inherent power, according to the United States Supreme Court); (3) to appoint ambassadors, other public ministers and consuls (U.S. Const. art. II, §2); (4) to receive ambassadors and other public ministers (U.S. Const. art. II, §3); (5) to serve as commander in chief of the army and navy (U.S. Const. art. II, §2). A famous example of a sole executive agreement was the Litvinov Assignment (1933) that settled the claims of United States nationals against the Soviet Union, thereby clearing the way for the two countries to enter into diplomatic relations (United States v. Belmont (1937)). It is not clear to what extent the president may enter into an executive agreement on the basis of his inherent power to conduct foreign affairs rather than under an express constitutional power. Nor is it settled whether a sole executive agreement can ever supersede an Act of Congress (United States v. Guy W. Capps, Inc., (1953) aff'd on other grounds (1955) (holding that one such agreement did not supersede an Act of Congress)).

In order to avoid a dispute with Congress, the president normally seeks its authorization for an executive agreement. Congressional-executive agreements are therefore by far the most common arrangement (Dames & Moore v. Regan (1981) (upholding the president's power to impose control over foreign assets, consistent with legislation and with acquiescence by Congress, under an executive agreement with Iran to end the hostage crisis of the late 1970s)). Another important example of an executive agreement is the Congressional grant of "fast track" authority for the North American Free Trade Agreement, the World Trade Organization package of agreements, and other trade arrangements. This procedure ensures that when the president submits a negotiated agreement to Congress, both houses will proceed expeditiously, with automatic discharge from committee, limited floor debate, and up-or-down votes without amendment.

Under the political question doctrine, federal courts generally refuse to decide whether a particular executive agreement unconstitutionally bypasses the treaty-making process (Made in USA Foundation v. United States (2001)). As guidance for determining whether formal treaty-making procedures are required in a particular instance, the State Department's Foreign Service Manual lists eight factors: (1) the extent to which the agreement involves commitments or risks affecting the nation as a whole; (2) whether the agreement is intended to affect state laws; (3) whether the agreement can be given effect without the enactment of subsequent legislation by the Congress; (4) past United States practice with respect to similar agreements; (5) the preference of the Congress with respect to a particular type of agreement; (6) the degree of formality desired for an agreement; (7) the proposed duration of the agreement, the need for prompt conclusion of an agreement, and the desirability of concluding a routine or short-term agreement; (8) the general international practice with respect to similar agreements.

[See also Presidency of the United States]

• Myres McDougal and Asher Lans, "Treaties and Congressional-Executive or Presidential Agreements: Interchangeable Instruments of National Policy," Yale Law Journal 54 (1945): 181, 534. Lawrence Margolis, Executive Agreements and Presidential Power in Foreign Policy, 1986.   —James A. R. Nafziger

EXECUTIVE POWER. The Constitutional Convention of 1787 invented the American *presidency, yet the president's powers, outlined in Article II, are both brief and unclear. "The Executive Power shall be vested in a President of the United States," "The President shall be Commander in Chief of the Army and Navy," and "he shall take Care that the Laws be faithfully executed."

In the years preceding the Constitutional Convention, Americans were bold and daring in their military challenge to the British. But when it came to designing governance arrangements, the *Constitution's framers exhibited caution. The presidency crafted was not a radical governmental institution; rather, it was in part a modified version of the English monarchy and in part a variation on the powers held by state governors in places such as New York in the 1780s.

The framers who gathered in Philadelphia had read the history of Magna Carta, the English Civil War, and the Glorious Revolution. On each occasion, English landowners had found it necessary to place a check on the monarchy, hoping to achieve a more equitable distribution of power. But even as the English system of governance moved toward a more representative form, the governance systems exported to the colonies were clearly less democratic.

Royal *governors operated with significant executive authority. Arguably more powerful than the monarch, some governors were able to control legislative agendas, establish taxes and tariffs by decree, and wield a veto over legislation. The reaction to this centralized authority was an equal centralization of resentment. As the Revolution progressed, citizens in the former colonies quickly adopted governance arrangements that lodged public power in a dominant legislative branch. With the exception of New York, governors served terms of one or two years, and were subordinate to the legislature. Many were selected by the legislature, some shared powers with an executive council, and strict limitations were placed on reeligibility.

The Articles of Confederation (ratified in 1781) at the national level also reflected this backlash against strong executive power. The Articles made no provision for a chief executive or an independent executive branch of government. In place of a formalized executive, the Continental Congress attempted to carry out the confederacy's executive responsibilities through ad hoc committees of its own members, which ultimately proved to be an unmanageable task. It became clear by the mid-1780s that dominant legislatures at the state and national level were ineffective systems for governing. Citizens developed reservations about the excesses of *legislative power, similar to their fear of executive rule in pre-Revolutionary days.

The framers came to the 1787 Constitutional Convention recognizing the need to balance a representative body of lawmakers with some kind of national executive. Still, the framers were not wholly in agreement as to how that balance might be struck or what form the executive might take. Suggestions ranged from an authoritative "Governor," who would serve a life term, to an executive committee directly elected by and responsible to *Congress.

One of the most important powers finally granted to the executive was that of the veto power, even if it was a qualified veto. (Congress can override it with a two-thirds vote in each house.) The framers also required the president to periodically give Congress information about the state of the Union and recommend measures the president deemed necessary. Through these two provisions, the framers ensured that the president would be more than a federal clerk, solely attending to the enforcement of laws passed by the legislature. The president was expected to be a partner in the legislative process, helping to set the legislative agenda, clarifying national priorities, and providing leadership in times of emergency.

When the framers made the president commander in chief of the armed forces, which would presumably be called into service only by Congress, they conferred an enormously important power on future presidents, particularly in the nuclear age. Some executive powers could be exercised only by the president, such as the power to grant pardons and reprieves for all federal offenses except in cases of impeachment. The other major executive powers decided on at Philadelphia were the power to nominate department heads and judicial officers (subject to Senate confirmation), the right to require written opinions from each of the department heads, the obligation to take care that the laws be faithfully executed, and the right to receive ambassadors and other public ministers.

While these enumerated powers have remained the same down through the years, the president's job as chief executive is different now from what it was more than 200 years ago. The dynamics of American democracy increasingly revolve around the presidency in ways the framers could not have foreseen. The presence of political parties, nuclear weapons, global communications, welfare, and world terrorism all demand greater efficiency and energy, which can be found more readily in the executive branch than in other parts of government.

The individual character and ambition of presidents, national and international emergencies, economic changes, and other factors such as advancements in technology, have also changed the office. While the power of the presidency grew dramatically during some presidents' tenure, it was eroded during others'. Periods of growth include the Civil War and the Great Depression, when Abraham *Lincoln and Franklin Roosevelt assumed powers that exceeded those of any previous president. Andrew Jackson energized the office by drawing legitimacy directly from the public. Other presidents, such as Theodore Roosevelt, were willing to assume greater prerogative powers, but served in times that only occasionally called for bold executive action.

Presidential power has at times waned. Reacting to the inevitable growth of executive power under Lincoln during wartime, and to the personal deficiencies of Lincoln's predecessor, the House of Representatives impeached Andrew *Johnson in 1868, thereby stripping him of his ability to oversee the South's reconstruction. Congress retained its strong influence over the executive branch for much of the remaining nineteenth century. Presidents Harding, Coolidge, and Hoover, who generally believed that laissez-faire market capitalism rather than the federal government should be the guiding hand in the nation's development, also oversaw a period of decline in executive power in the 1920s. In the 1970s, in the wake of the Vietnam War and Watergate, Congress attempted to reassert itself in budgetary, war-making, and other policy areas.

Beyond the impact of individual presidents and events, the *Supreme Court has shaped presidential power. This practice began in 1803 with *Marbury v. Madison, in which Chief Justice John *Marshall carefully positioned the Court, as opposed to the president, as the final arbiter of the Constitution. But unlike Marbury, which limited the powers of the presidency, most of the Court's decisions have expanded executive authority. One of the first major tests came in the Prize Cases (1863), when the Court was asked to decide whether President Lincoln had the power to make war without a Congressional declaration of war. The Court decided that a president may determine the existence of an emergency and take whatever steps are necessary to deal with it. In In re Neagle (1890), the Court used sweeping language to establish the president's right to use broad executive powers to "faithfully execute" the laws of the land. In United States v. Curtiss-Wright Export Corp. (1936) the Court ruled that for the "important, complicated, delicate and manifold problems [of foreign policy], the president alone has the power to speak or listen as a representative of the nation." Justice George Sutherland went even further in dicta, calling the president the "sole organ of foreign affairs."

Many have accused the Court of overstepping itself with this opinion, yet the Court's intent was clear in this and related cases. The president must have the necessary latitude to meet the challenges of governance—especially in emergencies and in national security matters.

Other Court decisions that have increased the powers of the presidency include United States v. Nixon (1974) and Immigration and Naturalization Service v. Chadha (1983). In Nixon, the Court affirmed, under certain circumstances, the president's right to withhold information from the public and Congress that has potential national security implications. But presidents do not have the exclusive right to determine when executive privilege is properly employed. In Chadha, the Court clarified the balance of power between Congress and the presidency. In ruling that Congress did not have the constitutional authority to exercise a *legislative veto when it was displeased with the manner in which the president was carrying out a Congressional mandate, the Court thereby expanded the prerogatives of the executive branch.

Despite the Court's long history in deferring to the executive branch, it has generally restrained presidents. After Marbury, the first significant check on presidential power came in Ex parte Milligan (1866), in which the Court ruled that Lincoln had overstepped the bounds of acceptable emergency powers when he sanctioned the establishment of military courts outside the war zone. In the 1930s, the Court rejected essential pieces of Franklin Roosevelt's "New Deal" recovery program. Roosevelt responded with his ill-fated *"court packing" scheme, but finally gained the Court's support by 1937. In *Youngstown Sheet and Tube Co. v. Sawyer (1952), the Court ruled that President Harry Truman had improperly invoked emergency powers. More recently, the Court limited the power of the presidency in 1997 by ruling unanimously that Bill Clinton, as a sitting president, was not immune to civil litigation.

The relationship between Congress and the presidency has been one of constant tension. The *impeachments of Andrew Johnson and Bill Clinton, and Richard Nixon's resignation, symbolize moments of notable strain between the branches. The most recent trend has been for the Congress to cede power, explicitly and implicitly, to the executive—for instance, with its war and budgetary powers. Fearing that presidents had established a precedent for waging war without its approval, the Congress passed the War Powers Resolution in 1973 to rectify the balance of power. The War Powers Resolution, however, has been largely ignored, and Congress has neglected to take action to ensure its enforcement. In the area of budgetary control, Congress passed the Budget Act of 1974 and the Graham-Rudman Act of 1985 to attempt to make Congress a stronger budgetary partner with the president. But neither of these initiatives produced the desired effect.

Congress took a major step toward increasing executive powers in 1996 with the passage of the Line Item Veto Act, which was designed to allow presidents to strike "pork-barrel" items from appropriations bills. But the Court ruled in *Byrd* v. *Raines* (1997) that the item veto was an unconstitutional violation of the *separation of powers doctrine.

The power of the executive has also grown dramatically as the size of the federal bureaucracy has increased. In 1802, only 588 people staffed the entire executive branch; today, over 4 million people work for the federal government. In an attempt to formalize the president's control over the expanding government, Franklin Roosevelt created the Executive Office of the President (EOP) in 1939. The EOP provides a stronger and more institutionalized White House staff, which allows the president to give more effective direction to the federal bureaucracy and thereby increases the president's power over the machinery of government.

The president's other powers include executive orders and executive privilege. An executive order is a presidential directive with the force of law. It can be used to set up agencies, modify rules, or give emphasis to certain laws. These orders are important because Congress often passes laws that, due to vague or imprecise language, require executive interpretation. And while executive orders are sometimes criticized as an attempt by the president to subvert the normal lawmaking process, they can be effectively challenged in the courts or overturned by the legislature itself or by subsequent presidents. Like executive orders, there is no explicit reference in the Constitution to executive privilege—the power of presidents to withhold information from the courts, Congress, and the public. Intended to allow presidents to protect vital information pertaining to national security, executive privilege has been used by nearly every administration, but abused on occasion, notably during the Watergate (Nixon) and Monica Lewinsky (Clinton) investigations.

An important Constitutional restriction on the presidency is the two-term limit established by the Twenty Second Amendment (1951). It is designed to ensure that the presidency's powers do not become centralized in a single individual as they did under Franklin Roosevelt, who was elected to four consecutive terms.

Under American *federalism, a state *governor shares many of the attributes of the presidency, including the duties of party leader, legislative leader, and commander in chief of state military forces. In general, though, governors have less power than presidents because of the smaller size of their constituencies and their restricted involvement in foreign affairs. Governors are also obliged to share power and responsibilities with other statewide elected officers such as secretary of state, attorney general, and treasurer. The executive power of local mayors is much smaller, and their powers are regulated by state constitutional and legislative provisions requiring that they share authority with separately elected school boards and regional authorities.

At every level of government, the United States continues to struggle with the paradox posed by combining executive authority and democratic idealism. If executives have too much power, they can become tyrants. On the other hand, if executives have too little power, they may be enfeebled. American public institutions do not depend on finding angels to run the government. The framers assumed that presidents and other leaders, even good ones, would need checks on their powers. James Madison's advice remains crucial: "A dependence on the people is, no doubt, the primary control of the government, but experience has taught mankind the necessity of auxiliary precautions." Thus the president and other executives work within a framework that calls for active participation of legislative bodies, the courts, political parties, the media, and concerned citizen groups to ensure that executive power is exercised in a constitutional and prudent manner.

• Charles C. Thach Jr., *The Creation of the Presidency, 1775–1789: A Study in Constitutional History*, 1923. Edward S. Corwin, *The President: Office and Powers, 1789–1957*, 1940. Joseph E. Kallenbach, *The American Chief Executive: The Presidency and the Governorship*, 1966. Thomas E. Cronin, ed., *Inventing the American Presidency*, 1989. Forrest McDonald, *The American Presidency: An Intellectual History*, 1994. Thomas E. Cronin and Michael A. Genovese, *The Paradoxes of the American Presidency*, 1998. Louis Fisher, *The Politics of Shared Power: Congress and the Executive*, 1998. Sidney M. Milkis and Michael Nelson, *The American Presidency, 1787–1998: Origins and Development*, 1999. Louis Fisher, *Congressional Abdication of War and Spending Powers*, 2000.   —Thomas E. Cronin and Neil G. Kornze

EX POST FACTO LAWS. Ex post facto law is the particular American (and British) implementation of the widely recognized *criminal law principles of *nulla crimen sine lege* (no act is criminal in the absence of law against it) and *nulla poena sine lege* (no punishment is imposed in the absence of law authorizing it). These principles are aimed at providing fair notice to citizens. They are part of many national constitutions, as well as international *human rights documents such as the International Covenant on Civil and Political Rights, the Universal Declaration of Human Rights, and the (proposed) Statute of the International Criminal Court.

The United States *Constitution's prohibitions of ex post facto laws in article 1, sections 9 and 10 (applying to Congress and the states, respectively), and similar provisions in state constitutions, are the principal guarantors against retrospective application of criminal laws in the American legal system. They are intended to ensure that all persons have notice of the kinds of acts that are prohibited by the criminal law and the punishments that may be imposed for them.

Justice *Chase of the U.S. Supreme Court set out the classic, four-part, American definition of ex post facto laws in *Calder* v. *Bull* (1798).

> 1st. Every law that makes an action done before the passing of the law, and which was *innocent* when done, criminal; and punishes such action. 2d. Every law that *aggravates* a *crime*, or makes it *greater* than it was, when committed. 3d. Every law that *changes the punishment*, and inflicts a *greater punishment*, than the law annexed to the crime, when committed. 4th. Every law that alters the *legal* rules of *evidence*, and receives less, or different, testimony, than the law required at the time of the commission of the offense, *in order to convict the offender.*

Thus criminal prohibitions may not be expanded retrospectively—that is, to cover acts done before the expansion. This applies to the creation of new crimes, expansion of the definition of old crimes, and abolition of defenses to crimes.

Punishments also may not be expanded retrospectively. Even adjustments to criminal sentencing such as abolishing early release credits are prohibited ex post facto laws, as applied to crimes committed before the law's enactment, if the adjustment works to disadvantage the offender affected by it (see CRIMINAL PUNISHMENTS).

New laws that allow conviction on less evidence than previously, such as eliminating a requirement that evidence of rape be corroborated, may not be applied ex post facto. However, changes to rules of evidence declaring previously incompetent witnesses (e.g., convicted felons) competent, may be applied retrospectively.

The Constitution's ex post facto clauses themselves apply only to changes in the text of statutes. But their principle of fair notice of what will be considered criminal has been incorporated into the interpretation of the Constitution's *due process clauses, to prevent unforeseeable retrospective expansion of criminal liability by court decisions.

Retrospective laws that are *civil* in nature, rather than criminal, are not prohibited by the ex post facto doctrine. Whether a given restriction imposed on a person is "punishment" or not is generally the most contentious issue in ex post facto law today.

• *Kansas* v. *Hendrix*, 521 U.S. 346 (1997). *Carmell* v. *Texas*, 529 U.S. 513 (2000).

—Kenneth S. Gallant

EXTRADITION. The term "extradition" was not used until the late eighteenth century, but the process of returning a fugitive from one political authority to another to face justice has been used since antiquity. For example, the Treaty of Peace of 1280 B.C. between Pharaoh Ramses II and the Hittite King Hattusili III contained an extradition provision.

The U.S. Constitution, art. IV, §2 requires one state's executive authority to extradite a person "who shall flee from justice" after being charged with a crime committed in another state whose executive authority demands his return (see EXECUTIVE POWER). The purpose of this provision was to promote comity among the various states in the criminal realm in the same way that the *"full faith and credit" clause promoted comity in civil matters. Congress implemented the extradition clause "for a fugitive from justice" in 1793 by further requiring that the requesting authority produce an indictment or an affidavit from the governor or chief magistrate stipulating that the fugitive had in fact been charged with the crime. The state giving asylum is required to arrest and hold the fugitive for up to six months until the police of the requesting state can return the fugitive to face criminal proceedings (18 U.S.C. §3182 (1994)).

The U.S. Supreme Court in *Michigan* v. *Doran* (1978) found that the extradition clause permitted a "summary and mandatory executive proceeding" only after the governor granted extradition. Thus a court in the asylum state reviewing the accused's request for *habeas corpus can release him only if the extradition papers are on their face defective or if the accused has not been charged, is not the person named, or is not a fugitive. Virtually all the states have enacted the 1936 Uniform Criminal Extradition Act (1995), which filled some procedural gaps in the federal legislation and extended cooperation among states to cases in which the accused did not flee the requesting state—for instance, when the crime occurred outside the state.

*International extradition, unlike interstate extradition, is based almost entirely on the many bilateral treaties the United States has with other nations. In addition, Congress has agreed that the federal executive has the discretion to refuse extradition. Courts cannot bind the secretary of state to grant extradition in contravention of this executive prerogative, which includes the obligation to protect *human rights. An international fugitive in the United States also has the right to *due process to resist extradition through judicial proceedings and to be represented by *counsel.

The requesting nation must show probable cause that the accused committed a crime and met the requirements of "dual criminality" and "speciality." Dual criminality requires that a fugitive be extradited only for conduct that is punishable in both the United States and the requesting nation. It is satisfied if the offense charged is "substantially similar" in each nation. The doctrine of speciality requires that there be a correspondence between the charges contained in the indictment and the facts presented to the extraditing judge. A person may not be prosecuted for any offense other than that for which he is extradited, which is determined by the crime's material elements.

[*See also* Criminal Law Principles]

• Christopher L. Blakesley, *Terrorism, Drugs, International Law and the Protection of Human Liberty*, 1992. M. Cherif Bassiouni, *International Extradition: United States Law and Practice*, 3d ed., 1996. Christopher L. Blakesley, "The Law of International Extradition: A Comparative Study," in *International Criminal Law and Procedure* (John Dugard and Christine van den Wyngaert, eds.), 1996. Wayne R. LaFave, Jerold H. Israel, and Nancy J. King, *Criminal Procedure*, 3d ed., 2000.

—Christopher L. Blakesley

EXTRALEGALITY. Scholars have posited that people obey the law when they perceive the government is legitimately formed and acts in fair and nondiscriminatory ways. Legitimacy can be provided by the moral and just actions of a government, but according to contractarians such as Hobbs, Locke, Rousseau, Kant, and Rawls, consent of the people is an important prerequisite for any legitimate government, regardless of those moral and just actions. However, the manner in which government acts is also important when analyzing why people obey the law. According to Tom R. Tyler, *Why People Obey the Law* (1990), although people are concerned that governments produce fair outcomes in specific situations, they are primarily concerned with being provided with an opportunity for meaningful participation. Through this participation, people assess the fairness of the legal or political procedures involved, and are more likely to obey the law when those procedures are fair and impartial.

Definition. "Extralegality" is a term used to define behavior by individuals and groups that strikes at the heart of this legitimacy. Extralegality is conceptually distinct from anarchy, which is defined as the absence of government. Essentially, these individuals and groups question the legitimacy of government, and advocate some form of drastic action to cure the perceived inadequacies. In contrast, anarchists advocate the overthrow of governments. The Whiskey Rebellion of 1794 was one such group, as were the Montana Vigilantes of 1864. According to David Ray Papke in *Heretics in the Temple* (1998), abolitionist William Lloyd Garrison, women's rights advocate Elizabeth Cady Stanton, socialist Eugene Debs, and the Black Panther party of the 1970s were all legal heretics who fought for significant change in our legal and political system, and whose behavior can be defined as extralegal.

Unlike the individuals and groups named above, modern extralegal groups fight not within the courts and legislatures, but on the Internet, in the realm of public opinion, and, in the more extreme cases, in armed conflicts against governmental officials. These include the more radical *militias, the common-law movement, and the *Posse Comitatus*, a blending of the antitax movement and Christian identity beliefs. Observers contend that over two hundred militia groups are active in the United States, while over thirty states have some form of common-law movements. Although the *Posse Comitatus* has lost explicit membership throughout the country, most common-law adherents and many of the more radical militia members have incorporated both the beliefs and activities of the movement. This article will discuss these modern groups in the context of their extralegal behavior.

In general, the militias, common-law movement and *Posse Comitatus* call for similar actions from their members. These range from the relatively innocuous rejection of the use of Social Security numbers, drivers licenses, license plates, and ZIP codes, to the more serious disobeying of gun laws, refusal to pay taxes, and the filing of frivolous (i.e. untrue) liens against public officials. Members also believe that the use of their incomplete name by the government creates a fictitious persona for the government to abuse. Finally, the common-law movement has created "common-law courts" that purport to issue their own divorce decrees, absolve members of traffic violations, and issue edicts to public officials that call for their death by hanging.

Members are organized in cell-like leaderless groups, and generally are more prevalent in rural areas throughout the United States. Heroes and martyrs of the groups include Gordon Kuhl, a tax evader and leader of the *Posse Comitatus* who killed three officials and was killed himself during a shootout, Ruby Ridge casualties Vicki and Samuel Weaver, wife and young son of armed fugitive Randy Weaver, and the Montana Freemen, twelve of whom surrendered to federal authorities in 1996 after a protracted stake out.

Foundations of Beliefs. Although far from homogeneous in their beliefs, members of these groups are in basic agreement regarding the underlying causes that brought them to this point of vocal dissent. The first and perhaps most fundamental cause was the farming crisis of the 1980s. In *Bitter Harvest: The Birth of Paramilitary Terrorism in the Heartland* (1995), James Corcoran writes that countless farmers defaulted on their loans and had liens placed against not only their farms but also their entire assets. In desperation, many farmers begged the federal government to grant a temporary moratorium on the foreclosures, but were largely unsuccessful in their efforts. As a result of this governmental inaction, many farmers joined the *Posse Comitatus*, the first of these extralegal groups. Governmental action at Ruby Ridge and Waco, Texas, is also cited as symptomatic of governmental intolerance, in this case of pro-gun groups, and have been used as rallying cries for the militia and common-law movements. These groups see the assault weapons ban and the Brady bill as further evidence of a tyrannical government (see ARMS CONTROL LAW). Finally, they point to the lack of personal accountability of federal officials and their allegedly demonstrated lack of understanding of the needs of rural America to show that the federal government has degenerated into state tyranny.

The militias, the common-law movement, and the *Posse Comitatus* have developed complex legal, and religious justifications for their positions. Legally, they rely on the Magna Carta, the Declaration of Independence, the United States *Constitution, the Uniform Commercial Code secs. 1–103 and 1–207, and on the United States Supreme Court case *Erie Railroad Co.* v. *Tompkins* (1938). While their reasons for justifying their positions with the Magna Carta and Declaration of Independence are not fully articulated, a rich body of literature has been developed regarding their concerns about the United States Constitution. The movements' reasoning centers on the Second and *Fourteenth Amendments, the latter of which is the foundational underpinning of the movements. Specifically, the movements claim that the Fourteenth Amendment recognizes two sources of citizenship. The more powerful of these types is the "sovereign citizen," who has full protection under the *Bill of Rights, and who has renounced his federal *citizenship by filing quiet title and showing proof of birth in the fifty states, not including the District of Columbia. The use of "quiet title" in this context is confusing, since an action to quiet title is a proceeding to establish one's legal title to land, and is accomplished by bringing into court adverse claimants to the land and forcing those claimants to either prove their claims at that time or renounce their ability to assert any such claims in the future. The second and weaker type of citizenship is termed "Fourteenth Amendment citizenship," and is composed of ex-slaves and those Americans who have not renounced federal citizenship. Rights under this second type may be rescinded by Congress at any time, and do not include the sovereign citizen's inalienable right to travel without hindrance of federal or state laws. Additionally, sovereign citizens assert their absolute rights to own weapons, and interpret the Second Amendment to uphold that right without restrictions.

These movements also contend that the Constitution recognizes three types of court jurisdictions: law, *equity, and *admiralty. In essence, they believe that all federal district courts only look to admiralty law and the Uniform Commercial Code, and have essentially renounced the Constitution. Because federal courts are perceived as relying on the Uniform Commercial Code, sovereign citizens can invoke Uniform Commercial Code sections 1–103 and 1–207 to allow them to revoke their contract with the government. This revocation echoes the implicit consent to be governed that Contractarians find to be a prerequisite to a legitimate government. Essentially, sovereign citizens take this consent to be quite literal, and believe that revoking this consent allows them to renounce government's authority over them.

Contractarians theorize that without this implicit consent to be governed, governments must rely on *natural law to provide legitimacy for their institutions. Sovereign citizens translate this "natural law" to mean "common law" given by God, and point to the U.S. Supreme Court case *Erie Railroad Co.* v. *Tompkins* (1938) to prove that the

United States government has illegally abolished *common law. In reality, this case held only that there is no federal general common law. However, this rejection of common law, coupled with their assertion that President Franklin D. Roosevelt suspended the Constitution in 1933, proves to sovereign citizens that the country has been in a state of lawlessness ever since 1938.

The movements also contend that their positions are supported by fundamental religious truths. The Christian identity group that pervades throughout the movements teaches that white Americans are the true Israelites, and the Chosen People of God. Another strain of belief identifies farmers as the Chosen People, and looks to Thomas Jefferson's writings espousing this idea. In addition, according to the Federal Bureau of Investigation's *Congressional Statement on the President's Fiscal Year 2000 Budget*, most militias do not follow the Christian identity's racist and anti-Semitic beliefs. These groups have tried to distance themselves from the religious bigotry, but recent intrusions into the Michigan militia, the largest in the country, may prove to be only the beginning of a blending of militia and Christian identity adherents. However, regardless of whether they embrace or disassociate from this racism and anti-Semitism, all strains of these movements maintain that there is a hierarchy of allegiance and power: God, People, and the United States Constitution. Finally, conspiracy theories within the movements abound. Many members believe that the United Nations has implemented a "New World Order" that will subjugate all Americans, and that Jews are planning through financial circles the downfall of the United States.

Government Response. Courts and legislatures have articulated a variety of responses. Legislatures have criminalized the simulation of legal processes in an effort to prohibit the common-law movement from holding common-law courts. State laws now allow public officials to reject nonconsensual liens, and provide for a streamlined process to remove bad-faith liens. The Montana Anti-Intimidation Act of 1996 punishes threats towards officials, and it has long been a felony to impersonate a judge in most jurisdictions. Finally, according to the Federal Bureau of Investigation's *Congressional Statement on the President's Fiscal Year 2000 Budget*, sixteen states prohibit militia groups in general, while seventeen prohibit paramilitary training.

Similarly, courts have increasingly issued sanctions and *injunctions for frivolous lawsuits brought by common-law members. Although only a few cases have been appealed, there are three important appellate decisions restricting the actions of members of these movements. In *Rice* v. *Paladin* (1997), Paladin Publishers published a book on how to murder using hit men. The victim's family of a subsequent murder brought suit against the publishers, and both sides stipulated to the publishers' intent to assist criminals, and that the murderer was following explicit instructions from the book. After a much publicized trial, the 4th Circuit upheld a finding of civil *liability for the murder. Earlier, the 7th Circuit in *U.S.* v. *Schneider* (1990) upheld a conviction of a common-law adherent, giving Schneider five years imprisonment for threatening a public official. In their opinion, the court held that disrespect for our law warrants extra punishment. Finally, the Eighth Circuit in *U.S.* v. *Moss* (1979) upheld a conviction of a tax protester and *Posse Comitatus* member who aided and abetted others in the filing of false withholding information when he gave seminars on tax evasion. It remains to be seen whether these legal measures will prevent the movements from such harassment of federal officials. Similarly, the armed militias are still a source of great concern for government officials, and continue to threaten violence towards the government.

[*See also* Civil Disobedience]

• Vicente Medina, *Social Contract Theories: Political Obligation or Anarchy?*, 1990. Tom R. Tyler, *Why People Obey the Law*, 1990. Thomas Halpern and Brian Levin, *The Limits of Dissent: The Constitutional Status of Armed Civilian Militias*, 1996. Susan P. Koniak, "When Law Risks Madness," *Cardozo Studies in Law & Literature* (1996): 65–107. Susan P. Koniak, "The Chosen People in Our Wilderness," *Michigan Law Review* (1997): 1761–98. Andrew P. Morriss, "Private Actors and Structural Balance: Militia and the Free Rider Problem in Private Provision of Law," *Montana Law Review* (Winter 1997): 115–66. William A. Edmundson, *Three Anarchical Fallacies: An Essay on Political Authority*, 1998. William A. Edmundson, ed., *The Duty to Obey the Law*, 1999. Francis X. Sullivan, "The 'Usurping Octopus of Jurisdictional/Authority': The Legal Theories of the Sovereign Citizen Movement," *Wisconsin Law Review* (1999): 785–823.   —Thomas J. Moyer

EXTRATERRITORIALITY. *See* Court Systems; Courts, Federal; Legislative Power.

F

FAIR SPEECH. *See* Speech and the Press, Freedom of.

FAIR TRIAL, CRIMINAL. Article III of the Constitution states that "the Trial of all Crimes, except in Cases of Impeachment, shall be by jury"; and the Sixth Amendment guarantees the right to a "speedy and public trial by an impartial jury." Before the U.S. Supreme Court applied the right to a *jury trial in criminal cases to the states in 1968 (*Duncan* v. *Louisiana*), cases involving state jury claims were decided under the *due-process clause of the Fourteenth Amendment. A defendant may claim the right only if the crime with which he or she is charged could result in imprisonment of more than six months (*Baldwin* v. *New York*, 1970). The Supreme Court has not required the states to follow the federal standards for jury size (twelve) and unanimity, however. The Court has upheld state verdicts of 10–2 and 9–3 in noncapital cases, and allowed juries with as few as six members (*Johnson* v. *Louisiana*, 1972; *Burch* v. *Louisiana*, 1979). Today, Louisiana and Oregon are the only states that allow less-than-unanimous verdicts (though some states allow the defendant to waive unanimity). Over thirty states use juries of less than twelve, at least for some offenses.

A defendant may also waive a jury trial in favor of a bench trial because of concerns about jury prejudice or the complexity of the case, so long as the waiver is made expressly, intelligently, and voluntarily. (Of course, *plea bargaining, which is a waiver of the right to a trial before the trial takes place, occurs in the great majority of cases for reasons of defense strategy and institutional overload.) However, the Sixth Amendment guarantees only a right to a jury trial, not a right to a bench trial. Consequently, the federal courts and most states allow the judge or the prosecutor to veto a waiver. The Supreme Court upheld such vetoes in *Singer* v. *U.S.* (1965).

Impartiality. A defendant is entitled to an impartial judge and jury. Thus, if a judge's interest in a trial is both personal and substantial, the defendant's due-process rights are violated. For example, the Supreme Court once invalidated an Ohio practice that allowed presiding judges to take a percentage of any fine they assessed in enforcing the state's prohibition law (*Tunney* v. *Ohio*, 1931). In an earlier case, however, the Court upheld a system in which half of the town's revenues came from fines and the mayor-judge had a fixed salary (*Dugan* v. *Ohio*, 1928).

Juries must also be impartial. Courts must screen potential jurors in the *voir dire* to filter out the negative effects of pretrial publicity (see below). Ensuring that jurors are drawn from a fair cross-section of the community is another method that attempts to promote impartiality. Before the 1960s, courts had not allowed intentional racial or gender discrimination in the formation of jury lists (see, e.g., *Ballard* v. *U.S.*, 1946). Exclusion in practice still prevailed, however. Responding to the *civil rights and women's movements, Congress passed the Jury Selection and Service Act in 1968. This act eliminated the "key man" system in federal trials, a system in which jurors were drawn from pools of community leaders (often white men). The new system required prospective jurors to be drawn from general voter lists, a method deemed more likely to reflect the new norm of "a fair cross-section" of the community. In a landmark 1975 case, the Supreme Court applied this logic to the states, holding that the Sixth Amendment guarantee of "impartiality" mandates that juries be drawn from a representative cross-section of the community (*Taylor* v. *Louisiana*). Only discrimination against "cognizable" or "distinct" groups violates the Sixth Amendment, including groups based on race, gender, religion, national origin, and economic status. The "young" are not a cognizable group (see *Barber* v. *Ponte*, 1985).

The cross-section norm has its fans and its critics. At its best, it enhances jury deliberation and fairness by broadening the voices on the jury. At its worst, it disparages the belief that individual jurors can rise above their group interests in common deliberation and pursuit of the truth—a form of interest-group politics applied to juries.

The Supreme Court has also limited the power of *prosecutors to use peremptory challenges during *voir dire* to exclude jurors on grounds of race and gender. Prosecutors and defense lawyers must explain their reasons for exclusion if the defendant makes a *prima facie* case showing that race or gender were factors (*Batson* v. *Kentucky*, 1986; *J.E.B.* v. *Alabama*, 1994). This rule has been applied to civil as well as criminal cases. These decisions are controversial, as they place the right to be on a jury ahead of the claims of the defendant, at least in this context.

Speedy Trial. The Sixth-Amendment right to a speedy trial encompasses three goals: to prevent unnecessary incarceration before trial; to lessen the anxiety that attends public accusation; and to limit the ways in which delay might hinder preparation of the defense. The defendant must invoke the right, which attaches only after the prosecution has accused someone of a crime. Lower courts have generally held that trials should be held within six to eight months of the charges; undue delay before an accusation violates the due-process clause (*U.S.* v. *Lovasco*, 1977). In adjudicating speedy trial claims, the Supreme Court has developed a three-part test that considers the length of the delay, the reasons for the delay, and the prejudice to the defendant (*Barker* v. *Wingo*, 1972). Though the remedy for a violation of the speedy-trial right is dismissal of the case with prejudice, *Barker* and other cases provide ample flexibility for trial-court justices to balance the competing interests at stake.

Barker stated that the length of time within which trials must commence is a matter of legislative discretion. Following *Barker*, Congress passed the 1974 Federal Speedy Trial Act, which covers only federal cases. The act requires district courts to develop plans for trying cases within one hundred days of arrest or a summons. Within a decade, over two-thirds of the states had passed similar legislation. The federal and state laws are riddled with exceptions, and courts are reluctant to exact the ultimate remedy. The defendant must show that undue delay is intentional; and commentators point out that the laws' provisions constantly rub up against the institutionalized delay that is endemic to the system.

The Right to Confront Witnesses. The right to a fair trial also embraces the right to confront and cross-examine *witnesses. The accused also has a right to be informed of the charges against him, in language with sufficient specificity to allow him to be able to prepare a defense (*Douglas* v. *Alabama*, 1965). Another preliminary right in this regard is the right to be present at one's trial, which means the right to be mentally competent and physically present at each critical stage in the trial process. The right may be waived, however, except in *capital cases. And defendants may also be removed from the courtroom for disruptive or abusive behavior. The defendant may waive the right to be present, but only if the trial court informs him or her of the potential consequences (*Taylor* v. *U.S.*, 1973).

Federal Rule of *Criminal Procedure 43 prohibits holding trials *in absentia*, that is, in which the defendant does not appear. (If the defendant leaves during the trial, that is another matter.) But the Court has not prohibited states from trying cases *in absentia*, so long as they can show a compelling enough reason (see *Tucan* v. *Arizona*, 1973).

The right to confront witnesses is designed to further the search for truth, as it is less likely that witnesses will lie in front of the defendant than when she is not present, and it gives the defendant a chance to question and challenge the witness. The right is also the constitutional backbone of the rules against hearsay (statements made by someone other than a witness who is testifying at a trial, which is offered to establish the truth of the matter asserted), which is difficult, if not impossible, to cross-examine. The Supreme Court, for example, has reversed convictions in which prosecutors read confessions of accomplices who refused to testify (*Douglas* v. *Alabama*, 1965). Nonetheless, the rule against hearsay is riddled with exceptions.

Cases involving child witnesses raise interesting problems. In 1988, the Supreme Court struck down an Iowa law that allowed alleged victims of child abuse to testify behind a screen. Justice Antonin Scalia wrote that "face-to-face presence may, unfortunately, upset the truthful rape victim or abused child, but by the same token it may confound and undo the false accuser, or reveal the child coached by a malevolent adult" (*Coy* v. *Iowa*). Later, however, the Court upheld letting an allegedly abused child testify in another room by closed-circuit television, and allowed the admission of hearsay statements by a child unable to testify on the grounds that the statements could be tested for their validity (*Maryland* v. *Craig*, 1990; *Idaho* v. *Wright*, 1990).

Prejudicial Publicity and Cameras in Court.
The Sixth Amendment right to a "public" trial and
the First Amendment right of public access to trials work together to protect against judicial bias
or tyranny. Sometimes, however, the two rights
are at odds, as when publicity before or during the
trial produces prejudice against the defendant,
thus violating due process. In two important cases
in the 1960s, for example, the Supreme Court
overturned convictions because of widespread
prejudicial publicity that included evidence that
would not have been allowed in court (*Irvin* v.
Dowd, 1961; *Sheppard* v. *Maxwell*, 1966). In response to such concerns, trial court judges resorted to issuing gag orders against the press or
participants, or not allowing the public access to
the trial in cases posing a "clear and present danger" of prejudicial publicity.

As the Supreme Court grew accustomed to
dealing with media, however, it limited the power
of trial courts to control the press. It required trial
courts to attempt less drastic remedies that fall
short of prior restraint—for example, outright
censorship, such as ordering a continuance of the
trial, questioning jurors about their reactions to
pretrial publicity, or sequestering the jury during
the trial (see *Nebraska Press Association* v. *Stuart*,
1976). Screening jurors during *voir dire* is helpful,
but the Court has ruled that the Constitution does
not require trial judges to question each individual
juror about publicity (*Mu' Min* v. *Virginia*, 1991).
Impartiality is not violated by jurors simply having
some knowledge or opinion of a case, but only
when they "have such fixed opinion that they
could not judge impartially the guilt of the defendant" (*Patton* v. *Yount*, 1984; see also *State* v. *Lau-
man*, New Hampshire, 1974). Though reversals of
convictions due to pretrial publicity are difficult
to attain, trial-court judges in prominent cases often bend over backwards to weed out jurors with
any meaningful knowledge of the case, leading
some critics to question their competence to be
jurors in the first place. The famous cases involving Bernhard Goetz, Lyle and Erik Menendez, and
Oliver North provide examples.

In extreme cases, defendants may ask for a
change of venue, as in the trial of Los Angeles
police officers for beating Rodney King (*Powell* v.
Superior Court, 1991) The Supreme Court has
overturned convictions because of a failure to
grant a change of venue, but today it is reluctant
to do so if trial judges attempt other methods of
ensuring jury impartiality (see *Patton* v. *Yount*,
1984).

The First Amendment prohibits trial-court
judges from closing a trial to the press or the public, although judges may restrict attendance in order to ensure a orderly trial (*Richmond Newspapers, Inc.* v. *Virginia*, 1980). Whereas a grand-jury
hearing is not open to the public, a preliminary
hearing must be open unless the defendant can
show a strong probability of prejudice. Juvenile
proceedings may also be closed. The Court has
given more leeway for judges to restrict the speech
of actual trial participants. Some lower courts use
a "clear and present danger" test in such cases
(see, e.g., *U.S.* v. *Regan*, 1989); and the *American
Bar Association Rules of Professional Responsibility prohibits lawyers from making statements out
of court that have the "substantial likelihood of
affecting the outcome of the trial" (ABA Rule
3.6(a)(b)).

A related issue is the presence of cameras in the
courtroom. Traditionally, courts did not allow
cameras in court. By the later 1970s, however, the
American Bar Association and the Conference of
State Chief Justices became more tolerant of cameras in court, and in 1981 the Supreme Court upheld Florida's policy of allowing television coverage despite a defendant's objection, as long as
judges employ the standard alternative means of
ensuring impartiality (*Chandler* v. *Florida*). Today,
most states allow televising of trials, whereas federal courts do not. The Judicial Conference of the
United States (which governs the lower federal
courts) gives federal appellate judges the discretion
to televise appellate arguments. The Supreme
Court does not allow cameras in its hearings, but
did allow delayed radio broadcasting of its two
hearings involving *Bush* v. *Gore*.

[*See also* Criminal Law Principles]

• Rita J. Simon, *The Jury System in America: A Critical
Overview*, 1975. Albert W. Alschuler, "The Supreme
Court and the Jury: Voir Dire, Peremptory Challenges,
and the Review of Jury Verdicts," *University of Chicago
Law Review* 56 (1989). Jeffrey Abramson, *We, the Jury:
The Jury System and the Ideal of Democracy*, 1994. Akhil
Reed Amar, *The Constitution and Criminal Procedure:
First Principles*, 1997. William T. Pizzi, *Trials Without
Truth*, 1999. Charles Whitebread and Christopher Slo-
bogin, *Criminal Procedure: An Analysis of Basic Concepts*,
2000.

—Donald A. Downs and Cristina Ruggiero

FAMILY LAW encompasses many areas: *adoption; assisted reproduction; *child custody, access,
and support (either in *divorce, paternity, or neglect proceedings); entry into *marriage with its
attendant rights, duties, and benefits; divorce,
*property division, and alimony; parentage ac-
tions; premarital and postmarital agreements; and
tort actions between family members. Some peo
ple include *juvenile justice in this area; others

categorize it as criminal law. Family-law issues overlap conflicts, contracts, torts, evidence, debtor-creditor, criminal law, property, civil procedure, constitutional law, estates, taxation, remedies, trusts, and other areas. Family law interfaces with other disciplines such as medicine, psychology, sociology, mediation, accounting, and appraising. Traditionally, family law has been based on widely accepted religious and cultural values. In England, ecclesiastical courts had exclusive jurisdiction over marriage and divorce until 1857. Today a more diverse populace challenges the ability to achieve consensus on many family law issues, which are debated often in terms of morality, religious doctrine, and cultural values.

Family law in the United States consists of fifty individual state law systems and federal laws. The Tenth Amendment to the U.S. Constitution provides that those items not reserved for the federal government are the exclusive province of the individual states. Until the 1970s nearly all family law matters were governed by state law. Congressional legislation in the past thirty years has resulted in federalization of several areas, especially child support enforcement, allocation of benefits provided by federal law, and health benefits required for children. Family law is also international law. The United Nations (UN) Universal Declaration of Human Rights 16(3) recognizes the family as the natural and fundamental group unit of society entitled to state protection. The UN Convention on the Rights of the Child has been adopted in 197 countries. The United States has ratified the Hague Convention on the Civil Aspects of International Child Abduction and the Hague Convention on Cooperation in Respect to Intercountry Adoption and participated in the drafting of two others affecting families.

Since the 1800s, federal courts have used a domestic relations exception to avoid hearing family law matters involving divorce, alimony, child custody, or child support. Beginning in 1965 the U.S. Supreme Court, using the Equal Protection Clause of the U.S. Constitution, has played an increasingly pronounced role in family matters by striking state statutes that impinge on rights as fundamental as the right to *privacy, the right to marry, and the right to bear and rear children. Congress has opened federal courts by granting both federal and state courts concurrent jurisdiction over Hague Abduction Convention cases.

Marriage. Marriage is both a *contract requiring consent of the parties and a status, conferring rights and obligations such as inheritance and support. England recognized common law or infor-

mal marriages with the ages of capacity being twelve (females) and fourteen (males). While more than thirty states recognized common-law marriage in 1900, less than ten still do. Most states have similar procedural and substantive requirements—the parties must obtain a license, have witnesses, and solemnize the marriage. The parties must be eighteen or have parental consent, be of the opposite sex, and not be closely related by blood (although twenty-one states allow first cousins to marry). Vermont in 2000 enacted the first statewide civil-union law granting same-sex couples the same benefits and rights as married couples.

The majority of states imported their marriage and property system from the *common law of England, which gave the husband control of his wife's person and property because of the fictional unity of husband and wife. The Married Women's Property Acts in the latter half of the nineteenth century removed many of the disabilities imposed on married women, by restoring to the married woman the rights to acquire, own, or transfer property, to make a will and enter contracts, to engage in business or be employed, to keep her own earnings, to sue and be sued, and to testify in trials. Spousal immunity, however, was not abolished until the 1990s.

The common-law doctrine of necessaries, based on the fictional unity of husband and wife, required a husband to support his wife in return for her domestic services. The U.S. Supreme Court has stricken gender-based jurisprudence as violating the Equal Protection Clause. States have chosen to either abolish the doctrine of necessaries, to make the spouse who incurs the expense primarily liable for repayment and the other spouse only secondarily liable, or made both spouses equally liable.

Nine states have community-property systems. California, Louisiana, and Texas started them at statehood, while Arizona, Idaho, Nevada, New Mexico, Washington, and Wisconsin adopted community-property laws after trying the common law. A married couple may hold three types of property: the wife's separate property, the husband's separate property, and community property. The "separate" property is owned and managed by the spouse who brought it into the marriage. Although originally the husband was the manager of the community property during the marriage, the wife now has equal status. As a general rule a spouse's separate property is not liable for a community debt absent an agreement.

Divorce. Until the 1960s states required a person to be a "domiciliary" (usually one-year residency showed intent of permanency) to seek a divorce based upon the "ground" that the other party committed a marital fault, that is, *adultery, cruelty, desertion, gross neglect of duty, or the like. By 1985 all states had enacted a basis for no-fault divorce such as incompatibility, irremediable breakdown of the marriage, or the parties living apart for a prescribed period pursuant to an agreement.

The determination of when alimony, also called maintenance or spousal support, can be awarded, and the appropriate amount, differs from state to state. While thirty years ago it was common to find an alimony award for a homemaker spouse until her death or remarriage, the trend is toward shorter, rehabilitative awards. Alimony is awarded primarily based on the need of the dependent spouse and the ability of the other to pay. Among the factors that courts look at are the ages, length of the marriage, the standard of living during the marriage, prospective earning capacities, responsibilities for children or others, and property owned. While marital fault remains a factor in only a few states, economic fault may be relevant in most.

What property is divided depends on whether the state is an equitable distribution state or a community-property state. A community property state divides only property acquired after the marriage with with most having a presumption of a fifty-fifty split. Separate property is set aside to the party who owns it. Traditionally, most common-law states awarded property to the named title-holder. In the 1970s common-law states adopted equitable distribution principles. Although the property does not have to be divided fifty-fifty, the law may presume equal distribution. Some states classify the couple's property as "marital" and "nonmarital" allowing division of only marital property, similar to community property states. Other states classify all property as "marital" once a divorce is filed so the judge can divide equitably all property, however titled and whenever acquired, with no requirement that specific property be set aside to the spouse who brought it into the marriage or holds title.

Child Custody. The parental preference doctrine requires a child to be placed with a parent unless the parent has been found unfit. Absent extraordinary circumstances, such as abandonment or abuse, a fit parent will be awarded custody and be allowed to determine with whom the child associates. At common law, fathers had superior rights to custody of children as the head of the family. Mothers, however, were entitled to custody of nonmarital children who had no right to get support or inheritance from their fathers. The consent of an unwed mother was all that was necessary for adoption until the 1970s when the U.S. Supreme Court found that when a father makes a good faith attempt to be a father, his rights cannot be cut off without his consent or a finding of parental unfitness. When, however, a father fails to assume support or parental responsibilities, to comply with requirements to sign a registry, to file an action to prove paternity, or when he waits too long to assert his parentage, a court may deem the father's consent to adoption unnecessary.

In the nineteenth century the tender-years doctrine presumed that it was in the best interest of a small child to be in the custody of the mother. Beginning in the 1970s the laws changed to give both mothers and fathers equal rights to custody based on the best interest of the child. All states authorize, and some prefer, joint legal custody. In awarding primary residential custody, judges look at who has been the child's primary caretaker, what the child's preference is, the child's relationship with each parent and siblings, which parent will be the most cooperative in fostering a relationship with the other parent, and the presence of *domestic violence. Morality is a factor only to the extent that the parents' conduct adversely affects the child. A nonresidential parent has a right to visit with his or her child unless there is evidence that visitation would endanger the child's health and welfare.

Most states have statutes authorizing grandparent visitation under certain circumstances, such as if the grandparent's child has died, the parents divorce, or the child was born out of wedlock. Some states allow "any person" to petition for visitation while others list stepparents, siblings, or others. Third parties must overcome presumption in favor of parents and will only be given court-ordered rights if they have had a substantial relationship and it would be in the child's best interest to continue the relationship or some say the child would suffer harm.

Paternity and Child Support. At common law the obligation to pay support depended on status— a father had no duty to support an illegitimate child. The law presumed that a child born to a marriage was the husband's and Lord Mansfield's Rule prevented either spouse from testifying to nonaccess by the husband. Beginning in 1968, the U.S. Supreme Court invalidated on *equal-protection grounds various state laws that discriminated on the basis of being born out of wedlock.

Today it is the parent-child relationship that gives rise to legal duties, rights, and obligations and is presumed in several situations, such as when the parents are married or have acknowledged paternity. If a child has a presumed parent, many states require a showing that it is in the child's best interest to order paternity testing.

All fifty states have child support guidelines that are used to set amounts of child support in a divorce or paternity case. A contract between parents that compromises or deprives a child of support is void and considered against public policy. Most states require child support through high school or until age nineteen, but do not require parents to pay for college or vocational school without a written agreement.

All states have immediate income withholding for child support. In addition to execution and garnishment, states can place liens on professional, occupational, and drivers' licenses, as well as on personal and real property. Federal law requires states to enforce child support orders entered in another state without modification. All fifty states have enacted the Uniform Interstate Family Support Act providing for continuing jurisdiction in the state that issued the original support order.

Family law is in a transformative period. Dramatic changes in family form and function have altered the American family and the law governing families. Disputes arise involving nonmarital cohabitants and participants in new assisted forms of reproduction, such as surrogate parenting and in-vitro fertilization. There are challenges to traditional definitions of marriage, parenting, property, and the family itself. What constitutes family law fifty years from now may be substantially different from what it is today.

[See also Gender and Law]

• William Blackstone, *Commentaries on the Law of England*, 1858. Homer Clark, *Domestic Relations*, 2d ed., 1988. Linda Henry Elrod, *Child Custody Practice and Procedure*, 1993; 2001. Allen Parkman, *No-Fault Divorce: What Went Wrong?*, 1992. Judith S. Wallerstein, Julia M. Lewis, and Sandra Blakeslee, *The Unexpected Legacy of Divorce: A 25 Year Landmark Study*, 2000.

—Linda Henry Elrod

FAMILY LAW PRACTICE. Family law has always differed from other areas of practice because it affects people's lives in personal, tangible, and deeply felt ways. The litigants have had an intensely personal relationship, either as spouses, parents, or family members. In addition to the legal claim, the parties need to resolve emotional, social, economic, parental, and psychological issues. Family legal problems reflect desires, aspi-

rations, disappointments, and griefs. There is a tension between family privacy and the protection of the interests of individual family members.

Thirty years ago most lawyers were male and practiced family law as part of a large general practice. The main resources were state specific—statutes, court decisions, and perhaps a legal treatise or encyclopedia. A lawyer represented one of the spouses who wanted a *divorce and routinely dealt with personal and in rem jurisdiction, the grounds and defenses for divorce and dividing *property, usually according to title. A homemaker wife could expect alimony until her death or remarriage. *Child custody was rarely litigated because custody was either awarded to the party not at "fault" or to the mother, based upon the tender years doctrine. The custodial parent had the authority to determine the child's school, residence, and religion. A child born to a *marriage was presumed legitimate, almost irrefutably. Paternity actions had short, often one-year, statutes of limitation because the evidence could get "stale." Child support amounts were discretionary, often very low and enforcement rarely happened, especially if the obligor left the state.

States began revolutionizing the laws of divorce in 1969. Consequently, the family law practice has become more driven by statutes and court rules than *common law and discretion. By 1985, all states had enacted a basis for a no-fault divorce, which eliminated trials over the grounds for divorce but moved trials to issues of defining, discovering, and valuing property. Property division became more complex as common law states moved to equitable distribution of assets and rehabilitative alimony replaced "permanent" alimony. Custody laws changed from the tender years doctrine to equal rights for both parents, based on the best interest of the child, with a preference for joint legal custody. Parents litigate primary residency, access, and relocation issues. Child support amounts are set by guidelines in every state and enforced within the state and out by income-withholding procedures.

The large volume of divorces and remarriages have resulted in actions by stepparents, grandparents, and others for access to children. The increase in cohabiting couples, same sex and heterosexual, has resulted in more litigation over division of assets when the unions break up. Because of dissatisfaction with state laws and concern over the permanence of the marriage, more couples are asking lawyers to draft premarital contracts. Because one-third of the country's children are born out of wedlock and statutes of limitation on paternity are unlimited because of DNA testing, paternity and custody litigation between unmarried parents has become more common. Artificial insemination, in vitro fertilization, and surrogate parenthood require lawyers to draft contracts and arrange adoptions, as well as litigate custody and access arrangements. The abolition of interspousal immunity has made tort litigation a part of family practice.

In addition to state statutes and cases, the lawyer needs to be familiar with decisions of the Supreme Court that have constitutionalized large areas of family law by recognizing a right to marital *privacy, individual privacy, and family autonomy; the fundamental right of parents to the care, control, and custody of their children; and the equal rights of fathers regarding the custody of their children. The Court has made parenthood the criteria for imposing obligations and granting rights so that children born out of wedlock are entitled to equal support from their fathers, and states cannot discriminate against them when the intent of legislation is to benefit children generally.

Since 1970, Congress has enacted numerous pieces of legislation affecting families. To a large extent, Congress has federalized the laws relating to establishment and enforcement of child support and paternity through the Child Support Enforcement Amendments of 1984 (CSEA); The Family Support Act of 1988 (FSA); and the Personal Responsibility and Work Opportunity Reconciliation Act of 1996 (PRWORA). The Parental Kidnapping Prevention Act of 1980 requires states to give *full faith and credit to sister-state custody decrees that meet certain jurisdictional requirements. Federal laws, such as the Employment Retirement Income Security Act of 1974 (ERISA); the Retirement Equity Act of 1984 (REA) allowing for the Qualified Domestic Relations Order (QDRO); and amendments to the Uniformed Services Former Spouses Protection Act (USFSPA) allow states to divide employee pensions on divorce. Congress overhauled the tax code for property division, alimony, and child dependency exemptions in 1984.

Nationalization and internationalization of family law make cases from other states and countries relevant resources. All fifty states have enacted the Uniform Interstate Family Support Act (UIFSA) and either the Uniform Child Custody Jurisdiction and Enforcement Act (UCCJEA) or the Uniform Child Custody Jurisdiction Act (UCCJA). Twenty-six states have the Uniform Premarital Agreement Act. Since 1980, the United States has ratified two Hague Conventions dealing with families and signed two others. The Hague Convention on the Civil Aspects of Child Abduction is now in force in over sixty-one countries. The International Child Abduction Remedies Act (ICARA) allows both federal and state courts to hear cases. The United Nations Convention on the Rights of the Child has been adopted in 197 countries, making it similar to an international common law rule, even though it is not in effect in the United States.

In the early twenty-first century, family law is a specialty comprising one of the most complex, challenging, and rapidly changing areas of law. Thirty-five states have a specialty designation for family lawyers and a handful have board certification. Many large firms now have a family law division, and there are firms which specialize in family law matters. "Family law" encompasses *adoption, assisted reproduction, child custody, divorce with its property division and alimony considerations, marriage, paternity, premarital and postmarital agreements, as well as support and visitation matters. The family law specialist engages in a wide range of "lawyering" activities, including counseling, drafting, negotiating, and litigating. Family law overlaps other areas of law including conflicts, contracts, torts, evidence, debtor-creditor, criminal law, property, civil procedure, constitutional law, estates, taxation, remedies, trusts, and others. Family law interfaces with other disciplines such as medicine, psychology, social work, accounting, appraising, and others.

The legal profession has more lawyers, more diversity, and more roles for a lawyer in family matters. Although a lawyer still may represent one of the divorcing parties in a traditional role, the lawyer may be a collaborative lawyer, may represent the child as a guardian ad litem, or attorney, or serve as a mediator, arbitrator, case manager, or in some other capacity.

[See also Legal Practice, Forms of]

• Mary Ann Glendon, The Transformation of Family Law, 1989. Linda D. Elrod, Child Custody Practice and Procedure, 1993, 2001 supp. William J. Goode, World Changes in Divorce Patterns, 1993. Laura Morgan, Child Support Guidelines: Interpretation and Application, 1996 and supps. Thomas Oldham, Divorce, Separation, and the Distribution of Property, 1998. American Law Institute, Principles of the Law of Family Dissolution, 2001.

—Linda D. Elrod

FAULT LIABILITY. "Fault" is a type of *liability in which the plaintiff must prove that the defendant's conduct was either negligent or intentional; fault-based liability is the opposite of strict liability.

[See also Torts]

—Mark F. Grady

F.B.I. See Federal Bureau of Investigation.

FEDERAL BUREAU OF INVESTIGATION. The Bureau of Investigation (formally renamed the Federal Bureau of Investigation in 1935) was created in July 1908, by order of Attorney General Charles Bonaparte, as the investigative division of the Department of Justice. At the time of its creation, the Bureau employed only thirty-four agents and had limited authority owing to the paucity of federal laws (dealing with, e.g., antitrust violations and crimes on Indian reservations) requiring prosecutive action. As Congress enacted new laws to prosecute interstate violations (White Slave Traffic Act, 1910; Stolen Motor Vehicle Act, 1919; laws on kidnapping and bank robbery, 1932–34) and to apprehend spies and detect *conspiracies to violently overthrow the government (Espionage Act, 1917; Foreign Agent Registration Act, 1939; Smith Act, 1940), the Bureau's personnel grew to 23,685 by 1997, when the Bureau had fifty-six field offices outside Washington, D.C., with hundreds of regional offices in smaller towns and thirty-six so-called legat offices in foreign capitals (e.g., London, Moscow, Paris, Mexico City).

Bureau operations were initially subject to close oversight by the attorney general or a designated assistant attorney general, but this changed during the 1930s. Dating from a secret oral directive of President Roosevelt in August 1936, FBI investigations began to focus as well on collecting "intelligence" (noncriminal information) about suspected "subversives" (who might not have violated any federal law). Such information was often relayed to the White House and to military and naval intelligence officials, ostensibly to further policymaking interests or for counterintelligence purposes. To minimize bureaucratic conflict and to avert military surveillance of domestic politics, delimitation agreements of 1940–42 instituted the FBI's central role in the internal security area. These agreements were reaffirmed and refined after 1949 following the creation in 1947 of the Central Intelligence Agency and the National Security Council.

First during the era of World War I and then radically and permanently during World War II and the Cold War eras, Bureau investigations expanded beyond law enforcement to include monitoring radicals and political dissidents. Questions about Bureau arrests of "slackers" (suspected draft evaders) in 1918, about the Bureau's extralegal role during the so-called Palmer Raids of January 1920 (enforcement of the alien deportation provisions of the 1918 *Immigration Act was the responsibility of the Immigration Bureau), and about the monitoring of labor union activities and then of members of Congress critical of the leasing of the

Teapot Dome naval oil reserve in 1921–24 led Attorney General Harlan Fiske *Stone in May 1924 to institute strict rules to preclude future Bureau abuses of power (banning *wiretapping and limiting investigations to violations of federal statutes). Stone's restrictions, however, were effectively rescinded during the 1930s and 1940s. President Franklin Roosevelt in 1936 and then in 1939 directed the FBI to monitor "fascist and communist" activities, and in 1940 he authorized wiretapping during "national defense" investigations (in effect circumventing the ban against wiretapping of the 1934 Communications Act). FBI Director J. Edgar Hoover, in addition, issued a series of secret directives between 1940 and 1949 that authorized clearly illegal break-ins as well as special records procedures (Do Not File, blue/pink/informal memoranda, JUNE Mail) to ensure that specially sensitive material would not be filed in the FBI's central records system (minimizing the risk of discovery in response to court orders).

President Roosevelt's executive directives of 1936–40 and requests for FBI reports had in effect bypassed the attorney general. An indirect result was to undercut departmental oversight. An emboldened FBI director first began to monitor noncriminal personal and political activities and then, after 1946, to disseminate information to favored members of Congress (e.g., Senators Joseph McCarthy and James Eastland), to congressional committees (the House Committee on Un-American Activities and Senate Internal Security Subcommittee), and to reporters and columnists and prominent citizens. The culmination came with the controversial COINTELPRO, a series of programs instituted between 1956 and 1968 to "harass, disrupt, and discredit" targeted radical organizations and their key leaders, and other formal programs (Mass Media, COMINFIL) to shape public opinion and monitor organizations and individuals suspected of being under Communist influence.

The scope of these surveillance and dissemination activities first became known during the course of a special Senate investigation into the *Watergate Affair (1973) and then during 1975 investigations by special congressional committees (the so-called Church and Pike committees) into the scope of and authority for activities of the FBI and other federal intelligence agencies. In response, Attorney General Edward Levi in March 1976 issued new guidelines to ensure tighter departmental oversight and to preclude future FBI monitoring of personal and political activities. In March 1983, however, Attorney General William French Smith issued new "domestic security/terrorism" guidelines that relaxed the Justice Department's oversight role and permitted an expanded FBI investigative role. At the same time, FBI investigative priorities were shifting to focus on *white-collar and *organized crime (FBI authority having been expanded through legislation legalizing wiretapping and to target racketeering activities, under the Omnibus Crime Control and Safe Streets Act of 1968 and the Racketeer Influenced and Corrupt Organization Act of 1970). New, more sophisticated procedures (e.g., profiling, DNA testing, undercover sting operations) were also implemented to apprehend and convict criminals.

The collapse of the Soviet Union and of Communist governments in Eastern Europe, the rise of religiously motivated dissident movements, and the emergence of militant *militia, antiabortion, and white supremacist movements led to an expanded FBI surveillance role during the 1980s and after, while also provoking controversy about FBI practices and the level of executive oversight. Disclosures during the 1980s about the FBI's Library Awareness program and monitoring of the Committee in Solidarity with the People of El Salvador (CISPES) were soon followed by the actions of the FBI's Hostage Rescue Team in 1992–1993 at Ruby Ridge (Idaho) and near Waco (Texas), raising further questions about the FBI's surveillance of political activities and use of excessive force. Concurrently, FBI investigations led to the apprehension and conviction of individuals responsible for terrorist bombings of the World Trade Center in New York (1993) and the Albert Murrah Building in Oklahoma City (1995). Widely varied in method, and with varying public and congressional support, FBI activities raised questions about the effectiveness of executive and judicial oversight, following disclosures that agents had monitored dissident groups and that FBI officials had withheld information when responding to media and congressional inquiries. Congress, however, did not enact legislation to govern FBI methods and authority, instead limiting itself to periodic hearings into publicized controversial actions.

[See also Police]

• Sanford Ungar, FBI, 1975. Frank Donner, The Age of Surveillance, 1980. Athan Theoharis and John Stuart Cox, The Boss, 1988. Tony Poveda, Lawlessness and Reform, 1990. Curt Gentry, J. Edgar Hoover, 1991. Ronald Kessler, The FBI, 1993. Athan Theoharis, ed., The FBI: A Comprehensive Reference Guide, 1999.

—Athan G. Theoharis

FEDERAL EMPLOYER LIABILITY ACT. See Labor Law: Workplace Issues.

FEDERALISM may be the chief contribution of the framers of the United States *Constitution to the science of government. Before 1787, political thinkers did not believe two governments could have direct authority over the same people. *Sovereignty was considered indivisible, and divided authority impossible. The framers, however, "split the atom of sovereignty" (U.S. Term Limits v. Thornton (1995), Kennedy, J., concurring), creating a system with two levels of strong, representative, and independent political power—the federal government and the states.

Federalism is deeply embedded in American law, politics, and culture. We have not just one system of laws but fifty-one, with the states adopting their own rules in areas that comprise the core of civil society—contract, tort, property, criminal law, domestic relations, corporate law, and the regulation of the professions. We have not just one political system but fifty-one, with state political parties frequently at arms length from their national counterparts, and state elected officials independently making and enforcing policies with respect to such key matters as education, policing, public health, transportation, and economic development. We define ourselves not simply as Americans, but as Vermonters and Virginians, Iowans, and Texans, with state loyalties and distinctive social, cultural, and political values shaped by, and reflective of, the states we live in.

Although federalism is embedded into our political and legal systems, tension between the federal government and the states "is perpetually arising, and will probably continue to arise, as long as our system exists" (*McCulloch v. Maryland (1817)). Power has shifted back and forth between the federal and state governments, while the role of the courts in resolving federal-state conflicts continues to be sharply debated.

Federalism and the Constitution. The American federal system consists of two levels of government, each with authority over the same people but independent of the other. The national, or "federal," government is often considered to be the "upper" level of government, in part because it encompasses the territory of all of the states, in part because of its powers under Article IV, the Supremacy Clause, of the U.S. Constitution. But the federal government is not always the hierarchical superior of the states. Rather, under the Constitution, federal and state governments are coordinate, each supreme within its own sphere, and each having a sphere in which it is supreme.

The federal government is not a creature of the states. Federal officials are directly elected by the voters, not by state governments. The president and vice president are chosen by an electoral college; although the Constitution authorizes the state legislatures to determine presidential electors, the long-standing practice has been for the voters to choose the electors. Under the Constitution as initially adopted, state legislatures did select United States senators, but since the ratification of the Seventeenth Amendment, senators have been popularly elected. Members of the House of Representatives have always been popularly elected.

Similarly, state governments are not creatures of the federal government. Each state government is organized under its own state constitution, adopted by that state, and its leaders are elected by the state's voters. Each state can revise and replace its constitution, enact laws, and raise revenues on its own without authorization from the federal Constitution or the federal government. State constitutions can and do differ from the federal Constitution. For example, many state constitutions authorize voter-initiated legislation, provide for the election of judges and the executive item veto, and require the provision of public education.

The Constitution links federal and state governments even as it separates them. States are basic component units of the federal government: congressional districts are created within the states, senators are elected from states, and the president is chosen by an electoral college composed of electors chosen by the voters of the states. *Constitutional amendments require ratification by supermajority (three-fourths) of the states. The Constitution in turn protects the territorial integrity of the states, and guarantees them a republican form of government and protection against invasion and domestic violence. The Constitution presumes the states will play an important role in domestic governance. In enumerating the powers of the federal government, the Constitution assumes that the states will have responsibility for those areas beyond the scope of the federal authority. The Tenth Amendment confirms that powers "not delegated by the Constitution, nor prohibited by it to the States, are reserved to the States, respectively, or to the people." As the supreme law of the land, the Constitution binds the states as well as the federal government.

Beyond vesting the federal government with exclusive responsibility for national defense, foreign affairs, and the currency, and barring the states from imposing import and export duties, the Constitution does little to demarcate federal and state roles. In many of the areas, most notably the regulation of interstate and foreign commerce, in which the Constitution authorizes federal action, the states continue to enjoy authority as well. When a state law conflicts with a federal law derived from one of the Constitutional grants of federal power, the Supremacy Clause requires that federal law prevail. But in the absence of a conflicting federal measure, the states may pass laws and regulate commercial activity.

The Constitution also governs the relationships between a state and its own citizens and between a state and the citizens of other states. The *Fourteenth Amendment's guarantees of *due process and *equal protection of the laws constrain a state's regulation of its own citizens. Equally, Article IV's *privileges and immunities clause requires states to respect the rights of citizens of other states.

The Role of the Supreme Court. The *Supreme Court has long been an arbiter of federalism conflicts. With respect to "vertical federalism"—disputes concerning the relative scope of federal and state powers—the Court has sought to protect the federal government from state interference, such as state efforts to tax federal instrumentalities (*McCulloch* v. *Maryland* (1819)), while preventing the federal government from acting beyond its authority. A central issue has been the scope of federal power under the Commerce Clause of the U.S. Constitution. For much of the nineteenth century and into the twentieth, the Court sought to confine federal power by defining commerce in terms of the physical movement of goods. In this era of so-called "dual federalism," the Court treated such areas as manufacturing and agriculture as reserved for the states and beyond the scope of federal regulation. These decisions were highly controversial, and often drew criticism, especially as the Court's actions limited the ability of the national government to regulate an increasingly national economy or to address the national economic and social consequences of the Great Depression.

In the 1930s, the Court sharply revised its approach, abandoned dual federalism, and adopted a much broader definition of commerce. Congress could regulate intrastate transactions that indirectly affected interstate commerce and matters that individually had little impact on commerce, but in the aggregate had implications for the national economy. From the mid-1930s into the 1990s, the Supreme Court largely left the allocation of federal and state roles to Congress. Only once in that period did the Court seek to limit federal power by immunizing core state and local government functions from federal wage and hour regulation. But the Court soon concluded there were no judicially workable criteria for determining which state and local government activities were beyond the Commerce power, and abandoned the effort. Instead, the Court embraced the theory famously advanced by Professor Herbert Wechsler ("The Political Safeguards of Federalism," *Columbia Law Review* 54 (1954): 543) that it is the Constitution, not *judicial review, that protects the interests of the states through the national political process.

In the 1990s, however, a narrow Supreme Court majority again sought to impose federalism limitations on Congress. In a series of cases, the Court held that the federal government may not require state and local governments to administer federal policies, and that Congress lacks the power to abrogate state sovereign immunity even in suits brought by individuals to enforce federally created rights. Most significantly, the Court imposed federalism limits on Congress's power to regulate private behavior, invalidating federal laws criminalizing the possession of a firearm within a certain distance of a school, and providing a federal civil remedy for victims of gender-motivated violence. The Court found that these were essentially noncommercial concerns that did not fall within the Constitution's Commerce Clause.

Although these decisions place new outer limits on federal action, the Court has left undisturbed its earlier decisions that expanded the definition of commerce, and recognized broad federal authority to spend federal funds to promote the general welfare. Today, the question of whether the federal or state government should act on economic and social issues such as health care, welfare, or business regulation is largely one to be settled in the political arena rather than by the dictates of constitutional law.

The Court's role with respect to "horizontal federalism"—conflicts among the states on interstate commercial issues—has been less controversial but no less important. Developing the notion of a "dormant" or "negative" Commerce Clause, the Court, starting in the nineteenth century, held that although the Clause is phrased as an affirmative grant of power to Congress, it can also act as a constraint on state action even in the absence of national legislation. The Court has invalidated state laws that it found to discriminate against interstate and out-of-state commerce or that burden the ability of goods, people, and businesses to cross state lines. The Court's decisions thus helped provide the legal framework for the emergence of a national domestic common market.

The Supreme Court also shapes federalism through its use of the Fourteenth Amendment to protect political and *civil rights from state infringement. The structure of state and local *legislatures, criminal justice, public education, and land use are largely state matters, but state autonomy in these areas has been constrained by Supreme Court decisions. When the Court finds that a matter affects constitutional rights, it effectively nationalizes the right in question, and concomitantly weakens state regulatory authority.

The Federal-State Balance. At first, the states dominated the federal system. Writing in the *Federalist Papers*, James Madison observed that the federal government's powers were "few and defined," limited primarily to "external objects, as war, peace, negotiation, and foreign commerce." The states had authority over "all the objects which, in the ordinary course of affairs, concern the lives, liberties and properties of the people, and the internal order, improvement, and prosperity of the State" (*The Federalist*, No. 45). The federal government played only a limited role in peacetime domestic life, and most government power was exercised at the state and local levels. As late as 1927, federal spending accounted for barely one-sixth of total domestic government spending, with the federal government providing few services and engaging in little regulation of domestic activity.

With the New Deal, the Second World War, and the Cold War, the federal government took on major new and costly responsibilities for income security, social welfare, economic stability, and national defense. New technologies in transportation, information, and communications created a national economy, facilitated interstate personal mobility, and contributed to an increasingly national political culture. Greater consciousness of civil and political rights, poverty, and environmental degradation led to calls for national action to address these issues. State governments, many with legislatures gerrymandered to favor rural interests or to exclude minority voters, often came in for criticism as antiquated and out of touch with contemporary concerns. The role of the federal government grew sharply, particularly during the 1960s and 1970s.

The states, however, enjoyed a resurgence in the final decades of the twentieth century. Due in part to federal interventions such as the one person, one vote doctrine, and the Voting Rights Act— which made the states more politically representative of, and accountable to, their own people, as well as to state-generated innovations that reformed the governing capacity of state institutions—the states again began to take the initiative in policymaking, regulation, and the provision of public services. Skepticism about the federal government's expanded role, and the federal budget deficit's effect in constraining federal spending, contributed to a modest shift in power and responsibility back to the states. The state and local share of total government spending rose, and some federal programs were partially devolved to the states.

Fiscal Federalism. Since World War II, the federal government has been an important source of financial support for the states. The federal government obtains about 70 percent of all tax collections—federal, state, and local—and through the income tax it has access to the most dynamic source of revenue growth in our fiscal system. States and localities, by contrast, rely far more on sales and property taxes, which do not grow as rapidly with the economy as the income tax does. Moreover, tax resources vary significantly across the states whereas the federal tax base is nationwide.

The greater federal revenue base has been a substantial factor in the enhanced federal role in domestic governance. Significantly, however, the federal government frequently does not use its funds to take over administration of a policy area, such as education or income assistance for the poor. Instead, it provides funds to the states to support the programs the federal government is interested in. Such federal grants-in-aid may be targeted to promote discrete federal goals, and may be accompanied by conditions and directives that control how the money is spent.

To some extent, this fiscal federalism bolsters the traditional federal system by combining federal funding with continued state administrative control and policymaking discretion. On the other hand, the strings attached to federal funds can and have been used to impose the federal government's agenda on the states. This stirs up state resentment, and may obscure accountability for administrative decisions nominally undertaken by state or local officials but ultimately attributable to federal grant conditions. Even more troubling to the states have been so-called unfunded mandates—that is, federal requirements, often linked to grant programs, that impose new costs on the states but fail to provide the funds necessary to defray those costs.

In the 1990s, the fraction of state budgets composed of federal aid declined, and in many areas the conditions accompanying federal aid were relaxed. The most famous instance of this was the 1996 welfare reform law, which gave the states broad new authority over federally funded welfare programs. Congress also passed the Unfunded Mandates Reform Act, which made it more difficult to impose costly new requirements on the states. On the other hand, most of the preexisting mandates that provoked the law remain on the books. Many of these mandates grow out of concerns with environmental quality, the prevention of discrimination, and workplace safety. Although the targeting of some federal financial assistance may be less fine-tuned than previously, federal grants-in-aid also continue to be accompanied by conditions and restrictions that give the federal government an important, albeit indirect, role in state decision-making.

The Values of Federalism. In the 1950s and 1960s, the defense of *"states' rights" was closely associated with resistance to school integration and opposition to political and civil rights for African Americans. Similarly, opponents of government economic regulation tend to be more critical of the federal government and to support the states. But views on federalism do not necessarily match up with a conservative-liberal continuum. Liberals may support state power when states stake out more aggressive positions on environmental protection or undertake initiatives in health care, campaign finance reform, or gay rights. Conservatives may seek to preempt state action with national rules when states seek to regulate industry.

Although conflicts over federalism are frequently linked to substantive disputes, federalism also raises basic questions of values. Federal action is more likely to be desirable to those who seek to regulate business or promote redistribution. Not only does the federal government have a greater tax base, but state *taxation and *regulation are inevitably constrained by the interstate battle for tax-paying investment, businesses, and residents. States are primarily dependent on state-level resources, so they may be reluctant to raise taxes or impose new regulations because they fear they will lose taxpayers to competing states. As the Supreme Court noted in sustaining a federal unemployment insurance compensation system, the failure of most states to adopt such a program was "not owing, for the most part, to the lack of sympathetic interest. Many held back through alarm, lest, in laying such a toll upon their industries, they would place themselves in a position of economic disadvantage as compared with neighbors or states" (*Steward Machine Co.* v. *Davis* (1937)). Interstate competition imposes a structural limitation on state taxation and business regulation. As a result, many forms of regulation, economic and otherwise, are likely to require a significant federal component. Federal action is also likely to be necessary to address problems such as air and water quality that cross state borders.

On the other hand, state-level action is likely to "increase" "opportunity for citizen involvement in democratic processes," "allow" "for more innovation and experimentation in government," and "make" "government more responsive by putting the States in competition for a mobile citizenry" (*Gregory* v. *Ashcroft* (1991)). State-level decision-making makes it possible for government to be more responsive to the diverse needs, preferences, and circumstances of our heterogeneous society. Different states may take different approaches—reflective of different local views—to the same problems. Indeed, many conflicts over federalism, particularly in the area of political and civil rights, often involve debates over whether a certain matter requires a uniform national standard or whether it can be left to varying state approaches that reflect continuing interstate differences in values, beliefs, and conditions.

Federalism also exemplifies the framers' concern with checks and balances. By creating multiple centers of power, federalism limits the ability of any one government to concentrate power to itself. Federalism may contribute to the protection of liberty even as it makes concerted government action more difficult.

The federal structure thus provides a vital mechanism for combining political power on a continental scale with attention to state-specific preferences, needs, and circumstances. It prevents our internal borders from interfering with personal mobility and economic life, while using those borders to provide opportunities for enhanced participation in political policy-making and for more varied governmental responses to our common problems. By allowing different states to pursue differing policies within a federal union, rather than forcing a national resolution on all issues, federalism avoids some conflicts. But by constantly asking which matters are for federal resolution, which for the states, and what to do when federal and state governments disagree, federalism generates conflicts. These conflicts of federalism are a central part of American democratic self-government.

[*See also* Government, United States]

• Robert A. Goldwin, ed., *A Nation of States: Essays on the American Federal System*, 1963. Aaron Wildavsky, ed., *American Federalism in Perspective*, 1967. George F. Break, *Financing Government in a Federal System*, 1980. J. Richard Aronson and John L. Hilley, *Financing State and Local Governments*, 1986. Daniel J. Elazar, *Exploring Federalism*, 1987. David B. Walker, *The Rebirth of Federalism*, 1995. David L. Shapiro, *Federalism: A Dialogue*, 1995. John D. Donahue, *Disunited States*, 1997. G. Alan Tarr, *Understanding State Constitutions*, 1998.

—Richard Briffault

FEDERAL RULES OF CRIMINAL PROCEDURE. *See* Criminal Procedure, Federal Rules of.

FEDERAL TRADE COMMISSION. *See* Regulation.

FEES, ATTORNEY. Attorneys, like other professionals, charge for their services and are entitled to a reasonable fee for their services. At the same time, however, for many people access to the legal system is a necessity. Increasingly, the complexity of our laws and administrative regulations make it virtually impossible to obtain basic services, such as unemployment compensation, Medicaid, housing, and criminal defense benefits or relief without legal assistance.

An individual's access to legal assistance and an attorney's need for adequate compensation are difficult interests to balance. Efforts by the legal profession to provide access to justice to the poor and unpopular can create ethical dilemmas for individual lawyers. The Comment to the ABA Model Rules of Professional Conduct (RPC) 1.2 states: "Legal representation should not be denied to people who are unable to afford legal services, or whose cause is controversial or the subject of popular disapproval." This Comment suggests an affirmative duty to represent any poor or unpopular client in need of services, but is unenforceable, since no corresponding disciplinary rule exists to compel such representation. Because resources are scarce, representation often is provided as a largely voluntary moral responsibility on the part of individual lawyers. There are no guidelines to enforce when an attorney should accept a client, particularly if doing so would be a financial burden, morally repugnant, or harmful to the attorney's reputation.

RPC 1.5 states that attorney fees must be "reasonable," providing factors that may be employed in the calculation of reasonableness, including: time and labor required, novelty and difficulty of the issues, expertise required, amount involved in the case, and the experience, ability and reputation of the lawyer. Traditionally, the most common form of fee agreement calls for calculation of the fee by multiplying the lawyer's hourly fee rate by the number of hours spent on the case. Recently, fixed or flat rate fee arrangements, where the attorney is paid an agreed upon amount for a particular representation, are becoming more common. The flat fee can promote efficiency and cost-effectiveness, since the attorney receives the same amount regardless of how much time was spent, or how many other attorneys or paralegals worked on the case.

RPC 1.5(c) also authorizes contingent fee arrangements, where the attorney fee is calculated as a percentage of a settlement or judgment for *damages. For example, under a 40 percent contingent fee arrangement, if the client loses the attorney is paid no fee; if the client wins a $10,000 judgment, the attorney is paid $4,000. State courts have placed a number of restrictions on contingent fee agreements, including the following: (1) the agreement must be in writing and state the method by which the fee is to be determined; (2) the client should normally have the option of basing the fee on the attorney's hourly rate; and (3) contingent fees are generally prohibited in criminal and divorce cases.

Contingent fees are one way of providing access to the courts. Individuals with legal claims who are unable to afford an attorney's hourly rate can still bring their claims if a lawyer is willing to take the case and advance the costs in the belief that the client will ultimately prevail. In addition, *class actions provide a mechanism for providing legal access to large numbers of individuals with claims too small to litigate individually. Class actions also expose defendants to *liability they might have avoided, thus improving the deterrent function of civil litigation. Litigating a case that can affect a class of poor people, as opposed to an individual poor person, may be the most efficient use of scarce legal resources. Contingency fee class actions have been criticized when the benefit to class members appears to be negligible compared to the attorney fees earned. Recently, judicial monitoring and restrictions have been established to keep the costs and attorney fees more reasonable.

Another means of providing legal access is through fee-shifting statutes that allow courts to award attorney fees as a portion of or in addition to the plaintiff's damages. Under the "American Rule," all parties in litigation pay their own attorney fees, regardless of who wins. In many other countries, the loser must pay the winner's attorney fees. Those countries do not permit contingent fees. In the leading case of *Alyeska Pipeline Service Co. v. The Wilderness Society* (1975), the United States Supreme Court reaffirmed the "American Rule" and rejected for federal courts a claimed equitable power to award attorney fees to a plaintiff solely on the ground of a presumed public interest in encouraging "private attorneys general" to undertake lawsuits to enforce statutory claims. In response to the Court's requiring Congressional authorization to award attorney fees to the prevailing party, Congress has since provided authorization in over one hundred statutes.

There are also various publicly funded and privately sponsored attempts to improve access to legal services. It is estimated over 60 percent of criminal defendants, all of whom are guaranteed a Sixth Amendment right to *counsel, are unable to retain private counsel. Therefore, state and nonprofit organizations provide public defense services. Access to legal assistance is not constitutionally guaranteed in most civil cases, however, even though the potential impact is often as significant as it is in criminal cases.

Public interest law organizations and privately organized legal assistance organizations under the auspices of the federally funded Legal Services Corporation undertake limited civil representation. Lawyer and law student clinics and nonlawyers can provide community-based, cost effective, and efficient legal services. Many of these nonprofit legal programs are subsidized through state bar IOLTA (Interest on Lawyers' Trust Account) funds. Many lawyers also provide pro bono services to these same organizations. Nevertheless, public interest cases may require substantial resources due to their complexity, novelty, and the financial assets of the adversary, and all these programs are severely underfunded.

Particular fee structures may implicate the ethical conduct of attorneys. The hourly fee may tempt an attorney to drag out the litigation, while the flat-fee attorney might prefer to settle more quickly than might otherwise be desirable. A contingency fee attorney may want to litigate a case in the hope of obtaining a greater recovery, despite the client's desire to settle, or may accept a high volume of quick settlements for inadequate sums in order to provide a good income without investing too much time or effort in each case. Attorneys ideally will resist such temptations and both choose and implement the fee structure most likely to provide access to justice and protect their clients' legitimate interests.

[*See also* Legal Practice, Forms of]

• Stephen Gillers, *The Rights of Lawyers and Clients*, 1979. Robert H. Aronson, *Attorney-Client Fee Arrangements: Regulation and Review*, 1980. Charles Wolfram, *Modern Legal Ethics*, 1986. David Luban, *Lawyers and*

Justice: An Ethical Study, 1988. Stuart M. Speiser, *Lawyers and the American Dream*, 1993.

—Robert H. Aronson

FELONY AND MISDEMEANOR

Historical Background. As a category of legal theory, the *criminal law is primarily concerned with assessing the blame of those who breach criminal rules. That the criminal law pays serious attention to the personal culpability of criminal offenders is a consequence of the distinctive nature of the criminal sanction—punishment. To be morally justifiable, only those who are to blame should be punished, and in a manner proportional in its severity to the degree of the offender's blameworthiness.

Assessing blame, or culpability as it is often described, is a function of two elements: the offender's degree of moral accountability and the offense's seriousness. For centuries, the criminal law attempted to rank the seriousness of offenses in order to dispense punishment in a fair manner.

Early in its origins, the criminal law drew a distinction between two classes of crimes, felonies and misdemeanors, which carried important substantive and procedural implications. The felony and misdemeanor distinction continues to play a variety of important roles in today's law. In addition to felonies and misdemeanors, the common law distinguished a third group of crimes, labeled *"treason."

Under English common law, the crimes of *homicide (eventually divided by statute into murder and manslaughter), *mayhem, *arson, rape, *robbery, *burglary, *larceny, prison breach, and rescue of a felon constituted felonies. Felonies were defined as crimes, the commission of which resulted in *forfeiture of lands and goods in addition to imposition of the death penalty, except for mayhem, which was punished by mutilation. However, while virtually all common law felonies were theoretically capital offenses, the defendant might avoid the death penalty by pleading "benefit of clergy," a device that originally transferred the case from the king's court to an ecclesiastical court, which did not impose the death penalty (see CAPITAL PUNISHMENT). Later, the benefit of clergy became available in the king's courts as well. Originally, only defendants who were members of the clergy could take advantage of the benefit of clergy, but as the device was extended to the king's courts it became available to any defendant who could read. The assumption was that one who could read must be a member of the clergy—that is, a clerk or cleric.

In time, as in the case of murder, for example, Parliament passed statutes eliminating use of the benefit of clergy for certain felonies. Thus, while virtually all *common law felonies were capital offenses, some were more likely than others in practice to result in the imposition of the death penalty. While the original list of common law felonies was short, Parliament eventually added a host of new felonies, so that by *Blackstone's time in the eighteenth century, the list of felonies extended into the hundreds. All of these felonies were punishable by forfeiture of land and goods and, theoretically, by death.

As distinguished from felonies, misdemeanors included at common law any crime that was not a felony (or treason). Generally, these were less serious offenses that did not merit the penalties of forfeiture or death. If the circumstances surrounding the commission of a misdemeanor were particularly egregious, the crime might be upgraded to a felony.

Apart from the severity of the penalty imposed, the felony and misdemeanor distinction was implicated in a variety of procedural rules. While these procedural differences were important historically under early common law, the traditional distinction has now been statutorily abolished in England.

American Jurisdictions. In the United States, the felony and misdemeanor distinction retains considerable vitality. In most American jurisdictions, felonies are often defined as crimes punishable by death or confinement in a *prison or penitentiary. Under such statutes, misdemeanors, in contrast, are generally defined as crimes punishable by fine or incarceration in a local jail, or both. Other jurisdictions draw the distinction explicitly on the basis of severity of punishment, with felonies commonly constituting crimes punishable by death or by imprisonment of more than one year, with misdemeanors being any other crime.

While many American jurisdictions operate within the common law tradition, others adhere to the *Model Penal Code. It is thus useful in understanding the role played by the felony and misdemeanor distinction in the substantive criminal law to separately discuss the common law and Model Penal Code systems.

Common Law Systems. Common law concepts have been statutorily codified in many American jurisdictions. In such systems, some crimes are defined with specific reference to the felony and misdemeanor distinction. For example, the common law "felony-murder rule" has been adopted in most American jurisdictions. Historically under this rule, a person was guilty of murder if he killed another person during the commission or attempted commission of any felony. In time, the common law courts limited application of the rule to "inherently dangerous" felonies. In many American jurisdictions, statutes list the potential predicate felonies, usually focusing on such dangerous crimes as rape, robbery, arson, and *kidnapping. In some jurisdictions, statutory lists are used in the definition of first-degree felony-murder, leaving open the possibility of prosecution for second-degree felony-murder if an offender kills while committing or attempting felonies not listed in the statute, as long as the unlisted felony is itself deemed "inherently dangerous."

Some jurisdictions embrace a rule analogous to felony-murder, variously labeled the "misdemeanor-manslaughter" or "unlawful act manslaughter" rule. Under the strictest form of this doctrine, an accidental homicide occurring during the commission of any misdemeanor constitutes involuntary manslaughter. However, some jurisdictions limit the rule to inherently dangerous misdemeanors, while others restrict its application to *mala in se* (conduct wrong on its face) misdemeanors, leaving *mala prohibitum* (conduct wrong only because legally proscribed) misdemeanors outside the scope of the rule.

Beyond homicide, the felony and misdemeanor distinction is used in the definition of a variety of other crimes. Burglary, for example, is traditionally defined as "breaking and entering the dwelling house of another at night with the intent to commit a *felony* therein." At common law, it is a crime to "compound a felony"—that is to agree not to prosecute or to keep quiet about a felony one knows has been committed. Moreover, at common law, parties involved in felonies are divided into "principals" and "accessories," with various consequences flowing therefrom, while all parties to misdemeanors are considered principals. Statutes sometimes punish *conspiracy or attempt to commit a felony more severely than if those crimes involve misdemeanors.

Recently, many American jurisdictions have enacted so-called "three strikes" laws, under which a person suspected of committing a felony can be charged and subjected to enhanced punishment upon conviction if he has been previously convicted of two or more felonies—that is, already had two or more "strikes." The statutes are limited to the commission of felonies, and are not triggered by prior convictions for misdemeanors. Some statutes spell out specific felonies that are necessary for strikes under the three-strike law. Some statutes require that the predicate felonies be "violent," while others permit statutory application in the context of all felonies. In jurisdictions without specific three-strike laws, sentencing procedures often permit prior felony (but not misdemeanor) convictions to be taken into account by judges in exercising sentencing discretion. Some jurisdictions have enacted statutes specifying that multiple convictions for the same misdemeanor constitute a felony.

The Model Penal Code System. Many American states have adopted, in whole or in part, the Model Penal Code. This classifies crimes as "felonies" (offenses punishable by death or imprisonment in excess of one year), "misdemeanors" (offenses so designated by the Code), and "petty misdemeanors" (offenses punishable by imprisonment for a maximum of less than one year). The Code involves a fourth category, "violations," which are offenses punishable by fine, or fine and forfeiture only, and do not constitute "crimes" under the Code system.

The Code divides felonies for sentencing purposes into three degrees. Felonies of the first degree are punished by a minimum of one to ten years imprisonment and a maximum of life imprisonment. Felonies of the second degree are punished by a minimum of one to three years imprisonment and a maximum of ten years imprisonment. Felonies of the third degree are punished by a minimum of one to two years and a maximum of five years imprisonment.

The Code allows for "extended terms" of imprisonment for the three degrees of felonies for "persistent offenders, professional criminals," offenders with drug or alcohol problems that require rehabilitative treatment "for a substantial period of time," and "multiple offenders." Under an alternative provision, the Code permits the death penalty for murder in certain circumstances in lieu of the felony first-degree penalty.

The Code allows imprisonment of up to one year for "misdemeanors," and up to thirty days for "petty misdemeanors." Similar to its treatment of felonies, the Code allows for extended periods of imprisonment for specially designated misdemeanants.

The Code rejects the felony-murder and misdemeanor-manslaughter doctrines, and defines burglary in terms of entering a building with the purpose of committing "a crime" rather than "a felony," as at common law. Under the Code, "compounding" is a crime if one agrees not to report any "offense," while compounding under some common law systems is limited to "felony" situations. The Model Penal Code, unlike the common law, draws no distinction between principals and accessories on the basis of whether the crime involved is a felony or misdemeanor, nor does the Code address the felony and misdemeanor distinction in its attempt and conspiracy provisions. The Code does not provide a "three-strike law."

Procedural Implications. The felony and misdemeanor distinction is relevant in a variety of procedural contexts. At common law, persons could be arrested without a warrant as long as the person making the *arrest had "reasonable grounds to believe" that a *felony* had been committed and that the person to be arrested had committed it. In the misdemeanor context, however, the common law rule required a warrant for an arrest, except in cases of breach of the peace occurring in the arresting officer's presence. The common law rule continues to be followed today, at least with regard to felony arrests. The United States Supreme Court has upheld the constitutionality of the felony arrest rule when the warrantless arrest takes place in public (*United States v. Watson* (1976)).

The jurisdiction of criminal courts is often defined in terms of whether the crime charged is a felony or misdemeanor. In some jurisdictions, felony charges must be initiated by grand jury indictment, whereas misdemeanors may be prosecuted by prosecutorial "information." Witnesses testifying in their own behalf may be impeached in some jurisdictions on the basis of a prior conviction for a felony, but not for a misdemeanor. Finally, accused felons must generally be present at their trials, but persons accused of misdemeanors may sometimes agree to be tried in their absence.

In the context of jury trials, the U.S. Supreme Court has held that while the right to trial by *jury is fundamental, it does not extend to "petty offenses," defined by the court as offenses punishable by imprisonment for six months or less (*Bloom v. Illinois* (1968)). In some jurisdictions, "petty offenses" may be synonymous with misdemeanors.

Outside the Criminal Law. The felony and misdemeanor distinction has important implications outside the area of criminal law and procedure. Felony (but not misdemeanor) convictions disqualify persons from holding public office in some jurisdictions. Conviction of a felony may also be grounds for losing the right to vote, disqualification from serving on a jury, or prohibition from practicing law. Moreover, in those jurisdictions re-

taining fault principles for divorce, conviction of a felony constitutes such a ground.

[*See also* Criminal Law Principles; Criminal Punishments]

• Theodore F. T. Plucknett, *A Concise History of the Common Law,* 5th ed., 1956. Glanville Williams, *Criminal Law, The General Part,* 2d ed., 1978. Rollin Perkins and Ronald N. Boyce, *Criminal Law,* 3rd ed., 1982. Joshua Dressler, *Understanding Criminal Law,* 2d ed., 1995. Wayne R. LaFave, *Criminal Law,* 3rd ed., 2000.

—Martin R. Gardner

FEMINIST LEGAL THEORY. During the 1960s, a women's movement reemerged in the United States with close connections to the civil rights movement, the antiwar movement, and other movements of the Left. As a result of the new wave of feminism, the number of women in law schools as students and as faculty increased dramatically in the 1970s. And for the first time, law schools offered courses on women and the law. During this initial period, feminist scholarship tended to be doctrinal, with little theory beyond the important insight that stereotypes and rigid sex roles are harmful, but it paved the way for the theoretical work which followed.

In the twenty-first century, there are many strands of feminist legal theory in the United States. All have been influenced by the *legal realist and *critical legal studies movements and by European postmodernism. Feminists agree with legal realists and critical legal scholars that law is politics. Feminists, like legal realists, critical legal scholars, and postmodern theorists see law as socially created out of categories and dichotomies that have little to do with reality and much to do with maintaining inequality. For example, all these intellectual approaches see the private–public dichotomy, which is central in traditional liberal legal thought in the United States, as not descriptive of a reality in which the two spheres are inextricably intertwined, and as conservative (supporting existing power structures enforcing much injustice, such as the existing distribution of property and women's work without pay in their own homes, seem beyond the reach of legitimate government).

Feminist legal theory in the United States began in 1979 with the publication of Catharine MacKinnon's first book, *Sexual Harassment of Working Women,* which not only offered a critique of formal equality but also an alternative. MacKinnon notes that formal equality gives rights only to women who look like men, and what it gives these unusual women is the right to equal treatment un-

der rules developed by and for men. Formal equality cannot give women the rights women need
when men do not share their needs. Further, as
MacKinnon points out in her 1987 book *Feminism
Unmodified,* men and women tend not to be similarly situated; if half the population is elevated
and the other half is denigrated, we are unlikely
to have a society without differences between the
sexes.

For MacKinnon, the root or cause of inequality
is sexuality as currently structured to eroticize
women's subordination. Although rigid sex roles
and norms constrain individual men as well as individual women, men come out on top, with sexual pleasure and much of social life defined in
terms of their needs and desires. MacKinnon proposes a dominance approach to determine
whether a rule or policy discriminates on the basis
of sex: the key question is not whether it treats
similarly situated women and men differently, but
whether it contributes to women's subordination
to men. Although formal equality dominates
American culture and courts in discussions of sex
*discrimination, MacKinnon's dominance ap-
proach is widely used within the academy.

Relational (or cultural) feminism can be traced
to the publication of Carol Gilligan's influential
book *In a Different Voice: Psychological Theory and
Women's Development* (1982). Gilligan posits an
alternative to the dominant method of resolving
moral dilemmas—application of abstract rules—
an alternative with a focus on relationships and
how best to preserve them in concrete situations.
Gilligan associates this different, more relational,
voice with women.

Relational feminism in legal theory today
stresses that one of the causes of inequality between women and men is undervaluation of feminine traits, such as nurturing, empathy, and caring for others, and overvaluation of masculine
traits, such as autonomy, aggression, and being
unemotional. Most women, unlike most men,
continue to spend significant portions of their
lives as primary caretakers of dependents, work of
great value but either unpaid (within the family)
or underpaid. Feminists in a variety of disciplines
have increasingly voiced the concern that without
better social supports for caretakers, women will
remain unequal. European countries with universal health care, publicly financed day care for pre-
school children, and other family supports, are often used as models (see Mary Becker, "Towards a
Progressive Constitution," *Fordham Law Review*
(2001): 2007).

Critical race feminism emerged during the
1980s as a critique of formal equality, dominance
theory, and relational feminism. Critical race feminists note that much feminism, though purporting to speak for all women, actually voices the
needs and concerns of privileged white women.
For women of color, racism, sexism, and other
problems (such as immigration status) interact in
complex ways, making solutions that may work
for privileged women of little relevance to their far
more pressing needs (see Kimberlé Crenshaw,
"Demarginalizing the Intersection of Race and
Sex," *University of Chicago Legal Forum* (1989):
139). Some of this work has had a postmodern
slant, arguing that the privileged white theorists
have been "essentialist," viewing all women as the
same (see Angela P. Harris, "Race and Essentialism in Feminist Legal Theory: A Black Feminist
Critique of Antidiscrimination Doctrine, Feminist
Theory and Antiracist Politics," *Stanford Law Review* (1990): 581).

Although formal equality began with little theory, some feminists have used postmodernism to
defend its lack. Postmodernism, for example, provides tools for deconstructing categories and dichotomies. Indeed, one strand of postmodern
feminism argues for formal equality on the ground
that women and men are not different in any essential way; existing differences are socially constructed. Any legal rule, however, recognizing differences is necessarily dangerous for women since
legal recognition of difference can be used to justify inequality and restrict women to traditional
roles. Yet another strand of postmodern feminism
in the United States tends to be entirely critical
both of law and of all proposals for reform
through law.

[*See also* Gender and Law]

• Victoria Nourse, "Passion's Progress: Modern Law Reform and the Provocation Defense," *Yale Law Journal*
(1997): 1331. Dorothy Roberts, *Killing The Black Body,*
1997. Robin West, *Caring for Justice,* 1997. Joan C. Williams, *Unbending Gender: Why Family and Work Conflict
and What To Do About It,* 2000. Mary Becker, Cynthia
Bowman, and Morrison Torrey, *Feminist Jurisprudence:
Taking Women Seriously,* 2d ed., 2001.

—Mary Becker

FEUDING. *See* Extralegality; Mob Violence and
Vigilantism.

FIELD, DAVID DUDLEY, JR. (13 February 1805–
13 April 1894), New York attorney, was born in
Haddam, Connecticut. Field attended Williams
College until 1824 when he was suspended. Ad-
mitted to the bar in 1828, Field practiced with
Robert Sedgwick and, at various times, with other

partners including his brother Stephen and his son David Dudley III.

A Jacksonian Democrat, Field joined the "Barnburner" faction of the party, which in 1849 opposed slavery and supported Martin Van Buren, the "Free-Soil" candidate for president. In 1856 he supported John C. Frémont, the Republican Party's first presidential candidate. In 1860 Field helped secure the Republican presidential nomination for Abraham *Lincoln. With Lincoln's victory, Field gained influence in the administration and used it to assure his brother Stephen's appointment to the U.S. Supreme Court.

After the Civil War, Field appeared in several significant cases before the Supreme Court. In *Ex parte Milligan* (1866) and *Ex parte McCardle* (1867) he argued against suspension of writ of *habeas corpus and trial of civilians by military tribunals. In *Cummings* v. *Missouri* (1867) he helped convince the Court to overrule Missouri's test oath law. In *U.S.* v. *Cruikshank* (1876), opposing the Enforcement Act of 1870, he argued that the *Fourteenth Amendment protected citizens from the states but not from the acts of private individuals. These cases demonstrated a commitment to liberty but they also revealed Field's disenchantment with the "Radical Republican" plan for Reconstruction. By 1876, when he was elected to one term in Congress, Field returned to his Democratic roots.

Perhaps Field is best known as a law reformer. He was a champion of *codification, a movement to supplant the complicated system of *common law inherited from England with a simpler set of procedural and substantive legal codes. These codes eventually became known as the Field Codes. Ironically, although many states adopted codification, Field was not fully successful in his home state of New York.

Field's career also had a darker side. He was said to be part of a group that in 1863 swindled John Frémont out of his California estate. He represented Jay Gould and Jim Fisk during the Erie Wars and their attempt to corner the gold market. Field defended Boss William Tweed on charges of corruption. Although he argued that an attorney should not be judged on the basis of the people he represents, Field made numerous enemies in political and legal circles. More than one critic complained that Field would take retainers from Satan himself. Nevertheless, by the end of his life David Dudley Field was one of the wealthiest and most prominent lawyers in New York.

• Duan van Ee, *David Dudley Field and the Reconstruction of the Law*, 1986. Philip J. Bergan, *David Dudley*

Field: A Lawyer's Life*, in *The Fields and The Law* (Joseph Franasaek et al, eds.), 1986. Henry M. Field, *The Life of David Dudley Field*, rpt., 1995.   —Paul Kens

FIELD, STEPHEN JOHNSON (1816–1899), associate justice of the U.S. *Supreme Court, was born in Haddam, Connecticut, to David Dudley Field, Sr. and Submit Dickinson. He married Sue Virginia Swearingen in 1859. They had no children.

Field graduated from Williams College in 1837. He studied law in New York with his brother David Dudley Field, and later joined his brother's practice. He left New York for the California Gold Rush in 1849, where he settled in the new town of Marysville. He was immediately elected to the Mexican-style office of Alcalde, a position that combined the functions of judge and mayor. Field, a Democrat, won election to the California Supreme Court in 1857, and became chief justice in 1859. In March 1863, when Congress enlarged the U.S. Supreme Court, President *Lincoln appointed Field as the tenth justice.

Although Field wrote opinions on a wide variety of topics, his legacy lies in promoting a doctrine of entrepreneurial liberty that would significantly limit government's power to regulate the economy. His innovative dissent in *The Slaughter-House Cases* (1873) contained the embryo of "liberty of contract," a theory that the *Fourteenth Amendment's protection of *liberty and *property established a constitutional right to enter into virtually any *contract one might desire. In the landmark case *Munn* v. *Illinois* (1877) he dissented from the majority ruling that government may regulate business "affected with public interest."

The doctrine that Field developed would restrict federal *regulation by narrowly construing Congress's power. Moreover, it would limit state power to enact only those regulations that promoted Victorian morality, promoted public health and safety, provided for orderly settlement of disputes, and smoothed the flow of commerce. Field's opinions reflected a distrust of majority rule and admiration of the law. He opposed laws in which he detected any undue interference with economic freedom, referring to them as "class legislation." He insisted that the court, rather than the legislature, had the final right to determine what regulations were legitimate.

Field resigned from the Court on 1 December 1897. He had spent a record thirty-four years on the Court, outlasting eight presidents and three chief justices.

[*See also* Due Process: Substantive]

• Carl Brent Swisher, *Stephen J. Field: Craftsman of the Law*, 1930. Paul Kens, *Justice Stephen Field: Shaping Liberty from the Gold Rush to the Gilded Age*, 1997.

—Paul Kens

FIFTH AMENDMENT. *See* Self-Incrimination, Privilege Against.

FILM. *See* Arts, Popular Culture, and Law: Entertainment Law; Media and the Law.

FINES. *See* Criminal Punishments.

FIRMS, LAW. The American law firm has profoundly influenced the evolution of the legal profession, exercised a significant influence on the nation's political, economic, social, and cultural life, and served as a model for the delivery of legal services abroad.

Historical Development. Until the late nineteenth century, most American *lawyers either worked alone or in partnership with no more than a few other attorneys. Even when lawyers were partners, their association usually involved little more than the sharing of overhead expenses such as office space and did not result in any significant division of labor. The rise of large-scale industrial and commercial enterprises, particularly railroads, created the need for regular delivery of highly sophisticated, labor-intensive *legal services that far exceeded the capacity of existing law offices. At first, large corporations hired staff attorneys to perform their burgeoning legal work. During the late nineteenth century, legal partnerships began to expand the scope of their operations to accommodate the growing needs of corporations.

The new law firm model was pioneered early in the twentieth century, by New York attorney Paul D. *Cravath. Shortly after joining a small firm that traced its origins to 1819, Cravath reorganized the firm to facilitate its ability to provide high-quality and cost-efficient legal services for large corporations. Under the so-called Cravath system, lawyers coordinated their work more closely, providing a full array of services to their corporate clients. Cravath also developed a distinctive procedure for recruitment, training, and promotion of lawyers. Rather than hiring experienced lawyers who would immediately become partners, Cravath hired recent graduates of prestigious law schools, who were slowly and carefully initiated into the intricacies of practice while they worked as salaried employees, or *associates*. Although they received little compensation and were expected to work long hours, their reward for diligent service was promotion to partnership. The Cravath system

was quickly emulated by other firms in New York before spreading to other major cities and finally to any town big enough to support a large firm.

The standardization of practices in large law firms was facilitated by the growth of professional organizations, particularly the *American Bar Association (founded in 1887). The ABA and its state and local counterparts drew a disproportionate share of their membership from the elite bar. Beginning in 1908, the ABA promulgated codes of *ethics that reflected the culture of large urban law firms. In particular, the prohibitions on advertising and tight restrictions on contingent fees reflected the distaste of bar leaders for the more competitive and presumably less dignified practices of solo practitioners who did not enjoy a secure base of wealthy clients.

Large law firms flourished as corporate business enterprises that valued their services continued to expand throughout most of the twentieth century. The growth of large firms during the twentieth century reflected the growth of the regulatory state. Landmark legislation such as the Pure Food and Drug Act of 1906, the Federal Employers Liability Act of 1912, the Clayton Antitrust Act of 1914, the Securities Act of 1933, the Securities Exchange Act of 1934, the Social Security Act of 1935, the Civil Rights Act of 1964, the Occupational Safety and Health Act of 1970, and the Employee Retirement Income Security Act of 1975 (ERISA) created the need for large numbers of lawyers to interpret such legislation for business enterprises and to litigate conflicts arising under the laws. The increase of income tax rates during most of the twentieth century and the steady growth of the complexity of federal and state tax codes likewise increased the need for highly trained attorneys. Between 1967 and 1992, the percentage of legal services consumed by businesses increased from 39 percent to 51 percent, and the income of law firms, adjusted for inflation, nearly doubled.

The proportion of lawyers in private practice who worked in law firms increased from one-third in 1960 to more than half by 2000, while the number of lawyers engaged in law firm practice increased from 70,000 to nearly 400,000. The number of lawyers working in firms with more than fifty lawyers increased from a few thousand in 1960 to 28,000 in 1980 to more than one hundred thousand by 2000. Meanwhile, the number of firms having more than fifty lawyers expanded from 287 in 1980 to 702 in 1995.

The growth of large firms is inhibited in part by ethics rules that limit the extent to which a firm is permitted to represent clients with conflicting interests. Although firms usually may represent such clients if the firm obtains the consent of the client, representation of a new client with a divergent interest may erode good relations between the first client and the firm even if the original client is willing to provide consent. If a firm finds that it represents clients that have conflicting interests, the firm normally must withdraw from representation of both clients. Some courts in some instances have ameliorated the harshness of these rules by permitting a firm to represent clients with conflicting interests if the firm builds a "Chinese wall" to separate the flow of information between attorneys who represent clients with conflicting interests.

Organization. The growth of firm size has required many firms to adopt a more hierarchical and professional management system that has departed from the consensus and collegiality that traditionally characterized law firms. Some firms have hired professional lay managers, although many firms have found that such managers have difficulty in exercising authority over attorneys who own the firm.

Until recently, most law firms were organized as partnerships rather than as *corporations, in part because corporate income is taxed twice insofar as a corporation itself must pay tax before it passes taxable income to its shareholders. Unlike a corporation, however, a partnership does not limit the liability of its principals. As malpractice actions increased during the 1980s and 1990s, all fifty states and the District of Columbia enacted legislation to permit lawyers and other professionals to form limited liability partnerships, known as LLPs, which shield partners from vicarious liability for the negligence of their fellow partners. Similarly, some law firms have availed themselves of recent state laws that permit professionals to form limited liability corporations, or LLCs, that afford even more protection than LLPs because they also relieve lawyers from personal liability for the debts of the firm.

During recent years, some attorneys have advocated the development of *multidisciplinary practices*, or MDPs, in which lawyers would enter into partnership with other professionals, such as accountants or investment advisors, to provide a fuller and more closely coordinated range of services to clients. Legislatures and bar associations have opposed such a step because they fear that MDPs would debase ethical standards by eroding confidentiality and creating conflicts of interest.

Although lawyers at large firms traditionally have prided themselves on being generalists rather than specialists, the growing need for specialization has led many attorneys to develop expertise on particular subjects, such as corporate mergers, or particular industries, such as railroads or utilities. Law firms typically are divided into several relatively informal departments in which attorneys specialize in business transactions, litigation, trust and estates, and tax.

The growing complexity and competitiveness of law firms also has been reflected in the growing specialization of attorneys. Since the 1980s, there has been a jump in the number of so-called boutique law firms that concentrate on defined specialties such as intellectual property or entertainment law. These firms generally remain small, typically having no more than twenty lawyers.

The decision of the U.S. Supreme Court in *Bates v. State Bar of Arizona* (1977) to relax prohibitions on advertising provided an impetus for the establishment of several large national law firms that have established a large number of small branch offices that provide counsel for relatively simple, often routine matters such as divorces, bankruptcies, wills, and personal injury and criminal cases for clients of modest means. These firms sometimes employ a management company to arrange the purchase of supplies, equipment, real estate, and advertising. Local attorneys typically are paid a salary and receive profits from business that they generate.

Although clients traditionally remained with the same firm for generations and even large corporations often gave nearly all their business to one firm, client loyalty began to erode during the 1980s as many companies increasingly emphasized results and cost-efficiency at the expense of long-standing personal ties. Client stability also was affected by the growth of corporate mergers since assignments to law firms were often reshuffled in the wake of a merger. The demise or decline of many manufacturing businesses also diminished the client bases of many law firms.

The decline of old client bases and the erosion of old concepts of client loyalty occurred at the same time that new businesses specializing in services, information, or technology were searching for firms to satisfy their heavy need for legal assistance. The result was a sharp increase in the competitiveness of law firms after 1980, particularly since businesses in the "new economy" did not feel bound by traditional concepts of long-term loyalty to law firms.

Services. Created largely to serve corporations, large firms generally have represented individuals only if they were wealthy and even then usually only in connection with trusts and estate work. Firms have tended to eschew cases involving such matters as divorce or personal injuries as déclassé, although some firms defend their corporate clients in *tort actions and sometimes represent officers of the corporations or wealthy individuals in divorce or tort actions. The bulk of work at large firms has consisted of rendering advice to clients about business transactions and ways to avoid litigation. Although litigation became a much more prominent feature of law firm practice during the 1970s as lawsuits among major corporations grew more common, most large firms engaged primarily in the pretrial aspects of protracted litigation that usually culminated in a settlement rather than trial.

Large firms pride themselves on their professional autonomy, perceiving themselves as performing a useful societal function by restraining their clients from pursuing illegal or antisocial actions and policies. Critics of large firms, however, have argued that most firms are so dependent on their wealthy and powerful clients for business that they exercise little meaningful influence over their clients, and that smaller firms or solo practitioners who represent individuals may be more independent. Critics of big firm practice also contend that lawyers at large firms so internalize the norms of their clients that they may be unaware of their own lack of professional autonomy.

In order to facilitate professional independence, firms attempt to develop a broad base of clients, avoiding dependency on any particular client. Although the most prominent client at some firms provide less than 10 percent of their revenue, a broad client base does not necessarily promote professional autonomy because individual partners often work almost wholly for a single client or a small group of clients.

Since partners are closely involved with the business affairs of their clients, they often serve as members of their clients' boards of directors. Lawyers therefore may become intimately involved in helping their clients to make business decisions and to establish corporate policy. Although some critics have warned that such close association with clients may diminish an attorney's professional judgment, advocates of such service contend that attorneys have often acted as a social conscience for large corporations and have succeeded in persuading their clients to enact measures that promote the public interest.

Lawyers at large firms traditionally have acted as intermediaries between government and private enterprise. In addition to guiding corporations through mazes of state and federal regulations, some law firms, particularly those in state capitals and in Washington, help to provide their clients with access to public officials and lobby for the enactment of legislation. Many lawyers move through the "revolving door," going back and forth between government positions and private practice at various times during their careers and using governmental service as a means of obtaining a lucrative partnership at a law firm, or making a law firm their base from which to launch a political career. A number of presidents and presidential candidates, including Charles Evans Hughes, John W. Davis, Franklin D. Roosevelt, Wendell Willkie, Thomas E. Dewey, Adlai E. Stevenson, Richard M. Nixon, and Walter F. Mondale, have held partnerships in prestigious law firms at various stages of their careers. Numerous partners at large firms, notably Abe Fortas, John J. McCloy, and Clark Clifford, have acted as key presidential advisors. A substantial number of Cabinet officers and most federal judges are drawn from the ranks of big firm partners.

Large firms have helped to shape the development of the law by crafting arguments in high profile cases that often result in precedent-making judicial decisions. Members of large law firms also are prominent in various organizations that influence legal development and reform, including national, state, and local *bar associations, and the *American Law Institute.

Recruitment, Training, and Promotion. Since law firms perform labor-intensive services, they have a constant need to efficiently recruit and train personnel. Prior to 1980, most large firms recruited attorneys only from a small number of law schools, typically the six or eight most elite national schools and the better schools in a firm's locality. The subsequent burgeoning of large firms while law school enrollment has remained stable has forced even the most elite firms to hire associates from a much broader range of schools and with lower rankings in their law school classes.

Associates at large firms traditionally have been willing to work long and unpredictable hours even though their salaries have not been differentiated for productivity because they hoped to become a partner. In order to stimulate the incentive of associates to work hard to become partners, firms have needed to promote a reasonable proportion of associates to partnership, which has required many firms to expand the size of their partnerships beyond levels that would maximize partner compensation.

Associates typically serve for six to eight years before a partnership decision is made. In the larger firms, only about 10 percent of associates become partners. The number of associates who become partner tends to be inversely proportional to the size of the firm and the size of the city in which the firm is located. Although senior attorneys in large firms traditionally have helped to train associates, many lawyers during recent years have complained that firms neglect such training, partly because partners are too busy generating and servicing business and administering the law firm. Critics of firms contend that such neglect has adversely affected clients since poorly trained associates often provide inferior or inefficient services. Some firms have tried to remedy the problem by assigning new associates to partners who are supposed to act as mentors.

Law firms traditionally helped associates who failed to become partner to find other jobs, particularly with clients. Placement of a former associate as in-house counsel with a client helped to assure that such client would continue to send business to the firm. Since the late 1970s, associates often have used executive recruitment agencies to find other jobs. By 2000, there were hundreds of legal recruitment firms.

Until the 1960s, law firms often permanently retained lawyers who failed to become partner. Such "permanent associates" later began to disappear as law firms concluded that the retention of such lawyers was bad for morale. Since the 1980s, however, more firms have given permanent tenure to attorneys who have useful technical skills but who lack the social skills to bring in business or interact with clients.

During recent decades, law firms increasingly have used the services of nonlawyers to assist with work that does not require law school training, such as organizing documents and conducting factual investigations. The number of such *paralegals has increased rapidly, to more than one hundred thousand by 2000. The background and training of paralegals differs widely. Some have no previous experience, while others are graduates of paralegal training courses and are certified by either of two paralegal organizations.

In order to cut costs, many law firms during the 1990s began to hire lawyers provided by agencies to work on a temporary basis during times of heavy work volume. For more sophisticated work, independent agencies have begun to offer legal research assistance to law firms on an ad hoc basis, using the services of highly trained specialists such as law professors who work as independent contractors for the research agencies under the supervision of lawyer-editors. Technological advances, particularly *computerized legal research and document delivery, have reduced the need for a permanent labor force insofar as attorneys may easily work in locations other than a law office.

The increasing competitiveness of law firms has been manifest in the large numbers of associates or partners who are laterally hired by other firms, a practice that was largely taboo until the early 1980s. Law firms also became much less tolerant of partners whose productivity declined, often reducing their compensation or forcing them into early retirement. Dismissal of partners, highly uncommon as late as 1980, became routine at many firms. Meanwhile, mergers among firms also became more common, and many of the old-line firms dissolved because of their inability to adjust to new business conditions, particularly the increasing mobility of clients.

Diversity. The social, ethnic, and gender composition of law firms has changed significantly during recent decades, with firms becoming more meritocratic. Until the 1950s, a disproportionate majority of the attorneys at elite firms were white Protestant males. Traditional barriers against Roman Catholics and Jews have subsequently almost vanished as the upward mobility of these groups removed prejudices based on social class, while the rapid diminution of religious and ethnic prejudices in society after World War II eroded bias based on religion and ethnicity. Large firms also suspended longtime unwritten prohibitions against non-whites and many began to actively recruit racial minorities as nonwhites entered law schools in larger numbers.

Opportunities for women also have rapidly expanded during recent decades as enrollment of women in law schools has increased from less than 3 percent in 1960 to nearly 50 percent in 2000, when 23 percent of all lawyers were women. Women lawyers, who as recently as the 1950s often were offered jobs only as secretaries in some large firms, now are routinely hired. They tend to join large firms in proportions only slightly lower than their numbers, but are proportionately less likely than men to become partners. By 2000, only 15 percent of the partners in firms with more than 250 lawyers were women, a disparity that may reflect continuing prejudices against women and the substantial familial responsibilities of many women. Although many firms have allowed women with young children to work part-time, such an arrangement usually removes the women from the partnership track or lengthens the timetable for partnership consideration.

Although large firms no longer discriminate on the basis of race, class, or gender, members of traditionally disadvantaged groups still may have difficulty rising in firms because they lack the social contacts that would help them to bring significant business to the firm. By 1996, only 1 percent of the partners at the nation's 250 largest law firms were African American, and only two percent were Asian American or nonwhite Hispanic. Moreover, black partners were less likely to be "equity" partners in firms having two-tiered partnerships.

Compensation. Large law firms typically receive substantial *fees for their services. Clients often are expected to pay a retainer fee before the firm performs any work. Such a fee may be nonrefundable, or it may be applied against future legal bills. Until the 1960s, most firms billed their clients irregularly, often with no more description of the work performed than the cryptic "for services rendered." After management experts argued that lawyers could enhance their compensation by keeping time records, large firms began to bill attorney services monthly at an hourly rate. Clients increasingly have demanded detailed accounts of how attorneys spend their time. Since the late 1980s, many clients have complained about various abuses of hourly billing, particularly bill padding and work of questionable utility that may be performed more to inflate bills than to serve the actual needs of clients. Widespread complaints about billing abuses stimulated the growth of a legal audit industry that has flourished since the 1990s. Meanwhile, many large corporations have attempted to control costs by promulgating "billing guidelines" that prescribe terms and conditions for billing practices and limit the amount of time or resources that firms are permitted to spend on certain types of activities.

Concerns about abuse of hourly billing during the 1990s led some clients to request their attorneys to charge contingent fees in litigation. Since many clients of large firms are defendants, some firms began to experiment with so-called reverse contingent fees, which enable a firm to recover a fee that is inversely proportional to the amount that a defendant client has to pay to the plaintiff. Many clients, however, continue to believe that contingent fees tend to erode an attorney's independence of judgment since he has a stake in the outcome of a lawsuit.

Disillusionment with hourly billing also increased the use of so-called flat fees, by which a client pays a predetermined sum for representation in a lawsuit or transaction, and task-based billing, by which a client pays for discrete legal services within a lawsuit or transaction. These alternatives, however, have remained relatively uncommon because of the inherent difficulty of calculating a reasonable fee before the work is actually performed. Moreover, flat fees and task-based fees may encourage attorneys to perform too little work, although professional pride and the advantages of satisfying the client should discourage such an abuse. Some clients have also experimented with so-called value billing, which blends an hourly rate with a premium if an attorney achieves superior results. This type of billing has remained rare because of the difficulty of assessing the amount of premium and the likelihood of conflicts between attorneys and clients in retrospective imposition of a fee. Flaws in the various alternatives to hourly billing have ensured that more than 90 percent of bills presented by large firms to corporate clients are based on an hourly rate.

Partner compensation typically is calculated largely on the basis of the revenue that the partner brings to the firm through client development or through billings. Some partners are predominately "rainmakers" who generate business but who perform few actual legal services, while others may bring in little or no business and spend their time servicing the clients brought into the firm by other partners. Larger firms typically can accommodate more partners who fail to generate business. In many firms, only partners who generate significant amount of business become *equity partners*, who divide the profits or losses of the firm among themselves and own the firm's assets. Other partners in firms having a two-tiered partnership are *income partners*, who merely receive a stipend for their services. In many firms, some attorneys serve as "of counsel," a salaried position usually reserved for elder attorneys who are retired partners or serve as a special liaison with a particular client.

Partnership compensation outpaced inflation throughout the 1990s, when shares of more than one million dollars per year became relatively common during an economic boom that increased the need for legal services. In 2000, the compensation of partners at the nation's hundred most profitable law firms averaged nearly $750,000.

The work of associates is "leveraged" insofar as approximately one-third of the revenue generated by an associate is allocated to partnership compensation, with one-third paying the associate's salary and one-third covering overhead. During recent years, many firms have increased the partner-to-associate ratio in an effort to enhance partner compensation.

Until well into the twentieth century, attorneys often worked for no compensation during their first few years as clerks in large firms and at relatively small salaries until they attained partnership. Since large firms drew most of their attorneys from the upper classes, neophyte attorneys generally were expected to live on independent means. By the middle of the twentieth century, the erosion of class barriers and the increased competition for legal talent required law firms to provide comfortable salaries for even the most junior associates. The increased competition for legal talent has resulted in salary increases that have much exceeded the cost of living. The starting salary for new associates in leading firms in 2000 was typically $125,000.

Public Roles. Attorneys at large firms traditionally have exercised important public roles. In addition to the many law firm partners who have been active in politics or have served as advisors to elected officials, partners also have been publicly prominent as leaders of local and national charitable and civic organizations, particularly hospitals, art museums, and symphony orchestras. In addition to providing legal services, lawyers have used their ties with wealthy clients to facilitate fund-raising.

Beginning in the early twentieth century, law firms began to support legal aid clinics. Emphasis on such *pro bono* work markedly increased during the 1960s, when it became mandatory at many large firms, reflecting society's growing concern for the disadvantaged. The increasingly competitive business environment of law firms may have caused pro bono work to wane. In 2000, about one-quarter of the lawyers at the nation's largest firms spent more than twenty hours on such work during a typical year.

As early as the nineteenth century, many commentators complained that lawyers were so engrossed in the business of their firms that they were relinquishing their traditional leadership roles in cultural, charitable, civic, and political activities. Present critics of law firms contend that pressure to generate more revenue through hourly billing has eroded involvement in public affairs.

Expectation of billings for associates at a typical firm increased from 1400 hours per year during the 1960s to 2000 per year by the end of the century, with partnership expectations increasing from 1200 to 1800.

Billing pressures have compounded morale problems that always have existed in law firms because many attorneys find the work tedious. Others are frustrated during their junior years by lack of autonomy that results from close supervision by senior attorneys or by the high level of compartmentalization that often prevents them from perceiving the broad structure into which their work fits. Although the depersonalization of work in law firms was explored as early as the 1850s by Herman Melville in his novella *Bartleby the Scrivener*, concern over morale became intense during the 1990s, when the booming technology industry led to a diversion of much legal talent away from law firms into more lucrative occupations such as investment banking. During the same period, applications to law schools declined. On the whole, however, law schools have continued to enroll a very high caliber of students and large firms have remained able to hire many of the brightest law school graduates. The ability of law firms to attract highly able persons was greater even at the height of the economic boom of the 1990s than it was during the Vietnam War, when hostility toward capitalist institutions soured many law graduates on corporate practice.

Law firms have also tried to improve public perceptions of their work by shedding their tradition of secrecy. Until the Supreme Court began to lift bans on advertising, law firms generally refused to reveal information about such sensitive subjects as client identity, revenue, partner compensation, and billing practices. Since the relaxation of advertising prohibitions, law firms have became more comfortable about providing information about themselves. Meanwhile, the rapid growth of law firms stimulated public interest, and a burgeoning legal affairs journalism began to provide more detailed, informed, and critical accounts of the internal operations of law firms. Many leading newspapers hired full-time legal affairs reporters, who often themselves were lawyers, and several new publications were devoted to reporting exclusively on legal affairs.

Once the news media began to publish extensive information about law firms, most firms found that they needed to cooperate more closely with journalists in order to correct misinformation and to compete with the publicity that their peers were receiving. Despite their continuing abhorrence of advertising, elite firms used the news media as a means of boasting about their attributes and keeping their names before present and potential clients. Meanwhile, many lawyers began to use media contacts as a means of publishing favorable information about their clients, and billing clients for public relations services became an accepted practice.

Despite the relaxation of restrictions on advertising, most large firms still do not formally advertise their services, partly because of the continued perception that advertising is undignified, but perhaps more because such advertising is not practicable since consumers of the types of services offered by large firms are not likely to shop for firms through the news media. Despite the continuing reluctance to advertise, some firms have retained marketing agencies to help them develop business and others have hired public relations specialists to burnish their public image.

International Presence. Toward the end of the twentieth century, an increasing number of firms began to establish branch offices, domestically and abroad. Originally begun on a small scale to service particular clients or facilitate political connections in Washington or other capital cities, branch offices have attempted to take advantage of opportunities in far-flung markets and have greatly grown in size while acquiring increasing autonomy from home offices. Some American law firms now have branch offices in Europe and Asia with more than one hundred lawyers. By 2000, sixty U.S. firms had London offices with a total of more than 1300 lawyers.

The development of foreign offices of United States firms has served as an influence for the creation abroad of indigenous firms based on the American model. In particular, Europeans and Asians during recent decades have developed much larger law firms, many of which have opened branches in other cities or countries. Emulating the American model, law firms abroad have begun to offer a broader array of legal services to their clients and lawyers at such firms have begun to play more important political and civic roles.

[See also Legal Practice, Forms of]

• Erwin O. Smigel, The Wall Street Lawyer: Professional Organizational Man?, 1964. Paul Hoffmann, Lions in the Street: The Inside Story of the Great Wall Street Law Firms, 1973. Jerold S. Auerbach, Unequal Justice: Lawyers and Social Change in Modern America, 1976. John P. Heinz and Edmund O. Laumann, Chicago Lawyers: The Social Structure of the Bar, 1982. Wayne K. Hobson, The American Legal Profession and the Organizational Society, 1880–1930, 1986. Nancy Lisagor and Frank Lipsius, A Law Unto Itself: The Untold Story of the Law Firm of Sullivan and Cromwell, 1988. Robert L. Nelson, Partners With Power: The Social Transformation of the Large Law Firm, 1988. Marc Galanter and Thomas Paley, Tournament of Lawyers: The Transformation of the Big Law Firm, 1991. Ralph Nader and Wesley J. Smith, No Contest: Corporate Lawyers and the Perversion of Justice in America, 1996. David B. Wilkins and G. Mitu Gulani, "Reconceiving the Tournament of Lawyers: Tracking, Seeding, and Information Control in the Internal Labor Markets of Elite Law Firms," Virginia Law Review 84 (November 1998): 1581–1681. Patrick J. Schlitz, "On Being a Happy, Healthy, and Ethical Member of an Unhappy, Unhealthy and Unethical Profession," Vanderbilt Law Review 52 (May 1999): 571–951. David B. Wilkins, "Partners Without Power? A Preliminary Look at Black Partners in Corporate Law Firms," Journal of the Institute for the Study of Legal Ethics 2 (1999): 15–48.

—William G. Ross

FIXTURES. *See* Property, Personal.

FLAG BURNING. *See* Civil Disobedience; Speech and the Press, Freedom of.

FOREIGN TRADE AND INVESTMENT LAW. Foreign trade law's international roots extend at least as far back as the Renaissance Italian city-states, with modern antecedents dating from efforts around the beginning of the twentieth century to address customs cooperation and discrimination in international trade. The culmination of government *regulation of imports and exports was reached in 1947 with the General Agreement on Tariffs and Trade (GATT). GATT forbids governments to discriminate against member countries (this is the most-favored-nation principle), to assess tariffs in excess of levels agreed on, to act to benefit domestic products over imports (the national treatment principle), or to restrict imports or exports. The GATT also contains limits on antidumping and countervailing duties—charges designed to neutralize sales of especially low priced and governmentally subsidized imports—and it contains various exceptions. The 1994 "Uruguay Round" agreements clarified certain GATT commitments, extending many beyond goods to services and intellectual *property, and established the World Trade Organization (WTO).

Regionally, the North American Free Trade Agreement (NAFTA) joined Canada, Mexico, and the United States in a liberal trade alliance in 1993. Among other things, it phases out tariffs, opens up investment opportunities, establishes special dispute settlement processes for antidumping and countervailing duty matters, and contains a side accord to address environmental consequences of NAFTA.

On trade law's domestic side, the United States has many legislative and regulatory measures implementing GATT/WTO commitments. These include amendments to the 1930 Tariff Act and legislation like the Uruguay Round Agreements Implementation Act. However, departures such as the 1974 Trade Act's section 301, which can be used to respond to what the U.S. considers unfair practices of foreign governments, do exist. NAFTA commitments are also implemented in U.S. law, principally through the NAFTA Implementation Act.

The contractual relationship between private parties involved in international sales is regulated through the 1980 UN Convention on Contracts for International Sale of Goods (CISG). The antecedents of CISG reside in efforts of UNIDROIT (International Institute for Unification of Private Law) in the 1930s and 1950s, of certain European states in the 1960s, and of UNCITRAL (UN Commission on International Trade Law) in the 1970s to unify private-trade transaction law. CISG speaks to issues of *contract formation, buyer and seller obligations and *remedies, and risk bearing in cases of loss or injury to goods in international trade. It applies when the contract is between businesses in countries party to CISG, though even then it may be escaped by specific contract terms. It also applies when choice-of-law (i.e., private *international law) rules favor the law of a CISG party. As permitted, the United States has declared it will not use CISG in the latter situation. When CISG is otherwise inapplicable, *conflict-of-law rules may then result in relevant U.S. state versions of the Uniform Commercial Code being used. CISG is considered a "self-executing" treaty in U.S. constitutional law, and has required no implementing domestic legislation.

Foreign investment law is represented by two branches, both far less developed than their trade law counterparts. The first is reflected in certain bilateral *treaties, regional agreements, and multilateral standards; the second, in domestic law affecting foreign nationals interested in investing within the borders of the United States.

The modern Bilateral Investment Treaty, assuring nondiscrimination and relief against expropriation, has antecedents in older treaties of friendship, commerce, and navigation. NAFTA's chapter 11 is the chief regional agreement. It requires nondiscrimination, security from expropriation, free conversion and transfer of currency, and a special claims process for NAFTA investors wronged by actions of a party state. Multilateral investment standards date from the Organisation for Economic Cooperation and Development (OECD) efforts in the 1960s and 1970s to develop conventions on foreign property protection and the conduct of multinational enterprises. Though the International Monetary Fund's Guidelines on the Treatment of Foreign Investment and the UN Code of Conduct on Transnational Corporations reveal current thinking, their merely recommendatory nature leaves unresolved the shortcomings plaguing most multilateral efforts. Prominent exceptions, however, include the convention of the International Centre for Settlement of Investment Disputes and the World Bank's multilateral investment guarantee agreement.

The domestic branch of foreign investment law aims at an open-door policy, but various national and state laws limit foreigners' investment opportunities. Nationally, limitations exist in the transportation, communication, and natural resources sectors. In addition, the 1988 Exon-Florio Amendment prohibits, or compels divestment of, acquisitions of U.S. businesses when national security concerns are present. The 1978 Agricultural Foreign Investment Disclosure Act establishes a reporting requirement in connection with foreign-owned U.S. agricultural land. On the state level, an interesting example of such limitations exists in Oklahoma's restriction on foreign ownership of land.

[See also International Law]

• John H. Jackson, *World Trade and the Law of GATT*, 1969. J. Eugene Marans et. al., eds., *Manual of Foreign Investment in the United States*, 1984. John H. Jackson, *The World Trading System: Law and Policy of International Economic Relations*, 1989. Jon Johnson, *The North American Free Trade Agreement*, 1994. Ralph H. Folsom and W. Davis Folsom, *Understanding NAFTA and its International Business Implications*, 1996. John Honnold, *Uniform Law for International Sales Under the 1980 United Nations Convention*, 3d ed., 1999.

—Rex J. Zedalis

FORENSICS. *See* Evidence; Science and Law.

FORFEITURE. Tracing its roots to biblical and ancient English traditions, forfeiture served to punish persons who had committed offenses through the assessment of fines, or, when they employed an instrument in the commission of an offense, by confiscation of the instrument. English common law recognized three distinct forms of forfeiture: (1) *deodand*, which provided for confiscation of an object that directly or indirectly caused a person's death; (2) forfeiture of all of the property of a person convicted of a felony or treason; and (3) statutory forfeiture, which provided for confiscation of instruments employed to commit offenses relating to custom and revenue laws. Only statutory forfeiture was recognized in the new American nation. Generally speaking, two types of statutory forfeiture became part of the American legal landscape: *in personam* and *in rem* forfeitures. *In personam* forfeitures punish the criminal offender by confiscating his property; *in rem* forfeitures confiscate property based upon the use of the property in illegal transactions, regardless of the property owner's guilt. *In rem* forfeitures are predicated on the legal fiction that the offending inanimate object deserves punishment apart from the owner's guilt.

Forfeiture remained dormant in the United States until the 1970s, when it was revived principally as a weapon against the drug trade. This occurred by passage of statutes, exemplified by the federal Comprehensive Prevention and Drug Abuse Control Act (1970), 21 U.S.C. § 801 et seq. (1994), which provides for the forfeiture of illegal *drugs, the instruments employed to transport drugs, money derived from drug transactions, and real *property purchased with proceeds from drug transactions. Such statutes, moreover, labeled such forfeiture as civil, not criminal, thereby lowering the threshold of proof necessary for the forfeiture of such property (see BURDEN OF PROOF, CRIMINAL AND CIVIL). Criminal forfeitures are based upon the guilt of the offender, characteristically impose fines on the offender, and require the government to establish guilt beyond a reasonable doubt. Civil forfeitures, on the other hand, merely require the government to establish probable cause that either money, instruments, or real property was linked to drug transactions. Therefore, such statutes allow the government to freeze the criminal defendant's assets pending the outcome of the criminal trial. In *Caplin & Drysdale Chartered* v. *United States* (1989) and *United States* v. *Monsanto* (1984) the Supreme Court rejected the argument that the federal Comprehensive Forfeiture Act (1984), 19 U.S.C. § 1589 et seq. (1994), prevented the government from freezing such funds because it would deprive the defendant of his right to hire a private attorney in violation of the Sixth Amendment right to *counsel.

Two other prominent issues have emerged in challenges to civil and criminal forfeiture statutes: whether *criminal punishment (incarceration or fine) for the offender as well as confiscation of his property constitute either a violation of the Fifth Amendment's *double jeopardy clause or the Eighth Amendment's ban against excessive fines. With a few exceptions, the Supreme Court has rejected such challenges, thus paving the way for the government to continue to rely upon the forfeiture statutes as powerful tools in the war on drugs.

[*See also* Criminal Law Principles]

• Jimmy Gurule and Sandra Guerra, *Law of Asset Forfeiture*, 1998.   —Alfredo Garcia

FORNICATION. *See* Adultery; Morality, Ethics, and Crime; Morals Offenses.

FOURTEENTH AMENDMENT. With the end of the Civil War and the abolition of *slavery by the Thirteenth Amendment (ratified 1865), the Confederate states sought readmission to the Union and to Congress. Under Article I, section 2 of the Constitution, a slave had been counted as three-fifths of a person for purposes of representation. Because of the abolition of slavery, southern states expected a substantial increase in their representation in the House of Representatives. The Union, having won the war, might lose the peace.

Reconstruction. In 1865–66, southern states and localities enacted *Black Codes to regulate the status and conduct of the newly freed slaves. The codes deprived blacks of many basic rights accorded to whites, including full rights to own property, to testify in court in cases in which whites were parties, to make contracts, to travel, to preach, to assemble, to speak, and to bear arms. To Republicans, the Black Codes were only the latest southern attack on individual rights. Before the war, southern states had suppressed fundamental rights, including free speech and press, in order to protect the institution of slavery. Although the Supreme Court had ruled in 1833 that guarantees of the Bill of Rights did not limit the states (*Barron* v. *Baltimore*), many Republicans thought state officials were obligated to respect those guarantees. The Court in *Dred Scott* v. *Sandford* (1857) had held that blacks, including free blacks, were not citizens under the Constitution and therefore were entitled to none of the rights and privileges it secured. Republicans rejected *Dred Scott* and maintained that the newly freed slaves were citizens entitled to all the rights of citizens.

The Fourteenth Amendment was proposed by Congress in 1866 and ratified by the states in 1868. It reflected Republican determination that southern states should not be readmitted to the Union and Congress without additional guarantees. Section 1 made all persons born within the nation citizens both of the United States and of the states where they resided (thereby reversing *Dred Scott*) and prohibited states from abridging *privileges or immunities of citizens of the United States and from depriving persons of *due process of law or *equal protection of the laws. Section 2 reduced the representation of any state that deprived a part of its male population of the right to vote, an indirect attempt to protect the voting rights of blacks. Other sections protected the federal war debt, prohibited payment of the Confederate debt, and disabled from holding office those who had sworn to uphold the Constitution but who had engaged in rebellion—unless Congress repealed the ban by a two-thirds vote. Section 5 empowered Congress "to enforce, by appropriate legislation," the preceding sections.

Early Interpretation. The first major interpretation of the Fourteenth Amendment's effect came in the *Slaughterhouse Cases* (1873), in which the Court suggested that most basic *civil rights and liberties of citizens remained under control of state law. In cases following *Slaughterhouse*, the Court limited the privileges and immunities of citizens of the United States referred to in the amendment to relatively narrow rights such as protection on the high seas and the right to travel to and from the nation's capital. These cases drastically curtailed the protection afforded by the amendment against state violations of fundamental guarantees of liberty. One reason for the Court's narrow construction of the amendment was its fear that a more expansive reading would threaten the basic functions of state governments, both by federal judicial action and through enforcement of federal statutes that might displace large areas of state law.

Contrary to the expectations of some of the amendment's framers, the Supreme Court held that the amendment did not overrule *Barron* v. *Baltimore* (1833) and require states and local governments to respect the guarantees of the *Bill of Rights. The Court also held that because the amendment provided that "no state shall" deprive persons of the rights it guaranteed, Congressional legislation protecting blacks and Republicans from Ku Klux Klan violence exceeded the power of the federal government. In the *Civil Rights Cases* (1883) the Court nullified provisions of the 1875 Civil Rights Act guaranteeing equal access to public accommodations. It held that the amendment reached only state action, not purely private action. In 2000, the Court held the Violence Against Women Act unconstitutional. The decision was based, in part, on the rule that the Fourteenth

Amendment does not give Congress power to reach private action as opposed to state action. (*United States* v. *Morrison*, 2000).

In *Plessy* v. *Ferguson* (1896) the Court held that state-mandated racial *segregation of railway cars did not violate the amendment's Equal Protection Clause. In 1898, it upheld a state statute requiring segregation of private colleges (*Berea College* v. *Kentucky*). Justice John Marshall *Harlan registered eloquent but lonely dissents to the Court's decisions sanctioning state-imposed segregation. The Court also held, in *Bradwell* v. *Illinois* (1873) and *Minor* v. *Happersett* (1875), respectively, that the amendment did not protect the right of women to practice law or to vote.

Although the Court first embraced a narrow reading of the amendment, the Court gradually read it expansively to protect corporate and property interests. In 1886, the Court declared that a *corporation was a "person" for purposes of the Fourteenth Amendment (*Santa Clara County* v. *Southern Pacific Railroad Co.*). By 1897, it had begun reading the amendment as protecting freedom of *contract, finding in *Allgeyer* v. *Louisiana* that a state statute restricting out-of-state insurance companies violated due process. In *Lochner* v. *New York* (1905), it held that a law limiting bakers to a sixty-hour week violated the liberty of contract secured by the amendment's Due Process Clause.

Liberty Protections. After the constitutional crises of 1937 (see COURT PACKING), the Court repudiated its decisions striking down economic regulation. But while the amendment shrank as a protection of economic interests, it grew as a protection of other liberty interests. Much of this modern growth has resulted from extension of the Bill of Rights to the states. Since World War II, the Equal Protection Clause has emerged from obscurity. Under it, the Court has subjected racial *discrimination to increasingly strict (usually fatal) scrutiny. In *Brown* v. *Board of Education* (1954), the Court found that segregated education denied minority schoolchildren the equal protection of the laws.

In *Reynolds* v. *Sims* (1964), the Court found that malapportioned state legislative districts also violated the Equal Protection Clause. Other discrimination, such as that against aliens, was also subjected to strict judicial scrutiny. While state legislation restricting fundamental rights is subject to strict judicial scrutiny, economic regulation is usually measured by a more relaxed test that merely requires the court to find some rational purpose for the classification—which it usually does. Discrimination based on sex or illegitimacy has been scrutinized less strictly than discrimination based on race, but more strictly than purely economic regulation.

By a broader reading of what constituted state action, from the 1940s to the end of the 1960s, the Court reached a wide range of action once considered private and therefore outside the protection of the Fourteenth Amendment. In *Shelley* v. *Kraemer* (1948), the Court outlawed judicial enforcement of racially restrictive covenants in housing. In *United States* v. *Guest* (1966), six justices in dicta indicated that congressional power under the Fourteenth Amendment could reach racially motivated private violence—a view since repudiated.

Another major area of expansion of the Fourteenth Amendment was in the application of the Bill of Rights to the states. As early as 1908, in *Twining* v. *New Jersey* (1925), the Court suggested that some Bill of Rights guarantees might limit the states through the Due Process Clause. In *Gitlow* v. *New York* (1925), the Court began to apply protections of speech, press, assembly, religion, and counsel to the states. The guarantees applied to the states were those the Court considered essential to ordered liberty (*Palko* v. *Connecticut*, 1937). A majority of the Court thought that many rights in the Bill of Rights—trial by jury and the privilege against self-incrimination, for example—did not meet that test. The incorporation of the Bill of Rights accelerated under the *Warren Court. By 1969, most Bill of Rights guarantees had been incorporated as limits on state power.

In addition to applying the Bill of Rights to the states, the Court found other fundamental rights, though not specifically set out in the Constitution, were entitled to protection under the Due Process Clause. These included a right to *privacy that embraced the right of married couples (*Griswold* v. *Connecticut*, 1965)—and later unmarried adults—to use birth-control devices, and the right of women to obtain an *abortion (*Roe* v. *Wade*, 1973). The abortion decision has been subjected to severe political attack. In 1986, in *Bowers* v. *Hardwick*, the Court held the right to privacy did not protect consenting adults from prosecution for homosexual conduct under state sodomy laws (see HOMOSEXUALITY AND THE LAW). The decision criticized prior privacy cases as having "little or no textual support in the constitutional language" and suggested that they were of questionable legitimacy.

By 1968, the Warren Court's decisions—particularly in areas of criminal procedure, school prayer, and civil rights—provoked political criticism. President Richard Nixon's appointees to the Court, followed by those of Presidents Ronald Reagan and George Bush have espoused a narrower view of guarantees of liberty, particularly as they affect the rights of the accused.

After many years of judicial appointments by Republican Presidents who called for "strict construction," the Court changed direction. After the abortion decision, both the *Burger and Rehnquist Courts seemed unwilling to further expand the class previously recognized of fundamental rights that are less explicitly set out in the text of the Constitution. These include the right to use birth control devices or to an abortion. For example, in a case challenging great funding disparities between poor and wealthy public school districts, the Court rejected the claim that there was a fundamental right to public education (*San Antonio School District* v. *Rodriguez*, 1973). In a case where terminally ill patients sought to employ medical assistance to end life, the Court found no such fundamental right (*Washington* v. *Glucksberg*, 1997). Similarly, the Court has been unwilling to expand the group of suspect classifications. Regulations based on suspect classifications must be justified by a compelling government interest and are narrowly aimed at the particular problem the government seeks to address. (For example, racial classifications are suspect and receive strict scrutiny). Still, the Court seems increasingly willing to find some non-suspect classifications to be irrational. In the cases of a zoning decision excluding a group home for the mentally retarded and a Colorado Constitutional Amendment that denied gays the benefit of laws forbidding discrimination based on sexual orientation, the Court has found the legislation irrational (*City of Cleburne* v. *Cleburne Living Well Center*, 1985; *Romer* v. *Evans*, 1996).

At one time it seemed that that the government had broader power to employ racial criteria to craft programs to assist those who had suffered from a history of discrimination. The Rehnquist Court, however, applied strict scrutiny to all racial classifications, whether they were employed to help or hurt members of minority groups. It has applied similar logic in the case of legislation drawing electoral districts based mainly on racial criteria (*Adarand Constructors, Inc.* v. *Pena*, 1995; *Miller* v. *Johnson*, 1995).

The Court has also limited the power of Congress to enforce the Fourteenth Amendment. When Congress sought to expand the substantive protections of the amendment beyond the boundaries set by the Court, the Court declared the effort beyond the power of Congress. For example, Congress could not, under the Fourteenth Amendment, create a test to protect free exercise of religion from generally applicable law, that was more protective than that established by the Court (*City of Boerne* v. *Flores*, 1997).

The Fourteenth Amendment remains, as it has been through most of its history, a center of controversy, and the Court's interpretations of it continue both to mirror and to shape changes in American society.

[*See also* Gender and Law; Race and Ethnicity]

• Michael Kent Curtis, *No State Shall Abridge: The Fourteenth Amendment and the Bill of Rights,* 1986. William E. Nelson, *The Fourteenth Amendment: From Political Principle to Judicial Doctrine,* 1988. Richard L. Aynes, "Constricting the Law of Freedom: Justice Miller, the Fourteenth Amendment, and the Slaughter-House Cases," *Chicago Kent Law Review* 70 (1994): 627. Raoul Berger, *Government by Judiciary: The Transformation of the Fourteenth Amendment,* 2d ed., 1997. Pamela Brandwein, *Reconstructing Reconstruction: The Supreme Court and the Production of Historical Truth,* 1999. Michael J. Perry, *We the People: The Fourteenth Amendment and the Supreme Court,* 1999.   —Michael Kent Curtis

FOURTH OF JULY. *See* Public Ritual, Law and.

FRANCHISE. A franchise is a special *privilege granted by government to an individual or a *corporation to engage in activities that are not a common right.

[*See also* Commercial Law]

—James W. Ely Jr.

FRANK, JEROME N. (1889–1957), lawyer, public official, and judge of the United States Court of Appeals for the Second Circuit, 1941–57.

Jerome New Frank was born in New York City on September 10, 1889, and died in New Haven, Connecticut on January 13, 1957. He graduated from the University of Chicago and its law school. In legal practice, he specialized in corporate finance and reorganization. His first book, *Law and the Modern Mind* (1930), was a critique of law based on psychoanalytical insights, and immediately established his reputation as a Legal Realist. He subsequently published five more books, including *Courts on Trial* (1949), and numerous articles.

Frank taught as a lecturer at the Yale Law School, and in 1933 became General Counsel to the Agricultural Adjustment Administration, then special counsel to the Reconstruction Finance Corporation, and finally commissioner of the Securities and Exchange Commission. He was elected SEC chairman in 1939, succeeding William O. *Douglas. In 1937, he was one of the cofounders of the *National Lawyers Guild.

Frank's principal contribution to American law came through his service as a Judge of the Court of Appeals for the Second Circuit, where he sat from 1941 to his death. He wrote influential opinions that shaped the law of obscenity, adhesion contracts, so-called "private attorneys-general," and labor relations, among others. He did not invariably decide cases in ways consonant with his earlier Legal Realist views, however. He voted to sustain the conviction of the Rosenbergs in the atomic espionage trial, and the conviction for contempt of counsel for the Communist Party leaders tried in *Dennis* v. *United States* (1951).

[*See also* Educator, Legal; Legal Realism]

• Robert J. Glennon, *The Iconoclast as Reformer: Jerome Frank's Impact on American Law,* 1985.

—William M. Wiecek

FRANK, LEO, CASE OF. The Leo Frank case, known formally as *Frank* v. *Mangum* (1915), concerned the heinous murder of a thirteen-year-old girl, the conviction of a man based on circumstantial *evidence, and a preposterous tale told by the prosecution's chief witness. The trial took place in an Atlanta courtroom with an almost total absence of any semblance of fairness.

On the morning of 27 April 1913, the night watchman of a pencil factory discovered a dead girl, whose body was covered with bruises. Police identified her as Mary Phagan and summoned the factory superintendent, Leo Frank. He recognized the corpse as that of the girl he had paid the day before and appeared quite nervous and ill-at-ease. Two days later, mostly because of public clamor for a culprit and Frank's odd behavior when he saw the dead body, the police arrested Leo Frank. For the next two months they incarcerated him while the solicitor general of Georgia, Hugh Dorsey, prepared a case against Frank. The fact that he was an industrialist, a Jew, and a northerner made it easier to prosecute Frank in this southern town.

The trial began on 28 July 1913. Because of the heat, the windows of the main floor courtroom remained open, and among the crowd who stood outside, those who could peered in. Their shouts could be heard throughout the room. Both the police and the prosecuting attorney had signaled earlier that there was no doubt that they had the man who killed the girl. They reached this conclusion in spite of the fact that the state's main witness, a black janitor named Jim Conley, had been caught previously in several lies and had given four successive affidavits indicating how he had assisted Frank in removing the dead body after Frank had committed the crime. The reason for the different affidavits was that after each one was published in May and June, reporters and others pointed out that some of the aspects noted in these documents could not possibly have happened the way Conley purportedly remembered them. Thus, each succeeding affidavit dealt with the criticisms. The main point of all of them, however, was that Frank was a sexual pervert (the nature of the perversion was never explained), had sex with teen-aged girls many times, and inexplicably had murdered Mary after abusing her.

In court, despite numerous witnesses for and against the defense, the verdict hinged on the acceptance of Conley's tale. The two lawyers for Frank were unable to disprove Conley's story. Those who witnessed Conley in the courtroom were convinced that he was either a fine actor or that he was telling what he knew. Bigots assumed that if Frank's attorneys could not get the black janitor to change his testimony then Conley had to be telling the truth. Frank's attorneys also elicited information from Conley about Frank's alleged lascivious conduct in the past. Sixteen hours of testimony later they discovered that they had mistakenly taken the wrong path of questioning, and asked to have the information stricken from the record. The presiding judge, however, allowed the remarks to remain. He noted that while the testimony relating to Frank's alleged previous conduct "may be extracted from the record . . . it is an impossibility to withdraw it from the jury's mind."

The trial ended with the defense attorneys agreeing to keep their client out of court when the *jury rendered its verdict. The populace outside had been vocally supporting the prosecution during the trial and shouts of "hang the Jew" were periodically heard in the courtroom. The presiding judge feared a riot and possible lynching if the jury rendered a verdict of not guilty. Therefore, in front of the members of the jury, he consulted with the chief of police and the head of the National Guard about how to keep order when the trial ended. Frank was found guilty, however, and outside of the building a mob of thousands "went wild with joy."

Frank's attorneys appealed the verdict on the ground that there was insufficient evidence to reach the jury's conclusion and that the nature of the irregularities both inside and outside of the courtroom constituted deprivation of *equal pro-

tection of laws for their client. In three successive appeals to the Georgia Supreme Court the petitioners' requests were turned down. Frank unsuccessfully sought a writ of error from the *Supreme Court, and then asked the federal courts to grant a writ of *habeas corpus on the grounds that the trial was dominated by a mob and amounted to a denial of *due process. The Supreme Court heard arguments on this last point, but a 7–2 majority ruled that during the trial none of Frank's constitutional rights had been violated. In a wringing dissent, however, Justices Oliver Wendell *Holmes and Charles Evans *Hughes wrote, "Mob law does not become due process of law by securing the assent of a terrorized jury."

Eight years later, in *Moore* v. *Dempsy* (1923), the Supreme Court reversed itself and indicated that the threat of mob violence deprived defendants of due process of law.

[*See also* Criminal Law]

• Leonard Dinnerstein, *The Leo Frank Case*, 1968. Eric M. Freedman, "Milestones in Habeas Corpus-Part II. Leo Frank Lives: Untangling the Historical Roots of Meaningful Federal Habeas Corpus Review of State Convictions," *Alabama Law Review* 51 (2000): 1467.

—Leonard Dinnerstein

FRANKFURTER, FELIX (1882–1965), Lawyer, Professor, Justice of the U. S. Supreme Court, 1939–1962. Felix Frankfurter was born 15 November 1882 in Vienna, capital of the Austro-Hungarian Empire, to a middling, Jewish household. In 1894, they emigrated to the United States taking up residence in New York City. Although young Felix only spoke Yiddish and Hebrew on arriving in the New World, he learned to master the new language sufficiently well to graduate City College and gain admittance to Harvard Law School, where he became a member of the prestigious *Harvard Law Review* and graduated first in his class. After a year in private practice in New York, displaying his talent for cultivating luminous professional friendships, he joined Henry L. Stimson in the U.S. Attorney's Office in 1906. From there he followed Stimson into private practice, then, in 1911, the U.S. War Department as counsel for the Bureau of Insular Affairs.

In 1914, he joined the Harvard Law faculty where he wrote or co-wrote several seminal books and articles on interstate commerce, federal courts, and administrative law including *The Business of the Supreme Court* with James M. Landis in 1927. Taking the place of his friend and mentor, Louis D. *Brandeis, when the latter received an appointment to the *Supreme Court, as legal advisor to the National Consumers' League, he argued several cases before the Court including *Bunting* v. *Oregon* (1917) and *Adkins* v. *Children's Hospital* (1923). He was also active in the American Zionist movement, the *Sacco and Vanzetti case, and other causes historians associate with the Progressive movement. In 1917, Frankfurter joined the war effort as an assistant to secretary of war where he specialized in mediating labor disputes, which led to his service as chair of the War Labor Policies Board in 1918. After several years of courtship, he married Marion A. Denman on 20 December 1919.

After participating in the Paris Peace Conference to conclude World War I as a Zionist representative, he returned to his busy schedule at Harvard. He played a highly active role in the early years of Franklin D. Roosevelt's New Deal (1933–37) helping to write the *Securities and Exchange Commission Act and supplying his so-called "Happy Hot Dogs," lawyers he sponsored that helped write the legislation for and staff the new regulatory agencies. In 1939, Roosevelt appointed Frankfurter to the seat on the Supreme Court vacated by the death of Benjamin N. *Cardozo. Frankfurter retired from the Court in 1962.

His career on the Court disappointed many of his friends and subsequent biographers who found that Frankfurter's adherence to the doctrine of judicial restraint left him on the sidelines of the rights revolution. He voted with the majority to allow the internment of Japanese Americans in *Korematsu* v. *U.S.* (1944), upheld compulsory flag saluting in *Minersville School District* v. *Gobitis* (1940), urged his fellow justices to go slow with desegregation, and dissented in redistricting in *Baker* v. *Carr* (1962). His *jurisprudence built strongly on the Brandeis inheritance of deference to legislators, respect for judicial process and balancing tests, and incorporation of the Bill of Rights, but Frankfurter left to Justices Hugo *Black, William O. *Douglas, and William *Brennan the extension of that legacy into new areas of civil rights and civil liberties. Justice Frankfurter died on 22 February 1965, three years after leaving the bench.

[*See also* Supreme Court of the United States]

• Leonard Baker, *Brandeis and Frankfurter: A Dual Biography,* 1984. Melvin I. Urofsky, *Felix Frankfurter: Judicial Restraint and Individual Liberties,* 1991.

—Williamjames Hull Hoffer

FRAUD. *See* White Collar Crime.

FRAUDS, STATUTE OF. *See* Statute of Frauds.

FREEDOM OF INFORMATION ACT. Although the U.S. *Constitution protects the freedom of the press from government interference, it does not establish for reporters or other citizens a right of access to government documents. In 1966, however, Congress passed the Freedom of Information Act, which requires government agencies to make their records available on request. The news media and government reform groups fought for the new law after they perceived that federal agencies were using the 1946 Administrative Procedure Act as authority to withhold public documents rather than as a mandate to release them. The Freedom of Information Act, or FOIA as it is often called, mandates that the federal executive branch, except for the White House and a few other agencies, disclose to the public all records that do not fall into one of nine categories: (1) national security, (2) agency rules and practices, (3) documents specifically closed by legislative action, (4) confidential business information, (5) the deliberative process of agencies, (6) personal information considered protected from an "unwarranted" invasion of *privacy, (7) law enforcement investigations, (8) banking reports, and (9) geological and geophysical information about wells. Neither Congress nor the courts must disclose documents under the act. Any person, citizen or not, can make a formal, written request for any tangible agency records, including computerized information. Agencies must respond to requests within twenty working days. Fees for documents can be waived if an agency determines the request "is in the public interest." Persons who have been refused documents can appeal to the head of the agency or file a complaint in federal district court.

[*See also* Civil Rights and Civil Liberties]

• James T. O'Reilly, *Federal Information Disclosure* (2 vols.) (updated regularly). Reporters Committee for Freedom of the Press, *How To Use The Federal FOI Act,* 8th ed., 1998.

—Bill F. Chamberlin

FREEDOM OF SPEECH AND THE PRESS. *See* Speech and the Press, Freedom of.

FTC. *See* Regulation.

FULL FAITH AND CREDIT CLAUSE. Article IV, § 1 of the U.S. *Constitution provides: "Full faith and credit shall be given in each State to the public acts, records, and judicial proceedings of every other state. And the Congress may by general laws prescribe the manner in which such acts, records and proceedings shall be proved, and the effect thereof." This provision was one of several constitutional clauses designed to create a single nation from a group of newly independent states. Scholars disagree, however, whether this goal was to be accomplished through obligations directly imposed on the states through the first sentence of the clause or through congressional enactments under the second sentence. Although *Congress has since enacted some implementing legislation, the U.S. *Supreme Court has played the most significant role in defining the scope of the clause.

The clause's greatest influence has been in the enforcement of state-court judgments in other states. The Supreme Court, in *Mills* v. *Duryee* (1813), interpreted the clause's 1790 implementing statute to require that state courts give the same effect to the judgments of other states as they would receive in their home states. This implementing statute still exists in amended form (See 28 U.S.C. § 1738 (1994)). Not covered by this "same effect" rule are judgments rendered without subject-matter or personal jurisdiction, nonfinal judgments, judgments obtained by fraud, and penal judgments. In addition, the clause does not require the states to give any effect to foreign-nation or federal-court judgments.

In the twentieth century, the Supreme Court interpreted the clause to require that states enforce the public acts, or statutes, of other states in certain circumstances. Early decisions imposed rigid restrictions on the states that appeared to incorporate the "territorial" or "vested rights" system of *conflict-of-laws rules then generally accepted in the United States. Later the Court discarded this approach and eventually arrived at a minimalist interpretation of the clause. Under this interpretation, the Court will not invalidate a state's decision to apply its own law under a "traditional" conflict-of-laws rule that is, one generally accepted at the time the states ratified the Constitution. Alternatively, the Court will not invalidate a state's choice of its own law if it employs a nontraditional, or "modern," conflict-of-laws approach, as long as the state has sufficient contacts with the parties and events to give it an interest in having its law applied. See *Sun Oil* v. *Wortman* (1988); *Phillips Petroleum Co.* v. *Shutts* (1985); *Allstate Ins. Co.* v. *Hague* (1981). Under these standards, the clause imposes few restrictions on the power of the states to apply their own, instead of other states', statutes.

Recently, Congress has been more active in creating implementing statutes under the clause, suggesting that it may play a more important role in defining the boundaries of the clause in the twenty-first century than in previous times. See 28 U.S.C. § 1738A (1994 & Supp. IV 1998) (child custody determinations); 28 U.S.C. § 1738B (1994 & Supp. IV 1998) (child support orders); 28 U.S.C. § 1738C (Supp. IV 1998) (same-sex marriages); 28 U.S.C. § 1739 (1994) (state and territorial nonjudicial records).

[*See also* Commercial Law]

• Walter Wheeler Cook, "The Powers of Congress Under the Full Faith and Credit Clause," *Yale Law Journal* 28 (1919): 421. Kurt H. Nadelmann, "Full Faith and Credit to Judgments and Public Acts: A Historical-Analytical Reappraisal," *Michigan Law Review* 56 (1957): 33. Ralph U. Whitten, "The Original Understanding of the Full Faith and Credit Clause and the Defense of Marriage Act," *Creighton Law Review* 32 (1998): 255. Luther L. McDougal III, et al., *American Conflicts Law*, 5th ed. 2000, chs 7, 9.   —Ralph U. Whitten

G

GAMBLING, or gaming, involves an agreement between two or more individuals to play collectively at a game of chance for a wager, which will become the winner's property. Gambling activities include lotteries, betting, and sometimes gaming machines. Given the puritanical roots of American society, it is not surprising that gambling has been a disfavored behavior, although at *common law it was only unlawful when it rose to the level of a nuisance. Gambling became a crime only if some legislature declared it to be a crime.

In the 1930s depression, Nevada's legislature legalized casino gambling, which gave birth to modern Las Vegas. Las Vegas casinos were largely financed by organized crime (most notably Bugsy Siegel's Las Vegas Flamingo). While organized crime's involvement in the Nevada casinos quelled other states' enthusiasm for casino gambling, New Jersey ultimately followed Nevada's lead in 1978 with the development of Atlantic City. In those states that have sanctioned casino gambling, its activities are highly regulated by state gaming commissions, which issue licenses for permitted activities. Criminal statutes frequently support such regulatory frameworks.

Most state legislatures today permit some form of gambling, most notably state lotteries, although there are a few exceptions, such as Idaho and Alabama, which permit only charitable gaming. In those states that criminalize all or some forms of gambling, the crime's basic elements are: 1) consideration; 2) a result dictated solely by chance; 3) a potential reward; and 4) in some circumstances, "for profit." Punishments typically include fines, imprisonment, or some combination of both.

Throughout U.S. history, gambling has been regulated at the state level. Nonetheless, the federal government can assert legislative jurisdiction by virtue of the U.S. Constitution's Commerce Clause. This it did in 1988 with the passage of the Indian Gaming Regulatory Act (Gaming Act). The Gaming Act allows Indian tribes to engage in ritual gambling without oversight, offer bingo and card game gambling with the oversight of the National Indian Gaming Commission, and open casinos if the Indian Tribes reach an agreement with their host states (see NATIVE AMERICANS AND THE LAW—NATIVE AMERICANS UNDER CURRENT UNITED STATES LAW). Today the gaming industry is the fastest-growing segment of the entertainment industry. Las Vegas is enjoying a renaissance and the travel industry is actively promoting gambling-oriented travel. Online electronic gambling will clearly be gaming's next legal frontier, presenting obstacles related to the "cross-border" and multijurisdictional nature of Internet-based gambling. Many states, in an effort to keep gaming proceeds within the state and to maintain regulatory control over in-state gambling-related activities, are taking steps to criminalize all or some forms of Internet-based gambling.

[*See also* Morals Offenses; Victimless Crime]

• Gambling and the Law. *www.gamblingandthelaw.com*

—Janet K. Levit

GAME THEORY. *See* Law and Economics, Theory of.

GANGS. *See* Organized Crime.

GARNISHMENT. A form of civil preliminary or postjudgment relief, garnishment is granted when the plaintiff asks the judge for an order that requires one who owes a debt (i.e., an employer to its employee, a bank to its account holder) to withhold paying it to the defendant until the court can determine whether the sum should be paid instead to the plaintiff to satisfy a *judgment.

[*See also* Debtor and Creditor]

—David S. Clark

GENDER AND LAW. The relationship between gender and American law is paradoxical. Law has been the source of significant gender inequality, reflecting a social and cultural consensus that justifies inequality as consistent with the natural order. Yet law has also been used as a tool for change, challenging both law and society to be true to the most idealistic principles of justice, equality, and liberty. Law reform has successfully dismantled formal structures of express inequality in the law, removing legal disabilities and expanding categories of harms and the definitions of rights.

But the limits of law as a vehicle for change are evident in the persistence of problems in precisely those areas where law reform has been the most successful. For example, while law can provide remedies, it has not successfully eliminated or significantly reduced employment *discrimination and gender-motivated violence. Furthermore, some law reform has unintended negative consequences in an ongoing context of inequality and gender neutrality. Mothers have been disadvantaged under shared custody rules that ignore actual care in favor of formal equality between parents. Mutual injunctions have been issued in *domestic violence situations, failing to distinguish batterers from victims or offensive injuries from defensive injuries. The availability of domestic violence remedies has also been used to sanction parents who fail to remove their children from violence, discouraging the use of domestic violence remedies because of these consequences. Moreover, the mere presence of laws does not insure their unbiased application. While women are viewed as equal citizens, they remain underrepresented politically and therefore a distinctly minority voice in the creation and administration of the law.

This coextensive positive and negative relationship is also evident in the practice of law. Historically, women were discouraged from the practice of law either by the refusal of state bars to admit them, of courts to permit them to practice, or of *bar associations to admit them to membership. Furthermore, when legal *education shifted to law schools, many would not admit women until well into the twentieth century. Women were viewed as unfit for the profession by their very nature, a practice validated by the U.S. Supreme Court in *Bradwell* v. *Illinois*, where the Court upheld the denial of the admission of a married woman to the bar on the basis of her sex. The famous concurrence of Justice Bradley found not only justification, but necessity, for women's exclusion. Bradley wrote in part:

[T]he civil law, as well as nature herself, has always recognized a wide difference in the respective spheres and destinies of man and woman. Man is, or should be, women's protector and defender. The natural and proper timidity and delicacy which belongs to the female sex evidently unfits it for many of the occupations of civil life.

While women continued to practice law, they were excluded within the professional culture. Beginning in the 1970s, however, increasing numbers of women began attending law school, and by the turn of the century, women constituted half of the students entering law school; in some law schools, women were a numerical majority. Despite this rapid and remarkable infusion of women into the profession, women have not then, and do not now, occupy a proportionate share of *law firm partnerships, state or federal judgeships, or academic positions. Even more remarkably, legal education has barely accommodated women's presence: despite qualitative and quantitative evidence of women's adverse reaction to traditional legal education, and their contrasting success in the undergraduate sphere, there has been relatively little change in pedagogy or substance in the curriculum. Coupled with this professional educational picture is the widespread evidence of gender bias in the legal system with respect to both the judicial and executive branches, as evidenced in state reports concluding that significant bias exists in the administration of the law by police, attorneys, and judges.

Over the course of this movement between law's conservative and progressive role, one can identify several notable patterns of the relationship between gender and law. First, American law has moved from being explicitly gendered—wedded to a patriarchal norm—to a norm of gender neutrality. Because that norm of neutrality exists in a context of gender inequality, however, it exposes the challenge of ongoing gendered norms in the law that foster, rather than challenge, ongoing inequality. Second, the subordination of women in and by law has varied dramatically for different women. Racial differences are particularly sharp, both historically and currently, in the relationship between women and the law. Class and sexual orientation are other differences among women, alone or in combination with racial identities, that vary significantly the relationship between gender and the law. Third, while the subordination of women has figured most prominently in the story of gender and law, men have not always benefited from the norm of male privilege. The price of that privilege historically has been a limited concept of masculinity, and particularly of fatherhood. And gender privilege has been more limited when *race and class are taken into account. Race and class may trump gender privilege if the man is not white and he is being compared with other men, although he may retain gender privilege in relation to women of the same race and class identities.

Similarly, the presumed male norm is heterosexual, and gay men have been explicitly targeted by the law for sanction (while lesbians, while disfavored, historically have largely been ignored rather than targeted). Finally, the development of feminist jurisprudence has challenged the law's objectivity and neutrality, while also using law to strategize social change. Feminists have radically critiqued and reenvisioned the law. Sometimes in conjunction with grassroots movements, academic feminists have intertwined theory and practice to challenge the law's professed neutrality, objectivity, and its omissions and hierarchies.

Moving from Difference to Gender Neutrality. The historical relationship between law and gender has been a relatively straightforward incorporation of patriarchy. Patriarchy was expressed as an acceptance of gender differences as essential to the nature of men and women, and the natural dominance of men because of their superior physical, emotional, and intellectual characteristics. In this respect, American law was indistinguishable from many other legal systems and traditions, including English *common law. Men's dominance was rational and natural according to the view of women as less than human, with characteristics of men used to define what it meant to be human. Men's role was to engage in public affairs, and therefore they were accorded full legal status. Women were presumed destined to marry and perform domestic roles, and the consequence of *marriage was, in *Blackstone's words, for husband and wife to merge as one—with the husband being the sole one to be accorded legal status. Married women were viewed as having no separate legal existence, and therefore could only act through their husbands. Their legal disabilities were used to justify their exclusion from the public sphere since they lacked the power to be recognized as independent and responsible.

Even more legally subordinate were women of color who were imprisoned by *slavery. Slave women did not benefit from the protection of marriage because they were not allowed to marry. They were not considered legally subordinate to men in the same sense as white women because they were not viewed as persons but rather as property. As property they were subject to restrictions on their liberty and power that included the inability to refuse sexual activity with white men and the inability to control their reproductive capability or protect their family. Slave children were considered a reproduction of property rather than human beings with familial connections. The subordinate status of women is clear in the U.S. Constitution. Proclamations of the equality of "men" were indeed gender-specific. Women were not considered full citizens, did not have the right to vote, and were not considered part of "we the people." Slaves also were not considered part of the political community, and the protection of slave "property" and slavery as an institution is expressed in several places in the Constitution. Other women of color, particularly Asian women, were similarly not treated as part of who could become the "people," by policies of exclusion that barred them from immigrating since they were not deemed to be valuable workers, as were Asian men. Even with the addition of the Civil War amendments to the U.S. Constitution, including the *Fourteenth with its guarantee of *equal protection of the laws, women were consistently excluded or treated differently in the public sphere on the basis of their perceived inherent differences.

A series of U.S. Supreme Court decisions beginning in the 1970s changed the analysis of sex discrimination. In place of the deferential rational basis standard and acceptance of stereotypical gender differences, the Court moved toward heightened or intermediate scrutiny under which sex-based classifications had to serve important governmental interests, and the means to achieve legitimate ends had to significantly serve those ends. Stereotypes no longer would do; there had to be a rational, scientific basis of "real" difference, or men and women had to be treated equally. The strongest expression of the Court's standard came in *United States* v. *Virginia* (1996), a case challenging the exclusion of women by the state of Virginia from an all-male military-type college. The Court's decision read in part:

> Parties who seek to defend gender-based government action must demonstrate an 'exceedingly persuasive justification' for that action. . . . [This standard] does not make sex a proscribed classification. But . . . such classifications may not be used, as they once were, to create or perpetuate

the legal, social, and economic inferiority of women.

Even this stronger constitutional standard applies only to intentional discrimination on the basis of sex. With the removal of most express gender classifications, therefore, constitutional protections have had limited impact, although they carry significant ideological weight. The greatest change in the law with respect to gender has come, rather, by means of statutory enactments at the federal and state level. Chief among such laws have been antidiscrimination provisions at the federal, state, and local levels prohibiting discrimination in employment, education, and services on the basis of sex; the enactment of federal and state parental-leave legislation; and pension and social security legislation. In addition, at the state level there has been significant change with respect to the definition of, and evidentiary rules regarding, sexual assault, as well as the recognition and enactment of various statutory schemes to combat domestic violence, including special injunction statutes, recognition of the battered women's syndrome as the basis for actions taken in self-defense, and development of proactive police and prosecution policies.

*Family law has also seen significant change in response to gender critiques of the patriarchal assumptions underlying marriage and divorce. The most significant changes have been reforms in the *divorce structure embodying a partnership conception of marriage rather than the old patriarchal family model, and a presumption of shared parenting rather than women having exclusive responsibility for household work and childcare. With the influx of women into the paid workforce, a presumption that women will work has undermined the traditional notions of alimony, and has shifted responsibility for child support. Under this model, it is presumed that both parents do paid work as well as nurturing—a model of equality and gender neutrality. The changes in family law have also been extended to nonmarital families, shifting dramatically the patriarchal assumptions concerning both nonmarital children and their fathers. Another significant shift in family law is *welfare reform, which has used the equality and gender neutrality norms and the entry of women into the paid workforce to limit the availability of financial support in amount and duration, under the rationale that women now routinely combine childcare and wage work and can obtain sufficient income from wage work under contemporary equality guarantees.

Despite these significant legal changes, men and women remain differently situated as measured by most economic, social, and political criteria. This deeper and more complex level of inequality has been more difficult to reach under current concepts of equality that focus on identifying perpetrators of discrimination rather than confronting and dealing with structural and cultural barriers. For example, in employment law, the full-time worker is the presumed ideal employee, defined in terms of traditionally male notions of combining work and family by being a breadwinner parent who does little care or backup care of children. Parents with significant childcare responsibilities are adversely affected by the employment structure, and that group remains disproportionately female. Parents who are expected to provide are expected to put work first, as breadwinners traditionally have done, and that group also remains disproportionately male. In family law, the divorce structure presumes actual economic equality between spouses, despite evidence of the consistent impoverishment of a significant proportion of women post-divorce linked to the consequences of marital decision-making and/or ongoing primary childcare responsibilities in conjunction with a sex-based differential in the employment opportunity structure. Men may benefit from this structure economically, but they frequently lose the opportunity for meaningful relationships with their children, both during the marriage and after divorce. Under welfare law, marriage is rewarded and encouraged as a means to leave welfare, presuming the welfare recipient is female and the new spouse can accomplish with marriage the fiscal stability that is not possible for a single mother. The ongoing gendering, or gendered nature, of law is thus linked to the presence of structures that perpetuate inequality and gendered roles and norms.

Differences Among Women. A second pattern in the relationship between gender and the law is that historically and currently, different women have been treated differently under the law. The gendering of law also means the privileging of some women over others, buying their allegiance and alliance with white men, even in a patriarchal structure. Although women as a group have been subordinated, particular women have been privileged over other women. White middle-class women have benefited from the oppression and subordination of women of color, beginning during slavery with rules of sexual access and objectification of women of color. The same pattern of hierarchy exists in women's employment. White middle-class women are more likely to be in professional and managerial jobs, while women of color and lower-class women predominate in low-wage service and retail jobs as well as providing childcare for middle- and upper-income white women.

White woman played a pivotal role in the oppression of enslaved African women, both participating in and condoning forced labor, physical abuse, sexual violation, and destruction of families. During the post-Emancipation era, middle-class women improved their status by protecting their domestic role while relying on Black women and immigrant women to provide cheap domestic labor to support the cult of domesticity. In an era of accepted gender difference, the ideal woman was limited by race. Sojouner Truth's famous question, "Ain't I a woman too?" truthfully would have been answered "no." Women of color were expected to work, and their families were expected to function without their presence. Their labor was essential to support the cultural ideal of mothers at home, an ideal limited to white women.

The political agenda of the women's movement also has reflected this split. While white women were involved in the abolitionist movement, they failed to join or support the anti-lynching and anti-violence campaigns initiated by African-American women. Racism also was explicitly involved in the quest for women's suffrage. One of the arguments for extending suffrage was the need to counterbalance the expansion of suffrage to black men under the Fifteenth Amendment to the U.S. Constitution. Legal reforms that have assisted women have sprung from the agenda of privileged middle-class women, not from the perspective of women of color or of lower-class women. The most obvious example of this is welfare reform. The tenor of the welfare debate and ongoing discourse regarding motherhood has been strongly influenced by framing black women's families as dysfunctional. Strong black women, particularly single black women, have been viewed as domineering matriarchs and promiscuous breeders who are unable to maintain "proper" family structures and thus became dependent on the state to support their families at hard-working taxpayers' expense. The movement to "end welfare as we know it" by removing welfare as an entitlement, and by imposing stringent qualifications for family support, echo the post-Emancipation assumption that black women and black families are not worthy, and therefore limitations on reproduction, and requirements to work even without structural support for childcare, are permissible.

Another area of difference among women is reflected in legal reforms aimed at sexual assault and domestic violence. In the area of sexual assault, the distinctive legacy of women of color is the legal system's administration of the law from the perspective that women of color are "Jezebels," sexually available and promiscuous, and therefore sexual assault is deemed legally impossible because consent and availability is presumed. At the same time, gender stereotypes of men of color have resulted in their over-prosecution and even false accusation when their alleged victim was white. Furthermore, legal strategies aimed at stronger police presence and prosecution are problematic from the perspective of communities with a conflicted, oppressive relationship with police. By the same token, shelters for domestic violence victims have failed to be inclusive of all women.

Differences among women, then, construct a complex set of relationships between gender and law. Gender does not operate unmodified, or singularly. It operates in complex relation with subordination and privilege. Even within the struggle against gender subordination those same strains of hierarchy are present. Finally, this pattern has a global component as well, in the dominance of American perspectives over the issues and analyses of the *human rights agenda.

Men, Gender, and Law. The relationship between gender and law not only reflects male norms, but also enforces limits on men. While men have been privileged by the explicit patriarchal bent of the law and the ongoing gendered nature of the law, their privilege is entwined with limits on their liberty and freedom. For example, men continue to be exclusively obligated to register for the military draft. Norms of male conduct embedded in the law also confine men to stereotypes. For example, self-defense norms reflect assumptions about male responses to challenge and violence; sexual-assault norms reflect men's presumed lack of sexual control in the doctrine of consent; and the resistance of discrimination law to consideration of sexual-orientation claims limits the conditions under which failure to conform to male stereotypes is actionable discrimination.

Another example of male subordination within a norm of male privilege is the treatment of fathers within the law. Fathers historically were all powerful, controlling the lives and wealth of wives and children. Their status meant that men were the preferred custodians of children, and that children without identified fathers, who had not been legitimated by their fathers if they were not born within marriage, were ostracized as illegitimate.

With respect to slaves, fathers had even fewer obligations or responsibilities attached to parenthood; instead, they had the power and legal right to treat their property as objects for sexual gratification, and their children by slaves as additional property with no claim to family rights. During the course of the nineteenth century, custodial preferences shifted to women, grounded in an ideology of domesticity, gender difference, and the essential nature of mothering to children. Although men retained patriarchal power in the family, they lost the right of custody and care of their children as custody preferences shifted to mothers. Although express mother-preference has disappeared from the law, replaced by gender neutrality, custody of children still remains overwhelmingly with mothers post-divorce. Men succeed in contested cases at a very high rate, but overall the distribution is strongly pro-mother. Some see that pattern merely as a reflection of disproportionate mother-care of children, but in some instances it reflects an inability to see fathers as nurturers (see CHILD CUSTODY).

The view that men are not primary caregivers is consistent with the law's view of men as breadwinners rather than as nurturers. Social and cultural conditioning reinforces the primacy of economic fatherhood, and legal rules also strongly support this construction of fatherhood. Unemployment compensation and social security support, for example, support breadwinner parents, presumed to be male. Modern notions of "responsible fatherhood" are linked strongly to payment of child support to fulfill the role of economic father.

Just as the analysis of women and the law necessitates looking at differences among women, especially differences of race and class as well as sexual orientation, the same is true for men. For men of color, for example, race virtually trumps patriarchal privilege, and has resulted in a depressing litany of statistics that show the negative intersection of men of color and the law, particularly the criminal justice system.

Feminist Theory and Methodology. The development of feminist theory has been one of the most vibrant movements in the law in the past several decades. No single theory has dominated, but rather a number of major lines of theory have been used in various contexts, reflecting a strong connection between theory and practice.

Formal equality theory, or liberal feminism, has strongly emphasized similarities between women and men. In contrast to historic notions of difference, liberal theory argued for sameness, and therefore that removing artificial barriers in favor of a single, neutral standard was essential to equality. One of the most powerful critiques of liberal theory, however, was the argument that differences matter, but in a different way from patriarchal assumptions. Women's differences represented the consequences of socialization and culture, and to deny those differences was to devalue things associated with women. Advocates of this position, "cultural feminists," argued that the key to gender equality was equal valuation of things culturally associated with women. To do otherwise, they argued, was not to achieve neutrality, but in fact to be granted equality only according to a male standard.

A third powerful theory rejects the sameness/difference debate and focuses instead on locating and describing the operation of gender power and privilege. This dominance theory, associated particularly with Catharine MacKinnon, centers analysis on identifying subordination. In particular, sexual subordination (and how subordination could be seen as "sexy") was seen as critical to understanding women's inequality. Two final important threads in classic feminist analysis were socialist feminism and postmodernism. Socialist feminists pointed to economic relationships and class analysis as critical to understanding inequality. Postmodernists challenged the possibility of grand theory, and suggested the provisional nature of gender analysis.

One core link between these theories was their acceptance of the essentialist notion of a universal "woman" or of women as a unified group. Essentialism assumes that the experience of women is unitary and universal. The essentialist critique disagrees that the categories "woman" or "female" are unitary and universal, that there is a single "essential" woman or a single culture or experience of womanhood. The essentialist critique also disputes the proposition that gender is a primary and separable aspect of identity.

Antiessentialist theory posits that women's differences are critical to feminist theory. Women's identities are composed, created and continually transformed by interactions of gender with other critical identity characteristics including race, class, and sexual orientation. Thus, antiessentialist feminist theory in a sense combines the best of classic feminism and the antiessentialism generated by race, class, and sexual orientation.

In summary, American law historically has been explicitly gendered, grounded in assumptions of gender difference and the devaluation of things feminine. Only recently has the presumption of inferiority been challenged, so that gender neutrality is now the norm in most areas of American law. However, gender neutrality has not degendered the law. Male norms and standards continue to pervade the law, and the subjects of legal concern reflect (1) issues that have dominantly concerned men, or (2) experiential modes that reflect the general expectations for men. This, then, is the challenge faced by current theorists, who are met with the belief that all gender has been eliminated from the law, that the framework for equality exists, and that it will simply take time and sociocultural change in order to achieve equality. In addition, they must reconceive real equality for all women, and therefore be conscious of the interaction of law and gender with other forms of subordination.

[*See also* Civil Rights and Civil Liberties; Feminist Legal Theory; Social Dimensions of Law]

• Carol Gilligan, *In a Different Voice*, 1982. Gilda Lerner, *The Creation of Patriarchy*, 1986. Catharine MacKinnon, *Feminism Unmodified*, 1987. Carol Smart, *Feminism and the Power of Law*, 1989. Patrica Hill Collins, *Black Feminist Thought*, 1990. Patricia J. Williams, *The Alchemy of Race and Rights*, 1991. Vicki L. Ruiz and Ellen Carol DuBois, eds., *Unequal Sisters: A Multicultural Reader in U.S. Women's History*, 2d ed., 1994. Martha Fineman, *The Neutered Mother, the Sexual Family, and Other Twentieth Century Tragedies*, 1995. Adrien Wing, ed., *Critical Race Feminism*, 1997. Dorothy E. Roberts, *Killing the Black Body: Race, Reproduction, and the Meaning of Liberty*, 1997. Linda K. Kerber, *No Constitutional Right to Be Ladies: Women and the Obligations of Citizenship*, 1998. Martha Chamallas, *Introduction to Feminist Legal Theory*, 1999. Joan Williams, *Unbending Gender: Why Family and Work Conflict and What to Do About It*, 1999.   —Nancy E. Dowd

GENERAL INCORPORATION LAWS. *See* Corporation.

GENEVA CONVENTION. *See* War, Law of.

GENOCIDE. *See* War, Law of.

GERMAN LEGAL PHILOSOPHY, INFLUENCE OF.

The nineteenth century was one of the most fertile periods in the history of European philosophy, especially in Germany. German law was, above all other systems, solidly founded in philosophy at that time. There remained some followers of the *natural law school who continued to study the works of Pufendorf and his contemporaries, but this was the age of romanticism, the historical school, and the Pandectists. It was during this period in Germany that the universities were dominated by the [great philosophical jurists]: Kant,

Savigny, Gans, Jhering, Hegel, and their contemporaries.

The German lawyer philosophers of the nineteenth century set about formulating basic concepts and advanced rules of law. They based these rules on both their study of Roman law, particularly the *Digest*, and on their vigorous debates about political and academic freedom. German legal philosophy was also beset by controversies. These lawyer philosphers generated a mass of scholarly literature debating some of the most pressing legal and philosophical problems of the day. An example is the great debate between the historical school and its opponents as to the appropriate sources of law: was law ultimately to be derived from society as understood in the notion of a *Volksgeist*, or was it, rather, a set of rules that could be derived from external sources, such as natural law? In this debate, Savigny and Hugo, the leaders of the historical school, produced a host of polemical texts, most notably Savigny's *Beruf unserer Zeit für Gesetzgebung und Rechtswissenschaft*, in support of their positions. These texts were widely circulated in Germany and abroad.

These developments were far more than theoretical. For instance, the historical school's theories were at the center of the very practical debate in Germany as to the wisdom of codification. Kant's legal and philosophical works were also influential throughout Germany and other European countries in the development of several areas of the law. His writings on the importance of the subjective will played an important role in the development of *contract law, and provided a theoretical underpinning to the discussion of whether the law of contracts, as it was then developing, should take a subjective or objective approach to interpretation. Hegel, in several of his works, including his *Elements of the Philosophy of Law*, provided a new theoretical framework for analyzing legal rules and a systematic basis for legal classification. This work provided a starting point for other jurists to develop the characteristically nineteenth-century "scientific" approach to the law.

The intellectual ferment of German jurisprudence and legal philosophy had an influence far outside Germany's borders, reaching Japan and the United States. During the American Revolution and the following decades, one of the most important influences on American law came from the philosophers of the French Enlightenment. The works of Montesquieu, among others, were known to the founding fathers, and deeply influenced the architects of the American Constitution. But by the beginning of the nineteenth century, the influence of the French philosophers was waning and that of the Germans was on the rise. The leading antebellum American jurists were both aware of, and influenced by, German law and philosophy. For example, Joseph *Story, an associate justice of the United States Supreme Court and a professor at the Harvard Law School, assiduously collected German texts on law and legal philosophy even though he could not read German. He went so far as to commission German graduate students to translate contemporary German works for him because he recognized how important these works were even to an American lawyer. Hugh Swinton Legare, a South Carolina lawyer and scholar who served as U.S. attorney general, commissioned an acquaintance who was traveling to Germany to obtain a copy of Savigny's work on *codification because it was not easily available to him in the United States. William Story, Joseph Story's son, biographer, and successor on the faculty at Harvard Law School, even traveled to Germany to meet the leading German philosophers and jurists, especially Savigny.

One of the great difficulties for American jurists who wished to study German legal philosophy during the first half of the nineteenth century was the fact that few of the basic texts were available in English and few of these lawyers knew German well enough to read the original texts. Even those who could read German, such as Hugh Legare or Rufus *Choate, found that it was often difficult to obtain German-language texts in the United States. But these jurists were persistent, as evidenced by their works. As the nineteenth century progressed, instruction in German became more common in the United States and more German texts became available to Americans in both the original language and in translation.

Equally important in the spread of German legal philosophy in the United States were the relationships of specific people. The United States was fortunate to have many talented German immigrants trained in law and philosophy at German universities. Among the most important of them were Francis Lieber and Charles Follen. Follen came to America in the 1820s, and within a few years was appointed to hold the first chair in German at Harvard College. He also became the first teacher of Roman law at the Harvard Law School. In his "Introductory Lecture" in 1831, Follen told his Harvard audience how much progress German scholars had made in fields such as law, philosophy, and science, and assured them they could benefit from this work if they so desired. Many took his advice. Lieber, who made many academic contributions to the United States as editor of the *Encyclopedia Americana* and as a professor at South Carolina College and Columbia University, served as an important bridge between Germany and the United States. His works on legal interpretation, political philosophy, and the laws of war, among others, helped shape the development of these areas in the United States in a decisive way.

The influence of German philosophy on the development of American law did not end with the Civil War. On the contrary, in the second half of the nineteenth century, German juristic science and legal philosophy were of even greater significance. It was during this period that German notions of individual freedom, for instance, found resonance with the growing American interest in freedom of contract. The historical school, with its approach to the sources of law, was particularly interesting to a number of American lawyers and jurists, including William Hammond and Oliver Wendell *Holmes Jr. At the end of the century, German philosophy played a decisive role in shaping the attitudes of a new generation of American legal scholars, including Roscoe *Pound, later dean of the Harvard Law School. The influence of German legal philosophy is to be found underlying page after page of the writings of these men. For instance, there is hardly a work of Holmes, including his seminal *The Common Law*, which does not show this influence.

While European, and especially German, philosophy was of great importance generally in the shaping of American law during the nineteenth century, it was of particular importance in several private law fields, including contract and *commercial law. The nineteenth century witnessed a vast expansion of American commerce, a growth that required constant legal development and innovation. American jurists were not satisfied to create their new law from whole cloth, nor were they willing to slavishly follow their British cousins. Instead, the development of American contract law can only be properly understood as a development that took place in a transatlantic context. In virtually every fundamental area of American contract law there can be seen European, and particularly German, traces. This is not to suggest that American lawyers and judges adopted European principles en masse. They did, however, consider European developments in formulating their own ideas; in certain cases, they adopted them.

It would be an exaggeration to claim that American law was "Europeanized" during the nineteenth century. But it would be equally misinformed to believe that American law developed independently of external *civil law influences. One need only look at the American legal periodicals of the period, or at the footnotes in many of the best legal treatises, to see that Americans were aware of the writings of the best German legal philosophers—Kant, Hegel, Hugo, and Savigny, for instance. Americans debated many of the same topics as the Germans did—that is, codification, contractual obligation, and legal classification, and often looked to their German counterparts for guidance and inspiration. While one cannot claim that there was a broad incorporation of German legal rules into American law during this period, we must accept the fact that American jurisprudence was formulated within a broad intellectual tradition built in part on European, and especially German, legal scholarship.

[See also Jurisprudence, American]

• M. Reimann, "German Legal Science," Boston College Law Review 31 (1990): 837–97. J. Q. Whitman, The Legacy of Roman Law in the German Romantic Era: Historical Vision and Legal Change, 1990. J. Gordley, The Philosophical Origins of Modern Contract Doctrine, 1992. M. Hoffheimer, Eduard Gans and the Hegelian Philosophy of Law, 1995. M. H. Hoeflich, Roman & Civil Law and the Development of Anglo-American Jurisprudence, 1997.   —Michael Harlan Hoeflich

GIDEON V. WAINWRIGHT, 326 U.S. 335 (1963). Clarence Earl Gideon, a prisoner in the Florida penitentiary, wrote to the U.S. Supreme Court in 1962 in pencil on lined prison paper. He had been tried without a lawyer, he said, and that was unconstitutional. In fact it was not unconstitutional when Gideon wrote, but it was when his case ended.

In 1932, in Powell v. Alabama, the Supreme Court had reversed the convictions of seven young black men sentenced to death for rape after hasty trials, without lawyers, in a hostile community. Due process of law guaranteed by the *Fourteenth Amendment, Justice George Sutherland said for the Court, required "the guiding hand of counsel" to be provided by the state for those too poor to afford their own lawyers. In 1938, in Johnson v. Zerbst, the Court refused to extend that rule to state trials. The Fourteenth Amendment, it said, required *counsel in noncapital cases only if the defendant suffered from some disability, such as mental illness. Justice *Black dissented.

In the Gideon case, decided in 1963, the Supreme Court unanimously overruled Betts v. Brady. Justice Black wrote the opinion of the Court. "The right of one charged with crime to counsel may not be deemed fundamental and essential to fair trials in some countries," he said, "but it is in ours."

Many aspects of Gideon v. Wainwright made it a legal and popular landmark: A poor, friendless prisoner had led the Supreme Court to reinterpret the Constitution. Justice Black vindicated his twenty-one-year-old dissent. The decision was one of a series in which the *Warren Court applied to state criminal proceedings the provisions of the *Bill of Rights that had applied only in federal cases.

The impact of the decision on social reality was, and is, more cloudy. All poor defendants in serious cases were now entitled to counsel, but competent counsel was a different question. In many places inexperienced or uninterested lawyers were paid derisive fees to represent the poor. Decades later, the promise of Gideon remains unfulfilled.

[See also Counsel, Right to]

• Anthony Lewis, Gideon's Trumpet, 1964.

—Anthony Lewis

GIFT TAX. See Taxation: Estate and Gift Taxes.

GOVERNANCE is a somewhat ambiguous term for social regulatory processes that directly or indirectly implicate the political system; it is analogous to the sociologists' term "social control." Its political sweep is captured in Harlan Cleveland's well-known admonition that what we need is "more governance and less government."

That aphorism represents a long-standing American attitude that government should operate as a mechanism of last resort. Even then the preference is for a loose regulatory scheme (governance) and local control. De Tocqueville describes, in 1838, that this priority in American life is already well established. Indeed, throughout the centuries American society had been seen as emphasizing self-help governance over tight government. By the twentieth century, however, more structured (often more national) associations grew at the expense of local volunteerism.

The constitutional concept of *federalism—two levels of authority, one acting directly and one regulating individuals—was conceptually and institutionally pioneering. Other American innovations include the presidential system (the separation of the *executive power from the legislature, with its potential for friction and paralysis) the emphasis on legalism, especially *judicial review, and the development of mass bourgeois parties.

The original colonization of America did not encourage volunteerism. The various settlements were established by charters—essentially contracts between Crown and grantee, whether a company or an individual. Charters were written at various times by different authorities and reflected diverse purposes. By and large, they were economic documents designed to allocate economic gain to the grantee in return for similar gain for the Crown. Like the home country, the colonies had extensive regulation of economic, sumptuary, and religious behavior. Mercantilism, the prevailing economic doctrine, emphasized governmental promotion of business. *Common law principles imported from England included inculcation of proper moral values and public demonstration of their significance. To the extent that *civil law influence from Dutch, French, and Spanish systems survived, their usage tended toward more rather than less formal regulation.

From the beginning, however, colonists insisted on their rights as Englishmen, based on established or developing law, and sometimes mythical law. Although Adam Smith's *The Wealth of Nations* was not published until 1776, marking the beginning of English laissez-faire doctrines, *Jefferson and no doubt others were well aware of the earlier, similar arguments of the French physiocrats. The founding fathers were mercantilists but the doctrine was decaying.

The conditions of the colonies and the early years of the Republic were difficult for the theory and practice of strict government. Poor transportation and an acute shortage of labor permitted local deviations and easy evasion by elopement, as indicated by the breakdown of the system of indenture. The slavery system was strengthened by skin color, but for those not easily identified, nonconformity to both government and governance was much easier than it had been at home. As de Tocqueville pointed out, the absence of feudalism meant there was no class structure reinforcing the system or performing services legitimizing it. Although lawyers and the clergy performed some of the functions of the nobility, their rewards and therefore their loyalties were localized. While clergy of the established church were often Tories, non-conformist ministers and largely self-made lawyers were at the heart of colonial resistance.

The U.S. *Constitution, like its framers, was mercantilist, providing for a governmental role in promoting arts and science, in using revenue for "the general welfare," and giving the national government both wide fiscal authority and the seminal congressional authority to "regulate commerce among the several states." One of Eldridge Gerry's objections to the Constitution was that it would permit national laws regulating incorporation, a power that seems clearly granted but has never been implemented to this day. Both supporters and opponents of the Constitution agreed upon the protection of private property, and it was clearly provided for in the *Bill of Rights as well as in the original document. The Anti-Federalists, however, wrestled from the confirmation process explicit protection of individual rights. Their amendments narrowed national power over criminal processes and added ambiguous provisions that buttressed *states' rights.

Time was on the side of the Anti-Federalists as laissez-faire economics prevailed over mercantilism and states' rights grew more prominent. The Democratic Party became the political vehicle for rejecting a national bank and protective tariffs, and was philosophically committed to localism or nongovernment. Those ideas and ideals have seized the imagination of subsequent generations as well. The American civic culture and views of government are Lockean, filtered largely through an Anti-Federalist prism.

Even the most enduring work of American political thought, *The Federalist Papers,* reflects that primacy. While Hamilton's essays on specific provisions and institutions remain influential, it is Madison's pregnant exposition of pluralism and geographic diversity (particularly in *Federalist* #10) that has been its most powerful voice.

Nevertheless, the new government pursued promotion of the economy and territorial expansionism. Often this was through granting concessions to private parties and quiet, informal cooperation between the national and state governments. The encouragement of farmers through land grants and the establishment of strategic monopolies in transportation was seldom questioned as a violation of laissez-faire. Labor regulation, including prohibitions against poaching employees through higher wages, and guild regulation, was a common carryover from older systems. Such regulations were highly local and contested as issues of state politics. Only where there was alleged discrimination against interstate commerce or usurpation of congressional authority over navigation or trade (e.g., *Gibbons* v. *Ogden* (1824)) was there an issue for federal courts or even the Congress.

Much the same pattern prevailed over what we now call civil liberties issues. States persisted in having established churches or privileging specific sects, since the Bill of Rights was held to apply only to the national government. While a secular trend toward greater tolerance slowly prevailed, it was hardly uniform. Freedom of expression about political issues and candidates was robust even in the eighteenth century and still more vigorous after the congressional remittance of the fines levied under the Alien and Sedition Acts. Still, southern states prohibited distribution of "incendiary material" about slavery and the federal concern was only whether the U.S. post office should buttress that prohibition by banning use of the mails. Eccentric and extreme viewpoints, such as anarchism or chiliasm (millenarianism), were largely tolerated in limited circles. Drawing attention to unorthodox views with wide-open meetings was risky. But there were routes open to those facing undesired *regulation. Workers could migrate. Religious bias could be avoided by going to a state favoring one's sect. Establishing an enclave community was also unusually easy and "heavens on earth," based upon religion or ideology, were common. Famous communities—Oneida, Amana, Shaker Town, Brooks Farm—usually decayed from internal problems rather than external ones.

But this localism and community isolation was undergoing change well before the Civil War. A growing populism was transforming politics. The presidential nominating convention removed control from the congressional caucuses, and the practice of permitting popular votes on electors allowed the chief executive to claim direct authority as "tribune of the people." The full effect of this was not felt until the twentieth century, but *Lincoln's aggressive use of the office would not have been possible during the nadir of presidential authority under Madison and Monroe. Local direct elections and short terms meant issues were widely considered by the populace, and a growing practice of legislatures choosing the winner of the popular vote for senator, although not fully institutionalized until the Seventeenth Amendment in 1913, gradually eroded the senate's role as a collection of ambassadors from the states and established it as another, often more thoughtful, national body.

The explosive issue of *slavery regionalized—even nationalized—the politics of the day. It also opened up a debate on the nature of property and how far a state could go in defining and prohibiting property. Paralleling this was the growing conflict over liquor and, in that instance too, whether state definitions could trump national provisions.

More quietly, the common law changed under the needs of a society growing exponentially in size and population. As Willard Hurst and Morton Horwitz have shown in different ways, American law reconfigured the common law to favor a dynamic use of *property when minor or indirect consequences fell on others. Subtle but actually significant and cumulative steps transformed and distinguished American and English practices to favor entrepreneurs over stand-pat property usage.

Underlying all of this was a change from an economy of small farms, medium-sized plantations, and small craft enterprises, to one dominated by growing regional and national financial enterprises and much larger industrial concerns. The Civil War intensified that transformation as well as the growing desire for better communication, transportation, and internal trade. The largest market in the world was growing and replacing a society supplying raw materials to Europe. New forms of government and governance were needed.

Perhaps the most far-reaching change of the nineteenth century—rivaled only by growing democratization—was the spread of the *corporation. In the nineteenth century, incorporation was achieved by individually crafted acts of state legislatures, which typically dealt with quite minute specifics. New York pioneered general statutes that provided uniform procedures and duties for all qualifying enterprises, which could, within broad limits, run their business as they saw fit rather than kowtow to the legislature's whims and maneuvers. This broadening of the corporation's scope and dynamism was dramatically enhanced by the idea of limited liability to investors. By 1860 most states had standardized incorporation and the heyday of industrialization had arrived.

The courts aided its rise with key decisions enhancing corporations' sway. Corporations were held to be legal persons (but not citizens) and to be able to conduct business in states other than where they were incorporated, with the protection of federal courts. The use of the *Fourteenth Amendment's language to establish federal court oversight to protect corporations, property rights, and freedom of *contract was resisted at first by the Supreme Court, but this approach came to prevail at the turn of the century. Beginning in 1925, the Amendment was also gradually transformed by the Supreme Court into a charter of human rights, even as property rights began to be de-emphasized.

The characteristic form of American capitalism had emerged by 1900: the corporation capable of nationwide and, as the twentieth century demonstrated, international operations. Some multinational corporations have subsequently accumulated resources greater than most nations, and their jurisdictional intricacies raise questions of which nation, if any, controls their loyalties. To its employees, suppliers, and consumers, a corporation's actions can have consequences more far reaching than the actions of governments.

The unleashing of such potential challenged a governmental structure habitually biased toward local control and piecemeal solutions. Growing majoritarianism empowered a population that generally supported economic dynamism but balked at some its consequences, particularly cyclical recessions. The *Civil War's firm assertion of national supremacy led to tension on the question of responsibility for economic regulation, and the continual, easy abuse of transstate regulation led to increased demand for national governmental action.

Faced with those contradictory impulses, the Supreme Court created ambiguous lines of governmental authority that permitted it to monitor the new system. At the state level it sanctioned the doctrine of "police power": authority to legislate for the "health, safety, welfare, and morals" of the community. This redundant legal formulation of state authority both expanded and cramped legislation at the state level. But it also drew a distinction between the states and the national government, which possessed no police power. While accepting some pragmatic consequences of the growing national scope of commerce, the Court distinguished between matters directly affecting commerce and those with indirect effects. The latter were inherently closed to national regulation, no matter how extensive their economic consequences. Above all, the Court gave great scope to the words *"liberty" and "property" under the Fourteenth Amendment, creating a sphere where the state governments were prohibited from infringing and the national government was totally barred from entry. At the core of that liberty was the right of adults to contract freely. In essence, the Court begrudgingly allowed some increases in governmental power, but strongly supported a basic autonomy for economic institutions. While a strong case can be made that such developments in the nineteenth century facilitated the burgeoning economy, most historians see continued court protection in the twentieth century as counterproductive. The special protection of freedom of contract seemed to indicate an almost perverse unwillingness of judges to acknowledge the growing authority of the corporation. These distinctions have been largely swept aside since 1937, but there is a growing school of legal thinkers, particularly rational choice advocates, that argue for restoration of some part of that tradition of federal court protection of property. Since 1990, protectionists have also won some victories in the courts, particularly focused on the takings clause.

The expansion of corporate power and the beginnings of regulatory power at the turn of the century altered the balance of volunteerism and social self-help. Other forces crystallized and became more structured, many with the aid of state-level government. Professional associations, often with delegated licensing powers emerged; the American Medical Association and the *American Bar Association began to regulate their members and their training. At the federal level, agricultural associations sponsored by county agents working for the Department of Agriculture to improve farm methods, moved into the political arena as lobbyists of the government that had spawned them. Both the consumer movement and the "voluntary" system of product standards emerged just after World War I from structures created originally by the National Bureau of Standards. The labor movement, mainly a weak structure of odds-and-ends craftsmen, such as house painters and cigar rollers, became a power much later when Roosevelt's New Deal embraced protection of craft and industrial unions' rights to organize and bargain collectively.

Another source of new governance was the onrush of *immigration and a new ethnic diversity in America. As non-English speaking newcomers from Eastern Europe, Italy, Scandinavia, and Central Europe came into the country, they formed associations, settlement houses, and neighborhood centers to facilitate absorption. The immigrants were as diverse in religion as in culture and language. They reinforced the strong American tradition of churches as sources of self-help and community life. While Progressives like Theodore Roosevelt denounced the emergence of "hyphenated–Americans," these new wave immigrants did not accept the ideal of being transformed by "the melting pot," but instead claimed they could both be Americans and retain their ethnicity. The strongest justification of this was by Horace Kallen, who argued for "cultural pluralism." His discussion remains the most impressive intellectual reformulation of diversity and multi-cultural enrichment, almost a century after he pronounced it. Robert Merton has suggested that big-city machine politics was also a by-product of immigration, and that the political machine and its preoccupation with votes and patronage was a mechanism for moving immigrants into the American mainstream.

Paralleling the ethnic diversity was the move to organize groups and use the courts to protect minorities. The courts were tested early over consti tutional rights of Asians in the late nineteenth century, with mixed results. Not surprisingly, restrictions on the right to pursue a living were invalidated, while most regulation of social relations was allowed. The most successful and far-reaching litigator was the American Civil Liberties Union, which adopted a broad agenda and helped establish many ethnic and religious litigating entities. The prototype, however, was the NAACP, which challenged such issues as segregated residences, restrictions on voting, and other forms of discrimination, culminating in the triumph of *Brown v. Board of Education in 1954 and 1955. Similar organizations included the American Jewish Congress and similar groups serving Japanese American, Native American, Italian American, and other communities. Their effectiveness drew the compliment of imitation, especially after World War II. Women's groups, veterans' groups, and special-cause advocates of environment, separation of church and state, and other interests have developed. In recent decades not only have business groups expanded their court activities, but right-wing groups have aggressively pursued a litigating strategy, and aided by a growing cadre of conservative judges have scored some notable successes. Once established as litigators, most organizations have expanded into legislative and executive lobbying as well.

The twentieth century witnessed a major growth of national governmental powers, with depressions, wars, and internationalization of the economy providing the impetus. Theodore Roosevelt's intervention in the United Mine Workers strikes in 1908 marked a growing expectation that the national economy would be a responsibility of the national government. New governmental structures such as the Federal Reserve Board and the Federal Trade Commission created under Wilson, and the Federal Deposit Insurance Corporation, Agricultural Administration Authority, Securities and Exchange Commission, and other agencies developed by the comprehensive New Deal system, are still in place. Both Presidents Hoover and Roosevelt tried to move governance in the direction of European regulation through "peak business" associations. The demise of the National Recovery Act in 1935 was the high-water mark for this type of centralized private-public cooperative structure. After 1936, in what has been called the "second New Deal," growing national power came through more traditional methods of working with localities and local interest groups.

As a consequence, state government has also expanded to provide social services demanded by a growing and increasingly urbanized population. Both levels of government have been under pressure to provide some measure of employment guarantees and old-age insurance, and control of the economic cycle, but they have resisted efforts to bring health insurance under governmental sponsorship, making U.S. unique among advanced industrial countries.

Perhaps the most distinctive feature of twentieth-century America has been the structured effort to protect individual *civil rights and achieve equality through the law. Beginning in 1925, but especially since 1937, the Supreme Court nationalized the protections of the Bill of Rights. Now federal constitutional law—not states with divergent laws and constituents—is the front-line for political and religious rights. The old Constitution, Edward Corwin suggests, was a Constitution of powers; now it is a vehicle of rights.

Increased concern for individual rights is in part a product of the growing power of government and the economic consequences of industry. But protection of the individual through organizations presents a paradox. While they exist in the tradition of American self-help, such organizations are also increasingly professionalized, official structures within which "members" participate almost exclusively by contributing financial support. Robert Putnam has argued that the decline of participatory, face-to-face structures constitutes a failure of governance, which he argues is ultimately the undergirding of democratic government. This problem is seen by many as a challenge not only to American volunteerism, but to all democracies.

A related issue is how to achieve privacy in an electronic world where governments, employers, hackers, and sellers have increasing means of eavesdropping, gaining access to records, and compiling files on individuals. Current thinking emphasizes aggressive government monitoring of such abuses, and martialing citizens to protect their rights through organizations, which also carries a paradoxical diminishment of the individual.

Control of the multinational corporation also looms ominously. Globalization involves giant multi-locale structures capable of assuming new guises, purposes, and states by means of simple electronic communication. With stockholders of diverse nationalities, or increasingly corporations, federations, or funds of differing registration, control by national jurisdictions is problematic. The potential for corporate relocation has led critics like Ralph Nader to extrapolate a "race to the bottom," in which nation-states are played against each other, weakening the protections for workers, the environment, and product safety currently enforced by governments. On the whole, careful scholarship has found many examples of "trading up" and few of lowering standards. Still, the logic of the position and its potential is frightening to activists opposing international governance, and to widespread segments of the population.

[*See also* Congress; Legislative Power; Presidency of the United States]

• Horace Kallen, *Cultural Pluralism and the American Ideal*, 1920. Adolph Berle and Gardiner Means, *The Modern Corporation and Private Property*, 1932. Alexis de Tocqueville, *Democracy in America* (Henry Reeves edn.), 1949. Edward S. Corwin, *A Constitution of Powers in a Secular State*, 1951. Willard Hurst, *Law and Conditions of Freedom in Nineteenth Century United States*, 1956. Robert Dahl, *Polyarchy: Participation and Opposition*, 1977. Morton Horwitz, *The Transformation of American Law, 1780—1860*, 1977. Lawrence W. Friedman, *History of American Law*, 2d ed., 1985. Michael Kammen, *Spheres of Liberty*, 1986. Kay Schlossman and John T. Tierney, *The Mischiefs of Faction: Organized Interests in American Politics*, 1987. David Vogel, *Trading Up*, 1998. Robert Putnam, *Bowling Alone*, 2001.

—Samuel Krislov

GOVERNMENT, UNITED STATES. The laws of the United States are, with the *Constitution itself, the supreme law of the land and take precedence over those of the states. The U.S. Constitution gives *Congress the power "to make all laws which shall be necessary and proper for carrying into execution" those powers assigned to it (Article 1, Section 8). The president "shall take care that the laws be faithfully executed" (Article 2, Section 3). The federal courts oversee "all cases, in law and equity, arising under the Constitution" (Article 3, Section 2). The Tenth Amendment reserves for the states those powers not delegated to the national government, with state laws operating intrastate, and federal laws regulating interstate activity. But the lines of demarcation between the three branches of the federal government and the states are far from distinct, and their overlapping powers and ambitions have caused recurring tension.

State governments held real power under the Articles of Confederation (1781–89), at a time when the national government consisted of a single legislative body with limited lawmaking capacity. Congress, under the articles, could make foreign policy and declare war, but could neither regulate foreign trade nor raise revenue through taxation. Nor could Congress force the states to comply with its directives. During the depression that followed the Revolutionary War, state legislatures responded to public outcries by enacting moratoria on tax payments, prohibiting creditors from collecting debts, and placing trade restrictions on goods from other states. Clashing state laws raised fears for the survival of the new nation. James Madison, a member of Congress from Virginia, then proposed "a republican remedy" for the problems inherent in a republican government. A new Constitution would divide power between the states and an enlarged national government to reduce the influence of any single faction or party.

The framers of the Constitution aimed to create a national government powerful enough to govern effectively but not so powerful as to reign arbitrarily. Abandoning the unicameral legislature that had operated under the Articles of Confederation, they divided power between the executive, legislative, and judicial branches of the government, and further divided the legislature into the House of Representatives and the Senate. Madison explained the logic of the division of powers and checks and balances in the federal system most simply: "Ambition must be made to counteract ambition."

At the Constitutional Convention of 1787, Madison failed to achieve a national *legislative veto of all state laws, which the other delegates thought would empower the central government too greatly at the expense of the states. Those who most feared a strong national government proposed a *bill of rights to protect individuals from federal power. Although the convention declined to include a bill of rights, the issue became so divisive during the Constitution's ratification that Madison pledged to amend the document in the first Congress. As a member of the House, Madison introduced the first ten amendments to the Constitution, now known collectively as the Bill of Rights. They prohibited Congress from enacting laws that would abridge the free exercise of *religion, freedom of *speech, freedom of the press, the right to assemble peaceably and to petition the government (see ASSEMBLY AND ASSOCIATION), and they guaranteed *due process of law.

The Constitution largely left it to Congress to establish the federal court system, the subject of the first major legislation that the Senate considered. The Federal Judiciary Act of 1789 organized the U.S. *Supreme Court and lower federal courts, whose rulings further augmented the power and authority of the federal government. Chief Justice John *Marshall (1801–35) transformed the Court into a powerful independent branch of the government, beginning with the case of *Marbury v. Madison (1803). When Madison as secretary of state declined to deliver commission from the previous administration appointing William Marbury as a justice of the peace, Marbury sought redress in the Supreme Court, under a provision of the Judiciary Act of 1787. In *Marbury v. Madison*, the Supreme Court ruled unanimously that it lacked the jurisdiction to order Madison to act. Justice Marshall observed that the Constitution had not included requests for court orders, such as the writ of mandamus, among the types of cases it specified that could be taken directly to the Supreme Court. By declaring that section of the Judiciary Act unconstitutional, the Court asserted the right of *judicial review—the power to determine whether laws passed by Congress were valid under the Constitution.

The Supreme Court again expanded the central government's authority in the case of *McCulloch v. Maryland (1819). The state of Maryland had attempted to tax a branch of the Bank of the United States, a private corporation chartered by Congress. The court found the creation of a national bank constitutional as an implied power of the government. Since the Constitution permitted Congress to issue money, borrow money, and collect taxes, the federal government could adopt any method "necessary and proper" to exercise those powers. Citing the preamble of the Constitution, Chief Justice Marshall observed that the federal government proceeded directly from the people rather than the states, making the national government "supreme within its sphere of action" rather than subordinate to the states. No state therefore could tax the federally created national bank.

A third pivotal ruling, in *Gibbons* v. *Ogden* (1824), struck down a state-granted monopoly on steamboat traffic on the Hudson River that had attempted to control shipping between New York and New Jersey. The Supreme Court declared this an unconstitutional effort by a state legislature to extend its power to interstate commerce, which the Constitution had assigned exclusively to the federal government. Marshall's expansive interpretation of the commerce clause meant that anything moving between states and crossing state boundaries, or "affecting" more states than one, was subject to federal control. Over time, this reasoning would justify a wide range of initiatives by the national government, from the regulation of railroads to the construction of highways and the abolition of racial segregation.

Those who believed in a stricter construction of the Constitution, *states rights, and a limited central government believed that Marshall's rulings had gone too far. John C. *Calhoun of South Carolina argued that the Constitution represented a compact between the states and that the national government was therefore a "creature" of the states. If the federal government imposed its power improperly on the states, a state should be able to nullify that federal law within its own boundaries. In 1832 a South Carolina convention acted to nullify a federal tariff it considered punitive. President Andrew Jackson, although also an advocate of states' rights, nevertheless rejected nullification. At Jackson's request, Congress enacted the Force Act, giving him military power to suppress any resistance to federal authority. The crisis ended when Congress repealed the offending tariff, but the ground had been laid that would provide the rationale both for the South's secession in 1861, and for President Abraham *Lincoln's determination to preserve the Union at all costs. Victory for the North in the Civil War (1861–65) more fully established the supremacy of federal law.

Congress holds the power to enact laws, subject to the approval of the president. Presidents can veto legislation, but vetoes can be overturned by a two-thirds vote in both houses of Congress. Congress can also pass concurrent resolutions to propose constitutional amendments, which require state ratification rather than a presidential signature. For a bill to become law, both the Senate and House must pass it in precisely the same language. Since the Constitution permits each house to establish its own rules of procedure, the two bodies proceed in similar but not necessarily identical fashion. As the larger body, with its membership apportioned according to population, the House sets rules to allow the majority to exert itself. Once a committee reports a bill, the House Rules Committee enacts a rule determining the length of the debate and the number and type of amendments the House can consider, thus preventing dilatory tactics. By contrast, the smaller Senate, where all states have two senators regardless of their size, gives greater voice to the minority. With the Senate conducting much of its work by unanimous consent, a lone senator can stop the proceedings by dissenting. The Senate also permits "unlimited debate," by which a minority of members can prevent a vote from occurring. Known as filibusters, such delays can now be ended by a clo-ture vote of three-fifths of the senators, which lim-its the time remaining for debate. If the two houses pass different versions of a bill, one house may accept the other's or may call a conference committee to forge a compromise version. Con-ference reports are then voted upon in both houses without amendments. The convoluted pro-cess ensures that only a fraction of the many bills introduced in each session in Congress become law. In 1939, Missouri Senator Harry Truman de-fined a good legislator not as someone who got things done quickly and efficiently, as an admin-istrator was supposed to do, but as one who pre-vented the enactment of "crazy and crackpot mea-sures" into law.

Once Congress has acted, the bill goes to the president, who may sign it into law or veto it. It takes a two-thirds vote in both houses of Congress to override a veto. A president may allow a bill to become law without his signature after ten days, so long as Congress remains in session. If Con-gress is not in session, and the president does not sign the bill within ten days, it is considered a pocket veto, which Congress cannot override. Congress also attempted to create a legislative veto by granting the president and executive agencies authority to create policies that would stand unless voted down by either the House or Senate. Orig-inated in 1932 to facilitate a presidential reorgan-ization of the executive branch, the legislative veto expanded over time to cover a wide range of ex-ecutive agency regulations. In *Immigration and Naturalization Service* v. *Chadha* (1983), the Su-preme Court struck down all legislative vetoes as unconstitutional, but the practice continues none-theless.

*Treaties negotiated by the executive branch and ratified by a two-thirds vote of the Senate also have the force of law and override state law. In two centuries the Senate has rejected only twenty treaties by outright vote, although some treaties were withdrawn or never acted upon. To improve the chances of a treaty's passage, the Senate can alter it by adding amendments (changing the lan-guage of the treaty), reservations (indicating a substantial change in interpretation), and under-standings (clarifying relatively minor aspects of treaty implementation). Such alterations require only a majority vote for passage, and help make the treaty palatable enough to achieve the required two-thirds approval. The Supreme Court upheld the Senate's right to alter treaties in its decision in the case of *Haver* v. *Yaker* (1869), reasoning that since the Constitution made a treaty the "law of the land," the Senate had the right to adopt, reject, or modify it like any other law.

Congressional approval is not required for pres-idential executive orders (directives that imple-ment or interpret the laws). Although executive orders deal mostly with the internal operations of the executive branch, presidents have used them to enlarge national forests, prohibit racial discrim-ination in federal contracting, pardon draft evad-ers, and freeze wages and prices. After it is pub-lished in the *Federal Register*, an executive order has the force and effect of law and is treated by the federal courts as the equivalent of a statute. It may, of course, be overruled by a subsequent act of Congress.

Until the late nineteenth century, government *regulation usually took place at the state and local level. States created railroad commissions, insur-ance and banking commissions, and boards of health. In *Wabash, St. Louis & Pacific Railway* v. *Illinois* (1886), the Supreme Court struck down state laws regulating railroads that crossed state boundaries, as a violation of the national govern-ment's sole authority over interstate commerce. That ruling spurred Congress to establish the In-terstate Commerce Commission in 1887. A weak agency initially, the ICC was later expanded and strengthened, and provided a model for other fed-eral regulation. The new independent agencies represented an admission by Congress that it could not devote sufficient attention to the com-plex issues of industrial growth, nor wait to meet each inevitable crisis separately. Refusing to cede its constitutional power to regulate commerce to the executive branch, Congress fashioned inde-pendent commissions that combined quasi-legislative, judicial and executive functions, rep-resenting a delegation of responsibility from elected to appointed officials. During the Progres-sive era (1901–16), activist presidents used such agencies to address social and economic ills at the federal level. When a decade of conservative re-trenchment followed World War I, reformers looked to the states as "laboratories for democ-racy." The Great Depression (1929–39) again re-versed the initiative to the national government, whose programs and bureaucracy grew at an un-precedented rate.

With that growth, agency rules and regulations became an ever-expanding portion of American law. Administrative law reflected the independent agencies' broad powers to investigate problems and issue regulations, as well as the need to establish some procedural constraints. State and federal courts have required administrative agencies to respect due process, including giving notice and conducting fair hearings to permit public participation in the agencies rule-making deliberations. The Administrative Procedure Act of 1946 imposed stricter form and procedure on the agencies to protect the rights of those with business before them, and forcing the independent boards to act more like courts.

Since no statute can anticipate every eventuality, and laws become cumbersome if overly detailed, Congress has granted executive agencies leeway in filling in the details of legislation. In *Hampton & Co. v. U.S.* (1928), the Supreme Court upheld delegations of power to the president to adjust tariffs, so long as the legislature promulgates rules, standards, goals, or some "intelligible principle" to guide the exercise of administrative power. The New Deal programs of President Franklin D. Roosevelt (1933–45), designed to end the Great Depression, expanded the federal government into agriculture, business, labor, finance, and welfare. The New Deal spawned an "alphabet soup" of administrative agencies to deal with these issues. The Supreme Court in *Schechter Poultry v. U.S.* (1935) struck down the National Industrial Recovery Act as an unconstitutional delegation of congressional power to an administrative agency, as well as an infringement on a state's right to regulate business within its borders. Roosevelt responded with a plan to increase the size of the Supreme Court, which his opponents denounced as *"court packing." The plan failed, but retirements from the Court soon allowed Roosevelt to appoint justices more sympathetic to government innovation and intervention in the economy.

The "power of the purse" also shapes federal policy. The constitutional requirement that Congress appropriate all federal funds allowed the legislative branch to make policy by earmarking funds for specific purposes and by conducting oversight hearings of the agencies it funds. Raising revenue was in itself a form of economic regulation. In the nineteenth century, the government obtained most of its operating funds through tariffs, which privileged certain industries and interest groups over others. Tariffs encouraged specific American manufacturing by making them more competitive against foreign imports. The Sixteenth Amendment (1913) permitted the federal government to collect income taxes, shifting the government's main form of revenue to personal and corporate taxes. The government has also imposed taxes on such products as cigarettes and yellow oleomargarine, as much to curtail consumption as to raise revenue.

Various social forces, from reform movements to organized crime, spurred the growth of a federal police power. The Eighteenth Amendment (1919) prohibited the production, sale, or transportation of alcoholic beverages. Widespread disregard of the amendment during the 1920s put greater demands on federal investigators and clogged the federal courts. The kidnapping and murder of aviator Charles Lindbergh's infant son contributed to the Crime Control Act of 1934, which expanded federal jurisdiction over criminals who crossed state lines, gave the federal government power to punish anyone who interfered with, assaulted, or killed a federal agent, and set a death penalty for kidnappers. The chief federal policing agencies included the *Federal Bureau of Investigation, the Bureau of *Alcohol, Tobacco, and Firearms, the Secret Service, and the Immigration and Naturalization Service.

The crusade to end racial *segregation also pressed the federal government into areas that previously had resided with the states. The Supreme Court struck down school segregation in the case of *Brown v. Board of Education of Topeka, Kansas* (1954). A bus boycott in Montgomery, Alabama, "freedom riders" who challenged segregation in interstate transportation, and voter registration drives among African Americans forced further federal action. In 1964, the Senate broke a lengthy Southern-led filibuster and passed the Civil Rights Act of 1964, which used the commerce clause to make racial segregation effectively illegal in public accommodations. Title VII of that Act prohibited discrimination in employment on account of sex as well as race, thereby promoting equal rights for women. Congress later expanded the federal definition of *civil rights to include the disabled in the Americans with Disabilities Act of 1990.

The massive expansion of federal authority, ranging from economic regulation to civil rights laws, both diminished the role of the states and triggered a backlash. Under Chief Justice Earl *Warren (1953–69) a more liberal Supreme Court applied the protections of the Bill of Rights to the states, strengthened the definitions of civil rights and civil liberties, and threw its support behind the national government. Critics objected to the judicial activism of the Warren Court, calling for restraint and a return to the "original intent" of the Constitution's framers. A conservative majority on the Supreme Court under Chief Justice William Rehnquist (1986–   ) initiated a shift in federalism, striking down more acts of Congress in an effort to return power from Washington to the states.

Similar tensions arose between the legislative and executive branches. The Cold War helped justify a massive enlargement of presidential power, until the excesses of the "Imperial Presidency" during the Vietnam War (1959–75) and the Watergate scandal (1972–74) encouraged Congress to reassert its authority. The presidencies of Richard Nixon, Jimmy Carter, and Ronald Reagan put emphasis on deregulation, block grants to states, and renewed federalism. A welfare-reform accord reached between President Bill Clinton and Republican majorities in Congress further shifted responsibilities back to the states. More often than not during the last decades of the twentieth century, the executive branch and legislature were controlled by opposite parties. Such "divided government" lent political reinforcement to the constitutional system of checks and balances.

[See also Courts, United States—Federal Courts; Executive Power; Legislative Power; Legislatures, Structure of; Presidency of the United States; Separation of Powers]

• James MacGregor Burns, *The Deadlock of Democracy: Four-Party Politics in America,* 1963. Lawrence M. Freidman, *A History of American Law,* 1973. Arthur M. Schlesinger Jr., *The Imperial Presidency,* 1973. William H. Riker, *The Development of American Federalism,* 1987. Morris P. Fiorina, *Congress: Keystone of the Washington Establishment,* 2d ed., 1989. D. Robert Kiewiet and Mathew D. McCubbins, *The Logic of Delegation: Congressional Parties and the Appropriations Process,* 1991. Robert A. Carp and Ronald Stidham, *Judicial Process in America,* 1993. Robert A. Katzmann, *Courts and Congress,* 1997. Louis Fischer, *The Politics of Shared Power: Congress and the Executive,* 4th ed., 1998.

—Donald A. Ritchie

GOVERNMENT LAWYERS play a central, often defining, role in the shaping of public policy. They draft *regulations and legislation, provide counsel to policymakers, and represent the government in court. Whether the issue is the possible breakup of the *Microsoft Corporation, the power of the federal government to regulate tobacco products, or the constitutionality of racial preferences and school vouchers, government lawyers set the terms of the debate.

Involvement on All Levels. In the United States, the federal government employs more than forty thousand attorneys (with approximately eleven thousand lawyers working in the Department of *Justice). State and local governments employ many times this number of lawyers. Moreover, given the scope and size of the administrative state, nearly every lawyer in the United States has dealings with government lawyers.

Government lawyers play a unique and highly influential role, in part, because of the division of power both among the three branches of government and between the states and federal government. In particular, with lawyers serving as counselors and advocates for each unit of government, these divisions of political power have led to a proliferation of legal offices. Furthermore, by involving lawyers in every stage of agency rulemaking and enforcement, the management of the administrative state is largely left to government lawyers. Correspondingly, American political culture is especially legalistic. Federal courts, for example, are often asked to strike down governmental decision-making on constitutional and/or statutory grounds. Indeed, the United States (represented by Department of Justice lawyers) is a party in roughly forty percent of all filings in federal district court.

The Attorney General. Notwithstanding the vast power that government lawyers now possess, the Constitution's framers envisioned a quite modest role for government lawyers. Most striking, the *attorney general (who today oversees 128,000 employees in 59 separate offices and divisions) had virtually no power during the nation's early years. Rather, with little legal work to do, the attorney general worked only part-time until 1857. In fact, Congress did not establish the Department of Justice until 1870.

History of the Office. Before the Civil War, Congress's reluctance to establish a cabinet-level Justice Department was largely a result of the paucity of legal work. But Congress's hesitancy was also a byproduct of lawmaker desires to control agency decision-making. Unlike the Justice Department (whose hierarchical, centralized structure facilitates White House control of legal policymaking), a system in which each agency is responsible for its own lawyering empowers Congress. Specifically, with Congress controlling an agency's purse strings and its legislative mandate, agency heads are more apt to listen to Congress than is the attorney general (especially since most attorneys general are confidantes to the president who appoints them). Indeed, before Franklin Delano Roosevelt reorganized the Justice Department in 1933 to give it exclusive authority over most government litigation, Congress continued to allow agencies to manage their own legal policymaking, including litigation.

Roosevelt's New Deal ushered in the modern era and, with it, transformed the role of government lawyer from bit player to central figure in the administrative state. On the eve of the New Deal, there were 900 federally employed attorneys, 115 of whom worked in the Justice Department. By 1968, the staff of the Justice Department had grown to 32,000 (from 250 in 1905). Nevertheless, Roosevelt's efforts to strengthen Justice Department control of legal policymaking were only partially successful. Although supporting Department of Justice control of most government litigation authority, Congress placed agencies in charge of the crafting of regulations, the launching of administrative enforcement actions, and a host of other lawyer-related counseling functions.

Role of the Attorney General. Department of Justice control of government litigation places the attorney general, who answers only to the president, above all government litigants. The White House and the Department of Justice endorse this conception of the attorney general's role because it enables the government to speak as a unified voice in court, and it places the president or his cabinet-level surrogate, the attorney general, in charge of that voice. The realities of attorney general control, however, diverge from this hierarchical scheme. Legislative grants of independent litigating authority allow the Senate's Office of legal counsel, most independent agencies, and some executive agencies to represent themselves in court. Thirty-five agencies possess significant litigation authority, including the Department of Labor, the Securities and Exchange Commission, the Federal Communications Commission, the National Labor Relations Board, and the Federal Trade Commission.

Through these statutory grants of litigation authority, Congress protects its prerogatives from Department of Justice centralization. In so doing, however, Congress also ensures that a significant number of intragovernmental disputes are publicly aired before the federal courts. For example, the Federal Elections Commission, the Federal Trade Commission, the Federal Communications Commission, and the Postal Service have all locked horns with the "United States" (represented by Department of Justice lawyers). Lawyers representing Congress have also battled with Department of Justice lawyers over the constitutionality of federal legislation as well as efforts by executive branch officials to withhold documents from congressional committees. Finally, lawsuits challenging federal legislation and regulation have been launched by both state attorneys general and government lawyers representing county and city officials. Indeed, state attorneys general participate in approximately fifty U.S. Supreme Court cases each year (filing roughly five hundred separate briefs).

Limitations on the Attorney General. With so many different entities representing their own interests in court, attorney general control of litigation sometimes seems more illusory than real. Furthermore, since the president cannot order Congress, independent agency heads, or state and local officials to follow his lead on legal policymaking, there is next to nothing that the Department of Justice or White House can do to see to it that government lawyers speak a unitary voice in court. Put another way, the "United States" (represented by Justice Department lawyers) is simply one of many governmental entities represented in court.

The attorney general's power to coordinate legal policymaking is further limited by internal divisions of power both among executive branch agencies and within the Department of Justice itself. In critical respects, the Justice Department is a mammoth decentralized bureaucracy. The department has six central divisions: antitrust, civil, civil rights, criminal, environmental, and tax. On occasion, these divisions disagree with each other. For example, in sorting out the meaning of employment discrimination protections, the Civil Division has a pro-defendant view (because it defends lawsuits filed against the government) whereas the Civil Rights Division typically has a pro-plaintiff view (because it initiates lawsuits against businesses as well as states and municipalities for violating civil rights laws). More significant, some offices within the Justice Department have a history of independence. The *solicitor general (which represents the United States before the Supreme Court) is typically left alone by both the Attorney general and the White House. United States Attorneys (located in each of the ninety-four federal judicial districts throughout the United States) also enjoy a great deal of independence, especially on criminal law matters. Indeed, Congress's support for decentralized enforcement of federal criminal statutes resulted in the Department of Justice's withdrawal of a 1993 initiative to have the head of the Environment Division, not the local U.S. attorney, approve environmental prosecutions.

Attorney general control is limited in another way. Agency lawyers write the regulations that Department of Justice lawyers defend in court. Consequently, agency lawyers act as agenda setters and, in this way, box-in Justice Department lawyers. Agency lawyers, moreover, refer enforcement matters to the Department of Justice. And while the Justice Department need not pursue all of these referrals, congressional overseers sometimes pressure (through appropriations and oversight hearings) the Justice Department to pursue them.

The Power Wielded by the Attorney General. Notwithstanding these various impediments to her control of litigation, the attorney general wields enormous power in shaping federal legal policymaking. Reflecting the view that litigation is part of the president's power to enforce the law, Congress—although frequently tinkering at the margins—generally leaves it to Justice Department lawyers to represent federal interests in court. The *separation of powers likewise explains the power of agency lawyers to counsel agency heads by, among other things, drafting programmatic initiatives and rules. In particular, agency attorneys perform a quasi-legislative task, filling in the details of delegations of lawmaking power from Congress to agency heads.

State Attorneys General. The divide between in-court lawyering and out-of-court counseling is not as sharp at the state and local level. State attorneys general, in addition to representing the state in court, frequently serve as legal counselors to state agencies. Also, local prosecutors (most of whom are elected) are responsible for nearly all criminal prosecutions. One explanation for differences between the federal and state systems is that nearly all state attorneys general are elected and, as such, are independent of the state's governor. In this way, the power of the governor/executive branch is not aggrandized when state attorneys general perform quasi-legislative tasks, e.g., drafting legislation and regulations, and advising government officials about legal issues.

Like their federal counterparts, however, state attorneys general are responsible for managing an ever-growing bureaucracy. From 1970 to 1990, state attorneys general offices grew at an exponential rate—outpacing in every state the growth of government generally. California, for example, now employs more than one thousand lawyers in its state attorney's general office. And with Congress delegating primary enforcement responsibility to states for a host of federal regulatory initiatives, it is likely that state attorneys general will increasingly play a significant role in defining the meaning of federal as well as state law.

State and Federal Checks and Balances. The division of power both among the branches of the federal government and between the federal government and the states is premised on the belief that independent political actors will check each other. The disunitary nature of government lawyering reflects that belief. For example, when implementing federal law (or, alternatively, when challenging the legality of federal mandates), state officials will not look to Washington, D.C., to sort out what is in the best interest of their client. Instead, most state attorneys general will look to their own conception of the public interest. Likewise, lawyers both for Congress and independent agency heads will not attempt to have their legal interpretations match those of either the president or the attorney general.

More striking, even for lawyers working in the same branch of government, government lawyering often appears disunitary. Agency lawyers, for example, sometimes see their client as either their agency head, the head of the division they work for, the Congress that wrote the statute they are enforcing, or the president who appointed their agency head. Lawyers in Congress too have a difficult time identifying their client. Is it the Congress, the committee they work for, or the member who hired them? Needless to say, this pattern repeats itself at the state and local level. When advising state lawmakers, for example, should lawyers working in the office of the state attorney general see their client as the state legislature or the attorney general?

One thing is clear, however: government lawyers play a pivotal role in shaping public policy in the modern administrative state. Whether it is writing legislation and regulations, litigating on behalf of the government, or counseling policymakers, government lawyers are engaged in every facet of policymaking. And with so many different legal offices representing so many different governmental interests, it is inevitable that government lawyers rarely think of their client as being the "United States" (or the state of California for that matter). This disunitariness, rather than a cause of concern, is simply a reflection of how the separation of powers and federalism spread power among many different governmental actors.

[*See also* Lawyers; Legal Practice, Forms of]

• Donald Horowitz, *The Jurocracy,* 1977. Geoffrey P. Miller, "Government Lawyers' Ethics in a System of Checks and Balances," *University of Chicago Law Review* (1987): 293. Nancy Baker, *Conflicting Loyalties: Law and Politics in the Attorney General's Office,* 1992. Cornell

Clayton, *The Politics of Justice: The Attorney General and the Making of Legal Policy*, 1992. "Symposium: Executive Branch Interpretation of Law," *Cardozo Law Review* (1993). Cornell Clayton, ed., *Government Lawyers: The Federal Legal Bureaucracy and Presidential Politics*, 1995. Neal Devins, ed., *Government Lawyering, Law and Contemporary Problems* 61, nos. 1, 2 (1998).

—Neal Devins

GOVERNOR. The view of a state governor as the U.S. *president writ small—exercising the same role in state *government that the president does in the national government—is incorrect. Historically, states have possessed weak governorships, although their powers in some states have increased over the last three to four decades. Still, considerable differences remain between governorship and the presidency and between governorships in different states.

Conceptually, a strong governorship means (1) an office that allows its occupant to exert significant influence over the behavior and policies of state government, and (2) an office comparable in power and influence to the other branches of state government, so that an effective system of checks and balances exists. Whether an office meets these standards is determined primarily by its formal authority—powers attached to the office by a state constitution or legislative statute. Such powers are multiple and varied, but three—tenure, appointment, and veto—are particularly important and provide concrete illustrations of the strengths and weaknesses of the office.

"Tenure" is how long a governor can serve in office, both the length of term (one, two, or four years) and how many times he can be reelected. Changing the behavior of any large organization—such as a state government—takes time. Governors with lengthy tenure have time to accomplish the following: fully assess the strengths and weaknesses of current programs, build popular and legislative support for new programs, guide a newly adopted program through its implementation by the bureaucracy, and ensure the continued political and financial support necessary for the program to succeed. With severely restricted tenure, a governor can do none of these things.

The power of appointment is central to the notion of a *chief* executive—the leader who directs subordinates. At the national level, the president selects, with senatorial approval, the heads of federal agencies and can replace them at will (see EXECUTIVE POWER). Federal judges follow the same process of presidential selection and senatorial approval, though with tenure during good behavior

once confirmed. Few governors have comparable appointment power. Most face a few, sometimes many, state agency heads selected by the legislature, independent boards, or the voters.

Finally, a chief executive needs a strong veto. It serves to check an overzealous legislature, and the threat of a veto can be an effective tool to modify legislative actions. The strength of a veto is determined by its type (regular, item, or amendatory) and by override requirements, which vary from an easy-to-obtain simple majority legislative vote to the federal practice of a two-thirds vote in each legislative house.

How have American governors fared on these traits over time? The earliest, colonial governors were often appointed directly by the British king to protect the interests of the crown. They served until recalled by the king and wielded extensive power, which included commanding the local armed forces, appointing judges and other governing officials (no legislative consent required), and granting *pardons from judicial actions. Essentially, governors *were* the colonial governments. In pre-Revolutionary times, legislatures, when they existed at all, were called by the governor to meet temporarily and provide advice on colonial needs. Neither the judiciary nor the legislature had independent sources of power allowing them to check the governor.

As the colonies matured, the emerging intellectual and economic leaders expected to play larger roles in colonial affairs. They served as delegates when legislative meetings were called and, over time, these colonial leaders used the legislative assemblies to complain about aspects of British rule. Eventually, legislatures became platforms for the rhetoric of revolution and independence, which led to immediate dissolution by the colony's governor.

With this history, it is not surprising that the Revolutionary era was one of little faith in executives, the symbols of British rule, but considerable faith in legislatures that historically spoke for popular needs. Suspicious of a chief executive and the power wielded by such an office, the first national government, the Articles of Confederation, contained no executive office. The legislature alone both established policies and operated the government.

The failure of this experiment gave rise to the federal Constitution, which strengthened the national government and created a chief executive within that government. Historians agree that the presidency was made possible by George Washington. The writers of the Constitution accepted a strong executive office only because they knew the dependable Washington would be its first occupant. The situation was not the same in the states. As they created their own post-Independence governments, all included a gubernatorial office, but most left it without much authority. Compared with the president's multiple four-year terms, early governors often served only one-year terms, with many forbidden to serve more than one term. Compared with the president's veto authority, only the constitutions of Massachusetts and New York gave their governors some veto over legislative actions. Compared with the carefully crafted checks and balances at the national level, the early American governorship, as observers usually described it, was an office with innumerable checks and few balances.

This situation could not last forever. Complex government activities require the leadership and coordination that only a strong chief executive can provide. The most populous states, with growing cities and complex economies, recognized early the need to strengthen their governments and governors. Rural states had less need for active governments and were content to keep their governors as weak figureheads. Normal economic and population growth would eventually have led these states to strengthen their governing institutions as well, but the *Civil War intervened. In its aftermath, nervousness about strong state executives was refueled.

At the end of the Civil War, Congress mandated harsh punishment for the former states of the Confederacy. During Reconstruction, southern states were treated as conquered territories. Power was concentrated at the state capital, and particularly in the governor's hands, so a few northern appointees could run the state regardless of popular will. Reconstruction was so despised by southerners that as soon as it ended they immediately rewrote their constitutions to strip their state governments, and especially their governors, of power. Gubernatorial tenure was limited, veto authority was weakened, and the concept of the plural executive was instituted. Post–Civil War southern constitutions typically required the election, not gubernatorial appointment, of many state agency heads; other agencies were governed by boards or commissions beyond the governor's direct influence. Observing the experience in the South, new western states added some of the same restrictions when writing their own constitutions.

By the beginning of the twentieth century only a handful of states had effective governorships, yet the country was quickly moving away from its rural heritage, becoming an industrial power among nations. Political, intellectual, and civic leaders across the country pushed to strengthen and streamline government structures at the city, county, and state levels. There were a number of successes at the city level, and some at the state level, but increasingly archaic state legislatures were an obstacle. States did not regularly redraw the boundaries of their legislative districts. Consequently, the vast population shift in the twentieth century from rural areas to the cities was not reflected in state legislatures. Containing only a minority of the state's population, rural districts often elected a majority of the legislators. Rural areas were not interested in new taxes supporting mass transit or pollution control, or in strengthening governors elected by the state's urban majority.

The 1960s and beyond were a time of massive upheaval in the states. Demands for new streets, schools, and prisons, urban growth and new federal programs drew the states into a variety of new activities. A series of U.S. Supreme Court decisions, beginning with *Baker v. Carr (1962), eliminated legislative malapportionment. Appearing in the state capitals were a new crop of legislators who reflected urban and suburban needs and a stronger executive branch that could effectively manage larger state programs.

Most governorships changed dramatically after 1960. New agencies created by the expanding states followed the federal model of gubernatorial nomination and senatorial approval for agency leaders. In 1964, fifteen states restricted their governors to two-year terms, and another fifteen limited the governor to a single term. By 1998, those numbers had dropped to three states and one state, respectively. Many states have given their governors item vetoes over budgetary matters, and a few are experimenting with amendatory vetoes— powers not possessed by the president. While a few small states retain their historically weak governorships, most governors are now chief executives of their states in fact as well as in name.

[See also Executive Power]

• Larry Sabato, Goodbye to Good-time Charlie, 1983. Alan Rosenthal, The Governor and the Legislature, 1988. Eric B. Herzik and Brent W. Brown, eds., Gubernatorial Leadership and State Policy, 1991. Marshall Kaplan and Sue O'Brien, The Governors and the New Federalism, 1991. Laura Van Assendelft, Governors, Agenda Setting, and Divided Government, 1997. Sarah McCally Morehouse, *The Governor as Party Leader*, 1998. Thad Beyle, "The Governors," in *Politics in the American States*, 7th ed. (Virginia Gray, Russell L. Hanson, and Herbert Jacob, eds.), 1999. Nelson C. Dometrius, "Governors: Their Heritage and Future," in *American State and Local Politics* (Ronald E. Weber and Paul Brace, eds.), 1999. Council of State Governments, "The Executive," in *The Book of the States*, biennial.

—Nelson C. Dometrius

GRAND JURY. *See* Prosecutor.

GRAND LARCENY. *See* Theft.

GREGG V. GEORGIA, 428 U.S. 153 (1976), decided 2 July 1976 by a vote of 7 to 2. Stewart announced the judgment of the Court in an opinion joined by Powell and Stevens; White, *Burger, Blackmun, and Rehnquist concurring; *Brennan and *Marshall dissenting. In his dissenting opinion in *Furman* v. *Georgia* (1972), Chief Justice Burger had noted that three of the five justices supporting the Court's holding had not ruled that *capital punishment under all circumstances was unconstitutional and that it may be possible for states to rewrite their laws to meet the "test of guided discretion."

Taking cues from this and the other dissents filed in *Furman*, many states set out to revise their death penalty laws. Among the new plans was one proposed by Georgia (and other states). At the heart of the law was the "bifurcated trial," which consisted of two stages—the trial and the sentencing phase. The trial would proceed as usual; if the jury's verdict was guilty, the prosecution could seek the death penalty at the sentencing stage, in which the defense attorney presents the mitigating facts and the prosecution presents the aggravating facts. Mitigating facts include the individual's record, family responsibility, psychiatric reports, chances for rehabilitation, and age. Such data are not specified in law. The prosecution, however, has to demonstrate that at least one codified aggravating factor was present.

The Georgia law specified ten aggravating factors, including murders committed "while the offender was engaged in the commission of another capital offense," the murder of "a judicial officer . . . because of the exercise of his official duty," and murders that are "outrageously or wantonly vile, horrible, or inhumane." After hearing arguments in mitigation and aggravation, the jury determines whether the individual receives the death penalty. By spelling out the conditions that must be present before a death penalty can be imposed, the law

sought to reduce the jury's discretion and eliminate the arbitrary application of the death penalty that the Court found unacceptable in *Furman*. As a further safeguard, the Georgia Supreme Court was to review all jury determinations of death. This new law was applied to Troy Gregg, and quickly challenged by groups opposed to capital punishment.

Gregg and a friend were hitchhiking in Florida. Two men picked them up, and later the foursome was joined by another passenger who rode with them as far as Atlanta. The four then continued to a rest stop on the highway. The next day, the bodies of the two drivers were found in a nearby ditch. The individual let off in Atlanta identified Gregg and his friend as possible assailants. Gregg was tried under Georgia's new death penalty system. He was convicted of murder and sentenced to death, a penalty the state's highest court upheld.

When the justices announced their decision in *Gregg* (along with decisions in four other capital punishment cases), the media characterized it the following terms: "The Supreme Court ruled that the death penalty is not inherently cruel or unusual." But a careful reading of the opinions reveals a more complex picture.

The plurality opinion of Justices Stevens, Stewart, and Powell consisted of two major components. The first, which drew heavily on Powell's dissent in *Furman*, sought to demonstrate that precedent, history, and the intent of the framers supported the conclusion that the death penalty was not *cruel and unusual per se. The opinion also indicated that evolving standards of decency did not support another outcome, nor did judicial restraint. Finally, the three adopted the rather controversial position that the death penalty may serve the legitimate government functions of retribution and deterrence. The second component explained why Georgia's law was constitutional. This boiled down to a matter of logic for the three justices: the basic "constitutional infirmity" of the laws at issue in *Furman* was that their "unbridled discretion" led to arbitrariness. Since the new plans called for guided discretion, for a consideration of the particular circumstances of the case, and for appellate review, the justices reasoned that the chances for arbitrary imposition had dissipated considerably.

Justices White, Burger, Rehnquist, and Blackmun concurred. Writing for Burger and Rehnquist, White wrote that Gregg's attorneys had failed to demonstrate that the new laws would produce arbitrary results. Further, in an attempt to reconcile his views here with those he expressed in *Furman*—that the death penalty was so infrequently imposed that it could not serve as a credible deterrent—White wrote "I cannot conclude at this juncture that the death penalty . . . will be imposed so seldom and arbitrarily as to serve no useful penological function."

Brennan and Marshall dissented. Brennan's dissent was short, mainly reiterating his position in *Furman* that the Constitution prohibits the imposition of the death penalty. Marshall's dissent was longer, focusing on the purpose of capital punishment. He challenged the position taken by the majority of his colleagues that it serves a legitimate government function and, like Brennan, concluded that it is an "unnecessary" and "excessive penalty" forbidden by the Constitution.

Many scholars have speculated on why the Supreme Court reached the decision it did in *Gregg*. Some suggest that the Court succumbed to public pressure in this area: Americans wanted the death penalty, and the justices caved in, the argument goes. Other analysts point to the difference in the laws at issue in 1972 and in 1976.

Whatever the explanation, many states have now adopted variations of Georgia's death penalty law (currently, thirty-eight states have death penalty laws on their books), and executions have increased accordingly. During the 1970s, only three people were legally executed in the United States; in the 1990s, that figure was more than 470. In 1999 alone, a record ninety-eight individuals were executed, and, as of December 2000, nearly 4,000 wait on death rows.

Between its 1976 and 1999 terms, the Supreme Court heard challenges to about sixty of these scheduled executions. And while it has occasionally ruled for the defendant (in roughly 40 percent of the cases), it has not veered from the position it took in *Gregg*—that capital punishment is not unconstitutional per se. Thus, today, the United States is one of ninety countries that retain the death penalty, though not many of the others use it with any regularity. Indeed, the 1,625 *known* executions occurring in 1998 took place in only thirty-seven nations—with China, the Democratic Republic of Congo, the United States, and Iran accounting for 80 percent.

[*See also* Criminal Punishments]

• Franklin E. Zimring and Gordon Hawkins, *Capital Punishment and the American Agenda,* 1986. Lee Epstein and Joseph F. Kobylka, *The Supreme Court and Legal Change: Abortion and the Death Penalty,* 1992. Herbert H. Haines, *Against Capital Punishment: The Anti-Death Penalty Movement in America, 1972–1994,* 1996. Stuart Banner, *Dangling between Heaven and Earth: A History of Capital Punishment in the United States,* 2001.

—Lee Epstein

GUARDIANSHIP. *See* Aging and the Law; Children's Rights; Family Law; Health Law.

GUILTY PLEA. *See* Procedure, Criminal.

GUN CONTROL. *See* Arms, Right to Bear.

H

HABEAS CORPUS. The writ of habeas corpus is a judicial *remedy available to litigants challenging the legality of their confinement. It is usually used as a post-conviction remedy by criminal defendants to challenge the legal sufficiency of the procedures used to convict, but it can also be used by other confined people. Unlike a direct appeal of a criminal conviction, the writ is a collateral civil procedure that may be filed in a trial court.

The "Great Writ" was part of the *common law tradition inherited by the United States from Britain. It was available as a remedy in colonial courts, and was so well established that after the Revolution, its suspension would be prohibited by Article I, Section 9, of the U.S. Constitution "unless, when in cases of Rebellion or Invasion the public Safety may require it." Similar provisions are included in all fifty state constitutions, with eleven states prohibiting its suspension outright.

Although the writ can be used to review state cases in state courts, and federal cases in federal courts, it is most conspicuously and controversially used in federal courts to review the sufficiency of state confinement and conviction procedures. The U.S. Constitution is silent as to whether federal courts have this power, but it can be plausibly argued that such review of state court proceedings for conformance with federal constitutional and statutory requirements is granted to the courts by the supremacy clause of Article VI. In any event, Congress expressly granted this power to the federal courts shortly after the Civil War. The use of this power grew dramatically with the so-called *Due Process Revolution of the twentieth century. As the procedural requirements imposed upon the state courts by the U.S. Supreme Court grew, so did the grounds upon which a habeas corpus petition could be based.

It is fairly simple to understand why a litigant would find federal habeas review preferable to a direct appeal from state to federal court. The only court in the federal system that can hear direct appeals from state courts is the U.S. Supreme Court. Because that court has an extremely limited discretionary docket and many applications for review, it is highly unlikely that it will choose to hear any given case. Thus, there are long odds against a state prisoner getting any federal review of his or her case on direct appeal.

A habeas corpus application, however, can be filed with the appropriate district court, and that court must consider the application. Until recently, there has also been no limitation on the number of habeas petitions that can be filed by the same litigant on the same case, nor has there been any requirement of timeliness. The writ can give the litigant several "bites of the apple" over long periods of time. Direct appeal, on the other hand, is generally a one-shot affair with strict timeliness requirements.

Obviously, the ease of access to the writ creates huge potential problems for the states. In theory, every inmate in a state could continuously file habeas petitions, cumulatively imposing great legal costs on that state. In practice, the filing of successive habeas petitions proved an especially effective device for delaying the imposition of the death penalty (see CAPITAL PUNISHMENT). Following an unsuccessful process of direct appeal, a condemned prisoner typically files a habeas petition in federal court, forcing the federal court to postpone the execution while the petition is considered. If the petition was denied at district court, the prisoner could then appeal the denial to the circuit court and then to the Supreme Court. If the petition failed at that level, the defendant could start the whole process over by filing a new petition in the district court, claiming a different constitutional violation.

Several statutes and judicially created doctrines have, however, limited the ability of prisoners to use habeas proceedings by imposing conditions for habeas review. These include requirements (among others) that: 1) the writ is based on a violation of federal constitutional or statutory provisions (not state law claims); 2) the prisoner has exhausted all state fora in which he might litigate this claim (although there is some disagreement in the case law as to whether this includes an application for review by the state's court of last resort); 3) that the relief not be based on law that was enacted or precedent created after the case was originally litigated, unless that law or precedent was intended to apply retroactively; and 4) successive habeas corpus applications by the same applicant cannot be based on the same claim or on new claims unless it can be shown that the claim is based upon the discovery of new facts or subsequent developments in the law that were meant to apply retroactively. The most significant recent statutory change, however, has been the enactment of the Antiterrorism and Effective Death Penalty Act of 1996, which imposes a one year limitation on applications for federal habeas review of state courts for the complicated provisions governing what actions toll the one-year clock. This limitation has been highly controversial among legal academics and professionals, but its true effects are rather hard to gauge.

Another major controversy is now arising concerning the use of the writ. Habeas corpus is generally a procedural remedy, not a forum for relitigating the facts of a case. As such, factual innocence is not, by itself, a basis for relief. In order for relief to be granted on the basis of innocence, the litigant must show that some sort of procedural insufficiency or governmental misconduct prevented the defendant from producing this evidence. With the discovery of new technologies such as DNA identification, however, there have been several cases of exculpatory evidence that was not available at the time of trial. Because the unavailability of this evidence at the time of trial did not result from government misconduct, however, habeas corpus review cannot generally provide a remedy in such cases. Under these circumstances, innocent inmates must rely on alternative forms of relief (such as a pardon), or hope that a judge can find a procedural pretext for granting relief.

[See also Criminal Law Principles]

• Emanuel Margolis, "Habeas Corpus: The No-Longer Great Writ," Dickinson Law Review 98 (1994): 557–627. Marshall J. Hartman and Jeanette Nyden, "Habeas Corpus and the New Federalism after the Anti-Terrorism and Effective Death Penalty Act of 1996," John Marshall Law Review 30 (1997): 337–87. James S. Liebman and Randy Hertz, Federal Habeas Corpus Practice and Procedure, 2 vols., 3d ed., 1998. Alan K. Chen, "Shadow Law: Reasonable Unreasonableness, Habeas Theory, and the Nature of Legal Rules," Buffalo Criminal Law Review 2 (1999): 535–634. Eric M. Freedman, "Milestones in Habeas Corpus: Part I: Just Because John Marshall Said It, Doesn't Make It So: Ex Parte Bollman and the Illusory Prohibition on the Federal Writ of Habeas Corpus for State Prisoners in the Judiciary Act of 1789," Alabama Law Review 52 (2000): 535–602. Lissa Griffin, "The Correction of Wrongful Convictions: A Comparative Perspective," American University International Law Review 16 (2001): 1241–1308.

—Daniel R. Krislov

HAND, LEARNED (born Albany, N.Y., 27 January 1872; died New York, N.Y., 18 August 1961), federal judge. Learned Hand enjoyed one of the longest tenures on the federal bench of any judge in this century. President William Howard *Taft, seeking to improve the federal bench, appointed Hand to the district *court in New York in 1909 upon the recommendation of Charles Burlingham. In 1924 Calvin Coolidge elevated Hand to the Court of Appeals for the Second Circuit; Hand served as chief judge of that court from 1939 until his nominal retirement in 1951, but he continued to carry a heavy load as a senior judge until his death.

Twice Hand came close to appointment to the U.S. Supreme Court. In the 1920s he was considered for every vacancy on the high court, but then Chief Justice William Howard Taft, still bitter at Hand's having backed Theodore Roosevelt's Bull Moose ticket in 1912, blocked his appointment. Then in the early 1940s Felix *Frankfurter lobbied incessantly to have Hand appointed, but Franklin D. Roosevelt wanted younger men and also resented Frankfurter's heavy-handed tactics.

Hand's reputation lies less in constitutional law, since at that time relatively few constitutional cases came before the Second Circuit, than in private law and statutory interpretation, in which he set high standards for clarity of expression and judicial craftsmanship. Yet his voice was also important in the ongoing debate over judicial activism and the expansion of constitutional liberties.

Like his good friend Felix Frankfurter, Hand believed that judges had a limited role to play, a philosophy that, like Frankfurter, he derived from his studies with James Bradley *Thayer at the Harvard Law School, from which he graduated in 1896. He would later claim that Thayer and others had taught him that the highest satisfaction a lawyer or a judge could derive came from knowing a job had been done in a craftsmanlike manner. Hand did not see judicial restraint as an abdication of responsibility, nor as an intellectually sterile enterprise. Within modest parameters judges had important work to do, exploring the underlying questions of law and creating legal rules appropriate to the times. Larger questions of policy, however, should be left to the elected branches.

Hand constantly expressed his dissatisfaction with the activist wing of the Court headed by Hugo *Black and William O. *Douglas, and in the Holmes lectures at Harvard in 1958 he questioned the propriety of judges enlarging the meaning of the *Bill of Rights. Years earlier he had attacked the majority decision in *Lochner v. New York (1905) for imposing conservative personal values in place of legislative wishes, and he now applied that same reasoning to the *Warren Court. Like Frankfurter, Hand believed that the extent of Bill of Rights protection, as well as its enforceability, should be left to the legislature.

Hand believed strongly in free *speech, and in 1917 handed down a highly controversial opinion in Masses Publishing Co. v. Patten, in which he argued that the First Amendment protected all speech short of direct incitement to illegal action. When the Supreme Court issued its first rulings in the wartime speech cases, Holmes's clear and present danger test in Schenck v. United States (1919) fell far short of Hand's standard. Hand criticized the Holmes test as too vague and assumed that the Court had implicitly rejected the Masses criterion.

This explains why, despite his lifelong commitment to free speech, Hand confirmed the conviction of eleven communist leaders in United States v. Dennis (1950), a case in which the clear and present danger test was watered down to allow the government to prosecute people for conspiring to teach the overthrow of the government, a far cry from the Masses test. But Hand in this case was carrying out what he saw as his role as a judge—adherence to precedent and deference to the elected branches of government; privately he still adhered to the Masses test. Eventually the Supreme Court moved away from Schenck and Dennis, and in Brandenburg v. Ohio (1969) adopted what many commentators believe is essentially Learned Hand's approach.

[See also Judge]

• Kathryn Griffith, Judge Learned Hand and the Role of the Federal Judiciary, 1973.   —Melvin I. Urofsky

HANDICAP. See Disabilities Law; Discrimination.

HARASSMENT is a general term in law used to describe behavior that is annoying, alarming, or threatening. Stalking, which consists of an ongoing course of conduct that causes the victim to fear for his or her safety, is one form of harassment.

The three most common scenarios for harassment involve stalking by former spouses or lovers (overwhelmingly women being stalked by ex-husbands or ex-boyfriends), celebrities stalked by obsessed fans, and people harassed by acquaintances such as neighbors or co-workers. Workplace harassment, particularly of a sexual nature, is common, but typically dealt with through civil rights laws that deal exclusively with employment relationships. Other types of harassment are addressed primarily through state criminal laws prohibiting harassment and stalking.

According to one study conducted by the National Institute of Justice, 8 percent of women and 2 percent of men have been stalked at some point in their lives; 1.4 million Americans are stalked each year. Stalkers engage in a variety of behaviors, including making harassing phone calls, sending written messages or objects, monitoring their victim's whereabouts, following or lying in wait for their victim, vandalizing property, and, more recently, sending threatening e-mail messages.

Celebrity stalking victims, who are often stalked by strangers, get the most press coverage but comprise a small minority of such incidents. Some celebrities, including John Lennon, singer Selena, and actress Rebecca Schaeffer, have been murdered by their stalkers.

Non-celebrity stalking victims are primarily young, adult women. Stalkers are primarily male, and their victims tend to be women with whom they have been in intimate relationships. Stalking occurs across racial and class lines.

Stalking is more likely to occur in relationships in which controlling or emotionally abusive behavior occurs. There is a demonstrated relationship between stalking and other types of violence. Eighty percent of women who are stalked by a husband or boyfriend are also physically assaulted by him; 31 percent are sexually assaulted. Stalking often escalates over time, sometimes resulting in fatal attacks. According to an FBI crime study, 30 percent of murdered women are killed by a husband or lover who first stalked them.

Stalking can take a severe emotional toll on its victims, causing many to become depressed or anxious, exhibit symptoms of post-traumatic stress disorder, seek counseling, miss work, carry a weapon, or take extraordinary steps to avoid contact with the stalker. Stalking lasts nearly two years on average, longer if the victim and perpetrator were once in an intimate relationship. Stalking is most likely to stop if the victim moves away or the perpetrator either finds a new target of attention or is deterred from further contact by a warning from the police.

Stalking often eludes traditional criminal and civil law. Many of the individual acts that comprise stalking—such as calling someone on the phone, watching from a distance, or sending written messages—are perfectly legal. The elements of many traditional criminal offenses, like *assault and battery, often cannot be made out because the harassment does not cause physical injury to the victim. Likewise, although service upon a stalker of a civil protection order (also called a restraining order) may sometimes deter future contact with the victim, such orders do not adequately address the problem because they are often only available against family members, are poorly enforced, and do not assure sufficient deterrence of future incidents.

Even before the enactment of legislation directed specifically to stalking behavior, some states had laws on the books criminalizing harassment, telephone harassment, or terroristic threats. Such statutes provided some protection against annoying or alarming behavior not captured by traditional criminal laws, such as obscene or crank telephone calls, abusive language, and threats of serious bodily harm. But the laws did not adequately address the problem of stalking because they were not broad enough to cover a course of conduct that did not include physical contact, express threats, or telephone communication, and because the offenses were only misdemeanors.

Several highly publicized cases of celebrity stalking led California to enact the nation's first anti-stalking law in 1991. Today, that law defines the crime of stalking as repeatedly following or harassing a person, making a credible threat of harm, and causing the person to have a reasonable fear for his or her safety. The first offense is punishable as a *felony, and penalties are more severe when the stalker acts in violation of a restraining order. California has also expanded its courts' jurisdiction to issue protective orders outside of family relationships, and enabled police to commence the process for entry of a protective order on behalf of a stalking victim.

In the last decade, every state and the District of Columbia has enacted an anti-stalking law of its own, many expressly modeled on the California law. Some states retain separate offenses of harassment and stalking, but many have merged them into a single offense. While every state requires more than a single instance of nonconsen-

sual communication, the states vary as to whether the conduct must be accompanied by a threat of harm, whether such a threat must be express or may be implied, how serious the threatened harm must be, and whether the perpetrator must intend to instill fear or simply intend to commit the act that in fact makes the victim fearful. Congress also passed a federal law banning interstate stalking in 1997.

Anti-stalking laws have been subjected to constitutional challenges under the *Fourteenth and First Amendments on grounds of vagueness and overbreadth. Vagueness challenges are premised on an individual's right to have fair notice of forbidden behavior and be protected from arbitrary enforcement of criminal laws. The overbreadth doctrine says that laws cannot be so broad as to punish constitutionally protected behavior, such as *speech protected by the First Amendment.

These challenges have been largely unsuccessful. Courts generally have upheld stalking laws, albeit sometimes by interpreting them narrowly to save them from constitutional attack. Although a few courts have struck down stalking laws, legislatures in those states have responded by rewriting or narrowing the laws to cure the deficiencies. At the same time, other states have expanded their anti-stalking laws to provide greater protection to victims. California, for example, amended its original statute to apply to implied threats of harm, reconciling its law with survey data suggesting that express threats are relatively uncommon in stalking relationships. Many states have also amended their laws to cover so-called cyberstalking—the use of electronic communication to instill fear in a victim.

Although it is too soon to evaluate the overall effectiveness of anti-stalking laws, victims today have more remedial options than they did a decade ago. Harassment victims may file criminal complaints against stalkers, which may result in an arrest. Victims may also, depending on state law, obtain a restraining order against the perpetrator, ordering him or her not to call or come within a certain number of feet. Laws directly targeting stalking seem to have improved the rate at which stalking is reported to the police, although there does not seem to be a similar effect on arrest rates.

Victims of harassment may also avail themselves of private forms of protection. Phone companies, for example, can place a block preventing the harasser from calling the victim. Privately run shelters may provide a safe haven for stalking victims, although most are available only to women. For celebrity victims, private bodyguards are often employed for protection against the stalker.

[See also Criminal Law Principles; Domestic Violence-Partner Abuse]

• Lenore Walker, The Battered Woman, 1979. Violence Against Women Grants Office, Domestic Violence and Stalking: The Second Annual Report to Congress under the Violence Against Women Act, 1997. Neil Jacobson and John Gottman, When Men Batter Women, 1998. Patricia Tjaden and Nancy Thoennes, Stalking in America, 1998.
—Joanna L. Grossman

HARLAN, JOHN MARSHALL (1833–1911), Supreme Court justice, 1877–1911. Harlan was a member of a prominent Kentucky family, his father a distinguished lawyer and leading Whig politician. After undergraduate education at Centre College, law study at Transylvania University, and reading law with his father, Harlan was admitted to the Kentucky bar in 1853. As the Whig Party collapsed, Harlan and his father briefly became leaders in the Know-Nothing Party, and he won election as a county judge on the Know-Nothing ticket in 1858. Harlan was initially an opponent of abolition and used racist and *states' rights appeals in stump speeches. He assumed the same stance in a successful bid to become Kentucky's attorney general near the end of the Civil War. But he was also a nationalist who fought with the Union during the war and in 1870 embraced the Republican Party and the goals of Reconstruction. Harlan lost two gubernatorial bids on the Republican ticket but played a key role in swinging the Kentucky delegation to Rutherford B. Hayes at the party's 1876 national convention. The next year Hayes rewarded him with a seat on the Supreme Court. However complex Harlan's past political leanings, as a justice he became an ardent and essentially consistent champion of racial and most other civil liberties claims. Felix *Frankfurter would later characterize Harlan as a constitutional "eccentric." But the modern Court has largely embraced many of the positions he advanced in ringing dissents, including incorporation of *Bill of Rights safeguards into the *Fourteenth Amendment's restrictions on state authority, broad construction of congressional power over *civil rights, and condemnation of *segregation laws in his *Plessy v. Ferguson (1896) dissent.

[See also Supreme Court of the United States]

• Loren P. Beth, John Marshall Harlan: The Last Whig Justice, 1992. Tinsley E. Yarbrough, Judicial Enigma: The First Justice Harlan, 1995.

—Tinsley E. Yarbrough

HARLAN, JOHN MARSHALL II (1899–1971), *Supreme Court justice, 1955–71. The grandson of the first Justice *Harlan he was raised in comfortable circumstances. Following education from his early youth at a Canadian boarding school, he enrolled at Princeton, where he compiled an outstanding academic record and was president of the student newspaper. His law studies consisted of two years at Oxford on a Rhodes scholarship and a year at New York Law School. Winning admission to the bar in 1924, Harlan rose quickly in the ranks of what was to become Dewey, Ballantine, one of New York's most prestigious Wall Street firms. Harlan became a master of his craft—a "lawyer's lawyer" in the eyes of his contemporaries. After World War II service with military intelligence, Harlan returned to his firm and an impressive array of corporate clients.

When Dwight D. Eisenhower became president, he appointed Harlan to the U.S. Court of Appeals for the Second Circuit and, in 1955, to a seat on the Supreme Court. On the bench, Harlan quickly allied with Felix *Frankfurter's restraintist bloc. Following Frankfurter's retirement in 1962, Harlan became the principal critic of liberal-activist trends on the *Warren Court, especially in criminal justice, domestic security, reapportionment, *federalism, and nonracial *equal protection cases. He was a vigorous opponent of the Court's *"incorporation" rulings, which applied most *Bill of Rights safeguards to the states via its interpretation of the *Fourteenth Amendment *due process guarantee. But Harlan embraced a flexible, *common-law approach to the *Constitution's meaning that sometimes led him in liberal-activist directions. In a Poe v. Ullman (1961) dissent, for example, he recognized a constitutional right of marital *privacy four years before a majority embraced that stance in the Griswold case. In Cohen v. California (1971), decided in his last term, Harlan spoke for the Court in rejecting governmental power to cleanse public *speech of offensive epithets.

[See also Supreme Court of the United States]

• "Mr. Justice Harlan: A Symposium," Harvard Law Review 85 (Dec. 1971). Tinsley E. Yarbrough, John Marshall Harlan: Great Dissenter of the Warren Court, 1992.

HATE CRIMES. Imagine that three husky fraternity members, out for a Saturday night drive, come across a lone African-American undergraduate walking home from the library. Deciding they do not like his looks, they slow down and yell: "Go back to Africa, you N. You don't belong on this campus." Their words target the victim because of his *race, and may constitute hate speech covered by a campus disciplinary code.

But suppose the three assailants go beyond merely shouting insults. They get out of the car and attack the undergraduate, sending him to the campus infirmary. Since they singled out their victim because of his membership in a racial minority group, their actions would qualify as a hate crime, if the state is one of the many that have enacted a statute covering such offenses.

Virtually every American state has provided for the punishment of this type of crime, in which the perpetrator singles out the victim because of his sex, race, ethnicity, national origin, or sexual orientation. The movement to enact hate laws began at the state level in the early 1980s, as a result of the upsurge in the incidence of hate crime and an increase in the activity of white supremacist groups. A number of highly publicized beatings and killings, such as those of Rodney King, Vincent Chin, Mathew Shephard, and the Central Park jogger, as well as the torching of black churches and shootings at synagogues added to public concern.

Legislatures have taken a number of different approaches to drafting hate crime legislation. Some have passed sentence-enhancement statutes that increase the severity of the sentence when the underlying crime was shown to have been committed with a particular racial or sexual animus. These piggyback on existing crimes, such as *assault or battery, and create no new offenses. Another approach punishes behavior in which the perpetrator selects a victim because of his membership in a vulnerable group. A third variety of hate crime statute singles out perpetrators who victimize others with a particular motivation, such as racial or ethnic hatred or a dislike of foreigners.

The differences among these approaches are sometimes significant. For example, a mugger might single out women, believing them easy marks, or target Japanese tourists, believing them likely to have a lot of money. Such a criminal may harbor no particular animus toward women or foreign tourists per se, and so would not qualify for punishment under an animus-based statute. He would qualify, however, under a statute that punishes behavior that singles out the victim because of membership in a protected group.

When hate crime statutes were first proposed, they attracted sharp criticism. Critics charged that such statutes violated *equal protection, mental privacy, or freedom of expression. Hate crimes were said to violate the norm of equality because they treated two similar offenses, such as assaults, differently merely because they were carried out with different motivations. These statutes were also said to punish thought or expression because the perpetrator of a hate crime is singled out for punishment because of something he says or thinks about the victim.

Defenders replied that legislation is needed because hate crimes are more serious than ones committed without this additional element. Hate crimes send a message to the entire minority, gay, or Jewish community, causing them to fear for their personal safety. They also have more lasting effects on victims, requiring a longer period before they feel safe in going about their daily affairs. And they are said to violate the norm of equality and equal citizenship and to erode the bonds that bind us together as a nation.

Doubts about the validity of hate crime statutes were largely laid to rest when the U.S. Supreme Court decided the case of *Wisconsin* v. *Mitchell* (1993). In that case, a nineteen-year-old black youth, Todd Mitchell, had encouraged some companions to attack a fourteen-year old white boy, Gregory Riddick. The group, which had just watched a movie about white violence against blacks, selected its victim because of his whiteness, and were charged under a Wisconsin bias crime statute that provided for an additional sentence of up to five years. The same crime without this feature would have drawn only a maximum two-year sentence. The prosecutor charged Mitchell under both provisions, so that his maximum possible sentence was seven years. The Supreme Court upheld his sentence, including the enhanced portion under which he had received an additional five years.

With the constitutionality of hate crimes laws now well established, different issues have moved to the fore. Social scientists are exploring why most perpetrators of hate crimes are men and why most victims are members of religious or racial minority groups, not of the white majority, as was the case in *Wisconsin* v. *Mitchell*. Scholars and public policy experts debate whether the United States should have a national hate crime law—as opposed to a patchwork of state laws—as many European countries do. At present, the federal government maintains statistics on hate crimes, but has not passed a bill punishing them. And scholars are investigating the relationship between hate speech and hate movements, such as the Nazi Holocaust. Building on a hypothesis first put forward by Gordon Allport in *The Nature of Prejudice* (1954), they are examining whether hate speech, hate literature, and hate movies vilifying minority groups create an environment in which hate crimes may flourish.

[*See also* Civil Rights and Civil Liberties; Gender and Law; Homosexuality and the Law; Speech and the Press, Freedom of]

• Jack Levin and Jack McDevitt, *Hate Crimes: The Rising Tide of Bigotry and Bloodshed*, 1993. Richard Delgado et al., *Words That Wound: Critical Race Theory, Assaultive Speech, and the First Amendment*, 1993. Frederick M. Lawrence, "The Punishment of Hate: Towards a Normative Theory of Bias Motivated Crimes," *Michigan Law Review* 93 (1994): 320. Lu-in Wang, *Hate Crimes Law*, 1997. Lu-In Wang, "The Transforming Power of Hate: Social Cognition Theory and the Harms of Bias-Related Crimes," *Southern California Law Review* 71 (1997): 647. Symposium, "Federal Bias Crime Law," *Boston University Law Review* 80 (2000): 1185–1449.

—Richard Delgado

HATE SPEECH. *See* Speech and the Press, Freedom of.

HAYMARKET TRIALS. The explosion of a bomb during a labor rally in Chicago's Haymarket Square on May 4, 1886, exacerbated tensions between labor unions and industrialists and had profound consequences for the incipient trade union movement.

The rally was organized by anarchists who had infiltrated Chicago trade unions, to protest the death of four persons three days earlier, when police had attacked some participants in a citywide general strike called to generate support for an eight-hour work day. The rally was initially peaceful, with various speakers denouncing capitalism. The bomb exploded shortly after police demanded that the protesters disperse. After the explosion, the police fired into the crowd for several minutes, killing an unknown number of civilians. One police officer was killed by the bomb and six others were killed by the stray fire of their fellow officers.

The bombing triggered a nationwide reaction against anarchists, socialists, and even the moderate elements of organized labor. Numerous businesses intensified efforts to discourage unionization, making more frequent use of lock-outs, blacklists, antiunion oaths, and strike-breakers. Courts also became more hostile toward labor, issuing an increasing number of injunctions against union activity and convicting more labor organizers of incitement and rioting. State legislatures enacted more stringent *conspiracy and anti-boycott laws to discourage unionization and for many years became more resistant to the eight-hour day.

Hostility toward organized labor also hastened the decline of the Knights of Labor, the nation's largest federation of trade unions. Even though its leaders strongly denounced the bombing, its opposition to capitalism brought it under increased suspicion during the wave of revulsion against socialism that followed the bombing.

Eight anarchists involved in the rally were brought to trial and convicted of conspiracy to commit murder, despite lack of evidence linking them with the bomb. Four were hanged and one committed suicide. The remaining three were pardoned in 1893 by Illinois Governor John Peter Altgeld, whose astringent denunciation of the tactics of the police, the judge, and the prosecutor doomed his prospects for re-election. The source of the bomb remains a mystery.

Since seven of the eight convicted anarchists were German-born, and many other anarchists and labor leaders also were immigrants, the bombing also exacerbated nativism and encouraged proposals to restrict *immigration. After an anarchist assassinated President William McKinley in 1901, Congress in 1903 barred the immigration of anarchists. The bombing also encouraged several states, including Illinois, to enact legislation restricting the right of aliens to own land.

The Haymarket bombing, however, may indirectly have promoted the long-term interests of organized labor. The injustice of the trial against the alleged conspirators intensified the dedication of many social reformers, and the executions created martyrs for the labor movement. More significantly, the widespread reaction against labor radicalism stimulated the growth of the American Federation of Labor (AFL), which was founded in 1886. In contrast to the Knights, the AFL accepted capitalism, and successfully sought to improve conditions for workers through collective bargaining. The AFL's amelioration of antagonism between labor and capital helped to reduce the tensions that precipitated the Haymarket tragedy.

[*See also* Criminal Law; Labor Law]

• Henry David, *The History of the Haymarket Affair: A Study in the American Social-Revolutionary and Labor Movements*, 1936. Paul Avrich, *The Haymarket Tragedy*, 1984.

—William G. Ross

HEALTH LAW is a large and disparate field consisting of the statutes, regulations, and judicial and administrative decisions pertaining to the health of individuals and communities. Much of health law involves the laws that relate directly to the provision of health services, but the field also includes other laws that affect the population's health.

Given the field's wide scope, it should not be surprising that it is inherently interdisciplinary. It cuts across and is comprised of numerous legal disciplines, such as torts, constitutional law, administrative law, tax and corporate law. Health law is also influenced by and relates to such nonlegal disciplines as medicine, nursing, psychology, economics, and philosophy. Traditionally, state law dominated the field. Since the enactment of federal health insurance programs in 1965, however, the federal government has played a large role. Determining the appropriate relationship between federal and state law is a major question in many areas of health law.

Although health law is too diverse and complex to be reduced to a simple summary, several major themes have been dominant. These include: professionalism, patient rights, access to care, cost of care, and public health.

Professionalism. Traditionally, U.S. health law has recognized and supported the authority of physicians over matters relating to health. Since the nineteenth century, state laws have licensed physicians and prohibited others from practicing *medicine without a license. Such laws were reaffirmed by the United States Supreme Court in *Dent* v. *West Virginia* (1889).

Medicine's prestige was also reflected in state *common law. As physicians became more critical to health care, they became vulnerable to malpractice suits. Courts responded by holding that medical custom established the legally mandated standard of care and that expert testimony was necessary to establish such custom. State laws banning the corporate practice of medicine also served to preserve the physician's dominance.

By the second half of the twentieth century, the civil rights and women's rights movements, as well as the high cost of medical care, began to weaken the law's deference to physicians. State courts began to reject the locality rule and hold physicians to a national standard of medical *custom. Courts also began to recognize that hospitals played a critical role with respect to patient care and could no longer be considered as simply theaters for physician practice. A significant plurality of states also held that physicians must provide a patient with the information a reasonable patient would find material in determining whether to undergo a medical procedure. And in some cases, such as

Helling v. *Carey* (Wash. 1974), courts went so far as to abandon medical custom as the legal standard of care. Other challenges to physician prestige have come from statutes and cases which have expanded the scope of practice of other health professionals, especially advanced practice nurses.

Despite these developments, U.S. law still confers considerable prestige and deference upon physicians. Many state legislatures have enacted *tort reforms that limit plaintiff's damages or make it more difficult for plaintiffs to reach a jury. Moreover, judicial decisions still echo the refrain of medical expertise and the need for courts to defer to medical judgment. Physicians continue to occupy a central and respected role in U.S. health law, but it is no longer as unimpeachable as it once was.

Patient Rights. If deference to professionalism was the initial theme of U.S. health law, the recognition of patient rights was its successor. Throughout the twentieth century, both state and federal law treated individual patients as rights-bearers with the legal right to control what happens to their body.

In 1914 Benjamin *Cardozo, sitting as a New York state court justice, proclaimed: "Every human being of adult years and sound mind has a right to determine what shall be done with his own body; and a surgeon who performs an operation without his patient's consent, commits an assault, for which he is liable in damages." *Schloendorff* v. *Society of New York Hospitals* (N.Y. 1914). The right of patients to control what happens to their body led many jurisdictions to require that physicians provide patients with the information they need to "meaningfully exercise their right to make decisions about their own bodies." *Truman* v. *Thomas* (Cal. 1980).

Respect for patient autonomy permeates other areas of the law. For example, it lies at the core of federal regulations governing human subject research. Although these complex regulations also embody other values (particularly the principle that harm should be in proportion to benefit), they most fundamentally demand that individuals be able to make an informed decision about participating in clinical trials supported by federal money.

Concern for individual autonomy has also been reflected in constitutional decisions about the beginning and ending of life. For example, in upholding a woman's right to choose an *abortion in *Roe* v. *Wade* (1973), the Supreme Court emphasized the right of a woman, as a patient, to make a decision with her doctor. And twenty years later in *Planned Parenthood* v. *Casey* (1992), in a plurality joint opinion, the Court affirmed a woman's right to choose an abortion, emphasizing her right to make autonomous decisions.

Similar respect for patient autonomy exists in the *"right to die" cases. As medicine became more technologically advanced, patients and their families began to question the value of extremely invasive procedures that prolonged life. In 1976, the New Jersey Supreme Court in *In re Quinlan* (N.J. 1976) first held that the family of such patients may assert their loved one's constitutional right to terminate treatment. In subsequent years, numerous state courts followed suit, setting forth different standards for determining the intent of an incompetent patient, but agreeing with the fundamental principle that patients have the right to end treatment, even if the result is death. State legislatures concurred, enacting living will and health care proxy statutes, each of which provides, in a different manner, for competent patients to control the health care decisions that will be made for them if and when they are no longer competent. In 1990, a majority of the justices of the United States Supreme Court suggested that competent individuals have the constitutionally protected right to have their wishes followed, although a different majority also held that the Constitution permits a state to require that a patient's wishes be determined by clear and compelling evidence (*Cruzan* v. *Director, Missouri Department of Health* (1990)).

Once the legislatures and courts had effectively settled the right to refuse treatment, debate turned to whether patients have the right to procure physician assistance in committing suicide. Here the law's recognition of patient autonomy appears to have stalled. Although Oregon enacted a law permitting physicians to assist with patient suicides under strictly defined circumstances, the Oregon Death With Dignity Act (1999), other states rejected such measures and the United States Supreme Court held unanimously in *Washington* v. *Glucksberg* (1997) that state laws prohibiting physician-assisted suicide are constitutional.

The right of patients to maintain the privacy of their medical records has also been the subject of great debate and conflicting legal standards. Although state common law principles provide some protection against a physician's disclosure of medical records, the law has not traditionally prohibited disclosures by others with access to medical records. This gap has become increasingly problematic as medical records contain more sensitive information (such as genetic profiles) and are

computerized and shared with health insurers, auditors, employers, and numerous other entities, many of whom have a legitimate and pressing need for the information. In 1996 Congress authorized the Department of Health and Human Services to develop regulations to protect medical records. In 2000, the Department promulgated the first set of nationwide medical record privacy protections (65 Fed. Reg. 82462; 28 December 2000). The complexity of these regulations affirms the difficulty of protecting confidentiality in a rapidly changing and increasingly integrated health care system.

Access to Care. In the United States there is no general legal right to access to health care or to the means to pay for it. This permits over forty million Americans to go without health insurance and often without health care. For them, the law's recognition of patient rights is illusory.

Most Americans under age sixty-five rely upon the workplace to provide them with access to health *insurance. This association between work and health care is supported by federal tax law that permits employees to forgo taxes on employer-provided health insurance premiums. The Employee Retirement Income Security (ERISA) Act of 1976 governs employer-provided plans and limits states' ability to regulate them. The boundaries between federal and state jurisdiction over so-called ERISA plans, and the torts they may commit, has become the subject of significant litigation.

In recent years Congress has increasingly regulated ERISA plans. The Health Insurance Portability and Accountability Act of 1996 ("HIPAA") limits the use of preexisting condition exclusions and waiting periods when employees change jobs and hence health plans. HIPAA also prohibits ERISA plans from discriminating on the basis of health status. But it does not require employers to provide insurance.

Government programs provide insurance for millions without private plans. The most significant programs are Medicare and Medicaid. Medicare is a federal *entitlement program that provides insurance for individuals over sixty-five plus many others with disabilities. Since its inception in 1965, it has grown enormously, and is expected to continue to grow as the population ages. Nevertheless, while the program provides nearly universal health insurance for those over sixty-five, it leaves many medical costs uncovered: including the cost of long-term care and prescription drugs. The enormous size and complexity of Medicare has led to an extensive body of federal regulations and administrative decisions regarding eligibility and coverage reimbursement.

Medicaid is a federal-state, needs-based program; however, not every poor person is eligible, only certain groups, such as children and pregnant women, as well as the elderly or disabled. Because Medicaid is a federal-state program specific eligibility criteria and benefits are determined by the states as well as federal law. A recent federal law, the Children's Health Insurance Program has given states the option of either expanding their Medicaid program to cover more children, or to undertake other measures designed to expand children's access to care. Nevertheless, this statute creates no entitlement. And despite the complex array of programs, millions remain uninsured. Some state and federal laws attempt to provide a safety net for those without insurance. For example, the Emergency Medical Treatment and Active Labor Act requires hospitals with an emergency room to screen and, if necessary, stabilize emergency patients regardless of their ability to pay. State common law decisions also provide a limited right to emergency care for the uninsured. Despite these safety-nets provisions, the stark fundamental fact of health law in the U.S. is the absence of a universal legal entitlement to care.

Cost Controls. For numerous reasons, including the aging of the population, inefficiencies in the health care marketplace, and the increasing technological sophistication of medical care, health care costs have risen dramatically over the last forty years. Controlling those costs has become a major preoccupation of U.S. health law.

Early responses to the rising cost of health care utilized "command and control" regulatory interventions. In the 1970s federal law required regulatory approval for the siting of health care facilities and many states imposed price controls on hospitals. The federal government also enacted laws designed to review and weed out inappropriate and unnecessary care in the Medicare program.

During the 1980s, policies began to favor a more "market-oriented" approach to cost-control. For example, Medicare changed the way it reimbursed hospitals, moving from a method based on the usual and customary fee (which provided no incentive for economic efficiencies) to one that paid hospitals a relatively flat rate for each "diagnostic related group," thereby encouraging providers to treat patients as inexpensively as possible.

Since the 1980s, there has been a steady rise in managed care. Encouraged by the 1973 Health Maintenance Act, which provided federal loans and tax benefits, managed care organizations (MCOs) initially offered comprehensive medical services for a flat fee. The goal was to integrate the provision of care with its financing, creating incentives to keep patients healthy and treat them economically.

In the 1980s and early 1990s, as the cost of care skyrocketed, MCOs increased their market share. This development was accelerated by President Bill Clinton's 1993 proposal to provide universal coverage via a plan that would have relied heavily upon the competition of various MCOs. Although that plan was never enacted, many employers moved their employees to MCO plans in anticipation of it. The federal government also began to permit states to enroll Medicaid beneficiaries in MCOs and to encourage Medicare beneficiaries to enroll in such plans.

By 2000, managed care dominated the health care marketplace, in many ways eclipsing the authority once held by physicians. Today, MCOs exist in various forms. Many are organized by for-profit corporations that establish complex "networks" of providers. Patients are generally required to use only providers within the network, often only with a referral from their primary care provider. Some MCOs use utilization review, which requires physicians to obtain approval for particular medical interventions. Many MCOs pass some of the economic risk of care to physicians. In *Pegram* v. *Herdrich* (2000), the Supreme Court held that such incentive schemes do not violate ERISA's fiduciary obligations. The ability of MCOs to exclude providers from their networks creates many federal *antitrust, tax law, and state law issues. Generally courts have been sympathetic to MCO attempts to control the composition of their network. Because MCOs have an incentive to reduce services, litigation has shifted from claims about unnecessary care to claims that necessary care has been denied. Many of these cases have been brought against ERISA plans. These cases have faced considerable jurisdictional hurdles, as the lines between state and federal jurisdiction remain contentious.

The belief of many providers and consumers that MCOs inappropriately limit care has led to numerous calls for "managed care reform." Most states have enacted legislation, providing patients with such protections as the right to an independent review of denied claims. The degree to which ERISA preempts such laws, however, remains unclear. In addition, Congress continues to debate a federal "patients bill of rights," but for now such legislation is stalled over whether MCOs should be liable for damages. Interestingly, any managed care bill will likely provide patients rights against insurers, not physicians, effectively reasserting some of the prestige and authority that physicians once held.

Public Health. Health law's focus on medical care and insurance threatens to obscure the importance of other laws that relate to and affect a community's health. Laws that pertain to sanitation, the quality of the food and water supply, infectious disease control, and hazardous products may all have a significant impact on a population's morbidity and mortality. Historically such public health laws were considered to be part of the states' police power, although as in other areas of health law, the federal government played an increasingly important role throughout the twentieth century.

Traditionally states protected public health by establishing departments of public health and vesting them with broad authority to take the steps necessary to protect health. At times this had led to conflicts with an individual's liberty. For the most part the courts have affirmed that individual freedoms may be restricted in order to prevent a public health risk. For example, in 1905 the Supreme Court held that states may require vaccination for smallpox if there is an epidemic (*Jacobson* v. *Massachusetts* (1905)). Courts have also generally upheld quarantines for communicable diseases, although in recent years, they have demanded that procedural protections accompany detention.

Two contemporary public health threats illustrate the key themes and challenges facing U.S. public health law. The AIDS epidemic has forced the law to revisit the conflict between individual rights and the public health. Since the advent of human immunodeficiency virus (HIV), legislatures and courts have recognized that individuals with HIV have often been the victims of irrational discrimination and that such discrimination may actually hamper efforts to contain the epidemic. As a result, antidiscrimination law (particularly *disability discrimination law) has been incorporated into the domain of public health law (*Bragdon* v. *Abbott* (1998)). More broadly, U.S. public health law has come to accept that individual rights are not always in conflict with public health; sometimes they may foster it.

The HIV epidemic has also highlighted the global nature of public health. The development of effective but expensive medications has raised profound conflicts between the legal protections for intellectual *property and the public health

problems facing developing nations. In a world where diseases know no borders and corporations are global, public health law must inevitably become international (see INTERNATIONAL LAW).

*Tobacco is another major public health hazard. Since the 1960s federal law has required warning labels on cigarettes and has limited their advertisement on electronic media. The Supreme Court has ruled (*Food and Drug Admin.* v. *Brown and Williamson Tobacco Corp.* (2000)), however, that the Food and Drug Administration lacks the authority to impose broader *regulations and that existing federal laws preempt state laws pertaining to cigarette labeling (*Cippolone* v. *Liggett Group* (1992)). Since the 1990s, tort cases have played an increasingly important role in tobacco policy. Although the first lawsuits brought against tobacco manufacturers for tobacco-related injuries were uniformly unsuccessful, by the 1990s, plaintiffs had some success, especially in using discovery to expose tobacco industry documents. In addition, state attorney generals brought cases against the tobacco companies seeking reimbursement for state health care costs associated with tobacco. These cases were settled in 1998 in a multistate settlement agreement that placed restrictions on certain marketing practices and provided for payments of over a billion dollars to the states. Many individuals, states and localities are pursuing a similar litigation strategy against other public health hazards, such as guns.

The Future. As the population ages and health care becomes more effective and more expensive, health law is likely to become even increasingly complex and interdisciplinary. In the years ahead it will likely oversee the struggles to restrain costs and improve health, while maintaining individual's rights in an increasingly global health care system.

• Judith Feder, *Medicare: The Politics of Federal Hospital Insurance,* 1977. Paul Starr, *The Social Transformation of American Medicine,* 1982. President's Commission for the Study of Ethical Problems in Medicine and Biomedical and Behavioral Research, *Summing Up: The Ethical and Legal Problems of Medicine and Biomedical and Behavioral Research,* 1983. Jay Katz, *The Silent World of Doctor and Patient,* 1984. George J. Annas, *The Rights of Patients,* 2d. ed., 1989. Harvard Medical Practice Study Group, *Patients, Doctors and Lawyers: Medical Injury, Malpractice Litigation and Patient Compensation in New York,* 1990. Mark Hall, *Health Care Corporate Law,* 1993. Peter Kongstvedt, ed., *Managed Health Care Handbook,* 3d. ed., 1996. Kenneth Wing, *The Law and the Public's Health,* 5th ed., 1999. Barry R. Furrow, Thomas L. Greaney, Sandra H. Johnson, Timothy Stoltzfus Jost, and Robert L. Schwartz, *Health Law,* 2d. ed., 2000.

Lawrence O. Gostin, *Public Health Law: Power, Duty, Restraint*, 2000. Jerry Menikoff, *Law and Bioethics: An Introduction*, 2001.   —Wendy E. Parmet

HIGHER LAWS. *See* Civil Disobedience; Ethics, Morality, and Law; Extralegality; Religion.

HIGHWAY PATROL (AND STATE POLICE). State law enforcement agencies that direct most of their attention to enforcing laws that govern the operation of motor vehicles on public roads and highways are typically designated as highway patrols. While traffic enforcement is the primary activity for highway patrols, in most cases they are charged with the investigation of crimes that occur on state property, state highways, or federal interstate highways. Their activities also include drug interdiction on interstate highways, especially those involving the use of public carriers.

Statewide agencies that have general *police powers and enforce state laws are usually designated as state police (e.g., New Mexico), or state troopers (e.g., Alaska). While traffic law enforcement on state and federal highways is a common activity of state police, they are also typically granted broad authority to investigate major crimes, to work independently of local police systems in gathering intelligence about organized crime, gambling, and drug trafficking, and to enforce the criminal laws of the state and nation.

Texas created the first statewide law enforcement agency with the establishment of the Texas Rangers in 1835. Initially its central role was to provide military-like service along the Mexican border. By the end of the nineteenth century only Delaware, Massachusetts, and South Carolina had followed Texas' lead. Between 1900 and 1920 law enforcement agencies with statewide jurisdiction were created in eighteen states, with most of that growth after 1910. Formal statewide police organizations existed throughout much of the nation by 1925. Law enforcement activities in all mainland states and the territory of Alaska were supported by a highway patrol and/or a state police by 1941.

Statewide law enforcement grew out of rapidly occurring societal changes. Population growth, territorial expansion, and changes in economic conditions produced extra pressures and responsibilities for a fee-based constable and *sheriff law system that had become more attentive to civil duties (e.g., town tax collection) than to legal duties of crime prevention and control. The earlier law system was soon recognized as ill equipped, especially for rural America. The growth in the development and use of roads and transportation

systems, in addition to expanding the reach and impact of crime beyond local communities, eventually required statewide regulation of highway traffic and the elimination of counties' and locales' control over such regulation. Population growth and expansion required that state highways supplement city and county roads. It became necessary for a state highway patrol to supplement the work of local law enforcement on those roads. Inadequate, and in many cases nonexistent, communication among communities made the crime and traffic work of local law enforcement that much more difficult. The establishment and growth of geographically unrestrained statewide law enforcement agencies with committed resources were a direct response to these new concerns.

Highway patrols (and state police) are generally thought of as the premier law enforcement agencies in the state. Their ranks are open to all U.S. citizens. Because their activities can affect citizens' civil liberties so directly, their work is scrutinized by the community and courts. Special emphasis is placed on legal procedure and constitutional safeguards during both the initial training academy experience and the continuous in-service training required of all highway patrol troopers and state police. All agencies maintain an office dedicated to the investigation of alleged misconduct among its personnel.

[*See also* Automobiles and Crime; Investigation, State Bureaus of]

• H. Kenneth Bechtel, *State Police in the United States: A Socio-Historical Analysis*, 1995.

—Matthew Zingraff

HISS, ALGER, TRIALS OF. The two trials of Alger Hiss for perjury in 1949–50 were perhaps the most symbolically significant of the McCarthy era. To conservatives this New Dealer and alleged spy symbolized "twenty years of treason" by the Roosevelt and Truman administrations. Liberals, on the other hand, considered the Hiss case a "red herring" that Republicans had manufactured to discredit the New Deal and divert attention from their own failings. Although Hiss's innocence was long an article of liberal faith, intercepted Soviet communications made public since the end of the Cold War show he did spy for the USSR.

Following his graduation from Harvard Law School in 1929, Hiss clerked for Supreme Court Justice Oliver Wendell *Holmes Jr., to whom he was recommended by a future justice, Professor Felix *Frankfurter. After a few years of private practice, like many of Frankfurter's proteges, Hiss went to Washington in the early days of the New Deal. There he worked for the Agricultural Adjustment Administration and the Senate's Nye Committee before joining the State Department in 1936. He rose rapidly at State and was part of the American delegations to the Yalta Conference and the 1945 meeting in San Francisco that organized the United Nations. In 1947 he left government service to head the Carnegie Endowment.

In 1948, while testifying before the Republican-controlled House Committee on Un-American Activities (HUAC), a *Time* magazine editor, Whittaker Chambers, claimed that in the 1930s he and Hiss had both been Communists and together had supplied government information to the Soviets. At first, Hiss denied Chambers's allegations. Subsequently, he acknowledged that a picture of Chambers looked like a journalist named "George Crosley," to whom he had once sublet an apartment and loaned a car. At a third HUAC session, arranged by Representative Richard Nixon, Hiss dared Chambers to make his allegations in public, where they would not be privileged. Chambers did so on *Meet the Press*. Hiss then sued him for libel. Chambers produced typed copies and microfilm of confidential State Department documents to which Hiss had had access in 1938, along with notes that appeared to be in Hiss's handwriting.

Hiss failed to convince a federal grand jury that these items were fakes or had come from someone else. Prevented by the running of the three-year statute of limitations from charging him with espionage, the grand jury indicted him for perjury. It alleged that Hiss had lied in saying he had never given government documents to Chambers and in stating he had not seen him after 1 January 1937.

Hiss was tried twice. Frankfurter, Justice Stanley Reed, and Illinois Governor Adlai Stevenson testified for him as character witnesses. The prosecution, however, produced letters done on a Woodstock typewriter once owned by the defendant's wife, Priscilla, the typing on which matched that on the documents Chambers had produced. The first trial, which began on 31 May 1949, ended six weeks later with a hung jury, split eight to four against Hiss. He was convicted in his second trial, which ended in early 1950. Hiss served forty-four months in a federal penitentiary.

• Allen Weinstein, *Perjury: The Hiss-Chambers Case*, 1978. Sam Tanenhaus, *Whittaker Chambers: A Biography*, 1997.
                                    —Michal R. Belknap

HISTORY AND LAW. The relationship between history and law can be understood from at least two fundamentally different perspectives. First, the relationship can be approached from the vantage point of law practice and judicial decision-making. Second, the relationship can be understood from the perspective of the scholarly study of law.

History can play dual roles in law practice and judicial decision-making. One role emerges through the legal doctrine of stare decisis, a key component in a *common law system, such as that of the United States. Stare decisis requires a court to consider and follow previously decided cases (or precedents) that sufficiently resemble an instant or current case. As it is sometimes phrased, courts should treat like cases alike. Stare decisis therefore requires a court to consider history: the history or tradition of analogous cases. The problem that arises, however, is that the similarity and dissimilarity between a prior case (or precedent) and a current case is almost always disputable. We might agree that like cases should be treated alike, but disagree about what cases are alike. For instance, is a case that questions the constitutionality of a publicly displayed crèche, standing alone, meaningfully different from an earlier case that also involved a publicly displayed crèche, but with other Christmas decorations? The answer is not self-evident. In short, the meaning of history, as manifested in the doctrine of stare decisis, is not a transparent or unambiguous given. Rather, the meaning of a prior case or series of cases is often the crux of a legal dispute.

History also sometimes plays a second role in law practice and judicial decision-making. Namely, lawyers and judges sometimes invoke historical arguments to support a particular legal or judicial conclusion. As a general matter, lawyers and judges typically accept certain types or modes of argument as being legitimate within the legal system. For instance, if a lawyer asserts the meaning of a legal text, such as a contractual or constitutional provision, the mode of argument—textual interpretation—is usually deemed to be legitimate within the legal system, even if the opposing attorney or the judge disagrees with the specifically asserted interpretation. Likewise, if a lawyer asserts that stare decisis requires a court to follow a particular case as precedent, the opposing attorney or the judge might disagree about the relevance of the particular case as precedent, but all participants will likely agree that stare decisis is a legitimate means of argument.

The use of history is another legitimate mode of argument within the legal system. History often plays a prominent role in constitutional law. In particular, attorneys and judges will assert that historical evidence reveals that the framers of a constitutional provision intended to achieve some desired goal. For instance, in *Everson* v. *Board of Education* (1947), the United States Supreme Court needed to interpret the establishment clause of the first amendment to the Constitution. In order to support its conclusion regarding the meaning of the establishment clause, the Court invoked history. James Madison and Thomas *Jefferson, according to the Court, had played leading roles in the drafting and adoption of the establishment and free exercise clauses (the first amendment *religion clauses). Moreover, historical materials revealed that Madison and Jefferson had previously led a political fight to disestablish the official church in the state of Virginia. Since their intentions regarding religious freedom supposedly could be gleaned from the historical materials relevant to the Virginia experience, the Court reasoned that it could justifiably conclude that Madison and Jefferson had similar intentions for the first amendment. They sought to construct a wall of separation between *church and state.

While the use of history as a means of legal argument is generally deemed legitimate, the specific invocations or interpretations of historical materials are typically controversial. Many critics charge lawyers and judges with disregarding the complexities of historical evidence. Lawyers and judges, in other words, will often invoke only those historical materials that support their desired conclusion, and will ignore any other evidence. For example, in the *Everson* case, one could reasonably criticize the Court for giving undue emphasis to the Virginia experience and disregarding other historical materials that might have complicated the story of religious freedom. Nonetheless, in the context of law practice or judicial decision-making, this type of simplified history is at least explicable. Lawyers and judges, after all, are constructing legal arguments rather than writing scholarly essays. When a legal scholar, on the other hand, presents simplified or conclusory historical arguments, it is just bad history.

Turning then to the relationship between history and law, as understood from the perspective of scholarly study, a so-called historical school of *jurisprudence emerged in America during the late nineteenth century. For various reasons, its long-term influence was limited. The most renowned proponents of a historical approach to law were Europeans from an earlier generation: Friedrich Carl von Savigny, who was German and published in the early 1800s, and Henry Maine, who was English and published his most famous work, *Ancient Law*, in 1861. From their perspective, law is like language: it develops slowly as part of a national culture. In America, the clearest proponent of the historical school was James Coolidge Carter. Carter was a prominent New York attorney and leader of the bar who strongly opposed efforts to codify the law in New York in the late nineteenth century. Consequently, except for one book published posthumously, his writings mostly were politically motivated speeches and reports printed in bar association pamphlets. To Carter, the historical approach rectified the hubris he saw in the *codification movement. The common law, which Carter referred to as "custom authenticated," necessarily evolved throughout a nation's history. It could not be suddenly controlled and remade, as the codifiers supposedly sought, without leading to "mischief" and "confusion" (Carter, 83, 209–10). In fact, earlier in the century, Savigny himself had similarly drawn upon his historical approach to oppose codification in Germany.

Nevertheless, Carter's ideas did not flourish in American legal thought. He may have weakened his own jurisprudential position when he extended his opposition to codification into a general antagonism toward legislation. He insisted that legislation was actually inconsistent with democracy. Even Christopher Columbus Langdell, Carter's contemporary and the influential dean of Harvard Law School, did not display such aversion to legislation. Langdell stressed the teaching of legal science, which demanded a strictly logical approach to common law subjects such as *contracts and *property, purified of any concern for history, philosophy, society, and so forth. Even so, Langdell believed that statutes were important and deserved careful study, just not in American law schools. Carter's more hostile viewpoint toward legislation obviously ran against the grain of American political thought with its ever-increasing emphasis on the sovereignty of the people.

The main themes of the historical school nonetheless resonated with certain other late-nineteenth-century thinkers in constitutional theory such as Thomas M. *Cooley and Christopher G. Tiedeman. The historical concerns of these legal scholars emerged as they struggled to synthesize natural rights with positive law. Unlike many of their post–Civil War contemporaries, Cooley and Tiedeman did not strongly repudiate *natural law and natural rights, yet neither did they rely on natural law and natural rights as a legal foundation or otherwise, as antebellum scholars had widely done. For both Tiedeman and Cooley, natural law and natural rights were meaningful only insofar as they had been adopted as positive law, and positive law evolved largely as a matter of the historical and cultural development of a people and nation. In a sense, then, natural rights continued to be significant only because the American people continued a tradition of supporting their positive enforcement and not because such rights existed in the abstract.

In the end, the historical school of jurisprudence was only of secondary importance in American legal thought because, ironically, it was insufficiently historicist—the historical school viewing history as generating and conservatively imposing normative values and customs. As such, the historical school tended to reinforce tradition, the status quo. The more modern historicist view, taking firm hold in most intellectual circles at the turn of the twentieth century, was to view history as disclosing the potential for endless progress inspired by human ingenuity. This modern historicist view corresponded with a confidence in human ability to control and reorder society for the general welfare. Thus, the greatest long-term significance of the historical school for American legal thought may have been its encouragement of a general historical awareness—an awareness that ultimately was embodied more fully in the modernist strains of historicism.

Whereas the long-term influence of the historical school was minimal, the same cannot be said for the jurisprudence of Oliver Wendell *Holmes Jr., also a contemporary of Carter and Langdell's. Holmes might even be considered the first American jurist to shift completely to a modern historicist sensibility, suggested in his most famous aphorism, "The life of the law has not been logic: it has been experience," which appeared on the first page of his magnum opus, *The Common Law*. Holmes stressed his concern for the interrelationship of law and history as he continued: "The law embodies the story of a nation's development through many centuries, and it cannot be dealt with as if it contained only the axioms and corollaries of a book of mathematics. In order to know what it is, we must know what it has been, and what it tends to become. We must alternately consult history and existing theories of legislation" (Holmes, 1).

Unsurprisingly, then, Holmes believed history revealed that society progresses and that humans can control and direct societal change. Holmes therefore recommended that judges openly acknowledge their lawmaking (or legislative) power and more consciously attempt to make law for the good of society. In discussing the mailbox rule of contract law, for instance, Holmes emphasized

pragmatic considerations, reasoning that a posted acceptance of an offer should be effective upon dispatch, rather than upon receipt, if that solution would be most practical or convenient. Langdell had reached the opposite conclusion by dismissing practical concerns and instead focusing on an abstract syllogistic proof grounded on axiomatic principles and definitions. Moreover, and again in contrast to Langdell, Holmes never conceived of the common law as a perfectly logical and conceptually ordered system. "The truth is," Holmes asserted, "that the law is always approaching, and never reaching, consistency. It is forever adopting new principles from life at one end, and it always retains old ones from history at the other, which have not yet been absorbed or sloughed off" (Holmes, 36).

Holmesian jurisprudence can be understood as a pragmatic historicism that anticipated the work of the American *legal realists, who were not to come on the scene for almost another half century. Writing in the 1920s and 1930s, realists such as Underhill Moore and William *O. Douglas, displayed the confidence of a full-blown historicist attitude. They conducted social-science-like empirical studies on legal problems, such as bankruptcy during the Great Depression, with the assuredness that their work would provide the knowledge needed to solve real and pressing problems. Their aim was to reorder society for the greater good. Despite the realist efforts in such matters, however, and despite their contributions to the New Deal, the realists did very little work that directly focused on the historical sources and development of law. Indeed, through much of the first half of the twentieth century, few legal scholars attempted to incorporate a historical perspective into their jurisprudential writings, though some historians, such as Perry Miller, occasionally wrote about the law or legal matters.

This jurisprudential neglect of history ended in the 1950s and 1960s with the emergence of the Wisconsin School of legal history. The intellectual progenitor and inspiration for this movement was J. Willard Hurst, with books such as *The Growth of American Law: The Law Makers* (1950) and *Law and the Conditions of Freedom in the Nineteenth-Century United States* (1956). The Wisconsin School legal historians tended to explain law and legal culture as the reflection of material and social interests. The law does not lead society; rather society leads the law. While Hurst may have been the progenitor of this approach, its most renowned practitioner has probably been Lawrence Friedman. His book, *A History of American Law*, first published in 1973, may very well have been the first effort at a comprehensive history of American law. Friedman's "Preface" unequivocally declared his historical method: "This book treats American law, then, not as a kingdom unto itself, not as a set of rules and concepts, not as the province of lawyers alone, but as a mirror of society. It takes nothing as historical accident, nothing as autonomous, everything as relative and molded by economy and society" (Friedman, 12).

Subsequent legal historians generally applauded the work of the Wisconsin School, but nonetheless criticized it as overly reductionist. *Critical legal historians such as Morton Horwitz and Mark Tushnet emphasized social conflicts and the function of law as an ideology that affects those conflicts. The law, in other words, not only mirrors social and material interests but rather is a partially autonomous system that itself influences the rest of society. More broadly, contrary to the Wisconsin School approach, many legal scholars today maintain that culture, including ideas (including those specifically related to law), can be a powerful causal factor in society. Culture and ideas, of course, are not necessarily good; they can be pernicious, such as the racist ideas emanating from the Social Darwinists during the late nineteenth and early twentieth centuries. Even so, such ideas matter. Friedman, though, following his Wisconsin School approach, has argued that the Social Darwinists' racist ideas should be understood as a reaction to, or reflection of, the social dislocations engendered by industrialization. Undoubtedly, Friedman is correct, in part. But just as surely, the Social Darwinists' ideas causally influenced American society, for example, by helping to nurture during the early twentieth century a political movement to restrict immigration to the United States. And such ideas have a genealogy, a history, in and from other ideas. The Social Darwinists' racist ideas, for instance, partly evolved from the ideas of earlier eras, including Darwin's theory of biological evolution, Hegel's philosophical emphasis on the importance of history, Christian anti-Semitic dogma, and the American antebellum intellectual defenses of slavery. Thus, a more eclectic approach to legal history—one that accounts for a variety of causal factors, including social interests, cultural symbols, legal ideas, and political ideologies—can be seen in the recent work of some legal scholars, such as G. Edward White, as well as in the works of some historians such as Gordon S. Wood and Laura Kalman, who focus on law or jurisprudence.

A similar eclectic approach is also evident in the work of those American legal scholars who emphasize our existence as historical creatures who live within communal traditions. Influenced by Continental social and philosophical thinkers, particularly Hans-Georg Gadamer, these scholars maintain, in other words, that we have a historical consciousness. As such, our interpretations of all texts, legal or otherwise, are both fostered and constrained by our prejudices and interests, as derived from our communal traditions. We never can directly access a meaning of a text, prior to the interpretive process, nor can we arbitrarily assign a meaning to a text, free of interpretive constraints. As historical creatures, we always experience and understand from within our historical and cultural contexts. If true, then legal interpretation is necessarily a historical exercise—a function of our historical consciousness. History and law, we might say, are inextricably entwined.

• Oliver Wendell Holmes Jr., *The Common Law*, Dover ed. 1991, 1st ed., 1881. James Coolidge Carter, *Law: Its Origin, Growth, and Function*, 1907. Gordon S. Wood, *The Creation of the American Republic, 1776–1787*, 1969. Michel Foucault, *Discipline and Punish*, Alan Sheridan trans., 1977. Morton J. Horwitz, *The Transformation of American Law, 1780–1860*, 1977. Lawrence M. Friedman, *A History of American Law*, 2d ed., 1985. Kermit L. Hall, *The Magic Mirror*, 1989. G. Edward White, *Intervention and Detachment*, 1994. Neil Duxbury, *Patterns of American Jurisprudence*, 1995. Laura Kalman, *The Strange Career of Legal Liberalism*, 1996. Stephen M. Feldman, *Please Don't Wish Me a Merry Christmas: A Critical History of the Separation of Church and State*, 1997. Stephen M. Feldman, *American Legal Thought From Premodernism to Postmodernism: An Intellectual Voyage*, 2000.   —Stephen M. Feldman

HISTORY OF AMERICAN LAW

Colonial Period
Antebellum Through Reconstruction
   (1801–1877)
Gilded Age to the Great Depression
   (1877–1929)
Great Depression to 1968
Since 1968

HISTORY OF AMERICAN LAW: COLONIAL PERIOD

Courts and Law in British North American Colonies. In the British North American colonies, law offered the hope and the semblance of stability. Men and women went to court to assert old values of social intercourse and test new ways of doing business. Law interceded between disputants, and intruded into the everyday lives of towns and parishes. Law kept order, although not everyone was equal under the law, nor benefitted from it equitably.

For much of the seventeenth century and into the first decades of the eighteenth, colonial law was written or spoken in a language ordinary people could understand. In the course of the eighteenth century, that informality was replaced by increasingly sophisticated technical pleading. Local elites still functioned as officers of the courts, but by the middle of the eighteenth century, law practice steadily became the preserve of trained lawyers trying to introduce the formalities of English legal practice. Despite its increasing resemblance to Old World texts and models over time, the law in the American colonies was always more liberal, individualistic, and open to reform than the law in the home countries.

Sources of Law and Structure of Courts. The sources of law and the structure of courts in individual colonies had a common form, but exhibited local variations, and changed over time. Most of the colonies had closer ties to the home countries than they did to one another, and there was no movement to unify inter-colonial law until the very end of the colonial period, during the Revolutionary crisis.

Sources of Law. The *Native American peoples who greeted the European newcomers to America had laws and courts employing an oral tradition and councils of elders, but Indian laws rarely influenced the final shape of colonial laws and courts. As long as the European population was small, Indians and Europeans relied on legal hybrids, compromises, and mutually acceptable legal fictions to do business, and met in quasi-diplomatic councils to settle outstanding legal differences. When Indian numbers declined and the European population swelled, the Europeans insisted on imposing their legal forms on the natives.

Thus, the most important sources of law in the colonies were English. Royal charters enabled merchant companies and individual proprietors of North American colonies to hold and govern land, and contained strictures on law. Later acts of Parliament, rulings of the king's attorney general, and English central court and Privy Council opinions were sources of law for the colonies. So were the special instructions the secretary of state for the southern department gave the colonial governors. In later years, decisions by crown courts on cases appealed from colonial courts joined the former sources of official transmission of law.

Law books constituted a second major source of law. Alphabetical abridgments of the law, such as those of Francis Bacon's and later Charles Viner's, were purchased by colonial assemblies or carried to the colonies by individuals. Abridgments brought together the major headings of the law. Legal dictionaries, such as John Cowell's *A Law Dictionary* (1708) and Giles Jacob's *A New Law Dictionary* (1736), and manuals for justices of the peace, such as Michael Dalton's *The Countrey Justice* (1618), were very commonly read, and expanded local editions, such as George Webb's *Virginia Justice of the Peace* (1736), were widely owned in individual colonies. These manuals were also alphabetical, but detailed the statutory basis for jurisdiction as well as the managerial functions of justices of the peace.

Finally, knowledge of Old World law arrived in the colonies with the immigrants themselves. If few among the settlers practiced law or acted as magistrates in England, over time the number of trained English lawyers and judges who went to the colonies grew. Many colonists had prosecuted cases or given testimony in English courts. Sometimes these men and women were unhappy with the legal system they had left behind, and carried with them to the New World a determination to reform the law and the courts. These reforms manifested themselves in the first legal codes of the Puritan colonies and the Quaker colonies.

Colonists also brought ideas of law from their experience outside of England. For example, the martial law employed to suppress Irish rebellions in the sixteenth century and police England's boundaries with Scotland and Wales came to early Virginia with a new governor, Sir Thomas Dale. Virginia's "Lawes Divine, Moral, and Martiall" were discarded after a generation, but the governors of all the royal colonies continued to be called "governors-general" and had military as well as civil and political functions.

Negative experience with English law could also be a formative influence on the settlers' legal arrangements. While still in England, harassed by church courts and threatened by civil courts, the Puritans called for a wholesale reformation of the law. Puritans called for simplification of the body of the law in codes that were clear and fair; all penalties were to be rationalized and procedure made more direct. A direct reflection of this dissent, Massachusetts' Body of Liberties of 1648, combined a frame of government, the prototype of a *bill of rights, and a penal code. Much of its language was based on earlier English declarations of rights, including the Great Charter (Magna Carta) of 1215 and the parliamentary Petition of Rights of 1628, but, unlike the latter, which left the prerogative of the crown intact, the Body of Liberties limited the discretion of Massachusetts' to prosecute crimes. "No man's life shall be taken away, no mans honour or good name shall be stained, no mans person shall be arested, restrayned, . . . no mans goods or estate shall be taken away from him . . . unlesse it be by vertue or equitie of some expresse law of the Country waranting the same, established by a general court and sufficiently published . . . Every person within this jurisdiction, whether inhabitant or forreiner shall enjoy the same justice and law, that is general for the plantation." The frequent recourse to the Bible in the Body of Liberties was more than window dressing, but less than an attempt to rebuild Jerusalem. In fact, it tracked English law, not Old Testament. Nevertheless, the deviations from English law in the direction of the laws of Moses told a story of their own. Although *adultery and blasphemy, misdemeanors in the *common law, were made capital crimes in Massachusetts, as was disrespect to parents, Massachusetts men and women were almost never prosecuted for these offenses, and even those few prosecuted very rarely suffered the prescribed penalty. The borrowing of Old Testament injunctions was primarily a solemn public warning to those at the edges of the Puritan community against violation of the deeper social mores that held the Puritan towns in the wilderness together.

Ethnic and Regional Variations in Law. Indians' relative lack of concern for personal *property, strong belief in sharing food and housing, concepts of group responsibility for crimes, and ideas of punishment—for example, Indians did not believe in *capital punishment for crimes—remained in force on the frontier long after English notions of law had established themselves on the seaboard, and traders or missionaries who lived among the Indians had to conform to these ideas or cede their influence. When Indians lived among the colonists, however, the latter insisted that the Indians obey colonial law. Thus Indian communal land-holding practices had to give way to colonial rules on individual possession. Disputes over land sales and indictments of colonists for crimes against Indians and of Indians for offenses against colonists went into the colonial courts.

The Dutch brought Dutch Roman law to their colony of New Netherlands, with its provisions for arbitration of disputes, joint property holding in marriage, and absence of juries. When the New Netherlands fell to the forces of the Duke of York, the English generously allowed the Dutch to retain their property and practice their religion. The Duke of York's laws allowed Dutch mayors courts to function in New York City and Albany, and made some concessions to Dutch customary law as well, but English lawyers gradually displaced the Dutch at the bar and in the courts. After a series of political upheavals, ending with Jacob Leisler's full-scale revolt in 1689, the legal system attained the form it would have for the rest of the colonial period. The law now conformed closely to English practice, and a central supreme court was established.

The two great waves of German immigration to the colonies in the late 1710s, and in the 1740s and 1750s, brought varieties of German customary law to America. Like Dutch law, German law was also influenced by Roman law precepts of joint property holdings and communal dispute resolution. The Germans resisted anglicization of their law more than the Dutch, but over time, the Germans bowed to English legal authority. Other non-English speaking peoples in the English colonies more readily accepted the legal forms of their new rulers—for example, the French Huguenots in New York and South Carolina.

In the Quaker colonies of East and West Jersey (unified as the royal colony of New Jersey in 1704) and Pennsylvania, the law varied from the English model, but the cause was not the large number of Welsh, Germans, and other non-English peoples in the colonies. Instead, the law stressed harmony and mediation because Quaker leader William Penn, a proprietor of the Jerseys and the founder of Pennsylvania, based the law on humane Quaker principles.

Courts. Colonial courts followed the contours of English models, but diverged in significant details. As in the home country, the structure of courts in the colonies was hierarchical in form—local courts handled claims for small amounts and less serious crimes, assize (circuit) or central courts determined cases that were more serious—but the differences were striking.

The courts in England had evolved over the course of 700 years from the Norman conquest of Saxon England, and displayed a bewildering pattern of overlapping jurisdictions and arcane functions. Old Saxon shire courts coexisted with Norman manorial courts and more recently established royal courts. Some cases took years to wander through the court system. Colonial courts were simpler, had general jurisdiction over persons and claims, and reached decisions more swiftly.

In one even more important respect, colonial courts differed from English courts throughout the colonial era. English *judges—particularly those sitting in the central courts—were well trained in the law. Many had practiced law themselves; some sought appointment as "prothonotaries" (chief clerks) or under-clerks in the central courts; others had been "serjeants at law" or "kings counsel," and represented the crown in important matters of law. Colonial high court judges were men of affairs and authority in their communities who were acquainted with law, but rarely trained in it. Moreover, they were never full-time jurists. At any given moment, the highest courts of Massachusetts and Virginia rarely included more than one well-educated lawyer. The legal skills of the judges in Pennsylvania were no greater. Only the Duke of York's province could boast a legally literate bench. This pattern continued well into the eighteenth century in most of the colonies. The result of having laymen on the high court benches might be swift and sensible justice. Massachusetts Superior Court justices, such as Samuel Sewall, were deeply moral men, concerned about the quality of their performance. Other colonial judges were not so ethical or able. Governor William Cosby of New York, who sat as its chancellor, disgraced himself by venality and partisanship.

Colonial courts were less elaborate than those in England, and colonial judges less well trained, but colonial courts and judges were still obeyed, and a larger proportion of the colonists turned to them for aid than did the people of England seek succor from its tribunals. In the colonies, legal pleading was in English, not Latin. A larger proportion of the adult male population participated in the operation of the colonial courts than was the case in England. The lowest level of colonial legal jurisdiction was the justice of the peace. He dealt with petty offenses and minor disputes. Although he was not required to keep a record of his actions—and few such records survive—the personal diaries of some of these justices suggest that justices relied on a system of fines and bonds that bound neighbors to keep the peace and obey the laws. This semi-private network of order-keeping drew strength from the homogeneity of the community and the hegemonic influence of leading figures in the village or parish. Often these men posted "sureties" that would be forfeit if the offender repeated the offense, indebting the of-

fender to them as they indebted themselves to the court. In addition, this "watch and warn" system was cheap to administer.

The justices of the peace also met at county courts much like the English quarter sessions courts to hear civil disputes. Civil disputants could pay for *jury trials if they wished. The same panel of justices sat at "sessions of the peace" to hear grand juries present men and women for such violations of law as drunkenness, sexual misconduct, failure to attend church, *assault, and battery. The accused might ask for a jury, but juries were expensive, and most suspects "put themselves upon the court." More serious crimes were reserved for the central courts. For example, in Virginia after 1705, local trial of felons gave way to a centralized system of trial only at the capital, Williamsburg. In the county, an examining court held a preliminary hearing, and on finding probable cause sent suspects on to the capital, where a grand jury and trial awaited them. Other colonies' supreme courts traveled once or twice a year on circuits from county seat to county seat, hearing civil cases and serious criminal causes.

Civil Law and Lawyers. The crucial element in the formalization of *civil law was the increasing prominence of professional *lawyers. These were attorneys in the first colonies who represented others in court, but they earned fees for pleading others' cases in the courts. The rise of the legal profession to an elite position in America commenced in the early eighteenth century. Increased litigation in the 1720s and 1730s made lawyering lucrative, and attracted able young men. Women were not accepted as apprentices in lawyers officers, nor were they licensed to practice law by the superior courts. By the 1730s, most of the statutory barriers to law practice enacted by colonial legislatures in the seventeenth century had fallen, brought down by consumer demand for trained assistance in litigation.

American lawyers most often trained by "reading" law as clerks and juniors in established lawyers' chambers or offices. A few had learned their craft in England's Inns of Court. *Bar associations created by the leading lawyers soon gained the approval of the colonial legislatures, themselves increasingly penetrated by members of the legal profession. *Bar examinations went hand in hand with licensing examinations by judges, the result of which was a more influential profession as well as a more English one.

Civil Procedure. Like the colonial courts in which the lawyers practiced, legal procedure varied from colony to colony. In general, pleading in the colonies in the eighteenth century followed enough of the English model to be recognizable to a lawyer from the mother country. The suit at common-law, called an "action," began with the filing in court of a "writ." Originally these writs were in Latin, and were quite specific—filing the wrong writ led to dismissal of the action. The purpose of common-law writ pleading in England and the colonies was to reduce the legal issue to a single "cause of action" and confine juries to deciding a narrowly defined factual question.

Once the "original" writ was filed, the colonial court informed the defendant that litigation had begun, and summoned the defendant to appear. In court, the plaintiff's declaration laid out one version of the facts. Defendants had to answer the declaration. They might confess *judgment; there the action ended, and payment of *damages and costs was arranged. They might deny all the facts, assert facts excusing them, challenge the technical correctness of the writ on which the action was brought, or admit that some or all of the factual allegations in the declaration were true, but insist that they were not sufficient to sustain the particular action brought by the plaintiff.

Back and forth the pleas went. If the plaintiff failed to appear in a colonial trial court, he was "non-suited." If the defendant failed to answer or appear, he was held in "default" and had to pay the judgment plus the court costs. In order to insure that defendants did not disappear or squirrel away their property, the plaintiff could obtain a variety of intermediate writs to "attach" the defendant's property or "arrest" his flight. Defendants jailed by the *sheriff were ordinarily freed on bail or given the right to move freely about the jailhouse and its environs.

Most suits did not go to trial. They were settled in the shadow of the courthouse by negotiation, confession and payment, or arbitration of some sort. If a trial began, the *evidence offered was primarily documentary. Witnesses could be called and examined under oath, but the testimony of persons who had any monetary interest in the suit was barred. Emphasis rested on a very narrow base of evidence, and there was little cross-examination of witnesses. The jury was expected to reach its verdict on its independent assessment of evidence, not on its judgment about who was telling the truth and who was lying.

After the trial verdict, judicial order, or the default, was entered; another, final, series of writs, paid for by the parties, started the "execution" of judgment. Sometimes a successful plaintiff had to pay for many rounds of writs before the sheriff found the defendant and obtained the damage award or took possession of the defendant's land and chattels and sold these at auction to pay off the plaintiff.

As procedure varied from colony to colony, so did substantive law, although no sharp boundary separated procedure from substance—a writ, for example, was both a procedural device and a substantive claim. In its overall contours, colonial substantive law was English law, but there were differences, and these are almost as important as the similarities.

Slavery. The law that turned men and women into chattels (personal property) was the most vivid divergence between English and colonial law. England recognized the status of persons in the law. Servants and apprentices, for example, were unfree laborers and could be jailed or corporally punished for leaving their employment. Some agricultural workers were bound to their land. But all persons had legal existence. No one was *property in the law.

In the colonies, by contrast, some men and women were property, and could be bought and sold, inherited, and used as though they were livestock, furniture, or tools. Much of the history of slave law belongs to a later period than covered here, but the introduction of *slavery in the colonies was inseparable from law—that is, slavery only existed where law abetted the institution. The Virginia Burgesses, later followed by the assemblies of the Carolinas and Georgia, had borrowed the slave law of the British West Indies, gradually but inexorably elaborating a system of chattel slavery that had no precedent in English law. These *"black codes" made color into the badge of slavery, and slaves into chattels, to be bought and sold, given away, and inherited. By the middle of the eighteenth century, slavery existed in all of the English colonies under laws that varied in their harshness. All made color a presumptive badge of slavery. Free men and women of color had to have freedom papers to prove that they had been emancipated or born free. In some colonies—for example, Virginia—the law did not allow manumission, although masters and mistresses who wished to free their slaves found loopholes in the law.

Slave law was not criminal law per se, for in law, slaves were property. At the same time, slaves were men and women capable of committing acts that were dangerous to their masters or to each other. The progressive debasement of Africans, and the elaboration of a separate and harsh code for criminalization of acts by these bondsmen and women, went hand in hand. For example, in 1669, the Virginia assembly prospectively exculpated masters who killed slaves in the course of "due correction" (punishment). In 1680, the legislature made it a *felony for slaves to carry a weapon, leave the plantation without a pass, offer resistance against any free person, or lurk about—the last an open-ended offense capable of infinite extension—and punishment of all of which might include thirty lashes on the back "well laid on." In all the southern colonies, slaves were tried by "freeholders" courts, effectually denying Africans and African Americans the basic rights of any white inhabitant of the English colonies: jury trial by peers when accused of a serious crime, compulsory process against accusers, the right to *counsel, and the right to address the court in their own behalf under oath.

Real Estate. The common lawyers had liberated much of English real estate and inheritance practice from the dead hand of feudalism by 1607, but the first magnates granted proprietorships in the colonies wanted to reestablish feudalism. The seven noble proprietors of the Carolinas, for example, believed they could send their estate managers and servants to America and rule in the style of medieval barons. In New York, leading Dutch and England families pried great swaths of land from the government to set themselves up as the lords of vast manors.

The feudal dreams of these men vanished when they came face to face with the labor shortage in the colonies. Even when the proprietors could find men and women to till the soil, there was so much land that no one need bind himself to serve another when the prospect of ownership of land beckoned. In Virginia, indentured servants whose labor contracts required them to work for their masters for a term of years, knew that the end of service would bring them ownership of a small farmstead. New York's great landowners were in reality landlords, not feudal barons. Their tenants had leases whose terms were based on contractual agreements. In Pennsylvania, the many tenants on the proprietors' manors had gained customary rights based on multiyear leases.

Early in the course of settlement, the colonists opted for a clean, straightforward approach to the transfer of title to lands. Almost all the colonies adopted the "deed" and "record" system. In "deed and record," title passed with the exchange of a deed, a memorandum of sale. The deed was then recorded in a county or colonial record book. The title was fully secure only with the record (a prior deed lost out to a later deed that had been re-

corded first). The deed described the property, giving its boundaries and extent. Subsequent sellers merely endorsed the deed over to new buyers; the latter bore the burden of recording the transaction.

Despite the availability of land, and the ease with which it could be bought and sold, possession of land was not evenly distributed among the settlers. Most land grants by the colonial and imperial governments took the form of patronage. Hundreds of thousands of acres in the colonies were tied up in this way, and courts in all the colonies became political arenas when political factions sought to test each others' control of land.

Inheritance. In the colonies, as in England, inheritance law was partly statutory, partly based on common law (judicial precedent). Many of the colonies created *probate courts or devoted separate portions of the superior courts' sessions to hear and approve the provisions of *wills. Commissioners were appointed to take inventories of *estates if one were not included in the will.

Wills reflected family strategies for building funds of capital or distributing accumulated wealth, sometimes concentrating the wealth in a few hands, more often distributing it among surviving spouses and children. In Bucks County, Pennsylvania, for example, testators tended to give equal shares to all their sons, and favored sons over daughters, though early in the county's settlement, daughters were also given some land. In the Tidewater South, testators generally treated their sons equally, and left nearly equal portions of their estates to their daughters, albeit tying these up in life estates or irrevocable trusts rather than allowing the daughter to take the property without strings.

When there was no will, widows of intestates retained a life estate (an estate that could not itself be devised) in one-third of the land and one-third of the personal estate. In New England, statutes provided for partible inheritance, with a double share—the biblical portion—going to the oldest son. In the Middle and Southern colonies, the English rule of primogeniture was retained, the oldest son getting all of the land, though he had to settle for an equal share of the personal property with his brothers and sisters.

Gender and Property. Colonial law discriminated against women. American courts retained the common law view of married women as "feme covert" whose legal rights and property were totally merged with her husband's. The wife could not sell off property without her husband's consent, nor could she bind herself by contract. Her husband had the right to sell off any or all of the couple's property without the consent of his wife, even if the property was brought into the marriage by her, though there were qualifications on this sort of sale. Husbands could not sell property the wife inherited, and if she appeared to consent to such a sale, she would be privately examined by a magistrate about her true feelings.

Some colonial courts would enforce pre-marital agreements under which women could protect their own property against coverture. These agreements often involved the creation of a "trust" into which brides-to-be put their property. Southern courts tended to be more solicitous of these agreements than Northern courts, and Southern chancellors protected the trust funds from the husbands' creditors. So, too, Southern chancellors insisted that the widow keep her dower (the one-third lifetime interest in the marriage's real estate) against all claims. Indeed, Southern courts assured widows a one-third portion of the personal property as well, enabling women to retain household goods and personal articles of value.

Marriage and Divorce. In the colonies, as in England before the Marriage Act of 1753, a man and a woman could enter into *marriage by mutual consent and open cohabitation. No formal steps were necessary, though many couples did engage in religious ceremonies.

Ending the marriage was much more difficult. In England, the church courts could annul marriages for cause (impotence, affinity, consanguinity) or allow separation on condition that the partners lived celibate until one or the other died. In 1670, Lord de Roos was able to obtain permission from the House of Lords to remarry after he proved his wife guilty of adultery. In effect, the Lords had granted him a legislative divorce. After de Roos's successful plea, legislative bills of *divorce were theoretically available, but there were still very few legislative divorces in England—about ninety between 1692 and 1785—and they cost more than a poor person could afford.

Divorce was easier and more frequent in many of the colonies. New England Puritans regarded marriage not as a sacrament but as a contract, which might be breached by misconduct by either partner. The Massachusetts General Court, and later the governor and his Council, took upon themselves the power to grant a divorce on grounds of adultery of either partner, as well as cruelty or desertion. At first, couples did not rush to the General Court to get divorces. In Massachusetts and Connecticut, whose divorce practices were even more liberal than Massachusetts, there

was rarely one petition per year in the seventeenth century. In the next century, however, the number of petitions steadily increased. The assemblies of Rhode Island and New Hampshire also severed marriages upon petition of one of the spouses and a finding of adultery or, more commonly, desertion.

New York and Pennsylvania allowed divorces, but only for adultery. Southern courts and legislatures refused to liberalize divorce, allowing only annulments and celibate separations. One could obtain legislative bills of divorce when one partner had disappeared, although these were sometimes disallowed by the Privy Council in England.

Church and State. English divorce law rested on the authority of the "established" church. Established churches, such as the Church of England in the Southern Colonies and the Puritan churches in much of New England, enforced a broad range of religious regulations running from sexual conduct to conformity in worship. Although the ministers did not prosecute misfeasors, the magistrates of justices of the peace, under colonial statutes, insured that public authority reinforced religious precepts.

Over time, the nature of settlement in the colonies undercut the relationship between civil and religious authority. The Puritans had no sooner fled the persecution of the high church in England than they attempted to reinstate the idea of religious uniformity in their new home. Rhode Island, a safe haven for Puritans driven out of Massachusetts, adopted a policy of official toleration—of Protestants only. This concession led not to harmony, but to campaigns by Baptists for full religious freedom. Connecticut attempted to achieve harmony by instituting synods of elders—in effect switching from Massachusetts' plan of Congregationalism to a form of Presbyterianism. The result was not uniformity but conflict over the proper form of church governance.

Pennsylvania was more tolerant of religious dissent than New England, which ironically fostered splits among the Quakers. The Quakers did not encourage immorality, but civil authorities, hard put to protect the settlers against Indian and European raiders, weakened by disputes over colonial autonomy with English authorities, and underfunded and understaffed from top to bottom, simply could not insist on strict conformity to any church regime.

The very mixed state of the ministry in the Southern churches, where Anglican worship was theoretically established—some ministers were able and wellborn, others were not so respectable or competent—did nothing to amend the colonies' unofficial but pervasive religious pluralism. In Virginia and South Carolina, Anglican ministers were often ill-paid. Vestrymen, chosen for their status in the community rather than their piety, were supposed to insure that the churches and the churchmen were well-kept. Instead, they often quarreled with their ministers over salaries. Some of these quarrels ended in the civil courts, where the juries joined with the vestrymen against the ministers.

The advent of the Great Awakening in the late 1730s, the first of many American revival movements, further disrupted religious orthodoxy throughout the colonies. Visiting Anglican preachers such as George Whitefield, and native-born reformers such as Jonathan Edwards and enthusiasts such as William Davenport, led revivals in churches. In the towns of New England, factions within congregations flew at each other, ministers were hastily hired and ignominiously fired, and new churches formed according to the worshippers' choice of minister. In the backwoods of Virginia, the authority of the Anglican parish swayed in the wind of Baptist preaching, the latter sometimes sweeping up slaves in its enthusiasm and lack of pretension. The statutes governing tithing, the choice and authority of ministers, and regulation of immorality remained on the books, but in practice, religious affiliation became a matter of individual volition.

Criminal Law and Law Enforcement. At all levels of the legal system, colonial lawgivers and judges shared two of the ruling assumptions of their English counterparts. The first was that there was no clear line of demarcation between crime and sin. The pious person was law-abiding; the dissolute of spirit would or had committed crimes. This association was natural in a society that prosecuted Protestant religious dissent and threatened Roman Catholics with death. What is more, sinful activities such as drunkenness, failure to attend church, and fornication made up the vast majority of criminal prosecutions in both the mother country and her North American colonies. The second assumption was that authorities in both locales assumed that sinful misconduct led to more serious crime. The profligate youth became the adult thief; the disorderly youth grew into the mature murderer.

In England and its North American colonies, criminal courts had a dual function—to keep order and determine guilt or innocence. These functions overlapped but did not perfectly coincide. In times of civil disorder, both England and its colonies used the criminal justice system to suppress dissent. On these occasions, the determination of guilt or innocence was sacrificed to the goal of defending the interests of the existing government. In addition, seventeenth-century colonial courts operated under different demographic conditions than those in England. English authorities wished to rid the realm of its surplus of wandering poor. In the colonies, labor was always scarce, and correspondingly valued. No colony ever duplicated the severity of punishment for petty crime on the English statute books, for no colony could afford to cripple its labor force.

Types of Crime. English and colonial *criminal law defined two general types of crimes: felonies and misdemeanors. Felonies were serious crimes, including murder, *treason, rape, *burglary, *robbery, counterfeiting, *arson, forgery, grand *larceny, and, after 1650 in England, a mixed group of offenses against property that included social protest acts such as breaking factory machinery.

The penalty for felony was death, but "benefit of clergy," transportation, *pardon, and jury mitigation averted *capital punishment for a host of offenses in England. Murder, treason, and a few other capital offenses were not "clergyable," but by the early eighteenth century, benefit of clergy was available for many offenses and could be pled by lay men and women as well as clerics. In eighteenth-century England, capital punishment was also mitigated by "transportation" for a term of seven or fourteen years. Transportees were sent to the colonies under guard, and placed with masters who paid for the convict's labor. Transportees could not return before their term expired, on penalty of death. Some of these convicts were political dissidents, others were poor farm laborers who had engaged in some form of protest against their working conditions—for example, wrecking agricultural machinery or burning crops.

Other convicted felons were pardoned by the crown. Upon the request of the home secretary and with the approval of the trial judge, the king issued pardons to more than 50 percent of those convicted of capital offenses. Such pardons were purely discretionary, a free gift of the king's grace. Its use reaffirmed his authority and his mercy. The promise of it could be used to turn offenders into informers; the threat of refusal of it hung over every unrepentant defendant. Juries regularly alleviated punishment for children and first offenders in theft cases by altering the value of the object taken and reducing the offense to petty larceny, not a felony. Judges went along with this common subterfuge.

Benefit of clergy and jury mitigation were practiced in those colonies where the list of capital offenses was similar to England's. Some colonies did not duplicate the severity of England's penal code, however. In New England, crimes against property, notably burglary and robbery, were not capital unless the convict was a repeat offender. The Quaker colonies of Pennsylvania and the Jerseys mitigated punishment for crimes against property with the aim of reforming the severity of English penal law. Murderers were hanged, but those convicted of other offenses were shamed, fined, sold into forced labor, whipped, or incarcerated for short terms.

Misdemeanors were by far the most commonly committed crimes in the colonies. The most common misdemeanors were assaults and batteries, rioting, sexual misconduct, abusing the constables or the magistrates, vagrancy, and violating any of the multitude of economic and moral regulatory statutes—for example, selling alcoholic beverages without a license, overcharging for bread, or failing to attend church (see MORALS OFFENSES). Punishment for a misdemeanor was usually a fine, corporal punishment, or some form of shaming— for example, standing in the "stocks" or wearing a letter denoting one's offense. Alternatively, or in addition, the offender might be required to post a bond for future good behavior. Sureties were required as well from neighbors, who would forfeit their bonds if the offender repeated the offense.

Elaboration of the Criminal Law after 1660. English criminal law changed markedly after the Restoration. Although a final civil uprising would drive the Stuarts from the throne, over the long course of time from 1660 to 1776, criminal law focused less on religious dissent and political disorder and more on protection of new forms of commercial, and later, industrial wealth. Strictures against vagrancy and wantonness gave way to statutes against breaking machinery as organized acts of violence against an emerging "monied" class increased. A criminal bar emerged, and began to take an active role in defending those accused of major crimes, a practice not fully sanctioned until an 1832 statute of parliament.

The transformation of colonial criminal law followed the changes in England, but distantly, and with an American twist. For example, after 1692, Massachusetts, under a new charter, began to adopt more English criminal law. The biblical cast of the old Body of Liberties never quite disappeared, but crimes against property became much more important, and crimes against religious and sexual rules declined in importance. A Supreme Court of Judicature, whose members were named by the crown, replaced the Assistants. Parliament authorized courts of vice-admiralty, similar to those in England, to sit in the colonial ports and hear cases of smuggling and evasion of customs duties. These courts did not have juries. Throughout the colonies the level of judicial expertise began to rise. Often politics and personal ambition undercut this development. For example, English-trained lawyer Nicholas Trott brought much needed order to South Carolina law, but soon after his accession to the chief justiceship in 1703, he began to line his own pockets with ill-gotten gains. For this, and his avid partisanship, the colonial assembly impeached him in 1719.

Yet even as criminal law in the colonies began to resemble English law much more closely, new elements of colonial criminal law were emerging. Prototype bills of rights, protecting the right to jury trial, legal counsel, public and speedy hearings of cases, and other familiar procedural guarantees, appeared in more than half of the colonies. The most striking of these provisions was that for counsel for the accused. Colonial law stipulated that criminal defendants had a right to be represented by lawyers, a signal advantage to the accused. The Massachusetts Body of Liberties, followed by Connecticut's Fundamental Laws, suggested that there was a right to counsel; the Concessions of the West Jersey Proprietors, in 1677, and the Frame of Government of Pennsylvania, in 1683, gave the same assurances. After the dissolution of the first charter, Massachusetts' General Court tried to reenact a guarantee of counsel in 1692, but for other reasons the statute was disallowed by the Privy Council. In 1701, the General Court repassed the criminal counsel provisions, and the courts, on occasion, appointed counsel for needy suspects in felony trials. The Connecticut General Court followed this practice. Pennsylvania in 1718, Delaware in 1719, and South Carolina in 1731 wrote an explicit provision for counsel in criminal cases into their laws. Some colonies resisted this reform—New York most notably—but by the 1760s, counsel was permitted for felony suspects in over half the colonies.

Criminal Procedure. Early modern Anglo-American criminal procedure supposedly exemplied the ideal of "rule of law," but the process of determining innocence and guilt was in fact greatly influenced by the status of the suspect and the victim. Modern criminal *procedure is ruled by concern for the rights of the accused. In colonial criminal justice, suspects had fewer rights, and determinations of cases were usually much swifter than they are today.

In seventeenth- and eighteenth-century England and its North American colonies, there were no police forces. Towns had watchmen, and rural areas were patrolled by the sheriffs's constables, but these men were neither eager to discover crime nor trained to ferret it out. Instead, reportage depended on the victims or alert neighbors. Often, suspects were tracked and caught after a "hue and cry" was raised by neighbors. The "dark figure" of unreported crime associated with this gap between precept and performance in criminal law varied over time and place in England and the colonies.

The community took a formal role in criminal procedure in the grand jury presentments of misdemeanors and indictments of suspected felons and the petty jury trial of defendants. The grand jury was an assemblage of men from the neighborhood who presented information on petty offenses to the court "on their own knowledge." The grand jurors also met to hear indictments against felons. When the grand jury found a true bill against a suspected felon, the suspect might try to bargain with the court for a lesser charge, or demand a trial. At any time before a verdict was brought in by a trial jury, the defendant could confess and seek the mercy of the court. Convicted, the offender was sentenced.

In Elizabethan and Stuart England, criminal trial was a straightforward matter. The defendant's life and limb depended on convincing a judge and jury that he or she was not guilty. The jury returned its verdict, often without retiring, and always without "meat nor drinke nor fire," on case after case. The community—in the form of the jurors—played a vital, sometimes a controlling, role in particular cases, as did judges, whose instructions to juries were on occasion tantamount to directed verdicts. Colonial juries played, if anything, a larger role in the outcome of trials than the juries did in England.

The criminal jury was a redoubt the colonists hotly defended against their own magistrates and English authorities, although few accused took advantage of their right to jury trial for petty offenses—they were heard "summarily" by the bench. Even in more serious crimes, Virginia defendants did not always insist on a jury trial. Less than half of all prosecutions that might have been heard by juries were in fact brought before the jury. Defendants were evidently busy *plea bargaining or trying to avoid the expense of a jury trial (they had to pay for it). In New England, defendants commonly, but by no means universally, asked for jury trial. In New York, upper-class

defendants sought jury trials, lower-class defendants only sometimes did the same.

By the eighteenth century, first in the colonies and later in England, new players strode upon the trial stage—counsel for the prosecution and the defense. These lawyers never appeared in more than a small portion of the total number of cases, but in their cut and thrust with each other, their colloquies with the judges, and their caustic, sometimes brutal, examination of witnesses, they began to build a recognizably modern trial procedure.

The last stage of criminal procedure, punishment itself, was ordinarily quite swift, unless a point of law was in doubt, or the defendant could give some other reason why punishment should be delayed. Among these, a pregnant woman could "plead the belly" and gain a respite from punishment until her child was born. The eighteenth-century procession of felons to the Tyburn gallows in London (now the "speakers corner" of Hyde Park) was a spectacle of punishment meant to impress the majesty of the law on potential felons that instead brought out the worst in English conduct. Colonial punishment had a similar message for potential felons, but never duplicated the disorder at Tyburn. For those convicted at trial, punishment was swift and highly visible, but much more solemn than in England. In New England, ministers' "gallows sermons" seemed to have more impact than in England, and many a convict would warn the crowd against duplicating his or her sins.

By the end of the colonial era, a powerful current of reform was beginning to sweep through ideas of sentencing and punishment. In England, under the influence of Enlightenment rationalism and direct experience of the bestial conditions of English prisons and public punishments, penal reformers such as Henry Fielding, David Colquhuon, Samuel Romilly, and James Bentham demanded rational schemes of punishment linked to the severity of the crime, and began to argue for punishment that would rehabilitate criminals.

In Revolutionary America, this program resonated with republican reformism, supporting the "penitentiary" movement underway in England. The new *prisons, incarceration in which would replace whipping and branding, were to be asylums for socially maladjusted men and women. In the penitentiary, the ways of crime would be replaced by habits of hard work and obedience to rules. Meanwhile, in the new state legislatures, reformers such as Thomas *Jefferson pushed for revision of criminal codes. These revisions would reserve capital punishment for murder, treason, rape, and arson.

Colonial law in the period just before the Revolutionary crisis was riven with paradoxes. With Anglicization in the law came needed sophistication and unwanted formality. Lawyers were everywhere abused for stirring contention and everywhere employed to bring suits. The openness and fluidity of the law gave rise to a litigiousness that flooded court dockets and delayed legal redress. The iniquities of private law became the inequities of public law in what seemed to contemporaries to be a spiral of private avarice and official corruption. The law promoted greater equality for some and progressively debased others into chattel slaves.

These tensions in American law could not be wholly contained within the colonial legal system. Popular dissent took many forms. Farmers and tenants in New York and the Carolinas demanded legal reform. In Virginia, grand jurors refused to serve. In a voluntaristic, face-to-face society, such indifference to public duties was calamitous. Parliament would shortly add to these local disorders the burden of almost unenforceable customs regulations and taxes. A crisis of law and order fast approached the colonies.

[See also Church and State; Criminal Punishment; Gender and Law; Homicide; Procedure, Civil; Religion]

• John M. Murrin, "The Legal Transformation: The Bench and Bar of Eighteenth-Century Massachusetts" in Colonial America: Essays in Politics and Social Development, (Stanley N. Katz, ed.), 1971. William E. Nelson, Americanization of the Common Law, The Impact of Legal Change on Massachusetts Society, 1760–1830, 1975. Douglas Greenberg, Crime and Law Enforcement in the Colony of New York, 1692–1776, 1976. A. G. Roeber, Faithful Magistrates and Republican Lawyers, Creators of Virginia Legal Culture, 1680–1810, 1981. N. E. H. Hull, Female Felons: Women and Serious Crime in Colonial Massachusetts, 1987. Bruce Mann, Neighbors and Strangers, 1987. Carol Shammas, Marylynn Salmon, and Michel Dahlin, Inheritance in America, From Colonial Times to the Present, 1987. John H. Baker, An Introduction to English Legal History, 3rd. ed., 1990. Peter Charles Hoffer, Law and People in Colonial America, 2d ed., 1998.
                                            —Peter Charles Hoffer

HISTORY OF AMERICAN LAW: ANTEBELLUM THROUGH
RECONSTRUCTION, 1801–1877

The Revolutionary War brought Americans the crucial goals of economic and political independence. During the next century, the personal, informal, and local dealings that typified the Revolutionary era yielded to an increasingly impersonal national and international commercial market economy based on regional specialization. At the same time, profound social changes, most notably the freeing of more than 4 million slaves following the Civil War, reshaped the nation and its legal culture. Throughout, the role of government, the law, and the legal profession became more pronounced in the day-to-day lives of Americans. As significantly, the sectional divisions that had plagued America before the Civil War, while hardly extinguished, were attenuated by a more robust Union, a more active national government, and, thanks in large measure to the *Civil War Amendments to the Constitution, a scheme of *federalism with a stronger national center.

Lawmakers and Economic and Social Transformation. Congress and state legislatures were the most important "lawmakers" of the nineteenth century, although the courts also played a critical role. These lawmakers enacted statutes either to promote or regulate the marketplace and to shape a host of social relations. Federalism gave differing scope to their actions, with the states intervening more frequently and forcefully than Congress. In neither instance did the level of activity match the depth of governmental involvement associated with the modern administrative state. Following a burst of activity in the first part of the nineteenth century, legislatively directed promotion and regulation waned while the scope of judicial power broadened.

The social consequences of these national economic initiatives affected groups in different ways. Congress in the Indian Removal Act of 1832, for example, displaced thousands of *Native Americans from their ancestral lands in the Southeast to poorer lands in the Indian Territory of present-day Arkansas and Oklahoma. Their "trail of tears" was a lawfully mandated policy designed to open the Indians' former lands to what the whites considered more profitable forms of farming and planting.

Other Congressional policies stirred controversy within the white community and along sectional and class lines. What was wanted in the West was not always best for the East; what served the interests of manufacturers did not necessarily benefit small farmers and laborers. Lurking behind these debates was a persistent concern that greater power for the federal government might lead to the national abolition of *slavery.

Sectional conflict over slavery in general, and the extension of slavery into the new territories in particular, formed the political and legal fault lines of the nation. The most dramatic evidence of this sectional tension surfaced in the Nullification Crisis of 1832, when a South Carolina convention adopted an ordinance declaring a federal tariff null and void. The nullifiers were motivated as much by fear of the disruption of the institution of slavery, whose fate they believed was tied to the strength of their economy, as by the direct economic effects of the tariff.

With secession in 1861, northern Republicans not only gained control of the Congress from Democrats, but they proceeded to enhance the traditional distributive economic role of the legislative branch. Republicans blended the abolitionists' stress on the positive responsibility of the federal government to advance individual rights with a healthy dose of economic nationalism. In theory, at least, the bounty of government activity was to fall broadly over the nation; in practice, Republican policies during the Civil War and Reconstruction laid the foundations for big business.

The riches that Congress bestowed were varied and generous. Congress, for example, was directly responsible for stimulating the growth of the railroads, the nation's single most important, and most feared, business during the late nineteenth century. By 1900, the amount of land given for the purpose of subsidizing railroads was as large as the state of Texas. Congress also passed tariff, banking, and homestead legislation. Tariffs protected emerging industries, such as steel, by placing a duty on imported goods. National banking legislation in 1863, which had not existed since President Andrew Jackson vetoed the rechartering of the Second Bank of the United States, facilitated credit arrangements and therefore the availability of capital necessary to the expansion of manufacturing. Homestead legislation encouraged permanent settlement of the national domain by clearing the West of Native Americans with the army and by authorizing extensive work on rivers and harbors to facilitate waterborne commerce.

Beginning in 1865 and continuing for the next decade, Congressional Republicans also invoked the lawmaking authority of the federal government in an ultimately failed attempt to reconstruct the social basis of southern politics. The three Civil War amendments—Thirteenth, *Fourteenth, and Fifteenth—embodied the spirit of this new constitutional order, redefining through federal authority the social and political position of blacks and the relationship of the central government to the states.

Of these amendments, the impact of the Fourteenth, ratified in 1868, was the most far-reaching. Three of the amendment's five sections dealt with punitive measures directed against the South, and a fourth gave Congress the power to pass necessary legislation to enforce the amendment. The first section, however, was the most important. It established national citizenship, and declared that *privileges and immunities, *equal protection of the laws, and *due process of law extended to all persons against state action. This configuration worked a powerful revolution in federalism and set aside Chief Justice Roger B. *Taney's opinion in *Dred Scott v. Sandford (1857). Former slaves became citizens protected, at least in theory, by the federal government.

The new amendment provided Republicans in Congress with the authority to implement a full-blown plan of reconstruction. Congress provided for a reformation in governance of the South, effecting the repeal of the *Black Codes, which limited the freedom of newly freed slaves, stemming the violence of the Ku Klux Klan, and asserting federal military, judicial, and legal power. Ultimately, however, the embedded racism of the Reconstruction era limited the scope of social change through the law. By 1877, the Republican party had grown weary of the costs associated with Reconstruction, and as the memory of the war slipped away, the Northern white public, which had little real interest in the fate of blacks to begin with, also lost interest.

The Supreme Court greeted these Republican initiatives skeptically, in large measure because they reversed the traditional primacy of the states. A closely divided Supreme Court in the Slaughterhouse Cases (1873) held that the privileges and immunities clause of the Fourteenth Amendment was to be narrowly construed, and that the amendment was meant to apply only to former slaves, a position that generated intense dissent from the minority. The dissenting view eventually prevailed. In Santa Clara County v. Southern Pacific Railroad (1886), for example, the justices concluded that *corporations had the same rights under the amendment as did natural persons. While the Court proceeded to extend the scope of the amendment to corporations, it narrowed its application to former slaves. In the Civil Rights Cases (1883), for example, the justices struck down the Civil Rights Act of 1875. The decision began a long cycle in which federal and state law discriminated against not only blacks, but also Native Americans and Chinese.

Congress had filled a modest regulatory role earlier in the nineteenth century. Perhaps its one most significant success involved steam-boating. In 1838 alone, at least 496 lives were lost as a result of steamboat explosions. Congress in 1852 passed the nation's first major regulatory act. It governed the operation of steamboats, set standards for boiler construction, and established boards to inspect, license, and investigate steamboat operators. It also contributed to a dramatic decline in steamboat accidents. The 1852 act was a straw in the wind rather than the harbinger of a vast new role for Congress.

The most important intervention in the economy came at the state level rather than the national level. Even though the laws governing each state's mixed economy were unique, general patterns did appear. Of these, one of the most important was the singularly American vision of the state as a commonwealth. The commonwealth idea was a quasi-mercantilist concept wrapped in a democratic framework. The state existed to ensure that the rights of the public took precedence over any individual interest. The commonwealth idea fitted well with federalism, because the federal Constitution reserved to the states the police powers to provide for the health, safety, morals, and welfare of their citizens.

Legislatures breathed life into the commonwealth idea through a veritable blizzard of economic regulations. Most of this legislation involved low-level economic relationships. Every state had laws regulating the sale of food products, setting standards for the conduct of peddlers and vendors, and directing manufacturers to include the name and place of manufacture. These measures helped to guarantee the quality of goods produced within the state, making that state's economy competitive with every other state in the national marketplace, and provided a modicum of protection to consumers against fraudulent commercial practices. The states also pioneered the development of bureaus and independent regulatory commissions, particularly to address the effect of the railroad. Much nineteenth-century *regulation, therefore, while driven by an economic purpose, also carried forward from the colonial era an ethical commitment to fair dealing.

In the Midwest, where Grange and Populist agitation was significant, legislators fashioned more powerful regulatory bodies. Illinois in 1871 passed Granger laws that established a commission with authority to ascertain whether railroads and warehouses were complying with the laws. The railroads, for their part, gravitated toward the position that federal supervision was an attractive alternative to a tangled web of state regulation.

State legislators, under the pressure of market capitalism, also structured important social relationships in the nineteenth century. Beginning in the 1830s, and continuing into the 1870s, state legislators sought to protect the viability of the family and the advancement of the economy through married women's *property acts. These laws protected wives from the pecuniary embarrassments of their husbands, especially during periodic upheavals in the economy. While they granted married women special treatment under the law, they provided *equity, not equality. In states with a strong *civil law tradition (e.g., California, Texas, and Louisiana), the community property system prevailed over the *common law practice of dower. The civil law provided that husband and wife each owned one-half of the property, although, just as in common law jurisdictions, the husband had an exclusive right to manage the property.

Beginning in the middle of the century, state legislatures and even Congress intervened in matters of birth control. In 1870, explicit restrictions on the dissemination of birth control information first appeared as a moral purity movement took hold. Anthony Comstock, a failed New York City businessman, mobilized the reform effort, and persuaded Congress in 1873 to pass the first national obscenity statute, which prohibited the dissemination of information about birth control and *abortion, and received constitutional validation by the Supreme Court in *Ex parte Jackson* (1877). Several states promptly passed "little" Comstock acts.

At the same time that state and federal legislators sought to regulate personal behavior, they also engaged actively in economic promotion. For example, the legislatures of New York, Ohio, and Pennsylvania adopted comprehensive plans for public construction of transport facilities. Aggressive state policies, however, frequently ended in fiscal debacles. Large-scale bankruptcies, swindles, and defalcations on bonds following the Depression of 1873 punctuated state promotion of railroads. When times were bad, legislators withdrew from promotional activity; when times improved, they returned, although direct aid became less and less significant.

State promotional activity appeared in other less direct but nonetheless critical forms. For example, state legislatures gave support to the development of what became the modern corporation. First, they began to enact corporate charters that specified limited *liability, a rule that proved the single greatest lure to would-be investors. Limited liability meant that individuals could pursue profit far in excess of the amount of their investment without fear that, should the venture fail, they would be held responsible for all of its debts. Second, the formation of corporations became easier. By the end of the Civil War, every state had adopted general incorporation laws. These laws standardized the means of obtaining a charter and doing corporate business, added continuity and predictability to corporate affairs, and made the advantages of incorporation available to all people. Third, the states also facilitated economic growth by easing the terms on which municipal corporations operated. The Missouri constitution of 1875 was the first to include a home-rule provision. Under it, a municipality was given control over its local affairs in return for a pledge to abide by certain legislative provisions, the most important of which involved the borrowing power of the municipality.

The rise of the corporate form was complemented, and in someways enhanced, by the broadened powers of eminent domain. The heyday of public expropriation of private property, one of the most glaring exceptions to laissez-faire ideology, lasted from about 1870 to 1910. Beginning in the 1870s, state legislatures, especially in the developing West, authorized private corporations to take private property for private purposes. Delegates to the Colorado constitutional convention of 1875–76 blazed the way, framing the first fundamental law in the nation to contain such a provision. The clash among farmers, ranchers, and miners typically had more to do with who would benefit from the power (either via irrigation to raise crops and livestock or via extraction of minerals) than whether the power should be used. Most Western states took an eclectic approach, giving a little bit to every interest.

State legislators also had to balance conflicting interests in another controversial area: *debtor-creditor relations. With the growth of corporations and the rise of the banking system, the entire scheme of debtor-creditor relations became more impersonal and accountable. Loans were made not on the basis of personal assessment, but on a measure of the borrower's record and future prospects for profit. The growing geographical scope of business activity further depersonalized credit relations, and the absence of a federal *bankruptcy statute added an element of uncertainty to national debtor-creditor relations. This condition was not relieved until Congress in 1898 passed meaningful national bankruptcy legislation.

Institutional Transformation and Professionalization of the Bar. By the outbreak of the Civil War, faith in the active state had eroded. The wish to curb legislative authority was strong everywhere. More than three-quarters of the states by 1877 either had rewritten existing *constitutions or had written new fundamental documents of government, and the states of the former Confederacy experienced a prolonged period of constitutional restructuring. These new organic laws attempted to rein in *legislative power by limiting state indebtedness and prohibiting state and local governments from aiding private enterprise. The new documents also placed stringent restraints on capital expenditures. Moreover, state constitutions, which had been viewed as fundamental laws half a century earlier, became code-like documents intended to limit governmental action. In addition, the role of state officials began to change significantly. *Governors gained increased authority through the veto power, the pardoning power, and the ability to make appointments, once the exclusive province of the legislature.

The most dramatic change came to the judiciary. "The Americans," Alexis de Tocqueville wrote in the 1830s, "have given their courts immense political power." Judges, who increasingly were trained lawyers elected for limited terms of office, proceeded gradually between the Revolution and Reconstruction to claim an extended sphere of operations. The change was apparent, for example, in the growing role of judges in settling questions of law, a task that had previously been left in many jurisdictions to juries. The autonomy gained by the jury over matters of fact was lost to the judiciary over questions of law.

The judiciary also extended its influence over legislatures. In the 1830s, Francis Hilliard and William Duane, two of the nation's most prominent lawyers, insisted that judges had an overtly political as well as judicial character. The incidence of *judicial review by state and federal appellate courts exploded after the Civil War as appellate judges fortified their growing role as economic and social policymakers. Earlier, the Supreme Court had resorted to judicial review in cases such as *McCulloch v. Maryland* (1819) and *Gibbons* v. *Ogden* (1824) to sweep away state impediments to the emerging national market economy.

Increasingly, judges reshaped the common law to suit the rapidly evolving American experience. For example, establishing the scope of corporate charter powers became a crucial function of antebellum courts. While state judges generally held that corporate charters should be narrowly construed, the federal Supreme Court embraced a more expansive doctrine in the landmark case of *Dartmouth College* v. *Woodward* (1819). Chief

Justice John *Marshall's majority opinion invoked federal constitutional authority to promote voluntary risk taking by creating a stable legal environment for the formation of private corporations. Moreover, Justice Joseph *Story's concurring opinion established the legal basis for distinguishing a public corporation from a private corporation.

The same state courts that approved the development of the corporate form of organization for investors eventually came to accept that some workers might protect their earning power through collective organization. By the 1840s, U.S. courts began to retreat from the English common law doctrine of labor conspiracy. Chief Justice Lemuel *Shaw of Massachusetts led the way in the case of *Commonwealth* v. *Hunt* (1842). Shaw concluded that the best interests of the commonwealth would be furthered through competition, and unions were one means of stimulating just such competition.

As the tempo of economic activity quickened in the early nineteenth century, traditional concepts of property rights, including vested rights and absolute domain, came under judicial scrutiny. For example, beginning in the 1830s, the doctrine of priority and prescription, which held that the best way to promote initial economic activity was to give a monopoly over the uses of land to those persons willing to undertake the risks of development, came under judicial attack. It was replaced by an instrumental concept of property law known as the reasonableness or balancing test. It stressed the efficient use of resources based on competition, and rejected as inefficient the monopolistic features of absolute domain.

The judicial acceptance of a dynamic view of property law based on economic efficiency and public rights doctrine was especially evident in the areas of water rights and eminent domain. In the case of water law, at least east of the Mississippi River, the antidevelopmental doctrine of natural flow declined, and was replaced by a doctrine of reasonable use. This doctrine held that some existing property holders along a water course had to suffer losses without a legal remedy in order that the community as a whole might benefit. In the arid West, water law turned on the principle that the individual who got to the water first had priority over all other users, as well as the power to sell it in whole or in part.

The judiciary also helped to shape the law of eminent domain. The Fifth Amendment to the Constitution, for example, provided that property shall not "be taken for public use without just compensation." Although the federal amendment was adjudged in *Barron* v. *Baltimore* (1833) not to apply against the states, state courts regularly invoked it along with clauses in their own constitutions to restrict the power of eminent domain. State court judges developed two important limitations that protected property rights: first, that property might be taken only for a "public purpose"; second, that the owner had to be given fair, or just, compensation.

Judges, however, also adopted a utilitarian perspective on the power of eminent domain. First, they gave wide play to the coercive feature of the power of eminent domain. They accepted, for example, the practice of "offsetting." Numerous legislatures mandated that the calculation of the presumed benefits to an individual attributable to construction of a canal, road, or railroad be used to offset the value of losses suffered as a result of having property taken. Second, judges also agreed that franchise corporations could exercise the power of eminent domain as long as they did so for a public purpose.

The worst fears of the proponents of vested property rights were realized in *Charles River Bridge* v. *Warren Bridge* (1837). Chief Justice Roger B. Taney, a Jacksonian Democrat recently appointed to the Court, endorsed the new pragmatic attitude that vested rights had to give way before new technological advances that promised economic growth. Taney held on the narrow legal issue that, contrary to *Dartmouth College*, no monopoly or other power should be viewed as implied in a corporate charter. But the opinion was even more important for the dictum Taney added. Only by preventing established capital from entrenching itself could economic growth based on new technology occur.

This same combination of expediency and principle spilled over into the new law of *contract and the so-called "will theory" that undergirded it. What counted was that the wills, or minds, of two independent and free individuals had met and that they had settled on the terms of the bargain between themselves. The equitable character of their agreement was not for the courts to consider; judges had only to establish objectively that the agreement had been made.

Judges, lawyers, and legal writers all participated in the transformation of the law of contract. Daniel Chipman, Nathan Dane, Joseph Story, and Guilian Verplanck published major treatises on the law of contract before the Civil War. The capstone of this literature appeared in 1844 when William Wetmore Story published *A Treatise on the Law of*

Contracts. Every contract, Story proclaimed, is founded on the mutual agreement of the parties.

The new contract theory had important implications for the economy. First, it stressed the significance of expectation damages in the context of national markets. Increasingly in the nineteenth century, agreements turned on the realization of a future return, the value of which would be dictated by the marketplace. Second, because it emphasized an objective approach to contract theory, the interpretation of an agreement was a matter of law rather than fact, sharpening the division of labor between judge and jury. Objectivity meant that judges ensured that agreements adhered to the usages of the marketplace rather than strictly considering equality of price.

Theory and practice never blended fully in nineteenth-century contract law. The idea that judges objectively analyzed contracts was illusory, because they continued to examine the terms of the contract. They had ample opportunity to infuse their beliefs and, as Peter Karsten has shown in *Head Versus Heart* (1997), their sense of fairness into the law. Moreover, as Karsten has also shown, while the doctrine of caveat emptor took on new authority, the old eighteenth-century sound-price doctrine—a sound price warrants a sound commodity—continued to have some vitality.

Judges also applied the new contract doctrines to the law of negotiable instruments. The federal courts were particularly important in molding this uniformity, and the role of Justice Joseph Story was especially significant. Story was not only the nation's leading authority on negotiable instruments, but he was also the author of the leading case, *Swift* v. *Tyson* (1842). In his opinion for the Court, Story concluded that federal judges in commercial cases were free to turn to the general principles and doctrines of commercial jurisprudence rather than being bound exclusively by existing state law. Story aimed to replace the indeterminacy in *commercial law with a unified body of rules promulgated by federal courts.

The Supreme Court also contributed, along with state judges, to the development of the nineteenth-century law of contract in other ways. The justices, for example, broadened the meaning of a contract, first in holding in *Fletcher* v. *Peck* (1810) that a grant made by a state was a contract, and then in *Dartmouth College* that a charter granted by a state was a contract.

The same issues of economic efficiency and moral conduct appeared in *tort law. The establishment of the fault principle was the most important tort law development before the Civil War.

American judges reexamined the meaning of tort liability within the context of a market economy dependent on new and often dangerous forms of technology and a society in which strangers increasingly came into contact with one another. The fault standard replaced strict liability, with Lemuel Shaw's decision in *Brown* v. *Kendall* (1850), the leading case. Shaw introduced the principle of blameworthiness: that there could be no *liability without fault. Injured people could no longer win damages merely by showing that a person had perpetrated the injury. They had to show as well that the action had been negligent. Furthermore, Shaw permitted a defendant to escape liability if he could show that his act had not directly caused the accident.

Shaw's decision contained another innovation: the idea of contributory negligence. Under it, a plaintiff could not collect damages if he was in any way responsible for (contributed to) the accident. The plaintiff's own negligence, even if slight, acted as a barrier to his recovery.

New technology, the factory system, and expanding markets increased the physical and psychological distance between employer and employee. Courts accepted the new reality of the workplace through the fellow-servant rule and the doctrine of assumption of risk, both of which Shaw articulated in *Farwell* v. *Boston and Worcester Railroad* (1842). The emerging law of industrial accidents in the nineteenth century generally favored capital over labor, and frequently distributed much of the costs of accidents onto the workforce (see LABOR LAW).

While it is clear that some courts used the fault standard to subsidize capital development, there were, as Karsten has shown, many instances when trial and appellate judges showed great solicitude for the victims of accidents. In *Spencer* v. *Campbell* (1845), for example, the Pennsylvania Supreme Court ruled that the owner of a public trade or business, which required the use of a steam engine, owed a duty to the public to be responsible for any injury resulting from its deficiency. Moreover, American judges continued to apply the doctrine of absolute liability to ultra-hazardous activities. The New York Court of Appeals in 1852 held in *Thomas* v. *Winchester* that the production of drugs was so inherently dangerous that the manufacturer was strictly liable for any damages done.

Judicial reconstruction of the common law was challenged by the *codification movement. In the first half of the nineteenth century, radical codifiers such as Robert Rantoul ridiculed both the practicality and suitability of judicial interpretation of the common law. They proposed to replace it with a scheme of codified written law that, like the civil law system, would be readily accessible and easy to interpret. More moderate voices, such as those of Timothy Walker, Justice Joseph Story, and David Dudley *Field, stressed the lack of uniformity and certainty in U.S. law. A code promised to unify law, to reduce the growing bulk of reports, and to speed the processing of commercial disputes by freeing lawyers from the technical encumbrances of the common law. The most notable achievement came in 1848 when Field delivered his Code of Civil Procedure to the New York legislature. The code aimed to simplify the trial process by giving greater weight to the substantive issues in a case rather than the manner in which lawyers presented them. The Field Code was adopted in Missouri (1849) and California (1851), and several other Western states also embraced it after the Civil War.

The debate over codification took place against a background of fundamental change in the legal profession. Until about 1830, the *lawyer class had been guildlike, based on local control and built on a restrictive system of personal alliances including marriage, paternal occupations, and extended apprenticeship. By the 1870s, however, the traditional features of law practice began to fade, as the role of the lawyer evolved from advocate to counsel, as large law *firms (five or more) grew, and as lawyers began to specialize to meet the soaring demands of the new industrial market economy.

The theme of professionalization also figured in the rise of the *American Bar Association (ABA), founded in 1878 by Connecticut Supreme Court Judge Simeon E. *Baldwin. The new association, like its local and state counterparts, was purposefully exclusionary and designed to rid the profession of ambulance chasers and ethnic immigrant lawyers. The leaders of the ABA also recognized that the profession of law had to share its prestige with others of the new "scientific" professions, such as economics.

The bulk of the nineteenth-century bar was drawn from white, middle-class males. Women were excluded from the bar before the 1870s, and their ranks grew only at a glacial pace through the 1920s. The most celebrated case was that of Myra Bradwell. Bradwell studied law and passed her examination, but was refused admission to the bar of Illinois in 1869. She appealed to the U.S. Supreme Court, arguing that the equal protection clause of the Fourteenth Amendment prohibited state legislation excluding her from practice. The Court unanimously disagreed. Justice Joseph P.

Bradley explained for the Court in *Bradwell* v. *Illinois* (1873) that women's place was inherently in the domestic sphere, not the courtroom.

Black males enjoyed only slightly greater access to the bar than did women. The 1870 census listed only three black lawyers in Massachusetts. The few practicing black lawyers in 1877 had a broad legal practice, handling both civil and criminal cases, although the most profitable cases went to white lawyers.

Most lawyers were trained through a practice of apprenticeship or reading law, although by the last quarter of the century, law schools were appearing in greater and greater numbers. Between 1850 and 1900, the number of law schools increased from 15 to 101, with an enrollment of over 10,000. The most important development came during the 1870s when Dean Christopher Columbus Langdell of the Harvard Law School permanently altered the course of legal *education. Langdell tightened admissions standards by requiring students without a college degree to take an admissions test; he lengthened the period of law training from one to three years; and he introduced year-end final examinations that students had to pass in order to move to the next year, and ultimately graduation. And most importantly, Langdell introduced the case method of instruction. Through its use, Langdell shifted the emphasis away from vocational training and toward the development of a scientific understanding of the law, one designed to help corporate and nationally oriented clients. The law, according to Langdell, was not just a vocation (something tawdry that craftsmen practiced), but a genuine branch of higher learning that required rigorous formal training. It was a profession, and a scientific one at that.

Instrumentalism, Formalism, and Judicial Power. The rise of legal professionalism, the acceptance of the case method, and the idea of a scientific approach to law were part and parcel of broader trends associated with the term "legal formalism." Instrumentalism was the older path, and its heyday was in the antebellum era. Instrumentalist legislators relied on the police powers to promote economic growth with some appropriate degree of regulation. Judges engaged in instrumental activity by using their common law authority to fashion doctrines that enhanced private business activity. This instrumentalist approach, as Karsten has shown, never died away, either on the bench or in legislatures. Moreover, its freewheeling nature was often balanced against traditional ideas of fairness, equity, and right conduct.

Formalism, on the other hand, held that law

was a whole body of knowledge that scientific legal thinkers could discern and properly trained judges could apply. Formalism, however, did not imply inactivity; to the contrary, appellate judges were supposed to be oracular, to propound impartially a set body of doctrine. Judge Thomas M. *Cooley summed up much of the formalist agenda in his famous *Treatise on the Constitutional Limitations Which Rest upon the Legislative Power of the States of the American Union.* First published in 1868, and appearing in twelve subsequent revised editions, *Constitutional Limitations* offered one simple message: legislatures were to steer clear of any regulatory efforts, and the courts, when legislatures did act, were bound to strike down such laws as unconstitutional.

As a result of these developments, the single most significant feature in nineteenth-century American legal culture was the steady rise of judicial authority. By the end of Reconstruction in 1877, federal and state courts had reduced the law-finding role of the jury, fashioned a distinctive American common law, and established the principle of judicial review. As a consequence, the courts emerged as economic policy-making institutions.

[*See also* Civil Rights and Civil Liberties; Economics and Law]

• J. Willard Hurst, *Law and the Conditions of Freedom in Nineteenth Century America,* 1964. Morton Horwitz, *The Transformation of American Law, 1780–1860,* 1979. Lawrence M. Friedman, *A History of American Law,* 1986. Michael Grossberg, *Governing the Hearth: Law and Family in Nineteenth-Century America,* 1988. Kermit L. Hall, *The Magic Mirror: Law in American History,* 1989. Morton Horwtiz, *The Transformation of American Law, 1870–1960: The Crisis of Legal Orthodoxy,* 1994. Peter Karsten, *Head Versus Heart: Judge-Made Law in Nineteenth-Century America,* 1997. Harry N. Scheiber, *The State and Freedom to Contract,* 1999.

—Kermit L. Hall

HISTORY OF AMERICAN LAW: GILDED AGE TO THE GREAT DEPRESSION (1877–1929)

The period from the 1870s through the 1920s saw great changes in both the practice and the substance of American law. Law was closely connected to commerce, and the nation's transition from a largely agricultural commercial society to an urban, industrial one made changes inevitable.

Courts, the Legal Profession, and a Changing Society. Because of their diverse backgrounds, lack of fixed social hierarchy, and great social and geographic mobility, Americans had in the mid-nineteenth century neither strong customary rules governing personal relationships nor many informal institutions to resolve disputes. Law and the courts provided the primary way in which Americans established mutual relations and resolved disputes. As the economy grew during the Gilded Age (1870–1900), a growing proportion of legal activity involved business relations, which eventually displaced the settlement of disputes among ordinary citizens as the courts' prime concern.

Well into the Gilded Age, courts continued to play the central role not only in enforcing the law and adjusting disputes but in setting *social and *economic policy. The courts settled disputes in accordance with *common law, adapting it to new developments. Courts rather than legislatures or administrative agencies made the first adjustments to the changing social and economic conditions of the Gilded Age. Statutes played a secondary role, remedying inadequacies in the common-law rules that courts developed or curing perceived injustices that resulted from their application. The result was that during a time of immense change, judges established the prevailing law and critics of their decisions had the handicap of trying to challenge it.

With law so important a part of the *commercial system, demands upon courts grew dramatically. A national transportation system of railroads and canals was completed in the 1870s and 1880s, creating a national market that fueled a tremendous economic expansion. Nationalization of the market led to an exponential growth in the work of the federal *courts, encouraged by congressional enactment of the Judiciary Act of 1875. Answering complaints from interstate businesses that local courts were biased against them, the new law authorized out-of-state defendants to transfer cases to the federal courts. The courts foundered under the load. In response Congress periodically modified and increased the size of the federal judiciary. Major Judiciary Acts in 1891 and 1925 restructured the federal courts and gave the *Supreme Court broad authority to decide what cases it would hear. An increasing number of lawyers found themselves practicing in federal as well as local courts.

Complaints about procedural complexities and delays in state and local courts also grew. As critics urged the creation of administrative agencies to relieve courts of the primary responsibility for applying rules to business activities, lawyers urged the creation of specialized courts. Likewise, business people and reformers complained about the wide legal disparities in different jurisdictions. In response, elite lawyers urged greater uniformity. Not until the 1910s and 1920s, however, were practical steps taken to provide guidance through restatements of the law and the promotion of uniform codes.

The difficulty of adjusting to a rapidly changing society through common-law adjudication altered the locus of change in the law. Between 1880 and 1920 statutes slowly replaced court decisions as the primary source of legal rules. With the creation of state railroad commissions in the 1870s, state legislatures (and later Congress) began to establish a number of administrative agencies whose decisions and regulations also became major sources of legal rules. The courts, as well as most lawyers, at first resisted this shift in legal authority. Administrative agencies were widely denounced for introducing alien sources of law and arbitrary procedures to the American system. Until the end of the nineteenth century, judges construed statutes so as to disturb common-law rules as little as possible. Judges insisted that administrative agencies meet common-law standards of due process, imposing *judicial review of administrative decisions. Although the courts became more accommodating to both statute and administrative decision-making in the twentieth century, tension continued, laying the basis for the confrontation between the courts and other branches of government during the New Deal.

Although a large part of lawmaking shifted from courts to legislatures and administrative agencies, lawyers continued to play a key role. Their role in state legislatures and Congress was crucial. Administrative agencies, subject to judicial review of their procedures and even the substance of their decisions, required legal expertise both in their administration and in the representation of parties appearing before them. Lawyers continued to represent clients in the courts, presenting arguments about how legal principles should be applied to cases or should be modified. The demand for lawyers and legal services burgeoned.

With the great expansion of commerce, the concerns of lawyers shifted. Increasingly they served business clients and dealt with commercial issues. Although the highly specialized practices that characterize large urban law *firms did not develop until the very end of the period, as early as the 1870s people referred to "railroad lawyers," experts in transportation law. Likewise, elite lawyers developed special expertise in the legal problems of banks and large financial institutions. From the 1870s to the turn of the century, businesses regularly called upon influential lawyers to provide legal opinions on business practices and decisions, virtually creating the field of *corpora-

tion law and foreshadowing the development of in-house counsel in succeeding decades. Devising *contracts and resolving contractual disputes augmented mere debt collection as a central concern of lawyers. The development of railroads and manufacturing led to a significant growth in personal injury, or *tort, law. The growing complexity of business led to the development of whole new fields of law, such as agency—the consequences arising out of the relationship between principals and those they employed or designated to act for them.

The Gilded Age also saw the beginnings of the trend toward larger law firms to service the complex needs of immense business clients. Although single practices and two-person partnerships remained the norm, by 1900 a few larger firms located in urban centers had as many as twenty partners and associates, with supporting staffs of twice that number.

Professionalization.   Professionalization was one of the defining characteristics of the Gilded Age and Progressive Era. It provided a sense of identity, drew distinct boundaries between those who shared particular expertise and those who did not, and established standards to be met by those who claimed membership in the profession. Lawyers developed bar associations to further these goals and established a professional identity long before most other occupational groups. A few *bar associations predated the Civil War, but most had been fleeting efforts. With the rise of the professional ethic generally, the times were right for more permanent efforts. Setting the pattern was the Bar Association of New York City, established in 1870. Lawyers in other jurisdictions followed suit. In 1878 a group of leading practitioners founded the *American Bar Association (ABA). These associations were selective rather than inclusive, designed to separate elite lawyers from mere pettifoggers. Only slowly did these organizations undertake to improve—to professionalize—the legal profession as a whole.

The elite lawyers who founded the first bar associations identified greater exclusiveness with higher standards. With apprenticeship the predominant form of legal training and admission to the bar turning on the recommendations of practitioners, established lawyers had been able to control entry. However, admission to a local bar generally secured the right to practice anywhere in a state. As late as 1890 fewer than one-third of the states and territories controlled admission to the bar through a central agency or their supreme courts. Most admissions were local, based on perfunctory oral examinations, with the recommendation of local practitioners counting for more than demonstrated knowledge. After 1890 this changed dramatically. A centralized bar examination became all but universal.

From the 1890s to well into the twentieth century, passing the bar examination remained the main requirement for becoming a lawyer. Educational requirements remained minimal. In 1890 fewer than half the jurisdictions in the United States required any formal legal preparation, whether in law school or a law office. In 1917, thirteen of the forty-nine jurisdictions still had no such requirement (and none required attendance at a law school). In 1921 the ABA called for higher pre-law educational standards, and the states slowly responded.

With centralized rather than local admission to the bar, minimal educational requirements, and the great demand for lawyers, whatever exclusiveness the old system of local bar admissions had fostered broke down by the later nineteenth century. The apprenticeship system, which had allowed lawyers some control over entry to the profession, was increasingly replaced by a growing number of law schools. By 1900 there were more than a hundred, many of them private, profit-making establishments offering courses at night and catering to any part-time student who paid. Many colleges acquired local proprietary law schools, some of them beginning to follow Harvard's example of upgrading standards—making law school a graduate program, requiring undergraduate experience for admission, and establishing a three-year curriculum. To encourage attendance at such schools, a few states enacted a "diploma privilege," directly admitting graduates to the bar. However, the trend was reversed when states adopted and toughened bar examinations after the 1890s. Despite its opposition to the diploma privilege, the ABA sporadically passed resolutions encouraging higher standards in legal *education. But in 1900 nearly twice as many students (about seventy-five hundred) attended part-time law schools offering primarily night courses as attended full-time law schools with stricter standards. In response, the ABA encouraged "reputable" law schools to establish the *Association of American Law Schools (AALS), founded in 1900. The motivation of the ABA, still an elite organization with barely fifteen hundred members, no doubt was partly to put obstacles in the way of aspiring lawyers with undesirable social and ethnic backgrounds. But while the number of member schools increased and the AALS consis-

tently raised standards—after 1907 requiring a three-year curriculum of all members—the proportion of law students attending AALS institutions shrank.

Not until the 1920s did the ABA and AALS, inspired by the medical profession's success in controlling education and licensing, launch an effective campaign to monopolize legal education. In 1921 the ABA endorsed a report that declared only law schools meeting high standards could provide an adequate legal education, two years of college should be required for admission to any law school, and law schools should phase out night courses aimed at part-time students. The campaign would bear fruit in the 1930s, when states mandated higher standards, the Depression put nonelite law schools under financial pressure, and student attendance shifted decisively toward institutions meeting ABA and AALS standards. As states finally established strict requirements for legal training, law schools requiring undergraduate degrees for admission and providing three years of rigorous training were in place to meet the states' mandates.

A growing number of women sought entry to the bar. The bar traditionally had been closed to women; only five women were identified as lawyers in the United States census of 1870. In 1869 the Illinois supreme court, relying on tradition, refused to admit Myra Bradwell, the able editor of the *Chicago Legal News*, to the bar. Her lawyers failed to persuade the Supreme Court in *Bradwell* v. *Illinois* (1873) that the refusal deprived her of the *privileges and immunities of American citizenship. Although Illinois and a number of other states changed this rule, few women were able to become lawyers. Established lawyers generally declined to train them in law offices, and law schools refused to admit them. African Americans faced similar obstacles. Howard University, established to provide higher education for black students, created a law school in 1868. As the school struggled for existence, unable to meet AALS standards until the 1930s, a few other law schools, primarily in New England, accepted black applicants. But most did not, even if they had no formal exclusionary policy.

The Science of the Law and Legal Education. Understandings of the nature of the law changed radically from the second half of the nineteenth century through the 1920s. The nineteenth century was preeminently an age of science, and in the first half of the century many elite lawyers insisted that law was a science too. However, in practice, common law had been an arcane body of rules and procedures based on an ancient and complex system of writs, each of which began a different action requiring a different pattern of pleadings. Through these complicated pleadings, the parties to a case would finally arrive at a key question of fact or law upon which the whole decision would turn.

This system proved entirely inadequate to cope with changing economic conditions in the United States. Results often turned on procedural technicalities unrelated to the substance of the dispute; they were inordinately dependent on the quality of legal counsel. The legal system lacked the predictability essential to a modern commercial system. As early as 1848 New York had adopted a new code of civil *procedure (the Field Code) simplifying the system, and a few other states followed suit. In the second half of the nineteenth century nearly all the western states adopted the code, while most eastern states enacted less radical reforms. The reforms led to the triumph of the proposition that law was a science—a development that had the welcome side effect of raising the prestige and status of the profession and promised the regularity and consistency commercial clients craved. Just as in any science, principles could be induced from a careful scrutiny of raw data—in this case, earlier cases, the raw materials of the law. Once established, the principle could be applied to the case at hand. Access to the reports of cases became crucial, and several new publishing firms began to specialize in making reports of cases available. In 1876 West Publishing Company established a National Reporter System, making the decisions of all jurisdictions available and linking like cases by cross-references of ever-growing sophistication. Digests and restatements of American law appeared, organizing the rules and principles of American law in logical structures, annotated with the cases from which the rules' principles were derived. Law schools established journals devoted to divining basic principles and to critiquing court decisions and hoary doctrines in the light of these principles.

The triumph of the scientific conception of the law had a powerful impact on legal training. Apprenticeship in a law office was not adequate for learning how to understand and apply a science. Like the other sciences, law required formal higher education. The method of training lawyers in elite law schools changed dramatically, establishing the foundation for legal education in the mid-twentieth century and after. Prodded by the example of Harvard Law School, where Dean Christopher Columbus Langdell first instituted the reform, laws schools replaced lectures with the casebook method of instruction. Instead of lecturing on a series of legal rules and practices, instructors queried students about the facts, holdings, and reasoning of specific cases, forcing them to draw more general principles from them. The result was to make legal instruction more an academic inquiry and less a mere vocational training.

The growing number and prestige of law schools also created an academic legal community. Law schools increasingly appointed instructors with relatively little experience as practitioners. They established publications in which teachers and students explored legal concepts and assessed whether court decisions conformed to them. With a strong interest in maintaining the academic credentials of their discipline, many academic lawyers at the most prestigious law schools sought to align law with the social sciences. And unfettered by obligations to clients, many of these academics stressed the public function of the law. Both characteristics of academic law prepared the way for yet another clash over the nature of the law.

The Substance of the Law. By the time of the Civil War, Americans saw the right to make contracts rather than the ownership of property as the hallmark of freedom and independence. The right to make voluntary agreements, to decide upon one's own obligations, to be responsible for one's own well-being, seemed the essence of *liberty. When the nation abolished slavery, the right to make contracts was specified in the Civil Rights Act of 1866, which defined the basic rights inherent in freedom. Reformers insisted that women could not be considered free until they had the same freedom of contract as men. State after state passed laws abolishing common-law restrictions of women's property and contractual rights.

Contract reflected the idea that the range of voluntary agreement should be maximized. There was strong pressure to minimize rules through which the law imposed responsibilities involuntarily or refused to enforce voluntary contracts because they appeared unfair to one of the parties. This attitude affected public policy. By the turn of the twentieth century, the Supreme Court held that the Constitution protected "liberty of contract" and that laws imposing constraints upon this liberty required special justification. The spirit of contract permeated other areas of law, putting pressure on rules that imposed involuntary obligations. The doctrine of "privity" limited the safety obligations of manufacturers and vendors toward those with whom they had no contractual relationship. The notion developed that employees took the dangers of working conditions into account when they negotiated their wages and thus assumed the associated risk.

In the nineteenth century, tort law was reconfigured around the concepts of *fault and negligence. In the absence of special agreements, people owed no more than reasonable care to others; they were at fault only when they were negligent. From this principle, legal analysts elaborated a number of rules that they believed enhanced personal responsibility for safety. The "fellow employee" rule made one's coworkers, not the employer, responsible for negligence in the workplace, thus making fault a matter of negligence not the status relationship between master and servant. According to the doctrine of "contributory negligence," an injured party could not win compensation for an injury that could have been avoided by greater care on her part.

Laissez-Faire Constitutionalism. The emphasis on the individual right to enter freely into one's own arrangements reinforced a growing suspicion of government. Most lawyers, academics, businessmen, and other elite groups in society strongly believed that voluntary contracts fairly reflected the supply and demand for goods and services in a free market. They saw growing demands for regulation of railroad rates, maximum-hours-of-labor laws, and minimum-wage laws as illicit efforts to benefit some interests at the expense of others. They insisted that such "class legislation" deprived its victims of liberty (especially liberty of contract) and of property with *due process of law, in violation of the Fifth and *Fourteenth Amendments.

By the 1880s and 1890s state and federal *courts accepted such arguments. Although judges sustained most laws regulating business practices and the use of property as valid exercises of governmental police power, they imposed significant restrictions on public policy. Where government agencies regulated business practices, especially transportation rates, the rules had to meet judicial standards of reasonability; unreasonable regulations unconstitutionally deprived the regulated parties of property without due process of law. The courts were especially stringent when they scrutinized *labor legislation. In the paradigmatic *Lochner v. New York (1905) the Supreme Court ruled maximum-hour legislation unconstitutional except in occupations traditionally recognized as dangerous. When states banned labor contracts that prohibited workers from joining unions, courts declared the laws unconstitutional violations of liberty of contract. The same was true of minimum-wage legislation. Courts acted forcefully

to protect the rights of employers and workers to enter into contracts free of labor union coercion, issuing labor injunctions to end boycotts, picketing, and intimidation of replacement workers. This constitutionalization of laissez-faire made judges the allies of conservatives who resisted the reforms championed by Populists and Progressives in the 1890s and the first two decades of the twentieth century.

The greatest exception to the law's commitment to maximizing individual freedom lay in the areas of *race and *gender. In the twenty years following 1890, the southern states deprived African Americans of the right to vote, serve on juries, and other basic civil and political rights through the discriminatory application of laws that were equal on their face. They imposed a system of racial *segregation in all areas of southern life, and aspects of the system spread to parts of the North as well. Although a few court decisions would nibble around the edges of this system, in *Plessy v. Ferguson (1896) the Supreme Court sustained the constitutionality of racial segregation, even though such forced separation imposed massive limitations on the freedom of individuals to establish their own relationships voluntarily.

The courts also gave legislatures wider latitude to impose obligations on women than on men. In Muller v. Oregon (1908) the Court held that women's role as mothers and their general dependence on men justified limits on contracts designed to protect them—in this case, a limit on the number of hours women could agree to work. While Progressive reformers celebrated the breach in the Court's adherence to "liberty of contract," feminists chafed at the idea that they were not entitled to the same contractual freedom—generally understood to be the most essential element of liberty—as men. In 1921 feminists celebrated the Court's decision in Adkins v. Children's Hospital, ruling unconstitutional a minimum-wage law applying only to women.

Sociological Jurisprudence and Legal Realism. As Populist and Progressive reformers blasted the courts for obstructing social and economic reform, critics within the profession began to complain that the law had become over-rationalized and too abstract. Courts were applying rules regardless of the real-world context in which people made laws, entered into contracts, and disputed rights. Critics such as Roscoe *Pound and Louis *Brandeis argued that judges should adopt a "sociological jurisprudence" that would provide a context in which to determine whether principles and rules still served their original functions. This was especially important in constitutional adjudication, where the constitutionality of statutes and administrative decisions turned on whether judges found them reasonable or arbitrary. Moreover, a better appreciation of the real world would lead judges to question just how "voluntary" agreements between parties of greatly disparate power really were. Recognition that many contracts did not really reflect voluntary agreements would undermine the sanctity of contract.

Other critics went further, applying a new realism to all legal relationships. As a law-review editor, law professor, state judge, and finally Supreme Court justice, Oliver Wendell *Holmes insisted that law grew out of experience; it could not be administered by applying logical syllogisms. It reflected the needs of society and the interests of those with the power to shape it. Pretending that the rules were "scientific" and divorced from those needs was a dangerous illusion. By the 1910s and 1920s *"legal realists" were insisting that all legal rights were no more than society's decision about the conditions under which people should have certain privileges and obligations.

During the so-called Progressive era (1900–20), these ideas encouraged a wave of social and economic legislation imposing new duties on businesses and employers and creating new administrative agencies to establish and administer regulations. In general, courts sustained the constitutionality of such legislation. However, in the 1920s more conservative ideas were revived, both in society generally and in the law. Many courts, and especially the U.S. Supreme Court, reverted to doctrines of laissez-faire constitutionalism, especially when considering labor legislation. The Court struck down laws establishing minimum wages, barring labor injunctions, and establishing mandatory arbitration of labor disputes. The conflict would come to a head during the crisis of the Depression and the New Deal.

• J. Willard Hurst, *The Growth of American Law: The Law Makers*, 1950. Wilfred E. Rumble, *American Legal Realism*, 1968. G. Edward White, *Patterns of American Legal Thought*, 1978. G. Edward White, *Tort Law in America: An Intellectual History*, 1980. Gerald L. Fetner, *Ordered Liberty: Legal Reform in the Twentieth Century*, 1983. Robert Stevens, *Law School: Legal Education in the United States from the 1850s to the 1980s*, 1983. Lawrence M. Friedman, *A History of American Law*, 2d ed., 1985. Charles A. Lofgren, *The Plessy Case*, 1987. Morton J. Horwitz, *The Transformation of American Law, 1870–1960*, 1992. Bernard Schwartz, *Main Currents in American Legal Thought*, 1993. Vivien Hart, *Bound by Our Constitution: Women, Workers, and the Minimum Wage*, 1994. William P. LaPiana, *Logic and Experience: The Origin of Modern American Legal Education*, 1994. David E. Bernstein, *Only One Place of Redress: African Americans, Labor Regulations, and the Courts: From Reconstruction to the New Deal*, 2001.

—Michael Les Benedict

HISTORY OF AMERICAN LAW, GREAT DEPRESSION TO 1968

The period from the Great Depression through the Great society is marked, more than anything else, by the growth of the federal government and accompanying administrative regulations, and in a related development, by the growth of state governments and rules. Although common law remained, and courts still heard cases for which there was neither a statutory nor an administrative law basis for decision, the great age of the common law had passed; courts now relied primarily on state and federal codes as well as administrative rules, and law school education reflected that change.

The Great Depression and the Emergence of Modern Legal Thought. The depression that lasted from 1929 to 1941 was the most severe in the nation's history, and did much to undermine the faith in industrial capitalism that had been the hallmark of American social and legal thought from 1870 through the 1920s. Conservative predilections could not easily be erased, however, and both bench and bar fought the New Deal's expansion of the administrative state. But it was a losing battle. Without the earlier faith in business, the older notions of laissez-faire that underlay classical legal thought could not be maintained.

Some of the changes that took place after 1930 originated earlier, such as the creation of the American Law Institute (founded in 1923) and the development of legal realism at schools like Yale and Columbia. The ALI had been created to address the growing complexity of the law, and its elite sponsors hoped that its results, the Restatements of Law, would reinforce the conservative economic and social views they held. Its more liberal sponsors, on the other hand, hoped that social science methodology could be imposed, and thus make law more of an objective science.

The ALI's first product, the Restatement of Contracts, appeared in 1932. Written primarily by Professor Samuel Williston of the Harvard Law School, it clearly reflected the so-called Langdellian view that law should be a science, and that through the application of scientific methods the basic principles of law could be clearly enunciated. The powerful logic of the Restatements, it was believed, would lead both bench and bar to follow the law as enunciated by the ALI. Between 1933 and 1945, the Institute issued eight other restatements, and it has continued its work up to the present, with Second and even Third Restatements issued from time to time.

But the Restatements never had the influence that its sponsors had expected. Some lawyers cited the Restatements as legal authority (which they were not); some judges referred to them in their decisions; and many law schools incorporated all or parts of various Restatements in teaching. But the supposed unity of the law as presented by the Restatements soon ran aground under the piercing criticism of scholars such as Arthur Corbin of Harvard, who pointed out that in many instances, one could find as many precedents arguing the opposite principle as the one adopted in the Restatement. Moreover, most judges refused to give up their discretion in choosing among precedents and rules just because certain law school professors claimed to know exactly what the law meant.

The quest for certainty also marked the dominant legal philosophy of the time, the school of thought known as "legal realism." This too began in the 1920s, and derived directly from the sociological jurisprudence of the Progressive Era. Where the ALI wanted to base its certainty on vast numbers of precedents, the realists wanted to find their certainty in the functional aspects of the law, how judges actually decided cases, and what non-case factors affected their decisions. In 1920, Judge Benjamin Nathan Cardozo had given the Storrs Lectures at Yale Law School, in which he acknowledged that judges made law and that a variety of factors influenced their decisions. Ten years later, Karl Llewellyn published a law review article, "A Realist Jurisprudence—The Next Step," and Jerome Frank, later to be a federal circuit court judge, published *Law and the Modern Mind*, which some scholars believe to be the most important book about modern American law. Both men rejected the objective, abstract basis of the ALI Restatements, and emphasized instead the prejudices and preferences that informed judicial decision-making. During the 1930s, the debate between the realists and the ALI/Langdellian model dominated academic journals. How fruitful a debate is unclear, and historians are still divided over both the merits and the importance of the two approaches.

In the end, as in so many other areas of law, two seemingly opposites eventually merged. The money for the empirical studies demanded by the realists dried up during the Depression, so they could never develop the body of statistical evidence necessary to prove their arguments. The rise of fascism abroad, and the deliberate perversion of law by the Nazis, also helped undermine realism, with its seeming moral relativism and lack of values. In the 1940s, Llewellyn joined the ALI, where he created what is arguably its greatest accomplishment, the Uniform Commercial Code. Rather than developing a restatement of prior decisions, Llewellyn and his team used past commercial law decisions to fashion a model statute based on market custom, one that has been adopted by nearly every state in the Union and which, as a result, has brought uniformity to a major area of American law. At the same time, many law professors, while eschewing overt realism, nonetheless adopted some of its psychological insights into their own teaching and research. Within a short time, what had seemed so radical in the 1920s became commonplace academic wisdom.

The New Deal and the Rise of the Administrative State. Although Herbert Hoover sought to ameliorate some aspects of the Depression, he could not abandon his basic belief that the government should not be involved in regulating the economy. When Franklin D. Roosevelt took office in March 1933, he called, in words that horrified conservatives, for "bold, persistent experimentation." Specific New Deal programs borrowed liberally from earlier reform efforts, especially from the Progressive notion of an orderly economy regulated by disinterested administrative agencies. In attempting to put such a philosophy into place, the New Deal ran headlong into entrenched legal and constitutional assumptions. A good example is that of the National Industrial Recovery Act (NIRA) of 1933.

Relying on the Constitution's Commerce Clause, the Act set up a system of industrial self-government codes under the neutral authority of the federal government. In cases where industries proved unable to develop an appropriate code of conduct, the president could establish codes and agencies, and delegate any of his powers to them to enforce the codes. The overall supervisory agency, the National Recovery Administration (NRA), had the responsibility for implementing both voluntary and imposed regulations on more than 3 million businesses. Above all, the NRA needed lawyers to draft, revise, and review thousands of codes, and during the early years of the New Deal, young lawyers flooded into Washington. Most of them came from elite law schools; 60 percent came from Harvard, Yale, and Columbia, where they had been imbued with the ideas of legal realism. Primarily liberal politically, they immediately set up a counterweight to the established bar operating through the American Bar Association. Moreover, the New Deal opened the corridors of powers to young Jews, Irish, blacks, and even female lawyers, groups that had previously been excluded by the conservative elite. If nothing else, the New Deal completely transformed the face of the American legal profession.

The NIRA had been hastily drawn up, and contained numerous internal contradictions; one clause, for example, declared that the antitrust laws would remain in effect, while another clause suspended their application to code-covered industries. The Supreme Court unanimously struck down the NIRA on May 27, 1935, holding that it exceeded the federal government's power under the Commerce Clause and that its excessive delegation of power violated the separation of powers. But the conservative majority's opposition to the New Deal collapsed following the constitutional crisis of 1937, in which Roosevelt unsuccessfully attempted to pack the Court. Within a few years, the four arch-conservatives on the Court had been replaced. From 1937 until the 1990s, not a single congressional statute was held invalid under the Commerce Clause. The result was a flood of congressional measures not only regulating the economy, but affecting education, welfare, health, and numerous other areas once believed beyond the reach of the federal government.

Federal programs, however, require bureaucracies to administer them, and federal regulations require administrators to enforce them. The expansion of federal agencies and bureaucracies begun during the first years of the New Deal expanded significantly during the Second World War, when many new war-related agencies, such as the Office of Price Administration, came into existence. This expansion of the administrative state continued until 1980, and administrative law, which had not even been a course in law schools until the mid-1920s, suddenly became an important elective for students who either wished to enter government service or go into private practice. Commercial clients especially needed lawyers to guide them through the administrative mazes, whether to secure approval from a local zoning board for a new plant, or endorsement by the Food and Drug Administration of a new medicine.

The administrative state also brought with it new volumes for judges, students, and scholars to rely on, and which vied for shelf space with the published decisional volumes. In early 1935, during oral arguments on one aspect of the NIRA, the defendant's lawyer told the Court that he had been unable to secure copies of the regulations his client had been accused of violating. An astounded Justice Louis Brandeis then grilled the government's attorney on whether this was true, and the government admitted it had no provision for publishing regulations. Soon after this case, the government began publishing the *Federal Register* to make new and existing government regulations easily available.

Tied in closely to the need to make regulations known was the need for a method of making the regulations themselves that would meet a due process challenge. Even as Congress created more agencies and charged them with creating a new body of administrative law, the problem arose as to how those rules would be made. The ABA, after an initial hostility to the new bureaucracy, realized it had come to stay, and took the lead in securing the passage of the Administrative Procedures Act of 1946, a federal law—soon copied in nearly every state—that imposed procedural rules on administrative agencies and, at the same time, expanded the already significant role of lawyers in the regulatory state.

In only one area did federal power diminish during this time, and that ironically involved the reach of the federal judicial power. Ever since *Swift* v. *Tyson* (1842), federal courts had been free to ignore state court decisions and to formulate a federal common law. As a result, large multi-state firms went "forum-shopping," looking for a federal court whose decisional rules would favor their case. In *Erie Railroad* v. *Tompkins* (1938), Brandeis held that the earlier decision had been unconstitutional, and ruled that federal courts had to follow both the statutory and decisional rules of the states in which they were located. Large commercial companies would no longer be able to forum-shop.

The Triumph of Legal Liberalism. From the end of the Second World War until the 1990s, the legal culture in the United States was decidedly liberal, and both the courts and the law schools fostered the belief that law could provide the remedy not only to private legal disputes but to larger questions of social injustice. This transformation had begun with the appointment of the so-called "Roosevelt Court," and came to a culmination in the latter years of the Warren Court. The men whom Roosevelt appointed to the Court between 1937 and 1943 believed that the federal government had ample power under the Commerce Clause to regulate the economy. But even as they took their seats, the dockets of state and federal courts began to shift from economic questions to issues of civil liberties and civil rights. And although some jurists, such as Felix Frankfurter, tried to stem the flood by claiming that not all grievances could be judicially resolved, the ideas of men such as Hugo Black and William O. Douglas carried the day. As a result, even during the war years, the Court began to look at questions of racial discrimination and due process, and while the courts bent with the winds of anti-communism in the late 1940s and early 1950s, in the end they reaffirmed—and more importantly—expanded basic constitutional rights.

At the heart of the controversy lay the question of incorporation—whether the Due Process Clause of the Fourteenth Amendment "incorporated" the guarantees of the first eight amendments and thus applied the Bill of Rights to the states as well as to the federal government. The question had first been articulated by Justice Brandeis in the early 1920s, and within a few years the First Amendment Speech Clause was held to apply to the states as well as to the federal government. By the early 1940s, two distinct schools had emerged. One, taking its cue from Justice Cardozo, called for "selective" incorporation of only those rights that are fundamental to a democratic and free society. The other, led by Justice Black, called for "total" incorporation of the Bill of Rights, and rejected selective incorporation as leaving too much power in the hands of judges to choose what rights were important. In the end, the Court never adopted Black's philosophy, but selectively applied practically every part of the Bill of Rights to the states. As a result, wide areas of state law previously considered to be outside the purview of federal oversight—such as criminal procedure, education, and libel—now came under judicial scrutiny. During the Second World War, for example, the Supreme Court voided local regulations regarding street corner orators and pamphlet distribution on the grounds that they violated the First Amendment. It held a mandatory flag salute in public schools unconstitutional, and closely scrutinized local police procedures regarding labor unions.

At the same time, the Court began explicating a footnote written by Justice Harlan Fiske Stone in an otherwise inconsequential commerce case. The footnote suggested that while the Court should apply only a minimal test of rationality in looking at economic regulations, it should impose a higher level of scrutiny when fundamental rights were at stake or where discrete, insular minorities were involved. The full articulation of this premise

came in 1954, when the Court, in *Brown v. Board of Education*, struck down racial segregation in public schools. Over its fifteen years, the Warren Court dismantled nearly every aspect of legally-enforced racial segregation, expanded the reach of the First Amendment Speech and Press Clauses, and imposed on the states a strict standard for matters of criminal procedure.

The Warren Court established a model for aspiring lawyers. The young men and women who graduated from law school starting in the 1960s saw the Warren Court as the embodiment of what justice under law meant. They had been taught by the very brightest products of American law schools in the 1950s and 1960s, mainly young men and a few women who had gone to Washington to clerk in the high court and then went on to take teaching positions at the nation's top law schools. As a result, Warren Court activism, so despised by conservatives, came to be seen as the norm in most American law schools.

The Litigious Society. The example of the NAACP Legal Defense Fund, Inc. in spearheading the civil rights cases that led to the end of segregation inspired other groups. Women, gays, Hispanics, and others created legal funds to pursue their agendas, although most of their cases would not reach the courts until the 1970s. The idea of using the courts to resolve public as well as private issues is not new in the United States; in the 1830s, the French traveler Alexis de Tocqueville noted that eventually all political issues become legal questions before the courts. But in the 1960s, the United States seemed to many a litigious society, as the number of cases filed in state and federal courts seemed to double every few years, a process that went on into the 1980s. People went to court not only over public matters such as segregation and free speech, but also over private matters, and the hitherto rarely used device of a class action suddenly came into vogue. Workers suffering from asbestos poisoning, for example, instead of individually suing their employers, now gathered together and brought action as a class of persons similarly situated. This gave them and their lawyers far more resources in the fight than if they had brought hundreds or even thousands of individual suits.

While many of these suits grew out of real grievances, and their resolution brought justified relief, many were frivolous, the result of petty personal disputes or a misguided notion that if someone else could sue a large company and win a hefty settlement, then they could as well. Judges complained that their dockets had become congested as a result of frivolous suits, which still took time and resources to dismiss. The reaction seemed to focus on lawyers who filed these cases, hoping for a big win from which they could claim their contingency fee. A public perception of lawyers as immoral became widespread, but efforts by bar associations to rein in such suits failed. Although legislatures passed laws penalizing the filing of totally unfounded suits, powerful trial lawyer associations managed to block any effective regulation of such suits.

The Legal Profession: Culture and Education. After the Second World War, law became a popular profession, and the GI Bill made it possible for many returning veterans, who might not otherwise have been able to do so, to attend college and professional school. By 1960, there were over 286,000 lawyers in the United States, and that number more than doubled in the next quarter of a century. America had one lawyer for every 350 people in the country, a ratio unrivaled anywhere in the world. White ethnic and religious groups had begun to enter the profession in greater numbers before the war, thanks in large measure to the New Deal; after the war, more blacks and women began to go to law school. Although only one in forty lawyers in the country in 1950 was a woman, by 1987 that figure had risen to one in seven, with the great upsurge coming in the late 1960s and early 1970s. Given the great strides made in civil rights, one might have expected larger numbers of African Americans to enter the profession. In 1969, blacks made up 12 percent of the population but only 1 percent of the bar, and while the numbers increased over the next two decades, they still accounted for less than 3 percent of the profession. Some of this can be attributed to the fact that this generation still carried with it the burden of inferior segregated education and limited opportunities for higher education. But even those who chose to enter the law faced discrimination, both in the law schools and in law firms.

Despite this blot, the profession as a whole grew more diverse and multicultural. Tinges of the anti-Semitism that marked the 1920s and 1930s still remained in some of the old-line elite law firms in the 1960s, but most of these biases had disappeared by 1968. In the law schools, Jewish names could be found out of all proportion to their numbers in the general population. The old adherence to laissez-faire also vanished, and in 1969 the American Bar Association adopted a new Code of Professional Ethics repudiating many of the restrictive and conservative views of prior codes. The one area where the new code seemed to be running counter to the times was in its insistence that the obligation to provide legal services remained a matter of individual responsibility; the ABA also opposed group clinical practice by salaried lawyers.

But the Johnson administration, as part of its War on Poverty, began to provide legal services for the poor, a step long advocated by the liberal National Lawyers Guild and stoutly opposed by the ABA. In 1964, when Congress created the Office of Economic Opportunity, it also initiated a small program that made grants to lawyers willing to set up storefront law offices in poor neighborhoods. Two years later, Congress made the program permanent when it created the Legal Services Office, which later became the Legal Services Corporation. Originally set up to help poor families with mundane daily legal issues such as wills and navigating the bureaucracy, the program soon antagonized conservatives by helping poor people launch suits against municipal and state governments to force them to increase the quality of education and other public services in poor neighborhoods.

The 1960s, in fact, may have been the acme of the public interest law movement, which saw the proliferation of government agencies, Legal Services and other storefront operations, and public interest groups such as Common Cause and the Sierra Fund, as well as young lawyers who demanded and won time from their large corporations to do pro bono work. Ideally—and idealistically—the public interest law movement aimed to make the United States a more democratic and equalitarian society by employing law in the service of civil rights, consumers, the poor, and the environment. Those involved often filed suits against large corporations as well as government, and their victories embittered conservatives, who eventually set up their own public interest agencies. At its height, more than 2,500 lawyers in 300 communities worked in Legal Services, and thousands more operated through other channels. When the Reagan Administration came into office, one of its earliest attacks focused on Legal Services, which it pared down to a shadow of its former self.

During this time, the practice of law also changed, as firms grew bigger and bigger. In 1951, three out of every five lawyers practiced alone; over the next quarter of a century, while more and more people entered the profession, fewer than a third now practiced solo. Where a "large" law firm at the turn of the twentieth century consisted of ten, or at the most, twelve lawyers and a few secretaries, by the early 1970s the trend was clearly for firms that not only had 200 or 300 associates, but often had offices in several cities and even in foreign countries. Law became a big business in its own right, and legal fees shot upward to cover the increased overhead involved in larger office space, clerical help, paralegals, book-keepers, and office managers.

Preparation for the bar also changed after the Second World War. With the GI Bill making it possible for more people to attend law school, legislatures finally agreed to long-standing demands of state bar groups that the educational standards for admission be raised. Where two years of college—or in some places none—had been the prerequisite for admission to law school, most states now mandated that admission to the bar required four years of undergraduate education followed by three years of law school. Although most states still allowed the old practice of reading for the law through apprenticeship, circumstances conspired to make that a very difficult option, and few people took advantage of it.

Despite this tightening of requirements, law school became, and remained, a very attractive option for many people after the war, so much so that the better law schools became more selective in their acceptances. Boalt Hall, the law school at the University of California Berkeley, accepted 70 percent of all applicants in 1950; in 1968, it took in only 34 percent.

Once in law school, the students found that the courses and teaching methods had not changed greatly from the law schools that their fathers or grandfathers had attended, with the Langdellian case method still supreme. Some teachers who believed in legal realism utilized non-case materials, but the law still revolved around precedent, not social science studies. The biggest change in the law school curriculum came with the introduction of legal clinics in the 1960s. Although the clinic, or practicum, had been created in 1928, it did not catch on until the 1960s, when students radicalized by the civil rights movement and Vietnam demanded that legal education include some real-life experience. Today most law schools have some clinics, but the battle remains between the purists, who believe law school should be for study and mastering the skills of case law, with practice skills developed later, and the clinicians, who believe that practical skills are a necessary part of the curriculum.

Nothing in the law schools in the 1960s approached the intellectual fervor generated by legal realism in the 1920s and 1930s. During the Scond World War, Harold Lasswell and Myres McDougal of Yale, the former a political theorist, the latter a property law teacher, published an article entitled "Legal Education and Public Policy," in which, while they argued for a Langdellian approach to case law, they also made the case that since law students would be the policy makers of the future, teachers had to imbue them not only with moral values but also a sense of social responsibility. In some ways, the two men laid the groundwork for the public interest law movement of the 1960s. Intellectually the most stimulating development in legal theory was the "law and economics" school, developed primarily at the University of Chicago Law School and led by Richard Posner. Its adherents believed that law should be based on the economic rules governing the efficient operation of the marketplace, and they believed that such anti-market policies as antitrust legislation could not succeed. The classical economic theory Posner and his colleagues utilized gave the law a sense of certainty (which the realists had rejected) as well as a unity of purpose that made it attractive, especially to conservatives.

Substantive Private Law after the Second World War. Where private law had once been wholly within the purview of private law, beginning in the 1930s more and more matters came under the control of statutes or administrative regulations. In trial courts, one saw a great increase in the number of criminal as opposed to civil cases, and within the latter a shift from commercial transactions to domestic and tort suits. (One reason is that businesses began to turn to nonjudicial proceedings, such as arbitration, to settle contractual disputes in a faster and less expensive manner.) The explosion of statutory and administrative law was phenomenal; where in the nineteenth century all of a state's laws might occupy one large volume, by the 1960s state codes took up twenty or more volumes, with fat "pocket parts" marking the addition of new laws between revisions.

If the constitutional revolution of the New Deal did away with substantive due process and freedom of contract as protections of traditional property rights, the founding of the welfare state brought about a new form of vested interest—entitlements. Veterans' benefits, welfare, social security, Medicare, unemployment compensation, and aid for children benefited millions of Americans, and during the 1960s courts heard numerous cases about whether entitlements were rights, which the state could not take away, or merely privileges, which could be withdrawn. Professor Charles Reich of the Yale Law School argued that these entitlements constituted a new form of property. Not until the 1970 case of *Dandridge* v. *Williams* did the Supreme Court resolve this dispute, holding that entitlements were a form of economic regulation that state and federal governments were free to give or withdraw, so long as they did so on a nondiscriminatory basis.

The civil rights movement spawned numerous public interest law firms that began to defend minorities and the poor against what they saw as economic exploitation, and in doing so invoked one of the basic tenets of the Uniform Commercial Code on their behalf. Section 3–302 articulated the doctrine of unconscionability, meaning that contractual provisions that took unfair advantage of one party, even if that party had agreed to them, would not be enforced by the courts. Public interest lawyers utilized unconscionability provisions to create protections for consumers, especially the poor, to nullify lease-purchase agreements that not only imposed usurious interest rates, but also tied in purchases so that collateral interest on items already paid for could be seized if a customer defaulted on payment for later purchases. Court decisions eventually led state legislatures to enact consumer protection statutes that required full and plain disclosure of all terms and limited the conditions under which goods could be repossessed.

Criminal Law. Perhaps the greatest explosion in law came in criminal matters, fueled by the Warren Court's due process revolution, in which the Court applied the protections of the Fourth, Fifth, and Sixth Amendments to the states. Local and state police were now held to the same standards of accountability as federal officers, and defendants could not only invoke these rights, but after the landmark decision of *Gideon* v. *Wainwright* (1964), would be ensured a lawyer to look after their interests. It is questionable whether crime itself increased at an exponential rate, but the rapid trials without juries that yielded convictions based on forced confessions and evidence seized without a warrant disappeared. In addition, the pandemic of drug abuse that infested not only the inner cities but the suburbs as well led to a host of new drug-related criminal statutes that in many cases clogged the courts.

Conclusion. The chief characteristic of the period extending from the beginning of the 1930s until the end of the 1960s was the growth of administrative law and the establishment of the regulatory/welfare state as an accepted fact in American life. Despite attacks by President Nixon in the late 1960s, and repeated by President Reagan in the 1980s, most Americans saw the regulatory state as an efficient method of governance, one that treated its citizens fairly. The years between 1946 and 1966 might in some ways be called the golden age of the regulatory state, with an almost universal agreement on the value of administrative governance. The judiciary, initially hostile to regulatory agencies, soon granted them broad fact-finding power and authority to resolve disputes within the established parameters of legislation and the Administrative Practices Act. Even during the Republican administration of Dwight Eisenhower, the bureaucracy expanded, as Americans looked more and more to the government for assistance in various areas of social and economic activity. Not until the end of the Great Society did a reaction set in.

• G. Edward White, *Patterns of American Legal Thought*, 1978. William C. Chase, *The American Law School and the Rise of Administrative Government*, 1982. Kermit Hall, *The Magic Mirror: Law in American History*, 1989. Morton J. Horwitz, *The Transformation of American Law, 1870—1960*, 1992. William LaPiana, *Logic and Experience: The Origins of Modern Legal Education*, 1994. Laura Kalman, *The Strange Career of Legal Liberalism*, 1996. Barry Cushman, *Rethinking the New Deal Court: The Structure of a Constitutional Revolution*, 1998. William M. Wiecek, *The Lost World of Classical Legal Thought*, 1998.   —Melvin I. Urofsky

HISTORY OF AMERICAN LAW: SINCE 1968

The headlines of 1968 reflected a society in a crisis of authority. Wide unrest over the Vietnam War shut down universities, as student demonstrators took over the administration buildings at Columbia University, followed in coming semesters by similar takeovers at Berkeley, Harvard, and numerous other campuses. The race riots in 1967 had given national prominence to the Black Panther Movement, which joined forces with antiwar extremists to call for violent insurrection. Public support for the war was evaporating, and President Lyndon B. Johnson announced in March that he would not seek reelection. Five days later, Martin Luther King Jr., was assassinated. In June, campaigning in Los Angeles to replace Johnson, Robert F. Kennedy was assassinated. Demonstrations and violence by police at the Democratic National Convention in Chicago underscored the fragility of the social fabric. America appeared close to anarchy.

Distrust of authority had been building for over a decade. The *civil rights movement prompted a reexamination of habits and institutions long taken for granted, revealing pervasive pollution, unsafe automobiles, and exclusionary treatment of other segments of society. The villains were easy to identify: public officials, corporations, judges, and others in authority who had tolerated practices now exposed to be intolerable.

In law, the crisis of authority directly translated into reforms to support the rights of individuals. The individual against what? Authority, wherever it lurked. Reforms were designed to minimize official discretion, referred to by federal judge J. Skelly Wright as "the soft underbelly of the American legal system." Congress, busy building a regulatory state to address lapses of corporate stewardship in areas like clean air (1970) and worker safety (1970), encouraged agencies to minimize official error by laying out precise rules for every conceivable situation. With detailed rules, there would be no more human error or bias. *Regulations began to multiply at an exponential rate. At one point, the worker safety agency had 140 rules dealing with wooden ladders.

Even the most diligent rule writer, however, could not write a rule for every possible dispute. Some legal mechanism was needed to make these decisions. But traditional sources of authority such as judges, bureaucrats, and school principals were no longer trusted. A new approach to decision-making, advocated by Harvard law professors Henry Hart and Albert Sacks, spawned the "legal process" movement that placed trust not in a decision-makers but in the adversarial process itself. Fairness in a diverse and distrustful society could be best achieved, they argued, by letting individuals make their own case in a neutral forum. The civil rights movement had shown the power of "rights" as a vehicle to overcome unjust practices. Why not adopt the legal vocabulary of "rights" to provide everyone with a forum purged of personal values and bias?

Until the 1960s, disputes hinged on rulings that interpreted principles like duty, discretion, and reasonableness. An individual seeking to invoke legal power against another citizen or to avoid an official act had to first establish the legal justification. Over the last four decades of the twentieth century, however, these traditional standards were supplanted by a focus on individual rights. Judges and other officials became reluctant to assert values at all, including who could sue for what. Individual rights became the focus of American law, and, after a while, of daily social interaction.

Civil Rights. The rights revolution did not begin as a movement to give power to individuals. The civil rights movement was intended to tear down walls that deprived an entire segment of the population from enjoying ordinary freedoms, such as using restaurants and public facilities. The prohibition against workplace *discrimination, enacted as Title VII of the Civil Rights Act in 1964, did not create affirmative rights to get or keep a job, but was meant to be a defense against systemic patterns. As one of its sponsors, Senator Harrison Williams, put it, "those who say that equality means favoritism do violence to common sense."

A series of class actions following the Civil Rights Act broke huge holes through the barriers of segregation. The NAACP brought suit against the State of Alabama because not one state trooper was African American, and a federal judge ordered one black to be hired for each white until the number of black troopers reached 25 percent of the total force. Confronted with a *class action showing that many blacks could not meet the regular hiring criteria of many corporations, the Supreme Court in 1971 held that discriminatory intent was not required for corporations to be liable; companies could be liable if their hiring policies had a "disparate impact" on blacks. In 1971, the Supreme Court ordered the immediate end of dual black and white school systems.

Reformers in other areas naturally began to look to rights as a vehicle for their own causes. In 1967 Congress passed an act forbidding discrimination on the basis of age. In 1972 Congress passed Title IX of the Education Amendments, prohibiting *gender discrimination in educational institutions. In 1973, Congress passed an act funding disabled services, and included, without discussion, a clause "prohibiting discrimination of the disabled." Did this mean that thousands of school libraries and transit systems had to be rebuilt to provide Braille and wheelchair access? No one even asked the question; rights were considered a kind of universal vaccine against unfairness. In 1975 Congress passed an act giving disabled children rights to "specially designed instruction . . . to meet the unique needs of a handicapped child." In 1990 the Americans with Disabilities Act broadened the right to "equal access" to residential dwellings and "reasonable accommodation" in the workplace.

It was largely left to the courts to determine how to implement these open-ended rights. Courts initially were expansive in their rulings. In the early 1970s, several lower federal courts began ordering busing of children to achieve racial balance, nearly causing riots in Boston. "Affirmative action," the practice of giving preferences to mi nority applications initially enjoyed wide support to remedy past injustice. A preference for one group, however, meant a prejudice against another, soon leading to bitter conflict. Probably the most controversial decision was *Roe v. Wade (1973), which upheld the right to an *abortion in the first trimester of pregnancy and in certain other situations. Large fissures began appearing in the ideology of rights, as opponents to abortion demanded a higher "right," the right to life.

By 1975, a majority of Warren Court justices had been replaced by Nixon and Ford appointees, including Chief Justice Warren *Burger (1969), Harry Blackman (1970), Lewis Powell (1972), William Rehnquist (1972) and John Paul Stevens (1975). The appetite of the Burger Court to overturn *Warren Court precedents proved to be greatly exaggerated, but the Court began to constrain the early rulings. In 1976, the Supreme Court held that "disparate impact" did not constitute unlawful discrimination if hiring criteria were reasonably related to job fitness. In 1978, in the Bakke case, the Court held that *affirmative action quotas in medical school admissions were unconstitutional, although the Court suggested that race could be considered as one factor.

For the next twenty years, the Supreme Court repeatedly surprised observers with rulings first on one side of the rights scale, and then on the other. Based on evidence that a union had deliberately dragged its heels on integration, the Court in 1986 upheld a ruling requiring the union to achieve a specific quota. On the other hand, in 1995, it held unconstitutional a common practice by government to "set aside" a certain proportion of contracts for minority vendors. In 1986, the Court upheld a state statute that essentially made *homosexuality illegal. In 1992, with the eight members of the Supreme Court now Republican appointees, the Court reaffirmed its abortion ruling in Roe v. Wade.

Congress in several instances passed laws to overrule the Supreme Court decisions that had restricted individual rights. In response to a decision that permitted employers to exclude pregnancy benefits, Congress enacted a law requiring pregnancy benefits in every health plan (1978). In 1991 the Civil Rights Act was amended to overrule a number of decisions that had restricted individual discrimination lawsuits. Congress specifically provided jury trials, treble damages, and attorneys fees "to encourage private citizens" to sue to ensure "a discrimination-free workplace."

The "Due Process Revolution." Until the 1960s, the *due process clause in the Constitution, which provides that no citizen can be "deprived of life, liberty or property" without "due process of law," had not been applied to ministerial judgments by officials about how to run a school or administer a government agency. The Supreme Court made a distinction between a "right," like personal property, and a "privilege," like government benefits or services. The distinction was famously articulated by Oliver Wendell *Holmes Jr., in a case brought by a Boston policeman who was fired for his political views: "Petitioner may have the constitutional right to talk politics," Holmes announced, "but he has no constitutional right to be a policeman." Courts always allowed claims for "abuse of discretion," but the presumption was in favor of the official who had the official responsibility.

Distrust of authority led to abandonment of the right/privilege distinction by the Supreme Court, however, and radical expansion of the due process protection to daily government choices. The early cases involved government acts that closely resembled deprivations of *property or *liberty. In 1970, in Goldberg v. Kelly, the Supreme Court held that welfare benefits were "property" within the meaning of the Constitution and could not be cut off without due process. With public schools, the first case also involved rights of a constitutional dimension. Five high school students in Des Moines were suspended after they wore black arm bands to protest the Vietnam War. The Supreme Court declared in 1969 that public schools would not be "enclaves of totalitarianism": Students, Justice Abe Fortas wrote for the majority, do not shed their "constitutional rights ... at the school house gate."

The Supreme Court did not draw the line at political speech, however. In 1975, four students physically attacked a security officer who was trying to stop a brawl in a lunch room. The principal, who witnessed the incident, suspended the students immediately. The Supreme Court overturned the suspension, holding that the status of being a student was like a "property right," and thus, under due process, "suspensions without notice or hearing" are unconstitutional. Also in 1975, the Supreme Court held that students who had been suspended for spiking the punch at a school party could sue school officials for monetary damages for violating their constitutional rights of due process.

Almost immediately, schools started creating manuals requiring procedures for discipline that resembled those of a criminal trial—allowing (and sometimes providing) lawyers, preparing written transcripts, requiring third-party witnesses, and so forth. Schools went out of their way to tell students that disciplinary decisions would be determined in strict conformity to stated rules and rights.

Constitutional protections were extended also to government employees. In 1972, the Court held that the status of having a government job could be "property" worthy of constitutional protection. The "opportunity for the employee to present his side of the case is ... of obvious value," Justice Byron White wrote in a 1985 decision.

In all these cases, the Court emphasized that the due process that was due would depend on the circumstances, and that only "some kind of hearing" was necessary. But no one knew how much and in what circumstances. The effect, probably unintended, was to shift the burden to officials to demonstrate why their choices were valid. Officials who were once autocratic became reluctant to do what was obvious. A "due process explosion," in the words of federal judge Henry Friendly, fundamentally altered the ability of government to manage schools and agencies.

Criminal Rights. Rights of criminal defendants had been dramatically expanded in the 1960s by the Warren Court, which effectively "federalized" criminal *procedure in the 1960s by holding that the *Fourteenth Amendment incorporated the basic protections of the Bill of Rights for criminal defendants in state proceedings. The Warren Court also revolutionized criminal rights, imposing the "exclusionary rule" which barred use of evidence from warrantless *searches and seizures, granting the right to *counsel in all except minor offenses and, in the 1966 *Miranda case, creating a right to be informed of all rights before *interrogation.

The Burger Court did not overturn these holdings, but reduced their force by, for example, permitting *arrests without a warrant in public (1976), creating a good faith exception to the exclusionary rule (1984), and permitting use of statements obtained in violation of *Miranda* for impeachment of witnesses (1971). In *Furman* v. *Georgia* (1972), the Court held that the Georgia death penalty was unconstitutional because it was capriciously imposed, but then, in 1976, upheld the death penalty after the Georgia statute was redrawn.

Private Lawsuits. The distrust of authority that underlay much of the rights revolution also affected private lawsuits for accidents and injuries. Under the common law, as expressed by judicial leaders like Oliver Wendell Holmes Jr. and Chief Justice Roger *Traynor of the California Supreme Court, judges had the responsibility to declare the "standard of care" in private cases, not leave decisions "to oscillating verdicts of juries." But judges in the age of individual rights did not feel they had the authority to declare standards limiting an individual's right to sue. As a prominent federal judge, Charles Wyzanski, said in 1973, "choosing among values is much too important a business for judges to do the choosing. That is something the citizens must keep for themselves."

In hindsight, the effect was predictable: without judicial control, damage claims and awards grew steadily. One poster case was the $2.9 million verdict in 1994 against McDonalds (later reduced to $640,000) when an elderly woman spilled hot coffee while driving away from a drive-through window. Practically any accident, it seemed, could be the basis of a lawsuit: baseball injuries, camp accidents, even disagreements over use of a sandbox. Almost any injured person, at least if the injury were reported in a police or hospital file, could also expect a solicitation from lawyers encouraging them to sue. This phenomenon flowed directly from a Supreme Court ruling in 1977 that invalidated, as a violation of lawyers' First Amendment rights, *bar association rules against lawyer advertising.

The amounts sued for also grew dramatically. In the 1970s, damages of $800,000 for ordinary accidents made headlines. By the 1990s headlines periodically would describe a verdict in the hundreds of millions or even billions. In 1999, for example, a jury returned a verdict of $4.9 billion against General Motors because one of its cars exploded when rear-ended by another car traveling at high speed. In 2001 a jury awarded a smoker in California a verdict of $3 billion. Most of these verdicts were reduced by judges or appellate courts after trial. The verdict for the California smoker, for example, was reduced to $100 million. Huge verdicts occurred only in a tiny fraction of all cases, but media attention to those cases reinforced the view that awards were possible that bore no connection to actual economic losses.

"Mass torts," class actions claiming compensation for injuries caused by side effects of modern products such as asbestos, smoking, breast implants, and pollution, were brought by entrepreneurial lawyers on a contingency basis on behalf of thousands and in some cases millions of people. Confronted with seemingly limitless asbestos claims, two dozen major corporations declared bankruptcy. On several occasions, the Supreme Court urged Congress to legislate solutions for these society-wide problems, to avoid "elephantine mass" of huge losses clogging courts and commerce alike. But the Supreme Court did almost nothing to limit claims, the one exception being a 1996 decision overturning as "grossly excessive" $2 million of punitive damages on a $4,000 claim against BMW for retouching the paint on a new car.

Rights in the Twenty-first Century. The original idea of the civil rights movement, that its rights could not "favor one group over another," remained the ideology of the reformed legal system. By the year 2000, however, rights had become a cacophony of conflicting claims and paradoxes.

In civil rights, so many rights had been created that one scholar calculated that, if all the protected categories were totaled, they would add up to 374 percent of the American population. Julian Bond, an original civil rights activist, asked how it is that the "victims of the African slave trade" ended up pushed aside and "how the road to civil rights became so crowded" including "white men over 40, short people, the chemically addicted, the left-handed, and the obese." "When short, fat old men step to the front of the line," Bond observed, "then our civil rights are as endangered as they were by Bull Connor and Sheriff Jim Clark."

The original group-wide goals of discrimination law were supplanted by a preoccupation with individual claims. By the 1990s, there were only a handful of class actions alleging discriminatory patterns, while individual discrimination claims had become 10 percent of the total federal caseload. The ability of any angry individual to invoke discrimination law chilled workplace relations, as "diversity workshops" trained employees not to be candid with each other. The more self-conscious people became, the greater the anger. The highest incidence of claims of unlawful discrimination was found in the Equal Employment Opportunity Commission itself, whose employees made claims against the agency at twenty-eight times the national average.

The Due Process Revolution, striving to avoid unfairness by school and government officials, inadvertently discouraged decisions altogether. How does a principal "prove" who is a good teacher and who is not? Where there had once been authority without accountability, there was now neither authority nor accountability. Rigid "zero tolerance" policies swept through schools in the 1990s, leading to automatic suspensions of innocent students caught with a nail file or aspirin in their purse, because no one had the authority to exercise the human judgment needed to distinguish between a nail file and a switchblade.

Judges in the 1970s and 1980s were criticized for being "activist" in pursuit of individual rights, such as ordering busing. The activism, however, basically went in one direction: to expand claims by individuals but not to limit them. The goal of expanding individuals' right to sue was intended to enhance everyone's freedom by assuring fair dealings. But fear of litigation began to hang over ordinary daily choices. Every school, hospital, church, and sporting league knew of lawsuits for what were once ordinary accidents and disputes. It did not matter who won or lost, or even if the likelihood of being sued were small. The fact that any self-interested person could unilaterally sue for almost any injury or gripe meant that people no longer felt free to do what they believed was right. Doctors began to practice "defensive medicine," ordering unnecessary tests that would provide proof in the case of a lawsuit. School boards started removing seesaws, diving boards, and jungle gyms. Warning labels began to appear on almost every product: "Caution: contents are hot."

By the year 2000, the reforms had almost come full circle. *Race relations were strained, government unresponsive, schools unmanageable and justice perceived as a game—almost like a lottery. In the place of officials who had been unfair, self-interested individuals bullied the rest of society. In the name of individual rights, legal fear had become a defining feature of daily life.

[*See also* Disabilities Law; Labor Law: Workplace Issues; Litigiousness]

• Lawrence M. Friedman, *Total Justice*, 1985. Kermit Hall et al., eds., *The Oxford Companion to the Supreme Court of the United States*, 1992. Mary Ann Glendon, *Rights Talk: The Impoverishment of Political Discourse*, 1993. Philip K. Howard, *The Death of Common Sense: How Law is Suffocating America*, 1995. Kermit L. Hall et al., *American Legal History*, 1996. Philip K. Howard, *The Collapse of the Common Good: How America's Lawsuit Culture Undermines Our Freedom*, 2002.

—Philip K. Howard

HOLDING COMPANY. *See* Business Organizations.

HOLMES, OLIVER WENDELL JR., (1841–1935), Associate Justice of the U.S. Supreme Court (1902–32). Few lawyers or judges have exercised the degree of dominance over legal culture as has Oliver Wendell Holmes Jr. Holmes was blessed by several significant advantages. He was born into one of the most prominent intellectual families in nineteenth-century Boston. His father, a professor at the Harvard Medical School, was one of the most popular authors of the century and the developer of the most widely used photographic devices of the period, the Holmes-Bates stereoscope. Oliver Wendell Holmes Jr. grew up among the intellectual and social elite of one of the most important American urban centers, attended Harvard College and Harvard Law School, was friends with men like the philosopher William James and the logician Charles Pierce (who with Holmes were principal members of the Metaphysical Club). Holmes fought bravely during the Civil War, was wounded several times and was imprisoned by Confederate forces, an imprisonment made famous by his father's writings in the *Atlantic*. Holmes successfully practiced law in Boston briefly, but his ambition and his ability assured a more illustrious career. The great turning point in his life came with the publication in 1881 of his book, based on a series of lectures, *The Common Law*. In this intellectual *tour-de-force*, Holmes provided a comprehensive philosophical and historical critique of the *common law, a critique which became the basis for much of the development of American *jurisprudence in areas such as *contracts, *torts, and *property law during the twentieth century. All his historical and analytic abilities were highlighted in this work, along with his pragmatic approach to life and the law. The work also displays another of Holmes's great gifts, one that would serve him well on both the Massachusetts and federal benches: his consummate writing style. Holmes was not only the master of the clear and insightful paragraph, he was also a consummate crafter of the maxim, a style of writing which struck chords both with the legal profession and with the general public. It was in *The Common Law* that Holmes's ability to encapsulate complex ideas into short pithy phrases shone through, as in "the life of the law is not logic, but experience." Holmes provided a basis for generations of readers to understand and easily adopt his approach to the law. The publication of Holmes's 1881 masterpiece led to rapid career advancement, He was appointed to the Harvard Law faculty but remained for only a brief time, since he was soon to take up an appointment to the Supreme Judicial Court of Massachusetts. He remained on this court for nearly two decades; his work on this court revolutionized several areas of American private law. In contracts, in torts, and in the law of property Holmes applied his pragmatic approach to the law consistently. In contract law, for instance, Holmes wrote countless decisions that not only shaped the law of his own state but which were soon followed in other states throughout the whole country. Holmes's opinions while on the Massachusetts

court are exemplars of judicial reasoning and style, and his reputation as a superb jurist grew during his tenure on that court. Holmes was not content, however, to simply be a judge. Throughout his period on the Supreme Judicial Court he was also a prolific author of law review articles and in this way was able not only to spread his fame as a jurist but also to carry the doctrines that he was creating into far greater spheres of influence. Indeed, Holmes was fortunate that it was precisely during the last quarter of the nineteenth century that the first of the most influential American law reviews, the *Harvard Law Review*, came into its own as a publication of national scope and influence. Holmes helped the journal establish its preeminence as a journal of legal scholarship and the *Review* provided Holmes with an outlet for his writing and a national platform with which to spread his influence.

Most men would have been content with Holmes's career as a legal scholar and state court judge, but at a time when most of his contemporaries were preparing for retirement, Holmes began a new career when he was appointed an associate justice of the U.S. *Supreme Court by President Theodore Roosevelt. Holmes, blessed both by extraordinary vigor and longevity entered this new career with enthusiasm. During his decades on the Court Holmes became an important factor in the development of public law and helped to shape a number of areas of great significance to later generations including such fields as *labor law. Holmes also established one of the most important institutions of the modern Supreme Court. From the beginning of his tenure on the Court Holmes appointed young law graduates to serve as his "secretary," a position which evolved into the modern judicial clerkship (see CLERK, LAW). It was soon apparent after his appointment, however, that Holmes was not to be the judge Roosevelt had hoped for: he would not be a follower of the majority decisions. Instead, he rapidly carved out a unique place for himself on that court through a series of forcefully written dissents, a habit that led to his being dubbed "the great dissenter." In many cases, within a few years Holmes's dissents became the basis for majority decisions and, as such, he left his indelible imprint upon many areas of American law. Unlike any other American jurist of his time, however, Holmes's fame expanded far beyond the confines of the judiciary and the bar. Holmes became a figure of national importance. His life and career became the basis for countless books including collections of his letters, his essays, and his occasional speeches. He was the subject for a number of laudatory biographies, one of which became a successful stage play and was made into a Hollywood movie. Over the years his many law secretaries, particularly, Felix *Frankfurter who served both on the Harvard Law faculty and the U.S. Supreme Court, did all that they could to ensure that Holmes's reputation would increase. Indeed, on his ninetieth birthday Holmes was the guest on a celebratory national radio broadcast. Holmes was, in many ways, the first modern judge to achieve celebrity status.

Holmes exercised enormous influence over the legal profession and American law for more than half century. Since his death, Holmes has been hailed by some legal scholars and condemned by others. He has been characterized as a liberal and a conservative jurist. But whatever characterization one may choose to apply to Holmes, there can be no debate that he was truly a giant in his profession, rivaled, perhaps, only by John Marshall in his national celebrity both during his life and after. Indeed, even more than half a century after his death, Holmes is still the subject of debate and frequent biographical and analytic studies. As long as there is an American legal system, an American judiciary, and an American bar, Oliver Wendell Homes Jr. will be, to use his own words in a different context, a "brooding omnipresence."

• M. A. De Wolfe Howe, *Oliver Wendell Holmes: The Shaping Years, 1841–1870*, 1957. M. A. De Wolfe Howe, *Oliver Wendell Holmes: The Proving Years, 1870–1882*, 1963. S. Novick, *Honorable Justice: the Life of Oliver Wendell Holmes*, 1989. L. Baker, *The Justice from Beacon Hill: The Life and Times of Oliver Wendell Holmes*, 1991. G. Edward White, *Justice Oliver Wendell Holmes: The Law and the Inner Self*, 1993. A. Alschuler, *Law without Values: the Life, Work and Legacy of Justice Holmes*, 2000.
—Michael H. Hoeflich

HOLOGRAPHIC WILL. *See* Estate; Trust.

HOMEWORK, INDUSTRIAL. *See* Labor Law: Workplace Issues.

HOMICIDE. The term homicide refers to any killing of a person. Such a killing may be a violation of *criminal law, or it may be excusable or justifiable. Because criminal law exists to identify, prevent, and punish harms that persons cause one another, and because killing is, by general consensus, the greatest harm that can befall a person, every system of criminal law takes homicide seriously. It is almost always among the most severely punished of crimes. Unintended killings, as well as intended killings, are often punished. Because

of the finality of death, legal prohibitions extend not only to intentionally taking life but to unusually risky and careless conduct that puts lives unjustifiably in jeopardy. *Liability for homicide can, in appropriate circumstances, be based even on non-action as well as action. One who has a duty to take care of another may be held liable if death results from a culpable failure to carry out that duty.

Murder and Manslaughter: Degrees of Seriousness. Modern homicide prohibitions distinguish at least two levels of homicide, murder and manslaughter. Murder, the more serious category, includes most instances of intentional killing, as well as those unintentional killings that show exceptional disregard for the life of others. Such disregard is usually present, for example, in an *assault with the aim of causing serious bodily harm.

Manslaughter includes unintended killings that result from unjustifiable conduct that places others at risk, conduct that either does or should alert the actor to the nature and degree of the risk. Manslaughter also includes intended killings for which there is mitigation, acts that are provoked by the victim, or that result from temporary and understandable circumstances that compromise the actor's normal responsibility. Such circumstances typically involve extreme emotional disturbance grounded in conditions that would affect most actors similarly situated. Mitigated intentional killings are charged as *voluntary*, rather than involuntary, manslaughter.

Homicide statutes in most states have additional gradations. Murder and manslaughter are usually subdivided into degrees of seriousness. In the United States, first-degree murder may be a capital offense, punishable by death. The way in which first-degree and second-degree murder are distinguished varies enormously among the states. Homicides less serious than manslaughter may be punishable as negligent homicide. Deaths caused by driving may be prosecuted under separate vehicular homicide statutes.

The law of homicide encompasses not only criminal prohibitions, but also defenses (excuses and justifications) that identify legally permissible killings. Accidental killings are excusable if the actor was neither reckless nor negligent. Defending oneself against a potentially deadly assault is justifiable even if the assailant is killed (see CRIMINAL LAW PRINCIPLES: DEFENSE PRINCIPLES). Justifiable killings may also occur during the defense of others—both by citizens and, more importantly, by the police, who are privileged to use deadly force in appropriate cases.

Common Law and Statutory Law. American *common law of crime has its origins in English common law, where the distinction between murder and manslaughter is long-standing. Traditionally, the requirement of "malice aforethought" was a condition of murder liability, but not of manslaughter. In the early history of English common law, this distinction alluded simply to the difference between a deliberate, or planned, killing and a spontaneous one. The former was punishable by death, the latter by lesser penalties.

As criminal law devolved to modern times, the inadequacies of the notion of malice aforethought became evident. Malice was easily confused with evil, a moral category—but evil was neither a necessary nor sufficient condition for a deliberate killing. The scope of planning needed to qualify as malice *aforethought* proved endlessly controversial. From a moral point of view, a spontaneous killing (a killing for thrills, for example) seemed, in many instances, no less inhumane, cruel, and harmful than a planned killing. Although some American jurisdictions, notably California, retain the term malice aforethought, most have adopted more illuminating criteria.

The notion of a *common law* of homicide, and of crime generally, is ambiguous. One meaning is the historical common law of England, prior to the middle of the seventeenth century, in which the death penalty was the exclusive punishment for murder and in which all planned killings were treated as murder. A second meaning of common law is the law of crimes as it evolved in American case law before it was codified, which has occurred in all American jurisdictions since the middle of the twentieth century. A third meaning is the *codified* case law of the various states, as contrasted with the widely promulgated statutory recommendations embodied in the *Model Penal Code (MPC), first made public by the *American Law Institute in 1962. The MPC has influenced criminal law reform in many states. Various debates about its suggested reforms illuminate the most controversial aspects of the evolved—now codified—common law of the states.

The Model Penal Code. Among the ways in which the MPC drafters rethought the law of homicide, three are of particular note. The first involves refining the standard for mitigating intentional homicide to voluntary manslaughter. Traditionally, intentional homicide is mitigated when it is a response to provocation. Accordingly, unjustified aggression by the victim serves as a partial justification for the intentional killing; it implies that the actor was prompted to act out of

character, and that blame for the ultimate result is shared by the victim. By contrast, the MPC recommends mitigation whenever the actor responds out of understandable, contextually based extreme emotional disturbance, regardless of the source. The victim may be blameless. Thus, mitigation in the MPC takes on the aspect of a partial excuse rather than a partial justification.

Second, most states retain the common law rule of felony-murder, whereby any killing, even an accidental one, caused while one is carrying out an inherently dangerous *felony, such as rape or armed robbery, is treated as first-degree murder. In such cases, it is said that the intention to kill is conclusively (if fictitiously) presumed or that the intention to carry out the felony is "transferred" to the homicide. The MPC rejects the felony-murder rule as unfair, adhering to the general requirement that unintentional homicides be treated as murder only when their circumstances show extraordinary disregard for life. Under the MPC, any presumption that such disregard is present when a felony results in death may be rebutted.

Third, the Model Penal Code addresses a theoretical tension that runs through the common law of homicide—and through all of criminal law. As George Fletcher has shown, many controversies within criminal law exemplify tension between incompatible theoretical patterns. One pattern, for example, bases the seriousness of a crime on the extent of harm caused. A different pattern assesses the seriousness of the crime by determining the actor's disposition to cause harm regardless of whether he succeeds. The historical roots of criminal law reflect the pattern of manifest harm. The evolution of criminal law is, in large part, one of taking the subjective or psychological dimension ever more seriously; perhaps the most significant aspect of the shift from common law to statutory law is the effort to fine-tune culpability to the nature and disposition of the actor. The MPC is a high-water mark in embracing both social science research and the moral significance of subjective states. Its preference for emotional disturbance over provocation as a basis for mitigation, and its rejection of the crude presumptions (fictions) that underlie the felony-murder doctrine, are examples of this trend.

To be sure, the pattern of manifest harm remains persuasive to many scholars, judges, and legislators. They stress the fact that any taking of life elicits an elemental demand for retribution, and that in appropriate circumstances (such as a felonious act), this demand justifies severe punishment even when the resulting death was accidental. They also argue that our moral responsibility not to kill transcends our psychological vulnerabilities. Accordingly, such theorists favor limiting such defenses as necessity and duress to crimes less serious than homicide. For the same reason, they oppose innovative extensions of self-defense, such as the battered spouse defense and other diminished-capacity arguments, in cases of homicide.

Sanctions. Imprisonment is by far the most common form of punishment for homicide. Terms may extend from a few years for involuntary manslaughter to as much as a life sentence for first-degree murder. Over the last twenty years, legislators in many states and the federal jurisdiction have responded to demands for more determinate sentences. The discretion of judges to craft sentences within a wide prescribed range has been undercut by statutes that prescribe fixed sentences, that involve mandatory minimums, and that require judges to use sentencing schedules with determinate aggravating and mitigating factors that have specific point values. Moreover, states have increasingly curtailed the power of parole boards to release prisoners after they have served little more than half their formal sentences. This trend toward determinate and predictable sentences—a shift of power from judges and parole boards to lawmakers—has its critics, who argue that it produces unfair results not tailored to the circumstances of the individual offense and offender.

Although some states have experimented modestly with alternative sentencing, they have used such innovations—prompted by both rehabilitative and cost-cutting aims—mostly for crimes less serious than homicide. The most significant recent change in American penal practice has been reinstatement of the death penalty, authorized in thirty-eight states and for some federal crimes. Between the late 1950s and the mid-1970s, the death penalty fell into disuse, and its constitutionality under the Constitution's Eighth Amendment prohibition against *"cruel and unusual punishment" was in doubt. The U.S. Supreme Court resolved these doubts in favor of constitutionality in *Gregg v. Georgia* (1976), requiring only that the penalty be imposed in accordance with standards that insure uniform application. The United States is the only Western democracy to use the death penalty for ordinary crimes committed during peacetime, and it has been criticized for being out of step with the moral standards of the world community. (see CAPITAL PUNISHMENT)

Federalism. Historically, the definition and prosecution of crimes that do not implicate a federal interest have been reserved to the states, and homicide cases are almost always matters of state jurisdiction. The main constraints on state practice are the various rights prescribed by the Fourth, Fifth, Sixth, and Eighth Amendments to the Constitution, applied to the states through the *Fourteenth Amendment under the *incorporation doctrine. An act of homicide may, however, be prosecuted as a federal crime if it violates antiterrorist laws or the federal civil rights statutes (in particular, 18 US Code §242), or if it constitutes obstruction of justice. Killing a witness to prevent him from testifying is an example of the latter (18 US Code §1513).

Comparative Perspectives. The broad parameters of homicide law in the United States are remarkably similar to homicide law in other cultures. Legal regimes vary among nations whenever they are determined by variations in economic systems, political history, or social arrangements. Homicide law, however, responds to a universal need to identify, deter, and punish intentional and reckless killings, a need that crosses borders. We all fear annihilation. Any kind of social order depends on controlling homicide.

A comparison of French, German, and Russian homicide law with American law implies that many of our preoccupations are historically determined and are explained by the age of our legal system. French criminal law, also a venerable system with a 200-year-old code, is characterized by similar controversies about severe penalties and a felony-murder presumption. Newer systems of codified criminal law, in Germany and Russia, for example, have laws that echo, in broad outline, the familiar revisions of the Model Penal Code.

[*See also* Criminal Punishments]

• Charles L. Black Jr., *Capital Punishment*, 1974. George Fletcher, *Rethinking Criminal Law*, 1978. Joel Feinberg, *The Moral Limits of the Criminal Law: Harm to Others*, 1984. Andrew Ashworth, *Principles of Criminal Law*, 1991. Wendy Lesser, *Pictures at an Execution: An Inquiry into the Subject of Murder*, 1993. Joshua Dressler, *Understanding Criminal Law*, 1995. Paul Robinson, *Criminal Law*, 1997. Samuel H. Pillsbury, *Judging Evil: Rethinking the Law of Murder and Manslaughter*, 1998.

—Thomas H. Morawetz

HOMOSEXUALITY AND THE LAW. In the United States, homosexuality and the law are best understood through the prism of the penal regulation of same-sex sexual activity. Legal prohibitions against consensual sodomy date to the nineteenth century and permeate both the criminal and civil law in their dealings with lesbians and gay men.

By the mid-twentieth century, all American states criminalized noncommercial sodomy among consenting adults in private as a *felony, with penalties ranging to twenty years in prison. Typically banning cunnilingus, fellatio, and anal intercourse, these statutes often revealed their Victorian roots by describing the forbidden acts merely as the "crime against nature." Although the statutes in theory applied to all people regardless of sexual orientation, sodomy proscriptions were selectively enforced against homosexuals. Prosecutions reached their zenith in the late 1940s and 1950s, with tens of thousands of lesbians and gay men ensnared.

Equally important, judges have used sodomy laws to justify denying *civil rights and liberties to lesbians and gay men. Research on American appellate courts indicated that the presence of consensual sodomy laws helped predict about 8 percent more negative judicial action regarding all lesbian-and-gay-rights claims than in jurisdictions without the prohibition. Accordingly, in addition to their criminal sting, sodomy statutes affect the home, cited, for instance, as good reason to refuse lesbian and gay parents custody of, and visitation with, their children (e.g, *Bottoms* v. *Bottoms* (1995)); *Ex parte D. W. W* (1998); and *Thigpen* v. *Carpenter* (1987)) (see CHILD CUSTODY).

Sodomy laws also infiltrate the workplace, with the ban on lesbian and gay military service members the most conspicuous example (*Dronenburg* v. *Zech* (1984)). In turn, other federal agencies have discriminated against homosexual civilians: the Central Intelligence Agency (*Doe* v. *Gates* (1993)), the Department of Defense (*High Tech Gays* v. *Defense Industrial Security Clearance Office* (1990)), the Federal Bureau of Investigation (*Padula* v. *Webster* (1987)), and the U.S. Information Agency (*U.S. Information Agency* v. *Krc* (1993)). At the state level, an attorney general's denial of employment to an otherwise qualified lesbian attorney was upheld in part because of a sodomy law [*Shahar* v. *Bowers* (1997)).

States have taken other antigay actions allegedly in deference to sodomy statutes. In 1995, Alabama passed a law forbidding the use of public funds by colleges and universities to support activities of groups fostering lifestyles proscribed by the state's sodomy law. Oklahoma adopted a law dismissing or suspending teachers engaged in the advocacy of homosexual conduct that might come to the attention of school children or employees. Federal courts struck down both statutes based on the First Amendment's prohibition of viewpoint discrimination (*Gay Lesbian Bisexual Alliance* v. *Pryor*

(1997)); *National Gay Task Force* v. *Board of Education of the City of Oklahoma City* (1984)). State universities have withheld formal recognition of lesbian-and-gay student organizations because school officials thought their approval would lead to sodomy-law violations, e.g., *Gay Lib* v. *University of Missouri* (1977)); *Gay Student Services* v. *Texas A&M University* (1984).

Ironically, this sodomy-law-based homophobia occurred during a sea change in American penal law. In 1955, the *American Law Institute voted to recommend decriminalization of consensual sodomy. Six years later, in adopting the ALI's Model Penal Code, Illinois became the first state to eliminate criminal sanctions for noncommercial sodomy among consenting adults in private. Twenty-four other states and the District of Columbia followed suit: Alaska (1978), California (1975), Colorado (1971), Connecticut (1969), Delaware (1972), District of Columbia (1994), Hawaii (1972), Indiana (1976), Iowa (1976), Maine (1975), Nebraska (1977), Nevada (1993), New Hampshire (1973), New Jersey (1978), New Mexico (1975), North Dakota (1973), Ohio (1972), Oregon (1971), Rhode Island (1998), South Dakota (1976), Vermont (1977), Washington (1975), West Virginia (1976), Wisconsin (1983), and Wyoming (1977). Further, the highest courts of Georgia (*Powell* v. *State* (1998)), Kentucky (*Commonwealth* v. *Wasson* (1992)), Montana (*Gryczan* v. *State*, (1997)), New York (*People* v. *Onofre* (1980)), and Pennsylvania (*Commonwealth* v. *Bonadio* (1980)) invalidated their states' laws, while lower courts did so in Arkansas, Maryland, Tennessee, and Texas. Moreover, the legislatures in seven states reduced consensual sodomy from felony to misdemeanor level: Alabama (1977), Arizona (1977), Arkansas (1977), Kansas (1969), Minnesota (1977), Missouri (1977), and Utah (1973).

Thus, in 2001, Idaho, Louisiana, Massachusetts (the law of which *Commonwealth* v. *Balthazar* (1974) attenuates), Michigan, Mississippi, North Carolina, South Carolina, and Virginia maintain felony-level sodomy statutes affecting both same-sex and opposite-sex partners, while Alabama, Arizona, Florida, Minnesota, and Utah do so at the misdemeanor level. Five states (Arkansas, Kansas, Missouri, Oklahoma, and Texas) penalize sexual activity only between same-sex partners, with just one (Oklahoma) at the felony level. In short, during the last four decades of the twentieth century, more than 80 percent of the states eliminated consensual sodomy as a felony.

The most consequential constitutional challenge to sodomy laws occurred in *Bowers* v. *Hardwick*

(1986). There, by a five-to-four vote, the Supreme Court rejected an extension of privacy rights granted heterosexuals in *Griswold* v. *Connecticut* (1965), and its progeny. Indeed, the *Hardwick* Court derided the privacy claim, characterizing the issue as "whether the Federal Constitution confers a fundamental right upon homosexuals to engage in sodomy" and then labeling that assertion as, "at best, facetious."

However, in *Romer* v. *Evans* (1996), the Court, by a six-to-three vote, upheld an *equal-protection attack on Colorado's Amendment 2, a popularly mandated state constitutional revision forbidding localities from enacting ordinances outlawing discrimination against lesbians and gay men. The *Romer* Court's analysis that "the amendment seems inexplicable by anything but animus toward the class that it affects" and thereby "lacks a rational relationship to legitimate state interests" implicitly overrules *Hardwick*, because sodomy laws, especially those criminalizing only same-sex conduct, are similarly flawed. In Oklahoma, for example, lesbian and gay adults are felons for performing the same private, consensual acts heterosexuals do, but without the prospect of ten years in prison.

State courts have agreed. In 1998, the Georgia Supreme Court struck down the law upheld in *Hardwick*, but on state, not federal, constitutional grounds (*Powell*, supra). In all, the appellate courts of eight states (among the twenty-five not decriminalizing consensual sodomy by legislative action) have declared their sodomy laws unconstitutional or otherwise inapplicable to private consensual activity among adults.

Military Ban. The United States is the only major western power to discharge military personnel because of their sexual orientation. Despite the "Don't Ask, Don't Tell" law adopted by Congress and the Clinton administration in 1993, the ban is the most blatant form of sexual-orientation apartheid in America, responsible for the annual separation of about one thousand lesbians and gay men from the armed forces. Diverse arguments against the taboo have been made to the federal courts of appeals for over twenty years, and every constitutional claim has failed (e.g., *Beller* v. *Middendorf* (1980); *Woodward* v. *United States* (1989); *Steffan* v. *Perry* (1994); *Walmer* v. *U.S. Department of Defense* (1995); *Richenberg* v. *Perry* (1996); *Philips* v. *Perry* (1997); *Holmes* v. *California Army National Guard* (1997); *Able* v. *United States* (1998)). The prominent exception to this vast panorama of ineffable personal tragedy is *Watkins* v. *U.S. Army*

(1989), where the service member prevailed on a nonconstitutional ground (equitable estoppel).

The Supreme Court itself has yet to rule on the policy's constitutionality. Many intermediate appellate decisions cite *Hardwick* as authority for the military ban. Nevertheless, *Romer's* presumptive overruling of *Hardwick* leaves the viability of the military's homosexual exclusion an open question.

Employment. Legislation in eleven states (California, Connecticut, Hawaii, Massachusetts, Minnesota, Nevada, New Hampshire, New Jersey, Rhode Island, Vermont, and Wisconsin), and in at least eighty-eight counties and municipalities of other states, prohibits discrimination based on sexual orientation in public and private employment. Executive orders protect public employees in Colorado, Iowa, Maryland, New Mexico, New York, Pennsylvania, and Washington. In contrast to sodomy laws, statewide gay-civil-rights provisions have helped predict success in appellate-court rulings on all lesbian-and-gay-rights claims by 13 percent more than in jurisdictions without the statutory protection.

In addition, many public and private employers have nondiscrimination policies that include sexual orientation. President Bill Clinton issued an executive order to that effect for civilian employees of federal agencies, and over half of the "Fortune 500" companies have employment rules not to discriminate against lesbians and gay men.

Gay Marriage. In *Baker* v. *State* (1999), the Vermont Supreme Court held that the Vermont Constitution required the state to extend to same-sex couples the common benefits, protections, and security flowing from *marriage. In response, the state legislature took the historic step of granting "civil unions" to same-sex couples, conferring about three hundred legal benefits and obligations on the newly de facto spouses. The Hawaii Supreme Court, in *Baehr* v. *Lewin* (1993), ruled that the exclusion of same-sex couples from the state's marriage statute constituted sex *discrimination under the Hawaii Constitution and was subject to strict scrutiny. The state legislature then passed the Hawaii Reciprocal Beneficiaries Act, a less comprehensive grant of legal benefits to same-sex couples than in Vermont, but nonetheless significant.

The Hawaii and Vermont court decisions also triggered hostile legislative responses. In 1996, Congress passed the Defense of Marriage Act (DOMA), defining marriage as not to include same-sex unions in the application of federal law and providing that states are not required to give effect to same-sex marriages contracted or solemnized in other states. The latter provision seeks to subvert the *Full Faith and Credit Clause of the federal Constitution, which requires states to recognize marriages validly performed in other states. In addition to DOMA, more than thirty states adopted laws prohibiting marriage between persons of the same gender.

Hate Crimes. *Hate crimes—offenses manifesting evidence of prejudice based on victims' status or condition—concern lesbians and gay men. The Federal Bureau of Investigation reported that hate crimes based on sexual orientation rose in the United States by almost 15 percent between 1997 and 2001, at the same time that the overall crime rate diminished. Twenty-three states and the District of Columbia have hate-crimes legislation that explicitly includes sexual orientation among other protected categories such as race and religion.

Constitutional Victories. Lesbians and gay men have savored some unequivocal, constitutionally based legal successes. Early triumphs in higher education came under the aegis of the First Amendment (*Gay Students Organization* v. *Bonner* (1974); *Gay Alliance of Students* v. *Matthews* (1976)). A notable later judicial win involved the constant verbal harassment and physical abuse of a gay public-school student by classmates, which mistreatment school officials habitually ignored. Relying on the Equal Protection Clause, a federal court of appeals held the Wisconsin school civilly liable for sexual-orientation discrimination [*Nabozny* v. *Podlesny* (1996), and the school district settled the suit for $900,000.

Lesbian-and-gay litigants have experienced even more reliable success in court when invoking state constitutions. In fact, court claims based on state constitutions have prevailed by a factor almost 75 percent more than those founded on the federal Constitution. For example, in *Tanner* v. *Oregon Health Sciences University* (1998), the state of Oregon gave health and insurance benefits to the spouses of heterosexual state employees, but denied the same perquisites to the unmarried domestic partners of lesbian and gay employees. In overturning this dissimilar treatment, the state court of appeals determined that the Oregon Constitution prohibited the state from granting privileges or immunities to one group of citizens that were not equally available to all and that lesbians and gay men were a "suspect" class, demanding a high level of judicial protection. In *Campbell* v. *Sundquist* (1996), the right to privacy of the Tennessee Constitution invalidated the state's consensual sodomy law. Similarly implementing state

constitutions, the supreme courts of Georgia (in *Powell*, supra), Kentucky (*Wasson*, supra), and Montana (*Gryczan*, supra) struck down their sodomy statutes.

Judicial Behavior. Research on appellate courts has disclosed the importance of attitudinal forces in the judicial resolution of lesbian-and-gay-rights claims. For instance, religious affiliation is crucial. Roman Catholic judges were 11 percent more likely to vote against lesbian-and-gay rights than Protestant colleagues and 21 percent more negative than Jewish judges. Additionally, African-American and Hispanic jurists voted 20 percent more favorably than others, while women judges were 12 percent more positively disposed than male counterparts. In cases involving child custody, visitation, *adoption and foster care, judges sixty years of age or older had a probability of voting against lesbian or gay litigants of 20 percent more than jurists under fifty years of age.

[*See also* Gender and Law]

• Ruthann Robson, *Lesbian (Out) law: Survival Under the Rule of Law*, 1992. Marc Wolinsky and Kenneth Sherrill, eds., *Gays and the Military*, 1993. William B. Rubenstein, *Cases and Materials on Sexual Orientation and the Law*, 1997. Lisa Keen and Suzanne B. Goldberg, *Strangers to the Law: Gay People on Trial*, 1998. William N. Eskridge Jr., *Gaylaw: Challenging the Apartheid of the Closet*, 1999. Evan Gerstmann, *The Constitutional Underclass: Gays, Lesbians, and the Failure of Class-Based Equal Protection*, 1999. Janet E. Halley, *Don't: A Reader's Guide to the Military's Anti-Gay Policy*, 1999. David A. J. Richards, *Identity and the Case for Gay Rights: Race, Gender, Religion as Analogies*, 1999. Patricia A. Cain, *Rainbow Rights: The Role of Lawyers and Courts in the Lesbian and Gay Civil Rights Movement*, 2000.

—Daniel R. Pinello

HOSTILE TAKEOVER. *See* Corporation.

HOUSTON, CHARLES HAMILTON (1895–1950), litigator, law school *educator, with a principal role in defining, planning, and implementing the legal phase of the African-American struggle for racial justice, 1930–50. Born in the District of Columbia to William LePre Houston, a lawyer, and Mary Ethel Hamilton Houston, a hairdresser and former school teacher, Houston would serve as a litigator, teacher, and mentor for nearly two decades. He trained hundreds of African-American law students at Howard University, collaborated with community leaders, and advised or worked with local African-American attorneys throughout the nation from 1924 to 1950. Although best known for his *equal-protection litigation pertaining to schools, his record as a litigator in connection with cases of employment and housing *discrimination prompted Justice William O. *Douglas (in a letter to J. Clay Smith, Esq., 19 April 1975) to describe Houston as "one of the top ten advocates to appear before [the U.S. Supreme] court."

As a child Houston attended the racially segregated public schools of Washington, D.C., graduating from M Street high school's college preparatory program in 1911. By 1915 he had graduated from Amherst College *magna cum laude* and had been inducted into Phi Beta Kappa. After a brief period of teaching at Howard University in Washington, D.C., and serving as an officer in the American Expeditionary Forces during World War I, Houston entered Harvard Law School. There he became the first African-American editor of the *Harvard Law Review* (1921), earned the LL.B. with honors (1922), and fulfilled the requirements for the doctor of juridical science (S.J.D.) degree (1923). He was admitted to the District of Columbia bar in 1924 and thereafter practiced in the firm Houston & Houston (with his father), focusing primarily on civil litigation, while teaching at Howard University's Law School. In the 1930s Houston's Howard students included African Americans who would become legal luminaries, among them Thurgood *Marshall, Oliver Hill, and William B. Bryant Under Houston's administrative leadership, Howard's Law School not only qualified for *American Bar Association accreditation and *Association of American Law Schools membership but also became a legal laboratory for *civil rights. Students at the school were trained to become "social engineers" who would skillfully advocate social change and civil rights for African Americans.

Charles Houston was invited to become the first salaried special counsel for the National Association for the Advancement of Colored People (NAACP) in 1934, and in that position he implemented his social engineering strategies. In many tasks, until he returned to private practice in 1940, Houston worked with local African-American attorneys, while Thurgood Marshall aided him in the role of NAACP assistant special counsel. Cases in Maryland and Missouri marked the beginning of the planned assault upon *Plessy v. Ferguson (1896), the famous "separate but equal" ruling of the Supreme Court that declared racial *segregation consistent with the *Fourteenth Amendment's equal-protection provisions. *Murray* v. *University of Maryland* (1936) and *Missouri ex rel Gaines* (1938) were important steps in dismantling *Plessy.*

In *Gaines,* Houston established the groundwork for *Brown* v. *Board of Education* (1954) by persuading the Supreme Court justices that each state's Fourteenth Amendment equal-protection obligation had to be fulfilled within its borders without exclusion of African Americans from educational opportunities afforded white citizens. The approach of dismantling segregation by establishing new equal-protection precedents before the Supreme Court continued with Houston's advice and counsel through *Sipuel* v. *Oklahoma Regents* (1948), *Sweat* v. *Painter* (1950), and *McLaurin* v. *Oklahoma Regents* (1950). With Houston's blessing, the direct attack on segregation was launched by Thurgood Marshall and Robert Carter, among others, for the NAACP and the NAACP's tax-exempt Legal Defense and Educational Fund.

Retaining his affiliation with the NAACP Legal Committee, but pursuing other civil rights litigation through his private practice, Charles Houston litigated successfully the landmark *Steele* v. *Louisville and Nashville* (1944) (with its companion case of *Tunstall* v. *Brotherhood of Locomotive Firemen* (1944)), which established the duty of fair representation. Later in the 1940s, Houston appeared in oral argument before the U.S. Supreme Court to oppose racially restrictive covenants in the District of Columbia's housing practices. NAACP-sponsored collaboration with social scientists and attorneys nationwide resulted in two rulings by the Supreme Court outlawing racially restrictive covenants in housing—for the states through *Shelley* v. *Kraemer* (1948) and for the District of Columbia through *Hurd* v. *Hodge* (1948).

After Houston's death from a heart attack in 1950, leaving his wife, Henrietta, and one son, Charles Houston Jr., his funeral was attended by many admirers, from parents of school children he had represented to Supreme Court justices before whom he had argued. In June 1950, the NAACP awarded its Spingarn Medal posthumously to Charles Houston for his contributions to the African-American struggle for freedom and justice. Among scholars and veteran civil rights lawyers, Houston is remembered as the first "Mr. Civil Rights" for his litigation and his conceptualization of a long-range strategic plan of litigation to eradicate constitutional support for racial segregation.

[See also Educator, Legal; Race and Ethnicity; Segregation]

• Conrad Harper, "Houston, Charles H.," in *Dictionary of American Negro Biography* (Rayford Logan and Michael Winston, eds.), 1982. Genna Rae McNeil, *Groundwork: Charles Hamilton Houston and the Struggle for*

Civil Rights, 1983. J. Clay Smith Jr., *Emancipation*, 1993. "Tributes to Charles Hamilton Houston," *Harvard Law Review* 111 (June 1998). —Genna Rae McNeil

HUGHES, CHARLES EVANS. Born Glen Falls, N.Y., 11 April 1862; died Cape Cod, Mass., 27 August 1948. Hughes was an associate justice of the *Supreme Court (1910–16) and chief justice of the United States. (1930–41). He graduated first in his class at Columbia Law School. After a brief stint as a professor at Cornell University, he plunged into the world of the corporate bar, where he earned both reputation and wealth.

In 1910, President William Howard Taft nominated Hughes, who had been a reform governor of New York, to the high court. He became an intellectual colleague of Justice Oliver Wendell *Holmes Jr., even though they often voted differently. In *Bailey* v. *Alabama* (1911), Hughes wrote the majority opinion that declared a state statute unconstitutional because it enforced peonage. Justice Holmes dissented. Hughes was a sentimental conservative in his reform impulses; Holmes was an equally unsentimental defender of legislative prerogative. The two dissented in *Frank* v. *Mangum* (1915), where they denounced the "lynch law" trial of a Jew. Hughes was also sympathetic to some efforts to regulate the new American economy. Thus, in *Coppage* v. *Kansas* (1915), he dissented when the majority voted that the state of Kansas could not outlaw the use of "yellow-dog" contracts.

Hughes reputation grew so strong that he became the Republic candidate for president in 1916. He lost to Woodrow Wilson and returned to the practice of the law. From 1921 to 1925, he served Presidents Warren G. Harding and Calvin Coolidge as secretary of state. Hughes also served briefly on the International Court of Justice before his appointment in 1930 by President Herbert Hoover as chief justice of the United States.

As chief justice, Hughes had to deal with Justice Holmes, who was in declining health, with the strong-minded liberal Louis D. *Brandeis, and with the Four Horsemen opposed to President Franklin D. Roosevelt's New Deal program. Hughes exercised diplomacy that helped sustain the Court against FDR's attacks. He was a moderate, but one capable of activism. He supported civil liberties, as his votes in *Stromberg* v. *California* (1931) and *Herndon* v. *Lowry* (1937) underscore, and he also favored civil rights, as indicated by his votes in the *Scottsboro* case and *Brown* v. *Mississippi* (1936).

But Hughes marched to the beat of his own drummer. He sided with the conservatives in opposing key elements of the New Deal program, although in other areas he was more accepting of state and federal efforts. When FDR decided after his re-election in 1936 to try to "pack" the Court, Hughes successfully moved the justices toward the center (see COURT PACKING). In *West Coast Hotel* v. *Parrish* (1937), Hughes wrote for a bare majority (5–4) in sustaining a state regulatory measure; in *National Labor Relations Board* v. *Jones & Laughlin Steel Corp.* (1937) he did the same (5–4) in upholding the National Labor Relations Act. Roosevelt thereafter scrapped his court plan.

Hughes retired in 1941. He left behind a legacy of skillful leadership during an especially turbulent period in the history of the Court and the nation.

• Samuel Hendel, *Charles Evans Hughes and the Supreme Court*, 1951. Merlo Pusey, *Charles Evans Hughes*, 2 vols., 1951. —Kermit L. Hall

HUMAN RIGHTS, INTERNATIONAL LAW AND. Human rights law has an ancient pedigree. Its origins can be traced to the *natural law doctrines of the Greeks and Romans. The emergence of human rights as part of modern domestic law dates back at least to John Locke's *Two Treatises on Civil Government*. In 1690, Locke argued that governments were bound in a covenant with the governed to protect an individual's natural rights to life, liberty, and property. Enshrined in 1776 in the American Declaration of Independence and in 1789 in both the French Declaration of the Rights of Man and Citizen and the United States Constitution's *Bill of Rights, human rights law has become an ordinary feature of many domestic legal systems, including that of the United States.

However, human rights law made a definitive appearance in *international law only in the middle of the twentieth century. Before then, international lawyers assumed that governments were ordinarily shielded by state *sovereignty from external scrutiny for acts commited within their own territories. The principal exception involved foreign nationals, who could be protected in international law by their national governments even when outside national territory. Moreover, legal positivism, then the prevalent philosophy of international law, assumed that only states, not individuals, could be subjects of international law. This assumption was decisively challenged on October 30, 1943, when the governments of the United States, the United Kingdom, France, and the Soviet Union put the world on notice that individual Germans, including German government officials, would be held individually responsible for atrocities committed during World War II. The 1945 Charter of the International Military Tribunal constituted the Nuremberg Tribunal, which in turn in 1946 found individual Germans guilty under international law for crimes against peace, war crimes, and crimes against humanity (see WAR, LAW OF). Finally, in 1948, the United Nations General Assembly issued the Universal Declaration of Human Rights, an instrument now generally accepted as part of customary international law. The Universal Declaration, along with the French Declaration of the Rights of Man and Citizen and the U.S. Bill of Rights, constitutes the foundation of modern human rights law. In the last half of the twentieth century, human rights law came to be accepted as an integral part of international law.

Although there is still no universal international human rights court, there are several regional human rights tribunals. Most prominent is the European Court of Human Rights in Strasbourg, which pursuant to the 1950 European Convention for the Protection of Human Rights and Fundamental Freedom has adjudicated more than a thousand cases involving forty three European countries. Its judgments have almost always been respected. There is also the Inter-American Court of Human Rights, based in Costa Rica. However, fearful for its sovereignty, the United States has refused to submit to this court's jurisdiction. The United States has participated on two ad hoc United Nations international criminal courts: one for the former Yugoslavia, the other for Rwanda. The United States, however, is not willing to permit its citizens to be subject to an international criminal court. Accordingly, the United States has refused to ratify the new Rome Convention that will establish an International Criminal Court. This position is, in part, responsible for the ouster of the United States in 2001 from the United Nations Human Rights Commission, a political body that considers violations of international human rights law.

Despite America's reluctance to submit to international systems protecting human rights, U.S. courts have sometimes found and applied international human rights law in U.S. domestic litigation. Most notable is the 1980 judgment of the U.S. Second Circuit in *Filartiga* v. *Pena-Irala*, where it was held that torture committed in Paraguay by a Paraguayan official against a Paraguayan was subject to punishment as a violation of international human rights law in the United States under the until-then long-dormant 1789 Alien Tort Claims Statute. U.S. courts have been more willing to apply international human rights law to foreign governments than to the U.S. government. For example, in *Sei Fujii* v. *California* (1952), the California Supreme Court held that the human rights provisions of the United Nations Charter were too general to be self-executing in U.S. law and that although a California statute escheating alien property violated the Fourteenth Amendment to the Constitution, the court would not find the statute in violation of international law.

[*See also* Civil Rights and Civil Liberties]

• Thomas Buergenthal, *International Human Rights*, 1988. Ian Brownlie, *Basic Documents on Human Rights*, 3d ed., 1992. Richard B. Lillich and Hurst Hannum, *International Human Rights*, 3d ed., 1995. Mark W. Janis, Richard S. Kay, and Anthony W. Bradley, *European Human Rights Law*, 2d ed., 2000. Henry J. Steiner and Philip Alston, *International Human Rights in Context*, 2d ed., 2000.   —Mark W. Janis

HUMOR. *See* Lawyers, Popular Perception of.

HUTCHINSON, ANN, TRIALS OF. The so-called "antinomian" or "free grace" controversy was one of the many religious disputes that spilled over into early Massachusetts politics. Established as a haven for dissenting reform English Protestants, sometimes called "Puritans," the colony promised a religious life that was supposed to be harmonious. The opposite proved to be true, as the trials of Ann Hutchinson for contempt of the ministers and public disorderliness demonstrated. But the crisis that culminated in her conviction and banishment did not begin with her or her views of Christianity and the role of the ministers. Instead, hers was the last act in a complex drama involving the foremost political and religious figures in the young colony.

In 1635, Henry Vane, a nobly-born Puritan, arrived in the colony. He won the governorship one year later with the help of the Boston freemen, including William Hutchinson and his wife, Ann Marbury Hutchinson, who had arrived in 1634.

They all subscribed to their minister John Cotton's views that those who doubted the sincerity of their faith must wait for some sign of divine approval before seeking membership in the church. Other ministers maintained that the biblical promise of salvation for the regenerate and the practice of "holy duties" sufficed for a start.

Hutchinson not only preferred Cotton's formulation, she applied it to the situation of the colony. In weekly meetings with other women to discuss Cotton's sermons, she argued that the covenant of works had never really been banished from some Massachusetts ministers' teachings. In her view, the doctrine was awfully close to "antinomianism," a heresy that implied true saints could get along without church discipline. The implication of this lesson was that such ministers should not be allowed to preach—a revolutionary thought in a colony built upon respect for the ministry.

The dispute might have quietly died had not her brother-in-law, John Wheelwright, delivered a sermon in January 1637 in which he seemed to state that some of the other ministers were holy hypocrites, fooling themselves that their show of piety proved their election to the kingdom of heaven. John Cotton drew back from the consequences of his own preaching, exposing Wheelwright and Hutchinson to the combined might of an infuriated clergy and an irritated government.

When Vane returned to England and Wheelwright was convicted of *treason by the General Court of the colony, near the end of 1637, the association of ministers turned its attention to Hutchinson. Her attackers argued that she had renounced the proper role for a woman, and become a "husband, magistrate, and minister"—all roles reserved for men.

She was tried in the General Court in November 1637 for defamation and civil disorder. Trading biblical exegesis with her accusers, she held up her end of the discourse admirably, but the court, packed with her adversaries, concluded that she had "disparaged all our ministers" and ordered her expelled from the colony. The following March, she faced a trial before her own ministers and congregation in Boston, at which she admitted to misstating her views, but would not concede that congregants could never criticize the ministry.

Hutchinson and her family left the colony in May 1638 and traveled to Rhode Island. After some controversial years in Rhode Island, she moved once again to a Puritan community on Long Island, where she and members of her family were killed in an Indian raid.

[See also Criminal Law]

• Mary Beth Norton, *Founding Mothers and Fathers*, 1997. Michael Winship, *Making Heretics: The Free Grace Controversy In Massachusetts, 1636–1639*, 2002.

—Peter Charles Hoffer

I

IBM LITIGATION. The federal government's landmark *antitrust case against International Business Machines (IBM) is most remarkable for the length of the trial and its inconclusive outcome. Robert Bork called it the Antitrust Division's Vietnam. The United States alleged that the giant manufacturer had illegally maintained a monopoly in the sale of general-purpose digital computers by engaging in several kinds of anticompetitive practices. After eight years of investigation and discovery, the trial began in May 1975 and ended nearly seven years later when the government dropped the case. Not only was the trial among the longest in antitrust history; more importantly, in no case of even roughly comparable magnitude had the government so close to the end of its proceedings simply dismissed charges.

The peculiar history of the IBM litigation was mainly a product of shifting ideology in antitrust law. The complaint was filed on 17 January 1969, three days before the end of the Lyndon B. Johnson administration. At that time, the federal law was hostile to dominant firms, holding that a firm with a large market share violated the Sherman Act simply by using aggressive tactics to maintain its position. The government challenged IBM's low and discriminatory pricing, its bundling of hardware, software, and support services, and its policy of preannouncing production schedules on new "phantom machines." IBM vigorously defended its practices and argued that the government had used an unduly narrow market definition that inflated the firm's market power.

By 1981, when Ronald Reagan was inaugurated as president, the law had changed, largely in response to criticism from the Chicago School. The U.S. Court of Appeals for the Second Circuit had ruled in *Berkey Photo, Inc.* v. *Eastman Kodak Co.* (1979) that even a monopolist has a right to compete aggressively. President Reagan's first Antitrust Division head, William Baxter, a Stanford law pro-

fessor and Chicago School scholar, concluded that although IBM probably had monopoly power in a relevant market during the complaint period, the government had not proven that the power resulted from predatory practices. Rather, IBM was dominant because it was more efficient than its rivals. Baxter also believed that no feasible remedy could be fashioned. Injunctive relief would be either irrelevant or insignificant, and a structural remedy, given the technological progress in the computer industry that was already eroding IBM's dominance, would be disproportionate to the offense and unnecessary. He dismissed the case on 8 January 1982.

[*See also* Anti-Trust Law]

• Franklin M. Fisher, John J. McGowan, and Joen E. Greenwood, *Folded, Spindled, and Mutilated*, 1983. Richard T. DeLamarter, *Big Blue*, 1986.

—John E. Lopatka

IMMIGRATION. Immigration has significantly shaped American society. From the perspective of the constitutional legal system, however, immigration law—the federal law related to the entry, residence, status, and rights of noncitizens—has long occupied something of an outcast status. The broad development of immigration law has been from a welter of autonomous state systems to a complex, relatively opaque, and highly discretionary federal bureaucracy generally subject to little judicial oversight.

One reason for its somewhat unusual constitutional status is that immigration was relatively open and unregulated by federal law until the late nineteenth century. Another factor is the unique way in which the Supreme Court ultimately defined the federal power to control immigration as outside the constitutional restraints normally applied to government actions. The baroque interrelationship between general questions of aliens' rights (e.g., the right to hold certain jobs, to open businesses, to vote, to work, to obtain welfare or state-subsidized medical care) and more central immigration concerns such as entry, deportation, and naturalization practices has also led to odd legal rules. Still, because immigration law is essential to the self-definition of the United States, both as a matter of demography and as a defining feature of national mythology, its legal history is infused with unusually deep social, cultural, and political currents.

The roots—and the conflicts—of U.S. immigration law long predate the Constitution. Colonies founded by European emigrants seeking religious freedom and economic opportunity generally encouraged the entry of others of similar background. Emigration was often actively supported by European governments—for reasons rarely, if ever, grounded in idealism. The British Parliament, for example, crafted legal inducements, and in some cases compulsions, to transport white emigrants to the New World to rid England of convicts, paupers, and others, to support the colonists' struggles against native American Indians, and to suppress slave revolts. Indentured servants were a major source of colonial immigration for which colonial legislatures developed various legal support mechanisms.

Even in this early period, however, immigration law and policy presented challenges. The diversity of the European immigrants—English, Dutch, French, Spanish, Portuguese, among others— caused tensions and led to calls by Benjamin Franklin, Thomas *Jefferson, and others to restrict at least certain types of immigration. The qualities for permissible immigration were often regulated by colonial legislatures. Laws sought to control and sometimes to prohibit the immigration of paupers, criminals, unpopular religious sects, and people suffering from disease.

Although the Declaration of Independence had cited the obstruction of immigration and naturalization by King George III as a justification for revolution, the Constitution does not mention immigration, either as a right held to be "self-evident" or as a delegated power of the federal government. The use of the term "migration" (Art. I, § 9, cl. 1) was clearly a tortured euphemism for *slavery.

The Constitution did contain a delegation of federal power relating to *citizenship, granting Congress the power to "establish an Uniform Rule of Naturalization" (Art. I, § 8, cl. 4). This power is best understood as arising from the framers' desire to reconcile potentially conflicting state citizenship laws. It was exercised by the Congress in

the first U.S. citizenship statute, passed in 1790, which authorized naturalization of any person who was free, white, resident at least two years in the United States and one year in the state of application, and of good moral character. The racial aspects of this naturalization law were not repealed until 1943. It was generally accepted also that the English *common law doctrine of *jus soli* applied to the new United States and provided for automatic citizenship by virtue of birth in U.S. territory. Justice Roger *Taney's controversial, racialized interpretation of this principle in the *Dred Scott* case, *Scott* v. *Sandford* (1857), led in part to the passage of the *Fourteenth Amendment, which clarified that "All persons born or naturalized in the United States, and subject to the jurisdiction thereof, are citizens of the United States."

The naturalization clause has not been held to be a delegation of federal power to control the admission of aliens. Indeed, through much of the nineteenth century, control of admissions to the United States was seen as a matter of state law, not federal law (e.g., *New York* v. *Miln* (1837)), upholding New York law regulating immigration). This pattern began to break down in the mid-nineteenth century as the increasing complexity of the U.S. economy and the developing power of the federal government led the Supreme Court, in the *Passenger Cases* (*Smith* v. *Turner* (1849)), to invalidate two state systems of taxes on immigrants as unconstitutional regulations of foreign commerce. By 1884, in the *Head Money Cases* (1884), the Court was sufficiently confident of the propriety of federal control of immigration under the Commerce Clause to uphold federal duties imposed on immigrants.

Although the Court saw certain kinds of immigration laws as part of Congress's power to regulate commerce with foreign nations, laws of exclusion and deportation presented deeper conceptual legal problems. Formal deportation of noncitizens, except as the historical punishments of "transportation" and "banishment" for crime (which also applied to citizens), seems not to have been a significant part of colonial or state law. The constitutional authority of the federal government to deport immigrants was fiercely debated as a result of the intense political turmoil engendered in the United States by the French Revolution and by the struggle between the Federalists and the Republicans, whose strongest advocate was Thomas Jefferson. Ostensible fears of foreign intrigue by French agents and Republican supporters led the Federalists to expand the naturalization residency period from two to fourteen years in 1798. In that same year, the so-called Alien Enemies Act and Alien Friends Act granted to the president unprecedented power to deport any alien whom he considered dangerous to the welfare of the United States. Though many were alarmed by the potentially despotic reach of these laws, the laws were not widely enforced and concerns about them passed with the election of President Jefferson in 1800.

Through most of the nineteenth century, as noted above, there was virtually no federal and little effective state regulation of immigration. Nearly 5 million European immigrants entered the United States from 1820 to 1860, some 2.5 million each decade from 1860 to 1880, over 5 million in the 1880s, and 16 million in the next quarter-century alone. Changes in the ethnic composition of immigrants, as well as economic and demographic factors, led to increasingly strident calls for federal immigration restrictions in the late nineteenth century. Anti-Catholic, anti-Irish riots occurred in many cities, and attitudes hardened against Italian, Jewish, eastern European, and other immigrant groups. Chinese immigration engendered the most severe reactions, however, as well as the most significant changes in the law. Large numbers of Chinese laborers had been sought during the 1848 California gold rush and later for various other types of menial work, in particular the construction of the Central Pacific Railroad in the late 1860s.

The first federal so-called Chinese Exclusion Law, passed in 1882, suspended the immigration of Chinese laborers for ten years. Mandatory identity certificate laws were soon passed for Chinese laborers who were in the United States or who wished to leave temporarily and return. In 1888 Congress passed a statute that prohibited the return of all Chinese laborers who had left the country, even those who had obtained the required certificates to guarantee their return. The Supreme Court upheld this law against a variety of constitutional challenges in the case of *Chae Chan Ping v. United States* (1889). Its most important legal holding, however, was that the power to exclude foreigners was described not as derived from the Constitution directly but as "an incident of *sovereignty." The implication of this idea was that this power is essentially subject to no constitutional restraint. This "plenary power doctrine," though much criticized by scholars and even by some Supreme Court justices, exists to this day. The internal limits of this doctrine were ex-

plored by the Court in the case of *Fong Yue Ting v. United States* (1893), which involved a deportation law with many apparent constitutional defects, including a requirement for a "credible white witness" to prove legal residence. The Court, however, upheld the law and stated that the power of the government to deport foreigners "rests upon the same grounds, and is as absolute and unqualified as the right to prohibit and prevent their entrance into the country." In later years, the Court mitigated somewhat the harshness of these doctrines by upholding the application of procedural *due process to deportation cases and even to admission cases that involved lawful permanent-resident aliens.

The general rule remains, however, that aliens seeking admission to the United States have virtually no Constitutional rights. Deportation cases (now formally known as "removal proceedings") must comport with due process, but, because deportation is generally considered to be a civil, nonpunitive sanction, various other constitutional protections—such as the *ex post facto clause, the Sixth Amendment right to *counsel, and the Eighth Amendment prohibition against *cruel and unusual punishment—have been held inapplicable. Also, only a minimalist interpretation of the Fourth Amendment's exclusionary rule applies in deportation proceedings.

Much of the development of immigration law, beginning in the twentieth century, is handled through statute and regulation. The current system derives from the comprehensive McCarren-Walter Act of 1952, which consolidated various laws into one statute. The law differentiated between "nonimmigrant" and "immigrant" visas and established a system of "preferences" for various family and employment visas. Essentially, close family relationships to U.S. citizens and job skills were given priority. These aspects of the law remain valid today.

The 1952 act also incorporated the "national origins quotas" of the 1920s, which had sought to maintain the ethnic and racial composition of the United States in ways that were sufficiently racist to compel President Truman to veto the 1952 act. The statute was passed over his veto, however. The watershed year for a nonracial approach to immigration quotas was 1965. Amendments to the immigration statute passed in that year finally abolished the national origins quotas, though they also significantly limited Western Hemisphere immigration, which until that time had been relatively unrestricted.

Significant changes to statutory immigration law occurred in 1986, with the passage of an amnesty law for undocumented aliens and an employer sanctions law that substantially increased the reach of federal power over the workplace. In 1996 Congress passed harsh new immigration laws that included strict restrictions on *welfare benefits for aliens, including lawful permanent residents (e.g., the Antiterrorism and Effective Death Penalty Act of 1996 and Illegal Immigration Reform and Immigrant Responsibility Act of 1996). Among many other provisions, these laws eliminated *judicial review of certain types of deportation (removal) orders, dramatically expanded many grounds of inadmissibility and deportation, retroactively expanded criminal grounds of deportation, eliminated some and limited other discretionary waivers of deportability, developed a system of mandatory detention for many classes of noncitizens, created expedited removal procedures for certain types of cases, and authorized vastly increased state and local law-enforcement involvement with immigration matters. Various amelioratory laws have been passed since 1996, including a restoration of welfare benefits for some noncitizens, an automatic citizenship law for certain minor children, and a series of targeted amnesty laws for specific groups. But the central features of the 1996 laws remain in force today, though many have been subject to judicial challenge.

The development of international *human rights law has paralleled that of immigration law since the end of World War II. Not until the Refugee Act of 1980, however, was a complete statutory system crafted for the admission of refugees and the processing of applications for political asylum in the United States. At present, a person who has been persecuted or who has a "well-founded fear of persecution" on the grounds of race, religion, nationality, political opinion, or membership in a particular social group may apply for refugee status or, if already in the United States, asylum. Recent limitations have been placed on asylum applications, including controversial provisions that apply at the border and time limits of one year for filing a claim. Conversely, however, administrative and judicial interpretations have rather liberally expanded the scope of U.S. asylum law in recent years to include cases such as persecution on account of sexual orientation or gender, female genital mutilation, and certain instances of interpersonal ("domestic") violence. Moreover, ratification of the Convention against Torture has resulted in the recent development of an important new form of relief from deportation, grounded in *international law.

[*See also* Citizenship]

• John Higham, *Strangers in the Land: Patterns of American Nativism, 1860–1925*, 1955. Oscar Handlin, *The Uprooted*, 2d ed., 1973. Select Commission on Immigration and Refugee Policy, *U.S. Immigration Policy and the National Interest Staff Report*, 1981. Ronald Takaki, *Strangers from a Different Shore: A History of Asian Americans*, 1989. Lucy Salyer, *Laws as Harsh as Tigers: Chinese Immigrants and the Shaping of Modern Immigration Law*, 1995. Gerald Neuman, *Strangers to the Constitution: Immigrants, Borders, and Fundamental Law*, 1996. Stephen H. Legomsky, *Immigration and Refugee Law and Policy*, 2d ed., 1997. Thomas Alexander Aleinikoff, David A. Martin, and Hiroshi Motomura, *Immigration and Citizenship: Process and Policy*, 4th ed., 1998. Peter H. Schuck, *Citizens, Strangers, and In-Betweens: Essays on Immigration and Citizenship*, 1998.

—Daniel Kanstroom

IMMIGRATION LAW PRACTICE. Immigration attorneys in the United States handle a wide variety of matters for citizens of other countries who seek temporary, habitual, or permanent residence in the United States. Because the U.S. immigration laws are complex, immigration attorneys must have specialized experience. Some states require their certification. Although private attorneys represent noncitizens, government attorneys represent the Immigration and Naturalization Service in administrative and judicial proceedings.

A few large law firms have immigration attorneys. However, most immigration attorneys work as sole practitioners or in small law firms specializing in immigration law. Because of the growing appreciation of the importance of immigration law and its complexity, the prestige of immigration law practitioners has risen in recent years.

The U.S. immigration laws create a variety of immigration "benefits" for noncitizens. Family-based visas are the centerpiece of the immigration laws. Attorneys may assist family members of U.S. citizens and lawful permanent residents, including but not limited to spouses and fiancés, to secure visas to immigrate to the United States.

Some immigration attorneys focus primarily on assisting noncitizens to obtain the proper documentation to work or do business in the United States. Employers often sponsor foreign workers seeking to obtain visas. Employment visas range from those for business visitors, which generally are routine, to visas for high-level corporate executives, professionals, academics, and skilled and unskilled workers, which may be quite complex.

The U.S. immigration laws permit persons fearing political and other persecution to seek asylum in the United States. In major metropolitan areas, such as Los Angeles, New York City, San Francisco, and Washington, an organized *pro bono publico* bar assists asylum seekers pursue their claims. Public interest attorneys also provide representation to asylum applicants. Because asylum applicants generally are of limited economic means, many cannot obtain representation. Some "voluntarily" return to their native country without pursuing their available legal rights.

For a variety of reasons, the U.S. government may seek to remove, or deport, a noncitizen from the country. Because of drastic changes to the immigration laws in 1996, increasing numbers of noncitizens, including some convicted of crimes many years ago, face possible removal from the country. Practitioners currently find it increasingly difficult to defend noncitizens in removal proceedings.

Lawful immigrants, known as lawful permanent residents, generally become eligible to naturalize and become citizens after five years of continuous residence in the United States. Attorneys may assist immigrants in filing the necessary naturalization petition and related paperwork.

The policies of the U.S. government toward immigrants have often been challenged through class action lawsuits, a legal device that permits many immigrants to be represented in one action. For example, class actions were filed in the 1990s challenging the U.S. government's policy of interdicting Haitian refugees on the high seas and returning them to the political violence in Haiti. Public interest organizations, such as the American Civil Liberties Union, the Mexican American Legal Defense and Education Fund, and other organizations, often bring class actions. In some instances, corporate law firms assist these organizations file class actions.

[*See also* Citizenship; Immigration; Legal Practice, Forms of]

• Bill Ong Hing, *Handling Immigration Cases,* 2 vols., 1995, and *Immigration and the Law: A Dictionary,* 1999.

—Kevin Johnson

IMPEACHMENT is the process prescribed by the *Constitution for removing the president, vice-president, and all "civil officers of the United States," including federal judges, from office. An impeachment power also exists in most state constitutions, albeit with variations both in law and practice from state to state. At the federal level, the power to impeach resides solely in the House of Representatives, and the exclusive responsibility for trying impeachments rests with the Senate. The constitutional text provides only a few other guideposts. Senators must be under oath during the trial, and conviction requires a two-thirds majority. When the president is the subject of impeachment, the chief justice of the Supreme Court presides. The most severe penalty the Senate may impose is removal from office and future disqualification from any office of "honor, trust, or profit," but impeachment does not preclude trial in other courts for crimes committed. Impeachable offenses are "treason, bribery, or other high crimes and misdemeanors."

The U.S. Supreme Court has ceded nearly all power over impeachment to the political judgment of *Congress (*Nixon* v. *United States* (1993)), and both the House and Senate, in their discretion, give substantial control to committees. The process involves several steps. A proposed impeachment action begins in the House, which refers the issue to its Judiciary committee. Acting essentially as a grand jury, the committee decides whether there is enough evidence to justify a full investigation. If the House agrees to launch an impeachment inquiry, the matter returns to committee for fact-finding and hearings. On that investigation, the committee makes the key decision whether to approve one or more articles of impeachment. Articles supported by a simple majority in the House go to the Senate for trial, where Representatives serve as prosecution "managers." Concerned in the past by lengthy trials and poor attendance by Senators, the Senate has given itself the option of sending the matter to a trial committee of twelve senators, with a final debate and vote by the full Senate. Otherwise, the full Senate conducts the trial. Removal from office is automatic upon conviction, but disqualification from future office is decided by an additional vote requiring only a simple majority.

In the nation's history, the House has voted to impeach sixteen people, including twelve judges, and the Senate has convicted seven. Impeachment has been contemplated many other times, often stalling in committee, and some officials have chosen to resign rather than face impeachment, but its rarity nevertheless highlights its seriousness as a remedy for misbehavior. Indeed, the attempted removal by impeachment of Presidents Andrew *Johnson, Richard Nixon, and Bill Clinton rank among the most momentous events in American history. Owing to its infrequent use and limited constitutional guidance, the law and norms for impeachment have developed case-by-case, with only a few fixed points of law and history.

Origin and Early Development. During the Constitutional Convention of 1787, delegates struggled to balance the power of separated branches of government and accountability to democratic authority. Concerned that the executive's limited term in office was not enough to protect against misuse of executive authority, impeachment arose as one check against, in James Madison's words, "the incapacity, negligence, or perfidy of the chief Magistrate." Impeachment was already well known to the Constitution's framers. English law stretching back to the fourteenth century provided impeachment as a tool for Parliament to remove judges and members of the King's court. In the colonial experience, impeachment was used relatively frequently, at first targeting corruption, and later increasingly aimed at other branches of government, especially royal officials. The framers adapted impeachment primarily as a check on presidential authority, over the objection that placing removal in the hands of the legislature would destroy the executive's independence.

After agreeing on the need for impeachment, the key questions for the delegates were the process and the standard. Various models were proposed. The Senate's power to try impeachments succeeded an earlier proposal giving that role to the Supreme Court, although having the Chief Justice preside over presidential impeachment trials avoided the obvious conflict of interest, with the vice-president's succession to the presidency depending on the outcome of the trial. More significant was the wording of the standard for impeachment. *Treason and bribery were unquestioned elements. A proposal to add "maladministration," a common phrase in state constitutions of the era, was criticized as too vague, at which point "other high crimes and misdemeanors" was suggested and approved. Even with the revision, the scope of the power raised concerns in the ratification debates, and numerous advocates reassured state conventions that impeachment was intended only for "great offenses" and "abuses of trust."

Early impeachments exposed the Constitution's gaps and vagueness while confirming potential concerns about the power. The first impeachment, that of Tennessee Senator William Blount in 1798, ended when the Senate declared that it "ought not to hold jurisdiction," a conclusion since taken to mean that members of Congress are not "civil officers" subject to impeachment. Then, in a key test of the political limits of impeachment, the House in 1804 presented articles of impeachment against Supreme Court Justice Samuel *Chase, immediately following the impeachment and conviction of Federalist judge John Pickering. The charges grew out of Congressional discontent with Chase's "intemperate" and "partisan" behavior while presiding over several trials and proceedings involving charges of treason and sedition, culminating in a controversial charge to a Baltimore grand jury in which Chase directly attacked Jeffersonian Republicans. Judged by modern standards, Chase's behavior certainly fell short of the ideal, but the Senate trial showed the articles of impeachment to be motivated by the same partisan excessiveness of which he was accused. The Senate fell four votes short of convicting Chase. His acquittal ended the early attempt to use impeachment as a political tool, and raised the standard for future attempts to remove federal judges.

High Crimes and Misdemeanors. The greatest controversy centers on the meaning of "high crimes and misdemeanors" as the standard for impeachment. The breadth given to its interpretation affects the independence of civil officers and the executive branch, in particular, from Congressional influence. Most scholars and politicians have been reluctant to take the view expressed by then-Congressman Gerald Ford during a drive to impeach Supreme Court Justice William O. *Douglas, when he said that an impeachable offense "is whatever a majority of the House of Representatives considers [it] to be at a given moment in history." By general consensus, many "crimes" such as jaywalking and parking violations would not justify impeachment. One unsettled issue concerns when an official's personal morality and private conduct can warrant impeachment: murder almost certainly, but lesser offenses spark disagreement. (Whether the President can or should be subject to criminal trial while in office remains unclear, but criminal convictions have been the basis of impeachment for other officials in the past.) In both theory and practice, the phrase "high crimes and misdemeanors" provides a highly flexible standard, and it is at least clear that no single category of crimes or misbehavior captures the range of possible meanings.

The minority view is that only "indictable crimes"—that is, violations of known laws committed with criminal intent—can qualify as impeachable offenses. That view has been consistently rejected in light of the meaning of "high crimes and misdemeanors" in early English and colonial impeachments and the intent of the Constitution's framers in adopting this language. Congress frequently has understood this history to mean that impeachable offenses include "political" wrongdoing that subvert the Constitution or do particular damage to the nation, and has successfully impeached individuals for behavior otherwise not indictable. For example, Congress removed Judge West Humphreys by impeachment in 1862 for advocating Tennessee's secession from the Union and accepting a judicial appointment in the Confederacy. In a less clear case, the Senate acquited Judge Halsted Ritter in 1936 of six charges alleging kickbacks and tax evasion, yet convicted him on a seventh condemning the "scandal and disrepute" he had brought onto his court, with the result of a loss of "public respect for and confidence in the Federal judiciary." How great "great offenses" must be in order to justify impeachment remains open to Congressional interpretation.

In rare cases, Congress has used censure—a resolution by one or both chambers disapproving of an impeachable official's conduct—as a less severe alternative to impeachment. The Senate passed such a resolution in 1834 to protest what it viewed as President Andrew Jackson's usurpation of power in opposing the National Bank. Since censure is not mentioned in the constitution, its legitimacy is uncertain, but lawmakers have considered it when it has been either legally or politically difficult to conclude that an official has committed "high crimes or misdemeanors."

Presidential Impeachments. The problems of definition strike most forcefully in the charged political context of presidential impeachment, justifying the concerns of some framers that impeachment would be used to pursue partisan ends. President Johnson's impeachment in 1868 was a partisan clash of the executive and legislative branches, growing directly out of the intense climate of post–Civil War reconstruction. Adopting President *Lincoln's generally conciliatory approach to the Southern states, Johnson ran into severe opposition from the strong Republican majority in Congress, made worse by Johnson's expansive interpretation of presidential powers. The principal charge lodged against Johnson was his removal of Secretary of War Edwin Stanton in violation of the Republican's Tenure of Office Act, which forbade removal without Senate consent. Following Johnson's impeachment by a partisan House, the Senate trial presented a fundamental argument between the branches regarding the limits of political power, with Congress attempting to

define Johnson's challenge to the Act as a "high crime." Many historians now sharply question the merits of the impeachment, as the Act was, in principle, declared unconstitutional in 1926. Further, accounts of the trial emphasize the clearly injudicious approach of Congress, with many Senators standing ready to convict before the trial began. By just one vote, the Senate fell short of the two-thirds majority needed. In the wake of the attempt, Congress enjoyed a sustained period of relative influence, although opinions vary whether Johnson's failures, other political forces, or merely the ebb and flow of power between the branches explains the succeeding decades of weakened presidencies.

The most enduring legacy of Johnson's impeachment was Congressional reluctance to use its power against the executive until until it felt justified by the clear case of President Nixon. The break-in at Democratic National Committee headquarters by political operatives associated with Nixon's 1972 reelection campaign, and the subsequent attempt to cover it up from Congressional investigation, displays all the attributes that converge at the core meaning of "high crimes and misdemeanors": serious indictable offenses, political in nature, assisted by the powers of the executive office. As more evidence came to light, a number of legislators from the president's party came to support the impeachment drive. In August 1974, the House Judiciary committee approved three detailed articles of impeachment to be sent to the House. Faced with almost certain impeachment and conviction, Nixon chose to become the first President to resign from office.

Compared with the Johnson and Nixon crises, the merits and lessons of President Clinton's impeachment in 1998 are much less clear. Clinton had been dogged by a lawsuit alleging sexual harassment and an *independent counsel investigation into other matters when his sexual relationship with a White House intern came to light. Driving his impeachment were, first, his misleading statements and false denials of the relationship made variously to the public, to friends and colleagues, and under oath in legal proceedings, and second, his possible attempts to lead the intern and key witnesses into giving false testimony about the affair. Unlike Nixon's case, the House impeachment proceedings and the Senate trial ending in his acquittal were marked by sharp partisan disagreements over the characterization of the president's behavior and the appropriate standard for impeachment. Critics of Clinton argued that perjury and obstruction of justice are indictable offenses that erode the trust placed in a public officer. Clinton's "private" conduct did not present a clear misuse of executive powers, his defenders answered. With almost exclusive attention to factual questions and the meaning of "high crimes and misdemeanors," Congressional debate did not reach the fundamental issues of executive power and democratic accountability. As with many cases in the nation's history, where Congress has not been able to overcome partisan conflict during the process, impeachment and conviction have been difficult to obtain.

[*See also* Executive Power; Legislative Power; Separation of Powers]

• Raoul Berger, *Impeachment: The Constitutional Problems,* 1973. Peter Hoffer and N. E. Hull, *Impeachment in America 1635–1805,* 1984. William Rehnquist, *Grand Inquests: The Historic Impeachments of Justice Samuel Chase and President Andrew Johnson,* 1992. Michael Gerhardt, *The Federal Impeachment Process: A Constitutional and Historical Analysis,* 1996. Richard Posner, *An Affair of State: The Investigation, Impeachment and Trial of President Clinton,* 1999. Emily Field van Tassel and Paul Finkelman, *Impeachable Offenses: A Documentary History from 1787 to the Present,* 1999.

—Patrick Schmidt

IMPRISONMENT. *See* Criminal Punishments; Prisoners' Rights; Prisons and Jails.

IN ABSENTIA, TRIAL. *See* Fair Trial, Criminal.

INCOME TAX. *See* Taxation: Income Tax.

INCORPORATION DOCTRINE. "Incorporation" is a constitutional law doctrine under which several provisions in the first eight amendments to the federal *Bill of Rights are implicitly included among the limits imposed upon state power by the Fourteenth Amendment. The terminology derives from the use of the phrase "incorporated by reference" to indicate that the contents of an earlier document are to be understood as though they had been rewritten in, and made part of, a later document.

The federal Bill of Rights, usually defined as the first nine (sometimes first eight or ten) amendments to the *Constitution, originally limited only the powers of the federal *government, not those of the states. That understanding was confirmed in 1833 when the Supreme Court ruled in *Barron* v. *Baltimore* that the *Takings Clause of the Fifth Amendment did not limit state power. However, at that time, the distinction between rights under federal or state law was generally of little import; most of the provisions of the federal Bill were understood to be equivalent to *common-law rights under state law. In fact, declarations of rights included in a number of the state constitutions adopted between 1776 and 1780 had provided the model for the federal Bill of Rights.

After the *Civil War, however, when Southern state governments threatened the liberties of former slaves, the Fourteenth Amendment was adopted to place limits on state power. At least some of that amendment's proponents intended its protection of citizens' *"privileges or immunities" to include the rights identified in the federal bill of rights; however, that understanding was blunted when the Supreme Court construed that clause very narrowly in 1873 in *The Slaughterhouse Cases.*

However, the Court subsequently began to read the Fourteenth Amendment's guarantee of *"due process" as a broad protection of individual rights. In that context, the Court recognized that the substance of some rights in the federal Bill were so "fundamental" to liberty as to be implicit in the "due process" required for state proceedings. Specifically, in *Chicago, Burlington and Quincy Railroad* v. *Chicago* (1897), the Court treated the protection of the Takings Clause of the Fifth Amendment as being required for "due process" regarding state government action—though it did not use the term "incorporation." Thereafter, the Court treated freedom of *speech, freedom of the press, freedom of *assembly and freedom of *religion—all addressed in the First Amendment—as being sufficiently fundamental to be part of the "due process" limits placed on state government power. Nevertheless, the Court consistently refused to treat the specific criminal justice provisions in the federal Bill as being necessary for "due process" in state proceedings.

In the 1930s, however, the Supreme Court began to recognize that the Fourteenth Amendment Due Process Clause set some minimal requirements for fair state criminal proceedings. It ruled in 1932 in the *Scottsboro case (*Powell* v. *Alabama*) that assistance of counsel might be so fundamental to a *fair trial, at least in a capital case, as to be required by due process. It also ruled in 1936 that brutally coerced confessions violated the Fourteenth Amendment's due process requirement (*Brown* v. *Mississippi*). Even so, the Court continued to refuse fully to apply to the states any of the criminal justice protections set out in the federal Bill. In 1937, it declined to apply the Fifth Amendment ban against *double jeopardy to state prosecutions, opining, in Justice *Cardozo's words, that Fourteenth Amendment due process protection extended only to rights that were so fundamental as to be "implicit in the concept of ordered liberty" (*Palko* v. *Connecticut*). The Court used the same rationale in 1947 when reiterating its refusal to apply the Fifth Amendment protection against compelled *self-incrimination (*Adamson* v. *California*).

Dissenting in *Adamson,* Justice Hugo *Black strongly advocated "total incorporation" of the first eight federal amendments into the Fourteenth Amendment, arguing that straightforward incorporation of those provisions would provide a more objective way to determine which constitutional protections applied to state criminal proceedings than the "fundamental" rights approach did. Although the Court never adopted Black's total incorporation theory, majorities of justices during the *Warren Court era "selectively" incorporated almost all of the federal criminal *procedure protections, starting in 1961 with the Fourth Amendment's *search and seizure protection (*Mapp* v. *Ohio*), followed shortly with the Sixth Amendment's right to counsel (*Gideon* v. *Wainwright* (1963)) and the Fifth Amendment's self-incrimination clause (*Malloy* v. *Hogan* (1964)). By the end of the 1960s, the justices had incorporated most of the federal criminal justice protections, including the right to a jury trial (*Duncan* v. *Louisiana* (1968)) and the right against double jeopardy (*Benton* v. *Maryland* (1969), which overruled *Palko*). The Court has also incorporated the Eighth Amendment ban against *"cruel and unusual punishments" (*Robinson* v. *California* (1962)) and has assumed the incorporation of that amendment's prohibition against excessive *bail (*Schilb* v. *Kuebel* (1971)). Thus, the selective incorporation theory provided the doctrinal basis for requiring state criminal proceedings to meet minimum federal constitutional standards. Although the incorporation of these federal protections regarding criminal justice was controversial as late as the Reagan administration, it now appears to be settled under stare decisis.

However, the Court has stopped short of incorporating all of the criminal justice provisions. It has never incorporated the Fifth Amendment grand jury indictment requirement—perhaps because contemporary prosecutor-dominated grand juries no longer appear to be a significant protection. Likewise, it has not addressed incorporation of the Eighth amendment's Excessive Fines Clause.

To date, the Court has not applied the incorporation doctrine beyond First Amendment rights and criminal justice protections. The Court has not incorporated the Second Amendment regarding the bearing of *arms (*Presser* v. *Illinois* (1886)),

the Third Amendment ban against quartering troops in houses (but see *Engblom* v. *Carey* (1982)), or the Seventh Amendment guarantee of jury trial in civil cases (*Walker* v. *Sauvinet* (1875)). The Court also declined to incorporate the broad protection afforded unenumerated rights in the federal Ninth Amendment when it struck down a state law prohibiting purchase of contraceptives as a violation of Fourteenth Amendment due process in 1962 in *Griswold* v. *Connecticut*—although some opinions in that case referred to the Ninth Amendment when discussing the right of *privacy. Likewise, the Court did not incorporate the Ninth Amendment when it ruled in *Roe* v. *Wade* in 1973 that the Fourteenth Amendment protected a right to an abortion; instead, the Court reverted to the earlier "fundamental" liberty approach to "due process." The Tenth Amendment presents a special case; because it reserves power to the states, it cannot be read to limit state power, so incorporation cannot apply to it.

[*See also* Criminal Law Principles; Fourteenth Amendment; *Mapp* v. *Ohio* (1961)]

• Charles Fairman, "Does the Fourteenth Amendment Incorporate the Bill of Rights? The Original Understanding," *Stanford Law Review 2* (1949): 5–139. Jerold H. Israel, "Selective Incorporation Revisited," *Georgetown Law Journal* 71 (1982): 253–338. Michael Kent Curtis, *No State Shall Abridge: the Fourteenth Amendment and the Bill of Rights,* 1986. Donald Dripps, "Akil Amar on Criminal Procedure and Constitutional Law: 'Here I Go Down That Wrong Road Again,'" *North Carolina Law Review* 74 (1996): 1559–1639. Ronald D. Rotunda and John E. Nowak II, *Treatise on Constitutional Law: Substance and Procedure* (sections 15.5–15.7), 3d ed., 1999. Wayne R. LaFave, Jerold H. Israel, and Nancy King, *Criminal Procedure*, chapter 2, 3d ed., 2000.   —Thomas Y. Davies

INCORPORATION LAWS. *See* Corporation.

INDEPENDENT COUNSEL. A legal brainchild of the post-Watergate era, the independent counsel was perhaps the most controversial feature of the Ethics in Government Act passed by Congress in 1978. Prior to Watergate, the responsibility for investigating executive-branch malfeasance fell to the *Justice Department, the *FBI, or occasionally to outside lawyers with temporary appointments (usually called *special prosecutors*) who were accountable to the Justice Department. Frustrated with actions taken by Watergate Special Prosecutor Archibald Cox, President Nixon ordered Justice Department officials to fire Cox in the now infamous "Saturday Night Massacre" on 20 October 1973. The president's well-publicized and controversial termination of the special prosecutor outraged the public and helped fuel the drive for extended *impeachment hearings. Stung by the entire Watergate episode, Congress sought to ensure greater public confidence in unbiased law enforcement by securing greater legal and political protections for outside counsels appointed to investigate allegations of misconduct by high-level federal officials. The Ethics in Government Act thus authorized a special division of federal judges—acting upon the official request of the *attorney general of the United States—to appoint an "independent counsel" charged with investigating (and where appropriate, prosecuting) allegations against certain officials designated under the Act. Unlike special counsels or prosecutors appointed in the past, duly appointed independent counsels enjoyed at least some protection from political reprisals: they could be removed by the attorney general only in those instances where "good cause" could be demonstrated. Detractors of the new office viewed this removal restriction as unwise, and potentially hostile to the system of checks and balances prescribed by the Constitution. But the U.S. Supreme Court cast aside this constitutional objection in *Morrison* v. *Olson* (1988), where it held that such a removal limitation did not impermissibly limit executive authority under Article II.

After passage of the 1978 Act, Congress reauthorized the independent-counsel law in 1983, 1988, and 1994. (Although Congress allowed the legislation to lapse in 1992, it reauthorized the legislation two years later.) In all, twenty independent counsels have been appointed under the act. Most of those officials whose actions have been scrutinized by independent counsels were never indicted: of the eighteen independent-counsel investigations whose details have been publicly disclosed, only seven resulted in criminal prosecutions of any kind. Still, multiple indictments were handed down in the two most notable investigations to date: (1) Lawrence Walsh's investigation of the Iran—Contra Affair from 1986–92; and (2) Kenneth Starr's combined investigation of the "Whitewater Affair" and President Clinton's alleged coverup of his relationship with White-House intern Monica Lewinsky.

Although the constitutionality of the independent-counsel provisions was eventually upheld, doubts about its value and practicality persist. Critics charge that because independent counsels enjoy more independence from the attorney general than other federal prosecutors, the new office's powers can be more easily abused.

The investigations conducted by Walsh and Starr, respectively, cost taxpayers tens of millions of dollars; in each case the attorney general was in no political position to rein in those costs, or even to demand some public accountability for the many expenses incurred. Public frustrations with the independent-counsel law reached a climax in 1998 when Kenneth Starr forwarded his lengthy report on the Clinton-Lewinsky affair to Congress. The report, made widely available to the public, featured enough lascivious details to raise questions for many about the manner in which Starr was conducting his investigation. Even some of President Clinton's harshest critics lamented that Starr's investigation had grown into a public-relations fiasco for all concerned.

Thus, with enthusiasm for the law waning, Congress allowed the independent-counsel provisions of the Ethics in Government Act to lapse in June 1999. Its refusal to act affirmatively to save the beleaguered legislation brought an end (at least for the time being) to all future independent-counsel investigations.

[*See also* Executive Power]

• Terry Eastland, *Ethics, Politics and the Independent Counsel: Executive Power, Executive Vice, 1789–1989,* 1989. Katy J. Harriger, *The Special Prosecutor in American Politics,* 2d ed., 2000.   —David A. Yalof

INDIANS, AMERICAN. *See* Native Americans and the Law.

INDIGENOUS PEOPLE'S RIGHTS, INTERNATIONAL LAW OF. Three sets of law govern United States indigenous groups: tribal law, federal Indian law, and *international law, which has thus far not played a major role. As indigenous peoples become increasingly disenchanted with federal Indian law, international law has the potential to become more important.

Both the United Nations and the Organization of American States have been active in this area. Within the United Nations, two major groups have taken the lead—the International Labor Organization (ILO) and the Working Group on Indigenous Populations (WGIP).

In 1959, the ILO became the first U.N. body to devote substantial attention to the status of indigenous groups with its Convention (No. 107) Concerning the Protection and Integration of Indigenous and Other Tribal and Semi-Tribal Populations in Independent Countries. This Convention focused on the now outdated idea of assimilating indigenous groups into the general populace. In 1989, the ILO adopted Convention

(No. 169) Concerning Indigenous and Tribal Peoples in Independent Countries, which is more reflective of the demands of indigenous groups, as it recognizes their distinctness and charges governments with protecting that separateness, while at the same time ensuring nondiscrimination. The United States has not ratified either convention. The current focus of indigenous groups is with the WGIP and the creation of a Permanent Forum on Indigenous Issues. The WGIP was created in 1982, and its parent body is the Sub-Commission on Prevention of Discrimination and Protection of Minorities, which reports to the Commission on Human Rights, a subsidiary of the Economic and Social Council (ECOSOC). The WGIP consists of independent experts and members of the subcommission and generally meets once a year. At these sessions, the WGIP hears from representatives of various countries, nongovernmental organizations, and indigenous groups, who advise on the WGIP's primary task, the Draft Declaration on the Rights of Indigenous Peoples. In 1994 the WGIP completed its work and transmitted the document to the subcommission, which accepted it with no changes and passed it along to the Commission on Human Rights.

The Draft Declaration is comprehensive, protecting, for example, rights to cultural and political identity and to lands and resources traditionally owned or occupied. The Draft Declaration is controversial, primarily with respect to the definition of "self-determination." This controversy is symbolized by the debate regarding the terminology used in referring to indigenous groups—indigenous "peoples" or indigenous "people."

The term used potentially carries great consequences, as the U.N. Charter calls for the self-determination of all peoples. Should indigenous groups have the same rights as a country? This possibility is obviously anathema to most countries. "Self-determination," however, can mean a variety of things. At one end of the spectrum is the ability to make rules for the group's own members, like any voluntary organization; at the other, the ability to secede and form an independent country—somewhere in the middle lies the ability to govern a specified territory, something akin to the states within the United States.

Many countries are attempting to avoid this debate by not defining indigenous groups as peoples, thus not triggering the right to self-determination. Indigenous groups, however, believe that achieving some form of self-determination is essential to their continued existence. The Draft Declaration itself is deliberately vague. Article 3 declares that "[i]ndigenous peoples have the right of self-determination," but does not define the contours of that right. Article 31 calls for indigenous peoples to have autonomy in internal affairs. It is unclear, however, whether Article 31 is a limitation on Article 3 or simply an articulation of one aspect of self-determination. Several more years' deliberation will be necessary before the status and language of the Draft Declaration is resolved.

The future of the WGIP is in doubt now that ECOSOC has passed Resolution 2000/22, creating the sixteen-member Permanent Forum on Indigenous Issues. Eight members will be nominated by governments and elected by ECOSOC, with the other eight members appointed by the President of ECOSOC after consultation with indigenous groups. The Permanent Forum serves as an advisory body to ECOSOC regarding indigenous issues, and as such will formally integrate indigenous groups into the U.N. structure.

The Organization of American States also addresses the rights of indigenous groups. In 2001, the Permanent Council convened a special meeting to allow its working group to continue examining the Proposed American Declaration on the Rights of Indigenous Peoples. This document attempts to resolve disagreements concerning self-determination by focusing on internal sovereignty. In the preamble, the document explicitly states that indigenous groups "are entitled to be part of the national identities of the countries of the Americas." At the same time, the document recognizes the distinctness of indigenous groups, protects both individual and collective rights, and prohibits forced assimilation.

[See also Native Americans and the Law: Native American Law and Tribal Sovereignty]

• S. James Anaya, *Indigenous Peoples in International Law*, 1996. Siegfried Wiessner, "Rights and Status of Indigenous Peoples: A Global Comparative and International Legal Analysis," *Harvard Human Rights Journal* (1999): 57–128. Maivân Clech Lâm, *At the Edge of the State: Indigenous Peoples and Self-Determination*, 2000.

—Melissa L. Tatum

INDUSTRIAL HOMEWORK. *See* Labor Law: Workplace Issues.

INFORMATION. *See* Technology and Law.

INFORMATION, RIGHT TO. *See* Sunshine Laws.

INFORMED CONSENT. *See* Health Law; Medicine and Law.

INITIATIVE. In a modern representative democracy, most laws are enacted by *legislatures—the representatives of the people—rather than by the people themselves. The initiative is an alternative process through which citizens themselves propose and vote on new laws directly. In states that allow use of this process, proponents, after drafting a proposal, generally must collect signatures in order to place their measure on the ballot.

The *initiative* should be distinguished from two other direct democracy devices—the **referendum* and the *recall*. In contrast to the initiative, which allows citizens to pass new laws, the referendum gives citizens a direct way to challenge laws newly passed by the legislature. By collecting the required number of signatures, citizens force a vote by the people on the statute. (The term *referendum* can be used in many ways and does not always refer to this particular procedure.) The recall allows citizens to remove elected officials before the end of their terms. After sufficient signatures are collected, the citizenry is asked to vote as to whether the officeholder shall be retained in office or recalled.

First used in Switzerland in the 1840s, the initiative burst onto the American scene in the 1890s when the Populist Party advocated it along with the referendum and the recall as a way to restore faith in democracy—a faith shaken in the minds of many by the extent to which special interests and political bosses controlled state legislatures. Carried forward by Progressives in the early 1900s, the initiative quickly attracted great support, particularly in the West. By 1918, eighteen states, mostly western, had adopted the initiative procedure. In 2000, twenty-four states and the District of Columbia made use of the procedure. States that use the initiative process at the statewide level generally authorize its use at the local level as well. Local use is permitted in some other states.

The initiative process varies considerably by state. Fifteen states allow citizens to propose either **constitutional amendments or statutes through the initiative. Six states and the District of Columbia limit proposals to statutes, while three states limit proposals to constitutional amendments. Five states require that all proposals be considered by the state legislature before any vote by the people ("indirect initiative"). Fourteen states and the District of Columbia, on the other hand, completely bypass the state legislature ("direct initiative"), and five other states use some kind of mixed system. In states using the indirect initiative, the legislature adopts the proposal in about 10 percent of the cases, so that it never goes on the ballot.

Signature requirements also vary greatly by state. Six jurisdictions using the direct initiative for statutes, for example, require signatures equal to 5 percent of the number of votes cast in the last gubernatorial race, while two require 10 percent. Of the sixteen states using the direct initiative for constitutional amendments, one requires signatures equaling 5 percent of the votes cast in the last gubernatorial race, while two require 15 percent. Signature requirements for the indirect initiative vary even more.

More than two thousand initiatives have appeared on statewide ballots in the United States since South Dakota first adopted the initiative in 1898. Over half have been in just six states—Arizona, California, Colorado, North Dakota, Oregon, and Washington. Each of these states has had over one hundred initiatives on statewide ballots. In some the initiative has become such an important institution that it has been called a fourth branch of government. Other states, such as Illinois, make little use of the procedure. Historically voters approve about 40 percent of the initiatives appearing on the ballot.

Initiatives have often played an important role in introducing new, leading-edge issues and in crystallizing state and national political agendas. Oregon initiative voters were in 1908 the first to institute presidential primaries and to demand the popular election of U.S. senators, and California's Proposition 13 launched a national tax revolt in the 1970s. The 1990s brought votes on term limits, the **right to die, and medical use of marijuana. Prominent issues in 2000 included school vouchers, campaign finance, and alternatives to imprisonment for drug offenders.

Initiative proponents not only generally have a free hand in drafting their proposals but are able also to avoid many of the pressures to compromise that legislative proposals face. As a consequence, initiative proposals tend to challenge the status quo much more than legislative measures on the same subject. Some find this potential for change a major advantage. Others see it as too confrontational, a dangerous bypass around the consensus-building process necessary for a working democracy.

Because initiatives often deal with important issues in controversial ways, they have frequently been challenged in the courts. By far the most basic challenge has been the claim that the initiative process itself violates the U.S. **Constitution's guarantee to every state "of a republican form of government." (Article IV, § 4.) Faced with this issue in 1912, the **Supreme Court, in *Pacific States Tel. & Tel. Co. v. Oregon* ruled that the question was "po litical" and that the Constitution allocated its resolution to the *Congress rather than the courts.

Initiative measures are also frequently challenged on the ground that they fail to conform to state rules concerning the initiative process. Many states, for example, limit initiatives to a single subject, require a proper title, or refuse to allow initiatives dealing with budget matters. Although the Supreme Court has never ruled on whether the U.S. Constitution (Article V) permits substitution of an initiative for the action of the state legislature in ratifying amendments to the Constitution or proposing a constitutional convention, a number of state courts have held that this can only be done by the legislature itself.

Because initiatives often push the boundaries of existing constitutional law, opponents frequently challenge their substantive provisions. Finding violations of equal protection of the laws, due process, or other constitutional provisions, the courts have overturned many measures. There are also some constitutional rules concerning the initiative process itself. The Supreme Court, for example, has ruled that states may neither prohibit paid petition circulators nor generally restrict the amounts that can be spent in support of or in opposition to a measure during the campaign on the measure. Such restrictions would violate the free-speech rights of the proponents or others.

[See also Constitutions, United States]

• David B. Magleby, *Direct Legislation: Voting on Ballot Propositions in the United States*, 1984. Betty H. Zisk, *Money, Media and the Grass Roots: State Ballot Issues and the Electoral Process*, 1987. Thomas E. Cronin, *Direct Democracy: The Politics of Initiative, Referendum and Recall*, 1989. Philip L. Dubois and Floyd Feeney, *Lawmaking by Initiative: Issues, Options and Comparisons*, 1998. Peter Schrag, *Paradise Lost: California's Experience, America's Future*, 1998. David S. Broder, *Democracy Derailed: Initiative Campaigns and the Power of Money*, 2000. —Floyd Feeney

INJUNCTION, LABOR. *See* Labor Law: Labor Relations.

INJUNCTIONS. Injunctions are either preliminary or permanent court decrees that order a defendant to act (or refrain from acting) in a particular way. Preliminary injunctions are usually granted to preserve the status quo in an emergency until the judge can determine the underlying issues. If the plaintiff later prevails on the merits, the judge may grant a permanent injunction as an equitable remedy where legal remedies are inadequate.

[See also Remedies]

—David S. Clark

INSANITY DEFENSE. *See* Criminal Law Principles: Defense Principles.

INSURANCE is generally understood as an arrangement in which an insurer, in exchange for a premium paid by or on behalf of an insured, promises to assume the insured's risk of loss. The insurer distributes the risk across a large group of similarly situated persons whose risk the insurer assumes in similar transactions. By taking advantage of the law of large numbers, the insurer can predict the frequency of loss within the group with a high degree of accuracy. This enables the insurer to set the premium at a level adequate to cover the anticipated losses and the insurer's overhead and expenses and (if the insurer is a for-profit enterprise) to earn a profit. The insured obtains economic security by substituting a predictable stream of periodic premiums for the uncertain possibility of a large, perhaps catastrophic loss. The obligations of the insured and insurer are usually articulated in a written *contract (insurance policy). Insurance as a private contract must be distinguished from "social insurance" arrangements (e.g., Social Security, Medicare). Social insurance combines elements of public welfare with revenue-collection mechanisms that mimic the payment of premiums in private insurance contracts but are essentially wealth transfers from one segment of the public to another.

Insurance law has two major divisions. One focuses on regulating entities that engage in the insurance business. This realm of insurance law is primarily a body of statutes enacted by state legislatures and administrative regulations promulgated by agencies (typically a department of insurance, headed by the insurance commissioner) that exist in every state. The other major division is a set of judicially articulated doctrines that regulate the relationship between an insurer and its policyholder. This aspect of insurance law is predominantly a specialized application of contract law, although *tort law (e.g., the law of bad faith) and agency law principles, as well as some statutes and administrative regulations, are sometimes relevant.

Categorizing Insurance. Because of its size and complexity, the insurance business can be categorized in several ways: (1) by line, which divides insurance into personal insurance (life, accidental death or dismemberment, disability, and *health insurance) and *property and casualty insurance (fire, ocean and inland marine, title, errors and omissions, various forms of *liability insurance, and various discrete forms of property coverage);

(2) by interests protected, which distinguishes first-party insurance (the policyholder insures her own interest in a person's life or property) and third-party insurance (liability insurance, which pays proceeds to a third party to whom an insured becomes liable); (3) by method of marketing, which distinguishes (*a*) between group policies, purchased by a group representative (e.g., an employer or professional association) for the benefit of members of the group, and individual policies and (*b*) among insurance entities based on the methods used to sell policies (e.g., through agents authorized to act for only one entity; through independent agents, commonly called "brokers," who represent several companies but typically with more limited authority; or through direct marketing techniques, such as Internet marketing); and (4) by insurer organization, which recognizes the myriad structures through which insurance entities operate (e.g., stock companies, mutual companies, reciprocal exchanges, Lloyd's associations, and various hospital and medical organizations).

Some insurance law principles apply consistently to different lines of insurance. For example, because insurance policies are often standardized forms drafted by the insurer and offered to the policyholder on a "take-it-or-leave-it" basis, ambiguities in the text are strictly construed against the insurer, and exclusions are construed narrowly while coverage grants are construed broadly. Similarly, a prerequisite to an insurance contract's validity is that the insured loss must be "fortuitous" in some sense, although the precise meaning of "fortuity" varies with the context.

Sometimes, however, insurance law principles have different ramifications in different lines. For example, in both life and property insurance, the owner of a policy must possess an "insurable interest" in the life or property insured as a prerequisite to the contract's validity, but what constitutes such an interest differs in the two lines because of the basic differences between property and lives. The principle of "indemnity," which holds that the benefit from an insurance contract cannot exceed the amount of the loss, is strong in property insurance but weak in life insurance, owing to the difficulties inherent in placing an economic value on an insured's life. A similar distinction is also evident with respect to "subrogation," an equitable principle (and sometimes a right afforded to the insurer by the contract) that enables one party (here, the insurer) who has paid, under some kind of legal compulsion (the contractual obligation imposed by the insurance pol-

icy), another's debt (the insured's loss for which a third party is legally obligated) to succeed to the creditor's (the insured's) claim against the third party. Subrogation, which in its application promotes indemnity, is commonly available in property and casualty insurance, where the principle of indemnity is strong, but not available in life, disability, and accidental death insurance, where the principle of indemnity is weak.

Regulation of Insurance Entities. The first insurance regulations were the restrictions placed by state legislatures in the charters granted to insurance *corporations. When the first general incorporation statutes appeared in the early nineteenth century, many states also enacted statutes governing the establishment of insurance companies. These statutes imposed requirements similar to those contained in a typical insurer's corporate charter, such as making periodic reports to state officials, avoiding certain kinds of investments, and maintaining minimum levels of capitalization and reserves. More onerous burdens were typically imposed on out-of-state insurers. By the 1860s, insurers tended to view the patchwork system of state regulation as burdensome, and the industry urged Congress to adopt national standards in which insurers would become federal institutions analogous to banks. This strategy, however, was foreclosed when the Supreme Court ruled in *Paul* v. *Virginia* (1869) that "issuing a policy of insurance is not a transaction of commerce," which effectively put the business of insurance outside Congress's regulatory authority and preserved the dominant role of the states.

By 1900 most states had adopted some kind of licensing procedure for insurers and agents, but state regulation was generally quite lax. Public concern over insurer abuses led to an investigation of the life insurance industry by a New York legislative committee. Its highly critical 1906 report prompted the enactment of remedial legislation in New York, which became a model for statutes in other states. By 1919, thirty-six states had created separate insurance departments vested with the authority to administer regulatory statutes. By 1930, insurance departments in most states were authorized to collect information from insurers, to protect insurer solvency, and to regulate reserve levels, valuation of assets, investments, policy forms, and unfair trade practices, such as rebating, misrepresentation, and discrimination. State regulation had become fairly comprehensive by 1944 in all areas except rate-making.

The Supreme Court, in *United States* v. *South-Eastern Underwriters Association* (1944), overruled *Paul* v. *Virginia* and held that insurance transactions could be subjected to federal regulation under the Commerce Clause. Ironically, by 1944 the insurance industry generally preferred state regulation to an unknown federal regulatory scheme and the possibility that federal *antitrust laws might be applied in ways detrimental to the industry. Industry lobbying and the efforts of the National Association of Insurance Commissioners led to Congress's enactment in 1945 of the McCarran-Ferguson Act. In this act, Congress declared that state regulation superseded federal law to the extent that states chose to exercise their regulatory authority over the business of insurance.

Shortly after passage of the McCarran-Ferguson Act, state insurance departments collaborated in an effort to propose state legislation to regulate the areas Congress indicated it would not enter if the states acted. By 1950, some form of rate regulation had been adopted in every state. A federal inquiry into advertising practices in the accident and health insurance industry in the mid-1950s led to the adoption of unfair trade practices legislation in all states. Public concern over automobile insurance rates in the 1960s and early 1970s prompted federal inquiries, and a majority of states adopted some form of automobile insurance reform (often "no-fault" legislation). By 2000, insurance was the largest U.S. industry (in 1999 employing 2.4 million persons and collecting $677 billion in premiums, exclusive of health insurance, accounting for 7.4 percent of gross domestic product) to have escaped significant federal regulation.

State regulatory frameworks have multiple objectives, each pursued through a variety of regulatory devices. Although each state has a unique insurance code, the National Association of Insurance Commissioners, which prepares and recommends model legislation and administrative rules, provides a unifying force for state regulation, and some general observations on regulation are possible.

To promote insurer solvency, state statutes limit the organizational structures in which the insurance business can be conducted; regulate relationships among insurers and their affiliates or holding companies; impose minimum capitalization, surplus, and reserve requirements; require disclosure of various kinds of financial information; regulate rates; control the kinds and proportions of investments insurers can make; and create guaranty associations to cover the financial obligations of insolvent insurers through assessments on all insurers. The solvency objective is also related to preventing excessive competition and monopoly pricing, both of which are sometimes cited as goals of insurance regulation.

To compensate for inadequate information in insurance markets, state statutes regulate the text and substantive content of insurance policies, require disclosures to consumers at the time of sale, and impose standards for accuracy in advertising. Much regulatory activity by state insurance departments might be explained as a government agency using its expertise to act as the consumer's proxy in the face of information neither accessible to nor understandable by the public. To correct unequal bargaining power, state statutes prohibit unfair trade and claims settlement practices. To promote market access, state statutes limit the ability of insurers to refuse to underwrite, cancel, or deny renewals of some kinds of insurance; prohibit insurers from withdrawing from the market; and create residual markets (e.g., access to coverage for high-risk persons).

Some insurance regulation is best understood as paternalism, manifested in the override of undesirable consumer choices. And some regulation is best seen as promotion of social goals not uniquely related to insurance, such as prohibiting underwriting practices that reinforce socially unacceptable or discriminatory classifications; increasing compensation for automobile accident victims by requiring vehicle owners to purchase minimum amounts of liability insurance; and promoting or endorsing (or discouraging or condemning) particular statuses or behavior by requiring (or proscribing) insurance coverage for particular losses (e.g., the costs of abortions or costs of infertility treatments for childless couples).

The Insurer–Policyholder Relationship. The relationship between insurer and policyholder is established in the insurance contract (or policy), a kind of "private law" stating the parties' reciprocal rights and duties. A typical policy contains coverage-granting provisions, exclusions, definitions, conditions and sometimes warranties (facts or circumstances the insured "warrants" to be true), and claims-processing provisions. In liability insurance, the insurer, in addition to promising to indemnify the insured against judgments or settlements of covered claims, promises to defend the insured against claims within the coverage—which means the insurer appoints an attorney to represent the insured and defend the claim made against the insured. The ability of insured parties to shift their responsibility for tort liabilities to insurance mechanisms has significant implications for the deterrence, corrective justice, and compensatory purposes of tort law. Some state statutes require those who engage in particular activities (e.g., owners of automobiles in almost all states;

those engaging in hazardous businesses, such as mining) to purchase liability insurance. The predominant rationale for such requirements is to provide a source of compensation for victims of accidents. By interpreting insurance contracts and making decisions about the relative rights and duties of insurers and policyholders, courts exert significant regulatory influence on the insurance business.

Some insurance law doctrines relevant to the relationship between insurer and policyholder exist outside the text of the contract. Examples include the requirement that the loss be accidental in some sense (the "fortuity principle"); rules that allocate proceeds among multiple parties having partial interests in insured property; rules that disqualify life insurance beneficiaries who intentionally kill the insured; and rules that provide the insurer with a defense if the policyholder fails to provide accurate information during the underwriting process or during claims processing.

Contemporary Issues. At the outset of the twenty-first century, insurance institutions and those who regulate them confront many challenging issues. The inappropriateness of race as a basis for insurance underwriting is no longer questioned, but no similar consensus exists on whether, or in what circumstances, it is appropriate for insurers to use gender, age, health status (such as HIV infection), the results of genetic tests, or zip code (a proxy for racial or ethnic classifications in some locales) for underwriting purposes. The blurring of boundaries between insurance, banking, and securities firms portends significant changes in the financial marketplace for consumers and new challenges for regulators. Increased development in coastal areas increases the likelihood of catastrophic losses from earthquakes and hurricanes, which strains the capacity of property insurers. Seemingly benign exposures that many years later are discovered to have caused massive losses and liabilities (e.g., exposure to asbestos, toxic substances, and pollutants) greatly stress the reserves of insurers and cause expensive litigation. Longstanding problems of health care cost, access, and quality directly implicate health insurance, and vice versa, and these issues are destined to persist for many years to come.

[See also Commerical Law]

• Edwin W. Patterson, *Essentials of Insurance Law: An Outline of Legal Doctrines in Their Relations to Insurance Practices*, 1957. Spencer L. Kimball and Herbert S. Denenberg, eds., *Insurance, Government, and Social Policy: Studies in Insurance Regulation*, 1969. John G. Day, *Economic Regulation of Insurance in the United States*, 1970. Kenneth S. Abraham, *Distributing Risk: Insurance, Legal Theory, and Public Policy*, 1986. Robert E. Keeton and Alan I. Widiss, *Insurance Law: A Guide to Fundamental Principles, Legal Doctrines, and Commercial Practices*, 1988. Robert H. Jerry II, *Understanding Insurance Law*, 2d ed., 1996. American Council of Life Insurers, *Life Insurers Fact Book 2000*, 2000. Roger C. Henderson and Robert H. Jerry II, *Insurance Law: Cases and Materials*, 3d ed., 2001. Insurance Information Institute, *The Fact Book 2001*, 2001.   —Robert H. Jerry II

INSURANCE, HEALTH. *See* Aging and the Law; Health Law; Medicine and Law.

INSURANCE, UNEMPLOYMENT. *See* Labor Law: Workplace Issues.

INTERNATIONAL CUSTOM. *See* Common Law.

INTERNATIONAL LAW consists of rules, norms, and principles that apply to nations in their dealings with one another. But it should not be thought of as rules imposed on the approximately 190 nations in the world today; rather the rules were generated by the nations (and their predecessors) themselves over the past 5,000 years.

One of the earliest of these rules was the immunity of ambassadors and envoys. The rule gives state A assurance that when it sends its ambassador into state B, the ambassador will not be personally harassed or injured. But state A must pay a price for this confidence: it must itself refrain from injuring or harassing B's ambassador. Behind every rule of international law is a similar cost-benefit component. The idea of cost-benefit in turn suggests two even more fundamental principles of international law—the principle of equality and the principle of reciprocity. Under the principle of equality, state A has the same rights and obligations under international law as state B. Thus, A may be an island state of one square mile and B may be a superpower; they have equal rights, duties, and obligations under international law. Under the principle of reciprocity, state A is put on notice that if it harms B's ambassador, state B may retaliate by harming, or at least arresting and holding hostage, A's own ambassador.

Rules of international law have arisen because states have perceived their national interest to be served by a set of rules, norms, and principles that are grounded in equality and reciprocity. Even though the international legal system has no legislature, no chief executive, and no court of universal jurisdiction, its rules are obeyed as much as, if not more than, the rules of law within any given state. International law is not more frequently violated than, for example, ordinary criminal law. Moreover, as the rules of international law increase in coverage and density over time, the overarching principle of reciprocity ensures that the rules will be treated as a package. Thus, if state A violates a particular rule of international law because it has decided that its self-interest requires the violation, state A may find that other states will retaliate by violating other rules that state A wants to preserve. In 1979, when Iran resorted to the historically unprecedented action of arresting fifty United States diplomats and consular officers, the United States retaliated by invading Iran's bank accounts and freezing $13 billion of Iranian assets. This invasion of a state's property was clearly a transgression of international law on its face, but it was justified as a "countermeasure" to force Iran to release the prisoners. Iran had no rational economic choice but to cave in. It returned the prisoners unharmed to the United States, and the United States unfroze the assets. The selection by a victimized state of a different rule of international law for its countermeasure is a variation of game theory's tit-for-tat strategy, which might be called "tit-for-a-different-tat." It is a fundamental principle that operates to reinforce the authority of the entire package of international rules.

In early times, when the rules of international law were few, resort to war was a more likely form of retaliation than it is today. As the rules of international law grew more dense with the passage of time, as more nations appeared on the scene, and as communication among states and people became easier, many more possibilities for tit-for-a-different-tat countermeasures have arisen. A victimized state today can select a countermeasure that is proportionate to the initial violation. A significant result is the lessening of the tendency of tit-for-tat retaliation to escalate. There is less need to resort to the ultimate countermeasure—war itself.

Sources. If a controversy arises between two states, where do we find the applicable rules? First we see if the states have entered into a *treaty that governs the dispute. If so, the treaty rules prevail in all cases except where the treaty itself may be illegal (for example, treaties concerning the transport of human slaves); illegal treaties are banned by the customary international law of *jus cogens*. If the treaty is ambiguous, the parties look to the customary international law of treaty interpretation, codified in the Vienna Convention on the Law of Treaties (1969).

If the controversy is not covered by a treaty, then the parties look to customary international law. This pervasive body of law, which may be viewed as the default rules of international law, is similar to common law, except that it developed through the practice of states and not primarily through judicial decisions. As states engaged in practices over a period of time, those practices became regarded as constituting norms, deviation from which was deemed unjustified or illegal. These norms were almost invariably in the long-term interests of the majority of states, or they would not have evolved and persisted.

After treaties and *custom, rules of international law may be found in various subsidiary sources. "General principles of law," reflecting the laws of most states, have been used as sources of procedural rules for international courts and tribunals. The decisions of national courts on questions of international law are not, strictly speaking, determinations of international law itself, but rather constitute authoritative expressions of the practice of the state in which the court sits. This practice, in turn, contributes to the formation of customary international law. *"Equity" has sometimes been championed as a source of international law, but the decision of the International Court of Justice in the *Continental Shelf Cases* put an end to that contention. A still-surviving subsidiary source of international law is the writing of international law scholars. It is felt that a person who devotes his life to the study of international law has achieved a measure of respect for the principles of reciprocity and equality that give some degree of authoritative weight to his conclusions about the content of various rules and norms.

Domain. The domain of present-day international law is vast. It includes:

The Oceans. Seventy-one percent of the earth's surface is *water*. International rules, codified in the United Nations Convention on the Law of the Sea (1994), prescribe the breadth of the territorial sea (12 miles) and the extent of the exclusive economic zone (200 miles), the determination of the continental shelf, fisheries and conservation regimes, preservation of endangered acquatic species, mineral exploitation of the seabed, identification of vessels, freedom of navigation and commerce, and many other areas.

Polar Regions. The Arctic Circle is a water mass, subject to oceanic rules. Antarctica is a continent divided into sectors in which some nations have established predominant claims, subject to general principles of international law respecting environmental management and mining activities.

Airspace. The subjacent state has sovereignty over its airspace, but extensive treaty regimes have carved out principles of identification, duress, over-flight, and liability for accidents.

Outer Space. Once considered open territory, all

space above the airspace and all extraterrestrial objects are now regarded as the "common heritage of mankind." The United States, for instance, does not own the Moon, even though it was the first to land a spaceship there.

Artificial Satellites. Increasingly, the stratosphere is being populated with artificial communications and reconnaissance satellites. International law has developed rapidly in this area. The satellites belong to the nations that send them up; other nations have no right to shoot them down. If they fall to earth, the nation owning them has strict liability to pay for all damages.

Global Environment. If state A builds a factory near its border with state B, and the factory emits pollutants that drift over state B, A is liable for damages. Any nation that degrades the global environment (for example, by spillage from an oil tanker) is responsible under international *environmental law to clean up the damage. Still controversial is the developing international law of state responsibility for preserving the environment in light of the desire of many nations for rapid economic growth. States so far have only been able to agree on a principle of "sustainable development," a nice-sounding but elusive concept.

Global Market. The transboundary movement of goods, services, and investment is governed by "private international law"—a complex interacting series of contractual arrangements. Yet the line between private and public international law is fuzzy; when there is a resort to default rules, they are the rules of public international law. For example, when governments engage in business transactions, are they shielded by sovereign immunity? Increasingly, the answer of public international law is "no." What about concession agreements—contracts between a government and a foreign corporation? The concession agreements themselves typically spell out their *conflict-of-law rules, but if the rules are ambiguous or incomplete, then public international law steps in. Recently, *antitrust rules have become a subject of international legal regulation. A state may want to regulate anticompetitive activities of subsidiary corporations abroad, yet this intrusive "legislative reach" is bounded by an international rule of reasonableness.

Global Communication. Some nations and religious groups want to regulate the content of international information disseminated over the airwaves and through the worldwide Internet. Content restrictions include advocacy of war or revolution, criticism of government officials or policies, regulation of advertising claims, and suppression of real or fictional depictions of pornog-raphy. International law in this area is developing rapidly. Its tendency is in the direction of freedom of information, with some clear exceptions such as child pornography.

International Crimes. The basic rules of international criminal law were developed in the great codification conventions of The Hague in 1899 and 1907 and Geneva in 1949. The Nuremberg and Far East Tribunals after World War II applied these rules to individuals. Nearly five decades later, these precedents have become salient again. The International Criminal Tribunal for Former Yugoslavia, established in The Hague, has been active in prosecuting and trying military and civilian leaders responsible for atrocities committed in Bosnia, Serbia, Croatia, and Kosovo. The public respect accorded this tribunal augurs well for the establishment of an International Criminal Court of universal jurisdiction. The jurisdiction of these special international tribunals over crimes including genocide, murder of civilians, deportation, persecution, rape, pillage, torture, and enslavement is not exclusive. National courts also can exercise jurisdiction over persons who have allegedly committed crimes against humanity or war crimes.

Terrorism and Hijacking. Both terrorism and hijacking are international crimes. But with the terrorist attacks on the World Trade Center in New York City on September 11, 2001, the United States and many of its allies have declared a "war on terrorism," a concept that expands the notion of "war" to include nonstate actors. The classic international law rules regarding belligerency and neutrality need to be revived in dealing with global terrorism. Under the old rules, a state loses its neutrality if it furnishes material support to one of the belligerents. These rules may now be applied to states that harbor terrorists, making such states a legitimate target in the war against terrorism.

Humanitarian Intervention. States may use military force for the limited purpose of preventing large-scale atrocities in other states. The American interventions in Granada (1983), in Panama (1989), and with NATO's assistance in Kosovo (1999), in varying degrees exemplify this rule. In order to be legitimate under international law, military intervention must satisfy the following minimal criteria: (1) the goal must be to prevent a significant human-rights abuse; (2) the means employed must be proportionate to this goal (in other words, the cure cannot be worse than the disease); (3) all means short of military intervention must have been tried first; (4) U.N. and multilateral support must at least be solicited; (5) it cannot be part of the goal of the intervenor to seek territorial aggrandizement for itself; (6) it cannot be part of the goal of the intervenor to seek a permanent change in the political independence of the target territory; (7) the intervenor must withdraw its forces as soon as the humanitarian goal is accomplished.

Human Rights. This is the most controversial extension of public international law. Under the classic concept, only states had standing under international law; people were invisible. But since the Holocaust of World War II, the Nuremberg trials, and Eleanor Roosevelt's superb drafting of a General Assembly resolution entitled "The Universal Declaration of Human Rights" (1948), people are demanding direct access to public international law. Prior to 1945, a state could do anything it wanted to its citizens within its own territory, including murdering them, without any international accountability. Today, genocide, torture, enslavement, and other crimes, possibly extending to persecution and deportation, are illegal under customary international law even if they occur entirely within the territorial boundaries of a state and involve the state's own nationals. The law of *human rights has a long way to go, but it is conceptually the biggest breakthrough in the 5,000-year history of international law. In effect, it is changing "international law" into "interpersonal law." One of the major sources of controversy concerns the hierarchy of human rights: are personal liberties more important than food and shelter? Are fair judicial procedures more important than the right to a job or the right to vacations with pay? Should *capital punishment be banned? What about capital punishment of *juveniles? Should *abortions be legalized throughout the world? Should women have equal legal rights as men in countries that wish to preserve their cultural and religious values that hold that women to be subservient to men? It is no wonder that law students are increasingly demanding courses in international human rights.

Group Rights. Among the claims asserted by various groups are the right to self-determination, autonomy, secession, native community practices, native language, and freedom of religious exercise. In the past, these claims were considered to be within the exclusive jurisdiction of the state containing a particular group. But today these claims are becoming internationalized as the result of multilateral conventions and the growing popular conviction that attacks on groups are a form of cultural genocide.

Nationality. The most important link between a person and a state is nationality or *citizenship. International law imposes the requirement of a "genuine link" for nationality to be effective. This concept applies particularly to the nationality of vessels, and rules out "flags of convenience" where there is no genuine link between the ship and its state of incorporation.

The State. Finally, and most fundamentally, international law defines the state itself. It sets forth the basic principle that a government that is in effective control over a defined territory, and owes allegiance to no other government, is a state. The form of government is immaterial; it can be a democracy, a dictatorship, or totalitarian. Once a state is recognized as such, it immediately obtains the benefits, and incurs the obligations, of all the rules, norms, and principles of international law in all the categories enumerated above. It is also bound by the international law of state succession. If government X of state A is overthrown by a revolutionary force, and a new government Y is installed, all the treaties and obligations entered into by the former government X remain binding because they were incurred on behalf of state A itself. Thus a revolutionary government cannot get rid of the state's previous treaties, as the Soviet Union partially attempted (but never succeeded) after the Revolution of 1917. States may no longer increase their size by aggression and conquest, as they used to centuries ago. Since the Kellogg-Briand Pact of 1928, acquisition of territory by force is illegal. Saddam Hussein learned this when he conquered Kuwait; the international community joined together in the Persian Gulf War to divest him forcibly of his conquest. But states may add to their territory by the consent of other states. An example is the purchase of Alaska from Russia in the nineteenth century.

International Law In National Courts. In some countries, such as Germany under article 25 of its Constitution, international law has the same standing in the courts as national law. In the United States, the relationship between international law and national law is more complex. Any treaty in which the United States is a party constitutes the supreme law of the land under article VI of the Constitution. Whether an individual may bring a lawsuit under a treaty depends on whether *or not* the treaty is "self-executing." A treaty that requires further legislation by Congress *for its implementation* is not self-executing.

Various statutes have expanded the international rights of American citizens in national courts. A person may sue a foreign country for expropriating his property without compensation;

a person who is tortured abroad may, with certain restrictions, bring suit in an American court. The former "sovereign immunity" of foreign countries in American courts has been restricted by the Sovereign Immunities Act of 1976, which provides a "commercial exception" to immunity. Finally, federal courts increasingly recognize international customary law as comprising part of federal *common law. But despite these advances, the United States seems to be moving slowly toward incorporating international law as part of its national law.

[See also Comparative Law; Foreign Trade and Investment Law; War Law of]

—Anthony D'Amato

INTERNET. See Computerized Research; Speech and the Press, Freedom of; Technology and Law.

INTERROGATION AND CONFESSION. "Interrogation" (or questioning) is the means by which *police officers extract a confession (admitting all elements of the crime) or an admission (admitting some elements of the crime) from a suspect, in writing or orally. The *prosecutor may present a written confession or admission to a jury at the defendant's trial, while a police officer may testify at trial that he heard the defendant make an oral confession or admission. Such *evidence is usually extremely damaging to the defendant's case, as the jury takes the defendant's own words admitting a crime very seriously.

Because of this, police officers might be tempted to use improper means to induce reluctant suspects to talk. While defense counsel is free to present evidence of those means to the jury in an effort to persuade them that the confession or admission was false, if the means are sufficiently improper, the judge will simply "exclude" the evidence (preventing the prosecutor from presenting the confession or admission to the jury), because use of such evidence would deny the defendant his right to *"due process of law."

"Coerced" Confessions. The United States Supreme Court has had a very difficult time regulating the interrogation process, because the justices have come to no clear consensus about which interrogation methods are "improper," and why. They agree that beatings and threats should not be allowed, but in recent years these primitive devices have given way to more sophisticated psychological techniques, which often involve a certain amount of deception. They cause no physical harm to the suspect, and they are often successful in extracting confessions and admissions that are later verified as true by corroborating evidence. Yet these techniques cause a suspect to "waive" his constitutional right not to incriminate himself, which some justices find disturbing.

In one of the Court's earliest cases, Brown v. Mississippi (1936), it held that a state conviction obtained by use of a coerced confession violated the *Fourteenth Amendment's due process clause. Brown's confession had been extracted by using a whip. It was easy to see the reason for excluding such a confession. A confession that is beaten out of the defendant might well be false, and its introduction into evidence would result in the conviction of an innocent man.

The cases that followed soon after Brown were similar, though not so extreme. In Ashcraft v. Tennessee (1944), the defendant was not beaten, but was interrogated for thirty-six hours straight. He might have confessed falsely, just to get some sleep. The Court reversed the conviction. Later cases held that a confession obtained by improper means must be excluded even if the confession was probably true—for example, where the confession included some details that were later verified. Here, the policy was not to prevent conviction of the innocent, but to discourage the police from beating and otherwise mistreating prisoners.

But when the police began using psychological rather than physical methods, it became more difficult for the Court to decide which methods were "improper"—and why. The Court began adopting vague terms, allowing interrogation as long as the police did not "overbear the will" of the defendant, thereby causing the resulting confession to be "involuntary" (or "coerced," or "the product of compulsion"). This decision would be based on the "totality of the circumstances." And this totality would involve what the police did (threats, promises, deprivation of food or sleep) and what the defendant was like (age, education, prior experience with police, knowledge of his right to remain silent).

In Crooker v. California (1958), for example, Crooker was arrested and subjected to three late-night interrogation sessions by several officers, who denied his request to see a lawyer. Crooker, however, was thirty-one-years old, a college graduate, and had attended one year of law school—where he had studied criminal law. As he probably knew of his right to remain silent, the Court found his confession to be "voluntary" and affirmed his murder conviction. On the other hand, in Spano v. New York (1959), the Court reversed the murder conviction of a young man who initially followed his lawyer's advice not to talk to the police, but then succumbed to eight hours of continuous questioning by several interrogators—one a police officer who had been Spano's childhood friend. Each of these cases was very "fact specific"—they turned, not on the application of "bright line" rules of law, but on the specific facts of the case.

There are several problems with this "involuntariness" test. The first is semantic. Calling a confession "involuntary," "coerced," or the product of an "overborne will" suggests that the defendant had *no choice* but to talk. But when a policeman tricks a suspect into talking (e.g., by pretending to despise the victim), does this deprive the suspect of the ability to choose not to talk? Perhaps, in one sense. Psychologically, the suspect might feel that he *should* say something in response to what the policeman said. However, this is true of *any* interrogation, and if the suspect was a sane, sober adult, he had the choice of refusing to talk. Calling the confession "coerced" or "uncoerced" does not flow naturally from the situation, but from the *policy* one wants to achieve by using these labels.

The second problem is determining just what policy the "involuntariness" test is intended to further. We do not want the police to beat or mistreat people, but why not allow them to use tricks just to get defendants to talk? Difficulties in defining "involuntary" increased in the late 1950s, when the police began to use interrogation manuals that recommended rather sophisticated psychological techniques, designed to get a reluctant defendant to start talking—but not to confess falsely.

In addition, the "totality of the circumstances" test required endless litigation (trial and appellate) to determine the validity of confessions. Since the test was so indefinite and depended on so many variables, neither the police nor trial lawyers could ever predict whether a court would find that a given interrogation met the test, so each doubtful case had to be litigated. By the mid-1960s, the Supreme Court was looking for a way out of this difficulty. It thought it found it, in *Miranda* v. *Arizona* (1966).

Miranda v. Arizona. Two new developments contributed to *Miranda.* One was the 1964 decision in *Malloy* v. *Hogan,* which applied the Fifth Amendment *self-incrimination clause ("No person . . . shall be compelled in any criminal case to be a witness against himself. . . .") to the states. However, *Malloy* did not involve police interrogation, and no previous case had held that the self-incrimination clause applied to police interrogation. Traditionally, courts had held that the use of the word "witness" in this clause meant a witness *in court,* not in the police station.

The other development was the extension of the Sixth Amendment right to counsel. In **Gideon* v. *Wainwright* (1963), the Court held that this clause applies to the states through the Fourteenth Amendment's due process clause, and therefore a state must provide an indigent felony defendant with a lawyer at trial. After *Gideon,* the Court applied the right to *counsel to any "critical stage" of a criminal case, which was deemed to include certain posttrial proceedings (such as appeals) and pretrial proceedings (such as arraignments and preliminary hearings). No case had yet held that this right applied to a pre-*court* proceeding, such as a police interrogation session. If it did apply, this might be a way of side-stepping the "totality of circumstances" dilemma: give the suspect a lawyer, and the lawyer will simply tell him not to talk.

In *Escobedo* v. *Illinois* (1964), the defendant was arrested for murder. During his interrogation, he asked to see his lawyer. The police ignored his request, and kept questioning him. Finally, Escobedo made certain admissions. Even though this interrogation occurred before any indictment or arraignment, the Court held that the police had violated Escobedo's Sixth Amendment right to counsel.

Escobedo set the stage for *Miranda,* where the defendant had neither the money to hire a lawyer nor the knowledge to ask to see a lawyer. The absence of such wealth or savvy could hardly be expected to be sufficient to cause the Court to rule differently. However, *Miranda* was not based on the Sixth Amendment, but on the Fifth. The Court summarized its holding as follows:

> The prosecution may not use statements, whether exculpatory or inculpatory, stemming from custodial interrogation of the defendant unless it demonstrates the use of procedural safeguards effective to secure the privilege against self-incrimination. By custodial interrogation, we mean questioning initiated by law enforcement officers after a person has been taken into custody or otherwise deprived of his freedom of action in any significant way. As for the procedural safeguards to be employed, unless other fully effective means are devised to inform accused persons of their right of silence and to assure a continuous opportunity to exercise it, the following measures are required.

Prior to any questioning, the person must be warned that he has a right to remain silent, that any statement he does make may be used as evidence against him, and that he has a right to the presence of an attorney, either retained or appointed.

The defendant may waive effectuation of these

rights, provided the waiver is made voluntarily, knowingly and intelligently. If, however, he indicates in any manner and at any stage of the process that he wishes to consult with an attorney before speaking there can be no questioning. Likewise, if the individual is alone and indicates in any manner that he does not wish to be interrogated, the police may not question him. The mere fact that he may have answered some questions or volunteered some statements on his own does not deprive him of the right to refrain from answering any further inquiries until he has consulted with an attorney and thereafter consents to be questioned.

Miranda seems to say that this problem had gone on long enough, and that the Court would resolve it once and for all. From now on, there would be a simple set of rules for the police to follow regarding interrogation, and these would be easy for courts to apply in assessing the admissibility of confessions. Things did not turn out quite that way. Courts have had considerable difficulty determining when warnings are required (what is "interrogation,"? what is "custody"?) and what is a "waiver"? And researchers have hotly debated whether *Miranda* in fact discourages confessions. Some contend that giving *Miranda* warnings reduces the number of confessions and convictions and enables criminals to elude justice. Others contend that the police have found ways to comply with the letter of *Miranda* while undermining its spirit (by blending the warnings into informal conversation, or by telling the suspect that the police are "not allowed to hear his side of the story" unless he first hears and waives his *Miranda* rights). Thus, the effect on confessions and convictions is minimal.

Miranda did not totally make the old "involuntariness" test unnecessary. If the police properly advise the defendant of his rights, and obtain a valid waiver, they may then proceed with the interrogation. During such interrogation, the same tricks and threats that sometimes occurred before *Miranda* might still occur, and *Miranda* does not give any guidelines for analyzing this situation. Although there is no violation of *Miranda*, there might be a violation of the old, pre-*Miranda* due process test of "coercion" looking at the "totality of the circumstances."

The due process test remains important for another reason. Suppose the police have violated *Miranda*, but the prosecution does not introduce the defendant's admissions in the prosecution's case-in-chief. If the defendant then takes the witness stand and denies that he committed the crime, the prosecutor may introduce his admissions to *impeach* defendant's testimony, even though the admissions were obtained in violation of *Miranda*, as long as the statements were "voluntary" under the pre-*Miranda* "due process" test (*Harris* v. *New York* (1971)).

[*See also* Criminal Law Practice; Criminal Law Principles]

• Joseph D. Grano, *Confessions, Truth, and the Law*, 1993. Stephen J. Schulhofer, "Reconsidering Miranda," *University of Chicago Law Review* 54 (1987): 435. Stephen J. Markman, "The Fifth Amendment and Custodial Questioning: A Response to Reconsidering Miranda," *University of Chicago Law Review* 54 (1987): 938. Schulhofer, "The Fifth Amendment at Justice: A Reply," *University of Chicago Law Review* 54 (1987): 950. Richard Leo, "Inside the Interrogation Room," *Journal of Criminal Law & Criminology* 86 (1996): 266. Richard Leo, "The Impact of Miranda Revisited," *Journal of Criminal Law & Criminology* 86 (1996): 621. Paul Cassell and Bret Hayman, "Police Interrogation in the 1990's: An Empirical Study of the Effects of Miranda," *UCLA Law Review* 43 (1996): 839. Paul Cassell, "Miranda's Social Costs: An Empirical Reassessment," *Northwestern Law Review* 90 (1996): 387. George Thomas, "Is Miranda A Real-World Failure? A Plea For More (And Better) Empirical Research," *UCLA Law Review* 43 (1996): 821, 831.   —Myron Moskovitz

INTERSTATE COMMERCE COMMISSION. *See* Regulation.

INVENTION. *See* Property: Intellectual; Technology and Law.

INVESTIGATION, STATE BUREAUS OF. State bureaus of investigation (SBIs) are typically independent agencies with statewide jurisdiction. SBIs provide assistance to the various branches of local, county, and state criminal justice (i.e., law enforcement, courts, and corrections) with direct investigative support and expertise. In addition to primary investigation, support is often provided to local and state law enforcement agencies in the form of extensive forensic crime laboratory services. Ordinarily, state bureaus of investigation do not have general law enforcement jurisdiction, and seldom does the SBI officially respond directly to citizen complaints. There are exceptions to this general rule, however. For example, Iowa law requires that the Division of Criminal Investigation provide primary enforcement of criminal activities associated with licensed liquor establishments.

Absent general law enforcement jurisdiction, requests for the investigative assistance of state bureaus of investigation must be made by officials of local, county, or state government. Requests are most common from *police chiefs, *sheriffs, and district attorneys. Governmental authorities such as the state attorney general or governor may also request assistance. In those areas of the criminal law where state bureaus of investigation have limited original and initial jurisdiction (for example, in an investigation of alleged financial fraud at a public university), SBI jurisdiction is usually concurrent with and not exclusive of local authorities.

The historical emergence of state bureaus of investigation followed closely the increasing magnitude of crime in the United States and its growing dispersion across all locales, especially rural America. Legislatures across the nation recognized that the increasing complexities of crime in their particular states after the turn of the twentieth century required greater and systematic statewide coordination of efforts. They recognized, also, that no matter how diligent the efforts of local law enforcement, few local communities had the resources needed for systematic investigations. Thus, state bureaus of investigation initially reflected the plainclothes *detective complement to the uniformed *highway patrol and state police organizations that developed between 1900 and 1935. Advancements in science enabled state bureaus of investigation to supplement on-site investigative activities with further laboratory investigations of forensic evidence (e.g., fingerprints, blood samples) and the use of statewide information systems pertinent to criminal activity (e.g., individual criminal histories, crime locations and patterns).

—Matthew Zingraff

INVOLUNTARY SERVITUDE. *See* Slavery, Law of.

J

JACKSON, HOWELL EDMUNDS (1832–1895), associate justice of the United States *Supreme Court, 1893–95. Son of a well-educated Tennessee doctor, Howell Jackson pursued an excellent classical education, followed by a law degree from Cumberland University.

Jackson opposed *secession but accepted a civilian post under the Confederacy. After serving a term in the United States Senate, President Cleveland appointed him to the Sixth Circuit Court of Appeals in 1886, and President Harrison elevated him to the United States Supreme Court in 1893.

Jackson's most prominent role on the Supreme Court was his dramatic return to Washington while gravely ill to participate in the re-hearing of the income tax (see TAXATION: INCOME TAXES) case, *Pollock* v. *Farmers' Loan & Trust Co.* (1895), and his dissent in favor of the tax's constitutionality.

[*See also* Supreme Court of the United States]

• Irving Schiffman, "Howell E. Jackson," in Leon Friedman and Fred L. Israel, eds., *The Justices of the United States Supreme Court 1789–1969*, vol. 2, 1969. Terry Calvani, "The Early Legal Career of Howell Jackson," *Vanderbilt Law Review* (1977): 41–45.

—David J. Langum

JACKSON, ROBERT HOUGHWOUT (b. Spring Creek, Pa., 13 Feb. 1892; d. Washington, D.C., 9 Oct. 1954) held various federal positions during the New Deal and served as associate justice of the United States *Supreme Court from 1941 to 1954. Preparing for the bar by a year of study at Albany Law School and a law office clerkship, Jackson was the last member of the Supreme Court to receive part of his legal education through the apprenticeship system. An active Democrat, he was named by President Franklin D. Roosevelt to a series of posts in the Treasury and Justice departments. Roosevelt appointed Jackson as *solicitor general in 1938, and two years later made him

*attorney general. Jackson published *The Struggle for Judicial Supremacy* (1941), in which he protested the tendency of a conservative Supreme Court to strike down economic legislation. That year Roosevelt named Jackson to the Supreme Court.

On the Court Jackson was supportive of governmental regulations and took an expansive view of congressional authority under the commerce clause. In *Wickard v. Filburn* (1942) he upheld federal control of agricultural production and broadly defined congressional power over commerce. Indeed, Jackson generally adhered to a philosophy of judicial self-restraint, sustaining measures to preserve public order and suppress domestic communism. In 1945–46 Jackson (on leave from the Court) served as chief counsel for the United States at the Nuremberg war crimes trials.

[*See also* Supreme Court of the United States]

• Eugene C. Gerhart, *America's Advocate: Robert H. Jackson*, 1958.

—James W. Ely Jr.

JAILS. *See* Prisons and Jails.

JAPANESE INTERNMENT. Beginning in early 1942 and lasting until the end of World War II, approximately 120,000 Americans of Japanese ancestry were excluded from their homes in the western United States and forcibly relocated to internment camps. The internment was justified on the grounds that Japanese-American citizens posed a security risk and might conduct acts of sabotage or espionage. In spite of the complete absence of proof to support these fears, and actually overlooking evidence to the contrary, all three branches of the federal government took part in the internment. Today, the internment is recognized as the product of wartime hysteria and racial antagonism directed at Japanese-Americans.

Immediately after the United States' entry into the war, President Franklin Roosevelt issued Executive Order 9066 that authorized the secretary of war to designate exclusion zones on the West Coast. Early in 1942, Congress implicitly ratified the Order by enacting legislation that made it a misdemeanor to violate any authorized exclusion order. Following these actions, the military commander in charge of the West Coast, General John DeWitt, imposed a curfew on Japanese-Americans. Later, DeWitt issued an exclusion order that led to the evacuation of West Coast Japanese-Americans to "relocation centers" in several western states. DeWitt justified the exclusion of all citizens of Japanese ancestry on the grounds that making individualized determinations of who presented a security risk was infeasible and too time consuming.

Two important legal challenges followed the issuance of DeWitt's orders. In the first, *Hirabayashi v. United States* (1943), the U.S. Supreme Court deferred to the views of the military authorities and upheld the curfew order. Chief Justice *Stone wrote for the Court that "[w]hatever views we may entertain regarding the loyalty to this country of the citizens of Japanese ancestry, we cannot reject as unfounded the judgment of the military authorities and of Congress that there were disloyal members of that population, whose number and strength could not be precisely and quickly ascertained." A year after *Hirabayashi*, the Court decided *Korematsu* v. *United States* (1944) and upheld General DeWitt's exclusion order. The Court again deferred to the military and rejected a Fifth-Amendment attack on the exclusion of Japanese-Americans.

The Japanese-American internment was the subject of intense scrutiny and criticism in the years following World War II. President Gerald Ford formally rescinded Executive Order 9066 that had authorized the exclusion orders. Congress established a Commission to investigate the internment, and, in an Act signed by President Ronald Reagan, provided $20,000 to former internees and issued a national apology. Finally, the Supreme Court's decisions in *Hirabayashi* and *Korematsu* have also come under attack. On the basis of newly discovered evidence that the U.S. Government may have misstated the extent of its evidence regarding espionage and sabotage by Japanese-Americans while litigating the cases, the convictions of Gordon Hirabayashi and Fred Korematsu were reversed using the writ of coram nobis. Finally, in *Adarand* v. *Pena* (1995), the Supreme Court itself recognized the legal errors in *Hirabayashi* and *Korematsu*, referring to the decisions as discredited and incorrect.

The exigencies of war frequently threaten constitutional liberties. Yet the existing consensus that the internment of Japanese-Americans during World War II was a nadir in the history of civil liberties in the United States, plus the time-hewn institutional constraints in the U.S. government, provide hope that the episode will not be repeated again.

[*See also* Civil Rights and Civil Liberties; Fourteenth Amendment]

• Martin Grodzins, *Americans Betrayed: Politics and the Japanese Evacuation*, 1949. Jacobus tenBroek, Edward Barnhart, and Floyd Matson, *Prejudice, War and the Constitution*, 1958. Peter Irons, *Justice at War*, 1983. Joel Grossman, "The Japanese American Cases and the Vagaries of Constitutional Adjudication in Wartime: An Institutional Perspective," 19 *University of Hawai'i Law Review* 649 (1997).   —David Weiner

JAY, JOHN, 1745–1829, lawyer and first chief justice of the United States, 1789–95. The eldest son of a wealthy New York merchant, John Jay matriculated in 1760 at King's College (now Columbia University) to deepen his knowledge of classics, public law, and political economy. Only in his final year at university did he decide to focus his attentions on law, both as a profession and as an avenue to public service. After graduation, he undertook a legal apprenticeship with the eminent New York lawyer Benjamin Kissam. One of Kissam's law clerks later testified that the young Jay exhibited "indefatigable application, and uncommon firmness of mind"; others characterized him as a restless law student who eagerly seized opportunities to visit the family estate in Rye, New York, and dive into studies in support of a master's degree in classics.

The Stamp Act crisis of 1765 propelled Jay into a maelstrom of revolutionary politics and accelerated professional activity. In 1768, after gaining admission to the prestigious New York bar, he opened a law office in the city with his friend Robert Livingston; a year later, he accepted his first public office, as a commissioner in a boundary dispute between New York and New Jersey. Initially, the politically conservative Jay resisted the necessity of independence. By 1775, however, he had concluded that the British Crown could no longer guarantee the safety of colonial trade and property, and therefore resolutely decided to support the rebellion.

Jay rose rapidly in patriotic ranks. He guided state committees of safety and correspondence, served in the first and second Continental Congresses, and helped draft key revolutionary documents—among them, the New York state constitution and the Olive Branch Petition. Until 1779, he sat without much distinction as chief justice of the New York superior court. In 1778, while still on the bench, Jay was elected president of the Congress; he then found himself in Europe, first as minister plenipotentiary to Spain and then as one of five commissioners charged with negotiating the Paris Peace Treaty with Great Britain. During these years, his reputation as a diplomat and political economist far surpassed his comparatively slight reputation as a jurist.

When Jay returned to New York City in 1784, he turned down a number of ambassadorships in favor of law practice and local politics. But within a few weeks he agreed to serve as secretary of foreign affairs—a position he held until 1789. Indeed, until March 1790, while the nation awaited Thomas *Jefferson's return from Paris to take up his post as the new nation's first secretary of state, Jay served informally in that position. In February of the same year, he accepted President Washington's commission to become the United States' first chief justice.

Jay's appointment partly reflected Washington's knowledge of his friend's familiarity with the Paris treaty, trade agreements, war contracts, and European dignitaries; without Jay's support the new republic would surely sink into the Atlantic. And, true to form, Jay initially tried to use the *Supreme Court as well as the district and circuit courts as instruments in pursuit of honorable relations with Europeans, particularly when individuals or states failed to honor the terms of treaties and other agreements. In *Chisholm* v. *Georgia* (1793), for example, Jay labored to persuade Georgians that the state treasury had to make good on revolutionary war debts, such as the value of Loyalist estates sequestered during the war. In the 1792 New York circuit court hearing in *Hayburn's Case*, and in several lesser-known rulings, the justices quietly began to develop the judiciary's controversial powers of *judicial review. Jay contributed mightily to public knowledge of the existence of a shadowy and controversial federal government with eloquent grand jury charges, reprinted widely in newspapers. But Jay's interests ultimately lay in foreign relations and abstract international "systems," not in the comparatively tedious work of inventing a federal judiciary, wresting review powers from suspicious states, staffing a federal bar, or working out rules, procedures, and conventions appropriate to an unprecedented system of national courts.

Not surprisingly, Jay's tenure as chief justice was brief. The associate justices whined incessantly about the rigors of circuit-riding; European friends complained about Americans' bad faith and Jay's apparent inability to force his countrymen to meet their obligations, and Anti-Federalists raised a clamor about the justices' apparent disdain for state courts, local law, and popular *sovereignty. Equally troubling, the state of Georgia not only refused to appear in federal court to defend itself in *Chisholm*—the Supreme Court's first constitutional case—but toyed openly with hanging federal officers. Georgia finally commenced a campaign in Congress to deprive the nation's highest court of jurisdiction whenever states might be called as defendants—a campaign that led to the adoption of the humiliating Eleventh Amendment in 1798.

Frustrated and disgusted with the judiciary as a weapon against disorder, lawlessness, and excessive democracy, Jay decided to pursue what he called "great objects of state" through diplomacy. In 1794, while seated as chief justice, he accepted a commission as *envoy extraordinaire* to defuse tensions with Great Britain over unpaid war debts and other violations of the Paris Treaty. The resulting Jay Treaty of 1795, while hotly contested in the Senate, assured Jay, in his own words, that "justice will finally be done."

Elected governor of New York in absentia, Jay resigned as chief justice in 1795. When President John Adams asked him to resume his judicial post in 1800, he tersely declined on the grounds that the supreme court utterly lacked "energy, weight and dignity." In 1801, Jay abandoned public life and retired to his farm in Westchester County, New York, where he devoted himself to the Episcopal Church, abolitionism, and an extensive correspondence—much of it in opposition to a rising tide of "Jacobinism" in the wake of Thomas Jefferson's election to the presidency.

[See also Courts, United States]

• Richard B. Morris, *John Jay, the Nation, and the Court*, 1967. William R. Casto, *The Supreme Court in the Early Republic: The Chief Justiceships of John Jay and Oliver Ellsworth*, 1995. Sandra F. VanBurkleo, "Honour, Justice, and Interest": John Jay's Republican Politics and Statesmanship on the Federal Bench," in *Seriatim: The Supreme Court before John Marshall* (Scott Gerber, ed.), 1998.
                                    —Sandra F. VanBurkleo

JEFFERSON, THOMAS. (1743–1826), author of the Declaration of Independence and third president of the United States, 1801–09. Born in Albemarle County in central Virginia, the son of Peter Jefferson and Jane Randolph, he was a member of the slaveholding gentry, colonial Virginia's social and political elite. Despite this aristocratic background, however, Jefferson championed individual rights and was an ardent opponent of privilege. As a leading figure in the Founders' generation, he authored many key documents in early American law and was instrumental in developing the philosophy of limited government that dominated American constitutional thought until the twentieth century.

Educated at the College of William and Mary and trained as a lawyer by Williamsburg attorney George Wythe, Jefferson was well versed in English radical Whig thought and its distrust of political power. In August 1774 he wrote proposed instructions for the Virginia delegates to the first Continental Congress. Published under the title *A Summary View of the Rights of British America*, Jefferson's essay stridently defended Americans' rights against Parliament, which he maintained had no authority to legislate for the colonies.

In 1775–76 Jefferson was a Virginia delegate to the Second Continental Congress in Philadelphia, where in June 1776 he drafted the Declaration of Independence, adopted by the Congress on July 4. In that document he not only justified American independence but also defined the American philosophy of government as premised on individual rights, the inherent natural rights of "life, liberty, and the pursuit of happiness." "To secure these rights," he wrote, "governments are instituted among men, deriving their just powers from the consent of the governed."

During the Revolutionary War, Jefferson helped to establish new republican governments both in his home state and in the United States. As a member of the Virginia House of Delegates during the years 1776–79, he served on the committee to revise the laws of the Commonwealth and drafted several important bills, among them the one subsequently enacted as Virginia's Statute for Religious Freedom. In 1779–81 he served two one-year terms as governor of Virginia; following his retirement from that office he wrote *Notes on the State of Virginia*, his only book-length publication.

After a brief return as a Virginia delegate to Congress in 1783–84, when he helped draw up the plan for settling the West that was later enacted as the Northwest Ordinance, Jefferson was appointed in 1785 to succeed Benjamin Franklin as minister to France. In Paris until October 1789, he witnessed firsthand the early events of the French Revolution, and advised his friend the Marquis de Lafayette on the formulation of a French constitution.

Although Jefferson was absent from the United States when the *Constitutional Convention met, he played a critical role in the Constitution's ratification during the years 1787–89. Although he maintained neutrality in the ratification debates—calling himself "neither a Federalist nor an Anti-Federalist"—Jefferson generally supported the new constitution. Through his transatlantic correspondence with James Madison and others, however, he helped push for the addition of the *Bill of Rights, which he considered "necessary by way of supplement," to assure that the national government not abuse the powers granted it under the Constitution.

During the 1790s Jefferson served as secretary of state in the presidency of George Washington and then, after a brief retirement from politics, as vice president under John *Adams. With his friend and collaborator, James Madison, Jefferson headed the Republican opposition to the Federalist administrations of Washington and Adams. Among his many political writings during this decade were his opinion on the constitutionality of the Bank Bill (1791), which advised Washington that the Constitution did not empower *Congress to charter a national bank, and the Kentucky Resolutions (1798), which Jefferson drafted anonymously to dispute the constitutionality of the Alien and Sedition Acts.

Jefferson was the first president of the United States chosen by the House of Representatives, due to a tie vote between Jefferson and his running mate, Aaron *Burr, which resulted from a peculiarity in the Electoral College system, subsequently corrected by the Twelfth Amendment. Despite this awkward start, his presidency has generally been regarded by scholars as successful. Critical of his predecessors' failure to respect the "chains of the Constitution," Jefferson set important precedents limiting presidential power. He refrained from exercising the veto power, which he believed ought to be used only against clearly unconstitutional legislation; and as commander in chief during the Barbary War in the Mediterranean, he ordered the navy to engage in defensive operations only until Congress authorized war. Refusing to issue a presidential proclamation for a day of prayer or thanksgiving, Jefferson gave as his explanation his famous view that the First Amendment's religious freedom clause built "a wall of separation between *Church and State." And, declining to deliver personally his annual message to Congress—a practice he disdained as too reminiscent of the British monarch's opening of a new Parliament—he instead sent it in writing, a practice that lasted until Woodrow Wilson's presidency.

Perhaps the most noteworthy event of Jefferson's first term as president was the Louisiana Purchase, which doubled the size of the United States. Critics, past and present, have decried the Purchase as inconsistent with his strict constitutionalism. Jefferson opened himself to the charge of hypocrisy by questioning the constitutionality of the Purchase and attempting to validate it explicitly by *constitutional amendment, thus "to set an example against broad construction." More troubling as a precedent for broad federal power, however, was the embargo policy Jefferson pursued during his second term in order to avoid U.S. involvement in the war between Britain and France.

Following his presidency, Jefferson retired again to Monticello, his home in Virginia, where he maintained through voluminous correspondence his keen interest in legal matters. He encouraged the "Old Republicans," a group of radical Jeffersonians in Virginia, in their protest against a series of decisions by the *Supreme Court, including *McCulloch* v. *Maryland* (1819), which they believed threatened to consolidate power at the national level. Although he accepted *judicial review, Jefferson regarded as "very dangerous" the doctrine that the Supreme Court was the ultimate arbiter of constitutional questions, arguing that the people themselves were the only "safe depository" of ultimate power.

He died at Monticello on July 4, 1826, the fiftieth anniversary of the Declaration of Independence.

[See also Bills of Rights; Executive Power]

• Dumas Malone, *Jefferson and His Time*, 6 vols., 1948–81. Merrill D. Peterson, *Thomas Jefferson and the New Nation*, 1970. Edward Dumbauld, *Thomas Jefferson and the Law*, 1978. Merrill D. Peterson, ed., *Thomas Jefferson: Writings*, 1984. Noble E. Cunningham, Jr., *In Pursuit of Reason: The Life of Thomas Jefferson*, 1987. David N. Mayer, *The Constitutional Thought of Thomas Jefferson*, 1994.   —David N. Mayer

JIM CROW LAWS. *See* Segregation.

JOHNSON, ANDREW, IMPEACHMENT TRIAL OF. The first *impeachment of a president, the trial of Andrew Johnson, established a touchstone for later proceedings. The Johnson impeachment grew out of the president's effort to defeat congressional legislation setting terms for reunion after the Civil War and securing equal civil and political rights for African Americans. The struggle over such fundamental issues tested the strength of democratic institutions. Johnson exacerbated the conflict with inflammatory rhetoric, claims of exclusive authority to decide the issue, and the use of *executive power to undermine enforcement of the law. At the same time, Johnson's political opponents identified their own policies with the national interest, identifying dissent with *treason.

Although most congressmen denied they were endorsing such a narrow view, Johnson's impeachment by the House of Representatives on 22 February 1868, primarily for his attempt to remove Secretary of War Edwin M. Stanton in violation of the Tenure of Office Act (1867), suggested that only a violation of law constitutes a "high crime or misdemeanor" required for impeachment. Johnson's acquittal by one vote in May, largely on the grounds that the law did not cover Stanton, reinforced this perception. The Senate treated the impeachment trial as analogous to a trial of law, although the senators acted as both judge and jury, deciding both matters of law and fact. The trial indicated how difficult it is to adhere to judicial impartiality in a proceeding that inevitably involves politics.

For nearly one hundred years the impeachment of Johnson was condemned as a vindictive congressional effort to gain supremacy over the Executive Department. Although some historians now view the impeachment as understandable and even justified, the long-held negative view has fostered the conviction that a president should be impeached only in the most extreme instances.

• Michael Les Benedict, *The Impeachment and Trial of Andrew Johnson*, 1973. William H. Rehnquist, *Grand Inquests: The Historic Impeachments of Justice Samuel Chase and President Andrew Johnson*, 1992.

—Michael Les Benedict

JOINDER. *See* Procedure, Civil.

JOKES, LAWYER. *See* Lawyers, Popular Perceptions of.

JOURNALISTS. *See* Media and the Law; Speech and the Press, Freedom of.

JUDGE. Those who adjudicate formal disputes between competing parties—judges—have long played a significant role in the American legal system. Because they serve at the federal, state, and local levels, judges in the United States exercise various degrees of authority and perform a variety of different roles. They sit primarily in three ways: as a group with other judges on appellate courts, where they decide cases usually by issuing written *opinions; with juries in civil and criminal trials, where they give instructions to jurors and decide questions of law; and alone in local courts, where they deal with such matters as *probate, small claims, and traffic offenses. Judges attain their positions by some form of popular election, appointment, or "merit selection," but regardless of how they gain office, as arbiters and decision-makers, judges often become enmeshed in *politics.

History in English Common Law. The historical roots of the American judicial office lie in English *common law, which developed during the Middle Ages. Angles, Saxons, and other Europeans who migrated to Britain during this era established a legal system based on custom and folkways rather than on a written code (see CODIFICATION). This common law system—in contrast to the *civil law that pervaded the European continent—gave great authority to judges. Their task was to draw upon previous decisions in order to fashion legal principles reflective of the values of the English people. The common law operated on two levels. First, it grew up around the central royal courts, where powerful jurists heard disputes involving the landed aristocracy. Over centuries the procedural rules that developed in these courts became increasingly complicated, thus requiring extensive legal training on the part of the bench and bar. Second, the common law functioned on the local level, where county, manor, and borough courts meted out justice on a daily basis for the vast majority of the English people. Although custom also shaped judicial rulings in these courts, the work of local judges had little or no impact on the high common law doctrine formulated by the great English jurists and later described in the eighteenth century by William *Blackstone. Custom, precedent, and tradition thus became the hallmarks of the English legal system and the guiding principles of English judges.

The Early Republic. When Americans constructed their own system of courts, they drew upon the basic elements of the English system while adapting their judicial structure to the unique conditions of their society. All the early American colonies established layered systems of courts, with legislative assemblies actually considered the highest "courts" within each colony, below which were superior and local tribunals. Colonists' distrust both of the legal profession and of concentrated power, combined with the lack of English-trained lawyers in the colonies, meant that most seventeenth-century judges had little formal training and expertise in the law. Although an expanding population and commercial economy fostered the growth of a more educated judiciary and more technical legal forms during the eighteenth century, not until the dawn of independence and the writing of new state constitutions did judges begin to function independently of the legislative branch. Many revolutionary-era state constitutions recognized the judiciary as a separate branch of government and granted judges tenure during good behavior, though legislatures maintained control over the selection of judges.

The *Constitution of the United States further contributed to the idea of an independent judiciary by establishing the U.S. *Supreme Court and authorizing the creation of a system of lower federal courts. The president possessed the power to appoint Supreme Court justices, with the "advice and consent" of the U.S. Senate, a mode of selection subsequently instituted for all federal judges. Both Supreme Court justices and judges of the lower federal courts were to serve during good behavior. From their eighteenth-century perspective, the founders probably never envisioned that the justices of the Supreme Court, nor their counterparts on the lower federal courts, would ever emerge as the powerful legal and political actors that they became. Article Three of the Constitution, which relates to the judiciary, is brief and vague compared to the articles pertaining to the other two branches of the national government. In the 78th *Federalist*, Alexander Hamilton described the courts as "the least dangerous to the political rights of the Constitution" and dismissed whatever popular fear existed of powerful judges. "The judiciary . . . has no influence over either the sword or the purse; no direction either of the strength or of the wealth of the society; and can take no active resolution whatever," he wrote. "It may truly be said to have neither FORCE nor WILL, but merely judgment."

Hamilton underestimated the power that the judiciary would come to wield in American life. During the 1780s and 1790s, state supreme courts in Rhode Island, North Carolina, and Virginia all asserted the power to declare legislative enactments unconstitutional, and the U.S. Supreme Court under Chief Justice John *Marshall followed suit in the landmark case *Marbury* v. *Madison* (1803). "It is emphatically the province and duty of the judicial department," Marshall argued, "to say what the law is."

Judges as Lawmakers. Although state supreme courts and the U. S. Supreme Court infrequently overturned legislative acts during the first half of the nineteenth century, judges assumed the power of *judicial review and thereby asserted their independence from the other branches of government. At the same time, appellate judges began to modify existing English common law doctrine in such areas as contracts and property to accommodate the demands of America's economy and society. The relatively informal character of legal *education and law reporting gave judges freedom to innovate. Most aspiring attorneys still learned the law by studying in the office of an established lawyer, and because appellate judges—even U.S. Supreme Court justices—spent much of their time riding the circuit, they usually had limited access to extensive collections of law books and to published decisions. Judges often crafted opinions in the "grand style," in which they frequently employed references to Blackstone and the Bible, as well as arguments based on history, moral philosophy, and *natural law. This florid style of opinion writing also reflected the public nature of the judicial role. Court sessions—both trial and appellate—drew large audiences during much of the nineteenth century, and judges served an important function as symbols of the authority of the law and the state. In short, during the nineteenth century judges asserted their independence from the other branches of government and became powerful lawmakers in their own right.

Selection of Judges. This creative flourish on the part of the judiciary coincided, however, with attempts to make judges more accountable to the electorate. During the late eighteenth and early nineteenth centuries, most state judges had been chosen by legislatures, but by the 1820s many states required that local trial judges be popularly elected. The removal of property qualifications for *voting and the rise of mass political parties during the ensuing decades invited fresh scrutiny of the increasingly powerful appellate judiciary. In 1832, Mississippi mandated the election of all its judges for limited terms of service, and by the time of the Civil War twenty-three of the thirty states had adopted the practice of popularly electing supreme court judges for limited terms, usually six or eight years. Although some states rescinded the practice of popular election after the Civil War and returned to an appointive system, popular election of state judges remained in place in a majority of states well into the twentieth century.

Eventually merit selection became the most common method of staffing the judiciary. In 1940 Missouri became the first state to adopt a merit plan for selecting judges, under which the governor appointed judges for an initial period of service, after which a judge was subject to a retention referendum. Since that time states have adopted a variety of merit selection plans, particularly for choosing appellate and state supreme court judges. Many of these schemes involve appointed, non-partisan nominating commissions, usually composed primarily of lawyers, who submit a short list of qualified judicial candidates to the governor or legislature for appointment. Currently, twenty-five states use nominating commissions to assist in the selection of judicial candidates for their supreme courts, and twenty states hold popular judicial elections. The remaining five states, including California, invest the power of judicial appointment in either the governor or legislature, without the aid of a nominating commission. Every state except Rhode Island (all of whose judges serve for life) requires that judges go through a retention process—usually a popular retention election, in which a judge runs against his own record—after a specific number of years of service. The appointment of federal judges has never involved a formal merit selection process, although since the mid-twentieth century the *American Bar Association Committee on the Federal Judiciary has rated the qualifications of prospective judicial nominees. Despite the trend toward merit selection, popular election remains the most common method of selecting local trial judges.

Education and Requirements. The rise of the merit plan of judicial selection reflected the ongoing professionalization of the bench by the early twentieth century. Rapid economic growth and the concomitant rise of the national regulatory state made understanding and practicing the law much more complicated than it had ever been before. As new specialized areas of law developed, legal education moved out of law offices and into law schools. By the early twentieth century the case method of instruction, originally instituted at Harvard Law School, became the standard in legal education, while *bar associations formed to restrict membership in the profession to those who met its standards of conduct and competency. This increased professional consciousness among lawyers resulted in new requirements for judicial service, although today they vary widely among the states. Most states mandate that judges be members of the bar of that particular state, usually for a specific number of years. Minnesota, however, requires only that judges "be learned in the law." Some states have minimum residency requirements, while Texas's constitution explicitly states that judges must be U.S. citizens. A few states require judges to be a minimum age; Michigan's constitution, in contrast, forbids anyone from being "elected or appointed to judicial office after reaching the age of 70 years." Although the U.S. Constitution contains no specific requirements for judicial service, professional competency is an established tradition. All federal appellate judges are and have been lawyers.

As Political Figures. Since the founding of the republic, American judges have struggled to reconcile their role as impartial legal actors, whose rulings must rely on established principles of law, with their place in the political sphere. During the nineteenth century, the issues of slavery and economic regulation caused judges great anxiety over the proper relationship between established law and personal convictions. In the early twentieth century, advocates of *sociological jurisprudence and *legal realism argued that judges needed to look beyond precedent to the underlying social and economic bases of the law. Legal realists in particular contended that a judge's political beliefs could not be separated from the judicial process. These jurisprudential theories, combined with the historic power of judicial review, contributed to a tide of judicial activism in the second half of the twentieth century. Judicial rulings regarding desegregation, abortion, and civil rights not only profoundly affected the development of public policy, they also spurred debate over the proper role of the judiciary in American life. The recent expansion of individual rights under federal law, with the passage of measures such as the Civil Rights Act of 1964 and the Americans with Disabilities Act of 1990, has especially conferred new authority upon federal judges to render decisions affecting the everyday lives of American citizens. With this authority, though, has come increased public debate over nominees for the federal bench, and U.S. senators' willingness to reject or delay action on judicial appointments based on nominees' partisan or ideological commitments represents the latest manifestation of this tension between the judge's role as both a legal and a political actor. The U.S. Supreme Court's controversial decision regarding the vote count in the 2000 presidential election means that political debate over federal judicial appointments will likely continue.

Despite partisan conflict surrounding the judiciary, the American public has and continues to hold its judges in high esteem. The U.S. Supreme Court typically earns higher marks for trustworthiness than Congress, while state and local judges nearly always win retention elections. Part of this respect for the judiciary stems from the trappings of the judicial office and the ceremony associated with the legal process. The wearing of judicial robes, the practice of rising when a judge enters a courtroom, the perfunctory forms of address used when speaking to a judge, and the emphasis on proper procedure in a court of law all lend an air of dignity and authority to the judicial office. Common law judges in general enjoy much greater prestige than those in the civil law countries of western Europe, where judges serve a more bureaucratic function and constitute part of the civil service system. Thus, the common law heritage, combined with the unique historical evolution of the judicial office in the United States, have made the American judge a significant and powerful legal actor.

[*See also* Courts, United States]

• Benjamin N. Cardozo, *The Nature of the Judicial Process,* 1922. Alexander Bickel, *The Least Dangerous Branch: The Supreme Court at the Bar of Politics,* 1962. Henry J. Abraham, *The Judicial Process: An Introductory Analysis of the Courts of the United States, England, and France,* 1968. Morton J. Horwitz, *The Transformation of American Law, 1780–1860,* 1979. John R. Schmidhauser, *Judges and Justices: The Federal Appellate Judiciary,* 1979. Lawrence Friedman, *A History of American Law,* 1985. G. Edward White, *The American Judicial Tradition: Profiles of Leading American Judges,* 1988. Kermit L. Hall, *The Magic Mirror: Law in American History,* 1989. Peter Karsten, *Heart versus Head: Judge-Made Law in Nineteenth-Century America,* 1997.

—Timothy S. Huebner

JUDGMENTS: the final authoritative disposition of a matter that may be in dispute before a court. Two quite different types of judicial proceedings produce judgments. In criminal proceedings brought by the state against persons (including juridical persons), the resulting judgment is either the conviction or the acquittal of the accused. In civil proceedings, brought by one party against another, the resulting judgment either grants the claiming party the relief sought or denies it.

A judgment is different from a *verdict, which is the decision of a jury on disputed issues of fact. Normally the judge will order judgment in accordance with a verdict, but not always. Courts have some power to order judgment notwithstanding the verdict (now called "judgment as a matter of law" in federal courts: Federal Rule 50) if the court is convinced the jury acted irrationally.

Judgments *in personam* are those that determine the rights and duties of the parties with respect to the matter in issue. An ordinary case in *tort or *contract seeking damages is such an action *in personam*. Before a court may adjudicate an action seeking such a judgment, the court must have jurisdiction over the parties. Judgments *in rem* are those that determine ownership of *property. A judgment in a "true" *in rem* action determines the claimant's ownership against all the world, such as in an action to obtain title registration to real property. A judgment *quasi in rem* determines interests in property as between named parties, such as in a *mortgage foreclosure.

A peculiar feature of the English legal system, implanted in the American colonies before their independence, was the existence of two separate sets of legal principles, procedures, and remedies. The *common law was administered by the courts of Common Pleas, Kings Bench, and Exchequer, while *equity was administered by the Chancery Court. In equity, there were no juries, and on appeal from equity decrees (not then called judgments), the determinations of fact as well as rulings of law could be reviewed. Common law judgments in general were only enforceable by execution against property. Equity decrees, on the other hand, could be enforced against the defendant's person by holding him in *contempt of court pending compliance with the decree.

Today in the United States, law and equity have been merged in all but a few states that still retain separate law and equity courts. However, vestiges of the old system remain everywhere. The right to *jury trial in civil cases, guaranteed by the United States Constitution's Seventh Amendment, does not extend to cases that were not triable to a jury in 1791, the year that amendment was adopted. The Seventh Amendment applies only in federal courts, but all states provide for jury trial in civil cases, and generally follow the federal doctrine. Decrees in suits with equitable issues generally do not use a jury and may still be enforced *in personam* through the court's contempt power, although in modern times some equitable *remedies have come to be enforceable against property as well. Equity judgments include, for example, *injunctions, decrees for specific performance of contract, trust accounting, and mortgage foreclosure.

In modern state court practice, it is possible to obtain a judgment that merely declares the rights and duties of the parties with no immediate coercive affect. Declaratory judgments in federal courts are governed by 28 U.S.C §2201 (1994) and Federal Rule of Civil Procedure 57.

Although a judgment is the end product of all litigation, not all cases require a trial. A trial is necessary only to resolve disputed facts. If the facts are not in dispute, the matter in controversy will turn on questions of law that can be resolved by the judge. If the claimant's pleading does not allege grounds for which the law provides relief, the defending party can move to dismiss the case (in some states called a "demurrer"). The demurrer's effect is to admit for purposes of the motion the truth of the claimant's allegations; it asserts that the law simply does not provide relief on those facts. In modern procedure in a majority of states, this defense is called a motion to dismiss for failure to state a claim on which relief can be granted (Federal Rule 12(b)(6)). If the demurrer or motion to dismiss is successful, the court may grant judgment against the claimant dismissing the action. Usually, however, the claimant will be given leave to amend the pleading to properly state the claim if that can be done.

A case may also be dismissed without trial if the claimant lacks credible evidence to prove some essential element of the case. If the claimant cannot produce such evidence, the defending party can move for summary judgment (Federal Rule 56) and the court may order judgment for the defending party. The hearing on this motion is not a trial: the judge does not weigh the evidence to see which side's case is stronger. The hearing merely tests whether there is any credible evidence to support the claimant's position. In unusual cases, a summary judgment may also be granted to the claimant. If the evidence available is so overwhelming that the court is convinced that no reasonable jury could find against the claimant, the court can order an immediate judgment.

If a defendant fails to respond to the plaintiff's pleading, the plaintiff may then move the court to order judgment by default against the defendant. Before granting such a judgment, the court may require the plaintiff to produce some evidence to support the claim and the amount of damages sought. Default judgments are generally disfavored, and even if granted in the court's discretion, the judgment may be later set aside if the defendant has some excuse for the default and a plausible defense on the merits (Federal Rule 55).

Once a judgment has been rendered, it must be entered in written form into the court's record, usually called a judgment docket (Federal Rule 58). The direct effect of a judgment against the claimant is dismissal of the action. The effect of a judgment for the plaintiff, except for a declaratory judgment, is to require the defending party to pay a sum of money (damages) or to do, or to refrain from doing, some specific act. If the defending party does not comply, the judgment can be enforced by seizing the defendant's nonexempt assets and selling them (in the case of a money judgment), or by holding the defendant in contempt of court subject to fine, or in some cases incarceration for further noncompliance.

Once a matter has been fairly litigated and resolved in a final judgment on the merits, that should end the matter. If a later lawsuit is brought raising the same matter, the first judgment may preclude further litigation. The first judgment may be preclusive in two distinct ways. It may preclude altogether a second lawsuit on the same claim, called "claim preclusion." The earlier judgment may also preclude relitigation of the issues that were adjudicated and decided in the earlier action, even if the second suit is on a different cause of action, called "issue preclusion." The term *res judicata* includes both of these actions. In earlier times, and in some courts even today, *res judicata* was often used to describe only the claim preclusion effect. "Estoppel" was the term used to describe the issue preclusion effect: direct estoppel if the second suit was on the same cause of action as the earlier one, collateral estoppel if the later suit was on a different cause of action. Because a second suit on the same cause of action was usually precluded altogether through claim preclusion, the term "collateral estoppel" came to be widely used for issue preclusion in general whether the second suit was on the same or a different cause of action.

To have claim preclusion effect, the judgment must be on the merits. The judgment in favor of the claimant is always a judgment on the merits, but a judgment for the defending party may not be on the merits. Dismissal of an action for lack of jurisdiction or for non-joinder of indispensable parties are examples of judgments without prejudice; they are not on the merits and do not preclude a later suit on the same claim.

Even a judgment without prejudice may have issue preclusion effect. If the same issue was actually litigated in a prior action, and the decision was necessary to the judgment rendered, that issue may be precluded. In a default judgment, nothing was actually litigated, so there would be no issue preclusion. A default judgment is a judgment on the merits, however, and so it would have claim preclusion effect. A dismissal for want of jurisdiction is not a judgment on the merits, and so has no claim preclusion effect. But if the jurisdiction issue was actually litigated by the opposing parties, the determination of lack of jurisdiction will have issue preclusion effect, since every court is deemed to have jurisdiction to determine whether or not it has jurisdiction. A consent judgment normally has no issue preclusion effect, although there are some cases holding otherwise.

There are some limitations on issue preclusion. Only parties, persons in privity with parties, or persons represented by parties can be bound by the issue preclusion effects of prior litigation. It was long held that the same limitation governed the question of who may take advantage of issue preclusion from former litigation. That mutuality doctrine is still the rule in several states, but in most states today, a person who was not a party to the prior litigation may invoke issue preclusion under some circumstances against one who was a party to that former suit. See *Parklane Hosiery Co. v. Shore* (1979).

By virtue of the constitutional *full faith and credit clause (art. IV, §1) and the broader federal statute (28 U.S.C. §1738 (1994)), jurisdictionally valid judgments of one court must be given the same effects in all other courts in the United States. The judgment of one state thus may be enforced in another state without examination of the merits by the second court. The same rule applies to the claim and issue preclusion effects of the first state's judgment, which must be recognized by all American courts.

[*See also* Procedure, Civil; Procedure, Criminal]

• Charles Wright, Arthur Miller, and Edward H. Cooper, "Res Judicata," *Federal Practice and Procedure* 18 (1981). American Law Institute, *Restatement (Second) of Judgments*, 1982. Susan Bandes and Lawrence Solum, "Effect of Judgment and Preclusion," *Moore's Federal Practice* 18, 3d ed., 1997. Robert C. Casad and Kevin M. Clermont, *Res Judicata: A Handbook of Its Theory, Doctrine and Practice*, 2001.   —Robert C. Casad

JUDGMENTS, RECOGNITION OF. *See* Conflict of Laws.

JUDICIAL REVIEW is the power of courts, in deciding specific cases before them, to refuse to recognize the constitutionality of acts of other departments of the federal government and of the states and their subdivisions. However, a declaration of unconstitutionality by the United States *Supreme Court usually has the effect of invalidating all applications of that policy because of the operation of stare decisis and the authority of the Supreme Court to review the decisions of other courts. Rulings of invalidity by state *supreme courts have a similar effect within their jurisdictions.

Judicial review has sometimes been characterized as the power to make policy, because broad statements defining the *Constitution may obligate federal and state officials who are not parties to litigation to act in specific ways or deny them the authority to do so. When the governor of Arkansas blocked the desegregation of schools in Little Rock, on the ground that his state had not been a party to *Brown* v. *Board of Education*

(1954), in which the Court had held racial segregation in schools to be contrary to the *Equal Protection Clause of the *Fourteenth Amendment, the Supreme Court responded in *Cooper* v. *Aaron* (1958), in an opinion signed separately by each of the nine justices, that "the interpretation of the Fourteenth Amendment enunciated by this Court in the *Brown* case is the supreme law of the land."

Critics argue that judicial review is not firmly founded either in the constitutional text or in history. In *Marbury* v. *Madison* (1803), the Supreme Court's first full exercise of the power to invalidate a federal law, Chief Justice John *Marshall for a unanimous Court argued that a written Constitution limits the authority of all branches of the government, that "it is emphatically the province and the duty of the judicial department to say what the law is," that the judiciary cannot enforce a law that conflicts with the Constitution, and that the oath taken by judges requires them to uphold the Constitution in making decisions that come before them. Nonetheless, the Constitution does not specifically fix in the judiciary the authority to interpret whether a law conflicts with the Constitution; and in many other democratic nations this task is left to the legislative branch. Since executive and legislative officials also take an oath to uphold the Constitution, this constitutional requirement does not specifically vest the final authority to interpret the Constitution in the judiciary.

A stronger claim for judicial review might rest in Article III, Section 2, which declares that "the judicial power shall extend to all cases . . . arising under this Constitution, the laws of the United States, and treaties made, or which shall be made, under their authority . . ." Skeptics claim that the judicial power could be interpreted to recognize the validity of interpretations of the Constitution inherent in the actions of other departments.

The Supremacy Clause of Article VI declares that the Constitution, laws of the United States, and treaties entered into by the United States "shall be the supreme law of the land; and the judges in every state shall be bound thereby, anything in the Constitution or laws of any state to the contrary notwithstanding." And the Judiciary Act of 1789, adopted by the First Congress that included many of the Constitution's framers, specifically authorized the Supreme Court to review decisions of state courts. Even if these provisions are read as authorizing courts to exercise judicial review of state actions, it does not follow that it authorizes them to strike down acts of *Congress and the president. And their silence on that matter

may imply an absence of such authority. Justice Oliver Wendell *Holmes emphasized the distinction between judicial review of state and federal authority in *Collected Legal Papers* (1920): "I do not think the United States would come to an end if [the Court] lost [its] power to declare an act of Congress void. I do think that the Union would be imperiled if we could not make that declaration as to the laws of the several states." Judicial review of state actions may protect national authority and assure uniform application of the Constitution throughout the nation. Judicial review of actions of Congress and the president serves no similar purpose.

The cause of judicial review has been weakened by the circumstances surrounding *Marbury* v. *Madison*. John Marshall was the secretary of state who signed the judicial commissions at issue in *Marbury*, and his authorship of the opinion is commonly regarded as a conflict of interest. The Judiciary Act of 1789, whose provisions were at issue, could readily have been interpreted to avoid the apparent conflict between the Constitution and the Act. Or the Constitution could have been interpreted as stating the minimum original jurisdiction of the Supreme Court, with extensions of that jurisdiction permitted by Congress, in which case the apparent conflict between the Constitution and a reading of the Judiciary Act that vested additional original jurisdiction in the Supreme Court would have been resolved.

Opponents and defenders of judicial review have both purported to find support in events leading up to adoption of the Constitution and in the intent of the framers. Edward S. Corwin, one of the twentieth century's leading constitutional scholars, came close to the mark in his characterization of these historical claims: "The people who say the framers intended it are talking nonsense, and the people who say they did not intend it are talking nonsense." The judicial power to strike down acts of the president and Congress is not explicitly stated in the Constitution. Indeed, the Constitutional Convention specifically rejected a proposed Council of Revisions, which would have included the president and judges, to revise laws that did not conform to the Constitution. Proponents of judicial review argue that the Convention rejected the Council because it breached the *separation of powers by mingling executive officials and judges in a single body, not because it sanctioned judicial review. In only a handful of instances before 1789 did state courts strike down state laws, and the outrage that followed showed that judicial review was not commonly accepted.

On the other hand, *Federalist Paper* No. 78 explicitly argued that the Constitution did authorize judicial review. But its author, Alexander Hamilton, played only a peripheral role in framing the Constitution. James Madison and several other framers explained that the Constitution included judicial review during debates in several state ratifying conventions, but this was apparently not argued in the majority of them. The Constitution was framed against some prior history of the British Privy Council and similar bodies' striking down of laws in the colonies that contradicted colonial charters or English law. A number of the most important framers are quoted in the years following ratification and *Marbury* as favoring judicial review, but retrospective statements, made in light of subsequent experience, may provide little insight into the intentions of the Convention itself.

If constitutional language and history are unclear, the repeated exercise of the power of judicial review for two centuries, and the apparent acceptance of that power by the public and by state and federal officials, have endowed the power with substantial legitimacy. By one count, the Supreme Court by the late 1990s had declared unconstitutional 135 provisions of federal law and 1,233 provisions of state laws and local ordinances.

The contemporary debate over judicial review has largely been driven by, in Alexander Bickel's phrase, "the countermajoritarian difficulty," which he explained as "the reality that when the Supreme Court declares unconstitutional a legislative act or the action of an elected executive, it thwarts the will of the representatives of the actual people of the here and now; it exercises control, not in behalf of the prevailing majority, but against it. [A]nd it is the reason the charge can be made that judicial review is undemocratic." This criticism of judicial review is heightened by the steady historical movement toward making other aspects of government in the United States more and more democratic: by the extension of the suffrage to women, African Americans, and those who attain age eighteen; by the elimination of poll taxes and property qualifications for voting; by the direct election, instead of appointment, of United States senators and presidential electors; by apportionment of congressional and legislative districts according to population; and by almost universal adoption of primary elections to nominate candidates for office.

A number of limits to modulate judicial review's countermajoritarian character have been urged:

first, checks by the other branches on the Court's power of judicial review. Second, doctrinal limitations on the Court's exercise of judicial review. Third, methods of interpreting the Constitution that limit the scope of judicial review. Fourth, limits on the functions of judicial review. Fifth, assertion of judicial review only to enhance democracy.

"Democratic checks" by elected officials may be (1) decision-curbing actions that overrule specific judicial decisions, or (2) court-curbing actions that alter the authority or structure of the judiciary. *Constitutional amendment, the most palpable decision-curbing authority, has been used on at least five occasions to overrule specific Supreme Court decisions. But it is hardly majoritarian: it requires extraordinary majorities in each house of Congress and ratification by legislatures or conventions in three-quarters of the states. A quite different check is congressional restriction of the Court's appellate jurisdiction. Endorsed once by the Court in 1869, jurisdiction-stripping measures have subsequently been greeted by some justices with reservations about whether the Court could be entirely denied appellate authority in any matter that falls within the judicial power of the United States.

Court-curbing measures have included legislation in 1802 delaying the Court's term, and at least five efforts to change the size of the Court to influence its policy direction. But the former measure has not been repeated, and its constitutionality is widely doubted. The number of justices was changed several times through 1870, but not since, despite a massive effort by Franklin D. Roosevelt to enlarge the Court in 1937 at the height of his political power and in the midst of a national economic crisis (see COURT PACKING). No justice has ever been removed from office, partly because of the extraordinary two-thirds vote required.

The power to make judicial appointments is the most important check on judicial policy, but it operates largely in the long term. In the modern era, vacancies on the Supreme Court have occurred only every twenty-four months, and at somewhat shorter intervals at earlier times. There seems to be constitutional warrant for the president and Senate to take nominees' views into account during the appointment and confirmation process, and they have usually done so, except for a period from 1894 to 1968, when few presidential nominations were subject to close scrutiny by the Senate. Justices may change their minds on issues once on the Court, however, and they are inevitably called upon to decide issues that neither the president nor the Senate could anticipate.

Throughout its history the Supreme Court has asserted certain doctrinal limitations on the exercise of judicial review—some rooted in the Constitution, others in canons of judicial prudence and self restraint. Hence, the Court has said it eschews decisions in cases that are moot, in cases whose facts are not fully "ripe," and in cases where parties do not have standing because they are not directly affected by the challenged governmental actions. The Court has sometimes declined to decide cases by invoking the "political question" doctrine, whose most important facets are the clear constitutional designation of decisions to other branches and the potential for judicial decisions to cause disarray in sensitive matters such as foreign policy and war-making. The justices have also said that they will avoid exercising the power of judicial review by deciding cases wherever possible on nonconstitutional grounds. One scholar has catalogued sixteen such judicially asserted rules of self-restraint. However, the rules of judicial abnegation are themselves open to widely differing interpretation by different justices, are not embraced by all who sit on the Court, and appear to be ignored when a majority of the justices are determined to exercise the power of judicial review.

Methods of constitutional interpretation have also been offered to diminish the countermajoritarian aspects of judicial review. Adhering closely to the original intentions of the framers, so as not to stray from the Constitution endorsed by the people, has been urged by many scholars and such officials as Justice Antonin Scalia and former Attorney General Edwin Meese. The difficulty of ascertaining original intent is formidable: records rarely illuminate the full scope of the framers' intent, and there may have been different intentions by different framers and by different framing bodies such as the Convention, the two separate houses of Congress in formulating amendments, and the thousands of members of state legislatures or ratifying conventions. It is likely that the framers had no intent about most matters that reach the Court. And constitutional language may be intended to change rather than ratify practices at the time of its adoption.

A second body of scholarly thought, generally called "interpretativism," urges that constitutional decisions be governed by the plain and ordinary meaning of the constitutional words. But the most frequently interpreted clauses of the Constitution—such as the *due process and equal protection guarantees of the Fourteenth Amendment—are so broadly phrased as to make literal interpretation impossible. A sharply different approach, most often associated with Justice William *Brennan, and called "developing constitutionalism," seeks to render decisions consistent with the underlying values or purposes of constitutional provisions. But the values underlying constitutional clauses are often as illusive as the original intent of the framers.

The Supreme Court has been urged to limit the scope of judicial review to matters involving individual rights and liberties. Both the Congress and the president have substantial powers to protect their constitutional authority from intrusion by the other, and both the national government and the states have ample political power to maintain the balance of American federalism. Individuals, by contrast, have no similar protection against government power except for judicial intervention on behalf of their liberties. Professor Jesse Choper's rendering of this functional limitation on judicial review seemed to reflect the Court's own direction for more than a half century beginning in the late 1930s. Since the late 1980s, however, the Supreme Court has again been actively deciding disputes between the national legislative and executive branches and has devised a series of doctrines that modify established *federalism doctrines. A functional limitation on judicial review finds little foundation in the constitutional text, and it has not reflected the realities of Supreme Court doctrine.

Finally, in an attempt to turn the countermajoritarian difficulty on its head, and building on Justice Harlan Fiske *Stone's provocative footnote four in *United States* v. *Carolene Products Co.*(1938), Professor John Hart Ely has argued that the Supreme Court should engage in judicial review to assure democratic politics—by deciding only cases relating to voting, candidacy, and apportionment, as well as to speech, petition, and association—and to protect minorities unable to effectively assert themselves politically because of widespread community prejudices. Apart from the difficulty of defining the rights essential to democratic politics or the minorities entitled to heightened solicitude because of prejudice, the Supreme Court's record of the exercise of judicial review through history, with a notable exception during the *Warren Court era, has not been notably protective of such rights.

Judicial review—the power of the courts to overturn laws enacted by elected officials on grounds of unconstitutionality—has become a fixed feature of American constitutionalism over two centuries, and has been adopted in a growing number of other nations, often with modifications that assure a measure of review by elected officials or the people. Its persistence in the United States has been rooted in a public vision of the Constitution as a law superior to ordinary acts of government and in public acceptance of a judicial institution to adjudicate claims of conflict between those two sources of law. Despite its contradiction of democratic principles, judicial review has persisted because the public is hesitant to alter the nation's constitutional structure or to sanction the use of political and constitutional means to curb the courts. Harsh burdens have been imposed on some Americans for extended periods throughout the nation's history by judicial decisions and policies, but the Supreme Court's exercise of judicial review has rarely, over time, altered the basic directions of national policy approved by the people's representatives.

[See also Courts, United States; Judge]

• Alexander Bickel, The Least Dangerous Branch, 1962. Clifton McCleskey, "Judicial Review in a Democracy: A Dissenting Opinion," Houston Law Review 3 (1966): 354–66. William Van Alstyne, "A Critical Guide to Marbury v. Madison," Duke Law Journal (1967): 1–47. Leonard Levy, "Judicial Review, History, and Democracy: An Introduction," in Judicial Review and the Supreme Court (L. Levy, ed.), 1967: 1–42. Jesse Choper, Judicial Review and the National Political Process, 1980. John Hart Ely, Democracy and Distrust: A Theory of Judicial Review, 1980. William O. Brennan, "The Constitution of the United States: Contemporary Ratification," Southwest Texas Law Review 27 (1986): 433–54. Edwin Meese III, "The Supreme Court of the United States: Bulwark of a Limited Constitution," Southwest Texas Law Review 27 (1986): 455–66. James O'Fallon, "Marbury," Stanford Law Review 44 (1992): 219–60.

—David Adamany

JURISDICTION, EQUITY. See Equity.

JURISPRUDENCE, AMERICAN

European Influence and Nineteenth-Century
American Jurisprudence.
The Revolt Against Formalism
1945–1970
1970–Present

JURISPRUDENCE, AMERICAN: EUROPEAN INFLUENCE AND NINETEENTH-CENTURY AMERICAN JURISPRUDENCE

When the thirteen colonies successfully fought the American War of Independence and cast off the yoke of British colonialism they also freed themselves to create a new *legal system and a new jurisprudence independent of the British *common law. This meant that they could move away from the parochialism of the common law and seek legal inspiration in other countries and other legal systems. The law of the new republic came to be marked by a jurisprudential syncretism far greater than that of its British forebears. During the crucial first century of American history, American law drew both substantive principles as well as legal philosophy from a wide range of sources, including the law of ancient Rome and of the European nation-states whose legal systems, drawn from Roman law, are generally characterized as *civil-law systems. Most important among these countries in their influence on the United States and its jurisprudence were Germany and France.

French and German Innovations. During the nineteenth century, both France and Germany were at the forefront in the development of new modes of legal thinking. France was the birthplace of the Code Napoléon, arguably the greatest and most influential legal *codification effort since Justinian's in the sixth century. Frenchman Robert Joseph Pothier was one of the most influential commercial jurists of the modern period and one of the most productive legal authors of the time. France was home, as well, to Baron de Montesquieu, whose seminal work the Esprit des Lois (1752) became a virtual bible for the American founding fathers in their quest for a new, democratic legal and political structure for the new nation.

Germany, also at the forefront of legal philosophy during the nineteenth century, was the origin of what has come to be known as the "historical" school of jurisprudence. C. J. A. Mittermaier was a pioneer in criminal law studies, Hugo and Friedrich Karl von Savigny were founders of the historical school, and a host of others published works on the history and philosophy of law that became highly influential across the Atlantic. A generation of German jurists and scholars who fled Germany's conservative political regime contributed enormously to U.S. legal development. Among these were Charles Follen, the first teacher of Roman law at Harvard, who helped to spread the study of German throughout the New England elite, and Francis Lieber, the author of the Legal and Political Hermeneutics (1839), a seminal work in legal interpretation and constitutional jurisprudence, and General Orders 100, the foundational doctrine for the modern laws of war from which was derived the modern Geneva Convention (see GERMAN LEGAL PHILOSOPHY, INFLUENCE OF).

Civil Law. Civil law was studied and used by some of the greatest American jurists of the nineteenth century. Joseph *Story, associate justice of the Supreme Court of the United States (1811–45) and Dane Professor of Law at Harvard, was one of the key figures in the transfer of European law to the United States. The author of some of the most important treatises on constitutional law, *commercial law, *conflicts of laws, and *equity, Story was steeped in the works of European jurists, works that he cited freely in his treatises. He was a frequent correspondent with Mittermaier and Lieber, and a colleague of Follen; from these scholars he was able to keep up with the latest developments in European jurisprudence.

Chancellor James *Kent of New York, the author of the *Commentaries on American Law*, referred to both Roman and French legal sources. Similarly, Gulian Crommelin Verplanck, a leader of the New York Bar, used these European sources in his treatise on contract law, a treatise that was quite influential in the antebellum period. Hugh Swinton Legare, a South Carolina lawyer who rose to be attorney general of the United States, was an expert on Roman law and learned German so as to keep up with the latest in German juristic writing. William Wetmore Story, Joseph Story's son, Harvard Law School professor, and legal author, traveled to Germany in part to meet German jurists, including Savigny. Rufus Choate, like Hugh Legare, believed that German was such an important language for the American lawyer that he, too, began to learn it in middle age.

The Availability of European Legal Sources. Crucial to the successful reception of foreign legal ideas into American jurisprudence was the diffusion of foreign legal materials into the United States. From an early date, American booksellers, especially in New York, Boston, and Philadelphia, listed books from France, Spain, Germany, Italy, and the Netherlands in their catalogs. The libraries of nineteenth-century American jurists were filled with works on foreign law. The cornerstones of the Harvard Law library, the Story and Livermore collections (the first belonging to Justice Story; the second bequeathed to Harvard by Samuel Livermore, a Harvard graduate and successful New Orleans attorney), were rich in foreign legal materials. By the middle of the nineteenth-century, American lawyers could purchase the main works of European jurisprudence from the American publishers Little, Brown, or Gould, Banks, as from a Parisian or Berlin bookseller.

Equally important to the spread of European legal ideas in the United States was the availability of many European legal works in English translation. Many of these works were translated in England and originally published there. Such was true, for instance, of the most common translations of Montesquieu's *Esprit des lois* (1749). These translations became common on the American market from the late eighteenth century on, and were often reprinted by American publishers and booksellers. There was also a remarkable group of American lawyers, several of whom were refugees from Europe, who provided additional legal translations for American lawyers. Peter S. DuPonceau, a French émigré who was with George Washington at Valley Forge, was both a successful lawyer and literary figure in Philadelphia. He was the translator of Cornelis van Bijnkershoek's *Quaestiones iuris publici libri duo* (1752), a volume on the law of war and of the sea, which has been cited by the United States Supreme Court more than one hundred times. Luther Stearns Cushing, a Boston lawyer and lecturer on Roman law at Harvard, translated one of Pothier's volumes on contract law, which was published by Little, Brown, and became an important source of American commercial jurisprudence.

The European Impact. Much of American law and legal thinking was influenced either directly or indirectly by European legal thought. European law was seen as an alternative to the English common law and was a source for legal principles in cases where American law had no models and where English law was either unsuitable or undesirable. Thus, much of American commercial law is derived from continental sources as popularized particularly in the works of Pothier. *Admiralty law and the law of the sea as developed in American courts was highly dependent upon the European treatises of the early modern period, especially such works as those written by Hugo Grotius and such compilations as the *Consolato del mare*. Even in such obscure fields as mining law, European models were of singular importance. One of the first American treatises, published in San Francisco in 1849, was a translation from a European original.

Many of the most important movements in American legal philosophy in the nineteenth century were influenced by European law and legal treatises as well. The influence of European writers on *natural law upon American writers during this period is well known. Francis Lieber's text on hermeneutics was quite important in the development of constitutional arguments about *slav ery in the antebellum period, and Lieber imported the ideas of many European jurists, such as those of Johann Kaspar Bluntschli, into the American juristic vocabulary through his writings on international law. At the time that the American codification movement was in full swing, the German debate over codification brought on by Savigny's small pamphlet, *Vom beruf unserer Zeit für Gesetzgebung und Rechtswissenschaft* (1814), was known in the United States in Abraham Hayward's translation under the title *On the Vocation of Our Age for Legislation and Jurisprudence.* Hugh Swinton Legare thought this work by Savigny was so important that he commissioned an acquaintance to find a copy and send it to him from Germany.

After the Civil War, many American lawyers and jurists began to utilize German legal concepts in their jurisprudential writings. It was during this period that the German historical school greatly influenced a generation of young lawyers and law reformers. During this period, too, German ideas on *contract law came to shift the focus of the traditional common-law approach. Oliver Wendell *Holmes Jr. in his pathbreaking lectures and in his *Common Law* (1881) saw in German legal antiquity many of the sources of Anglo-American concepts of *liberty and private law.

Roman law and the European legal systems derived therefrom were also of great importance in the development of a more precise common-law legal terminology. The pioneer in this effort was the English legal philosopher John Austin, who imported many Roman and civil law terms into the common law, and especially into jurisprudential discussions. The works of Austin and his followers were known in the United States, and a number of American jurists, like William Gardner Hammond and Roscoe *Pound, used foreign legal language to improve their own common-law discourse.

Although the vast majority of the United States followed the common law, one state, Louisiana, adopted a legal system based upon an amalgam of Spanish and French law. Other states, particularly California, Texas, and Florida, although common-law jurisdictions, adopted specific doctrines from the Spanish and French traditions that had been established in the period before they became part of the United States. Thus, for instance, these states adopted a legal regime for matrimonial property based upon the community property ideas of the Spanish legal system rather than the English common-law concepts of community property.

Implementation of European Ideas. Through-out the United States there were a number of attempts to introduce European legal ideas into the American common law, particularly in private law, and to supplant common-law doctrines, but most of these attempts were doomed to failure. Generally, even the American jurists who were most interested in European law, like Joseph Story, were not willing to replace common-law doctrines with civil-law doctrines. They were willing to supplement the common law by the importation of civilian legal ideas and theories, but not to supplant it. In a few cases, European legal theory was able to make significant inroads and modify American law. This was the case, for instance, in American contract law. During the nineteenth century the philosophical underpinnings of American contract law were expanded to include an objective approach to the interpretation of contracts as well as a subjective approach. This expansion was due, in large part, to the importation of German ideas and, especially, the "will theory" of contractual obligation developed in Germany in mid-century.

In some cases, where there was no native tradition, American jurists were even more expansive in their borrowing from European law. For example, in the early nineteenth century there were virtually no American decisions on the conflict of laws, a subject that was becoming of increasing importance due to the interaction of the laws of the various states with each other and with the federal system. The first two American treatises on the subject were both very much derived from Roman and civil law. The first of these, Samuel Livermore's *Dissertations on the Questions Which Arise from the Contrariety of Laws* (1828), was, for all intents and purposes, a summary of European legal learning on the subject. The second, and best known, Joseph Story's *Commentaries on the Conflict of Laws* (1834), was derived from Livermore's treatise as well as from an even greater selection of European sources. The European cast of American conflicts law, even today, is very much a product of this nineteenth-century borrowing.

It was not only a small handful of jurists who believed that European law was important to American lawyers during the nineteenth century, as R. H. Helmholz has demonstrated, Roman and civil law was routinely cited in American courts. Further, many American legal periodicals, like the *American Jurist and Law Magazine*, published in Boston between 1829 and 1843, made it a practice to list newly published European legal texts, even when these had not been translated. Harvard included foreign materials in its recommended law curriculum from an early date, as did David Hoffman in his influential *Course of Legal Study* (1836).

[*See also* Critical Legal Studies; Law and Society Movement; Publishing, Law]

• Roscoe Pound, "The Influence of French Law in America," *Illinois Law Review* (1909): 354–63; and *The Formative Era of American Law,* 1938. Peter Stein, "The Attraction of the Civil Law in Post-Revolutionary America," *Virginia Law Review* (1966): 403–34. Daniel R. Coquillette, "Justinian in Braintree: John Adams, Civilian Learning, and Legal Elitism, 1775–1778," in *Law in Colonial Massachussetts, 1630–1800* (F. S. Ellis, ed.), 1984. M. H. Hoeflich, "The Americanization of British Legal Education in the Nineteenth Century," *Journal of Legal History* (1987): 244–59; "Transatlantic Friendships and the German Influence on American Law in the First Half of the Nineteenth Century," *American Journal of Comparative Law* (1987): 599–611; and *Roman and Civil Law and the Development of Anglo-American Jurisprudence,* 1997.   —Michael H. Hoeflich

JURISPRUDENCE, AMERICAN: THE REVOLT AGAINST FORMALISM

Jurisprudential thinking in nineteenth-century America failed both to keep pace with changing social, political, and economic conditions and to develop original ways, commensurate with American experience, to look at law and the legal system. In part this was because the expositors of jurisprudential ideas in the nineteenth century were busy attorneys and judges. The Thomas *Cooleys and Christopher Tiedemans whose treatises dominated post–Civil War thinking were concerned with practical law, not theory. Reformers like John Norton Pomeroy and David Dudley *Field had narrow objectives. They did not try to reconceptualize the law, merely to make it more efficient. The classics of jurisprudence, like John Austin's lectures, were still widely read, supplemented by German historical writers like Friedrich Karl von Savigny and Rudolf Von Ihering, who debated endlessly the relative value of Roman law and Germanic customs. The younger German writers seemed to appreciate the role of social and economic context, but they made little impression here. Our own lawyer-jurisprudents were out of touch with the new academic disciplines that were coming to dominate the curriculums at the elite universities. They still clung to a *natural-law order, colored with the idea of progress.

Oliver Wendell *Holmes Jr., in his lectures on *common law at Lowell Institute, later revised and expanded as *The Common Law* (1881), recognized that the life of the law was change and that logical formalism of the Langdellian sort only obscured the changes. Holmes knew Peirce's work on prag-

matism slightly, but was not very much taken with it. Instead, he offered a "grab-bag of other 'forces' that shaped the law": necessity, history, public policy, moral consensus, and even the prejudices of particular judges, yes—logic, no. Holmes did not assay any jurisprudence; certainly nothing more original than a combination of John Austin's positivism (the law is the command of the state) and Jeremy Bentham's instrumentalism (the command of the state should better the condition of the people), though later in life Holmes decided that he was sympathetic to Dewey's social pragmatism. Holmes's contribution to jurisprudence was to couple historical subjects to instrumental objects, a feat of scholarship that made Holmes the patron saint of the next generation of modernists but did not really move formalism from its pedestal.

Against the bedrock of formalism flowed higher and higher tides of social and economic controversy. It was a perfect Kuhnian situation of a paradigm under assault—the paradigm still stands, but more and more observations contradict its central tenets. A court that denied political and social reality would (and did) have a hard time dealing with new forms of political and social organization and new ideas of political and social right. The purpose of jurisprudence was to aid lawmakers in understanding what they did, but the old jurisprudence was helpless and, when the forces of reaction in the courts came to light, formalist jurisprudence changed from a bumbling anachronism to a sinister coconspirator in the eyes of reformers.

Christopher Columbus Langdell, Harvard Law School's pathbreaking dean from 1870 to 1895, may be best remembered today as the promulgator of the casebook method of law study. But perhaps equally important as his impact on legal education and jurisprudence in America well into the twentieth century was his innovation in appointing and arguing for a professional academic law professor class—the single most important precondition of the new jurisprudence. Though exogenous anomalies were daily shaking the old jurisprudential verities, only a new kind of insider, a new cadre of professional academics, could refashion jurisprudence in any profound and thoroughgoing way.

Langdell's persistence, in the face of dwindling classes and puzzled students, was remarkable. But in the end he triumphed. Full-time professors of law were to have no allegiance to a particular client's perspective; they were to be intellectually free to explore and argue the rules of law as they saw fit. As members of a university community they were also encouraged to apply emerging academic disciplines and ideas to fundamental questions about law. Finally, as academics, freed from court-imposed deadlines, client meetings, and other practical chores, they were to have more time to simply think about the law, its problems and its place in American society. The greatest irony of Langdell's successful innovation in creating this professional legal academic jurisprudent would be that the professors would mount an ultimately successful revolt against the jurisprudential formalism Langdell himself espoused.

Roscoe *Pound was not the first of these law professors, but he studied under them, and saw, as practioner-professors did not, where academic jurisprudence might go. The common law gave to judges the power (and Pound implied, the duty) to uphold the *property rights of individuals, no matter how bent by reality (for the workers who "bargained" for longer hours and accepted jobs with dangerous working conditions had little choice, in reality), and that made common law the defender of an old and now dangerous view of society. The inference led Pound to a powerful social insight: the conception of law as a means toward social ends and the doctrine that law exists to secure interests, social, public, and private requires the jurist keep in touch with life. By upholding these interests, Pound argued, and creating rights to secure them, law is very likely to be something made rather than found. So much for formalism or a jurisprudence of concepts, as Pound derisively termed the old paradigm.

To his side in this quest he summoned philosophy, sociology, history, and the more traditional sources of legal study—a bricolage of disciplines. Pound fabricated from the bits and pieces of old jurisprudence and modern case law a powerful restatement of what was wrong with American jurisprudence. The new jurisprudence must be utilitarian. It should limit the use of private property in the common good; prevent outrageous claims of liberty of *contract, establish the duties of public utilities, and protect the virtuous *debtor. The new jurisprudence even pointed to a return to *strict liability. Overall, social interests were now being recognized.

The agenda of the antiformalist jurisprudence that emerged at the end of the nineteenth and the beginning of the twentieth centuries included social scientific studies of the "actual social effects" of legal doctrines and how the law worked. Holmes and Pound's initial revolt against the formalism of the era inspired others to examine and question earlier legal thought. Joseph Bingham, in 1912, answered the question "What is Law?" with the revolutionary proposal that it is a mental or psychological construct. Jerome *Frank would take Bingham's insight much further in 1930 in his best-selling jurisprudential tome *Law and the Modern Mind*. Pound, himself, turned to *sociology to ground law as a social institution worthy of social scientific study, an idea he tried to apply in the data heavy analysis of the Cleveland Crime Study he headed with Felix *Frankfurter. Karl *Llewellyn, with Jerome Frank one of the second generation of antiformalists who came to be known as "realists," would look at economics and later anthropology for social scientific support for his jurisprudential ideas.

The effect of all these approaches and challenges to formalism was to remove law from the untouchable realm of discovered principles by supposedly neutral judges to that of a living entity deeply connected to and influenced by the society in which it operates. This insight then opened the way to progressive reform of the law, an explicit or implicit objective of all these antiformalist challengers to the jurisprudential order. Over the course of five decades, from Holmes through the work of Pound, Bingham, and Benjamin *Cardozo, who writing from the judge's perspective in *The Nature of the Judicial Process* borrowed from the trail blazers and expanded on their message, to the more boldly, even irreverently, critical work of the realist agitators of the 1930s like Llewellyn and Frank, the revolt against the conservative formalist jurisprudence took shape and demolished the outmoded paradigm. All the jurisprudence of the remainder of the twentieth century acknowledged and responded to the revised landscape of antiformalism.

[*See also* Education, Legal; Educator, Legal; Legal Realism; Social Dimension of Law]

• Roscoe Pound, "Mechanical Jurisprudence," *Columbia Law Review* (1908): 101. Joseph W. Bingham, "What is the Law," *Michigan Law Review* (1912): 22. Benjamin Nathan Cardozo, *The Nature of the Judicial Process,* 1919. Jerome Frank, *Law and the Modern Mind,* 1930. Laura Kalman, *Legal Realism at Yale, 1927–1960,* 1986. Morton Horwitz, *The Transformation of American Law, 1870–1960,* 1992. John Henry Schlegel, *American Legal Realism and Empirical Social Science,* 1995. N. E. H. Hull, *Roscoe Pound & Karl Llewellyn: Searching For An American Jurisprudence,* 1998.   —N. E. H. Hull

JURISPRUDENCE, AMERICAN: 1945–1970

During the disruptive period immediately following the American Revolution, law was uniquely positioned to be a source of order and continuity in the unruly new republic. With state legislatures expressing their anti-elitist zeal with measures like expansive debt relief, Federalist leaders looked to legal traditionalism to provide a "reasoned" check to democratic "passion." The *Constitution, in particular, seemed a perfect mediator between democracy and authority, serving simultaneously as the declared expression of popular *sovereignty and as a distinctly *legal* text, to be interpreted only by those learned in the law. In an ornate vocabulary drawn largely from the natural law tradition, lawyers of the early Constitutional period described themselves as "trustees" of the virtue of the republic and "priests at the temple of justice," placed as sentinels on the dangerous outposts of defense to guard the nation from the specifically democratic threats of irrational legislation and mob rule.

While law was a source of reason and authority, however, its precise content was uncertain. In the early colonies "law" meant a stable set of religiously based obligations, but each colony had adopted the precise forms of the English *common law to suit its own economic and geographic conditions and its own social and religious assumptions. Although the disparate and quirky procedural forms of the common law writ system still gave law most of its content and predictability, and lawyers their claim to expertise, by the early 1800s there was no single "common law." Moreover, traditional cohesive religious obligations were challenged by a variety of factors: economic expansion, especially in transportation; population growth; ethnic/religious pluralism; and celebration of individual freedom and entrepreneurship. Meanwhile, sources for law included not just common law, but also *natural law (traditional religious/ethical obligation as well as the secular Enlightenment's formulation of natural rights, so rhetorically powerful during the Revolution), statutory law, and the recently ratified Constitution. The appropriate role of each source in relation to the others was by no means obvious.

Early nineteenth century jurists confronted the challenge of disparate sources and a changing reality with self-confident activism. The Supreme Court of Chief Justice *Marshall deftly blended common law and natural law traditions to justify broad protection of *property, *contract, and *corporation rights, while rooting ultimate authority in the Constitution. Meanwhile, private law judges elided the potential conflict between common law and natural law, as well as between tradition and market freedom, by employing two interpretive techniques: "liberality" and "implication." Liberality meant interpreting the strict, outmoded forms of common law with a flexible progressive spirit and with a special concern for commercial utility. This liberality, jurists claimed, had always been part of the "changing changelessness" of the common law tradition, evidence of its reasonableness and hence of its consistency with natural reason and the whole natural law tradition.

The technique of implication meant linking the notion of free subjective choice, basic to the growing commercial importance of contract law, to a set of discrete relationships (bailment, sales, labor), each with its own set of assumed expectations and goals. Judges interpreted private intent in light of quasi-public policies and principles, thereby muting the conflict between subjective self-interested choice (with the relativity of values that implied) and a more cohesive conception of community obligation.

In retrospect, the activism of the pre–Civil War period had a robust pragmatic character, but it was ill-suited to the model of liberal political legitimacy then gaining dominance—the model of the individual as absolute rights bearer, protected by the "rule of law" from a potentially oppressive sovereign power. The thrust of later nineteenth century law was toward a universalized and rationalized conceptualism which would render coherent the liberal model of political legitimacy. Particularized categories based on the procedural forms of the common law writ system and on distinct social groupings gave way, after the Civil War, to a unified conceptual scheme of absolute rights and powers within spheres whose boundaries were objectively derived by judicial reference to a few highly abstracted doctrinal categories.

This structure, which dominated the "classical" turn-of-the-century period, postulated a boundary between the private realm, within which individuals owned property and made freely willed choices, and the public realm, within which the state exercised its legitimate police power. This structure, in turn, was marked by a high level of analogic uniformity. For example, property rights an individual could claim as against another individual were identical to those that could be claimed as against either the state or the national government—a uniformity inconceivable in the early nineteenth century. Moreover, the crucial boundary between public and private reproduced itself at every level of legal analysis, generating a vast proliferation of strictly bounded dualities: (private) *tort law was now wholly distinct from (public) *criminal law, as was (fault-based) negligence from the more "public" *strict liability side of torts, as was contract from the more public tort law, as was the freely bargained contract from the more tort-like quasi-contract, etc.

To classical jurists the very meaning of liberty itself lay in the judicial protection of bounded dualities, especially the boundary between the public sphere of state action and the private sphere of individual freedom. That protection, in turn, meant the exercise of judicial reason—a reason now described, not as embodying moral principles or commitment to the public good, but simply as the application of objective methodology to the task of boundary definition. While others could, within their spheres, exercise unbridled will in pursuit of moral, political or economic goals, judges must exercise only reason, for the specific task of "finding" correct boundaries.

That methodology, in turn, depended upon the coherence of a few key categories (e.g., property, free contract) central to Constitutional law's definition of protected *liberty. Classical jurists were confident that those categories could be found within a now highly rationalized private law doctrine. For example, Williston's monumental treatise on contracts demonstrated that all of contract doctrine could logically be derived from the basic premise of free contract itself, the same premise protected by the Constitution. Upon the supposed objectivity of this conceptualism hinged the liberal faith that the rule of law could resolve the tension between freedom as unfettered private right and freedom as the republican ideal of public participation and civic virtue.

During the classical period, however, the concepts that supposedly defined "liberty"—free contract especially—seemed starkly at odds with a reality of unrestrained industrial power and impoverished workers living in squalor and disease. For a time classical legalism's zeal for conceptualism had seemed consistent with the post–Civil War search for general principles in both natural and social science, and also with the Darwinism invading social theory. By century's end, however, academic social scientists, influenced by the Progressive movement, had started to emphasize inductive empiricism and data gathering as the only way to study the complex interrelationships of a modern industrial, urban society. Meanwhile, Progressive political theorists, urging public regulation of business and worker protection, challenged the coherence of the notion of purely "private" property or wholly "free" contracting. When the Supreme Court, during the infamous *Lochner era, overturned popular wage and hour regulations and early New Deal legislation as unconsti-

tutionally invading free contract rights, the Court appeared to be overreaching its authority for the sake of promoting laissez-faire economic ideology.

The legal realists, who came to be associated with the New Deal, carried on with gusto the Progressive critique of classical conceptualism, attacking the coherence of the categories upon which the whole structure depended. Collapsing the crucial public/private distinction, the realists described "property" and "free contract" as simply a delegation of the (public) power to exclude or withhold. Similarly, they described "rights" as the self-referencing outcome of legal decision-making, with no essentialist content and always subject to equally logical but wholly contradictory claims of competing right. Moreover, the realists demonstrated that the application of rules and precedents to new cases could never be neutral and objective; inevitably, interpretation involved choices about relevance which were inherently value-laden.

As associated with the New Deal *legal realism meant embracing the growing role of government, especially administrative agencies, in regulating an advanced economy. As applied to private law, realism meant eschewing abstract formalism and doing a fact-based, policy-oriented "justice" in the particular case. This policy-orientation required the collection of social and economic data for the sake of making sensible policy choices, and also for understanding the role of law within the institutional structures of a complex economy. The realists thus removed law from its sphere of autonomous, objective logic, placing it within a larger set of social and political systems.

After World War II, however, with communist totalitarianism expanding abroad, the complacent realist assumption that lawyers should simply be elite policymakers for the regulatory state seemed far from satisfying. Classical legalism had held out the promise that the rule of law could effectively protect a realm of civil freedom from totalitarian statism. In the wake of the realist assault, jurists were left searching among the doctrinal ruins, so to speak, in an effort to reconstruct a still-coherent basis for that promise.

During the 1950s many reconstructive efforts were based on the Hart and Sacks legal process materials, which optimistically described an America in which people shared their confidence, not in particular substantive legal categories, but in the process by which decision-making took place within various institutions, each with is own distinct competency. The special competency of judging was "reasoned elaboration," as opposed to the "unbuttoned" discretion exercised by legislatures.

The shift from substance to process seemed to satisfy the realist critique of substantive rights, while also recognizing the importance of doctrinal vocabulary as a culturally (if not logically) constraining force. Still, the precise distinction between discretion and reasoned elaboration remained elusive in the absence of objective doctrinal categories or modes of interpretation; during the 1960s and 1970s, with Vietnam War and civil rights protests, the complacent worldview of shared values ran counter to reality.

Most post-realist reconstruction has been less ambitious than Hart and Sacks', but its techniques now pervade modern law. Typically, key realist insights are conceded, then incorporated as strengths in an otherwise intact structure: the indeterminacy of rules becomes "flexibility," and the collapse of rights into contradiction is recast as "competing interests" requiring enlightened judicial balancing. Similarly, the collapse of clear conceptual categories led, not to the abandonment of doctrine or the public/private distinction, but to a recognition of blurred rather than absolute boundaries, an approach which now cuts across all doctrinal lines. So too, standards of reasonableness and justice pervade modern treatises and opinions, leaving unresolved an inherent tension between rules and general standards.

Meanwhile, during the New Deal the Supreme Court finally abandoned to the legislature the field of economic *regulation. That abandonment left uncertain the status of other rights, and led to a serious reexamination of *judicial review. In the 1970s Alexander Bickel called for "prudence," meaning Supreme Court deference to legislative bodies in all areas, while Herbert Wechsler advocated instead a return to general and neutral principles as the only legitimate basis for judicial review. Even as legal academics called for judicial restraint or reasoned justification, however, the *Warren Court expanded the scope of liberty and equality rights more dramatically than had any Court in history.

In defense of an activist Court, liberal academics fought back the call for prudence or neutrality by invoking a variety of justifications: versions of natural law, sophisticated reassertions of shared values, frank invocation of extralegal ethical norms, return to radical republicanism, and "representation reinforcement" on behalf of the marginalized and excluded. Despite some critical neo-realist skeptics, many academics shared a fresh faith that Constitutional law could be a source for a new era of justice and equality.

Dashing that faith, however, the Supreme Court soon retreated from activism into what some consider an almost classical reliance on reference to ahistoric conceptualism and federalist spheres of distinct powers. At the same time many fear that the judicial appointments process has become so politically driven that the ideal of neutral or objective judging has lost all meaning.

Some have now filled the void left by the lost faith in conceptual coherence with a law and economics methodology which ignores doctrinal categories for the sake of reaching efficient results— i.e., results that mimic unhampered market exchange. Meanwhile, a promising direction from left scholars, has been to accept the bankruptcy of objective conceptualism and to pay attention to those traditionally excluded from mainstream legal thought—women, the poor, and persons of color. This outsider jurisprudence understands rights only in relation to moral practice and as situated in historical context. The insights now emerging are a hopeful sign for the future.

[*See also* Civil Rights and Civil Liberties; Legal Reasoning]

—Elizabeth B. Meusch

JURISPRUDENCE, AMERICAN: 1970–PRESENT

Ronald Dworkin began his career in jurisprudence as a critic of positivism. In his 1967 article "The Model of Rules," he advanced an interesting and, in the view of many legal scholars, successful criticism of legal positivism, specifically the positivism of H. L. A. Hart. The essence of Hart's positivism, as presented in his pathbreaking book, *The Concept of Law* (1961), had two principal elements: his theory of law, advanced as a critique of the then-reigning view of John Austin, and his account of adjudication.

Hart argued that law is essentially a matter of rules. He divided rules into two categories, primary and secondary. Primary rules are rules setting forth obligations and prohibitions. Secondary rules, which regulate the application of primary rules, include rules for changing primary rules. The most important secondary rule is the "rule of recognition," which functions as a basic norm for the legal system. The "validity" of the rule of recognition is grounded in social acceptance. The validity of all other secondary rules and primary rules depends on their connection to the rule of recognition.

In Chapter 7 of *The Concept of Law*, Hart stated that law is expressed in language and is, for that reason, subject to judicial interpretation. He argued that legal concepts have both a core (uncontroversial) and a penumbral (disputed) meaning.

It is in the application of legal concepts that judges sometimes have to exercise their discretion in deciding whether a given case falls within the purview of a concept.

Dworkin contested both aspects of Hart's positivism. Hart's ontology of law was incomplete, Dworkin maintained, because the law contains principles as well as rules. As an example Dworkin used, among others, the famous case of *Riggs* v. *Palmer* (1889). Elmer Palmer killed his grandfather by poison in order to obtain money earmarked for Elmer under his grandfather's will. In a split decision, New York's highest court found the principle "no person should profit from his own wrongdoing" to take precedence over straightforward application of the language of New York's Statute of Wills, and Elmer was denied his legacy. According to Dworkin, this showed that Hart's ontology of law was impoverished and, for this reason, positivism must be rejected.

Dworkin also disputed Hart's account of the role of discretion in adjudication. In a move that would prefigure what many take to be Dworkin's central contribution to jurisprudence, he argued that law and morality are joined at the deepest level of political theory. In his argument that law is a "seamless web" of principle, Dworkin used political theory as the basis for his claim that, no matter how difficult the task, judges do not have discretion and are always required to do their best to find the right answer in every case.

In 1986, Dworkin published his first full-length account of law, *Law's Empire*. In this work, he maintained that law is an "interpretive" practice. Citing and alluding to the hermeneutical tradition in German philosophy, he advanced the argument that all understanding of law is ultimately a matter of interpretation. Dworkin used the figure of a fictional judge—Hercules—to illustrate the three stages of legal interpretation. In the first, pre-interpretive stage, the judge gathers together legal materials all would agree are relevant to the question at hand. In the second, interpretive stage, the judge advances a justification for the materials assembled in the first stage. In the third, post-interpretive stage, the judge decides on a justification that puts the law "in its best light."

In *Law's Empire* Dworkin expanded his earlier claims about the nature of law and law's relationship to political theory. In addition to reaffirming (albeit in a less enthusiastic way) his claim that every legal decision has a right answer, Dworkin continued to argue for the superiority of his view of law against positivism. In fact, *Law's Empire* contains thorough critiques of both legal positivism and *law and economics, two leading schools of jurisprudence. Dworkin's work remains absolutely essential for anyone working in any aspect of legal theory. While his views are quite controversial, no one denies their relevance.

Law and economics is another leading school of jurisprudence. Some law and economics work of interest is in the public law arena (e.g., public choice theory), but the bulk of law and economics scholarship is in the area of private law. Richard Posner, though not without his critics, is generally viewed as the pioneer in the use of economic analysis in law. Beginning with his 1972 book *Economic Analysis of Law*, and throughout his career as a law professor and judge, Posner has done more than any individual to advance the cause of the economic approach to law.

It is difficult, perhaps impossible, to reduce law and economics to a few propositions. Law and economics scholars, especially scholars of private law, are interested in "explaining" the law. What is meant by "explanation" is not always clear, but one way of expressing the aspiration of law and economics scholars is to say that law and economics seeks to identify the "goals" of a given area of law.

Consider *tort law. When asked for the elements of a cause of action in tort, every lawyer will answer "duty, breach of duty, causation, and injury." A law and economics explanation of tort law can identify the goals of tort law that include, but are not limited to, deterring risky conduct and compensating victims of wrongful acts. Thus, the law and economics "explanation" of tort law is an account of how tort law can and should go about the business of discouraging risk and compensating for injuries.

Another central concept of law and economics scholarship is "efficiency." Various formulations of efficiency are advanced by scholars, in both descriptive and prescriptive forms. For example, one might ask whether a given regulation or body of legal doctrine achieves efficiency in transactions (e.g., *contract law). Similarly, law and economics scholars frequently criticize existing legal doctrine for failure to achieve efficient outcomes. It is not unusual to see legal scholarship from the economics perspective that argues for complete overhaul of a given body of law.

Despite trenchant and long-standing criticism of its premises, law and economics is now the dominant form of private-law theory in the legal academy. The dominance of law and economics has made itself felt in all areas of law and has made its way into the daily pedagogical activities of law professors. Nevertheless, its scope and usefulness remain subjects of great consternation and debate.

*Critical legal studies began at the University of Wisconsin in 1977. After a small group of law professors, disenchanted with conventional doctrinal scholarship, met to discuss their mutual frustrations, they decided to pursue their interests in a systematic and ongoing fashion. The movement known as critical legal studies has changed from its heyday in law schools during the 1970s and 1980s. Today, "traditional" critical legal studies has given way to critical feminist theory (see FEMINIST LEGAL THEORY) and *critical race theory, each of which arose out of particular dissatisfactions with mainstream critical legal studies. Nevertheless, mainstream critical legal studies has had lasting effects on legal academia.

The central intellectual figure in critical legal studies is Roberto Mangabeira Unger. A student and then a professor at Harvard, Unger has written some of the most significant books in legal theory. In 1975 he published Law and Politics the first complete critique of liberal political and legal theory by a member of the critical legal studies movement. It marked Unger as the doyen of the movement and guaranteed his place in the history of critical legal studies.

Also prominent in critical legal studies is the work of Duncan Kennedy. Kennedy argued that legal doctrine is "indeterminate" and, for that reason, any legal outcome could be justified. The "indeterminacy thesis" remains a hotly contested aspect of critical legal studies. There is now substantial disagreement over what exactly the "thesis" was and the extent to which anyone or everyone adhered to it. Nevertheless, anyone associated with virtually any aspect of critical legal studies identifies it as the movement that gave birth to the idea of legal indeterminacy.

Legal formalism is best represented today in the work of Ernest Weinrib. In a series of articles spanning several decades, Weinrib developed an original approach to private law. In a unique synthesis of the work of Aristotle, Aquinas, Hegel, and Kant, he has shown how tort law is a conceptual unity held together by a necessary conceptual structure. In The Idea of Private Law (1995), Weinrib presents a systematic account of the nature of private law. Following Hegel, he argues that private-law ordering is a matter of certain basic concepts structuring the entire process of legal justification. For example, there can be no *liability

without fault, for the very concept of liability "implies" the concept of fault. The act of a tortfeasor (one who commits a tort) can be regarded as a wrong only when the tortfeasor inflicts injury in a way that violates a preexisting duty owed to another.

With this scheme, Weinrib rejects *strict liability as a form of tort law. He also uses his conception of private law to reject the premises of law and economics. For example, economic analysis might explain tort law with the argument that the goal of tort law is compensation of victims for personal injury. Weinrib points out that such an explanation fails to explain why the tortfeasor and not a third party is the one properly required to pay compensation. Weinrib believes that the bipolar nature of the civil lawsuit is dictated by juridical concepts necessarily implicated by tort law. Failing to account for all these concepts is a central fault of the economic approach to law.

The later philosophy of Ludwig Wittgenstein has been immensely influential in philosophical circles. In recent jurisprudence, two scholars have made great use of Wittgenstein's philosophical achievements to advance debate in legal philosophy on the fundamental issues of legitimacy, justification, and truth. The most original example of this work is that of Philip Bobbitt in constitutional law. Bobbitt argues that constitutional argument—indeed, all legal argument—uses six forms of argument (he refers to them as "modalities") to show the truth of legal propositions. These six forms (textual, doctrinal, historical, ethical, structural, and prudential) exhaust the argumentative possibilities for law. Bobbitt shows how the debate over the so-called countermajoritarian objection in constitutional law is a red herring, one that disappears when we see that legitimacy in constitutional argument is not a matter of results but depends upon the use of the forms of legal argument to show the truth of legal propositions. Bobbitt's work in constitutional theory is not uncontroversial, but it is among the most original recent work in the field of constitutional law and jurisprudence in general.

In Law and Truth (1996), Dennis Patterson takes Bobbitt's work in constitutional theory and expands it into a jurisprudential theory he refers to as "practice theory." Patterson shows that the forms of argument are part of a wider discursive structure of legal argument. Starting from the observation that law is a Wittgensteinian language game, Patterson shows how the truth of legal assertions is ultimately a matter of forms of argument. There is, Patterson maintains, no legal truth outside this system of argument.

[*See also* Fault Liability]

• Ronald Dworkin, *Taking Rights Seriously*, 1973. Roberto Unger, *Knowledge and Politics*, 1975. Philip Bobbitt, *Constitutional Fate*, 1982. Philip Bobbitt, *Constitutional Interpretation*, 1991. Richard Posner, *The Problems of Jurisprudence*, 1991.
                                    —Dennis Patterson

JURY

Right to a Jury Trial
Juries

JURY: RIGHT TO A JURY TRIAL

The Right to a Jury Trial in Historical Perspective. The right to trial by jury is deeply rooted in history. Allusion to the idea of utilizing ordinary citizens to decide the legal culpability of those accused of committing crimes or wrongfully harming others has been detected in the annals of ancient Greek and Roman civilizations. But the first clear-cut recognition of the right to judgment by laypersons occurred in 1215 when England's King John was forced by the nobility to sign the Magna Carta, a document that forbade the imposition of imprisonment, exile, or a death sentence without judgment by peers. Although a secret and arbitrary administrative court known as the Star Chamber sometimes supplanted jury trials from the fifteenth through the seventeenth century, entrusting judgments about guilt and innocence to a jury drawn from the community ultimately became enshrined in the British jurisprudential system.

The American colonists quickly adopted the jury system. So cherished was the right to a jury trial that it was the only procedural right included in the original U.S. *Constitution: Article III, Section 2, states that "the trial of all crimes, except in cases of impeachment, shall be by jury." The Sixth Amendment to the Constitution, adopted in 1791, which enumerates various rights of the accused, reaffirms the right and further stipulates that the jury be an impartial body drawn from the district where an alleged crime took place. The Seventh Amendment extends the right to a jury trial to all civil cases involving a dispute over twenty dollars or more.

Some state constitutions also include the right to jury trial, but often in attenuated form, limiting applicability to a restricted set of cases such as serious *felonies. Compounding matters was the constitutional doctrine of *Barron* v. *Baltimore* (1833) that rights protected in the first ten amendments only applied to cases heard in federal court.

This meant that the Sixth and Seventh Amendments were rather hollow protections, because the vast majority of criminal and civil litigation is based on state law and takes place in state courts. Essentially this left defendants at the mercy of state legal systems that had widely varying practices concerning the boundaries of the right to a jury trial.

This situation changed dramatically in 1968, when the U.S. Supreme Court ruled in *Duncan* v. *Louisiana* that the *due process clause of the *Fourteenth Amendment guaranteed the right to a jury trial to any person tried in state court who would be so entitled if the case had arisen in federal court. Subsequent decisions have established that anyone subject to at least six months imprisonment may demand a jury trial. The Supreme Court has also ruled that the right to a jury trial in civil cases is not a fundamental right, and that states are at liberty to determine the extent to which (if at all) defendants being sued for civil wrongs, such as negligence or breach of contract, must be afforded the opportunity to have the case decided by a jury.

While the right to a jury trial is now embedded in constitutional law doctrine, the Supreme Court has permitted variations in the nature of jury structures and processes. The court has ruled that juries that are smaller than the twelve-person jury utilized in federal criminal cases are permissible, as long as there are at least six jurors (*Ballew* v. *Georgia* (1978)). It has been held that state court juries need not be unanimous to reach a noncapital verdict, which is a departure from the federal rule that requires unanimity (*Johnson* v. *Louisiana*; *Apodaca* v. *Oregon* (1972)). Flexibility has also been allowed regarding other aspects of the jury trial, such as whether the foreperson must be chosen by the entire jury, whether jurors can take notes, and the extent to which jurors in deliberation may review the trial transcript. Disparities in jury processes are rooted in American *federalism, the fundamental constitutional principle establishing some national rules binding on all the states while leaving substantial room for diversity at the state level.

The American Jury's Role in Adjudication. At one time the jury made both legal and factual determinations in deciding verdicts. Gradually, however, *judges took over the role of lawgiver; it is now the case that jurors at the federal level and in all but two states (Maryland and Indiana) are mandated to follow the legal instructions given by a judge at the end of a trial. Jurors are told what must be proven in order for defendants to be convicted of specific charges (the "elements of a crime") as well as the applicable standard of *proof that must be applied. They are also given general instructions about interpretation of *evidence and the drawing of inferences.

The jury's role is therefore now primarily one of fact finder. Its province is to determine whether persons charged with crimes did what they were alleged to have done, whether their actions violated the law as defined by the judge, and whether they had the state of mind that the law requires to find culpability (e.g., intentionality, recklessness, premeditation). If the jury acquits, its word is final—no matter how dubious the verdict. A conviction is somewhat less final because it can be overturned on *appeal if there were prejudicial legal errors made at the trial or if the defendant's rights had been violated.

One problematic aspect of the jury's role is the issue of jury nullification—the refusal to convict in the face of clearly incriminating evidence because the jury dislikes a law or the uses to which it is being put. Both colonial and early American juries occasionally engaged in this practice and in fact were at times told by judges of their right to do so. A New York jury acquitted anti-British publisher Peter Zenger of seditious libel in 1735 despite conclusive proof that he had printed articles in his newspaper that were indisputably libelous. Some pre–civil law juries in the North similarly acquitted persons who had unquestionably harbored runaway slaves in violation of the fugitive slave laws.

In 1896, however, in *Sparf and Hansen* v. *United States*, the Supreme Court repudiated the right of jurors to set the law aside. More recently, the United State Court of Appeals for the Second Circuit in *United States* v. *Thomas* (1997) said potential jurors could be excluded from the jury if they revealed a willingness to acquit someone who was clearly guilty out of contempt for the law or to avert a perceived injustice. While jury nullification is thus proscribed, juries still have the power to do as they please even if they lack formally the right to do so. Because juries have the last word and do not give reasons for their verdict, they can de facto acquit those who are truly guilty if they think the substantive law is unduly harsh (as in minor marijuana cases) or if they feel that the context in which a crime took place absolves the defendant of moral responsibility (as when a battered woman exceeds the bounds of the doctrine of self-defense in killing her batterer).

In all but a few states, juries play no role in the punishment process. They are in fact normally told expressly by presiding judges that sentencing is the sole province of the judge and that legal culpability must be determined without regard to the fate that a defendant might suffer. Juries are usually long gone from the courthouse when the judge, after a special hearing, pronounces the sentence.

There is, however, a major exception to the exclusion of the jury from sentencing: capital cases. The Supreme Court has ruled, in *Gregg* v. *Georgia* (1976) and other cases, that death sentences can only be imposed or recommended by juries after a special hearing where aggravating and mitigating circumstances are considered. If the prosecution seeks *capital punishment (provided for in specific categories of cases by the federal government and thirty-eight states), there is a bifurcated trial. The jury first decides whether the defendant is guilty, and then after hearing new evidence on the opprobrium of the defendant's deeds decides whether or not to sentence a defendant to death. In many states, the jury's decision to impose the death sentence or to spare the defendant's life is conclusive, but in some states the presiding judge can overturn it.

Civil cases are also usually divided into two stages. Based on the applicable law as explained by the judge, the jury first decides whether the defendant is liable for the harm allegedly befalling the plaintiff. If it rules for the plaintiff, another hearing is held to provided evidence about money damages. The jury can award compensatory damages, the monetary equivalent of the injuries inflicted on the plaintiff; and in certain kinds of cases it can also award punitive damages, an additional penalty assessed to punish the defendant for particularly egregious conduct. While the jury can theoretically award millions (and even billions) of dollars, not only do judges have the right to reduce excessive damage awards but some states have placed maximum limits on the amounts of punitive damages awards.

Jury Selection Principles. The Constitution says little about the composition of juries other than that they must be "impartial" and drawn from the district where an alleged crime was committed. However, constitutional law as well as changes in statutory law have stipulated specific procedures that must be followed and practices that must be avoided in order to assure that proper juries are constituted. There are three guiding principles governing methods of jury selection: 1) all citizens have a legal duty to serve on juries if called unless they are exempted or excused; 2) the jury pool must be a cross-section of the community; and 3) biased jurors who might decide cases subjectively must be precluded from serving.

Early jury selection mechanics relied on jury commissioners who selected persons of sound mind and good character to serve on juries; this was known as the "key man" system. Because this approach not only vested such commissioners with almost unfettered discretion in their choices but in practice limited jurors to a small spectrum of the population, it was replaced by a system relying on voting lists from which names of candidates for jury service were randomly generated. But this method too was skewed because of differential rates of voting registration based on demographic traits such as age, race, and income. Consequently, multiple source lists are now normally utilized to include rosters of licensed drivers, tax rolls, and records of welfare recipients. Jurisdictions that continue to rely on narrow samples of the population run the risk of having convictions overturned because jurors were selected from panels that were unrepresentative.

To further insure maximum inclusivity, many categorical exemptions from jury service have now been rescinded; lawyers, police officers, physicians, morticians, and members of other occupational groups are no longer automatically kept off the jury. Across-the-board exclusion of parents with primary child-care responsibilities without regard for individual circumstances was a particularly limiting feature of jury selection procedures, because it disproportionately removed women from the ranks of those called for jury duty and thus contributed to the predominance of male jurors; it has been abolished in most states. One persisting exclusion, that of convicted felons, has been constitutionally questioned on the grounds that it disqualifies an inordinate number of blacks and Hispanics from serving, but this challenge has yet to be sustained by the courts.

Those who arrive at the courthouse prepared for jury duty are assigned by lot to a specific trial and are then vetted by the presiding judge and the attorneys to ascertain whether they have bias that would preclude them from serving. Both defendants and prosecutors have the right to prevent persons called to court from serving on a particular jury if they demonstrate bias. A process called the *voir dire* (meaning "to speak the truth") is part of the empaneling of any jury: potential jurors are asked a number of questions by lawyers and/or the judge intended to ferret out biases and preconceptions. Those who are in some way personally connected to the parties to the trial may be struck

from the jury by the judge. More significantly, those who demonstrate to the satisfaction of the judge that they have prejudices regarding issues involved in the case (e.g., the use of drugs) or negativity towards groups of people relevant to the case (e.g., racial prejudice or homophobia) may be removed. These requests for exclusion, called challenges for "cause," are only partially successful in making the jury ultimately selected truly objective because the questioning process is often quite superficial and some jurors who pass muster in reality harbor underlying preconceptions that prevent open-mindedness.

One controversial use of the challenge for cause occurs in capital cases. Jurors who state that they are unequivocally opposed to the death penalty under any and all circumstances can be (and normally are) removed from the jury. Although it has been contended that this tilts the jury in favor of those who are pro-prosecution because death penalty opponents are also more liberal in general, the Supreme Court ruled in *Lockhart* v. *McCree* (1986) that those voicing scruples about inflicting the death penalty can be eliminated because their sentiments would preclude them from heeding arguments in favor of death at the punishment phase of the trial.

A venerable practice of American courts is the granting to both sides in criminal cases a certain number of opportunities to remove jurors without any rationale whatsoever; these are called "peremptory challenges." The theory behind giving this carte blanche chance to eliminate jurors who have not necessarily evidenced bias is that it allows both the prosecution and the defense to rely on hunches and intuition to eliminate prejudiced people who are able to conceal their convictions. It has been thought that such exclusions provide for a cleansing of the jury of people who have made up their minds or who lean in a specific direction even before the trial starts.

This practice, however, came under constitutional attack some years ago because lawyers would use peremptory challenges to "shape" juries by purging entire segments of the community, thus diminishing jury representativeness. In *Batson* v. *Kentucky* (1986) the Supreme Court accepted this argument, ruling that *race could no longer be used in criminal cases as a basis for striking jurors without cause; this doctrine has been extended to civil cases. Subsequently, in *J.E.B.* v. *Alabama ex rel. T.B.* (1994), the Court held that peremptory challenges could not be used to remove women if *gender alone was the basis for the removal. While the leeway afforded both sides has thus been constitutionally constricted, in practice it has proved difficult to determine whether the impermissible criteria of race and gender were in fact the bases of peremptory challenges since by definition such challenges need not be explained or justified. To assist judges with the task of identifying wrongful uses of the peremptory challenge, special "mini" hearings are now held to explore attorneys' rationale for excluding jurors.

Legal Procedures for Enhancing Jury Fairness. During the course of trials, judges rely on established practices and the use of sound judgment in an attempt to assure that juries will be objective in their decision-making. Introduction of evidence and questioning of witnesses is constrained by complex legal rules; jurors are taken out of the courtroom when arguments are being presented about trial procedures; lawyers and witnesses are constrained if they use inflammatory language; spectators and the media are required to maintain a low-key presence; and jurors are admonished at many points about their sworn duty to rely exclusively on the evidence in deciding cases.

In addition to these and other routine protocols, there are several specific options available to judges (and sometimes legally required) to enhance the fairness of adjudication. First, if virtually the entire jury pool of a jurisdiction is slanted toward conviction because of passionate reactions to a crime and feverish media coverage, the venue of the trial can and must be changed. The trial of Timothy McVeigh for the murder of 168 people in the Oklahoma City bombing case was moved to Denver, Colorado, because it was thought to be impossible to empanel a fair jury in the city where so many were affected by the heinous crime that was committed.

Second, contrary to the standard practice of having jurors identify themselves by name and other means, juries can be empaneled anonymously if it is thought that they might be intimidated by defendants and their associates. Those fearing retaliation if they convict dangerous people might be hesitant to subject themselves to such risk, so the law permits judges to hide jurors' identities by conducting the voir dire in private and expurgating names and addresses from public records. This approach, which has been used in a good number of trials involving organized crime or violent gangs, has been approved by higher courts.

Finally, judges may order sequestration of the jury to protect it from being affected by intense media coverage. This process entails the removal of jurors from their normal life: jurors are kept together as a group; they eat their meals together; they spend nights at hotels under the surveillance of court officers; access to television or newspapers is severely limited; and they are barred from virtually all contact with anyone but each other. Sequestration may cover the entire trial, from start to finish; or it may be limited to the deliberation period. While judges are reluctant to order sequestration because it can impose acute hardships on jurors, defendants can request it in celebrated cases where passions run high. Thus former football star and television sportscaster O. J. Simpson was acquitted of murdering his wife and her friend by a jury that wound up being sequestered for 266 days pursuant to the interest of providing a fair jury trial.

Conclusion. Although the jury system has suffered much criticism in the aftermath of a number of hotly debated verdicts, the right to a jury trial remains fixed in American jurisprudence. The percentage of jury trials has diminished in both criminal and civil adjudication; most criminal cases are disposed of by guilty pleas, most civil cases by settlements, and virtually no misdemeanor cases are decided by peers. But the mere fact that trial by jury flourishes as a constitutionally guaranteed option in serious criminal cases is a constraint on the disposition of the bulk of cases that are decided without trial. Every aspect of pretrial decision-making by the law enforcement and judicial system is impacted by the ultimate recourse defendants have of taking their case before a jury and by predictions made about how jurors will behave.

There are certainly imperfections in the actual functioning of juries and occasional verdicts that do not bear scrutiny. But the right of the accused to judgment by one's peers in the United States is every bit as profound today as it was when granted in Britain by King John nearly eight hundred years ago. It is a right that has over the years been enhanced in many ways, especially in the broadening of participation to include citizens from every walk of life as jurors. Trial by jury continues to be a linchpin in the American scheme of justice.

[*See also* Courts, United States; Criminal Law Principles; Procedure, Court]

• Valerie P. Hans and Neil Vidmar, *Judging the Jury*, 1986. Jeffrey Abramson, *We, the Jury: The Jury System and the Ideal of Democracy*, 1994. Norman J. Finkel, *Commonsense Justice: Jurors' Notions of the Law*, 1995.

"The Jury: Research and Reform," *Judicature* 79 (March–April 1996). Clay S. Conrad, *Jury Nullification: The Evolution of a Doctrine*, 1998. Barry Latzer, *Death Penalty Cases: Leading U.S. Supreme Court Cases on Capital Punishment*, 1998.   —James P. Levine

JURY: JURIES

There are two kinds of juries in the American legal system. One is the petit jury (normally shortened to "the jury"), which decides whether defendants in criminal cases are guilty; it also determines whether people being sued in civil cases are liable and how much they must pay. Its name derives from its relatively small size: federal court juries hearing criminal cases have twelve members; federal juries dealing with civil cases have six members; and state court juries vary between six and twelve members.

The petit jury has its origin in medieval England. King John in 1215 established the right to trial by jury in the Magna Carta, a right which was ultimately transported to the American colonies. Both Article III of the original U.S. Constitution and the Sixth Amendment guarantee the right to trial by jury in federal criminal cases; the Seventh Amendment provides for it in civil cases heard in federal court. In *Duncan* v. *Louisiana* (1968), the U. S. Supreme Court held that the *Fourteenth Amendment requires state courts to provide for a jury trial in all serious cases. Although most criminal cases never go to a jury because they are dismissed or *plea-bargained at a pretrial state of adjudication and most civil cases are settled out of court, the hovering right to a jury trial that can be invoked has a bearing on dispositions without trials.

The grand jury is a larger body, generally comprised of sixteen to twenty-three members. Its role is to determine whether there is a sufficiently strong case against a defendant to warrant an indictment, formal allegations that require the defendant to stand trial on criminal charges. Unlike the petit jury, whose decisions must be unanimous or near-unanimous (depending on jurisdiction), the grand jury can indict by a simple majority vote. Because nearly all requests for indictments are granted after very brief presentation of evidence by the *prosecutor, the grand jury's role has become somewhat perfunctory. It has therefore been abolished in many states including California where prosecutors and judges determine whether criminal trials are justified. Although the Fifth Amendment to the Constitution requires action by a grand jury in capital cases and other "infamous" cases, the courts have ruled that this guarantee is only applicable in the federal judicial system and is not binding on the states.

The jury's mission is a seemingly simple one: apply the law as explained by the judge to the facts revealed by the evidence presented at trial. But despite careful instructions, the law can be ambiguous (e.g., what is "premeditation"?) and the facts are rarely indisputable even after a painstaking trial. The very nature of the American adversary system, which entails two sides presenting conflicting versions of the truth, complicates the jury's tasks. Consequently, jury decision-making is anything but mechanical; it is a complex judgment process.

For centuries, the juror's mind seemed impenetrable; speculation about what lay behind verdicts abounded. This all changed in 1966 when Harry Kalven Jr., and Hans Zeisel published *The American Jury*, a pathbreaking nationwide study of 3,576 verdicts in criminal cases. While juries were deliberating, cooperating presiding judges wrote down the verdict they would have reached had they been deciding the cases. These hypothetical judgments were compared to the jury's *actual* verdicts, and where differences resulted the judges were asked to proffer reasons for the discrepancy.

Their finding that judges and juries agreed in 79 percent of all cases suggested to them that most of the time, juries were guided by facts. Subsequent empirical research involving interviews with jurors and simulated juries reacting to mock trials has validated this; jurors' thinking is evidence-driven. Jurors, true to their sworn duty, do in fact endeavor to get the facts right—who was lying and who was telling the truth, whose eyewitness testimony was most credible, which alibis were sound, and what inferences can be legitimately drawn from physical evidence. Jurors reconstruct events to come up with the most plausible story of what really happened.

That one-fifth of the cases studied by Kalven and Zeisel resulted in disagreements led them to recognize that subjectivity was another unmistakable facet of jury behavior, a conclusion that has subsequently also been affirmed beyond dispute. The legal and factual uncertainties that remain despite good-faith efforts to resolve matters objectively liberate jurors to rely on personal values and predispositions in reaching a verdict. It is not that they disregard the evidence; rather, they subconsciously rely on their predilections as a guide to deciphering it. These penchants vary from juror to juror, from community to community, and from era to era—thus accounting for variability in juror verdicts that *cannot* be attributed to differences in the facts alone.

The desire for outcomes that square with jurors' moral codes or at least do not violate them egregiously is a particularly keen underpinning of their judgments. While jurors on the one hand are obsessed with facts, they are also in a quest for *justice—seeing to it that people get what they deserve. They will at times twist the law and bend the facts to achieve a morally satisfying result.

This is a subtle process. Jurors bring to bear a range of aggravating and mitigating circumstances in deciding whether to arrive at what British scholar Patrick Devlin, in *The Enforcement of Morals* (1959), called "a merciful view of the facts." For example, the law renders principals and accessories to crimes equally culpable, but jurors are inclined to treat those who played minor roles less harshly. Similarly, the right of self-defense vanishes once the victim of a crime is out of danger; but jurors may well give the benefit of the doubt to someone who attacks a fleeing assailant. Verbal provocations and obscene gestures directed at another are never a legal justification for assault, but in sorting things out, jurors are not oblivious to the assault victim's responsibility for what happened. In their search for justice based on common sense, jurors will contextualize crimes to arrive at more nuanced decision-making than the law allows.

Jurors will sometimes go beyond stretching or twisting the law; they will purposefully disregard it. This is the process known as "jury nullification," the acquitting of those who jurors think are factually guilty because they think the law is wrong or the particular application of the law is unwise. Juries who thought it was foolish to ban liquor manufacturing and sales in the 1920s acquitted many people charged with violating prohibition laws. In the 1970s some Vietnam War protesters and selective service resisters who clearly had engaged in illegal activities were exonerated by juries who thought such forms of *civil disobedience should go unpunished. Jury nullification, however, is a rare phenomenon, since jurors normally respect the laws on the books or feel morally compelled to heed the law despite having misgivings about it.

A more global set of values that almost invariably affects jurors is their political ideology. Where jurors stand on the conservative-liberal spectrum can affect their propensity to convict. Those who deem tough law enforcement a very high priority will be more prone to convict, while those who are more concerned with protecting individual rights will likely acquit. Because the standard of proof necessary to convict, "guilt beyond a reasonable doubt," is quite amorphous, jurors have considerable discretion in selecting the probability of guilt that must be demonstrated to permit conviction.

Another dimension of these ideological postulates are jurors' attitudes toward *police officers. A pro-police perspective will enhance the persuasiveness of the prosecution's case, which often is dependent on police testimony (especially in *drug cases); hostility toward the police may result in a skepticism about their assertions on the witness stand. However, this set of biases will be reversed if police officers themselves are on trial: police boosters will be less likely to convict than critics.

When Kalven and Zeisel did their study in the late 1950s, jurors were a source of leniency; they were more likely to acquit than judges. However, the national drift toward conservatism on questions of "law and order" in the 1970s and beyond was reflected in changing jurors mind-sets as well. The same political views that led to an embracing of *capital punishment, life sentences for multiple offenders, and "zero tolerance policing" led to a rise in jury conviction rates that has not yet abated.

Yet another segment of the constellation of attitudes that may intrude on jurors' judgments is outright prejudice. Racial, ethnic, religious, and other forms of bigotry toward victims can lead to the acquittal of defendants in the face of incontrovertible incriminating evidence. The reverse also happens: juries have been known to convict on the basis of very flimsy evidence out of hatred for the kind of person on trial. While such prejudicial decision-making is no longer consciously engaged in very often, negativity toward groups of people can and does distort some jurors' construal of the evidence.

A related set of values that can impinge on juror thinking is ethnocentrism, the identification with and glorification of one's own ethnic group. Jurors who feel a bond with defendants based on a common heritage may show partiality toward them in reviewing the evidence. If it is the victim to whom jurors feel ethnically tied, they might be inclined to scapegoat the defendant to avenge the wrong done to someone with shared roots.

Jury selection entails a screening of those who have been summoned to court for jury duty, having been drawn from sources such as lists of registered voters. Prosecution and defense lawyers question prospective jurors (a process known as the "voir dire"). Some may be eliminated for cause, if they have revealed significant biases. Others can be eliminated through peremptory challenges, the almost unfettered right of both sides to exclude persons without giving reasons.

This process ostensibly is used to make the jury more objective by removing those who harbor preconceptions. In reality, both sides try hard to get a sympathetic jury. Not only do lawyers have intuitions about the directionality of jurors' values, but there is increased reliance on psychological and sociological research on juror attitudes to get a more accurate portrait of a favorable juror for a particular case. Although lawyers primarily impact verdicts with their effectiveness in case preparation and trial advocacy, they also play a role in trying to skew the jury. Jurors will abide by the facts if they are crystal clear, but if they are murky, the tilting of the jury one way or the other can affect the outcome.

Jury verdicts are more than a composite of individual views; they are rather a product of a complex interactive process among individual jurors. When the trial is over, there is usually at least some disagreement within the jury. Jurors are left to their own devices in trying to reconcile them. In most jurisdictions they must reach unanimity to convict, although a number of states allow some dissent. If the jury fails to reach the required accord, it is deemed a "hung jury" and the result is a mistrial. This is a costly and unsatisfying outcome, because the case must either be dismissed altogether or retried before an entirely new jury.

The most dominant feature of jury deliberations are attempts at persuasion. Jurors rely on their recollection of the evidence, on logic, on acquired knowledge, and on personal experience in attempts to sway others to their point of view. Exchanges within the jury room often become emotional, but the focus of attention almost always remains on the details of the case.

Usually the initial majority within the jury prevails, especially if it is a sizable majority. Peer pressure, the urge within groups to conform to dominant sentiments, plays a considerable role in converting those in the minority. Put otherwise, the discomfort associated with being part of a tiny faction or (even worse) being a single individual at odds with an emerging consensus normally produces a reexamination of one's own views. It is difficult for jurors to remain steadfast in their opinions when a succession of presumably level-headed co-jurors are not only challenging the minority position but sometimes claiming it is dead wrong. Although there are dissenting jurors who hold out indefinitely despite vehement pressuring, rarely do one or two jurors change the minds of all others as happened in the popular movie *Twelve Angry Men*; at most they hang the jury, causing a mistrial.

Another means of resolving conflict besides outright capitulation to the majority is negotiation. Most trials present more than the simple dichotomous option to convict or acquit. Rather, the presence of more than one defendant, the opportunity to consider various charges of greater or lesser severity, and the proffering of multiple counts produces many possible verdict outcomes— a situation that provides grist for give-and-take among jurors. Hard-liners on the jury who would like to "throw the book" at those on trial can compromise with their more lenient colleagues who are oriented toward acquittal. The most central figures implicated in crimes can be convicted while minor accomplices are absolved; defendants can be convicted on lesser charges (e.g., manslaughter instead of murder); there can be convictions on some counts but not others. Such trade-offs almost never result from blatant bargaining, but a veiled signaling process entailing the loosening of viewpoints sometimes results in the reaching of a brokered verdict that can get everyone's assent.

Judges have some control over the deliberation process. First, if a trial produces substantial publicity they can order sequestration—the removal of jurors from normal life, which among other things entails spending nights at a hotel until a verdict is reached. This can have the effect of intensifying the desire to arrive at a mutually acceptable verdict in order to end the unpleasantness and distress that sequestration occasions.

The length of time a jury is required to continue deliberating is also in the hands of the judge. Judges can accept a jury as hopelessly deadlocked after one or two days or they can keep the jury working for extended periods. The longer the deliberations, the greater the pressure on the minority to abandon their resistance to the verdict being urged by the majority and the greater the incentive to find common ground.

One way or another, jury-room interactions are successful in obtaining verdicts. Only about five percent of all trials result in hung juries, a quite notable result given the diversity of backgrounds and perspectives represented on the typical jury. Jury deliberation, a complex blend of intellectual discourse and group dynamics, does the job of producing cloture in criminal and civil cases that go to trial.

Jury behavior is a mix of objectivity and subjectivity. In most cases, jurors strive valiantly to get the facts right and apply the law faithfully. But the ambiguity inevitably occasioned by most trials engenders a certain degree of juror reliance on their own predilections. No matter how committed jurors are to leaving their personal feelings outside the courthouse door, and no matter how rigorous the jury selection process, political views of jurors wend their way into the decision-making process. The history of the American jury and copious empirical research on jury functioning confirm the conclusion reached in 1835 by Alexis de Tocqueville in his classic work *Democracy in America*: "The jury is, above all, a political institution and it must be regarded in this light in order to be duly appreciated."

• Reid Hastie, Steven D. Penrod, and Nancy Pennington, *Inside the Jury*, 1983. Valerie P. Hans and Neil Vidmar, *Judging the Jury*, 1986. James P. Levine, *Juries and Politics*, 1992. Reid Hastie, ed., *Inside the Juror*, 1993. Jeffrey Abramson, *We, the Jury: The Jury System and the Ideal of Democracy*, 1994. Norman J. Finkel, *Commonsense Justice: Jurors' Notions of the Law*, 1995.

—James P. Levine

JUSTICE. What is justice, and what is the relation of justice to the idea of law? Justice centers on the imperative that people are to receive what they are due. Justice can be a personal virtue: a settled disposition to consider and act on what others are due. But it is as a virtue of institutions, not of persons, that justice connects most closely to the idea of law.

Considered as a virtue of institutions, there is a basic distinction between corrective justice and distributive justice. Corrective justice concerns what is due to a person as a matter of punishment. For institutional practices of punishment to be just, those practices must satisfy at least three conditions: the practices must mete out punishments only to those found to have violated a law; they must demonstrate procedural equality, for example punishments must be uniformly imposed; and whatever punishments they mete out must be proportional to the gravity of the legal violation that triggered them.

American legal scholars differ widely, however, on the question of how punishments in pursuit of corrective justice are to be justified. Some see the justification in heightened deterrence, others as a requirement of retribution, and still others see "punishment" as a form of moral education. These rival forms of justification generate divergent interpretations of how culpability and proportionality are to be assessed, and even about the form that punishment should take. Thus, there is a rich literature on the question of how moral limits should be affixed to the criminal law. In the Anglo-American tradition, debates about the relation of morality and *criminal law have centered on the notion of harm to others, and on related dilemmas about whether harm to oneself, harmful but consensual activities, and harmless but offensive behaviors should properly fall within the purview of corrective justice.

The other institutional branch of justice is that of distributive justice. Distributive justice concerns the allocation of social goods that are due to a person. In the modern conception, these social goods include the rights and liberties that people are recognized as holding as citizens, and not just material benefits they may be owed by others. Distributive justice is thus a broader, more foundational concept than corrective justice. Theories of distributive justice address themselves to the ordering of a society's basic institutions. Such theories offer themselves as criteria for evaluating not just judicial decisions, or particular laws or policies, but the constitutional essentials of society itself. Public debates in America—among academics and public intellectuals, within courts, and at the level of the general electorate—are animated in part by divergent underlying conceptions of distributive justice. These disparities run deep, offering rival visions of the purview of law and of the nature of American society itself.

Modern Theories of Distributive Justice. A utilitarian conception of justice is rooted in the work of Jeremy Bentham and John Stuart Mill. In this view, allocations of social goods are just if those allocations maximize utility (whether aggregately or per capita), where utility is defined as pleasure, satisfaction, or the realization of preferences. The protean quality concepts of "maximization" and of "utility" have allowed utilitarianism to be used to support very different visions of the well-functioning American social world. The minimalist conception of American government advocated by F. A. Hayek, for example, is justified on utilitarian grounds. Still, the impulse of utilitarianism in America has historically been progressive. It has blended well with American pragmatism, providing grounds for an optimistic view of the capacity of the social world to be improved by the direct application of human reason.

John Rawls, by contrast, argues for a conception of justice fairness. Allocations of social goods are just if they are determined according to principles that are fair. Fair principles are ones people would agree to in a choice situation designed to reflect their reciprocal recognition of one another as free and equal beings. Rawls most famous argument for this position proceeds by way of a hypothetical social contract. To find fair principles, Rawls imagines parties in an "original position" behind a "veil of ignorance" (to prevent them from tailoring principles to suit whatever contingent advantages each may have), selecting from a range of candidate principles that will order the basic institutions of the society in which they are to live. This fairness-tracking device leads Rawls to affirm a conception of distributive justice with two lexically ordered principles: the first affirms basic rights and civil liberties (e.g., freedoms of association and speech), and the second requires equal opportunity as well as a distribution of social benefits and burdens that improves the position of the least well off members of society. Rawls's view has been called "welfare liberalism" or "Great Society" liberalism because of its presumed affinity with expansive public policies such as those of Lyndon B. Johnson. Justice as fairness sees the purview of justice as including not only freedoms from interference but also a strong positive commitment to full equality of opportunity, including a concern for the material bases that make liberties of any sort valuable. Rawls's theory of justice offers a philosophical foundation for the inclusivist, activist conceptions of public policy associated with the progressive wing American Democratic party.

Robert Nozick offers an entitlement theory of justice. In Nozick's view, justice is not some pattern of material distribution that centralized institutions must quickly get a society into and then maintain. Rather, the entitlement theory conceives of justice as historical. People receive what they are due if their holdings—whatever the overall social pattern of such holdings—arise from a process of voluntary transfers, provided those holdings were justly acquired in the first place. Nozick's view is libertarian. His conception of justice could be thought of as a contemporary affirmation of the U.S. Supreme Court case *Lochner v. New York (1905), and the run of cases surrounding it. The Lochner-era Court affirmed "liberty of contract" and "substantive due process" as trumping much of the progressive New Deal legislation that was then emerging from the states (for example, laws dictating maximum hours or minimum wage laws). Nozick's entitlement theory, rooted in ideas traceable at least as far back as those of John Locke, is a justification for capitalism, for strong freedoms of person and exchange, and thus provides one set of grounds for arguing against the ambitions of progressive state planners.

In yet another variation, Michael Walzer defends a communitarian conception of distributive justice. According to Walzer, there can be no single overarching answer to the question of what distributive justice requires. Goods only acquire their value within social practices. Different social goods thus generate different spheres of justice. The criterion of distribution that is appropriate for each type of good is internally related to how each community interprets the value of that good. In the American context, the institutional valence of this approach to social justice is indeterminate: communitarianism has been described as a political theory bereft of political advocates (although Etzioni argues otherwise). The general emphasis is on the importance of contextualizing values. Communitarian conceptions of justice thus give local communities or state legislatures, for example, a greater ballast against the procedural abstractions of federal courts. In this approach to distributive justice, the question of what people are due is a local one—a question to be answered social good by social good, political community by political community.

The Subjects of Justice. Justice is giving people what they are due. But this formulation contains not just one ambiguity—concerning the specification of what counts as "due"—but two: to *whom* (or what) is justice, on any of these specifications, owed? The scope of the imperative of full political equality has expanded slowly, often painfully, throughout American history: from a recognition of white males, to the recognition of white females, of black Americans, members of minority national and ethnic groups, and to that of gays and lesbians. Boundary questions about the scope of justice seem likely to continue setting the agenda for American *jurisprudence for some time. One cluster of boundary questions is developmental: are fetuses "constitutional persons"? What rights do children have? Can claims of justice be made on behalf of the dead, or even on behalf of generations of people as yet unborn (concerning, for example, claims to the preservation of natural resources)? Other boundary problems ask us to consider the moral standing of nonhuman animals, whether as whole species or even as individual living creatures.

A crucial further set of boundary problems concerns the moral significance of state boundaries themselves. Americans are increasingly challenged to think of themselves as citizens of the world and not just as citizens of the United States. As Americans commit themselves to considering, and acting on, what others are due, the question of what human beings in other counties are due becomes increasingly vivid. Are there basic *human rights? If so, do such rights require supranational legal institutions to see that they are recognized? We may be on the verge of a great fluorescence of legal and philosophical scholarship in which the rivalries Americans have witnessed between domestic theories of distributive justice—utilitarian, Rawlsian, entitlement based, and communitarian—are played out yet again, but this time on a global stage.

[See also Civil Rights and Civil Liberties; Criminal Punishment; Equity; Liberty]

• Joel Feinberg, The Moral Limits of the Criminal Law Oxford, 1987. John Stuart Mill "Utilitarianism" in Collected Works of John Stuart Mill, vol. X, J. M. Robson, ed. 1969. John Rawls, A Theory of Justice, 1971. Robert Nozick, Anarchy, State and Utopia, 1974. Michael Walzer, Spheres of Justice: A Defense of Pluralism and Equality, 1983. Amitai Etzioni, The Monochrome Society, 2001 Martha Nussbaum and respondents, For Love of Country: Debating the Limits of Patriotism, Joshua Cohen, ed., 1996. Thomas Pogge, "Cosmopolitanism and Sovereignty," Ethics 103, no. 1 (1992): 48–75. Henry Shue, Basic Rights: Subsistence, Affluence and U.S. Foreign Policy, 2d ed., 1996. Charles Beitz, Political Theory and International Relations, 2d ed., 1999.

—John O. Tomasi

JUSTICE, UNITED STATES DEPARTMENT OF. The Department of Justice (DOJ) is the chief federal law enforcement agency in the United States. Established by Congress in 1870, it is one of the "four great departments" in the executive branch (along with State, Defense, and Treasury). It is responsible for prosecuting federal criminal and civil laws, defending the federal government in judicial proceedings, providing legal counsel to the President and the executive branch, and overseeing federal policing and corrections.

Prior to 1870, the government's legal work was conducted primarily by the *Attorney General, an office established by the Judiciary Act of 1789. As its administrative head, the Attorney General holds almost complete administrative authority over the DOJ's statutory functions and powers, although certain statutory and conventional restraints shield some of its operations from direct political control.

The DOJ was established in an effort to consolidate control over the federal government's legal work. The Judiciary Act of 1789 created separate U.S. Attorneys offices in each of the federal judicial districts; many executive branch departments and agencies also had established separate legal counsels offices of their own. Prior to 1870, the Attorney General had little supervisory authority over the activities of these offices. The surge of litigation following the Civil War forced Congress to create a central legal department in an effort to bring coherence and efficiency to the government's legal work. Amos T. Ackerman was the first Attorney General to head the new DOJ. Under the 1870 act, the district attorneys came under the supervision of the Attorney General. Offices of the *Solicitor General and two separate Assistant Attorneys General were also created to serve as administrative assistants. Although agency legal counsels' offices were not brought into the DOJ, most of their litigating authority was gradually transferred to the new department. Eventually a functional division of labor emerged in which the DOJ has almost complete authority over federal litigation and prosecutions, while agency legal counsels continue to advise their respective agencies on routine legal matters. Official opinions of the Attorney General, however, are binding on executive branch departments and agencies.

The DOJ's growth has reflected expansions in the federal regulatory state. By 1900, Congress had established nine separate Assistant Attorneys General positions. In 1909, Attorney General George Wickersham reorganized the DOJ, creating its first permanent bureaus and divisions. By 1919, Attorney General A. Mitchell Palmer established the DOJ's modern structure, creating eight functionally based divisions, each headed by an Assistant Attorney General.

In fiscal year 2000, the DOJ had 128,000 employees and a budget of $21 billion. It was divided into more than forty major offices and divisions. A Deputy Attorney General serves as a general administrative assistant to the Attorney General. An Associate Attorney General and the Solicitor General have more specialized administrative responsibilities. The latter has evolved into an elite barrister's office, responsible for conducting appellate litigation. As the lawyer for the "United States" and as the most frequent litigant before the Supreme Court, the Solicitor General enjoys a unique and influential relationship with the Court. He is sometimes popularly referred to as the "tenth justice," a term suggesting both the office's extraordinary influence with the Court and the quasi-judicial norms that surround its functions.

The DOJ has six central legal divisions, each headed by an Assistant Attorney General: Antitrust, Civil Rights, Land and Natural Resources, Criminal, Civil, and Tax. Additionally, the Office of Legal Counsel, also headed by an Assistant Attorney General, is responsible for authoring the official opinions of the Attorney General and issuing legal advice on matters concerning the executive's constitutional prerogatives. These divisions are the department's primary "lawyering" divisions. They employed approximately 5 percent of the department's personnel in fiscal year 2000. Another 8 percent of its personnel were employed in the federal district attorney's offices located throughout the United States. The bulk of the department's personnel, however, were located in its policing and corrections divisions. The most important of these include the *Federal Bureau of Investigation (22 percent of personnel), the Immigration and Naturalization Service (25 percent), the Bureau of Prisons (27 percent), the Drug Enforcement Administration (7 percent), and the Marshal's Service (3 percent).

Few countries combine in a single agency (1) responsibilities for the government's lawyering activities, which are connected to broad policy concerns and over which political accountability is thought to be necessary, with (2) responsibility for routine criminal prosecution and policing, over which political control is often thought to be less appropriate. The tensions produced by combining these roles in a single agency has intensified during the twentieth century as larger areas of criminal law have become federalized and as more complex government ethics laws have emerged. The DOJ's central role in political corruption scandals—Teapot Dome, Watergate, Iran-Contra, and Whitewater—has periodically focused public attention on this problem, and made the DOJ the subject of repeated reform efforts.

During the early 1970s, for example, the FBI was reformed after having been controlled by a single director, J. Edgar Hoover, for nearly fifty years. In an effort to balance institutional independence with accountability, Congress changed the Director's appointment to a ten-year term that overlaps presidential administrations. Similarly, following the *Watergate scandal in the Nixon administration, Congress considered proposals to reestablish the DOJ as an "independent" agency, severing it from presidential control. These proposals were eventually rejected. In 1978, however, Congress passed the *Independent Counsel Act in an attempt to create an independent mechanism for investigating and prosecuting allegations against high-ranking members of the president's administration. Independent Counsels were appointed by a special division of the courts, and were not directly accountable to the Attorney General. Controversy surrounding the Independent Counsel's investigation of the Whitewater scandal and the 1999 *impeachment of President Clinton, however, led to the office's disestablishment. Nevertheless, Attorneys General may still appoint "special prosecutors" inside the DOJ and grant them functional independence from political supervision.

Efforts to reform the DOJ have faced two obstacles. First, the Constitutional doctrine of *separation of powers complicates any attempt to buffer important law enforcement functions from presidential supervision. Although the Supreme Court has recognized limited exceptions to the doctrine, such as when it upheld the constitutionality of the Independent Counsel Act in *Morrison v. Olson* (1988), it is usually presumed to vest exclusive Constitutional authority over federal law enforcement in the President. Second, efforts aimed at "depoliticizing" the administration of justice often fail to find a practical way to distinguish between proper and improper forms of political influence. Even when this is possible, removing White House influence over the administration of justice may only shift, rather than remove, improper influences. A primary criticism of the Independent Counsel's office, for instance, was that it had become a partisan weapon for opponents of the administration.

[*See also* Executive Power]

• Hommer Cummings and Carl McFarland, *Federal Justice*, 1937. Luther Huston, *The Department of Justice*, 1967. Donald Horowitz, *The Jurocracy*, 1977. James Einstein, *Counsel for the United States*, 1978. Cornell W. Clayton, *The Politics of Justice: The Attorney General and the Making of Legal Policy*, 1992. Rebecca Mae Salokar, *The Solicitor General: The Politics of Law*, 1992. Katy J. Harriger, *The Special Prosecutor in American Politics*, 2000.

—Cornell W. Clayton

JUSTICE OF THE PEACE. *See* Judge.

JUSTIFICATION AND EXCUSE. *See* Criminal Law Principles: Defense Principles.

JUVENILE COURTS. *See* Courts, United States: Juvenile Courts.

JUVENILE DELINQUENCY. *See* Courts, United States: Juvenile Courts; Juvenile Law.

JUVENILE LAW. Children's underlying needs, not their misdeeds, guided the formation of a separate body of laws governing juveniles. This body of juvenile law accommodated children's developing moral and cognitive capacities, acknowledging that juvenile offenders may be less responsible for their actions than are adults and may be in need of state protection. Although the United States has federal laws covering individuals under eighteen years of age who are charged with committing a federal crime, most juvenile offenders fall under the jurisdiction of state law. Each state has a juvenile code, laws encompassing a variety of rights and procedures applicable to juveniles.

Juvenile offenders, defined as those under eighteen years old in most states, are perceived as more amenable to rehabilitation than adult criminals and thus deserving of treatment in a separate juvenile justice system. The dividing line between juveniles and adults is socially and culturally constructed (e.g., in Sri Lanka, the age of adulthood is fourteen for girls and sixteen for boys; in Iran it is nine lunar years for girls and fifteen lunar years for boys). In the United States, the age at which a young person is considered an adult varies by state.

Historical Background in English Law: The Age of Culpability. The foundation of the American juvenile justice system, beginning in 1899, lies in English *common law. From the thirteenth century on, there was general agreement that children's criminal responsibility included both absolute and conditional categories. Under "the rule of responsibility of infants," children under seven were guiltless and those above fourteen were considered adults. For individuals between seven and fourteen, there was a rebuttable presumption of the capacity of the "infant" to commit a crime. Children near the younger end of this age range (*proximi infantiae*) were generally absolved while those at the upper end (*proximi pubertate*) were often deemed criminally responsible. This guide was only approximate, given that children's exact ages were not known until the beginning of parish registration of baptisms in the early sixteenth century (under Henry VIII). Without knowing the exact age of a child, English judges often used their intuition when deciding a case.

In sixteenth- and seventeenth-century England, a primary duty of the legal system was to act as a surrogate parent by caring for and seeking apprenticeship training for poor children. As the church became less active in providing for the social needs of the poor, greater concern arose about an emerging class of vagrants and criminals. In response, Parliament passed the Statute of Artificers (1562), which allowed the government to override parental wishes and apprentice poor children older than ten years to a local resident until their age of majority. The apprenticeships helped provide an adequate labor supply and a cost-effective means of supervising children deemed to have idle or un-Christian parents or to lack good

breeding. The underlying philosophical justification was related to the English chancery doctrine of *parens patriae*, in which the state acted as a surrogate parent in the child's best interest.

The Refuge System and Reformatories. In Colonial America, communal legal sanctions were guided by common law. Juveniles (most often those from the lower classes) deemed sinful and in need of strict control or punishment for such common offenses as rebelliousness and disobedience were warned, were shamed, or received corporal punishment, before being returned to family control. More serious offenders were treated as adults. As the population grew, mobility increased, and traditional forms of social control diminished, wayward or dependent juveniles needed an institutional setting.

The housing of juveniles with adults in *prisons raised concerns about corrupting youth (a concern that also resulted in some juries refusing to convict youth offenders guilty of serious crimes). The effects of poverty were also considered, especially among immigrant children. The "house of refuge" movement was launched in 1825 to address vagrancy, other minor offenses, and the needs of neglected children. In some cases, parents turned their ill-behaved children over to the state. Once housed in the refuges, children worked a full eight-hour day at trades and attended school for another four hours. More serious child offenders tended to remain in the adult system, however. By 1860, sixteen houses of refuge dealt with delinquent children who had committed minor offenses and dependent children (i.e., those children whose parents or guardians a court has judged to have provided care that is below a legal standard of proper care, that is, care deemed to be abuse or neglect).

Ex parte Crouse (1839) was a landmark case upholding the refuge system and the state's power to make decisions in the child's best interest. Without a trial, the mother of Mary Ann Crouse committed her purportedly recalcitrant daughter to the Philadelphia House of Refuge. The father's appeal for his daughter's return was denied for three main reasons: (1) the house was not a prison (even though Mary Ann was not free to leave); (2) the child was there for her own reformation through industry and moral teaching and to separate her from her formerly corrupting environment; and (3) no punishment was being inflicted (despite her probable oppressive treatment). The court's decision is credited with originating *parens patriae* in the United States and providing the foundation of juvenile law through the mid-1960s.

Concerns that houses of refuge did not curb delinquency led to state-supported reformatories in 1848. These institutions had harsher conditions and required intensive child labor. In accordance with *parens patriae*, some youths in overcrowded facilities were apprenticed, often in "uncorrupted" rural areas, until the age of twenty-one. Although the reformatory experiment was abandoned in 1910, it left an important legacy for corrections, including the indeterminate sentence, conditional release, and education and vocational training.

The Founding of a Separate Juvenile Justice System. Middle-class reformers founded both the houses of refuge and the United States' first separate juvenile justice system, begun by the 1899 Illinois Juvenile Court Act. The nation's first juvenile code targeted impoverished dependent or delinquent children under the age of sixteen. Progressives who declared that children were vulnerable and lacked criminal responsibility were upset by the placement of youths in deplorable facilities with adults. They were also concerned about controlling immigrant children, as immigration into the United States from eastern and southern Europe increased. Although misbehavior by middle-class youths was to be handled by concerned families, lower-class youths were to be reformed under *parens patriae*.

In addition to giving the juvenile courts jurisdiction over children charged with crimes, the Illinois act also gave them jurisdiction over children exhibiting a variety of behaviors and conditions, including minor offenses (so-called status offenses such as truancy and disobedience), and children living in distressing conditions.

The Illinois court established a policy of confidentiality of records to minimize stigma and required the separation of incarcerated juveniles from adults. Children under the age of twelve were barred from jails, and court procedures were to be informal. Different terminology was used for juvenile offenders (e.g., "adjudicated as delinquent" rather than "found guilty"; "hearing" rather than "trial").

By 1925, forty-six states, three territories, and the District of Columbia had juvenile courts. In addition, parents could commit their children to the Prison Association, even though the children were merely hard to control, not necessarily delinquent. Treatment of juveniles concluded when they were rehabilitated or turned twenty-one, whichever came first. Because the goal was rehabilitation, no formal hearing was necessary to justify a child's loss of liberty. Civil liberties were suspended in favor of policies that controlled undesirable members of society.

Changes in Juvenile Law in the 1960s. Although the criminal-law revolution of the *Warren Court era emphasized all defendants' *due process rights, juvenile law changed markedly, becoming more formal and more like the adult system. The public and policymakers believed that family, police, schools, and courts could not check rising delinquency. In addition, some thought that the juvenile courts' informality and focus on treatment without full regard for due process ignored juveniles' rights.

In *Kent* v. *United States* (1966), the U.S. Supreme Court ruled that Morris Kent was denied his due process rights by the failure of the trial judge to hold a hearing before transferring the sixteen-year-old to adult court for trial. Also, Kent's lawyer lacked access to the social information used by the court. The court ruled that there must be an opportunity for a hearing on the issue of transfer to adult court, that counsel must have access to the social records considered by the juvenile court in making its decision, and that the court must explain in writing its waiver (transfer) order.

A year after the *Kent* decision, the Supreme Court decided *In re Gault* (1967), perhaps the most significant juvenile case of the twentieth century. Gerald Gault was a fifteen-year-old charged with making obscene telephone calls to a female neighbor living in the same trailer park; he asked, "Do you have big bombers? Are your cherries ripe today?" Gault was convicted by a juvenile court in Arizona and committed to a juvenile correctional facility for an indeterminate period not to extend beyond his twenty-first birthday—a marked contrast to the maximum sentence for such an offense by an adult: a fifty dollar fine or two months in jail.

The Supreme Court ruled for the first time that juveniles have a right to adequate notice of the precise nature of the charges against them, to be advised of the right to *counsel and the right to confront and cross-examine *witnesses against them, and to have (and be informed of) the privilege against *self-incrimination. The due process rights stemming from this case (and regarding adjudications where loss of liberty was involved) demarcated a change from the informality of *parens patriae*.

In 1968, the National Conference of Commissioners on Uniform State laws drafted the Uniform Juvenile Court Act, to foster the development of youth with treatment and training. The act's stipulation that juveniles were "taken into custody" rather than arrested meant that police were encouraged to settle disputes and complaints informally, especially given that police handle mostly minor offenders. Judges (or masters or referees) also were given great discretion in how to dispose of a case.

Although juveniles have a right to a court-appointed attorney only when they face commitment to a secure state (or federal) facility, such defense attorneys' role is short-term. Probation staff serve as advocates; the act notes the need for competent probation staff with a limited workload. During an *interrogation, however, asking for a probation officer does not assert the privilege against self-incrimination, nor is it the equivalent of asking for an attorney (*Fare* v. *Michael C.* (1979)). Probation officers counsel youths on probation and link them to other community services. *Probation, the most common disposition of juvenile court, has been officially recognized as an option of the court since 1878.

Developments in the 1970s. In 1970 the Supreme Court ruled that guilt beyond a reasonable doubt (and not just a preponderance of evidence) was to be the standard of *proof in juvenile cases. The next year, however, the Supreme Court ruled that a *jury system was not required for juveniles, given their differences from adults. By 1975 the Supreme Court had essentially concluded its revolution in the procedural aspects of juvenile justice. These changes led to more protection of children but, by making changes that approximated the adult system, made children more accountable for their transgressions.

In 1974 Congress passed the Juvenile Justice and Delinquency Prevention Act, which required states seeking to qualify for federal juvenile justice funding to deinstitutionalize status offenders and separate juveniles from adult offenders. Juveniles had to be housed either in separate facilities or in the same facility with "sight and sound separation," such that juveniles and adults could neither see each other nor converse. In addition, federal law pertaining to abuse and neglect was developed, such as a court-appointed guardian for every child, judicial oversight hearings, and monitoring responsibilities conducted by each state and overseen by the federal Office of Juvenile Justice and Delinquency Prevention (OJJDP).

The Modern Era. After 1975, compassion for delinquents diminished as sensational juvenile violence grabbed the headlines. Legislators rather than social scientists or child professionals led the charge for change, in particular for more juvenile accountability and severer punishment. Changes included increased use of waivers to adult court (especially for minorities), less use of probation as a sanction, and less use of treatment in institutions. Programs that provided top-rated educational and vocational programs risked censure for "rewarding" delinquents who are "undeserving" (as occurred with a model Pennsylvania program, Glen Mills, that serves gang members from across the country). Public fear governed policy.

In the 1980s, public perception that the juvenile justice system was too lenient led to changes such as the automatic waiver of certain serious juvenile offenders to the adult system and legislation on juvenile executions. In *Schall* v. *Martin* (1984), the Supreme Court allowed preventive detention (keeping juveniles in custody before trial because they might pose a future danger to the community or themselves), raising questions about whether the juvenile's or the community's interests are paramount. The Supreme Court in *Thompson* v. *Oklahoma* (1988) forbade the execution of those under sixteen years of age at the time of the crime, but a year later the justices, in *Stanford* v. *Kentucky* (1989), left to states the option of executing those age sixteen and older.

Legislation of the 1990s was driven by publicized statistics about burgeoning juvenile-committed homicides. Even though the rate of homicide by juveniles declined in the mid-1990s, the drive to toughen laws applicable to juveniles continued. Guns seemed to be an equalizer, making juveniles as dangerous as adults. Publicity about violence in schools led to suspensions or expulsions for any kind of weapon, such as a pocketknife or a paint-ball gun. Already existing provisions for juveniles to be transferred to the adult system were expanded in forty-five states. In most states, once a juvenile had been convicted in the adult system, any subsequent crimes had to be prosecuted in adult court.

Modification or elimination of juvenile confidentiality laws in forty-seven states allowed the proceedings of waived cases to be more visible to the public. Twenty-two states added laws augmenting the role of victims in the processing of juvenile offenders. Blended sentences permitted juveniles to fulfill their sentence in the juvenile justice system, then face adult sanctions. Case dispositions were based more on the offense than on the offender, emphasizing retribution and deterrence rather than rehabilitation.

The "war on drugs" has led to Supreme Court decisions that deemphasize civil liberties. Students have a lowered expectation of *privacy at school, school searches do not require probable cause or warrants, and random drug testing of student athletes is permissible. A policy known as zero tolerance has punished juveniles sharing nonprescription pain relievers.

A wave of laws during the 1990s made parents accountable for their children's misbehavior, an echo of *parens patriae* at the turn of the century. Unfit parents could be criminally liable when their children were truant, violated curfew, or broke other laws. The laws targeted gang offenders, raising questions about selective application of the law to minority families—reminiscent of earlier laws aimed at children of immigrants. The emphasis in modern times, however, is less rehabilitative.

Juveniles can "knowingly and voluntarily" waive their right to counsel, opening the possibility of being questioned about serious crimes without a parent or attorney present. Given that it is legal for police to manipulate suspects (e.g., falsely claim that they have an eyewitness implicating the suspect), preteen juveniles without an adult advocate are at risk of being pressured into making false confessions. The public is torn between the desire for retribution for juveniles who commit violent crime and recognition that the developing maturity of juveniles necessitates their legal protection as they pass through the justice system.

With a few exceptions (e.g., jury trials, speedy and public trials), the treatment of juvenile offenders increasingly parallels that of adults, blurring the distinction between juveniles and adults. The culpability and dispositions of felonious juveniles resemble those of more than a century ago, before the passage of the 1899 Illinois juvenile court statute.

[*See also* Courts, United States-Juvenile Courts; Criminal Law Principles; Family Law]

• "The Juvenile Court," *The Future of Children* 6 (winter 1996) (www.futureofchildren.org). Samuel M. Davis, Elizabeth S. Scott, Walter Wadlington, and Charles H. Whitebread, *Children in the Legal System: Cases and Materials*, 2d ed., 1997. "A Centennial Celebration of the Juvenile Court 1899–1999," *Juvenile and Family Court Journal* 49 (fall 1998). John C. Watkins Jr., *The Juvenile Justice Century: A Sociolegal Commentary on American Juvenile Courts*, 1998. U.S. Department of Justice, Office of Justice Programs, Office of Juvenile Justice and Delinquency Prevention, *Juvenile Justice: A Century of Change*, December 1999 (www.ojjdp.ncjrs.org). John C. Watkins Jr., *Selected Cases on Juvenile Justice in the Twentieth Century*, 1999.   —Lauren Dundes

K

KENT, JAMES (b. Putnam County, N.Y., 31 July 1763; d. 12 Dec. 1847) was a legal educator, distinguished jurist, and influential treatise writer. Educated at Yale University, Kent prepared for the New York bar by apprenticeship. In the mid-1790s, after the private practice of law proved disappointing, Kent became the first professor of law at Columbia College. He then served on the New York Supreme Court from 1798 to 1814, becoming chief justice in 1804. Kent was appointed chancellor of New York in 1814 and held that post for nine years. While on the bench, Kent was instrumental in bringing about the publication of judicial *opinions in New York.

As a judge, Kent championed the independence of the judiciary from legislative interference. He also sought to incorporate principles of *equity, as developed in England, into American law. Convinced that security of *property ownership promoted individual *liberty and economic development, Kent restricted state authority in order to safeguard the rights of property holders. For instance, in *Gardner v. Village of Newburgh* (1816) he ruled that payment of compensation when property interests were taken by governmental action was a fundamental element of *due process.

Kent's most significant contribution to American law was the publication of his monumental *Commentaries on American Law* (1826–30). Modeled on the famous work of William *Blackstone, Kent's treatise helped to define law in the new republic by gathering and analyzing a wide range of legal authorities. Highly successful, the *Commentaries* was reprinted in numerous editions throughout the nineteenth century.

[*See also* Constitutional Commentators]

• James Theodore Horton, *James Kent: A Study in Conservatism, 1763–1847*, 1939. John H. Langbein, "Chancellor Kent and the History of Legal Literature," *Columbia Law Review* 93 (1993): 547–94.

—James W. Ely Jr.

KIDNAPPING is aggravated false imprisonment. The seventeenth-century common law of kidnapping required the violent abduction or confinement of a person with movement to another country. The crime has evolved from a misdemeanor punishable by fine or pillory to a *felony.

In the United States, kidnapping is a crime now proscribed by state and federal law. In general, kidnapping requires the taking or confining of a person, without consent, to gain some benefit. Secrecy, although common in kidnapping, is usually not required (unless the victim is not moved). Movement has been satisfied when a person was compelled to move to another room. Kidnapping for ransom, or injury to the victim, is considered aggravated, and in some jurisdictions formerly could carry the death penalty. The federal statute has a commerce clause-based jurisdictional requirement that the victim be moved across state lines (1994).

Kidnapping was only a state crime (often a misdemeanor) until 1932. In the 1920s and early 1930s the crime was endemic. Kidnappers targeted children of the rich, oftentimes obtaining high ransoms, yet leaving their victims dead. Efforts to combat kidnapping were hamstrung by state jurisdictional limits, which criminals used to their advantage. Public outcry for federal intervention occurred when a kidnapper brazenly abducted the infant son of Anne and Charles Lindbergh from his crib in 1932. The culprit escaped with a hefty ransom, but weeks later the child was found dead. Congress responded with the kidnapping statute known as the "Lindbergh Law."

Ransom kidnapping is rare in the United States today, even though the elements to convict for kidnapping have broadened to included any unlawful restraint or movement of a person, regardless of the offender's motive. The victim's lack of consent is presumed if he is taken by force, threat, or trickery, or when a child or incompetent is taken without the parent's or guardian's consent.

The federal statute excludes parental kidnapping, but "child abduction" by a parent is a federal offense. Most states penalize parental kidnapping, which occurs when a parent removes a child in violation of the other parent's custody rights. The Uniform Child Custody Jurisdiction Act and the federal Parental Kidnapping Prevention Act (1994) were promulgated to deter child abduction.

About 50,000 people annually are "trafficked" for sex trade, often kidnapped, within or to the United States. In 2000, Congress enacted the Victims of Trafficking and Violence Protection Act to combat this crime.

The official abduction of fugitives is illegal under *international law. The U.S. Supreme Court, however, held in *Frisbie* v. *Collins* (1952) that an illegal abduction across state lines does not bar jurisdiction to prosecute. This rule was extended in *United States* v. *Verdugo-Urquidez*, (1990) to the abduction of foreigners outside the United States: abductors may now stand trial here and evidence may be admitted that was illegally seized, since the Fourth Amendment does not extraterritorially apply to foreigners. Also, the Ninth Circuit Court of Appeals held in *United States* v. *Verdugo-Urquidez* (1991) that if the foreign government objects, an applicable *extradition treaty, may deprive the American court of jurisdiction.

[*See also* Child Custody; Criminal Law; Lindbergh Kidnapping Case]

• Caroline Moorehead, *Hostages to Fortune: A Study of Kidnapping in the World Today,* 1980. Rollin M. Perkins and Ronald N. Boyce, *Criminal Law,* 3d ed., 1982. Charles E. Torcia, *Wharton's Criminal Law,* 15th ed., 1994, and Supp., 2000. Christopher L. Blakesley, "Comparativist Ruminations From the Bayou on Child Custody Jurisdiction: The UCCJA, the PKPA, and the Hague Convention on Child Abduction," 58 *La. L. Rev.* 449 (1998).
—Christopher L. Blakesley

KING, RODNEY, CASE OF. On 3 March 1991, Los Angeles police officers were led on a high-speed automobile chase by twenty-five-year-old Rodney Glen King. Once apprehended, King was restrained by four LAPD officers who shot him with Taser stun darts, beat him with batons, and kicked their prostrate suspect. Placed under arrest, King was taken by police to a hospital where he was treated for skull fractures and kidney injuries.

Unknown to the officers who apprehended him, King's beating had been videotaped by a local resident. On 4 March, George Holliday provided his tape to a Los Angeles television station, which then broadcast what would become one of the most controversial videotapes ever recorded.

King was African American; the LAPD officers who beat him were white. The racial tension that runs like a red thread through the history of American criminal justice was a crucial factor contributing to the sensational impact of the Rodney King case (see RACE AND ETHNICITY). Four officers were arrested and charged with *assault and use of excessive force. Defense attorneys sought, and were granted a change of venue which moved the trial from Los Angeles to suburban Simi Valley, in Ventura County, from which a predominantly white jury, (there were no African Americans) was drawn and sworn.

While instructed by the judge to assess the behavior of the LAPD defendants objectively, applying as a standard the conduct of a reasonable peace officer, the jury was invited by defense lawyers to see the King arrest subjectively, from the point of view of the particular officers who beat King—defendants who testified they believed he was under the influence of the powerful drug phencyclidine, or PCP. On April 29, 1992, the jury acquitted three officers on all charges, and a mistrial was declared as to the fourth.

Upon announcement of the verdict, a riot exploded in Los Angeles. A twenty-five-square-block section of the central city was torched. Gang members and looters, as well as demonstrators, roamed the streets and Reginald Denny, a thirty-six-year-old white truck driver, was dragged from his vehicle and severely beaten. These riots, like the King beating itself, were videotaped; scenes of violence saturated the media. A curfew was imposed, and national guardsmen as well as federal officers were dispatched to Los Angeles. More than forty people died in the civil disturbance, nearly ten thousand were arrested, and property damage estimates reached a billion dollars. On the third day of rioting following the initial not-guilty verdicts, King famously begged the people of Los Angeles to try to get along with each other.

The officers who had beaten King were then prosecuted by federal authorities for *civil rights violations. On April 17, 1993, a federal trial jury convicted two of them, Sergeant Stacey Koon and Officer Laurence Powell. The court sentenced the officers to thirty months in prison; both served most of their sentences. The prosecution of Koon and Powell did not violate the *double jeopardy clause of the U.S. Constitution because under rulings of the Supreme Court state and federal trials are regarded as prosecutions for different offenses (offenses under different penal codes). On April

19, 1994, the jury in Rodney King's civil damages suit returned a judgment of almost four million dollars against the city of Los Angeles.

[See also Civil Rights and Civil Liberties; Criminal Law Practice]

• Jerome H. Skolnick & James J. Fyfe, *Above the Law: Police and the Excessive Use of Force*, 1993. Mark Baldassare, ed., *The Los Angeles Riots: Lessons for the Urban Future*, 1994.   —Anthony Chase

KUNSTLER, WILLIAM M. (1919–1995), lawyer who defended controversial causes and radical clients. The son of a New York doctor, Kunstler had the advantages of a middle-class upbringing. He majored in French at Yale, served as an officer in World War II, and attended Columbia Law School. In 1943 he married Lotte Rosenberger, had two daughters, and maintained a conventional law practice in New York City. He also served as a radio host, taught as an adjunct law professor, and authored several books. Kunstler's first marriage ended in divorce, and in the early 1970s he married Margie Ratner, with whom he had two more daughters.

In 1961, he threw himself into the *civil rights movement, representing many different types of protestors, becoming more radical and more op-posed to racism. In the 1960s, Kunstler represented the Black Power advocate H. Rap Brown. The disruptive Chicago Seven trial (1969–70) catapulted Kunstler into the national spotlight, although the trial was not representative of his usually civil manner of trying cases. He went on to represent the Attica prisoners, the Indian defendants in the Wounded Knee uprising, and such Arab defendants as Nosair, an alleged rabbi-killer, and the World Trade Center defendants. Among his last major cases, he briefly represented Colin Ferguson, the Jamaican shooter on the Long Island Railroad, raising a controversial "black rage" defense.

Kunstler always tried to deflect culpability from the defendant and put the government on trial. He sought to use criminal proceedings as opportunities to publicize the political nature of the governmental or economic system that underlay the particular prosecution. His tactics attracted many fans but even more bitter enemies.

[See also Chicago Conspiracy Case; Civil Rights and Civil Liberties]

• William M. Kunstler with Sheila Isenberg, *My Life as a Radical Lawyer*, 2d ed., 1996. David J. Langum, *William M. Kunstler: The Most Hated Lawyer in America*, 1999.   —David J. Langum

L

LABOR ARBITRATION. *See* Arbitration and Mediation; Labor Law: Labor Relations.

LABOR LAW

Labor Relations
Workplace Issues

LABOR LAW: LABOR RELATIONS

Rationales for Regulation. As a generalization—and certainly by comparison with the laws of other industrialized nations—the employment relationship is not pervasively regulated in the United States, even to this day. Absent a specific statute or express *contract, employment in this country is considered "at will"; both the employee and employer are free to terminate the relationship with or without cause. It is argued that reliance on market forces will best serve the joint interests of employers and workers. Under an "at will" rule, employers face lower costs in hiring workers because they can easily terminate the relationship if it proves unsatisfactory. Workers also benefit from a system that allows them to quit at any time. An unfair employer will not be able to keep able workers and will have trouble recruiting new ones. Such an employer also must deal with the threat that workers dissatisfied with their conditions will form trade unions.

Over the course of the twentieth century, however, public policy in the United States has shifted in favor of a system that mixes reliance on market forces with *regulation. Three rationales are often offered for government intervention. First is a concern that contracts formed between employers and individual workers will systematically favor employers because of the limited bargaining power of workers. Under this view, workers often will endure long hours, unsafe conditions, and poor pay because they are dependent on employers for their livelihood, and are not able easily to pull up stakes and seek opportunities elsewhere. Indeed, for unskilled workers in relatively stable manufacturing jobs, there may be few such alternative opportunities. Regulation is thought to be needed *to correct this imbalance of bargaining power* by protecting the right of workers to form unions and engage in collective bargaining, and by writing certain terms into every employment contract such as maximum hours of work, limits on the use of child labor, and guarantees of safe workplaces.

A second rationale for regulation is that society can properly insist that employment takes place only in conformity with *evolving social norms of fair conditions*. This justification would apply to maximum hours, child labor laws, and occupational safety laws. Rules barring *discrimination because of race, religion, sex, age, or handicap can also be viewed as an expression of social value judgments about the permissible grounds for evaluating human beings.

A similar argument is that the law may seek to alter the values of workers and firms. For example, occupational safety laws may encourage workers to change their expectations of the proper conditions for work—expectations that form a new baseline for employment contracts. Similarly, the discrimination laws have forced employers to reevaluate early assessments of the costs of hiring black and female workers because anticipated adverse reactions of customers or coworkers did not materialize.

A third justification for regulation is *to correct deficiencies in the operation of labor markets*. Under this view, labor markets are not perfectly competitive, and some forms of regulation may actually improve efficiency in labor markets. Unemployment insurance and adjustment assistance laws require employers to absorb some of the costs of their termination decisions; in the absence of such laws, these costs would be imposed on society. The mobility of workers, and hence their ability to pursue market options, can be enhanced by laws making pensions and other benefits portable rather than dependent on continued service with the same employer. Collective bargaining laws can also be viewed as a mechanism for producing "collective goods" such as grievance systems, if employees can bargain on a collective basis. In individual bargains, such terms may be underproduced because the costs to the firms of such systems (which cannot be confined to individual workers) may be greater than the benefits to the individual worker.

However, regulation is not cost-free. There are the costs of administering the scheme (including the risk that fear of liability may discourage employers from making socially desirable judgments). Moreover, employers will attempt to shift the costs of regulations to workers, in the form of lower wages or smaller wage increases. To the extent that such cost-shifting occurs and mandatory minimum terms do not capture what workers want, these workers may be worse off than they would be in the absence of regulation. Even when such laws benefit those who have (and retain) jobs, they may create disincentives to hire additional workers. Imposing excess costs on employers may also affect the competitiveness of U.S. products and services in world markets.

Here we examine collective bargaining and union organization law in the private sector. Historically, the American labor movement distrusted state intervention, and preferred self-help through union organization and collective bargaining to promote the welfare of workers. This policy, termed *voluntarism*, arose as a response to judicial hostility to protective legislation secured by labor groups. This preference was reflected in a labor and employment law that emphasized protections for collective bargaining over mandatory minimum terms of employment. However, with the decline of union organization in private firms from a high point of 35 percent of private workers in 1954 to less than 10 percent today, and the rise of civil rights movements challenging racial and other forms of discrimination, legal intervention increasingly takes the form of expansions of employment law and discrimination law.

Federal Structure. Regulation of the employment relationship in the United States is divided between the federal government and the states. The federal government's authority to regulate the behavior of private parties is limited to matters affecting interstate commerce. Since 1937, however, Congress's power to legislate under the commerce clause of the Constitution has been given an expansive reading.

Because Congress has regulated only in certain defined areas, the states play an important role in filling out the terms of the employment relationship. States administer the unemployment insurance and workers' compensation systems; maintain their own safety, minimum wage, overtime and maximum hour rules; and set the terms for hiring and firing workers. Even where Congress has legislated in the area, with the exception of laws governing labor relations and employee benefits, most federal statutes allow the states to enact more protective worker standards.

In the area of labor relations, however, the states generally have limited authority over employees and employers that are within the reach of the two major statutes, the Railway Labor Act of 1926 (RLA), which covers the airlines and railroads, and the National Labor Relations Act of 1935 (NLRA), which covers all other industries affecting commerce. These laws broadly preempt any state regulation of activity they arguably protect or prohibit, any conduct that Congress wishes to leave entirely unregulated (such as peaceful economic strikes), or any claims whose adjudication requires the interpretation of collective bargaining agreements. States may regulate where federal labor boards cede jurisdiction back to them, or where they deal with aspects of conduct that reflect deeply held state concerns and are only peripherally the concern of the federal statutes. Examples in this category include state regulation of violent or mass picketing and libel actions for knowingly or recklessly false statements made in the course of labor disputes.

Some states have enacted "mini Wagner Acts" for industries not regulated by federal law, and public sector labor relations laws for the employees of state and local governments. The federal government has a separate labor relations statute for its employees.

Union Organization and Collective Bargaining Law. Although once the fountainhead of American employment law, union organization and collective bargaining have receded in importance with the decline of union representation in private firms.

Underlying Premises. The American labor relations system differs from its European counterparts in a number of ways. First, the system is based on an adversarial model. Unions obtain bargaining rights in contested elections administered by a federal agency. In such election contests, management has a right to, and often does, speak out in opposition to the union. Companies are permitted no role in initiating and supporting "labor organizations," a term that is broadly defined to include any mechanism by which employees "deal with" their employer on terms and conditions of employment. The labor laws are based on a fundamental division of interest between labor and management: unions can seek bargaining authority on behalf of nonmanagerial and nonsupervisory workers, but managers and supervisors are deemed representatives of the firm who have no right to form unions and insist on collective bargaining. The scope of bargaining also reflects this division between spheres of influence: the parties must bargain over wages, hours, and working conditions, but decisions involving the disposition of assets and the strategic position of the firm, including plant closings, are deemed to be part of management's realm of unilateral action.

Second, collective bargaining is highly decentralized. Unions acquire bargaining authority on a plant-by-plant basis, even often among a subgroup of workers in the plant. Unlike the German, French, and Swedish systems, regional bargaining between labor federations and multiemployer organizations in the United States is exceptional. Multiemployer bargaining units are formed only by consent. Unions attempt to maintain "pattern" settlements across firms competing in the same product market, but are finding this increasingly difficult in the face of a growing nonunion sector and the competitive pressures of global markets.

Third, unions are predominantly multiemployer organizations representing employees of competing firms. Independent employee associations representing only the employees of a particular firm are rare, and tend over time to affiliate with national labor organizations that are members of the central labor federation, the American Federation of Labor-Congress of Industrial Organizations (AFL-CIO). Enterprise-based works councils—found in most continental European countries—are nonexistent in the United States. However, U.S. unions typically negotiate agreements with single companies, often applicable only to a particular facility. Even national agreements between, say, General Motors and the United Automobile Workers (UAW), a member of the AFL-CIO, make provision for local bargaining over plant-specific issues.

Finally, U.S. unions are institutionally insecure. The unions' vulnerability comes from the growing

nonunion sector, and various legal mechanisms for ensuring union responsiveness to the rank-and-file employees. These mechanisms include decertification elections; the employer's ability to test the union's continued majority support; duty of fair representation suits brought by employees complaining of the union's representation in grievances or collective bargaining; the rights of nonunion members to seek rebates of union dues used for noncollective bargaining purposes; and union democracy requirements for the conduct of internal union election and union discipline.

Administrative Framework. In the early twentieth century, the federal courts were often hostile to union activity. The Norris-LaGuardia Act of 1932 narrowed the grounds on which federal judges could issue injunctions in labor disputes, thereby reducing the role of the judiciary. In part as a consequence of this history, administrative agencies play an important role in the administration of the federal labor laws. In the case of the NLRA, the National Labor Relations Board (NLRB) has exclusive authority over the representation procedures and unfair labor practice provisions of the NLRA. The role of the courts is limited to judicial review of final NLRB orders in unfair labor practice cases, and suits to enforce collective bargaining agreements. In the case of the RLA, the National Mediation Board (NMB) conducts representation elections and plays an important role in mediating disputes.

Under the NLRA, charges of unfair labor practices (ULPs) are filed with regional offices of the NLRB. If, after investigation, the charges are believed to be meritorious, the General Counsel issues a complaint on the government's behalf. An adversary, trial-type proceeding is then conducted before an *administrative law judge, who after hearing the testimony and reviewing the evidence makes initial findings of fact and conclusions of law. If no appeal is taken, the ALJ's determination becomes the ruling of the agency. If a party appeals, the five-member NLRB (usually sitting in panels of three members) considers the record and briefs. The final decision of the NLRB is reviewable in the federal courts of appeals. The reviewing court must uphold the agency's decisions if its findings of fact are supported by "substantial evidence" on the record "considered as a whole," and its rulings of law are in conformity with the NLRA. Further review is possible, on writ of certiorari, to the U.S. Supreme Court. Such writs of certiorari are rarely granted. By contrast, under the RLA, the NMB's adjudicative authority is limited to representational disputes; the parties go directly to the federal district court to enforce other statutory obligations.

Both statutes are based on the principles of *exclusivity* (employees have a right to be exclusively represented in bargaining by representatives chosen by a majority of the employees in a unit); a *legally mandated duty to bargain* (both the exclusive bargaining representative and the employer are legally obligated to bargain in "good faith"); *free collective bargaining* (after exhaustion of the duty to bargain, the parties are free to press their disagreements in the form of strikes and lockouts); and *arbitration* of disputes arising under collective bargaining agreements (provided for by contract rather than statute, as in Canada).

Selection of Exclusive Bargaining Representatives. Unions typically seek exclusive bargaining status either by securing voluntary recognition from the employer upon a showing of majority support or petitioning the NLRB or the NMB to hold a secret-ballot representation election. Such petitions require a preliminary showing of interest. The agency conducts a hearing to resolve any contested issues concerning the bargaining unit or eligibility of voters, and then schedules an election to determine if a majority of the employees desire union representation. (The NLRB requires that a majority of employees voting affirmatively select union representation; the NMB also requires that a majority of the eligible electorate cast valid ballots.) After the election is held, the agency considers challenges based on the conduct of the election campaign. If the petitioning union was selected by a majority of the employees, and the agency has rejected challenges to the conduct of the campaign, the agency certifies the union as the exclusive bargaining representative.

In the election campaign, the employer is permitted to voice his opposition to the union. The employer may not discharge or discipline employees because of their support of the union, engage in threats of reprisal, or change the terms and conditions for the purpose of affecting the election outcome. Such conduct would provide grounds for setting aside the election (if the majority of employees voted "no union") or holding the employer to have engaged in unfair labor practices. Under the NLRA, if employers are guilty of egregious ULPs that so mar the environment that a fair rerun election cannot be held, the NLRB may order the employer to bargain with a union that previously demonstrated majority support on the basis of authorization cards signed by a majority of the unit.

The Process of Collective Bargaining. Under the NLRA, once the union has been certified, the parties are under a duty to meet at reasonable times and engage in "good faith" bargaining. There is no legal obligation to make concessions or reach agreements. The duty to bargain is limited to "wages, hours and working conditions." These are considered "mandatory" subjects over which the parties must bargain and are free to press disagreements to the point of "impasse." Bargaining is not required over subjects such as plant closings, advertising budgets, and capital investments that are considered to lie within the realm of "entrepreneurial control"; subjects that affect the union's relationship with its members such as strike and contract ratification votes; or subjects that alter the established framework of negotiations, such as proposals to bargain with coalitions of unions or to submit disagreements (over the content of the new contract) to arbitration. These are considered "permissive" subjects over which the parties have no duty to bargain and may not be a basis for deadlock over mandatory subjects.

If the parties have reached "impasse" over mandatory subjects, the NLRA permits a resort to self-help after notice is given to the Federal Mediation and Conciliation Service (FMCS) and a sixty-day "cooling off" period has expired. The employer may lockout its employees and/or unilaterally implement its final offer to the union. The union may strike. The right to strike is legally protected. However, although the employer may not discharge workers, it can, in the interest of maintaining operations, hire permanent replacements. Even if permanent replacements have been hired, strikers remain "employees" and have preferential rights to job openings as they occur once the strikers have offered unconditionally to return to work. If the strike is in protest over the employer's unfair labor practices, the employer may not hire permanent replacements, and returning ULP strikers displace replacement workers. If the employer resorts to a lockout, locked-out employees may not be permanently replaced.

Although employers have enjoyed the ability to hire permanent replacements as a means of staying in business at least since 1938, the decade of the 1980s witnessed a significant increase in the use of this bargaining tactic. Bills to outlaw the hiring of permanent replacements have not mustered the necessary support in Congress.

The framework for collective bargaining in the railroad and airline industries resembles that of the NLRA, but differs in at least two important respects. First, bargaining typically occurs on a carrier-wide basis (airlines) or multiemployer basis (railroads). Second, there are substantial statutory impediments to changing agreements. The parties to a collective bargaining agreement are under a statutory duty "to exert every reasonable effort to make and maintain agreements." A party commences the process of seeking changes in agreements by serving the other side with what is called a "Section 6 notice" containing its proposals. The parties are then obligated to engage in direct negotiations. If no agreement is reached, either party may request mediation by the NMB, or the agency can intervene on its own. The NMB has the authority to prolong bargaining (virtually free of judicial review) as long it believes further talks may be productive. As a practical matter, the NMB determines when the parties are at impasse by making a proffer of voluntary binding arbitration of the dispute; if the offer is refused, the agency declares that its mediation efforts have failed. The parties are then obligated to maintain the status quo for thirty days, during which time the president may establish an emergency board. If the president fails to establish an emergency board, the parties are free after the conclusion of the thirty-day period to engage in economic action to attempt to resolve the dispute. Emergency boards are common in rail disputes, but have seldom been appointed in airline disputes since the 1960s.

The Process of Administering the Labor Agreement. Once the parties have entered into a collective bargaining agreement, some mechanism is needed to resolve disputes arising under the agreement—of necessity, a general document that cannot contain rules for all disputes that might develop. Such disputes typically involve discharges and other discipline challenged by the union under the "just cause" provisions of the labor agreement, or disagreements over the meaning of particular terms governing seniority, overtime assignments, and the use of subcontractors. The preferred mechanism under U.S. labor law for resolving such "rights" disputes is a contractual grievance machinery involving, in the first instance, stages of negotiations between union and management representatives, and should disagreements persist, arbitration before a neutral arbiter. Typically, unions agree not to strike over "rights" disputes during the life of the agreement, in exchange for which employers agree to "final and binding" grievance arbitration.

Arbitrators are chosen by the parties. Some agreements provide for regular resort to the same arbitrator or a panel of arbitrators. More commonly, arbitrators are selected on an ad hoc basis. Under the RLA, the parties are required to establish boards of adjustment to hear grievances (for railroads, the statute establishes an industry-wide grievance apparatus, the National Railroad Adjustment Board).

Hearings before arbitrators are seen as informal, quicker, and less costly than proceedings in court. The arbitrator's award is considered a "final and binding" resolution. The legal bases for challenging an award are limited. Absent bias, an indefinite award, or a strong showing that the arbitrator clearly exceeded his authority under the contract, the court must enforce the award.

In a trio of 1960 rulings decided the same day, the Supreme Court established rules strongly supportive of labor arbitration. The Court announced a "presumption of arbitrability" under which any facially plausible claim of a contract violation within the scope of the arbitration clause of the agreement is presumed arbitrable, absent clear evidence in the agreement that the parties intended to exclude a particular subject from the promise to arbitrate. The Court also made clear that since the parties bargained for their own special dispute-resolver, the courts may not set aside an award absent clear proof that the arbitrator strayed beyond his contractual authority. Even where an award is claimed to be in conflict with "public policy," the Court has insisted that in order to overturn an award, the award must be in "explicit conflict" with other "laws and legal precedents" rather than simply in tension with an assessment of "general considerations of supposed public interests." Moreover, even where employees engage in conduct violative of public policy, such as working under the influence of drugs, arbitrators have considerable latitude to reinstate such workers, absent proof that the reinstatement itself violates public policy.

There can be situations where a challenge to an employer's decision, such as a discharge, can be framed both as a breach of the collective bargaining agreement and as an unfair labor practice under the NLRA. The NLRB's policy in such cases is to require the employee (or the union) to exhaust the contractual grievance procedure before the agency will exercise its statutory jurisdiction. After completion of the grievance procedure, the agency will generally defer to the results of the labor arbitration if the statutory claim involves the same facts as the contractual claim, and the arbitration award is not "clearly repugnant" to the policies of the labor law.

Individual Rights and the Collective Agreement. Once the employees have selected an exclusive bargaining representative, their ability to negotiate individual employment contracts is severely curtailed.

Concerning disputes arising under the labor agreement, individual workers file grievances with their union representatives. The union ultimately controls which grievances are taken to arbitration. If a grievance is taken to arbitration, the arbitrator's award will be preclusive of any court action by the employee against his employer for breach of contract. Even if a grievance is not taken to arbitration, it is normally "final and binding" and precludes a court action. There are two exceptions to the preclusive effect of labor arbitration. The first is where the union breached its duty of fair representation; if such a breach is shown, the court action for breach of contract against the employer may proceed. The second exception is where the employee's claim is based on a public law creating individual rights not waivable by the collective bargaining representative, such as claims under the federal antidiscrimination laws.

Union Democracy. Federal labor law does not require workers to become members of labor unions, even in firms where unions are the exclusive bargaining agency. Indeed, the law prohibits "closed shops"—that is, agreements requiring workers to become union members as a condition of being hired for a position. However, "union shop" clauses are lawful (except in states which have enacted so-called "right to work" laws barring such provisions). Under a typical "union shop" clause, the employer is permitted to hire whomever it wishes, but the individual hired must within thirty days pay dues representing the costs of collective representation. This is a financial obligation rather than an obligation to join the union as such.

For individuals who are union members, the federal Labor-Management Reporting and Disclosure Act of 1959 (LMRDA or Landrum-Griffin Act) imposes rules of internal union democracy. Under the LMRDA, union members have enforceable rights of free *speech at union meetings and to run for union office free of unreasonable restriction. The NLRA also limits what unions can do to discipline their members. Union members can be subject to reasonable fines but cannot lose their jobs because of a violation of internal union rules. They also have the right to resign their union membership, even in the midst of a strike.

Labor Law and Business Change. As a general matter, companies seeking to merge with other firms or to sell all or part of their assets are under no duty to bargain over the decision itself, although there is a duty to bargain over the "effects" of the decisions. "Effects" bargaining must be in time to permit "meaningful" bargaining, but can take place after the decision is made.

In mergers and sales of stock, the surviving entity or purchaser will generally be held to assume the obligation to bargain with the union and to comply with the terms of the unexpired labor agreement—absent a strong showing that employment conditions with the surviving entity or stock purchaser will so radically alter the preexisting employment relationship that the union cannot be considered any longer to be the exclusive representative of the workers in an appropriate unit.

In the case of assets purchases, however, the purchaser's obligations are substantially relaxed. The purchaser is free to hire an entirely independent workforce, absent proof of refusal to hire the seller's workers because of their union status. The purchaser is under no obligation to assume the predecessor's labor contract—unless it hires substantially all of the predecessor's employees without predicating offers on changes in terms and conditions and without making substantial changes in the operation. The purchaser is also under no obligation to bargain with the predecessor's union unless a majority of the purchaser's employees come from the ranks of the predecessor's workforce. This determination is made at the time the purchaser hires a "substantial and representative" complement, rather than at a later point when its "full" complement has been hired.

Conclusion. U.S. labor and employment law presents a mix of reliance on market forces and regulation. With private-sector unions and collective bargaining on the decline, public policy has shifted away from an emphasis on private bargaining toward a regulatory model of how best to pursue public objectives in the employment arena. The laws governing labor organization and collective bargaining remain important for represented workers, workers actively seeking representation, and nonunion workers benefiting from favorable working conditions granted by employers seeking to avert unionization.

[See also *Commonwealth* v. *Hunt* (1842); Economics and Law; Haymarket Trials]

• Samuel Estreicher and Daniel G. Collins, *Labor Law and Business Change: Theoretical and Transactional Perspectives*, 1988. Samuel Estreicher, "Labor Law Reform in a World of Competitive Product Markets," *Chicago-Kent Law Review* 69 (1993): 3. Samuel Estreicher and Michael C. Harper, *Labor Law: Cases, Materials, and Problems*, 4th ed., 1996. Julius G. Getman, Bertrand B.

Pogrebin, and David L. Gregory, *Labor Management Relations and the Law,* 2d ed., 1999.

—Samuel Estreicher

LABOR LAW: WORKPLACE ISSUES

While formal regulation of employer-employee relations is ancient (Deuteronomy 24:14–15), America witnessed an explosive growth in the scope of such laws during the twentieth century.

Preventing Injury and Disease Among Workers. In 1877 Massachusetts enacted the first factory inspection law. Other states followed, and for the next ninety years, industrial safety was largely a matter of state law; a few federal safety statutes affected specific industries, such as railroads. Dissatisfaction with uneven administration of state laws, and with their confusingly different requirements, led Congress to enact the Occupational Safety and Health Act (OSHA) of 1970. This statute dominates the field, but has not brought state activity to an end. States may reassume responsibility for occupational safety and health by submitting to the secretary of labor a plan that meets standards developed under the act. Roughly twenty states have done so. Most of these closely track the provisions of OSHA, and state performance is monitored by federal inspectors.

OSHA imposes two principal duties on employers: The general duty clause requires an employer to furnish "employment and a place of employment which are free from recognized hazards that are causing or are likely to cause death or serious physical harm. . . ." The standards clause requires each employee to "comply with occupational safety and health standards promulgated under" the Act by the secretary of labor.

OSHA is enforced by an inspection-citation system, administered by the Occupational Safety and Health Administration (also known familiarly as OSHA). The agency selects workplaces to inspect either by using an administrative plan that emphasizes relative safety records of different industries and employers, or on the basis of specific complaints. An employer can refuse to submit to a warrantless inspection, but warrants can be obtained not only on the basis of traditional Fourth Amendment probable cause, but also on the basis of administrative probable cause—roughly, a demonstration that the general agency inspection plan is reasonable.

If the inspection reveals OSHA violations, the agency issues a citation, identifying each violation, assessing a civil penalty, and setting a time scheme for abatement of the violation. An employer may contest the citation before the Occupational Safety and Health Review Commission, whose decisions are subject to review by federal circuit *courts. How successful OSHA has been is frequently debated. Labor critics point to consistent underfunding of the agency, too few inspections and slow development of new standards. Management commentators criticize the agency as too aggressive and the standards as unduly demanding.

The specialized laws that apply to specific industries—mining, railroading, shipping, nuclear power—have created less controversy, perhaps because the hazards involved are easier to appreciate. One difference is that inspectors enforcing these, and some state plans, have a "red tag" power that permits them to halt operations they find particularly dangerous.

Both the federal and state governments make special efforts to protect the health and safety of very young workers. The Fair Labor Standards Act forbids employment of most children under fourteen in virtually all pursuits other than family businesses, some agricultural settings, and entertainment.

Benefits for Injured Workers. Injured workers can seek compensation for disabilities under three major systems: *tort law, workers compensation, and the disability benefits provisions of the Social Security Act.

Tort. In the nineteenth century, a worker bore the full burden of a job injury unless he could successfully sue his employer or some third party in a tort action, usually for negligence. In theory, tort law protection should have been fairly good, since the courts articulated a number of specific employer duties: to provide a safe place for work, to hire a reasonable number of competent fellow workers, and to set reasonable rules for the conduct of work. Actions against employers rarely succeeded, however, because of three defenses: contributory negligence; the doctrine of assumption of risk; and the fellow servant rule. The last of these became commonplace in the United States largely because of the influential opinion of Chief Justice Lemuel *Shaw in *Farwell* v. *Boston & Worcester Ry.* (1842); it denied recovery to a worker injured by the negligent acts of a fellow employee. Despite these defenses, and perhaps because of gradual modification of them, actions against employers multiplied early in the twentieth century, as did social protest against poor working conditions.

Two types of statutes were adopted to change the common law situation, employers liability laws and workers compensation statutes. The former statutes modify tort law; the latter largely supplant it, so far as actions against employers are concerned. Even after a workers compensation statute is in place, an injured worker can still recover damages under tort law against her employer for intentional torts, or if the workers compensation law does not cover the employer (many statutes exclude domestic service, for instance). It is also possible to recover against parties other than the employer, such as a manufacturer that sold negligently made equipment to be used in the workplace.

Employer Liability Acts. Only one major example of an employers *liability law remains on the books, the Federal Employers Liability Act (FELA). It applies to railroad workers and (under the Jones Act) to seafarers. This federal statute does away with contributory negligence in favor of a comparative negligence regime, and essentially abolishes the other two defenses. The Supreme Court has generally given the FELA an employee-friendly reading, setting a low burden of proof for plaintiffs on causation issues and finding the violation of any safety-related statute by a defendant should usually result in liability.

Workers Compensation Laws. Workers compensation laws are a substitute for tort law. For most workers, the applicable statute will be a state law, but there are three important federal statutes. One covers the federal government's own employees. The second, the Longshore and Harbor Workers Compensation Act, applies not only to the named occupations, but is often used by Congress for other private sector workers in federal enclaves. A third, the Black Lung Benefits Act, applies only to coal miners. Developed from earlier English and German models, American workers compensation statutes do not use employer fault as a basis for liability. Instead, an injured worker is entitled to benefits if she can prove that her injury was sufficiently connected to her work. The phrase used in the early statutes was "arising out of and in the course of employment." In all but a handful of states, and in the federal statutes, an administrative agency rather than a court decides whether the employer is liable under this formula, although limited judicial review is available.

The typical statute provides three categories of benefits: medical care, income replacement for the disabled worker or his surviving dependents, and rehabilitation benefits. The employer usually bears the full burden of medical care costs. Escalation of these costs has led to heavy lobbying for provisions that would cut these expenses, such as allowing employers to use Health Management Organizations (HMOs) to provide the care. Income replacement benefits for injured workers traditionally fell into four categories: temporary partial, temporary total, permanent partial, and permanent total disability benefits. Benefits are ordinarily paid in weekly increments. A typical figure is two-thirds of the worker's average weekly wage prior to the injury, subject to a cap that varies substantially from one state to another. Permanent benefit claims are often hard fought. Some statutes continue to use "schedules" to fix the number of weeks of permanent partial disability benefits. Loss of a leg might be rated at 200 weeks; loss of an arm, 100. Impairments not listed in the schedule would be dealt with by assigning a number of weeks to the "body as a whole" and then estimating the relative severity of the particular injury, often using a set of guidelines developed by the American Medical Association. More recently, an increasing number of statutes require economic factors to be taken into account, in addition to (or to some extent instead of) physical impairment. Actual wage loss is usually the most important. Permanent total benefits are paid in two circumstances: First, most statutes require such benefits in cases of truly severe impairment, such as loss of two limbs, even if the individual continues to work. Second, all statutes provide such benefits to a person who can demonstrate that her impairment in fact prevents any further opportunity to work, given her age, education, and experience. Most statutes allow either a claimant or an employer to ask for a reevaluation of the seriousness of an injury from time to time. If a worker dies from an injury, a surviving spouse and minor children receive benefits, usually without needing to prove dependency. Vocational rehabilitation benefits vary widely from state to state.

In exchange for the virtual certainty of receiving benefits for injury, the worker loses the right to sue her employer for damages in tort, under a provision in all the laws known as the exclusive remedy clause.

Social Security. A claimant under the disability benefits program of social security must establish that she worked in employment subject to the Social Security Act for a long enough period, and that she suffers from a severe disability. Only disabilities that will prevent the claimant from working at all for a substantial period are covered. The claim process is administrative, but benefit denial is subject to limited judicial review.

Tenure of Employment. Most employment in America is "at will." An employee may quit at any time or an employer can discharge at any time without liability. This general concept has given rise to at least three principal doctrines: (1) In any action for breach of an employment *contract, the party asserting that the contract was for a term rather than at will bears the burden of proof; (2) An employment contract that uses nonspecific words about the term of the agreement, such as "permanent," will be construed to provide for employment at will; (3) An employer may fire an employee for reasons "morally wrong" without being liable for damages. Since the 1970s, each of these has been modified in one or more states.

The most noted change has been to allow employees fired for reasons that violate a clearly defined public policy to recover damages from the employer. A majority of states now likely allow recovery, for example, if an employer fires an employee because that worker has filed a workers compensation claim, or has refused to lie in order to get out of jury duty. There is less uniformity in "whistle-blower" cases, in which a discharged worker alleges his firing was the result of reporting the employer for violating a safety statute, or filing false claims with the government. In such cases, courts often analyze not just whether the employee had the facts right, but also the motive for the complaint, and whether the worker followed an appropriate procedure. Several states now have whistle-blower statutes.

While no court has yet abandoned the position that the burden of proving employment is not at will remains on the proponent, there seems to be greater willingness than before to find contract-term promises in sources such as employee handbooks, bulletin board notices, and correspondence.

Some states and commentators have toyed with the notion that an employer owes a "duty of good faith and fair dealing" to employees, which in turn means that a long-term employee ought not to be discharged without reason. When the Montana Supreme Court adopted a version of this approach, its legislature responded by enacting the nation's only broad wrongful termination statute.

Regulating Employee Compensation. An employee's compensation has three principal components, each regulated to some extent by law: wages, government-mandated benefits, and contract-based benefits. The federal Fair Labor Standards Act (FLSA), sets the minimum wages for most workers, and also requires premium pay (time and one-half the employee's regular rate) for hours worked over forty in a week. This 1938 statute was upheld as constitutional in *United States v. Darby* (1941). The original statute covered only workers "engaged in commerce or in the production of goods for commerce." Under this language, one of two employees hired by the same firm, performing essentially the same work, might be protected while the other would not be. These anomalies were ended in 1961 by extending coverage to all those "employed by an enterprise engaged in commerce or in the production of goods for commerce." Despite this, much FLSA litigation continues to involve coverage issues, often focusing on the complicated definition of "enterprise," sometimes on the complex exemptions from coverage. Coverage of public employees has also been a battleground at the Supreme Court. Currently, employees of state governments are protected by the statute, but whether they can enforce their rights depends upon whether their employer state has waived sovereign immunity (see SOVEREIGNTY). For private sector employees, on the other hand, there can be enforcement by the secretary of labor or by private right of action. Wages of employees who work for firms that provide goods and services to the federal government are regulated not just by FLSA but by statutes, such as the Davis-Bacon Act (protecting construction workers), that require payment of "prevailing" wages. Employers who violate these requirements are subject to civil penalties, and in extreme cases to being barred from bidding on more government contracts. Another statute, Title II of the Consumer Credit Protection Act, limits how much of a worker's wages can be garnished by creditors, and forbids an employer to fire a worker because of a single garnishment.

State and local governments are free to set higher minimum wage rates than those under FLSA, and a handful do. Most states have laws requiring that wages be paid regularly and in cash. Many have prevailing wage laws applying to state contracts. Only a few nonwage benefits are required by law. Social security, Medicare, unemployment compensation, and workers compensation are the principal mandated benefit programs for most workers. Social security and Medicare taxes are paid by the vast majority of workers and their employers. The funds created by these taxes provide old-age income benefits, income benefits for seriously disabled workers, and medical care for persons eligible for either old-age or disability payments. The pension amount is based on the taxable wages an individual has received over a career, using a computation method that favors lower-paid workers. Unemployment compensation programs exist in every state, under a joint federal-state program. They are financed by payroll taxes that include an experience rating element, so that employers with heavy turnover pay somewhat more. Benefit amount and duration are based on the beneficiary's work experience. The typical maximum duration is twenty-six weeks. Workers compensation is mandatory for most private sector employment. Under the Family and Medical Leave Act employers of fifty or more must provide unpaid leave up to twelve weeks to most of their employees for purposes of childbirth and adoption, and also for the care of seriously ill family members, or for the employee's own medical disability. This last coverage overlaps at times with benefits provided by workers compensation or requirements under the Americans with Disabilities Act.

No law requires employers to provide such contract-based benefits as medical care or pensions, but for over half a century tax laws have encouraged developing such programs. Prior to the passage of the Employee Retirement Income Security Act (ERISA) in 1974, day-to-day regulation of plans was left to the states. ERISA changed that situation, replacing state law with federal standards. For pension plans, the statutory standards are substantial and detailed. Pension plans must be adequately funded, and the funds prudently invested. Any pension plan contribution an employee makes must vest immediately, and employer contributions must vest within a defined period.

Discriminating against an employee in order to prevent pension rights from vesting is forbidden. ERISA also regulates non-pension plans, such as employment-based group health care. The standards for these plans are not nearly so detailed as for pensions, and there continues to be widespread criticism of the decision to preempt most state law regarding benefit plan administration, without providing an adequate substitute. Individual beneficiaries may bring actions against employers, administrators or trustees for various wrongs, but damages are limited.

Who is an Employee or Employer? Most workplace law applies only to employers and employees. Despite the fact that these words are used commonly, they have proved slippery. Millions of Americans regularly confront the problem when trying to decide whether the once-a-week house cleaner who sets his own schedule and brings his own supplies, but uses the homeowner's vacuum cleaner, is an employee on whose behalf the homeowner must pay social security taxes, or an independent contractor who pays all that tax himself. All courts seem to agree that in deciding which label to apply, a long list of factors must be

considered, and that no one factor is determinative. The factors that get the heaviest weight are the extent to which the alleged employer controls the physical details of the work to be done, how much economic freedom the alleged employee has, and whether the work is of the sort usually done by independent business persons.

To complicate matters further, it is sometimes hard to decide whose employee a worker may be. When is a parent corporation the employer of its wholly owned subsidiary's workers? If two businesses share the services of a worker, are they joint employers at all times, or does the worker's status shift constantly back and forth? When a farmer hires a crew of harvest workers through a labor contractor, are those workers employees of the farmer only, the contractor only, or both? Questions such as these abound, and concepts such as *joint employer* and *borrowed employee* are maddeningly hard to apply. They are likely to be put to even more severe tests as more and more work is done in a "virtual workplace" through the Internet.

Other Concerns. Through job applications, personnel records, and medical examinations, employers—particularly large employers—acquire a lot of information about their employees. Until recently, employers have been able to use this information freely. During the last few years, however, there have been scattered lawsuits by former employees claiming they have been defamed or placed in a false light by their ex-employer's disclosures of reasons for dismissal. There are now statutory limits on the extent to which employers can listen in on their employees' phone conversations. A number of bills have been introduced to try to deal with privacy issues on the Internet. New regulations governing the release of medical information were issued in the closing days of President William Jefferson Clinton's administration. There have been an increasing number of employee protests over electronic surveillance by employers, particularly in rest rooms. All this is likely ultimately to be reflected also in courts' understanding about what constitutes a "reasonable expectation of privacy" in the workplace, an expectation that will in turn be protected by tort law and for some public employees by the Constitution.

Another current debate concerns what role employee and employer interests should play in *immigration law. It is clear that in some areas of the nation, the work of noncitizens is important to the functioning of the economy. It is also clear that some employers both exploit undocumented aliens in their employ and also use their availability as a means to avoid hiring citizens and paying them adequate wages. The Immigration Reform and Control Act of 1986 was the first statute to impose sanctions on employers for employing aliens who lack work permits. How successful that statute has been is hotly debated, but it is clear many abuses continue.

• John R. Commons, David J. Saposs, Helen L. Sumner, E. B. Mittelman, H. E. Hoagland, John B. Andrews, and Selig Perlman, *History of Labor in the United States, 1926–35*. Gary Z. Nothstein, *Law of Occupational Safety and Health*, 1981. Barbara J. Coleman, *Primer on ERISA*, 4th ed., 1993. Robert N. Covington and Kurt H. Decker, *Individual Employee Rights in a Nutshell*, 1995. Arthur Larson and Lex Larson, *Larson's Workers Compensation Law*, 1997. Mark A. Rothstein, Lea S. VanderVelde, Elinor P. Schroeder, Elaine W. Shoben, and Charles B. Craver, *Employment Law*, 1999. Social Security Administration, *Social Security Handbook*, 14th ed., 2001. (Electronic version at www.ssa.gov takes precedence.)

—Robert N. Covington

LABOR UNION. *See* Labor Law: Labor Relations.

LACHES. *See* Equity.

LAND. *See* Property, Real.

LANDLORD-TENANT. A revolution occurred in landlord-tenant law in the 1960s and 1970s. That revolution occurred is remarkable because landlord-tenant law is a part of the law of *property, which traditionally changes only gradually. Many important and long-standing doctrines— generally favoring the landlord—were replaced by rules more favorable to the tenant. Although courts led this reform effort by announcing a new theoretical vision of the nature of a lease, legislatures and law reform commissions raised important voices in favor of the work begun by the courts. Economically, the revolution's beneficiaries were residential tenants. Politically, the revolution in landlord-tenant law exemplified the spirit of the times, in which reformers viewed government as a positive force in people's lives and law as an appropriate vehicle for political and economic change. Ideologically, the revolution embraced government intervention—legislative and judicial—rather than market dynamics to correct the deficiencies of a housing market, rife with overpriced and declining properties and widely perceived to be malfunctioning.

No revolution accomplishes all of its goals. Some important doctrines governing residential leases survived the era largely intact. Moreover, the revolution bypassed commercial leases almost entirely, leaving traditional rules in place. Modern landlord-tenant law thus reflects both the important changes launched in the 1960s and '70s and longstanding *common-law rules.

Institutions of Change. The revolution in landlord-tenant law was produced by a combination of judges and legislators who contributed to the resulting body of new governing doctrines and policies. Throughout its history, landlord-tenant has been a common-law subject, one whose existence and development depended on private parties to formulate a dispute and present it to a court for resolution. Accordingly, the judiciary played a vital role in the transformation of that law: usually following the lead of one or two preeminent state or federal courts, the *supreme courts in virtually every American state adopted the major reforms. However, at least equally important have been the state legislatures, which can regulate an area broadly and comprehensively in contrast to courts, which are limited in their reform efforts by the timing and the nature of the disputes brought to them.

In addition to courts and legislatures, two prestigious associations of judges, lawyers, and law professors promulgated major documents in the field of landlord-tenant law in the reform era. The National Conference of Commissioners on Uniform State Laws produced the Uniform Residential Landlord and Tenant Act (URTLA) in 1972. The *American Law Institute selected the area of landlord and tenant as the subject of its initial effort in the second round of restatements, producing the Restatement (Second) of Property (Landlord and Tenant) in 1977. Although the formulations and pronouncements of these bodies are not binding, they are nevertheless widely respected and influential: the restatement rules are often adopted by courts, while the URLTA has been enacted in fifteen states, thus moving from the status of model act to binding legislation.

Doctrines: The Paradigm Shift. Throughout most of its history, the law of landlord and tenant imposed few duties on the landlord. The landlord owed no duty to the tenant to guarantee the habitability of the dwelling leased to the tenant. The tenant likewise continued to owe rent if, through act of God such as by fire or flood, the premises became unavailable for use or occupancy; the landlord had no duty to repair, or in general to concern himself with the success or failure of the tenancy. The rent obligation remained intact if the tenant abandoned the premises, even if the landlord, although having ample opportunity, failed to find a new tenant and avoid a loss. In cases in which the landlord obligated himself by an express promise in the lease, such as a promise to repair the premises, the landlord's failure to perform that promise did not excuse the tenant from the obligation to continue paying rent, and consequently did not provide the tenant with a legal basis for withholding rent to secure compliance with the promise; the tenant's obligations were regarded as independent of the landlord's obligations.

A historically oriented interpretation of this situation would trace its source to a particular conceptual view of the lease arising from the predominantly agricultural society in which landlord-tenant law originated. A yeoman farmer who leased land as a means of livelihood would not care greatly about the lack of repair, or even the continued existence, of buildings on the land, so long as the land itself remained to support agriculture. And the tenant who possessed the land could not blame the landlord even if the tenant's crop failed. The paradigm of land served well enough in its agricultural heydey; it became awkward when the underlying social conditions changed: when the lease, moving into the city, became a central legal arrangement for housing rather than the means of producing the tenant's livelihood. Urbanization marked the point at which the failure of the old lease paradigm of land to coincide with social reality became noticeable; the second half of the twentieth century marked the point at which it became unbearable enough to bring about widespread changes in the rules.

The major conceptual basis for change was a paradigm shift away from the concept of a lease as a conveyance of land to the concept of a lease as a *contract, an exchange of promises in which, in return for the tenant's promise to pay rent, the landlord obligated himself to deliver a "package of goods and services" to the tenant. Viewing a lease as a contract, courts derived opposite conclusions from those that had previously existed on all of the doctrines mentioned above: habitability, frustration of purpose, mitigation of *damages, and dependency of promises. By agreeing to lease the premises to the tenant, the landlord (it was now held) impliedly undertook a duty to furnish liveable premises at the outset of the lease and to maintain them at the standard of habitability during the term of the lease. Now, the destruction of the premises by fire or other casualty excused the tenant from the remaining rental obligation. The landlord who stood idly by his vacant premises after the tenant abandoned them suffered a deduction from the remaining rent of whatever sums

the landlord could have received by finding another tenant. And, the landlord's breach of an express promise to repair, or of the implied warranty of habitability, justified the tenant in remaining in possession, withholding rent, and getting a judicially determined abatement in the amount of rent due.

Legislative Efforts. Although courts took the lead in modernizing the doctrines canvassed above, legislatures also played an important part, sometimes by adopting a warranty of habitability when the state courts refused to, more usually by giving specifics and boundaries to issues that the courts had only sketched in broad outline. Some important reforms of the era, however, owe their existence almost exclusively to legislation. The federal Fair Housing Act of 1968 (amended 1988) and its state counterparts modify the landlord's common law right to rent to whomever he pleases by imposing prohibitions on *discrimination based on a wide range of characteristics, including disability (see DISABILITIES LAW).

The most significant example of legislative intervention into the operation of the market, however, is regulation that limits the central contractual provision of the lease bargain: the amount of rent that the landlord charges for use of the premises. Although based on a variety of considerations, rent control legislation is centrally premised on the same consideration underlying the judicial implementation of the implied warranty of habitability: in a housing market characterized by scarcity and lack of consumer bargaining power, significant numbers of the urban poor and middle class would be unable to afford, or would spend a disproportionate part of their income for, housing were it not for rent controls. On the other side, opponents of rent control see market *regulation as an illicit redistribution of wealth and a counterproductive initiative that will reduce the stock of housing by discouraging capital investment in the housing market. Touching as it does on opposing views of the proper roles of government and free enterprise, rent control legislation will remain controversial as long as it exists. It is symptomatic of the controversy generated by rent control that it exists today in only a handful of jurisdictions, such as New York City, having never been adopted in many states, and abandoned in others.

The Unfinished Revolution. The revolution left a sizeable agenda of theoretical and doctrinal issues requiring work. As to theory, more than one commentator questioned whether the contractual paradigm on which so much of the reform effort was based was adequate to the task assigned it. Two examples suffice. Courts that imposed an implied warranty of habitability on the landlord almost without exception held that the warranty could neither be disclaimed in the lease (by an "as is" provision) nor waived by the tenant's conduct (for example, taking possession in the face of obvious defects in the premises). In contract law generally, however, goods and services can be sold according to whatever terms the parties agree upon. Again, after announcing that the tenant had a right to habitable premises, the courts universally held that the dependency of the tenant's promise to pay rent on the landlord's performance of the habitability promise required that the tenant be allowed to withhold rent (i.e., completely cease to perform his own obligation) until a judicial resolution of the dispute, which could occur months after the tenant's withholding began. In contract law, the complete cessation of one's performance is only justified when the party aggrieved by the other's breach terminates the contract; the aggrieved party is not allowed to retain its benefits, as in the tenant's remaining in possession, without rendering at least some of the counterperformance called for by the terms of the bargain. The recited doctrinal difficulties show that the fit between the courts' stated theoretical bases for their decisions and the actual results reached is less than snug. A lease is partly a contract and partly a conveyance of a possessory interest in land (or a building) to the tenant. It is no more possible to derive all of the necessary rules to govern the relationship of landlord and tenant from the law of contracts than from the law of property. At the level of doctrine, important issues remain from the era of reform; a few of the most important can be mentioned here. Courts and legislatures generally have not addressed the important question of the tenant's entitlement to possession itself. Under the traditional rule, the landlord is not required to renew a term lease at its expiration, or to continue a month-to-month tenancy for any prescribed duration. Fair housing laws bar discriminatory conduct by the landlords; but that legislation does not offer the tenant the right to retain a tenancy until such time as the landlord has good cause to end it. New Jersey has gone the farthest in this direction by adopting a comprehensive statutory scheme that assures almost all residential tenants a right to continued occupancy during good behavior. It remains to be seen whether the New Jersey initiative will be followed in other states.

In contrast to the remedy of rent reduction when the landlord breaches the warranty of hab-

itability, the tenant's damages remedy for personal injury resulting from the condition of the premises raises the possibility of potentially ruinous *liability on the landlord (either through juries' high damages awards or costly liability insurance). Consequently, courts moved much more cautiously during the 1960s and 1970s in delineating the *tort liability of the landlord than in imposing a warranty of habitability. Although some courts in residential lease cases adopted the general standard of tort liability (reasonable care under all of the circumstances) the older approach (a rule of nonliability punctuated by a few exceptions) has in the main survived the era of reform. The general negligence (reasonable care) standard has much to recommend it.

Although this essay focuses on residential leases, it deserves mention that some aspects of the law of commercial leases would profit from further study. Commercial tenants are often large-scale enterprises well able to take care of themselves, and commercial leases are often fully negotiated and lengthy documents presenting, when a dispute arises, garden variety issues of contract interpretation rather than any unique property questions. However, many nonresidential leases are held by tenants operating modest enterprises; for those tenants, an implied warranty of suitability, based on the idea of disparity of bargaining power between the landlord and tenant, is a plausible extension of the law applying to residential lessees. So is the extension to at least some nonresidential tenants of the residential tenant's remedy of rent withholding, when the landlord fails to perform any promise constituting an inducement to the tenant to enter into the lease. There are a few isolated cases establishing those doctrines in commercial leases, but they have not had the galvanizing effect on the courts of other states that the leading cases had in the area of residential leases.

Reference has already been made to the passage in the 1960s and '70s of antidiscrimination legislation; one widely publicized issue is whether the landlord whose religious scruples condemn sex outside of marriage is guilty of discrimination in refusing to rent to unmarried couples. The question has divided courts in different states, and no consensus appears imminent. Landlord-tenant law remains an unsettled and exciting field. As long as the question of where one lives remains important, along with the questions how and with whom, it could hardly be otherwise.

[See also Consumer Law; Contract Law]

• Glen Weissenberger, "The Landlord's Duty to Mitigate Damages on the Tenant's Abandonment: A Survey of Old Law and New Trends," *Temple Law Quarterly*

(1980): 1–46. James Casner, "Restatement (Second) of Property as an Instrument of Law Reform," *Iowa Law Review* (1981): 87–100. Olin L. Browder, "The Taming of a Duty—The Tort Liability of Landlords," *Michigan Law Review* (1982): 99–156. Mary Ann Glendon, "The Transformation of American Landlord-Tenant Law," *Boston College Law Review* (1982): 503–76. John A. Humbach, "The Common-Law Conception of Leasing: Mitigation, Habitability, and Dependence of Covenants," *Washington University Law Quarterly* (1983): 1213–90. Edward H. Rabin, "The Revolution in Residential Landlord-Tenant Law: Causes and Consequences," *Cornell Law Review* (1984): 517–84. Edward Chase and E. Hunter Taylor Jr., "Landlord and Tenant: A Study in Property and Contract," *Villanova Law Review* (1985): 571–699. Gerald Korngold, "Whatever Happened to Landlord-Tenant Law?" *Nebraska Law Review* (1998): 703, 707–08.
—Edward Chase

LAND USE PLANNING. *See* Zoning.

LARCENY developed as the common law's first nonviolent crime against *property, distinguished from *robbery, which criminalized the taking of another's property by force or threat of force. Larceny is traditionally defined as (1) the wrongful or "trespassory" (2) taking (3) and carrying away (4) of the personal property (5) of another (6) with the intent to deprive him of it permanently. Today, larceny, along with the newer crimes of embezzlement and false pretense, constitute alternative ways of committing the consolidated crime of *theft. The *Model Penal Code also recommends use of the term "theft" for the broader crime.

Larceny's wrongful or "trespassory" element requires that the perpetrator enjoyed no right to take the property.

"Taking" requires that the larcenist actually seize control of the property. Unlike robbery, the taking does not have to be from a person by force. The perpetrator can take unattended property, left temporarily in a public or private location. The wrongful appropriation of property by a person already entrusted by its owner with possession is not a taking. The crime of embezzlement addresses this wrongdoing. Courts expanded the concept of trespassory takings to include not only stealthful snatching, but taking property by trickery. This includes the taking and failure to return lost goods, or the failure to return misdelivered property.

Traditionally, the property must be "carried away." This third element has been construed to impose only the most minimal ["asportation"] requirement, such as moving a motel air conditioner four inches from its base. Some jurisdictions and the Model Penal Code have rejected the [asportation] element.

The requirement that the perpetrator take "personal property" at *common law precluded criminal liability for taking undomesticated animals as well as real property, including trees, growing vegetables, and gravestones attached to the land. Intangible property, such as stocks and certificates of deposits, were also excluded. Modern larceny statutes, however, routinely include such items. Today, scholars debate whether larceny should include stealing information, such as trade and government secrets, or computer time. The economic implications of not protecting trade secrets argue for expanding larceny to cover stealing information. On the other hand, overzealous prosecution could result in unfairly chilling an employee's move to another company or a journalist's legitimate efforts to learn information some would prefer to keep secret.

The property subject to larceny must be the property of "another." The victim need not own the property, but merely have a right of possession superior to that of the perpetrator. Contraband, and even a thief's loot, can be stolen from him.

The perpetrator of larceny must have the intent to deprive a person of his property permanently. Permanently means a significant portion of the stolen property's useful life. This requirement precludes unauthorized borrowing. In most instances, borrowing without permission may be antisocial, even tortious, but not criminal without special statutes, such as laws against "joyriding" in automobiles, which supplement the crime of larceny.

Furthermore, since the perpetrator must also intend to deprive the "property of another," he is not guilty of larceny if she honestly believes the property is hers or believes she is entitled to it. Larceny requires intentional wrongdoing to impose criminal *liability.

[*See also* Criminal Law Principles]

• Jerome Hall, *Theft, Law and Society*, 2d ed., 1952. George P. Fletcher, *Rethinking Criminal Law*, 1978. Wayne R. Lafave and Austin W. Scott Jr., *Criminal Law*, 2d ed., 1986.
—John L. Diamond

LAW AND ECONOMICS, THEORY OF. Perhaps no branch of legal scholarship has enjoyed greater influence during the last half century than the economic analysis of law. Although its conceptual kernel can be traced at least to the English jurist and philosopher Jeremy Bentham (1748–1832), the field of law and economics did not hit full stride until the 1960s. This timing is no coincidence, arriving on the heels of the *legal realism movement, which had made a serious case that law was not an independent discipline, but rather an institutional intersection of disparate and competing social forces, ideas, and agendas. This realist criticism set the stage for constructive and interpretive theories of law emanating from external disciplines (including economics). What is coincidental, however, is that economics was simultaneously undergoing its own transformation, from a largely philosophical discourse to an elegant mathematical approach for analyzing social and private ordering. Energized by this intellectual transformation, economic-minded scholars (particularly at the University of Chicago) soon began to seek out institutional applications for this methodology. Law proved an inviting target.

Most law and economics analysis falls into one of two subspecies: (a) positive theory, which uses economic analysis to explain observed social behavior, or to predict (for example) how behavior will respond to a change in legal regime; and (b) normative theory, which evaluates the social desirability of observed behavior or predicted changes thereto. Positive theories are the simplest, yet still depend on some core assumptions about individual behavior. Most central: they posit that individuals respond to economic incentives in systematic and predictable ways. This assumption—known generally as "rationality"—maintains that individuals behave as if they were attempting to maximize their happiness, or "utility." As long as one's underlying preferences are sufficiently well behaved, the argument goes, a mathematical "utility function" exists that faithfully embodies those preferences. When a collection of rational individuals interact with one another, the predicted outcome that results is called an "equilibrium."

Normative theories go a step further, explicitly evaluating which equilibrium outcome (or collection thereof) is socially most desirable. To make this assessment, the theorist must provide a method for aggregating and comparing individuals' welfare. A number of methods are possible here, ranging from the relatively weak notion of Pareto efficiency (ranking as efficient all outcomes that cannot be altered to increase someone's utility without reducing someone else's) to the stronger notion of Kaldor-Hicks efficiency (identifying efficient outcome as those for which there exists no alternative that, when compared, confers greater monetized benefits on winners than it does on losers). Although most tractable notions of efficiency require one to compare individual utilities, Kenneth Arrow's "impossibility theorem" has demonstrated that it is frequently (though not always) impossible to make such comparisons coherently without also being dictatorial. Consequently, normative theorists frequently must wield their conclusions with measured caution.

The law has proven an extremely fertile field for applications of economic theory. Perhaps the first—and most durable—is due to Ronald Coase, whose Coase theorem asserts that if individuals are rational, well informed, and can negotiate effortlessly, private bargaining will allocate *property rights efficiently irrespective of their initial distribution. Indeed, the theorem (which has positive and normative implications) posits that if a legal rule were to create an inefficient distribution of rights, there is (by definition) an opportunity for individuals to reallocate them in a way that makes everyone better off. Nevertheless, because the predicate assumptions of the Coase theorem often fail to hold in practice, much scholarly effort (including Coase's own article) since has focused on how courts should craft law efficiently in the presence of impediments to efficient bargaining.

*Criminal law and *tort law were also early subjects for law and economics scholars. Much of Gary Becker's work in the field formalized modern theories of deterrence, arguing that there was a fundamental trade-off between the severity of legal sanctions and the intensity of harm detection by either public or private enforcers. These theories remain influential in the early twenty-first century.

Another well-known application of economic analysis to law concerns whether legal precedents, like competitive markets, evolve efficiently. Although the argument seems plausible when judges themselves are motivated by efficiency goals, some early scholars argued that even without judicial assistance, inefficient rules would be challenged (and therefore overturned) more frequently. Such arguments are increasingly viewed with significant skepticism in light of conflating factors such as decisions to sue, settlement, and informational failures.

More recently, law and economics scholars have employed approaches from game theory to analyze law. An outgrowth of conventional economics, game theory attempts to analyze how a rational actor behaves when her economic "environment" consists of strategic counterparts forming their own strategies and expectations, often within an environment of private information. This approach has proven to be powerful in recent years, spawning applications ranging from criminal law (through the well-known "prisoner's dilemma"), to administrative law, civil procedure, *contract law, corporate law, and even extralegal norms of behavior. A particularly salient observation from game theory is that legal rules designed to improve one actor's incentives may create perverse incentives for another (e.g., making companies liable for securities fraud may increase frivolous litigation). Such "rent-seeking" behavior represents an attendant cost to any legal rule deserving of independent consideration.

Although law and economics has proven a powerful methodology, it is not without criticism. For example, even though nothing in theory requires individuals to be wholly self-interested in their preferences, such an assumption is perhaps too common within existing law and economics scholarship. In addition, "economic efficiency" need not be coterminous with wealth maximization, many legal scholars too frequently equate the two concepts. Moreover, existing scholarship has been relatively inattentive to how the analysis might change when individuals do not have well-behaved preferences, or are subject to cognitive biases that induce them to act against their own interests. A new generation of law and economics scholars is now in the midst of pushing these (and other) issues to the front of the agenda. Although the success of such efforts remains to be seen, if nothing else they have renewed the intellectual energy that sustained the discipline for the last half century.

[*See also* Law and Society Movement]

• R. H. Coase, "The Problem of Social Cost," *Journal of Law and Economics* (1960): 1–44. G. S. Becker, "Crime and Punishment: An Economic Approach," *Journal of Political Economy* (1968): 169–217. S. Shavell, *Economic Analysis of Accident Law,* 1987. A. M. Polinsky, *An Introduction to Law and Economics,* 2d ed., 1989. D. Baird, R. Gertner, and R. Picker, *Game Theory and the Law,* 1994. R. D. Cooter and T. Ulen, *Law and Economics,* 2nd ed., 1997. R. A. Posner, *Economic Analysis of Law,* 5th ed., 1998.
— Eric Talley

LAW AND LITERATURE, THEORY OF. The contemporary law and literature movement began with the publication of James Boyd White's *The Legal Imagination* (1973). Arguing for the inclusion of literary studies in legal *education, White urged that law is best understood as an art, not as a social science. Articulating justice, White suggests, requires a hybrid act of imagination drawing on the precedents of fiction, poetry, and drama, as well as those of case and code. The idea that literature might play a role in shaping a society's *jurisprudence has a long history. From Plato to the present, philosophers, poets, novelists, and jurists have considered the connections between the literary and the legal, the aesthetic and the juridical. As the most recent installment in this line of inquiry, the law and literature movement originates in law schools and English departments and is one of several 'law ands,' such as *law and economics and *law and society, centrally concerned with the possibility that the study and practice of law might benefit from exposure to other disciplines.

Most law and literature scholarship seeks to challenge the notion that law is, or should be, an autonomous language of rules and analytical methods. The advent of a formalist approach to law as largely isolated from extralegal influences and concerns represents a turning point in the history of American law. At the nation's inception, this story begins, the founding fathers did not distinguish between law and literature. These early republicans saw law and literature as part of the rational and humanistic venture to express the basis of a just and coherent social order, which was the responsibility of all citizens. Over the course of the nineteenth century, however, law became increasingly professionalized, as alien to the average citizen as medicine or any other specialized discipline. This trend did not go unchallenged. Abolitionists, suffragettes, progressives, and legal realists argued that law is, and must be, shaped by such extrinsic considerations as ethical convictions and economic or political interests. The law and literature movement, like *Critical Legal Studies and *Critical Race Theory, is a descendant of these earlier critiques of law's autonomy. Ironically, one of law and literature's best-known texts, Judge Richard Posner's *Law and Literature: A Misunderstood Relation* (1988) contends that there is no substantive interaction between law and literature. For Posner, literature provides lawyers and judges with little more than instruction in reading and writing. In many respects, the rest of the field defines itself against Posner's views.

Contemporary law and literature studies can be divided into four categories. First, there is the argument that literature teaches lawyers and judges important moral lessons. In a heterodox and heterogeneous culture, literature furnishes, for the humanist law and literature scholar, an important repository of public values. Reading literature, Martha Nussbaum's *Poetic Justice* (1995) argues, can move judges and lawyers to chasten their implementations of legal doctrine with sympathy. Robin West stresses the value of literary texts as a medium of jurisprudential debate. West uses Kafka's *The Trial* to illuminate the impracticability and unethical nature of Judge Posner's 'scientific' approach to human conflict. Second, law and literature scholars with a hermeneutic bent apply lessons learned in literary and critical theory to challenge traditional accounts of legal interpretation. Stanley Fish provocatively disputes the notion that judges neutrally and objectively construe legal rules. Whether interpreting a statute or a poem, the reader does not *find* meaning; instead, she or he *creates* a meaning that fits with the expectations of the community to which the reader belongs. This account, Owen Fiss and Ronald Dworkin charge, amounts to a kind of interpretive nihilism. Third, a considerable number of law and literature studies focus on the narrative aspects of law. Taking their cue from Robert Cover's influential argument that legal doctrine requires broader cultural narratives to give it meaning, law-as-narrative scholars, such as Robin West and Patricia Williams, urge that we recognize the key role played by storytelling in shaping law. Focusing on narrative, one can observe how both the prosecution and defense of a woman on trial for killing her abusive spouse crucially depend on the kinds of narrative details included or excluded by the rules of evidence, as well as the larger cultural narratives about marriage and women influencing the judge and jury. Critical Race Theorists, such as Richard Delgado, argue that the unofficial stories of the disenfranchised can effectively contradict and undermine the official story of citizenship told by the law.

While scholars working in these first three categories of law and literature tend to ask what *might* happen to law if one viewed it as comprised of ethics, interpretive theory, or narrative, as well as rules and rulings, the fourth category of law and literature scholarship takes a different tack, investigating historical interactions between law and literature. Robert Ferguson has shown, for instance, how the radical abolitionist John Brown merged the conventions of the literary romance with the varied narrative and dramatic materials of the criminal trials to craft a charismatic self-portrait as a sacrificial hero, and Brook Thomas describes how legal and literary figures of the late nineteenth century found in contract doctrine a secular means for consensually deriving basic social values.

Law and literature scholars often note or even lament the limited practical impact their movement has had, especially when compared with its interdisciplinary cousin, the law and economics movement. Whatever accuracy this perception has probably results, at least in part, from the fact that, wanting to be pragmatic, American jurists are more willing to acknowledge the legal influence of economics, which seems reliable and scientific compared with the study of literature and culture. The limited impact of the law and literature movement should not, however, obscure the impact that literary, cultural, and philosophical texts have often had on the law, such as the influence of James Joyce's *Ulysses* on legal definitions of obscenity or the influence of Frederick Douglass's advocacy on the course and content of such Reconstruction measures as the Civil Rights Act of 1875.

• Robert Ferguson, *Law and Letters in American Culture*, 1984. Sanford Levinson and Steven Mailloux, *Interpreting Law and Literature: a Hermeneutic Reader*, 1988. Patricia Williams, *The Alchemy of Race and Rights*, 1991. Richard Weisberg, *Poethics and Other Strategies of Law and Literature*, 1992. Robin West, *Narrative, Authority, and Law*, 1993. Brook Thomas, *American Literary Realism and the Failed Promise of Contract*, 1997. Guyora Binder and Robert Weisberg, *Literary Criticisms of Law*, 2000. Gregg Crane, *Race, Citizenship, and Law in American Literature (forthcoming)*.   —Gregg Crane

LAW AND SOCIETY ASSOCIATION. The Law and Society Association (LSA) was founded in 1964 by a small group of social scientists and law professors. Today it has about 1,600 members, most of whom are in university or college faculties or are graduate students. The membership is drawn from many academic disciplines. Sociology, political science, and law make up the largest portion, with a smaller number from anthropology, history, psychology, economics, and the humanities.

In addition to being multidisciplinary, LSA has in recent years become substantially more international. About 20 percent of its members are outside the United States. In 1991, recognizing the increasing globalization of legal issues and expanding opportunities for cross-national research, LSA began holding its annual conferences in Europe on a regular basis—Amsterdam (1991), Glasgow (1996), and Budapest (2001). In Budapest, scholars from fifty-seven countries participated in the conference.

The primary activities of LSA are publishing its journal, *Law & Society Review*, now in its thirty-fifth year, holding annual conferences at which scholars present their research, and running educational workshops for graduate students and junior faculty. LSA is a member of the Consortium of Social Sciences Associations and the American Council of Learned Societies.

For decades prior to the founding of LSA, universities had departments of social science and schools of law, with little interaction between them. Since then, several academic programs in law and society have been created. Perhaps best known are the law and society graduate programs at the University of California at Berkeley, Arizona State University, New York University, and Northwestern University, and the strong law and society presence in the law school faculties of the University of Wisconsin, SUNY at Buffalo, Denver University, and Miami University. More common has been the development of undergraduate programs in law and society, which now number about sixty; notable among them are Amherst College, the University of Massachusetts-Amherst, Ramapo College of New Jersey, and the University of California at Santa Barbara.

Outside the academic setting, the American Bar Foundation in Chicago is a major research center for law and society scholarship. In Europe, Asia, South America, and Australia, law and society scholars are more typically found in law schools, which, unlike in the U.S. and Canada, are undergraduate programs, and where sociology of law is often part of the required curriculum. LSA draws heavily from these various programs for its membership. Even so, the majority of law and society scholars are found in traditional disciplinary departments and traditional law schools.

The founders of LSA had a rather narrow vision of what they hoped to accomplish with the Association. In the late 1950s and early 1960s, the social sciences were in academic ascendence after having adopted some of the powerful new statistical sampling and analytical methods developed in mathematics and the sciences. Law schools, however, were largely stagnant and closed to outside perspectives, preoccupied with the production of lawyers for traditional practices. However, the emerging social activism of the courts and the government in that period (which later came to be called the "rights revolution") appeared to present social science with an opening in law to assist in progressive social change. But few law students, lawyers, or judges had been trained in social science research methods or had the ability to evaluate scientific research. The place to start was the law school curriculum. Backing this objective were two charitable foundations, Russell Sage and Walter E. Meyer, which made substantial grants to four universities (Wisconsin, the University of California at Berkeley, Denver, and Northwestern) to begin the effort. While programs in law and social science remain in some form at each of these universities, they were never able to get law schools to accept social science in the required curriculum, nor did the idea spread. (Ironically, greater success in this effort came later to the discipline least represented in the law and society movement, economics. The success of economics has been attributed to its affinity, like law, to political conservatism, whereas other social sciences

were seen as more aligned with liberal politics that faded after the sixties. *Law and economics has its own academic association and journal.) While LSA's founders' original objectives were unsuccessful, still they helped launch what has proven to be a vibrant field of research and scholarship, largely outside of law schools.

Prior to the launch of the *Law & Society Review* in 1966, there were no journals in law and social science. Now there are a half dozen journals with this focus, and many more disciplinary journals that regularly include work in the law and society tradition. Where law faculties once had few members with multidisciplinary graduate training, now joint holders of JD/PhDs in a social science are common. Where there were once few treatises and no texts on law and society, several academic publishers now have long lists of books under this heading.

For LSA, the success of the *law and society movement has come in its support for the development of individual scholars to research law and legal systems using the tools of social science. LSA's work has been largely oriented to individual career development and support: through mentorship, networking, collegial critique and research assistance, presentation opportunities, publishing, assistance in research grant applications, and support of local seminars. The understanding now is that a larger critical mass of law and society scholars must be built before institutional innovation can emerge. This has begun to happen, particularly in the development of undergraduate programs in law and society and in many traditional social science departments and law schools, which now include law and society among their specialities. It is also seen in traditional disciplinary societies. The social sciences, which once considered law little more than an illustration of more important social processes (e.g., social control, social cohesion, criminology, public policy, regulation, politics, and so on), have all now established divisions on law to accommodate the subject as a distinct area of inquiry rather than one merely subsumed under other categories.

Perhaps the most interesting consequence of LSA's emphasis on the development of individual scholars is that the field of law and society is constantly changing as new members bring in their research and existing members move on to new areas of inquiry. The research remains the most advanced, the boundaries of the field stay amorphous, and the multidisciplinary interaction continues to create excitement and creative thinking for the participants. The ultimate goal is to continue to provide the scholarly community, governmental institutions, and the public with knowledge and useful information on how law and legal systems are working in the United States and other societies.

[*See also* Education, Legal; Publishing, Law]

• Law and Society Association web site: http://www.lawandsociety.org. Bryant Garth and Joyce Sterling, "From Legal Realism to Law and Society: Reshaping Law for the Last Stages of the Social Activist State," *Law & Society Review* 32:2 (1998): 409–71. Felice J. Levine, " 'Goose Bumps and The Search for Signs of Intelligent Life' in Sociolegal Studies: After Twenty-Five Years," *Law & Society Review* 24:1 (1990): 7–33. Susan S. Silbey, "From the Editor," *Law & Society Review* 34:4 (2000): 859–72. Christopher Tomlins, "Framing the Field of Law's Disciplinary Encounters: A Historical Narrative," *Law & Society Review* 34:4 (2000): 911–72.

—Ronald M. Pipkin

LAW AND SOCIETY MOVEMENT. The term "law and society" refers to an association of scholars, a journal of academic research, and a collection of empirical approaches to understanding how law works. As an intellectual movement, law and society scholars often locate themselves at the margins of legal scholarship, looking at what law does rather than what law ought to do. Adopting a distinctly empirical approach, law and society scholars tend to avoid the normative projects of traditional legal scholars. By employing what are believed to be the more reliable and powerful resources of social scientific inquiry, law and society scholarship professes to be both value free, in terms of particular policies and parties, and yet critical because it is independent of the authority and interests of the legal profession or the state.

Because law is a system of both symbols and action, structured reason and constrained force, the social scientific study of law has roots in diverse intellectual traditions. Attention to the relationship between law and society, the role of reason, and the regulation of force can be found in ancient and medieval works of philosophy from Plato, through Hobbes and Locke, to Montesquieu's canonical work *The Spirit of the Laws* (1748). The cultural and social action dimensions of law became more prominent in the nineteenth century *jurisprudence; for example, in 1831 when Friedrich Karl von Savigny described law as the slow, organic distillation of the spirit of a particular people, or Sir Henry Maine described the development of *social relations over the millennia as a movement from status to contract.

At the beginning of the twentieth century, European and American legal scholars began devoting even more attention to the sociological aspects of law. Oliver Wendell *Holmes Jr., American judge and jurist, provided an icon of the movement toward social understanding of law when he wrote in *The Common Law* (1881) that the life of the law is not logic but experience. In 1913 the Austrian scholar Eugen Ehrlich described what he called "the living law," the complex system of norms and rules by which the members of organizations, communities, and societies actually live. Formal law emanating from the state is dependent in large part, he argued, on its concordance with the living law. Roscoe Pound, Dean of the Harvard Law School, pushed this perspective further in 1910 when he named the informal practices of legal institutions "the law-in-action," contrasting it to "the law-in-the-books," formally enacted legal doctrine. American *legal realists, writing in the 1920s and 1930s, made the exploration of this gap between the formal law and the law-in-action the central focus of their research. Alongside their efforts to expose the illogic of ostensibly logical legal principles and precedents, the legal realists laid a foundation for the law and society movement, which would emerge three decades later, to describe how the law really works.

By the end of World War II, the social sciences had developed empirical tools for data collection and analysis (surveys of legal use and need, statistical analysis of court records, interviews with jurors and judges) that moved the study of the law-in-action forward. Social scientists could also draw upon their own disciplinary traditions to authorize this attention to law. The most important social theorists writing in the nineteenth and early twentieth century had recognized law as a central feature of rationalized coordination and regulation in modern societies, no longer governed as tightly by *custom and religion. Looking closely at how law accomplished this role as the general societal manager, they drew upon Emile Durkheim's theory of the association of law with varying divisions of labor, and sought out evidence of repressive law and restitutive law in less or more industrialized societies. Following Weber, others described patterns of litigation and legal doctrine to the variation in types of legal rationality associated with different types of economy and cultural social development.

In 1964, a group of sociologists, political scientists, psychologists, anthropologists, historians, and law professors formed the Law and Society Association; in 1967, they began publishing a research journal, the *Law and Society Review*. Following two national meetings in the 1970s, conferences have been organized annually from 1980 to the present. The early years of the association and journal, as well as four interdisciplinary research centers located on the campuses of Berkeley, Denver, Northwestern, and Wisconsin, were created with support by generous grants from the Russell Sage Foundation whose interest in social policy and change found a happy target in this nascent intellectual movement. Recognizing law as the central governing mechanism, and language, of the modern state, the foundation sought to explore ways in which the legal profession might, or might not, provide leadership for progressive social change. Drawing on the diverse historical sources, their own research projects, and the pioneering work of contemporaries such as Philip Selznick at Berkeley, Harry Kalven, Hans Zeisel, and Rita Simon at Chicago, and Willard Hurst at Wisconsin, the birth of the law and society association signaled an organized, long-term commitment to interdisciplinary empirical work that would transcend the limitations of traditional legal research and jurisprudence.

In its more than thirty-five-year history, this multidisciplinary movement has produced a body of durable knowledge about how the law works, while institutionalizing its field of scholarship. Although the sociology of law in Europe remains a predominantly theoretical and normative enterprise, it is, nonetheless, a required subject for the *education and training of lawyers. In the United States, the original centers of law and society research in the law schools of Berkeley, Wisconsin, Denver, and Northwestern remain strong, with additional concentrations at UCLA, Buffalo, Michigan, Santa Barbara, and New York University. Nonetheless, law and society research has flourished more conspicuously outside of law schools in colleges and universities. The appearance of an increasing number of synthetic texts for undergraduate students, research journals, dictionaries and encyclopedia entries, of the more than five dozen undergraduate programs and the half dozen Ph.D. programs in existence, and demands for international meetings and collaborations, testify to an increasingly mature and institutionalized field.

[*See also* Critical Legal Studies; Critical Race Theory]

• Leon Lipson and Stanton Wheeler, *Law and the Social Sciences*, 1986. John Henry Schlegel, *American Legal Realism and Empirical Social Science*, 1995. Bryant Garth and Joyce Sterling, "From Legal Realism to Law and Society: Reshaping Law for the Last Stages of the Social Activist State," *Law and Society Review* (1998): 409–71. Christopher Tomlins, "Framing the Field of Law's Disciplinary Encounters: A Historical Narrative," *Law and Society Review* (2000) 911–72.   —Susan S. Silbey

LAW CLERK. *See* Clerk, Law.

LAW COMMUNES. *See* Legal Services, Provision of.

LAW DAY. Law day is celebrated in the United States on May 1. The idea for the observance originated in the Cold War era. Some argued that the Soviet bloc devalued legal institutions and the rule of law and suggested that a celebration of law on May 1 would nicely contrast with Communist celebrations of May Day on the same date. Dwight D. Eisenhower established the date via presidential proclamation on 30 April 1958, saying, "It is fitting that people of this nation should remember with pride and vigilantly guard the great heritage of liberty, justice and equality under law which our forefathers bequeathed to us." Congress passed a joint resolution in 1961, permanently designating May 1 "Law Day U.S.A."

In subsequent years countless civic groups, government offices, schools, and communities have hosted and promoted Law Day celebrations. The *American Bar Association, more than any other organization, has become an eager sponsor. Each year the association announces a theme for the observance, e.g., the 2000 theme of "Protecting the Best Interests of Children." The association also provides planning guides, classroom strategies and lessons, and camera-ready art, which can be downloaded. The association's "Law Day Store" sells Law Day lapel pins, T-shirts, mugs, and mouse pads.

Despite formal government proclamations and the efforts of the American Bar Association, Law Day seems not to have been embraced by the general public. Given the powerful and central role of law in American life, what might explain this? Contributing factors include the very abstraction of the Law Day notion; the decline of a Cold War animus determined to contrast the American rule of law with Communist totalitarianism; and reportedly rampant cynicism regarding law, lawyers, and legal institutions. Constitution Day (September 17) has attracted even less public enthusiasm than Law Day.

• Law Day materials are available from the Public Education Division of the American Bar Association, 541

N. Fairbanks Court, Chicago, IL 60611-3314; www. abanet.org/publiced/lawday/home.html/. Wilbur Zelinsky, *Nation Into State: The Shifting Symbolic Foundations of American Nationalism*, 1988.

—David Ray Papke

LAW FIRM. *See* Firm, Law.

LAW OFFICES, NEIGHBORHOOD. *See* Legal Services, Provision of.

LAW PROFESSOR. *See* Educator, Legal.

LAW PUBLISHING. *See* Publishing, Law.

LAW SCHOOL ADMISSION TEST. *See* Education, Legal.

LAW SCHOOL CLINICS. *See* Legal Services, Provision of.

LAWSUIT. *See* Complex Litigation; Procedure, Civil.

LAWYERS. Alexis de Tocqueville observed nearly two centuries ago that in the United States, lawyers were the "arbiters between the citizens," and were, at the same time, "the political upper class and the most intellectual section of society. . . . It is at the bar or bench that the American aristocracy is found" (*Democracy in America*, J. P. Mayer, ed., 1969; 264, 268). Tocqueville was prescient in uncovering the importance of lawyers for both the political and social order of American constitutional democracy. Lawyers have been important in the United States because, in his words, "[t]here is hardly a political question in the United States which does not sooner or later turn into a judicial one" (*ibid.* 270). The importance of lawyers in shaping American society has been present since the founding of the country, when lawyers dominated the processes that formed our Constitution and governmental structure. Lawyers have also been influential in the development of private power, historically through land ownership and, more recently, corporate organizational representation. Nevertheless, American lawyers have also been distinguished from lawyers from other countries by their commitment to public interest issues, representation of unpopular causes and people, and the protection of *liberty, equality, and *human rights.

The history of the structure of the American legal profession illuminates a number of contradictory themes. The American lawyer as protector of private property or defender of human rights and public responsibilities is one such contradic-

tory theme. Whether the bar was ever truly unitary or homogeneous as a professional class is another question. For at least the first century of American lawyering, most lawyers came from similar social origins—from relatively well-off landed gentry or urban merchant classes—and learned their craft by apprenticing in law offices. By the end of the nineteenth century, however, the legal profession began to be transformed as, increasingly, immigrant groups entered the profession, and entrance to it was increasingly regulated both by enhanced educational requirements (eventually requiring a graduate degree in law beyond collegiate studies) and by professional *bar associations that sought to limit entry as a means of preserving social privilege and economic monopoly over the delivery of legal services.

Although for most of American history, lawyers were generalists serving both individual and organizational clients in both law office counseling and litigation matters in courts, within the last fifty years the legal profession has been characterized by the development of highly specialized subject-matter practices and what is known as the "dual hemispheres" of representation—those who represent individuals and those who represent large entities, such as corporations, unions, or governmental institutions. Entrance to the profession is now controlled by a hierarchical educational system, mandatory *bar examinations, and professional association control and discipline. Lawyers are admitted to practice at the state level—there is at present no "national" or "federal" bar in the United States, just as there is no official recognition of the international or "global" practice of law, which serves an increasing number of multinational private and public entities.

Despite the sociological diversification of the bar in function, demography, and social stratification, the United States, unlike many other legal regimes, does not officially divide its bar between solicitors (law office counselors) and barristers (litigators or courtroom lawyers) or between private and governmental or civil service functionaries. Once admitted to a state bar, a lawyer may practice in any setting. A few states have formally recognized some forms of specialization through certification programs in such fields as taxation, workers' compensation, domestic relations or family law, bankruptcy, patent or copyright (intellectual property), and criminal law, among others. Because of the growing complexity of law in the United States, however, most lawyers develop expertise in only a few particular areas.

Transactional or corporate lawyers ("deal" lawyers) seldom appear in court. While prestige in the legal profession was formerly associated with dramatic trial work (and is still the most likely depiction of lawyers in literature and popular culture), higher social and economic status is now associated with corporate lawyers who prepare the documentation and planning for corporate activities, including mergers, acquisitions, public offerings of securities, and venture capital and financial planning, as well as general tax and government compliance services.

Organization of legal work is increasingly performed in large work units, whether in the "megalaw firms" of more than 200 lawyers or in-house in large corporations or in legal departments in government agencies; at the same time, the relative number of *sole practitioners continues to decline. The American model of the large law *firm with departmental expertise has been exported to other countries, and every major capital city in the world now has either a branch office of a large American law firm or its own national equivalent of a large law firm.

Issues facing the American legal profession are also becoming common issues for the legal profession in other countries—multinational practice, multijurisdictional practice (such as in the multinational European Union and in other "federalized" states), the use of conditional or contingent fees, competition with other professions, such as accountants ("multidisciplinary" practice), financing and provision of *legal services for the indigent, access to justice, and lawyers' roles in human rights and other legal and social *"causes." Whether the legal profession is to be self-regulating for admission, discipline, quality control, and continuing education requirements (through membership in professional associations) or regulated by government agencies continues to be a point of contest at the state and national levels in the United States as well as in other countries.

Demographics and Social Structure. Over time, the legal profession in the United States has been changing in its composition and structure. There are almost 1 million lawyers in the United States in 2001, a three-fold increase in the last three decades. The United States is well known for having more lawyers than almost any other country. The ratio of population to lawyers has decreased from 695:1 in 1951 to 303:1 in 1995. Much of the growth in the profession can be attributed to an increase in the number of law schools to about 170 full-time schools at present, and much of the increase in the numbers of graduates can be at-

tributed to the rapid influx of women into the profession. Women now constitute about half the total number of law students admitted to American law schools each year, and constitute about one-quarter of the entire profession. Minorities in the profession continue to be just that—a minority. The total population of ethnic or racial "minority" lawyers (including Blacks, Hispanics-Latinos, and Asian-Americans) is still only about one-tenth of the total profession, despite much larger numbers in the general population. The American legal profession has been growing somewhat younger as well, given the growth of law school admissions within the last twenty years, although this development will likely abate in the next few years. Female lawyers are, on average, considerably younger than their male counterparts. In 1995, the average age of all male lawyers was forty-five and of women, thirty-seven.

The vast majority of American lawyers (74 percent) are employed in private practice (including both large and small practice units), but the nature of that private practice is changing. Within the last twenty-five years, the size of major law firms has increased exponentially, and law-firm practice, like much of corporate economic life, has been characterized by mergers and acquisitions as smaller firms are brought into larger ones, and large firms, often from different cities, merge with each other. While the single biggest category of practice location remains solo practice (46 percent of all practitioners), more and more lawyers are working in firms of over 100 lawyers, and lawyers now work in firms with several hundred lawyers, with multijurisdictional office settings, including many cities in the United States, as well as abroad.

Despite these general trends toward the large private law firms, there are several other specific patterns of professional location. Both female and minority lawyers are much more likely to work in the public sphere as government lawyers, prosecutors, public defenders, or legal services lawyers (for the poor) than their white male counterparts. While 75 percent of male attorneys work in private-practice settings, females were represented disproportionately in government practice locations (and were over represented by about 41 percent in that sector, based on their total numbers in the profession). Both women and minorities are disproportionately located in the "associate," not partnership, rank in the large law firms. For example, women still constitute less than 15 percent of all partners in law firms, and the figure for minorities is even lower. Occupational sociologists continue to study the "push-pull" effects of these phenomena. Are women and minorities "pushed" into government and legal aid positions because they are systematically excluded from or discriminated against by the private sector, or are they "pulled" by choice into work with greater social justice potential because of their own commitment to such work? Empirical research on these questions remains inconclusive since both factors seem to operate simultaneously. In early periods of entrance to the profession, minorities (starting with Jews and Catholics and now including Blacks and Hispanics-Latinos) and women founded their own firms to serve their own populations. More recently, such entrance strategies appear to be declining as all minorities and women seek more integrated practice locations and the official body of American lawyers, the *American Bar Association, seeks to promote greater equality for diverse lawyers within the profession and greater access to justice for all members of the population. Both of these goals remain works-in-progress.

There is evidence of widening income disparities in the profession. Incomes at the top level of the profession have increased to yearly partnership shares of more than 1 million dollars for lawyers in the largest firms in the largest cities. At the same time, there is evidence that income levels at the solo or small-firm end have remained stable in absolute dollar amounts, which actually represents a decline in income value. Salaries are lower for women and minorities at virtually every level of practice, and while the disparities are decreasing, they continue to exist.

Issues Facing the Profession. Despite the tremendous growth in the numbers of lawyers in the United States (the growth in the legal profession surpasses any other profession), there is some concern about increased dissatisfaction with the demanding life of a lawyer. Surveys of both young and older lawyers continue to reveal patterns of dissatisfaction both with the profession itself and with the particular legal positions held (about 25 percent of the lawyers surveyed expressed some dissatisfaction with their lives as lawyers). While most lawyers are relatively happy with their choice of life's work, two major concerns continue to reappear in such surveys—quality of life (including the balance of time for work and family and stress levels of the job) and the ability to contribute to the social good (a motivating factor for many choosing law as a career). Others are concerned that lawyers may increasingly have to compete with other professions (accountants, real estate brokers, bankers, trusts officers, and paralegals) for their livelihood, and are torn between increased regulation to prevent competition or more flexible arrangements under which lawyers might deliver their services alongside other complementary professionals (accountants, social workers, estate planners and financial advisors, and psychologists) in what has come to be known as "multidisciplinary" practice. American lawyers are also performing new roles themselves, including serving in non-representational capacities such as mediators, arbitrators, and public-policy consensus builders, to facilitate resolution of disputes or prevent legal problems before they ripen into major conflicts (see ARBITRATION AND MEDIATION).

And while the number of lawyers is increasing, many believe there is still not adequate access to justice for many Americans. With so many lawyers choosing to do private corporate work, there are not enough lawyers to provide criminal defense work (especially, but not exclusively, in death penalty cases), and general civil legal services for the underserved middle and working classes of American society, as well as our nation's poorest citizens, who often have many legal problems. A recent study documents that four-fifths of the civil needs of the poor and two- to three-fifths of the civil needs of middle-income individuals remain unmet by America's legal system. In a nation that claims "equal justice for all," legal services are allocated primarily by wealth, leaving many people without access to lawyers to accomplish some basic human needs—including divorce, custody, home purchase, economic counseling and consumer credit, access to governmental benefit programs and criminal defense—that greatly affect the well-being of American citizens. For many years, bar associations, law schools, and other professional groupings have urged more *pro bono publico* (free legal services for the public good) requirements for lawyers, and some state and local associations and law schools are now requiring lawyers to do more to equalize access to legal services.

American lawyers have historically been active in the most important political and policy issues facing the nation, including equality in education, employment, and public accommodations. Lawyers helped create the civil rights movement, the war on poverty, and the feminist movement, and are now active in a variety of other legal causes, including abolition of the death penalty, same-sex marriage rights and civil rights for gays, abortion and women's rights, disability civil rights, immigration law, and international human rights. American lawyers invented the "test case" and "*class action" to force courts to decide important legal rights cases; they have also been active in promoting social reform legislation. These inventions of American lawyers are now being exported to other nations, where new constitutions, new rights, and increased consciousness about human rights are being developed in a wide variety of legal regimes and new states. American lawyers have probably been among the most proactive of professionals, doing more than simply "serving" individual clients. American lawyers have expanded the *common law system to create new "causes of action" and legal claims (such as sexual harassment and discrimination, property entitlements to government benefits, and new forms of entities for both corporate and political action), but this role has always been controversial, especially among more conservative practitioners, who see the lawyer's role as one of responding to client needs for already existing legal categories.

American lawyers are increasingly diverse in their demographic characteristics, their choice of career and work locations, and their political commitments. The profession faces the challenge of whether it really will remain a "unitary" profession, a challenge that is currently being played out in the debates about appropriate ethical and disciplinary rules to be applied to lawyers performing such different roles and tasks in so many different locales. Given the wide variety of client needs and lawyers' important roles in American culture in debating and litigating on behalf of social and legal causes, it is likely that the American legal profession will continue to play an important role in how society treats its important issues. Legal resolution of social and political issues remains one of the most dominant cultural forms in the United States, guaranteeing the continued significance of American lawyers in American society.

[See also Education, Legal; Fees, Attorney; Government Lawyers; Legal Practice, Forms of]

• Jerold Auerbach, Unequal Justice: Lawyers and Social Change in America, 1976. John Heinz and Edward Laumann, Chicago Lawyers: The Social Structure of the Bar, 1982. Richard Abel, American Lawyers, 1989. Richard Abel and Philip Lewis, eds., Lawyers in Society: Vol 1: The Common Law World; Vol. 2: The Civil Law World; Vol. 3: Comparative Theories, 1989. Anthony Kronman, The Lost Lawyer: Failing Ideals of the Legal Profession, 1993. J. Clay Smith, Emancipation: The Making of the Black Lawyer, 1844–1944, 1993. Robert Nelson, "The Futures of American Lawyers: A Demographic Profile of a Changing Profession in a Changing Society," Case Western Law Review 44 (1994): 345. Carroll Seron, The Business of Practicing Law: The Work Lives of Solo and Small-Firm Attorneys, 1996. Richard Abel, ed., Lawyers: A Critical Reader, 1997. Virginia G. Drachman, Sisters in Law: Women Lawyers in Modern American History, 1998. Austin Sarat and Stuart Scheingold, eds., Cause Lawyering: Political Commitments and Professional Responsibilities, 1998. American Bar Foundation, The Lawyers' Statistical Report: The U.S. Legal Profession in 1995, Clara N. Carson, 1999. Deborah Rhode, In the Interests of Justice: Reforming the Legal Profession, 2001.

—Carrie Menkel-Meadow

LAWYERS, POPULAR PERCEPTIONS OF. Historically, American lawyers have been respected, although their public approval ratings never matched those of physicians or the clergy. After all, the lawyers' most publicized role is criminal defense; many people will never view with approval a profession that they believe puts dangerous criminals back on the street.

Nevertheless, during most of American history, people thought that lawyers could be trusted and that the profession had considerable prestige. Writing in the 1830s, Alexis de Tocqueville stated: "as the lawyers form the only enlightened class whom the people do not mistrust, they are naturally called upon to occupy most of the public stations." No one would dream of writing that today. In the last twenty-five years, the public's opinion of lawyers has turned sharply negative. Nowadays, American lawyers are distrusted and despised.

This assertion is supported by a large amount of polling data. One source, the Harris Poll gathers data each year about the public's confidence in various institutions. In 1973, 24 percent of the public had confidence in law firm leadership, a figure which placed law *firm leadership ahead of most institutions of government. The figure plunged to 7 percent in 1997, far below all other major institutions including such suspect groups as the leadership of Wall Street, organized labor, big business, or the military, as well as the White House, Congress, and the press. Indeed, the 7 percent figure was the lowest number ever recorded by Harris in the thirty years it has been taking this particular poll.

Reasons for the Decline in Public Perception of Lawyers. What might account for the precipitous decline in public esteem for the legal profession? No one really knows the answer to this question, but there are a number of likely possiblilities. Probably each of these factors accounts for some part of the decline and, collectively, they probably account for most of it.

During the 1980s and 1990s, the income of lawyers, particularly in law firms, rose sharply; the staggering fees awarded to the plaintiffs' lawyers in the *tobacco litigation exacerbated the problem. In the past, data about lawyer incomes was secret but the media now routinely publish information about law firm profits. Many people feel that lawyers are vastly overpaid, and that the amount of income diverted to lawyers is harmful to the economy. During those decades, the commitment of big firms toward pro bono activity declined steadily. To many, in and out of the legal profession, law has become much more a profit-making business than an honorable profession. Needless to say, this perception does not enhance the public's confidence in the profession.

Moreover, during this time, the number of lawyers rose sharply and, at least in popular perception, the amount of litigation increased dramatically. Moreover, the public perceived that there was a great increase in frivolous litigation (the famous McDonald's coffee case is often cited as an example) (see LITIGIOUSNESS).

Many people think that the decline in public esteem for the profession began with the *Watergate scandal in 1973; in that imbroglio, nearly all of the protagonists were lawyers. This trend was exacerbated by such publicized trials as the O. J. *Simpson case in 1995, in which defense lawyers like Johnny Cochran were widely blamed for what some of the public saw as a miscarriage of justice. Saturation media coverage of famous trials brings them into millions of homes, and irresponsible news analyses of the trials oversimplifies them, treating them as entertainment.

During the 1980s and 1990s, there were sharp increases in the rates of crime, divorce, and bankruptcy. As a result, more people came into contact with lawyers in intensely unpleasant situations; lawyers took part of the blame for the crime wave. During this time, government regulation of business became more intrusive; many business people blame lawyers for this unwelcome development. More generally, many people came to distrust all institutions and power centers; certainly the bar was not immune. During this period also, mass communications changed; the prominence of radio talk shows and internet bulletin boards seems to have intensified the negativity of criticism of many elements of society, lawyers definitely not excepted.

During this period, the costs, delays, and complexity of litigation worsened. People think that lawyers behave less ethically and more uncivilly than before and the discovery process has become much more costly, protracted and unpleasant.

An important contributor to the public's negative attitude toward the legal profession may be widespread television advertising that seems to encourage people to invent phony personal injury claims, weasel out of their debts, or escape the consequences of drunk driving. Television advertising went from zero in the late 1970s to hundreds of millions of dollars per year today. While TV advertising soared, public esteem for lawyers plunged.

The legal profession became the target of well-organized and funded public relations campaigns. Big business attacked *personal injury lawyers, particularly those representing claimants in products liability cases. Some government officials got on the bandwagon, broadly condemning the legal profession for the lack of American economic competitiveness.

Bad Lawyers in Popular Culture. Evidence of the public's venomously negative view of lawyers and the legal profession is plain for all to see. Everyone has heard lawyer jokes, many of them quite nasty. It is no accident that lawyer jokes repeatedly describe lawyers as shark bait or road kill. Jokes directed at racial or national groups or at women are no longer socially acceptable, but jokes aimed at lawyers are considered in impeccable taste.

The media of popular culture, especially movies and print, have strongly and consistently reflected the bad public image of lawyers. Prior to the 1980s, the vast majority of lawyers in film were portrayed very positively. Not all the movie lawyers were as skillful, admirable, and heroic as Atticus Finch in *To Kill a Mockingbird*, Paul Biegler in *Anatomy of a Murder,* or Henry Drummond in *Inherit the Wind,* but many came close. On television, Perry Mason and Matlock saved innocent people from prison every single week by discovering the real killer in the back of the courtroom. On *The Defenders,* two noble and selfless lawyers tackled every possible social and legal problem on behalf of their clients. In print, lawyers were favorably portrayed in countless novels, including *To Kill a Mockingbird, Peyton Place,* and *By Love Possessed.*

Beginning in the 1970s, however, the portrayal of lawyers in popular culture changed sharply. In film, the vast majority of lawyers were repulsive human beings, unethical or incompetent lawyers, or both. Consider first three path-breaking films of the late 1970s and early 1980s—*The Verdict,* . . . *And Justice for All,* and *Body Heat.* In the *Verdict,* plaintiff's lawyer Frank Galvin is a washed-up drunk, soliciting business at strangers' funerals and totally neglecting a malpractice case that is about to come to trial. Defense lawyer Ed Concannon tries every dirty trick in the book, including planting a sexual spy in the opponent's camp and bribing an expert witness to disappear. . . . *And Justice for All* lampoons the criminal justice system; nearly all the attorneys and judges are dishonest, uncaring, or repulsive people—some of them are outright criminals themselves. In *Body Heat*, lawyer Ned Racine is lazy, greedy, incompetent, and easily persuaded by the alluring Matty Walker to help do away with Matty's husband.

Countless movies followed in the footsteps of these three films. In *The Firm*, a respected tax law firm turns out to be a front for the mob, and the partners are vicious killers. In *Liar Liar*, attorney Fletcher Reede is pathologically incapable of telling the truth either in court or in his personal life. He thinks nothing of putting on perjured testimony; his law firm consists of a bunch of dishonest sharks. *The Devil's Advocate* took the demonization of lawyers to its logical extreme; law firm managing partner John Milton is the devil himself. As Satan, he explains that being a Wall St. lawyer is the "ultimate backstage pass. It's the new priesthood." In *The Star Chamber*, a group of embittered judges form a vigilante group to kill criminal defendants who escaped the criminal justice system through legal technicalities. In *Philadelphia*, a law firm fires a young lawyer who is stricken with AIDS and lies to cover it up. And there are many, many others.

In print, recent years have seen a veritable tsunami of lawyer novels. Leading the pack is John Grisham, currently the best selling writer in the world. In numerous smash hit novels, including *The Rainmaker, The Firm, The Partner, The Runaway Jury*, and *The Brethren*, Grisham portrays nearly every practicing lawyer, prosecutor, or judge as a greedy and dishonest scoundrel. Grisham's lawyers lie, cheat, and steal, usually with impunity. In his books, with few exceptions, the only worthy characters are law students or professors, lawyers working for free, or lawyers who have just entered the profession and have not yet been tainted by it. Many other novelists have followed Grisham's example, writing legal thrillers in which the killers generally turn out to be lawyers. Yet, not all the lawyers in print are evil; Scott Turow's fine novels are more balanced and contain some quite positive lawyer portrayals. But on the whole, print lawyers are a scummy lot.

Things are different on television, however. The most important law show of the late 1980s and early 1990s was *L.A. Law*, the first lawyer show on television to focus on a law firm as opposed to a solo lawyer. Especially in its early years, *L.A. Law*

was an enormous critical and popular success. On *L.A. Law*, some of the lawyers such as managing partner Douglas Brackman or family law specialist Arnold Becker were unpleasant characters, but the rest of the lawyers were very favorably portrayed. On the whole, *L.A. Law* represented the world of lawyers and law firms as challenging, exciting, and financially rewarding; yet it was a world in which lawyers did a great deal of good.

L.A. Law has been followed by numerous other lawyer shows, all of which portray lawyers favorably. *Law and Order* paints a very positive picture of prosecutors; *The Practice* does the same for defense lawyers. *JAG* portrays military lawyers favorably, as does *Family Law* for family lawyers and *Picket Fences* for a small-town solo practitioner. *Ally McBeal* is harder to classify; this is a female buddy show that happens to be set in a law firm, but the public likes and empathizes with the zany lawyer characters.

It is interesting to speculate on why law and lawyers on television differ so sharply from law and lawyers in film and print. The explanation, probably, lies in the nature of weekly television series. In order for a series to be successful, the public must like and empathize with most of the characters. Nobody wants to invite into their living rooms every week a cast of repulsive, dishonest creeps. This is not a problem with movies or print, however; here the emphasis is on a good story. Every good story requires a good antagonist and if that antagonist is a slimeball lawyer, so much the better.

Clearly, the portrayal of lawyers in film and in print reflects the public's stridently negative attitude toward attorneys. This is unsurprising; popular culture can usually be relied upon to mirror public opinion. Filmmakers are trying to sell tickets, so films are unlikely to trash popular characters such as grandmothers, algebra teachers, pharmacists, or rabbis. But unpopular groups are definitely fair game; if people hate lawyers, writers will write about hateful lawyers, and producers and investors will select such stories from the vast array of choices available to them.

A more interesting question is whether the consistent and harshly negative treatment of lawyers in film and print might be one of the causes for the public's hatred of the legal profession. There is every reason to believe that negative stereotypes in popular culture can create and intensify negative beliefs in the consumers of the culture. As a thought experiment, ask yourself what it was like to fight the Germans or Japanese in the Second World War. Undoubtedly even if you had a vast amount of information on the subject, your perception came not from history books or discussing the war with people who were there, but instead from fictitious films like *Saving Private Ryan*. Popular culture is a powerful teacher—perhaps the most powerful ever known.

If that is true, it seems likely that ordinary people are obtaining much or even most of their information about law, lawyers, and the legal system from fictitious stories in film, television, and books. This theory is supported by psychological studies of the "cultivation effect." Cultivation theorists show that in making quick judgments (such as answering questions in a poll), people draw heavily on what they learned from television or film. Heavy television watchers, for example, believe in a "meaner" world than light viewers; they think the crime rate is higher and there are far more police officers, lawyers, or prostitutes, more alcoholism and drug abuse, than do light viewers of television.

Cultivation theorists believe this is no accident; they contend that heavy exposure to television actually changes people's opinions. They analogize the mind to a series of files or bins; when someone is asked a question, they mentally pull information from the relevant bin. Information drawn from popular culture is deposited in the bins along with information drawn from personal experience or other sources. However, people do not "source discount," meaning they do not differentiate between information derived from real events and fictitious stories. These bins are accessed from the top down. Whether an individual accesses a particular piece of data in the bin depends heavily on whether the item has been encountered frequently, and recently and how vividly it was communicated.

Research on the television show *L.A. Law* strongly supported the application of the cultivation effect to information about law and lawyers. The investigators found that heavy watchers of *L.A. Law* had more favorable opinions about attorneys than people who never or seldom watched the show. Heavy consumers of the program gave lawyers a more favorable rating on such characteristics as composure, physical attractiveness, power, presence, and sociability than did nonviewers of the show. The same even held true for lawyers; those who watched the show had more favorable opinions of lawyers in general than lawyers who never watched it.

Since lawyers in film and in novels are presented in a strongly negative way, and such presentations are both frequent and vivid, it seems likely that these portrayals do negatively influence people's opinions of lawyers. On the other hand, lawyers on television are usually presented favorably; these representations may well offset the negative effect of the movies and books.

Conclusion. It is an unfortunate fact of life that Americans hate lawyers and the legal profession. It is unfortunate because this attitude often affects actual behavior—as jurors, voters, or legislators. In California, for example, Governor Pete Wilson in 1988 withdrew funds from the state bar, bringing to a grinding halt all bar activities such as attorney discipline, continuing education, and client protections. The governor stated that this action was the most popular thing he had done during his eight-year incumbency.

There are undoubtedly many reasons why lawyers have fallen so far and so fast in public esteem. Many of these reasons reflect serious problems with the legal profession. There may well be too many lawyers and too much litigation; lawyers' fees and incomes may be too high; legal advertising showcases the profession at its worst; all too often, lawyers make litigation costlier and more unpleasant than it needs to be; and lawyers often act in a rude and uncivil way toward each other and toward litigants and witnesses. Perhaps the negative portrayal of lawyers in film and in print is yet another reason why people hate lawyers, although surely not among the most important.

The profession could do much to restore public opinion. Finding ways to speed up and simplify litigation (such as by sharply limiting the discovery process) would be a good place to begin. As mentioned before, improving the civility of lawyer interactions with other lawyers and witnesses would be very desirable. The profession's image would undoubtedly be enhanced if the flow of lawyers entering the profession were curtailed. Finally, American lawyers should make a renewed commitment to render pro bono legal services to the poor (such commitments have been declining for many years). If lawyers become sufficiently concerned about their public image, the profession can begin to take steps to improve it.

[*See also* Ethics and Professional Responsibility, Legal; Fees, Attorney]

• Lawrence M. Friedman, "Law, Lawyers and Popular Culture," *Yale Law Journal* (1989): 1579. Gary A. Hengstler, "Vox Populi—The Public Perception of Lawyers: ABA Poll," *American Bar Association Journal* (1993): 30. George Gerbner et al., "Growing Up With Television: The Cultivation Perspective," in *Media Effects: Advances in Theory and Research*, Jennings Bryant and Dolf Zillman, eds. (1994): 17. Michael Pfau et al., "Television Viewing and Public Perceptions of Attorneys," *Human Communications Research* (1995): 307. Paul Bergman and Michael Asimow, *Reel Justice: The Courtroom Goes to the Movies*, 1996. Harris Poll, no. 37, (11 August 1997). Richard J. Cebula, "Does Lawyer Advertising Adversely Influence the Image of Lawyers in the United States? An Alternative Perspective and New Empirical Evidence," *Journal of Legal Studies* (1998): 503. Barbara Mahan, "Who Killed the State Bar?" *California Lawyer* (1998): 33. American Bar Association, *Perceptions of the U.S. Justice System*, 1999. Michael Asimow, "Bad Lawyers in the Movies," *Nova Law Review* (2000): 533. Deborah L. Rhode, *In the Interests of Justice*, 2000. Michael Asimow, "Embodiment of Evil: Law Firms in the Movies," 48 *UCLA Law Review* (2001): 1339.

—Michael Asimow

LEGAL AID. *See* Legal Services, Provision of.

LEGAL EDUCATION. *See* Education, Legal.

LEGAL EDUCATOR. *See* Educator, Legal.

LEGAL ETHICS. *See* Ethics and Professional Responsibility, Legal.

LEGAL MALPRACTICE. *See* Ethics and Professional Responsibility, Legal.

LEGAL PRACTICE, FORMS OF. The principal forms of the practice of law include the private practice of law, employment by a for-profit entity (known as corporate or in-house counsel), and government practice. A smaller number of lawyers work as public-interest lawyers, as public defenders, and as staff personnel in the judiciary. Other law jobs that are related to the practice of law include work as a member of the judiciary (whether as a municipal judge, trial or appellate judge, or Supreme Court Justice) and work as a teacher of law (in a law school, undergraduate and graduate education, or in elementary or secondary schools).

Most *lawyers who practice law do so as private practitioners. The private practice of law has been the dominant form of legal practice since the beginning of the American legal profession in the early eighteenth century. Although the percentage of lawyers engaged in the private practice of law declined from 89 percent of the legal profession in 1948 to 68 percent in 1980, it rose to 74 percent in 1995. The private practice of law includes lawyers (1) engaged in providing legal services to one or more clients, and (2) who are self-employed, members of a partnership consisting of two or more lawyers, or members of a professional or limited liability corporation in which all the shareholders are lawyers.

The traditional and current understanding of the private practice of law in the United States limits the ownership of firms that offer legal services to lawyers. Although this is now the subject of intense discussion, nonlawyers are not allowed to own any part of a firm that offers legal services in the United States. In Europe, Australia, and much of the rest of the world, providers of legal services have joined with providers of accounting, business, lobbying, and consulting services to form multidisciplinary practices.

A lawyer in private practice is hired to resolve the legal problems of a client, who ordinarily pays the lawyer's fees for those services. The work of lawyers in private practice includes, among other tasks, litigating on behalf of clients, advising and counseling clients about the legal consequences of anticipated actions, and drafting legal documents for clients. These three tasks are usually only performed by licensed law practitioners. Lawyers in private practice also perform other tasks for clients, such as lobbying legislators, offering business advice, and monitoring governmental regulatory action. The work of private practice lawyers is extraordinarily varied, and that has led many private practice lawyers to specialize in particular tasks, doctrines, or types of client. The provision of legal services by private practitioners is a multibillion dollar service industry.

The organizational settings of the private practice lawyer encompass self-employed *sole practitioners, small law *firm partnerships and limited liability corporations, and large law firms, the last of which may comprise over one thousand lawyers. Lawyers in law firms are generally either partners or associates. Partners own and control the business of the firm, either as shareholders of a corporate entity, or as part of a partnership. Partners are responsible for generating and supervising client business, and their compensation is based on the profits generated by the firm. Associates are salaried employees of the firm. Associates do not control the business of the firm, and may or may not have a responsibility for generating business from clients. Associates are generally hired on a partnership track, which lasts anywhere between four and twelve years (the higher side of that range is the norm), and most associates hired at large law firms will not be offered promotion to partner. Although lawyers who failed to obtain a partnership offer were in the past asked to leave their firms, the difficulty in replacing the skills possessed by these lawyers has resulted recently in the creation of more categories of law firm lawyers. Lawyers may be asked to accept the position of "permanent associate" or "non-equity partner." These attorneys are offered greater employment security than other associates, but they remain employees rather than owners of the firm. Other related law-firm positions include "junior partner," "senior attorney," and "participating associate," all of which designate employment rather than ownership status. Some law firms hire lawyers on a temporary basis to complete specific assignments in a particular matter.

Legal work in law firms is usually performed by small groups of partners and associates, as well as by nonlawyer *paralegals (professional staff trained to perform certain legal work under the supervision of lawyers). These groups generally number between two and five lawyers, although major matters (including some litigation, mergers and acquisitions, and antitrust matters) may involve many more lawyers. Some firms are departmentally organized by area of practice or client, and assign associates to that department, other firms rotate lawyers among different departments at the beginning of their employment, and still others allow partners to assign projects to associates in a relatively unorganized fashion.

In theory, the legal profession in the United States is a unitary profession. There is no formal division of the bar, as in Great Britain, between solicitors, who advise clients and conduct matters out of court, and barristers, who argue cases in court. All lawyers in this country must meet the same licensing requirements imposed by the state in order to practice law, and all lawyers are required to abide by the duties imposed upon them by the state through its rules of professional conduct. However, the legal profession is, in practice, not a unitary profession. A majority of sole practitioners and law firms of ten or fewer lawyers offer legal services to individuals, and most large law firms offer their legal services to corporations and other institutions. The result is a clearly divisible legal profession within the private practice of law.

The federal government began to regulate the economy more extensively after the end of World War II, resulting in the hiring of more lawyers by the federal government. The largest percentage of lawyers in the federal government is employed at the Department of *Justice, but lawyers are found throughout all federal executive departments, as well as in the Internal Revenue Service, the Veterans Administration, the Federal Trade Commission, and other administrative agencies. Federal *government lawyers advise Congress and the executive branch about proposed legislation, assist in the drafting of statutes and administrative regulations, and litigate challenges to those statutes and administrative regulations. Department of Justice and United States attorneys prosecute violations of federal criminal law, and government lawyers litigate tort, contract, and other civil claims.

Just over half of all federal government lawyers work in the Washington, D.C., area. Although nearly half of all government lawyers in 1960 were employed by the federal government, about 60 percent of all government lawyers are now employed by state and local governments. Many of these state and local government lawyers are employed as criminal *prosecutors. A substantial number of state and local government lawyers engage in civil litigation, and advise public officials about statutes, municipal ordinances, and state administrative regulations. In addition to prosecutorial offices, other major places of employment include state *attorney general offices, county and municipal governments, and state administrative departments. Government lawyers constitute approximately 8 percent of all lawyers.

Lawyers employed in private industry are known as corporate, or in-house, counsel. In 1948, only 3 percent of all lawyers were employed in private industry, most of them employed by large corporations. As of 1995, about 8 percent of all lawyers were employed as corporate counsel. Corporate counsel traditionally acted as business counselors and advisors to their employers concerning routine legal issues; more complex legal issues were handled by the corporation's outside counsel. For this reason, the position of corporate counsel until the 1960s was considered less prestigious than that of partner of a large law firm. The job of corporate counsel is now well regarded, and is reflected in the substantial compensation paid to these lawyers. Due to the high cost of outside legal fees, corporate counsel are now expected to complete much of the more complex legal work formerly reserved for the corporation's outside lawyers, including litigation matters. Many corporate counsel have imitated large law firm lawyers by limiting their work to particular areas of legal specialization. In addition to working as corporate counsel, a substantial number of lawyers are employed by corporations in a nonlegal capacity.

Public-interest lawyers practice a policy-driven advocacy. These lawyers are interested in using the legal system to effect changes in public policy, and often choose to clients on the basis of the congruence of the client's interests and those of the lawyer or organization that employs him. Although these lawyers claim to represent the interests of the public, they are required by the code of lawyering to put the interests of their clients before the interests of the public-interest organization that employs them or funds the litigation. This requires public-interest lawyers to make an informed decision about which clients to represent. Public-interest lawyers are often employed by nonprofit organizations whose purpose is to advance particular social goals. The most famous of such organizations are the National Association for the Advancement of Colored People Legal Defense Fund and the American Civil Liberties Union.

Beginning in the early 1970s, the number of public-interest law firms mushroomed with the financial support of the Ford Foundation. One recent development in public-interest law is the rise of a number of politically conservative public-interest organizations, possibly as a counterweight to longer-existing politically liberal public-interest organizations. Public-interest lawyers make up less than 1 percent of all lawyers, and although not well paid, they often derive much job satisfaction from achieving their policy goals through the practice of law.

The public defender is a state-employed criminal defense attorney. An indigent person charged with a crime for which imprisonment is a possible sentence is constitutionally guaranteed legal *counsel. Some states responded to this Supreme Court-imposed mandate by creating public defender offices, as did the federal government. A public defender is required to represent his or her clients as an independent advocate, and states are constitutionally required to respect the professional independence of the public defender. Public defenders represent a little more than one half of one percent of all lawyers, and their median annual income is substantially less than the median annual income of practicing lawyers. Unlike private practice lawyers, public defenders do not generate their income through legal fees.

Approximately 4 percent of all lawyers are employed in the judiciary. One-quarter of those lawyers are staff personnel, including staff attorneys (permanent employees), law *clerks (recent law school graduates who work for a judge on a one- or two-year appointment), and other court personnel. The remaining lawyers employed in the judiciary are *judges. The vast majority of judges are employed by state governments rather than the federal government.

Lawyers employed by educational institutions make up about 1 percent of all lawyers. Most of these lawyers teach in law schools, although lawyers teach and work as administrators in colleges and universities, community colleges, and elementary and secondary schools. Another 1 percent of lawyers are employed by private organizations, including trade associations and unions.

[See also Cause Lawyers; Educator, Legal]

• Charles W. Wolfram, Modern Legal Ethics, 1986. Richard L. Abel, American Lawyers, 1989. Marc Galanter and Thomas Palay, Tournament of Lawyers, 1991. Robert L. Nelson et al., eds., Lawyers' Ideals/Lawyers' Practices: Transformations in the American Legal Profession, 1992. Clara N. Carson, The Lawyer Statistical Report: The U.S. Legal Profession in 1995, 1999.   —Michael Ariens

LEGAL REALISM. "Legal Realism" is best understood as the reaction of a group of individuals centered at Columbia, Johns Hopkins, and Yale to (1) the collapse of the Progressive movement after World War I, (2) the decisions of the Supreme Court invalidating state or federal economic *regulation on grounds of either substantive *due process or interference with vested contractual rights, and (3) the general shift of the United States to the political right after World War I.

Scholars regularly identified with the movement include Thurman Arnold, Charles Clark, Walter Wheeler Cook, William *Douglas, Jerome *Frank, Walton Hamilton, Karl *Llewellyn, Underhill Moore, Herman Oliphant, and Hessel Yntema. Others associated with Legal Realism include Adolph Berle, Walter Bingham, Felix Cohen, Morris Cohen, Leon Green, Robert Hale, Robert Hutchins, Edward Robinson, Max Radin, Fred Rodell, and Wesley Sturges.

Intellectually, the Realist movement is an outgrowth of the Sociological Jurisprudence of Rudolph von Jhering as expounded by Roscoe *Pound and the thought of Oliver Wendell *Holmes Jr. However, the "realism" in Legal Realism is best understood in reference to artistic and literary naturalism's desire to describe the realities of daily activities, and not as a reference to any particular legal sociology. Instantiating this sense of realism, the Legal Realists joined in activities directed at critique of the doctrinal results of nineteenth-century legal formalism, at understanding judicial decision-making, at empirical research in law, and at the reform of legal *education.

The Realist's critique of nineteenth-century legal formalism is exemplified by Cook's continuing work on what courts were really doing in *conflict-of-laws doctrine and by Green's parallel work on *torts doctrine. Other examples include the work of Arnold and Robinson on the symbolic uses of law, Llewellyn's work on commercial practice, Hutchins' work on the psychological underpinnings of evidence law, and Berle's work on corporate governance. All of this scholarship simultaneously implied three critiques of nineteenth-century understandings of judicial decision-making—logical, psychological, and sociological.

The logical critique argued that legal concepts were not a constraining force to law. Here, Realists relied on Wesley Hohfeld, who argued that legal concepts inappropriately treated various discrete legal relationships as unitary; on Judge Benjamin *Cardozo, who asserted that there was more than one method for deciding a case; on Cook, who claimed that legal rules "hunt in pairs"; and on Llewellyn, who identified a great range of acceptable techniques for dealing with a legal precedent. These observations suggested that legal concepts did not produce necessary results, but rather permitted judges a choice of results.

Similarly, the psychological critique argued that judicial opinions hid the real sources for decisions. Here, Realists relied on Judge Joseph Hutchinson, who argued that most cases were decided on the basis of a "hunch" about the appropriate result, and on Frank, who argued that a judicial opinion was but a rationalization of a decision reached otherwise. These observations suggested that judges obscured the real factors that operated in particular cases behind a web of false necessity.

The sociological critique attempted to identify the factors at work behind the facade of the judicial opinion. Here, the most common argument drew on the work of William Ogburn, who posited that social understandings of the world commonly lagged behind the practices that these understandings purported to describe. Versions of this concept of "cultural lag" were offered to explain how it was that judges utilized an "outdated" economic theory to understand labor conditions or commercial transactions, an "outdated" psychological theory to understand witness testimony, or an "outdated" political theory to limit governmental economic regulation.

The Realists relied on their sociological critique to draw together their attacks on both substantive and decision-making formalism by positing that the major problem with law was the lack of relationship between legal doctrine and the "realities" of modern life. Closer attention to these realities would focus efforts at law reform on institutions, including the courts, and on the functions that these institutions performed. Such an analysis would disclose when the law needed to be updated because of its lag behind social practice, and would also expose circumstances where the law was dysfunctional—where a body of doctrine was ineffective—and so force law to develop effective and appropriate social policy for the conditions of modern life.

Empirical work by the Realists was designed to examine legal and social institutions for this purpose. At Yale, Clark, Douglas, and Moore focused on the activities of the federal courts in civil, criminal, and bankruptcy cases, on the activities of bankers, on compensation for the victims of auto accidents, on the efficacy of parking regulations, and on the legal needs of citizens of modest means. At Hopkins, Oliphant, Yntema, and Leon Marshall focused on the operation of state courts in civil, criminal, divorce, and justice of the peace cases.

Much of the impetus behind Legal Realism was educational. The Realists were mostly law professors for whom the question of how to present the materials of law study was a daily concern. They drew all of their scholarly interests together in an attempt to reform legal education by translating their critique of the efficacy of legal categories into a reorganization of the law school curriculum, bringing their interest in judicial decision-making into classroom discussion and expanding the materials of law study to include the results of their formal and informal empirical research, all in the interest of examining appropriate social policy.

Though none of these attempts was wholly successful, it is in the area of education that Legal Realism had its greatest impact. The critique of formalism utterly changed the way that law was justified in the law-school classroom. From a formalism based on assertedly logical derivation from the nature of a given legal category, the justification of legal rules has shifted to a realism based on assumed knowledge of social conditions to which law is applied in the pursuit of supposedly agreed-upon social policy. As a result, the law professors and their students now talk the language of the bureaucrats in Washington and in various state capitals.

[See also Jurisprudence, American—The Revolt Against Formalism]

• William Twining, *Karl Llewellyn and the Realist Movement*, 1973. Laura Kalman, *Legal Realism at Yale*, 1986. Morton J. Horwitz, *The Transformation of American Law, 1870 1960*, 1992. Neil Duxbury, *Patterns of American Jurisprudence*, 1995. John Henry Schlegel, *American Legal Realism and Empirical Social Science*, 1995. N. E. H. Hull, *Roscoe Pound and Karl Llewellyn*, 1997.

—John Henry Schlegel

LEGAL REASONING. Lawyers and legal decision-makers engage in two major kinds of legal reasoning: deductive reasoning and reasoning by analogy. In deductive, or syllogistic, reasoning a general legal proposition is identified, the relevant facts of the case are marshaled in support of the proposition, and a conclusion is drawn (the legal consequence of the particular facts). For example, the prosecutor in a case under the Malicious Damage Act might reason as follows: an element of the crime is that the defendant's act must be malicious; the defendant stated, "I'll get even with Jones by burning his house down"; therefore, the defendant acted maliciously. The general legal proposition can be derived from the terms of a statute or from the holdings of one or more precedents.

Reasoning by analogy or by example involves comparing the facts of the particular case with the facts of an earlier case with a known result. Since no two cases are ever completely identical, the key issue in analogous reasoning is whether the cases are "distinguishable," whether the disparities are strong enough to require a different outcome. If, for example, the highest court in the jurisdiction affirmed the Malicious Damage Act conviction of a defendant who stated, "I'm going to get even with Smith by destroying his boat," the prosecutor in the case of the burned-down house will reason that the two cases are indistinguishable because the difference in the nature of the destroyed item is insignificant to the analysis.

Although in the abstract these two processes appear to be the application of basic logical reasoning, in practice they are not. In legal deductive reasoning, the meaning of the general legal proposition—even when set forth in a statute—is not always clear. The "maliciousness" element, for example, can mean actual intent to harm property, reckless disregard for whether harm will occur, or any unlawful act that harms property. Because law serves social purposes and arises in particular factual contexts, reasoning about the meaning of a legal rule often requires more than the mechanical application of the general words in the text. As Justice Oliver Wendell *Holmes stated in his dissenting opinion in *Lochner* v. *New York* (1905):

"General propositions do not decide concrete cases. The decision will depend on a judgment or intuition more subtle than any articulate major premise." The meaning of a legal rule may require any analysis of different policy considerations: traditional *customs in the community, historical changes since the original adoption of the rule, economic efficiency, social welfare, basic principles underlying the legal system, and the competency of the decision-maker to make the ultimate judgment as to the rule's meaning.

Similarly, the analysis of whether a case is distinguishable from an earlier case may depend, at least in part, on consideration of policy. As Judge Benjamin N. *Cardozo wrote in applying prior cases concerning the sale of inherently dangerous articles, such as poisons and explosives, to the purchase of a negligently manufactured automobile: "Precedents drawn from the days of travel by stage coach do not fit the conditions of travel to-day. The principle that the danger must be imminent does not change, but the things subject to the principle do change. They are whatever the needs of life in a developing civilization require them to be" (*MacPherson* v. *Buick Motor Co.* (1916)).

Depending on the position of their clients, lawyers develop different textual and policy arguments and case comparisons to urge the decision-maker to adopt either a narrow or an expansive definition of the legal rule, and decision-makers, relying on their own understanding of the relevant texts, precedents, and policy, develop their own interpretations. Although some lawyers and courts often couch their reasoning in terms of applying fixed rules, the process is far more indeterminate. Moreover, most legal scholarship—for example, in the areas of economic analysis of the law, *critical legal studies, *critical race theory, and feminist jurisprudence—focuses on the relationship between social policy and legal rules rather than the description of fixed rules.

Law students are introduced to these legal reasoning processes by reading appellate decisions and relevant statutes in different areas of the law. Professors pose hypothetical cases based on these materials, and students are required to decipher the general legal propositions from their readings and, using deductive reasoning, apply those rules to the facts of the hypothetical cases. They are also asked to reason by analogy, comparing the precedents with the hypotheticals. Throughout these discussions, students are shown how policy considerations affect legal reasoning.

[*See also* Feminist Legal Theory; Law and Economics, Theory of]

• Oliver Wendell Holmes Jr., "The Path of the Law," *Harvard Law Review* 10 (1897): 457–78. Benjamin N. Cardozo, *The Nature of the Judicial Process*, 1922. Jerome Frank, *Law and the Modern Mind*, 1930. Edward H. Levi, *An Introduction to Legal Reasoning*, 1949. Henry M. Hart Jr. and Albert M. Sacks, *The Legal Process: Basic Problems in the Making and Application of Law*, 1994.

—Stefan H. Krieger

LEGAL SECRETARY. *See* Paralegal and Legal Secretary.

LEGAL SERVICES, PROVISION OF. The legal profession in the United States enjoys a monopoly over the provision of legal services, and it delivers these services primarily through unregulated private markets. Large organizational clients obtain legal representation from highly compensated lawyers in private law *firms and from lawyers employed directly by industry. Individuals and small businesses are served by lawyers in smaller private firms and *sole practices. Alternative practice organizations, including franchise law firms and group legal service plans, compete for some of the more routine aspects of this business. Those who cannot afford legal services must rely on legal aid programs, public defender services, and free or reduced-fee work provided by lawyers in private practice.

Until the early twentieth century, almost all lawyers were independent sole practitioners. Since then, lawyers have moved into larger practice settings and different practice roles. In 1995, 74 percent of American lawyers worked in private practice—a much higher percentage than in most Continental legal systems. Ten percent of American lawyers worked in government, 9 percent in private industry, and 1 percent in legal aid and public defender programs. Of those lawyers in private practice, 47 percent were in solo practice and 53 percent in firms. Approximately one in ten lawyers worked in firms of 100 or more lawyers.

The American legal profession is highly stratified by types of clients served. In a landmark study of the Chicago bar in 1975, Heinz & Laumann found that the legal profession is divided into two fairly distinct "hemispheres." One hemisphere serves primarily large organizations and wealthy individuals, and the other serves individuals and small businesses. These hemispheres correspond to two social classes of lawyers divided by socioeconomic and ethno-religious backgrounds, educational credentials, practice settings, political values, and social networks. Lawyers serving corporate clients are more likely to have attended elite law schools, to practice in large law firms, to earn large salaries, and to exercise influence in the profession. Lawyers serving individual clients and small businesses are much more likely to have attended local law schools, to work in sole practice or small law firms, to earn modest incomes, and to handle work perceived to be less prestigious. A follow-up study in 1995 showed a similar division of the bar by types of clients served, although it found greater specialization within each of these groups.

Corporations. Since the early twentieth century, lawyers for corporations have worked primarily in large private law firms, where they exercise substantial influence within the profession and participate in disputes and transactions that powerfully shape the American economy and society. Until the 1970s, these firms enjoyed stable relationships with corporate clients and handled all but the most routine legal services for them. However, the market for corporate legal services has undergone substantial restructuring during the past few decades. A significant expansion of federal law and litigation between corporations greatly increased the demand for specialized corporate legal services. During the same period, large law firms' traditional practice eroded. Inside counsel began to assume functions previously served by private law firms, and firms saw their long-term relationships with corporate clients replaced by competition among firms on a case-by-case, transaction-by-transaction basis. Corporate clients began to exert control over the cost of legal services, closely monitoring fees and demanding detailed accounting of services rendered.

As their traditional bases of practice have disappeared, large law firms have competed aggressively for the lucrative, specialized work of the corporate market. High stakes in corporate litigation and transactional work lead some corporate clients to pay premiums to obtain representation from the top firms. To compete in this market, large law firms recruit the best law students from elite law schools, merge with other firms to acquire new expertise, and hire partners away from other firms. In trying to maintain relationships with corporations that are expanding internationally, law firms have established overseas offices. Firms have expanded dramatically in the past two decades to meet the needs of existing clients and to acquire new ones. In 1980, 13,000, or 7 percent of lawyers in firm practice worked in firms of more than 100 lawyers. In 1995, more than 76,000, or 23 percent of lawyers in firm practice worked in firms of more than 100 lawyers.

Lawyers employed directly by corporations as

in-house counsel also play an important part in the provision of legal services to the corporate sector. In-house counsel were once consigned primarily to routine tasks, with most of the important corporate work delegated to outside firms. As corporations have sought to economize on legal services and to obtain undivided loyalty from their lawyers, they have increased the size of in-house counsel offices and moved important legal work inside.

Other types of professional service providers, including accounting firms and their affiliated law firms, have recently made small inroads in the market for legal services to corporate clients, particularly with respect to tax matters.

Middle-income Individuals and Small Businesses. The lawyers who serve middle-class consumers of legal services work primarily in small firms and sole practices. These lawyers mainly handle a few substantive areas: wills and trusts, estate probate, family law, personal bankruptcy, house closings, and corporate matters for small businesses. Some lawyers in sole and small firms also handle personal injury litigation, usually on a contingency basis, and some more highly compensated work on family law matters for wealthier clients. Much of the work handled by lawyers in sole practice and small firms is fairly routine and standardized.

A flood of new entrants into this field in recent years has spurred intense competition and declining incomes in this sector of the legal services market. Supreme Court decisions invalidating *bar associations' minimum fee schedules, prohibitions on group plans, and blanket bans on advertising have eliminated significant market barriers. Some of the competition for routine work in the personal sector of the legal services market has come from franchise law firms and group legal-service plans. Franchise law firms employ efficient production and marketing systems and offer routine services at competitive flat fees rather than hourly rates. These firms rely heavily on advertising to attract clients and on standardized services, large portions of which can be delegated to secretaries. Prepaid legal-services plans work through a network of lawyers who agree to address the needs of clients who join the plan. Plan members pay membership fees in return for access to attorneys who handle their work free or for reduced fees. Lawyers who work for prepaid legal services plans typically have independent practices and work in their own offices. These trends toward greater competition have been reinforced by the availability of legal forms that enable people to handle simple legal matters themselves—for example, drafting their own simple wills and filing for divorce.

The Poor. During most of American history, legal services for the poor have consisted primarily of individual lawyers in private practice representing individual indigent clients for reduced fees or no fees. (Reduced fee, or no fee, work for the poor is called pro bono, from *pro bono publico*, for the public good.) The pro bono tradition reflects a view that lawyers, as officers of the court, have special obligations to ensure that the legal system works well. Representing indigent clients who otherwise would not receive representation is one aspect of that general obligation. A related rationale is the legal profession's obligation to contribute to the fair functioning of the legal system in return for its monopoly on law practice and its privilege of self-regulation.

In the late nineteenth and early twentieth centuries, groups of lawyers and bar associations began to establish legal aid societies to supplement the pro bono contributions of the private bar and to provide better-organized legal services for the poor. Bar associations initially opposed legal aid societies because many lawyers viewed legal aid lawyers as competitors for scarce business. Legal aid societies responded by excluding services that the private bar might profitably provide. In 1919, Reginald Heber Smith's *Justice and the Poor* documented the ways poor people were disadvantaged in the legal system. His dire assessment of America's justice system helped muster support within the elite bar for expanding legal aid. Widespread concern about the influx of immigrants from Southern and Eastern Europe and the prospect of social unrest in urban ghettoes allowed proponents of legal aid to promote it as a way to teach immigrants about American institutions and the legal order.

In the mid-1930s, Karl *Llewellyn, a Columbia law professor and prominent Legal Realist, became the leading advocate for low-cost legal services for people of modest incomes. He argued that individualized legal aid and ad hoc pro bono services were poorly suited to the conditions of modern urban life, and he proposed that metropolitan bar associations establish a network of neighborhood law offices staffed by young unemployed lawyers or junior law firm associates working pro bono. The proposal did not receive the endorsement of the mainstream bar, but chapters of the *National Lawyers Guild in Philadelphia and Chicago attempted to implement the neighborhood law office proposal on a small scale.

The pro bono and legal aid models of legal services to the poor emphasized service to individual clients rather than law reform. A more aggressive, collective approach to the representation of poor people grew out of the civil rights movement and began to compete with the legal aid model. In the 1940s and 1950s, the NAACP and the NAACP Legal Defense and Education Fund, Inc. (known as the "Inc. Fund") litigated and lobbied against racial segregation. Other civil rights organizations in the early 1960s enlisted lawyers to help dismantle racial segregation and enforce civil rights. In the mid-1960s, the shortage of legal services for the poor became part of the debate about the causes of poverty. Edgar and Jean Cahn proposed establishing neighborhood law firms staffed by lawyer activists who would advocate institutional reform. A new War on Poverty program—OEO Legal Services—was established in 1965 to provide legal services to the poor and to pursue social reform through litigation and other aggressive legal rights activities. In 1974, the Legal Services Corporation Act established an independent Legal Services program.

Since its inception, Legal Services has been a lightning rod in controversies over the purposes of legal services for the poor. The program immediately encountered opposition from sole and small-firm practitioners who feared that Legal Services lawyers would take away their business. Some critics advocated the alternative of a "judicare" system, used in many other countries, in which eligible poor people select their own private lawyers, who then receive payment from the state. Other critics opposed Legal Services' law reform aspirations and its violation of traditional ethical prohibitions on the representation of groups. Suits by legal services programs against state agencies and programs also generated enormous controversy. Political battles over Legal Services in the 1970s resulted in restrictions designed to discourage class action litigation and to ensure that Legal Services lawyers did not engage in political organizing. In the early 1980s, President Reagan tried, but failed, to eliminate funding for the Legal Services Corporation. His administration succeeded in obtaining new prohibitions on certain types of representation, including matters involving aliens in deportation and other immigration matters, and voter redistricting cases. In the mid-1990s, Congress sharply cut funding for Legal Services and imposed additional restrictions on the activities of Legal Services lawyers, including prohibitions on lobbying, filing class actions, and suing to challenge new federal and state welfare laws and regulations.

The organized bar, initially skeptical about legal aid, became a strong advocate for the creation of the OEO Legal Services and the Legal Services Corporation in the 1960s. The bar also strongly opposed attempts in the 1980s and 1990s to eliminate the federal Legal Services Corporation and to limit its lawyers' activities.

Legal services to indigent criminal defendants in the United States have traditionally been provided primarily through the assignment of counsel by the courts. The first public defender programs, staffed by salaried lawyers with expertise in criminal matters, began to appear in very small numbers in the early 1900s. In the mid-1960s and 1970s, hundreds of public defender programs were established in the wake of *Gideon v. Wainwright* and its progeny, which held that defense *counsel were constitutionally required. The United States has no unified system for representing indigent defendants. Instead, state and local governments have assembled a patchwork of assigned counsel and public defender programs whose quality varies tremendously.

Free or subsidized legal services comprise a very small proportion of legal work in the United States. Just 1 percent of lawyers work in legal aid or public defender's offices. The bar's ethical codes urge lawyers to provide pro bono services, but they do not require such pro bono contributions. Although most lawyers participate in some pro bono work, very few donate services to indigents. Various studies of unmet legal needs suggest that the high cost of legal services significantly impedes access to justice for poor people. Laws prohibiting the unauthorized practice of law discourage external competitors from attempting to provide legal services.

[*See also* Civil Rights and Civil Liberties; Fees, Attorney; Ethics and Profesional Responsibility, Legal; Legal Practice, Forms of]

• Jerold S. Auerbach, *Unequal Justice: Lawyers and Social Change in Modern America*, 1976. Joel F. Handler, et al., *Lawyers and the Pursuit of Legal Rights*, 1978. John P. Heinz and Edward O. Laumann, *Chicago Lawyers: The Social Structure of the Bar*, 1982. Robert L. Nelson, *Partners with Power*, 1988. Richard L. Abel, *American Lawyers*, 1989. Richard H. Sander and E. Douglas Williams, *Why Are There So Many Lawyers? Perspectives on a Turbulent Market*, Law and Social Inquiry 14 (1989): 431–79. Marc Galanter and Thomas Palay, *The Tournament of Lawyers*, 1991. Carroll Seron, *The Business of Practicing Law: The Work Lives of Solo and Small-Firm Attorneys*, 1996. Jerry Van Hoy, *Franchise Law Firms and the Transformation of Personal Legal Services*, 1997. Clara N. Carson, *The 1995 Lawyer Statistical Report*, 1999.

—Ann Southworth

LEGAL SERVICES CORPORATION. *See* Legal Services, Provision of.

LEGAL SYSTEMS. In the Western legal tradition, of which the American legal system is a part, the English word "law" has a moral dimension, a *social dimension, a political dimension, and a historical dimension. Each of these dimensions may at certain times predominate, but over time all four interact with each other.

Moral, Social, and Political Dimensions of Law. The moral dimension of law is expressed more vividly in other European languages, which have two words for law, one referring to law in general, called "right" (in Latin *jus*, in French *droit*, in Italian *diritto*, in German *Recht*, in Russian *pravo*), the other referring to a particular law (*lex, loi, legge, Gesetz, zakon*) or, in the plural, particular laws. The question whether a particular law is valid and binding—is "law"—if it violates principles of law in general, principles of "right," has been answered in different ways in different legal systems; in the United States such "laws" may be held to be void because they violate Constitutional guarantees of *"due process of law," a phrase that originated in the fourteenth century as an English equivalent of the Latin *jus naturale*, "natural law," signifying principle of law, or right, inherent in human nature. Also in that earlier time the word "right," or "rights," came to be used to refer to the entitlement of persons to the enforcement of legal duties owed to them. Thus in European languages other than English the word for "the law" in general is the same as the word for "a right" of a person under "the law."

Regardless of linguistic differences, however, in all Western legal systems, and perhaps in all other legal systems as well, both the law in general and particular laws purport to promote virtue and discourage vice. Anthropologists report that in every known culture there are rules forbidding some forms of the *moral offenses proscribed by the last five of the Ten Commandments: murder, sexual acts that violate family relations, stealing, slander, and appropriation of what belongs to others. Moreover, in every culture, indeed, in every stable community, there are principles of morality that correspond to what in Western societies, at least, have come to be called principles of law. Even a child will say, "That's my toy"—asserting a primitive right of property; "you promised me"—asserting a primitive right of contract; "he hit me first"—corresponding to a plea of justification in criminal law; "daddy said I could"—an appeal, in effect, to constitutional law. Moreover, in addition to serving external principles of morality, law has

its own internal morality, expressed vividly in the fundamental requirement that persons who claim or defend their legal rights are entitled to a fair hearing by an impartial tribunal.

Whether or not fundamental legal principles are derived from an innate morality, as proponents of a theory of *natural law contend, the specific forms that they take in different societies, and the specific institutions that are created to support them, are a product of social experience. The social dimension of law is strikingly reflected in the customary norms that the people of a society create for the informal settlement of their disputes, enforcement of their obligations, and government of their social relations generally. Sociologists of law have stressed the fundamental importance of such unofficial customary law not only in tribal societies, where virtually all law may be customary law, but also in modern highly developed societies, whose legal systems rest in part on the foundation of unofficial customary social norms.

The legal systems of modern highly developed societies consist, however, not only of underlying moral and social norms but also of official norms promulgated by political authorities in the form of statutes, judicial decisions, and administrative regulations, applied by practicing lawyers, and analyzed by legal scholars. Legal systems thus reflect and reinforce the political dimension of law insofar as they effectuate the policies of the governmental authorities that make and apply them.

The Historical Dimension of Law. The distinction between the political dimension of law and its moral and social dimensions is especially relevant to the emergence and early development of modern legal systems in Western Europe in the late eleventh and twelfth centuries. Prior to that time there was a legal order in each of the local, tribal, and territorial polities that existed in Western Europe, in the sense that each was governed by unofficial moral and social norms of a legal character. Official law, however, was rudimentary. After the final collapse of the Western Roman Empire in the fifth century, the highly developed system of Roman law, which continued to flourish in the Eastern Roman Empire, only barely survived in the West, and then not as a legal system but only in fragments. There were also, to be sure, some official legal institutions and occasional official collections of customary laws, but even in the more highly structured Frankish Empire of the ninth to eleventh centuries there was no professional judiciary, no professional class of lawyers, and virtually no professional body of legal literature. Very little of the law was in writing. The same was true in the Western church, which, like the secular realm, was largely decentralized, with the local priesthood appointed by local lords and leading bishops appointed by the Frankish Emperor and, outside the empire, by kings and other rulers. Indeed, kings were sacral figures, and the emperor, who was called vicar of Christ, appointed the bishop of Rome, who was called vicar of St. Peter.

In the late eleventh and twelfth centuries all this changed "with marvellous suddenness," to use the phrase that the great legal historian F. W. Maitland applied to the transformation of Anglo-Saxon law during that period. Every country of Europe created for the first time professional courts, a body of royal legislation, a legal profession, a science of law. The primary impulse for this development came from the assertion of the supremacy of the bishop of Rome over the entire church and the emancipation of the church from the control of emperors, kings, tribal rulers, and feudal lords. This was a revolution, declared in 1075 by Pope Gregory VII; supporters of the papal party fought it out against imperial and royal forces in bloody wars for almost fifty years. Ultimately, the Papal Revolution, as it has come to be called, resulted in the separation of the ecclesiastical and the secular powers throughout Western Europe. This, in turn, led to the creation of the first modern Western legal system, the *canon law of the Roman Catholic Church, and to the gradual development of parallel systems of royal, feudal, mercantile, and urban law. The coexistence of ecclesiastical and secular courts, with separate but in some matters concurrent jurisdiction, and of diverse royal, feudal, mercantile, and urban courts within the secular sphere, also with concurrent jurisdiction in some matters, lay at the foundation of the emergence of modern Western legal systems.

The systematization of the canon law of the Church, called at the time *jus novum*, "the new law," was reflected in the great treatise of the Bolognese monk Gratian, written in approximately 1140, characteristically entitled "A Concordance of Discordant Canons." This treatise was the first attempt to present the entire law of a given polity as a single integrated body of legal norms, in which all parts are reconciled with each other and are viewed as interacting to form a whole. Gratian's work was—indeed, still is—treated as authoritative by the hierarchy of Roman Catholic courts of bishops and archbishops culminating in the papal curia.

One of the virtues of Gratian's treatise was that it included canons issued by church councils and leading bishops from early times, resolving conflicts among them and adapting them to the new historical circumstances. Also the older canons were replenished and modified by new legislation enacted by twelfth-and thirteenth-century Lateran Councils convened by the papacy. Thus the historical dimension of law, its self-conscious continuity and ongoing development in time, was emphasized in the new system of canon law. A historical dimension was also introduced into the secular legal systems that began to be created, partly in response to the new separation of ecclesiastical and secular jurisdictions. Also within the secular realm there were separate royal, feudal, mercantile, and urban jurisdictions, each with its own developing body of law. Thus cooperation and competition between subsystems of law within larger polities characterized the emergence of legal systems in the West. This, in turn, was both a cause and a consequence of the strong emphasis that was placed on the historical dimension of law, its historicity, its self-conscious evolution over generations and centuries. It was also a source and a reflection of the belief in the capacity of law to resolve political conflicts within a pluralist society—a belief in what came to be called "the rule of law."

In later centuries the pluralism of legal subsystems within each national legal system was overshadowed by the increasing centralization of state power. Yet as late as 1765 William *Blackstone could write in his famous *Commentaries on the Laws of England*—a book that had an even greater impact in the American colonies, and later, in the United States, than it had in the mother country—that there prevailed in England the following kinds of law: natural law, divine law, the law of nations, the English *common law, local customary law, Roman law, ecclesiastical law, the law merchant, statutory law, and the *equity of the Court of Chancery. Not all of these kinds of law were legal systems or subsystems in the sense in which those terms are used here. Yet the English common law, statutory law in aid of the common law, and the Chancellor's equity, taken together, constituted such a subsystem, as did the law of nations (which at that time included maritime law as well as other branches of transnational customary law), Roman law, ecclesiastical law, and mercantile law ("law merchant"). Each of these autonomous subsystems of law co-existed with the others. Taken together, they constituted the English legal system.

Blackstone's reference to Roman law needs explanation. It is usually said by contemporary scholars who compare legal systems that in England the common-law system prevails, whereas in continental European countries the Roman-law system—also called the civil-law system—prevails. In this context the term "Roman law" refers to the massive collection of texts compiled in the sixth century under the auspices of the Eastern Roman Emperor Justinian, constituting over four thousand pages in a modern English translation, which only came to the attention of the West in the 1070s and was then seized upon by adherents of the competing imperial and papal parties in the hope of finding legal support for their respective causes. In 1087 the first European university was founded in Bologna, Italy, primarily in order to study those texts, which contain a multitude of extracts from the diverse and often conflicting opinions of Roman classical and postclassical jurists on a wide variety of legal questions. The outlook of a new class of Western legal scholars dictated that they "gloss" the Justinian texts so as to construct from them a single body of law, a *corpus juris*, which was called civil law to distinguish it from the canon law of the Church. Thereafter Roman law came to be treated in European countries as a subsidiary law, available to fill gaps and resolve ambiguities in prevailing customary and statutory law. Although Roman law eventually came to play a much greater role in the development of other European legal systems, it had a substantial effect on English law as well, especially in the separate English courts of ecclesiastical law, maritime law, and equity, as well as in the application of the law of nations. It also became—and this is what Blackstone was referring to—the law governing the universities of Oxford and Cambridge. In the courts of King's Bench and Common Pleas, however, which in the late seventeenth century became supreme over all other English jurisdictions, there developed a body of case law called the common law, based on decisions of those courts and on the reasons given by the judges for those decisions. Although the English common-law courts often borrowed Roman-law concepts and doctrines, the more empirical method of the largely judge-made English law differed in important respects from the more conceptual and doctrinal method of the legal systems of most other European countries, in which judge-made law played a lesser role and systematization was brought about not primarily by judges but primarily by professors trained in Roman law and eventually by legislative codification.

The historical dimension of law is specially emphasized in the English common-law tradition, as courts look back to earlier analogous cases, called precedents, for principles to be applied in the similar case at hand. The historical dimension is also present, however, in other Western legal systems, which place stress on continuity with past legislation and past scholarly interpretations of legal doctrines.

The American Legal System. The American legal system has been called the most complicated legal system in the world. It has also been said that there is no single American legal system—that not only does federal law differ from state law but also the laws of the fifty different states, the District of Columbia, and the territories differ in important respects from each other. Moreover, in both federal and state law the complexities are magnified by the lawmaking role of the respective hierarchies of courts, which have developed large bodies of authoritative precedents in the various branches of law. A French, German, or other continental European lawyer who confronts a difficult legal question may find the answer in the relevant provisions of a national code as interpreted in an authoritative scholarly treatise; the American lawyer may have to search for the answer in many volumes of federal and state reports containing judicial opinions explaining decisions in analogous cases. Even English law is much simpler, not only because it lacks the diversity of federal and state law but also because its courts play a less creative lawmaking role.

Despite its complexities, however, it would be foolish to suppose that law in America is, in Tennyson's derisive phrase, "a wilderness of single instances." Taken together, the subsystems of federal and state law are interrelated parts of a larger whole. Also the various sources of federal and state law in *constitutions, statutes, administrative regulations, and judicial decisions are interrelated with each other in a common structure. Complex it is, to be sure, but certainly less so than the political or the moral or the social systems of which it is a part.

It is the historical dimension of the American legal system that serves best to unravel its complexities. Indeed, the best introduction to an understanding of American law is an examination of how it came to be, what it is, and what direction it is now taking, for its history is built into it. Each of the major periods of its historical development contributes to its present character: the colonial period, the period from the American Revolution to the Civil War, the post–Civil War period to the Great Depression, and the New Deal of the 1930s to the present and the future.

The English colonists in America in the seventeenth and eighteenth centuries brought with them the English common law. From the beginning of the colonial period, however, there were important innovations in the law made both by the colonists and by their superiors in the mother country. The royal charter of each colony contained a clause stating that English law was to be applicable only so far as it was suitable to the colony's conditions. Different colonies modified the law of the mother country in different ways. For example, some colonial governments, in view of the great abundance of land in the new continent, eliminated the rule of primogeniture in English inheritance law, that in the absence of a will the oldest son was to inherit the decedent's entire landholding. Such changes were subject, however, to the approval of the English Privy Council (later, of the Board of Trade). And the colonies were not to have the benefit of new English statutes unless they were specially named in them, or of old English statutes enacted before settlement. Thus the colonists were deprived of many basic rights of British subjects, and this was a principal cause of the movement for independence in the 1760s and 1770s. The Declaration of Independence listed in detail oppressive restrictions imposed on the colonists by the Crown: the absence of representation in Parliament, the absence of an independent judiciary, rule by governors appointed by the Crown, denial of the benefits of such common-law statutes as Magna Carta, the Habeas Corpus Act, and the 1689 Bill of Rights, and many other disabilities that were not imposed on their brethren in England. The uprising of the colonists, however, was only in part a War of Independence for the purpose of obtaining the full benefits of the English system of law and government. It was also a Revolutionary War to establish a new kind of constitution and a new legal system that would reflect the new beliefs that were adumbrated in the first paragraph of the Declaration of Independence and were associated with what has come to be called the eighteenth-century Enlightenment: democratic beliefs as contrasted with prevailing English aristocratic beliefs, individualist beliefs as contrasted with English communitarian beliefs, rationalist utilitarian beliefs as contrasted with prevailing English traditionalist beliefs, and Deist beliefs as contrasted with prevailing Anglican and Puritan beliefs.

The tension between the two belief systems, and the combination of them, were dramatically reflected in the new system of law established in 1787 by the United States' Constitution. Members of the United States Senate, elected for long terms and, at first, by the state legislatures, were supposed, like members of the English House of Commons, to represent the nation as a whole, while members of the House of Representatives were supposed to represent their particular constituencies. Justices of the Supreme Court, appointed for life, resembled the law lords of the English House of Lords, who constituted England's supreme judicial body. The president, in foreign policy at least, was a kind of monarch, albeit not a hereditary monarch. The United States Constitution, to be sure, established democratic principles, but the meaning of its words was subject to development by continuous judicial interpretation in the light of earlier judicial interpretations, and so a historicity was established that reflected the British stateman Edmund Burke's concept of government as a partnership of successive generations over time.

Yet the same persons who carried over and adapted English traditions to the new republic—such as James Wilson and James Madison—also introduced into the United States Constitution liberal ideas associated with the eighteenth-century European Enlightenment that culminated in the French Revolution of 1789. These included, for the first time, the idea of a written constitution, separation of legislative, executive, and judicial powers (see SEPARATION OF POWERS), and the theory of a government responsible to the public opinion of the electorate, as well as guarantees of freedom of *religion, *speech, press, and *assembly, and universal and equal rights of life, *liberty, and *property.

What was new in American constitutional law was not restricted, however, to a combination of the two opposing belief systems that were also competing with each other in Europe: conservative and liberal, republican and democratic, late-seventeenth-century English and late-eighteenth-century French. Wholly new, wholly original, was American *federalism, with its complex system of interaction between the states and the federal authority and among the states themselves. Also wholly new was what might be called continentalism—the implicit provision for an expanding polity of continental scope, "America," with freedom of movement across state borders and unlimited absorption of immigrants from different European countries. Wholly new also was the establishment of a federal government of delegated powers, together with a hierarchy of federal courts whose jurisdiction was concurrent with that of state courts in disputes between citizens of different states (see COURTS, UNITED STATES). Inevitably connected with these complexities was the exalted role given to the judiciary, including the extraordinary power of judicial annulment of congressional legislation that violates the Constitution. This, too, was wholly new. Indeed, the words "constitutionality" and "constitutionalism" were American inventions of the late eighteenth and early nineteenth centuries.

Changes in American criminal and civil law were less drastic and came more slowly than changes in constitutional law. Both *criminal law and civil law remained in large part, though certainly not entirely, in the competence of the individual states rather than of the federal government, and the individual states left them in large part, though again not entirely, to be developed case by case by the state courts rather than by legislation. With the exception of the state of Louisiana, which inherited first Spanish and then French law, all the states "received" the English common law—again, as in the colonial charters, to the extent that it was applicable to their conditions. In practice, the period before the Civil War was a period of considerable judicial creativity as the courts of various states interpreted English precedents broadly in adapting their holdings to new circumstances. They were guided in this by what may be called an integrative *jurisprudence, which sought to combine emphasis on the political dimension of law with emphasis on its moral, social, and historical dimensions. Among the exponents of an integrative jurisprudence in the early nineteenth century were such great American jurists as New York Chancellor James *Kent, who taught law at Columbia College (as it then was), and U.S. Supreme Court Justice Joseph *Story, who taught at Harvard Law School. These jurists were steeped not only in the English common law but also in the law of nations, Roman law, and European legal history. They brought their learning not only into the classroom, thereby influencing future leaders of the bench and bar, but also into their books and into their judicial opinions.

The efforts of leading legal scholars and judges to give a new systematization to the changing American civil and criminal law were hampered, however, by its heritage in the English common law. In civil matters, the English common law was systematized not in terms of broad legal concepts such as *"property" and *"contract" and *"tort" but in terms of numerous procedural remedies, called "forms of action." A person whose legal rights were violated was to obtain a writ categorizing his claim: a writ of trespass to land, or of trespass to chattels, or of trespass to the person for direct injury, or of trespass on the case for indirect injury, a writ of covenant for breach of a sealed promise, or of special assumpsit for certain types of undertakings, or of general assumpsit for various kinds of enrichment at the expense of another, or one of many other kinds of writs. Within such categories a formal system of written pleadings was designed to enable the parties to a lawsuit to join issue on a particular set of facts to be proved on trial to a jury. The technicalities were treacherous.

In criminal law as well, prosecution and defense had to be brought within traditional judge-made definitions of *felonies and misdemeanors, whose precise scope was left to judicial interpretation. The principle that it was not for the courts but for democratically elected legislatures to make criminal law was, indeed, early adopted by the United States Supreme Court for federal crimes, making all federal criminal law statutory, but most states continued to apply the common law of crimes. Also federal criminal statutes continued to use the traditional terminology of common-law felonies and misdemeanors, leaving broad discretion to the federal courts in interpreting their scope.

In the mid-nineteenth century there was a strong movement to codify the entire civil law of the states and thus to remove some of the complexities and anomalies of the English heritage. Although some states adopted codes of civil procedure, simplifying the writ system, and a few far-Western states did adopt civil codes, the codification movement as a whole failed, and even those few states that adopted civil codes assimilated them to the traditional judge-made common law. The *codification movement did, however, presage the emergence of a new type of systematization of civil and criminal law in the decades following the Civil War.

Thus in the pre–Civil War period the formal system of judge-made civil and criminal American law remained essentially English, although within that system the more creative role of the courts, especially in interpreting earlier precedents, facilitated the judicial creation of new law that reflected American moral and social values. Many cases reflected the strongly Protestant Christian belief system that dominated American moral and social legal norms in the pre–Civil War period. State courts enforced Sunday laws that forbade commercial and other secular activities on the Christian Sabbath. In an 1811 New York case the criminal defendant had said that "Jesus Christ was a bastard and his mother must be a whore." He was convicted of blasphemy, and Chancellor Kent, writing the opinion in the case, said "that we are a Christian people, and the morality of the country is deeply integrated upon Christianity." In the words of David Hoffman, a leading legal scholar of the period, whose legal textbook *Course of Legal Study*, published in 1817 and again in 1830 was viewed as authoritative by lawyers and judges as well as by statesmen, the Bible "is the foundation of the common law of every Christian nation. The Christian religion is a part of the law of the land and, as such, should certainly receive no inconsiderable portion of the lawyer's attention."

It should be emphasized in this connection that Negro *slavery also remained "the law of the land" in the Southern states and was there also held to be justified by "the Christian religion," while at the same time Christianity was a powerful factor in the Northern movement to abolish slavery.

This period, which has been called "the Golden Age" of American legal history, was a time of creative constitutional decisions of the U.S. Supreme Court. Famous are the powerful opinions of Chief Justice John *Marshall, speaking for a unanimous court, in cases that established judicial supremacy in controlling the system of checks and balances among the legislative, executive, and judicial branches, and the supremacy of the federal union over the constituent states. Also of importance were Marshall's opinions in cases that supported freedom of economic enterprise. Thus the Marshall Court interpreted the Constitution's clause forbidding a state to impair the obligations of contract as prohibiting a state from changing the charter of a corporation against the will of its trustees, and the Constitution's clause giving the federal government the power to regulate interstate commerce as prohibiting a state from granting a monopoly to a river steamboat company engaged in transporting persons and goods from one state to another.

In contrast to the Golden Age of American law, the post–Civil War period from 1870 to the early 1900s has been called the Age of High Formalism. At both the federal and state level, and in constitutional law as well as civil and criminal law, an effort was made to establish a system of substantive and procedural rules that would help to give stability and predictability to the legal system. The earlier integrative jurisprudence, which stressed the interaction of the moral, social, political, and historical dimensions of law—its links with justice in the broad sense of fairness, with customary norms of social relations, with official governmental structures and policies, and with an evolving tradition—gave way to a more narrow positivism, which stressed the nature of law as an official body of fixed rules handed down by law-making authorities, whose main function was to maintain order in society. The chief emphasis both of courts and legal scholars and also, though to a lesser extent, of legislatures, was on bringing coherence and consistency to the various branches of law and to the legal system as a whole.

In the legal scholarship of the post–Civil War period a relatively sharp distinction was made between public law and private law, and in private law the forms of action were categorized in terms of property law and obligations, and the law of obligations, in turn, was divided into contract, tort, and unjust enrichment (called quasi-contract). These categories were taken largely from continental European legal science; traditionally, the English common law had combined public and private law, and its forms of action overlapped property and obligations. The new scholarly categorization was associated with a new systematization of the various individual branches of law. Treatises were written on the law of contracts (including quasi-contracts), the law of torts, the law of property, civil procedure, criminal law, business associations, and other branches of law, and casebooks were published for use in law school courses in those fields, containing what were called "leading cases," that is, court decisions whose holdings were accepted as authoritative and which served as binding precedents.

The new scholarly systematization of case law accompanied the judicial development of a strict doctrine of precedent, called *stare decisis*, "to stand by the decisions." In the eighteenth century a great English judge had said, "It is the reason and spirit of cases that make law, not the letter of particular precedents." In the late nineteenth century, in both England and America, the contrary doctrine was introduced: "the letter of particular precedents"—the narrow holdings of individual "leading cases"—were treated as authoritative and thus a body of strict judge-made rules, was created in each of the various branches of law, having an effect similar to that of codification. Through legislation as well, some individual branches of law, including the law of sales and the law of negotiable instruments, were in effect codified in separate statutes, called uniform laws, that were adopted in virtually all the states. Thus private law was increasingly systematized as a self-contained body of fixed rules, one of whose principal purposes in a rapidly expanding market economy was to foster private economic initiatives and to facilitate security of transactions. In a famous law-school classroom interchange in the early 1900s, in which a student questioned the justice of the decision in the particular case being analyzed, the professor responded, "If it's justice you're interested in, you should have gone to the divinity school!"

In the decade before and the decade after the First World War there were movements to liberate the American legal system from what came to be called "conceptualism" and "mechanical jurisprudence," and to make it more receptive to "progressive" social and political movements. It was only with the New Deal of the 1930s, however, in response to the Great Depression and the failures of uncontrolled capitalist enterprise, that fundamental changes were introduced which continued throughout the twentieth and into the twenty-first century. These include, in public law, the predominant role of national legislation and national administrative agencies in the regulation of the economy and in the administration of social welfare programs. Federal legislative and administrative regulation of the stock market, banking, labor-management relations, relief of unemployment and poverty, security in old age, manufacture of food and drugs, and a variety of other matters, created a constitutional crisis that was only resolved in the late 1930s by a closely divided United States Supreme Court in favor of what has eventually come to be called an "administrative state" and a *"welfare state."

In private law as well, governing most aspects of property relations, contract relations, personal injuries caused by defects in manufactured products, management of business enterprises, and other legal matters in which the state is not directly involved, there has been since the 1930s a breakdown of traditional legal categories and traditional legal rules in light of public policy considerations. Courts look back less and less to the English heritage of American law, and also less and less to nineteenth-century and early twentieth-century American precedents. At the same time, judicial creativity—judicial activism, as it has come to be called—has increased markedly, both in public and in private law. Indeed, the distinction between the two legal categories "public" and "private" has become blurred. Especially in the period since the Second World War, as the American legal system has moved toward a marked expansion of *civil rights, much of what was once considered the domain of private law is now subject to public-law rules of nondiscrimination on the ground of color, creed, ethnic background, gender, age, or physical disability.

The relative ease with which the United States moved in the twentieth century to establish new forms of state control of the economy, state programs of social *welfare, and state protection against *discrimination on the ground of congenital or cultural differences, may be attributed in large part to the character of the American legal system. In some countries, state economic planning, state programs of social welfare, and state protection against ethnic and gender discrimination were only instituted in the twentieth century by a violent political and ideological revolution, with most painful results. Less radical forms of these developments were instituted in the United States (a) by interaction of the executive, legislative, and judicial branches within a framework of cooperation between federal and state governments, and (b) within a legal tradition in which final authority to oversee such interaction, and to resolve its complexities, is vested in the judiciary, whose decisions, being based on law, are ultimately acceptable to the nation as a whole.

At the same time, the scope of the transfer to statutory and administrative regulation of matters that had previously been resolved by the common law greatly affected the nature of the judicial process itself. The necessary infusion of explicit considerations of public policy into judicial decisions in matters of private law contributed to a breakdown in the stability of law and in the coherence of its various branches. Courts themselves became seriously divided in their judgments in many types of cases. Some legal scholars and some leading practitioners began to speak and write of a crisis of law in the United States.

The word "crisis" is appropriate if it is understood in its original Greek sense as a "turning-point." That the American legal system for almost a century has been at a turning-point must be understood, however, in the context of its entire history, in which turning-points have recurred more than once.

In 1840 Alexis de Tocqueville famously wrote that "[t]here is hardly a political question in the United States which does not sooner or later turn into a judicial one." This, in his view, counteracted the tendency of democracy toward "tyranny of the majority." It is also a consequence of the complexity of the American legal system itself. In its moral dimension, the American legal system must respond to the complex moral convictions of a multireligious, multicultural people. In its social dimension, the American legal system must respond to the complex customary social and economic norms of a continental multiethnic nation of mobile immigrants. In its political dimension, the American legal system must respond to the complex interactions between a sovereign union and once-sovereign states and between the different branches of government within each. And in its historical dimension, the American legal system must respond to the collective national memory of successive transformations during almost four centuries—a memory that is preserved in the historical character of American law, manifested especially in its case law and its flexible doctrine of judicial precedent.

In the pluralism of jurisdictions and the existence of subsystems within it, and in its sources in morality, social *custom, political structures, and historicity, the American legal system is rooted in the Western tradition of legal systems. It is chiefly these characteristics that make it possible to speak of the rule of law over arbitrary exercise of power as a basic characteristic of the Western legal tradition. What is perhaps unique, however, among the nations of the West is America's great size and diversity and its complex history, which have led to its belief in law as a unifying force, a common faith, and in the judiciary as the high priesthood of that faith.

[See also Civil Law in America; History of American Law; Jurisprudence, American; Politics and the Law]

• Carleton Kemp Allen, Law in the Making, 3rd ed. rev., 1939. Karl N. Llewellyn, The Common Law Tradition: Deciding Appeals, 1960. Edgar Bodenheimer, Jurisprudence: The Philosophy and Method of the Law, 1962. Lon L. Fuller, The Morality of Law, rev. ed., 1969. Grant Gilmore, The Ages of American Law, 1977. J. Willard Hurst, Law and Social Order in the United States, 1977. Harold J. Berman, Law and Revolution: The Formation of the Western Legal Tradition, 1983. Lawrence M. Friedman, A History of American Law, 1985. Alexander Bickel, The Least Dangerous Branch: The Supreme Court at the Bar of Politics, 2d ed., 1986. Kermit Hall, The Magic Mirror: Law in American History, 1989. Anthony T. Kronman, The Lost Lawyer: Failing Ideals of the Legal Profession, 1993. Peter Stein, Roman Law in European History, 1999. —Harold J. Berman

LEGISLATIVE POWER

Legislational Lawmaking
Legislation, Federal
Legislation, State and Local

LEGISLATIVE POWER: LEGISLATIONAL LAWMAKING

Modern lawmaking assemblies grew out of the prolonged struggle over the power of monarchs. Originally, monarchs summoned representatives of the "estates" of the realm (the nobility, clergy, landed gentry, and town officials) to arrange "ways and means" (revenues) to fill the royal treasury. These bodies—called parliaments—gradually wrested power from the monarchs. While the North American colonies were founded in the seventeenth century, the British parliament was consilidating its control over lawmaking.

Lawmaking in the colonies mirrored that of the British parliament. Local affairs were managed for the most part by elected assemblies. Crown-appointed *governors looked after British interests, usually by making their peace with the colonists. Vetoes of the assemblies' enactments from London were few in number and often tardy, given the difficulties of transatlantic communication. When Britain decided in the 1760s to tighten its control over the colonies, the native assemblies naturally sided with their constituents, who in turn claimed the rights of Englishmen.

Responding to the British threat, the colonial assemblies sent delegates to two continental congresses (1774, 1775–76). National lawmaking in America began on 5 September 1774, when all but one colony sent delegates to the first Continental Congress, convened in Philadelphia. Reacting to further British provocations, the colonists began to work for common cause. The Second Continental Congress (1775–76) adopted Thomas *Jefferson's resolution proclaiming independence.

The new states gave their legislatures almost total governing power. The first national Constitution, the Articles of Confederation, created a *Congress but no executive or judicial branches. The weakness of this scheme brought delegates to Philadelphia in 1787, where they wrote a new *Constitution with powers shared by three branches.

The First Congress (1789–91) created three executive departments, organized the judicial branch, devised an orderly process for admitting territories as new states, adopted a financial plan for retiring the Revolutionary War debt, drafted twelve *constitutional amendments for the states to ratify (ten of which became the *Bill of Rights), and fixed the site of the new capital on the Potomac River between Maryland and Virginia. Early congresses passed laws aiding industry (patents and copyrights), scientific advancement (for example, the Lewis and Clark expedition), and internal improvements (roads and canals).

During its first century, Congress's greatest failure was its inability to resolve the *slavery question through legislation. Following the *Civil War, however, Congress gained new powers through the so-called Civil War Amendments—Thirteen through Fifteen—and the Sixteenth Amendment (1913), which gave Congress the power to levy an income tax.

Each two-year period, or Congress, enacts several hundred statutes (many of them revisions of earlier laws). Such laws must be processed by each chamber, approved by them in identical language, and signed by the president (or, if vetoed, passed by two-thirds of each chamber). The twentieth century saw three periods of especially intense legislative activity: the Progressive-Era enactments during Woodrow Wilson's first term (1913–17); the torrent of Depression-era laws during Franklin D. Roosevelt's first term (1933–37); and a period of liberal activism, roughly framed by President John F. Kennedy's assassination (1963) and the Watergate scandal's aftermath (1974).

Because of its constitutional independence, its complex organization and staffing, and the experience of its members, the U.S. Congress can itself draft and process most legislative enactments. Modern presidents present legislative programs and lobby for their enactment. Congress is only one of thousands of lawmaking bodies in the nation, however. State legislatures, county boards, and city councils, not to mention thousands of special-district entities (school boards, for example), have lawmaking authority in their respective jurisdictions.

[See also Governance]

• Charles O. Jones, *The Presidency in a Separated System,* 1994. Walter J. Oleszek, *Congressional Procedures and the Policy Process,* 5th ed., 2001.

—Roger H. Davidson

LEGISLATIVE POWER: LEGISLATION, FEDERAL

Article I of the *Constitution creates a bicameral federal *legislature, outlines procedures for selecting members and enacting legislation, and establishes some rules for meeting and for disclosing records. Perhaps most importantly, Article I, Section 8, contains a lengthy list of topics upon which *Congress can legislate, and Section 9 contains a shorter list of limitations on congressional powers. Several *constitutional amendments have modified this initial outline by placing new limits on congressional powers, adding to Congress's enumerated powers, or modifying election procedures. Because of some important and controversial evolutionary changes in legislative power, however, the constitutional text provides only the starting point for understanding the range of federal legislation in place today.

A first important evolutionary change has been a dramatic expansion in topics over which Congress legislates, much of which has taken place in the last hundred years. Federal legislation today regulates nearly all parts of the economy and much private conduct. Congress raises revenues and funds visible projects such as highways and the military. It also regulates, among other things, the environment, banking and securities exchanges, energy, transportation and international trade, the workplace, food and medicines, and a growing range of criminal offenses. Congress also provides social services through Social Security, Medicare, Medicaid, veterans' benefits, and subsidies for housing and education. The Senate ratifies treaties, and Congress passes legislation that structures U.S. obligations under international agreements.

The expansion of federal power has been controversial, because the Constitution created a federal *government of enumerated powers, that is, a government that can exercise only those powers specifically listed in the Constitution, or fairly inferred from those listed powers. The growth of federal legislation has led some critics to complain that Congress has gone beyond the powers originally enumerated in the Constitution. However, supporters of federal power point out that the Constitution enumerates broad legislative powers in general terms, that changing conditions have altered the significance of some of the original grants of federal power, and that several amendments to the Constitution have enumerated new congressional powers.

The expansion of federal power is often associated with the New Deal, but its roots lie in the earliest days of the republic. In the nineteenth century, state governments assumed many of the responsibilities for regulating economic activity and individual conduct that are today exercised by the federal government. That system of local control became unstable as industrialization and improvements in transportation produced a more integrated national economy. Regional tensions over advantages created by competing state regulatory systems (including competing slave- and free-labor systems) eventually resulted in the *Civil War. That war and its aftermath laid the foundation for a new constitutional system of expanded federal power. Reconstruction-era legislation established new federal bureaucracies that regulated local activities and provided social services. More importantly, the Civil War resulted in three transformative constitutional amendments, each of which enumerated new congressional powers and established broad new limits on state governments. Although Congress abandoned much of the Reconstruction program after 1876, the process of building the modern national state continued, with the Progressive, New Deal, and Great

Society eras providing the greatest periods of growth.

The Supreme Court has occasionally struck down federal laws after rejecting an expansive reading of Congress's enumerated powers. Because the Court constricted congressional powers under the Civil War amendments, Congress has justified much new legislation under the Constitution's original grant of power to regulate interstate commerce. The Court used a narrow reading of the commerce power to strike down some federal legislation in the early twentieth century, but by the late 1930s the Court switched to an expansive reading of the commerce power. Until very recently, this expanded reading seemed to allow Congress to pass legislation on almost anything, including activities only loosely connected to commerce. (Compare *Hammer* v. *Dagenhart* (1918), *Wickard* v. *Filburn* (1942), and *United States* v. *Morrison* (2000).)

Another important evolutionary change concerns the role that Congress has created for the executive and judicial branches in the modern administrative state. Over the past hundred years, Congress has set up a large number of new cabinet departments, bureaus, and independent regulatory agencies to implement the expanding range of federal legislation. Current federal statutes often state only very general goals and thus allow agencies outside Congress to create more specific rules from Congress's broad outline. Delegation has become so prevalent that Congress today spends more time on oversight of the executive branch and on constituent casework than on new legislation.

Critics complain that delegation allows Congress to escape responsibility for important decisions. While delegation was initially justified in part because it allowed neutral experts to make technical decisions, critics have shown that delegated decisions are more political than technical and that attempts to insulate experts from politics have failed. However, critics have had less success convincing judges that delegation is unconstitutional. In response to Supreme Court decisions striking down New Deal statutes on the grounds of excessive delegation (e.g., *Schechter Poultry* v. *United States* (1935)), Congress developed more structured procedural safeguards for delegated power. Judges now routinely allow Congress to delegate much rulemaking power, in part because the Administrative Procedures Act (1946) guarantees public scrutiny and judicial oversight of administrative decision-making.

Judges also play a crucial role as interpreters of federal legislation. Ambiguous legislative language often forces judges to resolve policy questions as they determine the meaning of statutes. Interpretive controversies are inevitable, in part because ambiguity is an essential tool for legislative compromise. Judges are supposed to choose an interpretation of a statute that matches Congress's intent, but there is considerable controversy about how judges should find that collective intent in the unruly records of messy congressional deliberations. However, the difficulties of determining Congress's intent are offset by congressional power to reverse court interpretations by enacting clearer statutes. Thus, while courts play an essential role in the development of legislative policy, Congress can have the final say over the meaning of legislation.

• Theodore J. Lowi, *The End of Liberalism: The Second Republic of the United States*, 2d ed., 1979. Stephen Skowronek, *Building a New American State: The Expansion of National Administrative Capacities, 1877–1920*, 1982. William J. Novak, *The People's Welfare: Law and Regulation in Nineteenth-Century America*, 1996. Roger H. Davidson and Walter J. Oleszek, *Congress and Its Members*, 7th ed., 1999. William N. Eskridge Jr., Philip P. Frickey, and Elizabeth Garrett, *Legislation and Statutory Interpretation*, 2000.   —George I. Lovell

LEGISLATIVE POWER: LEGISLATION, STATE AND LOCAL

In general, the structure of state governments parallels the system of the federal government. Popular elections determine the composition of a bicameral congress. State legislatures are organized into various committees that set about the task of enacting laws that further the *governor's program or further the will of the legislature. An elected governor, empowered by a state *constitution, operates as the head of the state administration. A governor creates a program for presentation to a convening legislature. The program provides direction for the legislature in the form of ideas that respond to the present needs of the constituents. The governor is a powerful figure in the legislative process with the power to veto and the attentive ear of the constituents

Local governments vary widely across the United States. The diversity arises, in part, from the rapid, piecemeal expansion of America. Once a country with a population initially concentrated along the eastern coast, America began sprawling out westward across uncertain territory. With each newly established town, there arose the necessity of developing a government capable of adapting to the changing needs of its citizens.

Modernly, local governments, alternatively called municipal governments, fall into three general categories: weak mayor-council plan, strong mayor-council plan, and council–city manager plan. The first two categories mainly differ as to the administrative and legislative power of the *mayor and the city council. In some systems, the mayor serves as an elected diplomat with no power to veto legislation presented by the council. The mayor may preside over council meetings or simply act as the principle figurehead of the city. In other systems, the mayor writes the budget and has the power to veto objectionable legislation offered by the city council. Still other systems are composed of a city manager and a city council. The city manager answers to the council and works in an administrative capacity to oversee the daily functions of city agencies as they carry out the laws passed by the council. The mayor and the members of the city council are generally chosen in a popular election while the city manager is appointed by the city council.

State and local legislation have similar components: a central authority in the form of a governor or mayor and a legislative body in the form of a state legislature or a city council. Each component has as its primary goal the duty of passing legislation reflecting the response of the current administration to the needs of its constituents. These needs predominately relate to the general health, safety, and welfare of the citizens.

Interest groups funded variously by citizens or businesses play an influential role in the legislative process at both the state and local level. Interest groups may lobby the governor, state legislatures, mayors, or members of the city council to give ear to their cause. The work of influence is carried out in publication and in person and an interest group's ready access to the media and thus to the electorate operates as a tremendous, if subtle, power on the legislative process.

The reach and subject matter of state and local legislation must always heed the express curtailment of its powers as provided for in the Tenth Amendment to the Constitution of the United States. The amendment decrees that the states retain only the powers not prohibited to them by the Constitution nor designated to the federal government. This Constitutional prohibition on certain action by state and local legislatures predominantly occurs in situations where the federal government has chosen an area in which to legislate and then passed legislation in that field. In such situations, the presence of federal legislation leaves no room for conflicting state or local legislation. As a result of the federal legislative occupation, any existing state or local legislation confronting a field occupied by the federal government is said to be preempted by the federal legislation.

[See also Legislatures, Structure of]

• Sho Sato and Arvo Van Alstyne, *State and Local Government Law*, 1977. Osborne M. Reynolds, *Handbook of Local Government Law*, 1982.

—Matthew J. Middleton

LEGISLATIVE VETO. Articles I and II of the Constitution set forth the procedures for how a bill becomes law. Both the Senate and the House of Representatives must approve the same bill, and that bill in turn is signed or vetoed by the president. If vetoed, the bill may become law if two-thirds of each house votes to override. These two critical lawmaking steps—bicameral approval and presentment to the president or Chief Executive—are found in state constitutions as well.

From the earliest days of the republic it has been recognized that the executive and judicial branches of government may make law under power delegated by Congress. Initially these delegations occurred in specialized areas, such as the adoption of judicial rules of procedure by the *Supreme Court or in areas where the president shared constitutional power, such as in the realm of foreign policy. These delegations of power to another branch did not pose any serious challenge to the primacy and breadth of *legislative power conferred on *Congress by Article I. Throughout the twentieth century, however, the nature of delegation changed significantly. Congress began to delegate to both the president and myriad new government agencies broad powers to regulate various aspects of the American economy and society. Additionally, Congress and the states charged new agencies with administering expansive social welfare programs in health care, unemployment, and social security.

Critics and proponents of these trends in American government have sought to explain why Congress and state legislatures transferred their powers. Some have charged that this allows Congress to claim credit for addressing a problem but avoid responsibility by leaving the hard choices to the agencies. Others argue that special-interest groups, sometimes aided by powerful legislators, set up agencies to benefit narrow interests. But some applaud this transfer of power, arguing that it allows expert agencies to address increasingly complex problems, and permits the forging of coherent regulatory policy under presidential control.

While Congress continued to delegate power to administrative agencies, it increasingly sought ways to control agencies. It proved unsurprising that even after power had been given to administrators, members of Congress and their constituents remained keenly interested in how the agency interpreted and implemented the law, either through agency rulemaking or agency adjudicative orders. What if Congress disagreed with an administrative agency on enforcement or interpretation? The obvious remedy could be found in the Constitution: Congress could pass a law and overturn the agency's decision. Congress realized, however, that passing a law is not costless or easy. Moreover, where the agency's decision reflected the preferences of the president, Congress would surely face a veto of any law it might pass. Hence, in some situations it became necessary to garner two-thirds of each house of Congress to overturn an agency decision.

In response Congress sought to experiment with new mechanisms for ex post control of agency actions. One of the most successful and prominent was the legislative veto, often classified as a one-house or two-house veto. With a one-house veto Congress could nullify a decision of an agency if either the Senate or the House of Representatives voted a resolution of disapproval. With a two-house veto a concurrent resolution of disapproval would overturn the agency's decision. These mechanisms gave Congress and its individual members a relatively inexpensive and fast way to respond to agency orders or regulations. Eventually, Congress enacted hundreds of legislative veto provisions, often as part of the original law that delegated power to the agency. In *INS* v. *Chadha* (1983) the Supreme Court invalidated the legislative veto. The Court concluded that an agency decision made under delegated power has the status of law, and therefore can be overturned only by enactment of a superceding law by Congress. Articles I and II of course permit a law to be enacted only by bicameral action and presentment to the president. According to the Court, the legislative veto, by not requiring bicameral approval and excluding any role for the president, violated the clear mandate of the lawmaking provisions of the Constitution.

The decision in *Chadha* has proven to be controversial. Some commentators applaud it, noting that legislative vetoes distorted the legislative power and gave disproportionate power to individually powerful members of Congress and interest groups. Others criticized *Chadha*, arguing that the entire concept of Congress delegating power to agencies is problematic, and the legisla-

tive veto allows for important legislative involvement.

States, as well, experimented with the legislative veto. Judicial results on the state level have been mixed. State, not federal constitutional law, controls these cases, hence the departure from *Chadha* in some states.

[*See also* Executive Power; Regulation]

• Harold H. Bruff and Walter Gellhom, "Congressional Control of Administrative Regulation," *Harvard Law Review* (1977): 1369. E. Donald Elliott, "INS v. Chadha: The Administrative Constitution, the Constitution, and the Legislative Veto," *Supreme Court Review* (1983): 125. Stephen G. Breyer, Richard B. Stewart, Cass R. Sunstein, and Matthew L. Spitzer, *Administrative Law and Regulatory Policy*, 4th ed., 1999.   —Nicholas S. Zeppos

LEGISLATURES, STRUCTURE OF. The roots of American legislatures, state and federal, extend to the colonial legislatures, and through them to the British parliament. The first colonial legislature met in Jamestown in 1619, and by 1690 almost every English colony in the Americas had one. As they developed, the colonial legislatures copied many of the forms and procedures of the parliament, but at the time of the Revolution new structures were chosen. In 1776, Virginia adopted a new constitution that provided for a bicameral legislature that was granted the lion's share of power relative to the governor. It had a larger Assembly (elected annually) and a smaller Senate, the latter with four rotating classes. Soon all the states except Pennsylvania followed suit with bicameral legislatures that had different bases of representation. (Following from these early precedents, today all state legislatures except Nebraska's are bicameral.) The new national government under the Articles of Confederation (ratified in 1781) was given a unicameral legislature of very limited powers, with each state having a single vote. Reflecting the causes of the Revolution, the intent was to restrict the power of the central government.

The Intent of the Framers. It quickly became apparent, however, that the national government did not have sufficient capability to deal with national problems, and so the constitutional convention was convened in 1787. After extensive debate, the delegates agreed to a stronger central government, but still one of limited, enumerated powers, with the *Congress as the primary branch. To protect the interests of both the large and small states, the framers agreed to a bicameral legislature with the seats in the House of Representatives apportioned on the basis of population (to be reapportioned after every decade's census). All the representatives were to be elected every two years. Representation in the Senate, on the other hand, was to be equal, with each state having two senators (with six-year terms) selected by the state's legislature. Senators were divided into three overlapping classes, so that only about a third would begin their terms at the same time.

The bicameral design of the Congress and its subsequent development illustrate the interaction of constitutional and statutory law, and legislative rules and customs in shaping American legislatures. First: the differences in representation between senators and representatives—individually and in the aggregate—have led to quite different legislative processes. Because the Senate has equal representation by state and consequently is much smaller (fewer than fifty senators for its first fifty years), it developed rules and procedures that vested significant power in each individual and protected the equality of senators. A salient example of this was the Senate's tradition of unlimited debate (a tradition unimaginable in a body as large as the House), and the weapon that evolved from it—the filibuster. In a filibuster opponents of legislation continue to talk, thereby preventing a final vote, and eventually either killing the proposal or extracting concessions from its supporters. Under current rules, most proposals require 60 members to cut off debate, with 41 senators having absolute blocking power. Furthermore, such an arrangement is difficult to alter because proposed rules changes can themselves be filibustered. Thus, the Senate has often been a major obstacle to positive legislative action, which is very much the role it was intended to play by the framers.

The House, on the other hand, was designed to be larger and more popularly responsive. Because of this difference, the House quickly developed rules and practices to manage the activities of a large body. In particular, formal rules assumed greater importance in the House, leading to a more hierarchical structure. The presiding officer (the Speaker), who is also the leader of the majority party, became the dominant figure in the chamber. The House rules were intended to guarantee that the legislative process could move forward smoothly and that no individual or small group of members could impede that. Thus the Speaker (and the majority party more generally) were able to use their control of procedures to advance and protect their party's legislative interests. Put another way, the House evolved into a majoritarian institution in which a majority (even a narrow one) could work its will. The Senate was not, and is not, such an institution.

Most fundamentally, the role of a legislature is to consider proposed laws and to deliberate about their adoption. In a bicameral arrangement, this task is shared by the two chambers. In the Congress, except for a few special powers granted to the Senate (such as approving presidential nominations and treaties), the legislative authority of the two chambers is the same, and the Constitution requires that bills pass both houses in the same form. This arrangement makes it relatively difficult for the federal government to adopt new policies (as the framers wished), and it compels compromise between the political forces reflected in the different bases of representation of the senators and representatives. These effects are magnified by the Constitution's granting to the president shared power over legislation. Similar effects are seen in many states because of similar constitutional arrangements, although there is considerable variation. Central to the historical influence of legislatures is their "power of the purse." That is, only the legislature can impose taxes or appropriate money. In the Congress, the Constitution has vested the power to initiate all tax proposals in the House, and by practice the same is true of appropriations measures.

The Committee System. One common institutional device used by American legislatures to deal with their legislative responsibilities is a committee system, in which the legislature's duties are parceled out among a set of committees (and often further divided among subcommittees). Committees use the advantages of division of labor and specialization to magnify the capabilities of a given number of members. Division of labor means that some members are given disproportionate responsibility over a portion of the chamber's legislative duties, while other members are allocated other portions. This can involve either or both considering proposals or gathering information through legislative investigations. Specialization means that members of a given committee focus more attention and effort on those responsibilities than on the rest of what the legislature does, developing greater expertise than other members.

How strong the effects of division of labor and specialization are on a legislature depends in large measure on its practices. In the federal House of Representatives, for example, a representative may serve for many years or even decades on the same committee, becoming progressively more influential over its subject matter. In many state legislatures, on the other hand, committee memberships are revised every two years. These alternative arrangements also lead, in turn, to other differences of practice. Because of members' long investments in individual committees in the U.S. House, the committee chairmen are usually the members of the majority party with the longest service on each committee. In state legislatures without long continuous committee service, committee chairs are often chosen anew every two years, even from members without previous committee service.

One consequence of the even distribution of legislative powers between two chambers is that the burdens of legislating fall more heavily on the members of the smaller body. In the Congress, for example, collective legislative responsibility is shared among 435 representatives in the House, but only among 100 senators. This means that, an average individual senator will serve on considerably more committees and subcommittees than a House counterpart, and consequently will be able to devote less time and attention to each of those committees. As a result representatives will usually have greater personal expertise on matters within their committee responsibilities, while senators will tend to have familiarity with a broader range of issues.

The Shaping of the Legislature. Another device for multiplying the capabilities of legislators is the use of staff. Most federal and state chambers employ professional staff for the legislature as a whole, for the chamber's committees, and for individual members. The amount of staff resources varies enormously across legislatures. Legislatures also vary in the average length of service among members, and this in turn also affects the amount of expertise legislators tend to have on issues. We term those legislature with long average service and large staff (and other) resources as "professional," while those at the other end of the spectrum are called "amateur." During the twentieth century, the general tendency had been toward more professionalized legislatures, until the 1990s when there was a populist movement toward constitutional term limits for government officials. States with *referendum capabilities adopted such limits, while the others (and the U.S. Congress) did not.

Term limits are only one example of the ways in which constitutional and legislative rules affect the process of electing legislators. Two other important ways are the laws on legislative districting and on campaign finance. These areas also draw the courts into shaping the legislatures. Until the 1960s, the drawing of district lines for both the state and federal legislatures was left almost entirely to the states. Then the U.S. Supreme Court promulgated its series of "one-man, one-vote" decisions that demanded that districts within a state be essentially equal in population, and the courts took on the role of overseers of this process. As a result, if state legislatures deadlock over district lines, or if they produce unsatisfactory results, the courts may intervene and make the decision. With regard to campaign finance, the Congress sought to regulate various aspects of federal elections during the 1970s. In particular, they sought to limit the amounts that could be donated and spent in a campaign, and to make public information on donations. States also tried to regulate similar matters related to their legislatures. Soon, however, the U.S. Supreme Court intervened and ruled that the First Amendment prevented restrictions on total spending for legislative elections, and on how much of their own money candidates could spend. More recently the courts have chipped away at the law's restrictions on spending by parties on their candidates' campaigns, although this area of the law is still in flux.

Political Parties. During much of the nation's history, political parties have played a preeminent role in the election of candidates. Party labels served as a cue to voters about the views of candidates on issues, and often are the basis for voters' choices. The party organizations frequently selected the candidates who would run for them, and provided money, workers, and organizational resources for the campaigns. During the twentieth century, the role of parties in elections gradually waned as voters' ties weakened and candidates became more independent. In recent years, however, parties have again assumed a larger role, primarily as a source of money, expertise, and candidate recruitment.

The influence of parties within legislatures tended to wax and wane with their influence in elections. In the nineteenth and early twentieth centuries, parties often played a dominant role in organizing legislative bodies and in choosing policies. Then as the electoral influence of parties declined, and as factional disagreements within them increased, their legislative influence also receded. This was particularly apparent in the Congress, where a split within the Republican Party in the House led to a revolt against the

Speaker in 1910. This produced a reduction in the powers of the majority party and (over subsequent decades) strengthened the influence over legislation of committees relative to parties. In the last thirty years, however, the pendulum has reversed again. As the electoral process produced congressional parties with greater internal agreement on policy and greater conflict between them, the members have tended to strengthen the influence of party leaders relative to committees. Because of its roots in the electoral process, this resurgence of partisan influence has been apparent not only in the Congress but in state legislatures as well.

Determining Factors. In summary, the applicable constitutional rules are the starting point in shaping legislative structure, particularly those that define the electoral incentives of members and the powers of the chamber(s). Beyond that, the principal determinants are the statutes and chamber rules created by the legislators themselves. These will define the main structural features of the body—the relationship between the parties (and their leaders) on one hand and the committee system on the other.

[*See also* Legislative Power]

• David R. Mayhew, *Congress: The Electoral Connection,* 1974. Barbara Sinclair, *The Transformation of the Senate,* 1989. David W. Rohde, *Parties and Leaders in the Postreform House,* 1991. Joel H. Silbey, ed., *Encyclopedia of the American Legislative System,* 1994. John H. Aldrich, *Why Parties? The Origin and Transformation of Political Parties in America,* 1995. Sarah A. Binder, *Minority Rights, Majority Rule,* 1997. Christopher Deering and Steven S. Smith, *Committees in Congress,* 3d ed., 1997. Alan Rosenthal, *The Decline of Representative Democracy: Process, Participation and Power in State Legislatures,* 1998. Walter J. Oleszek, *Congressional Procedures and the Policy Process,* 5th ed., 2000.

—David W. Rohde

LEOPOLD AND LOEB CASE. Two wealthy, brilliant, and highly educated Chicago youths, Nathan Leopold (1904–1971) and Richard Loeb (1905–1936), brutally murdered a fourteen-year boy in 1924 for no apparent reason other than a bizarre desire to commit an undetectable crime.

Leopold and Loeb used a chisel to kill Bobby Franks, a casual acquaintance, after he accepted their offer of a ride home from his private school. After mutilating Franks's corpse and hiding it in a culvert under a remote railroad embankment, the murderers sent a note to their victim's millionaire father demanding a ransom of ten thousand dollars. Before Mr. Franks could pay the ransom, a railroad worker discovered Bobby's body. Leopold and Loeb were linked to the crime by a pair of eyeglasses that Leopold accidentally left near Franks's corpse and by the typewriter used for the ransom note.

The case generated massive national publicity because the crime was so wanton and the defendants had squandered such promising futures. Both had graduated from elite colleges while still in their teens and were engaged in advanced studies at the University of Chicago at the time of the murder. To many Americans, the crime symbolized the decadence of an era in which materialism had corroded traditional values.

Pleading guilty in order to avoid a jury trial, Leopold and Loeb were sentenced to life imprisonment rather than death after their attorney, Clarence *Darrow, argued passionately in opposition to *capital punishment of *juveniles. Although Darrow did not contend that the defendants were insane, he insisted that they suffered from mental disturbances and emotional immaturity that should mitigate their sentence.

While the case did not establish any important legal precedent, it was one of the first in which substantial psychological testimony was offered. It also provided an illustration of how the criminal justice system has often favored wealthy defendants: the Leopold and Loeb families could afford to hire Darrow, the most famous trial lawyer of the day.

The case has continued to fascinate in ways that reflect changing social attitudes. At the time of the trial, Leopold and Loeb were widely derided as freaks who helped to validate the now-discredited theory that criminal tendencies are made manifest by physical characteristics. Later, they were portrayed as victims of deficient parenting. More open discussion of homosexuality during recent decades has produced speculation that Leopold participated in the crime in order to win the affections of Loeb. Darrow's argument against execution of juveniles received renewed attention during the 1980s as many states began to reinstitute the death penalty for minors. Psychologists continue to study Leopold and Loeb for clues about criminal personalities.

Leopold has often served as an example of the possibilities of criminal rehabilitation. An exemplary prisoner who worked hard to help educate his fellow inmates, he spent much of his time after his release in 1958 as a medical researcher. Loeb was stabbed to death in prison in 1936.

[*See also* Civil Rights and Civil Liberties]

• Hal Higdon, *The Crime of the Century: The Leopold and Loeb Case*, 1975. Paula S. Fass, "Making and Remaking an Event: The Leopold and Loeb Case in Popular Culture," *Journal of American History* 80 (December 1993): 919–51.   —William G. Ross

LIABILITY is a broad concept that encompasses various types of legal oblicagion It includes the responsibility for *torts, the duty to pay debts and taxes (see TAXATION), and the obligations arising from *contracts.

[*See also* Fault; Torts]

                —James W. Ely Jr.

LIABILITY, LIMITED. *See* Corporation.

LIABILITY INSURANCE. *See* Insurance.

LIBEL. *See* Torts.

LIBERTIES, CIVIL. *See* Bill of Rights; Civil Rights and Civil Liberties.

LIBERTY, usually used synonymously with freedom, has always been at the center of American political discourse, yet its precise meaning has often been contested. The rhetoric of liberty invariably amounts to a claim that some state of affairs is preferable because it maximizes the ability of people to do things they wish to do. But the claim is used in so many contexts, and with such radically different assumptions grounding the claim, that an ordering of its possible variants is needed before considering the history of its use in America. These variants on the concept result from, and embody, a number of crosscutting considerations and questions. Is liberty the attribute of individuals or of communities? Is the concept essentially philosophical, theological, political, legal, or simply pragmatic? Does it refer to all humans, to humans who have achieved a certain way of life, to humans who have organized themselves in certain ways according to certain rules, to members of a particular group or nationality, to people who have certain beliefs, or to humans who can successfully make the claim? Is it a modern term or an ancient one? Is it defined by the presence of something, or the absence of something—that is, is it something positive or something negative? Is liberty something that can be defined objectively so that we can agree on its presence after using certain empirical or moral standards, or is it subjective to the extent that anyone who feels the need to make the claim is not in fact free? The answer to each of these possibilities for liberty has been "yes," and the various yeses have been ar-

rayed in differing combinations. A brief reprise of some of the prominent definitions for liberty will illustrate the difficulties as well as lay out the basic claims that have been made in American history.

There seems to be broad agreement that liberty can be used, at a minimum, to describe an exemption or release from captivity, bondage, or *slavery. Liberty is often placed in opposition to slavery such that the perceived absence of the former is deemed the latter. However, freeing American slaves from bondage did not in fact remove the claim that these people lacked liberty. Mere physical and legal liberty did not constitute a sufficient basis for former slaves to relinquish the claim for additional changes if they were to be able to do what they wanted to do. That is, the simple absence of bondage did not end the need for something else of perhaps a more positive nature if they were to feel free.

A usage related to moral slavery suffers a similar problem, and offers additional insights into the complexity of liberty. Many colonists came to America for religious freedom, which they would easily have defined as the absence of impediments to each person's following his or her own conscience. However, these people did not view liberty as simply the absence of restraints. For one thing, they tended to believe in what is termed "federal liberty." One component of federal liberty is the belief that God created the universe, with one corner of freedom where his creation does not automatically follow the Eternal Law governing creation. This corner of the universe is comprised of humans on Earth, who alone retain the ability to say yes or no to God's will. That is, God, the sovereign of the universe, grants an exemption to the automatic execution of the Eternal Law for humans. Humans who choose to follow God's laws will prosper on earth and be rewarded in Heaven. If not, the contrary occurs. These believers therefore sought to remove themselves from the bondage of sin so as to make the correct choice. The removal of sinfulness was a common goal of those in the community, and those in the community were expected to assist each other in achieving the common goal. As a result, government was viewed as a "scourge to the wicked," and the members of the community bound themselves to the goal of achieving what they could not achieve alone. This positive view of liberty rested on the colonial charters given to a religious people—charters that included a provision to establish and run their own local government. Positive liberty was thus associated with an active, interventionist government.

There are several interesting features to this view. For one thing it equates sin with slavery, whereas following the restraining moral laws of God is true liberty. For another, it parallels the English *common law definition of liberty as a privilege or exceptional right granted to a subject by a sovereign power; or an exemption from the law. The colonial charters were each in essence a privilege granted by the Crown to a group of people to create and run local colonies, and thus constituted an exemption from being directly dependent on parliamentary law. On the eve of independence, the colonists would claim their liberty in part on the grounds of the common law exemption of liberty granted by their charters, in part on the grounds that because humans have the ability to say yes or no to God, they have the ability to say yes or no to a government in pursuing God's will. Another feature of the colonial view was that it blended freedom *from* governmental interference in matters of conscience for individuals with the freedom of communities *to* achieve mutual goals associated with running a godly community—"a city upon a hill" to serve as a beacon for humankind.

One result was to create local governments that were often based on what amounted to popular consent by a people striving to "walk in the ways of the Lord." Freedom of conscience required that each person be involved in making the laws, or in selecting those who did, and these laws were supposed to aid the members of the community to achieve the positive aims of federal liberty. Every charter provided for local government in the colonies, so common law liberty was in this instance consonant with federal liberty. The liberty available to all humans was thus actualized only among a people who were properly organized politically, and liberty came to include, for the colonists, the ability to create their own government and to control it through popular consent. One important side effect of this approach was to allow inclusion of anyone who came later and consented to community values, opening the political system to newcomers on an equal footing.

Colonists who did not participate in this religious view were still left with another common law notion of liberty, which included the rights of Englishmen that the charters explicitly said the colonists took with them. In colonies originally established as joint-stock companies, inhabitants who owned land were stockholders with voting rights, which made liberty in one view a heritable possession. *Property rights were strong in English common law, and anyone who owned a certain amount of property, and who could thus be taxed, had the right to vote. Whereas in England this enfranchised 8 to 12 percent of adult males, cheap and plentiful land in America led to the same English common law provision enfranchising three times that percentage in southern colonies and upwards of 75 percent further north. For one reason or another, then, liberty came to include what increasingly came to resemble popular sovereignty in all of the colonies. That is, individual liberty based on freedom of conscience was easily transformed into political freedom for a community.

By the mid-eighteenth century, these various notions of liberty had evolved into a full-blown civil liberty defined as the exemption or freedom from arbitrary, despotic, or aristocratic rule or control. The English common law notion of no taxation without consent had given way to freedom from all laws to which one had not consented. While communitarian liberty was strongest in New England, it had become a common view of liberty throughout Anglophone America. That communal liberty rested on individual liberty did not seem paradoxical as it does to some today. The libertarian notion that individual rights have precedence over communal rights was yet in the future. At least into the early nineteenth century, it was expected that individual rights would give way, whenever necessary, to the needs of the community. Modern liberalism, embryonically present during the founding era, would not reach full tide until the second half of the nineteenth century. Nor was this development materially aided by the American appropriation of major liberal thinkers such as John Locke. Locke distinguished natural liberty—the state in which every individual is free to act as he or she sees fit subject only to the laws of nature—from civil liberty—where natural liberty is so far restricted by established law as is expedient or necessary for the good of the community as determined by the majority. The condition of being able to act in any desired way without hindrance or restraint was commonly termed licentiousness.

Even further down the road was the notion of freedom from the control of fate or necessity—a largely twentieth-century concept of liberty made possible through scientific and technological development that produced medical cures for age-old diseases, the taming of nature with dams and agricultural advances, and the expectation that any human ill, social or natural, was susceptible to manipulation, even to the point of altering human genes. There is still no proper term for this last notion of liberty, but we will here term it "total libertarianism" as distinguished from the standard libertarian concern for minimal interference in individual lives from government or society. Libertarianism is essentially negative freedom, freedom from interference, whereas total libertarianism is the positive freedom to do almost anything that humans can deem desirable. That is, the libertarianism that seeks freedom from governmental intrusion has gradually been joined by a broader libertarian view that liberty also requires freedom from interference by non-governmental sources. Put another way, it gradually came to be realized that behind a free government there must be a free society, and a free society came increasingly to be viewed as one where an individual could even pursue ends that had in the past been prohibited by the laws of biological nature.

The difference between positive and negative freedom, famously described by Isaiah Berlin, is embedded in the words "liberty" and "freedom." The deep root for liberty is found in the latin term "liberalia," which was an ancient Roman festival in honor of Liber and Libera. Liber and Libera were ancient Italian gods of wine that were often identified with Bacchus, from which was derived, among other things, the term bacchanal. Those who participated in bacchanals were termed "libertines." Freedom, on the other hand, is derived from a word that in Middle German, and thus in Middle English, described someone who was in a blood relationship with the head of the household, and thus not a slave. To be free therefore meant not only that one was not a slave, but a member of a community with positive rights the way a child's status is related to that of his or her parents. The equating of liberty with freedom mixes the positive notion with the negative. The ease with which negative liberty could be construed as licentiousness explains why the seventeenth- and eighteenth-century view tended to restrain liberty by placing it either in the context of the common law, to which a limited exemption had to be explicitly given by the sovereign, or by some overarching moral order enforced communally.

The relationship between positive and negative liberty has become increasingly complex. The positive, communitarian view is that one is not at liberty to break a law precisely because one is at liberty to consent to those laws. But what constitutes consent, and what limits, if any, are there to the laws that can be adopted consensually? The Supreme Court ruling of "one man, one vote" is a relatively non-controversial protection of liberty whether viewed individually or communally, as is the move to grant *voting rights to all adults. The evolved American notion of liberty requires that freedom be available equally to all citizens. At a minimum, therefore, the rule of law requires that citizens be viewed as equivalent to the extent that laws do not distinguish among citizens. But what if this is not enough? What if government must intervene to create a level of equality sufficient for citizens to be indistinguishable in pursuing their respective life goals? And what if pursuit of a "level playing field" impinges on individual property rights, or the right to be treated as indistinguishable? For example, the perceived need for positive liberty to assist those living with the legacy of racial *discrimination keeps running into the perceived need to protect the negative liberty of those who feel unfairly put upon by government regulations sometimes associated with *"affirmative action."

Positive and negative liberty run into each other in other ways. Are consenting adults free to engage in any activity they wish? Put another way, to what extent may government or society restrict or impede the activities of citizens in pursuit of commonly desired goals? *Environmental laws, in pursuing the positive goals of clean air and water invariably impinge on the activities and property rights of those who are perceived to pollute. Americans have come to see the need for positive laws such as these, as well as those regulating food, pharmaceuticals, and vehicular traffic. On the other hand, Americans also continue to see the need for safeguarding negative liberty by tending toward the elimination of laws dealing with sexual activity among adults. The continuing mixture of positive and negative liberty results in the definition of liberty remaining at the center of American politics. Moral standards of local communities, based on the positive right of communities to base government on majority consent, keep running into first amendment standards that now are used to protect the social as well as the political liberty of individuals.

The complexity of liberty for modern Americans seems to result from several ongoing trends. The need for free government to rest on a free society has greatly broadened the relevance of claims for liberty. At the same time, the deepening of individualism during the twentieth century makes claims of liberty almost limitless. Using the language of rights that is centuries old on the North American continent, individuals feel less and less restrained in claiming the liberty of engaging in any activity that is viewed positively. Technological advances, and the expectation of continuing advances, leads to claims that are less and less relevant to formal political activity, but that have become politicized. One has a right to a college education because without it one's life possibilities are reduced. Does this include the right of admission to any institution of higher education one might choose? To what extent does the threat of injury justify the claim that one ought to be free from all such threats? Is the death of 100 people in a population of almost 300 hundred million a justifiable basis for laws attempting to make such deaths zero? Is there such a thing as the liberty from premature death of any kind? What if premature death or injury results from activities individuals have freely chosen, such as smoking, piloting private aircraft, skydiving, driving on freeways at high speeds, or following unhealthy diets? To what extent must a population bear regulations designed to affect a relative few who engage in such risky behavior? Does liberty, in other words, void all individual responsibility? Increasingly, positive and negative liberty, individual and group liberty, and political and social liberty collide in the political arena. One person's liberty of expression is another person's "slavery" to the consequences of pornography, and one person's ability to control her body may conflict with another person's ability to live her faith that proscribes *abortion.

The concept of liberty is at the center of American political culture. At the same time, inherent in the concept are a number of ambiguities that have ripened into a growing set of problems without easy solutions. The difficulty of the situation is compounded by controversies regarding the appropriate protector of liberty. An elected legislature was once at the center of liberty claims. Increasingly, courts have become involved, and many Americans look to the executive branch for relief. In the end, perhaps it is perfectly appropriate that a free people argue most passionately over the meaning of liberty and what it implies.

[See also Civil Rights and Civil Liberties; Jurisprudence, American; Morals Offenses; Religion]

• Isaiah Berlin, Four Essays on Liberty, 1969. Michael Kammen, Spheres of Liberty: Changing Perceptions of Liberty in American Culture, 1986. Daniel T. Rodgers, Contested Truths: Keywords in American Politics since Independence, 1987. John Phillip Reid, The Concept of Liberty in the Age of the American Revolution, 1988. Mary Ann Glendon, Rights Talk: The Impoverishment of Political Discourse, 1991. Orlando Patterson, Freedom, 1991. Richard H. King, Civil Rights and the Idea of Freedom, 1992.
—Donald S. Lutz

LIBERTY OF CONTRACT DOCTRINE. See Contract Law.

LICENSES. See Property, Real.

LIFE, RIGHT TO. See Abortion and Reproductive Decisions.

LIFE INSURANCE. See Insurance.

LIMITED LIABILITY. See Corporation.

LIMITED PARTNERSHIP. See Business Organization.

LINCOLN, ABRAHAM (1809–1865), Lawyer, congressman, and president of the United States, 1861–65. The only son of a subsistence farmer, Lincoln was born in Hardin County, Kentucky, and moved with his family to Indiana in 1816. He worked as a farmhand and boatman along the Ohio River until his family again moved, to Macon County, Illinois, in 1830. Settling in New Salem, Illinois, in 1831, Lincoln labored as a farmhand, riverman, surveyor, soldier, store clerk, and failed merchant as he strove to find a livelihood. From his court-watching days as an Indiana youth, Lincoln had always considered becoming a lawyer. But his scant two years of formal education curtailed his ambition to rise above the laboring class.

Invited by a justice of the peace, to informally comment on cases before his court, Lincoln was soon writing simple law documents from form books and giving legal advice to neighbors. In 1832, future law partner John T. Stuart encouraged Lincoln to study law during their service in the Black Hawk War. Two years later, Lincoln won a seat in the state legislature on his second attempt, and, with fellow legislator Stuart's support and loaned law books, diligently studied on his own to enter the Illinois bar in March 1837.

Lincoln practiced in three partnerships during his twenty-four-year career in Springfield, Illinois: serving as junior partner with John T. Stuart, 1837–41, and Stephen T. Logan, 1841–44; and heading his partnership with William H. Herndon, 1844–61. Unlike most beginning lawyers, Lincoln did not hang his shingle and wait for business. Both Stuart and Logan maintained successful firms and were well connected politically and socially in the state capitol. Colleagues considered Logan the finest lawyer in the state, and under his guidance Lincoln, though not an avid student of the law, became as skilled in preparing and presenting his cases as his mentor.

The vast majority of the 5,669 cases Lincoln's

firms handled before the state and federal courts mirrored the growing pains of antebellum Illinois: debt collection, contract disputes, land squabbles, slander, divorce, and notably fewer cases of violent crime than previously thought by historians. However, by the 1850s expanding commerce and manufacturing, especially railroad transportation, greatly transformed Lincoln's law career. For example, when most fees ranged from 5 dollars to 20 dollars Lincoln received 5,000 dollars in the 1855 McLean County tax case for winning tax-exempt status for the Illinois Central Railroad. Lincoln earned about 800 dollars during the first year of the Stuart-Lincoln partnership and peaked at an annual income between 3,000 dollars and 5,000 dollars during the decade before the Civil War.

Railroad cases were not the sole source of Lincoln's increasingly successful legal career during the 1850s, but they illustrate the status he reached within the Illinois bar. Lincoln's successful argument before the state supreme court in 1851 made it difficult for stock subscribers to void their contracts to capital starved railroad companies.

By 1860 Lincoln's reputation as a lawyer stretched beyond the borders of Illinois. The day after delivering his famous Cooper Union address on 27 February 1860 in New York City, Lincoln met with Erastus Corning, president of the New York Central Railroad. Corning offered Lincoln the lucrative position as general counsel for the company. Lincoln politely declined and returned to Springfield.

[See also Executive Power; Lawyers, Popular Perceptions of]

• John P. Frank, *Lincoln as a Lawyer*, 1961. Martha L. Benner and Cullom Davis, eds., *The Law Practice of Abraham Lincoln: Complete Documentary Edition*, 2000.

—William Beard

LINCOLN ASSASSINATION TRIALS. The trials of those who allegedly conspired with John Wilkes Booth early in 1865 to assassinate President Abraham *Lincoln served as outlet for Northern anger against the South and its leaders and resulted in one of the few federal executions of a woman. Their origin lay in a plot to kidnap Lincoln. After it misfired twice, Booth changed his objective to assassinating the president, vice president, and secretary of state. He managed to kill Lincoln at Ford's Theater on April 14, 1865, but was captured and killed twelve days later near Port Royal, Virginia.

On May 10 the government brought to trial eight individuals it alleged had conspired with Booth. Lewis Paine had stabbed, but failed to kill, Secretary of State William Seward. David Herold was supposed to accompany Paine and guide him to a rendezvous point, but he panicked, deserted his accomplice, and fled with Booth. Although assigned to kill Vice-President Andrew Johnson, George Atzerodt lost his nerve and never even tried to do so. Samuel Arnold and Michael O'Laughlin, paroled ex-Confederate soldiers, had participated in the *kidnapping plot, but broke away from Booth before the assassination. Edward Spangler, a scene mover at Ford's Theater, allegedly helped the assassin escape from the theater, and Dr. Samuel Mudd set Booth's leg while he was a fugitive. Mary Surratt owned a Washington, D.C. boarding house where Paine stayed under an assumed name and where he, Herold, and Atzerodt met frequently with Booth during the early months of 1865. Mrs. Surratt also delivered a package for Booth on the day of the assassination. Her son, John, a Confederate courier and participant in the kidnapping plot, was also accused of involvement in the assassination *conspiracy but was not tried with the others because he had fled to Canada.

The conspirators stood trial before nine army officers, the most famous of whom was Major General Lew Wallace, the author of *Ben Hur*. Although the large number of Confederate sympathizers in Washington might have made obtaining a civilian jury that would convict these defendants difficult, trial by military commission was problematic. The Supreme Court subsequently ruled in *Ex parte Milligan* (1866) that it was unconstitutional to try civilians before such a body where the civilian courts were open and functioning.

After hearing a case put together by Secretary of War Edwin Stanton and Judge Advocate General Joseph Holt, which included some quite dubious evidence, such as testimony from three witnesses later determined to have perjured themselves, the court convicted all of the accused. It sentenced Paine, Herold, Atzerodt, and Mrs. Surratt to death. Her execution is highly controversial, for the case against her was weak, and Stanton and Holt suppressed favorable evidence and may have kept Andrew Johnson from learning that five members of the court had recommended granting Mrs. Surratt clemency. Mudd, Arnold, and O'Laughlin received life sentences and Spangler got six years. O'Laughlin died in prison, but in 1869 Johnson pardoned all of the others.

John Surratt, who was apprehended in Egypt and tried before a civilian court in Washington in June 1867, fared even better. The jury could not agree upon a verdict, and on June 22, 1868, the government dropped the case against him.

[*See also* Criminal Law Principles]

• Guy W. Moore, *The Case of Mrs. Surratt: Her Controversial Trial and Execution for Conspiracy in the Lincoln Assasination*, 1954. Thomas Reed Turner, *Beware the People Weeping: Public Opinion and the Assassination of Abraham Lincoln*, 1983.   —Michal R. Belknap

LINDBERGH KIDNAPPING CASE. In May 1927, Charles Lindbergh captured the world's attention by his solo flight from New York to Paris in the *Spirit of Saint Louis*. Lindbergh subsequently married Anne Morrow, daughter of wealthy financier and diplomat Dwight Morrow and a gifted writer in her own right. The couple's first child, Charles Jr., was born on 22 June 1930, to considerable public fanfare. Seeking seclusion, the Lindberghs purchased an estate in the Sourland Mountain area of New Jersey. On the evening of 1 March 1932, a kidnapper seized the baby from his crib by using a ladder to enter a window on the second floor.

Using a retired Bronx schoolteacher, Dr. John F. Condon, as intermediary, the kidnapper demanded a ransom from Lindbergh, using a series of crudely written notes that betrayed a poor grasp of English. Working closely with Condon, who did not know the kidnapper (he met with him under the cover of darkness at a Bronx cemetery), Lindbergh paid the $50,000 ransom in marked bills. The corpse of the Lindbergh baby was discovered a little more than a month later near the Lindbergh estate.

An intensive investigation by the New Jersey State Police focused on the Lindbergh and Morrow family servants, as the kidnapper's knowledge of the location of the baby's nursery suggested an inside job. In the wake of the discovery of the child's body, President Herbert Hoover ordered FBI director J. Edgar Hoover to coordinate a federal effort to aid the New Jersey State Police in solving the case. Because *kidnapping was not then a federal offense, J. Edgar Hoover, though eager to become as involved as possible, legally could play only a supporting role. Congress soon remedied the problem, however, by passing the so-called Lindbergh law on 22 June 1932. The measure provided for federal criminal jurisdiction in cases involving kidnapping and ransom notes. The Lindbergh case thus became a significant landmark in the evolution of American criminal justice.

The breakthrough in the Lindbergh investigation came on 18 September 1934, after a series of marked ransom-money bills turned up in the Bronx. Authorities then arrested German immigrant Bruno Richard Hauptmann, who had used a $10 gold certificate to purchase gasoline at a Bronx filling station. A subsequent search of the twenty-five-year-old carpenter's garage revealed $14,600 in marked Lindbergh bills and a small loaded pistol.

Newspaper and radio reports blared out the arrest of Hauptmann, whom the public presumed guilty from the outset. Jailed for thirty-two hours without food, sleep, or the presence of an attorney, Hauptmann was also beaten by police—who nonetheless failed to elicit a confession.

Beginning in January 1935, the Hauptmann trial was conducted in a carnival atmosphere as hundreds of people, including celebrities, descended on the tiny New Jersey town of Flemington. Massive pretrial publicity, virtually all of which assumed Hauptmann's guilt, undermined the effort to mount a credible defense. A cameraman filmed Lindbergh's sensational testimony and the grilling of Hauptmann by prosecutor David T. Wilentz, the New Jersey attorney general. In the wake of the Hauptmann trial, a committee of the American Bar Association issued a special report condemning "the commercialization of the administration of justice." The committee urged that cameras and sound equipment be barred from American courtrooms. As a result of the sensational case, states began to pass and strengthen laws against the use of photographic and recording devices during courtroom proceedings.

Evidence of Hauptmann's guilt included the ransom money, incriminating financial records, handwriting analysis of the ransom notes, eyewitnesses, and expert testimony linking wood used in constructing the kidnap ladder with wood found in the attic of Hauptmann's Bronx home. While the evidence of Hauptmann's guilt was abundant, it is equally clear that he did not receive a fair trial. Determined to secure the death penalty, overzealous New Jersey and federal officials withheld exculpatory evidence, used perjured testimony, and manufactured evidence used at the trial. These actions, which would clearly constitute prosecutorial misconduct today, called into question the outcome of the Hauptmann trial for generations to come. Despite the overwhelming evidence of Hauptmann's guilt, resolution of the Lindbergh kidnapping cannot be counted as a triumph of American justice.

[*See also* Media and the Law]

• Lewis M. Seidman, "The Trial and Execution of Bruno Richard Hauptmann: Still Another Case That Will Not

Die," *Georgetown Law Journal* 66 (1977): 1–38. Walter L. Hixson, *Murder, Culture, and Injustice: Four Sensational Cases in American History*, 2001.

—Walter L. Hixson

LINEUP. A lineup, called an "identification parade" in Britain, is a procedure that enables the *police to determine if a victim or eyewitness to a crime can identify one or more of the persons who committed it.

Lineup Procedures. Usually several people are placed in a line facing the witness, who is then asked to identify the perpetrator. The police place in the lineup a suspect—the person they believe committed the crime—along with several other people whom they know did not commit the crime (because they are police officers or prisoners who were in custody at the time of the crime). Police choose these other people because they are of the same sex and race as the suspect and have similar physical features. The witness might be placed behind one-way glass, so the witness cannot be seen by lineup participants, to avoid possible retaliation or the fear of such. The people in the lineup might be ordered to speak, walk, or otherwise display certain physical characteristics that the witness observed at the time of the crime.

If the witness fails to identify the suspect, the suspect might be released. If the witness does identify the suspect, a prosecutor often files charges against him.

If the case goes to trial, the witness normally testifies and is asked if she sees in court the man who committed the crime—whereupon she usually points to the suspect she identified at the lineup, now the defendant. Juries tend to be heavily influenced by eyewitness testimony and are more likely to convict in this situation.

Thus, it is very important that police conduct lineups properly, to avoid misidentification. But misidentifications do happen, resulting in the conviction of innocent people. Police might improperly suggest to the witness that a certain person in the lineup is in fact the crime's perpetrator. A police officer might tell the witness, "We believe that the man on the right did it," or he might express the same belief more subtly, e.g., by directing the witness's attention to this man, or by ensuring that this man stands out from the others in his appearance or treatment (height, facial hair, clothing, or handcuffs). A "show-up"—a one-man lineup—is particularly suggestive, as presentation of a single suspect implies that the police think, "This is the guy that did it."

Witnesses tend to trust the police, believing that they are expert at catching the right man through independent investigation. So any suggestion by the police that they believe a certain individual in the lineup is the criminal is likely to taint the witness's judgment.

Lineup Identification Reliability. At trial, defense counsel may challenge the witness's identification by presenting to the jury any available evidence that the lineup was conducted in a suggestive manner. If, however, the resulting identification is so "unreliable" as to present "a very substantial likelihood of irreparable misidentification" (*Neil* v. *Biggers* (1972)), the judge will simply exclude this evidence. To allow the jury to hear testimony about the lineup or an in-court identification would deny the defendant his right to due process of law. If the prosecutor has no other evidence against the defendant, the case must be dismissed.

The question of reliability turns on two considerations. First, how suggestive were the police? Second, what was the effect of this suggestion on the witness? On this second question, the court will consider whether the witness had a good look at the criminal at the time of the crime—as shown by the witness's opportunity to view the criminal, the witness's degree of attention, the accuracy of the witness's prior description of the criminal, the witness's level of certainty, and the length of time between the crime and the lineup. These factors might show that police suggestion is unlikely to have had much effect on the witness. Recent studies indicate that witnesses have difficulty identifying people of a different race, sex, or age, so it would seem that these factors also should be taken into account.

Right to Counsel at Lineups. Does the suspect have a right to a lawyer at a lineup? One might not think so, because a lineup does not lend itself to a lawyer's usual roles. While a lawyer may serve as an advocate at trial, he cannot be much of an advocate at a lineup, where there is no judge or jury to rule on his arguments. While a lawyer may serve as an advisor during interrogation (usually advising his client not to speak to the police), the suspect's privilege against *self-incrimination gives him no right to refuse to appear in a lineup since his appearance is not "testimonial."

Nevertheless, the Supreme Court held in *Wade* v. *United States* (1967) that the suspect does have a right to *counsel at a lineup to protect his Sixth Amendment right to confront *witnesses at trial. The Court reasoned that the lawyer could better cross-examine the witness who identified the defendant if the lawyer were present at the lineup and observed any suggestive police activity. The Court overlooked the fact that if the witness denies that such activity occurred, the lawyer could present his own observations only by testifying himself—which is generally considered improper. The lawyer's credibility would be weakened by his bias in favor of his client. Also, it would be awkward for him to question himself on the witness stand, and it would be even more awkward to have him argue for his own credibility in the closing argument to the jury.

Possibly for these reasons, the Court later substantially limited the application of *Wade*, holding that the right to counsel during a lineup applies only "after the initiation of adversary criminal proceedings—whether by way of formal charge, preliminary hearing, indictment, information, or arraignment" (*Kirby* v. *Illinois* (1972)). Because most lineups occur soon after the defendant is arrested and before any formal charge is filed, counsel are now required less often at a lineup.

No counsel is required at a photograph identification (e.g., where the witness is shown a "mug book"), because the danger of suggestion is lower here than in a lineup. Nevertheless, if the judge finds that the photo identification is "unreliable," any resulting testimony will be excluded from the trial.

[*See also* Criminal Law Practice]

• Neil Colman McCabe, "The Right to a Lawyer at a Lineup: Support from State Courts and Experimental Psychology," *Indiana Law Review*. 22 (1989): 905. Elizabeth F. Loftus and James M. Doyle, *Eyewitness Testimony: Civil and Criminal*, 1992. Gary L. Wells and Amy L. Bradfield, " 'Good, You Identified the Suspect': Feedback to Eyewitnesses Distorts Their Reports of the Witnessing Experience," *Journal of Applied Psychology* 83 (1998): 360. LaFave, Israel, and King, *Criminal Procedure*, 3d ed., 2000.   —Myron Moskovitz

LITERATURE AND LAW

A History of the Interrelation between Literature and Law. Few twinned fields hold as much promise for interdisciplinary inquiry as law and literature. Although law is a profession, while literature is an art—and lawyers practice a functional craft designed to resolve their clients' problems and bring a measure of closure to contentious situations, while literary theorists participate in an open-ended discourse that is seemingly averse to resolution—law shares a virtual identity with both the telling and the interpretation of stories. Without these two components, law would be drained of its quality as a distinctive and authoritative enterprise. Conversely, stories aspire to law in their obsessive representations of law throughout the ages, through mimetic or dramatic re-codifications of justice on earth.

Both law and literature involve a narrativized attempt to account for various human activities and conditions. Both function exclusively within the confines of structured language. The two seemingly disparate pursuits invite comparison through their common fascination with problems of language: structure, rhetoric, ambiguity, interpretation, and the quest for meaning through linguistic signs. Both law and literature, moreover, depend on abstract formulations and on patterns of associative thinking to attain humanistic judgment. Thus the expressive and conceptual processes of both resemble each other, and the two fields form a natural and mutually sustaining partnership.

Many historical periods and cultural epochs so unite law and literature as to feel no reason to speak self-consciously of such an "interrelation." Whether in the Mosaic stories, or the Code of Hamurabi, or the rhetorics of Cicero, or the Icelandic family sagas, or American public oratory from the colonies through the end of the Civil War, law and literature find identity in the preeminent discourse of the day. No special need existed in those periods to define or argue for the identity of law to literature. In the antebellum American period, many lawyer-orators were also writers (Ferguson, 1984) and law schools then and prior to the 1870s trained budding professionals to write well and to learn the law by reading Shakespeare, the Bible, and the legal scholar Blackstone. In these and many other periods, stories either become law or represent law as a formally allied activity integral not only to the thematics but also to the structure itself of the work of art.

As the disciplines defined themselves in the modern European and American university, and as law practice became more specialized and less "humanistic," law and literature largely lost their sense of identity; on the contrary, both lawyer and literary theorist saw every reason to deny similarities that other periods deemed self-evident. Law, perhaps more in England and America than on the continent of Europe or elsewhere in the world, increased its economic power in the society by mystifying its language and reasoning so as to be inaccessible to the nonprofessional. The law school curriculum, once defined by the literary arts and skills, now innovated a kind of "scientific" curriculum based on the exclusive source of the judicial opinion. Meanwhile, various literary methodologies stressed the insular nature of the text, gradually closing off theory's permeability to the structures of history and justice as they played against the story or poem.

Nonetheless, during this period—the latter third of the nineteenth century until the present day—stories themselves exhibited a profound fascination for the law. Drawing on but intensifying the preoccupation of some earlier nineteenth century novelists (Balzac, Dickens, Thackeray, Trollope, Austen, Flaubert, and many others), storytellers contradicted in their obsession for law the practical and theoretical distancing of law from literature. Our greatest storytellers aspired to *justice in their most central works: from Dostoevsky to Twain to Melville—whose genial "Billy Budd, Sailor" remains at the top of the "Law and Literature charts" (Weisberg, 1984)—and on to Kafka and Camus and numerous American writers, both "serious" and "popular," literature kept the twinned flame alive.

So the storyteller's periodic infatuation with things legal (lawyers, trials and investigations, the often-disappointed but universal aspiration for justice) provides perhaps the best (and certainly the most delightful) "evidence" of the identity status of these fields during the modern era of alienation and strict disciplinarity. Perhaps for this reason, the distinguished law professor John H. *Wigmore, in his *List of Legal Novels* (1908), took time to identify in a famous article the one hundred stories he felt all lawyers had to read to be both proficient and humane in their practice. Wigmore's four categories of literary representations of law may be helpfully recast for the incoming scholar, teacher, or student of Law and Literature as follows:

A. Works in which a full legal procedure is depicted, sometimes exclusively a "trial scene," but just as frequently the preliminary investigations leading to the trial.

B. Works in which, even in the absence of a formal legal process, a lawyer is a central figure in the plot or story, frequently, but not always, the protagonist

C. Works in which a specific body of laws, often a single statute or system of procedures, becomes an organizing structural principle.

D. Works in which, in an otherwise nonlegal framework, the relation of law, justice, and the individual becomes a central theme.

The purely schematic nature of Wigmore's approach should not trivialize his message: lawyers need training that includes both the stylistic modeling and the (potential) humane absorption of stories about law. Beyond these elements, however,

reading stories like these brings two additional benefits: to the legal community, a critique and deconstruction of legal reasoning unavailable from other sources; and to the literary community, a formal or structural raising of the stakes as to textual meaning.

Later in the twentieth century, Wigmore's schematic re-association of *Law and Literature was immeasurably enhanced by two developments. First, Judge Benjamin N. *Cardozo published an influential 1931 essay associating the judicial act with the finest elements of literary sensitivity and style. Taking up the titular theme of "Law and Literature" (Hall, ed., 1947), Judge Cardozo proved the centrality of style—of a sense of narrative and form (which he calls "architechtonics")—to the judge's task of rendering justice. Second, various strains in poststructuralist theory tended to break down the sharp disciplinary borders that had separated one discourse from another. Literary scholars began working not only with representations of law within stories, but also with the very "stuff" of law itself. Remarkable work in intellectual property, authorship theory, women's property rights, and other areas formerly considered the exclusive domain of lawyers has emerged from the community of literary scholarship and theory. (See Weisberg, ed., CSLL.) The "new historicism"—in its various evocations—has further encouraged the mining of literary texts for formal, thematic, and rhetorical elements explicitly connected to law.

More for descriptive than theoretical reasons, the late twentieth century tended to "divide" the field of Law and Literature into "law-in" and "law-as" literature, the former examining the manifold "uses" by story-tellers of legal themes, devices, and representations, the latter reading traditional legal texts as narrative. Although the bifurcation is weak theoretically (Weisberg, 1992), it has helped the entering scholar or inquirer to understand differing approaches to the revivified field. This approach is followed for the remainder of this article.

The Law in Literature. Many components of the "law-in" side of the interrelation emerge through consideration of a single text, Dostoevsky's *The Brothers Karamazov*. For decades, traditionalists did little or nothing with the one-fourth of the story that represents in great detail a criminal procedure, the inquiry into the murder of old man Karamazov. The rewards are many of refocusing on this "legalistic" side of the tale, which includes compellingly satiric depictions of lawyers and—quintessentially—an inquiry into the relationship of justice to the individual. Dostoevsky's 1881 *chef d'oeuvre* adopts the paradigmatic tripartite structure of the legalistic novel, influencing other writers well into the late twentieth century. A contentious event (usually, as here, a criminal act) is narrated at least three times in such novels: first, the unmediated narration of a transgressive event; then the preliminary investigation into that event; and third, a trial (or its equivalent) that brings legal closure but rarely full satisfaction to the individuals and community affected by the original transgression. Often in such stories, the process ends in error (Holdheim, 1969).

The criminal procedure almost precisely parallels the literary procedure within the novel. Both move from an exposition of the facts of the crime (the "Preliminary Inquiry" being the equivalent of the novel's early rendition of the events) to the narrative articulation of a theory of reality predicated on those facts (the trial, which even includes a restatement by the defense lawyer of the Karamazov family situation). In this way, the erroneous outcome of the trial attains an immense self-critical significance. If the legal process ends in falsehood by finding Dmitri guilty of the murder, so the novelistic attempt to recreate a given reality into a verbal form may also result in deception. The lawyers' collective narrative produces a falsehood that reflects the distortion of the grand narrative itself (Weisberg, 1984).

Indeed, lawyers in many works of fiction contrive to use their verbal gifts to transform an anterior and hitherto unformulated reality into an enduring, and largely fictive, narrative frame. Their task, therefore, duplicates that of the novelist who has created them. Dostoevsky took the time to learn the small as well as the large areas of the law that so compellingly held his interest, thereby influencing such twentieth-century writers as Kafka, Faulkner, Camus, Solzhenitsyn, John Barth, Durrenmatt, E.L. Doctorow, Katherine Anne Porter, and a host of pop-culture bestsellers.

The Law as Literature. Just as literature continues to find fertile soil on the lawyer's home ground, so the craft of law draws on the skills of narrative to assist the individual client and also to render the doing of justice in a court of law.

Like the inquiry into "law in literature," that into "law as literature" may be divided into four sections. Seen as analogous academic pursuits, law and literature share a grounding in style and rhetoric (including the narrative expression of a vision of reality), hermeneutic function, value awareness, and imagination. Were it not for the uses to which we put the law, on the one hand, and literature, on the other, we would be struck immediately by their common epistemologies. Narrative organizes reality into a truth-seeming form that is (in both endeavors) highly subjective. As perhaps the most "poetic" of all lawyers, Judge Cardozo once noted, in a statement about his function that recalls some of Gustave Flaubert's theories of narrative art, the struggle between "truth and subjectivity":

> The important thing . . . is to rid our prepossessions, so far as may be, of what is merely individual or personal, to detach them in a measure from ourselves, to build them, not upon instinctive likes and dislikes but upon an informed and liberal culture, a knowledge (as Arnold would have said) of the best that has been thought and said in the world, so far as that best has relation to the social problem to be solved. Of course, when our utmost effort has been put forth, we shall be far from freeing ourselves from the empire of inarticulate emotion, of beliefs so ingrained and inveterate as to be a portion of our very nature. "I must paint what I see in front of me," said the elder Yeats to his son, the poet. "Of course, I shall really paint something different because my own nature will come in unconsciously." There is nothing new in all this.

The legal process, like the literary, moves from an experience in life toward a narrative re-creation of that experience. However tightly bound to evidence and the logic of events, the re-creation needs the bridging or collating powers of the imagination to put together the scene, or the picture, in all its details (James Boyd White, 1974). Statute writing, too—although lacking traditional narrative elements—can and should be the place for the most rigorously literary of stylistic pursuits (Llewellyn, 1978). Forming what we might call the legal "literature of narrative" are, in descending order of definitive articulation, the judicial opinion, the legal brief, the parties' and witnesses' formal statement of fact (in affidavits, pleadings, or statements in court or at depositions), and the parties' informal accounts of the situation, usually to their attorneys. Ironically, the chain linking legal narrative to an event becomes authoritatively strong only as it achieves distance from the event. The ultimate statement, both of what originally occurred and of what the law of the case should be, comes from one or more judges whose rendition of the event is vicarious and sometimes fictional. Like the novelist, the appellate judge, furthering the fictive chain initiated by one or the other party's lawyers, employs the stuff of vicarious experience to forge an enduring reality in narrative prose. Cardozo's highest praise went to *Holmes and John *Marshall; as he said of another great stylist, Louis D. *Brandeis, "his writing is communication rather than self-expression."

But appellate judges far less luminary than these, or less conscious of their re-creative powers, also use style, rhetoric, and form to narrate experience. Cardozo put it this way:

> We find a kindred phenomenon in literature, alike in poetry and in prose. The search is for the just word, the happy phrase, that will give expression to the thought, but somehow the thought itself is transfigured by the phrase when found. There is emancipation in our very bonds. The restraints of rhyme or metre, the exigencies of period balance, liberate at times the thought which they confine, and in imprisoning release.

So we contrast the effects of legal and literary prose only at our peril and only by narrowing our definition of "literature" to texts consciously created as such. Particularly when we consider that every legal document expresses the values of the surrounding culture itself, we may begin to ponder why we limit the uses of literature and law as we do.

Practicing lawyers, for their part, are constantly interpreting, always bridging the hermeneutic gap and expressing values, consistently bringing an audience closer to their own perceptions of a text, an individual, or a reality. Most of the lawyer's work involves the imaginative (and goal-oriented) re-casting of a prior reality into narrative form. A legal document such as a will expresses the entire humanity—the desires, quest for power, even the fantasies—of the testator. Aside from the jargon, as well as the stultifying repetition of synonyms that sometimes characterizes the legal idiom (Mellinkoff, 1963), even ordinary legal correspondence requires legal writers to interpret and understand the perspectives of a variety of possible readers of their texts (Weisberg, 1987). Admittedly, the interplay of the lawyer's subjective vision with the objective law (which may exist in a judicial opinion) should not dominate the final draft of a will, contract, or securities prospectus. These, to be sure, far less than the courtroom argument or judicial opinion, are palpably works of "literature" in the sense of being organized imaginative writings. Still, some of their genre achieve a higher "literary" status through the lucid transformation of the client's desires into prose, through the near-poetic discipline of the expert legal draftsperson

or through the convincing exposition of a human drama. These, too, as stylized acts of interpretation, are narrative art.

Judge Cardozo, from the pinnacle of judicial artistry, realized that the framing of his decision, structurally and linguistically, would often decide whether the intended audience would accept his legal reasoning. In his famous "Law and Literature" essay he put it this way: "The opinion will need persuasive force, or the impressive virtue of sincerity and fire, or the mnemonic power of alliteration and antithesis or the terseness and tang of the proverb, and the maxim; neglect the help of these allies, and it may never win its way."

When Cardozo speaks of an opinion's ability to "win its way," he is referring to its chances of convincing the other judges on the case and of gaining authority within the professional community. Much the same can be said about any piece of literature or criticism. In these twinned narrative pursuits, the effective use of style can gain credibility for the idea proposed and lasting acceptance for its author. Let us not forget that Cicero won the acquittal of a mass murderer of kin with his eloquence.

To this extent, the advocate and judge are artists far more than logicians or technicians. Cardozo adds: "The judge or advocate is expounding a science or a body of truth which he seeks to assimilate to a science, but in the process of exposition he is practicing an art. The Muses look at him a bit impatiently and wearily at times. He has done a good deal to alienate them, and sometimes they refuse to listen and are seen to stop their ears. They have a strange capacity, however, for the discernment of strains of harmony and beauty, no matter how diffused and scattered through the ether. So at times when work is finally done, one sees their faces change; and they take the worker by the hand. They know that by the lever of art the subject the most lowly can be lifted to the heights."

Conclusion. The area of Law and Literature (not only in modern generic modes), then, can evoke a panoply of interpretive investigations, shape a vast panorama of study, all the more fertile because it remains (despite a quarter-century of explosive growth) relatively unexplored. However, the theoretical parameters of the field by now have been worked through, and the novice can enter the interdiscipline via works already cited here.

[See also Education, Legal]

• Karl Llewellyn, "On the Good, the True, the Beautiful in Law," University of Chicago Law Review 9 (1942): 224–56. David Mellinkoff, The Language of the Law,

1963. Margaret Hall, ed., *Law and Literature: Selected Essays of Benjamin N. Cardozo,* 1947. W. Wolfgang Holdheim, *Der Justizirrtum als literarische Problematik,* 1969. James B. White, *The Legal Imagination: Studies in the Nature of Legal Thought and Expression,* 1973. Robert Ferguson, *Law and Letters in American Culture,* 1984. Richard Weisberg, *The Failure of the Word: the Protagonist as Lawyer in Modern Fiction,* 1984. Richard Weisberg, *When Lawyers Write,* 1987. Richard Weisberg, *Poethics, and Other Strategies of Law and Literature,* 1992. Richard Weisberg, ed., *Cardozo Studies in Law and Literature* (CSLL), vols. 3, 7. —Richard Weisberg

LITIGATION. *See* Complex Litigation; Litigiousness; Procedure, Civil.

LITIGATION EXPLOSION. *See* Litigiousness.

LITIGIOUSNESS. The concept of litigiousness—the propensity to litigate—was developed in the United States to describe the high rate at which Americans use the courts to resolve civil disputes. In the 1970s litigiousness became a public policy issue under the metaphor of a "litigation explosion." At the same time, court administrators collected caseload statistics, including figures on litigation rates, for the more mundane task of managing judicial resources and addressing perennial complaints about court delay. Scholars became interested in these issues and more generally in the role of courts in American society. Attention also turned to other countries to learn how they handled individual disputes and resolved the larger social problems then being addressed in federal courts in the United States.

In 1967, Quintin Johnstone and Dan Hopson speculated in *Lawyers and Their Work* about the greater rate of litigation in the United States than in England. They attributed this difference to several factors. First, the United States is a wealthier nation, generating more disputes out of more economic transactions. Second, the United States has greater social disorganization, since its citizenry is less homogeneous. At that time the United States had higher rates of crime and family instability and greater racial tensions, although by the twenty-first century other countries seem to have become "Americanized" in this respect. Third, Americans insist on procedural *due process in dealing with organizations and government, and courts seem willing to grant it. Finally, Americans generally distrust executive bureaucracies, believing many are incompetent or corrupt, and put more confidence in courts to correct inequities in government administration.

In the early 1970s a new slogan, "access to justice," became common among some lawyers in the United States, Europe, and elsewhere. It arose after a period of political turmoil, including student riots at universities and racial conflicts in the streets. In the name of equality and fairness, access to justice called for legal institutions to be more responsive to citizens' needs. For most proponents this meant an increase in civil litigation. There should be more legal aid for the poor, possibly through state-paid attorneys; poor people would thus become more aware of their legal rights. Furthermore, mechanisms should be created to represent the public's wide range of interests in an aggressive enforcement of the new social rights that legislatures and courts had created.

During the 1970s and 1980s the number of civil cases filed in American and European courts climbed significantly. By the late 1970s, however, the access to justice movement generated its dialectical antithesis, a growing alarm (at least in the United States) over the "litigation explosion." Books, articles, and the popular press described the United States as the most litigious nation in human history. Americans brought a range of cases to court, from petty grievances to mammoth social problems beyond the courts' ability to resolve. Doctors complained about litigation impeding their ability to practice effective medicine. Company executives told stories about litigation impairing their business, putting them at a competitive disadvantage in the worldwide search for profits, and thereby harming the United States.

In the early 1980s Marc Galanter surveyed the limited historical and comparative data available and concluded that the hysteria over litigation was not supported by the evidence. The litigation rate in seventeenth-century Virginia was much higher than anywhere in the United States in the 1980s. Moreover, although Japan had a very low civil litigation rate and was the opponents' favorite example of a harmonious society, a few other countries had high rates. The statistics themselves, however, could not answer the question of whether, overall, American civil litigation benefited society. At the high point of litigation, in 1991, plaintiffs filed about 5,960 cases per hundred thousand inhabitants. About one-quarter of these cases dealt with *family law and another quarter were small claims cases. In Germany, the rate was 3,800 per hundred thousand, and there was no significant "legal explosion" rhetoric. German judges had an excellent reputation for speedy case processing and for following the relevant legal norms in resolving all types of civil disputes.

In the 1980s some observers argued that Americans were too individualistic and unwilling to accept the social status quo or the political system's response to it. Americans looked to the courts to blame someone else when harmed, even when they themselves were partly responsible. Moreover, lawyers and the procedural system were too adversarial, stimulating a society of litigants. These arguments generated support for a more communitarian dispute-resolution system, perhaps more on the Asian model, in which disputants listened to a mediator or conciliator who could help them resolve their differences. Lawyers, with their aggressive discovery and cross-examination, would be outside this new world or would have to learn new techniques of dispute resolution.

Lawyers decided they would rather not lose potential clients to these "alternative dispute resolution" processes, and they embraced the movement. Today, dispute resolution courses are taught at most law schools. This has been one factor in reducing civil litigation. Another is that Congress reduced federal financial support for legal aid in civil cases.

Corporations, health care organizations, and other defendant groups exposed to large liability judgments in product liability and malpractice *tort lawsuits also sought to reduce litigation. They have been successful in some state legislatures and supreme courts in changing tort or procedure rules to reduce or cap the size of damage awards. Furthermore, American procedural law in general has changed to give judges more managerial control over their cases, to increase the risk that plaintiffs might have to pay defendants' attorney fees if they lose, and to reduce the intrusiveness of discovery, all of which may discourage some litigants.

The controversy over litigiousness demonstrates that access to civil justice is fundamentally a political question, similar to the more visible debates about the criminal justice system. American civil justice may have serious problems, but an explosion of cases is no longer one of them. From 1988 to 2000 the annual number of civil and administrative cases in federal courts remained constant at about 203,000, although in 2000 there were 10,000 fewer administrative cases involving the U.S. government and a comparable increase in nongovernmental civil cases. Over this twelve-year period, the number of federal civil rights cases terminated annually increased by 20,000, while cases based on state law with parties from more than one state declined by 16,000 since Congress raised the minimum dispute value for these cases to $75,000.

The great majority of civil cases are filed in state courts: 20.1 million in 1996 (one-quarter of which dealt with family law). Approximately 51 percent of the states' civil (including administrative) caseload is heard in general jurisdiction courts. States' civil court filings peaked in 1991 at 5,900 filings per hundred thousand inhabitants, then declined to 5,600 in 1996. Tort cases have followed this same pattern of decline.

[See also Law and Society Movement; Lawyers, Popular Perception of]

• Marc Galanter, "Reading the Landscape of Disputes: What We Know and Don't Know (and Think We Know) about Our Allegedly Contentious and Litigious Society," UCLA Law Review 31 (1983): 4–71. David S. Clark, "Civil Litigation, Access to Justice, and Social Change: Research Issues in Longitudinal Court Studies," Southern Illinois University Law Journal 12 (1988): 713–29. David S. Clark, "Civil Litigation Trends in Europe and Latin America since 1945: The Advantage of Intra-country Comparisons," Law and Society Review 24 (1990): 549–69. David S. Clark, "Civil and Administrative Courts and Procedure," American Journal of Comparative Law 38, suppl. (1990): 181–206. Brian J. Ostrom and Neal B. Kauder, Examining the Work of State Courts, 1996: A National Perspective from the Court Statistics Project, 1997. Adrian A. S. Zuckerman, ed., Civil Justice in Crisis: Comparative Perspectives of Civil Procedure, 1999. David S. Clark, "Civil Procedure," in Introduction to the Law of the United States (David S. Clark and Tugrul Ansay, eds.), 2001.

—David S. Clark

LIVING WILL. *See* Right to Die.

LLEWELLYN, KARL NICKERSON. Karl Nickerson Llewellyn was born on 22 May 22 1893 in Seattle, Washington, and died on 14 February 1962 in Chicago, Illinois. He was educated at Yale College and Yale Law School after a short stint at gymnasium in Schwerin, Germany. He taught at Yale Law School briefly, at Columbia Law School until 1951, and then at the University of Chicago Law School. He was married three times, the last time to Soia Mentschikoff, also a law professor and later a dean. His major works included essays on *legal realism, whose greatest proponent he was, legal *education, *commercial law, *Native American law, and judicial reasoning. He was chief reporter for the Uniform Commercial Code, and one of its strongest proponents. He published a number of poems, some under pseudonyms, and a casebook on sales that anticipated the *"law and society" movement's emphasis on actual practices rather than on arcane formal principles of law.

Llewellyn was an impulsive correspondent and conversationalist as well as a broad-ranging writer. He loved to share his ideas with other people in lectures, and to be in their company. His teaching was a kind of networking, for there was no distance, literal or figurative, between him and his students. He could be abrasive and demanding, but he was always "all there," according to one former student. Llewellyn was by nature gregarious and a hard worker, which enabled him to keep the *Law Journal* going at Yale when most of the students went off to fight in the First World War.

Llewellyn, particularly in his early jurisprudential writings, publicly acknowledged various thinkers upon whom he had drawn to compose his own view of *jurisprudence. This first list of acknowledgments appeared in an article he wrote for the *American Economic Review* in 1925, and included such diverse figures as the conservative anthropologist William Graham Sumner, the liberal economists John R. Commons and Thorstein Veblen, Justice Oliver Wendell *Holmes Jr., and fellow jurisprudent Roscoe *Pound. Llewellyn included another eclectic list of thinkers in his contribution to the 1930 *Law and the Modern Mind* symposium in the *Columbia Law Review*—Commons, Veblen, Sumner, and Holmes were joined by Max Weber as thinkers "to whom [Llewellyn is] particularly indebted."

Llewellyn was capable of brilliant innovation in legal thinking. The first law and economics texts were produced by realists like Llewellyn, *Douglas, and Wesley Sturges in the 1920s. So, too, the first work of the law and literature movement was Karl Llewellyn's poetics. There were some false turns in his thought. Although he was a strong defender of democratic institutions, a believer in diversity of thought and freedom of expression, he was never the most generous of critics, often finding fault with others.

Llewellyn was best known as one of the founders of the American jurisprudential movement called legal realism. In 1930, when he was challenged by Roscoe Pound to define legal realism, Llewellyn simply wrote to every other academic whom he thought might be classified a legal realist. Many replied. Scholars still debate the contours of that movement, seeing it variously as a turn away from formal legal doctrine to social science empiricism, or as a rejection of philosophical formalism in favor of pragmatism, or as a mode of teaching law based on study of how actual transactions took place in the real world. When pressed, Llewellyn backed away from a formal definition, and depicted it as a diverse but collective effort of law professors such as Charles E. Clark, Arthur *Corbin, Walter Wheeler Cook, William O. Douglas, Underhill Moore, and Herman Oliphant.

But Llewellyn was ever mistrustful of abstractions and dry rules. He decried philosophers and

philosophy dictating jurisprudence. He told his students that "Jurisprudence ought to be for lawyers and not for philosophers." Philosophizing in general terms was the antithesis of Llewellyn's method. He told his students, "I take no ideas as ideas. This is a course which is a course in Jurisprudence. And Jurisprudence, for my money, is of the nature of law; and law has no purposes, generalities, or other things unconnected with measures and with the concrete." He neither admired nor participated in legal philosophizing: "I want fellows who talk Jurisprudence to lawyers, not to philosophers and leave the philosophers to do their own work." In his last statement on the subject, *The Common Law Tradition* (1960), he maintained that "Realism was never a philosophy."

Once we reconceptualize Llewellyn as a "*bricoleur,*" a craftsman who assembled novelty from old pieces, not a devotee of social science, nor a secret conservative defending custom against democratic regulation, nor a theorist inspired by German neo-positivist philosophy, we can begin to recover the motives of his academic enterprise. He wanted a sturdy, pragmatic method to refashion and reform divorce, commercial law, and legal education. He was from start to finish an applied jurisprudent, cobbling together the bits and pieces in the universe of law and social science around him.

[*See also* Educator, Legal]

• William Twinning, *Karl Llewellyn and the Realist Movement*, 1973. John Henry Schlegel, *American Legal Realism & Empirical Social Science*, 1995. N. E. H. Hull, *Roscoe Pound and Karl Llewellyn: Searching for an American Jurisprudence*, 1997.   —N. E. H. Hull

LOCHNER V. NEW YORK, 198 U.S. 45 (1905).

In 1895, New York passed a law limiting the hours of work in bakeries to 10 hours per day and 60 hours per week. Spearheaded by the bakers' union and tenement house reformers, this provision reflected the labor movement's long struggle to achieve shorter work hours. Typically paid $12 per day, bakers of that era had usually been required to work 12 hours per day, 6 or 7 days per week in shops located in filthy tenement house cellars.

In 1902, Utica bakeshop owner Joseph Lochner was fined for violating the new hours law. Appealing to the United States Supreme Court, Lochner claimed the statute violated the *Fourteenth Amendment guarantee that no person shall be denied life, liberty, or property without *due process of law. This constitutional right to due process was originally considered a guarantee of correct judicial procedure. But under the theory of substantive due process, courts assumed the power to examine the content of legislation as well as the means by which it was enforced. Thus, courts could invalidate any type of state economic or reform legislation determined to be in conflict with a constitutionally protected right.

Voting 5–4, the Supreme Court overruled Lochner's conviction and held the bakeshop law unconstitutional. Justice Rufus Peckham's majority opinion reasoned that among the liberties protected by the Fourteenth Amendment was "liberty of contract." This included the right of the employee and employer to agree on the number of hours the employee would work. A state might interfere with that liberty, Peckham admitted, but only if its *regulation fell under the legitimate police powers of the state. Peckham defined the police power narrowly, saying the bakeshop law could only be upheld if it protected public health. A mere assertion that the law related to the bakers' health was not enough, he continued. The state had the burden of proving the law was reasonable.

Dissenting, John M. *Harlan agreed that a shorter hours law might violate liberty of *contract, but argued that the burden should be on those challenging the legislation to prove "plainly, palpably, beyond all question" that the law was unconstitutional. Oliver Wendell *Holmes's dissent went further. Attacking the majority's underlying premise, he argued that the Court had based its decision on laissez-faire economic theory rather than the Constitution. He charged that the court had merely substituted its own judgment for that of the state legislature.

Critics viewed the decision as an abuse of judicial power and usurpation of legislative authority. Until *Lochner* was overruled by *West Coast Hotel* v. *Parrish* (1937), countless attempts to reform social and economic conditions through legislation were challenged on the basis of *Lochner*. Many of these regulations were upheld, but so many reform statutes were invalidated that the history of constitutional law during that time is commonly called "the *Lochner* era." Although some historians have argued that Justice Peckham's opinion was not based on laissez-faire theory but free labor and Jacksonian ideals, the *Lochner* case remains important today as a symbol of unrestrained judicial activism.

[*See also* Civil Rights and Civil Liberties; Economics and Law; Labor Law]

• Howard Gillman, *The Constitution Besieged: The Rise and Demise of Lochner Era Police Power Jurisprudence*, 1993. Paul Kens, *Lochner v. New York: Economic Regulation on Trial*, 1998. —Paul Kens

LOCKWOOD, BELVA ANN (born Royalton, N.Y., 24 October 1830; died Washington, D.C., 19 May 1917). She graduated from Genesee College (later Syracuse University) in 1857 and began a career teaching, moving to Washington, D.C. in 1866 where she founded her own school. Two years later she married Ezekiel Lockwood, who took over the school. Belva then turned to the study of law, enrolling at National University Law School in 1871 after being refused admission to the law schools at Columbian College (now George Washington University), Georgetown University, and Howard University. She graduated in 1873 and was admitted to the bar, but was refused, based on the custom of the time, an opportunity to speak before the U.S. Supreme Court.

Lockwood became a proponent of women's rights. After being denied admission to the Supreme Court in 1876, she successfully lobbied Congress to pass legislation that resulted in her becoming, in March 1879, the first women to be admitted to practice before the Court.

In 1884 and 1888 she ran unsuccessfully for president on the National Equal Rights Party ticket, but played an active role in politics throughout her life. Lockwood was instrumental in persuading Congress to add amendments to the statehood bills for Oklahoma, New Mexico, and Arizona that granted women in those states the vote. She also pursued a vigorous legal practice. Her most important case resulted in the Cherokee Nation receiving $5 million in damages from the U.S. government for encroaching on tribal territory.

[*See also* Gender and Law; Lawyers]

• Barbara Babcock, *Belva Ann Lockwood: For Peace, Justice, and President* (1997). —Kermit L. Hall

LOITERING. *See* Victimless Crime.

LSAT. *See* Education, Legal.

LYNCHING. *See* Extralegality; Mob Violence and Vigilantism; Race and Ethnicity; Segregation.

M

M'NAUGHTEN RULE. *See* Criminal Law Principles: Defense Principles.

MAFIA. *See* Organized Crime.

MAGISTRATE. *See* Judge.

MALPRACTICE. A professional's failure to exercise the level of knowledge and skill that would be employed under the circumstances by an ordinary, reasonable member of the profession. Also known as professional negligence.

[*See also* Lawyers; Liability; Torts]

—Sally F. Goldfarb

MALPRACTICE, MEDICAL. *See* Medicine and Law.

MALPRACTICE INSURANCE. *See* Insurance.

MANN ACT. Illustrative of the Progressives' penchant for using government to suppress vice and immoral behavior were the two Mann Acts, which were designed to suppress prostitution and sexual immorality. The first act, passed on 26 March 1910, dealt with immigrant women; the second, passed on 25 June 1910, focused on American women. Both made it a *felony to transport women into the United States or across state lines "for the purpose of prostitution or debauchery, or for any other immoral purpose, or with the intent and purpose to induce, entice, or compel such woman or girl" to participate in such an act. The commerce clause was used as a constitutional hook to regulate what was usually considered an offense, to the extent that it was an offense, against state law. Transportation in these circumstances was a felony, "whether with or without her consent." Thus, if two unmarried adults had consensual sex after crossing state lines the man involved could be prosecuted under the act. The act doubled the punishment, to ten years in jail and $10,000 fine, if the female in question was a minor. The acts specifically abolished the *common law rule that wives could not be forced to testify against husbands. The Supreme Court upheld the acts in *Hoke* v. *U.S.* (1913).

The ostensible purpose of the laws was to prevent the trafficking in women and girls by prostitution rings in what was called the "white slave trade"—however, the law was often used to punish "immoral" behavior. The most famous prosecution under the act involved the first African-American heavyweight champion of the world, Jack Jackson. He was convicted under the act for bringing his white girlfriend (whom he later married) to Chicago. There was no contention that he had an interest in prostitution, but the Wilson administration, which had introduced segregation into the federal government, used the law to prosecute a famous black man, for flaunting his relationships with white women. The act was also used, in *Caminetti* v. *United States* (1917) against a California man who crossed interstate lines with his girlfriend, and Utah polygamists in *Cleveland* v. *United States* (1946). Dissenters on the Supreme Court in these cases argued that the purpose of the act was to suppress prostitution, not consensual sex among adults.

[*See also* Criminal Law; Morals Offenses; Victimless Crimes]

• Roberts, Randy, *Papa Jack: Jack Johnson and the Era of White Hopes*, 1983. Finkelman, Paul, ed., *Religion and American Law*, 2000.

—Paul Finkelman

MANSFIELD, ARABELLA (born Burlington, Iowa, 23 May 1846; died Aurora, Ill., 2 August 1911). Born Belle Aurelia Babb, she subsequently became known as Arabella. She graduated from Iowa Wesleyan College in 1866 and two years later married John M. Mansfield. Together they studied law, she for two years in the office of her brother in Mount Pleasant, and taught at Iowa Wesleyan.

In 1869 she passed the bar examination in Henry County and sought admission along with her husband. The Iowa Code, however, specifically limited admission to the bar to white males. Francis Springer, a progressive judge, granted Mansfield's application by relying on an Iowa statute that provided that words importing the masculine gender could be extended to women as well. As a result, she became the first officially recognized woman lawyer in the United States.

Mansfield never formally practiced law, but instead put her energies into suffrage reform and education. She served as chairperson and secretary of the first Iowa Suffrage Association state convention in 1870. Mansfield campaigned relentlessly to lower the barriers for women to vote and gain an education. She earned an M.A. in 1870 and an LL.B from Iowa Wesleyan in 1872.

In 1879 she moved with her husband to Greencastle, Indiana and joined the faculty of Asbury University (now De Pauw University). She became dean of the school of art and music at De Pauw, a position she held until her death.

[See also Gender and Law; Lawyers]

• Eileen Babb Sumner, Famous Iowa Babbs, 1998.

—Kermit L. Hall

MANSLAUGHTER. See Homicide.

MAPP V. OHIO, 367 U.S. 643 (1961). In Mapp v. Ohio, the United States Supreme Court held that state courts must exclude from their trials *evidence obtained through "unreasonable searches or seizures." While neither the Fourth nor Fourteenth Amendment to the Constitution mention this remedy, the Court nevertheless held that this "exclusionary rule" must be inferred, because other remedies failed to deter the police from committing such violations and because exclusion is necessary to preserve the integrity of the judiciary.

Both reasons are questionable. The Court failed to show that exclusion will deter police misconduct, and when a judge excludes relevant evidence and this results in the release of an apparently guilty defendant, this diminishes the integrity of the courts in the eyes of many people.

For these reasons, later cases have limited the scope of Mapp—for instance by allowing illegally seized evidence to impeach the testimony of a defendant who testifies, and by admitting evidence obtained through an invalid *search warrant that the police believed in good faith was valid.

Nevertheless, Mapp remains the most important *search and seizure case ever decided. The exclusionary rule is the gateway to the large body of cases setting out the substantive rules establishing when the police may search and seize evidence and persons. These rules are taught in police training programs and are enforced by trial court judges throughout the country.

[See also Fourteenth Amendment; Incorporation Doctrine]

• Wayne R. LaFave, Jerold H. Israel and Nancy J. King, Criminal Procedure, 3d ed., 2000.

—Myron Moskovitz

MARBURY V. MADISON, 1 CRANCH (5 U.S.) 137 (1803). Marbury v. Madison is regarded by legal scholars as the leading precedent for U.S. *Supreme Court authority to disregard acts of *Congress that violate the *Constitution. This is the power of *judicial review. In Marbury, the Court, for the first time in an unanimous decision accompanied by a fully reasoned opinion, refused to enforce an act of Congress because of constitutional problems in the act.

The case arose in 1801 when William Marbury and three others who had been appointed justices of the peace in the District of Columbia by outgoing President John Adams failed to receive their commissions on the eve of Thomas *Jefferson's inauguration. The new administration refused delivery of the commissions. The four would-be judges sued for writs of mandamus in the Supreme Court to force newly appointed Secretary of State James Madison to produce them. Political infighting developed over these and other eleventh-hour Federalist judicial appointments in the months after Jefferson assumed office. Among other things, this infighting led to the Republican Senate's refusal to produce records of the confirmations, and to congressional suspension of the Court's 1802 terms, causing Marbury's case not to be tried until 1803.

In its Marbury opinion, the Court (per Chief Justice John *Marshall) ruled that Section 13 of the Judiciary Act of 1789, by empowering the Court to issue writs of mandamus in original (trial) jurisdiction to any "persons holding office under the authority of the United States" (1 Stat. 73, at 81), had impermissibly enlarged the Court's jurisdiction beyond the terms of Article III, Section 2 of the Constitution, which restricts the Court's original jurisdiction to cases involving ambassadors, public ministers, consuls, or states. This meant that, although Marbury had a legal right to his commission that was violated by Madison's failure to perform a ministerial duty, the Court could not provide the requested relief because the congressional act upon which Marbury relied was unconstitutional.

In the final pages of his *Marbury* opinion, Chief Justice Marshall justified the Court's constitutional analysis, arguing that the courts must "say what the law is," that the Constitution is "superior," "paramount" law, and that a legislative act in conflict with the Constitution is void.

After establishing the principle that unconstitutional legislative acts are void, Marshall carefully restricted the Court's power to invalidate such acts to cases in which the Court is forced to ignore either the Constitution or the statute in order to decide the case before it. Thus *Marbury*-style judicial review is very limited in scope. This is the reason why the case was largely ignored by courts and legal commentators until the late nineteenth century.

Beginning in the 1880s, when the case was first cited as a precedent for judicial review by the Supreme Court, *Marbury* began its rise to prominence as a symbol in the Progressive-era controversy over the constitutional role of the courts. It was during this era that the Court began to invalidate acts of Congress with greater frequency. *Marbury's* case became a useful precedent. Since that time, the case has become an icon of American constitutional law. Throughout the twentieth century, the case has been cited not only more frequently, but often in support of sweeping declarations of judicial supremacy that contrast sharply with the more modest *Marbury* of John Marshall's Court.

• Robert Lowry Clinton, *Marbury v. Madison and Judicial Review*, 1989. William E. Nelson, *Marbury v. Madison: The Origins and Legacy of Judicial Review*, 2000.

—Robert Lowry Clinton

MARITIME INSURANCE. *See* Insurance.

MARITIME LAW. *See* Admiralty and Maritime Jurisdiction.

MARRIAGE is an important legal and social status that affects the parties' financial rights and duties and many other aspects of their lives. Despite the continuing practical and symbolic importance of marriage, state regulation of entry into marriage has declined greatly in the last hundred years.

Marital Property Rights. Marital *property systems are grouped into two major categories—*common law or community property. Community property states are Arizona, California, Idaho, Louisiana, Nevada, New Mexico, Texas, Washington, and Wisconsin.

Before the mid-nineteenth century, a married woman's personal property in common law property states became her husband's. He had the right to manage and use her real property for the duration of the marriage and, if the couple had children, for his life. If a wife outlived her husband, she reclaimed her real property and received a third of his real property for life. Married women could not make *wills or sue or be sued and they were not liable for their owns debts or those of their husbands.

In the mid-1800s, all states adopted married women's property acts, which eliminated these rules. Under these acts, which remain the law today, each spouse owns the property he or she earns from labor or investment and property that he or she is given or inherits. Joint ownership of property arises by deliberate act and not by operation of law. The system is formally equal, but one who does not work in the marketplace has no independent means of acquiring property and has no automatic right to property that the other spouse acquires.

In community property states, all property that either spouse acquires after marriage is presumed to be jointly owned as community property. Separate property is property owned before marriage or acquired after marriage by gift or inheritance. The community property states have varying rules to characterize increases in value of, and income from, separate property.

Control of property usually follows ownership. Thus, in both common law and community property states, each spouse controls his or her separate property, and the spouses have equal or joint control over jointly owned property. In addition, in most states, spouses have a legal duty to support each other financially, meaning that both spouses may be held liable by creditors for family expenses.

Other Legal Consequences of Marriage. Marriage historically was important in order to confer legitimacy on children, which meant giving the children access to the resources of the parents and perhaps the extended family. Today, legal discrimination against nonmarital children has mostly been abolished, but marriage is still important for determining a child's legal father. The law of all states presumes that a child born to a married woman is her husband's child. In most states, blood test or other evidence may rebut that presumption.

State laws may alter criminal rules and personal injury law when the parties are spouses. For example, under traditional principles, a man could not be held legally liable for raping his wife, though this rule has been abolished in many states. Similarly, under traditional principles, spouses could not sue one another to recover for personal injury, though many states have abandoned this limitation.

Marriage Formation. State law regulates marriage formation. In general, a marriage that is valid where it was entered into will be recognized as valid elsewhere. This rule is subject to an important, if vague, limitation: if recognizing a marriage as valid would violate a strong public policy of the state asked to recognize it, the state will not do so. For example, a state might refuse to recognize as valid a polygamous marriage, even though the parties entered into the marriage in a Moslem country that allows polygamy.

The law of marriage regulation has changed greatly over the last hundred years, with a strong trend toward decreased regulation. Among the social changes associated with this trend are growing acceptance of *divorce and unmarried unions, the relative decline in the social importance of religion, and women's increased economic and social independence.

Competence to Marry. The prohibition against having more than one spouse at a time is among the oldest and most widespread of marriage regulations. In England and the United States, the Mormons, who believed that they had a religious obligation to practice plural marriage, presented the only serious challenge to this rule. The social response to Mormon plural marriage was overwhelmingly negative; people feared that polygamy would reintroduce patriarchy and despotism into the new republic. Other major concerns were that polygamy would mean that only wealthy men could marry, that polygamy degraded women, and that dependent women and children would not be cared for adequately. Mormon challenges to bans on polygamy, based on First Amendment freedom of religion, failed in the nineteenth century and breakoff groups failed again in the 1980s (*Reynolds* v. *U.S.* (1978); *Potter* v. *Murray City* (1985)). However, Americans today practice polygamy in the sense of serial monogamy. If serial monogamy is defined as polygamy, Americans are more polygamous than many people living in "polygamous" cultures are.

Bigamy (having more than one living spouse at a time) is commonly a crime. Most states have laws that provide a defense to a criminal bigamy charge. These laws say that if, at the time of second wedding the defendant believes (1) that the first spouse is dead, (2) the circumstances justify this belief, and (3) the spouse has been absent without explanation for a set period of time, the defendant is not guilty. However, the second marriage is not valid.

In most states, one must be eighteen to marry without parental consent; in some states, persons as young as fourteen may marry with parental consent, though sixteen is a more common minimum age. Statutes in some states provide an exception to the minimum age limit or to the requirement of parental consent when the girl is pregnant. Below some fixed age, it is assumed that children can neither physically consummate marriage nor intellectually understand its significance. The common law boundaries were twelve for girls and fourteen for boys. At *common law, people older than the minimum age but younger than twenty-one could marry only with parental consent. In the late nineteenth century, minimum age limits for marriage were raised. Higher age limits survive today in part because of the belief that youthful marriages are unstable.

By statute or common law, all jurisdictions provide that a person who lacks the mental capacity may not validly marry. Like the age restrictions, mental requirements have sometimes been justified as protecting individuals from their own poor judgment and from being imposed on. They have also been justified in eugenic terms, and today some argue that they insure family stability and protect children. The test for mental capacity to marry is whether a person can understand the meaning of marriage. A disabled adult is often considered to have legal capacity to marry even though he or she seems to understand marriage less well than a teenager who cannot marry. Commitment to an institution for the mentally ill is not determinative of capacity to marry, nor is appointment of a conservator to manage a person's property.

In the late nineteenth century and through much of the twentieth, many states also barred people with certain communicable diseases, especially venereal disease, from marrying. Other states required blood tests as a prerequisite to getting a marriage license. Testing requirements were in decline until the onset of the AIDS epidemic.

Limits Based on Relationship. Laws that forbid marriage between people related to one another by blood or marriage are the most widespread kind of barrier to marriage in the world, though the contours vary significantly from society to society. Typical U.S. rules prohibit marriage between a person and his or her ascendants or descendants, siblings, and aunts or uncles. Some states extend the bar to first cousins.

Voluntary Consent. Besides having adequate mental capacity to marry, a person must enter marriage freely. Traditionally, fraud duress had to be quite extreme to warrant a finding that the marriage was invalid. These restrictive definitions were said to protect society's interest in preserving the indissolubility of marriage. As divorce laws have been relaxed, the definitions of fraud and duress have become correspondingly more liberal. Traditionally, duress meant the use or threats of physical force, and only misrepresentations of willingness and ability to have sex and children, and, for women, of chastity, constituted fraud. Modern cases expand the concept of fraud so that a person is entitled to an annulment if he or she cannot live in the marriage because of the deceit. Still, false representations of financial status or the like are typically not enough.

Joke and Limited Purpose Marriage. Sometimes people participate in an apparently valid marriage ceremony but then later claim that they did not intend to be married because the whole thing was a joke or because they only intended to obtain some legal benefit of marriage without taking on all the rights and duties. The latter is sometimes called "limited purpose marriage." While older cases generally denied annulments on such facts, modern courts tend to grant annulments, saying that public policy does not require forcing people to be married against their will.

The cases are more complex when the issue is whether a limited purpose marriage is effective for obtaining legal benefits of marriage. Case law clearly establishes that even though a domestic relations court might refuse to annul the marriage, the "marriage" may not be valid for obtaining some ancillary benefit (*Lutwak* v. *U.S.* (1952)).

Formalities and Common Law Marriage. All states have statutes prescribing formalities for ceremonial marriage. In most states, this is the exclusive way of marrying. In a handful of states, the alternative is common law marriage.

The usual required marital formalities are a license, a fee, a waiting period, and a ceremony. Statutes may prescribe who may officiate at the ceremony, and its form. If people fail to comply with all the statutory formalities, and the validity of the marriage is later questioned, courts usually conclude that the parties are validly married because of the social interest in protecting expectations arising from the belief that the parties were married.

In the District of Columbia and eleven states, parties may enter into a common law marriage. If parties have a common law marriage, such a marriage has all the effects of ceremonial marriage. To enter into a common law marriage, the parties must be eligible to marry each other, and must intend to be married, live together, and represent themselves to the world as married. Contrary to popular belief, most states do not impose a minimum time of cohabitation for common law marriage. These requirements have been modified by statute in some states.

People rarely deliberately enter into common law marriage. Instead, the parties have usually lived together, sometimes for years, and someone raises the claim of common law marriage when the relationship ends. The issue is whether the relationship will be given the legal effect of marriage for purposes of divorce, inheritance, survivors' benefits, and the like, or whether the parties will be treated as mere roommates.

Courts' receptivity to common law marriage varies greatly. A finding of common law marriage validates the expectations that arise from the parties' conduct, but often the parties' conduct is ambiguous. To the extent that courts are reluctant to accept claims of common law marriage, they are emphasizing the importance of the voluntary assumption of marital duties and protection against fraudulent claims.

The states that allow common law marriage are Alabama, Colorado, Iowa, Kansas, Montana, Oklahoma, Pennsylvania, Rhode Island, South Carolina, Texas, and Utah. Parties who have a substantial connection with one of these states and who validly enter a common law marriage there are also regarded as married in other states. Some cases require that the parties be permanent residents of a state in order to enter into a common law marriage there, while others require that people who visit regularly have sufficient connection.

Same-Sex Marriage. All American states prohibit same-sex couples from marrying. While this bar has been challenged on constitutional grounds a number of times, only two challenges have succeeded in part. In *Baehr* v. *Lewin* (1993), the Hawaii Supreme Court held that statutes that prevent a person from marrying someone of the same sex might violate the state constitution. While the case was still in the courts, however, the Hawaii legislature proposed an amendment to the state constitution to allow the legislature to ban same-sex marriage, but also enacted a law allowing couples ineligible to marry to register as reciprocal beneficiaries and to receive many of the benefits formerly available only to married couples. In *State* v. *Baker* (1999), the Vermont Supreme Court held that the state constitution required that same-sex couples have access to the same benefits under state law that married couples have. In response, the state legislature enacted a civil union law that gives same-sex couples the same rights as married couples but does not allow them to marry formally (see HOMOSEXUALITY AND THE LAW).

Procedures for Challenging the Validity of a Marriage. An annulment is a judicial declaration that a purported marriage is invalid. In earlier times, when divorce was rare, annulment was important as the only legal way for a person to get out of marriage and be eligible to remarry. Today, most states provide that the children of an annulled marriage are legitimate. In some states, a court's authority to divide property or award alimony at annulment is less than at divorce, but in many others, a court has the same authority whether the action is for annulment or dissolution.

The validity of a marriage may also be attacked in some other legal proceeding when the rights of the parties depend on whether the marriage was valid. For example, after one "spouse" dies, the decedent's heirs may claim that the "surviving spouse" is not entitled to a share of the estate because the marriage was invalid.

Invalid marriages were traditionally classified as either void or voidable. In theory, a void marriage never had any legal effect; a voidable marriage is legally effective until declared invalid by a court. However, because courts apply these labels inconsistently, people who have purported to enter into a prohibited marriage should not assume that the marriage has no legal effect. If they want to end the relationship, they should obtain an annulment or a divorce.

Constitutional Right to Marry. Constitutional protection for the right to marry dates from the civil rights movement of the 1960s. *Loving* v. *Virginia* (1974) held that a statute forbidding racial intermarriage violated the equal protection provisions of the U.S. Constitution. Though the Supreme Court in *Loving* called marriage a "fundamental right," the rationale of the case is unclear because the statute also involved an explicit race-based rule. *Zablocki* v. *Redhail* (1978) defined the constitutional status of the right to marry more clearly. The Supreme Court reiterated that marriage is a fundamental right, which means that rules denying access to marriage must be substantially related to important state interests. While the Court held that the statute challenged in *Zablocki* failed this test, it noted that other regulations, such as age limits, would probably not. A year earlier, in *Califano* v. *Jobst* (1977), the Supreme Court

held that a rule that burdens marriage, and indirectly makes marriage more difficult, is treated more deferentially. So long as the rule is rational, it is constitutional.

[*See also* Children's Rights; Family Law]

• William Q. deFuniak and Michael J. Vaughan, *Principles of Community Property*, 1971. Mary Ann Glendon, *The New Family and the New Property*, 1981. Michael Grossberg, *Governing the Hearth: Law and the Family in Nineteenth-Century America*, chs. 3, 4; 1985. Homer H. Clark Jr., *The Law of Domestic Relations in the United States*, chs. 2, 3, 6, 7, 10; 1988. Mary Ann Glendon, *The Transformation of Family Law: State, Law, and Family in the United States and Western Europe*, chs. 2, 3; 1989. John DeWitt Gregory, Peter N. Swisher, and Sheryl L. Scheible, *Understanding Family Law*, chs. 2, 3 4, 6; 1993. Dagmar Coester-Waltjen and Michael Coester, *International Encyclopedia of Comparative Law*, vol. IV, ch. 3, "Formation of Marriage," 1997. Leslie J. Harris and Lee E. Teitelbaum, *Family Law*, chs. 1, 2, 3; 2000.

—Leslie J. Harris

MARSHAL. *See* Court Officers.

MARSHALL, JOHN (1755–1835), chief justice of the United States, 1801–35, was born on September 24, 1755, in Fauquier [then Prince William] County, Virginia. He was the eldest of fifteen children of Thomas Marshall, a planter and county leader, and Mary Randolph Keith, a clergyman's daughter descended from one of Virginia's first families. At age fourteen Marshall spent a year at an academy in a neighboring county, which was followed by a year of study at home with the local parish priest. These two years of formal schooling provided him the rudiments of a classical education.

Marshall entered military service at the onset of the War of Independence, rising to the rank of captain in the Continental army. He saw action at Brandywine Creek, Germantown, Monmouth, and Stony Point and survived the winter's encampment at Valley Forge in 1777–78. On temporary leave from the army, Marshall in 1780 attended a course of law lectures by George Wythe at the College of William and Mary. Wythe's lectures constituted the future chief justice's only formal law study and supplemented his self-education.

Marshall commenced his law career in earnest after moving permanently to Richmond in 1784. He rapidly ascended the professional ladder, distinguishing himself among the small fraternity of lawyers who practiced in the state superior courts. During the 1780s and 1790s he served periodically in the state legislature. He was a delegate to the state ratifying convention of June 1788, where he made a notable speech defending the judiciary article of the *Constitution. After the new government began operation in 1789, Marshall repeatedly declined offers to run for Congress or to accept a federal appointment, not yet ready to give up a lucrative law practice.

Marshall attracted public notice as the leading Virginia defender of the Washington administration. He was warmly received when he traveled to Philadelphia to argue the case of *Ware* v. *Hylton* (1796) in the *Supreme Court. In his only appearance as a lawyer in that court, Marshall acquitted himself well in a losing cause. In 1797 he accepted a diplomatic appointment to France. The publication of his dispatches detailing the abortive "X, Y, Z" negotiations made him a national hero on his return home in 1798. Elected to Congress the following year, Marshall proved to be a formidable spokesman for the Adams administration. In May 1800 the Virginian entered the cabinet as secretary of state, a post he held until the end of Adams's term. With the resignation of Oliver Ellsworth as chief justice in October 1800, Adams turned to his secretary of state. Marshall took the oath of office as the fourth chief justice of the United States on February 4, 1801.

During the next three decades, Marshall laid the foundations for the Supreme Court's institutional role as the preeminent interpreter of the Constitution and as the arbiter of conflicts arising from the clash of federal and state *sovereignties. In *Marbury* v. *Madison* (1803) and in subsequent cases, the chief justice successfully affirmed the Court's duty to consider the Constitution as paramount law in its ordinary exercise of adjudicating cases and to invalidate acts held to be repugnant to that law. His principal contribution to American constitutional law was to solidify the practice of *judicial review by adapting the traditional methods of *common law interpretation to the novel task of expounding the Constitution.

Except for *Marbury*, which struck down a portion of the federal judiciary act, Marshall invoked judicial review exclusively against acts of the state legislatures. In one line of cases he applied the *contract clause to void state laws and uphold vested rights. *Fletcher* v. *Peck* (1810) extended the clause's reach to public grants of land; *Dartmouth College* v. *Woodward* (1819) brought corporate charters within the clause's protection; and *Sturges* v. *Crowninshield* (1819) ruled that state bankruptcy acts discharging a debtor from full *liability unconstitutionally impaired the obligation of contract. Marshall insisted that the contract clause embraced prospective as well as retrospective

bankruptcy laws, but a Court majority upheld the former in *Ogden* v. *Saunders* (1827)—which brought forth Marshall's only dissent in a constitutional case. In another line of cases the chief justice employed with equal effect the supremacy clause to invalidate state legislation. Here the leading opinions were *McCulloch* v. *Maryland* (1819), which disallowed a state tax on the Bank of the United States, and *Gibbons* v. *Ogden* (1824), which set aside New York's laws creating a monopoly over steamboat navigation on the state's waters.

Marshall construed the Constitution broadly not only to restrict state powers but also to give full effect to the powers conferred on the federal government. *McCulloch* affirmed Congress's authority to charter a national bank as a legitimate exercise of its discretion to choose the means for executing its express powers. *Gibbons* expansively defined Congress's power to regulate interstate commerce. In *Cohens* v. *Virginia* (1821) and in *Osborn* v. *Bank of the United States* (1824), Marshall contended that the Constitution conferred broad jurisdiction on the federal judiciary to decide cases arising under the Constitution and federal laws. These nationalizing opinions also set forth other propositions that became settled principles of American constitutional law, namely, that the Constitution was the constituent act of the people of the United States, not a compact among sovereign states; that the Constitution created a real government, one of enumerated powers yet supreme within its sphere of action; and that the Constitution, as merely a general outline designating only the important objects, was to be construed in an enlarged sense, not in a restrictive sense appropriate to a detailed legal code.

Marshall died in on July 6, 1835 in Philadelphia, where he had sought medical treatment for a liver problem.

[*See also* Supreme Court of the United States]

• George L. Haskins and Herbert A. Johnson, *Foundations of Power: John Marshall, 1801–15*, 1981. G. Edward White, *The Marshall Court and Cultural Change, 1815–35*, 1988. Charles F. Hobson, *The Great Chief Justice: John Marshall and the Rule of Law*, 1996. Jean Edward Smith, *John Marshall: Definer of a Nation*, 1996. Herbert A. Johnson, *The Chief Justiceship of John Marshall, 1801–1835*, 1997. David Robarge, *A Chief Justice's Progress: John Marshall from Revolutionary Virginia to the Supreme Court*, 2000.   —Charles F. Hobson

MARSHALL, THURGOOD (1908–1993), civil rights lawyer and Supreme Court justice, 1967–91. Marshall's father was the chief of staff at an elite private club; his mother, an elementary school teacher. After attending the African-American Lincoln University in Pennsylvania, Marshall went to Howard Law School rather than the segregated University of Maryland Law School.

While at Howard, Marshall became one of Charles Hamilton *Houston's protégés. The law school's academic dean, Houston revitalized the school by insisting that its students adhere to the highest academic standards in the course of learning how to use law as a tool for "social engineering." Marshall assisted Houston in the defense of George Crawford, an African-American handyman charged with murder in northern Virginia. During the course of his work for Houston, Marshall learned the importance of detailed investigation of facts and careful preparation for trial, traits that came to characterize his work as a lawyer.

After graduating first in his class from Howard in 1933, Marshall opened his own law practice in Baltimore. Struggling to make a living during the Great Depression, Marshall attracted a few important clients from the African-American community, including the publisher of the local African-American newspaper, and devoted a great deal of his time helping build the local chapter of the National Association for the Advancement of Colored People (NAACP). His first major *civil rights case was a successful challenge to *segregation at the University of Maryland Law School.

Working as the NAACP's special counsel, Houston elaborated a plan for systematic attacks on segregation that included challenges to segregation in higher education and unequal salaries paid to teachers in African-American schools. Marshall enthusiastically promoted Houston's plan, using Maryland as the site for some of the earliest salary challenges. Houston encouraged Marshall to move from Baltimore to the NAACP's headquarters in New York, where Marshall served as Houston's assistant and then, when Houston returned to Washington and his private practice in 1938, as the NAACP's principal lawyer.

From the late 1930s through 1961 Marshall coordinated the NAACP's legal activities. Ultimately Marshall won twenty-nine Supreme Court cases. He was one of the NAACP's most charismatic figures, whose speeches throughout the country served to build the NAACP's membership. His most important activities involved the attack on segregated education. He pursued Houston's strategy of attacking segregation in higher education, using victories in university cases to develop theories that could eventually be used in challenging segregation in elementary and secondary educa-

tion. The Supreme Court ruled in the NAACP's favor in a series of cases from 1938 through 1950, when the Court's decision invalidating segregation in Texas's law school provided Marshall with a solid theory to attack segregation in elementary and secondary schools.

Marshall oversaw five NAACP school segregation cases and was the trial lawyer himself in one of them. The cases reached the Supreme Court under the name *Brown v. Board of Education. Argued twice on the merits and then, after the Court found segregation unconstitutional, once more on the question of *remedy, the cases were Marshall's greatest victory and secured him a place in the history of American constitutional law.

The South resisted complying with Brown and several states launched attacks on the NAACP and its lawyers. Much of Marshall's time in the late 1950s was devoted to fending off those attacks. His first wife died in 1955; Marshall remarried and soon began a family. Drained by the burdens of travel and wanting to spend more time with his young sons, Marshall accepted President John F. Kennedy's appointment to the federal Court of Appeals for the Second Circuit in 1961. Marshall served on that court, for four years. In 1965 President Lyndon B. Johnson appointed Marshall *solicitor general, the government's representative in the Supreme Court. Both Johnson and Marshall anticipated that Johnson would appoint Marshall to the Supreme Court when the opportunity arose. In 1967 Marshall was nominated and confirmed as the first African-American justice of the Supreme Court, where he served until 1991.

Marshall joined a Court dominated by liberals, including Chief Justice Earl *Warren. The Court's composition changed rather quickly, and by 1972 Marshall had become one of the Court's persistent liberal dissenters. Along with Justice William J. *Brennan, Marshall was a consistent opponent of *capital punishment; as the Court's only member who had represented defendants facing the death penalty, Marshall regularly insisted to his colleagues that capital punishment could not be administered fairly. Marshall's opinion for the Court in Stanley v. Georgia (1969) emphasized the connection between speech and *privacy; his opinion in Police Department of Chicago v. Mosley (1972) articulated the rule that distinctions among types of speech based on their content or viewpoint were particularly questionable.

Marshall's most substantial contribution to constitutional jurisprudence was his theory of the *equal protection clause. The Court's stated doctrine divided equal protection claims into two rigid 'tiers,' one involving suspect classifications like race and constitutionally protected rights, the other involving all other classifications and claims. According to the Court, equal protection claims in the higher tier almost always succeeded while those in the lower tier almost never did. Marshall argued that this two-tier structure did not accurately describe the Court's own decisions or provide a sensible structure for constitutional analysis. Instead, he argued, the Court should adopt a "sliding scale" approach, in which the Court's examination of equal protection claims varied according to the nature of the interest adversely affected and to the basis on which the classification was made. Most academic commentators agreed that Marshall's analysis was sensible, but the Court continued to use the "two tier" approach.

Marshall brought a unique perspective to the Supreme Court. An accomplished raconteur, Marshall used anecdotes and personal recollections to prod his colleagues into acknowledging the social reality of the way in which justice was administered in the United States. When Marshall retired, his colleagues commented on the importance his presence had for them in reminding them that the law made a difference in people's lives. Still, his role among his more conservative colleagues remained the dissenter's. Marshall's close friend William J. Brennan retired in 1990; finding the job increasingly difficult as he aged, and without Brennan's companionship, Marshall himself retired in 1991. He died of heart failure in 1993. His body lay in state at the Supreme Court, where thousands of people streamed past.

[*See also* Supreme Court of the United States]

• Jack Greenberg, *Crusaders in the Courts: How a Dedicated Band of Lawyers Fought for the Civil Rights Revolution*, 1994. Carl Rowan, *Dream Makers, Dream Breakers: The World of Justice Thurgood Marshall*, 1994. Mark Tushnet, *Making Civil Rights Law: Thurgood Marshall and the Supreme Court, 1936–1961*, 1994. Mark Tushnet, *Making Constitutional Law: Thurgood Marshall and the Supreme Court, 1961–1991*, 1997. Juan Williams, *Thurgood Marshall: American Revolutionary*, 1998. Mark Tushnet, ed., *Thurgood Marshall: His Speeches, Writings, Arguments, Opinions, and Reminiscences*, 2001.

—Mark V. Tushnet

MARTIAL LAW —the control of civilians by their own military forces in emergency circumstances— must be distinguished from military government, in which armed forces exercise control over a belligerent's territory, and from military law—(the internal regulation of the armed forces). Further, a distinction must be made between the domestic use of troops in aid of civil authorities, under the doctrine of *posse comitatus*, and their use to enforce a proclamation of martial law. When martial law is proclaimed it may be absolute, a complete suppression of civil authority by the military, or qualified, in which some operations of government remain in civilian hands. Finally, any discussion of martial law must recognize the consequences of its application in a federal system.

In each state the *governor is the commander in chief of the National Guard, a term that has come to be synonymous with "militia." Few state constitutions expressly provide authority for a declaration of martial law but many provide that the governor may employ the state's militia to suppress insurrection, repel invasion, and execute the laws. Governors and, in some states, local officials, may exercise their *police power by calling on the guard to suppress riots or protect property in the aftermath of a natural disaster. When troops act in aid of the civil authority they are not acting "under martial law," but the judge-made rules regulating their behavior do not distinguish between the two classifications. Most important martial law judicial opinions involve the militia or the guard carrying out their state constabulary functions. In *Luther* v. *Borden* (1849), the Supreme Court ruled that Rhode Island authorities accused of *trespass could justify their right of entry on private *property by citing a declaration of martial law in order to combat insurrection in that State. Although the Court in *Borden* and in *Moyer* v. *Peabody* (1909) spoke of the conclusiveness (i.e., unreviewability) of a State's decision to proclaim martial law, its ruling in *Sterling* v. *Constantin* (1932) distinguished incidents where breach of the peace demanded immediate action from those in which there was no threat of violence. In the latter situation, executive decisions to proclaim martial law were subject to *judicial review as to their necessity.

Between 1880 and 1930 state and federal troops were routinely used to put down industrial disorders. State law suits seeking injunctive relief were rare. Most reported cases involved claims that the petitioner's right to a writ of *habeas corpus* had been denied by the military authorities; a few involved *tort claims or criminal prosecutions. State reports from Colorado, Montana, Idaho, West Virginia, and Pennsylvania offer particularly useful sources although those decided before the *Constantin* decision overly emphasize the nonreviewability of executive action (see EXECUTIVE POWER).

Although the term "martial law" does not appear in the Constitution, commentators and courts agree that federal authorities are implicitly authorized to impose military rule in states or territories in order to repel invasion, suppress insurrection, or execute federal law. Supreme Court decisions during the *Civil War and World War II established the present contours of the federal doctrine and, by implication, state law as well. In *Ex parte Merryman* (1861) Chief Justice Roger B. *Taney, sitting on circuit, ruled that only *Congress, not the president, could suspend the writ of *habeas corpus*. The president ordered the army not to respond to the writ and Congress subsequently delegated its authority to the president. In *Ex parte Milligan* (1866), decided after the Civil War, a sharply divided Supreme Court concluded that military commissions (courts established under martial law declared by the president) could not be employed to try civilians unless civilian courts were actually closed and, in *dicta*, concluded that Congress could not authorize trial by commission if civil courts were open. *Merryman* and *Milligan* were the only two instances of presidential action, but subordinate federal officers, both military and civilian, have invoked martial law powers. The most famous incident involved the suspension of *habeas corpus* and establishment of military commissions by the governor of Hawaii in World War II. In *Duncan* v. *Kahanamoku* (1946), the last martial law case decided by the Court, seven justices agreed that, under the circumstances, the governor had exceeded his authority. They did not agree on the criteria to be used in deciding such cases.

Many instances described as the imposition of martial law involve use of federal or state troops in aid of federal or state civil authorities. The 1957 use of federal troops in Little Rock, Arkansas, to enforce federal *civil rights laws, and their 1992 mobilization to suppress rioting and protect property in Los Angeles did not involve the dissolution of civil authority. The use of federal troops for law enforcement is subject to the Posse Comitatus Act, passed in 1878, which supplemented earlier statutes by requiring explicit presidential approval before federal troops could be used to enforce laws at the request of local and state officials or federal marshalls. Federal troops, and state troops called into federal service under the Calling Forth provisions of the Constitution have, with one noteworthy exception, remained under federal civilian control. The Army's official history identifies the Coeur d'Alene (Idaho) 1899 labor disturbances as the sole occasion where a local military commander violated *Milligan* principles and failed to follow the Posse Comitatus Act. There is no similar history of state use of military forces but the

sources available do not suggest that militia commanders routinely abused the authority granted them by their governors. Thus, the legal problem posed by martial law and its variants is not civilian control over the military but judicial control over the executive and legislative branches' delegation of authority to the armed forces. The history of judicial review in the United States belies the Duke of Wellington's apothegm that martial law is nothing more nor less than the will of the general.

[*See also* Military Justice]

• William Winthrop, *Military Law and Precedents*, 2d ed., 1920. Charles Fairman, *The Law of Martial Rule*, 1930. Frederick Bernays Wiener, *A Practical Manual of Martial Law*, 1940. Robert W. Coakley, *The Role of Federal Military Forces in Domestic Disorders, 1789–1878*, 1988. Clayton D. Laurie and Ronald H. Cole, *The Role of Federal Military Forces in Domestic Disorders, 1877–1945*, 1997. William H. Rehnquist, *All The Laws But One: Civil Liberties in Wartime*, 1998.

—Michael F. Noone Jr.

MARXIST AND POST-MARXIST THEORIES OF LAW. It is impossible to speak knowledgeably about the embedded nature of law in society without addressing the central notions of Karl Marx's political theory. What distinguishes Marx from all other Western philosophers is that he argued that the point of all philosophy is not to merely *interpret* the world, but to *change* it. Karl Marx (1818–1882), born in Trier, Germany, located in the Rhineland and home of German socialism, and raised in a Jewish family, is best known as the author of *Das Kapital* and co-author with Friedrich Engels of the *Communist Manifesto*, works that have earned him a reputation as a revolutionary advocate of world communism and emancipator of the working class.

Marx belongs to an elite set of Western thinkers like Vico, Schelling, and Hegel, who attempted to make sense of every sphere of social life. Trained as a philosopher, Marx wrote on such diverse subjects as law, history, anthropology, and, most brilliantly, on economics. In an age steeped in religious dogma, Marx maintained the necessity of an economic interpretation of history that some have criticized for being materialistic or scientific. Nevertheless, contrary to the critics who read Marx as a crude reductionist, Marx sought to unveil the economic conditions that shape the legal and political institutions of modern capitalist societies. Marxist theory is no more materialistic nor scientific than any other attempt to account for the historic process of capitalist development, as the liberal economist Joseph A. Schumpeter has recognized.

Marxist theory can be understood in terms of two propositions about the economic foundations of human development. First, Marx identified economic conditions of class struggle as a fundamental determinant of history and culture. Second, he viewed the entire modern history of capitalist societies as bound up with the relationship between labor and capital. From these two propositions of history and sociology, Marx proclaimed the revolutionary insight that legal and political institutions represent the "superstructure" of class interests. At the "base" stands the relationship of production and the site of struggle of social class on which the "superstructure" of legal and political institutions and the ideology of the state itself rests. From this insight, Marx was able to proclaim that social practices cannot be fully grasped without the insights of a concrete historical description of the dynamic role of capital accumulation and labor conditions.

Karl Marx was thus the first to comprehend the importance of the relationship between law and *economics. In *Das Kapital*, Marx comprehensively examined how legal institutions function with the intention of producing economic results at every stage of the economic process. No other scholarly work, either before or after Marx, has provided more detailed analyses of the important connection between law and economics in the development of modern society. Marx tries to show how the forms or conditions of production require legal structures, attitudes, and actions that change according to the necessities inherent in economic conditions. In his famous essay "On the Jewish Question," Marx explains how modern legal institutions debilitate human freedom by distinguishing and splitting the state and civil society, public and private interest. According to Marx, only when the meaning of *abstract citizen* is taken back into the individual and lived in everyday life as a *species-being* will the individual recognize and organize power as *social* power no longer alienated from the *political* power needed to make human emancipation complete.

Marx's historic critique of Western capitalism and the relationship between labor and capital were given intellectual support and power by a group of Marxist theorists who built on his early work and gave it a new intellectual foundation. Hence, Georg Lukacs's theory of reification and Antonio Gramsci's concept of hegemony bring to Marxist theory a new psychological and phenomenological explanation, allowing Marxist theory to be relevant to virtually everything that organizes modern societies. Lukacs and Gramsci and the next generation of Marxists helped to give rise to new forms of Marxism that promised to transcend both the instrumental and structural accounts of capitalist societies.

A new breed of post-Marxist theorists have more recently attempted to move Marxist theory beyond the view of law as the instrument of the ruling class (instrumentalism) or the Marxist view of law that equates legal institutions with the inevitable logic of the conditions of production (structuralism). Post-Marxist theory, as illustrated in the work of Fredric Jameson, for example, attempts to transcend the dialectic method of Marxist theory as the foundational method of all critiques of capitalism, and instead to contemplate the possibility of a critique of capitalism without foundations. This postmodern or poststructuralist form of criticism attempts to bring out the importance of race, gender, and ethnic culture in late capitalism, where differences reconfigure in a multitude of ironic relations. Working class alliances with conservative politicians who support capitalists, for example, are the new "transitional" categories in the development of late capitalist society, which post-Marxists seek to explain and describe. Globalization phenomena and information technology are also thought to mark a new millennium in the development of late capitalism. A number of post-Marxists apparently believe that postmodern phenomena are working to transcend the very categories between labor and capital that Marx sought to explicate.

In contemporary legal theory, post-Marxist accounts of law can be found in the work of *critical legal studies and feminist and legal race scholars who have emphasized the importance of race, gender, and class in the progressive critique of law. The effort of critical legal studies and feminist and race theory is aimed at advancing Marx's insight about the inherent interaction between the law and legal institutions and the conflict arising in other spheres of social life. Recent interest in revealing the "politics of law" in the American legal academy reflects the continuing relevance of Marxist thought. Thus the spirit of Karl Marx remains alive, and provides inspiration for guiding the important task of unveiling the economic and social functions of law embedded in contemporary society.

[*See also* Critical Race Theory; Feminist Legal Theory; Jurisprudence, American]

• Karl Max, *The Communist Manifesto*, 1948. Karl Marx, *"On the Jewish Question,"* in *Karl Marx: Early Writings* (T. B. Bottomore, ed.), 1964. Karl Marx, *Capital,* vols. I–III, 1969–72. Joseph A. Schumpeter, *Marx the Sociol-*

ogist, in *Karl Marx* (T. B. Bottomore, ed.), 1973. David Kairys, ed., *The Politics of Law*, 1982. Fredric Jameson, *Postmodernism, or The Logic of Late Capitalism*, 1991.

—Gary Minda

MASSACRE, WARTIME. *See* War, Law of.

MAYHEM at English common law was a form of aggravated battery in which the victim was dismembered or some bodily member was permanently disabled in such a way that the victim was less able to fight. The rationale underlying the crime was the desire to preserve the king's right to the military services of his subjects. Thus the removal of or permanent disablement of an arm, hand, finger, leg, or foot constituted mayhem, but it was not mayhem to merely disfigure a person by inflicting a permanent scar on his face.

All modern forms of mayhem abolish the emphasis on the military significance of the injury, while extending the crime to encompass permanent disfigurement as well as dismemberment and disablement. The modern rationale underlying the crime is to protect and preserve the completeness and normal appearance of the human face and body.

Many jurisdictions have replaced the common-law crime of mayhem with statutory forms of aggravated *assault and battery. These statutory offenses eliminate the requirement for dismemberment or disfigurement, but require that the defendant actually cause or create a risk of some form of serious injury. For example, the aggravated battery of malicious wounding occurs whenever the defendant shoots, stabs, cuts, or wounds any person with the intent to maim, disfigure, disable, or kill. Other modern statutes prohibit specific types of aggravated assaults. Examples include assault with intent to commit a dangerous felony (like rape, robbery, or murder), felonious assault (that is, intent to inflict serious injury), and assault with a deadly weapon.

[*See also* Criminal Law Principles]

• Wayne R. LaFave, *Criminal Law*, 3rd ed., 2000.

—Ronald J. Bacigal

MAYOR. Since the beginning of European settlement, the office of mayor has been a feature of North American municipal government. During the colonial era, municipal corporations along the Atlantic seaboard conformed largely to the English model, with no separation of *legislative, *executive, and *judicial powers. The mayor, who was either appointed by the colonial *governor or chosen by aldermen, presided over the muncipal council and served with the aldermen as a magistrate on the mayor's court.

During the century after the Revolutionary War, however, the office of mayor in the United States developed into an executive position independent of the council and with diminishing judicial responsibilities. Influenced by the notion of *separation of powers and by the three-part structure of the state and national governments, city charters refashioned the office of mayor into one resembling that of governor or president. Indicative of this change was the shift to popular election of mayors. By the third and fourth decades of the nineteenth century, election was becoming the norm, with Boston and St. Louis adopting the practice in 1822, Detroit in 1824, New York City in 1834, and Philadelphia in 1839. Mayors were no longer simply chief aldermen selected by their fellows on the governing boards but popularly chosen spokesmen for the city as a whole. Moreover, mayors gradually acquired powers similar to those of the governors or presidents. As early as 1797 Baltimore's charter granted the mayor veto power, though this negative could be overridden by a two-thirds vote of both chambers of the city council. Over the next sixty years, some other cities followed the example of the federal government and authorized this executive power. In 1830 New York City's mayor acquired a veto, and in 1854 both Boston and Philadelphia embraced the mayoral negative.

In the mid-nineteenth century, however, the mayor's office in the United States remained a mix of the old and new. Most mayors continued to preside over the city councils and to exercise judicial powers in mayor's courts. They wielded little control, however, over most of the expanding administrative departments. The city council or independent commissions oversaw the administration of most municipal services. Thus the older English model of the mayor as chief alderman and ceremonial head of the city survived, but drafters of city charters were grafting onto that model some of the characteristics of the executive as found in the state and federal *constitutions.

During the late nineteenth century the trend toward separation of powers continued, with the mayor winning greater control over municipal departments and the city council's administrative role diminishing. By the 1890s most municipal reformers agreed that the key to better city government was a "strong" mayor. Thus new charters authorized the chief executive to appoint an increasing number of department chiefs and denied the council any role in the process. In 1882, for example, the mayor of Brooklyn was granted absolute authority to select department heads, without confirmation by the council. Two years later New York City also relieved the municipal *legislature of its confirmation power, as did a number of other cities during the following twenty years. Neighborhood representatives on the city council adopted ordinances, subject to mayoral veto, but an executive elected at large was increasingly in charge of administration. By 1900, moreover, mayors in many of the largest cities no longer exercised judicial powers, leaving the municipal executive with a role in local government comparable to that of the president in national government.

This practice deviated from the European pattern. In Europe and the British dominions the notion of separation of powers had not influenced municipal government, and city councils, not the electorate, generally selected the mayor. In Britain and France the mayor was a member and presiding officer of the city council, and in Britain and Canada council committees were primarily responsible for overseeing municipal departments. Many smaller American cities retained this "weak" mayor structure. But the strong mayor plan, characterized by an executive veto and absolute mayoral appointment power, was becoming the norm for America's largest cities.

During the first two decades of the twentieth century, however, two new plans of municipal rule challenged the strong mayor scheme. In 1901 Galveston, Texas, pioneered the commission plan, which defied traditional notions of separation of powers. A body of five commissioners, elected at large, exercised all executive and legislative authority, with each commissioner in charge of one area of municipal administration. One of the commissioners would be designated mayor, but this was strictly a ceremonial post, with no more authority than that of the other commissioners. During the second decade of the century an alternative reform scheme, the city manager plan, won increasing acclaim among good-government advocates. The manager plan retained the traditional city council but shifted authority over municipal administration to a hired manager, ideally a nonpartisan expert recruited from outside the city. Under the manager plan, one of the members of the city council would be named mayor with authority to preside over the council and perform ceremonial tasks; this mayor resembled the British counterpart, playing primarily a legislative role.

The city manager plan soon superseded the commission scheme on the reform agenda, and by the 1990s few cities retained commission government whereas council-manager municipalities actually outnumbered mayor-council cities. Many of the nation's largest cities retained the strong mayor structure, but the manager plan's weak mayor was a feature of government in over 3,200 municipalities with populations of 2,500 or more. Thus in the twentieth century American municipalities freed themselves from the nineteenth-century preoccupation with reproducing the office of governor or president at the local level; instead, at the close of twentieth century, thousands of mayors were not executives but officers presiding over municipal legislatures.

[*See also* Executive Power]

• John A. Fairlie, *Municipal Administration,* 1901. Russell McCulloch Story, *The American Municipal Executive,* 1918. William Bennett Munro, *Municipal Government and Administration,* 1925. Jon C. Teaford, *The Unheralded Triumph: City Government in America, 1870–1900,* 1984. Melvin G. Holli, *The American Mayor: The Best and the Worst Big-City Leaders,* 1999.

MCCARREN-FERGUSON ACT. *See* Anti-Trust Law.

McCULLOCH V. MARYLAND, 4 WHEATON 17 U.S. 316 (1819). The case of *McCulloch* v. *Maryland* played the leading role in defining the relationship between the national and state governments. In *McCulloch,* the United States *Supreme Court, unanimously and for the first time in a fully reasoned opinion, explored the reach of implied congressional authority under the Necessary and Proper Clause of the Constitution (Art. I, § 8).

The case arose when McCulloch, cashier of the Baltimore branch of the Second Bank of the United States, refused to pay a tax levied on the bank's assets by the state of Maryland, claiming that it was not within the power of a state to tax a congressionally chartered instrument of the national government. Maryland sued and won in its own courts, and McCulloch appealed to the U.S. Supreme Court. Counsel for Maryland presented the Court with two major arguments. First, the state contended that Congress had no power to charter a national bank in the first place, given that no such power is specified in Article I, Section 8, or anywhere else in the Constitution. Second, the state contended that even if Congress had such power, the state was acting within its legitimate taxing authority when it taxed a bank doing business in its territory.

On the issue of the bank's constitutional legitimacy, the case turned on the Court's reading of the word "necessary" in Article I, Section 8. After enumerating the assigned powers of Congress in the first seventeen clauses of that article, the Constitution adds, in Clause 18, an "implied" power to enact laws that are deemed "necessary and proper" for making the other powers of the national government effective. Maryland's argument, in effect, amounted to a restriction of the implied power to laws that are "absolutely necessary" for accomplishing the objects of the assigned powers. However, Chief Justice John *Marshall's opinion for the Court pointed out that the framers intended the clause to enlarge rather than to restrict the power of Congress, holding that the words "necessary" and "proper" must be read together to mean "appropriate" or "conducive to" the accomplishment of those objects. The bank, then, was viewed as an appropriate extension of the fiscal, monetary, and other powers of the national government. Marshall also strongly suggested that the Court's decision was compelled by considerations of judicial self-restraint, since the choice of appropriate "means" to accomplish legitimate constitutional objectives was within the discretion of Congress, not that of the courts.

On the issue of the state's power to tax the bank, the Court ruled that such a tax would amount to *taxation without representation, in effect allowing the citizens of one state to tax citizens of other states not represented in Maryland's legislature. Again, the Court strongly suggested that considerations of judicial self-restraint were important, since allowing states to tax instrumentalities of national government would inevitably require judges to draw the line between "allowable" and "destructive" taxation with great precision—a task more suitable for legislatures than for courts.

McCulloch proved to be one of the most controversial decisions in Supreme Court history. The Court's opinion inspired a set of newspaper critiques so vigorous that John Marshall himself felt compelled, pseudonymously, to reply to the Court's critics extrajudicially.

[*See also* Judicial Review; Legislative Power]

• Gerald R. Gunther, *John Marshall's Defense of McCulloch v. Maryland,* 1969.

—Robert Lowry Clinton

MEDIA AND LAW. The law governing the mass media has largely developed since 1930, and most particularly in the second half of the twentieth century. Much of the law comes from the U.S. Supreme Court's interpretation of the First Amendment, "Congress shall make no law . . . abridging the freedom of . . . the press." The au-

thors of the *Bill of Rights, on balance, were more narrowly concerned that public officials not censor newspapers and books before publication than they were about many of the legal issues involving the media today, including protection for news-gathering activities, access to government information, libel and *privacy suits, regulation of the electronic media, advertising, and copyright.

The most important ruling for the press prior to World War II came in *Near* v. *Minnesota* (1931), in which the Supreme Court said that the First Amendment's prohibition against government abridgement meant government officials could not prevent magazines and newspapers from being published, even when authors and editors persisted in publishing racist rhetoric (see SPEECH AND THE PRESS, FREEDOM OF). The government could punish such publications only after the offending articles appeared in print. More recently, the Court affirmed its reluctance to tolerate prior restraint when the administration of President Richard Nixon tried to prevent publication of news stories about a classified history of the Vietnam War that became known as the "Pentagon Papers." The Court also ruled unconstitutional a judge's order that reporters not print information about a Nebraska murder they had learned about in an open courtroom.

The Court also has been extremely reluctant to punish the media for publishing or broadcasting truthful information about public affairs that was lawfully obtained, even when statutes prohibited publication. The Court stated, for example, in *Florida Star* v. *B.J.F.* (1989), that the First Amendment prevented newspapers from being successfully sued for printing the name of a rape victim contrary to a Florida statute. The statute violated the First Amendment, because the state law provided for punishment only of the media and not other forms of communication that might infringe on a rape victim's privacy and threaten her safety. The statute also allowed courts to consider individual case circumstances, such as whether a rape victim's name was already widely known. The Court has not generally provided First Amendment protection for the gathering of news, particularly when that would mean extending a privilege to the press that is not available to other citizens. The Court has consistently said that journalists cannot break laws while gathering news. In its opinion in *Branzburg* v. *Hayes* (1972), the Court established that journalists do not have a First Amendment right to refuse to testify before grand juries about criminal activities they have witnessed, any more than do other citizens. The

Court said individual state legislatures could decide to protect journalists' sources when such individuals might want to talk to the press but feared retribution from employers or public officials they were exposing. A little more than half of the state legislatures have adopted such "shield laws." In addition, sometimes courts have decided that a journalist who has not directly witnessed criminal activity can refuse to testify if the person seeking the information from the journalist cannot demonstrate that the information is specifically relevant to a court case, vital to the case, and not obtainable from other sources.

The Supreme Court has established that the First Amendment does not require that government officials provide to journalists information that is not available to the public generally. For example, the Court ruled in *Pell* v. *Procunier* (1974) that the First Amendment mandate that government not abridge freedom of the press did not require government officials to provide reporters with special access to meet with prisoners, access that would not be granted to other members of the public for security reasons.

The only right of access to information granted by the Supreme Court under the First Amendment has been the right to attend court proceedings, a right also available to other citizens. Beginning with *Richmond Newspapers, Inc.* v. *Virginia* (1980), the Court decided in a series of cases that the press and the public had a constitutional presumption to attend criminal trials, the jury selection at criminal trials, and even pretrial hearings. For a court proceeding to be closed, a judge has to be convinced that an overriding interest, such as the right of a defendant to a *fair trial, is at risk and that the interest cannot be protected short of closure. Proceedings can be closed only long enough to serve the overriding interest at stake. The Supreme Court's decisions, however, do not mean that courts cannot protect from disclosure either proceedings or court records that may infringe on economic and social values such as privacy and trade secrets.

The lack of general constitutional protection for newsgathering has led the federal government and all the states to adopt statutes that allow both the press and the public to attend government meetings and obtain government records. The statutes attempt to balance the need for public knowledge about government activities with the need for government—and the businesses and individuals who deal with government—to protect some information from public disclosure. For example, in the *Freedom of Information Act passed in 1965,

Congress gave to the federal executive branch the authority to classify information that, if disclosed, could endanger national security (see EXECUTIVE POWER). Congress and state legislatures protect from public disclosure many aspects of executive branch decision-making and many details involving criminal investigations. Both the federal and state governments also frequently restrict access to personal information, such as medical reports and personnel records, held by the government. Legislatures often are particularly sensitive to releasing the identity and location of crime victims, in order to protect their safety. They protect from release the names of juveniles who have committed crimes, in the hope that protection from public scrutiny will allow them to be punished but not permanently scarred by a public criminal record. On the other hand, many states have mandated the public disclosure of the whereabouts of criminal sexual offenders, even after they have served their sentences.

Individuals who believe the media have published unauthorized personal information about them can sue, but they seldom win such suits, especially after appeals. Courts usually rule that the information, unless it is medically related, is of legitimate public interest. Individuals also can sue the media for publishing false information about them. They can sue journalists for physically intruding on their privacy by unauthorized entry onto private property or physically putting the safety of family members at risk. Individuals also can sue the media for using their names or likenesses for commercial use without permission.

Individuals can sue the media for damaging their reputations, although First Amendment protections often make it difficult for public officials and public figures to win cases. Libel law changed significantly in *New York Times Co.* v. *Sullivan* (1964), when the Supreme Court said that the importance of a widespread public debate in a democratic society required some tolerance for error when discussing the performance of public officials. The Court then stated, in a series of rulings, that in order to win a libel suit, public officials or other persons who have widespread recognition, or who have voluntarily injected themselves into the discussion of a public controversy, must prove that journalists either knowingly published falsehoods or acted with reckless disregard for the truth. Other persons can successfully sue if they can establish that journalists acted with negligence. All persons suing the media must demonstrate that a story that has been published or broadcast contains false allegations that identify them individually and damage their reputation in a provable way.

The media also have substantial freedom under the First Amendment to report court proceedings, primarily because of the importance the Supreme Court places on journalists' role in public oversight of the judicial system. At the same time, the courts have tried to protect the Sixth Amendment right of a criminal defendant to trial by an impartial jury. Since the 1940s, in such cases as *Bridges* v. *California* (1941), the Supreme Court has given the media wide leeway to comment on court proceedings without being subject to contempt-of-court rulings. However, in the 1950s and 1960s, at least in part because of the development of television news coverage, the Court decided that at least a few defendants had been tried by juries inappropriately influenced by either pervasive media coverage or disruptions involving media personnel inside the courtroom. Finally, in the landmark case of *Sheppard* v. *Maxwell* (1966), the Supreme Court insisted that trial court judges ensure that defendants be tried by juries making decisions based only on evidence presented inside the courtroom. In the case involving Dr. Sam Sheppard, the case that launched the television series *The Fugitive* and multiple movies, the Supreme Court said that judges could issue orders preventing participants in court proceedings from talking to the press and could limit press activities inside the courtroom. The Court said judges also could move a trial away from pervasive local publicity, question potential jury members about their attitudes toward a defendant before they were selected to serve, and isolate jurors during a trial so they were not exposed to discussion of the case in the community and in the press.

The tension between the First Amendment rights of the press and Sixth Amendment rights of criminal defendants was exacerbated in the 1960s with increased media interest in photographing and televising trials, a practice discouraged by the American Bar Association since the 1930s. The Supreme Court first ruled in *Estes* v. *Texas* (1965), in the early years of television news coverage, that the presence of television cameras so disrupted court proceedings and distracted trial participants that cameras must be banned from courtrooms. However, about a decade and a half later, the Court decided in *Chandler* v. *Florida* (1981) that states could permit cameras in court unless defendants could prove that their Sixth Amendment rights to a fair trial would be violated. By 2001, all but one state permitted cameras in state courts, although cameras were still restricted in federal court proceedings.

When adjudicating the issue of cameras in the courtroom, the Supreme Court recognized that different reporting techniques posed different legal problems and therefore could be treated differently under the First Amendment. The Court also has often said that the different attributes of different media require different First Amendment treatment. For example, the Court has decided that government officials ordinarily cannot interfere with decision-making processes of print media editors. In *Miami Herald Publishing Co.* v. *Tornillo* (1974), the Supreme Court said that the paper could not be required to print the reply of a union leader to editorials criticizing him. In *Reno* v. *American Civil Liberties Union* (1977), the Court seemed to say that content on the Internet would be subject to the same minimal regulation as content in newspapers.

Radio and television broadcasters, however, are required to serve the public interest in their programming. In *Red Lion Broadcasting Co.* v. *FCC* (1969), the Supreme Court stated that content regulation of the broadcast media passed First Amendment muster because broadcasters serve a fiduciary role for other citizens. Limited broadcast frequencies mean that not everyone who wants to broadcast can do so. Therefore, those who obtain broadcast licenses must recognize the First Amendment rights of viewers and listeners to receive adequate information about social, political, aesthetic, and moral ideas and experiences. Broadcasters are required, for example, to provide airtime to federal candidates for public office and to provide equal opportunities on the air for political candidates running for the same office. Broadcasters also must provide educational programming for children. In addition, the Supreme Court said in *FCC* v. *Pacifica Foundation* (1978) that because broadcast signals were a "pervasive presence" intruding on the privacy of Americans and "uniquely accessible to children," the FCC could restrict "indecent" programming to times when children are less apt to be listening and watching.

The Supreme Court decided in *Turner Broadcasting System, Inc.* v. *FCC* (1997) that cable programming was not subject to the same regulation as broadcasting, because cable did not use the limited electromagnetic spectrum. However, consistent with the First Amendment, cable operators could be required, for example, to carry the signals of local broadcasters, because cable systems usually could, as a practical matter, control the video programming that most households receive.

Telephone companies have traditionally been regulated as common carriers, companies required to carry the communications of anyone who wants to send a message. Telephone companies have not been allowed to monitor, or interfere with, the messages sent by businesses and individual citizens. The Telecommunications Act of 1996, in fact, protected Internet service providers, such as America Online, from legal liability for content sent through their systems by other businesses or individuals.

Advertising on all media is subject to the regulation of the Federal Trade Commission, which restricts false and deceptive ad content. The Supreme Court has said that advertising receives First Amendment protection only if the ads are truthful and not misleading and if the advertising promotes legal activity. If the advertising truthfully promotes a legal activity, then governments can regulate it only if the regulation satisfies a substantial public interest and is tailored so that it does not infringe on constitutionally protected expression.

The mass media also have to conform to legislation adopted by Congress under its constitutional authority to "promote the Progress of Science and useful Arts" through copyright law. The 1976 Copyright Act protects the ability of authors and artists to receive income for their creative activities. No one, including the media, can use large amounts of someone else's creative work without permission. However, only the style of the artist can be copyrighted, not facts or ideas. The courts and Congress have established, in an attempt to reconcile protection of artists with the need to disseminate information broadly, a "fair use" doctrine that allows the use of copyrighted works in a limited way, usually for creative or educational uses. A use is less likely to be a fair use if a substantial amount, or the most important portions, of a work are copied and if the copy has a significant impact on the market of the original work. The courts also consider the nature of a work, such as whether the small size of a poem makes any copying "substantial copying" or whether a work is unpublished, when evaluating conflicts over fair use.

Even though they experience some constraints, journalists have more protection from government interference and punishment in the United States than anywhere else in the world. Journalists in the United States also, under legislation and constitutional interpretations, have more access to information about their government than do journalists anywhere in the world.

[See also Speech and the Press, Freedom of]

• Leonard Levy, *The Emergence of a Free Press*, 1985. Bruce W. Sanford, *Libel and Privacy*, 2d ed., 1994. Vincent Blasi, "The Checking Value in First Amendment Theory," *American Bar Foundation Research Journal* (1997): 523. Fred Cate, *Privacy in the Information Age*, 1997. C. Thomas Dienes, Lee Levine, and Robert C. Lind, *Newsgathering and the Law*, 2d ed., 1999. Harvey L. Zuckman, Robert L. Corn-Revere, Robert M. Fricden, and Charles H. Kennedy, *Modern Communication Law*, 1999. James C. Goodale, ed., *Communications Law*, 2000. Kent R. Middleton, Robert Trager, and Bill F. Chamberlin, *The Law of Public Communication*, 2001.

—Bill F. Chamberlin

MEDIATION. *See* Arbitration and Mediation.

MEDIATION, LABOR. *See* Labor Law: Labor Relations.

MEDICAL EXAMINER. Medical examiners are public officers charged with investigating sudden, unexplained, unnatural, or otherwise suspicious deaths. Their responsibilities usually include the performance of autopsies and assisting the government in prosecuting criminal cases. Accordingly, medical examiners are almost always licensed physicians and/or forensic pathologists, trained to provide accurate, legally defensible determinations of the manner and cause of suspicious deaths.

In many jurisdictions, the medical examiner has replaced the official "coroner," a title of English origin once bestowed on public officers who performed similar investigative functions. Yet by tradition, coroners traditionally enjoyed substantially greater authority than do modern-day medical examiners. In old England, coroners were the principal conservators of peace in their respective jurisdictions. The office was essentially judicial or ministerial, as coroners conducted full-blown "inquisitions" into the causes and circumstances of death in a "coroner's court," often with the assistance of a jury. There the coroner would hear counsel and evidence on both sides and formally charge the jury to inquire how the deceased came by his or her death. If any individuals were found guilty of murder or homicide at the inquest, the coroner would certify the inquisition, together with the evidence, to the Court of the King's bench. By contrast, medical examiners today act primarily as expert officials in a support capacity: their principal role is to assist police, prosecutors, and other government officials who must independently make critical decisions concerning who—if anyone—is to be charged with a *homicide.

Although no one set of death-investigation procedures applies in the more than three thousand criminal jurisdictions in the United States, there are some common elements to nearly all medical examiners' investigations. Upon arriving on the death scene, the medical examiner ("ME") attempts to document and evaluate any relevant facts concerning the scene itself, and check whether any artifacts or contamination were introduced. At this point, the ME's responsibilities may include collecting and inventorying all relevant evidence, and interviewing relevant witnesses at the scene. After evaluating the death scene, the ME normally establishes and records the decedent's profile information, including his or her medical and mental health and social histories. A full autopsy is then conducted in cases where the ME's office concludes it is in the public interest, or if the prosecuting attorney formally requests an autopsy. Finally, the ME may be responsible for securing transportation of the body prior to releasing it into the jurisdiction of the family.

The system for selecting and retaining medical examiners also varies considerably from state to state. In most states, the chief medical examiner (or "coroner," as the office is still called in some states) is an appointed position: appointment powers may reside in a county board of supervisors, the relevant medical or safety commission in that jurisdiction, the state secretary of health, the governor, or some other political official. By contrast, in a handful of states the chief coroner or medical examiner is chosen by general election. Finally, some states continue to maintain separate offices for an elected coroner and an appointed chief medical examiner, dividing up responsibilities between the two positions.

[*See also* Criminal Law]

• Office of Justice Programs, U.S. Department of Justice, *National Guidelines for Death Investigation: Research Report*, 1997.
—David A. Yalof

MEDICARE AND MEDICAID. *See* Health Law.

MEDICINE AND LAW

Medicine and Law
Medical Malpractice

MEDICINE AND LAW

American law and medicine have had an increasingly complex relationship as each has evolved independently and interdependently during the last century. Traditionally, medical research, and the concomitant development of new medical treatments that have shaped the practice of medicine, had little impact on the law—and vice versa. Until the early 1900s, physicians and hospitals provided medical services with little external regulation and oversight; instead, private researchers and provid-

ers and their professional organizations monitored patient services. But the practice of medicine in the United States changed dramatically in the twentieth century. The early emphasis on the art of healing was supplanted in the late nineteenth century with the rise of medicine's scientific side as a result of advances in medical research. As surgery and other invasive technologies entered the doctor-patient relationship, so too did the questions of where best to care for patients, who should make course-of-care decisions, how much care is medically appropriate, and, increasingly, how to pay for it all. The hospital became the locus for treatment in the twentieth century, and the high cost of that venue led to the creation of health care insurance, first from nonprofit entities such as Blue Cross and Blue Shield and other private, for-profit insurance companies, and later from public insurance such as Medicare and Medicaid. Likewise, hospitals became the place for training new providers, doing medical research, and the creating and testing of innovative medical techniques and technology.

As David J. Rothman chronicled in *Strangers at the Bedside: A History of How Law and Bioethics Transformed Medical Decision Making* (1991), the American law of bioethics developed as these changes altered the relationship between medicine and society. As doctors and treatment in hospitals became more distanced from patients' communities, and a common sense of values could not be assumed, doctors' discretion became increasingly circumscribed by a growing number of public and private regulations. Nowhere is this more clearly in evidence than in medical research. Decades after the widespread acceptance of the Nuremberg principles governing research on human subjects, the 1970s saw the U.S. Public Health Service's forty-year syphilis study at Tuskegee exposed, as well as numerous unethical research practices at Harvard Medical School. In response, Congress passed the National Research Act in 1974, which required the establishment of institutional review boards (IRBs) for research funded by the federal government. While this structure of legal regulations made a significant step at curbing abuses inherent in a system in which the medical investigators themselves determined whether subjects were properly selected and advised, the system continues to struggle with the fast-paced changes in medical research and human experimentation wrought by the limitless benefits of gene therapy.

The relationship between medicine and law continues to become increasingly complex at the start of the twenty-first century, for the practice of medicine has shifted once again. This time, treatment in the outpatient arena—outpatient surgery, alternative, non-Western therapies, home health care—has led corporate providers to integrate hospitals, providers, home care, and other health services to offer a full continuum of care. Thus, Paul Starr's prophecy in his Pulitzer Prize winning book, *The Social Transformation of American Medicine* (1984), about the corporatization of medicine has come true. Now three major changes are poised to affect the way that medicine operates and the way the law responds to it. First, the organization of medical care delivery in the post–managed care age prompts policymakers to question the role of health *insurance in medical treatment and the need to strengthen patients' rights. Second, the continuing movement of the fine line dividing the living and the not living—either at the start or the end of our lives—has forced law to constantly keep up with science. Finally, the mapping of the human genome and the multiple ways genetic information can be used and abused have already provoked legislative responses and court challenges in both the civil and criminal realms.

From major medical insurance to managed care, the changing legal structures of health insurance have had a profound impact on the practice of medicine. While providers in private practice once had an incentive to deliver more medical treatment, cost-containment measures in health maintenance organizations can create conditions for under-treatment, and thereby create a conflict in interest between the physician's duty of loyalty to the patient and the bottom line of the health plan. The United States Supreme Court recently recognized this conflict in *Pegram* v. *Herdrich* (2000), but nonetheless ruled that a patient injured by a cost-containment decision that affected her medical treatment did not have a claim for breach of fiduciary duty under the Employment Retirement Income Security Act (ERISA). Congress is now actively considering an HMO Patients' Bill of Rights to enable patients to hold managed care corporate entities legally accountable for medical treatment decisions made by the plan's physicians.

Advances in medical research and technology that affect the beginning of life have forced the law to adapt as the science has evolved. For example, the progress made in helping women to begin a pregnancy, via a variety of assisted reproduction techniques, has shaped how courts and legislatures approach the regulation of this area of medicine. Whether artificial insemination, in vitro fertilization, or surrogacy—what looked futuristic and outlandish two decades ago is now largely accepted by the public, although courts and legislatures have only just begun to establish rules. Increasingly, courts get involved when couples divorce and the legal status of pre-embryos must be determined. Compare *Davis* v. *Davis* (Tenn., 1992) with *Kass* v. *Kass* (N.Y. App., 1998). Surrogacy, which captured the public's attention in the late 1980s with the Baby M case (*In the Matter of Baby M* (N.J., 1988)), spurred almost half the states to adopt statutes regulating it by 2000. A recent case from California perhaps most vividly portrays the brave new world that science has created for the law regulating *family relations. In *In re Marriage of Buzzanca* (App., 1998), a child was born with five potential parents because it was created by anonymous egg and sperm donors, then gestated by a surrogate mother for two intended parents who divorced soon after the child was born.

Research and treatment developments in neonatology have likewise had an impact on the decision to end a pregnancy. Fetal viability played an important role in *Roe* v. *Wade* (1973) in determining the appropriateness of state *abortion regulation. But viability in 1973, estimated at twenty-eight weeks, has shifted as fetuses survive outside their mothers' wombs at earlier ages. By 1992, advances in neonatal medicine had enabled a fetus as young as 23½ weeks to exist outside its mother's body. Consequently, the United States Supreme Court post-*Roe* has abandoned the trimester approach used earlier; as *Planned Parenthood of Southeastern Pennsylvania* v. *Casey* (1992), made clear, although the Court continues to support the right to an abortion, it also allows states an ever-increasing regulatory role pre-viability as long as no "undue burden" is placed on the mother.

At the end of life, the very definition of death has changed as has medical knowledge. Largely fueled by advances in organ transplantation (and the concomitant need for more organ donations) and the technology that can keep hearts and lungs functioning ad infinitum, medicine and law have come to recognize cessation in brain function as defining the moment of death. This contrasts with the traditional definition—cessation of heart and lung function. In 1979, President Carter appointed medical researchers and practitioners, ethicists, attorneys, and members of the public to participate in the President's Commission for the Study of Ethical Problems in Medicine and Biomedical and Behavioral Research, which urged all United States jurisdictions to accept a Uniform Determination of Death Act. This Act establishes "irreversible cessation of all brain functions" as the definition of death, and this definition has been approved by the American Medical Association, the American Bar Association, and the Uniform Law Commissioners.

Responding to the technological ability to be kept alive, many patients have sought to control decision-making at the end of their lives. The United States Supreme Court, in *Cruzan* v. *Director, Missouri Department of Health* (1990), clearly announced that a patient's right to refuse unwanted medical treatment was inherent in a competent adult's liberty interest. Similarly, the New Jersey Supreme Court had permitted a patient's family to use its substituted judgment to end mechanical ventilation almost fifteen years earlier in *In the Matter of Karen Ann Quinlan* (1976). During the time between *Quinlan* and *Cruzan*, both state and federal legislatures enacted laws sanctioning advance directives such as living wills, durable powers of attorney for health care decision-making, and health care proxies. By the 1990s, all but a small handful of states had enacted statutes that permitted all three kinds of legal documents. Moreover, in 1990, Congress passed the Patient Self-Determination Act (PSDA), which required health care institutions such as hospitals and nursing homes that receive federal funds to provide patients information about advance directives.

But both state and federal legislators and judges have stopped short in determining that the U.S. Constitution provides a federal right to physician-assisted suicide (PAS). In *Washington* v. *Glucksburg* (1997) and *Vacco* v. *Quill* (1997), the United States Supreme Court held that the states' interest in protecting life extends to deciding whether a doctor may aid a patient in committing suicide. So far, only the voters in Oregon have made PAS available, passing the Death With Dignity Act, first in 1994, and then again in 1997 after a court challenge and repeal effort. In contrast, the Netherlands quietly legalized PAS in 2001, becoming the first nation to allow doctors to end the lives of terminally ill patients. The law formalizes a practice discreetly used for decades, making guidelines adopted by parliament in 1993 legally binding requirements. Several countries, including Switzerland, Colombia, and Belgium, tolerate PAS, and Britain, France, Switzerland, and Belgium are considering similar legislation.

Interestingly, while legal policymakers have debated the effect of medical technology on the end of a patient's life, leaders of the medical community have actively opposed the involvement of medicine in executions. In the United States, thirty-eight states continue to impose the death penalty, and physician participation in the execution process is required in many of them. This requirement has created much debate in both law and medicine, focused primarily on whether a physician's participation in the actual execution of criminals is ethical, and whether it is ethical for a psychiatrist to provide assessment and treatment to inmates, who must be found competent in order to be put to death. The major argument against physician participation at any stage is that an execution is a harm, and thus runs counter to a physician's ethical commitment to do no harm. In fact, the American Medical Association has deemed physician involvement in executions unethical. Similarly, a psychiatrist has a duty to prevent harm and cure mental disease, and thus assessing or providing treatment to a prisoner who, if found competent will be executed, presents an ethical dilemma. As execution techniques such as lethal injection become more medicalized in the interests of avoiding *"cruel and unusual" punishment, the debate between law and medicine becomes even more poignant (see CAPITAL PUNISHMENT).

The criminal justice system has also witnessed developments in forensic medicine that have fueled numerous changes in the law. Forensic identification science is unlike most conventional sciences; in the legal system, it uniquely requires the individualization of various samples and the study of abnormalities and irregularities in order to differentiate one source from another. Forensic science methods include fingerprints, dental impressions, handwriting identification, toolmarks, striations on bullets, hair and fiber comparisons, voice spectrograms, neutron activation analysis, blood-grouping, and serum-protein and enzyme typing, as well as the latest technique, DNA profiling.

Clearly the development of DNA evidence in the mid-1980s has had a profound effect on the criminal justice system. First introduced in a 1986 criminal case, this complex and rapidly evolving technology has gained widespread acceptance. The ability to identify a person from the cellular matter in a speck of blood or skin to the exclusion of anyone else except an identical twin is considered the most significant advance in forensic science since the introduction of fingerprinting almost a century ago. But this ultimate forensic ability has created a new evidentiary reality. By 1990, the use of DNA typing as forensic evidence was being seriously challenged, for its use must meet the same criteria for admission as other types of forensic evidence. There are two main standards used to determine the admissibility of scientific evidence at trial: the "general-acceptance" test of *Frye* v. *United States* (1923) and the "sound-methodology" test of *Daubert* v. *Merrell Dow Pharmaceuticals, Inc.* (1993). *Frye* requires that the underlying theory and methodology of the scientific evidence admitted be generally accepted in the scientific community; *Daubert* requires federal judges to review the evidence for its validity rather than solely taking the word of an expert witness. Although the *Frye* method is the accepted standard relied on for DNA admissibility, the *Daubert* standard has effectively disqualified other types of forensic evidence. The choice of the admissibility standard, and new evidence rules, affect the future of the development of new scientific methods. Similarly, new scientific methods will shape admissibility standards and evidence rules.

Beyond questions of admissibility in court, state legislatures have responded quickly to shape the investigative uses of DNA evidence. At the pretrial phase, the use of DNA databases for mass sampling of collected specimens has raised questions about who must submit samples and who should have access to them. At least five states have either expanded the number of crimes for which offenders must submit DNA samples, or lengthened the statute of limitations on crimes where DNA may be present; four more are considering DNA submission. Curiously, the availability of databanks has spawned the "DNA warrant," where prosecutors have a suspect's DNA profile but lack his or her name; thus far, these warrants have permitted prosecutors to avoid statute of limitation problems while continuing to search for the name that matches the DNA. Post-trial, DNA's capacity to exonerate an innocent prisoner raises questions about how long DNA should be kept. By January 2001, DNA testing had exonerated eighty-two prisoners, including ten on death row. These exonerations have not only shaken some people's faith in the criminal justice system, but have impugned the reliability of other types of evidence, from eyewitness identification to hair sampling. In response, at least nine states have enacted laws that provide for post-conviction testing when inmates claim to be innocent, or require the preservation of DNA evidence as long as the prisoner remains in custody. At least eighteen other states and Congress are considering similar legislation.

[*See also* Health Law; Malpractice; Right to Die]

• Paul Starr, *Social Transformation of American Medicine*, 1984. David J. Rothman, *Strangers at the Bedside: A History of How Law and Bioethics Transformed Medical Decision Making*, 1991. Paul R. Billings, ed. *DNA on Trial: Genetic Identification and Criminal Justice*, 1992. Philip Kitcher, *The Lives to Come: The Genetic Revolution and Human Possibilities*, 1997. Judith W. Leavitt, and Ronald L. Numbers, eds., *Sickness and Health in America: Readings in the History of Medicine and Public Health*, 3rd ed., 1997. Leslie J. Reagan, *When Abortion Was a Crime: Women, Medicine, and Law in the United States*, 1997. Martha C. Nussbaum and Cass R. Sunstein, eds. *Clones and Clones: Facts and Fantasies About Human Cloning*, 1999. Le Fanu James, *The Rise and Fall of Modern Medicine*, 2000. American College of Medicine, ed., *Legal Medicine*, 5th ed., 2001. Jay Katz, *Silent World of Doctor and Patient*, reprint 2001.

—Tracy Bach

MEDICINE AND LAW: MEDICAL MALPRACTICE

The medical malpractice system (the "System") is a subcategory of America's *common law, fault-based *tort system. Medical malpractice actions provide a legal venue for imposing financial *liability on physicians, dentists, hospitals, health care organizations, and other health care providers ("Providers") for iatrogenic injuries to patients or third parties that arise directly or vicariously from the provision of medical treatment.

The primary policy rationale for medical malpractice is the promotion of injury compensation and injury prevention. Injury compensation achieves corrective justice by requiring persons responsible for injuries to compensate those injured. Ethicists ponder the efficacy of corrective justice in a system that compensates only some injured patients, and who will ultimately receive only a fraction of their judgments after litigation overhead. Moreover, taxpayers may end up absorbing more of the expense of malpractice, through their payment for inflated medical costs, than the providers who are responsible for the injuries.

The system also promotes injury prevention by deterring providers from delivering substandard health care to patients. Litigation is a costly investment of time, money, and professional reputation. Suits may last three to five years within the civil court system. Injury prevention, as a means of avoiding litigation, is viewed as the system's predominant efficiency rationale.

Economists argue that a no-fault malpractice system provides greater efficiency by spreading litigation and premium costs among all physicians and distributing compensation to more injured patients. This approach compensates all injured patients regardless of provider fault. Virginia and Florida are among the states that have enacted limited no-fault schemes. Countries such as New Zealand and Sweden have adopted broader systems.

Provider liability is premised on the omission

or commission of some act while treating patients. Negligence is the hallmark action of malpractice cases. Plaintiffs must prove that defendant breached a duty of care owed to the patient, and that this breach was the proximate cause of an injury for which compensable damages are payable.

As early as 1898, the courts recognized that every physician owes an implied duty of care to exercise reasonable knowledge and skill common within the medical profession (*Pike* v. *Honsinger* (N.Y., 1898)). The existence of a physician-patient relationship is pivotal in determining whether a duty of care arises. Relationships are recognized when a physician undertakes the responsibility of a patient's care and the patient assents to treatment. Malpractice claims are also available as intentional torts, such as assault and battery and defamation, where a provider intentionally acts in a manner that harms a patient during treatment.

Failure to obtain a patient's informed consent is actionable in negligence and intentional tort. A patient's right to determine his own medical treatment is premised on the common law of self-determination (*Schloendorff* v. *Society of New York Hospital* (N.Y., 1914). The informed consent doctrine requires patient assent to all risk-bearing surgeries, medical interventions, procedures, and treatments (*Canterbury* v. *Spence* (1972)). Providers must also disclose financial interests related to a patient's care (*Moore* v. *Regents of University of California* (Cal., 1990)).

Vicarious liability of hospitals and other health care provider organizations for injuries to patients caused by individual providers is based on the nature of the employment relationship between the parties, particularly the degree of control the entity exercised or appeared to have exercised over a provider's treatment of patients. The doctrines of responde at superior and ostensible agency are central in resolving questions of when employers will be held liable for the wrongful conduct of employees.

Damages recoverable in malpractice actions include economic losses (wages and medical expenses); noneconomic *damages (pain, suffering, and emotional distress); and punitive damages (for malicious or reckless conduct). Provider liability for damages may be absolved or adjusted by affirmative defenses of contributory or comparative negligence if it is proven that the patient caused or contributed to his injury. Likewise, statutes of limitations completely bar legitimate malpractice claims where plaintiff fails to timely file his lawsuit. The immunity doctrine shields state and federal governments from malpractice liability unless immunity is statutorily waived, as in The Federal Tort Claims Act, 28 U.S.C.A. §2671 *et seq.*

Malpractice actions are preeminently a matter of state statutory and common laws that reflect the public policies of state courts and legislatures. State courts often provide plaintiffs with more favorable and accessible judicial forums. In recent years, Health Maintenance Organizations (systems responsible for the delivery, quality, and payment of basic and supplemental health services to a segmented population on a prepaid basis) have escaped vicarious liability for state malpractice claims against their affiliated physicians because of the federal preemptive provisions of the Employment Retirement Income Security Act, 29 U.S.C.A. §1144 (a) (2001), where patient care is provided under a qualified employer health plan. Judicial misinterpretation of this provision created a jurisdictional liability loophole that Congress never intended (*Duke* v. *U.S. Healthcare, Inc.* (1995), but see *Pegram* v. *Herdrich* (2000)).

President George W. Bush successfully lobbied the United States House of Representatives to pass a national Patients' Bill of Rights on 3 August 2001 that allows plaintiffs to sue Health Maintenance Organizations in state court under federal law. This bill must be reconciled with the broader version passed by the Senate on 3 June 2001.

Since the early 1970s, the rising costs of medical liability *insurance and health care have spurred on reform. A national health care crisis threatened at times when insurers left the malpractice insurance industry, leaving physicians uninsured or uninsurable. Insurers demanded reforms that provided market predictability in light of unprecedented malpractice jury verdicts and awards.

Reform antagonists criticize reforms (damage capitations and collateral source offsets) as governmental overtures that violate the *equal protection and *due process clauses of the U.S. Constitution. Courts uphold reforms, such as compensation schemes, that are rationally related to a legitimate state interest (*Fein* v. *Permanente Medical Group* (1985)).

[*See also* Health Law]

• Patricia M. Danzon, *Medical Malpractice: Theory, Evidence, and Public Policy*, 1985. Paul C. Weiler, Howard H. Hiatt, Joseph P. Newhouse, William G. Johnson, Troyen A. Brennan, and Lucian L. Leape, *A Measure of Malpractice: Medical Injury, Malpractice Litigation and Patient Compensation*, 1993.   —Gloria J. Banks

MEGAN'S LAW. *See* Media and the Law; Sex Offenses; Sunshine Laws.

MENS REA, the subjective element for criminality, requires that a defendant have both a culpable state of mind (for instance, not be insane or coerced) and the particular mental state, such as intent, knowledge, recklessness, or negligence, required for the commission of a specific crime.

[*See also* Actus Reus; Criminal Law Principles]

—David S. Clark

MERCY KILLING. *See* Homicide; Medicine and Law.

MERGER. *See* Anti-Trust Law; Corporation.

MILITARY COURTS. *See* Military Justice.

MILITARY DRAFT. *See* War, Law of.

MILITARY JUSTICE began with the founding of the United States. Indeed, the first federal courts were courts-martial conducted within George Washington's army, and they predate establishment of federal civil courts by more than a decade. Yet the Articles of War adopted by the Continental Congress in 1775, and revised in 1776, emphasized military discipline rather than military justice. The revisions were largely the work of John *Adams, supported by Thomas *Jefferson. The two future presidents were well aware of the need for discipline within the military, if only because the success or failure of the Revolution might well depend on it, affecting in turn their careers if not their lives. Thus, Adams drew heavily upon the existing British Articles of War. As revised in 1776, with minor alterations in 1786 and 1806, the American Articles of War remained essentially unchanged until after World War II.

National concern with military justice has been infrequent in American history, while emphasis on discipline and obedience to orders has been consistent. This is understandable, given the role that rank, and tradition play in the military environment. The perennial tension between military justice and discipline however, exists in tandem with a larger uneasiness between the military and the civilian order that it serves. Distrust may be too strong an adjective, but our history is replete with incidents that reflect this uneasiness—even though it is not widely articulated. Thus, analysis of military justice must begin with an awareness of how the framers confronted the place of military authority within the new American republic. They worried about power, and their concerns extended to authority within the military.

Civil Versus Federal Control. Their resolution of this issue boiled down to two essentials: first, that the military would always be subject to civilian control, and second, that this civilian supremacy would not reside in a single federal department. Thus, although the president is commander in chief, the military that he "commands" is shaped, clothed, fed, paid, and regulated by Congress. There can be no doubt that this tradition of civilian control over the military is well established, even though some may question its actual effectiveness. But the tradition of real civilian control of military justice has been much more arduous to incorporate. Two reasons explain this condition.

Throughout American history, the extent of justice within an atmosphere of military discipline has been difficult to define as well as determine. It is a truism that the military environment cannot be equated with civilian society. In the former, one must be prepared to die upon order of the state, and rights which one might take for granted in the latter do not apply. Yet, given the fact that for more than twenty years, the armed services have relied only upon volunteers to join their ranks, the question arises as to what rights did (and does) an American serving in the armed forces retain? While American legal history may provide some clues, it does not offer definitive answers.

Moreover, any issue of civilian control concerning military justice is complicated by the extent of separation between civilian and military judicial sectors. Although there is no evidence that Congress intended the two to be separate, by mid-nineteenth century, they were. Military justice had come to be seen as being completely within the purview of the military, and thus apart from jurisdiction of federal civilian courts. Consider, for example, the Supreme Court decisions in *Dynes* v. *Hoover* (1858) and *Ex parte Vallandigham* (1864). In both instances the Court declined to intervene in a case instituted by the military. On the other hand, in the famous case of *Ex parte Milligan* (1866), the Court barred a military commission from proceeding against a civilian as long as civil courts were operating unimpeded. In the twentieth century, the Court has, for the most part, supported the government's position.

Thus, in actuality it is unimportant to ascertain whether Congress actually decreed that military justice be separate from its civilian counterpart—the Supreme Court has in practice reached such a conclusion. Importantly: while this separation might be considered logical in the context of a military environment, and conservative and hierarchical by nature, it resulted in one area where military justice lagged far behind its civilian counterpart. This was in the matter of *appeals within military justice. By mid-nineteenth century an appellate process was well established both in state and federal jurisdictions, but it had no counterpart in military justice. There was no formal process of appeal by which an accused within the military could seek reversal or relief from a court-martial verdict after it had been approved by the commanding authority. Even when the president reviewed a court martial record, as Abraham *Lincoln did with greater frequency than any of his predecessors, he could not reverse the decision. Although he could indeed issue a pardon, and/or set the verdict aside, such action was not the same as a reversal of a guilty finding upon appeal.

Benefits of Civilian Control. A civilian appellate process represented an opportunity where independent judges could examine the record of a case, and in a context of timely reflection—without haste—consider the facts and law involved, the issues raised, and come to a decision. The process was one that required reasoned deliberation. Military justice, on the other hand, was designed to be rapid in its operation and rigorous in its effects. Moreover, it required flexibility in location as well as finality in its procedure. A court-martial held within the field of conflict where troops might well be on the move, by its nature could not have that aspect of stability that a federal courthouse might reflect. Finally, military justice was seen primarily as an adjunct to command, and thus much less important than the primary military objective—victory.

Drawbacks of Military Control. Those who supported this view insisted that military justice was only a tool to enhance military discipline. The actual procedure of a court martial reflected this perception, which was not seriously questioned until 1917. Thus the commander had unusual authority over the trial, even though he did not actually participate in it. In the first place, the commander selected the members of the court, all of whom were usually subordinate to him in rank. Further, if not satisfied with the verdict, he could "instruct" them to recommend a harsher penalty. Commonly known as "command influence," this procedure can be described as the "bane" of military justice. It was employed by General (later President) Andrew Jackson, and immortalized by Herman Melville in his classic novella *Billy Budd.* Finally, the commander had to approve the sentence before it could go into effect. In the period prior to World War II, it was not unusual for com-

manders to insist on harsher punishment, only to reduce it after the court-martial's conclusion; thus appearing, especially to the accused, as a merciful, rather than a harsh officer.

The accused had no right to counsel as is commonly understood by this term. Historically, the Judge Advocate General (JAG) in addition to prosecuting the case was also responsible for advising the defendant, albeit to a very limited extent. Although the incongruity of having the same party responsible for the success of the prosecution and at the same time the welfare of the defendant was obvious, the system resisted change. Moreover, although the JAG might be a lawyer, in general the individual representing the defendant was not. Nor was there any requirement that legal counsel had to be provided. Although the military insisted that every officer detailed to represent a defendant had to study a booklet of court martial instructions, what Edmund Morgan (later the chairman of the committee that drafted the Uniform Code of Military Justice) wrote in 1919 was more explicit. Defendants in courts-martial, he noted, were often prosecuted by "officers of low rank who wouldn't know a law book from a bale of hay, and as frequently defended by a chaplain who is hardly able to distinguish between a rule of evidence and the Apostle's Creed." (*New York World*, 4 April 1919)

This procedural weakness in courts-martial was matched by another problem, the shocking inconsistencies in penalties meted out by different military courts for the same offense. As with the lack of an appeals process, so here too the system had endured even as the United States gained victory in two world wars. Its imperviousness to change may have been based on the popular perception that one did not want to change military justice in time of war, and in time of peace, the need for such change had vanished. Nevertheless, by 1945, an American generation nurtured by a long tradition of law, litigation, and rights, found these flaws no longer acceptable.

Unified Code of Military Justice. In the wake of World War II, these problems could at last be remedied. After unification of the armed forces in 1947–48 under the Department of Defence, it no longer made sense to have the three branches under different rules of procedure (see PROCEDURE, COURT). A single federal statute applicable to all branches of the military was drafted during 1948–49, and in 1950 Congress enacted the Uniform Code of Military Justice (UCMJ), still in effect today. Passage of the statute with its accompanying appeals courts occurred at a time when a number of European countries were moving towards greater civilian oversight of military justice. It might be noted that American reforms of military justice came even as one totalitarian regime (Nazism) had been destroyed, while another (communism) had been strengthened.

Among other things, the new code established two levels of appellate procedure; first, an intermediate appellate court located within each armed service, with its judges appointed by the Judge Advocate General, and second, a civilian appeals court with three judges (now five) appointed by the president and confirmed by the Senate. The United States Court of Appeals for the Armed Forces has been in operation since 1951, and in most cases is the court of last resort for military justice. In addition, the UCMJ mandated that counsel in a general court martial had to be a trained attorney.

The court's jurisdiction is worldwide, as it can accept cases from courts-martial arising from wherever American armed forces personnel may be stationed. There is little doubt that within its limited purview, the court has made a positive difference in the quality of appellate military justice. Over the years, it has undertaken to bring military justice procedures in line with their civilian counterparts, to the extent compatible with the military mission. It has, for example, dramatically strengthened the authority of the military judge, at the expense of the commanding authority.

On the other hand, the court as an institution is administered by the Department of Defence, and although Congress has insisted that its judges be treated on a par with other federal appellate jurists in terms of salary and perquisites—it has repeatedly declined to grant them life tenure. Although the legislators have glorified this court as the equal of all other intermediate federal appellate tribunals, their action in denying tenure to its judges, and limiting their terms to fifteen years, has inevitably set this judicial body apart from other federal courts. Moreover, senatorial consideration of appointees to its bench rests with the Senate Armed Services Committee, a group not distinguished by its concern for the judicial quality of nominees that come before it.

Further, there are some basic differences between military justice and its civilian counterpart, although it would be a serious mistake to assume without critical examination that military justice is either a contradiction in terms, or markedly inferior to its civilian counterpart. It is impossible to separate the "military" from military justice. And while today courts-martial are viewed more

as legal proceedings rather than adjuncts to command, the constituency they serve is fundamentally different from civilian society, and has unusual requirements and needs. Of necessity, *"due process" means something different in a court-martial than in a civilian trial.

Nevertheless, in some respects the procedures mandated under the UCMJ are markedly superior to their civilian equivalent. Two such examples may be cited here. The military equivalent to a grand jury proceeding, for example, is conducted on a much fairer level than in state and federal courts. Although there is no common standard, in general state grand juries are secret, and subjects of the investigation may not hear what other witnesses testify. Thus, there is no right of cross examination. In the military, the equivalent procedure is public, lawyers may be present, and witnesses may be cross examined. Also, in a court-martial, under certain conditions supervised by the presiding judge, the members of the court (the jury) may ask questions of the witnesses.

Supreme Court Involvement. Since 1951, with one very conspicuous exception, in general federal "civil" courts have not been consistently involved in military justice. The one exception to this pattern is a controversial case *O'Callahan* v. *Parker* (1969), decided by a divided Supreme Court. Speaking for a bare majority, Justice William O. *Douglas rejected court-martial authority concerning an army sergeant who while on leave had committed a felony (attempted rape) off base. This offense was not related in any way to the military, the victim was a civilian, and the assault had been committed at a location under civil jurisdiction. Under these circumstances, the court-martial that had found O'Callahan guilty was without authority to try him. This case is unique as it is one of the very few in which the Court interfered with a court-martial of a member of the military. (The examples cited above in the Civil War era had involved civilians prosecuted by the military.)

But *O'Callahan* turned out to be a very weak precedent, and although it did not overrule the case until 1987, in fact the Court began a slow retreat from its holding almost immediately. Especially obvious under Chief Justice William H. Rehnquist, the Court's tendency has been what can be called one of excessive deference to the governmental claim concerning military necessity. In the years since 1987 one can find very few, if any, Supreme Court holdings that have sustained an appellant's appeal from military authority. Such deference, however, has not deterred the Court from insisting that constitutional rights do apply to members of the armed services, even as it has consistently declined to identify what is included, and to specify when they may be applicable. Thus a member of the armed forces can point to few specific parameters where, for example, the first amendment freedom of *speech applies. In general, the Supreme Court has contented itself with generalities rather than specifics.

Moreover, the relatively few cases the Supreme Court has heard concerning military justice indicate a definite lack of interest in this field. This unfortunate tendency has been reflected in Congress as well. In 1990, for example, that body quietly deleted the requirement that changes in military justice regulations had to be reported to it. The unfortunate implications of such disinterest for effective civilian oversight of military justice speak for themselves. But the extent of civilian disinterest in military justice goes much further. With few exceptions, the subject is not taught in law schools, nor—apparently—does a legal career within the military appeal to our most capable law school graduates. Although public interest always will be aroused by a colorful if not lurid case, in general these are exceptions to the rule. For the most part, and with a skill honed from many years of practice the military leadership has managed very effectively, to isolate its military justice system from sustained civilian scrutiny.

Future Directions. On balance, American military justice represents a system that confronts both potential and peril. On the one hand, the system has succeeded, but it can also be argued that the military's absence of sustained interest in a democratic process, in which it is held in strict subordination to the civil authority, may well be dangerous. Lack of judicial interest can lead to a loss of judicial involvement; thus giving further credence to the dubious assumption that Congress had always intended the military justice system be isolated from civilian oversight. To remedy this situation, civilian courts, especially the United States Court of Appeals for the Armed Forces, remains always ready to intervene where it feels such action is warranted. There appears little doubt, however, that the more effective American military justice is, the more effective will be our armed services. American military justice well warrants continued interest and involvement on the part of the external legal order.

[*See also* Criminal Law; Procedure, Criminal]

• Harrison Hayford, *The Somers Mutiny Affair*, 1960. Homer F. Moyer Jr., *Justice and the Military*, 1972. Richard Kohn, *Eagle and Sword: The Federalists and the Creation of the Military Establishment in America, 1783–1802*, 1975. Thomas Turner, *Beware the People Weeping: Public Opinion and the Assassination of Abraham Lincoln*, 1982. Alan R. Milett and Peter Maslowski, *For the Common Defense: A Military History of the United States of America*, 1984. Russell F. Weigley, *The History of the United States Army*, 1984. Theodore J. Crackel, *Mr. Jefferson's Army: Political and Social Reform of the Military Establishment, 1801–1809*, 1987. Mark E. Neely Jr., *The Fate of Liberty*, 1991. Jonathan Lurie, *Arming Military Justice: The Origins of the United States Court of Military Appeals*, 1992. Jonathan Lurie, *Pursuing Military Justice: The History of the United States Court of Appeals for the Armed Forces, 1951–1980*, 1998. Jonathan Lurie, *Military Justice in America: The United States Court of Appeals for the Armed Forces, 1777–1980*, 2001.
—Jonathan Lurie

MILITARY POLICE. The military police (called MPs in the army and air force and Shore Patrol in the navy) have as their primary function the enforcement of military discipline and order.

Military forces have always assigned personnel to constrain stragglers, deter or capture deserters, take custody of prisoners, and when deemed necessary, contain rowdiness or criminal action by service members. The British Army had provost units for such functions, and in 1778, during the American Revolution, the Continental Army adopted British practice by creating such a unit. After the Revolution, however, from 1783 to 1861, the small U.S. Army simply detailed regular troops temporarily to perform military police functions as needed.

The huge armies of citizen soldiers in the Civil War often proved unruly in the field, in encampment, and sometimes in civilian areas. Both the Union and Confederate Armies created extensive if temporary systems of provost marshals. In 1861, the Union Army established regimental provost marshals to serve as a permanent police force with the duties of preventing riotous conduct, controlling stragglers, and preventing looting and personal violence against civilians as the army advanced into the South. In 1863, the army created a Provost Marshal department, which extended the role of the provost marshals to include operation of the conscription system and control of local government in occupied Southern states.

In World War I, a temporary Military Police Corps was created, with assigned soldiers wearing the "MP" armbands. It garnered American soldiers absent without leave, guarded enemy prisoners of war, and investigated desertion, draft evasion, and related military prisons and prisoner-of-war camps in the United States. In 1920, Congress refused a permanent MP corps, but authorized reserve MP units.

The navy for most of its history has relied primarily upon temporary assignment of regular personnel to maintain order and discipline. The navy assigns sailors to Shore Patrol duty to prevent disorder between off-duty crew members and local civilians. Longer-term security is provided by naval masters-at-arms or by Marines, who are assigned to guard the "brig," the secure prison area aboard ship or ashore.

When the army began mobilization for World War II, Secretary of War Henry Stimson authorized a Military Police Corps on September 26, 1941, and it has remained a permanent part of the U.S. Army ever since. Nearly 210,000 officers and enlisted personnel served in the army's MP Corps during the war, and an MP school was established. During World War II and the wars in Korea, Vietnam, and the Persian Gulf, MPs secured movement in and out of theaters of operation, processed and guarded hundreds of thousands of prisoners of war, and provided protection for military facilities.

Military police operate under and enforce military law—originally the Articles of War and since 1950 the Uniform Code of Military Justice. Military offenses range from disrespect and disobedience, to desertion, insubordination, misbehavior before the enemy, or mutiny. The military codes and regulations were designed primarily to enforce discipline, but increasingly in the last century have sought also to maintain justice within the military.

In regard to criminal offenses (such as robbery, assault, rape, and murder) by service members against American civilians, such cases are tried in civil courts (but in military courts when the crimes by service members are against military personnel or government property). When U.S. service personnel are deployed in allied nations, jurisdiction over such offenses committed against local nationals is generally determined under bilateral treaties. U.S. attempts to persuade host countries to allow the United States to try military personnel accused of the rape or murder of a local civilian have, however, remained a continual source of controversy.

[*See also* Police]

• Brent L. Richens and Russell B. Shor, "18th Military Police Brigade, Three Years in Vietnam," *Military Police Journal* 19 (September 1969): 5. Mary R. Hines, "Military Police Duties in the Federal Army," *Military Police Journal* 11 (Summer 1984): 20. Thomas J. Johnson and Mary R. Hines, "The Battle of the American Embassy," *Military Police Journal* 11 (Summer 1984): 6. U.S. Army Military Police School, *Military Police Corps Regimental History*, 1986.   —John Whiteclay Chambers II

MILITIA. *See* Arms, Right to Bear.

MILITIA MOVEMENT. The Militia Movement is the most recent example of a right-wing paramilitary movement in modern American history. Although the antigovernment attitudes at the core of such movements have deep roots in American political culture, the Militia Movement has departed from earlier organizations in several respects. The emergence of a distinctive ideology associated with this movement was facilitated by several developments, most notably the confrontation with the federal government at Ruby Ridge, Idaho, in 1992 and the siege of the Branch Davidian compound at Waco, Texas, 1993. Members of the movement view themselves as part of the unorganized militia of the states—in effect, as the guardians of the "original" vision of the Constitution. Central to this vision is a revisionist interpretation of the Second Amendment. Although the meaning of the Second Amendment had been fairly settled as a matter of law, supporters of the Militia Movement claim that their understanding of the amendment is truer to the original meaning of the text. This particular populist variant of the constitutional philosophy of originalism, drew as much from the Anti-Federalist opponents of the Constitution, as it did from the Federalists. Supporters of this view not only believe in an individual's right to own weapons, including military-style weapons, but they see the unorganized militia as part of the founders effort to provide a popular check on government tyranny.

The Militia Movement's understanding of gun rights and its radical new view of the Second Amendment is part of a larger change in the ideology of America's gun culture. More mainstream gun rights organizations such as the NRA echoed the same rhetoric as the Militia Movement, attacking agents of the Bureau of *Alcohol, Tobacco, and Firearms as "jack-booted thugs." At the same time, a small but highly vocal group of constitutional scholars advocated a new insurrectionary theory of the Second Amendment that argued that one purpose of the amendment was to allow individual citizens the right to own weapons to check government tyranny.

The Militia Movement's ideology is also heavily shaped by conspiracy theory. The fear of secret government plots to disarm the population is one result of the general disillusionment with the federal government in the aftermath of the Watergate era. The rise of new age millennial ideas about secret government conspiracies exemplified by popular television shows such as the *X-Files* also fueled conspiracy theories. Members of the movement believed that the federal government's gun control policies were the first step to the creation of a police state. Secondly, conspiracy theorists saw American involvement in the United Nations as part of an effort to establish a New World Order in which American sovereignty and liberty would be destroyed. Popular scrutiny of the ideas of the Militia Movement was intensified after the bombing of a federal office building in Oklahoma City in 1995. The arrest of several prominent members of the movement for possession of explosives and illegal weapons caches has further weakened the movement.

The Militia Movement continues to take advantage of the new technological powers afforded by the Internet to spread their ideas and coordinate their activities far more effectively than was possible for earlier right-wing groups. The power of the Internet continues to sustain the movement even as popular interest in its ideas has waned.

[See also Arms, Right to Bear; Civil Rights and Civil Liberties; Terrorism]

• D. J. Mulloy, Homegrown Revolutionaries: an American Militia Reader, 1999. Mark Pitcavage, "Camouflage and Conspiracy: The Militia Movement from Ruby Ridge to Y2K," American Behavioral Scientist 44 (2001): 957–81.

—Saul Cornell

MINIMUM/MAXIMUM HOURS LAWS. See Labor Law: Workplace Issues.

MINIMUM WAGE. See Labor Law: Workplace Issues.

MIRANDA V. ARIZONA, 384 U.S. 436 (1966) is one of the most important criminal *procedure cases ever decided by the United States *Supreme Court.

Before Miranda, the Court was plagued with a difficult question: when is a confession "coerced" (i.e., when have the police obtained a confession by improper interrogation of a suspect)? The Court had used a vague "totality of circumstances" test, considering the methods used by the police and the sophistication of the suspect who was the object of such methods. Because these factors vary from case to case, it was difficult for litigants and lower court judges to determine whether a particular confession was obtained in compliance with constitutional standards.

In Miranda, the Court sought to bypass this problem by enhancing the suspect's ability to "freely" waive his right to silence. The Court required the police, before engaging in "custodial interrogation," to give the suspect certain warnings: "Prior to any questioning, the person must be warned that he has a right to remain silent, that

any statement he does make may be used as evidence against him, and that he has a right to the presence of an attorney, either retained or appointed."

The defendant may "waive" these rights, expressly or implicitly—although subsequent cases suggest that any indication by the suspect that he understands his rights and is nevertheless willing to talk will constitute a waiver. During the *interrogation, if the suspect clearly asserts his right to silence or to a lawyer, the interrogation must cease.

The Miranda Court hoped that the warnings would diminish the need to determine whether confessions were "coerced" under the Court's earlier test—in part because the warnings might dissuade suspects from confessing. This hope has not been fully realized. While some researchers claim that Miranda has substantially reduced the number of confessions obtained by the police, others contend that the reduction is small, partly because the police have found effective ways to comply with the letter of Miranda while undermining its spirit (e.g., by working the warnings into "friendly" conversation with the suspect). Also, in later cases, the Court provided the police with an incentive to continue interrogation even after the suspect has asserted his right to silence or *counsel: the police may use any statements obtained in violation of Miranda to impeach the defendant's credibility if he chooses to testify at his trial (as long as the police did not "coerce" the suspect, under the old test).

[See also Civil Rights and Civil Liberties; Criminal Law Principles; Self-Incrimination, Privilege Against]

• Joseph D. Grano, Confessions, Truth, and the Law, 1993. Richard Leo, The Impact of Miranda Revisited, Journal of Criminal Law and Criminology 86 (1996): 621.

—Myron Moskovitz

MISDEMEANOR. See Felony and Misdemeanor.

MOB VIOLENCE AND VIGILANTISM. Mob violence and vigilantism share a common trait: the use of violence to impose social control or to achieve popular *justice. These forms of violence involve an appeal to shared notions of higher law when the law enacted by the state is seen as morally wrong, inadequate to the task, or nonexistent. Mobs are social groups having no decision-making structure and coming together for political or economic reasons. They often form spontaneously, generally last only a brief time, and are united by a sense of shared interests and purposes.

Mobs can involve dominant groups subordinating less privileged groups, the less privileged protesting against their oppressors, or both groups united against a common perceived enemy. Vigilante groups generally last longer than mobs and take the law into their own hands in situations where the official legal institutions are seen as failing.

Throughout late-eighteenth-century America, mob action spread in reaction to the Stamp Act of 1765, by which the British imposed a stamp tax on all legal documents. For many poor laborers and seamen, the Stamp Act riots offered opportunities to demonstrate pent-up antagonisms toward rich merchants or wealthy officials who abused power. But many merchants, lawyers, and other colonists of more comfortable means saw the issue as *taxation without representation and believed that *property damage hurt the cause. Middling merchants and leading mechanics organized the Sons of Liberty, appealing to popular demonstrations but seeking to limit misconduct and to protect property. Nevertheless, mobs at times exceeded the bounds that the Sons of Liberty sought to set. Rioters in Newport, Rhode Island, for example, moved from the usual hanging of effigies to the destruction of homes, and rioters in New York focused on images of wealth and pretension. By the end of 1765, stamp distributors in all the colonies had resigned their posts.

The subsequent Boston Tea Party played a particularly powerful role in uniting Americans of different classes. The lower classes viewed tea drinking as a symbol of the wealth of an intrusive British military presence that kept the rich in power. The more propertied classes saw resistance to the British tax on tea as a protest against colonial exclusion from British liberty and against an assault—in the form of taxation—on colonial property. On 16 December 1773, five thousand people gathered at the Old South Meeting House in Boston. That evening, selected members of the meeting dumped the contents of 342 tea chests into Boston Harbor. The British reacted by adopting the Coercive Acts (1774), which virtually established martial law in Massachusetts, and by closing Boston's port and sending in troops, thus further fanning the fires of colonial resistance.

If Revolutionary era mob actions and riots such as these encouraged the common man to see himself as politicized, entitled to some role in governing, that new role did not include slaves. Mobs came to play a special role in the South's struggle to maintain its "peculiar institution." Suspected abolitionists were tarred and feathered in the South or ridden out of town on a rail. Northern mobs in the mid-1830s joined the repression, breaking up abolitionist meetings, assaulting abolitionists, even killing them, all without fear of prosecution by the law.

Despite the violence, the abolitionist cause was ultimately vindicated with the end of *slavery in 1865 with adoption of the Thirteenth Amendment. Southern resistance to the new order continued for many decades, often in the form of the lynch mob, southern whites lynching blacks suspected of crimes or of insults to whites. The lynchings served to vindicate southern honor and to reassert white dominance in a way that resort to the formal processes of the law could not.

Lynchings also took place for reasons unconnected with race, such as the "necktie parties" in western states for the summary disposal of thieves, rapists, murderers, and desperados, and the frenzied mob attacks on villainous white men in the North and East. In the twentieth century, race continued as an important theme underlying mob action. In the early part of the century, the pattern continued primarily to involve white-on-black assaults. This pattern changed in the 1960s as African-American rage at white racism exploded.

Riots were sparked in 1964 and 1965 in Florida by the killing of a black woman and by a bomb threat against a black high school; and in Cleveland, by the killing of a white minister who had blocked a bulldozer to protest the exclusion of blacks from construction work. A massive riot in the Watts section of Los Angles, arising from perceived police abuses, followed. The greatest urban riots of American history swept black ghettos in 1967, mob anger focusing on symbols of authority and property associated with white society. A subsequent report of the National Advisory Committee on Urban Disorder blamed the 1967 riots on antiblack discrimination and *segregation in employment, education, and housing and on the growing impoverishment of urban black communities. Congress reacted by passing the Civil Rights Act of 1968, presumably strengthening the laws prohibiting violence against blacks but also criminalizing interstate travel or use of interstate facilities to encourage or participate in a riot.

Vigilantism differs from mob violence in the degree to which it is an organized movement whose members take the law into their own hands. Upper-class frontiersmen who sought to establish in the frontier states the values of the property-holding societies of the more developed areas usually led vigilante actions. The middle classes were the movement rank and file, with the lower classes and outlaws being the vigilantes' targets. Vigilante roundups of ne'er-do-wells and outlaws involved flogging, expulsion, or killing. Usually, organized "vigilance committees" led the violence. Most often such committees were small, perhaps having twelve to fifteen members, but thousands joined the San Francisco Vigilance Committee of 1865.

Vigilantism often arose where regular law enforcement was absent or ineffective because of fear, friendliness to the accused, or bribery and corruption, leading juries to acquit or law enforcement to refuse to act. Lack of jails or their flimsy construction made it hard to stop escapees, and limited law-enforcement resources and arduous transportation made the capture of fugitives difficult and expensive.

But vigilantism also appeared where law enforcement was capable of functioning effectively. This existence of parallel legal and extralegal systems came about because vigilantism was cheaper, keeping down the taxes required to expand law enforcement. Vigilante hangings also more powerfully reinforced frontier society's commitment to re-creating the stable social structure of the developed areas from which its members had migrated. Parallel structures were also used as a way to retake control of a government captured by competing groups or to achieve political and fiscal reform.

Despite the elite leadership of vigilante groups and their conservative goals, their ideology was that of popular *sovereignty: the people are the real sovereigns; whenever those to whom they have delegated authority fail, it is the people's right to take back that authority into their own hands.

[See also Civil Rights Legislation; Extralegality]

• Richard Maxwell Brown, "Violence and Vigilantism in American History," in American Law and the Constitutional Order: Historical Perspectives (Lawrence M. Friedman and Harry N. Scheiber, eds.), 1978. Paul A. Gilje, The Road to Mobocracy: Popular Disorder in New York City, 1763–1834, 1987. Larry May, The Morality of Groups: Collective Responsibility, Group-Based Harm, and Corporate Rights, 1987. Howard Zinn, A People's History of the United States, 1999. Michael Kent Curtis, Free Speech, "The People's Darling Privilege": Struggles for Freedom of Expression in American History, 2000. Ray Raphael, A People's History of the American Revolution: How Common People Shaped the Fight for Independence, 2001.   —Andrew E. Taslitz

MODEL PENAL CODE. The publication of the Model Penal Code (MPC) in 1962 marked the beginning of modern American *criminal law. Along with the Uniform Commercial Code, the MPC is the most significant law reform achievement of the *American Law Institute (ALI), a non-governmental organization of distinguished lawyers, judges, and law professors founded in 1923.

The MPC has influenced criminal law reform in almost all American jurisdictions. It has been cited in over 2,000 state court opinions as well as in hundreds of U.S. Supreme Court decisions. Outside the United States, the MPC is frequently consulted by criminal law reform commissions and cited by legal commentators, particularly in *common law countries.

The MPC was drafted in the 1950s by an interdisciplinary group of experts under the leadership of Professor Herbert Wechsler of Columbia University Law School. The MPC's origins, however, reach back to the first years of the ALI. Soon after its foundation, the ALI undertook a study of the American criminal justice system, which found that a fundamental reform of the entire system was needed. Unlike other areas of law, such as contracts or torts, where a mere "Restatement" of existing law sufficed, criminal law and criminal *procedure required "Model Codes" to guide comprehensive legislative reform. In 1930, the ALI published the Model Code of Criminal Procedure, but the MPC project was not taken up in earnest until after World War II, under Wechsler's direction and with the Rockefeller Foundation's financial support.

The MPC was the first systematic American criminal code. Before the MPC, American criminal law was largely a common law creature, a centuries-long string of judicial precedents emanating from English, and later American, courts. The MPC transferred criminal law from the judiciary to the legislature, enunciating the general principles of criminal *liability in its "general part" and defining specific offenses in its "special part."

American criminal law before the MPC had no general part; it was content to leave the definition of many offenses to the courts. Moreover, state legislatures failed to systematize the offenses they did define in any particular way, other than perhaps by placing them in alphabetical order. The MPC codified basic principles of criminal liability that apply to all offenses, such as *actus reus, *mens rea, and causation, as well as defenses such as necessity, self-defense, duress, infancy, and insanity.

In its special part, the MPC organized offenses by the interests they protected, including those of the person, *property, family, public administration, and public order and decency. Important substantive reforms included a radical revision of the law of *homicide, the curtailment of strict liability offenses, and the elimination of *morals offenses such as *adultery and fornication. In homicide law, the MPC replaced the common law's convoluted system of offenses with three types of homicide: murder, manslaughter, and negligent homicide. It also limited the scope of the traditional felony murder doctrine, which transforms any death caused in the course of a felony, no matter how accidentally, into full-blown murder. Strict liability was restricted to a new category of non-criminal offenses called violations.

[See also Criminal Law Principles]

• American Law Institute, *Model Penal Code: Official Draft and Revised Commentaries,* 1980. Sanford H. Kadish, "Codifiers of the Criminal Law," in *Blame and Punishment: Essays in the Criminal Law,* 1987.

—Markus Dirk Dubber

MONOPOLY. *See* Anti-Trust Law; Economics and Law; Regulation; Technology and Law.

MORALITY. *See* Ethics, Morality, and Law.

MORALS OFFENSES lie at the outskirts of American *criminal law. At the same time, American criminal law would not be the same without them. Their history is one of both steady decriminalization and remarkable resilience. They are as numerous and varied as their scope is difficult to define. Morals offenses are *morals* offenses because they deal with conduct, and sometimes character traits, considered immoral. For that reason, they occupy an awkward position in liberal legal systems, which pride themselves in maintaining a clear distinction between law and morality. In these systems, immorality may deserve social disapproval, and even censure, but it is none of the state's, and therefore the law's, business.

Morals offenses are *offenses* in two senses. They are criminalized precisely because they are offensive. While they do not harm anyone in particular, they may offend the multitudes. For this reason, morals offenses are often described as *victimless. Not only do they not inflict harm on anyone, but they often involve private consensual interactions among two or more people. Since none of these people will have any reason to complain about being victimized, the enforcement of morals offenses tends to rely on undercover agents, informers, and surveillance, electronic or otherwise.

Morals offenses are also offenses in that they tend not to be full-fledged crimes. So some modern reformers, among them the drafters of the *Model Penal Code, decided to put many morals offenses in a special category of non-criminal offenses, or violations. That does not mean, however, that there are no morals offenses that *have been* (for example, sodomy) and *continue to be* (for example, *drug offenses) classified as very serious crimes.

Morals offenses remain crimes, no matter how they might be formally reclassified. They are defined in criminal codes and are punished with criminal sanctions, however light. That is what distinguishes them from, say, licensing programs or regulatory schemes. They do not regulate conduct; they punish it. And it is this residual criminal aspect that continues to attract criticism. For it is one thing to say that the state may protect the moral fiber of the community. It is another to permit the state to employ its sharpest weapon, the criminal law, in pursuit of that goal.

The state's authority to proscribe morals offenses is derived from its general *police power. The power to police is the power to promote the general welfare of the community, including its moral well-being. "Any practice or business, the tendency of which is to weaken or corrupt the morals of those who follow it or to encourage idleness instead of industriousness is a legitimate subject for regulation or prohibition by the state" (*Fernandez* v. *Alford* (1943)).

Although morals offenses have always resisted clear definition, they may be thought of as criminalizing the failure of self-control, or the failure to resist temptation. Many can be traced back directly to the seventeenth century "blue laws" of American theocratic colonies, deriving their name from the blue paper on which they were printed. Morals offenses that openly enforce a particular religious morality (see RELIGION) generally have fallen out of favor, though "Judeo-Christian" values continue to be invoked in support of sexual morals offenses in particular (*Bowers* v. *Hardwick* (1986)). Nonetheless, "blue laws" persist in some jurisdictions in the form of laws proscribing commercial activity on Sunday.

Morals offenses also have their roots in the sumptuary legislation of medieval Europe, which devoted a great deal of energy to the maintenance of status distinctions. These regulations were designed to keep people in their place by regulating what they could wear, eat, and do according to their societal status. Sumptuary legislation in its original form no longer exists. Yet morals offenses, in their application, if not on their face, continue to control certain segments of society that are considered dangerous, or at least offensive, by the majority.

Morals offenses, in this sense, are one way of using the criminal law to define and combat deviance. To act immorally, or simply to be immoral, is also to be deviant in the sense of deviating from the moral norms of the community, however defined. Morals offenses are "offenses against public sensibilities." They offend and annoy; they are moral *nuisances. And as nuisances, the argument goes, they need to be abated not only to prevent offense to the public, but also to ensure the survival of the moral community.

In addition to their role in upholding religious and social morality, morals offenses have always enforced sexual morality. Sexual morals offenses still play an important role in American criminal law in some jurisdictions. They include, among others, prostitution, pornography, nude dancing, *adultery, fornication, *abortion, contraception, bigamy and polygamy, incest, underage sex, and various forms of "unnatural" or "deviant" *sex acts, including sodomy (anal and oral sex, heterosexual or homosexual), and sex with animals (bestiality) or dead persons.

American law has come a long way since the theocratic laws of its early colonies, and even from the founding fathers' pride in the moral health of a supremely virtuous America free from the corruption of the Old World. Yet the decriminalization of morals offenses in the United States has not kept pace with developments in other Western countries. American law continues to punish conduct that is no longer criminal elsewhere (particularly sexual morality) or punishes more harshly conduct that remains criminal abroad (especially drug-related offenses). While some American morals offenses are rarely enforced (adultery, for example), the criminalization of moral deviance remains an important, and increasingly distinctive, feature of American law.

Blue Laws. Several American states prohibit certain activities, commercial or not, on Sunday. The Alabama Criminal Code, for instance, in a chapter devoted to "Offenses Against Public Health and Morals," threatens with punishment of up to three months' imprisonment anyone who "compels his child, apprentice or servant to perform any labor on Sunday, except the customary domestic duties of daily necessity or comfort, or works of charity or who engages in shooting, hunting, gaming, card playing or racing on that day, or who, being a merchant or shopkeeper, druggist excepted, keeps open store on Sunday."

Sunday blue laws have a long history in Anglo-American criminal law. They have been traced as far back as a 1237 statute of Henry III, which forbade the frequenting of markets on Sunday.

The Supreme Court has repeatedly upheld their constitutionality, most notably in *McGowan* v. *Maryland* (1961). The defendants in that case had been indicted "for the Sunday sale of a three-ring loose-leaf binder, a can of floor wax, a stapler and staples, and a toy submarine." That same year, blue laws survived another constitutional challenge, this one by Orthodox Jewish merchants from Philadelphia who argued that their livelihood depended on their Sunday business since they closed on Saturdays for religious reasons (*Braunfeld* v. *Brown* (1961)).

Gambling. Throughout American history, the unauthorized sale of lottery tickets has been condemned in law as injurious to public morals. In the nineteenth century, it was punishable even in the absence of statutory authority, as a *common law misdemeanor. See, for example, *People* v. *Jackson* (1846). *Gambling continues to be criminalized throughout the United States. In New York, an entire article of the Penal Law is dedicated to "Gambling Offenses," including promoting gambling, possession of gambling records, and possession of a gambling device, with maximum penalties ranging from one to four years' imprisonment.

Strictly speaking, only *unauthorized* gambling is prohibited. Several states have authorized various forms of gambling, including on- and off-track racehorse betting, dog racing, and even casino gambling. State lotteries have proved similarly popular, ever since New Hampshire opened the first one in 1964.

Intoxication. Public intoxication remains a crime in many American jurisdictions. Even in the Model Penal Code, which generally disfavors morals offenses, it is a violation for a person to "appear in any public place manifestly under the influence of alcohol, narcotics or other drug, not therapeutically administered, to the degree that he may . . . annoy persons in his vicinity." Public intoxication statutes so far have withstood constitutional attack (*Powell* v. *Texas* (1968)).

Private intoxication is not a crime, nor was it one even during Prohibition (1920–33). Prohibition did, however, criminalize the private possession of liquor with intent to sell it. Public possession of alcohol is still criminalized today, under so-called open container laws.

While private drunkenness is not a morals offense per se, American criminal law has traditionally expressed disapproval of drunkenness, private or public, in another way, by severely restricting intoxication as a defense. As a famous nineteenth-century American judge, when confronted with a defense of intoxication, put it: "This is the first time, that I ever remember it to have been contended, that the commission of one crime was an excuse for another. Drunkenness is a gross vice, and in the contemplation of some of our laws is a crime; and I learned in my earlier studies, that so far from its being in law an excuse for murder, it is rather an aggravation of its malignity" (*Montana* v. *Egelhoff* (1996), quoting *United States* v. *Cornell* (1820) (Justice Joseph Story)).

Possessing drugs is a far more serious morals offense than possessing alcohol. For over a century, drugs have been considered "an insidious and demoralizing vice, injurious alike to the health, morals, and welfare of the public" (*Ex parte Mon Luck* (1896) (opium)). Possessing drugs is criminal even in private, and even without the intent to use them in one way or another, with punishments up to life imprisonment without the possibility of parole (*Harmelin* v. *Michigan* (1991)).

Vagrancy. At least since sixteenth century England, vagrancy statutes have been a popular mechanism for policing social misfits, including various and sundry immoral persons. Though not a morals offense on its face, vagrancy has thus played an important role in the enforcement of public morality. Notice the cast of immoral characters in this Florida municipal ordinance: "Rogues and vagabonds, or dissolute persons who go about begging, common gamblers, persons who use juggling or unlawful games or plays, common drunkards, common night walkers, thieves, pilferers or pickpockets, traders in stolen property, lewd, wanton and lascivious persons, keepers of gambling places, common railers and brawlers, persons wandering or strolling around from place to place without any lawful purpose or object, habitual loafers, disorderly persons, persons neglecting all lawful business and habitually spending their time by frequenting houses of ill fame, gaming houses, or places where alcoholic beverages are sold or served, persons able to work but habitually living upon the earnings of their wives or minor children shall be deemed vagrants."

The Supreme Court struck down this ordinance in 1972 on the grounds of vagueness. (*Papachristou* v. *City of Jacksonville* (1972)). Similar offenses survive to this day, though they have become less explicit in their focus on immoral activities and characters. The Model Penal Code, for instance, contains the following vagrancy successor statutes: "loitering or prowling," "disorderly conduct," and "open lewdness."

Sexual Morality. Disorderly conduct is frequently disorderly because it violates communal standards of sexual morality, which is why the line between vagrancy, loitering, disorderly conduct, and lewdness is fluid. Those "that be not of good fame," in the words of an old English statute, are often prostitutes, johns, and pimps. These are the "common night walkers," the "lewd, wanton and lascivious persons," and of course those "habitually spending their time by frequenting houses of ill fame."

Among public affronts to public morality, prostitution is the most visible. Prostitution remains criminal throughout the United States. As with gambling, though on a smaller scale, some local governments have replaced criminal prohibition with administrative regulation, following the example of other Western countries, including England (Street Offences Act (1959)). In some Nevada counties, registered prostitutes can work out of licensed brothels, while streetwalking remains illegal.

The drive to criminalize prostitution in American law has been so strong that it contributed significantly to the expansion of federal criminal law. When federal criminal law was in its infancy, the *Mann Act of 1910 made it a federal crime to transport in interstate commerce "any woman or girl for the purpose of prostitution." But the Act was not targeted against white slavery, or forced prostitution, alone. It launched an all-out, nationwide, assault on sexual immorality, criminalizing the interstate transportation of women for "debauchery, or for any other immoral purpose," including "becoming a concubine or mistress" (*Caminetti* v. *United States* (1917)). A 1986 Congressional amendment limited its scope to "any sexual activity for which any person can be charged with a criminal offense."

Other public offenses against sexual morality might include, as in New York, public lewdness (intentionally exposing one's private parts in a lewd manner), exposure of a person (exposing one's private parts in a lewd manner, with a breastfeeding exception), promoting the exposure of a person (maintaining a public place where someone exposes his or her private parts), and public display of offensive sexual material (displaying pictures of "a person or a portion of the human body that predominantly appeals to prurient interest in sex"). These offenses, which provide for penalties ranging from a fine to one year's imprisonment, are classified as "offenses against public sensibilities," along with another nonsexual morals offense, called simply "offensive exhibition." Offensive exhibition includes organizing dance marathons and similar endurance contests, exposing a person "to ridicule or contempt by voluntarily submitting to indignities such as the throwing of balls or other articles at his head or body," and putting on a show where a "firearm is discharged or a knife, arrow or other sharp or dangerous instrument is thrown or propelled at or toward a person."

Public morals are so well guarded that offenses against it also reach into the private sphere, provided the sexual deviance is sufficiently pronounced. As recently as 1965, American criminal statutes prohibited the use and distribution of contraceptives, to protect public morals by preventing premarital sex. Only in 1965 and 1972 were they struck down by the Supreme Court on the grounds that they improperly interfered with the right of *privacy, of married and of unmarried couples, respectively (*Griswold* v. *Connecticut* (1965); *Eisenstadt* v. *Baird* (1972)). The right of privacy, in conjunction with the First Amendment, also brought down a criminal statute proscribing the possession of obscene material in one's home (*Stanley* v. *Georgia* (1969)).

The right of privacy has played its most celebrated role in the context of constitutional attacks on another offense tinged with sexual morality, abortion. Unlike the use and distribution of contraceptives and, arguably, the possession of obscene materials, abortion is not merely a morals offense; it also involves the question of the fetus's rights. Nevertheless, the proscription of abortion was always also seen as deterring sex that for one reason or another deviated from a norm of marital procreative sex. As a result, the fight for the legalization of abortion was also the fight against the legitimacy of enforcing this norm through criminal morals offenses (*Roe* v. *Wade* (1973)).

Privacy, however, has been no barrier to the criminal prohibition of certain other deviations from sexual morality, so adultery and fornication remain crimes in many American jurisdictions. Adultery is nonmarital sex between two persons, at least one of whom is married to another; fornication is nonmarital sex. By last count, adultery was a crime in twenty-four states, fornication in seventeen. The statutes, however, are rarely enforced, and were not included in the Model Penal Code.

Every American jurisdiction continues to criminalize bigamy, polygamy, incest, and corruption of minors ("statutory rape"). While other considerations also come into play, these crimes are morals offenses insofar as they punish individuals for deviating from the sexual and social norms of the community. In the case of incest, it should be kept in mind that it broadly punishes anyone—regardless of age—who, to use the Model Penal Code's

formulation, "marries or cohabits or has sexual intercourse with an ancestor or descendant, a brother or sister of the whole or half blood or an uncle, aunt, nephew or niece of the whole blood." "Statutory rape" statutes typically continue to treat as a felony, nonmarital sexual intercourse between anyone over twenty and anyone under seventeen, regardless of consent. The Model Penal Code also provides for the crime of "seduction," which criminalizes sexual intercourse with "a female who is induced to participate by a promise of marriage which the actor does not mean to perform."

American jurisdictions persist in criminalizing private consensual sexual intercourse that is considered "deviate" or "unnatural." States differ on what is considered deviate or unnatural. Under the Model Penal Code, "deviate sexual intercourse" is "sexual intercourse per os or per anus between human beings who are not husband and wife, and any form of sexual intercourse with an animal." New York defines it in much the same way, but excludes bestiality. Bestiality is a crime in all jurisdictions, including in New York. So is sex with a dead person, another type of behavior criminalized as "sexual misconduct."

In the Model Penal Code, private consensual "deviate" sex between persons is not a crime. In New York, however, and in many other states, consensual sodomy statutes remain on the books. The U.S. Supreme Court upheld one of these statutes against a federal constitutional challenge based on the right of privacy (*Bowers* v. *Hardwick* (1986)). Nonetheless, consensual sodomy laws are rarely enforced, and state courts have begun to strike them down on state constitutional grounds. See *Powell* v. *State* (1998).

[*See also* Criminal Law; Sex Offenses; Victimless Crimes]

• Joseph Gusfield, *Symbolic Crusade: Status Politics and the American Temperance Movement*, 1963. Herbert L. Packer, *The Limits of the Criminal Sanction*, 1968. Richard A. Wasserstrom, ed., *Morality and the Law*, 1971. Edwin M. Schur and Hugo Adam Bedau, *Victimless Crimes: Two Sides of a Controversy*, 1974. National Institute of Law Enforcement and Criminal Justice, *The Development of the Law of Gambling: 1776–1976*, 1977. American Law Institute, *Model Penal Code: Official Draft and Revised Commentaries*, 1980. David A. J. Richards, *Sex, Drugs, Death and the Law*, 1982. Joel Feinberg, *The Moral Limits of the Criminal Law*, 1984. Lawrence M. Friedman, *Crime and Punishment in American History*, 1993. Alan Hunt, *Governing Morals: A Social History of Moral Regulation*, 1999.   —Markus Dirk Dubber

MORTGAGE. Because land is immovable and generally increases in value, it has been used as security for loans and other obligations since antiquity. American mortgage law traces its lineage to the earliest English laws; during the twelfth century in England, the *mort gage* was used to create security interests in land. Unfortunately, mortgage law has never been thoroughly overhauled and modernized. Instead, as problems have surfaced, courts and legislatures have fashioned piecemeal solutions.

Today, a security interest in land is created, depending on the state where the land is located, by a mortgage, deed of *trust, or deed to secure debt. Despite some differences in form, these three are so similar that they often are described generically as mortgages. Mortgages include a variety of provisions designed to preserve the land's value. For example, the borrower ("mortgagor") is commonly required to maintain the *property and to keep it insured.

If the mortgagor defaults in its obligations, the primary remedy for the lender ("mortgagee") is foreclosure. Foreclosure procedures vary among the states but generally require a public auction of the land. The foreclosing mortgagee uses the sale proceeds to recover the secured debt. Any excess is paid to those whose rights in the lands are extinguished by the foreclosure, such as the mortgagor. In every state, a mortgagee can foreclose by judicial action, in which a court determines whether a default in the loan has occurred and orders a sale of the property. Approximately half the states permit nonjudicial foreclosures in accordance with specified statutory procedures. These are faster and cheaper than judicial foreclosures and are more commonly used when available.

A major flaw in both methods is that the foreclosing mortgagee normally is the only bidder at the sale, and generally bids no more than the debt amount, regardless of the land's value. Therefore, no surplus proceeds are generated to pay others. In an attempt to prevent abuse of the foreclosure process, states have enacted a variety of rules, often adopted during periods of economic depression. Some states, for example, permit the borrower to keep possession of the land for some time after the foreclosure and to invalidate the sale by repaying the foreclosure sale purchaser ("statutory redemption"). Some states limit the foreclosing mortgagee's right to sue the mortgagor if the foreclosure does not generate enough money to pay the entire debt ("antideficiency legislation").

Although mortgage law traditionally has been state law, the federal government has become increasingly active. Today, mortgagees routinely sell their mortgages in the secondary mortgage market. Stock markets around the world sell shares in pools of these mortgages. This market is facilitated by the use of standard forms and procedures. Therefore, the federal government is attempting to enact uniform procedures, such as a national foreclosure method. In this way, the government hopes to maximize the amount of capital available for mortgage loans, which benefits borrowers, lenders, builders, and the other participants in the real estate market.

[*See also* Property]

• Grant S. Nelson and Dale A. Whitman, *Real Estate Finance Law*, vol. 3, 3d ed., 1994. Richard R. Powell, *Powell on Real Property* (ch. 36 & 37), 1997.

—Ann M. Burkhart

MOVIES. *See* Arts, Popular Culture, and Law: Entertainment Law; Media and the Law.

MULTINATIONAL CORPORATION. *See* Business Organizations; Corporation.

MURDER. *See* Homicide.

MURDER MYSTERY. *See* Literature and Law.

N

NARRATIVE JURISPRUDENCE. *See* Law and Literature, Theory of.

NATIONAL BAR ASSOCIATION. The National Bar Association was established on 1 August 1925 in Des Moines, Iowa. On that day, George H. Woodson and eleven other African-American lawyers, including one woman, met to (as stated in the association's charter) "advance the science of jurisprudence, uphold the honor of the legal profession, promote social intercourse among the members of the bar, and protect the civil and political rights of all citizens of the several states of the United States." Today, the National Bar Association represents the interests of minority lawyers and the larger minority community through its programs and resolutions. Given the widespread discrimination against minority groups throughout American history, the National Bar Association devotes much attention to protecting constitutional rights and civil liberties.

Following the Civil War and Reconstruction, America's lawyers began organizing *bar associations for the purpose of increasing professional standards and improving the public's perception of attorneys. Moreover, business corporations increasingly sought out professionals with the competence to provide legal counsel in an industrializing society. Founded in 1878, the *American Bar Association was the country's primary organization for legal professionals, but in 1912 the association officially began excluding black lawyers when it became known that the group had unwittingly admitted three black members.

Denied membership in mainstream bar associations, black lawyers decided to form an organization dedicated to protecting minority rights and improving *race relations within the legal profession: thus they formed the National Bar Association. Many of the association's objectives were similar to those of the American Bar Association. By restating these goals in their charter, the National Bar Association's lawyers drew attention to the American Bar Association's failure, as a group, to promote equality within the legal profession and society.

The National Bar Association has argued that greater diversity on the federal bench is needed to maintain the public's faith in the judiciary's impartiality, reasoning that a racially segregated bench cannot fully convince the oppressed that all people are treated equally before the law. Under the leadership of Elmer C. Jackson, in 1960 the association persuaded both Democratic presidential candidate John F. Kennedy and Republican candidate Richard M. Nixon to pledge to nominate an African-American lawyer to the United States district courts. After winning the 1960 presidential election, Kennedy promptly nominated Joseph Dolan, an African-American attorney, as United States deputy assistant attorney general and James B. Parsons as the first African-American U.S. district judge within the continental United States.

Since the 1960s, the National Bar Association has continued to promote the advancement of *civil rights and civil liberties through the courts by filing amicus curiae briefs in cases where the interests of minorities and oppressed people are at stake. These briefs allow the association to articulate the concerns of Americans whose opinions the courts may not otherwise hear. As a national organization, the association has local affiliates in all fifty states and the District of Columbia. Most of these affiliates conduct pro bono legal services and other volunteer work in communities neglected by mainstream lawyers.

[*See also* Lawyers; National Lawyers Guild]

• Geraldine R. Segal, *Blacks in the Law: Philadelphia and the Nation*, 1983. J. Clay Smith, *Emancipation: The Making of the Black Lawyer 1844–1944*, 1993.

—David Kenneth Pye

NATIONAL LAWYERS GUILD. The National Lawyers Guild was established in 1937 as a progressive alternative to the *American Bar Association, which was dominated by corporate lawyers and opponents of the New Deal. The Guild's organizers were a small group of liberal lawyers, including Morris Ernst, Frank Walsh, Jerome *Frank, and Karl *Llewellyn. Its first members included a diverse group of liberal and radical attorneys, including establishment lawyers with close ties to the Roosevelt administration, lawyers involved in the labor movement, and ethnic minorities frustrated by their restricted professional opportunities. Unlike the American Bar Association at that time, the Guild opened its membership to all lawyers, regardless of race or ethnicity.

During its early years, the Guild was torn between liberals and radicals and between those who believed the organization should function as a trade group pursuing members' narrowly defined professional interests and those who sought to engage the organization in broader political goals. Almost immediately after its founding, the Guild endorsed Roosevelt's *court-packing plan, opposed the Taft-Hartley Act of 1947, challenged the application of the Neutrality Act of 1794, which prohibits private military activity against a foreign state, to the Spanish Civil War, and criticized the work of the House Committee on Un-American Activities. Guild lawyers also were active in the defense of Communist Party members charged with violating the Smith Act of 1940 that prohibited subversive activity.

During the two decades after its founding, internal discord, anticommunist attacks by bar leaders, and federal government investigations nearly extinguished the Guild. In 1939, Guild members linked to the Roosevelt administration proposed adding a statement to the group's constitutional preamble denouncing "dictatorship of any kind, . . . whether Fascist, Nazi or Communistic." Guild leaders rejected this pledge, and many liberal lawyers resigned. In the late 1940s, the American Bar Association recommended anticommunist loyalty oaths for all lawyers and urged state *bar associations to expel lawyers who were Communist Party members. The association also strongly criticized Guild proposals to provide public funding for low-cost legal services, equating such proposals with communist subversion. Beginning in the 1940s, the Federal Bureau of Investigation began an extensive campaign to monitor and disrupt Guild activities. In 1950, the House Un-American Activities Committee denounced the Guild as "the foremost legal bulwark of the Communist Party, its front organizations, and controlled unions," and in 1953 Herbert Brownell, President Eisenhower's attorney general, recommended that the Guild appear on the attorney general's list of subversive organizations. The Guild's five-year battle to avoid being listed as a subversive group ended in 1958 when a new attorney general withdrew the recommendation. The fight nevertheless sapped the Guild of financial resources and many of its most prominent members.

By 1960, the National Lawyers Guild had only about six hundred members nationwide and only four active chapters. Membership rebounded during the mid-1960s as the group became more active in the *civil rights and antiwar movements. In 1964, the Guild established a committee of lawyers to represent civil rights demonstrators and to assist in prosecuting civil rights suits. The next year it passed a resolution opposing the United States' involvement in Vietnam, and Guild lawyers began counseling and representing draft resistors and antiwar protestors.

In the late 1960s and 1970s, the Guild was consumed by internal divisions by class, race, gender, and age. Some minority members criticized the group's antiwar activities as benefiting primarily middle- and upper-income whites, and women challenged the group's mostly male leadership. A proposal to admit law students, legal assistants, and "jailhouse lawyers" (prisoners who use legal procedures to seek release but have no formal legal training) as full voting members generated contentious debate between older members, who were committed to the Guild's distinctive character as a bar association, and younger members, who questioned its emphasis on legal expertise. As the younger generation took control of the Guild, many older members retreated from involvement in the organization.

In the late 1970s and 1980s, the National Lawyers Guild turned its attention to affirmative action, the antinuclear movement, opposition to U.S. intervention in Central America, and international *human rights. The group's projects of the 1990s included advocating workers' and *prisoners' rights, opposing globalization, fighting the death penalty, and monitoring police misconduct. By 2001 the organization had approximately six thousand members, one hundred lawyer chapters, and one hundred student chapters nationwide.

• Jerold S. Auerbach, *Unequal Justice: Lawyers and Social Change in Modern America*, 1976. Ann Fagan Ginger and Eugene M. Tobin, *The National Lawyers Guild: From Roosevelt to Reagan*, 1988.

—Ann Southworth

NATIVE AMERICAN REMOVAL. Both the surrender of tribal lands and the relocation of Indian peoples were significant elements of Indian policy from the earliest days of the American Republic. However, the original *treaty negotiation system proved too slow in the face of increased demands from land-hungry settlers. Thus, Thomas *Jefferson proposed the removal of Native Americans from their traditional homelands east of the Mississippi River to newly established "Indian Territories" in the West.

As Indian tribes increasingly resisted pressure to surrender their lands by individual treaties of cession, the government accelerated a federal policy of removing Indians. Although advocated by Jefferson, the first transfers were not concluded until after the War of 1812. Congress did not formally adopt the Removal Policy until after the election of Andrew Jackson who, in 1829, called for "voluntary removal" in his first annual message.

The Indian Removal Act narrowly passed Congress in 1830. It authorized exchange of "public lands" or territory, often claimed by other tribes, located west of the Mississippi for tribal lands occupied by tribes in the east. The Indian removal debate was fierce. Jacksonians argued that the policy was "humanitarian and civilizing." Removal, they believed, protected Indians from the corrupting influence of white settlers, while opening "unused" tribal hunting lands to productive agricultural use. The opposition countered eloquently by supporting the sanctity of treaty promises and Native American human rights. Caught in the middle, Indians soon discovered that to refuse to emigrate might mean the end of federal annuities, and protection and recognition of their negotiated treaty rights, as well as the transfer of tribes to state jurisdiction.

Native American removal remained the heart of United States Indian policy from 1830 until the emergence of the post–Civil War allotment and reservation policy. This policy had the most dramatic impact among the Southern Indian Nations, particularly the Cherokees, Choctaws, Chickasaws, Creeks, and Seminoles, whose forced removal became known as "The Trail of Tears." Tribes from other sections of the country, such as the Potawatomi, became victims of Indian removal. The Delaware, Kickapoo, and Quapaw were also driven west, as were the Winnebago, Sauk, and Fox. In later times, Navajo, Cheyenne, and Nez Perce were moved in similar tragic treks known by names such as the Long Walk.

The Cherokee experience has come to symbolize American Indian removal. The nation learned of this conflict when the tribe brought their case before the U.S. Supreme Court in *Cherokee Nation* v. *Georgia* (1831) and *Worcester* v. *Georgia* (1832). Although Chief Justice John *Marshall's ultimate decision supported the Cherokees, Andrew Jackson used troops and agents with the power to enforce their interpretation of the removal policy.

The Cherokee experience mirrors the tragedy of other tribes forced to abandon their ancient lands and march westward on their individual "Trail of Tears." The Cherokee journey of a thousand miles from Georgia to present-day Oklahoma during the winter of 1838–39 lasted six months. Sixteen thousand Cherokees began the trek; only twelve thousand finished it.

Jacksonians saw Native American removal as a policy designed to benefit both Native peoples and the growing Republic. Much contemporary scholarship, however, looks upon removal as "genocide-at-law," with one-quarter to one-third of removed Indians dying from the forced migration and resettlement.

[*See also* Native Americans and the Law]

• Grant Foreman, *Indian Removal: The Emigration of the Five Civilized Tribes*, 1932. Ronald N. Satz, *American Indian Policy in the Jacksonian Era*, 1975.

—Rennard Strickland

NATIVE AMERICANS AND THE LAW

History
Native American Law and Tribal Sovereignty
Native Americans under Current United States Law

NATIVE AMERICANS AND THE LAW: HISTORY

The peoples who originally inhabited the lands that became the United States have had unique legal relationships among themselves and with the various colonial elements that evolved into the current American federal and state governments. This evolution of legal relationships is characterized by at least three thematic developments. First, despite numerous attempts to retain their legal practices and systems, the indigenous peoples of North and Pacific America (American Indians, Native Hawaiians, Samoans, and Native Alaskans) have had forced upon them by the various non-native powers a variety of *legal systems. This has resulted in a legal maze that defies easy generalization and often employs both a native and another legal institution in a dual dispute-resolution process. Each native community or reservation attempt to varying degrees to practice traditional law-ways in conjunction with or in competition with laws imposed from the outside. Second, legal relationships between the conqueror and the conquered have centered around control of land and *sovereignty; this has required a variety of legal mechanisms, the best known being the treaty. Third, the desire of the colonial power not only to take the land but to steal the mind of the Native American has resulted in confrontations over cultural rights and freedoms. The history of Native Americans and law is a most complicated affair that continues to evolve.

The Years before the Constitution, 1492–1787. Colonial relationships can be traced to the variety of European nations that ventured to North America during the fifteenth, sixteenth, and seventeenth centuries. The Spanish, French, English, Swedish, Dutch, and Russians all tried to conquer and control the land and its peoples. Each nation had unique legal characteristics that it sought to implant, and each witnessed success and failure. Eventually the English prevailed, and along the way, a hybrid legal system—mostly Anglo-Saxon—was put in place.

A primary objective of the English was the development of a legal system that extinguished indigenous land titles in favor of English land titles and regulated colonial trade with Indians. These two important elements in establishing control over North America dominated English law in the colonies in the seventeenth and eighteenth centuries and the legal system of the new American nation in the nineteenth century.

With the replacement of Indians on the land by white settlers, a theory was put into practice through *common law that Indians had no claim to their land because they did not use it properly. "Proper use" in English jurisprudence meant farming. And even when the English happened upon farmers, such as the Cherokee or the Seneca, their use of farming methods other than European methods discounted their claims to the land. Consequently, European legal theorists rationalized the Americas as an unclaimed land awaiting possession. These mythic rationales confronted the reality of indigenous occupation and use of the land. The Europeans, with the English and Spanish in the lead, agreed among themselves on the rights of discovery, by which the "discoverer" claimed the right to the soil from natives in the region, by purchase, if the peoples were willing to give up the land in exchange for something else, or by conquest.

To facilitate the transfer of land claims, colonial nations engaged in treaty-making with indigenous nations. Individual colonists also made land agreements, but these activities ultimately did not receive the sanction of colonial law. *Treaties are nation-to-nation agreements, and a variety of kinds of treaties were negotiated between various indigenous groups and European nations. Some anomalies evolved in the treaty-making process. For example, the Russians did not make any treaties with the Indians, Aleuts, or Inuit of Alaska. And there are no treaties between the United States and Native Hawaiians. Some Indian tribes made treaties of friendship or alliance but never forsook their land titles. Others made treaties that gave up not their homelands but the lands of others, something they did not have the power to do. Once the United States emerged as the central power over North America, the federal government consolidated its power to make treaties.

The earliest confrontations in English America involved treaty and sovereignty disputes, and two of these disputes resulted in legally significant events. The first war between English colonists and the Powhatan Confederacy became a struggle over the land. Lasting from 1622 to 1644, the war was particularly debilitating for both sides. The English eventually prevailed, and they forced the remaining Powhatans onto reservations in western Virginia in order to use them as buffers against other potentially hostile native nations. Eastern Virginia became the rightful preserve of English colonists. A similar result with a different method occurred in New England, where the Pequot war in 1637 resulted in the near annihilation and expulsion to the Caribbean of most of the Pequots. The Connecticut Valley was thus cleared for occupation by English colonists.

The size and significance of European trade with Indians fostered the development of legal regulations. To be deemed legal, colonial traders required a license, and licensed traders were to abide by certain rules and regulations administered by appointed commissioners. These laws were particularly strict regarding guns and alcohol, but most attempts to enforce the regulations were frustrated by the difficulty of establishing law enforcement. This exacerbated the already tense relationships among the various parties.

The Declaration of Independence cited Native Americans as one of the reasons justifying revolution against the British Crown. American revolutionaries hoped to prevent Indians from bolstering British forces once the war began. The Articles of Confederation gave Congress "the sole and exclusive right and power of . . . regulating the trade and managing all affairs with the Indians, not members of any of the States, provided that the legislative right of any State within its own limits be not infringed or violated." In 1786 Congress passed the Ordinance for the Regulation of Indian Affairs, which created Indian departments, each administered by a superintendent; the primary purpose of the departments was to regulate trade.

The New American Nation and Early Indian Laws, 1787–1871. American Indians are mentioned only twice in the Constitution. Article I, Section 2, provides that "Representatives and direct Taxes shall be apportioned among the several states which may be included within this Union, according to their respective Numbers . . . excluding Indians not taxed." Section 8 of the same article granted Congress the power "to regulate Commerce with foreign Nations, and among the Several States, and with the Indian Tribes." Elsewhere in the Constitution, provisions regarding treaties ensured that preexisting treaties with American Indians would be honored. The Bill of Rights did not universally apply to America's indigenous peoples, because of their unique status.

The first major statute to affect the relationship of American Indians with the new nation was the Trade and Intercourse Act of 1790. This law instituted a licensing system for trade with Indians— something the British had also tried—and reserved the purchase of Indian land for the federal government. The law also asserted that crimes by non-Indians against Indians could be prosecuted within the jurisdiction of American courts. This movement to use treaties to restrict sovereignty and implement trade policy culminated in the revised Trade and Intercourse Act of 1834, expanding federal jurisdiction into Indian country.

A more direct confrontation with Indian sovereignty came with passage of the Indian Removal Act of 1830, urged by President Andrew Jackson. The Cherokee challenged their removal before the Supreme Court, in *Cherokee Nation* v. *Georgia* (1831) and *Worcester* v. *Georgia* (1832). In *Cherokee Nation*, Chief Justice John *Marshall held that the Court did not have original jurisdiction, since Indian tribes were "domestic dependent nations" rather than sovereign nations. This set the tone for all subsequent litigation affecting indigenous peoples. One year later, Marshall seemed to soften his pronouncement when he denied any state jurisdiction in Indian territory and ordered the state of Georgia to stop its incendiary action toward the Cherokee. Indians were "distinct, independent political communities, retaining their original natural rights," and only the federal government could legally deal with Native Americans. Jackson ignored the Court's ruling and sanctioned Georgia's violation of Cherokee sovereignty when the state asserted control over Cherokee lands. Ultimately many of the Cherokee were forced to relocate to what would become Oklahoma, thousands of them perishing in the winter walk across half of the United States along the Trail of Tears.

Following the Civil War, the United States refocused its expansive energies on the trans-Mississippi west. With Indian–white warfare gripping the Plains, Congress in 1867 created the Indian Peace Commission, whose task was to negotiate peace treaties with Indian tribes west of the Mississippi River. The objective of these treaties was to confine Indians to reservations in order to secure safe resettlement for non-Indians and to implement a forced assimilation program on the now concentrated Indian populations. These treaties proved tenuous in securing peace, but the momentum for reform continued from Washington, D.C. In 1869 the Board of Indian Commissioners was formed to assist the secretary of the interior in the administration of federal Indian policy. Most significantly, the board criticized the treaty system and recommended its abolition; its recommendations reflected public sentiments. In 1871 Congress abolished all future treaty-making between the United States and indigenous peoples.

This era highlighted the legal complexities of trying to place within a democratic legal system the byproducts of colonialism. Trade was regulated but at the cost of sovereignty for indigenous peoples; treaties were signed but seldom honored; and treaty-making was abolished while retaining sovereignty. "Domestic, dependent, nations," the three words of Chief Justice Marshall designed to summarize these legal relationships, proved to be unlikely modifiers that courts and legislatures still struggle to define.

The Era of Allotments and Assimilation, 1871–1928. When Congress ended the treaty system in 1871, it signaled a wholesale assault on the remaining native lands, tribal cultures, and Indian sovereignty. After the warfare of the 1870s between the United States and most Indian nations west of the Mississippi River, Native Americans were confined to reservations. Here indigenous peoples experienced heightened pressures on their remaining land base and their existing cultures.

The history of the Supreme Court case of *Ex parte Crow Dog* (1883) demonstrates this trend. When Crow Dog murdered Spotted Tail, revered leader of the Brulé Lakota, according to Sioux legal custom a significant payment of restitution was paid by the killer's relatives to the victim's family.

Even so, the U.S. district attorney for Dakota Territory believed Crow Dog should be prosecuted in federal court. The prosecution proceeded, and Crow Dog was convicted and sentenced to hang. Upon appeal, the Supreme Court ruled that no legislation gave federal courts any jurisdiction over Indian-on-Indian crime and threw out the conviction.

Congress responded by passing the Major Crimes Act of 1885, which made it a federal offense for an Indian to commit certain felonies against Indians on reservations or designated Indian lands. This represented a major assault on tribal sovereignty and Indian law-ways. The act would be amended several times in the twentieth century to include many more crimes than the original seven. Supreme Court decisions in the 1880s witnessed the invocation of the plenary power doctrine. With treaty-making officially ended, the Court granted to Congress all powers over Indian policy.

The federal government implemented legislation intended to foster cultural assimilation of American Indians while at the same time reducing the reservation land base. A reform impulse overtook Indian policy in the 1880s, and it was a legal nightmare for America's indigenous peoples. Its high watermark is embodied in the General Allotment Act of 1887, also known as the Dawes Severalty Act. Promoted by Senator Henry L. Dawes of Massachusetts, the General Allotment Act divided reservation lands into separate allotments of 160 acres each (modeled after the Homestead Act of 1862) for heads of Indian households and individuals. The reformers intended to break up communal land ownership and inculcate the value of private *property upon Native Americans; they hoped to usurp tribal culture by dividing tribal lands. Others who did not share the reform's lofty intentions simply wanted to acquire the land that would be declared "surplus" by the government following reservation allotments.

The greed of allotment did not go unchallenged. The Kiowa, led by Lone Wolf, refused to give up their lands. The Jerome Commission used bribes and coercion to secure a contrived agreement. Congressional approval of the fraudulent Kiowa allotment triggered a lawsuit by Lone Wolf and others against Ethan A. Hitchcock, secretary of the interior, challenging the proposed allotment of their reservation. The case of Lone Wolf v. Hitchcock (1903) proved a disaster for indigenous rights, as the Supreme Court held that congressional power was supreme over tribal land despite treaties and despite fraud and corruption. This decision eroded tribal land sovereignty and reinforced the plenary power of Congress over Native Americans.

In the post–Civil War era, the United States purchased Alaska from Russia. Alaska was home to Native Alaskans, such as the Aleuts (on the Aleutian Islands and parts of the mainland), the Inuit, and American Indians (such as the Tlingit and Haida in southern Alaska's panhandle). In 1884 the Alaska Territory was created, and Native Alaskan land claims were protected until Congress passed future legislation. In 1906 the Alaska Native Allotment Act, patterned after the Dawes Severalty Act, provided allotments of up to 160 acres for heads of families; efforts to set up reservations were never completed.

The turn of the nineteenth century found the United States expanding its domain beyond California's borders into the Pacific Ocean. As a result of the Spanish-American War the United States gained possession of a number of Pacific Islands, including Guam, which was set up as an unincorporated territory. Competition for other islands resulted in the United States and Germany dividing them up, with the Americans claiming six islands in the Samoan group, the largest being Tutuila. Fortunately for the indigenous islanders, Americans ignored Samoa except as a harbor for the U.S. Navy. Two treaties of cession were eventually approved by Congress in 1929, and they took the most unusual tack of prohibiting land sales to non-Samoans. This factor more than any other helped preserve the traditional culture of Native Samoans.

The Hawaiian Islands also were annexed during this era. The annexation was really a coup d'état during which American sugar plantation owners overthrew Queen Lili'uokalani and the Native Hawaiian monarchy and created a republic in 1893. Hawaii was annexed by the United States five years later. During these early years, cultural attacks were committed on Native Hawaiians. They were prohibited from using their native language, and a great many indigenous Hawaiian lands were confiscated. Unlike the Native Samoans, who successfully prevented the loss of their lands, Hawaiian courts introduced by missionaries and American lawyers over the thirty years preceding annexation initiated a process that made land available to non-Hawaiians.

The first two decades of the twentieth century brought further attacks on American Indians. These assaults took several forms, from the Indian Citizenship Act passed in 1924 to restrictions on American Indian *religion. In 1921 the head of the

Indian Service issued administrative orders out-lawing Indian dancing. Indians were restricted from leaving their reservations. Indian children were taken, sometimes forcibly, from their families and placed in Indian boarding schools, where they were prevented from speaking their language, practicing Indian religions, or even wearing traditional Indian clothing or hair styles.

Opposing this cultural war were many Indian leaders and John Collier, a New York City social worker who left the city to work with the Pueblos in 1920. Collier and others criticized policies that harmed Native American rights, and they sought to demonstrate their adverse effects. Those who opposed the federal Indian agency bureaucracy worked to gather greater information on the state of Indian America. This resulted in one of the most exhaustive collections of data on indigenous peoples in the United States ever compiled.

Secretary of Interior Hubert Work requested that the Institute for Government Research, a private research organization, conduct a thorough examination of American Indian economic and social conditions. The institute appointed Lewis Meriam, a Harvard Law School graduate, to lead the study. The researchers conducted on-site visits to reservations, agencies, Indian hospitals and schools, and off-reservation Indian communities. Commonly referred to as the Meriam Report, this study, *The Problem of Indian Administration* (1928), revealed the impoverished, hideous conditions under which American Indians lived, and it condemned the Indian Service. Forced acculturation as a government policy had failed, and this report provided the basis for the subsequent legal reforms to be known as the Indian New Deal.

Era of Indian Reorganization, 1928–40. The Great Depression facilitated reform and legal experimentation. It fell to the new administration led by Franklin Roosevelt to implement basic changes.

John Collier was appointed the new commissioner of Indian Affairs for Roosevelt's New Deal government. He was instrumental in crafting the Indian New Deal's hallmark legislation, the Indian Reorganization Act (IRA) of 1934. Not all the measures Collier wanted were approved, but allotment was abolished, surplus lands were restored to tribes, new governments were encouraged on reservations, and attacks on Indian culture were halted.

Of particular note was the creation of new tribal governments. Each tribe was required to vote on whether to extend the IRA to their reservation through a new governmental framework. This in-volved creating tribal constitutions with tribal councils and tribal chairmen. One hundred and seventy-four tribes approved of the Indian New Deal governments, seventy-two rejected the constitutions, and seventeen with a majority rejecting the IRA governments had to live under the new governments, because the number who did not vote (their nonvotes were counted as yes votes) pushed approval into the majority. The largest Indian nation, the Navajo Nation, rejected the IRA referendum.

By the late 1930s the favorable climate for the Indian New Deal had ended, and Congress slashed funding for Indian programs. With the onset of World War II, the Indian New Deal died from a lack of financial and political support.

Termination and Reaction, 1940–68. In part because of the heroic contributions of Native Americans to the war effort, in 1946 Congress created the Indian Claims Commission (ICC) legislation. Before establishment of the commission, Congress had (in 1855) created the Court of Claims, which provided the only legal recourse for tribes contesting treaty violations. The Court of Claims could hear treaty complaints only if Congress authorized a specific case, so Native Americans had very limited access to the court as a result. The Indian Claims Commission Act authorized the commission to hear all claims, to be filed before 1951. It had the power to recommend monetary compensation, to be appropriated by Congress, for illegal takings of tribal lands. Limiting financial restitution, the act detailed that compensation would be determined by the value of the land at the time of the taking and that the value of federal funds and property already given to tribes would be deducted from the financial award as gratuitous offsets. First created to last ten years, the ICC was in operation until 1978 because so many cases were filed. Moreover, the ICC generated a number of investigations into the recognition of tribes. An entirely new area of law emerged, setting the criteria for official recognition.

Shortly after creation of the ICC, the Cold War began, and one of its side effects was to hamper the ICC and other Indian programs. Once again there were attempts to destroy Indian culture, which was seen as suspect by the majority of Americans. This time, greater use was made of the law and the damage to indigenous peoples was significant.

The ICC soon became an agent to prepare tribes for "abolition." The commission was to clean the slate of all outstanding legal disputes, and once this was accomplished, all federal–tribal legal relationships would be terminated and Native Americans would be ready to assume a fully assimilated American life. No legal exceptions were to be made; the trust relationship was to be terminated. Federal services were to be stopped and reservations abolished. Congress enacted Termination, and the process of tribal termination began on an individual tribal basis in 1954.

Termination was authorized from 1954 to 1966. During this period, 109 tribes and bands, comprising 11,500 Indians, were terminated, and in the process they lost more than 1.3 million acres of land. The largest tribes affected were the Menominee of Wisconsin and the Klamath of Oregon, who were thrown into abject poverty.

Together with Termination, Congress adopted two other programs that had significant impacts on Indian peoples. The most successful attempt to limit Indian sovereignty came with passage of Public Law 280. Under this statute, selected state governments could take criminal and civil jurisdiction away from Indian courts on Indian reservations without Native American consent. In a federal program called Relocation, young Indians had to leave reservations and take up residence in cities. They were supposed to be given housing and job training, but the housing tended to be ramshackle ghetto apartments and the training proved to be for nonskilled and, all too often, nonexistent jobs. The combination of Termination, Public Law 280, and Relocation constituted the strongest legal attack on Indian rights and sovereignty since the adoption of the Constitution. The 1950s were the nadir of American Indian law.

Era of Self-determination, 1968–Present. The 1960s and beyond represent a revival in legal recognition and protection of Native American rights and sovereignty. Much of this revival originated in the American Indian communities with the rise of Red Power movements, pan-Indian organizations, Indian lawyers, and the Native American Rights Fund. At the same time, the majority society, the courts, and the federal government realized the failures of Termination and Relocation and moved toward implementing greater self-determination for Native Americans.

The Civil Rights movement of the 1960s and 1970s resulted, for Native Americans, in the Indian Bill of Rights, an amendment to the Civil Rights Act of 1968. The Indian Bill of Rights differed slightly from the Bill of Rights in order to accommodate cultural differences, and despite its good intentions, it potentially infringed upon tribal sovereignty. In *Santa Clara Pueblo* v. *Martinez* (1978), the Supreme Court recognized tribes as quasi-sovereign nations and stopped appellate court expansions of the Indian Bill of Rights at the expense of the power of tribal governments.

Indigenous water rights were also protected. Building upon *Winters* v. *United States* (1908), which guaranteed Indian reservations a right to water, the Supreme Court ruled in *Arizona* v. *California* (1963) that Indian reservations had rights to as much water as would be needed for successful irrigation. Similarly, tribal fishing rights were preserved against the rights of states seeking to regulate them in the Pacific Northwest during the 1970s.

Native Hawaiians have sought recognition as Native Americans, with access to programs that serve Indians and Alaska Natives. Congress has approved Native Hawaiian rights to autonomy in their internal affairs, a right to reorganize a Native Hawaiian governing body, and the general right of self-determination and self-governance.

Rights were also accorded to Native Samoans and Native Alaskans. In 1960 a constitution was approved that provided a legal basis for Samoa's government. Eventually Samoans elected a governor and created a two-chambered assembly, or fono. Samoan government is a combination of American and traditional Samoan governance structures. Samoa, like Guam, retains limited territorial sovereignty as an unincorporated territory administered by the Department of the Interior.

When Native Alaskans submitted claims for hundreds of thousands of acres they had lost to the state of Alaska and the federal government, it became obvious that Congress needed to deal with this issue in a more comprehensive manner. Congress passed the Alaska Native Claims Settlement Act in 1971. Native Alaskans gained direct access to forty million acres of public domain. Under the act, native regional corporations were set up with close to a billion dollars in reserves to administer the lands and other economic activities for the bands, tribes, and villages. Not all worked out well. For example, a cap was placed on oil and mineral royalties for Native Alaskans that prevented more than a 2 percent return.

In the 1970s the process of restoring recognition of terminated American Indian tribes began, and through the cooperation of tribes and states Public Law 280 was retroceded. The Indian Self-Determination and Education Assistance Act became law in 1975. The Indian Child Welfare Act of 1978 protected Indian children from being taken from Indian families and placed in nonindigenous environments. Indian religious freedom was also strengthened. The American Indian Religious Freedom Act was passed in 1978. And when the Supreme Court, in *Employment Division, Department of Human Resources of Oregon* v. *Alfred L. Smith* (1990), restricted the ability of the Native American Church to use peyote in its ceremonies, Congress passed legislation that further enhanced Indian freedom of religion.

Economic freedoms were expanded for Indian tribes when the Supreme Court, in *Cabazon Band of Mission Indians* v. *California* (1988), allowed Indian commercial *gambling. This was followed by the Indian Gaming Regulatory Act of 1988, which created the National Indian Gaming Commission to regulate gaming and protected the establishment of casinos on Indian land from state authorities.

The era of self-determination also resulted in Indian tribes gaining greater rights to run their own governments and avoid interference from the Bureau of Indian Affairs. However, by the 1990s Supreme Court decisions were steadily undercutting self-determination by allowing states to gain greater access to regulation over reservation lands and tribal court jurisdictions. Self-determination resulted in several legal breakthroughs for indigenous Americans, but they are not firmly established and are subject to destruction by any one of the three primary branches of the federal government.

[*See also* American Revolution, Legal Impact of; Civil Rights and Civil Liberties; Native American Removal]

• Wilcomb Washburn, *Red Man's Land/White Man's Law*, 1971. Russel Lawrence Barsh and James Youngblood Henderson, *The Road: Indian Tribes and Political Liberty*, 1980. Vine Deloria Jr. and Clifford Lytle, *The Nations Within: The Past and Future of American Indian Sovereignty*, 1984. Francis Paul Prucha, *The Great Father: The United States Government and the American Indians*, 2 vols., 1984. Charles F. Wilkinson, *American Indians, Time, and the Law: Native Societies in a Modern Constitutional Democracy*, 1987. Mari J. Matsuda, "Law and Culture in the District Court of Honolulu, 1844–1845: A Case Study of the Rise of Legal Consciousness," *American Journal of Legal History* 32 (1988): 16–41. Robert D. Craig, *Historical Dictionary of Polynesia*, 1993. Sidney L. Harring, *Crow Dog's Case: American Indian Sovereignty, Tribal Law, and United States Law in the Nineteenth Century*, 1994. John R. Wunder, "*Retained by the People*": *A History of American Indians and the Bill of Rights*, 1994. John R. Wunder, ed., *Native Americans and the Law: Contemporary and Historical Perspectives on American Indian Rights, Freedom, and Sovereignty*, 6 vols., 1996. David E. Wilkins, *American Indian Sovereignty and the U.S. Supreme Court*, 1997. Sally Engle Merry, *Colonizing Hawai'i: The Cultural Power of Law*, 2000.

—John R. Wunder and John P. Husmann

NATIVE AMERICANS AND THE LAW: NATIVE AMERICAN LAW AND TRIBAL SOVEREIGNTY

Law as it applies to Indians in the United States is complex, not least because of the multiplicity of overlapping jurisdictions and the history regarding the European conquest of North America. There are about 350 federally recognized Indian tribes in the contiguous states, and some 500 if Alaska is included. These numbers do not include the many groups claiming tribal existence, but which are not recognized as such by the United States. The federal government is continually evaluating the claims of different groups and granting, or denying, federal recognition. Nor do these numbers include native Hawaiians, who inhabit a place in the law both ethnically and historically different from the tribes of North America.

This area of the law is further complicated by the nascent body of *international law that applies to *indigenous people, which theoretically may have an impact on the domestic law of the United States with respect to Indians. In addition, the existence of American federalism means that state law comes into play, though certainly within American law the federal government holds the dominant role.

There is more diversity among the tribes of North American than there is among the present nations of Europe, a condition that would certainly have been even more dramatic prior to the arrival of Europeans in America. Hence, generalizations regarding the legal systems of the various tribes, either precontact or today, are dangerous, and tend to evolve too quickly from generality to stereotype. Nevertheless, a few broad observations can be made.

First, most modern tribes are small, homogeneous communities, with resulting small, rather informal governments. American-style separation of powers does not exist in pristine form on many reservations. Matters such as conflict of interest and nepotism are of necessity tolerated and managed on reservations.

Second, tribal judicial systems tend to be more informal than off-reservation systems, and methods of dispute resolution called *"alternative" off-reservation are more likely to be "primary" under traditional law.

Third, Indian tribes have suffered a long series

of attempts by Europeans and their descendants to destroy tribal customary and traditional law. Nevertheless, these kinds of indigenous laws in fact survive, and are subject to modern resurgence, especially in the reapplication of tribal common, or customary, law.

Fourth, notwithstanding the above, the on-reservation influence of off-reservation law has been great. Tribal judicial systems have become increasing like their off-reservation analogs, at least partly in an attempt to have off-reservation courts recognize tribal judgments as legitimate.

Regarding the laws internal to tribes, then, it is plain that tribes vary greatly among themselves, such that generalizations about internal tribal *custom, law, and practice are difficult. Yet it is fair to say that tribes generally retain and exhibit important legal differences from the states, the United States, and foreign nations about legal matters.

Without diminishing the importance of internal tribal law to the governing of tribes, the dominant law regarding tribes in the United States is federal law. There are seven well-established principles of domestic federal Indian law.

First, tribes are governments. Before the United States became a country, and in the republic's early days, North American tribes were treated by the Europeans as sovereign entities, entitled to self-government. This recognition began with the state-to-state negotiations that led to the making of treaties between the United States and the tribes. In the Supreme Court case of *Cherokee Nation* v. *Georgia* (1831), Chief Justice John *Marshall characterized the tribes as "domestic dependent nations." While subsequent Courts have defined and redefined the domestic limits on tribal *sovereignty, the principle of tribal self-government remains the essential characteristic of federal Indian law.

Second, tribal sovereignty is inherent. The right of self-determination reflected in the first principle does not derive from the United States, but has existed since time immemorial in the tribes themselves. The Supreme Court affirmed this principle in *United States* v. *Wheeler* (1978), holding that a prosecution by the Navajo Tribe was not a federal prosecution, so that a later prosecution by the United States was not *double jeopardy.

The inherent tribal sovereignty recognized under federal law in the two principles mentioned make the station of Indians and their tribes unique among American ethnic groups. Members of other groups must participate in American government as individuals, or as members of private, voluntary organizations. Only American Indians are recognized to be members of their own governments.

Third, the United States Constitution does not bind the actions of tribal governments. The U.S. Supreme Court decided in *Talton* v. *Mayes* (1896) that the general terms of the Constitution—the Fifth Amendment in that case—do not control the activities of tribal governments. This is a sensible result, as the tribes were not parties to the Constitution's ratification, either originally, or through the process of statehood. The Constitution applies to state action, meaning state or federal action, not tribal action.

It is important to note that the third principle does not mean that individual Indians do not have rights protected by the United States Constitution. They do. But neither they, nor non-Indians, have those rights against a tribal government. In those relationships, both Indians and non-Indians have the protections of the Indian Civil Rights Act, 25 U.S. Code §§ 1301–1303 (1994), which contains many of the protections of the federal *Bill of Rights and the *Fourteenth Amendment. Non-Indians dealing with tribal governments have the additional protection of an expanding federal *common law doctrine flowing from Supreme Court authority that limits the powers of tribes over non-Indians, in cases such as *Oliphant* v. *Suquamish Indian Tribe* (1978) and *Nevada* v. *Hicks* (2001).

Fourth, Congress has plenary power over Indian affairs. The Supreme Court has rarely stricken a Congressional enactment affecting tribes as beyond the constitutional power of Congress to act. Most agree that the constitutional source of this power comes from article I, section 8, clause 3, the Indian commerce clause. It was under this power that Congress enacted the Indian Civil Rights Act. Whether the present Court will limit the reach of the Indian commerce clause, concomitantly with its limitation of the reach of the interstate commerce clause, is an active question in American Indian law, but such a limitation has not yet come.

Fifth, state law has only limited application to Indian country. This result flows both from the supremacy clause of the Constitution in article VI, and from the so-called dormant Indian commerce clause in article I. Both of these clauses have application well beyond American Indian law. When Congress passes a statute that lies within its power to pass, or the executive branch properly promulgates a regulation, then inconsistent state laws fall under the supremacy clause. There are many Indian cases applying this doctrine, such as *White Mountain Apache Tribe* v. *Bracker* (1980) and *Montana* v. *Blackfeet Tribe* (1985), often involving state attempts to tax reservation activity.

There are times when state law is preempted even when Congress has not acted, by the force of the Indian commerce clause alone. The famous "infringement test" from *Williams* v. *Lee* (1959), supplies the law: the question is "whether the state action infring[es] on the right of reservation Indians to make their own laws and be ruled by them."

Between these two modes of analysis—preemption by positive Congressional acts and infringement under the dormant commerce clause—the courts prefer the former, as in *McClanahan* v. *Arizona State Tax Commission* (1973). There are many more cases striking down state laws because they are inconsistent with federal statutes than there are cases striking down state laws because they infringe on tribal self-government.

It is noteworthy that two of the most visible aspects of American Indian law—the laws regarding reservation casino *gambling and those governing the *adoption of Indian children—flow from the two principles discussed earlier. Gambling is largely regulated by state law, not federal law, and those state laws do not generally apply on reservations, as the Court found in *California* v. *Cabazon Band of Mission Indians* (1987). Congress responded to this situation by enacting, under its plenary power, the Indian Gaming Regulatory Act, 25 U.S. Code §§ 2701–2721 (1994). Likewise, the rules of adoption are state, not federal. Reacting to what it saw as too aggressive Indian-child adoptions, Congress passed the Indian Child Welfare Act, 25 U.S. Code §§ 1901–1963 (1994), which places jurisdiction over non-divorce-related custody and adoption matters concerning Indian children under the jurisdiction of tribal courts.

Sixth, *treaties are valid and enforceable agreements, binding on the United States. The United States entered into treaties with the tribes from the earliest days of the nation. Treaty-making ended in 1871, although agreements between the federal government and the tribes still continued past that date, usually embodied in the form of executive orders. These treaties, like international treaties, are the "supreme law of the land" under the Constitution, and are enforceable as such. Treaties, in fact, are a large part of the federal "preemption package" that tribes use to challenge the on-reservation application of state law.

Notwithstanding the general validity of Indian treaties, there are many Supreme Court cases accepting as legitimate the abrogation of those treaties by the United States acting alone. Such an abrogation can come expressly through Congressional action, as in *South Dakota* v. *Yankton Sioux Tribe* (1997) and *Rosebud Sioux Tribe* v. *Kneip* (1977), or by implication, when Congress enacts a law in apparent conflict with a tribe's treaty right, as in *United States* v. *Dion* (1986). The *Dion* case established a strong test for these latter abrogations: it is essential to this case that Congress actually considered the conflict between the statute and Indian treaties, and chose to abrogate the treaty.

Tribes are not without a remedy when their treaties are abrogated. In *United States* v. *Sioux Tribe of Indians* (1980), the Court affirmed a large award from the Court of Claims in favor of a tribe whose treaty was abrogated in the 1870s.

Seventh, a *trust responsibility exists between the federal government and the Indian tribes. "Humanity," wrote John Marshall in 1823, "acting on public opinion, has established as a general rule, that the conquered shall not be wantonly oppressed." (*Johnson* v. *M'Intosh* (1823)). A few years later, the Chief Justice, in *Cherokee Nation* v. *Georgia* (1831), wrote further that the relationship of the United States to the tribes was like that of a guardian to its ward. These pronouncements led to the early common-law establishment of a trusteeship between the two, a trusteeship that was later made statutory, in part, by the General Allotment Act, 25 U.S. Code § 348 (1994).

The parameters of this trust responsibility are such that it is similar to the usual law as it pertains to private fiduciary duties. The fact that the United States, as fiduciary, is also a government, subject to sovereign immunity, has caused the Supreme Court some trouble in the past, as in *United States* v. *Mitchell* (I) (1980) and (II) (1983). It is because of this complication that the Court in the *Sioux Tribe of Indians* (1980) found difficult the question of whether a unilateral abrogation of an Indian treaty is compensable, and established a good faith test. Because the government is the fiduciary for the tribes, the Court noted, some abrogations might be mere management of the beneficiary's property, while others might be plain treaty violations. The distinction, then, turned on whether the government made a good faith attempt to compensate the Indians for the abrogation. If so, then the abrogation was not compensable. In *Sioux Tribe*, the Court found that the government had abrogated the treaty without good faith, and affirmed the Claims Court judgment.

In summary, this from the Supreme Court of the United States: "It must always be remembered that the various Indian tribes were once independent and sovereign nations, and that their claim to sovereignty long predates that of our own Government" (*McClanahan* v. *Arizona State Tax Commission* (1973)).

• Karl N. Llewellyn and E. Adamson Hoebel, *The Cheyenne Way: Conflict and Case Law in Primitive Jurisprudence*, 1941. Wilcomb E. Washburn, ed., *The Indian and the White Man*, 1964. Rennard Strickland, *Fire and the Spirits: Cherokee Law from Clan to Court*, 1975. Charles F. Wilkinson, *American Indians, Time and the Law*, 1987. William C. Canby Jr., *American Indian Law in a Nutshell*, 2d ed., 1988. Robert A. Williams Jr., *The American Indian in Western Legal Thought: The Discourses of Conquest*, 1990. Francis Paul Prucha, *American Indian Treaties: The History of a Political Anomaly*, 1994. Frank Pommersheim, *Braid of Feathers: Pluralism, Legitimacy, Sovereignty, and the Importance of Tribal Court Jurisprudence*, 1995. Jo Carrillo, ed., *Readings in American Indian Law: Recalling the Rhythm of Survival*, 1998.

—Robert Laurence

NATIVE AMERICANS AND THE LAW: NATIVE AMERICANS UNDER CURRENT UNITED STATES LAW

Native American tribal governments are an integral part of the political fabric of the United States. As the Supreme Court of the United States determined in *Cherokee Nation* v. *Georgia* (1831), tribal governments are not "states" in a constitutional sense, nor are they "foreign states," at least for purposes of Article III original jurisdiction. Instead, they are "domestic dependent nations," with many sovereign powers retained from the pre-European contact period. As tribal governments have grown in political and economic power, the Supreme Court, the United States Congress, the federal executive, and the tribes have engaged in an increasingly important discussion to determine the scope of the tribes' powers. States, municipalities, and individual citizens have all contributed to this conversation. The result is a legal regime of fascinating complexity.

The United States government recognizes more than 500 tribal governments. Some have large membership bases and control vast domains. The Navajo, the largest federally recognized tribe, comprise a population of nearly 300,000 and govern lands totaling in excess of 15 million acres spread over three southwestern states, while the Cherokee Nation, the second largest tribe, has about 200,000 citizens. Most tribes, however, have fewer than 1,000 members. Approximately 40 percent of all federally recognized tribes are village groups in Alaska. The smallest tribal reservation is less than 100 acres. The state with the largest Native American population is California, with Oklahoma a close second. Alaska is the state with the highest percentage of Native Americans living within its borders.

Each tribal government operates according to its own constitutional rules. Most tribes have written *constitutions. Many of these are modeled after form constitutions prepared by the United States Department of the Interior pursuant to the Indian Reorganization Act (IRA) of 1934, a New Deal initiative designed to strengthen tribal government. Tribes that operate under these constitutions are called "IRA" tribes. By electing, according to the terms of the Indian Reorganization Act, not to opt out of the Act's coverage, these tribes were empowered by Congress to borrow funds for economic development and form tribal *corporations. Some tribes, most notably the Navajo, voted to opt out of the IRA's coverage. The Oklahoma tribes were not covered by the Act; instead, they were made subject to a similar statute, the Oklahoma Indian Welfare Act. IRA tribes ordinarily have strong executives, although constitutional amendment has replaced many of these with balanced executives, legislatures, and judiciaries.

Tribal governments exercise power that has been diminished over time by acts of the federal government. Congress, which has "plenary" power over Indian affairs, *Lone Wolf* v. *Hitchcock* (1903), has repeatedly acted to limit the scope of tribal power. Perhaps the most dramatic instance occurred in 1968 with the passage of the Indian Civil Rights Act. As non-parties to the United States Constitution, tribes are not subject to the restrictions contained in the *Bill of Rights or subsequent amendments (*Talton* v. *Mayes* (1896)). Thus tribes have been free historically to legislate to the extent allowed by their own constitutions. Many of these constitutions contained provisions analogous to the provisions of the Bill of Rights. Nevertheless, in 1968, inspired by the *Civil Rights movement, Congress passed the Indian Civil Rights Act, imposing on tribal governments many (but not all) of the provisions of the Bill of Rights and other limitations as well, for example, the 1968 Act affords individuals *equal protection and *due process protections, but does not prohibit the establishment of *religion by tribal governments. The ICRA also denies tribal courts the power to impose sentences in criminal cases in excess of $5,000 or one year in jail. This restriction has made it difficult for many tribal courts to address criminal activity in their jurisdictions. The Indian Civil Rights Act provides statutory, but not constitutional, limitations. Individuals who feel their Indian Civil Rights Act rights have been violated by a tribal government cannot bring a federal civil rights suit to challenge that action. Instead, as the Supreme Court made clear in *Santa Clara Pueblo* v. *Martinez* (1978), persons may bring Indian Civil Rights Act claims only in tribal court, and then only if the tribe has accorded that court jurisdiction.

Congress has also limited the power of tribes by making tribal governments subject to certain laws of general application—for example, environmental protection laws. Where these laws fail to mention tribes, and their application impinges on treaty rights, courts must make individual determinations to assess whether a given law applies to a tribe. Congress has the power to abrogate Indian *treaty rights, but when it does so it is liable to pay the tribe compensation under the Fifth Amendment to the United States Constitution. Before a court will find a Fifth Amendment taking to have occurred, it will look to Congress's intent. Some federal circuit courts have found tribal accountability under the Occupational Safety and Health Act and federal collective bargaining laws.

Since the late 1970s, the Supreme Court has also been an active participant in placing limits on the scope of tribal sovereign power. The Supreme Court is the architect and custodian of a federal common law doctrine called the "discovery doctrine." Introduced in *Johnson* v. *M'Intosh* (1823), the doctrine provided that at the European arrival in the "New World," by agreement of the European sovereigns, title to all discovered lands vested in the discovering European sovereign, while the tribes retained an occupancy right alienable only to the same sovereign. Discovery thus deprived the tribes of the power to alienate their lands freely. In *Oliphant* v. *Suquamish Indian Tribe* (1978), the Supreme Court held that discovery also deprived the tribes of the power to conduct criminal prosecutions of non-Indians. The *Oliphant* holding was expanded in *Duro* v. *Reina* (1990), to proscribe tribal criminal prosecutions of nonmember Indians. The *Duro* decision prompted a federal legislative override; the constitutionality of this override has been questioned, and its effect remains uncertain. Other discovery-related limitations on tribal power involve the exercise of civil jurisdiction. In the key case in this line, *Montana* v. *United States* (1981), the Court held that tribes

could not exercise civil regulatory jurisdiction over non-Indian activities on non-Indian-owned lands within the boundaries of reservations unless the non-Indian had some commercial relationship with the tribe or the activity threatened or had some direct effect on the tribe's political integrity, economic security, or health or welfare. Recently, in *Nevada* v. *Hicks* (2001), the court expanded this rule to deny a tribal court the right to hear a *tort claim brought by a tribe member against a non-Indian state officer for acts committed on tribally owned lands within the reservation.

Tribes exercise jurisdiction over Indian Country, as defined in 11 U.S. Code §1151 (1994). Indian Country includes all land within the limits of Indian reservations, all "dependent Indian communities," and all restricted Indian allotments— that is, individual restricted parcels formerly part of reservations but allotted to individual tribal members pursuant to the General Allotment Act of 1887 or by similar statutes. Reservations, for the most part, resulted from *treaties. Conceptually, "reservations" were not lands given to the tribes, but tribal lands reserved by the tribes from larger tracts, other parts of which were ceded to the United States. This applies to other treaty rights as well: where the rights, for example, to hunt and fish, are not expressly ceded by the tribe, they are deemed "reserved." In most instances—the lands of the Five Civilized Tribes in Oklahoma and the Pueblos are the most notable exceptions—the tribes do not own the underlying fee title to reservation land. Instead, that title is held to have passed to the United States by way of the original European discovery of the land.

The situation of the Alaska Natives is different. In 1971, Congress settled tribal claims to most of Alaska by passing the Alaska Native Claims Settlement Act (ANCSA), under which, in exchange for relinquishing their claims to 365 million acres, Alaska Natives received land selection rights to 44 million acres plus cash payments equaling $963 million. Title to these new native lands was vested not in tribal governments, but in tribal village corporations, chartered under state law, and individual Alaska Natives became corporate shareholders. According to the Supreme Court, most Alaska Native land ceased at that time to be Indian Country (*Alaska* v. *Native Village of Venetie Tribal Government* (1998)).

The United States is trustee or guardian for the tribes. This role traces back to the Supreme Court's 1831 opinion in *Cherokee Nation* v. *Georgia.* Chief Justice John *Marshall wrote that the relationship of the tribes to the United States resembles that of a "ward to its guardian." Because of this role, the United States holds the underlying fee title to tribal lands in *trust for the tribes. For this reason, they are styled "trust lands." The role of the United States as guardian or trustee has several consequences. When managing tribal or individual Indian property, the United States is held to a high standard of care. The tribal status as ward entitles tribes to sue officers of the United States when that standard of care is violated. In addition, because they are federal wards, tribes may seek United States assistance in litigating against states or private parties. As the Supreme Court decided in *United States* v. *Kagama* (1886), the guardianship responsibility also serves as an extraconstitutional source of authority for Congress to pass legislation affecting Indians.

The Bureau of Indian Affairs (BIA) in the Department of the Interior is the principal federal agency charged with carrying out the trust responsibility. The BIA is headed by the Assistant Secretary for Indian Affairs. Other offices charged with carrying out the trust responsibility include the Indian Resources Section in the United States Department of Justice's Environment and Natural Resources Division. The trust responsibility runs to all federally recognized tribes. Some tribes are not federally recognized, although many of these are recognized by the states in which they are located. Some groups are not officially recognized by either state or federal governments. The Department of the Interior has established a procedure whereby such groups can petition for federal recognition by demonstrating political cohesiveness and continuity. Currently, the Branch of Acknowledgment and Research of the Bureau of Indian Affairs oversees the process. Alternatively, non–federally recognized tribes can petition Congress for recognition.

Tribal status is a political classification. Thus statutes and regulations providing different treatment for Indians as enrolled tribal members are not subject to challenge as race *discrimination under the *Fourteenth Amendment's equal protection clause (*Morton* v. *Mancari* (1974)). Statutes affecting Indians and Indian tribes are for the most part collected in the U.S. Code's Title 25. Federal agencies also issue regulations affecting Indians and tribal governments.

Not all substantive tribal rights, however, are located in statutes and regulations. Prior to 1871, the federal government dealt with tribes by treaty. Many of these pre-1871 treaties remain in force. Treaties were routinely negotiated in ways disadvantageous to tribes. United States negotiators frequently worked into these documents legal concepts and terms unfamiliar to tribal negotiators, binding tribes to obligations they did not fully understand. Treaties were often executed by tribal signatories appointed by the United States. Language difficulties confounded many tribal negotiators. For these and other reasons, when courts interpret these treaties today, they employ canons of construction similar to those used when courts interpret long corporate-form adhesion *contracts: ambiguous terms are interpreted in favor of the Indians; treaties are interpreted as the Indians would have understood them; and treaties are liberally construed in favor of the Indians. Application of these canons does not always meet with popular approval. In 1974, when a U.S. district court ruled that the treaties at issue in *United States* v. *Washington* (1974), must be interpreted to allow the tribes 50 percent of the anadromous fish run in Washington, the federal judge was hanged in effigy.

Perhaps the most complicated interaction in federal Indian law is that between the tribes and the states. The Supreme Court, in *Worcester* v. *Georgia* (1832), attempted to establish a bright-line rule that would disallow any state authority in Indian Country. This rule has been eroded over time, however, and while *Worcester* still provides a benchmark, other analytical methods are employed to determine whether a state's purported exercise of jurisdiction is valid. The Court introduced one such method in *Williams* v. *Lee* (1959). *Williams* involved a state court's attempt to exercise jurisdiction over a breach of contract claim brought by a non-Indian storeowner against a Navajo couple for failure to pay an on-reservation store account. The Court held that the state had no authority to exercise jurisdiction over an on-reservation transaction if to do so would infringe on the "right of reservation Indians to make their own laws and be governed by them." In 1980, the Court identified federal preemption against the backdrop of tribal sovereignty as an additional ground for denying state jurisdiction. If the United States heavily regulates timber harvesting on a reservation, for example, a state cannot impose taxes on non-Indian truck operators using Bureau of Indian Affairs' roads to carry timber off the reservation under contract with the tribe (*White Mountain Apache Tribe* v. *Bracker* (1980)). The difficulty of applying these tests and enforcing the exercise of state jurisdiction even where appropriate has led many states, with the Court's encouragement, to enter into compacts with tribes setting forth the terms of resolution of jurisdictional disputes. These compacts cover a wide area, from tax-revenue sharing to water rights sales.

Perhaps the most publicly discussed state-tribal compacts today are those involving Indian gaming. Indian gaming as an industry began modestly in the 1970s. At that time, California moved to shut down the Cabazon Band's bingo operation. The tribe took the case to the Supreme Court, which ruled that California had no authority to prohibit or regulate the operation (*California* v. *Cabazon Band of Mission Indians* (1987)). Overnight, other tribes moved to establish gaming facilities. In 1988, Congress responded to complaints from states that without some regulation, lawlessness would result. It passed the Indian Gaming Regulatory Act, which divides gaming into three classes: Class I (traditional tribal games with nominal prizes); Class II (bingo and like games); and Class III (other games, including slot machines, horse racing, and card games played against the house). Before a tribe can open a facility offering Class III games, it must compact the terms of operation (including law enforcement) with the state. In addition to tribal supervision and compacted state supervision, Indian gaming facilities are subject to federal supervision through the National Indian Gaming Commission. As a result, Indian gaming facilities are heavily regulated. While only a minority of tribes are located in areas sufficiently close to large urban areas to draw a large number of customers, many tribes receive some economic benefit from gaming. These benefits pass directly to tribal members and the surrounding community as a result of federal requirements that revenues go to public functions (see GAMBLING).

Federal Indian policy has long expressed support for tribal economic development. In the Indian Reorganization Act of 1934, Congress provided for the creation of tribal corporations to carry out development projects. Since that time, Congress has amended restrictive legislation to allow tribes more flexibility in developing their economies. The Indian Mineral Development Act of 1982, for example, allowed tribes for the first time to enter into joint ventures and other types of agreements with outside mineral development partners. Because of their remote locations and various statutory limitations, including the restraint on land alienation, which precludes mortgaging, tribes have had to be creative in economic development planning. One natural avenue has been the sale of duty free items subject to high taxation by the states. These products (including cigarettes) are sold off-reservation at inflated tax rates, partly to discourage use. To the extent that tribes can sell them on-reservation without these taxes, they can sell them at competitive prices and draw business to their remote locations. In a series of decisions, the Supreme Court has held that while tribes can sell tax-free to their members, they cannot sell tax-free to nonmembers. Difficulties in working out a mechanism to enforce the collection of taxes on nonmembers has led many states, such as Oklahoma, to compact with the tribes terms for tax revenue collection and distribution that are intended ultimately to benefit both tribe and state (see TAXATION).

One modern trend that has facilitated tribal economic development is the transfer of responsibility for the management of federal programs for tribes from the federal government to the tribes themselves. The Self-Determination and Education Assistance Act of 1975 established a procedure for tribes to apply to the U.S. Department of the Interior to take over control of existing BIA programs in Indian Country. Congress subsequently expanded this program to allow certain tribes (designated "Self Governance" tribes) to create their own programs using federal funds.

Tribal economic, political, and cultural development has also been encouraged by federal Indian education legislation. The most important of these statutes, the Indian Education Act of 1972, established the Office of Indian Education and the National Advisory Council on Indian Education and made federal funds available for Native American educational initiatives at all grade levels.

A final, and increasingly important, tribal political initiative that has facilitated tribal economic development is the creation of tribal judicial systems. Tribal courts hear both civil and criminal cases and often provide non-Indians their first exposure to tribal political culture. Not all tribal courts are equally busy. Some states (the so-called "Public Law 280" states) assumed jurisdiction over criminal and civil causes arising in Indian Country during the 1960s pursuant to federal legislation, and in these states, on-reservation disputes are routinely litigated in state court. Other states, on the other hand, including Oklahoma, have made provision for tribal court decisions to be recognized in state courts, thus making possible greater participation of tribal courts in the national justice system.

• Felix S. Cohen, *Handbook of Federal Indian Law*, 1982. Charles F. Wilkinson, *American Indians, Time and the Law: Native Societies in a Modern Constitutional Democracy*, 1988. Stephen L. Pevar, *The Rights of Indians and Tribes: The Basic ACLU Guide to Indian Tribal Rights*,

2d ed., 1992. Frank Pommersheim, *Braid of Feathers: American Indian Law and Modern Tribal Life*, 1997. William C. Canby Jr., *American Indian Law in a Nutshell*, 3d ed., 1998. David H. Getches, Charles F. Wilkinson, and Robert A. Williams Jr. *Cases and Materials on Federal Indian Law*, 4th ed., 1998. Monroe E. Price, Robert N. Clinton, and Nell. J. Newton, *American Indian Law: Cases and Materials*, 4th ed., 2001.

—Lindsay G. Robertson

NATURAL LAW. *See* Legal Systems.

NATURAL LAW THEORY. Theories of natural law have played an important role in the development of Western *jurisprudence for more than two millennia. Both Plato and Aristotle developed their legal and political theories in part on the assumption that there were laws of universal applicability, found in nature, that were both unchangeable and a standard against which all human, positivist laws could be measured. These theories of natural law were adopted and adapted by the Roman lawyers, and played some role in Roman legal theory. They are found both in the writings of the Roman jurists contained in the *Digest,* one of the constituent parts of the *Corpus Iuris Civilis,* and especially in the legal and political writings of Cicero.

During the Middle Ages, natural law theories were further adopted into the laws of the Catholic Church, and became the basis for the theoretical elaboration of law in the writings of Thomas Aquinas. In the early modern period, natural law continued to be a vital force in legal theory on the European continent. Jurists such as Grotius, Puffendorf, and Suarez used natural law as a platform on which to develop their theories of *international law. Macchiavelli and Hooker used natural law for their theoretical elaboration of notions of *sovereignty. Indeed, no European jurist prior to the beginning of the nineteenth century was able to ignore natural law theory. One could argue whether there was such a thing as natural law, but the strength of the natural law tradition was so great that no writer on legal or political subjects for more than two thousand years could fail to deal with it.

In England and the United States, interest in natural law theory was also strong. Many of the crucial debates between Edward Coke and Francis Bacon on the nature of sovereignty and the authority of the *common law centered on their differing conceptions of the relationship between natural law and common law. Especially important in these debates and the development of natural law theories in the common law world was the tradition, dating back to Roman law, of seeing natural law as an embodiment of "pure reason" [*recta ratio*]. This notion of natural law as pure reason, combined with the concept that common law, too, was the embodiment of reason, permitted common law jurists to develop a working theory of the congruence between natural law and common law.

In the sphere of public law, natural law theories were of particular importance. The use of natural law theories as a basis for developing concepts of sovereignty in the sixteenth and seventeenth centuries led to the later transformation of these theories into a basis for the development of theories of inherent "natural rights." The works of political theorists such as Montesquieu, Hobbes, and above all, John Locke, wrestled with the crucial issues of whether natural law bestowed certain inalienable natural rights upon individuals, rights that could not be abrogated by positivist laws created either by monarchs or legislatures. Thus, natural law theory in the hands of men such as Locke could be used to create a consistent theory of the right of individuals and groups in order to resist the imposition of positive laws that were in derogation of inalienable rights. Natural law was thus able to be used by jurists and political theorists as a basis for justifying the revolutionary movements of the late eighteenth century. Natural law was, in the words of Edward S. Corwin, a principal source for the "higher law" theories that helped formulate a distinctively American constitutional jurisprudence and the ideas of "inalienable" rights, particularly to *liberty and *property and the correlative right of *due process, which underlies so much of American constitutional law.

Natural law theories were well known to American lawyers and jurists in the eighteenth and nineteenth centuries. The works of Montesquieu, Locke, and Grotius were well known to the founders and succeeding generations. Puffendorf's writings were in countless antebellum American libraries. The natural law theories of the Roman jurists were available to Americans in the 1756 English translation of Justinian's *Institutes* by George Harris and the 1812 American revision of Harris by the emigre president of South Carolina College, Thomas Cooper. And, of course, Cicero's writings, so greatly influenced by the Stoics and by natural law theories, were a constant companion of many of the founders and their intellectual heirs. Thus, antebellum American jurists and politicians had available to them both the ancient writings on natural law and the more recent writings of the early modern period and the European Enlightenment.

One area where natural law presented particular problems to American jurists concerned the "peculiar institution" of *slavery. Although slavery was known to the ancients and permitted in Roman law, the Romans did not believe that slavery was a part of natural law, but was instead solely a creation of man-made positivist law. Much of the abolitionist writing both in England and the United States during the eighteenth and early nineteenth century began from the position that slavery as an institution contravened natural law and the inherent natural rights of human beings and therefore was illicit and invalid. Such a theory to proponents of slavery was anathema, for it could lead not only to the eventual prohibition of slavery but also to a legal justification of armed insurrection, if necessary, to achieve that end.

Natural law was also used as a justification for legal decisions regarding private law in the antebellum United States. With the rupture from England and the growing need to develop an American jurisprudence, many judges were unwilling to rest their decisions solely on English precedents. But judges did not then—as they do not now—wish to be seen to be deciding cases on personal prejudice or whim. Thus, many judges sought other sources of authority that might be used to justify holdings when there were no relevant American precedents and when they chose not to cite or follow English law. Natural law was one of these authoritative sources, and proved to be of great value. For example, Chief Justice John *Marshall, in an important case (*Laidlaw* v. *Organ*) on *contract law and the obligation of disclosure arising from the blockade of New Orleans during the War of 1812, based his decision primarily on natural law and reason. Many of the best antebellum judges followed Marshall's lead and utilized natural law as the embodiment of reason, as a justification for private law decisions.

Natural law theories met with strong opposition in the latter part of the nineteenth century and the beginning of the twentieth with the rise of new jurisprudential movements such as pragmatism and the historical school. Some of the most prominent American jurists, particularly Oliver Wendell *Holmes Jr., vehemently argued against the legitimacy of natural law. While natural law theories did not disappear from the legal horizon, they were certainly in eclipse. In the twentieth century, however, they enjoyed something of a limited renaissance. The importance of these theories to the development of American public law was highlighted in particular by Edward S. Corwin's seminal study *The Higher Law Background of American Constitutional Law*. The so-called "rights revolution" of the second half of the twentieth century owes much to the later-eighteenth-century theories of natural law, and the influence of Locke and other theorists is clear in the development of the law in several areas, including, for instance, the development of the idea of a constitutional right to *privacy. At the end of the twentieth century, natural law theory found several new champions, particularly those in the Catholic tradition, such as the legal philosopher John Finnis.

• Edward S. Corwin, *The "Higher Law" Background of American Constitutional Law*, 1955. Carl J. Friedrich, *The Philosophy of Law in Historical Perspective*, 1958. Alexander Passerin D'Entreves, *Natural Law: An Historical Survey*, 1965. John Finnis, *Natural Law and Natural Rights*, 1980. Michael H. Hoffheimer, *Justice Holmes and the Natural Law*, 1992.   —Michael H. Hoeflich

NEGLIGENCE. *See* Torts.

NEGOTIATION is a strategic communication process used to put deals together or resolve conflicts. Each element of that definition reflects a dimension of significant negotiation activity in American legal culture.

Negotiation always involves communication—whether it is in writing, on the telephone, across the conference table, or by e-mail. Sending and receiving messages is fundamental to the process. If effective, that communication is strategic; it reflects thought and deliberate action with a clear objective in mind. Finally, negotiation, as a communication dynamic, is a process. To a large extent, it can be studied, defined, and predicted.

The process of negotiation is a cornerstone of the American legal system. While images of "law" typically reflect the drama of courtroom adjudication, the legal system's reality is dependent on negotiation. In the United States, more than 90 percent of all civil cases are resolved short of a full trial, usually through a negotiated settlement. Most criminal defendants serving time in prison are there not as the result of a trial and conviction, but as the result of a particular negotiation called a *"plea bargain." When one adds to that picture the realization that virtually all transactions resulting in legal agreements emanate from this communication process, the reality is clear. In America, the normative way legal disputes are resolved and transactions occur is through the dynamic of negotiation.

Negotiation strategy generally reflects two approaches. "Competitive negotiation" usually takes place when parties have opposing positions on a matter, or perceive that there is a limited resource—such as money, time, or authority—that must be divided between them. Competitive negotiation tends to be more adversarial because one party's gain often results in the other party's loss.

"Cooperative negotiation" generally occurs when parties are motivated to find an agreement, often one that can more completely meet both parties' needs. While real differences exist, parties embrace a problem-solving approach in an attempt to find a more creative and satisfactory outcome.

Neither approach is inherently good nor bad. Either may be effective in achieving a desired outcome. But the strategies involved, the nature of the communication, and the focus of the process may be quite different.

The negotiation process is central to the American judicial system. First, most courts now require that parties to legal disputes attempt to settle their differences before adjudication at trial. Usually that requirement results in a negotiated settlement. If private settlements did not take place in cases where they were appropriate, courts would not be able to process the cases that need adjudication in a timely manner. Thus the legal system depends on negotiation.

Second, to promote the private resolution of disputes, most jurisdictions protect settlement discussions as a policy matter by designating them as privileged or protected communications. In most cases, the content of settlement negotiations is not subject to judicial inquiry or to testimony by the parties. This protection promotes the free exchange of information and, ultimately, more settlements.

[See also Alternative Dispute Resolution]

—L. Randolph Lowry

NEIGHBORHOOD LAW OFFICES. See Legal Services, Provision of.

NEUTRALITY. See War, Law of.

NEW PROPERTY. See Entitlement.

NEW YORK TIMES CO. V. SULLIVAN, 376 U.S. 254 (1964). L. B. Sullivan, a city commissioner in Montgomery, Alabama, sued the New York Times for libel for an advertisement that criticized Alabama officials for their treatment of civil rights workers. The advertisement contained some minor factual errors—such as alleging that Rev. Martin Luther King Jr. had been arrested seven times, when in fact he had only been arrested four times.

In response to a complaint by the governor, the Times issued a retraction. However, this did not satisfy Sullivan, or ten other officials, who collectively won $5.6 million in judgments against the Times, a sum sufficient to bankrupt the paper. These suits were part of a concerted effort by Alabama officials to stifle reporting of the civil rights movement, which depended on Northern and national media to inform the nation of the horrors perpetrated on civil rights workers by the police in the South.

The U.S. Supreme Court viewed this case as part of an attempt to impose seditious libel on the news media in the guise of civil lawsuits. The Court held that while these were civil actions on their face, they were really attempts by public officials to suppress the press through heavy damages brought by local juries made up entirely of whites who were opposed to integration.

Three justices were willing to declare that public officials could never sue for libel, if the alleged defamation was based on official conduct. The rest of the Court would not go that far. But in the end the Court, in an opinion by Justice William *Brennan, nevertheless made it almost impossible for a public official to win a libel suit. Brennan said that recovery was only possible if the official could prove "actual malice," which Brennan defined as "knowledge that the [publication] was false" or that it was published "with reckless disregard of whether it was false or not." The Court held that this was to be proved by "clear and convincing proof," and unlike most factual issues, was subject to appellate review. In other words, the Court would not allow local juries to punish newspapers for exposing the wrongdoing of popular local officials.

[See also Speech and the Press, Freedom of; Torts]

• Harry Kalven, "The New York Times Case: A Note on 'The Central Meaning of the First Amendment'," Supreme Court Review (1964): 191–221. Anthony Lewis, Make No Law: The Sullivan Case and the First Amendment, 1991.

—Paul Finkelman

NO-FAULT INSURANCE. See Insurance.

NORRIS-LA GUARDIA ACT. See Labor Law: Labor Relations.

NUCLEAR REGULATORY COMMISSION. See Regulation.

NULLIFICATION, JURY. See Jury.

NUREMBERG TRIALS. See War, Law of.

O

OBSCENITY. *See* Harassment; Morality, Ethics, and Crime; Morals Offenses; Organized Crime; Speech and the Press, Freedom of;.

OFFICERS, CORPORATE. *See* Corporation.

OFFICIALS, COURT. *See* Court Officials.

OPTIONS CONTRACTS. *See* Contract Law.

ORATORY, LEGAL. Legal oratory is the art by which an attorney applies facts to the applicable law in an attempt to convince the listener that his client should prevail. The style of legal oratory has evolved over time; as society has changed, so too have the advocates. In the seventeenth and eighteenth centuries, before the advent of radio, motion pictures, and television, Americans were entertained by theater troupes, the Bible was widely read, and public speeches were much valued for political discourse, as well as the inherent spectacle. Florid speaking styles were much admired, and brevity was not desired. To the modern reader, legal arguments from this period seem stilted and filled with what are now obscure quotations and literary references, traits that marked the speaker as knowledgeable and trustworthy but now seem quaint and impenetrable. Nineteenth- and early twentieth-century jurors listened to lawyers who quoted liberally from the Bible—often in Latin—and spoke for hours, if not days.

The all-male, homogeneous jury of the past has been replaced by a more varied but more narrowly educated jury pool. Modern juries are not as well read or as tolerant of the windy rhetoric of yesteryear's speakers (neither are judges). Short attention spans demand shorter speeches.

In law, two vastly different audiences are routinely addressed through oral argument: judges and juries. The skillful practitioner of legal oratory must alter her method and practice based upon her audience. The jury trial is the most familiar forum for the practice of legal oratory; many Americans have served on a jury, and most have seen Hollywood's versions of courtroom practice portrayed in film and television. Successful practitioners of trial law quickly learn that the most effective courtroom advocates tailor their style and delivery to the audience. In practical terms, this means the attorney must establish a horizontal dialogue with the jury, neither speaking down to them nor using stilted language and legal jargon to obscure the path to the desired verdict.

There are four phases in a jury trial that involve the use of legal oratory: jury selection, opening statement, direct and cross-examination of witnesses, and closing argument. Perhaps no part of the trial better showcases the skilled legal orator than the closing argument.

During the closing argument, the attorney finds a compelling theme, weaves together the testimony of the witnesses, reminds the jurors of significant testimony, and highlights subtle points made by the attorney but perhaps overlooked by the jury. The attorney tells jurors how the law applies to the facts, using rhetoric—or even rhyme—to explain a subtlety of the law. One of the finest examples of this took place in the trial of *Silkwood* v. *Kerr-McGee* (1979). Attorney Gerry Spence, renowned for his folksy style and cowboy attire in the courtroom, was explaining the concept of *"strict liability" to the jury, in order to convince them they should hold a giant corporation liable for contaminating the plaintiff's deceased daughter (Karen Silkwood) with plutonium. Likening the radioactive metal to a dangerous beast that had escaped from a cage in Merry Olde England and injured a neighbor, Spence told the jury that plutonium was the lion; Kerr-McGee was the owner; and Karen Silkwood was the neighbor. Spence told the jury, "If the lion gets away, Kerr-McGee has to pay." Repeated throughout the closing argument, Spence's rhyme helped the jury understand the concept of strict liability and convinced them to make Kerr-McGee pay for its negligence.

In "law and motion," or appellate law, the lawyer must prepare written legal briefs, attempting to lay out all relevant legal issues and provide the judge or justices with the applicable law; then must apply the facts of the case and explain by use of analogy why the controlling cases support the advocate or, conversely, distinguish the legal cases that appear to undercut the attorney's case, and explain why they should not control the outcome (see APPEALS).

This type of oral argument differs significantly from that used in a jury trial, because of the target audience. The lawyer presenting an oral argument to a court is rarely allowed simply to deliver a speech, as in a jury trial, uninterrupted and at his leisure. He is instead cut off in mid-sentence, aggressively questioned by skeptical judges, and forced to refocus his argument to address the concerns of the court. The attorney who triumphs is one who always answers the question, explains why the court's interpretation is incorrect or spot on, then makes a smooth transition back into his original argument.

[See also Jury: Juries; Media and the Law]

• Joseph Wesley Donovan, *Skill in Trials: Containing a Variety of Civil and Criminal Cases Won by the Art of Advocates; With Some of the Skill of Webster, Choate, Beach, Butler, Curtis, Davis, Fountain, and others, Given in Sketches of Their Work, and Trial Stories*, 1982 [1899]. Joseph Wesley Donovan, *Modern Jury Trials and Advocates: Containing Condensed Cases, with Sketches and Speeches of American Advocates; the Art of Winning Cases and Manner of Counsel Described, with Notes and Rules of Practice*, 1985 [1908]. Francis Lewis Wellman, *Day in Court, or, The Subtle Arts of Great Advocates*, 1986 [1914]. Michael S Lief, H. Mitchell Caldwell, and Benjamin Bycel, *Ladies and Gentlemen of the Jury: Greatest Closing Arguments in Modern Law*, 1998. David Paul Brown, *The Forum: Or Forty Full Years of Practice at the Philadelphia Bar*, 2000 [1856].   —Michael S Lief

ORGANIZED CRIME. Until a decade ago, the tenacity of organized crime in the United States made clear that it was more than a mere outlaw way of life. Organized criminal conduct thrives by performing services and providing goods that social conventions may condemn and laws prohibit but which, nonetheless, people crave. Much of the public's fascination with and ambivalence about the American underworld may be seen as a consequence of the intangible links between the law-abiding and law-breaking. Unless someone is a direct victim of a gangster, uncompromising public hostility toward organized crime has always been muted. Criminal groups frequently have been used by business people to break employee strikes and to participate in commercial wars over retail and wholesale markets. Gangs have been used by legitimate business to frustrate competition and ruin rivals. At the same time, organized crime groups have played important roles in assisting labor unions to resist employers and in putting together the multiethnic labor force. In these roles, gangsters acted as "padrones," as labor disciplinarians, and as gatekeepers for industrialists concerned with keeping prices stable, controlling labor costs, and limiting the number of competitive firms in the industrial arena. Thus, it is naive to suppose that businesses were simply preyed upon as victims. Indeed, the putative victims used the victimizers for their own ends.

Along with their infiltration of legitimate business through extortion and their more conventional vice activities, organized criminals have enjoyed lucrative relationships with political parties and their urban "machines," as Robert Merton has noted. Many gangsters became "political merchants" and entrepreneurs and played significant roles in urban politics by terrorizing voters and manipulating votes in local elections and by working around and through government bureaucracies, subverting them or using their natural inertia to stymie reforms. As consorts of greedy and unscrupulous businesspeople and cynical politicians, organized criminals represent one element in an illicit and mutually beneficial link that reaches deeply into many social institutions. These relationships tend to blur the distinction between legitimate society and the underworld. Thus, the determination to destroy organized crime is necessarily blunted by the underworld and the "upperworld" of American society being dependent upon each other and so intertwined that isolating one from the other is almost impossible.

The successful prosecutions of La Cosa Nostra, Italian American crime families, in the 1980s and 1990s say much about organized crime and its future. Scholarly and popular writing allots much space to the Mafia or Cosa Nostra—the terms are used interchangeably—because the historical record plainly demands such emphasis. Such a focus, however, distorts the contexts in which crime operates and has meant that gangsters of other ethnic backgrounds and in social settings not usually thought of as criminal milieus have been relatively neglected. However, the relentless use of the Racketeer Influenced and Corrupt Organization Act (*RICO), also known as the Organized Crime Control Act of 1970, in prosecutions has revealed the possibility of broadening the scope of organized crime to include criminals of other ethnic backgrounds as well as *white-collar and corporate offenders.

The idea that organized crime occurs in office suites as well as on the impoverished streets has always been a leading theme of radical criminologists such as Alan Block and William Chambliss. Consequently, a significant number of modern scholars, such as Stephen Fox, focus on the conditions that breed organized criminality, the structure and organization of criminal groups, the environments in which they operate, and their ties to the larger, legitimate upperworld of American society. While social scientists concentrate their energies on structural factors that give rise to the phenomenon, law enforcement tends to include in its operational models and definitions the notion of ethnicity as a key dimension of organized crime. This is not to say that the government's emphasis on ethnicity is misguided. Sufficient evidence is abundantly available to warrant such an inclusion at this time. But a preoccupation with ethnicity to the exclusion of other factors that generate this type of crime unduly circumscribes and constrains the field of investigation.

Presently, organized crime is popularly understood as a function of three major factors: *conspiracy, enterprise, and ethnicity. Perhaps more than in any other area of crime in America, ethnicity matters—in affecting the methods of criminal activities, establishing power, sustaining associations, and developing criminal specialties. For many observers, ethnicity is a delicate topic to be discussed carefully with many qualifying statements. However, gangsters have never felt bound by such discretion. Mafia defector Joseph Valachi said at the 1963 government hearings (where the term "La Cosa Nostra" was first heard publicly), "I'm not talking about Italians . . . I'm talking about criminals"—a vital distinction for any discussion of organized crime.

Defining Organized Crime. American prisons are filling up with gangsters of every ethnic background convicted of a wide variety of criminal offenses, yet until fairly recently a debate still raged about the meaning of "organized crime." Though this may seem odd and even trivial given the intensity of law-enforcement activity and prosecutions, no one definition seems to have satisfied both practitioners and scholars.

There are good reasons for wanting to define organized crime clearly and comprehensively. From the law-enforcement standpoint, an authoritative definition enables government to measure the extent of such crime and to determine how resources may be allocated in attacking it. If it cannot be defined, it cannot be measured, and if it cannot be measured, assessing the effectiveness of anticrime control efforts will be difficult.

The statutory definitions of organized crime at all levels of government contain many characterizations that are distinguished by their variety and inconsistency. The research literature, by comparison, presents relatively few notions, which are generally of a purely descriptive nature, as Michael Maltz has shown. In any case, "organized crime" is not an appropriate label to apply to all illegal enterprises and acts involving more than one individual. Robbery of a small grocery store by two or three youths waving guns and threatening patrons cannot be considered on the same level with illegal *gambling operations covering several states and involving millions of dollars or with international drug-trafficking activities. There must be some qualitative distinctions to qualify some acts as instances of organized crime. The hijacking of a truck is not by itself an organized crime as this term is ordinarily understood. But if, for instance, an employee of the trucking firm has been bribed or has conspired to provide information on cargo content and route or has been persuaded to take the vehicle to a prearranged location, and if the stolen cargo makes its way through a maze of "fences" and eventually into legitimate outlets, then the criminal event qualifies as an organized crime because it exhibits the characteristics normally associated with this type of criminal behavior. The important factors in the robbery illustrate that the discrete individual acts of bribery, armed robbery, and receiving stolen goods are interconnected, making their combination more dangerous in sum than the acts themselves.

Social scientific approaches to organized crime seek to elaborate empirically these main features, thereby avoiding the ambiguity and rigidity of legalistic definitions. The problem encountered in defining organized crime stems not from the word "crime" but from the word "organized." Beyond the sensational examples of the Cosa Nostra, there is no standard consensus as to when a criminal group is "organized" or how well organized it may be. The fact that organized crime is not always well organized complicates the definitional process. Moreover, because organized crime has become so interwoven into American politics and economic life, not everyone agrees about the seriousness of particular manifestations of it. A variety of activities officially defined as organized crime—extortion, sports betting, loan-sharking, labor racketeering, for example—are not seen by everyone as equally criminal or socially harmful.

The issue of definition, which seems essential for law-enforcement purposes but less so for scientific analyses, can be dealt with by asking what organizational characteristics permit some gangs to pose threats to society that oblige us to pay special attention to them. The threats are those of coercion and the capacity to force others, criminal and noncriminal alike, to comply with illegal commands with or without physical violence being exercised. Some groups or gangs possess the reputation and resources to exert their will in this fashion, others do not. Further, to make threats of contingent violence fully effective and believable, those threatened must believe that a criminal group can either corrupt legitimate authority or ensure that it can evade apprehension by law enforcement. Credible threats, the power to enforce them, and the ability to neutralize law enforcement are the defining features of organized criminal groups that distinguish them from ordinary street gangs and criminal entrepreneurs. Clearly it is easier to identify the attributes of organized crime than to define it with legalistic precision.

Although the complexity and variety of organized criminal activities seem to defy strict definition, some consensus has emerged in the literature about what constitutes organized crime. Organized crime may be defined as a continuing criminal conspiracy that derives profits from illegal activities and goods that the public demands. The existence and the structure of criminal groups are sustained through the use of violence, corruption of police and public officials, intimidation, credible threats, and control of particular illicit markets in *drugs, gambling, loan-sharking, and extortion.

It is noteworthy that organized crime is not restricted to the activities of the conventional and fairly well-known criminal groups such as the Mafia, La Cosa Nostra, the Triads (Chinese crime groups), Colombian drug cartels, the Yakuza (Japanese crime organizations), or other ethnic or racial criminal syndicates. In the savings and loan scandal of the 1980s, for example, there were criminal conspiracies between savings and loan officials, including accountants, lawyers, and real estate developers. Such criminal collusion, when compared with traditional organized crime conduct involving no-show construction jobs or protection payoffs, reveals more similarities than differences.

Such examples illustrate that much organized crime is committed by otherwise legitimate and official agencies and is as harmful as the crimes of recognized criminal enterprises. Still, over the decades, commissions, Congressional investigative committees, law-enforcement agencies, and the media have used the term "organized crime" to describe a formally structured nationwide conspiracy involving thousands of criminals organized to gain control over whole sectors of legal as well as illegal activities.

Groups with some type of organizational structure engaging in continuing criminal enterprises, whose primary purposes are profits, constitute the general contours of criminal organizations labeled "organized crime." These components are instrumental in operating durable enterprises, but more fundamentally they reflect the ways in which the group determines the most efficient manner to implement the capacities for violence noted above.

Organized crime flourished in the absence of serious opposition. Local police departments and prosecutors lacked the resources and tools to mount sustained investigations and prosecution of powerful organized-crime figures. Prosecutions such as those conducted by racket buster Thomas Dewey in the 1930s and 1940s in New York City were successful but failed to disrupt Cosa Nostra's operations and power bases.

Despite the important work of the Kefauver and McClellan Committees of the U.S. Senate, which exposed a powerful Cosa Nostra, the *Federal Bureau of Investigation paid scant attention to the Mafia's existence. This egregious intransigence may be explained in part by the federal law-enforcement agency's lack of a crime control program and of a legal instrument to combat the crime syndicate. In 1970, all that changed when Congress passed RICO, the most important substantive anti–organized crime statute in history, which, among other things, legally defined organized crime and made it a crime to acquire an interest in, to participate in the affairs of, or to invest the profits acquired from an enterprise through a pattern of racketeering activity.

Prior to passage of the Organized Crime Control Act of 1970, the investigation and prosecution of organized criminal groups had not been conducted in a coordinated manner. Congress passed RICO with the specific intent of combating the infiltration of organized crime into legitimate businesses. Providing a wide range of criminal and civil sanctions to control organized criminal activities, prosecutors employ RICO to imprison heads of crime families, to exact *forfeiture based on criminal earnings, and to treble the penalties associated with racketeering. Other techniques and tools such as the witness security program (witness protection and relocation), electronic surveillance, immunity from prosecution, cultivation and recruitment of informants, and antiracketeering laws such as the Money Laundering Control Act of 1986 provide additional support and serve to challenge the status of American organized crime.

With RICO it became possible, in a single trial, to prosecute an entire crime family or gang. The defendants are crime family members who participated in the affairs of the same enterprise through a pattern of criminal activity. RICO penalties are draconian as G. Robert Blakey, the law's principal architect, has made clear. Once the Supreme Court gave the green light to use the law against criminal enterprises, almost every significant organized crime prosecution was brought under the statute. In New York City, Rudolph Giuliani, the U.S. attorney for the city's southern district in the mid-1980s, brought the bosses of all the families (known as "The Commission") to trial on RICO charges and convicted them all on patterns of racketeering activity. The "Commission Case" (Cosa Nostra Commission Prosecution) is probably the most famous and important organized crime prosecution in U.S. history.

The History of Organized Crime in the United States. To understand the rise of organized crime, we need to know something of the changes and conditions in American society that facilitated its development and evolution. Organized crime thrived in the United States long before the country became fixated with the menace of the Mafia. The outlaw gangs of the nation's western frontier in the nineteenth century ravaged the Native American population and preyed mercilessly on new settlers. That early tumultuous history passed into American social history and has been sanitized in the country's romantic legends and myths of its pioneer heritage.

The modern concern with crime is not associated with bandits such as Jesse James raiding trains and stagecoaches but more with cities filling up with immigrants. Nineteenth-century American history is replete with suspicions of newcomers whose exploitation produced crime, which in turn laid the foundations for xenophobic reactions and repressions. That legacy of fear of the immigrant persists today.

For some European arrivals in the nineteenth and early twentieth centuries, and for some contemporary waves of immigrants from Central America and the Caribbean rims, the quick, illicit money to be gained from crime often represents opportunities for rapid advancement up the first rungs of the ladder of social mobility that promised, then as now, an escape from the squalor of slum life. Of course, the bulk of immigrants patiently put up with the indignities of poverty and remained law abiding, as they do today. A small percentage of immigrants gravitated into crime, and a similar proportion of Asians, Caribbeans, and others from Latin America find crime attractive and justifiable as a means of skirting the problems that assimilation and acculturation entail.

The history of this ethnic succession in crime describes a relationship among politics, crime, and minority social status. It first infected the Irish, who formed notorious street gangs in the large cities where they settled. By the end of World War I, the Irish virtually dominated crime and big city politics. Eventually the political influence they nurtured enabled them to shift into legitimate occupations in construction, trucking, public utilities, and the burgeoning civil services, where Irish ethnicity became synonymous with police work.

The aftermath of the war also brought Prohibition, a defining moment in the American crime scene. The Volstead Act forbade the sale and distribution of alcoholic beverages for personal consumption. From a moral standpoint, the law was intended by its authors and supporters to rescue the masses, mainly workers and immigrants, from enslavement to liquor, which it did to some degree. At the same time, Prohibition helped to create unprecedented criminal opportunities for Jewish, northern European, Italian, and other ethnic gangsters who cooperated and competed with the Irish underworld. The subsequent outbreak of murder and mayhem, the "Roaring Twenties," saw vicious and violent competition for control of the illegal alcohol business.

La Cosa Nostra. Until the Crime Commission trials and the defection of major figures in the American Mafia, La Cosa Nostra (literally, "our thing") was the largest, most sophisticated, and most powerful crime syndicate in the history of the United States, as Donald Cressey has described. It is unlikely in the foreseeable future that any crime organization will achieve anything approximating the influence of the Cosa Nostra in the country's economic and political life.

In different places and at different times, the Cosa Nostra, or Mafia, was identified as "The Outfit," "The Combination," and "The Honored Society." The Cosa Nostra is a variation on the Sicilian Mafia and Neapolitan Camorra, which Italian immigrants brought with them as part of their cultural heritage when they arrived in huge numbers at the turn of the last century. The Cosa

Nostra became the center, the main source of continuity and power in the affairs of American organized crime in the mid-1930s, when competing Italian criminal factions settled their differences in what has become known as the Castellammarese War. The bloody showdowns of gang warfare, which began in New York City, stretched all the way to Chicago to involve Al Capone's powerful syndicate and allies of the warring Sicilian gangsters in major cities in the Midwest and along the eastern seaboard.

When the fighting stopped, the two leading antagonists in the struggle, Salvatore Maranzano and Joe ("Joe the Boss") Masseria were dead, and the survivors, under the leadership of Charles ("Lucky") Luciano, crafted and installed an organization that sustained the central cultural features of the Mafia. Only those of Italian descent could be inducted as members ("made men"), and the individual "soldier"/member was subordinated to and for the group and its leaders. Oaths of secrecy and modes of defiance were also retained. What did change, according to Francis Ianni, were the ways in which the Cosa Nostra restructured itself: the tradition of an autocratic "Boss of all Bosses" (Capo di Tutti Capi) was abandoned in favor of a national commission consisting of the leaders or representatives of the leading families across the nation. No one man dominated; decisions were reached through consensus, similar to the operational style of administration in modern business organizations. Each Mafia family was autonomous on its own turf; the commission's authority lay in its role as a forum rather than a board of directors, and over time the commission gave the Mafia an expansive new scope, stability, and impact.

In the groundbreaking presidential commission report *Task Force Report: Organized Crime* of 1967, based on testimony from defectors such as Joseph Valachi (who coined the term "La Cosa Nostra") and law-enforcement experts, several issues were elaborated in an attempt to understand the structure and operations of the Cosa Nostra. First, the major components of organized crime in the United States were organized in a nationwide alliance of at least twenty-four tightly knit crime families. Second, all members of these families were Italians and Sicilians or of Italian descent. Third, the crime families (usually named after their founders or bosses) were organized in terms of statuses and functional roles, including a boss (don), who directed the illegal and legal activities of the members, an underboss (sotto capo), section leaders (capos), and, at the bottom of the hierarchy, soldiers. In the pyramid of power, the bosses were protected by layers of subordinates from responsibility for the crimes committed on their orders. The Cosa Nostra families were held together by violence and a circle of secrecy—known as *omerta* (code of silence).

Over time federal and local law-enforcement agencies developed tools to undermine the social glue that kept the Cosa Nostra intact and coherent as an organization. Immunity from prosecution for evidence, victim security programs to protect witnesses and their families, sophisticated electronic eavesdropping, and the power of RICO to compel evidence dealt the Cosa Nostra some lethal blows. But, as Robert Kelly and James Jacobs have described, the Cosa Nostra's authority and reputation in the affairs of organized crime remained intact through the 1980s. From 1950 to 1985 the Cosa Nostra gathered vast, unpublicized power not only in strictly criminal activities but in the allied fields of labor racketeering and urban machine politics, which deteriorated rapidly under the pressure of relentless RICO prosecutions. Even though the Cosa Nostra has been battered by intense law-enforcement efforts, it would be premature to write its obituary.

The Future of Organized Crime. Organized crime has not disappeared from American cities. While the Mafia may live off its vaunted reputation, new ethnic gangs from Latin America, East Asia, and eastern Europe have become wealthy through their control of large-scale illicit drug-distribution systems.

These gangs are also effective extortionists in their own communities. Whether the new groups will take on Mafia-like styles and capabilities can only be conjecture at this point. So far, although the Colombian cocaine traffickers and the Chinese groups organized by Tongs (versions of Hong Kong Triads) have exhibited some Mafia-type entrepreneurial abilities, they have not branched out into other activities in the United States. They have not been able or have not chosen to diversify as widely as did the Mafia into mainstream political and social institutions outside their own communities.

Black, Asian, Hispanic, and indigenous multi-ethnic crime groups seem to be burgeoning and doing well in the United States. They represent a broader spectrum of players than previously imagined; drugs, especially, have rewritten the formulas for participants and their strategies. The developing consensus among specialists is that organized crime is organized in more numerous and complicated ways than it used to be, and that the Cosa Nostra families continue to play some part in it—

decisive in some illegal markets but marginal in others.

As the President's Commission on Organized Crime noted in 1986, the highly profitable and dangerous business of drug trafficking has attracted younger ethnic criminals along with lower-echelon members of Cosa Nostra crime families. In a twist on the traditions bequeathed by Prohibition, many of the new criminals are recent immigrants to the United States. Chinese, Vietnamese, Jamaicans, Mexicans, Russians, Colombians, Dominicans, and even Sicilians turn to crime not because the society is closed off to them but because it is so wide open. In many cases, the new immigrants who turn to crime come from societies, riddled with systemic poverty, that are noted for draconian police methods. Thus, the relative freedom and anonymity possible in the United States with its diffusion of law enforcement are inviting to those who wish to skirt legitimacy, make money as quickly as possible doing whatever it takes, and hide themselves from police scrutiny in the protective cocoons of ethnic enclaves.

As Rufus Schatzberg and Robert Kelly have observed, given the numerous witnesses that provided the President's Commission with extensive testimony about large-scale sophisticated heroin-trafficking networks in African-American communities, managed by African Americans, the lack of attention to this phenomenon was indeed puzzling. The testimony suggested a highly structured level of organization.

The black underworld is far from a monolithic, homogeneous structure of power wielded only by native-born black Americans. Nor is it a mere ghetto appendage of Cosa Nostra rackets and businesses. Since the late 1960s in many major U.S. cities, the Jamaican Rastafarian "Posses" have operated successful drug rings alongside native blacks engaged in traditional vice activities.

For African-American and Hispanic ghetto dwellers, one of their most important problems—one confronting white ethnic immigrants decades earlier—is how to escape through socially approved means, when these means are virtually closed. This problem is resolved to some extent by crime activities. For most ghetto dwellers, the provision of illegal goods and services or the illegal provision of legal goods and services is tolerated because it is not seen as intrinsically evil or socially disruptive. Poverty provides its own moral climate for organized criminality in the ghetto, with the exception, perhaps, of drug peddling. And even here, escape from the bondage of poverty provides emotional pressure and an acceptable if ambiva-lent context for widespread drug use. It is, then, the pervasive persistent poverty of the ghetto and its collective despair that is at the basis of recruitment into criminal networks.

Crack cocaine is to the ghetto gangster what illegal alcohol was to the white ethnic groups during Prohibition. Crack is the lucrative *modus vivendi* of today's ghetto drug dealers, the currency of the informal economy. Crack has helped minority criminals generate impressive amounts of criminogenic assets such as guns, illegal capital, distribution networks, and credit with major cocaine producers. These elements have enabled cocaine gangs to develop street gangs that are much more than juvenile delinquents hanging around street corners seeking the thrills of combat with other youth gangs for control of delinquent "turf."

The rise of black gangs in the mid-1980s, primarily the Crips and the Bloods, originating in the Los Angeles ghettos, is due in large part to crack. The Crips, estimated in the 1980s and 1990s at thirty thousand strong, spread eastward principally as purveyors of crack. By 1991, the U.S. Department of Justice located the Crips and the Bloods (a drug gang some ten thousand strong) in 113 cities across thirty-two states. These gangs are reflections of a demographic bulge in those age cohorts (fifteen to twenty-five years old) that are more criminally prone. Coupled with high unemployment rates among young black males, the conditions for the expansion of minority crime are present.

There is little reason to believe that the crime economy of the new gang culture will stop growing, whatever the scale of repression mounted by law enforcement, or that it will stay confined to black ghettos. Although the epicenter remains in the ghetto, which is the zone of hard-core unemployment and utter disillusionment, the gang mystique has spread into middle-class black areas, where people are close to panic or vigilantism.

Transnational Organized Crime. Crime has become increasingly international over the past two decades, especially in the 1980s in the wake of the Cold War. The post–Cold War environment witnessed the growing integration of the world's economic systems and institutions; the easing of barriers to trade, migration, and travel; and the sophistication of technologies that support global commerce and communications. All these factors have also increased criminal opportunities across national borders for individuals and organizations worldwide. In recent years, the United States and other countries have devoted significant resources to the investigation and control of "transnational organized crime." At this point in time, however, reliable knowledge about the phenomenon of transnational crime is scarce and whether it is indeed a global threat to democracy and free enterprise, as it is often portrayed to be, is an important issue that remains unresolved. The literature and data on transnational offenses are just beginning to emerge, and the complexities of law-enforcement and political responses are only beginning to be understood.

For the last quarter-century, heroin and cocaine have caused great damage to the nation. Also, large-scale smuggling of illegal immigrants into the United States has become more prominent. This type of crime, unconstrained by boundaries, appears to have been affected by a number of factors. The rise in the numbers of immigrants is unprecedented. The vast improvement in communications technologies make borders permeable—indeed, criminal activities can be carried out in the United States without anyone stepping across a border. These factors undoubtedly have played a role in the American crime picture of the past, but they are very pronounced in the opening decade of the twenty-first century. A sufficient number of incidents have occurred to give substance to general anxieties about uncontrollable foreign crime impinging upon everyday life in the United States.

Transnational organized crime has attracted a good deal of media attention. Politically there has been some very visible activity in response to the issue. President Clinton in two speeches before the UN General Assembly observed that transnational organized crime and terrorism were serious problems that threatened the integrity of all nations. He issued Presidential Decision Directive Number 42 in October 1995, authorizing government agencies to develop initiatives against such crime. In addition, at the 1995 meeting of the Group of Seven nations, control of transnational organized crime was a principal item on the agenda. Other policy initiatives emerging from these decisions at the programmatic level have included efforts to help other governments (e.g., Italy, Russia, and Colombia) deal with crime organizations that pose a threat both to their own countries and to the United States. During the 1990s and onward to the milestone meeting of the United Nations in Palermo in 2000, the U.S. Department of Justice became interested in international crime problems and the ways in which they affect domestic crime in the United States. The U.S. government is strengthening its links through participation in a worldwide network of criminological institutes af-filiated with the United Nations. With these sources of information and analyses, the United States will be able to determine the seriousness of international crime. The issues now are to estimate the kind of knowledge needed to prevent and control this type of organized crime.

[*See also* Criminal Law; Race and Ethnicity]

• U.S. Senate Special Committee to Investigate Organized Crime in Interstate Commerce (Kefauver Committee), *Final Report*, 1951. Robert K. Merton, *Social Theory and Social Structure*, 1957. U.S. Senate Select Committee on Improper Activities in the Labor or Management Field (McClellan Committee), *Final Report*, 1960. President's Commission on Law Enforcement and Administration of Justice, *Task Force Report: Organized Crime*, 1967. Donald R. Cressey, *Theft of the Nation*, 1969. Francis A. J. Ianni, *A Family Business*, 1972. Thomas E. Dewey, *Twenty against the Underworld*, 1974. Alan Block and William Chambliss, *Organizing Crime*, 1981. President's Commission on Organized Crime, *The Impact: Organized Crime Today* (Report to the President and the Attorney General), 1986. Stephen Fox, *Blood and Power*, 1989. G. Robert Blakey, "RICO: The Federal Experience (Criminal and Civil) and an Analysis of Attacks against the Statute," in *Handbook of Organized Crime in the United States* (Robert J. Kelly et al., eds.), 1994. Michael Maltz, "Defining Organized Crime," in *Handbook of Organized Crime in the United States* (Robert J. Kelly et al., eds.), 1994. Rufus Schatzberg and Robert J. Kelly, *African-American Organized Crime*, 1997. James B. Jacobs, *Gotham Unbound*, 1999. Robert J. Kelly, *The Upperworld and the Underworld*, 1999.

—Robert J. Kelly

OSHA. *See* Labor Law: Workplace Issues.

OUTLAWS, POPULAR. Popular outlaws or social bandits were criminals with kinship networks, active supporters, and passive sympathizers who helped them to thwart the efforts of law enforcement officials to arrest them. These social bandits were not part of popular justice movements or crime control vigilantes who used extralegal proceedings to enforce law outside of legal institutions. Rather these criminal gangs targeted banks and railroads thought to be gouging local residents as well as the working poor in general. Included within this category are Billy the Kid, John Wesley Hardin, Sam Bass, Joaquin Murieta, and the James-Younger, Dalton, and Doolin-Dalton gangs of the nineteenth century.

The local support of these criminals made them popular and the romantic images created in the nineteenth-century pulp press and dime novels, and the twentieth-century film and television media maintain the image of outlaws robbing from the rich capitalists and giving to the poor, honest working class locals in need. The image and the reality seldom converge. In addition to kin, the outlaws and their gangs frequently drew support from people they knew personally. This base of support combined with passive sympathizers converted outlaws into local heroes. By concentrating their robberies on the rich, particularly railroads and banks, they avoided harming local people. Further, in agricultural communities farmers and ranchers frequently believed that the railroads were extorting rates and banks usurious interest. The outlaw gangs returned this ill-gotten gain to local economies in the form of cash for horses, feed, supplies, and lodging.

Despite this class conscious definition of popular outlaws, it is clear that the outlaws and their sympathizers came from market-oriented groups, not from the dirt poor. The James-Younger gang members had Confederate origins like the elder offspring of well-to-do slave holding farmers who supported them. When Frank James was brought to trial for murder, a jury of well-to-do farmers from one of the richest counties in Missouri acquitted him. When he left the outlaw trail, he toured the country making money off of his outlaw past telling crowds that crime did not pay while pocketing their money. The social bandit created an image that reached beyond his Confederate, outlaw past. In the 1890s Frank James preached a capital-labor struggle and a national contest between greed and manhood. The rhetoric played well amidst economic turmoil.

Popular outlaws also gained public support in areas where local populations had little faith in the honesty and competency of public law officers. This was particularly true in postwar Missouri and Oklahoma in the 1890s. The James-Younger gang benefited in Missouri and the Dalton and Dalton-Doolin gangs in Oklahoma. In Missouri, ex-Confederates thought Union *sheriffs the enemy. In Oklahoma, settlers distrusted United States deputy marshals who used their office to secure the best lands, prosecuted settlers for minor liquor offenses in Indian country, and lived off of fees paid by locals.

The cultural definition of masculinity also benefited the popular outlaws. They were strong men who could protect their people and revenge themselves with firearms, the symbol of equality and great leveler of the nineteenth century. Their sympathizers saw attributes they admired such as bravery and daring despite the odds, freedom from social restraint, shrewdness, loyalty to kin and cause, generosity to those most in need, and genuine politeness born of country living and respect for elders. These men were not simply common criminals, but men who used criminal acts to right wrongs unredressed by law or politics.

[*See also* Criminal Law]

• Gordon Morris Bakken and Brenda Farrington, eds., *Law in the West*, 2000.   —Gordon Morris Bakken

OVERSIGHT, REGULATORY. *See* Regulation.

OWNERSHIP, CONCURRENT. *See* Property, Real.

P

PACIFISM. *See* Civil Disobedience; Ethics, Morality, and Law; Religion; War, Law of.

**PALSGRAF V. LONG ISLAND RAILROAD CO.,
248 N.Y. 339 (1928).** While waiting for a train, Helen Palsgraf, a ticket-holder, stood on the platform of the Long Island Railroad. Perhaps thirty feet away, a man carrying an unmarked package containing fireworks jumped onto a train leaving the platform. Two of the train's conductors steadied him, but knocked the package to the tracks. It exploded and the concussion toppled a large scale onto Palsgraf.

Chief Judge Benjamin N. *Cardozo ordered dismissal of Palsgraf's negligence suit on the basis of a "proper plaintiff" requirement embedded in the duty element of negligence. The conductors may have acted carelessly toward those near the man, but they were not careless with respect to Palsgraf, standing far away. Because the plaintiff failed to establish a breach of any duty of care owed to her, she was not entitled to sue. Dissenting, Judge William S. Andrews argued that, when conduct is unreasonable, it is unreasonable to "the public at large," not to particular persons. The live issue for him was proximate cause: whether common sense or policy required the court to limit *liability given the freakishness of the accident.

Palsgraf is canonical because it poses the perennial puzzle of responsibility for bizarre consequences, and because realist scholars (see LEGAL REALISM) seized on it as demonstrating the aridity of traditional *legal reasoning. The Cardozo-Andrews dispute, they argued, is irresolvable on its terms because concepts like duty and proximate cause are empty labels that merely mask exercises of judicial discretion. More recent scholarship, however, suggests that *Palsgraf* raises a genuine and fundamental question: Is *tort rightly understood as regulatory law, or as a law of private redress? Andrews rejected the proper plaintiff requirement because he thought it hindered tort law's ability to deter antisocial conduct and compensate the injured. By contrast, because Cardozo viewed tort as enabling the wrongfully injured to seek redress against their wrongdoers, he required Palsgraf to prove a breach of a duty owed to her, not merely a wrong to others that happened to harm her.

[*See also* Regulation]

• William L. Prosser, "Palsgraf Revisited," *Michigan Law Review* (1953): 1–32. Benjamin C. Zipursky, "Rights, Wrongs and Recourse in the Law of Torts," *Vanderbilt Law Review* (1998): 1–100

—John C. P. Goldberg

PARALEGAL AND LEGAL SECRETARY. Also known as a legal assistant, a paralegal assists licensed attorneys in the delivery of legal services. Paralegals obtain their knowledge of law through training, experience, and education. Although a paralegal is not permitted to practice law, paralegals may perform legal work under the direct supervision of a *lawyer.

Beginning in the late 1960s, largely in response to demands by clients that legal services become more cost-effective, law *firms delegated more responsibilities to support staff. Those tasks included work formerly completed by lawyers. The time spent on legal work by these staff members, originally called legal paraprofessionals, was billed to the clients, thus making legal paraprofessionals profit centers rather than cost centers in law firms. In the early 1970s, the term paralegal was coined to describe this emerging category of law firm employees.

Although a few states have granted legal assistants the authority to act without lawyer supervision in some particular legal matters, legal assistants are almost never permitted give legal advice, represent a client in court, or accept a case. Paralegals perform myriad tasks for lawyers, from investigating facts and interviewing witnesses to drafting pleadings and motions to researching relevant statutes and cases to writing memoranda to aid attorneys handling cases. Paralegals assist in drafting contracts and trust and estate planning instruments, and may aid lawyers in preparing tax returns.

There are more than 136,000 paralegals employed in the United States. Most paralegals work in private law firms, and smaller numbers are employed by corporations and the government. A small but growing number of paralegals are self-employed and work for lawyers on a contract basis.

In most states, there are no educational or licensing requirements to be a paralegal. However, most paralegals have graduated from some paralegal educational program. The types of paralegal educational programs range dramatically, varying from certificate programs to two-year associate degree programs and four-year baccalaureate degree programs. A few institutions offer a master's degree. About 800 institutions offer paralegal training of one type or another, of which about 240 are certified by the ABA. A paralegal may obtain certification as a certified legal assistant (CLA) or as a registered paralegal (RP) from voluntary associations of paralegals.

Legal secretaries traditionally performed such tasks as taking dictation, typing, and retyping draft legal documents. Legal secretaries also screened the lawyer's telephone calls, kept the lawyer's calendar, and managed all or most of the files generated by the lawyer's work product. The advent of the personal computer and introduction of powerful word-processing and other software programs have dramatically altered the job of the legal secretary. The legal secretary now spends less time revising and filing documents, and more time using his or her organizational and technological skills to manage aspects of the modern law office, making the legal secretary more like a legal assistant.

[*See also* Legal Practice, Forms of]

—Michael Ariens

PARDON, REPRIEVE, AND COMMUTATION.
A pardon is an act of grace from the sovereign that cancels or releases a person from punishment for a *criminal offense. It is "an act of public conscience that relieves the recipient of all the legal consequences of the conviction" (*Schick* v. *Reed* (1974)). As the U.S. Supreme Court explained in *Schick*, pardons may be absolute or conditional. Since conditions attached to the pardon may be

more objectionable than the punishment itself, courts have no power to force the pardon upon the individual. Pardons do not affect the rights of third parties. Unlike a full pardon, commutation is simply the change of a punishment to one which is less severe. A commutation does not absolve the beneficiary of most of the legal consequences of an offense. A reprieve is simply the postponement of punishment. Forgiveness and mitigation, both within the rubric of clemency, fall outside the traditional checks and balances of a representative government, but each has been a fundamental part of Western criminal justice systems.

The power to pardon and commute punishment is of ancient origin. Greece and Rome espoused their uses to promote civil peace and advance political purposes. The pardoning power was consolidated in the Crown of England by Parliament in 1533. The great legal commentator, Blackstone, considered the crown's use of the pardon power one of the advantages of a monarchy over other forms of government, because it moderated the harsh application of general law.

The English crown delegated to the *governors of American colonies the power to pardon. The colonies' charters often endorsed the power; however, some, wary of unfettered discretion in the hands of a ruler, placed restrictions upon the governor's ability to pardon. Not surprisingly, the debates and compromises of the 1787 Constitutional Convention questioned which branch should be given the power of pardons and whether the legislative branch would have veto power over presidential or gubernatorial acts of mercy. Soon after the adoption of the 1789 Constitution, many state constitutions vested the authority solely with the governor. Some states still require clemency recommendation from an independent administrative panel as a condition precedent to executive action, but primarily it is left to the governor to make what some have called a 'lonely' and 'Godlike' decision. Pardons were also part of Native American restorative justice, under which material reparation was much less important than emotional or symbolic reparation. When peace was made, the wrongdoer was pardoned.

The U.S. *president is vested in Article 2 with the constitutional "Power to grant Reprieves and Pardons for Offences against the United States, except in Cases of Impeachment." The U.S. pardon attorney is supposed to review all claims for clemency. However, as illustrated by former President Clinton's controversial pardons on his last day in office in January 2001, this may not occur and the president makes the final decision. Some states have similar executive staff. Individual acts of clemency inherently call for discriminating choices by the executive, because no two cases are ever the same. This grant of power has been interpreted to be equivalent to that power possessed by the English monarch, and its operation and effect has been evaluated by reference to English interpretations (*United States* v. *Wilson* (1833)).

Presidents have issued pardons for a variety of reasons and a variety of offenses. Pardons and commutations have been issued in "justice neutral" situations: to serve the public good, to serve political friends, to procure testimony, to restore order, and to heal divisions among factions within a state. They have also been used in "justice enhancing" situations: to rectify miscarriages of justice in cases of procedural unfairness, disproportionate punishment, and actual innocence or uncertain guilt. They have been used as pure acts of mercy, out of pity, or in recognition of a wrongdoer's rehabilitation or redemption.

Because only a few states require the pardoning authority to abide by statutory or administrative standards, governors typically exercise unreviewable discretion. Although *judicial review of pardons occurs, the power to pardon is generally left intact. However, the Supreme Court has warned that *impeachment is a proper remedy for abuse of pardoning discretion (*Ex parte Grossman* (1925)).

The exercise of state executive clemency does not implicate the U.S. Constitution, so Supreme Court case law is not binding on a governor (*Herrera* v. *Collins* (1993)). A petitioner for executive mercy has neither a *due-process right nor an entitlement to mercy. Neither does she have a right to an explanation of a denial of pardon or commutation (*Connecticut Bd. of Pardons* v. *Dumschat* (1981)). Theorists have advocated the imposition of procedural reform or more objective substantive standards to obviate caprice or bias in *executive power.

The U.S. Supreme Court has rarely addressed clemency. In *Gregg* v. *Georgia* (1976), the Court approved, for the first time in several decades, a state death-penalty statute. It did so because a statute guided the jury's discretion in imposing such a sentence. The Court required narrowly tailored guidelines focusing on the offense and the character of the accused, including a consideration of both mitigating and aggravating circumstances. Most state courts prohibit jury instructions, evidence, or argument on a capital defendant's prospects for parole, pardon, or commutation of sentence, but in *California* v. *Ramos*, the Supreme

Court upheld the constitutionality of informing jurors about the possibility of future clemency (1983). The chance of eventual release may unduly influence jurors, contrary to the Court's pronouncement that "the decision of whether a man deserves to live or die must be made on scales that are not deliberately tipped toward death" (*Witherspoon* v. *Illinois* (1968)).

Despite the controversy surrounding clemency, and its long history, its use for *capital punishment has dramatically declined. Six thousand four hundred prisoners were sentenced to death between 1973 and 1998: 146 state sentences were committed, but there were no federal commutations. Early in the twentieth century, clemency was as common as execution. Current views of punishment as retribution, rather than as a means of rehabilitation, may account for the less frequent tender of mercy today.

[*See also* Criminal Law]

• Capital Punishment @http://www.ojp.usdoj.gov. W. H. Humbert, *The Pardoning Power of the President*, 1941. Kathleen Dean Moore, *Pardons: Justice, Mercy, and the Public Interest*, 1989. Daniel T. Kobil, *The Quality of Mercy Strained: Wresting the Pardoning Power from the King*, 1991. Clifford Dorne and Kenneth Gewerth, *Mercy in a Climate of Retributive Justice: Interpretations from a National Survey of Executive Clemency Procedures*, 1999. Elizabeth Rapaport, *Symposium on Law, Psychology, and the Emotions: Retribution and Redemption in the Operation of Executive Clemency*, 2000.

—Lorraine A. Schmall and Steven M. Thiede

PARENS PATRIAE DOCTRINE. *See* Anti-Trust Law.

PARENTAL RIGHTS. *See* Abortion and Reproductive Decisions; Adoption and Termination of Parental Rights; Aging and the Law; Domestic Violence.

PAROLE. *See* Probation and Parole.

PARTICIPATION, POLITICAL. *See* Voting and Political Participation.

PARTNERS, DOMESTIC. *See* Domestic Violence: Partner Abuse; Family Law; Homosexuality and the Law; Marriage.

PARTNERSHIP. *See* Business Organizations.

PASSIVE RESISTANCE. *See* Civil Disobedience.

PATENT. *See* Property, Intellectual; Technology and Law.

PATENT LAW PRACTICE. Patent law is a major branch of intellectual *property law, which also includes copyright, trademark, and trade secret law. Attorneys who specialize in patent law practice engage in a wide variety of legal work including investigating the potential patentability of inventions at the behest of clients; preparing patent applications for protecting inventions; filing the applications with the U.S. Patent & Trademark Office (PTO); prosecuting the applications before the PTO to secure the grant of patents; licensing patents; litigating patents in federal courts against infringers; determining whether clients may be infringing the patents of others; securing foreign patent protection and advising clients of potential infringement of foreign patents; and advising clients how best to manage their patents. Patent attorneys also often practice in areas of intellectual property, including trademark law (e.g., obtaining trademarks for patented products); copyright law (particularly with the advent of copyright protection of computer software); trade secret law (protecting and licensing valuable but not patented information); and law relating to the internet, which may cut across the other areas mentioned.

Patent attorneys practice in a variety of relationships, ranging from the *sole practitioner (rare) to small- or medium-size firms that specialize in patent law (probably the most common) to large full-service law firms that include a patent or intellectual property unit. Many corporations, universities, research laboratories, and government agencies also employ patent attorneys.

Patent law deals with *technology—indeed the most advanced technology—whatever its nature: mechanical, electrical, chemical, bio-technical, computer. Thus, specialized training in technology is highly desirable for an attorney practicing patent law. Practice before the PTO requires training in engineering or *science (usually a bachelor's degree or equivalent) and passing an examination administered by the PTO. (One does not have to be an attorney to take this examination.) However, attorneys who are not registered to practice before the PTO may, and often do, practice in other areas of patent law, particularly litigation, licensing, and business development. A number of law schools now place considerable emphasis on intellectual property law, recognizing its importance and the need to educate specialists in this area.

Clients of patent attorneys typically are corporations, and long-term relationships are not unusual as patent attorneys may be intimately involved in the technological developments of their clients. Patent attorneys do represent independent inventors, but this does not typically constitute the bulk of their practice.

The prestige and compensation of patent attorneys are commensurate with the talents and training they must possess. Indeed, patent attorneys are among the highest compensated of any specialty in the law. At present, there is a significant demand for patent attorneys, particularly those with technical expertise in evolving fields of technology.

Patent practitioners in foreign countries often are not lawyers but are technically trained individuals who have been authorized to practice before particular patent offices. These practitioners enjoy considerable professional status, and U.S. patent attorneys transact legal matters with them relating to foreign patents on a regular basis.

[*See also* Property]

• American Bar Association, Section of Intellectual Property Law, Careers in Intellectual Property Law, www.abanet.org/intelprop/patprep.html. United States Patent and Trademark Office, General Requirement Bulletin for Admission to the Examination for Registration to Practice in Patent Cases Before the United States Patent and Trademark Office, www.uspto.gov/weboffices/dcom/olia/oed.   —A. Samuel Oddi

PATIENTS RIGHTS. *See* Aging and the Law; Health Law.

PENNZOIL V. TEXACO, 481 U.S. 1 (1987). The clash of two commercial giants in *Pennzoil Co.* v. *Texaco Inc.* resulted in one of history's largest jury verdicts. By the time the case reached the Supreme Court, it involved a clash between two equally great legal principles: the availability of federal *courts to protect federal rights, and the deference owed by federal courts to proceedings that are already underway in the state courts.

In February 1984, Pennzoil sued Texaco in a Texas state court alleging that Texaco's offer to purchase Getty Oil had unlawfully interfered with an existing stock purchase agreement between Getty and Pennzoil. The jury returned a verdict for Pennzoil of over $10 billion. Texaco immediately filed suit in federal court in New York, claiming that the Texas verdict violated various of its federal rights; among them that the enormous cash bond required by Texas law to secure an *appeal violated the Constitution.

Federal courts rely on a doctrine called abstention to resolve the tension between opening the doors of federal courts to hear claims of federal rights violations, and proper respect for ongoing state court proceedings. In *Pennzoil* v. *Texaco*, the Supreme Court applied the doctrine of abstention to hold that Texaco's federal suit should be dismissed. This was the first time that the Supreme Court had ordered a federal court to abstain in a *civil lawsuit between two private parties, sharply limiting the availability of federal courts to protect federal rights.

[See also Corporations: For-Profit Corporations]

• Thomas Petzinger Jr., *Oil and Honor*, 1987.

—Barry Friedman

PEONAGE. *See* Slavery, Law of.

PEREMPTORY CHALLENGE. *See* Jury.

PER SE RESTRAINT. *See* Anti-Trust Law.

PERSONAL INJURY LAW PRACTICE. Personal injury (PI) lawyers, also called plaintiffs' lawyers or contingency fee lawyers, devote most of their practices to representing individuals injured in accidents. They service these clients on a contingency basis, taking their fees from a percentage of the proceeds from any damage award or settlement.

PI practices vary. Most center on low-value (as low as $2,000) frequently occurring accidents, like automobile accidents. The majority of these lawyers work as *sole practitioners or in small firms (fewer than five lawyers) with small support staffs. The size of the typical practice is modest (perhaps 100 to 150 cases per year), and because it is built on representing victims of individual accidents, the normal lawyer-client relationship is a one-time affair. Doing this work on a contingency fee basis places a premium on the lawyer's ability to maintain a steady flow of clients. Despite often expressed concerns about advertising and direct solicitation, the primary method of obtaining clients is word-of-mouth referral from former clients. As a result, most lawyers are concerned with the quality of service they provide, because poorly served clients are unlikely to recommend them to someone else.

While most PI lawyers fit this general pattern, not all do. One exception is the small percentage of lawyers with high-volume practices. They too focus on low-value cases and work in small firms. However, in order to handle the high volume they have sizeable support staffs and highly routinized organizations. To generate the high volume they rely on direct marketing in one form or another, such as direct mail solicitation, billboards, television, and the Internet. The largest of these practices handle more than 2,500 cases a year and rely

on saturation advertising, spending as much as $1 million per year.

Both the typical PI lawyer and the high-volume lawyer are likely to settle most of their cases rather than take them to trial. Part of the reason is economic—it is in no one's interest to spend the money a trial costs, which may exceed the potential winning. Some lawyers also avoid trials because they are not capable litigators, and there has long been a division among PI lawyers between those who actually litigate and those who do not.

Another exception to the general pattern is the specialist. Few in number, specialists have fundamentally different practices focusing on a small number of complex, higher-value cases (sometimes in the millions of dollars). Some specialize in a particular type of case, like medical *malpractice, and develop significant expertise in that area. Others handle a variety of higher-value cases that go to trial, their specialization being high-stakes litigation itself. The specialists' firms are small, usually no more than ten or twelve lawyers. The largest may have thirty to forty, still far smaller than the major legal-defense firms. Specialist firms, however, have larger support staffs than those of the typical PI lawyer, often with staff members who are professionals or specialists—as when a medical malpractice lawyer has registered nurses on staff.

No specialized training is required to enter the personal injury field, but some lawyers do seek it once they have done so. Those who try cases seek training in trial practice or in the substantive aspects of emerging areas of personal injury. The *Association of Trial Lawyers of America—the PI lawyers' professional organization—offers a wide variety of training and continuing education programs through its National College of Advocacy, as do state *bar associations and state-level PI lawyers' organizations. Some state and professional organizations offer certification to lawyers with training in trial practice, and a small percentage of lawyers do become certified. Additionally, a handful of lawyers bring specialized, nonlegal training with them when they enter the field. There are, for instance, lawyers who are medical doctors specializing in malpractice, and lawyers who are engineers specializing in particular type of products *liability.

Because personal injury practice requires no specialized training, there is no dominant avenue for entry. Some lawyers try to establish a practice in this field on leaving law school, usually with little success. Others seek employment with an established PI lawyer, gain experience, and then go out on their own. There is no associate-to-partner system, as there is in large law firm practice, in the personal injury field. Alternatively, some lawyers start with an *insurance defense firm in order to learn the field and then switch to handling plaintiffs' cases. Others work first for a local prosecutor or governmental agency in order to gain trial experience.

PI lawyers rank at or near the bottom of the legal profession's prestige hierarchy. Their work is perceived as unsavory and less than intellectually challenging, and they tend to represent clients who have little prestige, power, or wealth. They are also criticized for reliance on the contingency fee, the stated fear being that the lawyer will bring frivolous cases just to collect a fee, or will be more concerned with his/her own financial interest rather then with the clients' best interest. The contingency fee is often defended, though, as the only way injured people can afford access to the *legal services they need to vindicate their rights and receive compensation, and many PI lawyers see themselves as representatives of the have-nots.

The most successful PI lawyers, especially the specialists, have among the highest annual incomes (well in excess of $1 million) in the legal profession. The typical PI lawyers' income, however, is much more modest, close to the median income for all lawyers in private practice (approximately $90,000–$100,000). In the wake of the political campaign for "tort reform" during the 1990s, the typical PI lawyer probably makes less today than ten years earlier, with some even abandoning this practice area.

[See also Legal Practice, Forms of; Torts]

• Jerome E. Carlin, *Lawyers on Their Own*, 1962. John P. Heinz and Edward O. Laumann, *Chicago Lawyers: The Social Structure of the Bar*, 1982. John A. Jenkins, *The Litigators: Inside the Powerful World of America's High-Stakes Trial Lawyers*, 1989. Jonathan Harr, *A Civil Action*, 1995. Carroll Seron, *The Business of Practicing Law: The Work Lives of Solo and Small-Firm Attorneys*, 1996. Barry Werth, *Damages: One Family's Legal Struggles in the World of Medicine*, 1998.

—Stephen Daniels

PHILADELPHIA LAWYER. *See* Lawyers, Popular Perceptions of.

PICKETING. *See* Labor Law: Labor Relations.

PINKERTONS. *See* Private Security Services.

PLANNING, ECONOMIC. *See* Property Rights.

PLEA, GUILTY. *See* Procedure, Criminal.

PLEA BARGAINING. Despite the high value American constitutional law and tradition assign to the formal procedures of a criminal trial, most criminal cases are not resolved by a jury trial, or by a trial of any kind. Instead, in about 90 percent of criminal cases, the defendant waives trial and pleads guilty. Some defendants, wishing to take responsibility for their criminal conduct, plead guilty without any prompting from judges or prosecutors. Most guilty pleas in serious cases, however, result from the practice of plea bargaining, in which the accused exchanges his plea for some explicit or tacit consideration from the *prosecutor, the court, or both. Usually the consideration consists of mitigation of the punishment imposed after conviction, or reduction of the charges, or more lenient treatment while charges are pending (for example, pretrial release on *bail or on the defendant's own recognizance), or some combination of all of these.

Plea bargaining is not the only way in which the letter of the *criminal law is tempered by official discretion. Informal processes dominate the entire criminal justice system. Police officers decide whether to arrest, prosecutors decide whether to file charges, and what charges to file, judges decide whether to sentence a convicted defendant to incarceration, and if so, for how long, parole boards decide whether to release a prisoner early, and parole and *probation officers decide whether to seek revocation of a defendant's release.

Plea bargaining is especially controversial because it substitutes a discretionary process largely hidden from public view for the formal, highly visible process of adjudication by jury trial, with all its familiar and respected protections for the accused. Moreover, the importance of plea bargaining has increased in recent years, as other opportunities for discretion in the criminal justice system have been limited, notably by the proliferation of mandatory sentences and the drastic curtailment of parole.

Forms of Plea Bargaining. Plea bargaining occurs in every American criminal trial court, both at the federal and state levels. But the practice takes different forms. Some plea bargaining consists of an open exchange between the defendant on the one hand and the prosecutors (and sometimes the judge) on the other. Judges may not participate too actively or too directly in plea negotiations, but they are permitted, and in some cases required, to approve the final agreement. But overt agreements are not always necessary. Often there is an unspoken understanding between judges and lawyers that criminal defendants who insist on going to trial will be treated more harshly. An incentive structure is built into the practices of the courthouse and buttressed by the long sentences increasingly mandated by statute: with a possible prison term frequently exceeding the length of a defendant's vigorous adulthood, the costs of failing to cooperate need not be made explicit.

Sometimes prosecutors and defendants agree that after a guilty plea a particular sentence will be imposed. The judge may formally approve the bargain before the defendant pleads guilty, ensuring that the agreed-upon sentence will in fact be imposed, or the prosecutor may simply promise to recommend a particular sentence. In theory, the judge is free to reject the prosecutor's recommendation and impose a higher sentence, but in practice this rarely happens.

Not all explicit plea bargains promise the defendant a particular or recommended sentence. Often prosecutors agree only to reduce the charges against a defendant, either by moving for dismissal of certain charges or by refraining from filing them in the first place. By pleading guilty to reduced charges, a defendant hopes to obtain a lighter sentence, either because the maximum sentence the judge can impose is thus reduced or simply because the reduced charges send a signal to the judge that the offense is less serious.

Most explicit plea bargaining in state courts is like a retail transaction: prosecutors in a given jurisdiction regularly make a standard offer to a broad category of defendants, and individual defendants can take it or leave it. There may be a going price, for example, to resolve a charge of aggravated assault by a defendant with no prior convictions. Often, no formal offer may be necessary, because the going price is well known to local defense attorneys.

Some federal defendants, particularly those accused of white-collar fraud or participation in major narcotics operations, encounter a different kind of plea bargaining, in which the terms are open for negotiation. Agreements with these defendants differ from standard plea bargains, not only because they are individually negotiated, but also because the defendant's side of the bargain often includes both a guilty plea and a promise to cooperate with prosecutors and investigators and to testify truthfully in the trials of any accomplices.

Concerns about Plea Bargaining. The Supreme Court has repeatedly made it clear that plea bargaining is fully constitutional. The Court has required that a guilty plea be accompanied by an admission of guilt in open court, after the judge has advised the defendant of his rights and explained the possible consequences of waiving them. Often, though, these requirements result in little more than a perfunctory exchange between the judge and the defendant, providing little assurance that the defendant is truly making an informed and intelligent choice. Moreover, the Supreme Court has permitted guilty pleas even from defendants who continue to assert their innocence; the judge only has to have grounds for believing the defendant is guilty. Although the constitutionality of plea bargaining is thus settled, concerns about the process are widespread. Four concerns are paramount.

First, many observers worry that guilty pleas produced by plea bargaining are not truly voluntary and that the process may extract guilty pleas from some defendants who are innocent. When going to trial entails the risk of a decades-long sentence—and in some cases the risk of execution—many defendants may feel they have no choice but to plead guilty, even if they have legitimate defenses. This kind of pressure can make the right to trial sound hollow, and is particularly troubling when it leads an accused to plead guilty despite a belief in his own innocence.

As the potential punishment becomes more severe, the price that will be paid for the defendant's insistence on the full assertion of his rights intensifies. The ironic result is that a potentially severe punishment motivates a defendant both to plead guilty and to avoid the most dire consequences of conviction. Instead of operating as an ameliorating reward for the cooperative defendant who does not resist the system, the plea becomes a way to avoid the unacceptable risk of an excessively severe system. Security and risk avoidance have a higher value for the prosecutor as well as the defendant. The prosecutor faces greater risks for losing cases as their severity increases, and so is inclined to reduce the risks by negotiating a plea bargain.

Second, plea bargaining is often criticized not for forcing guilty pleas from defendants who may be innocent, but rather for letting guilty criminals get off lightly. Prosecutors with heavy caseloads may be too eager to cut deals in order to avoid trials, and standard plea bargains may thus confer unwarranted leniency on offenders who deserve stiffer sentences.

Third, plea bargaining creates certain inequities. Because plea bargaining is an inherently discretionary process, defendants of comparable culpability often receive starkly different treatment—either because they are charged in different jurisdictions, or because they face different prosecutors, or because the prosecutor simply feels differently about them. The discretion that is at the heart of the system also leaves it more vulnerable to racial *discrimination and other forms of bias.

Fourth, plea bargaining is largely hidden from public view. The prevalence of plea bargaining reduces the frequency of direct confrontation between constitutional doctrine and everyday law-enforcement practices, particularly since prosecutors are more likely to settle cases in which the legality of police behavior may be challenged by means of motions to suppress evidence. Plea bargaining also obviates the public's ability to observe the difficulties inherent in the exercise of assessing criminal liability in a full trial.

The Future. Despite these serious concerns about plea bargaining, the practice continues unabated, largely because the practicalities of criminal litigation require it. Some have suggested that with additional resources and streamlined trial procedures, plea bargaining could and should be abolished. But at present, the American criminal justice system relies heavily on the practice. Prosecutors and judges have grown accustomed to disposing of cases without trial in the vast majority of cases. Prosecutors also have come to rely on the testimony they obtain from accomplices in exchange for favorable plea bargains. Whether or not taxpayers realize it, they too have grown to depend on plea bargaining: there are very few communities in which local budgets are adequate to bring most criminal cases to trial. This is in part because plea bargaining has allowed American courts to operate with trial rules that might prove unworkable if applied in all criminal cases; with fewer criminal trials, it has become less important that they proceed efficiently.

[See also Criminal Law Practice; Criminal Punishments]

• The President's Commission on Law Enforcement and Administration of Justice, *Task Force Report: The Courts*, 1967. Arthur Rosett and Donald Cresses, *Justice by Consent: Plea Bargains in the American Courthouse*, 1976. Stephen J. Schulhofer, "Is Plea Bargaining Inevitable?" *Harvard Law Review* 97 (1984): 1037. Gerald Lynch, "Our Administrative System of Criminal Justice," *Fordham Law Review* 66 (1998): 2117. Mary E. Vogel, "The Social Origins of Plea Bargaining: Conflict and the Law in the Process of State Formation," *Law and Society Review* 33 (1999): 161. George Fisher, "Plea Bargaining's Triumph," *Yale Law Journal* 109 (2000): 855. Ralph Wenham, " 'Truth in Plea-Bargaining': Anglo-American Approaches to the Use of Guilty Plea Discounts at the Sentencing Stage," *Anglo-American Law Review* 29 (2000): 1.

—Arthur Rosett and David A. Sklansky

PLEADING. *See* Procedure, Civil.

PLEDGE OF ALLEGIANCE. *See* Public Ritual, Law and.

PLESSY V. FERGUSON, 163 U.S. 537 (1896). The case of *Plessy* v. *Ferguson* placed the Supreme Court's judicial stamp of approval on the emerging Jim Crow *segregation system in the South. Until *Plessy*, the Court had distinguished between state action and individual acts of *discrimination, maintaining that the federal government could protect the rights of black citizens in cases of discriminatory state laws. Now the Court adopted a formalistic logic that allowed some appearance of impartiality while ignoring the reality of the situation. Segregation laws, Justice Henry Billings Brown wrote for the Court, did not "necessarily imply the inferiority of either race to the other." If blacks considered such laws discriminatory, it was only because they chose to look at them that way.

Plessy made its way to the Supreme Court as a deliberate challenge to Louisiana's 1890 Separate Cars Act, which required "equal but separate" railroad cars and forbade blacks to sit with whites. A group of New Orleans Creoles engaged Albion Tourgee, a leading voice for black rights, to help them. By prearrangement with railroad officials, Homer Plessy, an octoroon with no visible African lineage, was evicted from the first-class car. When the state courts upheld the law, Plessy appealed to the U.S. Supreme Court.

The justices deemed the segregation statute a "reasonable regulation" under the police powers of the state. Relying on the 1883 *Civil Rights Cases* (1883), Justice Brown rejected Tourgee's Thirteenth Amendment argument that segregation was a badge of servitude, then turned to the *Fourteenth Amendment equal-protection claims. Brown shrewdly relied on a Massachusetts case (*Roberts* v. *City of Boston* (1849)) that permitted segregated public schools to demonstrate that if segregation was legal in Boston when the Fourteenth Amendment was written, Congress could not have meant to abolish racial distinctions. Indeed, Brown stressed that distinctions between the races "must always exist," because they were grounded in the natural order of things. The law was "powerless to eradicate racial instincts or to abolish distinctions based upon physical differences." Reflecting the values of their own time, the Supreme Court justices, most of them former railroad lawyers who came to the bench after Reconstruction, sacrificed the constitutional rights of

African Americans to the notions of "scientific racism."

Justice John Marshall *Harlan stood alone for the rights of black Americans. A former Kentucky slaveholder with twenty years of experience on the Supreme Court bench, Harlan had firsthand knowledge of racism's ugly hold on the South. Thus he castigated the majority for its legalization of caste through the "thin disguise" of equal accommodations. Harlan maintained that the Reconstruction amendments "removed the race line from our governmental systems." Segregation laws violated a color-blind Constitution. Predicting that the *Plessy* ruling would perpetuate racial antagonism, Harlan prophesied accurately that the decision would "prove to be quite as pernicious as the decision made by this tribunal in *Dred Scott v. Sandford.*"

Freed from constitutional restraints, southern states moved boldly to institute a system of segregation at every level of society. The separate-but-equal doctrine established in *Plessy* upheld the Jim Crow system until the *Warren Court ruled in *Brown* v. *Board of Education* (1954) that "separate educational facilities are inherently unequal."

[*See also* Civil Rights and Civil Liberties; Race and Ethnicity]

• Charles A. Lofgren, *The Plessy Case: A Legal-Historical Interpretation*, 1987. Brook Thomas, ed., *Plessy v. Ferguson: A Brief History with Documents*, 1997.

—Lou Falkner Williams

POLICE. The United States has the most decentralized police system in the world, with more than twenty thousand different forces. The variety in American policing is in part attributable to the social, political, cultural, and economic context in which it developed. The roots of American policing can be traced to the transplantation of European institutions to the New World, beginning in the seventeenth century.

The word "police," has its origins in the Greek word *politeia*, which described all affairs that affected the survival and order of the state. By the eighteenth century, European states used "la police" (in France) and "die Polizei" (in Germany) to refer to the internal administration, safety, protection, and surveillance of a territory. The English eschewed the word "police" because of its absolutist connotations, but the term gained increasing currency in France. By the end of the eighteenth century the term was in more common use in England, and as a preventive police force developed in the first decades of the nineteenth century the term seemed to lose much of its stigma.

Before the establishment of professional police in the nineteenth century, most cities in America and Europe depended on a variety of peace officers, a combination of night watchmen and constables, with *sheriffs in the more rural environs. There was little innovation in the early American colonies, with most preferring what they were familiar with—some incarnation of the English parish constable, night watchman, and county sheriff.

A relic of the medieval world, night watchmen were notoriously inefficient. Their main duties included watching out for crime, making regular announcements of the time and weather conditions, and spotting fires. Night-watch duties in America varied from city to city, with southern watchmen expected to observe slaves and indentured servants on the streets after dark. Early constables were responsible for delivering warrants, surveying lands, and even regulating weights and measures. By the eighteenth century constables were required to supervise the evolving watch and ward system (night and day police). Constables have now diminished in importance in the law-enforcement network, and in 1976 the word "police" was dropped from the title of the National Police Constables Association. Today, constables perform duties similar to sheriffs, tasks that include transporting prisoners, collecting back taxes and debts owed the government, serving legal papers, and providing emergency assistance when necessary. Currently thirty-seven states utilize the office of constable. Unlike the sheriff, the modern-day constable is no longer imbued with traditional peacekeeping and investigatory powers that it once had.

Policing in the Colonial Era. Between 1608 and the end of the American Revolution (1781), most sheriffs and constables were appointed by colonial governors and performed the same tasks as their English counterparts. The office of sheriff, an ancient law-enforcement position first established in Anglo-Saxon England before the Norman Conquest of 1066, made its appearance in America in the early colonial period. Sheriffs in colonial America served process papers, maintained law and order, collected taxes, and maintained jails prior to the Revolution.

While the town constable was the most familiar peace officer in New England, the sheriff played a more significant role in more sparsely settled Virginia. The job was often won through patronage, the traditional bane of honest policing. Sheriffs were expected to fulfill a wide assortment of services ranging from organizing courts and calling elections to running the jail and keeping county records. Sheriffs could not meet their obligations without the assistance of a coterie of under-sheriffs, deputies, jailers, county clerks, and executioners.

In the more urban reaches of the country, such as Boston, New York, and Philadelphia, the British night-watch system was adopted to complement the duties of the constable. During the 1630s the dim outlines of American policing were beginning to take shape in Boston, where America's first night watch was established.

As slavery flourished in the South during the eighteenth century, the colonies responded by organizing slave patrols to suppress insurrections and crime. The first slave patrol was established in South Carolina in 1704, initially part of the colonial militia. All ambulatory men between the ages of eighteen and fifty were expected to volunteer for duty. Typical tasks included inspecting highways and inns and being alert for runaway slaves. Imbued with many traditional police powers, slave patrols may have been the progenitors of modern policing.

Colonial law enforcement saw few improvements between 1607 and the late eighteenth century. The demand for more and better policing resulted from the massive social and political unrest in the colonies, which led to an increase in crime in the second half of the eighteenth century. The French and Indian War (1756–63) was followed by a major economic depression, one that impoverished many Americans. Property and street crimes became more common, and the need for a better system of law enforcement was evident. From the beginning, the colonies were committed to local peacekeeping rather than a centralized system of policing. Today's decentralized police system and lack of a national police force are a testament to this earlier tradition.

Development of Professional Police Forces. Law enforcement and criminal justice figured little in the founding fathers' discussion of which direction the nation would take in creating police forces. The only mention of law enforcement in the Constitution is the power of the president during national emergencies. In a country with little if any concern about establishing a national police force, future events would lead to an increasingly decentralized police system.

The early development of police forces in Europe was stimulated by the affiliation of policing with the state. France introduced the office of lieutenant of police as early as 1667. Charged with suppressing crime, this office became a political position of considerable importance in the Na-poleonic era (1799–1815) under minister of police Joseph Fouché.

Following the Napoleonic wars, London faced a growing crime problem. With high unemployment and the transition to a factory-based economy that favored machine over human labor, social and economic conditions deteriorated and pressure grew for more professional policing. Despite some support for a standing police force, most British people opposed it. With a tradition that ran counter to the centralized police system in vogue on the European continent, British reformers envisioned a preventive police system rather than one in the oppressive tradition of the Napoleonic police. A firm proponent of preventive policing, Britain's home secretary Robert Peel led the passage of the bill that created the police force in 1829. The London "bobbies" or "peelers" patrolled regular beats, wore uniforms, and were paramilitary in structure and discipline.

The history of early American policing was the history of distinctly different forces in different cities. By the early nineteenth century, policing was firmly rooted in the English system of part-time magistrates, sheriffs, constables, and the occasional paid watchman. As American cities grappled with the exigencies of industrialization, urbanization, and immigration, communities began to create civil police forces, making the transition from unpaid watchmen to more formal arrangements, and began a number of experiments in policing. Southern cities such as New Orleans and Charleston tried instituting uniformed city guards, with sporadic success. Philadelphia became one of the first to establish separate day and night police forces in the 1830s, but the day force was soon disbanded. Boston also took hesitant first steps toward police reform during the incessant ethnic rioting that marked the 1830s.

In 1845, New York City became the first city outside the British Empire to adopt a police force based on the London model. With a long-established antipathy for uniforms, the original officers objected to wearing special costumes. Worried that the uniforms infringed on traditional American freedoms, opponents feared the dangers of a standing army. So a compromise was reached in which New York City police officers wore eight-point star-shaped copper badges over their left breasts instead of a complete uniform—hence their identification as the "star police," "coppers," or just plain "cops." The development of American policing after 1845 was hampered by a lack of consensus about wearing uniforms, whether police should be armed, and the use of force.

Between 1845 and 1865 major American cities established professional police forces that emphasized prevention over detection. As early as the 1850s, while cities such as New York could boast uniformed police on the London model, in other regions fears of a standing army led to informal vigilante groups, particularly in the trans-Mississippi west after 1850. Although there is little disagreement that a breakdown in social order caused by immigration and urbanization contributed to the development of policing in urban America, creation of urban police forces, according to Eric Monkonnen (in his 1981 book *Police in Urban America, 1860–1920*), may have been an attempt by municipal authorities to first control the "dangerous classes" and then to manage cities more efficiently. Refuting the notion that modern policing developed in response to rioting and rising crime rates, Monkonnen argued that if this had been the case, cities that experienced neither problem would not have established police forces.

The development of modern urban police was a slow process, occurring gradually in most cities. Initially, the new police forces used a syncretic approach, which assimilated part of the old watch system before making the transition to totally new strategies. By 1851 Chicago had adopted a police system similar to that of New York City, followed by New Orleans and Cincinnati (1852), Philadelphia (1855), St. Louis (1856), Newark and Baltimore (1857), Detroit (1865), and Buffalo (1866).

In order to prevent the police from becoming separate and remote from the citizens they served, some cities instituted residency requirements to ensure that police officers were members of the community. As immigration politics became inextricably linked with policing in cities such as New York and Boston, Irish immigrants and Irish Americans became the most common ethnocultural group in police forces in the mid-nineteenth century. This is best explained by the Irish predilection for partisan politics and the spoils system that went along with it.

Although the London police model inspired many American police forces, because of the inherent differences in the two societies this model was seldom closely imitated. In England, police officers were recruited from the military and from laborers on the fringes of London. After joining the force, officers accepted the restriction of many personal liberties. Married officers were not allowed to live in certain parts of town, and bachelors were assigned to barracks. Barred from voting, London bobbies were ultimately responsible to Parliament rather than to local constituents. The intricacies of the American system would never permit such restrictions of individual liberties.

During the Civil War, U.S. marshals were mainly concerned with arresting suspected traitors and Confederate sympathizers. Their role in supporting Lincoln's suspension of the writ of *habeas corpus made the marshals objects of derision in many quarters.

Following the war, marshals were confronted with protecting recently freed slaves and helping reimpose federal authority in the South. Meanwhile, Ku Klux Klan groups spread their campaign of terror across much of the South in defiance of the Civil Rights Act of 1866. Marshals soon found themselves at the center of the struggle as they supervised polling places and protected politically active blacks from white violence.

In the 1860s and 1870s, Indian police forces were created to suppress criminal activity on the reservations. In 1878 the federal government authorized the establishment of Indian police on most reservations, and by 1890 fifty-nine reservations could boast Indian police, with seventy officers and seven hundred privates. The Indian police were chiefly responsible for keeping the peace, protecting property, discovering and returning stolen property, and arresting whisky peddlers and horse and cattle thieves. Poorly paid and ill-equipped, the Indian police were often unwilling to wear police uniforms.

Perhaps the greatest development in federal law enforcement, the creation of the U.S. Secret Service in 1865, was a last-gasp attempt to counter the longstanding counterfeiting problem. During the service's first year of operation, field offices were set up in eleven cities and were credited with establishing a measure of monetary stability in the decade following the war. However, not until after two more presidential assassinations after Lincoln's (Garfield in 1881, McKinley in 1901) did the Secret Service become officially responsible for protecting the president.

Throughout the nineteenth century there was little support for statewide policing. Americans favored decentralization of policing in an era that placed considerable value on a republican ideology, which endorsed local control of policing. Texas and Massachusetts were the only states to experiment with state policing in the nineteenth century. Credited as the United States' first statewide police force, the Texas Rangers were created in 1823, but did not appear in official legislation as the "Texas Rangers" until 1874; during the nineteenth century the Rangers had an off-and-on existence. Beginning in 1865 Massachusetts embarked on a series of state police experiments. Throughout its early existence, the powers and duties of the state's police force targeted Irish immigrants and Irish Americans, focusing most of its attention on enforcing liquor laws.

Between 1870 and 1900, police reform efforts were led by local politicians, state legislatures, and chiefs of police. In the 1870s the New York City police force was reorganized and a new set of standards implemented, including requirements that police candidates be U.S. citizens, residents of the state for at least one year, and without a criminal record. But in 1894 a more sinister side of the police force was revealed, when the Lexow Committee to investigate corruption discovered a menu of bribes required for officers to rise through the ranks of New York City's "finest." The following year, future president Theodore Roosevelt was appointed as one of four newly installed police commissioners. Over the next two years he played an instrumental role in weeding out corruption and is credited with introducing a policing system with promotion based on merit rather than patronage, more stringent physical and mental qualifications, and more progressive recruitment.

In the years before an effective federal police apparatus and the birth of the *Federal Bureau of Investigation (FBI), banks, railroads, and other enterprises often avoided local law enforcement by hiring private agents to cross jurisdictions to apprehend wide-ranging criminal gangs such as the James Gang and the Younger Brothers.

During the nineteenth century, the history of private policing is closely tied to the development of the Pinkerton National Detective Agency. The Pinkertons came to prominence when they foiled a plot to assassinate President Lincoln and later served as counterespionage agents during the Civil War. Following the war, agency founder Allan Pinkerton returned home to Chicago and to new challenges ranging from pursuing train robbers to strikebreaking. By the 1870s the Pinkertons claimed to have assembled the largest collection of mug shots in the world as well as having created a criminal database for agents.

A variety of private police services were established during the early twentieth century to compete with the Pinkertons and traditional police forces. Among the most prominent was Burns National Detective Agency, founded by William J. Burns in 1904. Burns had earlier worked for the U.S. Secret Service. In 1921 he was selected to head the Bureau of Investigation, the precursor to the FBI.

Policing, Politics, and Law in the Twentieth Century. Before 1914, violations of the Fourth Amendment's protection against unreasonable *search and seizure were perceived as common-law trespassing. In order to keep seized evidence from being admitted at trial, a defendant only had to petition for the property to be returned and then could sue the responsible police officer for damages. In *Weeks* v. *U.S.* (1914), the U.S. Supreme Court held for the first time that a violation of the Fourth Amendment in itself could justify excluding *evidence from trial. This ruling had a profound impact on the admissibility of evidence seized by police in federal trials.

Weeks v. *U.S.* was a landmark case, but its greatest limitation was that it did not apply to the states. However, in a practice known as the "silver platter," if state or local police conducted the search and turned over otherwise illegally obtained evidence to federal officials, the evidence was declared admissible. This exception to the exclusionary rule meant local prosecutors could use illegally seized evidence in trial under state law (if the state allowed it).

During the first decades of the twentieth century, the world of work began to change under the influence of radical politics and unionization. While police work had more responsibilities than most jobs, it shared many of the concerns of other wage-earning occupations. In the early decades the typical patrolman worked twelve-hour days and received low wages. Between 1910 and 1920 police officers began to take an active role in creating labor unions and police organizations. This crusade reached a crescendo of sorts in Boston in 1919: when the police commissioner prohibited officers from joining a union, 1,117 of the 1,544 members of the force went on strike. But the subsequent crime wave and civil disorder lost police any support they may have had. All the strikers were eventually fired and a new force was recruited. If anything came of the strike, it was the setting back of the police union movement until the 1960s.

Berkeley, California, police chief August Vollmer was the preeminent proponent of police professionalism during the Progressive era. Among his earliest achievements was establishing a department code of ethics that barred the acceptance of gratuities and favors under penalty of dismissal. Vollmer rose to prominence for his requirement that prospective police officers pursue a college education, in an era when most police departments did not even require a high school diploma.

The onset of the Depression stimulated the state

police movement, leading to the creation of fifteen state police forces between 1929 and 1941. Of these, twelve were based on the highway patrol model. A new pattern also developed in which earlier state forces were reorganized into larger forces. By the end of 1941 each state had developed either a highway patrol or a force based on the state police model.

During the 1920s and 1930s crime emerged as one of the nation's greatest social issues, as popular attention was focused on the exploits of bootleggers, gangsters, public enemies, and crime wave hysteria. By the 1930s law enforcement became a national obsession, thanks to the publicity-minded genius of FBI director J. Edgar Hoover. In response, Congress broadened the mandate of federal law enforcement to include the policing of prostitution, *drugs, and the sale of alcohol.

Among the most significant challenges to search and seizure laws during the 1920s was *Carroll et al. v. United States* (1925). In this case the Supreme Court upheld the conviction of a bootlegger after illegal liquor was found in his car, finding that the search of a moving vehicle is not the same as search of a home, because crucial evidence can be moved quickly in moving vehicles and thus lost forever. Therefore, given probable cause of illegal activity, under what is known as the "Carroll Doctrine" police can conduct a search of a vehicle such as a car or a boat without a warrant.

The federal government became increasingly involved in crime fighting in the years between the World Wars. Paralleling the growth of most federal agencies during the New Deal was the expansion of the FBI, its crime-fighting powers augmented to include kidnapping (1932), crossing state lines to avoid prosecution (1933), interstate transportation of stolen goods (1934), and marijuana prohibition (1937)

In 1929 President Herbert Hoover selected former U.S. attorney general George Wickersham to chair the National Commission on Law Observance and Enforcement. Between 1929 and 1931 the "Wickersham Committee" produced a fourteen-volume report, the most important findings related to policing appearing in two volumes, *Report on Lawlessness in Law Enforcement* (no. 11) and *Report on Police* (no. 14). According to the first of these, the use of the third degree to extract confessions was a violation of constitutional privileges. The police-sanctioned brutality of the pre-Miranda rights era was often mentioned in the report in carefully coded words and phrases, such as "shellacking," "massaging," or "breaking the news." *Report on Police* was a critique of police

administration and bore the stamp of August Vollmer, who was credited with directing the report and even writing several chapters himself. In its conclusions, the report inveighed against the corrupting influence of politics on police organizations. Despite the noble intentions of the Wickersham Commission, most of the suggestions went unheeded. Among its harshest critics were police executives, who found many of the conclusions hastily drawn.

Along with the well-documented expansion of the FBI, the duties of other federal agencies also expanded in response to the exigencies of Prohibition- and Depression-related crime. Between 1920 and 1933 the Bureau of *Alcohol, Tobacco, and Firearms, which traces its origins to 1862 (Alcohol, Tobacco, Tax Unit), saw considerable action in disposing of illegal whiskey and arresting bootleggers. Meanwhile, the Customs Service was kept busy trying to stem the flow of illegal liquor into the country by boat. The Internal Revenue Service enjoyed perhaps its finest hour with the conviction of Al Capone on income tax evasion in the 1930s. And in 1940, the Immigration and Naturalization Service became part of the Department of *Justice.

Also reflecting the influence of police professionalism was the emphasis placed on professional police training programs at various levels of government. State police forces led the way in implementing professional training programs in the 1930s. As early as 1931, San Jose State College boasted the first major program in police training, and in 1935 the FBI introduced an academy for training local police officers.

One unanticipated result of the growth of the FBI was the diminution in importance of U.S. marshals, America's first federal crime-fighters. By the time Prohibition ended in 1933, the FBI had reached national prominence. Under Hoover's direction, the FBI became increasingly specialized and professionalized. Unable to keep pace with these developments, U.S. marshals were forced to make the transition to little more than process servers and court policemen. In the 1940s and 1950s, police departments across the nation continued the trend toward professionalism, as police administrators began to upgrade standards for new officers while casting off the yoke of political interference and manipulation of police forces by political bosses and ward leaders. Police reformers such as Los Angeles police chief William H. Parker and Chicago police commissioner Orlando W. Wilson personified the model of professional impartial law enforcement.

The 1960s and 1970s: Changing Police Roles and Practices. One of the most turbulent eras in American history, the 1960s and 1970s were marked by *civil rights and war protests, race riots, and domestic terrorism. The police establishment would be challenged on many fronts. In an attempt to understand the rising crime rates and create strategies for suppressing crime, the federal government launched a variety of official inquiries. Among the most significant was the President's Commission on Law Enforcement and Administration of Justice, which concluded that the police had become increasingly isolated from the communities they served. Its 1967 report, *The Challenge of Crime in a Free Society*, concluded that city officials had given police chiefs too much latitude in running their departments. In an era of rising concerns over the role of police in contemporary society, the extensive report suggested more than two hundred recommendations on reform, including raising educational requirements and improving training programs for police officers.

The Omnibus Crime Control and Safe Streets Act of 1968 affected the criminal justice system in a number of ways. Building on *Katz* v. *United States* (1967), the Supreme Court decision that limited the use of electronic eavesdropping because of concerns about invasions of privacy, the Omnibus Crime Control Act prohibited lawful interceptions except by warrant or with consent.

The turbulence and social conflict that shook the United States in the 1960s had important consequences for the police. A revolution in civil rights law, championed by the U.S. Supreme Court, would place limitations on police work by challenging longstanding police customs and practices, including search and seizure, brutality, and in-custody investigations.

In the landmark case of *Mapp* v. *Ohio* (1961), the Supreme Court greatly increased the ability of criminal defendants to defend themselves by ruling that evidence secured by the police through unreasonable searches must be excluded from trial. The decision was shortly followed by the *Escobedo* v. *Illinois* (1964) and *Miranda* v. *Arizona* (1966) decisions by the Warren Court, credited with significantly changing the way police officers carried out interrogations and at the same time guaranteeing the rights of the accused.

Building an appeal based on the 1914 *Weeks* decision, which held that the Fourteenth Amendment barred the use of evidence secured through illegal search and seizure, Mapp's conviction in *Mapp* v. *Ohio* was overturned in 1961. In the process the exclusionary rule was extended to the states. *Miranda* v. *Arizona* substantially altered American police practices in the interviewing of suspects. Lauded by civil libertarians, *Miranda* was roundly criticized by law enforcement and was later modified under the more police-friendly Burger Court in the 1980s.

These court rulings have come under fire in recent years, with police officers arguing that the decisions have placed unreasonable burdens on them. Many legal experts believe the decisions will be modified. *Terry* v. *Ohio* (1968) began that process by validating a police officer's right to stop, question, and even search a person who acts suspiciously, as long as the officer has reasonable grounds for doing so. During a decade notable for placing restrictions on police powers, *Terry* v. *Ohio* clearly augured a new climate favorable for enhancing them.

During the 1960s the police establishment was increasingly tested by a wide variety of mass confrontations. The urban riots of the 1960s were unprecedented in the destruction of property and communities. According to the findings of the National Advisory Commission on Civil Disorders, better known as the Kerner Commission, the torpid police response to many riots often allowed civil unrest to flare out of control. The subsequent Kerner Report reserved its greatest criticism for the lack of police training in riot control.

Running on a "law and order" platform in 1968, Richard Nixon castigated the Kerner Commission for blaming "everybody for the riots except the perpetrators." After taking office in 1969, Nixon recommended more funding for the Law Enforcement Assistance Administration in order to supply police departments with tanks, armored cars, helicopters, riot control equipment, and a national computerized identification system for fighting crime. A reflection of the new administration's support for policing was its increased funding for the Law Enforcement Assistance Administration, from $63 million in 1969 to $700 million in 1972. In order to seem tough on crime, Congress was coerced by the White House to pass questionable bills such as the "no-knock" provision, which allowed police to break into a house without a *search warrant, and preventive detention, which allowed judges to jail suspects for sixty days before trial.

One of the most memorable images of the 1960s was the beating of antiwar demonstrators by Chicago police during the 1968 Democratic Convention. A subsequent investigative commission later described police tactics as a "police riot." Police work changed dramatically in the 1960s and

1970s. Rising crime rates, urban riots, and antiwar violence led police executives and political leaders to examine the role of police as crime-fighters. Although a number of police authorities blamed the rising crime problem on the limitations imposed on them by *Miranda, Mapp,* and *Escobedo,* a more convincing explanation perhaps can be found in the number of fifteen- to twenty-four-year-old males in these years—an age group traditionally responsible for most violations of the law.

Beginning in the 1970s, research in several cities demonstrated that increasing the number of police officers on random patrol or increasing the speed of their response had little effect on crime reduction. Since the inception of the London bobbies in the 1820s, routine police patrol had been considered a hallmark of modern preventive policing. The notion that crime could be prevented or at least suppressed by a highly regular and visible police presence was a long-held belief. Beginning in 1972, a one year study was conducted in Kansas City to test this conviction. The controversial *Kansas City Preventive Patrol Experiment* report of 1974 found that police patrols, whether stepped up or diminished, had no significant impact on crime. With traditional methods of policing under such scrutiny, new concerns about the role of police in society sent experts back to the drawing board for answers.

The first documented occurrence of women with police powers can be traced back to 1910, but women made few inroads as crime-fighters in the male-dominated profession until the 1960s. The federal government led the way in removing impediments to the entry of women into the police ranks. The creation of the Equal Opportunity Commission in 1968 provided the impetus for giving women fuller roles in policing. Passage of the Equal Employment Opportunity Act of 1972 prohibited discrimination by public and private employers. Another barrier fell when the federal government amended the 1964 Civil Rights Act in 1972. Women and minorities continued to enter policing in increasing numbers in the 1980s. And by the end of the decade, New York City, Atlanta, Chicago, and Houston were among the major cities boasting African-American police chiefs.

The Crime Control Decade. During the 1980s police forces made concerted attempts to improve their tarnished image. Among the public relations strategies enlisted were crime prevention programs that encouraged citizen cooperation with the police.

When Ronald Reagan ascended to the presidency in 1980 he took advantage of his opportunity to appoint conservative-minded justices to the Supreme Court. The new Court leadership did not totally abandon the advances of the due process revolution of the 1960s and 1970s, but subsequent rulings tended to favor the prosecution.

In 1983 the Court ruled in *Gates* v. *Illinois* that police could obtain a search warrant based on an anonymous tip, rather than going through an extensive investigation to corroborate the reliability of the information through independent sources. Another important decision reflecting the new "get tough" approach on crime and the conservative bias of the Court was *United States* v. *Leon* (1984), which held that the exclusionary rule did not apply to evidence seized by police using a warrant unsupported by probable cause. This in effect allowed police to use warrants with factual errors and inadequate probable cause.

Attempts at improving the often rancorous relationships between police departments and the communities they served were widely heralded in the 1980s. Better police-community relations were given a high priority by most departments, particularly after the publication in 1982 of "Broken Windows: The Police and Neighborhood Safety." In this widely read article in *Atlantic Monthly*, two justice policy experts, James Q. Wilson and George Kelling, articulated a vision for improving police relations by what they called the "broken windows model." According to this theory, neighborhood disorder creates fear and neighborhoods give out crime-promoting signals such as broken windows, graffiti, and run-down housing. Offenders often target these neighborhoods because they interpret such conditions as signs of vulnerability. Police, then, need the cooperation of citizens if they intend to reduce fear and successfully fight crime in these environments.

The endorsement of "broken windows" by police administrators represented a major step toward enlisting communities in the war against crime by reverting to an earlier model of policing. Since the Progressive era, August Vollmer, and the introduction of the police car, the patrol officer has been increasingly removed from the mainstream community. Rather than encouraging citizen confidence and cooperation, generally the reverse was occurring. Although police cars maintained a presence, ensured rapid response to crime, and covered a wider area, they also alienated community members.

In the 1980s some urban police departments returned to an earlier style, when police walked a beat or foot patrol and maintained intimate contact with the neighborhood they served. The implementation of community policing took officers out of patrol cars and put them on a walking beat to strengthen ties to the community. Although early studies indicated that foot patrols did not decrease crime rates, residents felt safer and less vulnerable to crime.

The 1990s: Policing at a Crossroads. Following a three-mile high-speed car chase in the early hours of 3 March 1991, Rodney *King was ordered to get out of his car by several Los Angeles police officers. In the subsequent struggle, a number of officers used batons and stun guns to subdue the African-American motorist. Unknown to the police, the beating was recorded on videotape. The eighty-one-second tape of police officers seemingly beating and kicking a supine citizen, while other officers stood and watched, resonated in the minority neighborhoods of Los Angeles, where tensions had continued to fester since the 1965 Watts riots. In a *Los Angeles Times* poll taken two weeks after the beating, 87 percent of African-American and 80 percent of Hispanic respondents reported incidents of brutality by Los Angeles police officers as either "common" or "fairly common."

Reflecting the conservative mood of the country, in the mid-1990s the New York City police department, under Mayor Rudolph Giuliani, embarked on a campaign to take illegal handguns off the streets. Although civil liberties groups claimed that the police targeted minorities with "street justice tactics," new police strategies were credited with reducing violent crime in New York City in the 1990s.

There is no consensus as to why violent crime dropped so dramatically in the 1990s nationwide. The police establishment has been quick to take credit for the reduction. New police strategies and the increased numbers of police officers on the streets certainly share credit for the decline, but other factors have also contributed, including declining unemployment rates, an aging population, and the decline in the crack cocaine trade. In urban America, the decreased trade in crack cocaine and greater police efforts to seize handguns should get much of the credit. The 30 percent drop in murders and shootings in New York City in 1995 was considered to be the result of police frisking efforts, which drove illegal guns off the streets. Despite criticism from civil libertarians, there is little doubt that police assertiveness in this arena made some contribution to the drop in crime.

Between 1997 and 1999, the proportion of police departments across the nation using routine foot patrols increased from 28 to 34 percent. In 1999, more than two-thirds of departments used some type of community-based police program. Despite a movement from reactive to proactive policing, there is little evidence that the new policy is responsible for suppressing criminal activity. Civil libertarians and police critics point to the emergence of paramilitary SWAT teams in police departments as an alarming departure from the community policing model. Supported by federal grants and forfeiture laws, these units were initially aimed at the drug trade.

[*See also* Criminal Law Practice; Detective]

• Wilbur R. Miller, *Cops and Bobbies: Police Authority in New York and London, 1830–1870*, 1973. James F. Richardson, *Urban Police in the United States*, 1974. David R. Johnson, *Policing the Urban Underworld: The Impact of Crime on the Development of the American Police, 1800–1887*, 1979. David R. Johnson, *American Law Enforcement: A History*, 1981. Frank Morn, *"The Eye That Never Sleeps": A History of the Pinkerton National Detective Agency*, 1982. Frederick S. Calhoun, *The Lawmen: United States Marshals and Their Deputies, 1789–1989*, 1991. H. Kenneth Bechtel, *State Police in the United States: A Socio-Historical Analysis*, 1995. Dennis C. Rousey, *Policing the Southern City: New Orleans, 1805–1889*, 1996. Hereward Senior, *Constabulary: The Rise of Police Institutions in Britain, the Commonwealth, and the United States*, 1997. Samuel Walker, *Popular Justice: A History of American Criminal Justice*, 1998. Mitchel P. Roth, *Historical Dictionary of Law Enforcement*, 2001.

—Mitchel Roth

POLICE PROCEDURES. The impact of American law governing four of its most prominent police investigatory procedures—searches for *evidence, *interrogation, identification procedures, and undercover work—is examined in detail, looking at (1) the historical development of American police forces and the sources of law that govern them, (2) mechanisms for enforcing that law, and (3) certain rules that govern police investigation.

Historical Overview. The antiauthoritarian origins of the United States heavily influenced both the organization of its police forces and the way those forces are regulated. Compared with European countries, police organizations in America developed slowly and in a decentralized fashion, and the most important rules governing police procedures today are much more likely to come from the courts rather than from majoritarian institutions such as legislatures, or from police departments themselves.

Formal police forces did not begin operating in the United States until the mid-nineteenth century, and even then only in municipalities such as Philadelphia and New York. State police forces were not established until the end of the nineteenth century, and federal police entities such as the *Federal Bureau of Investigation were not created until even later. Within municipalities, police power was often divided. Today, some urban areas host over one hundred different police organizations, and there are more than seventeen thousand such organizations nationwide.

Given this diversity, uniform rules of police procedures were not likely to come from the police themselves. Nor were federal or state legislative bodies willing to promulgate rules regulating local police powers. Even the courts were initially reticent to do so. Although the judiciary possessed the power of review—the authority to overturn statutes and prohibit government practices believed to violate the United States Constitution—until the mid-twentieth century it rarely exercised this power in a way that affected the police.

This relative passivity on the part of the courts changed abruptly in the 1960s with a string of decisions by the U.S. Supreme Court during the time Earl *Warren was Chief Justice. The Warren Court for the first time established nationwide rules regarding various aspects of police work, including searches for evidence, interrogations, and use of identification procedures such as *lineups, and also adopted, as the mechanism for enforcing these rules, the exclusion of unconstitutionally obtained evidence. One reason for the new activism toward police regulation was the realization that regulating the trial process, which had been the focus of much of the Court's criminal law *jurisprudence up to that time, did little good if the evidence presented there was obtained by abusive or otherwise improper methods. A second, more important reason for the new judicial attitude was the Court's perception that the poor and disadvantaged, in particular racial minorities, were usually the focal point of police abuse and that lacking political power, this group's only hope for protection from such abuse was the courts. In a sense, the Court's famous decisions regulating police practices were descendants of Court opinions on school desegregation and other civil rights matters handed down during the 1950s.

When Earl Warren and three other justices left the Court between 1969 and 1973, President Nixon appointed justices who were more concerned about crime control than protecting the disadvantaged. Since that time, the Court, while not overturning the Warren Court's landmark decisions, has tended to limit them, with the result that the police have been subject to less constitutional scrutiny. At the same time, an important

legacy of continued judicial attention to police practices is that both federal and state legislatures have for the most part abdicated their role in establishing rules in this area.

The judiciary has not created its rules out of whole cloth, however. Most of the important limitations on police authority in the United States are based on interpretations of four provisions of the *Bill of Rights. The Fourth Amendment prohibits the government's "unreasonable" *search and seizure, and sets out the requirements for *arrest and *search warrants. The Fifth Amendment states that "[no] person . . . shall be compelled in any criminal case to be a witness against himself," language that has been construed to prohibit coercive practices during police interrogation. The Fifth Amendment (and the *Fourteenth Amendment, ratified after the Civil War) also contains the *"due process" clause, which prohibits deprivations of life and liberty "without due process of law." Courts have construed this language to require the government to act fairly when it exercises its power to punish and, in the context here, have held that the clause places limits on the conduct of interrogations, identification procedures, and undercover operations. Finally, the Supreme Court has construed the Sixth Amendment's guarantee of the "assistance of counsel" during "criminal prosecutions" to require *counsel during interrogations and lineups that take place after a defendant is formally charged.

The Exclusion Remedy. Probably the most conspicuous aspect of the Warren Court's attempts to regulate police practices is the mechanism it adopted to sanction unconstitutional actions by the police—namely, the exclusion or "suppression" of evidence that is unconstitutionally obtained through a search, seizure, interrogation, or lineup. The Warren Court appeared to view the exclusion remedy primarily as a means of avoiding judicial complicity in police illegality, but in more recent years the Court has made clear that the remedy's sole purpose is to deter police misconduct. Whatever its rationale, a successful suppression motion can often lead to dismissal of charges against the accused for lack of evidence, with estimates of convictions lost because of exclusion ranging from a [half] percent to over [two] percent of all arrests. That result has made the exclusionary rule controversial; most other countries resort to other means of regulating the police.

To the extent the rationale for exclusion is deterrence of police misconduct, empirical support for the remedy is not particularly strong. In the vast majority of cases in which police seize or search a person, for instance, no arrest is made, and thus the rule has no impact. Even when an arrest and prosecution occurs, the legality of the arrest and any accompanying search or interrogation is seldom litigated because the vast majority of cases are resolved through *plea bargaining, often before a suppression hearing can take place. When the constitutional issues are litigated, police know that their version of the action is much more likely to be given credence than the suspect's, and they also know that the fact that evidence was found (which is always the case in a suppression hearing) influences judicial decisions about the legality of the conduct in their favor. On those rare occasions when exclusion occurs, months may have passed since the illegal action, undermining any deterrent effect. More importantly, the party harmed by exclusion is not the officer but the prosecutor; the primary job of the police is to get a "collar," not ensure conviction. Although some proponents of the rule argue that it has at least prompted police departments to improve the training of their officers, research indicates that police understanding of the Fourth and Fifth Amendment's rules is minimal at best.

On the other hand, there is no doubt that without exclusion, the rules governing searches, interrogations, and other investigatory procedures would be violated even more frequently, given the pressure on the police to combat crime. Other means of ensuring that the Constitution is followed have proven futile, as the Court pointed out in *Mapp* v. *Ohio* (1961), the case that adopted the exclusionary rule in Fourth Amendment cases. Damages against the police and police departments are difficult to obtain, largely because juries tend to favor the police, and police departments are seldom willing to impose sanctions on their own members for violations of abstract constitutional rules. The exclusionary remedy, flawed as it is, may be the most effective means of enforcing the Constitution.

Searches and Seizures. The Fourth Amendment drafters were principally interested in curtailing the use of the "general warrant," which had given British soldiers wide-ranging authority to search at their whim for seditious literature and uncustomed goods. Thus, the Amendment includes a "warrant clause" that requires that warrants be based on probable cause and spell out with particularity the place to be searched and the things or persons to be seized. The "reasonableness clause" declares that "the right of the people to be secure in their houses, persons, papers and effects

from unreasonable searches and seizures shall not be violated."

As interpreted by the Warren Court, these two clauses express a preference that arrests and searches be authorized by a warrant, issued by a "neutral and detached magistrate" who has found probable cause (akin to a more-likely-than-not level of certainty). However, in practice, only about 5 percent of all searches and arrests are based on warrants, given the numerous exceptions to the so-called "warrant requirement" developed over the past 200 years. For instance, if police enter a house in hot pursuit of a suspect, no warrant is required. Furthermore, virtually any public arrest, and almost all searches outside the home, including those involving searches of arrested persons and vehicles, may be conducted without a warrant. Research on the warrant process indicates that it may not provide significant protection against arbitrary actions in any event, since magistrates often review warrant applications in a cursory manner.

The courts have also held that seizures short of arrest, as well as some types of searches, not only do not require a warrant, but also need not be based on probable cause. Stops (brief detentions) and frisks (patdowns) require only reasonable suspicion, a level of certainty less than probable cause. Seizures considered even less significant, such as roadblocks, do not require any individualized suspicion, although they must still be conducted in a reasonable manner (e.g., with notice to drivers, and placement controlled by central office authorities). Finally, police actions that are not considered "searches," because they do not infringe "reasonable expectations of privacy" (e.g., going through garbage, flying over backyards, use of binoculars to look at open fields), or "seizures" (e.g., brief, casual questioning) need not even be "reasonable" because they do not involve the Fourth Amendment at all. The same is true of searches authorized by voluntary consent, which constitute a large proportion of police intrusions onto private property, suggesting that not all of these consents are entirely "voluntary."

Probably the most controversial aspect of modern search and seizure law is the concept of "aggressive patrolling," a means of using stop and frisk authority to make the police presence felt in certain neighborhoods, remove weapons and drugs from the streets, and turn targets into informants. Because arrests are rarely made in this context, the exclusionary rule is almost useless as a deterrent. An analogous strategy occurs in connection with traffic stops. Because there are so many traffic laws—governing speed, turning signals, equipment, and the like—the police can stop almost any driver for a violation, and then search the car if something suspicious is spied in plain view, consent is obtained, or if the occupant can be arrested for a custodial offense (which the Court has held authorizes search of the entire car's interior). Although such traffic stops might serve merely as a pretext to check out the officer's "hunch" that the occupant is engaged in more serious crime, the Supreme Court has held that the officer's hidden agenda is irrelevant to Fourth Amendment analysis. Some view these police techniques as necessary tactics in the war on drugs and gangs, while others believe they are reminiscent of the general warrants that gave rise to the Fourth Amendment in the first place.

Interrogation. During the nineteenth century, confessions obtained by the police were occasionally excluded as unreliable under state or federal evidentiary law, but it was not until 1936 that the U.S. Supreme Court held that the due process clause prohibits the admission of confessions that were "involuntary" in the "totality of the circumstances." In a series of cases, the Court applied the involuntariness doctrine to invalidate confessions obtained through torture, threats against family members, and deprivation of basic amenities. By the 1960s, however, the Court felt that the voluntariness test failed to provide police and judges sufficient guidance. In 1964, it decided that under the Sixth Amendment, defendants who are formally charged are entitled to counsel during any questioning by the state. Two years later, the Court decided *Miranda* v. *Arizona* (1966), which held that the Fifth Amendment privilege against self-incrimination requires the police to tell anyone subjected to custodial interrogation—even interrogation that occurs prior to formal charging—that he has a right to remain silent, that anything he said can be used against him, that he has a right to counsel during interrogation, and that counsel will be supplied if he cannot afford one.

Dire predictions that *Miranda* would end custodial interrogation never materialized. Indeed, it has done very little to curtail police abuse of the interrogation process. The post-1966 confession rate during custodial interrogation appears to be almost identical to the pre-1966 rate (between 50 percent and 60 percent). There is less physical coercion during interrogation today than when *Miranda* was decided, but that is probably part of a longer term trend resulting from greater profes-

sionalization of the police and pre-*Miranda* decisions outlawing force. Most importantly, the same techniques the *Miranda* Court had criticized as part of the "inherently coercive" atmosphere of custodial interrogation—including the "good cop-bad cop" routine, the "pretended friend" technique, and exaggeration and falsification of evidence against the suspect—are still endorsed by police manuals today.

Other means of regulating interrogation have been proposed, including mandatory presence of counsel, taping of interrogations, and even a return to judicial questioning (which was the primary means of interrogating suspects in colonial times given the absence of police forces). But the Court's reaffirmation of *Miranda* in 1999 may ironically have ensured that these alternatives are never seriously considered in most jurisdictions. In the meantime, foreign countries have adopted all or part of the *Miranda* requirements, and added their own protections. For instance, interrogations in the station house in England must be taped, and affirmative misrepresentations by the police in Germany are prohibited.

Identification Procedures. Procedures used to determine the identity of the perpetrator involve either comparison of specimens (such as fingerprints, blood type, or DNA) or eyewitness identifications using lineups, photo arrays, and show-ups (one-on-one confrontations). Comparison procedures require careful attention to the specimen "chain of custody," as well as use of scientifically reliable tests. Eyewitness identification procedures are even more prone to error. Research has shown that perception and memory deficits, especially in connection with stressful events involving weapons, can be significant. Gaps in memory may then be filled by the conscious and unconscious suggestions of police and other individuals.

Accordingly, the Warren Court held that the due process clause prohibits unnecessarily suggestive identification procedures, such as "sore thumb" lineups, where the suspect is the only obvious selection, or one-on-one confrontations that could have been avoided. It also held that defendants subjected to lineups are entitled to counsel. However, later Court decisions held that unnecessarily suggestive procedures are not unconstitutional as long as the resulting identification can be shown to be reliable, and that the right to counsel only attaches when the defendant has been formally charged, which often occurs well after most identifications have taken place. Under these rules, few identifications are excluded, even though, in contrast to situations involving violations of the Fourth Amendment or *Miranda*, suggestive procedures are more likely to produce unreliable evidence.

Undercover Investigation. As crime became more clandestine and organized during the late nineteenth century, police turned increasingly to sting operations, informants, and other types of undercover activity. Such activity is subject to very little regulation. The Supreme Court has held that citizens assume the risk that their acquaintances are working for the government, and thus they are not protected from undercover intrusions by the Fourth Amendment, which as noted earlier is only implicated by infringements of "reasonable" expectations of privacy. Nor does questioning by a covert agent violate the Fifth Amendment, since no coercion is involved, or the Sixth Amendment, if it occurs before formal charging occurs, which it usually does. The only constitutional limitation on pre-charge undercover work comes from the due process clause, which bars law enforcement conduct that "shocks the conscience." While the Court has suggested that threats of violence by an undercover agent would violate due process, typical undercover activity is unlikely to do so.

Another limitation on undercover activity is the common-law defense of "entrapment." As defined in the federal courts and most states, such a defense is available only if the defendant can show he was not predisposed to commit the crime proposed by the undercover agent. Because most individuals approached by government agents have prior records, this defense is rarely successful. But it does prevent undercover police from offering strong inducements to otherwise innocent people to commit crimes.

The effectiveness of undercover law enforcement techniques is unclear. Studies of large-scale sting operations have generally failed to show a significant reduction in crime, perhaps because the operations capture criminals who would have been caught in any event using overt methods, or perhaps because they often involve creation of opportunities to commit crime (e.g., fencing operations). On the other hand, there is no doubt that a large percentage of arrests and searches are based on information from "confidential informants," whose identities are protected by the police because of their involvement with other criminals who might retaliate. The disadvantage of relying on such individuals is that they will sometimes lie in order to obtain money or avoid prosecution. Moreover, because these informants are "confi-

dential," judges have difficulty verifying that they exist; in some cases, police have fabricated the existence of informants in support of a warrant application.

Future Challenges. The increasing randomness of crime, and the continuing perception that society must vigorously pursue the "war on drugs," has ensured the continuous development of new policing techniques. These include "community policing," which emphasizes close police-citizen contact and mutual problem-solving, fine-tuned "loitering" laws designed to permit removal of gang members and other undesirables, community roadblocks as a means of cordoning off high-crime areas, and pervasive video surveillance, sometimes using magnification and illumination capacities. Some of these techniques may well prove to be very effective in crime prevention. But each also presents potentially significant threats to *privacy and autonomy.

[*See also* Criminal Law Principles; Police]

• Herbert Packer, *The Limits of the Criminal Sanction*, 1968. James Q. Wilson, *Varieties of Police Behavior*, 1968. Nathan A. Sobel, *Eyewitness Identification: Legal and Practical Problems* 1972. Jerome Skolnick, *Justice Without Trial*, 1972. Richard Van Duizend, L. Paul Sutton, and Charlotte A. Carter, *The Search Warrant Process: Preconceptions, Perceptions and Practices*, 1985. Gary T. Marx, *Undercover: Police Surveillance in America*, 1988. Michael Tonry and Norval Morris, eds., *Modern Policing*, 1992. David H. Bayley, *Police for the Future*, 1994. Joseph D. Grano, *Confessions, Truth, and the Law*, 1996. Akhil Amar, *The Constitution and Criminal Procedure: First Principles*, 1997. George Thomas and Richard Leo, *The Miranda Debate*, 1999. Wayne R. LaFave, Jerold H. Israel, and Nancy J. King, *Criminal Procedure*, 2000. Charles Whitebread and Christopher Slobogin, *Criminal Procedure: An Analysis of Cases and Concepts*, 2000.

—Christopher Slobogin

POLITICAL SCIENCE AND LAW. Law was once central to the study of government. Scholars of "public law" in the academic departments that predated the discipline of political science taught American *politics in legal terms (constitutional law and administrative law) to college students for generations. They employed historical and case analysis to teach about the practices of government and they lectured on the nature of politics. Institutions were the core curriculum and doctrine was their methodology. Critical scholars like Charles Beard tied the political thought of men such as James Madison, Thomas Jefferson, and Alexander Hamilton to economic interests, challenging the emerging notion that selfless idealists wrote and ratified the Constitution.

The last of the great doctrinalists was Edward S. Corwin, who retired in the 1950s. Corwin wrote the first compendium on constitutional interpretation and described the "Higher Law" background of American Constitutional law. The study of government began to be called political science in the early twentieth century. With its new name, the subject of study broadened to include international politics and the attitudes of ordinary people. At the same time, the methodology narrowed and the discipline moved away from mere descriptions of the institutions to inquiry and theory meant to stand with the social sciences.

This move coincided with the emergence of the professional legal academy within the university from its traditional place in the law practice. Law study became situated in a postgraduate, professional, university setting that became known as the law school. With this move, authoritative commentary on the law and the work of the courts shifted to these schools. Even constitutional law eventually became the province of the lawyers in the academy. Political science now involved scholarship on the politics in courts, learning how law is implemented, and the emerging study of law in society. Methodologically the shift is from descriptive doctrinal studies to behavioral, sociological, and economic analysis of law. Institutional practices were still described but they became less central to developing academic reputations.

C. Herman Pritchett was the founder of the behavioral school, which flourished in political science after the Second World War and demonstrated that judges are political. His approach evaluated the array of dissenting votes on the Supreme Court and used them to describe the ideological orientation of the justices. More contemporary scholars such as Harold Spaeth and Jeff Segal continue to develop what is now known as the attitudinal model.

Another version of the scientific study of law is sociological jurisprudence, which showed how court decisions impact society, described the activity of interest groups producing litigation and submitting amicus curiae briefs, and analyzed the process for selecting judges, including the role of the American Bar Foundation and the attorney general. The work of Sheldon Goldman is important here.

Institutional studies, dubbed New Institutionalist to distinguish them from their less sophisticated forebears, emerged from this social scientific milieu as a return to the practices of government and politics. This led to work on the emergence of the administrative state, citizenship, and the system of entitlements that characterized the welfare state. Some scholars working in the institutional tradition looked again at the nature of the Supreme Court and proposed how it might be understood as part of the cultures of authority in America.

Some political concerns in law such as the social status of women, people of color, and the disenfranchised are characteristic of law in political science. Catharine MacKinnon, reconceptualized the authority of law as well as the law on pornography, equality, and harassment by rereading the traditions in political theory. Other legal issues such as monopolization in the computer industry or the regulation of intellectual property have received relatively little attention in political science and remain the province of the law schools.

Economic or "public choice" analysis of law is a recent development. First evident in the work of Walter Murphy in the 1960s, it found new life in the modeling associated with utility maximization and calculations of economic self-interest. With government funding, Lee Epstein and colleagues have developed this essentially conservative approach and claimed a special place for it as science.

Having once held a more central position in the cultural life of law, political science scholars now seem largely content with their secondary status. They take pride in their initial insight about the political nature of judging and appreciate that it has become conventional wisdom. Motivated by the conflicting aspirations to be scientific and to comment on public policy, this disciplinary approach to law lacks coherence while the vitality of its subject keeps it alive.

[See also Economics and Law; Law and Society Movement; Social Dimensions of Law]

• Walter Murphy, The Elements of Judicial Strategy, 1964. Sheldon Goldman and Thomas P. Jahnige, The Federal Courts as a Political System, 1985. Stephen Skowronek and Karen Orren, Studies in American Political Development, 1986. Catharine A. MacKinnon, Toward a Feminist Theory of the State, 1989.

—John Brigham

POLITICS AND THE LAW. Working to illuminate the links between politics and law, we consider politics and, of, and in law. Conventionally we speak of politics "and" law. But the conjunction "and" does not really join; it is disjunctive. Law and politics are generally seen as opposites that contest and subvert one another. They may be two sides of the same coin, but they are the opposite sides. The prepositions are less distinct and used a bit more randomly. To say that there is a politics "of" law is generally seen as being more critical. This statement is offered as a reluctant truth about law, a sort of sad and resigned sense that law has been subverted or infiltrated by the corrupting influence of politics. In the United States, the belief that there is a politics of law appears to be widespread, yet not particularly unsettling. Proposing that there is politics "in" law is challenging and a little more disruptive. "In" law is an uncommon usage suggested here as a way of highlighting the interpenetration between law and politics that is difficult to comprehend. Politics in law is a perspective that takes us back to the beginning, and challenges the disjunction. We conclude with the notion that there is a politics in separating law from politics and there is a politics in putting them back together again.

Legal institutions provide a forum and a crucible for hammering out questions of public policy. They also help frame these questions and they suggest the answers we may consider. In thinking about the relationship, we address events and institutions that have shaped the most important policy questions in our history. Politicians and *judges play important roles, but those who have commented on the relationship—the theorists of law—have done the most to determine how we speak about these two spheres. From the beginnings of the American experience to the world at large today, the related spheres of law and politics have shifted with events and affairs of state. With each shift, someone can usually be credited with articulating what the relationship means. We start with what is supposed to be the traditional understanding, and move on to suggest that this is simply a way of making the present seem compelling. We conclude by suggesting the limits to these conventions shown by contemporary legal research.

And the Law. Politics and law, law and politics; it doesn't seem to matter which way you arrange these elements. The meaning is the same either way. *Jurisprudence, the study of legal theories, teaches that this is the conventional wisdom. We are encouraged to think that law and politics incorporate two different spheres and that they share relatively little. The idea is that when they overlap, it is to the detriment of law. By this relationship, law is elevated and politics is seen as a bad influence. Politics, as an activity that is opposite to law, is the basis for the hope that America can be a government of law and not of men. The phrase has varied uses and significance in American history.

Stated by John *Adams in his draft of the Massachusetts Constitution of 1780, the aspirational phrase assumes a divergence between the two spheres, and suggests the hierarchy. At the beginning, the relationship appears to have been fluid. Adams, arguing a decade later that Massachusetts should ratify the United States *Constitution, and specifically the notion of two legislative houses, saw in the mixing of institutional powers a sense of the limits to the dichotomy. He quoted Aristotle to the effect that "a government where the laws alone should prevail, would be the kingdom of God." This was not a reasonable aspiration. It appears that Adams' reference to the kingdom of God was in recognition, along with others in the founding generation such as James Madison in Federalist No. 10, that Americans, who once hoped to build a society divine in its purity, ought no longer believe that this was likely. Instead, the conventions of law came to be understood as checks on human frailty. They would work to the extent that the arrangements kept the frailties in balance.

The aspiration to be a government of laws and not of men gets a prominent restatement from the Chief Justice of the United States, John *Marshall, in *Marbury v. Madison in 1803. This is the case that addresses the authority of a judicial reading of the Constitution for the political branches of government. Marshall asserts his authority, as a judge, by telling the *Congress that it has acted beyond its authority in providing direct access to the *Supreme Court. The power of the law is preserved, at least in part, because Congress is not a party to the case and does not have to respond. In this case, Marshall, the most political of justices, builds on the distinction between law and politics as a way of buttressing his power as a figure with particular capacity in reading the law. This happened in a case where Marshall had been involved, and from which he should have recused himself. Perhaps because of these frailties, Marbury is a benchmark for both the separation of law and politics, and the sense that the distinction gives power and authority to the judge.

That there should be politics on the one hand and law on the other, that there should be separate spheres, has had distinguished supporters throughout American history, and has come to be an idea associated with the constitutional system of *government. At every level of American government—local, state, and federal—one can find those who proclaim their devotion to this concept that law and politics are two different spheres of life, which is often called "formal" or "formalistic." Crime in a local context brings defendants before a judge sworn to uphold the law whose robes and separation from the proceedings behind the bench are meant to reinforce the notion that he is the embodiment of law and not of his more mundane, human self. In America, the decision to charge is made by the local *prosecutor, and no matter how many variables he or she must weigh in an undeniably political process, all prosecutorial decisions will be presented as if dictated by the law rather than politics.

At the national level, Americans owe their identity not to ethnicity or to geography but to legality, to being born under the Constitution. The formal power of law is much more in what we take for granted than it is a resolution for contested political questions. We debate the status of *immigrants coming to America without the proper documentation, but for the bulk of Americans carrying a passport the law divides citizen from alien. We debate who will be the president, but seldom what it means to be thirty-five years old. States contest with each other and with the national government, but we generally know that California and Massachusetts are states and Puerto Rico and Canada are not. We have one president, two houses of Congress, and a Supreme Court, whose interpretation of the law receives special attention.

Florida provided a vivid example of law and politics contesting at the level of the American states in the presidential election that pitted the Republican George W. Bush against the Democrat Albert Gore. There, the arcane details of paper ballot counting, normally reserved for the most expert of election lawyers, demonstrated the aspirations for a legal conclusion to the controversy. Indeed, the extraordinary closeness of the contest, and the sense that all the states but Florida had been decided, raised the stakes in this contest. Fear of a "constitutional crisis" in which the familiar law would no longer govern drew people to a resolution even as nearly everyone in the country became a potential authority on the relevant law, and their interpretations tended to reflect their political orientations. In the end, the Supreme Court in Washington decided the election of 2000 with finality amounting to all the authority it needed for a nation grown weary and slightly nervous about a continuing stalemate.

Thus, as much as it is supposed to exist in fact, the dichotomy often breaks down in the American experience. The Declaration of Independence was a challenge to the legally constituted authorities governing America in the 1700s. But the Declaration has a distinctively legal form. It is a "bill of particulars" that lists grievances following a major premise that seeks to justify a popular uprising. Charles Beard shocked Americans that followed his economic orientation and the Progressive Era. He offered the observation that economic considerations, not purely legal ones, were driving the founding fathers. Some considered calling too much attention to motives of a material sort unseemly. On the other hand, Beard's career was distinguished, and in his time the link to *economics made sense to many people. When Abraham *Lincoln entered the national stage as president, he was transformed from a local politician about whom little was known other than that he had doctrinaire views on *slavery, the issue of the day. As president, he mobilized the nation and took many actions that challenged the conventions of law, particularly the notion that the federal government could impose its will on a state or group of states by armed force.

In contemporary American jurisprudence, politics and law are increasingly linked, not simply as the two sides of the same coin, but as corollaries. The consensus depends on the notion that this wasn't always the case. It is a common belief in America that in some not so distant past, law was a check on politics. We repeat the mantra "a government of law not of men" as an aspiration with increasing skepticism.

Sometimes called "formalism," sometimes "mechanical jurisprudence," we now often hear that it was in earlier times that naive figures in American legal life believed that you could separate politics from law. Scholars in the 1960s called attention to the claim by Justice Owen Roberts that when he considered constitutional questions, all he had to do was lay the Constitution down next to a statute and see if "the former squared with the latter." A more sophisticated example is Felix *Frankfurter, a justice of the Supreme Court who lived from 1882 to 1965. Frankfurter is seldom held up to the sort of criticism we associate with Roberts and formalism, but the implications of his view of law are much the same. There are still some believers around. We hear about them in the judiciary and in the law schools, but seldom is the claim in jurisprudential circles made this boldly.

Often the claim that law can stand apart from politics is buttressed with other considerations such as "the original intent of the Founders" or the "economic analysis of law." In Richard Posner's book *The Economic Analysis of Law*, the techniques of economics are used to buttress law. Some believe that law has relatively little authority of its own; others simply see economics as more compelling these days. These claims give reason for us to believe that law can stand outside politics and for us to have confidence in its authority. They also suggest that the question of the relationship between law and politics is perennially interesting.

Of the Law. The law of politics, the politics of law—in this case, if you change the order of the words, the statement doesn't seem to mean the same thing. The law of politics might be election law, including term limits and campaign finance, which is not the subject here. It might include gerrymandering and the gingerly forays by the Supreme Court into the formerly forbidden arenas called "political questions," which is more closely tied to the subject of "politics and law".

We learned that politics effects law as part of the realist critique (see LEGAL REALISM). In jurisprudence, this contemporary incorporation of politics into law is often set against a background of formal legal control. Jerome *Frank, an academic and a judge, called attention to the contentious nature of American law. He also led the charge in the academy to bring to life Oliver Wendell *Holmes' notion that the "law is what the judges say it is."

We have an extension of the realist perspective in the behavioralists in political science. When we think of Pritchett's work demonstrating that when justices of the Supreme Court dissented, they did so often according to political inclinations they most likely brought with them to the Supreme Court.

A modern way to incorporate the insight of the past is to recognize that legal institutions serve as a forum and crucible for hammering out questions of public policy. There are institutional channels and checks that are not themselves totally dependent on politics.

In the late 1970s and early 1980s, a movement emerged in the legal academy known as *Critical Legal Studies. It sought to extend the "Realist" project in law by pushing its implications to the extreme. The results were published in numerous law reviews and as *The Politics of Law*. This book was divided into various areas, often reflecting divisions in the law. The critique had considerable influence on progressives in law school, and for a time it challenged the conservative *law and economics orientation and the Federalist Society.

In a fashion at once similar as critique and different in its implications, feminist theorist Catharine MacKinnon developed the patriarchal critique of law as male politics. Law was phallic, and its categories equally centered on male standards of rationality. But MacKinnon went further. In a substantial challenge to the liberal presumptions of law, she transcended the political, the "of," to suggest the politics in the nature of law. She is a transitional figure.

In the Law. Meddling with the order of presentation again, as a way to continue this inquiry, the law in politics means something different from politics in law. The law in politics would be about representation and voting, about elections and campaigns. Politics is often grounded in law. This was the case in the struggle over whether the Constitution would be ratified, the abolitionist efforts that led to the *Civil War, even the effort by President Franklin D. Roosevelt to control the Supreme Court and protect the New Deal. Roosevelt's *"Court-packing" plan was initially an attempt to place a number of new justices on the Supreme Court to counteract the conservative tendencies of many of the occupants. It was developed by his *attorney general, who had instituted a similar plan to add one justice for each justice over the age of seventy to the lower federal courts. But the plan came to be seen as excessively political, and its failure ultimately symbolized the stature of the Supreme Court in twentieth-century American life.

The law in politics seems about the same as the law of politics, although it sounds a little stranger. The politics in law is another thing all together, and it operates at two different levels. One of these we have already discussed as the legal realism initially associated with Jerome Frank and developed by political scientist C. Herman Pritchett and appearing with new enthusiasm most recently in the Critical Legal Studies movement in law schools. In fact, what was presented as critique or insurgency in the 1930s and again in the 1980s has become the orthodoxy throughout much of the legal community. As doctrine, there is a need to understand that politics is a characteristic part of the law, and that the authority of law comes from acceptance of this doctrine, a key aspect of which is that the law cannot be separated from politics.

This suggests the importance of saying something about the politics in "law." This is in part the politics of widespread acceptance that there is a tension between law and politics. This is the basis for the larger, more imperial sense of a politics in "the law." This is what makes sense to look at when we think of politics *in* law. The politics in law is a politics in what we take for granted, the tension between law and politics and the institutions in which the tension is felt. With the Declaration of Independence, and then in the move to a constitutional system, Americans spent a dramatic period in the late eighteenth century engaging in politics while creating a legal system. In America, the story of independence begins with a statement of principles about what men might expect of government, and concludes with a Constitution that specifically lays out how they should proceed.

Today, global constitutionalism continues that politics by extending an American conception of markets through law to the rest of the world. Nelson Mandela, the first President of South Africa elected with Black African votes, appears to have imagined a constitution only roughly based on the American model, with economic rights guaranteed. The international community wouldn't permit it, and he had to back down. Similarly, the United States' effort to preserve the Western liberal government of Colombia in the face of fifty years of rebel insurgency has demanded American institutions of law such as a prosecutorial system and more stringent criminal codes.

An aspect of the contemporary perspective is recognition that politics, in the form of legal institutions and legislation, produces law, but also that law, in the form of shared understandings and aspirations, produces politics.

[See also Bush v. Gore; Law and Society Movement]

• C. Herman Pritchett,The Roosevelt Court, 1948. Walter Murphy, The Elements of Judicial Strategy, 1964. Felix Frankfurter, Law and Politics, 1971. Jerome Frank, Courts on Trial, 1973. Richard Posner, The Economics of Justice, 1983. Charles A. Beard, An Economic Interpretation of the Constitution of the United States, 1986. Catharine MacKinnon, Feminism Unmodified: Discourses on Life and Law, 1987. Ronald Dworkin, Law's Empire, 1988. Mari Matsuda, Words That Wound: Critical Race Theory, Assaultive Speech, and the First Amendment, 1993. John Brigham, The Constitution of Interests, 1996. Helena Silverstein, Unleashing Rights: Law, Meaning, and the Animal Rights Movement, 1996. David Kairys, The Politics of Law: A Progressive Critique, 1998.

—John Brigham

POPULAR CULTURE AND LAW. See Arts, Popular Culture, and Law; Entertainment Law.

PORNOGRAPHY. See Morality, Ethics, and Crime; Morals Offenses; Organized Crime; Technology and Law; Victimless Crimes.

POSSESSION, ADVERSE. See Property, Real.

POSSESSION, EXCLUSIVE. See Property, Real.

POUND, (NATHAN) ROSCOE (born Lincoln, Nebraska, 27 October 1870; died 1 July 1964, Cambridge, Massachusetts). Pound's father, Stephen, and mother, Laura Biddlecombe, were New Yorkers who relocated to Lincoln, where Stephen practiced law and entered politics. They schooled Nathan Roscoe and his two sisters at home until they were old enough to attend the preparatory department of the University of Nebraska. Neither sister married. Louise, the elder, became a professor at Nebraska. Olivia was a high-school teacher and principal. At fourteen, Pound entered the University of Nebraska where he studied botany; he received his bachelor's degree in the subject in 1888 and completed a master's degree the following year. Then he succumbed to his father's importuning to study law, but he convinced his father that he should do so at Harvard Law School. While Pound's enthusiasm for law study may have only been lukewarm at the time he left for Harvard, his experience during his year there converted and transformed him. From his first moment in Cambridge, he virtually moved into the law library.

Pound returned to Lincoln after one year of study, read law in his father's firm, and was admitted to the bar in the year 1890. He devoted nights to study of *jurisprudence, stealing time from what he called a "long and tedious" law practice. It may have been the drudgery of practice in these early years that inspired him to go on with his botanical studies—he earned a Ph.D. in botany in 1897—and join the Nebraska Botanical Survey, but by that time he had made up his mind that he preferred the study and teaching of law.

In 1895, he was asked to teach jurisprudence and Roman law at the University of Nebraska. Four years later he was appointed an assistant professor. By 1903 he was dean. He left in 1907 to teach at Northwestern Law School for two years, then at the University of Chicago School of Law, and the next at Harvard, where he taught until his death, in 1964. He was dean of the school from 1916 to 1936.

Although he grew into a socially conservative man of fastidious personal taste, Pound's personal conservatism was part of a dual strain in his jurisprudential nature. A liberal Republican in politics and temperament, Pound always despised violent change and lauded systemization and classification, but he also espoused a progressive pragmatic doctrine of jurisprudence that fused together European ideas of the social origins of law and liberal Republican progressive impulses into a "sociological jurisprudence."

Pound rejected what jurisprudence would later call "formalism," the idea that the law was a series of fixed concepts from which rules could easily and aptly be derived. Instead, he argued that law was rooted in social and political realities, changed with the times, and was a product of discrete and sometimes partisan human choices. His sociological approach to law took on great importance in this era of legal contests between organized labor and corporate capital on the one hand, and conservative politics against progressive reform on the other.

In 1904, he tied "The Need of a Sociological Jurisprudence" to a crisis in Americans' confidence in law, whose "fault must be laid largely to the law and to the matter in which law is taught and expounded." Teachers of law could no longer dismiss "sociological principles" and apply them "to the problems of state and municipal life." Data must be collected on the actual administration of law "in a scientific apprehension of the relations of law to society and of the needs and interests and opinions of society of to-day." For law "is a means, not an end," and Pound judged that end to be "away from the older individualism" and "property rights" toward a larger goal. Modern legislation limiting the independence of large employers and providing insurance to workers, repudiating contributory negligence doctrines, showed that way.

Rejecting the U.S. Supreme Court's idea of liberty of contract in *Lochner* v. *New York* (1908), Pound instead called for deference to democratically elected legislatures.

Pound had some misgivings about calling his approach "sociological jurisprudence," but as he wrote in 1919, "The word 'sociological' seems to me important because it necessarily associates itself in men's minds with this element of change." Sociology was then the most progressive and innovative of the emerging social sciences and this was the "pioneering" era of American sociology.

The high-water mark of Pound's liberal prescriptions came in his *Interpretations of Legal History*, a series of lectures that Pound gave at Trinity College, Cambridge, in 1922. He wrote, "Let us think of jurisprudence for a moment as a science of social engineering, having to do with that part of the whole field which may be achieved by the ordering of human relations through the action of political organized society." Jurisprudence was not supposed to just explain, it was supposed to tutor action. Even more important was Pound's proffer of a new theory of law, what may be termed a "demand side" or consumer view of the legal pro-

cess. Law (and its interpreters, both official and academic) were in the business of "satisfying human demands." It had struck Pound that in the 1920s, for the first time, consumption rather than production—what critics called "consumptionism"—had become the chief concern of the market. Until now, lawmakers, under the cloak of formalism or conceptualism (the later a term Pound had introduced nearly two decades before), had "covered up what the legal order really was and what court and law-maker and judge really were doing—weighing social interests." In each of these calculations, there was no abstract process of pure *legal reasoning, but a series of compromises of social interests, dressed up as legal form and intent.

Pound had claimed for the progressive pragmatic jurists the role of lawmaker. The search for an American jurisprudence had led to its progressive-pragmatic conclusion. One would expect from him now a law program, but that was not what Pound wanted to do. Instead, he gradually retreated into a pallid pedantry. In an era in which he admitted that other jurists were "becoming more confident in the efficacy of intelligent effort to improve the law" and projects for " 're-statements of the law' are in the air," Pound took little role in these reform efforts. In fact, from the middle 1920s on, Pound's involvement in data gathering and policy-planning projects, from his sponsorship of a study of criminal justice in Cleveland at the end of the 1920s to his attempt to write a system of laws for Nationalist China after World War II, did not advance the progressive agenda. Courted in the late 1920s and thereafter by the very elite corporate interests he had shunned in his youth, he became an outspoken critic of the New Deal and a severe critic of President Franklin Delano Roosevelt's *court-packing plan.

But he remained a staunch supporter of legal *education and the community of scholars in the law schools. In fact, Pound did almost all of his legal writing and thinking within the framework of institutional associations and affiliations, principally the schools where he taught. What he wrote for public consumption he often first tested extensively in private correspondence with other academics, creating a network of colleagues, former students, and intellectuals. By so doing, Pound linked Harvard Law School to the rest of what was becoming the foremost research university in the country.

In his declining years, Pound traveled and lectured. He loved both. With no children, his legacy became his long-awaited five-volume encyclopedia of jurisprudence, published in 1959. It was replete with the schools and movements of the law, with interests and obligations, but it lacked the inner vision that had made his earlier, far shorter, forays into jurisprudence so galvanizing.

[*See also* Educator, Legal]

—N. E. H. Hull

POWER OF ATTORNEY. A power of attorney is a written document that gives an agent the power to act for the signer (principal). The power of attorney confers upon the agent the power to legally bind the principal by the agent's acts, and assures third parties that the agent has the power to act for the principal. An example of an ordinary business use of a power of attorney is in a residential real estate transaction where the sellers have already moved from the jurisdiction. The sellers can give a power of attorney to their agent, such as a lawyer or realtor. This document allows the agent to act for the sellers at the closing and sign all the necessary documents. In addition to specific powers of attorney, which limit the agent's representation to a specific task, a general power of attorney allows a principal to give an agent the ability to act for any purpose.

At *common law a power of attorney automatically ceased to operate if the principal became incapacitated, on the theory that the principal could no longer consent to the agent's actions. In order to avoid this result most states have passed laws allowing *durable* or *springing* powers of attorney, which allow an agent to continue to act pursuant to the power of attorney. Durable powers of attorney specifically state that they will continue to operate if the principal becomes incapacitated. Springing powers of attorney do not become effective unless the principal becomes incapacitated. The purpose of these two forms of powers of attorney is to allow the agent to make medical decisions and to take care of the principal's affairs during a period of incapacity. The durable power of attorney is the better instrument for dealing with the problems caused by the principal's incapacity. A springing power raises the question whether the principal is really so incapacitated that the agent can use its powers. Conservative third parties, such as financial institutions, might refuse to recognize an agent's power in ambiguous situations.

The competent principal can take comfort from having executed a durable power of attorney in favor of a reliable agent. In the event of the principal's incapacity, the appointment avoids the cost and delay of a court hearing to determine whether the principal is incapacitated. A power of attorney also allows the principal to choose an agent instead of having the court appoint a guardian who might not have been the principal's choice. The agent can make decisions about medical treatment in order to comply with the principal's desires. In particular, if the principal has strong feelings about using life-prolonging medical treatments, an agent with a power of attorney is in the best position to make sure that medical personnel honor the principal's wishes. The agent can also handle the business affairs of the principal so as to conserve assets and pursue matters where time is of the essence. For these reasons, modern estate planners use the durable power of attorney to protect their client's interests in the event of incapacity.

[*See also* Procedure, Criminal]

• William W. Brown, *Estate Planning: A Practical Guide*, 1991.

—R. Ben Brown

PREJUDICIAL PRETRIAL PUBLICITY. *See* Fair Trial, Criminal; Media and the Law; Speech and the Press, Freedom of.

PRESIDENCY OF THE UNITED STATES. Many countries have adopted the United States presidency as a model, but rarely with success. They learned that it is not enough to borrow text from another constitution and hope for comparable results. The U.S. presidency created in 1787 responded to specific domestic needs, and gained sustenance from a unique political and legal culture. The energy and independence called for in the American executive has been controlled by public and institutional checks not found in other political systems.

Creation of the Presidency. When President George Washington took office in 1789, he had the good fortune to inherit an administrative structure that had been building after America declared its independence from England in 1776. At first, the national government consisted of a single branch: the Continental *Congress. For several years it carried out all three functions of government, passing necessary legislation, sitting in committees to handle administrative work, and creating other committees to resolve judicial disputes. It became obvious that executive and judicial duties had to be delegated to outside bodies. Judicial questions were farmed out to a Court of Appeals in Cases of Capture. For executive matters, Congress experimented with boards made up of people outside the legislative body. These multi-member boards were so slow and unreliable that Congress, in 1781, created single executive officers to supply better accountability: Secretary for Foreign Affairs, Secretary at War, and Superintendent of Finance.

This administrative structure provided a solid foundation for the new national government in 1789. John Jay served as Secretary for Foreign Affairs from 1784, and remained in that post as Acting Secretary of State under Washington's first administration, until Thomas *Jefferson assumed the duties of Secretary of State in 1790. General Henry Knox was elected Secretary at War in 1785, and continued in that office until 1794.

During this period, there developed a preference for single executive officers over multimember boards. The experience under the Continental Congress convinced most lawmakers in 1789 that the board system lacked responsibility, energy, and order. Congress voted for single executives to head the departments. A similar principle guided the delegates at the Philadelphia Convention in 1787, where it was proposed that there be three members of the Executive "to be drawn from different portions of the Country." The delegates voted 7–3 in favor of a single president to serve a term of four years after being chosen indirectly by an Electoral College. To protect the president's independence, Congress was prohibited from increasing or diminishing the president's compensation during his term in office.

The powers assigned to the president are relatively few. He is commander-in-chief of the armed forces, grants *pardons except in cases of *impeachment, gives a state of the union message to Congress, and recommends measures that he shall judge necessary and expedient. Other powers are shared with the Senate, such as the power to make *treaties and to nominate and appoint public officers. Congress may remove the president from office after impeachment and conviction of *treason, bribery, "or other High Crimes and Misdemeanors." Impeachment is by majority vote in the House; conviction requires a two-thirds vote of the Senate.

The Growth of Presidential Power. The Constitution states that the "executive Power shall be vested in a President." Scholars have long debated whether the words *"executive power" suggest a grant of broad, discretionary authority of all powers conceivably executive in nature, ranging beyond those specifically enumerated in the Constitution. As part of his administrative responsibilities and his duty to faithfully execute the laws under the "take care" clause, it was early recognized that the president has the implied power to remove certain executive officials. Similarly, the

Supreme Court in *United States* v. *Nixon* (1974) recognized a limited executive privilege to retain information within the executive branch.

Apart from the concept of enumerated and implied powers, each of which is grounded in the Constitution, do presidents possess an extra-constitutional authority or prerogative power? May they act in response to an emergency—in the absence of law or even in conflict with it—for the public good? Having acted outside the law, the president must then go to Congress and receive retroactive authorization. When President Abraham *Lincoln took extraordinary actions at the start of the Civil War, while Congress was in recess, he acknowledged that some of his actions may have lacked legal authority, and therefore turned to Congress for retroactive approval.

The part of presidential power that has grown the most beyond the framer's intent is the war power. Congress is given specific power in the Constitution to declare war and to provide for the armed forces. It may declare war or authorize it, as it did with the Quasi-War against France in 1798. In *Talbot* v. *Seeman* (1801), Chief Justice John *Marshall acknowledged the broad constitutional authority of Congress to decide to initiate hostilities, whether by declaration or not: "The whole powers of war being, by the constitution of the United States, vested in congress, the acts of that body can alone be resorted to as our guides in this inquiry."

The delegates at the Philadelphia Convention recognized an implied power for the president to "repel sudden attacks." The president's independent power was therefore limited to defensive, not offensive, actions, and for almost a century and a half the president and executive advisers understood that the decision to take the country to war lay with Congress. Matters changed fundamentally in 1950 when President Harry Truman went to war against North Korea. At no time did he ask Congress for authority, either in advance or afterward. In *Youngstown Sheet and Tube Co.* v. *Sawyer* (1952), the Supreme Court struck down Truman's seizure of steel mills to prosecute the war, but the precedent had been established for unilateral action by the president to bring the country into large-scale military operations.

In 1973, Congress passed the War Powers Resolution to ensure that the "collective judgment" of both branches be applied to the introduction of U.S. forces into hostilities. The statute has had no such effect. Presidents continued to exercise the war power without seeking authority from Congress. President Bill Clinton went to war against

Yugoslavia in 1999 solely on his own authority, even though there was no claim of acting in a defensive manner or to protect American lives. Efforts by members of Congress to litigate these actions and restrain presidential power have been unsuccessful. Judges typically tell lawmakers they lack standing and failed to use the institutional powers available to them.

The president makes treaties "by and with the Advice and Consent of the Senate." Some presidents, such as Woodrow Wilson, decided that the negotiation of a treaty is purely a presidential matter, with the Senate brought in only after the draft treaty has been completed. This theory proved to be disastrous with the Versailles Treaty, which the Senate rejected after Wilson refused to accept legislative amendments. Other presidents recognize the wisdom of having lawmakers participate in the drafting of a treaty, as was done with the successful negotiations over the NATO treaty in 1949.

The Senate is the only branch of Congress formally recognized in the Constitution as having a role in treaties. However, since most treaties require appropriations and other implementing legislation, the House often has a co-equal role with the Senate in deciding the scope and meaning of a treaty. In some cases, when two-thirds of the Senate has failed to ratify a treaty, presidents have turned to Congress as a whole to accomplish the same purpose by obtaining a simple majority in each House for a joint resolution. The annexation of Texas and Hawaii and the adoption of the St. Lawrence Seaway plan were accomplished in this manner.

Administrative Duties. The president's appointment, removal, and other administrative duties are often shared with Congress in ways not obvious from the constitutional text. In legal theory, according to *Marbury* v. *Madison* (1803), the president's power to nominate is the "sole act of the president" and "completely voluntary." In fact, Congress can stipulate the qualifications of appointees, and legislators frequently select the names of federal judges, U.S. attorneys, and marshals for their state. In such cases, the roles are reversed: Congress nominates and the president "advises and consents." If the names submitted by Congress are unacceptable to the executive branch, the White House and the *Justice Department can object and request substitute proposals.

The framers realized that the Senate would not always be in session to give advice and consent to presidential nominations. To cover these periods, article II authorizes the president to make recess appointments: "The president shall have Power to fill up all Vacancies that may happen during the Recess of the Senate, by granting Commissions which shall expire at the End of their next Session." The executive branch interprets the word "happen" broadly to mean "happen to exist," even if a vacancy occurs while the Senate is in session. The meaning of "recess" remains uncertain, triggering charges by Congress that the president abuses this power. Legislation was enacted in 1863 to restrict payment in certain cases, and has been modified since that time.

Although the Constitution provides no express authority for the president to remove executive officials, it was agreed by the first Congress that responsible government requires the president to dismiss incompetent, corrupt, or unreliable administrators. These debates of 1789 were interpreted by the Court in *Myers* v. *United States* (1926) to leave not the "slightest doubt" that the power to remove officers appointed by the president and confirmed by the Senate is "vested in the President alone." Yet the debates in 1789 revealed deep divisions among House members and produced close votes on the Senate side. The decision in 1926 was later modified in such cases as *Humphrey's Executor* v. *United States* (1935) to permit Congress to limit the president's power to remove commissioners with quasi-legislative and quasi-judicial powers. Moreover, through the passage of non-binding resolutions, committee investigations, the contempt power, and other legislative pressures, Congress can precipitate an official's resignation or removal.

During the 1930s, executive officials wanted to "make law" without passage of a statute. President Herbert Hoover obtained authority to reorganize the executive branch without having to submit a bill to Congress for hearings, amendments, and enactment by both houses. Congress agreed only on the condition that either house could reject a reorganization plan by passing a resolution of disapproval. Through this accommodation was born the "legislative veto." By the 1970s, executive officials decided that this procedure, which had spread to such areas as immigration, arms sales, impoundment, and agency regulations, no longer favored the president. The Justice Department supported a test case, *INS* v. *Chadha* (1983), in which the Supreme Court held the *legislative veto unconstitutional. However, the decision did not, and could not, eliminate the conditions that gave rise to the legislative veto: the desire of executive officials for broad delegation of power, and the insistence of Congress that it control those dele gations without having to pass another public law. The executive-legislative accommodation that prevailed before *Chadha* continues to exist, sometimes in the form of committee and subcommittee vetoes. The executive branch tolerates these legislative "encroachments" because they want the discretionary authority.

Presidents occasionally advise members of Congress that they cannot have certain executive documents, but this assertion of "executive privilege" can be successfully rebuffed if Congress wants to use various tools at its disposal: the power of the purse, the power to issue subpoenas and hold executive officials in contempt, and ultimately the impeachment power. In these confrontations, the two branches usually work out a satisfactory compromise. The major executive privilege case— *United States* v. *Nixon* (1974)—did not involve a Congressional request for executive documents. The request came from the courts as part of the effort to prosecute Watergate crimes. A unanimous Court rejected the argument that the decision to release such documents is left exclusively to the president.

[*See also* Governance; Legislative Power]

• David Gray Adler and Larry N. George, eds., *The Constitution and the Conduct of American Foreign Policy*, 1996. Thomas F. Eagleton, *War and Presidential Power: A Chronicle of Congressional Surrender*, 1974. Martin L. Fausold and Alan Shank, eds., *The Constitution and the American Presidency*, 1991. Louis Fisher, *Presidential War Power*, 1995. Louis Fisher, *Constitutional Conflicts between Congress and the President*, 4th ed., 1997. Jordan J. Paust, "Is the President Bound by the Supreme Law of the Land?: Foreign Affairs and National Security Reexamined," *Hastings Constitutional Law Quarterly*, 9 (1982): 719–72. Christopher H. Pyle and Richard M. Pious, eds., *The President, Congress, and the Constitution*, 1984. Peter M. Shane and Harold H. Bruff, *Separation of Powers: Cases and Materials*, 1996. Robert J. Spitzer, *The Presidential Veto: Touchstone of the American Presidency*, 1988.
—Louis Fisher

PRESS. *See* Media and the Law.

PRESS, FREEDOM OF THE. *See* Speech and the Press, Freedom of.

PRIOR RESTRAINT. *See* Media and the Law; Speech and the Press, Freedom of.

PRISONER OF WAR. *See* War, Law of.

PRISONERS' RIGHTS. In 1876, in its opinion dismissing the claims of a convict in the state prison, the Virginia Supreme Court wrote, "[the prisoner] is for the time being a slave of the State" (*Ruffin*

v. *Commonwealth* (1876)). Eighty years later, the language was different, but the results were the same. Prisoners "had no standing," the issues they raised were "not justiciable," courts were bound by a "hands-off" doctrine. Thus in 1956, a federal court could dismiss a petition of an Illinois prisoner who claimed he had been savagely beaten, held in solitary confinement for two months without clothes or blankets, had his mail withheld from him, and had been deprived of food for periods up to five days, on the basis that "... it is well settled that it is not the function of the courts to superintend the treatment and discipline of prisoners in penitentiaries" (*U.S. ex rel. Atterbury* v. *Ragen* (1956)).

Twenty years later all this had changed. Prisons in virtually every state were under court orders; many were in virtual receivership. The sea-change from 1956 to the mid-1970s is dramatized in the Supreme Court's decision in *Wolff* v. *McDonnell* (1974), in which the U.S. Supreme Court ruled that prisoners could not be deprived of "good time" credit for disciplinary infractions without written notice, a hearing of some sort, and a written statement of reasons for the decision. Speaking for a unanimous Court, Justice White proclaimed the end of the "hands-off" doctrine, and declared that "[t]here is no iron curtain drawn between the Constitution and the prisons of this country."

Three interrelated developments account for this transformation between the mid-1950s and the mid-1970s: the continued development of the "Constitutional rights revolution," the expansion of professionalization within correctional administration, and the rise of national policymaking and the decline of *federalism. We review each of the factors below.

Beginning in the early 1960s courts began to recognize First and *Fourteenth Amendment rights of prisoner inmates. In a series of decisions, federal courts ruled that Black Muslim inmates should have the same access to religious materials and services that are available to other (Christian) inmates, that Muslims had a right to a pork-free diet, that prisoners should not be segregated on the basis of *race, and the like. Then, beginning in the mid-1960s courts began to impose *due process and fair hearing requirements on parole board decision-making, prison disciplinary policies, classification decisions, and the like. Similarly, the courts held that administrators cannot prevent inmates from communicating with their attorneys, contacting the courts, and gaining access to and using legal materials.

As important as these rulings were, none of

them addressed in a central way what many prisoners and prison reform advocates believed were the central problems of the prisons: in many places terror, torture, brutality, and degradation, and, nearly everywhere, abysmal conditions and services. Thus the impetus for the final stage of prisoners' rights litigation: reliance on the Eighth Amendment's prohibition against *"cruel and unusual punishment," a provision that hitherto had not been interpreted by the courts in this context. In the first such case, *Holt* v. *Sarver* (1969), Judge J. Henley Smith found that the Arkansas state prisons countenanced widespread torture, brutality, and indifference to suffering to such an extent that the "totality of the conditions" in the state's prisons violated the Eighth Amendment. This set in motion massive judicial intervention that touched every facet of the administration of the prison system and that lasted over twenty years. Immediately after *Holt*, federal judges elsewhere began issuing similar orders. The most expansive cases occurred in the South, whose prisons were explicitly modeled after slave plantations and were expected to operate at low or no cost to the state. However, far-reaching prisoners' rights judgments, perhaps more appropriately called structural reform cases, were handed down against prisons and jails in virtually all fifty states.

Despite the importance of these court decisions, it would be a mistake to think of the creation and expansion of prisoners' rights solely as product of litigation. At the outset, the prisoners' rights "movement" was a mass movement, a loose coalition of social activists, labor unions, lawyers, and others who shared the belief that prison inmates were people with rights and should at least be counted among society's "have-nots," who deserved a better deal. In many states, more enlightened penological practices and more rights for prisoners emerged from legislative and administrative decision-making, not litigation. The American Correctional Association, the national organization of correctional administrators, was instrumental in fostering the idea of prisoners' rights, and since the 1950s, had published standards for prison administration, which included an appreciation of the "rights" of inmates.

The third important factor in promoting prisoners' rights is a consequence of the transformation of American political policymaking in the mid-twentieth century. The history of prisons is a history of scandal and neglect, and public officials and the informed public had always known that prisons were terrible places. What was different in the 1960s was not that the public finally learned the truth about prisons or that the judges had become more squeamish. Rather, it was the rise of a national political community and the corresponding decline of federalism. With the success of the civil rights movement, *states' rights were accorded much less deference. Traditionally, the running of prisons had been an exclusive function of state and local governments, but with the decline of federalism, national policymaking in several areas, including prisons, was possible. It was not only the federal courts that sought structural changes in prisons; Congress and the executive branch did so as well. In the mid-1960s, the U.S. Department of Justice initiated investigations of allegations of abuse and discrimination in Southern prisons. In 1967, Congress authorized a federal program to develop national goals and standards for criminal justice, including prison administration. And in 1981, it adopted the Civil Rights for Institutionalized Persons Act (CRIPA), which provided inducements for state correctional systems to adopt national standards for prisons and authorized federal intervention when they were not complied with them. Thus the federal courts moved in concert with the other change agents and the other federal branches to create and establish prisoners' rights. However, it is important to note that many of the rights are now firmly ensconced in the U.S. Constitution as well as in state administrative regulations and laws.

[*See also* Civil Rights and Civil Liberties; Criminal Law Practice; Prisons and Jails]

• Ben M. Crouch and James W. Marquart, *An Appeal of Justice: Litigated Reform of Texas Prisons*, 1989. John J. DiIulio Jr., ed., *Courts, Corrections, and the Constitution*, 1990. Malcolm M. Feeley and Edward L. Rubin, *Judicial Policy Making and the Modern State: How the Courts Reformed America's Prisons*, 1998. Wayne Welch, *Counties in Court: Jail Overcrowding and Court-Ordered Reform*, 1995.
—Malcolm M. Feeley

PRISONS AND JAILS. The practice of detaining accused offenders can be traced to the earliest days of civilization and governments around the globe. By contrast, the practice of incarcerating offenders in prisons for the purpose of punishment is a relatively recent phenomenon. As late as the eighteenth century in Europe, the punishment imposed on offenders did not involve imprisonment. Instead, a dual system of punishment meted out vastly different penalties that depended on the offender's social status and the prevailing economic interests of those inflicting the punishment. For example, members of the nobility found guilty of violating the laws and customs of the realm were either fined or sentenced to forfeit some or all of their land and property. More serious crimes committed by members of this class brought forced labor and banishment, often for life. By contrast, members of the lower classes bore the brunt of the early penal policies, especially if they had offended against the interests of the upper classes. Torture, mutilation, branding, flogging, and execution became their lot. During these early days, punishment was administered in public and was, more often than not, unmatched in its cruelty. Furthermore, the type of punishment inflicted on commoners was more closely related to the prevailing supply and demand of labor than to the nature of the crimes they committed. For example, when oarsmen were needed for military or merchant ships, or when there was a need for the production of goods, offenders were sentenced to work in ship galleys, workhouses, and houses of correction. But in times of surplus labor, these types of sanctions would quickly lose favor, while *capital punishment, banishment, and transportation to the colonies in America and Australia became the options of choice.

Development of Prisons and Jails in the United States. Reflecting the legacy of their European ancestors, the American colonists made extensive use of corporal punishment, with death, mutilation, branding, and whipping decreed for serious offenses, and public ridicule, such as the stocks, the pillory, the public cage, or the ducking stool, imposed for lesser offenses. In general, the colonial penal system was harsh, exacting, and motivated principally by revenge. Even though colonial America did not have penal institutions in the modern sense, over time, some of the early settlements developed workhouses for debtors and petty offenders and jails, then known as "gaols," for detainment of offenders awaiting trial. Local *sheriffs or marshals were invested with the authority to control the jails and to keep the peace in the community. Conditions in most jails were dreadful. Indiscriminate mixing of the old with the young, men with women, and the mentally ill with criminals created a hellish environment. Inmates were literally at the mercy of their jailers, most of whom ran their facilities for profit. While food and other necessities could be purchased by inmates with means, the poor were left to the mercy and caprice of their keepers.

Jails persisted in their highly limited role in the colonies until the end of the eighteenth century. The historical pertinacity of these early institutions is evident in their persistence, along with the institution of "sheriff," to this day as the prevailing form of local correction and law enforcement in most states.

Incarceration practices changed in the second half of the eighteenth century, when noted European social philosophers, scholars, and scientists—among them Montesquieu, Voltaire, Beccaria, Rousseau, and *Blackstone—began to reject the brutality of the prevailing system of punishment for humanitarian reasons and in the interest of social reform. Reflecting the mainstream thought of their era, these Enlightenment thinkers took a rational and scientific approach to the religious, political, economic, and social issues of their day. Expressing supreme confidence in humans' rationality and amenability to be guided by reason, they opposed the special privileges enjoyed by the clergy and nobility and decried the abuses inflicted on the common people. Attacking the dogmatism and intolerance of their day, they professed an unerring belief in the equality of men, not in terms of status or assets but before the eyes of God and in terms of equality and rights under the law.

In 1764, the eminent Italian criminologist and jurist Cesare Beccaria published his famous *Essay on Crimes and Punishments*, in which he incorporated the basic tenets of the Enlightenment into a foundation for the development of a new penal policy. Beccaria's views were further expounded by the noted English philosopher and utilitarian Jeremy Bentham, the English law reformer Samuel Romilly, and many others. Together, these concepts formed the basic elements of "classical" *criminal law and embody the basic structure of modern Western penal codes.

Emergence of the Penitentiary: An American Creation. After the Revolutionary War, reform-minded colonists began to experiment with new criminal codes. They also embarked on a course of penal reform that would not only affect America but eventually spread throughout the world. Imbued by the ideas of the Enlightenment thinkers, and reflecting upon their own adverse experiences with British *justice, first in their homeland and later in the colonies, the colonists were particularly influenced by the writings of English sheriff John Howard. Considered one of the greatest prison reformers of all time, Howard published his classic work *State of Prisons* in 1777. His reforms included the humane treatment of prisoners, the development of secure and sanitary housing, and the provision of training and pay for jailers. Howard was also one of the first prison reformers to advocate the reformation of prisoners while they were incarcerated.

By 1787, the confluence of these ideas strongly

affected a small group of concerned citizens in Pennsylvania who wanted to reform the existing penal structure. The group included Benjamin Franklin, Dr. Benjamin Rush, and other like-minded reformers. Together, they organized the Philadelphia Society for Alleviating the Miseries of Public Prisons. Rejecting the wretched conditions of the gaols and opposing the public degradation of prisoners while working on chain gangs, the society advocated the solitary confinement of prisoners and hard labor as the most effective means for reforming criminals. The society's efforts were aided by the Pennsylvania Quakers, whose religious beliefs forbade violence in any form. The Quakers provided significant support for the society's proposed prison reforms. One hundred years after its founding, the society shortened its name to the Pennsylvania Prison Society. It continues to this day as a force for penal reform.

By 1789, the Pennsylvania General Assembly accepted the main proposals and recommendations of the Philadelphia Society. With the passage of appropriate legislation, the American penitentiary system was born. The immediate effect of the new legislation was the renovation of the Walnut Street Jail in Philadelphia. First constructed in 1776, this jail had all the hellish characteristics of its predecessors. The renovation implemented in 1790 turned the jail into the young nation's first penitentiary. A cell house was added, with sixteen solitary cells designed to hold hardened offenders. Licentiousness, debauchery, and brutality came to an end. Debtors were separated from convicted felons, men from women, and children were no longer kept at the facility. Corporal punishment was banned. Food and clothing were provided at the Commonwealth's expense. The new rules developed by the Philadelphia Society and codified by the legislature shifted the focus from the physical punishment of offenders to their reform. Following the religious precepts of the Quakers, convicts were now serving their sentences in solitary confinement and at hard labor. Inmates were given a bible and religious instructions to facilitate the contemplation of their errant and sinful ways. After due penitence and much discipline imposed to teach self-control, the offenders, so it was reasoned, might reform their evil ways and eventually be permitted to return to society as law-abiding citizens.

The rules drawn up by the Prison Society and the Pennsylvania legislature were the first ever written for a penal institution in the United States. They represent a monumental step in the evolution of American and Western penology. Although

the Walnut Street jail closed down in 1835, largely due to politics, crowding, and a lack of financial resources, it left its imprint on world penology.

Prison and Jail Development in the Early Nineteenth Century. In spite of the ultimate failure of the Walnut Street Jail, the concept of reform and punishment through solitary confinement took root and became Pennsylvania's official penal policy. Two penitentiaries opened in quick order. The Western Penitentiary, opening in Pittsburgh in 1826, was a round building modeled after Bentham's Panopticon. Cells were arranged like spokes around a hub, from which the prisoners could be constantly watched. The Eastern Penitentiary opened in Philadelphia in 1829; it consisted of seven wings, also connected to a central hub. Inmates were housed in single cells and provided with a workbench and bible. A small garden space was attached to each cell. Massive granite walls prevented any visual or auditory contact. The prison design unmistakably emanated a monastic influence, the architecture reflecting the new treatment philosophy of the age. Although founded on the best of intentions, the Pennsylvania system proved to be expensive for the government and disastrous for the inmates. The total lack of human contact led to psychoses, other forms of mental and physical illness, and suicide.

The Pennsylvania system was not the only penal experiment vying for the attention of prison reformers in the first quarter of the nineteenth century. A rival emerged in 1819, when the state of New York built a new penitentiary at Auburn. In design and programming, it was almost the opposite of the Philadelphia prison design. Known as the Auburn system, it featured congregate labor during the day and solitary confinement at night. It was also known as the "silent system," because inmates were prohibited from talking or even looking at one another. They were marched in lockstep to their workstations, to the mess hall, and to religious services. Discipline was extremely severe and designed to break a person's spirit before he could be expected to accept reformation. The architecture of Auburn prison consisted of a new "inside" cell configuration. Cells were much smaller than those of the Pennsylvania system, arrayed in tiers and surrounded by fortress-like walls.

The two models competed for decades for the approval of prison reformers around the globe. The Europeans favored the Pennsylvania system, because they saw solitary confinement as more conducive to reformation. As a result, prisons built in Europe, Latin America, and later even Asia reflected that design. By contrast, the Auburn system prevailed in the United States, largely because it was more cost-effective and exacted a somewhat lower human toll on the inmate population.

By the close of the nineteenth century, the most populous U.S. states had constructed one or more large prisons in which convicted felons served their sentences under state control. By contrast, cities and county seats had constructed their own jails, where accused offenders were held pending trial and criminals convicted of lesser offenses, such as misdemeanors, were incarcerated as punishment. Jails were under the control of locally elected and sometimes appointed sheriffs.

The Purposes of Imprisonment. Historically, penal objectives have been succinctly summarized by four key words: retribution, incapacitation, deterrence and rehabilitation.

Retribution has long been a central objective of punishment. The concept is deeply rooted in the earliest legal codes. Recognized as the "eye-for-an-eye doctrine," it is based on the ideas that offenders deserve to be punished for wrongdoing and punishment serves the interests of justice by reaffirming society's strongly held beliefs and values. Incapacitation restrains the offender from doing further harm. Capital punishment obviates the possibility of further crimes. Corporal punishment, maiming, and branding have historically served to stigmatize offenders as transgressors, making the commission of future crimes more difficult. With the advent of prisons, authorities were given unprecedented opportunities for incapacitation. Offenders could now be completely isolated from society for as long as they were perceived to be a threat to public safety. Deterrence is based on the idea that an odious or painful penal experience will deter future crimes. Individual deterrence rests on the assumption that offenders, having experienced the pains of imprisonment or other punishment, will refrain from future wrongdoing. General deterrence assumes that observing the punishment of convicted offenders will serve as an example to others and thereby deter them from crime. The penal objectives of retribution, incapacitation, and deterrence continue to serve as valid purposes of incarceration. They also furnish the main justifications for the perpetuation of prisons around the globe.

Reformation as a penal objective rests on two basic premises: first, the belief that crime is caused by some deficiency or abnormality in the criminal, and second, the assumption that with proper treatment and tending these failings can be modified, reforming and changing the offender into a law-abiding citizen. The objective of reformation was an integral part of the earliest conceptualizations of the penitentiary in the United States. Both the Pennsylvania and the Auburn systems embodied a treatment philosophy not only in their programs but also in their architectural designs.

Unfortunately, the prisons that followed in their wake found it increasingly difficult to adhere to the founding precepts of Auburn and Pennsylvania. Many became overcrowded, mismanaged, and brutal. Violence and scandals brought frequent investigations. Political interference with prison management became rampant. Among the more influential critics were French politician and writer Alexis de Tocqueville and French social critic Gustave de Beaumont. In their widely acclaimed book *On the Penitentiary System in the United States, and Its Application in France* (1833) they tacitly observe that while some of the American penitentiaries they visited might serve as models for other countries, others were "everything which ought to be avoided." Disillusionment with the sorry state of prisons and disagreements over the best way of implementing reform brought forth new strategies promulgated by yet another generation of penal reformers.

Prisons and the Reformatory Movement. The nation's first state reformatory, built in Elmira, New York, in 1876, represents another landmark in American penology. Under the leadership of Zebulon R. Brockway, the prison was specifically designed for young offenders, perceived to be more amenable to reform than were older and hardened criminals. Elmira became a model prison emulated by many other states and is generally recognized as the beginning of the "reformatory movement" in American corrections. Architecturally, Elmira was similar to its Auburn predecessor. But it differed programmatically by placing great emphasis on the reform of its inmates through education, vocational training, and work. In addition, Elmira is credited with many other significant penal advances. It adopted a new indeterminate *sentencing system, under which inmates received a maximum prison term but were given the opportunity to earn early release on parole through hard work and good behavior. It implemented a classification system for inmates based on their conduct. And it embraced the "mark system" originated by the noted English prison reformer Alexander Maconochie, when he became superintendent of Australia's penal colony at Norfolk Island in the early 1840s. In the mark system, inmates earned marks or chits for good behavior and forfeited the same for misbehavior.

Inmates were able to exchange marks for less restrictive prison conditions, transfers to less secure prison environments, and ultimately their release.

Of all the major penal objectives, the goal of reform proved to be the most elusive. Against all the expectations and hopes of its founders, the Elmira reformatory system, like its predecessors, failed. The reasons for failure are multiple. Too many inmates returned to a life of crime after discharge, thus calling into question the lofty promises of the reformatory movement. High recidivism rates, scarce resources, overcrowding, the lack of professionally trained personnel to teach and train inmates, and an increasingly abusive and corrupt prison staff combined to end yet another noble experiment in penology.

From Reformation to the Industrial Prison. The period between 1890 and 1930 brought a mixture of progress and regression in the nation's prison systems. On the positive side, a new breed of penal reformers decided to modernize the prisons. Programming included education, vocational training, family visits, library and correspondence privileges, and even some outdoor recreation in the prison yard. Inmate labor begun under the Auburn system expanded. On the negative side, liberalizing the previously oppressive controls brought disciplinary problems, inmate violence, and increasing security concerns. Growing inmate populations swelled correctional budgets. Prison administrators, under pressure to reduce rising costs, turned to expanding the prison workshops, not only to offset some of their expenses but also to show profits. This quest coincided serendipitously with a growing conviction among the new reformers that prison work was uniquely suited to infuse the inmates with self-discipline and personal responsibility.

Given these developments, industrial prisons proliferated during the first quarter of the twentieth century. Convict labor took various forms. Between 1910 and 1945 chain gangs were popular, as in most states legal provisions allowed some state and, more often, county convicts to work on public roads. Chain gangs were most common in the South. Wearing leg irons, convicts would work in small groups, linked together with long iron foot chains. But for the most part, prisoners in state systems worked in the new industrial prisons. Among the better-known and still operational institutions are San Quentin in California, Sing Sing in New York, and the Illinois State Penitentiary at Statesville. Given the new emphasis on manufacturing and production, the prisons produced materials and goods needed by the military, the gov-

ernment, and the private sector. Demand for prison products accelerated during World War I.

The income generated by inmate labor, however, was not sufficient to cover the rising costs of operating correctional facilities. Without independent oversight and monitoring, the convict labor system gradually eroded into corruption and bribery. Moreover, private industry soon complained about being forced to compete with prison industries, which had a clear advantage due to the very low inmate wages. The emerging labor unions also opposed cheap prison labor. The final blow to prison industries came with the Great Depression, when jobs were scarce or nonexistent. Congress responded to the combined pressures of the economy, organized labor, and private interests by passing legislation that first curtailed and then prohibited convict labor. Passage of the Ashurst-Summers Act in 1935 effectively ended prison industries by prohibiting the interstate transport and sale of prison goods in states with laws proscribing them. Most states passed similar legislation prohibiting prison industry from competing with the private sector.

Deprived of meaningful activities, prisons became warehouses during the decade that followed. Prison administrations, lacking constructive alternatives for their inmates, returned to a regimen of harsh discipline, custody, security, and punishment. Indolence and frustration soon led to violence and riots, leading the National Commission on Law Observance and Enforcement, better known as the Wickersham Commission, to make a series of recommendations to President Hoover. First, the commission urged that prison classification systems differentiate inmates by security risk and that less serious offenders be placed into forestry camps and prison farms. Second, it strongly recommended that prisons return to a program of rehabilitation, education, and vocational training. Third, it proposed an expansion of the parole system. These recommendations, combined with a general dissatisfaction with the state of the nation's prisons, set the stage for the next phase in prison reform, the era of treatment.

Modern Prisons and Jails: 1945 to the Present. The early goals of reformation under the Pennsylvania and Auburn systems were reborn as the "medical model" in corrections, developed in the early twentieth century. This model was based on a treatment orientation, which combined the basic premises of physical medicine with those of the newly emerging discipline of psychology. By applying the medical profession's creed of diagnosis, treatment, and cure to the perceived psychological, social, physical, educational, vocational, and moral inadequacies of offenders, the medical model promised to rehabilitate criminals through a process of diagnosis, assessment, and treatment. As such, proponents of the medical model placed the causes of crime squarely on the individual offender. The emergence of this model is a reflection of the growing influence of science in general and the social sciences in particular during the first half of the twentieth century. In short order, prison systems developed new classification systems for the assessment and evaluation of inmates. This diagnostic process resulted in the formulation of individualized treatment plans. It also formed the basis for assigning inmates to facilities and housing on the basis of perceived security risk.

In the mid-1970s the treatment era ended, largely because of widespread disenchantment with the rehabilitation model. Rising crime rates, accompanied by a groundswell of academic attacks on rehabilitation, raised serious questions about its efficacy. High recidivism rates, defined here as the rate at which offenders returned to prisons for new crimes, supported the growing chorus of scholars who saw serious if not fatal flaws with rehabilitation. A new penology emerged that was distinctly hard-line. Offenders were to be held responsible for their actions. Individualized treatment was to be replaced by swift and certain punishment. States soon began changing their sentencing structure. Indeterminate sentences gave way to flat, fixed, presumptive, and mandatory sentences. Within one decade, the usually inert criminal justice system was transformed. Offenders were sentenced to prison in unprecedented numbers and for long periods of time. Parole and community-based options were seriously curtailed. Several states, including Alabama and Florida, even revived chain gangs. The totality of these developments shows clearly that the prison system and justice administration had come full circle, returning to the classical precepts of Beccaria.

By 2001, the nation's prisons and jails incarcerated about two million persons. Two-thirds of the inmates are located in the fifty state penal systems, the District of Columbia, and the Federal Bureau of Prisons. The remaining third of prisoners are held in local jails. During the 1990s, the rate of incarceration in all of the nation's penal facilities jumped from 1 in 218 to 1 in 142 residents. In spite of their highly diverse composition, prison and jail inmates share certain characteristics. With few exceptions, the people are poor, undereducated, and unemployed and belong to minority groups. The disproportionately high incarceration rate of African Americans and Hispanics is especially troubling. An analysis by the Bureau of Justice Statistics in 2001 found that an estimated 12 percent of African-American males and 4 percent of Hispanic males in their twenties and thirties were incarcerated. The comparable percentage for white males of this age group was 1.7 percent. Female incarceration rates, while much lower than male rates at every age, reveal similar racial and ethnic disparities. Almost half of all inmates in state prisons are incarcerated for violent crimes (murder, robbery, assault, rape and other sexual assaults). The remainder were sentenced for property crimes, *drug offenses, and crimes against the public order.

To accommodate their growing inmate populations, most states and the Federal Bureau of Prisons have been constructing new facilities in record numbers. Between 1998 and 1999 alone, the nation's corrections systems initiated the construction of 162 large new prison projects and launched 675 major renovations of existing facilities. These efforts will add fifty thousand new bed spaces to the existing stock. Annual operating budgets for state and federal prisons exceed thirty billion dollars, not counting capital budgets set aside for construction.

The prisons constructed during the 1980s and 1990s look very different from the old fortress prisons. Today's penal facilities incorporate the latest architectural and security advances. With modular designs, they look more like school campuses, complete with schools, vocational training centers, libraries, and chapels. Housing is dispersed in small residential pods, usually with direct supervision. Educational, vocational, and industrial facilities are on a par with those of modern technical schools. Vastly improved classification systems have facilitated the assignment of many inmates to a variety of prison settings characterized by different degrees of security. Serious, high-risk offenders continue to be housed in close-custody prisons. Others are placed in medium- and minimum-security prisons, which generally provide more humane environments and more extensive programs.

A growing trend for the federal and most state prison systems is to place their most violent and disruptive inmates into a "super-max" prison. The mission of these prisons is to incapacitate these offenders by keeping them in locked cells twenty-three hours a day, with one hour for recreation and showers. But even in these austere and harsh environments, there is some focus on controlling and changing inmate behavior through programs and staff contacts. Programming is initially provided by closed-circuit television and, if necessary, directly by staff. As inmates adapt, program offerings increase, ranging from basic education to more sophisticated curricula, such as anger management, prison life skills, and cognitive behavioral change.

Do Prisons Rehabilitate? Assessing the true relationship between imprisonment and rehabilitation is difficult because of prisons' multiple objectives, ranging from retribution, incapacitation, and deterrence to rehabilitation. Nonetheless, the existing body of criminological research warrants at least some provisional statements on the subject.

First, imprisonment does reduce the nation's crime rate through deterrence and incapacitation, but that reduction is probably more moderate than most prison advocates suggest. Recent declines in the national crime rates are better explained by the interaction of demographic and macroeconomic forces. Second, the severe criticism of prison-based rehabilitation programs was probably justified to the extent that they involved compulsory treatment or coercive programs. But recent advances in rehabilitation programming show that carefully designed institutional and community-based treatment programs can and do reduce recidivism. Interestingly, much of the new evidence comes from outside the United States. Canada, Denmark, Sweden, and Finland have developed a number of successful intervention and crime-prevention programs. In some cases, the effectiveness of these treatment programs is on a par with treatment results obtained by the medical field. For example, programs that target offenders' needs and high-risk cases, and focus on improving the cognitive and social skills of inmates, effectively reduce recidivism rates by 30 percent or more. Third, the enormous costs of maintaining and constructing the nation's prisons and jails raise questions of efficacy. Do the public benefits of incarceration outweigh the costs? The answer is probably not. Prisons and jails are clearly overused and overloaded. The high cost of imprisonment diverts scarce public resources from more productive alternatives. The evidence shows that community-based programs are consistently more effective than prison-based programs. Low-risk offenders, such as substance abusers, needlessly clog the prisons and jails. Prison advocates fail to consider the high social and political costs of their recommendations. In sum, current high imprisonment rates do not serve the long-run interests of societal protection.

Legal Safeguards of Prisons and Jails. Most prison litigation revolves around rather mundane issues of prison life: food, shelter, sanitation, space, programming, personal safety, and medical care. Inmates began to challenge the constitutionality of many prison rules and practices by appealing to the rights guaranteed under the provisions of the First, Fourth, Sixth, Eighth, and *Fourteenth Amendments to the U.S. Constitution. The decades that followed brought major relief to prison and jail populations, including, among other things, the right to treatment, *equal protection, *due process in prison discipline, freedom of *religion, legal defense and access to lawyers (see COUNSEL, RIGHT TO), and due process protections against arbitrary management decisions.

Litigation about prison conditions involves a determination of whether prison and jail conditions are so inadequate that they constitute *cruel and unusual punishment. Using the "totality of conditions" or the "totality of circumstances" test, the courts began to examine virtually all aspects of the penal facilities. A recent count by the Criminal Justice Institute found almost 200 prisons and jails under court orders to improve the conditions of imprisonment, another 150 with imposed inmate population caps, and about 100 under the guidance of court-appointed masters. The history and extent of prison litigation speaks volumes about legislative and executive neglect of the nation's penal facilities. In that light, the nation's court system appears to be the only effective tool for curbing neglect and abuse in prisons and jails.

Prison Privatization in the Twentieth Century. "Privatization" refers to the shifting of government function, programs, responsibilities, and assets from the public to the private sector. The privatization of correctional services can assume several forms. In its most frequently used form, privatization is the contracting out of specific services, such as medical and mental health services, programs, food services, and maintenance, and entails the competition of private bidders. In these outsourcing types of arrangements, the government provides all the financing and retains full management and policy control over the institution. Another form of private sector interest in corrections is the involvement of private industry, in which industries are brought into the prison to produce goods to be sold by the private interest. A third form of private involvement, which grew in the 1980s, involves the government transfer of ownership of assets, commercial enterprises, and management responsibilities to the private sector.

Private corporations may finance and construct prisons. A private contractor may manage and operate a whole correctional facility, an arrangement common in juvenile corrections and community-based programs such as halfway houses and drug rehabilitation centers and other diversion programs. In these types of arrangements, government has limited or no involvement in the financial support, management, or oversight of the correctional institution. This latter form of privatization is the most controversial.

By the mid-1970s, governments, faced with expanding prison populations and a more conservative, antigovernment ideology, became more interested in the potentials of private partnerships. The process of privatization began in earnest in the 1970s, with juvenile corrections. Massachusetts' great experiment with deinstitutionalization began by closing state reformatories and placing its youthful offenders into a vast array of private institutional and community-based programs. By the early 1980s, the *Immigration and Naturalization Service was among the first government agencies to take advantage of the growing interest in private prisons. Many of its detainees were placed in private facilities pending hearings and deportation. The first county- and state-level contracts with private correctional corporations were also made in the mid-1980s.

Pressures on the prison system due to skyrocketing incarceration rates, prison overcrowding, and rising correctional costs contributed greatly to the use of private penal facilities as an acceptable political and correctional option. But large political and economic influences also helped set the stage for privatization. The public increasingly demanded government downsizing and lower taxes, while at the same time demanding increased quality of services. Lacking confidence in the quality of correctional services provided by governments, and believing that the public sector is inept and corrupt, the public saw private business as more efficient and effective. Policymakers turned to the private sector as a means of providing publicly mandated services of higher quality and at lower cost, while private entrepreneurs were willing to accommodate their needs. Unlike the nineteenth-century experiments with private involvement in corrections, which almost always involved local businesses, the twentieth-century incarnation involves large corporations, some of which are traded on the world's stock exchanges. One of the first corporations to enter the private prison business was the Corrections Corporation of America. It can be traded on stock exchanges with ten other private prison businesses, which altogether generate about a billion dollars a year in revenues. These corporations stimulated policy reformers' interest in privatization by promoting their own proposals to governments sorely in need of solutions.

Correctional privatization grew throughout the 1980s and 1990s, first in the United States and more recently in the United Kingdom, Australia, and South Africa. Between 1987 and 1998, the number of inmates housed in private facilities worldwide grew from 3,000 to over 132,000. In the United States alone, private prisons have the capacity to house more than 117,000 inmates. Private prisons are now operating in thirty states, the District of Columbia, and Puerto Rico. Most such facilities are concentrated in the southern and western parts of the country. In addition, there are more than five hundred privately operated nonsecure facilities, such as halfway houses, residential drug treatment, and juvenile facilities.

Many issues have been raised about the processes, operations, and consequences of prison privatization. The three primary areas of concern relate to costs, quality of services, and legal questions. Research on the effectiveness of private prisons in these areas is sparse, and there are serious methodological difficulties in comparing the results of studies on public versus private prisons. The evidence that is available on the effectiveness of private prisons and jails shows that they provide no or only marginal improvement over public facilities. The costs of operating private facilities are also similar to those of public facilities. Private prisons may provide more services and sometimes even better services, but they do not show great improvements over public prisons, especially if the physical condition and size of the public agency is taken into consideration. Privatization of prisons and jails is neither a panacea nor an anathema to the solution of incarceration issues in western societies in the early twenty-first century.

[See also Criminal Law Practice]

• Daniel Glaser, The Effectiveness of a Prison and Parole System, 1964. William G. Nagel, The New Red Barn: A Critical Look at the Modern American Prison, 1973. Michel Foucault, Discipline and Punish (Alan Sheridan, trans.), 1978. Michael Ignatieff, A Just Measure of Pain: The Penitentiary in the Industrial Revolution, 1750–1850, 1978. David J. Rothman, Conscience and Convenience: The Asylum and Its Alternatives in Progressive America, 1980. Charles H. Logan, Private Prisons: Cons and Pros, 1990. Ted Palmer, A Profile of Correctional Effectiveness and New Directions for Research, 1994. David Shichor, Punishment for Profit: Private Prisons/Public Concerns,

1995. Michael Tonry, *Malign Neglect—Race, Crime, and Punishment in America*, 1995. Paul Gendreau, Tracy Little, and C. Goggin, "A Meta-analysis of Predictors of Adult Offender Recidivism: What Works!" *Criminology* 34, no. 4 (1996). Daniel S. Nagin, "Deterrence and Incapacitation," in *The Handbook of Crime and Punishment* (Michael Tonry, ed.), 1998. Michael Tonry and Joan Petersilia, eds., *Prisons*, 1999.

—Edith E. Flynn and Margaret Zahn

PRIVACY. In 1890, when overeager journalists attempted to crash the events hosted by Boston lawyer-socialite Samuel Warren, he and his business partner wrote a pathbreaking article arguing that people had a "right to be let alone." The partner was Louis D. *Brandeis, who would later be named to the Supreme Court, and their article would be cited by Harvard Law School Dean Roscoe Pound as doing "nothing less than add[ing] a chapter to our law."

Justice Brandeis extended the chapter of the law dealing with privacy even further in his dissent in the wiretapping case of *Olmstead* v. *United States* (1929). There he argued, in phrases frequently quoted in today's privacy decisions, that the founders "conferred, as against the Government, the right to be let alone—the most comprehensive of rights and the right most valued by civilized men."

But the word "privacy" does not in fact appear in the *Constitution. When the Supreme Court first declared, in *Griswold* v. *Connecticut* (1965), that there is nonetheless a constitutionally protected right to privacy, Justice William O. *Douglas wrote for the majority that it was to be found in the "penumbras" cast by the First Amendment's right to communication, the Third Amendment's prohibition against quartering soldiers in private homes during peacetime, the Fourth Amendment's right to be free from unreasonable *searches and seizures, the Fifth Amendment's right against *self-incrimination, and the Ninth Amendment's reservation of unenumerated rights to the people.

Other justices have since spoken about the right to privacy as located in the "liberty provision" of the Fifth and Fourteenth Amendments' *due process clauses (*Roe* v. *Wade* (1973)), while yet other jurists have questioned whether it is in the Constitution at all. Judge Robert Bork, for instance, told the Senate Judiciary Committee that ultimately rejected his 1987 nomination to the Supreme Court that the right of privacy "comes out of nowhere and doesn't have any rooting in the Constitution."

One reason for the societal argument about the notion of a constitutional right to privacy lies in the uses to which it has been put. The *Griswold* case and subsequent rulings held that privacy extends to the right to acquire and use contraceptives. But the furor over privacy did not erupt until the Court decided in *Roe* v. *Wade* that the right encompasses a woman's decision to have an *abortion and that neither the federal nor state governments can interfere with it. The state can regulate the circumstances under which abortions are performed and can prohibit abortions once a fetus has become viable, but it cannot deny the right. Even toward the end of pregnancy, *Roe* held, a woman has a constitutionally protected right to abort her fetus if doing otherwise will endanger her health or life.

The decision outraged and mobilized those members of society who believe that life begins at conception or very early in pregnancy and that abortion therefore is murder. A rash of pro- and antiabortion rights organizations came into existence and began agitating, respectively, for an extension of *Roe* or for its demise. The national debate took on added significance when Ronald Reagan was elected to the presidency in 1980 in part on a promise to end legalized abortion (the promise was not fulfilled). As the Supreme Court later noted, *Roe* brought the Court "under fire" in an "intensely divisive controversy" that was equaled only by the outcry raised by opponents of *Brown* v. *Board of Education* in 1954.

Many states responded to the anti-*Roe* anger by enacting statutes that restricted abortion rights by, for example, prohibiting abortions without a husband's consent, requiring abortions to be performed in hospitals rather than clinics, requiring health personnel to give women requesting an abortion specific information about fetal development, and mandating a twenty-four-hour waiting period after a request for abortion. The Court of the 1970s and 1980s struck down most such provisions (*Planned Parenthood* v. *Danforth* (1976), *Bellotti* v. *Baird* (1979), *Akron* v. *Akron* (1983), *Thornburgh* v. *American College of Obstetricians* (1986)).

In 1989, in *Webster* v. *Reproductive Health Services*, the Court began moving in a new direction, upholding a ban on the use of public facilities for nontherapeutic abortions and a requirement that physicians ascertain fetal viability before performing an abortion during the second trimester of pregnancy. In 1992, in *Planned Parenthood* v. *Casey*, however, the Court reaffirmed *Roe*'s central holding but gave the states greater leeway to regulate access to abortion as long as the regulations do not constitute an "undue burden."

The federal government reacted to the public debate by passing laws prohibiting the use of Medicaid or other federal funds for abortions and forbidding workers in federally funded facilities from discussing abortions with their clients. The Supreme Court upheld these limitations, as well as similar prohibitions in some states (*Maher* v. *Roe* (1977), *Harris* v. *McRae* (1980), *Rust* v. *Sullivan* (1991)).

At the same time, the Court has extended privacy in new ways, gradually coupling it with a right to "personal autonomy and bodily integrity." In *Cruzan* v. *Director* (1990), the Court announced that the privacy/autonomy right applied to the right to die, so that hopelessly ill but mentally competent people who want to die, or have indicated before falling into a vegetative state that they would not wish to go on living in that way, cannot be forced by the government to remain alive. Troubled about possible abuses of an asserted right to assisted suicide, the justices subsequently declined to recognize such a right but indicated that they might look more favorably on a specific case in which "an interest in hastening death is legitimate" (*Washington* v. *Glucksberg* (1997)). The Court has not yet decided whether autonomy rights apply to yet another area of asserted privacy, private homosexual conduct (see HOMOSEXUALITY AND THE LAW), and its decision in *Planned Parenthood* v. *Casey* suggests that is may be moving away from the idea that privacy is a "fundamental right" requiring a high level of judicial protection.

Federal courts have long recognized a right to privacy in the criminal justice area, interpreting the Fourth Amendment's search and seizure clause to prohibit such governmental intrusions as *wiretapping without a warrant (*Katz* v. *U.S.* (1967)) or monitoring people and conversations in situations with a "reasonable expectation of privacy" (*Terry* v. *Ohio* (1968)). In the 1990s there was increasing awareness that, as computerization allowed the centralization of huge quantities of information about citizens, governments and other large institutions would have access to personal data.

Large portions of the public began to demand that legislatures and courts give them the right to access and control specific information such as credit ratings, medical records, social security numbers, the results of DNA testing, and so on. Polls taken in the 1990s showed that more than 80 percent of Americans were concerned about privacy and believed they had already lost control over their personal information. The potential harm caused by erroneous computerized data was discussed in *Arizona* v. *Evans* (1995), in which the Supreme Court in effect held that good faith errors by law-enforcement personnel relying on erroneous data entries could not be punished, even when they resulted in a mistaken arrest. Justice John Paul Stevens protested that the Court ignored "the reality that computer technology has changed the nature of threats of citizens' privacy," and Justice Ruth Bader Ginsburg, also in dissent, noted that "inaccurate data can infect not only one agency, but the many agencies that share access to the database." Increasing societal awareness of the dangers of technological error suggests that the issue of wrongs suffered as a result of inaccurate computerized information is likely to be revisited by the Court in the near future.

A host of other privacy-related problems have begun to work their way into the courts. Some center on the Internet, as when a federal court ruled that a company has the right to monitor e-mail communications of its employees (*Smyth* v. *Pillsbury* (1996)). Others concern the increasingly common tendency of employers to test their workers for drugs. The Supreme Court upheld the federal government's power to test some workers randomly (*Skinner* v. *Railway Labor Executives' Association* (1989), *National Treasury Employees Union* v. *von Raab* (1989)), but courts in the ten states with constitutions guaranteeing a right to privacy (Alaska, Arizona, California, Florida, Hawaii, Illinois, Louisiana, Montana, South Carolina, and Washington) struck down random drug testing of employees.

The "right to be let alone" delineated by Brandeis and Warren clearly has become relevant to areas far removed from their concerns and has been joined by an asserted right to informational privacy. Both aspects of privacy rights will no doubt continue to be explored by the courts as values change and technological development continues.

[See also Civil Rights and Civil Liberties; *Roe* v. *Wade* (1973)]

• David M. O'Brien, *Privacy, Law, and Public Policy*, 1979. Dorothy J. Glancy, "The Invention of the Right to Privacy," *Arizona Law Review* 21 (1979): 1–39. Richard F. Hixson, *Privacy in a Public Society: Human Rights in Conflict*, 1987. John Gilliom, *Surveillance, Privacy, and the Law: Employee Drug Testing and the Politics of Social Control*, 1994. Anne Wells Branscomb, *Who Owns Information? From Privacy to Public Access*, 1995. Priscilla M. Regan, *Legislating Privacy: Technology, Social Values, and Public Policy*, 1995. Karen O'Connor, *No Neutral Ground? Abortion Politics in an Age of Absolutes*, 1996. Mark A. Rothstein, ed., *Genetic Secrets: Protecting Pri-*

vacy and Confidentiality in the Genetic Era, 1998. Philippa Strum, *Privacy: The Debate in the United States Since 1945,* 1998.

—Philippa Strum

PRIVATE SECURITY SERVICES. Since the early 1970s, an escalating share of the responsibility for crime control in the developed world has shifted from public law enforcement agencies to private security companies. The trend has been especially pronounced in the United States. The American private security industry today employs far more guards, patrol personnel, and *detectives than the federal, state, and local governments combined, and the disparity is growing. Increasingly, private security firms police not only factories and stores, but also office buildings, airports, bus and train stations, sports and entertainment centers, shopping centers, parks, government facilities, and even entire commercial districts and residential neighborhoods. On any given day, many Americans are far more likely to encounter a security guard than a *police officer.

In some ways law enforcement has come full circle. Crime control in America was mostly a private affair—supplemented only by poorly funded, semiamateur constabularies and night watches—until the rise of professional public police departments in the nineteenth century. Even then, police departments emphasized patrol and prevention, leaving the task of investigation largely to private firms such as Allan Pinkerton's National Detective Agency. In the twentieth century, police departments and newly formed agencies such as the *Federal Bureau of Investigation took over many of the investigative functions previously performed by companies like Pinkerton's. The private firms reacted by gradually shifting their business to patrol and prevention, functions increasingly deemphasized by public agencies. Today private firms have taken over much of the "beat patrol" work once thought to be the most basic job of the police.

The legal rules governing private security firms differ from those applied to public law enforcement organizations. The constitutional restrictions on the police do not apply to private firms, nor does the exclusionary rule, which often bars prosecutors from relying on evidence the police obtain illegally. On the other hand, private security employees facing civil *damage claims do not share the immunity that public law enforcement officers enjoy for actions conducted in "good faith." And private guards lack most of the special authority granted to the police to carry out searches and arrests; most private guards have only the *arrest powers of ordinary citizens.

The growing role of private security firms has been controversial. There are perennial complaints that the firms are inadequately regulated and their employees unqualified. Police departments deemphasized patrol in part because it is expensive, and private security firms have been able to fill the void in part because private guards earn much less than police officers. But the pressure to keep salaries low has made it difficult for private security firms to attract qualified candidates, to screen them carefully, and to train them well. In addition, private security firms answer to their customers, not to the community as a whole. In some respects this makes the firms more responsive than modern police departments often criticized for excessive independence and insularity—but it also means they are not subject to direct democratic control. It remains unclear, moreover, to what extent private security firms simply supplement public policing, and to what extent they partially supplant it, dampening support, at least among their customers, for spending more tax dollars on law enforcement.

• Brian Forst and Peter K. Manning, *The Privatization of Policing: Two Views,* 1999. David A. Sklansky, "The Private Police," *UCLA Law Review* (1999): 1165–1287.

—David A. Sklansky

PRIVILEGES AND IMMUNITIES. The *Constitution of the United States declares in Article IV, Section 2, Clause 1, that "the Citizens of each State shall be entitled to all Privileges and Immunities of Citizens in the several States," and in Amendment XIV, Section 1, that "no state shall make or enforce any law which shall abridge the privileges and immunities of citizens of the United States." Both clauses were designed to secure certain rights of national *citizenship. Despite these grand intentions, the privileges and immunities clause of the *Fourteenth Amendment is the lost tribe of American constitutionalism. Five years after the amendment was ratified, the Supreme Court in *The Slaughter-House Cases* (1873) declared that the privileges and immunities of citizens of the United States were limited to those "which owe their existence to the federal government, its national character, its Constitution, or its laws." These rights included the right to travel between states and the right to protection overseas (rights generally thought to have been protected by the antebellum constitution), but, crucially, did not include such fundamental liberties as freedom of *speech and freedom of *religion. One consequence of this decision was that constitutional litigants stopped pleading privileges and immunities, pinning their hopes for protection of civil liberties and rights on the *due process clause of the Fourteenth Amendment. The Supreme Court in *Saenz* v. *Roe* (1999) declared unconstitutional on privileges and immunities grounds California's effort to place durational requirements on welfare benefits, but this is the only case that is still good law that relies on that constitutional provision.

The privileges and immunities clause of Article IV has been the subject of a little more commentary and litigation, protecting rights of out-of-state residents to certain commercial opportunities, but not much more.

[*See also* Bills of Rights; Civil Rights and Civil Liberties]

• Akhil Reed Amar, *The Bill of Rights,* 1998.

—Mark A. Graber

PROBATE. Probate generally means proving, but it is usually used to refer to the specific process of proving to the satisfaction of a court that a document is a deceased person's last *will and testament.

[*See also* Estate]

—John V. Orth

PROBATION AND PAROLE. Probation is a criminal sentence imposed in lieu of incarceration. Parole is the discretionary release of an inmate by a parole board before the expiration of his sentence, although it is also frequently used to describe non-discretionary early release. Many states combine probation and parole in the same agency, whose officers supervise both probationers and parolees. Officers monitor an offender's behavior while providing social services to aid rehabilitation.

Probation originated in Boston in the decade before the Civil War. Its use spread with the popularity of juvenile courts, beginning in Chicago in 1899. Probation eventually became the standard sentence for all less serious offenders, juvenile and adult. In the late twentieth century, as a result of prison overcrowding, probation had extended to cover more serious *felony offenders.

While parole has English antecedents, its use in the United States dates back to the establishment of Elmira Reformatory in New York.

Elmira Reformatory. The first American Prison Association (APA) convention met in Cincinnati in 1870, where the possibilities of a system of parole and the idea of indeterminate sentences were discussed. The APA urged New York to adopt these ideas at the planned Elmira Reformatory. In 1876, New York enacted a statute under which young first offenders would be sent to Elmira under an indeterminate sentence not to exceed the maximum term already in place for non-reformatory offenders. The board of managers set the actual release date based on the inmate's institutional behavior. After an inmate had accumulated a certain number of marks based on appropriate institutional behavior, and with the assurance of employment, he could be released. Paroled inmates remained under the jurisdiction of reformatory authorities for an additional six months, during which the parolee was required to report every month to his "appointed guardian" (from which the parole officer evolved) and provide an account of his situation.

Although most states had a mechanism in place for parole based on the Elmira system prior to 1929, the great impetus for the system's expansion was pressing economic conditions. The Great Depression led to federal legislation that effectively abolished the economic exploitation of convict labor, which had kept down imprisonment costs under the so-called Auburn system. Additional factors were the high cost of constructing *prisons and concern about prison overcrowding and riots.

Corrections. Toward the end of World War II a new approach to criminal behavior called "corrections" emerged in California, whereby scientific methods would be used to "correct" criminals. Borrowing from Elmira Reformatory, all prison sentences in California became indeterminate, with a minimum and a maximum term; inmates were eligible for parole after completing their minimum sentence. Parole boards reviewed the effects of prison treatment to determine if the offender was sufficiently rehabilitated to be paroled to the supervision of a parole officer. This approach was eventually adopted by every state.

From its inception in California, the corrections approach continued without serious opposition into the 1970s. Criticism came primarily from conservatives, who saw it as "coddling" criminals. Liberals also argued that indeterminate sentences and parole rested on a view of crime as pathology to be "cured" by treating individual criminals. This downgraded societal factors such as poverty, discrimination, and lack of employment opportunities. Furthermore, liberals argued, even if the corrections approach were valid, behavioral sciences did not offer a sufficient scientific basis for rehabilitation.

The Pendulum Swings. Criticism of corrections and parole reached a critical point in 1974 when the sociologist Robert Martinson published a summary review of correctional treatment efforts entitled *What Works?* Martinson's answer: virtually nothing. Proposals to eliminate the indeterminate sentence and abolish parole gained support. By 1980, eight states had already abandoned parole by adopting some form of determinate sentencing, including the pioneering state of California (in 1977). Since then, the federal government and many other states have either abolished or severely limited the indeterminate sentence and parole release.

In the absence of indeterminate sentencing and parole, prison inmates serve their entire sentence less any time taken off for good behavior ("good time"), which can range from 15 to 50 percent. In most states without parole, an inmate released under good time provisions is placed under the supervision of a parole officer. However, in the absence of discretionary release—that is, release by a parole board's decision—the incentive for adequate funding of offender supervision is often absent. No one, not the governor or parole board, can be criticized for the serious misconduct of mandatory releasees.

The Parole Board. Governors usually appoint parole board members for six-year terms. Qualifications vary, but typically include a college degree and some relevant criminal justice experience. Boards hold release hearings in the state's prisons. This aspect of parole release may be handled by hearing examiners, who interview inmates and report back to the board with a recommendation. The U.S. Supreme Court has determined that an inmate does not have a constitutional right to be released on parole or any constitutional rights during the parole release process, since no "liberty interest" is at stake (*Greenholtz* v. *Inmates of Nebraska Penal and Correctional Complex* (1979)). Accordingly, inmates considered for release are not entitled to representation by counsel at parole hearings.

Parole boards usually consider the crime, the length of time served, the inmate's age, prior criminal history, substance abuse, and institutional record. Prison behavior has not proven to be a good predictor of post-prison behavior. Some parole boards may also request a recommendation from the prosecutor in the original trial. All certainly consider opposition to an inmate's parole from the police and the news media. More than thirty states permit victims or their next of kin to appear before the parole board, and about a dozen others permit written statements to be considered at the parole hearing. Many states include a victim-impact statement as part of the documentation considered by the parole board.

Probation and Parole Violations. Every probationer and parolee is required to sign an agreement to abide by certain general conditions, which typically involve restrictions on travel, association with other offenders, weapons possession, and drug use, as well as special conditions tailored to the individual offender. For example, persons with a history of sex offenses against children will be prohibited from areas where children typically congregate, such as playgrounds; persons with a history of alcohol abuse may be prohibited from using alcohol or being in facilities, such as bars, where alcohol is consumed. In recent years, some agencies have required the payment of restitution and supervision fees.

There are two types of probation and parole violations: (1) technical violations that occur when one or more conditions have been violated, and (2) "new offense" violations that involve an arrest and prosecution for the commission of a new crime. In practice, new offense violations often involve technical violations.

The Supreme Court has held that decisions about probation violations require a judicial process (*Gagnon* v. *Scarpelli* (1973)), while parole violation determinations are deemed sufficient with an administrative process typically devoid of court involvement (*Morrissey* v. *Brewer* (1972)). A probationer or parolee is not entitled to the same *due process rights as a criminal defendant, since only conditional, not total, freedom is at issue. But he is entitled to challenge the alleged violations with a limited right to confront and cross-examine adverse *witnesses and to present evidence on his own behalf. The offender may use legal counsel, although the state is not constitutionally required to provide an attorney (see COUNSEL, RIGHT TO). As opposed to the rules of *evidence in the criminal process, the use of hearsay is admissible at violation hearings, and the level of evidence is considerably less than the criminal trial standard of "beyond a reasonable doubt."

The violation process usually has two steps. First, a preliminary hearing determines if there is probable cause to believe that the offender has violated a condition of supervision. Second, a positive finding leads to a revocation hearing to determine if the violation is serious enough to require incarceration.

Conclusion. Parole release has been under attack since the 1970s as a device for releasing criminals back into the community, an option that is never politically popular. While parole eventually became intertwined with the concept of corrections, its essential function is to serve as a device for controlling the prison population. In the absence of parole release, states have increased their use of probation, as well as resorted to devices such as boot camp prisons, extra good time awards, and extended furloughs to avoid creating dangerously overcrowding prisons and violating the Eighth Amendment's prohibition against "cruel and unusual punishment." It was analogous conditions earlier in the twentieth century that led to the establishment of parole boards to serve as a more rational mechanism to determine when and which inmates should be released from prison.

[*See also* Criminal Law Practice]

• Robert Martinson, " 'What Works?' Questions and Answers about Prison Reform," *Public Interest* 35 (1974): 22–54. Douglas Lipton, Robert Martinson, and Judith Wilks, *The Effectiveness of Correctional Treatment: A Survey of Treatment Evaluation Studies*, 1975. Howard Abadinsky, *Probation and Parole: Theory and Practice*, 7th ed., 2000.
                                    —Howard Abadinsky

PRO-BONO LEGAL SERVICES. *See* Legal Services, Provision of.

PROCEDURE, CIVIL

    Pretrial
    Trial
    Appeal

PROCEDURE, CIVIL: PRETRIAL

Like all law, civil procedure can be seen as a series of expedients to influence, punish, reward, and authoritatively explain human behavior. Substantive law typically addresses the behavior of human and artificial members of society. Procedural law, in contrast, addresses a much smaller group: *lawyers, as agents for these members, and *judges. It is about litigation behavior.

Litigation resembles a sports game. Litigants are like players—the plaintiff initiates the game by suing a defendant. Judges are like umpires. The litigation game in America is remorselessly competitive and is often thought to have winners and losers. Civil procedure represents, in this sense, the rules of the litigation game. Like the rules of many other games, civil procedure is difficult to understand in the abstract. It takes life and meaning from the litigation game itself.

Litigation, however, bears a greater burden of justification than lighthearted sport. Most games exist for the pleasure they give to participants or spectators. So long as they are relatively harmless, they are not difficult to justify. In contrast, the litigation game is likely to impose onerous cost upon the parties, courts, and the public. It often has only one enthusiastic player, the plaintiff. As the burden of justification for lawsuits increases in our society, the idea of litigation as a sport becomes more difficult to maintain, and the corresponding search for cost-saving alternatives to formal civil litigation intensifies.

On the other hand, the purpose of civil procedure is to make real for society's members the rights secured for them by substantive law. To deny plaintiffs opportunities to become effective players in the litigation game might make those rights meaningless.

The plaintiff initiates the civil lawsuit with a pleading, called the complaint, and files a copy with the court. Pleadings set out a litigant's factual and legal position in the case. The complaint becomes the first in a series of documents that will make up the official file or record in the case. The plaintiff also requests a *sheriff or process server to deliver the complaint to the defendant. This is accompanied by a summons, a notice from the court officially designating the recipient as a defendant and requiring him to appear and respond in the case within a certain time.

The purpose of service of the process and complaint is to give notice to the defendant of the nature of the plaintiff's claim against him. The complaint alleges facts indicating that the defendant has behaved toward the plaintiff in a way entitling him to a judicial *remedy such as money *damages or an *injunction against the defendant. The plaintiff thus tries to allege facts in the complaint that (if proven at trial) will establish a claim or cause of action against the defendant.

A cause of action is a legal formula created by substantive law. The story the plaintiff tells through the allegations of his complaint must conform to the elements of that formula. For example, to establish a *tort claim for battery, the plaintiff must allege that the defendant deliberately touched him without his consent. When the complaint's allegations fail to support any claim, the defendant may immediately move to dismiss the plaintiff's case for failure to state a claim upon which relief can be granted. At the same time, the plaintiff will not be required to prove the truth of facts alleged in the complaint until later. It is enough for the complaint that, in good faith and after prudent investigation by the plaintiff's lawyer, there is reason to believe that it may be possible to prove the facts at trial.

The defendant usually also files a pleading, called the answer. It must respond to the complaint by either admitting or denying the plaintiff's factual allegations. The answer may, in addition, contain two other types of material.

First, it may contain one or more affirmative defenses. These offer further factual allegations supporting a legal rule capable of nullifying the plaintiff's claim. For example, proof that the defendant touched the plaintiff deliberately and without his consent is insufficient to create a claim for the plaintiff if we add the fact that the defendant acted out of reasonable fear for his safety. In other words, self-defense is an affirmative defense capable of defeating a cause of action for battery.

Second, the answer provides an opportunity for the defendant to make claims as well. The most common are counterclaims, claims in the answer directed back against the plaintiff. In many disputes (for example, those arising from traffic accidents), each disputant has a claim to make against the other. The disputant who gets to court first becomes the plaintiff and makes his claim in the complaint. The other disputant makes his claim as a counterclaim in his answer. Defendants may also make claims in the answer against co-parties, called cross-claims. And defendants may claim against one not previously a party for reimbursement, should the defendant be required to pay a *judgment in favor of the plaintiff. The defendant may be required to place the latter claim in a separate document, called a third-party complaint. Those against whom counterclaims, cross-claims, or third-party claims are directed must in turn file a responsive pleading, admitting or denying the allegations offered to support the claims made against them. These responsive pleadings may spark a new round of further claims, and so the process may continue.

There are other procedural means for enlarging the number of claims and parties. For example, procedural rules permit a claimant to join several claims together against the same opponent, or permit joinder of multiple persons as co-plaintiffs or as co-defendants in the same case. The most ambitious complex litigation device is the *class action. The number of persons in the class may be as high as several million. The scale of class-wide damage recoveries can be correspondingly great.

Factual investigation is an important pretrial function. It is the search for facts supporting a client's position; lawyers may offer these facts as admissible evidence at trial. A lawyer can obtain many of these facts from cooperative sources (the client or those supportive of the client's interests) or from public records. Other facts, however, may be in the exclusive control of uncooperative sources (the opposing side, those supporting opposing interests, or third parties who do not wish to give the appearance of cooperating with either side). Lawyers will not be able to obtain these facts without judicial assistance.

A lawyer becomes eligible for that assistance by serving various types of formal discovery requests on those withholding information, and filing copies of the requests with the court. If the targets of the discovery refuse to respond by disclosing information that they have, the lawyer can then apply for a court order requiring them to respond. Unless those resisting discovery can demonstrate that the information sought is privileged or factually unimportant to the case, the judge or magistrate will usually compel discovery.

Discovery tools include oral depositions (live testimony of persons taken outside the court), interrogatories (written questions directed to such persons), and requests to produce documents or other things. Much discovery, like interrogatories and requests to produce, may only be directed against opposing parties in the case. The most recent discovery development has been the limited use of mandatory disclosure, which requires the parties to automatically disclose certain types of information at the outset of the case.

The American emphasis on discovery sets its procedural law apart from that of civil law systems in Europe, Japan, and elsewhere. The differences are most apparent in the far greater latitude permitted for exploration in American discovery, and the extent to which it is attorney-initiated rather than tightly controlled by the judge.

The great majority of civil cases never reach trial. Many of these end by the defendant's default, the failure to respond, and many end by settlement. This occurs when the opposing parties agree to end the litigation. The plaintiff's incentive is the certainty of receiving some money from the defendant, although less than the amount sought as damages in the complaint. The defendant gives up the possibility of winning the case (whereby the plaintiff would have gotten nothing) in exchange for reduced *liability exposure. Both sides save litigation expense.

Cases may also end during the pretrial period by some court order. The defendant may succeed in getting the case dismissed for a procedural defect (e.g., want of subject matter jurisdiction). Such dismissals are usually without prejudice. That is, the plaintiff remains free to refile the action in a way curing the defect. Other pretrial dispositions are with prejudice. That is, dismissal precludes re-litigation of the case. For example, the plaintiff or defendant may move for summary judgment upon a showing that there is no contested issue requiring trial and that the moving party is entitled to judgment as a matter of law.

Finally, pretrial conferences will either facilitate settlement or coordinate final preparation of the case for trial. One or two such conferences may be mandatory. Courts use them to encourage parties to explore possibilities for settlement, to ascertain which matters raised in the pleadings will actually be tried in the case, to rule on as many anticipated trial issues as possible, and to set an agenda for the submission of evidence. Like discovery, pretrial conferences operate to minimize mystery and surprise concerning the trial and make that part of the game fairer.

[*See also* Criminal Law Principles; Criminal Law Practice]

PROCEDURE, CIVIL: TRIAL

Most civil cases do not reach trial; instead, they are settled, voluntarily withdrawn, or decided on the merits prior to trial. Cases not settled in these ways must go to trial. The idea and prospect of trial shape procedure for all civil cases, whether they reach trial or not. Pleadings and pretrial proceedings set the bounds of inquiry for trial; discovery and less formal means of investigation prepare the parties for trial; and trial can be either a specter that facilitates or an enticement that blocks settlement. Trial is the focal event in American civil litigation. It has no functional counterpart in the civil law systems of other countries, where fact determinations occur over a series of smaller, incremental stages.

Civil trials perform three essential functions in the American legal system. First, they determine the truth of facts contested in litigation—or at least, what is most likely to be true given the *evidence. Second, they resolve the case for the plaintiff or the defendant, depending on the law applicable to the determined facts. The first function concludes with a jury *verdict or, in cases tried without a jury (bench trials), with the judge's findings of fact. The judge always performs the second function. Third, trials constitute a public ceremony by which litigants are afforded their proverbial "day in court." This public witness of the government's administration of justice through its courts is important for the parties and for the entire society.

The defendant may attempt to avert trial by questioning the court's authority to hear the case. The two most significant bases for this challenge are lack of personal jurisdiction and lack of subject matter jurisdiction.

A state or federal court has personal jurisdiction over a defendant if the defendant is a resident of the forum state, or is found and served there, or has consented to service in that state. Otherwise, personal jurisdiction usually exists only where the forum has minimum contacts (connections) with the defendant. The "minimum contacts test" restricts state courts, because it derives from the *due process clause of the *Fourteenth Amendment. The same test usually binds federal courts as well, because their personal jurisdiction is in most cases limited by rule to the corresponding reach of the state court where the federal court is sitting (see COURTS, UNITED STATES).

The minimum contacts test examines the extent to which the defendant has purposefully directed activity into the state where the court is located. Activity related to the controversy satisfies the test through creation of a form of personal jurisdiction called "specific jurisdiction." The defendant must direct more extensive activity toward the forum to satisfy the minimum contacts test if none of the defendant's activity is related to the controversy; this form of personal jurisdiction is called "general jurisdiction."

Subject matter jurisdiction concerns the competence or power of a court to hear a particular kind of case. It is rarely a concern in state litigation, because a state's law gives its courts power to hear any sort of civil case. Subject matter jurisdiction is, in contrast, a major concern of the federal courts, which are courts of limited jurisdiction. Their power to hear a particular case must be (1) authorized under the language of Article III of the Constitution and (2) authorized by a state. Most issues of federal subject matter jurisdiction involve questions of statutory interpretation.

Factual determinations at trial are made either by a *jury or by the *judge sitting in the absence of a jury. Any litigant may claim a jury trial in those types of cases for which the right to a jury exists. The Seventh Amendment confers a right to jury trial in virtually all federal court cases for damages. The right to a federal jury trial may also be conferred by statute. Similar arrangements exist in state courts, controlled by state constitutions and statutes. The responsibilities of the judge in jury cases are to rule on the admissibility of evidence and to limit applications of the jury's fact findings to those permitted by law.

Jury trials follow (with minor variations) a traditional ceremony or sequence of events. Trials without a jury may be more abbreviated. The jury trial begins with the attorneys' opening statements, in which they describe the evidence they hope to submit in a manner that conveys to the jury their side of the story. The plaintiff and defendant then submit their evidence, which may take the form of tangible things (e.g., documents, photographs) or oral witness testimony. The importance given to the latter in American procedure stands in contrast to the distrust and very limited use of oral testimony in the civil law of other countries. Following the submissions of evidence, the attorneys make their closing arguments to the jury. These afford each side the opportunity to place the evidence admitted at trial in its most favorable light. The judge then instructs the jury on how to weigh the evidence, and the jury retires to start its deliberations. Once the jury has reached and reported a verdict, the judge enters a *judgment that usually implements the verdict.

Attorneys may, in appropriate cases, move for termination of the trial prior to jury deliberation (for directed verdict) or for a judgment opposite to that reached by the jury verdict (for judgment notwithstanding the verdict). Both types of motion accentuate the legal requirement that the jury's factual determination must have some reasonable basis in the evidence. When a party has finished presenting the evidence for his case, and before the jury has been given the case for deliberation, the opposing party may move that the court direct a verdict in her favor. The court may grant the motion if satisfied that the evidence is incapable of supporting a verdict in favor of the party against whom the directed verdict is sought. If a party's motion for directed verdict is denied, it may be renewed as a motion for judgment notwithstanding the verdict, if the jury in fact returns a verdict against that party. Even if the evidentiary record is strong enough to enable a verdict to withstand the latter motion, the party against whom the verdict is rendered may make a third type of motion: for a new trial. The court has the discretion to grant a new trial following a verdict against the clear weight of the evidence, following jury mistake or misconduct, or for other reasons.

Trials culminate in a judgment for the plaintiff or defendant. Winning plaintiffs thus obtain a measure of the relief or remedy they sought in the case. The three types of *remedies available in American civil litigation are *damages, equitable relief, and declaratory judgments.

To win at trial in an action for damages, the plaintiff must establish by a preponderance of the evidence that the defendant failed to act as he had a legal duty to act toward the plaintiff and that the plaintiff suffered compensable harm as a result. Damage actions are usually compensatory in character—that is, they attach monetary value to the difference between what the plaintiff's situation is and what it would have been if the defendant had performed a legal duty owed to the plaintiff. Courts may on occasion also award either nominal damages, which are symbolic and do not require proof of particular harm, or punitive damages, which are penal and may greatly exceed the assessed amount of actual harm. While English courts usually require the losing party to pay the victor's attorney *fees, the United States has a strong tradition against this practice. Subject to a few exceptions, created by statute, each side pays its own litigation costs.

The principal form of equitable relief dispensed by American courts is the *injunction, a court decree that controls the behavior of the defendant by requiring that he either act or refrain from acting in a certain way. Trial issues in damage actions address the past: what the defendant did and what his action cost the plaintiff. But trial issues in injunction cases concern the future: what the defendant will do to the plaintiff, absent an injunction. Injunctions obtain their force from the prospect that defendants who violate them may be liable for contempt. *Contempt sanctions for violating an injunction include compensation to the opposing party, daily fines or incarceration to ensure future compliance, and fixed penal fines or imprisonment. The first and second types of sanctions are associated with civil contempt, the third with criminal contempt.

The declaratory judgment remedy differs from damages and injunctions in that it is not a coercive remedy—it does not produce either an enforceable judgment for damages or a binding injunctive decree. Declaratory judgment trials merely determine an issue contested by the parties. That alone, however, has value. Issues determined by declaratory judgment bind the parties in any further litigation. Declaratory judgment and injunctive remedies are alike in that courts have considerable discretion to withhold the remedies, even when the plaintiff has established a case. In contrast, damage action awards are usually mandatory upon proof of the plaintiff's case.

PROCEDURE, CIVIL: APPEALS

Appeal is the judicial process by which a court ruling is reviewed by a higher court. Appeals serve two purposes. First, they monitor the correctness of lower court rulings. This purpose is reflected by the availability in most judicial systems of at least one layer of mandatory review—appeal by right. Even when appellate decisions do not display a greater understanding of the case than does the lower court, they bolster the authority of the decision. As Justice Robert H. Jackson candidly observed in *Brown* v. *Allen* (1953): "We are not final because we are infallible, but we are infallible only because we are final." A second purpose of review is to make the application of law more uniform and to furnish guidance to lower courts. This purpose is most often served by the Supreme Court, which today is largely able to pick and choose its cases in order to unify aspects of disputed law.

Tension exists between the pursuit of correctness and uniformity through the appellate process and two additional procedural objectives: efficiency and finality. The latter objectives are frustrated by the delay and expense that appeals generate. Consequently, the law of appeals must balance a desire for correctness and uniformity against concerns about efficiency and finality.

The judicial systems of most states are three-tiered. Immediately below the state's highest court (e.g., the California Supreme Court) is a series of coequal intermediate appellate courts (e.g., the California courts of appeals). Each appellate court is usually responsible for reviewing the work of state trial courts—the third and bottom tier—from a particular geographic region of the state. The structure is like a pyramid in that the number of judges at the trial level greatly exceeds the number in the intermediate, appellate tier, which in turn greatly exceeds the number of judges at the top.

In the federal court system, the pyramid consists of the United States *Supreme Court, courts of appeals, and district courts. In addition, the U.S. Supreme Court exercises significant appellate review over state courts when the latter rule on important questions of federal law.

As is evident from the pyramidal design of American court systems, there is an insufficient number of second-and top-tier judges to adjudicate fully all the cases heard by the tier below. Appellate judges tend as a result to be more burdened with cases than their colleagues on the trial bench. Two factors keep appellate courts from becoming overwhelmed. First, the losing parties at trial often decide not to prolong the expense and frustration of litigation by appealing. Second, appellate courts refuse to reexamine many types of trial court decisions and may give only summary treatment to the cases they do review.

American procedure gives a losing party one appeal by right from a final *judgment on the merits of the case. The appellant court may designate a number of rulings by the trial court—for example, refusal to grant a pretrial motion to dis-

miss, a trial ruling on the admissibility of evidence, or the giving of an erroneous jury instruction—as reversible error. Appellate courts will review only those rulings in which an error could have affected the outcome of the case—that is, prejudicial as opposed to harmless error. If the reviewing court fails to find a prejudicial error, it will affirm the judgment of the court below. If the court does find a prejudicial error, it will either reverse the judgment and order entry of judgment for the appellant or will vacate the judgment (render it void) and remand the case to the trial court for further proceedings consistent with the higher court's decision. Reversal is appropriate when the record indicates that correction of the error must lead to judgment for the appellant. But when it is not clear from the record how the case would have been decided without the error, the appellate court can only vacate the decision and order the lower court to complete the trial of the case.

Appellate courts also give parties a limited amount of review of trial court rulings that are made prior to final judgment, a process called interlocutory review. Interlocutory review is, as a general matter, more difficult to justify than review of a final judgment, because interlocutory review interrupts the progress of the case and because final judgment may obviate (render harmless) the ruling challenged by the interlocutory appeal. Justification for interlocutory review is greatest when the trial court ruling has immediate and irreparable consequences, in which case the cost of possible error outweighs the cost of an extra appeal, and when there can be no effective later appeal at final judgment. For example, federal rules permit certain interlocutory appeals of a district court order denying the plaintiff a temporary *injunction.

Appellate courts show varying degrees of deference to the trial court when conducting review. The most stringent review comes when the trial court ruling is challenged on the basis of an error or misunderstanding of the law. Appellate courts are expositors of the law and guardians of its uniform application, and thus they will review pure questions of law *de novo*, without any deference to the prior decision of the trial court. At the other extreme, appellate courts are reluctant to disturb a judge's findings of fact, and even more reluctant to disturb a jury verdict. Such matters are committed to the sound discretion of the fact finder—that is, they will not be overturned unless the record reveals flagrant error.

Many types of trial court rulings represent mixed issues of law and fact—for example, the question of whether to grant a new trial because the jury's *verdict was against the clear weight of the *evidence. Appellate courts speak of such rulings as "discretionary," but their deference to trial courts in considering appeals of these rulings is not as great as it is with findings of fact.

[See also Appeals; Courts, United States; Supreme Courts, State]

• Karl N. Llewellyn, The Common Law Tradition: Deciding Appeals, 1960. Robert A. Leflar, Appellate Judicial Opinions, 1974. Robert M. Cover and Owen M. Fiss, The Structure of Procedure, 1979. Robert E. Keeton, Judging, 1990. Daniel John Meador, American Courts, 1991. Roger S. Haydock, David F. Herr, and Jeffery W. Stempel, Fundamentals of Pretrial Litigation, 2d ed., 1992. Geoffrey C. Hazard Jr. and Michelle Taruffo, American Civil Procedure: An Introduction, 1993. Gene R. Shreve and Peter Raven-Hansen, Understanding Civil Procedure, 2d ed., 1994. Charles Alan Wright, The Law of Federal Courts, 5th ed., 1994. Jonathan Harr, A Civil Action, 1995.
—Gene R. Shreve

PROCEDURE, COURT. Each of the American judicial systems—state, federal, and territorial—has its own procedural law governing the conduct of civil and criminal cases. In their major features, these procedures are similar, although they differ in detail. They are descendants of the legal order developed in England before the Revolutionary War, an ancestry still discernable despite numerous changes in American judicial procedure over the past two centuries.

English Origins. For centuries after the Norman invasion in 1066, the legal scene in England was pluralistic, with a patchwork of local and special courts. But in the thirteenth century, two separate sets of central royal courts began to emerge—the *common law courts (Common Pleas, King's Bench, Exchequer) and the *equity court (Chancery). Eventually these courts became the dominant judicial tribunals in England. The practices and substantive doctrines developed in those courts ultimately formed the basis of the legal order in the North American colonies.

The common law courts held sessions in Westminster Hall in London, but their judges also rode circuit to conduct civil and criminal trials. In civil actions, a plaintiff could get one of two kinds of *remedy: an adjudication that defendant owed money to compensate plaintiff for the injury suffered, or an adjudication that plaintiff was entitled to possession of *property, real or personal, wrongfully possessed by defendant. Contested factual issues were resolved by *juries. Juries were also used in criminal prosecutions.

Alongside those common law courts sat the Court of Chancery. It had its roots in the authority of the crown to do justice, as a matter of discretion, to give relief to persons asserting that the remedies provided in the law courts were not adequate in their particular case and that extraordinary relief was necessary. The court was presided over by the chancellor, the chief royal official. Equity dealt with matters of conscience and breaches of trust; it had a strong moral element, heightened by having ecclesiastical figures as chancellors in its early years. Whereas the law courts rendered judgments that had to be executed by the sheriff, and did not order the defendant to do anything, the chancellor's decrees, generally called *injunctions, directly ordered individuals to do or not do something. There was no jury; the chancellor decided all issues. Violation of a decree could be punished by *contempt proceedings, through which a person could be fined or imprisoned to compel compliance or be punished for noncompliance. In having separate courts and procedures for law and equity, the English legal system was in sharp contrast with those of *civil law countries in continental Europe, whose roots were in Roman law, in which there was no separation of law and equity.

The English common law courts functioned through writs known as "forms of action." There was a separate form for each kind of injury—for example, *trespass (direct injury to person or property), trespass on the case (indirect injury to person or property), trover (wrongful conversion of personal property), detinue and *replevin (recovery of possession of personal property), and ejectment (recovery of possession of real property). Each form had its own substantive and procedural features. If a plaintiff proceeded under a form that did not fit the facts, he would lose the case. The procedures and substantive doctrines developed in these courts were known collectively as the "common law," to be distinguished from "equity," developed in the Chancery Court.

Transplantation and Nineteenth-Century American Reform. This body of common law and equity was transplanted to the North American colonies by the English colonial authorities and colonists in the seventeenth and eighteenth centuries and formed the basis of the states' legal systems after the adoption of the Federal *Constitution in 1789. The one exception was Louisiana's legal system, which was derived from Spanish and French law. Two works published in England and studied by nearly every American lawyer were highly influential in the transplantation process:

Sir Edward Coke's *Institutes for the Law of England* (1648) and Sir William *Blackstone's *Commentaries on the Laws of England* (1765–69). Before the Revolution, dozens of Americans studied law in the Inns of Court in London and returned home to become members of the bar, imbued with English common law and equity practice. Versions of the English forms of action were widely used, and separate systems of common law and equity continued, although in some states they were administered in the same court.

Hyper-technical pleading requirements and the rigidity of the writ system made many of these inherited procedures increasingly ill-suited to a growing American society. This prompted efforts for reform, which were influenced by the writings of Jeremy Bentham in England. These efforts culminated in the enactment in 1848 by the New York legislature of a Code of Civil Procedure, the major American procedural reform of the nineteenth century. The Code was developed under the leadership of David Dudley *Field, a New York lawyer. The Field Code's key provisions abolished the forms of action, and united law and equity into a single civil action to be conducted under the same procedure in the same court. All the rights and remedies at law and equity were preserved; they were simply merged procedurally. However, juries continued in common-law cases, but not in equity cases. Pleadings were simplified and stripped of useless legal jargon. Plaintiffs were required only to set forth facts that entitled them to relief under some legal or equitable theory. The Field Code was copied in numerous states over the ensuing decades, mainly in the Midwest and Far West. But restrictive legislative amendments and limiting judicial interpretations rendered the Code a less effective reform than Field had intended. Moreover, numerous states still retained the old common law and equity practices.

Twentieth-Century Reforms. The advent of the twentieth century brought renewed interest in judicial reform. Influential in that respect was a 1906 address to the *American Bar Association by Roscoe *Pound entitled "Causes of the Popular Dissatisfaction with the Administration of Justice." After explaining that discontentment ran far back in history, Pound criticized the American judicial process for being overly contentious, for its "sporting theory," and for the rigid application of rules of evidence and procedure, causing unnecessary retrials. A similar reformist spirit motivated the establishment of the *American Judicature Society in 1913, a national organization devoted to improving state courts through nonpartisan merit selection of judges.

The most significant procedural reform since the Field Code came in 1938 with the promulgation of the Federal Rules of Civil Procedure by the U.S. Supreme Court. Until then, under a Congressional statute known as the Conformity Act, each federal district court followed the procedures of the state courts in the state where it sat. The new rules established a nationally uniform procedure for the federal district courts in civil cases. They incorporated the key concepts of the Field Code by abolishing the forms of action and merging law and equity into a unified civil action. In addition, they introduced numerous innovations in pretrial processes. Pleadings as the primary means of defining contested issues were downgraded; henceforth, pleadings would serve only to give generalized notice of claims and defenses. The task of defining issues was shifted to devices later in the pretrial stage, chiefly pretrial conferences conducted by the judge with opposing counsel, aided by greatly expanded discovery procedures. Those new discovery procedures enabled parties to examine each other, as well as any witnesses, under oath, and to obtain documents and other evidence from their opponents. The objective was to increase fairness by eliminating surprise as a factor in litigation—in theory, all parties would be equally informed of the facts and have access to the same evidence—thereby promoting settlement through negotiation. Liberalized rules of joinder of claims and parties were introduced, with the aim of having all aspects of a controversy, as to all persons involved, litigated in a single action, something not possible under the Field Code and other earlier procedures.

Over the years, those new federal rules were widely copied in the states. In some states, they were adopted in their entirety; in others, portions were adopted. Today they represent the prevailing pattern of civil procedure in American courts. Although highly innovative in their time, they have spawned new problems. The relaxed rules of pleading have given rise to criticism that controversies are too ill-defined initially. The wide-ranging discovery permitted by the rules is said to have been abused in some cases, adding costs and delays. These criticisms have prompted efforts to tighten pleading requirements and limit discovery, but these efforts have produced only modest changes.

The success of these civil rules, developed through an advisory committee of distinguished judges, lawyers, and law professors, led to the formulation, through similar advisory committees, of the *Federal Rules of Criminal Procedure (1946), the Federal Rules of Appellate Procedure (1968), and the Federal Rules of Evidence (1975). (The latter were enacted into statute by Congress.) Like the civil rules, these rules have been influential among state courts, and serve as models in their fields.

In criminal procedure, the most significant changes in the second half of the twentieth century have been effected through decisions of the U.S. Supreme Court interpreting the *due process and *equal protection clauses of the *Fourteenth Amendment to the Constitution. Those decisions have expanded the rights of criminal defendants in state courts, especially the rights of indigents. They include, among others, a right to *counsel at trial and on *appeal at state expense, a right against self incrimination, a right to be informed by the prosecution of any exculpatory evidence, and protection against the knowing use of perjured testimony and involuntary confessions. As a result, state criminal procedure has, to a considerable extent, become federalized.

The Adversary System and the Rise of Case Management. A pervasive feature of civil and criminal litigation in American courts, inherited from England, is the so-called adversary system. Under that system, in its purest form, each party is responsible solely for presenting the facts and legal theories supporting its position, with no obligation to assist opposing parties. The judge is a passive umpire, with no responsibility to develop the facts or to assist any party, but only to rule on motions and objections made by opposing counsel. This system is in contrast to the so-called inquisitorial system found in civil law countries, under which trial judges actively participate in the proceedings, affirmatively directing the assembling of evidence and in moving the case along toward disposition; lawyers play a correspondingly lesser role.

The strict adversary system has been modified in several ways in American courts during the twentieth century. The discovery provisions in the 1938 federal civil rules and their state counterparts introduced a significant modification by permitting a party to obtain from opposing parties evidence that under the pure adversary process could not be known. Some trial judges, viewing themselves as having an obligation to see that justice is done, will, in exceptional circumstances, depart from a passive role by making rulings on evidence and other matters on their own motion, especially to protect a defendant's rights in criminal cases.

The rise of judicial case management in the late twentieth century has also altered the adversary nature of civil litigation. Trial judges, in varying degrees, now exercise affirmative control over civil actions by setting timetables and limits on discovery and the filing of motions and by holding periodic conferences to monitor the progress of the pretrial stage; many judges also actively involve themselves in encouraging settlement, with the aim of avoiding trial. Lawyers' control over the pace and scope of litigation has thus been curtailed.

Such judicial case management emerged as a response to the unprecedented growth in litigation that began in the 1960s, and has continued (see LITIGIOUSNESS). Courts were threatened with unacceptable backlogs and protracted delays; litigation expense was also rising. Judges and legal scholars came to believe that the opposing lawyers could not be relied on, left to their own devices under the adversary process, to move cases along expeditiously. This affirmative judicial case management has brought many American trial courts closer to the inquisitorial model of the civil law, although counsel still play a more important role in American civil proceedings than counsel in civil law countries.

Judicial case management, now widely practiced in the busiest trial courts, has been, and continues to be, controversial. One criticism is that the lawyers for the parties know more about the case than the judge and thus should have greater latitude in managing the proceedings. Another criticism is that in aggressively managing cases, judges exercise too much unchecked discretion; there are few rules governing the judge's actions, and what is done is not a matter of record and thus not reviewable on appeal. Special criticism is directed at judges who actively intrude themselves into the settlement process, with the risk of losing their impartiality and of forcing parties to give up positions they are entitled to under the law. Another criticism is that there is no uniformity of practice among judges; some affirmatively manage cases more actively than others, resulting in unequal treatment of litigants. Despite these objections, case management seems here to stay, sustained by the felt need to move huge volumes of cases through the courts with minimum delay and expense.

Case management has become especially necessary in *class actions and other complex suits involving a host of widely dispersed persons. Such large-scale litigation, which proliferated in the late twentieth century, is ill-suited for traditional judicial processes, and can be rationally conducted only under the firm control of a judge.

Appellate Procedure. The procedures described here concern the conduct of litigation in trial courts—courts of first instance in which cases are initiated, evidence offered, contested issues resolved, and judgments entered, awarding or denying relief to the parties. Above this level in the judicial structure are the appellate courts. In the federal system, and in all but a few state judicial systems, there are two appellate tiers: the intermediate courts, and, above them, the court of last resort, usually called the supreme court. The primary role of the intermediate courts is to provide losing litigants an opportunity for a review of the trial proceedings to ensure there was no prejudicial error. By contrast, the main role of the supreme court is to maintain uniformity in the law and to develop the case law in a sound fashion. In that role, it typically reviews intermediate court decisions, taken up at its discretion. In addition, some state supreme courts also hear designated categories of appeals directly from the trial courts, bypassing the intermediate court. Appellate review is based on the record made at trial—typically embodied in a printed transcript of witnesses' testimony—and in other documents; no new evidence can be offered. As an appellate court's concern is with legal issues, it accepts the factual determinations of the trial court, unless they are considered clearly erroneous. While a trial court is presided over by a single judge, an appellate court functions through multiple judges, usually three at the intermediate level, and more in the supreme court.

Under the traditional procedure, followed by state and federal appellate courts in almost every case until the 1960s, parties file written arguments called briefs. Then the judges sit together to hear counsel present oral argument, after which the judges gather in conference to discuss the case. One of the judges drafts an opinion analyzing the issues and giving the court's decision and the reasons for it. When the opinion is agreed on by a majority of the judges, it is issued and becomes part of the court's binding case law, published in the court's reports. In the traditional process, each judge personally studies the briefs and drafts opinions, assisted by law clerks, personal assistants who do library research and make editorial suggestions on the judge's opinion drafts.

This traditional process has been altered for many appeals as a result of the growth of litigation that began in the 1960s, an increase in judicial business that has had a disproportionately greater impact on appellate courts than on trial courts. In response, to avoid unacceptable backlogs, intermediate courts have taken two innovative steps. One is to employ central staff attorneys to assist the court by reviewing appeals for defects in jurisdiction, preparing memoranda for the judges analyzing the issues, and, in some courts, drafting proposed opinions. Although judges long had personal law clerks to assist them, a central staff working for the court as a whole was novel and initially controversial as posing a risk of undue delegation of judicial responsibility. The other, related innovation is the introduction of differentiated decisional processes through which appeals are screened and put on different tracks. Appeals deemed simple, with a predictable result, are put on a fast track and decided without oral argument and court conference, typically on the basis of a staff attorney's memorandum and a short opinion deemed to have no precedential value. Other appeals receive the traditional process of oral argument, court conference, and fully explained opinion. Only the latter opinions are published in the court's reports.

Procedural Change. Under a regime of law, courts must themselves function under law, acting through established procedures that embody the essential due-process elements of notice and opportunity to be heard. As circumstances in society evolve, the nature of controversies changes, and procedure must be adapted to those changes if courts are to remain effective protectors of the rule of law. But because procedural rules are often compromises between competing social and political interests, change is difficult and slow, usually lagging behind the needs of the day. However, throughout American history, adaptations have been made, preserving American courts as vibrant agencies of governance and suggesting that judicial procedure will continue to evolve pragmatically to fit ever-changing conditions.

[*See also* Court Systems; Courts, United States: Federal Courts; Courts, United States: State and Local Courts; Procedure, Civil; Procedure, Criminal]

• "Addresses Delivered at the National Conference on the Causes of Popular Dissatisfaction with the Administration of Justice," *Federal Rules Decisions* 70 (1976): 79–246. Paul R. Connolly, Edith A. Holleman, and Michael J. Kuhlman, *Judicial Controls and the Civil Litigative Process: Discovery*, 1978. Lawrence M. Friedman, *A History of American Law*, 2d ed., 1985. Fleming James Jr., Geoffrey C. Hazard Jr., and John Leubsdorf,

Civil Procedure, 4th ed., 1992. Daniel J. Meador and Jordana S. Bernstein, *Appellate Courts in the United States*, 1994. Federal Judicial Center, *Manual for Complex Litigation, Third*, 1995.   —Daniel J. Meador

PROCEDURE, CRIMINAL

Pretrial
Trial
Appeals

PROCEDURE, CRIMINAL: PRETRIAL

Criminal procedure in the early period of American colonial history was informal and local. For example, one neighbor might accuse another of theft before the elders of the local church. The penalties were most often fines or public apologies, but could also include branding, whipping, or the stocks. Prisons, professional prosecutors, defense lawyers, and police forces were nonexistent, and jury trials were rare. Criminal justice officials, including judges, were often volunteer laymen.

The colonies began to rely more on English procedure as they grew larger and more established. Unlike the civil law system, in which a judge presides over a series of meetings in an investigative process, English procedure focuses on an adversarial trial before a lay jury. A grand jury would investigate serious charges and, if there was probable cause, it would turn the case over to a "petit," or trial, jury to determine guilt or innocence. As in England, the defendant during the colonial period was not allowed to testify under oath or have the assistance of a lawyer. The judge was there to protect the defendant's rights and provide the jury with an understanding of the relevant law. A few colonies in the 1730s allowed defendants to have trial counsel, but defendants were not allowed to testify under oath until the 1860s.

The United States Constitution's Bill of Rights both codified *common law procedural rights and reformed them in response to perceived abuses of the English system. For example, Fourth Amendment *search and seizure restrictions are explicitly designed to prevent writs of assistance, which gave colonial governors sweeping rights to search for contraband.

During the nineteenth century industrial revolution, migration made the cities more populous, anonymous, and ethnically diverse, and the old volunteer system of constables and nightwatchmen no longer sufficed to keep the peace. By the 1840s, some large cities began to establish professional *police forces, largely in response to mob violence. Professionalization of other legal actors followed, and the legal system transformed itself into a bureaucratic case-processing apparatus. For the most part, negotiated guilty pleas replaced trials, and imprisonment, rather than shaming punishments, became the norm. During this period, states began to codify their criminal laws and procedural rules.

Contemporary state criminal procedure still varies greatly from state to state. The federal Constitution as interpreted by the United States Supreme Court provides a common baseline of procedural protections for defendants, but state constitutions and statutes may provide various additional protections.

Investigation. The criminal process begins with the investigation of crime. Patrolling officers may discover criminal activity on the street, citizens may call to report a crime, or, more rarely, criminal activity will be uncovered as a result of a long-term investigation. In these latter cases, sometimes involving government corruption or complex financial crimes, a grand jury may be involved in a continuing investigation. The federal grand jury is composed of at least sixteen citizens, drawn from the same pool as the more familiar petit jury. Black men were formally included on juries after *Strauder* v. *West Virginia* (1880), and women were included after *Ballard* v. *United States* (1946), though informal methods of exclusion remained. Grand jurors meet in a secret session with *prosecutors, who bring before them testimony and documentary *evidence of criminal activity. The grand jury has the power to subpoena witnesses and documents, and members may play either an active or passive role in the investigation, depending on the case and the prosecutor involved. Ultimately, the grand jury has the power to determine whether the evidence establishes probable cause to indict (formally charge) a defendant. Some scholars question the fairness of grand jury secrecy and the substantial extent to which prosecutors direct the jury's decision-making.

Though law enforcement agents may conduct investigations without any judicial intervention, they are restricted by limitations on searches and seizures derived from the U.S. Constitution's Fourth Amendment, by limitations on police *interrogation derived from the Fifth Amendment right against *self-incrimination and the Sixth Amendment right to *counsel, by common law rules against entrapment, and by federal and state statutory limitations on certain investigative tech nologies (electronic surveillance and wiretaps, for instance). Within these constraints, there is no general constitutional requirement that law enforcement agents have a reason to target a potential defendant before investigating him.

Arrest and Formal Charge. The Fourth Amendment provides that a defendant may not be arrested unless there is probable cause to believe he has committed a crime. Probable cause may be determined before arrest by a grand jury or a judge's imprimatur on an *arrest warrant, or it may be determined by a magistrate after the arrest. Warrantless arrests are restricted by the Fourth Amendment, especially arrests in one's own home.

Interrogation after arrest must be preceded by a *Miranda warning to the defendant, that he has the right to remain silent, that anything he says may be used against him in court, and that he has the right to an attorney who will be paid for by the state if he cannot afford to hire one.

The Miranda warning was the most visible and controversial requirement set down in a series of U.S. Supreme Court criminal procedural decisions in the 1950s and 1960s under Chief Justice Earl *Warren. In part, the new criminal procedural protections of this era were a response to police brutality and abuses of poor and minority defendants brought to prominence by the civil rights movement, and in part the decisions were a continuation of an earlier, more timid, extension of *Bill of Rights protections to state defendants. The Bill of Rights was initially interpreted to apply only to federal prosecutions, but as early as 1908 the Court suggested that some of these rights might be part of the *"due process" required in state trials by the post–Civil War *Fourteenth Amendment. The constitutional basis of Miranda, however, remained controversial, but was reaffirmed in Dickerson v. United States (2000).

Bail Hearing. An arrest may be made before or after a formal charging procedure. If the police initiate the charge, it is called a "complaint." Defendants who are arrested must be brought promptly before a magistrate for an initial probable cause examination to determine the legality of the arrest (if made without a warrant) and for an opportunity to receive *bail and counsel. This hearing is often called the "first appearance," and the magistrate sets bail and assigns counsel to an indigent defendant if the matter is serious enough to involve jail time. The right to state-funded counsel for indigent defendants was established by *Gideon v. Wainwright (1963), another Warren Court reform, although incompetent, underfunded defense counsel remain a serious problem.

Defendants may waive counsel, although this is not common, and have a constitutional right to proceed pro se (Faretta v. California (1975)). After counsel is assigned, the police normally may not interrogate the defendant about the case without his lawyer present, so the period between arrest and the first appearance is the prime opportunity for police interrogation.

Preliminary Hearing. In colonial America, and now under the U.S. Constitution's Fifth Amendment, grand jury evaluation of probable cause is required for a formal *felony charge to be brought against a defendant. This provision has not been applied to the states, however, and many states allow a prosecutor to bring a formal charge without a grand jury's imprimatur, often called an "information." When a grand jury procedure is not used, however, a substitute procedure called a "preliminary hearing" requires a magistrate to determine whether there is probable cause to continue the prosecution. Unlike grand jury proceedings, a preliminary hearing generally occurs in the defendant's presence and may, depending on state law, allow the defense to present evidence or cross-examine prosecution witnesses. Federal law and other grand-jury states also provide for hearings to ensure that there is a forum for promptly determining probable cause to prosecute in the event that grand jury indictment is delayed.

Discovery and Plea. After a formal charge is brought, the defendant must plead guilty or not guilty. During this period, plea negotiations with the prosecutor may take place (see PLEA BARGAINING), and defendants may undertake their own investigation of the charges. Although defendants have the right to subpoena witnesses and documents in their defense, they have very limited rights to discover the prosecutor's case in most jurisdictions. The Supreme Court's interpretation of the due process clause only requires prosecutors to turn over evidence that tends to exculpate a defendant (Brady v. Maryland (1963)). In federal criminal trials, defendants need not receive a prosecution witness's prior statements until after that witness testifies at trial (Jencks v. United States (1957), later codified as the "Jencks Act"). Federal law requires that prosecutors disclose the defendant's prior statements and other material documentary or tangible evidence, including the results of experts' examinations and tests, but there is no requirement that the prosecution disclose any other inculpatory evidence (Federal Rules Of Criminal Procedure 16). Most discovery in criminal cases is left to the prosecutor's discretion, and prosecutorial custom varies from an "open file" policy to minimal disclosure. The lack of complete discovery imposes the greatest hardship on indigent defendants, who may have state-compensated lawyers but no additional funds for investigators or professional testing. The Supreme Court has required states to fund expert testing in some cases, *Ake* v. *Oklahoma* (1985), but there is otherwise little provision for investigative services for the indigent.

Pretrial Motions. The decision to plead guilty or not guilty may also be contingent on the outcome of a pretrial challenge to the arrest, search, or interrogation procedures, or the sufficiency or propriety of the charging document. Pretrial hearings may include motions to suppress evidence on the ground that it was obtained in violation of Fourth or Fifth Amendment rights, motions to challenge a lack of specificity or accuracy in the indictment, or motions to dismiss the prosecution because of entrapment, delay, or because the defendant has already been acquitted or convicted of the crime charged (a violation of the constitutional prohibition against *double jeopardy). The question of the defendant's mental competency may be raised by a court itself and resolved pretrial after a court-ordered mental examination.

The remedy of evidence-suppression for abusive or unconstitutional investigative practices continues to be controversial, since critics claim that its costs in public safety outweigh its benefits to public privacy. They call into doubt its constitutional pedigree, or they argue that judicial oversight is misplaced. However, many commentators point out that other remedies for police overreaching are not effective.

The constitutional protection against double jeopardy has its roots in the common law tradition and is intended to prevent both multiple punishments for the same offense and the anxiety, expense, and harassment caused by multiple trials for the same offense. Though simple in principle, its application is complicated by overlapping statutes and by similar crimes that may be prosecuted by different jurisdictions.

A prosecution may also be dismissed for delay. The Sixth Amendment requires a speedy prosecution, though the constitutional case law mandates only a balancing of the length and reason for the delay against the prejudice to a defendant who has demanded a quick resolution. The Federal Speedy Trial Act (1994) and comparable state statutes provide strict time periods within which a case must be prosecuted, though the defendant may waive those protections.

Finally, additional pretrial motions may be made "in limine," at the threshold of a trial in order to solve evidentiary disputes before a jury is convened. These motions usually involve nondispositive disputes over the introduction of certain kinds of evidence (such as vivid pictures of a victim's injuries) or testimony (such as hearsay or coconspirator statements). The judge's resolution of these disputes is usually intimately connected to the management of the trial itself.

[*See also* Criminal Law Practice; Criminal Law Principles]

• Anthony Lewis, *Gideon's Trumpet*, 1964. John H. Langbein and Lloyd L. Weinreb, "Continental Criminal Procedure: 'Myth' and Reality," *Yale Law Journal* 87 (1978): 1549. Bernard Schwartz and Stephan Lesher, *Inside the Warren Court*, 1983. Lawrence M. Friedman, *Crime and Punishment in American History*, 1993. John H. Langbein, "The Historical Origins of the Privilege Against Self-Incrimination at Common Law," *Michigan Law Review* 92 (1994): 1047. Carol S. Steiker, "Second Thoughts About First Principles," *Harvard Law Review* 107 (1994): 820. Akhil Reed Amar, *The Constitution and Criminal Procedure: First Principles*, 1997. William J. Stuntz, "The Uneasy Relationship Between Criminal Procedure and Criminal Justice," *Yale Law Journal* 107 (1997): 1. Wayne R. LaFave, Jerold H. Israel, and Nancy J. King, *Criminal Procedure*, 3d ed., 2000.

—Linda Ross Meyer

PROCEDURE, CRIMINAL: TRIAL

American criminal trial procedure has several elements that distinguish it from criminal procedure in other nations. These elements include prosecutorial discretion, *bail, *jury trial, legal aid, discovery, the exclusionary rule, and guilty pleas.

Prosecutorial Discretion. Article II, Section 3, of the United States Constitution provides that the executive branch of the federal government "shall take Care that the Laws be faithfully executed." Most state constitutions contain similar provisions. At both the state and federal level, one manifestation of this faithful execution of laws falls on *prosecutors. Tradition ally prosecutors have been given wide-ranging, but not absolute, authority to decide whether or not to prosecute. Thus, prosecutorial decisions are subject to constraint under both *equal-protection and *due process principles. Equal protection is violated if a defendant is intentionally selected for prosecution from among similarly situated offenders for an arbitrary reason or based on a suspect classification. Due process is violated if the prosecutor's charging decision is a vindictive response to the defendant's exercise of a legal right.

Bail. The money bail system in the United States carried over from the English practice of allowing an accused person to be released to a third party of her own choosing following arrest for most crimes. If the accused did not appear for trial, the third party would be required to surrender himself to custody or, in later times, surrender property or money. In modern times, a *bail bondsman generally serves as the third-party surety. The bondsman takes a percentage fee for securing the temporary release of the accused and searches for the individual if she is absent at trial.

Jury Trial. The right to a trial by jury has roots deep in English *common law. This right was recognized as essential as early as Magna Carta. In medieval England, the jury trial functioned more like a modern grand jury, and such a jury could be punished if its verdict was contrary to law. During the early days of the American Republic, citizens revered the trial jury as a group of peers acting as a buffer between the criminal accused and the state. As such, the framers of the Constitution were committed to making the jury trial an indispensable part of the criminal justice system. Article II, Section 2, of the Constitution provides that "the trial of all crimes, except in cases of impeachment, shall be by jury." Furthermore, the Sixth Amendment reads: "In all criminal prosecutions, the accused shall enjoy the right to a . . . trial, by an impartial jury." The Supreme Court has implemented the Sixth Amendment's impartiality requirement by mandating that the jury should be a cross-section of the community.

Jury selection takes place in several stages. A jury pool, generally compiled from voter registration lists or telephone directories, is designed to be a diverse cross-section of the community from which to pick potential jurors. The pool is whittled down to a smaller jury panel (venire) through a random process. At this stage, potential jurors are excused if they fall within any of the statutory exemptions for jury duty, such as not meeting the minimum age requirement or not being able to speak English. The next step is voir dire, which helps in the selection of an impartial jury. This process allows the parties in the case to inform themselves about the potential jurors so that they can exclude, through challenges, those they find unsuitable. Each party may excuse any potential juror that admits to having a bias or who appears to be biased. Such challenges "for cause" are unlimited in number. Moreover, each party has the right to exercise a limited number of peremptory challenges, which allow the removal of a panel member for any reason without explanation.

Although the Sixth Amendment speaks only of juries, the Supreme Court has held that the due process clause also guarantees the defendant an impartial *judge, regardless of whether the judge sits with or without a jury. There are three mechanisms for ensuring the impartiality of a judge. The first two parallel the voir dire mechanisms for removing biased jurors. First, a judge can be removed for cause if it is shown that she is biased toward a particular party. Second, some jurisdictions allow the peremptory removal of a judge; such a trial would automatically be transferred to another judge, who would be subject to removal only for cause. Finally, a judge is required by the code of judicial ethics to recuse or disqualify herself if (1) she has a personal bias or prejudice concerning a party or has personal knowledge of disputed evidentiary facts concerning that proceeding; (2) she or a former law partner served as a lawyer or material witness in the controversy; (3) she or a close relative has a financial or other substantial interest in the outcome of the proceeding; or (4) she is related, directly or by marriage, to one of the parties or lawyers.

Legal Aid. The right to *counsel at trial developed over many decades, beginning with case-by-case analysis under the Fourth Amendment's Due Process Clause in 1932. Later Supreme Court decisions applied the Sixth Amendment, which today guarantees counsel at any trial that may result in the deprivation of liberty. The Court held in *Gideon* v. *Wainwright* (1963) that the Sixth Amendment's guarantee of counsel for indigent criminal defendants was fully incorporated by the Fourteenth Amendment. Justice Hugo *Black, for the Court, concluded that lawyers in criminal courts are necessities, not luxuries.

Discovery. Prior to the 1946 adoption of Rule 16 in the Federal Rules of *Criminal Procedure, there were few formal provisions permitting discovery in criminal cases. Rule 16 permits the defendant, upon request, to discover from the prosecution (1) any written statements or transcriptions of oral statements made by the defendant that are in the prosecution's possession; (2) the defendant's prior criminal record; and (3) documents, photographs, tangible objects, results of physical and mental examinations, and test reports in the prosecution's possession that the prosecution intends to use as *evidence or that is deemed material to the defense's trial preparation. Additionally, under Rule 16 a prosecutor served with a discovery request that falls within either of the latter two categories is entitled to reciprocal discovery: he may request inspection of documents, objects, and test results that the defense intends to introduce at trial.

Some state rules are more expansive in scope, requiring the prosecution and defense to provide lists of all possible witnesses as well as copies of any statements they may have made pertaining to the case. Discovery by the prosecution is subject to limitation by the Fifth and Sixth Amendments. Under the Fifth Amendment privilege against *self-incrimination, a criminal defendant cannot be compelled to provide inculpatory statements from his own mouth. Moreover, a defendant may not invoke the Sixth Amendment to avoid providing discoverable documents, claiming that doing so would deprive him of his right to effectively confront witnesses for the prosecution.

The Exclusionary Rule. The primary remedy available to the criminal defendant who has been aggrieved by the police is the exclusionary remedy. The doctrine of exclusion flows from the Fourth Amendment, which proscribes unreasonable *searches and seizures. The exclusionary remedy renders inadmissible any evidence that was originally obtained in an illegal manner by the police in conducting their investigation. The Supreme Court's decision in *Mapp v. Ohio (1961) made this rule binding on the states. The Court reasoned that although the rule would allow some criminals to go free, the overriding imperative of judicial integrity demanded that the *remedy be available to criminal defendants.

The exclusionary rule counterbalances its social costs by retaining a reasonable, good faith exception for three situations. The first is the exception for reliance on a defective warrant. Evidence that is seized by an officer armed with a *search warrant is admissible even if that warrant is subsequently found to be unsupported by probable cause, so long as the officer objectively believed the underlying warrant to be valid at the time of execution and the warrant was originally issued by a neutral and detached magistrate. Second is the exception for reliance on a statute that is later found to be unconstitutional. Evidence seized by an officer relying on a statute in good faith is admitted even if that statute is later found to be invalid by a court. Third is the exception for reliance on court-generated records and reports. For example, a police officer, in arresting an individual following a routine traffic stop based on an outstanding warrant list generated by the state's computer, discovers contraband in the person's automobile. If that warrant had been quashed by the court but this information not yet updated in the computer system, the contraband is admissible at trial because of the officer's good faith reliance on what she believed to be a valid list of outstanding warrants.

Exclusion applies not only to tangible evidence taken in violation of an individual's Fourth Amendment rights but also to statements taken in violation of his Fifth Amendment right to counsel. This right springs from the defendant's assertion of his desire to retain counsel in order to help with the process of *interrogation and thus is a separate right to counsel not contained in the Sixth Amendment. The Supreme Court's decision in *Miranda v. Arizona (1966) canonized the Fifth Amendment right to counsel and has today become a part of popular culture. The Miranda decision requires a person subject to custodial interrogation to be given the following warning: "You have the right to remain silent; anything you do or say can and will be used against you in a court of law; you have the right to an attorney; if you cannot afford an attorney, one will be appointed for you by the court; you may terminate this interrogation at any time." A criminal defendant may waive these rights, but such a waiver must be voluntarily, knowingly, and intelligently made. Any confession taken from a suspect during custodial interrogation without the Miranda warning, or with an invalid waiver of the suspect's rights, is excluded as evidence against the accused.

Guilty Pleas. The overwhelming majority of criminal cases never go to trial before a jury or a judge. These cases are dealt with in a four-step procedure: arrest, confession, guilty plea, and sentencing; this serves the purpose of expediting the criminal justice process, whose limited resources do not allow for the trial of every criminal case. Additionally, by choosing to *plea-bargain, a defendant has an opportunity to receive a lesser sentence than would result from a trial. A criminal defendant may choose to plead guilty or to enter a plea of nolo contendere. The legal effects of these pleas are identical, except that a nolo contendere plea may not be used against a defendant in subsequent civil proceedings pertaining to the alleged act.

Federal Rule 11(c), which has served as a model for many states, provides that the court may not accept a guilty plea until it has determined that the defendant understands (1) the nature of the charge or charges to which the plea is offered; (2) the maximum sentence for each offense to which the plea is offered; and (3) the rights he will be waiving if he pleads guilty—that is, the rights to be tried by a jury, to the assistance of counsel at trial, to confront and cross-examine *witnesses against him, and to avoid compelled self-incrimination.

• Herbert Packer, *The Limits of the Criminal Sanction*, 1968. Barbara Babcock, "Voir Dire: Preserving 'Its Wonderful Power,'" *Stanford Law Review* 27 (1975): 545. Stephen A. Saltzburg, "Foreword: The Flow and Ebb of Constitutional Criminal Procedure in the Warren and Burger Courts," *Georgetown Law Journal* 69 (1980): 151. Yale Kamisar, "The Warren Court (Was It Really So Defense-Minded?), The Burger Court (Is It Really So Prosecution Oriented?) and Police Investigatory Practices," in *The Burger Court: The Counter-Revolution That Wasn't* (V. Blasi, ed.), 1983. Peter Aranella, "Rethinking the Functions of Criminal Procedure: The Warren and Burger Courts' Competing Ideologies," *Georgetown Law Journal* 72 (1984): 185. Lilly Graham, "Notes on the Confrontation Clause and *Ohio* v. *Roberts*," *University of Florida Law Review* 36 (1984): 207. Akhil Amar, *The Constitution and Criminal Procedure: First Principles*, 1997. William J. Stuntz, "The Uneasy Relationship between Criminal Procedure and Criminal Justice," *Yale Law Journal* 107 (1997): 1. Charles H. Whitebread, "Selecting Juries in High Profile Criminal Cases," *Greenbag 2d* 2 (1999): 191.   —Charles H. Whitebread II

PROCEDURE, CRIMINAL: APPEALS

A criminal appeal typically involves an appellate court's examination of trial court records in an effort to ascertain whether the lower court properly applied the relevant substantive and procedural law. Sometimes the appellate proceeding is a new, independent trial in a superior court. In either case, appeal procedure gives a convicted offender the opportunity to obtain one judicial review of his conviction by a tribunal other than that in which he was tried. Although most states, as well as the federal system, provide at least one appeal as of right and one level of discretionary appeal (i.e., at the discretion of the appellate court), the *Supreme Court has never given constitutional status to the opportunity to appeal. Several Supreme Court decisions have supported the proposition that although a state need not provide an appeals process, if it does so it may not unfairly inhibit the use of that process. These decisions have precipitated a set of rights available to every criminal defendant seeking appeal.

First, indigent defendants are entitled to receive complete trial transcripts, free of charge. The Supreme Court, in *Griffin* v. *Illinois* (1956), reasoned that all defendants should be allowed access to trial transcripts in order to perfect their appeals and that a state may not grant the right to appeal "in a way that discriminates against some convicted defendants on account of their poverty."

Second, the Supreme Court has interpreted the Sixth Amendment right to *counsel as applying only to criminal prosecutions and thus not to the appellate process. However, in applying the *due process and *equal-protection clauses, the Court has determined that the state must provide an indigent defendant with counsel for an appeal as of right. A discretionary appeal does not carry the right to counsel.

Third, the criminal defendant has the right to pursue any nonfrivolous argument on appeal. In the event that the defense counsel reviews a case and finds that no such argument exists, she may withdraw from the case by filing a brief in accordance with the Supreme Court's decision in *Anders* v. *California* (1967). Such a brief (*Anders* brief) refers to anything in the record that might arguably support an appeal. Furthermore, counsel must submit a statement to the court as to why any possible issues lack merit. After appellate review of the *Anders* brief, the appellate court determines the appropriateness of counsel's withdrawal.

Finally, a criminal defendant has the right to pursue an appeal without fear of retaliation by the state. In *North Carolina* v. *Pearce* (1969), a defendant who had successfully appealed a conviction received a heavier sentence at retrial than that meted out at his original trial. The Supreme Court held that such conduct by the sentencing court gave rise to a presumption of vindictiveness. Thus, as a general rule, the defendant may not be given a harsher sentence on retrial after successful appeal.

The presumption of vindictiveness applies to sentencing and charging authorities that have some vindictive motivation toward a given defendant and thus does not generally apply if, for instance, the disparate sentences are handed down by different judges. To overcome the presumption, the state must prove identifiable conduct occurring after the original sentencing proceeding that would indicate a justification for the enhanced sentence.

Besides appealing after conviction and sentencing, a defendant may appeal certain pretrial decisions, as long as they comport with the "final judgment rule." This rule, observed in most jurisdictions nationwide, discourages inefficient pretrial litigation by allowing only the trial court's final decisions to be appealed. A few states permit interlocutory appeal, which is a pretrial appeal, and many more permit pretrial appeal of certain issues. The questioned pretrial ruling must involve an important right that would be lost if review were to await conviction and must involve an issue that either is independent of the original cause of action or is so inherently limited to the specific defendant that it could not be raised by another defendant. Examples of appealable rulings include those concerning *bail or *double jeopardy. Examples of nonappealable rulings under the final judgment rule include those concerning the Fourth Amendment right against unreasonable *searches and seizures, matters dealing with grand juries.

The prosecution may not appeal any judgment that determines there is insufficient evidence upon which to convict the defendant, as guaranteed by the Constitution's double jeopardy clause. However, certain statutory provisions allow the state to appeal other types of rules without violating double jeopardy, including certain crucial pretrial rulings that do not go to the merits of the case, such as motions for discovery, speedy trial, and change of venue.

In nineteenth-century England, the so-called Exchequer Rule created a presumption of prejudice whenever there was error at the criminal trial; error of any type would result in a new trial. American courts rejected this rule and all have adopted some type of "harmless error" rule, which allows convictions to stand despite error. The reasoning is that some errors are so insignificant that they do not have any substantial impact on the outcome of cases. The Supreme Court has enumerated standards for determining the relative harmlessness of error. For nonconstitutional error at the trial level, the Court stated in *Kotteakos* v. *United States* (1946) that error was harmless only when "the error did not influence the jury, or had but very slight effect." For a constitutional error, however, the Supreme Court announced a more stringent test. In *Chapman* v. *California* (1967), the Court held that the prosecution must prove "beyond a reasonable doubt that the error complained of did not contribute to the verdict obtained."

According to the Supreme Court's decision in *Chapman*, some constitutional errors involve "rights so basic to a fair trial that their infraction can never be treated as harmless error." Examples include the use of coerced confessions, the denial of trial counsel, and denial of the right to an impartial judge. Moreover, various Court decisions have suggested that violations of the right to speedy trial, the double jeopardy clause, and the right to a representative trial jury or grand jury should not generally be viewed as harmless.

[*See also* Appeals; Courts, United States; Fair Trial, Criminal]

• Roger J. Traynor, *The Riddle of Harmless Error*, 1970. Stephen Saltzburg, "The Harm of Harmless Error," *Virginia Law Review* 59 (1973): 988. Martha A. Field, "Assessing the Harmlessness of Federal Constitutional Error—A Process in Need of a Rationale," *University of Pennsylvania Law Review* 125 (1976): 15. Peter C. Erlinder and David C. Thomas, "Prohibiting Prosecutorial Vindictiveness while Protecting Prosecutorial Discretion," *Journal of Criminal Law and Criminology* 76 (1985): 341. Marc Arkin, "Rethinking the Constitutional Right to a Criminal Appeal," *UCLA Law Review* 39 (1992): 503. Daniel Meltzer, "Harmless Error and Constitutional Remedies," *University of Chicago Law Review* 51 (1994): 1.   —Charles H. Whitebread II

PRODUCTS LIABILITY. See Consumer Law; Torts.

PROFESSIONAL CORPORATION. See Business Organizations.

PROFESSIONALISM, LEGAL. See Ethics and Professional Responsibility, Legal.

PROFESSOR, LAW. See Educator, Legal.

PROMISSORY ESTOPPEL. A promise that reasonably and foreseeably induces an action or forbearance to another's detriment that a court will enforce to avoid injustice.

[*See also* Contract Law]

—Williamjames Hull Hoffer

PROPERTY, as conceptualized in American law, consists of rights regarding things that are binding upon others and that are endorsed by the state. The objects of property include tangibles, such as land and automobiles; intangible claims to wealth, such as corporate stock; and inventions and literary works, now termed "intellectual property." The most important property rights are those of use, dominion, and alienation. Use rights permit the owner to employ the resource for economic benefit or personal satisfaction. Dominion rights permit the owner to exclude others. Alienation rights permit transfer of the owner's use and dominion rights by sale, gift, or testamentary disposition. This view, that property consists of a bundle of rights with respect to others, differs sharply from the everyday notion that property consists of things that one owns.

In general, American law treats rights in most valuable resources as property. It presumes that property is held by individuals, as opposed to family or communal groups or the state. Its preference for practical finality over theoretical perfection is manifest in the concept of adverse possession, by which a person occupying land without permission for a modest number of years acquires a fresh title that is superior to old claims of ownership. The American legal concept of property has no fixed meaning or clear-cut structure. It has developed from a multitude of European and indigenous sources, the most important being the English *common law. As the notions of utility and *justice that have shaped it continue to evolve, the concept of property evolves as well.

Pre-Colonial Sources. The sources of American property rights include the classical Roman law (c. A.D. 1–250) which recognized ownership (proprietas) of tangible things. Roman occupation of Britain (55 B.C.–c. A.D. 410) was terminated by Angles, Saxons, and Jutes, who came from the Danish peninsula and north Germany. Chieftains of these riding bands granted tracts of land to their followers. As the Anglo-Saxon concept of kingship developed, this customary practice was regularized through the issuance of charters granting occupation of land in exchange for payments and services.

Anglo-Saxon rule in turn was overthrown in 1066 by William the Conqueror, whose Norman French invaders had their origins in Norway. While the Normans never adopted Anglo-Saxon landholding practices in a formal sense, these practices formed the basis of immemorial custom that shaped the early common law. William's grants of land differed from previous practice in that they generally were conditioned upon personal oaths of fealty and promises to supply specified numbers of knights for battles. Over the next two centuries, paid armies replaced knights and the economic value of land was increasingly recognized. Correspondingly, feudal obligations of military service were replaced by money rents, and the Statute Quia Emptores (1290) permitted landholders to sell their estates. Over time, the cost of royal wars led to continued strife with Parliament, but by the Glorious Revolution of 1688 English law had evolved so even the king was subject to the rule of law.

Property in American Colonial Times. The American concept of property was shaped by economic and political developments during the colonial period (1607–1776). In England, land title ultimately was vested in the crown. Those who held land through royal grants of tenure formed a highly concentrated elite. In America, land was plentiful and colonial proprietors had to lure immigrants with the promise of absolute title. Also, colonists had absorbed the teaching of the English and Scottish Enlightenment that government was

a compact among individuals for the preservation of their liberties. The most influential Enlightenment author was John Locke, whose *Second Treatise of Government* (1688) proclaimed that men had property rights in themselves and in those natural resources fashioned into usable things through their labor.

By and large, the indigenous Indian tribes were hunters and gatherers; they did not build permanent structures or delineate individual landholdings. While such communal use of land was sensible given the lack of towns and intense agricultural development, it was not recognized by Europeans as creating property. Thus, European nations distributed lands without regard for customary American Indian rights (see NATIVE AMERICANS AND THE LAW: HISTORY).

The Development of Property from Independence Through the New Deal. When the colonies achieved independence, the English common law of property was received as the law of the new states. The ratification of the United States Constitution in 1787 did not substantially affect the common law basis of property, since the Constitution provided the federal government with only limited powers. Furthermore, the framers regarded the protection of property as a great object of the Constitution and a necessary condition for the preservation of *liberty.

The powers delegated to Congress enhanced the importance of property by establishing a national common market. Among them were the power to coin money; to regulate interstate, foreign, and American Indian commerce; to establish post offices; to grant patents and copyrights; and to regulate *bankruptcy (Article I, Section 8). Similarly, among the few prohibitions imposed upon the states were the coinage of money and the impairment of *contracts (Article I, Section 10). The Fifth Amendment to the Constitution) prohibited the taking of private property by the federal government without just compensation and similar provisions were incorporated in all state constitutions. State statutes facilitated the incorporation of businesses and placed on a firmer footing the rights of investors whose tangible property consisted of shares of corporate stock.

During the rapid industrialization that followed the Civil War, states responded to perceived abuses by businesses with legislation regulating railroad and utility rates as well as labor conditions. (In so doing they relied upon the police power, the inherent right of the sovereign to protect the public health, safety, and welfare.) Late in the nineteenth century the Supreme Court held that such regulations must present a reasonable return on investments in regulated property and, more fundamentally, that the right to contract to enter into a lawful occupation or to acquire property was a liberty interest, protected by the *due process clause of the Fourteenth Amendment. In cases such as *Lochner v. New York (1905), which came to epitomize the Court's approach, it would ascertain independently whether a regulation was necessitated by the public health, safety, or welfare, or whether it deprived business or employees of their property or contract rights arbitrarily and in violation of their substantive right to due process of law. In the wake of the Great Depression and the New Deal, the Court backed away from this approach. Ever since its decision in United States v. Carolene Products Co. (1938), the Supreme Court has permitted the government wide latitude to impose economic and social regulations, shifting its closer scrutiny to such rights as freedom of speech and freedom from racial discrimination.

A problem inherent in the Court's post–New Deal jurisprudence is that the legal concept of property encompasses both dominion rights and use rights. The value of the right to exclude others from land, for instance, may be insignificant without the owner's additional right to use the land. In monetary terms, the value of a thing used in commerce depends upon the anticipated income generated by that use. Therefore, there is an internal inconsistency in the familiar assertion that property (dominion rights) is protected from uncompensated seizure by the Fifth Amendment's *takings clause, while the business activity (use rights) that generates income may be regulated stringently under the police power.

Property in Contemporary America. A marked attribute of contemporary American property law is its growing complexity. At the beginning of the twentieth century, property was conceptualized as real property (land and buildings), personal property (other tangible things), and intangible rights, such as stock, patents, and copyrights. By the end of the century these concepts had changed significantly.

Over a millennium, real property had acquired a unique legal status and claim on popular affections. For many centuries, real property was the basis of family wealth and power. Given its relative permanence, real property ownership had to be tracked over long periods of time. For these reasons, changes in the few permissible variations from complete ownership of land, such as life *estates and leases, came slowly. As a basis of economic self-sufficiency, real property ownership re-

duced the need to remain in favor with the king and thus facilitated the quest for political rights.

Through the early twentieth century, ownership of land used for commercial purposes was embodied in the simple deed of the equity owner, and the simple *mortgage protecting the lender who advanced funds for the land's purchase. These relationships have been transformed by the growth of modern financial institutions, including pension and mutual funds, and the proliferation of distinctions in tax law. Now hundreds of ownership rights might exist in a shopping center or office complex project, each tailored to the time horizon, aversion to risk, and tax status of a particular type of investigator.

The residential lease, which earlier was conceptualized as the transfer of ownership of a land for a term of months or years, has been reconceptualized by the *landlord-tenant revolution of the mid-twentieth century into a contract for the provision of housing services. This change permits courts to read into leases various "implied warranties" by landlords that never were part of traditional property law. In fact, these warranties result from police power regulation rather than contract, since the implied provisions cannot be disclaimed even by tenants' most explicit agreements. As in feudal times, the rights of residential landlord and tenant are determined by their status rather than by their bargain.

Property rights in residences, farms, and other lands occupied by their owners have been reconceptualized as well. In the United States, ownership of land traditionally has been viewed as carrying with it the right to make economically useful improvements. To be sure, owners could not commit acts of nuisance, which deprived neighbors of the right to reasonable enjoyment of their lands. Beyond this, however, owners could not be required to leave land undeveloped simply to provide open space for the community. In many European nations, on the other hand, use rights in land are limited to existing uses. Subsequent development is predicted upon obtaining permission from local planning authorities.

Comprehensive *zoning was approved by the U.S. Supreme Court in Village of Euclid v. Ambler Realty Co. (1926). It was adopted rapidly by almost all American cities. Although predicated on the notion of sound planning, zoning has mostly served to segregate residential from industrial and commercial districts and to protect property values and aesthetics in homogenous suburban communities. While the more blatant forms of exclusionary zoning against disfavored socioeconomic groups have been prohibited in some states, zoning is inherently exclusionary. In recent years, a few states have adopted state-wide or regional growth-management programs, which generally have been upheld by the courts. These typically create urban growth boundaries, beyond which most development is precluded. The goal is to establish sharply defined and densely populated towns surrounded by green belts, reconceptualizing American land use rights along the European model. The recent demand for "smart growth" legislation may hasten this trend.

Many landowners have attempted to coordinate the use of their respective parcels through private agreements. These create easements (nonpossessory rights in the land of another), and equitable servitudes (similar promised binding as a matter of fairness). While the distinctions among these devices are somewhat arcane, owners might choose one device over another to ensure either flexibility or rigidity in the enforcement of their agreements over time. The recent *Restate (Third) of Property, Servitudes* (2000) would collapse these devices into the servitude, which would be enforced by courts in light of reasonableness. For some, this is a welcome change. For others, it represents another reconceptualization of traditional property, which is capable of serving owners with precision if used with care into another domain of public policy, governed by amorphous standards of fairness.

As the legal concept of property becomes increasingly complex and less set apart from other bodies of law, it moves farther from the laypersons' view of property as the tangible thing in which the owner might vest care and affection. The effects of these developments upon the historic links between property and the creation of wealth and property and the preservation of individual liberty remain to be determined.

[*See also* Patent Law Practice]

• Forrest McDonald, *Novus Ordo Seclorum: The Intellectual Origins of the Constitution,* 1985. Jeremy Waldron, *The Right to Private Property,* 1988. Ellen Frankel Paul and Howard Dickman, eds., *Liberty, Property, and Government: Constitutional Interpretation Before the New Deal,* 1989. Jennifer Nedelsky, *Private Property and the Limits of American Constitutionalism: The Madisonian Framework and Its Legacy,* 1990. Robert C. Ellickson, *Order without Law: How Neighbors Settle Disputes,* 1991. Margaret Jane Radin, *Reinterpreting Property,* 1993. James W. Ely Jr., *The Guardian of Every Other Right: A Constitutional History of Property Rights,* 2d ed., 1998. William B. Stoebuck and Dale A. Whitman, *The Law of Property,* 3d ed., 2000.   —Steven J. Eagle

PROPERTY, INTELLECTUAL. Intellectual property is a general category of rights that protect commercially valuable, intangible products of human intellect. The category includes copyright, trademark, and patent rights as well as trade secret, publicity, and unfair competition protections. Despite its intangible nature, intellectual property (IP) can be sold, transferred, or leased. Revenue from the commercial use of intellectual property represents an increasingly large percentage of the global economy.

Intellectual property is regulated on both a national and international level. A patent, copyright, or trademark generally must be registered in each market where it is sold, licensed, or leased, and most countries have their own laws governing the requirements and terms of protection. While these laws have general similarities, they can vary greatly in their registration requirements and enforcement.

The increasing globalization of markets has encouraged efforts to standardize intellectual property protections. These efforts have been initiated through intellectual property unions and more recently through international organizations such as the World Intellectual Property Organization (WIPO) and the World Trade Organization (WTO). WIPO promotes the international protection of intellectual property and supervises administrative cooperation among the Paris and Berne Conventions and other intellectual property treaties. The WTO has adopted the Trade Related Aspects of Intellectual Property Agreement (TRIPS). TRIPS establishes minimum substantive standards for protecting intellectual property, requires that members establish enforcement mechanisms to protect those rights, and provides sanctions for violations of the agreement.

Copyright. Copyright grants a monopoly of exclusive rights to creators of original artistic, literary, musical, and dramatic works. The monopoly includes the rights to publish, reproduce, display, or perform the work as well as the right to make subsequent derivations using the original. Copyright can exclude third parties from such things as reproducing copies of a sculpture, performing a play, adapting a novel for film, or copying computer code. Copyright is a dynamic area of law, and its subject matter and protections have evolved with changes in technology.

The ability of the printing press to create multiple copies of written works prompted England's passage of the first statutory copyright protection in 1710. The Statute of Anne granted authors the exclusive right to make copies of their works ("copy rights"). The Statute offered the protections to incentivize new works in order to promote the public welfare through the dissemination of knowledge. Balancing the interests of authors and the public, the statute granted an author the sole right to publication during a term but provided that upon the term's expiration the protected work would pass into the "public domain," such that the public was then free to use the formerly protected work without restrictions.

England's focus on the public benefits of copyright protection contrasted with the approach of other European nations that focused on the protection of the creator's rights. These nations treat *droit d'auteur,* or author's rights, not as statutory creations but products of natural justice. Protecting a creative work is therefore essential to protecting the author's bodily integrity. Accordingly, the civil law in these nations tends to be more sympathetic to authors' interests and protective against subsequent alteration or destruction of copyrighted works.

Copyright in the United States follows the English tradition and is granted solely as a matter of statute. In *Wheaton* v. *Peters* (1834) the Supreme Court held that there was no common law right in literary property. Copyright does not seek to protect the bodily integrity of the author but to provide market incentives to encourage the dissemination of knowledge and the progress of science. This economic rationale stems from Article I, Section 8 of the U.S. Constitution, which authorizes Congress to create a national copyright system to "promote the Progress of Science and useful Arts, by securing for limited Times to Authors . . . the exclusive Right to their . . . Writings."

Congress first passed a copyright law in 1790. The modern copyright system is based on the Copyright Acts of 1909 and 1976. The 1976 Act defines copyrightable subject matter. It states that "Copyright protection subsists . . . in original works of authorship fixed in any tangible medium of expression, now or later developed, from which they can be perceived, reproduced or otherwise communicated, either directly or with the aid of a machine."

A copyrightable work must be original and fixed. Originality does not require that the work be exceptionally creative or unique, only that it possess a mere modicum of creativity and is the product of independent creation. The underlying facts and ideas of a work are not copyrightable, although the manner of expression and the selection and arrangement of facts may be sufficiently original to receive protection. Fixation requires a sufficiently permanent and tangible recording. Examples include a handwritten notation of a song or the capture of an image on film. The copyrighted work need not be directly perceptible from its source of fixation. The 1976 Act provides that a machine, such as a computer, may assist in the perception of a work from a fixed source.

The Copyright Act recognizes several categories of copyrightable works: literary, musical, and dramatic works; pantomimes and choreographic works; pictorial, graphic, and sculptural works; motion pictures and other audiovisual works; and sound recordings. The list is not exhaustive, and the categories are generally broad and flexible—as is evident by the inclusion of computer programs in the category of literary works. The categorization a work receives is important, however, in determining the rights the author receives with her copyright.

The Copyright Act grants creators of original works of authorship exclusive rights of reproduction, adaptation, distribution, performance, display, and sound recording of digital audio transmissions. This bundle of rights is infinitely divisible—each right can be transferred, owned, and enforced individually. The author of a play can transfer to different individuals the rights to perform the play, produce written copies of its script, and adapt a film version. Each transferee can then sue to enforce his right. Those rights not transferred remain with the author. Copyrights are subject to limitations including the term of the copyright, the doctrine of fair use, and compulsory licenses. The 1976 Act, as amended, sets the general term for copyright protection at life of the author plus seventy years.

The doctrine of fair use is a defense to claims of copyright infringement and permits third parties to use copyrighted materials without the consent of the copyright owner. Fair use analysis examines (1) the purpose of the use, (2) the nature of the copyrighted work, (3) the amount of the work copied, and most significantly (4) the effect of the use on the potential market for, and value of, the copyrighted work. Noncommercial uses of smaller segments of a copyrighted work that do not affect the copyright holder's market for the work generally qualify for the fair use defense. Examples include the unauthorized use of copyrighted materials for education, parody, or commentary. Finally, certain categories of works are subject to compulsory licenses that permit third parties to utilize a copyrighted work without the permission of the author, so long as the user pays a standard fee.

The emergence of digital technology has presented new challenges to traditional copyright law. First, the emergence of digital technology has significantly reduced the effort and expense needed to reproduce and transmit copyrightable works. Digital technology enables copyright holders to produce copies of images, songs, books, and other artistic works by translating the works into a series of 0s or 1s which can be read by a computer. The digital copies can then be reproduced without deterioration in copy quality and widely distributed over the Internet or through CD-ROM. The ease of digital reproduction and transmission has also eased the ability to pirate, or illegally copy and distribute, copyrighted works. The problems have been exacerbated by the emergence of peer to peer ("P2P") filing sharing networks. P2P networks allow users to index and "swap" files over the Internet without the digital transmission traveling through any central commercial server.

Advances in digital technology have also raised issues regarding the ability of copyright holders to gain additional protections through contracting. These protections have been criticized because they often come at the expense of the "rights" the Copyright Act and international agreements afford consumers of copyrighted works. A copyright holder, for instance, may insist through its license that users disclaim their traditional fair use rights for research or education even though those rights may be protected under a country's copyright legislation.

The issue has been raised in the particular case of electronic databases. Digital technology has reduced the cost of information storage and encouraged the creation of large databases of information. These databases often have significant market values; yet copyright does not protect the database's facts and information. It can only protect the original selection and arrangement of the data. As a result, database owners have attempted to obtain through sales contracts rights they do not have under copyright. Their license agreements often contain clauses that restrict a purchaser's ability to use the underlying facts and data as well as require the purchaser to disclaim recognized fair use rights. The licenses generally are not open to bargaining and can be accepted online by simply clicking through various prompt screens on a computer.

Trademark. Trademarks are visible symbols that distinguish the goods of one business enterprise from another. Trademarks can include letters, words, numbers, names, the presentation of products or packaging, color combinations, and product design. Recognized trademarks include the corporate name Microsoft, the pink color of Dow-Corning insulation, and the classic Coca-Cola bottle. Trademarks serve to protect both manufacturers and consumers. They protect manufacturers from unfair competition by preventing third parties from passing off their own goods as those of a recognized manufacturer and protect customers by allowing them to rely on a mark to indicate that a product is of certain origin and quality.

Trademark law has evolved from *common law roots to national statutory protections, although state trademark regulation through unfair competition law still offers substantial protections. Trademarks are created through use, not formal registration—although ownership of a trademark is generally acknowledged only after the mark has been registered. Recognized trademarks are the property of the mark holder and are transferable through sale or lease. The licensing of marks allows third parties to manufacture and sell a recognized product provided the product meets the specifications and qualities consumers associate with the mark.

Not all identifiable marks are trademarks. First, a trademark must be distinctive. The requisite distinctiveness can either be present when a mark is first used or can develop through continued use by a manufacturer that creates a secondary meaning in the minds of consumers. A mark must not lose this distinctiveness. When the public comes to associate a once distinctive mark like Kleenex or Aspirin with a general class of products, the requisite distinctiveness can disappear and the trademark lose its validity. There accordingly is a duty on the part of mark holders like Xerox to take affirmative steps to ensure their marks are not used to generically refer to the other members of its product class. The United States adheres to this vigilance requirement, though internationally many countries do not.

Second, a mark holder must actually use the trademark. In the United States, a trademark is abandoned if not used for three consecutive years. Other countries follow similar time frames. The requirement of constant use, however, is offset by the fact that trademarks can enjoy indefinite protection. Whereas other forms of IP rights—copyright and patents—expire after set periods, those trademarks that are consistently used and which retain their distinctiveness can warrant continuous protection and recognition.

Finally, based on the distinctiveness requirement, a single trademark can be owned by more than one party. Trademark protections can be limited to geographic areas and product classifications. Trademark law permits there to be both an American Insurance Company and an American Airlines as well as a Blue Note Jazz Club in New York and a Blue Note music club in Memphis. The geographical distance or difference in the products ensures that each use remains distinct and there is not a significant likelihood of consumer confusion.

A trademark entitles its holder to various legal protections. The primary protection is against infringing uses of the mark that are likely to create consumer confusion. A trademark holder can seek damages and enjoin a third party from using a mark that is likely to cause consumer confusion as to the origins and quality of the product. The test for likelihood of confusion generally considers the type of mark at issue, the similarity of the two marks, the similarity of the parties' products or services, the similarity of the parties' retail outlets and target consumers, the intent of the alleged infringer, and evidence of actual confusion.

A second protection is against dilution of a mark. Dilution occurs when the unauthorized use of a trademark or other mark lessens the value of the trademark to its holder. Dilution does not require consumer confusion, and in the United States, can occur through *blurring* or *tarnishment* of the registered mark. Blurring occurs when the value of a trademark is diminished by use on dissimilar products. Tarnishment occurs when the trademark's value is diminished due to unwholesome portrayal or association with inferior products or services.

If a registered trademark goes uncontested by claims of prior use for a period of typically seven years, the owner's rights to the mark are presumptively uncontestable. In the United States, the Lanham Act governs the legal registration and recognition of trademarks. Under the Act, trademark rights are not granted, but similar to copyright and unlike patent, originate with qualifying use. The Patent and Trademark Office ("PTO") does, however, register trademarks, which creates procedural and substantive advantages for trademark holders. Also, registration provides a right to enhanced *remedies in suits for infringement. The PTO will only register marks that are (1) not deceptive, (2) not confusingly similar to other registered marks, (3) more than merely descriptive of the goods, (4) not misdescriptive of the goods, (5) not geographically descriptive or misdescriptive, and (6) not merely a surname. Historically, the United States only registered marks that were in

actual use. Following other countries, the United States now will permit registration if the applicant attests that it intends to use the mark in the near future.

As with copyright, the emergence of the Internet has raised new issues in trademark law. Domain name disputes have been of particular prevalence. A domain name is a text-based address that users enter in an Internet browser to reach a website. Examples include http://www.amazon.com or http://www.yahoo.com. In the real world, geographic distance and the contrast of different products often permits more than one individual to register the same mark. Yet on the Internet there can only be one "american.com." To settle disputes over the priority to a domain name, a dispute resolution mechanism has been established through ICANN, an international group that grants domain names.

Another trademark issue arising in the online context is *cybersquatting*. Cybersquatting is the practice of registering a domain name based on a popular trademark before the legal holder of the mark does. The registrant, or cybersquatter, then offers to sell the domain name to the trademark holder at an exorbitant price. This "ransoming" can infringe on a trademark holder's use of their mark and potentially dilute its value. The registration system for domain names originally permitted such behavior, but recently has given preference in the sale of domain names to holders of recognized trademarks. The United States, moreover, has enacted a statute, the Anti-Cybersquatting Act, to restrict the practice.

Patent. A patent grants its holder the exclusive right to use or sell a product or process for a limited time. Patentable items must be novel products or processes that embody a nonobvious advance in the current art and are capable of industrial application. Patentable subjects include new machines, chemical compounds, foods, and product designs. Discoveries of natural occurrences generally are not patentable, although patents are awarded to bioengineered plants and foods.

Unlike copyrights and trademarks, patents do not originate in creation or use. They are granted by statutory authority. An inventor must file a patent application detailing the proposed product or process and the way in which the product or process is novel and useful. Novel items represent significant advances in the state of the art and go above and beyond obvious ideas. The standard of novelty is higher than the originality requirement of copyright and is intended to avoid protecting inventions that only slightly modify existing works. In exchange for this higher standard, patents offer the strongest form of IP protection. A patent precludes a second party from asserting independent creation—copyright does not.

In the United States, Article I, Section 8 of the Constitution authorizes Congress to "promote the Progress of Science and useful Arts" by creating a national patent system to secure "for limited Times to . . . Inventors the exclusive Right to their respective . . . Discoveries." Congress has delegated authority to the Patent and Trademark Office to scrutinize patent applications and grant patents to items that are novel and useful. Most countries utilize a patent approval process similar to the PTO's. However, the degree of requisite novelty and usefulness often vary.

Patents have limited duration. In the United States, the PTO recognizes three general types of patents: utility patents, plant patents, and design patents. The terms for utility and plant patents run twenty years from the date of application; design patents fourteen years from the date of their grant. Patent duration is considerably shorter than copyright duration, and these periods mirror those granted internationally. After a patent expires, the invention falls into the public domain.

During its lifetime, a patent grants its owner the rights to exclude others from making, using, or selling the patented invention. The patent holder can enforce her rights by suing for monetary damages as well as by seeking a court order to stop unauthorized use of the invention. Patents and their accompanying rights are also transferable. A patent holder can license its invention or sell the patent outright. The United States does not require that the patent holder ever use, manufacture, or license a patented invention. Many other nations, in contrast, require that a patent holder "work," or use, the patent to maintain protection.

Patents are also subject to compulsory licenses. A compulsory license enables a third party to use a patented product or process without the permission of the patent holder, provided that the third party pays a set royalty rate and makes a reasonable effort to obtain a standard license through good faith bargaining.

Advances in technology have raised new issues in patent law. The United States and other nations have issued patents for sequences in the DNA structures of humans. It is controversial whether these are scientific discoveries and not the subject of patent protection. Finally, challenges have been raised regarding the applicability of patent protections during times of national crisis. The Africa AIDS crisis led several African nations to challenge the validity of U.S. pharmaceutical patents for AIDS treatment drugs. The nations have proposed suspending their recognition of foreign patents to enable them to produce the medications at low cost. They have sought to grant compulsory licenses to manufacture the drugs at lower costs. Challenges have also been made to patents granted to online business models. The United States has issued patents for "one-click" online shopping, which opponents argue not only affords protection to an obvious idea, but grants a monopoly over a process that could have enormous efficiency value if better allocated.

[See also Patent Law Practice; Technology and Law]

• Donald S. Chisum, *Intellectual Property: Copyright, Patent and Trademark*, 1980. Earl Kinter and Jack Lahr, *An Intellectual Property Law Primer*, 1982. Lester Nelson, *Digest of Intellectual Property Laws of the World*, 1997. Debora J. Halbert, *Intellectual Property in the Information Age*, 1999. —Steven Hetcher

PROPERTY, PERSONAL. The *common law distinguished between personal property and real property, or the rights in land. Personal property is any object susceptible of ownership that is not real property. The object is often described as a good or a chattel, and objects in their totality are referred to as goods or personalty. Personal property may be either tangible (e.g., physical objects) or intangible (e.g., bank accounts). Because there is no widely used system for recording the title to personal property in public records, the basis for ownership of personal property is typically a right to possession of an object.

There are fewer forms of ownership in use for personalty than for real property. Sometimes a life estate is involved, and often objects are placed in trust by one person for another. Full title to an object is known as absolute ownership.

Acquisition. Personal property issues typically involves one of the law's basic concepts—possession. A person acquires possession by (1) intending to and (2) actually seizing possession of an object. For example, the initial possession of wild animals may be gained by hunters who kill or capture them. (Possession of wild animals, so often discussed to introduce American law students to the concept of possession, is a part of the common intellectual culture of American lawyers.)

Later possessors are also entitled to some legal protection, and cases protecting them have been particularly influential in evolving rules to protect possession. The leading case on the subject is English—*Armory* v. *Delamirie* (King's Bench 1722), which pitted a lowly chimneysweep who had found a jewel against a famous jeweler. The sweep won, the court holding that the finder of a lost object may acquire a right to possession good against everyone, except the owner. From this, courts have derived the rule that prior possessors, like finders, may acquire a right good against everyone except the owner. So prior possessors prevail over later possessors of the same object; thus a first finder of an object has a right of possession superior to that of a second finder. Prior possessors may elect to recover either the object itself (in a *replevin lawsuit) or the value of the object (in a suit in trover).

Because objects are often found by persons on land that they do not own, the right to possession is often claimed by both the finder and the landowner. In a suit between these parties, the fact that the finder was trespassing or did not report the find to the landowner, can mean that the landowner prevails. American cases seem to favor nontrespassing, honest finders, giving expression to the maxim "finders keepers." This is often the result of statutes, enacted in many states, for the disposition of lost and found objects.

No matter the number of later possessors, an owner may either recover an object or sue for its value, on the basis either of proof of title or prior or superior possession. An owner may sue for an object's value on a theory that courts may force a later possessor to buy it; in this "forced sale," the measure of *damages is the value of the object at the time of the sale. An owner may also sue for damage to an object, on the theory that the assertion of rights associated with ownership by a later possessor represents a conversion of the owner's rights.

Transfer. Possession or title to personalty may be transferred in six ways. Three are voluntary—gift, bailment, and sale. Three are involuntary—adverse possession, accession, and confusion.

A inter vivos gift is a gratuitous transfer of an object and requires its delivery by the donor to the donee. Delivery is the transfer of a right or title to an object by (1) its physical transfer, with (2) an intent to transfer the object to a transferee. The delivery must also be (3) accepted by the transferee. When the object is too bulky or heavy to be delivered physically, a transferor may substitute a symbolic delivery, as when the keys to heavy piece of furniture are delivered. Delivery may also be constructive, meaning that the transferor denies himself future control over an object, as when handing over the keys to a locked box is a transfer of possession of the objects in the box.

If the object given is capable of physical delivery, it must be so delivered; courts are suspicious otherwise. Indeed, courts are generally suspicious of gifts—the law's underlying assumption is that people do not usually give their things away.

Such suspicions are particularly evident when the gift involved is a gift causa mortis, a gift made in contemplation of the donor's impending death. This type of gift is typically regarded as conditional and revocable: thus, if the death does not occur from the cause contemplated, the gift is automatically revoked. Another type of gift regarded as conditional involves engagement rings. If there is no wedding, the ring generally must be returned.

A gift initially made subject to an oral condition, however, usually becomes unconditional once a delivery occurs. If the condition is to survive the delivery, it must be written in a deed of gift.

A bailment is a delivery of possession of an object for a limited purpose, without a transfer of ownership. Commercial bailments are everyday transactions. They arise when someone brings clothes to a cleaner, or a watch to a jeweler for repair. In such situations, the transferees, or bailees, have a duty to treat the bailed objects as their own and to exercise due care under the circumstances. Bailees are not insurers of the objects, but the extent of their duty of care is traditionally determined by defining whether the bailment benefited the bailor, the bailee, or both. When the bailor is the beneficiary, the bailee is liable only for gross negligence. A bailee who alone benefits is liable for a failure to use extraordinary care. If the bailment is for mutual benefit, the bailee must use ordinary care or diligence. Special statutory rules govern the *liability of warehousemen.

Bailments are regarded as governed by a blend of *contract and property rules; thus bailors and bailees may establish liability by contract, except that bailees may not exculpate themselves from gross negligence. At a bailment's end, the bailee has an absolute duty to redeliver the object to the bailor, a duty imposed whether or not the bailee's inability to redeliver is due to negligence, although today it too may be the subject of an agreement otherwise.

A sale is a transfer for money or other legal consideration. It is again accomplished by delivery, accompanied typically by the delivery of a deed transferring the title to, or a bill of sale for, the object. The deed or bill of sale identifies what is sold and states the purchase price and the terms of the sale. A seller may not convey (a word referring to a transfer by deed) a better title than he has—a rule today found in the Uniform Commercial Code, § 2–403, enacted in all states except one. For example, a thief has no title to convey, thus has a void title. Such a title cannot be made absolute in the hands of any subsequent buyer. In the same vein, a conditional donee can only convey subject to the condition, and a bailee has only a limited possessory right to transfer.

These rules are subject to three exceptions necessary to give security and certainty to commercial transactions. One involves acquisition of an object from its owner not by theft but by dishonesty (e.g., by paying with a bad check), in a situation indicating that the owner meant to deal with the buyer. In this situation, the buyer acquires a voidable title. When that buyer resells the object to a person who pays for it and takes delivery in good faith, without knowledge of the seller's earlier dishonesty, the owner may not thereafter recover it. The second buyer is known as a bona fide purchaser.

The focus of two further exceptions is on the owner instead of the buyer. The first involves the doctrine of estoppel, under which conduct of the owner prevents him from reasserting ownership. A second exception involves the entrustment of an object to a merchant who regularly deals in objects of the type sold to a bona fide purchaser. When any of these three exceptions applies, the right and title of an owner can be defeated by a later buyer.

Title may also be transferred by its adverse possession. Every American jurisdiction has a statute of limitations requiring that lawsuits to recover personalty be brought within a certain number of years from the time the cause of action accrued. Thus the possession of an object by a person without a previous right or title for the period of adverse possession runs out the statute of limitations in two respects. It not only bars the owner from bringing a lawsuit to assert superior right to possession, but also transfers both the right and the title to the object to the adverse possessor. These statutes have been given a judicial gloss, requiring that an adverse possessor make an (1) actual, (2) exclusive, (3) continuous, (4) hostile, and (5) open and notorious use of the object throughout the period during which the owner may bring a lawsuit to recover it. (These five requirements for adverse possession are the same for real property as for personalty.) The "open and notorious" requirement is often a stumbling block for persons attempting to hold personalty adversely. For example, hanging a valuable painting on the wall of a private residence may not be open and notorious

enough for many courts. Adverse possession is a means of assigning ownership to the person who actually uses an object—the twin underlying assumptions being that the actual, long-continuing user merits protection, and that a non-using owner has no use or cares little for the object.

The time when the right to bring suit against an adverse possessor begins has been the subject of two distinct legal rules. The first rule states that the adverse possession period does not begin at the time of the true owner's loss, but is delayed until the owner either discovers, or should have discovered the whereabouts of the object. This delay is granted only so long as the owner exercises diligence in attempting to discover the whereabouts of the object. The second rule is that the period does not begin until the owner makes a demand for return of the object and is refused, without regard to other evidence of the owner's lack of diligence.

Another method of transfer of an object by operation of law involves its accession. An accession is the physical attachment of an object as a component of another, more complicated product, so that it is not severable without damage to the product—as for example when ink and paper are combined to produce this essay. Auto parts may be incorporated into an engine or an engine into an automobile. When the goods or objects of two or more different owners are incorporated together, the title to the component is given to the owner of the principal object produced. Who gets title is often determined by the relative values of the component and the product. Thus, even if an artist steals a canvas, once he has painted a valuable picture on it, the painting (including the canvas) is his. Accession is a means of assigning title to one owner so as to simplify and centralize ownership and management decisions about the resulting product.

Related to the doctrine of accession is that of confusion, or the combination of two similar substances into a uniform mass—as when the wheat crops of several farmers are put in the same silo—so that the separate identity of each is lost. Here the need to place title in a single person is trumped by the ease of allocating each owner a respective share of the resulting mass; so all contributors own the mass in common. While accession is a doctrine meant to vest title in a single owner, confusion is not.

Finally, personalty may become a fixture. That is, an object may be attached and adapted to real property, with an intent that it be permanently affixed, so that it is not severable without damage to the property as a whole. Courts view the intention to affix personal property as the most important element. For example, a house can be attached to land and become a fixture on it, and a furnace can be attached to the house, and become a fixture in it. So may a stove, or a refrigerator, become a fixture. At some point, however, the object alleged to be a fixture is light enough, moveable enough, or replaceable enough, so that the law will not classify it as a fixture. Moreover, under the trade fixture rule, tenants are usually allowed to remove trade items upon the expiration of a lease.

Many areas of personal property law overlap. For example, possession and delivery have both subjective (intent) and objective (seizing or actually delivering) aspects. A finder may be regarded as a gratuitous bailee. A bailment for the bailee's benefit may sometimes come close to a gift. Accessorizing and fixturizing have similarities. These and other, similar relationships make personal property law simultaneously simple and complex.

• Oliver Wendell Holmes Jr., *The Common Law* 162–194 (Lecture VI, "Possession") 1881, reprinted 1963. Mark DeWolfe Howe and William T. Fryer, eds., *Readings on Personal Property,* 3d ed., 1938. Walter Raushenbush, *The Law of Personal Property by Ray Andrews Brown,* 3d ed., 1975. Barlow Burke, *Personal Property in a Nutshell,* 2d ed., 1993. Bruce Welling, *Property in Things in the Common Law System,* 1996.

—Barlow Burke

PROPERTY, REAL. The rules of property regulate human relationships that involve things of value. In the *common-law system, these rules are divided into those applying to personal property, meaning movable assets (intangible or tangible), and those applying to real property, assets regarded as immovable, notably land. This distinction was based on the view of land as a sufficiently unique asset to warrant separate legal treatment. Unlike chattels (tangible, movable property), land is deemed to endure forever, and thus it requires a legal system that accounts for future interests in a far more complex fashion than does personal property law. And the immobility of land—the impossibility of moving it from one jurisdiction to another—gives the rules of real property a flavor that is both more insular and less responsive to demands for national uniformity than is so for many other branches of the law.

"Land" is frequently used as a synonym for "real property," but in terms of legal principles it is not to be confused with the soil located on the land in that place. Soil is readily removed and can be taken elsewhere and so is only an approximate equivalent of the land where it is situated. Real property, or land, is best understood in terms of spatial dimensions, measured above and below the surface and along compass lines on the surface itself. Because rights in land extend "to the heavens above and the depths below," ownership may be above or below the surface (as in a second floor condominium or a basement garage) as well as at ground level, and trespasses may occur by unpermitted overhead or underground activity (air flights or slant wells) as well as by surface entries.

Real property also includes "fixtures," chattels that were personal property until they became affixed to land in a permanent fashion so as to thereafter be recharacterized as land. A conveyance (transfer) of title (legal ownership) to land carries with it not only the soil within the described boundaries but also the structures built thereon, as well as built-in fixtures, even when none of these are mentioned in the deed. Crops grown on the land represent a reverse transition from real to personal property, once they are severed.

Estates in Land. As real property has diminished as the dominant form of wealth in the United States, and as land is regarded more as a commodity than as the primary vehicle for preserving and transmitting wealth to future generations, both the forms and the rules of "estates" in land have been considerably simplified.

To say that a person "owns" land means more precisely that he has an estate in that land. From a commercial point of view, what is most important is the location and spatial dimension of the land; but from a legal perspective, the temporal element is more important: the duration of one's interest in the land—whether for five years, or life, or potentially (through heirs) forever. The same rules are generally as applicable to a small parcel of land as to an extensive area. Thus, the major categories of ownership interests in land have always involved time.

Depending on whether a person is entitled to present or only future possession of some land, her interest is referred to as a "present estate" or a "future interest" in that land. "Future" is somewhat misleading, since the interest has a present value and may be sold or transferred (much as a stock option); it is only the right of possession of the property that is postponed.

Present estates in land were traditionally divided into "freeholds" and "nonfreeholds" and subject to different rules and judicial procedures. Consistent with the primacy of temporal considerations, only freehold estates were regarded as featuring a lack of any ascertainable termination date. Thus, an estate for life was deemed a freehold and therefore more valuable than a nonfreehold estate of a fixed term, even though that term might be 999 years. The law of nonfreehold estates has developed into *landlord-tenant law.

The present freehold estates in land consist of the "fee simple," inheritable by the heirs of the owner, and the "life estate," which terminates on the death of the owner. (An earlier intermediate estate, the "fee tail," inheritable only by the lineal descendants of the owner and not by her general heirs, has almost entirely disappeared from the American estate system.) Future interests arise whenever the present estate held by the owner does not constitute the complete (absolute) fee simple. Thus if O, owning a fee simple absolute, conveys a life estate to A, O retains a future interest—known as a reversion—that entitles O (or her heirs) to take possession of the property upon the death of A. If, instead, O conveys her fee simple estate "to A for life, and then to B and his heirs," B's future interest is called a remainder (in fee simple) and replaces the reversion held by O in the first example.

Future interest may be conditional, as in "to A for life and then to B and his heirs if B is married at the time of A's death." In this case, B has a "contingent remainder" (rather than a vested remainder), because it is uncertain whether B will ever be entitled to take possession of the property. Remainders are also considered to be contingent when they are given to unascertained persons, as in "to A for life and then to his widow." A future interest that is not vested may be subject to legal destruction if its remoteness (in time) makes title to the property too unmarketable for present purposes, such as the ability to convey it or to borrow money on it. The Rule against Perpetuities (1682) invalidated any interest that was capable of vesting more than twenty-one years after some life then in being, as in "to A for life and then to her first child who marries," since that child might be as yet unborn and might not marry thereafter until A has been dead for more than twenty-one years. Because the common-law version of the rule too often frustrated legitimate goals, it has been widely replaced by new versions that invalidate future interests only when they fail to vest within ninety years (and "wait and see" whether that will happen) or that abolish the old rule altogether.

Co-ownership. When two or more people share concurrent ownership of the same land, special rules regulate the many aspects of their relationship. Although such rules often appear complicated and unnecessary, they eliminate the need for the parties to draft lengthy agreements covering all possible future contingencies. The American legal system has created several forms of concurrent ownership of land. The two usual forms are "tenancy in common" and "joint tenancy." (These interests can be held by more than two persons—that is, title can be held by three or four tenants in common or joint tenants—but for convenience co-ownership is treated here as encompassing only two.) When the two parties are married to one another, they may have the further options of holding the land as "tenants by the entirety" or as "community property."

Tenancy in common is the loosest and most general form of co-ownership. Any two or more persons may hold title in this way, and this is the form of ownership presumed to exist unless another concurrent interest is expressly indicated. Although the interests of tenants in common are undivided—that is, none can claim that any particular part of the land belongs to him rather than the others—the fractional shares are separately owned, e.g., if A and B are tenants in common, on the death of A, her interest will pass only to her heirs or devisees, free of any ownership claim by B. The shares of each tenant are independently transferable, and there is no requirement that they be equal.

A condominium project generally involves participants who share ownership of the common features of the project (external walls, common hallways) as tenants in common and at the same time separately own an individual unit, which may itself be owned in tenancy in common or otherwise. For example, A and B may own unit 101 as joint tenants among themselves, while owning the common parts of the entire project as tenants in common with the owners of all the other units. In a cooperative project, title to an entire apartment building generally is held by a corporation, and owners acquire the right to possess individual units through acquisition of stock in the corporation together with proprietary leases to those units.

Joint tenancy creates a closer relationship between owners by imposing the principle of survivorship at death: the share of the first joint tenant to die belongs to the surviving tenant, even if another party may have been named in the will or qualified as the heir of the decedent. Joint tenancy generally requires explicit language identifying it as such in the creating document. Individual joint tenants, like tenants in common, may convey (transfer) their interests without the consent of the other; however, a conveyance by one joint tenant to a third party severs the joint tenancy, and the new owner becomes a tenant in common with the existing other owner.

Tenancy by the entirety is a form of joint tenancy between married tenants. The unity of person that characterized the marital state in common law, combined with the unity of title in joint tenancy, creates an even more intertwined estate. Tenants by the entirety cannot sever their estate by unilateral conveyance to a third party; the estate terminates only on *divorce (when it becomes either a joint tenancy or tenancy in common). This type of estate has been eliminated in many jurisdictions, especially those adopting community property principles.

Community property is an alternative system for spouses to hold title; it is borrowed from French and Spanish law and applies in seven western states and in Louisiana. In community property jurisdictions, spouses may continue to take title as tenants in common or as joint tenants, but there is a presumption that any property they acquire during the *marriage (except that acquired from gift, devise, or descent) is community rather than separate property, even though the nominal title may suggest otherwise. Like tenancy by the entirety, such shared ownership is terminated only by divorce, and any deed or mortgage must be executed by both spouses to be effective. Some nonwestern jurisdictions have created a somewhat comparable form of ownership through adoption of a Marital Property Act.

As is evident, then, the various types of estate co-ownership differ in terms of what happens to ownership on death, on transfer while living, and on divorce. These differences are of considerable significance to creditors, whose ability to reach all or half (or none) of the title of an asset held by both parties to satisfy a debt incurred by one of them may depend on the form of title. For instance, community property is generally liable for the debts of either spouse, whereas, conversely, tenancy by the entirety may be immune from the reach of creditors of either spouse (see DEBTOR AND CREDITOR).

Co-ownership also has consequences for accountings. Income received by one co-tenant for rental of the entire property is generally regarded as belonging to all the co-owners, but each co-owner is entitled to free possession of the entire property and is not liable for rent to the others for such sole occupancy. With regard to expenditures, a co-owner who pays expenses necessary to preserve the property (such as property taxes and joint *mortgage payments) is generally allowed to recover a proportionate share from the other owners, although perhaps only by way of a deduction from rental income received or from proceeds arising from sale or division of the property. Recovery for repairs and improvements is less likely, although, again, such expenditures may be taken into consideration if there is income to be distributed or if the property sells for an increased amount because of these improvements.

"Partition of the title" between the owners may result from an agreement between them or by court order when the parties can no longer manage the property in unison. "Partition in kind" occurs when each owner receives some physical part of the common property (thereby transforming the parties from undivided owners of a larger parcel into neighboring, separate owners of adjacent smaller parcels). If such physical partition is not possible, a court may order the property sold and the sale proceeds divided instead.

Landlord and Tenant. Current landlord-tenant law is far removed from its feudal origins, which treated the lease as a conveyance of a nonfreehold estate in land from landlord to tenant. Today, the lease is viewed as a *contract more than a conveyance, a contract involving an exchange of rent from the tenant in return for possession of the property and related services from the landlord. For residential leases, however, legislation and judicial intervention go well beyond even that approach, generally rejecting the notion of freedom of contract in the context of scarce urban housing.

The two basic types of nonfreehold estate in common law were the "term of years" and the "periodic" tenancy (a third category, the "tenancy at will," has no real legal significance). These differ in their method of termination: the term of years ends automatically on the termination date stated in the lease (a week, a month, ten years, etc.), whereas the periodic tenancy is automatically renewed at the end of each period unless proper notice of termination was given by either side. However, the "just cause" requirement of many rent-control ordinances may eliminate all right of a landlord to terminate an existing residential tenancy, either at the end of the lease term or, in the case of periodic tenancy, by advance notice; this has, de facto, created a new form of tenancy.

With the common-law emphasis on treating a lease as a conveyance of an estate in land, it was generally irrelevant whether the tenant stayed in possession during the lease term. A tenant who abandoned during the term of the lease could generally be held liable for the rent for the entire balance of the term (as it fell due) on the ground that the abandonment did not terminate the tenant's leasehold estate in the land. Correspondingly, the landlord was not entitled to relet the premises to a third party after abandonment, since the abandoning tenant still officially held the possessory estate in the property. Modern contract analysis of this situation frequently requires a landlord to mitigate damages by attempting to relet after tenant abandonment.

The converse situation occurs when the tenant fails to leave at the end of the tenancy. Common law gave the landlord the right to compel a "holdover" tenant to stay for another entire term, usually as a periodic tenant, regardless of how long the initial holdover lasted; this remedy does not receive much judicial acceptance today. The landlord's alternative right is to compel a holdover tenant to vacate the premises. Statutes in every jurisdiction generally deny the landlord the right to evict the tenant himself (self-help eviction) but make available a speedy action (usually known as "summary dispossess" proceedings) to accomplish this. Such actions are brought either when the tenant holds over after the natural termination of the term of years or periodic tenancy or when the tenant's estate is terminated prematurely by the landlord because of a default, usually in the payment of rent. The abbreviated nature of the proceedings has generated constitutional concerns about whether the tenant has been denied due process with regard to potential defenses.

The common-law view of the lease as a conveyance implied that the landlord had no obligations to the tenant for the condition of the premises. There was no liability for preexisting defects, since the principle of caveat emptor required the tenant to make an inspection before taking the lease; conversely, the obligation to correct problems that arose during the term of the lease fell on the tenant, since he was the one in possession. The only exceptions to these general principles of landlord nonliability were fraud and express warranties. Even when the landlord breached actual promises about the condition of the premises, however, the common-law doctrine that covenants in leases were independent meant the tenant was not entitled to quit or terminate the lease for that reason. This consequence has been mitigated through the judicial fiction of constructive eviction, which treats the landlord's failure to honor covenants in her lease as a breach of her covenant of quiet enjoyment and allows the tenant to quit and terminate her interdependent covenant to pay rent.

The tenant's obligations for the condition of the premises were determined by the doctrine of "waste," which compelled a tenant to treat the premises in a prudent way and to repair damage caused by his own activity (active waste) or damage arising from external causes but for which a small repair would have avoided a larger loss (passive waste), such as failing to board up a broken window during a rainstorm. In the residential field, an implied warranty of habitability is now a matter of public policy (i.e., without regard to what the lease provides) and entitles a tenant residing in substandard housing to withhold all or part of the rent (based upon diminution of value) for as long as the condition goes uncorrected.

When personal injuries resulted from a condition of the premises, the landlord historically had no liability because of the lack of any basic duty to repair. However, so many exceptions to this rule now exist—for example, where the landlord concealed the defect from the tenant, or promised to repair or was required by local law (building codes) to repair, or where injury occurred in a common area or common facility—that landlord liability is generally more common than nonliability. Commercial landlords especially are at risk for failing to protect their tenants from assaults and accidents occurring even outside the premises (such as in the building's parking garage) that might have been avoided by better security systems or other protective steps.

Leasehold transfer is one feature of landlord and tenant law that is not much changed from its feudal origins. As an estate in land, a leasehold is freely transferable by the tenant, although contrary restrictions in leases are upheld against charges that they constitute invalid restraints on alienation, at least where the landlord's power to consent to the transfer is not to be unreasonably withheld.

An "assignment" by a tenant transfers the entire remainder of his leasehold estate to an assignee, creating a new "privity of estate" between landlord and assignee, although not automatically terminating the old "privity of contract" between the tenant/assignor and his landlord. Hence, the landlord may recover rent from the old tenant if the assignee fails to pay it.

A tenant may also sublease his premises by giving a shorter term to the transferee than he holds himself (thereby technically retaining a reversion). When property is sublet, there is no direct landlord—tenant relation between the landlord and the subtenant, and their rights and duties may need to be enforced indirectly through the medium of the tenant.

A landlord is generally free to transfer (or encumber) her reversion, without requiring the tenant's assent, although it is common for the tenant to "attorn," i.e., acknowledge and accept, the new party. A transfer of leased property has no effect on the leases themselves.

Nonpossessory Interests in Land. The interests in land described thus far may be generally characterized as possessory, entitling their holder to occupy land to the fullest extent possible, including the right to exclude others from the land. But the "bundle of sticks" principle that characterizes most property analysis permits division of rights in land into smaller and more refined categories. It is not uncommon for a nonpossessor to have rights to use the land or to restrict the possessor in his use of the land.

Nonpossessory rights in land are generally termed "servitudes" when they arise from an agreement between the possessor and the holder of the right. When a third person is privileged to perform acts on the land that would otherwise be unprivileged (i.e., trespassory), for example, to walk across it, she is said to have an "easement" in the land. If she is entitled to compel the possessor to perform acts on his land that he would otherwise be free not to perform (e.g., to allow his tree to go untrimmed), she is said to hold a "covenant running with the land" (or "equitable servitude" or "restrictive covenant" or "real covenant"). If she is entitled to compel the possessor to refrain from performing acts on his land that he would otherwise be privileged to perform (e.g., to erect a structure that would block her view), she may hold either a negative easement or a negative covenant (in the following discussion treated as a covenant rather than an easement).

An easement does not entitle its holder to possess the land involved; it entitles her only to engage in some activity on it. The possessor of the property, the "servient owner" (or "servient tenant"), thus loses the right to prohibit the "dominant tenant" from engaging in that activity. Generally, an easement is created when the servient owner conveys that particular right in land to the other person. If the right may be exercised by the dominant tenant only in conjunction with her ownership of a particular parcel of land—usually neighboring land—her parcel is referred to as a "dominant tenement" and the easement is said to be "appurtenant" rather than "in gross" (meaning that the exercise of the easement is unconnected with the dominant tenant's ownership of any particular parcel of land).

Because an easement constitutes an interest in land, its proper creation generally requires compliance with the *Statute of Frauds, that is, proper execution and signature of an appropriate document. If only a revocable or short-term interest in land is intended, such as the right to visit a house for a party or to enter a theater to see a performance, the interest is referred to as a "license" and a written document is not required. Many easements are created as part of the subdivision of a larger parcel, wherein the subdivider "grants" to the owner of the newly created lot an easement for some use over the subdivider's retained part; alternatively the subdivider "reserves" from his grant an easement for a use by him over the granted part and for the benefit of his retained part.

When a subdivision has created two or more parcels, courts may infer that the parties intended to grant or reserve easements even though explicit language to that effect is missing from the deeds. Courts may hold that an easement by implied grant or implied reservation has been created when a similar usage (a "quasi-easement") existed before the land was divided, which was sufficiently obvious and permanent as to justify the inference that the parties intended this arrangement should survive the subdivision. Similarly, if a use was explicitly granted but only orally, so that only a license rather than an easement arose, detrimental reliance by the licensee may bar the licensor from revoking it, thereby converting the license into an easement. Finally, in some cases, although no consensual act of creation of an easement may have ever occurred, a wrongful activity on land by a stranger may have continued so long that it has imposed the bar of the statute of limitations on the servient owner, thereby creating for the wrongdoer an easement by prescription, on principles similar to adverse possession.

For a covenant to bind successor owners of the property ("run with the land"), a court generally must determine that the initial parties intended the covenant to have such an effect and that the covenant "touches and concerns" the land—that is, it relates to the land in such a way as to justify the inference that it should benefit and burden subsequent owners of the parcels involved, even though these owners were not privy to the original contract.

The transfer of the benefits and burdens of easements occurs automatically in connection with the transfer of the affected estates, especially with regard to easements appurtenant. The transferee of the dominant estate receives the benefit of the easement along with the estate itself, and the transferee of the servient estate takes it subject to the burden of the easement.

With regard to real covenants and equitable servitudes, older technical requirements severely impeded their ability to run with the land and affect successor owners. It was required that the original contracting parties be in "privity of estate" with one another (thus prohibiting ordinary neighbors from creating enforceable covenants). And it was also required that successor owners succeed to their entire estates of the original parties (making it difficult to bind or benefit tenants of the original parties). Courts of equity generally rejected those requirements in cases of equitable servitudes, and the new Restatement of Property (Third)—Servitudes formally proposes their elimination. If this policy is accepted, real covenants will bind and burden later owners of land in the same fashion as easements.

Because these situations involve limited usufructuary rights (rights of use) rather than unrestricted possessory rights, the most common disputes concern whether either party is violating the easement or covenant. Locational issues are perhaps the easiest to deal with: an easement of defined location cannot be enlarged or relocated by the dominant tenant. However, she may subdivide her existing parcel and thereby confer the benefit of the easement upon all of her partial grantees, as long as this does not unreasonably burden the servient tenant. Other claimed violations are harder to deal with, such as a dominant tenant's attempt to increase the number of trips and the type of vehicle used for travel. Courts generally assume that the original parties anticipated changes and intended to tolerate such changes as are consistent with normal development in the area and do not unreasonably burden the servient owner. In the case of easements, a servient tenant is considerably less restricted in scope than is a dominant tenant. He is free as a possessor to engage in any lawful activity that does not unreasonably interfere with the dominant tenant's rights.

The duration of servitudes is not generally different from that of possessory interests in land. Easements are commonly held in fee or for a term of years and subject to terminating conditions. When the date or event of termination occurs, the interest ends. Because servitudes always involve the existence of two owners of rights in the same land, the return of one party's interest to the holder of the other interest leads to the natural termination of the servitude. Thus an easement is terminated by its conveyance from dominant to servient tenant or by acquisition of the dominant land by the owner of the servient land (a termination by merger), since, by definition, a person cannot have an easement in his own land. The same is true for a release of a covenant executed by covenantee to covenantor, or their successors.

Informal forms of release may also be effective, as when the dominant tenant orally states that she no longer intends to use a right of way and then confirms that statement by constructing a fence blocking the old path. Less certain, but still possible, is a statement of intent to abandon supported by a long period of nonuse. Nonuse alone without the support of confirming words will not terminate the interest, since a person is not required to continue using an easement in order to preserve it, nor is a person required to continue demanding that a covenantor comply with his covenant when there is no indication of any breach of it.

Covenants also terminate when courts determine that enforcement is no longer appropriate. Common situations, especially when subdivision restrictions are involved, include cases in which the enforcing parties are themselves guilty of similar breaches ("unclean hands"), or have tolerated others' engaging in similar breaches without complaint ("acquiescence"), or have delayed too long in seeking enforcement ("prescription" or "laches"). If external developments have made a restriction more burdensome to one party than it is beneficial to the other, the defense of changed conditions may apply.

• Robert C. Ellickson, Carol M. Rose, and Bruce A. Ackerman, eds., *Perspectives on Property Law*, 2d ed., 1995. Richard H. Chused, ed., *A Property Anthology*, 2d ed., 1997. Roger Bernhardt and Ann M. Burkhart, *The Black Letter Law of Real Property*, 3d ed., 1998. G. W. Thompson, *Commentaries on the Modern Law of Real Property*, 2d ed., 1998. John G. Sprankling, *Understanding Property Law*, 2000. William B. Stoebuck and Dale A. Whitman, *The Law of Property*, 3d ed., 2000. Roger Bernhardt and Ann M. Burkhart, *Real Property in a Nutshell*, 4th ed., 2001. Herbert Hovenkamp and Sheldon F. Kurtz, *The Law of Property: An Introductory Survey*, 5th ed., 2001. Liebman, ed., *A Concise Restatement of Property*, 2001. Joseph William Singer, *Introduction to Property*, 2001.

—Roger Bernhardt

PROPERTY RIGHTS. Anglo-American constitutional thought has long assigned a high place to the rights of property owners. Magna Carta, a document venerated by colonial Americans, protected owners against deprivation of property except by "the law of the land." The property-conscious tenets of English *common law were reinforced in colonial America by the availability of land. A large number of colonists became landowners, strengthening the appeal of doctrines that safeguarded property rights. The *natural law philosophy of John Locke stressed the link between private property and political *liberty. According to Locke, private property existed before the formation of government, and a principal purpose of government was to safeguard property rights. Strongly influenced by Locke, colonial Americans came to associate property and liberty, and to regard respect for property rights as a bulwark against arbitrary rule.

This keen attachment to private property did not, however, preclude any restrictions on the use of property and on economic behavior. Consistent with the prevalent mercantilist policy, colonial governments sought to regulate markets and to promote economic development. But regulations were difficult to enforce and there was persistent pressure for a free market in goods and wages. Moreover, colonial lawmakers generally awarded compensation when land was taken by eminent domain for roadways or other public projects.

The American Revolution produced seemingly contradictory behavior toward private property rights. On one hand, Revolutionary rhetoric frequently linked political liberty and property ownership. Early state constitutions contained provisions to safeguard property rights; a number, for instance, affirmed the natural right of "acquiring, possessing and protecting property." The Massachusetts constitution of 1780 expressly required compensation when private property was taken for public use. On the other hand, the Revolution generated wholesale interference with private property. State legislatures enacted bills of attainder that confiscated property owned by Loyalists, and took steps to repudiate debts owed to British creditors.

Attacks on the rights of property owners continued in the post-Revolutionary era. State lawmakers repeatedly interfered in debtor-creditor relations, most notably by issuing depreciated paper currency. Many political leaders became convinced that the state governments could not be relied upon to protect economic rights.

The establishment of stronger safeguards for property ownership was one of the main objectives of the Constitutional Convention of 1787. The framers expressed the Lockean view that

property was the basis of civil society and essential for political liberty. In addition, they emphasized the economic utility of private property, believing that security of property and respect for contractual arrangements would promote national prosperity by encouraging capital investment.

Accordingly, numerous provisions of the Constitution and Bill of Rights relate to property rights. The contract clause prevented the states from passing any law "impairing the Obligation of Contracts." Even more significant was the Fifth Amendment, which declared that no person should be "deprived of life, liberty, or property, without due process of law; nor shall private property be taken for public use, without just compensation." The Constitution also contained provisions to safeguard property in slaves and to prevent Congress or the states from confiscating property by means of bills of attainder. Further, it authorized Congress to protect intellectual *property by the award of copyrights and patents to authors and inventors. The federal Constitution and Bill of Rights strongly influenced later state constitutions. Many states, for example, added takings and *contract clauses to their fundamental law. These developments at the state level strengthened the standing of property in the constitutional culture.

At times invoking the precepts of natural law, federal courts early manifested their willingness to curtail state infringement of property and contractual rights. In *Vanhorne's Lessee* v. *Dorrance* (1795), for instance, Justice William Paterson declared: "The preservation of property . . . is a primary object of the social compact." Such constitutional rulings anticipated the jurisprudence of the Supreme Court under John *Marshall (1801–35).

In a far-reaching line of decisions the Marshall Court molded the contract clause into a powerful guard of property interests. Marshall held in *Fletcher* v. *Peck* (1810) that a state was barred from impairing its contracts, and that hence Georgia could not rescind a land grant. The most significant application of the contract clause by the Marshall Court, though, occurred in *Dartmouth College* v. *Woodward* (1819), which determined that a corporate charter was a constitutionally protected contract. Rendered at a time when Americans were increasingly relying on corporate enterprise to achieve economic growth, *Dartmouth College* assisted business interests by curtailing public control of corporations through charter revocation or amendment. Similarly, the Marshall Court invoked the contract clause to prevent state legislatures from revoking grants of tax immunity and discharging debts incurred before enactment of insolvency laws.

This judicial insistence on the sanctity of contract secured private arrangements and encouraged reliance on the private ordering of the economy. During much of the nineteenth century the states were the primary source of regulation; decisions limiting the exercise of state authority meant, for all practical purposes, that economic activity would be governed by market forces.

In contrast to its vigorous application of the contract clause, the Marshall Court declared that the takings clause of the Fifth Amendment did not bind the states. In *Barron* v. *Mayor and City of Baltimore* (1833), the justices held that the Bill of Rights limited only the power of the federal government. Consequently, states took the initiative in fashioning eminent domain law. Antebellum state courts generally adopted a broad definition of public use and sustained the delegation of eminent domain powers to canal and railroad companies. They also grappled with the vexing issue whether physical invasion or diminution in the value of land resulting from public improvements constituted a taking.

State judges additionally began to fashion due process into a substantive restraint on legislative authority over economic rights. Thus, in *Wynehamer* v. *People* (1856), the New York Court of Appeals struck down a prohibition statute, as applied to liquor on hand when the law took effect, as a deprivation of property without *due process. Such decisions foreshadowed the development of a substantive reading of the due process clause of the Fourteenth Amendment (ratified in 1868) to protect property rights.

The Civil War and the adoption of the Thirteenth Amendment in 1865 destroyed *slavery as a form of property. Wartime exigencies had forced the federal government to assume greater responsibility with respect to the economy. In order to finance the war, Congress had levied the first income tax and issued a large amount of paper money, known as greenbacks. The Supreme Court upheld these steps toward national control of the currency and fiscal policy.

Industrialization proceeded rapidly in the decades following the Civil War. Legislators sought to restrain the unfettered operation of the market, to assist farmers, and to mitigate employment conditions. In response, business interests increasingly turned to the courts as a safeguard against laws that entrepreneurs felt were an arbitrary interference with their economic rights. They argued

that the due process clause of the Fourteenth Amendment provided a basis for federal courts to review state laws. At first the Supreme Court rejected this view. In *Munn* v. *Illinois* (1877) the justices upheld a statute that regulated rates for storing grain in elevators, and seemingly allowed the states latitude to control the use of private property "devoted to a public use."

During the 1880s, however, the Supreme Court, as well as state courts, began to view state *regulation of business enterprise more skeptically. This new outlook reflected the influence of leading constitutional theorists, such as Thomas M. Cooley and Christopher G. Tiedeman, who were critical of most governmental involvement in the economy. Equally important was an enlarged understanding of property. Courts and commentators recognized that property ownership went beyond physical possession and encompassed the right to use property for economic gain. Federal and state courts increasingly took the position that, under the due process clause, they could scrutinize both the purpose behind state regulations and the means employed to achieve the stated goals. Developing this concept of substantive due process, courts assessed regulations against a reasonableness standard and struck down measures deemed unduly restrictive of property rights.

During the chief justiceship (1888–1910) of Melville W. Fuller the Supreme Court showed considerable solicitude for the rights of property owners. Wielding the doctrine of substantive due process, the Fuller Court insisted that regulated industries, such as railroads, were entitled to a reasonable return on investment, which implied limiting state regulatory authority. It developed the liberty of contract principle, and ruled that states could not interfere with contractual freedom. The Fuller Court also gave a new vitality to the takings clause, holding that the just compensation requirement was an essential element of due process applicable to the states. In *Pollock* v. *Farmers' Loan & Trust Co.* (1895) a divided Court invalidated the 1894 federal income tax as an unconstitutional direct tax. Although dedicated to economic liberty as a vital constitutional value, the Fuller Court nonetheless upheld many health and safety regulations.

After 1900 the Progressive movement sought to address problems associated with the new industrial and urban society by promoting a more active role for government in regulating the economy. These regulations necessarily circumscribed traditional property rights and free-market ordering.

The Supreme Court closely reviewed such legislation, but sustained workers' compensation laws and statutes limiting the working hours of women. Even as the Court accommodated a degree of heightened control of economic life, though, it continued to treat unfavorably laws that regulated labor-management relations (see LABOR LAW: LABOR RELATIONS), imposed barriers to new businesses, or set minimum wages.

Land use controls gained popularity in the early decades of the twentieth century. In *Buchanan* v. *Warley* (1917) the Supreme Court voided residential *segregation laws as a deprivation of property without due process, and some state courts in the early 1920s were initially hostile to *zoning ordinances as an interference with owners' use of their land. Yet the Supreme Court sustained the constitutionality of comprehensive zoning in *Village of Euclid* v. *Ambler Realty Co.* (1926). In practice, zoning tended to stabilize neighborhood property values, and put a premium on majority preferences, not the rights of individual owners. For decades after *Euclid* most courts deferred to the regulation of land use by local governments.

As states more vigorously controlled land use, the Supreme Court also ruled that a regulation might be so severe as to effectuate a *taking of property for which compensation was required. Thus, Justice *Holmes stated in *Pennsylvania Coal Co.* v. *Mahon* (1922): "The general rule at least is, that while property may be regulated to a certain extent, if regulation goes too far it will be recognized as a taking." The Court, however, proved reluctant to apply this doctrine for decades.

The Great Depression and the political triumph of the New Deal marked a watershed in the constitutional protection accorded property rights. The New Deal hoped to alleviate economic distress and promote general social welfare by enlarging governmental responsibility and redistributing wealth. The Supreme Court, adhering at first to the traditional constitutional values of limited government and respect for private property, invalidated a number of New Deal measures in 1935 and 1936. Under great political pressure, however, several justices changed their position and looked more favorably on expanded governmental control of the economy.

Even more significant, the Supreme Court relegated property rights to a secondary position in the constitutional order. In *United States* v. *Carolene Products Co.* (1938), the justices fashioned a dichotomy between property rights and other personal liberties, and established a higher level of judicial review for the preferred category of personal rights. The dubious distinction between property rights and other liberties represented a sharp break with the Constitutional framers' belief that economic rights and political freedom were inseparable. But the upshot was that property rights were virtually removed from the constitutional agenda for years.

The concept of constitutionally protected property rights evolved in seemingly contradictory ways after World War II. Governmental regulation of business expanded, and the drive for *environmental protection generated new and often sweeping restrictions on land use. State and federal courts upheld a broad exercise of eminent domain power to achieve public purposes. The Supreme Court, in *Nollan* v. *California Coastal Commission* (1987), began to scrutinize land use regulations and to put teeth into the regulatory takings doctrine. Likewise, a number of states enacted laws that mandate the payment of compensation when governmental action has diminished the value of property under certain circumstances. At the start of the twenty-first century judges and legislators continued to adjust the perceived need to regulate economic behavior with the Constitution's express protection of property ownership. Although property receives less constitutional protection than at earlier times in American history, private ownership still enjoys a degree of judicial solicitude.

• Stuart Bruchey, "The Impact of Concern for the Security of Property Rights on the Legal System of the Early American Republic," *Wisconsin Law Review* (1980): 1135–58. Richard A. Epstein, *Takings: Private Property and the Power of Eminent Domain*, 1985. Jennifer Nedelsky, *Private Property and the Limits of American Constitutionalism*, 1990. James W. Ely Jr., *The Chief Justiceship of Melville W. Fuller, 1888–1910*, 1995. Carol M. Rose, "Property as the Keystone Right," *Notre Dame Law Review* 71 (1996): 329–66. James W. Ely Jr., *The Guardian of Every Other Right: A Constitutional History of Property Rights*, 2nd ed., 1998. Gregory S. Alexander, *Commodity and Propriety: Competing Visions of Property in American Legal Thought, 1776–1970*, 1997. Richard Pipes, *Property and Freedom*, 1999.

—James W. Ely Jr.

PROPERTY TAX. *See* Taxation: Property Taxes.

PROPRIETORSHIP, SOLE. *See* Business Organizations.

PROSECUTOR. The prosecutor occupies a unique position in the American criminal justice system. She is expected to serve both the victim and the accused and adhere to the formal rules of the legal system while also reflecting state and local values.

Charged with formal responsibilities in the administration of justice, the prosecutor necessarily also weighs the social and political implications of decisions.

Though much of American law descends from the British *common-law tradition, the English system relied on private prosecution, a practice never adopted in the American colonies. Early in American history, and continuing throughout the seventeenth century, the authority to bring criminal actions in the thirteen colonies was vested in the *attorney general. After the Revolutionary War, the system became increasingly professional, as all states (beginning in the 1830s) established a generally elected office of public prosecutor. A connection between prosecutors and the electorate promoted both local control of the administration of justice and the nation's geographic expansion

As the nation grew in size, population, and complexity, so too did the domain of the prosecutor, thus allowing, indeed *requiring*, increased prosecutorial discretion. *Police and prosecutors eventually replaced *judges and juries as the essential agents of case disposition in the twentieth century. The expanded prosecutorial role, and consequent passivity of judges, has been criticized by some scholars, but this transfer of power—enlarging the domain of authority, increasing discretion, and demarcating the prosecutor as an active and visible legal/political figure in the community—is essential to understanding the modern prosecutor as the central actor in the criminal justice system.

Moreover, to appreciate the position and influence of the American prosecutor, we must note that the United States has nearly 3,000 prosecutorial systems—an office in each of the ninety-four federal districts (varying widely in size, structure, and values: compare the U.S. attorney's office in Wyoming with that in the Southern District of New York), a system in each of the fifty states (as most cases involve violations of state law), and 2,700 offices at the county level. Consistent with American *federalism, and in contrast to, for example, the French system of public prosecution as a nationwide service, prosecutorial duties in the United States are divided between the U.S. attorneys (and the two thousand assistant U.S. attorneys), who address violations of federal law (mostly drug, white-collar, and corruption cases); the state attorneys general, whose powers and prosecutorial agendas vary across states and political environments; and the multitude of prosecutors at the county level, who process the large majority of cases. Given that prosecutors are generally elected officials at the county and state level (except in New Jersey and Connecticut), and bearing in mind that each state has an elected attorney general and that federal prosecutors (appointed by the U.S. attorney general's office) can be replaced with a change of executive administration, the office of prosecutor—and the motives, behavior, obligations, and decisions of the actors themselves—must be understood in a legal and political sense.

Charged with the responsibility to prosecute all crimes and civil actions to which the local, state, or federal government may be party, American prosecutors enjoy considerable freedom of choice in the day-to-day execution of their official duties. Thus, in contrast to the German system, for example, in which prosecutors are required to prosecute all offenders, the American system both permits and promotes a regulated degree of prosecutorial autonomy. And thus, although the American system is an amalgam of European models—and the American prosecutor shares some characteristics with European officers—the discretion, localism, and authority inherent to the office ensure that the prosecutor in the United States has no exact or even approximate counterpart in the world.

In carrying out their duties, prosecutors receive much of their education "on the job." Pledged to the enforcement of the law, but increasingly aware of the realities of the system, prosecutors learn that they not only must depend on the cooperation of the police and other actors in the system but must also, at times, perform the function of the judge or law-enforcement agents. Thus, in their perceived responsibility to satisfy competing interests, in their capacity to set the agenda, frame the issues, and shape the values of their office and of the community in general, prosecutors are the principal agents in the administration of justice. Prosecutors specify what charges to file (if any), what charge revisions to accept during the *plea-bargaining process, what kinds of cases to concentrate on, and, by their rhetoric, disposition, and actions, what the "complex of values" in their office (and community) will be.

Yet, like any public official, prosecutors are also shaped by the communities in which they serve—feeling, for example, the need to be the voice of the community's demand for retribution—as they take cues from, and structure policies consistent with, perceived social roles and responsibilities. This discretion, like any imprecise grant of authority, is subject to potential abuse; but nonetheless, this concern is "trumped" by the gains associated with affording prosecutors substantial discretion—discretion that is essential if the prosecutor is to facilitate the disposition of cases by encouraging negotiated settlements.

In general, then, discretion, if used "correctly," allows for the exercise of prudence and judgment at the intersection of competing social values, interests, roles, and the formal law. (Consider, for example, the practice of "plea bargaining," an essential method of "extralegal" negotiation in the criminal justice system, considered and sanctioned by the United States Supreme Court in *Santobello* v. *New York* (1971) and *Bordenkircher* v. *Hayes* (1978).) Only by understanding the exercise of prosecutorial discretion can we appreciate the centrality of the prosecutor to the American criminal justice system. And only by evaluating how this discretion is used can we assess the consequences and propriety of the enormous power exercised by prosecutors in both the state and federal systems.

[*See also* Criminal Law Principles]

• Milton Heumann, *Plea Bargaining: The Experiences of Prosecutors, Judges, and Defense Attorneys*, 1977. Joan Jacoby, *The American Prosecutor: A Search for Identity*, 1980. George Cole, *The American System of Criminal Justice*, 7th ed., 1995. David Johnson, "The Organization of Prosecution and the Possibility of Order," *Law and Society Review* 32 (1998): 247–308. H. W. Perry Jr., "United States Attorneys—Whom Shall They Serve?" *Law and Contemporary Problems* 61 (1998): 129–48. Lara Beth Sheer, "Prosecutorial Discretion," *Georgetown Law Journal* 86 (1998): 1353–65.

—Milton Heumann and Brian K. Pinaire

PROSECUTORIAL DISCRETION. *See* Procedure, Criminal.

PROSSER, WILLIAM. William Prosser was born in New Albany, Indiana in 1898. He graduated Harvard College in 1918 and the University of Minnesota Law School in 1928. Between 1928 and 1948, he practiced law and taught at the University of Minnesota and Harvard Law Schools. In 1948, he accepted the deanship at the University of California–Berkeley Law School, a position he held until 1961. When he retired from Berkeley in 1963, he joined the Hastings College of Law, where he taught until his death in 1972.

Prosser was the most influential *torts scholar of his generation. His first major publication, a treatise titled *Handbook of the Law of Torts* (1941), won an immediate following. His casebook, *Cases and Materials on Torts* (1952), was one of the most widely adopted teaching tools in legal education. His articles on intentional infliction of mental distress, *strict liability for defective products, and the right of privacy, are among the most fre-

quently cited law review articles ever written. Prosser also substantially reconceptualized and redirected American tort law as the Reporter for the *American Law Institute's Restatement (Second) of Torts from 1955 to 1970.

Part of Prosser's influence was due to his personal qualities and abilities as a prose stylist. He was a gifted teacher and natural showman. His wide-ranging interests, talents, and humor placed him at the center of every group. In an era of turgid and technical academic prose, Prosser's writing was lucid, lively, and vivid. In Prosser's writings, striking examples frequently complement abstract statement.

Most of his eminence, however, flowed from the way his approach to torts meshed with the jurisprudence of mid-century America. Prosser blended the insights of *Legal Realism with the legal profession's reemerging interest in comprehensive doctrinal frameworks. As a Realist, he treated tort doctrine as judicially created law that sought to promote social welfare by providing accident victims with fair compensation. As a doctrinalist, he presented tort law as an evolving set of formulas whose application was sufficiently rigid to allow lawyers to predict case outcomes, yet sufficiently flexible to do justice in the every case. In Prosser's view, legal doctrine distilled the wisdom of countless cases and reflected the consensus of American society on problems of accident law. What distinguished Prosser was his formulation of tort law as an expression of America's distinctive and widely held values at a time when the search for consensus values dominated many areas of American intellectual life.

[*See also* Educator, Legal]

• G. Edward White, *Tort Law in America: An Intellectual History*, 1980 (139–79). David Jung, "Commentary on William Lloyd Prosser, Strict Liability to the Consumer in California," *Hastings Law Journal* 50 (1999): 681–99.

—Stephen A. Siegel

PROSTITUTION. *See* Morality, Ethics, and Crime; Morals Offenses; Organized Crime; Victimless Crimes.

PROTEST, PUBLIC. *See* Civil Disobedience.

PSYCHOLOGY AND LAW. With the publication of Hugo Munsterberg's *On the Witness Stand* (1908), modern scientific psychology entered the courtroom. However, it was not until the late 1960s that the discipline of psychology and law began to flourish. The field now has its own journals, *Law and Human Behavior* and *Psychology*,

Public Policy, and Law, and supports several graduate programs leading to joint degrees in psychology and law. It has also spawned two distinct subfields. Forensic psychology involves the study of issues at the intersection of clinical psychology and the law: insanity, offender risk assessment, and offender competencies. Legal psychology involves the application of social, cognitive, and developmental psychology to legal issues such as jury decision-making, eyewitness identification, and child witness behavior.

Civil litigation includes several areas in which the expertise of clinical psychologists, who are trained to assess and treat mental disorders, may benefit the court. In child custody disputes, psychologists are often appointed to evaluate those involved in the dispute to determine what parenting arrangement might be in the best interest of the child. In civil commitment procedures, psychologists evaluate a person's mental state and provide evidence about whether the defendant is a risk to self or to others. The new laws that allow for the indefinite commitment of sexually violent predators who pose an ongoing risk to the community have provided a new arena in which psychologists' assessments of future risk are needed. Finally, when plaintiffs seek compensatory *damages for psychological harm they have suffered, clinical psychologists may evaluate these plaintiffs to determine the severity of psychological damage or to investigate whether psychological harm is due to trauma that predates the current litigation.

Experimental psychologists who specialize in determining the cognitive and social factors that influence human behavior also have provided information that is useful in civil litigation. Psychologists who study prejudice and *discrimination sometimes testify about workplace characteristics that may increase the likelihood of discriminatory employment practices and *sexual harassment. Psychology has also provided courts with information on the factors that influence how jurors award compensatory and punitive damages, and whether proposed reforms such as caps on pain and suffering awards reduce variability in damage awards.

Experimental psychologists have provided expertise that improves criminal investigations. Cognitive psychologists have developed techniques for eliciting more information from witnesses of a crime without reducing accuracy, and have trained law enforcement personnel in the use of these techniques. Psychologists have also identified several methods of conducting *lineups that decrease the likelihood of mistaken identifications without decreasing the rate of correct identifications. These methods include: instructing the witness that the culprit may not be in the lineup, matching the nonsuspect members of a lineup to the witness's description of the perpetrator and not to the suspect, and presenting the lineup members sequentially rather than simultaneously. In addition, the lineup administrator should not know the identity of the suspect. New Jersey has adopted these procedures for conducting lineups and it appears as if several other states will soon follow New Jersey's lead.

Psychological practitioners also have a role to play in criminal litigation. Whether juvenile offenders are transferred to adult jurisdiction is based in part on their amenability to treatment and their risk for future violence. Psychologists are uniquely positioned to evaluate juveniles on these dimensions. Psychologists have also developed assessment tools for evaluating whether criminal defendants are competent to waive their *Miranda rights, to stand trial, and to plead guilty. In the rare cases in which a criminal defendant relies upon the insanity defense, psychologists may opine whether the defendant realized the wrongfulness of his or her conduct at the time of the offense. Psychologists working as trial consultants may survey the community in which a trial is going to occur to determine whether pretrial publicity has tainted the potential jury pool, suggesting the need for a change of venue.

Some areas of psychology cut across criminal and civil litigation. Psychologists may assist attorneys in jury selection and trial preparation, using community surveys to find demographic and attitudinal predictors of verdict or successful evidence presentation strategies. Finally, psychologists have studied how juries make decisions, whether they can disregard inadmissible evidence that they have heard but have been instructed to disregard, and whether jurors understand legal instructions.

[*See also* Law and Society Movement]

• Brian L. Cutler and Steven D. Penrod., *Mistaken Identification: The Eyewitness, Psychology, and the Law,* 1995. Allen K. Hess and Irving B. Weiner, *The Handbook of Forensic Psychology,* 2nd ed., 1999. Ronald Roesch, Stephen D. Hart, and James R. P. Ogloff, eds., *Psychology and Law: The State of the Discipline,* 1999. Kirk Heilbrun, *Principles of Forensic Mental Health Assessment,* 2001. James R. P. Ogloff, ed., *Taking Psychology and Law into the Twenty First Century,* 2002.

—Margaret Bull Kovera

PUBLIC ADMINISTRATION. *See* Regulation.

PUBLIC CHOICE. *See* Economics and Law; Law and Economics, Theory of; Regulation.

PUBLIC DEFENDERS. *See* Criminal Law Practice.

PUBLIC FIGURE. *See* Defamation.

PUBLIC INTEREST. *See* Environmental Law; Property Rights.

PUBLIC INTEREST LAWYERING. *See* Cause Lawyers.

PUBLICITY, PREJUDICIAL PRETRIAL. *See* Fair Trial, Criminal; Media and the Law; Speech and the Press, Freedom of.

PUBLIC LAW. *See* Legal Systems.

PUBLISHING, LAW. The law publishing business in the United States has been marked by the steady process of specialization of the industry and proliferation of products to meet the unique needs of the legal profession. From its roots in the small-scale efforts of individuals creating limited runs of texts for a subscription market, the law publishing business today is dominated by a few multinational corporations with revenues in the hundreds of millions of dollars. A profound influence on this business is the fact that the primary market for its products—the practicing bar—has sufficient means to pay for legal resources, thus spurring innovation and the creation of a dizzying array of resources.

The law publishing industry offers a wide range of products in response to the special needs of the bar, the courts and academics. Included in this array are (1) court reporters, for publication of judicial decisions, (2) codes, which are subject-arranged compilations of currently in-force statutes or administrative regulations, and (3) "secondary" sources, such as treatises, digests, looseleaf services, and periodicals, which assist the researcher in locating the "primary" sources of law (case law, statutes and regulations). The need for currency is crucial in legal research, and the publishing industry has responded in a variety of ways. For example, the "pocket part" was developed as an efficient method of providing current updates to bound volumes of codes, legal encyclopedias, and other categories of legal texts. A pocket part is a softbound supplement that fits inside a sleeve on the back cover of a hardbound volume. Other devices, such as "slip laws" and "advance sheets," were introduced as a temporary means of quickly distributing the text of new law before the more permanent bound volumes could be produced.

Another product born of the special needs of the legal profession is the citator. Because of the importance of "stare decisis," or precedent, it is essential to discover how a judicial decision has been treated by subsequent decisions. A citator is a research tool that compiles subsequent citations to court decisions resulting from later decisions from that same court or a different court. The Shepard's company long ago established itself as the leading producer of citators, and indeed had essentially no competition in the field until the advent of a competing computer-based service in the late 1990s.

Legal periodical literature desires special mention. Periodical literature comes in a variety of forms, such as law journals, magazines, newspapers, and newsletters. This literature serves both the current awareness needs of the profession, and the scholarly needs of legal academics. The first law journal was the *American Law Journal*, established in 1808. A large number of journals and newsletters were developed in the nineteenth century, though few survive today. One of the first law school journals was the *Harvard Law Review*, founded in 1887. A unique feature of American legal scholarship is that law reviews are edited by law students. Every law school now produces one or more student-edited law journals; as a result, more than 250 journals are now published.

The sheer volume of legal periodicals makes gaining access to articles challenging. In response, several indexes were developed to cope with this situation. In 1908, the H. W. Wilson Company created its *Index to Legal Periodicals* (ILP). The ILP was the only comprehensive periodical index for periodicals until the creation of the *Current Law Index* in 1980. Both indexes continue to be published, and have been made available electronically, greatly improving their usefulness.

Early History. The history of American law publishing must begin with a look at the type of texts in use during the colonial period. Courts in the colonies applied English law and used English law books. The colonial lawyer was largely limited to books produced in the home country. English court reports and works such as *Blackstone's Commentaries on the Laws of England*, published in 1765, were very influential in the colonies (and for many years after independence). It should be kept in mind that the practice of law prior to independence was typically very local in character, with a small number of lawyers often relying on handwritten notes and summaries of cases decided in their region.

Gradually, an indigenous law book publishing industry took root in colonial America, as it was a necessity to publish and distribute colonial laws. Through the efforts of a small number of printers, colonial statutes and, to a lesser extent, case reports, began to appear. The 1648 publication of the *General Lawes and Libertyes* of Massachusetts Bay in Boston is credited as being the first law book printed in America.

The independence of the United States stimulated the rapid development of a native law publishing industry. In addition to the need to publish the statutes and cases emanating from the now independent state legislatures and courts, there was a general perception that the United States must sever its dependence on English authorities. The first reports from an American jurisdiction were Ephraim Kirby's Connecticut *Reports*, which appeared in 1789. A Connecticut Congressman, Zephaniah Swift, published the first American legal treatise. His *System of the Laws of Connecticut* appeared in 1795 and was sold by subscription. Swift wanted to establish American law as independent from its English origins, although the text, by necessity, relied heavily on the citation of English authorities.

The reporting of decisions of the *Supreme Court deserves special mention, as it illustrates some important aspects of the history of law book publishing. Because of the importance of these decisions, the Court's holdings were reported almost from the beginning. In 1793, a lawyer named A. J. Dallas published the first reporter volume containing decisions of the Court. Since the Court at that time did not issue written decisions, but read its decisions from the bench, there is room for debate on the accuracy of these reports. Following Dallas, a number of other private individuals continued the practice of publishing the decisions of the court, with Henry Wheaton becoming the first "official" reporter in 1817. In 1834, the Supreme Court ended the practice of issuing oral opinions, and thenceforth submitted prepared opinions to the reporter. The publication of Supreme Court decisions was eventually standardized by the creation of an official publication, the *United States Reports*.

The early decisions of the Supreme Court were reprinted many times, and one such effort at republishing led to the lawsuit of *Wheaton* v. *Peters* (1834), in which Wheaton claimed copyright protection in an attempt to block republication of decisions he had reported. The Supreme Court endorsed the principle that no copyright should exist in the laws governing the nation, since their wide dissemination is essential. This precedent was of great importance in the development of the law publishing industry.

The Founding of West Publishing Company. Until the middle of the nineteenth century, the American law book publishing industry was largely a local affair. Nationalization of the industry resulted largely from the emergence of West Publishing Company. West was founded in 1872 in St. Paul, Minnesota, by John B. West. The first West product was *The Syllabi*, a weekly summary of Minnesota court decisions. This publication was expanded into the National Reporter System, which was the first attempt to develop a comprehensive, standardized method of reporting case decisions from both the federal and state systems.

The National Reporter System was revolutionary not only because of the breadth of its coverage, but also for the way the the decisions were enhanced with editorial information. As eventually developed by West, the decisions reported in the National Reporter System contained headnotes that were linked to a system of West "digests." The digests were the finding tool that provided subject access to the very large volume of reported cases. For the first time, lawyers could purchase an integrated set of reporters and digests that provided dependable access to the full text of the nation's appellate decisions.

The National Reporter System was so successful that competitors gradually disappeared, with West often displacing even official state court reports of their decisions. No official reporter for decisions of the United States Courts of Appeal or the District Courts was ever developed, probably because the West system of reporting was sufficient. Not until the appearance of online access to court decisions was this dominance of West in reporting case law challenged.

During the first few decades of the twentieth century, the law publishing business experienced a rapid growth in the number of publications in parallel with the growth of the population and commercial activity of the nation. The New Deal era of the 1930s further increased the output of legal material being produced by the courts, legislatures and, increasingly, the regulatory agencies of the country. As the output of law increased, so did the complexity of legal research and the need for better finding aids. This surge in the output of primary sources was a boon to the legal publishing industry, increasing the size of law libraries and the demand for tools to help researchers cope with this flood of material. While West continued to be the major publisher in the United States, dozens of other companies also had significant shares of the market.

Computer-based Legal Resources. The development of computer-based resources has had a tremendous impact on the legal publishing industry. The field of law has arguably the finest array of computer-based research resources of any profession. Today, access to computer-based legal material is moving increasingly to the web.

Computer-based legal research began in earnest with the development of the LEXIS online database. The LEXIS system traces its origins to 1967 when a group of Ohio attorneys developed a prototype online retrieval system for Ohio caselaw. This effort was soon taken over by Mead Data Central, Inc., which expanded the database and made the LEXIS system available nationwide.

In response to this challenge, West in 1975 introduced Westlaw, a database that has been in competition with LEXIS since then. Westlaw and LEXIS both offer an enormous amount of legal and nonlegal information. While the current owners of the LEXIS and Westlaw databases still produce an impressive number of print products, the legal publishing industry is increasingly steering its customers toward databases accessed through the Internet.

This increased reliance on online access to legal information has had a very important benefit for nonprofessional users of legal information. State and local governments, which had largely abandoned publication of their laws in print, have been active in putting statutes, ordinances, case law, and regulations on the Internet. This has been a welcome development, as citizens now have indisputably better access to this material than in years past. The federal government, which had a long tradition of making its law available to the public, has also been active in creating websites to expand access to legal material.

Consolidation of the Publishing Industry. The mid-1990's saw an unprecedented degree of acquisition activity in the legal publishing industry, leaving two international firms in control of the bulk of the U.S. market. In 1994, Reed-Elsevier, an English-Dutch conglomerate, purchased the LEXIS-NEXIS database, thus positioning itself as the supplier of about half the online legal research services in the United States.

In 1996, West was bought by the giant Canadian publisher, the Thomson Corporation. This deal faced hurdles, however, as the United States Justice Department launched an anti-trust investigation that focused on the potential anticompetitive implications of such a deal. Thomson was already a major player in the American law book market, having purchased the Lawyers Cooperative Publishing Company in 1989.

By virtue of a consent degree, Thomson agreed to divest itself of approximately fifty of its legal publications and to license the West system of paginating its court reporters. This latter point was of great interest since West had long claimed copyright protection in the pagination of its court reporters, a practice that critics claimed was an unfair and monopolistic practice. Reed-Elsevier acquired the fifty divested legal titles from Thomson, further concentrating the legal publishing industry into the hands of the two multinational giants. This concentration of the industry has been met with considerable skepticism by the profession as the decrease in the number of publishers has been accompanied by a substantial increase in the price of legal materials.

The present state of law publishing is characterized by the dominance of two large corporations that produce a wide array of material, often available in multiple formats. This marks a dramatic return to control of the law market by general publishers that produce much more than legal materials. It is especially remarkable that the commercial market for legal materials is controlled almost wholly by two corporations based outside the United States.

[*See also* Computerized Research; Property, Intellectual]

• Erwin C. Surrency, *A History of American Law Publishing*, 1990. Thomas A. Woxland and Patti J. Ogen, *Landmarks in American Legal Publishing: An Exhibit Catalog*, 1990. Thomas A. Woxland, ed., *Symposium of Law Publishers*, 1991. George S. Grossman, ed., *Legal Research: Historical Foundations of the Electronic Age*, 1994. Morris L. Cohen, *Bibliography of Early American Law*, 1998.
                                    —Roy M. Mersky

PUNISHMENT. See Capital Punishment; Criminal Punishments; Cruel and Unusual Punishment; Electric Chair; Forfeiture.

R

RACE AND ETHNICITY are social categories that have been embedded in American law throughout U.S. history. Although the ambiguous nature of these categories is recognized by society in general, many *civil rights policies reflect these cognitive understandings. Numerous laws have sought to guarantee the rights of minorities, such as *voting rights acts, fair housing laws, and others; many of the most contentious social issues revolve around the proper interpretation of *equal protection of the laws, and the question of which groups ought to be considered protected.

In the late nineteenth century race was treated as though it were a biological reality. European thinkers published works using pseudoscientific ideas to try to prove the fundamental inequality among races, including Arthur de Gobineau in *Essay on the Inequality of the Human Races* (1853–55) and Houston Stewart Chamberlain in *The Foundations of the Twentieth Century* (1899, 1911). The objective was to legitimize the Aryan myth, the false claim that northern Europeans were superior to southern and eastern Europeans and to peoples in African and Asia. In the United States, similar notions appeared in widely read books such as Madison Grant's *The Passing of a Great Race* (1917) and Lothrop Stoddard's *The Rising Tide of Color Against White-World Supremacy* (1920). In addition, leaders in the eugenics movement, such as the English gentleman and cousin of Charles Darwin, Sir Francis Galton (who coined the term eugenics for "good genes"), and his American counterpart, Charles Davenport, popularized the idea that racial differences were genetically determined and that some races were superior to others. Eugenicists promoted the use of intelligence quotient (IQ) tests whose results demonstrated a discrepancy attributed to race rather than cultural bias in the test. Decades later, Arthur Jensen revived this debate over racial testing, which has continued to reemerge periodically in American public discourse. The falsity of these claims has been exposed by many scholars, perhaps most persuasively by Stephen Jay Gould in his powerful study *The Mismeasure of Man* (1981).

Increasingly, the validity of characterizations attributable to race has been called into question. In particular, *Critical Race Theory (CRT), an intellectual movement at law schools in the 1990s, has revealed the extent to which racial categories are largely social constructs. Some of the leading figures associated with CRT are Derek Bell, Kimberle Crenshaw, Richard Delgado, Charles Lawrence, Ian Haney-Lopez, Mari Matsuda, and Adrien Wing. Their scholarship demonstrates the profound racial bias that exists in the American legal system.

There is also a vast literature on ethnicity, and scholars have divergent conceptualizations of it. Ethnicity, usually considered distinct from class, refers to a social classification of individuals whose culture differentiates them from other social groups. The anthropologist Frederik Barth, in *Ethnic Groups and Boundaries: The Social Organization of Cultural Difference* (1969), emphasized the boundary as defining the group as opposed to the culture shared by members of the group. A long-standing debate in the literature on American ethnicity focuses on the relative merits of the assimilation or melting pot model and the cultural pluralism model (terms coined by Israel Zangwill (1908), and Horace Kallen (1924), respectively). Milton Gordon's classic conceptualization of the relationship between the models is found in his book *Assimilation in American Life* (1964), which concerns the extent to which immigrants conform to Anglo-American standards.

Although the precise relationship between race and ethnicity is somewhat unclear, some analysts regard race as a biological designation, and ethnicity as a social status. Another view is that ethnicity is the larger category, which subsumes race: all races are ethnic groups, but not all ethnic groups are races. Some, like Omi and Winant, take issue with this position because racial groups can be ethnically differentiated.

In legal policy debates there has been an unfortunate tendency to conflate race and ethnicity. Furthermore, religious minorities and indigenous groups also suffer from the imposition of social classifications that often seem ambiguous, at the very least, if not altogether arbitrary. For instance, in the United Kingdom a determination had to be made as to which groups constituted "ethnic" groups for purposes of litigating under the Race Relations Act (1976). While Sikhs, a religious minority group from India, were regarded as an "ethnic group" in *Mandla* v. *Dowell Lee* (1983), Rastafarians, a religion whose members came from the Caribbean, were not seen as constituting such a group, as in *Dawkins* v. *Crown Suppliers* (1991).

In the United States, membership in particular social groups has been crucial for legal status. Among American Indians, for instance, only those belonging to federally recognized tribes have been entitled to apply for social programs. The U.S. government used the notorious "blood quantum" standard, among other seemingly scientific criteria, to determine who could claim Indian identity (see NATIVE AMERICANS AND THE LAW). Arbitrary racial and ethnic classifications continue to be used in the U.S. census, whose categories continue to evolve, and even in policies such as *affirmative action programs, which were established to benefit disadvantaged groups.

While many different groups have suffered *discrimination, much of the civil rights scholarship has tended to emphasize the experience of African Americans. In the late twentieth century, scholars in the field of race and ethnic politics urged other scholars and policymakers to move beyond the black/white paradigm. Although this call for a wider scope of analysis is important, it in no way diminishes the significance or magnitude of the suffering in the African-American community.

The study of race in American law begins with *slavery. That the country was founded on this institution demonstrates the centrality of race to American legal history. Slaves had no legal standing. They could not marry except through customary law ("jumping the broom"), they could not enter into business contracts, and they could not testify except against another slave. When the U.S. Supreme Court had the opportunity to consider the slave question directly in the famous *Dred Scott* case (1857), it rendered one of its worst decisions. Dred Scott was a slave who was taken by his master into a free state and argued that this journey made him free. The Court concluded that Scott had no standing to sue in federal court because federal *citizenship permanently excluded blacks, and in any event rejected his argument that he was made free by going to the free state. This unfortunate decision provided a major impetus for the Civil War.

After the Civil War, new legal standards were established to help pave the way to racial justice. Some were struck down, as in the *Civil Rights Cases* (1883), which invalidated the Civil Rights Act of 1875. In the vast case law on race, decisions have been based on civil rights laws and the Fifteenth Amendment, but many of the crucial ones hinged on the interpretation of the equal protection clause of the *Fourteenth Amendment. One landmark equal protection decision that addressed discrimination against Chinese Americans was *Yick Wo* v. *Hopkins* (1886). The Supreme Court held that a law requiring that persons operating wooden laundries obtain a license violated equal protection because the board of supervisers refused to issue any licenses to those of Chinese ancestry.

In another important decision rendered during World War II in *Korematsu* v. *U.S* (1944), Fred Korematsu challenged Executive Order 9066, issued by President Franklin D. Roosevelt, to incarcerate 120,000 Japanese Americans whose loyalty was thought to be in question. Although the Court ruled that laws containing a racial classification should be reviewed under the "strict scrutiny" standard and could be sustained only if "narrowly tailored" and justified by a "compelling state interest," the Court upheld the internment policy on the basis of military necessity. This was one of the rare occasions when the Court authorized the use of a racial classification, which led constitutional scholar Gerald Gunther to say that the strict scrutiny test is "strict in theory, but fatal in fact." Although Korematsu's conviction was vacated in a *coram nobis* lawsuit several decades later, the precedent has never been overturned (see JAPANESE INTERNMENT).

At the turn of the twentieth century, southern states enacted Jim Crow laws mandating racially separate institutions. Many of the most important legal decisions concerning race, in fact, dealt with *segregation. For example, Homer Plessy who was an "octoroon" (one-eighth black), challenged the

Louisiana Separate Car Act by riding in a railway car reserved for whites only. In *Plessy v. Ferguson (1896) the Supreme Court upheld the now infamous "separate but equal" doctrine. This remained the law of the land for many decades.

The National Association for the Advancement of Colored People (NAACP) laid the foundation for a major Supreme Court decision overturning Plessy through a series of lawsuits documented in the magnificent study, Simple Justice, by Richard Kluger. Charles Houston instigated the litigation in *Brown v. Board of Education (1954), although the case was ultimately argued before the Supreme Court by Thurgood *Marshall, who would later become the first black justice on the U.S. Supreme Court. In Brown the Supreme Court accepted the NAACP theory that "separate but equal" was "inherently unequal." The overturning of the Plessy precedent was facilitated by the doll experiments of psychologists Kenneth and Mamie Clark. Their research demonstrated that black children suffered psychic injury as a consequence of being required to study in segregated educational institutions.

Basing a legal argument on social science evidence was regarded as perilous by some. In a famous article, Herbert Wechsler argued that one should not base something as important as the interpretation of a constitutional principle on something as "flimsy" as social science. In his view, it is better to ground arguments in "neutral principles," although it is not obvious how one could reinterpret the meaning of equal protection in the abstract, considering the existence of the legally binding Plessy precedent. Because of the controversial nature of the argument, the Court deemphasized it, mentioning it only in footnote 11 of Brown.

The Court realized that there would be considerable resistance to its decision and therefore declined to provide a remedy immediately. A year later in Brown II, the Court ordered desegregation "with all deliberate speed," an oxymoronic formula. In the years following Brown the Court repeatedly found too much deliberation and not enough speed. The Supreme Court tried to expedite the process but cases like Cooper v. Aaron (1958) demonstrated the sorts of obstacles that had to be faced. Questions emerged over what methods of implementing the mandate of Brown were acceptable: what were the permissible affirmative uses of the race line? Although the Supreme Court considered busing a legitimate tool for desegregation, busing had limited success, in large part because of residential patterns. For instance, the Court refused to allow interdistrict busing in

Milliken v. Bradley (1974), though that was the only way to achieve any semblance of racial balance in the Detroit area, where the litigation occurred. Years later, because Brown generated massive resistance and created a backlash, some questioned whether it was really the victory many proclaimed.

A difficulty emerged in equal protection litigation involving challenges to "facially neutral" laws, those that did not mention race explicitly but whose use led to discrimination. In Washington v. Davis (1976), a black police officer challenged the use of a written test that had the effect of keeping African Americans from joining the police force. The Court held that plaintiffs must show that those who adopted the policy intended to discriminate. A disparate impact is insufficient to prove a violation of equal protection. Of course, not only is it difficult to determine what policymakers were thinking when they formulated a new policy, but the intent standard presupposes that individuals are conscious of their own motives. In a devastating critique of the intent standard, Charles R. Lawrence notes that discrimination is often "influenced by unconscious racial motivation" (1987: 322), which means that proving a conscious intent will often be impossible.

The use of equal protection analysis continues to be debated. In applying the analytic framework established for race, scholars have considered how far to extend the logic. Although there are no reasons for distinguishing among different races, the question is whether there can ever be valid reasons for treating women differently from men, for treating homosexuals differently from heterosexuals, and so forth. In order to determine which groups deserve more protection, courts often invoke the language of "discrete and insular minorities" taken from footnote 4 of the Carolene Products (1938) case to defend greater legal protection for groups lacking access to political processes.

One of the more contentious issues has been whether affirmative action policies are consonant with equal protection. The Supreme Court authorized the use of the policy in Regents of the University of California v. Bakke (1978), a case in which a white student challenged the U.C. Davis admissions program, which allocated sixteen spaces for minorities for whom different standards applied. Although the Court thought strict numerical quotas violated equal protection, and concluded that Bakke had to be admitted to the U.C. Davis medical school, it accepted the proposition that race or ethnicity can be a legitimate factor in admissions decisions, along with geographical background, athletic prowess, musical talent, and other accepted considerations. The Court's decision (5–4) was so highly fragmented that commentators were unsure whether there was a consensus on much of anything. In the aftermath of the decision it appeared that the Court declined to use the strict scrutiny standard, according to which policies based on racial classifications are almost automatically struck down, and instead resorted to a lesser standard known as the intermediate standard of review. This analysis suggests a recognition that the use of racial classifications to help groups that have suffered discrimination differs significantly from invidious racial categories designed to exclude or incarcerate minorities.

Despite the continuation of affirmative action programs, many opposed them, including groups benefiting from them, sometimes because they felt stigmatized. Anglo students might erroneously assume that minority students had weaker academic qualifications simply because a university had an affirmative action program. Conservative Anglo students objected to affirmative action because they felt that they were victims of discrimination. Some, such as Ronald Dworkin, have argued that it is a "piece of intellectual confusion" to regard affirmative action as discrimination against whites, the group in power. That is, whites are not rejected because they belong to a group that is hated. Nevertheless, the view that affirmative action violates equal protection has become increasingly more influential. In *Hopwood* v. *Texas* (1996), a federal appellate court, invoking the strict scrutiny test, struck down the admissions program at the University of Texas law school as violative of equal protection. Even though the decision was binding only on educational institutions in the Fifth Circuit's jurisdiction, the ruling reverberated across the United States. Colleges and universities reexamined their affirmative action policies to determine whether they would withstand constitutional challenges. The change in public sentiment was clear, as, for example, California voters rejected affirmative action, and the U.C. Regents discarded that state's use of it.

The use of race in other areas of law also reflects an increasing discomfort on the part of the courts. The move to apply strict scrutiny to affirmative action programs has also been made in the employment realm. At every level of government, the use of race conscious criteria to increase the number of contracts going to minority businesses has been invalidated (see *City of Richmond* v. *Croson* (1989); *Adarand* v. *Pena* (1995)). Likewise, the use of race in drawing electoral districts has been limited as well (*Shaw* v. *Reno* (1993)).

Race and Ethnicity in the Criminal Justice System. Race has also been a salient issue in the criminal justice system. For instance, the *Black Codes, adopted by former slave states between 1865 and 1866 to limit the rights of blacks, often included a requirement that juries be all-white. In *Strauder* v. *West Virginia* (1880) the Supreme Court found that *jury discrimination of this sort violated equal protection. This victory did not, however, prevent lawyers from using peremptory challenges to excuse blacks from serving on juries. In *Swain* v. *Alabama* (1965), a black who had been sentenced to death by an all-white jury for raping a white woman challenged the discriminatory use of peremptory challenges that removed all blacks from the jury pool during jury selection or voir dire; the Court, however, declined to find a violation of equal protection. In 1986 the Court finally overturned *Swain*. In *Batson* v. *Kentucky* (1986) it said that after the defense makes a *prima facie* showing that the prosecutor exercised peremptory challenges in a discriminatory fashion, the burden shifts to the prosecutor to provide a nonracial reason for exercising peremptory challenges to exclude racial minorities. Unfortunately, the well-intentioned decision met with limited success because lawyers learned how to manufacture seemingly neutral reasons for their behavior.

Batson was a significant case nonetheless; the doctrine was subsequently extended to apply to civil cases, misconduct by defense counsel, and exclusion of women from juries, but not to exclusion based on language ability. In *Hernandez* v. *New York* (1986), a case where the prosecution removed all Spanish-speaking prospective jurors, the Court found no violation of equal protection because the nexus between ethnicity and language ability was not considered close enough to constitute a violation of equal protection under *Batson*. The logic was that some non-Latinos might be fluent in Spanish whereas some Latinos might not speak Spanish at all. Even though the principle that one should be judged by a jury of one's peers is not written in the Constitution, many regard it as a fundamental principle. The ability of lawyers to manipulate the voir dire process to exclude jurors of a particular ethnic group threatens to undermine the legitimacy of the justice system.

The American legal system has also come under attack for sentencing disparities. One issue concerned guidelines requiring prosecution in federal court for possession of cocaine, rules whose enforcement effectively meant that minorities would be subject to much harsher punishments than white-collar Anglo drug users. Although disparities exist with respect to punishment for many offenses, it is the unequal application of the death penalty that has especially given cause for alarm. Social science research, in particular the famous Baldus study, demonstrated that minorities are much more likely to receive the death penalty than Anglo Americans; the study also found that those who killed white victims were more likely to be subject to *capital punishment. This data led to an argument that capital punishment violated the equal protection guarantees of the Fourteenth Amendment. However the Supreme Court rejected the systemic inequities argument in *McCleskey* v. *Kemp* (1987), holding that even if the statistical study demonstrated patterns that were nearly irrefutable, the research could not prove that racial bias had influenced the particular trial of the defendant in question. While this position struck some as unbelievable (if bias was pervasive, why wouldn't it have affected the disposition of the defendant's case), had the Court ruled in favor of McCleskey, all death penalty rulings would have been called into question. Some speculated that the Court was not prepared for the magnitude of such a ruling. Interestingly, a similar systemic inequities argument was advanced much earlier in the Inter-American Commission of Human Rights.

When defendants argue that race tainted the trial, they may point out that some of those involved in the case made reference to racial epithets, stereotypes, or images which may have influenced the jury to convict. In a thought-provoking study, "Racial Imagery in Criminal Law," Sheri Lynn Johnson proved that courts have generally not taken these racist remarks seriously. On appeal, courts frequently invoke the "harmless error" rule, according to which there is no need for reversal provided the trial judge admonished the jury to disregard the racist comments just made. Johnson proposes a race shield law that would operate as a "per se" rule, meaning that any mention of a racial stereotype would automatically require instigating a new trial. While this policy proposal might strike some as far-fetched, it would probably deter the utterance of racist remarks in court.

The U.S. Federal Sentencing Guidelines (1987) forbid any reference to race or ethnicity during the sentencing phase of the trial, presumably to avoid unjust increases in punishment. While this policy was designed to minimize discriminatory practices in federal cases, it is unclear whether this would preclude judges from reducing or "departing downward" because of cultural considerations. Because the guidelines disallow the consideration of race, ethnicity, or national origin, some judges worry about whether that encompasses cultural heritage. It seems illogical to equate national origin with cultural heritage because immigrants might be completely assimilated and individuals born in the United States might strongly identify with the ethnic group of their parents. Nevertheless, it remains to be seen whether the guidelines will be interpreted to prevent considerations of cultural differences that would mitigate punishment.

At the end of the twentieth century there remained widespread concern about racial justice in the American legal system. The criminal prosecution of the police officers who assaulted Rodney *King, which resulted in their acquittal, confirmed the suspicions of many that the system was biased. (An oddity of the case was that it was called the "Rodney King" trial, even though he was the victim, not the defendant.) Widespread civil unrest in the Los Angeles area in the aftermath of the verdict exposed deep-rooted anger over injustices in the American legal system. Another trial whose meaning for racism was widely discussed was O. J. *Simpson's trial for the murder of his wife. Simpson's prosecution received extraordinary media coverage, and he had remarkably adept legal representation. The reaction to his high-profile acquittal seemed to differ along racial lines.

Many issues of race and ethnicity demonstrate inadequacies in existing legal policies, some of which pertain to the workplace. For example, civil rights laws do not afford sufficient protection to African-American women. Title VII of the 1964 Civil Rights Act is a major policy tool that has enabled minorities to challenge discrimination in the workplace, and it does not allow employers to claim a bona fide occupational qualification as a defense if charged with racial discrimination. Although the law has served its purpose well, there have been some difficulties. For instance, African-American women who choose to wear cornrows and are threatened with termination of employment as a consequence cannot successfully invoke Title VII. Paulette Caldwell outlines their dilemma in her celebrated essay "A Hair Piece," which shows how civil rights policies covering race, *gender, and national origin are inapplicable to the cornrows litigation. The point is that the experience of African-American women is not adequately addressed in antidiscrimination law designed for race or gender categories.

Antidiscrimination law has not been applied to language issues with a great degree of success. For the most part, courts have not been receptive to challenges to "English-only" policies in the workplace or to claims of accent discrimination. Because of a tendency not to view language discrimination as a violation of either equal protection or of Title VII, ethnic minorities whose problems are associated with linguistic barriers may find themselves without recourse.

At the end of the twentieth century minorities sought redress of their grievances through reparations. Although the call for reparations at first won little support in the mainstream, it has gained wider acceptance. Although Japanese Americans who were imprisoned in concentration camps during World War II received a mere twenty thousand dollars, if they were still alive, few other groups have received any restitution for historic injustices. In the late twentieth century some called for reparations for African Americans for the violence they suffered and for the massive injuries associated with slavery. Congressman John Conyers has introduced reparations bills in Congress, but as of 2001 his proposed legislation had not won sufficient support to be made law.

Some question the proposal for reparations, charging that the injustices occurred long ago, that individuals who suffered the harms are no longer alive, and that it would be impossible to calculate a proper sum for restitution. Proponents argue, in response, that the descendants of slaves still suffer from the lack of wealth that their relatives would have accumulated had they been compensated for their labor. They also maintain that economists can compute lost wages by means of various formulas; hence the impracticability argument is simply misguided. The main difficulty with reparations policy in the American legal context is Americans' deeply entrenched individualism. Ordinarily, only those who themselves suffer the injury have standing to sue for *damages. It is often difficult to prove that those related to the victims also suffer the injury. To the extent that the American legal system refuses to recognize group harms (as well as group rights), acceptance of reparations policies is unlikely.

It is noteworthy that some groups have won restitution. For example, in 1994 the Florida legislature authorized payment of more than $2 million for victims of the racist arson and massacre that had terrorized the African-American community in Rosewood, Florida, decades earlier. Another way in which victims of racial violence have sought justice is through civil rights lawsuits. For example, Morris Dees of the Southern Poverty Law Center has successfully sued white supremacist organizations, winning multimillion-dollar judgments for the families of victims of hate crimes.

Another complexity in the American legal system is the refusal to outlaw hate speech. Americans tend to embrace the folk view that "sticks and stones can break my bones, but words can never hurt me." Critical race theorists questioned the wisdom of this view in *Words that Wound*. However the United States has declined to reconsider its position on hate speech. When the U.S. ratified the International Covenant on the Elimination of All Forms of Discrimination Based on Race (1994), it declined to accept the provisions forbidding hate speech. The U.S. position differs dramatically from that of most other countries that outlaw the advocacy of race hatred. The United States, as of 2001, has chosen to favor freedom of expression over racial equality. Although the Supreme Court struck down a hate speech ordinance in *R.A.V.*, in large part because it was poorly drafted, there is no reason to suspect the Court will accept regulations of hate speech in the future. In the twenty-first century new questions concerning race and ethnicity will have to be answered. When, if ever, is racial profiling consistent with the law? Should individuals who falsely accuse another of a crime because of his race, e.g. Susan Smith and Charles Stuart, be subject to prosecution for racial hoaxes? The members of the United Nations, including the United States, will have to find more effective ways to enforce international *human rights standards to halt genocidal killing, known as "ethnic cleansing." Although law can be an effective tool for social change and protection of rights, the legal system is inadequate to the task of combating prejudice and discrimination on its own.

[*See also* Hate Crimes]

• Gordon Allport, *The Nature of Prejudice*, 1958. Boris Bittker, *The Case for Black Reparations*, 1973. Frank F. Chuman, *The Bamboo People: The Law and Japanese Americans*, 1976. Don Fehrenbacher, *The Dred Scott Case: Its Significance in American Law and Politics*, 1979. Stephen Jay Gould, *The Mismeasure of Man*, 1981. Ronald Dworkin, "Bakkes's Case: Are Quotas Fair?" in Dworkin, *A Matter of Principle*, 293–303 (1985). Charles R. Lawrence III, "The Id, the Ego, and Equal Protection: Reckoning with Unconscious Racism," *Stanford Law Review* 39 (1987): 317–88. Robert N. Clinton, Nell Jessup Newton, and Monroe E. Price, *American Indian Law: Cases and Materials*, 3rd ed., 1991. Sandy Coliver, ed., *Striking the Balance: Hate Speech, Freedom of Expression, and Non-discrimination*, 1992. Abraham L. Davis and

Barbara Luck Graham, *The Supreme Court, Race, and Civil Rights*, 1995. Richard Delgado, ed., *Critical Race Theory: The Cutting Edge*, 1995. Alison Dundes Renteln, "A Psychohistorical Analysis of the Japanese American Internment," *Human Rights Quarterly* 17 (1995): 618–48. Gerald Rosenberg, *The Hollow Hope*, 1995. Werner Sollors, ed., *Theories of Ethnicity: A Classical Reader*, 1996. James B. Jacobs and Kimberly Potter, *Hate Crimes: Criminal Law and Identity Politics*, 1998. Katheryn K. Russell, *The Color of Crime: Racial Hoaxes, White Fear, Black Protectionism, Police Harassment, and Other Macroaggressions*, 1998.

—Alison Dundes Renteln

RACE HATE CRIMES. *See* Hate Crimes.

RADIO. *See* Arts, Popular Culture, and Law: Entertainment Law; Media and the Law.

RAPE. *See* Sex Offenses.

REAL ESTATE. *See* Property, Real.

REASONING, LEGAL. *See* Legal Reasoning.

RECOGNITION OF JUDGMENTS. *See* Conflict of Laws.

RECORDING. *See* Property, Real.

REFERENDUM. Citizens in modern democracies often vote on issues in addition to voting for candidates. Such votes may concern the adoption or amendment of a *constitution, passage of a new law, or deciding what country or state should govern the jurisdiction where the voters live. Even totalitarian regimes hold referendums—a way of generating support for their policies or leadership rather than as a method for determining popular sentiment. Each of these different kinds of votes, and a dizzying number of others, fall within the term "referendum." In its broadest sense, the term refers to any vote by the people on a decision relating to government other than an election for candidates.

Voters in Massachusetts and New Hampshire were the first to vote on their state constitutions—turning down proposals in 1778 before approving later revisions. In 2000, nearly every U.S. state constitution has been approved by the voters in a referendum. Connecticut was the first state to require popular approval of *constitutional amendments (1818)—a practice now followed by every state but Delaware. Many states also require that certain kinds of laws (such as bond measures) be submitted to the citizenry for a vote. In addition to these mandatory kinds of referendums, many states give their legislatures the option of referring particular proposals to the people.

One special kind of referendum affords citizens a grassroots method for challenging newly passed laws. To use this procedure, citizens must collect the required number of signatures from other citizens. Submission of these signatures to the appropriate authority suspends the new statute until it is voted on by the people. Originated in Switzerland in the first half of the 1800s, this "protest" kind of referendum—along with the *"initiative" (a grassroots method allowing citizens to propose new laws) and the "recall" (a grassroots method for voting elected officials out of office)—was promoted by the Populist Party in the 1890s as an antidote to special-interest control of state legislatures. This grassroots mechanism is also called a "referendum"—making it difficult to distinguish it from broader uses of the term.

Twenty-four U.S. states had laws allowing this protest type of referendum at the statewide level in 2000. All but three—Kentucky, Maryland, and New Mexico—also authorize use of the initiative. Although very important in Switzerland, statewide protest referendums have been used infrequently in the United States—partly because it is difficult to collect the signatures necessary within the time limits, often as short as ninety days. At the local level, timing is less important as an issue, and protest referendums are much more frequent. Zoning, fluoridation, antidiscrimination ordinances, gay rights, and public school financing have often been referendum issues.

The referendum is often used as a mechanism to settle ad hoc issues of importance, nationally and internationally. Danish voters in 2000, for example, rejected adoption of the Euro as that nation's currency. A few countries, such as Switzerland and Italy, use the protest referendum as part of their regular national lawmaking machinery. There has been little political support for a national referendum in the United States, although the subject has been discussed at times.

[*See also* Governance]

• David Butler and Austin Ranney, eds., *Referendums: A Comparative Study of Practice and Theory*, 1978. David Butler and Austin Ranney, eds., *Referendums Around the World*, 1994.

—Floyd Feeney

REFORMATION is a civil remedy to reformulate a document such as a *contract, usually to reflect the parties' intent after the plaintiff proves fraud or mistake, but sometimes to meet minimum fairness standards (e.g., if unconscionable terms were used) or other legal standards (e.g., to avoid restraint of trade). Once a contract is reformed, the plaintiff often shows that as rewritten it was breached, and requests restitution.

[*See also* Procedure, Civil]

—David S. Clark

REGIONALISM. Though often obscured by the unifying features of American law—the *Constitution, Supreme Court decisions, and congressional enactments—regionalism represents a significant strain in the nation's constitutional and legal development. Long before the American colonies achieved nationhood, European settlers' ideas about law and governance both shaped and responded to the unique geographic, social, and cultural characteristics of the communities and regions that they settled. Even after the American colonies united to win their independence and establish a new government, regional understandings of law and constitutionalism flourished during the nineteenth century, helped bring about the American *Civil War, and continued to affect twentieth-century constitutional and legal development.

Regional variations in the law emerged during the colonial era. Although settlers in the New England and the Chesapeake regions, for example, shared a common legal heritage and patterned their court systems after those in England, the distinct climates and cultures of the two regions influenced their substantive legal development. In the Chesapeake, a tobacco economy and slave-labor system first found expression in a 1662 Virginia law that declared that children of slave mothers would themselves be slaves, and by 1705 the colony implemented the first comprehensive slave code in North America. Other southern states, where cash-crop agriculture and *slavery also took root, followed a similar path. North Carolina operated special "Negro courts" for slaves during much of the eighteenth century, while South Carolina enacted a particularly harsh slave code in 1740 in response to a slave rebellion. New England, in contrast, settled mostly by Puritans with a religious vision for their society, attempted to establish a legal system based on political and moral consensus. The *Book of the General Lawes and Libertyes* of Massachusetts Bay Colony, written in 1648, codified Puritan ideals about proper behavior and cited biblical authority for offenses and punishments. Because the region's topography and climate made it ill-suited for plantation agriculture, commerce emerged as the lifeblood of New England, and laws regarding bills of exchange, for example, proved much more significant in the re-

gion's early legal development than codes governing the small number of slaves.

After the colonies won their independence, region played a significant role in the shaping and ratifying of the Constitution. Historians have long emphasized conflicts over representation between the most populous and least populous states at the Constitutional Convention of 1787. James Madison believed regional conflict posed a serious threat to national unity. "The difference of interest in the United States lay not between the large and small, but the Northern and Southern states," he noted during the convention. Slavery and *commercial regulation, in particular, divided the delegates. Debate specifically focused on how slaves were to be counted for purposes of taxation and representation, the future of the African slave trade, and the extent of congressional control over commerce. The founders eventually compromised on all these matters. Delegates decided that a state's total population consisted of the "whole number of free persons" plus "3/5 of all other persons," meaning slaves. The Three-Fifths Clause proved to be an important issue in national constitutional debate for decades, as northerners charged that it gave unwarranted power to the southern states in *Congress and the Electoral College.

Debates about the scope of congressional power over slavery and other forms of commerce resulted in another compromise: Congress would possess the power to regulate commerce "with foreign nations and among the several states" but would have no such similar control over the slave trade. Not until 1808, under the Constitution, would Congress have authority to prohibit the importation of slaves. These provisions satisfied northerners who favored congressional power over commercial regulation, but preserved some southerners' hopes that the slave trade would continue. Southerners, moreover, succeeded in gaining a prohibition on taxation of exports, which they saw as benefiting their agricultural-export economy. Finally, southern delegates to the convention argued for a clause protecting the fugitive slave property of masters. Ironically, this clause—which later proved to be the most divisive portion of the Constitution pertaining to slavery—engendered little debate, and northern delegates received nothing in return for its inclusion in the document.

Despite these compromises at the founding, regional differences in legal development and constitutional interpretation became increasingly apparent over the next few decades. As the Northeast outpaced the South in population growth, urbanization, and commercial expansion, northeastern judges and lawyers accelerated economic change by shaping the law of *contract, *tort, and *property to conform to emerging social and economic realities. Instrumentalist judges such as Lemuel *Shaw and Theophilus Parsons Jr. of Massachusetts, who viewed law as a tool of social change, championed the fellow-servant rule, the doctrine of caveat emptor, and a dynamic conception of property. Decisions such as *Farwell* v. *Boston and Worcester Railroad* (1842), in which Shaw ruled that a railroad company could not be held responsible for an injury to an engineer caused by another railroad employee, served the interests of business and spurred commercial and industrial development. These doctrinal innovations in private law generally fit with the political and constitutional ideals advanced by northeasterners in the Federalist and, later, the Whig Parties: protection of creditors and propertied interests, a national program of economic development, and a popular-sovereignty constitutional argument that emphasized the possibilities rather than the limits of federal power.

Another Massachusetts native, Supreme Court Justice Joseph *Story, personified New England's vision of law and constitutionalism. From his seat on the nation's highest court and his professorship at Harvard Law School, Story attempted to systematize American jurisprudence through writing legal treatises and educating law students. In this way, Story hoped to shape American legal and constitutional development in the image of New England, particularly by promoting the ideals of contract that he viewed as the basis for a social and moral order. During the early decades of the nineteenth century, southern control of the White House and the decline of the Federalist Party imbued Story and fellow New Englanders with an urgent desire to shape the nation's legal culture.

As northeasterners and their ideals migrated westward, the Midwest emerged as a burgeoning new region of the country. Initially formed out of the territories north of the Ohio River, where Congress had banned slavery under the Northwest Ordinance of 1787, the Midwest experienced rapid population growth and economic development during the first half of the nineteenth century. Hoping to promote new economic ventures that served the public interest, midwestern legislators and judges fostered the building of canals, railroads, and factories. By the 1850s, as American political and constitutional debates grew increasingly divisive, a cadre of midwestern Republican lawyers and political leaders, including Salmon P.

*Chase of Ohio and Abraham *Lincoln of Illinois, joined northeasterners in blending entrepreneurial ideals, antislavery principles, and an ideology of national supremacy. Northern victory in the Civil War represented the triumph of these values and led to adoption of the Reconstruction amendments to the Constitution. Although the amendments abolished slavery, restricted state power, and protected *civil rights and *voting rights, tepid enforcement of these constitutional guarantees demonstrated the limits of the northern commitment to racial justice.

More significant in the midwestern legal experience were the competing views of economic regulation that emerged during the late nineteenth century. Michigan Chief Justice Thomas *Cooley, a renowned legal thinker and treatise writer, championed judicial oversight of state regulation of economic activity, which he believed interfered with the liberty to contract. Cooley's ideas helped facilitate the expansion of judicial power, as well as the growth of a corporate capitalist order. Contrary to the values articulated by Cooley, the agrarian and progressive reform movements of the late nineteenth and early twentieth centuries also had their roots in midwestern soil. Farmers pushed legislators to enact granger (farmer or homesteader) laws, regulating railroad rates and grain elevator charges, while progressives championed greater accountability on the part of government and health and safety measures for workers. Wisconsin, the birthplace of such innovations as the state initiative and referendum, enacted a progressive reform agenda that served as a model for the nation. Midwestern legal ideals, in short, spread far beyond the region's boundaries.

The South followed its own path of social, legal, and constitutional development. The invention of the cotton gin at the end of the eighteenth century solidified the region's ties to slavery and plantation agriculture. These distinctive features of southern society manifested themselves in the development of a whole body of slave law, both statutory and judicially created, to govern the social and economic relationships arising out of the institution. Legal treatment of slaves and free blacks varied widely across the South and over time. Nowhere was this more apparent than in southern state judicial opinions, which ranged from North Carolina Chief Justice Thomas *Ruffin's blunt assertion in *State* v. *Mann* (1829) that the "power of the master must be absolute to render the submission of the slave perfect" to Tennessee Chief Justice Nathan Green's eloquent pronouncement in *Ford* v. *Ford* (1846) that "a slave is not in the condition of a horse or an ox. . . . [He] is made after the image of the Creator." The relative harshness of statutes and judicial decisions regarding slavery often reflected the tenor of national political debate and the degree of fear of slave insurrection at any given time.

Slavery and the South's agrarian-commercial economy helped to shape other aspects of the region's legal development. The South's large debtor population, for example, prompted Mississippi to enact the nation's first married woman's property law in 1839, under which the real property of a married woman remained her separate estate. This measure abrogated the common-law disability of coverture and in effect protected a wife's property from her husband's creditors. Likewise, Texas and other southern sates in the antebellum era created homestead exemption statutes that protected one's home from seizure by creditors.

By far the most significant expression of the South's unique constitutional and legal heritage was evident not in its statutes or judicial decisions but in the arguments of its political leaders. As early as the 1820s, when southerners began to fear becoming a minority in the national government, regional constitutional theorists such as South Carolina's John C. *Calhoun articulated the compact theory of government: that the Constitution was a contract among several equal, sovereign states, thus making them the locus of power within the American constitutional system. On this theoretical foundation of state *sovereignty rested the doctrines of nullification and *secession that threatened the survival of the Union. When eleven southern states seceded and formed the Confederate States of America in 1861, they wrote a constitution that explicitly protected slavery, established state sovereignty, prohibited protective tariffs, and invoked the favor of God. After the Civil War, southerners attempted to preserve white supremacy by placing a variety of legal restrictions on African Americans and engaging in extralegal activities such as lynching. By the turn of the twentieth century, southern states assured their control over African Americans through legal *segregation and disfranchisement.

Resistance to federal power and the expansion of rights continued to characterize the South well into the twentieth century. Although a series of Supreme Court decisions and congressional enactments gradually undermined segregation and protected voting rights during the 1950s and 1960s, southerners reasserted state-sovereignty constitutional arguments. In the Southern Manifesto of 1956, a congressional statement against desegregation and judicial activism, southern members of Congress invoked state autonomy over education under the Constitution's Tenth Amendment. During the next decade, southern states passed laws designed to circumvent desegregation, while southern members of Congress unsuccessfully fought the passage of the Civil Rights Act of 1964. Opposition to women's rights also had a uniquely southern flavor. Nine of the ten states that refused to ratify the Nineteenth Amendment, which granted suffrage to women (1920), had been a part of the old Confederacy, and southern states constituted the bulk of those that refused to ratify the *Equal Rights Amendment in the latter half of the twentieth century.

The trans-Mississippi West exhibited its own regional peculiarities. When settlers first moved across the Appalachian Mountains and into the Mississippi River Valley during the late eighteenth century, the West emerged as both an American ideal and a geographic reality. Those seeking land, gold, opportunity, and adventure continually pushed westward, and by the end of the Civil War the region stretched from the Mississippi to the Pacific, a vast territory marked by great variation in climate, terrain, and cultures. In addition to white settlers with common-law values, the region was home to large groups of Native Americans, Asian immigrants, Mexicans, and Mormons. The struggles involving these competing cultures left their marks on the western legal landscape. In former civil-law jurisdictions where Mexican and Spanish community property principles remained influential, married female property owners gained legal protections, while in California, where large number of Asians settled, state lawmakers excluded the Chinese from voting and prohibited their employment in public works. The peculiar demands of *environment, particularly the allocation of resources, also was a critical component of western law. In the arid and semi-arid regions of the Southwest, appellate judges discarded traditional *common-law definitions of riparian rights that had emphasized equitable apportionment and the "natural uses" of streams and rivers. Instead, in order to accommodate the needs of manufacturers and miners, judges advanced the doctrine of prior appropriation, which allowed individuals to claim the right to use water on a first come, first served basis. Western legal innovation also came in other forms, particularly the treatment of farmers, workers, and women. The region's lawmakers stood with midwesterners at the vanguard of the Populist and Progressive reform movements. State constitutions in Utah and

Washington, for example, contained provisions that favored workers and regulated business, while Oregon's legal protections for working women precipitated the landmark Supreme Court case of *Muller* v. *Oregon* (1905). Western states, moreover, were the first to grant women the right to vote.

Despite these legal innovations indigenous to the American West, the federal presence also significantly shaped the social and economic order. During the second half of the nineteenth century alone, Congress enacted legislation providing cheap land for western homesteaders, offering generous land grants to railroad companies in exchange for the laying of track, controlling the region's Native American population, restricting Chinese immigration to the United States, and forcing Utah's Mormons to end polygamy as a precondition for statehood. Federal legislation continued to profoundly affect western states during the twentieth century, particularly in the areas of *immigration, agriculture, and environmental regulation. Today, the extensive amount of western land still owned by the federal government and the huge bounty the region receives in the form of federal dollars and employment have ensured a continuing federal presence unlike in any other region of the United States. Despite the benefits of such largesse, antigovernment attitudes have found fertile soil in the western states, with the recent formation of "common-law" courts and *militia movements being the most extreme examples.

The effects of regionalism on American legal development, of course, should not be exaggerated. Much evidence points to a broadly held commitment to the ideals of legalism and constitutionalism across the nation—from the Overland Trail of the American West to the courtrooms of the Old South. Moreover, the professionalization and nationalization of American legal culture by the late twentieth century, in addition to increasing economic integration, will perhaps eventually eliminate the significance of region in American law. Still, even today the effects of region remain, particularly in the South, where for the past several decades rates of violent crime, incarceration, and *capital punishment have exceeded those in the rest of the nation.

[*See also* Governance]

• Morton J. Horwitz, *The Transformation of American Law, 1790–1860*, 1977. John Phillip Reid, *Law for the Elephant: Property and Social Behavior on the Overland Trail*, 1980. David J. Bodenhamer and James W. Ely Jr., *Ambivalent Legacy: The Legal History of the South*, 1982. Kermit L. Hall, "The 'Magic Mirror' and the Promise of Western Legal History at the Bicentennial of the Constitution," *Western Historical Quarterly*, 18 (1987): 429–35. R. Kent Newmyer, "Harvard Law School, New England Legal Culture, and the Antebellum Origins of American Jurisprudence," *Journal of American History* 75 (1987): 814–35. David Hackett Fischer, *Albion's Seed: Four British Folkways in America*, 1989. Kermit L. Hall, *The Magic Mirror: Law in American History*, 1989. Kermit L. Hall and James W. Ely Jr., *An Uncertain Tradition: Constitutionalism and the History of the South*, 1989. Thomas D. Morris, *Southern Slavery and the Law, 1619–1860*, 1996. Timothy S. Huebner, *The Southern Judicial Tradition: State Judges and Sectional Distinctiveness, 1790–1890*, 1999. Paul Finkelman, *Slavery and the Founders: Race and Liberty in the Age of Jefferson*, 2001.

—Timothy S. Huebner

REGULATION. Richard Hofstadter once noted that America, the land of the trusts, is also the land of *antitrust. Similarly, a nation renowned for its dedication to free enterprise and faith in markets is also exceptional for the scope and rigidity of its regulation of the private sector. A variety of recent studies have found that American regulation is more stringent, legalistic, adversarial, and punitive and more fraught with uncertainty, delay, and transaction costs than regulation in Western Europe and Japan. One reason for this apparent paradox is that imposing demands on the private sector has proved a politically popular alternative to direct public spending or public ownership. Moreover, American distrust of centralized bureaucratic power has produced a plethora of detailed rules and constraints, multiple opportunities of public participation and *judicial review, and overlapping rules issued by state, federal, and local officials. The study of regulation in the United States demonstrates that American political culture and our political institutions are not nearly as hostile to activist government as we are usually led to believe.

Defining the boundaries of "regulation" is not an easy task. One key feature of regulation is that it involves government directives backed by the threat of coercion. For this reason in the U.S. regulation has almost always been accompanied by *due process guarantees, judicial review, and complaints about overzealous bureaucrats. Moreover, because regulation involves enforcing rules and orders rather than distributing money, the elaborate budget mechanisms developed over the years by Congress and the president offer them only limited control over the operation of regulatory programs. Consequently, presidents and members of Congress have searched for alternative methods for supervising administrative action, and have frequently lamented their alleged inability to do so.

As the scope of American regulation has expanded, its boundaries have blurred. In 1955 Marver Bernstein could define the field as "Regulation of Business by Independent Commissions." Regulation meant the work done by the Interstate Commerce Commission (ICC), the Federal Communications Commission (FCC), the Federal Trade Commission (FTC), the Securities and Exchange Commission (SEC), the Civil Aeronautics Board (CAB), and other "alphabet soup" agencies known more for their ponderous, courtlike procedures than for their accomplishments. These agencies—typically multimember boards insulated from direct presidential control—issued rules on business practices and distributed valuable licenses allowing firms to market goods and services. Typically regulation was aimed at a particular sector of the economy—such as railroads, trucking, broadcasting, the stock market, or banking—that was vulnerable to "market failure" (such as monopoly power, externalities, moral hazard, and imperfect information). This industry-by-industry approach created the danger that regulators would become "captured," that is, more attentive to the interests of the regulated industry than to the welfare of consumers.

Over the past thirty years a number of changes in the politics of regulation have made this familiar picture anachronistic. Independent regulatory commissions have not quite gone the way of manual typewriters, but their significance has declined precipitously. A few, most notably the ICC and the CAB, have been abolished. Most new regulatory programs have been entrusted to single-headed agencies squarely within the executive branch. These regulatory bodies typically regulate a wide variety of businesses rather than a particular industry. They promulgate broad, legislative-style rules and rarely used adjudicatory procedures rather than narrow licenses or orders. Moreover, business firms are just one of the many targets of the "social" regulation of recent decades. Contemporary regulation frequently attempts to change the behavior of subnational governments, federal public works agencies, the nonprofit sector (universities, hospitals, and foundations), and millions of private citizens. To complicate matters even more, the line between regulatory and spending programs has blurred as Congress, administrators, and judges have applied more and more "strings" to federal grants and invented new mechanisms for ensuring compliance.

The protean nature of regulation makes it a useful window for examining changes in American political culture, institutional arrangements, and political coalitions. Over the past 150 years the United States has experienced three surges of regulatory activity. Each era produced regulatory programs distinctive in their purpose, their form, and their effectiveness.

During the Populist-Progressive era (roughly 1887–1917) the federal government engaged in extensive economic regulation for the first time. New bodies such as the ICC and the FTC were charged with taming the huge new business entities—commonly known as the "trusts"—that transformed economic life during this period of rapid industrialization. The limited legal authority and administrative capacity of these regulators exposed the enormous barriers to aggressive action by the national government in the early twentieth century.

A second burst of regulatory activity came during the 1930s. Here, of course, the chief concern was coping with the Depression by stabilizing markets and increasing employment. The depth of the crisis and the commitment of the Roosevelt Administration to building expert agencies insulated from judicial oversight added significantly to the power and effectiveness of regulatory bodies.

The third wave of regulation hit rather unexpectedly around 1970. Congress enacted a wide array of demanding *health, safety, *environmental, and *consumer protection laws. At about the same time, administrative and judicial interpretations of Reconstruction-era laws, the Civil Rights Act of 1964, and subsequent nondiscrimination statutes expanded federal regulation of private employment practices and a variety of programs run by state and local governments. In contrast to earlier eras, both Congress and the courts were committed to enhancing the administrative capacity of regulatory agencies, and advocates of aggressive regulation were able to sustain political support for their programs. Although some commentators have described the 1980s and 1990s as a period of "deregulation," such a characterization is misleading. To be sure, deregulation of transportation, telecommunications, energy prices, and financial services was an important and largely successful policy development. But the dismantling of some forms of traditional "economic" regulation was matched by the steady expansion of environmental regulation, new rights for the disabled (see DISABILITIES LAW), a myriad of mandates on health care providers, and ever greater restrictions on the *tobacco industry. Social regulation has proven politically popular and resilient.

Populist/Progressive Regulation: New Challenges, Old Constraints. No regulatory agency embodied both the hopes and the pitfalls of traditional economic regulation more fully than the Interstate Commerce Commission. Established in 1887, the ICC became the prototype for regulatory commissions. Its creation was a response both to widespread discontent about the railroads' control over the fortunes of farmers, merchants, and shippers and to limits the U.S. Supreme Court placed on the states' authority to control railroad rates. The five-member ICC was given authority to prevent pooling and price discrimination as well as to require that rates be "reasonable and just." Monitoring the thousands of rates set by railroads throughout the country without clear legislative standards of what constituted "discrimination" or "just" was an imposing task for a small, inexperienced regulatory body. Moreover, the ICC suffered defeat after defeat in the Supreme Court, leaving it virtually powerless. Legislation passed during Theodore Roosevelt's administration increased the power of the ICC, but also contributed to the declining financial health and physical condition of the railroads. After a brief period of nationalization during the First World War, new legislation in effect shifted the mission of the ICC from protecting customers to reestablishing the health of the industry. This often meant protecting the railroads from competition. By the 1920s the ICC had indeed been "captured" by the railroad industry, but the process had taken decades, a world war, and a substantial shift in congressional sentiment.

Ambiguous legal standards, pro-business judges, weak administrators, and dashed expectations characterized antitrust as well. The Sherman Antitrust Act of 1890—the statute that was used to attack John D. Rockefeller's Standard Oil in 1911 and Bill Gate's Microsoft in 2000—relied on the courts to define and enforce the prohibition on "combinations in restraint of trade." Rather than specifying the difference between ordinary business practices and illegal "restraint of trade," legislators took refuge in the politically appealing myth that common law principles provided answers to the convulsing problems of the "trusts." The famous "rule of reason" announced by the Supreme Court in key antitrust cases left the Court with considerable discretion to distinguish "good" trusts from "bad." Not surprisingly, the Court set a high standard for winning antitrust suits. The Wilson administration and Congress responded by creating the Federal Trade Commission (FTC), which was charged both with developing the expertise needed to prosecute complex antitrust cases and with establishing rules for business conduct that would prevent monopolies from forming in the first place. Despite the optimism of Louis Brandeis and other progressive reformers, devising rules to ensure competition remain an elusive goal. Indeed, before long the FTC was devoting most of its energy to protecting local businesses against price competition from larger chain stores. From the 1920s until its brief revival in the 1970s, the FTC earned its reputation as "the little old lady of Pennsylvania Avenue." The first wave of federal regulation thus exposed both the limited administrative capacity of the national government and the frailty of the political coalitions supporting more aggressive government action.

New Deal Regulation: Building Economic Security and Administrative Capacity. Coping with the consequences of the Great Depression and preventing similar economic catastrophes in the future was, of course, the overriding aim of the multitude of regulatory programs created during the New Deal. On the old question of concentration of economic power the New Deal was, to put it mildly, ambivalent. On the one hand, many New Deal programs sought to cartelize various sectors of the economy, reducing "excessive" competition in order to stabilize the economy and allow the chosen firms to survive. This goal was at the heart of the ill-fated National Industrial Recovery Act, airline regulation by the Civil Aeronautic Board, and shipping regulation by the Federal Maritime Administration. On the other hand, the bitterly contested Public Utilities Holding Company Act (1935) successfully attacked large power companies, Thurman Arnold's Antitrust Division in the Department of Justice vigorously pursued antitrust cases in court, and a variety of other programs sought in one way or another to reduce the power of those FDR described as "economic royalists" and "princes of property."

The New Deal produced two highly significant regulatory success stories, which indicate how much stronger the federal government had grown since the Progressive Era. The first was the Securities and Exchange Commission (SEC). As Thomas McCraw has emphasized in *Prophets of Regulation,* the Securities Act of 1933, "the quintessential sunshine law," worked well because it gave "every person involved—executive, accountant, broker, banker—a stake in helping to enforce the law." The second success story, the National Labor Relations Act of 1935, recognized unions' rights to organize, negotiate, and strike. It created the National Labor Relations Board

(NLRB) to clarify and enforce these rules, and to prohibit "unfair labor practices." Within four years the NLRB had conducted 2500 union elections and settled about 2000 strikes; by 1939 union membership had nearly doubled. To the delight of New Dealers and old Progressives, the NLRB successfully displaced the federal judiciary as the chief arbiter of *labor disputes. Passage and successful administration of the NLRA played a major role in cementing the New Deal coalition. In later years NLRB policy swung back and forth from pro-labor to pro-management, depending largely on the party affiliation of the president appointing a majority of members.

The success of many New Deal programs and the influence of its newly created agencies can be attributed not just to the depth of the Depression and the longevity of the Democratic coalition, but to FDR's firm conviction (announced in his 1932 Commonwealth Club address) that "the days of enlightened administration had come." Roosevelt sought to build a powerful national administrative apparatus under the control of the president. A key element of this project was defanging the federal judiciary, which had not only eviscerated previous regulatory programs, but threatened to declare virtually the entire New Deal unconstitutional. The constitutional crisis that peaked in 1937 was resolved when Roosevelt's appointments filled the Supreme Court. Along with the best-known jurisprudential shifts of the new Roosevelt Court—an end to the use of *due process clause to strike down economic regulation and an open-ended reading of Congress's power under the Commerce Clause—came much more deferential review of administrative action by the federal courts. The New Deal's devotion to administrative expertise was closely tied with its hostility to an activist judiciary.

Perhaps the most important product of the bitter battle between the New Deal and the federal judiciary was the Administrative Procedures Act of 1946 (APA), the statute that establishes generic administrative procedures and outlines the scope of judicial review. For many years the Roosevelt Administration sought to enact legislation giving administrative agencies broad rule-making power, freeing them from cumbersome adjudicatory procedures and from meddling by federal judges. According to the New Deal model of the administrative process, agencies would have broad discretion to issue legislative-style rules rather than narrow, judicial-style orders. The *American Bar Association, reflecting the views of its corporate clients, sought to circumscribe administrative power with elaborate court-like procedures and searching judicial review. The legislation finally enacted by Congress represented a compromise: agencies could use either "informal rule making" (the New Deal model) or "formal adjudication" (the ABA's alternative). Congress would decide on an agency-by-agency basis which model would apply. Or Congress could devise hybrid procedures, which it frequently did. Over the next several decades, rule making eventually displaced adjudication as the dominant form of decision-making by regulatory agencies. Ironically, just as the heirs of FDR were winning this battle, the federal courts were becoming more aggressive in overseeing administrative action.

Social Regulation after 1970: Multiplying Goals, Multiplying Constraints. Despite the success of significant elements of New Deal regulation, by the 1960s the regulatory commissions and the regulatory process were under attack once again. But this time condemnation came primarily from liberal reformers and intellectuals, not business or its allies. The criticisms were many: parochialism, lack of standards, ponderous procedures, the revolving door between agencies and industry, agency reliance on information supplied by industry, lack of participation by consumers and "the public," stifling of competition and innovation, and, above all, the "capture" of regulatory agencies by the regulated industry. As applied to bodies such as the ICC, CAB, FCC, and state occupational licensing boards, these harsh descriptions were largely accurate. This was hardly surprising since many of these commissions had been established or reconstituted with the express purpose of promoting the regulated industry by limiting competition.

This powerful political and academic critique of the regulatory process had two long-term consequences. First: combined with substantial technological change, it contributed to the movement that culminated in the partial deregulation of transportation, financial services, and telecommunications in the late 1970s and 1980s. The deregulation coalition included an odd array of free-market economists, Naderite consumer advocates, mainstream liberal Democrats, presidents looking for ways to reduce inflation, and business entrepreneurs searching for ways to enter previously closed markets. Although the transition to relatively unregulated markets did not always proceed smoothly—consider the savings-and-loan debacle of the 1980s—phasing out old-style economic regulation generally increased competition, lowered prices to consumers, and stimulated innovation.

This deregulation impulse coexisted with a far stronger movement to expand health, safety, environmental, consumer, and anti-discrimination regulation. The critique of regulatory process summarized above played a crucial rule in shaping this new "social" regulation. Determined to avoid the pitfalls of the past, those who wrote the new regulatory statutes, designed the new regulatory agencies, and oversaw the implementation of the new regulatory programs instituted a wide variety of reforms. Among them were the following: detailed statutes with multiple deadlines; agencies with authority to regulate a wide variety of industries; extensive rule-making authority; tough conflict of interest rules; public participation requirements, at times accompanied by intervenor funding for public-interest groups; sufficient appropriations for agencies to develop their own technical expertise; authority for agencies to issue orders and fines without first going to court; citizen suit provisions allowing individuals and public-interest groups to sue an agency for failing to perform a "nondiscretionary duty" or a business firm for violating agency rules; and aggressive oversight by congressional committees and subcommittees.

The most notable feature of the new "social" regulation that emerged after 1970 was its unprecedented scope. Clearly public expectations about the role of government in general and the federal government in particular had undergone a sea-change since the passage of the Interstate Commerce Act eighty years before. With each expansion of the government's agenda, the next step became less extraordinary and easier to justify. Few mainstream politicians, officials, or journalists any longer doubted that the constitutional power of Congress extended to every commercial transaction in the county—and to a wide variety of noncommercial transactions as well. Few problems failed to generate demands for new public programs. At the same time, the cost and intrusiveness of the accumulating government policies produced chronic antagonism between regulators and the regulated as well as frequent demands for regulatory relief. Heated political battles over regulation, once merely episodic, became a regular feature of American politics.

The number and complexity of the regulatory programs initiated over the past thirty years make it difficult to describe them adequately in a brief essay. The paragraphs that follow will briefly describe four categories of social regulation, emphasizing both their broad sweep and their innovative design. Three themes regularly reappear. The first is risk reduction. Social regulation is an ambitious effort to make the lives of citizens more secure by reducing or eliminating a wide variety of the risks of everyday life. The second theme is egalitarianism. This is most apparent in regulation outlawing various forms of discrimination. But behind almost all social regulation lies an effort to reduce the power of large institutions over the lives of average Americans. The third theme—rather paradoxical in light of the huge expansion of government responsibility—is distrust of administrative power. Gone was the New Deal and Progressive faith in "enlightened administration." In its stead came a wide array of efforts to limit bureaucratic discretion without crippling regulatory programs.

Environmental Protection. The most expensive and extensive regulation of this era—or any other era in American history—was the vast set of rules established to protect the environment. Most federal pollution control efforts are administered by the Environmental Protection Agency (EPA). Created by executive order in 1970, EPA is by far the largest regulatory agency in the U.S., employing over 12,000 people, not counting the thousands of state and local administrators who share responsibility for administering federal environmental programs. EPA is charged with administering the Clean Air, the Clean Water Act, the Safe Drinking Water Act, Superfund, and federal statutes establishing complex regulatory regimes for solid waste, pesticides, toxic chemicals, and oil spills. Among those subject to EPA rules are 40,000 major sources of air pollution, 68,000 point sources of water pollution, 650,000 generators of hazardous waste, 27,000 abandoned hazardous waste dumps, 79,000 public water systems, and hundreds of millions of cars, trucks, motorcycles, and planes. The annual cost of complying with environmental regulation is $150–200 billion or 2.5–3 percent of GDP.

Despite the formidable difficulty of formulating precise emission limitations for thousands of sources of pollution and forcing business firms and municipalities to spend millions of dollars to comply with them, EPA and the states have succeeded in reducing industrial and automotive pollution during a period of substantial economic growth. But environmental agencies have had no time to rest on their laurels. New challenges arose faster than old ones were met. Love Canal, the Exxon Valdez oil spill, spotted owls and snail darters, radon, acid rain, Alar, dioxin, asbestos, ozone depletion, wetland destruction, global warming—just to mention a few items—remind us how ubiquitous environmental issues have become.

Not only has the media been eager to call attention to new environmental problems, but environmental groups have become adept at using media attention to build political support for further government action.

During the 1970s and 1980s the Democrats who controlled Congress frequently included strict—even utopian—standards and deadlines in environmental statutes. They also authorized public-interest groups to go to court to enforce these requirements. Often described as "technology forcing," these rigid rules allowed Democrats on the Hill to claim they were "greener" than Republicans in the White House—and to castigate Republican administrations whenever statutory goals were not achieved on schedule. Divided government fueled the growth of environmental regulation as both parties tried to appeal to swing voters in the suburbs. Since the EPA had neither the administrative capacity nor the political support needed to meet all these legislative demands, its priorities were often set by the vagaries of litigation. Especially in the 1970s the courts were more inclined to castigate regulators for excessive delay and insufficient zeal than to condemn them for exceeding their statutory mandate.

A different form of environmental regulation placed new restrictions on the use of federal lands and the conduct of state and federal development agencies. The National Environmental Policy Act (NEPA), perhaps the most famous of all the environmental enactments of this era, requires federal administrators to assess the "environmental impact" of all major governmental actions and to integrate these factors into their decision-making. NEPA, the Endangered Species Act, and a variety of other "cross-cutting" regulations were aimed not at private parties, but at government agencies whose actions significantly affected the environment—which sooner or later includes nearly every unit and level of government. Because it is difficult for one federal agency to force another to comply with its rules, enforcement of these "cross-cutting" regulations usually fell to citizen groups acting through courts. The federal courts played an especially active role in interpreting and enforcing NEPA's procedural and citizen participation requirements, blocking a wide array of actions by the Forest Service, the Corps of Engineers, the Federal Highway Administration, and the Atomic Energy Commission.

Health and Safety Regulation. Other regulatory programs established in the 1970s focused on health and safety risks associated with particular dangerous technologies or the locations. No federal agency managed to provoke such opposition from business as the Occupational Safety and Health Administration. Established in 1972 after an aggressive legislative campaign by labor unions, OSHA ran into a firestorm of criticism when it announced a host of detailed safety rules and adopted a rigid enforcement policy. From its vinyl chloride, benzene, and cotton dust rules in the 1970s to the ergonomic rules announced in the waning days of the Clinton administration, OSHA has promulgated stringent rules that have generated extensive litigation, scrutiny from White House economists, and grumbling in Congress, but little change in its legislative mandate or mission. As is often the case with health, safety, and environmental regulation, small business had more difficulty complying and complained more bitterly about overregulation than did larger firms.

While OSHA regulates a wide variety of employers, other health and safety agencies have narrower jurisdictions. The National Highway Traffic Safety Administration—the agency that brought us padded dashboards, interlocking seat belts, airbags, and hundreds of recalls of thousands of vehicles—has focused almost exclusively on the design of the automobile. The Nuclear Regulatory Commission was split off from the old Atomic Energy Commission in 1975 in order to make it a more effective watchdog of the nuclear power industry. Congress also steadily added to the jurisdiction of the granddaddy of all health and safety regulators, the Food and Drug Administration. That the FDA was created in 1906 shows that health and safety regulation was hardly an innovation of the 1970s. But the scope and stringency of this regulation and the extent to which the federal government rather than the states took the lead distinguish the social regulation of the 1970s from the health and safety regulation of previous eras.

Consumer Protection. The 1970s also witnessed an outpouring of initiatives to protect consumers from faulty products and deceptive practices. Some of these initiatives—such as the creation of the Consumer Product Safety Commission, the Moss-Magnuson Warrantee Act, the Truth-in-Lending Act, and the Consumer Credit Protection Act—were the result of congressional action. Senator Warren Magnuson, chair of the Senate Commerce Committee in the 1970s, and his peripatetic aide Michael Pertschuk, raised the visibility of consumer issues and tirelessly pushed new legislative initiatives. They personified the policy entrepreneurship that characterized congressional politics in this period. At the same time the FTC and the Antitrust Division were launching "structural" antitrust actions against some of the nation's largest companies, including IBM, ITT, Exxon, and Kellogg. In the late 1970s the FTC announced controversial new rules on used cars, the funeral industry, and lending practices. When the FTC launched an investigation of TV advertisements aimed at children, it discovered that it had exhausted its political support in Congress. Soon thereafter President Reagan appointed to the FTC market-oriented economists who were much more skeptical of such consumer-protection programs.

While the FTC was drawing media attention and political heat, state court judges were quietly establishing a new regime in *tort law that shifted liability for accidents from consumers to producers. Following the advice of experts at prestigious law schools and the lead of appellate judges in California and New Jersey, between 1965 and 1976 the majority of state supreme courts adopted *"strict liability" rules in product liability cases. This was just one of the many ways in which judges shifted the burden from plaintiffs to defendants in tort suits. As a result, the number of tort cases filed, the number of awards to plaintiffs, the size of these awards, and the cost of liability insurance all increased dramatically. This serves to remind us that a substantial amount of regulation comes not just from legislatures and administrative agencies, but from *common-law judges as well.

Nondiscrimination Rules. Although few people realized it at the time, the Civil Rights Act of 1964 significantly expanded federal regulation in two ways. First, Title VII of the Act prohibited racial *discrimination in the workplace and created the Equal Employment Opportunity Commission (EEOC) to monitor employers' compliance. As originally drafted, Title VII was limited to intentional discrimination against racial minorities (see RACE AND ETHNICITY). It did not take long, though, for its scope to expand. The House immediately added a provision outlawing *gender discrimination by employers. Within five years a complex combination of judicial rulings and administrative decisions had transformed Title VII into an affirmative action program complete with specific "goals and timetables." Although Congress never endorsed this new understanding of nondiscrimination, it steadily increased the powers of the EEOC and the number of groups protected by federal law. In 1976 it prohibited employers from discriminating on the basis of age

(see AGING AND THE LAW). In 1990 Congress enacted the Americans with Disability Act, requiring employers to make "reasonable accommodations" for employees with disabilities. In recent years the EEOC and the federal courts have relied upon Title VII's prohibition of gender discrimination to establish federal rules on sexual harassment in the workplace.

Title VI of the Civil Rights Act prohibited racial discrimination in any "program or activity" receiving federal funds. This meant that federal agencies that made grants to state and local governments had to define and monitor compliance by recipient institutions. Here, too, "structural" discrimination soon replaced intentional discrimination as the guiding legal standard. The federal courts put teeth into Title VI regulation by authorizing private parties to file suit to enforce its provisions. Congress followed the Title VI model in banning gender discrimination by educational institutions receiving federal funds (Title IX of the Education Amendments of 1972), prohibiting discrimination against the handicapped (section 504 of the Rehabilitation Act of 1974), and requiring state and local school systems to provide each handicapped child with a "free and appropriate public education." (Education for All Handicapped Children Act of 1975). By 1980 the Office of Management and Budget listed nearly 60 "cross-cutting" federal regulation binding on all subnational governments receiving federal funds. Despite intense criticism from state and local officials, Congress continued to add new strings, mandates, and other instruments of "regulatory federalism" to legislation passed in the 1980s and 1990s.

As the United States enters the new century there is no sign that the expansion of government regulation is abating. The Patient's Bill of Rights is just the latest of a long series of federal rules governing the medical-industrial complex. Between 1994 and 1997, nearly all of the attorneys general of the state governments brought suits against the major cigarette manufacturers, the individual and collective settlements of which produced a new regime to tobacco regulation as well as the promise of more than $200 billion in payments to state governments. Congressional Republicans have apparently lost their initial zeal for rolling back environmental protection laws and at times have endorsed moderate expansion. While it is hazardous to try to predict political trends in so vast an arena, most social regulation seems firmly entrenched.

Regulation American Style. If a comparison between the United States in 1960 and the United

States today highlights the enormous scope of social regulation, a comparison between regulation in the United States and regulation in Western Europe draws attention to this country's peculiar regulatory style. In *Regulatory Encounters* Robert Kagan summarizes the key features of what he has termed American "adversarial legalism":

> American regulatory programs involve more detailed and complex bodies of rules, harsher penalties, a more legalistic enforcement style, more fragmented institutional structures, and more frequent recourse to courts to challenge administrative decisions. Liability laws and civil litigation are more frequently employed in the United States than in Western Europe, Japan, and British Commonwealth nations, and those processes are more punitive, more expensive, and more unpredictable.

Although the substance of health, safety, and environmental laws is often similar in these countries, companies doing business in the United States experience much higher transaction costs and substantially more regulatory delay. This seems to be true of almost all American regulatory programs.

Three factors contributing to American "adversarial legalism" are readily apparent in the preceding description of post-1970 social regulation. One is the profusion of sources of legal rules and regulations. Congress, federal agencies, federal courts (stretching from the Supreme Court to the thirteen courts of appeal to 512 district court judges), the White House, state legislatures, state agencies, state courts, local governments—all can and do issue rules binding on business firms, private citizens, and other government agencies. Not surprisingly, these rules often overlap and conflict with one another. Judges, legislators, and administrators then struggle to formulate new rules that explain which regulations have priority. Second: many of these disputes eventually end up in the courts, which are both highly decentralized and subject to extensive delay. The unusual power of courts in the United States contributes to the uncertainty of the regulation and makes lawyers (and high legal costs) central to the regulatory process. Third: since 1970 heightened public expectations about government protection and assistance have gone hand-in-hand with dwindling public trust in government. Advocates of social regulation have attempted to resolve this dilemma by sharply limiting bureaucratic discretion and multiplying opportunities for public,

legislative, and judicial oversight. From the head of EPA to the lowliest enforcement officer, administrators are expected to "go by the book" rather then negotiate informal arrangements with regulated firms. This is in stark contrast to other advanced industrial democracies, which tolerate far more informal bargaining both in establishing regulatory standards and in enforcing them.

Given the diversity and complexity of regulatory programs in the United States, it is not difficult to find exceptions to many of the generalizations offered in this essay. Each program has its own distinctive history, political coalition, achievements, dangers, and conundrums. That is why case studies of regulatory behavior are so rich and informative. Looking at the broad outline of regulatory development over the past century and a quarter, though, helps us appreciate how much public expectations of government have changed and how the distinctive features of our political institutions have shaped the policies that so directly affect our daily lives.

[*See also* Administrative Law Judge; Commercial Law; Securities Law]

• Marver Bernstein, *Regulating Business by Independent Commission*, 1955. James Q. Wilson, ed., *The Politics of Regulations*, 1980. Stephen Breyer, *Regulation and its Reform*, 1982. R. Shep Melnick, *Regulation and the Courts: The Case of the Clean Air Act*, 1983. Thomas K. McCraw, *Prophets of Regulation*, 1984. Martha Derthick and Paul Quirk, *The Politics of Deregulation*, 1985. Donald F. Kettl, *The Regulation of American Federalism*, 1987. Martin Shapiro, *Who Guards the Guardians? Judicial Control of Administration*, 1988. Morton Keller, *Regulation a New Economy: Public Policy and Economic Change in America, 1900–1933*, 1990. Peter H. Schuck, ed., *Tort Law and the Public Interest: Competition, Innovation, and Consumer Welfare*, 1991. Marc Landy, Marc Roberts, and Stephen Thomas, *The Environmental Protection Agency: Asking the Wrong Questions*, expanded ed., 1993. Richard Harris and Sidney Milkis, eds., *The Politics of Regulatory Change: A Tale of Two Agencies*, 2d ed., 1996. Robert Kagan and Lee Axelrad, *Regulatory Encounters: Multinational Corporations and American Adversarial Legalism*, 2000.

—R. Shep Melnick

REGULATION, INSURANCE. *See* Insurance.

REGULATION, SECURITIES. *See* Securities Law.

REGULATORY TAKING. *See* Takings.

RELIANCE loss is one of three generally recognized measures of damages that a plaintiff may recover in a civil action against the party who has breached a *contract. This recovery reimburses the plaintiff for losses he has suffered in reliance on the defendant's contractual promise and is distinguished from expectation damages or restitution.

—David S. Clark

RELIGION. On its face, law has much in common with religion. Like religion, law is a means of regulating human conduct. It defines a society's vision of "good" and "evil." Indeed, laws enacted by government often reflect moral and religious values. Sometimes they do so in a very overt manner. Massachusetts, for example, passed a law in 1782 punishing blasphemy. This law held that any person "wilfully blaspheming the name of God or denying him, or . . . cursing or contumeliously reproaching him or any part of the Trinity, or the Bible" could be imprisoned for up to a year or whipped. As late as 1835, a newspaper editor named Abner Kneeland, who denied Jesus's virgin birth and resurrection, called clergy hypocrites, and derided the sacredness of marriage, was convicted of blasphemy in Massachusetts. The state's Supreme Judicial Court, in *Commonwealth* v. *Kneeland* (1838), upheld his sentence of sixty days in prison.

Because the U.S. Supreme Court did not "incorporate" (make binding on the states) the Establishment Clause of the First Amendment of the Constitution until 1947 (in *Everson* v. *Board of Education*), the Massachusetts blasphemy law and others like it continued to be constitutional after the 1791 ratification of the First Amendment. Indeed, before *Everson*, the First Amendment prevented only the national government from establishing a religion; states remained free to do so. Seven states (Connecticut, Georgia, Maryland, Massachusetts, New Hampshire, South Carolina, and Vermont) retained some form of religious establishment. All had multiple or general establishments rather than the establishment of a single denomination, but none included *all* religions. For example, the 1780 Massachusetts constitution, drafted by John *Adams, created a multiple establishment of all Protestant churches. Adams called this a "mild and equitable establishment" of religion. According to Article II of the Massachusetts constitution: "It is the right as well as the duty of all men in society, publickly, and at stated seasons to worship the SUPREME BEING, the great Creator and preserver of the Universe," because, as Article III explained, the "public worship of GOD and instructions in piety, religion, and morality . . . promote their happiness, and secure . . . the good order and preservation of their government."

Disestablishment did not come to Massachusetts until 1833.

Many laws reflect religious values in a less overt manner. For example, states have routinely passed laws protecting *marriage and regulating other forms of sexual conduct. In early U.S. history, some states severely punished sexual activity outside marriage. In 1785 Massachusetts law called for public whipping of a man or woman found guilty of *adultery and death for homosexual intercourse (see HOMOSEXUALITY AND THE LAW); Virginia law called for those found guilty of bigamy to be executed. Many states continue to make adultery a misdemeanor. In Idaho, it can still be deemed a *felony leading to imprisonment in the state penitentiary for up to three years. As of 1999, ten states continued to punish sodomy as a felony and an additional nine punished it as a misdemeanor.

Although laws regulating sexual conduct often seem to be rooted in religious views, the recent move toward enacting laws prohibiting *discrimination based on sexual orientation and recognizing same-sex marriage has turned the issue on its head. Some religious groups have objected to such laws. In response to these concerns, Congress passed the Defense of Marriage Act in 1996. Signed into law by President Bill Clinton, the act purportedly gave states the legal authority to refuse to recognize same-sex marriages performed in other states (in fact, no state permits same-sex marriages). The act also withheld from same-sex couples those federal benefits (e.g., tax, welfare, and pension benefits) that are offered to married heterosexual couples. Nonetheless, the Vermont Supreme Court ruled in *Baker* v. *State* (1999) that the state constitution entitled same-sex couples to "the common benefits and protections that flow from marriage under Vermont law." That case led the Vermont legislature to pass a law in April 2000 giving gay and lesbian couples the right to join in "civil unions," a status equivalent to marriage. The law took effect in July and led social and religious conservatives in Vermont to wage a "Take Back Vermont" campaign during the 2000 election season.

Sunday Closing Laws also have religious roots, although a secular argument can be used to justify them. The U.S. Supreme Court, in *McGowan* v. *Maryland* (1961), upheld a Maryland Sunday Closing Law used to prosecute employees of a department store chain who worked on Sunday on the grounds that the law was motivated by the secular concern of providing "a uniform day of rest for all citizens" and therefore bore "no relationship" to the establishment of religion. In *Braunfeld* v. *Brown* (1961), the Court likewise rejected a Free Exercise claim against a Pennsylvania closing law. Abraham Braunfeld, an Orthodox Jew, opened his retail clothing and home furnishing store on Sunday because he closed it on Saturday—his Sabbath. The Court agreed that the Pennsylvania law made the practice of Braunfeld's religious beliefs more expensive for his business but concluded that it did not violate the Free Exercise Clause of the First Amendment. Neither case has been overruled, but Sunday closing laws, for cultural and political reasons, have either been repealed or are not enforced.

Braunfeld and the Vermont civil union law are just two of many examples that illustrate the tension between religious values and legal choices. Many individuals feel that laws infringe in one way or another upon their religious beliefs or reflect values that they do not hold. Religious pacifists, for example, have objected to draft laws. Supreme Court decisions have also provoked opposition on religious grounds. School prayer is a notable example. In *Engel* v. *Vitale* (1962), the Court ruled that a prayer written by the New York State Board of Regents to be recited aloud each morning by students in New York's public schools violated the Establishment Clause. New York courts had upheld the prayer as long as a student's participation in the recitation was voluntary. The Supreme Court, however, ruled that any state-sponsored prayer was unconstitutional—even if it was nondenominational and participation in its recitation was voluntary. Reaction was swift. Barry Goldwater, Republican senator from Arizona, said the Court had "ruled against God." Members of Congress introduced more than a hundred proposed *constitutional amendments to allow school prayer. Although many Americans were opposed to the ruling, Congress also received a flood of letters supporting it. Moreover, a wide array of organized religious groups testified against such constitutional amendments when the House Judiciary Committee held public hearings on the issue in 1964. Among those organizations opposing a constitutional amendment to allow prayer in public schools were the American Baptist Convention, the American Jewish Congress, the American Lutheran Church, the Episcopal Church, the National Council of Churches of Christ, the Synagogue Council of America, and the United Presbyterian Church.

Attempts to amend the Constitution failed, and the Supreme Court extended its ruling in subsequent cases. In *Abington School District* v. *Schempp* (1963), the Court ruled that the policy of beginning the public school day by reading Bible verses was unconstitutional, as were recitations of the Lord's Prayer. In *Wallace* v. *Jaffree* (1985), the Court struck down an Alabama law authorizing public schools to set aside a minute of every school day for silent prayer or private meditation. In *Lee* v. *Weisman* (1992), the Court struck down clergy-led prayer at public school graduation ceremonies. And in *Santa Fe Independent School District* v. *Doe* (2000) the Court ruled that a public school district's policy of permitting student-led, student-initiated prayer at football games also violated the Establishment Clause.

Such decisions still provoke controversy. President Ronald Reagan stated in the 1980s that the Court had ruled wrongly on school prayer, and his attorney general, Edwin Meese III, in a speech before the American Bar Association in July 1985, criticized the Supreme Court for departing from the "original intent" of the framers of the Constitution on such issues as school prayer. When Republicans took control of the House of Representatives in the 1994 midterm elections, there was renewed talk of a constitutional amendment to allow school prayer. In an effort to ward off such an amendment, President Clinton issued a memorandum in 1995 to disabuse the assumption that religious expression of any type is either inappropriate or explicitly forbidden by the Court's decisions. He pointed out that students are free to engage in private religious speech including individual and nondisruptive group prayer, that they may read their Bibles or other scriptures, and participate before or after school in religious activities (such as a prayer club). He noted that although local school authorities have wide discretion to impose rules of order and other pedagogical restrictions on student activities, they cannot use such rules to discriminate against students' religious activity or speech. In 1998 the House voted 224 to 203 in favor of an amendment allowing voluntary school prayer. This fell short of the required two-thirds majority by sixty-one votes, and the Senate failed to act on it.

Other aspects of education have also sparked religious debates. One example is the teaching of evolution, which has been opposed by those who believe it conflicts with the Biblical version of creation found in the Book of Genesis. Some states have passed laws prohibiting the teaching of evolution in public schools. In 1927, John T. *Scopes, a twenty-four-year-old high school teacher in Dayton, Tennessee, was tried for violating a 1925 Tennessee law that prohibited the teaching of "any theory that denies the story of the divine creation as taught in the Bible." Although Scopes was ultimately convicted for teaching evolution in the famous "Monkey Trial" (*Scopes* v. *State* (1927)), the judge fined him only a hundred dollars and, on appeal, the conviction was overturned on a technicality. Although similar laws remained on the books in "Bible Belt" states, they were not enforced and were eventually struck down by a unanimous Supreme Court in *Epperson* v. *Arkansas* (1968). In *Edwards* v. *Aguillard* (1987), the Court also struck down the Louisiana Balanced Treatment for Creation-Science and Evolution-Science in Public School Instruction Act, which prohibited the teaching of evolution unless accompanied by the teaching of "creation science."

The Supreme Court's *abortion decisions have been particularly controversial and have also provoked opposition on religious grounds. In *Roe* v. *Wade* (1973), a majority of the Court attempted to balance a woman's constitutional right of *privacy to control her own body (including the decision about whether or not to abort her fetus) and the states' interest in protecting a fetus's potential right to life. *Roe* became one of the most controversial Supreme Court rulings of recent times. Conservative religious activists, in particular, saw the ruling as a liberal enactment that conflicted with their strongly held belief in the sanctity of human life (which, according to many of them, began at conception). In the ensuing years, abortion became a major issue in Supreme Court confirmation hearings. The Senate rejected President Reagan's nomination of Robert Bork to the Court in 1987 in large part because of his stated opposition to *Roe*. Had he been confirmed, Bork would have provided the decisive fifth vote necessary to overturn it. A divided Supreme Court reaffirmed the "central tenet" of *Roe* by a vote of 5–4 in *Planned Parenthood of Southeastern Pennsylvania* v. *Casey* (1992). A plurality of the Court went on to abandon *Roe*'s trimester framework and replace it with an "undue burden" standard that said women have a right to choose abortion before viability of the fetus "without undue interference from the state." Opposition to *Roe*, as modified by *Casey*, remains a major objective of religious groups such as the Christian Coalition and the Catholic Church.

[*See also* Civil Rights and Civil Liberties]

• Kenneth M. Dolbeare and Phillip E. Hammond, *The School Prayer Decisions: From Court Policy to Local Practice*, 1971. Leonard Levy, ed., *Blasphemy in Massachusetts: Freedom of Conscience and the Abner Kneeland Case*, 1973. Frank J. Sorauf, *The Wall of Separation: The Constitutional Politics of Church and State*, 1976. Stuart Taylor Jr., "Meese in Bar Group Speech, Criticizes High Court," *New York Times*, 10 July 1985, A13. John T. Noonan Jr., *The Believer and the Powers that Are: Cases, History, and Other Data Bearing on the Relation of Religion and Government*, 1987. Leonard Levy, *The Establishment Clause: Religion and the First Amendment*, 2d ed., 1994. Bill Clinton, *Public Papers of the Presidents*, vol II, 1995 (1083–85). Edward J. Larson, *Summer for the Gods: The Scopes Trial and America's Continuing Debate over Science and Religion*, 1997. John Witte Jr., *Religion and the American Constitutional Experiment*, 2000.

—John Anthony Maltese

REMEDIES

Legal and Equitable
Pretrial

REMEDIES: LEGAL AND EQUITABLE

A remedy in the law involves the resolution of a lawsuit or an issue in a lawsuit, and provides redress to aggrieved parties or protects the integrity or efficiency of judicial proceedings. There are different types of remedies and many rules about when and how those remedies may be awarded, and like other rules, they reflect values in the society.

A remedy may be classified as legal, equitable, or declaratory, or as pretrial, trial, or appellate. If a remedy is declaratory, the plaintiff obtains a court ruling about his or her status, but does not recover tangible relief. Legal and equitable remedies are defined by contrasting them. One difference between the two is in their form. A legal remedy is a court judgment that a plaintiff (or another party, even the defendant) is entitled to something. Lawyers refer to legal actions as either *in rem,* relating to interests in *property, or *in personam*, creating an obligation for a particular person.

Legal remedies usually involve an award of money damages to substitute for what the plaintiff lost. This may be for personal injury, which can include compensation for past and present medical expenses, lost earnings, and pain and suffering, all with adjustments for inflation and interest. Any award projecting future losses will be reduced to its present value in current monetary terms. A legal award will compensate for future losses because judgments are final awards. Thus, it is only fair to take into account damages both from the past and those that are likely to occur in the future. Damages that are speculative, however, will not be awarded. Money damages are also awarded to substitute for damaged property, or to compensate for harm to one's reputation, or because someone did not perform contractual duties. A return of personal property (*replevin) or land (ejectment) that the plaintiff owns is also a legal remedy.

Equitable remedies are court orders to a person or institution to do or not do something. As mentioned, these equitable actions are *in personam*. Equitable orders can cover myriad situations, such as court orders to officials to desegregate schools, to corporate actors to stop mergers or acquisitions, to development companies to stop construction pending an environmental review, to an employer to reinstate someone wrongfully fired, or to a *contract breacher to keep his or her promise. All but the last of these court orders are referred to as injunctions. Where enforcement of a contract is ordered, the equitable remedy is called specific enforcement. Sometimes the court's equitable order can involve the payment of money, such as orders to pay child support. Because the order is equitable, if circumstances change, one or the other of the parties can return to the judge and ask for a change in the order. A legal judgment, however, is final once the time for appeal has run out.

A simple example illustrates the difference between legal and equitable remedies. Suppose two people contract for the sale of a painting for $10,000. If the seller refuses to sell, the buyer has two options, to seek legal relief or equitable relief. Legal relief will compensate the buyer for his or her lost expectation in the value of the contract. The court will award him or her the difference between the value of the painting, minus the $10,000 he or she expected to pay. Thus, if the painting is worth $10,000, the buyer will not have any expectation of damages, and will merely be excused from having to pay $10,000. If the buyer has already paid, he or she can recover the seller's unjust enrichment of $10,000, for which the seller gave no value—that is, the painting. If, however, the buyer had not paid, but the painting is actually worth $15,000, then he or she had made a good bargain and is entitled to the $5,000 expected gain.

If the plaintiff only wants the painting, he or she will need a court to order the defendant to convey the painting to the plaintiff. To get that equitable order, the plaintiff will have to show that the legal remedy is inadequate; therefore, equitable relief is not automatic. Typically, the plaintiff would be able to say that the legal remedy is inadequate if the painting were unique. Why must the plaintiff make such a showing to get equitable relief? The answer lies in part in the historical roots of actions at *equity and in law.

Over a period of centuries in England, the delivery of justice evolved into two systems, equity courts and law courts. Each court had its own jurisdiction. If a plaintiff were in the wrong court, his or her suit would be dismissed and he or she would have to bring the suit again in the correct court. In the meantime, the statute of limitations might have run out, making his or her suit untimely. In the United States, the Federal Rules of Civil Procedure, first written in 1938, merged legal and equitable actions into one action, the civil action. The distinction between law and equity was thus abolished as a matter of jurisdiction for federal courts and in most states, but remains for some procedural issues, and at the remedial stage of the action.

The first consequence of this remaining distinction concerns the right to a *jury trial. The Seventh Amendment to the United States Constitution states: "In Suits at common law . . . the right of trial by jury shall be preserved." The exclusion of the word "equity" means that there are no federal jury trials in actions in which equitable relief is sought. If the action combines both legal and equitable remedies, a jury will determine the facts and the legal remedy, and a judge will determine the equitable remedy.

Another important consequence of whether a remedy is legal or equitable concerns the way remedies are enforced. Because an equitable order is an order from a judge to a person to do or not do something, if that person does not comply, he has disobeyed the judge. The judge can enforce the order with *contempt. On the other hand, since a legal judgment is not an order to a person, if the defendant does not comply, he or she will not be subject to contempt. If the defendant does not comply with the judgment voluntarily, the plaintiff can take the judgment to a *sheriff or marshall. Pursuant to the jurisdiction's execution procedures, the officer will attach and sell the defendant's assets to satisfy the judgment.

This enforcement mechanism illustrates another reason why courts typically require that the legal remedy be inadequate before an equitable remedy becomes appropriate. Legal remedies do not require the judge's continued supervision, and thus preserve judicial resources. A court's equitable contempt power can also be onerous, and should not be invoked frequently. Contempt puts a range of powerful tools into the hands of the judge. Contempt can be either civil or criminal. If the contempt is criminal, the contumacious defendant (who did not comply with the order) can be punished with imprisonment or a fine. The defendant will have a hearing in which it must be proven that he or she knew about the injunction and violated it, having had the capability to comply. At the hearing, the defendant will be entitled to criminal protections, such as the right against *self-incrimination. If the possible imprisonment is more than six months, or if the possible fine is substantial, the defendant will be entitled to a jury trial.

If the contempt is civil, it is either coercive or compensatory. Coercive contempt is designed to make the defendant comply with the court's order. The court might imprison or fine the defendant until he or she complies. The civil coercive imprisonment or fine is different from the criminal sanction. While a criminal sanction is determinate in time, a coercive contempt is indeterminate because it will last only as long as needed to make the defendant comply. In civil coercive contempt, the defendant "has the keys to the jail in his [or her] pocket." If the defendant chooses not to comply, the sanction can be onerous.

With compensatory contempt, the disobedience may have already occurred, leaving nothing that can be remedied by coercion. The plaintiff can seek compensation at the contempt hearing for the damage caused by the defendant's non-compliance with the order. Ironically, to get the original injunction, the legal remedy must have been inadequate. Once a plaintiff is seeking damages in a contempt hearing, however, the plaintiff is seeking what looks like a legal remedy—money damages— but without a jury trial. The irony here is only superficial, however, because the fact that damages would have been inadequate before the harm occurred does not mean that the plaintiff should go uncompensated if the defendant does not comply with the injunction.

Equitable remedies can be preliminary and temporary. A court can order a defendant to do or not do something pending a trial. Such temporary relief can be in the form of a temporary *restraining order (TRO), which typically lasts only a matter of days, or in the form of a preliminary injunction, which will last until a final decision is reached after trial. An appellate court can also issue temporary equitable relief. It can order a stay (a reversal pending appeal) of a lower court's order, or order an injunction pending appeal if one were denied by the trial court. To obtain a TRO, a preliminary injunction or a stay from a judge or an appellate court, the plaintiff must show that he or she is likely to succeed at trial or on appeal, that he or she will be irreparably harmed if the injunction or stay is not issued, that the defendant will not be harmed as much, and that the injunction or stay is in the public interest (or at least does not harm it).

Courts will often issue this temporary relief to preserve the status quo for the trial, but it is sometimes difficult to see where the status quo lies. For example, in December 2000, the U.S. Supreme Court in *Bush v. Gore stayed the Florida Supreme Court's order to the county election boards to count the presidential votes that machines had not registered. With that stay, the status quo might have been the certified machine tally showing that George W. Bush had won the electoral votes of Florida and thus the presidential election. Or the status quo might have been the ongoing count, which might have reversed Bush's narrow margin of victory over Albert Gore. When the Supreme Court heard the appeal a few days later, it decided that the Florida Supreme Court's order violated the *Fourteenth Amendment's *due process and *equal protection clauses because of problems in how to interpret the same type of ballots from county to county. The Court's opinion said, however, that "The only disagreement is as to the remedy." Five justices held that no standard for counting disputed ballots could be devised or could be devised in time; four justices would have ordered the counties to continue to count the votes. Thus the U.S. Supreme Court's determination about the impracticability of an equitable remedy in Bush v. Gore may have affected the outcome of the 2000 presidential election.

[See also Procedure, Civil; Torts]

• Dan B. Dobbs, Law of Remedies 1–3, 2d ed., 1993. Doug Rendleman, Remedies, 6th ed., 1999. Robert Leavell, Grant Nelson, Jean Love, and Candace Kovacic-Fleischer, Equitable Remedies, Restitution and Damages, 6th ed., 2000. Douglass Laycock, Modern American Remedies, 3d ed., 2002.

—Candace Saari Kovacic-Fleischer

REMEDIES: PRETRIAL

American courts recognize a variety of remedies that are available in appropriate circumstances prior to trial. These may be used either to keep a party from disposing of *property before a final *judgment is obtained or to prevent irreparable harm to a party before trial. In addition to these legitimate purposes, pretrial remedies can also be used to obtain a tactical advantage over an adversary by, for example, depriving the adversary of the property's possession pending trial. Since they are awarded prior to judgment, pretrial remedies are provisional and thus subject to modification before the lawsuit's conclusion.

Pretrial remedies, reflecting their historical origins, may conveniently be divided into legal and equitable remedies. The legal remedies that are available before trial include *attachment, *garnishment, *replevin, and ejectment. The equitable pretrial remedies include preliminary *injunctions, temporary *restraining orders, and receivership. Another pretrial remedy that may be used in actions to recover title to real property is *lis pendens*.

There is considerable variation among states in the grounds for which pretrial remedies are available, the procedures for obtaining them, and even in the terminology used to refer to them. This non-uniformity also exists in the federal courts, because Rule 64 of the Federal Rules of Civil Procedure adopts the law of the state where the district court is located for all pretrial remedies involving the seizure of property for the purpose of securing a judgment's satisfaction. In contrast, Rule 65 provides uniformity for federal courts with respect to preliminary injunctions and temporary restraining orders.

Attachment is a procedure by which the court orders the *sheriff to take control of the defendant's property for the period while an action is pending. Personal property is attached by the sheriff's taking physical possession of it, while real property is attached by recording a writ of attachment in the land records of the county where the real property is located. Attachment is available only in an action seeking a money judgment, and its purpose is to safeguard the defendant's property for the eventual satisfaction of a judgment in favor of the plaintiff. While state law varies, there generally must be some actual or threatened conduct of the defendant to jeopardize the enforceability of the plaintiff's potential judgment. In addition, the plaintiff is generally required to post a bond as security, and depending on the particular state, attachment may be limited to *contract, as opposed to *tort, creditors (see DEBTOR AND CREDITOR).

Historically, attachment was also used as a means of acquiring territorial jurisdiction over a nonresident defendant through seizure of the defendant's property in the state. Since the Supreme Court's decision in *Shaffer* v. *Heitner* (1977), however, minimum contacts have been required for all state court assertions of territorial jurisdiction; accordingly, attachment may no longer be used to acquire so-called quasi *in rem* jurisdiction over a nonresident, except in very limited circumstances.

Garnishment is a procedure in which a third party, who either owes the defendant money or has possession of his property, is required to hold the money or property during an action's pendency and not pay or return it to the defendant. Typical third parties who are subject to garnishment are employers and banks. With garnishment, in contrast to attachment, the money or property is held by the third party rather than the sheriff.

Replevin is a *common law procedure in which the court orders specified personal property that is in the defendant's possession returned to the plaintiff, who has an ownership interest. Ejectment is the analogous procedure for real property. With replevin, in contrast to attachment, the plaintiff rather than the sheriff takes possession of the property while the action is pending.

A preliminary injunction is a court order directing a party to either perform or refrain from performing one or more acts during an action's pendency. Notice and a hearing are required before the court may issue a preliminary injunction, and a bond is generally required for security. To obtain a preliminary injunction, a plaintiff must prove (1) a likelihood of success on the merits, (2) irreparable harm unless the injunction is issued, and (3) that the probable harm to the plaintiff if the injunction is not issued outweighs the probable harm to the defendant if the injunction is issued. Maintenance of the status quo is an additional factor that favors a preliminary injunction's issuance. A temporary restraining order differs from a preliminary injunction in that its duration is limited to ten days, and it may be issued without notice to the defendant upon a showing that the plaintiff would suffer irreparable harm before notice can be given.

A receivership is a pretrial remedy in which the court orders a receiver, who is designated by the court, to take possession of specified property of the defendant's to preserve it during an action's pendency. Issuance of an order appointing a receiver requires a showing that there is a danger of injury to the property, which would cause irreparable injury to the plaintiff.

Finally, *lis pendens* involves recording a notice of an action's pendency concerned with the title to specified real property in the county land records. Once the *lis pendens* is recorded, subsequent purchasers and mortgagees are subject to the court's eventual determination of title to the real property in its final judgment.

Prior to 1969, most of these remedies were available ex parte, meaning that no prior notice was required to be given to the defendant before seizure of his property. Consequently, these remedies could give plaintiffs an important tactical advantage and cause serious hardship to defendants. For example, the Wisconsin garnishment statute scrutinized in *Sniadach* v. *Family Finance Corp.* (1969), permitted one half of a defendant's wages to be frozen without advance notice to the defendant. In *Sniadach*, the United States Supreme Court held that the Wisconsin garnishment statute violated *due process of law because it did not provide for prior notice and a hearing before the garnishment's issuance. In a line of cases since *Sniadach*, the Supreme Court has ruled that prior notice and a hearing are not necessary for invoking pretrial remedies such as attachment, garnishment and replevin if the following requirements are satisfied: (1) a judge, rather than a clerk, issues the order for the pretrial remedy, (2) the plaintiff submits a detailed affidavit, (3) a prompt postdeprivation hearing opportunity is provided, and (4) the plaintiff shows exigent circumstances to justify the pretrial remedy (*Connecticut v. Doehr* (1991)).

• Mary Kay Kane, *Civil Procedure In a Nutshell*, 3rd ed., 1991. Fleming James Jr. et al, *Civil Procedure*, 4th ed., 1992. Richard L. Marcus et al., *Civil Procedure: A Modern Approach*, 4th ed., 1992. Jack H. Friedenthal et al., *Civil Procedure*, 3rd ed., 1999. Geoffrey C. Hazard Jr. et al., *Pleading and Procedure: State and Federal*, 8th ed., 1999. Larry L. Teply and Ralph U. Whitten, *Civil Procedure*, 2d ed., 2000.   —Charles W. Adams

REORGANIZATION, CORPORATE. *See* Bankruptcy: Business; Corporation.

REPLEVIN is a form of preliminary civil relief, with which the plaintiff recovers specific movable *property wrongfully seized. The judge requires the plaintiff to post a bond to reimburse the defendant for damages if it is finally determined that the defendant is entitled to the property.
[*See also* Commercial Law]
          —David S. Clark

REPORTER, COURT. *See* Court Officers.

REPRIEVE. *See* Pardon, Reprieve, and Commutation.

RESCISSION is a remedy to avoid or undo a *contract, frequently due to mutual mistake or fraud, that is generally followed by restitution by both parties. It may be accomplished by mutual agreement, unilateral rescission at law (usually the plaintiff suing for restitution of money), or judicial rescission in *equity (often requiring the defendant to bring a document to court for cancellation or amendment).
          —David S. Clark

RESEARCH, LEGAL. *See* Computerized Research.

RESISTANCE, PASSIVE. *See* Civil Disobedience.

RES JUDICATA determines the effects that prior adjudication, ending in a valid final *judgment, has in either binding or precluding a common party as to the same issues or claims raised in a later civil action.
[*See also* Jurisprudence, American]
          —David S. Clark

RESTITUTION. *See* Criminal Punishments; Forfeiture.

RESTRAINING ORDER. Most restraining orders are temporary civil court orders, similar to preliminary *injunctions, to protect constitutional, personal, or property rights. The plaintiff must show irreparable injury without the order and often that future harm is imminent.
[*See also* Remedies]
          —David S. Clark

RESTRICTIVE COVENANT. *See* Segregation.

REVERSE DISCRIMINATION. *See* Affirmative Action; Discrimination; Fourteenth Amendment; Race and Ethnicity.

REVIEW, JUDICIAL. *See* Judicial Review.

REVOLUTION, AMERICAN. *See* American Revolution, Legal Impact of.

REVOLVING DOOR. *See* Regulation.

RICO. The Racketeer Influenced and Corrupt Organizations Act (RICO) was enacted in 1970 to combat infiltration of legitimate businesses by *organized criminals. By providing a broad federal structure for imposing criminal and civil *liability on a wide range of conduct, RICO has succeeded in reaching much criminal activity that is beyond the scope of other statutes. Many prominent organized crime figures have received substantial prison sentences as the result of successful RICO prosecutions, particularly in cases involving illegal *drugs, fraud, and misuse of labor union funds.

RICO is violated if a person has used a "pattern of racketeering activity" to infiltrate an interstate business by investing income from such racketeering activity in the business, acquiring or maintaining an interest in the business through racketeering, or conducting the business through racketeering. The statute defines a pattern of racketeering activity as at least two instances of various activities in which organized criminals commonly engage, including narcotics trafficking, bribery, extortion, *gambling, mail fraud, prostitution, money laundering, and embezzlement.

Plaintiffs in civil RICO lawsuits also must demonstrate that they suffered injury to their business or property as the result of a RICO violation. RICO permits civil plaintiffs to recover three times the amount of their damages, and to recover their costs and legal fees.

Criminal penalties imposed by RICO include imprisonment, fines, and mandatory forfeiture of assets obtained in violation of the law. When ill-gained property is unavailable, RICO permits seizure of substitute assets.

Even though RICO was designed as a weapon against organized crime, civil RICO has been used against legitimate businesses that have committed minor or technical offenses that can be wedged into RICO's racketeering definition. The statute's provision for treble damages makes such litigation more attractive than traditional actions for negligence or mismanagement and has encouraged some questionable litigation. Lower courts tried to create barriers to the use of RICO against such businesses, but the United States Supreme Court held in *Sedima, S.P.R.L.* v. *Imrex Co.* (1985) that the statute's language did not warrant such limitations.

Civil RICO also has been invoked in a number of noncommercial contexts, including controversial cases in which it has provided the basis for liability against antiabortion protesters. Some civil libertarians fear that the use of RICO against public advocacy groups may increase.

Both civil and criminal RICO have withstood a wide range of constitutional challenges, including allegations that the statute is too vague and that it violates the First Amendment's freedom of association, the Fifth Amendment's protection against double jeopardy, and the Eighth Amendment's prohibition of cruel and unusual punishment and excessive fines.

Although RICO applies only to interstate crime, this limitation is not significant because most organized crime activities cross state lines. Thirty-two states have enacted so-called little RICO statutes that resemble the federal statute and are designed to complement it or to reach the relatively rare organized crimes that do not involve interstate activity.

• Gregory P. Joseph, *Civil RICO: A Definitive Guide,* 2d ed., 2000. Jed S. Rakoff and Howard W. Goldstein, *RICO: Civil and Criminal Law and Strategy*, 2000.

—William G. Ross

RIGHT TO DIE. The right to die is a relatively recent phenomenon, although its roots lie deep in *common-law proscriptions against unwanted touching. The notion of an individual right first burst into national prominence in the case of *In re Quinlan* (1976), in which Karen Ann Quinlan's parents won court approval to turn off life support for their daughter, who had been in a persistent vegetative state for months.

In essence, the right to die consists of two basic premises. The first is that any competent adult may knowingly and voluntarily decide to stop medical treatment, even if that decision brings on death. In *Quinlan* the New Jersey court based its decision on common-law rulings against unwanted touching and ruled that such a doctrine had long applied to medical treatments in general. The court also relied upon the newly enunciated constitutional right to *privacy, as expressed in *Griswold* v. *Connecticut* (1965). The parameters of privacy, the court held, included an individual's decision about whether or not to submit to medical treatments.

The second premise is that if a person is incapable of making such a decision, the law will allow a surrogate to make that judgment, providing certain legal criteria are met. The most common standard is whether the now-incompetent person drew up a so-called living will when still competent. The living will, or durable *power of attorney, allows a surrogate to carry out the wishes of the person, even if it means turning off life support.

Most of the initial cases establishing a right to die took place in state courts and were often collusive in nature. Typically a patient, recognizing the futility of treatment, wanted to be taken off life support; the doctors and the hospital, while agreeing with the patient on the course of action, worried about future liability. So the patient or the patient's family would sue the hospital, and the courts would grant the patient's wish while clearing the medical staff of liability. Eventually all fifty states enacted legislation regularizing this procedure and allowing the existence of either a living will or the clearly established wishes of the patient to be determinative.

Most states have a relatively simple evidentiary test, but three states insist on a higher level in order to ensure that the lives of their citizens are not ended prematurely or by accident. One of these states is Missouri, and a challenge to that state's law led to the Supreme Court's constitutionalizing the right to die.

Mary Beth Cruzan had been injured in an automobile accident and left in a persistent vegetative state. Her parents sought to have feeding and hydration tubes removed so their comatose daughter could die. The problem was that Mary Beth was an adult and had never signed a living will, nor was there the clear and convincing evidence required by Missouri law that she would have wanted to be taken off life support.

In *Cruzan* v. *Director, Missouri Department of Health* (1990), the Supreme Court, with the exception of Antonin Scalia, agreed that a constitutionally protected right to die was embedded in the personal autonomy protected by the *Due Process Clause of the *Fourteenth Amendment. But five members of the Court, led by Chief Justice William H. Rehnquist, ruled that this right was balanced by the state's interest in preserving life and that Missouri's evidentiary rule was not an undue burden on the right. The four members of the minority, speaking through Justice William J. *Brennan, would have struck the balance more in favor of the individual. Only Scalia thought this was not a constitutional matter and ought to be left to the states.

Following this case, some groups began pressing for what they considered the next logical step: allowing people who are not on life support but are in great pain or terminally ill to receive assistance from doctors to end their lives. Advocates of physician-assisted suicide managed to win their point in the Ninth Circuit (on due process grounds) and in the Second Circuit (on an equal-protection argument), but the Supreme Court, in the companion cases of *Washington* v. *Glucksburg* (1997) and *Vacco* v. *Quill* (1997), ruled that there was no constitutional right to assisted suicide. Five members of the Court, however, filed concurrences in the result that read as dissents. While willing to allow the states to work things out for the moment (Oregon had already passed a law allowing limited physician-assisted suicide), the five justices warned that if the states made end-of-life choices too narrow they would be willing to revisit the issue.

[*See also* Civil Rights and Civil Liberties; Medicine and Law]

• Melvin I. Urofsky, *Letting Go: Death, Dying and the Law*, 1993. Peter G. Filene, *In the Arms of Others: A Cultural History of the Right-to-Die in America*, 1998. Jennifer M. Scherer and Rita J. Simon, *Euthanasia and the Right to Die: A Comparative View*, 1999. Melvin I. Urofsky, *Lethal Judgments: Assisted Suicide and American Law*, 2000.
—Melvin I. Urofsky

RIGHT TO LIFE. *See* Abortion and Reproductive Decisions.

RIGHT TO WORK LAWS. *See* Labor Law: Labor Relations.

RIOTING. *See* Extralegality; Mob Violence and Vigilantism.

RISK ASSESSMENT. *See* Economics and Law.

RITUAL. *See* Public Ritual, Law and.

ROBBERY is a crime that combines the elements of an offense against a person with those of an offense against *property. Robbery was a *felony that predated *larceny under the *common law. Today, robbery is, in one form or another, a statutory felony in all fifty states. Robbery generally contains the following elements: (1) a *trespass, and (2) a taking (3) away from (4) the person, or in her presence, (5) the personal property of (6) another with (7) violence or putting in fear with (8) the intent to steal the property. The contours of these elements have been developed under the common law, and vary from jurisdiction to jurisdiction. However, these elements essentially describe larceny, with the addition of the requirements that the property be taken from the victim's presence or person and that the taking occur by force.

Robbery, then, is a combination of an *assault (and perhaps a battery) with a larceny. However, unlike larceny, the definition of robbery tends not to vary by virtue of the amount taken. Instead, grades of robbery are identified by the amount and kind of force used. Thus, while "aggravated robbery" is a more serious offense than simple robbery, the "aggravating" factors are often the use of a firearm or other "deadly weapon," or some other factor relating to the degree of force used, such as whether the act resulted in serious physical injury to the victim. Consistent with this focus on the aspect of force, in some cases, even a robbery that fails to net the robber any property at all will be treated as an attempt, which carries the same penalty as if the robbery had been completed.

Similarly, because robbery statutes are intended to deter and punish the forcible aspect of the taking more than the deprivation of property itself, the element of taking "away" (asportation) is interpreted fairly loosely, or dispensed with altogether. In contrast, the requirement that a robbery involve a physical confrontation of some kind—the use of force against the person or the threat of force—is what distinguishes robbery from other types of *theft. The threat may be accomplished by some sort of trick, such as the use of an unloaded gun, but it will nevertheless be sufficient to qualify the theft as a robbery. Moreover, the threat may not be one that would suffice in every case, with every person. It is usually enough that the threat of force was sufficient to cause the victim real apprehension of harm. Here, "apprehension" means the victim's prediction or belief that harm would result from a failure to comply. It does not necessarily mean an emotional state equaling "fear."

Every state has one or more robbery statutes, and there are a number of federal robbery statutes, the most prominent of which are those dealing with bank robbery. However, there are additional federal robbery statutes dealing with robbery that interferes with interstate commerce or the mail, robbery on the high seas, and robbery in various military contexts.

[See also Criminal Law; Crminal Law Principles]

• Paul H. Robinson, *Criminal Law*, 1997. Wayne R. LaFave, *Criminal Law*, 2000.   —Tamara R. Piety

ROBINSON-PATMAN ACT. *See* Anti-Trust Law.

ROE V. WADE 410 U.S. 113 (1973), symbolizes for friend and foe alike the legalization of *abortion across the entire United States. The reality is somewhat more complicated. *Roe* and its companion decision *Doe* v. *Bolton* did, however (in a 7–2 vote) establish the legality of abortion in that vast majority of American states where abortions remained a violation of criminal law as of 1973. In 1970 the legislatures of four states—New York, Hawaii, Alaska, and Washington—spurred by the women's rights movement that had begun in the late 1960s, legalized abortion. Federal or state judges in nine other states (California, Texas, Wisconsin, Georgia, Illinois, Florida, New Jersey,

Connecticut, and South Dakota) during 1969–72 had struck down those states' abortion statutes as unconstitutional, although many of those decisions were on appeal. Most of these lower court precursors to *Roe* had extrapolated a right to procure abortion from the logic of *Griswold* v. *Connecticut* (1965). That decision had declared that married couples have a constitutional right to *privacy from government interference in their decision whether or not to use contraceptives. In December of 1971, the Supreme Court—reduced by retirements to only seven justices—first heard oral arguments in *Roe* and *Doe*, the appeals, respectively, of the Texas and Georgia decisions. Three months after hearing these arguments, the Court ruled four to three in *Eisenstadt* v. *Baird* (1972), "If the right to privacy means anything, it is the right of the *individual* married or single, to be free of unwarranted governmental intrusion into matters so fundamentally affecting a person as the decision whether to bear or beget a child." This decision clearly indicated the signposts of the ruling the Court would map out in detail with *Roe* and *Doe*.

The *Roe* and *Doe* pair declared explicitly (in the majority opinion by Justice Blackmun) not only that "The right of privacy . . . is broad enough to encompass a woman's decision whether or not to terminate her pregnancy," but also indicated which governmental interests might be compelling enough to justify state restrictions on this constitutional right. The Court noted that a state's interest in protecting the potential life embodied in the growing fetus becomes compelling at the point of viability, that is, the point at which the fetus is able to survive (with or without artificial assistance) outside its mothers body. At this point, said the Court, legislatures may ban all those abortions not necessary for safeguarding the mother's life or health. The Court also allowed that protecting the mother's *health amounted to a compelling interest; that, as such, it justified a requirement that abortions be performed only by licensed physicians; and that, at the stage in pregnancy where abortion became more dangerous for the woman than continuation of the pregnancy to childbirth (which in 1973 was approximately the end of the first trimester of pregnancy) the state might adopt more substantial restrictions on abortion practice that were reasonably related to the goal of protecting maternal health. The legalization of abortion in the United States, beginning in 1970, stimulated an active antiabortion, or "pro-life" political movement, which intensified its activity after *Roe* v. *Wade*. The pro-life movement continues to demonstrate outside the U.S. Supreme Court building on the anniversary of the decision, January 22.

[*See also* Gender and Law]

• Marian Faux, *Roe v. Wade*, 1988. Leslie F. Goldstein, *Contemporary Cases in Women's Rights*, 1994.

—Leslie Friedman Goldstein

ROSENBERG ESPIONAGE TRIAL. In a one-month trial that began on 6 March 1951, Julius Rosenberg, his wife Ethel, and Morton Sobel were convicted of *conspiracy to commit espionage for allegedly stealing atomic secrets for the USSR. The principal witness against them was Ethel's brother, David Greenglass, who, while stationed at the Los Alamos test facility during World War II, made crude drawings depicting the implosion principle used to detonate one of the first atomic bombs. Greeenglass testified that he was collecting information for Julius.

After Judge Irving Kaufman sentenced Sobel to thirty years in prison and both Rosenbergs to death, the United States Court of Appeals for the Second Circuit twice refused to overturn their convictions. A bitterly divided Supreme Court repeatedly declined, over the protests of Justices Felix *Frankfurter and Hugo *Black, even to hear the case. Justice William O. *Douglas did grant the Rosenbergs a stay of execution, but the rest of the Court dissolved it. The Rosenbergs were put to death on 19 June 1953.

The trial and execution of the Rosenbergs triggered worldwide protests. Most were organized by their fellow Communists. Because the trial took place during a period of anti-Communist hysteria, however, many non-Communists also considered them victims of political persecution. Allegations that they were victims of anti-Semitism were unfounded. Once-secret Soviet and American archival material, opened up since the end of the Cold War, has established that Julius did in fact engage in espionage. Ethel was only marginally involved, however. She was given the death penalty because the FBI hoped that Julius would expose other members of his spy ring in order to save her.

[*See also* Capital Punishment; Criminal Law; Treason]

• Ronald Radosh and Joyce Milton, *The Rosenberg File: A Search for the Truth*, 2d. ed., 1997. Michael E. Parish, "Revisited: The Rosenberg 'Atom Spy' Case," *UMKC Law Review* 68 (2000): 601–21.

—Michael R. Belknap

RUFFIN, THOMAS CARTER (1787–1870), lawyer, judge. Born in King and Queen County, Virginia, Ruffin was the son of a Methodist minister. He enrolled at the College of New Jersey (Princeton), graduating in 1805, and then read law with prominent attorneys, first in Virginia and later in North Carolina. He settled in Hillsborough, North Carolina, where in 1808 he was admitted to the bar.

Ruffin succeeded both in the practice of law and in state politics, including sporadic involvement with elected office. He served terms in the lower house of the state legislature, two short periods as a judge of the superior court, and for less than a year as president of the state bank. The income earned from private practice lured him away from sustained public service. In 1829, however, the state senate elected him to the supreme court, where he served until 1852, the last twenty years as chief justice. Other than a short return to the court, the last years of his life were devoted to farming and public life outside the judiciary. An opponent of *secession, he was one of North Carolina's delegates to the Peace Conference in Washington, D.C., in early 1861. He eventually supported North Carolina's withdrawal from the union, based on the right of citizens to revolt to reform their system of government.

Ruffin wrote more than fourteen hundred judicial opinions, at a time when state courts were at the forefront of legal development in the nation. Although the country was on the cusp of industrialization, litigation in North Carolina continued to reflect the predominance of a rural society. The signal decisions of Ruffin's court reveal the agonies of a society and of individuals attempting to deal with *slavery. The most prominent of Ruffin's opinions was *State* v. *Mann* (1829). For the court, Ruffin wrote an opinion reversing Mann's conviction for assault on a slave. In bold language, Ruffin acknowledged the harsh conditions of slavery and emphasized the dominion of the master, while admitting his personal dislike of the institution. But he felt constrained by his sense of a judge's duty to support the society around him. He therefore looked to the legislature for change.

Ruffin's other most notable decision was *Hoke* v. *Henderson* (1833), in which he sought to preserve the Supreme Court from the attacks of Jacksonian reformers. Invoking the term "law of the land" in the North Carolina bill of rights, in a way not unlike later generations of judges would use the concept *"due process," Ruffin established both the principle of *judicial review and that of

judicial independence from legislative interference.

[*See also* Lawyers]

• Joseph G. de Roulhac Hamilton, ed., *The Papers of
Thomas Ruffin*, 4 vols., 1918.

—Walter F. Pratt Jr.

RULEMAKING, AGENCY. *See* Regulation.

RULE OF REASON. *See* Anti-Trust Law.

RULES OF EVIDENCE. *See* Evidence; Procedure,
Court.

S

SACCO AND VANZETTI CASE. Nicolo Sacco and Bartolomeo Vanzetti were executed in Massachusetts in 1927 for murder and robbery in a highly politicized case that remains controversial. Even after numerous exhaustive studies of the case, opinion remains divided as to whether one or both of the men were guilty, or whether they were the victims of bigotry because they were working-class Italian immigrants who professed political radicalism.

Many studies of the case conclude that Sacco and Vanzetti did not receive a fair trial because they were convicted on the basis of largely circumstantial *evidence and because their poor command of English caused them to mistakenly give incriminating answers during preliminary investigations. Their guilt also is questionable because they were denied a new trial even after a convicted murderer confessed to the crime, offered inside information about it, and exonerated Sacco and Vanzetti.

Numerous intellectuals, labor unions, religious groups, and journalists passionately defended Sacco and Vanzetti, contributing funds to their defense and rallying public opinion to their cause. Sacco and Vanzetti became symbols of the hostility toward immigrants and leftists that swept the nation in the wake of the Russian Revolution and the isolationism that followed World War I.

Studies concluding that Sacco and Vanzetti were guilty contend that the courts scrupulously observed standards of *due process because the proceedings were closely watched. In 1962, a forensic study linked a bullet found in one of the murder victims with a gun found on Sacco's person. Although the guilt or innocence of Sacco and Vanzetti is likely to remain a source of disagreement, the case remains a reminder of the danger of injustice against weak and unpopular minorities.

[*See also* Capital Punishment; Civil Rights and Civil Liberties; Criminal Law]

• William Young and David E. Kaiser, *Postmortem: New Evidence in the Case of Sacco and Vanzetti*, 1985.

—William G. Ross

SAFETY, WORKPLACE. *See* Labor Law: Workplace Issues.

SALEM WITCHCRAFT TRIALS. In the summer of 1692 all of eastern Massachusetts trembled in fear as neighbors and kinfolk accused one another of practicing witchcraft. Hundreds were jailed, and in the first round of the ensuing trials from June 2 to September 21, 1692—the most extensive mass trials of suspected criminals in the colonial period of our history—all of the defendants were convicted by juries and sentenced to death by hanging by the special court of oyer and terminer empaneled to hear the cases. Fifteen women and four men were hanged, and one eighty-year-old defendant was pressed to death with heavy stones for refusing to accept the authority of the court. Four of the indicted and detained suspects had died in jail and many more had sickened. But when the trials resumed in the winter of 1693, juries refused to convict an overwhelming majority of the defendants and by May of that year Governor William Phips had pardoned all those still in custody. Decisions about the law of evidence and trial procedure were largely responsible for both the initial round of convictions and the later pattern of acquittals.

In terms of established colonial legal procedure, the trials presented little of novelty. All of the defendants were indicted by grand juries and faced trial by *jury, according to Massachusetts and English law. None had counsel to represent them, but this in itself was not unusual in Massachusetts or England. Massachusetts had added a right to *counsel provision to its laws in the early 1690s, but these laws had been previously disallowed by the English crown.

Special courts of oyer and terminer to hear criminal cases were widely used in the colonies. Governor Phips could have waited for the first session of the new General Court (assembly) under the revised charter to meet and create regular courts, but the times and the situation seemed to call for immediate action. The empire was at war with France, and the war had come to the northern and western borders of the Massachusetts colony. The jails were filled to overflowing (indeed the overflow had enabled some suspects to escape while others were beginning to suffer from the ailments that close confinement and overcrowding precipitated).

It was clear from the records of the trials that the judges bullied some jurors, witnesses and defendants, but this too was common in seventeenth-century criminal proceedings. In the absence of counsel, *judges had immense power to control the pace of the trials and the admission of evidence. Judges were expected to protect the procedural rights of the accused but when judges believed, as the bench did in Salem, that the Devil was behind the supposed witches, defendants could not count on the kindly intervention of the court.

In a key decision made at the outset of the trials, the court had allowed the admission of spectral evidence—in particular the uncorroborated testimony of a group of adolescent girls that they had been visited and tormented by otherwise invisible wraiths. This evidence had already been admitted by the magistrates presiding over the initial inquiries and grand jury hearings. What is more, spectral evidence was widely used in English witchcraft trials until the latter portion of the seventeenth century. Such notable English jurists as Sir Matthew Hale believed it an invaluable aid in catching witches.

But the decision to admit spectral evidence was not based on accepted standards of law. In fact, English jurists, following currents of rationality and *science sweeping through European thought, increasingly rejected accusations of spectral harm. Cultural and religious norms particular to the colony weighed against the modernist turn away from the spirit world. All but one of the judges on the court (along with almost all of the learned men and women in the colony, the accusers, the witnesses, and most of the defendants) believed that there was a Devil and that he contracted secretly with men and women to do evil in the colony. Borrowing this power from Satan, witches thus had, at least in theory, the ability to leave their bodies and in spectral form assault their victims.

What freed the judges to retain the older concept of causation was that there were few of the rules of *evidence regarding the admissibility of prejudicial matters that modern legal practitioners would recognize. Indeed, these rules only began to come into trial practice in the early eighteenth century, and were usually pressed on courts by trained counsel. Although the more restrictive rules of admissibility of evidence were discussed in elite English legal circles by the 1690s, to the court of oyer and terminer Phips had named laymen who, though they had experience on high courts under the old charter, had no advanced training in law.

The result of the judges' initial decision to admit spectral evidence was that the Salem events became a worst-case example of unthinking panic and religious excess even in their own time. One of the judges, Nathaniel Saltonstall, was so appalled at the effects of admitting spectral evidence, and the spectacle of the girls' testimony in court, that he quietly resigned from the bench. The leading ministers (except for Cotton Mather, who publicly approved the conduct of the trials) increasingly protested against the proceedings and convinced minister Increase Mather, Cotton's father, to turn their criticism into a tract on the dangers of believing spectral evidence. He agreed that spectral visitations might be the Devil's instrument to fool the credulous and cast blame on the innocent.

Increase Mather's essay convinced Phips to stop the trials. They would reconvene in the winter, but this time spectral evidence was not allowed. In the winter and spring of 1693 juries acquitted all but three of the fifty defendants, and these, along with all others still in jail, Phips pardoned in May 1693. The end of the Salem witchcraft trials brought to an end prosecution for witchcraft in New England. Although the ghosts and demons of the spirit world remained a staple of folk culture and folk tales, examining magistrates and trial courts no longer admitted spectral evidence. Neighbors still complained to the magistrates that so and so was a witch, but officials did not credit the story. Indeed, in the early 1700s ministers and magistrates cooperated to expose an episode of fraudulent and spiteful accusations. Even Cotton Mather became convinced that mistakes were made.

[*See also* Criminal Law Practice]

• Paul S. Boyer and Stephen Nissenbaum, *Salem Possessed: the Social Origins of Witchcraft*, 1974. John Demos, *Entertaining Satan: Witchcraft and the Culture of Early New England*, 1982. Carol F. Karlsen, *The Devil in the Shape of a Woman: Witchcraft in Colonial New En-*

gland, 1987. Richard Godbeer, *The Devil's Dominion: Magic and Religion in Early New England*, 1992. Peter Charles Hoffer, *The Devil's Disciples: The Makes of the Salem Witchcraft Trials*, 1996.

—Peter Charles Hoffer

SALES TAX. *See* Taxation: Sales Taxes.

SANCTIONS, INTERNATIONAL. *See* War, Law of.

SCIENCE AND LAW. Participants in both law and science sometimes speak of a "culture clash" between the two spheres: science is portrayed as a truth-seeking, objective, descriptive enterprise; law, as normative, process-oriented, and adversarial, committed to justice as much as to truth. Scientific conclusions are provisional, while law requires closure. Science focuses on facts; law instantiates values. The sometimes turbulent relations between the two domains are often attributed to these disparate worldviews. Legislators, lawyers, judges and policymakers often want to inject "good science" into legal decision-making and become frustrated when science fails to provide the clear answers that are sought.

Scientists, for their part, can resent legally imposed fetters on free exploration or inquiry, and object to legal, administrative and legislative decisions that seem to fly in the fact of accepted scientific wisdom. Sociologists of science, however, have challenged this view of a culture clash as too simplistic, arguing that the sites of intersection often generate unease precisely because they reveal the limitations of each realm's self-conception. Scholars agree, however, that law and science have become deeply and permanently, if not always comfortably, intertwined.

The multifaceted relation between law and science can be usefully divided into two components: 1) the use of scientific knowledge within legal determinations, and 2) the mechanisms by which the legal system spurs, constrains, and regulates scientific research. This entry will first consider how law makes use of science and then how law affects science.

The Use of Science by Legal Decision-makers. The use of science by legal decision-makers raises important questions about the nature of expertise and the relation between scientific knowledge and broader democratic values. To what extent should juries, judges, administrative agencies, and legislatures defer to the judgments of scientists? Should a jury be permitted to reach a verdict that flies in the face of accepted science, as did a 1946 jury that recognized Charlie Chaplin's paternity even though blood tests revealed that he could not have been the biological father? How should administrative agencies negotiate between their policy objectives and scientific research? When law uses science for its own purposes, to what extent should it be bound by the views of scientists?

The Anglo-American adjudicatory system has long attempted to incorporate the special knowledge of skilled witnesses and scientific experts. In the nineteenth century, the use of experts selected by the parties within the adversarial system became both commonplace and controversial. Experts were viewed as unduly partisan: unconsciously influenced by the party that hired them, or worse, unscrupulous mouthpieces, quacks, and charlatans who would say anything for a price. Moreover, expert testimony was seen as confusing and contradictory, and lay juries were thought to lack the ability to choose sensibly which expert to believe. Many lawyers, judges, and experts argued for neutral experts appointed by the court rather than the parties. Despite some faltering legislative efforts in this direction at the turn of the twentieth century, party control of experts remained the norm. Ensuring that the legal system uses legitimate, valid expertise and concerns over whether lay fact finders can meaningfully evaluate the substance of expert testimony is still a vital concern, the result of the awkward fit between expert knowledge and an adversarial system with lay jury decisionmakers. What we expect from jurors with respect to expert testimony is not wholly clear: Do we want experts to educate the jurors to make their own assessment, or do we intend the fact finder to defer to the expert's claims? Some scholars doubt the ability of juries rationally to assess the testimony of competing experts, especially on highly complex, technical matters, while others claim that jury comprehension of expert testimony is satisfactory.

More generally, developing a system for the use of neutral rather than adversarial experts is frequently recommended but difficult to implement: How would neutral experts be selected? What would happen when there were multiple "camps" within the scientific community rather than a dominant viewpoint? Is the hoped-for neutrality that such experts could provide illusory? Moreover, in criminal cases, the use of neutral experts in place of party-called experts could raise Sixth Amendment constitutional concerns. Under the Federal Rules of Evidence and in nearly all the states, judges have the power to appoint neutral experts as a supplement to a party's experts, but in practice, they rarely do so. While many civil law countries typically use a single expert who reports to the court rather than to the litigants, the adversarial expert is likely to remain a permanent feature of litigation in this country.

The central question for judges assessing expert "evidence is what standard to use to decide whether expert evidence should be admissible in court. In *Frye* v. *United States* (1923), a case involving an early version of the lie detector, the Washington, D.C., Court of Appeals held, "Just when a scientific or discovery crosses the line between the experimental and demonstrable stages is difficult to define. Somewhere in this twilight zone the evidential force of the principle must be recognized. . . . [T]he thing from which the deduction is made must be sufficiently established to have gained general acceptance in the particular field in which it belongs." Though little noticed at the time, this *Frye* test of "general acceptance" by the relevant scientific community came to be the dominant test for evaluating whether novel scientific evidence should be admitted. However, despite lip service paid to *Frye* in the 1970s and 1980s, there was generally no rigorous judicial screening of scientific evidence; indeed, some commentators vociferously (and controversially) criticized the rise of so-called junk science in the courtroom.

In *Daubert* v. *Merrell Dow* (1993), a case involving a drug, bendectin, alleged to cause birth defects, the Supreme Court ruled that the Federal Rules of Evidence did not implicitly incorporate the *Frye* rule of "general acceptance." The court emphasized that judges were nonetheless expected to act as "gatekeepers," evaluating the reliability of expert evidence and permitting it into evidence only if it were both helpful to the fact finder and scientifically valid. The court listed a set of possible criteria as guidelines for judges to use in assessing scientific evidence, including whether the method or theory had been tested or subjected to efforts to falsify it; whether there was a known error rate; whether it had been peer reviewed; and whether it was generally accepted by the relevant scientific community. Some critics have argued that *Daubert* asks judges, typically not trained extensively in science, to do something beyond their institutional competence. Others view *Daubert* as an important positive development that improves the quality of expert evidence. Although *Daubert* has been influential in the state courts, a number of jurisdictions continue to use *Frye's* general acceptance test instead. In 1999, in *Kumho Tire* v. *Carmichael*, the Supreme Court made clear that judges' gatekeeping role extends to all kinds of expert evidence, whether scientific, technical, or based on experience. However, the case offered judges little guidance about how practically to determine whether nonscientific expert evidence is reliable enough to warrant admissibility.

The Supreme Court's recent holdings have not quieted debate over the admissibility of scientific evidence, especially in torts cases and in criminal cases. Legal challenges have arisen to long-used forms of forensic science, like expert handwriting identification evidence, that have never before been subjected to rigorous scrutiny, and if strictly applied, *Daubert* would limit much medical and psychiatric evidence as well. In toxic *torts cases, there is often only limited available research about whether a substance causes a particular harm. How much scientific evidence supporting causation should be required for an injured plaintiff to bring a case before a jury? The debates about toxic torts cases are not simply about the quality of the scientific evidence, but equally over the question of how and whether legal decision-making should proceed in the face of genuine scientific uncertainty. Generally, the practical effect of *Daubert* has been to provoke increasing scrutiny of plaintiffs' expert evidence in torts' cases, while less has changed in the criminal arena.

The most significant new form of scientific evidence to emerge in recent years is DNA profiling. This technique can determine whether extremely small quantities of biological matter, such as blood or semen left at the scene of a crime, match the DNA taken from a particular suspect, or whether the DNA matches that of anyone in ever-growing databases. The first judges to consider the new identification technique welcomed it wholeheartedly, but controversy soon erupted over both the adequacy of care taken in laboratory procedures and the population genetics research that underlay the statistical match probability that the test could provide. Over time, and after National Research Council panels issued two reports on the matter, these concerns diminished. DNA profiling is now routinely admitted in courts in every jurisdiction. In addition to providing a powerful investigation tool and a persuasive form of evidence, it has had several broader effects on perceptions of the adequacy of our trial process. Post-conviction DNA testing has drawn explicit and troubling attention to the limitations of other forms of evidence, including other kinds of forensic science such as serological evidence and hair identification techniques, and, especially, eyewitness identification. As of August 2001, at least sixty-three convicted felons have been exonerated through DNA tests, including several prisoners on death row. Some commentators suggest that the revelation of these erroneous convictions may be reducing popular support for the death penalty.

In addition to the widespread use of scientific evidence in court, scientific findings are also critical to the work of administrative agencies, and legislative decisions are also frequently informed by research. In these settings, there is often a tension between deference to scientific expertise and the incorporation of broader values. The Office of Technology Assessment (OTA) used to provide Congress with detailed and relatively nonpartisan reports about scientific issues and policy alternatives, but the OTA was eliminated by budget cuts in 1995. While Congress has no official source for scientific information, experts frequently testify before subcommittees and legislators may also seek out whatever scientific sources they choose to inform their views.

Scientific knowledge plays an enormous role within the administrative agencies that run the regulatory state. Agencies rely extensively on scientific research both through their own, often extensive, technical and research staff and by convening outside scientific advisory panels. Agency determinations affect ordinary citizens' lives in myriad ways: what food additives will be permitted, what pesticides will be allowed, what safety features an automobile will be required to include, and how much of a particular chemical can be ingested in the workplace, to give just a few examples. One of the many difficult aspects about agencies' efforts to protect the public's health, safety, and the environment, is that the scientific basis for assessing the risk of various substances is often lacking. Risk assessment is an inexact process at best, and agencies often make determinations at the frontiers of science in the face of enormous uncertainty. Also, there is the risk that agencies may be "captured" by the industry they regulate or by other political-interest groups. Agencies often seek input from outside advisory committees, who can provide independent peer review. When the agency's judgment coincides with the reviewers' views, it can enhance the legitimacy of the outcome. But when these outside reviewers disagree with the agency, it raises difficult questions: have these outside scientists found troubling flaws with the scientific basis for the agency's judgment, or does their disagreement merely reflect legitimate policy differences? Courts also frequently review both the substance and procedural aspects of agency decisions. Over time, however, agency's scientific judgments have generally been treated with increasing deference by the courts.

The Influence of Law on Scientific Research. The primary mechanism by which law spurs scientific and technological development is the intellectual *property system. Our intellectual property regime provides incentives for inventors to innovate or, as the Constitution puts it, "to Promote the Progress of Science and useful Arts." Unlike tangible property, intellectual property is "nonrivalrous"; possession by one person does not impede possession by others. Unlike real property, ideas can be shared freely without dissipating their value. Without protection, useful inventions or creative works would be imitated by others. Because these rivals did not have to invest the human capital to innovate, they could charge less than the original creator, thereby preventing her from recouping the costs of invention. This would result in a disincentive to spend money on research or an effort to keep inventions hidden from potential competitors, both of which would be socially undesirable. Intellectual property protection, therefore, is not intended as a reward to the inventor, but rather as a benefit to society as a whole. However, because creators are granted a limited monopoly, and can exclude others from using or building on their work without permission, protection too broad in scope or too lengthy can also hinder innovation. Whether the current system offers the proper degree of protection is an open question that scholars have debated, but the idea is to provide a private right for the public good, to encourage investment in innovation.

The statutorily created patent system, the main form of intellectual property protection for scientific and technological inventions, exchanges a limited monopoly for disclosure to the public of the details of the invention. Patents last for twenty years from the application date, and they confer the exclusive right to use, make, sell, or license the specified invention or device. In order to qualify for a patent, the invention must be both novel and nonobvious; it must be an identifiable advance on the prior art in the field. The subject matter must be an invention rather than a discovery, a product of human ingenuity rather than a product of nature, though these boundaries are not always clear. The definitions of what is patentable have changed over time. For example, a mathematical algorithm—an abstract idea rather than an invention—cannot receive a patent. Computer software, essentially a collection of algorithms, was therefore initially viewed as outside the scope of patent protection, and through the 1980s, the dominant way to gain intellectual property protection for software was via copyright. (Copyright, used for artistic and literary products, provides longer-term but weaker protection. It does not protect an idea, but only the author's particular expression of the idea. An independently developed work with similar ideas will therefore not be deemed infringing, whereas a patent protects its holder even if another inventor made the same invention wholly independently.) In recent years not only have the patent office and the courts granted computer software patent protection, but it has become the fastest-growing category of patents.

In *Diamond* v. *Chakrabarty* (1980), the Supreme Court held that a genetically engineered bacterium was patentable, sanctioning for the first time a patent on a life-form. Genetically modified life forms, including not only bacteria but also animals now fall within the patent system's purview. Patents on genes within the human genome are also commonplace, even when researchers do not yet fully understand the function and utility of the gene. As of December 2000, more than one thousand such patents had been granted with twenty thousand applications pending. In 1998, a scientist applied for a patent on a human-animal "chimera," a proposed blend of chimp and human cells feasible but never actually made, in order to provoke debate about patenting life. The patent was denied, but the issue seems likely to arise again in the future.

Critics of the patent system say that approval by the patent office is too easily gained, especially within high-technology fields like software and biotech. Patents can be challenged in court, but such challenges are expensive and time-consuming. Currently, physicians, medical researchers, and bioethicists worry that the stampede to patent human genes provides corporations with more protection than is needed to encourage innovation and will limit access to genetic testing and increase the costs of genetic research. Other critics contend that the easy availability and excessively broad scope of software and business-methods patents threatens innovation in e-commerce and cyberspace more generally.

In addition to offering intellectual property protection, the federal government has, since the Second World War, provided significant funding support for basic and applied research, most of which is distributed through administrative agencies such as the National Science Foundation (NSF), the National Institute of Health (NIH), the Department of Defense (DOD), and many others. Some agencies pursue research directly, through government-run laboratories, while others provide funding through grants and contracts. Courts generally do not meddle with or monitor agency decisions about funding and grant recipients; these are viewed as matters within the agency's discretion. While both direct research funding and intellectual property protection promote scientific and technological development, law also constrains scientific research in significant ways. There can be a tension between scientific freedom of inquiry and the risk to public safety or to a research subject's health. More generally, there are sometimes moral or ethical concerns about research that has become technologically feasible, as the current debates over human cloning illustrate. In the most extreme cases, certain kinds of research can be legally prohibited. In the early twenty-first century, for example, several states have passed statutes banning human cloning, establishing civil penalties for undertaking certain kinds of research. Sometimes the scientific community has engaged in self-regulation, as with a temporary moratorium on recombinant DNA research in the early 1970s. Generally, however, outright bans on broad categories of scientific research are extremely rare. Instead, the main mechanisms through which scientific research are constrained are, first, by federal regulation; and second, by the requirement that experiments on human test subjects go forward only with the informed consent of the participants.

Many kinds of research and their applications are heavily regulated. For example, in order to test a new experimental drug on human subjects, extensive animal testing must first be completed, and an application must be filed with the Food and Drug Administration (FDA), which has the authority to prevent the testing from taking place. If the FDA approves an application, the subsequent clinical testing will be conducted with continued significant agency oversight. While the FDA has authority over clinical drug trials regardless of whether any federal funding is involved, federally funded research is often subject to especially stringent regulation. For example, any research involving recombinant DNA and gene therapy conducted by an institution funded by the NIH must comply with NIH's extensive guidelines. Regulation may also prevent sharing research results or marketing products internationally, especially when there are national security concerns; cryptography, for example, has faced strict export controls.

Finally, any research involving human test subjects must be predicated on the informed consent of the participants. Over the course of this century, atrocities have been committed in the name of scientific research, ranging from the experiments conducted by Nazi doctors on concentration camp victims to the Tuskegee syphilis study in Alabama, in which African-American men with syphilis were purposefully left untreated in order to study the late-stage effects of the disease. There have been numerous efforts to describe, in broad terms, the requirements for ethical research on humans. Particularly influential examples include the Nuremberg Code, drafted during the Nuremberg War Crimes Trials, which treats voluntary consent as absolutely essential to ethical research, and the 1979 Belmont Report, emphasizing broad principles like "respect for persons," and the need to maximize research benefits while minimizing harm. Institutions that receive federal research funding must maintain institutional review boards that enforce compliance with informed consent and examine and approve any study involving human subjects. In addition, a failure to comply with informed consent requirements can subject a researcher to tort liability. Especially tricky questions arise when researchers attempt to balance the rights of cognitively impaired patients, who may not be capable of providing consent, with a desire to advance research into life-threatening conditions.

[*See also* Technology and Law]

• Sheila Jasanoff, *The Fifth Branch: Science Advisers as Policymakers,* 1990. Sam Gross, "Expert Evidence, Expert Evidence," *Wisconsin Law Review* (1991): 1113–1232. C. P. Snow, *The Two Cultures,* reissue ed., 1993. Steven Goldberg, *Culture Clash, Law and Science in America,* 1994. Sheila Jasanoff, *Science at the Bar,* 1995. David L. Faigman, David H. Kaye, Michael J. Saks, and Joseph Sanders, *Modern Scientific Evidence: The Law and Science of Expert Testimony,* 1997 and 1999 supp. Kenneth R. Foster and Peter W. Huber, *Judging Science: Scientific Knowledge and the Federal Courts,* 1997. Robert P. Merges, *Patent Law and Policy,* 1997. Robert P. Merges, Peter S. Menell, Mark A. Lemley, and Thomas M. Jorde, *Intellectual Property in the New Technological Age,* 1997. Helge Kuhse and Peter Singer, *A Companion to Bioethics,* 1998. David L. Faigman, *Legal Alchemy: The Use and Misuse of Science in the Law,* 1999. Federal Judicial Center, *Reference Manual on Scientific Evidence,* 2000.   —Jennifer Mnookin

SCOPES TRIAL. What was to become a sensational test case of antievolution law was instigated in May 1925 by the ACLU to challenge a new Tennessee state statute making it a misdemeanor, punishable by a maximum penalty of $500, to teach the theory of human evolution in the state's public schools. The statute represented the first major victory of a national educational and political campaign against the Darwinian theory of evolution launched by Protestant fundamentalists around 1920. Their effort gained momentum when popular politician and orator William Jennings Bryan lent his voice to the cause.

After passage of the Tennessee antievolution statute, the ACLU invited state teachers to challenge its legality. Dayton, Tennessee, science teacher John Scopes accepted this invitation at the urging of publicity-minded town leaders, including local school officials. Famed litigator Clarence Darrow led a team of nationally prominent attorneys and scientists in defense of Scopes and the alleged right to teach science. Bryan joined the prosecution in supporting the state's purported authority to control the public-school curriculum and questioning the Darwinist theory.

The confrontation produced a show trial that captured the nation's attention. Hundreds of reporters covered the eight-day event, which was broadcast over the radio and filmed for newsreels. Although hailed as a battle royal between science and *religion, no clear winner emerged. The court denied the defense's motion to strike the statute as unconstitutional and sustained the prosecution's objections to expert testimony regarding theory of evolution. Despite sparring by the lawyers over larger matters of science versus religion and academic freedom versus legislative control over public education, the court narrowed the legal issue to whether Scopes ever taught the theory that humans descended from other species. The defense conceded this fact and asked jurors for a conviction to facilitate an appeal on the law. Ruling in 1927, the Tennessee Supreme Court upheld the statute but overturned Scopes's conviction and directed prosecutors not to retry him.

The Scopes trial highlighted the issue of evolutionary teaching and helped to make it a flashpoint in the culture wars between the proponents of modern secularism and champions of traditional religion. Many publishers responded to the heightened controversy by deemphasizing the theory of evolution in high-school textbooks for a generation. Protestant fundamentalism was widely ridiculed for opposing science and turned inward. The Scopes trial thus had a profound cultural impact despite its legal insignificance.

By 1968, when the United States Supreme Court in *Epperson* v. *Arkansas* declared anti-evolution statutes to be an unconstitutional establishment of religion, the Scopes trial had entered the nation's folklore as an American equivalent of Galileo's persecution by the Church. Later religious opponents of evolutionary theory attempted to distance themselves from the cultural associations of the Scopes trial by promoting classroom instruction in their theories of creation or intelligent design of nature rather than focusing on the elimination of evolution teaching. For many others, the Scopes trial remained an object lesson in the danger to public science and private freedom posed by popular religion.

[*See also* Civil Rights and Civil Liberties; Lawyers, Popular Perceptions of]

• Ray Ginger, *Six Days or Forever? Tennessee v. John Thomas Scopes*, 1958. Edward J. Larson, *Summer for the Gods: The Scopes Trial and America's Continuing Debate Over Science and Religion*, 1997.

—Edward J. Larson

SCOTTSBORO TRIALS. The series of legal proceedings associated with alleged rapes on a train near Scottsboro, Alabama, marks the collision between sexualized racial violence and *due process of law and *civil rights. At the end of the nineteenth century, white fears of African-American sexuality led to increasingly brutal racial violence (see RACE AND ETHNICITY). White mobs tortured to death thousands of African-American men and justified their violence as made necessary by an alleged tendency toward sexual violence on the part of African-American men. When whites did not torture African-American males to death in the street, they subjected them to kangaroo courts where jurors dared not defy the mob outside, or inside, the courtroom.

The Scottsboro case began on March 25, 1931 when a young woman named Ruby Bates told a deputy sheriff that she and Victoria Price had been raped by nine African-American male youths while hoboing on a freight train. Authorities arrested the youths, preventing a lynching only with assistance from the Alabama National Guard.

At first the state of Alabama prosecuted the nine youths with little outside scrutiny. Prosecutors hurried the nine through a succession of trials, quickly winning death sentences for eight defendants. Jurors could not reach a verdict in Roy Wright's case only because seven jurors insisted he be sentenced to death even though the state had only asked for life imprisonment for Wright, aged thirteen.

The Communist International Labor Defense (ILD) sent agents to Scottsboro and learned that, contrary to the locally written accounts, the boys had been poorly represented. The ILD decided to finance a lawyer for the Scottsboro defendants and turned them into international celebrities, bringing attention to their plight through rallies and numerous newspaper and magazine articles. The National Association for the Advancement of Colored People (NAACP) had failed to see the propaganda potential in the case soon enough and suffered a setback. For a time, it appeared the ILD was more effectively committed to civil rights than the NAACP.

In *Powell* v. *Alabama* (1932) the Supreme Court threw out the convictions on the grounds that the due process clause of the *Fourteenth Amendment required that indigent defendants have adequate legal *counsel in capital cases. Justice George Sutherland complained that the boys had received only a pro forma defense and that the Alabama Supreme Court had known this was so when it approved the verdict.

At their new trials a New York lawyer named Samuel Leibowitz defended the nine young men. Leibowitz persuaded many journalists of his clients' innocence. He even convinced one Alabama judge. But he had little luck with Alabama juries. In *Norris* v. *Alabama* (1935) the Supreme Court again reversed a death sentence on grounds that African Americans were systematically excluded from the grand and trial juries.

In 1937 Alabama dropped its case against four of the defendants. Eventually the other defendants were released. A symbol of racial discrimination in the administration of criminal justice, the Scottsboro trials did much to start the process of constitutionalizing state criminal procedures.

[*See also* Criminal Law Principles]

• Dan Carter, *Scottsboro: A Tragedy of the American South*, 1969. James Goodman, *Stories of Scottsboro*, 1995.

—Philip Abbott

SEARCH AND SEIZURE. Police authority to *arrest and search is regulated primarily by judicial interpretations of the Fourth Amendment to the Constitution, which applies directly to federal officers and indirectly, through the *incorporation doctrine, to state officers. State courts sometimes also apply state constitutional standards. Because search and seizure requires balancing citizens' rights to *liberty and *privacy against the government's interest in effective law enforcement, it is especially susceptible to shifts in the ideological balance among Supreme Court justices. During the 1960s, the *Warren Court emphasized protection of citizens from excessive government intrusions. More recently, during the "war on drugs," the *Burger and Rehnquist Courts have favored aggressive law enforcement.

Scope of Fourth Amendment Protection. The Fourth Amendment requires that the police justify all "searches and seizures" by government agents of "persons, houses, papers, and effects." Not all police conduct constitutes a "search" or "seizure." Police arrests or temporary detentions are treated as "seizures" under the amendment, but police officers do not make a "seizure" when they simply approach a person in a public place and ask questions. Police conduct is a seizure that must be justified under the Fourth Amendment only if police officers assert their authority over a person, the person submits or is actually controlled by the police, and the person's liberty is significantly limited (*California* v. *Hodari D.* (1991)).

Whether an action by the police is a "search" subject to Fourth Amendment standards usually depends upon whether the police have intruded upon premises or information in which a person has a "reasonable expectation of privacy" (*Katz* v. *United States* (1967)). A reasonable expectation of privacy can exist in a house or other building not open to the public and in an auto or other personal property. However, a reasonable expectation of privacy cannot exist in "open fields" (an outside area beyond the "curtilage," the area immediately around a house). In addition, a person can expect privacy only if she has not exposed a place or information to others. Thus, if she shares financial information with her banker, that information is no longer protected by the Fourth Amendment. Similarly, if a normally private area can be observed from outside—for example, through an open window or from a helicopter—the expectation of privacy is lost. Police observation of something in plain view from a place in which they lawfully can be present does not constitute a police search that must comply with Fourth Amendment standards (*Florida* v. *Riley* (1989)).

Fourth Amendment protection can also be given up by consent to a search. Such consent must be voluntary, not merely acquiescence to an assertion of authority by the police. However, police are not required to inform persons of their right to refuse to consent to a search of their person, house, or automobile (*Schneckloth* v. *Busta-monte* (1973)).

Use of Warrants. According to modern search and seizure doctrine, the Fourth Amendment's reference to a right against "unreasonable searches and seizures" creates a broad requirement that police intrusions be "reasonable." In earlier periods, "Fourth Amendment reasonableness" was sometimes construed as creating a presumption that police should obtain a written judicial warrant prior to making a search. Use of warrants was preferred because "neutral and detached" magistrates were thought to be less likely than police officers to approve of hasty or poorly justified intrusions.

To be valid, a warrant must satisfy two explicit standards in the Fourth Amendment. First, the warrant must be supported by a sworn showing of "probable cause." Traditionally, probable cause was defined as information sufficient to warrant a prudent person's belief that the wanted individual had committed a crime (for an arrest warrant) or that *evidence of a crime or contraband would be found in a search (for a search warrant). By 1960 it was settled that a police officer could make a sworn showing of probable cause on the basis of hearsay from reliable informants. The standard was lowered, however, when the 1983 decision *Illinois* v. *Gates* redefined probable cause as information indicating "a substantial chance" or "fair probability" of criminal activity. *Gates* also directed reviewing courts to be deferential to the issuing magistrate's judgment that there was probable cause to support the warrant. In addition, a police factual error does not invalidate probable cause provided it was reasonable in the circumstances (*Illinois* v. *Rodriguez* (1990)). Thus, probable cause is now a relatively low threshold for justifying arrests or searches.

The second explicit standard for a valid warrant is that it must "particularly describe" the place to be searched and the person to be arrested or the items to be searched for. This particularity requirement is usually met if a search warrant states the address of a building to be searched and identifies the nature of the contraband or evidence sought.

Warrantless Arrests and Searches. In theory a search made without a warrant is presumed to be unreasonable unless the police conduct falls within a recognized exception to the requirement for a warrant (*Katz* v. *United States*). Police must sometimes obtain a warrant to lawfully enter a house or other private building (*Payton* v. *New York* (1980)). However, contemporary doctrine inclines toward a generalized, relativistic assessment of police reasonableness based upon the "totality of the circumstances," and the Supreme Court has recognized a number of exceptions to the warrant requirement that apply in most situations in which police officers make arrests or searches.

For example, police can intrude without a warrant when there is an "exigency," such as hot pursuit of a fleeing suspect, an immediate danger someone might suffer bodily injury, or imminent danger that evidence might be destroyed. In addition, police do not need a warrant to make an arrest in a public place (*United States* v. *Watson* (1976)). Police officers who make a lawful arrest are also permitted to make a warrantless search of the arrestee's person, as well as the area in the immediate vicinity of the arrestee or the passenger area of an auto the arrestee has recently occupied. Police can also make a warrantless inventory search of an arrestee's person and belongings during the arrest booking process. If an arrestee was driving a car and it was impounded, police can also make an inventory search of the car (*Florida* v. *Wells* (1990)).

As with arrests, the overwhelming proportion of police searches are made without a warrant. In particular, automobiles and any containers in them may be searched without a warrant if there is probable cause—information indicating a substantial chance that the auto contains contraband or evidence of a crime (*California* v. *Acevedo* (1991)). Generally, searches made under one of the exceptions to the search-warrant requirement must be based upon probable cause that contraband or evidence of a crime may be found. However, inventory searches, which are justified by administrative and safety considerations rather than law enforcement purposes per se, do not require probable cause.

Police "Stops" and "Frisks." Police officers may make an arrest—that is, take a person into custody to await criminal court proceedings—only if they have probable cause to believe that the person has committed a crime. However, under the 1968 decision *Terry* v. *Ohio*, police who lack probable cause to arrest may nevertheless stop, detain (i.e., temporarily seize), and question a person if they have "reasonable suspicion" of criminal activity. Reasonable suspicion requires less information than probable cause; it is met if the police officer can articulate some specific reason, beyond a mere hunch, for his suspicion. However, if police do not develop probable cause to arrest during the brief detention, they must allow the person to go on her way, otherwise a lawful detention becomes an illegal arrest.

During a *Terry* detention, a police officer may also frisk the suspect for weapons if she reasonably suspects the detainee may be armed or dangerous and may also inspect a car from which the person alighted for weapons. If an officer discovers a weapon, she may take control of it and, depending on the law of the jurisdiction, may have probable cause to arrest the person for illegal possession of a weapon. However, a frisk is permitted only for weapons; a fuller search is illegal unless there is probable cause to arrest.

Police encounters with citizens often begin with a traffic stop. Under the 2001 decision *Atwater* v. *City of Largo Vista*, the Fourth Amendment itself does not prohibit a full arrest for even the most minor traffic offense. Thus, local law can empower an officer who observes a traffic infraction to exercise discretion about whether to issue a traffic citation or to arrest the driver. If the police officer arrests a driver for a traffic violation, he can search her person and auto based upon the arrest. Because courts are permitted to inquire only whether police conduct was objectively valid, not whether it was pretextual, police officers who have a hunch that a car is engaged in criminal activity are free to follow the vehicle until they observe a traffic violation, stop the car, and then either obtain consent to search it or arrest and search as described above (*Whren* v. *United States* (1996)).

Although police are not permitted to establish road checkpoints solely to enforce drug-possession or other criminal laws, they may establish checkpoints and briefly stop autos on a systematic basis to identify intoxicated drivers or to check for valid license and registration. If an officer develops reasonable suspicion or finds probable cause of crime during the checkpoint stop, this permits further investigation or arrest and search. Because a sniff by a trained drug-dog is not deemed a "search," police may use drug-dogs at any checkpoint; if the dog detects drugs in a car, this constitutes probable cause to search the vehicle (*Edmonds* v. *Indianapolis* (2001)).

"Special Needs" Searches. Government officers or employees other than police sometimes conduct searches for purposes other than ordinary law enforcement. Such searches usually are subject to the Fourth Amendment, but they are assessed according to the "special needs" arising from the particular context—for example, effective regulatory enforcement, public safety, or the preservation of discipline in educational institutions. Such searches are usually subject to less stringent standards than the probable cause standard. In some instances, special needs may permit random searches that are not based on any individualized suspicion (*Vernonia School District* v. *Acton* (1995)).

Exclusion of Unconstitutionally Seized Evidence. In the absence of police brutality, the qualified official immunity doctrine usually protects police from civil liability for illegal arrests or searches (*Anderson* v. *Creighton* (1987)). In addition, *injunctions generally may not be issued to remedy abusive police practices (*Lyons* v. *California* (1983)). Instead, defendants who have been subjected to unconstitutional police conduct may request the suppression or exclusion from evidence of any items or information obtained as a result of a police violation of the Fourth Amendment. An illegal arrest usually has no legal consequence unless it resulted in a search in which incriminating evidence was discovered; in that case, the evidence is excluded as "fruit of the poisonous tree."

Until the 1970s, items or information obtained through unconstitutional arrests or searches were excluded from virtually any use as evidence (*Mapp* v. *Ohio* (1961)). However, the 1974 decision *United States* v. *Calandra* rejected earlier treatments of exclusion as a constitutional right of the victim of police illegality and redefined exclusion simply as a policy aimed at deterring future police illegality. Subsequent decisions purporting to weigh the "costs" against the "deterrent benefits" of excluding evidence have permitted unconstitutionally obtained evidence to be freely used in many legal proceedings. Although unconstitutionally obtained evidence is still excluded from the prosecutor's case-in-chief in a criminal trial, the government can use such evidence in preliminary hearings, to obtain grand jury indictments, to impeach a defendant who testified in his own defense at trial, to increase the sentence imposed, in probation or parole revocation hearings, and in related civil proceedings such as deportation hearings or tax penalty suits.

The Supreme Court has also created several exceptions that allow the government to make unrestricted use of unconstitutionally obtained evidence even in the prosecutor's case-in-chief. Evidence seized under unconstitutionally issued warrants is almost always admissible under a so-called "good-faith mistake exception," because the bad warrant is deemed the fault of the issuing magistrate rather than the police (*United States* v. *Leon* (1984)). A similar exception applies to evidence seized unconstitutionally because of an error in court records (*Arizona* v. *Evans* (1995)). To date, however, the court has not recognized a good-faith mistake exception for warrantless searches involving only police officers. The Court has also recognized an "inevitable discovery" exception that applies if the government can establish that the police would have found evidence legally independent of an unconstitutional police intrusion (*Murray* v. *United States* (1988)). Another exception permits the government to call a person as a witness even though he was identified only as a result of an unconstitutional search (*United States* v. *Ceccolini* (1978)).

Enforcement of the Fourth Amendment protection is often limited by the "standing" doctrine. Only a person whose own liberty or own privacy was violated can challenge the constitutionality of an arrest or search; no one can seek to exclude evidence that incriminates him only because someone else's rights were violated. Thus, police can obtain evidence that incriminates person A by deliberately conducting an unconstitutional search of person B's house, papers, or property, and A usually cannot challenge the admissibility of the unconstitutionally obtained evidence in his trial (*United States* v. *Payner* (1980)).

Commentators have concluded that exclusion is also limited, as a practical matter, by police perjury regarding the circumstances in which evidence was obtained and by the willingness of many judges to stretch search standards to allow incriminating evidence to be admitted in criminal trials. It is now widely accepted that only a very small percentage of arrests for serious crimes, and hardly any for violent crimes, are dropped because of exclusion of unconstitutionally seized evidence. When the limitations and exceptions to exclusion are coupled with the relatively weak standards for police searches and seizures, it appears that current Fourth Amendment doctrine exerts little influence on police conduct and offers little protection to citizens' liberty and privacy.

[*See also* Civil Rights and Civil Liberties; Criminal Law Principles]

• Thomas Y. Davies, "A Hard Look at What We Know (and Still Need to Learn) about the 'Costs' of the Exclusionary Rule," *American Bar Foundation Research Journal* [now *Law & Social Inquiry*]1983: 611–90. Yale Kamisar, "Does (Did) (Should) the Exclusionary Rule Rest on a 'Principled Basis' Rather than an 'Empirical Proposition'?" *Creighton Law Review* 16 (1983): 565–667. Albert W. Alschuler, " 'Close Enough for Government Work': The Exclusionary Rule after Leon," *Supreme Court Review* (1984): 309–58. Yale Kamisar, "*Gates*, 'Probable Cause,' 'Good Faith,' and Beyond," *Iowa Law Review* 69 (1984): 551–615. Craig M. Bradley, "Two Models of the Fourth Amendment," *Michigan Law Review* 83 (1985): 1468–1501. Myron W. Orfield Jr., "Deterrence, Perjury, and the Heater Factor: An Exclusionary Rule in the Chicago Criminal Courts," *Colorado Law Review* 63 (1992): 75–161. Akhil Reed Amar, "Fourth Amendment First Principles," *Harvard Law Review* 107 (1994): 757–819. Joshua Dressler, *Understanding Criminal Procedure*, 2d ed., 1996. Wayne R. LaFave, *Search and Seizure: A Treatise on the Fourth Amendment*, 3d ed., 5 vols., 1996. Tracey Maclin, "The Complexity of the Fourth Amendment: A Historical Review," *Boston University Law Review* 77 (1997): 925–74. Thomas Y. Davies, "Recovering the Original Fourth

Amendment," *Michigan Law Review* 98 (1999): 547–750.
—Thomas Y. Davies

SEARCH WARRANT. The search warrant, an intrinsic part of the Fourth Amendment, has come to play an integral role in defining and restricting the scope of *police investigations in modern America. The framers of the Fourth Amendment set forth the requirements for a valid search warrant: that "no Warrants shall issue, but upon probable cause, supported by Oath or Affirmation, and particularly describing the place to be searched and the persons or things to be seized." In large part, the warrant clause was drafted to counter what the early Americans perceived to be the abusive British practice in colonial times of issuing general warrants and writs of assistance. General warrants gave the British authorities indiscriminate authority to search homes and publishing houses for evidence of seditious libel. Writs of assistance afforded British agents the unfettered right to ransack homes or businesses in search of prohibited items or goods avoiding customs duties.

A lively academic debate has emerged regarding the correct interpretation of the warrant clause. Some scholars believe that the first part of the Fourth Amendment, which contains a prohibition against unreasonable *searches and seizures of houses, persons, papers, and effects, is separate and distinct from the warrant clause. They argue that the framers did not mean to imply through the warrant clause that all searches without warrants were unreasonable. They point to the historical evidence that prompted the framers to include the warrant clause in the Amendment—the abusive practices associated with British general warrants and writs of assistance. Warrants would now require probable cause before they could be issued. By contrast, other academics maintain that the two clauses of the Amendment are indivisible. To safeguard against unreasonable searches or seizures by government agents, the search warrant is necessary as a check on police authority by subjecting police conclusions about probable cause to search a place and seize items to judicial supervision. Expressing a preference for warrants, the Supreme Court in *Katz* v. *United States* (1967) held that searches performed without warrants are unreasonable, subject to a few well-defined exceptions. As a response to the more recent rise in crime and, particularly, the scourge of drugs in American society, the Court has substantially diluted the warrant requirement by creating numerous and wide-ranging exceptions.

In *Johnson* v. *United States* (1948), the Court elaborated on the essential purpose of the search warrant by noting that it is not designed to prevent the police from drawing inferences concerning probable cause about criminal activity, but rather to interpose the magistrate's neutrality on the normally "competitive enterprise of ferreting out crime." Accordingly, the Court has invalidated search warrants based on lack of neutrality by the judge issuing a warrant. For example, the attorney general of a state who issued a search warrant for a murder suspect's home and automobile was not detached or neutral, thereby invalidating the warrant. Similarly, a magistrate who received money for approving a search warrant application, and no compensation if he did issue the warrant, was not sufficiently neutral. In another instance, a magistrate who accompanied police agents to the site of the search became a partisan of the investigation, abdicating his neutrality.

The validity of search warrants depends on compliance with the restrictions set forth in the language of the Fourth Amendment. In short, search warrants must be based on probable cause that items linked to criminal activity will be found in the place searched, and that those items are subject to seizure. In some circumstances, a person may be searched pursuant to a warrant if there is probable cause to believe he may have an item relating to a crime on his person. On the other hand, *seizure* deals with the authority of the police to seize an item when executing a search warrant. Furthermore, law enforcement agents seeking a warrant must swear to the facts justifying its issuance. A search warrant must also meet the particularity requirement—it must with a certain degree of precision describe the place to be searched and the things to be seized. Constitutional, statutory, and court rule constraints govern the timing, manner, and execution of search warrants.

The threshold proof required for the issuance of a valid search warrant is probable cause. The Supreme Court has described that *burden as a fair probability, or substantial chance, that evidence of criminal activity or contraband will be found in the place to be searched. Therefore, the burden encompasses a less than 50 percent chance that the item will be found in the place to be searched. Rooted in both history and cultural practice, this low threshold might appear susceptible to abuse. To a large extent it represents a concession by the modern Court to police efforts to combat crime in general and the *drug trade in particular. Search warrants, moreover, are often based on information furnished to the police by informants who themselves are, or have been, involved in criminal activity. When relying on such informants to establish probable cause, police agents need to set forth their credibility or the basis for their knowledge. A logical corollary to this doctrine is that hearsay information may be employed to establish the probable cause necessary for the issuance of a warrant, as long it is corroborated by independent police investigation.

The particularity requirement protects citizens against unwarranted and mistaken invasions of their homes by law enforcement agents. It also restricts the scope of the search by compelling the police to look only in those places where the items for which they have the authority to search and seize could be located. Nevertheless, the police need not be perfect in the description of the search target. Rather, they only need to be as precise as is reasonably possible given the information they gather prior to the execution of the search warrant. And the nature of the items to be seized defines the scope of particularity. For example, a warrant authorizing the search of a business for documents relating to a complex fraudulent scheme might require less particularity in the description of the items than the search for the gun and fruits of an armed bank robbery. An item not described in the warrant may nonetheless be seized if it is in plain view, the police have probable cause to believe it is linked to criminal activity or is contraband, and if the police have not exceeded their authority before they come across the item. Finally, particularity serves to safeguard the property interests of the targets of a warrant by restricting the items the police may seize during the execution of a warrant.

Execution of search warrants must be reasonably prompt. Given the nature of probable cause to search for and seize items subject to movement, warrants have a tendency to go stale. Again, staleness varies with the nature of the crimes triggering the request for a warrant as well as the nature of the items subject to seizure. To protect residents of a home that is subject to being searched pursuant to a warrant, the Court has constitutionalized the common law practice of requiring police officers to knock and announce their presence before entering the premises to execute the warrant. This prerequisite, however, is flexible; if the police have reason to believe that knocking and announcing will threaten either their safety or that of persons inside the premises, they may dispense with that requirement. Similarly, the police do not need to knock before executing the warrant if they have a reasonable suspicion that by doing so the items they will be looking for (for example, drugs) will be destroyed. Finally, special circumstances and prior judicial approval are necessary if the police intend to serve a warrant during the night.

The principle remedy for violation of search warrant rules is the exclusionary rule, under which the prosecution will be barred from introducing the items seized to establish the accused's guilt. The violation may occur because the warrant was issued without probable cause, because it was overly broad in its description, or because the police exceeded the scope of authority conferred by the warrant while executing it. The Supreme Court, however, has carved out exceptions to the exclusionary rule. In *United States* v. *Leon* (1984), for example, the Court created a good-faith exception to the rule; that case stands for the proposition that if the police in objective good faith secure a warrant that is invalid because it lacks probable cause, the items seized still will be admissible to establish the defendant's guilt. Employing a cost-benefit analysis, the Court concluded that the costs of excluding probative evidence outweighed the benefits of exclusion, since deterrence of police misconduct was not a factor when law enforcement agents acted in the objective good-faith belief that their conduct was constitutionally permissible.

[*See also* Criminal Law Principles]

• Nelson B. Lasson, *The History and Development of the Fourth Amendment to the United States Constitution*, 1937. Anthony G. Amsterdam, "Perspectives on the Fourth Amendment," *Minnesota Law Review* 58 (1974): 349–477. Craig M. Bradley, "Two Models of the Fourth Amendment," *Michigan Law Review* 83 (1985): 1468. Christopher Slobogin, "The World Without the Fourth Amendment," *UCLA Law Review* 39 (1991): 1–107. William J. Stuntz, "Warrants and Fourth Amendment Remedies," *Virginia Law Review* 77 (1991): 881–943. Akhil Reed Amar, "Fourth Amendment: First Principles," *Harvard Law Review* 107 (1994): 757–819. William W. Greenhalgh and Mark J. Yost, "In Defense of the 'Per Se' Rule: Justice Stewart's Struggle to Preserve the Fourth Amendment's Warrant Clause," *American Criminal Law Review* 31 (1994): 1013–98. Wayne R. LaFave, *Search and Seizure*, 3d ed., 1996.

—Alfredo Garcia

SECESSION. The withdrawal of membership from an existing state by a portion of its citizenry is both an essential democratic right and a doctrine inconsistent with the maintenance of stable political authority. The legality of secession was widely debated in the United States until the end of the *Civil War. These debates were undertaken without explicit judicial direction, although arguments were frequently framed as a constitutional question. During and after the Civil War, courts addressed issues associated with southern secession although no consistent legal doctrine was employed.

In the United States, the question of secession has constituted a portion of the more general question concerning the relationship between federal and state governments. The authors of the *Federalist Papers* devoted several essays to the issue of secession. Should a new constitution not be adopted, John *Jay and Alexander Hamilton argued that the United States would likely dissolve into three or more separate states. The question, however, of the new relationship between the states and the federal government was described as partly federal and partly unitary, and thus left open the question of whether secession existed as an implicit legal option on the part of the states. Debate about secession revolved on upon whether federal–state relationships should be characterized as a compact among states that was legally dissolvable, as a compact among states that did not include secession rights or as a union best theorized on other terms.

The compact-secession model was utilized in the Kentucky-Virginia Resolutions (1798–99), drafted by Thomas *Jefferson and James Madison respectively. In opposing the Alien and Sedition Acts, the resolutions asserted the rights of states to nullify federal legislation. Nullification, as an act of selective secession, was advanced in the Kentucky Resolutions as the "rightful remedy" in "cases of an abuse of delegated powers" since "as in all other cases of compact among powers having no common judge, each party has an equal right to judge for itself, as well of infractions as to the mode and measure of redress." Federalists maintained that the judicial branch of the federal government was the only appropriate institution to decide constitutional disputes. Although James Madison later argued that the compact model did not imply secession, these resolutions were often cited in the nullification crisis of 1832 and by southern secessionists in the 1850 and 1860s as support for their positions.

The compact-secession model was also advanced in 1814 by a wing of the Federalist Party, named the Essex Junta by opponents. Members of this group raised the question of secession in opposition to the Embargo Act of 1807 and successfully persuaded state legislatures in Massachusetts, Rhode Island, and Connecticut to authorize delegations to meet to discuss "public concerns and grievances" arising from disputes over participation of state militias in the War of 1812. Although the final report of the Hartford convention did not recommend secession, John C. *Calhoun and other southerners referred to the convention as a precedent for their interpretation of the right to secession.

The Union model was dramatically presented by Daniel *Webster in his famous second reply to Robert Hayne in 1830. The occasion for the Senate debate was legislation dealing with public land policy in the West but the debate broadened to one over the nature of the *Constitution. Webster argued that the compact model in general was inadequate to the character of a union which had already proved to be a "copious fountain of national, social and personal happiness." In addition to this evocation of nationalistic sentiment, Webster contended that the Constitution was not a compact among states authorizing what Hayne described as the "right of constitutional resistance" on the part of states to unconstitutional legislation. Instead it was a "people's Constitution" in which both the federal and state governments were agents of the citizens at large.

As the question of *slavery and its expansion dominated the national political agenda in the 1850s, the debate over the three models was further expanded. Southern secessionists claimed that the right of peaceful exit was implied by the compact model. Some abolitionists, including William Lloyd Garrison, advanced a similar position and argued that a union that included slavery was no longer possible. At the state secession conventions of 1860–61, some southerners, known as cooperationists, either adopted a compact without secession model or claimed that threats to *states' rights were not yet so severe to justify secession. The outgoing president, James Buchanan, argued from a compact without secession model in his Annual Message to Congress (December 1861). He claimed that if secession was a constitutional remedy, "it must be on the principle that the Federal government is a mere voluntary association of states, to be dissolved at pleasure by any one of the contracting parties." However, neither the Congress nor the president had the authority to forcibly oppose secession since "the power to make war against a state is at variance with the whole spirit and intent of the Constitution."

When Abraham *Lincoln took office in 1861, he advanced a panoply of arguments against secession, significantly enhancing the union model. He presented a series of legal arguments including the claim that the original compact was not signed by states since the moment of incorporation occurred during the Revolution, the claim that the compact was made in perpetuity, the claim that the Declaration of Independence was the obligatory text rather than the Constitution in itself. It was Lincoln's centering of the Declaration in his analysis that was the anchor of his antisecessionist position. As the Civil War continued, Lincoln added powerful rhetorical elements to his model. He suggested that the war itself constituted an expiation of guilt for the tolerance of slavery and forcible opposition to secession was a test of not only the principle of majority rule but also of the stability of free government in general.

Lincoln thus defined the Confederate States of America (CSA) in terms of an insurrection. For example, in the blockade of Southern ports in 1861, he refused to recognize the belligerent status of the CSA and referred to infractions as acts of piracy. The Supreme Court in the *Prize Cases* (1862) both acknowledged the CSA as a belligerent power and described the Civil War as an insurrection. In subsequent cases regarding the status of property in the CSA, courts continued to accept a dual account of secession. In *Williams* v. *Bruffy* (1877), Justice Stephen J. *Field contended that the recognition of the belligerent status of the CSA was a humanitarian gesture that was operational only during hostilities and that the United States never acknowledged "in any form" the "lawfulness of the rebellious organization or the validity of any of its acts . . ." Jefferson Davis, the President of the defeated CSA, continued to defend the compact-secession model in *The Rise and Fall of the Confederate Government* (1881).

The Civil War and the southern defense of slavery discredited secession in the United States as a constitutional remedy for conflict. To the extent that the compact model survives as a legal doctrine, secession as an option remains only a theoretical possibility.

• James M. McPherson, *Battle Cry of Freedom*, 1988. Elizabeth R. Varon, "*United States* v. *Steinmetz*: The Legal Legacy of the Civil War, Revisited," *Alabama Law Review* (1995): 725–62. Philip Abbott, "The Lincoln Propositions and the Spirit of Secession," *Studies in American Political Development* (1996): 103–29. Percy B. Lehning, ed., *Theories of Secession*, 1998. Garry Wills, *A Necessary Evil*, 1999. David F. Ericson, *The Debate Over Slavery*, 2001.   —Philip Abbott

SECOND AMENDMENT. *See* Arms, Right to Bear.

SECRECY, CORPORATE. *See* Corporation.

SECRETARY, LEGAL. *See* Paralegal and Legal Secretary.

SECURED TRANSACTIONS. *See* Consumer Law.

SECURITIES LAW. Securities are different from most other commodities in commerce in that they have no intrinsic value; they merely represent rights in something else. Most goods are produced, distributed, and used or consumed; governmental *regulation for these goods focuses on protecting the *consumer against dangerous goods, false advertising, and unfair or noncompetitive pricing practices. Securities are different from goods in many respects, and these differences are reflected in the federal securities laws.

Securities represent nothing more than intangible rights in a company or some other entity. Unlike goods, securities are not produced; they are merely created by the entity issuing the securities. Securities can be issued in unlimited amounts, virtually without cost for the very reason that they are nothing in themselves and represent only an interest in something else. An important focus of securities laws, therefore, is assuring that when securities are offered to the public, investors have an accurate idea of what this "something else" is and how much of an interest in it the particular security actually represents. Purchasers of securities do not consume securities.

Securities are a form of currency, traded in the so-called "secondary markets" at fluctuating prices determined by supply and demand. Securities law is designed to ensure that there is an efficient market for securities based on a continuous flow of information into the market place concerning the company or other entity whose securities are being traded. Disclosures are required whenever holders of securities of public companies are being asked to vote, or make some other decision, with respect to the securities they own. The trading markets for securities are susceptible to manipulative and deceptive practices. Securities laws contain general "antifraud" provisions, which apply to trading by "insiders" on the basis of nonpublic information and to various kinds of misstatements by corporate management and others. The regulation of brokers, dealers, and professional traders is designed to ensure that these professionals do not use their superior experience to take advantage of investors. Securities laws provide for a variety of governmental sanctions against those who violate the antifraud, antimanipulation, and registration requirements. The securities laws also create civil *liability to persons injured by violations. In addition to the statutes' expressed remedies, the courts have recognized implied rights of action.

The federal securities laws consist of six separate statutes enacted between 1933 and 1940, and a seventh enacted in 1970. These securities acts have been amended over the years.

The Securities Act of 1933 regulates public offerings of securities. With certain exemptions, the Act prohibits offers and sales of securities that are not registered with the Securities and Exchange Commission. Registration requires that securities be offered only through the use of specified disclosure documents. The Act prohibits fraudulent practices in any offer or sale of securities. The rationale underlying the Act and the other federal securities laws that followed was to require full disclosure in order to enable investors to make an informed investment decision. The federal law rejected the legislative approach taken in many states—popularly known as "blue sky" laws—of trying to regulate the merits of securities offerings and prevent the sale of stock in fly-by-night companies.

The Securities Exchange Act of 1934 extended federal regulation to trading in the secondary markets of securities that are already issued and outstanding. The Act established the Securities and Exchange Commission (SEC) and gave it responsibility for administration of the federal securities laws. The Act contains a number of distinct disclosure and registration provisions aimed at different participants in the securities markets. The Act regulates securities of publicly held corporations; prohibits various "manipulative or deceptive devices or contrivances" in connection with the purchase or sale of securities; restricts the amount of credit that may be extended for the purchase of securities; requires brokers and dealers to register with the SEC and regulates their activities; and provides for SEC registration and supervision of national securities exchanges and associations, clearing agencies, transfer agents, and securities information processors.

The Public Utilities Holding Company Act of 1935 was enacted to correct abuses then existing in the financing and operation of electric and gas public utility holding company systems. The SEC's functions under this Act were substantially completed by the 1950s. There has been increasing pressure to repeal this outmoded Act.

The Trust Indenture Act of 1939 applies generally to bonds and other debt securities publicly issued by companies. Although the offering is registered under the 1933 Act, the indenture covering these debt securities must also be qualified under the 1939 Act, which imposes standards of independence and responsibility on the indenture trustee, and requires other provisions to be included for the protection of the security holders.

The Investment Company Act of 1940 imposes regulation on publicly owned companies, usually mutual funds, engaged primarily in the business of investing and trading in securities. The 1933 and 1934 Acts also apply to those companies. The 1940 Act regulates the composition of the management of investment companies, their capital structure, approval of their advisory contracts and changes in investment policy, and requires SEC approval for any transactions by these companies with their directors, officers, or affiliates.

The Investment Advisers Act of 1940 requires registration and regulation of investment advisers who are not broker-dealers registered as such under the 1934 Act. As of 1996, the SEC regulated investment advisers with more than $25 million in assets under their management; advisers with less than $25 million under management are regulated by their home states.

The Securities Investor Protection Act of 1970 was enacted to protect customers of insolvent brokerage firms. The Act established the Securities Investor Protection Corporation (SIPC), which provides insurance for customers, and has the power to supervise the liquidation of insolvent firms and arrange for the payment of customers' claims.

[See also Contract Law]

• Louis Loss Joel Seligman, Securities Regulation, 3d ed., 1989. Jerry W. Markham and Thomas L. Hazen, Broker-Dealer Operations Under Securities and Commodities Law: Financial Responsibilities, Credit Regulation, and Customer Protection, 2001. Thomas Lee Hazen, Treatise on the Law of Securities Regulation, 4th ed., (forthcoming).   —Thomas Lee Hazen

SECURITY SERVICES, PRIVATE. See Private Security Services.

SEDITION. The willful and knowing encouragement to overthrow or destroy by force an established government, sedition is as old as the United States, and ironically, was imported directly from England. Because the crime does not necessarily involve an overt *actus reus, but merely a *conspiracy or agreement, to revolt or use force against a government, sedition as a crime has repeatedly clashed with free *speech, a fundamental pillar of U.S.-style democracy. The history of sedition, therefore, has been contentious exchange between those believing in the need to fully protect the U.S. government through serious criminalization of seditious behavior and those championing the importance of free speech in a democracy.

The Sedition Act of 1798, enacted in the midst of the Adams administration and the French Revolution, stated:

> That if any person shall write, print, utter, or publish . . . malicious writing or writings against the government of the United States, or either house of the Congress, or the President of the United States, with intent to defame the said government. . . . or to bring them . . . into contempt or disrepute; or to excite against them, . . . the hatred of the good people of the United States,

then such person shall be punished with a fine or imprisonment. John *Adams and his supporters aggressively used the act to quiet Thomas *Jefferson's advocates. When Jefferson became president, he allowed the "over-reaching" Sedition Act to expire and pardoned all those prosecuted under it early in his administration.

Sedition laws have been more important when the nation is threatened. Both the Confederacy and the Union Government used sedition legislation prior to and during the Civil War to quell opposition. The Sedition Act of 1918, enacted during the First World War, criminalized a wide range of seditious activity, including those who shall "willfully utter, print, write, or publish any disloyal, profane, scurrilous, or abusive language about the form the government of the United States, or the Constitution of the United States, or the military or naval forces of the United States." Following both the Civil War and World War I, these sedition statutes were repealed, or scaled back in great part, in the name of the U.S. Constitution's First Amendment speech and press freedoms.

Seditious conspiracy remains a crime under federal law, and most states now have similar statutes. The current federal statute criminalizes any conspiracy (agreement) to: 1) overthrow or destroy the U.S. government by force; 2) oppose by force the authority of the U.S. government; 3) or delay by force the execution of any U.S. law. While seditious conspiracy does not necessarily involve an overt act, intent to oppose the government by "force" is an essential element. It is force that typically determines what constitutes a seditious act, as opposed to an act of free speech protected under the First Amendment.

Today, the government uses seditious conspiracy in the context of terrorism. For example, several Puerto Ricans affiliated with the F.A.L.N. were prosecuted and convicted for seditious conspiracy in the early 1980s. In 1995, a Muslim sheik and several other Muslim radicals were convicted of seditious conspiracy for a plot to bomb several New York landmarks, including the United Nations, the Holland and Lincoln tunnels, the George Washington Bridge, and several federal buildings.

Several federal criminal statutes are related to sedition, including: *treason (requiring an overt act); the Smith Act (prohibiting one to teach about overthrowing the U.S. government or to hold membership in an organization that advocates the overthrow of the United States government); and the Espionage Act (prohibiting acts of spying).

—Janet K. Levit

SEDITION ACT TRIALS. In 1798, at the height of American fears that contagion from the radicalism of the French Revolution or from Irish immigrants would roil America, Congress passed the Alien and Sedition Act. The Act made it a federal crime to write or publish "any false, scandalous, and malicious, writing or writings, against the government of the United States, or either house of congress of the United States, or the president of the United States, with intent to defame." There was already some case law authority holding that the federal government had a common law power to punish the crime of "seditious libel," but by erecting a firm statutory basis, the Adams administration hoped to thwart critics of such prosecutions. Further, the statute liberalized the *common law rule, by making clear that truth was an affirmative defense and that the issue of criminal intent was for the jury, not the judge. Nevertheless, the Act met with massive opposition from the Jeffersonians, and the prosecutions brought under it, virtually all against Jeffersonian sympathizers, triggered one of the first widespread debates on the nature of freedom of *speech in the early Republic.

There were twenty-five arrests, twelve trials, and eleven convictions under the Act until its expiration, by its own terms, on March 3, 1801. The most notable Sedition Act trials were those of Matthew Lyon, Thomas Cooper, and James Thompson Callender.

Lyon was a Jeffersonian Republican congressman from Vermont. He had made speeches critical of the Adams administration, implying that it was only interested in furthering its own welfare and had been unfair to the French. Lyons indicated that the president belonged in a "mad house." The Federalists, noting Lyon's Irish birth, deemed him a "seditious foreigner," and the jury found him guilty of violating the statute. Supreme Court Associate Justice William Paterson, presiding over the trial, sentenced him to four months of imprisonment and fined him $1,000.

Thomas Cooper, an English immigrant and a partisan writer allied with Thomas *Jefferson, was indicted for having published statements that the Adams administration was imposing a standing army on America, had paid too high a rate of interest during peacetime, and had improperly interfered with the judiciary. Justice Samuel Chase presided over Cooper's trial, and while Cooper raised the affirmative defense of the truth of his charges, Chase imposed the burden of requiring Cooper to prove his charges true "beyond a marrow." At least one of Cooper's charges (that regarding improper interference with the judiciary) was manifestly untrue, and the others, at best, were matters of opinion. Following Chase's instructions, the jury found Cooper guilty, and Chase sentenced him to pay a fine of $400 and to be imprisoned for six months.

The most important trial was that of James Thompson Callender, more because of the conduct of the presiding judge, again Samuel Chase, than because of Callender's "crimes." The Scottish immigrant Callender, like Cooper, had enlisted in Jefferson's cause, and had written a book critical of the Adams administration, in which the kindest thing said about Adams was probably that he was "a hoary headed incendiary." The most important charge for which Callender was prosecuted was the suggestion that Adams, who allegedly betrayed the interests of his own country when vice president, voted to break a tie and pass a statute favoring the interests of British creditors. Callender's lawyers were much more interested in scoring political points against the irascible Chase than they were in effectively defending their client, and Callender was found guilty, sentenced to nine months imprisonment, and fined $200. This provided the Jeffersonians with ammunition in their later efforts to impeach Chase.

Most historians view the 1798 Act as an outrageous attempt by the Federalists to silence an opposition press, but it seems equally possible that the Act was only designed to reign in the more mendacious of the radical critics of the Adams administration. Four of the leading Republican newspapers were silenced, but Cooper and others were quickly pardoned by President Thomas Jefferson. The Act expired in 1801, and the Supreme Court eventually ruled in *United States* v. *Hudson & Goodwin* (1812) that there was no federal common law that could support prosecutions for seditious libel. Most important, the Jeffersonians were able to use the prosecutions against Republican writers to rally sentiment against the Federalists, and Jefferson defeated Adams for the Presidency in 1800, beginning the end of the Federalist party.

[*See also* Criminal Law Principles]

• James Morton Smith, *Freedom's Fetters: The Alien and Sedition Laws and American Civil Liberties,* 1956. Stephen B. Presser, *The Original Misunderstanding: The English, the Americans and the Dialectic of Federalist Jurisprudence,* 1991. Gregg Costa, "John Marshall, the Sedition Act, and Free Speech in the Early Republic," *Texas Law Review* 77 (1999): 1011.

—Stephen B. Presser

SEGREGATION. Race *discrimination became embedded in American law with the emergence of slavery in the colonial period. Before the Revolution, some statutes singled out African Americans, even if free, for special punishments or special legal disabilities. However, a system of statutory segregation did not emerge until after the American Revolution. In the 1790s, public schools in New York, Boston, and other northern cities closed their doors to blacks. By the mid-nineteenth century, various private enterprises in the North and the South—steamboats, trains, inns, restaurants, theaters—either refused service to blacks or made them sit in separate areas. Meanwhile, in much of the North, and all of the South, public educational facilities were segregated by statute or custom.

Blacks and white abolitionists challenged the decision of the Boston school committee to segregate blacks into their own school, but Chief Justice Lemuel *Shaw of the Massachusetts Supreme Judicial Court upheld the policy in *Roberts* v. *City of Boston* (Mass., 1849). While losing the case, these early civil rights activists did not give up, and by 1855 the Massachusetts legislature had banned segregation in the state's public schools. In the late nineteenth century, most northeastern states had passed *civil rights laws to guarantee blacks access to most public accommodations as well as to public schools. However, private discrimination, racism, and weak enforcement created a regime of de facto segregation in much of the North. This segregation became intensified during and after World War I, as blacks began to move north. By the 1950s, most northern blacks lived in neighborhoods that were mostly segregated, and thus attended schools with a majority of minority students. This ghettoization led to some political clout for blacks, who soon had a smattering of seats in Congress and a number of seats in state legislatures and on city councils. In some places, such as New Jersey and Illinois, school boards deliberately, and in violation of state law, created segregated schools for blacks. However, most northern segregation was a function of private decision-making, racism, black poverty, and governmental actions, but not specific laws requiring segregation.

During the *Civil War, the United States initially refused to allow blacks to serve in the military, but this changed in late 1862, when blacks were allowed to enlist into segregated units. The United State Army would remain segregated until the end of World War II, when war manpower replacement needs led to some minor instances of integration. During the war, Japanese-American soldiers were also forced to serve in segregated units. In 1948, President Truman began the integration of the military with Executive Order 8802, but as late as the 1970s blacks complained bitterly about mistreatment and segregation within the Army and Navy.

After the Civil War, federal bureaucracies and federal facilities were integrated, and remained so until 1913, when the administration of President Woodrow Wilson began to segregate facilities in public buildings in Washington. The administration began to purge blacks from federal jobs, and soon required photo IDs for job applicants as a way of screening out blacks. The president himself declared: "I do approve of the segregation that is being attempted in several of the departments." Washington remained a wholly segregated city until the Roosevelt administration, and most private business in the city remained segregated until the 1960s. As a southern city, Washington reflected its region.

The main thrust of segregation was in the South, where free blacks faced numerous restrictions before the Civil War. In most of the South, they could not practice certain professions (such as pharmacist, gunsmith, printer), congregate in groups, attend churches without white supervision, or even attend school. Immediately after the War, the millions of former slaves faced segregation and repression through harsh *black codes passed by legislatures dominated by former Confederates. Northern reaction against these laws led to the Civil Rights Act of 1866, the three Civil War amendments to the U.S. Constitution, and other acts to protect black freedom. During Reconstruction, most of the black codes were repealed, and

in some places, such as Louisiana, civil rights laws mandated equality, and even integration.

With the end of Reconstruction and the return to white rule, the South began to institute increasingly rigid rules for the separation of the races. At first, institutions such as schools, hospitals, prisons, and various asylums were segregated. Starting in the 1890s, de jure segregation began to spread to all aspects of southern life, while de facto segregation (as well as some de jure segregation) appeared in many northern settings.

In the South, segregation was more than just a legal system; it was a way of life, supported by laws, private actions, and cultural norms. As Adam Fairclough has noted, southern states adopted a "plethora of segregation laws" that "marked the birth of a new social order" in which "segregation became a matter of faith among white Southerners." Southern law makers, at the state, county, or municipal level, seemed to constantly look for, and find, ways to segregate, oppress, and humiliate blacks. Joining them were individual store owners, who imposed their own rules or regulations for black patrons. In a series of decisions, including *The Slaughter-House Cases* (1873), *Hall* v. *DeCuir* (1878), *The Civil Rights Cases* (1883), *Louisville, New Orleans & Texas Railway Co.* v. *Mississippi* (1890), and *Plessy* v. *Ferguson* (1896), the U.S. Supreme Court gave its blessing to segregation. The virtual disfranchisement of blacks in the South between 1890 and 1910 set the stage for the creation of a harsh regime of segregation and inequality.

By 1920, virtually every facet of life in the South had been segregated. Southern blacks faced discrimination at every turn in their lives. Those born in hospitals entered the world in separate hospitals; they would be buried in segregated cemeteries. All schools, public and private, from nursery school to college were segregated throughout the period 1900 to 1954. When Berea College, a private institution in Kentucky, attempted to integrate, the state intervened, and the Supreme Court upheld Kentucky's laws mandating that private colleges be segregated. Toward the end of this period, the Supreme Court forced a few graduate and professional schools to desegregate. But these cases were won only because the states did not have a similar program for blacks. In fact, many southern states completely ignored the education of its black citizens. Louisiana, for example, created some twenty "trade schools" between 1934 and 1949, all of them for whites.

If arrested, blacks went to segregated jails. In

Florida, it was illegal for any sheriff or other law enforcement officer to handcuff or chain blacks and whites together; in Georgia, black and white prisoners were to be kept separate "as far as practicable." In most southern states, African Americans with a hearing problem, or a mental illness, went to special institutions for blacks only. Ironically, even state schools for the blind were segregated in the South.

Everywhere, public accommodations were segregated by law, separate, but almost never actually equal. The South required there be separate drinking fountains, restrooms, motels, hotels, elevators, bars, restaurants, and lunch counters for blacks. Trains had separate cars for blacks, and buses reserved the last few rows for blacks, always keeping them, symbolically, at the back of the bus. Waiting rooms at bus and train stations were also separate. At theaters, blacks sat in separate sections at the back or in the balcony.

Beyond public accommodations, blacks faced discrimination at every turn. South Carolina required separate entrances for blacks and whites working in the same factories, as well as separate stairways, restrooms, doorways, and pay windows. Georgia led the way in segregating its parks, and Louisiana required separate ticket windows and entrances at circuses and tent shows. Southern states banned interracial meetings of fraternal orders, and cities and states followed Birmingham's segregation of "any room, hall, theater, picture house, auditorium, yard, court, ball park, or other indoor or outdoor place." Mobile had a 10:00 p.m. curfew for blacks, Florida stored textbooks from black and white schools in different buildings, and New Orleans segregated its red light district. Most southern states banned interracial sporting events and boxing matches. In Louisiana, it was illegal for blacks and whites to reside in the same dwelling, and the existence of "separate entrances or partitions" would not be a defense to a charge under this law. Oklahoma provided for segregated telephone booths, Tennessee required that houses of worship be segregated, and Texas banned interracial boxing matches. As Judge William H. Hastie, the first black to serve as a federal judge noted: "The catalog of whimsies was long." These "whimsies," codified by law, reminded blacks, over and over again, that in the American South, and much of the North, they could not expect equal treatment anywhere in society, even in houses of worship.

Beyond the statutes, the "whimsies" manifested themselves as customs and extralegal forms of segregation. C. Vann Woodward noted that southern courts kept separate Bibles for black and white witnesses, even though no statute required this form of segregation. But, as Woodward noted, writing in 1956, with italics in the original:

> "[I]t is well to admit, and even to emphasize, that *laws are not an adequate index of the extent and prevalence of segregation and discriminatory practices in the South.* The practices often anticipated and sometimes exceeded the law. It may be confidentially assumed—and it could be verified by present observation—that there is more Jim Crowism practiced in the South than there are Jim Crow laws on the books."

The Supreme Court had allowed segregation under a theory of "separate but equal." However, in the segregated South, nothing was ever equal. Public schools illustrate the inequality. Expenditures for blacks education were always much lower than for whites. In 1938, the U.S. Office of Education noted that, on average, the southern states spent forty-five dollars a year for the education of whites, but less than twenty dollars for blacks. Similarly, in 1949, Clarendon County, South Carolina spent $179 per pupil for white school children, but only $43 for its black children. The school buildings for the 2,375 white children were valued at $673,850, but the schools for the 6,531 black children were worth only $194,575. Similar statistics, with greater or lesser disparities, could be found for every school district in the South, and for many in the North. In some places in the South, school districts even refused to build high schools for blacks.

Starting in the 1930s, the NAACP and other civil rights organizations began to chip away at segregation, concentrating first where the separate systems were clearly most unequal. Thus, in a series of cases, the U.S. Supreme Court ordered the integration of law schools and graduate schools in states that either did not provide them at all for blacks, or provided institutions that were so obviously inferior that no plausible argument of "equal" facilities could be made. The key case in this line was *Sweatt* v. *Painter* (1950) in which the Court ordered the integration of the University of Texas School of Law. Finally, in *Brown* v. *Board of Education* (1954) the Supreme Court declared that "separate but equal" education was "inherently unequal," and began the slow and painful process of dismantling the South's dual education system. In *Brown*, the Court specifically declared that it was not striking down other forms of segregation, but by 1967 the Court and Congress had effectively destroyed the legal apparatus of segregation. The 1964 Civil Rights Act banned segregation in enterprises involved in interstate commerce; the 1965 voting rights act finally put teeth, and federal enforcement, behind the promise of political equality found in the Fifteenth Amendment; and the 1968 open housing act prohibited discrimination in most forms of rentals and home sales.

Despite new civil rights laws, court victories, and federal enforcement, America remained a largely segregated society. Blacks had lower incomes, higher infant mortality rates, less educational opportunity, and lower life expectancy than whites. School integration worked in smaller cities outside the South, but in large cities, residential housing patterns (the result of complex forces and history) made school integration difficult or impossible. Where schools were integrated, whites often moved to suburbs, in effect creating black majority cities. The Supreme Court refused to order cross-district busing in places where there had not been a history of de jure segregation. The result was that by the year 2000, blacks in most cities, North and South, attended mostly black schools. Meanwhile, in the small towns and cities of the South, mostly segregated public school systems emerged as whites sent their children to segregated private schools. Although the laws creating segregation were no longer in force, the social structures that these laws reflected and created remained in place in much of the nation. Integration was a success for many as it brought millions of blacks into the middle class, and opened doors in higher education and many professions. But a half century after the Supreme Court declared separate but equal to be unequal, much of America remained segregated.

[See also Race and Ethnicity]

• Gunnar Myrdal, An American Dilemma, 1944. C. Vann Woodward, The Strange Career of Jim Crow, 1956. William H. Hastie, "Toward an Equalitarian Legal Order, 1930–1950," The Annals of the American Academy of Political and Social Science 407 (May 1975): 18. Richard Kluger, Simple Justice, 1975. John Hope Franklin and Alfred A. Moss Jr., From Slavery to Freedom: A History of African Americans, 7th ed., 1994. Adam Fairclough, Better Day Coming: Blacks and Equality, 1890–2000, 2001.   —Paul Finkelman

SELF-DEFENSE. See Criminal Law Principles: Defense Principles.

SELF-DEFENSE, NATIONAL. See War, Law of.

SELF-INCRIMINATION, PRIVILEGE AGAINST. The Fifth Amendment to the United States Constitution provides in part that "No person . . . shall be compelled in any criminal case to be a witness against himself." Under currently prevailing interpretations, this self-incrimination clause prohibits the introduction in a criminal proceeding of self-incriminating disclosures that were obtained through "compulsion" by the state and are "testimonial in nature." Notwithstanding the language of the Fifth Amendment itself, the privilege can be invoked by a witness in a criminal or civil case, at an agency hearing, or anywhere else where he is asked to testify under oath. And by "taking the Fifth," a witness can avoid interrogation altogether in a criminal trial in which he is the named defendant.

The broad interpretation of the self-incrimination clause that prevails in the early twenty-first century bears little resemblance to the interpretations of the clause that predominated for most of this nation's history. An absolute "right" or "privilege" against self-incrimination was not a phrase known to the framers of the Fifth Amendment; they spoke more generally of a right for each person not to be a witness against himself in a court of law. Thus the provision originally provided little real obstacle to policemen seeking to coerce confessions outside of court. When the Supreme Court first overturned a state conviction based upon an involuntary confession in Brown v. Mississippi (1936), it did so not based on the self-incrimination clause, but on the grounds that state authorities had violated the defendant's *due process rights. Brown and its progeny required that courts apply a "totality of the circumstances" test to determine whether a confession was involuntary, and thus inadmissible on due process grounds. Factors to be considered included evidence of physical abuse, psychological pressure, the age and experience of the defendant, and whether he had been informed of his rights. Meanwhile, the self-incrimination clause was deemed inapplicable to such circumstances because the "compelled testimony" had not occurred under oath.

Two landmark *Warren Court decisions in the 1960s vaulted the self-incrimination clause to its current place as a cherished right for criminal defendants. In Malloy v. Hogan (1964), the high Court applied the self-incrimination clause to all fifty states by incorporating it in the *Fourteenth Amendment's due process clause. Two years later, the Warren Court gave new life to the privilege in the controversial decision, *Miranda* v. *Arizona* (1966). In *Miranda,* the Court abandoned the totality-of-the-circumstances test then governing the admissibility of out-of-court confessions in favor of specific procedural steps that would thereafter apply to all "custodial interrogations." Specifically, the Court provided that before any official questioning begins, a suspect in custody must be clearly advised that (1) he has the right to remain silent; (2) anything he says can be used against him in court; (3) he has the right to a lawyer; and (4) a lawyer will be appointed to assist him if he cannot afford to retain one. The suspect is free to remain silent or engage counsel at any time prior to or during such *interrogation.

The *Miranda* opinion touched off a heated debate over the purpose of the self-incrimination clause that continues even today. Prior to *Miranda,* the clause had been thought to serve a "corrective" function for the legal system, protecting innocent people from being wrongfully convicted on the basis of questionable or inherently unreliable and coercive confessions. In *Miranda,* the Court articulated a more controversial justification for the privilege: its purpose was now "to preserve the integrity of the judicial system" in which even the guilty are not to be convicted unless the prosecutor "shoulders the entire load." When acting in conjunction with the exclusionary rule, which excludes from criminal trials most unlawfully obtained *evidence, *Miranda*'s dictates often work to favor the factually guilty. Additionally, the Court stressed that the clause protects defendants against both psychological and physical coercion. Despite the controversy that has surrounded the decision in the decades that followed, the Supreme Court has never backed off the elaborate set of procedural rules it first established in *Miranda*. Indeed, as recently as in 2000, the Court reaffirmed its commitment to the precedent, noting that "*Miranda* has become embedded in routine police practice to the point where the warnings have become part of our national culture."

Despite the protections afforded by *Miranda,* authorities have still been able to solicit confessions from suspects by resorting to a number of tried and tested techniques. Because *Miranda* only applies to confessions during custodial interrogation, policemen have become expert at "interrogating" suspects without warnings in their homes, at their offices, or in other locations where the individual is theoretically "free to leave." In the station house itself, detectives often walk a thin line in urging suspects to "voluntarily" waive their rights in return for vague promises of "leniency" at some unspecified time in the future. Finally, the Fifth Amendment does not prevent policemen from employing trickery (lying about evidence, recruiting jailhouse "snitches," and so forth) to secure confessions from suspects.

At the trial itself, the self-incrimination clause forbids prosecutors from forcing unwilling defendants to testify, or even from commenting, during the state's closing argument, on the defendant's failure to testify. (If the defendant chooses to take the witness stand on his own behalf, he waives the privilege and is thereafter subject to cross-examination). Still, prosecutors may force reluctant witnesses to answer questions under oath if one of two other conditions is met. First: a witness who has received a sufficient grant of immunity from prosecution may be compelled to testify. Although prosecutors sometimes grant immunity from prosecution for the transaction to which the compelled testimony relates ("transactional immunity"), the Fifth Amendment requires only a grant of immunity against using the incriminating statements themselves, including any evidence derived therefrom, in a future prosecution ("use immunity"). Second: a witness may be forced to testify if there is no further possibility of his being incriminated, such as when the applicable statute of limitations for his crime has already been tolled, or when he has already been acquitted in a criminal case and thus may be required to testify in a subsequent civil proceeding.

[*See also* Bills of Rights; Criminal Law Principles]

• Leonard Levy, *Origins of the Fifth Amendment,* 1968. Peter W. Tague, "The Fifth Amendment: If an Aid to the Guilty Defendant, an Impediment to the Innocent One," *Georgetown Law Journal* (1989): 1. John H. Langbein, "The Historical Origins of the Privilege Against Self-Incrimination at Common Law," *Michigan Law Review* (1994): 1047. Akhil Reed Amar, *The Constitution and Criminal Procedure,* 1997.   —David A. Yalof

SENTENCING. *See* Criminal Punishments.

SEPARATION OF CHURCH AND STATE. *See* Church and State.

SEPARATION OF POWERS. The pitfalls of communication are nowhere more evident than in governments with separated powers. It is difficult to avoid one misinterpretation without simultaneously committing another. Without separation, one branch might aggrandize power and threaten individual liberties. Yet in a system of literal and strict separation, each branch might spin independently and ineffectively in its own orbit, also endangering individual liberties. The framers of the U.S. *Constitution tried to strike a workable, middle ground.

Why Keep Powers Separate? Governmental powers are kept separate in order to preserve liberties, but too much stress on separation can destroy liberties. The historical antagonism in France between executive and legislature, characterized by an oscillation between administrative and representative forms of government, is a classic example of the danger of extreme separation. The French constitutions of 1791 and 1848 embraced a pure separation of powers. The first effort produced the Committee of Public Safety, the Directory, and the reign of Napoleon Bonaparte. The second experiment led to Louis-Napoleon, reaction, and the Second Empire. The pure doctrine of separation ended in absolutism.

Is a system of separated powers supposed to be efficient? In *Myers* v. *United States* (1926), Justice Louis *Brandeis made this claim: "The doctrine of the separation of powers was adopted by the Convention of 1787, not to promote efficiency but to preclude the exercise of arbitrary power." He spoke a half-truth. The framers met at the Philadelphia Convention to design a *government that would work more effectively than the discredited Articles of Confederation. They looked for ways of ensuring greater administrative efficiency and more reliable government machinery. They knew that inefficient government is a breeding ground for revolution.

Much is made of the influence of the French political theorist Montesquieu on the drafting of the Constitution. He was cited frequently at the Philadelphia Convention, the state ratifying conventions, and in the *Federalist Papers*, where he is praised as "the celebrated Montesquieu" and the "oracle" who guided the framers on the separation doctrine. The framers did refer to such foreign writers as Montesquieu, David Hume, and William *Blackstone, but they did so to embellish an argument, not to prove it. The argument itself was grounded on what had been learned at home. Theory played a role, but it was always circumscribed and tested by experience.

Historical and Philosophical Background. The framers drew their principles of government from a variety of sources and continually redefined those standards in the light of changing political conditions. The principle of "mixed government" as a technique for stabilizing government goes back at least to Plato and Aristotle, who proposed a combination of monarchy and democracy to form a well-governed city and a stable state. Polybius advocated a mixture of kingship, aristocracy, and democracy to produce checks and balance: "the force of each being neutralized by that of the others, neither of them should prevail and outbalance another, but . . . the constitution should remain for long in a state of equilibrium like a well-trimmed boat."

The concept of balance appears both in mixed governments and in the separation doctrine, but the mixed state divides the sovereign power among different social classes: the king, the nobility, and the people. The U.S. system allocates authority among different functions—executive, legislative, and judicial—with each function assigned to a distinct body. Montesquieu provided for legislative, executive, and judicial branches, but his system was partly a throwback to mixed government by relying on a balance between distinct social classes. One branch of the *legislature was reserved for the people, with the second legislative house set aside for nobles with hereditary privileges. No such class distinctions exist for the two chambers of Congress. The U.S. Constitution explicitly forbids the federal government and the states from granting titles of nobility.

Although Montesquieu saw the need for some overlapping of the branches, for the most part he kept them separate. He maintained that the legislative body should not impeach the executive, for the "moment he is accused or tried there is an end of liberty." The framers supported *impeachment of executive officials, including the president. Montesquieu allowed the executive to reject legislation but opposed any other executive participation in the legislative process. The Constitution empowers the president to make treaties with the advice and consent of the Senate (with self-executing treaties considered the supreme law of the land), and it authorizes the president to recommend such measures as "he shall judge necessary and expedient."

Colonial governments in America also learned about the need for political balance, with governors and elected assemblies checking one another and the branches charging each other with encroachment. After achieving their independence from England, many of the states wrote into their constitutions explicit guarantees for a separation between the branches of government, but the meaning of "separation" varied from state to state and became a constant source of misunderstanding.

The Philadelphia Convention. Only one branch of the national government existed before 1787:

the Continental Congress. There was no executive or judiciary. After legislating, members of Congress had to serve on committees to administer and adjudicate what they had passed. To relieve committees of administrative details, Congress turned to boards staffed by people outside the legislature and later to single executives. Congress also established the beginnings of a national judiciary by setting up Courts of Admiralty to decide all controversies over naval captures and the distribution of war prizes.

By 1787 there was broad agreement that the new government needed three separate branches. However, the Virginia Plan presented on May 29 made no reference to "separate and distinct" or any other formulation of the separation doctrine. Late in July, the convention adopted a resolution explicitly affirming the separation doctrine, stating that the three national branches were to be kept distinct and independent, except in specified cases. However, the version presented on August 6 by the Committee of Detail omitted the separation clause, and the Constitution was adopted in September without reference to separation.

Although the separation doctrine is not expressly stated in the Constitution, it is implied in the allocation of *legislative powers to *Congress in Article I, *executive powers to the *president in Article II, and judicial powers to the *Supreme Court in Article III. Several provisions help reinforce the separation. Article I, Section 6, prohibits members of either house of Congress from holding any other civil office (the Incompatibility Clause). The same section prohibits members of Congress from being appointed to any federal office created during their term of office or to any federal position whose salary has been increased during their term of office (the Ineligibility Clause). The framers were aware that members of the British Parliament had been corrupted by appointments to office from the Crown. Other safeguards for the separation doctrine exist. Congress is prohibited from reducing the compensation of the president and members of the judiciary. Congress may not pass bills of attainder (legislative acts that inflict punishment without judicial proceeding). The Speech or Debate Clause provides legislative immunity to protect members of Congress from executive or judicial harassments.

Several sections of the Constitution produce combinations, not separations, of the branches. The president may veto legislation, subject to a two-thirds override vote of each house. The president nominates officers, but the Senate confirms.

The president submits treaties that the Senate must approve. The House of Representatives may impeach executive and judicial officers, subject to the Senate's conviction at a trial presided over by the chief justice of the Supreme Court (for presidential impeachments). The courts decide criminal cases, but the president may pardon offenders and Congress may pass amnesty legislation for general classes of people.

These mixtures led to objections at the state ratifying conventions that the branches had been intermingled rather than kept separate. By the time of the Philadelphia Convention, however, the doctrine of separated powers had been overtaken by the system of checks and balances. One contemporary pamphleteer dismissed the separation doctrine, in its pure form, as a "hackneyed principle" and a "trite maxim." In the *Federalist Papers*, Madison devoted several essays to the need for overlapping powers, claiming that the concept was superior to the impractical partitioning of powers demanded by some of the Anti-Federalists. Montesquieu, he said, could not possibly have meant that the three powers of the British government were actually separate. Madison turned to the state constitutions for further support, pointing out that in no instance were the several departments of power kept absolutely separate and distinct. The intent of Montesquieu, Madison concluded, could be no more than this: "that where the *whole* power of one department is exercised by the same hands which possess the *whole* power of another department, the fundamental principles of a free constitution are subverted."

Opponents were not satisfied. Three states—Virginia, North Carolina, and Pennsylvania—insisted that a separation clause be added to the national *Bill of Rights. They proposed that no branch could exercise the powers vested in the others. Congress rejected that proposal, as well as a substitute amendment to make the three departments "separate and distinct."

Implied Powers. Strict constructionists regard the Constitution as one of enumerated powers. They oppose the notion of implied powers, inherent powers, powers derived from *custom, or any other extraconstitutional power not explicitly granted to one of the three branches. Although there is legitimate concern about the scope of implied powers, all three branches find it necessary to exercise powers not stated in the Constitution. Congress has the power to investigate, issue subpoenas, and hold executive officials in contempt as a necessary function of its legislative power. The president may remove certain administrative officers to maintain executive accountability and responsibility. The Supreme Court has acquired the power to review legislative, executive, and state actions on questions of federal constitutionality.

The framers understood the need for implied powers. As Madison noted in *Federalist* No. 44: "No axiom is more clearly established in law, or in reason, than that whenever the end is required, the means are authorized; whenever a general power to do a thing is given, every particular power necessary for doing it is included." The history of the Tenth Amendment underscores the need for implied powers. The Articles of Confederation gave great protection to the states, which retained all powers except those "expressly delegated" to the national government. When that phrase was proposed for the Tenth Amendment, Madison objected to the word "expressly" because the functions and responsibilities of the federal government could not be delineated with such precision. It was impossible, he said, to confine a government to the exercise of express powers, for there "must necessarily be admitted powers by implication, unless the Constitution descended to recount every minutiae."

The boundaries between the three branches are also strongly affected by the role of custom and acquiescence. When one branch engages in a certain practice and the other branches acquiesce, the practice gains legitimacy and can fix the meaning of the Constitution. Justice Felix *Frankfurter, in *Youngstown Co.* v. *Sawyer* (1952), explained how executive power can grow when unchallenged: "A systematic, unbroken executive practice, long pursued to the knowledge of the Congress and never before questioned, engaged in by Presidents who have also sworn to uphold the Constitution, making as it were such exercise of power part of the structure of our government, may be treated as a gloss on 'executive Power' vested in the President by § 1 of Art. II."

The Supreme Court has adopted several conflicting models of the separation doctrine, ranging from the functional and pragmatic to approaches that attempt a doctrinaire and purist formulation. Fortunately, many of the principal disputes involving separation of powers are resolved outside the courts. The majority of these controversies never reach the courts or, if they do, are quickly pushed back to the executive and legislative branches for nonjudicial answers.

[*See also* Governance]

• William Bondy, *The Separation of Governmental Powers in History, in Theory, and in the Constitution* (Studies in History, Economics, and Public Law, vol. V, no. 2), 1896. Benjamin F. Wright Jr., "The Origins of the Sep-

aration of Powers in America," *Economica* 13, no. 40 (1933): 169–85. W. B. Gwyn, *The Meaning of the Separation of Powers* (Tulane Studies in Political Science, vol. IX), 1965. M. J. C. Vile, *Constitutionalism and the Separation of Powers*, 1967. Robert A. Goldwin and Art Kaufman, eds., *Separation of Powers—Does It Still Work?* 1986. Dean Alfange Jr., "The Supreme Court and the Separation of Powers: A Welcome Return to Normalcy?" *George Washington Law Review* 58 (1990): 668–761. Louis Fisher, *Constitutional Conflicts between Congress and the President*, 4th ed., 1997. Peter M. Shane and Harold H. Bruff, *Separation of Powers: Cases and Materials*, 1997. Louis Fisher, *Constitutional Structures: Separation of Powers and Federalism*, 2001.

—Louis Fisher

SEQUESTRATION. *See* Fair Trial, Criminal; Jury.

SERVITUDE, INVOLUNTARY. *See* Slavery, Law of.

SEX OFFENSES. The most serious sex offense is rape, now called sexual assault in many jurisdictions. Traditionally, our criminal laws have followed *Blackstone's definition of rape as "carnal knowledge of a woman forcibly and against her will." The force element has generally been restricted to the use or threat of physical force, thus raising problems of proof in cases that do not involve a weapon—which describes the vast majority of rapes, especially those involving acquaintances, (which are believed to account for at least half of all rapes). Although several commentators have observed a *gender gap in perceptions of what constitutes force, the courts have generally ignored that issue—with one notable exception, *People* v. *Evans* (1975), which took the position that the defendant's intent and perceptions are controlling.

Given the traditional association of force with physical force, the crime of rape has not encompassed cases in which defendants used threats of nonphysical force to obtain sex—for example, where a guardian threatened to return his 14-year-old ward to a detention home, *Commonwealth* v. *Mlinarich* (1988), or a high school principal threatened to prevent a student from graduating, *State* v. *Thompson* (1990). Recently, however, a few state legislatures have broadened the definition of force and criminalized sex obtained by certain nonphysical forms of coercion. Consistent with the traditional view, one who makes a fraudulent misrepresentation to induce sex is generally not guilty of rape, although the crime does include cases involving deception as to the nature of the act itself—for example, where a woman is unexpectedly penetrated during a gynecological exam.

The dual requirements of force and lack of consent have proven controversial in several cases where courts reversed rape convictions after concluding that the element of non-consent was proven, but not the element of force. In *State* v. *Alston* (1984), the defendant had previously battered the victim and, shortly before intercourse, "threatened to 'fix' her face," but the court concluded that while these factors may have "induced fear" in the victim, they were "unrelated to the act of sexual intercourse." Although *State ex rel. M.T.S.* (1992) held that the force requirement could be satisfied by the force incidental to non-consensual penetration, almost all jurisdictions disagree and continue to require independent proof of both force and lack of consent. Recently, however, a number of state legislatures have enacted statutes making nonconsensual, non-forcible intercourse a lesser offense than rape.

Rape laws also traditionally required proof that the victim resisted, on the theory that lack of resistance was evidence of consent. Although no jurisdiction still adheres to the requirement that the victim must have resisted "to the utmost," some states require some reasonable resistance unless the force exercised by the defendant prevented the victim from resisting. Influenced by studies finding that some rape victims do not physically resist, either because they are paralyzed by fear or lack experience in physical combat, and that resistance can be dangerous for the victim, other states have repealed any statutory requirement of resistance.

Traditional definitions of rape contained no explicit mental state requirement, and today, *mens rea* issues in rape cases revolve almost exclusively around the element of non-consent. In *Director of Public Prosecutions* v. *Morgan* (1976), the British House of Lords held that a defendant could not be convicted of rape if he believed that the victim consented, even if that belief was unreasonable. The case—which involved a forcible rape by the victim's husband and three of his friends, who had been told by the husband that they should not be "surprised if his wife struggled a bit" since she was "kinky" and this was the only way she could get "turned on"—generated a great deal of controversy, and ultimately led Parliament to enact a statute defining rape to include cases where the defendant was reckless as to whether or not the victim was consenting. In the United States, most jurisdictions follow the approach taken in *People* v. *Mayberry* (1975), recognizing a defense only if the defendant's mistaken belief in the victim's consent was both honest and reasonable. A few jurisdictions have refused to attach any *mens rea* requirement to the element of non-consent, reasoning that the crime is established by proof of force and lack of consent, so that even an honest, reasonable mistake is no defense.

Given the *common-law doctrines treating a woman as her husband's property, merging her identity into his at the time of *marriage, and viewing marriage as an irrevocable consent to sex, a husband traditionally could not be convicted of raping his wife. The marital rape exemption has now been completely abolished in most states, although a significant minority still treat spouses differently from other defendants—either by punishing marital rape more leniently than nonmarital rape, by criminalizing only certain aggravated types of marital rape, or by bringing charges only if the spouses were living apart.

Historically, a number of special procedural rules were applied exclusively in rape cases: a prompt-complaint requirement barred prosecution unless the victim promptly reported the crime; a jury instruction warned juries to view the victim's testimony with caution because rape charges are easily made and not so easily defended; and a corroboration requirement mandated that evidence be introduced to corroborate the victim's testimony in order to support a conviction. Although these procedural rules have now been relaxed or rejected in most jurisdictions, they are endorsed by §213.6 of the *Model Penal Code.

In addition, most state legislatures enacted rape-shield laws during the 1970s. Their content varies widely from state to state, but generally they are designed to limit the admissibility of the victim's sexual history, which was traditionally introduced both to support the defendant's claim of consent and to cast doubt on the victim's credibility.

Somewhat less controversial than forcible rape, the crime of statutory rape punishes even consensual sex with minors. Although this crime was traditionally justified as a means of preserving an unmarried girl's economic value to her father, today it is seen as a way of protecting vulnerable children. The age of consent varies between twelve and eighteen years, depending on the jurisdiction, with sixteen being the most popular choice—although many statutes also require that the defendant be at least a certain age or a certain number of years older than the victim. Most contemporary statutory rape laws (like most forcible rape laws) are gender-neutral, although the Supreme Court in *Michael M.* v. *Superior Court* (1981) upheld the constitutionality of statutory rape laws following the traditional model, which punished only males who have sex with young women. Historically, chastity was an element of statutory rape, but today the crime is proven simply by establishing sexual conduct and the victim's age. The majority of states treat statutory rape as a *strict liability crime, and therefore do not recognize a defense, even when the defendant made an honest and reasonable mistake about the victim's age.

[*See also* Assault and Battery; Criminal Law; Morals Offenses]

• Frances Olsen, "Statutory Rape: A Feminist Critique of Rights Analysis," *Texas Law Review* 63 (1984): 387–432. Susan Estrich, *Real Rape*, 1987. Dorothy E. Roberts, "Rape, Violence, and Women's Autonomy," *Chicago-Kent Law Review* 69 (1993): 359–88. Patricia J. Falk, "Rape by Fraud and Rape by Coercion," *Brooklyn Law Review* 64 (1998): 39–180. Stephen J. Schulhofer, *Unwanted Sex*, 1998.   —Kit Kinports

SEXUAL HARASSMENT is a form of sex *discrimination that is common in American workplaces and educational institutions, as well as in prisons, on the street, and in a variety of other contexts. The term "sexual harassment" includes a range of unwelcome sexual behavior, from sexual jokes, comments, or pictures, to rape.

Since the 1980s, sexual harassment has been an important issue for feminists and one that has played a prominent role in American politics. For example, in 1991, then-Supreme Court nominee Clarence Thomas faced allegations of sexual harassment from a former employee, Anita Hill. The allegations concerned his conduct when he was chairperson of the Equal Employment Opportunity Commission (EEOC), which is, ironically, the agency charged with implementing Title VII of the Civil Rights Act of 1964, the federal antidiscrimination law that prohibits sexual harassment. Although Justice Thomas was confirmed to the Court despite the allegations, the controversy about that case and the issue of sexual harassment remained in the forefront of public discussion. Subsequent high-profile cases, like Paula Jones's 1994 suit against then-President Bill Clinton (a case that ultimately led to his impeachment by the U.S. House of Representatives) kept the subject of sexual harassment in the limelight.

Employment. Despite the proliferation of anti-harassment policies and other preventative measures over the last decade, sexual harassment in the workplace has proven to be an intractable problem. Surveys find that harassment occurs in all industries and affects individuals across age, racial, and socioeconomic class lines, and that 90 percent of sexual harassment complainants are women. Surveys in the early 1980s reported that four in ten women had been sexually harassed at work within the preceding two years; a 1994 up-date of one of those surveys found the number had risen to 44 percent.

Sexual harassment imposes enormous costs on victims and employers. Victims of sexual harassment report emotional and physical consequences like depression, anxiety, nausea, and headaches; many have high rates of absenteeism, either due to depression, illness, or injury, or because they are trying to avoid the harasser. Employers report significant costs attributable to absenteeism, job turnover, and lost productivity (by both the victim and the harasser), as well as those attributable to the monetary outlays involved in taking preventative measures, defending themselves against lawsuits, and paying out judgments.

Researchers in a variety of disciplines including law, sociology, psychology, and industrial organization have increasingly focused on the problem of sexual harassment and how to address it. Research suggests three possible causes of sexual harassment, rooted in biology, differing perceptions, and power differentials. The first explanation, sometimes termed the sex-role spillover effect, posits that sexual harassment is a function of sexual desire—men's harassment of women is a manifestation of an allegedly greater sex drive and tendency toward sexual aggression. The second explanation posits that men and women perceive sexual conduct differently and that sexual harassment occurs as a result of boundary differentiation problems. The third and best-supported explanation suggests that men's harassment of women is a manifestation of, and a way of reinforcing, male domination and female subordination. Organizational structure plays a role in making sexual harassment more or less likely to occur.

Sexual harassment litigation has risen dramatically over the last decade. With respect to internal grievances, a survey of employers reported that the number of complaints doubled between 1995 and 1998. Administrative complaints have increased as well. In 2000, the EEOC processed nearly 16,000 charges of sexual harassment, a 50-percent increase since 1992. The EEOC has successfully litigated sexual harassment cases on behalf of scores of female employees against employers like Mitsubishi Motor Company and Trans World Airlines, collecting over fifty million dollars in damages in 1999 alone.

Sex discrimination in employment is prohibited by Title VII, as well as by many state employment discrimination laws. Because Title VII only applies to employers with at least fifteen employees, state laws are often used in suits against smaller employers. The first cases in which plaintiffs argued that sexual harassment was a form of illegal sex discrimination were brought in the mid-1970s, without much success. Courts in that era were generally hostile to the idea that unwelcome sexual advances at work constituted a civil rights violation, believing instead that such behavior was a natural and unavoidable consequence of women entering the workforce.

In 1979, Catharine MacKinnon published *The Sexual Harassment of Working Women*, a groundbreaking book that used the term "sexual harassment" for the first time to describe the sexual conduct working women endured but rarely talked about. It also theorized about the role of power in sexual harassment and the degree to which sexual harassment oppressed women. This book became the blueprint for courts in the 1980s as they began to recognize sexual harassment as a cognizable harm. That trend culminated in the U.S. Supreme Court's decision in *Meritor Savings Bank* v. *Vinson* (1986), which held that sexual harassment is a form of intentional sex discrimination and therefore prohibited by Title VII.

Sexual harassment in the workplace comes in two forms. The first, sometimes called quid pro quo harassment, occurs when a supervisor conditions an employment-related benefit or detriment on a subordinate employee's willingness or refusal to submit to sexual advances. "Sleep with me or you're fired" is the classic example of this type of harassment, although in reality the threats are often more subtle. The essence of quid pro quo harassment is the misuse of supervisory authority to coerce sexual submission.

The second and more common form of harassment is called hostile environment harassment. It occurs when any employee or related third party engages in unwelcome conduct of a sexual nature that is severe or pervasive enough to alter the terms or conditions of employment for an employee. There is no requirement that there be a disparity in workplace authority between the perpetrator and the victim, though harassment by a supervisor is often more threatening and therefore more likely to be actionable. But surveys suggest that coworker harassment is more common than supervisory harassment.

A hostile environment may be created by any combination of physical (pinching, groping, grabbing, or sexual assault), verbal (sexual advances, sex talk, or sexual epithets), and visual acts (nude pictures, or graphic notes, pictures, and e-mail). A claim of sexual harassment may also be premised on conduct that is not necessarily sexual in nature. Verbal or written conduct evincing animosity toward women or demeaning them because of their gender may also be actionable.

To constitute a legally hostile environment, the harassing conduct must be both unwelcome and either severe or pervasive. Physical conduct is almost always considered severe by courts and, therefore, it need not happen more than once to be actionable. Verbal, written, and visual conduct, on the other hand, typically need to be part of a pattern.

Pursuant to the Supreme Court's holding in *Harris* v. *Forklift Systems, Inc.* (1993), sexual harassment may be actionable even though it does not cause tangible, psychological injury. But because Title VII only bans discrimination that alters the terms or conditions of employment, harassing conduct must have the effect of creating a working environment that is both subjectively (to the victim) and objectively (to a reasonable person) hostile, offensive, or abusive.

The Supreme Court in *Harris* was urged to adopt a so-called "reasonable woman" standard, which would have required judges and juries to consider whether the environment was objectively hostile from the vantage point of a reasonable woman rather than a reasonable person. The theory behind this proposed standard is that women are more likely to experience unwelcome sexual conduct as harassing than men are. The Supreme Court did not adopt the reasonable woman standard in *Harris*, although it did refer to the "reasonable victim," which arguably broadens the inquiry sufficiently to encompass different perspectives.

The requirement that hostile environment harassment be either severe or pervasive in order to be actionable has proven to be a substantial obstacle to sexual-harassment plaintiffs, particularly because courts tend to look at each incident in isolation rather than in the aggregate. A better approach might be to find all harassment actionable, but determine the amount of damages based on the severity or pervasiveness of the conduct.

Sexual-harassment claims are also hard to prove because of the difficulty in distinguishing between normal social interaction and harassment. Courts are reluctant to set down rules of conduct that resemble a civility code. Moreover, much of the conduct that may contribute to a hostile environment is perfectly legal and appropriate if it is welcome, but actionable if it is unwelcome. But empirical studies show that victims rarely voice their objections to harassment or confront their harassers; instead, typical responses include submitting to the harassment, rationalizing or denying the harasser's conduct, or avoiding the harasser. The reality of victim response to harassment makes unwelcomeness another obstacle to plaintiffs' success.

Title VII protects both men and women against same- and opposite-sex harassment. The Supreme Court confronted the issue of same-sex harassment in *Oncale* v. *Sundowner Offshore Services* (1998), holding that it is actionable under Title VII as long as the victim can prove the conduct was undertaken "because of sex." That standard can be satisfied with proof that the harasser was motivated by sexual desire, that he was attempting to enforce gender stereotypes (e.g, by punishing a man for behaving too effeminately), or that the harasser, in fact, only targeted victims of one sex.

Title VII also prohibits harassment on bases other than sex. Courts have applied the principles developed in the context of sexual-harassment law to hostile-environment claims based on race, national origin, ancestry, and religion. These claims are in some sense easier to prove because there is not a zone of otherwise permissible behavior that courts are trying to protect.

A successful claim of sexual harassment may entitle the victim to compensatory *damages (designed to compensate for actual losses suffered), punitive damages (designed to punish the responsible party), attorneys' fees, and any other equitable *remedy necessary to make the victim whole.

To prevail in court, victims of sexual or any other form of harassment need to prove not only that they were harassed in violation of state or federal law, but also that someone should be held liable for the harassment. While individual harassers cannot be held liable under Title VII, employers can. Some state laws do, however, permit individual liability.

The Supreme Court decided a trilogy of cases relating to employer *liability in 1998 and 1999. In *Faragher* v. *City of Boca Raton* (1998) and *Burlington Industries* v. *Ellerth* (1998), the Court confirmed that employers are only liable for coworker harassment when they knew or should have known about the harassment and failed to take prompt and effective remedial action. The Court also held that employers are strictly liable for sexual harassment committed by supervisors when it results in a tangible employment action. Thus, when a supervisor fires, demotes, or otherwise punishes an employee for refusing to submit to his sexual advances, the employer will be held liable for that conduct.

But when the harassment does not result in a tangible employment action, the employer has the opportunity to prove a two-pronged affirmative defense in order to escape liability or damages. The first prong asks whether the employer exercised reasonable care to prevent and correct sexual harassment. To satisfy this prong, employers need to enact and maintain effective sexual harassment policies that clearly prohibit harassment and provide potential victims with adequate grievance procedures. The second prong asks whether the victim failed to make use of available grievance procedures. To satisfy this prong, the employer needs to demonstrate that, despite the existence of an accessible and workable grievance procedure, the victim failed to complain entirely or waited too long to complain.

The following year, the Supreme Court decided *Kolstad* v. *American Dental Association* (1999), which held that employers cannot be made to pay punitive damages for harassment if they made a good-faith effort to comply with Title VII. *Kolstad*, like *Faragher* and *Ellerth*, gives employers an incentive to develop and implement strong antiharassment policies.

In response to these three cases regarding employer liability and the ever-increasing number of sexual harassment lawsuits, employers have hastened to enact antiharassment policies and to provide employees and supervisors with harassment training. Because these same rules of liability apply to all forms of illegal harassment (e.g., racial or religious harassment), many employers have chosen to provide diversity training as well. An increasing number are taking out employment-practices insurance policies, which provide coverage against losses caused by claims of discrimination and harassment.

In responding to harassment complaints, employers sometimes also face lawsuits by the accused. Employees accused of harassment have brought so-called whipsaw liability cases, suing employers for their involvement in investigating or taking action against them in response to a sexual harassment claim by another employee. These cases typically involve claims of wrongful discharge, breach of contract, or defamation, but they have been largely unsuccessful, particularly when employers have followed their own internal procedures in investigating claims and avoided unnecessary publicity of the allegations. Although some commentators have speculated that public employers may run afoul of the First Amendment by enforcing sexual harassment policies, there is little or no case law to support that theory.

Education. Sexual harassment in education has also proven difficult to eradicate. Two 1993 surveys showed a significant problem of sexual harassment in elementary and secondary schools. A substantial majority of students reported experiencing at least occasional unwanted or unwelcome sexual behavior that interfered with their lives. Most complained of peer rather than teacher-student harassment. A 2001 update of one of those surveys revealed that four in five students—both boys and girls—between eighth and eleventh grade reported experiencing unwanted sexual attention; one in four students reported that they experienced such conduct frequently.

Title IX of the Education Amendments of 1972 prohibits sex discrimination by educational institutions that receive federal funding. The earliest cases brought under Title IX involved teacher-student harassment. Courts in these cases disagreed about whether schools should be held financially responsible for such harassment. In 1992, the Supreme Court held in *Franklin* v. *Gwinnett County Public Schools* that Title IX prohibited sexual harassment and, although the statute did not expressly say so, that victims could sue schools for money damages.

In 1998, the Supreme Court established a restrictive standard of liability for money damages, holding in *Gebser* v. *Lago Vista School Board* that a school can be held liable for teacher-student harassment only where it has actual notice of the harassment and responds with deliberate indifference. This extremely high standard has made it difficult to impose liability on schools. The following year, the Supreme Court applied that same standard to claims of peer harassment in *Davis* v. *Monroe County Board of Education* (1999).

As in the employment context, educational institutions have been quick to respond to these cases by adopting written harassment policies and instituting training and other educational and preventative programs. Some schools have reacted to concerns about litigation by punishing conduct that falls far short of harassment. One school, for example, suspended a six-year-old boy for kissing a girl on the playground, producing a national media frenzy. But, at the same time, many schools have continued to ignore student complaints about harassment.

Concerns about academic freedom make the regulation of sexual harassment in colleges and universities even more complicated. Faculties, acting through unions or other representative bodies, have objected to sexual-harassment policies that purport to regulate their speech or conduct; universities, in turn, have been skittish about imposing penalties on tenured faculty members.

Sexual harassment today remains a serious social problem. The law relating to harassment and discrimination generally has been thoroughly developed in the last two decades, but social change has lagged behind. Much of the focus now is on how to change institutional culture to eliminate the problem of harassment.

[*See also* Civil Rights and Civil Liberties; Gender and Law]

- Lin Farley, *Sexual Shakedown: The Sexual Harassment of Women on the Job*, 1978. Barbara A. Gutek, *Sex and the Workplace: The Impact of Sexual Behavior and Harassment on Women, Men, and Organizations*, 1985. U.S. Merit Systems Protection Board, *Sexual Harassment in the Federal Workplace*, 1995. Michele A. Paludi, *Sexual Harassment on College Campuses: Abusing the Ivory Power*, 1996. Rosemary Skaine, *Power and Gender: Issues in Sexual Dominance and Harassment*, 1996. Margaret S. Stockdale, ed., *Sexual Harassment in the Workplace*, 1996. William O'Donohue, ed., *Sexual Harassment: Theory, Research, and Treatment*, 1997. AAUW Educational Foundation, *Hostile Hallways: Bullying, Teasing, and Sexual Harassment in Schools*, 2001.

—Joanna L. Grossman

SHAW, LEMUEL (1781–1861), lawyer, judge. Born in West Barnstable, Massachusetts, the son of a Congregationalist minister, Shaw was admitted to Harvard in 1796 and graduated in 1800, Phi Beta Kappa; the following year he began the study of law in Boston. For twenty years Shaw had an active practice as well as modest involvement with local politics. In 1830 he reluctantly accepted appointment as chief justice of the Supreme Judicial Court of Massachusetts. Once on the court, Shaw took full advantage of the forum, writing some twenty-two hundred opinions, only one of which was a dissent. The court over which Shaw presided faced some of the most critical issues in a society that was changing its economic base from agriculture to manufacturing. Without the fetters of a substantial body of precedent, Shaw wrote with sweeping assurance, becoming the most influential state court judge in antebellum America.

Shaw's opinions revealed a dedication to individual freedom, tempered by reverence for positive law. The theme of freedom dominated in *Commonwealth* v. *Aves* (1836), an opinion in which Shaw reasoned that since freedom was the natural state for humans, *slavery could exist only by positive law. Consequently, any slave brought into Massachusetts would be immediately freed on account of the lack of positive law establishing slavery in the commonwealth. Likewise, in *Commonwealth* v. *Hunt* (1842), he stressed freedom in analyzing the legality of workers organizing a labor union. Rather than hold that concerted action was criminal, as other courts had done following *common-law precedent, Shaw reasoned that a union was nothing more than the collective action of individuals, action that they were free to take. Similarly, in *Brown* v. *Kendall* (1850), he held that individuals could not be held liable for injury to others unless the individual had been negligent, a holding which became the key principle in *tort law for much of the next century.

But history has not favorably judged all Shaw's work, particularly his opinions in *Roberts* v. *City of Boston* (1849) and *Farwell* v. *Boston and Worcester Railroad* (1842). In *Roberts*, Shaw upheld the power of the city to have segregated schools, an opinion that would later be used to support the "separate but equal" principle in national constitutional law. *Farwell* essentially created the fellow-servant rule, under which an employee injured while working could not recover from the employer if the accident had been caused by the conduct of a fellow employee.

Both *Brown* and *Farwell* had the effect of encouraging industrial development, by limiting *liability for accidents. In his assured reliance on eighteenth-century concepts of individual freedom, however, Shaw occasionally failed to sense fissures developing in a society moving toward collective actions to deal with social problems.

• Leonard W. Levy, *The Law of the Commonwealth and Chief Justice Shaw: The Evolution of American Law, 1830–1860,* 1957.   —Walter F. Pratt Jr.

SHEPPARD, SAM, CASE OF. Marilyn Sheppard, the wife of Dr. Samuel H. Sheppard, was murdered in the early hours of 4 July 1954. The state alleged that Sam Sheppard bludgeoned his wife to death. The defense countered that an intruder broke into the Sheppard home and murdered Mrs. Sheppard. Following a highly publicized trial in Cleveland, Ohio, Sheppard was convicted of murder. After various appeals to state courts failed, Sheppard's attorney sought and won a writ of *habeas corpus from a federal district *court. The federal court of appeals reversed that decision.

However, in *Sheppard* v. *Maxwell* (1966) the Supreme Court granted a retrial, finding that Sheppard had not received a *fair trial due to "massive, pervasive and prejudicial publicity" resulting in a "carnival atmosphere at trial." From the beginning, Cleveland newspapers pointed at Sheppard as the murderer. The Court found that the heavy media focus denied Sheppard his right to a fair trial. The Court balanced the media's right to report public events against the right of a criminal

defendant to be tried only on *evidence introduced at the trial and found that the trial process had violated Sheppard's constitutional right. At his trial, the small courtroom had a table inside the bar for fifteen media representatives. Twenty more media representatives sat in three rows of seats outside the bar. During the six-week trial the jurors heard and read daily reports about the trial.

At the retrial, a jury found Sheppard not guilty.

The Sheppard case served as the basis for *The Fugitive* television series, featuring "Dr. Kimble" and his search for his wife's murderer; the series ran from 1963 to 1967. In 1993, the movie *The Fugitive* relied on the same theme.

In 2000, thirty years after Sheppard's death, his estate filed a state wrongful imprisonment lawsuit. That case focused on Richard Eberling as the murderer. In 1989 Eberling had been convicted of murdering an elderly woman, and he was linked to at least two other deaths of elderly women. Eberling periodically worked in the Sheppard home in 1954.

The jury declined to find that Sheppard was a wrongfully imprisoned person.

[*See also* Criminal Law Practice; Criminal Law Principles; Speech and the Press, Freedom of]

• Cynthia L. Cooper and Sam Reese Sheppard, *Mockery of Justice,* 1995. Walter L. Hixson, *Murder, Culture, and Injustice: Four Sensational Cases in American History,* 2000.   —J. Dean Carro

SHERIFF. The office of sheriff is of English origin and has been associated with county government in England since the late Anglo-Saxon period. After the Norman Conquest of 1066, the "shire-reeve" replaced the earl as the king's primary representative in each English county. Appointed at the pleasure of the king, he was responsible for collecting the king's revenues for the county, preserving the king's peace, serving and returning the king's writ, and presiding over the county court. Gradually, some of these functions were transferred to the king's courts and to other officials. The English colonists brought the office of sheriff and his basic responsibilities with them to America, and it is presently found in some form in every state.

The modern office of sheriff, served also by deputy sheriffs working under the sheriff's direction, retains two important functions of its medieval predecessor: law enforcement in the county and custody of the courthouse and jail. Sheriffs are therefore officials both of the court and of the county executive. They are usually the primary official involved in serving judicial processes that are directed to them on persons within their county and also are responsible for returning such processes to the courts. Sheriffs ordinarily have custody of those convicted of a crime until such persons are given over to other authorities or are due for release. They may also be responsible for the sale of property seized by a court. As law-enforcement officers, sheriffs are responsible for preserving the peace and making arrests.

Most county sheriffs in the United States are chosen by direct election, a residue of their historical role as chief executive officer in the English county. This makes them unique among chief law-enforcement officers; most others, such as *police chiefs and directors of state and federal law-enforcement agencies, are appointed. Many argue that the political nature of the office requires the sheriff to be more responsive to the needs of the community by developing programs aimed at the modern needs of communities, and some evidence suggests that county sheriff's departments have been more effective than nonelected law-enforcement agencies in these areas. However, others claim that electing the sheriff makes county law enforcement unnecessarily political. Voting for the sheriff generally has low salience among most members of the electorate, and as a result it may be difficult to ensure that the most qualified law-enforcement officer is chosen as the county sheriff.

In rural areas of the United States, which lack municipal police departments, sheriffs are often the only major law-enforcement officers. In addition to their common-law and statutory duties, many sheriff's departments have initiated programs to aid in crime prevention, such as anti-drug and anti–domestic violence efforts and presentations to schools and community groups. Some sheriff's departments have implemented special programs for children and the elderly. Still others are engaged in crime research in their communities. Again, these efforts may well be a response to the office's dependence on the electorate.

Like other law-enforcement agents, sheriffs are under careful legal scrutiny for their actions. They are generally immune from *liability for acts committed in the discharge of their official duties and from suits arising out of their discretionary functions; however, they may be liable for wrongful acts or acts that exceed the scope of their authority. These principles also apply to sheriffs' responsibilities as agents of the court, particularly regarding the service of judicial process. Laws on the civil liberties of those accused of crimes, such as the rights granted by the Supreme Court in the case of *Miranda* v. *Arizona* (1966), apply also to sheriff's actions.

In some areas, efforts have been made to curtail the powers of the sheriff or dispense with the office altogether. Responsibility for jail administration, for instance, has been removed from the control of sheriffs and given over to a dedicated public agency. Proponents of such measures claim that the political nature of the office makes sheriffs poor officials to handle the difficult business of detention of criminals. And in a few scattered counties across the United States, efforts have been made to abolish the office of sheriff. Although sheriffs have been largely successful in demonstrating their importance in serving the public as elected law-enforcement officers, the movement to abolish the office in some areas is likely to reemerge.

• L. A. Morris, *The Medieval English Sheriff to 1300*, 1927. George A. Billias, *Law and Authority in Colonial America*, 1965. Jacqueline Pope, *Bounty Hunters, Marshals, and Sheriffs: Forward to the Past*, 1998. Daniel R. Coquillette, *The Anglo-American Legal Heritage: Introductory Materials*, 1999. William Mack and Donald J. Kiser, "Sheriffs and Constables," in *Corpus Juris Secundum*, 1999.
—Seth W. Whitaker

SHERMAN ANTI-TRUST ACT. *See* Anti-Trust Law.

SHYSTER. *See* Lawyers, Popular Perceptions of.

SIMPSON, O. J., TRIALS OF. The O. J. Simpson criminal trial (*People of the State of California* v. *Orenthal James Simpson* (1995)) was the longest and most sensational trial in American history. The nationally televised trial revealed deep divisions over *race relations and raised troubling questions about the ability of the criminal justice system to function effectively in such a heavily mediated courtroom setting.

Simpson, a former National Football League Hall of Fame running back, pleaded not guilty to the savage murders of his ex-wife, Nicole Brown Simpson, and her friend Ronald Goldman, both of whom were found stabbed to death on 12 June 1994. Although the physical and circumstantial evidence arrayed against Simpson was compelling, police and prosecution errors combined with widespread distrust of the Los Angeles Police Department (LAPD) set the stage for Simpson's acquittal.

The murder trial of Simpson, an African American, unfolded in a city already seething with racial tension. On 30 April 1992, violent riots erupted in

Los Angeles when a predominantly white jury in Simi Valley acquitted four white LAPD police officers of brutality charges in the apprehension of African-American suspect Rodney *King, despite an amateur videotape, seen nationwide, that showed King undergoing brutal treatment. The subsequent outcome of the Simpson case stemmed directly from the profound mistrust on the part of the African-American community not only of the police but of the entire criminal justice system. While the Simpson *crime* had no apparent connection with race, the Simpson *case* was decided in a community and nation riven by racial tensions.

Simpson's defense, spearheaded by attorney Johnnie Cochran, emphasized police racism, corruption, and incompetent handling of evidence. Superior Court Judge Lance Ito gave the defense wide latitude, including allowing into evidence testimony that one of the LAPD officers involved in the Simpson investigation, Mark Fuhrman, repeatedly had used the racial epithet "nigger." Defense attorneys Barry Scheck and Peter Neufeld, experts on the use of DNA evidence, mounted a successful campaign to discredit the devastating blood evidence against Simpson amassed by the prosecution. Blood evidence at the crime scene, at Simpson's home, and in his motor vehicle had left the defendant's genetic fingerprints all over the crime. The defense argued that the evidence had been planted by police in a vast conspiracy against the former athlete and celebrity.

Cameras in the courtroom provided the public with complete access to the Simpson trial. Networks and stations offered "gavel-to-gavel" coverage of the unprecedented year-long murder trial. Sequestered for almost a full year, the Simpson jurors heard more than a score of attorneys as well as an astonishing sixteen thousand objections. When the case was finally turned over to them on 29 September 1995, the jury quickly returned a 12–0 vote for acquittal. The main reason for Simpson's acquittal was the total absence of LAPD credibility, not only among the predominantly African-American jurors but within the black community of Los Angeles.

Across the country, the unrestrained jubilation of African Americans contrasted sharply with the outrage expressed by most whites, who considered the evidence against Simpson overwhelming. According to one poll, 85 percent of blacks concurred with the verdict, compared with 32 percent of whites. The Simpson case traumatized Americans, not simply because of the verdict rendered but because it brought into the open deep divisions over race.

Although he won acquittal of the murder charges and obtained his freedom after spending sixteen months in jail, Simpson did not escape unscathed. On 4 February 1997, following a civil trial (*Fred Goldman* v. *O. J. Simpson*), a Santa Monica jury issued three judgments against Simpson on behalf of the Brown and Goldman families totalling $33.5 million.

[*See also* Media and the Law]

• Jeffrey Toobin, *The Run of His Life: The People v. O. J. Simpson*, 1996. Walter L. Hixson, *Murder, Culture, and Injustice: Four Sensational Cases in American History*, 2001.
—Walter L. Hixson

SLANDER. *See* Torts.

SLAVERY, LAW OF. Slavery flourished in most of the New World before 1600, but the British colonists were slow to adopt it, in part because slavery was unknown in seventeenth-century Britain and no legal structure was in place to protect this peculiar form of *property. Initially, the landowning and elite English colonists relied on indentured servants for labor. The British treated the first Africans, who arrived on a Dutch ship in 1619, as indentured servants; some of the Africans gained their freedom, and there is no evidence of overt discrimination against blacks.

By the 1630s the legal system was singling out Africans for distinctly different treatment. In 1640 a Virginia court sentenced a black indentured servant who had run away to "serve his said master or his assigns for the time of his natural Life here or elsewhere." No white runaway indentured servant in Virginia ever received such a sentence. By the 1650s court records regularly referred to "slaves." Further, a 1662 act declared that "all children born in this country shall be held bond or free only according to the condition of the mother." This legal rule, known as *partus sequitur ventrem* (the offspring follows the mother), was based on Roman law and was a complete reversal of English law; it was adopted throughout British America. The rule meant that the children of enslaved black women would be slaves, even if their fathers were free. It facilitated the sexual exploitation of female slaves, because any illegitimate children became slaves owned by the mother's master.

In 1705 Virginia enacted its first comprehensive statute on slavery. The law provided for the taxing and registration of slaves, explained when runaways or rebellious slaves "may be killed" and listed other punishments that might be inflicted on slaves. The law equated blacks with slaves, although the colony contained hundreds of free blacks. By 1750 all the Southern colonies, and most of the Northern ones, had adopted similar slave codes. In the process they created an entirely new area of law, unknown in England, to support slavery.

Under these early codes, slaves had virtually no legal rights. In most areas they could be executed for crimes that were not capital offenses for whites. Their testimony was restricted in legal cases and could not be used either for or against whites. Trials of slaves were usually by special courts. Slaves could not own property, move about without the consent of their owners, or legally marry. Throughout the South, the killing of a slave was not murder. Killing a slave who was resisting white authority, rebelling, or even, in some circumstances, running away was not a crime. By the end of the colonial period slaves were considered chattels, or movable property. Throughout the colonial South a master could not manumit (voluntarily free) a slave. By 1775 slavery was legal in all thirteen colonies.

The Declaration of Independence undermined the basis of slavery by articulating the principle that "all men are created equal." During and after the Revolutionary war, northern patriots took this new ideology seriously and took steps to end slavery. Pennsylvania (1780), Connecticut (1784), Rhode Island (1784), New York (1799), and New Jersey (1804) adopted gradual emancipation statutes. While no existing slaves gained freedom as a result, these laws set the stage for an end to bondage by providing that the children of all slave women would be born free, subject to indenture until adulthood. Massachusetts (1780), New Hampshire (1784), and the fourteenth state, Vermont (1791), ended slavery outright in their new state constitutions.

The Revolution also affected slavery in the South. For example, in 1791 North Carolina made it a capital offense to murder a slave; the preamble to this statute acknowledged the changes brought about by the Revolution. In 1782 Virginia allowed for the voluntary manumission of slaves by masters, although in 1806 it modified the law by requiring newly freed slaves to leave the state. Other Southern states eased restrictions on voluntary manumission. Virginia and Maryland also prohibited the importation of slaves. However, none of the Southern states considered ending slavery or

taking steps to find a long term solution to the problem of human bondage.

The Southern delegates to the Constitutional Convention reflected the region's commitment to slavery, fighting throughout the convention, with great success, to protect slavery. The final document counted slaves for apportioning representatives and electoral college votes; protected the African slave trade for at least twenty years; guaranteed that masters could recover their fugitive slaves; prohibited an indirect tax on slavery by banning export taxes; and guaranteed that the national government would suppress insurrections, including those led by slaves.

Finally, the entire constitutional structure protected against national emancipation. Constitutional amendments required approval by three-fourths of the states for ratification, giving the slave states a perpetual power to block an amendment ending slavery.

Southern Slave Law in the Nineteenth Century. After the Revolutionary period, the law in the South strengthened slavery as an institution. Ironically, one way of strengthening slavery was to make it less harsh, because this would make slave rebellions less likely and undercut abolitionists' critiques of the institution. Thus, in the 1820s South Carolina prohibited branding, dismemberment, castration, and other barbaric forms of punishment that had been legal in the colonial period. Similarly, by 1860 all Southern states recognized that anyone, even a master, who killed a slave in cold blood could be charged with murder. In *State v. Hoover* (1839) the North Carolina Supreme Court upheld the death sentence for a master who tortured his slave to death. Shortly before the Civil War, a few Southern states made rape of a slave a crime, although there is no instance of a white man being prosecuted for such a crime.

Along the same lines, Southern states provided *due process protections for slaves accused of crimes. Courts throughout the South overturned convictions of slaves who were denied a lawyer, were coerced into confessing a crime, were improperly prohibited from calling witnesses, or were incorrectly charged. Such procedural victories helped few slaves charged with crimes. Most slaves accused of criminal offenses were given quick trials and harsh punishments.

Slaves were at all times to be made subordinate to whites, and the southern legislatures and courts readily accepted this idea. As North Carolina's Chief Justice Thomas Ruffin declared in *State v. Mann* (1829): "The slave, to remain a slave, must be made sensible, that there is no appeal from his master; that his power is in no instance usurped, but is conferred by the laws of man at least, if not by the law of God."

By 1860 almost all the states that would join the Confederacy had either prohibited manumission or made it extremely difficult. Most slave states made it a crime to teach a slave to read. In most of the South, circulating antislavery literature was a crime and, in the 1850s, the national best-seller *Uncle Tom's Cabin* was banned. Slaves could organize their own worship services only if whites were present. Many of these restrictive laws were also applied to free blacks in the South—more than a quarter of a million by 1860.

Northern Law. By 1830 slavery had disappeared in much of the North, although a few aging slaves could be found in Pennsylvania, New Jersey, Connecticut, and Illinois. In the three decades before the Civil War, northerners passed laws to protect their free black neighbors from kidnapping and gradually, although grudgingly, offered them some social, political, and economic rights.

Most Northern states passed personal liberty laws, designed to frustrate, where possible, attempts by southerners to reclaim fugitive slaves. Before *Prigg* v. *Pennsylvania* (1842) outlawed the practice, these laws granted jury trials to alleged fugitives. After 1842 northern states simply withdrew their support and refused to aid slave catchers.

Northern states also freed slaves taken into their states by visiting masters. In England in 1772, in *Somerset* v. *Stewart* the Court of Kings Bench in London ruled that if a master brought a slave into the country, the slave became instantly free. This ruling was part of the *common law of the colonies at the time of the Revolution. In *Commonwealth* v. *Aves* (1836), the Supreme Judicial Court of Massachusetts held that slaves became free the moment they were brought into the North. But Southern states began to arrest free blacks who entered their jurisdictions. Before the 1830s about half the slave states did recognize the freedom of slaves who had lived in the North, but by 1860 only a few Southern states did so.

Slavery and National Law. After adoption of the Constitution, Congress and the Supreme Court generally supported slavery. In 1793 Congress passed the first fugitive slave law, to help masters recover runaway slaves. The Fugitive Slave Law of 1850 provided federal help to masters and harsh penalties for anyone interfering with the return of runaway slaves.

In 1808 Congress banned the importation of slaves. This was not necessarily an antislavery act, however. Many slave owners in Virginia and Maryland favored such a ban because it would increase the value of their slaves. Not until the *Civil War did Congress and the executive branch effectively enforce the ban. Meanwhile, in *The Antelope* (1825) the Supreme Court upheld the legality of the international slave trade. In *United States* v. *Amistad* (1841) the Court ordered a group of slaves taken from Africa to be set free, but only because they had been illegally imported to Cuba in the first place.

In the Northwest Ordinance (1787) Congress banned slavery in the Northwest Territory. In the Missouri Compromise (1820) it banned slavery in all the western territories north and west of the southern boundary of Missouri. Congress modified this ban in the Compromise of 1850 to allow slavery in most of the territories ceded to the United States after the Mexican–American War. In the Kansas–Nebraska Act (1854) Congress repealed most of the ban on slavery in the west. This led to a mini-civil war in Kansas, in which Congress and the administrations of Presidents Franklin Pierce and James Buchanan consistently sided with slave owners.

In *Dred Scott* v. *Sandford* (1857) the Supreme Court ruled that *all* bans on slavery in the territories were unconstitutional, because Southerners had a constitutional right to take their slaves into any federal territories. The Court also ruled that blacks had no legal rights under the Constitution and that they could never be citizens of the United States. *Dred Scott* was followed by an extraordinary backlash in the North. Abraham *Lincoln's sharp critique of the decision helped propel him to the Republican nomination for president in 1860.

The eleven slave states that seceded in 1860–61 did so to protect slavery from a national government controlled by Lincoln. As Confederate Vice President Alexander Stephens noted, slavery was "the cornerstone" of the Confederacy. The Confederate states maintained slavery almost exactly as it had been before the war, while the Confederate government violated accepted rules of international law by enslaving, or murdering, black U.S. soldiers captured in battle.

The nation effectively overruled *Dred Scott* during and after the Civil War. During the war, Congress banned slavery in the territories, abolished slavery in the District of Columbia, and with the enlistment of black troops, starting in 1862, acknowledged that African Americans could indeed be part of the nation's citizenry. Lincoln's Emancipation Proclamation (1863) ended slavery everywhere in the Confederacy that U.S. troops entered. The final reversal of *Dred Scott* came with the adoption of the Thirteenth Amendment (1865), ending slavery everywhere in the United States, and the *Fourteenth Amendment (1868), declaring that all people born in the United States were citizens of the nation and of the state in which they lived.

[*See also* Civil Rights and Civil Liberties; Race and Ethnicity; Segregation]

• William M. Wiecek, *The Sources of Antislavery Constitutionalism in America, 1760–1848,* 1977. Don E. Fehrenbacher, *The Dred Scott Case: Its Significance in American Law and Politics,* 1978. A. Leon Higginbotham, *In the Matter of Color: Race and the American Legal Process, the Colonial Period,* 1978. Judith Kelleher Schafer, *Slavery, the Civil Law, and the Supreme Court of Louisiana,* 1994. Thomas D. Morris, *Southern Slavery and the Law, 1619–1860,* 1996. Paul Finkelman, *Dred Scott v. Sandford: A Brief History with Documents,* 1997. Paul Finkelman, *Slavery and the Law,* 1998. Paul Finkelman, *Slavery and the Founders: Race and Liberty in the Age of Jefferson,* 2d ed., 2002.   —Paul Finkelman

SMOKING. *See* Drugs, Illegal; Health Law; Insurance; Tobacco Litigation.

SOCIAL CONTROL. *See* Custom and Law; Extralegality; Mob Violence and Vigilantism.

SOCIAL DIMENSIONS OF LAW. The study of law's social dimensions may be likened to a seismic science. Like seismology, a historical *sociology of law looks beneath the surface of legal formations to the undercurrents of their sources, to the volatile activity that causes new formations to emerge, and to the unseen, unknown, and underappreciated causes of legal developments. The legal sociologist digs for the social origins of law in order to determine the exact influences that shape formal law: law is not a self-contained system but is a part of the vast complexity of society as a whole; law is a product of the larger social, *economic, and political forces that surround it. In short, an appreciation of the social dimensions of law is necessary to understand not only why formal laws take shape but also the impact of these laws on social life.

One way to answer the question "What *is* a historical sociology of law?" is to appreciate what it is not. Most importantly, it is not a formalistic, case-by-case summation of legal doctrines. The formalistic study of legal doctrine does not reach legal sociology's central concern of how society has shaped law and vice versa. Unlike formalistic case studies, the study of law and society does not abstract formal law from the historical environment in which it developed; nor does it attribute formal law solely to intellectual insights. The study of law and society therefore examines law from many different perspectives, including those of legislator, administrative agent, judge, juror, executive, and citizen. By viewing law formation from these vantages, the legal sociologist emphasizes law's chronology and context, as well as the influence of changing circumstances on the course of legal development. In short, *law-and-society scholarship appreciates that law cannot be understood apart from the larger social world within which it exists; and it recognizes that the historical development of law stems from the interplay of formal law and social growth—that laws are rooted in a particular context and cannot be properly studied without reference to the *culture, economy, and legal customs that prevail when a law is adopted.

Early American *property law clearly demonstrates the historical development of law in response to social circumstances. The early American colonists adopted English *common law as the foundation of their colonial legal systems; yet, over time, this common law began to reflect American rather than English values and concerns. For example, the royal charters that established certain New World colonies provided that the colonists would pay a specified fee to the king for the land they used; but the open, abundant land in America made collection of these fees far more difficult than it had been in England: the threat of eviction, which had worked so well in land-scarce Britain, had little effect in land-abundant America. Therefore, the centuries-old English tradition of paying land fees to the king died almost immediately in the New World—thereby demonstrating that when old laws are transplanted to a new society, such transplantation is the beginning, not the end, of legal evolution.

Culture can have a substantial impact on legal development. American culture may be defined as the shared values implicit in the symbolic practices of American society; and attention to cultural context can shed light upon laws that cannot be explained simply by the cash nexus. Legal scholars who believe American law merely responds instrumentally to the imperatives of a free-market economy overlook the possible religious, social, and cultural explanations for the passage of laws that cannot be explained solely on the basis of market imperatives. Economic factors alone, for example, cannot explain why Sunday-closing laws were enacted nationwide in the late nineteenth century. Sunday-closing laws required businesses and merchants to close on the Christian Sabbath. As participants in a free-market economy, some merchants found it disadvantageous to sacrifice one day of profits weekly. Religious leaders, on the other hand, favored and promoted Sunday-closing laws without regard to economic consequences. Influenced by their desire to foster Sabbath-keeping and church attendance, clergymen petitioned and lobbied their legislators to pass Sunday-closing laws. Other reasons also help explain these laws, such as the desire for a national day of rest for workers, advocated by *labor reformers. Hence, legal historians and sociologists are keenly aware that laws have multiple, not single, causes. A society's *politics, *religion, and other cultural characteristics—not just its economy—shape the context of laws and therefore influence their creation.

American private-law topics—for example, property, *family law, and *torts—often clearly display the ways in which sociocultural factors influence legal change. As mentioned earlier, American property law came to differ from its English origins because of the abundant and inexpensive property available in America. Under English common law, social status was a central determinant of property ownership: English laws that restricted use, tenancy, conveyance, and inheritance protected a scarce resource—land—from the unprivileged. In America, however, scarcity did not mandate protection of the vital resource of land. With the new abundance of land came a change in scarcity-conscious British property law. For example, early nineteenth-century America saw the legislative abolition of common-law primogeniture (inheritance of land by the eldest son), thereby allowing persons to bequeath their property freely, regardless of the heirs' standing in the family or society.

Furthermore, the abundance of land, and the preeminence of economic efficiency as a cornerstone of social values, along with political pressure brought by land-hungry settlers, combined to undermine common-law security of title and absentee landlordism in America. The traditional common-law requirements mandating precise descriptions of boundaries became obsolete as pioneers outpaced government surveyors and created new ways of marking property for themselves, such as tree-blazing and the planting of crops. These pioneers, as members of the *voting citizenry, placed pressure on local lawmakers to pass laws supporting squatters' rights and preemption. The notion that squatters could acquire land belonging to an owner-by-deed was readily acceptable in a society that valued economic efficiency over the nonuse of land. As a result, state *legislatures responded to the settlers' political pressure by enacting laws that favored possession and use of property over mere title. Politicians in Kentucky, for example, passed laws that not only protected an occupant's rights to his improvements on privately owned land but also established his right to acquire title through undisturbed possession and use of that land. Thus, no longer could absentee landlords expect to retain ownership of their land simply by virtue of paper title. These legal innovations stood in direct conflict with the common law of "conveyance and title by contract," but they met the needs (and desires) of an acquisitive and expanding American society.

Just as property law eventually conformed to the abundance of land, so did American family law conform to society's changing attitudes toward marriage. Once widely perceived as a unit of socialization and economic production, by mid-twentieth century the American family was coming to be regarded as a collection of individuals in pursuit of goals grounded in purely personal fulfillment. In keeping with this changed view of the family, new legal attitudes toward divorce emerged as marriages came to be seen as a site for individual satisfaction rather than selfless devotion to child rearing and other family responsibilities. Responding to this cultural change of the 1960s and 1970s, legislatures began to pass no-fault divorce laws. Unlike previous divorce legislation, no-fault divorce laws allowed easier access to divorce decrees without the financial and social repercussions previously attached to divorces. In sum, then, American family law changed as the family changed.

American tort law changed in large measure on account of social imperatives spawned by the new industrial advances of the nineteenth century. Early nineteenth-century American tort law focused primarily on issues of *trespass, assault and battery, and defamation; but with the emergence of the transportation and industrial revolutions, tort law had to provide remedies for injuries to innocent strangers arising from new events such as industrial accidents, train wrecks, and steamboat explosions. From these novel disasters, the notion of negligence emerged as the dominant standard for tort actions arising from carelessness; and because no comprehensive body of law existed to govern negligence, judges in nineteenth-century America felt free to create laws that favored entrepreneurial growth. During the 1840s, for example, courts began to decide certain tort cases according to the fellow-servant rule. This rule shielded employers from *liability in cases where employees were injured by the negligent acts of co-employees, thus rejecting employers' vicarious liability for worker injuries caused by coworkers. By placing such limits on employer liability, courts promoted commercial enterprise and investment through doctrines that placed the responsibility for workplace safety not upon business and industry but upon the employees themselves. Employees were required to conduct their activities so as to protect themselves and their fellow employees from injury or to absorb the losses. Thus, American tort law evolved to meet the needs of a developing and capital-scarce American economy.

The legal traditions in which lawmakers are trained can also have a substantial influence on the formation of laws. Many lawmakers, especially judges, share a common language: the rubric and axioms of their taught legal tradition. Hence lawmakers, even when dedicated to innovation, are guided by legal tradition, for they do not possess the ability, expertise, or insight to shape a novel legal order. To this end, legal tradition can actually inhibit or prevent new ideas or social expectations from changing the law. For example, American legislatures in the early nineteenth century adopted, by rote, European *civil-law tenets of *water-rights law. Roman water-rights law, which provided that bodies of water could not be owned by individuals, conflicted with the traditional common-law concept that a landowner's domain extends from the depths of the earth to the heavens—a concept readily embraced by American landowners. Many states nevertheless adopted the Roman law principle that waterways cannot be privately owned, even though it was contrary to the concerns and needs of riparian property owners. Thus, lawmakers who have been trained as *lawyers often tend to rely more on their appreciation of the commands of the legal tradition than on the express desires or necessities of their society.

Just as society and legal tradition have had a substantial impact on the formation of laws, so also can laws have two determinable effects on society: they can produce either intended or unintended results. Intended results are those that the lawmaker anticipated and, in fact, aimed to produce in drafting a particular law. The antebellum Married Women's Property Acts provide concrete evidence of laws achieving their intended results. Prior to these acts, husbands were the owners of all assets and debts of the marital regime, including whatever property, assets, and debts the wife brought to the marriage. The chief purpose of the acts was to remove obstacles that impaired the speed and efficiency of the market in land: because under the common law a husband was legally responsible for his wife's marital and premarital debts, his own land could be declared unmerchantable on account of the wife's creditors enforcing their rights against the husband's property. With passage of the Married Women's Property Acts, which granted women sole ownership of their own property (assets and debts), a husband was no longer liable to his wife's creditors, thus removing those clouds from his land titles.

Laws can also produce unintended consequences. Consider, for example, late nineteenth- and early twentieth-century property taxes levied in New Orleans and San Francisco, which were based on the frontage of residential property instead of the total square footage. The result was a popular residential design, extremely narrow on the front side and extending back a substantial distance from the street. This unique oblong architectural norm arose, then, not for aesthetic reasons but as a tax avoidance measure—an unintended but architecturally pleasing consequence of a simple revenue measure.

In sum, the legal sociologist appreciates law and social history not as separate academic disciplines but as part of an integrated legal sociology. The recognition of the formal sources of law is only the starting point of inquiry as the legal sociologist probes for law's purposes and influences by studying its historical evolution through social growth.

• Leonard W. Levy, *The Law of the Commonwealth and Chief Justice Shaw*, 1957. James Willard Hurst, *Law and Social Order in the United States*, 1977. Lawrence Meir Friedman, *A History of American Law*, 2d ed., 1985. Alan Watson, "The Transformation of American Property Law: A Comparative Law Approach," *Georgia Law Review* 24 (1990): 163. Richard H. Chused, *Private Acts in Public Places: A Social History of Divorce in the Formative Era of American Family Law*, 1994. Andrew J. King, "Sunday Law in the Nineteenth Century," *Albany Law Review* 64 (2000): 675. Joseph M. Hawes and Elizabeth I. Nybakken, eds., *Family and Society in American History*, 2001. Christopher L. Tomlins and Bruce H. Mann, eds., *The Many Legalities of Early America*, 2001. Melvin I. Urofsky and Paul Finkleman, *A March of Lib-*

erty: A Constitutional History of the United States, 2d ed., 2002. —James Étienne Viator

SOCIAL JUSTICE. *See* Justice.

SOCIAL SECURITY. *See* Aging and the Law; Entitlements; Health Law; Insurance; Taxation; Welfare.

SOCIOLOGICAL JURISPRUDENCE. The legal philosophy "sociological jurisprudence" is an approach to adjudication that views law as a means to promote social welfare, requiring legislators and judges who will make law in light of society's constantly evolving needs and interests. Although sociological jurisprudence has roots in European legal thought, particularly in the writings of Rudolf von Inhering, Eugene Ehrlich, and Hermann Kantorwicz, it is, in America, most fully defined by Roscoe *Pound, Dean of the Harvard Law School from 1916 to 1936, and Benjamin *Cardozo, judge of the New York Court of Appeals from 1914 to 1932 and justice of the United States Supreme Court until his death in 1938. Pound first described sociological jurisprudence in a 1906 address to the *American Bar Association. He discussed and defended his views in a two-part article, "The Scope and Purpose of Sociological Jurisprudence," published in the Harvard Law Review in 1911–12. Cardozo elaborated this new jurisprudence in his Storrs Lectures at Yale, which were published as *The Nature of the Judicial Process* (1921). Many other legal scholars, such as Jerome Hall and Julius Stone, carried forward Pound's and Cardozo's insights until mid-century.

Pound's and Cardozo's development of sociological jurisprudence was part of the general movement in American social thought that Morton White described in *The Revolt Against Formalism* (1949) (see JURISPRUDENCE, AMERICAN: THE REVOLT AGAINST FORMALISM). Since the Civil War, American law had been dominated by formal modes of analysis. Legal formalism taught that law was an apolitical science modeled on the physical and mathematical sciences. Formalist jurists believed that judges and legal scholars could empirically study legal cases, induce the abstract legal principles that governed how appellate courts decided them, and deductively apply these principles in all subsequent controversies. For formalists, law was geometrically shaped: the myriad legal rules were the logical and nondiscretionary elaboration of a few fundamental principles. Formalists developed their supposedly apolitical approach to law into such constitutional and private law doctrines as liberty of *contract, contributory negligence, and privity of contract that limited state power to regulate private *property and exempted businesses from *liability to their workers and customers. Legal formalism was the jurisprudence of conservative jurists who generally favored laissez-faire economics.

In contrast, sociological jurisprudence was the legal expression of Progressive reform in American politics. In the late-nineteenth and early twentieth centuries America became industrialized and urbanized; developed national markets, transportation, and communication networks; and through massive immigration became ethnically diverse. Although these developments produced some radical ferment, the dominant response was progressive in character. Progressive reformers accepted the new social and economic conditions but sought to curb the abuses associated with them. Sociological jurisprudence sought moderate reform that would make law more responsive to the needs of *consumers and workers.

Sociological jurisprudence also was the legal expression of the pragmatic turn in American philosophy. In the early twentieth century, the pragmatists William James and John Dewey believed that ideas were "right" or "true" if they functioned well when put into practice. Sociological jurists used pragmatism as a basis to criticize legal formalism as a "mechanical" jurisprudence that incorrectly preferred law's logical form to its ability to promote social well-being. Sociological jurists thought of law not as an end in itself, but as a "means to an end," to fulfill human needs and values. As pragmatists, sociological jurists conceived law as an evolving set of principles, whose application should always be responsive to the ever-changing context in which they were applied. Sociological jurists approached law as the conscious pursuit of social welfare, as social engineering not doctrinal geometry.

Sociological jurisprudence involved a three-part program. First, since the purpose of law was to satisfy community needs and desires, a study of the "social facts" of American society was required as a step toward making appropriate law. Second, sociological jurists analyzed the actual social effects of legal rules rather than their logical symmetry. Sociological jurists thought legal rules should be considered from the point of view of how they functioned. Law must effectively influence social life in desirable directions. Third, sociological jurists insisted that every legal case required individualized consideration to take account of the diverse circumstances of each dispute. Law should be premised not on strictly drawn rules but on ambiguous standards, such as "good faith" and "reasonableness." Standards made the prediction of case outcomes less certain, but fairer.

Although sociological jurisprudence influenced American law, it never was America's dominant philosophy. When, during the Great Depression, legal formalism was finally displaced as America's dominant approach to law, sociological jurisprudence was itself under attack by the two newer schools: *legal realism and legal process. Legal realists criticized sociological jurisprudence for its restraint in appraising legal formalism: society changed more rapidly and was more heterogeneous. Consequently, legal doctrine always lagged behind social need and could not satisfy the desires of society as a whole. Legal realists also thought that abstract legal doctrine hardly ever determined legal disputes. It was naive to believe, as the sociological jurists did, that if legal doctrine were properly updated and clearly stated, judges could apply it faithfully in subsequent controversies.

Legal process jurists believed that the sociological jurists correctly viewed law as involving debatable policy choices. Accordingly, judges should generally defer to legislative, administrative, and executive policymakers. Judges should rarely and circumspectly make law. In general, they should intervene only to establish correct procedures for legislative, administrative or executive lawmaking.

By mid-century, sociological jurisprudence was an outmoded approach to law. It had proven insufficiently radical for some American jurists and too political for others. In breaking with legal formalism, and giving birth to legal realism and legal process jurisprudence, sociological jurisprudence was an important, but transitional, approach to American law.

[See also Brandeis, Louis Dembitz; Economics and Law; Holmes, Oliver Wendell, Jr.; Social Dimensions of Law]

• Roscoe Pound, 'The Scope and Purpose of Sociological Jurisprudence," Harvard Law Review (1911): 591; Harvard Law Review (1912): 489. Benjamin Cardozo, The Nature of the Judicial Process, 1921. Julius Stone, The Province and Function of Law, 1946 (391–785). G. Edward White, "From Sociological Jurisprudence to Realism: Jurisprudence and Social Change in Early Twentieth-Century America," in G. Edward White, Patterns of American Legal Thought (1978): 99–135. James Herget, American Jurisprudence, 1870–1970, 1990.

—Stephen A. Siegel

SOCIOLOGY AND LAW. The essential insight underlying all sociological approaches to law is that law is a social phenomenon that should, therefore, be studied sociologically. Beyond this core unifying orientation, sociology and law, otherwise known as the sociology of law, or law and sociology, consists of a variety of different approaches, assumptions, and attitudes.

This internal proliferation of approaches is the product of diversity at two different levels. First: sociology and law are contrasting bodies of knowledge. Sociology is a social science focused on the study of society, and like all such disciplines its overarching goal is the gathering of knowledge. Law, in contrast, is a practical activity that focuses on completing certain fundamental tasks, including promulgating and enforcing rules, responding to disputes, and maintaining order. Second: each of these contributing bodies of knowledge is in its own way internally driven, with sociology divided among various competing schools of thought and law divided among practitioners and theorists (adhering to competing schools of thought). When sociology and law are brought together, the differences between them, and the internal divisions that characterize each, are manifested in the combination of the two.

In the United States, the primary academic influences in bringing sociology to law were philosophical pragmatism, *sociological jurisprudence, and *legal realism; the key figures were Oliver Wendell *Holmes Jr., Roscoe *Pound, and Karl *Llewellyn. These schools of thought and figures were leaders in the critique of formalistic approaches to the law that dominated at the end of the nineteenth century and early twentieth century. Under formalist views, law was a gapless, logically coherent self-contained system that could be discovered and applied exclusively through consideration of legal concepts, principles, and rules, without regard to social context or consequences. The figures identified above argued, to the contrary, that law was the product of social forces, that it was neither gapless nor systematic, that one could not move mechanistically from principle to application (choices had to be made), and that judges were influenced by the social background in their interpretation and application of law. Most important: they argued that law, far from being autonomous and self-standing, was above all else an instrument to serve social needs. An important social-political influence on their thought was the social programs of the New Deal, which resorted to law as the key mechanism for implementing social policy.

It follows this cluster of views that the efficacy of law, and its social consequences, must be carefully evaluated. Hence the call for the application of sociology to law. The early agenda for sociology ranged from studying the gap between "law in the books" and "law in action," to discovering the social influences on the making, the application, and the interpretation of law, to learning whether law is effective in achieving social policy, and how it can be made more effective when it is not. Many sociological studies of law, from the study of crime to influences on judicial decision-making, were conducted to meet this call. Under the influence of sociologist E. A. Ross, law came to be understood as a mechanism of social control, and the thrust of many studies was to make law more efficient and effective in accomplishing this task.

A backlash against this jurisprudence-dominated agenda gradually developed from the sociological standpoint, which decried the instrumental use of sociology as a "handmaiden to law." As the science of society, the application of sociology to law, it has been argued, should take place in the context of general theories about society, with proper attention paid to epistemological and methodological concerns. The classical sociological theories about law—famously including Émile Durkheim's view of law as the essential element integrating modern society, Max Weber's ideal-type analysis of the kinds of law found relative to kinds of societies, and Karl Marx's characterization of law as determined by economic forces, serving the dominant class (see MARXIST AND POST-MARXIST THEORIES OF LAW)—all possessed these qualities. A modern sociological theory of this type of law is Donald Black's view, which assumes a positivistic stance of measuring law in quantitative terms, and articulates a series of "laws" of legal behavior based upon patterns he observes relating to factors like degree of social stratification.

A different current source of criticism of the jurisprudence-influenced approach to sociology and law comes from critical schools of sociolegal theory, including "critical empiricists" and "post-empiricists," which reject positivism and many of the epistemological underpinnings of classical sociology (including the fact/value distinction). Adherents criticize sociology and law as currently practiced as a conservative tool that serves to preserve the status quo by enhancing the efficiency of law and by failing to scrutinize and reveal the institutional structures and ideological beliefs about law circulating in society which perpetuate (class-based, gender-based, and/or race-based) oppression and domination. Sociological approaches to law, according to this view, must reject the agenda set by jurisprudence, and instead seek to expose all forms of domination perpetuated through law.

Sociology and law thus encompasses divergent perspectives on law. Despite significant internal schisms, a growing community of scholars and body of discourse has developed around the combination of sociology and law, united by the shared commitment to view law as a social phenomenon that must be examined in sociological terms.

[See also Law and Society Movement]

• Donald Black, The Behavior of Law, 1976. Alan Hunt, The Sociological Movement in Law, 1978. Roger Cotterrell, The Sociology of Law: An Introduction, 1992. Kahei Rokumoto, Sociological Theories of Law, 1994. Brian Tamanaha, Realistic Socio-Legal Theory: Pragmatism and a Social Theory of Law, 1997.

—Brian Z. Tamanaha

SODOMY. See Homosexuality and the Law; Morals Offenses; Sex Offenses.

SOLE PRACTITIONERS. The sole practitioner is a self-employed *lawyer engaged in the private practice of law.

From the beginning of the eighteenth century, when the rudimentary elements of a legal profession were established in colonial America, through the first half of the twentieth century, most practicing lawyers were sole practitioners. Although some lawyers might employ a scrivener (a professional copyist) or other office assistant, most lawyers did not associate professionally with other attorneys during the nineteenth century and the first half of the twentieth. From the post–World War II era to the present, the percentage of sole practitioners within the legal profession has dropped substantially, although sole practitioners still remain a plurality of lawyers in the private practice of law.

During the first sixty or so years of the nineteenth century, the minority of lawyers who deviated from this standard, such as Abraham *Lincoln, practiced law in a partnership of two lawyers. A common division of labor in the two-man partnership was for one partner to handle the work in court, and for the other to take care of the office-based work. For example, in the decade-long partnership of Abraham Lincoln and William Herndon, Lincoln ordinarily performed the court work, and Herndon managed the office and did much of the legal research. Like many partnerships at this time, Lincoln and Herndon worked together on many matters, yet they also worked independently of one another, as well as with other lawyers on occasion. Before 1870, only a minuscule number of lawyers were members of a law *firm consisting of four or more lawyers. Although some current law firms can date their origins to well before the Civil War, as of 1872, there were merely fourteen law firms consisting of four or more lawyers in the ten largest cities in the United States. By 1903, there was a tenfold increase in the number of law firms with four or more lawyers.

The initial shift in the private practice of law from sole practice to law firm practice was accompanied both by a change in the ideal lawyer type, and a change in the American economy. During the first half of the nineteenth century, the orator, or advocate, was the prototypical lawyer. The prominent antebellum lawyer was one who earned his reputation in the skilled handling of litigation. Leading lawyers of the early nineteenth century were lauded for their unique forensic abilities. At the midpoint of the century, the image became that of the railroad lawyer, a trial lawyer who might also counsel the railroad on some of the many legal problems it faced. Beginning about 1870, the industrial revolution in the northern United States, coupled with the rise of finance capitalism, created a need for lawyers skilled in counseling and reorganizing businesses. The business counselor rarely went to court. His expertise lay in advising corporations and financial institutions. He was seen as an ideal lawyer type by the end of the nineteenth century, although there was a marked dissension within the profession about this appellation.

The increase in the number and complexity of the legal matters of corporations created a need for a further division of legal labor, and paved the way for the rise of the large law firm at the end of the nineteenth century. One advantage of the large law firm, claimed its defenders, was that it included both legal generalists and specialists in relatively narrow fields of law. A second claimed advantage was the so-called "Cravath system." The Cravath law firm hired graduates of elite law schools and required them to work solely on the firm's business. In exchange for devoting all of their time to Cravath's business, these associated lawyers were paid a salary by the firm, and were not required to generate their own legal business. The associates were trained in the firm's work by other lawyers in the firm, which promoted some of them to partner after a lengthy period of seasoning.

Although the large law firm was a fixture in many large cities by 1900, this change in the form of the practice of law created anxiety about the future of the legal profession and about the role of lawyers in an industrialized economy. The ideal lawyer was one who possessed a thorough knowledge of the law and an independence from both clients and the market in the practice of law. The sole practitioner symbolized this ideal lawyer type, and the rise of the large law firm lawyer was a challenge to this ideal. The sole practitioner also symbolized the individualist temperament of American society, and represented stability and the belief in incremental change in an era in which revolutionary changes appeared commonplace. From 1870–1910, the United States was transformed from a rural, agrarian nation to an urban, industrialized country, its population increasing from 39 million to nearly 92 million. During this time, the number of law schools increased almost fourfold, and the number of lawyers almost tripled. The effort to install the business lawyer as the ideal lawyer type thus appeared to signal the disappearance of the independent lawyer. Critics of the business counselor claimed that the corporate lawyer was merely a hired man, an instrument. Those opposed to the rise of the large law firm quoted the late robber baron Jay Gould: "[B]rains were the cheapest meat in the market."

Large law firms worked mainly for corporate and institutional clients, and sole practitioners and small law firms worked on behalf of individuals. This difference in type of client suggested a fractured legal profession, not a unitary bar. In 1913, the *American Bar Association asked the Carnegie Foundation to investigate the system of legal *education in the United States in the hope of making a reality the ideal of a unitary bar. Eight years later, *Training for the Public Profession of the Law* (commonly known as the Reed Report) was published. The Report concluded that a unitary bar was nonexistent, and that the widely varying existing types of legal education well served the differing interests of differing types of clients. Although the Report was rejected by elite sectors of the American legal profession, the verbalization of a heterogeneous legal profession made more distinct the professional distance between the sole practitioner and the large law firm lawyer.

From the 1940s through the 1980s, the percentage of sole practitioners declined substantially. In 1948, three out of every five lawyers were sole practitioners. By 1980, only one out of three lawyers was a sole practitioner. More lawyers in the private practice of law practiced in the law firm setting, and greater numbers of lawyers chose legal careers in government and corporations. The advent of the administrative state in the 1930s slowly but surely increased the number of lawyers in government service. Further, the dramatic expansion of the economy in the post–World War II era, combined with an increase in governmental regulation of the economy, resulted in an increasing number of lawyers employed by private industry (corporate, or in-house, counsel). In 1948, more than 89 percent of all lawyers were engaged in the private practice of law. By 1980, only 68 percent of all lawyers were engaged in the private practice of law. Within that sector, the number of sole practitioners declined from about two-thirds of all private practitioners to just under 45 percent between 1960 and 1990.

During this post–World War II era, the reputation and prestige of sole practitioners began to decline. A prominent criticism of the sole practitioner beginning in the 1950s was that the sole practitioner attempted to practice in all areas of law. Traditionally, this breadth of knowledge indicated a strength of the legal profession. The traditional argument was then turned on its head; the attempt of sole practitioners to practice in all areas of law made them less professionally capable than the law firm lawyer specializing in a few areas. The institution of the large law firm, through specialization, economies of scale, and diversification, its supporters declared, was the only institution capable of providing legal services to institutions. This criticism of sole practitioners was arguably buttressed by surveys indicating that sole practitioners earned less than partners in law firms and corporate counsel. Additionally, sole practitioners were disproportionately the subject of professional discipline and legal malpractice cases. The sole practitioner, critics claimed, was a jack-of-all-trades and master of none, in an era in which specialization was fast becoming the professional norm.

Through most of the 1980s, large law firms had much greater accessibility to legal knowledge than sole practitioners. Large law firms offered clients not only the diverse knowledge of the partners of the firm, but also the ability to obtain legal information more quickly than the sole practitioner, through the employment of associates, *paralegals, and law librarians. In addition, economies of scale made it much more possible for a large law firm than a sole practitioner to pay the costs of maintaining an extensive law library. As a result, there were thirteen times as many law firms with more than fifty lawyers in 1985 than in 1960. In 1988,

149 firms were larger than the largest firm in 1968. By 2001, at least seven law firms were comprised of more than 1,000 lawyers, and 250 law firms consisted of more than 150 lawyers.

The 1990s saw an increased democratization of the practice of law, which may have resulted in the first increase in the percentage of sole practitioners in forty years. The percentage of lawyers in private practice rose from 68 percent in 1980 to 74 percent in 1995, even as the number of lawyers increased to 858,000. That growth was driven by a disproportionate increase in the number of sole practitioners, who in 1995 constituted 47 percent of all private practice lawyers. The advent of *computerized legal search services during the 1980s and 1990s slowly altered the informational advantage enjoyed by large law firms. Although proprietary legal search services were too expensive for many sole practitioners and small firm lawyers during the 1980s, those services, along with other services found on the Internet, became economically accessible to most sole practitioners during the 1990s. The reduction in the disparity of access to legal information, the relatively low cost of electronic communication technology, the rise of the price of legal services at large law firms, the weakening bonds of loyalty among partners at large law firms, and the growing dissatisfaction with the quality of life available to lawyers working in large law firms have all made the option of small firm and sole practice attractive.

Many sole practitioners remain legal generalists who serve a variety of legal needs of individuals. Many other sole practitioners are specialists, either by type of practice or by type of client, and those practitioners serve both individuals (in areas such as criminal defense, bankruptcy, elder law, family law, and personal injury) and institutions (in areas such as tax law, health law, and labor law). The ratio of sole practitioners to practicing lawyers since 1980 has remained stable despite predictions of the end of the sole practitioner. The evidence suggests that both the generalist and the specialist sole practitioners are likely to remain a significant part of the American legal profession.

[See also Legal Practice, Forms of]

• Alfred Z. Reed, *Training for the Public Profession of the Law*, 1921. James Willard Hurst, *The Growth of American Law: The Law Makers*, 1950. Jerome E. Carlin, *Lawyers on Their Own*, 1962. John P. Heinz and Edward O. Laumann, *Chicago Lawyers: The Social Structure of the Bar*, 1982. Richard L. Abel, *American Lawyers*, 1989. Robert L. Nelson et al., eds., *Lawyers' Ideals/Lawyers' Practices: Transformations in the American Legal Profes-*

sion, 1992. "Know the Law: A History of Legal Specialization," *South Carolina Law Review* 45 (1994): 1003–61. Joel P. Bennett, ed., *Flying Solo: A Survival Guide for the Solo Lawyer*, 2d ed., 1994. Clara N. Carson, *The Lawyer Statistical Report: The U.S. Legal Profession in 1995*, 1999.
—Michael Ariens

SOLE PROPRIETORSHIP. *See* Business Organizations.

SOLICITOR GENERAL. The solicitor general of the United States is a political appointee who serves as the chief practicing appellate lawyer for the national government. The solicitor general is responsible for most litigation involving the government as a named party before the U.S. *Supreme Court. The solicitor general also decides whether the United States will file an amicus curiae brief in Supreme Court cases where the government is not a party to the suit. When the government loses a case at the trial level, the solicitor general is also responsible for authorizing further litigation before an appellate court other than the Supreme Court.

Modeled after the English tradition of the king's solicitor, the position of solicitor general was established by the Judiciary Act of 1870 in response to increased governmental litigation following the Civil War and a growing dependence on private counsel that became quite costly. As of January 2001, there have been forty-one solicitors general. Of these, five became justices of the Supreme Court (William Howard *Taft, Charles Evans *Hughes, Robert H. *Jackson, Stanley Reed, and Thurgood *Marshall), while others were, before and after, legal scholars in the academic community (Francis Biddle, Charles Fahy, Archibald Cox, Erwin Griswold, and Robert Bork, for example).

The Office of the Solicitor General is managed like a small law firm with four deputy solicitors general, seventeen staff attorneys, and a professional support staff. The workload is significant in terms of the number of cases the office handles, as well as the substance of the subject matter of the litigation. For the October 1999 Supreme Court term, the Office of the Solicitor General prepared and filed briefs in over 250 cases at the petition stage, participated as a named party in 28 cases decided on the merits, and filed twenty-four amicus curiae briefs. Research has shown that the government's presence in a case serves as a cue to the Court in selecting cases for review. Moreover, the solicitor general is unusually successful at all stages of litigation.

The solicitor general plays an important role for both the Court and the executive branch. As an officer of the Court, the government's attorney serves as a gatekeeper in identifying important cases for the justices and presenting well-reasoned legal arguments that are often incorporated into the Court's decisions. That the justices recognize the solicitor general's expertise is boldly evident when they invite the office to file an amicus brief at the petition stage of litigation. But the solicitor general is also an integral member of the executive branch and helps in shaping the Administration's policy agenda by both selecting cases that will further the political goals of the White House and by presenting legal arguments that coincide with the ideological predilections of the president. While typically viewed as an independent member of the Department of *Justice and rarely subjected to direct partisan pressures, the solicitor general is chosen on the basis of personal ideology as well as legal expertise, and ultimately is subject to the directions of the *attorney general. As a result, the solicitor general works across the blurred constitutional borders of the executive and judicial branches, balancing the rule of law with the motives of partisan politics.

• Charles Fried, *Order and Law*, 1991. Rebecca Mae Salokar, *The Solicitor General: The Politics of Law*, 1992. Stephen S. Meinhold and Steven A. Shull, "Policy Congruence Between the President and the Solicitor General," *Political Research Quarterly* 51 (June 1998): 527–37.
—Rebecca Mae Salokar

SOLICITORS. *See* Legal Practice, Forms of.

SOVEREIGNTY. The term "sovereignty" expresses the idea that there is a supreme power somewhere in the political community, as well as implying the idea that this final authority is somehow limited. This paradox of sovereignty is captured in the original French where *souverain* implies simultaneously something above, superior, or supreme with respect to others of its kind in terms of rank; and something that excels, surpasses, or is better than others of its kind in terms of worth. When applied to a monarch, the second aspect of the term took on a distinctly moral connotation. The king as sovereign was supposed to be both supreme in power and morally of the highest order. The model for a sovereign was God, who was omnipotent and at the apex of the moral order. A monarch worthy of the title was supposed to be a stand-in for God on Earth, which combined his secular supremacy with the need that he be limited by God's law since God was the true sovereign. A popular sovereign would, properly speaking, also need to be highly moral.

Origin. Published in 1576, Jean Bodin's *Six Bookes of a Commonweale* contains the first systematic analysis of sovereignty in western political thought. However, that there must be a supreme power somewhere in the political community was generally taken for granted by most political theorists before Jean Bodin. The problem addressed by sovereignty is as old as politics. Every system of rule rests on some method of legitimating the ruler as well as some pattern of accountability that the ruler observes. It is in this observation of a pattern of accountability that legitimate rule has always been distinguished from mere political power. Historically, the concept of sovereignty has been used by those who sought to buttress older forms of legitimation and accountability as well as by those who have hoped to justify new means for converting power into authority. Whenever we encounter pre-Bodin discussions in which there is an attempt to marry supreme power with institutions and practices that limit the operation of that ultimate power we are in the presence of a discussion about sovereignty.

Aristotle captured the paradoxical double thrust of sovereignty in his inclination to ground the limits on supreme power in some transcendent order. He suggested that superiority in the political community should be vested in the rational principle embodied in laws handed to men by the gods rather than in any person or persons in the community. Aristotle's formulation, as codified by Cicero in the idea of *natural law, became the standard formulation until supplanted by the modern positivist view of lawmaking. Aristotle's view supported the idea that law is found, not made, and thus the sovereign is automatically limited by this higher law. Christianity would gloss this position by declaring God the one and only true sovereign, so that His representative(s) on Earth were always bound by His will. Aristotle's approach also stands as a precursor to constitutionalism since a community organized around an effective but limited supreme power is the essence of constitutionalism.

The idea of sovereignty implicit in Aristotle was worked out institutionally in the ancient Roman Republic. Under the Republic all magistrates enforced the law in the name of the *populus Romanus*. In the same way, *imperium* denoted a power to rule conferred by the Roman people on specific individuals who then became public officials in the service of the people. By making the various magistrates creatures of the *populus Romanus,* the Roman Republic effectively declared

the people as a whole to be sovereign. Every magistrate had at least one other person with an equivalent title or similar power. There were, for example, two consuls, four praetors, two quaestors, multiple aediles, and two tribunes. Since the various civic powers were divided between at least a dozen people, no one agent of the *populus Romanus* could claim supreme power. At the same time, the *populus* who signified supreme power was itself circumscribed in ways that are in line with the limits implied by sovereignty. For example, the law in republican Rome was not supposed to rest on the will of the people, but on the higher morality, which Cicero identified as the natural law. This subservience of the people's will to a higher law was expressed and supported both culturally and institutionally. In sum, the Roman Republic, while it remained a republic, was profoundly constitutional, and the effective use of an implicit doctrine of sovereignty stood at the center of its constitution.

Bodin's Definition. Medieval Europe was dominated by the struggle for sovereignty between the Pope and Holy Roman Emperor, a struggle that took place in the context of the "Two Sword Theory." The Two Sword Theory was an attempt to implicitly preserve the unified singularity that sovereignty requires, while reflecting the reality that two different men arguably had what could be termed "sovereignty." The legal fiction rested upon both men being subservient to God's will, who was the true sovereign, and thus the Pope and Holy Roman Emperor were only agents of the sovereign. A long, complicated process during the fifteenth and sixteenth centuries produced both empires and nation-states in Europe. Jean Bodin and Hugo Grotius were instrumental not only in codifying sovereignty, but also in codifying it primarily in terms of nation-states. As a result, although the concept of sovereignty does not require a nation-state, today we inevitably link the two.

Bodin described sovereignty as viewed from inside the political system, whereas Grotius described it as viewed from outside the political system. From the inside, sovereignty is experienced as a limited supreme power, whereas from the outside sovereignty is experienced primarily in terms of supreme power limited only by the ability to project that power. The study of international relations, which focuses on the external interaction of states, necessarily ignores the limited aspect of sovereignty, just as in the current historical context it tends to make sovereignty an attribute only of nation-states. As an external attribute of a nation-state, sovereignty refers to the ability to maintain internal order within a delimited geographic area, to speak for that order, and to exclude foreign powers from interfering with that internal order. Sovereignty is thereby usually linked with the successful maintenance of geographical boundaries, which is itself a characteristic of a nation-state. Thus, for example, the long-standing three-mile offshore limit to a nation's "sovereignty" was predicated upon the standard, effective range of coastal defenses. More modern, missile and aircraft-based defenses have resulted in the convention of a two-hundred-mile offshore boundary for defining the limits of a nation's sovereign space.

Bodin says "Majesty or Sovereignty is the most high, absolute, and perpetual power over the citizens and subjects in a Commonweale." "Majesty" and "sovereignty" are treated as equivalent terms, an equivalence that is pregnant with implications. Majesty is rooted in the Latin term *majestus*, which was used in classical Rome to signify the power and dignity of the people, especially with respect to offenses against it. *Majestus* was the primary attribute of the *populus Romanus*, and was thus the Latin equivalent of the modern term sovereignty as Bodin correctly puts it. This supreme power, he says, can be discovered by tracing back grants of power to the entity that stands behind them all. Those who speak of parliamentary sovereignty, for example, would need to remember that since any parliament worth the name has its power from the people who elect and can unelect it, the people in a parliamentary system are de facto sovereign regardless of the legal fiction. By the same token, the pre–Civil War debate in America over state sovereignty was really over the relationship between a national people and state peoples, since neither state nor national governments were understood to be sovereign under the prevailing understanding of popular sovereignty.

Bodin declared there was no natural designate of God's sovereignty. Sovereignty lay with whomever could successfully claim they possessed the essential character of sovereignty—a power that is "most high, absolute, and perpetual." Whoever can enforce their claim is sovereign, but the sovereign can "put in trust," "pawn," "loan," or "lease" the execution of sovereignty to some agent or agents who act under the authority of the sovereign. The agent(s) has absolute power, it does not have "most high and perpetual power." Bodin thereby draws a distinction between the holders of sovereignty and the executors of sovereignty. In his terms, although the terms "parliamentary sovereignty" and "state sovereignty" are acceptable uses of the term, his admonition to trace back grants of power leads in both the British and American contexts to the true sovereign, the people. There is always, Bodin says, a covenant, compact, or agreement of some sort at the beginning of each regime, and the terms, conditions, or content of this original agreement is crucial. Thomas Hobbes, John Locke, and Jean-Jacques Rousseau are in this way prefigured. There are reasons why a people might want to completely alienate their sovereignty, and primary is the notion that we are better off with some supreme power, no matter its nature, than with none at all, which prefigures one of the dangers in sovereignty exemplified in Hobbes' *Leviathan*.

A Twenty-First Century View. With a robust concept of popular sovereignty we can view a mixed regime, *federalism, and *separation of powers in Bodin's terms. In each case we push beyond the multiple executors of sovereignty to the entity that is "most high, absolute, and perpetual," the people. The people are now viewed as a single entity created by a covenant, a single entity that is the "greater force," and thus the ultimate power. The people, through the constant and endless replacement of members as individuals die and new individuals are born, are perpetual, thus satisfying one of Bodin's key requisites for a sovereign. And finally, the covenant as *constitution creates a self-limiting people with all of the necessary characteristics of a true sovereign. This popular sovereign can then distribute pieces of its power to a variety of agents acting in its name. Institutions like separation of powers, mixed government, and federalism are like multiple pipelines of power sent to various agents acting in the name of the popular sovereign.

Part of Bodin's overall theoretical contribution was to emphasize that the most fundamental characteristic of a sovereign was the ability, some said the right, to make laws. If a sovereign establishes a commonweale, and a commonweale is defined by a set of citizens governed by a common set of laws, then the requirements for a common set of laws determines the necessary characteristics of a sovereign. A sovereign must be a single entity, or there will be conflicting laws. A sovereign must be absolute in the sense of having no competitor or the laws will not be enforceable. A sovereign must be perpetual or the laws will be mutable and therefore unstable and unpredictable. A sovereign must be limited or there will be no laws, since there will be nothing beyond the sovereign's changing, capricious will.

[*See also* Governance; States' Rights]

• Charles E. Merriam, *History of the Theory of Sovereignty since Rousseau*, 1900. Hans Kelsen, *General Theory of Law and State*, 1949. Bertrand de Jouvenal, *Sovereignty: An Inquiry into the Political Good*, 1957. Jean Bodin, *Six Books of a Commonweal*, 1962. F. H. Hinsley, *Sovereignty*, 1966.   —Donald S. Lutz

SPACE LAW, as a discipline, came into existence in 1951 with the publication of an article by John Cobb Cooper of Princeton's Institute for Advanced Study. Entitled "High Altitude Flight and National Sovereignty," the article explored the legal issues presented by spaceflight. Cooper asked, as did other authors, whether national sovereignty would extend to outer space, making orbiting spacecraft trespassers when they crossed national borders, and whether the first nation to reach the Moon would be able to claim that body as its national territory.

Though Cooper's article seemed absurdly visionary at the time, humans were to walk on the moon in fewer than twenty years. By the time they did so, many of Cooper's questions had been answered by the developing body of *international law of outer space. More recently, space law has expanded into domestic regulatory law, governing private companies that launch rockets and operate satellites for profit.

International Law. Coming as it did in the middle of the Cold War, the dawn of the space age created two major fears. The first was that space might become an arena for expanded military conflict, with nuclear bombs stationed in orbit, ready to be dropped at short notice on those below. The second was that a scramble for territory and resources in space, akin to the scramble for African colonies in the late nineteenth century, might increase tensions to the point where they would touch off a nuclear war on earth.

These issues were addressed by the 1967 Outer Space Treaty. In addition to addressing a number of important issues regarding liability, registration of spacecraft, and treatment of stranded astronauts, the Treaty had two major provisions. Article II provided that outer space would not be subject to "national appropriation," meaning that nations could not claim the Moon or other celestial bodies as national territory. And Article IV provided that nations could not place nuclear weapons or other weapons of mass destruction in orbit or on celestial bodies. The provision was drafted this way so as to permit ballistic missiles, which pass through space but do not enter orbit.

The Outer Space Treaty prohibited national appropriation, but not private *property rights. The 1979 Moon Treaty sought to ban private property rights in outer space, and to subject any resource extraction to international controls. Although that treaty is now in force, its signatories include no space powers, making its impact minimal. At present, although national appropriation is forbidden, private claims to space resources remain possible. This is likely to become an issue of importance by the second decade of the twenty-first century, as private space missions grow more ambitious and more capable.

Domestic Space Law. Beginning with the 1984 Commercial Space Launch Act, the United States actively encouraged the development of commercial space launch industries: that encouragement was strengthened after the *Challenger* explosion led to the retirement of the space shuttle as a launch vehicle for commercial cargoes. Subsequent statutes expanded the range of activities considered appropriate for the private sector, such as remote sensing (satellite imagery), expanded communications and positioning satellites, and space tourism.

Private space activities are regulated by the Federal Aviation Administration under the auspices of its Associate Administrator for Commercial Space Transportation. That office regulates space activities in order to ensure safety and to ensure that the international obligations of the United States are met.

The Discipline. Though once primarily an academic subject, space law is now a recognized area of legal practice, with its own journals, bar association sections, and law firms. Hundreds of lawyers now practice in the field, and space law is taught at more than thirty law schools and several nonlegal institutions such as the U.S. Air Force Academy. Like admiralty law, space law is a legal discipline organized around the needs of an industry with a small but enthusiastic corps of practitioners. Its ranks are likely to grow substantially.

[*See also* Governance]

• John Cobb Cooper, "High Altitude Flight and National Sovereignty," *International Law Quarterly* 4 (1951): 411. Nathan Goldman, *American Space Law: International and Domestic*, 1989. Glenn H. Reynolds and Robert P. Merges, *Outer Space: Problems of Law and Policy*, 2d ed., 1998.   —Glenn Harlan Reynolds

SPECIALIZATION, LEGAL. *See* Lawyers; specific specialties.

SPECIAL PROSECUTOR. *See* Independent Counsel.

SPECIFIC PERFORMANCE is a nonmonetary *remedy for breach of *contract, common in land

and unique movable *property purchase cases, which puts the plaintiff in the position accorded him or her in the defendant's promise.

—David S. Clark

SPEECH AND THE PRESS, FREEDOM OF. Freedom of speech and the press is perhaps the best-known principle of American law. The First Amendment epitomizes the limitations placed on government by the *Bill of Rights. Jurists and philosophers expend much ink debating the principle's foundation and scope, and controversies about the meaning and scope of free speech and a free press continue to occupy the courts and the public arena. American constitutional principles of free speech, as they have developed over more than two hundred years, have had a marked influence on the constitutionalism of other countries and on the conception of international *human rights.

Freedom of speech assumed its modern cast as a result of developments in seventeenth- and eighteenth-century England, from which the United States derived most of its legal and political forms. The problems of religious toleration informed the famous disquisitions on free thought of John Locke and John Milton, as did the problem of seditious libel (criticism of the government). In his *Commentaries*, William *Blackstone announced the doctrine that prior restraints—licensing and censorship schemes that required submission of a writing to a government censor before publication—were impermissible, although subsequent punishment of "pernicious" publications remained available. This "prior restraint" doctrine, seemingly libertarian in its censure of licensing schemes but unlibertarian in its approval of subsequent punishment, exerted an important influence on American law until its decisive rejection in the twentieth century.

The Seventeenth and Eighteenth Centuries. Issues of free speech and a free press figured episodically during the colonial and Revolutionary eras. As is amply demonstrated by the banishment of Anne *Hutchinson and Roger Williams from Massachusetts Bay Colony and by the *Salem witch trials, freedom of belief (and therefore of expression) was not a primary value even among the religious dissenters who had founded the colony. Eventually, disputes over secular political speech—the right to criticize government—broke out in the colonies. The most celebrated instance was in 1735, when, in a blow for expressive freedom, a jury acquitted John Peter *Zenger of the charge of seditious libel in publishing a newspaper critical of the authorities in the colony of New York. While freedom of speech was not specifically mentioned in the Declaration of Independence, it is clear that the habit of free political expression, exemplified by the numerous political pamphlets that appeared in the colonies beginning in the 1760s, had an enormous influence on revolutionary ideology.

The devotion to free speech, however, is always purer among dissenters than among those in power. The *Constitution of 1787 was amended in 1791 by the addition of the Bill of Rights, including the First Amendment. Nevertheless, the governing Federalists enacted the *Sedition Act of 1798. Prosecutions carried out pursuant to this law attempted to punish critics of the Adams administration for their (sometimes vituperative) attacks. The adoption and clumsy application of these laws aroused such an outcry that they became a permanent symbol of the failed elitism of the Federalists, and of the importance of free speech.

The Nineteenth Century. Freedom of speech and the press played a lesser role in nineteenth-century American politics, but it did emerge in the context of the *slavery issue. The House of Representatives, controlled by southerners and others sympathetic to slavery, in the 1830s adopted a notorious "gag rule" forbidding consideration by that body of any petitions that requested antislavery measures. The federal government banned abolitionist literature from the mails, a fate that also befell literature advocating free love and reproductive freedom under the "Comstock laws" later in the century. At the local level, fervent opponents of slavery were frequently subjected to violent reprisals for their antislavery agitation. Free speech and a free press, usually understood today as a limitation on government action, in the nineteenth century probably suffered more from vigilante justice and private ostracism than from government actions.

The Twentieth Century. Numerous other actors besides the U.S. Supreme Court—legislators, presidents, scholars, political activists and agitators of every stripe, and even persnickety litigants of no great personal attractiveness—have played important roles in the development of ideas about free speech. The constitutions of all fifty states incorporate their own free-speech principles. But the Supreme Court assumed the leading role in explicating free-speech jurisprudence beginning in the late 1910s, when American entry into World War I raised as a national issue the problem of political dissent in wartime. When the United States criminally prosecuted individuals who dissented from the nation's war policy, the Supreme Court was faced for the first time with the task of giving meaningful content to the strictures of the First Amendment. In a series of opinions handed down in 1918, Oliver Wendell *Holmes Jr. coined the famous "clear and present danger" test in upholding the government's prosecutions. Holmes's enigmatic formulation suggested that, while the First Amendment seemed to speak in absolute terms, the Court would uphold any punishment of speech that reasonably could be thought to lead to harmful consequences, such as disruption of the war effort. This gave the government virtual *carte blanche* to punish dissidents.

The government campaign to stamp out radical dissent, and the Court's validation of these actions, helped galvanize greater public awareness, particularly among political liberals, about the dangers of repression and the importance of free thought and expression. While the Court continued to uphold federal and state government prosecutions of political dissenters for their speech through the 1920s, Holmes (joined by fellow Justice Louis D. *Brandeis) adopted a more libertarian position. In a 1919 case involving the twenty-year prison sentence of several foreign-born anarchists for their role in distributing leaflets advocating an end to the war, Holmes dissented from the majority's upholding of the convictions, arguing that there must be a true "marketplace of ideas" predicated on the freedom to speak. Amidst the illiberal decisions of the 1920s was a ruling that would have important libertarian consequences: in 1925, the Court ruled that the First Amendment, by way of its *"incorporation" through the *Fourteenth Amendment, applied to the acts of the states as well as to those of the federal government.

In the 1930s and 1940s, totalitarianism abroad cast new light on the dangers of government repression. The Supreme Court adopted a far more protective interpretation of the First Amendment. One of the most dramatic decisions of this period was a 1943 case in which the Court, at the height of the American public's commitment to winning World War II, struck down as unconstitutional the requirement of the West Virginia public school board that students salute the American flag each morning.

In the late 1940s and 1950s, the United States witnessed its most sustained crisis of civil liberties with the onset of the Cold War and the pervasive fear of communist influence. Numerous free-speech cases came before the Supreme Court as a result of this fervor, including the government's prosecutions of officials of the American Communist Party, restrictions imposed on labor union officials suspected of communist affiliation, and disbarment of lawyers and dismissal of public school teachers by state and local governments. The Court, while never validating wholesale the more illiberal government measures during this period, retreated somewhat from the libertarian jurisprudence it had created during the previous decades. Not until the *civil rights movement of the late 1950s and 1960s—when spirited protests, rallies, and public advocacy provided free expression with a face more palatable to political liberals than that of communist advocacy—did the Court restore a more protective free-speech jurisprudence. In an important 1964 decision, the Court reversed a libel judgment against the *New York Times* and in favor of a southern sheriff who claimed to have been defamed by an advertisement in the *Times* protesting the treatment of civil rights protesters by southern law-enforcement authorities. With this decision, the Court effectively established the primacy of free speech and a free press in criticism of the government. In 1969 the Court issued an opinion virtually ruling out all statutory attempts to criminalize seditious or subversive speech.

In the last thirty years, the number and variety of free-speech problems presented to the courts have multiplied exponentially. Historically, free-speech jurisprudence in the United States was forged in the image of the persecuted political dissenter, but such subversive advocacy is no longer at the center of the free-speech docket. Rarely today does the government seek to punish speech that criticizes it. More common is the case in which the government acts in a way that either directly or incidentally places some burden on free speech, although the government's own motivation is not principally the suppression of ideas. The following sections cover just a small fraction of free-speech issues of current importance.

Content and Viewpoint Discrimination. "Content discrimination" by the government—a law that singles out for regulation or prohibition speech on a particular topic—is strongly disfavored by the Supreme Court and is upheld only after demonstration of a compelling interest by the government. Thus, for example, the Court in 1990 struck down a federal law forbidding the burning of the American flag, which appeared to the majority of the Court to single out for punishment a particular expressive act. (The repeated and, thus far, unsuccessful efforts to submit to the States a *constitutional amendment reversing this decision is one of the few occasions on which the general public has concerned itself with issues of free speech.) Even more suspect from the Court's perspective is so-called "viewpoint discrimination," in which the government regulates speech on one side of an issue but not on another. The concepts of content and viewpoint discrimination are elusive and erratically applied, but the Court has often relied on them in distinguishing valid from invalid regulations of speech.

Methodology: Categorization versus Balancing. The Supreme Court has sometimes taken a "categorical" approach to scrutinizing government action that burdens speech, holding that certain types of speech by their very nature are unprotected by the First Amendment or are entitled to limited protection under it. This approach is preferred by some libertarians because, by limiting the unprotected types of speech to a finite set of categories, one can maintain the strict protection given to the protected categories. By contrast, a "balancing" approach, in which the Court simply weighs in an individual case the importance of permitting the speech against the government's interest in regulating it, can over time vitiate the importance of the free-speech principle. The categorical approach is at work in the Court's view that such types of speech as defamation, "obscenity," and "fighting words" lie outside the First Amendment.

Obscenity and Pornography. From the late 1950s through the early 1970s, the Supreme Court wrestled, with almost comic fractiousness, with the problem of government efforts to prosecute vendors and users of "obscene" materials, such as sex magazines and films. In 1973 the Court established a standard permitting states and localities to regulate and punish the sale or use of such materials if the jury in an individual case found such materials to violate "community standards" of decency and to lack redeeming artistic, literary, political, or scientific value. This decision assumed that the free-speech problem was one of weighing the injury to public morality against the public interest in making available materials with redeeming social or artistic value. In the 1970s and 1980s, however, feminist theorists devised a critique of "pornography" and a theory of its regulation by the state that distinguished it from traditional conceptions of "obscenity." Under this theory, pornography is not merely an insult to community standards of morality but is also sex discrimination, a violation of the civil rights of women, who are portrayed in dehumanizing ways. This theory has not been accepted by the courts,

and in 1986 the Supreme Court summarily struck down an Indianapolis anti-pornography ordinance embodying it (see MORALS OFFENSES).

Racist Speech and Hate Speech. In 1942 the Supreme Court held that abusive speech or "fighting words" fell outside any category of protected speech and thus raised no constitutional problems when punished. A decade later, confronted not with face-to-face abusive speech but with so-called "group defamation"—a local pamphlet using racist terms to urge citizens to resist "black aggression"—the Court narrowly upheld a state "group libel" ordinance punishing such speech. This decision seemed out of tune with the generally libertarian decisions of the Court during the 1960s. In the 1980s and 1990s, however, the problem of racially motivated "hate speech" received a sharper critique from scholars and activists, who pointed out the devastating and exclusionary effects such speech could have on those against whom it was directed. This development was prefigured in the late 1970s when the American Nazi Party successfully petitioned for a permit to march through the streets of Skokie, Illinois, a community with a large Jewish population, including concentration camp survivors. While the local courts upheld the Nazi Party's right to obtain such a permit on First Amendment grounds, the incident raised serious questions about an absolutist approach to regulating speech that might not merely be "offensive" to listeners but cause significant psychological distress. In the 1990s such issues came before the courts more frequently as states, localities, and public educational institutions began to adopt rules and ordinances prohibiting or punishing "hate speech"—usually, speech directed in a hostile or hurtful manner toward racial minorities, women, and homosexuals.

The question of regulating hate speech presented a dilemma for traditional liberals, who had long associated themselves with both civil libertarianism and the rights of women and minorities. The Supreme Court has come down firmly against government attempts to protect minorities by the enactment of hate speech ordinances. In 1992 it struck down under the First Amendment an ordinance in St. Paul, Minnesota, under which several teenagers had been prosecuted for placing a burning cross in the fenced yard of a black family. This decision suggests that the current Court has not accepted the argument that the harm associated with the use of abusive speech against minorities justifies such ordinances.

Commercial Speech. In a capitalist society, a free-speech principle inevitably confronts the question of speech (such as paid advertising) that appears to consist of commercial information or to be motivated by profit or both, rather than the archetypal "political" or "literary" expression. In the early 1940s, the Supreme Court resolved the problem of reconciling free speech with state power to regulate *commercial activity by simply defining "commercial speech" as outside the protection of the First Amendment. Today this distinction between commercial speech and political speech is widely seen as untenable, and the Court's more recent decisions have recognized that a great deal of seemingly commercial expression conveys information of great consequence, not only to *consumers as consumers but to the public as an ingredient of their knowledge of public affairs. At the same time, false or misleading information can sometimes lead to great harm if unregulated. Thus, the federal government's regulation of cigarette advertising and labeling of food and drug products has been held to be consistent with the First Amendment, but state bans on advertising of lawyers' services, the prices of prescription drugs, and availability of abortion services have been struck down. Today the Court is more likely to regard *regulation of economic or commercial information not as a salutary protection of the consumer but as a suspect intervention by the government into the marketplace in order to direct consumers' choices.

Free Speech and the Electoral Process. Why do we have a free-speech principle at all? The most consistent and durable motif in the Supreme Court's free-speech opinions in the twentieth century is that free speech is vital to the nation's democratic politics, and not simply a protection of the individual. The notion that a rigorous free-speech principle finds its strongest justification in the integrity of the political process has led some to ask whether, in a society where inequalities of wealth and power render some voices louder than others, speech might not at times have to be curtailed or regulated in order to preserve a genuine "marketplace of ideas." Of particular importance is the question of campaign finance reform. In 1976 the Court struck down part of a major congressional campaign finance law. The act had limited the amounts of both individual contributions to political campaigns and individual expenditures on behalf of a candidate. The Court struck down the limitations on expenditures but upheld those on contributions, reasoning that individual, independent expenditures (but not contributions) were a basic form of political expression and that Congress's asserted interest in diminishing the appear-

ance of corruption was not sufficient to justify the restriction. Significantly, the Court declared that "the concept that government may restrict the speech of some elements of society in order to enhance the relative voice of others is wholly foreign to the First Amendment." Critics have derided the Court's decision as establishing the principle that "money is speech," although the Court was undoubtedly correct that there is *some* important element of political expression in individual expenditures. The Court's distinction for constitutional purposes between contributions and expenditures has contributed to a Byzantine structure of campaign financing that has ultimately done nothing to reduce the role of money in politics.

Freedom of the Press. Much of the foregoing discussion on free speech is applicable also to freedom of the press; many of the seminal free-speech cases were actually press cases, involving the right of the press to publish vituperative criticisms on matters of public interest. But some First Amendment issues are particular to the press, because "the press" is the only nongovernment institution specifically recognized in the Constitution. The press is not constitutionally exempted from generally applicable legal duties and burdens, such as taxation. But, in the area of reportorial investigation, may a reporter subpoenaed by a grand jury refuse to reveal her sources (a privilege not available to other citizens)? The Court held in 1972 that a reporter may not do so, despite arguments that protecting the identities of confidential sources may sometimes be crucial to the press's carrying out its investigative and "watchdog" functions. On the whole, the Court has resisted the notion that the press *as an institution* has special exemptions not available to other citizens or businesses.

In other contexts, the press has fared better. The law of libel has been liberalized considerably from the days in which the publication even of truthful revelations could subject a newspaper to civil or criminal *liability if such revelations harmed a person's reputation without "good cause." It is now the plaintiff's burden in a libel proceeding to establish the falsity of any defamatory statements. More important, the Supreme Court has ruled that, where the subject of the publication is a "public figure"—one in whom the public legitimately has an interest, such as a political officeholder—that person can win a libel judgment only by demonstrating that the defendant published the defamatory material with knowledge of its falsity or "reckless disregard" of its possible falsity. Some have argued that the very existence of libel law is an affront to the First Amendment, and, despite the slow liberalization of libel law, the prospect of expensive libel litigation frequently "chills" the tone and content of publications.

Information Technology. Technologies of communication have changed so profoundly that traditional images of the press have become anachronistic models on which to found a free-press jurisprudence. The sheer size of newspapers (many of them owned by media conglomerates) and television networks has prompted many to worry that inequality of access to these all-powerful media organizations stultifies and skews our public debate. At the same time, the advent of the Internet and inexpensive wireless and cable transmission has made entrée into that debate available to almost anyone with a personal computer. In the 1960s, when television viewers in most communities were served at best by the three major networks and one or two local stations, the Federal Communications Commission applied a "fairness doctrine" (upheld by the Supreme Court), requiring television stations to grant equal time to opposing viewpoints when matters of public interest were ventilated. By the 1980s, with the proliferation of cable stations and the partial demise of the "spectrum scarcity" argument that had justified the fairness doctrine, this policy seemed anachronistic and was replaced. (The Court had declared in 1974 that such a state-compelled "right-of-reply" or "equal access" law violated the First Amendment when dealing with newspapers, for which no such argument about spectrum scarcity argument could be made.)

The Internet is the most rapidly changing medium of communication. The most pressing legal issues arising from this new *technology revolve not around the newsgathering and reporting enterprises of the traditional *media but around such issues as *privacy, the availability of sexually explicit materials on the Web, and the property rights of those whose copyrighted material can be more easily pirated than ever before. In 1997 the Court struck down Congress's attempt, in the Communication Decency Act, to criminalize the knowing transmission of sexually explicit materials to minors over the Internet. Similarly, in 2000 it struck down Congress's requirement that cable operators scramble, during certain hours, channels that featured sexually explicit programming. Efforts to regulate these rapidly changing media of communication will clearly generate free-speech and free-press issues for years to come.

[See also Property, Intellectual]

• Alexander Meiklejohn, *Free Speech and Its Relation to Self-Government*, 1948. Thomas I. Emerson, *The System of Freedom of Expression*, 1970. Fred W. Friendly, *Minnesota Rag: The Dramatic Story of the Landmark Supreme Court Case That Gave New Meaning to Freedom of the Press*, 1981. Frederick F. Schauer, *Free Speech: A Philosophical Enquiry*, 1982. Leonard W. Levy, *Emergence of a Free Press*, 1985. Harry Kalven Jr., *A Worthy Tradition: Freedom of Speech in America*, 1988. C. Edwin Baker, *Human Liberty and Freedom of Speech*, 1989. Edward de Grazia, *Girls Lean Back Everywhere: The Law of Obscenity and the Assault on Genius*, 1992. Catharine A. MacKinnon, *Only Words*, 1993. Mari J. Matsuda et al., *Words That Wound: Critical Race Theory, Assaultive Speech, and the First Amendment*, 1993. David M. Rabban, *Free Speech in Its Forgotten Years*, 1997. Michael Kent Curtis, *Free Speech, "The People's Darling Privilege": Struggles for Freedom of Expression in American History*, 2000.
                                              —Clyde Spillenger

SPEEDY TRIAL. *See* Fair Trial, Criminal.

SPORTS LAW is not a body of substantive law in the traditional sense: it consists instead of two separate but related fields of study. First, it is the study of the way many various substantive bodies of law (such as *contracts, *antitrust, *labor law, constitutional law, *torts, intellectual *property, business enterprises law, etc.) that were created in a much broader social or business context apply and interface with one another in the unique context of the sports industry. Second, it is several "bodies of law" and *"legal systems" that have been privately created, each within a sports organization, to govern the relationships and operation of that entity. An explanation and some illustrations will clarify the nature of sports law.

The sports industry, with its great variety of sports and organizational models for governing each, is one of the most unusual industries in the economy. While the "product" is a form of entertainment characterized by athletic competition, that competition on the field or court must be regulated and governed so that it is honest, played within a defined set of rules, and reasonably balanced so that the outcome is not predetermined. This produces a subculture in which many of the normal rules by which society and economic activity are governed do not sensibly apply. The first prong of sports law is the study of how these normal rules must be adapted and applied to this subculture.

To illustrate, it is difficult to apply tort and *criminal law principles that seek to deter violent physical contact to a subculture in which violent physical contact is either an inherent part of the game or is often an unavoidable occurrence. It is difficult to apply traditional labor law principles that encourage trade unionism and uniform treatment of workers in order to prevent economic exploitation to an industry where the "workers" each vie in a highly competitive marketplace to negotiate their own individual salaries that make them the highest paid unionized employees in the world. It is difficult to apply traditional antitrust principles that condemn agreements among separate businesses to increase market power to an industry where a natural monopoly league of wholly integrated but separate teams is a prerequisite to the making of the product in the first place. Similar gaps between the social and economic institutions for which traditional bodies of law were designed, and the reality of sports organizations, can be cited in every substantive area of sports law.

The diversity of the analytical inquiry necessary to study sports law can be demonstrated by the five sports law cases that the U.S. Supreme Court heard during the 2000–2001 term. *The PGA Tour* v. *Martin* involved two issues related to the application of the Americans With Disabilities Act (ADA) to sports governing bodies: (1) whether the field of players in a professional golf tournament constitutes a "place of public accommodation," so that the ADA applies to the body that governs the tournament, and (2) by what standard should the courts judge whether allowing participating golfers to ride in an electric cart rather than walk the course, as the rules require, would constitute a fundamental change in the nature of the sport. *Brentwood Academy* v. *Tennessee Secondary Schools Athletic Association* raised the issue of whether an association that sets rules for the conduct of all high school athletics in a state is a "state actor," so that its rules are subject to free speech, freedom of religion, due process, equal protection, and privacy challenges under the U.S. Constitution. *Cleveland Indians Baseball Co.* v. *United States* involved the income tax question of whether damages payments made by a professional baseball team because it unlawfully underpaid players in violation of its collective bargaining agreement are to be assessed ancillary employment taxes for the year in which the income should have been earned by the players or in the year in which the damages were actually paid. Provisions of the ADA, the Constitution, and the Internal Revenue Code were all triggered in such complex ways, because of the unique context presented by the sports industry, that the Supreme Court had to step into the case. *Major League Baseball Association* v. *Garvey* addressed

the standards of review that a court should use in hearing an appeal from an arbitrator's decision. Finally, *Cedrick Kushner Promotions* v. *Don King* involved whether an individual boxing promoter could personally be sued for unlawful racketeering for conduct carried on under the rubric of a wholly owned corporation.

This is not to suggest that there are no statutes or *common law doctrines targeted specifically for sports. There is the Sports Broadcasting Act of 1961, 15 U.S. Code §§1291–1295, which gives sports leagues an express antitrust exemption for pooling the member teams' television rights if sold for "sponsored telecasting." There is the Curt Flood Act of 1998, 15 U.S. Code §27, that expressly applies the antitrust laws to the rules of Major League Baseball governing major league players. This statute was the outgrowth of several Supreme Court decisions determining that the antitrust laws did not apply to the business of baseball, which was neither interstate nor commerce. There are statutes in twenty-eight states that regulate the business of athlete-agents. There are statutes at both the state and federal level that regulate the business of boxing. There is the Ted Stevens Amateur Sports Act, 36 U.S. Code §§373 et seq., that establishes the structure for the governance of all Olympic sports in the United States. There are other examples. But this body of sport-specific law is scattered and not comprehensive. The laws that govern sports are overwhelmingly laws of general application that must be tailored to the unique circumstances of sports. Sports law in its first incarnation is largely the study of this process.

The second prong of sports law is the study of the various bodies of privately created "laws" and legal systems, each of which governs one sport or sports entity. These private legal regimes include constitutions and bylaws establishing the various leagues and governing bodies (such as the NFL, the PGA Tour, the International Olympic Committee, and the NCAA), collective bargaining agreements between leagues and their players' certified collective bargaining representative, and agent-certification regulations established by the various professional sports unions. A detailed body of law has grown up that relates solely to the article in the NFL's collective bargaining agreement that establishes the maximum amount teams may spend on player costs in a given year (the "salary cap"), and sets the penalties for violation. The same is true for the system of salary arbitration in Major League Baseball and the National Hockey League. The complex set of rules, and the internal mechanisms for interpreting them established in the NCAA's bylaws, is perhaps the most prominent example of such a private system of law, all of which is encompassed under the rubric of this second prong of sports law.

[*See also* Entertainment Law]

• Gary A. Uberstine, ed., *Law of Professional and Amateur Sports*, 1988. Michael J. Cozzillio and Mark S. Levinstein, *Sports Law*, 1997. Paul C. Weiler, *Leveling The Playing Field: How The Law Can Make Sports Better For Fans*, 2000. Ray Yasser, James R. McCurdy, C. Peter Gopplerud, and Maureen A. Weston, *Sports Law*, 4th ed., 2000. Paul C. Weiler and Gary R. Roberts, *Sports And The Law*, 2d ed., 1998, with 2001 Supplement.

—Gary Roberts

SPOUSAL SUPPORT, also called alimony or maintenance, is a post-divorce obligation of a person to provide economically for his or her former spouse. Support is usually paid periodically, often monthly; lump-sum support orders are permitted in some jurisdictions. The need of the recipient and the payer's ability to pay are the primary criteria for determining when spousal support is awarded and in what amount. Marital fault may be considered in awarding spousal support in almost half the states. However, because both "need" and "ability to pay" are far from objective standards, spousal support awards vary greatly from jurisdiction to jurisdiction and even from case to case. Relatively few former spouses, less than 20 percent of the total, have ever been awarded spousal support.

Alimony was originally developed by the English ecclesiastical courts as part of the law of legal separation, which authorized spouses to live apart because of the serious marital fault of one of them. Because legally separated spouses were still married, a husband was still legally obliged to support his wife unless the separation was her fault. When American jurisdictions began to allow full *divorce, they used the fault-based grounds and the alimony principles that had been developed in the context of legal separation.

When fault divorce was replaced by no-fault divorce in the 1970s, spousal support lost its foundations. No-fault divorce is based on the idea that marital breakdown is ordinarily a complex process rather than the result of one spouse's misconduct. Therefore, the goals of the new divorce regime were to end failed marriages with civility and, to the extent possible, to end all personal and economic ties between the former spouses. These goals, in conjunction with the increasing acceptance of the ideal of *gender equality, implied that both spouses should become equal and independent social and economic actors after the divorce. Nevertheless, the divorce reformers recognized that in some circumstances the economic disparity between the former spouses would be so great or the needs of one spouse would be so apparent that some form of spousal support needed to be available. The law in most states at this time disfavored alimony and allowed it only when necessary to provide for a spouse incapable of self-support and only long enough to allow that person to become economically independent. During the 1970s and 1980s a number of states enacted statutes that limited the duration of spousal support awards, and the majority of court orders for spousal support in this period were for a limited duration. During this same time the Supreme Court ruled that a traditional spousal support law, which only authorized courts to order former husbands to pay support to former wives, violated *equal protection, in part because it was based on outdated gender stereotypes (*Orr* v. *Orr* (1979)).

Less than ten years after the beginning of the no-fault divorce revolution, critics began to argue that the revolution had caused economic disaster for the women and children of divorce. One of the most prominent critics was Lenore Weitzman, who argued in *The Divorce Revolution* (1985) that no-fault divorce caused the poor economic plight of women, because it reduced their power to bargain for favorable divorce settlements and gave judges more discretion, which they exercised to women's disadvantage. Although later studies undermined Weitzman's claims about the relationship between divorce grounds and the post-divorce economic position of men and women, no one doubted that, in general, women and children suffered economically after divorce.

Increased awareness about the economic consequences of divorce led many to reconsider the clean-break theory of divorce that had seemed so attractive in the 1970s. Reformers argued that marriage can have lasting economic consequences for former spouses that are often unequal. In many marriages today, spouses still adopt gender-based roles that affect their ability to earn money in the market. Wives still do the majority of the home and child care, which does not bring them wages or skills that are readily transferable to well-paid market work, and husbands are still the primary breadwinners in many families and so develop their market skills. When the parties separate, a spouse who has worked in the market is likely to be more capable of self-support than one who has devoted significant effort to homemaking. In addition, the homemaker spouse is more likely to have the primary care of children after the divorce, which further limits her ability to earn money in the marketplace.

These arguments form the basis for the reexamination of spousal support. Realizing that most divorcing couples do not have enough property to provide support for dependent spouses and children, lawmakers and scholars have developed a new theory of spousal support. This theory provides for the more economically capable spouse to compensate the other for contributions to the family and to the payer's career, as well as to help the recipient enhance her workplace skills. The arguments for ordering spousal support more often and in greater amounts have not gone unanswered. Spousal support obligations can severely limit the choices and opportunities of payers, since few workers earn enough money to support two households comfortably. Those who believe that spousal support should not be routinely awarded point out that much of the difference in the earning capacity of men and women results from wage discrimination in the workplace, not roles in marriage. Further, they argue, even if spouses did assume very different roles during the marriage, it is likely that the two agreed to this arrangement, making it less clear that one should compensate the other for lost opportunities when the marriage ends. Still other opponents argue against the new support theory because they believe that it encourages women to become economically dependent.

Even if the compensation theory of spousal support becomes widely accepted, questions remain about how much impact it will have. The theory is more likely to support the claims of spouses who have been married for a long time than of those married for only a short while. However, most marriages that end in divorce are of short to medium duration. Of all divorcing couples, 63 percent have been married for less than ten years and only 12 percent for twenty years or longer.

[See also Family Law]

• National Conference of Commissioners of Uniform State Laws, Uniform Marriage and Divorce Act, 1973, § 308. Marygold S. Melli, "Constructing a Social Problem: The Post-Divorce Plight of Women and Children," American Bar Foundation Research Journal (1986): 759. Mary Ann Glendon, The Transformation of Family Law: State, Law, and Family in the United States and Western Europe, ch. 5, 1989. National Center for Health Statistics, Department of Health and Human Services, Monthly Vital Statistics 43, no. 9, suppl. (22 Mar. 1995). American Law Institute, Principles of the Law of Family Dissolution: Analysis and Recommendations, Proposed Final Draft Part I, ch. 1, 5; 1997. Leslie J. Harris and Lee E. Teitelbaum, Family Law, ch. 5, 2000.

—Leslie J. Harris

SPOUSE. See Divorce and Annulment; Domestic Violence: Partner Abuse; Family Law; Homosexuality and the Law; Marriage; Spousal Support.

STALKING. See Harassment.

STATES' RIGHTS is the doctrine that the American states retain constitutionally protected authority that can be exercised free of federal interference, or even in the face of conflicting federal claims. Asserted in response to the elastic concept of federal power, according to which Congress can legislate in any area of law or policy by finding a "necessary and proper" rationale relating to the Commerce or Taxing and Spending Clauses, "states' rights" has been more often a political doctrine than a judicial doctrine. Anchored in the Tenth Amendment's declaration that "The powers not delegated to the United States by the Constitution, nor prohibited by it to the States, are reserved to the States respectively, or to the people," and implicit in the equal representation of the states in the Senate and the states' role in ratifying *constitutional amendments, states' rights remains a perennial issue in American constitutionalism, though not always under that name.

"States' rights" was the rallying cry of the Jeffersonians. In his First Inaugural Address, *Jefferson promised "the support of the State governments in all their rights, as the most competent administrations for our domestic concerns and the surest bulwark against anti-republican tendencies." Before the Civil War, opposition to the *Sedition Act, to the national bank, and to federal efforts to restrict the institution of *slavery was couched in states' rights. The most serious use of the doctrine was to justify independent state authority to interpret the *Constitution, and even to resist contrary assertions of federal authority. This included the purported right to interpose state *sovereignty and to nullify unconstitutional federal statutes, and even to secede from the Union if the constitutional compact was deemed broken, and therefore void. The issue of *secession having been settled on the battlefields of the Civil War, the states' claims of independent authority became for a time a matter of constitutional law rather than one of political assertion. In the late nineteenth and early twentieth centuries, the Supreme Court occasionally struck down federal legislation that it thought exceeded the powers of Congress though usually in the name of protecting the states' police powers rather than their rights. With the expansion of congressional power in the New Deal, and the accompanying "Constitutional Revolution" in judicial doctrine, states' rights seemed eclipsed by pragmatic *federalism, which at once diminished the role of the states and insisted on seeing federal-state relations as a matter of political negotiation, not constitutional right. The use of the old rhetoric of states' rights by defenders of state *segregation statutes in the 1950s and 1960s further discredited the doctrine. Nevertheless, in a series of cases decided by a bare majority in the 1990s, the Supreme Court has again protected states' sovereign immunity from federal lawsuits and states' *legislative and *executive powers from federal commandeering. The Court has stressed the independence of the states, and restricted the scope of federal authority. Whether this new judicial federalism, with its moderate recognition of states' sovereign rights, survives or is abandoned remains to be seen.

• Forrest McDonald. *States' Rights and the Union: Imperium in Imperio, 1776–1876*, 2000.

—James R. Stoner Jr.

STATUTE OF FRAUDS. The defining feature of the act, which appeared in 1677, is the requirement of a writing signed by the party against whom enforcement is sought (known as "the party to be charged"). Statutes of frauds (many jurisdictions have more than one) usually arise in the context of real estate conveyances, *wills, and, importantly, certain classes of *contracts. Numerous exceptions to the Statute of Frauds have developed since its inception. These exceptions, coupled with relentless academic criticism, have served to diminish but not eliminate the scope and effect of the statute.

[*See also* Probate]

—Dennis M. Patterson

STATUTORY RAPE. *See* Sex Offenses.

STONE, HARLAN FISKE (born Chesterfield, N.H., 11 October 1872; died Washington, D.C., 22 April 1946). He was a legal educator, lawyer, associate justice (1925–41), and chief justice (1941–46) of the U.S. *Supreme Court. Stone was the single university professor ever to serve as chief justice and, like Democrat Edward White, one of only two chief justices appointed by a president from a different party. Republican President Calvin Coolidge first appointed Stone associate justice; Democrat Franklin Roosevelt el-

evated the Republican Stone to the chief justiceship.

Stone's legal career developed along two paths. Perhaps the most important was his service in the legal academy, culminating with his appointment as dean of the Columbia Law School in 1910. Stone remained in that position until 1923. As a law professor, Stone wrote as an active law reformer on rights of *trust beneficiaries, bankers' duties, and specific performance of *contracts. As dean, Stone's most important legacy was building a strong research faculty and defending the rights of free *speech by professors and socialists. At the same time, Stone had a secondary career as a practicing corporate lawyer with the firm of Sullivan and Cromwell, whose department of litigation he headed from 1923 until his appointment in 1924 as attorney general under Secretary Calvin Coolidge.

As an associate justice, Stone dissented vigorously, along with Justices Louis D. *Brandeis, Oliver Wendell *Holmes Jr., and Benjamin N. *Cardozo, against the Four Horsemen, a group of justices that routinely objected to Roosevelt's New Deal measures. Stone's dissents proceeded from three basic principles. First, he believed that the Constitution gave the appropriate level of government the power to govern. Second, he insisted that the power to govern had to change to meet changing conditions, a point he made emphatically in *Morehead* v. *New York ex. Rel. Tipaldo* (1936). Third, and finally, when a matter of constitutional doubt arose about the power of government to remedy economic problems, that doubt had always to be resolved in favor of the legislative branch and not the courts. By the late 1930s, Stone's dissents were becoming the law of the land.

As chief justice, Stone moved his colleagues away from issues of economic regulation and toward matters of *civil rights. Indeed, despite his brief service as chief justice (the briefest since 1801), Stone began the process of developing the affirmative implications of Footnote 4 of his most famous opinion, *U.S.* v. *Carolene Products* (1938) and led the effort to abolish the all-white primary (*Smith* v. *Alwright* (1944)). When *executive powers collided with civil liberties during World War II, Stone was usually a defender of the latter. Nevertheless, Stone did uphold the punishment of Americans of Japanese ancestry for disobeying curfew laws (*Hirabayashi* v. *United States* (1943)) and their banishment to concentration camps (*Korematsu* v. *United States* (1944)) (see JAPANESE INTERNMENT).

Stone urged the justices to reason cases out at length, a technique markedly different from his predecessors. Greater discussion, however, produced more dissent and increased judicial backbiting on the bench, neither of which Stone was able to alleviate. Indeed, high levels of dissent on the modern Court date from Stone's tenure as chief justice.

• Herbert Wechsler, "Mr. Justice Stone and the Constitution," *Columbia Law Review* 46 (1946): 764. Alpheus T. Mason, *Harlan Fiske Stone: Pillar of the Law,* 1956.

—Kermit L. Hall

STORY, JOSEPH (1779–1845), *Supreme Court justice, political advisor, law professor, and legal scholar. Story absorbed nationalism and a dedication to public service from his parents, Elisha Story, a physician, and Mehitable Pedrick, the daughter of a merchant. He graduated second in his class in 1798, read law under Samuel Sewell, a future chief justice of Massachusetts, and was admitted to practice in 1801.

Story served in the Massachusetts House of Representatives (1805–1808, 1811) and the U.S. Congress (1808–1809). In 1810 Story successfully argued the Yazoo land case, *Fletcher* v. *Peck*. Nominated to the Supreme Court by President James Madison on 15 November 1811 and confirmed on 18 November, the thirty-two-year-old Story was the youngest person ever placed on the Court.

On the Court he was an ally of John *Marshall, supporting judicial nationalism and an expansive reading of the *Constitution while opposing *states' rights. Story found implied powers throughout the Constitution, declaring in a circuit court opinion in *United States* v. *Brainbridge* (1816) that "whenever a general power to do a thing is given, every particular power necessary for doing it is included." Story persistently argued for extensive federal powers and sought to create general federal question jurisdiction for the U.S. courts as well as a federal *common law for criminal, civil, and admiralty cases. In his first few years on the Court he tried unsuccessfully to create a federal common law in admiralty, diversity, and criminal cases. In *Swift* v. *Tyson* (1842), however, Story gained the support of the Court to create a general federal common law for civil *procedure and *commercial litigation. *Swift* allowed all entrepreneurs in the nation relatively clear certainty about how contracts and commercial notes would be interpreted in the federal courts. The case remained viable law until 1938.

Story's first important attack on states' rights was in *Fairfax Devisee* v. *Hunter's Lessee* (1813), where he used the Supremacy Clause to reverse a Virginia decision that violated American treaties with Britain. When the case came back to the Court as *Martin* v. *Hunter's Lessee* (1816), Story presented his greatest statement of federal supremacy, arguing that under Section 25 of the Judiciary Act of 1789 the Supreme Court was the final authority in interpreting the Constitution in disputes between the states and the federal government. Here Story denounced states' rights, pointing out that the Constitution was not created "by the states in their sovereign capacities, but emphatically, as the preamble of the Constitution declared, by 'the people of the United States.'" Story reminded Virginia, and the nation, that the Constitution was "to endure through long lapses of ages," and therefore had to be interpreted with flexibility to provide for the "exigencies of the future."

In *Prigg* v. *Pennsylvania* (1842), Story tied his attacks on states' rights to his strong nationalism, as he upheld the constitutionality of the Fugitive Slave Law of 1793. Story also created a common law right of recaption for masters seeking fugitive slaves. Although personally opposed to *slavery, Story wrote this proslavery decision in *Prigg* in order to nationalize power over fugitive slave rendition. His striking down Pennsylvania's personal liberty law in *Prigg* dovetailed with his desire to strengthen the national government at the expense of states' rights. Story hoped to prevent the free states from interfering in the return of fugitive slaves, which Story feared would then lead to southern hostility towards the Union. To achieve these goals Story was willing to accept the possibility that some free blacks might be illegally enslaved under the 1793 law or the common law right of recaption that he found in the Constitution. Story's nationalism, as well as his personal distaste for slavery, led him to vigorously enforce the federal laws for the suppression of the African slave trade.

In addition to his numerous circuit court opinions, Story wrote 268 majority opinions for the Supreme Court. But, he rarely wrote opinions in the most important cases because throughout his career Story served under two very strong chief justices, John Marshall and Roger B. *Taney.

In his concurring opinion in *Dartmouth College* v. *Woodward* (1819), Story provided extra intellectual support for Chief Justice Marshall's opinion, while articulating modern notions of the role of *corporations and their relationship to the government. Story's dissents in *Briscoe* v. *Bank of the Commonwealth of Kentucky* (1837), *Mayor of New York* v. *Miln* (1837), and *Charles River Bridge* v. *Warren*

Bridge (1837), reflect his initial disagreements with Chief Justice Taney and Jacksonian Democracy.

By 1839 Story was once again able to exert enormous influence on the Court. He wrote the Court's opinion in the politically sensitive case, *United States* v. *Amistad* (1841), which involved international relations (with Spain) and the illegal African slave trade (1842).

Story's nonjudicial activities—as political actor, legal scholar, and law professor—by themselves would have made him a major figure in American legal history. He was a close confidant of Daniel *Webster. Story colluded with Webster in developing a strategy for bringing *Dartmouth College* v. *Woodward* to the Supreme Court. Story lobbied for judicial and political appointments of friends and proteges and was in constant contact with members of Congress, often sending them drafts of legislation. His draft of a federal *criminal law became the basis for the Federal Crimes Act of 1825. While service on the bench normally precludes political activity, in 1820 Story won election to the Massachusetts Constitutional Convention and in 1836–37 he served on a state commission to consider a *codification of Massachusetts law. He served on two Harvard boards but never recused himself from cases involving Harvard, like *Charles River Bridge* (1837), or cases involving other organizations he was involved in.

Story was also the nation's most important and prolific legal scholar and the major professor at Harvard Law School, where he helped train a generation of new lawyers. By training lawyers and writing legal treatises that argued for constitutional nationalism and the perpetuation of conservative legal and economic values, Story clearly hoped to counter Jacksonian democracy, and the rise of southern politicians who advocated states' rights, and the anti-nationalist sentiments of the president and his followers.

Before joining the Court he published works, including *A Selection of Pleadings in Civil Actions* (1805), that helped "Americanize" the common law. His most important book was his three-volume *Commentaries on the Constitution of the United States* (1833), which provided an intellectual basis for his judicial nationalism. He also wrote or edited more than ten other treatises and commentaries on such legal topics as *conflict of laws, *equity, and bailments. In 1840 he published a one-volume edition of the *Commentaries*, entitled *A Familiar Exposition of the Constitution*. Attorneys throughout the nation, unable to get even recent reports of the cases, relied on Story's *Commentaries* for their understanding of the law. In these writings, even more than in his court opinions, Story shaped the development of American law. As the Dane Professor at Harvard Law School, Story permanently altered the institution. In 1828 only one student registered for the University's law program. The following fall Justice Story helped attract 28 new students. By 1844 Harvard, under Story, was the premier law school in the nation, and one that was truly national with 156 students from twenty-one states. Story used his professor's podium to instill a sense of constitutional nationalism in his students.

In 1843 Story was too ill to sit with the Court—the only time in his judicial career that he was absent. Story returned for the 1844 term, but was ill and unhappy. He planned to resign as soon as a successor could be named, but he became ill and died on 10 September 1845.

[*See also* Constitutional Commentators; Educator, Legal]

• William Wetmore Story, *The Life and Letters of Joseph Story*, 2 vols., 1851. Roscoe Pound, "The Place of Judge Story in the Making of American Law," *American Law Review* (1914): 676–97. Gerald T. Dunne, *Justice Joseph Story and the Rise of the Supreme Court*, 1970. R. Kent Newmyer, *Supreme Court Justice Joseph Story: Statesman of the Old Republic*, 1985. Paul Finkelman, "Story Telling on the Supreme Court: *Prigg* v. *Pennsylvania* and Justice Joseph Story's Judicial Nationalism," *Supreme Court Review* 1994 (1995): 247–94.   —Paul Finkelman

STRICT LIABILITY. Imposed, in *tort law, even if the defendant did not intend to cause harm and acted with reasonable care. Its most significant use is in products *liability.

[*See also* Fault Liability]

—Jay M. Feinman

STRIKE. *See* Labor Law: Labor Relations.

SUBROGATION. *See* Insurance.

SUICIDE. *See* Medicine and Law.

SUIT. *See* Complex Litigation; Litigiousness; Procedure, Civil.

SUMMARY JUDGMENT is the early resolution of part or all of a civil action on the basis of either party's pretrial motion offering to show the judge by affidavits or other evidence that there is no genuine issue as to any material fact, so that the applicant is entitled to a *judgment as a matter of law.

[*See also* Procedure, Civil]

—David S. Clark

SUMMONS, SERVICE OF. *See* Procedure, Civil.

SUMPTUARY LEGISLATION. *See* Morals Offenses.

SUNSET LAWS. A sunset law is a statute or provision in a statute that requires periodic review of the rationale for the continued existence of that particular law, administrative agency, or other governmental function. The U.S. Congress sometimes specifies an end date when it establishes federal agencies or programs. If an affirmative decision is not made to continue to support an agency or program, then the "sun sets" on them and they are automatically terminated.

The process of sunsetting is a legislative solution to the problem of "legal obsolescence," a term used to describe the reduced usefulness or applicability of a statute, regulation, or agency. An automatic sunset provision ensures that a regulation remains in place only if it is justified and necessary.

The sunset process is unique in that it mandates that the regulation or agency end on a specified date unless the legislature determines the regulation or agency is useful and necessary by reenacting the legislation. The burden of proof is on those persons seeking reenactment and not on those seeking its repeal.

Congress has not passed a government-wide sunsetting statute. Although it passed a large number of sunset provisions in the late 1970s, following the post-Watergate antigovernment sentiment that was prevalent throughout the country. Congress passed the "Sunset Act of 1977," however, it was never signed into law. Congress made another attempt at passing sunset legislation in 1995, titled the "Regulatory Sunset and Review Act of 1995," but it failed as well.

Laws become obsolete for a number of reasons. First, some laws are created in response to particular problems or crisis. Once the problem no longer exists, or the crisis has passed, the law becomes obsolete. Second, particular problems with laws may not manifest themselves for decades. Third, some laws become obsolete in today's world of international competition and fast-moving technology.

Sunset laws were adopted in thirty-six states in the late 1970s and early 1980s. These laws vary in terms of types of entities and programs covered by the law, the source of staff to conduct reviews, the responsibility for overseeing the conduct of reviews, and the responsibility for managing sunset bills in the legislature. A number of states have repealed their sunset statutes since then, because of the time and money involved in the review process, among other issues.

[*See also* Governance]

• Guido Calabresi, *A Common Law for the Age of Statutes,* 1982.
                                                    —Sandra F. Chance

SUNSHINE LAWS. Although government openness is essential in a democracy, neither the First Amendment nor the *common law has been interpreted as requiring access to American government meetings. In fact, James Madison excluded the public from meetings deliberating the First Amendment itself. Thus, public meeting or "sunshine" laws must define meetings, describe exemptions, and provide remedies for violations.

The 1976 Government in the Sunshine Act (5 U.S.C. sec. 552b) complements the federal *Freedom of Information Act in requiring about fifty agencies, including the Federal Communications, Federal Trade, and Securities and Exchange commissions, to meet in public. Since passage of the 1972 Federal Advisory Committee Act (5 U.S.C. App. sec. 1), advisory boards have also been required to hold public meetings.

Under the Sunshine Act, agencies must publish in the *Federal Register,* at least one week in advance, the time, place and purpose of a meeting, along with any plans for closure (exclusion of the public). Seven of the ten exemptions parallel those of the FOIA, including national security, administrative rules, statutory exemptions, trade secrets, personal *privacy, law enforcement, and financial issues. Additionally, closure is allowed for investigations of individual criminal activity or censuring of individuals, certain financial matters, and discussion of litigation or arbitration.

Any portions of meetings from which the public is excluded should be followed with publication of results of any votes taken. And although the law allows the public to observe meetings not exempted, nothing in the law mandates public participation.

According to the U.S. *Constitution (Art. I, sec. 5), although both houses of *Congress must publish records of meetings, they may decide which sessions are open: most sessions of both the House and Senate are public. The House voted in 1995 to open most meetings, and Senate rules require openness unless a majority votes for closure. Both chambers allow coverage of their open meetings by C-SPAN.

SUPREME COURT OF THE UNITED STATES   771

A few states include access requirements in their constitutions, and all fifty have passed sunshine laws. However, definitions of "meeting" vary, from any meeting of two or more to only those with a quorum. Virtually all states allow closure for "executive sessions," with exemptions some times found in laws other than the state sunshine law. Closure may be allowed for discussions of land acquisition, personnel matters, or pending litigation. Most states exempt their legislatures from sunshine laws, although some state constitutions require openness of legislative sessions.

Some citizens have expressed dissatisfaction with the enforcement of sunshine laws. Anyone can sue a federal agency that violates the Sunshine Law, but there are no penalties for violators, and violations do not invalidate action taken in closed meetings. Some state laws provide for criminal or civil remedies as well as for invalidation of actions taken in secret; prosecution of violations, however, is expensive and time consuming.

Several organizations, including the Reporters Committee for Freedom of the Press and the Society of Professional Journalists, keep people informed of public record and sunshine law cases. In addition, the National Freedom of Information Coalition funds public-access projects.

[See also Governance; Speech and the Press, Freedom of]

• Reporters Committee for Freedom of the Press, *Tapping Officials' Secrets*, 1997 (updated on the Internet at *www.rcfp.org*). Sandra Chance, "Access to Public Documents and Meetings," in Wat Hopkins, ed., *Communication and the Law*, 2001, 327–43.

—S. L. Alexander

SUPREME COURT OF THE UNITED STATES. The U.S. Supreme Court and the power of *judicial review together are one of the greatest yet most controversial contributions of the *Constitution. Article 3 of the Constitution simply provides that, "The judicial Power of the United States, shall be vested in one supreme Court, and in such inferior Courts as Congress may from time to time ordain and establish." That power was not further defined because the framers' experience was too limited and the power of judicial review did not exist in England.

The framers also differed over the role of the Court. Some, like James Wilson, anticipated the exercise of judicial review—the power to strike down any congressional or state legislation or other official government action deemed inconsistent with the Constitution and federal law. By con-

trast, Alexander Hamilton, in *The Federalist*, No. 78, claimed that the judiciary was "the least dangerous branch" since it had "no influence over either the sword or the purse."

Chief Justice John *Marshall (1801–35) provided the classic justification for judicial review in *Marbury v. Madison* (1803). There, a section of the Judiciary Act of 1789 was struck down as inconsistent with Article 3. Chief Justice Marshall reasoned that the Constitution, as provided in the Supremacy Clause of Article 6, is "the supreme Law of the Land;" that judges take an oath to uphold the Constitution; and therefore they must authoritatively interpret the Constitution and enforce only those laws pursuant to it. Since *Marbury*, the power of judicial review has grown in both score and frequency. The Court has exercised judicial review over acts of *Congress about 150 times, invalidating some 956 congressional statutes, and it has struck down 1,068 state and local laws.

Institutional Development. The power of the Court has grown with the changing business coming before it and with its institutionalization as a coequal branch. In its first decade, the Court had little business, frequent turnover in personnel, no chambers, and no fixed customs or institutional identity. When the Court initially convened, only Chief Justice John *Jay (1789–95) and two other justices arrived at the Exchange Building in New York City. When the capital moved from New York City to Philadelphia, the Court met in Independence Hall and in the Old City Hall for ten years, until the federal government moved to its permanent home in Washington, D.C. Most of the first justices spent their time riding circuit, for the Judiciary Act of 1789 required them twice a year to hold circuit court in the company of district judges (see COURTS, UNITED STATES: FEDERAL COURTS).

Although the national capital moved to Washington, D.C. in 1801, no courtroom was provided. Between 1801 and 1809, the justices met in the basement of the Capitol. In 1810, they shared the Orphans' Court of the District of Columbia, but the British destroyed it in 1814 and for two years the Court met in a tavern. In 1817, the Court moved back into the Capitol and finally in 1819 returned to its restored courtroom, where it met for almost half a century.

Along with the Court's move into the Capitol, John Marshall assumed the chief justiceship. He established regularized procedures and a tradition of collegiality. By making certain the justices roomed in the same boardinghouse, he turned the disadvantage of transiency into an opportunity for achieving unanimity in decision-making, and thereby promoted the Court's legitimacy. After a day of hearing oral arguments, the justices would dine together and then discuss cases.

After 1860, the Court met upstairs in the old Senate Chamber but the justices still had no offices or staff. Following the Civil War, the caseload steadily grew and the Court's terms were lengthened to accommodate the increasing workload. The justices also began holding conferences on Saturdays to discuss and vote on cases, with announcements of decisions on Mondays.

By the twentieth century, the justices resided in the capital and largely worked at home, where each had a library, a messenger, and a secretary. The Court's collegial procedures had evolved into institutional norms based on respect for each justice's independence and on decision-making by majority vote. Chief Justice William Howard *Taft (1921–30) lobbied Congress for the construction of a building for the Court. Nonetheless, when the building that now houses the Court was completed in 1935, none of the sitting justices moved in. Upon his appointment in 1937, Justice Hugo L. *Black was the first to move in and the other appointees of President Franklin D. Roosevelt (FDR) followed. Even when Harlan Fiske *Stone was elevated by FDR from associate to chief justice (1941–46), he continued to work at home. The Court under Chief Justice Fred Vinson (1946–53) was the first to see all nine justices regularly working in the building.

The "marble palace," as the Supreme Court's building is often called, stands for more than a symbol of the modern Court. Once again, the institutional life of the Court changed. The building buttressed the Court's prestige and reinforced the norms of secrecy, tradition, and collegiality that condition the work of the Court. The justices continued to function independently, like "nine little law firms." But the work of the Court gradually grew more bureaucratic. Along with the rising caseload in the decades following World War II, the number of law *clerks more than tripled and the number of other employees increased as well.

Law clerks have become central to the work of the modern Court. In 1882, Justice Horace Gray initially hired a "secretary" or law clerk. When Justice Oliver Wendell *Holmes Jr. succeeded him, he continued the practice, and other justices gradually did as well. By Chief Justice Stone's time, each justice had one clerk. During the chief justiceships of Fred Vinson and Earl *Warren (1953–

69), the number increased to two. In the 1970s under Chief Justice Warren E. *Burger (1969–86), the number grew to three and then four per justice. Five justices also began pooling their clerks— in a "cert. pool"—in order to screen cases and receive recommendations on which cases should be granted. All the justices, except for Justice John Paul Stevens, now pool their clerks for screening cases.

The justices have also delegated more opinion-writing to their clerks and incorporated modern office technology into their work. In addition to law clerks, five officers and their staffs assist the justices. The Office of the Clerk collects filing and admission fees; receives and records all motions, petitions, briefs, and other documents; circulates those necessary items to each justice's chambers; and maintains the oral-argument calendar.

There was no official reporter of decisions during the first quarter-century of the Court. Early reporters worked at their own expense and for their own profit. In 1922, Congress established the present arrangement: the Reporter of Decisions has responsibility for supervising the publication of the Court's opinions and writing headnotes or syllabi that accompany each decision.

U.S. marshals preserved order in the courtroom until 1867, when Congress created the Office of the Marshal. The Marshal not only maintains order in the courtroom and times oral arguments but also oversees building maintenance and serves as the business manager for Court employees. The fourth officer of the Court is the Librarian. The justices acquired their first small library in 1832, and in 1948, Congress created the Office of the Librarian, which employs several research librarians to assist the justices with legal research.

Unlike other members of the Court, the chief justice has special administrative duties. Over eighty statutes confer duties ranging from chairing the judicial conference to supervising the Administrative Office of the U.S. Courts to presiding over the Smithsonian Institute. Chief Justice Burger is credited with pushing judicial reforms and bringing Taft's marble palace into the world of modern technology and managerial practices. He also lobbied Congress to create a fifth legal officer of the Court, the Administrative Assistant to the Chief Justice, who has been instrumental to the Court's acquiring computers for use in its work.

The Court also has a public information office, and in 2000, set up a Web site at http://www. supremecourtus.gov, on which opinions are available the same day they are handed down, along with transcripts of oral arguments.

Trends in the Business of the Court. Along with the institutionalization of the Court and the increasing delegation and bureaucratization of its work, four other trends are notable. First, the nature of the business before the Court has changed. During its first decade, the Court had little important business and fewer than thirty cases arrived annually. Over 40 percent consisted of *admiralty and prize cases. About half raised issues of *common law; the remaining dealt with matters like *equity. By the late nineteenth century, though, the Court's business had gradually changed in response to developments in American society. The number of admiralty cases declined sharply and, although about 40 percent of the cases still dealt with disputes at common law or questions of jurisdiction, over 40 percent involved interpreting congressional statutes. That increase in statutory and constitutional interpretation reflected the impact of the industrial revolution and the growing *regulation of social and economic relations. Throughout the twentieth century, the trend continued. About 45 percent of the cases now involve matters of constitutional law and around 38 percent deal with the interpretation of congressional statutes. The remaining cases involve administrative law, *taxation, and practice and *procedure.

Second, the amount of business coming to the Court grew phenomenally. That, in turn, led to an expansion of the Court's discretionary jurisdiction. During most of the nineteenth century, the Court had to decide every appeal that came before it. But that proved problematic as its caseload grew. The Civil War and Reconstruction, both great sources of legal conflict, and the late-nineteenth-century business boom dramatically swelled the docket to 2,000 filings a year.

By the 1880s the Court confronted a growing backlog of cases and Congress provided relief in the Evarts Act of 1891, which created judgeships for the circuit courts of appeals. The act preserved access to the Court by providing, instead of mandatory rights of appeal, for petitions for writs of *certiorari*, which the Court could refuse to grant. For the first time the Court had some discretionary review.

In the early twentieth century, the Court's docket grew again. Economic changes and World War I brought a rash of disputes over war contracts and suits against the government. A large measure of the Court's congested docket was nonetheless due to expanding congressional legislation and regulation. Once again the Court could not stay abreast of its caseload. Chief Justice

Taft campaigned for relief and Congress enacted the Judiciary Act of February 13, 1925, known as the "Judges' Bill." That act further replaced mandatory review of appeals with discretionary review of *certiorari* petitions. At the time, though, Congress remained concerned that important cases might be denied review. Hence, the justices adopted an informal "rule of four"—that is, cases are granted review on the basis of four justices' votes, although the Court operates on a majority vote on all other matters.

After World War II, the Court's business increased yet again. In the 1970s, Congress provided further incremental relief by eliminating still more provisions for mandatory review. Finally in 1988, Congress passed the Act to Improve the Administration of Justice, eliminating virtually all non-discretionary appellate jurisdiction. The only mandatory *appeals that the Court now must review involve reapportionment, some *antitrust matters, and cases under the *Civil Rights and *Voting Rights Acts and the Presidential Election Campaign Fund Act. About 99 percent of the Court's current docket is now discretionary and *certiotari* may simply be denied.

The Court's power to decide what to decide from a very large docket enables it to set its substantive agenda as well. The largest number of cases involve indigents' claims and issues of criminal procedure. Yet, few are granted. Cases raising other issues of constitutional law tend to be selected, as are those involving statutory, administrative, and regulatory matters. The Court functions like a superlegislature in selecting and deciding only cases of national importance; it is not its job merely to correct injustices to litigants in the lower courts.

A third, recent trend under Chief Justice William H. Rehnquist (1986–) has been a sharp decline in the number of cases granted review and, thus, a decline in the Court's supervisory role over lower federal and state courts. In the 1970s and early 1980s the docket was reaching 5,000 cases and between 150 and 185 cases were decided each term. The docket is now close to 9,000, yet the justices decide only about 80 cases a year, or less than 1 percent. That is the same number decided in the 1950s when the docket had not yet reached 2,000.

Even if the Court were to continue deciding as many cases as it did in the 1970s and 1980s, the percentage would decline due to the continued growth in the caseload. Still, the diminished plenary docket is striking and reflects factors both internal and external to the Court. Early in his chief justiceship, Burger expanded the size of the oral-argument calendar in order to accommodate twice as many cases, because of concerns about the Court's declining supervisory capacity. During his tenure, the discipline of the rule of four was also weakened by the emergence of the practice of casting "Join-3" votes—that is, instead of voting to grant or deny, justices voted to "Join-3" and thus provide a fourth vote for granting review, if three others voted to grant. That practice lowered the threshold established by the rule of four. As the Court's composition changed in the late 1980s and 1990s so did the justices' voting practice when deciding what to decide: Join-3 votes became less commonplace and the justices became more tolerant of conflicting lower-court decisions.

In addition, the Act to Improve the Administration of Justice eliminated virtually all nondiscretionary appellate jurisdiction, thereby increasing the Court's "managerial capacity" for controlling the nature and size of the plenary docket. Finally, the *cert.* pool may have contributed because more justices now rely on their clerks' memos on whether cases should be granted. Hence, there is less independent review by the justices and, as Justice Stevens has emphasized, the clerks tend to be "risk averse" when recommending whether cases should be granted review.

Finally, a fourth trend has been the demise of consensual norms. Institutional opinions for the Court's decisions became devalued due to the rise of individual opinions—opinions concurring, dissenting, or both concurring and dissenting in part. Throughout the nineteenth century, there were few separate, concurring, or dissenting opinions. The norm of consensus forged by Chief Justice Marshall remained the established practice throughout the nineteenth century.

That norm broke down in the late 1930s and 1940s with the publication of increasing numbers of individual opinions. Whereas throughout the nineteenth century, opinions for the Court accounted for 80 to 90 percent of all opinions annually issued, the percentage steadily fell, and from 1960 through the 1990s rarely rose above 50 percent of the total number of opinions handed down. When compared to the practice a half century earlier, there are approximately ten times as many concurring opinions, four times more dissenting opinions, and seven times the number of separate opinions.

What explains the rise of individual opinions? In *The Roosevelt Court: A Study in Judicial Politics and Values* (1948), C. Herman Pritchett traced the rise of individual opinions to FDR's nine appointees between 1937 and 1943. Disagreement rates increased and the percentage of opinions for the Court of the total opinions issued plunged and continued to fall for several decades. Why? Simply put, the New Deal justices brought the force of American *Legal Realism and liberal legalism to bear on the Court. FDR's appointees not only constituted a majority but embodied the intellectual forces of a generation of progressive liberals who revolted against the legal formalism of the old constitutional order. Legal realism highlighted the indeterminacy of the law, taught that judges make law, and advocated judicial pragmatism or the balancing of competing values. As a result, consensus became more difficult to achieve, while the premium on justifying the Court's decisions was raised.

Moreover, liberal legalism lacked coherence. On the bench, liberal legalism inherited from Justices Holmes and Louis D. *Brandeis, and perpetuated by FDR's appointees, fragmented the justices. Holmes stood for judicial self-restraint and deference to legislatures, while Brandeis championed progressive legal reform. Although dominating the Court, FDR's justices split into two camps: Justices Felix *Frankfurter, Stanley Reed, and Robert H. *Jackson stood for judicial self-restraint and became more conservative, while Justices Black, William O. *Douglas, Frank Murphy, and Wiley Rutledge pushed toward more progressive judicial activism. These two camps in turn further fragmented over where and how to draw the line between judicial self-restraint and activism in constitutional interpretation. Consequently, they were inclined to articulate their distinctive views in individual opinions.

Later justices, then, were socialized into higher rates of individual expression. By the 1970s, the norm of consensus had effectively been transformed into one of individual expression, which continued during the more conservative Burger and Rehnquist Courts.

The Court and Constitutional Politics in Historical Perspective. The role of the Court has changed with changes in its composition and socioeconomic forces in the country. Along with establishing the power of judicial review, the Marshall Court defended broad powers of the national government in *McCulloch* v. *Maryland* (1819), for example, and promoted a national economic common market by striking down state laws discriminating against the flow of interstate commerce, in cases like *Gibbons* v. *Ogden* (1824). The importance of the Marshall Court in this regard has led to comparisons to the European Court of

Justice's rulings that helped forge a common market in Western Europe in the latter half of the twentieth century. In addition, the Marshall Court reinforced the basis for capitalism by broadly construing the Contract Clause in *Fletcher* v. *Peck* (1810) and *Dartmouth College* v. *Woodward* (1819), among other decisions.

The Taney Court (1836–64) was less nationalistic and more concerned with balancing national and state regulatory powers over contracts and commerce, in leading cases such as *Charles River Bridge Company* v. *Warren Bridge Company* (1837) and *Cooley* v. *Board of Wardens of the Port of Philadelphia* (1852). But, Chief Justice Roger B. Taney remains largely remembered for his infamous ruling in **Dred Scott* v. *Sandford* (1857), holding that blacks could not be citizens of the United States or bring suits in federal courts, and striking down the Missouri Compromise of 1820. That decision damaged the Court's reputation for decades and contributed to the *Civil War. After the Civil War the Court further advanced the doctrine of dual *sovereignty and *citizenship, in the *The Slaughter-House Cases* (1873), as well as limiting the application of the Reconstruction Amendments (the Thirteenth, *Fourteenth, and Fifteenth Amendments), largely returning control over *race relations to the states in *The Civil Rights Cases* (1883).

The late nineteenth and early twentieth century is known as a period of legal formalism and the Court's defense of laissez-faire capitalism against progressive regulation of working conditions and economic relations. By drawing and enforcing formalistic distinctions between "production" and "distribution," and direct versus indirect effects on interstate commerce, the Court curbed congressional and federal regulatory powers in, for example, *United States* v. *E. C. Knight Company* (1895), *Hammer* v. *Dagenhart* (1918), and *Schechter Poultry Corporation* v. *United States* (1935). Although upholding some progressive state laws when deemed to advance public health and the general welfare, often the Court invalidated such laws as protectionist measures for special interests or for running afoul of principles of laissez-faire capitalism. Indeed, the period became identified as "the Lochner era" because **Lochner* v. *New York* (1905) struck down a New York law limiting the hours bakers could work. There, a bare majority held it to violate an unenumerated "liberty of contract" protected by the Fourteenth Amendment's *Due Process Clause.

The confrontation between the Court and Congress reached a "constitutional crisis" in 1937. After his landslide reelection in 1936 and bitter over the Court's invalidation of early New Deal legislation, FDR proposed to increase the number of justices from nine to fifteen, thereby securing a favorable majority. Before the Senate voted on his plan, however, the Court in the spring of 1937 repudiated earlier doctrines in *National Labor Relations Board* v. *Jones & Laughlin Steel Corporation* (1937) and *West Coast Hotel* v. *Parrish* (1937), and thereafter upheld the New Deal, in *United States* v. *Darby Lumber Company* (1941) and *Wickard* v. *Filburn* (1942).

For almost sixty years after the New Deal crisis, the Court upheld Congress's expansive powers in enacting the Civil Rights Act of 1964 and the Voting Rights Act of 1965. The Court also became more protective of claims to individual rights. Most of the guarantees of the *Bill of Rights were incorporated into the Fourteenth Amendment's Due Process Clause and applied to the states. Along with the landmark school desegregation ruling in **Brown* v. *Board of Education* (1954), the Warren Court forged a "reappointment revolution" and a "due process revolution," with rulings such as **Mapp* v. *Ohio* (1961), **Gideon* v. *Wainwright* (1963), and **Miranda* v. *Arizona* (1966). Although the Burger Court became more conservative, it extended the constitutional "right of *privacy," proclaimed in *Griswold* v. *Connecticut* (1965), and in its ruling on *abortion in **Roe* v. *Wade* (1973). The Court also upheld most *affirmative-action programs and extended the *Equal Protection Clause to gender and other nonracial classifications.

In the 1990s, however, a bare majority of the Rehnquist Court, composed of the chief justice and Justices Sandra Day O'Connor, Anthony Kennedy, Antonin Scalia, and Clarence Thomas, limited congressional power in a series of rulings—notably, in *United States* v. *Lopez* (1995), *Printz* v. *United States* (1997), *City of Boerne* v. *Flores* (1997), and *United States* v. *Morrison* (2000). In defending its view of *states' rights and *federalism, the Court also resurrected the Eleventh Amendment to protect states from lawsuits aimed at forcing their compliance with federal law. Affirmative-action programs and the creation of minority-majority voting districts were also made harder to defend. Except for First Amendment freedoms, the Rehnquist Court has proven less willing to recognize new claims to individual rights. It has generally made exceptions to past rulings on the rights of the accused, though reaffirming the constitutionality of the controversial *Miranda* ruling in *Dickerson* v. *United States*

(2000) and in *Planned Parenthood of Southeastern Pennsylvania* v. *Casey* (1992) and declining to overrule *Roe* v. *Wade*.

Judicial Independence and Accountability. Although the framers did not foresee this growth in judicial power, they laid the foundation in providing for judicial independence. Justices are appointed by the *president, after Senate confirmation, and basically hold lifetime tenure. Their salaries may not be diminished and they may be removed only upon *impeachment by the House of Representatives and conviction by a two-thirds vote of the Senate. Justice Samuel *Chase (1796–1811) was the only member of the Court to be impeached and that effort failed to result in a conviction.

Presidents invariably try to infuse their political philosophy into the Court through their appointments. Because vacancies have historically become available about every two-and-a-half years, presidents may influence the direction of the Court, particularly if they make several appointments or fill the seats of pivotal justices. FDR's appointees moved the Court in more liberal directions, while those appointed by Republican Presidents Ronald Reagan and George H. W. Bush pushed the Court in a more conservative direction. Thus, presidents may hold the Court accountable for past decisions through their appointments, though subject to confirmation by the Senate, which has rejected or forced the withdrawal of twenty-eight nominees for the Court.

Scholars differ on how much power the Court wields. Gerald N. Rosenberg, in *The Hollow Hope: Can Courts Bring About Social Change?* (1991), contends that the Court rarely brings about major social changes. Others, like William Lasser in *The Limits of Judicial Power: The Supreme Court in American Politics* (1988), disagree. In the end, the Court's power rests, as Chief Justice Edward D. White (1910–21) observed, "solely upon the approval of a free people."

• Walter Murphy, *Elements of Judicial Strategy*, 1964. Bernard Schwartz, *Super Chief: Earl Warren and His Supreme Court*, 1983. Bernard Schwartz, *A History of the Supreme Court*, 1993. William E. Leuchtenburg, *The Supreme Court Reborn: The Constitutional Revolution in the Age of Roosevelt*, 1995. Lawrence Baum, *The Puzzle of Judicial Behavior*, 1997. Henry J. Abraham, *Justices, Presidents, and Senators: A History of the U.S. Supreme Court Appointments from Washington to Clinton*, 1999. Cornell W. Clayton and Howard Gillman, eds., *Supreme Court Decision-Making: New Institutional Approaches*, 1999. Terri Jennings Peretti, *In Defense of A Political Court*, 1999. Robert G. McCloskey, revised by Sanford Levinson, *The American Supreme Court*, 3d ed., 2000. David M. O'Brien, *Constitutional Law and Politics*, 2 Vols., 4th ed., 2000. David M. O'Brien, *Storm Center: The Supreme Court in American Politics*, 5th ed., 2000.

—David M. O'Brien

SUPREME COURTS, STATE. The state supreme court serves as a state's court of last resort for *appeals in civil cases and criminal cases. Forty-eight states vest this ultimate appellate authority in a single court, denominated the Court of Appeals in Maryland and in New York, the Supreme Judicial Court in Maine and in Massachusetts, and the Supreme Court in all other states. Texas and Oklahoma have divided this authority, establishing a Court of Criminal Appeals, which has final responsibility for appeals in criminal cases, and a separate Supreme Court, which bears that responsibility in civil cases.

The Distinctiveness of State Supreme Courts. State supreme courts differ from the United States *Supreme Court in several respects. One difference involves size. Whereas the U.S. Supreme Court has nine justices, only six states have that large a supreme court. Twenty-six state supreme courts have seven justices, another eighteen courts have five justices, and the Oklahoma Court of Criminal Appeals has only three. A second difference involves the selection and tenure of these justices. Justices on the U.S. Supreme Court are appointed by the president and confirmed by the Senate, and they hold office during "good behavior," which in practice has meant until retirement or death. The states, in contrast, employ a variety of methods for selecting justices, and most justices serve fixed terms—the median is an eight-year term—after which they must be reappointed or reelected. A third difference relates to the workload of state supreme courts. The United States Supreme Court has virtually complete discretion in determining what cases it will hear, which means that it can focus its energies on what it believes are the most important legal issues confronting the nation. However, state *constitutions and state statutes mandate that the state supreme court hear certain types of cases; states that enforce *capital punishment, for example, usually require the justices to review the conviction of any defendant sentenced to death. Whereas the U.S. Supreme Court in recent years has decided fewer than one hundred cases per term, most state supreme courts, partly as a result of their mandatory jurisdiction, have heard more than two hundred cases per year. Collectively, state supreme courts decide more than ten thousand cases annually.

Finally, the issues addressed by state supreme courts differ somewhat from those confronted by the U.S. Supreme Court. The U.S. Supreme Court deals almost exclusively with matters of federal law, whereas state supreme courts deal primarily with matters of state law. (However, state supreme courts also hear cases raising issues of both federal and state law; for example, when a litigant claims that a state law violates her rights under both the federal *Bill of Rights and the state constitution.) In addition, the U.S. Supreme Court for most of the twentieth century focused on cases raising constitutional issues; more than half the Court's cases concern whether federal or state statutes or the actions of public officials have violated the federal Constitution. In contrast, state supreme courts deal with constitutional challenges in a relatively small proportion of their cases. Typically less than fifteen percent of the cases before state supreme courts raise issues under either the state constitution or the federal Constitution. Many of these constitutional cases involve appeals by defendants in criminal cases, claiming that *police officers infringed on their rights in collecting the evidence that led to their conviction or that they did not receive a *fair trial. In most cases, however, state supreme courts are called upon to interpret and apply state statutes and administrative regulations, rather than to assess their constitutionality. These cases can involve important issues, for example, the Florida Supreme Court in the aftermath of the presidential election of 2000 had to determine whether Florida election statutes should be interpreted to require a recount of votes by hand in several counties. State supreme courts are also called upon to elaborate the *common law, that is, to fashion legal standards for resolving disputes in the absence of legislative enactments or administrative regulations. Examples of common-law cases include *tort cases such as *medical malpractice suits and personal-injury suits resulting from defective or dangerous consumer products. Whatever the issue, if a case does not involve federal law, then the state supreme court issues the final and determinative ruling in the case.

Justices and Judicial Selection. The membership of state supreme courts has tended to reflect the composition of the American legal profession. For most of the nation's history, this has meant that justices have been white, male, middle-aged, and middle- or upper-class. However, as the composition of the legal profession has changed, so too have the demographics of state supreme courts. The first woman appointed to a state supreme court was Florence Allen, who served on the Ohio Supreme Court from 1922 to 1933, but it was not until 1958 that another female justice was selected. As of 1980, there were only ten fe-

male justices, but by 1996, there were sixty-six, including four chief justices. The appointment of Judge Sandra Gardebring to the Minnesota Supreme Court in 1991 made it the first supreme court to have a female majority. The racial composition of state supreme courts has also changed somewhat. In 1975, only one African American served on a state supreme court, but by 1996 there were twenty-five. Other groups have also made gains: in 1996, there were six Asian-American and four Hispanic-American justices.

Despite these demographic shifts, the backgrounds of current state supreme court justices resemble those of past justices. Most justices are natives of the state in which they serve, attended law school there, and have been active in state or local politics. This is not altogether surprising: prospective judges who develop good contacts within the state and have been politically active are more likely to secure a seat on the state high court, regardless of the mode of judicial selection in the state.

Currently, states employ five systems for selecting state supreme court justices. In South Carolina and Virginia, the legislature elects the justices. In four states, the governor appoints justices, usually with the advice and consent of the state senate. Nine states elect their justices in partisan elections, and another thirteen states elect them in nonpartisan elections, that is, with no party affiliation indicated on the ballot. Finally, twenty-two states employ what is called merit selection or the Missouri Plan, after the state that first adopted it. Under merit selection, when a vacancy occurs on the state supreme court, a nominating commission, comprised of lawyers selected by the state *bar association and nonlawyers chosen by the governor, submits to the governor a list of three-to-five candidates to fill the slot, and the governor is obliged to appoint a justice from that list. After a short period of service, the justice so selected runs in an uncontested retention election, which allows voters to decide whether or not the justice should remain in office.

These differences in judicial selection tend to follow a regional pattern. Gubernatorial appointment is most common in the Northeast, partisan election in the South, nonpartisan election in the northern tier of states from Michigan to Washington, and merit selection in the rest of the West. Thus, shared political values within regions of the country and the tendency to emulate the laws and institutions of neighboring states explain some of the interstate variation. The interstate diversity also reflects the waves of political reform that have periodically swept the American states. During the late eighteenth century, all thirteen states selected their justices by either gubernatorial appointment or legislative election. Indeed, those states in which legislatures elect justices have retained that system for over two centuries. The presidency of Andrew Jackson (1829–37) ushered in an era of democratic reform, including a move toward election (rather than appointment) of most governmental officials. This movement encouraged states to adopt a system of popular election of justices— by the Civil War, twenty-four of the thirty-four states in the Union had shifted to partisan election, and every state that entered the Union from 1846 to 1912 instituted judicial elections. Most states that currently elect their justices in partisan elections adopted the system during the nineteenth century. During the early twentieth century, however, a new set of reformers—the Progressives—sought to remove judicial selection from politics. They claimed that partisan election prevented the best-qualified persons from serving as justices, because political machines controlled who would appear on the ballot, and that the justices' connections to those political machines undermined their independence. As an alternative, the Progressives advocated nonpartisan judicial elections, arguing that "there is no Democratic or Republican way to administer justice," and they also proposed that sitting justices run unopposed in retention elections, in which voters would determine whether they should remain in office. The thirteen states that elect justices in nonpartisan elections adopted this system during the early decades of the twentieth century. The most recent campaign for reform—spearheaded by the *American Judicature Society, the *American Bar Association, and other legal groups—has championed merit selection of judges. Since Missouri pioneered this system in 1940, twenty-two states have adopted merit selection for state supreme court justices. In recent years, however, this reform movement has lost momentum—from 1980– 2000, only Rhode Island switched to merit selection.

Whether they reach the bench by election or merit selection, given their fixed term of office, most justices must periodically seek reelection in contested or retention elections. Since 1980, elections for seats on the state supreme court have become increasingly contentious and expensive. In some instances, controversial rulings in cases involving the death penalty, the rights of defendants, or abortion have prompted campaigns to oust sitting justices. For example, in 1986 conservative groups in California—incensed by a series of rul-

ings overturning death sentences in murder cases— spent $5 million to defeat Chief Justice Rose Bird and two associate justices in a retention election. More recently, an unpopular vote in a death penalty case cost Justice Penny White her seat on the Tennessee Supreme Court. In other instances, interest groups have supported candidates for state supreme courts that they believed would rule favorably for their clients. A particularly egregious example occurred in Texas: while an $11 billion lawsuit by Pennzoil against Texaco was pending before the Texas Supreme Court, Texaco representatives made campaign contributions totaling $72,000 to members of the court, and Pennzoil's lawyers responded with contributions of more than $315,000 to the justices. In a number of states, groups of *personal-injury lawyers and insurance companies have each lavished financial support on judicial candidates whose views they favored. In the 2000 election, for example, the Chamber of Commerce spent more than $1 million in an unsuccessful attempt to defeat an Ohio justice that it deemed hostile to its interests.

The inflamed rhetoric and extraordinary expenditures found in some recent state supreme court elections underscore a key point: what state supreme courts do matters a great deal. Of particular importance have been state supreme court rulings expanding rights based on state constitutions (known as the "new judicial federalism") and elaborating the common law in cases involving injuries from accidents, consumer products, or medical malpractice (tort law).

State Supreme Courts and the New Judicial Federalism. Since the early 1970s, state supreme courts have increasingly looked to the guarantees found in state bills of rights to develop a body of state law protecting civil liberties (such as freedom of *speech, the right to *privacy, and the rights of criminal defendants) against violation by state and local governments. The emergence of this "new judicial federalism" confirms that state supreme courts can play an important role, independent of the U.S. Supreme Court, in securing liberties. But it also reveals how developments on the Supreme Court affect the rulings of state supreme courts. From the 1930s through the 1960s, the U.S. Supreme Court took a more expansive view of civil liberties than did state supreme courts. This was particularly true during the chief justiceship of Earl *Warren (1953–69), when an activist Supreme Court significantly expanded the scope of rights protections under the federal Bill of Rights. The Warren Court's activism encouraged litigants who sought to protect or expand rights to file their suits in federal courts, rather than in state courts, or to base their claims in state court on the federal Constitution. However, the appointment in 1969 of Warren *Burger to succeed Earl Warren as chief justice appeared to signal a change in direction of the U.S. Supreme Court. Faced with a less receptive Supreme Court, civil-liberties advocates sought to safeguard and extend their gains by looking to state supreme courts, arguing that state bills of rights often provided more expansive protections for rights than were available under the federal Bill of Rights, at least as interpreted by the Burger Court. During the early 1970s, the supreme courts of California, New Jersey, Oregon, and a few other states proved receptive to those arguments, announcing pioneering civil-liberties rulings under state bills of rights. What began as an effort to circumvent Burger Court rulings soon was transformed into a national phenomenon. By the beginning of the twenty-first century, state supreme courts throughout the nation regularly announced rulings based on the rights guarantees of their state constitutions, and this willingness to recognize claims based on state constitutional guarantees encouraged litigants to continue to bring such claims to state supreme courts.

One area in which state supreme courts have been particularly active under the new judicial *federalism has been public school finance. Historically, states have relied primarily on local property taxes to fund elementary and secondary schools. As a result, the level of funding for public education has varied from school district to school district, depending on the value of taxable property in the district and on the rate at which it is taxed. In the late 1960s, reformers began to challenge this system of school finance, charging that the disparities in funding among school districts violated the rights of students in property-poor districts. In 1973 the U.S. Supreme Court rejected a challenge to Texas's system of school finance, which was based primarily on local property taxes, ruling that the resulting disparities did not violate the federal Constitution. However, shortly after the Supreme Court's ruling, the New Jersey Supreme Court in *Robinson* v. *Cahill* (1973) ruled that New Jersey's system of school finance (which closely resembled Texas's) did violate the New Jersey Constitution. Other state supreme courts soon followed New Jersey's lead. From 1970–2000, the supreme courts in twenty-nine states considered claims that their states' system of school finance were inconsistent with the state constitution, and in fifteen states they have upheld those claims. Having invalidated the existing system of school

finance, most state supreme courts declined to get involved in the details of educational policy, a task for which they were ill-suited. Instead, they left it to the governor and legislature to devise a new system for financing public education in their states, while making clear that they would intervene once again if a satisfactory system was not developed. Often these state supreme court rulings were controversial. They certainly had a dramatic effect on politics in those states, elevating the task of creating a new and constitutionally adequate system of school finance to the top of the political agenda.

A second important area of state supreme court activity has involved the rights of gays and lesbians. Although the U.S. Supreme Court has upheld state sodomy laws, a number of state supreme courts have struck down laws regulating consensual sexual activity as in violation of the state constitutional right to privacy. In addition, the Hawaii Supreme Court in 1993 ruled that a state statute restricting marriage to opposite-sex couples violated the state constitutional ban on *discrimination, a ruling later reversed by a state constitutional amendment. Finally, the Vermont Supreme Court in 1999 ruled that same-sex couples could not be denied the same benefits available to opposite-sex couples. The court's ruling impelled the Vermont Legislature to reexamine the issue, and in 2000 it enacted a statute that gave gay and lesbian couples the right to join in civil unions, a status equivalent to marriage (see HOMOSEXUALITY AND THE LAW).

State Supreme Courts and Tort Law. Tort law suits deal with noncriminal wrongs that result in death, personal injury, or property damage. Examples include suits for *damages arising from automobile accidents, medical malpractice, and dangerous consumer products. For the most part, state legislatures have left tort law to the judiciary, permitting state supreme courts to prescribe the rules that govern the resolution of tort-law cases through their decisions elaborating the common law. Since the 1960s, these rules have changed dramatically. State supreme courts have transformed the legal standards for determining *liability, so that plaintiffs no longer have to prove that their injuries were caused by negligence on the part of those being sued. The courts have also facilitated recovery for injuries from products whose design made them dangerous. State supreme courts have abolished longstanding immunities that protected charitable organizations, municipalities, and others from suit. Finally, courts have reduced or eliminated various other barriers to plaintiffs recovering damages for the injuries they have suffered, such as bans on recovery when injured persons to some extent contributed to their injuries. Taken altogether, these judicial innovations have transformed tort law, particularly as it relates to products-liability, that is, the responsibility of manufacturers or sellers for the injuries suffered by consumers of their products.

Critics of these state supreme court rulings—among them, insurance companies and manufacturers—have charged that the decisions have unleashed a flood of frivolous and unjustified suits and that juries have responded with damage awards far in excess of injuries suffered. To combat against these evils, these critics have sought protection from state legislatures, seeking caps on damage awards, limits on attorney fees, and penalties against attorneys who file frivolous suits. During the 1980s and 1990s, many state legislatures enacted "tort reform" statutes to safeguard producers. However, trial attorneys and others have challenged these statutes, arguing that many violate the right to jury trial and other rights protected by state bills of rights. In a number of states, these arguments have succeeded, and state supreme courts have declared tort reform statutes unconstitutional. The continuation of this battle—in state legislatures, on state supreme courts, and in elections for seats on those courts—demonstrates that state supreme courts are inevitably enmeshed in the politics of their states.

[See also Civil Rights and Civil Liberties; Judge; Litigiousness]

• Henry R. Glick, Supreme Courts in State Politics, 1971. Robert A. Kagan, Bliss Cartwright, Lawrence M. Friedman, and Stanton Wheeler, "The Evolution of State Supreme Courts," Michigan Law Review (1978): 961–1005. Mary Cornelia Porter and G. Alan Tarr, eds., State Supreme Courts: Policymakers in the Federal System, 1982. Susan P. Fino, The Role of State Supreme Courts in the New Judicial Federalism, 1987. Stanley Friedelbaum, ed., Human Rights in the States, 1988. G. Alan Tarr and Mary Cornelia Aldis Porter, State Supreme Courts in State and Nation, 1988. Paul Finkelman and Stephen E. Gottlieb, eds., Toward a Usable Past: Liberty Under State Constitutions, 1991. G. Alan Tarr, ed., Constitutional Politics in the States, 1996. G. Alan Tarr, "The New Judicial Federalism in Perspective," Notre Dame Law Review (1997): 1097–1118. Charles H. Sheldon and Linda S. Maule, Choosing Justice: The Recruitment of State and Federal Judges, 1997. Robert F. Williams, State Constitutional Law: Cases and Materials, 3d ed., 1998.

—G. Alan Tarr

SWIFT V. TYSON Swift v. Tyson (1842) was a diversity action to compel payment of a bill of exchange drawn by a speculator in Maine lands under circumstances suggestive of fraud. The bill was accepted by Tyson, a New York investor, and endorsed to Swift, who took it in payment of a pre-existing debt. Was the debt valuable consideration such that Swift took the bill free from defenses? That question had enormous practical importance. Specie was in chronically short supply, and there was no uniform paper currency. The more freely commercial paper could be negotiated, the greater the volume of business.

The Supreme Court, in an opinion by Justice Joseph *Story, held unanimously in favor of negotiability, applying general principles of *commercial law. Because state judicial decisions were found not to be "laws" within the meaning of the Rules of Decision Act, federal courts in diversity cases were not bound by them. The spottiness of case reports, the proliferation of new states, and the risk to interstate commerce of balkanized commercial law doctrines gave strong practical support to Story's reasoning, which contained the potential for a uniform commercial jurisprudence.

However, Swift also contained the seeds of a general federal *common law for diversity cases. By the 1880s, the Court had converted Swift into a broad mandate to protect out-of-state creditors from the effect of state laws in a wide range of subject matter. Swift became identified with the Supreme Court's expansive notions of liberty of *contract and substantive *due process—the "brooding omnipresence in the sky." Story's opinion came under scholarly criticism as his concept of law was being undermined by the growing pull of positivism. Swift had become, in Grant Gilmore's words, "a headless monster, marked down for destruction by all right thinking men" by the time it was overruled on constitutional grounds in Erie Railroad Co. v. Tompkins (1938).

• Grant Gilmore, The Stages of American Law, 1977 (31–93). Tony A. Freyer, Harmony and Dissonance: The Swift and Erie Cases in American Jurisprudence, 1981.

—Hugh Macgill

T

TAFT, WILLIAM HOWARD (1857–1930), lawyer, twenty-sixth president of the United States, 1909–13, chief justice of the United States *Supreme Court, 1921–30. William Howard Taft holds a unique position in United States legal history in that he is the only person to have served as both president and chief justice. Although he is best remembered for his significant efforts to reform the federal judiciary, his contribution to American law is not inconsequential. Unfortunately for Taft, his legal and judicial values and approach fell out of favor in the early 1930s with the onslaught of the New Deal.

Born on 15 September 1857 in Cincinnati, Ohio, Taft graduated from Yale University in 1878 and attended the University of Cincinnati Law School before being admitted to the bar. Taft spent much of his life in public service. He served as solicitor general of the United States; in 1892, President Benjamin Harrison appointed him to the United States Court of Appeals for the Sixth Circuit, where he began to make a name for himself as a protector of industrial *property and an opponent of organized *labor. Thereafter Taft chaired the Philippine Commission. In 1904, President Theodore Roosevelt chose Taft as his secretary of war, and Taft became Roosevelt's handpicked successor to the White House in 1908. Although the incumbent, Taft lost a three-way election for the presidency in 1912. After the death of Chief Justice Edward D. White, President Warren G. Harding appointed Taft to the chief justiceship on 30 June 1921, and the Senate approved his nomination that same day.

Taft's major contribution to American law came in the reform of the administration of the federal *courts. He successfully lobbied for enactment of the Judicial Reform Act of 14 September 1922. This statute created a conference of nine of the senior circuit federal judges plus the chief justice with power to realign the federal districts to meet the demands for federal courts. Further, this statute directed the conference to develop an annual survey of the business of the federal courts and to recommend further judicial changes to Congress. These reforms altered how the federal courts administered themselves by providing more and better information to the senior judges and Congress. Based on this information, the flexibility, accountability, and responsiveness of the federal courts increased.

Taft's other major accomplishment in judicial reform came in the form of the Judiciary Act of 1925, popularly called the Judges' Bill. Under the Judges' Bill, the Supreme Court gained the authority to select its own caseload through the writ of *certiorari*, a writ that allows the Court wide authority to hear or reject cases as it sees fit. Recognized as a dramatic reform at the time, this ability to pick and choose the issues it wishes to consider in any particular term has proven to be the key to keeping the Supreme Court at the center of major constitutional questions.

Taft believed that cordial relations played a key role in "massing" the justices on a decision, and the positive relationships among the justices during Taft's chief justiceship can be directly credited to Taft's charm and persuasion. Enduring evidence of Taft's considerable ability as a judicial lobbyist is the Supreme Court building itself. Distressed at the cramped quarters for the Court, Taft lobbied Congress for its own building: the marble judicial palace behind the Capital is a tribute to William Howard Taft's tenure as chief justice.

While Taft receives high marks for his efforts for judicial reform and administration, on doctrinal issues Taft falls short. Steeped in the traditional legal culture of the late nineteenth century, Taft saw the justices' role as defending private property from undue governmental interference, and maintaining law and order. Over the course of the eight terms he served on the Supreme Court, Taft authored 249 opinions for the Court, dissented twenty times, and submitted written dissents in only four cases. Yet few of Taft's opinions survived far into the twentieth century because of the rise of judicial liberalism. Nevertheless, some of his decisions deserve attention for what they suggest about Taft and an earlier conception of judicial behavior and legal values. Taft's first major decision was *William Truax* v. *Corrigan* (1921), a case regarding an Arizona statute that limited state courts' ability to issue *injunctions in labor controversies. Taft's majority opinion held that such restraints on injunctions in labor cases denied *due process and *equal protections of law to the property owners being picketed by the labor agitators and consequently the state statute was unconstitutional. This opinion demonstrated Taft's long-standing suspicion of the labor movement and his belief that a key role for the state and federal judiciaries was to protect private property rights. This suspicion of workplace regulations can be further seen in the second child labor case, *J. W. Bailey* v. *Drexel Furniture Company* (1922), which involved the chief labor tax law. Taft's court struck down this legislation as an abuse of the federal taxing power, a threat to private property rights, and a threat to the rights of the states to regulate businesses as they saw fit.

Nevertheless, on occasion Taft supported the powers of Congress to craft reasonable regulations of the national economy based on the commerce clause. In the case of *Stafford* v. *Wallace* (1922), Taft broadly interpreted the commerce clause in finding the Packers and Stockyards Act of 1921 constitutional, and ruled that Congress could regulate stockyards. This decision foreshadowed later judicial decisions that provided Congress an almost unlimited free hand in regulating the national economy through the federal commerce clause.

In one of his few written dissents, Taft opposed the majority's decision in the *Adkins* v. *Children's Hospital of the District of Columbia* (1923), a case in which the majority struck down a federal minimum wage for women as a violation of the "liberty of contract."

Taft considered his most important decision to be his majority opinion in *Myers* v. *United States* (1926), which dealt with the president's powers of removal. Taft and the majority of the Court held that the president could remove persons who held office in the executive branch of the federal government without the advice and consent of the Senate, and could do so without violating the fundamental constitutional principle of the *separa-

tion of powers. The majority decision no doubt influenced by Taft's previous service as president, *Myers* settled a long-disputed area of constitutional law.

Given Taft's conservative nature as a person and as a judge, it is not surprising that he favored strict enforcement of the criminal law. This value can be seen in his majority opinion in *Olmstead* v. *U.S.* (1928), upholding federal wiretapping against the argument that this practice violated the Fourth Amendment rights against unreasonable *search and seizure. Taft and the majority disagreed. They narrowly held that spoken conversations picked up on wiretaps were not similar to an entry into a building or the opening of an envelope; therefore, none of the defendant's Fourth Amendment rights were violated.

Thus while William Howard Taft left a physical mark on the American law—the building of the United States Supreme Court—he also left his mark on the federal judiciary; for example, the Judges' Bill of 1925 provided the Supreme Court full discretion over its docket. Taft's opinions did not significantly influence twentieth-century jurisprudence. But his personal example of grace, charm, organizational skills, and political acumen defined a key role for future chief justices and set a standard against which later chief justices would be judged.

[*See also* Presidency of the United States]

• Alpheus Thomas Mason, *William Howard Taft: Chief Justice*, 1964. Henry F. Pringle, *The Life and Times of William Howard Taft*, 1939, reprint, 1986.

—Thomas C. Mackey

TAFT-HARTLEY ACT. *See* Labor Law: Labor Relations.

TAKEOVER, HOSTILE. *See* Corporation.

TAKINGS. The power of the sovereign to take private *property for public purposes through eminent domain has existed for many centuries. By the time of American independence, however, payment of compensation to owners had become customary. That approach was embodied in the Fifth Amendment of the United States Constitution, which provides "... nor shall private property be taken for public use, without just compensation." This provision originally applied only to the federal government, but was held applicable to the states through the *due process clause of the *Fourteenth Amendment (1868) in *Chicago, Burlington & Quincy Railroad Co.* v. *City of Chicago*

(1897). The constitutions of all of the states contain similar provisions.

Just compensation is defined as the market value of the property taken, which might be land, personal items, or intangible rights. Nevertheless, just compensation hardly ever is full compensation, since most owners have customized property used in business or have sentimental attachment to their homes. Moving also carries significant costs and disruption. The public use requirement limits eminent domain to situations when legitimate governmental needs compel its exercise, thereby avoiding arbitrary takings from some private individuals for the benefit of others and reducing uncompensated losses. In *Hawaii Housing Authority* v. *Midkiff* (1984), however, the Supreme Court effectively eliminated the public use requirement by equating public use with the general constitutional standard that government regulations advance the public health, safety, or welfare. This has led to the invocation of eminent domain for the benefit of private businesses, so long as some public benefit is shown.

In *Pumpelly* v. *Green Bay Co.* (1871), the Supreme Court held that the permanent flooding of private land behind a public dam was an exercise of eminent domain, in spite of the fact that the landowner never had been deprived of title. Likewise, in *Pennsylvania Coal Co.* v. *Mahon* (1922), Justice Oliver Wendell *Holmes observed that the imposition of regulations could constitute a taking where the regulations went "too far." What constitutes a regulatory taking has been in dispute ever since.

The Supreme Court has ruled that permanent physical occupation of land constitutes a taking in *Loretto* v. *Teleprompter Manhattan CATV Corp.* (1982), and that regulations that deprive land of all economically viable use constitute takings in *Lucas* v. *South Carolina Coastal Council* (1992). Beyond these relatively clear situations, the Court has employed a balancing test that takes into account the character of the regulation, its economic impact on the owner, and whether the owner has "investment-backed expectations" that are defeated, as in *Penn Central Trans. Co.* v. *City of New York* (1978).

Numerous questions continue to swirl around the *Penn Central* standards, including whether they should be applied to all of the claimant's property or to some lesser "relevant parcel"; whether property rights, which primarily arise from state *common law and statutes, might be amended by statute so as to preclude takings claims; and whether the relationship between expectations and property is irredeemably circuitous. Several states have enacted private property rights laws, which require payment of compensation when government action has reduced the value of property in certain situations. Until the Supreme Court comprehensively defines property rights, it is unlikely that regulatory takings issues can satisfactorily be resolved.

[*See also* Constitutions, United States; Sovereignty]

• Richard A. Epstein, *Takings: Private Property and the Power of Eminent Domain*, 1985. Steven J. Eagle, *Regulatory Takings*, 2d ed., 2001.   — Steven J. Eagle

TANEY, ROGER BROOKE, born 17 March 1777, Calvert County, Maryland, died 12 October 1864, Washington, D.C.

Taney's parents, Michael Taney and Monica Brooke Taney, came from a long line of wealthy Maryland tobacco planters. Taney was valedictorian of Dickinson College in 1795, and was admitted to the bar in 1799. In 1806 he married Anne Key, sister of the prominent Maryland attorney Francis Scott Key. Taney was a Roman Catholic, the first to serve on the U.S. *Supreme Court.

Before joining the Court, Taney practiced law, freed the few slaves he had inherited, and held various offices in Maryland. He began his career as a Federalist, but by 1825 he was a fervent Jacksonian. As attorney general (July 1831–September 1832) he drafted part of Andrew Jackson's message vetoing the recharter of the Bank of the United States and wrote an unpublished opinion arguing that free blacks could not be citizens of the United States. While ad interim secretary of the treasury (September 1833–June 1834) he began taking all federal funds out of the Bank of the United States. Jackson rewarded his loyalty by nominating him for chief justice in December 1835. He was confirmed in March 1836 and held his seat until his death, serving longer than any other chief justice except John *Marshall.

Taney led the Court in a direction that favored *states' rights, local economic development, and slavery, and generally disfavored a nationalist interpretation of the Constitution. Under Taney, the Court moved away from Chief Justice Marshall's expansive nationalist reading of the Constitution. Taney often assigned key decisions to other justices, but he was clearly the leader of his court, and set its tone and direction.

Charles River Bridge Co. v. *Warren Bridge Co.* (1837) illustrates Taney's economic jurisprudence. The Charles River Bridge Company claimed that

Massachusetts violated its charter by allowing the Warren Bridge Company to build a competing bridge across the Charles River. The Charles River Company argued that its charter implied it had a monopoly, and that in granting a charter to the Warren company the state effectively violated the contract clause of the Constitution. Speaking for the Court, Taney disagreed, concluding that "any ambiguity in the terms of the contract, must operate against the adventurers [stockholders] and in favor of the public."

This decision was not a radical departure from Chief Justice Marshall's economic jurisprudence, but rather it simply recognized that the public good required a balance between private interests and public need, as reflected by the legislature. *Charles River Bridge* and subsequent cases also reflected Taney's states' rights proclivities. The *Charles River Bridge* opinion deferred to the needs of the states in promoting economic development and in controlling local industries. Similarly, in *Briscoe* v. *Bank of Kentucky* (1837) and *New York* v. *Miln* (1837) the Taney court upheld the right of states to regulate their economic affairs, even when the *regulations seemed to impinge on national power. In *The License Cases* (1847) the Taney court upheld state bans on the importation of liquor, denying that these laws infringed on the Congress's commerce clause powers. In *Cooley* v. *Board of Port Wardens of Philadelphia* (1851) the Court upheld a Pennsylvania law requiring that ships entering Philadelphia take on a local pilot. This decision, written by Benjamin R. Curtis, also reflected Taney's general deference to the states.

Taney was overwhelmingly proslavery and equally hostile to free blacks. His most famous opinion, in *Dred Scott* v. *Sandford* (1857), illustrates his proslavery racism and his hostility to national power. Here Taney struck down the Missouri Compromise (1820) on the ground that Congress had no power to regulate slavery in the Territories. He also held that blacks had no legal rights under the Constitution, and even free blacks living in states where they could vote and hold office could not be considered citizens under the Constitution. In fugitive slave cases like *Ableman* v. *Booth* (1859) Taney backed away from his support for states' rights, and instead supported a strong national government, because here a strong nationalist position dovetailed with a proslavery position.

Taney did his best to undermine the *Lincoln administration during the Civil War, opposing almost every governmental policy. He was seen, correctly, as a Confederate sympathizer, and for the most part Lincoln ignored him, as when he tried as a circuit court justice in *Ex parte Merryman* (1861) to prevent Lincoln from suppressing a Marylander from organizing troops for the Confederacy. Similarly, a majority of the Court voted against him on most war-related issues. He died personally embittered and despised by most of the nation. Senator Charles Sumner of Massachusetts expressed the sentiments of most Americans when he opposed placing a bust in the national capital for Taney, because of his proslavery and anti-Union sentiments.

[*See also* Race and Ethnicity; Slavery, Law of]

• Carl B. Swisher, *The Oliver Wendell Holmes Devise History of the Supreme Court of the United States, vol. 5, The Taney Period,* 1974. Don Fehrenbacher, *The Dred Scott Case: Its Significance in Law and Politics,* 1978. Harold M. Hyman and William M. Wiecek, *Equal Justice Under Law,* 1982. Paul Finkelman, " 'Hooted Down the Page of History': Reconsidering The Greatness of Chief Justice Taney," *Journal of Supreme Court History 1994* (1995): 83–102.   —Paul Finkelman

TAXATION

Overview
Estate and Gift Taxes
Income Taxes
Property Taxes
Sales Taxes

TAXATION: OVERVIEW

The United States *Constitution provided the new federal government with broad taxing powers: Article I, Section 8, of the Constitution empowered the new federal government "to lay and collect Taxes, Duties, Imposts, and Excises." Under the Articles of Confederation, the federal government had been unable to solve a fiscal crisis during the 1780s because it lacked the power to tax and had to rely on voluntary state contributions. In light of the traditional powers of the states, the framers of the new constitution wished to make it clear that the federal government could collect all manner of taxes "to pay the Debts and provide from the common Defence and general Welfare of the United States."

The Constitution, however, also imposed some restrictions. First, Article I, Section 8, specified that "all Duties, Imposts, and Excises shall be uniform throughout the United States." This clause prevented Congress from singling out a particular state or group of states for higher rates of taxation on trade, and reflected the hope of the framers that the new Constitution would foster the development of a national market. Second, Article I, Section 9, limited federal taxation of *property by specifying: "No capitation, or other direct Tax shall be laid, unless in Proportion to the Census." The framers of the Constitution never clearly defined "direct" taxation, but they regarded property and poll taxes as direct taxes. The framers' goals were to protect the dominance of state and local governments in property taxation and to shield special categories of property, particularly slaves, against discriminatory federal taxation.

Under the leadership of Secretary of the Treasury Alexander Hamilton, the new federal government made extensive use only of the taxation of imports. These taxes provided substantial revenues while minimizing tax revolts such as the Whiskey Rebellion of 1794, caused by federal excises on distilled spirits.

State and local governments, meanwhile, forged revenue systems that relied heavily on property taxation. Most states created general property taxes designed to reach not only real estate but also "intangible" property such as cash and securities. Some states added to their constitutions provisions for uniformity (requiring that properties of equal value be taxed at the same rate) and universality (requiring that all property be taxed). However, the instruments of the federal government remained beyond the reach of state and local governments. In *McCulloch v. Maryland (1819), the Supreme Court, led by Chief Justice John *Marshall, ruled unconstitutional a Maryland tax on the Baltimore branch of the Bank of the United States. In Weston v. Charleston (1823), the Marshall Court likewise found unconstitutional state or local taxes on federal bonds.

During the *Civil War the federal government exercised in earnest the wide range of tax instruments possible under the Constitution. Republican administrations enacted high tariffs, a wide range of sales taxes (excises) on domestic consumption, and a progressive income tax. Congressional leaders regarded the income tax as an indirect tax in the sense that it did not directly tax property values. In Pacific Ins. Co. v. Soule (1868), the Supreme Court upheld the taxation of the gross receipts of corporations. Following the war, Republican Congresses phased out most of the excise taxes and allowed the income tax to lapse. But they kept high tariffs as a source of revenue and protection. They also left in place "sin" taxes on alcohol and tobacco.

Between the Civil War and the First World War, the economic and social stresses of industrialization fueled democratic pressures for taxation according to "ability to pay." Coalitions of farmers and middle-class property owners complained that tariffs were regressive and encouraged monopoly power, and that the general property tax had failed to reach intangible personal property.

Tax reform, however, moved slowly. State and local governments worried that increasing taxes on the wealthy would discourage investment. In 1894, Congress adopted a progressive income tax; but, the Supreme Court in Pollock v. Farmers' Loan and Trust Co. (1895) declared the tax unconstitutional. The Court concluded that the income tax was a direct tax and that, because the federal government had failed to allocate the tax across the states according to population, the tax was unconstitutional.

In 1909, bipartisan leaders in Congress, including conservatives who wished to blunt the threat of radical taxation, proposed the Sixteenth Amendment, which explicitly granted the federal government the power to adopt income taxation. The amendment was ratified in 1913, and Congress passed a modestly graduated tax on nearly all income, both personal and corporate.

A major exception, however, was the interest income earned by state and local bondholders. The 1913 legislation exempted such income and, in fact, some proponents of the legislation even argued that the Constitution itself protected owners of state and local bonds from federal taxation. The Supreme Court adopted this position, known as the doctrine of reciprocal intergovernmental immunity, which held that the Constitution shields the federal government and state government from discriminatory taxes on each other's activities.

The federal government would have moved slowly to expand income taxation had it not been for American entry into the First World War. Wartime mobilization created a need for huge revenues, and President Woodrow Wilson and the Democratic leadership of Congress embraced "soak-the-rich" taxation in the form of steep taxation of corporate "excess-profits," and of the personal income and estates of the nation's wealthiest citizens.

After the First World War, Secretary of the Treasury Andrew Mellon presided over fiscal policy under the Republican "return to normalcy." Mellon led in the eradication of the excess-profits tax and the reduction of the progressiveness of the income tax. But the Republicans retained the income tax rather than adopt a national sales tax. Mellon recognized the broad popular support for the progressive income tax. Moreover, he saw opportunities for carving out loopholes (deductions and exemptions) in the tax code.

During the 1920s, while the federal government consolidated the income tax, state governments replaced their crumbling systems of state property taxation with new arrays of sales taxes (such as gasoline taxes), user charges (such as motor-vehicle fees), and special taxes on corporations and incomes. Local governments continued to rely on real property taxation but abandoned any serious effort to tax personal property.

The Great Depression revived "soak-the-rich taxation." The New Deal increased marginal income tax rates, closed many income-tax loopholes, and enacted a graduated tax on undistributed corporate profits. Offsetting the progressiveness of the New Deal's income tax reforms, however, was the regressiveness of payroll taxes that President D. Roosevelt embraced to fund Social Security benefits. And, following the Recession of 1937–38, a conservative Congress to killed the undistributed profits tax.

During the Great Depression, under the pressures of an eroding tax base, state governments diversified their tax systems. They increased their use of special sales taxes and, between 1932 and 1937, thirty-three states adopted general sales taxation.

The Second World War brought about a personal income tax that was both broadly based and progressive. The Revenue Act of 1942 taxed middle-class wages and salaries and raised the highest marginal rates of taxation on personal incomes to over 90 percent. The progressiveness of the new tax, the popularity of the war effort, a withholding system of taxpaying, and general deductions, such as for interest on home *mortgages and payments for state and local taxes, all helped win support for mass-based taxation of incomes.

After the Second World War, the nation's system proved resilient and stable. The various levels of government continued to rely on the forms of taxation they had developed earlier and rarely engaged in any challenges over intergovernmental taxing powers or the distribution of the tax base. In *South Carolina* v. *Baker* (1988) the Supreme Court reduced the scope of intergovernmental tax immunity and held that income from state and municipal bonds may be taxed. Congress has not yet done so. Since the end of the Second World War until the 1990s, economic growth and episodes of inflation enabled the federal government to use its revenue both to fund growing military and civilian programs and to provide significant tax cuts. At the beginning of the twenty-first century, the tax system of the United States, in comparison with those of the world's other large econ-omies, relies less heavily on consumption taxes, particularly value-added taxes and gasoline taxes, and more heavily on payroll taxes and the progressive income tax.

[*See also* Economics and Law; Governance]

• Edwin R. A. Seligman, *The Income Tax: A Study of the History, Theory and Practice of Income Taxation at Home and Abroad*, 1914. W. Elliot Brownlee, *Federal Taxation in America: A Short History*, 1976. Robert A. Becker, *Revolution, Reform, and the Politics of American Taxation, 1763–1783*, 1980. Robert Stanley, *Dimensions of Law in the Service of Order: Origins of the Federal Income Tax, 1861–1913*, 1993. Sven Steinmo, *Taxation and Democracy: Swedish, British, and American Approaches to Financing the Modern State*, 1993. Glenn W. Fisher, *The Worst Tax? A History of the Property Tax in America*, 1996.
—W. Elliot Brownlee

TAXATION: ESTATE AND GIFT TAXES

Taxes on the gratuitous transfer of *property at death date back to ancient times. They come in two forms. Estate taxes are levied on the aggregate value of a decedent's property, whereas inheritance taxes are imposed on what individuals receive from a decedent by *will or intestate succession. Typically, marginal tax rates rise as the size of an *estate or inheritance increases. The two taxes may sometimes have identical effects, but often they do not. Because inheritance tax schedules begin anew with each recipient, the overall tax burden of a progressive inheritance tax is lighter the more pieces an estate is broken into. Estate taxes do not depend on how finely an estate is divided. Gift taxes are imposed on gratuitous transfers by living donors.

History. Federal taxes on property transfers at death were intermittent and fairly low through the first third of the twentieth century. Their fitful use reflected the government's shifting revenue needs, particularly the cost of waging war. In 1797, when relations with France deteriorated, Congress levied a stamp duty on decedents' possessions, exempting shares passing to spouses or descendants. The duty was repealed in 1802, once war no longer threatened. Likewise, in 1862, Congress began taxing estates progressively to raise funds to fight the Civil War. Those taxes ended in 1872, when most wartime bills had been paid. In 1898, a tax on inheritance was enacted to help fund the United States' military clashes with Spain—a tax discontinued in 1902 when the military menace had disappeared.

In the late nineteenth century, pressure built for more robust death taxes aimed at leveling great fortunes. Progressives agreed with industrialists such as Andrew Carnegie that huge disparities of wealth destroyed equality of opportunity; in their view, more uniform starting places for the young benefited not only society but those individuals forced to struggle for economic preeminence. By 1906, President Theodore Roosevelt proposed a progressive gift and inheritance tax on the very rich. Congress initially balked, finally passing an estate tax in 1916 only when war was imminent. Estate tax rates were lowered after World War I, then rose and fell by turns until 1931, as defenders and foes gained the upper hand. A gift tax also was introduced, repealed, then reinstated, to block evasion of the estate tax.

Throughout the 1930s and 1940s, as the egalitarian goal of reducing inherited fortunes gained broader acceptance, rates rose steadily. By 1954, the marginal tax on estates above $10 million was 77 percent. Lower rates applied to gifts, nudging the wealthy to divest themselves while alive, which nonetheless few did. From 1976 on, gifts and estates were taxed using a single set of rates, although lifetime gifts still enjoyed a tax advantage. Congress reduced estate and gift taxes substantially in 1986. In 2001, it lowered them much further over ten years, repealing the estate tax in 2010 (but not the gift tax, which was deemed necessary to reduce income tax avoidance). In 2011, the law will automatically return to its form as of early 2001. Experts expect Congress to intervene before then to alter that result. Whether the United States will join Australia, Canada, and Israel in repealing the estate tax permanently is uncertain.

Since the nineteenth century, many states have imposed inheritance taxes at low rates. Few states now levy taxes higher than the amount the federal government permits executors to credit against a decedent's federal estate tax liability. This may change if, as planned, the credit for state death taxes is replaced by a deduction in 2005.

Current Federal Law. There are three federal wealth transfer taxes: a gift tax, an estate tax, and the generation-skipping transfer tax (an additional 55 percent tax on aggregate gifts above $1.06 million per donor to persons who are two or more generations younger). In 2000, only about 1.5 percent of decedents owed any federal estate tax, and large estates supplied most of the approximately $30 billion collected. The 2001 tax bill enacted sweeping changes, phased in over ten years.

Gifts to each recipient in excess of $10,000 annually are potentially subject to tax. They are added to the total of a person's gifts above that amount, and taxed at graduated rates. The top rate, now 60 percent, will be reduced to 35 percent after the estate tax is repealed in 2010.

Estate taxes are imposed on the total value of a decedent's property, not counting gifts to charity or a surviving spouse. The first $675,000 of combined lifetime gifts and estate property is exempt from tax in 2001—an amount due to increase from $1 million in 2002 to $3.5 million in 2009, before the tax ends in 2010. Rates currently range from 37 percent to 60 percent. The top rate will fall to 45 percent between 2003 and 2007.

Policy Issues. Three main arguments support wealth transfer taxes. First, they are said to advance equality of opportunity by reducing the unmerited advantages of being born to parents with money. Second, they are alleged to profit society by breaking up dangerous concentrations of wealth, which imperil economic markets and democratic politics. Third, they purportedly generate revenue without serious disincentive effects or high costs, because at nonconfiscatory levels they do not deter work effort or saving, and earners rarely feel the sting of the tax, as most people are dead when it is collected.

Opponents of wealth transfer taxes dispute these assertions. They contend that communities may not justly tax people's decisions to give property to others to consume in the donor's place; taxpayers' after-income-tax earnings are theirs to savor or to let others enjoy. They further argue that estate taxes have altered the overall distribution of wealth only slightly, and that more precise tools should be used to tackle anticompetitive or politically corrupting behavior. Finally, they maintain that wealth transfer taxes discourage work and saving considerably (though nobody has successfully measured by how much) and that the high costs of tax planning—perhaps over $10 billion annually—make the tax glaringly inefficient.

• Louis Eisenstein, "The Rise and Decline of the Estate Tax," *Tax Law Review* 11 (1956): 223–59. Mark L. Ascher, "Curtailing Inherited Wealth," *Michigan Law Review* 89 (1990): 69–151. W. Leslie Peat and Stephanie J. Willbanks, *Federal Estate and Gift Taxation: An Analysis and Critique*, 2d. ed., 1995. *U.S. Master Estate and Gift Tax Guide*, 2002.   —Eric Rakowski

TAXATION: INCOME TAXES

Income taxes impose levies on rents, interest, profits, salaries, and wages. Defining such income has always been difficult, as has been discovering the actual incomes that particular individuals receive.

Until the twentieth century American governments preferred to levy property taxes rather than income. Governments appreciated the ability of property taxes to reach the form of wealth—real estate—that accounted for most of the assets in an agricultural society and the ease with which they could verify the property values. The earliest precedents for the income tax in America were the "faculty taxes" that many colonial and early state governments assessed on the implicit incomes of people in trades or businesses. By the 1770s most colonies had adopted such taxes and during the Revolution they generally expanded their use of faculty taxes. However, the great difficulties in defining and verifying what "faculties" were worth led the new states to abandon the taxes or turn them into license fees for trades and professions.

The political leaders of the new nation never discussed taxes on actual incomes until 1799, when Great Britain, to finance the wars against Napoleon, adopted a general income tax. Subsequently, American governments occasionally considered income taxes as emergency measures during fiscal crises. For example, in 1815, near the end of the War of 1812, President James Madison's secretary of treasury, Alexander J. Dallas, proposed adopting an income tax based on the British model. During the 1840s, in the depression that followed the panic of 1837, and again during the Civil War, several states adopted income taxes, on an emergency basis, to balance budgets and provide some tax relief to agriculture. Except for Pennsylvania, all these states were in the South. None of these taxes defined incomes in any systematic way, and only Virginia's raised substantial revenues.

During the Civil War, which caused the greatest fiscal crisis of the United States of the nineteenth century, the federal government launched its first major experiment in income taxation. Congress adopted a graduated tax on personal incomes that reached a maximum rate of 10 percent. Once again, policymakers regarded income taxation as an emergency measure. The commissioner of internal revenue had to rely heavily on voluntary compliance. He lacked both the legal authority and the administrative capacity to obtain earnings reports from farms and small businesses, where most Americans earned their income. But the law required corporations to collect taxes on dividends and interest and did require the federal government to collect taxes on the salaries it paid. By the end of the war, more than 15 percent of all Union households in the industrial and commercial northeast states paid an income tax. The complaints of affluent citizens led Congress to allow the income tax to expire in 1872.

Between the Civil War and the First World War, popular interest grew in income taxation as a way of taxing the richest Americans. At the state and local level, the general property tax had clearly failed to reach "intangible" personal property (for example, stocks, bonds, *mortgages, and cash), which turned out to be even more difficult to assess than incomes. At the federal level, tariff revenues, which were the mainstay of public finance, seemed to many Americans to have become regressive and protective of monopoly power. And, as large *corporations expanded dramatically, they created the organizational capacity for the federal government to assess the incomes of increasing numbers of wealthy Americans.

The movement for income taxation, however, progressed slowly. State and local governments generally believed that they would be unable to administer income taxation or worried that an income tax on the wealthy would ruin commerce. In 1894 Congress adopted a progressive income tax based on the Civil War tax, but the Supreme Court, in *Pollock* v. *Farmers' Loan and Trust Co.* (1895) declared the tax unconstitutional. In what amounted to a reversal of the position the Court had taken after the Civil War, it now ruled that an income tax was a direct tax and thus, following the requirement of Article I, Section 9, of the Constitution, must be allocated among the states according to population.

Support for income taxation continued to grow, however, and in 1909, bipartisan leaders in Congress proposed the Sixteenth Amendment, which explicitly granted to the federal government the power to adopt income taxation. In 1911 Wisconsin passed the first modern income tax. Wisconsin rigorously defined the meaning of income, used corporations to collect taxes on wages, salaries, and interest payments, and taxed corporate profits. The Sixteenth Amendment was ratified in 1913 and Congress passed a modestly graduated tax on nearly all forms of income, both personal and corporate.

Income taxation became a major source of federal revenue during the First World War. The administration of Woodrow Wilson and the Democratic leaders of Congress embraced steep taxation of corporate "excess-profits" and of the personal income of the nation's wealthiest citizens. This represented a conjunction of a political desire to "soak-the-rich" and the inability of the federal government to establish machinery for taxing wages, salaries, and the profits of small businesses and farmers on a mass basis. The only feasible income taxes were ones that focused on profits, interest, and large salaries as reported by corporations.

The income tax survived the First World War

and became the central feature of the federal tax system. The Republican administrations during the 1920s, under the financial leadership of Secretary of the Treasury Andrew Mellon, recognized the broad popular support for income taxation, but they were able to reduce the progressiveness of the income tax by creating exemptions and deductions. These deductions were valuable to taxpayers who faced high tax rates, but they lent the income tax code in the United States an exceptionally complex "swiss-cheese" quality.

The Great Depression intensified "soak-the-rich taxation." New Deal Congresses increased marginal income tax rates and closed many income-tax loopholes. However, the New Deal also introduced a regressive variant of an income tax. Congress adopted a flat rate tax on wages and the payrolls of employers to fund the new Social Security system in what became a pay-as-you-go system.

The Second World War was the occasion for the introduction of a personal income tax that was, for the first time, both progressive and broadly based. The Revenue Act of 1942 raised the marginal rates of taxation on high personal incomes to over 90 percent and also taxed middle-class wages and salaries. A withholding system that relied on corporations and the information-collection procedures provided by the Social Security system helped the federal government administer the mass-based taxation of incomes. By the end of the war about 60 percent of the labor force paid income taxes, usually in the form of withheld wages and salaries.

After the Second World War, the income tax proved resilient and stable. Economic growth and episodes of inflation enabled the federal government to use its tax revenue to fund growing programs, to provide significant tax cuts designed to stimulate economic expansion (in 1964, 1981, and 2001), and, during the late 1990s, to reduce the size of the national debt.

Social Security payroll taxes, meanwhile, increased relentlessly. In 2000, three-fourths of Americans taxpayers paid more Social Security payroll tax than income tax. Even so, many forecasts suggested that payroll taxes would prove inadequate to fund the Social Security benefits of the "baby-boom" generation, and the generation to follow, especially if the federal government abandoned a "pay-as-you-go" system in favor of creating individual retirement accounts.

• Edwin R. A. Seligman, *The Income Tax: A Study of the History, Theory and Practice of Income Taxation at Home and Abroad*, 1914. W. Elliot Brownlee, *Federal Taxation in America: A Short History*, 1976. John Witte, *The Politics and Development of the Federal Income Tax*, 1985. Eugene Steuerle, *The Tax Decade, 1981–1990*, 1992. Robert Stanley, *Dimensions of Law in the Service of Order: Origins of the Federal Income Tax, 1861–1913*, 1993. Sven Steinmo, *Taxation and Democracy: Swedish, British, and American Approaches to Financing the Modern State*, 1993.
—W. Elliot Brownlee

TAXATION: PROPERTY TAXES

Property taxes are annual levies on the assessed value of *property. Although unpopular, they remain the major source of local government revenue in the United States.

Imposts based on the ownership of property were used in ancient times, but the modern tax has roots in feudal obligations owed to British and European kings or landlords. In the fourteenth and fifteenth centuries, British tax assessors used ownership of property to estimate ability to pay. In time the tax came to be regarded as a levy on the property (in rem) itself. In the United Kingdom the tax developed into a system of "rates" based upon the annual (rental) value of property.

The growth of the property tax in America was closely related to economic and political conditions on the frontier. In precommercial agricultural areas the tax was a feasible source of local government revenue, and equal taxation of all wealth was consistent with the prevailing egalitarian ideology.

Anglo-American property law distinguishes real or immovable property (basically land and buildings) from personal (movable) property. Personal property is further subdivided into tangible and intangible property. Intangible personal property may represent a claim or right to wealth (e.g., *mortgages and corporate securities) or may be valuable in its own right (e.g., copyrights, *patents, goodwill). Equal taxation of wealth requires that the latter be taxed, but taxing intangible property risks double taxation.

Many nineteenth-century state constitutions required equal taxation of all property, real and personal, except property owned or used by governments, charities, or religious or educational institutions. By the end of the nineteenth century, however, many believed that the tax, as administered, was not taxing wealth equally. Disagreements over assessed value, the inconveniences of making large annual payments, and the belief that property owners were penalized for keeping buildings in good condition added to the unpopularity of the tax. States began to seek other sources of revenue, such as income and sales taxes, to reduce the property tax or to replace the tax on intangibles. Nevertheless, the property tax continued as the main, albeit controversial, source of local tax revenue. Today intangible property and many forms of tangible personal property are exempt in most states.

Appraised value is usually defined by statute as fair market value or the price that a willing buyer would pay a willing seller in an open market. The tax base may be the appraised value or some portion thereof. Unique properties, however, or properties in changing neighborhoods are difficult to assess even with modern methods. Many assessments are contested before tax appeal boards or in the courts.

Proposition 13, an amendment to the California constitution approved by voters in 1978, is often cited as the beginning of a tax revolt that continued through the 1980s and into the 1990s. This amendment limited property taxes to 1 percent of 1975–76 assessed value. Increases in the value of properties that had not changed ownership were limited to the inflation rate or 2 percent a year, whichever was smaller.

The California amendment, which became the model for limitations in several states, had far-reaching consequences. It weakened local government by reducing revenue, and projected the state legislature into local budgeting as it attempted to ration the one-percent levy among several overlying levels of local government. The provision limiting assessment increases on individual parcels created a tax base determined by market value, the inflation index, and ownership history. Proposition 13 thus created confusion and conflict that resulted in dozens of additional *constitutional amendments and *legislative acts clarifying or modifying the results of the original amendment.

Since 1978 many other states have adopted property tax relief measures. Assessments or taxes have been rolled back, frozen, or limited. Exemptions or special rates have benefited farmers, low income persons, homeowners, veterans, the elderly, and the disabled. Businesses have benefited from a variety of provisions aimed at job creation and economic development. Together, these changes have transformed the uniform, ad valorem property tax into a hybrid tax based partly on value, and partly on ownership history, the personal characteristics of the owner, or the use of the property.

In *Rodriguez* v. *San Antonio Independent School District* (1973), the U.S. *Supreme Court held that the Texas system of local school finance did not violate the *equal protection clause. Nonetheless, the case foreshadowed decisions in many jurisdictions holding that the state constitution makes the state, not local districts, responsible for providing adequate education of every child in the state. The quality of education, it was determined, could not depend upon the wealth or assessment practices in a particular district.

In response, many state legislatures modified school finance systems to provide additional funds to poorer districts. Many developed an equalization formula using assessed value per student as a measure of local effort. In other cases, uniform statewide property tax levies were imposed. Fair application of either approach requires uniform assessment in the various school districts. States, often under court order, are active supervisors of the assessment process. Many utilize statistical measures to assure the quality of assessment or to adjust school aid formulas to redress inequalities.

The constitutional requirement that direct taxes be apportioned among the states by population is a serious barrier to federal property taxation. Federal property taxes imposed in 1798, 1812, and at the beginning of the Civil War created much controversy but produced little revenue. The Sixteenth Amendment (ratified 1913) authorized the federal government to impose an income tax without apportionment, but property taxes remain subject to the apportionment requirement.

The property tax is most highly developed in former British colonies, but Great Britain has eliminated local rates based on rental value. A Council Tax, based on a band of values derived from market values with certain personal exemptions, helps support local governments; business property is subject to a uniform national tax. In Australia taxes are on land alone. Many countries include property as an element in another tax. For example, Japan combines office floor space and salaries of employees in the base of its Office Business Tax. The property tax continues to provide local governments with an autonomous source of revenue.

• Joan M. Youngman and Jane H. Malme, *An International Survey of Taxes on Land and Buildings,* 1994. Joan Youngman, *Legal Issues in Property Valuation and Taxation: Cases and Materials,* 1994. Glenn W. Fisher, *The Worst Tax: A History of the Property Tax in America,* 1996. Bartley W. Hildreth and James Richardson, eds., *Handbook on Taxation,* 1999, (91–117, 119–48).

—Glenn W. Fisher

TAXATION: SALES TAXES

Most states and many local governments levy taxes on the production, use, or consumption of goods and services. Such taxes include general retail sales taxes (the most common), special sales (or excise) taxes, use taxes, and gross receipts taxes.

General sales and gross receipts taxes were products of the Great Depression, being introduced in 1932 at the state level in Mississippi and at the local level in New York City and New Orleans. Special sales (or excise) taxes, however, were imposed as early as 1790, in the form of the whiskey tax.

Today, forty-five states, as well as the District of Columbia, impose a sales tax. Indeed, sales and gross receipts taxes are the largest state revenue source. In general, local governments adopted sales taxes later than their states did, but today the local governments in two-thirds of the states levy sales taxes. Local sales taxes are especially important in states that severely limit local property taxes, for example California and Louisiana.

Sales and gross receipts taxes have increased in popularity because of strong public pressure to reduce income and property taxes without a corresponding decrease in public services. Consumption taxes are attractive because taxpayers sense greater control over their tax burden (by purchasing fewer goods and services), and the tax burden can be shared with the nonresidents who make purchases in the jurisdiction.

General Sales Taxes. The general retail sales tax is imposed at the time of retail sale in the taxing jurisdiction of tangible personal *property and of taxable services. Retail sale usually is defined as transfer by a person engaged in business of the ownership of tangible personal property in exchange for something of value, to a purchaser for use or consumption (i.e., not for the purchaser's subsequent resale as tangible personal property). Transactions subject to this tax typically include retail sale of consumer goods, entertainment admission charges, payments for public accommodations (e.g., hotels, restaurants), utility charges, payments for commercial transportation (e.g., airlines, railroads), and many rental fees for tangible personal property. Most states exclude professional and many personal services from the retail sales tax; indeed, attempts to tax professional services have generated substantial controversy.

Statutes authorizing retail sales taxes contain detailed provisions concerning the imposition and administration of the tax, which place the burden of collecting the tax on the seller under one of two general theories. Under the privilege tax theory, the tax is imposed on the retail seller's gross receipts as a charge for the privilege of doing business within the state. Under statutes based on this theory, seller is primarily liable for the tax, but can pass it on to purchasers. Under the transaction theory, the sales tax is imposed on the purchaser. Although the seller collects the tax, the purchaser is primarily liable for payment of the tax. Under either theory, sellers are not permitted to absorb the tax but must separately state it and add it to the purchase price. Sellers then must remit to the taxing jurisdiction the taxes they collect on a periodic basis (usually quarterly).

Though most statutes contain broad language purporting to cover any retail sale and any transfer, they also contain many specific exclusions and exemptions. Thus, states often expressly exclude sales of intangible personal property, sales of personal property for the purpose of resale, purchases of materials and/or machinery for use in manufacturing or fabricating tangible personal property for sale, sales of personal property to charitable organizations, and sales of containers and packaging materials.

The exemption categories are quite detailed and vary considerably from state to state, but in general they are designed to exclude from taxation sales of goods intended for resale, equipment and machinery used to produce goods for retail sales, sales in interstate commerce, and sales to tax-exempt organizations and governmental entities. In addition, certain exemptions, especially the common ones for unprepared food and drugs, are intended to lessen the regressivity of the sales tax. (A tax is regressive if its burden is greater for persons with lower incomes or wealth than for persons with higher incomes or wealth.)

Use Taxes. The use tax, sometimes called the compensating use tax, is imposed upon the privilege of using, storing, or consuming tangible personal property within the taxing jurisdiction. It is not a property tax but rather an excise tax imposed upon the enjoyment of personal property brought into the state or local jurisdiction by purchasers. The use tax is designed to protect the sales tax base by offsetting purchasers' attempts to avoid the state and local sales taxes by buying products outside the jurisdiction. In addition, the use tax ordinarily compensates for revenue that would otherwise be lost because of commerce clause limitations on the taxation of sales of goods purchased outside the state but used in the state.

Use taxes are usually applied as a percentage of the retail sales price, generally at the same rate as the sales tax. If a sales tax has been paid on a particular item in another jurisdiction, a credit usually will be allowed, or the item may be exempted from the state or local use tax. *Liability for the tax is imposed on the person using, storing, or consuming the property, but responsibility for actually collecting the tax and remitting it to the state is often that or the seller of the goods (e.g., some catalog sales companies).

Excise Taxes. In addition to the broadly applicable general retail sales tax, most states levy special sales taxes, also known as excise taxes, targeted at purchases of specific items, especially tobacco products, motor fuel, and alcoholic beverages. Typically, the items subject to these excises are not also taxed under the general retail sales tax. Special sales taxes usually are imposed only by state governments, but some states authorize local governments to levy certain excises.

Gross Receipts Taxes. Gross receipts taxes are levied upon the total revenues of a business on a periodic basis, usually annually. A typical example of a gross receipts tax is the occupational license tax, which is imposed on foreign and domestic *corporations for the right to do business in the state. It is measured as a percentage of the total gross revenues of such a corporation during the specified period.

Unlike the corporate income tax, which taxes only a corporation's profits (revenues minus allowable expenses), the gross receipts tax is levied on the total revenues received by the business. The gross receipts tax is levied on only the business activity itself—not the consumption of goods produced by that activity—and, therefore, it is sometimes treated as a license tax. Furthermore, this tax is assessed as a percentage of the revenues received, regardless of the source.

(This article draws heavily from the authors' book, Gelfand, Mintz, & Salsich, *State and Local Taxation and Finance in a Nutshell* (2nd ed., 2000), with the permission of its publisher, the West Group.)

• Paul Hartment, *Federal Limitations on State and Local Taxation*, 1981. M. David Gelfand, ed., *State and Local Government Debt Financing*, vol. 2, 1991. Jerome R. Hellerstein and Walter Hellerstein, *State and Local Taxation: Cases and Materials*, 6th ed., 1997. M. David Gelfand, Joel A. Mintz, and Peter W. Salsich, Jr., *State and Local Taxation and Finance in a Nutshell*, 2nd ed., 2000.

—M. David Gelfand and Joel A. Minty

TECHNOLOGY AND LAW. Our age is noteworthy for the development of a range of powerful technologies. During the past century, new modes of transportation opened up opportunities for traveling over great distances. During the coming decades, advances in medical and biotechnology are likely to significantly change our understanding of the human body and the treatment of disease. Affecting all these technologies, and important in its own right, are information technologies that have emerged rapidly during the past few years.

New technologies allow old things to be done in new ways, and new things to be done that were not possible before. Elizabeth Eisenstein called the technology of printing that developed in the fifteenth century "an agent of change." This label might be applied to all new technologies. Whether the technology is perceived as beneficial and creating efficiencies and opportunities, whether it is conceived of as threatening and damaging, or whether it is recognized to have applications with both positive and negative potential, law will be looked on to manage change.

Because they are agents for change, even new technologies that are welcomed positively will be disruptive. People and institutions that are comfortable with and benefit from the status quo will feel threatened. As James Lardner observed, "technological history is a constant struggle between pioneers and protectionists—between those who are trying to introduce new devices and those who are trying to guard and exploit existing ones." Law is often in the middle of this, trying to fashion ways to exploit the new while also working to preserve the past.

Technology significantly affected the development of law in numerous ways during the nineteenth century. The invention of the steamboat, for example, revolutionized travel on inland waterways. This innovation encouraged navigation on fresh water lakes and rivers, and rendered obsolete the traditional English rule that *admiralty jurisdiction was limited to waters within the ebb and flow of the tide. In *Propeller Genesee Chief* v. *Fitzhugh* (1851), the Supreme Court, in an opinion by Chief Justice Roger B. *Taney, enlarged federal admiralty jurisdiction and noted that legal doctrine must accommodate the growth of new technologies. Similarly, the advent of railroading exemplified the close relationship between the legal sytem and emerging technology. The railroad industry compelled the formation of new legal rules governing such diverse fields as industrial accidents, eminent domain (see TAKINGS), duties of common carriers, *labor relations, administrative law, and the reorganization of insolvent businesses (see BANKRUPTCY: BUSINESS). Railroad diverted business from existing canal and turnpike systems, but in *Charles River Bridge* v. *Warren Bridge* (1837), the Supreme Court rejected the argument that original corporate charters conferred implied exclusive rights. It pointed out that such a principle would stymie improvements in transportation. At the same time, legislators and courts early recognized the need to regulate railroad activities to protect public safety. The technology of railroading was therefore a catalyst for major changes in American law.

When the Internet was largely used by academics and researchers, some thought it would be different from other technologies in that the need for formal law would be limited. It was hoped that by expanding communication, conflicts that arose could be resolved in a non-adversarial way. This was a false hope, and it is clear that the Internet will be anything but a harmonious place. While part of the explanation for this can be traced to persons committing intentionally harmful acts online, a large part is simply a result of cyberspace's being an extremely active, competitive, and lucrative environment. Conflict can be a result of failed transactions, but conflict can also be a reflection of a rapidly growing environment. When a new technology is successful, when change is accelerated, when creative energies are unleashed, and when transactions multiply and relationships expand, disputes will inevitably occur and law will be called upon to establish standards of behaviors and to structure a dispute-resolution process for them.

While the Internet has not proven to be different from other technologies in requiring legal attention, it is different in one critically important way from even the most complex of other new technologies. For most emerging technologies, the law can be expected to be challenged to design appropriate policies for an array of novel problems. The manner in which law is enacted and applied, however, may not be different in any significant way from the manner in which legal responses to problems typically occur. New technologies can lead to new questions that need to be answered, some of which may be particularly vexing if there are ethical implications. Some problems may also demand a faster response than the law typically provides now. Fashioning a workable legal response to issues raised by any new technology, in other words, can become highly challenging, but it does not mean that there is a need for inherently different legal approaches and frameworks.

The emergence of networked information technologies brings with it the same need to adapt legal doctrines to new problems. It also presents us with something else, something that distinguishes information technologies from other technologies. This is that as the new information technologies take root, the law will not only respond to change, but will itself change. Information technologies are an "agent of change" for the law along with other institutions, providing the law with new resources to implement doctrine and resolve conflict, as well as creating conditions in which new tools will be needed. At the same time as legal standards of behavior need to be established or clarified, and rising levels of conflict need to be addressed, new tools and resources are being provided for guiding behavior and resolving conflict.

Any new technology is a moving target in the sense that early forms and applications of the technology are never final forms. It is for this reason that *regulation is difficult, and ongoing monitoring of any new regulatory process is necessary. The appearance of new means for working with information also turns the law into something "moving" and changing. Change in the law will not be as fast as in many other institutions, but the depth of change may be as great.

We may not be as familiar with the information-oriented nature of law as we are with visible symbols of the law such as courthouses, lawyers, and the police. New technologies of communication are rare enough that they become embedded in legal thinking and practice at a deep level, and their significance is generally invisible to persons who are not legal professionals. We may be aware of sayings such as "fine print" and "black letter law" that suggest some connection between law and the technology of printing, but less likely to be noticed, even though it is considerably more important, is the link between printing and the centuries-old concept of precedent. Judicial respect for precedent requires that great weight be given to how similar cases were handled in the past. This is a practice that took hold only after the development of printing, when multiple copies of a judge's ruling could be published, when it could be taken for granted that all copies were identical.

Legal Process and Dispute Resolution. All dispute resolution processes involve obtaining information, evaluating it, and drafting it into an agreement. Those who recognized the power and potential of computers early assumed that the main impact of the new information technologies would be increased efficiency in the operation of the courts. By automating some tasks and enabling the electronic filing of pleadings and motions, costs of various kinds could be reduced, time could be saved, and access to information and justice improved. Introduction of technology into the courts, however, has not occurred rapidly. Electronic filing, for example, has not yet been adopted widely. Some applications—for example, the use and assembling of evidence on CD-ROMs and the presentation of visual simulations during trials—have been growing in use. The new media are unlikely to replace the trial or the oral argument, but an electronic informational infrastructure is slowly being put in place, and some added efficiencies in court operations will be achieved.

Courts are an institution where change has been slow, partly because of limited funding, and partly because existing practices are strongly rooted. A much more rapid adoption of technology has occurred with dispute resolution processes out of court. *Alternative dispute resolution processes can be designed by the parties to meet their needs, and technology can generally be employed in any manner the parties wish. Mediation and *arbitration employ a "third party," a neutral person who can work with the parties. Technology has been called the "fourth party," not a tool to replace the third party, but something that can be used to provide new resources for dispute resolution, allow communication and interaction in between face-to-face meetings, identify and explore options, and assist in decision-making. Alternative dispute resolution typically focuses on a hearing or face-to-face meeting, inevitably a communications-rich environment. While the use of technology allows some disputes to be settled by online means exclusively, it may be most often used in between face-to-face meetings, time that is not used efficiently at present.

Alternate dispute resolution has grown because many disputes involve misunderstandings, accidents, or other situations where getting the problem resolved quickly is more important than placing blame. Rather than seeking revenge or the enforcement of rights, disputes may involve parties who see some possibility of working together in the future, and removing hostility might even be more valuable than getting compensation. Frequently, getting something resolved quickly is important because taking too much time will cost more than the value of whatever is involved in the dispute. In the Internet environment and in information-related industries, these factors are likely to be even more important. Where the value of information declines quickly over time, and where parties are located far apart, litigation becomes an even less desirable option.

The use of the word "alternative" suggests that there is a primary model for settling disputes—namely, litigation in court. What are considered the *alternatives* offline, however, might become the primary models of dispute resolution online. Litigation still occupies a central place in our thinking about dispute resolution, and this is so even though the reality is that relatively few disputes end up being settled via a trial. With cyberspace-related disputes, there is even less reason to think that courts will be the choice of first resort.

Legal Profession. The growing number of conflicts does not necessarily lead to greater reliance on the courts. As discussed earlier, while technology can bring new efficiencies to traditional modes of processing disputes, it can also support the development of new systems and approaches that may have been costly or not even possible before. The impact of technology on the legal profession can be considered with a similar perspective. It is certainly possible that services performed by lawyers will increase as the number of transactions increases and disputes grow, and it is also possible that tasks performed by lawyers will be more efficiently and more widely available. It is also possible that the new technologies will damage the authority of the legal profession, a profession oriented around control of a specialized body of knowledge called law. This could occur as new tools for accessing information and processing information allow various functions and activities to be performed in novel ways by nonlawyers.

The initial attraction of computers for the profession, as it was for the courts, was to more efficiently manage informational and communication activities. Efficiencies in legal research, in assembling and managing documents, and in communicating with clients are already quite routine. Networks have allowed lawyers and firms to extend their reach to new geographical areas, and to work with clients who are similarly trying to extend the reach of their businesses. At the same time, expanding the reach of one's practice may also increase the number of one's competitors, and bring the profession into contact with persons performing discrete roles that were previously exclusively the province of the legal profession.

The novel qualities of electronic communication present lawyers with new opportunities and new threats. The opportunities derive from increases in the complexity and number of transactions and relationships that the online environment makes possible. Managing conflict and complexity is a traditional role of lawyers, and the demand for their expertise in some areas can be expected to grow. The new media, however, by weakening the boundaries between legal and nonlegal work, raise serious questions about what the "practice of law" means and who is entitled to perform it. As information from outside the world of law becomes more accessible, and lawyers attempt to move beyond traditional boundaries of legal practice, others will attempt to expand into the domain of the legal profession.

Legal Doctrine. As cyberspace is put to new uses, the number of doctrines in which judicial or legislative activity is being generated is continually expanding. Here is one framework for understanding the areas most affected:

• Doctrines designed to protect property
• Doctrines designed to protect values
• Doctrines designed to protect people

Protection of property. Those creating something of economic value wish their investments to be protected. New opportunities to create intellectual *property and the new difficulties in enforcing intellectual property laws were among the earliest lessons of cyberspace. The constituent parts of intellectual property doctrine, copyright, trademark, and patents all give rights to a certain group to control the use of some information. Powerful capabilities for obtaining, communicating, and working with information are both a stimulus to creative endeavors, and something that makes control of the protected work more challenging than in the past. The manner in which information is communicated on the Internet also increases the challenge considerably since communication online always occurs by making and sending a copy, not by sending the original.

The initial period of technological impact is much more likely to lead to an ongoing series of controversies and fluctuating doctrine than any clear and stable standard. The *Napster* case (2001) represented a victory for musicians, music publishers, and others who thought that new models of distribution reduced the value of their creations. As even newer models of distribution spread, legal doctrine will have to come to a new accommodation among many competing interests. In the intellectual property area, unlike some other areas identified below, technological solutions may, in the end, be more influential than legal solutions.

The link between new forms of communicating and processing of information and the need to reconsider intellectual property doctrine is direct. A less direct impact occurs as the use of technology spreads, and transactions and other activities begin to occur in novel ways. The clearest current example is electronic commerce, in which relationships formed online and at a distance may lack some of the elements of trust that traditionally support relationships among people or companies that do not know each other well. For example, substitutes are necessary for signatures and other forms of authentication that are not present in the online environment but are typically part of contract formation. Legislation regarding such a substitute, a digital signature, is only one of many additions to commercial law that will be put in place to reduce risk for those wishing to participate in long-distance relationships and endeavors.

Protection of values. Free expression and *privacy are two fundamental concerns that directly involve the regulation of information. The former generally involves limiting controls placed on communication, while the latter, often defined as the control of information about oneself, requires placing controls on the use of information. Neither is protected absolutely, and, as with intellectual property, the new technologies are generating conflict over how much legislation is needed and how quickly it is needed.

The new technologies have expanded opportunities for communication, thus supporting the key purpose of the First Amendment. Yet the ability to communicate often depends upon new intermediaries such as Internet Service Providers and new quasi-public entities such as the Internet Corporation for Assigned Names and Numbers (ICANN). Restrictions imposed by nonstate intermediaries are not easily challenged under the traditional First Amendment framework. In addition, harmful and hateful speech can be delivered more quickly than ever before over a wider area, thus generating attention that the same content might not have generated before. Places such as libraries and schools that were able to control access to information when it was in print form are challenged to do so in an environment where the same machine can bring valuable health information by pressing one set of keys and violent obscenity by pressing another set.

Privacy may represent the most challenging of the legal doctrines touched by cyberspace. Economic growth depends on the acquisition, use, and reuse of information by large numbers of institutions, and these processes are occurring at a fast pace. The erosion of privacy has as much to do with the rising economic value of information and with efficient new techniques for collecting, processing, and distributing information as it does with law enforcement and the actions of government.

We may have a right to control information about ourselves, but the ability to control such information is diminishing rapidly. If government served as the original focus of concern for privacy, as evidenced by the Fourth Amendment, and the news *media have been an added concern during the past century, the diffusion of information in cyberspace will require new understandings and definitions of privacy. As with copyright, the effort cannot solely be to enforce standards that emerged out of our experience with the print media. Privacy is a concept with boundaries that are not rigid and that has changed over time as our experiences with media have changed.

While the new media allow for intrusions into what might have previously been thought to be private, they also provide unprecedented opportunities to individuals to obtain information; in that sense, the private space available to individuals is expanding. Our experience with printing shows a medium that made possible glaring instances of invasions of privacy, but which also led to a clearer and more broadly accepted concept of privacy. Print thus encouraged the existence of and appreciation of privacy as well as its invasion. The new media are likely to lead us down a similar path.

Modern privacy law grew out of a changed communications environment, and we can expect the future of privacy law to reflect the new communications environment. This is an environment that greatly accelerates acquiring, sharing, and distributing information. Writing and print conditioned us to think of information as being "contained" on pages of paper or in files. Information stayed put unless it was physically carried or sent by someone to another place. When information is in electronic form, the resting state of information is more temporary than it used to be. As this occurs, our expectations about "containing" information will change, and our concept of privacy, which is neither particularly clear nor very old, will change as well.

It would be a mistake to assume that even if it were possible to do so, we would desire to extend existing laws to cover every situation that in the past might have been considered an an invasion. More likely to occur, as we become more aware of the almost continuous movement of information about ourselves, is the redefinition and reorientation of the legal concept of privacy in a way that is compatible with the promotion, protection, and enhancement of the options provided by the new media to individuals to choose and select information, to find out information about others, and, by so doing, distinguish ourselves from oth-

ers. Our experience with information is thus changing; as a result, so too are our values and concerns. This may be more obvious today to those concerned with the increasing availability of sexually explicit materials and to those affected by illegal copying, but the same difficult challenges will also have to be faced by those wishing to use law in the future to promote individual privacy.

Protection of people. Computer crime was originally assumed to refer to crimes against computers. The most serious computer-related crimes, it was thought, would involve damage to property, to hardware, to software, and to networks rather than to people. Many traditional categories of criminal activity require some kind of physical contact, something that networks would seem to protect us from. One of the earliest pieces of legislation directed at criminal activity, the Computer Fraud and Abuse Act, focused on interference with the running of computers and the network. Our experience with the Internet and with the powerful machines connected to it have made us aware that many crimes against people can indeed occur at a distance. The growing range of activities that are possible online has led to the new creative and commercial opportunities described earlier, and, unfortunately, to new techniques for causing injury. The clues that a face-to-face meeting give to the identity of those meeting and to the degree of potential danger in the encounter are not as easy to find online. The same tools that allow anonymity or creating a new identity for purposes of expressing unpopular views also allow one to participate in online conversations for less desirable purposes.

Those categories of crimes that involve information and communication are facilitated by the online environment, but new resources for dealing with criminal activity are also part of the same environment. While total anonymity is possible, it is also extremely difficult to achieve, since computer use almost always leaves electronic tracks. Sophisticated use of encryption is possible, but would also be a warning to those who might be victims. Unfortunately, the online environment is unfamiliar enough to many users that many will miss cautionary signs that are clear signals to experienced online participants. Thus, threatening behavior, child pornography, and unlicensed online health care, very different kinds of crimes but all involving communication, are on the increase, and will probably continue to do so, at least for the near future.

Conclusion. The "rule of law" requires not merely *rules* of law but processes for the law to be enforced, for laws to be changed or initiated, and for law to be implemented even in the face of some resistance. While the content of any rule—for example whether the scope of child pornography includes images that show virtual children but not real children—may be the focus of public attention and of courts, there always lurks in the background the issue of who has the right to be making the rules and whether they can be enforced.

Cyberspace is not independent of territorially based states, but cyberspace also does not map easily onto a world made up of territorially based states. This makes it difficult, and at times impossible, for any one state to impose its own standards and solutions. Cyberspace should be viewed as a shared environment, with stakeholders that include nation-states and other entities, including individuals. Economic and other entities are struggling to adapt traditional practices to such an environment, and law can be expected to engage in the same kind of struggle.

It is often assumed that new technologies are synonymous with new tools and that the goal of any legal response is to establish standards for the use of these tools. We are learning that our new information technologies should be considered to be environments or spaces as well as tools, and that these spaces not only allow speedy and long-distance interactions, but interactions that raise questions about jurisdiction and enforcement and about the power and role of law. Justice Oliver Wendell *Holmes once stated that "the law is behind the times. And that is as it should be." What Holmes was concerned with was the possibility of too frequent changes in the law and the possible sacrifice of long-held traditions and values. Holmes's dictum is worth remembering, but it also needs to be remembered that when change in society and technology is rapid, even the law must react more quickly than it may be accustomed to, or its authority and ability to protect people, property, and values, may be permanently diminished.

[See also Computerized Research; Economics and Law; Science and Law]

• Elizabeth Eisenstein, The Printing Press as an Agent of Change, 1979. Ithiel de Sola Pool, Technologies of Freedom, 1983. Richard Susskind, Expert Systems in Law, 1987. Ethan Katsh, The Electronic Media and the Transformation of Law, 1989. William Mitchell, City of Bits, 1995. Ethan Katsh, Law in a Digital World, 1995. Richard Susskind, The Future of Law, 1996. Mike Godwin, Cyber Rights: Defending Free Speech in the Digital Age, 1998. Lawrence Lessig, Code and Other Laws of Cyberspace, 1999. Ray Kurzweil, The Age of Spiritual Machines, 1999. Ethan Katsh, Online Dispute Resolution, 2001. Stuart Biegel, Beyond Our Control: Confronting the Limits of Our Legal System in the Age of Cyberspace, 2001.

—Ethan Katsch

TELECOMMUNICATIONS. See Media and the Law; Speech and the Press, Freedom of; Technology and Law.

TELEPHONE. See Harassment; Technology and Law.

TELEVISION. See Arts, Popular Culture, and Law; Entertainment Law; Media and the Law.

TENANT. See Landlord-Tenant.

TERMINATION OF PARENTAL RIGHTS. See Adoption and Termination of Parental Rights.

TERRITORIES AND POSSESSIONS. In 1820, Chief Justice John *Marshall said that the term "United States of America" refers not simply to the states that are united. Rather, "It is the name given to our great republic, which is composed of States and territories. The district of Columbia, or the territory west of the Missouri, is not less within the United States, than Maryland or Pennsylvania. . . ." (Loughborough v. Blake).

The United States has had territories since its inception. The Northwest Territory was a part of the nation when the *Constitution was ratified. Congress has plenary power to legislate for the territories under the territorial clause of the Constitution, which provides that "The Congress shall have power to dispose of and make all needful rules and regulations respecting the territory or other property belonging to the United States. . . ." (Article IV, Section 3, Clause 2).

The United States today has five permanent territories (using the term territory in the generic sense). Puerto Rico and Guam were acquired as a result of the Spanish-American War, in 1898. American Samoa, the only U.S. territory south of the equator, was ceded to the United States by the matai (chiefs) of the islands in 1900 and 1904. In 1917, on the eve of World War I, the United States purchased what is now the U.S. Virgin Islands from Denmark. Finally, in 1976, the people of the Northern Mariana Islands, situated north of Guam and formerly a part of the United Nations Trust Territory of the Pacific Islands, voted overwhelmingly in a plebiscite to become a part of the United States. Those islands now constitute the

Commonwealth of the Northern Mariana Islands (CNMI).

Residents of each of the territories, except American Samoa, are United States citizens at birth. American Samoans are United States nationals by birth, but may obtain immediate United States *citizenship upon establishing a domicile in any U.S. state (which they, along with other territorials, have an absolute right to do). Official and unofficial referenda in the territories consistently indicate that large majorities in each favor continued affiliation with the United States.

In *American Insurance Co.* v. *356 Bales of Cotton, David Canter* (1826), Chief Justice Marshall held that Congress, acting under the territorial clause, can create courts in territories that combine the functions of Article III federal courts and those of state courts. Unlike Article III judges, the judges of such courts typically do not have life tenure.

Early court decisions considering the application of the Constitution in the territories generally followed the *ex proprio vigore* (by its own force) doctrine, which was summed up in the phrase, "the Constitution follows the flag." In the *Insular Cases* (1901), especially *Downes* v. *Bidwell*, the U.S. Supreme Court moved toward the *incorporation doctrine, which became settled law by the time of *Balzac* v. *Porto Rico* (1922). Under the incorporation doctrine, the Constitution is not fully applicable in a territory unless that territory has been "incorporated into and made a part of the United States." None of the current territories are deemed to be incorporated.

While the Supreme Court has not overruled the incorporation doctrine, lower courts have considered it modified by cases such as *Reid* v. *Covert* (1957) (which held that the Sixth Amendment right to trial by *jury applied on a U.S. Air Force base in Great Britain). At least two federal Circuit Courts of Appeals have adopted a rule of construction which holds that in any case arising in a territory, there is a presumption that the Constitution applies, but that presumption can be rebutted by proof that a particular application is "impractical" (that it would not work because of cultural differences) or that it would be "anomalous" (that it would be destructive of the indigenous culture). For example, the United States Court of Appeals in *Wabol* v. *Villacrusis* upheld a law of the CNMI prohibiting sale of land to non-Marianans against a charge of unconstitutional "reverse" racial *discrimination. Deeming the law one designed to protect the indigenous culture, the court stated that the Constitution is not "a genocide pact, whether we define genocide as physically destroying a people or killing their culture."

In addition to the distinction between incorporated and unincorporated territories, there is a distinction between organized and unorganized territories. An organized territory has an organic act—an act of Congress that establishes its government. An unorganized territory was traditionally governed under the authority of the president of the United States. Today, American Samoa is the only territory with a substantial indigenous population that is "unorganized." American Samoa has protection for its local self-government, however, in that federal law now provides that no changes can be made in the Samoan constitution without the approval of the Congress. Thus, the distinction between organized and unorganized territories has become less significant.

Puerto Rico and the CNMI are formally designated *commonwealths*. The principal identifying characteristic of a commonwealth is that the organic act is in the form of a covenant or compact between the U.S. government and the people of the territory. In general, Congress has respected these agreements. The federal courts have held, however, that acting under the territorial clause, Congress can enact valid legislation that is inconsistent with the covenants.

The United States is in a relationship of *free association* with the Federated States of Micronesia and the Republic of Palau (both in the Caroline Islands, in the Western Pacific) and with the Republic of the Marshall Islands (just east of the Carolines). These island nations (along with what is now the CNMI) were formerly the UN Trust Territory of the Pacific Islands, for which the United States was trustee. The relationship between the United States and these islands is still close. The U.S. government is pledged to defend the free association states as if they were part of the United States, and has a veto over any action of any of their governments if the United States considers such action inconsistent with its obligation to defend them. Nevertheless, the three are recognized as sovereign and independent nations by the United Nations (see SOVEREIGNTY). The terms of the compacts of free association are periodically renegotiated.

• Stanley K. Laughlin, *The Law of United States Territories and Affiliated Jurisdictions*, 1995 with 1997 Supplement). Stanley K. Laughlin, *United States Territories, Their Political Status, Government and Legal Systems*, 2002.
—Stanley K. Laughlin

TERRORISM. There is no generally agreed upon definition of "terrorism." On the contrary. During the days of the cold war, and before the collapse of the Soviet Union, one would often read or hear the statement, "One man's terrorist is another man's freedom fighter." This reflected the unpleasant reality that some countries, including the former Soviet Union and radical third-world states, refused to recognize certain acts as illegitimate that others regarded as terrorism—including, for example, hostage taking or the bombing of civilians—if they approved of the cause of the perpetrators, such as communist revolution or the overthrow of the apartheid government in South Africa.

Under the United States Criminal Code, by contrast, there is a definition of "international terrorism," 18 U.S. Code §2331(1), which states:

(1) the term "international terrorism" means activities that—
(A) involve violent acts or acts dangerous to human life that are a violation of the criminal laws of the United States or of any State, or that would be a criminal violation if committed within the jurisdiction of the United States or of any State.
(B) appear to be intended—
(i) to intimidate or coerce a civilian population;
(ii) to influence the policy of a government by intimidation or coercion; or
(iii) to affect the conduct of a government by assassination or kidnapping; and
(C) occur primarily outside the territorial jurisdiction of the United States, or transcend national boundaries in terms of the means by which they are accomplished, the persons they appear intended to intimidate or coerce, or the locale in which their perpetrators operate or seek asylum.

Nonetheless, at least at the federal level, there is no crime of "terrorism" per se. Federal prosecutors do not wish to have the burden of proving terrorist motivation in addition to the traditional intent necessary to prove murder or other violent crimes. Instead, U.S. legislation incorporates the elements of terrorism as a limitation on prosecutorial discretion. That is, if a U.S. national abroad is killed or seriously injured, no prosecution may be undertaken unless the attorney general or his designate certifies that the act "was intended to coerce, intimidate, or retaliate against a government or a civilian population" (18 U.S. Code §2332(d)).

At the local level, several states, such as Pennsylvania, provide criminal penalties for "terroristic threats," patterned after the *Model Penal Code §211.3. It provides that

a person is guilty of a felony . . . if he threatens to commit any crime of violence with purpose to terrorize another or to cause evacuation of a building, place of assembly, or facility of public transportation, or otherwise to cause serious public inconvenience, or in reckless disregard of the risk of causing such terror or inconvenience.

Such statutes, while not widely applied, have been upheld against constitutional attack.

It is noteworthy that terrorism has been responsible for relatively few deaths. Why, then, the great concern with terrorism? The reason is that the political goals of terrorists often are contrary to the vital interests of democratic countries, including the United States and its closest allies. Terrorism in the Middle East, for example, aims to prevent the peace process between Israel and the Palestinians from succeeding and to induce renewed armed conflict between Israel and its neighbors.

Moreover, there has been a disturbing trend toward terrorist acts that kill large numbers of people, such as the bombings of U.S. embassies in Kenya and Tanzania, the Oklahoma City federal building, and the World Trade Center. There is also increasing concern that terrorists will resort to so-called "catastrophic terrorism"—that is, terrorism using weapons of mass destruction—nuclear, chemical, or biological. Biological weapons in particular, such as anthrax, the smallpox virus, or the plague microbe, are viewed as a threat because of the widespread dispersal of knowledge among governments and private terrorist groups about how to create and use biological weapons. Similarly, law enforcement officials worry that terrorists might employ computers to attack energy sources or transportation systems in such a way as to cause substantial loss of life and create widespread panic and chaos.

The increased concern about catastrophic terrorism illustrates what may be the greatest threat terrorism poses: governmental overreaction that destroys fundamental liberties and violates bedrock values such as privacy. The Soviet Union, after all, had little to fear from terrorism because of its totalitarian control over the population.

If terrorism is international, the difficulties in preventing and punishing it are compounded, and new legal issues arise. For instance, when terrorism has been supported by a foreign country, the issue is not so much how to punish the individual perpetrators, but how to deal with the country that has sponsored the terrorism. Authorities have to be cognizant of the UN Charter's limitations on countries resorting to armed force.

It may also be much more difficult for law enforcement officials to arrest the perpetrators or to obtain the evidence necessary to convict them if the terrorism is international instead of domestic. Under *international law, one country's law enforcement officials cannot operate in the territory of another without that government's permission. To help alleviate this problem, the United States and other countries have entered into international *treaties that classify certain manifestations of terrorism—for instance, hijacking airplanes or taking hostages—as international crimes. This requires the treaty parties to make the covered crimes punishable under their own law, regardless of where the crimes may be committed. The United States has also ratified mutual legal assistance treaties that facilitate cooperation between law enforcement officials in transnational cases, as well as extradition treaties that require a country in which an alleged perpetrator of terrorism has been apprehended to extradite him to the United States for trial.

Current trends in terrorism, however, may make the prosecution of these crimes more difficult. Specifically, the number of aircraft hijackings and hostage takings have declined, since the perpetrator is often apprehended, but bombings that result in large number of casualties and the escape of the perpetrators are increasing. Terrorists frequently are not identified or, if identified, not prosecuted or punished, sometimes because the governments of other countries fail to cooperate. A major focus of U.S. antiterrorism policy in the twenty-first century will be to improve such cooperation.

[See also Criminal Law]

• John F. Murphy, *Punishing International Terrorists*, 1985. John F. Murphy, *State Support of International Terrorism*, 1989. United States Department of State, *Patterns of Global Terrorism—1999*, 2000. Report from the National Commission on Terrorism: *Countering the Changing Threat of International Terrorism*, 2000. Max Taylor and John Horgan, eds., *The Future of Terrorism*, 2000. Laurie Garrett, "The Nightmare of Bioterrorism," *Foreign Affairs* (2001): 76–89.   —John F. Murphy

THAYER, JAMES BRADLEY (1831–1902), lawyer, law professor, and legal writer. Born in Haverhill, Massachusetts, the second son of Abijah Wyman Thayer and Susan Bradley, James Thayer grew up in a family of modest means. Through the financial assistance of family friends he attended Harvard College, graduating with honors in 1852. Fol-

lowing a brief stint of teaching, he entered Harvard Law School, and after completing his legal studies in 1856 he was admitted to the Boston bar. In 1861 he married Sophia Bradford Ripley; they raised two sons and two daughters. Thayer died in Cambridge, Massachusetts.

For the first eighteen years of his professional career, Thayer practiced law in eastern Massachusetts. Then, in 1874, he made a major career move: he accepted an offer from Christopher Columbus Langdell, dean of Harvard Law School, to join the faculty at his alma mater. Langdell had recently introduced the "case method," a form of instruction destined to revolutionize the teaching of law in the United States. Initially relying upon lectures in his teaching work, Thayer eventually became one of the staunchest practitioners of the case method in courses on evidence and constitutional law. Like his better-known colleagues James Barr Ames and John Chipman Gray, Thayer was convinced that law teaching should be a vocation in itself, as opposed to something lawyers could do in their spare time or in retirement.

As much as Thayer loved teaching, it was his influence as a writer that made his reputation in legal circles. His book *A Preliminary Treatise on Evidence at the Common Law* (1898) is generally credited with linking the rules of evidence to the development of trial by jury in England and the United States. As its title indicates, the volume was intended as an introduction to a comprehensive history of the law of *evidence. Although Thayer collected the cases and materials for this larger project over many years, he died before he could produce the definitive legal work on the law of evidence. It fell to Thayer's student J. H. *Wigmore to publish the multivolume magnum opus on evidence, *A Treatise on the System of Evidence in Trials at Common Law* (1904–5).

In the field of constitutional law, Thayer was best known for his strongly held belief that a legislative enactment should not be struck down by a court unless it was clear beyond question that the law violated a constitutional provision. Thayer's best known exposition of this position was an 1893 *Harvard Law Review* article, "The Origin and Scope of the American Doctrine of Constitutional Law." Such legal luminaries as Roscoe *Pound and Oliver Wendell *Holmes would later credit Thayer's writings as the intellectual stimulus for their own abhorrence of *judicial review.

[See also Constitutional Commentators; Educator, Legal]

• David Wigdor, *Roscoe Pound: Philosopher of Law*, 1974. Jerold S. Auerbach, *Unequal Justice: Lawyers and Social Change in Modern America*, 1976. Robert Stevens,

Law School: Legal Education in America from the 1850s to the 1980s, 1983.   —John W. Johnson

THEFT is a *property crime. To the extent that there are a number of ways to appropriate the property of another, the term "theft" does not usually describe a specific crime, but rather refers to a crime genus that encompasses most appropriations of someone else's property—embezzlement, *larceny, fraud, conversion, extortion, and blackmail. These are all specific crimes that involve what might more colloquially be called theft. The severity or grade of the crime (*felony or misdemeanor, or some subcategory) is, absent the use of force, primarily dependent on the amount or value of the property taken. Thefts of large amounts are felonies: thefts of smaller amounts are misdemeanors.

Originally, under the *common law, there was no single crime entitled theft. Rather the term was used as an umbrella to define at least three distinct, but overlapping, crimes: larceny, embezzlement, and false pretenses. Larceny involved taking someone's property from his possession without his consent. Embezzlement involved the misappropriation of property where the perpetrator already had lawful possession, but then used that possession to appropriate the property to his own use. False pretenses involved taking or transferring the property by some sort of fraud or trick. Because these three separate offenses overlapped to some degree, numerous variants of these offenses evolved. This led to confusion. Sometimes a court would acquit a defendant or reverse a conviction on the grounds that while the evidence may have been sufficient to prove one of these crimes—for instance, larceny—the crime charged by the prosecutor or grand jury was embezzlement, and hence not the one proven.

In response to these and other difficulties, many jurisdictions passed statutes that subsumed larceny, embezzlement, and false pretenses into the single crime of theft. The *Model Penal Code went even farther. Under the Code, theft includes receiving stolen property, blackmail, and extortion. Many states have followed this approach. This consolidation reflected the mid-twentieth-century tendency, seen also in the development of the Federal Rules of *Criminal Procedure, to eliminate the proliferation of technical requirements that could result in unintended loopholes for offenders, as well as traps for the unwary, in favor of a broader "standards" approach.

Interestingly enough, the late twentieth century saw the creation of an increasing number of statutory crimes (particularly federal crimes) with in-creasingly complex elements, such as the federal Racketeer Influenced and Corrupt Organizations Act (*RICO). RICO crimes are what might be called "compound" offenses, of which a theft crime is merely one element. Thus, the simplifying impulse that led to the creation of a crime for theft appears to have been superceded once more by the urge to create crimes requiring extremely complex and specific pleading of the sort that the creation of theft was meant to eliminate.

[*See also* Criminal Law; Criminal Law Principles]

• George Fletcher, *Rethinking Criminal Law*, 1978. Joshua Dresser, *Understanding Criminal Law*, 2001.

—Tamara R. Piety

TITLE INSURANCE. *See* Insurance.

TOBACCO LITIGATION. Over time, lawsuits against the tobacco industry have proceeded on a variety of grounds. In the first wave of the tobacco litigation, individual smokers sued the industry in *tort (as a wrongful act but not a breach of contract) based upon smoking-related disease. This first wave culminated in *Cipollone* v. *Liggett Group, Inc.* (1992), in which the Supreme Court held that federal legislation specifying the content of cigarette warnings precludes, in substantial part, lawsuits against the industry by smokers. The Court, however, left open the possibility of lawsuits based upon allegations of fraud.

The second wave of the tobacco litigation exhibits two distinctive features: a focus upon nicotine addiction in addition to smoking-related disease; and the use at trial of internal documents that detail the industry's awareness of the risks posed by its products as well as its extensive efforts to mislead the public concerning those risks. The signal development of this second wave came in a *class action in Florida state court that resulted in a $144.8 million punitive damage verdict against the industry. In addition, state governments sued for reimbursement of the sums that they previously had expended in connection with smoking-related disease. These state suits led to a settlement under which the industry is obligated to pay $240 billion to state governments by the year 2025.

Some observers applaud the tobacco litigation for bringing to light the misconduct of the industry, and for forcing it to address the toll that its products take upon both public *health and the coffers of the government. Other observers sharply criticize the litigation on several grounds. Practical objections include the claim that the multibillion-dollar state settlement amounts to little more than an indirect tax on cigarettes to be paid by future smokers. A related practical objection is that the litigation is likely to be less effective than direct *regulatory measures to control the health risks of smoking, particularly by teenagers. Some see the litigation as a troubling effort to use tort law as a vehicle to punish the tobacco industry, without regard to whether its past misconduct actually caused the injuries of which smokers complain. Finally, some cultural critics frame the litigation as the product of a society in which individuals seek to transfer responsibility to others for the adverse consequences of their own risk-decisions.

• Richard Kluger, *Ashes to Ashes*, 1996. Richard A. Nagareda, "Outrageous Fortune and the Criminalization of Mass Torts," *Michigan Law Review* 96 (1998): 1121–98.

—Richard A. Nagareda

TORTS. "Tort" comes from a Latin word meaning "twisted" or "turned aside," so a tort is an act that is turned aside from the standard of proper conduct—a wrongful act. A punch in the nose, careless driving that causes an accident, defective design of a product that injures a consumer, or a fraud are all wrongful acts for which the victim can sue for an award of money *damages.

The central issue in tort law is defining what type of behavior is wrongful. Some cases are easy—for example, an unprovoked punch in the nose. Many cases are more difficult, because facts are complex and the concept of wrongfulness is vague. In that respect, it is useful to think of tort law as both a body of principles and a decision process. An essential element of tort law is the application of general principles to particular cases. The litigation system, in which judges and juries share decision-making authority, is the institutional structure through which the principles are applied.

History. Tort law has ancient roots. By the middle of the thirteenth century, the English *common law had developed the writ of *trespass, the first civil *remedy for a tort. Trespass provided a remedy for injury that the defendant caused by direct physical contact with the plaintiff or the plaintiff's *property, whether the injury was caused intentionally or inadvertently. Within a hundred years, a new writ was created, called "trespass in a similar case," through which a plaintiff could recover for indirect injury as well.

For practical purposes, however, there was very little tort law until the nineteenth century. Tort law is primarily the law of personal injury, and in pre-industrial society there was relatively little opportunity for people to seriously injure each other. Industrialization brought the railroad and the factory, and later the automobile and mass-manufactured consumer products, all of which increased the incidence of personal injuries and created a demand for a response by the legal system.

Scholars still dispute the precise role of tort law in responding to industrialization, but many agree that the emerging tort law served to nurture emerging industry by creating rules that protected industry from *liability for the injuries it caused, thereby requiring victims to subsidize economic expansion. One notorious example was the "fellow servant rule." Ordinarily an employer was liable for injuries caused by his employee in the course of the performance of the employee's duties. The owner of a business would therefore bear the cost of injuries caused by a worker. The fellow servant rule created an exception for injuries caused by one worker to another. The rule effectively immunized employers for workplace accidents; in a factory or in the operation of a railroad, a worker could only be injured by the actions of another worker—a fellow servant—so the owner would not be liable (see LABOR LAW: WORKPLACE ISSUES).

Tort law through the middle of the nineteenth century consisted of scattered cases extending older common law precedents. After 1870, leading scholars and judges, notably the great Oliver Wendell *Homes, Jr., began to first define general concepts of tort law and then to systematize the body of cases and doctrines. They defined the negligence principle—with its requirement of fault as the violation of a general duty owed to all persons whom a person might injure—as the organizing concept for many of the disparate cases. They also identified three separate categories of torts, which we still use today: intentional torts, negligence, and liability without fault, or *strict liability.

From the 1920s onward, judges and scholars transformed tort law by reconstructing the classical doctrines and emphasizing tort law's social context. Progressive judges and legal realist scholars pointed out that tort law, like other law, was an application of social policy, not simply the explication of legal principle, so courts ought to be concerned with the circumstances giving rise to accidents and the effects of the doctrines and decisions on those circumstances. These scholars, notably Leon Green, also emphasized that tort law is a process, and the allocation of power between judge and jury is a central element of the process. In 1941, William L. *Prosser published the first edition of his treatise, *The Law of Torts*, which summarized existing law and created new categories for understanding developing areas of the law, while recognizing the complexity and inconsistency that the cases presented. Beginning in the 1960s, approaches to the subject became much more diverse. An economic approach that emphasized the efficiency of the tort system became especially widespread; an early contribution to this approach, Guido Calabresi's *The Costs of Accidents* (1970), introduced into common use the concept that liability ought to fall on the "cheapest cost avoider," the party who could most efficiently avoid an accident. Rights-based, feminist, and critical approaches also contributed different understandings to the subject.

Tort Policies. Tort law has three essential purposes. First, it provides incentives for good conduct and disincentives for bad conduct, thereby deterring wrongful conduct and reducing the incidence of injuries. Second, it provides compensation for victims of injuries. Third, by requiring that wrongdoers compensate their victims, it serves our sense of fairness.

Tort law is not the only governmental mechanism that serves these purposes. Criminal law and administrative regulation also provide incentives for conduct. Social Security, welfare, and other insurance systems compensate victims. But the tort system has certain advantages over other mechanisms.

First, tort law permits private persons to take the lead in implementing its policies through civil litigation. Thus, the tort system does not require a large administrative bureaucracy to formulate rules, investigate wrongdoing, and pursue complaints.

Second, tort law is made up of relatively general rules, such as a rule that a person must act with reasonable care. What that means is fleshed out in the context of individual cases, so it does not require the law to specify in detail in advance every situation with which a person may be faced.

Third, tort law links the deterrence and compensation policies to the objective of fairness by requiring that the compensation to the victim come from the wrongdoer. Once an injury has occurred, it seems right that the wrongdoer should be punished and the victim should be made whole. There is a symmetry to the mechanism that accomplishes both objectives at the same time.

Whether tort law works as it is supposed to is one the most controversial issue in the law. Beginning around 1975, businesses, doctors, and insurance companies initiated the "tort reform" movement to do away with some basic tort doctrines and cut back on many others, arguing that the law had become unbalanced in favor of serving the compensation policy of tort law, with too little re-

gard for fairness and proper incentives. Increasingly, they asserted, the overwhelming impulse of courts in making tort rules and juries in individual cases is to compensate the injured victim and to disregard the need to prove the defendant's fault before imposing liability. The consequence of these actions is a system of too much tort liability and the ever-present threat of even more. This raises the cost of many goods and services and undermines personal responsibility.

Defenders of the tort system point out that the system has been a great success in improving the safety of the American people. Tort law has had a significant effect in providing incentives for safety, particularly in the area most under attack by the tort reformers—the manufacture of defective products. The prospect of tort liability encourages manufacturers to research the potential dangers of their products and to develop safer products. Many dangerous products have either been taken off the market, restricted in use, or improved. And the issue of personal responsibility is a complicated one; making the plaintiff assume liability for his conduct is often achieved only by letting the defendant not bear responsibility for his.

This debate is ongoing, but it has had its effects. For example, most of the state legislatures adopted tort reform measures such as limitations on damages and restrictions on medical malpractice liability. The United States Supreme Court also established constitutional limitations on the award of punitive damages.

Tort Doctrines. The most commonly-litigated torts concern physical injuries to a person, or actions that can be analogized to such injuries. These torts are subdivided into three categories: intentional torts, negligence, and strict liability. In intentional torts, the person causing the harm meant to do so. Negligence involves carelessness. Strict liability holds the actor responsible even though he did not mean to harm the victim, and exercised care in trying to avoid the harm.

The prototypical intentional tort is known as battery. A person commits a battery when he intentionally causes harmful or offensive contact with another person—a punch in the nose, for example. As with other concepts in tort law and law generally, the elements of battery expand beyond the prototype. The intent requirement can be satisfied by something less than the desire to cause harm An intent to cause an offensive contact renders the actor liable for any harmful consequences that follow, and acting with the knowledge that a harmful contact is substantially certain to occur, even if the actor does not mean for it to occur, is enough. Similarly, a battery can occur through contact that is not physically harmful but offends the victim's dignity, as with a light slap or an unwanted kiss.

Other intentional torts show similar expansions of the basic concepts. *Assault is the imminent apprehension of a battery. Here the harm is not physical injury but the threat that such injury might occur, and the line the law must draw is what constitutes a sufficient threat to be legally actionable. False imprisonment protects a person's freedom of movement in the same way that battery protects freedom from bodily invasion, by making it wrongful to restrain a person through force or threats. Intentional infliction of emotional distress protects emotional security just as battery protects physical security. Extremely outrageous conduct that causes emotional harm, such as unwarranted, threatening visits from a bill collector, are actionable. Here the difficulties are defining which conduct is too outrageous and making sure that the tort does not infringe on free *speech protected by the Constitution.

There are a number of defenses to intentional torts, the most common of which is consent. If the victim consents to a contact, for example, no battery has been committed. Issues arise in determining whether consent has been manifested and what is the scope of the consent. Silent acquiescence can, but does not always, indicate consent, particularly in ambiguous settings such as sexual contact. Consent to a degree of bodily invasion is not consent to any bodily invasion; in a sports contest, for example, the participants have consented to a certain degree of violence, perhaps even violence that violates the rules of the game, but not to conduct far outside the scope of the contest.

Although intentional torts may be the easiest to understand, negligence is the core of modern tort law. The core idea of negligence is that people should exercise reasonable care when they act by taking account of the potential harm they might foreseeably cause to other people. It is only an idea, not a rule, though, because its elements ("reasonable," "foreseeably") give courts great flexibility. Accordingly, a key element in determining negligence is the interaction between judge and jury.

The first part of the negligence inquiry is whether a general duty to act with reasonable care in a class of cases exists. The duty question is always a question of law for the judge. In many cases, it is clear that a duty of reasonable care exists because there is a direct relationship between

the dangerous conduct and the potential harm to the victim. An automobile accident caused by careless driving is an obvious example. It is foreseeable that careless driving may cause injuries, and it serves the policies of tort law to impose liability. By doing so, the law deters the conduct and provides an avenue of compensation for the victim.

In other cases, whether there should be a duty to exercise reasonable care is more controversial. Four traditional classes of "no-duty" issues deserve mention. First, there is no duty in cases in which the harm is too remote from the carelessness. A favorite case of law professors, *Palsgraf* v. *Long Island Railroad Co.* (1928), in an opinion authored by one of the great American judges, Benjamin *Cardozo, illustrates no duty. As Palsgraf was waiting on a railroad platform, a train arrived at the station. A conductor on the train reached forward to pull up a passenger attempting to board the train, while another conductor on the platform pushed him from behind. The conductors' pushing and pulling dislodged his package containing fireworks, causing it to fall and the fireworks to explode. In the explosion or the ensuing panic, scales at the other end of the platform fell on Palsgraf. Even assuming that the conductors were negligent in pushing and pulling the passenger carrying the package, the court concluded, the railroad was not liable, because the possibility of injury to her was too remote from the conductors' carelessness.

Second, the duty to prevent economic harm is much more limited than the duty to prevent physical harm. If a driver carelessly causes an accident that blocks a highway, people who are late for work and have their wages docked have no remedy against the driver. An exception arises in cases involving large environmental disasters. When the Exxon Valdez oil tanker broke up off the Alaska coast and spilled millions of gallons of oil, courts engaged in difficult line-drawing issues to determine to which of the parties indirectly injured Exxon owed a duty of care.

Third, the duty to protect against emotional harm is also less extensive than the duty to protect against physical injury. A family member or friend of an accident victim may suffer extreme emotional harm upon seeing or learning of the accident, but only in narrow circumstances can that person recover against the person who caused the accident.

Fourth, there is no duty to act affirmatively to prevent harm that might befall another person. The duty of reasonable care is imposed on those who enter into a course of conduct, not those who refrain from acting altogether. Starting down the path of imposing affirmative obligations would present line-drawing problems that traditionally have been regarded as better avoided altogether.

Once it has been determined that the defendant owed the plaintiff a duty of reasonable care, what the specific content of the duty is, and whether the defendant violated it is a question for the jury, constrained by the judge's instructions on the law and by a variety of special rules, such as the requirement of expert testimony in a malpractice case. The definition of reasonable care is vague, and the courts have attempted to help juries by giving it more content. One of the best known attempts to define reasonable care came in the case of *United States* v. *Carroll Towing Co.* (2d Cir 1947). Judge Learned *Hand provided an algebraic expression: Negligence occurs where the probability of harm multiplied by the gravity of the resulting injury is greater than the burden of taking precautions to prevent the harm. Another common attempt at definition is to provide the model of the reasonable person, who acts the way people always should act, cautiously and responsibly though not perfectly.

These attempts at definition give the jury access to the policies underlying tort law. The law provides incentives for exercising the right amount of care, but not too much. Where the defendant has taken too little account of the victim's interests, it is fair to require that compensation be paid.

Professional *malpractice cases require special rules for the determination of negligence. Ordinarily, the jury's common knowledge is sufficient to evaluate the evidence presented and determine if the defendant exercised reasonable care. Some issues are more complicated, however, and require expert testimony, including expert opinions about the defendant's negligence, to aid the jury in reaching its decision. In medical malpractice cases, for example, when the victim alleges that a physician was negligent in diagnosing an illness or carrying out a medical procedure, the jury's common knowledge is inadequate to evaluate the physician's conduct, so expert testimony is required to inform the jury about the relevant standard of care (see MEDICINE AND LAW: MEDICAL MALPRACTICE).

When the victim's own carelessness mixed with the defendant's negligence to cause the injury, the traditional rule of contributory negligence barred the victim from recovering altogether. The unfairness of this absolute bar led courts and legislatures to limit the scope of the doctrine. The great majority of states have adopted a rule of comparative negligence. Under comparative negligence, the plaintiff's fault reduces but does not entirely eliminate the defendant's liability for the plaintiff's injury. The jury is assigned the task of quantifying the degree of fault, and the damages are based on the percentages they come up with. Under a pure comparative negligence system, the victim can always recover some amount, even if the defendant is only 1 percent responsible. Under modified comparative negligence, the victim can only recover if he is not as responsible (50 percent) or more responsible (51 percent) than the defendant.

One other situation involving the plaintiff's contribution to the harm arises when the plaintiff engages in assumption of the risk of harm. As with intentional torts, when someone consents to a dangerous activity and agrees to absolve someone else from liability if the actor is injured, that act removes the wrongfulness of conduct. Therefore, releases signed at ski resorts or health clubs often are held to be enforceable.

The third major area of tort liability for physical harm is strict liability—liability that is imposed even in the absence of intent to injure or negligence. One of the earliest strict liability cases was *Rylands* v. *Fletcher* (LR 3 HL 330), decided by the House of Lords in 1868. The defendants had built a reservoir on their property on top of an abandoned mine. The water in the reservoir broke through the abandoned mine and flooded the connecting mine of an adjoining landowner. Although the defendants were not negligent because they did not know the mine was there, some activities, such as building a reservoir to hold a large quantity of water, are abnormally dangerous even if they are performed with due care. Holding the actor liable without fault for all damages that flow from the act encourages a heightened degree of care and imposes on the actor the duty to pay all of the costs associated with the activity. Today, strict liability is imposed especially for activities that are not only dangerous but are unusual for their locale.

The area in which strict liability is used most often involves manufactured products. Strict liability for defective products—products liability—was one of the major developments in tort law in the twentieth century. It is also the area in which large corporations, *insurance companies, and their lawyers have mounted the strongest attack on the tort system under the banner of tort reform.

Liability for defective products expanded gradually for a hundred years beginning in the late nineteenth century, and then exploded in the

1960s. The process involved judicial creativity, scholarly rethinking of the subject, and new social and economic circumstances. Judges gradually extended liability by analogy and then by a leap, in two key ways. Liability was detached from its roots in contract warranty law and moved firmly into the realm of torts, and then the tort theory shifted from negligence to strict liability. Scholars justified and pressed for the shift as they reconceptualized the law from its basis in fault in the individual case to a social problem of producing safer products and compensating for product injuries. The circumstances with which they dealt also had changed. No longer was the paradigm of product injury an isolated accident caused by the carelessness of a small producer; instead, the typical case was a newly developed, technologically complex product that was mass-manufactured by a huge corporation.

Strict products liability developed for three basic reasons. First, in many cases the defect in a product is caused by the manufacturer's negligence, but the negligence is difficult or impossible to prove. The physical evidence may be destroyed or inconclusive, or the information about the manufacturing process that is required to prove negligence may be uniquely within the control of the manufacturer. Second, negligence liability alone provides insufficient incentives to induce manufacturers to make safe products. When considering how much to invest in careful product design, manufacture, and quality control, a manufacturer should calculate the cost of all of the injuries caused by its products, and figure those damages into the cost of the product. Third, even if the manufacturer has acted reasonably, the victim of the product accident is still injured. If the cost of the injury is shifted to the manufacturer, the manufacturer will in turn distribute the loss among all of its customers. The cost of each product increases slightly, so that each purchaser is in effect buying insurance against being the unlucky product user who otherwise would suffer a catastrophic loss.

Strict products liability, therefore, is imposed for manufacturing defects, as when a product is improperly made. More important are two other situations: When the product has a design defect and when the manufacturer fails to warn about a risk created by the product.

With a design defect, the product is made exactly as the manufacturer intended, but the problem is with the design of the product itself. Courts traditionally have used two alternative tests to find a design defect. A product is defectively designed if it is more dangerous than users of the product ordinarily expect it to be (called the consumer expectations test) or if the dangers created by its design outweigh the benefits of the design (called the risk-utility test). The Restatement (Third) of Torts: Products Liability, adopted in 1998 by the *American Law Institute, substitutes a test of whether a reasonable alternative design that would reasonably have reduced the foreseeable risks of harm was available to the manufacturer, in effect reinstating an enhanced negligence standard. The Restatement provision has been very controversial, and its mixed reception in the courts illustrates the fundamental dispute about the extension of strict products liability.

Even if a product is not defectively manufactured or designed, the manufacturer can be strictly liable for failing to warn the user of the product of some risk associated with it. The required warning can take one of two forms: instructions that are necessary so that the product may be used safely, or a warning of inherent dangers of the product that cannot be eliminated.

Finally, a class of products liability cases that provides some of the most controversial issues in the field are cases in which the risks of the product are alleged to outweigh its benefits even though there is no alternative design or alternative product that would serve essentially the same need and even though the manufacturer has warned the consumer of the products' dangers. This area is known as generic liability because the generic class of products is arguably defective despite the lack of alternatives and the presence of a warning. The litigation over cigarettes and handguns illustrates the controversial nature of generic liability.

Paradoxically, it is in the area of products liability that American tort law has had its greatest influence in other countries, at the same time as the law has narrowed in the United States with the adoption of the Restatement (Third). The European Community's 1985 Directive on Products Liability adopts a strict liability rule and a standard for defective products that approximates the law in the United States prior to the Restatement, with particular emphasis on a consumer expectations test. The Japanese Products Liability Act of 1994 also adopts liability without fault, supplanting the previous legal requirements of negligence or breach of contract. Both of these measures used the American experience as a model for expanding liability.

Several important issues cut across intentional torts, negligence, and strict liability. The first is damages. The law cannot undo the physical consequences of an injury. What it does instead is award money damages in an attempt to compensate the injured plaintiff for the loss suffered at the hands of the defendant. These compensatory damages include lost earnings and medical expenses, to the time of trial and projected into the future. More controversial are damages for noneconomic loss, such as pain and suffering and the diminished quality of the victim's life. Traditionally, courts have concluded that an award of damages for pain and suffering serves several purposes. It provides some measure, however inadequate, of the plaintiff's loss, affirming the significance of the plaintiff's injury and requiring that the defendant bear the full cost of its wrongdoing. It also provides the plaintiff a fund for activities and pleasures that can reduce his pain and make up for his loss of enjoyment. Finally, damages for pain and suffering provide a fund for the plaintiff's attorney's *fees, which allows the award for economic loss to remain intact. Beginning in the 1970s, the tort reform movement persuaded a number of state legislatures to limit damages for noneconomic loss, particularly in medical malpractice cases. As a result, in a number of jurisdictions the victim's recovery is limited no matter how serious the injuries or what the jury awards.

Also controversial are punitive damages. Punitive damages can be awarded where the defendant's conduct "shocks the conscience," is "outrageous," or demonstrates a "willful and wanton disregard" for the safety of the plaintiff. Because of the narrowness of the standard, punitive damages are awarded in only one or two percent of the tort cases that go to judgment. In those cases, they serve two purposes. They punish the defendant for its wrongdoing and they enhance the deterrent effect of tort law. In some cases, the defendant's conduct is so outrageous that the award of compensatory damages seems insufficient to deter it. In other cases, compensatory damages are inadequate because all of the injured victims will not sue or recover. In both situations, punitive damages reduce the defendant's incentive to engage in wrongful conduct.

A second general issue is causation. In a typical case, there is a direct, obvious causal connection between the wrongdoer's act and the victim's harm. More esoteric claims can present problems, though, and courts responded by moving from a strict requirement that the harm would not have occurred but for the defendant's act to a more reasonable concern that the defendant's conduct be a substantial factor in causing the harm.

There is an important class of cases in which even this solution does not adequately tie the victim's injury to the negligence of a particular wrongdoer, as with drugs that increase the incidence of harm that may have other causes and that do not show their effects until a long period of time has elapsed. To solve these problems, courts ordinarily allow statistical evidence as the basis for liability, and impose some form of market share liability. In market share liability, there is no need to match an individual wrongdoer and an individual victim; instead, liability is imposed on a manufacturer based on its share of the relevant market for the drug that injured the victim.

Social and economic factors in the torts process shape the workings of the law of personal injuries as much as the rules of law themselves. Insurance may be the most pervasive of these factors. The ideal of the tort system matches an individual victim against an individual wrongdoer, with each potentially bearing the costs of its actions and shaping its behavior accordingly. In practice, however, both parties are likely to carry insurance. For the victim of an injury, the incentive to sue is reduced to the extent that medical insurance, property insurance, and disability insurance provide the compensation that otherwise only could come from tort damages. For the wrongdoer, liability insurance attenuates the deterrent effect of tort law. The rules of law assume that an actor will calibrate the potential liability costs of injuries from pursuing a course of conduct and vary its behavior accordingly. In fact, an insured wrongdoer has less incentive to do so, particularly when, as is often the case, the insurance premiums are not precisely rated to account for the individual's experience of loss.

Insurance plays another important role, as a substitute for whole areas of tort law. The earliest example was the adoption of workers' compensation plans at the beginning of the early twentieth century. Workers' compensation bars workers from suing their employers for injuries on the job; in return, workers are compensated for workplace injuries without having to prove the employer was at fault, with the amount of compensation based on a prescribed schedule. In theory, the system provides smaller but certain compensation for a potentially larger but less certain award, with savings in the cost of litigation. Although the theory has not always worked well in practice, the model has been adopted for automobile no-fault schemes, sports injuries, and side effects of childhood vaccines.

Two other areas of tort law deserve brief mention: torts to land and economic and dignitary torts. In early English law, invasions of land were of particular concern to the law as threats to social order. The concern lead to the development of torts that are still with us. Trespass is an unauthorized entry into another's land, and a trespass can be the basis for an injunction or a damage award. The common law stated that a landowner's rights extended from the center of the earth to the heavens, but courts accommodated the doctrine to technological development, so constructing a building that overhangs a neighbor's property is a trespass, but flying over in an airplane is not.

Nuisance is a different invasion of an interest in land, in which the land is not physically invaded but its use is made less valuable because of some activity of an adjoining landowner. The activity typically takes the form of generating noxious odors, particulates, excessive noise, or the carrying on of disruptive activities. When the activity uniquely affects a private landowner, the appropriate remedy is for private nuisance. When the activity affects the public at large or a public resource, as pollution of a stream, the remedy is available to public officials for public nuisance. In a crowded society with shifting mores, the determination of what constitutes a nuisance is difficult.

Although the core of tort law is physical injury, harm to economic and dignitary interests without physical injury also are important, particularly in business litigation. Defamation, formerly called libel and slander, involves damage to a person's reputation by the uttering or publication of a false statement. A major concern in this area has been reconciling the desire to provide a remedy for harm to reputation with free speech interests in promoting robust debate on public issues. With respect to public officials and other persons involved in public issues, the law of defamation has contracted as constitutional protection has expanded.

Torts figure prominently in business litigation in defining the appropriate scope of behavior in the marketplace. The law of misrepresentation defines how truthful one must be in the conduct of business relations; intentional deception regarding an important fact is always wrongful, and concealment, nondisclosure, and negligence may give rise to liability as well. The tort of intentional interference with contract or prospective advantage defines the limits of competition for employees or clients. Market competition requires that businesses entice each other's employees or clients, but the law imposes limits to provide for some stability in relationships.

[*See also* Fault Liability; Personal Injury Law Practice]

• G. Edward White, *Tort Law in America: An Intellectual History*, 1980. Peter A. Bell and Jeffrey O'Connell, *Accidental Justice: The Dilemmas of Tort Law*, 1997. Marshall S. Shapo, *Basic Principles of Tort Law*, 1999. Dan B. Dobbs, *The Law of Torts*, 2000. Jay M. Feinman, *Law 101: Everything You Need to Know About the American Legal System*, 2000.
—Jay M. Feinman

TRADEMARK. *See* Property, Intellectual.

TRAYNOR, ROGER (1900–1983), California Supreme Court Justice, 1940–70. Roger John Traynor was born to a working class Irish immigrant family on Feb. 12, 1900, and grew up in the Utah mining town of Park City. He entered the University of California at Berkeley in 1919, and later enrolled there as political science graduate student. Upon taking a course from the influential legal realist Thomas Reed Powell, he decided also to seek a law degree. Traynor excelled in law school, and completed his J.D. and Ph.D. degrees simultaneously in 1927.

From 1930 to 1940, Traynor served on the Boalt Hall faculty, where he became known as a '*taxation expert. In 1940, Governor Culbert L. Olson appointed him to the California Supreme Court after Olson's first choice was blocked for being "too liberal" by then Attorney General Earl *Warren. Traynor remained a justice for thirty years, serving the last six as chief justice. Subsequently, he continued to teach and write until his death on May 13, 1983.

Traynor was the most important state judge of the mid-twentieth century. On the bench, he embodied the aspirations of those legal realists who believed that academically minded judges could undertake enlightened, broad law reform in deciding individual cases. His scholarly *opinions helped shape many of the most recognizable features of modern American law. In civil *procedure, Traynor expanded the use of collateral estoppel. In *conflicts of law, he oversaw the adoption of "governmental interest" analysis. In contracts, he rejected plain meaning interpretation, and extended *promissory estoppel. In constitutional law, he endorsed the exclusionary rule in criminal cases and wrote an early opinion striking down anti-miscegenation laws.

Traynor's greatest legacy, however, lies in *tort law. His concurrence in *Escola* v. *Coca-Cola Bottling Co.* (1944), and his opinion for the court in *Greenman* v. *Yuba Power Products, Inc.* (1963), served as catalysts for the nationwide judicial transformation of products *liability law. The uncertainties of negligence and warranty law, Traynor reasoned, must give way to a strict liability regime that would provide consistent compensation to the injured and promote product safety. In similar fashion, he reasoned that the courts ought to recognize the new tort of intentional infliction of emotional distress. In negligence Traynor supported the elimination of traditional immunity doctrines, and the plaintiff-status categories in premises liability cases. Traynor's confidence in the ability of judges did not carry over to juries. He displayed considerable willingness to take assessments of unreasonableness and damages away from jurors, as well as reluctance to permit them to hear claims for negligent infliction of emotional distress.

[*See also* Judge]

• G. Edward White, *The American Judicial Tradition*, 1976. G. Edward White, *Tort Law in America: An Intellectual History*, 1980.   —John C. P. Goldberg

TREASON. The essence of treason is the violation of the duty of allegiance owed by a subject or citizen to the sovereign. It is the highest crime known to law. Earliest accounts of treason in England date back to King Edward I, who classified levying war against the king as high treason. The Treason Act of 1351 punished high treason by death and defined it to intend death or bodily harm to the sovereign or his heirs, to levy war against the king in his realm, and to adhere to the king's enemies in the realm and to give them aid and comfort. The English definition also included counterfeiting the great seal or coin and killing a judge while in exercise of his office. The statute gave rise to prosecutions for "constructive treason," whereby a case could be based merely on opinions expressed rather than to actual acts.

During the colonial era, England used the law of treason against protests of the 1765 Stamp Act, boycotts of British imports, and Sons of Liberty clashes with British troops. The American Declaration of Independence was often referred to as the "ultimate act of treason." At the Constitutional Convention, the framers carefully weighed the definitional scope of treason with the historical record of its application. They sought language that would prevent political disagreements from escalating into charges of treason and the abuses of treason law as practiced by British authorities. The *Constitution's Article III, Section 3 confines treason to "levying war" against the United States or to "adhering to the enemies, giving them aid and comfort." No one accused of treason may be convicted unless two witnesses testify to the same overt act or the accused confesses in open court. Congress, which is granted the power to decide on the punishment for treason, decided that one who is guilty shall suffer death or be imprisoned for not less than five years and fined not less than ten thousand dollars, and shall be ineligible to hold any U.S. office.

Guided by the constitutional design, the Supreme Court has kept treason prosecutions within narrow bounds. Thus, it held that "levying war" does not mean merely laying plans to go to war, "but the actual assembling of men for treasonable purpose," and that "adhering to" means that the accused has the intent to aid the enemy. Criticizing the government, even out of sympathy for the enemy, is not treason if the speaker did not intend to betray the nation. The government must prove through direct testimony of two witnesses that the accused gave "aid and comfort" by an overt act. This act must be intentional, and intended to facilitate betrayal. An American citizen owes allegiance to the United States wherever he may reside. If an alien is domiciled in the United States, he owes it allegiance and may be liable for treason. Dual nationality is not a bar to prosecution for treason.

While the treason clause limits Congress's and the Court's ability to change the definition of treason or the requirements of proof, it does not bar Congress from providing punishment for acts dangerous to national security that fall short of treason. State constitutions frequently make it a crime to commit treason against the state, but there have been very few prosecutions.

[*See also* Burr, Aaron, Trial of; Rosenberg Espionage Trial]

• Brandley Chaplin, *The American Law of Treason: Revolutionary and Early National Origins*, 1964. James Willard Hurst, *The Law of Treason in the Unites States: Collected Essays*, 1971.   —Tayyab Mahmud

TREATIES. A cornerstone of *international law is the axiom that treaties and other international agreements are binding as law (*pacta sunt servanda*). To be enforceable within United States jurisdiction, however, a treaty obligation must satisfy constitutional requirements, or at least the Bill of Rights (*Reid* v. *Covert* (1957)). As the supreme law of the land (U.S. Const. art. VI, cl. 2.) a treaty is binding on federal, state, and local governments for as long as it remains in effect.

Treaty making in the United States normally involves seven stages: (1) negotiation and approval of a draft; (2) publication of the final version; (3) signature within a specified period of time; (4) advice and consent of the Senate; (5) ratification; (6) exchange or deposit of a ratification instrument by the president to provide formal notice to the outside world; and (7) proclamation. Normally, negotiations are conducted by diplomats or other designated officials. Either the president or his designee may sign a treaty. Under international law, a signature without subsequent ratification is not legally binding on a party but does constrain it from taking any acts which would defeat the objects and purposes of the treaty.

Prior to ratification, the United States Senate must give its advice and consent to a negotiated treaty by a two-thirds vote. The Senate then submits a resolution of consent to the president. He may then sign an instrument of ratification or similar attestation, to which the secretary of state customarily affixes the Seal of the United States. After this step, the country becomes a party to the treaty within its terms. An instrument of ratification may, however, attach reservations, understandings, or declarations that qualify obligations. These are acceptable as long as they are not expressly prohibited or excluded by the treaty and are not incompatible with the objects and purposes of a particular treaty.

The Constitution and constitutional practice both confirm and qualify a treaty's status as the supreme law of the land. The qualifications include the constraints of federalism as between federal and state authority, the dualist theory of enforceability, the "later-in-time" principle to resolve a conflict between a treaty and an Act of Congress, and a requirement of separate implementing legislation to enforce "non-self-executing" treaties.

Constraints of Federalism. The Constitution's advice-and-consent requirement reflects an original intent of the framers that the states, through their senators, should be actively involved in all phases of treaty making, even the negotiation process. From the beginning of the Republic, however, the direct role of the states in treaty making has seemed unfeasible. By now, the role of the states has been marginalized by the powers the full Senate has assigned to the Foreign Relations Committee and its chair, which are frequently at odds with the president in his leadership of the treaty making process. After the senate rejected the Treaty of Versailles concluding World War I, for example, President Wilson branded the senate as the "graveyard of treaties."

Given that the states' role in treaty making has diminished, the federal government's exercise of its treaty making power might seem to threaten the constitutionally reserved powers of the states in areas of mutual or overlapping authority. A treaty can, indeed, confer upon the federal government, as against the states, a power to regulate activity otherwise within state authority, as, for example, *Missouri* v. *Holland* (1920), which held that a migratory bird treaty, as the supreme law of the land, preempted the normal authority of a state to manage wildlife within its territory. More extravagant extensions of federal powers, however, are politically and constitutionally controversial.

The Dualist Theory, as opposed to the monist theory, posits that international law and domestic law constitute two separate legal orders. Within the domestic order, treaty obligations may therefore compete with a conflicting Act of Congress because of their coequal status under the supremacy clause of the Constitution (U.S. Const. art. VI, cl. 2). When that happens, the treaty obligations may be unenforceable within United States jurisdiction. On the international level, however, the treaty continues to be binding on the United States. To help avoid the resulting contradiction, a famous opinion of Chief Justice *Marshall in 1804 established that "an act of Congress ought never to be construed to violate the law of nations if any other construction remains" (*Murray* v. *The Schooner Charming Betsy* (1804)). State legislation, state and federal regulations, and judicial decisions are subject to the same rule of construction.

The "Later-in-Time" Principle. The supremacy clause of the Constitution does not prioritize between federal statutes and treaties. Both constitute the supreme law of the land. Under the "later-in-time" principle, however, an Act of Congress will, for domestic purposes, supersede conflicting provisions of a preexisting treaty. Conversely, a subsequent treaty trumps a preexisting statute (*Whitney* v. *Robertson* (1888)). To minimize the resulting contradiction, federal and state law must be construed so as to comply with treaty obligations whenever possible.

The Self-Execution Requirement. Constitutional practice has established that a treaty cannot take effect as domestic law when it would achieve what lies within the exclusive law making power of Congress. Accordingly, certain treaty provisions, such as those requiring an appropriation of money or establishing crimes of international significance, are unenforceable without separate legislative action because they involve the exercise of powers reserved by Congress, according to the Constitution. Even in the absence of express powers, only "self-executing" treaties constitute domestic law without separate implementing legislation. Thus, "[w]hen the terms of the stipulation import a contract, when either of the parties engages to perform a particular act, the treaty addresses itself to the political, not the judicial department; and the legislature must execute the contract before it can become a rule for the Court" (*Foster & Elam* v. *Neilson* (1829)). In practice, whether a treaty is self-executing depends in part on the design and purpose of the drafters of the treaty, in part on whether it imposes rules that are feasible for courts to apply without further legislative action, and in part on the constitutional allocation of powers and prerogatives among the three branches of the federal government and between it and the states. Despite good arguments in favor of a presumption that treaties generally should be regarded as self-executing, recent practice indicates the contrary.

Courts generally have held that the United Nations Charter, perhaps the best-known treaty, is non-self-executing. This interpretation has been significant, primarily in inhibiting efforts to apply the human rights clauses of the Charter as law, particularly in domestic litigation. Provisions of the Charter, including those requiring promotion and protection of human rights, have been instrumental, however, in guiding the interpretation, application, and development of domestic law. Indeed, the Charter played a role in defining the constitutional rule of equal protection at the beginning of the modern civil rights movement in the United States. (See, e.g., *Namba* v. *McCourt* (Or. S. Ct. 1949)).

• Lord McNair, *The Law of Treaties,* 1961. Louis Henkin, *Foreign Affairs and the Constitution,* 1972. Kenneth Randall, "The Treaty Power," *Ohio State Law Journal* 51 (1990): 1089. Paul Reuter, *Introduction to the Law of Treaties,* 2d ed., 1995. Thomas M. Franck, ed., *Delegating State Powers: The Effect of Treaty Regimes on Democracy and Sovereignty,* 2000.

—James A. R. Nafziger

TRESPASS is the unauthorized and unprivileged intentional physical intrusion onto the land of another. At *common law, trespass was not a crime. It was only a *tort, subjecting the perpetrator to civil *liability. Many modern statutes and the *Model Penal Code now impose criminal liability for trespass. Nevertheless, these statutes are often quite limited, and unlike civil tort liability, impose criminal liability only under specified circumstances.

For example, the Model Penal Code limits criminal trespass culpability to cases in which there is an intrusion into a building, other occupied structure, or land that has notice posted, or otherwise communicated, precluding trespass. Under the limitations of the Model Penal Code, even intrusions into a dwelling would not be criminal under the common law unless the requisite elements of *burglary, including felonious intent, were present. Prosecutors, for example, were unable to successfully convict, for either trespass or burglary, an uninvited intruder who entered Buckingham Palace and visited Queen Elizabeth II in her bedroom.

The civil law has many cases analyzing at what height or depth an intrusion onto land constitutes trespass. Tort law also regularly holds that the perpetrator need not personally enter the *property, but can commit trespass by intentionally causing a physical substance to enter the victim's property. Such issues are often dealt with differently by specific criminal statutes.

The absence of a common law crime of trespass may come as a surprise to most people, who assume that when land is privately owned, the public is excluded. The common law developed in an environment in which the use of land, even if privately owned, was far less exclusive than it is today.

[*See also* Criminal Law Principles]

• Rollin M. Perkins and Ronald N. Boyce, *Criminal Law,* 3d ed., 1982.
—John L. Diamond

TRIAL, CIVIL. *See* Procedure, Civil.

TRIAL, CRIMINAL. *See* Procedure, Criminal.

TRIAL BY JURY. *See* Jury: Right to Jury Trial.

TRUST. Although generally connoting faith and confidence, trust has a special meaning in the law of *property: an enforceable arrangement whereby property is committed to a specific purpose by dividing ownership between a trustee and one or more beneficiaries. Sharing some features with institutions known to Roman law and its continental European successors, the trust is unique to England and countries sharing the English legal tradition. Originating in the Middle Ages, trusts have met an astounding variety of needs over the centuries, and continue to serve important functions, among them providing for persons unable to manage property, assisting wealthy individuals in planning their estates, and endowing charities.

Historical Roots. The trust, at first called a "use," was the product of a peculiar history and division of labor between medieval English courts. The *common law courts, which had originally shown great creativity in developing English land law, reached a stage of development beyond which they proved unwilling to advance. A parallel system of courts, known as chancery or *equity courts, then emerged and demonstrated a willingness to enforce intention in ways previously unrecognized. The use, at that time enforced only in equity, served many needs of medieval society that were difficult or impossible to address using only common law forms. Knights leaving on a crusade, for example, could transfer title to their estates to persons who became legal owners but who held the title "to the use of"—that is, for the benefit of—those named by the original owners, typically family members. Monasteries of friars sworn to poverty could be endowed with lands transferred to persons who held the property on their behalf. Although wills were not at that time permitted by law, their functional equivalent could be achieved in equity by transfers to uses to be declared later.

By the sixteenth century, a cumbersome but workable system had evolved, and might have continued indefinitely had not uses become a major means of evading certain feudal payments known as "incidents" that were of great value to the Crown. In 1535, King Henry VIII forced through parliament the Statute of Uses designed to prevent the further evasion of feudal incidents by converting ("executing," as it was called) uses into legal estates. A belated companion act, the Statute of Wills in 1540, specifically authorized wills of land for the first time.

Although the Statute of Uses put an end to most uses, the device had facilitated so many convenient arrangements apart from the evasion of feudal incidents that it proved impossible to suppress. In the years after the Statute of Uses, an important distinction was drawn between uses in which the person to whom title was transferred had merely a passive role—to which the statute applied—and uses in which such person had active management duties. In the latter case, the equity courts continued their enforcement role. About this time, the word trust began to be generally used in describing the enforceable arrangement.

The English equity courts became notorious in the nineteenth century for their costs and delay, abuses vividly illustrated by Charles Dickens's novel *Bleak House*, involving a trust embroiled in litigation for generations, and finally completely consumed by fees. In colonial America, equity courts were unpopular because they functioned without juries and were identified with royal power. The reform of equity and its eventual merger with law was, however, no more fatal to the trust than the Statute of Uses had been.

Modern Reality. The essence of the modern trust, as of the medieval use, is the legal effectuation of intention respecting property, largely without regard to technical forms. The process by which a trust is created involves the transfer of property by an owner, known as the settlor, to a trustee to hold in trust for one or more beneficiaries. The trust may be self-settled—that is, the settlor may retitle the property so that the settlor now holds as trustee; the settlor may even be one of the beneficiaries. The trust may be created during the lifetime of the settlor, in which case it is called an inter vivos or living trust, or it may be created at the settlor's death by means of a *will, in which case it is called a testamentary trust. Inter vivos trusts may remain revocable by the action of the settlor, or they may be made irrevocable.

In some states, specialized trusts created by so-called deeds of trust serve as the functional equivalent of *mortgages, and are routinely used in the financing of real estate purchases; in such cases, the trustee does not take possession, but merely holds technical title as security for the repayment of the loan. Like its medieval ancestor, the modern trust may also serve as the functional equivalent of a will, and can be used to avoid *probate. A common arrangement of modern estate planning is the creation of a revocable inter vivos trust in combination with a will that transfers or "pours over" any remaining assets into the trust at death. Under some circumstances, particularly as part of family arrangements, trusts can be used to defer or reduce estate taxes (see TAXATION: ESTATE AND GIFT TAXES).

The legal effect of the typical trust is to transfer the settlor's title to the trustee, who manages the property on behalf of the beneficiaries. The trustee holds legal title, but because the beneficiaries can enforce the duties owed to them by the trustee, the beneficiaries are said to hold an equitable or beneficial title as well. This arrangement, separating management from enjoyment, is of obvious utility for the settlement of property on behalf of persons unable to manage property as effectively themselves. Although originally created as a device for holding title to land, trusts today are more often funded with investment securities. At one time, trusts were extensively used to organize business monopolies, but this function of trusts was ended by various "trust-busting" measures, beginning with the Sherman Antitrust Act of 1890. Modern trusts serve almost exclusively purposes of private wealth management.

Under the most common trust terms, trustees are obligated to manage the trust property in return for a fee, usually calculated with respect to the value of the trust funds, or the amount of income generated, or both. So lucrative is the business of trust management that specialized trust companies have emerged, either as independent entities or, more commonly, as departments of banks or other financial institutions. The legal standard by which to evaluate a trustee's performance is generally referred to as "the prudent investor rule," although the content of this standard has changed over time. Originally formulated in the early nineteenth century, the prudent investor rule, really only a specific application of the prudent person rule in the law of *torts, once strictly limited trust investments to conservative, income-producing *securities. Today, the Uniform Prudent Investor Act, adopted by many states, permits diversification of trust investments by evaluating the trust's total investment portfolio, not each individual security.

The interests of beneficiaries in a trust are defined by the settlor when the trust is created, and may take many forms. A common arrangement is for a settlor to create a trust for the benefit of the settlor's surviving spouse for life, with the remainder to be distributed to the settlor's children. In such case, the trustee's duty to deliver the trust income to the spouse for life and the trust principal to the children at the spouse's death is mandatory. Another possibility is the creation of a trust to provide a beneficiary with whatever support it takes to maintain a certain standard of living; again, the trustee's duty is mandatory. A trustee may, alternatively, be given wide discretion in the distribution of trust property; specifically, the trustee may be authorized to distribute only as much income or principal to a particular beneficiary as the trustee sees fit. Giving a trustee so much discretion may be useful if the settlor is not confident the beneficiary is able to manage his affairs wisely; discretionary trusts may be particularly helpful in reducing income and estate taxation.

Throughout history, trusts have been created almost exclusively by and for the wealthy. Trusts are most common in well-established financial centers where wealthy elites, advised by skilled lawyers, seek to secure their economic and social position. Observing an early burst of trust creation in Boston almost 200 years ago, Oliver Wendell Holmes Sr., the witty father of the famous Supreme Court justice, advised the well-to-do: "Don't put your trust in money, put your money in trust."

One of the more controversial developments of trust law, specifically designed to serve wealthy set-tlors, is the spendthrift trust, first recognized in the last half of the nineteenth century, and resoundingly criticized at its inception by Harvard Law School Professor John Chipman Gray for its dilution of individual responsibility. The object of a spendthrift trust is to protect the beneficiaries, even profligate ones, from the consequences of their own improvidence. The essential provision is a disabling restraint, preventing the sale or mortgage of the beneficial interest in the trust; the trustee of a spendthrift trust must pay the beneficiary personally, and cannot be compelled to pay any creditors. In defense of the arrangement, it may be said that the settlor has no legal duty to give the beneficiary anything at all, and so may make a specially restricted gift. Spendthrift trusts must ordinarily benefit someone other than the settlor—that is, they may not generally be used by a settlor to shield assets from the settlor's own creditors. Recently, generous exemptions in estate tax law have led to the development of another device for the preservation of wealth within the family, the so-called dynasty trust, designed to avoid estate taxation and provide income to descendants of wealthy individuals over many generations.

Trusts may also be used by the wealthy for purposes other than the preservation of family fortunes. Charitable trusts, dedicated to purposes such as the advancement of education, religion, or public health, or the relief of poverty, have been endowed with vast assets. Unlike most private trusts, charitable trusts are permitted to last in perpetuity; over time, changing social needs can lead to some difficult questions in the administration of older trusts. Because there are no individual beneficiaries of charitable trusts, supervision of the trustees is the task of the various state law officers; abuse by charitable trustees in a few instances have occasioned notable scandals. Recently, charitable trusts have lost favor with philanthropists, who have instead created charitable foundations organized in corporate form.

Created by the decisions of equity courts, trust law was long predominantly judge-made law. Creative chancellors such as Lord Chancellor Nottingham in England or New York Chancellor James Kent in the United States laid the foundations in their decisions of individual cases. In the twentieth century, academic commentary became increasingly important as scattered state courts with no particular expertise in equity matters confronted complex trust questions. The series of restatements of the law of trusts produced by the *American Law Institute has greatly influenced judicial decisions as well. In the last few decades, uniform acts such as the Uniform Prudent Investor Act have been proposed, and have provided some much-needed standardization.

An instrument of almost breathtaking simplicity, the modern trust serves many needs. It provides a convenient means for separating the management of property from its enjoyment, and allows the settlor's intention to continue to govern the use of property long after the settlor is dead. The future of the law of trusts is certain to be long, although impossible to predict in detail; trust purposes are, as Austin Scott once observed, "as unlimited as the imagination of lawyers."

• Frederic Maitland, *Equity: A Course of Lectures* (John Brunyate, 2d ed.) 1936. George G. and George T. Bogert, *Trusts and Trustees,* 2d ed., 1983. Austin W. Scott, *Trusts* (William F. Fratcher, 4th ed.) 1989. American Law Institute, *Restatement (Third) of Trusts,* 1992.

—John V. Orth

U

ULTRA VIRES. *See* Corporation.

UNCONSCIONABILITY. *See* Contract Law.

UNEMPLOYMENT INSURANCE. *See* Labor Law: Workplace Issues.

UNIFORM COMMERCIAL CODE. *See* Commercial Law.

UNION, LABOR. *See* Labor Law: Labor Relations.

UNITED NATIONS, U.S. OBLIGATIONS TO.

United States obligations to the United Nations stem from three principal sources: the United Nations Charter, the Convention on the Privileges and Immunities of the United Nations, and the United Nations Headquarters Agreement. The first two are multilateral treaties to which the United States became a party in 1945 and 1970, respectively. The Headquarters Agreement is a 1947 bilateral agreement between the United States and the United Nations, entered into by the president pursuant to a Congressional joint resolution.

The U.N. Charter is the law of the land under the United States Constitution, even though individuals could enforce few, if any, of its provisions in U.S. courts. The Charter imposes several obligations on all U.N. members, including the United States. Foremost is the duty under article 2, paragraphs 3 and 4, to settle international disputes peacefully, and to refrain from the threat or use of force against the territorial integrity or political independence of any country or in any other manner inconsistent with U.N. purposes. These purposes include maintaining international peace and security, as well as achieving international cooperation in solving international problems. Article 2 notwithstanding, article 51 permits the use of force for individual or collective self-defense if an armed attack occurs against a U.N. member, until the U.N. Security Council has taken measures necessary to maintain international peace and security.

Article 2, paragraph 5, requires all members to give the U.N. assistance in any action it takes under the Charter. For example, if the Security Council authorizes a peacekeeping mission, the United States is required to cooperate, though the form of assistance is not spelled out in the Charter. It does not include a duty to provide U.S. armed forces unless a special agreement to do so has been reached under article 43 of the Charter. No such agreements have ever been concluded. For the United States to enter into any such agreement, Congress would have to approve it.

Article 25, in conjunction with articles 48 and 49, requires the United States and other members to carry out the decisions the Security Council makes for the maintenance of international peace and security. Consequently, when the Security Council imposes a trade embargo on a country that the Council finds to be threatening or breaching the peace, the United States is required to observe the embargo as a matter of *international law embodied in the Charter. As a matter of U.S. constitutional law, however, Congress can override the international law obligation. This has occurred, but rarely. When the Security Council imposed a trade embargo in 1968 on the former Southern Rhodesia, Congress enacted legislation directing the United States to continue importing Rhodesian chrome. The United States Court of Appeals for the D.C. Circuit upheld the legislation in *Diggs* v. *Shultz* (1972). What was thus lawful under U.S. law was unlawful under international law.

Article 17, paragraph 2, says, "The expenses of the [U.N.] shall be borne by the Members as apportioned by the General Assembly." This provision creates a binding international obligation on member states to pay the assessments the General Assembly apportions to them. For many years, the United States has been substantially in arrears under this obligation, largely because of disagreement between Congress and the U.N. over the share of the regular and peacekeeping budgets that should be apportioned to the United States. Even after an accommodation was reached in 2001, resulting in the release of $582 million in U.S. back dues, a substantial arrearage remained.

Under article 94, each member undertakes to comply with the decision of the International Court of Justice (the World Court) in any case to which it is a party. The United States has seldom been a party to an ICJ case. An exception was *Nicaragua* v. *United States* (1986), where the Court—after rejecting U.S. defenses to its jurisdiction—held that the United States had violated international law in several respects by its actions in support of rebel forces against the Sandinista government of Nicaragua. The Court decided that the United States had an obligation to make reparation to Nicaragua. The United States contended that the Court lacked jurisdiction, and thus did not concede that it had an obligation to comply with the decision on the merits.

In the LaGrand case (2001), the World Court held that the United States had violated an obligation to comply with the Court's previous order of provisional measures calling for a stay of execution of a German national who had been convicted of murder in Arizona, but whose rights under the Vienna Convention on Consular Relations had been violated before he was prosecuted. He was executed a few hours after the Court issued the order of provisional measures. The Court also held that in future cases where such rights have been violated, the United States by means of its own choosing must allow review and reconsideration of the conviction and sentence. It remains to be seen whether U.S. courts will consider this decision to be authoritative within the U.S. legal system.

U.N. Charter articles 104 and 105 obligate all members to grant the U.N. such legal capacity, and such *privileges and immunities, as are necessary to fulfill its purposes and exercise its functions. The Convention on the Privileges and Immunities of the United Nations implements these provisions by giving the U.N. the capacity to contract for, acquire, and dispose of property; bring legal proceedings, and have absolute immunity from legal process unless it expressly waives its immunity. In addition, representatives of U.N. member states, as well as officials of the U.N. and experts on missions for the U.N., enjoy a range of immunities from legal process and other interference with their official functions while in the United States. Such individuals who have abused their privileges of residence may be required to leave the country.

The Headquarters Agreement obligates the United States not to permit federal, state, or local officials to enter U.N. headquarters in New York City without U.N. consent. The Agreement also requires the United States to give principal resident representatives of U.N. member states, and certain resident members of their staffs, the same privileges and immunities it gives diplomats. The United States may not impose any impediments on transit to or from U.N. headquarters on representatives of members, U.N. officials, and other persons on U.N. business.

In 1987, Congress enacted legislation forbidding the Palestine Liberation Organization (PLO) from maintaining any premises in the United States. Consequently, the attorney general of the United States ordered the PLO's observer mission to the United Nations to close, even though the State Department conceded that doing so would violate the provision in the Headquarters Agreement on transit to or from the United Nations. In a suit brought by the United States to compel the PLO to vacate its office, the court agreed with the State Department, and held that Congress had not unequivocally expressed an intent to close the mission if the closure would violate the Agreement (*United States* v. *Palestine Liberation Organization* (1988)). The mission remained open.

• Ruth B. Russell and Jeannette E. Muther, *A History of the United Nations Charter*, 1958. Leland M. Goodrich, Edvard Hambro, and Anne Patricia Simons, *Charter of the United Nations*, 3d ed., 1969. Harold G. Maier, ed., "Appraisals of the ICJ's Decision: Nicaragua v. United States (Merits)," *American Journal of International Law* 81 (1987): 77–183. Panel Discussion, "The Palestine Liberation Organization Mission Controversy," *American Society of International Law Proceedings* 82 (1988): 534–52. Frederic L. Kirgis, *International Organizations in Their Legal Setting*, 2d ed., 1993 (19–121). Louis Henkin, *Foreign Affairs and the United States Constitution*, 2d ed., 1996 (250–59).

—Frederic L. Kirgis

V

VAGRANCY. *See* Nuisance Offenses.

VANDERBILT, ARTHUR T. (1888–1957), lawyer, reformer, dean of New York University School of Law, 1943–48, and chief justice of New Jersey, 1948–57. Born in Newark, New Jersey, the son of Lewis Vanderbilt, a telegraph operator, and Alice Leach Vanderbilt, Arthur T. Vanderbilt grew up in a family of limited means. He was student-body president at Wesleyan University, where he received an A.B. in 1910 and an M.A. in 1912. Wesleyan's president later remarked that Vanderbilt was the most unusual and gifted student he had ever known.

Vanderbilt was tireless, working his way through Wesleyan then Columbia, where he received his LL.B. in 1913. After law school, he built a thriving practice while also teaching at New York University's law school and participating in New Jersey reform politics. As a result of his reform efforts, New Jersey adopted a new constitution in 1947 that modernized the court system. Meanwhile, at the national level, Vanderbilt was instrumental in the passage of the Administrative Procedure Act (1946) and the promulgation of the Federal Rules of *Criminal Procedure.

In 1943 Vanderbilt was tapped to become dean of New York University School of Law. He used this role to spread his message of continuous reform to future generations of lawyers. For example, he introduced programs stressing public service and added courses to the curriculum on such subjects as the legislative process and judicial administration. Vanderbilt became the chief justice of New Jersey in 1948. He is best known for using that position to improve the quality of judicial administration in the state.

Vanderbilt died in Summit, New Jersey, a year before his planned retirement.

[*See also* Constitutional Commentators; Judge]

• William J. Brennan Jr., *New York University Law Center Bulletin* 6 (1957): 7. Arthur T. Vanderbilt, *Selected Writings of Arthur T. Vanderbilt*, 2 vols. (Fannie J. Klein and Joel S. Lee, eds.), 1965. Arthur T. Vanderbilt II, *Changing Law: A Biography of Arthur T. Vanderbilt*, 1976. —Mary Brigid McManamon

VEHICULAR HOMICIDE. *See* Automobiles and Crime.

VEIL, PIERCING THE CORPORATE. *See* Corporation.

VENUE. *See* Fair Trial, Criminal; Procedure, Civil; Procedure, Criminal.

VERDICTS. A verdict is the jury's resolution of a civil or criminal case. Civil verdicts may be: (1) general, where the jury finds without explanation for the plaintiff (and awards *damages) or the defendant; (2) special, where the jury only answers interrogatories submitted by the judge, who decides the case based on the answers; and (3) general, accompanied by answers to interrogatories, where the judge determines whether the verdict and answers are sufficiently harmonious to enter a *judgment. Criminal verdicts either acquit the defendant or find him or her guilty, but some courts also permit jury interrogatories.

[*See also* Criminal Law Practice; Criminal Law Principles —David S. Clark

VICTIMLESS CRIME. In the 1960s, some prominent criminologists argued that certain illegal activities categorized as "vices"—primarily drug-taking, *gambling, and prostitution—might better be seen as "victimless crimes." These reformers contended that because of "over-criminalization," the police department vice squads charged with suppressing this illicit behavior were intruding upon private conduct that was "not the law's business." Some sins were not crimes; it was futile to try to coerce virtue and "legislate morality" because of the practical limits of criminal sanctions.

Branding activities as morally offensive "vices" reflects condemnation, but the expression "victimless" implicitly questions the wisdom of legal prohibitions. A more neutral formulation of the issue would characterize drug-taking, gambling, and commercial sex as "crimes without complainants." What these outlawed actions share is that they arise from a consensual exchange between a willing buyer and seller of an illicit product (controlled substances) or service (placing a bet, selling sex), usually after a face-to-face meeting. Once the agreed-upon transaction is completed, neither party considers himself as a victimizer or victim, and neither files a complaint with the authorities.

To gather *evidence usable in court, law enforcement agencies rely on informants or undercover agents. Besides the temptation of corruption—extortion and bribery to look the other way—there is the danger of the entrapment of innocents. Ineffective suppression strategies also enable *organized crime families to develop virtual monopolies over black market goods and services. Cutthroat competition among gangsters seeking to control these lucrative rackets as well as buyer-seller conflicts settled by force add to the level of violence surrounding these voluntary but illicit activities. Furthermore, according to labeling theory, intense law enforcement pressures drive participants deeper into deviance, as they adapt to rejection by internalizing a stigmatized identity and negative self-image. Many participants band together—for example, pimps and prostitutes taking part "in the life." Additionally, the problem of secondary deviance arises whenever desperation for cash drives addicts and compulsive gamblers to steal.

Crimes without complainants fall under the heading of *mala prohibita*—wrong only because they have been outlawed at a particular time or place—as opposed to offenses that are *mala in se*—which are universally forbidden because the harm to unwilling innocent parties is self-evident, intolerable, and abhorrent. Mala prohibita consensual behavior suggests that "no act is inherently criminal," and that "all crimes are socially defined." The charge that victimless behaviors have been outlawed as a result of campaigns waged by powerful special-interest groups supports the conflict theory about the origins of criminal laws, as opposed to the consensus view that views legisla-

tion as representing the will of the majority. Moral entrepreneurs lead periodic crusades against vice as part of a process called "boundary maintenance," in which they seek to uphold traditional values by discrediting their opponents as dangerous deviants. Stigma contests break out whenever the targeted group (such as prostitutes, who view themselves as sex workers) tries to reject the negative labeling and argues that its alternative lifestyle should not be subjected to coercive legal sanctions: arrest, prosecution, incarceration, and compulsory treatment.

The contention that wagering, commercialized sex, and drug-taking actually are victimless can provoke a number of distinct policy responses. The first is a morality-based insistence on holding the line against any toleration of sinful and perverse conduct. Resigned acceptance is denounced as surrender, "permissiveness," and "defining deviance down."

During the 1990s, many jurisdictions adopted a zero-tolerance policy of stepped-up arrests for quality-of-life infractions carried out in plain view, including drug-selling and consumption, solicitations by streetwalkers, and outdoor gambling. These vice crackdowns were said to be necessary on strictly pragmatic grounds, in accord with the "broken windows" theory that removing blatant signs of neighborhood disorder discourages troublemakers from committing more serious offenses.

Another interventionist response arose from a different motivation—that members of a compassionate society are indeed "their brother's keepers." This paternalistic outlook argues that nonparticipants should not stand idly by as self-destructive adults engage in reckless risk-taking, but should try to save them from destroying themselves. From this perspective, so-called victimless crimes actually inflict serious physical harm, financial losses, and psychological damage on the participants, their families, and communities, even if the negative effects are subtle or deferred. For example, prostitution undermines family values, spreads diseases, imperils the providers (who may be assaulted by their customers and abused by their pimps), and lowers property values. Intervention is also justified by "the medicalization of deviance," which contends that drug abusers, alcoholics, compulsive gamblers, and sex addicts are not "evil doers" who deserve punishment, but are "sick" and need treatment.

A hands-off libertarian stance proceeds from the laissez-faire assumption that it is not the government's responsibility to prevent its citizens from harming themselves. Autonomous individuals have *liberty interests and *privacy rights to discretely pursue what they consider to be pleasurable. They should be free from state interference and control as long as their activities do not intrude on the rights and comfort of others.

Although the "war on drugs" rages unabated, gambling has been legalized to such an extent that the illicit forms (betting with bookmakers or backroom poker games) pale in comparison to the socially acceptable, state-promoted, and corporate-run opportunities for wagering (sweepstakes, lotteries, off-track and sports betting, and casino and Internet games of chance). Legalization has not proceeded very far for other victimless crimes. A limited number of licensed brothels operate in certain jurisdictions within Nevada, and houses of prostitution proliferate in officially designated red-light districts in many foreign cities. Coffee houses serve marijuana in Amsterdam. And drug users are not treated as criminals in many countries.

A compromise position called "harm reduction" has developed between the two extremes of vice suppression and vice acceptance. For example, the goal of harm-reduction policies for drug-taking is to minimize the collateral damage inflicted on heavy users of controlled substances, as well as on society as a whole. Strategies include methadone maintenance clinics, which dispense a substitute narcotic to heroin addicts so they will not feel compelled to steal to support their habits, and needle-exchange programs for intravenous drug injectors, who then will not share contaminated hypodermic syringes and spread AIDS to each other and their sex partners.

[See also Drugs, Illegal; Morals Offenses]

• Edwin Schur, Crimes Without Victims: Deviant Behavior and Public Policy—Abortion, Homosexuality, and Drug Addiction, 1965. Edwin M. Schur and Hugo Adam Bedau, Victimless Crimes: Two Sides of a Controversy, 1974. Alexander Smith and Harriet Pollack, Some Sins Are Not Crimes, 1975. Gilbert Geis, Not The Law's Business: Examination Of Homosexuality, Abortion, Prostitution, Narcotics and Gambling in the United States, 1979. Donal MacNamara and Andrew Karmen, Deviants: Victims Or Victimizers?, 1983. Piers Beirne and James Messerschmidt, Criminology, 3d ed., 2000.

—Andrew Karmen

VIGILANTISM. See Mob Violence and Vigilantism.

VOIR DIRE. See Jury.

VOTING AND POLITICAL PARTICIPATION. The history of voting in the United States has not been characterized by smooth and inexorable progress toward universal suffrage and widespread political participation. It has instead been much messier, littered with periods of both expansion and retraction of the franchise with respect to many groups of potential voters. Throughout this checkered history, those who controlled existing institutions had the ability to manipulate democratic processes and outcomes, and they used that ability, first and foremost, to preserve their own control. This, in turn, meant that less powerful segments of society, including racial and ethnic minorities, faced long, difficult struggles for meaningful political participation.

The *Constitution initially contained little guidance on the question of suffrage: there was no express right to vote, and there were few provisions that even related to the exercise of the franchise. Article I, Section 2, mandated that voters for members of the House of Representatives (the only directly elected federal body under the original Constitution) meet the same qualifications as voters for the most numerous branch of the state legislature, and Article II, Section 1, granted the states discretion to choose the procedure for selecting members of the electoral college. Under the Constitution, then, the breadth of the right to vote for both state and national elections was fixed by state law. And at the time of ratification, this meant that many people—including most women, African Americans, Native Americans, and propertyless white men—could not vote.

The first half of the nineteenth century witnessed a dramatic expansion of the right to vote, but most of its benefits were reserved for white men. Property qualifications, already eroding at the time of the Revolution, were gradually dismantled; by 1850, only two such requirements remained in force, and both were specifically targeted—one applied to blacks in New York and the other to foreign-born residents of Rhode Island. As property qualifications were phased out, states sometimes replaced them with tax-paying requirements, but those, too, after peaking around 1830, were swept aside in the democratic upsurge of the period. By the middle of the century, most formal economic barriers to voting had been eliminated.

This dramatic expansion of the franchise had no parallel in Europe, perhaps because upper classes in America had less to fear from a newly franchised agricultural or industrial underclass. Most agricultural labor in the United States was done by slaves, not peasants, and the slave vote was not yet an issue. Similarly, elimination of tax-paying requirements did not unleash a horde of factory workers as it would have in England, for America remained a largely agrarian society. Thus, the decoupling of economic status from the right to vote opened the possibility of democratic participation to a burgeoning urban population of largely middle-class men, not to lower-class factory workers, and certainly not to slaves. Indeed, the democratic expansion did not even result in the ready franchisement of existing minority groups to which it could have applied. A large number of states, as they removed the economic restrictions on voting, formally excluded free black men, and by the middle of the century, only five states (Maine, Massachusetts, New Hampshire, Rhode Island, and Vermont) did not formally discriminate against blacks.

In the middle of the nineteenth century, millions of immigrants from Asia, Ireland, and Southern and Eastern Europe began to arrive to farm, work in factories, and build the railroads. Most of the country, with the exception of some of the new Midwestern states that were hungry for settlers, was apprehensive about the prospect of immigrants at the polls. While early nativist movements achieved some success in combating immigrant electoral power, the great waves of *immigration in the latter half of the nineteenth and early twentieth centuries provoked a more widespread reaction. Many states rejected proposals that allowed for alien suffrage, and states that had once actively courted immigrant settlers began to repeal laws that allowed certain aliens to vote. States adopted devices purportedly aimed at combating fraud—such as lengthy waiting periods and requirements that naturalized citizens show their naturalization papers to election officials before registering or voting—that discouraged or prohibited immigrants from voting. The use of literacy tests and the rise of the secret ballot (which was a de facto literacy test since it required the voter to be able to read the ballot) also took their toll on immigrant participation.

While few blacks could vote before the Civil War, the end of the conflict ushered in a brief period when black political participation flourished. The Military Reconstruction Act of 1867 required Southern states to grant the vote to all men—including recently emancipated black men—as a condition of reentry into the Union. An early question about whether the Thirteenth Amendment, abolishing *slavery, formed a sufficient basis for enlarging the franchise became moot with the ratification of the *Fourteenth and Fifteenth Amendments.

The first section of the Fourteenth Amendment addressed the subject of the black vote somewhat obliquely, granting citizenship to those born or naturalized in the United States and preventing states from depriving any person of *equal protection of the laws. The second section of the amendment confronted the subject of voting more directly, providing that any state that denied participation in state or federal elections to "any of the male inhabitants of such State, being twenty-one years of age, and *citizens of the United States . . . except for participation in rebellion, or other crime," should have its allocation of representatives and presidential electors proportionately reduced. This preserved the states' entitlement to discriminate with respect to voting but imposed a substantial penalty—loss of federal representation—for doing so. This second provision, though fairly specific, has never been used; the equal protection clause, however, was later the source of a tremendous amount of voting-rights jurisprudence.

With Ulysses S. Grant's narrow victory in the 1868 presidential election, the Republican Party, realizing that the black vote was critical to its future success, drafted the Fifteenth Amendment to deal with the issue of black suffrage more directly. The amendment, ratified in 1870, guarantees that a citizen's entitlement to vote could not be "denied or abridged by the United States or by any State on account of *race, color, or previous condition of servitude." Shortly after it went into effect, Congress exercised its power to effectuate the amendment through the Enforcement Act of 1870, which criminalized interference with the new right to vote, and the Force Act of 1871, which established the infrastructure—in the form of federal election supervisors—to ensure access to the polls.

The Southern reaction to these efforts to safeguard the black vote was swift and, at times, vicious. Some states attempted to take the bite out of the black vote: Georgia, for example, passed a statute that prohibited blacks from holding public office. There was also widespread violence. Between the April gubernatorial election and November presidential election of 1868, Louisiana Democrats killed over a thousand people, mostly blacks.

But with the new federal legal machinery in place—and the occupying Union army to enforce it—the South witnessed a tremendous upsurge in black political participation. Moreover, with access to the polls safeguarded, black candidates experienced a marked degree of electoral success. Between 1869 and 1901, the South sent twenty blacks to the U.S. House of Representatives, and even produced two black senators. Although no Southern state elected a black governor, three states—Louisiana, Mississippi, and South Carolina—elected black lieutenant governors, and over seven hundred African Americans were elected to state legislatures.

The Compromise of 1877 and withdrawal of military troops marked the beginning of the end of black political participation in the South. Although the Reconstruction Amendments were still in place, the Supreme Court gutted the Enforcement Act and the Force Act in two 1876 cases, *United States* v. *Reese* and *United States* v. *Cruikshank*. These cases, combined with the withdrawal of the Union army, crippled the ability of Congress to enforce the Fifteenth Amendment against public and private incursions. Southern whites responded with a combination of force and ballot-box fraud to reduce the number of black voters and, more significantly, the impact of the black vote on elections. To the same end, Southern legislatures instituted a range of practices such as blatantly gerrymandered districts and at-large elections in areas where blacks were in the minority. As a result, while blacks continued voting in fairly substantial, though decreasing, numbers through the 1880s, they were no longer able to elect many of their own candidates to office.

Although the Fifteenth Amendment prohibited outright race discrimination at the polls, it was not interpreted to prevent states from imposing facially neutral measures that served as proxies for race. From 1890 to 1910, the Southern white political leadership closed the book on black voting altogether through a series of state statutory and constitutional provisions imposing devices such as poll taxes and literacy tests. Such devices were intended to prevent poor and illiterate blacks—and in Texas, Mexican Americans—from voting, and the provisions gave officials broad discretion to determine whether a particular voter met the requirements. As a result, political participation in the South plummeted; in Louisiana alone, the number of registered blacks dropped from more than 130,000 in 1896 to fewer than 1,500 by 1904. Other Southern states were similarly successful in their efforts to disenfranchise blacks, and the Supreme Court, most notably in *Giles* v. *Harris* (1903), turned a blind eye to the problem.

Another highly effective discriminatory practice was the white primary, which involved closing the Democratic primaries—the only real election in most Southern political races—to blacks. In a series of cases out of Texas, the Supreme Court initially invalidated state-sponsored white primaries,

but in *Grovey* v. *Townsend* (1935), it upheld a refinement involving the exclusion of blacks by vote at the party convention because it was sufficiently detached from state action to escape constitutional scrutiny. *Grovey*, though, was overruled just nine years later by a reconstituted Court in *Smith* v. *Allwright* (1944), based on the integral role of the primary in the state's voting process.

Although the end of the white primary had some positive effects on black political participation, the constitutional and statutory roadblocks erected around the turn of the century continued to keep most Southern blacks away from the polls. In the North, while more blacks registered and voted, they did not do so at the same level as whites, and recent immigrants continued to face significant obstacles to achieving meaningful representation. And while the ratification of the Nineteenth Amendment in 1920 opened the polls to women, black and immigrant women continued to face the same hurdles as their male counterparts. The relative calm of the first half of the twentieth century, though, came to an end with the momentous constitutional and statutory changes in voting-rights law in the 1960s.

Black migration from the rural South and immigration from southern and eastern Europe fueled population growth in urban areas in the early part of the twentieth century. Political boundaries, however, were not redrawn to maintain districts of roughly equal population and, as a result, the voting power of those in growing urban districts was numerically diluted while that of their rural, largely white counterparts was correspondingly concentrated. State legislatures, dominated by rural interests, refused to grant the concessions needed to achieve more equitable district sizes, and the Supreme Court was initially reluctant to intervene in what Justice *Frankfurter termed the "political thicket" of legislative reapportionment.

The Supreme Court, however, soon entered that thicket in *Baker* v. *Carr* (1962), where it found unequal apportionment to be a justiciable constitutional claim. Soon thereafter, the Court mandated an equiproportional or "one person, one vote" standard for congressional districts in *Wesberry* v. *Sanders* (1964) and for state legislative districts in *Reynolds* v. *Sims* (1964). Because *Reynolds* required both houses of state *legislatures to be based on population, the structure of most state *governments was dramatically altered. *Baker* and its progeny also resulted in a massive shift of political power from rural areas to the cities and suburbs.

After a series of ineffective attempts to open the

political system to blacks in the South in the *Civil Rights Acts of 1957, 1960, and 1964, Congress took a new approach in the Voting Rights Act of 1965. The act, designed to enforce the Fifteenth Amendment, quickly became one of the most successful pieces of civil rights legislation in the nation's history. Some provisions applied to the entire country. Section 2, for example, tracked the language of the Fifteenth Amendment in prohibiting voting qualifications or practices that denied or abridged the right of any citizen to vote on account of race or color. Other provisions focused on the unique problems of the South by using a neutral formula to select certain jurisdictions for special treatment; the formula captured many of the worst offenders, including Alabama, Louisiana, Mississippi, South Carolina, Virginia, and parts of North Carolina.

The "covered" jurisdictions were subject to two principal constraints. First, they were prohibited from using devices, such as literacy tests and character tests, that discriminated against minority voters. Second, they were required to submit any proposed change in election procedures—from moving the location of a polling place to wholesale redistricting—to the *attorney general or to the federal district court for the District of Columbia for "preclearance" before making the change. The Supreme Court, in *Allen* v. *State Board of Elections* (1969), gave a broad interpretation to the preclearance section, finding that it included changes that diluted black votes as well as those that disenfranchised black voters. Changes would only be approved if they did not have the purpose or effect of abridging the right to vote on the basis of race. This essentially meant that any change in voting procedure in the covered jurisdictions, including those involving attempts to evade the purpose of the act, had to go through Washington.

The Voting Rights Act of 1965 had an immediate and lasting effect on black political participation in the South. Within the space of a couple of years, the percentage of eligible blacks registered in the covered jurisdictions rose from an average of 29 percent to over 52 percent. The initial gains were most dramatic in the jurisdictions of some of the worst offenders: in Mississippi, for example, black registration rose from a disgraceful 6.7 percent in 1964 to nearly 60 percent in 1968. And, over the next several decades, black voter participation continued its upward climb, slowly reducing the gap between white and black voter registration.

In the years after its passage, the Voting Rights Act of 1965 was extended and strengthened. As part of its reauthorization in 1970, the ban on literacy and character tests was extended nationwide. In 1975, the Act was amended to provide protection to foreign-language minorities, and has been used quite successfully on behalf of Hispanic voters. Thus, while the Voting Rights Act originally targeted the problem of black political participation in the South, it has since been extended to protect most racial and ethnic minorities in all jurisdictions.

The Voting Rights Act, however, was not the only significant legal change that cleared the way for minority political participation. The Twenty-Fourth Amendment, ratified in 1964, barred the use of poll taxes in federal elections; the Supreme Court followed suit in *Harper* v. *Virginia Board of Elections* (1966), prohibiting their use in state elections. More significantly, the Fourteenth and Fifteenth Amendments were used to challenge districting schemes and other devices that, while not denying minority voters access to the polls or numerically diluting their votes, nonetheless hindered their ability to participate and elect representatives of their choice. In *White* v. *Regester* (1973), for example, the Supreme Court found that use of multimember state legislative districts in Texas violated the equal protection rights of black and Hispanic voters by diluting their voting power. The multimember districts in question, the court found, were used to submerge the minority voters in a sea of white voters, effectively precluding them from electing their preferred representatives.

These "qualitative" vote dilution claims (as opposed to the "quantitative" claims involving numerical dilution) were soon expanded to other, more ingenious districting schemes. Most litigation under the Constitution, though, ground to a halt when the Supreme Court found in *City of Mobile* v. *Bolden* (1980) that a party alleging qualitative vote dilution under the Fourteenth or Fifteenth Amendments must demonstrate that the challenged procedure was established or maintained with discriminatory intent. The *Bolden* decision, however, set off a storm of protest that culminated in passage of an amendment to Section 2 of the Voting Rights Act when it came up for reauthorization in 1982. The amendment decoupled Section 2 claims from constitutional claims of vote dilution, and specifically eliminated the requirement of discriminatory intent. As amended, Section 2 has become the weapon of choice in voting rights litigation.

The development of the Voting Rights Act and aggressive use of its preclearance requirements by the Justice Department in the 1990s led to creation of a number of districts in which minority groups comprised an effective majority of the voting-age population. While these majority-minority districts proved crucial to ensuring the electoral success of minority candidates, the future of such districts was dealt a blow by *Shaw* v. *Reno* (1993), in which the Supreme Court allowed white voters to challenge the constitutionality of a majority-black Congressional district in North Carolina with a "bizarre" shape. Writing for a 5–4 majority, Justice O'Connor found the proposed district so irrational on its face that it could only be understood as an attempt to segregate voters based on race.

The Court clarified the *Shaw* standard in *Miller* v. *Johnson* (1995). While not outlawing majority-minority districts per se, the Court promoted a colorblind view of the districting process by insisting that race could not be the predominant factor in drawing district lines. But, given that race is strongly correlated with political party preference in the United States, the impact of these recent opinions may be lessened as plaintiffs find it difficult to prove that race, and not party affiliation, is the predominant consideration in redistricting decisions.

Although racial and ethnic minorities now experience greater opportunities for political expression than at many other times in the nation's history, there are still significant legal roadblocks to more widespread participation. Most states, for example, prohibit those convicted of serious crimes from voting, many for the period of incarceration, and some for life. Such restrictions are estimated to keep about four million people from the polls, and because some groups experience higher rates of conviction and incarceration, a disproportionate number of them are black and His-

panic. Nationwide, 14 percent of black men are disenfranchised by such laws; in some states, such as Alabama and Florida, almost one in three black men is barred from the polls. Immigrants, too, continue to fight an uphill battle. Millions of legal and illegal aliens fully participate in the economic and social life of the nation, but are barred from participating in its political life by requirements that they be citizens in order to cast a ballot. Such rules, like many throughout our history, are neutral on their face with respect to race and ethnicity, but clearly impede the ability of many minority groups to express their preferences at the polls and illustrate the continuing challenge they face in their struggle to fully participate in our political institutions.

[*See also* Governance]

• Chilton Williamson, *American Suffrage: From Property to Democracy, 1760–1860*, 1960. William Gillette, *The Right to Vote: Politics and the Passage of the Fifteenth Amendment*, 1965. Robert B. McKay, *Reapportionment: The Law and Politics of Equal Representation*, 1965. Marchette G. Chute, *The First Liberty: A History of the Right to Vote in America, 1619–1850*, 1969. J. Morgan Kousser, *The Shaping of Southern Politics: Suffrage Restriction and the Establishment of the One-Party South, 1880–1910*, 1974. Steven F. Lawson, *Black Ballots: Voting Rights in the South, 1944–1969*, 1976. Bernard Grofman, Lisa Handley, and Richard G. Niemi, *Minority Representation and the Quest for Voting Equality*, 1992. Chandler Davidson and Bernard Grofman, eds., *Quiet Revolution in the South: The Impact of the Voting Rights Act, 1965–1990*, 1994. Keith Reeves, *Voting Hopes or Fears?: White Voters, Black Candidates & Racial Politics in America*, 1997. J. Morgan Kousser, *Colorblind Injustice: Minority Voting Rights and the Undoing of the Second Reconstruction*, 1999. Alexander Keyssar, *The Right to Vote: The Contested History of Democracy in the United States*, 2000.

—Grant M. Hayden

W

WALL STREET LAWYERS. *See* Lawyers, Popular Perceptions of.

WAR, LAW OF. These rules traditionally fell into the categories of state of war, relations between belligerents and neutrals, and limitations on the conduct of war.

State of war largely concerned questions about the lawfulness of initiating war (that is, "just" versus "unjust" war), or determining whether certain measures taken by one country against another constituted war.

Belligerent-neutral relations centered on the principles governing the interaction between states not joining particular military hostilities and those states actually engaged in combat (for example, trade with belligerents). With the 1907 Hague Convention prohibiting war for collection of contract debts, the 1927 Kellogg-Briand Treaty outlawing war in relations between states, the post–World War II Nuremburg International Military Tribunal Charter characterizing "aggressive war" as a crime against peace, and finally, the UN Charter's prohibition on the use of force except in self-defense, matters of state of war and belligerent-neutral relations have become inconsequential.

The law of war now revolves around limitations on the conduct of war. That subject consists of rules dealing with either the weaponry and tactics used in combat, or with the protections to be accorded to various individuals and property affected by military operations.

Rules addressing the weaponry and tactics employed in combat implement the notion that force used should be only that necessary to accomplish a legitimate military purpose. The 1868 Declaration of Saint Petersburg and the 1899 Hague Conventions, representing some of the earliest efforts in that direction, aim at prohibiting weapons and tactics that needlessly aggravate the suffering of soldiers. Along the same lines, the 1925 Geneva

gas and bacteriological protocols (which emerged from the experience of World War I when over 91,000 deaths and 1.2 million injuries were suffered by troops exposed to substances like chlorine gas, phosgene, xylyl bromide, and mustard gas) strike at battlefield use of poisons and toxins.

The 1907 Hague Regulations on land warfare provide the foundation for the modern law on the subject. Article 23's prohibition of weapons that cause unnecessary suffering, and articles 25 to 27's prohibition on unnecessary bombardment and destruction are especially significant. As a state-party to that international agreement, the United States has incorporated the Regulations' basic standards into its armed services operation manuals. The United States is also a party to the so-called 1993 Chemical Weapons Convention, the most recent statement on that matter. It forbids not only use of such weapons, but also calls for disposal of stockpiles and prohibits production.

With regard to protections for individuals and property affected by military operations, the rules fall into two categories: those concerned with injured, sick, or captured combatants, and those concerned with noncombatants and their property.

Current law is contained in four 1949 Geneva Conventions, which apply between states-parties even though not all the nations involved in hostile operations are signatories, and two 1977 Additional Protocols. The Geneva Conventions on sick and wounded armed forces in the field or at sea, and the Geneva Convention on prisoners of war, seek humane treatment for relevant enemy combatants and provide various mechanisms to enhance observance of the Conventions' requirements and to punish violations. The antecedents of these conventions' basic principles date from articles 4 to 21 of the 1907 Hague Regulations and various 1929 Geneva conventions on wounded and sick soldiers and prisoners of war.

The 1949 Geneva law protections have little applicability to guerrilla forces or civil war. The 1977 Additional Protocols provide for such an extension. Their controversial nature, however, has lead to reluctance on the part of the United States to formally take on these new obligations, unlike the United States' willingness shortly after World War II to comply with the basic 1949 Geneva law.

The 1949 Geneva Convention on protection of civilians during war time and the 1907 Hague Regulations establish much of the controlling law for noncombatants and their property. Many of their basic rules can be traced at least as far back as General Orders No. 100, issued in 1863 and designed to govern activities of Union forces during the American Civil War. The Geneva Convention on protection of civilians applies regardless of whether war is declared, and whether all or part of another party's territory is occupied without resistance. Some of its requirements forbid forcible transfers of population, discrimination based on ethnicity, religious belief, or political persuasion, and reprisals or collective penalties against civilians.

The Hague Regulations protect private property, though an occupying belligerent is entitled to seize property that is war material, or requisition property for appropriate compensation. Works of art and other cultural artifacts are protected, whether they are privately or publicly owned. Under the Hague Regulations, immovable property of the occupied state may be used, but not appropriated; movable property capable of being used for military operations may be appropriated by a belligerent.

[See also International Law; Terrorism]

• U.S. Army Field Manual 27–10, *The Law of Land Warfare*, 1956. Myers McDougal and Florentino Feliciano, *Law and Minimum World Public Order*, 1961. *United States v. William Calley* (1977). Antonio Cassese, ed., *The New Humanitarian Law of Armed Conflict*, 1979. Fritz Kalshoven and Yves Sandoz, eds., *Implementation of International Humanitarian Law*, 1989. John Jones, *The Practice of the International Criminal Tribunal for the Former Yugoslavia and the International Criminal Tribunal for Rwanda*, 3d ed., 1997.   —Rex J. Zedalis

WAR CRIMES. *See* War, Law of.

WAR ON DRUGS. *See* Drugs, Illegal; Organized Crime.

WARRANTIES. *See* Contract Law.

WARREN, EARL, born 19 March 1891, Los Angeles, California, died 9 July 1974, Washington, D.C. Warren's greatest impact on America law was as chief justice of the United States (1953–69). He also affected legal developments as governor of California (1943–53), attorney general of California (1939–43), and district attorney of California's Alameda County (1925–38).

The son of Scandanavian immigrants, Christine (Crystal) Hernlund Warren and Erik Methias (Matt) Warren, a railroad repairman who later became a small landlord, Warren earned undergraduate and law degrees from the University of California at Berkeley in 1912 and 1914.

In college, Warren worked in the successful gubernatorial campaign of Progressive Party candidate Hiram Johnson. Politically, he remained a "progressive," although always running for office as a Republican. His later jurisprudence reflected the Progressive Party's values of protecting the weak in society, reigning in powerful institutions, rationalizing government, and destroying corruption.

He served stateside in World War I, rising from private to first lieutenant. In May 1920, he became a deputy district attorney in Alameda County, and in 1925 married Nina Palmquist Meyers, a young widow. Warren subsequently adopted Nina's son, and they had five children of their own. In 1953, *American Magazine* named the Warrens the "Family of the Month," and other national magazines featured the Warrens as the quintessential all-American family.

As district attorney (1925–38), Warren gained a national reputation for his scientific law enforcement in fighting crime and political corruption. In contrast to his civil libertarian jurisprudence on the Supreme Court, as district attorney Warren prosecuted "radicals" under California's syndicalism act, using red-baiting tactics to gain public support for his cases, and won convictions with possibly coerced confessions, warrantless wiretapping, and an interrogation conducted after the District Attorney's office refused to allow a suspect to see a lawyer.

During Warren's tenure as chief justice, the Court would strike down such police and prosecutorial practices through such decisions as *Silverman* v. *United States* (1961), overturning a conviction based on evidence gathered with a spike microphone placed without a warrant, and **Miranda* v. *Arizona* (1966), requiring that a suspect be allowed to see an attorney before being interrogated. On the Supreme Court, Warren rejected red-baiting, and in his opinions in *Watkins* v. *United States* (1957) and *United States* v. *Robel* (1967), and in *Yates* v. *United States* (1957), where he was in the majority, Warren helped overturn convictions of radicals and communists as violations of freedom of expression.

In 1938, Warren won election as attorney general of California with 80 percent of the popular vote. He concentrated his law-enforcement efforts on suppressing political corruption, gambling, dog racing, prostitution, and organized crime. He also attacked aliens and what he perceived as alien ideologies, supporting anticommunist mini-witchhunts led by Assemblyman Samuel Yorty, and constantly sparred with Governor Culbert L. Olson, a Democrat with strong ties to labor and liberal causes. Warren denounced Olson's pardon of the labor hero Tom Mooney and other labor radicals, and successfully opposed Olson's attempt to appoint Professor Max Radin, an outspoken civil libertarian, to the California Supreme Court.

Shortly after Pearl Harbor, Warren publicly advocated the internment of the *Japanese-Americans, arguing that they were a "fifth column" and the "Achilles heel" of the United States. He later declared, "Our treatment of Japanese-American citizens during the war was regrettable," and that he was "conscience-stricken" over the results, but he also asserted that he supported the internment in order "to keep the security of the state" (*Memoirs*, p. 149). In a 1972 interview, Warren cried when discussing his role in the internment, but throughout his life he defended the right of the government to restrict personal liberty during wartime.

In 1942, Warren ran for governor of California, winning 57 percent of the vote. In 1946, he won reelection by a margin of more than two to one. In 1950, he won an unprecedented third term, defeating James Roosevelt, son of the late president, by more than a million votes, and carrying every county in the state.

In 1950, Warren opposed the firing of University of California professors who refused to sign a McCarthy-era loyalty oath, which the Board of Regents had adopted over his objections. His attempt to protect academic freedom at the university stands out in the face of the rising tide of red-scare paranoia led by Richard Nixon and other California Republicans. But Warren did endorse a Regents policy against the employment of communists, and after the outbreak of the Korean War, he supported and signed the Levering Act, which required loyalty oaths for all state employees.

In 1948, Warren was the Republican nominee for vice president of the United States. In 1952, he hoped to be a compromise presidential candidate in a deadlocked Republican national convention. He later campaigned for the Eisenhower–Nixon ticket despite his belief that Nixon was dishonest, untrustworthy, and dishonorable. After the election, Eisenhower considered Warren for cabinet positions at Interior or Justice, but in the end, called the governor, telling him, "I want you to know that I intend to offer you the first vacancy on the Supreme Court" (*Memoirs*, p. 260). In July 1953, in preparation for that appointment, Eisenhower offered Warren the job of *solicitor general. Warren was making plans to come to Washington for that position when Chief Justice Fred M. Vinson died. In late September, Eisenhower made Warren chief justice in an interim appointment. On 1 March 1954, the Senate finally confirmed the new chief justice.

In May 1954, Warren delivered his most famous and most important opinion in *Brown* v. *Board of Education of Topeka* (1954), holding that *segregation in public education was unconstitutional. More than the opinion itself, Warren's ability to bring unanimity to the decision in *Brown* was probably his greatest accomplishment.

The key to *Brown*'s success was its unanimity. The Court was overturning the legality of all the school systems in seventeen states, and local school systems in a few others. Moreover, *Brown* was clearly the tip of the iceberg for the American South. If segregation was illegal in schools, it was only a small step to finding segregation unconstitutional in all other areas of public life. In the next decade and a half, this happened. In *Johnson* v. *Virginia* (1963), the Court, by then known as the Warren Court, declared "it is no longer open to question that a State may not constitutionally require segregation of public facilities."

In *Brown,* Warren displayed the strengths that made him the most important Supreme Court justice since John *Marshall. The Court under Warren heard *Brown* in December 1953. At the first conference after the arguments, Warren declared his belief that there could be no justification for segregation, unless it was that blacks were actually inferior to whites. He pointed out that the skillful presentations before the Court by Thurgood *Marshall and other black attorneys in the case made such a position untenable. Warren essentially preempted the debate by making it impossible for any of the justices to defend segregation. Warren also acknowledged the need to go slowly in ordering the South to integrate. This was Warren as a skilled, even brilliant, politician. He then succeeded in convincing the entire Court to join him.

When Warren read the opinion of the Court in May 1954, he slipped the word "unanimously" into the text when he declared that "segregation of children in the public schools solely on the basis of race" deprives minority children "of equal educational opportunities." Thus the Court unanimously held that "in the field of public education the doctrine of 'separate but equal' has no place." This unanimity shocked most Court watchers, but gave the decision enormous credibility. Warren wrote in his *Memoirs*, "When the word 'unanimously' was spoken, a wave of emotion swept the room; no words or intentional movement, yet a distinct emotional manifestation that defies description" (*Memoirs*, p. 3). At the time, everyone realized that the unanimity was the result of Warren's personal and political skills.

Warren's *Brown* opinion revealed his ability to see that the central issues of American law are often social and political, and that the *Supreme Court must persuade not only lawyers and judges, but the people of the nation. *Brown* is short, easy to read, nontechnical, and accessible to lay persons. It is an opinion for people and politicians, not law professors. It is a simple opinion, declaring that segregation based on race is morally wrong and particularly damaging to young children. This is both its great strength and its weakness.

Between his opinions in *Brown* (1954) and *Loving* v. *Virginia* (1967), which struck down all laws prohibiting interracial marriage, Warren was able to gain a unanimous vote for all cases involving statutory segregation. At no time before or since has the Supreme Court acted with such unanimous determination in any area of law. Warren's political skills brought about this unanimity. Justice William *Brennan recognized this skill, noting, "To those who served with him, Earl Warren will always be the Super Chief" (Schwartz, p. vii).

Unlike the nation's other "super chief," John Marshall, Warren did not insist on writing the opinions in the most important cases of the period. Indeed, in his fifteen years on the bench he wrote only 168 opinions of the Court, 56 dissents, and 11 concurrences. Warren supported and helped shape, but did not write, many of the great "Warren Court" opinions, including *Mapp* v. *Ohio* (1961), excluding evidence seized without a warrant; *Engel* v. *Vitale* (1961), prohibiting state-mandated or state-sanctioned prayers in public schools; *Gideon* v. *Wainwright* (1963), guaranteeing the right to *counsel to all criminal defendants; *New York Times* v. *Sullivan* (1964), reshaping the law of freedom of the press; *Heart* of *Atlanta Motel, Inc.* v. *United States* (1964), upholding the *Civil Rights Act of 1964; *Griswold* v. *Connecticut* (1965), striking down Connecticut's ban on the use of birth control devices or pills, even by married women, and creating a right to *privacy; *In re Gault* (1967), guaranteeing basic *due process rights to minors tried in juvenile courts; *Jones* v. *Mayer* (1968), prohibiting racial *discrimination in the sale of housing on the basis of the 1866 Civil Rights Act; and *Tinker* v. *Des Moines School District* (1969), upholding freedom of expression rights for children in public schools. Warren did not write the opinion in *Baker* v. *Carr* (1962), the first reapportionment case, even though he considered it "the most important case of my tenure on the Court" (*Memoirs*, p. 306). In *Baker*, the Court paved the way for the "one person, one vote" rule in legislative apportionment.

Besides *Brown*, Warren's most significant opinion was in *Miranda* v. *Arizona* (1966), where he set out a series of principles for how police should treat suspects after their arrest known as the "Miranda warning," starting with the right to remain silent and the right to have an attorney. While many law enforcement officials initially disliked *Miranda*, they endorsed Warren's opinion in *Terry* v. *Ohio* (1968), upholding the right of an officer to stop and frisk someone for weapons on the basis of a suspicion that the person stopped was carrying a concealed weapon.

In *Reynolds* v. *Sims* (1964), the second reapportionment case, Warren articulated the need for legislative districts based on population size. He noted that "Legislators represent people, not trees or acres. Legislators are elected by voters, not farms or cities or economic interests." He declared that the right to be represented equally in a legislature was the "bedrock of our political system."

In *South Carolina* v. *Katzenbach* (1966), Warren wrote a strongly worded majority opinion, upholding the *Voting Rights Act of 1965. Like the reapportionment cases, *Katzenbach* expanded the political power of citizens. But, unlike those cases and *Brown*, the Court did not really make new law. In *Katzenbach*, it merely upheld a recent Act of Congress.

As he had in *Brown*, Warren spoke for a unanimous Court in *Loving* v. *Virginia* (1967), striking down Virginia's antimiscegenation law and by extension all such laws in other states. These antimiscegenation laws were the last vestiges of statutory segregation.

The "Warren Court" is remembered for modernizing and rationalizing criminal *procedure, striking down almost all forms of racial discrimination, strengthening the wall of separation between *church and state, and expanding individual *liberty in such areas as privacy, *speech, and political expression.

The sense that most Americans had of Warren as a man of unimpeachable ethics and honesty led to the strangest and least successful endeavor of his public life—his chairmanship of the Commission to investigate the assassination of President John F. Kennedy. Warren initially declined President Johnson's request that he chair the Commission, arguing that this extra-judicial role was inappropriate. The president appealed to Warren's patriotism, saying the country needed him to help end the wild rumors of a conspiracy to kill Kennedy.

For a variety of reasons, Warren and his Commission did a poor job of investigating the Kennedy assassination. Warren wanted to finish the work of the Commission as soon as possible, and thus rushed his staff. The Commission's work was unsatisfying, and in the end fueled the very rumors it was designed to quell.

For Warren, the Assassination Commission was a ten-month interlude in his career as a justice. After the Commission, he remained on the bench for another five years. During this period, he faced constant criticism from self-promoting "conspiracy buffs" who offered increasingly fantastic theories of a conspiracy to kill Kennedy and silence any investigation of the murder. At the same time, Warren became the focus of right-wing political attacks. The John Birch Society began placing billboards around the country calling for Warren's impeachment. Warren never responded to these attacks, and his Court continued to press forward, vindicating individual liberties, striking down racially discriminatory legislation, and upholding the central themes of the Bill of Rights.

On 1 April 1968, President Lyndon Johnson announced he would not seek a second full term. At the time, Richard Nixon, Warren's lifelong political enemy from California, was the frontrunner for the Republican presidential nomination. Fearful that Nixon would appoint his successor, Warren notified President Johnson of his plan to resign, at Johnson's pleasure.

Ultimately this strategy backfired. Johnson nominated Justice Abe Fortas to replace Warren and Judge Homer Thornberry to replace Fortas. However, a scandal surrounding Fortas's financial dealings forced Fortas to resign from the Court. Warren then remained Chief Justice until Richard Nixon appointed his successor in 1969. Much of Nixon's presidential campaign had been directed at Warren. Nixon pledged to appoint judges who would reverse the Warren Court in every way. (Ironically, Warren's successor's very name, Warren Earl *Burger, was a reversal of Earl Warren's name.) But, in important ways, the Burger court did not reverse the Warren Court. In some areas, such as the right to privacy, the Burger Court expanded what Warren had started.

In retirement, Earl Warren lectured, wrote his posthumously published memoirs, publicly opposed legislation to limit the power of the Court, and privately condemned Richard Nixon during the *Watergate scandal.

• Leo Katcher, *Earl Warren: A Political Biography*, 1967. John D. Weaver, *Warren: The Man, The Court, The Era*, 1967. Richard Kluger, *Simple Justice: The History of Brown v. Board of Education and Black America's Struggle for Equality*, 1976. Earl Warren, *The Memoirs of Chief Justice Earl Warren*, 1977. G. Edward White, *Earl Warren: A Public Life*, 1982. Bernard Schwartz, *Super Chief: Earl Warren and His Supreme Court, A Judicial Biography*, 1983. Gerald Posner, *Case Closed: Lee Harvey Oswald and the Assassination of JKF*, 1993. Mark Tushnet, ed., *The Warren Court in Historical and Political Perspective*, 1993.
　　　　　　　　　　　　　　　　—Paul Finkelman

WATERGATE. It is a measure of the place of law in America that when the country experienced Watergate, the worst political crisis in its history save for the Civil War, the passions inflamed by the event flowed swiftly and surely into the channel of legal combat. The law tamed Watergate's partisan hatred and mistrust. That mistrust, in turn, had its effects, good and bad, on the law itself.

What was to become the greatest scandal of American history began as a minor event. On June 17, 1972, agents of the reelection campaign of President Richard Nixon were arrested breaking into the offices of the Democratic National Committee in the Watergate Office Building. Their aim was to photograph documents and install listening devices to gather information for the campaign. For more than two years, the White House attempted to conceal its involvement in the crime. This effort led to the conviction of a large number of senior Nixon administration officials and, on August 9, 1974, the first resignation of a president in American history.

Although many factors played a role in creating Watergate, none was more important than the Vietnam War. President Nixon came into office in 1968 believing, as his predecessors Kennedy and Johnson had believed, that the United States, in order to succeed in its relations with the Soviet Union and China, had to present both the appearance and the substance of strength. To do so, Nixon believed, it was necessary that the United States conclude a peace agreement in Vietnam that would leave South Vietnam capable of defending itself. This belief led Nixon to prolong the war amid rising public opposition.

Nixon also believed, again like his predecessors, that it was vital to protect the secrecy of America's negotiations with adversary governments. In Nixon's case, this legitimate concern expanded into doubtful, then illegitimate, areas as the domestic conflict over the war intensified.

In the spring of 1969, major leaks of classified national security information appeared in *The New York Times*, revealing America's secret bombing of Cambodia and its fallback position in arms limitation talks with the Soviets. In response, Nixon directed the FBI to initiate wiretaps, seventeen in all, of administration officials suspected of leaking the information. Though the president's power to order electronic surveillance on his own authority was then unclear, the FBI, as during the Johnson years, conducted the presidentially ordered wiretaps without court order (see WIRETAPPING AND ELECTRONIC EAVESDROPPING).

In May 1970, Nixon ordered the invasion of Cambodia in order to curtail attacks on U.S. and South Vietnamese forces by the North Vietnamese, who were using Cambodian territory for sanctuaries. The invasion spurred massive protests at home, which led to the killings at Kent State University, a shutdown of leading American universities, and large antiwar demonstrations in major cities, including Washington, where the White House found itself in a virtual state of siege.

That summer, Nixon authorized the so-called Huston Plan, a proposal for investigations to be conducted by intelligence agencies in the Executive Branch using wiretaps, break-ins, and opening of mail. The plan aimed to identify sources of support for antiwar activity, including possible involvement by foreign governments. But FBI director J. Edgar Hoover opposed the plan for his own personal and bureaucratic reasons; as a result, the plan was never implemented.

At the time the Huston Plan was being debated, the law governing investigative surveillance was still ambiguous, but beginning in 1971, the state of the law started to clarify. In January 1971, in a federal prosecution of a conspiracy by a group called the "White Panthers" to bomb a CIA office in Ann Arbor, Michigan, U.S. District Court Judge Damon J. Keith, over Department of *Justice opposition, granted a defense motion to compel production of transcripts of government wiretaps.

The Court of Appeals affirmed. In June 1972, the Supreme Court affirmed the lower courts (see *United States* v. *United States District Court for the Eastern District of Michigan*). In the Keith case, as the White Panthers case became known, the Supreme Court did not rule on the government's claim of inherent power to conduct national security wiretaps without court order. Instead, the Court ruled more narrowly that the government's concerns in the case before it did not justify departing from the Fourth Amendment requirement for a court order.

The lower courts had already ruled against the government in the Keith case by June 1971, when former Defense Department consultant Daniel Ellsberg delivered the Pentagon Papers to *The New York Times*. The Justice Department moved to enjoin publication, but the Supreme Court ruled in favor of the *Times* on First Amendment grounds (see *New York Times Co.* v. *United States*).

Nixon was thus frustrated by resistance from the courts and his own bureaucracy. He responded by creating the White House Special Investigations Unit, known as the "Plumbers," to deal with problems of classified information and leaks.

The objective of the Plumbers was essentially that of the derailed Huston Plan. However, instead of being a well-trained national security bureaucracy, as had been envisioned by the Huston Plan, the Plumbers were a small, informal operation, ad hoc and unsupervised. The operational directors of the Plumbers were G. Gordon Liddy, Treasury official and former FBI agent, and E. Howard Hunt, former CIA agent and veteran of the aborted Bay of Pigs invasion. The Plumbers' first sortie was a burglary of the office of Daniel Ellsberg's psychiatrist, aimed at obtaining information about Ellsberg that would tarnish his reputation and undermine his defense to pending criminal charges. The mission was unproductive, as were others the Plumbers undertook. The group was terminated before the end of 1971.

At President Nixon's direction, the focus of White House information gathering now shifted to the 1972 reelection campaign and the acquisition of political intelligence. Liddy and Hunt were assigned to the Committee to Re-elect the President for the purpose of preparing plans to gather such intelligence. In the spring of 1972, campaign director and former Attorney General John Mitchell authorized Liddy and Hunt to spend $250,000 on intelligence operations, which came to include the break-in at the Watergate. The burglary failed, and the burglars were arrested.

The Watergate coverup started immediately after the arrests. The White House distanced itself from the break-in by blanket denials, meanwhile assigning the White House counsel, John Dean, to orchestrate details of the coverup. Those details included perjury by campaign personnel such as deputy campaign director Jeb Magruder. President Nixon's personal counsel, Herbert Kalmbach, was enlisted to deliver payments for counsel fees and family support to the Watergate burglars, whose silence was essential to the success of the coverup. President Nixon himself was involved in the coverup as early as June 23, 1972, when he conferred with White House Chief of Staff H. R. Haldeman about seeking CIA assistance in the enterprise. Nixon issued false public statements asserting that neither he nor anyone else in the White House knew about the break-in.

Meanwhile, Nixon had incurred added political antagonism for reasons other than the Vietnam War. Beginning in 1971, the president had made clear his intention to alter the traditional balance of federal power by creating an "administrative presidency," which would centralize Executive Branch power more completely in the White House. Shortly after his 1972 election victory, with the coverup still under control, Nixon named four cabinet officials to supervise relations between the federal bureaucracy and Congress in the interests of White House control. This assertion of power increased the hostility of Nixon's antagonists and undermined support among his traditional allies, weakening him for the impeachment crisis to come.

The coverup collapsed in stages. First, evidence of corrupt political activities, including illegal fundraising and dirty tricks, was discovered and made public by a press that at first had hesitated to report the Watergate story, but eventually made it the most massively reported political event in American history. Next, persons at criminal risk, such as James McCord and John Dean, made decisions to speak about their involvement to the court and to prosecutors. Then, Senate Watergate Committee investigators broke into the inner circle of the president's defenders, forcing the resignations of Haldeman and presidential assistant John Ehrlichman. Finally came the disclosure of the self-incriminating presidential taping system and the evidence it revealed of the president's personal involvement in the coverup.

On October 20, 1973, Attorney General Elliot Richardson and Deputy Attorney General William Ruckelshaus resigned rather than carry out the president's order, which they believed without sufficient cause, to discharge Archibald Cox, the special prosecutor investigating Watergate. The res-ignation, known as the Saturday Night Massacre, generated mounting pressure for production of presidential tapes. The pressure continued until the Supreme Court's decision in *United States* v. *Nixon, President of the United States* (1974), which denied the president's claim of executive privilege regarding the tapes. This decision resulted in the discovery of the incriminating tape of June 23, 1972, which revealed Nixon's involvement in the coverup and rendered him unable to resist *impeachment. Richard Nixon made his resignation address to the nation on August 8, 1974, and left the White House the next day.

Thus Watergate ended, and the post-Watergate era began. The consequences of Watergate for American law and politics were immeasurable. Even though existing checks and balances had succeeded in removing Nixon from office, reformers took the opposite lesson from the crisis, demanding wholesale change. Congress created the now-defunct Office of the *Independent Counsel (see *Morrison* v. *Olson* (1987)). New legislation imposed stringent financial reporting requirements on officials, limited the contacts between ex-officials and their old agencies and colleagues, and tightened the rules on campaign contributions. Congress created an Office of Government Ethics and counterparts within individual departments and agencies. The investigative apparatus in the Executive Branch grew exponentially in size. There was an explosion of investigative reporting, based on the conviction that what was newsworthy was whatever government officials did not want the public to know.

As a result, the federal government became superficially cleaner than government before Watergate. But government service became less attractive. People who wished to evade the new rules still found ways to do so. The conviction became widespread that the power of money in politics was greater than ever before.

Thus the lessons of Watergate were less clear than they had seemed, and some of those lessons were yet to be learned.

[*See also* Executive Power; Governance; Media and the Law]

• John Osborne, *The Last Nixon Watch*, 1975. J. Anthony Lukas, *Nightmare: The Underside of the Nixon Years*, 1976. Richard Nixon, *The Memoirs of Richard Nixon*, 1978. Henry A. Kissinger, *Years of Upheaval*, 1982. Stephen E. Ambrose, *Nixon (Vols. 1–3)*, 1987, 1989, 1991. Stanley I. Kutler, *The Wars of Watergate: The Last Crisis of Richard Nixon*, 1990. Suzanne Garment, *Scandal: The Culture of Mistrust in American Politics*, 1992. H. R. Haldeman, *The Haldeman Diaries: Inside the Nixon White House*, 1994.

—Leonard Garment

WATER RIGHTS. Two distinct systems of water rights operate in the United States. The doctrine of riparianism, followed in the eastern states, grants rights of water use to one who owns land on the bank of a stream or lake. A riparian owner must share the common resource with other riparians without regard to priority of use. In stark contrast stands the prior appropriation doctrine used in the arid western states. Under prior appropriation, one who first appropriates water for a beneficial use has the right, pursuant to a state-issued permit, to continue such use based on the priority of the appropriation and irrespective of ownership of land adjacent to the stream.

Riparianism, as developed in preindustrial England, embraced a natural flow theory under which each riparian had a natural and equal right to receive the flow of the stream undiminished in quantity or quality. While appropriate in water rich England in an era when navigation and fishing were the prime uses of water, the absolutist natural flow doctrine inhibited development and did not survive long in the United States. A young country required a doctrine of water rights with greater flexibility.

In the mid-nineteenth century, American courts began a transition from the absolutist natural flow doctrine to a relativist reasonable use doctrine. Under this approach, each riparian landowner is entitled to a reasonable use of the water, provided that in making such use no material injury is inflicted on other riparians. When disputes arise courts balance the challenged use against the interests of, and harms to, other riparians and society in general. This balancing test results in ad hoc determinations that lack predictability. Even the victor in a case lacks certainty with respect to the quantity of water that can be used and does not know how the balance will be adjusted in the future, when new demands by other riparians are made.

Interbasin transfers of water are particularly controversial. Growing urban centers increasingly seek what they regard as underused water from rural areas. However, transporting water from one geologic basin to another runs afoul of the traditional restrictive riparian rule that limits use of water both to the riparian tract and to the watershed that drains into the source river or lake. Some courts, recognizing development pressures, have relaxed this limitation, and many states permit interbasin transfers by statute.

Acknowledged inefficiencies in riparianism have led to the introduction of permit systems in a growing number of eastern states. These permit systems have the advantage of giving private users certainty and of better protecting the public interest in this common pool resource. State statutory regimes usually regulate, rather than replace, riparian rights. This is in part due to the recognition that legislative abolition of such rights may be found to be a *taking of *property within the meaning of the Fifth Amendment, requiring the state to pay just compensation.

In the West, courts early concluded that the arid nature of the land dictated a different rule. During the nineteenth-century western expansion, farmers diverted water from streams to irrigate land without regard to whether it abutted a stream. Gold miners also used water to run sluices. In *Coffin* v. *Left Hand Ditch Co.* (1882), the Colorado Supreme Court, recognizing the necessity of continuing these practices if the state were to be settled, declared that riparianism, which limited water use to land abutting a stream, had never been the law there. Under this Colorado doctrine, followed by a number of states, right of use depends solely on priority of appropriation. Some western states employ a mixed riparian and appropriation doctrine.

Prior appropriation rights are acquired by physically diverting water from a stream for beneficial uses. Traditionally, these include only irrigation and other consumptive uses. Instream flow was not recognized as a beneficial use. For environmental and recreational reasons, however, some states now establish minimum instream flows. Under pressure from junior appropriators and environmentalists, state agencies may require greater efficiency from users with early appropriation dates who maintain out-of-date irrigation systems. In contrast to riparian rights, appropriation rights are lost if not used.

Riparianism and prior appropriation apply to surface waters that flow in a natural channel and to lakes. Different legal regimes cover rights to groundwater and diffuse surface water (rainwater).

• A. Dan Tarlock, *Law of Water Rights and Resources*, 2000. *Waters and Water Rights*, 7 vols., 1996.

—Thomas E. Roberts

WEBSTER, DANIEL (1782–1852), lawyer and politician, born in Salisbury, New Hampshire. After graduation from Dartmouth College in 1801, Webster followed the traditional path to a legal career by reading law in the office of Thomas W. Thompson in rural New Hampshire. Despite misgivings about his choice of profession, he finished his clerkship in Boston with Christopher Gore. After admission to the Boston bar in March 1805,

Webster returned to New Hampshire to begin a career in the law. During his nearly fifty years of legal practice Webster became a much sought after counselor and an advocate before the United States *Supreme Court where he argued over 170 cases. In 1807 Webster moved his practice to Portsmouth, New Hampshire, then the state's principal city. Elected to the U.S. House of Representatives in 1812 because of his opposition to the War of 1812, he served until 1817. Realizing that his New Hampshire practice was peaking, Webster moved to Boston in 1816 where he built a *commercial law practice that served Massachusetts's merchant and manufacturing elite. Webster represented Massachusetts in the U.S. House of Representatives (1823–26) and the Senate (1827–41; 1844–50).

His victory in the *Dartmouth College Case* (1819) established his reputation as a constitutional lawyer. In that decision the Court turned the *Contract Clause of the *Constitution into a legal bulwark to protect private *property from the ambitions of state legislatures. Webster also argued many of the major cases of the Supreme Court's *Marshall and Taney years. Among these were *McCulloch* v. *Maryland* (1819; necessary and proper clause); *Gibbons* v. *Ogden* (1824; commerce clause); *Ogden* v. *Saunders* (1827); and *Charles River Bridge* v. *Warren Bridge* (1837; contract clause); *Thurlow* v. *Massachusetts* (1847) and *Norris* v. *Boston* (1849; commerce clause), and *Luther* v. *Borden* (1849; guaranty clause).

Webster's oratory was not limited to the courtroom. From his earliest years in New Hampshire he had gained distinction as a gifted speaker. His reputation grew in Massachusetts after he delivered orations at Plymouth (1820) and Bunker Hill (1825) in which he spoke eloquently about the uniquesness of the American political system. The Americans had created a new form of government—a republic—in which the people were sovereign and the government one of delegated powers. His renown reached its zenith in the famous senatorial Webster-Hayne debates during 1830 over *states rights and nullification. When Webster proclaimed "Liberty *and* Union, now and forever, one and inseparable!" he propounded the theory that the people, through the Constitution, had founded a sovereign federal government over which the Supreme Court acted as arbiter of government power. Following publication of the speech he was hailed as "Defender of the Constitution."

As secretary of state (1841–43; 1850–52) he negotiated the Treaty of Washington (1842) that set- tled the Maine boundary dispute with Great Britain. Though Webster and Henry Clay helped found the Whig Party in the 1830s, and despite an intense interest in the presidency, Webster was never able to win his party's nomination. Webster died in Marshfield, Massachusetts, on 24 October 1852.

[*See also* Lawyers; States' Rights]

• Alfred J. Konefsky and Andrew J. King, eds., *The Papers of Daniel Webster: Legal Papers*, 3 vols., 1982–89. Maurice G. Baxter, *One and Inseparable, Daniel Webster and the Union*, 1984.   —Andrew J. King

WELFARE. The American welfare state emerged during the twentieth century. Over the course of a hundred years, the nation fashioned a complex web of social insurance and means-tested programs, financed and administered at all levels of government. Today, most Americans share a commitment to protecting the most vulnerable from extreme economic hardship. What has yet to emerge is a true consensus about how that commitment should be balanced against a variety of other social policy goals that Americans value, such as a belief in limited government and the primacy of individual responsibility. Moreover, the American welfare state remains less extensive and less generous than those in most other industrialized nations.

The oldest roots of American social welfare policy are in England, in the Poor Laws of 1601 and 1834. American antipoverty policy was, in its colonial origins, a patchwork of locally administered programs offering minimal assistance to the most obviously blameless among the destitute. Administrators were preoccupied with the social dangers of "pauperism," a dispirited dependency among the poor. While the programs reflected a salutary symbolism of public concern with the poor, in practice they were inadequate to the challenges of industrial society.

The 1900s ushered in the Progressive Era and a wave of new public efforts to prevent poverty and protect children. Many states created programs of social *insurance, including workers' compensation and unemployment insurance; in part, they hoped to induce employers to take better care of their workers. Moreover, the "Child Saving Movement" led most states to enact "mothers' pensions," to help morally upright widows survive without abandoning their children. None of these programs, however, could address the suffering brought on by the Great Depression of the 1930s, which left one-fourth of the workforce unemployed in 1933.

Franklin Delano Roosevelt's New Deal made so-cial welfare policy an overarching concern of the federal government. The Federal Emergency Relief Administration provided funds to state govern-ments to help the poor. The Civil Works Admin-istration provided public employment of last re-sort during the winter of 1934. And the successor Works Progress Administration created many low-wage, means-tested jobs.

The Supreme Court invalidated some New Deal legislation, such as the National Industrial Recov-ery Act (*A.L.A. Schecter Poultry Corp.* v. *United States* (1935)) and the Railway Pension Act (*Rail-road Retirement Board* v. *Alton Railroad* (1935)). Undeterred, Congress pressed forward with an ambitious interventionist agenda. Roosevelt pro-posed to "pack" the Court with sympathetic jus-tices, and under political pressure the Court un-derwent a change of philosophy, allowing the national government a greater role in economic affairs (*NLRB* v. *Jones & Laughlin Steel Corp.* (1937)) (see COURT PACKING).

The signature enactment of the New Deal was the Social Security Act of 1935. Responding in part to a political crusade led by Francis Townsend, the Act created a federally financed and administered retirement insurance program of "old age pen-sions" for people who had worked in certain sec-tors of the economy and had, along with their em-ployers, paid payroll taxes on their wages. The Act also created a federally financed but state-administered unemployment insurance program. The Act created means-tested programs to assist the elderly poor and the blind poor, in each case run by the states but partially financed by the fed-eral government under a structure known as "co-operative federalism." And the Act created Aid to Dependent Children ("ADC," later to become Aid to Families With Dependent Children, or "AFDC"), a program of cooperative *federalism designed to support certain needy children.

ADC authorized states to provide support for the children of divorced, separated, and never-married mothers, as well as the children of wid-ows. But, at least initially, states were not required to take full advantage of that authority. They could choose to offer benefits only to those families where the mother maintained a "suitable home." Most states used that discretion to manage the sexual conduct and workforce participation of their clientele.

ADC is the paradigmatic "welfare" or "relief" program: when Americans speak of "welfare," they are usually alluding to ADC and its successor pro-grams. From the outset, the design and imple-mentation of ADC highlighted the central conflicts of welfare policy. Issues of *race, *gender, work, and parenting style were, then as now, matters of great social tension. Those tensions created many disputes over whether a home was indeed "suita-ble" within the meaning of the Act.

From 1935 until 1960, changes in the structure of the welfare state took the form of relatively mi-nor expansions of social security for widows and the disabled. Then, during the Kennedy adminis-tration, poverty was "rediscovered" and a new set of policy goals came to the fore. Policymakers be-gan to speak of creating equal opportunity for all to compete in the marketplace, and of "rehabili-tating" the poor by eliminating artificial barriers imposed by the circumstances of birth.

In his 1964 State of the Union address, Presi-dent Johnson declared "unconditional war on poverty." He proposed a series of new legislative initiatives intended to usher in a "Great Society." They included creation of the Office of Economic Opportunity, which was to provide the poor themselves with "maximum feasible participation" in antipoverty programs, creation of Medicare to provide health insurance for the elderly, and cre-ation of Medicaid to provide health care for the poor. The Legal Services Corporation was estab-lished to provide legal representation for the poor in noncriminal matters.

In the late 1960s, major cultural shifts trans-formed the country and put pressure on the fed-eral government to further expand the welfare state. Popular movements pressed the legal, polit-ical, and social cases for civil rights for African Americans, for women's equality, and against the war in Vietnam. A "welfare rights" movement ad-vanced the claim that welfare was not an act of public charity, but instead an *entitlement of the poor.

Legal Services lawyers, working collaboratively with welfare rights advocates, initiated a series of lawsuits that made the Supreme Court, under the leadership of Chief Justice Earl *Warren, a major actor in welfare policy. The welfare rights trilogy (*King* v. *Smith* (1968), *Townsend* v. *Swank* (1971), and *Carleson* v. *Remillard* (1972)) interpreted the Social Security Act in ways that substantially re-duced states' discretion to condition welfare eli-gibility on conformity with caseworkers' views about proper behavior. *Shapiro* v. *Thompson* (1969) interpreted the Constitution to limit states' authority to deny welfare benefits to new resi-dents. *Goldberg* v. *Kelly* (1970) interpreted the Constitution to prohibit states from terminating welfare benefits without *due process.

The combination of Great Society legislation and welfare rights litigation sparked an expansion of the welfare rolls from about four million people in the mid-1960s to about six million by 1969, leading to proposals for welfare reform. Ever since, whether and how to curb welfare spending has been a prominent feature of political and legislative debate.

In 1969, President Nixon proposed the Family Assistance Plan (FAP) as a replacement for AFDC. FAP included a national minimum welfare benefit coupled with a work requirement, but mothers of preschool-age children were to be exempt. FAP and similar negative income tax (NIT) plans emphasized the extension of welfare to two-parent families, the establishment of a national minimum welfare benefit, the reduction of work disincentives arising from AFDC's high marginal tax rate on earnings, and the decoupling of cash assistance and social services. The NIT plans reflected the view that welfare recipients did not need assistance from social workers so much as they needed cash, and that increased benefits were all that was required to reduce their poverty. FAP itself failed to gain legislative approval, but the Food Stamp program evolved into a kind of NIT that provided a national benefit in food coupons that varied by family size, regardless of state of residence, living arrangements, or marital status.

As for the Supreme Court, its activism was short lived, and changes in the Court's membership during the early 1970s brought a different approach to welfare law. Cases such as *New York State DSS* v. *Dublino* (1973) restricted the scope of the welfare rights trilogy. *Mathews* v. *Eldridge* (1976) limited the scope of *Goldberg* v. *Kelly*. *Wyman* v. *James* (1971) and *San Antonio* v. *Rodriguez* (1973) rejected efforts to use other provisions of the Constitution to claim additional economic or procedural rights for the poor.

To be sure, the American judiciary did not become wholly irrelevant to welfare policy after the end of the Warren Court. In *Saenz* v. *Roe* (1999), for example, the Supreme Court struck down California's effort to limit the level of benefits it provided new residents to whatever they would have been receiving in their state of origin. And when Congress attempted to prevent Legal Services lawyers from using the courts to promote systemic welfare reform, the Supreme Court held that attempt unconstitutional, concluding that it constituted a form of "viewpoint discrimination" that is prohibited by the First Amendment (*Legal Services Corporation* v. *Velasquez* (2001)). Still and all, it is fair to say that since the early 1970s, Congress has been the dominant actor in the evolving American welfare state.

In 1977, President Carter proposed the Program for Better Jobs and Income (PBJI), a NIT with one income guarantee for those not expected to work and a lower guarantee for those expected to work, with the latter group also eligible for minimum-wage public service employment (PSE) in a job of last resort. As would have been true under FAP, a single mother with a child under seven years old would have been exempted from work. Only those single mothers whose youngest child was over age fourteen would have been expected to work full time. By providing jobs of last resort and supplementing low earnings, PBJI was a precursor to proposals articulated in the United States in the late 1980s, and by the Blair government in the United Kingdom in the late 1990s to "make work pay."

Yet PBJI, like FAP before it, failed in Congress. Unlike the academic policy community, Congress and the public never embraced the notion of a guaranteed income, not even when the income guarantee was linked to an expectation of work. Moreover, the plan would also have increased total federal welfare spending substantially, by expanding the welfare rolls and providing expensive PSE jobs.

Despite the rejection of FAP and PBJI, the income maintenance system expanded substantially between the late 1960s and the late 1970s, as new programs were introduced, benefit levels were increased, and eligibility requirements were liberalized. The number of AFDC recipients increased from about six to eleven million and the Food Stamp program assisted nineteen million recipients during this period. As higher cash and in-kind benefits became available to a larger percentage of poor people, more and more concern was expressed about the various costs of welfare programs. The public and policymakers viewed increased welfare recipiency as evidence that the programs were subsidizing dependency, encouraging idleness, and enabling nonmarital childbearing.

With the arrival of the Reagan Administration, the 1980s began as an era of welfare retrenchment. Early on, a ten-year-old federal PSE program (the Comprehensive Employment and Training Act) was repealed, on the theory that it was intruding unnecessarily into the labor market. Ironically, that meant fewer welfare recipients were working at all, which only heightened public dissatisfaction with welfare. During the remainder of the 1980s, concern mounted over whether the welfare system was doing enough to encourage mothers to obtain paid employment.

Real spending on cash welfare for the *nonworking* poor was cut back, but at the same time spending on programs to help the *working* poor increased. A program that had been enacted in 1975 to raise the effective wage of low-income workers, the Earned Income Tax Credit (EITC), continued to draw bipartisan support. New welfare-to-work experiments were initiated by the states with federal backing, such as the Community Work Experience Program. And when evaluations of those experiments proved promising, a broad political consensus supported the Family Support Act (FSA) of 1988.

The FSA broadened the safety net in exchange for tougher AFDC work requirements. Drawing on the experience with the prior demonstration projects, it required state governments to establish a new training and education program: Job Opportunities and Basic Skills (JOBS). States were expected, through JOBS, to offer a range of education, skills training, job placement, and support services, and to extend them to a greater proportion of the caseload.

Moreover, FSA required more mothers to participate in JOBS, even earlier in their children's growth and development. Once her youngest child reached age three, a mother had to participate for up to twenty hours per week; once that child reached age six, a mother could be required to participate for up to forty hours per week. Participating meant agreeing to a reasonable "employability plan" that the state devised, as long as the state provided child care, transportation, and other work-related expenses. Refusal to participate could lead to serious sanctions for the recipient family.

Significantly, the political consensus at the end of 1980s stressed the concept of *mutual* responsibility. The government had a responsibility to provide education, training, and work opportunities. Welfare recipients had the responsibility to take advantage of those opportunities and to lead a generally responsible personal life. If the state did not appropriate sufficient funds to provide a JOBS slot (and many states did not), the recipient was not sanctioned for the state's failure.

Shortly after the FSA was enacted, the economic expansion of the 1980s came to an abrupt end, and the welfare rolls jumped from eleven to fourteen million recipients. Critics of the welfare state became more vocal, renewing arguments that welfare programs might be creating incentives for individuals to engage in socially irresponsible behavior. They argued that the welfare system was discouraging recipients from seeking paid employment. In addition, some argued that the rise in nonmarital childbearing since the mid-1970s was also attributable to the growing generosity of the welfare state. In the context of these criticisms, presidential candidate William Jefferson Clinton made welfare reform one of his central commitments, promising if elected to "end welfare as we know it."

Four years later, legislation was passed, and its provisions made clear how much had changed since 1988. The Personal Responsibility and Work Opportunity Reconciliation Act of 1996 (PRWORA) ended the nationwide entitlement to cash assistance that had begun with the Social Security Act. It replaced AFDC with Temporary Assistance for Needy Families (TANF), a decentralized program of block grants to the states. Each state now determines which families are eligible for benefits, subject only to a requirement that they receive "fair and equitable treatment."

PRWORA left very few boundaries around the exercise of state and federal discretion. It freed the federal government from any obligation to increase expenditures in response to future population growth, economic downturns, or inflation. The federal government promised only to make an annual block grant to each state, equal to what the federal government had given to the states as its contribution to welfare expenditures in 1994. For their part, the states were required only to maintain total expenditures for needy families equal to 75 percent of their 1994 level of expenditures on AFDC, JOBS, child care, and Emergency Assistance.

Of course, states were also free to create an even more supportive safety net than existed before. Subject to only a few specific limitations, they were free to design whatever kind of program they chose. In the strong macroeconomic environment of the late 1990s, however, almost all states chose to concentrate on reducing the size of the welfare caseload.

The most important boundary that PRWORA established around state discretion was its time limit. As a general rule, the statute prohibited states from using federal block grant funds to provide more than a cumulative lifetime total of sixty months of cash assistance to any welfare recipient, no matter how hard she may be trying to satisfy public behavioral expectations. Even that general rule was subject to an exception: states may grant exceptions to the lifetime limit and continue to use federal funds for up to 20 percent of their total caseload.

With respect to procreative behavior, early legislative proposals would have made children born out of wedlock completely ineligible for cash assistance. But as it was finally enacted, PRWORA ultimately imposed few constraints on state discretion. It offered modest rewards for states that reduce nonmarital childbearing without increasing abortion rates. And it encouraged states to make rule changes that promote marriage.

With respect to work, PRWORA imposed more constraints. Continuing the trend of all welfare reform legislation since the 1960s, PRWORA required more mothers who receive federal money to work, still earlier in their children's growth and development. A single parent with no children under age one is expected to work at least thirty hours per week. And states may push the age even lower. Indeed, some states now exempt a mother for only thirteen weeks following childbirth.

PRWORA also backed away from any strong requirements that states provide educational and training services at the early stages of job placement for welfare recipients. As the legislation was being crafted, much attention was being given to the experience of Riverside, California. In its welfare-to-work experiment, Riverside had implemented a "work first" program, which required participants to pursue private-sector employment *before* they could receive any training services, and the program had proved relatively successful in getting recipients into jobs. Many people found attractive the "work first" philosophy that any job is a good job and that the best way to succeed in the labor market is to develop work habits and skills on the job.

In the first five years since PRWORA was enacted, the American welfare state has changed significantly. First, PRWORA itself "ended welfare as we knew it" more decisively than most policy analysts expected when the legislation was signed. Welfare caseloads dropped so dramatically that by 2001 the number of recipients had fallen to 5.8 million, the smallest fraction of the population since 1965.

Second, the economic and policy environment around PRWORA has also changed, so that welfare recipients face different incentives than did their predecessors. Most significantly, the financial rewards for moving from welfare to work have increased substantially. The EITC has been expanded and the minimum wage has been raised. In 1997, Congress enacted the Children's Health Insurance Program, and childcare subsidies have been increased. As a result, the dramatic caseload decline has not caused the surge in poverty or homelessness that many critics of the 1996 Act predicted. Even though many who have left welfare are not working full time, year round, and many are working at low-wage jobs, a significant number are earning at least as much as they had received in cash welfare, and some now have higher net incomes because of the expanded income supplements.

Third, despite the large caseload reduction, the national poverty rate has fallen rather little. Many who have left welfare for work remain poor and continue to depend on other forms of government assistance. In recent years a great deal of evidence has been accumulated about welfare recipients whose prospects for stable unsubsidized private sector employment are limited by personal issues such as poor physical or mental health, or limited skills. For those welfare recipients, there does not yet appear to be a successful and replicable programmatic alternative to cash support.

Fourth, we do not yet know how welfare reform will play out during a recession. Because PRWORA placed a five-year, lifetime limit on the receipt of cash assistance, women still receiving welfare are at risk of "hitting their time limits" during a period of slow economic growth or recession. If more than 20 percent of any state's caseload comprises recipients whose personal attributes prevent them from securing stable unsubsidized private sector employment, the states themselves will have to consider providing extended cash benefits or PSE jobs without any contribution from the federal government whatsoever.

PRWORA will be reauthorized by Congress in 2002. While it is unlikely that major changes will be legislated, it will clearly be a time for renewed debate about the ultimate goals of welfare policy. Once again, it is fair to expect that the subtle balance among those goals will be readjusted in search of a new consensus.

[*See also* Economics and Law; Social Dimensions of Law]

• Charles Reich, "The New Property," *Yale Law Journal* 73 (1964): 733. Charles Murray, *Losing Ground*, 1984. William Julius Wilson, *The Truly Disadvantaged*, 1987. David Ellwood, *Poor Support*, 1988. Christopher Jencks, *Rethinking Social Policy*, 1992. James Patterson, *America's Struggle Against Poverty in the Twentieth Century*,

2000. Sheldon Danziger and Robert Haveman, eds., *Understanding Poverty*, 2002.

—Sheldon H. Danziger and Jeffrey S. Lehman

WHITE COLLAR CRIME is a familiar but ill-defined concept. First coined by sociologist Edwin Sutherland in 1939, the term *white collar crime* originally meant a species of criminal conduct defined primarily by the social status of the offender and the circumstances surrounding the offense. In Sutherland's view, white collar crimes were crimes committed during the course of employment or occupation by respectable citizens who enjoyed high social status. Later scholars found this definition problematic because it was divorced from the conduct constituting the crime and from the resulting social harm. Thus, Sutherland's nebulous criteria encompassed an undifferentiated range of crimes that, to some, lacked a coherent organizing principle.

Despite intervening decades of academic debate, white collar crime is still an evolving concept that eludes precise definition. Apart from the definitional dilemma, it is hard to generalize about what the universe of white collar crime includes because it is so vast and varied. While reasonable minds may disagree, many scholars would define white collar crime to include: crimes committed by a person who abuses his position of institutional power or trust; economic crimes involving fraud or deceit; occupational crimes committed by one who has substantial operational authority or responsibility; crimes committed by organizations; and a host of regulatory crimes. These broad and often overlapping subgroups include crimes like price fixing, mail fraud, insider trading, financial institution fraud, embezzlement, bribery, public corruption, and currency reporting violations, to name but a few.

As is true in other criminal law contexts, some white collar crimes have relatively limited impact. A shady car dealer who rolls back the odometer on a used car or a dishonest bank manager who embezzles $500 are minor figures in the grand scheme of things. But white collar crimes are also capable of inflicting widespread harm. In the last two decades of the twentieth century, for example, white collar crime led to the collapse of the savings and loan industry, to loss of investor confidence in the nation's financial markets, to systemic fraud and corruption in the health care industry, to an international banking scandal that caught one of the world's largest banks laundering drug money on a magnificent scale, and to a worldwide price-fixing cartel in the feed additive industry that affected more than $1 billion in sales.

Although white collar crimes may seem relatively benign when compared with violent street crime, the harm they cause often extends beyond the merely economic. Criminal violations of occupational safety and health regulations or *environmental laws can result in death or serious physical injury, for example. To illustrate: a producer illegally exports tons of toxic fertilizer micronutrient with a 30-percent lead content to Bangladesh, where laborers apply it directly to crops by hand; managers of a company that processes spent x-ray film allow clouds of toxic hydrogen cyanide gas to accumulate in a poorly ventilated plant, causing a worker's death by acute cyanide poisoning; after a steam pipe explosion spews two hundred pounds of asbestos into a residential area, the power company that owns it falsely denies that asbestos was released—thus misleading investigators who prematurely allow evacuated residents to return to their homes; and a passenger jet crashes as a result of a fire fueled by oxygen generators illegally shipped in its cargo hold.

While the occupational safety and environmental contexts provide a useful baseline for comparison with violent crime, fraud and other garden variety white collar crimes can endanger life and limb as well. Government contractors who provide defective springs for use in critical assemblies in military aircraft or who supply machine gun parts that will cause the guns to jam aptly illustrate the point.

White collar crime can be a matter of state or federal concern. Although state criminal codes include crimes that can be classified as white collar crimes, the limits of state criminal jurisdiction put state prosecutors at a relative disadvantage. State authority to exercise criminal jurisdiction is grounded in principles of territoriality. A state's criminal enforcement authority is thus limited to conduct that is committed (or causes harm) within its geographical bounds.

Federal criminal jurisdiction, in contrast, is breathtaking in its reach. First, the sheer volume of federal criminal laws (which number in the thousands) signals coverage of a much more comprehensive range of criminal conduct. Second, Congress has considerable authority to invoke federal criminal jurisdiction. It has the power to make conduct a federal crime if it implicates a special federal interest (e.g., defrauding the federal government or stealing from a federally insured bank) and to regulate the United States mails (e.g., mail fraud). It takes little imagination to comprehend just how sweeping these jurisdictional bases may be.

But the commerce power is the source of even more extensive jurisdictional authority. Under the commerce clause of the U.S. Constitution, Congress can regulate (and hence criminalize) activity that occurs interstate (e.g., shipping adulterated food across state lines), intrastate activities that substantially affect interstate commerce (e.g., fraudulent land sales), and use of the facilities of interstate commerce (e.g., telemarketing fraud via interstate telephone lines). Thus, commerce clause jurisdiction is a virtual Pandora's box. It provides Congress almost limitless regulatory power as long as there is a demonstrable federal interest in exercising it. In consequence, when white collar crimes have interstate dimensions or are national or international in scope, the federal government is uniquely suited to prosecute them.

Since many white collar crimes involve sophisticated schemes, deceit, or concealment, they are generally more difficult to detect. Hence, white collar investigations may require pursuit of more rigorous investigative techniques such as tracing an obscure and complex paper trail to document fraud or performing costly laboratory analyses to detect environmental pollutants. Effective intervention may thus require greater resources and specialized technical assistance. Because the federal government can draw expertise and manpower from the Justice Department, the FBI, the United States Attorneys' offices, and specialized administrative agencies, its effectiveness in addressing large-scale white collar crime is enhanced by its superior evidence gathering ability. Advantageous use of these unique resources can also confer the additional benefit of promoting coordinated enforcement efforts nationwide.

[See also Criminal Law; Organized Crime; RICO]

• Edwin Hardin Sutherland, *White Collar Crime*, 1949. Stanford H. Kadish, "Some Observations on the Use of Criminal Sanctions in Enforcing Economic Regulations," *University of Chicago Law Review* 30 (1963): 423. Stanton Wheeler, Kenneth Mann, and Austin Sarat, *Sitting in Judgment: The Sentencing of White-Collar Criminals*, 1988. John C. Coffee Jr., "Does 'Unlawful' Mean 'Criminal'?: Reflections on the Disappearing Tort/Crime Distinction in American Law," *B.U.L. Rev.* 71 (1991): 193. Leonard Orland, ed., *Corporate and White Collar Crime: An Anthology*, 1995. "Fifteenth Survey of White Collar Crime," *American Criminal Law Review* 37 (2000): 145.
                                    —Kathleen F. Brickey

WHODUNIT. See Literature and Law.

WIFE. See Divorce and Annulment; Domestic Violence: Partner Abuse; Family Law; Marriage; Spousal Support.

WIGMORE, JOHN HENRY (1863–1943). John Henry Wigmore was born March 4, 1863, in San Francisco, California, one of several children of John and Harriet (Joyner) Wigmore. He received his early education at San Francisco's Urban Academy, and attended Harvard, where he earned A.B. (1883), A.M. (1884), and LL.B. (1887) degrees.

Wigmore practiced law in Boston for two years following his graduation from law school. He then embarked on an academic career with his first appointment as professor of Anglo-American law at Keio University in Tokyo, Japan.

While at Keio, Wigmore immersed himself in the study of *comparative law, and became a distinguished student of Japanese law. A major legacy of his tenure at Keio was a program of research into the law of the Tokugawa era and a resulting series of publications edited and issued under the collective title, *Materials for the Study of Private Law in Old Japan*.

Wigmore accepted an offer to teach at Northwestern University, and joined the faculty of its School of Law in 1893. He remained affiliated with Northwestern for the rest of his life serving as Dean of the School of Law from 1901 to 1929. In this capacity, he assembled a distinguished faculty, reformed and added breadth to the curriculum, promoted research into developing areas of legal scholarship, and supported the establishment and publishing efforts of significant legal journals.

Within the legal profession, Wigmore was widely known for his multivolume work, *A Treatise on the System of Evidence in Trials at Common Law, Including the Statutes and Judicial Decisions of All Jurisdictions of the United States* (1904–5), commonly called the *Treatise on Evidence*. Wigmore's *Treatise*, published in several editions, was one of the most frequently cited law texts of its day.

The *Treatise* remains the foundation for Wigmore's reputation as a scholar, but is by no means his only significant contribution to the legal literature. Major publications on other topics include synthetic and comparative works such as *A Panorama of the World's Legal Systems* (3 vols., 1928) and *A Kaleidoscope of Justice* (1941). Wigmore was an editor of considerable energy and renown. Titles and series published under his editorial control or with his assistance include *Modern Criminal Science Series* (9 vols.), *Select Essays in Anglo-American Legal History* (3 vols.), *Modern Legal Philosophy Series* (12 vols.), *Continental Legal History Series* (10 vols.), *Evolution of Law Series* (3 vols.), *Sources of Ancient and Primitive Law* (1915), and *Science and Learning in France* (1917). He also authored scores of law review articles, comments, and notes, as well as topical pieces and book reviews.

Wigmore was tirelessly involved in the work of academic organizations and professional associations of the legal community. He figured prominently in the American Association of University Professors and was a leading member of the *American Bar Association. He was the first chairman of the ABA's Section of International and Comparative Law. He organized the National Conference on Criminal Law and Criminology in 1909, out of which came the American Institute of Criminal Law and Criminology. Wigmore served as its first president. He was influential in the development of the *American Judicature Society and contributed to the work of the National Conference of Commissioners on Uniform State Laws.

Wigmore married Emma Hunt Vogl (July 26, 1860–August 22, 1943) of Cambridge, Massachusetts, in 1889. John Henry Wigmore died in Chicago on April 20, 1943.

[*See also* Criminal Law Principles; Educator, Legal]

—Kevin B. Leonard

WILL. A will is an expression of intention, but it has a special meaning in the law of property: intention concerning the disposition of *property after the death of the owner, expressed in a manner that renders it legally enforceable.

[*See also* Estate; Probate]

—John V. Orth

WILL, LIVING. *See* Right to Die.

WILLISTON, SAMUEL R. Samuel R. Williston (1861–1963), was, with Arthur *Corbin, one of the two giants of twentieth-century *contract law. Williston's father, Lyman Richards, adopted his Puritan foster parents' surname. As a youthful professor at Amherst, Lyman converted to Unitarianism, forsaking Puritanism and his job. Young Samuel admired his foster grandfather but wrote that it was odd that he was "agonized with fear that he was not one of the elect, and that,

irrespective of the propriety of his conduct, he was, nevertheless, fated to eternal damnation. . . ." Samuel was no Puritan, but Puritanism is difficult to shed, and a strong moralistic streak permeated his writings.

Williston suffered periodically from what he termed "nervous breakdowns" marked by sleeplessness, debility, and inability to concentrate. Harvard carried him during long absences. Despite these episodes, he dominated his field, and wrote what were the leading treatises on contracts and sales in the English-speaking world. He also wrote much legislation and was the principal author of the first *Restatement of Contracts*. He was honored with the ABA's first gold medal for "conspicuous service to American Jurisprudence" and his alumni formally heralded his achievements as "Olympian."

Williston associated with professionals and businessmen. He viewed law from a business perspective, concentrating on finding the right balance among businesses, exemplified by his work in preparing legislation on bills of lading, balancing the rights of sellers, buyers, and carriers. His predominance was attacked, beginning in the 1930s, by the legal realists who advocated, among other things, the scrapping of general rules in favor of the grouping of legal issues into narrower compartments than had been customary (see LEGAL REALISM). Williston, however, deemed that the law already suffered from too much uncertainty. Uniform general rules, he held, produce certainty thereby reducing litigation with its uncertainties of outcome and frequent injustices.

A different spate of Williston bashing occurred in the 1960s and 1970s. Members of the *critical legal studies movement demonized him for his formalistic approach to the law and his alleged rigidity. Freudians might explain the ferocity of these criticisms as extreme outbreaks of Oedipal rage. Learned *Hand painted a more accurate picture. He described Williston's traits as "scepticism, tolerance, discrimination, urbanity, some—but not too much—reserve towards change, insistence on proportion, and, above all, humility before the vast unknown."

Corbin's treatise on contracts eclipsed Williston's in the second half of the twentieth century. Williston had taught Corbin to play golf. "Younger and stronger than I," Williston wrote, "he would generously carry my clubs; but as often happens, it was not long before the caddy's game was far superior to that of the man whose clubs he had carried"—a sporting compliment that may be taken as a metaphor for larger things. But the eclipse is far from total. Williston's works were cited in more than two hundred reported cases and law review articles in 1999.

[*See also* Educator, Legal]

• Samuel Williston, *Life and Law*, 1940. "Williston," *Current Biography* (1954): 651–53.

—Joseph Perillo

WIRETAPPING AND ELECTRONIC EAVESDROPPING. The practice of standing under the eaves of a house to surreptitiously eavesdrop on conversations inside was a nuisance at *common law. In the twentieth century, electronic eavesdropping was feasible by planting tiny microphones, or "bugs," in a room. Parabolic microphones allow the interception of conversations without planting a bug; other devices register the vibration from conversations within a room that are transmitted through the room wall, windows, building frame, air conditioning ducts, water pipes, and heating vents.

At the beginning of the twentieth century, states began to pass statutes prohibiting wiretapping, the secret interception of telephone conversations. By 1927, more than twenty-five states had criminalized wiretapping, which was accomplished by connecting to the telephone wire carrying the conversation. Today, however, telephone conversations can be intercepted without connecting to the telephone wire by using an induction coil. This two-cubic-inch device, when placed near the telephone or near a wire carrying the voice signal, can draw off the signal if it is within the magnetic field of the telephone conversation.

The Fourth Amendment provides protection against government intrusion, including electronic wiretapping and eavesdropping, to obtain *evidence. In *Olmstead* v. *United States* (1928), the United States Supreme Court considered the extent to which wiretaps violated the Fourth Amendment. Telephones in the homes of four defendants and in an office building were tapped. The taps were executed by inserting small wires along telephone lines in the street outside the defendants' homes and in the basement of the office building. The Court held that the wiretaps did not violate the Fourth Amendment because there had been no physical intrusion, and the conversations were not protected while en route. In his dissent, Justice Oliver Wendell *Holmes called wiretapping a "dirty business."

While roundly criticized, *Olmstead* was not overruled until 1967 by *Berger* v. *New York* and *Katz* v. *United States*. In *Berger*, the Court held that a New York eavesdropping statute violated

Berger's Fourth and *Fourteenth Amendment rights because it allowed "a trespassory intrusion into a constitutionally protected area." Pursuant to the New York statute, an eavesdrop court order was obtained that allowed the installation of a recording device in an attorney's office for sixty days. Based on evidence from the first device, a second eavesdrop order allowed the installation of a recording device in another man's office.

The *Berger* Court explained that the overbroad New York statute violated the Fourth Amendment because it failed to require evidence that a particular crime had been or was being committed, it failed to require a description with particularity of the conversations to be intercepted, it allowed extension of the original two-month eavesdropping period with no further proof of its necessity, it failed to require evidence of exigent circumstances, and it failed to require a return on the warrant.

In *Katz*, the Court held that "[t]he Government's activities in electronically listening to and recording the petitioner's words violated the privacy upon which he justifiably relied while using the telephone booth and thus constituted a 'search and seizure' within the meaning of the Fourth Amendment." FBI agents had attached a listening and recording device to the outside of a glass-paneled telephone booth. Using the device, the agents overheard Katz speaking on the telephone in the booth. Katz was convicted of transmitting wagering information based on the interceptions. The Court reasoned that "[w]hat a person knowingly exposes to the public, even in his own home or office, is not a subject of Fourth Amendment protection. . . . But what he seeks to preserve as private, even in an area accessible to the public, may be constitutionally protected." In his concurrence, Justice *Harlan explained that the Fourth Amendment protects conversations as long as two requirements have been met: "first that a person have exhibited an actual (subjective) expectation of privacy and, second, that the expectation be one that society is prepared to recognize as 'reasonable.' "

Prior to *Berger* and *Katz*, Congress attempted to deal with the advances in technology that threatened communications privacy. Section 605 of the 1934 Communications Act provided that "no person not being authorized by the sender shall intercept any communication and divulge or publish the existence, contents, substance, purport, effect, or meaning of such intercepted communication to any person." Some interpreted this statute to preclude any violation unless wiretapping was coupled with disclosure of wiretapped information to outsiders. The U.S. Supreme Court interpreted the statute to make evidence obtained in violation of §605, or derivative of a violation of §605, inadmissible in federal court, even if by law enforcement officers.

Congress failed to pass any additional legislation protecting communications privacy until 1968, when the Omnibus Crime Control and Safe Streets Act was drafted to conform to the constitutional standards set forth in *Katz* and *Berger*. It attempted to balance the individual's right to privacy in communication against law enforcement and national security concerns. The 1968 Act protects certain types of communications against interception, but allows law enforcement officers to intercept communications pursuant to a court order. The protected conversations are those made on landline telephones ("wire communications") and face-to-face as long as the individuals have a reasonable expectation of privacy ("oral communications"). In 1986 and 1994, the Act was amended to protect cellular and cordless telephone conversations and electronic communications, such as email, display pagers, and other digital transmissions.

The electronic wiretapping or eavesdropping court order authorized by the federal statutes is a special type of warrant that must comply with the Fourth Amendment. The application necessary for the court order is quite detailed. The order is limited to obtaining evidence of a specified list of crimes. A high-ranking official in the Justice Department or in a state prosecutor's office must authorize the application for the court order. The application must contain the targeted offense, the place where the communication is to be intercepted, a description of it, and the identity of the person whose communication is to be intercepted. The court order authorizes interception for no longer than thirty days, although extensions may be granted. At the end of the interception, the recording must be made available to the judge who issued the court order, and the recording must be sealed.

Federal statutes prohibit law enforcement interception of oral, wire, and electronic communications except upon court order. However, they do allow surreptitious tape recording of a conversation by a party to the conversation. The party to the conversation may be a private individual, a law enforcement agent, or a police informant. This consent exception to the federal statutes is in line with U.S. Supreme Court decisions. Illegally intercepted oral and wire communications are inadmissible in court proceedings. Federal statutes authorize a civil action by anyone whose communication has been intercepted in violation of these statutes.

Although every state but Vermont has statutes prohibiting electronic eavesdropping or wiretapping or both, there is substantial variation in their statutory language. The *Model Penal Code classifies electronic eavesdropping and wiretapping as a violation of privacy, protecting activities in a "private place" and telephone conversations. The Code provides exceptions as "authorized by law," and punishes a violation as a misdemeanor. Some state statutes track the federal language. Several statutes contain wording similar to the Model Penal Code.

State statutes may provide the individual the same or greater privacy protection than the federal statutes, but not less privacy. For example, a dozen states have statutes requiring all parties to a conversation to consent to taping; this varies from federal statutes and other state statutes that allow taping upon the consent of one party to the conversation. Federal statutes control the question of whether a tape recording is admissible in federal court even if a state's statute would not allow the tape recording to be admissible in state court.

[*See also* Criminal Law Practice; Federal Bureau of Investigation; Police; Search and Seizure]

• Alan F. Westin, *Privacy and Freedom*, 1967. Ruth Gavison, "Privacy and the Limits of Law," *Yale Law Journal* 89 (1980): 421–71. Clifford S. Fishman and Anne T. McKenna, *Wiretapping and Eavesdropping*, 2d ed., 1995. Priscilla M. Regan, *Legislating Privacy: Technology, Social Values, and Public Policy*, 1995. Carol M. Bast, "What's Bugging You? Inconsistencies and Irrationalities of the Law of Eavesdropping," *DePaul Law Review* 47 (1998): 837–942. David Banisar and Simon Davies, "Global Trends in Privacy Protection: An International Survey of Privacy, Data Protection, and Surveillance Laws and Developments," *John Marshall Journal of Computer and Information Law* 18 (1999): 1–111.

—Carol M. Bast

WITNESS, RIGHT TO CONFRONT. The right of a criminal defendant to confront witnesses against him/her is one of the fundamental principles of the adversary system of justice. This system presumes that truth can best emerge through vigorous cross-examination, and with the witnesses generally present. The Sixth Amendment to the U.S. *Constitution illustrates this commitment to confrontation, reading in part: "In all criminal prosecutions, the accused shall enjoy the right . . . to be confronted with the witnesses against him (and) to have compulsory process for obtaining witnesses in his favor. . . . " All fifty U.S. state constitutions contain identical or similar provisions. The language of the Sixth Amendment seems absolute ("all criminal prosecutions"), but in practice, U.S. courts have been willing to limit this right depending on circumstances.

The history of the right to confront one's accusers stretches back at least to ancient Hebrew and Roman law. The right became part of English *common law over time, with its strongest expression in the sixteenth and seventeenth centuries. In this period, the Crown attempted to convict various opponents, including Sir Walter Raleigh, with ex parte affidavits alleging guilt from witnesses who did not appear at trial for questioning. Use of these affidavits was one of the abuses of the Star Chamber. The public outcry led to the abolition of the Star Chamber, and English jurists ever since have treated confrontation as a fundamental legal principle. *Blackstone's *Commentaries* describes confrontation as an integral part of a public trial.

In continental Europe, the *civil law system's preference for depositions and a written record instead of a public trial has minimized the importance of the right to confront. However, this right is a part of the European Convention on Human Rights, and is beginning to be used to overturn criminal convictions in member countries.

In the United States, even though the Sixth Amendment clearly articulated the right to confront witnesses, the U.S. Supreme Court had little need or desire to further interpret the provision for over one hundred years. As was true for the rest of the *Bill of Rights, it was not applied against state governments until relatively recently. In *Pointer* v. *Texas* (1965), the Court first asserted that the *Due Process Clause of the Fourteenth Amendment incorporated the Confrontation Clause against the states.

Since *Pointer*, the Court has had to grapple with the relationship between the Confrontation Clause and another long-established principle of the adversary system—the exclusion of hearsay statements from trial. Both the Clause and the principle have the goal of ensuring effective cross-examination by the defense. There are many exceptions to the hearsay rule, however. The Clause cannot realistically be absolute, either (for example, in a financial fraud case, does the prosecution have to call a witness to merely state what the price of a stock was on a given day?). It is tempting, therefore, for the courts to interpret the Confrontation Clause as incorporating traditional hearsay rules, reading the two doctrines as mu-

tually supportive. To an extent, the U.S. Supreme Court has done this.

The leading case in Confrontation Clause jurisprudence is *Ohio* v. *Roberts* (1980). In this case, the Court established a test to determine admissibility of *evidence against the Clause. It ruled that the Clause first requires a showing that the witness is unavailable for trial. The issue of availability has been contested as well. The Court has ruled that a witness who asserts his/her Fifth Amendment right against *self-incrimination should usually be considered "unavailable" to testify against another accused. A few circuit courts, however, have been willing to grant court-ordered immunity to allow a witness to testify for the defense in limited circumstances.

The Court has also set up basic guidelines regarding the testimony of child witnesses in sex abuse cases, since in some circumstances the legal process itself could be damaging to the child. In *Coy* v. *Iowa* (1988), the Court overturned the conviction of a defendant convicted in part by testimony from children speaking from behind a one-way screen in the courtroom (the children could not see, but could be seen). The Court voided the Iowa statute allowing this *procedure because there was no individualized finding of harm to the child from testifying. In *Maryland* v. *Craig* (1990), however, the Court upheld a conviction under a courtroom procedure allowing one-way closed circuit television testimony and cross-examination, with the defense lawyer in the room with the child witness. The trial judge was required to make an individualized finding, though, that the child would be traumatized by the standard courtroom procedure.

Assuming that the witness is ruled unavailable for trial, the *Roberts* standard will only allow hearsay testimony if it bears "indicia of reliability." These indicia can be shown in two ways: either they fall within a "firmly rooted" hearsay exception, or there are other "particularized guarantees of trustworthiness" of the testimony. Regarding these guarantees, the Court has not fully defined what they might be, but in *Idaho* v. *Wright* (1990) (a child sex abuse case), the Court ruled that the testimony must be shown to be trustworthy on its own: the attorney may not offer corroborating evidence of otherwise questionable hearsay, in order to prevent a "bootstrap" of unreliable evidence. Some courts have been willing to allow seemingly uncoerced videotaped statements to law enforcement officials as inherently reliable, though, even if the child is subsequently unavailable at trial.

Regarding "firmly rooted" hearsay exceptions,

the Court in *Roberts* identified four in particular: cross-examined testimony in previous court proceedings; so-called "dying declarations" (the subject of *Mattox* v. *U.S.* (1895), the Court's first significant Confrontation Clause case); statements by co-conspirators; and business and public records. In *White* v. *Illinois* (1992), the Court added two more "firmly rooted" exceptions: statements made for the purpose of medical treatment, and so-called "excited utterances," or statements made without time for reflection. (Note: this doctrine has received some criticism from feminists, particularly in rape cases.) In *Lilly* v. *Virginia* (1999), however, the Court refused to declare that statements against penal interest, or hearsay testimony that would tend to inculpate the witness, counted as a firmly rooted exception, even though many states' hearsay rules would allow the testimony. The Court feared that witnesses might testify in a way that would mildly inculpate themselves while shifting the bulk of the guilt to an accomplice.

At the state level, some state supreme courts have interpreted their own constitutions to guarantee broader rights to confront than their federal counterparts. In part, this is due to differing constitutional provisions: in eighteen states, the right to confront must be "face to face," likely stemming from this phrase's use in the Pennsylvania Constitution, used as a model by other state drafters. In the 1990s, at least four state supreme courts (Indiana, Pennsylvania, Ohio, and Illinois) voided convictions in child sex-abuse cases where closed-circuit television was used, relying on the "face-to-face" language. The legislatures in two of these states (Pennsylvania and Illinois) responded by overturning the decisions through constitutional amendment. In fact, many state legislatures have passed legislation creating a hearsay exception allowing qualified adults to testify regarding what children have told them about abuse.

In Montana, the state supreme court read its "face-to-face" provision to require the author of a state crime lab report to testify personally, without forcing the defense to call him/her as a witness (*State* v. *Clark* (1998)). Opponents argue that personal testimony will add nothing to a scientific report prepared months ago by a technician with no direct knowledge of the case, but supporters point to various abuses and errors by lab technicians to justify cross-examination.

Given the flexibility of Supreme Court doctrine in this area, it seems likely that courts will be faced with Confrontation Clause issues for some time to come.

[*See also* Criminal Law Principles]

• Stanley Goldman, "Not So 'Firmly Rooted': Exceptions to the Confrontation Clause," *North Carolina Law Review* 66 (1987): 1–47. Randolph Jonakait, "The Origins of the Confrontation Clause," *Rutgers Law Journal* 27 (1995): 77–108. Roderick Ingram, "A Clash of Fundamental Rights: Conflicts Between the Fifth and Sixth Amendments in Criminal Trials," *William and Mary Bill of Rights Journal* 5 (1996): 299–321. Akhil Amar, *The Constitution and Criminal Procedure*, 1997. Richard Friedman, "Confrontation: The Search For Basic Principles," *Georgetown Law Journal* 86 (1998): 1011–43. Elizabeth Strobel, "Play It Again, Counsel: The Admission of Videotaped Interviews in Prosecutions for Criminal Sexual Assault of a Child," *Loyola University of Chicago Law Journal* 30 (1999): 305–56. Sarah Heisler, "My Brother, My Witness Against Me: The Constitutionality of the 'Against Penal Interest' Hearsay Exception in Confrontation Clause Analysis," *Northwestern School of Law Journal of Criminal Law and Criminology* 90 (2000): 827–73.
—Matthew H. Bosworth

WORCESTER V. GEORGIA, 31 U.S. 515 (1832). *Cherokee Nation* v. *Georgia* (1831) and *Worcester* v. *Georgia,* together known as the "Cherokee Cases," form the foundation for Native American law. These cases must be seen against the backdrop of the 1820s and 1830s, which includes the Cherokee constitution's adoption, the discovery of gold on Cherokee land, President Andrew Jackson's election, Georgia's enactment of laws extending jurisdiction over tribal treaty lands within state boundaries, and the Cherokee Nation's tribal government abolition.

Georgia enacted laws making it a criminal offense for whites to reside in the Cherokee Nation without a state license and an oath of allegiance to the state. Two white missionaries, Samuel Worcester and Elizure Butler, were indicted under these laws for living in that part of the Cherokee country over which Georgia claimed jurisdiction. Worcester pleaded that the United States acknowledged the status of the Cherokees as a sovereign nation in its treaties with the Cherokees; consequently, state laws could not be applied on Cherokee lands. The two missionaries were tried by the Georgia courts, convicted, and sentenced to four years in prison.

The case was appealed to the U.S. Supreme Court. Georgia refused to appear. Taking jurisdiction, the Court reversed, and held that Georgia laws were constitutionally void. They violated treaties, the Indian nation's sovereign authority, and the U.S. Constitution's contract and commerce clauses. Chief Justice John *Marshall determined that Indian tribes were distinct nations—sovereign political communities with independent rights. In response to the *Worcester* decision, President Jackson supposedly said: "Marshall has made his law, now let him enforce it." The constitutional crisis over enforcement of the *Worcester* decree came to an end in 1833 when Georgia Governor Lumpkin pardoned the missionaries in exchange for their agreement to leave Georgia.

[*See also* Native Americans and the Law; Sovereignty]

• Joseph C. Burke, "The Cherokee Cases: A Study in Law, Politics, and Morality," *Stanford Law Review* 21 (1969): 500. Rennard Strickland and W. Strickland, "The Supreme Court and the Trail of Tears," *Yearbook of the Supreme Court Historical Society* 20 (1979).

—Rennard Strickland

WORKER'S COMPENSATION. *See* Labor Law: Workplace Issues.

WORKPLACE. *See* Labor Law: Workplace Issues.

WORLD COURT. *See* International Law; United Nations: U.S. Obligations to; War, Law of.

Y

YOUNGSTOWN SHEET & TUBE CO. V. SAW-YER, 343 U.S. 579 (1952). The power of the president to take extraordinary measures in the face of national emergencies expanded rapidly during Franklin Roosevelt's administration (1933–45). Roosevelt pushed the limits of executive power in dealing with the Great Depression and in preparing for and fighting World War II. Harry S. Truman inherited this expanded role of the presidency. Furthermore, his own personal philosophy of decisive action made him a proponent of even greater presidential powers. The *Supreme Court thus found itself ruling on just how expansive these presidential powers were in *Youngstown Sheet & Tube Co.* v. *Sawyer* (1952).

In December 1951, the United Steel Workers of America gave notice of intent to strike for higher wages. President Truman referred the matter to the Federal Wage Stabilization Board. The board's investigation avoided a strike until April 1952, but failed to resolve the issues. The union then called a nationwide strike for April 9.

President Truman found himself unable to use presidential war powers and unwilling to invoke statutory procedures to deal with this crisis. He could not invoke his war powers because he had initiated military action in the Korean Peninsula without a congressional declaration of war. Moreover, his ties to organized labor were such that he was politically foreclosed from invoking the Taft-Hartley Labor Act to delay the strike. In order to avoid a complete shutdown of the steel industry, Truman relied on the implicit powers of the presidency. He claimed that powers embedded in the *Constitution justified an executive order directing the secretary of commerce to take possession of the steel mills and run them under federal control. The steel industry immediately challenged this order in federal court and obtained an injunction. The Supreme Court agreed to hear an expedited appeal of the issue.

A divided Court rejected the president's claim for expansive power. Justice Hugo L. *Black wrote that the president's power must issue either from an act of *Congress or from the Constitution itself. He rejected the idea that the role of commander in chief gave the president control over civilian industries. No other provisions of the Constitution gave the president the power to take actions not in conformity with federal statutes. Since the president's actions attempted to make law rather than execute laws, he was acting beyond his authority, and the Court granted an injunction against this seizure order.

Justice Robert H. *Jackson, in a concurring opinion, categorized presidential power. When the president acted pursuant to express or implied congressional authorization, his authority was at the maximum. When the president acted in a way incompatible with the will of Congress, however, his power was greatly restricted. Justice Jackson found that Truman's failure to make use of the various statutory enactments governing management-labor relationships placed this seizure in the latter category. With this opinion, the Court put limits on presidential powers and began to reestablish equality between the branches.

[*See also* Executive Power; Labor Law: Labor Relations]

• Maeva Marcus, *Truman and the Steel Seizure Case: the Limits of Presidential Power*, 1977.

—R. Ben Brown

Z

ZENGER, PETER, TRIAL OF. In 1733, shortly after his arrival in New York, Governor William Cosby summarily removed from office the colony's longtime chief justice, Lewis Morris. In November 1733 allies of Morris, including attorneys James Alexander and William Smith, soon launched an anti-Cosby newspaper—the first opposition paper in America—which was printed by John Peter Zenger. The paper attacked Cosby with satire, humor, and biting irony, and published serious essays from the English libertarian philosophers on the nature of government. Using innuendo and acerbic wit, the paper compared Cosby (but not by name) to a monkey; his leading advisor, to a spaniel. In January 1734 the new chief justice, James DeLancey urged a grand jury to indict Zenger for libel without success. The sheriff arrested Zenger in November 1734, and Zenger's supporters declined to offer bail—believing that he would be let out at the end of December—because they correctly understood that no grand jury would indict him. In January however, Zenger was charged with the misdemeanor of libel. During preliminary arguments DeLancey disbarred Alexander and Smith for challenging the legitimacy of his appointment.

On the day of the trial in July 1735 Andrew Hamilton of Philadelphia, the most important attorney in the colonies, appeared to represent Zenger. Working with a brief supplied by the now disbarred James Alexander, Andrew Hamilton startled the court when he admitted that Zenger had published the newspapers, but then argued that the printer should be permitted to prove the truth of his allegedly libelous publications. This was counter to English law, which held that a defamatory publication was libelous whether it was true or not. Speaking directly to the jury, Hamilton argued that the precedents disallowing truth as a defense came from the hated Star Chamber, and that the jury should ignore them. Here he made important political arguments on the differences between England and America. He further urged that the jury should be free to reach a general verdict of not guilty, rather than follow the traditional English practice in libel cases of deciding only the "facts" of publication, and leaving to the court the right to decide whether the publication was libelous. Ignoring Chief Justice DeLancey's instructions, the jury acquitted Zenger.

This case did not change the law of libel in America or Britain, but did set the stage for later legal arguments. Although not a legal precedent, it was surely a political one, which put colonial governors on notice that American juries would be supportive of those printers who spoke "truth to power" by attacking the governors.

[See also Speech and the Press, Freedom of]

• Paul Finkelman, ed., *A Brief Narrative of the Case and Tryal of John Peter Zenger: Printer of the New York Weekly Journal,* 1997; 1999.   —Paul Finkelman

ZONING. The most prevalent method of local land use controls in the United States is zoning. Other methods include subdivision controls, housing codes, building codes, historic preservation and aesthetics, and natural resource protection (such as coastal zones). The exercise of local land use controls is firmly rooted in the police power—the power to regulate in order to protect the health, safety, morals, and welfare of the people. In most jurisdictions, that power is delegated from the state—the repository of police power—to units of local government through enabling statutes.

History of Zoning and the Police Power. Zoning developed very late in American history, but its roots go back several centuries. Indeed, land use controls can be traced back to seventeenth-century England. Laws in the American colonies dealt extensively with land use controls for more than the abatement of *common-law nuisance;

some of these took the form of building laws. Some commentators point to the use of restrictive covenants running with the land in the early regulation of land use in the United States as a basis for later public controls. Land use restrictions on building heights were upheld by the Supreme Court as early as 1909. The bulk of land use controls by local zoning came after 1900, with increasing urbanization. During the nation's first century, the abundance of land coupled with a largely agrarian economy and a strong belief in private *property rights combined to confine most land use disputes to those involving nuisance. But it is in the *police power, not the common law of *nuisance, that land use controls are firmly grounded.

New York City enacted the first comprehensive zoning ordinance, in 1916, though more rudimentary forms had appeared in both Boston and Los Angeles at least ten years earlier. The New York law divided the city into zones according to permitted uses of land, minimum lot size, and maximum building heights. The Supreme Court decision in *Village of Euclid* v. *Ambler Realty Co.* (1926) upholding the general authority to impose zoning under the police power, coupled with promulgation of the Standard Zoning Enabling Act gave land use controls a strong impetus. The drafting of a standard zoning-enabling act, its dissemination by the U.S. Department of Commerce, and its adoption by dozens of states were principally responsible for the spread of land use controls throughout the nation. The act was the product of an advisory commission appointed by Herbert Hoover, then secretary of commerce; the first printed version of the act (1924) sold over fifty-five thousand copies. By 1923, 208 municipalities with 22 million inhabitants, representing 40 percent of the urban population of the United States, were zoned. By 1930, forty-seven states had adopted zoning-enabling legislation in accordance largely with the Standard Zoning Enabling Act, and 981 municipalities, representing 67 percent (46 million) of the urban population, had adopted the zoning ordinance as the most useful technique to control the use of land.

The 1920s also saw the judicial creation of a limitation on land use controls, based on the theory that a land use regulation, if too onerous, constituted a taking of property without compensation, contrary to the Fifth Amendment to the Constitution. The Supreme Court in *Pennsylvania Coal Co.* v. *Mahon* (1922) held that Pennsylvania had "taken" property without compensation by passing a law forbidding the mining of coal under private property in a way that caused the land surface to subside. In the now famous words of Justice Oliver Wendell *Holmes: "The general rule at least is, that while property may be regulated to a certain extent, if regulation goes too far it will be recognized as a taking."

After five decades of silence on this topic, the Court suggested in *Penn Central Transportation Co.* v. *City of New York* (1978) that the economic effect of regulations on a landowner, together with the landowner's "distinct, investment-backed expectation," would figure prominently in deciding regulatory *takings cases. In *Lucas* v. *South Carolina Coastal Council* (1992), the Court held that a *regulation leaving landowners with no "economically beneficial use" constituted a regulatory taking regardless of such expectation, unless the regulating government could prove that the regulation either abated a nuisance or reflected a "background principle" of the state's law of property, in which case the right to use land contrary to the regulation was not a part of the landowner's title to begin with.

The Elements of Zoning. State zoning-enabling acts or statutes permit, but do not require, local governments to divide the land area in their jurisdiction into districts, or zones, and to list permitted uses, their permitted height and density ("bulk" regulation), and conditional uses in each zone. The map upon which the districts are drawn is called the "zoning map," and the lists of uses and bulk regulations are collectively called the "text." The text also contains administrative regulations setting forth how the zoning ordinance restrictions on a particular piece of property may be changed and, usually, a section dealing with uses permitted at some past date but no longer conforming to the existing land use regulations for the district, called collectively "nonconformities." The principal vehicles for administration and enforcement of a local zoning ordinance are the zoning officer or administrator, the zoning board of appeals, the local legislative body, and the plan commission.

Among the troublesome issues confronting early zoning ordinance draftsmen were the potential hardships caused to individual property owners by the literal application of the zoning ordinance to a particular piece of property. This problem is addressed through the "variance" (sometimes called a variation or special exception). The Standard Zoning Enabling Act provided for a local zoning board of appeals for the particular purpose of granting variances after a hearing, but some jurisdictions converted such boards into hearing agencies only, with the variance granted by the local legislative body.

Variances are usually granted in cases of special or unique hardship, and the zoning regulation is varied only to the extent necessary to relieve the applicant of that hardship. Hardship usually is determined by a three-step test: (1) the land cannot yield a reasonable return if used only for the permitted use; (2) the proposed use will not alter the community's essential character; and (3) the need for the variance is due to unique circumstances and not general neighborhood conditions.

The rapid spread of comprehensive zoning to most urban areas of the United States after the *Euclid* case resulted in many structures and uses no longer permitted in the new use districts in which they found themselves. Nonconformities may be created by a rezoning or map amendment or by changes in the list of permitted or special uses in an existing district. To qualify for nonconformity status, a use or structure must have been legally commenced or used *ab initio*. Most state zoning-enabling acts provide expressly for such nonconformities, and local governments are generally prohibited from immediately eliminating most nonconforming uses and buildings. The law of nonconformities has assumed increased importance in recent years owing to the current prominence of vested rights issues and cases, the theories for which grew directly from the law of nonconformities.

While courts originally held that nonconformities must be permitted until they slowly wasted away, most jurisdictions now permit the termination of certain nonconformities over time. The validity of such termination often depends upon such factors as the type and value of the nonconformity, its useful life, and whether it is a nonconforming use or a nonconforming structure. Junkyards and nuisance-type nonconformities appear to be particularly vulnerable to quick termination, as are relatively low-value uses such as signs and billboards. Of particular use in the elimination of nonconformities is the technique of amortization, whereby the nonconformity is terminated after a period during which the user is theoretically able to recapture all or part of the investment therein. Courts have generally upheld the concept as applied to signs, junkyards, billboards, sites of adult entertainment, and similar structures.

Subdivision Controls. The regulation of land and the dedication of public improvements through the subdivision process is a relatively modern land use control technique. The modern subdivision ordinance developed from local responses to so-called "plat acts," by which, as legislative policy, no parcels of land should be divided and sold without the filing of a "plat"—a scaled drawing of the parcel showing the division or divisions into which it had been carved. The purpose of such plat acts was to aid "conveyancing," or the process of buying and selling land.

At first, subdivision ordinances dealt primarily with an increasing volume of design standards, such as width and composition of streets and sidewalks, perimeter linkage, and uniformity of building setback from the street. Street and road standards often came from formally referring to and incorporating the language and illustrations in an "official map" showing where the community had decided to place its streets. From the design and location of public facilities needed to serve new subdivisions, it was an easy step to require construction of such facilities as a condition of subdivision approval. Thus, many state enabling acts directed local subdivision codes to require the building and dedication to the community of the streets, sewers, water mains, sidewalks, and other public facilities. By the 1950s the subdivision ordinance was well on its way to becoming a development code.

A logical step from regulating the design and dedication of public facilities was the "mandatory showing" of open space and public building sites on subdivision plats. The first step—the showing of such public uses and consequently the prohibition, even if for a short time, of an owner's developing such sites—was both common and practical. After all, increasing residential construction logically increases the need for schools, police and fire stations, and parks.

The next step was more problematic: the required "dedication" of such park, public-building, and school sites. The theory was much the same as that supporting public-improvement requirements and dedication: if an owner of property sought to develop it in such a fashion as to add to the population of a local government area in a particular section of its jurisdiction, that property owner should provide its share of the park, school, and public-building needs thereby generated. If the subdivision was too small to generate the need for a "whole" such site, then cash would do, to be paid into a fund for the purchase of the site as other subdivisions were approved. Indeed, in a spate of recent cases, such mandatory dedication schemes have been upheld in a number of jurisdictions, usually so long as the dedication of land is required to fill a need attributable to the developer being asked to make the dedication or cash contribution. Such subdivision "exactions" are therefore increasingly commonplace and are often viewed as an acceptable growth-management tool.

"Takings" and Land Development Conditions. The requirements to dedicate streets, roads, and similar public facilities have generally been upheld on the grounds that the subdivision is creating the need for such facilities and that the facilities will benefit the subdivision almost exclusively. Exactions of land, money, or both for other facilities and services pose significant "taking" problems, particularly if these exactions are for public facilities extrinsic to the development. Land developments often generate a need for off-site improvements and facilities. This, together with drastic reductions of available federal government funds for such facilities and citizen revolts against increases in property taxes (the other major source of local government funds), led to the creation of the "impact fee." An impact fee is levied upon a land development to pay for public facilities, the need for which is generated by that development. The developer must therefore pay a proportionate share of the cost of the facility that is attributable to the development. This is called the "rational nexus test." Approved by many state courts in the 1970s, the test was boosted considerably when the Supreme Court in *Nollan* v. *California Coastal Commission* (1987) used an "essential nexus test" in deciding that a state agency could not require the dedication of lateral public-beach access across the rear of a private beachfront lot in exchange for granting permission to the owner to rebuild a beach house. The Court reasoned that there was no connection or essential nexus between the condition—access—and the problems, if any, that rebuilding the house would cause. The Court followed this decision with *Dolan* v. *City of Tigard* (1994), in which it added that the condition or dedication must be "roughly proportional" to the need generated by the proposed land development. Impact fees are accordingly used to fund such facilities as streets and roads, water, wastewater, solid waste, schools, parks, public libraries, police and fire facilities, and even public housing. The fees commonly add from a few hundred to over ten thousand dollars per unit to the cost of residential development.

State and Regional Land Use Controls. While traditional zoning and other local land regulatory ordinances continue to be the primary method of controlling the use of land, a "quiet revolution" in land use controls in the 1960s and 1970s moved much of the broad policy decision-making to the states in many developing regions. Essentially, the states took back some of the powers delegated to their local governments by zoning- and planning-enabling legislation so as to exercise a variety of state and regional land use controls themselves. They did so for a variety of reasons, principally (1) a perception that local governments were unwilling or unable to make decisions of supra-local impact except on narrow, parochial grounds; (2) a response to a crisis regarding a particularly large development or a particularly critical natural feature or resource threatened by actual or pending land development; and (3) the threatened imposition of federal land use controls.

There are many such systems of state control of land today, but four—those in Hawaii, Vermont, Florida and Oregon—have achieved particular notoriety, due in part to their unique but disparate features, the frequent challenges thereto, and their considerable impact on growing populations. The systems have several common threads, one of the most prominent being a reliance on statewide planning of some sort as an initial or later addition to the basis for exercising land use controls. All four systems supercede in some fashion the local land use regulatory function, and all have running or incipient controversies over plan "conformance." All attempt to preserve certain identified critical natural resources and to control developments that would have a regional impact.

• Fred P. Bosselman and David L. Callies, *The Quiet Revolution in Land Use Controls*, 1971. Robert H. Freilich and Michael Schultz, *National Model Subdivision Regulation, Planning, and Law*, 1995. Richard F. Babcock, *The Zoning Game*, 1996. Barry Cullingworth, *Planning in the U.S.A.*, 1997. Julian Juergensmeyer and Thomas E. Roberts, *Land Use Planning and Control Law*, 1998. David L. Callies, Robert H. Freilich, and Thomas E. Roberts, *Cases and Materials on Land Use*, 3d ed., 1999. Robert Meltz, Dwight Merriam, and Richard Frank, *The Takings Issue*, 1999. Patrick Rohan, *The Law of Planning and Zoning* (Eric Damian Kelly, ed.), 10 vols., 2001.
—David L. Callies

CASE INDEX

For an explanation of the reports that have been used to provide case citations, see the Introduction, pp. x–xi.

INDEX

For all cases mentioned in this book, please see the Case Index on p. 851.

uniformity of federal courts, 705
U.S. Supreme Court, 648
Federal Rules of Criminal
  Procedure, 195–197, 654, 801,
  817
Federal Rules of Evidence, 196,
  281, 649, 714–715
Federal Securities Act (1933), 169
Federal Securities and Exchange
  Act (1934), 169
Federal Speedy Trial Act (1974),
  292
Federal Speedy Trial Act (1994),
  653
Federal Tort Claims Act, 558
Federal Trade Commission Act
  (1914), 29, 30, 156
Federal Trade Commission (FTC),
  29, 32, 238, 253, 343, 500, 553,
  694, 698. *See also* regulation
Federal Wage Stabilization Board,
  845
Federal Water Pollution Control
  Act (1948), 260, 261
federalism, 299–303
  citizenship, 104
  conflict of laws, 138
  Erie Railroad v. *Tompkins*, 271–
    272
  federal system, 545
  governance and, 333
  history of American legal system
    and, 510
  homicide and, 400
  judicial, 778–779
  judicial review, 443
  rise of, 374
  sovereignty and, 757
  states' rights and, 767
  treaties and, 810
  U.S. Supreme Court, 775
The Federalist Papers
  as commentary on Constitution,
    147–150
  federalism, 301
  Hamilton, 63, 436, 442, 771
  implied powers, 736
  influences, 334
  Jefferson, 434
  Madison, 142, 151
  secession, 725
  separation of church and state,
    99
  separation of powers, 734, 735
Federalists, 146, 409, 434, 563
Federated States of Micronesia, 798
Feinberg, Joel, 276
Feingold, Russ, 206
Feinman, Jay, 203
"fellow servant rule," 749, 802

felonies and misdemeanors, 305–
  307
  burglary, 74
  capital punishment and, 371
  in the colonies, 372
  criminal codes and, 186
  defined, 190
  double jeopardy, 227
  harassment, 352
  history of American legal system
    and, 511
  homicide, 305–306, 399, 567
  juries, 454
  kidnapping, 469
  morals offenses and, 570
  probation and parole, 640
  sodomy, 401
feminism and feminist theory
  antiessentialist feminist theory,
    330
  critical legal studies and, 204
  critical race theory and, 308
  equal rights amendment, 268–
    270
  feminist jurisprudence, 149, 327,
    503
  feminist legal theory, 40–41, 307–
    308
  feminist movement, 222
  feminist theory, 330
  free speech and, 114
  heat of passion defense and, 195
  law profession, 494
  postmodernism and, 308, 330
  relational feminism, 308
  See also abortion; women's issues
Feminism Unmodified
  (MacKinnon), 308
Ferguson, Robert, 488
feudalism, 129
Field, David Dudley Jr., 109, 120,
  126, 196, 308–309, 380, 447, 648
Field, Stephen Johnson, 120–121,
  309–310, 726
Field Code, 380
Fielding, Henry, 373
Fifteenth Amendment
  Black, Hugo Lafayette, 66
  civil rights and, 111
  federal authority and, 375
  segregation and, 732
  U.S. Supreme Court, 775
  Voting Rights Act (1965) and,
    822
  voting rights and, 146, 218, 820,
    822
  women's suffrage and, 329
Fifth Amendment
  Burger on, 74
  civil rights and, 113

"class legislation," 385
compensation for property, 847
conspiracy, 145
criminal law, 186, 193, 655
double jeopardy, 227–228
due process, 192, 232
eminent domain, 378
forfeiture, 318
homicide and, 400
incorporation doctrine, 415, 416
interrogation and confession,
  428
Japanese-American Internment,
  432
juries, 458
Native American compensation,
  584
police procedures, 618
property rights, 674
RICO statutes and, 707
right to counsel and, 172
self-incrimination, 617, 637, 651,
  655, 733, 842
slavery and, 82
takings clause, 659, 782
water rights and, 831
See also self-incrimination
*Fifty Resolutions in Regard to
  Professional Deportment*
  (Hoffman), 277–278
"fighting words," 761
filibusters, 340, 519
film, 42, 496–498
finance
  community property, 274
  elderlaw, 250
  labor law, 472
  landlord-tenant law, 482
  law firms, 599
  property, 659
  trusts, 813
  victimless crimes and, 818
  See also business and commerce;
    economy and economics
fingerprints, 617
Finnis, John, 588
First Amendment
  assembly and association, 43–44
  Black, Hugo Lafayette, 66
  canon law, 83
  children's rights, 96, 97
  civil rights and, 112
  conspiracy, 145
  court publicity, 293
  culture and, 207
  dissident political expression
    and, 213–214
  entertainment and, 256
  harassment, 352
  incorporation doctrine, 415–416